বাংলা একাডেমী
CW01081866

BANGLA ACADEMY BENGALI-ENGLISH DICTIONARY

Bangla Academy
Bengali-English Dictionary

EDITORS

Mohammad Ali

MA (Dhaka), MA (Oxon)

Professor, Department of English, Chittagong University, Chittagong

Mohammad Moniruzzaman

MA (Dhaka), PhD (Dhaka)

Professor, Department of Bengali, Dhaka University, Dhaka

Jahangir Tareque

MA (Dhaka), MA (Sorbonne), MA (Paris), PhD (Paris)

Professor, Institute of Modern Languages

Dhaka University, Dhaka

COMPILERS

Latifur Rahman

MA (Dhaka)

Jahangir Tareque

MA (Dhaka), MA (Sorbonne), MA (Paris), PhD (Paris)

BANGLA ACADEMY DHAKA

Bangla Academy Bengali-English Dictionary

First Edition
Ashar 1401/June 1994

Manuscript
Compilation Department

BA 4800
First Reprint
Kartik 1401/October 1994
Twenty Seventh Reprint
Magh 1416/January 2010

Published by
Shahida Khatun
Director
Establishment, Training & Planning Division
Bangla Academy, Dhaka

Printed by
Mobarak Hossain
Manager
Bangla Academy Press
Bangla Academy, Dhaka

Cover Design
Quayyum Chowdhury

Print Run : 15,000 copies

Price : ৳.275.- only.

ISBN 984-07-4808-1

প্রসঙ্গ-কথা

Bangla Academy English-Bengali Dictionary প্রকাশের পর পাঠক সমাজের ব্যাপক সাড়া আমাদেরকে গভীরভাবে আনন্দিত ও উৎসাহিত করে। ইংরেজি-বাংলার মতো একটি বাংলা-ইংরেজি অভিধানও বাংলা একাডেমীর থাকবে—এ প্রত্যাশা আমাদের সবার। Bangla Academy Bengali-English Dictionary সে প্রত্যাশা পূরণে কিছুমাত্র সক্ষম হলে আমরা নিজেদের ধন্য মনে করবো।

ভাষার নিজস্ব পরিমণ্ডল আছে, সেই পরিমণ্ডলে প্রতিটি শব্দের এক বা একাধিক অনুষঙ্গ সৃষ্টি হয়। শব্দের সে অনুষঙ্গকে ভিন্ন ভাষায় হুবহু রূপান্তর করা সম্ভব নয়। আমাদের এই বেঙ্গলি-ইংলিশ ডিকশনারিতে বাংলা শব্দের নিকটতম ইংরেজি অর্থ এবং ব্যঞ্জনা তুলে ধরার চেষ্টা করা হয়েছে। এ চেষ্টায় আমাদের সাফল্যের চাইতে ব্যর্থতাই হয়তো বেশি। এ ব্যর্থতাকে স্বীকার করে নিয়েই আমরা ভাষা-ব্যবহারকারীর প্রয়োজনে 'হাত বাড়ালেই খানিকটা সাহায্য পাওয়া যায়' এমন একটা গ্রন্থ উপহার দেবার চেষ্টা করেছি। বাকিটা বিচারের ভার রইলো পাঠক-সমাজের উপর।

যে-কোনো বাংলা-ইংরেজি অভিধানে প্রথম সমস্যা হলো, বাংলা বাগ্‌বিধির সঠিক ইংরেজি প্রতিরূপ নির্দেশ করা। এ অভিধানে আমরা তেমন অভিব্যক্তিগুলোকে যথাসম্ভব পরিহার করার চেষ্টা করেছি, যা ষোলোআনা আদলে ইংরেজি হলেও আসলে বাংলা বাগ্‌বিধির অক্ষম ইংরেজি প্রতিরূপ। বাংলা ভাষায় 'মরা' শব্দটির অর্থ যাই হোক না কেন, 'মরাকান্না', 'মরমে মরা', 'মরা মুখ দেখা', 'মরে বাঁচা', 'মরতে মরতে বাঁচা' ইত্যাদি অভিব্যক্তিগুলোর অর্থ নির্ণীত হয় প্রয়োগ অনুসারে। তাই 'মরা' শব্দের আক্ষরিক অর্থ এসব ক্ষেত্রে খুঁজে পাওয়া নাও যেতে পারে। এ জাতীয় অভিব্যক্তির ক্ষেত্রে আমরা ইংরেজিতে ইংরেজি-রীতি অনুসারেই শব্দার্থ নির্ণয় ও উপস্থাপনের চেষ্টা করেছি। কাজটি খুব দুরূহ এবং সঙ্গত কারণেই কিছু ত্রুটি থেকে যাবে, সেটাই স্বাভাবিক। সহৃদয় পাঠক যদি এ সম্পর্কে কোনো পরামর্শ দিতে এগিয়ে আসেন, তাহলে আমরা কৃতার্থ বোধ করবো।

অভিধান মুদ্রণের অন্তঃপর্বে বাংলা একাডেমীর পরিচালকবৃন্দ সর্বজনাব শামসুজ্জামান খান, গোলাম মঈনউদ্দিন, সুব্রত বিকাশ বড়ুয়া ও মুহম্মদ নূরুল হুদা ত্রুটি সংশোধন এবং পরিমার্জনার কাজে যে বিপুল শ্রম দিয়েছেন তার তুলনা হয় না। আমাদের অনুরোধে জনাব

জামিল চৌধুরী এবং ড. হাবিবুর রহমানও এ-কাজে সাহায্য করে আমাদের অশেষ ঋণে আবদ্ধ করেছেন। জনাব আজহার ইসলাম এবং জনাব ওবায়দুল ইসলাম বর্ণানুক্রম অনুযায়ী ভুক্তিবিন্যাসের ত্রুটিনির্দেশ ও সংশোধনের কাজ করে দিয়েছেন।

বাংলা একাডেমীর কর্মকর্তাদের মধ্যে যাঁরা এ-কাজে পেশাগত কারণে সবচেয়ে বেশি সংশ্লিষ্ট ছিলেন, তাঁরা হলেন সর্বজনাব সেলিনা হোসেন, ওবায়দুল ইসলাম, স্বরোচিষ সরকার, লতিফুর রহমান ও মিজানুর রহমান। প্রাথমিক পর্যায়ে প্রুফ সংশোধনের কাজে জড়িত ছিলেন সর্বজনাব মোহাম্মদ ইব্‌রাহিম, আবদুল হান্নান ঠাকুর, আ.ব.ম. শামসুদ্দিন, আমিরুল মোমেনীন, মোবারক হোসেন ও আবদুল বারি। কম্পিউটার কম্পোজে সহায়তা করেছেন সর্বজনাব সাইদুর রহমান, মিন্টু কুমার সূত্রধর, নজরুল ইসলাম ও এমদাদুল হক।

অভিধানটির প্রকল্প-প্রণয়ন পর্বে জনাব সেলিনা হোসেনের ঐকান্তিক আগ্রহ ও নিষ্ঠার কথা বিশেষভাবে উল্লেখযোগ্য। কম্পোজ ও মুদ্রণ পর্বে জনাব ওবায়দুল ইসলাম সনিষ্ঠ শ্রম দিয়েছেন।

এঁদের সকলকে জানাই ধন্যবাদ ও কৃতজ্ঞতা।

এ অভিধানের সম্পাদকত্রয়—প্রফেসর মোহাম্মদ আলী, প্রফেসর মোহাম্মদ মনিরুজ্জামান, প্রফেসর জাহাঙ্গীর তারেককে এ জাতীয় একটি অভিধান সম্পাদনা করার জন্যে আন্তরিক ধন্যবাদ জানাই। সবশেষে, বাংলা একাডেমীর সাম্প্রতিকতম এই অভিধানটি ইংলিশ-বেঙ্গলি ডিকশনারির মতোই গুণ ও মানের বিচারে সুধীসমাজে সমাদৃত হবে এবং এ দেশের মানুষের দেশপ্রেমে অভিষিক্ত হবে—এই আশা।

মোহাম্মদ হারুন-উর-রশিদ
মহাপরিচালক

ভূমিকা

বাংলা–ইংরেজি অভিধান সংকলনের ইতিহাস দীর্ঘ দিনের— প্রায় দুই শত বছরের। এ দেশে ইংরেজদের আগমন, ধর্ম প্রচার ও শাসন প্রতিষ্ঠার সঙ্গে এর নিবিড় সম্পর্ক রয়েছে। অষ্টাদশ শতাব্দীর থেকে এ দেশে যেসব বাংলা-ইংরেজি অভিধান রচিত হয়েছে, তার বেশির ভাগকেই শব্দ-নির্ঘণ্ট বলা চলে। এসব অভিধানে কোনো অভিন্ন নীতি অনুসৃত হয়নি এবং অন্তর্ভুক্ত শব্দের সংখ্যায়ও রয়েছে বিপুল তারতম্য। বাংলা ভাষায় নিত্য ব্যবহৃত প্রচুর আরবি-ফারসি শব্দের অনুপস্থিতি এসব অভিধানে লক্ষ্য করা যায়।

কেবল বিশুদ্ধ জ্ঞানচর্চায় নিয়োজিত বিদ্বৎ-সমাজের ব্যবহার ও সহায়তার জন্য নয়, বাংলাভাষী সকল শিক্ষিত ব্যক্তির দৈনন্দিন জীবনের পেশাগত অথবা ব্যবসায়িক প্রয়োজনে, বাংলা গদ্যের ইংরেজি রূপান্তরে অথবা বাংলাভাষী শিক্ষিতজনের ইংরেজি রচনার কাজকে সহজতর করার উদ্দেশ্যে বাংলা একাডেমীর বর্তমান অভিধানটি প্রণীত। প্রাতিষ্ঠানিক শিক্ষায় নিয়োজিত বিদ্যার্থীরাও এর থেকে উপকৃত হবেন বলে আমরা আশা করি।

সমাজের প্রয়োজনে ভাষার বিকাশ ও বিবর্তন ঘটে। একটি ভাষাগোষ্ঠীর মনীষা ও চারিত্রের প্রতিফলন ঘটে ভাষার দেহে। প্রত্যেক ভাষার নিজস্ব একটি মেজাজ রয়েছে' যা অনুবাদে বা ভাষান্তরে হারিয়ে যাবার আশঙ্কা থাকে। বাংলা থেকে ইংরেজিতে অনুবাদ করার প্রক্রিয়ায় বাংলা ভাষার শুধু শাব্দিক অর্থ নয়, ব্যঞ্জনটুকুও যাতে ইংরেজি ভাষায় যথাসম্ভব সঞ্চারিত হয়, তার দিকে লক্ষ্য রাখা প্রয়োজন। বর্তমানে অভিধান প্রণয়নকালে এই দিকটির প্রতি বিশেষ লক্ষ্য রাখা হয়েছে।

বর্তমান অভিধান সংকলনকালে বাংলাদেশের বৃহত্তর জনগোষ্ঠীর ভাষা–ব্যবহারের প্রতি বিশেষ দৃষ্টি রাখা হয়েছে। এ অভিধানে শব্দার্থের সঙ্গে শব্দের উৎস-নির্দেশ, পদবিন্যাস, শব্দ ব্যবহারের পরিপ্রেক্ষিত, প্রয়োগবাক্য ইত্যাদি সন্নিবেশিত আছে। শব্দ থেকে জাত বাগ্‌বিধি, প্রবাদ-প্রবচন্ শব্দের সমাসবদ্ধ রূপ প্রভৃতি উপভুক্তিরূপে গৃহীত হয়েছে। যেক্ষেত্রে একই শব্দের একাধিক অর্থ রয়েছে, সেক্ষেত্রে সংখ্যানির্দেশ করে অর্থগুলোকে বিন্যস্ত করা হয়েছে। ভুক্তির মধ্যে ব্যবহৃত ঢেউ (~) চিহ্ন মূল ভুক্তির পরিবর্তে ব্যবহৃত। বানানের ভিন্নতা সত্ত্বেও অর্থ এক হলে তা নির্দেশ করা হয়েছে সমান (=) চিহ্ন দিয়ে। একইভাবে দ্রষ্টব্য অর্থে ব্যবহৃত হয়েছে তীর (⇒) চিহ্ন। চতুর্ভুজ (❑) চিহ্ন ব্যবহৃত হয়েছে পদান্তর নির্দেশের ক্ষেত্রে। বাংলা শব্দের বানানে যথাসম্ভব বাংলা একাডেমীর বানাননীতি অনুসৃত। এ অভিধানের আর একটি বৈশিষ্ট্য হলো, এতে হর-হামেশা-ব্যবহৃত আঞ্চলিক ও নিত্যব্যবহার্য প্রচুর আরবি-ফারসি শব্দ ভুক্তিরূপে গৃহীত হয়েছে।

এ অভিধান রচনায় একদিকে যেমন অভিধানবিজ্ঞানের সাম্প্রতিকতম ধারণাসমূহের ব্যবহার হয়েছে তেমনি শীর্ষশব্দ অন্তর্ভুক্তির সময়ে শব্দের সমকালীন প্রচলন বা ব্যবহারের উপর জোর দেওয়া হয়েছে। শব্দচয়নের আর একটি দিক সম্পর্কেও কিছু বলা দরকার। সাংস্কৃতিক ও সামাজিক রুচিবোধের পরিবর্তনের সঙ্গে সঙ্গে ভাষাও পরিবর্তিত হয় এবং বহু নতুন শব্দ ব্যবহারিক মর্যাদা পায়। শব্দ চয়নে এ দিকেও লক্ষ্য রাখা হয়েছে।

বাংলা একাডেমীর বাংলা–ইংরেজি অভিধান প্রকল্পটি হাতে নেওয়া হয় ১৯৯১ সালের মাঝামাঝি সময়ে। যে কোনো অভিধান সংকলনের কাজ খুব দুরূহ এবং সময় সাপেক্ষ। নির্ধারিত সময়ের মধ্যে এ ধরনের কাজ সম্পন্ন হওয়ার পথেও অনেক বাধা। তা সত্ত্বেও সংকলকদ্বয়ের সহযোগিতায় আমরা যথাসম্ভব অল্প সময়ের মধ্যে পাণ্ডুলিপি প্রণয়নের কাজ সমাপ্ত করেছি।

অভিধানটি প্রকাশের ব্যাপারে যাঁর কৃতিত্ব সর্বাধিক তিনি হলেন একাডেমীর সুযোগ্য মহাপরিচালক প্রফেসর মোহাম্মদ হারুন-উর-রশিদ। তাঁর ক্লান্তিহীন কর্মপ্রেরণা, সম্পাদক ও সংকলকদের যুগপৎ অনুপ্রাণিত ও তাড়িত করার অশেষ ক্ষমতা এ অভিধান রচনাকে সম্ভব করেছে।

প্রকল্পটি বাস্তবায়নে জনাব সেলিনা হোসেনের সক্রিয় ভূমিকা ও আন্তরিক প্রচেষ্টা বিশেষভাবে উল্লেখযোগ্য। জনাব ওবায়দুল ইসলাম এ অভিধান সংকলনের শেষ পর্বে এ উপবিভাগের দায়িত্বে এসে বিশেষ নিষ্ঠার সঙ্গে এর প্রকাশনার সার্বিক দায়িত্ব পালন করেছেন। সংকলন ও প্রকাশনা তত্ত্বাবধানের দায়িত্ব পালনে জনাব লতিফুর রহমান ও ডক্টর স্বরোচিষ সরকার উভয়েই শুধু যে কঠোর শ্রম স্বীকার করেছেন তা নয়–তাঁদের

দুজনের কাজে তাঁরা বিরল নিষ্ঠা ও জ্ঞানস্পৃহার পরিচয় দিয়েছেন। প্রুফ-পঠনে বিশেষ সহায়তা করেছেন জনাব মিজানুর রহমান। জনাব সাইদুর রহমান, জনাব মিন্টু কুমার সূত্রধর, জনাব মোহাম্মদ এমদাদুল হক ও জনাব মোহাম্মদ নজরুল ইসলাম-এর অক্লান্ত পরিশ্রম অভিধানটির কম্পোজের কাজ ত্বরান্বিত করেছে এবং তাঁদের কাছ থেকে আমরা অকুণ্ঠ সহযোগিতা পেয়েছি। এঁদের সকলের কাছে আমরা ঋণী।

অভিধানটি বাংলাদেশের সুধীসমাজে আদৃত হলে এবং ব্যবহারিক প্রয়োজনে কাজে লাগলে আমাদের শ্রম সার্থক হবে।

১৬ আষাঢ়, ১৪০১
৩০ জুন, ১৯৯৪

মোহাম্মদ আলী
মোহাম্মদ মনিরুজ্জামান
জাহাঙ্গীর তারেক

বর্ণানুক্রম

সাধারণ বর্ণানুক্রম

অ আ ই ঈ উ ঊ ঋ এ ঐ ও ঔ ক খ গ ঘ ঙ চ ছ জ ঝ ঞ ট ঠ ড ঢ ণ ত থ দ ধ
ন প ফ ব ভ ম য র ল শ ষ স হ ড় ঢ় য় ৎ ং ঃ ঁ

এই অভিধানে ব্যবহৃত বর্ণানুক্রম

অ আ ই ঈ উ ঊ ঋ এ ঐ ও ঔ ং ঃ ঁ ক খ গ ঘ ঙ চ ছ জ ঝ ঞ ট ঠ ড ড় ঢ
ঢ় ণ ৎ ত থ দ ধ ন প ফ ব ভ ম য য় র ল শ ষ স হ

যুক্তাক্ষরের বর্ণানুক্রম

ক্ক ক্ট ক্ত ক্ষ ক্স গ্‌ণ গ্ধ ঙ্ক ঙ্ক্ষ ঙ্খ ঙ্গ ঙ্ঘ ঙ্ম চ্চ চ্ছ চ্ছ্র জ্জ জ্‌ঝ জ্ঞ
ঞ্চ ঞ্ছ ঞ্জ ঞ্ঝ ট্ট ড্ড ড়্গ ণ্ট ণ্ঠ ণ্ড ণ্ঢ ণ্ন ণ্ম ত্ত ত্থ দ্গ দ্ঘ দ্দ দ্ধ দ্ভ ধ্ব ন্ট ন্ঠ
ন্ড ন্ঢ ন্ত ন্থ ন্দ ন্ধ ন্ন ন্ম প্ট প্ত প্প প্স ব্জ ব্দ ব্ধ ব্ব ভ্র ম্প ম্ফ ম্ব ম্ভ ম্ম
ল্ক ল্গ ল্ট ল্ড ল্প ল্ভ ল্ম ল্ল শ্চ শ্ছ ষ্ক ষ্ট ষ্ঠ ষ্ণ ষ্প ষ্ফ ষ্ম স্ক স্খ স্ট স্ত
স্থ স্প স্ফ হ্ল হ্ন হ্ম

কার চিহ্ন

া ি ী ু ূ ৃ ে ৈ ো ৌ

ফলা চিহ্ন

্ন ্র ্য ্ম ্ল ্ব

স্বরবর্ণ, অনুস্বর, বিসর্গ ও চন্দ্রবিন্দুর বিন্যাসের নমুনা

ক কঅ কআ কই কঈ কউ কঊ কঋ কএ কঐ কও কঔ কং কঃ কঁ কঁক কঁখ ... কা কাঅ
কাআ কাই কাঈ কাউ কাঊ কাঋ কাএ কাঐ কাও কাঔ কাং কাঃ কাঁ কাঁক কাঁখ কাঁগ...
কি কিঅ কিআ কিই কিঈ কিউ কিঊ কিঋ কিএ কিঐ কিও কিঔ কিং কিঃ কিঁ কিঁক কিঁখ
কিঁগ ... কু কুঅ কুআ কুই কুঈ কুউ কুঊ কুঋ কুএ কুঐ কুও কুঔ কুং কুঃ কুঁ কুঁক কুঁখ
কুঁগ.... কৃ কৃঅ কৃআ কৃই কৃঈ কৃউ কৃঊ কৃঋ কৃএ কৃঐ কৃও কৃঔ কৃং কৃঃ কৃঁ কৃঁক কৃঁখ কৃঁগ...

অভিধান ব্যবহারের নির্দেশিকা

এই অভিধানে শব্দের অর্থ, পদ পরিচয়, অর্থান্তর, প্রয়োগ প্রভৃতি কিভাবে নির্দেশ করা হয়েছে নিম্নলিখিত নির্দেশিকায় তা পরিস্ফুট করার চেষ্টা করা হলো :

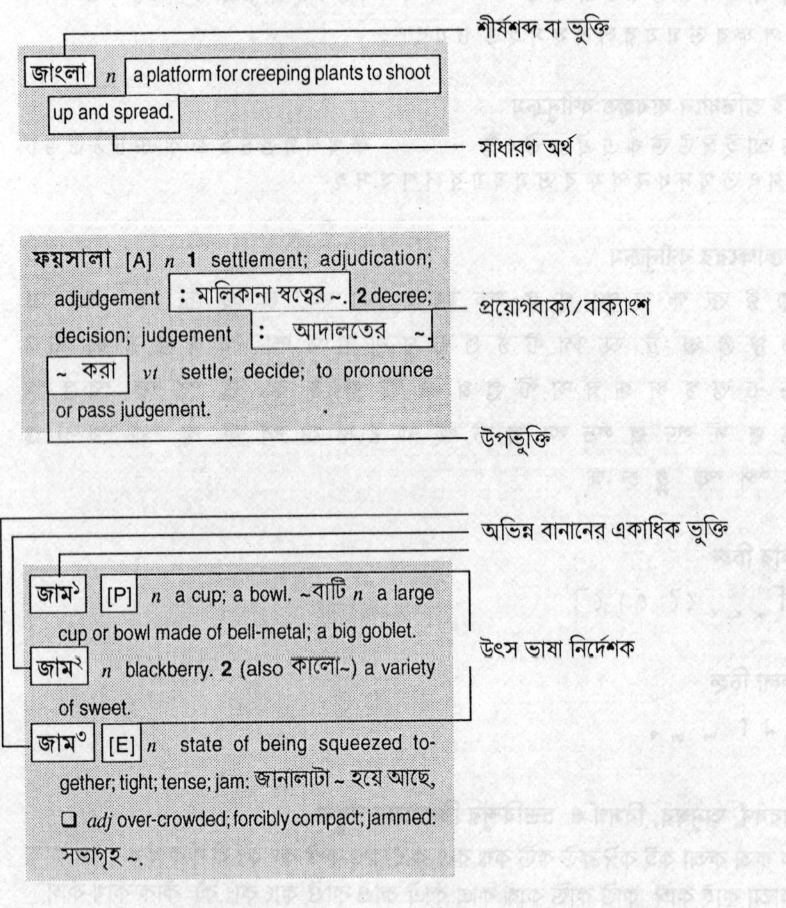

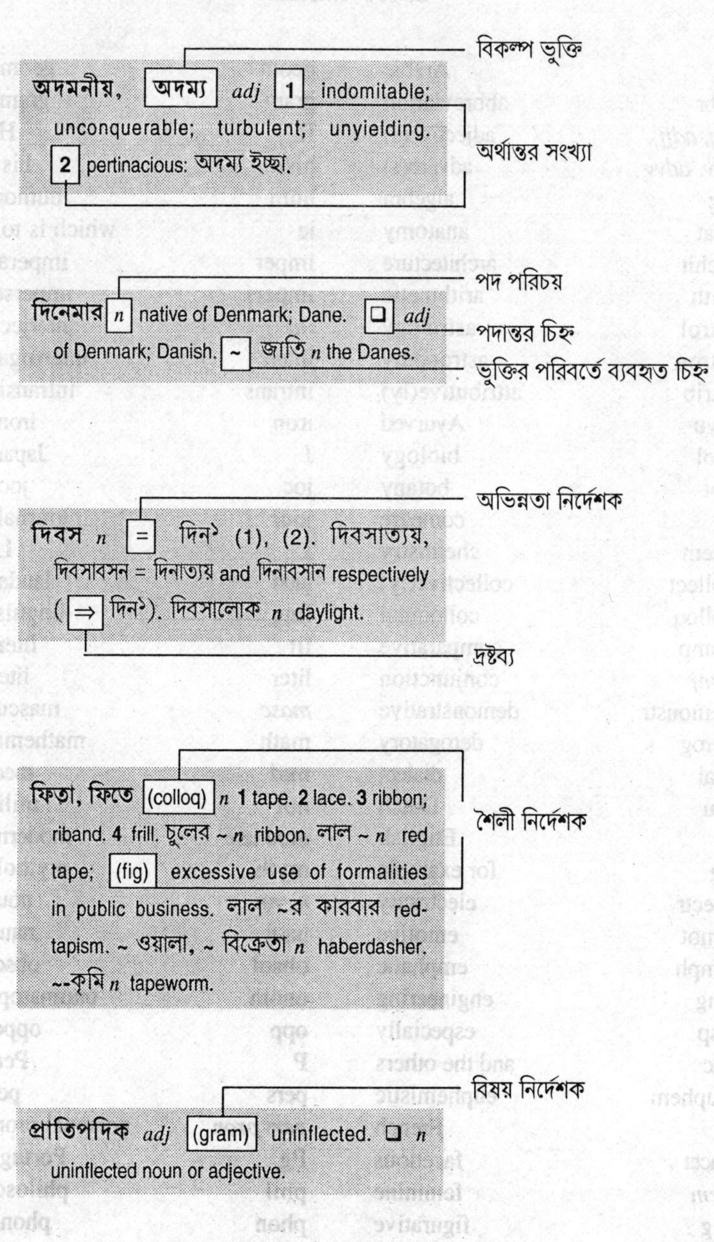

বিকল্প ভুক্তি
অদমনীয়, অদম্য adj 1 indomitable; unconquerable; turbulent; unyielding. 2 pertinacious: অদম্য ইচ্ছা.
অর্থান্তর সংখ্যা
পদ পরিচয়
দিনেমার n native of Denmark; Dane. ❑ adj of Denmark; Danish. ~ জাতি n the Danes.
পদান্তর চিহ্ন
ভুক্তির পরিবর্তে ব্যবহৃত চিহ্ন
অভিন্নতা নির্দেশক
দিবস n = দিন১ (1), (2). দিবসাত্যয়, দিবসাবসন = দিনাত্যয় and দিনাবসান respectively (⇒ দিন১). দিবসালোক n daylight.
দ্রষ্টব্য
ফিতা, ফিতে (colloq) n 1 tape. 2 lace. 3 ribbon; riband. 4 frill. চুলের ~ n ribbon. লাল ~ n red tape; (fig) excessive use of formalities in public business. লাল ~র কারবার red-tapism. ~ ওয়ালা, ~ বিক্রেতা n haberdasher. ~-কৃমি n tapeworm.
শৈলী নির্দেশক
বিষয় নির্দেশক
প্রাতিপদিক adj (gram) uninflected. ❑ n uninflected noun or adjective.

শব্দসংক্ষেপ ও সংকেত
abbreviations

A	Arabic	geom	geometry
abbr	abbreviation	gram	grammar
adj, adjj	adjective(s)	H	Hindi
adv, advv	adverb(s)	hist	history
alg	algebra	hum	humorous
anat	anatomy	ie	which is to say
archit	architecture	imper	imperative
arith	arithmetic	impers	impersonal
astrol	astrology	*int*	interjection
astron	astronomy	interr	interrogative
attrib	attributive(ly)	intrans	intransitive
Ayu	Ayurved	iron	ironical
biol	biology	J	Japanese
bot	botany	joc	jocular
cf	compare	jour	journalism
chem	chemistry	L	Latin
collect	collective(ly)	laud	laudatory
colloq	colloquial	ling	linguistics
comp	comparative	lit	literally
conj	conjunction	liter	literary
demonstr	demonstrative	*masc*	masculine
derog	derogatory	math	mathematics
dial	dialect	med	medical
Du	Dutch	mil	military
E	English	mod use	modern use
eg	for example	myth	mythology
electr	electricity	*n, nn*	noun(s)
emot	emotive	naut	nautical
emph	emphatic	obsol	obsolete
eng	engineering	onom	onomatopoeia
esp	especially	opp	opposite
etc	and the others	P	Persian
euphem	euphemistic	pers	person
F	French	*pers pron*	personal pronoun
facet	facetious	Pg	Portuguese
fem	feminine	phil	philosophy
fig	figurative	phon	phonetics
G	Greek	phr	phrase
geol	geology	phys	physics

physiol	physiology	sb	somebody
pl	plural	*sing*	singular
poet	poetic	sl	slang
pol	politics	sth	something
poss	possessive	*suff*	suffix
pref	prefix	superl	superlative
pres t	present tense	T	Turkish
pron	pronoun	trig	trigonometry
psych	psychology	U	Urdu
pt	past tense	usu	usual(ly)
reflex	reflexive	*vi*	verb intransitive
rel	relative	*vt*	verb transitive
rhet	rhetorical	vulg	vulgar
sarcas	sarcastic	zoo	zoology

Bangla Academy Bengali-English Dictionary

অ[1] *n* the written form of the first vowel sound and 1st letter of the Bengali alphabet. Unlike other vowels অ has no shortened sign (like া ি ী). অ-আ, অ-আ-ক-খ *nn* **1** the letters of the Bengali alphabet. **2** elementary knowledge; the rudiments of learning; ABC: ব্যাকরণের অ-আ-ক-খ.

অ[2] *pref* used before *nn*, *adjj* and *advv*, it indicates negation, absence, want, shortage, contrariety, and hostility (eg অবাঙালি, অকারণ, অযত্ন, অপরিণত, অঘাট, অধর্ম) and is equivalent to various negative prefixes in English, ie, non-, un-, il-, im-, in-, ir-, dis-, mis-, etc; when prefixed by a word beginning with a vowel, অ is replaced by অন, eg অ+অভিজ্ঞ=অনভিজ্ঞ, অ+ঐক্য=অনৈক্য, অ+উর্বর=অনূর্বর, etc.

অওরত⇒ আওরত

অংশ *n* **1** portion or piece of a whole; a section; a constituent or organic part: দেহের অর্ধাংশ (অর্ধ+~); যন্ত্রের অংশ (যন্ত্রাংশ); শহরের পশ্চিমাংশ (পশ্চিম+~); সমাজের বুদ্ধিজীবী ~, the intellectual section of the society. **2** an incomplete portion; a fragment or decimal fraction: ভগ্নাংশ (ভগ্ন+~) ($\frac{1}{5}$, 0·20). **3** a region or geographical division: পার্বত্য ~. **4** a share or allotment: সম্পত্তির ~, কারবারের ~. **5** (geog) $\frac{1}{360}$th part of the earth's circumference; a degree: অক্ষের ~ (অক্ষাংশ). **6** (astrol) $\frac{1}{12}$th part or one of the 12 signs of the zodiac: রাশিচক্রের ~ (রাশি). **7** begetting power of male deities: অবতার দেবতার অংশে জাত, an Avatara is begotten/born of a god. **8** incarnation or personation: বিষ্ণুর ~রূপে ধরাধামে আবির্ভূত, incarnation of Vishnu on earth. **9** point(s) of consideration; any aspect(s) of sth: কোনো কোনো অংশে, in some respects. **~ক** *n* (alg) fractional part of a logarithm; a mantissa; a kinsman; a day. **~ করা** *vi,vt* divide into parts or shares; distribute. **~গত** *adj* included in the rightful or inherited share; relating to a share or portion. **~গ্রহণ** *n* taking part; participation. **~গ্রহণ করা** *vi,vt* take part/ participate (in). **~গ্রাহী** *adj* taking a share; sharing; participating. ❑*n* co-sharer; shareholder; participant; a party. **~ত** *adv* in part; partly; partially: ~ত দায়ী. **~ন** *n* act of dividing/apportioning; apportionment. **~নামা** *n* a deed of partition. **~নীয়** *adj* divisible into parts or shares; to be divided. **~ভাগী** *adj* having a claim to a share; entitled to a share.

অংশাংশ *n* **1** fraction of a share. **2** different shares.

অংশাংশি, **অংশা-অংশি** *n* division into respective shares. ❑*adv* according to respective shares; part by part.

অংশানো *vi,vt* descend/devolve on as an inheritance.

অংশিত *adj* divided into parts or shares; partitioned.

অংশী *adj* constituted (or composed) of parts. ❑*n* **1** one who shares (the sorrows of) or feels (pity for): আমার দুঃখের ~. **2** an associate in business or ownership; partner; co-sharer; shareholder; party; participant. **~দার** *n* one having a share in a property or business. **~দারি** *n* partnership. ❑*adj* relating to partnership.

অংশু *n* **1** ray of light; beam; glow. **2** a fine fibre. **~ক** *n* piece of cloth; fine cloth. **~পট্ট** *n* silk cloth. **~ময়ী** *adj fem* dazzling; luminous; radiant. **~ময়** *mas.* **~মালী** *n* the sun. ❑*adj* blazing; luminous. **~ল** *adj* having rays; full of rays; radiant. **~শিরা** *n* animal having arteries spread all over from one centre like the sun rays; rayed animal; the radiata.

অংশ্যমান *adj* in the process of being divided.

অংস *n* the joint by which the arms are connected with the body; the shoulder. **~কুট**, **~কূট** *n* the hunch on the shoulder of a bull; bull's hump. **~ত্র** *n* protective covering for the upper part of the body worn by soldiers in former times; coat of mail. **~ফলক**, **~ফলকাস্থি** *nn* (anat) the shoulder-blade; the scapula. **~ভার** *n* **1** the load or burden on the shoulder. **2** (fig) being accountable; duty; responsibility. **~ল** *adj* having massive or robust shoulders; broad-shouldered. **~লা** *fem.*

অকচ *adj* having no or not much hair on the scalp; bald; bald-headed. অকচা *fem.*

অকটু *adj* not pungent or bitter; sweet.

অকঠোর *adj* **1** not harsh or severe; mild. **2** easy; simple.

অকণ্টক *adj* **1** thornless; with no pricks. **2** (fig) free from troubles or obstacles; safe and peaceful. **অকণ্টকে** *adv* without let or hindrance; in peace and safety.

অকথন *adj* what cannot be explained or expressed in words; inexplicable: ~ বেদন. ❑*n* abusive, unjust or obscene utterance. **অকথনীয়** *adj* not proper to say; unseemly or indecent to speak.

অকথা *n* abusive, indecent or filthy language (also ~-কুকথা).

অকথিত *adj* unspoken; not pronounced, disclosed or revealed.

অকথ্য *adj* unutterable; unseemly or improper to say: ~ খবর; beyond expression in words: ~ যন্ত্রণা. **~-কথন** *n* improper utterance; abusive words; revile. ❑*adj* indescribable; inexpressible.

অকনিষ্ঠ *adj* without a younger or the youngest son/brother.

অকপট *adj* frank; open; sincere; free from angularities; candid; unreserved. **~তা** *n* frankness; candour. **অকপটে** *adv* frankly; without hiding anything. **~-চিত্ত** *adj* open-hearted; simple-natured; frank. **~চিত্তে** *adv* open heartedly; frankly; freely; sincerely.

অকবজ *adj* not mastered; not acquired.

অকবি *n, adj* one without the genius of a poet; not fit to be called a poet.

অকমনীয় *adj* **1** not to be wished for; undesirable; unwelcome. **2** ungraceful; uncouth; ugly.

অকম্প, অকম্পিত, অকম্প্র *adj* not tremulous or timorous; steady; undaunted; unmoved; unperturbed. **অকম্পনীয়** *adj* not affected by tremors; not sensitive to shaking.

অকর *adj* **1** (of landed estate) rent-free; free-hold; not-liable to taxes. **2** having no hands; handless; armless. **3** without a ray of light; having no radiation.

অকরণ *n* **1** state of being inactive; inactivity; inaction; indolence. **2** illegal act; improper action. **অকরণী** *n* (math) rational quantity; a quantity commensurable with natural numbers, eg, $\sqrt{81}=9$. **অকরণীয়** *adj* what should not be done; not becoming to do. **অকরণীয় ঘর** *n* a family not acceptable or suitable for matrimonial alliance.

অকরুণ *adj* lacking in/not showing kindness; unkind; merciless; cruel.

অকরোটি, অকরোটী *n* the species of animals with partial or no scalp; the acrania.

অকর্কশ *adj* **1** not rough or harsh; soft; tender. **2** smooth to the touch; glossy; slippery.

অকর্ণ *adj* **1** having no ear; deaf. **2** without a helm or rudder: ~ নৌকা. ❑*n* a snake; a serpent.

অকর্তব্য *adj* what ought not to be done; improper to do.

অকর্তা *n* one who is not the doer or performer; not the master of a house or family. ❑*adj* not the principal or chief; secondary; minor. **অকর্তৃত্ব** *n* lack of authority or controlling power.

অকর্ম *n* **1** want of work; inaction, inactivity. **2** a misdeed; a mischief. **~ক** *adj* **1** (gram) a verb not governing any object (intransitive verb). **2** unemployed; out of job. **~-কাণ্ড** *n* spectacular display of misdeeds. **~ণ্য** *adj* **1** disabled; inefficient; ineffective. **2** not in working order; unserviceable. **~ণ্যতা** *n* incompetence; inefficiency; uselessness; worthlessness. **অকর্মা** *adj* **1** good for nothing. **2** lazy; idle; averse to labour. ❑*n* an evil-doer; a mischief-maker. **অকর্মার ধাড়ি** *adj* a great idler; an inveterate bungler.

অকর্মিষ্ঠ *adj* **1** engaged in wrong-doing or mischief-making. **2** inefficient; incompetent; worthless.

অকর্ষিত *adj* unploughed; uncultivated; fallow.

অকলঙ্ক *adj* unblemished; taintless; innocent; pure; graceful. **অকলঙ্কি, অকলঙ্কী** *adj* unblemished; unsullied; undefiled; pure; innocent. **অকলঙ্কিনী** *fem.*

অকলুষ *n* absence of sin or corruption. ❑*adj* sinless; uncorrupted; unsullied; undefiled; innocent (also অকলুষিত).

অকল্পিত *adj* **1** not imaginary; not fancied; real; existing. **2** unexpected; unthought of; sudden.

অকল্যাণ *n* evil; harm; injury; woe; misfortune. **~কর** *adj* harmful; injurious; inauspicious; woeful. **~কারিণী** *fem.*

অকষ্টকল্পনা *n* a thought or supposition arrived at without strain or exertion; free and spontaneous thought or (literary) composition. **অকষ্টকল্পিত** *adj* not laboured or far-fetched; free and spontaneous.

অকস্মাৎ *adv* suddenly; unexpectedly; unwarrantedly; all at once. **~ বজ্রাঘাত** a bolt from the blue; sth quite unexpected.

অকাজ *n* useless, unnecessary or undesirable act; a mischief; a wrong-doing. **অকাজের কাজি** a mischief-monger.

অকাট[১], আকাট *adj* thorough; downright; out-and-out; arrant: ~ মূর্খ, arrant fool.

অকাট[২] *adj* what cannot be disputed; incontrovertible; irrefutable: ~ সত্য।

অকাট্য *adj* what cannot be refuted; irrefutable: ~ যুক্তি; unanswerable; conclusive: ~ প্রমাণ.

অকাঠা *n* timber of inferior quality; trashy wood.

অকাতর *adj* **1** not distressed or afflicted; not stricken with grief; unworried; unagitated. **2** sound of body; free from disease; hale. **3** liberal; ungrudging; unhesitating; unperturbed; unflinching; untiring. **অকাতরে** *adv* **1** with no hesitation in the mind; unflinchingly; liberally; bountifully: অকাতরে দান করা, to bestow liberally. **2** without strain; easily; ungrudgingly; untiringly; spontaneously: অকাতরে পরিশ্রম করা, to work ungrudgingly or untiringly. **3** with carefree ease; calmly; profoundly: অকাতরে ঘুমানো, to sleep profoundly.

অকাম[১] *adj* **1** having no desire or wish. **2** not given to sensual pleasures; not voluptuous/profligate/lustful; having no sex-urge.

অকাম[২], **আকাম** *n* a condemnable or disputable act; an act deserving to be censured.

অকাম্য *adj* not to be wished for; undesirable; unwanted; unwelcome.

অকায় *adj* **1** incorporeal; having no form or physique. **2** eclipsed; ill-fated. **3** the Supreme Being; God.

অকার *n* the letter or the vowel sound 'অ'. **অকারান্ত** *adj* ending with the vowel sound 'অ'.

অকারণ *adj* **1** without any cause or justification. **2** without use, value, meaning or result. ❑*adv* unnecessarily; for nothing. **অকারণে** *adv* = অকারণ *(adv)*.

অকার্য *n* a useless act; a misdeed; a mischief; a bungle. **~কর** *adj* ineffectual; ineffective; futile; not producing the result(s) desired; serving no purpose.

অকাল *n* **1** inopportune/unsuitable/unusual time: ~ বর্ষণ, untimely rain; ~পক্বতা, precociousness; precocity. **2** scarcity; famine; hard times: অকালে কি না খায়, necessity knows no law. **3** an inauspicious time; a time not suitable or appropriate for an auspicious or solemn function. ❑*adj* untimely. **অকালে** *adv* at an inauspicious or unsuitable time; out of time; aforetime. **~কুষ্মাণ্ড** *n* **1** a gourd grown out of season. **2** (fig) a stupid or worthless person. **~জ, ~জাত** *adj* born at an unusual time; untimely or prematurely born. **~পক্ব** *adj* **1** prematurely ripened. **2** behaving like an old man in one's childhood; prematurely clever; precocious. **~বার্ধক্য** *n* premature aging. **~বৃদ্ধ** *adj* gone old prematurely. **~মৃত্যু** *n* untimely or premature death.

অকিঞ্চন *n* one who is utterly poor, destitute or indigent. ❑*adj* inferior; insignificant; worthless; lowly. **~তা, ~ত্ব** *n* indigence; misery; lowliness.

অকিঞ্চিৎ, অকিঞ্চিৎকর *adj* of no importance; insignificant; trivial; worthless. **অকিঞ্চিৎকরতা** *n* insignificance; triviality; worthlessness.

অকীর্তি *n* a disgraceful act; infamy; notoriety. **~কর** *adj* inglorious; infamous; disgraceful.

অকীর্তিত *adj* not celebrated or publicized; unsung and unhonoured.

অকু, অকুআত [A] *n* occurrence; accident; riot; criminal act. **অকুস্থল, অকুস্থান** *n* the place of occurrence of an incident or accident; the venue of a criminal offence.

অকুটিল *adj* open in manner; direct in speech; frank; simple; above-board. **অকুটিলা** *fem.* **~তা** *n* frankness; candour; naivete; naivety.

অকুণ্ঠ, অকুণ্ঠিত *adj* **1** not showing signs of uncertainty or unwillingness in speech or action; unhesitating. **2** unfailing; unhindered; uninterrupted. **3** not distracted, agitated or aggrieved. **অকুণ্ঠিতা** *fem.* **~-চিত্ত** *adj* open-hearted; open-minded; liberal. **~চিত্তে** *adv* unhesitatingly; ungrudgingly; with open mind.

অকুতোভয় *adj* endowed with rare daring; undaunted. **অকুতোভয়া** *fem.* **~তা** *n* a rare feat of daring; complete fearlessness.

অকুল *n* low family; a family not fit for matrimonial alliance.

অকুলন, অকুলান *n* want; shortage; deficit; insufficiency.

অকুলীন *adj* not born of a high family; not aristocratic; having no family status.

অকুশল *n* evil; misfortune; danger. ❑*adj* not adroit or skilful; inexpert.

অকুস্থল, অকুস্থান ⇒ অকু

অকূল *adj* **1** having no limit; boundless; endless; vast. **2** deep; thick; dense. ❑*n* (fig) a great crisis; an extremely critical situation; a very crucial problem. **অকূলে পড়া** *vt* (fig) be in unending crises. **~ পাথার** *n* **1** (lit) an unchanging stretch of land or sea with no sign of human presence; a vast uncharted ocean. **2** (fig) extreme danger; hopeless situation; utter helplessness. **~-ভাসা** *adj* floating on a boundless sea; being in unending affliction. **অকূলে কূল পাওয়া** *vt* get out of danger; be rid of a great jeopardy. **অকূলে ডোবা, অকূলে ভাসা** *vt* meet with an extremely difficult situation; be in inescapable danger. **অকূলের ভেলা** *n* a haven or refuge in utter helplessness.

অকৃত *adj* **1** not done or performed. **2** without results or success; fruitless; useless. **~কর্মা** *adj* unskilled; inefficient; incompetent. **~কার্য** *adj* unsuccessful. **~কার্যতা** *n* failure. **~দার** *adj* unmarried. ~ধী *adj* not resolute; fickle-minded. ~নামা, ~নাম্নী *adj* one whose name is not famous; obscure. ~বিদ্য *adj* uneducated; illiterate.

অকৃতঘ্ন *adj* one who is not ungrateful to one's benefactor; grateful. ~তা *n* gratitude.

অকৃতজ্ঞ *adj* ungrateful. ~তা *n* ingratitude.

অকৃতাদর *adj* **1** a visitor not received with cordiality or attention; unwelcome. **2** one who has not shown cordiality to a visitor.

অকৃতাপরাধ *adj* one who is free from the responsibility for wrong-doing; not guilty; innocent.

অকৃতার্থ *adj* **1** one who has failed to achieve the desired object; unsuccessful in effort. **2** poor; unsuccessful in earning livelihood.

অকৃতিত্ব *n* incapacity; inefficiency; incompetence.

অকৃতী *adj* unworthy; unfit; undeserving.

অকৃত্য *adj* unfit or improper to be done. ❑*n* an improper act; a wrong-doing; a misdeed. ~কারী *adj* a wrong-doer; a mischief-maker.

অকৃত্রিম *adj* **1** real, not pretended; pure; true; genuine; unadulterated: ~ প্রণয়, ~ বন্ধু. **2** natural; not artificial. **3** frank; sincere; not feigned: ~ হাসি. ~তা *n* sincerity; frankness; genuineness; absence of artificiality.

অকৃপণ *adj* **1** not niggardly; liberal; openhanded; generous. **2** extravagant; prodigal; lavish in expenditure. **3** abundant; plentiful; profuse. ~ প্রশংসা *n* commendations without reserve. ~তা *n* liberality; generosity.

অকেজো *adj* **1** unfit for any work; disabled. **2** not in working order; unserviceable; useless.

অকেলাস *adj* not crystallized.

অকেশ *adj* hairless; bald. অকেশী, অকেশা *fem.*

অকৈতব *adj* showing clearly the thoughts and feelings; open; frank; simple; undeceitful.

অকোপ *n* absence of anger. ❑*adj* free of anger or rage.

অকৌশল *n* **1** want of skill or tact; lack of dexterity or adroitness. **2** ill-feeling; quarrel; bad blood.

অক্কা *n* (derog) death. ~ পাওয়া *vi* to die. ~প্রাপ্তি, ~লাভ *n* death; demise.

অক্টোপাস *n* **1** an eight-armed ferocious sea mollusc; octopus. **2** (fig) anything having wide power of causing harm.

অক্টোবর *n* October, the tenth month of the Christian calendar.

অক্ত[১] *adj* (used as *suff)* smeared, covered or marked with oily or sticky substance: কর্দমাক্ত, তৈলাক্ত, লবণাক্ত.

অক্ত[২]⇒ ওক্ত

অক্রম *n* absence of serial order; disorder.

অক্রমিক *adj* without continuity; disordered; unofficial.

অক্রিয় *adj* **1** (of persons) without work; unemployed. **2** not enterprising; lethargic; inactive. **3** out of order; inoperative; not working. ~তা, ~ত্ব *n* inaction; inactivity; indolence. ~কর্মা *adj* given to mischief-making. ❑*n* an evil-doer; a mischief-maker.

অক্রিয়া *n* **1** absence of work or employment; inaction. **2** an improper act; a wrong-doing; a misdeed. ~নিষ্ঠা, ~ন্বিত, ~রত, ~সক্ত *adj* given to mischief-making. ~চরণ *n* misbehaviour; improper conduct.

অক্রীত *adj* **1** not purchased. **2** not for purchase.

অক্রুর *adj* not crooked or cruel; frank; straightforward. ❑*n* (myth) Akrura, an uncle of Sri Krishna.

অক্রেয় *adj* too expensive; extremely dear or costly; unpurchaseable. ~তা *n* costliness; dearness; unpurchaseability.

অক্রোধ *n* absence of anger. ❑*adj* free from anger. অক্রোধিত, অক্রোধী *adj.*

অক্লান্ত *adj* showing no sign of tiredness; unwearied; untiring; indefatigable. ❑*adv* unremittingly; untiringly. ~কর্মা *adj* untiringly laborious; extremely hard-working.

অক্লিষ্ট *adj* **1** not feeling weary; unwearied; untired; indomitable. **2** ceaseless; continuous; undiminished; unfading. ~ শোভা unfading beauty. ~ স্নেহ undiminished affection. ~কর্মা *adj* ungrudging in labour; accomplishing one's job without difficulty.

অক্লীব *adj* **1** having the qualities expected of a man; manly; virile; sexually potent. **2** patient; enduring; forbearing.

অক্লেশ *n* absence of trouble or difficulty. ❑*adj* not troublesome or painful. অক্লেশে *adv* without trouble or difficulty; easily.

অক্ষ *n* **1** a die for gaming; any of the dice in games of chance. **2** the earth's axis. **3** a bead; a perforated seed used as a bead in a rosary. **4** latitude or the angular distance of any place from the equator measured in degrees. **5** a sense organ; the eye: নলিনাক্ষ. **6** political connection (not necessarily alliance) between two or more states. ~ ক্রীড়া *n* game of dice; dice-play. ~পাদ *n* Gautama, the sage, author of a logical treatise. ~বাট *n* **1** wrestling ground; a gymnasium for wrestling. **2** a rendezvous for dice-play. ~বিদ, ~বিৎ, ~বেত্তা *adj* versed in law or diplomacy; clever at dice. ❑*n* a lawyer; a diplomat; an expert dice player. ~বৃত্ত, ~রেখা *n* the parallels of latitude. ~মালা, ~সূত্র *n* a string of beads; a rosary. ~শক্তি *n* the Axis Powers of Germany, Italy and Japan in the World War II.

অক্ষটি⇒ আখেট

অক্ষত *adj* **1** not hurt, wounded or injured: ~ দেহ. **2** unblemished; unimpaired; intact. **3** uncleft; unsevered; entire. ❑*n* sunned rice. ~দেহ, ~ শরীর *adj* one whose person bears no wound; unhurt; unwounded. ~যোনি *adj (fem)* a woman in the state of virginity; having had no sexual intercourse yet; virgin; maiden.

অক্ষম *adj* **1** powerless; weak. **2** incapable; inefficient; incompetent. **3** unfit. **অক্ষমা** *fem.* ~তা *n* inability; impotence; incompetence.

অক্ষমা[1] *n* **1** anger; want of forbearance. **2** intolerance.

অক্ষমা[2] ⇒ অক্ষম

অক্ষয় *adj* **1** undecaying; undying; immortal; eternal. **2** inexhaustible. ~ **কীর্তি** *n* **1** any glorious deed that physically exists for ever. **2** everlasting fame. ~**ভাণ্ডার** *n* inexhaustible stock. ~**তৃতীয়া** *n* the third day of the lunar half of the month of Vaishakh, sacred to the Hindus. ~**লোক** *n* the eternal abode of the blessed; heaven.

অক্ষর *n* **1** a character or letter of alphabet. **2** a syllable. **3** a leaden type. ~**জীবী**, ~**জীবিক**, ~**জীবক** *n* person who earns his bread by writing; a scribe; a copyist; a printer or compositor; a writer. ~ **ডম্বর** *adj* an ostentatious show of a great crowd of letters. ~ **পরিচয়** *n* **1** knowledge of the alphabet. **2** first lessons; initiation into the art of learning. **3** rudimentary learning. ~**বিন্যাস** *n* arrangement of letters; putting in black and white; writing. ~**বৃত্ত** *n* a metrical pattern in Bengali versification. ~**মালা** *n* the alphabet. ~**যোজক** *n* person who arranges words, sentences, pages, etc for printing; a compositor. **অক্ষরে অক্ষরে** *adv* literally; verbatim; to the letter; word for word. **অক্ষরে অক্ষরে পালন করা** *vt* to act strictly (according to advice); carry out (instructions) to the letter; to obey rigorously or with strict exactitude. **অক্ষরান্তরীকরণ** *n* writing (a word, name, sentence, etc) in the alphabet of a different language or system; transliteration. **আক্ষরিক** *adj.*

অক্ষাংশ *n* one of the degrees of latitude; latitude.

অক্ষারলবণ *n* common salt as found in mines, not in the sea; rock-salt.

অক্ষি *n* the eye. ~**কাচ** *n* a lens of spectacles, cameras, microscopes, etc. ~**কোটর** *n* socket of the. ~**তারকা** *n* the pupil or apple of the eye. ~**পক্ষ্ম**, ~**লোম** *n* eye-lash. ~**পট** *n* the retina. ~**পটল** *n* cataract of the eye. ~**পুট** *n* the eye-lid. ~**বিভ্রম** *n* illusion. ~**ভিষক** *n* an oculist; an ophthalmic surgeon. ~**শালাক্য** *n* ophthalmic surgery.

অক্ষীয় *adj* of or concerning the axis of the earth; axial; axile; angular.

অক্ষুণ্ণ[1] *adj* not offended or aggrieved: ~চিত্ত. ~**চিত্তে** *adv* without regret, repining or displeasure.

অক্ষুণ্ণ[2] *adj* **1** unhindered; unchecked; unrestricted; uninterrupted: ~ গতি. **2** uncurbed; undisputed; unopposed: ~ প্রতাপ. **3** untainted; untarnished; undamaged: ~ সতীত্ব. **4** unbroken; unabated; undiminished: ~ মনোবল. **5** unaffected; unimpaired; in force: ~ স্বাস্থ্য. **6** unused; intact: ~ মূলধন.

অক্ষুব্ধ *adj* **1** not perturbed or disturbed; calm; placid: ~ হৃদয়. **2** unruffled; still; tranquil: ~ সাগর. ~ **চিত্ত** *adj* having a steady state of mind; composed. ~ **চিত্তে** *adv* with an undisturbed/unperturbed mind.

অক্ষোভ *n* absence of distraction, perturbation or agitation. ❑*adj* not aggrieved or disgruntled; placid.

অক্ষৌহিণী *n* **1** (myth) an army consisting of 2, 18, 700 combatants. **2** (fig) a vast army.

অক্সিজেন *n* oxygen, an elementary gas.

অখণ্ড *adj* **1** unbroken; undivided; in one piece: ~ সংকলন. **2** unquestioned; undisputed; supreme: ~ প্রতিপত্তি. **3** thick; intense; compact; dense: ~ অন্ধকার. **4** untouched; unused; intact: ~ মূলধন. **5** (math) integral; forming a necessary part of a whole; not fractional: ~ সংখ্যা. ~**তা** *n* integrality; indivisibility; unity. ~**নীয়** *adj* **1** irrefutable; indisputable: ~নীয় যুক্তি. **2** indivisible. ~**নীয়তা** *n* indisputability.

অখণ্ডিত *adj* **1** (of a hoof) unsevered; undivided: ~ ক্ষুর, uncloven hoof. **2** unrefuted: ~ মত.

অখর্ব *adj* not short; tall.

অখল *adj* simple and direct; artless; naive; ingenuous.

অখাত, আখাত *adj* (of watercourses) undug; not made by digging; not excavated; natural.

অখাদ্য *adj* **1** inedible; not fit to be eaten. ❑*n* **1** unwholesome food. **2** forbidden food.

অখিল *adj* **1** entire; whole. **2** vast; huge. ❑*n* the universe; the world. ~**প্রিয়** *adj* loved and respected all over the world.

অখুশি *adj* not satisfied; displeased. ❑*n* dissatisfaction; displeasure.

অখ্যাত *adj* **1** not famous; obscure. **2** negligible; insignificant. **3** despicable; contemptible. ~**নামা** *adj* not famous by name; unknown; obscure.

অখ্যাতি *n* ill-repute; infamy; disgrace; scandal. ~**কর** *adj* disgraceful; scandalous.

অগণন *adj* too many to be counted; countless; innumerable.

অগণনীয় *adj* **1** not countable; innumerable. **2** insignificant; trivial; fit to be ignored.

অগণিত *adj* **1** too many; innumerable. **2** what has not been counted.

অগণ্য *adj* **1** uncountable; innumerable. **2** trifling; trivial; insignificant; negligible.

অগতি *n* **1** helpless person: ~র গতি, the only resort of the helpless; the only way out. **2** adversity; distress; misery; wretchedness. **3** want of proper performance of a dead man's obsequies. ❑*adj* motionless; immobile; static. **~ক** *adj* disadvantageous; awkward. ❑*n* helpless/unfavourable/awkward situation; a tight corner.

অগত্যা *adv* as an unavoidable consequence; having no alternative course left.

অগন্তব্য *adj* **1** (of places) difficult of access or approach; inaccessible. **2** out of bounds; outside the limits of areas that one is allowed to enter.

অগভীর *adj* **1** not deep; shallow. **2** superficial; not profound: ~ জ্ঞান.

অগম *adj* **1** = অগন্তব্য (1). **2** inaccessible; out of bounds. **3** unfathomable; bottomless; too deep. **4** motionless; static. ❑*n* inaccessible place.

অগম্য *adj* = অগন্তব্য (1, 2). **অগম্যা** *adj fem* one with whom sexual intercourse is prohibited.

অগরু⇒ অগুরু

অগস্ট⇒ আগস্ট

অগস্ত্য *n* **1** (astron) the Canopus, a bright star in the southern constellation. **2** a mythological sage of India. **~ যাত্রা** *n* **1** (fig) the ultimate journey; a journey from which one never returns. **2** the first day of the month of Bhadra. **3** (fig) an inauspicious day (usually the first day of a month) to set out on a journey.

অগা, অগাকান্ত, অগাচণ্ডী, অগারাম *adj* **1** (colloq) grossly stupid or ignorant. **2** good for nothing; worthless.

অগাধ *adj* **1** so deep that the bottom cannot be reached; unfathomable: ~ সমুদ্র. **2** without limits; unbounded; unlimited; endless: ~ আকাশ. **3** profound; immense; immeasurable: ~ শান্তি. **4** more than enough; plentiful; inexhaustible: ~ ভাণ্ডার. **5** everlasting; eternal.

অগীত *adj* unsung: ~ সঙ্গীত.

অগুণ *adj* having no worth or qualification. ❑*n* fault; guilt; offence.

অগুনতি *adj* countless; innumerable.

অগুরু[1] *n* the *Dulbergia sisoo* or its timber; a kind of fragrant wood.

অগুরু[2] *adj* one having no spiritual guide or preceptor.

অগোচর *adj* beyond comprehension; out of the range of sense-organs; invisible; unknown. **অগোচরে** *adv* invisibly; without being noticed.

অগোপন *adj* not hidden or concealed; open. **অগোপনীয়** *adj* what cannot or should not be concealed.

অগৌরব *n* **1** dishonour; disgrace. **2** infamy; ill-repute.

অগ্নি *n* **1** fire; flame; blaze. **2** power; force; strength. **3** digestive power; hunger: জঠরাগ্নি. **4** worries; afflictions; mortifications: শোকাগ্নি. **~কণা** *n* a spark. **~কর্ম, ~সংস্কার, ~ সৎকার** *n* cremation of the dead according to Hindu rites. **~কল্প** *adj* **1** fire-like; extremely hot. **2** terribly angry; furious with rage. **~কাণ্ড** *n* **1** destructive fire that burns houses and properties; conflagration. **2** (fig) a boisterous quarrel. **~কুণ্ড** *n* enclosed fireplace; a furnace. **~কোণ** *n* the south-east. **~গর্ভ** fiery; impregnated with fire. **~-গিরি** *n* a volcano. **~চূর্ণ, ~চূর্ণক** *n* explosive substance; gun-powder. **~তপ্ত** *adj* heated with fire; as hot as fire. **~তুল্য** *adj* fire-like, fiery, furious. **~দগ্ধ** *adj* burnt; consumed by fire. **~দাতা** *n, adj* one who sets fire to the mouth of a deceased Hindu at cremation. **~দাত্রী** *fem.* **~দাহ** *n* 1 conflagration. **2** the heat of fire. **~দাহ্য** *adj* capable of catching fire; combustible. **~পক্ব** *adj* **1** cooked on fire; hardened at a fire. **~পরীক্ষা** *n* **1** (fig) a very severe test. **2** an ordeal by fire according to Hindu beliefs. **~পুরুষ** *n, adj* one as vigorous as fire. **~প্রবেশ** *n* the Hindu rite of mounting the funeral pyre of the husband by a widow. **~প্রস্তর** *n* a hard stone from which fire is struck with steel; a flint. **~বর্ণ** *adj* crimson; red as fire. **~বর্ধক** *adj* promoting hunger or digestion. **~বাণ** *n* **1** (myth) fire emitting arrow. **2** (fig) the hardest blow or stroke. **~বৃদ্ধি** *n* stimulation of appetite or digestion. **~বৃষ্টি** *n* **1** (fig) a spell of extreme heat. **2** shower of shells or bullets. **~মন্ত্র** *n* **1** a doctrine having the power of fire. **2** cult of fire; an extremely dangerous or difficult resolve or vow. **~মান্দ্য** *n* loss of appetite; indigestion; dyspepsia. **~মূর্তি, ~শর্মা** *adj* violently angry; livid with rage. **~শর্মা হয়ে ওঠা** *vt* flare up with rage. **~মূল্য** *adj* extremely dear; prohibitive. **~যুগ** *n* (fig) the age of revolution. **~শিখা** *n* a flame of fire. **~শুদ্ধ** *adj* purified by burning in fire. **~শুদ্ধি** *n* purification by burning. **~-সহ** *adj* fire-proof. **~সেবন** *n* warming oneself at the fire; basking in the heat of fire. **~স্ফুলিঙ্গ** *n* spark of fire. **~হোত্র** *n* the Vedic rite of daily oblation. **~হোত্রী** *n* one who performs the above rite.

অগ্ন্যুৎপাত *n* **1** a volcanic eruption. **2** the fall of a meteor, shooting-star or thunderbolt from the sky.

অগ্ন্যুৎসব *n* the display of a fire; out-door merry-making; a bon-fire.

অগ্র *adj* **1** the first or foremost; chief: ~নায়ক. **2** before in time; born before: ~জ. ❑*n* **1** the upper part; the top; the summit; the peak; the apex. **2** an end or extremity: সূচ্যগ্র. **3** the front; the fore-part. **4** an aim; a purpose: একাগ্র. **~গণ্য** *adj* fit to be considered on a priority basis; most important. **~গতি, ~গমন** *n* **1** onward movement; advancement. **2** progress; promotion; development. **~গামী** *adj* moving to the front; going before; leading. **~গামিনী** *fem.* **~জ** *adj* **1** elder brother. **2** born earlier; senior in age; older. **~জা** *fem.* **~জিহ্বা** *n* the small piece of fleshy matter at the root of the tongue, which prevents food from entering the windpipe; the uvula; the epiglottis. **~নী** *adj* leading; prominent; important; principal. ❑*n* a leader; a pioneer. **~দানী** *n* a fallen Brahmin who receives offerings at the obsequies of a Hindu deceased. **~দূত** *n* **1** a leader; a pioneer. **2** a fore-runner; a precursor; a harbinger. **3** (mil) an escort. **~নেতা** *n* a leader; an army commander. **~পথিক** *n* one who goes before in point of time or place; a guide; a precursor. **~পশ্চাৎ** *adv* **1** from beginning to end; alpha and omega. **2** (fig) good and bad; right and wrong. **3** (fig) the past and the future. **~বর্তী** *adj* situated at the front; that which is leading. **~বর্তিনী** *fem.* **~ভাগ** *n* **1** the top or the peak. **2** an extremity or end. **3** the first part or share. **~মহিষী** *n fem* the queen-consort. **~সর** =~গামী. **~সূচনা** *n* a presage; a foreboding; a preface; a foreword. **~স্থ, ~স্থিত** *adj* situated in the front/on the top/at the end.

অগ্রহণীয় *adj* not fit to be supported or agreed to; unacceptable.

অগ্রহায়ণ, অঘ্রান *n* the eighth month of the Bengali calendar.

অগ্রাধিকার *n* priority; the right to have or do sth before others.

অগ্রাহ্য *adj* **1** not fit to be accepted or approved. **2** fit to be slighted or ignored. **3** rejected; not approved.

অগ্রিম *adj* **1** advance; paid or payable in advance. **2** first; chief. **3** eldest. **~ক** *n* the part of cost or charge paid as advance or earnest money. **~ চুক্তি** *n* forward contract.

অগ্রিয়, অগ্রীয় *adj* **1** chief; best; first. **2** concerning the front or top. **3** advance. **~ প্রদান** *n* part payment made in token of a bargain; payment on account.

অগ্রে *adv* **1** in advance; in the first place. **2** before; in front: বিচারকের ~.

অগ্র্য *adj* **1** former. **2** first. **3** best.

অঘ *n* **1** irreligiousness; a sin. **2** blemish; scandal. **3** sorrow; misery.

অঘটন *n* **1** unlikely or unusual incident: ~ যদি ঘটেই . **2** non-occurrence. **~ঘটনপটিয়সী** *adj fem* skilled in making the impossible possible. **অঘটনীয়** *adj* not likely to occur. **অঘটিত** *adj* what has not occurred.

অঘর *n* family of lower status and so unfit for matrimonial connection.

অঘা, অঘাচণ্ডী, অঘারাম=অগা

অঘাট, আঘাট *n* **1** a place by a watercourse not fit to be used as a landing stage. **2** out of the way place.

অঘোর[১] *adj* **1** deep; profound: ~ নিদ্রা. **2** terrible, awful: ~ বাদল. **অঘোরে পড়ে থাকা** *vi* lie unconscious. **অঘোরে** *adv* deeply; profoundly; unconsciously.

অঘোর[২] *adj* not terrible; calm; quiet. ❑*n* god Shiva of the Hindus: ~-মন্ত্র. **~পন্থী** *n* a sect of Shiva worshippers practising abominable rites.

অঘোষ *adj* (phon) unvoiced; voiceless. **~ বর্ণ** *n* the consonant sounds that do not produce usual vibration in the vocal cords (eg, ক খ চ ছ ট ঠ ত থ প ফ).

অঘ্রাত⇒ অনাঘ্রাত

অঘ্রান⇒ অগ্রহায়ণ

অঙ্ক, অংক *n* **1** (math) a sum; an arithmetical problem: ~ কষা. **2** (math) number; digit; figure. **3** counting; calculation. **4** the lap: মাতৃ ~. **5** an act of a play: একাঙ্ক নাটিকা. **6** blemish; spot: কলঙ্ক. **6** an ornament; decoration. **~ কষা** *vt* to do or work out a sum; to count or calculate. **~গত** *adj* **1** lying on or in the lap (of). **2** in possession or under control (of). **~দেশ** *n* **1** the lap. **2** the surface of the belly; the ventral surface. **~পাত** *n* **1** placing figures or numbers. **2** doing sums. **3** marking with signs; impression: আমার উপদেশ তার মনে কোনো ~পাত করেনি, my advice made no impression on his mind. **~পাতন** *n* (math) system of signs or symbols representing numbers as in algebra; notation. **~বাচক** *adj* cardinal: ~বাচক সংখ্যা, cardinal numbers, eg 4, 5, 6 (contrasted with ordinal numbers, eg 4th, 5th, 6th). **~বিদ, ~বিৎ, ~বেত্তা, ~শাস্ত্রবিৎ, ~শাস্ত্রবেত্তা** *n* mathematician. **~বিদ্যা, ~শাস্ত্র** *n* mathematics. **~লক্ষ্মী** *n* wife; the mistress of a house. **~লগ্ন** *adj* **1** placed on the lap. **2** proximate; close (to). **~শায়ী** *adj* lying on the lap; (fig) enamoured. **~শায়িনী** *fem.* **~স্থিত** *adj* **1** situated on the lap. **2** very close (to). **3** under control or in possession.

অঙ্কন *n* **1** drawing or painting. **2** marking; impression. **3** writing down of figures or numbers. **4** (geom) act of plotting; construction. **অঙ্কনি** *n* drawing or painting implements (pencil, brush, etc). **অঙ্কনীয়** *adj* **1** to be marked, drawn or painted. **2** (geom) to be plotted or constructed.

অঙ্কিত *adj* **1** marked; written. **2** drawn; painted; carved; engraved. **3** described or portrayed: ~ চরিত্র. **4** imprinted: মানসপটে ~. **5** (geom) plotted; constructed.

অঙ্কুর *n* **1** seedling; sapling; sprout: বীজাঙ্কুর. **2** origination; germination; first stage: ভাবের ~. **3** root; source; commencement. **4** an end or tip: তৃণাঙ্কুর, কুশাঙ্কুর. **5** a bud; a blossom. **অঙ্কুরে বিনাশ করা** *vi,vt* to nip in the bud.

অঙ্কুরিত *adj* **1** sprouted; germinated. **2** published; revealed. **অঙ্কুরোদয়, অঙ্কুরোদ্গম** *n* **1** sprouting; blossoming; germination. **2** commencement; beginning. **~ হওয়া** *vi,vt* sprout; germinate; come out.

অঙ্কুশ, অঙ্কুষ *n* iron goad used by an elephant driver.

অঙ্কোপরি *adv, prep* on the lap.

অঙ্গ *n* **1** the body; physique. **2** appearance; shape; form. **3** an organ of the body; a limb: চলার ~, ie foot. **4** a part; a portion: নিম্নাঙ্গ. **5** state; condition; feature: উচ্চাঙ্গের রচনা. **6** scale; measure: উচ্চাঙ্গ সঙ্গীত. **7** an ingredient or element; a component; an item: যৌতুকের ~. **~গ্রহ** *n* **1** convulsion of the body; muscular spasm. **2** tetanus. **~গ্লানি** *n* **1** physical exertion; tiredness of the body. **2** filth, dirt or soil of the body. **~চালন** *n* **1** the movement of the body or limbs. **2** physical exercise. **~চ্ছেদন, ~চ্ছেদন** *n* **1** amputation of a limb. **2** removal or separation of a part; mutilation. **~জ.** *n* offspring; children; progeny. ❑*adj* born of one's body. **~জা** *fem.* **~ত্র, ~ত্রাণ** *n* armour; a coat of mail. **~ন্যাস** *n* act of touching parts of the body while uttering charms and incantations. **~প্রত্যঙ্গ** *n* different limbs and appendages of the body. **~প্রসাধন, ~রাগ** *n* **1** dressing, decoration or embellishment of the body. **2** toiletry or cosmetics. **~প্রায়শ্চিত্ত** *n* purification of the body for remission of sins; expiatory rite of the Hindus to remove the taint of the body. **~বিকৃতি** *n* deformity. **~বিন্যাস** *n* posing; posture; a gesture. **~বিহীন** *adj* **1** wanting in one or more limbs; crippled; deformed. **2** bodiless; formless; incorporeal. **3** imperfect; incomplete. **~বিহীনা** *fem.* **~ভঙ্গি ~ভঙ্গিমা** *n* a physical gesture for communicating one's intention; a beckoning. **~মর্দক** *n* a masseur. **~মর্দিকা** *fem.* masseuse. **~মর্দন** *n* massage. **~মোটন** *n* stretching or straightening of the body for removing inertia, lethargy or weariness. **~সংস্কার** *n* **1** meticulous dressing of the body. **2** scouring or scrubbing of the body. **~সেবা** *n* **1** massage of the body. **2** act of beautifying the body with cosmetics. **~সৌষ্ঠব** *n* beautiful symmetry or shapeliness of the body. **~হানি** *n* **1** loss or damage of a limb. **2** omission; imperfection or defect in any part of a thing.

অঙ্গন *n* **1** the compound of a house; a courtyard. **2** a vestibule; a terrace. **3** (fig) the body; physique: প্রাণের ~.

অঙ্গনা *n fem* **1** a woman. **2** a beautiful wife; a graceful woman.

অঙ্গাঙ্গি *adj* co-related like the mutual attachment of different limbs of a body: ~জড়িত. ❑*n* preferential treatment or partiality towards a party-man. **~ভাব, ~সম্বন্ধ** *n* inseparable intimacy; intimate friendship. **~ভাবে** *adv* inseparably.

অঙ্গাবরণ *n* covering for the body; a garment.

অঙ্গার, অংগার *n* **1** solid, black, fossil substance used as fuel; coal; cinder; charcoal. **2** (fig) person causing shame or disgrace: কুলাঙ্গার. **~ক** *n* chemical element denoted by C; carbon. **~ক রসায়ন** *n* branch of chemistry dealing with carbon compounds. **~ক মণি** *n* the white or reddish hard substance found in tropical oceans; coral. **~কৃষ্ণ** *adj* coal-black; black as coal. **~তুল্য** *adj* having the qualities of charcoal. **~ধানী, ~ধানিকা** *n* an incense-pot; a censer. **অঙ্গারিত** *adj* carbonized; turned into coal. **অঙ্গারীয়** *adj* related to coal; carbonaceous. **~যৌগিক** *n* carbon compounds.

অঙ্গারাম্ল *n* carbonic acid.

অঙ্গিকা *n* bodice; a modesty vest.

অঙ্গী *adj* having a body or form; corporeal. **অঙ্গিনী** *fem.*

অঙ্গীকরণ *n* promising or making a pledge.

অঙ্গীকার *n* **1** a promise or undertaking; a pledge. **2** consent; acceptance; approval. **~ করা** *vi,vt* make a promise/pledge. **অঙ্গীকারাবদ্ধ** *adj* bound by a promise; promise-bound.

অঙ্গীকৃত *adj* promised; bound by promise; under a pledge: ~ অর্থ.

অঙ্গীভূত *adj* embodied; incorporated; included in the body. **~ করা** *vi* take in; include; make a part (of): বিজিত অঞ্চল রাজ্যের ~ করা, to annex the conquered territory.

অঙ্গুরি, অঙ্গুরীয়, অঙ্গুরীয়ক *n* a finger ring; an ornamental ring for the finger.

অঙ্গুলি, অঙ্গুলী *n* any of the five digits of the hand or foot; a finger or toe. **~ত্র, ~ত্রাণ** *n* a metal cap or covering for the finger-tip used while sewing or playing on musical instrument; a thimble. ~সঙ্কেত, ~হেলন, ~নির্দেশ *n* act of beckoning or directing with the finger. ~মোটন, ~স্ফোটন *n* snapping of the finger.

অঙ্গুষ্ঠ *n* the thumb.

অঙ্গুস্তানা, অংগুস্তানা, অঙ্গুষ্ঠানা *n* **1** thimble used for protection of finger in sewing or in playing on musical instruments. **2** a strap or piece of leather used for sharpening razors.

অচকিত *adj* **1** not alarmed or perturbed. **2** not surprised or taken aback.

অচক্রী *adj* free and open in speech and manner; frank; candid; above-board.

অচঞ্চল *adj* **1** not restless/ fickle/impatient. **2** unwavering; firm; steady; calm.

অচতুর *adj* **1** not clever. **2** not adroit; guileless; artless.

অচন্দ্রচেতন *adj* having no sexual urge; asexual.

অচপল *adj* not fickle; unwavering; steady; firm. অচাপল্য *n* steadiness; firmness.

অচরিতার্থ *adj* **1** not gratified; unfulfilled; unsuccessful.

অচল *adj* not moving; stationary; motionless. **2** not current; gone out of practice; obsolete: ~ প্রথা. **3** counterfeit; forged; fake: ~ টাকা. **4** outcast; ostracized: সমাজে ~ **5** not fit to be used; unserviceable: ~ ঘড়ি. **6** not throbbing; what cannot be kept going: ~ ব্যবসা. **7** not pulsating; still: ~ নাড়ি. **8** untenable; unacceptable: ~ যুক্তি. **9** not practicable; impractical: ~ প্রস্তাব. ❑*n* a mountain; a hill. ~অবস্থা, অচলাবস্থা *n* a position from which there is no way out; impasse; deadlock; stalemate. ~ন *n* the condition of being antiquated ; obsoleteness. ~নীয় *adj* not suitable to be introduced or circulated. ~প্রতিষ্ঠ *adj* firmly established. অচলিত *adj* out of date; antiquated; obsolete; not in current use,

অচলায়তন *n* unprogressive or reactionary institution. ❑*adj* unprogressive; unchanging; still.

অচলা *adj fem* firm in standing or position; constant in mind and purpose; unwavering: অচলা ভক্তি. ❑*n* the earth.

অচাঞ্চল্য, অচাপল্য *n* absence of restlessness; steadiness; calmness.

অচালনীয়, অচাল্য *adj* what cannot be conducted or transferred.

অচিকিৎসক *n* a quack; a charlatan.

অচিকিৎসা *n* want of medical treatment; faulty medical treatment; quackery. **অচিকিৎস্য, অচিকিৎসনীয়** *adj* what cannot be cured; incurable; irremediable.

অচিকীর্ষু *adj* averse to work, indolent; lazy.

অচিন *adj* (dial) unknown; unidentified: ~ পাখি. ❑*n* an outsider; a stranger; one who is unfamiliar.

অচিন্তনীয়, অচিন্ত্য *adj* unthinkable; beyond imagination. অচিন্তনীয়া *fem.*

অচিন্তিত, অচিন্তিতপূর্ব *adj* what could not be conceived of before; unthought of; unexpected.

অচির *adj* not durable; transitory; brief; short. ~তা *n* the condition of being transient; transitoriness. ~কালে *adv* within a short time; before long; shortly; soon. ~জীবী *adj* not everlasting; perishable; transient; ephemeral. ~দ্যুতি, ~প্রভা *n* flash of light that precedes thunder; lightning. ~স্থায়ী *adj* not permanent; transitory; momentary. অচিরে *adv* without delay; soon; immediately.

অচিহ্নিত *adj* unmarked; without an identifying mark. ~কর্মচারী *n* uncovenanted employee.

অচিরাৎ *adv* in no time; soon; immediately; suddenly.

অচূর্ণ, অচূর্ণিত *adj* **1** not pulverized; not reduced to dust. **2** not destroyed; intact; whole; entire.

অচেতন *adj* **1** senseless and motionless; unconscious; fainted. **2** without life or animation; inanimate. **3** wanting sensibility; insensate; stupefied. **4** enchanted; bewitched; affected with an illusion. **5** ignorant; foolish.

অচেনা *adj* unknown; unfamiliar. ❑*n* an unknown person.

অচেষ্ট *adj* **1** having no initiative; unenterprising; effortless. **2** benumbed; stupefied. **অচেষ্টিত** *adj* **1** unattempted; untried. **2** not examined or sought for.

অচৈতন্য *adj* unconscious; senseless; fainted. ❑*n* ignorance; stupefaction.

অচ্ছ *adj* **1** transparent; crystalline. **2** translucent; allowing light to pass through but not transparent. ❑*n* transparent natural substance like quartz; crystal.

অচ্ছদ, অচ্ছন্ন *adj* uncovered; roofless; open.

অচ্ছিদ্র *adj* **1** having no hole or opening. **2** free from defect or loophole; perfect; flawless.

অচ্ছিন্ন *adj* not cut or divided; not torn; intact; whole. ~ত্বক *adj* (of male person) one whose foreskin has not been removed; uncircumcised.

অচ্ছুত, অচ্ছুৎ *adj* untouchable; unclean; low-caste Hindu community considered untouchable by higher castes: ~ জাতি.

অচ্ছেদ্য *adj* what cannot be cleft or split; uncleavable; inseparable: ~ বন্ধন.

অচ্ছোদ *adj* clear; transparent: ~ সরসী নীরে.

অচ্যুত *adj* not fallen or detached.

অছি [A]*n* a trustee having the charge of an orphan's property; a guardian; a custodian; a regent; an administrator; an executor.

অছিঅত, অছিয়ত [A] *n* **1** one's death-time advice or direction. **2** a will and testament. **~নামা** (অছিয়ত A+নামা P) *n* the letter or document appointing a trustee or executor; a deed of will saying how one's property is to be administered or divided after one's death.

অছিলা [A] *n* **1** an occasion; medium. **2** a pretext; a plea; an excuse; a pretence.

অজ১ *adj* (derog) thorough; downright; utter: ~ মূর্খ. ~ **পাড়াগাঁ** *n* a backward village.

অজ২ *n* **1** the billy-goat; the ram . **2** (astrol) the Ram, the Aries. **অজা** *fem.*

অজ৩ *adv* unborn; self-existent; eternal.

অজগর *n* a python or boa-constrictor; a large non-poisonous snake that can swallow up a goat or a deer.

অজচ্ছল *adj* more than enough; profuse.

অজন্ত *adj* (a word) ending with a vowel sound.

অজন্মা *n* failure of crops; scarcity; famine. ❑*adj* bastard; illegitimate.

অজপা⇒ অজিফা

অজবুক=উজবুক

অজয় *n* **1** absence of victory. **2** defeat; discomfiture. ❑*adj* unconquerable; invincible.

অজর *adj* not subject to old age; not decaying.

অজরামর [অজর+অমর] *adj* not subject to decrepitude and death; never aging or dying.

অজস্র *adj* innumerable; abundant; profuse. ❑*adv* incessantly; always.

অজা⇒ অজ২

অজাগর১= অজগর

অজাগর২ *adj* asleep; in a sleeping state.

অজাচার*n* insincerity; sexual promiscuity; incest.

অজাত *adj* **1** bastard; illegitimate. **2** low-born. ❑*n* **1** what is not yet born. **2** family of lower status. **~শত্রু** *adj* one whose enemy is not yet born; having no enemy. ❑*n* the name of the son of Bimbishar, the king of ancient Magadha. **~শ্মশ্রু** *adj* one whose beard has not yet grown; not yet grown to manhood.

অজানত⇒অজান্তে

অজানা, অজানিত *adj* **1** unknown; unfamiliar. **2** unknowable; beyond knowledge or comprehension.

অজান্তে, অজানত (archaic)*adv* **1** unknowingly; unconsciously. **2** secretly; surreptitiously; stealthily.

অজিজ্ঞাস *adj* uninquisitive; unwilling to know.

অজিজ্ঞাসিত *adj* unasked; one who has not been questioned. **অজিজ্ঞাস্য** *adj* not fit for asking; not to be inquired.

অজিত *adj* unconquered; unbeaten; unsurpassed.

অজিতেন্দ্রিয় *adj* (liter) of uncontrolled passion; having no control over the senses; intemperate.

অজিন *n* **1** the skin of a goat or deer or wolf. **2** hides; a seat made of leather.

অজিফা, ওযীফা [A]*n* **1** a selection of Qoranic verses which a Muslim reads or recites at the end of canonical prayers. **2** food and clothing; maintenance.

অজীর্ণ *n* indigestion; dyspepsia. ❑*adj* undigested.

অজু, ওজু, ওযু [A]*n* ablution; ceremonial washing for saying prayers, according to Islam.

অজুরদার *n* [A আজর+দার P] a labourer; one who works for wages; wage-earner.

অজুরা⇒আজুরা

অজুহাত, ওজুহাত [A] *n* **1** cause; reason; ground. **2** a plea; an excuse; a pretext; a pretence.

অজেয় *adj* unconquerable; invincible; insuperable.

অজৈব *adj* not belonging to an organism; inorganic: ~ রসায়ন; mineral: ~ লবণ, ~ সার.

অজ্ঞ *adj* ignorant; uninformed; foolish. **~তা** *n* ignorance; stupidity; foolishness; want of education. **~তামূলক** *adj* proceeding from or caused by ignorance.

অজ্ঞাত *adj* unknown; unpublished; secret, mysterious. **~কুলশীল** *adj* one whose family and antecedents are not known; of obscure origin. **~নামা** *adj* not famous by name; unknown; unidentified. **~পরিচয়***adj* one whose identity is not known. **~পূর্ব** *adj* not known before; hitherto unknown. **~বাস** *n* livinig incognito. **~ রাশি** *n* (math) unknown quantity. **~সারে, অজ্ঞাতে** *adv* secretly; imperceptibly; unawares, beyond one's knowledge.

অজ্ঞান *adj* **1** ignorant; illiterate; foolish. **2** unconscious; fainted; infatuated. ❑*n* **1** want of knowledge; lack of education; ignorance. **2** (phil) illusion; delusion; false idea or belief. **~তা** *n* ignorance. **~কৃত** *adj* done through ignorance; committed unknowingly or unconsciously. **~ত, অজ্ঞানে** *adv* unknowingly; through ignorance. **~তিমির** *n* gloom of ignorance. **~তিমিরাচ্ছন্ন** *adj* wrapped up or enveloped in (the gloom of) ignorance.

অজ্ঞেয় *adj* unknowable; incomprehensible.

অজ্ঞেয়বাদ *n* (phil) the belief or doctrine that nothing can be known about God or of anything except material things; agnosticism.

অঝোর, অঝর *adj* incessant; unceasing: ~ বাদল. **অঝোরে, অঝরে** *adj* ceaselessly; profusely; in torrents.

অঞ্চল *n* **1** the loose end or marginal portion of a woman's sari. **2** a region or locality: পাহাড়ি ~. **3** border; brim: নয়নক অঞ্চল চঞ্চল ভাণ. **~প্রভাব** *n* domination or influence of the wife over the husband; petticoat government.

অঞ্চিত *adj* **1** what has been curved; tortuous(কুঞ্চিত). **2** worshipped. **3** raised; thrilled (রোমাঞ্চিত). **4** strung; composed; woven; collected (সঞ্চিত). **5** decorated; dressed; adorned; ornamented. **~ ভ্রূ** *adj* one with curved eye-brow.

অঞ্জন, আঞ্জ, আঞ্জন *n* **1** eye-salve; antimony; collyrium. **2** gloom; dimness; dullness; darkness; blemish (নিরঞ্জন). **3** various minerals described in the Ayurvedic science (রসাঞ্জন, নীলাঞ্জন).

অঞ্জনি *n* kind of small tumour or sore.

অঞ্জনিকা *n* a small boil or tumour on the edge of the eyelid; a sty.

অঞ্জলি *n* **1** palms of hands put together; hands cupped together as a token of respect. **2** a handful. **3** worship; adoration; devotion. **4** offering before an idol; oblation. **~পুট** *n* cavity formed by clasped palms. **~পুটে** *adv* with clasped palms or folded hands. **~বদ্ধ** *adj* having the palms folded or cupped together. ❑*n* act of folding or cupping the palms of hands. **~ বন্ধন** *n* act of forming cavity by clasping of the palms.

অটবি, অটবী *n* **1** forest. **2** tree.

অটল *adj* **1** unshaken; firm; steady; fixed. **2** unperturbed; unflinching; resolute.

অটুট *adj* **1** unbroken; intact; whole; entire. **2** flawless; unimpaired; sound.

অটো [E] *n* otto, a kind of perfume; attar.

অটোগ্রাফ [E] *n* autograph, ie a person's own handwriting, esp his signature.

অট্ট *adj* very loud. **~নাদ, ~নিনাদ, ~রব, ~রোল** *n* a very loud sound; uproar. **~হাস, ~হাসি, ~হাস্য** *n* very loud or roaring laughter.

অট্টালিকা *n* a big building; an edifice; a palace; a mansion.

অডিকোলন [F] *n* eau de cologne, a French perfume.

অডিট [E] *n* audit or examination of accounts by authorized experts; official examination of accounts. **অডিটর** *n* authorized examiner of accounts; auditor.

অড়হর, অড়র *n* a variety of pulse.

অঢেল, আঢেল *adj* plentiful; enough; immense; sufficient; inexhaustible: ~ সম্পদ.

অণিমা *n* **1** fineness; subtlety; the condition of being extremely slender. **2** faculty or power acquired by yogic practices which, it is believed, enables one to assume an atomic form and move about everywhere invisibly.

অণু *n* minutest particle of matter; atom; molecule. **2** ❑*adj* a little; a bit: ~ পরিমাণ. **~মাত্র** *adj* just a little; infinitesimal; least: ~মাত্র সংশয়. **~ বীক্ষণ** *n* an optical instrument for magnifying; microscope.

অণুচ্ছেদ⇒অনুচ্ছেদ

অণ্ড *n* **1** an egg. **2** either of the two scrotal glands; testicles. **~কোষ** *n* the scrotum; the scrotal sack. **~জ** *adj* born of an egg; oviparous. **অণ্ডাকার, অণ্ডাকৃতি** *adj* egg-shaped; oval. **অণ্ডালু** *adj* having eggs; oviparous.

অত, অতো *adj* so much; so many: ~ টাকা নেই. ❑*adv* in great amount; in plenty: ~ খেয়ো না. ❑*pron* that much: ~ দেবো না. **~শত** *adj* detailed; elaborate: ~শত দেখতে হবে না. ❑*adv* very thoroughly: ~শত বুঝি না.

অতএব *conj* hence; so; therefore; consequently.

অতঃপর *conj* hereafter; henceforth; after this; afterwards; then.

অতট *n* a steep surface; a plateau; a table-land; a river-bank high above the water level. ❑*adj* **1** without shore or bank. **2** vast; extensive.

অতথ্য *adj* inaccurate; inexact; improper; untrue; false.

অতদবির [অ+A তদবির] *n* non-supervision; absence of effort; want of enterprise. **অতদবিরে** *adv* in the absence of supervision or enterprise.

অতনু *n* Madana, the Hindu god of love. ❑*adj* **1** incorporeal; having no body or form. **2** not slender; large. **~রতি** *n* sex-urge; amorous sport.

অতন্দ্র, অতন্দ্রিত *adj* **1** sleepless; not sleeping, awake: ~ নয়ন. **2** untiring; unceasing; non-stop: জ্ঞানচর্চায় ~. **3** watchful; vigilant; attentive: ~ প্রহরী. **4** bright; shining; luminous; radiant. ❑*adv* indefatigably; diligently; actively and energetically. **অতন্দ্রিতা** *adj fem* sleepless; awake.

অতর্ক *n* useless or futile argument; bad or fallacious reasoning. **~নীয়** *adj* what cannot be settled by reasoning; not debatable or arguable.

অতর্কিত *adj* unthought of; unanticipated; unnoticed; sudden; surprise: ~ আক্রমণ. **অতর্কিতে** *adv* suddenly; in a surprising manner; in an unguarded state; unawares.

অতল *n* the hollow or bowels of the earth; (myth) one of the seven underworlds. ❑*adj* **1** bottomless; unfathomable; abysmal; extremely deep. **2** inaccessible; unapproachable; unknowable; out of reach.

অতলস্পর্শ *adj* extremely deep; having a bottom that cannot be touched or reached.

অতলন্ত⇒অতলান্ত

অতলান্ত, অতলন্ত [E] *n* the Atlantic ocean.

অতশত⇒অত

অতসী *n* **1** a kind of yellow flower. **2** linseed; flaxen. **3** the linseed plant; flax.

অতি *adv, prep* used as *pref* in the sense of excessive, improper, over, etc: ~মাত্র, অত্যাচার. ❑*n* excess; superabundance; extremity; intensity: অতির কিছুই ভালো নয়, too much of a thing is no good. ❑*adj* **1** improper; unreasonable; unjustifiable; unbecoming: ~মান, ~বাড়. **2** excellent: ~নাগর. ❑*attrib adj* too much; too many; great excessive: ~গরম. **~কথা** *n* exaggeration; hyperbole. **~কায়** *adj* gigantic; huge; enormous; monstrous. **~ক্ষণিক** *adj* transitory; transient; momentary; short-lived. **~ঘরন্তি** *adj fem* a woman whose household is her be-all and end-all; skilled or adept in house keeping. **~চার** *n* quick movement; (astrol) the fall or deviation of a planet at an unusual pace. **~চালাক** *adj* over-clever; much too crafty: ~চালাকের গলায় দড়ি, too much cunning overreaches itself; the fox must pay his skin to the furrier. **~জন** *n* the majority. **~জীবন** *n* long life; survival. **~জীবিত** *adj* long-lasting; stable for a long time; durable; enduring. **~তপ্ত** *adj* superheated. **~দর্প** *n* too much vanity; extreme haughtiness; excessive arrogance: ~দর্পে হত লঙ্কা, pride goeth before destruction; pride hath its fall. **~দৈব** *adj* unworldly; unearthly; supernatural; superhuman; miraculous; transcendental. **~পরিপক্ব** *adj* precocious; prematurely ripe. **~পাত** *n* spending (of time); passing one's days (দিনাতিপাত, কালাতিপাত). **~প্রসঙ্গ** *n* over-statement; frequent repetition; exaggeration. **~প্রাকৃত, অপ্রাকৃত** *adj* supernatural. **~বড়ো** *attrib adj* **1** very great; very big: ~বড়ো বিজ্ঞানী. **2** very much; too much: ~বড়ো বৃদ্ধ. **3** bitterest; severest: ~বড়ো শত্রু, ~বড়ো শাস্তি. **4** very intimate: ~বড়ো বন্ধু. **5** (derog) very great; very important: ~বড়ো দরদি. **~বল** *adj* very strong or powerful; mighty. **~বাড়** *n* overgrowth; growing extremely haughty or arrogant: ~বাড় বেড়ো নাকো ঝড়ে পড়ে যাবে, don't grow too high lest a storm should make you stumble down; (fig) pride will have a fall. **~বাদ** *n* **1** exaggeration. **2** unpleasant talk; harsh words. **~বাহন** same as ~পাত. **~বিনীত** *adj* much too courteous: ~বিনীত বক্তৃতা. **~বেগুনি, ~বেগুনী** *adj* ultraviolet. **~ভক্তি** *n* **1** excessive devotion. **2** (fig) insincere reverence: ~ভক্তি চোরের লক্ষণ, too much courtesy, too much craft. **~ভুজ** *n* (geom) the side of a right-angled triangle opposite the right angle; hypotenuse. **~ভোজন** *n* over-eating; surfeit; gluttony. **~ভোজী** *adj* voracious. ❑*n* a gourmand; a glutton. **~মন্দা** *n* (trade) sudden depression in business; slump. **~মাত্র, ~মাত্রায়** *adj* very much; excessive. **~মান** *n* excessive vanity. **~মানব, ~মানুষ** *n* a man of exceptional qualities or powers; a superman. **~মানবিক** *adj* superhuman; spiritual; divine. **~রঞ্জন** *n* exaggeration. **~রিক্ত** *adj* more than what is necessary. **~রেক** *n* abundance; excess. **~লোভ** *n* overgreediness. **~সার, অতীসার** *n* an intestinal disease; diarrhoea; dysentery.

অতিক্রম, অতিক্রমণ *n* crossing; passing over; going beyond; supersession; taking the place of another; surpassing; violation. **~করা** *vi,vt* to exceed; to violate; to excel; to outdo; to surpass. **~নীয়, অতিক্রম্য** *adj* what can be or is to be passed over; violable; surpassable. **অতিক্রান্ত** *adj* **1** passed; past. **2** overstepped; surpassed; violated; slighted; transgressed.

অতিথি, অতিথ (colloq) *n* a guest; a visitor; a caller. **~পরায়ণ** *adj* affording shelter and hospitality to guests and strangers; hospitable. **~সৎকার, ~সেবা** *n* hospitality. **~শালা** *n* **1** guest house. **2** inn.

অতিষ্ঠ *adj* extremely annoyed or vexed; irritated.

অতীত *adj* **1** gone by; passed away; past: ~ঘটনা. **2** concluded; ended; closed; finished: সে স্বপ্নসাধ এখন ~. **3** beyond the range (of); lying outside or beyond: ধারণার ~, আশার ~. ❑*n* **1** past times; ancient days; the past. **2** (gram) the past tense.

অতীন্দ্রিয় *adj* not perceptible by the senses; beyond the range of the eyes, ears, etc; transcendental. **~তা, ~বাদ** *n* mysticism; transcendentalism.

অতীব *adv* very much; too much; exceedingly; excessively.

অতীসার⇒অতি

অতুল, অতুলনীয় *adj* what admits of no comparison with others; incomparable; matchless; peerless; unparalleled; unequalled. **অতুলনীয়া** *fem.*

অতুষ্ট *adj* not satisfied; unappeased; displeased; discontented. **অতুষ্টি** *n* dissatisfaction; displeasure; discontent. **অতুষ্টিকর** *adj* displeasing; irritating; unsatisfactory.

অতৃপ্ত *adj* **1** unsatisfied; unappeased. **2** insatiated. unfulfilled: ~কামনা. **অতৃপ্তি** *n* lack of satisfaction or gratification. **অতৃপ্তিকর** *adj* unsatisfactory; not pleasing or gratifying.

অত্যধিক *adj* excessive; extreme; very great. ❑*adv* exceedingly; extremely; very much; too much.

অত্যন্ত *adj* excessive; extreme. ❑*adv* extremely; highly; beyond limit. **~গামী** *adj* extremely swift or fast.

অত্যয় *n* **1** passing away or elapsing (কালাত্যয়). **2** death; destruction; annihilation (প্রাণাত্যয়). **3** danger; hazard; distress; suffering. **4** a sudden or unexpected danger; emergency. **~পত্র** *n* an emergency certificate. **~সংচিতি** *n* emergency reserve.

অত্যল্প *adj* very little; very few; scanty.

অত্যহিত [অতি + অহিত] *n* extreme harm or injury; total destruction.

অত্যাচার *n* **1** oppression; tyranny; persecution; outrage. **2** intemperate or irregular habit of eating, sleeping and working: শরীরের উপর ~. **3** taking undue advantage of one's goodness, affection or courtesy. **~ করা** *vi* oppress; tyrannize. **অত্যাচারী** *n* an oppressor; a tyrant. **অত্যাচারিণী** *fem.* **অত্যাচারিত** *adj* oppressed; harassed; persecuted; victimized.

অত্যাজ্য *adj* what cannot be disowned or given up /away; not to be abandoned, deserted or relinquished.

অত্যাবশ্যক, অত্যাবশ্যকীয় *adj* urgently or absolutely necessary; very urgent; essential; important.

অত্যাশ্চর্য *adj* most astonishing or amazing; very wonderful; miraculous.

অত্যাসক্ত *adj* very much addicted (to); strongly attached (to). **অত্যাসক্তি** *n* strong attachment; extreme addiction (মদ্যাসক্তি).

অত্যুক্তি *n* exaggerated statement.

অত্যুগ্র *adj* **1** extremely rough or haughty. **2** very strong: ~ বাসনা, ~ গন্ধ.

অত্যুচ্চ *adj* very high; lofty.

অত্যুজ্জ্বল *adj* extremely bright or shining; very brilliant or luminous.

অত্যুৎকৃষ্ট *adj* super-excellent.

অত্যুৎপাদন *n* over-production.

অত্যুষ্ণ *adj* extremely hot or warm; excessively heated.

অত্র *adj* here; in this place. **~ত্র,~স্থ** *adj* of this place.

অথই, অথৈ *adj* very deep; unfathomable.

অথচ *conj, adv* yet; still; inspite of; nevertheless; nonetheless; but.

অথবা *conj* or; alternatively; on the other side/ hand.

অথর্ব *adj* **1** seized with the infirmities of old age; unable to move or use the limbs because of decrepitude; senile. **2** disabled; ineffective. ❑*n* the last one of the four Vedas.

অদক্ষ *adj* unskilled; inexpert: ~ শ্রমিক.

অদণ্ডনীয় *adj* not to be punished; unpunishable.

অদন *n* **1** eating. **2** edible article; food.

অদন্ত *adj* toothless; edentate. ❑*n* a toothless man.

অদমনীয়, অদম্য *adj* **1** indomitable; unconquerable; turbulent; unyielding. **2** pertinacious: অদম্য ইচ্ছা.

অদরকারি *adj* unnecessary; unimportant; not essential; dispensable.

অদর্শন *n* absence from sight; disappearance. ❑*adj* out of sight; vanished.

অদল[1] *adj* having no petal; leafless.

অদল[2] [A] *n* act of changing. **~ বদল** *n* **1** exchange; interchange. **2** changing; alteration; modification.

অদহনীয় *adj* not combustible.

অদান *n* an unworthy bestowal or gift.

অদাহ্য= অদহনীয়

অদিতি *n fem* **1** the earth. **2** (myth) the mother of gods.

অদিন *n* **1** inauspicious day. **2** hard times; days of hardship.

অদীক্ষিত *adj* not introduced to the elementary instruction or secret knowledge of (a group, etc); uninitiated.

অদূর *adj* not distant; not far off; near; close. **~দর্শিতা** *n* lack of foresight; imprudence. **~দর্শী** *adj* having no foresight; imprudent. **~দর্শিনী** *fem.* **~বর্তী** *adj* near-by.

অদূরে *adv* not far off; close by; near.

অদৃশ্য *adj* **1** what cannot be seen; invisible. **2** transcending knowledge acquired by experience; transcendental. **~ হওয়া** *vt* become invisible; go out of sight; vanish.

অদৃষ্ট *adj* not seen; unseen. ❑*n* fate; luck; fortune; destiny. **~ক্রমে** *adj* by chance; as luck would have it. **~পুরুষ** *n* destiny. **~পূর্ব** *adj* not seen before. **~বাদ** *n* the belief that all events are predetermined by fate; fatalism. **~বাদী** *n* one who believes in fatalism; fatalist. **~ লিপি** *n* the unseen writing of fate. **অদৃষ্টের পরিহাস** *n* irony of fate. **হা অদৃষ্ট !** *int* dear me!; good heavens!

অদ্ভুত *adj* **1** strange; queer; astonishing; amazing; wonderful. **2** sudden; unexpected. **3** extra-ordinary. ❑*n* (rhet) a sort of literary flavour that strikes the reader with its extraordinary strangeness (also ~ রস). **~কর্মা** *adj* **1** having the power of performing miraculous deeds. **2** endowed with extraordinary capabilities. ❑*n* (derog) one who is in the habit of doing odd things.

অদ্য *n, adv* **1** now. **2** recent. **3** today. ❑*n* now-a-days.

অদ্যাপি *prep* **1** still now; even at present; as yet.

অদ্যাবধি *adv* **1** till today; till now. 2 from today; hereafter.

অদ্রব *adj* insoluble; undissolved.

অদ্রাব্য *adj* insoluble.

অদ্রি *n* a mountain.
অদ্রোহ *n* non-violence; amity; amicability.
অদ্বয় *adj* having no equal; unparalleled; absolute. ~বাদ *n* monism; monotheism; the belief of teaching that there is only one God.
অদ্বিতীয় *adj* having no second or parallel/ equal; absolute; unique, supreme.
অদ্বৈত *adj* (theol) having no second or diversity; non-dual; monistical; unitarian; absolute. ❑*n* a prominent follower of Sri Chaitanya. ~বাদ *n* the doctrine that the embodied soul and the Supreme Soul/Spirit are one and the same as advocated by Shankaracharya. ~বাদী *adj* believing in the doctrine of ~বাদ.
অধ, অধঃ (in compound) *adv, prep* below; beneath; under. অধঃকৃত *adj* 1 defeated; vanquished. 2 felled; lowered; cast downwards; thrown down. অধঃক্রম *n* descending order. অধঃপতন, অধঃপাত *n* downward trend; degeneration; degradation; downfall. অধঃপতিত *adj* downfallen; degraded; degenerated. অধঃপাতে যাওয়া *vt* go to the dogs; to be ruined morally or otherwise. অধঃস্থ, অধঃস্থিত *adj* 1 lying or placed under; lower. 2 of lower grade; subordinate.
অধম *adj* inferior; vile; mean; despicable; abominable. অধমাঙ্গ *n* lower part of the body; the foot or leg. অধমাধম *adj* worse than the worst; vilest of the vile.
অধমর্ণ *n* a debtor; a borrower.
অধর *n* 1 the lower lip. 2 the lips. ~পল্লব *n* lips as tender and attractive as young shoots. ~মদিরা /সুধা lips as intoxicating as wine.
অধরামৃত (অধর+অমৃত)= অধর মদিরা. ~ পান করা *vt* 1 (fig) have a sucking or intoxicating kiss.
অধরোষ্ঠ (অধর+ওষ্ঠ) *n* the lips.
অধর্ম *n* irreligion; impiety; sinful act. ❑*adj* that which contravenes scriptural or moral laws; irreligious; impious; sinful. ~চারী, অধর্মাচারী, ~নিষ্ঠ, ~পরায়ণ *adj* given to vice; committing sins; unrighteous. ❑*n* a sinner; a wicked person. অধর্মাচরণ *n* anything done in contravention of recognized religious or moral standard; a sinful or unrighteous practice.
অধর্ম্য *adj* irreligious; unjust; abominable; heinous.
অধস্তন *adj* 1 lying low; lower; junior; later in time; posterior: ~ পুরুষ, later generation; posterity. 2 belonging to the lower stratum; inferior; subordinate: ~ কর্মচারী.
অধার্মিক *adj* irreligious; impious; sinful. ~তা *n* irreligiousness; impiety.
অধি *pref* indicating prominence, domination, authority, superiority, etc: ~কর্তা.
অধিক *adj* more; more than; exceeding: পাঁচের অধিকা *fem* (প্রাণাধিকা). ~তম *adj* most; greatest in number, degree, etc: ~তম দীর্ঘ, the longest. ~তর *adj* more; greater in number, quality, etc: ~তর সস্তা, cheaper. ~স্তু *conj* more over; farther; besides; in addition. ~ সন্ন্যাসীতে গাজন নষ্ট too many cooks spoil the broth.
অধিকরণ *n* 1 (gram) the locative case. 2 occupation or taking possession. 3 a place; an office; a court of justice (ধর্মাধিকরণ).
অধিকর্তা *n* the highest officer in charge of a concern or department; a director.
অধিকাংশ *adj* greater part (of). ~ ক্ষেত্রে/স্থলে *n* in most cases; mostly.
অধিকার *n* 1 ownership; right; title. 2 occupation; control. 3 knowledge; experience: শাস্ত্রে ~. 4 domination; authority; rule: তুর্কি ~কালে বঙ্গভাষার প্রভূত উন্নতি সাধিত হয়. 5 competence; claim: শিক্ষার ~. 6 jurisdiction; extent of authority. অধিকারী *n* 1 owner; lord; king. 2 manager or proprietor of an opera-party: যাত্রাদলের অধিকারী. 3 a family title; surname. 4 a high official; the holder of a high position. ❑*adj* having ownership, right or authority. অধিকারিণী *fem.*
অধিকৃত *adj* what has been taken possession of or brought under occupation; conquered; occupied. 2 acquired by culture; learned.
অধিগত *adj* 1 obtained; gained; earned. 2 learned; acquired by study; mastered.
অধিগম, অধিগমন *n* acquisition; attainment.
অধিগম্য *adj* 1 accessible; comprehensible. 2 what can be gained, acquired or possessed.
অধিজন *n* the majority. ~ সম্প্রদায় n the majority community.
অধিত্যকা *n* (geog) a plateau; a table-land.
অধিদেব, অধিদেবতা *n* presiding or guardian deity.
অধিনায়ক *n* a leader; a chief; a commander; the captain or skipper of a sports team. ~ত্ব *n* leadership; captaincy; command.
অধিপ, অধিপতি *n* an owner; a master; a lord; a king.
অধিবাস[১] *n* an abode; a dwelling place; a house.
অধিবাস[২] *n* ritualistic performance preliminary to any solemn Hindu ceremony: বরের ~ পূজার ~.
অধিবাসী *n* an inhabitant; a native; a resident.
অধিবিদ্যা *n* branch of philosophy dealing with the nature of existence, truth and knowledge; metaphysics. অধিবিদ্যক *adj* metaphysical. অধিবিদ্য *adj* erudite; learned.
অধিবৃত্ত *n* (math) a parabola or plane curve formed by intersection of a cone with a plane parallel to its side.

অধিবৃত্তি *n* extra remuneration to employees or extra dividend to shareholders; a bonus.

অধিবেত্তা⇒অধিবেদন

অধিবেদন *n* act of taking a second wife while the first wife is living. **অধিবেত্তা** *n* a person marrying a second wife during the lifetime of the first. **অধিবিন্না** *n fem* the living first wife of one having two wives.

অধিবেশন *n* the sitting or session of a body of persons; a meeting. ~ **ডাকা** *vi,vt* convene a meeting/session.

অধিভূ= অধিপ

অধিমাংস *n* **1** an abscess; a boil. **2** an eye-disease.

অধিমূল্য *n* a price above par. **অধিমূল্যে** *adv* above par.

অধিযান্ত্রিক *n* a mechanical foreman.

অধিযাচন *n* act of requiring; demand; requisition. ~**পত্রী** a requisition slip.

অধিযুগ *n* an epoch; a period of time in history.

অধিরথ *n* (myth) **1** a chariot-driver. **2** a charioteer who fights countless foes simultaneously. **3** the foster-father of Karna.

অধিরাজ *n* an emperor; a suzerain; an overlord. **অধিরাজ্ঞী** *fem* an empress.

অধিরাজ্য *n* a dominion or constituent part of an empire.

অধিরূঢ় *adj* mounted; seated upon; ascended: সিংহাসনে~.

অধিরোপণ *n* **1** act of making (sb) mount/ ascend. **2** act of charging a bow with an arrow.

অধিরোপিত *adj* placed (upon); charged (with).

অধিরোহণ *n* act of mounting / ascending/ riding/ climbing. ~ **করা** *vi, vt* to mount/ ascend/ ride/ climb. **অধিরোহণী, অধিরোহিণী** *n* a ladder; a flight of steps; a staircase. **অধিরোহী** *adj* mounted; ascended; boarded. ❑*n* a climber; a rider; a passenger. **অধিরোহিণী** *fem*.

অধিষ্ঠাতা *adj* dwelling; living; staying; being seated. ❑*n* a president; a governor; a director; a controller. **অধিষ্ঠাত্রী** *fem*.

অধিষ্ঠান *n* **1** act of staying or dwelling; existence (in a place, person or thing): কুলাচারে ~. **2** appearance; presence. **3** a dwelling place; a resort: দেবতার ~. **4** act of sitting or taking possession.

অধিষ্ঠিত *adj* **1** occupying; possessing; inhabiting. **2** appeared; present. **3** possessed; affected; attacked; surrounded; encompassed.

অধীত *adj* what has been read, perused or studied: ~ বিষয়ে গভীর ব্যুৎপত্তি. **অধীতি** *n* study; reading; pursuit of knowledge: সার্থক সাহিত্য সৃষ্টিতে গভীর অধীতি আবশ্যক. **অধীতী** *n, adj* one pursuing knowledge; well-educated; learned; erudite.

অধীন *adj* **1** subjugated; tamed: আজ্ঞার ~. **2** included (in); comprised (in); brought under authority: শাসনের ~. **3** obedient; devoted; dependent; subordinate: ~ জন. ~**তা** *n* subjection; subordination; bondage.

অধীর *adj* **1** restless; agitated; uneasy. **2** impatient; excited. **3** eager; anxious. **4** worried; alarmed; concerned. **অধীরা** *fem* . ~**তা** worry; impatience; eagerness; restlessness.

অধীশ্বর, অধীপ *n* **1** an owner; a master; a lord. **2** a king; an emperor.

অধুনা *adv* now-a-days; at present; in recent times. ~**তন** *adj* of recent times; present-day; modern.

অধৈর্য *n* impatience; restlessness; uneasiness. ❑*adj* impatient; restless; anxious; uneasy.

অধোগতি, অধোগমন *n* **1** downward motion; the state of falling downwards; descent. **2** the process of growing worse; deterioration; degeneration; downfall: মুঘল বংশের ~, degeneration of the Mughal dynasty. **অধোগামী** *adj* descending; degenerating ; deteriorating; declining.

অধোদৃষ্টি *adj* looking downwards; having downward looks. ❑*n* downward look. **অধোদৃষ্টিতে** *adv* with downcast looks.

অধোদেশ *n* the lower portion; the lower part of the body.

অধোবদন *adj* looking downwards; having the head bent down; having the face downcast. **লজ্জায় ~ হওয়া** *vt* to hang down one's head in shame.

অধোভুবন, অধোলোক *n* the underworld; the lowest of the three worlds spoken of in Hindu Purana; the world of the dead.

অধ্যক্ষ *n* **1** principal of a college or institution; speaker or president of a legislative assembly. **2** manager; superintendent; chief executive (কোষাধ্যক্ষ, মঠাধ্যক্ষ).

অধ্যবসায় *n* **1** act of continuing steadfastly in one's aim or activity; perseverance; steadfastness. **2** firm confidence or conviction. **অধ্যবসায়ী** *adj* persevering; steadfast.

অধ্যয়ন *n* assiduous study or reading. ~**শীল** *adj* given to absorbing study; studious. ~**শীলতা** *n* studiousness.

অধ্যাত্ম *adj* **1** pertaining to the Supreme Being/Soul. **2** pertaining to the individual soul; spiritual. **3** physical, bodily. ~**জ্ঞান**, ~**তত্ত্ব** *n* **1** knowledge about God. **2** knowledge about soul; metaphysics. ~**তত্ত্ববিদ** *n* one who has knowledge about God or the soul; a metaphysician. ~**বাদ** *n* the doctrine that all knowledge concerning the Creator arises from the mind without the aid or influence of anything external to the mind, ie, from subjective or personal experience; subjectivism; spiritualism.

অধ্যাত্মিক = আধ্যাত্মিক

অধ্যাদেশ *n* an ordinance; an order made by authority; a decree.

অধ্যাপক *n* a teacher ; an advisor; a professor of a college/university. **অধ্যাপিকা** *fem.*

অধ্যাপন, অধ্যাপনা *n* act of teaching or advising.

অধ্যায় *n* a chapter or section of a book.

অধ্যুষিত *adj* inhabited; colonized : ব্যাঘ্র ~, infested with tigers; মুসলিম ~ দেশ, country inhabited by Muslims.

অধ্রুব *adj* not stable; transitory; uncertain.

অন *pref*⇒ অ[২]

অনক্ষর *adj* unlettered; illiterate.

অনগ্ন *adj* not naked; dressed; covered.

অনঘ *adj* **1** holy; pure; innocent. **2** free from danger; safe; secure; sorrowless. **3** pleasant; charming; captivating.

অনঙ্গ *n* **1** the Hindu god of love. **2** sex-passion; lust. ❑*adj* incorporeal.

অনচ্ছ *adj* not crystal; opaque; turbid.

অনটন *adj* want; shortage; poverty. **অভাব-~** *n* pecuniary distress; stringency.

অনড় *adj* **1** motionless; immobile; still. **2** unchangeable; irrevocable: ~ প্রতিজ্ঞা.

অনত *adj* proud; haughty; insolent.

অনতি *adj* not much; little: ~দূর. **~কাল** *n* not a long time; a short time. **~কাল মধ্যে** *adv* before long; in a short time; shortly. **~দীর্ঘ** *adv* not very long: ~দীর্ঘ পথ; not very tall: ~দীর্ঘ দেহ. **~দূর** *adv* not very far; a little away. **~দূরে** *adj* not very far; not to a great distance. **~পক্ব** *adj* **1** of tender age; very young. **2** not fully ripe. **~পূর্ব** *adj* not of long before. **~পূর্বে** *adv* not long before; a short while ago. **~বিলম্বে** *adv* before long; shortly; soon. **~রিক্ত** *adj* not very excessive. **~ক্রম, ~ক্রমণ** *n* not passing beyond or over; not transgressing/infringing/violating. **~ক্রমণীয়, ~ক্রম্য** *adj* what cannot be overcome; impassable; inviolable; insuperable. **~ক্রান্ত** *adj* what has not been crossed/violated/infringed; not overcome or surmounted; unbeaten.

অনতীত *adj* not yet gone by; not passed.

অনধিক *adj* **1** not exceeding; not more than: ~ চার. **2** not much. **3** a little; a small amount.

অনধিকার *n* absence of right or claim. ❑*adj* not rightful; undeserving. **অনধিকৃত** *adj* not captured or seized; not occupied. **~চর্চা** *n* interference; unwarranted meddling. **~ প্রবেশ** *n* intrusion; trespass. **~ প্রবেশ করা** *vi, vt* intrude; trespass; encroach; transgress; infringe.

অনধিগত *adj* **1** not studied or learnt. **2** not acquired or earned.

অনধিগম্য *adj* **1** not comprehensible; unknowable: ~ রহস্যলীলা. **2** inaccessible; unapproachable: ~ গিরিশৃঙ্গ.

অনধীত *adj* not studied or perused.

অনধ্যায় *n* rest from study; a school holiday.

অননুকরণীয় *adj* not to be imitated; inimitable.

অননুভূতপূর্ব *adj* not felt or perceived before.

অননুমত, অননুমোদিত *adj* unapproved; not sanctioned/permitted.

অননুমোদন *n* absence of approval or sanction. অননুমোদিত⇒অননুমত.

অননুশীলন *n* absence of regular practice or exercise. **অননুশীলিত** *adj* not practised or cultivated; uncultivated.

অননুষ্ঠিত *adj* not performed or accomplished; outstanding.

অনন্ত *adj* **1** without limits; boundless; endless; infinite; unlimited. **2** imperishable; inexhaustible; eternal: ~কাল. ❑*n* **1** ornament for arms; armlet: সোনার ~. **2** the sky. **~কাল** *n* time without end; the future life; eternity. **~কাল ব্যাপী, ~কাল স্থায়ী** *adj* eternal; everlasting. **~নিদ্রা** *n* (fig) eternal sleep; death. **~মূল** *n* a medicinal root. **~রূপ, ~রূপী** *adj* having endless forms or manifestations. **~শীর্ষ** *adj* having many heads; hydra-headed; (fig) a thing hard to extirpate.

অনন্তর *adv, conj* then; thereafter; afterwards.

অনন্য *adj* **1** of unusual quality; singular; unique. **2** incomparable; peerless; having no equal or second. **অনন্যা** *fem.* **~কর্মা** *adj* engaged in no other work than; solely absorbed in. **~গতি** *adj* having no way out; having no alternative than. **~চিত্ত** *adj* single-minded; intent on nothing other than. **~চিত্তা** *fem.* **~চিত্তে** *adv* with undivided attention. **~চিন্তা** *adj* having no other thought in the mind than; meditating single-mindedly. **~দৃষ্টি** *adj* looking at nothing other than. **~মতি, ~মন, ~মনা, ~পরায়ণ** *adj* not devoted to anything other than. **~বৃত্তি** *adj* occupied solely in. **~ব্রত** *adj* performing no task other than. **~সাধারণ, ~সুলভ** *adj* uncommon; unique; singular; extraordinary.

অনন্যোপায় *adj* having no means or resource other than; having no alternative.

অনন্বয় *n* rhetoric in which the simile and the object compared are one and the same. ❑*adj* (gram) lacking in sequence or agreement; (phil) not governed by the law of causation; irrelevant; incoherent.

অনপত্য *adj* having no offspring; childless.

অনপনেয় *adj* indelible; ineffaceable: ~ কলঙ্ক.

অনপরাধ *n* innocence; guiltlessness. অনপরাধী, অনপরাধ *adj* free from the responsibility of criminal act; impeccable; innocent.

অনপেক্ষ *adj* impartial; unbiased; independent. ~তা *n* impartiality; independence. অনপেক্ষিত *adj* unexpected.

অনবকাশ *n* absence or want of leisure. ❑*adj* having no leisure or respite.

অনবগত *adj* uninformed; unaware.

অনবগুণ্ঠিত *adj* not veiled; uncovered. অনবগুণ্ঠিতা *fem.*

অনবচ্ছিন্ন *adj* without break; non-stop; continuous.

অনবচ্ছেদ *n* absence of intermission; continuity.

অনবদ্য *adj* flawless; impeccable; perfect.

অনবধান *n* absence of attention; carelessness; inadvertence. ❑*adj* inattentive; careless; inadvertent. ~তা *n*=অনবধান. ~তাবশত *adv* owing to inadvertence; inadvertently.

অনবরত *adj* ceaseless; unremitting; continuous. ❑*adv* incessantly; continuously; always; ever.

অনবরুদ্ধ *adj* not confined or besieged; free. অনবরোধ *n* freedom from restriction.

অনবসর *n* absence of leisure.

অনবসিত *adj* not finished or completed; incomplete; unfinished.

অনবস্থ, অনবস্থিত *adj* unsettled; unstable; restless. অনবস্থিতচিত্ত *adj* fickle-minded.

অনবস্থা *n* 1 lack of order; unsettled state; confusion. 2 (logic) a regress in reasoning; illogical argument.

অনবহিত *adj* 1 inattentive; unmindful. 2 incautious; unguarded. 3 uninformed; unaware. 4 careless.

অনভিজাত *adj* not aristocratic /high-born; having no family background.

অনভিজ্ঞ *adj* inexperienced; inexpert; unskilled. অনভিজ্ঞা *fem.* ~তা n inexperience; lack of skill.

অনভিপ্রায় *n* unwillingness; contrariety to one's wishes. অনভিপ্রেত *adj* undesirable; not to one's liking.

অনভিব্যক্ত *adj* not expressed/revealed; implicit.

অনভিভূত *adj* not overwhelmed; undefeated.

অনভিলষণীয় *adj* not to be desired; undesirable. অনভিলষিত *adj* undesired. অনভিলাষ *n* absence of desire; unwillingness. অনভিলাষী *adj* unwilling; not desirous of; having no desire for.

অনভ্যস্ত *adj* unaccustomed; not used to; unfamiliar.

অনভ্যাস *n* lack of practice.

অনমনীয় *adj* inflexible; rigid; obstinate.

অনম্বর *adj* having no clothes; bare; naked. ❑*n* 1 the sky. 2 a group of Buddhist monks.

অনর্গল *adv* incessantly; fluently. ❑*adj* unrestrained; unhindered; free.

অনর্ঘ *adj* having no known price; priceless; invaluable.

অনর্থ *n* 1 harm; mischief; injury. 2 mishap; reverse; trouble. 3 misinterpretation; distortion. 4 fruitlessness; futility; failure.

অনর্থক *adj* 1 futile; useless: ~ চেষ্টা. 2 for nothing; unreasonable: ~ বিলম্ব. ❑*adv* without cause or provocation: ~ বকা.

অনর্থকর *adj* injurious; harmful; full of mischief.

অনর্থদর্শী *n* one who believes that everything will turn out for the worst; a believer in the philosophical doctrine of pessimism; pessimist. অনর্থদর্শিনী *fem.*

অনর্থপাত *n* occurrence of an accident; disaster; trouble.

অনল *adj* fire. ~প্রভ *n* as radiant as fire. ~বর্ষণ *n* showering or emitting of fire; (fig) fiery eloquence. ~বর্ষী *adj* showering fire; (fig) emitting fire of eloquence: ~বর্ষী বক্তা, fire-brand (speaker)

অনলস *adj* not indolent; diligent; industrious. ~ভাবে *adv* diligently.

অনল্প *adj* not small in quantity /amount.

অনশন *n* starvation; fasting. ~ক্লিষ্ট *adj* stricken with starvation; famished. ~ ধর্মঘট *n* hunger-strike. ~ ব্রত *n* abstinence from food under a solemn vow.

অনশ্বর *adj* not perishable; indestructible; immortal. ~তা *n* indestructibility; immortality.

অনসূয় *adj* free from malice or envy. অনসূয়া *fem.*

অনস্বীকার্য *adj* what cannot but be admitted; undeniable .

অনহঙ্কার, অনহংকার *n* absence of pride/ arrogance. অনহঙ্কারী *adj* not proud/ arrogant/conceited; unassuming; polite; modest.

অনা *pref* indicating want, indecency or nastiness (অনাসৃষ্টি).

অনাকর্ষণীয় *adj* not attractive. অনাকর্ষণ *n* want of attraction.

অনাকার *adj* 1 having no form, shape or appearance. 2 dense; deep; intense: ~ অন্ধকার.

অনাক্রমণ *n* absence of aggression; non-aggression: ~ চুক্তি.

অনাক্রম্য, অনাক্রমণীয় *adj* very hard or difficult to attack; immune from attack.

অনাগত *adj* 1 future: ~ কাল. 2 absent; not yet come: ~ জন. অনাগতা *fem.* ~ বিধাতা *n, adj* one who makes provision for the future; far-sighted.

অনাঘ্রাত, অঘ্রাত *adj* 1 unsmelt: ~ ফুল. 2 what has not been enjoyed; unenjoyed. 3 undefiled; unstained. অনাঘ্রাতা *fem.*

অনাচার *n* **1** immoral/abominable practice. অনাচারী *adj* **1** given to abominable practice. **2** given to amorous life. **3** transgressing the established code of morality.

অনাচ্ছাদিত *adj* uncovered; having no roof; unthatched; bare.

অনাছিষ্টি=অনাসৃষ্টি

অনাটন=অনটন

অনাড়ম্বর *adj* unostentatious; simple.

অনাত্ম *adj* having no personality or individuality; impersonal. ~জ্ঞ *adj* ignorant of one's own self; not conscious of one's own position or status.

অনাত্মীয় *adj* **1** having no blood relationship or matrimonial connection (with). অনাত্মীয়া *fem.*

অনাথ *adj* in need of help; helpless; shelterless. ❑*n* orphan. অনাথা, অনাথিনী *adj fem* **1** helpless; shelterless. **2** without a husband or protector; widowed. অনাথাশ্রম, ~নিবাস *n* orphanage; asylum for the helpless; poor-house.

অনাদর *n* **1** lack of cordiality or care. **2** inattention; disregard. **3** slight; dishonour. disrespect; humiliation. ~ করা *vt* neglect; disregard; slight. ~নীয় *adj* unworthy of being respected /loved. অনাদৃত *adj* neglected; slighted. অনাদৃতা *fem.*

অনাদায় [অন+A আদায়] *n* non-realization; non-recovery. ❑*adj* unrealized; outstanding; due. অনাদায়ী *adj* =অনাদায় (*adj*). অনাদায়ীপাওনা *n* debt or dues unlikely to be paid; bad debt.

অনাদি *adj* **1** without a beginning; having no cause or origin; self-existent. **2** old; ancient; eternal. ~ কাল *n* time immemorial.

অনাদৃত⇒অনাদর

অনাদেয় *adj* unrealizable; that cannot be realized.

অনাদ্যন্ত *adj* without a beginning or end; self-born ; eternal; immortal.

অনাবশ্যক *adj* unnecessary; needless; redundant; superfluous : এ কথা বলা ~, it is needless to say; it hardly needs mention.

অনাবাদি *adj* uncultivated; not cultivable /arable; fallow.

অনাবাসিক *adj* **1** not residing; non-resident: ~ ছাত্র. **2** non-residential: ~ বিদ্যালয়.

অনাবিল *adj* **1** unmixed; unadulterated: ~ প্রেম, ~ আনন্দ. **2** clean; clear; translucent. অনাবিলা *fem* untainted; unstained; spotless; pure.

অনাবিষ্কার্য *adj* what cannot be traced or discovered.

অনাবিষ্কৃত *adj* not yet discovered/invented; unknown.

অনাবিষ্ট *adj* unmindful; inattentive ; heedless.

অনাবৃত *adj* uncovered; bare; open.

অনাবৃষ্টি *n* absence or shortage of rainfall; drought.

অনাব্য *adj* not navigable.

অনাময় *n* recovery from illness. ❑*adj* free from disease; healthy.

অনামিকা *n* ring-finger.

অনায়ত *adj* not broad; narrow.

অনায়ত্ত *adj* not mastered; not in one's power.

অনায়াস *n* ease; easiness. ❑*adj* demanding no exertion; effortless; easy. ~কৃত *adj* easily done. ~লভ্য *adj* easily available/obtainable. ~লব্ধ *adj* obtained without exertion; easily gained. ~সাধ্য *adj* easy to do; not hard to accomplish. ~সিদ্ধ *adj* easily performed/accomplished. অনায়াসে *adv* without difficulty; easily.

অনারব্ধ *adj* what has not (yet) commenced; not (yet) undertaken.

অনারারি [E] *adj* honorary; conferring honour.

অনারেবল [E] *adj* honourable; worthy of honour.

অনারোগ্য *n* state of illness. ❑*adj* incurable;

অনার্দ্র *adj* not wet; dry; (chem) free from water; anhydrous. ~ ব্যারোমিটার *n* a barometer for measuring air-pressure; an aneroid barometer.

অনার্য *n* a non-Aryan. ❑*adj* **1** other than Aryan. **2** uncivilized; uncultured; discourteous; rude (a connotation intentionally imposed by the Aryans. Non-Aryan civilization obtaining in South India or elsewhere in the sub-continent testifies to the falseness of the Aryan claim. Hence the use of the word আর্যামি to ridicule the Aryan hegemony).

অনার্যোচিত *adj* befitting a non-Aryan; uncouth; rude.

অনালোচনীয়, অনালোচ্য *adj* not fit to be discussed; not to be considered.

অনাশ্রয় *adj* shelterless. ❑*n* want of shelter. অনাসক্ত *adj* having no attachment for; indifferent.

অনাসক্তি *n* indifference; apathy.

অনাসৃষ্টি, অনাছিষ্টি *adj* **1** strange; queer; bizarre. **2** ugly; disorderly; abominable . ❑ *n* anything queer or strange.

অনাস্থা *n* **1** no-confidence; unreliability. **2** disregard; neglect. ~ প্রস্তাব *n* no-confidence motion. ~ভাজন *adj* untrustworthy; unreliable. ~সূচক মত *n* vote of no-confidence.

অনাস্বাদ *n* absence of taste; tastelessness. ❑ *adj* void of good taste; tasteless. অনাস্বাদিত *adj* not tasted; unenjoyed. অনাস্বাদিতপূর্ব *adj* not tasted/enjoyed before.

অনাহত *adj* **1** unhurt; unwounded; unbeaten. **2** unstruck; not played upon: ~ বীণা.

অনাহার *n* fasting; starvation. অনাহারী *adj* fasting; starving. অনাহারে *adv* without food; in fasting. অনাহারে কাটানো *vi,vt* go without food; fast; starve.

অনাহূত *adj* not invited; uninvited; unsolicited; uncalled for.

অনিকেত, অনিকেতন *adj* having no home/ shelter; homeless.

অনিচ্ছা *n* 1 unwillingness. 2 disrelish; distaste; dislike: আহারে ~. 3 indifference; aversion. 4 dissent; objection; protest. ~কৃত *adj* unintentional; not deliberate. ~পূর্বক *adv* unwillingly; reluctantly. ~ সত্ত্বেও *adv* despite unwillingness; against one's will. ~ সহকারে *adv* with reluctance. ~ প্রকাশ করা *vi, vt* to express unwillingness or reluctance. **অনিচ্ছুক, অনিচ্ছু** *adj* unwilling; reluctant.

অনিত্য *adj* not everlasting; transitory; mortal; perishable. ~ দেহ *n* mortal body. ~ সংসার *n* transitory world. ~তা *n* transience; transitoriness; impermanence.

অনিদ্রা *n* sleeplessness. ~ রোগ *n* insomnia. **অনিদ্র** *adj* sleepless.

অনিন্দনীয়, অনিন্দ্য *adj* 1 not blameworthy. 2 impeccable; unimpeachable; flawless. 3 beautiful; perfect; admirable.

অনিন্দিত *adj* 1 not censured; unreproached; unblemished. 2 perfect; beautiful. **অনিন্দিতা, অনিন্দ্যসুন্দরী** *adj fem* exquisitely beautiful.

অনিপুণ *adj* 1 unskilled; inexpert; not adroit. 2 of a disorderly type; irregular; messy; unsystematic; unmethodical. **অনিপুণা** *fem.*

অনিবার *adj* what cannot be prevented/resisted. ❑*adv* again and again; repeatedly; always. **অনিবার্য** *adj* 1 unpreventable; irresistible. 2 inevitable; unavoidable; sure to happen. **অনিবার্যতা** *n* inevitability; unavoidableness. **অনিবার্য কারণে** *adv* owing to unavoidable reasons; under unavoidable circumstances.

অনিমেষ, অনিমিষ *adj* (of eyes) not winking; steadfast. ~ নেত্রে, ~ লোচনে *adv* with a steadfast look.

অনিয়ত *adj* 1 unbridled; uncontrolled; unrestrained. 2 irregular; unsteady; indefinite. **অনিয়তাকার** *adj* having no definite shape; amorphous.

অনিয়ন্ত্রিত *adj* not regulated; uncontrolled.

অনিয়ম *n* 1 irregularity; indiscipline; disorderliness. ~ করা *vi* be irregular; violate a rule or break discipline. **অনিয়মিত** *adj* irregular. **অনিয়মিতভাবে** *adv* irregularly.

অনিরুদ্ধ *adj* 1 unchecked; unhindered; unobstructed; self-willed; free. 2 open. ~ পথ *n* free passage; the sky.

অনির্ণীত *adj* undefined; not determined/ ascertained; (math) indeterminate.

অনির্ণেয় *adj* not to be ascertained/fixed; indeterminate.

অনির্দিষ্ট *adj* not specified; indefinite. ~ কালের জন্য sine die (L); without a date fixed; for indefinite period.

অনির্দেশ *n* absence of direction/ instruction; uncertain state. **অনির্দেশ্য** *adj* that cannot be specified/determined; indeterminable.

অনির্ধারিত *adj* 1 unscheduled; out of schedule. 2 not settled or decided.

অনির্বচনীয় *adj* unspeakable; inexpressible; indescribable: ~ আনন্দ.

অনির্বাণ *adj* 1 deprived of Nirvana or salvation in the hereafter. 2 inextinguishable; blazing for ever: শিখা ~. 3 unceasing; unreceding; restless.

অনিল *n* air; wind; breeze.

অনিশ্চয়, অনিশ্চয়তা *n* uncertainty; doubt; doubtfulness; suspense. **অনিশ্চিত** *adj* uncertain; indefinite; doubtful; precarious. **অনিশ্চিতভাবে** *adv* without certainty; without being sure; indecisively.

অনিষ্ট *n* harm; injury; evil; mischief. ~কর *adj* harmful; injurious; mischievous; pernicious. ~কারী *n, adj* one who causes harm/injury; an evil-doer; a wrong-doer. ~ করা *vt* to harm; to cause harm (to); to do mischief. ~চিন্তা *n* evil design; mischievous thought; malevolence. ~চেষ্টা *n* mischievous or harmful activities. ~পাত *n* occurrence of a mishap; befalling of a calamity.

অনিষ্ঠা *n* absence of devoutness; lack of confidence; want of reverence; disbelief.

অনিষ্পন্ন *adj* unfinished; incomplete: outstanding.

অনীক *n* army; armed force; troops.

অনীকিনী (myth) a division of the army.

অনীতি *n* immorality; corruption; wrong policy or want of policy.

অনীপ্সিত *adj* unwanted; undesired; undesirable.

অনীশ্বর *adj* Godless; atheistic. ~বাদ *n* belief that there is no god; atheism. ~বাদী *n* atheist; unbeliever. ❑*adj* atheistic.

অনীহ⇒**অনীহা**

অনীহা *n* lack of energy/effort; apathy. **অনীহ** *adj* lacking in energy or effort; apathetic.

অনু *pref* denoting succession, similarity, extent, dependence, repetition, etc, eg অনুগমন, অনুরূপ, অনুক্ষণ, অনুগত.

অনুকম্পন *n* thrill; shiver; shaking; tremor.

অনুকম্পা *n* compassion; sympathy; mercy; kindness.

অনুকরণ *n* 1 act of copying; imitation. 2 following; going after; pursuit. ~ করা *vt* imitate/copy/follow/go after. ~কারী *n, adj* imitator; mimic; mimester. ~পটু *adj* skilled in imitating. ~প্রিয় *adj* fond of imitating or mimicking. ~প্রিয়তা *n* imitativeness. ~ বৃত্তি *n* habit /faculty of imitation. ~শীল *adj* habitually imitative. **অনুকরণীয়** *adj* worthy of being imitated; imitable; ideal; exemplary. হীন ~ *n* aping; apery. হীন ~ করা *vt* imitate foolishly like an ape; play the ape.

অনুকল্প *n* **1** alternative; choice between two things. **2** substitute; person or thing taking the place of another. **3** secondary injunction. ~ বিধি *n* theory of substitution.

অনুকার *n* imitation; copying. অনুকারী *n, adj* one who imitates; a follower, a mimic . ~ শব্দ *n* onomatopoeic word.

অনুকীর্তন *n* publicity or proclamation of a previous event or subject.

অনুকূল *adj* **1** favourable; helpful; propitious. **2** kind; compassionate; gracious; benignant. ❑*adv* favourably; graciously. ~তা, আনুকূল্য *n* favour; help; grace; compassion. ~ হওয়া *vi,vt* be of help; be helpful/favourable; become propitious. ~ বায়ু *n* favourable wind.

অনুকৃত *adj* imitated; copied; mimicked; followed. অনুকৃতি *n* imitation; mimicry.

অনুক্ত *adj* **1** not said or uttered; unmentioned; unexpressed. **2** (gram) implied; understood: ~ কর্তা. ❑*n* gap; blank space: ~ পূরণ.

অনুক্রম *n* **1** serial order; sequence; succession. **2** programme; list of item or events in serial order. ~ণ *n* indexing. ~ণিকা, ~ণী *n* (of books) introduction; preface; index. অনুক্রমিক *adj* following in order; sequential; serial. অনুক্রমে *adv* in order of; sequentially; serially.

অনুক্ষণ, অনুখন (poet) *adv* at every moment; ever; always; constantly.

অনুগ *n* follower; companion; attendant. ❑*adj* following; succeeding; according to; conforming to (নিয়মানুগ).

অনুগণক *n* **1** calculator; person who calculates. **2** a calculating machine.

অনুগণনা *n* act of calculating; calculation.

অনুগত *adj* **1** obedient; dependent; devoted; faithful . **2** adhering to the view (of); professing the tenets (of). আনুগত্য *n* obedience; fealty; allegiance.

অনুগমন *n* **1** act of following or going after. **2** act of travelling together or accompanying. **3** act of dying together or burning oneself to death on one's husband's funeral pyre. ~ করা *vt* follow; accompany.

অনুগামী *adj* following; attending; accompanying. ❑*n* follower; adherent; companion; attendant. অনুগামিনী *fem.* ~ হওয়া *vt* follow; be obedient/faithful; adhere to.

অনুগৃহীত *adj* benefited; favoured; protected; obliged. অনুগৃহীতা *fem.*

অনুগ্র *adj* **1** not strong/pungent/acrid: ~ সৌরভ. **2** not haughty; gentle; polite.

অনুগ্রহ *n* **1** kindness; mercy; grace. **2** help; favour; benefit. **3** happiness; satisfaction. ~ করা *vt* treat with kindness; accord favourable treatment; take pity. ~পাত্র *n* a favourite. ~ভাজন *adj* enjoying favour; favoured. ~পূর্বক *adj* kindly; graciously; benignantly. ~প্রার্থী *adj* soliciting favour. ❑*n* one who seeks favour. অনুগ্রাহক, অনুগ্রাহী *adj* kind; gracious; favourable. ❑*n* a patron.

অনুঘটক *n* (chem) substance that causes catalysis; catalyser; catalyst. অনুঘটন *n* act of aiding a chemical process by a substance that does not itself undergo any change; catalysis.

অনুচর *n* **1** follower; companion. **2** servant; attendant . ❑*adj* attending; accompanying; following. অনুচরী *fem.* ~ বর্গ *n pl* suite or train of attendants/followers; retinue.

অনুচিকীর্ষা *n* desire for imitation. অনুচিকীর্ষু *adj* desirous of imitating/copying.

অনুচিত *adj* improper; unbecoming; unreasonable. ~ ভাবে *adv* wrongly; unjustifiably.

অনুচিন্তন, অনুচিন্তা *n* contemplation of the past; backward view; retrospect.

অনুচ্চ *adj* **1** not high or lofty; low: ~ কণ্ঠ. ~ স্বরে *adv* in a low voice; in an undertone.

অনুচ্চারণীয়, অনুচ্চার্য *adj* **1** what cannot be or is not to be pronounced: ~ বর্ণ. **2** unutterable; unspeakable; inexplicable. অনুচ্চারিত *adj* not pronounced; unspoken; unuttered.

অনুচ্ছেদ, অণুচ্ছেদ *n* (of books, etc) a paragraph; a section.

অনুজ, অনুজন্মা *n* younger brother.

অনুজা *fem.* অনুজাত *adj* born later.

অনুজীবী *adj* employed in another's service; one dependent on another for maintenance. ❑*n* servant; attendant; follower; adherent. অনুজীব্য *adj* worthy of being served.

অনুজ্জ্বল *adj* **1** not bright; dim; dull: ~ দীপ. **2** not sharp; not brilliant: ~ প্রতিভা.

অনুজ্ঞা *n* **1** order; command; permission; sanction. **2** commission; employment. **3** (gram) imperative mood. ~ত *adj* ordered; commanded; permitted; licensed. ~ধারী *n* a licensee. ~পত্র *n* a permit; a licence.

অনুতপ্ত *adj* repentant; penitent; remorseful; contrite.

অনুতাপ *n* repentance; penitence; contrition. ~ করা *vt* repent. অনুতাপী *adj* repentant; penitent. ❑*n* repenter.

অনুত্তম *adj* **1** best; excellent: পরোপকার ~ ধর্ম. **2** inferior; worst: ~ বংশ.

অনুত্তর *adj* **1** not responding/answering; silent. **2** what or who has no superior; best; supreme; final. **3** not belonging to the north; southern.

অনুত্তীর্ণ *adj* **1** failed; unsuccessful: ~ ছাত্র. **2** unsurmounted; unconquered: ~ বিপদ. **3**

uncrossed; untraversed: ~ পথ. **4** unexpired: ~ কাল. ~ **হওয়া** *vt* fail or be unsuccessful.

অনুৎপাদী *adj* that produces nothing; unproductive.

অনুদান *n* government grant. **সহায়ক ~** *n* grant-in-aid.

অনুদার *adj* not liberal; ungenerous; mean; niggardly; miserly. **~তা** *n* niggardliness; narrow-mindedness.

অনুদিন *adv* day after day; daily; every day.

অনুদৈর্ঘ্য *adv* along length; lengthwise. ❑*adj* longitudinal. **~ তরঙ্গ** *n* longitudinal wave.

অনুদ্গত *adj* not sprung or grown; not projecting.

অনুদ্ঘাটিত *adj* not open: closed: ~ দ্বার; not revealed; undiscovered: ~ রহস্য.

অনুধাবন *n* **1** running after; pursuit. **2** reflection; consideration. **3** attention; concentration. **4** seeking; searching. **~ করা** *vt* run after; pursue; ponder; reflect; consider; understand.

অনুধ্যান *n* continuous thinking or remembrance; reflection; meditation; recollection. **~ করা** *vt* recollect; meditate; wish for. **অনুধ্যায়ী** *adj* thinking; recollecting; wishing good : তিনি আমার শুভানুধ্যায়ী [শুভ + অনুধ্যায়ী].

অনুনয় *n* earnest request; entreaty; prayer; supplication. **~ করা** *vi,vt* entreat; solicit; beseech; supplicate. **~ বিনয়** *n* entreaties; solicitations; importunities. **অনেক ~ বিনয়ের পর** *adv* after great importunity. **~কারী** *n* the supplicant.

অনুনাদ *n* sound reflected or rebounded; echo; resounding; resonance; reverberation. **~ক** *n* a resonating device; resonator; sound box. **অনুনাদিত** *adj* **1** echoed; resonated; reverberated; resounded. **2** sounded at a time; sounded simultaneously. **3** sounded. **অনুনাদী** *adj* echoing; resonant; reverberant; resounding; having a similar sound; sounding simultaneously.

অনুনাসিক *adj* nasal; uttered through the nose. ❑*n* (gram) nasal sound or letter representing this sound (ঙ, ঞ, ণ, ন, ম, ং). **~ সুরে** *adv* in a nasal tone or voice.

অনুন্নত *adj* **1** backward: depressed: ~ সম্প্রদায়. **2** lacking in progress; underdeveloped: ~ দেশ. **3** not high or elevated; low.

অনুপকার *n* disservice; harm; injury. **~ক** *adj* harmful ; injurious. **~ করা** *vi,vt* do (one) harm/mischief; injure.

অনুপকারিতা *n* harmfulness.

অনুপকারী⇒অনুপকারক

অনুপম *adj* without a peer; peerless; matchless; excellent; best. অনুপমেয় *adj* incomparable; too great to be compared with.

অনুপযুক্ত *adj* **1** not appropriate; inappropriate; unjustified: ~ কথা. **2** unfit; incompetent; unworthy; unqualified: ~ ব্যক্তি. **3** insufficient; incompatible with what is necessary: ~ মূল্য. **~তা** *n* unfitness; incompetence; insufficiency.

অনুপযোগিতা *n* **1** inappropriateness; uselessness. **2** incompetence; incapability; unworthiness. **অনুপযোগী** *adj* unfit; unsuitable.

অনুপস্থিত *adj* **1** not present; absent. **2** non-existent; unborn; lacking; wanting. **~ থাকা** *vi* absent oneself. **অনুপস্থিতি** *n* absence; want; inexistence.

অনুপাত *n* (math) ratio; (geog) proportion; rate; incidence. **অনুপাতে** *adv* in the ratio of; in proportion to; at the rate of.

অনুপান *n* anything to be taken with a dose of medicine to make it effective.

অনুপায় *n* want of means or resource; helplessness. ❑*adj* helpless; resourceless.

অনুপূরক *adj* **1** what makes sth complete; complementary. **2** extra; additional; supplementary: ~ বাজেট.

অনুপূর্ব *n* serial order; succession; method. ❑*adj* following due order or succession; orderly; successive.

অনুপ্রবেশ *n* **1** gradual interpenetration made unobservedly; infiltration; penetration. **2** grasping; understanding; realization. **অনুপ্রবিষ্ট** *adj* infiltrated; penetrated; gone into the depth (of).

অনুপ্রভ *adj* giving out light without burning; phosphorescent. **অনুপ্রভা** *n* phosphorescence.

অনুপ্রস্থ *adj* lying or placed across; crosswise; latitudinal; transverse. ❑*adv* across; latitudinally; transversely. **~ ছেদ** *n* transverse section.

অনুপ্রাণন *n* infusion of life or spirit. **অনুপ্রাণনা** *n* inspiration; invigoration; stimulus; incentive. **অনুপ্রাণনা দেওয়া** *vt* inspire; stimulate; invigorate. **অনুপ্রাণিত** *adj* inspired; stimulated; invigorated.

অনুপ্রাস *n* (rhet) repetition of a sound or letter in a succession of words; alliteration (নূপুরের নিক্বণ).

অনুপ্রেরণা *n* inspiration; enthusiasm; encouragement. **অনুপ্রেরিত** *adj* inspired; encouraged.

অনুবচন *n* (gram) component part of a complex sentence; a clause.

অনুবৎসর *n* lunar year.

অনুবন্ধ *n* **1** act of initiating; introduction. **2** request; solicitation. **3** attempt; effort; endeavour. **4** occasion; purpose. **5** contextual connection. **6** bond; tie. **7** correlation. **অনুবন্ধী** *adj* **1** related; connected; associated. **2** (gram) syntactically connected; inseparable; conjugate. **~ ব্যাস** *n* (geom) a conjugate diameter.

অনুবর্তন *n* **1** act of pursuing or following : পুরনো ধারার ~. **2** act of attending or serving. **3** act of leaving for a new abode. **~ করা** *vt* to follow/pursue; to attend/serve; to imitate; to leave for a new place. **অনুবর্তী** *adj* following; attending; obeying; complying. ❑*n* a follower. **অনুবর্তিনী** *fem*. **অনুবর্তিতা** *n* obedience; acquiescence; compliance; subservience. **অনুবর্তী হওয়া** *vt* to follow/succeed/obey.

অনুবল *n* grace; mercy; compassion. **2** power; influence. **3** one who renders assistance; a patron : "সেই কালে কেবা মোর হবে অনুবল." ❑*adv* according to one's capabilities; as much as power and ability permit.

অনুবাদ *n* act of rendering sth from one language to another; translation. **~ক** *n* translator. **অনুবাদিত**⇒অনূদিত. **অনুবাদী** *adj* **1** translating. **2** musical note other than বাদী, বিবাদী and সংবাদী. **3** corresponding; similar.

অনুবার *adv* again and again; repeatedly.

অনুবাসন *n* act of perfuming; fumigation. **অনুবাসিত** *afj* perfumed; fumigated. **অনুবাসিত করা** *vt* perfume/fumigate.

অনুবিদ্ধ *adj* set in; joined to; strung; imbedded.

অনুবিধি *n* (legal) a proviso; a clause.

অনুবৃত্তি *n* **1** act of following or pursuing. **2** imitation. **3** contextual connection (পূর্বানুবৃত্তি). **4** attending upon; serving.

অনুবেদন *n* **1** knowledge of the future. **2** sympathy; compassion. **3** imparting knowledge; enlightenment.

অনুভব *n* **1** perception; feeling; experience; realization. **2** influence; majesty; nobility; high-mindedness. **~ করা** *vi,vt* feel; perceive; realize; learn.

অনুভাব *n* **1** majesty; glory; power; influence. **2** feeling of happiness/pleasure/contentment. **3** (rhet) physical expression of permanent emotions, eg, tears, sighs, frowning, etc. **4** hint or gesture indicating ardent love or attachment. **~না** *n* reflection; recollection; well-wishing.

অনুভূত⇒অনুভূতি

অনুভূতি *n* feeling; realization; intuition; sense-perception. **অনুভূত** *adj* felt; perceived; realized; understood.

অনুভূমিক *adj* parallel to the horizon; horizontal.

অনুমতি *n* leave; permission; consent; approval; sanction; authorization. **~ দেওয়া** *vi,vt* permit; grant leave; allow; authorize. **~ লওয়া** *vi,vt* get/take permission; take leave; be allowed or authorized. **~পত্র** letter of authority; permissive note; permit; pass; licence; letters-patent. **~ প্রাপ্ত হয়ে** *vt* being authorized. **~সূচক** *adj* permissive; indicative of approval/consent.

অনুমান, অনুমিতি *n* **1** supposition; conjecture; guess; hypothesis. **2** deduction; inference; corollary. **3** (rhet) figure of speech corroborating the general by the particular or the particular by the general; corroboration. **~ করা** *vi,vt* suppose; guess; infer; conjecture. **অনুমিত হওয়া** *vi* seem; appear. **অনুমেয়** *adj* what can be supposed; inferable; deducible; conjecturable. **অনুমিত** *adj* what has been supposed, guessed, inferred, conjectured or taken as a hypothesis.

অনুমোদন *n* **1** consent; support; confirmation. **2** approval; sanction; authorization. **~সাপেক্ষ** *adj* subject to approval/sanction. **অনুমোদিত** *adj* **1** consented; agreed; permitted. **2** (govt level) sanctioned; authorized; affiliated; commissioned. **অনুমোদিত বিদ্যালয়** *n* affiliated school. **অনুমোদিত ব্যয়** *n* authorized expenditure.

অনুযায়ী *adj* like; similar; after the example of; consequent upon. ❑*adv* according to; in accordance with.

অনুযোগ *n* **1** imputation of a fault; act of blaming; finding fault with; complaint; accusation; recrimination. **2** admonition; reproach; reproof. **~ করা** *vt* complain; censure; reprove; admonish. **অনুযুক্ত** *adj* **1** worthy; deserving; fit; appropriate competent. **2** blamed; accused; censured; admonished. **অনুযোগী** *adj, n* one who complains/blames/reproves/reproaches/admonishes. **অনুযোগিনী** *fem*. **অনুযোগ্য** *adj* accusable; blamable; censurable; warranting reproach or reproof.

অনুরক্ত *adj* devoted; attached (to); having love and affection (for). **অনুরক্তা** *fem*. **অনুরক্তি** *n* devotion; attachment; love; affection.

অনুরঞ্জক⇒অনুরঞ্জন

অনুরঞ্জন *n* **1** act of pleasing or giving satisfaction; adulation : প্রজাকুলের অনুরঞ্জনে নিবেদিত প্রাণ. **2** act of dyeing or applying colour. **অনুরঞ্জক** *adj, n* **1** one who gives delight and satifaction; cultivating love and affection (প্রজারঞ্জক). **2** one who dyes or applies colour; dyer. **অনুরঞ্জিত** *adj* **1** what has been given delight or pleasure; delighted; pleased. **2** dyed or coloured.

অনুরণন *n* resonance; reverberation; echo. ❑*vi,vt* resound with echo and re-echo.

অনুরণিত *adj* resounded; resonated; reverberated; echoed.

অনুরত *adj* devoted; attached to; fond of: কর্ম~. **অনুরতি** *n* devotion; attachment; fondness; loyalty.

অনুরাগ *n* **1** love; devotion; passion. **2** caress; affection; fondling. **3** inclination; liking; propensity to; attraction for (ধর্মানুরাগ). **4** (music) subsidiary raga, ie, musical notes: ~ যেসব রাগিণী. **5** (archaic) consequence; a fault/

flaw//blemish. ❑*adv* (archaic) according to one's desire/ free-will; at pleasure. **অনুরাগানল** *n* fire of love; flame of passion. **অনুরাগান্ধ** *adj* blinded with passion/ love. ~**বশে** *adv* out of love. **অনুরাগী** *adj* devoted; impassioned; having attraction (for) **অনুরাগিণী** *fem.*

অনুরুদ্ধ *adj* **1** one who has been requested. **2** that for which a request has been made.

অনুরূপ *adj* **1** of the same kind; like; similar; resembling; corresponding. **2** suitable; worthy; appropriate. ~**ভাবে** *adv* accordingly; similarly.

অনুরোধ *n* expression of desire for sth; request; entreaty; solicitation; recommendation. ~ **করা** *vt* request; entreat; implore; recommend. **অনুরোধে** *adv* at the request/ instance of; for the sake of; on account of.

অনুর্বর *adj* **1** not fertile; barren; unproductive. **2** having no merit; not sharp: ~ মস্তিষ্ক. **অনুর্বরা**. *fem.*

অনুলঙ্ঘন *n* non-violation; non-transgression. **অনুলঙ্ঘনীয়,অনুলঙ্ঘ্য** *adj* inviolable; insurmountable; what cannot be/ is not to be transgressed / violated.

অনুলম্ব *adj, adv* standing upright; altitudinal; vertical.

অনুলাপ *n* telling sth repeatedly; tautology.

অনুলিখন, অনুলিপি, অনুলেখ *n* **1** dictation. **2** writing (sth) in the alphabet of a different language; transliteration. **3** facsimile or duplicate copy of a manuscript . **অনুলেখক** *n* copyist.

অনুলিপ্ত *adj* **1** anointed; besmeared with perfume, etc; dyed; coloured. **2** engaged/ employed/ occupied (in).

অনুলেখ, অনুলেখক⇒অনুলিখন

অনুলেপ, অনুলেপন *n* an ointment; act of coating or smearing. ~ দেওয়া *vi, vt* apply a coating or ointment (to); coat or smear(with).

অনুলোম *n* descending order; regular succession. ❑*adj* favourable; helpful; propitious. ~ **বিবাহ** *n* marriage of a Hindu bridegroom with a bride of lower caste. **অনুলোমে**, ~**ক্রমে** *adv* in regular succession; according to the best method.

অনুশাসন *n* **1** a legal rule; an order; an edict. **2** advice; dictum; teaching instruction. **অনুশাসক** *adj* ruling; governing. ❑*n* ruler; governor; director. ~**পত্র** *n* writ of ordinance; warrant.

অনুশিষ্য *n* disciple of the second degree; disciple of a disciple.

অনুশীলন *n* culture; cultivation; studies. ~ **করা** *vi,vt* study; peruse; culture; undergo training. **অনুশীলনী** *n* exercise; repeated study or practice. **অনুশীলনীয়** *adj* what has to be studied/ practised repeatedly. **অনুশীলিত** *adj* **1** what has been studied/ practised. **2** cultured; cultivated; chaste; elegant.

অনুশোচন, অনুশোচনা *n* sorrow for wrongdoing; repentance; repining; contrition. ~ **করা** *vi* regret; repent. **অনুশোচনীয়** *adj* regrettable; warranting repentance. **অনুশোচিত** *adj* what has excited repentance; regretted; repented.

অনুষঙ্গ *n* **1** context; connection; relation. **2** love; amour; affection: আত্মীয়তার ~. **3** kindness; compassion. **অনুষঙ্গী** *adj* connected with; attached to. **আনুষঙ্গিক** *adj* accompanying; concomitant; incidental.

অনুষদ *n* faculty; grouping of related departments of a university.

অনুষ্ঠাতা, অনুষ্ঠাত্রী⇒অনুষ্ঠান

অনুষ্ঠান *n* **1** act of initiating; introduction; arrangement. **2** celebration; function; festival. **3** sitting/ session of an association. **4** ritual; religious ceremony. ~ **করা** *vi, vt* perform; celebrate; observe; execute. **অনুষ্ঠাতা** *adj* one who initiates/ introduces/ executes/ performs. ❑*n* introducer; organizer; performer; promoter. **অনুষ্ঠাত্রী** *fem.* **অনুষ্ঠিত** *adj* performed; celebrated; executed; observed. **অনুষ্ঠেয়** *adj* what is to be/ should be performed/ observed/ celebrated/ held.

অনুসন্ধান *n* **1** search; seeking; inquiry. **2** research; investigation. ~ **করা** *vi, vt* search; investigate; examine. **অনুসন্ধানী** *adj* efficient in investigating; engaged in searching/ examining. ❑*n* inquirer; searcher; investigator; scrutinizer. **অনুসন্ধাতা, অনুসন্ধায়ক, অনুসন্ধায়ী** *adj* searching; researching; investigating. **অনুসন্ধেয়** *adj* worthy of research/ investigation/ scrutiny. **অনুসন্ধানী দৃষ্টি** *n* searching eye.

অনুসন্ধিৎসা *n* inquisitiveness; curiosity.

অনুসন্ধিৎসু *adj* eager to know; inquisitive; curious: ~ পাঠক.

অনুসন্ধেয়⇒অনুসন্ধান

অনুসরণ *n* **1** following; pursuit. **2** imitation. ~ **করা** *vi, vt* go after; follow; pursue; imitate. ~**কারী** *n, adj* one who follows/pursues/ imitates/ succeeds. ~**কারিণী** *fem.*

অনুসার *n* **1** following; pursuance. **2** similar; accordance; imitation; conformity. **3** supposition; conjecture; hint; gesture. **4** aim; motive; purpose: ভিক্ষার অনুসারে. **অনুসারী** *adj* **1** following; pursuing. **2** conforming; similar. **অনুসারিণী** *fem.* **অনুসারে** *adv* accordingly; according to; in accordance with; in conformity with; in pursuance of.

অনুসিদ্ধান্ত *n* (geom) sth self-evident after sth else has been proved; corollary.

অনুসূচক *adj* indicating; signifying; denoting. **অনুসূচি, অনুসূচী** *n* schedule; time table; programme.

অনুসূচন *n* **1** act of indicating. **2** a token; a sign; an evidence.

অনুসূচনা *n* **1** function; ceremony; ritual. **2** discussion; movement.

অনুসূর *n* (astron) point in a planet's orbit at which it is nearest to the sun; perihelion.

অনুসৃত *adj* followed; pursued; repeated; imitated.

অনুসৃতি, অনুসরণ *n* act of following/ pursuing/ imitating.

অনুস্বর, অনুস্বার *n* the vowel sound ং; the letter representing the nasal sound ং

অনুস্মরণ, অনুস্মৃতি *n* recollection. **~ করা** *vi, vt to* recollect.

অনুস্মারক *n* sth that makes one remember; reminder.

অনুস্যূত *adj* sewn or strewn together; affixed.

অনুস্রবণ *n* (of liquid) passing slowly through small pores; percolation.

অনূঢ় *adj* unmarried. **~ পুরুষ** *n* a bachelor. **অনূঢ়া নারী** *n* spinster; maid. **অনূঢ়ান্ন** *n* pre-wedding meal given to a Hindu bride.

অনূদিত, অনুবাদিত *adj* rendered from one language to another; translated.

অনূপ *adj* watery; moist; marshy. ❑*n* swamp; bog; marsh. **~ দেশ** *n* country of rivers and canals.

অনূর্ধ্ব *adj* not more than; under: ~ পাঁচ.

অনৃত *adj* not true; false. ❑*n* falsehood; untruth. **~বাদিতা** *n* untruthfulness. **~বাদী, ~ভাষী** *adj* untruthful; lying. ❑*n* liar **~বাদিনী, ~ভাষিণী** *fem.*

অনেক *adj* **1** many; too many; various : ~ সন্ন্যাসীতে গাজন নষ্ট, too many cooks spoil the broth. **2** much; enough : ~ টাকা, much money; ~ হয়েছে enough of it; সে ~ কথা; it is a long story. ❑*n* **1** many people; many a one : ~ গবা কালে গোবর্ধনবাবু হয়, many a ragged colt may make a good horse. **2** the universe : অনেকের পতি, the lord of the universe. **অনেকত্ব** *n* plurality; multiplicity. **~ কাল আগে** *adv* long ago. **~ দিনের আশা** *n* long cherished hope. **~ প্রকার, ~বিধ** *adj* of various kinds. **~বার** *adv* on several occasions. **~ রাতে** *adv* late at night. **অনেকাংশে** *adv* largely; to a great extent; in many respects. **অনেকানেক (~-~)** *adj* numerous/ manifold/various. **অনেকে** *pron* many persons; many a one.

অনৈক্য *n* **1** absence of unity; disunion; discord; animosity. **2** disagreement; difference of opinion.

অনৈচ্ছিক *adj* against one's will; involuntary.

অনৈতিক *adj* contrary to morality; immoral.

অনৈতিহাসিক *adj* not connected with important in history; unhistoric; unhistorical.

অনৈপুণ্য *n* lack of skill/ dexterity; incompetence.

অনৈসর্গিক *adj* not natural; supernatural.

অনৌচিত্য *n* impropriety; improper act or utterance.

অনৌদার্য *n* narrowness; inferiority complex.

অন্ত[১] *suff* used to form present participial, *adjj* or present progressive tense, eg, উঠ+অন্ত = উঠন্ত, চল+অন্ত = চলন্ত, etc.

অন্ত[২] *n* **1** end; termination(দিনান্ত, নিশান্ত). **2** border; limit; terminus (বনান্ত, সীমান্ত). **3** death; destruction: ~কাল. **4** intention or intrinsic nature: তার অন্ত পাওয়া ভার, he is too deep to sound. ❑*adv* upto; till (পক্ষান্ত, মাসান্ত). **~কাল** *n* death-time; the moment of termination/ destruction. **~ত, ~তঃ** *adv* at least. **~স্থ** *adj* lying within or in between.

অন্তঃ (অন্তর) *pref* denoting the heart, depth, within, inside, etc. **~করণ** *n* heart; mind; will. **~কোণ** *n* (geom) interior angle. **~পট**⇒**অন্তস্পট**. **~পাতী** *adj* lying in; situated within; included/ compressed in. **~পুর** *n* the inner portion of a dwelling house; zenana; harem; seraglio. **~পুরচারী, ~পুরচারিণী** *adj* confined to the inner apartments. ❑*n* one who keeps to the harem. **~পুরিকা** *n* lady in the harem. **~প্রবেশন** *n* literary interpolation. **~শত্রু** *n* **1** internal foe; an enemy within one's own kith and kin. **2** one who is culpable of treason; a quisling; fifth columnist; traitor. **3** passions regarded as veritable enemies of man. **~শিলা** *adj* that which contains stone within it. **~শীল** *adj* lying in the depth/ heart of a person/ thing; unrevealed; hidden. **~শীলা** *fem* . **~শুল্ক** *n* excise duty. **~সত্ত্বা** *adj fem* pregnant; in the family way. **~সংজ্ঞা** *n* subconscious mind or its activities. **~সলিল, ~সলিলা** *adj* having underground or subterranean water. **~সার** *n* substance/ essence/ kernel of anything; ❑*adj* having substance. **~সারশূন্য** *adj* having no substance within; useless; empty; hollow; insincere: ~সারশূন্য কথা. **~স্তর** *n* substratum (*pl*. substrata). **~স্থ** lying/ situated within; internal. **~স্থ বর্ণ** *n* the consonant letters য র ল ব which play the part of semi-vowels. **~স্রাবী** *adj* (med) making substances (hormones) which are poured directly into the bloodstream of the body; endocrine. **~স্রাবী গ্রন্থি** *n* endocrine gland.

অন্তকাল, অন্তত, অন্ততঃ⇒**অন্ত**

অন্তর *n* **1** the heart; the mind. **2** interior; depth. **3** distance; intervening space. **4** difference; contrariety (মতান্তর). **5** end; termination. **6** intimate relative: ~তম. ❑*adj* different; other (দেশান্তর). **~টিপুনি** *n* secret pinching of one's heart by another; secret prodding or surreptitious blow; home-thrust. **~জ্ঞ** *adj* **1** having intuition or introspection. **2** far-sighted; prudent. **~স্থ** *adj* lying/ dwelling in one's heart

~ হওয়া *vi* go away; vanish. **অন্তরে** *adv* at heart; in the depth of.

অন্তরঙ্গ, অন্তরংগ *n* **1** intimate friend; relative. **2** internal limb or part. ❑*adj* very intimate. ~ **বন্ধু** *n* bosom friend.

অন্তরণ⇒অন্তরিত

অন্তরা *n* (music) middle stave of a song.

অন্তরাত্মা *n* **1** individual soul. **2** inward spirit.

অন্তরাপত্যা *adj fem* pregnant.

অন্তরায় *n* obstacle; barrier; hindrance; bar; impediment.

অন্তরায়ন *n* act of imprisoning one or restraining one's freedom of movement; internment. **অন্তরায়িত** *adj* interned.

অন্তরাল *n* place out of sight; concealment; distance: দৃষ্টির অন্তরালে. ~**বর্তী** *adj* lying out of sight. ~**বর্তিনী** *fem.* **অন্তরালে** *adv* behind; in the background.

অন্তরিক্ষ⇒অন্তরীক্ষ

অন্তরিত *adj* **1** vanished; hidden. **2** covered; overcast; overwhelmed. **3** removed; driven away. **4** segregated or confined under authority of government. **অন্তরণ**=অন্তরায়ন.

অন্তরীক্ষ, অন্তরিক্ষ *n* the space above the earth; the sky. ~**চারী** *adj* residing or moving about in the sky. ❑*n* heavenly bodies; birds. ~**বাসী**, ~**বাসিনী** *adj* dwelling in the sky; aerial; ethereal. ~**মণ্ডল** *n* the atmosphere; the celestial region.

অন্তরীণ *n* person who is interned; internee. ~ **করা** *vt* intern. ~ **হওয়া** *vt* be interned.

অন্তরিন্দ্রিয় *n* inner sense; the mind.

অন্তরীপ *n* (geog) a cape; a promontory. **উত্তমাশা** ~ *n* the Cape of Good Hope. **কুমারিকা** ~ *n* Cape Comorin.

অন্তরীয়, অন্তরীয়ক *n* lower garment; skirt; underwear.

অন্তরে⇒অন্তর

অন্তর্গত *adj* [অন্তর+গত] included in; comprised in.

অন্তর্গূঢ় *adj* dormant in the heart; concealed within the heart/mind; unrevealed; secret.

অন্তর্ঘাত *n* willful damaging of machinery, buildings, etc to hinder the enemy's activity during a period of war or disturbance; sabotage. ~**ক** *n* saboteur; fifth columnist. **অন্তর্ঘাতী** *adj* sabotaging.

অন্তর্জগৎ *n* inner region; the realm of the mind; spiritual world.

অন্তর্জল *n* **1** mid-water. **2** middle of land and water. ❑*adj* situated in water. ❑*adv* inside water; between land and water. ~ **জাহাজ** *n* a submarine.

অন্তর্জলি, অন্তর্জলী *n* the Hindu rite of immersing the lower part of the body of a dying person in a river for spiritual salvation.

অন্তর্জাতীয়, অন্তঃরাষ্ট্রীয় *adj* of or concerning more than one nation; international.

অন্তর্দর্শন *n* (psych) examination of one's own thoughts and feelings; introspection. **অন্তর্দর্শী** *adj* introspective.

অন্তর্দাহ *n* **1** great affliction; mental agony. **2** the fire of envy; heart-burning. **অন্তর্দাহী** *adj* causing heart-burning.

অন্তর্দৃষ্টি *n* **1** intuition; insight. **2** (psych) introspection. ~**সম্পন্ন** *adj* endowed with insight or intuition; intuitive; introspective.

অন্তর্দেশ *n* **1** the inner part or region; the heart. **2** the inland; a valley. **অন্তর্দেশীয়** *adj* situated in the interior of a country; inland.

অন্তর্ধান *n* disappearance; vanishing. ~ **করা/হওয়া** *vi* disappear; vanish; go into concealment.

অন্তর্নিবিষ্ট, অন্তর্নিহিত *adj* placed within; lying in the heart; implanted; deep-rooted; deep-seated; inherent; latent: ~ শক্তি.

অন্তর্বর্তী *adj* in between; intermediate; interim: ~ সরকার.

অন্তর্বত্নী *adj fem* pregnant.

অন্তর্বাণিজ্য *n* trade within a country; inland trade.

অন্তর্বাষ্প *n* suppressed tears. ❑*adj* with suppressed tears.

অন্তর্বাস *n* **1** under-garment; underwear.

অন্তর্বাহ, অন্তর্বাহী *adj* flowing inward.

অন্তর্বিগ্রহ, অন্তর্বিপ্লব, অন্তর্বিরোধ *n* **1** internal feud; internecine quarrel. **2** civil war.

অন্তর্বিবাহ *n* marriage within own's group; endogamy.

অন্তর্বিরোধ⇒অন্তর্বিগ্রহ

অন্তর্বেদনা *n* mental anguish; suppressed feeling of agony.

অন্তর্বেদি, অন্তর্বেদী *n* plain land between two rivers; a river valley.

অন্তর্ভুক্ত, অন্তর্ভূত *adj* included/ comprised (in). ~ **করা** *vt* include; absorb.

অন্তর্ভেদী *adj* able see and understand quickly and deeply; penetrating: ~ দৃষ্টি.

অন্তর্মাধুর্য *n* internal beauty; sweetness of the heart.

অন্তর্মুখ, অন্তর্মুখী *adj* introspective; spiritual.

অন্তর্যামী *adj* knowing the mind: ঈশ্বর ~. ❑*n* God.

অন্তর্হিত *adj* disappeared; vanished; out of sight. ~ **হওয়া** *vi* disappear; go out of sight.

অন্তস্তর *n* (geol) a level (stratum) lying beneath another in the earth; sub-stratum (*pl* sub-strata).

অন্তস্তল *n* **1** the bottom or lower part of anything. **2** the heart; the mind.

অন্তস্থ⇒অন্ত

অন্তস্পট, অন্তঃপট *n* screen; curtain; cover.

অন্তিক *adj* adjacent; proximate; near; contiguous. ❑*n* 1 proximity; nearness. 2 the extreme; extremity.

অন্তিম *adj* 1 last; ultimate. 2 of the time of death; dying. ~ অবস্থা/দশা *n* dying state. ~ কাল *n* the time of death; last moment. ~ শয্যা/শয়ন *n* death-bed.

অন্তেবাসী *n* 1 pupil or disciple boarding at the master's house. 2 a neighbour. 3 the untouchable Hindu community who dwell in the outskirts of villages. ❑*adj* nearby; adjacent.

অন্ত্য *adj* 1 last; final; ultimate. 2 extreme; base; low . ❑*n* person of the lowest caste among Hindus. ~জ *adj* 1 low-born; base; mean. 2 depressed; abandoned. ❑*n* low-caste; depressed class. ~দেশ *n* the last extremity. ~ বর্ণ *n* 1 the last letter of a word. 2 the last of the four Hindu castes, ie, the Shudra. ~ সম্ভার *n* closing stock. ~স্থিতি *n* closing balance.

অন্ত্যেষ্টি, অন্ত্যেষ্টিক্রিয়া *n* obsequies; funeral ceremony; cremation.

অন্ত্র *n* 1 bowels. 2 intestines. ক্ষুদ্রান্ত্র *n* small intestine. বৃহদন্ত্র *n* large intestine. ~বৃদ্ধি *n* hernia. ~জ্বর *n* enteric fever. ~ প্রদাহ *n* a painful infection of the bowels; enteritis.

অন্দর, অন্দরমহল (P অন্দর+A মহল) *n* inner apartments of a dwelling house; female quarters; harem.

অন্ধ *adj* 1 blind; sightless. 2 extremely dark or gloomy. 3 ignorant; illiterate. ~কূপ *n* a dark pit; a black hole. ~কূপ হত্যা *n* (hist) the Black-hole Tragedy. ~তম *adj* extremely dark; darkest. ~তমস *n* utter darkness; blind darkness. ~ত্ব, ~তা *n* blindness; ignorance. ~বিশ্বাস *n* blind faith. ~ভাবে *adv* blindly; indiscreetly. ~ হওয়া *vi vt* go blind with; become blind of; (fig) be blind to sth. অন্ধের যষ্টি *n* (lit) a blind person's stick; (fig) only means of support to a helpless person. অন্ধের কিবা দিন কিবা রাত day and night are alike to a blind man.

অন্ধকার *n* absence of light; darkness; gloom. ❑*adj* full of darkness: ~ রাত; darkened with dejection: ~ মুখ; ill-fated; having no happiness in life: ~ জীবন. ~ দেখা *vt* be at one's wit's end; be confused/ bewildered. ~ দেখানো *vt* overwhelm or bewilder with threat; make one cowed with fear. অন্ধকারে ঢিল মারা take a leap in the dark. অন্ধকারে থাকা *vi,vt* be in the dark (about). অন্ধকারে হাতরানো vt grope in the dark. অন্ধকারাচ্ছন্ন, অন্ধকারাবৃত *adj* 1 overcast with darkness. 2 (fig) enveloped in the gloom of ignorance.

অন্ধানুকরণ *n* servile imitation. ~ করা *vt* follow without discrimination.

অন্ধিসন্ধি *n* 1 a fissure or cleft made by splitting of parts; hole; chink; cavity. 2 ins and outs; secrets; secret intention. 3 inclination; design; whereabouts: মনের ~. 4 effort; endeavour; enterprise; a means; a way.

অন্ধ্র *n* 1 the Andhra state of India. 2 the ancient Dravidian people inhabiting this part of india.

অন্ন *n* 1 boiled rice. 2 food; edible things. ~ উঠা *vt* 1 out of luck for food. 2 approach one's death. ~কষ্ট, অন্নাভাব *n* 1 want of food. 2 scarcity; famine. ~কুট, ~কোট *n* stupendous heap of rice. ~গত প্রাণ *adj* (derog) unable to go without food. ~চিন্তা *n* bread-problem. ~চিন্তা চমৎকারা bread-problem preying heavily on the mind; bread-problem being the chief problem. ~ছত্র, ~সত্র, ~ক্ষেত্র *n* centre for charitable distribution of food/ rice; poor-house. ~জল *n* food and drink. ~জল ওঠা *vt* run out one's longevity or term of employment. ~দা *adj fem* 1 bread-giving . 2 Hindu goddess Durga. ~দাতা *n* one who maintains or supports. ~দাত্রী *fem.* ~দাস *adj* slave to another for food and maintenance. ~নালী *n* alimentary canal; gullet; oesophagus. ~পথ্য *n* first rice-meal after recovery from illness. ~পানি *n* food and drink. ~পায়ী *adj* incapable of chewing solid food; one who swallows his food. অন্নপূর্ণা *n fem* 1 Hindu goddess Annapurna. ❑ *adj* full of rice or food. ~প্রাসন *n* the ceremony of giving rice to a child for the first time. ~বস্ত্র *n* food and clothing. ~ভোজী *adj* living on rice. ❑*n* rice-eater. ~ময় *adj* brimming with food. ~মুষ্টি *n* a morsel of food; a small quantity of food. ~রস *n* fluid derived from digested food; chyle. ~লোভাতুর *adj* hungry for food; extremely desirous of having food. ~সংস্থান *n* provision for food/ maintenance; means of livelihood. ~হীন *adj* starving; famished; hungry. ❑*n* beggar.

অন্য *pron* other. ❑*adj* some other; any other; different. ~-~⇒ অন্যান্য . ~কৃত *adj* done by some other person. ~কেউ *adj* some one else. ~গত *adj* 1 depending on others. 2 devoted/ attached to another. ~জন, ~জনা *pron* other people. ~ত *conj* 1 from the other. 2 in a different way. ❑*adv* somewhere else; in a different place. ~তম *adj* one of a number; any one of several persons/ things. ~তর *adj* one or either of the two; the other. ~ত্র *adv* elsewhere; in some other place. ~থা *adv, conj* otherwise. ❑*adj* contrary; different. ❑*n* the contrary; contrariety ; opposition; violation; exception; infringement. ~থা করা *vi,vt* do/act otherwise; disobey; violate; infringe. ~থা হওয়া *vi,vt* be contrary to/ different from. ~থাচরণ *n* acting/ doing otherwise. ~দীয় *adj* belonging to another person; regarding others. ~পূর্বা *adj fem* formerly betrothed or married to someone else. ~পূর্ব *mas*. ~প্রকার/ বিধ *adj* of other/different kind(s). ~প্রকারে, ~ভাবে *adv* in a different way. ~মতে *adv* according to a different view. ~মনস্ক, ~মনা *adj* not attentive; absent-minded; preoccupied with some other thought. ~মনস্কতা *n* inattention; absent-mindedness. ~সাপেক্ষ *adj* related to some other person/ thing; relative.

অন্যান্য *adj pl* 1 others. 2 different; various.

অন্যায় *n* 1 improper act; unjust action. 2 injustice; a wrong; a misdeed. ❑*adj* unjust; improper; unreasonable; wrongful. ~ করা *vt* do an injustice/ a wrong; act improperly. ~কৃৎ *n* wrong-doer; mischief-maker. ~ত, ~তঃ *adv* unjustly; improperly; unreasonably; wrongfully. অন্যায়াচরণ *n* improper conduct; unlawful action. অন্যায়াচারী *adj* behaving improperly; acting unjustly/ unreasonably. ❑*n* a wrong-doer.

অন্যায্য *adj* not just or fair; unjust; unreasonable; improper. ~তা *n* unjustness; impropriety; unreasonableness.

অন্যার্থ [অন্য+অর্থ] *n* another or a different meaning. ~ক *adj* having another/ different meaning.

অন্যাসক্ত [অন্য+আসক্ত] *adj* attached/ devoted to a woman other than wife. অন্যাসক্তা *adj fem* unfaithful (to husband); unchaste.

অন্যূন *adj* not less than; at least; in the least.

অন্যোন্য, অন্যোহন্য, অন্য-অন্য *adj* mutual; reciprocal; each other; one another. অন্যোন্য নির্ভর, অন্যোন্যাশ্রয় *n* interdependence; mutual dependence.

অন্বয় *n* (gram)1 relation; syntax; (rules of) sentence construction. 2 connected line of ideas, etc; sequence. 3 succession; serial order. 4 agreement; concord. অন্বয়ী *adj* related; connected; connecting; agreeing; concordant.

অন্বর্থ *adj* appropriate; consistent; significant; real; true. ~নামা *adj* having a name appropriate to one's nature/ qualities/ properties.

অন্বিত *adj* 1 possessed of; endowed with (আশান্বিত). 2 mutually related/ connected; (gram) sequential; syntactic: ~ বাক্য.

অন্বিষ্ট *adj* sought for; looked for.

অন্বীক্ষণ *n* 1 thought about the past; retrospection. 2 searching.

অন্বীক্ষা *n* philosophy; logic.

অন্বেষক⇒অন্বেষণ

অন্বেষণ *n* inquiry; search; quest; investigation. অন্বেষিত *adj* searched; sought; researched; investigated. অন্বেষক *n* researcher; investigator.

অপ *pref* used to mean animadversion, reprehension, opposition, etc: ~কর্ম, ~দেবতা. ~কর্ম *n* 1 a misdeed; a mischief. 2 wrongful/harmful act; a crime. ~কর্ম করা *vt* make mischief; do a misdeed; commit a crime. ~কর্মা *adj* 1 doing mischief/misdeeds. 2 committing crimes. ❑*n* a mischief-maker; a criminal; a miscreant; a wrong-doer. ~কলঙ্ক *n* a false imputation; slander; calumny. ~কীর্তি *n* ill-fame; infamy; disrepute; disgrace. ~ক্রান্ত *adj* removed; shifted; withdrawn; transferred. ~ক্রিয়া *n* wrongful act; harm; injury; crime. ~ঘাত *n* 1 unnatural death; death by accident. 2 accidental injury to one's person. ~ঘাতক, ~ঘাতী *adj* one who/what /which causes accidental death/injury. ~চ্ছায়া *n* 1 a fancied vision; a phantom; an apparition. 2 a ghost; a ghostly illusion. ~জাত *adj* having lost the original qualities; degenerate. ❑*n* degenerated race; base community. ~জাতি *n* same as ~জাত*(n)*. ~দেবতা, ~দেব *n* a ghost; an evil spirit. ~পাঠ *n* inaccurate reading; misreading; slip of the pen; error in copying. ~প্রয়োগ *n* misuse; improper use; misapplication; wrong application. ~প্রয়োগ করা *vt* misuse; misapply; use with improper motive/in an improper way. ~মিশ্রণ *n* adulteration.

অপকর্ষ *n* 1 deterioration; degeneration; decline; retrogression. 2 inferiority; baseness.

অপকলঙ্ক⇒অপ

অপকার *n* harm; injury. ~ক, অপকারী *adj* harmful; injurious. অপকৃত *adj* one who has suffered a loss/damage; harmed; injured; wronged. অপকৃতি same as অপকার.. ~ করা *vt* do harm; cause damage; injure.

অপকীর্তি⇒অপ

অপকৃত, অপকৃতি⇒অপকার

অপকৃষ্ট *adj* 1 base; inferior; low; mean. 2 degenerated; deteriorated. ~ ধাতু *n* base metal; non-precious metal.

অপকেন্দ্র *adj* (phys) tending away from the centre; centrifugal. ~ বল *n* centrifugal force.

অপক্রান্ত, অপক্রিয়া⇒অপ

অপক্ব *adj* 1 not ripe; immature; raw; green. 2 unboiled; part-boiled. ~তা *n* unripeness; immaturity; rawness; state of being uncooked/unboiled.

অপক্ষপাত *n* impartiality; neutrality; absence of bias/prejudice. ❑*adj* impartial; unprejudiced; neutral. অপক্ষপাতী *adj* 1 neutral; impartial. 2 just; even-handed. অপক্ষপাতিত্ব, অপক্ষপাতিতা same as অপক্ষপাত *(n)*.

অপক্ষয় *n* ruin; destruction ; extinction; extermination; elimination.

অপক্ষেপ *n* rejection. ~ করা *vt* refuse to accept; reject. অপক্ষিপ্ত *adj* rejected.

অপগত *adj* **1** passed away; departed; eliminated; removed. **2** dead. ~ হওয়া *vi* retreat; be withdrawn/ eliminated. অপগমন, অপগম *n* departure; disappearance; retreat.

অপগা *adj* going downwards; approaching the sea. ❑*n* a river.

অপগ্রহ, অপঘাত, অপঘাতক, অপঘাতী⇒অপ

অপচয় *n* **1** waste; wastage; misuse. **2** loss; decrease; decay; dissipation. ~ করা *vt* misuse; waste; squander away; fritter away. অপচিত *adj* **1** misused; wasted. **2** decreased; decayed; dissipated; lost. অপচীয়মান *adj* in the process of decay/ decrease/ misuse; decaying; waning.

অপচায়িত *adj* wasted; misused; squandered away.

অপচার, অবচার *n* **1** violation of the traditional course; improper conduct. **2** indigestion; dyspepsia. অপচারী *adj* behaving in an improper way; causing harm/ injury.

অপচিকীর্ষা *n* malice; ill-will; desire to injure others. অপচিকীর্ষু *adj* mischievous; malicious.

অপচিত, অপচিতি, অপচীয়মান⇒অপচয়

অপচ্ছায়া, অপজাত, অপজাতি⇒অপ

অপটু *adj* **1** unskilled; inexpert; incompetent. **2** indisposed; disabled.

অপঠিত *adj* not perused; unread; unstudied.

অপণ্য *adj* not marketable/ fit to be sold; unsaleable.

অপণ্ডিত *adj* not learned; illiterate; ignorant.

অপত্নীক *adj* **1** one whose wife is dead; widower. **2** unmarried.

অপত্য *n* child; son or daughter. ~নির্বিশেষে *adv* without discriminating between one's own children and another's; like one's own children. ~স্নেহ *n* parental love; affection for one's children. ~হীন *adj* childless; without issue.

অপথ *n* **1** evil way; foul method. **2** wrong path; a place which does not take one to his destination.

অপথ্য *adj* wrong diet; unsuitable as diet for a patient.

অপদ *adj* having no feet or legs.

অপদস্থ *adj* insulted; humiliated; disgraced. ~ করা *vt* insult; humiliate; embarrass; put to shame. ~ হওয়া *vt* be embarrassed/ insulted/ abased.

অপদার্থ *adj* **1** having no value; worthless. **2** incompetent; unfit. **3** useless; good-for-nothing.

অপদেব, অপদেবতা⇒অপ

অপনয়, অপনয়ন *n* removal; elimination. ~ করা *vi, vt* remove; take out; refute; eliminate.

অপনীত *adj* removed; eliminated; refuted. অপনেয় *adj* removable; effaceable. অপনোদন *n* removal; refutation; allaying; alleviation. দুঃখ ~ করা *vt* alleviate suffering.

অপনোদিত *adj* wiped out; eliminated; alleviated.

অপপণন *n* selling things on the black-market; black-marketing.

অপপাঠ, অপপ্রয়োগ⇒অপ

অপবর্গ *n* emancipation of the soul; salvation; liberation.

অপবাদ *n* bad name; ill-repute; defamation; slander; calumny. ~ দেওয়া *vt* defame; slander; make false accusation. ~ক *adj* defaming; slandering. ❑*n* one who defames; slanderer; accuser.

অপবিত্র *adj* unholy; impure; profane. ~ করা *vt* desecrate; profane; outrage. ~তা *n* unholiness; profanity; impurity.

অপব্যবহার *n* **1** misconduct; misbehaviour. **2** misuse; abuse; wrong use. ক্ষমতার ~ *n* abuse/ misuse of power. অর্থের ~ *n* wastage of money. ~ করা *vt* misuse; abuse; waste.

অপব্যয় *n* wrongful/ imprudent spending; wastage; unnecessary expenditure. ~ করা *vt* squander away; waste; abuse. অপব্যয়িত *adj* ill-spent; wasted; squandered. অপব্যয়িতা *n* prodigality; extravagance. অপব্যয়ী *adj* prodigal; extravagant. ❑*n* squanderer; spendthrift.

অপভাষ *n* infamy; slander; word of censure.

অপভাষা *n* obscene/ slang language; vulgar speech.

অপভূ, অপভূবিন্দু *n* (astron) position in the orbit of a planet when it is at its greatest distance from the earth; apogee.

অপভ্রংশ *n* **1** dialects descended from classical language. **2** corruption of a word. **3** ungrammatical or incorrect word. **4** act of slipping off; a fall. অপভ্রষ্ট *adj* **1** incorrect; corrupt: অপভ্রষ্ট শব্দ. **2** fallen; dislodged.

অপমান *n* insult; dishonour; disgrace; humiliation; affront. ~ করা *vt* insult; affront; slight; hurt one's feelings, esp in public. ~ বোধ করা। *vt* feel insulted/ humiliated/ disgraced. অপমানিত *adj* insulted; dishonoured; defamed; treated with insolence. ~কর *adj* insulting; humiliating; disgraceful. ~সূচক same as ~কর.

অপমিশ্রণ⇒অপ

অপমৃত্যু *n* accidental/unnatural death.

অপযশ, অপযশঃ *n* infamy; ill-repute; disgrace; discredit; bad name. অপযশস্কর *adj* disgraceful; scandalous; infamous.

অপয়া *adj fem* **1** ill-omened; ominous. **2** inauspicious; unlucky.

অপর *adj* **1** other; another: ~ ব্যক্তি. **2** opposite: নদীর ~ তীর. **3** later; coming after (পূর্বাপর আলোচনা); last; terminating (অপরাহ্ণ). ❑*pron* someone else: অপরের কথায়. **~ কেহ** *pron* somebody else. **~পক্ষে** *adv* on the other side/ hand. **~ সকলে** *pron* all others. **অপরঞ্চ** *adv, conj* more over; further; in addition. **অপরত্র** *adv, conj* elsewhere; somewhere else. **অপরন্তু**=অপরঞ্চ. **~ লোক** *n* the next world. **অপরা** *adj fem* other; another. ❑*pron* the other woman. **অপরাপর** *adj* the others; all others.

অপরাজিত *adj* unbeaten; unconquered; undefeated. **অপরাজিতা** *adj fem* undefeated; unrivalled. ❑*n* name of a flower or creeper. **অপরাজেয়** *adj* unconquerable; invincible; unrivalled: অপরাজেয় সুরশিল্পী.

অপরাধ *n* offence; crime; guilt; sin. **~ করা** *vt* commit a crime/ an offence/ a sin. **~জনক/মূলক** *adj* criminal; offensive; sinful. **~বোধ** *n* sense of guilt. **অপরাধী** *adj* offending; criminal; guilty. ❑*n* offender; criminal; guilty person. **অপরাধিনী** *fem.*

অপরাপর⇒অপর

অপরার্ধ *n* the other half.

অপরাহ্ণ *n* afternoon. **অপরাহ্ণে** *adv* in the afternoon. **আজ অপরাহ্ণে** this afternoon. **কাল অপরাহ্ণে** tomorrow afternoon. **গতকাল অপরাহ্ণে** yesterday afternoon.

অপরিকল্পিত *adj* unplanned; unthought-of; not designed; off-hand. **~ ভাবে** *adv* in an unplanned way.

অপরিগ্রহ *n* refusal; rejection; non-acceptance. ❑*adj* unmarried.

অপরিচয় *n* non-acquaintance; unfamiliarity. **অপরিচিত** *adj* unknown; unfamiliar; strange; **অপরিচিতা** *fem* **অপরিচিত ব্যক্তি** *n* a stranger.

অপরিচ্ছন্ন *adj* **1** unclean; dirty; slovenly; untidy. **2** (fig) impure: ~ মন. **~তা** *n* uncleanness; dirtiness; impurity.

অপরিচ্ছিন্ন *adj* undivided; continuous; incessant; endless; unlimited.

অপরিজ্ঞাত *adj* unknown; unfamiliar; unstudied; strange.

অপরিজ্ঞেয় *adj* unknowable; incognizable; inscrutable; incomprehensible.

অপরিণত *adj* **1** immature; young: ~ বয়স. **2** not ripened; green; raw. **~ বয়স্ক** *adj* **1** tender-aged. **2** one who has not attained the age of puberty. **3** minor. **~ বুদ্ধি** *adj* **1** of immature judgement. **2** frivolous. **3** childish; puerile.

অপরিণামদর্শী *adj* lacking in foresight; unforeseeing; imprudent. **~তা** *n* want of foresight; imprudence.

অপরিণীত *adj* unmarried; unwedded. **অপরিণীতা** *fem.*

অপরিতুষ্ট *adj* not satisfied; dissatisfied; discontented.

অপরিতৃপ্ত *adj* insatiated; unsatisfied; ungratified; unfulfilled: ~ আকাঙ্ক্ষা.

অপরিত্যাজ্য *adj* not to be forsaken/ given up; indispensable; essential.

অপরিপক্ব *adj* **1** not ripe; green; raw. **2** immature; inexperienced. **~তা** *n* unripeness; immaturity; inexperience.

অপরিপাক *n* indigestion.

অপরিপাটি, অপরিপাটী *adj* untidy; not well-arranged; out of order. ❑*n* untidiness; slovenliness.

অপরিপূর্ণ *adj* **1** not thoroughly filled; not full. **2** incomplete; unfulfilled; defective.

অপরিবর্তন *n* absence of change/ alteration : ❑*adj* correct; exact; accurate; unwavering. **~শীল** *adj* not subject to change; unchanging; immutable. **অপরিবর্তনীয়** *adj* unchangeable; invariable; fixed.

অপরিবর্তিত *adj* unchanged; unaltered.

অপরিবাহী *adj* not conducting heat or electric current; non-conducting. ❑*n* non-conductor.

অপরিমাণ *n* plenty; abundance; affluence. ❑*adj* immeasurable; innumerable; profuse; plentiful. **অপরিমিত** *adj* **1** countless; boundless; unlimited; immoderate. **অপরিমিতাচার** *n* intemperance; overindulgence. **অপরিমিত ভোজন** *n* over-eating.

অপরিমেয় *adj* that which cannot be measured.

অপরিষ্কার *n* uncleanliness; impurity; dirtiness. ❑*adj* unclean; dirty; impure; (fig) indistinct; vague. **অপরিষ্কৃত** *adj* what has not been cleaned; unrefined; unpurified.

অপরিসর *adj* not wide or spacious; narrow.

অপরিসীম *adj* unlimited; unbounded: স্রষ্টার ~ অনুগ্রহ.

অপরিস্ফুট *adj* not clearly expressed; not manifest; indistinct.

অপরিহার্য *adj* indispensable; unavoidable. **~ দ্রব্য** *n* necessaries.

অপরীক্ষিত *adj* not examined/ tried/ tested; untried/unexamined.

অপরূপ *adj* **1** never having happened before; unprecedented; incomparable. **2** strange; wonderful; queer. **3** deformed; ugly. **4** awkward; odd-looking.

অপরোক্ষ *adj* not indirect; with nothing/ none in between; straight; direct; immediate. **~ অনুভূতি** *n* (phil) direct perception. **~ উক্তি** *n* (gram) direct speech.

অপর্ণা *n fem* Aparna, appellation of Hindu goddess Durga.

অপর্যাপ্ত *adj* **1** more than enough; abundant; plentiful. **2** (also used in opposite sense) insufficient; inadequate. **অপর্যাপ্তি** *n* abundance.

অপলক *adj* (of eyes) winkless; steadfast. **~ নেত্রে** *adv* with a steadfast look.

অপলাপ *n* **1** the act of denying; denial. **2** suppression; concealment. **3** prevarication; false statement. **4** dishonour; detraction: সত্যের ~.

অপসরণ *n* **1** exit; retreat; withdrawal. **2** act of fleeing; flight; escape. ~ **করা** *vi,vt* move away; withdraw.

অপসারণ *n* shifting; transference; removal. ~ **করা** *vi,vt* remove; shift; dismiss. **অপসারিত** *adj* removed; dismissed; cancelled.

অপসারী *adj* (phys) that diverges; divergent.

অপসৃত=অপসারিত

অপহত *adj* perished; destroyed.

অপহন্তা *n* person committing an assassination; assassin; murderer.

অপহরণ *n* carrying off; stealing; theft; misappropriation. ~ **করা** *vt* rob sb of sth; misappropriate; steal; abduct. **অপহারক, অপহারী** *adj* robbing; stealing; plundering. ❑*n* robber; thief; plunderer. **অপহৃত** *adj* what is stolen/ robbed/ plundered.

অপহারক, অপহারী⇒অপহরণ

অপহৃত⇒অপহরণ

অপাঙ্‌ক্তেয়, অপাংক্তেয় *adj* **1** socially debarred from sitting at the same table with others; of lower status. **2** outcaste; ostracized.

অপাঙ্গ *n* outer corner of the eye. ~ **দৃষ্টি** *n* side-glance; looking askance.

অপাচ্য *adj* (of food) which cannot be easily digested; indigestible.

অপাঠ্য *adj* (of books, etc) not worth-reading; obscene; indecent.

অপাত্র *n* unworthy/ undeserving person.

অপাদান *n* (gram) ablative case.

অপাপ *adj* sinless. ~**বিদ্ধ** *adj* never committing any sin; innocent.

অপার *adj* boundless; endless; immense.

অপারগ *adj* not able; incapable. ~**তা** *n* inability; incapacity.

অপার্থিব *adj* unearthly; heavenly; supernatural.

অপার্যমানে *adv* in case of inability.

অপিচ *conj* moreover; besides; further.

অপুত্রক *adj* without a son; having no issue.

অপুষ্ট *adj* undeveloped; under-nourished.

অপুষ্টি *n* want of nutrition; malnutrition.

অপুষ্পক *adj* unflowering; flowerless; (bot) belonging to the cryptogamia class of plants; cryptogamous. ~ **উদ্ভিদ** *n* a cryptogam.

অপূর্ণ *adj* **1** not full/filled; incomplete; unfinished; imperfect. **2** unsatisfied; unfulfilled: ~ বাসনা. ~**তা** *n* incompleteness; imperfection.

অপূর্ব *adj* **1** unprecedented; not known/ seen previously. **2** remarkable; extra-ordinary; uncommon. **3** excellent; wonderful.

অপেক্ষমাণ⇒অপেক্ষা

অপেক্ষা *n* **1** act of awaiting/ waiting for. **2** dependence; reliance: বৃষ্টির অপেক্ষায় চাষাবাদ স্থগিত. **3** expectation; anticipation: সুদিনের ~. **4** care for; be concerned with/ dependent on: আমি কারো অপেক্ষায় বসে নেই. ❑*conj* than; in comparison to/with: চন্দ্র অপেক্ষা পৃথিবী বড়ো. ~ **করা** *vi,vt* await; wait for (sb). **একটু ~ করো** wait a little. **আর ~ করে লাভ নেই** its no use waiting any more. **আমি তার আসার ~ করছি** expect his arrival; I expect him to arrive or come. **অপেক্ষমাণ** *adj* awaiting. ~**কৃত** *adv* comparatively; relatively: ~কৃত বড়ো.

অপেয় *adj* what cannot/ should not be drunk; undrinkable.

অপোগণ্ড *adj* **1** baby; infant. **2** under-age; minor. **3** not more than fifteen years of age; not past fifteen. **4** unfit; incompetent; unworthy.

অপৌরুষ *n* unmanliness; cowardice; shame; infamy.

অপ্রকাশ *adj* **1** not known; obscure; hidden. **অপ্রকাশিত** *adj* unrevealed; undisclosed; unpublished. **অপ্রকাশ্য** *adj* what should not be/ is not to be made public; private: অপ্রকাশ্য স্থান.

অপ্রকৃত *adj* not real/ genuine; spurious; artificial.

অপ্রকৃতিস্থ *adj* unbalanced; insane; crazy; mentally deranged.

অপ্রচলিত *adj* not in vogue; gone out of use; obsolete; archaic (word).

অপ্রতিদ্বন্দ্বী *adj* unrivalled; matchless; unique.

অপ্রতিভ *adj* perplexed; embarrassed; non-plussed; confused. ~ **হওয়া** *vt* be abashed/ perplexed.

অপ্রতিম *adj* not comparable; unparalleled; matchless.

অপ্রতিহত *adj* unresisted; uninterrupted; unimpeded. ~**ভাবে** *adv* uninterruptedly; irresistibly.

অপ্রতুল *n* **1** insufficiency; absence of abundance. **2** want; shortage; deficiency; dearth; indigence.

অপ্রত্যক্ষ *adj* not perceptible by the sense organs; imperceptible; invisible; transcendental; indirect: ~ নির্বাচন, ~ করা রোপণ, indirect taxation.

অপ্রত্যাশিত *adj* unexpected; sudden; accidental. ~**ভাবে** *adv* unexpectedly; suddenly; by chance.

অপ্রয়োজন *n* want of necessity; needlessness. **অপ্রয়োজনীয়** *adj* unnecessary; needless; useless.

অপ্রশস্ত *adj* **1** not wide or spacious; narrow. **2** unfavourable. **3** inauspicious; unsuitable.

অপ্রসন্ন *adj* **1** displeased; dissatisfied; unhappy. **2** unfavourable; gloomy: ~ ভাগ্য. ~**তা**

n displeasure; sadness; bad grace. ~চিত্তে *adv* with dissatisfaction; with a bad grace.

অপ্রস্তুত *adj* **1** disconcerted; embarrassed; out of countenance. **2** not yet made or prepared. **3** unready; unprepared. **4** (fig) absent; irrelevant. ~ **করা** *vt* put one out of countenance; disconcert; embarrass; abash.

অপ্রাকৃত *adj* unnatural; supernatural; uncommon; extra-ordinary.

অপ্রাপ্তবয়স্ক *adj* under-age; minor.

অপ্রাসঙ্গিক *adj* irrelevant; out of place; not incidental/ to the point.

অপ্রীতিকর *adj* unpleasant; offensive.

অপ্সরা, অপ্সরী *n fem* (according to Hindu belief) celestial nymph of voluptuous beauty with exceptional gifts in music and dancing.

অফিস [E] *n* building(s) where the affairs of a government department or any other organization are conducted; an office.

অফিসার [E] *n* a person with a position of authority and trust in an office or organization; an officer.

অফুরন্ত, অফুরান *adj* unending; endless; inexhaustible.

অব *pref* indicating inferiority, baseness, downwards, inwards, certainty, expanse, absence, etc (অবক্ষয়, অবক্ষেপ, অবমূল্যায়ন ইত্যাদি).

অবকাশ *n* **1** leisure; respite; recess. **2** vacation: গ্রীষ্মাবকাশ. **3** necessary time/ opportunity for doing sth: কাজের ~. **4** scope; room; ground: সন্দেহের ~.

অবক্ষয় *n* waste; erosion; depreciation; decadence.

অবক্ষিত⇒অবক্ষেপ

অবক্ষেপ *n* act of throwing down or scattering; sarcasm; ridicule. **অবক্ষিপ্ত** *adj* thrown down; cast downwards; precipitated.

অবগত *adj* informed; aware of; acquainted with. ~ **করা** *vi,vt* inform; apprise; intimate. ~ **হওয়া** *vi,vt* learn; come to know; be aware of. **অবগতি** *n* information; knowledge; awareness.

অবগাহন *n* bathing by immersion in a pond/ river.

অবগুণ *n* absence of virtue; disqualification; blemish; fault; defect.

অবগুণ্ঠন *n* veil for the head and face used by women. **অবগুণ্ঠিত** *adj* veiled; hidden. **অবগুণ্ঠিতা** *fem.*

অবচেতন *adj* subconscious; beyond conscious knowledge; the hidden level of the mind and thoughts: ~ মন.

অবজ্ঞা *n* disregard; disrespect; slight; scorn; contempt; neglect. ~ **করা** *vt* slight; neglect; ignore; disregard. **অবজ্ঞাত** *adj* slighted; scorned; neglected. **অবজ্ঞেয়** *adj* contemptible; despicable.

অবতরণ *n* act of going or coming down; descent; landing down. ~ **করা** *vi* get down; descend; disembark: জাহাজ থেকে ~ করা; alight: বিমান থেকে ~ করা. **অবতরণিকা** *n* **1** (of books) preface; introduction; prologue; preamble; prelude. **2** ladder; staircase.

অবতল *adj* curved inward; like the inside surface of a hollow ball; concave. ~ **দর্পণ** concave mirror.

অবতার *n* incarnation; personation. **দয়ার** ~ mercy incarnate; kindness personified. ~**বাদ** *n* the doctrine of incarnation.

অবতারণ *n* causing to get down; putting up a proposal. **অবতারণা** *n* introduction; proposal; preface; foreword.

অবতারবাদ⇒অবতার

অবতীর্ণ *adj* one who has got/ come down; that which has been sent down: কোরআন আরবি ভাষায় ~ হয়. ~ **হওয়া** *vi,vt* descend; alight; come/step down; appear on earth as an incarnation. **যুদ্ধে ~ হওয়া** *vt* go to war; appear in the battle-field.

অবদমন *n* repression (of desires). ~ **করা** *vt* repress. **অবদমিত** *adj* repressed.

অবদান *n* contribution; noble achievement; heroic performance: বাংলা সাহিত্যে নজরুলের ~ অবিস্মরণীয়.

অবধারণ *n* determination; fixation; settlement. ~ **করা** *vi,vt* determine; fix; settle; discern.

অবধারিত *adj* **1** that which is sure to happen; certain; inevitable; unavoidable. **2** determined; ascertained; settled.

অবধি *prep, adv* **1** since; from: জন্ম ~. **2** till; upto: আজ ~. ❑*n* limit; end; termination: তার দুর্গতির ~ নেই. ~**-বাধিত** *adj* (legal) barred by limitation.

অবনত *adj* **1** bent down; humble. **2** degraded; downfallen. ~ **জাতি** *n* depressed class. ~ **মস্তকে** *adv* with the head bent down; meekly; humbly. ~**মুখী** *adj* downcast; having the face hung down. **অবনতি** *n* downfall; degradation; deterioration; humiliation.

অবনমিত *adj* laid low; humbled.

অবনী, অবণি *n* the earth; the world; the land. ~**তল** *n* the surface of the earth; the earth. ~**পতি** *n* king; emperor. ~**মণ্ডল** *n* the universe. ~**শ্বর** *n* king; emperor.

অববাহিকা *n* the basin of a river.

অবমাননা *n* insult; dishonour; disrespect; affront.

অবয়ব *n* **1** limb; member; body. **2** figure; form. **3** constituent part; portion. **অবয়বী** *adj* having a body; corporeal.

অবরুদ্ধ *adj* **1** obstructed; barricaded: ~ পথ. **2** confined; imprisoned. **3** blockaded; besieged: ~ নগর **4** checked; frustrated: ~ বাসনা. **~ করা** *vt* close; shut; blockade; besiege; imprison.

অবরোধ *n* **1** obstruction; hindrance. **2** harem; zenana: ~বাসিনী. **3** siege; blockade: নগর ~. **4** purdah system: ~ প্রথা. **5** detention; confinement. **~ করা** *vt* lay siege; besiege. **~ক** *adj* besieging. ❑*n* besieger. **~কারী সেনাদল** *n* besieging army. **~বাসিনী** *adj fem* confined in the harem. ❑*n* lady of the harem.

অবরোহ *n* **1** getting down; descent. **2** (logic) reasoning from a general idea to particular one; deduction. **3** deterioration; degradation. **4** (music) descending scale of notes. **~ণ** *n* descending; dismounting; coming down. **~ণ করা** *vi,vt* descend; get down. **~ণী** *n* flight of steps; ladder; escalator. **~ প্রণালী** *n* deductive method.

অবরোহী *adj* one who is coming down; (logic) deductive.

অবর্ণনীয় *adj* beyond expression in words; indescribable.

অবর্তমান *adj* **1** inexistent; absent. **2** dead; departed; past. **অবর্তমানে** *adv* in the absence (of); after one's death/ departure.

অবলম্বন *n* **1** act of having recourse to/ adopting: সন্ন্যাসাবলম্বন. **2** act of holding oneself in: ধৈর্যাবলম্বন, ধর্মাবলম্বন. **3** dependence; support; prop: যষ্টি ~. **~ করা** *vt* resort to; adopt; takeup; depend on; hold.

অবলা *adj fem* weak; feeble. ❑*n* woman. **~ জাতি** *n* the weaker sex. **অবলার মুখই বল** a woman's weapon is her tongue.

অবলীলা *n* absence of strain; dalliance; ease. **~য়, ~ক্রমে** *adv* unhesitatingly; playfully; in a carefree manner; easily.

অবলুপ্ত *adj* vanished; effaced; extinct. **~ হওয়া** *vi* vanish; disappear; become extinct.

অবলোকন *n* act of looking at; surveying; observation. **~ করা** *vi,vt* look at; set eyes on; observe.

অবশ *adj* **1** beyond control; unruly; refractory; untamed; unmanageable. **2** insensitive; paralysed; benumbed. **~ করা** *vt* paralyse; benumb; anaesthetize; etherize.

অবশিষ্ট *adj* remaining; residual; surplus; outstanding. ❑*n* the rest; remainder; a residue or surplus. **অবশিষ্টাংশ** *n* remaining portion; remainder; remnant; residue. **~ ক্ষমতা** *n* residuary power. **~ ব্যক্তিগণ** the rest; the remaining others.

অবশেষ *n* **1** end; termination. **2** the last stage/ portion: দিনের ~. **3** remnant; remainder: ধ্বংসাবশেষ. **অবশেষে** *adv* at last; at length; ultimately; in the end.

অবশ্য[1] *adj* who or what cannot be subdued; untameable; uncontrollable.

অবশ্য[2] *adv* **1** surely; certainly; inevitably: কেয়ামত ~ ঘটবে. **2** always; ever; by all means: ধূমপান ~পরিত্যাজ্য. **3** compulsorily; without fail: কোরআন ~পাঠ্য. **4** of course; undoubtedly; needless to say: আমি ~ তোমার অমঙ্গল চাই না. ❑*int* of course. **~কর্তব্য** *adj* obligatory. **~ম্ভাবী** *adj* inevitable. **~ম্ভাবিতা** *n* inevitability.

অবসন্ন *adj* fatigued; exhausted; wearied; dejected; extremely tired. **~ হওয়া** *vi,vt* sink down; be spent up; be exhausted/ dejected/ wearied. **~তা** *n* exhaustion; fatigue; lassitude.

অবসর *n* **1** leisure; respite. **2** opportunity: কথা বলার ~. **3** retirement: চাকুরি থেকে ~. **~ক্রমে** *adv* at one's leisure. **~ গ্রহণ** *n* retirement. **~প্রাপ্ত** *adj* retired. **~বিনোদন** *n* recreation.

অবসাদ *n* fatigue; weariness; exhaustion. **~গ্রস্ত** *adj* depressed; downcast; wearied; fatigued.

অবসান *n* termination; conclusion; end. **~ হওয়া** *vi,vt* terminate; come to an end; conclude.

অবস্থা *n* **1** state; condition. **2** temperament; mood: মনের ~. **3** circumstance: ~ বুঝে ব্যবস্থা. **4** financial position: তার ~ ভালো নয়. **~গতিকে** *adv* being compelled by circumstances. **~ঘটিত** *adj* circumstantial. **~ ফিরানো** *vt* improve one's financial condition; better one's fortune. **অবস্থাপন্ন** *adj* well-to-do; rich; solvent. **~ভেদে** *adv* in different circumstances.

অবস্থান *n* **1** staying; residing. **2** abode; dwelling place; location; situation. **~ করা** *vi,vt* stay; dwell; be positioned/ located. **~ ধর্মঘট** *n* stay-in strike.

অবস্থিত *adj* situated; located. **অবস্থিতি** *n* situation; location; presence.

অবহিত *adj* **1** attentive; absorbed; occupied. **2** informed; aware. **3** careful; watchful; alert.

অবহেলা *n* neglect; disregard; disrespect. **~ করা** *vt* neglect; slight; disrespect. **~ভরে** *adv* neglectfully; slightingly. **অবহেলিত** *adj* neglected; slighted; treated with disregard.

অবাক *adj* **1** destitute of the faculty of speech; dumb; mute; silent. **2** astonished; amazed; surprised. **~ হওয়া** *vi,vt* be amazed/struck with wonder.

অবাঙালি *adj* **1** other than Bengali-speaking. **2** non-Bengali; contrary to Bengali culture.

অবাধ *adj* unhindered; unobstructed; unrestricted; free. **2** unlimited; unbounded. **~ নীতি** *n* the principle allowing people's activities to develop without control; laissez-faire. **~ বাণিজ্য** *n* free trade. **অবাধে** *adv* freely; easily; without let or hindrance; uninterruptedly; incessantly.

অবাধ্য *adj* 1 disobedient; insubordinate; unruly; obstinate. 2 inevitable; unavoidable. ~তা *n* disobedience; obstinacy; recalcitrance.

অবান্তর *adj* 1 irrelevant; extraneous; beside the mark.

অবারিত *adj* unchecked; unbarred; open; free. ~-দ্বার *adj* with doors open; easily accessible. ~ দ্বার *n* free access; liberal hospitality.

অবাস্তব *adj* 1 not real or material; imaginary; fanciful: ~ কল্পনা. 2 not based on realities; unpractical; impracticable: ~ পরিকল্পনা. 3 non-existent; inexistent; unreal; illusory; false. ~তা *n* unreality; impracticability; inexistence.

অবিকল *adj* exact; whole; entire; precisely the same; true to the original: ~ বিবরণ. ❑*adv* exactly; precisely. ~ নকল *n* facsimile; true copy. ~ সত্য *n* perfect truth.

অবিকল্প *adj* that has no alternative/substitute.

অবিকৃত *adj* 1 unchanged; unaltered; exact. 2 unmixed; unadulterated; pure; genuine. 3 not deteriorated/decayed/decomposed; intact.

অবিকৃতি *n* the state of changelessness; uncorrupted or unperverted state.

অবিক্রীত *adj* that could not be sold; unsold.

অবিক্রেয় *adj* not marketable/salable; unstable.

অবিক্ষত *adj* unhurt; uninjured; unimpaired.

অবিক্ষিপ্ত *adj* 1 not scattered; orderly. 2 not perturbed/distracted; calm; composed.

অবিক্ষুব্ধ *adj* not agitated/distracted; calm; placid.

অবিচক্ষণ *adj* unwise; imprudent; indiscreet ~তা *n* imprudence.

অবিচল, অবিচলিত *adj* unshaken; unmoved; unperturbed; calm; firm: অবিচল বিশ্বাস. অবিচলিত কণ্ঠে *adv* in an unshaken voice; without hesitation. অবিচলিতচিত্তে *adv* firmly; calmly; unfalteringly.

অবিচার *n* injustice; unfairness; lack of justice. ~ করা *vi,vt* do injustice; judge unfairly.

অবিচ্ছিন্ন *adj* 1 unseparated; unsevered; entire. 2 continuous; uninterrupted. ❑*adv* ceaselessly; continually; incessantly.

অবিচ্ছেদ *n* 1 inseparation. 2 contiguity; continuity; conjunction. ❑*adj* 1 undivided; entire. 2 continuous. অবিচ্ছেদ্য *adj* inseparable; indivisible.

অবিচ্যুত *adj* not detached or fallen apart; undetached; unsupported; firm; intact.

অবিজ্ঞ *adj* unwise; injudicious; imprudent. ~তা *n* imprudence; injudiciousness.

অবিজ্ঞেয় *adj* incomprehensible; unintelligible; unknowable.

অবিত্ত *adj* insolvent; indigent. ❑*n* an insolvent person; a pauper.

অবিদিত *adj* unknown; uninformed; unaware.

অবিদ্যমান *adj* not present/existing; absent; inexistent.

অবিদ্যা *n* absence of education; ignorance.

অবিদ্বান *adj* uneducated; illiterate; ignorant.

অবিধান, অবিধি *n* a repressive or unjust law; a black act or ordinance.

অবিধেয় *adj* not proper to do; improper; unbecoming; unjust. ~তা *n* impropriety.

অবিনয় *n* lack of courtesy/politeness/civility; rudeness; indecorum; incivility; arrogance. অবিনয়ী *adj* discourteous; impolite; arrogant; uncivil; haughty.

অবিনশ্বর *adj* which will always exist or cannot wear out; imperishable; immortal; eternal.

অবিনাশী=অবিনশ্বর

অবিনীত *adj* impolite; discourteous; rough; uncivil. অবিনীতা *fem.*

অবিন্যস্ত *adj* 1 not well-arranged; unsystematic. 2 slovenly; messy; disorderly.

অবিবাহিত *adj* unmarried; unwedded. অবিবাহিতা *fem.*

অবিবেচনা *n* 1 lack of consideration. 2 injustice; impropriety; imprudence.

অবিভক্ত *adj* undivided; unsevered; whole; entire.

অবিভাজ্য *adj* indivisible. ~তা *n* indivisibility.

অবিমিশ্র *adj* unmixed; unadulterated; pure.

অবিমৃষ্য *adj* indiscreet; injudicious; imprudent. ~কারী *adj* rash; foolhardy; impetuous; headstrong. ~কারিতা *n* rashness; thoughtlessness; imprudence.

অবিরত *adj* ceaseless; incessant. unremitting; constant; continuous. ❑*adv* ceaselessly; incessantly; constantly; continuously; always.

অবিরল *adj* continuous; unceasing; incessant. ❑*adv* continually; ceaselessly. ~ ধারে *adv* in a continuous flow; intermittently; ceaselessly.

অবিরাম *adj* non-stop; unremitting; continual. ❑*adv* without intermission; ceaselessly; continuously. ~ গতি *n* perpetual motion. ~ জ্বর *n* remittent fever.

অবিরোধ *n* absence of opposition; accord; agreement; amity. অবিরোধী *adj* not opposed/antagonistic. অবিরোধে *adv* in the absence of opposition/hostility.

অবিলম্ব *n* absence of delay; haste; hurry. ❑*adj* immediate; prompt. অবিলম্বে *adv* without delay; immediately; at once.

অবিশ্বস্ত *adj* not trustworthy; unreliable; unfaithful. ~তা *n* untrustworthiness; unreliability; faithlessness; perfidy.

অবিশ্বাস *n* want/lack of faith; incredibility; suspicion; incredulity. ~ করা *vt* distrust; disbelieve; suspect; not to trust. অবিশ্বাসী *adj* 1 untrustworthy; unfaithful; unreliable. 2 (phil) sceptical; lacking in conviction/ faith. ❑*n* doubter; disbeliever; sceptic. অবিশ্বাস্য *n* incredible; unbelievable. ~যোগ্য *adj* unworthy of credit/ belief.

অবিশ্যি (dial) corrupt of অবশ্য[২]

অবিশ্রাম *n* want of rest. ❑*adj* unceasing.

অবিশ্রান্ত *adj* untiring; unremitting; non-stop; ❑*adv* untiringly; without rest/ break.

অবিসংবাদ *n* absence of opposition/ hostility; unanimity; amicability. অবিসংবাদিত *adj* undisputed; unopposed; unchallenged; unquestionable. অবিসংবাদিতরূপে *adv* indisputably; undisputedly. অবিসংবাদিত সত্য *n* irrefutable/ indisputable truth. অবিসংবাদে *adv* without opposition; peacefully.

অবিস্মরণীয় *adj* unforgettable; memorable.

অবিহিত *adj* contrary to what is enjoined/ prescribed; illegal; unlawful; improper.

অবীর *adj* **1** not heroic; timid; cowardly; weak. **2** without a hero. অবীরা *fem.* অবীরোচিত *adj* not becoming a hero; unheroic.

অবুঝ *adj* **1** incapable of understanding; not amenable to reason; unreasonable. **2** foolish; stupid.

অবেলা *n* inconvenient/ unsuitable hour of the day; late afternoon.

অবৈতনিক *adj* not serving for pecuniary benefit; honorary: ~পদ. ~বিদ্যালয় *n* free school.

অবৈধ *adj* **1** unlawful; illegal: ~ সমাবেশ. **2** unscriptural; forbidden in scripture: ~ খাদ্য. **3** illicit: ~ প্রণয়; illegitimate: ~ সন্তান. **4** improper; unfair: ~ উপায়. ~তা *n.*

অবোধ *adj* **1** lacking in judgment: ~ শিশু. **2** unreasonable; inconsolable: ~ মন. **3** foolish; stupid; dull-headed.

অবোধ্য *adj* which cannot be understood; unintelligible; incomprehensible.

অব্দ *n* year; calendar year: খ্রিস্টাব্দ, বঙ্গাব্দ.

অব্যক্ত *adj* **1** not manifest; hidden. **2** indistinct. **3** inexpressible; indescribable: ~ বেদনা.

অব্যবস্থা *n* disorder; mismanagement.

অব্যবহার্য *adj* not fit to be used; unserviceable; out of use.

অব্যবহিত *adj* being next to; adjoining; contiguous; immediate; next. ~ পরে *adv* immediately after. ~ পূর্বে *adv* immediately before.

অব্যয় *adj* not subject to change or decay; imperishable; immortal; eternal. ❑*n* (gram) word not varied by inflection; indeclinable word (ie, preposition, conjunction or interjection). অব্যয়ীভাব *n* (gram) system of forming a compound word by adding a noun to an indeclinable word (eg, অনু+রূপ= *অনুরূপ,* যথা+ অর্থ= *যথার্থ*).

অব্যর্থ *adj* (of things) never failing; infallible; sure to be effective: ~ ওষুধ. ~তা *n* effectiveness; unfailingness.

অব্যাহত *adj* uninterrupted; unhindered. ~রূপে *adv* unopposed; without hindrance.

অব্যাহতি *n* **1** state of being exempted; exemption: কর থেকে ~. **2** condition of being found not guilty; acquittal: খুনের দায় থেকে ~. **3** release: জেল থেকে ~. ~ দেওয়া *vt* acquit; exempt; release; relieve. ~ পাওয়া *vi, vt* escape; get rid of; be acquitted/ exempted/ released.

অভদ্র *adj* uncivil; unmannerly; discourteous. ~তা *n* discourtesy; incivility. অভদ্রোচিত *adj* unmannerly; impolite; ungentlemanly.

অভয় *n* **1** fearlessness; courage. **2** assurance of safety. অভয়ে *adv* without fear/ hesitation. ~ বাণী *n* pledge of safety/ security.

অভাগা *adj* luckless; unlucky; unfortunate. অভাগী, অভাগিনী *fem*: অভাগা যেদিকে চায়, সাগর শুকিয়ে যায়; once unlucky, always unlucky.

অভাজন *n* unworthy/ undeserving person; poor/ wretched fellow.

অভাব *n* **1** want; absence; non-existence. **2** shortage; scarcity; indigence; deficiency. ~গ্রস্ত *adj* needy; poverty-stricken; indigent. ~ পূরণ করা *vt* meet the want/need; make-up for deficit; become free from poverty/ want. অভাবে স্বভাব নষ্ট **1** Want is at the root of corruption. **2** Necessity knows no law.

অভাবনীয় *adj* **1** unthinkable; unimaginable; inconceivable. **2** unusual; unexpected; amazing. ❑*n* anything unexpected.

অভাবিত, অভাবিতপূর্ব *adj* unforeseen; unthought of.

অভি *pref* denoting proximity, similarity, front, approach, frequency, etc.

অভিকর্ষ *n* (phys) gravitational attraction.

অভিকেন্দ্র *adj* tending to move in the direction of the centre; centripetal. ~ বল *n* centripetal force.

অভিক্ষেপ *n* standing out beyond an edge or surface; projection. ~ তল *n* plane of projection.

অভিজাত *adj* aristocratic; high-born. ~তন্ত্র *n* government by the aristocracy.

অভিজ্ঞ *adj* **1** specialized; expert. **2** wise; experienced; well-versed; veteran. অভিজ্ঞা *fem.* ~তা *n* experience; skill.

অভিজ্ঞা[১] ⇒ অভিজ্ঞ

অভিজ্ঞা[২] *n* intuition; memory. ~ন *n* token of recognition; keepsake. ~ন-পত্র *n* letter of introduction; identity card.

অভিধা *n* **1** name; appellation; title. **2** connotation/denotation of a word.

অভিধান *n* dictionary; lexicon. ~ দেখা *vi, vt* consult/ look up a dictionary. ~ রচনা করা *vt* compile a dictionary. ~কার *n* lexicographer.

অভিনন্দন *n* **1** an expression of joy for someone's success, good luck, etc; congratulations; felicitations. **2** tribute of respect paid at formal reception; felicitous eulogy. ~ জানানো *vt* congratulate; felicitate. ~পত্র *n* an address of welcome. অভিনন্দিত *adj* congratulated; felicitated; received with honour.

অভিনব *adj* **1** new and novel; recent. **2** newly devised/ produced; new-fashioned. **3** never having happened before; unprecedented. ~ত্ব, ~তা *n* novelty; the quality of being new.

অভিনয় *n* theatrical performance; acting in the role of a dramatic character. ~ করা *vi,vt* play the part/ act the role of a dramatic character. অভিনেতা/অভিনেত্রী *n* actor/ actress.

অভিনিবেশ *n* **1** attention. **2** concentration; single-mindedness; •rapt attention. **3** assiduity; earnest exertion. অভিনিবিষ্ট *adj* absorbed in; deeply engrossed. ~পূর্বক *adv* with rapt attention.

অভিনেতা,অভিনেত্রী⇒অভিনয়

অভিন্ন *adj* **1** not different/ dissimilar; identical. **2** not separate; one and the same. **3** not severed/ detached; undivided. ~তা, ~ত্ব *n* identity; sameness; entirety; uniformity; similarity. ~ পরিবার *n* joint family. ~হৃদয় বন্ধু *n* bosom friend.

অভিপ্রায় *n* **1** a feeling of having or doing sth; wish; desire. 2 that which is aimed at; aim; intention; object; purpose; design. **3** meaning; significance; purport. **4** opinion. ~ করা *vt* desire; intend; mean; signify; design.

অভিপ্রেত *adj* desired; intended; meant; contemplated; designed; purported.

অভিবাদক⇒অভিবাদন

অভিবাদন *n* salutation; greeting; obeisance. ~ করা *vt* salute; greet; bow; make obeisance. অভিবাদক *adj* one who greets/ salutes.

অভিবাসন *n* settling into another country; immigration. অভিবাসী *adj* immigrant.

অভিব্যক্তি *n* **1** unfolding; expression; manifestation. **2** gradual development; evolution. অভিব্যক্ত *adj* unfolded; made clear/ apparent; developed; expressed; evident অভিব্যক্ত করা *vt* express; make known/ manifest. ~বাদ *n* theory of evolution.

অভিব্যপ্ত *adj* overspread; diffused. অভিব্যাপ্তি *n* diffusion.

অভিভাবক **1** guardian; regent; custodian. **2** one who gives shelter/ refuge.

অভিভাষণ *n* an address; a public/ platform speech.

অভিভূত *adj* **1** overcome; defeated. **2** attacked; overwhelmed; embarrassed; non-plussed; bewildered. **3** deeply impressed.

অভিমত *n* **1** desire; intention; choice. **2** opinion. ❑*adj* approved; permitted.

অভিমান *n* **1** offended state of mind; pique; sensitiveness; mental perturbation (caused by undesirable conduct of a near and dear one). **2** pride; conceit; egoism. **3** sense of self-respect. ~ করা *vi* be in a huff; take a pique at sb. অভিমানী *adj* sensitive; proud; haughty. অভিমানিনী *fem.*

অভিমুখ *n* the direction of approach: ঢাকা অভিমুখে যাত্রা. ❑*adj* facing; moving towards; bound for: গৃহাভিমুখ. অভিমুখী *fem* =অভিমুখ (*adj*). অভিমুখে *adv* in the direction of; to; towards: সে ঢাকা অভিমুখে যাত্রা করলো, he started for Dhaka.

অভিযান *n* expedition for military conquest or adventurous exploration: এভারেষ্ট ~.

অভিযুক্ত *adj* **1** accused; charged; one against whom a charge has been brought. **2** defendant in a criminal case. **3** respondent in a civil suit. অভিযোক্তা *n, adj* accuser; complainant; plaintiff. ~ করা *vt* charge; accuse; prosecute; bring an action/ lodge a complaint against. ~ হওয়া *vt* be accused of/ charged with/ prosecuted.

অভিযোগ *n* complaint; accusation; charge; allegation; legal prosecution. ~ করা *vt* complain; lodge a complaint; accuse; bring a charge/ legal action; prosecute in a court of law. ~কারী same as অভিযোক্তা (⇒ অভিযুক্ত). ~পত্র *n* charge-sheet.

অভিরুচি *n* **1** wish; desire intention. **2** inclination; liking; taste; pleasure. আপনার যেরূপ ~(হয়) as you please.

অভিলষণীয় *adj* desirable; covetable.

অভিলষিত⇒অভিলাষ

অভিলাষ *n* wish; desire; intention; pleasure. ~ করা *vt* desire; wish for; long/ yearn for. অভিলষিত *adj* desired; wished for; intended. অভিলাষী *adj* desirous; wishful; wishing; craving. অভিলাষিণী *fem.* অভিলাষী হওয়া *vt* be desirous of; crave for.

অভিশপ্ত *adj* under a curse/ interdiction; cursed; accursed; doomed. ~ হওয়া *vt* be cursed.

অভিশাপ *n* curse; imprecation; malediction. ~ দেওয়া *vi, vt* curse; imprecate.

অভিষিক্ত⇒অভিষেক

অভিষেক *n* **1** ceremony connected with coronation; installation; inauguration. **2** appointment; induction; initiation; enthronement; ~ করা *vt* crown; install; inaugurate. অভিষিক্ত *adj* crowned; installed. যুবরাজ রাজপদে অভিষিক্ত হলেন The prince was crowned king.

অভিসম্পাত=অভিশাপ

অভিসার *n* love tryst; appointment of lovers; a lover's journey to the place of assignation. ~**ক, অভিসারী** *adj* lover on his journey of love. **অভিসারিকা, অভিসারিণী** *fem.*

অভিহিত *adj* **1** designated; named; called; entitled. **2** referred to; mentioned.

অভীষ্ট *adj* **1** desired; intended; wished for; aimed at. **2** beloved; cherished; longed for. ❑ *n* object of desire. ~ **লাভ** *n* gratification/fulfilment of desire; attainment of an objective.

অভুক্ত *adj* **1** unfed; fasting; starving. **2** uneaten; unconsumed.

অভূত *n* **1** not having been born/ taken place; non-existent. **2** not gone by or passed. ~**পূর্ব** *adj* unprecedented; novel.

অভ্যন্তর *n* the interior; the inside/ inner part. **অভ্যন্তরীণ, আভ্যন্তর** *adj* **1** internal; inner. **2** interim. **3** mental. **অভ্যন্তরে** *adv* within; inside.

অভ্যর্থনা *n* **1** reception; entertainment; welcome. **2** felicitation. ~ **করা** *vt* welcome; give a reception. ~ **সমিতি** *n* reception committee. **অভ্যর্থিত** *adj.*

অভ্যস্ত⇒অভ্যাস

অভ্যাগত *n* **1** visitor; caller. **2** invitee. **অভ্যাগতা** *fem.*

অভ্যাস *n* settled practice of a person; habit. ~**গত** *adj* habitual. **অভ্যস্ত** *adj* habituated; accustomed; used to (sth).

অভ্যুত্থান *n* **1** a sudden or violent seizure of state power by a small group; coup d'etat: সামরিক ~. **নিস্ফল/ব্যর্থ** ~ abortive coup. **নিরক্ত** ~ bloodless coup. **2** rising into power/ prominence: রাজনৈতিক ~. **3** uprising; insurrection; revolt: গণ ~. ~ **করা** *vi,vt* rise in rebellion; take up arms.

অভ্যুদয় *n* advent; appearance; emergence.

অভ্র *n* **1** mineral substance; mica. **2** cloud. **3** the sky. ~**ভেদী** *adj* shooting through the sky; very lofty. ~**মালা** *n* row/range of clouds. ~**লেহ** *adj* lofty; sky kissing.

অভ্রান্ত *adj* unerring; correct; accurate: ~ লক্ষ; infallible: ~ সত্য.

অমঙ্গল *n* evil; harm; danger; misfortune. ~ **চিহ্ন** *n* evil omen. ~**জনক**, ~**সূচক** *adj* ominous. ~ **হতে অমঙ্গলের উৎপত্তি** Evil begets evil.

অমত *n* absence of approval/ consent; disapproval; disagreement. **অমতে** *adv* without one's consent/ sanction; against one's wishes.

অমন *adj* like that. *adv* so; such. ~**ই** *adj* just like that; just so.

অমনি *adv* **1** unreasonably; for nothing: ~ রাগ করা. **2** empty-handed: আত্মীয় বাড়িতে ~ যাওয়া যায় না. **3** without price; gratis: ~ পাওয়া. **4** without effort/ labour: পরীক্ষায় পাশ ~ হয়না. **5** without any work/ employment: সে ~ বসে আছে. **6** without necessary accompaniment or support: ~ ভাত খাওয়া যায়? **7** instantly; at once: ~ এসে পড়লো. ❑*adj* **1** like that; such: ~ সুন্দর. **2** uncovered; bare: ~ গায়ে থেকো না. **3** neither good; nor bad; so so: ~ এক রকম. **অমনি অমনি** *adv* without any cause; for nothing. **অমনি এক রকম** neither very good nor bad; moderate.

অমনুষ্যত্ব *n* lack of human qualities; inhumanity.

অমনোযোগ *n* **1** lack of attention; inattention; indifference; inadvertence. **2** neglect; heedlessness; disregard. **অমনোযোগী** *adj* inattentive; unmindful; careless; indifferent; negligent. **অমনোযোগী হওয়া** *vi* be inattentive/ unmindful/ careless.

অমর *adj* **1** not subject to death or decay; immortal; imperishable; undecaying: ~খ্যাতি. **2** eternal; unforgettable: ~ কীর্তি. ❑*n* divine being; deity. ~**তা**, ~**ত্ব** *n* immortality; imperishability. ~**ধাম**, ~ **লোক** *n* heaven; paradise.

অমর্যাদা *n* **1** disregard; disrespect; slight. **2** lack of cordiality; inattention. **3** violation; non-observance: চুক্তির ~.

অমল *adj* free from dirt; clear; stainless; pure.

অমলধবল *adj* exquisitely white; snow-white; milk-white.

অমলিন *adj* **1** unstained; free from dust/dirt. **2** bright; shining. **3** undecaying; undecayed; unfaded: ~খ্যাতি. **4** unblemished; untarnished; pure: ~ চরিত্র.

অমাত্য *n* courtier; minister; councillor.

অমানিশা *n* dark night of the new moon.

অমানুষ *n* a brute; a base fellow. ❑*adj* devoid of humanity; beastly. **অমানুষিক** *adj* **1** not expected of a human being; supernatural: **অমানুষিক** পরিশ্রম. **2** inhuman; brutal: **অমানুষিক** অত্যাচার.

অমান্য *adj* unworthy of honour/ obedience. ~ **করা** *vt* refuse to comply with; disobey; dishonour; violate.

অমাবস্যা *n* the last day of the dark fortnight.

অমায়িক *adj* **1** plain and honest; frank; candid; open-hearted. **2** unpretentious; unassuming. **3** loving; affectionate. **4** polite; courteous; amiable.

অমার্জিত *adj* **1** uncivil; unmannerly; indecorous; vulgar. **2** unrefined; uncouth; impolite; rough.

অমিত *adj* **1** that cannot be measured; immeasurable. **2** very much; immense. ~**তেজা** *adj* of immense strength and spirit. ~**বল** *adj* immensely powerful. ~**ব্যয়**, ~**ব্যয়িতা** *n* extravagance; prodigality. ~**ব্যয়ী** *adj* lavish in expenditure; extravagant; prodigal. ~**ভাষী** *adj* talkative; garrulous. ~ভোজন *n* over-eating; surfeit. ~ভোজী *adj* given to intemperate eating. ❑*n* a glutton; a gourmand.

অমিতাচার *n* intemperance in habits and conduct. **অমিতাচারী** *adj* intemperate immoderate.

অমিত্রাক্ষর *adj* (poet) rhymeless; unrhymed. ~ ছন্দ *n* blank verse.

অমিয় *n* nectar; honey; ambrosia. ❑*adj* as sweet as honey: ~ বাণী.

অমিল *n* 1 absence of similarity; dissimilarity; disagreement. 2 absence of rhyme. 3 discord; dissension. 4 scarcity; non-availability: মাছের ~.

অমিশ্র *adj* 1 unmixed; unadulterated; pure; genuine. 2 (math) simple: ~ যোগ বিয়োগ. 2 (math) whole (number).

অমীমাংসিত *adj* undecided. ~ খেলা *n* drawn match. ~ প্রশ্ন *n* unresolved question.

অমুক *adj* a certain; not definite. ❑*n* a certain person. ~ অমুক *n* such and such persons; so and so.

অমূলক *adj* baseless; groundless; unfounded; false: ~ সন্দেহ; ~ ভয়.

অমূল্য *adj* priceless; invaluable; too costly to afford.

অমৃত *n* 1 (myth) highly delicious and invigorating drink that makes the drinker immortal; nectar; ambrosia. 2 delicious food. 3 heaven; paradise. ❑*adj* invigorating; life-giving; immortalizing. ~ভাষী *adj* sweet-tongued; fair-spoken. ~ ভাষিণী *fem.*

অমোঘ *adj* 1 unfailing; infallible: ~ ঔষধ. 2 peremptory; compulsive: ~ আদেশ.

অম্বর [A]*n* 1 a kind of incense; ambergris. 2 the sky. 3 clothes; apparel (পীতাম্বর).

অম্বরি, অম্বুরি *adj* scented with ambergris. ❑*n* tobacco scented with ambergris.

অম্বরী *n* woman's sari (নীলাম্বরী).

অম্বল *n* 1 sour taste; a kind of sauce. 2 (path) acidity due to indigestion; heart-burn.

অম্বু *n* water. ~জ *adj* aquatic; water-born. ~জা *n fem* goddess Lakshmi. ~দ *n* the cloud. ~নিধি *n* the sea; the ocean.

অম্ল *n* 1 sour taste; sourness; acidity. 2 sour curry; any thing tasting sour. 3 a kind of disease; hyper-acidity. 4 (chem) an acid. ~তা *n* acidity; sourness. ~পিত্ত *n* gastric acidity; acidity of the stomach; acidosis. ~মধুর *adj* having a mixed taste of sour and sweet.

অম্লজান *n* elementary gas having no colour, taste or smell; oxygen.

অম্লান *adj* 1 unfaded; unfading. 2 not saddened; cheerful. 3 unhesitating; unperturbed. ~ বদনে *adv* without hesitation. সে ~বদনে মিথ্যা কথা বললো: He lied without batting an eyelid.

অযত্ন *n* 1 want of care or attention. 2 neglect; indifference. ~ করা *vi* treat with neglect/indifference. **অযত্নে** *adv* carelessly; negligently; without taking pains.

অযথা *adj* 1 unnecessary; unreasonable; unwarranted: ~ কলহ. 2 baseless; groundless; false: ~ নিন্দা. 3 extravagant; wasteful; fruitless: ~ খরচ. 4 exaggerated; inappropriate: ~ প্রশংসা. ❑*adv* without cause; unnecessarily ; unreasonably; for nothing.

অযথাযথ *adj* inaccurate; inexact; inappropriate.

অযথার্থ *adj* untrue; unjust; unreal; false.

অযাচিত *adj* unasked; unsolicited. ~ উপদেশ *n* advice gratis. ~ভাবে *adv* gratuitously; voluntarily.

অযোগ্য *adj* 1 unworthy; unfit; incompetent; unmerited; undeserving. 2 disabled. 3 unusable; unserviceable; out of order.

অযৌক্তিক *adj* unreasonable; illogical; contrary to reason. ~তা *n* unreasonableness; untenability; absurdity.

অয়ন *n* 1 a path; a route; a course. 2 (astron) the sun's movement or course: দক্ষিণায়ন; উত্তরায়ণ. 3 the ground; the earth; a homestead; a dwelling. 4 a passage through a battle order. 5 religious scriptures. ~বৃত্ত, ~মণ্ডল *n* the path along which the sun seems to move; ecliptic.

অরক্ষিত *adj* 1 not under protection; unprotected; unguarded; open. 2 undefended; defenceless. 3 not accumulated/preserved.

অরণ্য *n* wood; forest; jungle. **অরণ্যানী** *n* a vast or extensive forest. **অরণ্যায়ন** *n* afforestation. **অরণ্যে রোদন** crying in the wilderness; crying in vain.

অরবিন্দ *n* the lotus.

অরসজ্ঞ, অরসিক *adj* devoid of artistic taste; lacking in sense of humour; unwitty; dull.

অরসিক⇒অরসজ্ঞ

অরাজক *adj* 1 without a king. 2 divested of law and order; lawless; anarchical. ~তা *n* anarchy; disorder; lawlessness.

অরাজি *adj* (অ+রাজি A) not consenting or agreeing; disagreeing; disapproving.

অরি *n* enemy; adversary; foe. ~ন্দম *adj* one who subdues or conquers enemies.

অরুচি *n* 1 apathy or aversion (to food/pleasure). 2 distaste/disrelish for food due to indigestion; loss of appetite; a kind of disease. ~কর *adj* disagreeable; distasteful; unpalatable. ~ ধরা *vi,vt* develop apathy/aversion (for sth).

অরুণ *n* 1 the sun. 2 the newly-risen sun; the morning sun. 3 the glow of the morning or evening sun. 4 purple or crimson colour. ❑*adj* dark-red; crimson; purple. **অরুণিমা** *n* redness; rosy tint. **অরুণোদয়** *n* sun rise; daybreak; dawn.

অরুন্ধতী *n* (astron) a dim star encircled by the Ursa Major.

অরূপ *adj* **1** formless; shapeless. **2** bereft of beauty; ugly. ❑*n* incorporeal God; Allah.

অরে *int* contemptuous address; hey! ho!

অর্ক *n* **1** the sun. **2** sunrays; ray of light. **3** rock crystal. **4** sun-plant; swallow-wort.

অর্গল *n* **1** metal or wood fastening for a door or window; a bolt; a bar. **2** a hindrance; a barrier; an obstacle.

অর্ঘ *n* **1** price; cost: মহার্ঘ. **2** offerings at the worship of Hindu deities; articles of worship. **3** worship.

অর্ঘ্য *n* **1** offerings at the alter of worship; articles of worship. **2** presentations offered to an honourable person as a mark of respect.

অর্চক *n* worshipper; priest.

অর্চনা *n* worship; adoration. **~ করা** *vi* worship; adore; pay homage. **অর্চনীয়** *adj* fit to be worshipped; adorable.

অর্জন *n* **1** earning; income. **2** acquisition; acquirement. **3** gain; attainment. **~ করা** *vt* earn; acquire; gain; attain.

অর্থ[1] *n* **1** money; wealth; property: অর্থোপার্জন. **অর্থই অনর্থের মূল** Money is at the root of all evils. **2** object; purpose: দেশ সেবার্থে দান. **3** truth; reality: যথার্থ. **4** aim; desire; prayer: বিদ্যার্থী. **5** the science of production and distribution of wealth; economics: **~শাস্ত্র**. **~কর, ~করী** *adj* money-earning. **~করী ফসল** *n* cash crop. **~করী বিদ্যা** *n* professional/ vocational training; technical education. **~কষ্ট** *n* pecuniary hardship; financial stringency. **~পিপাসু** *adj* greedy; avaricious. **~পিপাসা** *n* greed for wealth; avarice. **~প্রদ** *adj* yielding money; money-earning. **~বান** *n* wealthy; rich. **~বিনিয়োগ** *n* investment. **~সঙ্কট** *n* financial crisis. **~সঙ্গতি** financial solvency.

অর্থ[2] *n* meaning; import; significance. **~ করা** *vi,vt* interpret; explain; expound. **~গৌরব** *n* (fig) depth of meaning; richness of import; significance. **~পূর্ণ, ~বহ** *adj* meaningful; significant. **~বিচার** *n* determination/ discrimination of meaning. **~ভেদ** *n* difference in interpretation. **~সঙ্গতি** *n* consistency in meaning. **~হানি** *n* misinterpretation. **~হীন** *adj* meaningless.

অর্থাগম *n* influx of money; income.

অর্থাৎ *conj* that is (ie=id est) that is to say; in other words.

অর্থান্তর *n* another meaning; different interpretation/meaning/significance. **~ন্যাস** *n* (rhet) figure of speech corroborating the general by the particular or the particular by the general; contrast of ideas; simile; metaphor; antithesis.

অর্ধ *n* half; any of the two halves. ❑*adj* divided into two parts; half done; incomplete. ❑*adv* half; partly; in part; partially; incompletely. **~চন্দ্র** *n* **1** crescent; half-moon. **2** (facet) act of pushing (one) out by the neck. **3** a system of battle array. **4** Muslim symbol in national flags; crescent. **~চন্দ্রাকার, ~চন্দ্রাকৃতি** *adj* crescent-shaped. **~নমিত** *adj* (of a flag) (lowered) at half-mast. **~নিমীলিত** *adj* (of eyes) partially closed; half-shut. **~পরিস্ফুট** *adj* half-articulate; indistinct. **~বয়স্ক** *adj* middle-aged. **~বৃত্ত** *n* semi-circle. **~ভূমণ্ডল** *n* a hemisphere. **~মৃত** *adj* half dead; almost dead; more dead than alive; dying. **~শয়ান** *adj* recumbent; reclining.

অর্ধাংগ⇒অর্ধাঙ্গ

অর্ধাংশ *n* half-share; one of the two parts; a moiety.

অর্ধাঙ্গ, অর্ধাংগ *n* **1** half of the body. **2** (facet) husband. **3** paralysis affecting one side of the body; hemiplegia. **অর্ধাঙ্গী, অদ্ধাঙ্গিনী** *n fem* wife; better half.

অর্ধাশন *n* half a meal; scanty food.

অর্ধেক *n* =অর্ধ

অর্পণ *n* **1** act of giving/offering/depositing; hand-over; make-over; committal; bestowal; delivery. **~ করা** *vt* give; offer; hand over; make over; give away; deliver. **অর্পয়িতা** *n* , *adj* one who gives/offers/delivers/hands over. **অর্পয়িত্রী** *fem*. **অর্পিত** *adj* handed over; delivered; deposited; bestowed; **অর্পিতা** *fem*.

অর্বাচীন *adj* **1** posterior; younger; new; modern. **2** immature; inexperienced; unwise; foolish.

অর্বুদ *n, adj* ten crores; one hundred million. ❑*n* a tumour; a kind of disease.

অর্শ *n* disease of the rectum; piles; hemorrhoids.

অর্হ *adj* worthy; deserving: দণ্ডার্হ. ❑*n* cost; price; value: মহার্হ.

অলংকরণ⇒অলঙ্করণ

অলংকার⇒অলঙ্কার

অলংকৃত⇒অলঙ্কৃত

অলংঘন⇒অলঙ্ঘন

অলক *n* **1** curling tress of hair; ringlet. **2** cloud of feathery appearance.

অলকনন্দা, অলকানন্দা *n* river in India.

অলকা *n* the kingdom of Kuvera, the Hindu god of riches. **~পুরী** *n* the palace of Kuvera.

অলক্ত, অলক্তক *n* the liquid dye of lac. **~রঞ্জিত** *adj* dyed with lac. **~রাগ** *n* the tinge/tint of lac.

অলক্ষণ *n* **1** bad omen; inauspicious sign; portent. **2** evil; harm. ❑*adj* ominous; inauspicious. **অলক্ষণা** *adj fem* ill-omened. **অলক্ষণে, অলক্ষুণে** *adj* inauspicious; ominous; portentous.

অলক্ষিত *adj* unnoticed; unobserved. **~ভাবে, অলক্ষিতে** *adv* **1** without being seen/

surreptitiously furtively/noticed. **2** beyond the range of sight. **3** suddenly; in an unguarded state/moment.

অলক্ষ্মী *adj* **1** graceless; not neat in works and activities. **2** unfortunate. ❑*n* misfortune. **~তে পাওয়া** *vt* get under the influence of unlucky star; get addicted to practices that bring misfortune and misery; be in constant misery. **~র দশা** *n* want; poverty; indigence. **~র দৃষ্টি** *n* the sinister look of a bad star; poverty; misery.

অলক্ষুণে (colloq)⇒ অলক্ষণ

অলক্ষে *adv* invisibly; stealthily; furtively.

অলক্ষ্য *adj* **1** invisible; unseen. **2** unknown. **3** indiscernible. ❑*n* **1** invisible place: ~ হইতে. **2** the sky; the heaven: অলক্ষ্যের পানে.

অলঙ্করণ, অলংকরণ *n* **1** materials for decoration. **2** decoration; ornamentation; adornment; illustration. **3** act of painting/ dressing. **4** artistic works or touches. **5** (lit) use of rhetoric. **~ করা** *vt* adorn; decorate; ornament; embellish; dress; paint; use rhetorical language. **অলঙ্কর্তা** *n* one who adorns/ornaments; a decorator/painter/ dresser. **অলঙ্কর্ত্রী** *fem.*

অলঙ্কার, অলংকার *n* **1** what adds to the beauty or glory; ornament; jewellery. **2** dressing; embellishment; painting. **3** mark or badge of honour. **4** beauty. **5** (fig) pride; glory: দেশের ~. **6** (lit) figure of speech (simile, metaphor, allegory, alliteration, etc). **~ক** adj that which adds to the beauty or glory. **~বর্জিত** *adj* (in lit) plain; bold. **~বহুল ভাষা** *n* florid/ornate language. **~শাস্ত্র** *n* the art of rhetoric. **অলঙ্কৃত** *adj* adorned; ornamented; embellished; decorated. **অলঙ্কৃত করা** *vt* adorn; decorate; bedeck; bring pride and glory to: জাতিকে অলঙ্কৃত করা.

অলঙ্ঘন, অলংঘন *n* **1** act of refraining from overstepping/disobeying; non-transgression; non-violation. **2** compliance; observance; fulfilment. **অলঙ্ঘনীয়, অলঙ্ঘ্য** *adj* **1** what cannot be/should not be violated/disobeyed: অলঙ্ঘনীয় আদেশ. **2** what cannot be crossed over; impassable: অলঙ্ঘনীয় বাধা. **অলঙ্ঘনীয়তা** *n* impassability; inviolability.

অলস *adj* **1** lazy; slothful. **2** indolent; effortless; dull-headed. **~তা** *n* laziness; indolence; effortlessness.

অলি১ *n* **1** bumble-bee. **2** scorpion. **3** wine: ~পান. **~কুল** *n* swarm of bees.

অলি২, ওলি [A]**1** guardian; custodian; trustee. **2** saint; fakir; ascetic. **অলি-অসি, অলি-অছি, ওলি-ওছি** *n* [A] guardian of a minor; trustee of a minor's property.

অলি গলি *n* lanes and bye-lanes; nook and corner.

অলিন্দ *n* balcony; porch; outer verandah; auricle.

অলিমা, ওয়ালিমা, ওলিমা *n* [A]**1** Muslim marriage feast. **2** marriage feast arranged by the groom's party.

অলী=অলি১

অলীক *n* falsehood; untruth. ❑*adj* false; baseless; empty; vain: ~ স্বপ্ন.

অলৌকিক *adj* **1** superhuman; supernatural; miraculous. **2** unworldly; unearthly.

অল্প *adj* **1** small in quantity/ amount; a little; a bit; a few. **2** frail; weak: ~প্রাণ. **3** illiberal; narrow-minded: ~মতি . **4** of short duration; ephemeral; short-lived: ~জীবী. **5** insufficient; inadequate; scanty; poor. **~বিদ্যা ভয়ঙ্করী** A little learning is a dangerous thing; Empty vessel sounds much. **অল্পেই** *adv* but little; hardly; scarcely; rarely; seldom; only a few/little. **~বিস্তর** *adv, adj* more or less. **~বুদ্ধি** *adj* dull-witted; unintelligent. **~ভাষী** *adj* reticent; taciturn; reserved. **~মূল্য** *adj* cheap. **~মূল্যে** *adv* at a low price. **~সংখ্যক** *adj* a few. **অল্পে অল্পে** *adv* little by little; gradually; slowly; by degrees.

অল্পাধিক *adj* more or less.

অল্পায়ু *adj* short-lived; ephemeral; transitory.

অল্পাহারী *adj* one who eats less; moderate in eating.

অশঙ্ক *adj* fearless; intrepid; brave. **~নীয়** *adj* not to be feared; not alarming. **অশঙ্কিত** *adj* undaunted; unafraid; unshaken.

অশন *n* **1** a meal; food. **2** eating. **~-বসন** *n* food and clothing; maintenance.

অশনি *n* thunder; thunderbolt; lightning. **~ সংকেত** *n* **1** flash of bright light produced by natural electricity between clouds in the sky or between clouds and the ground; lightning followed by thunder. **2** (fig) sth that signalizes an imminent danger/trouble. **~সম্পাত** *n* thunder-clap; crash of thunder.

অশরণ *adj* homeless; shelterless; resortless.

অশরীরী *adj* incorporeal; spiritual. **~ দেহ** *n* ethereal body. **~ বাণী** *n* voice from heaven; divine revelation.

অশান্ত *adj* not calm or tranquil: ~ সমুদ্র; restless; agitated; naughty: ~ বালক. **অশান্তি** *n* want of peace; disorder; disturbance; confusion.

অশিক্ষিত *adj* uneducated; illiterate; untrained. **~ কারিগর** *n* unskilled artisan.

অশিষ্ট *adj* uncivil; impolite; discourteous; rude. **~তা** *n* incivility; rudeness; haughtiness; arrogance. **অশিষ্টাচার** *n* rude behaviour; discourteous conduct.

অশীতি *n* eighty. **~তম** *adj* eightieth. **~পর** *adj* octogenarian: ~পর বৃদ্ধ.

অশীল *adj* uncivil; unmannerly; ill-behaved.

অশুচি *adj* unholy; impure; unclean; profane.

অশুদ্ধ *adj* **1** incorrect; erroneous; wrong. **2** unholy; impure. 3 unrefined; unpurified. **4** unsanctified; not permitted in scriptural law. **অশুদ্ধি** *n* impurity; uncleanness; mistake; error. **অশুদ্ধিপত্র** *n* list of errata; corrigendum (*pl*-da).

অশুভ *n* evil; misfortune; calamity. ❑*adj* ominous; inauspicious; baleful; harmful. ~ **ক্ষণ** *n* inauspicious moment/hour. ~ **ক্ষণে** *adv* in an evil hour/inauspicious moment. ~ **লক্ষণ** *n* evil/ill omen.

অশেষ *adj* **1** endless; unending; infinite; boundless. **2** various; numerous. ~ **প্রকারে** *adv* in various ways.

অশোক[১] *adj* free from grief. ❑*n* kind of deep red flower or its tree.

অশোক[২] *n* the famous emperor of ancient Magadha. ~**লিপি** *n* inscriptions of Ashoka. ~**চক্র** *n* the symbolic wheel connected with emperor Ashoka; the emblem of the official flag of India. ~**স্তম্ভ** *n* pillar erected by Ashoka with inscription of Buddhist teachings.

অশোভন *adj* **1** unbecoming; indecorous; inelegant. **2** improper; unsuitable. **3** indecent; ugly. ~**তা** *n* unbecomingness; impropriety; indecency.

অশ্রদ্ধা *n* **1** lack of respect; disrespect; disregard; irreverence. **2** contempt; hatred. **3** disgust; distrust; disbelief; apathy. ~ **করা** *vt* treat with contempt; despise; disregard. **অশ্রদ্ধেয়** *adj* unworthy of respect; contemptible; despicable.

অশ্রান্ত *n* **1** incessant; continual. **2** untiring; untired; unwearied. ❑*adv* incessantly. ~**ভাবে** *adv* unweariedly; indefatigably. incessantly; continually.

অশ্রান্তি *n* tirelessness; ceaselessness; continuity.

অশ্রাব্য *adj* not worth hearing; unpleasant; indecent; obscene. ~ **ভাষা** *n* vulgar/filthy language.

অশ্রু *n* tear; tears. ~ **গদগদ,** ~ **ভারাক্রান্ত** *adj* choked with tears. ~ **গদগদ কণ্ঠে** *adv* in a voice choked with tears; in a sobbing voice. ~**ধারা** *n* stream of tears. ~**নয়নে,** ~**লোচনে** *adv* with tearful eyes; with tears in the eyes. ~**পাত,** ~**বর্ষণ,** ~**বিসর্জন** *n* shedding of tears. ~**পাত করা** *vt* shed tears; weep. ~**পূর্ণ** *adj* full of tears; tearful. ~**পূর্ণ নয়নে** *adv* with tearful eyes; with eyes full of tears. ~ **প্লাবিত** *adj* suffused/flooded with tears; tearful. ~**বিগলিত** *adj* moistened with tears; blubbering. ~**সংবরণ** *n* checking/suppression of tears. ~**সংবরণ করা** *vt* check/suppress one's tears. ~**সিক্ত** *adj* bathed in tears.

অশ্রুত *adj* unheard of. ~**পূর্ব** *adj* unheard of before; unprecedented.

অশ্লীল *adj* obscene; indecent; vulgar. ~ **চিত্র** *n* obscene or blue picture; pornography. ~ **বাক্য** *n* filthy words; bawdy talk. ~ **সাহিত্য** *n* obscene literature; pornography. ~**তা** *n* obscenity; vulgarity. ~**ভাষী** *adj* given to filthy/bawdy talk.

অশ্লেষা *n* (astrol) a star considered inauspicious by astrologers.

অশ্ব *n* the horse. **অশ্বা, অশ্বী, অশ্বিনী** *fem.* mare. ~**কোবিদ,** ~**বিৎ** *adj* skilled in horsemanship. ❑*n* horse-trainer; horse-breaker; an equestrian. ~**খুর** *n* **1** a horse's hoof. **2** kind of plant used as perfume. ~**গতি** *adj* swift as a horse. ❑*n* the pace of a horse; a gallop. ~**গন্ধা** *n* a medicinal plant *Withania somnifera.* ~**ডিম্ব** *n* non-existent or trashy thing; mare's nest; a hoax. ~**তর** *n* cross bred of horse and donkey; a mule. ~**তরী** *fem.* ~**শক্তি,** ~**ক্ষমতা** *n* (mech) horse power. ~**শালা** *n* a stable. ~**শাবক** *n* a colt; a foal (*fem* filly). ~**সাদী** *n* a horseman or horse-soldier; a cavalier.

অশ্বত্থ *n* a variety of large tree; peepul.

অশ্বারোহণ *n* mounting a horse; riding. ~ **করা** *vi,vt* ride a horse.

অশ্বারোহী *n* rider; cavalier. ~ **বাহিনী** *n* the cavalry.

অষুধ, অষুধ করা, অষুধ ধরা⇒ঔষধ

অষ্ট *n, adj* eight. ~**ক** *n, adj* collection or set of eight. ~**কোণ** *n* (geom) an octagon. ❑*adj* octagonal (also ~কোণী). ~**ধা** *adv, adj* eight times; eight fold. ~**পাদ** *adj* having eight arms. ❑*n* a spider. ~**প্রহর** *n* a whole day and night; all day performance. ❑*adv* throughout the whole day and night. ~**ভুজ** *adj* having eight hands; eight handed. ❑*n* an octagon. ~**ভুজা** *n fem* Hindu goddess Durga. ~**মাংশ** *n* one-eighth; the eighth part. ~**মী** *n* eighth day of either fortnight of a lunar month. ~**রম্ভা** *n* (vulg) mare's nest; mere nothing; a hoax (indicative of failure).

অষ্টাত্রিংশ *n, adj* thirty-eight. ~**তম** *adj* thirty-eighth.

অষ্টাদশ *n, adj* eighteen. **অষ্টাদশী** *adj fem* eighteen years old.

অষ্টাবিংশ *n, adj* twenty-eight. ~**তিতম** *adj* twenty-eighth.

অষ্টাশি *n, adj* eighty -eight.

অষ্টেপৃষ্ঠে⇒আষ্টেপৃষ্ঠে

অসওয়াসা [A] *n* bad/evil counsel.

অসংকুচিত⇒অসঙ্কুচিত

অসংকোচ⇒অসঙ্কোচ

অসংখ্য, অসংখ্যক *adj* innumerable; numberless; countless; infinite.

অসংগত⇒অসঙ্গত

অসংযত *adj* unrestrained; uncontrolled; unbridled.

অসংযম *n* lack of self-control; intemperance. self-indulgence; sensualism. **অসংযমী** *adj* lacking in self-control; given to sensual pleasure; intemperate.

অসংস্কৃত *adj* unrefined; inelegant; other than Sanskrit.

অসংহত *adj* not concentrated/consolidated; scattered; incoherent. **অসংহতি** *n* disunity.

অসকাল *n* inopportune moment; improper time; evening or close of the day.

অসঙ্কুচিত *adj* **1** not contracted. **2** unhesitating; unwavering.

অসঙ্কোচ *n* **1** absence of hesitation. **2** width. **অসঙ্কোচে** *adv* without hesitation; unhesitatingly.

অসচ্ছল *adj* not well-off; hard-up; indigent. **~তা** financial stringency; poverty; indigence.

অসৎ *adj* dishonest; wicked; obscene; rude: অসদাচরণ. **~ উপায়** unfair means. **~ কর্ম** misdeed. **~পথ** evil way. **~ সঙ্গ** bad/evil company.

অসতর্ক *adj* careless; incautious; unguarded; unwary. **~ মুহূর্তে** in an unguarded moment. **~তা** *n* carelessness; inadvertence. **~তাবশত** owing to inadvertence.

অসতী *n fem* unchaste; unfaithful to one's husband.

অসত্য *adj* untrue; false. ❑*n* untruth; falsehood. **~বাদী** *adj* untruthful.

অসদাচরণ *n* **1** misbehaviour; ill-treatment; **~ করা** *vi,vt* misbehave; treat rudely.

অসদ্ব্যবহার *n* **1** discourteous or rude behaviour; improper conduct; ill-treatment. **2** misuse; abuse.

অসদ্ভাব *n* want of amity; unfriendliness; ill-feeling; bad blood; quarrel.

অসন্তুষ্ট *adj* displeased; dissatisfied; vexed; discontented. **~করা** *vt* vex; displease. **অসন্তুষ্টি, অসন্তোষ** *n* displeasure; discontent.

অসন্দিগ্ধ *adj* unsuspecting; unsuspicious. **~ চিত্তে** *adv* without hesitation/misgivings.

অসবর্ণ *adj* not of the same caste/colour. **~ বিবাহ** *n* inter-caste marriage.

অসভ্য *adj* uncivilized; uncultured; uncivil; rude; vulgar. **~ জাতি** *n* barbarous or savage people. **~তা** *n* barbarity; incivility; rudeness; lack of culture.

অসম *adj* **1** unequal. **2** dissimilar; different; incongruous. **3** uneven; rugged; undulating.

অসমঞ্জস *adj* inconsistent; asymmetrical; dissimilar; irrelevant. **অসামঞ্জস্য** *n* inconsistence; dissimilarity; irrelevance.

অসমতল *adj* uneven; rough; not plain.

অসমতা *n* inequality; unevenness; difference.

অসময় *n* **1** improper/inopportune time. **2** out of season: অসময়ের ফল. **3** hard times; time of stress: অসময়ের বন্ধু. **অসময়ে** *adv* at an inopportune/inauspicious time; untimely; prematurely; in time of need.

অসমর্থ *adj* **1** unable; incapable. **2** weak; powerless; disabled. **3** incompetent. **~তা, অসামর্থ্য** *n* inability; incapability; incompetence; disability.

অসমসাহস *n* rare feat of daring; uncommon courage; overboldness. ❑*adj* over-daring; over-bold; daredevil; absolutely fearless; rash. **অসমসাহসিক** *adj* of uncommon courage/rare feat of daring. **অসমসাহসিকতা** *n* overboldness; bravado.

অসমান *adj* **1** not equal or similar; unequal; dissimilar. **2** uneven; rugged; undulating. **3** not straight; curved.

অসমাপিকা *adj fem* not making complete. **~ ক্রিয়া** (gram) infinite verb; verb in the participile form.

অসমাপ্ত *adj* incomplete ; unfinished. **অসমাপ্তি** *n* incompletion; unfinished state.

অসমীচীন *adj* **1** improper; indiscreet; unbecoming. **2** unjust; injudicious; wrongful.

অসম্পূর্ণ *adj* **1** incomplete; unfulfilled; unfinished. **2** imperfect; defective. **~তা** *n* incompletion; incompleteness; unfinished state; imperfection.

অসম্ভব, অসম্ভবপর *adj* **1** not possible; impossible; improbable. **2** absurd; incredible; uncommon. **অসম্ভাব্য** *adj* unlikely to occur; improbable.

অসম্মত *adj* unwilling; dissenting; declining. **~ হওয়া** *vi,vt* disagree; decline; be unwilling/reluctant. **অসম্মতি** *n* dissent; refusal; disapproval.

অসম্মান *n* **1** dishonour; disrespect. **2** slight; neglect; insult. **~কর** *adj* disgraceful; ignominious; insulting. **~ করা** *vt* dishonour; neglect; insult. **অসম্মানিত** *adj* insulted; disgraced; slighted.

অসহ *adj* **1** unbearable; intolerable. **2** intolerant; impatient; unforgiving. **~নীয়** *adj* unbearable; unendurable; insufferable.

অসহযোগ, অসহযোগিতা *n* absence of co-operation; non-cooperation. **অসহযোগী** *adj* non-cooperating. ❑*n* non-cooperator.

অসহায় *adj* **1** helpless. **2** resourceless; destitute. **3** lonely; solitary. **~ বোধ করা** *vt* feel helpless.

অসহিষ্ণু *adj* impatient; intolerant; restless. **~তা** *n* impatience; intolerance; restlessness.

অসহ্য *adj* unbearable; intolerable; unendurable; insufferable.

অসাড় *adj* **1** insensate: **~** প্রকৃতি. **2** benumbed; bereft of all feelings: **~**দেহ. **3** torpid; callous. **~তা** *n* numbness; torpidity. **অসাড়ে** *adv* unconsciously; unknowingly; unaware.

অসাধারণ 1 uncommon; unusual; rare. 2 distinguishing; distinctive; extra-ordinary. 3 (logic) not general; particular; specific. **~তা, ~ত্ব** *n* uncommonness; rareness; peculiarity; particularity.

অসাধু *adj* evil; bad; wicked; dishonest; corrupt. **~তা** *n* dishonesty; wickedness; corruption.

অসাধ্য *adj* 1 impracticable; unpractical; hard to accomplish. 2 incurable; irremediable. **~ সাধন** *n* making the impossible possible.

অসাবধান *adj* careless; incautious; inattentive. **~তা** *n* carelessness; inadvertence; negligence. **~তাবশত** *adv* through carelessness/oversight; inadvertently.

অসামঞ্জস্য⇒অসমঞ্জস

অসামরিক *adj* non-military; civil. **~ জাতি** *n* non-martial race.

অসামর্থ্য⇒অসমর্থ

অসামাজিক *adj* 1 not pertaining to the society; not in conformity with social tradition. 2 unsocial; unsociable; anti-social.

অসামান্য *adj* 1 uncommon; unusual; extra-ordinary. 2 deep; profound: ~ জ্ঞান.

অসাম্প্রদায়িক *adj* 1 non-communal; non-sectarian. 2 free from communal feeling or prejudice; liberal; cosmopolitan. **~তা** *n* non-communalism; liberality; universality.

অসার *adj* 1 unsubstantial; pithless; sapless: ~কাঠ. 2 pointless; futile: ~তর্ক. **~ সংসার** *n* vain world. **অসারের তর্জন-গর্জনই সার** Barking dogs seldom bite; empty vessels sound much.

অসি[১] *n* a sword; a scimitar. **~যুদ্ধ** *n* sword-fight. **~যোদ্ধা** *n* a swordsman.

অসি[২]⇒অছি

অসিয়ত, অছিয়ত, অছিয়ত, ওসিয়ত⇒অছিঅত

অসিলা, অছিলা⇒অছিলা

অসীম *adj* 1 unbounded; unlimited. 2 infinite; endless. 3 vast; immense; profound. ☐*n* eternity.

অসুখ *n* 1 grief; distress, unhappiness. 2 illness; ailment; disease. **অসুখী** *adj* distressed; unhappy; displeased.

অসুন্দর *adj* not beautiful; ungraceful; ungainly; uncouth; ugly.

অসুবিধা *n* inconvenience; disadvantage; difficulty. **~জনক** *adj* inconvenient; disadvantageous; incommodious; difficult; troublesome.

অসুস্থ *adj* unwell; ill; indisposed; sick. **~তা** *n* indisposition; sickness; illness; ailment.

অসৌজন্য *n* 1 want of courtesy or decorum; discourtesy; impoliteness. 2 incivility; unmannerliness.

অস্ত *n* 1 the setting of the sun, moon, etc. 2 the end; the fall. **~গমন** *n* act of setting. **~গামী, অস্তাচলগামী** *adj* going to set; setting.

অস্ত্র *n* 1 weapon; missile; arms. 2 tools/instruments: ডাক্তারি ~. **~চিকিৎসক** *n* surgeon. **~চিকিৎসা** *n* surgery. **~ত্যাগ** *n* surrender of arms. **~ ত্যাগ করা** *vt* surrender/give up arms. **~ ধারণ করা** *vt* take up arms. **~সংবরণ** *n* cease-fire; cessation of fighting; withholding of arms.

অস্ত্রাগার *n* armoury.

অস্ত্রোপচার *n* surgical operation. **~ করা** *vi, vt* operate (upon).

অস্থাবর *adj* (of property) movable; no fixed.

অস্থায়ী *adj* not permanent; temporary; transient; unstable.

অস্থি *n* bone; skeleton. **~চর্মসার** *adj* all skin and bone; reduced to a skeleton. **~পঞ্জর** *n* bones and ribs; skeleton. **~বিজ্ঞান** *n* osteology. **~বিজ্ঞানী** *n* osteologist.

অস্থিতিস্থাপক *adj* inelastic. **~তা** *n* inelasticity.

অস্থির *adj* 1 uneasy; unsteady; unstable. 2 agitated; excited; perturbed; impatient. 3 fickle; frivolous, restless. **~চিত্ত, ~মতি** *adj* fickleminded; frivolous; impetuous. **~চিত্ততা** *n* fickle-mindedness; restlessness; impatience.

অস্পষ্ট *adj* 1 not clear; indistinct; dim: ~ আলো. 2 obscure; vague. 3 inarticulate: ~ বুলি. 4 illegible: ~ লেখা. **~তা** *n* indistinctness; obscurity; lack of clarity; inarticulateness.

অস্ফুট *adj* indistinct; inarticulate; not expressed; not in bloom. **~ কণ্ঠে, ~ স্বরে** *adv* in a whisper; in an undertone; in a murmur. **~ বুলি** *n* lispings.

অস্বচ্ছ *adj* not transparent; opaque. **~তা** *n* lack of transparency; opaqueness; turbidity.

অস্বস্তি *n* uneasiness; discomfort; trouble.

অস্বাভাবিক *adj* unnatural; unusual; abnormal. **~তা** *n* unnaturalness; abnormality.

অস্বাস্থ্য *n* ill-health; illness; ailment. **~কর** *adj* unhealthy; unhygienic.

অস্বীকার *n* refusal; denial; dissent; repudiation; rejection; non-compliance. **~ করা** *vt* refuse; deny; decline; reject; repudiate. **অস্বীকৃতি** *n* same as অস্বীকার.

অহঙ্কার, অহংকার *n* self-conceit; pride; vanity; vainglory. **~ করা** *vi, vt* pride oneself on; be proud of; boast. **অহঙ্কারী** *adj* proud; arrogant; haughty; boastful; vainglorious. **অহঙ্কারে মত্ত** puffed up/intoxicated/mad with pride.

অহমিকা *n* egoism; self-conceit; vanity; pride.

অহরহ, অহরহঃ *adv* daily; everyday; day in and day out; always; constantly.

অহর্নিশ *adv* day and night; at all hours; always; incessantly.

অহি⇒ওহি

অহিংস *adj* not malignant/violent; non-malignant; non-violent; in-offensive harmless. ~ অসহযোগ *n* (hist) non-violent non-cooperation.

অহিংসা *n* absence of malice/violence.

অহিত *n* harm; injury. ~কর *adj* harmful; injurious. ~কারী *adj, n* one who causes harm/injury.

অহিফেন *n* opium; poppy-plant. ~সেবী *n* opium-taker.

অহেতু, অহেতুক *adj* causeless; groundless; unreasonable. ❑*adv* unnecessarily; without any provocation; for nothing.

অহো *int* oh! alas! good heavens!

অহোরাত্র *adv* day and night; always. ❑*n* period from sunrise to sunrise.

আ

আ[1] *n* second vowel of the Bengali alphabet. When it joins a consonant letter it takes the form 'া', eg; ম + আ=মা.

আ[2] *int* expressing sorrow, pain, anger, aversion, surprise, relief, delight, etc; oh! ah! alas!: আ মরি বাংলা ভাষা, আ! বাঁচা গেল, আ, কি ছিরি!

আ[3] *pref* denoting "a little": আনত নয়ন; 'starting from': আজন্ম; 'up to': আকণ্ঠ; 'throughout'/'during the whole of': আজীবন, etc. It also implies negation, contrariety, perversion, etc, eg আগমন, আঁকাড়া, আঘাট, আকাল, আকথা.

আইন [P] *n* law; the body of rules established and administered by authority; any of those rules; an act; a statute; an ordinance. ~ করা *vi* legislate; enact a law; make a rule. দেওয়ানি ~ *n* civil law. ফৌজদারি ~ *n* criminal law. সামরিক ~ *n* martial law. ~-কানুন *n* [P + A] rules and regulations. ~কার, ~কর্তা *n* legislator; law-giver. ~গত *adj* legal; statutory. ~জীবী, ~-ব্যবসায়ী *n* a legal practitioner; a lawyer; a pleader; an advocate; a barrister; an attorney; a solicitor. ~জ্ঞ *adj* versed in law. ❑*n* a jurist. ~ত *adv* legally; according to law. ~ পরিষদ *n* legislative assembly; a legislature. ~ পেশা *n* legal profession. ~ প্রণয়ন *n* enactment of laws; legislation. ~মাফিক, ~মোতাবেক *adj* lawful; legitimate. ❑*adv* legally; according to law. ~ শাস্ত্র *n* the science or knowledge of law; jurisprudence.

আইবুড়ো *adj* unmarried. ~ মেয়ে *n* spinster.

আইয়াম, আয়াম [A] *n* **1** the days. **2** time; season. **3** proper time; opportune moment. ~বেজ, ~বীজ *n* the bright fortnight days; the 13th, 14th and 15th day of lunar months.

আউওল=আউয়াল

আউয়াল, আউওল [A] *adj* **1** first; original. **2** best; excellent.

আউলা *adj* (colloq) untidy; dishevelled (also ~ ঝাউলা). ~নো *vt* (of hair and clothes) dishevel. ❑*adj* dishevelled; untidy.

আউলিয়া, আওলিয়া [A] *n* Muslim saint.

আউশ *n* variety of paddy harvested in the rainy season.

আওড়ানো ~ *vi, vt* pronounce; recite; chant. ❑*n* repeated pronouncement or recitation.

আওতা[1] *n* shade; sunshade.

আওতা[2] **1** influence. **2** guardianship; custody; control.

আওতা[3] *n* jurisdiction; purview.

আওয়াজ [P] *n* **1** sound; noise. **2** voice. ~ তোলা *vi, vt* raise voice.

আওরত, আউরত [A] *n* **1** woman. **2** wife.

আওলাদ, আউলাদ [A] *n* children; offspring; progeny.

আওলিয়া=আউলিয়া

আংটা *n* metal ring affixed to sth as a handle.

আংটি *n* finger ring; ornamental ring for finger.

আংশিক *adj* partial; relating to a part/share. ~রূপে *adv* in part; partially.

আঃ[1], **আহ্** *int* expressing surprise, anger, irritation, vexation, grief, relief, etc.

আঃ[2] *n* abbreviation of the phrase "আলাইহিস্ সালাম" ie, "peace be on him" expressed or used after the names of prophets.

আঁইস[1]⇒আঁশ[1]

আঁইস[2] *n* scales of fishes.

আঁক *n* a mark or sign; (arith & alg) a problem or sum. ~ কষা *vt* do or work out a sum.

আঁকা *vi, vt* draw; paint; describe; trace; mark; delineate. ❑*adj* drawn; painted; traced; marked; described; delineated.

আঁকা বাঁকা *adj* crooked; zigzag; tortuous; serpentine.

আঁকিয়া-বাঁকিয়া=এঁকে-বেঁকে

আঁখি *n* the eye. ~জল *n* tears. ~ঠার *n* wink. ~ঠারা *vi, vt* wink or blink at. ~পুট *n* eyelid.

আঁচ[1] *n* **1** hint; presage. **2** guess; surmise; conjecture; anticipation. ~ করা *vt* guess; surmise; conjecture; anticipate.

আঁচ[2] *n* heat; warmth; glow; blaze.

আঁচড় *n* bruise; scratch; mark. ~ কাটা *vt* make a mark/scratch with finger-nails or claws.

আঁচল *n* the loose end of a woman's sari. ~ ধরা *adj* (of man) submissive to one's wife; (of boys) very much dependent on mother.

আঁচিল *n* mole; wart; pimple.

আঁজলা *n* a handful.

আঁট, আট *adj* tight; close-fitting. ❑*n* tightness; compactness. **কথার ~** reason or cogency of one's say. **~ করা** *vi, vt* tighten; make tight. **~সাঁট** *adj* tight; not loose; compact.

আঁটকুড়া, আঁটকুড়ে *adj* childless; without any issue.

আঁটি[১], আটি *n* a bundle of corn tied together in a stack.

আঁটি[২], আঁঠি, আঠি *n* the seed/stone of a fruit.

আঁত *n* **1** entrails; intestines; bowels. **2** heart; feelings. **আঁতে ঘা দেওয়া** (fig) comment on one's weak point; attack one with words that prove effective; touch the sore point.

আঁতকানো, আঁৎকানো *vt* be startled; feel sudden alarm. **আঁতকে ওঠা** *vt* be shocked with surprise/alarm.

আঁতাত *n* friendly understanding between nations; entente.

আঁতুড়, আঁতুড় ঘর *n* lying-in room; labour-room; house or room of confinement of a woman at child-birth.

আঁধার *n* darkness; gloom. ❑ *adj* dark; gloomy. **~ ঘরের মানিক** (fig) a darling son/daughter who brings joy to a cheerless home. **আঁধারে ঢিল মারা** make a blind guess; take a blind chance. **আঁধারে হাতড়ানো** grope in the dark.

আঁশ[১], আঁইশ *n* fibre/threadlike membranes in some fruits, plants, etc.

আঁশ[২]=আঁইস[২]

আঁস্তাকুড় *n* rubbish-dump; dustbin. **আঁস্তাকুড়ের পাতা** *n* rubbish; refuse; sweepings; (fig) undesirable/mean person.

আকণ্ঠ *adv* **1** upto the throat. **2** in full; completely. **~ ভোজন** *n* voracious eating; surfeit. **~ ভোজন করা** *vt* eat to excess. **~ নিমজ্জিত** *adv* almost submerged: তিনি ঋণে ~ নিমজ্জিত, He is over head and ears in debt.

আকথা-কুকথা *n* slang words; ominous talk.

আকনি⇒ আখনি

আকন্দ *n* sun-plant; swallow-wort.

আকবর [A] *adj* the great; almighty. ❑*n* Akbar, the Great Mughal emperor. **আকবরি** *adj* of emperor Akbar or his reign.

আকর *n* **1** a mine; a quarry. **2** (fig) rich or abundant source: জ্ঞানের ~. **আকরিক** *adj* **1** of mines; mineral. **2** relating to source: আকরিক গ্রন্থ.

আকর্ণ *adv* upto the ear; as far as the ear.

আকর্ষণ *n* attraction. **~ করা** *vt* attract; draw; pull. **আকর্ষণী শক্তি** *n* power of attraction; magnetism. **আকর্ষণীয়** *adj* attractive.

আকস্মিক *adj* sudden; unexpected; accidental. **~ ঘটনা** *n* chance; occurrence; accident. **~ দুর্ঘটনা** *n* mishap; accident.

আকাঙ্ক্ষা *n* desire; longing; wish. **~ করা** *vt* wish. for; long for; desire; expect. **আকাঙ্ক্ষিত** *adj* desired; wished-for, asked-for.

আকাট *adj* out and out; down-right; thorough; arrant: ~ মূর্খ.

আকাটা *adj* uncut. **~ হীরা** *n* rough diamond.

আকাঠ, আকাঠা *n* inferior quality wood.

আকাড়া *adj* (of rice) which is not husked/polished white; unrefined.

আকামত, ইকামৎ [A] *n* formal call to stand in rows for congregational prayers.

আকায়িদ⇒ আকায়েদ

আকায়েদ, আকায়িদ *n* [A] articles of faith in Islam.

আকার[১] *n* form; shape; appearance. **~-ইঙ্গিত** *n* gestures and signs; not in so many words. **~ প্রকার** *n* the way of behaving; demeanour.

আকার[২] *n* addition of the vowel sound আ or its symbol to consonants. **আকারান্ত** *adj* (of words) ending with vowel sound আ.

আকাল *n* scarcity; famine; hard times.

আকালী *n* a sect of the Sikhs.

আকাশ *n* **1** the sky; the space above the earth. **2** the heavens: ~-পাতাল. **3** weather: আকাশের অবস্থা খারাপ. **~-কুসুম** *n* castle in the air; day-dream; visionary object. **~-কুসুম কল্পনা করা** *vt* (fig) build castle in the air. **~চুম্বী** *adj* sky-scraping; cloud-kissing; very lofty. **~চুম্বী অট্টালিকা** *n* sky-scraper. **~ থেকে পড়া** *vt* **1** be struck with amazement/astonishment; be taken aback. **2** feign amazement/astonishment. **~পাতাল** *adv* **1** from the heaven to the earth. **2** everywhere; in all respects. **~পাতাল তোলপাড় করা** *vt* move heaven and earth. **~পাতাল প্রভেদ** *n* difference as between heaven and hell. **~পাতাল ভাবা** *vt* be in a maze; be at sea. **~ ভেঙে পড়া** (fig) be faced with sudden danger or serious problem. **~মণ্ডল** *n* the celestial sphere; the atmosphere. **আকাশের চাঁদ হাতে পাওয়া** (fig) attain one's cherished object unexpectedly; unexpectedly obtain a precious thing without effort.

আকিক, আকীক [A] *n* precious stone; agate.

আকিকা [A] *n* ceremony of naming a new-born Muslim child.

আকিঞ্চন *n* **1** desire; craving. **2** attempt; exertion; endeavour. **3** poverty; indigence.

আকিদা, আকীদা [A] *n* **1** article of faith (sing). **2** single-mindedness; devoutness.

আকীক⇒ আকিক

আকীকা=আকিকা

আকীদা⇒ আকিদা

আকীর্ণ *adj* bestrewn; overspread; scattered: কন্টকাকীর্ণ.

আকুঞ্চন *n* contraction; contortion; shrinking. **আকুঞ্চিত** *adj* slightly curled; shrunk; wrinkled.

আকুতি *n* entreaty; yearning; longing; wistfulness; fervidity; intense desire.

আকুল *adj* **1** anxious; eager; agitated; distraught. ভেবে ~ distracted with anxiety. **2** distressed; stricken (with): পিপাসাকুল. **3** nonplussed; bewildered: বিস্ময়াকুল. **~তা** *n* anxiety; bewilderment; agitation; restlessness. **আকুলি-বিকুলি** *n* extreme anxiety or worry. ❑*adv* very anxiously; ardently; fervently.

আকৃতি *n* shape; form; appearance.

আকৃষ্ট *adj* attracted; charmed; fascinated. enticed.

আক্‌দ, আক্‌ত [A] *n* **1** marriage; marriage tie. **2** a contract; an agreement. **~-রসুমাত** [A] *n* the ceremony of marriage; the social formalities of marriage.

আক্কেল [A] *n* (corrupt of আক্‌ল) common sense; wit; wisdom; consideration. **~ হওয়া** *vt* come to one's senses. **~ গুড়ুম** *n* confusion; bewilderment. **~ গুড়ুম হওয়া** *vi* be confused; be at one's wit's end. **~-দাঁত** *n* the wisdom tooth. **~সেলামি** *n* penalty paid or loss suffered on account of one's folly or inexperience.

আক্রমণ *n* (mil) an offence against an enemy; attack; invasion. **~ করা** *vi, vt* attack; fall upon; invade. **~কারী** *n* aggressor; invader.

আক্রা *adj* high-priced; dear; costly. **~ গণ্ডার দিন** *n* hard times.

আক্রান্ত *adj* attacked; invaded; assaulted. **শত্রুদ্বারা ~** attacked by enemy. **জ্বরে ~** attacked with fever.

আক্রোশ *n* grudge; malice; wrath; ill-feeling. **~বশে** *adv* out of malice/ill-feeling.

আক্ষরিক *adj* of letters; literal; to the letter: ~ অর্থ, ~ অনুবাদ.

আক্ষেপ *n* **1** regret; repentance; repining. **2** convulsion (esp muscular); spasm. **~ করা** *vt* regret; repine. **আক্ষেপের বিষয়** matter of regret.

আখ, আক *n* the sugarcane.

আখড়া *n* meeting-place; a club; a gymnasium; a monastery.

আখতার [P] *n* the stars.

আখনি [P] *n* solution prepared by boiling water with spices for cooking 'pilau'.

আখবার [A] *n* newspaper (*sing* খবর).

আখরোট *n* the walnut.

আখলাক [A] *n* good manners; etiquette.

আখির, আখিরি ⇒ আখের

আখিরাত ⇒ আখেরাত

আখের, আখির [A] *n* **1** end; termination; conclusion. **2** consequence. **3** future; the hereafter; the next world; the Day of Judgement. **~ খাওয়া, ~ নষ্ট করা** *vt* blight the future; come to grief in the long run. **আখেরে পস্তানো** *vt* repent in the long run. **আখেরে ভালো হওয়া** *vt* be paying in the long run. **আখেরি, আখেরী** [A] *adj* last; final: আখেরি নবী. prophet Muhammad (sm).

আখেরাত, আখিরাত [A] *n* the next world; the hereafter; the Day of Judgement.

আখেরি, আখেরী ⇒ আখের

আখ্যা *n* appellation; designation; name; title; epithet. **আখ্যাত** *adj* named; called; denominated; entitled; designated. **আখ্যান** *n* tale; narrative; legend; fiction; fable; history.

আখ্যায়ক *n* narrator; story-teller. **আখ্যায়িকা** *n* tale; story; narrative.

আগ[1] [H] *n* fire; flame; blaze.

আগ[2] *n* the forepart. ❑*adj* foremost; topmost. **~ডাল** *n* the topmost branch of a tree. **~দুয়ার** *n* the front door. **~ বাড়া** *vi* go ahead; step forward.

আগড়-বাগড় [H] *n* **1** trashy or worthless things; rubbish. **2** idle talk.

আগড়ম-বাগড়ম *n* meaningless chatter.

আগত *adj* one who/that which has come/arrived. **~প্রায়** *adj* coming soon; imminent; impending.

আগন্তুক *n* **1** visitor; guest; caller. **2** stranger; newcomer. ❑*adj* adventitious; incidental.

আগপাছ *n* pros and cons. **~ ভাবা** *vt* consider the ins and outs carefully.

আগমন *n* arrival; coming. **আগমনী** *n* song of welcome. ❑*adj* relating to arrival.

আগরবাতি *n* incense; aromatic vapour.

আগলা *adj* uncovered; unbolted; open.

আগলানো *vt* take care; look after; keep watch; protect.

আগস্ট *n* August, the 8th month of Christian calendar.

আগা[1] *n* top : গাছের ~; tip : ফুলের ~; end; extremity: লাঠির ~. **~গোড়া** *adv* from beginning to end; from head to foot.

আগা[2] [T] *n* lord; honourable person.

আগাছা *n* unwanted wild plants; weeds.

আগাম *adj* given in advance. ❑*adv* in advance. ❑*n* advance.

আগামী *adj* next; ensuing; coming. **~ কল্য** tomorrow. **~ পরশু** day after tomorrow. **~ মাস** next month: ~ মাসের ১৫ তারিখ, the 15th proximo.

আগার *n* house; room; container.

আগিলা *adj* preceding; previous; former.

আগুন *n* fire. **~ জ্বালা** *vi, vt* kindle; make/light a fire. **~ নিভানো** *vt* put out/extinguish a light. **~ ধরা/লাগা** catch fire. **~ লাগানো** *vi, vt* set fire to; set on fire. **~ হওয়া** *vi* (fig) flare up; fly into a rage. **রেগে ~** burning with rage. **সংসারে ~ লাগানো** fill the house with discord.

আগুয়ান *adj* forward; leading; going ahead. **~ হওয়া** *vi, vt* advance; go ahead; take the lead.

আগে *adv* **1** at first; formerly; in the beginning. **2** in front; before. আগে আগে *adv* in front. **আগের,**

আগেকার *adj* of the past. আগেভাগে *adv* in advance; at the outset.

আগ্নেয় *adj* producing fire; fiery; igneous. ~গিরি *n* a volcano. ~ দ্বীপ *n* volcanic island. ~ শিলা *n* igneous rock. আগ্নেয়াস্ত্র *n* fire-arms.

আগ্রহ *n* **1** eagerness; earnestness; zeal. **2** craving; longing. **3** attachment; fondness; attention. আগ্রহী, আগ্রহান্বিত *adj* eager; zealous; earnest; intent.

আঘাত *n* blow; stroke; hit; shock; beating. ~ করা *vi,vt* give a blow or blows; strike; hit. ~ পাওয়া *vi, vt* **1** receive/sustain a blow; be struck/hit/beaten. **2** be mortified.

আঙিনা, আঙ্গিনা *n* courtyard; compound.

আঙুর, আঙ্গুর *n* grape. ~ খেত *n* vineyard; grapery. ~ গাছ/লতা *n* vine. ~ ফল টক Grapes are sour.

আঙুল, আঙ্গুল *n* (হাতের) finger; (পায়ের) toe; ~ মটকানো *vi* snap one's fingers. হাতের বুড়া ~ *n* the thumb. পায়ের বুড়া ~ *n* the great toe. বুড়া ~ দেখানো *vi* (lit) show the thumb in defiance; (fig) defy; disregard. ~ ফুলে কলাগাছ *n, adj* one who has suddenly risen to eminence and so lacks refinement; upstart, nouveau riche.

আঙ্গিক *adj* **1** relating to the body limb(s); bodily. **2** technique. ❑*n* **1** dramatic motions/poses. **2** structure; form.

আঙ্গিনা⇒ আঙিনা

আঙ্গুর=আঙুর

আঙ্গুল=আঙুল

আচকান [P] *n* kind of long coat for men.

আচমকা *adj* sudden; unexpected. ❑*adv* suddenly; unexpectedly.

আচম্বিত *adj* unforeseen; unexpected; sudden. আচম্বিতে *adv* suddenly; all at once.

আচরণ *n* **1** conduct ; behaviour; treatment; dealing. **2** custom; practice; observance. ~ করা *vi vt* behave; deal (with); treat. আচরণীয় *adj* to be practised; fit for use. আচরিত *adj* observed; practised.

আচানক [H] *adj* strange; unforeseen. ❑*adv* suddenly; all on a sudden.

আচার[1] [P] *n* sauce; pickle.

আচার[2] *n* religious or scriptural rites; custom; usage; practice. ~চ্যুত/ভ্রষ্ট *adj* deviating from established practices/rules of conduct. ~নিষ্ঠ/বান *adj* observant of religious rites/established practices. ~নিষ্ঠ ব্যক্তি *n* ritualist. ~বিরুদ্ধ *adj* contrary to practice; unconventional. ~ ব্যবহার/বিচার *n* customs and manners.

আচার্য *n* **1** preceptor; spiritual guide; professor. **2** title of Brahmins.

আচ্ছন্ন *adj* covered; concealed; pervaded. ঘুমে ~ sleepy; drowsy; somnolent. মেঘে ~ overcast with clouds.

আচ্ছা *int* yes; very well; all right; let it be so. ❑*adj* good; excellent; fine: ~ বুদ্ধি; perfect: ~ লোক. ❑*adv* thoroughly : ~ মতো. ~ হয়েছে rightly served.

আচ্ছাদক *adj* what covers/conceals/affords shelter. ❑*n* cover; lid; case.

আচ্ছাদন *n* covering; cover; lid; clothing; garment. আচ্ছাদিত *adj* covered; concealed.

আছড়ানো=আছড়ান=আছাড় দেওয়া⇒আছাড়

আছাড় *n* slip; fall to the ground with force; tumbling. ~ খাওয়া *vi* slip and fall; tumble down. ~ দেওয়া/মারা *vi* throw down/dash to the ground violently.

আছি *vi* (1st pers) am; are.

আছিনু *vi* (poet) (1st pers) was; were.

আছিল *vi* (poet) (3rd pers) was; were.

আছিলে *vi* (poet) (2nd pers) were.

আছে, আছেন *vi* (3rd pers) is; are: সে আছে, তিনি আছেন.

আছো *vi* (2nd person) are: তুমি কেমন আছো?

আজ, আজকে (colloq), আজি (poet) *adv* to-day; at present; now. ❑*n* today; this day; the present time. আজকাল *adv* at present; now a days. আজকাল করা *vt* delay action; putting off; procrastinate. আজ নয় কাল *n* procrastination. আজপর্যন্ত *adv* till today; to this day; to date. আজ বাদে কাল *adv* shortly; soon. আজ খেতে কাল নেই live from hand to mouth.

আজকার[1], আযকার [A *pl n*] remembrance of God. জেকের, যিক্‌র *sing:* জেকের আজকার.

আজকার[2], আজকের, আজিকার *adj* of today; today's.

আজগুবি, আজগবি [P,A আয+ গয়বী] *adj* incredible; fantastic. ~ গল্প *n* cock and bull story.

আজনবি [A] *n, adj* stranger; foreigner.

আজন্ম *adj* life-long. ❑*adv* since one's birth; from birth onward. ~ কাল *adv* for life; all along.

আজব [A *pl* আজায়েব] *adj sing* strange; queer; amazing. ~ কাণ্ড *n* strange or queer incident. ~ দুনিয়া *n* strange world. ~ দেশ *n* wonderland.

আজবতর [A, P আজব + তর] *adj* wonderful; marvellous.

আজম[1], আযম [A] *adj* greatest. উজিরে~.

আজম[2] *n* [A] other than Arabia or the Arabs: আরব ~.

আজমায়েশ=আজমাইশ

আজরাইল, আজরাঈল [A] *n* the angel of death.

আজাজিল, আযাযীল [A] *n* Satan; devil.

আজাড় *adj* unloaded; emptied. ❑*n* leisure; opportunity.

আজাদ, আযাদ [P] *adj* free; independent. আজাদি *n* freedom; independence.

আজান, আযান [A] *n* muezzin's call to congregational prayers. ~ **দেওয়া** *vi* call to prayer.
আজানু, আজানুলম্বিত *adv* reaching up to the knees; down to the knees.
আজাব, আযাব [A] *n* punishment; suffering.
আজি⇒আজ
আজীবন *adv* as long as life lasts; for life. ❑*adj* life-long.
আজুরা, অজুরা [A] *n* wages for labour; service-charge.
আজেবাজে *adj* trashy; worthless; of little value. ~ **কথা বলা** *vi* talk nonsense.
আজ্ঞা *n* command; order; decree; mandate; injunction. ~ **করা** *vi* command; order. ~ **দেওয়া** *vi* command; give an injunction/order. ~**কর্তা** *n* one who orders or commands; commander. ~**ক্রমে,** ~**নুক্রমে** *adv* in obedience to/in accordance with an order or command. ~**ধীন,** ~**নুবর্তী** *adj* subservient; subordinate; obedient. ~**নুবর্তিতা** *n* subjection; subordination; obedience. ~**নুযায়ী,** ~**সারে**=~ক্রমে. ~**পত্র,** ~**লিপি** *n* writ of command; warrant; permit. ~ **পালন করা** *vi,vt* obey orders; comply with orders. ~ **লঙ্ঘন করা** *vi, vt* disobey orders; violate an order.
আজ্ঞে *int* polite response to a superior's inquiry/order; yes, sir. যে ~, ~ হ্যাঁ as you please, sir; yes, sir.
আঞ্চলিক *adj* local; regional.
আঞ্জাম, আনজাম [P] *n* arrangement; management.
আঞ্জুমান [P] *n* an association; a society; a club; a meeting.
আট[1]⇒আঁট
আট[2] *adj, n* eight. **আটই, আটুই** *n* the eighth day of a month. (**আহ্লাদে**) ~**খানা হওয়া** be beside oneself (with joy). ~**পহর,** ~**পর** (dial) *n, adv* the whole day and night. ~**পৌরে** *adj* for constant wear; for rough use; ordinary; commonplace.
আটক *adj* detained; confined; imprisoned. ❑*n* detention; confinement; restraint. ~ **হওয়া** *vi* be detained/confined.
আটকপালে *adj* ill-fated; unfortunate. **আটকপালি** *fem.*
আটকা *adj* detained; confined. ~ **পড়া** *adj* stranded.
আটকানো *vi, vt* check; restrain; prevent; detain: এতে আটকাবে না, this won't be a hindrance/won't stand in the way. **আটকে যাওয়া** *vi* get stopped/blocked/clogged.
আটকুড়িয়া= আঁটকুড়া
আটঘাট *n* ins and outs; details. ~ **বাঁধা** *vi* be prepared to meet any eventuality.
আটচল্লিশ *adj, n* forty-eight.
আটত্রিশ *adj, n* thirty-eight.
আটপহর⇒আট
আটপৌরে⇒আট
আটষট্টি *adj, n* sixty-eight.
আটা *n* coarse flour. ~ **মাখা** *vi* knead flour. **পেষা করা** *vi* press one hard.
আটাত্তর *adj, n* seventy-eight.
আটানব্বই *adj, n* ninety-eight.
আটান্ন *adj, n* fifty-eight.
আটাশ *adj, n* twenty-eight.
আটাশে আটাশ *n* the twenty-eighth day of a month.
আটি=আঁটি
আটুই⇒আট
আঠা *n* adhesive substance; gum; glue; paste.
আঠারো *adj, n* eighteen. ~**ই** *n* eighteenth day of a month. ~ **মাসে বছর** let the grass grow under one's feet; procrastination; tardiness.
আঠালো, এঁটেল *adj* sticky; viscid; gluey. **এঁটেল মাটি** *n* clayey earth.
আঠি= আঁটি[2]
আড়[1] *adj* squint; oblique; crooked: ~চোখ. ~ **ভাঙা** *vi* straighten a thing. ~ **চোখে চাহনি/চাউনি** sidelong look; oblique glance. ~ **চোখে চাওয়া** *vi, vt* look askance.
আড়[2] *adj* other; opposite.
আড়[3] *n* width; breadth. ~**কাঠ** *n* cross-beam. **আড়ে-দিঘে** *adv* in length and breadth. ~**ভাবে** crosswise; obliquely.
আড়[4]**, আইড়** *n* kind of fish without scales.
আড়ং, আওরংগ [P] *n* mart; market; entrepot; fair; store house.
আড়কাঠি, আড়কাটি *n* **1** recruiter of labourers. **2** pilot. **3** weaver's shuttle.
আড়ঙ্গ=আড়ং
আড়ত *n* warehouse; wholesale depot; godown. ~**দার** *n* the owner/keeper of a warehouse; wholesale merchant. ~**দারি** *n* **1** wholesale business. **2** commission of a wholesale merchant.
আড়মোড়া *n* stretching and rolling of the body to remove inertia.
আড়ম্বর *n* **1** pomp; grandeur; splendour. **2** pride; vanity. ~**শূন্য** *adj* not pompous; unostentatious; simple.
আড়ষ্ট *adj* benumbed; cramped; inert. ~**তা** *n* numbness.
আড়াআড়ি *adv* across; crosswise; athwart. ❑*n* mutual ill-feeling; rivalry. ~ **করা** *vi* compete or vie with.
আড়াই *adj, n* two and a half.
আড়াল *n* anything that intercepts the view; concealment; screen; cover. ~ **করা** *vt* keep out of view; conceal; hide. **আড়ালে** *adv* aside; behind the back/bush. **অন্ধকারের আড়ালে** under cover of darkness. **আড়ালে আবডালে** *adv* secretly; in concealment. **আড়ালে থেকে কল টেপা** pull the wires from behind.

আড়ি *n* sulky mood; quarrel; dropping of friendship. ~ **দেওয়া** *vi* terminate friendship. ~ **পাতা, ~ পেতে শোনা** *vi* overhear secretly; eavesdrop.

আড্ডা *n* **1** meeting place; haunt; rendezvous; den; club. **2** company of idle talkers. ~ **দেওয়া** keep company of idle talkers.

আণবিক *adj* molecular; atomic. ~ **আকর্ষণ** *n* molecular attraction. ~ **তত্ত্ব** *n* atomic theory. ~ **বিপ্রকর্ষণ** *n* molecular repulsion. ~ **বোমা** *n* atomic bomb.

আণুবীক্ষণিক *adj* microscopic.

আণ্ডা *n* egg. ~**বাচ্চা** *n* (facet) one's offspring or all children collectively.

আতঙ্ক *n* terror; dread; apprehension; panic; phobia. ~**গ্রস্ত, আতঙ্কিত** *adj* alarmed; terrified; panic-stricken.

আততায়ী *adj* assailing; attempting to kill. ❑*n* assailant; aggressor.

আতপ *n* sunshine; sunlight. ~ **চাউল** *n* sunned rice; rice obtained from sunned (and not boiled) paddy.

আতর [A] *n* perfume; essence of flowers; attar; otto. ~**দান** *n* container for otto or attar.

আতরাফ, আৎরাফ [A] *adj* low-born; lower strata of society: আশরাফ আতরাফ.

আতশ, আতস *n* fire, heat. ~**বাজি** *n* fire-works. **আতশী কাচ** *n* flint-glass; burning-glass.

আতা *n* custard-apple.

আতালিপাতালি, আথালিপাথালি *adv* above and below; everywhere; all about. helter-skeller.

আতিথেয় *adj* hospitable. ~**তা** *n* hospitality.

আতিথ্য *n* hospitality. ~**গ্রহণ** *n* acceptance of hospitality as a guest. ~ **স্বীকার করা** become a guest.

আতিশয্য *n* excess; superabundance; intensity.

আতুর *adj* sick; afflicted; distressed. ~-**ঘর** *n* labour room. **আতুরাশ্রম** *n* hospital; poor-house.

আত্তি *n* display of kinship; showing sympathy or affection. **যত্ন ~ করা** *vi* be all care and attention; treat with kindness and affection.

আত্তীকরণ *n* the process of absorption; assimilation.

আত্ম *adj* related to one's ownself; own. ❑*n* self. ~ **রেখে ধর্ম** Charity begins at home. ~**কলহ** *n* internal discord; domestic quarrel; civil war. ~**কৃত** *adj* done or performed by one's ownself. ~**গত** *adj* self-centred; self-possessed. ~**গরিমা** *n* self-conceit; vanity. ~**গর্বী** *adj* self-conceited; vain. ~**গোপন** *n* concealment of one's identity; self-disguise. ~**গোপন করা** *vi* go into hiding; live in disguise. ~**গৌরব** *n* self-glorification; vanity. ~**গৌরব করা** *vi,vt* glorify one's ownself; brag. ~**গ্লানি** *n* self-reproach; remorse. ~**ঘাতী** *adj* self-destroying; suicidal; prejudicial to one's own interest. ❑*n* self-murderer. ~**ঘাতিনী** *fem*. ~**ঘাতী নীতি** *n* suicidal policy. ~**চিন্তা** *n* thinking of self-interest; introspection; spiritual culture. ~**চেতনা** *n* self-consciousness. **আত্মজ** *adj* self-begotten. ❑*n* son. **আত্মজা** *fem* . ~**জীবনী** *n* autobiography. ~**জ্ঞ** *adj* self-knowing; learned; wise. ~**জ্ঞান** *n* spiritual or metaphysical knowledge. ~**জ্ঞানী** *adj* having spiritual knowledge. ❑*n* spiritualist; metaphysician. ~**তুষ্ট, ~তৃপ্ত** *adj* self-satisfied; self-complacent. ~**তুষ্টি, ~তৃপ্তি** *n* self-complacency; self-content. ~**ত্যাগ** *n* self-sacrifice; self-abnegation; self-denial. ~**ত্যাগী** *adj* self-abnegating; self-sacrificing. ~**দমন** *n* self-restraint; self-control. ~**দমন করা** *vi* restrain one's passions. ~**দর্শন** *n* introspection; self-realization. ~**দর্শী** *adj* introspective; self-realizing. ~**দান** *n* self-sacrifice. ~**দান করা** sacrifice oneself. ~**দোষ** *n* one's own fault. ~**দোষ স্খালন (খণ্ডন) করা** clear oneself from a charge; justify one's own conduct. ~**দ্রোহ** *n* self-torment; self-castigation. ~**দ্রোহী** *adj* self tormenting. ❑*n* self-tormentor. ~**নিগ্রহ** *n* self-repression; self-torture. ~**নিবিষ্ট** *adj* egocentric; self-absorbed. ~**নিবেদন** *n* self-dedication; self-devotion. ~**নিয়ন্ত্রণ** *n* self-control; self-determination. ~**নিয়োগ** *n* self-appointment. ~**নিয়োগ করা** *vt* devote oneself. ~**নির্ভর** *adj* self-reliant. ❑*n* self-reliance. ~**নির্ভরশীল** *adj* self-confident; self dependent. ~**পর** *n* friend and foe. ~**পরায়ণ** *adj* selfish. ~**পরিচয়** *n* one's identity. ~**পরিচয় দেওয়া** *vt* introduce oneself. ~**পরীক্ষা** *n* self-examination; self-scrutiny. ~**প্রকাশ** *n* self-revelation; self-assertion; public appearance. ~**প্রকাশ করা** *vi* appear/come out in public. ~**প্রতারণা, ~প্রবঞ্চনা** *n* self-deception. ~**প্রত্যয়** *n* self-confidence. ~**প্রশংসা** *n* self-praise. ~**প্রশংসা করা** *vi* blow one's own trumpet. ~**প্রসাদ** *n* self-satisfaction; self-complacence. ~**বলি, ~বলি দান** *n* self-sacrifice; dedication of one's own life; martyrdom. ~**বিকাশ** *n* manifestation or development of one's self. ~**বিলোপ** *n* self-effacement. ~**বিশ্বাস** *n* self-confidence. ~**বিশ্বাসী** *adj* self-confident. ~**বিসর্জন** *n* self-sacrifice; self-abnegation. ~**বিস্মৃত** *adj* self-oblivious; absent-minded. ~**বিস্মৃত হওয়া** *vt* forget oneself. ~**মর্যাদা** *n* self-respect. ~**মর্যাদাজ্ঞান, ~মর্যাদাবোধ** *n* sense of self-respect. ~**ম্ভরি** *adj* self-seeking; egotistical. ~**ম্ভরিতা** *n* extreme selfishness; egotism. ~**রক্ষা** *n* self-protection; self-defence. ~**রক্ষা করা** *vt* protect/defend oneself. ~**শুদ্ধি, ~শোধন** *n* self-purification. ~**শ্লাঘা** *n* self-praise; boasting; bragging. ~**সংযম** *adj* self-restrained; continence. ~**সংযমী** *adj* self-restrained; continent. ~**সংবরণ** *n* act of checking oneself. ~**সমর্পণ** *n* surrender; capitulation. ~**সমর্পণ করা** *vi,vt* surrender; capitulate; give up oneself.

~সমাহিত *adj* self-absorbed. ~সম্মান/সম্ভ্রম =~মর্যাদা. ~সর্বস্ব *adj* self-centred; selfish. ~সাৎ *n* illegal arrogation of something to oneself; misappropriation. ~সাৎ করা *vt* misappropriate. ~হত্যা *n* suicide. ~হত্যা করা *vi* commit suicide. ~হত্যাকারী, ~হন্তা *adj* self-murderer; suicide. ~হারা *adj* lost in oneself. ~হারা হওয়া be beside oneself (with).

আত্মা *n* soul; spirit; life.

আত্মানুসন্ধান *n* self-investigation; self-criticism.

আত্মাভিমান *n* self-conceit; pride; vanity.

আত্মারাম *n* (lit) inner soul imagined as a bird encaged in the body. ~ খাঁচাছাড়া হওয়া (facet) be extremely alarmed/afraid.

আত্মাশ্রয়ী *adj* self-dependent; independent.

আত্মাহুতি *n* self-sacrifice; dedication of one's life.

আত্মীয় *adj* related by blood or marriage. ❑*n* relative kinsman. আত্মীয়া *fem*. ~স্বজন *n* friends and relations; kith and kin. ~তা *n* relationship; kinship.

আত্মোৎকর্ষ *n* self-elevation; self-development.

আত্মোৎসর্গ=আত্মাহুতি

আত্মোন্নতি=আত্মোৎকর্ষ

আত্মোপম *adj* like oneself; equal to oneself.

আত্যয়িক *adj* urgent; emergent; critical. ~ অবস্থা *n* emergent situation. ~ ক্ষমতা *n* emergency power.

আথালি-পাথালি=আতালিপাতলি

আদত, আদৎ *adj* genuine; real. আদতে *adv* in reality; as a matter of fact.

আদপে *adv* **1** really; in truth. **2** at all; in the least.

আদব [A] *n* etiquette; good manners. ~কায়দা *n* forms of etiquette; laws of courtesy.

আদম [A] *n* Adam, the first man.

আদমশুমার, আদমশুমারি *n* census; official enumeration of population.

আদমি, আদমী *n* progeny of Adam; man. কালা ~ *n* (derog) coloured man; blackie.

আদর *n* **1** caress; fondness; love; affection. **2** respect; reverence; honour. ~ করা *vt* fondle; caress. **3** show respect/honour. ~-অভ্যর্থনা/আপ্যায়ন *n* cordial reception and entertainment to guests; warm welcome.

আদরিণী, আদরী *adj fem* beloved enjoying too much indulgence; favourite.

আদর্শ *n* one who or that which is to be followed as an ideal/model/specimen. ~ চরিত্র *n* exemplary character. ❑*adj* having an exemplary character. ~ পুস্তক *n* model book. ~ স্ত্রী *n* ideal wife. ~ লিপি *n* copy-book. ~স্থানীয় *adj* exemplary; ideal.

আদল *n* similarity; resemblance.

আদা *n* ginger. ~ জল খেয়ে লাগা be up and doing; undertake to do something tenaciously. আদায় কাঁচকলায় *adv* at daggers drawn. আদার ব্যাপারী petty trader; (fig) one who does not count in public affairs. আদার ব্যাপারীর জাহাজের খবর কেন? The cobbler must stick to his last.

আদান *n* act of receiving or taking. ~প্রদান *n* act of giving and taking; barter; exchange; matrimonial alliance.

আদায় *n* realization/collection (of bills, taxes, etc). ~ করা *vi, vt* realize; collect; levy. ~পত্র *n* realization of rents, taxes, etc.

আদালত [A] *n* court of justice. উচ্চ ~ *n* High Court. উচ্চতর ~ higher court. নিম্ন ~ *n* lower Court. ছোট ~ *n* small causes court.

আদি *adj* first; original; fundamental. ❑*n* beginning; origin; source. ❑*suff* and the others; et cetera. ~ কারণ *n* the first cause; the Supreme Being. ~কাল *n* ancient times. ~ কোষ *n* embryonic cell. ~পুরুষ *n* the progenitor of a family/race. ~বাসী *n* the aborigines. ~রস *n* (rhet) emotion of love; sex-passion; erotic sentiment. ~ রূপ *n* the original model; archetype.

আদিখ্যেতা *n* ostentatious attention to unimportant things; undue affectation; feigning.

আদিম *adj* **1** first; primitive, original. **2** aboriginal; ancient. ~ অধিবাসী *n* aborigines.

আদিষ্ট *adj* ordered; directed; advised.

আদুরে *adj* petted; brought up with excessive indulgence and hence spoilt. ~ গোপাল *n* spoiled child of indulgent parents.

আদৃত *adj* honoured; treated cordially.

আদেখলা, আদেখলে *adj* one who is so eager to see or have a thing that it seems one has never seen anything like it before; covetous; greedy.

আদেশ *n* order; command; decree; directive; ordinance; injunction. ~ করা/দেওয়া *vi vt* order; command; enjoin; direct. ~ক্রমে *adv* as per/according to/in obedience to an order. ~ পালন করা carry out an order/decree. ~ প্রার্থনীয় for favour of orders.

আদেষ্টা *n* one who orders or commands.

আদৌ *adv* at all; in the least, ~ সত্য নয়, not at all true.

আদ্য *adj* **1** first; prime; primeval. **2** chief; best; primary. ~ন্ত *n* beginning and end; alpha and omega. ❑*adv* from beginning to end; from first to last. ~শ্রাদ্ধ, ~কৃত্য *n* obsequies performed in memory of a Hindu deceased.

আদ্যিকাল *n* ancient times; primitive days: আদ্যিকালের বুড়ি, old-fashioned aged woman.

আদ্যোপান্ত *adv* from first to last; from top to bottom; all over; all through.

আধ, আধা *adj* half. ❑*n* one-half. আধ-আধ *adj* indistinct; inarticulate; babbling; mumbling.

❑*adv* indistinctly; imperfectly; babblingly; mumblingly. ~~বুলি *n* lispings; baby-talk.
আধকপালে *n* violent headache affecting one side only; hamicrania. ~খেঁচড়া *adj* 1 incomplete; half-done. 2 dishevelled; disorderly. ~পাগলা *adj* half-mad; crazy; eccentric. ❑*n* madcap; crank. ~পেটা *adj* 1 insufficient to satisfy one's hunger. 2 half-fed. ~পোড়া *adj* half-burned; partly baked/roasted. ~বয়সী *adj* middle-aged. ~বুড়া/বুড়ো almost old. ~বুড়ি *fem.* ~মরা *adj* 1 half-dead; almost dead. 2 lacking vigour and energy; weak; feeble; dull.
আধলি⇒ আধুলি
আধা⇒আধ. ~আধি *adj* half; almost half; fifty-fifty. ❑*adv* half-and-half; by halves; in two equal shares. ~সরকারি/সরকারী *adj* demi official. ~সরকারি প্রতিষ্ঠান *n* semi government concern.
আধার[১] *n* 1 container; vessel; case. 2 place; shelter; support.
আধার[২] *n* food (esp of birds or fish).
আধাসরকারি⇒ আধা
আধি[১] *n* mental agony; anxiety; worry. ~ক্লিষ্ট *adj* suffering from worries and anxieties; mentally distressed/afflicted. ~ব্যাধি *n* mental and physical ailments.
আধি[২] *n* system of sharecropping; arrangement under which a land owner and a cultivator share the crop on fifty-fifty basis.
আধিকারিক *adj* relating to ownership/legal claim. ❑*n* high ranking official.
আধিক্য *n* 1 excess; abundance. 2 predominance; intensity.
আধিখ্যেতা =আদিখ্যেতা
আধিজৈবিক *adj* concerning life on earth; earthly; worldly. ❑*n* worldly affairs; material things.
আধিদৈবিক *adj* providential; supernatural; natural. ~ বিপদ *n* natural calamity.
আধিপত্য *n* 1 mastery; supremacy; authority; suzerainty; overlordship. 2 predominance. 3 rule; government. ~ করা *vi,vt* dominate; rule; govern.
আধিভৌতিক *adj* pertaining to organic life; organic; biological; material.
আধুনিক *adj* of present times; modern; recent; current. আধুনিকা *fem.* ~তা *n* modernism.
আধুনিকীকরণ *n* modernization. ~ করা *vt* modernize; bring (sth) up to date.
আধুলি, আধলি *n* fifty-paisa coin; half a taka coin.
আধেক *adj, adv* half.
আধোআধো=আধআধ
আধ্যাত্মিক *adj* 1 pertaining to spirit; spiritual. 2 relating to God or the Supreme Being; theological; metaphysical. 3 intellectual; mental. ~তা *n* spiritualism.
আন[১] *adj* (poet) other; another; different. ❑*adv* 1 otherwise; in a different way. 2 more; else.
আন[২] *vt* bring; get.
আন[৩] [P] *suff* indicating plurality (eg, মালিক + আন = মালিকান, শরিক + আন ≡ শরিকান).
আনকোরা [H] *adj* 1 quite new: ~ প্রতিষ্ঠান. 2 brand-new; unused; unsoiled; unwashed: ~ কাপড়. 3 fresh; untarnished; unstained: ~ নোট. 4 inexperienced; unskilled: ~ অভিনেতা.
আনচান [B আন+Pচয়েন] *adj* anxious; restless; uneasy; passionate; fervent: প্রাণ ~ করা. ❑*adv* very anxiously/worriedly; ardently; fervently. ~ করা *vi,vt* feel uneasy or restless; show signs of impatience.
আনজাম ⇒ আঞ্জাম
আনত *adj* 1 bent down; inclined. 2 obeisant; bowed; polite; submissive. ~ হওয়া *vi,vt* bend the head or body as a sign of respect/as a greeting; stoop in obeisance. আনতি *n* obeisance.
আনন *n* 1 face; countenance. 2 mouth.
আনন্দ 1 joy; delight; cheerfulness: আনন্দের ঢেউ. 2 happiness; contentment. 3 pleasure; satisfaction; gratification; propitiation; gladness. 4 merriment; amusement; hilarity; joviality: ~ করা. ~ করা *vi,vt* rejoice; make merry . ~কর *adj* delightful; pleasant; gladdening. ~জনক/দায়ক *adj* what causes joy; delightful; pleasant. ~ন *n* 1 act of producing joy/delight. 2 greeting; words of welcome. ~বিহ্বল *adj* overwhelmed with joy; beside oneself with joy. ~ময় *adj* joyful; delightful; happy; cheerful; merry. ~ময়ী *adj* 1 *fem* of ~ময়. 2 Hindu goddess Durga. ~-লহরি *n* 1 wave of joy; surge of delight. 2 one-stringed musical instrument.
আনন্দাশ্রু *n* tears of joy.
আনন্দিত *adj* delighted; happy; glad; pleased; merry.
আনন্দোচ্ছ্বাস *n* burst of joy; ecstacy of happiness.
আনমন *n* act of bending down/curving slightly; inclination.
আনমনা *adj* unmindful; absent-minded; unaffected; indifferent. আনমনে *adv* listlessly; inattentively; absent-mindedly.
আনমিত *adj, adv* slightly bent down; inclined.
আনম্র *adj* polite; courteous; modest.
আনয়ন *n* act of bringing/fetching. ~ করা *vt* bring; fetch.
আনসার [A] *n* 1 helper; volunteer. 2 the people of Medina who helped the immigrants from Mecca under the leadership of Prophet Muhammad (sm).
আনা[১] *vt* bring; fetch. ❑*n* coming: ~ গোনা. ❑*adj* brought forth: তোমার ~ কাপড়. ~নো *vt* have sth brought by sb; make sb bring sth.

আনা[২], **আনি** *n* one-sixteenth part of a thing: এক আনা/আনি.
আনা[৩] *n suff* indicating one's conduct or position: বাবুয়ানা, গরিবানা.
আনাগোনা *n* act of coming and going. **~ করা** *vt* go often (to a place).
আনাচ-কানাচ *n* nook and corner; lanes and by-lanes; secluded/neglected places.
আনাজ *n* green-stuff; vegetables. **~-পত্র** *n* spinach and vegetables fit for cooking.
আনাড়ি *adj* **1** untrained; unskilled; inexperienced. **2** ignorant; foolish. ❑*n* novice; quack. **~পনা** *n* inefficiency; awkwardness; clumsiness.
আনানো⇒আনা[১]
আনাম [corrup of Arabic আমান)] *adj* entire; the whole একটা ~ কেক.
আনার [P] *n* the pomegranate. **~কলি** *n* **1** the bud of the pomegranate; green pomegranate. **2** a famous place/bazar of Lahore.
আনারস [pg] *n* the pineapple. **আনারসি** *adj* of sweet acid taste.
আনি = আনা[২]
আনীত *adj* brought forth; fetched.
আনীল *adj* slightly blue; bluish; light-blue.
আনুকূল্য *n* **1** favour; patronage; support. **2** help; aid; assistance. **~ করা** *vt* support; favour; patronize.
আনুগত্য *n* **1** loyalty due to a ruler or government; allegiance; fealty. **2** loyalty to one's mash; obedience; subservience; faithful adherence. **3** adulation; obsequiousness. **~ স্বীকার করা** *vi, vt* owe allegiance (to); submit (to). **আনুগত্যের শপথ** *n* oath of allegiance/fealty.
আনুতোষিক *n* **1** monetary gift (in addition to pay) to a retiring employee in acknowledgement of service; a gratuity. **2** tip (for service).
আনুপদিক *adj* following; succeeding.
আনুপাতিক *adj* (math) proportional; corresponding in degree or amount.
আনুপূর্ব, আনুপূর্ব্য *n* sequence; due succession/order. **আনুপূর্বিক** *adv* serially; in regular order; from beginning to end. ❑*adj* **1** serial; continuous; successive. **2** entire; complete. **আনুপূর্বিক বর্ণনা করা** *vt* describe in detail. **আনুপূর্বিকতা** *n* continuity; seriality.
আনুমানিক *adj* **1** probable: ~ ব্যয়; inferential. **2** approximate: ~ দু'শ লোক. ❑*adv* probably; nearly; approximately.
আনুরূপ্য *n* similarity; likeness; resemblance.
আনুষঙ্গিক, আনুষঙ্গ *adj* **1** accompanying; concomitant (with); incidental: ~ খরচ. **2** secondary; minor; unimportant: ~ বিষয়গুলো পরে বিবেচনা করা হবে.
আনুষ্ঠানিক *adj* **1** relating to ceremonies; ceremonial; formal: ~ উদ্বোধন. **2** according to rules, customs and conventions; formal: ~ স্বীকৃতি. **3** of religious rites; ritual; ritualistic: ~ ত্রুটি. **~তা** *n* formalities: বিবাহের ~. **~ভাবে** *adv* ceremonially; formally; ritually.
আন-আন⇒আন
আন্ত *adj* relating to inside.
আন্তঃনগর *adj* intercity
আন্তঃপ্রাদেশিক *adj* inter-provincial; inter-state: ~ যোগাযোগ.
আন্তরযন্ত্র *n* (anat) internal organs of the body, eg, the stomach, intestines, heart; lungs, etc; viscera. **আন্তরযন্ত্রীয়** *adj* visceral.
আন্তরিক *adj* **1** sincere; cordial; candid; genuine; hearty; heart-felt. **2** mental; inner; inward; hidden. **3** relating to the heart; cherished in the heart. **~তা** *n* candour; cordiality; sincerity.
আন্তরীক্ষ *adj* **1** of the sky; skyey; heavenly; celestial. **2** aerial; ethereal; atmospherical: ~ বিপদ. ❑*n* the sky; the cloud.
আন্তরীণ *adj* internal; inside.
আন্তর্জাতিক, আন্তর্জাতীয় *adj* **1** of different countries; concerning all nations: ~ সমস্যা. **2** current/in vogue among all nations; international: ~ বাণিজ্য.
আন্তর্বিদ্যালয় *adj* inter-school.
আন্তর্মহাদেশীয় *adj* inter-continental: ~ ক্ষেপণাস্ত্র.
আন্ত্র, আন্ত্রিক *adj* intestinal; duodenal; enteric. **আন্ত্রিক জ্বর** *n* enteric fever.
আন্দর, আন্দরমহল⇒অন্দর
আন্দাজ [P] *n* **1** guess; conjecture. **2** realization; perception; feeling: ঘুমের মধ্যে ~ পাচ্ছিলাম ট্রেন দ্রুতবেগে চলছে. ❑*adj* **1** similar; according to; proportional: আধাসের ফুটানো পানি, সেই ~ গুড় ও লবণ. **2** approximate; conjectural: ~ দু'গজ. **আন্দাজি** *adj* baseless; false: আন্দাজি খবর. ❑*adv* by a mere guess: অন্ধকারে আন্দাজি খোঁজাখুঁজি. **আন্দাজে** *adv* by guess/surmise/conjecture.
আন্দেশা, আনদেশ [P] *n* **1** fear; apprehension; doubt. **2** thought; imagination.
আন্দোলন *n* **1** agitation; turmoil: ছাত্র ~. **2** united actions and efforts of a group of people in favour of some change/plan; movement: ভাষা ~. **3** swinging; oscillation; vibration. **4** controversy; cogitation; thoughts; reflections. **~ করা** *vi, vt* agitate; start (or take part in) a campaign to gain a special object.
আন্ধা-চক্কর *n* state of confusion/bewilderment; maze; labyrinth: তিনি এক আন্ধা-চক্করে পড়েছেন.
আন্ধার⇒আঁধার
আন্নাকালী *n* name given to unwanted female children by Hindus literally imploring goddess Kali not to give any more female issue.
আপ [H] *n* one's ownself. ❑*adj* one's own. **~ ভালা তো জগৎ ভালা** to the pure all things are pure. **~ রুচি খানা পর রুচি পরনা** eat to please

thyself, but dress to please others.

আপকাওয়াস্তে, আপকেওয়াস্তে [U]*adv* **1** for your own self. **2** for one's ownself. ❑*adj* flattering; adulatory; self-seeking; selfish.

আপখোরাকি *adj* without food: ~ দিনমজুর.

আপ-টু-ডেট [E] *adj* up-to-date; modern; fashionable: ~ পোশাক.

আ-পড়া *adj* **1** what has not been read; unread. **2** uneducated; illiterate.

আপণ *n* **1** shop; sales emporium. **2** commercial centre; market; entrepot. **আপণিক** *adj* **1** of merchandise/trade. **2** shop-keeper; trader.

আপৎ, আপৎকাল⇒আপদ

আপতন *n* **1** the fact of falling upon; incidence: ~ কোণ, angle of incidence. **2** unexpected event; unintended action. **3** mishap; misfortune; casualty; calamity; accident. **আপতিক** *adj* accidental; incidental; casual. **আপতিত** *adj* **1** fallen by chance/accident. **2** suddenly happened. **3** accrued; incident: আপতিত রশ্মি.

আপত্তি *n* **1** objection; dissent; a plea; an excuse. **2** protest; expostulation; remonstrance. ~ **করা** *vi,vt* object; protest; remonstrate. ~ **তোলা/দেওয়া** *vt* raise/file an objection. ~**কর/জনক** *adj* open to objection; objectionable.

আপদ[1]⇒আপাদ

আপদ[2], **আপৎ** [A] *n* **1** danger; hazard; adversity. **2** disaster; mishap; misfortune. **3** one who/that which is irritating/ vexatious/ disgusting. **আপৎকাল** *n* time of danger/emergency. **আপদগ্রস্ত** *adj* involved in trouble/difficulty/ calamity. **আপদ্ধর্ম/আপদ্ধর্ম** *n* emergency measure (usu not honest). **আপদ-বালাই** [A] *n pl* sorrows and sufferings; dangers and difficulties. **আপদবিপদ** *n* storm and stress.

আপন, আপনার *adj* **1** own; one's own; of one's own. **2** relative; kinsman; friend: তুমি যে আমার কত আপনার. **3** direct; immediate: আপন মামা. **আপনপর** *n* far and near ones; friend and foe. **আপনভোলা, আপনহারা** *adj* indifferent to one's own interests; beside oneself; absent-minded. **আপনসর্বস্ব** *adj* self-centred; selfish. **আপনার ঢাক আপনি বাজানো/পিটানো** *vi* praise one's ownself; blow one's own trumpet. **আপনার পায়ে কুড়াল মারা** *vi* harm one's own interests; dig one's own grave.

আপনা *n* one's ownself: ~ থেকে. ❑*adj* one's own; relative; kinsman: ~ লোক. ~**আপনি** *adv* by/of one's own self/accord/free will; spontaneously. ❑*n* one's own people; kinsman: ~আপনির মধ্যে বিবাহ.

আপনার⇒আপন

আপনি *pron* **1** you; respectful form of *pron* of the 2nd per. **2** one's ownself. ~ **বাঁচলে বাপের নাম** self-preservation is the first law of nature.

আপন্ন *adj* **1** affected with; involved in (বিপদাপন্ন). **2** *(suff)* gained; acquired (শরণাপন্ন; অবস্থাপন্ন). ~**সত্ত্বা** *adj fem* pregnant; big with child. ❑*n* pregnant woman.

আপরাহ্ণিক *adj* of the afternoon/evening.

আপরুচি⇒আপ

আপশান, আপসান⇒আফসান

আপশোষ⇒আফসোস

আপস[1]=ওয়াপস

আপস[2] =আপোস

আপসে[1] *adv* **1** mutually; reciprocally; among one another: ~ বিবাদ করা. **2** amicably; by arrangement: ~ মিটমাট করা.

আপসে[2], **আপ্‌সে** *adv* **1** of one's own; spontaneously. **2** automatically; without any outward aid.

আপসোস⇒আফসোস

আপা [T] *n* **1** elder sister. **2** word used to address elderly women/unfamiliar ladies/school mistresses.

আপাকা *adj* **1** not yet ripe; raw. **2** not thoroughly ripe.

আপাণ্ডুর *adj* slightly pale/yellowish/blanched.

আপাত *n* **1** present moment; the time being: ~ মধুর. ❑*adj* apparent: ~ গতি. ❑*adv* seemingly; apparently: ~ কঠিন. **আপাতত** *adv* for the present/time being. ~ **দৃষ্টিতে** *adv* at first sight; apparently. ~**সুন্দর** *adj* seemingly/apparently nice (but not so in the long run).

আপাদ, আপদ *adv* **1** to the feet. **2** from the feet. ~**লম্বিত** *adj* pendent upto the feet; hanging down to the feet. ~**মস্তক** *adv* from head to foot; from top to bottom.

আপান *n* wine-shop; bar.

আপামর *adv* down to/including the lowest; all irrespective of high and low. ~ **জনসাধারণ** *n* people of all classes from the highest to the lowest.

আপিঙ্গল *adj* brownish; slightly copper-coloured.

আপিল, আপীল [E] *n* **1** (legal) appeal; prayer for re-trial by higher court. **2** prayer; petition; representation. ~ **করা** *vi* prefer an appeal; appeal. ~-**আদালত** *n* appellate court. ~**কারী** *n* appellant. **আপিলে খালাস** *vt* acquitted/released on appeal.

আপেক্ষিক *adj* **1** comparative. **2** (phys) relative; specific: ~ গতি, relative motion; ~ গুরুত্ব, specific gravity. ~**তা** *n* comparativeness; relativity. ~ **তত্ত্ব** *n* (phys) the theory of relativity.

আপেল [E] *n* kind of fruit; the apple.

আপোস, আপস [U] *n* **1** compromise. **2** amicable settlement. ~ **করা** *vi,vt* compromise; settle amicably. ~-**রফা** *n* amicable settlement; compromise. ~**হীন মনোবৃত্তি** *n* mentality of not compromising with the opposite party;

uncompromising attitude.

আপ্ত[১] *adj* **1** obtained; possessed. **2** free from errors; authentic; authoritative: ~বাক্য/বচন. **3** friend; relative: ~জন. **4** reliable; trustworthy; confidential: ~ করণিক, confidential clerk. **~কাম** *adj* one whose desires have been fulfilled/gratified.

আপ্ত[২] *adj* own; one's own. **~গরজি/গরজে** *adj* self-seeking; selfish. **~পর** *n* friend and foe.

আপ্যায়ন *n* **1** entertainment; hospitable reception. **2** tribute of respect; felicitation. **~ করা** *vt* welcome; entertain; felicitate. **আপ্যায়িত** *adj* **1** welcome; entertained; felicitated. **2** given pleasure/satisfaction; gratified.

আপ্রাণ *adj* tooth and nail. ❑*adv* to one's utmost; to the best of one's power/ability; to the last breath: ~ চেষ্টা.

আপ্লুত *adj* **1** drenched; bathed; inundated: হৃদয় আনন্দরসে ~.

আফখোরা⇒আবখোরা

আফগান, আফঘান [P] *n* inhabitant of Afghanistan; an Afghan. ❑*adj* of Afghanistan/Afghans. **আফগানি** *adj* born of Afghanistan.

আফঘান⇒আফগান

আফজল⇒আফযল

আফতাব[১] [P] *n* the sun.

আফতাব[২], **আফতাবা** [P] *n* ewer; jug with a spout.

আফতাবা⇒আফতাব[২]

আফযল, আফজল [A] *adj* comparatively good; better.

আফলাক [A] *n* the sky; the celestial sphere; the wide expanse of the heavens; the atmosphere.

আফলাতুন [A] *n* **1** Greek philosopher Plato. **2** intelligent; wise.

আফশাঁ, আফশা *n* [P] kind of sparkling powder of silvery or golden colour used by woman in decorating face and hair.

আফসর [A] *n* **1** officer; commander. **2** crown; coronet; diadem.

আফসানো, আপসানো [P] *vi,vt* **1** make a boast; brag; bluster; boast; vaunt. **2** express disappointment/annoyance on account of failure; regret; lament. **আফসানি** *n* **1** boasting; vaunting. **2** remorse; regret.

আফসোস, আপসোস [P] *n* remorse; regret; repentance; penitence. **~ করা** *vt* repent; regret; feel compunction.

আফিং⇒আফিম

আফিঙ্গ⇒আফিম

আফিম [P আফয়ূন cf opuim (lat); opion (G)] *n* drug obtained from poppy seeds and used as sedative/narcotic/intoxicant/stimulant; opium. **~খোর** *adj* addicted to opium. ❑*n* opium-taker.

আফিস=অফিস

আফুটন্ত, আফোটা *adj* **1** not in bloom. **2** not full-blown.

আফুটা *adj* not thoroughly boiled; parboiled:. ~ ভাত.

আফেন্দি [T] *n* honourable/respectful surname; master; lord.

আফোটা⇒আফুটন্ত

আফ্রিকান [E] *adj* of Africa. ❑*n* an African.

আফ্রিদি, আফ্রিদী *n* tribal people inhabiting the north-west frontier of Pakistan.

আব[১] [P] *n* water.

আব[২] *n* abnormal cell-growth in any part of the body; tumour.

আব[৩], **আভ** *n* **1** cloud. **2** mica, a mineral silicate.

আব-ই-কওসর⇒আবে কওসর

আব-ই-হায়াত⇒আবে হায়াত

আব-এ-জমজম⇒আবে জমজম

আবওয়াব, আবোয়াব, আবুয়াব [A] *n* illegal cesses/extra charges exacted by landowners from tenants.

আবকার, আবগার [P] *n* **1** manufacturer of alcoholic spirits; distiller. **2** dealer in intoxicants. **আবগারি, আবকারি** *n* **1** trade in intoxicating drugs. **2** tax imposed on the manufacture and sale of intoxicants; excise duty. **3** public department in charge of collecting excise duty; excise department. ❑*adj* **1** relating to alcoholic spirits/ intoxicating drugs. **2** relating to excise duty/ department.

আবখোরা, আফখোরা [P] *n* kind of large vessel/cup/glass for drinking.

আবছা *adj* indistinct. ❑*adv* indistinctly: ~ দেখা.

আবছায়া *n* shadowy/indistinct figure; phantom;

আবডাল *n* cover; screen; stealth; shelter: আড়ালে-আবডালে.

আবড়া-থাবড়া⇒এবড়ো থেবড়ো

আবদার[১] *n* childish insistence on having sth; unreasonable/capricious demand (as a child does). **~ করা** *vi* make an impossible/ unreasonable demand. **আবদেরে, আবদারে** *adj* insisting obstinately on having sth; importunate.

আবদার[২] [P] *adj* bright; radiant; sparkling; glittering: ~ মুক্তা.

আবদারে⇒আবদার[১]

আবদাল [A] *n* a class of Muslim ascetics/ saints.

আবদেরে⇒আবদার[১]

আবদ্ধ *adj* **1** besieged; confined: ঘরে ~. **2** closed; shut: ~ দরজা. **3** tied; bound (শৃঙ্খলাবদ্ধ). **4** involved; engaged: কাজে ~. **5** pledged; mortgaged. **~ করা** *vt* shut; confine; bind; involve; mortgage. **~ হওয়া** *vi* be confined/ bound/involved/pledged/ mortgaged.

আবরণ *n* **1** act of covering/veiling. **2** clothing; garment. **3** covering; lid. **আবৃত, আবরিত** (archaic) *adj* covered.

আবরা [P] *n* cover of pillow, quilt, etc.

আবরু, আব্রু [P] *n* **1** woman's honour; modesty; chastity. **2** privacy; screen; veil. **3** civility; courtesy; decency. **বে-আবরু** *adj* disgraced; insulted; put out of countenance; shameless.

আবরোঁয়া [P] *n* delicately woven cotton fabric; kind of Muslin cloth that seems watery when wet.

আবর্জন *n* **1** act of giving/throwing away; total abandonment. **2** act of bending down/controlling/ regulating. **আবর্জিত** *adj*.

আবর্জনা *n* **1** sweepings; rubbish; waste/refuse matter. **2** undesirable/mean person.

আবর্ত *n* **1** whirling motion/shape; any ring-like object (দক্ষিণাবর্ত). **2** (of water) circular or spiral movement; whirlpool; vortex; eddy. **3** act of whirling/revolving/rotating. **4** name for whirling cloud: ~ মেঘ. ❑ *adj* that which is revolving/reeling/rolling: ~ গতি. **আবর্তিত** *adj*. ~ **বাত্যা** *n* cyclone; whirlwind.

আবর্তদণ্ড⇒আবর্তন

আবর্তন *n* **1** act of whirling/ revolving/rolling. **2** return; repetition; reappearance; rotation. **3** act of stirring/churning; gyration. **আবর্তনী, আবর্তদণ্ড** *n* churning rod; pestle for churning. **আবর্তমান** *adj* that which is whirling/revolving/ rotating/ gyrating. **আবর্তিত** *adj* repeated; revolved; rotated; gyrated. **আবর্তিত হওয়া** *vi, vt* whirl; revolve; rotate; be repeated.

আবলতাবল⇒আবোলতাবোল

আবলী, আবলি *n* **1** row; line; range (বৃক্ষ + আবলী=বৃক্ষাবলী). **2** series; group; collection (নিয়মাবলী, রচনাবলী).

আবলুস, আবলুশ [P] *n* hard dark-coloured wood; ebony: ~ কাঠ ~**-কালো** *adj* deep black; as black as ebony.

আবশ্যক *n* need; necessity. ❑*adj* **1** necessary; important. **2** essential; unavoidable. ~ **ব্যবস্থা** necessary action. ~ **হলে** if required; if need be. ~**তা** *n* need; necessity. **আবশ্যকীয়** *adj* necessary; essential.

আবশ্যিক *adj* what must be done; compulsory: ~ পাঠ্য.

আবহ *adj* **1** carrying; bearing (শোকাবহ). **2** producing; begetting (ভয়াবহ). ❑*n* **1** the gaseous envelope of the earth; atmosphere; weather. **2** surroundings; circumstances; environment. ~ **চিত্র** *n* weather-chart. ~ **বিজ্ঞান/বিদ্যা** *n* meteorology. ~**বিদ, ~বিৎ** *n* meteorologist. ~**মণ্ডল** *n* the atmosphere. ~**-সংবাদ** *n* meteorological/weather report. ~**-সঙ্গীত** *n* background music. ~**-সূচনা** *n* weather forecast.

আবহমান *adj* passing/flowing on; ever-continuing; ever-existent; traditional. ~**কাল (ধরে)** *adv* ever since the beginning; from time immemorial.

আবহাওয়া [P] *n* climate; weather conditions of a region.

আবা [A] *n* kind of open-breast long shirt.

আবাগা⇒আবাগে

আবাগী *adj, n fem*⇒আভাগী, অভাগিনী) ill-fated; unfortunate; wretched.

আবাগে, আবাগা *adj, n* unlucky; unfortunate.

আবাদ [P] *n* **1** cultivation, tillage: ধানের ~. **2** cultivated land; land developed for cultivation. **3** human habitation; process of settling people in a new place; a settlement. ~ **করা** *vt* **1** cultivate; till. **2** prepare land for the raising of crops/settlement of human habitation. **আবাদি** *adj* **1** fit for cultivation; arable. **2** cultivated; tilled.

আবাবিল, আবাবীল [A] *n* species of small birds spoken of in the Qoran as having destroyed the invading army of Abraha. The Holy Book used the word only in the sense of "swarms of birds". It has no singular form.

আবার *adv* **1** again; once more. **2** moreover; further; besides: জ্বর ~ আমাশয়. ❑*int* expressing uncertainty/distrust/negation: ব্যাঙের ~ সর্দি, সে ~ কি করবে?

আবাল [A] *adj* **1** underage; destitute of judgement; helpless. **2** adolescent; teenaged. ❑*n* foolish/ignorant person. ❑ *adv* down to (including) the boys. ~**বৃদ্ধ** *n* the young and the old. ~**বৃদ্ধবণিতা** *n* men, women and children; (fig) one and all.

আবাল্য *adv* from childhood/infancy.

আবাস *n* residence; abode; dwelling place; habitation.

আবাসিক *adj* residential; resident; residing: ~ ছাত্র. ~ **বিদ্যালয়** *n* school where the students have to stay compulsorily at the attached hostels; residential school.

আবাহন *n* **1** invocation; call. **2** invitation. **আবাহিত** *adj*. **আবাহনী** *adj* invocatory; relating to invocation/invitation. ❑ *n* song of welcome.

আবিদ, আবেদ [A] *adj* worshipping; worshipful; devotee; devout.

আবিয়ে *adj* (rare) unmarried.

আবির *n* (S cf A আবীর) kind of perfumed red powder which the Hindus throw at each other during the Holi festival.

আবির্ভাব *n* **1** appearance; coming into view: চাঁদের ~. **2** outbreak: কলেরার ~. **3** advent; arrival; birth, উনবিংশ শতাব্দীতে এক মহান সমাজ সংস্কারকের ~ ঘটে: **আবির্ভূত** *adj* appeared; become manifest; come into existence. **আবির্ভূত হওয়া** *vi* appear; arrive; be born; become manifest; install oneself.

আবিল *adj* **1** defiled; polluted. **2** dirty; filthy;

foul. ~তা *n* dirtiness; filthiness; turbidity; foulness.

আবিষ্কার *n* **1** act of discovering/inventing. **2** the thing discovered/invented. ~ করা *vt* discover; invent; explore. **আবিষ্কর্তা, আবিষ্কারক** *n* discover; inventor; designer; explorer. **আবিষ্কর্ত্রী** *fem*. **আবিষ্কৃত** *adj* discovered; invented; brought to light.

আবিষ্ট *adj* **1** overwhelmed (with) (বিস্ময়াবিষ্ট). **2** thoroughly engrossed or absorbed in. **3** possessed (by) (ভূতাবিষ্ট). **4** overcast/pervaded (with) (মেঘাবিষ্ট).

আবীর=আবির

আবু [A] *n* father.

আবুয়াব⇒আবওয়াব

আবৃত *adj* **1** covered; enveloped; veiled. **2** surrounded; encircled. **3** concealed; overcast/pervaded with (মেঘাবৃত). **আবৃতি** *n* covering; fencing; enclosure.

আবৃত্তি *n* **1** recitation; recital. **2** act of reading over and over again. **3** repetition; return; recurrence (পুনরাবৃত্তি). ~ করা *vi, vt* recite; reproduce from memory; repeat.

আবে কওসর, আব-ই-কওসর [P আব +A কওসর] *n* water of the heavenly spring, Qawser (described in the Qoran).

আবেগ *n* **1** impulse; emotion; passion (ভাবাবেগ). **2** anxiety; worry; mental agitation (শোকাবেগ). **3** eagerness; haste; speed: মনের আবেগ. ~**পূর্ণ** *adj* impassioned; passionate. ~**শূন্য**, ~**হীন** *adj* passionless; dispassionate. **আবেগোচ্ছ্বাস** *n* outburst of passion; passionate outburst.

আবে-জমজম, আব-এ-জমজম [আব P+A যম্‌যম] *n* water of the holy Zamzam well of Mecca.

আবেদ⇒আবিদ

আবেদক *adj* one who submits a prayer/petition/application. ❑*n* applicant; petitioner; plaintiff.

আবেদন *n* **1** prayer; solicitation. **2** petition; application; representation. **3** plaint; allegation. **4** captivation/fascination of the mind; appeal: সুরের ~. ~ করা *vi, vt* pray; petition; apply; make an application. ~**কারী** = আবেদক. ~**কারিণী** *fem* . ~**পত্র** *n* application; petition.

আবেশ *n* **1** state of being obsessed by/with sth; obsession; engrossment; absorbedness; intense mental preoccupation (ভাবাবেশ).

আবেষ্টক *n* enclosure; fence; wall. **আবেষ্টন** *n* **1** act of surrounding/enclosing. **2** fence; wall. **3** surroundings; environment. **আবেষ্টনী** *n* that which encloses; enclosure. **2** surroundings; environment.

আবেষ্টিত *adj* surrounded; enclosed; encircled.

আবেস্তা *n* holy book of the Zoroastrians; Avesta.

আবে হায়াত, আব-ই-হায়াত [P আব + A হায়াত] *n* elixir of life.

আবোয়াব⇒আবওয়াব

আবোল-তাবোল, আবল-তাবল *n* **1** incoherent/irrelevant/meaningless talk; nonsense; delirium; abracadabra; gibberish. ~ **বকা** talk nonsense; talk through one's hat.

আব্বা, আব্বু [A আব, U আবু] *n* father.

আব্রু⇒আবরু

আভরণ *n* decoration; ornament; jewellery.

আভা *n* **1** lustre; glow; glaze. **2** beauty; grace. **3** colour; hue; tinge (স্বর্ণাভা).

আভাঙা , আভাঙ্গা *adj* **1** unbroken; unground; integral; whole: ~ ডাল, ~ গম. **2** intact. **3** unused.

আভাষ *n* **1** preface; prologue; introductory talk. **2** conversation; address; speech; talk.

আভাস *n* **1** an indirect indication or suggestion; hint; idea: ~ পাওয়া . **2** reflection; semblance; shadow. ~ দেওয়া *vi, vt* hint; give hints; suggest an idea.

আভিজাতিক *adj* **1** aristocratic; of noble birth. **2** pertaining to/indicative of high birth. **আভিজাত্য** *n* noble birth; aristocracy; nobility.

আভিধানিক *adj* relating to lexicography; lexicographic; lexicographical.

আভূমি *adv* down to the ground: ~ নত.

আভোগ *n* **1** the verse(s) in a song containing the author's name and preface. **2** the fourth or the last metre of a music. **3** completeness; fulness; expanse; extent. **4** act of enjoying; enjoyment.

আভ্যন্তর, আভ্যন্তরিক, আভ্যন্তরীণ⇒অভ্যন্তর

আম[১] *n* the mango. ~ **আচার, আমের আচার** *n* mango pickle. ~**চুর**, ~**শি** *n* slices of green mango dried and preserved in sugar and vinegar. ~**সত্ত্ব** *n* mango-pulp dried and preserved in cake forms.

আম[২], **আওয়াম** [A *sing* আম *pl* আওয়াম] *n* the common people; the public. ❑*adj* general; public: আম দরবার; of/for the general public. ~**খাস** *adj* (আম + A খাস) common and distinguished; high and low. ~**লোক**, ~**লোগ** *n* the common people; the general public.

আম[৩] *n* slimy substance secreted by the intestines; mucus. **2** disease of the intestines; dysentery. ~ **রক্ত** *n* blood dysentery.

আমড়া *n* the hog-plum. ~ **করা** *vi* (fig) do nothing harmful; be able to do no harm. ~ **কাঠের ঢেঁকি** *n* (fig) worthless person. ~**গাছি করা** *vi* laud/flatter one with some motive; coax/cajole one into or out of doing a thing. ~ **গাছে আম হয় না** (fig) you cannot make a silk purse out of a sow's ear.

আমতা আমতা *adv* in a hesitating/faltering manner. ~ **করা** *vi* falter in speech; hesitate to say.

আমদানি [P] *n* **1** bringing from abroad; import. **2** income; sale proceeds: আজকের ~ কত? **3** gathering; assemblage: বহুলোকের ~. ❑*adj* brought from abroad. ~ **করা** *vt* bring from abroad; import. ~-বাণিজ্য *n* import trade. ~ **রপ্তানি** *n* import and export. ~ **শুল্ক** *n* import duty.

আমন *adj* of winter; wintry: ~ ধান. ❑*n* paddy of winter variety.

আমন্ত্রণ *n* **1** asking sb to come somewhere; invitation. ~ করা *vt* invite; one (to come somewhere). request one's presence (some where). ~ **গ্রহণ করা** *vi* accept an invitation. **আমন্ত্রয়িতা** *n* one who invites; an inviter; a host. **আমন্ত্রয়িত্রী** *fem.* **আমন্ত্রিত** *adj* **1** invited: আমন্ত্রিত অতিথি, a guest. **আমন্ত্রিতা** *fem.*

আমপারা [A আম্ম +Pপারা] *n* the 30th or the last part of the Holy Qoran which begins with the word 'আম্ম'.

আমবাত *n* sort of skin disease; nettle-rash; urticaria.

আমমোক্তার [A আম্ম + মুখ্‌তার] *n* law-agent; legally appointed attorney. ~**নামা** *n* [A আমমোক্তার+P নামা] document giving power-of-attorny.

আময় *n* disease; illness (উদরাময়, নিরাময়).

আমরণ *adv* till death; throughout one's life.

আমরি (আ মরি) *int* expressing praise, enchantment, ridicule, etc: ~ বাংলা ভাষা.

আমল [A] *n* **1** reign; rule; regime: সুলতানি ~. **2** age; time; period: হাল আমলের ঘটনা. **3** heed; attention; indulgence: সে ওসবে ~ দেয় না. **4** practice; performance: ~ **করা** *vt* practise what one professes ~**দস্তক** *n* [A আমল+P দস্তক] *n* document giving title/right to property. ~**দারি** [আমল+P দারি] *n* **1** control; administration. **2** land-revenue. **3** the post of revenue collector. ~**নামা** *n* **1** document giving right to property. **2** record of man's virtue and vice.

আমলকী, আমলক *n* kind of small sour fruit or its tree; myrobalan.

আমলা[1] [A] *n* ministerial staff; government officer. ~**তন্ত্র** *n* system of government by officials; bureaucracy. ~ **তান্ত্রিক** *adj* bureaucratic. ~**তন্ত্রবাদী** *n* bureaucrat. ❑*adj* bureaucratic. ~-**ফয়লা** (আমলা+A ফয়লা) *n* clerical and executive staff.

আমলা[2]=আমলকী

আমহুকুম [A আম + হুকুম] *n* general order.

আমা[1] *adj* half-burnt; not thoroughly burnt: ~ ইট.

আমা[2] (archaic) *pron* **1** I; me. **2** I myself; myself. **3** me; to me.

আমাকে, আমায় *pron* me; to me.

আমাতিসার *n* dysentery; amoebic/bacillary dysentery.

আমাদিগকে *pron* us; to us.

আমাদিগের *pron* of us; ours.

আমাদের *pron* our; of us; ours; us; to us.

আমান[1] [A] *n* security; shelter; protection: ফি আমানিল্লাহ্‌ [~ + আল্লাহ্‌]. let Allah protect you.

আমান[2] [A] *n* whole; entire; unbroken; uncut: ~ কেক.

আমানত [A] *n* deposit; credit; trust property. ❑ *adj* deposited; placed in one's custody. **আমানতি, আমানতী** *adj* what has been placed under custody. ~ **করা/রাখা** *vt* deposit; place in one's custody. ~**দার** [A আমানত+P দার] *n* one in whose custody sth is placed; one who keeps sth in trust.

আমামা [A] *n* head-dress; turban.

আমার *pron* my; mine.

আমাশয়, আমাশা (colloq) dysentery.

আমি *pron* I. ❑*n* **1** the soul; the ego. **2** egoism; pride; vanity.

আমিন[1], **আমীন**[1] [A] *n* **1** land surveyor. **2** supervising officer; overseer; superintendent. ❑*adj* truthful; trustworthy.

আমিন[2], **আমীন**[2], **আমেন** [A] *int* so be it; be it so; amen.

আমির, আমীর [A] *n* **1** wealthy nobleman; rich and high-born Muslim. **2** title of the king of Afghanistan. **3** prince; courtier; Amir; Ameer. ~-**ওমরা/উমরাহ** [A] *n pl* (*sing* আমির, *pl* ওমরা) princes; courtiers; noblemen. ~-**জাদা** [A আমির+P যাদা] *n* son of an Amir; prince. ❑*adj* (ironic) lazy; averse to work.

আমিরানা, আমিরি *n* high style/ostentatious way of living; show of wealth: গরিবের আবার অত ~ কেন?

আমিরুল মুমেনিন [A] *n* **1** leader of the faithful. **2** appellation of the caliphs who succeeded Prophet Muhammad (sm).

আমিল [A] *n* officer; employee.

আমিষ *n* **1** meat. **2** non-vegetarian/protein food. ~**প্রিয়** *adj* fond of meat, fish, egg, etc/protein food. ~**ভোজী, আমিষাশী** *adj* carnivorous; non-vegetarian.

আমীন⇒আমিন

আমীর⇒আমির

আমুদে⇒আমোদ

আমূল *adv* **1** to the root; root-and-branch; thoroughly; fundamentally; radically; completely. ❑*adj* complete; thorough; radical: ~ সংস্কার.

আমৃত্যু *adv* till death; all through one's life.

আমেজ [P আমিয] *n* **1** tinge; touch; after-image; after-taste: সুরের ~, ঘুমের ~.

আমোদ *n* **1** joy; delight; amusement. **2** fun; festivity; recreation; merriment; rejoicings. ~ **করা**, ~-**প্রমোদ করা**, ~-**আহ্লাদ করা** *vi,vt* rejoice; recreate; make merry. ~**প্রিয়, আমুদে** *adj* sportive; gay; jolly; fond of/given to merriment; fun-loving.

আম্বর [A] *n* ambergris; aromatics.
আম্বরি [A] *adj* fragrant; scented: ~ তামাক.
আম্বিয়া [A] *n pl* (*sing* নবী) divine messengers; prophets.
আম্মা, আম্মাজান [A উম্ম] *n* mother.
আম্র *n* **1** the mango. **2** the mango tree. **~কানন, ~কুঞ্জ** *n* mango-grove.
আম্রাত, আম্রাতক, অম্রাত *n* **1** tropical tree bearing plum-like fruits. **2** the hog-plum.
আম্ল, আম্লিক *adj* acid; sour; acidic.
আম্লা, আম্লিকা *n fem* the tamarind-tree or its seed-pods containing acid pulp.
আযকার⇒আজকার
আযম⇒আজম[১]
আযমাইশ⇒আজমাইশ
আযরাঈল⇒আজরাইল
আযল, আজল [A] *n* **1** the past. **2** fate; luck. **3** a method of birth control allowed in Islam.
আযাদ⇒আজাদ
আযাদী⇒আজাদ
আযান⇒আজান
আযাব⇒আজাব
আযাযীল⇒আজাজিল
আয় *n* **1** income; earning. **2** profit; revenue. **~কর** *n* tax on income; income tax. ❑*adj* profit-giving; profitable. **~ব্যয়** *n* **1** income and expenditure. **2** (accounts) debit and credit; receipt and payment. **~ বুঝে ব্যয় করা** live within one's means; (fig) cut one's coat according to one's cloth.
আয়ত *adj* **1** large; wide: ~ লোচন . **2** extensive; expanded: নীল ~ আকাশ. **3** (geom) oblong; rectangular. **~ক্ষেত্র** *n* rectangle.
আয়তন *n* **1** (geom) measurement of an area; area. **2** (phys) amount of solid mass; compass; dimensions; volume. **3** house; abode; institution (মিলনায়তন, শিল্পায়তন).
আয়ত্ত *n* ownership; possession; control; grip; power: আয়ত্তের মধ্যে/বাইরে. ❑*adj* subject; subjugated; controlled; acquired; mastered. **~ করা, আয়ত্তে আনা** *vt* acquire; master; bring under control/possession/subjugation.
আয়ন-বায়ু *n* wind blowing continuously towards the equator from the SE and NE; the Trade wind.
আয়না [P আইনাহ্] *n* **1** mirror; looking-glass; speculum. **2** glass; quartz.
আয়ব্যয়⇒আয়
আয়মা, আয়মাদার⇒আয়েমা
আয়স *adj* of/made of iron; ferrous. ❑*n* iron. **আয়সী** *n fem* coat-of-mail made of iron.
আয়া [Pg] *fem* nurse-maid; waiting maid; midwife. **~গিরি** [Pg আয়া+গিরি] *n* the job of an aya.
আয়াত [A] *n* a verse of the Holy Qoran.
আয়াম⇒আইয়াম
আয়াশ⇒আয়েশ
আয়াস *n* **1** effort; endeavour; care; labour: **~লব্ধ**. **2** strain; exhaustion; fatigue. **3** trouble; difficulty; pain; suffering. **~সাধ্য** *adj* strenuous; toilsome; arduous; laborious.
আয়ু *n* **1** span of life; longevity: ~ শেষ. **2** life; lifetime: তার ~ শেষ, his days are numbered. তার ~ ফুরিয়েছে, his time is up. **~প্রদ, ~স্কর** *adj* life-giving; rejuvenating. **~ষ্মান** *adj* long-lived. **~ষ্মতী** *fem* . **~ রেখা** *n* (astrol) life line.
আয়ুর্বেদ *n* the science of medicine as taught in the Atharvaveda; Indian system of medicine. **~জ্ঞ, ~ বেত্তা** *adj* versed in the Ayurvedic medical system. **আয়ুর্বেদীয়** *adj* pertaining/ according to the Ayurvedic science.
আয়ুস্কর⇒আয়ু
আয়ুষ্মতী, আয়ুষ্মান⇒আয়ু
আয়েন্দা, আএন্দা [P আইন্দাহ্] *n* the future.
আয়েব, আএব [A] *n* infamy; scandal.
আয়েমা, আএমা, আয়মা [A] *n pl* rent-free estates granted by Muslim rulers to distinguished scholars and preachers. **~দার** [A + P] *n* a receiver of this grant.
আয়েশ, আয়াশ [A আয়শ্] *n* **1** ease; comfort; luxury. **2** recreation; rejoicings; merriment. **3** joyful/delightful life. **আয়েশি** *adj* ease-loving; easy-going; pleasure-seeking: ~ মানুষ.
আয়োগ *n* special committee set up by authority for investigation, etc; a commission.
আয়োজক⇒আয়োজন
আয়োজন *n* arrangement; preparations; provision. **~ করা** *vt* make preparations/ arrangement. **আয়োজক** *adj* one who takes necessary steps/ makes necessary arrangement for a purpose. ❑*n* organizer; promoter.
আয়োজিত *adj* arranged.
আয়োডিন [E] *n* tincture of iodine.
আর *conj* **1** and: তুমি ~ আমি. **2** or; alternatively: কথা বলো ~ না বলো. **3** but: শক্তের ভক্ত ~ নরমের যম. ❑*adv* **1** now; at present: ~ সেদিন নেই. **2** henceforth; hereafter; again; in future: ~ যেন ভুল না হয়. **3** else; besides; in addition: ~ বলার কি আছে? **4** at the same time; simultaneously: আমরা খেটে মরি ~ তোমরা আরাম করো. **5** on the other hand; contrary-wise: ~ যদি যেতেই হয়. **6** ever; at any time: টাকা কি ~ অমনি আসে. **7** certainly; of course: তুমি তো ~ আমার পর নও. **8** yet; still now; upto/even to this time: ~ আশা করা বৃথা . **9** since then: সেই যে গেলো ~ ফিরলো না. **10** as soon as; no sooner than: আমিও উঠলুম ~ গাড়িও ছাড়লো. ❑*adj* **1** other; another; different: ~ কেউ, ~ কিছু . **2** past; last: সে ~ বছর এসেছিল. **3** a second; another one: এমন মেয়ে ~ পাবে না. **4** more than this: ~ একটু. ❑*pron* other/another/different person or thing: একে চায় আরে পায়. **~ ~** *adj* others; all other. **আরো, ~ও**

adj more; greater in number, amount, quality ,etc: ~ও টাকা, আরো ভালো. ❑*adv* still more; further; more over; besides/apart from/ in addition to this: ~ বলছি শোনো.

আরক [A আর্‌ক] *n* **1** extract; essence; juice. **2** arrack; spirit; tincture; alcohol.

আরকান [A] (*sing* রুকন) *n pl* **1** fundamental principles. **2** employees.

আরক্ত, আরক্তিম *adj* **1** reddish; slightly red. **2** deep-red; scarlet; crimson. **~-নয়ন, ~-লোচন** *adj* **1** with blood-shot eyes; angry. ❑ *n* angry look. **~ বদন, ~ মুখ** *adj* flushed with bashfulness; abashed in flush of chastity.

আরক্ষ, আরক্ষক *n* **1** police/military station or outpost. **2** defence force; national guard. **আরক্ষা বিভাগ** *n* police department. **আরক্ষিক, আরক্ষী** *n* constable; police picket.

আরজ, আরয [A আর্‌য] *n* prayer; petition; plaint. ~গুজার [A আরজ+P গুজার] *n* petitioner; plaintiff. ~বেগ, ~বেগি [A আরজ+T বেগ] *n* person who presents or places before; bench-clerk of the court.

আরজি, আর্জি [A] *n* **1** formal request for sth; application; petition. **2** fervent request; entreaty; begging (sth of sb).

আরজু [P] *n* wish; desire; longing: মনের ~.

আরণ্য *adj* of forest(s); grown in forest; forest born; wild. **~ক** *adj* living in forests; wild. ❑*n* **1** officer in charge of a forest; a forester. **2** concluding section of the Vedic literature Brahmana.

আরতি[১] *n* cessation; termination; stoppage.

আরতি[২] *n* the Hindu religious rite of worshipping an idol by waving lamps, etc in the evening: সন্ধ্যা ~.

আরতি[৩] *n* desire; craving; prayer.

আরতি[৪] *n* deep attachment; devotion.

আরদালি, আর্দালি [E] *n* servant in attendance on an officer (or master) to carry his orders; orderly; bearer.

আরফাত⇒আরাফাত

আরব [A] *n* **1** Arabia. **2** inhabitant(s) of Arabia. **3** the people of Arab nationality; the Arabians; the Arabs. **আরবি** *n* **1** the language of Arabia; Arabic. **2** the people of Arabia; the Arabians/Arabs; an Arabian/Arab. ❑*adj* **1** pertaining to Arabia. **2** grown/born in Arabia: ~ ঘোড়া. **~ গঁদ** *n* gum Arabic. **আরব্য** *adj* of Arabia; born in the Arab world : ~ উপন্যাস, the Arabian Nights.

আরব্ধ *adj* what has been started/undertaken for completion: ~ কাজ

আরব্য⇒আরব

আরমান [P] *n* **1** wish; desire; longing.

আরমানি *n* inhabitant of Armenia; Armenian. ❑*adj* of Armenia.

আরম্ভ *n* **1** commencement; inception; origin. **2** introduction; prologue; preface. **~ করা** *vi,vt* start; commence; begin; introduce. **~ হওয়া** *vi,vt* originate; commence; start.

আরয⇒আরজ

আরশ, আরস [A আর্‌শ] *n* **1** the all-pervading seat of Allah; the highest heavenly position. **2** throne.

আরশি *n* mirror; looking glass.

আরশুলা, আরশোলা⇒আরসোলা

আরস⇒আরশ

আরসোলা, আরশুলা, আরশোলা *n* the cockroach; the black-beetle.

আরাধক *n* worshipper; devotee.

আরাধন, আরাধনা *n* **1** prayer; worship; adoration. **2** service. **~ করা** *vi,vt* pray; worship; adore. **আরাধ্য** *adj* to be worshipped; adorable.

আরাধ্য⇒ আরাধনা

আরাফাত, আরফাত [A] *n* the celebrated plain near Mecca where pilgrims assemble on the 9th of Zilhajj to perform rites connected with the annual Hajj.

আরাম[১] [A] *n* grove; garden; park; small wood.

আরাম[২] [P] *n* **1** ease; comfort. **2** rest; relaxation. ❑*adj* cured of /relieved of/recovered from illness. **~-কেদারা** (P + Pg), **~-কুর্সি** [P + A] *n* chair with side support for the arms; arm-chair; easy-chair. **~প্রিয়** *adj* ease-loving; fond of ease and comfort.

আরারুট, এরারুট *n* [E] starchy food obtained from the roots of a species of plants; arrowroot.

আরূঢ় *adj* mounted; seated on (অশ্বারূঢ়).

আরে *int* **1** expressing fear, shame, anger, astonishment, etc: ~ একি ! **2** (used in addressing) ho! halloo! oh! eh!

আরেফিন [A] *n pl* (*sing* আরিফ) spiritualists.

আরো⇒ আর

আরোগ্য *n* **1** cure; recovery from illness. **2** sound health; health. **~ করা** *vt* cure; heal; bring round. **~ লাভ করা** *vt* recover; come round; be cured; be restored to health.

আরোপ, আরোপণ *n* **1** act of ascribing/ attributing sth (দোষারোপ). **2** (phil) the seeing of sth as different from the reality; attribution of the quality of one thing to another. **3** act of placing/putting upon; imposition; emplacement. **~ করা** *vt* ascribe; attribute; impose; implant; bestow. **ধনুকে জ্যা ~ করা** string the bow. **আরোপিত** *adj* attributed; imputed; imposed; placed; planted.

আরোপ-পত্র *n* record of offence; charge-sheet.

আরোহ *n* **1** (phil) method of reasoning from particular instances to general principles; induction (opp অবরোহ). **2** ascent (দুরারোহ). **3** height; altitude. **4** buttock (esp of a woman) (বরারোহ). **5** grade; ladder. **~ণ** *n* **1** ascent; ascension (স্বর্গারোহণ). **2** mounting; climbing;

riding (অশ্বারোহণ). ~ণ করা *vi, vt* get up; ascend; mount; climb; ride; board (a ship, etc). ~ণী *n* stair; stair-case; ladder; lift; escalator. **আরোহিত** *adj* mounted upon. **আরোহী** *adj* **1** ascended; mounted; boarded. **2** (of musical notes) gradually increasing in pitch: ~ সুর. **3** (phil) using induction; inductive. ❑*n* **1** climber; rider; passengers (of train, ship, etc). **2** musical notes which gradually increase in pitch. **3** (phil) inductive method. **আরোহিণী** *fem.*

আর্ক *adj* pertaining to the sun; solar. ~**ফলা** *n* **1** the symbol of letter র (´) on the head of a consonant indicating a preceding '-r' sound. **2** sun-ray. **3** tuft of hair maintained by conservative Brahmins on the top of the head.

আর্কিড, অর্কিড [E] *n* varieties of wild plant having flowers of vivid colours and curious shapes; parasitic plant; orchid.

আর্জি⇒আরজি

আর্ট [E art] *n* **1** creation or expression of beauty in the form of literature, painting, sculpture, music, dramatic performance, etc. **2** fine skill or aptitude applied to the work of creative imagination. **3** work of visual arts that appeals to the sense of aesthetic beauty: হস্তলিপি সে যুগে একটা আর্ট হয়ে উঠেছিল.

আর্ত *adj* **1** afflicted/distressed/stricken with bodily or mental trouble; aggrieved; oppressed; sick; ill. **আর্তি** *n*. ~**ত্রাণ** *n* relief of the distressed; saving/succouring the afflicted. ~**নাদ** *n* scream; groaning; sharp cries of fear or pain; outcry. ~**সেবা** *n* relief work. ~**স্বর** *n* piteous cry; outcry of affliction. ~**স্বরে** *adv* in a piteous tone/voice; piteously.

আর্তত্রাণ⇒আর্ত

আর্তনাদ⇒আর্ত

আর্তব *n* menstrual discharge; menstruation. ❑*adj* **1** menstrual: ~ ব্যাধি. **2** seasonal.

আর্তসেবা⇒আর্ত

আর্তস্বর⇒আর্ত

আর্তি *n* **1** mental agitation/urge. **2** illness; ailment; disease. **3** pain; trouble; misery.

আর্থ⇒আর্থিক

আর্থনীতিক *adj* pertaining to financial policy/economics; economic.

আর্থিক, আর্থ *adj* **1** financial; pecuniary; monetary. **2** pertaining to private property/ financial position: ~ অবস্থা.

আর্দালি, আর্দালী=আরদালি

আর্দ্র *adj* **1** wet; moist; damp; humid. **2** soft; tender; touched/moved by compassion: দয়ার্দ্র চিত্ত. ~**কণ্ঠে**, ~**স্বরে** *adv* in a choked voice. ~**তা** *n* humidity.

আর্দ্রা *n* (astron) the star Orionis.

আর্মানি = আরমানি

আর্মেচার *n* [E] coil(s) of an electric motor; armature.

আর্য *n* the Aryan race; an Aryan. ❑*adj* **1** venerable; respectable. **2** civilized. ~**তা** *n* **1** Aryanism; the quality of being an Aryan. **2** civilized conduct. ~**পুত্র** *n* husband (a form of address by ancient Hindu Women). ~**সমাজ** *n* a sect of modern Hindus founded by Dayananda Saraswati.

আর্যা[1] *fem* of আর্য

আর্যা[2] *n* **1** kind of metre used in Sanskrit verse. **2** any of the rhymed arithmetical formulae.

আর্যাবর্ত *n* the Indo-Gangetic plain or upper India where the ancient Aryans settled (opp দক্ষিণাপথ).

আর্যামি *n* (facet) Aryanism. (⇒অনার্য)

আর্শি= আরশি

আল[1], **আইল** *n* demarcation line between agricultural plots; boundary. ~ **বাঁধা** *vi* set up a ridge of earth (to mark the limit of a plot of land).

আল[2] **1** the sting of insects, etc: মৌমাছির ~. **2** the sharp point of anything: তীরের ~. **3** pointed tool for making holes in leather, wood, etc; an awl: জুতা সেলাই-এর ~. **4** (fig) taunt; jeer: কথার ~. **5** a head or apex made on a piece of wood to fit it to another by means of dove-tailing. ~**কাটা** *vi* cut a notch/notches on wood/iron as a means of joining two pieces. ❑*adj* grooved; notched; serrated.

আল-কোরান, আল-কুরআন⇒কোরান

আলওয়ান⇒আলোয়ান

আলংকারিক⇒আলঙ্কারিক

আলকাটা⇒আল[2]

আলকাতরা [pg আলকাতরাও, A আল-কৎর] *n* thick and sticky black liquid obtained from coal, etc used as coating on wood and in the preparation of road surface; tar.

আলকেমি [A] *n* the science of chemistry.

আলখাল্লা, আলখেল্লা [A] *n* longskirted tunic; loose cloak.

আলগা *adj* **1** free; separate; detached: ~ কাপড়. **2** loose; lax; untied: খোঁপা ~ করা. **3** unfastened; unbolted: ~ দরজা. **4** slack; not tight: ~ গেরো. **5** bare; naked: ~ গা. **6** insincere; unnecessary; uncalled-for: ~ সোহাগ. **7** uncontrolled; unrestrained; unbridled: ~ জিভ. **8** unconnected; unrelated: ~ লোক. ❑ *adv* away; at or to a distance: ~ থাকা. ~~ **থাকা** *vi* to keep a distance.

আলগোছ *adj* **1** untouched; without contact: আলগোছে রাখা. **2** without support. **আলগোছে** *adv* cautiously; with circumspection.

আলঙ্কারিক, আলংকারিক *adj* **1** pertaining to rhetoric; rhetorical; figurative. **2** versed in poetics/rhetoric. **3** author of a treatise on rhetoric. ❑ *n* **1** rhetorician. **2** (rare) jeweller.

আলজিভ, আলজিহ্বা *n* small piece of fleshy matter at the root of the tongue; the uvula; the epiglottis.

আলতমগা [T] *n* **1** royal signature or seal. **2** an estate held in return for military service; a fief. **3** a medal.

আলতা *n* lac-dye used by women to paint the borders of the feet.

আলতারাফ [A] *n* metal fastening for closing a door, window, etc; a hasp; a clasp.

আলতু-ফালতু *adj* of little value/importance; worthless: ~ লোক; meaningless; useless: ~ কথা.

আলতো *adj* soft; light; not forceful: ~ হাতে. ❑*adv* (also ~ভাবে) loosely.

আলনা [E] *n* stand for clothes; dress-stand; clothes-horse.

আলপনা, আলিপনা *n* **1** auspicious white paint on the floor, walls, etc with liquid pigment of rice-powder according to indigenous traditon.

আলপাকা [E] *n* **1** Kind of sheep found in S America; the alpaca. **2** cloth made of the alpaca-wool: ~ কোট.

আলপিন *n* [Pg] pointed piece of steel wire with a round head used for fastening pieces of paper, etc; a pin.

আলফাজ, আলফাজ [A] *n pl* (*sing* লফয) words.

আলবত, আলবৎ [A] *adv* certainly; of course; surely: ~ দেবো.

আলবাল *n* ridge of earth set up round the root of a tree for watering.

আলবেদা [A] *n* farewell; separation; parting.

আলবোলা [P] *n* hookah with a flexible smoking tube.

আলম [A] *n* the earth; the world. ~ **গির/গীর** *n* **1** the greatest man on earth. **2** title of the Mughol emperor Aurangzeb.

আলমপানাহ্ [A + P] *n* king of kings; the emperor.

আলমারি [Pg] *n* chest of drawers; almirah; cupboard; locker.

আলমাস [A] *n* diamond.

আলম্ব *n* shelter; support (নিরালম্ব). ~**ন** *n* **1** act of taking shelter; support used to keep sth up; a prop. **2** (rhet) person/cause that gives rise to a sentiment. **আলম্বিত** *adj* **1** supported; protected. **2** suspended; hung down.

আলয় *n* **1** house; home (বিদ্যালয়). **2** a dwelling place; a resort (লোকালয়). **3** a container; a store (হিমালয়).

আলসে[১]⇒আলিসা

আলসে[২] *adj* lazy; slothful; sluggish; indolent. ~**মি**, ~**মো** *n* idleness; sluggishness; indolence; sloth; lethargy.

আলস্য=আলসেমি⇒আলসে[২]. ~ **ত্যাগ করা** *vi* shake off lethargy/indolence.

আলহামদুলিল্লাহ্ [A] praise be to Allah; expression of gratefulness to God.

আলহামরা [A] *adj* the red one. ❑*n* the famous palace in Spain built during the Muslim rule.

আলহেলাল [A] *n* the new moon.

আলা[১] [A] *adj* the first; the chief; the highest; the greatest: উজিরে ~.

আলা[২] *adj* bright; resplendent; illuminated. ❑*n* light.

আলা[৩] =ওয়ালা

আলাইকুম = আলায়কুম

আলাই-বালাই [A] *n pl* **1** dangers and difficulties. **2** diseases; harms; evils.

আলাদা, আলাহিদা [A] *adj* **1** different; separate; detached; distinct. ❑*adv* separately; in a different way. ~ **করে দেখা** *vi* **1** consider as outsider/unrelated/unfriendly. ~ **হওয়া** *vi* be separated.

আলান[১] *n* **1** pillar or post to which an elephant is tethered; a tying post. **2** peg or stake for tethering domestic animals.

আলানো, আলান[২] *vi* **1** dishevel; spread out: ধান ~. **2** open : বই ~.

আলাপ *n* **1** conversation; talk; discussion. **2** acquaintance: তার সাথে আমার ~ নেই. ~ **করা** *vi,vt* talk; converse; confer; discuss; make acquaintance; be acquainted. ~**চারিতা** *n* **1** a private conversation between two people; tete-a-tete. **2** small talk between two persons. ~**-পরিচয়** *n* acquaintance; familiarity; speaking terms. ~**-সালাপ** *n* (colloq)

আলাপী *adj* fond of talking and mixing with others; friendly; sociable.

আলাভোলা *adj* **1** absent-minded; forgetful. **2** artless; guileless; simple.

আলামত [A] **1** sign; evidence; testimony; proof. **2** supernatural/unnatural event. **3** feeling that some trouble is coming; foreboding.

আলায়কুম, আলাইকুম [A ওয়ালায়কুমুস্ সালাম] *n* reply to Muslim salutation আস্সালামু আলায়কুম, meaning "peace be on you too".

আলাল *n* a wealthy man. **আলালের ঘরের দুলাল** son of a rich family spoilt by over-indulgence. **আলালী** *fem.*

আলাহিদা⇒আলাদা

আলি[১], **আলী** [A] *adj* great; noble; generous. ~**শান** *adj* **1** huge; enormous; gigantic. **2** high-minded; noble; sublime. **3** high-born; honourable; respectable; venerable. ~**হুকুম** *n* general/unrestricted order; carté-blanché.

আলি[২] *n* row; line; series (গীতালি).

আলিঙ্গন *n* **1** embrace. **2** (fig) eager welcome/greeting: মৃত্যুকে ~.

আলিম⇒আলেম

আলিসা, আলসে *n* **1** edge of the roof; cornice. **2** parapet/protective wall around the roof of a building.

আলী, আলি *n* [A] **1** component word of a Muslim's name. **2** the fourth Caliph of Islam and son-in-law of Prophet Muhammad (sm).

আলীহুকুম⇒আলি[১]

আলু[১] *n* famous vegetable plant with rounded tubers. গোল~ *n* potato. মিষ্টি~ *n* sweet potato.

আলু[২] *suff* denoting nature, propensity, tendency, etc (দয়ালু, নিদ্রালু).

আলুথালু *adj* **1** dishevelled: ~ কেশ. **2** disorderly: ~ বেশ.

আলুনি, আলুনী *adj* **1** [of cooked food] deficient in salt; salt-free. **2** (fig) insipid; tasteless.

আলুফা [A] *n* food received without price. ❑ *adj* easily available.

আলুফাদার [P] *n* holder of a lucrative post.

আলুবোখারা [P] *n* acidic fruit from Bokhara; sort of dried plum; prune.

আলুলায়িত *adj* loose; untied; dishevelled: ~ কেশ.

আলেখ্য *n* picture; portrait; painting.

আলেম, আলিম [A] *adj* learned in religion. ❑*n* theologian; scholar; learned man.

আলেমুল গায়েব [A] *n, adj* one who knows the secret; All-knowing: আল্লাহ্ ~.

আলেয়া *n* **1** luminous marsh-gas; will-o-the-wisp; ignis fatunus. **2** (fig) ray of false hope; delusion. ~র আলো *n* (fig) false allurement; tempting object.

আলো *n* **1** light; beam; gleam. **2** lamp; lantern. **3** beauty: রূপের ~. **4** lustre; effulgence. ~ করা *vi* light up; lighten; brighten; illuminate. ~ দেখানো *vi* **1** show light. **2** (fig) guide; give hope. ~ আঁধারের খেলা interplay of light and shade.

আলো-আঁধারি *n* **1** mixture of light and shade; semi-darkness; twilight. **2** treatment of light and shade in painting; chiaroscuro.

আলোক *n* light; beam; ray; lustre; effulgence. ~গৃহ *n* tower emitting powerful light to direct navigation or aviation at night; lighthouse. ~চিত্র *n* a photograph; photography. ~চিত্রকর *n* photographer. ~চিত্রবিদ্যা *n* the art or process of producing images by the action of light; photography. ~চ্ছটা *n* flush/beam of light. ~-তড়িৎ *n* photo-electricity. ~-তাড়িত *adj* photo-electric. ~-বিজ্ঞান the science of light and vision; optics. ~ময় *adj* lighted; luminous. ~লতা *n* parasitic creeper. ~সঙ্কেত *n* signal of lights; beacon. ~সজ্জা *n* decoration with light; illumination. আলোকিত *adj* lighted; illuminated. আলোকিত করা *vi* lighten up; illuminate. আলোকিত হওয়া *vi* be lighted/ illuminated.

আলোচনা *n* **1** discussion; study; culture (জ্ঞানালোচনা). **2** examination; criticism (কাব্যালোচনা). **3** movement; deliberation; thought; consideration: এ বিষয়ে উত্তপ্ত ~ চলছে. ~ করা *vt* discuss; deliberate; consider. আলোচিত *adj* discussed; considered; deliberated.

আলোচ্য *adj* placed for/under consideration; to be examined/discussed.

আলোছায়া *n* Interplay of light and shade.

আলোড়ন *n* **1** churning; stirring. **2** agitation, movement. ~ করা *vi* stir; churn; excite, agitate.

আলোড়িত *adj* stirred; churned; agitated.

আলোনা *adj* salt-free: ~ মাটি.

আলোময়⇒ আলো

আলোয়-আলোয় *adv* by daylight; whilst there is light.

আলোয়ান [A] *n* woollen wrapper; shawl.

আল্লা⇒ আল্লাহ

আল্লামা [A] *n* the most learned man: ~ ইকবাল.

আল্লামি [A] *n* **1** the most learned. **2** appellation given to Abul Fazal by emperor Akbar.

আল্লাহ্, আল্লা [A] *n* Allah, the Creator, Nourisher and Sustainer of the universe as described in the Qoran; the incorporeal and only object of adoration by the Muslims; Omnipotent, Omnipresent and Omniscient. আল্লাওয়ালা *adj* one who has made absolute submission to Allah; intensely devoted and God-fearing. আল্লার কসম/কিরা a vow in the name of Allah. আল্লার কুদরত *n* supernatural/unnatural thing or event. আল্লার গজব *n* punishment/punitive action from Allah.

আশ[১] *n* eating; food (প্রাতরাশ).

আশ[২] *n* (colloq) **1** hope; expectation; longing. **2** desire; wish. ~ মিটানো *vi* satisfy/gratify one's desire.

আশকারা⇒আস্কারা

আশঙ্কনীয়⇒ আশঙ্কা

আশঙ্কা *n* **1** doubt; apprehension; suspicion. **2** fear; alarm; dread. ~ করা *vi* doubt; fear; apprehend; suspect. আশঙ্কনীয় *adj* fearful; dreadful; alarming. ~স্থল *n* object of fear/suspicion/ doubt/apprehension. আশঙ্কিত *adj* afraid; alarmed; fearful; suspicious. আশঙ্কিত হওয়া *vi* be afraid/alarmed/suspicious/ fearful.

আশনাই [P] *n* **1** love; devotion. **2** illicit love; secret amour.

আশ-পড়শি *n pl* neighbours.

আশপাশ *n* **1** surroundings; environs; neighbourhood: ~ থেকে. আশপাশে, আশেপাশে *adv* around; on all sides; in the outskirts/neighbourhood; hither and thither.

আশমান⇒আসমান

আশয় *n suff* **1** container; receptacle (জলাশয়). **2** indicative of heart, character, intention, etc (নীচাশয়, সদাশয়). **3** wealth; property: বিষয় ~.

আশরফি [P] *n* gold coin; unit of money in

medieval Iran.

আশরাফ [A] *n pl* [*sing* শরীফ] aristocratic/ respectable people: ~ আতরাফ. ~**উল-আম্বিয়া** *adj* 1 greatest of the Prophets. 2 appellation of Prophet Muhammad (sm). **আশরাফুল মখলুকাত** [A] *n adj* the acme of creation: মানুষ আশরাফুল মখলুকাত.

আশা *n* 1 hope; expectation: ছেলের উপর ~. 2 assurance; reliance; confidence, trust: তিনি একটি চাকুরির ~ দিয়েছেন. 3 wish; desire; longing: যাওয়ার ~ আছে. ~ **করা/রাখা** *vi, vt* hope; expect; trust; rely upon; long for. ~ **দেওয়া** *vt* assure; give hope. ~**তিরিক্ত**, ~**তীত** *adj* beyond expectation. ~**নুরূপ** *adj, adv* upto the expectation. ~**ন্বিত** *adj* hopeful. ~ **পোষণ করা** cherish hopes; look forward/wait in expectation. ~**প্রদ** *adj* hopeful; encouraging. ~**বাদ** *n* confidence in success; optimism. ~**বাদী** *adj* optimistic. ❑*n* optimist. ~**ভঙ্গ** *n* disappointment; frustration. ~**ভরসা** *n* hopes and expectations. ~**হত** *adj* frustrated; disappointed. ~**হীন** *adj* hopeless.

আশাবরী *n* a musical mode: সানাইতে ~ সুর বাজে.

আশি *n, adj* eighty.

আশিস *n* blessing; good wishes.

আশী[১]=আশি

আশী[২] *n* the fang or venom-tooth of a snake. ~**বিষ** *n* snake; serpent.

আশীর্বাদ, আশীর্বচন=আশিস. ~ **করা** *vt* bless. **আশীর্বাদক** *n, adj* one who blesses. **আশীর্বাদিকা** *fem.* **আশীর্বাদী** *adj* presented in token of good wishes. ❑*n* a presentation with one's good wishes.

আশু[১]⇒ আউশ

আশু[২] *adj* early; speedy; quick: ~ নিরাময়. ❑*adv* early, quickly; immediately; without delay. ~**গতি**. ~**গামী** *adj* quick-moving; swift. ~**তোষ** *adj* quickly/easily appeased. ❑*n* appellation of Hindu deity Shiva.

আশুরা, আশূরা [A] *n* the tenth day of the lunar month Muharram.

আশেক, আশিক [A] *n mas* lover; suitor: ~ মাশুক.

আশেপাশে⇒আশপাশ

আশৈশব *adv* since infancy/childhood.

আশ্চর্য *adj* 1 strange; queer; surprising: ~ ব্যাপার. 2 astonished; surprised; amazed. ❑*n* astonishment; surprise; wonder: পৃথিবীর সপ্ত ~, seven wonders of the world. ~ **করা** strike with astonishment/wonder/amazement; take one by surprise. ~ **হওয়া** be struck with wonder/astonishment. ~**জনক** *adj* astonishing; surprising; wonderful. **আশ্চর্যান্বিত**=আশ্চর্য *adj* (2). **আশ্চর্যের কথা** it is surprising/a matter of surprise.

আশ্বস্ত *adj* assured; consoled; comforted; encouraged. ~ **করা** *vt* assure; console. ~ **হওয়া** *vt* be assured/consoled/comforted.

আশ্বাস *n* 1 assurance. 2 consolation; comfort. ~ **দেওয়া** *vt* make sure; assure. ~ **পাওয়া** *vt* be assured. ~ **বাণী** *n* words of hope/ encouragement/assurance.

আশ্বিন *n* Aswin, the sixth month of the Bengali calendar. **আশ্বিনে** *adj* of Aswin: ~ ঝড়.

আশ্রম *n* 1 hermitage; monastery. 2 a residential institution; an asylum (অনাথাশ্রম). 3 the four stages of life of a Hindu as enjoined in the Vedas (চতুরাশ্রম). ~ **ধর্ম** *n* duties of the inmates of an asylum. ~**বাসী**, **আশ্রমী** *n* inmate(s) of a hermitage/asylum.

আশ্রয় *n* 1 shelter; resort; refuge: গরিবের ~. 2 help; support, protection. 3 dwelling house; residence; abode : ~হীন. 4 adoption; taking resort to: চাতুরীর ~. 5 embodiment: সর্বগুণের ~. 6 container; store; receptacle. ~ **নেওয়া/গ্রহণ করা** *vt* adopt; take shelter (in)/resort or recourse to. ~ **দেওয়া/দান করা** *vt* shelter; give shelter/protection. ~ **দান** *n* act of sheltering. ~**দাতা** *n, adj* one who gives shelter/protection; shelterer; protector. ~**পুষ্ট** *adj* nourished in shelter/support/ protection (of). ~**প্রার্থী, আশ্রয়ার্থী** *adj* seeking shelter. ❑*n* refugee. ~**প্রার্থিনী, আশ্রয়ার্থিনী** *fem.* **আশ্রয়ী** *n, adj* one who has taken shelter or is living under protection. ~**হীন** *adj* without shelter; shelterless. **আশ্রিত** *adj* sheltered; under protection. **আশ্রিত রাজ্য** *n* protectorate.

আশ্রুত *adj* 1 pledged; promised. 2 heard.

আশ্লিষ্ট *adj* 1 related/connected (with); involved (in). 2 embraced. 3 permeated; pervaded. 4 sarcastic; taunting; mocking.

আশ্লেষ *n* 1 embrace; union; connection. 2 sarcasm; taunt.

আষাঢ় *n* 1 Ashar, the third month of Bengali calendar. 2 (fig) the monsoon; the rainy season. **আষাঢ়ে** *adj* 1 of/occurring in Ashar. 2 false; incredible; fabulous; fantastic: আষাঢ়ে গল্প , cock-and-bull-story.

আষ্টেপৃষ্ঠে *adv* on all sides; all over the body; thoroughly : লজ্জা যেন তাকে ~ বেঁধে নিয়েছে, it seems, as if; he/she is possessed by bashfulness.

আসওয়া⇒আসোয়ার

আসকে *n* kind of cake made of liquefied rice-powder.

আসক্ত *adj* greatly enamoured (of); in deep love (of) (প্রণয়াসক্ত). 2 addicted to (মদ্যাসক্ত). ~ **হওয়া** *vt* be enamoured of/addicted to. **আসক্তি** *n* 1 deep love; amour. 2 devotion; attachment. 3 addiction.

আসঙ্গ *n* 1 association; union; company; social intercourse. 2 desire to enjoy; sexual intercourse: ~লিপ্সা. **3** love; attachment; fondness. **4** close attention; absorption. **~লিপ্সা** *n* desire for company/union/sexual intercourse. **~লিপ্সু** *adj* desirous of company/union/sexual intercourse.

আসছে *adj* that which is coming; next; ensuing: ~ সোমবার.

আসত্তি *n* **1** connection; proximity; nearness. **2** (gram) proximity of related words within a sentence: ~ দোষ.

আসন *n* **1** anything to sit on; a seat (কাষ্ঠাসন). **2** an office or post: সদস্যদের ~. **3** honour; prestige: বিদ্বানের ~ সর্বত্র. **4** dwelling place; abode; house (ভদ্রাসন). **5** postures of sitting in yoga (eg পদ্মাসন). **~ গ্রহণ** *n* act of sitting; taking of a seat. **~ গ্রহণ করা** *vi,vt* take one's seat; be seated. **~পিঁড়ি** *n* the posture of sitting with one's legs drawn up crosswise to the body; the posture of squating.

আসন্ন *adj* imminent; impending; approaching: ~ বিপদ. **~কাল** *n* time of death/disaster; crisis; critical time. **~প্রসবা** *adj fem* about to be confined/delivered; parturient.

আসব *n* distilled spirit; alcoholic beverage; wine. **আসবিক** *adj* alcoholic.

আসবাব [A] *n* articles of equipment, such as chairs, tables, beds, etc; furniture. **~পত্র** *n* furniture and fittings; goods and chattels.

আসবিক⇒ আসব

আসমান, আশমান [p] *n* the sky. **~জমিন** *n* heaven and earth. **~জমিন ফারাক** *n* difference as between heaven and earth; poles apart; poles asunder. **আসমানি** *adj* **1** skyey; sky-blue; azure. **2** heavenly; divine: আসমানি কিতাব. **3** of/relating to the sky. **আসমানের চাঁদ হাতে পাওয়া** get/come by a rare/scarce thing.

আসমুদ্র *adv* extending from/upto the ocean. **~হিমাচল** *adv* extending from the ocean to the Himalayas.

আসর[1] [A] *n* a gathering/ sitting/party: গানের ~. **~ গরম/সরগরম/গুলজার করা** *vi* enliven/warm up a party with oratory or humour; put a gathering into good humour. **~ জাঁকানো** *vi* make oneself the centre of interest in an assembly by artfulness or gift of the gab. **আসরে নামা/অবতীর্ণ হওয়া** *vi* make one's appearance on the stage/before the public.

আসর[2], **আছর**[1] [A] *n* **1** afternoon. **2** one of the five canonical prayers in Islam: আসরের নামাজ.

আসর[3], **আছর**[2] [A] *n* effect; influence; possession: জিনের ~.

আসল [A] *adj* **1** pure; genuine; unadulterated: ~ সোনা. **2** true; real; actual: ~ ঘটনা. **3** authentic; original: ~ দলিল. **4** free from all charges; nett: ~ আয়. **5** principal or capital money: সুদে আসলে. **~ কথা এই** the fact is. **আসলি** *adj* pure; unmixed; unadulterated: ~ সোনা. **আসলে** *adv* actually; in fact: ~ লোকটি সৎ.

আসশেওড়া *n* kind of wild tree.

আসহাব [A] *n pl* (*sing* সাহাবী?) companions of Prophet Muhammad (sm).

আসহাব-এ-কাহাফ, আসাব কাহাফ [A] *n pl* according to Semitic tradition, seven people entered a cave and remained asleep for ages, and when they woke up and came out they found themselves in a world completely transformed.

আসা[1] *vi* **1** to come; arrive; reach: বাড়ি ~. **2** rise; occur; crop up: মনে ~. **3** commence; begin: বৃষ্টি ~. **4** set in: বর্ষা ~. **5** be available : বাজারে সব জিনিসই আসে. **6** occur; take place: বিপদ ~. **7** accustom (oneself) to; make used to; be able to : বক্তৃতা আমার আসে না. **8** come to be on the point of: ফুরিয়ে ~. **9** spread; increase; rise upto : উঠান পর্যন্ত পানি এসেছে. **10** be earned : কিসে দু পয়সা আসে. ❑*adj* that which has come: হাতে আসা. ❑ *n* act of coming : আমার কাছে আসার কি কারণ? **উঠে ~** *vi* come up; come off : ছাল উঠে আসা. **কাজে ~** *vi* be of use; be useful/serviceable. **কান্না ~** move to tears. **নিয়ে আসা** bring; fetch: বইটি নিয়ে এসো, fetch me the book. **নেমে ~** *vi* come/get down; alight; descend; dismount. **ফিরে ~** *vi* come back; return. **ফেলে ~** *vi,vt* leave behind. **~ যাওয়া** *n* **1** coming and going; frequentation: ~ সার. **2** communication; intercourse; speaking terms : আমাদের মধ্যে ~যাওয়া নেই. ❑ *vi* be of importance: এতে কিছু আসে যায় না, it does not matter.

আসা[2], **আশা** [A] *n* **1** stick; staff; club. **2** ceremonial rod; mace; sceptre. **~নড়ি** *n* stick. **~বরদার** [A + P] *n* person carrying an official mace; mace-bearer. **~সোঁটা** [A + S] *n* royal mace; ornamental mace carried by a monarch as an emblem of authority; sceptre.

আসান, আছান [P] *n* **1** relief; mitigation: রোগের ~. **2** termination; end: মুস্কিল ~. **3** convenience; advantage : তুমি সাথে থাকলে আমার কাজে অনেকটা ~ হতো.

আসানি [P] *n* comfort; ease.

আসাব কাহাফ⇒আসহাব-এ-কাহাফ

আসামি[1] *n* **1** accused; defendant. **2** debtor.

আসামি[2], **অহমিয়া** *adj* **1** born in Assam. **2** pertaining to Assam. ❑*n* **1** inhabitant of Assam. **2** language of Assam; Assamese.

আসাসোঁটা⇒আসা[2]

আসীন *adj* **1** seated; sitting. **2** placed; situated.

আসুর, আসুরিক *adj* **1** of the Hindu mythological demons. **2** like or comparable to the demons. **3** savage; terrible; demoniac. **4** vile; unholy. **5** according to the customs of the mythological demons. **আসুরী** *fem*. **~ বিবাহ** *n* form of marriage in which the bride is purchased for money.

আসেচন *n* act of watering; besprinkling with water.

আসোয়ার, আসওয়ার [P] *adj* mounted; riding. ❑*n* rider.

আস্কারা, আশকারা [P] *n* **1** indulgence; over-indulgence : তুমি ওকে ~ দিচ্ছ. **2** successful investigation of a crime. **~ করা** *vt* unravel a crime; detect a criminal. **~ দেওয়া** *vi* treat with over-indulgence; give undue indulgence.

আস্ত *adj* **1** whole; entire; unbroken; intact. **2** thorough; stark sheer; out-and-out; downright: ~ পাগল. **3** real; hardened: ~ চোর. **4** terrible; dangerous: ~ কেউটে. **~ না রাখা** *vi,vt* (fig) beat up severely. **~ পাগলামি** *n* midsummer madness.

আস্তব্যস্ত *adj* very busy.

আস্তর, আস্তরণ *n* **1** covering; bed-sheet; bed-cover. **2** lining of a garment. **3** cement plaster. **4** carpet or ornamental cloth used on the back of an elephant for the rider.

আস্তাগফেরুল্লাহ্‌ [A] I beg pardon of Allah—expression enjoined on Muslims when guilty of committing a sin.

আস্তানা [P] *n* **1** haunt; resort: পীরের ~. **2** abode; dwelling place. **~ গাড়া** *vi* put up somewhere temporarily. **~ গুটানো** *vi* leave/depart from a place for good.

আস্তাবল [P] *n* stable (for horses, elephants, etc).

আস্তিক *adj* one who believes in God and in the life hereafter. ❑*n* a believer in theism; a theist. **~তা** *n* belief in the existence of God as the creator and ruler of the universe; theism.

আস্তিন [P] *n* part of a garment that covers the arm; sleeve. **~ গুটানো** *vi* **1** roll up the sleeves. **2** (fig) prepare (oneself)/be ready to challenge or fight an opponent/rival.

আস্তীর্ণ *adj* **1** spread/stretched out. **2** extended; extending. **3** covered by; pervaded/strewn with (কুসুমাস্তীর্ণ).

আস্তে [P] *adv* **1** slowly: ~ ঘুরাও. **2** carefully; lightly: ~ রাখো. **3** light-footedly: ~ হাঁটো. **4** in an undertone: ~ কথা বলো. **5** noiselessly; without being noticed: ~ বের হয়ে আসবে.

আস্তেব্যস্তে *adv* in a great hurry; in haste; helter-skelter.

আস্থা *n* **1** confidence; reliance; trust. **2** faith; devotion: ধর্মে ~. **~ রাখা** *vi, vt* have faith/confidence (in); have regard (for); be devoted (to). **~বান** *adj* one who has faith/confidence (in); confident; faithful; devoted. **~ভাজন** *adj* **1** worthy of trust/confidence. **2** trustworthy.

আস্পদ *n* who/what contains, holds or deserves; recipient or object (of) (স্নেহাস্পদ, প্রেমাস্পদ).

আস্পর্ধা *n* **1** audacity; arrogance. **2** boast; vaunt; pride.

আস্ফালন *n* act of bragging/boasting/ vaunting /brandishing. **~ করা** *vi* brag; boast; vaunt.

আস্ফোট *n* **1** sound of collision or thrashing. **2** act of slapping on one's own arms (as in wrestling). **3** act of blooming/manifestation.

আস্বাদ *n* taste; savour; relish. **~ন** act of tasting/enjoying/experiencing. **~নীয়** *adj* to be tasted; enjoyable. **আস্বাদিত** *adj* what has been tasted/eaten/enjoyed/relished/experienced.

আহওয়াল [A] *n pl* (*sing* হাল) state; condition.

আহত *adj* **1** hurt; wounded; injured. **2** (of musical instruments) sounded; played on.

আহব *n* war; battle; fight.

আহবাব [A] *n pl* [*sing* হবীব] friends and associates.

আহরণ *n* **1** procurement; collection; accumulation. **2** compilation. **3** act of earning. **4** preparation. **5** dowry; wedding gift. **আহরণী** *n* an anthology.

আহরণীয়, আহর্তব্য *adj* to be collected/ accumulated.

আহরিৎ *adj* slightly green; greenish.

আহর্তব্য⇒আহরণীয়

আহর্তা *adj* one who collects/ procures/compiles. ❑*n* collector; compiler.

আহ্লে⇒আহেল

আহা *int* expressing sorrow, sympathy, etc; ah! oh! alas! **~ মরি** *int* expression of praise or ridicule. ❑*adj* excellent; admirable; praiseworthy : ~ মরি রূপ.

আহাদ, আল-আহাদ [A] *n* Allah, the One and Only object of adoration.

আহাদিল *adj* afflicted; wounded.

আহাম্মক, আহাম্মুক [A] lacking in common sense; foolish. ❑*n* a fool; a dunce. **আহাম্মকি, আহাম্মুকি** *n* folly; idiocy; stupidity. **আহাম্মকের ধাড়ি** an inveterate fool.

আহার *n* **1** act of eating. **2** food; meal; diet. **~ করা** *vi,vt* eat; dine. **~ দেওয়া** *vi,vt* feed; give food. **~দাতা** *n* provider of food; feeder; (fig) maintainer, supporter. **~দাত্রী** *fem*. **~নিদ্রা** *n* food and sleep. **~ ও বাসস্থান** *n* food and lodge; bed and board. **~বিহার** *n* food and pleasures. **আহারান্তে** *adv* after the dinner/meal. **আহারার্থ** *adv* for eating/dining. **আহারার্থী, ~প্রার্থী** *adj* seeking food. **আহারী** *adj* **1** eating. **2** voracious; gluttonous.

আহার্য *n* article of food. ❑ *adj* **1** eatable; edible. **2** fit to be collected/procured.

আহিক *n* a snake-charmer.

আহুত *adj* what has been sacrificed as burnt-offering. **আহুতি** *n* burnt-offering; an oblation.

আহূত *adj* invited; summoned; invoked. **আহূতি** *n* invitation; call; invocation.

আহৃত *adj* **1** collected. **2** compiled. **3** earned.

আহলে, আহ্‌লে [A] *adj* **1** pure; unmixed; original: ~ বিলাত, pure European. **2** new; raw. ❑*n* **1** family; lineage: ~ হাশিম. **2** inhabitant: ~ আরব. ~ **ইসলাম** *n* followers of Islam; the Muslims. ~ **কেতাব** *adj* those who are followers of revealed scriptures; people of the Book.

আহ্নিক *adj* daily; diurnal. ❑*n* daily ritual of the Hindus. ~ **গতি** *n* diurnal rotation of the earth.

আহ্বান *n* invitation; call; summons: সভা ~ করা. ~ **করা** *vi,vt* **1** call; convene; invite; summon. **2** challenge : যুদ্ধে/প্রতিযোগিতায় ~ করা.

আহ্বায়ক *n* convener. আহ্বায়িকা *fem.*

আহ্লাদ *n* **1** joy; delight. **2** indulgence; fondling. ~ **করা** *vi,vt* rejoice; take delight. ~ **দেওয়া** *vi* give indulgence. **আহ্লাদিত** *adj* delighted; joyful. **আহ্লাদী** *adj fem* seeking indulgence. **আহ্লাদে আটখানা** beside oneself with joy. **আহ্লাদে মাথায় চড়া** become impudent/be spoilt as a result of over-indulgence.

ই

ই *n* third vowel of the Bengali alphabet. It is a short vowel and is equivalent to English 'i' in 'bit'. Added to a consonant letter, it changes its form to 'ি', eg ক+ই=কি.

-ই *suff* denoting **1** certainty: আমি যাবই যাব, go I must. **2** emphasis: তুমিই একাজ করেছ, it is you who have done it. **3** singularity: ধনীরাই সুখী, The rich alone are happy. **4** slight/contempt: সে যা-ই বলুক তাতে কিছু আসে যায় না, no matter whatever he says. **5** excess/abundance: যতই করিবে দান তত যাবে বেড়ে, the more you will give it, the more will it increase. **6** a condition/ stipulation/ qualification: যদি সে আসেই, if he comes at all. **7** the motivating force of an act: এতে করেই তো ঝগড়াটা বেঁধে গেল, this is exactly what led to the quarrel.

-ই as an inflexion (as also a *suff*) added to *nn*, *pron* and *adjj*, it helps formation of derivatives indicating various meanings eg **(a)** character or quality of an object (লম্বাই, খাড়াই); **(b)** profession of a person (ডাক্তারি, মাস্টারি); **(c)** dates in a month from the 5th to the 18th (পাঁচই, ছয়ই, সাতই ...); **(d)** origin of anything (ঢাকাই, পাটনাই); **(e)** similarity (বড়লোকি, ছেলেমানুষি).

ইউনানি [A] *adj* **1** of Greece; Greek. **2** pertaining to the Muslim system of medicine/the profession of a hekim: ~ দাওয়াখানা.

ইউনিফর্ম [E] *n* uniform dress worn by all members of an organization or institution: পুলিশের ~.

ইউনিভার্সিটি [E] *n* institution for advanced learning and research and for conferring degrees; a university.

ইউনিয়ন [E] *n* **1** association formed by the uniting of persons or groups: ট্রেড ~. **2** lowest/administrative unit comprising a number of villages: ত্রিশাল ~. ~**কাউন্সিল** *n* council formed by representatives of the union population for local government.

ইউরেশিয়া *n* Europe and Asia. **ইউরেশীয়** *adj* **1** of mixed European and Asiatic descent; Eurasian. **2** of Europe and Asia. ❑*n* a Eurasian.

ইউরোপীয় *n* native of Europe; a European. ❑*adj* **1** of Europe; European: ~ দেশ. **2** produced in/connected with/extending over Europe: ~ সাধারণ বাজার.

ইংকার⇒ইঙ্কার

ইংগবংগ⇒ইঙ্গবঙ্গ

ইংগিত⇒ইঙ্গিত

ইংরেজ [Pg] *n* native of England; an Englishman. ~ **জাতি** *n* the English.

ইংরেজি *n* the English language; English. ~**নবিশ** *n, adj* one who can read and write English. ~**য়ানা** *n* blind imitation of the Englishmen; Anglomania.

ইংরেজি *adj* **1** pertaining to the English. **2** produced in England: ~ মদ্য. **3** according to the Christian calendar: ~ নববর্ষ. ~ **কেতা** *n* the habits and customs of the Englishmen; English style.

ইংলন্ড *n* England. **ইংলন্ডীয়** *adj* of/belonging to England; English.

ইঃ *int* expressing sorrow, anger or wonder; eh! hey!

ইঁচড়, ইচড় *n* green or unripe jackfruit (cooked as food). **ইঁচড়ে-পাকা** *adj* **1** prematurely clever; precocious. **2** (fig) talkative; saucy; impudent.

ইঁচা *n* the prawn or the shrimp: ~ মাছ.

ইঁট⇒ইট

ইঁদারা, ইন্দারা *n* masonry-well; draw-well.

ইঁদুর, ইন্দুর *n* the rat; the mouse.

ইকরা [A] *vi* perform the act of reading; read; the first word of the earliest Revelation to Prophet Muhammad (sm) asking him to read.

ইকরাম⇒একরাম

ইকরার⇒একরার

ইকমিক কুকার [E] *n* cooking stove made of metal and worked with charcoal; an icmic cooker.

ইকামত⇒আকামত

ইকার *n* symbol of the vowel 'ই' giving ই-sound to consonants. **ইকারাদি** *adj* (of words) beginning with ই or ই-sound (ইলিশ, কিতাব). **ইকারান্ত** *adj* (word) ending in ই or ই-sound (কড়াই, কলি).

ইক্ষু *n* the sugar-cane. ~ **দণ্ড** *n* the plant or stick of sugar-cane. ~**নেত্র** *n* knob, node or joint of a sugar-cane. ~ **বিকার,** ~**সার** *n* treacle or thick syrup got out of sugar-cane juice; molasses.

ইখতিয়ার⇒এখতিয়ার

ইখতিলাফ⇒এখতেলাফ

ইন্‌কার, ইংকার [A] *n* **1** denial; refusal to admit; dishonour (of a trust/commitment). **2** slight; contempt; dislike; detestation; abhorrence. ~ **করা** *vt* **1** deny; refuse; **2** hate; despise; look down upon.

ইঙ্গবঙ্গ *adj* **1** having a mixture of English and Bengali words; Anglo-Bengali. **2** (of anglomaniacs) Bengalees imitating English way of life; Anglo-Bengalee; Anglophil.

ইঙ্গ-ভারতীয় *n* **1** person of British descent living or having lived in India. **2** person of mixed British and Indian blood; an Anglo-Indian. ❑*adj* of/pertaining to England and India or Anglo-Indians.

ইঙ্গিত *n* **1** expressing (one's) mind by means of beckoning or gesticulation; a wink; a sign, a hint. **2** sign used for distant communication as an information or warning; signal: ঝড়ের ~. ~ **করা** **1** *vt* hint; suggest. **2** *vi* announce/ communicate by signalling. **ইঙ্গিতে বলা** *vt* hint at; allude to. ~**পূর্ণ** *adj* tending to suggest (sth); suggestive; significant; meaningful; allusive. **ইঙ্গিতে** *adv* by a hint/ gesture/ allusion.

ইচড়⇒ইঁচড়

ইচ্ছা *n* **1** faculty by which we determine to do or not to do sth; wish; will, volition: কালই যাওয়ার ~. **2** taste; tendency; inclination; liking: খাওয়ার ~. **3** aim; object; the thing desired/intended: সবই আল্লাহর ~. ~ **করা** *vt* determine by choice; wish; desire; intend. ~**কৃত** *adj* wilful; intentional (~কৃত অপচয়). ~**ক্রমে** *adv* according to (one's) desire/wish; at (one's) will/pleasure. ~**কৃত ভাবে** *adv* intentionally; wilfully; with a motive. ~**ধীন,** ~**নুগ** *adj* that which depends on (one's) liking; optional. ~**নুযায়ী,** ~**নুসারে** *adv* as one pleases/desires/wills; according to one's choice/liking. ~**নুরূপ,** ~**মতো** *adj, adv* to one's liking/satisfaction. ~**পূর্বক** *adv* willingly; voluntarily. ~**শক্তি** *n* control exercised over one's impulses; will-force; will-power. ~ **থাকলে উপায় হয়** where there's a will, there's a way. **ইচ্ছায় হোক আর অনিচ্ছায় হোক** *adv* willingly or unwillingly; willy-nilly.

ইচ্ছু, ইচ্ছুক *adj* **1** having a wish; feeling desire; desirous; longing (মিলনেচ্ছু). **2** willing; agreeing; consenting: চুক্তি সম্পাদনে ইচ্ছুক.

ইছবগুল⇒ইসবগুল

ইজতিহাদ, ইজতেহাদ [A] *n* **1** effort/exertion for perfection, esp in the knowledge of law. **2** method of deducing new laws in the light of the Qoranic principles and prophetic traditions, recognized as one of the sources of law in Islam.

ইজমা, এজমা [A] *n* (legal) consensus of opinion among the learned in Islamic law.

ইজমালি⇒এজমালি

ইজলাস⇒এজলাস

ইজা *n* (account) the total of receipt or payment of the previous page brought forward to the next page. ❑*adj* brought forward.

ইজাব [A] *n* consent given to what is proposed; consent given by a Muslim bride to the proposal of her marriage. ~**কবুল** *n* [A] consent of the bride and acceptance by the groom.

ইজার [A] *n* garment for the lower part of the body; pair of loose trousers; pantaloons. ~**বন্দ** *n* ribbon or band used for fastening the trousers at the waist.

ইজারা [A] *n* letting of land for a certain time for a stipulated money payment; a lease or a tenure hold by lease. ~**দার** [A+P] *n* a tenant under a lease; a lessee; a leaseholder. ~ **দেওয়া** *vt* let on lease; lease out; farm out. ~**পাট্টা** *n* lease-deed. ~**মহল** *n* property held by a lessee.

ইজিচেয়ার [E] *n* soft arm-chair designed for rest and relaxation; easy chair.

ইজ্জত, ইজ্জৎ [A] **1** honour; prestige; dignity: ইজ্জতের ভয়. **2** chastity; modesty: নারীর ~. ~ **নষ্ট করা** *vt* **1** treat with indignity; dishonour. **2** violate (one's) chastity. ~**হানি** *n* **1** dishonour, loss of prestige. **2** violation of chastity.

ইঞ্চি, ইঞ্চ [E] *n* **1** measure of length; a twelfth of a foot; an inch. **2** (of rainfall) a quantity sufficient to cover a surface to the depth of an inch: গতকাল পাঁচ ~ বৃষ্টিপাত হয়েছে.

ইঞ্জিন, এঞ্জিন [E] *n* machine for converting natural power such as heat, gas, steam, into mechanical energy; an engine: রেল ~.

ইঞ্জিনিয়ার [E] *n* **1** an expert in engineering. **2** person engaged in engineering work.

ইঞ্জিনিয়ারিং [E] *n* **1** science concerned with the principles, design and development of engines, manufacture of mechanical, chemical and other scientific products and with the designing and construction of the works of utility like roads, bridges and buildings; engineering. **2** the technology, work or profession of an engineer.

ইঞ্জিল, ইঞ্জীল [A] *n* the Arabic name for the Bible.

ইট, ইঁট *n* block of clay baked hard and used as building stone; brick. ~ **পাটকেল** *n* broken pieces of brick; brick-bats. ~ **পাটকেল মারা/ছোঁড়া, ইটানো** *vi, vt* pelt (sb/sth) with brick-bats. ~**খোলা** *n* field where brick-clay is obtained and moulded into bricks; brick-field; brick-yard. **ইটের পাঁজা/ভাটা** *n* kiln for baking bricks; brick-kiln. ~**টি মারলে পাটকেলটি খেতে হয়** an injury for an injury; tit for tat.

ইতঃপূর্বে *adv* before this; previously.

ইতর *adj* **1** base; mean; vile: ~ লোক. **2** belonging to the animal kingdom: ~ জীব. **3** ordinary; common: ~ জন. **4** other; other than; different from: মানবেতর জীবন, life more like that of an animal than that of a human being. **5** vulgar: ~ ভাষা, slang. **ইতরামি/ইতরামো** *n* meanness; vulgarity. **ইতরামি করা** *vi* behave meanly; put up ignoble conduct. ~**বিশেষ** *n* difference; distinction; disparity. ~**বিশেষ করা** *vi* make a distinction. ~**বিশেষ হওয়া** *vi* be different; differ. **ইতরেতর** *adj* one with another; mutual; reciprocal: ইতরেতর দ্বন্দ্ব. ❑*adv* mutually; reciprocally.

ইতস্তত *adv* here and there; hither and thither; up and down; all around: ~ বিক্ষিপ্ত. ❑*n* hesitation; wavering. ~ **করা** *vi* **1** hesitate; falter; pause doubtfully; show signs of uncertainty/unwillingness. **2** feel delicacy/shy. **3** procrastinate; dilly-dally; be dilatory.

ইতি indeclinable word used at the end of a correspondence meaning termination or conclusion. ❑*adv* this much; this is all. ~ **করা/টানা** *vi, vt* **1** complete; conclude; finish: এখানেই ~ টানছি. **2** put an end to (sth); settle up: বিবাদের ~ টানা.

ইতিকথা *n* story not based on fact; a tale; a fable. **2** traditional story of oral origin based more on fancy than on fact; a legend. **3** account of past times and events; chronicle; history; annals.

ইতিকর্তব্য, ইতিকর্তব্যতা, ইতিকর্তব্যজ্ঞান *n* the decision on or knowledge of what is proper to be done; the propriety of anything. **ইতিকর্তব্য বিমূঢ়** *adj* one who is at a loss what to do; perplexed, non-plussed; bewildered. **ইতিকর্তব্য বিমূঢ়তা** *n* confusion; perplexity; nonplus; bewilderment.

ইতিকাহিনী, ইতিবৃত্ত, ইতিহাস *n* narrative of past events recorded chronologically; study of human activities— social, political or economic; history. **ইতিবৃত্তকার, ইতিহাসকার** *n* author of a book on history; historian; chronicler.

ইতিপূর্বে corrupt form of ইতঃপূর্বে

ইতিবৃত্ত, ইতিবৃত্তকার⇒ইতিকাহিনী

ইতিমধ্যে inc form of ইতোমধ্যে

ইতিহাস, ইতিহাসকার⇒ইতিকাহিনী

ইতিহাসবিদ, ইতিহাসবেত্তা *n* one versed in history; a historian.

ইতোমধ্যে *adv* meanwhile, in the meantime.

ইত্তেফাক *n* [A] **1** concord; harmony; amity; unity. **2** Bengali Daily of Dhaka.

ইত্তেলা⇒এত্তেলা

ইত্তেহাদ [A] *n* **1** unity. **2** friendship.

ইত্যনুসারে *adv* according to this; accordingly.

ইত্যবসরে *adv* in this interval; taking this opportunity; meanwhile; in the meantime.

ইত্যাকার *adj* of this shape; like this; such.

ইত্যাদি *adv* and so on; and so forth; and others; et cetera.

ইথার [E] *n* **1** upper regions of air above the clouds. **2** (Phys) hypothetical medium for the transmission of light and radio waves. **3** (chem) liquid anaesthetic made from alcohol; colourless volatile liquid.

ইদানীং *adv* of late; now-a-days; at present. **ইদানীন্তন** *adj* of modern times; recent.

ইদুজ্জোহা, ইদুলফিতর⇒ঈদ

ইদ্দত, ইদ্দৎ [A] *n* period of waiting obligatory on a Muslim widow/divorced woman for re-marriage.

ইনকাম [E] *n* earning; income. ~ **ট্যাক্স** *n* tax on income; income tax.

ইনকার⇒**ইঙ্কার**

ইনকিলাব [A] *n* **1** replacement of established authority/social order by a radically progressive one; a radical change; revolution: ~ জিন্দাবাদ. **2** united action or agitation of a group of people in favour of some change; a movement. **3** a Bengali Daily published from Dhaka.

ইনজিল⇒ইঞ্জিল

ইনজেকশন [E] *n* **1** forcing medicinal fluid into sb/sth by means of a syringe; injection. **2** medicinal preparation to be injected. ~ **দেওয়া** *vi* inject (medicinal preparation)

ইনশা আল্লাহ [A] *adv* if Allah wishes; if it is the will of Allah: ~ কাল বাড়ি যাব.

ইনশিওরেন্স⇒ইনস্যুরেন্স

ইন্সপেক্টর, ইনসপেক্টর [E] *n* an official whose duty it is to visit and see that work is done properly, etc; an Inspector: স্কুল ~.

ইনসান [A] *n* human being. **ইনসানিয়াত** *n* humanity.

ইনসাফ [A] *n* justice; equity. ~ **করা** *vt* do justice to; treat with justice.

ইনস্যুরেন্স, ইনসিওরেন্স, ইনশিওরেন্স *n* [E] undertaking by a company to pay under specified conditions a sum of money in case of accident, damage, loss, injury or death in return for a stipulated premium; insurance.

ইনাম, এনাম [A] *n* recompense for service or merit; reward; gift; grant; tip.

ইনি *pron* (respectful reference) this gentleman/lady/person; he; she.

ইনিয়ে বিনিয়ে *adv* **1** elaborately; in so many words; with repetitions/exaggeration: ~ নালিশ করা. **2** in an entreating way; entreatingly; imploringly; with importunity: ~ কাজ হাসিল করা.

ইন্তেকাল, এন্তেকাল [A] *n* death; demise.

ইন্তেখাব, এন্তেখাব [A] *n* the act of electing; election.

ইন্তেজাম⇒এন্তেজাম

ইন্তেজার⇒এন্তেজার

ইন্দারা⇒ইঁদারা

ইন্দিরা *n* appellation of goddess Lakshmi.

ইন্দু *n* the moon. **~নিভ** *adj* like the moon; as beautiful as the moon: **~নিভাননা, ~নিভাননী** *fem*. **~মতী** *n fem* day of the full moon; the full moon (personified). **~মুখী** *n fem* woman having a moonlike face.

ইন্দুর⇒ইঁদুর

ইন্দো *pref* (in compounds) Indo=Indian. **~-ইউরোপীয়** *adj* Indo-European; of the family of languages spoken in Europe and parts of Asia, esp Iran, Pakistan, India and Bangladesh. ❑*n* **1** the original language from which these related languages have evolved. **2** a member of a race speaking one of these languages.

ইন্দ্র *n* [Hindu myth] Indra the king of gods and goddesses. **~জিৎ** *adj* one who has won victory over Indra. ❑*n* appellation of Meghnad, son of Ravana, the King of Lanka. **~ত্ব** *n* **1** dignity or office of Indra. **2** sovereignty over the gods. **3** royalty; supremacy. **~পুরী, ~লোক** *n* **1** abode/city of Indra; heaven. **2** (fig) a splendid mansion; a royal palace.

-ইন্দ্র *suff* denoting chief; king or sovereign (নর+ইন্দ্র=নরেন্দ্র, বীর+ইন্দ্র=বীরেন্দ্র).

ইন্দ্রজাল *n* art of producing effects by superhuman means; magic; sorcery; enchantment; witchcraft. **ইন্দ্রজালিক, ঐন্দ্রজালিক** *adj* **1** pertaining to magical feats; magical; illusive; unreal. **2** infatuating; enchanting; charming: হাস্যরসে তিনি ছিলেন প্রকৃত ঐন্দ্রজালিক.

ইন্দ্রজিৎ⇒ইন্দ্র

ইন্দ্রত্ব⇒ইন্দ্র

ইন্দ্রধনু *n* **1** [lit] the bow of Indra. **2** the rainbow (also রংধনু, রামধনু).

ইন্দ্রপুরী⇒ইন্দ্র

ইন্দ্রলোক⇒ইন্দ্র

ইন্দ্রাগার *n* draw-well; masonry well.

ইন্দ্রাণী *n fem* wife of Indra; Sachi.

ইন্দ্রায়ুধ *n* **1** the rainbow. **2** the bow of Indra.

ইন্দ্রাসন [ইন্দ্র+আসন] *n* royal seat; a throne.

ইন্দ্রিয় *n* a part of the body performing a function, eg, the ear or eye; a sense-organ. **~গম্য, ~গোচর, ~গ্রাহ্য** *adjj* perceptible by/within the purview of the senses. **~গম্যতা, ~গোচরতা, ~গ্রাহ্যতা** *nn* state of being within sense-perception. **~গ্রাম** *n pl* all the senses/sense-organs collectively. **~জয়, ~দমন, ~ সংযম** *nn* **1** restraint of the desires and passions; control of the senses/sensual appetites; continence. **2** practice of lifelong celibacy; abstinence from sexual and secular pleasures although one's life; the unmarried state for life. **~জয়ী, ~জিৎ** *adj* one who has successfully subdued or mastered his passions; continent. **~জ্ঞান** *n* faculty of perception; knowledge gained through the senses of sight, hearing, smelling, feeling and tasting. **~তৃপ্তি** *n* **1** gratification of the senses; sensual pleasures. **2** sexual intercourse; cohabitation; copulation. **~দোষ** *n* lustfulness; licentiousness; lewdness. **~পরায়ণ, ~সেবী, ইন্দ্রিয়াসক্ত** *adjj* given to self-indulgence; voluptuous; licentious. **~বৃত্তি** *n* functions of the sense-organs. **~লালসা, ~লিপ্সা** *nn* sensual desires; sexual appetite. **~সুখ** *n* sensual pleasures. **~সেবা** *n* indulgence in sensual pleasures; voluptuousness; debauchery; profligacy.

ইন্ধন *n* **1** fuel; fire-wood; kindling. **2** inpetus; incitement; encouragement. **~ দেওয়া, ~ যোগানো** *vi* feed with fuel; enkindle; inflame; (fig) encourage; add fuel to the flame.

ইন্নালিল্লাহ [A] *int* surely, we are for Allah.

ইফতার, এফতার [A] *n* breaking of Ramadan or unobligatory fasting after sunset with snacks and cold drink. **ইফতারি, এফতারি** *n* the snacks and drink with which fasting of a day terminates.

ইবরানি [A] *n* the Hebrew language.

ইবলিস [A] *n* **1** evil spirit; Satan. **2** Arabic name for Devil.

ইবাদত⇒এবাদত

ইবারত⇒এবারত

ইমতিহান⇒এমতেহান

ইমন [A] *n* musical mode.

ইমান, ঈমান [A] *n* **1** belief in the articles of faith in Islam. **2** faithfulness. **~দার** *adj* [A+P] **1** steadfast (in religion); pious; devout. **2** faithful; trustworthy. **~দারি** *n* righteousness; piety; faithfulness.

ইমাম [A] *n* **1** leader of the religious congregation: নামাজের ~. **2** exponent of scriptural law: ~ আবু হানিফা. **~তি** *n* **1**

leadership in the canonical prayers; leading the congregational prayer. **2** leadership. ~বাড়া *n* [A+H] house where the shiite festival of Muharram is celebrated: হুগলির ~বাড়া.

ইমাম মেহদি, ইমাম মাহদী [A] *n* the last Imam or ruler of the Shia sect who, according to Shia belief, is to reappear on earth before the Day of Judgement for the reformation of Islam.

ইমারত [A] *n* a masonry/brick-built house; a building; an edifice.

ইয়ত্তা *n* **1** quantity; measure. **2** limit; definiteness. ~ করা *vt* ascertain the extent/limit; measure. ~ রহিত *adj* innumerable; unending.

ইয়া *attrib adj* so much (big); of this size: ~ বড় কাঁঠাল.

-ইয়া Bengali *inflexion*: হলুদ+ইয়া=হলুদিয়া, yellowish.

ইয়াল্লাহ্ [A] *int* **1** invocation of Allah. **2** expression of fear; sorrow or wonder.

ইয়াংকি, ইয়াঙ্কি [E] *n* native of New England; citizen of United States; Yankee.

ইয়াকুত [A] *int* precious stone or gem of red colour; red jewel; ruby.

ইয়াজুজ মাজুজ [A] *n* Gog and Magog spoken of in the Holy Qoran who would make their appearance on earth before the Day of Judgement.

ইয়াদ [P] *n* remembrance; recollection. ~গার *n* a memorandum; a memorial; a monument. ~দস্ত, ~দাস্ত *n* memorandum; notebook; diary.

ইয়া নাফসি [A] *int* Alas! what will happen to me!

ইয়ার [P] *n* **1** boon companion; intimate friend. **2** a witty person; a humorist. ~বকসি, ~বন্ধু *n* chums and comrades; friends and associates. ~কি⇒ইয়ার্কি.

ইয়ারিং [E] *n* ring or ornament worn in the ear.

ইয়ার্কি, ইয়ারকি *n* jocularity; jesting; waggishness. ~ করা, ~ দেওয়া *vi* cut jokes; have a joke/make fun with sb.

ইয়াসমিন, জেসমিন [P] *n* fragrant shrub with white or yellow flowers; the jasmine.

ইয়ে *int* expression used when an appropriate word is not readily forthcoming or is not proper to utter.

ইরম্মদ *n* **1** the flash of lightning. **2** the elephant.

ইরশাদ⇒এরশাদ

ইরশাল [A] *n* **1** payment of rent/revenue. **2** rent; revenue; tax.

ইরা *n* **1** the earth. **2** the power of speech. **3** water. **4** food. **5** wine.

ইরাক [A] *n* country in western Asia; ancient Mesopotamia or the land of two rivers—Tigris and Euphrates. ইরাকি *adj* pertaining to Iraq. ❑*n* inhabitant(s) of Iraq.

ইরাদা⇒এরাদা

ইরান [P] *n* Iran, the native name of Persia. ইরানি *adj* pertaining to Iran. ❑*n* inhabitant(s) of Iran.

ইরাবতী *n* river Ravi in the Punjab; river in Burmah (or Myanmar).

ইলজাম⇒এলজাম

ইলশা, ইলসা (colloq)=ইলিশ

ইলশাগুঁড়ি, ইলশেগুঁড়ি *n* drizzle; fine rain (suitable for good catch of hilsa fish): ~ বৃষ্টি.

ইলশে, ইলসে (colloq)=ইলিশ

ইলহান⇒এলহান

ইলহাম⇒এলহাম

ইলা *n* **1** the earth. **2** the cow. **3** water.

ইলাহি⇒এলাহি

ইলিশ *n* hilsa, the famous river fish of Bangladesh.

ইল্লত, ইল্লৎ [A] *n* **1** dirt; filth; ordure. **2** meanness; baseness. ~খানা *n* latrine; lavatory; privy. ইল্লুতে *adj* filthy; mean: ইল্লুতে কাজ. ~ যায় না ধুলে black will take no other hue.

ইশ, ইস *int* expressing sorrow, pain, amazement, etc.

ইশকাপন *n* [D] playing card of black suit; spade.

ইশতেহার⇒ইস্তাহার

ইশপিশ *n* restlessness; state of being impatient.

ইশাদি [A] *n* one who gives evidence in anything; a witness.

ইশারা [A] *n* beckoning; a wink; a sign; a hint. ~ করা *vt* beckon; hint; make a sign/wink.

ইষু *n* an arrow.

ইষ্ট *adj* **1** desired; cherished: ~ কর্ম. **2** beneficial: ~ চিন্তা. **3** adored; worthy of adoration: ~ দেবতা. **4** related by blood; dear: ~ কুটুম্ব. ❑*n* welfare; prosperity.

ইষ্টক *n* brick; building stone.

ইষ্টকুটুম্ব, ইষ্টিকুটুম *n pl* kith and kin; friends and relations.

ইষ্টানিষ্ট [ইষ্ট+অনিষ্ট] *n* gain or loss; good or evil. ❑*adj* good or bad.

ইষ্টি *n* wish; desire.

ইষ্টি *n* Vedic rite of sacrifice; an oblation.

ইষ্টি *n* (colloq) relative.

ইসপগুল, ইসবগুল, ইশবগুল [P] *n* medicinal seeds used as an antidote for dysentery.

ইসমাইলি, ইসমাঈলী [A] *n* followers of Ismail, the seventh Imam of the Shia; a sect of the Shia.

ইসলাম [A] *n* **1** Islam, the Arabic name for the religion of peace as preached and practised by Prophet Muhammad (sm). **2** (lit) submitting to the will of/making peace with the Creator.

ইসলামিয়াত, ইসলামিয়াৎ [A] *n* the scriptural law of Islam. **ইসলামি** *adj* **1** relating to Islam: ইসলামি শিক্ষা. **2** according to Islamic scriptural law: ইসলামি অনুশাসন.

ইসলাহ্ [A] *n* **1** correction; reformation. **2** purity; genuineness.

ইস্‌মে আজম [A] *n* Divine words, the utterance of which can work wonders.

ইস্রাফিল, ইস্‌রাফিল [A] *n* one of the four chief angels according to Islamic belief.

ইস্তক [U] *adv* **1** till; upto: কেয়ামত ~. **2** from: জন্ম ~. **3** including: জুতা পালিশ ~ সব কাজই সে করে. ❑*n* the king and the queen of the trump-card. **~ নাগাদ, ~ লাগাৎ** [U+A] *adv* from beginning to end; althrough; all along: বৃটিশ আমল থেকে ~ নাগাদ এই দুর্নীতি চলে আসছে.

ইস্তফা [A] *n* **1** relinquishment; giving up; resignation: চাকুরিতে ইস্তফা, resigning ones job. **2** end; termination; cessation: লেখা-পড়ায় ~ দেওয়া. **~ দেওয়া** *vt* resign; give up; relinquish; terminate.

ইস্তাহার, ইশতেহার [A] *n* public announcement; proclamation; communique; circular notice. **~ দেওয়া** *vi* issue a communique/circular.

ইস্তিরি, ইস্ত্রি [Pg] *n* **1** utensil for smoothing cloth/clothes; smoothing-iron. **2** smoothing linen with an iron; ironing. **~ করা** *vi, vt* smooth clothes with an iron; iron.

ইস্তেকবাল [A] *n* welcome; reception; greeting felicitation: সম্মানিত অতিথির ইস্তেকবালের জন্য সমবেত হলাম.

ইস্তেগফার [A] *n* act of begging pardon of Allah; apology to Allah.

ইস্তেনজা⇒এস্তেনজা

ইস্তেমাল⇒এস্তেমাল

ইস্পাত [Pg] *n* hard form of iron, produced by addition of carbon; steel. **~কঠিন** *adj* **1** hard as steel. **2** (fig) firm; unshaking; unwavering: ~ কঠিন সংকল্প.

ইহ *adv* **1** here; in this place; in this world; at this time; now. **~কাল** *n* the duration of this life; present life; the earthly or mortal life. **~জগৎ, ~লোক, ~সংসার** *nn* this world; the earth; the material world. **~জন্ম, ~জীবন** *n* this life. **~জন্মে, ~জীবনে** *adv* in this life; ever in this life: ~ জন্মে দেখিনি.

ইহা *pron* it; this. **~কে, ~ ছাড়া, ~ ব্যতীত, ~ ভিন্ন** besides; besides this. **~তে** *pron* in it; on it. **~দিগকে** *pron* them. **~দের, ~দিগের** *pron* their, theirs. **~র** *pron* its. **~র অধিক** more than this. **~র পূর্বে** before this; formerly; previously. **~র মধ্যে** in the meantime. **~রা** *pron* they.

ইহুদি [A] *n* **1** the Jewish community; the Jew. **2** the ancient religious community of Judea; the Hebrew.

ইহরাম⇒এহরাম

ইহসান⇒এহসান

ঈ *n* fourth vowel of the Bengali alphabet. As an aspirate or long vowel, it gives the sound of 'ee' as in 'geese'. It joins a consonant letter with its symbol 'ী' eg, ক+ঈ=কী.

-ঈ used as an inflexion, it serves several purposes, eg **(a)** transforming a *n* into an *adj* (দামী, রাগী, রেশমী); **(b)** giving feminine form to *nn* (নানী, চাচী, মানবী, বানরী); **(c)** denoting one's nationality or homeland (বিহারী, পাঞ্জাবী, পাকিস্তানী, বাংলাদেশী); or **(d)** indicating the special nature of work one is engaged in কেরানী, শাঁখারী, কাঁশারী, etc.

ঈঃ *int* expressing pain, anger, contempt, etc.

ঈ-কার *n* **1** symbol of the vowel 'ঈ' used with consonants. **2** the vowel ঈ. **ঈকারাদি** *adj* (of words) beginning with ঈ or ঈ-sound (গীত, ঈদ). **ঈকারান্ত** *adj* (of words) ending in ঈ. (নদী, মানবী, ধনী, উপযোগী).

ঈক্ষণ *n* **1** sight; vision; seeing. **2** the eye. **ঈক্ষিত** *adj* seen; viewed; observed.

ঈগল [E]*n* large bird of prey with strong curved beak; the eagle. **~স্বভাব** *adj* ferocious as an eagle.

ঈথার=ইথার

ঈদ [A] *n* **1** famous Muslim festival celebrated twice a year. **2** (lit) joy; happiness; festivity. **~গা/গাহ্** *n* open field where the Muslims assemble for saying Eid prayers. **ঈদুজজোহা, ঈদুল আজহা** *n* [A] the festival of sacrifice celebrated on the 10th of Jilhajj. **ঈদুল ফিতর** *n* [A] Eid or festival on the first day of Shawal to celebrate the end of the month of Ramadan.

ঈদৃশ *adj* like this; similar to this. **ঈদৃশী** *fem*.

ঈপ্সা *n* **1** desire to have (sth); longing; yearning. **2** covetousness; greed; temptation. **ঈপ্সিত** *adj* desired; longed for; wished for. **ঈপ্সু** *adj* wishing; desirous; covetous.

ঈর্ষা *n* pain or discontent excited by anothers good fortune; envy; jealousy. **2** malice; ill-will; ill-feeling; enmity. **3** suspicion in love. **~ করা** *vi,vt* envy; be affected with envy; feel envy of; cherish malice/ill-feeling/enmity against. **~তুর, ~ন্বিত** *adj* animated with envy/malice; envious; malicious; jealous. **~নল** *n* (fig) fire of envy. **~বশে** *adv* out of envy/malice.

ঈশ *n* **1** God (জগদীশ, পরমেশ). **2** lord; master; husband (প্রাণেশ). **3** king; overlord (নরেশ). **~ত্ব** *n* lordship; leadership. **~প্রাণতা** *n* devotion to God.

ঈশক⇒এশক

ঈশা⇒ঈসা

ঈশান *n* the north-east. ~ **কোণ** *n* north-east quarter.

ঈশিতা, ঈশিত্ব *n* **1** divinity. **2** one of the eight attributes of divinity. **3** lordship; mastery; supremacy.

ঈশ্বর *n* **1** God; Allah. **2** the Creator; the Lord of the universe. **3** owner; master; ruler; king (দিল্লীশ্বর). ~**ত্ব,** ~**তা** *n* the attributes of God; divinity. ~**দত্ত** *adj* God-given. ~**নিষ্ঠ,** ~**ভক্ত** *adj* devoted to God; pious; devout. ~**নিষ্ঠা,** ~**প্রেম** *n* devotion to God; piety; religiosity. ~**বাদ** *n* belief in God; theism. ~**বাদী** *adj* one who believes in God. ❑*n* a theist. ~**ভীরু** *adj* God-fearing.

ঈষৎ *adj, adv* a little; a bit; slight; slightly. **ঈষদচ্ছ** *adj* allowing rays of light to pass through but not transparent; translucent. **ঈষদুচ্চ** *adj* of moderate height; not very high. **ঈষদুষ্ণ** *adj* neither very warm nor cold; luke-warm.

ঈষিকা, ঈষীকা *n* **1** species of tall grass used for making mats. **2** painting-brush. **3** the eyeball of elephants.

ঈসা [A] *n* Jesus Christ, founder of Christianity. ~**য়ী** *adj* **1** according to the Christian system: ~য়ী সন. **2** followers of Jesus Christ. ❑*n* The Christians.

উ

উ *n* fifth vowel of the Bengali alphabet. It is a short vowel and is pronounced like 'u' as in bush. When joined to a consonant letter it takes the form of its symbol, eg, ক+উ=কু.

-উ as an inflexion it has several uses, eg, **(a)** transforming a *n* into an *adj* (চাল+উ=চালু, ঢাল+উ ঢালু); **(b)** changing the form of a word without changing its meaning (নীচ+উ=নিচু, উন+উ=উনু); or **(c)** expressing fondness (দাদু, নানু, আব্বু).

উই, উইপোকা *n* group of ant-like insects having membranous wings which are commonly called white ants and which are very destructive to timber, textiles, etc; termite. ~**চারা,** ~**ঢিপি,** ~**টিবি** *n* cone-shaped pile of earth thrown up by white ants in making their nest; ant-hill. ~**ধরা, উয়ে ধরা,** ~**লাগা** *vi* be attacked with/eaten up by white ants.

উইচিংড়া⇒উচ্চিংড়া

উইল [E] *n* legal testament in which a person declares how his property is to be used or distributed after his death.

উঃ, উহ *int* expressing pain, amazement, worry, anxiety or restlessness.

উঁ *int* used as a response in short to someone's call.

উঁকি *n* a look through a small opening; a glimpse or hasty view taken esp in secret; a peep. **ভোরের** ~ (fig) peep of day. ~**ঝুঁকি** *n* repeated peeping without exposing oneself. ~**দেওয়া,** ~**মারা** *vi* peep into sth; take a secret glance of sth.

উঁচকপালি, উটকপালি *adj fem* **1** woman with a protuberant forehead and so ugly to look at. **2** attended with misfortune; ill-omened. **উঁচকপালে, উচকপালে, উটকপালে, উঁচাকপাল** *adj mas* **1** one having a protuberant forehead. **2** having good fortune; fortunate.

উঁচল *n* **1** separating corn from stalks. **2** sifting/separating chaff from corn by winnowing or by means of a sieve.

উঁচলানো, ওঁচলানো *vi* separate or blow away husks, dust, stones, etc from grain; winnow: চাল ~.

উঁচা, উচা, উঁচু, উচু *adj* **1** high; tall; lofty. **2** elevated; exalted; noble: ~ মন. **3** loud; harsh; rough: ~ স্বর. **4** excellent; fine; surpassingly good of the kind: **উঁচু দরের** প্রসাধনী. **উঁচানো, উচানো, ওঁচানো** *vt* raise/lift up sth heavy. ❑*n* act of raising/lifting/heaving up (eg, a staff) ❑*adj* swelled; raised; going up ~ গোঁফ. ~**নিচু,** ~**নিচা** *adj* uneven; undulating. **উঁচিয়ে উঠা** *vi* increase in wealth/position from an insignificant state; thrive.

উহুঁ *int* expressing a negative reply.

উক *n* (colloq) the sugarcane.

উক , উকা *n* **1** flying sparks of fire (as from an oven). **2** fire. **3** a flambeau or ceremonial torch.

উকড়া, উকড়ো, উখড়া *n* pop-rice coated/ sweetened with sugar or molasses.

উকা *n* fishing-trap made of bamboo. or cane.

উকার *n* symbol of the vowel 'উ'. **উকারাদি** *adj* (word) beginning with 'উ' or its symbol (eg, উঠান, রুটি). **উকারান্ত** *adj* (word) ending with 'উ' or উ-sound. (eg বউ, কচু)

উকালত, উকালতি, উকালতনামা⇒ওকালত

উকি, উক্কি *n* **1** convulsive catch of the respiratory muscles resulting in a coughing sound; hiccup; hiccough. **2** vomiting tendency. ~ **তোলা** *vi* hiccup; hiccough; have the hiccups; ~ **ওঠা** *vi* be attacked with hiccups.

উকিল [A] *n* **1** professional representative in legal cases; a lawyer; a pleader; an advocate; a barrister. **2** agent or representative in a Muslim marriage who discharges the responsibility of conveying the bride's consent to the marriage to the bridegroom.

উকুন *n* parasitic of hair; the louse (*pl.* lice).

উক্ত *adj* **1** what has been said/expressed. **2** mentioned; referred to. **3** uttered.

উক্তি *n* expression of a fact or opinion; that which is stated; a statement.

উখড়নো, উখড়ানো, ওখড়ানো *vi* uproot. ❑*n* extirpation. ❑*adj* uprooted; extirpated.

উখা *n* **1** cooking pot. **2** oven.

উখা *n* metal tool having sharp serrated surface used for scraping; a coarse file; a rasp.

উগলানো, ওগরানো *vt, vi* **1** eject from the throat; disgorge; vomit. **2** (fig) give up; hand over, surrender (sth taken wrongfully): চোরাইমাল ~. **3** (fig) give out/confess secrets. **4** (fig) put down in an answer-script what has been committed to memory (without serious study).

উগ্র *adj* **1** easily angered; peevish; impatient: ~ স্বভাব. **2** strong; bitter; deadly; fatal: ~বিষ. **3** severe; excessive; terrible: ~ তাপ. **4** harsh; hoarse; rough: ~কণ্ঠ. **5** cruel; hard-hearted; merciless. **6** extreme; most violent: ~পন্থী, উগ্রা *fem.* **~কণ্ঠ, ~স্বর** *adj* having a hoarse or grating voice; raucous. **~কণ্ঠে, ~স্বরে** *adv* in a harsh/angry voice; raucously. **~কর্মা** *adj* one who performs cruel or violent deeds at ease/without feeling qualms of conscience. **~চণ্ডা, ~চণ্ডী** *n fem* **1** hot-tempered and quarrelsome woman. **2** appellation of goddess Durga in a terrible form; ❑*adj fem* terrible; violent. **~তা** *n* severity; sharpness; fierceness; extremity. **~পন্থী** *n* one holding extreme trims or advocating extreme action; extremist. **~মূর্তি** *adj* having an angry-look.

উচক্কা *adj* **1** advancing to manhood; adolescent. ~ **বয়স** youthful age; adolescence. **2** unruly; unmanageable; obstinate: ~ ছোঁড়া. ❑*adv* suddenly; all at once: ~ আগমন.

উচল *adj* (poet) high; lofty.

উচাটন *adj* anxious; agitated; restless: ~ মন. ❑*n* anxiety; worry.

উচিত *adj* **1** what is proper to be done; right. **2** fitting; becoming; worthy. **3** apt; appropriate; just. **ঔচিত্য** *n*. ~ **কথা** the right thing; the truth. ~ **বক্তা** straightforward in speech; outspoken. ~ **ব্যবহার** just treatment; fair deal.

উচ্চ *adj* **1** elevated; high; lofty: ~ পর্বত. **2** exalted; generous; noble: ~ মন. **3** high-born; aristocratic: ~ বংশ. **4** costly; dear: ~ মূল্য. **5** elevated in rank or office; senior; superior: ~ পদ/কর্মচারী. **6** high-pitched; loud: ~ স্বর. **~ আশা** *n* desire for prosperity/superiority; ambition. **~কণ্ঠ** *n* high-pitched voice. ❑*adj* having a high-pitched tone/voice. **~কণ্ঠে** *adv* at the top of one's voice; loudly. **~গ্রাম** *n* (music) higher scale of a note. **~তম** *adj* (superl) highest; loftiest. **~তর** *adj* (comp) higher; loftier. **~তা** *n* height; altitude; elevation. **~নাদ** *n* loud sound/noise. **~নাদী** *adj* high-sounding; loud. **~নীচ** *adj* high and low; up and down; undulating. **~পদ** *n* high office; exalted position: **~পদস্থ কর্মচারী** high/higher/top-ranking officer. **~বাচ্য** *n* **1** act of responding; response. **2** protest; objection. **3** raising a proposal or claiming sth. **~বাচ্য না করা** make no comment; raise no objection; keep quiet/silent. **~রোল** *n* loud noise; clamour; uproar. **~হার** *n* high rate. **~হারে** *adv* at a high rate. **~হাসি/হাস্য** *n* loud laugh; laughter.

উচ্চকিত *adj* **1** anxious; worried. **2** agitated; restless.

উচ্চগ্রাম⇒উচ্চ

উচ্চণ্ড [উৎ+চণ্ড] *adj* **1** violent. **2** angry; hot-tempered. **3** fierce; furious; outrageous. **4** terrible; severe.

উচ্চবাচ্য⇒উচ্চ

উচ্চাকাঙ্ক্ষা *n* ardent desire for some high attainment; ambition; aspiration. **উচ্চাকাঙ্ক্ষী** *adj* ambitious; aspiring; **উচ্চাকাঙ্ক্ষিণী** *fem.*

উচ্চাভিলাষ=উচ্চাকাঙ্ক্ষা, **উচ্চাভিলাষী** *adj.* **উচ্চাভিলাষিণী** *fem.*

উচ্চারণ *n* **1** act of oral expression; articulation; utterance: এমন কথা ~ কোরো না. **2** mode of pronouncing; pronunciation: ~বিভ্রাট. **3** manner or style of speaking. ~ **করা** *vi, vt* utter; pronounce; express; speak out. **~তত্ত্ব** *n* linguistic study dealing with the sounds of speech; phonetics. **~বিভ্রাট** *n* **1** wrong or corrupted pronunciation. **2** perversion in spelling or meaning due to wrong pronunciation. **~স্থান** *n* part of the mouth that produces a particular speech sound; point of articulation. **উচ্চারণীয়, উচ্চার্য** *adj* that which is to be/should be pronounced or uttered. **উচ্চারিত** *adj* uttered; pronounced; spoken. **উচ্চার্যমান** *adj* what is being uttered/pronounced/expressed.

উচ্চিংড়া *n* **1** insect that makes a creaking sound; the cricket. **2** (fig) person of quick-temper.

উচ্চৈঃ *adj* indicating elevation, loftiness, abundance, excess, etc. **~স্বর** *n* vocal utterance of high sound; loud voice; shout; outcry. **~স্বরে** *adv* aloud; loudly; at the top of one's voice.

উচ্ছন্ন=উৎসন্ন

উচ্ছল *adj* **1** that which is overflowing/surging up/swelling up. **2** spread/diffused all over; all-pervading. **3** passionate; emotional; throbbing; restless: ~যৌবন. **~ন** *n* act of surging/swelling up. উচ্ছলিত *adj* that has surged/swelled up.

উচ্ছিষ্ট *n* (of food) left-overs/remains of a meal; scraps of food (also উচ্ছিষ্টান্ন. ~ভোগী *adj* **1** one who eats the remains of another's meal. **2** (fig) hanging on others.

উচ্ছৃঙ্খল [উৎ+শৃঙ্খল] *adj* **1** one who is not disciplined in his day to day life; irregular unregulated. **2** unrestrained; licentious; wayward; perverse. **3** one whose mode of living is unconventional/Bohemian. ~তা *n* **1** licentiousness; perversity. **2** disorderliness; indiscipline; lawlessness.

উচ্ছে *n* kind of vegetable having bitter taste.

উচ্ছেদ *n* **1** eviction; ejectment. **2** eradication; extirpation; destruction; abolition. ~ করা *vt* evict; uproot; eradicate; extirpate; destroy. সমূলে ~ করা uproot; eradicate; destroy root (one) from hereditary homestead. ~ক *adj* one who/that which ejects/evicts/eradicates. ❑*n* ejector; evictor; eradicator; extirpator; destroyer.

উচ্ছোসন *n* **1** act of sucking/drying up. **2** act of causing affliction; afflicting. উচ্ছোসিত *adj* **1** sucked/dried up. **2** afflicted. উচ্ছোসক *n* blotting paper.

উচ্ছ্বসিত *adj* seized with over-mastering delight or sorrow; swollen; inspired ~ ক্রন্দন, ~ প্রশংসা.

উচ্ছ্বাস *n* **1** emotional or passionate outburst; strong emotion/passion. **2** joy; jubilation; delight. **3** manifestation; expression.

উছল, উছলিত *adj* **1** that which is swelling up/surging out; overflowing. **2** seized with emotion/anxiety; swollen; overwhelmed. উছলানো, উছলনো *vi, vt* increase in size, bulk or volume; swell up (with); be puffed up (with).

উজবক, উজবুক [T] *n* native of Tartary; a Tatar (or Tartar). ❑*adj* **1** stupid. **2** uncouth.

উজাড় [H] *adj* **1** exhausted; emptied: যা ছিল ~ করে দিয়েছি. **2** depopulated; desolate: মহামারীতে গ্রাম ~ হয়েছে.

উজান *n* **1** course against the stream; upstream course. **2** high tide; flow tide. ~ভাটি *n* flow-tide and ebb-tide; flow and ebb. উজানো *vi* **1** go or sail upstream/against the current; take a contrary course. **2** get over; cross. উজানে *adv* up a river; against the stream; upstream.

উজির [A] *n* a minister or adviser to a Muslim king (Sultan) (as in former times). উজিরে আলা Chief Minister. উজিরে আজম Prime Minister.

উজ্জয়িনী *n* ancient city in India; capital of king Vikramaditya.

উজ্জীবন *n* **1** infusion of new life; being alive again. **2** revival from disuse/inactivity, etc. উজ্জীবিত *adj* infused with a new life; regenerated; resuscitated; rekindled. উজ্জীবিত করা *vi, vt* breathe fresh life (into); revive; resuscitate; re-animate.

উজ্জ্বল *adj* **1** reflecting/giving out light; glittering; bright; luminous. **2** giving signs of success; promising: ছেলেটির ভবিষ্যৎ ~. **3** excellent; glorious: দেশসেবার ~ নিদর্শন. **4** famous; celebrated: সাহিত্য জগতের ~ জ্যোতিষ্ক. celebrated luminary of the literary world. ~ করা *vt* **1** give light to; throw light on; light up; illuminate. **2** give or bring honour and glory to; make famous; glorify: দেশের মুখ ~ করা. ~তা, ঔজ্জ্বল্য *n* brightness; lustre; splendour; beatuty; glory.

উঞ্ছ *n* act of gleaning/picking up scattered grains left by the reapers in the harvest field for one's livelihood; living by odd means. ~জীবী *adj* one who earns a living by shifts. ~বৃত্তি *n* subsistence by gleaning scattered ears of corn; mean livelihood. ~বৃত্তি করা *vi* live as the parasite of/be meanly dependent on (person for thing).

উট *n* large quadruped animal with a hump, used in desert regions for transport; the camel. ~চোখো *adj* having small eyes like the camel. ~পাখি *n* large flightless long-legged running bird found in Australia, Africa, Arabia and South America; the ostrich.

উটকপালি, উটকপালে⇒ উচকপালি

উটকা, উটকো *adj* **1** unknown; unfamiliar; new comer: ~ লোক. **2** strange; queer; incredible: ~ কথা. **3** unbelievable; undependable; baseless: ~ খবর. **4** unexpected, unthought of; sudden ~ ঘটনা. **5** disagreeable in appearance; ugly ~মুখো. ❑*adv* all at once; suddenly: ~ এসে হাজির হলো.

উটজ *n* small country house thatched with straw; thatched hut. ~ শিল্প *n* industry that can be carried on in cottages; cottage industry.

উটপাখি⇒উট

উঠতি *n* rise; growth; development; prosperity. ❑*adj* **1** rising; flourishing. ~ অবস্থা rising/flourishing state. **2** young; tender-aged; adolescent: ~ বয়সের ছেলে. ~পড়তি *n* rise and fall; boom and slump.

উঠন্ত *adj* **1** growing/increasing in power, etc. **2** advancing to adult years: ~ বয়স. **3** appearing above the horizon; rising: ~সূর্য, rising sun. ~ মূলা পত্তনেই চেনা যায় (prov) morning shows the day.

উঠবোস, ওঠবোস *n* **1** mode of physical exercise by a continuous process of sitting and standing. **2** sitting and standing alternately as a sort of punishment.

উঠা, ওঠা *vi* **1** get up from a lying or sitting position; rise; arise: (a) সে আমাকে স্বাগত জানাতে

উঠে এলো, he rose to welcome me. (b) আমাকে এখন উঠতে হবে. I must leave now. **2** get up from sleep; get out of bed: সে ভোরে ওঠে, he rises early. **3** appear above the horizon; rise: সূর্য উঠেছে, the sun is up. **4** come out; grow; cut: খোকার দাঁত উঠেছে the baby is teething/cutting teeth. **5** fall off: তার চুল উঠছে, his hair is falling off. **6** be promoted: সে নবম শ্রেণীতে উঠেছে. **7** be collected: চাঁদা ওঠা. **8** wash out: এ দাগ উঠবে না this spot will not wash out. **9** fade away/go off: এ রং উঠবে না will not fade/go off. **10** be available: বাজারে ~. **11** grow; sprout: চারা উঠছে the seeds have sprouted. **অন্ন ~ 1** loose one's source of subsistence. **2** die. **গাছে ~** climb a tree. **গাড়িতে ~** get into a carriage/car. **ঘোড়ায় ~** mount/ride a horse. **চোখ ~** have inflammation of the eye esp conjunctivitis. **জ্বর ~** catch/develop fever. **ট্রেনে/জাহাজে/প্লেনে ~** board a train, etc. **পাহাড়ে, ~** ascend a hill. **~নামা** *n* **1** upward and downward movement; ascent and descent. **2** elevation and depression. **~পড়া** *n* **1** rise and fall. **2** promotion and demotion. **উঠি-কি-পড়ি** *adv* in disorderly haste; helter-skelter: লোকটি উঠি-কি-পড়ি করে ছুটতে লাগলো, began to run helter-skelter. **উঠে পড়ে লাগা** *vi* engage oneself doggedly (in); be up and doing. **উঠে যাওয়া** *vt* **1** remove oneself/shift (from a place). **2** be abolished: স্কুলটি উঠে গেছে, has been abolished. **3** wind up: কারবারটি উঠে গেছে, has wound up. **4** be closed down: দোকানটি উঠে গেছে. **5** be out of practice: এ নিয়ম এখন উঠে গেছে is out of practice now. **উঠতে বসতে** *adv* every now and then; always.

উঠান, উঠোন *n* inclosure in which a house stands; courtyard; compound.

উঠানো *vi, vt* **1** raise (sth/sb) to a higher level or position; lift up. **2** set erect: খুঁটিটি উঠাও খোড়া করো set the pole erect. **3 ডাঙায় ~** haul up. **4 পতাকা ~** hoist a flag. **5 ব্যাংক থেকে টাকা ~** withdraw cash from a bank. **6 প্রস্তাব/প্রশ্ন/কথা ~** put up a proposal/raise a question/initiate a discussion topic. **7** pull out; extract: দাঁত ~. **8** wash out; efface; remove: দাগ ~. **9** awake; rouse: ঘুম থেকে ~. **10** tear up by the roots; uproot: আগাছা ~. **11** eject; evict: প্রজা/ভাড়াটে ~. **12** include in a list; enlist: তালিকায় ~. **13** গাড়িতে ~ pick up: আমরা তাকে গাড়িতে উঠিয়ে নিলাম, we gave him a lift.

উড্ডয়ন *n* act of soaring and moving in the air; flying; flight.

উড্ডীন, উড্ডীয়মান, উড্ডয়মান *adj* flying in the air. **উড্ডীনোন্মুখ** *adj* eager or ready to take flight.

উড়কি *n* variety of paddy.

উড়তি *adj* **1** (of news, etc) in the air; passing from man to man: ~ খবর. **2** what is flying/streaming out in the air (synonym for উড়ন্ত and উড্ডীয়মান).

উড়নচণ্ডী *adj* of disorderly habit; spendthrift; prodigal; extravagant. ☐*n* person who spends money extravagantly; spendthrift; squanderer. **~ ভাব** *n* prodigality; extravagance.

উড়ন্ত⇒উড়তি (2).

উড়শ, উড়ুশ *n* small, flat, blood-sucking insect; the bug.

উড়া ⇒উড়ো

উড়া, ওড়া *vt* **1** move through air by wings; fly: পাখি উড়ছে, birds are flying. **2** flutter: পতাকাটি পতপত করে উড়ছে the flag is fluttering in the breeze. **~-~** *adv* without certainty: ~-~ শোনা যাচ্ছে there are rumours in the air that ... **উড়ে আসা** *vi* **1** come suddenly/all on a sudden. **2** come with thundering speed. **3** come unwantedly: উড়ে-আসা লোক, stranger; unwelcome guest/visitor. **উড়ে এসে জুড়ে বসা** to come as an intruder and dig in with firmness; usurp someone else's rights. **উড়ে যাওয়া** *vi* **1** fly away; run fast; escape: পাখিটা উড়ে গেছে, has flown away/escaped. **2** disappear; escape detection: কলমটা কোথায় উড়ে গেল? where can the pen go? **3** be spent up quickly: টাকাগুলো দুদিনেই উড়ে গেল! the money vanished in two days! **4** be blown away by the wind: বাতাসে মেঘ উড়ে গেল. **5** breath one's last প্রাণপাখি উড়ে যাওয়া. **6** খবর শুনে প্রাণ উড়ে গেল lost heart at the news.

উড়ানো, ওড়ানো *vt* **1** cause to fly; fly: সে ঘুড়ি উড়ায়, flies kites. **2** waste money; squander: সে টাকা উড়ায়, makes his money fly; spends it quickly and recklessly. **উড়িয়ে দেওয়া** *vt* **1** let fly in the sky (by setting free): তিনি এক ঝাঁক কবুতর আকাশে উড়িয়ে দিলেন, he let a flight of pigeons loose; set them free. **2** cause to vanish; vanish: যাদুকর তাসটি উড়িয়ে দিলো, vanished the card. **3** neglect; disregard; slight; pay no heed/attention to: কথাটা উড়িয়ে দিয়ো না, don't take it lightly.

উড়াল *n* act of flying. **~ দেওয়া** *vi* take flight: পাখিটি ~ দিলো, took flight; flew away.

উড়ি-উড়ি *adv* about to take flight: বকটি ~ করছে, is about to fly/take flight.

উড়িয়া *n* native of the Indian state of Orissa.

উড়িষ্যা, ওড়িয়া *n* the Inidan state of Orissa.

উড়ু উড়ু *adj* **1** ready to take flight. **2** restless; impatient; fidgety. **~ করা** *vi* be restless/distracted; show signs of impatience: মনটা কেমন ~ করছে, I am in a listless mood. ☐*adv* extremely impatient to go away: তার মন ~ করতে লাগলো, he was miles away in thought/in an abstract mood/with an apathetic or depressed mind.

উড়ো, উড়া *adj* **1** what flies/is capable of flying/is in the course of flight: ~জাহাজ,

aeroplane; airship. **2** not reliable; uncertain; unconfirmed: ~ খবর, unfounded report; unconfirmed news; rumour; hearsay. ~ চিঠি letter without a name or with a name not known to anyone; an anonymous letter.

উতরাই *n* a declivity or downward slope; the descent of a mountain/hill: cf চড়াই.

উতরানো *vi,vt* **1** come/get down; descend. **2** reach/attain the goal. **3** be up to the mark; pass a test: রান্নাটা উতরেছে. **4** attain the set standard; turn out fairly well: লেখাটা উতরেছে. **5** be successful; pass the examination: পরীক্ষায় ~. **6** pass away; come to an end: সময় উতরে গেছে. **7** get/cross over: নদী ~. **8** pull oneself through; pass through: জীবন উতরে গেছে. **9** accomplish what one attempts; make good; prosper: জীবন সংগ্রামে সে উতরে গেছে. **10** (of liquids) boil over: দুধ ~. ❑*n* **1** act of crossing a river/traversing a way. **2** act of being successful.

উতরোল *n* noise; uproar; tumult. ❑*adj* showing signs of impatience; anxious; agitated; restless.

উতলা *adj* **1** troubled with anxiety; worried: ~ হয়ো না, আল্লাহ্ আছেন. **2** overwhelmed with emotion; excited; agitated. **3** very eager for sth; impatient; not enduring delay: খাবার জন্য এত ~ কেন? **4** in a state of perplexity; non-plussed; bewildered; confounded: এখন ~ হওয়ার সময় নয়.

উৎ *pref* denoting 'above', 'excessive', 'contrary', etc, eg উৎ+ক্রম=উৎক্রম, against the serial. উৎকট too strong; excessive.

উৎকট *adj* **1** that which is unbearable; terrible; abnormal: ~ গরম. **2** too strong; odd: ~গন্ধ. **3** hideous; monstrous; frightful: ~ চেহারা. **4** acute; incurable; malignant: ~ ব্যাধি. **5** excessive; hard; unjustified: ~দণ্ড. **6** misguided; perverted; vexatious: ~ রুচি. **7** violent; wild: ~ আনন্দ. **8** intense, profound: ~ আগ্রহ. **9** severe; excessive; acute: ~ ব্যথা. **10** too much; aggressive: ~ স্বাদেশিকতা chauvinism.

উৎকণ্ঠ *adj* anxious (about news, events, decisions, etc).

উৎকণ্ঠা *n* anxiety; mental uneasiness.

উৎকণ্ঠিত *adj* anxious; worried. ~ **হওয়া** *vi* be in a state of anxious suspense.

উৎকর্ণ *adj* all ears; very eager to hear. ~ **হয়ে শোনা** *vi* be all ears; listen attentively.

উৎকর্ষ *n* meritorious quality; notable proficiency; superiority; excellence. ~ **সাধন করা** *vi,vt* cause to become better/ superior/ excellent; improve; ameliorate.

উৎকল *n* old name for Orissa, the Indian state.

উৎকলিকা *n* **1** anxiety. **2** embryonic growth of a flower; a bud. **3** a wave or swell on the water surface.

উৎকলিত *adj* **1** quoted/extracted (from). **2** anxious. **3** wavy; billowy; undulating.

উৎকীরণ *n* act of engraving/carving/inscribing.

উৎকীর্ণ *adj* **1** engraved; carved; inscribed. **2** painted; drawn. **3** pierced; perforated. **4** thrown up or tossed up. ~ **লিপি** *n* inscription.

উৎকীর্তন *n* **1** proclamation; announcement; publicity. **2** propagation; dissemination. **3** laudation; high praise. **উৎকীর্তিত** *adj* what has been proclaimed, lauded or propagated.

উৎকুণ *n* the louse (*pl* lice).

উৎকৃষ্ট *adj* **1** good; excellent; fine. **2** elevated; exalted. ~**তা** *n* excellence; eminence; superiority. ~**রূপে** *adv* excellently; in an excellent manner.

উৎকেন্দ্রিক *adj* **1** (of persons) peculiar in habits and behaviour; not normal; eccentric. **2** (of circles) not having the axis in the centre; eccentric. ~**তা** *n* **1** strange/unusual acts and habits, eg in dress, etc; eccentricity. **2** a wheel with its axle not co-axial with the exact centre of the wheel; the condition of being eccentric.

উৎকোচ *n* illegal gratification; a bribe. ~ **দান** *n* bribery. ~ **দেওয়া** *vi* bribe. ~ **নেওয়া** *vi* receive a bribe. ~**ক** *n* a briber. ~ **গ্রাহী** *adj, n* one who accepts a bribe.

উৎক্রম *n* **1** break of order/sequence; exception. **2** inverse or reverse order. **3** deviation; violation; infringement. **4** act of sprouting or shooting up. **5** act of coming or going out. **6** departure of the soul from the body; death. ~**ণ** *n* **1** an inverse or reverse movement. **2** a reversion of order; disorder. **3** ending of life; decease; death. **4** (gr) disorderly transposition of words within a sentence.

উৎক্রান্তি *n* **1** shooting forth; sprouting. **2** surpassing or transgressing. **3** gradual rising or ascension. **4** act of coming or going out. **5** extinction of life; death; demise.

উৎক্রোশ *n* **1** large kind of hawk; the sea-eagle; the osprey. **2** a shout, scream or uproar.

উৎক্ষিপ্ত *adj* **1** thrown up into/through the air. ~ **হওয়া** be launched. **2** torn up by the roots; uprooted.

উৎক্ষেপ, উৎক্ষেপণ *n* act of throwing up, tossing up or launching. ~**ক** *adj* what throws up/launches (eg, a rocket).

উৎখাত *adj* **1** torn up by the roots; uprooted. **2** destroyed; eradicated; extirpated. **3** divested (of); deprived (of); removed (from); ejected; evicted: ক্ষমতা থেকে ~ deposed; divested of/removed from powers. ~ **করা** *vt* root out;

uproot; destroy; eradicate; extirpate; eject; evict; remove (from power).

উত্তপ্ত *adj* **1** very hot/heated. **2** hot with anger; enraged; excited.

উত্তম *adj* **1** good; fine; excellent. **2** having good qualities in the highest degree; best. **3** highly pleasing; delightful; delicious. ❑*adv, int* well; good. **উত্তমা** *fem* **~ পুরুষ** *n* (gr) the first person. **~ মধ্যম** *n* (facet) good beating; drubbing. **~ মধ্যম দেওয়া** *vi* give a sound drubbing.

উত্তমর্ণ *n, adj* one to whom a debt is owed; creditor; money-lender: (opp অধমর্ণ).

উত্তমাঙ্গ *n* **1** the head. **2** the upper portion of human body; the principal part of the body from the head to the waist.

উত্তমাশা [উত্তম+আশা] *n* the South African promontory called the Cape of Good Hope.

উত্তর *n* **1** answer; reply; retort: প্রশ্নের ~, answer to a question; চিঠির ~, reply to a letter; অপমানের সমুচিত ~, the retorting of insult for insult; **সমুচিত ~ দেওয়া** *vi, vt* retort; make a fitting retort; reply back in retaliation. **2** response; answer to a call. **3** the north; the opposite of 'দক্ষিণ'. **4** solution of an arithmetical sum; result of working with figures. **5** (legal) reply to/refutation of a charge or pleading; a rejoinder. ❑*adj* **1** future; that is to be/to come: ~ পুরুষ, future generation(s). **2** later; subsequent; succeeding: যুদ্ধোত্তর (যুদ্ধ+উত্তর) পুনর্গঠন, post-war reconstruction. **3** rare; uncommon; extraordinary; super-human: লোকোত্তর লোক+উত্তর প্রতিভা extra-ordinary genius. **4** (of a chapter of a book) concluding; last; final: উত্তর কাণ্ড, concluding chapter; final act; last incident/affair. ❑*adv* immediately after; thereafter; afterward: স্বাধীনতা ~ কালে, in the post-liberation period. **~ করা** *vt* **1** retort; argue. **2** respond. **~ দেওয়া** *vt* **1** answer; reply. **2** respond. **~কাল** *n* the future; the subsequent/succeeding age. **~কালীন** *adj* of the future/subsequent time: ~কালীন মানুষ, the future generation(s). **~কালে** *adv* in future; subsequently. **~ক্রিয়া** *n* last rites; funeral obsequies. **~চ্ছদ** *n* **1** outer garment. **2** bed-sheet; bed-cover. **3** a scarf; a wrapper. **~পত্র** *n* script containing the answers of an examinee; answer-script. **~পশ্চিম** *n, adj* (the) north-west; north-western: ~পশ্চিম সীমান্ত, the north-western frontier. **~পশ্চিমে** *adv* to or towards the north-west: ঢাকার ৩০ মাইল ~ পশ্চিমে, 30 miles north-west of Dhaka. **~পুরুষ** *n* the descendants; the posterity; the succeeding generation(s). **~পূর্ব** *n* the north-east. ❑*adj* north-eastern. **~পূর্ব দিকে** *adv* to the north-eastern direction: ২০ মাইল ~ পূর্বে অবস্থিত, situated 20 miles north-east. **~প্রত্যুত্তর** *n* reply and counter-reply; altercation; bandying of words. **~প্রত্যুত্তর করা** *vi* altercate; wrangle. **~বেতন** *n* stated monthly allowance drawn by an employee on completion of the term of service; pension. **~মেরু** *n* the north extremity of the earth's axis; the North Pole; the frigid zone round the North Pole. **~সাধক** *n* **1** a devotee or votary of the later time. **2** the chief assistant of a 'Tantrik' religious teacher. **~সাধিকা** *fem.* **~সূরি** *n, adj* spiritual descendant; (poet or wiseman) of the later time.

উত্তরঙ্গ *adj* full of waves: ~ সাগর, the billowy sea.

উত্তরণ *n* **1** act of crossing a river or sea. **2** act of reaching the destination.

উত্তরাধিকার *n* right of inheriting the property of a deceased; legal right to succeed to a title or property when the owner dies; inheritance. **~সূত্র** *n* the chain of succession through blood relationship. **~সূত্রে** *adv* by way of inheritance. **উত্তরাধিকারী** *n* heir; inheritor; successor. **উত্তরাধিকারিণী** *fem* .

উত্তরাপথ *n* northern part of India lying between the Himalayas and the Vindhyas; Upper India: cf দক্ষিণাপথ.

উত্তরায়ণ *n* the gradual movement of the sun to the point farthest north of the equator; the period during which this northward movement takes place, ie., between 22nd December and 21st june; the Summer solstice. **উত্তরায়ণান্তবৃত্ত** *n* the line of latitude 23° 27′ north; the Tropic of Cancer.

উত্তরিয়া=উত্তুরে

উত্তরীয়, উত্তরী *n* outer garment; a wrapper.

উত্তরোত্তর *adv* gradually; by degrees; successively: ~ শ্রীবৃদ্ধি.

উত্তল *adj* having a surface curved like the outside of a ball; of the shape of a half-circle; convex.

উত্তাপ *n* **1** heat; warmth. **2** warm emotion; ardour; zeal. **উত্তাপিত** *adj* **1** that has been heated; warmed-up. **2** excited; roused. **উত্তাপিত করা** *vi, vt* **1** heat up; warm up. **2** stir up the feelings; excite.

উত্তাল *adj* **1** very high: ~ তরঙ্গ, high waves. **2** billowy; violent; dreadful: ~ সমুদ্র, billowy sea. **3** noisy; boisterous; roaring. **4** emotionally aroused; agitated; upset: ~ হৃদয়. **~তা** *n.*

উত্তীর্ণ *adj* **1** one who has become successful: পরীক্ষায় ~. **2** that which has passed beyond/elapsed: সময় ~. **3** one who has crossed/got over: নদী ~, পথ ~, বিপদে ~. **~ হওয়া** *vi, vt* **1** be successful; pass: সে পরীক্ষায় ~ হয়েছে has passed/come out successful in the examination. **2** cross (a river, a distance etc.). **3** get over (a difficulty, etc). **4** be over/up: সময় ~ হয়েছে the time is up.

উত্তুঙ্গ *adj* very high; lofty. ~ শৃঙ্গ lofty peaks. ~**তা** *n.*

উত্তুরে, উত্তরিয়া *adj* coming from the north; northerly: ~ হাওয়া.

উত্তেজক *adj* producing excitement; exciting: ~ ঔষধ. ❑*n* anything that increases bodily or mental activity; stimulant.

উত্তেজন *n* **1** act of causing excitement/ sensation. **2** act of encouraging or stimulating.

উত্তেজনা *n* state of being excited; excitement; sensation; agitation: আমাদের বিজয়ের সংবাদ জনসাধারণের মধ্যে প্রবল ~ সৃষ্টি করে, the news of our victory caused a great sensation among the people. ~**কর সংবাদ** sensational/ thrilling/ exciting news. **চাপা** ~ mental or emotional strain; tension.

উত্তেজিত *adj* excited; agitated. ~ **করা** *vt* **1** incite; agitate; induce: শ্রমিক নেতাগণ শ্রমিকদের ধর্মঘট করার জন্য ~ করছে, the labour (union) leaders are inciting the workers to strike work. **2** cause to be active; stimulate/rouse (sb to sth/to do sth); encourage. ~ **হওয়া** *vt* be excited/encouraged.

উত্তোলন *n* act of raising or lifting up. **ভারোত্তলন** *n* lifting of weight; weight-lifting. ~ **করা** *vt* raise; lift up.

উত্তোলিত *adj* that which has been raised/lifted up/placed high.

উত্যক্ত *adj* one who is being annoyed/ vexed/ harassed. ~ **করা** *vt* cause annoyance or vexation to sb. ~ **হওয়া** be vexed/annoyed.

উত্থান *n* **1** rising from the sitting or lying position: গাত্রোত্থান (গাত্র+~). **2** coming into prominence; flourishing movement ; rise; emergence. **3** coming of the dead to life; resurrection: পুনরুত্থান (পুনঃ+~). **4** rising in rebellion; insurrection; insurgence: মুঘল সাম্রাজ্যের বিরুদ্ধে মারাঠাদের ~, the rising of the Marhattas against the Mughal empire. ~**পতন** rise and fall.

উত্থাপক *adj* one who puts up/moves/brings forward (a proposal, etc.). ❑*n* a proposer or a mover.

উত্থাপন *n* act of introducing/moving (a bill, proposal, etc.) ~ **করা** *vi, vt* introduce; propose; move (a bill, etc.). **আপত্তি ~ করা, প্রশ্ন ~ করা** raise an objection, etc. **উত্থাপনীয়** *adj* (fit) to be raised/moved/brought forward. **উত্থাপিত** *adj* that has been raised/put up.

উত্থিত *adj* **1** that has got up; risen. **2** that which/has come out/sprouted. **3** high; exalted; increased. **4** one who has stood against (sb/sth). ~ **হওয়া** *vi, vt* rise; occur; get up; crop up.

উৎপত্তি *n* **1** starting-point; beginning; source; origin: মানস সরোবর ব্রহ্মপুত্রের ~ ক্ষেত্র, the Brahmaputra originates/has its sources at the Manas Sarobar. **2** birth; begetting generation: অনিষ্ট থেকে অনিষ্টের ~, evil begets evil. **3** source from which knowledge of sth is derived; origination: জ্ঞানের ~. ~**মূল** *n* source of origin. ~**স্থল,** ~**স্থান** *n* the source; the place of origin.

উৎপন্ন *adj* **1** that has grown/been produced from the soil: ~ ফসল, crops grown. **2** goods manufactured at factories; industrial product. ~ **করা** *vt* give birth (to); grow; produce; manufacture. ~ **হওয়া** *vt* be born, created, produced or manufactured. **কৃষি-~ দ্রব্য** agricultural produce. **শিল্প- ~ দ্রব্য** industrial products.

উৎপল *n* the water-lily; the lotus: নীলোৎপল (নীল+~) the blue lotus. **উৎপলাক্ষ** *adj* having eyes like the petals of a lotus; lotus-eyed; blue-eyed. **উৎপলাক্ষী** *fem.*

উৎপাটক *n, adj* one who/that which pulls up sth by the roots; (fig) one who eradicates or destroys sth.

উৎপাটন *n* act of tearing up by the roots; uprooting; extirpation; eradication. ~ **করা** *vt* root out, uproot; eradicate; (fig) destroy; evict; remove. **উৎপাটনীয়** *adj* fit to be uprooted or destroyed.

উৎপাত *n* **1** thing, person, act, etc that causes damage, hindrance, injury, annoyance, etc; a nuisance: মশার ~, বাচ্চাদের ~. **2** natural calamity; Act of God (eg., earthquake, flood etc). ~ **করা** *vt* cause annoyance, irritation, disturbance or damage. **উতপেতে** *adj* causing nuisance.

উৎপাদক *adj* **1** one who creates, grows, produces or manufactures sth. **2** one who begets or gives existence as father. **3** that which generates sth (eg, electricity); generative. ❑*n* (arith) whole number by which a larger number can be divided exactly; a factor. **উৎপাদিকা** *fem.*

উৎপীড়ক *adj* oppressive; tyrannical; persecuting. ❑*n* one who treats with injustice and cruelty; an oppressor.

উৎপীড়ন *n* the condition of being oppressed; oppression; tyranny; persecution. ~ **করা** *vt* oppress; tyrannize; persecute.

উৎপীড়িত *adj* oppressed; tyrannized; persecuted; tortured. ~ **হওয়া** *vt* be oppressed etc.

উৎপেতে⇒উৎপাত

উৎফুল্ল *adj* **1** highly delighted; elated; jubilant; exultant. ~ **হওয়া** *vu,* be delighted/ cheerful/ elated. **2** blooming; blown; unfolded.

উৎরাই⇒উতরাই

উৎস *n* **1** starting point; source: ক্ষমতার ~. **2** a fountain; a spring; a cascade or waterfall. ~**মুখ** *n* **1** the source of a fountain; fountain-head. **2** the place of origin; the source.

উৎসন্ন, উচ্ছন্ন *adj* **1** gone to the dogs; spoilt; ruined. **2** downfallen; deteriorated; debased. **উৎসন্নে/উচ্ছন্নে যাওয়া** *vi* go to the dogs; be spoiled.

উৎসব *n* that which gives pleasure; a ceremonial function on some occasion, eg, marriage; birth-day, etc, a festival; festivities: বিবাহ ~, marriage ceremony; ঈদ ~, Eid festival. ~ **করা** hold a function. ~ **পালন করা** observe/celebrate an occasion. ~**মুখর** *adj* festive and joyous.

উৎসর্গ *n* **1** act of dedicating sth by sb for a noble cause: তিনি দেশের সেবায় জীবন ~ করেন, he dedicated his life to the service of his country. **2** offering of sth precious to a deity; sacrifice. **3** gift or foundation for public welfare. **4** dedicating a book by its author to someone. ~ **করা** *vi, vt* dedicate; offer as an oblation; sacrifice **উৎসর্গীকৃত** *adj* dedicated; sacrificed.

উৎসারণ *n* **1** act of throwing upwards. **2** act of removing/eliminating. **উৎসারিত** *adj* **1** thrown or pressed upwards (as by a spring). **2** removed; eliminated.

উৎসাহ *n* **1** eagerness in work; enterprise. **2** passionate ardour; zeal; enthusiasm. ~ **দেওয়া** *vt* inspire with courage; encourage; give confidence to. ~**দাতা** *n* one who encourages; encourager. ~**জনক/ব্যঞ্জক** *adj* inspiring confidence; encouraging. **উৎসাহিত** *adj* animated with confidence; encouraged. **উৎসাহিত হওয়া** *vt* be inspired with hope and confidence; be encouraged. **উৎসাহী** *adj* zealous; energetic; enthusiastic. ❑*n* an enthusiast.

উৎসুক *adj* **1** keenly desirous; eager: আমরা ~ হয়ে গল্পটি শুনলাম, we listened to the story with eager attention. **2** eager to know or learn; inquisitive; curious: ~ পাঠক এ বই থেকে উপকৃত হবেন, curious/inquisitive readers will benefit from this book. ঔৎসুক্য *n.*

উথল=উথাল

উথলানো *vt* **1** become greater in volume; swell up: দুধ ~. **2** surge up; roll on like waves: তার টাকা উথলে উঠেছে, he is rolling in wealth. **উথলে ওঠা** *vt* (fig) rise to affluence; become wealthy. **উথলিত** *adj* puffed up; swollen; over-flowing.

উথাল *adj* **1** swollen; billowy: ~ সমুদ্র. **2** very high: ~ তরঙ্গ. ~**-পাথাল** *adj* (of the surface of sea, etc) stirred up/agitated/lashed into fury by rolling waves.

উদ, উদ্বিড়াল *n* fish-eating aquatic animal; the otter.

উদগ্র [উৎ+অগ্র] *adj* **1** keen; strong: ~ বাসনা). **2** severe; fierce (~ তাপ). **3** extreme; radical: ~ রাজনীতি.

উদজ *adj* growing in water; water-born; aquatic.

উদ্‌জান *n* the gaseous elementary substance which combines with oxygen to form water; hydrogen. ~ **বোমা** *n* a variety of atomic bomb.

উদম⇒উদাম

উদয় *n* **1** rise; appearance: চন্দ্রোদয় (চন্দ্র+~). **2** dawning: তার মনে আশার ~ হলো. ~**কাল** *n* the time of sunrise.

উদয়াচল *n* horizon where the sun begins to rise.

উদয়াস্ত *n* **1** time from sunrise to sunset; day-time. **2** sunrise and sunset. ❑*adv* from sunrise to sunset; all day long; throughout the day.

উদর *n* **1** part of the body which contains the bowels; the belly. **2** female organ in which offspring is conceived; the womb. ~**সর্বস্ব** *adj* given to too much eating; voracious; gluttonous. ~**স্থ** *adj* eaten up; swallowed. ~**স্থ করা** *vt* eat up; swallow. **উদরান্ন** (~+অন্ন) *n* indispensable food; living; livelihood.

উদরাময় (উদর+আময়) *n* disease of the intestines causing frequent evacuation; diarrhoea.

উদলা *adj* with no clothing on the upper part of the body; uncovered; bare: ~ গা.

উদাত্ত *adj* **1** loud and sonorous; powerful: ~ কণ্ঠ, clarion voice; ~ আহ্বান, clarion call, stirring invitation. **2** noble; kind; generous; bountiful; বিশ্বব্রহ্মাণ্ড স্রষ্টার ~ মহিমা কীর্তন করে, the universe proclaims the glorious majesty of the Creator. ❑*n* (music) **1** high or sharp tone.

উদাম *adj* uncovered: খাবার ~ রয়েছে, the food is uncovered.

উদার *adj* **1** generous; liberal; open-hearted: দুঃস্থ ও দরিদ্রের প্রতি তিনি সর্বদা ~, always generous to the poor and the needy; তিনি দুর্গতদের সাহায্যে ~ হস্তে দান করেন, donated to the welfare of the distressed with open-handed liberality. ~**মতবাদ** liberal views; ~ **উপহার** a generous gift. **2** noble-minded; high-minded; magnanimous; munificent: ~চরিত, ~চিত্ত, ~চেতা. **3** open; wide; high: ~ আকাশ, ~ সমুদ্র. ~**তা** *n* greatness of heart; nobility of mind; liberality; generosity, magnanimity; munificence.

উদারনৈতিক *adj* liberal. ❑*n* member of the Liberal Party of Great Britain. ~ **দল** *n* the Liberal party; the Liberals.

উদারপন্থী=উদারনৈতিক

উদারা *n* (music) the first of the three musical notes (উদারা, মুদারা, তারা).

উদাস *adj* **1** having no wish or interest in worldly affairs; indifferent; apathetic; free from attachment. **2** low-spirited; sad; melancholy. ~ **হওয়া** be in a listless state of mind/in an abstract mood. ~ **দৃষ্টি** vacant look.

উদাসিনী⇒উদাসী, উদাসীন

উদাসী *adj* in a state of apathy/indifference; callous; disinterested. **উদাসিনী** *fem.*

উদাসীন *adj* having no interest in; neither for nor against; indifferent. **উদাসিনী** *fem.* **উদাস, উদাসী** and **উদাসীন** are often synonymous; but the first two are generally used in the sense of inattentiveness; while the third in the sense of indifference.

উদাহরণ *n* example; instance: বদান্যতার ~, instance of generosity. **উদাহৃত** *adj* cited or presented as an instance.

উদিত *adj* **1** risen; risen up: সূর্য ~ হয়েছে, the sun is up. **2** grown; shot up: চারা ~ হয়েছে, the seeds have shot up. ~ **হওয়া** *vt* rise; appear; come up.

উদীচী *n* the north. ~ **উষা** *n* luminous phenomenon seen at night in the northern sky especially in the regions of the North Pole; Aurora Borealis (cf অবাচী ঊষা). **উদীচ্য** *adj* belonging to the north.

উদীয়মান *adj* **1** rising; ascending: ~ সূর্য. **2** promising; flourishing; likely to get on or succeed: ~ কবি.

উদো *adj* dull-witted; stupid. ❑*n* a dunce; a dullard; a dolt. **উদোর পিণ্ডি বুধোর গাড়ে** (prov) one doth the scath and another hath the scorn; the boot is on the wrong leg; make a cat's paw of a person.

উদ্‌গত *adj* sprung up; sprouted. *n* **উদ্‌গম** sprouting; shooting forth. ~**কর্ম** *n* (sculpture) art of carving in which the figures stand out from the background; relief-work.

উদ্‌গাতা *n* reciter of the prayers of Sama Veda. ❑*adj* singing in a loud voice; (fig) exponent of a message, etc: **মুক্তিমন্ত্রের মহা** ~. **উদ্‌গাত্রী** *fem.*

উদ্‌গার *n* **1** ejection of wind, etc from the stomach; a belch; a hiccup; eructation; vomitting. ~ **তোলা** *vt* belch; eruct; eructate; hiccup; vomit. **2** emitting of smoke, etc.: ধূম্রোদ্‌গার (ধূম্র+~). **3** venting or expressing (grievances, etc): বিষোদ্‌গার (বিষ+~).

উদ্‌গিরণ *n* act of casting out; vomiting; belching; eructation. ~ **করা** *vt* disgorge, vomit, eructate; belch.

উদ্‌গ্রীব *adj* showing strong desire (for sth); extremely eager; full of curiosity; anxious.

উদ্‌ঘাটন *n* **1** act of unlocking/uncovering; ceremonial opening: দ্বারোদ্‌ঘাটন (দ্বার+~). **2** bringing to light; revelation; discovery. ~ **করা** *vt* open; unveil; reveal; bring to light.

উদ্‌ঘাটিত *adj* opened; unveiled; revealed.

উদ্দণ্ড *adj* with a raised stick in hand; ready to inflict punishment. ~ **নৃত্য** *n* wild dance with hands uplifted.

উদ্দাম *adj* **1** uncontrollable; indomitable: ~ বাসনা. **2** unrestrained; uncontrolled; unbound; intractable: ~ কেশপাশ. **3** wilful; self-willed; wanton violent. ~**তা** *n* recklessness; waywardness; indiscipline; impetuosity.

উদ্দিস্ট *adj* that has been aimed at; desired; intended; wished for.

উদ্দীপক *adj* **1** having the power to stimulate/encourage/inspire; stimulating; encouraging; inspiring. **2** provoking; inciting: হাস্যোদ্দীপক (হাস্য+~), ক্রোধোদ্দীপক (ক্রোধ+~). ❑*n* stimulus; stimulant; incentive.

উদ্দীপন *n* act of stimulating/encouraging/inspiring. **উদ্দীপনা** *n* **1** encouragement; impetus; inspiration. **2** enthusiasm; exuberance: বিজয় দিবসে জনতার মধ্যে প্রবল উদ্দীপনা লক্ষ করা যায়, the people showed great enthusiasm/exuberance to celebrate the victory day; তাঁর কথায় আমাদের প্রাণে উদ্দীপনার সঞ্চার হয়েছে, His words infused great enthusiasm in our hearts. **উদ্দীপিত** *adj* enkindled; animated/infused with. **উদ্দীপিত করা** *vt* enkindle; animate/infuse with.

উদ্দীপ্ত *adj* **1** that has been enkindled or illuminated. **2** flared up; incited; excited. ~ **করা** *vt* inflame; enkindle; flare up.

উদ্দেশ *n* **1** that which is aimed at; aim; intention; direction; purpose: নদী নিরন্তর বয়ে চলে সাগরের উদ্দেশে, a river flows on to meet the sea. **2** presence or existence of sb/sth; trace: নিরুদ্দেশ (নিঃ+~), traceless; missing. **3** the place for which sb/sth in bound; destination: নিরুদ্দেশ যাত্রা, a journey without a destination.

উদ্দেশ্য *n* **1** the desired result of one's efforts; aim: তোমার জীবনের ~কী? what is your aim in life? **2** that which urges a person to act in a certain way; motive; design; intention: খুনের ~, motive behind a murder. **3** the meaning or significance of anything. **4** (gram) subject in a sentence, ie, noun; pronoun, etc. ~**মূলকভাবে** *adv* with a motive. ~**হীনভাবে** *adv* aimlessly.

উদ্ধত *adj* **1** proud and disdainful; impolite; insolent. **2** haughty; arrogant; obstinate; stubborn; headstrong. **ঔদ্ধত্য** *n* .

উদ্ধার *n* **1** act of delivering sb from confinement; danger or evil পতিতা ~; deliverance; rescue. **2** recovery of anything lost or forgotten: সম্পত্তি ~. ~ **করা** *vt* deliver; rescue; recover. ~ **পাওয়া** *vt* get rid; become free. ~**কর্তা** *n* one who saves a person or people from danger or evil; deliverer; rescuer; saviour.

উদ্ধৃত *adj* quoted or cited as from some author. ~ করা *vi, vt* quote or make a quotation; cite or repeat a passage, etc already published. উদ্ধৃতাংশ *n* passage quoted from a writing; an extract; an excerpt. উদ্ধৃতি *n* that which is quoted; a quotation.

উদ্বন্ধন *n* death by hanging. উদ্বন্ধনে প্রাণত্যাগ করা *vi, vt* (commit suicide) by suspending oneself by the neck; উদ্বন্ধক *n* one who commits suicide by hanging.

উদ্বায়ী *adj* subject to quick evaporation; readily diffusible in the atmosphere; volatile.

উদ্বাসন *n* expulsion from one's native country; deportation; exile.

উদ্বাস্তু *n* person who has been forced to flee from danger, eg from floods; war; political persecution, etc; one who flies for refuge; refugee: ~ সমস্যা, ~ পুনর্বাসন.

উদ্বাহ *n* marriage; wedding ~ন *n* act of giving away in marriage. ~-বন্ধন *n* bond of wedlock; marriage tie. উদ্বাহিক, ঔদ্বাহিক *adj*.

উদ্বাহু *adj* one with hands uplifted.

উদ্বিগ্ন *adj* suffering mental distress; worried anxious; concerned. ~তা *n* worry; anxiety.

উদ্বিড়াল ⇒ উদ

উদ্বুদ্ধ *adj* 1 moved by inspiration; inspired: দেশপ্রেমে ~, inspired by patriotism. 2 enlightened; awakened. ~করণ *n* act of motivating (sb into sth); motivation.

উদ্বৃত্ত *n, adj* excess beyond what is required; excess of receipts over expenditure; surplus; balance: ~ রাজস্ব.

উদ্বেগ *n* concern about some uncertain event; state of being anxious; anxiety; worry. উদ্বেগাকুল (~+আকুল) *adj* overwhelmed with mental distress.

উদ্বেল, উদ্বেলিত *adj* 1 flowing over the bank; overflowing; crossing the limit. 2 effusive (with love; emotion, etc): উদ্বেলিত হৃদয়.

উদ্বোধন *n* act of opening/inaugurating/with suitable ceremonies: ~ অনুষ্ঠান, opening ceremony. ~ করা *vt* inaugurate. উদ্বোধনী *adj* relating to the opening ceremony: উদ্বোধনী সঙ্গীত.

উদ্ভট *adj* 1 out of the ordinary; unusual; peculiar: ~ কাণ্ড. 2 bizarre; fantastic; eccentric: ~কল্পনা.

উদ্ভব *n* the process of being originated; the act of coming into existence; rise; origin; birth.

উদ্ভাবন *n* act of inventing or contriving new things. ~ করা *vt* devise or produce sth that did not exist before; invent; contrive; design. উপায় ~ করা find a way of doing sth. উদ্ভাবক *n* an inventor; a contriver; a designer. উদ্ভাবিত *adj* invented; devised; designed; produced.

উদ্ভাস *n* brightness shooting in rays; lustre; radiance; glow; illumination. উদ্ভাসিত *adj* brightened up; illuminated. উদ্ভাসিত করা *vt* illuminate; brighten up.

উদ্ভিজ্জ *adj* produced or derived from a plant/vegetables. ~ তেল vegetable oil. উদ্ভিদ *n* that which grows or shoots up from beneath the surface of the earth; trees; plants; shrubs; vegetables, etc. ~ বিদ্যা *n* the science which treats of plants; Botany.

উদ্ভিন্ন *adj* 1 sprouted; germinated. 2 fully developed; full-blown. ~ যৌবন *adj* in the bloom of youth. ~যৌবনা *fem.*

উদ্ভূত *adj* what has arisen/developed/sprung up. ~ হওয়া *vi* arise; spring up; develop; come into view. ~ পরিস্থিতি *n* circumstances as obtaining. ~ পরিস্থিতিতে *adv* in the prevailing circumstances.

উদ্ভেদ *n* 1 a shoot of a bud, plant, etc; act of shooting/blooming: পুষ্পোদ্ভেদ (পুষ্প+~), অঙ্কুরোদ্ভেদ (অঙ্কুর+~). 2 outcrop of a boil; tumour, etc. over the skin. 3 revelation; appearance; manifestation (যৌবনোদ্ভেদ).

উদ্‌ভ্রম *n* mental aberration; bewilderment.

উদ্‌ভ্রান্ত *adj* bereft of senses; bewildered; nonplussed; confused: ~ প্রেম, overwhelming/frantic love. ~ভাবে *adv* wildly; madly; distractedly.

উদ্যত *adj* 1 ready/prepared/about to (do sth); on the point of (doing a thing): আঘাত করতে ~. ~ হওয়া *vt* attempt (to do sth). 2 raised; lifted; held up: ~ কৃপাণ

উদ্যম *n* 1 ardent zeal; enthusiasm; perseverance (ভগ্নোদ্যম). 2 effort; endeavour; enterprise; attempt; exertion (নিরুদ্যম). ~শীল, উদ্যমী *adj* enthusiastic; enterprising; persevering; diligent.

উদ্যান *n* a garden, park or grove; a delightful spot for recreation. ~পালন *n* the act or art of cultivating gardens; horticulture; gardening.

উদ্‌যাপন *n* 1 ceremonial observance/ celebration (of an event; occasion, etc): আন্তর্জাতিক শিশুদিবস ~, বিবাহ বার্ষিকী ~. ~ করা *vt* mark an event with public or private rejoicings; celebrate. উদ্‌যাপিত *adj* (an occasion, etc) observed with appropriate solemnity; celebrated.

উদ্যোক্তা *n* one who takes the initiative or makes necessary preparations for doing sth.

উদ্যোগ *n* effort; endeavour; enterprise. ~ গ্রহণ করা, উদ্যোগী হওয়া *vi* take the initiative.

উদ্রেক *n* incitement; rousing; excitement: ঘৃণার ~, ক্ষুধার ~. ~ করা *vt* cause to feel; stir up the feelings; excite; incite; rouse.

উধাও *adj* **1** vanished; disappeared. **2** out of sight; traceless. ❑*n* that which has taken an upward flight/flown away. ~ **হওয়া** *vi* flee/slip away; disappear; go out of sight.

উন⇒উন

উনচল্লিশ *n, adj* thirty-nine.

উনআশি *n, adj* seventy-nine.

উনত্রিশ *n, adj* twenty-nine.

উনন (dial)⇒উনান

উননব্বই *n, adj* eighty-nine.

উনষাট *n, adj* fifty-nine.

উনা, উনো *adj* less; least; minimum. **উনোভাতে দুনো বল** (prov) eat less and gain more strength. **উনা বর্ষা দুনা শীত** the year with less rainfall is doubly cold.

উনান, উনুন *n* an oven; a furnace; a stove. ~ **ধরানো** *vi* light an oven; make a fire.

উনাশি *n, adj* (colloq) seventy-nine.

উনি *pron* (respectful, cf সে) person in front; person referred to; he; she: ~ বড়োলোক.

উনিশ *n, adj* nineteen. ~**-বিশ** *n* negligible difference. ~**-বিশ করা** *vi, vt* treat with partiality. ~**-বিশ হওয়া** differ slightly. **উনিশে** *n* the nineteenth day of a month. ❑*adj* (of date) nineteenth.

উন্নত *adj* **1** (of moral excellence) noble; great; generous: ~মনা, high minded. **2** high; tall; lofty; elevated: ~ শৃঙ্গ. **3** prosperous; advanced; flourishing: ~ দেশ, ~ অবস্থা. **4** polished; refined: ~ রুচি.

উন্নতি *n* flourishing state; success; prosperity. ~ **(সাধন) করা** *vi* increase in wealth, etc; thrive; prosper. ~**শীল** *adj* flourishing; thriving; prosperous.

উন্নয়ন *n* **1** the act or action of developing; the state of being developed. **2** development; uplift. ~ **প্রকল্প** *n* (economic or other) project for development; development project. ~**শীল দেশ/জাতি** *n* a developing country/nation.

উন্নাসিক *adj* lofty with pride; haughty; overbearing; supercilious; snob. ~**তা** *n* snobbery; snobbishness.

উন্নীত *adj* **1** one who has been elevated or uplifted. **2** promoted; upgraded. ~**করা** *vi* **1** raise; lift; elevate. **2** cause to improve/prosper/flourish.

উন্মত্ত *adj* **1** highly overwrought with passion or emotion; frantic; crazy; frenzied. **2** drunk; intoxicated. **উন্মত্তা** *fem*. ~**তা** *n* craziness; craze; frenzy; intoxication; loss of self-possession.

উন্মনা *adj* **1** mentally agitated; listless; indifferent; absent-minded. **2** worried; anxious.

উন্মাদ *adj* **1** mentally ill; uncontrolled by reason; mad; insane; lunatic. **1** frenzied; frantic; furious. ~ **হওয়া** *vi* go mad; ~ **আশ্রম** *n* lunatic asylum. **উন্মাদিনী** *fem*.

উন্মাদনা *n* great enthusiasm (for sth); violent excitement.

উন্মীলন *n* opening (as of eyes); blooming; unfolding. ~ **করা** *vt* unfold; open.

উন্মীলিত *adj* opened; unclosed; blown; exposed.

উন্মুক্ত *adj* **1** not shut, covered or blocked; open. **2** released; liberated; set free; at liberty. **3** not restricted; accessible. **4** frank; candid; liberal; bounteous. ~ **করা** *vt* open; unsheathe; release.

উন্মুখ *adj* **1** keenly desirous; eager; anxious. **2** looking forward; on the tip-toe of expectation. **3** ready; prepared.

উন্মূলন *n* act of tearing up by the roots; eradication; extirpation. ~ **করা** *vt* uproot; eradicate; extirpate. **উন্মূলিত** *adj* uprooted; eradicated; destroyed.

উন্মেষ, উন্মেষণ *n* act of opening the folds of; unfolding; budding; blooming: ভাবের ~, rise or striking of an idea in the mind; ভালবাসার ~, growth/appearance/manifestation of love in one's heart. **উন্মেষিত** *adj* unfolded; manifested.

উন্মোচন *n* **1** act of unveiling or uncovering. **2** act of untying or setting free. ~ **করা** *vt* unveil; uncover; untie; release. **উন্মোচিত** *adj* unveiled; uncovered; untied.

উপ *pref* indicating nearness, similarity, subordination, incompleteness, shortcoming, etc and is equivalent to sub-, under-, deputy-, assistant-, etc, eg উপাধ্যক্ষ (~+অধ্যক্ষ).

উপকণ্ঠ *n* outer areas/outlying parts (esp of a city); outskirts; suburb: নগরীর ~.

উপকথা *n* old story handed down from the past having little possible base in truth; a legend; a folk tale; a fable.

উপকরণ *n* the ingredients or constituent parts that make up a thing: পূজার ~.

উপকার *n* **1** doing good; benefaction; favour; help. ~ **করা** *vi* do good (to); favour; help. **উপকারিতা** *n* usefulness or advantage given by sth; helpfulness; benefit; beneficence. **উপকারী** *adj* **1** one who has given friendly help; benefactor. **2** (of things) (also ~ক) helpful; useful: খেলাধুলা স্বাস্থ্যের জন্য উপকারী. **উপকারিণী** *fem*. **উপকারে আসা** *vi* be of use to sb/sth; be helpful/beneficent (to).

উপকূল *n* coastal belt; seashore; beach.

উপকৃত *adj* one who has been benefited.

উপক্রম *n* preparations serving as a prelude to sth; state of being on the point (of): বৃষ্টির ~ দেখা যাচ্ছে. ~ **হওয়া** *vt* be on the point of; be about to (do sth).

উপক্রমণিকা *n* 1 beginning; commencement; prelude. 2 introductory chapter of a book; a prologue; a preface.

উপগত *adj* in the state of sexual intercourse. ~ হওয়া *vi* make love.

উপগমন *n* 1 (lit) act of going near. 2 mating; sexual union.

উপগম্য *adj* worthy of being sexually united/mated. উপগম্যা *fem*.

উপগ্রহ *n* heavenly body moving round a planet; a satellite: চন্দ্র পৃথিবীর ~.

উপচয় *n* (opp অপচয়) 1 increase; prosperity; affluence; nourishment. 2 increase in the value of property; appreciation. 3 excess of what is necessary; abundance. 4 (astrol) the third, sixth, tenth and eleventh houses of the astrological zodiac. উপচিত *adj* increased; expanded; nourished.

উপচানো *vi, vt* flow over the edges (of); go beyond the limit (of). ☐*adj* over-flowing.

উপচার *n* 1 articles of Hindu religious offering: নানা উপচারে পূজা. 2 medical treatment; surgical operation: অস্ত্রোপচার (অস্ত্র+~).

উপচিকীর্ষা *n* desire or inclination to do good to others. উপচিকীর্ষু *adj* disposed to charity; of benevolent disposition.

উপচিত ⇒ উপচয়

উপচিতি *n* a heap or pile, amassment; accumulation.

উপচীয়মান *adj* in the process of being amassed/accumulated/collected; developing; flourishing; prospering.

উপচ্ছদ *n* a covering; a lid.

উপজনন *n* coming into existence; birth; origin; production.

উপজাত *n* subsidiary article produced incidentally in the manufacture of some other article; an incidental product; a by-product.

উপজাতি *n* a subclass; an aboriginal tribe. উপজাতীয় *adj* tribal.

উপজিহ্বা *n* the cartilage at the root of the tongue; the uvula; the epiglottis.

উপজীবিকা *n* 1 means of living; a profession; a trade. 2 subsidiary source of income.

উপজীবী *adj* living by a profession: ভিক্ষোপজীবী (ভিক্ষা+~).

উপজীব্য *n* means of subsistence; support.

উপজ্ঞা *n* spontaneous or natural impulse; intuitive feeling; instinct.

উপড়ানো *vt* root out; uproot: আগাছা ~.

উপঢৌকন *n* gift or present.

উপত্যকা *n* a low tract of land between hills; a valley.

উপদংশ *n* a contagious venereal disease; syphilis.

উপদিষ্ট *adj* advised; instructed or directed.

উপদেবতা *n* (myth) half a god or demi-god.

উপদেশ *n* 1 authoritative direction; command. 2 counsel; advice; instruction. 3 admonition. ~ দেওয়া *vt* advise; instruct; admonish. ~মূলক *adj* containing instruction; instructive.

উপদেষ্টা *adj* imparting advice or instruction. ☐*n* an adviser; a teacher; a preceptor.

উপদ্বীপ *n* land-mass bounded on three sides by water; a peninsula: আরব ~.

উপদ্রব *n* state of being annoyed or disturbed; a trouble; irritation or pesterment: চোরের ~, বখাটেদের ~. ~ করা *vt* give trouble; cause annoyance/disturbance/irritation. ~কারী *adj, n* one who gives trouble or causes disturbance (to sb).

উপদ্রুত *adj* affected by disturbance or natural calamity: ~ অঞ্চল.

উপধা *n, adj* (gram) (letter) before the last one in a word; penultimate (letter).

উপনগর *n* township in the outskirts of a big city; satellite town.

উপনদ, উপনদী *n* stream/river that flows into a larger stream or river; a tributary.

উপনয়ন *n* ritual ceremony among caste Hindus for investing a boy with the holy thread.

উপনাম *n* name given informally instead of one's actual name usually in jest or contempt; a nickname.

উপনায়ক *n* character in a play, poem or story next in importance to the hero; secondary hero.

উপনিবেশ *n* country or territory occupied and controlled by foreign settlers; a colony. ~ স্থাপন করা *vt* establish a colony in; migrate to and settle in as inhabitants; colonize. উপনিবেশিত *adj* colonized.

উপনিষদ *n* Hindu religious book containing Vedantic philosophy.

উপনীত *adj* 1 arrived; alighted; reached; brought: অবশেষে নগরীতে ~ হলাম, At last I arrived at the city; মৃতদেহ গোরস্তানে ~ হলো, was brought to the graveyard. 2 invested with the holy thread. ~ হওয়া *vt, vi* reach; arrive at; be brought; be invested with the sacred thread.

উপনেতা *n* a leader second in command; assistant or deputy leader.

উপন্যাস *n* a book of fiction; a novel. ~কার, ~ লেখক *n* a novelist.

উপপতি unlawful lover of a married woman; a paramour.

উপপত্নী *n fem* woman who lives with a man without being lawfully married to him; a concubine; a mistress.

উপপদ *n* (gram) the first of two words compounded into one.

উপপাদন *n* solution (of a proposition) with the help of reason and argument. উপপাদ্য *n* (geom) a proposition to be proved; a theorem.

উপবন *n* an artificial forest; a garden/park/grove.

উপবাস *n* abstinence from food; fast. ~ **করা** *vi* abstain from food; fast. **উপবাসী** *adj* abstaining from food; fasting.

উপবিধি *n* a rule or regulation framed by a local authority in consonance with the law of the land; by-law; bye-law.

উপবিষ্ট *adj* seated; sitting. ~ **হওয়া** *vi* be seated; sit down; take one's seat.

উপবীত *n* the holy thread of a Brahmin.

উপবৃত্ত *n* an oval figure; an ellipse. **উপবৃত্তাকার** *adj* oval or elliptical in shape.

উপবেশন *n* act of sitting/taking one's seat. ~ **করা** *vi* take one's seat; sit.

উপভাষা *n* the idiom or manner of speaking of a language peculiar to a locality; a dialect.

উপভোক্তা *n* one who uses or enjoys; a consumer. ❑*adj* eating; using; enjoying.

উপভোগ *n* **1** act of enjoying with satisfaction. **2** eating. **3** using. **উপভোগ্য** *adj* capable of being enjoyed by eating or using; to be enjoyed; enjoyable.

উপম *adj* (in compound) like; equal; similar; resembling: প্রাসাদোপম (প্রাসাদ+~); like a palace; palatial.

উপমহাদেশ *n* a mass of land large enough to be reasonably called a continent but not actually classed as one; sub-continent: দক্ষিণ এশীয় ~.

উপমা *n* **1** likeness; resemblance; similar; appearance; similitude: অনুপম (অ+উপম), peerless. **2** (rhet) a figure of speech in which one thing is compared with another; a simile. ~ **দেওয়া** *vi* find a simile for. ~**ন** *n* the object with which a simile is drawn; (logic) analogy.

উপমিত *adj* illustrated by comparison; compared. **উপমিতি** *n* **1** a simile; an analogy. **2** knowledge acquired by analogy. **উপমেয়** *adj* comparable; compared. ❑*n* that which is compared; an object of comparison.

উপযাচক *n, adj* one who begs sth of sb importunately; importuner. ~ **হয়ে** *adv* without being asked/invited; uncalled for; officiously; importunately.

উপযাচন *n* pressing solicitation; importunity.

উপযাচিকা *adj fem* a woman making advances for love or asking for making love.

উপযুক্ত *adj* **1** appropriate; fitting; befitting; proper: ~ শাস্তি. **2** possessing necessary ability or worth; deserving; equal; worthy; competent: কাজের ~, ~ পাত্র. **3** grown-up; adult; capable of earning one's living: ছেলে ~ হয়েছে. ~ **হওয়া** *vi* suit; deserve; be worthy of or equal to: সে একাজের ~ নয়, He is not suitable for this job. ~**তা** *n* suitability; fitness; propriety; competence.

উপযোগ *n* use; utility; application; applicability; fitness.

উপযোগিতা *n* suitability; usefulness; necessity; propriety; fitness. **উপযোগী** *adj* suitable; fit; appropriate; proper; useful.

উপযোজন *n* act of accommodating/appropriating; adaptation; adjustment.

উপর *n* the top (of anything); space over or above anything; the surface; the roof. ❑*adj* upper: ~ দিক, ~ ঠোঁট. ❑*prep* **1** on, upon; over; over and above; against: মাথার ~, on/over the head; এর ~ আর কথা চলে না, nothing to say against this; পাঁচ মাইলের ~, more than five miles. **2** to; with; towards: গরিবের ~ দয়া, charity to the poor; সে আমার ~ রাগ করেছে, angry with me.

উপরঅলা *adj* superior. ❑*n* superior officer; boss; (fig) God.

উপরতলা *n* upper storey or floor of a building; (fig) upper class of the society: তিনি ~র লোক, He belongs to the upper class; সে ~য় থাকে, He lives upstairs/on the upper floor.

উপরন্তু *adv* in addition (to this); more over; besides; over and above.

উপরা-উপরি *adv* one after another; successively; consecutively.

উপরি[1] *adj* **1** extra; additional (illegal income, eg tip, bribe, etc): ~ আয়. **2** uninvited; unestimated: অনেক ~ লোক খেয়েছে. **3** incidental; casual; subsidiary: ~ খরচ. **4** unexpected; not looked for; sudden : ~ লাভ.

উপরি[2] *adv* over; on; upon; above. ~-~ *adv* one upon another; one after another; consecutively; superficially. ❑*adj* consecutive. ~**ভাগ** *n* the top; the surface; the upper part. ~ **ভাগে** *adv* on the top of. ~**লিখিত** *adj* written above; above-mentioned; aforesaid. ~**স্থ**, ~**স্থিত** *adj* placed/situated above; lying/standing above.

উপরুদ্ধ *adj* solicited; requested. ~ **হওয়া** *vt* be requested. ~ **হয়ে** *adv* being requested; on being asked/requested.

উপরে *adv,prep* **1** on; upon; above; on the top. **2** upstairs. **3** on high; in the sky.

উপরোক্ত *adj* above-mentioned.

উপরোধ *n* persistent request. **উপরোধে ঢেঁকি গেলা** (prove) perform a difficult task unwillingly.

উপর্যুপরি *adv* successively; repeatedly.

উপল *n* **1** stone, rock; pebble. **2** gem; jewel.

উপলক্ষ *n* **1** aim; motive; purpose; need. **2** an occasion; a pretext; an excuse; an opportunity. **উপলক্ষে** *adv* on the occasion of.

উপলক্ষ্য=উপলক্ষ

উপলব্ধ *adj* **1** apprehended by sense-organs or by the mind; perceived; realized; felt; appreciated. **2** gained; obtained; known.

উপলব্ধি *n* perception; realization; appreciation; acquisition; knowledge. ~ **করা** *vt* realize; perceive; feel; appreciate; know; understand.

উপশম *n* ease or mitigation of suffering; relief; alleviation; cure (of a disease). ~ **হওয়া** *vi* be relieved.

উপশিরা *n* delicate blood-vessel; subsidiary vein: শিরা ~.

উপসংহার *n* state of being concluded; the end or concluding section (of a book, etc); conclusion or a summary. ~ **করা** *vt* conclude; sum up. **উপসংহারে** *adv* in conclusion; in fine.

উপসর্গ *n* **1** an accompanying complaint of a disease; a symptom of a disease. **2** natural calamity, eg earthquake, flood, etc or any sort of trouble/disturbance/impediment: নানা ~ এসে জোটে. **3** (gram) a prefix.

উপসাগর *n* part of the sea enclosed in a curve of the land; a bay; a gulf: বঙ্গোপসাগর (বঙ্গ+~), the Bay of Bengal.

উপস্থাপন *n* act of introducing or conducting a musical or discussion programme before the audience. ~ **করা** *vt* introduce or bring forward. **উপস্থাপক** *adj* one who introduces or conducts such a programme. **উপস্থাপিত** *adj* what has been presented.

উপস্থিত *adj* arrived or present at the place talked of. ~ **হওয়া** *vi* arrive; be present.

উপস্বত্ব *n* income from real property or business.

উপহার *n* a complimentary gift or present. ~ **দেওয়া** *vi* give (sb) a present; present (sb) with a gift.

উপহাস *n* mocking at (sb); ridicule; taunt. ~ **করা** *vi* mock at; jeer at; make fun of; ridicule. **উপহাসাস্পদ** *adj* object of ridicule/taunt/ fun/unkind laugh. **উপহাস্য** *adj* fit to be laughed or jeered at.

উপহৃত *adj* given/offered as a present: প্রধানমন্ত্রী কর্তৃক ~, presented by the Prime Minister.

উপহ্রদ *n* shallow lake connected with the sea; a lagoon.

উপাখ্যান *n* an incidental narrative; account of an event in a chain of events; an episode. **2** story having no base in truth; a fable. **3** a narrative account; a description.

উপাঙ্গ *n* [উপ+অঙ্গ] part of a limb.

উপাচার্য [উপ+আচার্য] the executive head of a university; vice-chancellor (the chancellor being only a figure-head).

উপাত্ত *n* facts from which a conclusion may be drawn; data. ❑*adj* **1** accepted; admitted. **2** obtained; earned.

উপাদান *n* **1** ingredient(s) of anything. **2** raw materials that make an industrial product.

উপাদেয় *adj* **1** pleasant to eat; palatable; delicious. **2** pleasing; delightful; enjoyable. ~**তা** *n* pleasantness; tastefulness; deliciousness.

উপাধান *n* cushion for supporting the head in bed; a pillow.

উপাধি *n* title used with the name of a person as a sign of rank, honour, status, profession, education, etc; an appellation; an academic degree. ~**ক**, ~**ধারী** *adj* holding a title; title-holder; degree-holder. ~-**পত্র** *n* an academic diploma/certificate; letter of investiture.

উপাধ্যক্ষ [উপ+অধ্যক্ষ] *n* vice-principal of a college.

উপান্ত [উপ+অন্ত] *n* border; extremity: আদ্যোপান্ত (আদি+~), from the beginning to the end; outskirts (of a town). **উপান্ত্য** *adj* lying on the border; next to the last; last but one; penultimate: উপান্ত্য বর্ণ, penultimate letter; উপান্ত্য টীকা, marginal note.

উপায় *n* **1** means of doing sth: এথেকে বেরিয়ে আসার কোনো ~ নেই, There is no way out of it. **2** redemption in the hereafter; salvation: এ পাপীর কী ~ হবে? What will happen to this sinner? **3** acquisition of wealth; earning; income: ~ কতো? **4** remedy of a disease; redress of an evil. **5** support; means of livelihood: বিধবার ~. **6** a contrivance; an expedient: ~ (উদ্ভাবন) করা, find a way out; devise some means for. ~**হীন** *adj* without means; helpless.

উপায়-উপকরণ *n* ways and means.

উপায়ান্তর *n* alternative means/course; other means. ~ **না দেখে** finding or having no other way/means.

উপার্জন *n* act of earning; earnings. ~ **করা** *vt* gain by labour; earn; acquire. ~**ক্ষম** *adj* capable of earning: পরিবারের একমাত্র ~ক্ষম ব্যক্তি, only earning member of the family. **উপার্জিত** *adj* earned; acquired; gained; obtained.

উপাস/উপোস=উপবাস

উপাসনা *n* **1** act of praying; prayer; worship; adoration. **2** meditation of God. ~ **করা** *vi* pray; worship; adore. **উপাসক** *n, adj* one who prays to God; a devotee. **উপাসিকা** *fem*.

উপাসী=উপবাসী ⇒ উপবাস

উপাস্থি [উপ+অস্থি] *n* the elastic tissue from which bone is formed; cartilage.

উপাস্য *adj* worthy of being worshipped; adorable. ❑*n* God.

উপুড়, উবুড় (opp চিত) *adj* lying with the face downwards: ~ করা কলস, pitcher turned upside down. ~ **হয়ে পড়া** *vi* tumble on one's face; fall prostrate.

উপেক্ষা *n* lack of care or proper attention; neglect; disregard; contempt. ~ **করা** *vi* neglect; ignore; disregard. **উপেক্ষিত** *adj* treated with disregard or contempt; neglected; disregarded; ignored. **উপেক্ষিতা** *fem*.

উপোস=উপবাস. **~ করে মরা** *vi* starve to death. **উপোসী** = উপবাসী⇒উপবাস..

উপ্ত *adj* (of seeds) planted or scattered on (a piece of land); sown; sowed. **উপ্তি** *n* act of sowing.

উবচানো=উপচানো

উবরানো *vt* be in excess; exceed; be surplus.

উবা (or **উবে যাওয়া**) *vt* disappear in the air; evaporate: কর্পূর উবে যায়, camphor evaporates.

উবু, উপু *adj* seated on one's heels or with legs drawn up to the body. **~ হয়ে বসা** *vi* squat.

উবুড়⇒উপুড়

উভ (poet) *pron* the two together; both. **উভচর** *adj* able to live both on land and in water; amphibious: উভচর প্রাণী, an amphibian. **উভলিঙ্গ** *adj* (esp of plants) being both male and female; androgynous. ❑*n* (gr) word in the common gender: ~লিঙ্গ.

উভয় *pron, adj* the one as well as the other; both. **~ দিক রক্ষা করা** follow a middle course or line of compromise; maintain neutrality; strike a balance. **~ত** *adv* in both cases; on either side/both sides. **~সঙ্কট** *n* difficult situation in which one has to choose between two courses of action, both undesirable; a dilemma.

উম *n* pleasant warmness (as under a quilt). **~ দেওয়া** *vt* incubate; hatch: ডিমে উম দেওয়া, hatch eggs.

উমদা [A] *adj* **1** excellent; exquisite. **2** tasteful; delicious. **3** charming.

উমর [A] age.

উমরা[1], **উমরাহ্** [A] *n pl* (*sing* আমীর) members of the nobility; the princes and nobles.

উমরা[2] [A] *n* performance of rites at the Holy Kaaba between Hajj seasons; lesser Hajj.

উমেদ, উম্মেদ, উমীদ [P] **1** hope; desire; expectation. **2** prayer; solicitation. **3** waiting.

উমেদার [P] *adj* **1** cherishing a hope; desirous; expecting. **2** seeking favour/ employment. ❑*n* mean flatterer; a sycophant. **উমেদারি** *n* act of soliciting favour or employment; job-seeking; flattery. **উমেদারি করা** *vi* flatter; seek employment.

উম্মত [A] *n* **1** follower; disciple; devotee. **2** community; nation: নবীর **~**.

উম্মি [A] *adj* unlettered; illiterate.

উরস, ওরস [A] *n* death anniversary of saints; celebration of such anniversary.

উর্ণনাভ=ঊর্ণনাভ

উর্দি [T] special dress or uniform worn by men-servants or orderlies in any office or organization.

উর্দু [T] **1** Hindustani language written in Arabic characters and having an abundance of Arabic and Persian words evolved during the Mughal rule in India; Urdu. **2** state language of Pakistan.

উর্বর, ঊর্বর [A] **1** *adj* (of land) rich in productivity; fertile. **2** (of men) full of ideas: ~ মস্তিস্ক. **উর্বরা** *fem*: জমির উর্বরাশক্তি, productivity of land.

উর্বশী, ঊর্বশী mythological nymph of eternal beauty and youth spoken of in the Purana.

উলকি *n* a pattern, picture or writing put on the skin by tattooing; a tattoo. **~ আঁকা** *vi* make a permanent pattern or picture on the skin by pricking with a pin and then pouring coloured dyes in; tattoo: তার বাহুতে তার নামটি ~ আঁকা ছিল, He had his name tattooed in his arm. **~-আঁকা** *adj* tattooed.

উলঙ্গ *adj* not having clothes on; naked; nude. **উলঙ্গিনী** *fem*.

উলট-পালট *adv* upside down; topsy-turvy. **~ করা** *vt* turn upside down; put into disorder; throw into confusion.

উলু[1] *n* sound raised by Hindu women by the moving of tongue on festive occasions.

উলু[2] *n* kind of grass growing in marshy land; reed. **~ খাগড়া** *n* **1** variety of reed. **2** (fig) ordinary innocent people: রাজায় রাজায় যুদ্ধ হয় ~ খাগড়ার প্রাণ যায়, (prov) Kings with one another vie, and the innocent people die. **~বনে মুক্তা ছড়ানো** (prov) Cast pearls before swines.

উলেমা [A] *n pl* (*sing* আলীম) men of learning.

উল্কা *n* transitory luminous body that shoots through the atmosphere; a shooting-star; a meteor. **~পাত** *n* fall of a meteor. **~পিণ্ড** *n* a meteorite. **~বেগে** *adv* at a thunderous speed.

উল্টা, উল্টো *adj* **1** overturned; upside down. **2** opposite; reverse; contrary. ❑*adv* on the contrary. **~ বোঝা** *vt* take sth amiss; take ill of sth. **~ বুঝানো** *vt* twist the meaning of sth to sb; misinterpret; misrepresent.

উল্টানো *vt* turn upside down; overturn; capsize: নৌকাটি উল্টে গেল, The boat capsized. **কথা ~** disown one's own word.

উল্টা-পাল্টা *adj* topsy-turvy; reversed.

উল্লঙ্ঘন *n* **1** act of passing over by leaping/jumping; crossing over. **2** infringement; transgression; violation. **~ করা** *vt* leap over; violate; transgress; infringe. **উল্লঙ্ঘিত** *adj* what has been jumped over/violated/transgressed.

উল্লম্ফন *n* act of leaping or jumping.

উল্লসিত *adj* elated with joy; delighted.

উল্লাস *n* joy; delight. **~ প্রকাশ করা** *vi* rejoice; take delight. **মনের উল্লাসে** being elated with joy; exultingly.

উল্লিখিত *adj* what has been mentioned or said before.

উল্লুক *n* **1** long-armed ape; a gibbon. **2** (colloq) an idiot.

উল্লেখ *n* mention; a direct reference to; an allusion. ~ **করা** *vt* mention; refer to; allude to. **উল্লেখ্য, ~যোগ্য** *adj* worth-mentioning; mentionable.

উল্লোল *n* high waves. ☐*adj* billowy; wavy.

উশখুশ=উসখুস

উশুল=উসুল

উষসী=ঊষসী

উস্কখুস্ক, উস্কোখুস্কো *adj* **1** dry; rough: ~ চেহারা. **2** (of hair) slovenly; untrimmed; untidy; dishevelled.

উষ্ট্র *n* the camel; (fig) the ship of the desert. **উষ্ট্রী** *fem*. **~চালক** *n* cameleer.

উষ্ণ *adj* **1** (of weather, atmosphere) hot and oppressive; sultry. **2** (of a country, region) very hot, tropical, torrid. **3** angry; enraged; indignant. ~ **হওয়া** *vi* **1** be heated. **2** get angry. **~তা** *n* heat; warmth. **~প্রধান** *adj* torrid; tropical: ~প্রধান অঞ্চল. **~মণ্ডল** *n* torrid zone.

উষ্ণীষ *n* head-dress; a turban.

উষ্ম, উষ্মা *n* **1** heat; warmth. **2** the summer. **3** anger; rage; passion. **উষ্মবর্ণ** (gram) *n* the four aspirated consonants in Bengali pronounced with full breath or with the sound 'h', eg শ ষ স and হ.

উসকানো *vt* **1** incite; instigate; goad (sb to do sth). **2** increase the light; brighten up: প্রদীপের শিখা ~, trim up the wick of a lamp. **উসকে দেওয়া** *vt* stir up; provoke; instigate. **উসকানি** *n* instigation; incitement.

উসখুস, উশখুশ *n* state of being impatient (at sth/for sth); impatience; restlessness: বাড়ি ফেরার জন্য মন ~ করছে. ~ **করা** *vt* be fidgety; become restless.

উসুল[1], **উশুল** [A] *n* realization of dues, etc. ~ দেওয়া *vt* realize rents; dues, etc. ~ **করা** *vt* pay off bills/dues/claims.

উসুল[2] [A *sing* আসল]*n pl* fundamental principles. **উসুলে ফিকাহ** *n* fundamentals of jurisprudence.

উস্তাগর *n* worker in stone and brick; a mason.

উস্তাদ=ওস্তাদ

উহ্, উঃ *int* expressing contempt, annoyance, extreme pleasure, etc.

উহা (old use) *pron* that (person or thing). **উহার** *adj* its. **উহারা** *pron pl* they. **উহাদের** *adj* their; theirs; of them.

উহু, উহুঃ *int* expressing pain, etc.

উহুঁ *int* expressing unwillingness or negative reply.

উহ্যমান *adj* in the state of being carried/ pulled/drawn.

ঊ *n* the sixth vowel of the Bengali alphabet pronounced like 'oo' in 'wood'. It joins a consonant with its symbol only eg ক+ঊ = কূ. **ঊকার** *n* the symbol of ঊ. **ঊকারাদি** *adj* (of words) beginning with ঊ or ঊ-sound. **ঊকারান্ত** *adj* (word) ending in ঊ or ঊ-sound.

ঊঢ় *adj* married; wedded. **ঊঢ়া** *fem*. (opp **অনূঢ়া**).

ঊন *adj* less; lesser; short; imperfect (ঊনবিংশ, কিঞ্চিদূন): ~ ভাতে দুন বল, ভরা ভাতে রসাতল.

ঊনআশি=ঊনআশি

ঊনচত্বারিংশ, ঊনচত্বারিংশত্তম *adj* thirty-ninth.

ঊনচল্লিশ=ঊনচল্লিশ

ঊনত্রিংশ, ঊনত্রিশ=**ঊনত্রিশ** *n, adj* twenty-nine.

ঊননবতি *n adj* eighty-nine.

ঊননব্বই=**ঊননব্বই**

ঊনপঞ্চাশ=**ঊনপঞ্চাশ**

ঊনপঞ্চাশৎ *n, adj* forty-nine **~তম** *adj* forty-ninth.

ঊনবিংশ *n, adj* nineteen. **~তিতম** *adj* nineteenth. **~তি** *n, adj* nineteen.

ঊনষষ্টি *n, adj* fifty-nine. **~তম** *adj* fifty-ninth.

ঊনষাট=**ঊনষাট**

ঊনসত্তর=ঊনসত্তর

ঊনসপ্ততি *n, adj* sixty-nine.

ঊনিশ=উনিশ

ঊরু, উরু *n* the thick part of the leg above the knee-joint; the thigh.

ঊর্ণনাভ, ঊর্ণনাভি *n* eight-legged insect that spins webs for catching its prey; the spider.

ঊর্ণা *n* wool. **ঊর্ণাময়** *adj* made of wool; woollen.

ঊর্দু=উর্দু

ঊর্ধ্ব *n* **1** upward direction: ঘুড়িটি অনেক ঊর্ধ্বে উড়ছে. **2** height: ঊর্ধ্বে তিনগজ, three yards in height. ☐*adj* **1** greatest in number or degree; most: ~পক্ষে, at the most. **2** higher in place; upper: ঊর্ধ্বাংশ. **~গতি** *n* an upward movement. **~গামী** *adj* going or moving upwards; ascending; soaring. **~চারী** *adj* **1** moving in the sky/air. **2** highly imaginative; full of sublime ideas; ambitious. **~তন** *adj* **1** higher; superior: ঊর্ধ্বতন কর্তৃপক্ষ. **2** former; going before: ~তন পুরুষ. **~পাতন** *n* (chem) distillation; sublimation. **~লোক** *n* the heaven. **~শ্বাস** *n* long breath; deep breath; last breath. **~শ্বাসে** *adv* breathlessly; pantingly: ~শ্বাসে দৌড়ানো run out of breath/very fast.

ঊর্বশী=উর্বশী

ঊর্মি *n* a wave; a surge; a billow. **ঊর্মিল** *adj* billowy; full of waves. **ঊর্মিমালা** *n* a row of waves. **ঊর্মিমালী** *n* a sea; an ocean.

ঊষর *adj* salty; barren: ~ মরুভূমি, barren desert.

উষসী *adj fem* **1** beauteous. **2** (fig) the dawn.
উষা *n* the break of day; the dawn.
উহ্য *adj* not expressed but understood; implied; elliptical.

ঋ

ঋ *n* the seventh vowel of the Bengali alphabet which gives 'r'-sound when joined with a consonant. Its symbol is 'ৃ' eg ক+ঋ = কৃ.
ঋক্ *n* Vedic hymn.
ঋগ্বেদ *n* the oldest Veda; Rigveda. ঋগ্বেদী *adj* learned in or obedient to the Rigveda.
ঋজু *adj* **1** straight; erect; uncurved; unbent. **2** frank; sincere; candid. ~কায় *adj* erect-bodied. ~তা *n* straightness; straight forwardness; simplicity; sincerity. ~প্রকৃতি *adj* frank and sincere by nature. ~রেখা *n* straight line.
ঋণ *n* **1** debt; loan; liability. **2** (math) the minus sign. ~ করা/নেওয়া *vi* borrow; incur debts; get into debt. ~ দেওয়া *vi* lend. ~গ্রস্ত *adj* indebted; run into debt. ~গ্রহণ *n* act of borrowing (money). ~গ্রাহক/গ্রহীতা *n* borrower; debtor. ~জাল *n* the meshes of debt: ~জালে জড়িত, over head and ears in debt. ~দাতা *n* lender; creditor. ~দান *n* lending of money. ~ পরিশোধ করা *vi* repay/pay off/discharge a debt. ~মুক্ত হওয়া *vi* be released/free from debt.
ঋণাত্মক [opp ধনাত্মক] *adj* implying absence, denial or negation; negative: ~ রাশি, negative quantity.
ঋণী *adj* indebted. ❑*n* debtor: আমি তোমার কাছে দুশ টাকা ~, I owe you Tk two hundred.
ঋতু *n* **1** natural division of the year on account of temperature, weather, etc; season: বাংলাদেশ ষড়ঋতুর দেশ. **2** the monthly course of a woman; menstruation. ~কাল *n* the period of menstrual discharge; state of passing the menstrual course. ~মতী *adj* menstruating; menstruous. ~মতী হওয়া *vi* have the menses; menstruate. ঋতুরাজ *n* the king of seasons; the spring. ~স্নান *n* bath on the termination of the menstrual period.
ঋত্বিক *n* the priest of a house; a family priest.
ঋদ্ধ *adj* prosperous; flourishing; affluent; fortunate. ঋদ্ধি *n* flourishing state; prosperity; affluence; fortune. ঋদ্ধিমান=ঋদ্ধ. ঋদ্ধিমতী *fem.* ঋদ্ধিলাভ *n* attainment of prosperity/affluence.
ঋষভ *n* **1** the ox; the bull. **2** (music) the second note of the musical scale. ❑*adj* chief; best; excellent.
ঋষি *n* a sage; a saint; a composer of Vedic hymns. ~কল্প, ~তুল্য *adj* saint-like; saintly.
ঋষ্ট *n* a species of deer; spotted deer. ❑*adj* inauspicious.
ঋষ্টি *n* evil influence of a star; evil; calamity.

এ

এ[১] *n* the eighth vowel of the Bengali alphabet. It is an aspirate. It joins a consonant with its symbol 'ে', eg., ক+এ=কে.
এ[২] *pron, adj, int* as a *pron* it is synonymous with 'this' and replaces a person as well as a material or immaterial object: এ কে? Who is this? এ ভালো নয়, this is not good. Used as *adj* it indicates anything under reference: এ-পথে যেও না, Don't go this way. 'এ' is also used as an *int,* eg এ ভাই! hallo, brother!
-এ as a case-ending 'এ' has its use in all the cases in Bengali grammer: পাগলে (পাগল+এ) কিনা বলে; ধীরে (ধীর+এ) কথা বল; তিলে (তিল+এ) তেল আছে আর কুসুমে (কুসুম+এ) সৌরভ, etc.
এই *pron* this, it: আমি ~ চাই, I want this. ❑*adj* sth near at hand; this: আমি ~ বইটিই হারিয়েছিলাম, This is the book that I lost. ❑*adv* without delay; immediately: ~ এলাম বলে, I'm just coming. ❑*int* expressing wonder, panic, terror, etc: ~ সেরেছে! ~ রে! good heavens! ~ অজুহাতে on this pretext/plea/excuse. ~ কতক্ষণ just a little while ago. ~ কারণে, ~জন্য for this reason; on account of this. ~ক্ষণে *adv* now, this (very) moment. ~ প্রকারে in this way/manner. ~ বেলা now that there is time; meanwhile. ~ মর্মে to this effect. ~মাত্র just now; this much; just this. ~বার this time; on this occasion. ~রূপ *adj* such; like this; similar. ~রূপে *adv* in this way/manner.
এইতো *adj* **1** just this: ~ চেয়েছিলাম This is just what I wanted. ❑*adv* just now: ~ এলাম, I've just arrived. ~ কলির সন্ধে It is just the beginning of the trouble.
এইসা *adj* such-like; of this type (cf H ঐসা).
এও *pron* **1** that which is said: এও কি সম্ভব? **2** person who is referred to: এও সঙ্গে যাবে.

এওজ, এওয়াজ [A] *n* **1** exchange: ~-বদল, mutual exchange. **এওজি** *adj* obtained by exchange: এওজি জমি. **এওজে** *adv* in lieu of; in exchange of.

এঃ *int* expressing displeasure, aversion, etc.

এঁচড়=ইঁচড়

এঁটে *adv* tightly; compactly: ~ বাঁধা, bind tightly.

এঁটেল *adj* **1** sticky; adhesive. **2** slippery: এঁটেল মাটি, clayey soil.

এঁটো, এঁঠো *n, adj* (of food) **1** scraps or left-overs in the plate; partly eaten. **এঁটো-কাঁটা** *n* leavings of a meal. **~খেকো** *adj* (abuse) depending on others' charity. **~পাত** *n* unwashed utensils after the meal is over. **~হাত** *n* uncleaned/unwashed hands after having the meal.

এঁড়ে *n, adj* male (young of cattle); bull-calf: এঁড়ে বাছুর. **এঁড়ে গলা** *n* heavy or husky voice. **~লাগা** *vi* suffer from dyspepsia or rickets.

এঁদের *pron* (respectful) their; theirs.

এঁদো, এঁধো *adj* giving no access to light; dark; gloomy: ~ বাড়ি; dark, dirty and narrow: ~ গলি; overgrown with weeds: ~ পুকুর.

এক *n* the number one. ❑*adj* **1** one and the same: ~ মায়ের সন্তান. **2** united: তোমরা ~ হও. **3** only one; absolute; unitarian: ~ আল্লাহর আরাধনা. **4** same in rank or status; equal: ~জাতি. **5** full; filled up: ~ হাঁড়ি ভাত. **6** a certain; indefinite: ~ ছিল রাজা. **7** one of a number: শিক্ষকদের একজন. **8** mixed up; amalgamated: চালে ডালে এক হওয়া. **~ আঁচড়ে বোঝা** understand by a cursory glance. **~ আন্দাজ জরিপ** survey of the entire estate at a time. **~ মন দুধে এক ফোঁটা চোনা** (fig) A little of sth odd or vicious can spoil the whole of a good thing. **~ কান দিয়ে ঢোকে, আর এক কান দিয়ে বেরোয়** in at one ear and out at the other. **~ক্ষুরে মাথা মুড়ানো** (fig) be of the same nature or luck. **~ গেলাসের ইয়ার** as intimate as one drinking from the same vessel; (fig) intimate friend. **~ চায় আর পায়** One sows, another reaps. **~ ঢিলে দুই পাখি মারা** kill two birds with one stone; (fig) achieve two goals with one strategy. **~ বারের রোগী আর বারের ওঝা** once a patient, the next time a physician; be trained in the school of experience. **~ মাঘে শীত যায় না** Chance of requital is never lost. **~ মুখে দুই কথা** going back (on) one's word; blowing hot and cold in the same breath. **~ যাত্রায় পৃথক ফল** Success or failure depends on individuals. **~ হাতে তালি বাজে না** It takes two to make a quarrel. **~ হেঁসেলে দুই রাঁধুনি, পুড়ে গেল তার ফেনগালুনি** A divided authority is never effective; Too many cooks spoil the broth.

একই *adj* one and the same; the/this very same: আমরা ~ পৃথিবীতে বাস করি We live under the same sun; ~ অবস্থা চলছে, there is no change. **~ কথা** all the same; just the same thing: তুমি যাও বা না যাও, ~ কথা, It is all the same whether you go or not; আমার ~ কথা, I am true to my word; ~ কথা বার বার বলো না, Don't harp on the same thing.

এক-এক *adj* **1** some; certain: এমন ~জন লোক আছে, there are some/certain people.... **2** different; diverse; various: ~দেশে ~ নিয়ম, There are different customs in different countries. **3** one after another; one by one: ~ করে. **~ বার** *adv* sometimes; at times; occasionally.

একক *adj* **1** lone; unaided; unaccompanied: ~ প্রচেষ্টা. **2** alone in its kind or class; resembling nothing else; unique: সাধারণ তবু ~. ❑*n* (arith) **1** the first digit of a number from the right. **2** quantity assumed as a standard; a unit: মুদ্রার ~, ওজনের ~. **~-সঙ্গীত** *n* piece of music performed by one person; solo.

এককড়া *n* a very small quantity; a particle; a bit; a little: এর ~ও দাম নেই. It is of no worth at all/altogether worthless. **~র কাজ** *n* trivial work; trifling matter.

এককথা *n* fixed/unalterable word; word that cannot be disowned. **~য় বলতে গেলে** in a word; in brief. **~র মানুষ** man of word; as good as one's word. **~য় দু কথায়** *adv* in the course of talking: ~য় দুকথায় ঝগড়া বেঁধে গেল.

এক্কা =এক্কা

এককাট্টা⇒একাট্টা

এককাঠি *n* a bit or measure of sth. ❑*adv* to the extent of a measuring rod. ~ **সরেশ** *adj* (facet) worse than any other person or thing.

এককাড়ি *adj* a heap of (sth); a lot of (sth): ~ টাকা, a good round sum.

এককালীন *adj* **1** what is to be done or given at a time/once: ~ চাঁদা; living or occurring at the same time. **2** contemporary; contemporaneous. ❑*adv* at a time; simultaneously: নৌ ও বিমান বাহিনীর ~ আক্রমণ.

এককালে *adv* **1** at the same time; simultaneously. **2** in bygone days; once upon a time. **3** only once; once for all.

এককুড়ি *n* a set of 20; a score. ❑*adj* twentieth.

এককেন্দ্রিক, এককেন্দ্রী, এককেন্দ্রীয় *adj* (of circles) having a common centre: ~ বৃত্ত.

একখান, একখানা *n* one; one piece.

একগলা *adj* as high as one's throat.

এক-গা *adj* (said of ornaments) covering the whole body: ~ গয়না.

একগাদা *adj* a heap of (sth); a great number or collection: ~ লোক.

একগামিতা *n* contentment with one wife only. একগামী *adj*.

একগাল *adj* mouthful: ~ ভাত, mouthful of rice. ~ **হাসি** *n* expansive or hearty laughter.

একগুঁয়ে *adj* self-willed; obstinate; headstrong: এঁড়ে গরুর চেয়েও ~. ~**মি** *n* obstinacy; wilfulness; waywardness.

একগুচ্ছ *n* **1** a cluster or bunch of fruits growing together: ~ আঙুর, a bunch of grapes. **2** a collection of things of the same sort fastened together: ~ চাবি, a bunch of keys.

একঘরে *adj* excluded from the privileges of social life (as a punishment); excommunicated. ~ **করা** *vt* excommunicate; ostracize.

একঘেয়ে *adj* uninterestingly repetitive and boring; lacking variety; monotonous: ~ খাবার আর ভালো লাগে না. ~**মি** *n* dull uniformity; want of variety; monotony.

একচক্ষু, একচোখো *adj* **1** blind of one eye; one-eyed. **2** looking to one side only; showing partiality; prejudiced: ~ নীতি, preferential treatment/policy. ~ **হরিণ** *adj* (fig) **1** whimsical; self-willed; wayward. **2** prejudiced; biased. একচোখোমি *n* partiality; bias; prejudice.

একচত্বারিংশ, একচত্বারিংশৎ, একচল্লিশ *n* the number forty-one. ❑*adj* forty-first.

একচালা *n, adj* (house) with only one slanting roof.

একচিত্ত *adj* absorbedly attentive; devoted to one thing; single-minded. ~**তা** *n* single-mindedness.

একচুল *adj* hair's-breadth; slight; slightest. ❑*adv* in the least: ~ এদিক ওদিক হবে না, There will be no deviation, not even by a hair's-breadth. সে একচুলের জন্য বেঁচে গেছে, He had a hair-breadth/narrow escape.

একচেটিয়া, একচেটে *adj* **1** maintaining sole privilege; tending to exclude others; exclusive: উচ্চশিক্ষার অধিকার ধনীদেরই ~, the rich alone have the privilege of higher education. **2** having no rival in enjoying exclusive privilege of trade, etc; monopolistic; monopolized. ~ **করা** *vt* monopolize. ~ **ব্যবসায়** trade over which one person or group has absolute control; monopoly. ~ **ব্যবসায়ী** *n* monopolist.

একচোখা, একচোখো⇒ একচক্ষু

একচোট *adv* **1** enough at one stroke: ~ শুনিয়ে দিলাম. **2** for a considerable duration: বেশ ~ ঝগড়া হয়ে গেল. **একচোটে** *adv* without break; in one attempt: একচোটে লেখাটা শেষ করলাম.

একচ্ছত্র *adj* having undisputed sway; paramount: ~ অধিপতি, paramount ruler; suzerain: হোসেন শাহ সারা বাংলায় ~ আধিপত্য প্রতিষ্ঠা করেন, Hussain Shah established his sovereignty/suzerainty/paramountcy over the whole of Bengal.

একছাঁচে *adv* in one form. ~ **ঢালা** *vt* cast or shape things in one mould. ❑*adj* cast or shaped in one mould.

একছার, একছের [P] *adv* directly; straight: কাউকে না দেখে ~ ঘরে ঢুকে পড়লাম, Seeing no one around, I entered straight into the house.

একছুট[১] *adj* single piece of cloth. **একছুটে** *adv* with a single piece of cloth on.

একছুট[২] *n* a non-stop run. **একছুটে** *adv* at a single run.

একজাই, একজায় *adj* **1** put together; assembled; united. **2** listed on a par. ❑*adv* repeatedly; incessantly; continually; over and over again: ~ বকা. ❑*n* sum total: বার্ষিক আয়ব্যয়ের ~. ~ **করা** *vt* unite; assemble; collect.

একজাতি *n* one nation/class/kind/species. **একজাতীয়** *adj* of the same species; homogeneous.

একজিবিশন *n* public show of things (eg of works of art) or display of commercial or industrial goods; exhibition.

একজোট *adj* **1** united in a group; combined as a party. **2** unanimous in views or ideas. ❑*n* group of people holding the same opinion. একজোটে *adv* in a body; unitedly.

একজ্বর, একজ্বরি *n* fever without remission; remittent fever.

একজ্বরী *adj* suffering from remittent fever.

একটা *adj* **1** one; single: ~ কলম. **2** a certain; any one: ~ লোক বললো. **3** one particular: ~ কথা বলি শোনো, Hear me, let me tell you one thing. ❑*adv* once; one time: ~ সই দাও, Please put your signature. ~ **কিছু** *n* sth unspecified or indefinite: ~-কিছু করতে হবে. ❑*adj* having existence but not definitely known; some: ~-কিছু ত্রুটি আছে, some fault/failing is there. ~-**না**-~ *adj* one or the other; at least one: ~-না-~ অসুখ লেগেই আছে. ~-**দুটো** *adj* one or two; a few.

একটানা *adv* **1** at a stretch; without break; continually; continuously; incessantly: ~ বৃষ্টি. **2** in a monotonous fashion; monotonously: ~ সুর ❑*adj* moving in one direction only: ~ স্রোত.

একটি=একটা. ~**মাত্র** *adj* but one; only one: বিপদ এড়াবার ~মাত্র পথ আছে, There is only one way out.

একটিনি *adj* [E acting] acting temporarily in place of a permanent employee.

একটু *adj* a little; some: ~ চা খাও. ❑*adv* **1** a little while: ~ দাঁড়াও. **2** once: ~ যাও না. ~ ~ **করে** *adv* bit by bit; little by little. ~**কু** *adj* slight; slightest. ~**কুতে** *adv* at the slightest provocation: তুমি ~কুতে রেগে যাও. ~**খানি** *adj* **1** little; small in size or amount: ~খানি দুধ. **2** of tender age: ~খানি মেয়ে. ❑*adv* a little while: ~খানি সবুর করো, Tarry a while; wait a bit.

একঠোকা=একরোখা

একত, একতঃ *adv* on the one hand/side.

একতন্ত্রী=একতারা

একতম *adj superl* one of/amongst more than two: সপ্ত আশ্চর্যের ~.

একতর[১] *adj comp* **1** one of two; either. **2** separate; different.

একতর[২] *adv* [PA এক+তর] of the same kind.

একতরফ *n* [PA এক+তরফ] one side/party.

একতরফা [P] *adj* **1** (legal) one-sided decree given in the absence of the defendant as per prayer of the plaintiff; exparte: ~ রায়. **2** spoken by one person: ~ বক্তৃতা.

একতলা, একতালা *adj* one-storeyed: ~ দালান. ❑*n* ground floor of a building.

একতা *n* condition of being united; agreement of aims and interests; Unity; identity. **~ই বল** unity is strength.

একতান *n* musical entertainment in which instruments are played in unison; concert. ❑*adj* absorbedly attentive; single-minded. **~মনা** *adj* closely attentive. **~মনা হয়ে** *adv* with rapt attention. **একতানে** *adv* **1** in one voice. **2** with undivided attention.

একতারা *n* one-stringed musical instrument (chiefly used by folk singers).

একতাল *n* musical measure of equal intervals; harmony in musical notes.

একতালা⇒একতলা

একতিল *adj* as little as a grain of sesamum; a bit of (anything): তার কথায় ~ সত্য নেই, There is not a bit of truth in what he says.

একত্ব *n* the state of being one complete whole; oneness; unity: আল্লাহ্‌র ~, unity of Allah.

একত্র *adv* in one place; together; in a body. **~ করা** *vt* gather; get/put together; collect; unite. **~ হওয়া** *vi* come together; meet; unite: কত লোক ~ হবে? How many people will gather? **একত্রিত** *adj* collected; assembled; brought together.

একত্রিশ, একত্রিংশ *n* thirty one. ❑*adj* thirty-first.

একত্রিশে, একত্রিশা *n* thirty-first day of a month.

একথোক *n* a lump. **একথোকে** *adv* in a lump.

একদম [P] *adv* thoroughly; out and out; utterly: ~ বাজে, utterly bad; ~ চলতে পারে না, utterly incapable of walking. **একদমে** *adv* in one breath; without stop.

একদা *adv* one day; at one time; once upon a time.

একদিক *n* one quarter; one side. **একদিকে** *adv* on one side; on the one hand.

একদিন *adv* on a day; some day: ~ এসো, Please come someday. ❑*n* **1** a certain time: ~ ছিল যখন, ... there was a time when ... **2** an ominous day: আজ তোরই ~ কি আমারই ~. **~ অন্তর ~** every other/alternate day. **~-না-~** one day or other; some day or other.

একদিল [P] *adj* (of two persons) having but one and the same soul; most intimate.

একদৃষ্টি *adj* having a fixed look; gazing; concentrated. ❑*n* a single glance.

একদৃষ্টে *adv* with a fixed look: ~ চেয়ে আছে, looking intently/steadfastly; gazing/staring at.

একদেশ *n* **1** a portion or region (esp of a country). **2** a country. **একদেশী** *adj* hailing from/living in the same country. **একদেশী লোক** *n* compatriot. **একদেশীয়** *adj* of/living in the same country.

একদেশদর্শী *adj* viewing or taking into consideration only one side of sth; biased; prejudiced. **একদেশদর্শিতা** *n* **1** partiality; bias; prejudice. **2** want of foresight; narrow-mindedness.

একদেহ *n* (of husband and wife) one body. ❑*adj* inseparably united; single-bodied. **~ একপ্রাণ** *adj* having common aims and interests; united in all intents and purposes.

একধর্মা *adj* having common qualities.

একধর্মী *adj* professing the same religion; belonging to the same religious community; homogeneous. ❑*n* co-religionist. **একধর্মিণী** *fem.*

একধা *adv* (opp বহুধা) **1** in one way or subject. **2** in one kind.

একনবতি *n, adj* ninety-one.

একনবতিতম *adj* ninety-first.

একনলা *adj* (of guns) having a single barrel; one-barrelled. **~ বন্দুক** *n* single-barrelled gun.

একনাগাড়, একনাগাড়ে *adv* at a stretch; continuously: ~ তিন ঘন্টা বৃষ্টি হলো, It rained for three hours at a stretch.

একনায়ক *n* **1** ruler invested with absolute authority; absolute ruler; dictator. **2** an absolute prince or sovereign who rules in a dictatorial and peremptory fashion; an autocrat. **~ত্ব** *n* absolute government by one person; dictatorship. **~তন্ত্র** *n* government by a single all-powerful ruler; autocracy.

একনিষ্ঠ *adj* **1** devoted or attached to only one; single-minded. **2** free from impure desires; chaste. **একনিষ্ঠা** *fem.* **~তা** *n* single-minded devotion; singleness of purpose.

একপক্ষ *n* **1** one side/party; either the plaintiff (বাদীপক্ষ) or the defendant (প্রতিবাদীপক্ষ). **2** a fortnight. **~কাল** *adv* for a fortnight. **একপক্ষে** *adv* on the one hand/side.

একপঙ্‌ক্তিক *adj* belonging to the same class.

একপঞ্চাশ *n* the number fifty one. ❑*adj* fifty-first.

একপত্নীক *adj* having one wife (at a time).

একপদ *n* **1** one foot; one step : ~ও অগ্রসর হয়ো না. ❑*adj* **1** one footed; crippled. **2** of the same part of speech. **একপদী** *n* narrow path passable for one person at a time. **একপদীকরণ** *n* (gram) compounding of two or more words into one.

একপাটি *n* **1** one of a pair (of shoes or boots). **2** one set: ~ দাঁত.

একপাদ *n* a fourth part; a quarter. ❑*adj* one-fourth.

একপাল *adj* **1** animals of the same kind flocked together: ~ ভেড়া, a flock of sheep; ~ গরু, a herd of cows. **2** (hum) of great number; numerous; many: ~ ছেলেমেয়ে.

একপাশ *n* one side. ❑*adj* resting on one side; slanting. ~ **করা** *vt* put on one side. ~ **হওয়া** *vi* turn to one side. **একপাশে** *adv* on one side.

একপুরুষ *n* a single step in the line of descent; a generation: এক পুরুষে বড়ো লোক.

একপেট *adj* a bellyful of. ❑*adv* to one's fill: ~ খেয়ে নাও, have your fill.

একপেশে *adj* **1** leaning to one side; one-sided; biased: তোমার ধারণাটা ~. **2** incomplete; partial: ~ বক্তব্য.

একপ্রকার *adj* of a type; of some sort or other. ❑*adv* in a way/manner; so so: আমি ~ আছি, I am so so. **একপ্রকারে** *adv* in the same way/manner.

একপ্রস্ত *adv* one time; once: ~ চা-নাস্তা হয়ে গেছে.

একপ্রাণ⇒একদেহ

একফালি *n* one piece; a long slice or strip: ~ চাঁদ.

একবংশীয় *adj* of the same blood; related by birth; consanguineous.

একবচন (gram) *n* the singular number.

একবয়সী *adj* of the same age.

একবর্ণ *adj* **1** of one colour or caste. **2** of one syllable consisting of a single letter: আমি এর ~ও বুঝতে পারছি না, I can't make any head or tail of it.

একবস্ত্র *n, adj* one having only one set of clothes to wear. **একবস্ত্রা** *fem*. **একবস্ত্রে গৃহত্যাগ** leaving home with no spare set of garments or any belongings.

একবাক্যে *adv* in one voice; unanimously: এটা সকলে ~ স্বীকার করে, it is admitted on all hands; All are unanimous on this point.

একবার *adv* **1** at one time; once: ~ যখন তার অসুখ হয়েছিল, once when he was ill. . .. **2** for once: ~ যাও না সেখানে, Please go there once.

একবারে *adv* at a time: কাজটি ~ করে ফেল, finish the job at a time.

একবিংশ, একবিংশতি *n* twenty-one. ❑*adj* twenty-first.

একমত *adj* of the same opinion; unanimous: এ বিষয়ে আমরা ~, we are unanimous on this point.

একমতাবলম্বী *adj* of the same faith or creed.

একমনা *adj* absorbed in one subject; single-minded.

একমনে *adv* with undivided or rapt attention.

একমাতৃক *adj* born of the same mother.

একমাত্র *adj* **1** one only; sole; single: ~ পুত্র, the only son. **2** absolute; unique; having no second: আল্লাহ্ই ~ উপাস্য.

একমাত্রা *n* **1** (med) quantity of medicine given at one time; one dose. **2** a rhythmic unit of speech sound.

একমাত্রিক *adj* of one syllable; monosyllabic.

একমুখি *adj* one-faced; having one face or opening.

একমুখে *adv* in one direction: সবাই ~ চলছে.

একমুখো *adj* having one direction; one-way: ~ রাস্তা, one-way road.

একমুষ্টি, একমুঠো *adj* small quantity; a handful of: একমুষ্টি চাউল, একমুঠো ভাত.

একযোগে *adv* **1** in a body; unitedly. **2** at a time; simultaneously: নৌ ও বিমান বাহিনীর ~ আক্রমণ.

একর [E] *n* measure of land; 4840 sq yards of land; an acre.

একরকম, একরূপ *adj* of the same type/kind/nature/appearance; similar: দেখতে সবগুলোই ~, All are similar in appearance. ❑*adv* in a way; somehow or other: দিন ~ কাটছে, pulling on somehow: আমি ~ আছি, I am so so.

একরঙা *adj* of one colour; dyed in one colour: ~ কাপড়.

একরত্তি, একরতি *n* very small quantity; one grain: সে আমাকে ~ও ভালোবাসে না, He doesn't love me, not in the least. ❑*adj* very young; of tender age: ~ মেয়ে.

একরাম, ইকরাম [A] regard; respect; honour: এনাম ~ সবই পেয়েছেন.

একরার, ইকরার [A] **1** act of confessing (one's guilt, etc). **2** solemn promise or pledge. **3** an agreement or pledge of action: আমি এই মর্মে ~ করছি যে, I do hereby promise/pledge that . . . . ~**নামা** [A+P] *n* deed of agreement.

একরাশ *adj* of a good number; many; abundant.

একরূপ⇒একরকম

একরেখীয় *adj* in the same straight line; collinear.

একরোখা *adj* self-willed; obstinate; headstrong.

একলপ্ত [P] *adj* touching one another; in contact; contiguous: একলপ্তে ত্রিশ বিঘা জমি.

একলসেঁড়ে *adj* **1** self-centred; unsocial. **2** selfish.

একলহমা *n* a moment; an instant. ~**য়** *adv* in a moment; in an instant; in a trice.

একলা (poet, colloq) *adj* unaccompanied; lone. ❑*adv* without others; alone: বড়ো ~ বোধ করছি. ~-**একলি** *adv* without anybody's help or support: ~-একলি কাজ করা. ~-**দোকলা** *n* one or two: এটা ~-দোকলার কাজ নয়.

একশত, একশো, একশ' *n* the number 100. ❑*adj* **1** 100th. **2** numerous; many: ~ কথা.

একশরণ *n* the only resort/recourse. ❑*adj* having or depending on an only recourse.

একশা [P] *adj* **1** mixed up together: চালে ডালে ~. **2** in a state of confusion and disorder.

একশিরা *n* disease causing inflamation of one of the testicles; orchitis.

একশেষ *n* **1** extreme condition; excessiveness: কষ্টের ~, extreme distress; trouble beyond measure: নাকালের ~, harassed beyond measure.

একষট্টি *n* number sixty-one. ❑*adj* sixty-first. ~**তম** *adj* sixty-first.

একসঙ্গে *adv* together; in company; simultaneously: ~পড়ি ও গান শুনি.

একসপ্ততি *n* the number seventy-one. ~**তম** *adj* seventy-first.

একসা⇒একশা

একস্থানে *adv* in one place; at the same place.

একহাঁটু *adj* knee-deep: ~ পানি.

একহাত *n* measure of length; eighteen inches; a cubit. ~ **দেখা** *vi* try to avenge a wrong. ~ **নেওয়া** *vt* teach one a lesson; retaliate.

একহারা *adj* slim; slender: ~ গড়ন

একা *adj* alone; solitary; unaccompanied. ❑*adv* singly; alone: সে ~ই একশো, He is a host in himself. **একা-একা** *adv* by oneself; single-handed.

একাংশ [এক+অংশ] *n* one part/portion.

একাকার [এক+আকার] *adj* **1** mixed up together. **2** having no difference/distinction; equal. **3** of the same shape or form. ~ **করা** *vt* mix up. ~ **হওয়া** *vt* be in a mess/confusion. **একাকারা** *fem*.

একাকী *adj* **1** lone, single. **2** helpless. ❑*adv* lonely. **একাকিনী** *fem*.

একাগ্র, একাগ্রচিত্ত *adj* having the mind bent on an object; closely attentive, intent on. ~**তা** *n* intentness; single-mindedness; concentration. একাগ্রচিত্তে *adv* intently; single-mindedly; with undivided attention.

একাট্টা [H] *adj* **1** united or associated in affections or principles; combined; concerted. **2** assembled or collected in one place.

একাডেমী, একাডেমি [E] *n* **1** centre for the culture and research in art, literature or science; academy: বাংলা ~, শিল্পকলা ~, ইসলামিক ~. **2** the garden in Athens where Plato lectured.

একাত্তর *n* the number seventy-one. ❑*adj* seventy-first.

একাত্মতা⇒একাত্মা

একাত্মবাদ *n* (phil) the Vedantic doctrine of universal Spirit; the doctrine that the universe is the immanence of Brahma; pantheism. **একাত্মবাদী** *n* believer in this doctrine; a monist.

একাত্মা *adj* (of groups of people) of one spirit; sharing the same views and ideas. **একাত্মতা** *n* oneness of spirit; identity of purpose; solidarity: ছাত্রগণ ধর্মঘটী শ্রমিকদের সাথে ~ ঘোষণা করে, The students declared solidarity with the striking labourers.

একাদশ *n* eleven. ❑*adj* eleventh.

একাদশী *n* **1** the eleventh day of the lunar fortnight. **2** the fast enjoined on the Hindus on this day. ❑*adj fem* eleven years old.

একাদিক্রমে *adv* **1** in serial order from the first. **2** in an uninterrupted sequence; consecutively; successively: ~ পাঁচ দিন, for five days consecutively.

একাধার *n* one and the same vessel/object/person. **একাধারে** *adv* in one and the same person or thing: তিনি একাধারে কবি ও সঙ্গীত শিল্পী.

একাধিক [এক+অধিক] *adj* more than one. ~**বার** *adj* more than once.

একাধিকার [এক+অধিকার] *n* exclusive rights; monopoly.

একাধিপতি [এক+অধিপতি] *n* the sole/sovereign/paramount ruler; one who is all in all. **একাধিপত্য** *n* undisputed sway; absolute rule; paramountcy; domination.

একানব্বই *n, adj* ninety-one.

একান্ত [এক+অন্ত] *adj* **1** extreme; overwhelming: ~ বিপদে পড়েই এসেছি. **2** sure; certain. **3** earnest; ardent: ~ অনুরোধ. **4** private; personal: ~সচিব. ~**পক্ষে** (also ~ই) *adv* **1** if at all. **2** in the least. **একান্তে** *adv* in private; privately; confidentially.

একান্তর *adj* every other; every second; alternate. ~ **কোণ** *n* (geom) alternate angle.

একান্ন[1] *n, adj* fifty-one.

একান্ন[2], **একান্নবর্তী, একান্নভুক্ত** *adj* living and eating jointly; living in one family. ~**বর্তী পরিবার** *n* descendants of a common ancestor living and eating jointly; a joint family.

একাবলী *n* **1** one-stringed necklace. **2** variety of Bengali metrical foot.

একামত⇒ আকামত

একার[1] *n* letter 'এ' or its symbol. **একারাদি** *adj* (word) beginning with 'এ': একারাদি শব্দ. **একারান্ত** *adj* (word) ending with 'এ' or its symbol: একারান্ত শব্দ.

একার[2] (poss case) *n* of one only: এটা আমার ~, This is mine only.

একার্থ, একার্থক *adj* **1** having one and the same meaning; synonymous. **2** having one and the same purpose. ~তা *n* synonymity. **~বোধক** *adj* having similar meaning; synonymic.

একাল *n* **1** present times; modern times. **2** the mortal life. ~ **ওকাল** *n* **1** the earthly life and the life hereafter. **2** the present or modern times and the ancient age. ~ **সেকাল** *n* the present and the past times.

একাশি *n, adj* eighty-one. ~**তম** *adj* eighty-first.

একাশ্রয় (এক+আশ্রয়) *adj* depending on only one for support; having no other means or alternative.

একাসন *n* the same and the only seat. ❑*adj* having no seat but one.

একাহ *n* the period of one day.

একাহার *n* a single meal in a day. **একাহারী** *adj* taking but one meal a day.

একি *int* expressing surprise or wonder: ~ অনাচার!

একিন, একীন [A] *n* **1** faith, belief, esp in religious doctrines. **2** confidence; trust: আমার উপর ~ রাখো.

একিনি, একীনী [A] *adj* free from doubts; firm; sound; steady.

একীকরণ *n* **1** act of levelling or equalizing; equalization. **2** act of unifying or amalgamating; fusion. **একীকৃত** *adj*.

একীভবন *n* **1** act of being levelled or equalized; reduction to equal position. **2** act of being mixed up together; amalgamation; fusion.

একীভাব *n* act of being united; unity. ❑*adj* act of being equalized or mixed up together.

একুন *n* sum total. **একুনে** *adv* in total; in all; altogether.

একুল-ওকুল *n* **1** the family or lineage of the father as also that of the father-in-law (of a woman); both resorts or both alternatives. **2** the mortal life and the life after death: ~ দুকুল হারা.

একুশ *n, adj* twenty-one. **একুশে** *n* the twenty-first day of a month.

একূল-ওকূল *n* both the banks of a river.

একে[1] *pron* him: একে তো চিনি না.

একে[2] *adv* on the one hand: ~ চুরি, তার উপর সিনাজুরি.

একেএকে *adv* one after another: ~ সবাই চলে গেল.

একেবারে *adv* thoroughly; completely: ~ শেষ. ❑*adj* extreme; thorough; downright: ~ শয়তান.

একেলা⇒একলা

একেশ্বর *n* only one God. ~**বাদ** *n* belief in one God; monotheism. ~**বাদী** *adj* monotheistic. ❑*n* a monotheist.

একোন [এক+ঊন] *adj* less by one: একোনত্রিংশৎ, twenty-nine; একোনচত্বারিংশৎ thirty-nine; একোনপঞ্চাশৎ, forty-nine.

এক্কা [H] one-horse carriage of two wheels; a gig.

এক্ষণ *n* this moment. **এক্ষণি, এক্ষুণি** *adv* this very moment; at once. **এক্ষণে** *adv* at this moment; now; this time.

এখতিয়ার, এক্তিয়ার [A] *n* **1** range of exercising authority; legal authority; jurisdiction: **2** right; power; ability. **3** one's power to decide or choose; will; wish; volition.

এখন *adv* **1** now; at this moment: ~ যাও, পরে এসো. **2** at present; now-a-days, currently: ~ সে ব্যবসা করে. **3** in the present circumstances/condition: ~ কী করা যায়? **4** in an inopportune moment when the need is over: ~ গিয়ে আর লাভ কি? **5** at last; after so long: ~ বুঝি তোর জ্ঞান হলো? **6** in fact; actually: ~, সেই লোক ছিল একটা ডাকাত. ❑*n* this time; present times: ~ শীতকাল. **~ই, এখনি** *adv* at once; instantly; immediately. **~ও, এখনো** *adv* **1** till now; to this day: ~ও তাকে দেখিনি. **2** even after this; notwithstanding this; still: ~ও কি বলতে চাও তুমি ভুল করোনি? **~কার** *adj* of this time; current; recent: ~কার খবর জানি না. **~তখন** *adj* on the point of death: রোগী ~তখন, . . . may die any moment.

এখান *n* **1** this place. **2** this earth; the earthly life: ~ থেকে চলে যাবার সময়ে কিছুই সঙ্গে যায় না. **~কার** *adj* of this place: ~কার পরিস্থিতি ভালো. **এখানে** *adv* at his place; here.

এগনো, এগোনো *vt* go forward; advance: কাজ এগোচ্ছে, The work is in progress; কাজ এগোচ্ছে না, is not progressing. **এগিয়ে দেওয়া** accompany sb for some distance to see him off. **এগিয়ে যাওয়া** *vt* **1** advance; go forward. **2** make progress.

এগানা [P] *n* relative; kith and kin: ~ বেগানা.

এগারো, এগার *n, adj* eleven. **~ই** *adj* eleventh.

এগুলো, এগুলি *adj, pron* these. ❑*n* these things.

এগোনো⇒এগনো

এঙ্কার⇒ইঙ্কার

এছমে আজম=ইসমে আজম

এজন্য, এজন্যে *adv* for this reason; hence.

এজমা⇒ইজমা

এজমালি, ইজমালি [A] *adj* (of property) shared or held by more than one: ~ সম্পত্তি, joint property.

এজলা [A] *adj* mean; vulgar; lowly.

এজলাস, ইজলাস [A] *n* **1** the seat of a judge. **2** the court-room.

এজাজত, ইজাজত [A] *n* assent; consent; permission. **~নামা** [A+P] *n* permit; licence.

এজাহার, ইজাহার [A] *n* complainant's deposition to the police in a criminal case; statement of the complainant.

এজিন [A] a bride's consent to the proposal of her marriage as required under Muslim law.

এজেন্ট [E] *n* **1** agent or representative of a commercial concern. **2** legally appointed attorney; a law-agent. **3** one appointed to act on behalf of or look after the business of another.

এজেন্সি [E] *n* instrumentality or means by which sth is accomplished; the office or business of an agent; agency.

এঞ্জিন⇒ইঞ্জিন

এটর্নি, এটর্নী [E] *n* **1** one who practises in the High Court. **2** one legally empowered to act for another; a solicitor; an attorney.

এটম [E] *n* the minutest particle of matter that can take part in a chemical change; atom. ❑*adj* atomic: ~ বোমা.

এটা, এটি *pron* this (person or thing); this one: ~ করিমের ভাই, This is Karim's brother.

এডভোকেট, অ্যাডভোকেট *n* [E] (legal) professional representative in a legal case; an advocate.

এডমিট কার্ড [E] *n* card giving sb access to somewhere esp a student to sit for an examination; admit card.

এডিট করা [E] *vt* make corrections, additions, alterations, etc and thus prepare another person's writing for publication; edit. **এডিটরি, এডিটারি** *n* act of editing; editorship.

এডিটর, এডিটার [E] *n* person who edits (a book, newspaper, periodical, etc) or is in charge of a publication; editor.

এডিটরিয়েল [E] *n* special article in a newspaper or periodical containing the views of the editor on a current affair; the editor's column or editorial.

এডিশন [E] *n* **1** the publication of a book as characterized by its form and editorial labours. **2** the total number of copies of a book issued at one time: নতুন ~, new edition.

এড়ানো, এড়ান *vt* **1** keep away from; avoid; shun: সে আমাকে এড়িয়ে চলে, He keeps away from me/shuns or avoids my company/fights shy of me. **2** slip away; escape: এতবড় একটা ভুল কি করে দৃষ্টি এড়ালো, How could such a gross mistake escape notice? **3** dishonour; ignore: আমার কথা এড়াতে পারবে না. **4** avoid by dexterity; evade; elude: এবার শাস্তি এড়াতে পারবে না. **5** make free; rid oneself of : মশার হাত ~.

এণ্ডা[1]=আণ্ডা

এণ্ডা[2] *n* the castor-oil plant.

এণ্ডায় গণ্ডায় *adv* by manipulation or by cooking up (an account). ~ **মিলানো** balance an account by manipulation.

এণ্ডি *n* coarse variety of silk cloth chiefly produced in the Indian state of Assam: এণ্ডির চাদর.

এত, এতো *adv* so much; so many: ~ টাকা, ~ লোক, ~ ঝামেলা. ❑*adj* excessive; too much: ~ বাড়া ভালো নয়. ~**টুকু** *adj* a little; a bit: ~টুকু লজ্জা নেই. ~**টুকু হয়ে যাওয়া** be embarrassed/ abashed/non-plussed; be put out of countenance.

এতৎ, এতদ্ *pron* this (person, thing or matter): এতৎসংক্রান্ত, pertaining to this.

এতদতিরিক্ত *adj* in addition to this; besides this; over and above this.

এতদনুযায়ী *adv* as per/according to/in accordance with this.

এতদর্থে *adv* to this effect; for this reason; wherefore: ~ এই অঙ্গীকারনামা লিখে দিলাম.

এতদুদ্দেশ্যে *adv* with this end in view; for this purpose.

এতদ্দেশীয় *adj* of this country.

এতদ্ব্যতীত *adv* apart from this; besides this.

এতদ্ভিন্ন⇒এতদ্ব্যতীত

এতদ্⇒এতৎ

এতদিন, এদ্দিন *adv* so long. **এতদিনে** *adv* after so long a time.

এতবার, এৎবার=এতেবার

এতলা=এত্তেলা

এতাদৃশ *adj* like this; such-like; similar to this. **এতাদৃশী** *fem.*

এতাবৎ *adv* this far; so far. ❑*adj* so much; so great. ~**কাল** *adv* so long.

এতিম [A] *n* **1** a child bereft of one or both of its parents; an orphan. **2** one who has none to help or protect. ~**খানা** *n* orphanage.

এতে=ইহাতে

এতেক (poet) *adj* this much. ❑*adv* upto this.

এতেকাদ, ইতিকাদ [A] *n* faith; belief; trust.

এতেকাফ, এহ্‌তেকাফ *n* living in the mosque for a particular period towards the end of the month of Ramadan for devotional exercises.

এতেবার, এতবার [A] *n* **1** quality or state of being credible; credibility: ইনিই যে সেই নামজাদা কবি তা ~ হয় না. **2** faith; trust: আমার কথায় ~ করো. **3** careful treatment; consideration.

এত্তেফাক=ইত্তেফাক

এত্তেলা, এতলা, ইত্তেলা [A] news; information; report: সদরে ~ পাঠানো হলো. ~**নামা** *n* summons; notice; written statement.

এত্তেহাদ, ইত্তেহাদ [A] **1** unity; concord. **2** amity; friendship.

এদিক *n* **1** this side/way/direction. **2** this place/region/country. **3** this party: এদিকের প্রস্তাবটি ভেবে দেখার মতো. ~**ওদিক**, ~**সেদিক** *n* all sides. ❑*adv* this way and that; here and there; all around. ~**ওদিক করা** *vi* be unsettled in decision; hesitate; vacillate; waver. ~**সেদিক করা** *vt* deceive or defraud sb. **এদিকে** *adv* **1** in this place/region. **2** on this side. **3** in these circumstances; in the meantime; on the other hand: সবাই রোগী নিয়ে ব্যস্ত, এদিকে চোর যে কখন ঘরে ঢুকেছে কেউ বুঝতে পারেনি.

এদ্দৎ=ইদ্দৎ

এদ্দিন=এতদিন

এধার [H]=এদিক

এনকার=ইংকার

এনকেলাব=ইনকিলাব

এনভেলাপ [E] *n* **1** covering for letters, etc; a wrapper. **2** stamped envelope of the postal service.

এনসান=ইনসান

এনাম=ইনাম

এনামেল [E] *n* glass-like substance in melted condition used for coating metal, porcelain, etc; enamel. ❑*adj* decorated with enamel.

এনায়েত, ইনায়েত [A] *n* grace; mercy; favour.

এনার্জি [E] capacity for/power of doing work; energy: বৈদ্যুতিক ~, electrical energy.

এন্তার [Pg] *adj* countless; profuse. ❑*adv* continuously; without break.

এন্তেকাল, ইন্তেকাল [A] *n* death, demise.

এন্তেখাব, ইন্তেখাব [A] *n* act of electing; election.

এন্তেজাম, ইন্তেজাম [A] *n* preparations; arrangement: খানাপিনার ~.

এন্তেজার, এন্তেজারি, ইন্তেজার, ইন্তেজারি [A] *n* act of waiting on; eager expectation: আপনার ~ করছি.

এপার *n* this side; this bank (of the river). ~ **ওপার** *n* both banks of a river. ~ **ওপার করা** *vi* cross and recross; ferry over.

এপাশ-ওপাশ *n* both directions; this side and that. ~ **করা** *vi* toss about or roll over (in bed).

এপিঠ-ওপিঠ *n* two sides; both sides; the top and the bottom; the head and the tail (of a coin).

এপ্রিল *n* the fourth month of the Christian Calendar; April.

এফতার⇒ইফতার

এফিডেবিট [E] *n* a written declaration signed upon oath before a magistrate or any appropriate authority; affidavit.

এফোঁড়-ওফোঁড় *adv* from one side to the other: ~ করা, pierce through.

এবং *conj* and. ~**বিধ, এবম্বিধ** *adj* of this kind, like this.

এবড়ো-খেবড়ো *adj* rugged; uneven; rough.

এবাদত, ইবাদত [A] *n* act of praying; prayer; religious exercises. ~**খানা** *n* **1** the famous religious seminary of emperor Akbar at Fatehpur Sikri. **2** place for worship; prayer house. ~ **বন্দেগি** [A+P] *n* religious practices.

এবার *adv* **1** this time; on this occasion: এবারের মতো ক্ষমা করে দিন. **2** this year: ~ ফসল ভালো হবে. **3** in the prevailing circumstances/ condition: ~ যাবে কোথায়? How can you escape now? ~**কার** *adj* **1** for this time/occasion: ~কার মতো স্থগিত. **2** of this year: ~কার দুর্ভিক্ষে বহুলোক মারা গেছে.

এবারত, এবারৎ [A] *n* **1** style of composition; idiom: ~ দেখেই বুঝতে পেরেছি কার লেখা. **2** the first sketch of any writing; a draft: ~ খুবই ভালো হয়েছে. **3** long statement; elaborate account.

এবে (poet) *adv* **1** now; at this moment. **2** thereafter; then. **3** at present; in these days; now-a-days.

এবেলা *adv* **1** at the present time; after this; things being so; now: নাও, ~ যাবার ব্যবস্থা করো. **2** in this part of the day: চাল যা আছে তাতে ~ চলবে. ❑*n* this part of the day; forenoon (opp ওবেলা). ~ **ওবেলা** *adv* twice daily; in the forenoon and afternoon.

এভিনিউ, এভিন্যু [E] broad roadway with trees on both sides; avenue.

এম. এ. [E] (abbr of Master of Arts) *n* **1** university degree of higher level in Arts; M.A. **2** a holder of this degree: তিনি একজন ~.

এম. এস-সি [E] (abbr of Master of Science) *n* **1** higher level university degree in science; M. Sc. **2** A holder of this degree.

এম-ডি [E] (abbr of Doctor of Medicine) *n* **1** university degree of higher level in Medical science; M. D. **2** one who holds this degree.

এমতেহান, ইমতেহান [A] *n* act of examining or being examined by question and answer (either orally or in writing); examination.

এমন *adj* **1** such; suchlike; similar: ~ সুযোগ আর আসবে না, ~ ভালো মানুষ হয় না. **2** (expression meaning) doubtful; uncertain: ~ কি আর ক্ষতি হয়েছে, ie the alleged harm/damage is not so much of consequence. ~**ই** *adj* so much so; so great: ~ই পোড়া কপাল যে . . . ., so great is my misfortune that . . . . ~**কি** *adv* (expressing a strong assertion) what is more; even: সে ~কি আমাকে বসতেও বলেনি, He didn't even ask me to sit down. ~**টি** *pron* such a one: ~টি আর কখনো দেখিনি. ~**তর** *adj* of this sort: ~তর বেহায়াপনা বড়োই নিন্দনীয়. ~**ভাবে** *adv* in this way/manner; thus. ~ **সময়** *adv, conj* at that time/moment; when: আমি বের হতে যাবো ~ সময় মেহমান এলো, I was just going out when a guest came in.

এমনি *adv* **1** without any cause/reason; for nothing: ~ কেউ কাউকে মারে না. **2** without taking anything with; empty-handed: আত্মীয় বাড়ি ~ যাওয়া যায় না. **3** without meeting the prerequisite; without effort: ~ কি আর পাশ করা যায়. **4** to such an extent; in such a manner (expressing the depth, gravity or seriousness of a thing): ~ ঘুম দিয়েছে যে . . . **5** without any particular purpose : ~ এলাম, ~ বললাম.

এম. বি. বি. এস. [E] (abbr of Bachelor of Medicine and Bachelor of Surgery). **1** university degree of Bangladesh in medical science. **2** a practising physician holding this degree.

এমুখো *adv* this way bound: সে আর এখন ~ হয় না.

এযাত্রা *adv* this time; on this occasion: ~ বেঁচে গেলাম.

এযাবৎ *adv* hitherto; uptil now: ~ কোনো অভিযোগ আসেনি.

এয়াকুত=ইয়াকুত

এয়াজুজ=ইয়াজুজ

এয়ার হোস্টেস [E]*n* a female attendant in an airliner; air-hostess.

এরণ্ড *n* the castor-oil plant.

এরশাদ,ইরশাদ[A]*n* command; order; instruction.

এরাদা,ইরাদা[A]*n* desire; determination; resolve.

এরারুট=আরারুট

এরূপ *n* this sort; this description : ~ আচরণ. ❑*pron* such a one: ~টি পেলে আনবে. ❑*adj* of this form/shape; such. ❑*adj* thus; so; in such a way. **এরূপে** *adv* in this manner/way; thus.

এরোড্রাম [E] *n* ground for the arrival and departure of aircraft usually smaller than an airport; aerodrome.

এরোপ্লেন [E] *n* mechanically propelled flying machine with one or two pairs of wings (monoplane or biplane); aeroplane.

এলজাম, ইলযাম [A] *n* blame; slander; calumny.

এলবাম [E] *n* a book with blank leaves on which may be affixed photographs, stamps, literary extracts, etc; album.

এলবার্ট [E] *n* (attrib) a particular fashion of shoe, hair-dressing, watch-chains, etc, introduced by Prince Albert: ~ জুতা.

এলহান, ইলহান [A] *n* voice; tone.

এলহাম, ইলহাম [A] *n* knowledge gained by intuition.

এলাকা, ইলাকা [A] *n* **1** the extent of a place; an area; a region. **2** limit; boundary; border. **3** judicial power; jurisdiction.

এলাচ, এলাচি *n* seed-capsules of the aromatic plant cardamom.

এলাজ, ইলাজ [A] *n* **1** (medical) treatment; act of healing; a remedy; cure. **2** preventive medicine. **3** reproof; admonition: বেতমিজটাকে ~ দেওয়া প্রয়োজন.

এলান[1]**, ইলান** [A] *n* announcement; notice; proclamation.

এলানো, এলান[2] *vt* **1** (of a woman's hair) untie/loosen/dishevel. **2** (of the body) spread out; relax. ❑*adj* disheveled; spread out : ~ খোঁপা.

এলাম (colloq) *vi* (1st person) *pt* of আসা: এইমাত্র ~.

এলাহি, ইলাহি [A] *n* Allah. ❑*adj* very big in size; huge: ~ কারবার.

এলুমিনিয়াম [E] *n* a very light metal of a silvery white colour; aluminium.

এলেম [A] *n* learning; knowledge; erudition; scholarship. **~দার** *adj* knowledgeable; erudite.

এলমেদীন *n* religious education; knowledge of the scripture. **এলমে দুনিয়া** *n* knowledge useful in day-to-day life; practical education. **তালেব~** *n, adj* one who is in quest of knowledge; seeker-after knowledge; a student.

এলো[1]**, এল** *vi* (3rd person) *pt* of আসা: এখনো এলো না. **এলো বলে** is just coming/coming in no time.

এলো[2] *adj* **1** (of the hair) hung down loosely and untidily; unkempt; dishevelled: **এলোকেশী** *n, adj fem* woman with unkempt/dishevelled hair.

এলোপাতাড়ি, এলোপাথাড়ি *adj* without order or plan; unmethodical; haphazard. ❑*adv* at random; haphazardly; confusedly; in a disorderly manner.

এলোপ্যাথি [E] *n* the usual method of curing diseases by applying medicines which produce results opposite to those produced by the disease to be cured: allopathy (cf homoeopathy).

এলোমেলো *adj* **1** of a disorderly kind; not neat or tidy; slovenly; messy: ~ সংসার. **2** (of speech, thought, ideas, reasoning) inconsistent, incoherent, irrelevant. **~ভাবে** *adv* in confusion; at sixes and sevens: জিনিসপত্র ~ভাবে ছড়িয়ে আছে, The articles are in a mess.

এশা, ইশা [A] *n* **1** the canonical late evening prayer. **2** the appointed hour for the late evening prayer.

এশিয়া [E] *n* the name of the largest continent of the world; Asia.

এশীয় *adj* **1** of the continent of Asia. **2** pertaining to Asia.

এশক, ইশক [A] *n* **1** the passion between the sexes; love. **2** warm affection; fond attachment.

এষণা, এষা[1] *n* **1** research/ investigation/ exploration undertaken in order to discover new facts or to get additional information. **2** wish; desire; longing.

এষা[2] *adj fem* **1** worthy of desire; desirable. **2** searchable; explorable. **3** fit to be remembered.

এসপার-ওসপার *n* **1** desperate decision; final settlement. **2** either this or that; either success or failure. **3** either good or bad: বিষয়টি আর ঝুলিয়ে না রেখে এর একটা ~ হওয়া উচিত.

এসরাজ *n* kind of musical instrument with five strings and played with a bow.

এসিড, অ্যাসিড [E] *n* (chem) sour substance containing hydrogen, which with certain other substances forms salts; acid.

এসেন্স [E] *n* extract of flowers obtained by distillation; scent; perfume; essence.

এসেসর, আসেসর [E] *n* **1** legal adviser who assists a magistrate or judge; assessor. **2** officer in charge of assessment of revenue.

এসোসিয়েশন [E] *n* group of people joined together for some common purpose; association: ফুটবল ~.

এস্টিমেট [E] *n* calculation of probable cost; valuation; estimate.

এস্টেট [E] *n* landed property; estate.

এস্তফা=ইস্তফা

এস্তেখারা [A] *n* mode of getting at a correct judgement through a dream/meditation.

এস্তেন্‌জা [A] *n* physical purification after having answered the call of nature.

এস্তেমাল [A] *n* act of using or applying; use; application. ~ **করা** *vt* **1** put to use; use. **2** be accustomed; get used to.

এহেন *adj* like this; such; similar.

এহ্‌রাম, ইহ্‌রাম [A] *n* ritual preliminary to the performance of Hajj.

এহ্‌সান [A] favour; benefaction; benevolence.

ঐ

ঐ[1] *n* the ninth vowel of the Bengali alphabet. It is pronounced as অই or ওই. It joins a consonant with its symbol ৈ. In the Bengali phonetics it is called diphthong.

ঐ[2] *adj* that or those (indicating sth in front or nearby. ❑*adv* over there; yonder. ❑*int* expressing regret for negligence, lapse of memory, etc: ঐ যা, একদম ভুলে গেছি.

ঐকতান *n* agreement in a design; concord; harmony; concert.

ঐকমত্য *n* agreement in opinion; unanimity.

ঐকান্তিক *adj* profound; intense; earnest: ~ বাসনা. ❑*adv* with sincerity and earnestness; absorbedly; single-mindedly: ~ প্রচেষ্টা. **ঐকান্তিকতা** *n*.

ঐকিক *adj* of or relating to a unit; unitary: ~ নিয়ম, (arith) the unitary method.

ঐক্য *n* **1** state of being one; unity; union. **2** similarity; likeness; affinity; resemblance. **3** agreement; concord; harmony. ~**বদ্ধ** *adj* united; combined. ~**সাধন** *n* act of establishing unity/concord.

ঐচ্ছিক *adj* **1** depending on one's own option or choice; optional; elective. **2** as one pleases; to one's liking.

ঐতিহাসিক *adj* **1** of or based on history; historical: ~ উপন্যাস. **2** of historical importance; historic: ~ ঘটনা. **3** versed in history. ❑*n* a writer or compiler of history; historian. ~**তা** *n* historical truth; reality.

ঐতিহ্য *n* **1** values, customs and accumulated experiences of earlier generations handed down to posterity; tradition: জাতীয় ~. **2** cultural heritage. ~**গত, ঐতিহ্যিক** *adj* traditional.

ঐন্দ্রজালিক⇒ইন্দ্রজাল

ঐরাবত *n* elephant; (myth) Indra's elephant.

ঐশিক *adj* relating to God. **ঐশী** *fem*. ঐশীবাণী.

ঐশ্বরিক *adj* of or belonging to God; divine.

ঐশ্বর্য *n* **1** wealth; riches. **2** pomp; splendour; magnificence. **3** power; authority; majesty. ~**গর্ব** *n* pride of wealth. ~**গর্বিত** *adj* proud of wealth. ~**শালী** *adj* wealthy; opulent; affluent.

ঐহিক *adj* **1** of this world; worldly; mundane. **2** of the present life; secular; temporal.

ও

ও[1] *n* the tenth vowel of the Bengali alphabet. It joins a consonant in the form of its symbol, eg ক +ও=কো.

ও[2] *conj* having the sense of adding sth to what has been said before and connecting words, clauses or sentences: একটি টেবিল ও দুটি চেয়ার.

ও[3] *pron* he; she; it; that (person or thing): ও কে? ওটা কি? ❑*adj* pointing to a person or thing mentioned or understood; that: ও কথা বলো না, ও লোকটি দুঃখী; the other: ওদিক, ওপার.

ও[4] *adv* moreover; further; besides; too; also; even: আমিতো যাবই, তোমাকেও যেতে হবে, আরও বিপদ আছে, সে থাকবে এবং খাবেও, নামও শুনিনি.

ও[5] *int* expressing a call; recollection, amazement, pity, etc: ও ভাই! ও, মনে পড়েছে, ও মা, এমনতো শুনিনি কখনো!

ও[6] 'ও' is also used as an inflexion to coin new words, eg ঝড়ো (ঝড়+ও), জলো (জল+ও), বুনো (বন+ও).

ওই=ঐ[2] *adj*

ওঃ *int* expressing regret, amazement, pain, derision, etc: ওঃ কী সাজ্ঘাতিক লোক!

ওঁ *n* the Hindu symbol of Supreme Being.

ওকার *n* the letter 'ও' or its symbol.

ওকালতনামা=উকালতনামা

ওকালতি=উকালতি

ওকুস্থল=অকুস্থল

ওখান *n* that place/region. **~কার** *adj* of that place. **ওখানে** *adv* there; in that place.

ওগরানো=উগরানো

ওজন [A] *n* **1** act of weighing; weight. **2** importance. **3** dignity; power; prestige. **~ করা** *vt* weight. **~-করা** *adj* measured: ~-করা কথা.

ওজর [A] *n* **1** objection; protest. **2** a plea; an excuse; a pretext. **বাজে ~** a lame excuse. **মিথ্যা ~** a false plea.

ওজস্বী *adj* **1** strong; vigorous, enthusiastic: ~ ভাষণ, fiery speech. **2** of florid character; ornate. **ওজস্বিনী** *fem*. **ওজস্বিতা** *n* strength; vigour; ornateness.

ওজারত [A] *n* the office of the minister.

ওজিফা=অজিফা

ওজু=অজু

ওজুহাত=অজুহাত

ওজোগুণ *n* (rhet) ornateness and vigour of style.

ওজোন *n* form of oxygen with a sharp and refreshing smell; ozone.

ওঝা *n* one who cures snake-bites or other morbidities by means of incantation.

ওটকানো=উটকানো

ওটা *pron* that (person or thing): ~ এখানে রাখো.

ওঠা=উঠা

ওড়না *n* modesty scarf for women.

ওড়া=উড়া

ওডিকোলন=অডিকোলন

ওত *n* act of lying in wait in order to surprise; ambush; ambuscade. **~ পেতে থাকা** *vt* lie in wait; wait in ambush; ambuscade.

ওতপ্রোত *adj* inseparably running in; thoroughly mixed up; pervasive. **~ভাবে** *adv* inextricably; inseparably.

ওদিক *n* **1** that side/direction. **2** the other party.

ওধার *n* the other side.

ওফাত [A] *n* death; decease.

ওবা [A] *n* **1** epidemic; pestilence. **2** contagious disease like cholera, smallpox, plague, etc.

ওমর, উমর [A] age.

ওমরা=উমরা

ওয়াকিফ, ওয়াকেব [A] *adj, n* one who knows; informed; experienced. **~হাল** one having particular knowledge about sth.

ওয়াক্‌ফ [A] *n* charitable or religious endowment under Muslim law. **~নামা** *n* deed of endowment.

ওয়াক্ত [A] *n* appointed hours for five-time canonical prayers.

ওয়াজ [A] *n* religious sermon; lecture on religious subjects. **~নসিহত** *n* lectures and instructions on religion.

ওয়াজিব, ওয়াজেব [A] *adj* **1** just; proper; right. **2** bounden; obligatory: ~ নামাজ. **3** necessary; essential.

ওয়াট [E] *n* unit of electrical power; watt (after James Watt, the inventor).

ওয়াড় *n* a pillow-case or a covering case for a quilt.

ওয়াতন [A] *n* birth-place; mother land.

ওয়াদা [A] *n* a pledge; a promise.

ওয়াপস [P] *n* act of coming back; return.

ওয়ারিশ, ওয়ারিস [A] *n sing* (*pl* ওয়ারিশান) successor to one's property; an heir or heiress.

ওয়ারেন্ট [E] document authorizing an officer to seize an offender; a warrant.

ওয়ালিমা=অলিমা

ওয়ালেদ [A] *n* the male parent; father.

ওয়াশিল, ওয়াসিল [A] *n* realization (of dues).

ওয়াহিদ, ওয়াহেদ [A] *adj* one; alone.

ওরফে [A] *adv* otherwise known as; alias.

ওল *n* edible bulbous plant akin to arum. **যেমন বুনো ~ তেমনি বাঘা তেঁতুল** (fig) measure for measure.

ওলকপি *n* vegetable of the turnip group; a kohlrabi.

ওলট-পালট=উলট-পালট

ওলন্দাজ [F] *n* native of the Netherlands/ Holland; a Dutch; a Hollander. ❑*adj* Dutch: ~ ভাষা.

ওলাউঠা *n* disease accompanied by purging and vomiting; cholera.

ওলান *n* the glandular organ of the cows in which the milk is produced; the udder.

ওষধি *n* plant that perishes after bearing fruit but for once.

ওষুধ *n* medicine; drug.

ওষ্ঠ *n* the upper lip; any of the lips. **ওষ্ঠাধর** *n pl* the two lips—upper and lower.

ওষ্ঠাগত *adj* what has neared the lips in order to come out; (fig) at the last gasp. **~প্রাণ** *adj* at the last gasp; at the point of death.

ওসিয়ত=অসিয়ত

ওস্তাগর [P] *n* an efficient artisan; a master artisan/mason/tailor.

ওস্তাদ [A, P] *n* master (in any art); preceptor; leader. ❑*adj* adept; expert. **ওস্তাদি** *n* mastery (of an art); skill; efficiency. **ওস্তাদি করা** *vt* parade one's skill/ability; show off one's tricks.

ওহাবি, ওয়াহাবি [A] *n* follower of Abdul Wahab, the 18th century religious leader of Arabia; Wahabi sect.

ওহি, ওহী [A] *n* Revelation from the Supreme Being to His prophets.

ওহে *int* used in addressing: hallo! Holla! Ho!.

ওহো *int* expressing recollection, surprise, amazement, regret, etc; good heavens! good gracious!

ঐ

ঐ *n* the eleventh vowel of the Bengali alphabet. When it joins a consonant it takes the form of its symbol, eg ক+ঐ=কৈ.

ঐকার *n* the letter ঐ or its symbol. **ঐকারাদি** *adj* (word) beginning with ঐ or ঐ-sound. **ঐকারান্ত** *adj* (word) ending in ঐ or its symbol.

ঐচিত্য *n* **1** state of being proper; propriety; fitness; justness. **2** truth; decorum; appropriateness.

ঔজ্জ্বল্য *n* **1** the quality of being bright; brightness. **2** lustre; glaze; glamour; splendour.

ঔৎকর্ষ=উৎকর্ষ

ঔৎসুক্য *n* **1** curiosity; inquisitiveness; ardour; zeal. **2** anxiety; worry.

ঔদরিক *adj* **1** given to excessive eating; gluttonous; voracious. **2** pertaining to the abdomen; abdominal. **~তা** *n* gluttony; voracity; voraciousness.

ঔদার্য *n* **1** greatness of soul; generosity; liberality; broadness of mind. **2** magnanimity; munificence.

ঔদাসীন্য *n* **1** indifference; disinterestedness; callousness. **2** absence of sympathy; apathy towards worldly interests.

ঔদ্ধত্য *n* **1** insolent bearing; arrogance. **2** rudeness; haughtiness; impudence; impertinent. **3** incivility; discourtesy; unmannerliness. **4** pride; vanity.

ঔদ্বাহিক *adj* **1** obtained through marriage. **2** marital; nuptial; matrimonial. ❑*n* marriage-portion; dowry.

ঔপনিবেশিক *adj* **1** pertaining to a colony; colonial. **2** settling in a colony; colonizing. ❑*n* colonist.

ঔপনিষদ *adj* of or relating to the Upanishad.

ঔপন্যাসিক *adj* relating to novels/a work of fiction. ❑*n* a novelist.

ঔরস *adj* born of one's semen and of the womb of one's wife; legitimate. ❑*n* **1** legitimate child. **2** semen. **~জাত** *adj* legitimately born; lawfully begotten.

ঔষধ, ওষুধ *n* that which cures a disease; medicine; drug; (fig) remedy to anything. **~ সেবন করা** *vi* take/use medicine. **~ সেবন করানো** *vi* administer medicine. **~ করা** treat medically. **~ ধরা** be effective; begin to act.

ঔষধালয় *n* a drug-store; a pharmacy; a dispensary.

ঔষধি *n* a medicinal plant.

ক

ক[১] *n* the first consonant of the Bengali alphabet. It is an unvoiced alveolar plosive sound.

ক[২] *vt* (in imperative mood) (colloq) say; tell: ক, কে ছিল তোর সাথে.

ক[৩] *pron* used as *adj* **1** some; several; a few; a number of: কদিন থেকেই যাবো যাবো করছি. **2** (short form of কত and কয়) how many; how much: ক' টাকা আছে?

ক[৪] (or **ক খ**) *n* the alphabet: এখনো ক খ শেখেনি; elementary knowledge (অর্থনীতির ক খ). **ক-অক্ষর গোমাংস** (one) to whom the alphabet is as detestable as beef to a Hindu; a grossly illiterate person; ignoramus.

-ক *suff* **1** (poet and colloq) ক is used as inflexion with certain words of negative purport (ie না, নাই, নাহি, নয়, নেই, নহে , নহি) which makes them sound sweet, eg "থাকব না ক বদ্ধ ঘরে". This ক sometimes takes the form of কো, eg যেও নাকো, খেও নাকো, etc. **2** ক was also in use as verb inflexion in the 19th century as an expression of respect in the imperative mood, eg, ২০ জন বসিবেক, খাইবেক, যাইবেক, etc.

কই[১], **কৈ**[১] *n* variety of fish famous for deliciousness when fried; the walking fish.

কই[২], **কৈ**[২] *adv* where: সে কই? ❑*int* **1** where (interrogative): কই, বইটাতো পাচ্ছি না. **2** (expressing dejection): সে এলো কই? he is not turning up, I see.

কই[৩] *vt* (1st Person) I say; I tell: মনের কথা কই.

কইতর=কবুতর

কইয়ে *adj* having the gift of the gab. ❑*n* a gifted speaker.

কউতর [P] *n* the pigeon.

কওম [A] *n* a community; a nation. **কওমি** *adj* of or concerning a nation; national: কওমি নিশান.

কওলা=কবালা

কওসর [A] *n* **1** nectar; ambrosia. **3** a stream; a current of water: আবে ~.

কংগ্রেস [E] **1** legislative assembly of the United states; one of the political parties of India, the Indian National Congress. **2** association; an organized party; a formal meeting of representatives of societies or countries to exchange information and opinion.

কংস, কংশ *n* bell-metal; white brass. **~-বণিক** *n* dealer in brass-vessels; a brazier.

ককানো, ককান *vi* sob; groan; moan. **ককানি** *n* act of sobbing; sob.

কক্ষ *n* **1** a room; an apartment; a chamber: শ্রেণী~. **2** the hollow underneath the arm-joined; armpit (also কক্ষপুট). **3** (astron) the path of a heavenly body. **~চ্যুত** *adj* (of heavenly bodies) deviated or fallen from one's orbit. **~তল** *n* the floor of a room; the floor. **কক্ষাধিপাল** *n* ward-master. **কক্ষান্তর** *n* another room; ante-chamber; private apartment.

ক-খ *n* the alphabet; elementary knowledge; ABC.

কখন *adv* **1** when; at what time. **2** long before: সেতো ~ চলে গেছে.

কখনো, কখনও, *adv* ever; at any time. **আর ~** ever afterwards. **আর ~ না** never again. **~ না** never. **~ ~** occasionally. **~ না ~** sometime or other.

কঙ্ক *n* large wading bird distinguished by its slender legs, long beak and neck; the heron.

কঙ্কণ=কাঁকন

কঙ্কর *n* coarse grain of stone; gravel; grit.

কঙ্কাল *n* the bony framework of an animal separated from the flesh; skeleton. **~সার** *adj* reduced to a skeleton; one who is only skin and bone.

কচ[১] [P] *n* **1** a curved projection of a piece of land or of a building. **2** the pointed end of a quill-pen; a nib.

কচ[২] *n* hair.

কচ[৩] *int* sound of cutting off or biting off sth at one stroke: ~ করে কাটা. **~ কচ** *int* repetition of this sound produced when sth soft (eg, an apple or a green mango) is crunched. **~কচে** *adj* giving the above sound when crunched ~কচে আম.

কচলানো *vt* wash by rubbing; cleanse; wring.

কচাল *n* dispute, quarrel; haggling; altercation. **~ করা** *vi* haggle; altercate.

কচালে *adj* (of a person) tending to dispute or argue; disputatious; contentious.

কচি *adj* (of plants and fruits) soft; tender; green: কচি ঘাস, কচি আম; (of children) young; delicate: কচি ছেলে, child in arms; babe; infant. **কচিখোকা** (facet) aged person but too much childish or innocent. **কচি খোকা আর কি** it seems you are a mere baby.

কচু *n* **1** famous esculent root; a sort of arum: কচুশাক, arum greens/ leaves. **2** (contemp) thing of no value; mere trifle; nothing: সে আমার কচু করবে, what hell he can do me? **কচুকাটা করা** cut down at will to pieces. **কচু-পোড়া খাওয়া** (abusive) get nothing after long expectation; be deprived of what was expected.

কচুরি *n* kind of pancake made of flour and pulses.

কচুরিপানা *n* water-hyacinth.

কচ্ছপ *n* reptile covered with a flattened shell; a tortoise; a turtle. **কচ্ছপী** *fem.*

কঞ্চি *n* a bamboo twig; a slip of bamboo.

কঞ্চুলিকা, কঞ্চুলী *n* modesty vest for women; bodice.

কঞ্জুস *adj* miserly; niggardly; close-fisted. ☐*n* miser. **~পনা, কঞ্জুসি** *n* miserliness; niggardliness.

কট *n* document pledging (a landed properly) as security for a debt; a deed of conditional sale; mortgage deed. **~কবালা** [S+A] mortgage deed.

কটমট *adj* hard; harsh; angry: ~ দৃষ্টি. ☐*int* denoting rudeness, frown, anger. **~ করে তাকানো**, look with fierce piercing eyes; look daggers; glare.

কটমটে *adj* difficult; complex; unintelligible.

কটরমটর *int* sound of crunching hard things like nuts, etc; crunching sound. **~ করে খাওয়া** *vt* crunch.

কটা *n* **1** brownish or yellowish colour. **2** roughness.

কটাক্ষ *n* **1** an oblique look; side-glance. **2** adverse reflection; oblique hint. **~ করা** *vi* look askance at; cast a reflection. **~পাত** *n* looking askance. **কটাক্ষে** *adv* with a meaningful look; by way of insinuation.

কটাল, কোটাল *n* the high tide which happens at the new and full moon; spring-tide. **ভরা ~** flow-tide; flood-tide. **মরা ~** flowing back of the tide; ebb-tide; neap-tide.

কটি *n* the part of the human body between the ribs and the hips; the waist (also কটিতট, কটিদেশ).

কটিত্র, কটিবন্ধ *n* the band of trousers, etc which encompasses the waist; a waistband; a belt; a girdle.

কটিবাত, কটিশূল *n* rheumatic affection of the muscles about the loins; lumbago.

কটু *adj* **1** sharp to the taste; bitter. **2** pungently aromatic; severe: ~ তৈল. **3** hard; stern; harsh; acrimonious: ~বাক্য, কটূক্তি.

কটুকাটব্য *n pl* abusive language; bitter reproaches.

কট্টর *adj* blindly attached to; inveterate; bigoted: ~ সমাজতন্ত্রী, diehard socialist.

কঠিন *adj* **1** firm; rigid; inflexible; unbending: ~ প্রতিজ্ঞা. **2** hard-hearted; merciless; heartless; pitiless: ~ লোক. **3** difficult; complicated; incurable: ~ রোগ. **4** complex; difficult to answer/ understand/ solve: ~ প্রশ্ন/ সমস্যা. **5** hard; solid: ~পদার্থ. **কঠিনত্ব, কঠিনতা, কাঠিন্য** *nn.*

কঠোর *adj* **1** strict; stern; rigid; stringent: ~ শাসন. **2** hard; arduous: ~ পরিশ্রম. **3** austere; steady; unflinching; zealous; earnest: ~ তপস্যা. **~তা** *n.*

কড়কড় *int* (onom) word denoting the sound of a crash of thunder: মেঘের ~.

কড়চা *n* **1** biographical sketch or a narrative. **2** a handbook; a diary: গোবিন্দদাসের ~. **3** an account book containing the details of rent payable by the tenants; a descriptive rent-roll.

কড়তা, করতা *n* the weight of the container (of a commodity for sale); tare: গুড়ের হাড়ির ~.

কড়মড় *int* (onom) suggesting a harsh grating noise: ~ করে চিবানো.

কড়া[1] *n* coin of the smallest value; (fig) anything negligible; a jot; a tittle; an iota: এক কড়ার মুরোদ নেই, having not an iota of power/ ability. **~য় গণ্ডায়** *adv* completely; entirely; to the last farthing. **~ হিসাব করা** go into minute details.

কড়া[2] *n* metal ring; ring attached to anything as a handle: দরজার ~.

কড়া[3] *adj* **1** harsh; rough; rude: ~ মেজাজ, ~ কথা. **2** sharp, severe: ~ রোদ্দুর. **3** strict; rigid; rigorous: ~ হাকিম, ~ আইন. **4** alert; watchful; careful: ~ পাহারা. **5** high; exorbitant: ~ সুদ. **6** strong; bitter; distasteful: ~ ওষুধ. **~কড়ি** *n* strictness; stringency.

কড়া[4] *n* small area on the skin hardened by constant rubbing or contact with sth; a corn: হাতে ~ পড়েছে.

কড়াই *n* bowl-shaped cooking utensil; frying pan; cauldron.

কড়ার [A] (colloq কড়াল) *n* a statement binding a person who makes it; promise; condition; stipulation. **কড়ারে** on condition. **কড়ারি** *adj* conditional; covenanted.

কড়ি[1] *n* money; riches; wealth: টাকা~. **কানা~** *n* coin which is unless as a medium of exchange; a trifle: এক কানাকড়ির মূল্য নাই.

কড়ি[2], **কড়িকাঠ** *n* a joist or beam supporting the ceiling of a structure/ building.

কড়ি[3] *n* musical note: ~ ও কোমল.

কড়ে *adj* small; little: ~ আঙুল.

কণা *n* a small particle of anything; an atom; a jot; a little grain: জল~, শস্য~. **~কার** *adj* consisting of or resembling a grain; granular. **~মাত্র** *adj* just a little grain. **কণিকা** *fem.*

কন্টক *n* **1** the spines or prickles of a tree or shrub; a thorn. **2** the bones of a fish. **3** (fig)a source of annoyance/ vexation/ impediment/ hindrance. **4** (fig) one who is an enemy/ antagonist: পথের ~. **~ময়** *adj* **1** full of thorns; thorny. **2** (fig) difficult of access/ approach. **~শয্যা** *n* **1** bed of thorns. **2** unbearable torment/ discomfort.

কন্টকাকীর্ণ *adj* **1** strewn with thorns of prickles. **2** (fig) difficult of approach. **কন্টকিত** *adj* full of thorns.

কণ্ঠ *n* **1** front part of the neck; the throat. **2** the windpipe; the esophagus. **3** voice; tone of voice. **~নালী** *n* the passage for the breath; the windpipe; the gullet. **~স্থ** *adj* what has been memorized. **~স্থ করা** *vt* commit to memory.

কণ্ঠা *n* the clavicle; the collarbone. **~গত** *adj* come up to the throat; about to get out of the mouth.

কণ্ডু, কণ্ডূ *n* skin disease; itch; scabies. **~য়ন** *n* itching; scratching. **~য়ন করা** *vi* itch; scratch.

কত, কতো *adj* **1** how much; how many: ~ক্ষণ, ~ টাকা, ~ দিন. **2** much, many: ~ করে বললাম. ~ নিশি হলো ভোর. ❑*adv* much; to a great extent: ~ কি দেখলাম, ~ কষ্ট, ~ সুখ. ❑*n* a great number/ amount: ~ এলো ~ গেল. ❑*pron* what; how much: ~ করে কিনলে, at what price. ~ **কিছু** sundries; varieties/ lots of things. ~ **শত** countless; innumerable. **এখন সময় ~ ?** what's the time now? **তার বয়স কত?** what is his age? How old is he?

কতক *adj* some; a little; a few. ❑*adv* in part; partially; to some extent. ❑*pron* some of it/ them: এ জিনিসগুলোর মধ্যে ~ দেশী, ~ বিদেশী, of these things, some are country made and some are foreign.

কতকটা *adj* some; a certain. ❑*adv* somewhat; to a certain extent. ❑*n* a part/ portion.

কতগুলো, কতগুলি *adj pron* some; a few; a number/ quantity of; how many.

কতটা *adj, pron* how much; how far.

কতটি *adj, pron* how many.

কতবেল *n* shelled fruit with sour pulp; wood-apple or elephant apple.

কতল [A] *n* beheading; decapitation. **~ করা** *vt* behead; decapitate; kill.

কতিপয় *adj* some; several; a number of.

কথক *n* person who recites or interprets legends and myths. **~তা** *n* the profession of such a person.

কথঞ্চিৎ *adv* **1** somehow; in some way. **2** slightly; partially.

কথন *n* act or mode of speaking.

কথা *n* **1** words spoken; utterance; discourse; talk. **2** mode of speaking; pronunciation: **তার** ~ জড়ানো (আড়ষ্ট). **3** subject; topic: **সে ~ পরে** হবে. **4** pledge; promise: ~ দেওয়া. **5** prayer; request; entreaty: ~ রাখা. **6** desire; aim; purpose: মনের ~. **7** heated dispute; wrangle; altercation: ~ কাটাকাটি. **8** subject or context of discussion; one's say: ~ শেষ তো? **9** one's opinion/ point of view: আমার ~ হলো যে. **10** a popular saying; a proverb: ~য় বলে. **~ কাটাকাটি** bandying of words; altercation. **~ কাটাকাটি করা** bandy words; altercate. **~ চালা/ চালাচালি করা** spread rumour. **~ দেওয়া** give one's word/ assurance; promise. **~ পাড়া** raise a topic; broach a subject. **~ প্রসঙ্গে** *adv* by the way; by the by; incidentally. **~ বলা** *vi* speak. **~ বাড়ানো** argue on; talk uselessly. **~ শোনা**

listen; obey; pay heed to. ~ শোনানো speak severely/ harshly. ~য় বলে the proverb goes; they say. ~র কথা 1 anything said incidentally/ by the way. 2 easy affair: একাজ করা কি ~র ~? ~র ফের jugglery of words; turn of language to evade the point in question; quibble. কথার মানুষ man of word/honour. ~র মারপ্যাচ jugglery of words.

কথাকলি *n* Kathakali, a folk dance of south India.

কথাক্রম *n* sequence of subjects.

কথাবার্তা *n* conversation; talk; chatting. ~ বলা *vi* talk; converse; chat.

কথাশিল্প=কথাসাহিত্য

কথাসাহিত্য *n* works written in prose, eg novels, stories, etc.

কথাসাহিত্যিক *n* author of prose fiction, stories, etc.

কথিকা *n* short story or talk.

কথিত *adj* 1 said; narrated. ~ আছে it is said; they say.

কথোপকথন *n* conversation; dialogue.

কথ্য *adj* 1 that which is to be spoken or told; speakable; utterable. 2 (of dialect) used in or suitable for ordinary conversation; not formal or literary: ~ ভাষা.

কদম[1] *n* variety of flower or its tree.

কদম[2] [A] *n* 1 leg; foot: কদমের ধূলি. 2 footstep: জোর কদমে, with quick steps. 3 pace of a horse; trot: কদমে চলা, trot. ~বুসি [A+P] *n* making obeisance to one by touching his/ her feet.

কদমা *n* variety of sweet.

কদম্ব=কদম[1]

কদর [A] *n* 1 respect; regard; honour: বিদ্বানের ~ সর্বত্র. 2 power; worth; value. 3 the holy night of 27th Ramzan called 'Lailatul Kadar' meaning the Night of power. The night is celebrated by Muslims with great reverence and prayer as being the one on which the Holy Qoran was first revealed to the Prophet. ~ করা *vt* respect; honour; have regard for; appreciate; receive with due honour. ~দান (A+P) *n* one who appreciates the worth of anything.

কদর্থ *n* perverted/ distorted meaning; misinterpretation. ~ করা *vt* pervert or distort the meaning (of); misinterpret.

কদর্য *adj* 1 disagreeable in appearance; ugly: ~ চেহারা. 2 base; mean; detestable: ~ স্বভাব, ~ রুচি. 3 miserly; niggardly. ~তা *n* ugliness; meanness; miserliness.

কদলী *n* plantain tree or fruit.

কদাকার *adj* ill-shaped; deformed; ugly.

কদাচ *adv* at any time; ever. ~ না never.

কদাচার *n* abominable habit or practice. কদাচারী *adj* given to abominable or loathsome habits and practice; wicked; profligate.

কদাচিৎ *adv* rarely; scarcely ever; seldom.

কদাপি=কদাচ

কদু *n* kind of vegetable marrow; a gourd.

কনক *n* precious metal used for making jewellery; gold. ❑*adj* having the lustre of gold; bright as gold; golden. ~চাঁপা *n* golden-coloured sweet-scented flower or its plant, ~প্রভ *adj* bright or shining as gold. ~প্রভা *n* the lustre of gold. ~বরণ *adj* golden-coloured. ~মুকুট *n* crown of gold; golden crown. ~লতা *n* creeping plant of golden colour; golden creeper.

কনকন *int* denoting aching pain, bitterness of cold or biting sensation. কনকনে *adj* aching; piercing; biting. কনকনে শীত biting cold.

কনিষ্ঠ *adj* younger in age; youngest: ~ ভ্রাতা, younger brother; সর্ব ~, youngest. কনিষ্ঠা *fem.*

কনুই *n* the bend or joint of the arm; elbow.

কনে *n* 1 girl about to be married; a bride. 2 a virgin of marriageable age. 3 a newly-married wife. ~বউ *n* 1 a newly-married wife. 2 a child-wife.

কন্দ[1] *n* a bulbous root; fleshy part of an underground stem with buds from which new plants will grow; tuber.

কন্দ[2] [A] *n* sugar-candy.

কন্দর *n* a mountain-cave; a cavern; (fig) the inside of a thing: হৃদয়-~.

কন্দর্প *n* Kamadeva, the Hindu god of love. ~কান্তি *adj* handsome as Kandarpa.

কন্না *n* that which a person is bound to perform; an obligation. ঘর~ *n* work of a housewife; housewifery.

কন্যা *n* 1 a female offspring; a daughter. 2 a virgin; a marriageable girl. 3 the heroine at a marriage festival; a bride: ~ পক্ষ. ~দান *n* act of giving a daughter in marriage. ~দায় *n* the responsibility of marrying a daughter; the state of being burdened with a marriageable daughter. ~দায়গ্রস্ত *adj* burdened with the responsibility of disposing a marriageable daughter whose marriage is long overdue.

কপচানো *vt* 1 utter or reproduce set words of speech like a parrot (ie without understanding the import of what is said). 2 learn sth by rote; memorize sth. 3 prattle empty words in order to parade one's learning.

কপট *adj* 1 given to deceiving; deceitful; hypocritical; insincere: ~ সাধু, ~ বন্ধু. 2 apt to deceive; delusive; false; fraudulent: ~ বেশ. ❑*n* trickery; chicanery; deceit. ~তা, কাপট্য *n*.

কপর্দক *n* 1 (fig) medium of exchange of the smallest denomination; a penny: আমি ~হীন, I am penniless. 2 the smallest amount of money/ riches: তোমাকে এক ~ও দেবো না.

কপাট, কবাট *n* 1 a door or the shutters of a door; door-panels: ~ খোলা, open a door; ~

লাগানো, shut a door. **2** a veil or cover of anything: মনের ~.

কপাটি১, কবাডি *n* sort of Bangladeshi outdoor game.

কপাটি২ *n* tetanus of the jaw; trismus; lock-jaw: দাঁত~.

কপাল *n* **1** the front part of the face above the eyes; the forehead: সুডৌল ~. **2** the bony case of the brain; the cranium; the skull: নর~, skull-bone. **3** luck; mere chance; fortune: ~ গুণে সে আজ কারখানার মালিক. **~ক্রমে** *adv* by luck/chance; luckily; fortunately. **~গুণে** *adv* **1** by good luck; fortunately. **2** unluckily; unfortunately. **~ খোলা** *vi* be lucky/ favoured with fortune: তার ~ খুলেছে, fortune has smiled upon him; his stars are in the ascendant. **~জোড়** *n* the favour of fortune. **~পোড়া** *vi* lose the favour of fortune; be unlucky. **~ ফেরা** *vi* be on the rise; begin to flourish. **ভাঙা ~ জোড়া লাগে না** lose luck is like a broken glass. **কপালের ফের** *n* the irony of fate. **কপালের লিখন** *n* the decree of fate. **হায় ~** *int* oh dear! Dear me!

কপালি *n* the horizontal part of the door or window frame; the lintel.

কপালী *n* a Bengali Hindu caste/ community.

কপালে, কপালিয়া *adj* lucky; fortunate.

কপি১ *n* small species of ape; the monkey.

কপি২ *n* kinds of kitchen vegetable; cabbage. **ওল~** *n* cabbage with turnip-shaped stem; kohlrabi. **ফুল~** *n* cabbage plant with a large flower-head; cauliflower. **বাঁধা~** *n* vegetable with a round heart of thick leaves; cabbage.

কপি৩ [E] *n* **1** a duplicate copy; a transcript; a facsimile. **2** matter for printing; copy. **~ করা** *vt* make a copy or duplicate of. **~-করা** *adj* copied.

কপিকল *n* a hoisting mechanism consisting of a grooved wheel in a block; a pulley.

কপোত *n* bird of the dove family; the pigeon. কপোতী *fem.* **~-মিথুন** *n* a pigeon-couple; a pair of male and female doves.

কপোতাক্ষ *n* the river Kobodak in the district of Jessore in Bangladesh famous for its association with the name of the great poet Michael Madhusudan Dutt who was born at Sagardari on the bank of the river.

কপোল *n* either side of the face below the eye; the cheek. **~-কল্পনা** *n* figments of the imagination; fanciful imagery. **~-কল্পিত** *adj* imaginery; fictitious.

কফ১ *n* viscid matter of the respiratory passage; the bronchial mucus; phlegm. **~ তোলা** *vi* cough out.

কফ২ [E cuff, A কাফ] *n* the lower portion of the shirt-sleeve; the strengthened band at the end of a sleeve.

কফি [E] *n* **1** evergreen shrub bearing small berries with highly-flavoured seeds. **2** these berries ground and roasted. **3** beverage made from this.

কফিন [E] *n* the chest in which a dead human body is buried according to Christian rite; a coffin.

কবচ১ *n* **1** a protective garment made from metal rings or plates worn as armour by soldiers in former times; coat of mail: দুর্ভেদ্য ~. **2** sth worn in the belief or hope that it will protect the wearer against evil, etc or cure him of a disease or bring him good luck; an amulet; a talisman; a trinket.

কবচ২, কবজ [A] *n* **1** a rent-receipt; a promissory note; a bond. **2** forceful occupation; seizure; grip: আজরাইল জান ~ করে.

কবজা, কব্জা [A] *n* the hook or joint on which the shutters of a door, etc hang and turn; the hinges.

কবয়ী=কই১

কবর [A] *n* a grave; a tomb. **~খানা, ~গাহ্** [A+P] *n* a graveyard; a burial-ground. **~ দেওয়া** *vt* bury; inter.

কবরী *n* coil of hair worn by women at the back of the head; lock or braid of hair; a chignon. **~বন্ধন** *n* braiding of hair; hair-dressing. **~ভূষণ** *n* items of decoration for the hair or chignon, eg, hairpin, hair-net or flowers.

ক-বর্গ *n* the consonants of the ক-group; the first five consonants, ie, ক-খ-গ-ঘ-ঙ.

কবল *n* **1** act of swallowing or devouring. **2** a sudden, clutching snatch; act of grabbing; a grip; a hold. **কবলিত** *adj* seized; gripped; possessed: ব্যাঘ্র কবলিত. **কালের করাল কবলে** sunk into the abyss of eternity.

কবাট⇒ কপাট

কবাটি=কপাটি

কবাব⇒ কাবাব

কবালা [A] *n* deed of sale; legal document embodying transfer of real property. **~ করে দেওয়া** *vt* make over (real property) by a deed. **কট~** *n* deed of conditional sale.

কবি *n* a person distinguished for poetic talents; one who consistently practises the art of poetry; a composer of verses; a poet. **~গান** *n* sort of Bengali folk song in which two parties led by their respective chiefs alternately present songs and verses on debatable themes in the form of questions and answers composed in the main extemporaneously.

কবিগুরু *n* the chief among poets.

কবিতা *n* a piece of poetry; a composition in verse; a poem. **গীতি~** *n* a poem written in a metre originally intended to be sung; a poem in manner or matter resembling a song; a lyric poem.

কবিত্ব *n* poetic imagination; the genius of a poet: ~ বিধাতার দান. **~পূর্ণ, ~ময়** *adj* full of poetry/poetical beauty. **~শক্তি** *n* poetical genius/ talent.

কবিয়াল *n* group leader of 'কবিগান'; a professional versifier.

কবিরা [A] *adj* attended with serious consequence; grave. ❑*n* a grave sin: ~ গুনাহ.

কবিরাজ *n* **1** medical practitioner who follows the Ayurvedic system of treatment; one versed in Ayurvedic system of medicine. **2** honourable title given to a poet in recognition of his poetic genius meaning the prince of poets.

কবিরাজি *n* the profession of an Ayurvedic physician. ❑*adj* Ayurvedic: ~ চিকিৎসা.

কবুতর [P] *n* the pigeon.

কবুল [A] *n* **1** consent to one's marriage proposal; acceptance of the terms of one's marriage contract. **2** the defendant's admission of the plaintiff's claims: আমি অন্যায় ~ করছি. **3** acceptance of an offer; granting of a prayer: হে আল্লাহ আমার মোনাজাত ~ করো. **~ করা** *vt* grant; accept; admit; confess.

কবুলিয়ত [A] *n* deed of agreement executed by a tenant undertaking to abide by the terms of the lease and pay the land owner the stipulated rent regularly.

কবে[1] *vi,vt* (colloq) will say/ tell: সত্য কথা ~.

কবে[2] *adv* when; at what time; on what day: ~ আসবে. ❑*int* long ago; many years back: ~ মরে গেছে! **~কার** *adv* **1** of what time: ~কার কথা? **2** of long ago: সেই ~কার কথা, আজ কি আর মনে আছে!

কব্জা⇒ কবজা

কব্জি, কবজি *n* the joint by which the hand is united to the arm; the wrist.

কভু *adv* ever; at any time.

কম [P] *adj* **1** small in size, amount or number; short; inadequate: পণ্যের বাজারে আমদানি ~, জিনিসের দাম ~ নয়, things are not cheap. **2** less (than); short of: একশ' টাকার ~ নয়. **3** inferior; inefficient; deficient: তুমিই বা ~ কিসে. **4** few; rare: এমন লোক ~ই দেখা যায়. **5** of little merit; ordinary: এটা ~ কথা নয়, its not a trifling matter/matter of joke. **~ করা, কমানো** *vt* lessen; reduce; decrease; abate; curtail: সংসার খরচ কমানো, cut down/ curtail one's household expenses. **~ পড়া** *vt* fall short (of). **~ হওয়া, কমে যাওয়া** *vt* fall off/ away; diminish: দর কমেছে, prices have fallen/ gone down. **~~** *adj* slightly less; not full/ filled up; incomplete. **~জাত** *adj* low-born; mean-minded; base. **কমজোর** *adj* weak; feeble; infirm. **কমজোরি** *n* weakness; feebleness; debility. **কমনজর** [P+A] *adj* **1** weak-sighted. **2** base; mean-minded. **কমবক্ত, কম্‌বখ্‌ত** *adj* **1** unlucky; unfortunate; wretched. **2** dull-witted; unintelligent. **কমবক্তি, কমবখ্‌তি** *n* lucklessness; misfortune. ❑*adj fem* luckless; unfortunate. **কমবেশ** *adj, adv* aproximate; approximately; more or less. **কম সে কম** [P+U], **কমপক্ষে** *adv* at least; at the minimum.

কমঠ *n* **1** =কচ্ছপ. **2** =কমণ্ডলু. **3** rat-like animal, about two feet long, covered with erectile spines; the porcupine.

কমণ্ডলু *n* metallic or wooden water-pot with a handle; the ascetic's bowl.

কমতি [P+U] *n* the state of being less than what is required; deficiency; inadequacy: রূপের ~ গুণে পোষায়.

কমনরুম [E] *n* room for use as a meeting-place of teachers or students at a school, college, etc; a common-room.

কমনীয় *adj* **1** having the power to give pleasure; charming; delightful; lovely; graceful. **2** soft; tender. **3** causing desire; worth having; desirable. **কমনীয়া** *fem.* **~তা** *n.*

কমপোক্ত [P] *adj* not yet fully developed; immature; not sufficiently strong; rather frail.

কমবক্ত, কমবখ্‌ত⇒ কম

কমর=কোমর

কমল *n* **1** that which enhances the beauty of water; the lotus; the water-lily. **2** (fig) water: কমলজ, born of water. **~কলি, ~কোরক, ~কোষ** *nn* a lotus-bud. **~দল** *n* a lotus-petal. **~নয়ন, লোচন** *adjj* lotus-eyed. **~নয়না, ~লোচনা** *fem.* ❑*n* an eye as beautiful as a lotus; lotus-like eye.

কমলা[1] (also **~লেবু**) *n* **1** the orange or its tree. **2** the reddish-yellow colour of this fruit.

কমলা[2] *n* an appellation of Hindu goddess Lakshmi. **~পতি** *n* appellation of Vishnu. **~সন** *n* appellation of Hindu god Brahma.

কমলিওয়ালা *n* Prophet Muhammad (sm); an ascetic in rag. ❑*adj* one wrapped in rag.

কমলিনী *fem.* **1** lotus. **2** a clump of lotuses.

কমলেকামিনী *n* manifestation of goddess Durga described as sitting on a lotus floating on the sea.

কমা[1] [E] *n* (gram) the mark of punctuation (,) used to mark off the phrases and clauses of a sentence; a comma.

কমা[2] *vi* decrease; abate; come down; diminish; fall: দাম ~. **~নো** *vt* cause to become less; lessen; lower.

কমি=কমতি

কমিটি [E] *n* a body of persons appointed to manage any matter; a committee.

কমিন [P] *adj* **1** evil in principle or practice; sinful; wicked; roguish. **2** low-born; humble in position of life; lowly. **কমিনা** *n, adj fem* unchaste or lewd (woman); a whore; a coquette; a flirt.

কমিশন [E] *n* **1** allowance made to an agent, etc for transacting business; commission: উচ্চহারে ~ দেওয়া হবে. **2** a body of men joined in an office or trust: বিশ্ববিদ্যালয় মঞ্জুরি ~. **3** body of persons given the duty of making an inquiry and writing a report: শিক্ষা ~. **~ এজেন্ট** *n* person who acts for, or who looks after the business of another for commission; commission agent. **~ এজেন্সি** *n* the office or business of a commission agent.

কমিশনার [E] *n* **1** the head of the administration of an administrative Division; the Divisional commissioner. **2** a member of a municipal committee. **3** member of an inquiry commission.

কমিশনি *n* service rendered for commission.

কমোড [E] *n* a chamber-pot or close-stool.

কম্প *n* an involuntary trembling; a shivering; vibration. **~জ্বর** *n* fever that develops with shivering of the body; an intermittent fever with cold fits and shivering; an ague. **~ দিয়া জ্বর আসা** have an attack of ague.

কম্পন *n* **1** a tremor; shivering; quaking; trembling: হৃৎ~. **2** vibration of the voice; tremulous effect in music. **কম্পিত, কম্পমান** *adj* one who/ that which is shivering or vibrating: কম্পিতশাখা. **কম্পিত/কম্পমান হওয়া** *vi* tremble; shiver; quiver; vibrate. **কম্পনীয়** *adj* to be shaken; shakable.

কম্পাউন্ড [E] *n* enclosure in which houses stand; house premises; a compound.

কম্পাউন্ডার [E] *n* a pharmacist who prepares a medicine as per prescription of a physician; a compounder. **কম্পাউন্ডারি** [E compounder+B ই] *n* the job of a compounder.

কম্পাস [E] *n* **1** an instrument with a needle that points to the magnetic north, and helps determining the course of ships, etc. **2** (geom) instrument for describing circles; a compass.

কম্পিটিশন [E] *n* contest for the same object; activity in which persons compete; a competition: বক্সিং ~, boxing competition; এসে ~, essay competition.

কম্পিত⇒ কম্পন

কম্পোজ [E] *n* setting up types in printing. **~ করা** *vt* compose or make up words, paragraphs, pages, etc in printing. **কম্পোজিটার** *n* one who composes type for printing; a compositor.

কম্পোস্ট [E] *n* fertilizer prepared from rotted organic matter by mixing with soil, manure, etc; a mixture of soil and various manure as a fertilizer; compost.

কম্প্র *adj* **1** that which is agitated; trembling; shivering. **2** trembling in fear; palpitating: ~বক্ষ. **3** vibrated; stirred; shaken.

কম্ফর্টার [E] *n* woollen muffler; comforter.

কম্বল *n* thick woollen blanket used as a wrap against cold; a rug used as a covering; a bedding item. **~সম্বল** *adj* (lit) having no earthly possessions; poor; indigent. ❑*n* religious mendicant who has forsaken pleasures of life.

কম্বলী-বাবা=কমলিওয়ালা

কম্বু *n* spiral shell of the marine mollusc; a small bivalve shell; a conch used as trumpet in Hindu temples. **~কণ্ঠ** *adj* having a voice very much like the sound made by the blowing of a conch. ❑*n* a voice as grave and loud as the sound of a conch. **~কণ্ঠী** *fem.* **~গ্রীব** *adj* possessing a neck marked with thread-like lines like a conch. **~গ্রীবা** *n* a neck so marked; a striated neck. **~নিনাদ** *n* the sound of the blowing of a conch. **~রেখা** *n* the striate markings on the conch.

কম্ম *n* (colloq)= কর্ম. কাজ-~ = ক্রিয়াকর্ম

কম্যুনিস্ট [E] *n* one who believes in the political theory of the socialists who aim at violent overthrowing of capitalism and establishing proletarian dictatorship for the realization of community of property; a communist. ❑*adj* pertaining to communism: ~ রাশিয়ার পতন হয়েছে.

কম্র *adj* **1** having the power of attracting; attractive; beautiful; lovely; graceful. **2** full of desire; desirous; eager to possess and enjoy. **3** inspired by lust/ sexual appetite; lustful; lewd; libidinous.

কয়[1] *adj* **1** (in interrogative sentences) how many: ~জন এসেছে. **2** few in number: ~দিন আর চলবে; 'কয়' is often shortened to ক⇒ক[3].

কয়[2] *vt* (colloq) corrup of কহে (= he says, they say).

কয়ড়া *n* iron chain; shackle; fetters: হাতে পায়ে ~ পড়ানো.

কয়লা *n* **1** black mineral used as fuel; coal. **2** any combustible substance in a state of ignition; charcoal: পাথুরে ~, কাঠ ~. **~ ধুলে ময়লা যায় না** (prov) black will take no other hue.

কয়াল [A] *n* one who weighs goods esp cereals for a wholesale dealer; a professional weigher/ weighman. **কয়ালি** *n* **1** the profession of a weighman. **2** weighman's charge/ fee/ toll.

কয়েক *adj* a few; some: ~দিন ভালোই কেটেছে.

কয়েতবেল=কতবেল

কয়েদ [A] *adj* sentenced to imprisonment; imprisoned; jailed; confined; under lock-up. ❑*n* imprisonment: ছয় মাসের ~ হয়েছে. **~খানা** [A+P] a prison; a jail; a lock-up.

কয়েদি, কয়েদী [A] *n* a prisoner; a captive.

কর[1] *n* 1 the extremity of the human arm below the wrist; the hand. 2 the trunk or proboscis of an elephant. **~কবলিত** *adj* come into one's possession; in one's grasp; under one's control. **~কমল, ~পদ্ম** *n* a hand as graceful as a lily. **~কোষ্ঠী** *n* 1 the lines or configurations on the palm that help read the horoscope. 2 horoscope determined by reading the lines on the palm. **~গ্রহ, ~গ্রহণ** *n* 1 acceptance of the hand (of a bride by a bridegroom) in marriage. **~জোড়** *n* folding the hands (in begging sth of sb). **করজোড়ে** *adv* with folded hands: ~জোড়ে প্রার্থনা করছি. **~তল** *n* the palm or inner surface of the hand. **~তলগত** *adj* (lit) caught in one's palm; got into one's clutches; (fig) under one's control; acquired; subjected: সমগ্র সিন্ধু উপত্যকা মুহাম্মদ-বিন কাশিমের করতলগত হয়. **~তাড়ন** *n* a blow with the open hand. **~তালি** *n* clapping of the hands in applause. **~তালি দেওয়া** *vi* applaud by claps; make claps in appluse. **~ত্রাণ** *n* cover for the hand; glove; a gauntlet. **~পল্লব** *n* a hand comparable with a young twig in softness and beauty. **~পুট** *n* folded hands; palms joined to make a fold as a token of respect. **~পুটে** *adv* with folded or cupped hands (in submission and humility. **~মর্দন** *n* shaking of hands in greeting/farewell. **~মর্দন করা** *vi* shake hands.

কর[2] *n* ray of sunshine; sunbeam, sun-ray: রবি ~.

কর[3] *n* contribution levied by authority for national purposes; revenue; a tax; a rate, duty imposed/charged on income/property: আয়~, শিক্ষা~, তীর্থ~, লবণ~. **~গ্রহণ** *n* collection of taxes, etc. **~গ্রাহী, ~গ্রাহক** *n, adj* one who collects taxes or revenue; a tax-collector; a revenue officer. **~দাতা** *n adj* one who pays revenue, taxes, etc; a tax-payer. **~নির্ধারণ** *n* 1 act of levying taxes; taxation **~নির্ধারণ** *n* act of assessing the value of anything for taxation; assessment. **~পীড়িত** *adj* fretting under the burden of high taxation; overtaxed; rack-rented. **~পীড়িত হওয়া** *vi* be burdened with over-taxation. **~মুক্ত** *adj* 1 not subject to taxation; exempt from taxation. 2 not liable to taxation; tax-free: ~মুক্ত সম্পত্তি. **~যোগ্য** *adj* liable by law to the assessment of taxes; taxable: ~যোগ্য আয়.

কর[4], করো *vt* command for doing sth: তোমার কাজ কর/ করো, তোর কাজ কর, do your work. **করলো** (*pt* of do in the 3rd person) (he) did.

কর[5] family name among certain Hindus.

-কর *suff* denoting an agent that creates or gives rise to sth: চিত্রকর, কষ্টকর, বিরক্তিকর. **-করী** *fem* :কার্যকরী, অর্থকরী.

করই⇒ কর[4]

করক *n* 1 the coconut-shell or fragment of it. 2 the pomegranate tree. **করকান্ত** *n* the milky juice of the coconut; coconut water.

করকচ, কড়কচ *n* salt made of sea water; sea-salt.

করকচি *adj* soft; tender: নারকেলের ~ শাঁস. ☐*n* green coconut.

করকমল⇒ কর[1]

করকর *int* 1 the sound suggestive of scraping (as the pulp of a coconut) or the crushing/ rubbing/ chewing of hard things. 2 word suggestive of a smarting sensation or irritation: চোখ ~ করছে, feel a smarting sensation in the eyes. **~ করা, করকরানো** *vi* give a sensation of scratching/ smarting/ burning/ paining. **করকরানি** *n* scratching; smarting or burning sensation. **করকরে** *adj* 1 giving out a sound of crushing grits as in food; gritty. 2 quite new; brand-new: করকরে নোট.

করকা *n* hail or snow mingled with rain; hail-stone. **~পাত** *n* fall of hail-stones; hail-storm.

করকোষ্ঠি⇒ কর[1]

করঙ্ক *n* 1 a casket for holding betel-leaves and con-comitant materials. 2 coconut shell; a beggar's bowl made of coconut shell. 3 the human skull. 4 metallic water-pot used by ascetics.

করঙ্গ=করঙ্ক (4)

করচা=কড়চা

করজোড়⇒ কর[1]

করঞ্জ, করঞ্জক *n* variety of sour fruit (also called করমচা).

করণ *n* 1 doing (of anything); execution; accomplishment: বিভক্ত~, একত্রী~, অভিযুক্ত~. 2 that which produces an effect; cause; motive. 3 instrument by which sth is done; (gram) the instrumental case: করণে তৃতীয়া. 4 (phil) sense organ: অন্তঃ~. 5 a place where business is carried on; an office.

করণ-কারক *n* (gram) the case called 'করণ'; the instrumental case⇒ করণ (3).

করণিক *n* one who is employed under another for a job like writing, copying and recording; a clerk.

করণী (math) 1 a quantity not exactly expressible in figures; an irrational number. 2 a root (√) that cannot be expressed in finite terms, as the square root of 2; a surd. **~ নিরসন করা** *vi* (math) clear from radical or irrational quantities; rationalize.

করণীয় *adj* 1 to be/ fit to be done. 2 fit for matrimonial alliance: ~ ঘর.

করণ্ড *n* 1 wicker-tray for flowers; a flower-basket. 2 bee-hive.

করণ্ডক *n* a diving bird; water-fowl; duck.

করত, করতঃ *adv* having done (it); after doing (it).

করতল, করতলগত⇒ কর[১]
করতা⇒ কড়তা
করতার *n* the creator of the universe; Allah; God.
করতাল, করতাল *n* basin-shaped musical instrument of brass, used in pairs; cymbal.
করতালি, করত্রাণ⇒ কর[১]
করদ *adj* paying tribute to another; subject: ~ রাজ্য, tributary state. **2** a stream that falls into another: ~ নদী.
করদাতা⇒ কর[৩]
করনা=কন্না
করবাল *n* weapon consisting of a long steel blade and hilt; a sword; a scimitar; a falchion.
করবী *n* an evergreen flowering shrub or its flower; the oleander flower: রক্ত~, শ্বেত~.
করভ *n* **1** the young of an elephant. **2** the camel or its young. **3** the mule. **করভী** *fem.*
করম[১] *n* (poet form of কর্ম) work; effort; labour. **2** luck; fortune.
করম[২] [A] *n* an act of grace; kindness; favour; mercy.
করমচা, করঞ্জা *n* = করঞ্জ. ❑*adj* red or crimson like the colour of ~.
করলা *n* kitchen vegetable having a bitter taste; *Mermordica cherantia.*
করহ *vi, vt* (poet) = কর[৪] (do).
করা *vt* **1** perform; accomplish or carry sth (an action, task or activity) to completion: পাঠ ~, কাজ ~, বিবাহ ~. **2** grow; produce: আবাদ ~, ফসল ~. **3** make; build; construct: রাস্তা ~, বাগান ~, বাড়ি ~. **4** make use of; employ: নিয়োগ ~, প্রয়োগ ~. **5** invent; devise: বুদ্ধি ~, কৌশল ~. **6** go/ attend regularly: অফিস ~, স্কুল ~. **7** look after; manage: সংসার ~. **8** exercise some profession; practise: ওকালতি ~, ডাক্তারি ~. **9** work out; calculate: হিসাব ~, অঙ্ক ~. **10** acquire; earn: টাকা ~, নাম ~. ❑*adj* what has been done: বাঁধাই ~ খাতা, a bound book. **সে কী করে?** what is he? **তিনি সরকারি চাকরি করেন** he is in government service. **বিড়ালটি মিউমিউ করছে** the cat mews. **আমি তার সাথে দেখা করেছি** I met him.
করাঘাত *n* a blow with the hand; a slap; a thump. **~ করা** *vt* strike with the open hand; slap. **দ্বারে ~ করা** knock at the door. **শিরে ~ করা** beat one's forehead.
করাত *n* cutting tool consisting of a thin blade with a serrated edge; a saw. **~ দিয়ে কাটা** *vt* cut with a saw; saw. **শাঁখের ~** *n* a saw having serrated edge on both sides used for cutting conch shells; (fig) situation when one is left with a choice between things that are equally undesirable; horns of a dilemma. **~কল** *n* a saw-mill. **করাতি, করাতী** *n* a sawyer.
করানো *vt* have sth done by another; cause sth to be done: তোমাকে দিয়ে কাজ ~ যাবে না.
করায়ত্ত (কর + আয়ত্ত) *adj* in one's grip; under one's control/ power/ sway; mastered; secured.
করার=কড়ার
করারদাদ [A] *n* that which is agreed or settled; a unanimous resolution; a deed of agreement; a contract.
করাল *adj* **1** filling with awe; awful; dreadful; terrible: ~ মূর্তি **2** having large teeth; dentate; toothed. **3** very high/ turbulent: ~ ঢেউ, ~ সমুদ্র. **~বদনা** *adj fem* of fearful aspect; hideous; ugly. ❑*n fem* appellation of Hindu goddess Kali. **করালী** *n* appellation of goddess Kali.
করাস্ফোট [কর + আস্ফোট] *n* keeping/ beating of musical measure by clapping one's hands.
করি-অরি *n* a lion.
করিও, কোরো *vt* a command or sanction for doing sth.
করিকর*n* the proboscis or trunk of an elephant.
করিডর [E] a long narrow passage in a building connecting the rooms on the same floor; a corridor.
করিতকর্মা, করিৎকর্মা *adj* well-experienced and highly skilled; adept; active.
করিম, করীম [A] *adj* having tenderness or goodness of nature; kind; benevolent. ❑*n* Allah, the Merciful.
করিষ্ণু *adj* in the state of doing.
করী[১] *n* one that has a proboscis or trunk; the elephant. **করিণী** *fem.* **করীন্দ্র** *n* (Hindu myth) the mount of Indra.
করী[২]⇒ কর
করীষ *n* dried cow-dung; cake of dried cow-dung.
করুক *vt* (imperative mood in passive voice) let (him) do; let it be done (by him).
করুণ *adj* **1** full of pathos; affecting the tender passions; causing pity, sympathy or sadness; pathetic: ~ রস. **2** affected by the feelings of others; sympathetic; compassionate: ~ হৃদয়. **3** causing grief; distressing; sorrowful; calamitous: ~ দৃশ্য. **~চিত্ত** *adj* tender-hearted; compassionate. **~ধ্বনি** *n* cry of woe; heart-rending cry; lamentation. **~ রস** *n* the literary quality which induces deep emotion such as moves one to sympathy; pathos. **~লোচন** *adj* having sympathetic eyes. **~ স্বর** *n* piteous tone; plaintive voice. **~ স্বরে** *adv* piteously; pitifully; in a plaintive voice.
করুণা *n* **1** a kindly act or deed; sympathy; benevolence: দুঃখীজন ~র পাত্র. **2** willingness to forgive someone in one's power; mercy; compassion; forbearance: **~ময়, ~নিদান, ~নিধান, ~নিলয়, ~ময়** *adjj* ocean of kindness; merciful; compassionate. ❑*n* Allah; God. **~র্দ্র** *adj* melted or moved with pity. **~র্দ্রচিত্ত** *adj*

tender-hearted. ~দ্রচিত্তে *adv* with a sympathetic heart, mercifully; compassionately. ~সাগর, ~সিন্ধু = ~ নিদান, etc.

করুণিমা *n* gloomy state of mind; melancholy; sadness; dejection.

করে, ক'রে [old use করিয়া] *infinite verb* after doing; having done: চেষ্টা ~ শিখেছি. ❑*adv* **1** by means of: with the help of: ট্রেনে ~, by train, বাসে ~, by bus. **2** in a way or manner: ভালো ~ পড়ো, read carefully/diligently: শক্ত ~ ধরো grasp it firmly. **3** by turns: দুজন ~, by twos. ❑*prep* with; in; on: হাতে ~, by hand, with the hands; মাথায় ~, on the head.

করেণু *n* the elephant. **করেণুকা** *fem.*

করোগেট, করোগেটেড আয়রন [E] *n* sheet iron formed into a series of parallel ridges and hollows, used for roofs; corrugated iron sheet.

করোট, করোটি, করোটী *n* the bony case which contains the brain; the skull.

কর্ক, কাক [E] *n* a stopple for a bottle made of the light bark of the tree called the cork-oak; a cork.

কর্কট, কককর্ট *n* **1** a ten-legged shellfish having a rounded body and strong claws; the crab. **2** (med) malignant growth in the body having the appearance of a crab which gradually consumes the tissues of the body; cancer. **3** (astrol) the constellation of the crab; the fourth sign of the zodiac; Cancer. ~**ক্রান্তি** *n* parallel of latitude 23° 27′ north of the equator; the Tropic of Cancer.

কর্কশ *adj* **1** not smooth or even; rough: ~ গাত্র. **2** grating to the ear; harsh; boisterous: ~ কণ্ঠ. **3** rugged in temper or manners; rude; haughty: ~ লোক. **4** unpleasant; stern; severe: ~ কথা; dry; arid; parched: ~ প্রকৃতি. ~ **ব্যবহার** *n* rude manners; impolite behaviour. ~**ভাবে** *adv* in a harsh manner; roughly; rudely. ~ **স্বরে** *adv* in a husky voice/ harsh tone. ~**তা** *n*

কর্কোট, কর্কোটক *n* **1** kind of snake. **2** kind of kitchen vegetable.

কর্জ [A] *n* that which is lent; a loan. **টাকা ~ দেওয়া** lend money at or without interest. **টাকা ~ নেওয়া** borrow money at or without interest. **কর্জে হাসানা**[A]*n* a loan the repayment of which is not insisted on; a loan that is advanced mainly to help the borrower or to ameliorate his sufferings. ~-**পত্র** *n* a bond; a promissory note; suffering a mortgage deed; a hand-note. ~ **শোধ করা** *vi* pay off a debt; repay a loan. ~ **নেই কষ্ট নেই** (prov) out of debt, out of danger.

কর্ণ[১] *n* the organ of hearing; the ear. ~**কুহর** *n* the ear-hole or audition passage in the ear. ~**গত** *adj* perceived by the ear; heard. ~**গোচর** *adj* what may be heard; within hearing; audible. ~**গোচর করা** bring to one's notice. ~**গোচর হওয়া** be heard; come to one's hearing. ~**পট**, ~**পটহ** *n* the thin membrane in the inner ear sensitive to sound vibrations; ear-drum; the tympanum (*pl* -s or -na) or middle ear. ~**পাত** *n* act of hearing/ listening (to). ~**পাত করা** *vt* listen to; lend ear to; pay heed to. ~**পাত না করা** pay no heed to; turn a deaf ear to. ~**বিবর** = ~কুহর. ~**বেধ** *n* act of boring the lobes of one's ears for wearing earrings etc. ~**ভূষণ** *n* any ornament for the ear. ~**মল** *n* waxy substance secreted in the ear; ear-wax. ~**মূল** *n* the root of the ear or auricular glands; inflammation of the auricular glands or mumps. ~**রন্ধ্র** = ~কুহর. ~**শূল** *n* pain in the inner ear; ear-ache. ~**হীন** *adj* wanting the sense of hearing; deaf. **কর্ণাকর্ণি** *n* speaking in a whisper; whispering. **কর্ণান্তর** *n* act of passing a piece of news to another/ others.

কর্ণ[২] *n* (geom) **1** the side of a right-angled triangle opposite the right angle; the hypotenuse. **2** straight line drawn between opposite angles of a quadrilateral figure; a diagonal.

কর্ণ[৩] *n* instrument by which a ship is steered; rudder; helm. ~**ধার** *n* the man at the helm of a ship; helmsman; a steersman; a pilot; (fig) a leader; a guide; a statesman.

কর্ণ[৪] *n* Mahabharata character Karna.

কর্ণিক *n* hand-tool used by masons for spreading mortar and plaster; a trowel (colloq কন্নি).

কর্ণিকা *n* **1** ornament for the ear; earring. **2** the pericarp or vessel containing the seeds of lotus. **3** the principal body of a plant, shrub etc; a stalk; a stem. **4** the writing tool; a pen.

কর্ণিকার *n* tree bearing yellow flowers or its flowers (colloq সোনালু).

কর্তন *n* **1** act of cutting/ chopping/ severing/ amputating. **2** (euphem) act of passing or spending time. ~ **করা** *vt* cut; sever; amputate; **কর্তনী** *n* pair of scissors; a cutting tool.

কর্তব্য *adj* **1** proper to do; fitting or appropriate for oneself to perform. **2** imposing an obligation to do sth; requiring performance of sth on the part of a person. ❑*n* that which a person is bound to perform; moral or legal obligation to pursue some action; one's business, service or office; a duty: পিতা মাতার প্রতি ~. ~ **করা** *vi* do/ discharge one's duty. ~**কর্ম** *n* a duty; an obligation. ~**জ্ঞান** *n* sense of duty. ~**নিষ্ঠ**, ~**পরায়ণ** *adj* regularly performing one's duties; devoted to duty; dutiful. ~**নিষ্ঠতা**, ~**নিষ্ঠা** *n* dutiful conduct; dutifulness. ~**পরাঙ্মুখ** = ~বিমুখ. ~**পালন** *n* performance of one's duties. ~ **পালন করা** *vi* perform/ do/ discharge one's duties. ~**প্রিয়** *adj* dutiful. ~**প্রিয়তা** *n* devotion to duty; dutifulness. ~**বিমুখ** *adj* averse to duty. ~বিমুখতা *n* aversion to duty. ~বিমূঢ়, কিং~বিমূঢ় *adj* at a loss what to do; perplexed; bewildered. ~বিমূঢ়তা *n* state of being perplexed/ bewildered; bewilderment. **কর্তব্যাকর্তব্যবোধ** *n* sense of right and wrong. **কর্তব্যানুরাগ** *n* devotion to duty. **কর্তব্যানুরোধে** *adv* for the sake of duty; out of the sense of duty.

কর্তরিকা, কর্তরী *n* heavy tool with a sharp edge for chopping meat, wood, etc; a chopper (⇒কাটারি).

কর্তা *adj, n* **1** one who does (things); a doer. **2** one who holds the authority to do things; the master of a house; the head of a family: ~-গিন্নি. **3** the chief or boss of office/ organisation: বড়ো ~. **4** the writer of a book; an author: গ্রন্থ~. **5** the spouse of a woman; a husband: স্ত্রী বললেন, কর্তা বাড়ি নেই. **6** owner of land or houses who has tenants under him; a landlord. **7** word meaning 'lord' or master used by servants in addressing their masters: ~, আমায় ডেকেছেন?. ❑*n* **1** the Lord of the universe; the Creator. **2** (gram) any word in the nominative case. **কর্ত্রী** *fem.* **~র ইচ্ছায় কর্ম** (prov) the master may do as he pleases; the master's will is law.

কর্তিত *adj* what has been cut off/ severed: ~ অংশ.

কর্তৃক *prep* referring to the agent by whom sth is done: বাংলা একাডেমী ~ প্রকাশিত (cf দ্বারা).

কর্তৃকারক *n* (gram) the case of a noun or pronoun when used as the subject of a sentence; the nominative case.

কর্তৃত্ব *n* **1** the power or legal right to give orders and be obeyed; authority; mastery; domination. **2** one's right to act independently without reference to others. **~ করা** *vi* exercise supreme authority. **~ ফলানো** *vt* make people feel one's authouity by being overbearing and insolent; exercise authority in a lordly and imperious style; domineer. **~ভার** *n* the responsibility attached to a position of authority. **কর্তৃত্বাধীন** *adj* under one's authority/ control/ management.

কর্তৃপক্ষ *n* group of persons having authority; the authorities: পৌর~, the municipal authorities; পানি ও বিদ্যুৎ উন্নয়ন ~, Water and power Development Authority (WAPDA).

কর্তৃপদ *n* the subject of a sentence; the nominative.

কর্তৃবাচ্য *n* (gram) voice implying action done to a person or thing; the active voice.

কর্ত্রী *adj, n fem* **1** holding authority. **2** a housewife. **3** the mistress of a house; a landlady. **4** the authoress of a book: গ্রন্থ~. **5** the chief of an organisation; the principal of an institution.

কর্দম *n* **1** soft, wet earth or soil; mud. **2** (fig) sth vile and contemptible. **~ময়, কর্দমাক্ত** *adj* mud-stained; muddy.

কর্নেল [E] (mil) *n* the chief commander of a regiment of troops; commanding officer below a Brigadier; a colonel.

কর্পূর *n* the well-known volatile substance, solid, semi-transparent and strong-smelling, prepared from a kind of plant-juice and used in medicine; camphor: বাবাকে দেখে তার সব সাহস ~ হয়ে উবে গেল.

কর্ম *n* **1** that which is done; a deed; an action. **2** anything a person is bound to perform; a duty; an obligation: ~ভার. **3** act of celebrating an occasion; a function, ceremony or ritual: ক্রিয়া~. **4** an appropriate or fitting job: যার ~ তারেই সাজে. **5** use; utility; service; usefulness: ঘড়িটি কোনো কর্মের নয়. **6** trade; profession; employment: ~স্থান. **7** that which happens to a person; fate; luck: ~ফল. **8** (gram) the case of the object; of a sentence: ~কারক. **9** (gram) the object of a transitive verb: কর্তা-~. **যেমন ~ তেমন ফল** (prov) as you sow, so you reap.

কর্মকর্তা *n* person invested with an office of a public nature; an officer; an executive.

কর্ম-কর্তৃবাচ্য *n* (gram) the quasi-passive voice, ie, the voice in which the object, in the absence of the subject, acts like the subject (জল পড়ে, পাতা নড়ে).

কর্মকাণ্ড *n* **1** the part of the Vedas dealing with rituals and ceremonies (opp জ্ঞানকাণ্ড). **2** *pl* actions and activities: উন্নয়ন ~ development activities.

কর্মকার *n* a smith who works in iron; blacksmith.

কর্মকারক *n* **1** one who performs an act; a worker. **2** (gram) the objective or accusative case.

কর্মকুণ্ঠ *adj* averse to work; lazy.

কর্মকুশল *adj* having expert resource and ability; dexterous; adroit.

কর্মক্লান্ত *adj* tired of bodily or mental exertion; fatigued.

কর্মক্ষম *adj* having ability/ physical fitness to work; possessing the power to act; active. **~তা** *n*.

কর্মক্ষেত্র *n* **1** the office or place where one works. **2** the sphere of activity one is involved in.

কর্মখালি *n* vacancy of post; situation vacant.

কর্মচারী *n* one who works for an employer; an employee; an officer/ official. **~বৃন্দ** *n pl* the staff of persons employed in an office; the personnel.

কর্মজীবন *n* the part of one's life characterized by activity; one's professional career; active life.

কর্মঠ *adj* industrious; hard-working; diligent.

কর্মত্যাগ *n* resignation of office; abandoning a work/job. ~ **করা** *vi* resign an office; give up a job.

কর্মদক্ষ *adj* efficient at one's work; capable; competent.

কর্মদোষ *n* **1** the evil consequence of one's own conduct; a wrong-doing; a sin. **2** ill-luck; misfortune. **কর্মদোষে** *adv* for one's own faults; owing to ill-luck.

কর্মধারয় *n* (gram) the name of the class of appositional or juxtapositional compounds in Bengali, which are formed by fitting an *adj* with a *n* thereby explaining or modifying the meaning of the *n* eg নীলোৎপল (নীল + উৎপল), চঞ্চল–অঞ্চল, etc.

কর্মধারা *n* method/ procedure of work.

কর্মনাশা *adj, n* one who/ that which spoils or bungles an action: তাস দাবা পাশা এ–তিন ~.

কর্মনিষ্ঠা *n* devotion to work; diligence; industry. **কর্মনিষ্ঠ** *adj* devoted to work; industrious; dutiful. **কর্মনিষ্ঠতা** *n* devotion to duty.

কর্মপথ, কর্মপদ্ধতি *n* the method or procedure in which sth is/is to be done; the line of action.

কর্মফল *n* the consequences of one's sins and misdeeds. **2** (according to Hindu belief) weal or woe in this life according to what one earned in a previous birth.

কর্মবশত *adv* on business; on account of duty.

কর্মবাচ্য *n* (gram) the voice in which the nominative is the object of some action or feeling; the passive voice.

কর্মবাদ *n* (phil) belief in action as the chief end of life (in contrast to mere thought); the doctrine of action. **কর্মবাদী** *adj, n* believing in action as the chief end of life; (one) professing the doctrine of action.

কর্মবিধি *n* rules and procedure.

কর্মবীর *n* one who has zealously devoted himself to the service of humanity and has earned undying fame for glorious achievements.

কর্মভূমি *n* place where one is engaged in a trade or profession; the scene of action; the earthly life.

কর্মভোগ *n* **1** suffering the consequenes of one's misdeeds. **2** unnecessary harassment. ~ **করা** *vi* suffer for nothing.

কর্মযোগ *n* performance of or devotion to wordly duties as a form of worship. **কর্মযোগী** *adj* one who is as diligent in worldly duties and obligations as an ascetic is to his religious devotion.

কর্মশালা *n* a shop or building where any craft or work is carried on; a workshop; a factory.

কর্মশীল *adj* disposed to action; active; diligent; industrious. ~**তা** *n* the condition of being active; active habits; deligence; industriousness.

কর্মসচিব *n* one who supervises the execution of any business; executive officer; a secretary.

কর্মসাধন *n* performance or implementation of an act; accomplishment of a job. ~ **করা** *vi* execute a work; accomplish a task.

কর্মসিদ্ধি *n* successful completion of an undertaking; accomplishment of a task.

কর্মসূত্র *n* the course of action.

কর্মস্থল, কর্মস্থান=কর্মক্ষেত্র

কর্মাকর্ম (কর্ম + অকর্ম) *n pl* works useful and useless; deeds and misdeeds.

কর্মাক্ষম (কর্ম + অক্ষম) *adj* incapable of doing any work; physically unfit for any job; invalid.

কর্মাধ্যক্ষ *n* the chief executive of an office or organisation; a superintendent; a secretary.

কর্মানুবন্ধ (কর্ম + অনুবন্ধ) *n* dependence upon action; the course of work; the urgency of business.

কর্মানুবন্ধী *adj* connected/ concerned with business.

কর্মানুরাগ *n* love of work; devotion to duty; diligence.

কর্মানুসারে *adv* according to one's action/ work.

কর্মান্তর *n* change of work/ job; another job.

কর্মার *n* a smith who works in iron; blacksmith.

কর্মারম্ভ [কর্ম + আরম্ভ] *n* beginning of daily activities; commencement of a work/ ceremony.

কর্মার্হ [কর্ম + অর্হ] *adj* fit for work; serviceable; useful.

কর্মিষ্ঠ *adj* showing zealous application to one's work; hard-working; assiduous.

কর্মী *adj* full of activities; hard-working: ~ পুরুষ. ❑*n* a worker; an employee.

কর্মেন্দ্রিয় (কর্ম + ইন্দ্রিয়) *n* organ of action, eg hands, legs, etc.

কর্মোদ্যম (কর্ম + উদ্যম) *n* enthusiasm or enterprise to engage or continue in an undertaking; perseverance.

কর্ষ[1] *n* measure of weighing gold or silver (= ·8 oz).

কর্ষ[2], **কর্ষণ** *n* act of tilling/ ploughing; cultivation: ভূমি–কর্ষণ. **কর্ষণ করা** *vi, vt* prepare the soil for seed; plough; till; cultivate. **কর্ষক** *adj, n* **1** one who ploughs the soil; a cultivator. **2** one who/ that which attracts or draws towards: বিপ্রকর্ষণ. **কর্ষণীয়** *adj* that which is to be cultivated; arable; cultivable. **কর্ষিত** *adj* ploughed; cultivated: কর্ষিত ভূমি.

কর্ষী *adj* having the power to attract; attractive. ❑*n* the iron piece of a bridle which sets in the mouth of a horse.

কল[১] *n* **1** the means by which some productive process is carried out; a mill; a machine: কাপড়ের ~, আটার ~. **2** a contrivance for catching unawares; a trap; a stratagem: ইঁদুরের ~. **3** a crafty device; a trick; an artifice; a knack or art: কলে কৌশলে. **কলে পাওয়া** catch one on the hip (ie get him at a disadvantage). **4** the trigger or lock of a gun; the switch or handle of a machine. **5** safety device to stop up or release water (or other liquid) in storage; water tap; hydrant: পানির ~. **কলকব্জা** *n pl* machinery; the component parts of a complex machine; machines in general. **~ টেপা, ~কাঠি নাড়া** *vi, vt* pull the wires from behind; to intrigue. **~ কারখানা** *n pl* mills and factories. **~কৌশল করা** have recourse to a trick; set a trap; intrigue. **কলে কৌশলে** *adv* by means fair or foul. **কলে পড়া** *vt* be entrapped; get into a trick. **কলের পুতুল** *n* a puppet moved by strings; spring-doll; a marionette.

কল[২] *n* sweet sound; a pleasing note (as the chirping of birds). ❑*adj* (of sound) pleasant to the ear; full of melody; melodious. **~কণ্ঠ** *adj* making a sweet sound; having a melodious voice; sweet-toned; (fig) composing sweet verses: ~কণ্ঠ কবি. **~কণ্ঠী** *fem.* ❑*n* **1** sweet tone; elegant voice. **2** the pigeon. **3** the cuckoo. **4** the swan; the gander. **~কথা** *n* melodious language. **~~** *n* **1** murmuring noise of running water. **2** the hum made by a number of people talking together. **3** chirping of the birds. **~কলানো** *vt* utter musically in a quavering manner; sing musically; carol; warble: খাবিদাবি ~কলাবি. **~কাকলি** *n* quavering melodious sound; sweet humming sound. **~কুঞ্জন, ~গুঞ্জন** *n* a low continued or repeated sound; sweet murmur. **কলতান** *n* sweet note; melodious tune. **~ধ্বনি** *n* a short shrill note of birds; chirping. **~নাদ** = ~ধ্বনি. **~নাদী** *adj* murmuring; sweetly warbling. **কলনাদিনী** *fem.* **কলনাদিনী স্রোতস্বিনী** murmuring stream. **~রব, ~রোল** *n* confused noise; uproar; tumult. **~স্বন, ~স্বর** *n* low musical sound: নদীর ~স্বন. ❑*adj* melodious in tune. **~স্বরে** *adv* melodiously; very sweetly. **~হংস** *n* the male of the duck or gander that makes the murmuring sound. **~হংসী** *fem.* **~হাস্য** *n* laughter with a sweet cackle; gentle burst of laughter. **~হাস্য করা** *vi* laugh cacklingly. **~হাসিনী** *n fem* one who laughs cacklingly.

কল[৩] *n* a shoot of a plant; a sprout. **~ গজানো** *vi* push out a shoot; sprout; germinate.

কল[৪] [E] *n* a call: ডাক্তার ~ দেওয়া. call in a doctor. **কলে যাওয়া** attend a call.

কল-কব্জা⇒ কল[১]

কলকা, কল্কা *n* ornamental design/ decorative embroidery on the borders of a sari or shawl. **~দার** *adj* having decorative embroidery. **~পেড়ে** *adj* having borders of ornamental design: ~পেড়ে শাড়ি.

কল-কারখানা⇒ কল[১]

কলকে, কল্কে *n* the bowl of a hubble-bubble which holds the tobacco and cinder. **~ পাওয়া** *vi* receive attention or recognition: তোমার মতো লোক যেখানে ~ পাবে না, won't be admitted to terms of equality.

কলগী [T] *n* the ornamental top of a crown or diadem; a jewelled headband or head-dress worn by women; a fillet; a tiara.

কলঘোষ *n* **1** sweet tone; melodious voice. **2** the cuckoo.

কলঙ্ক *n* **1** a disgrace, disrepute, scandal or stigma. **2** a sullying mark; a spot; a stain; a tarnish: কুলে ~ দেওয়া. **~কর** *adj* disgraceful infamous; scandalous. **~কালিমা** *n* the black stain of infamy; infamy. **~রটানো** *vi* spread scandal; calumniate; vilify; defame; traduce. **~ভঞ্জন** *n* vindication of one's good name/ honour; removal of stigma; exoneration. **~ভঞ্জন করা** *vt* exonerate one of his stigma. **~ভয়** *n* fear of scandal. **কুলের ~** *n* black sheep of a family.

কলঙ্কষ *n* the king of beasts; the lion. **কলঙ্কষা** *fem.*

কলঙ্কিত *adj* one who has been disgraced or stigmatized. **কলঙ্কিতা** *fem.* **~ করা** *vt* bring disgrace upon; stigmatize.

কলঙ্কিনী *adj fem* (woman) of bad name; unchaste.

কলঙ্কী *adj* stained; tainted. **~ চাঁদ** *n* the spotted moon.

কলত্র *n* the spouse of a man; wife.

কলধৌত *n* what has been washed or purified; gold; silver: **~ বাহিনী.**

কলধ্বনি⇒ কল[২]

কলন *n* **1** act of counting; enumeration. **2** act of collecting; collection. **কলিত** *adj* **1** counted. **2** collected; gathered. **উৎ~** *n* act of quoting. **উৎকলিত** *adj* quoted; collected.

কলন্তর *n* percentage of profit from money lent or invested; interest.

কলন্দর [A] Muslim ascetic moving from place to place.

কলপ [A] *n* **1** blackish paste for grey hair; hair-dye. **2** granular carbohydrate used for stiffening linen; starch. **চুলে ~ দেওয়া** blacken grey hair with a wash. **কাপড়ে ~ দেওয়া** stiffen clothes with starch.

কলব [A] *n* the primary organ of the body propelling the blood through the veins by its pulsations; the heart; (fig) the seat of emotions and affections; the mind.

কলভ (=করভ) **1** the young of an elephant/camel. **2** the thorn-apple or its fruit or flower; the stramonium.

কলভাষণ *n* baby-talk.

কলম[১] [A] *n* **1** writing tool made formerly of a feather; but now a metal nib fitted into a handle; a pen. **2** a writing; a decree: বিধাতার ~ খণ্ডাবে কে? who can alter the Decree of God? **~চি** *n* one who writes what another dictates; an amanuensis; a copyist. **~দান, ~দানি** *n* a tray or stand for keeping pens; a pen holder; a pen-stand. **~ ধরা** *vi* wield a pen; write: নজরুল সর্বপ্রকার শোষণের বিরুদ্ধে ~ ধরেন, Nazrul wielded his pen against all sorts of exploitation. **~পেশা** *n* clerkship. **~ পেষা** *vi* work as clerk. **~বাজ** *n* one living by his pen; a forceful or creative writer. **~বাজি** *n* the use of the pen; forceful writing; penmanship. **~ রদ করা** *vi* abrogate or nullify a decision. **কলমের খোঁচা** *n* stroke of the pen. **কলমের জোর** *n* ability to write forcefully. **কলমের এক খোঁচায় বাতিল করা** cancel with a single stroke of the pen.

কলম[২] *n* a shoot from a plant transplanted into another, to form a new growth; a graft: আমের ~, লেবুর ~. **~ করা** *vt, vi* put a graft in or on; graft one variety on into another.

কলম[৩] [E] *n* **1** a pillar supporting an arch or roof; a column. **2** a perpendicular section or vertical division of a page of type; a column of a newspaper.

কলম[৪] *n* variety of paddy.

কলমা=কলেমা

কলমি *n* edible aquatic plant; bindweed. **~ শাক** *n* the leaves of this plant cooked and eaten as spinach.

কলম্ব *n* **1** an arrow. **2** the stalk of spinach.

কলম্বিকা, কলম্বী=কলমি

কলরব⇒কল[২]

কলরোল⇒কল[২]

কলস, কলসি, *n* a metal or earthenware jar with a fat belly for holding water; a pitcher.

কলস্বন, কলস্বর⇒ কল[২]

কলহ *n* that which disturbs peace; a quarrel; a brawl; a dispute; a contention; a strife. **~ বাধানো** kick up a row; set (persons) by the ears; pick a quarrel (with sb). **~ করা** *vi* quarrel (with sb) (about sth); be engaged/take part in a quarrel. **~প্রিয়** *adj* apt to quarrel; inclined by temperament to quarrel; quarrelsome. **কলহান্তরিতা** *n* heroine suffering mental pain in separation after having dismissed her lover.

কলহাস্য *n* a sweet cackling laughter.

কলা[১] *n* **1** a lunar digit or one-sixteenth part of the moon's disc; a phase of the moon: ষোল~, the full moon; (fig) fulfilment; accomplishment: আমার সাধ ষোল~য় পূর্ণ হলো, my longings have come to fulfilment. **2** varieties of art, eg music, ballet, drawing, painting, sculpture, needlework, coiffure, etc; an art; a fine art. **বাগ্মিতা/ শিক্ষকতা একটি কলা** oratory/teaching is an art. **3** group of related disciplines eg history, literature, philosophy, etc contrasted with science subjects: কলা অনুষদ, faculty of Arts. **4** faculty or act of using stratagem; cunning; trickery; artifice: নাগর ভুলানোর ~, stratagem used by a woman to attract a lover. **ছলা~** *n* skilful way of doing sth; artifice; ingenuity; trickery; craftiness. **~কুশল** *adj* skilled in arts and crafts; adept in many arts. **~কৌশল** *n* artistic skill. **~বৎ** *adj, n* one who is versed in classical vocal music. **~বতী** *fem.* **~বিদ** *n* a skilled artist; an artcritic. **কাব্য~** *n* poetic art; poetry. **কারু-~** *n* **1** arts and crafts that save human labour; industrial art; mechanical art. **2** manual craft; handicraft. **চিত্র~** *n* art of painting. **ললিত~** *n* arts cultivated for their aesthetic, not utilitarian qualities; fine arts (music, painting, etc).

কলা[২]⇒ কদল *n* **1** the famous all-season fruit growing in tropical and semi tropical countries; the banana. **2** the plant or tree that bears banana; the plantain tree. **3** word expressing slight or contempt: সে আমার ~ করবে, he can do me little harm. **~ খাওয়া** (sl) be deceived/disappointed. **~ দেখানো** (sl) point the thumb at; show scorn; defy; evade a payment. **~পোড়া খাও** (sl) go to the dogs; be down and out; be ruined. **~র কাঁদি** *n* cluster of plantains. **~র ছড়া** *n* a bunch of bananas.

কলাই[১] *n* leguminous seeds of pulse; beans.

কলাই[২] [A] *n* substance of the nature of glass used for coating metal for decoration or as a protection; enamel. **~ করা** *vt* lay enamel on; paint in enamel; enamel. **~-করা** *adj* enamelled. **~কর** *n* one who enamels; an enameller; an enamellist. **~য়ের বাসন কোশন** *n* enamel ware.

কলানাথ, কলানিধি *n* the moon.

কলানুনাদী *n* **1** a small specie of bird; the sparrow. **2** the species of bird that in poetic imagination doesn't drink but rain water; the swallow. **3** large kind of hairy bee with a loud hum; the bumble-bee.

কলাপ *n* **1** the fine fan-shaped tail of the peacock: ~ মেলি করে সে কেলি. **2** jewellery esp one worn round the waist. **3** a collection of anything held together, eg a tuft of hair: কেশ~. **4** the famous work of this name on Sanskrit grammar.

কলাপী *n* the peacock. **কলাপিনী** *fem* the peahen.

কলাবউ *n* a banana plant dressed as a bride and conceived as goddess Durga worshipped by Hindus. **2** (euphem) an awkwardly bashful woman, such as with a long veil.

কলার [E] *n* part of a masculine garment that surrounds the neck; turned-over neckbond of a shirt.

কলালাপ *n* **1** a pleasant talk or talker. **2** the bumble-bee. **3** discussion about fine arts.

কলি[১] *n* **1** an embryonic growth of compact leaves or flower breaking out of the main stem; a half-opened flower; a bud. **2** a painting on one's face with sandal-paste after the Vaishnabic style: রস~. **3** a foot of a verse or song. **4** piece of cloth or a lace cut in the shape of a Vaishnabic কলি for setting on a garment as a decoration: ~দার পাঞ্জাবি.

কলি[২] [A] *n* composition of powdered lime or chalk and water, used for whitening walls, ceilings, etc; whitewash. **~চুন** *n* special quality lime made of oyster-shell or cockle-shell, used in white wash for brightness. **~ফিরানো** *vt* cover with whitewash; whitewash.

কলি[৩] *n* the fourth or last age of creation according to the Hindu Purana: ~যুগ, ~কাল. **~দেব, দেবতা** *n* the presiding deity of this age. **ঘোর ~** *n* devilish age full of sins. **~র সন্ধ্যা** the beginning of the age of irreligiousness: সবে তো ~র সন্ধ্যা, This is just the beginning of the approaching doom.

কলিকা[১]=কলি[১] (1)

কলিকা[২] pedantic form of কলকি.

কলিঙ্গ *n* old name of the region in India now including the state of Orissa and the adjoining area.

কলিজা, কলজে [H] *n* organ in the abdomen, which secrets the bile; the liver. **2** strength of character to resist danger, hardship, etc without flinching; stout-heartedness; courage. **3** the heart; the mind: দুর্গতদের অবস্থা দেখলে ~ ছিঁড়ে যায়, My heart rends at the suffering of the afflicted.

কলু *n* an oilman by caste. **কলুনী** *fem.* **~র ঘানি** *n* oilman's mill run by a single bullock. **কলুর বলদ** oilmans bullock; (fig) person who drudges for others without any benefit for himself.

কলুষ *n* **1** moral offence; a sin; a guilt. **2** defilement; stain; dirt; suli;. ❑*adj* filthy; foul; turbid. **কলুষিত** *adj* what has been defiled/stained/sullied.

কলেজ [E] *n* educational institution for the post secondary stage; a college.

কলেজা=কলিজা

কলেবর *n* the bulk or extent of anything; the body: পুস্তকের ~.

কলেমা, কলমা [A] *n* **1** the basic article of faith that makes one a Muslim. In it a Muslim declares that there's none worthy of worship but Allah and that Muhammad (sm) is His messenger: ~ তৈয়ব, ~ শাহাদাৎ **~ পড়া** *vi* **1** recite the basic article of faith in Islam. **2** marry in a legal way. **~ পড়ানো** *vi* conduct a marriage ceremony in the way as required under the law.

কলেরা [E] *n* malignant disease characterized by violent vomiting, diarrhoea and intense thirst; cholera.

কলোচ্ছলিত [কল +উচ্ছলিত] *adj* bulging with a sweet sound; full of melody.

কলোনি [E] *n* **1**= উপনিবেশ. **2** part or area of a town containing a cluster of houses owned or occupied by people of the same occupation; a housing estate: আজিমপুর ~, রিফিউজি ~

কল্কা⇒ কলকা

কল্কি, কল্কী *n* the last of the incarnations of Vishnu (কল্কি অবতার), expected in the Purana to appear on earth at the end of the *kaliyuga* (কলিযুগ) to put an end to irreligiousness. **~পুরাণ** *n* one of the Puranas dealing with কল্কি অবতার.

কল্কে, কলকি, কলিকা⇒ কলকে

কল্প *n* **1** a day and night of Brahma which according to Hindu belief is equal to a period of 432 million solar years of mortals: কল্পান্ত, কল্পান্তর. **2** one of the six Vedangas or sacred writings treating of rites and ceremonials in Hinduism (also কল্পসূত্র). **3** (gram) inflexion or *suff* denoting approximation or resemblance: মৃতকল্প, পিতৃকল্প, অমৃতকল্প. **4** an aim; an object: রক্ষাকল্পে, উদ্ধার কল্পে, উন্নতিকল্পে. **~তরু, ~দ্রুম** *n* (Hindu myth) heavenly tree that generously grants anything one wishes; (fig) a highly liberal and generous person. **~লতা** *n* wish-yielding creeper of the paradise. **~লোক** *n* a fancied land full of good things; a dreamland; a Utopia.

কল্পন *n* **1** act of planning, devising or thinking. **2** act of resolving or taking a decision. **3** a supposition.

কল্পনা *n* **1** forming a picture of sth in the mind; poetic imagination: কবি~. **2** unfounded opinion or belief; a fancy. **3** a conjecture; a surmise; an inference. **4** the power of creating beauty; the genius of a poet. **~ করা** *vt* form a mental image; imagine; fancy; conceive, contrive; invent. **~কারী** *adj* able to imagine/conceive/contrive/invent. ❑*n* one who imagines; a fancier; a thinker; an inventor. **~চিত্র** *n* forms of the fancy; an imaginary portrait. **~প্রবণ** *adj* given to fancy;

fanciful. ~বিলাসী *adj* having visionary ideas; dreamy. ~শক্তি *n* faculty of imagination/ invention. কল্পনীয় *adj* that which can be fancied/imagined; imaginable.

কল্পিত *adj* imaginary; fancied; invented contrived.

কল্পী *adj* imaginative; imagining; inventing; contriving.

কল্প্য *adj* what can be imagined/fancied; conceivable; devisable

কল্মষ *n* moral impurity; sin; guilt; dirt; filth. ❑*adj* sinful; vicious; foul; dirty.

কল্য *n* **1** the day after the present; tomorrow. **2** the day before this one; yesterday. আগামী~ *n, adv* tomorrow. গত~ *n, adv* yesterday. আগামী~ রাত (বা রাতে) *adv* tomorrow night. গত~ রাতে (গত রাতে) *adv* last night. আগামীকল্যকার/ গতকল্যকার *adj* of tomorrow/ yesterday.

কল্যাণ *n* well-being from point of view of health, wealth or happiness. **2** generosity; support; favour; patronage: আপনার কল্যাণে বেঁচে আছি, its your munificence that keeps me going. **3** name of a musical mode: ইমন~. ❑*adj* benign; gracious; auspicious. ~ করা *vi,vt* do good (to). ~ কামনা করা wish (one) good or happiness; bless (one): তোমার ~ হোক, may you be happy; may you prosper. ~কর *adj* beneficial; benignant; benevolent. ~ময় *adj* beneficent; bountiful. ~ময়ী *fem*. কল্যাণাস্পদ *adj* one who deserves good wishes (word uttered while addressing or referring to a younger person deserving affection).

কল্যাণীয় *adj* one whose well being is to be wished. কল্যাণীয়া *fem*.

কল্যাণীয়বর্, কল্যাণীয়বরেষু, কল্যাণবরেষু form of address used in a letter to one who is an object of affection.

কল্যাণীয়েষু *n* form of address in a letter to a junior. কল্যাণীয়াসু *fem*.

কল্লা[1] [P] *n* the head: বাবা জানতে পারলে ~ থাকবে না (অপরাধের বিষয়), father will inflict a severe punishment when he comes to know of (the crime); the head of a fish, goat etc: মাছের কল্লা, খাসির ~.

কল্লা[2] [B] *adj* quarrelsome; wicked; conspiring: ~ লোক. ❑*n* a quarrel; a dispute.

কল্লিদার [B কলি >কল্লি+দার P] *adj* inlaid with decorative piece of cloth or lace: ~ কোর্তা.

কল্লোল *n* **1** the babble of a running stream; a roaring wave: জল~. **2** a great joy or delight. **3** a loud confused noise; a tumult: জন~. কল্লোলিত *adj* full of din and bustle; clamorous; tumultuous: নানা পাখিনাদে কল্লোলিত বন, a forest resounding with the twitter of birds. কল্লোলিনী *adj fem* clamorous. ❑*n* a stream; a rivulet.

কশ [P] *n* **1** the two points joining the upper and the lower lips: ~ দিয়ে পানের পিক গড়াচ্ছে. **2** a projecting extremity; a corner; a nook.

কশফ [A] *n* heavenly inspiration; revealed truth; revelation.

কশা[1] [⇒কশ, কশা] *n* a whip; a lash. ~ঘাত *n* whipping; lashing. ~ঘাত করা *vt* whip; lash; flog.

কশা[2] *vt* **1** whip; lash; flog. **2** strike with the open hand; slap: চড়~.

কশিদা [P] *n* embroidered work on cloth; variegated needlework; embroidery.

কশেরু *n* the backbone; the spine; the vertebral column. ~ক *adj* having a backbone; vertebrate. ❑*n* the backbone; the vertebral bone. ~কা *n* the vertebral bone; the backbone.

কষ[1] *n* **1** astringent juice of some plants or fruits: আমের ~, গাবের ~, কলাগাছের ~. **2** stain caused by this juice: ~ লাগা. **3** tannic acid or tannin obtained from the bark of oak trees, and used in the manufacture of ink and in converting raw hides into leather.

কষ[2] *n* dark-coloured siliceous stone used in testing gold and silver; a touchstone.

কষণ[1] *n* **1** act of testing gold or silver by a touchstone. **2** the converting of hides into leather by the use of tan; tanning. কষিত *adj* **1** tested on a touchstone. **2** tanned. কষিত কাঞ্চন *n* tested gold; pure gold; (fig) person of a tried ability or integrity.

কষণ[2], **কষন** *n* **1** act of fastening sth tightly; making tight or tighter; tightening; (fig) act of enforcing rules and regulations (or discipline) with strictness; enforce strictness. **2** act of braising meat, fish, etc with oil and spices (ie, without gravy).

কষা[1] *vt* **1** try the purity of gold or silver by rubbing with a touchstone. **2** haggle or with a seller about the price of sth: দর ~. **3** work out a mathematical sum: অঙ্ক ~. **4** put on the brakes (of a bicycle, motorcar, etc): ড্রাইভার হঠাৎ করে ব্রেক কষে, the driver braked (his car) suddenly. **5** fasten sth (eg a belt by pulling (or pressing) it to the utmost: কষে বাঁধা. ❑*n* constipation.

কষা[2] *adj* **1** high in price; costly. **2** miserly; niggardly; close-fisted: ~ লোক. **3** fitting close or too close; tight: ~ জামা.

কষাকষি [P] *n* **1** bargaining between two parties over sth: দর ~. **2** estrangement between two persons: মন ~. দর ~ করা *vi* settle price by higgling; higgle; haggle. মন ~ করা *vi* estrange oneself from.

কষায় *n* **1** harsh or astringent taste. **2** astringent juice. **3** extraction obtained by boiling a substance in water; decoction. **4** tannic acid used for tanning hides. **5** reddish colour.

কষায়িত *adj* reddened: রোষ-কষায়িত লোচন, eyes reddened with anger.

কষি ⇒কষণ[১]

কষে, কষিয়া *adv* tightly; soundly; thoroughly: কষে কাজ করো, work in right earnest/wholeheatedly; কষে মারো টান/কোপ, pull/strike as hard as you can.

কষ্ট *n* **1** hardship; privation; destitution; want: কষ্টের সংসার. **2** toil; labour; hard work: কষ্টার্জিত. **3** bodily suffering; pain; trouble; diligent effort: কষ্টসাধ্য, কষ্টসহিষ্ণু. ☐*adj* strained: not genuine or natural: ~ কল্পনা. **~ করা** *vi* take trouble/pains; labour hard; toil. **~ দেওয়া** *vt* give trouble; cause suffering to; harass. **~ পাওয়া** *vi* suffer (from); be harassed/distressed. **~কর** *adj* troublesome; toilsome; distressing; painful. **~কল্পনা** *n* a forced or far-fetched idea; laboured concept/thought. **~কল্পিত** *adj* strained, not natural; far-fetched. **~ সহ, ~ সহিষ্ণু** *adj* inured to fatigue; painstaking; hardy. **~সাধ্য** *adj* difficult to accomplish; hard to achieve/attain. **কষ্টার্জিত** *adj* acquired with difficulty; hard-earned.

কষ্টি, কষ্টিপাথর=কষ[২]. **কষ্টি পাথরে যাচাই করা** test the purity of (eg gold) on a touchstone.

কষ্টে সৃষ্টে *adv* with great difficulty. **~ সংসার চালানো** manage one's domestic expenses with great difficulty.

কস[১] =কশ

কস[২]=কষ[১]

কসব [A] *n* **1** prostitution; harlotry. **2** trade; business. **কসবি** [A] *fem* a prostitute; a harlot; a whore. **কসবিপনা** *n* a harlots's way of behaviour.

কসবা [A] *n* **1** large and prosperous village with advantages of a town. **2** a small town; an administrative headquarters under the Turkish rule.

কসম [A]*n* an oath; a swearing. **~ খাওয়া** *vi* take an oath; swear. **~ দেওয়া** *vi* charge an oath; adjure. **খোদার ~** *int* in God's name; by God.

কসর [A] *n* **1** residence of a king or prince; a palace. **2** making short or shortening one's canonical prayer during a journey: সফরকালে নামাজ ~ পড়তে হয়.

কসরত, কসরৎ [A] *n* **1** physical exercise; athletic feat. **2** adroitness in an action; skill; tact; a trick. **3** practice in an art: গলার (গানের) ~. **4** earnest endeavour to achieve sth in a difficult situation: এর জন্য অনেক ~ করতে হয়েছে. **~ করা** *vt* practise; exercise.

কসাই, কশাই [A] *n* **1** one who kills animals for market: a butcher; a meat seller. **2** one who delights in bloody deeds; a very cruel person. **3** (fig) a selfish person always on the look out to prey on others: বরের বাপ তো একটা ~. **~খানা** *n* slaughter-house; butchery. **~গিরি** *n* **1** the trade of a butcher. **2** a cruel treatment, such as behoves only a butcher. **কসাইয়ের হাতে পড়া** fall a prey to a cruel person.

কসীদা=কাসীদা

কসুর [A] *n* **1** a fault; a guilt; an offence: ~ হয়েছে, মাফ করে দিন, I admit my fault, please excuse me. **2** carelessness; negligence: মেহমানের যত্নের ব্যাপারে কোনো ~ করা হয়নি. **3** failure or omission to do sth required: ভদ্রলোককে জব্দ করতে চেষ্টার কোনো ~ করেনি দেখছি. **~ করা** *vi* commit an offence; fail or neglect to do sth required.

কস্তা *adj* of a bright-red colour; scarlet. **কস্তাপাড়** *n* wide scarlet border. **কস্তাপেড়ে** *adj* having a broad scarlet border: কস্তাপেড়ে শাড়ি.

কস্তুর, কস্তুরা *n* deer of central Asia, the male of which yields the perfume musk; the musk-deer.

কস্তুরী, কস্তুরিকা *n* a strong-scented secretion from the musk-deer, used in perfumes; musk: **~ মল্লিকা** *n* sort of flower giving out musky fragrance.

কস্মিনকালে *adv* at any time; ever (used for emphasis): এমন কথা ~ও শুনিনি, have never heard of such a thing.

কস্য *pron* (used in legal deeds) whose; of such and such person.

কহ *vt* (poet) tell; narrate; answer.

কহতব্য *adj* **1** utterable; worth-mentioning; speakable. **2** fit to be expressed. **~ নয়** unspeakable; unutterable.

কহন [কথন] *n* act of saying/speaking/relating. ☐*adj* utterable; speakable.

কহর [A] *n* **1** imprecation of evil; curse: খোদার ~ পড়বে তোমার উপর. **2** misfortune; disaster; natural calamity: দেশে ~ পড়েছে. **3** oppression; tyranny.

কহা (old use) *vt* to say; to tell (modern use: বলা).

কাই *n* a mass in a semi-fluid state; a mixture or paste of flour for bread; dough.

কাইট *n* sediment of oil, etc.

কাউকে *pron* (colloq) whom.

কাউন *n* kind of food crop.

কাউন্সিল [E] *n* an assembly for consultation; a body of men designated to advise an executive head/body; a council.

কাউর *n* a skin disease; eczema.

কাএদা=কায়দা

কাওয়াজ [A] *n* military display; parade. **কুচ~** [P+A] *n* training in the art of warfare.

কাওয়ালি, কাওয়ালী [A] *n* devotional song of the sufi fraternity; the mode and measure of this music. **কাওয়াল** *n* one who sings কাওয়ালি; a master musician.

কাওরা *n* a down-trodden Hindu caste.

কাংস, কাংস্য, কাংস্যক *n* **1** a mixture of copper and tin, used for bells; bell-metal; white brass. **2** a bell-metal plate used as a sort of musical instrument struck with a stick. **3** bell-metal utensil. **~কার** *n* one who works in bell-metal or white brass; a brassier.

কাঁক *n* long-necked bird of the crane family; the heron.

কাঁকই, কাঁকুই *n* large size comb with thick teeth.

কাঁকড়া =কর্কট (1). **~-বিছা** *n* the scorpion; a small animal of the spider group with a jointed tail terminating with a poisonous sting. **~র খোলা** *n* the carapace.

কাঁকন *n* an ornamental band for the wrist worn by women; a bangle; a bracelet.

কাঁকর=কঙ্কর

কাঁকরোল *n* a kind of kitchen vegetable.

কাঁকলাস *n* **1** species of lizard with a long extensile tongue and a prehensile tail, and the power of changing its colour according to its background: the chameleon. **2** (fig) a very lean person (also ~-মূর্তি).

কাঁকুড় *n* the green melon.

কাঁখ *n* **1** the part of human body between the ribs and the hips; the waist: কাঁখের কলসি. **2** the hollow underneath the arm at the junction with the shoulder; the armpit; the axilla (also কাঁখতলি).

কাঁচ=কাচ

কাঁচকড়া *n* **1** the shell of a tortoise. **2** the soft bony part in the jaw of a whale. **3** superior vulcanized rubber; ebonite; vulcanite.

কাঁচকলা *n* a species of plantain chiefly used in its green state as vegetable. **আদায় ~য়** *adv* in a state of estrangement; at daggers drawn (with sb); at loggerheads with.

কাঁচপোকা *n* species of bright green beetle with a hard covering on its tail, the bits of which are used by women as decoration for the forehead.

কাঁচলি=কাঁচুলি

কাঁচা *adj*, **1** not ripe; unripe; green: ~ আম. **2** uncooked; unboiled; raw: ~ মাংস, ~ দুধ. **3** immature; young: ~ বয়স. **4** made of mud or earth and not brick or stones: ~ ঘর, ~ রাস্তা. **5** lacking; wanting; weak; deficient: অঙ্কে ~. **6** inexperienced; inexpert: ~ হাত. **7** temporary; provisional: ~রসিদ. **8** undried; unsunned; unseasoned: ~ কাঠ, ~ হলুদ. **9** not permanent; not fast: ~ রং. **10** faulty; defective; carelessly done: ~ কাজ. **~ কলা**=কাঁচকলা. **কাঁচা কাজ** *n* **1** unwise act. **2** faulty work. **~~** *adv*, *adj* in the state of growing; not fully ripe or mature. **~গোল্লা** *n* round sweet made of posset, not dipped in syrup. **~ ঘুম** *n* sleep in the primary stage. **~ চুল** *n* hair not yet grey; black hair. **~ টাকা** *n* metal money. **~ পয়সা** *n* money obtained by unfair or underhand means; easy money. **~বাজার** *n* market where fish, meat and other perishables are sold. **~ মরিচ** *n* green chillies. **~মাল** *n* the raw materials of industry. **~মিঠা** *adj* sweet though unripe; sweet in the unripe state. **কাঁচা রাস্তা** *n* unmetalled road. **~ লেখা** *n* **1** not a set hand in writing. **2** writing which is not of a mature literary standard. **~ সোনা** *n* pure gold. **~হলুদ** *n* turmeric which is raw and not yet dried. **~ হাত** *n* unskilled hand, not practised. **~ হিসাব** *n* rough account or estimate.

কাঁচি[1] [H] *n* cutting tool consisting of two blades each crossing the other and fixed at a pivot; (pair of) scissors. **আমার ~ কোথায়?** where are my scissors? **~টি কোথায়?** where is the pair of scissors?

কাঁচি[2] *adj* **1** short of or below the standard: ~ওজন (formerly in use). **2** (of cloth) very closely woven: ~ ধুতি. **3** (curd) made of unboiled milk: ~ দই.

কাঁচু-মাচু *adj* shrunken with extreme modesty or fear, etc; embarrassed; hesitant; shame-faced. **~ হয়ে বলা** speak with delicacy/diffidently/hesitatingly.

কাঁচুলি *n* women's close-fitting undergarment for the bosom.

কাঁচ্চা *n* measure of weight of the smallest denomination prevalent before the introduction of the metric system.

কাঁটা *n* **1** a spike, spine or prickle on the stem or branch of a tree or shrub; a thorn: গোলাপের ~. **2** the skeleton of a fish: মাছের ~. **3** the hand of a clock or watch: ঘড়ির ~. **4** small pointed piece of metal with a flat head to be driven into timber, leather, etc; a pin or small nail: জুতায় ~ মারা, fasten the sole or stud it with nails. **5** the pointer of compass or of a balance: কম্পাসের ~, দাঁড়িপাল্লার ~. **6** implement with a handle and two or more prongs (points) used for lifting food to the mouth; a fork: ~-চামচ. **7** sort of implements used by women for dressing the hair: চুলের ~. **8** (fig) a source of trouble or obstruction: পথের ~. **কারো পথের ~ হওয়া** (phrase) be a thorn in one's flesh/side. **গায়ে ~ দেওয়া** have a gooseflesh (ie, prickly roughening of the skin): ভয়ে আমার শরীর ~ দিয়ে উঠলো, fear made my flesh creep. **~ দিয়ে ~ তোলা** set a thief to catch a thief; befool one enemy by another. **~তার** *n* barbed wire. **~বন** *n* a bush of prickly shrubs. **~ময়** *adj* thorny prickly. **~য় ~য়** *adv* (of clock) just in time; punctually.

কাঁঠাল, কাঁটাল *n* juicy fruit with sweet kernels inside and a thorny outer covering; the jack-fruit. **কাঁঠালের কোয়া/কোষ** *n* kernel of the jack-fruit (containing a stone inside). **কাঁঠাল-চাঁপা** *n* yellow flower giving the smell of a ripe jack-fruit. **কাঁঠালের আমসত্ত্ব** (fig) sth impossible; a mare's nest. **পরের মাথায় ~ ভাঙা** (fig) use a person as a tool for one's own benefit; (phrase) make a cat's paw of a person.

কাঁড়া *vt* separate husk from rice; unhusk. ☐*adj* husked. **আঁ~** *adj* unhusked. **ভিক্ষার চাল ~ আর আ~** beggars can't be choosers; ie, must accept whatever is offered them.

কাঁড়ি *n* mass of material piled up; a heap; a collection. **~~ টাকা** heaps of money.

কাঁথা *n* a thick bed-cover or a rag made of patched cotton cloth; a quilt. **ছেঁড়া ~য় শুয়ে লাখ টাকার স্বপ্ন দেখা** have a day-dream, ie, impracticable ideal or plan; (phrase) build castles in the air.

কাঁদ-কাঁদ, কাঁদো-কাঁদো *adj* almost weeping; in tears; mournful.

কাঁদন *n* weeping; lamentation.

কাঁদা *vi, vt* manifest grief by shedding tears; weep; wail; lament. ☐*n* weeping; wailing; lamentation: জীবনে অনেক কাঁদা কেঁদেছি, I've had much wailing in my life. **~-কাটা, ~-কাটি** *n* **1** crying complainingly in a loud shrill voice; wailing. **2** earnest entreaty or supplication: ছেলেটিকে একবার দেখার জন্য বৃদ্ধ অনেক ~কাটি করলো. **গুমরে ~** *vi* weep in a suppressed manner. **ডুকরে ~** *vi* weep without restraint/aloud. **ফুঁপিয়ে ~** *vi* weep in convulsive gasps under mental distress; sob. **ইনিয়ে বিনিয়ে ~** *vi* (derog) weep elaborately making an exaggerated show of grief.

কাঁদানো *vi, vt* cause (one) to weep or cry.

কাঁদি *n* a bunch of fruits growing together/from the same stem; a cluster: কলার ~.

কাঁদুনি=কাঁদা *n*. **~ গাওয়া** *vi* express distress or relate grievances while weeping and talking through the nose like a hurt child asking for pity; express with a whine.

কাঁদুনে *adj* given to crying or weeping at trifles; whining. **~ গ্যাস** *n* gas that causes severe watering of the eyes; tear-gas. **~ সুরে** *adv* in piteous tone/plaintive voice; plaintively.

কাঁধ *n* the part of the body where the arms are joined to the trunk; the shoulder. **~ দেওয়া** *vt* (lit) shoulder a burden/load; (fig) shoulder a task or responsibility for sth. **~ বদলানো** *vt* transfer a load to another's shoulder or to one's other shoulder by turns. **কাঁধে নেওয়া** *vt* shoulder a load or a responsibility for sth. **কার কাঁধে দশটা মাথা** (said when a great risk is involved in sth) who will risk his head? who dares ?

কাঁধাকাঁধি *adv* shoulder to shoulder: ~ দাঁড়ানো. **~ বহন করা** *vt* carry on the shoulder.

কাঁপ, কাঁপন, কাঁপুনি=কম্পন (1)

কাঁপা *vi* tremble, shiver; quake. **ভয়ে ~** tremble with fear. **শীতে ~** shiver with cold.

কাঁপানো *vt* cause one to tremble or shiver: বখাটেরা সাড়া পাড়াটিকে কাঁপিয়ে তুলেছে.

কাঁসর *n* disc of bell-metal with a turned rim giving a resonant note when struck with a stick; a musical instrument; a gong.

কাঁসা *n* alloy of copper and tin; bell-metal; white brass: ~র বাসন. **কাঁসারি** *n* maker of brass, copper or bell-metal utensils; a brazier; a coppersmith.

কাঁসি =কাঁসর. **~দার** *n* one who beats or plays on a gong or bell-metal disc. **~ দেওয়া** *vi* play on a gong in tune/concert with other instruments.

কাঁহা *adv* at or in what place; where; whither.

কাঁহাতক *adv* **1** to what or which place: ~ যাওয়া যায়, how far to go. **2** how long; to what extent: এমন উপদ্রব ~ সহ্য করা যায়, how long to endure this nuisance.

কাক *n* black bird with a harsh cry living in human habitation; the crow. **~চক্ষু** *adj* as transparent as a crow's eyes: ~চক্ষু জল, ~চরিত্র. **~জ্যোৎস্না** *n* faint moonlight of the night-end which the crow mistakes for daylight and wakes up. **~তন্দ্রা, ~নিদ্রা** *n* short sleep; light sleep; wary nap; a slumber. **~তাড়ুয়া** *n* anything in the shape of a human figure set up to scare crows from crops; sth terrifying to birds but without danger; a scarecrow. **~তালীয়** *adj* (of two events)**1** founded upon the supposed connection of the crow (কাক) with the fall of the palmyra fruit (তাল) which is actually a case of coincidence. **2** coincidental and not related as cause and effect. **~তালীয় ন্যায়** *n* a fallacious argument based on the supposition " after it, so because of it." **~পক্ষ** *n* curl of hair like the wings of crow, hung down beside the ear on both sides: the love-locks. **~পদ** *n* a caret mark like crow's foot (ie, ^) placed below a line in writing or in proof correcting to indicate that sth has been omitted and is to be added at that place. **~পুচ্ছ** *n* bird having wings like those of a crow; the cuckoo. **~পুষ্ট** *n* a bird the young of which is reared up by a crow; the cuckoo. **~বন্ধ্যা** *n* woman who bears but one child. **~স্নান** *n* a brief bath as a crow takes by sprinkling only a small quantity of water. **~ কোকিলের সমান দর** inability to discriminate, eg, between good and bad/right and wrong.

কাকের ছা বকের ছা, কাকের ঠ্যাং বকের ঠ্যাং (fig) handwriting which is bad and utterly illegible. **তীর্থের ~** (fig) a servile person who like a crow in a sacred place, waits expectantly for others' favour. **বেল পাকলে কাকের কী** (lit) It matters little to a crow whether the wood-apple is ripe or not/in any case, he cannot eat it; (fig) state of total frustration. **দাঁড়~** *n* a raven. **ভাত ছড়ালে কাকের অভাব হয় না** (fig) have means enough to call the tunes. **কাকের মাংস কাকে খায় না** one raven will not pluck another's eyes.

কাকলি, কাকলী *n* low and sweet murmur; chirping of the birds.

কা-কা *n* onomatopoeic word denoting the cry of a raven or crow; cawing of a crow. **~ করা** *vi* utter the cry of a crow or raven; caw.

কাকা *n* paternal uncle; father's younger brother. **কাকী** *fem.*

কাকাতুয়া *n* a highly coloured bird of the parrot family, characterized by a crest of feathers on the head; a cockatoo.

কাকুতি=অনুনয়. **~মিনতি**=অনুনয়-বিনয়. **~মিনতি করা** *vi, vt* entreat or beg humbly for.

কাকুবাদ *n* words of entreaty; humble and earnest prayer.

কাকে (colloq) *pron* whom: ~ দিয়েছো? whom did you give (it)?

কাকোদর *n* a snake; a serpent.

কাগজ [P] *n* **1** substance manufactured from pulped vegetable or wood fibre, linen rags, etc in the form of sheets, used for writing, printing, packing, etc; paper. **2** legal documents (also ~পত্র). **3** a newspaper: আজকের কাগজে খবরটা বেরিয়েছে. **~ওয়ালা** *n* newspaper hawker; people connected with newspapers. **~পত্র** *pl* written records, documents, etc: মোকদ্দমার ~পত্র ঠিক আছে তো? **কাগজে কলমে** *adv* in writing or in print; in black and white. **খবরের ~** *n* newspaper. **পরীক্ষার ~** *n* examination scripts. **স্বচ্ছ ~** *n* strong transparent paper on which tracings are made; tracing-paper.

কাগজি *adj* **1** made of paper: ~ ফুল. **2** having a paper-like thin skin: ~ লেবু. ❑*n* paper manufacturer or seller. **~ মুদ্রা** *n* paper money; bank-note.

কাঙাল, কাঙ্গাল *n* one who is destitute of the means of subsistence; a beggar: কাঙালি ভোজ, feeding the poor; কাঙালি বিদায়, distribution of alms among the poor. ❑*adj* **1** destitute of means of comfortable subsistence; poor; indigent; poverty-stricken and therefore greedy of gain; covetous; avaricious: কাঙালিপনা. **2** ardently desirous (of sth): নামের (যশের) ~, hankering after fame; সন্তানের ~, desirous of children. **কাঙালিনী** *fem.* **কাঙালের ঘোড়া রোগ** to be too ambitious in one's plans; (prov) beggars on horseback will ride to the devil.

কাঙালি, কাঙ্গালী=কাঙাল, কাঙ্গাল

কাঙ্ক্ষণীয় *adj* desirable; to be wished for/longed for. **কাঙ্ক্ষা** *n* wish; desire; longing. **কাঙ্ক্ষিত** *adj* desired; wished for; longed for: কাঙ্ক্ষিত সাহায্য. **কাঙ্ক্ষী** *adj* desirous; longing for.

কাচ *n* **1** hard transparent and fragile substance made by the fusion of silicates with alkalis, used for manufacturing mirrors, bottles and drinking or other kinds of vessels; glass. **2** transparent natural substance; rock-crystal or quartz used as jewel. **কাঞ্চন দিয়ে ~ কেনা** to pay gold in exchange of glass, ie, to pay to dear for one's whistle.

কাচা *vi, vt* wash or make clean in water with or without soap (as clothes).

কাচি (colloq)=কাস্তে

কাচকি *n* a species of small fish.

কাচারি=কাছারি

কাচ্চা বাচ্চা *n pl* little ones; offspring: ~ রেখে মারা গেছে.

কাছ *n* state of being near to; proximity; nearness. **~-ছাড়া** *adj* separated; away from one. **~-বরাবর** *adv* near; close upon. **কাছাকাছি** *adv* near to (each other) close upon; near about: একশো টাকার কাছাকাছি, near about 100 taka. **কাছাকাছি আসা/হওয়া** *vt* approach to; draw near (to each other); approximate. **কাছে** *adv*, *prep* near to; in the vicinity of; beside: কাছে বসো, sit by (me). **হাতের কাছে** within reach of. **তার কাছে টাকা নেই** he has no money with him. **কাছে কাছে** *adv* close to: কাছে কাছে থেকো, keep close to.

কাছা *n* the end of a *dhuti* (loin-cloth) which the wearer tucks behind at the waistband between the legs.

কাছাড় *n* steep bank of a river.

কাছারি, কাচারি *n* court house; court of justice.

কাছি *n* thick rope for mooring boats and ships; mooring rope.

কাছিম=কচ্ছপ

কাজ *n* **1** mental or physical action regularly performed to earn a living; work; labour; trade; business; employment: তার কোনো ~ নেই, he is out of employment/without a job. **2** necessity; usefulness: এটা কোনো কাজে আসবে না, it will be of no use. **3** anything done; a deed; an act or action: ~টি ভালো হলো না. **4** a piece of work imposed by authority or by legal or moral code; task; duty; responsibility: রাজার ~ প্রজা পালন. **5** one's habit, character or mental inclination: পরচর্চাই তার ~. **6** the power to produce or bring the desired result; effectiveness: ওষুধে ~ হয়েছে. **7** the propriety or advisability of doing sth: তোমার সেখানে গিয়ে ~ নেই, you need not go there; you'd better not go there. **8** artistic skill; artistry: দেয়ালে রঙের ~ হচ্ছে. **9** motive or purpose behind anything: কি কাজে এসেছো? what brings you here? **~ আদায় করা** make (one's subordinates) work in full capacity by exacting methods; be a hard task master. **~ আনা** secure or obtain an order/work. **~ দেখা** *vi* supervise a work. **~ দেখানো** *n* show off one's activity; give a good account of oneself. **~ বাগানো** manage to obtain sth gainful. **~ বাড়ানো** *vi* to spoil (a thing) by inexpert handling; to botch or bungle. **কাজের কথা** *n* matter of importance; business talk. **কাজের লোক** *n***1** an active person; a practical man. **2** a servant. **কাজের সময়** business hours. **কাজের মতো ~** useful job; the right thing. **কাজের সময় কাজি, কাজ ফুরালে পাজি** to get rid of one who has served the purpose; give a dog a bad name and hang him. **আমার অনেক ~ আছে** my hands are full. **আমার অন্য কাজ আছে** I have other fish to fry. **আমার কথায় তোমার কাজ কি?** you need not poke your nose into my affairs? **তার কথায় ~ কী?** **1** why talk of him? **2** no use talking of him. **নিজের ~ করো** mind your own business.

কাজ-কর্ম *n* business; activities.

কাজল *n* kohl, cosmetic preparation used in the East to darken the eye-lids. **~কালো** *adj* as black as kohl; dark-black.

কাজলা *adj* black: ~ গাই, ~ মেয়ে. ❑*n* **1** sugarcane of reddish variety. **2** a wedge used by sawyers when sawing timber. **3** variety of paddy.

কাজি, কাজী [A] *n* **1** a dispenser of justice under Muslim law/rule; a judge. **2** registrar of marriages under Muslim law.

কাজেই, কাজে কাজেই *adv* for that or this reason; consequently; therefore.

কাঞ্চন *n* **1** that which has lustre; gold. **2** variety of flower. **3** wealth; riches: ~ কৌলীন্য, aristocracy of riches, not of blood or culture. **4** variety of paddy. ❑*adj* made of gold; gold coin: ~ মুদ্রা. **~প্রভ** *adj* having the lustre of gold. **~সন্ধি** *n* a treaty or agreement concluded on equal terms and so likely to be happy and enduring. **মণি~ যোগ** *n* a connection or union as beautiful and desirable as that between gold and jewel.

কাট [E] a cutting or design: জামার ~.

কাটখোট্টা *adj* **1** rough, uncouth and ill-mannered. **2** lacking in sense of humour/refined taste: বিজ্ঞানের আলোচনা বড়ই ~. **3** unfeeling; unsympathetic outspoken: ~ কথাবার্তা.

কাট ছাঁট *n* addition or alteration.

কাটতি *n* (of a commodity) sale; demand.

কাটনা *n* **1** act of spinning. **2** a spinning wheel. **~ কাটা** *vi* spin.

কাটনী *n* a spinner.

কাটমোল্লা *n* a bigoted and illiberal Muslim cleric.

কাটলেট [E] *n* a fried slice of meat cut from the rib-bones; a cutlet.

কাটা *vt* **1** cut sth down; to fell: গাছ ~, গাছের ডাল কাটা, lop off a branch. **2** dig; excavate: পুকুর ~. **3** to bite: সাপে ~. **4** pen through; strike off: লেখা/নাম কাটা. **5** pass over: বিপদ কাটা. **6** mend or sharpen পেন্সিল ~. **7** pinch or pick: পকেট ~. **8** disperse: মেঘ ~. **9** chop or hew: মাংস ~. **10** gather; harvest: ফসল ~. **11** operate on (sb/sth): ফোঁড়া/ ছানি ~. **12** pass away; elapse: সময় ~, দিন ~. ❑*adj* cut; severed; lopped off. **~কুটা, ~কুটি** *n* penning through (a writing) frequently for corrections and alterations. ❑*adj* untidy on account of frequent additions, alterations and corrections; injury done by a cut; open wound; festering wound. **~ ঘায়ে নুনের ছিটা** hurting a person's feelings who is already in pain of some injury; adding insult to injury. **কাপড় ~** *vi* **1** cut out cloth according to definite measurements for making garments, etc. **2** be eaten up by moths. **~ কাপড়** *n* piece goods. **আঁচড় ~** *vi, vt* **1** to scrape with the finger nails; make a scratch. **2** to make an impression on sb's mind: এতে তার মনে আঁচড় কাটলো না, this didn't make a mark/have any effect on his mind. **কথা ~** *vi* refute an argument, opinion, etc (prove it to be wrong or mistaken). **কথা ~কাটি** *n* argument and counter argument; altercation. **~কাটি মারামারি** *n* a violent affray; a tumultuous brawl or bloodshed. **কান~** *n, adj* one who has suffered disgrace or indignity/has been humiliated. **খাল ~** dig/excavate a canal; (fig) do sth that places the enemy at an advantage. **খাল কেটে কুমির আনা** bring on a calamity by one's own imprudence. **গলা ~** *vi* to charge exorbitant price for a commodity: গলা~ দাম. **গাঁট ~** *vi* to pick a pocket. **গাঁট-~** *n* a pick-pocket. **ঘোড়ার ঘাস ~** (fig)**1** be engaged in sth that is not worth-doing or paying. **2** while away one's time. **ঘোর ~** (inertia, illusion, etc) be disillusioned. **তার ঘুমের ঘোর তখনো কাটেনি** his drowsiness was not yet over. **চিমটি ~** *vt* to pinch. **চেক ~** *vi* write out or draw a cheque. **ছড়া ~** *vi* to cap verses. **ছানা ~** *vi* to turn (milk) into posset. **জাবর ~** (of animals) chew the cud. (fig) **1** repeat sth again and again like chewing the cud. **2** reflect/ponder over sth of the past. **জিভ ~** press the tip of the tongue between the teeth. **টেরি ~** parting the hair. **ঠোঁট ~** *adj* (fig) saying freely what one thinks; outspoken. **ডানা ~ পরী** (sarcas) as pretty as a fairy the only difference being the absence of wings. **তাল ~** (music) to make a slip in measure; fail to maintain musical time or measure: হঠাৎ ~ কেটে গেল, There was a sudden breach of measure. দাগ ~=আঁচড় ~ (2). **নাক কান ~ যাওয়া** be extremely humiliated. **ফাঁড়া ~** be out of the woods; get out of danger. **বুক-~** *adj* (of a garment) open at the front; open-breast: বুক-~ জামা. **মাথা-~** *adj* without a top; topless. **মাথা ~ যাওয়া** be extremely ashamed of. **মেঘ ~1** *vi* (of coads) be dispersed. **2** (of doubts) be dispelled. **সময় ~** (of time pass on: আমার সময় কাটে না, time hangs heavy on my hands. **সাঁতার ~***vi* swim. **সিঁথি ~** *vi* part one's hair. **সিঁধ ~** *vi* break into a house to commit burglary; burgle. **সুতা-~***vi* twist (wool , cotton, silk, etc) into threads; spin. **হাতা-~** *adj* (of shirts, etc) having sleeves upto the elbow or having no sleeves. **কাটানো** *vt* **1** cause sth to be cut/ dug/ chopped. **2** pass or spend: সময় ~. **3** get over; overcome: ফাঁড়া/ বিপদ ~..

কাটারি *n* tool for chopping wood, meat, etc; a chopper; a billhook.

কাটিম=কাঠিম

কাটুর কুটুর *int* denoting the sound of cutting or scratching with the teeth as by mice.

কাট্য *adj* what may be refuted or disproved; refutable (opp অকাট্য).

কাঠ *n* the substance of the trunk and branches of a tree; timber; wood. ❑*adj* **1** dry like wood: গলা শুকিয়ে ~. **2** motionless like a log of wood: ভয়ে ~ হওয়া. **3** lean and thin; reduced to a skeleton; bony: শরীর শুকিয়ে ~. **~কয়লা** *n* coal made by charring wood; charcoal. **~কুড়ানি** *n fem* woman who lives by collecting and selling twigs; pauper. **~খড়** *n* **1** materials for making fire; wood and hay; fuel. **2** (fig) preparations necessary for doing sth. **~খড় পোড়ানো** *vi* undergo various troubles and expenses to achieve an end: অনেক ~খড় পুড়িয়ে তবে লাইসেন্সটি পেয়েছি, secured the license for a great amount of trouble and expenses. **~খোলা** *n* frying pan used without sand or oil. **~গড়া** *n* enclosure in a law court in which an accused/ a witness stands while facing trial /giving evidence; a witness-box. **~গোলা** *n* yard where logs of wood, planks, boards, etc are stored; lumber yard; lumber-mill. **~ঠোকরা** *n* a variety of bird that clings to the bark of trees and pecks it to find insects; woodpecker. **~পিঁপড়া** *n* black long ant; wood-ant. **~ফাটা রোদ** *n* scorching rays of the sun. **~বিড়ালি** *n* small cat-like tree-climbing animal with bushy tail and grey fur; the squirrel. **~মল্লিকা** *n* a variety of sweet scented jasmine flower; wild jasmine.

কাঠা[১] *n* **1** measure of land (720 sq feet): পাঁচ ~ জমি. **2** a receptacle for measuring grains, etc.

কাঠা[২], কাঠুয়া *n* animal with a soft body protected by a shell; tortoise; the sea-tortoise; the turtle.

কাঠামো, কাঠাম *n* **1** that part of a structure that gives shape and support; a frame-work: ঘরের ~. **2** a fabric on which sth is based: ইউরোপীয় দর্শন মুসলিম দর্শনের ~র উপর প্রতিষ্ঠিত.

কাঠি *n* a small chip of wood, bamboo or metal (eg a match stick or tooth pick). **চাবি~** *n* an essential part of anything; sth which controls other things; a key. **জীয়ন~** *n* magic wand of the folk tale having the power to revive a dead person.

কাঠিন্য *n* **1** the quality of being hard, solid or inflexible. **2** hard-heartedness; severity; cruelty.

কাঠিম *n* a small cylinder or reel on which thread, wire, etc is wound; a bobbin; a spool.

কাঠুয়া=কাঠা[২]

কাঠুরে (colloq) *n* man who cuts down trees; a wood-cutter by profession.

কাড়ন *n* act of snatching away/ seizing by force; loot; plunder.

কাড়া[১] *vt* **1** snatch away; seize by force; grab; usurp: সিংহাসন ~, usurp a throne. **2** rouse feelings of interest in a person; win one's heart; attract; charm: মন ~. **কাড়াকাড়ি** *n* act of scrambling; very eager contest for sth. **কাড়াকাড়ি করা** *vi, vt* struggle to get as much or as many as possible of sth from competitors; scramble for sth.

কাড়া[২] *n* hollow cylindrical instrument of music beaten with sticks; a drum (used as a correlative of নাকাড়া which is smaller than কাড়া): ~ নাকাড়া.

কাণ্ড *n* **1** the main body or trunk of a tree. **2** (bot) part of a plant, eg cane, sugarcane, bamboo, etc between two nodes (joints). **3** an affair causing surprise: একি ~! how strange! **4** a part or chapter of a book; a division of an epic poem; a canto: সপ্ত ~ রামায়ণ. **~ কারখানা** *n pl* **1** events or affairs. **2** anybody's peculiar way of doing things: দেখো তার ~ কারখানা, just see how he acts. **~জ** *adj* shot from the trunk or stem. ❑*n* an offshoot from the trunk of a tree/ stem of a plant. **~জ্ঞান** *n* qualities that enable a person to choose the right course of things; practical common sense. **কাণ্ডা~ বোধ** *n* sense of right and wrong / propriety and impropriety. **~জ্ঞানহীন** *adj* devoid of/ lacking common sense.

কাণ্ডার *n* the helm or the steering mechanism of a boat or ship.

কাণ্ডারি, কাণ্ডারী *n* the man at the helm; the steersman; the helmsman; (fig) one at the helm of affairs; a leader. **বিপদের ~** *n* one's guide or resort in peril. ভবের ~ *n* pilot in the voyage of life.

কাত, কাৎ *n* slanting position: ~ হয়ে শোয়া, lie on one's side; গাছটি ~ হয়ে দাঁড়িয়ে আছে, stands in a slanting position. ~ ফেরা *vi* turn on one's other side. ~ করা *vt* cause to come into a sloping position; tilt; incline: খুঁটিটি ~ করো না, don't slant/ incline/ tilt the pole. ❑*adj* 1 frightened (of); afraid: এক ধমকে ~. 2 laid with: জ্বরে ~, defeated; knocked down: কুপোকাত.

কাতর *adj* 1 stricken with grief or sorrows; distressed: ~ প্রাণে ডাকা, call in a piteous voice. 2 struck / overwhelmed with: ভয়ে ~. 3 extremely solicitous; eager; intent: ঘরে ফেরার জন্য ~, homesick. 4 unwilling; disinclined; reluctant: অর্থব্যয়ে ~. কাতরোক্তি (~+উক্তি) *n* piteous / plaintive cry. ~তা *n*.

কাতরা, কাৎরা [A] *n* very small quantity of liquid; a drop: এক ~ পানি.

কাতরানো *vi* utter a low rumbling sound through pain; moan; groan: জ্বরে ~. কাতরানি *n* cry of anguish; moaning; groaning.

কাতল *n* 1 large variety of fresh water fish. 2 a wooden body sloping to a thin edge at one end used by sawyers; a wedge.

কাতলা *n*=কাতল (1). রুই-~ *n pl* (fig) 1 men of status and influence; rich people. 2 big chances: সে রুই-~ মারে, চুনোপুঁটি ছোঁয় না.

কাতা *n* rope or thick cord made of coir.

কাতান *n* long handled tool with a curved blade used for cutting branches of trees; a bill-hook.

কাতার [A] *n* number of persons or things in a line; a row: ~ করে দাঁড়াও. ~বন্দি [A+P] *adj* arrayed in lines/ rows. কাতারে কাতারে *adv* in rows/ lines/ files.

কাতারি *n* pair of scissors (or shears) for cutting gold and silver sheets / foils; jeweller's cutting tool.

কাতি *n* shell-cutter's saw with serrated edges on both sides.

কাতুকুতু *n* the act or the sensation of tickling; titillation. ~ দেওয়া *vi* excite the nerves at a sensitive part of the body (esp the armpit) to cause spasms or laughter; tickle; titillate. ~ দিয়ে হাসানো (fig) (satirical) try to please the readers' sense of humour without having the necessary intrinsic value.

কাত্যায়নী *n* an appellation of Hindu goddess Durga.

কাদম্বরী *n* famous work of Sanskrit literature by Banabhatta.

কাদম্বিনী *n* a collection of clouds.

কাদা *n* soft wet earth; mud; clay. ❑*adj* covered with mud; muddy. ~খোঁচা *n* bird with a long bill, which frequents marshes; the snipe.

কান *n* 1 organ of hearing; the ear. 2 the ear-like keys for tightening the strings of violin, etc. 3 sort of jewel for the ear; earrings. ~কথা *n* secret talk; malicious talk; back-biting. ~ কাটা যাওয়া *vi* suffer humiliation. ~ খাড়া করা *vi* prick up ones ears; pay sharp attention to sth being said. ~ ঝালাপালা করা *vi* 1 disturb one by making harsh noise; grate on one's ears. 2 (fig) have an irritating effect on a person, his nerves. ~ দেওয়া *vt* pay attention / heed to; listen to what one says. ~ না দেওয়া *vt* turn a deaf ear to; pay no heed to. ~ ধরা *vi* pull one by the ear; insult a person. ~ পাকা *vi* have infection in the ear. ~ পাতা *vi* listen secretly to private conversation; eavesdrop. ~ ভাঙানো, ~ ভাঙানি দেওয়া attempt to bias one's mind; poison one's ears against another. ~মলা দেওয়া/ মোচড়ানো twist one's ears. কানে আঙুল দেওয়া refuse to hear. কানে আসা/ওঠা (শ্রুত হওয়া) reach the ear (of); be heard. কানে কম শোনা be hard of hearing. কানে কানে *adv* in whispers. কানে খাটো hard of hearing. কানে তালা লাগা have a deafening effect on the ears. কানে লাগা be sweet to the hearing. কানের খইল *n* waxy substance secreted in the ear; ear-wax.

কানন *n* 1 an area of grassland with flower or fruit trees around a house; public recreation ground with plants and trees; a garden; a park. 2 an extensive and uncultivated tract of wood; a forest. ~-কুসুম *n* flowers of a garden or forest. ~বাসী *adj* dwelling in a forest. ❑*n* a forest dweller.

কানা *adj* 1 blind of one-eye; one eyed. 2 destitute of sight; blind. 3 having a hole or hollow place and so useless: ~ হাড়ি. কানি *fem.* ~কড়ি *n* a paisa (coin of the smallest denomination) having a hole at the centre (as prevalent in former times) or anything worth no more than it: ~কড়ির দাম নেই. ~ করে দেওয়া *vt* foil/ baffle/ spoil (sth). ~ কলসির জল (fig) anything not likely to be durable. ~ খোঁড়ার একগুণ বাড়া (fig) when one organ is defective, the others become more active; a worthless person is often full of vanity; (prov) empty vessel sounds much. ~ গরুর ভিন্ন পথ (fig) a fool or an ignorant person often strays away from the safe path as a blind cow does. ~গলি *n* an alley with an opening at one end only; a blind alley; (fig) a place or position from which there is no way out; an impasse; a dead lock. ~ ছেলের নাম পদ্মলোচন giving the name 'lotus-eyed' to a blind boy, which is as ridiculous as awarding honours on a worthless person. ~মাছি *n* a game in which one player, who is blindfolded, tries to catch and identify one of the others who push him about; blindman's buff. ~মাছি খেলা *vi* play the blindman's buff.

কানা[2] *n* 1 the rim of a thing (eg a pitcher, a pot, etc.) 2 the bank or brim of a river. ~য় ~য় *adv* upto the brim. ~য় ~য় ভরা *adj* full to the brim; quite full.

কানাই=কৃষ্ণ

কানাকানি *n* talking sth about another person that he wishes to be kept secret; communication of sth in whisper. ~ করা *vi* talk sth not based on definite facts; spread rumour/ scandal.

কানাঘুষা *n* hearsay; gossip; common talk; what one has heard others say. ~ করা *vi* spread spiteful rumours about the private concerns of others.

কানাচ *n* the backside of a house compound. ঘরের কানাচে *adv* just behind the house.

কানুন [A] *n* body of rules prescribed by authority for the proper regulation of a society or for correct conduct in life; legal rules; law. আইন ~ *n pl* laws and customs relating to social behaviour: দেশে আইন ~ আছে.

কানুনগো [A+P] *n* **1** officer in charge of land survey and settlement. **2** audit officer in the department of land revenue.

কানেস্তারা [E] *n* small box with a lid used for holding tea, coffee, etc; a canister.

কান্তা *n fem* the consort of a man; a wife; a beloved; a beauty.

কান্তার *n* very dense and inaccessible forest; an impenetrable wilderness: দুর্গম গিরি ~ মরু.

কান্তি *n* **1** the quality of being pleasing; grace; charm; beauty. **2** brightness; radiance; splendour. ~মান *adj* graceful; charming. ~মতী *fem*. ~বিদ্যা *n* the branch of philosophy concerned with qualities which connote beauty; the philosophy of taste; aesthetics.

কান্দা=কাঁদা

কান্না *n* act of weeping/crying (as by children). ~কাটি *n* **1** effusive or continuous weeping; lamentation; wailing. **2** earnest request; supplication; entreaty: অনেক ~কাটি করেও কোনো ফল হলো না. ~কাটি করা *vi* **1** weep effusively or in a noisy manner. **2** beg earnestly; beseech; entreat. ~ আসা/পাওয়া feel like weeping.

কাপ [E] small porcelain vessel with a handle for drinking tea, coffee, etc; a cup.

কাপড় *n* **1** material woven from cotton , wool, silk , etc; a piece of cloth or fabric used for garment: ৩ গজ ~. **2** coverings for a person's body; dress; garment; clothes; clothing. **3** a sari or length of cloth worn round the body by women in the Indian subcontinent. ~ ছাড়া *vi* put off one's clothes; change dress. ~ পরা *vi* put on one's clothes; dress oneself. ~ পাট করা *vi* fold up a dress/garment. আটপৌরে ~ *n* dress/ clothes/ sari for indoor use. তোলা ~ *n* quality clothes used occasionally when necessary. থান ~ *n* an entire length or sheet of a woven fabric; a length of cloth without borders worn by Hindu widows. ~-চোপড় *n pl* clothes; apparel; garments.

কাপালিক *n* a class of ascetics worshipping goddess Kali in an awful manner.

কাপাস=কার্পাস

কাপুড়ে *n* dealer in cloth; cloth merchant.

কাপুরুষ *n* a person who wants courage to meet danger or hardship; a coward. ❑*adj* destitute of courage; faint-hearted; weak-spirited; dastardly. ~তা, ~ত্ব *n* want of courage; cowardliness; cowardice. কাপুরুষোচিত *adj* like a coward; cowardly; mean; base. কাপুরুষোচিতভাবে *adv* in the manner of a coward.

কাপ্তান, কাপ্তেন [E] *n* **1** a naval officer immediately below a rear-admiral in rank. **2** an army officer immediately below a major. **3** commanding officer of a merchant ship. **4** the leader of a sports team or any such group of people. কাপ্তেনি করা *vt* act as a captain of (a football team, etc).

কাফন [A] *n* pieces of new cloth in which the dead body of a Muslim is wrapped up for burial; burial cloth; a shroud.

কাফফারা [A] *n* an expiatory measure to absolve one of a sin according to the Islamic Shariah: a money penalty paid as a means of absolution from a sin. ~ দেওয়া *vi* pay a penalty for committing a sin.

কাফে [F] *n* a coffee house; a restaurant; a cafe.

কাফের, কাফির [A] *n* **1** one who denies the truth or rejects Islam. **2** one who is a worshipper of idols; an idolater; an infidel.

কাফেলা [A] *n* **1** a company of travellers associated together for safety; a caravan. **2** a company of pilgrims. ~ সালার [A+P] the leader of a caravan.

কাফ্রি, কাফরি [Pg] *n* a member of one of the black-skinned African tribes living to south of the Sahara or a descendant of any of the tribes living elsewhere; a Negro.

কাবলি=কাবুলি

কাবা [A] *n* the Holy Kaaba, the centre of Muslim pilgrimage in Mecca, containing the sacred Black Stone, and in which direction Muslims all over the world offer their prayers. Also known as Baitullah, the House of Allah.

কাবাডি *n* country game of Bangladesh (also called *hadudu*).

কাবাব [A] *n* a dish of small pieces of meat seasoned and roasted. ~চিনি [A+P] *n* kind of spice akin to black pepper.

কাবার [Pg] *n* **1** the state of being exhausted; end; termination: গল্পে গল্পে রাত ~ হলো. **2** the final state; the last day: মাস কাবারে এসো. ~ করা *vt* spend; finish; exhaust. ~ হওয়া *vi* be finished/ exhausted / terminated.

কাবিন, কাবীন [A] *n* the dowry payable to a bride at a Muslim marriage. **~নামা** [A+P] *n* the deed of marriage contract under Muslim law.

কাবিল [A] *adj* possessing worth; deserving; suitable; fitting: এতেবারের ~, worthy of trust. ~তি *n* worthiness; fitness; suitability.

কাবু [T] *adj* **1** lacking in strength; weak; feeble. **2** conquered; subdued; prostrate; under one's control. **~ করা** *vt* defeat or overpower; bring under control. **~ হওয়া** *vi* go down; be defeated/ cornered / overpowered.

কাবুলি [P] *adj* of or relating to Kabul; born in Kabul or Afghanistan. ❑*n* a national of Afghanistan; man from Kabul (also ~ওয়ালা).

কাবেজ [A] *adj* **1** caught in the palm of one's hand; got into one's clutches; acquired; in one's possession: জান ~ করা.

কাব্য *n* **1** creative writing in verse form expressing an imaginative or deeply felt experience in a heightened style. **2** creative literature in the elevated style of prose expressing deep feeling or noble thought; polite literature. **3** a book of verse. **~কলা** *n* the art of poetry; the poetical art; poetics. **~কার** *n* a writer of verses; a poet. **~গ্রন্থ** *n* a book of verse. **~চর্চা** *n* cultivation or study of poetry. **~জগৎ** *n* the realm of poetry; the society of poets. **~বিশারদ** *adj* skilled in poetry. ❑*n* one versed in poetic literature. **~রস** *n* the beauty of poetry; the aesthetic value of poetry. **~রসিক** *n* one who appreciates poetry; a connoisseur of poetical art. **গদ্য ~** *n* composition in prose containing literary beauty. **গীতি~** *n* poetry based on deep personal feeling and intended to be sung; lyrical poetry. **খণ্ড~** *n* neither an epic, nor a short poem. **মহা~** *n* poetic account in an elevated style describing the adventures and achievements of one or more great heroes, or a nation's past history; an epic.

কাম[1] (colloq)=কাজ. **~চোর** *n* one who evades responsibility; a shirker.

কাম[2] *n* the Hindu god of love and lust called variously as Ananga, Kandarpa, Madana or Kama.

কাম[3] *n* **1** desire to have sex with sb: কামাতুর, stricken with the desire for sexual intercourse/ love-making; love-sick. **2** eagerness to obtain or enjoy; strong longing; aspiration: সিদ্ধ~, one who has attained his goal. **3** love; devotion; attachment. **~কলা** *n* the art of love-making. **~কেলি** *n* amorous sport; sexual intercourse; copulation. **~গন্ধ** *n* taint of lust/ sex. **~চর** *adj* one who can travel wherever he wills; moving at will: ~চর নারদ. **কামাচার** *n* act of doing as one wishes; wilfulness; wantonness; sensuality. **কামাচারী** *adj* lacking moral discipline; licentious; profligate. ❑*n* a dissipated and depraved person. **কামাচারিণী** *fem.* **~জ** *adj* **1** born of the unlawful union of one's father and mother. **~জ্বর** *n* inordinate desire for sexual union. **~দ** *adj* granting/ having the power of granting whatever one desires. **~দা** *fem.* **~ধেনু** *n* (myth) cow that grants any desire; wishing-cow. **~পীড়িত** *adj* love-sick; **~পীড়িতা** *fem.* **~প্রবৃত্তি** *n* sex urge; sexual appetite. **~মোহিত** *adj* overwhelmed with sexual desire. **~মোহিতা** *fem.* **~শাস্ত্র** *n* science relating to sexual passion; the art of lovemaking.

কামঠ *n* the meat of tortoise. ❑*adj* of or relating to the tortoise.

কামড় *n* gripping with the teeth; act of biting: সাপের ~, snake bite. **2** a wound made by a sting: মশার ~, mosquito bite. **3** a sharp or shooting pain: মাথার ~, পেটের ~. **4** (fig) an exorbitant or merciless demand: বরের বাপের ~. **~ দেওয়া** *vt, vi* pierce or wound with the teeth or sting; bite. **~ ধরা** *vi* have a sharp or shooting pain like that of biting. **কামড়ে ধরা** *vt* grip with the teeth. **মরণ ~** *n* the last bid of the vanquished.

কামড়ানো *vi, vt* **1** pierce or grip with the teeth. **2** wound with the sting (as by a mosquito). **3** have a biting sensation: পেট ~, stomach-ache; হাত-পা ~. **কামড়ানি** *n* act of biting; biting.

কামনা *n* **1** =কাম[3] (2). **2** the object of desire. **~ করা** *vt* wish for the possession or enjoyment of. **~ নাশ** *n* annihilation of desire. **~ সিদ্ধি** *n* fulfilment of a desire.

কামরা [Pg] *n* apartment in a house; a room.

কামরাঙা, কামরাঙ্গা *n* kind of sour fruit; *Averrhoa carambola.*

কামলা[1] *n* a disease characterized by yellowness of the eyes and skin, loss of appetite and general lassitude; jaundice.

কামলা[2] *n* one who earns his bread by labouring on daily basis; a day labourer.

কামাই[1] *n* that which is earned by labour; emolument which one receives for employment; earning. **~ করা** *vi* acquire by work; earn.

কামাই[2] *n* **1** absence from work/duty: অফিস ~ করে খেলা দেখেছি. **~ করা** *vi vt* absent oneself from duty. **2** cessation; termination; respite: বকবকানির ~ নেই. **কাজও নেই কামাইও নেই** no work, no leisure; one who is without a job/ unemployed.

কামাক্ষী *n fem* appellation of Hindu goddess Kamakhya so called because of her beautiful eyes (কাম beautiful+অক্ষি eyes).

কামান [E] *n* the well-known heavy fire-arm; cannon: ~ বন্দুক. **~ দাগা** *vi* fire a cannon; bombard with a cannon. **~ দেগে চূর্ণবিচূর্ণ করা** *vt* batter with cannon shots; cannonade. ~-গোলা *n* a cannon-ball.

কামানো *vt* **1** gain (money) by labour; earn: পয়সা ~. **2** cut off hair from the skin; shave: দাঁড়ি ~. **3** (sl) abusive word used to express anger or temper: এতক্ষণ কামাচ্ছিলে নাকি? what hell have you been doing so long?

কামার=কর্মকার

কামাল [A] *n* uncommon success; extraordinary achievements. ~ **করা** *vi* achieve wonderful success/ rare distinction: কামাল তুনে ~ কিয়া ভাই.

কামিজ [A] *n* garment for the upper part of the body; a shirt.

কামিনী *n* **1** an adult female; a woman. **2** the consort of a man; a wife. **3** a lustful woman. **4** a variety of sweet-scented flower. ~**সুলভ** *adj* befitting a woman; womanly: ~সুলভ কোমলতা.

কামিয়াব [P] *adj* attaining the desired success; successful: তুমি ~ হবে. **কামিয়াবি** *n* the achievement of a desired aim; success.

কামিল=কামেল

কামী *adj* **1** inspired by lust or the sexual appetite; lewd; lustful. **2** (chiefly used as a *suff*) desirous of: eager to have: শান্তি~. **কামিনী** *fem.*

কামুক *adj* one who is slyly and powerfully sexual; lascivious; wanton. **কামুকা, কামুকী** *fem.*

কামেল [A] *adj* one who has attained his end. ❑*n* person who has attained divine grace through austere religious practices; a saint; a sage: ~ ফকির.

কামোদ *n* a musical mode.

কাম্য *adj* **1** worthy of desire; desirable. **2** worth having; enjoyable. **3** what is to be performed for the realization of one's end: ~ কর্ম. ~ **ফল** *n* the result or outcome of one's desire.

কায় *n* **1** the human body. ~**কল্প** *n* an Ayurvedic system of therapy for rejuvenation of youth or prolongation of life. ~**ক্লেশ** *n* physical labour. ~**ক্লেশে** *adv* with toils and tribulations; with great difficulty: ~ক্লেশে জীবন ধারণ. ~**ক্লেশে দিন কাটানো** manage to live with great difficulty; live from hand to mouth. ~**মনোবাক্যে** *adv* (lit) with the body, mind and words; heart and soul; wholeheartedly.

কায়কারবার [P] *n* everyday duties; duties that are performed regularly.

কায়দা [A] *n***1** the knack or cleverness enabling one to do sth skilfully: দায়ে পড়লে ~ বেরোয়. **2** the means or mode of doing sth: রাতে আর ওপারে যাবার ~ নেই. **3** the first primer of Arabic alphabet and spelling. **আদব** ~*n* good manners; etiquette. ~ **করা** *vi* get one into the grips; be in an advantagious position: ~ করে আদায় করা. ~-**কানুন** forms and convention; formalities. ~**মাফিক** as per rules; according to formalities. ~**য় পাওয়া** get one at a disadvantage; catch one on the hip.

কায়স্থ *n* a caste among the Hindus.

কায়া *n* physical structure; the body.

কায়িক *adj* physical; bodily: ~ পরিশ্রম.

কায়েত (colloq)=কায়স্থ

কায়েম [A] *adj* firmly established; durable; permanent. ~ **করা** *vt* establish/ put on a firm footing; give a permanent basis. ~ **হওয়া** be in force; be firmly established.

কায়েমি *adj* permanent; lasting; abiding: ~ **স্বত্ব.** ~ **স্বার্থ** *n* vested interests; rights which, under the law, are securely in the possession of a person or group of persons.

কার[1] (colloq) =কাহার

কার[2] [P] *n* trouble; difficulty; scrape: কারে পড়া, get into trouble/ a scrape. **কারে পড়ে সাধুতা দেখানো** make a virtue of necessity.

-**কার** *suff* used in compounds: স্বর্ণ~, গ্রন্থ~, রূপ~. **2** indicating relation with sth: আগে~, of old; এদিক~, of this side; ভিতর~, of the inside.

কারক *n* (gram) the relation of a noun or pronoun to another word in a sentence; the case. ❑*adj* (used as *suff*) one who or that which performs or brings about sth: হিত~, অনিষ্ট~. **কারিকা** *fem.*

কারকুন [P] *n* **1**(lit) one who does (a duty). **2** a steward or caretaker of a landed estate. **3** an officer of the revenue department under Muslim rule in India.

কারখানা [P] *n* building(s) where commercial goods are manufactured; a workshop; a factory.

কারগো [E] *n* goods carried in a ship, aircraft or other vehicle; cargo.

কারচুপি, কারচুবি [P] *n* **1**a tricky device; an artifice; a fraud: ওজনে ~. **2** artistic work; handiwork. **কারচোব** *n* needle-work on cloth.

কারণ *n* **1** that which produces an effect; a person, a thing or an event that makes sth happen; a cause: শোকের ~, নালিশের ~. **2** source; root; origin: সৃষ্টির ~. ❑*conj* for the reason that; because; since; for; as: সে ভাত খায়নি, ~ সে অসুস্থ, he hasn't had his meal, because he is ill.

কারদানি=কেরদানি

কারফিউ [E] *n* a fixed time (under martial law) by or during which all persons must remain indoors; curfew.

কারবাইড [E] compound of carbon; carbide.

কারবার [P] *n* **1** buying and selling; trade; commerce; business: পাটের ~. **2** a business firm; a mercantile concern. **3** an occurrence; an affair: একি ~. **কারবারি** [P] *n* a trader.

কারবালা *n* **1** the wilderness near the Euphrates in Iraq and scene of the historic martyrdom of

Imam Hussain in his fight against the caliph of Damascus. **2** (fig) a place where water is not to be had.

কারসাজি [P] *n* fraud; cheating; artifice: প্রকাশকের ~তে একই বই বিভিন্ন নামে প্রকাশিত.

কারা[1] (colloq)=কাহারা

কারা[2] *n* confinement in prison. **~গার, ~গৃহ** *n* place of confinement; a prison; a jail; a gaol (GB). **~কক্ষ** *n* a prison-cell; a prisoner's cell. **~দণ্ড** *n* a sentence to imprisonment; incarceration. **~দণ্ড দেওয়া** *vt* sentence to imprisonment; imprison. **সশ্রম ~দণ্ড** rigorous imprisonment. **বিনাশ্রম ~দণ্ড** simple imprisonment. **~পাল** *n* superintendent in charge of a jail or the prisoners in it; jailer; gaoler (GB).

কারাভান [E]=কাফেলা

কারি [E] *n* flavoured fluid preparation of meat or fish with or without vegetables seasoned with spices; curry (cf তরকারি).

কারিকর=কারিগর

কারিকা *n* **1** a treatise containing couplets with various meanings. **2** a work of art. ❑*adj fem* of কারক.

কারিগর [P] *n* skilled workman in industry or trade; an artisan; a mechanic; a handicraftsman; an artist. **কারিগরি** *n* workmanship; artistic skill; artistry. ❑*adj* pertaining to workmanship/ handicrafts: কারিগরি শিক্ষা.

কারী, ক্বারী [A] *n* one whose recital of the Holy Qoran is perfectly faultless and accurate.

-কারী *suff* denoting a doer or performer of sth: হিত~, আড্ডা~.

কারু one skilled in a trade or mechanical art; an artisan; an artist; a craftsman. **~কলা, ~শিল্প, ~কার্য** *nn* artistic work in wood, metal, etc; art or craft needing skill with the hands. **~শিল্পী**= কারু. **~-সমবায়** *n* society of artisans for helping one another or for promoting their trade; guild organization.

কারুণিক *adj* ready to pity; sympathizing; compassionate.

কারুণ্য *n* kindness; compassion; mercy.

কারেন্সি নোট [E] *n* piece of paper money issued by authority of government; currency note.

কারোয়া [P] *n* aromatic plant whose seeds are used to flavour bread, cake, etc. car(r)away.

কার্টিজ=কার্তুজ

কার্ড [E] *n* **1** a piece of pasteboard printed or unprinted: ইনভাইটেশন~. **2** a post-card.

কার্তিক *n* **1** the seventh month of the Bengali calendar. **2** (Hindu myth) son of Mahadeva and Parvati. ❑*adj* (of men) good-looking; having virile beauty; handsome: দেখতে একেবারে ~. **নব~** (sarcas) extremely handsome. **লোহার ~** (sarcas & fig) of fine appearance but no worth; worthless person. **কার্তিকে** *adj* growing or happening in Kartik: কার্তিকে ফসল, কার্তিকে ঝড়.

কার্তুজ [Pg] *n* case (of metal, cardboard, etc) containing the charge of a gun or any firearm; cartridge.

কার্নিভ্যাল [E] *n* public merrymaking connected with a festival; a revel; carnival.

কার্নিস [E]*n* (archit) projecting part above the frieze, above a column; a cornice: দালানের ~

কার্পণ্য ⇒ কৃপণ

কার্পাস *n* the cotton plant; cotton. ❑*adj* made of cotton: ~ বস্ত্র.

কার্পেট [E] *n* thick woven fabric for covering floors; carpet.

কার্বন [E] *n* **1** non-metallic substance existing, other than in compounds, as charcoal, graphite and diamond; chemical element denoted by C. **2** a charcoal pencil used in electric arc-lamp. **3** a copy reproduced by carbon paper. **4** (also ~ পেপার) sheet of thin paper coated with coloured matter, used between sheets of writing paper for making copies.

কার্বলিক [E] *n* antiseptic and disinfecting acid obtained from coal-tar; carbolic acid. **~ সোপ** *n* a soap containing carbolic acid.

কার্য *n* **1** labour of mind or body; work; action; activity. **2** a purpose; a motive; an object: কোন কার্যে আগমন? **3** result; effect; benefit: ঔষধে কোনো ~ হয় নাই. **4** a rite or ceremony on an occasion: বিবাহ~. **5** that which a person is bound to perform; a duty: অবশ্য~. **~কর** *adj* capable of producing the desired result; effective; effectual; useful. **~করতা, ~কারিতা** *n* the condition of being effective; effectiveness; effectualness. **~করী** *adj* **1** what has taken effect. **2** that which manages the affairs (of some institution/ organization: ~করী সংসদ. **~কলাপ** *n pl* doings; functions; activities. **~কারণ সম্বন্ধ** *n* the relation of cause and effect; the principle that nothing can happen without a cause; causality. **~কাল** *n* **1** tenure of office; the period of one's professional career. **2** working hours in an office or factory. **~ক্রম** *n* a list containing the order of events of a cultural function or any such gathering; a programme. **~ক্ষম** *adj* fit for work; capable; competent. **~গতিকে** *adv* in course of business. **~ত** *adv* in effect; as a matter of fact; actually. **~নির্বাহ** *n* execution of a work/ order. **~ নির্বাহ করা** *vi* carry out/ execute/perform a work. **~নির্বাহক** *adj* executive. **~পরম্পরা** *n* sequence of events. **~প্রণালী** *n* the procedure of work. **~বশত** *adv* on business; on account of business. ~বিবরণী *n* proceedings (of a meeting, etc). ~সিদ্ধি *n* accomplishment of a work/ task. **কার্যারম্ভ** [কার্য+আরম্ভ] *n* commencement of a work. **কার্যোদ্ধার** [কার্য+উদ্ধার]=কার্যসিদ্ধি.

কাল[1] *n* **1** period of time; season: প্রাতঃ~, বর্ষা~. **2** a brief space of time; a moment: ক্ষণ~. **3** great or long period of time with special characteristics or events: প্রাচীন ~, আধুনিক ~. **4** any of the stages of human life: শৈশব ~, যৌবন ~. **5** the cause of one's misfortune or ruination: সেই বন্ধুত্বই অবশেষে তার ~ হলো. **6** (gram) the time of the action indicated by a verb; the tense: অতীত ~, বর্তমান ~. **7** time without end; eternity: মহা~. **কালের কবলে পতিত হওয়া** sink into the abyss of eternity. **~ কাটানো** *vi* pass or spend time. **~ হওয়া** *vi* be the cause of one's ruination. **~ক্রমে** *adv* **1** in course of time. **2** in later times. **~ক্ষেপ, ~ক্ষেপণ** *n* act of spending/ misusing time. **~ক্ষেপ করা** *vi* kill or misuse time. **~গ্রাস** *n* jaws of death. **~গ্রাসে পতিত হওয়া** *vi* fall into the jaws of death; be dead; die. **~ঘাম** *n* **1** excessive perspiration (due to overwork); profuse sweating. **2** sweating at the time of death. **~চক্র** *n* cycle of time. **~চিহ্ন** *n* sign of death. **~ধর্ম** *n* the spirit or trend of an age. **~প্রবাহ** *n* the unceasing flow of time; the passage or efflux of time. **~প্রভাব** *n* influence of the times. **~বিলম্ব** wasting of time. **~বিলম্ব না করে** not to waste time; without wasting any time. **~বৈশাখী** *n* strong gale that blows accompanied by thundershower in the afternoon of Baishakh (April-May); nor'-wester. **~রাত্রি** *n* inauspicious night; night of destruction. **~স্রোত** *n* the flow or passage of time. **অন্তিম ~** *n* the time of death. **দিন~** *n* the prevailing socio-political condition. **তিন ~ গিয়ে এক কালে ঠেকা** be old after having passed three stages of life—childhood, youth and manhood. **কালেভদ্রে** *adv* rarely; seldom: তিনি এখানে কালেভদ্রে আসেন, his visit here is few and far between.

কাল[2] *adv* **1** on the day after the present; tomorrow. **2** on the day before the present: yesterday. **~কার, ~কের** *adj* of tomorrow; of yesterday. **~কের ছেলে** (contempt) an inexperienced person; a mere child.

কাল[3], **কালো** *n* the black colour. □*adj* black. **~কিষ্টি** *adj* pitch-dark; jet-black; extremely soiled and dirty. **~চিটা, কালচিটে** *n* black stain. **~ বাজার** *n* illegal buying and selling of government controlled commodities; place where such trading is carried on; black market. **~ মুখ** *n* the face of one who has earned a disrepute; a face sullied with a scandal: এ ~ মুখ আর তাকে দেখাবো না. **~মেঘ** *n* medicinal plant used in the preparation of liver tonic. **কালশিরা, কালসিটা** *n* black stain or bruise on the skin caused by a blow or knock. **মেরে কালশিরা/কালসিটা পড়ানো** beat black and blue.

কালনাগ *n* species of venomous snake; black cobra. **কালনাগিনী** *n fem* female of black cobra; (fig) a treacherous woman.

কালনেমি *n* (myth) maternal uncle of Ravana, the king of Lanka. **~র লঙ্কাভাগ** (prov) try to enjoy a thing before acquiring it, just as Kalanemi was thinking which half of the kingdom of Lanka he would have if he could fulfil the stated condition of killing the Hanuman (character of the Ramayana).

কালপেঁচা *n* **1** kind of owl that screeches instead of hooting; a screech-owl, a barn-owl. **2** (fig) (derog) an extremely ugly person.

কালবেলা *n* (astrol) inauspicious time.

কালা[1] *n* hard of hearing; deaf.

কালা[2] *adj* **1** black; dark. **2** in disrepute; stigmatized: ~ মুখ. **3** soiled; dirty: ~ কাপড়, ~ আদমি, brown-skinned people or the easterners. **~কানুন** *n* law that aims at repressing the people; Black Act.

কালাকাল *n* proper or improper time; auspicious or inauspicious moments. **~ জ্ঞান** *n* sense about right time for anything.

কালাচাঁদ *n* an appellation of Sri Krishna given in endearment.

কালাজ্বর *n* tropical fever of the deadly type visiting particularly Assam in India; Kala-azar.

কালাতিপাত [কাল+অতিপাত] *n* **1** passing of time. **2** passage or efflux of time. **~ করা** *vi* pass or spend time.

কালাপানি *n* **1** the sea or the sea water. **2** the sentence of deportation (such as to the Andamans during the British rule in India).

কালাপাহাড় *n* **1** person of a gigantic stature and ferocious nature. **2** (fig) person who attacks popular beliefs or established customs which he thinks mistaken or unwise; an iconoclast. **3** (hist) a Brahmin who, after having embraced Islam during the Turkish rule, turned into a zealous iconoclast and destroyed many Hindu temples and idols.

কালাম [A] *n* a message; a revelation. আল্লাহর ~. কালামুল্লাহ [কালাম+আল্লাহ] *n* revelation from Allah; the Holy Qoran.

কালাশুদ্ধি *n* (astrol) unpropitiousness of time (to be avoided for any religious ceremony).

কালাশৌচ *n* the period of mourning observed among the Hindus following the death of any of the parents or a near kinsman.

কালি[1] *n* **1** black or other coloured liquid used in writing; ink: কালো ~ লাল ~. **2** thick black or coloured paste used for printing/ polishing shoes: ছাপার ~, জুতার ~. **3** mental depression; dejection; gloom: মনের ~. **4** (fig) person who is the cause of disgrace, discredit or shame: কুলের ~. **~ঝুলি** *n* black powder left by smoke on surfaces; stains made by bits of soot, dirt, etc; soot and smut. **চুন~** *n* disgrace; scandal; dishonour. **মুখে চুন~ পড়া** bring disgrace on oneself (by committing a crime, etc). **হাড় ~ হওয়া** (fig) live in extreme poverty and hardship.

কালি[২] old use *adv* tomorrow or yesterday **আজি~** *adv* in a day or two; soon.

কালি[৩] *n* (math) cubic measure; square measure: বিঘা~, কাঠা~. **~ করা/কষা** *vt* find the measurement of an area.

কালিক *adj* of or pertaining to time; temporary: সমাজের স্থানিক ও ~ রূপ বিধৃত হয় তার সাহিত্যে.

কালিকা *n* Hindu goddess Kali. **~ পুরাণ** *n* part of the Hindu Purana that narrates the feats of Kalika.

কালিজিরা *n* a variety of cumin seed; black cumin.

কালিদাস *n* the famous poet and dramatist of ancient India and one of the nine gems who adorned the court of king Vikramaditya.

কালিমা *n* **1** darkness of prospect; sadness; gloom: মনের ~. **2** a mark of dishonour; a blemish: চরিত্রে ~ লেপন করা, blemish or tarnish the character of one.

কালিয়া [A] *n* a juicy preparation of fish or meat with spices and turmeric; a curry.

কালী *n* Hindu goddess Kali, wife of Shiva.

কালীন, কালীয় *adj* (used as a *suff*) of a particular time: সম~ সমাজ, the contemporary society: তৎ~ অধ্যক্ষ, the then Principal: গ্রীষ্ম~ ছুটি, summer vacation.

কালে *adv* **1** in future; in due course: ছেলেটি ~ একজন বড়ো বিজ্ঞানী হবে, will make a great scientist in due course. **2** in an age (of history): প্রাচীন ~, আধুনিক ~. **~ কালে** *adv* **1** in course of time; with the passage of time: ~-~ কতোই দেখবো. **~ভদ্রে** *adv* not often; seldom; rarely: তিনি এখানে ~ভদ্রে আসেন, he seldom comes here; his visit here is few and far between.

কালেকটার [E] *n* the officer in charge of revenue administration of a district; a collector. **কালেকটারি** *n* the office of the collector; collectorate; collectorship.

কালোচিত *adj* befitting the age/ occasion; timely; opportune.

কালোয়াত *n* person who is an expert in Indian classical music. **কালোয়াতি** *n* **1** proficiency in classical music. **2** (sarcas) act of parading one's knowledge in anything.

কাল্পনিক *adj* **1** existing only in the mind or imagination; imaginary; visionary ~ কাহিনী. **2** falsely devised; fabricated; fictitious; false: ~ অভিযোগ. **3** unreal; unpractical; fanciful.

কাশ[১] *n* species of tall grass with tuft of soft downy white flowers; common reed.

কাশ২, কাশি *n* **1** act or sound of coughing; cough. **2** matter expectorated by coughing; phlegm. **~ দেওয়া** *vi* utter a cough or a series of coughs; cough. **~ দিয়ে তোলা** *vt* expel phlegm by coughing; expectorate.

কাশন্দি=কাসুন্দি

কাশা *vi, vt* send out air from the lungs violently and noisily to expel phlegm; expectorate.

কাশী *n* Vanaras or Varanasi, the famous place of Hindu pilgrimage. **~ প্রাপ্তি/লাভ** *n* **1** death at Kashi (Vanaras). **2** (fig) ascension to heaven (according to Hindu opinion).

কাষ্ঠ=কাঠ. **~কুট্ট**=কাঠঠোকরা⇒কাঠ. **~পাদুকা** *n* (pair of) wooden sandal. **~পুত্তলিকা** *n* a doll or puppet made of wood; (fig) person who is only a figurehead with no real authority. **~ফলক** *n* **1** a flat broad piece of sawed timber; a plank. **2** a plate or board of wood as used for a name-plate, etc. **~বৎ** *n* dry as wood. **~মঞ্চ** *n* a wooden platform. **~মণ্ড** *n* soft mass of wood fibre as used for making paper; wood-pulp. **~মার্জার**=কাঠবিড়ালি⇒কাঠ.[১] **~হাসি** *n* a silly or affected smile; a forced smile.

কাষ্ঠা *n* the limit or extent of sth. **পরা~** the acme or the highest excellence (of anything): তিনি ধৈর্যের পরা~ প্রদর্শন করেন.

কাসুন্দি, কাশন্দি *n* sort of pickle made of slices of green mango with mustard and salt; mango pickle. **পুরনো ~ ঘাটা** (fig) raise up an old and unpleasant topic.

কাসেদ [A] *n* person carrying a message; a messenger.

কাস্তে *n* scythe.

কাকে, কাহাকে *pron* (interr) (the objective case of 'কে', ie who) whom: ~ আসতে বলেছো? whom did you ask to come?

কাহার, কার *pron* (interr) the possessive case of কে; whose: এটা ~ জামা? whose shirt is this?

কাহারবা [H] *n* a musical measure.

কাহিনী [H] *n* **1** an account of past events; a real or feigned story; a tale; a fiction; an episode; an anecdote. **2** the details of an incident: তোমার ~ শুনবার সময় নেই.

কাহিল [A] *adj* **1** lacking in strength; weak; feeble: শরীরটা ~ হয়েছে. **2** emaciated by long illness or undernourishment; lean and thin; slim; slender: মেয়েটা না খেয়ে না খেয়ে ~ হয়েছে. **3** affected with sickness; frequently sick; sickly. **4** (fig) lacking confidence or enthusiasm; disheartened: মামলায় হেরে গিয়ে ওদের এখন ~ অবস্থা.

কি auxiliary word used in interrogative sentences: সে ~ বাড়ি আছে? Is he at home? সেকি how is it? একি what!

কিউ [E] *n* a file of persons waiting in the order of their arrival, to be served in a shop or to get into a carriage; a queue.

কিংকর=কিঙ্কর

কিংকর্তব্য *n* that which is proper to be done. **~বিমূঢ়** *adj* at a loss to determine what to do (in a situation arising out of fear, shame or surprise); bewildered; perplexed. **~বিমূঢ়তা** *n* perplexity; bewildered; perplexed. **~বিমূঢ়তা** *n* perplexity; bewilderment; nonplus.

কিংখাপ, কিংখাব [P] a silk or satin stuff ornamented with designs in gold and silver thread; brocade.

কিংবদন্তি, কিংবদন্তী *n* **1** traditional story of some incident; popular talk; rumour; hearsay: ~ আছে যে..., hearsay has it that ....

কিংবা *conj* either .... or; whether ... or; on the otherhand; alternatively.

কিংশুক *n* **1** a variety of red flower beautiful to look at but without scent, or its tree (পলাশ). **2** (fig) person without merit or virtue like the scentless কিংশুক: নির্গুণ ~.

কিঙ্কর *n* a slave; a servant; an attendant. **কিঙ্করী** *fem*.

কিঙ্কিণী a girdle for ankles set with small bells producing sweet jingling sound used in dancing.

কিচকিচা *int* denoting deep black colour: কালো ~ দাড়ি.

কিচমিচ, কিচিরমিচির *n, int* sound denoting the chirping, twittering, chattering or screeching as by birds, rats or monkeys. **~ করা** *vi* chirp; chatter; screech.

কিছু *adj* some; a little; any: ~ দুধ, ~ টাকা. ❑*pron* something: একটা ~ করো. ❑*adv* somewhat: রোগীর অবস্থা ~ ভালো. **অনেক ~** many things . **অল্প ~** just a little; something. **কত ~** various things. **~ই না** nothing whatever. **~~** something; a small number/ amount of. **~তে** in anything. **~তেই** under any circumstances; by any means; at all. **~তেই না** by no means. **~ না** nothing. **~ না ~** something or other; at least something. **~মাত্র** hardly any. **কোনো ~** something; anything. **সামান্য ~** just a little.

কিঞ্চিৎ *adv, adj* a little; some. **কিঞ্চিদধিক** *adj* little more than. **কিঞ্চিদপি** *adv* only a little **কিঞ্চিদুষ্ণ** *adj* moderately warm; lukewarm; tepid. **কিঞ্চিদূন** *adv* a little less than. **কিঞ্চিন্মাত্র** *adj* only a little; even a little.

কিড়মিড়, কিড়িমিড়ি *int* indicative of grinding or gnashing of teeth. **দাঁত ~ করা** grind/gnash the teeth.

কিড়া, কীড়ে *n* the larva of an insect; a maggot; a parasite: কাঠের ~. **মাথায় ~ ঢুকেছে** (fig) affected with a mania; one who is suffering from some morbid craving; one who has gone crazy.

কিতাব, কেতাব [A] *n* a book. **~ কোরান** *n* religious scriptures, evidential documents, etc. **কেতাবি** *adj* **1** of books; bookish: কেতাবি বিদ্যা. **2** (people) professing revealed religious, ie the Jews, the Christians and the Muslims.

কিনডারগার্টেন [G] *n* infant school in which amusements are systematically combined with instruction.

কিনা[1]=কেনা

কিনা[2] [P] ill-will; malice; rancour: মনে কোনো ~ রাখবেন না.

কিনা[3] *adv* **1** whether or not: সে যাবে ~ জানি না. **2** this is why; because; since; as ··· so for this reason: জ্বর হয়েছে কিনা তাই আসেনি, as he is ill, so he could not come. **3** used in interrogation: কথাটা ঠিক ~, isn't it right ?

কিনারা, কিনার [P] *n* **1** a bank (of a river): নদীর ~, river bank/side. **2** the edge or side (of sth) রাস্তার ~ , roadside. **3** provision; remedy; redress: বিধবার একটা ~ করো. **4** settlement or solution (of a problem, etc). **~ করা** *vi, vt* find out a solution. **~ করতে না পারা** fail to find a way out. **কূল~** settlement; solution; termination.

কিন্তু *conj, adv* **1** but; still; yet; nevertheless; notwithstanding; however; গরিব ~ সৎ, poor but honest. **2** then; in the case; only if: আজই যাবো, ~ টাকা পেলে , I will go today only if money is arranged. I may go today in the case fund is available. ❑*adj* hesitating; wavering: ~~ করো না, don't be hesitating. ❑*n* objection; a point to be considered: এর মধ্যে একটা ~ আছে.

কিন্নর *n* (myth) sweet-toned musician of the heaven. **কিন্নরী** *fem*.

কিপটে, *adj* (colloq) miserly; niggardly; closefisted. **~মি** *n* miserliness; niggardliness. **হাড় ~** one who in wealth acts as if suffering from poverty; extremely miser in habits.

কিফায়েত [A] *n* **1** a cut in/ reduction of expenditure. **2** cheapness; a gain in parchase: দরে ~ হয়েছে.

কিবলা=কেবলা

কিবা *int* **1** (poet) used in praise: ঐ ~ ধবধব তুঙ্গতুঙ্গ শৃঙ্গ সব. **2** what else; what more: ~ বলার আছে. **3** expressing sameness or equality: ~ রাত ~ দিন.

কিমত=কিম্মত

কিমতে *adv* (poet) how; in what manner.

কিমা [P] *n* meat chopped finely for making chops, etc; forcemeat; mince-meat.

কিমাকার *adj* (lit) of what shape or form (used in derogatory senses: কিম্ভূত ~, ugly in appearance).

কিমিয়া [A] chemical science of olden days; alchemy.

কিম্মত [A] *n* **1** price; cost. **2** worth; importance; prestige; value. **কিম্মতি** *adj* costly; valuable; prestigious: কিম্মতি চিজ.

কিয়ৎ *adj* a small amount/ number of; a little; a few. **কিয়দংশ** (~ + অংশ) *n* a part; a portion. **কিয়দ্দিন** (~ +দিন) *n* some days . ❑*adv* for some days. **কিয়দ্দূর** (~+দূর) *n* a short distance. ❑*adv* to a short distance. **কিয়দ্দূরে** *adv* at a little distance; not far off.

কিয়াম=কেয়াম

কিয়ামত=কেয়ামত

কিয়াস [A] *n* **1** (lit) analogical deduction. **2** framing of new rules and regulations in the light of the main principles contained in the Qoran and Hadith. **3** one of the sources of Muslim law.

কিরণ *n* a ray or column of light emitted by the sun, moon, or other luminous body; a beam. **~চ্ছটা** *n* the glow of rays. **~পাত/সম্পাত** *n* emission of rays; radiation. **~সম্পাত/ বিকিরণ করা** *vi, vt* shine forth; radiate; issue in rays. **সূর্য ~-সম্পাত করে** the sun radiates/emits/ sheds rays of light. **~ময়** *adj* emitting or diffusing light; glowing; luminous; lustrous. **~ময়ী** *fem.* **~মালী** *n* the sun.

কিরপিন (colloq)=কৃপণ

কিরা, কিরে *n* an oath; a swearing. **~ কাটা** *vi, vt* to swear (by sth). **~ দেওয়া** *vi, vt* bind one to an oath; force an oath upon.

কিরাত=কেরাত

কিরিচ [P] *n* a short sword with a curved blade used mostly in Malay peninsula; a falchion.

কিরীট *n* a crown; a coronet; a diadem; a headdress. **কিরীটী** *adj* **1** wearing a crown; crowned; coroneted. **2** an appellation of Arjuna of Mahabharata.

কিরূপ *adj* of what form/sort. **কিরূপে** *adv* how; in what manner/way; by what means.

কিরে[1]=কিরা

কিরে[2] *int* used in addressing a friend, or a person of lower status, or one who is on affectionate term: ~ ! কেমন আছিস, hallo! How are you?

কিল *n* a blow with the fist. **~ মারা** *vi, vt* strike with fist. **~ খাওয়া** *vt* be struck with the fist. **~ খেয়ে ~ চুরি করা** (fig) endure an insult or humiliation in silence/without protest. **~গুঁতা** *n* beating and prodding; (fig) rough and humiliating treatment: ~গুঁতা খেয়েও কাজ করে যাচ্ছি **~ দাগড়া** one whose back bears the marks of repeated beating. **কিলাকিলি** *n* fighting with the fists; fisticuffs. **কিলিয়ে কাঁঠাল পাকানো** (fig) be unreasonably flurried or bustling to get a result/ achieve an end before the stage is set for that. **ভাত দেবার মুরোদ নেই কিল মারার গোঁসাই** an over assertive master who is prompt to take his subordinates to task without having the mind or means to pay them.

কিলবিল *int* suggesting movement in a swarm (as of fish) or the crawling of reptiles (esp the young ones): সাপের বাচ্চাগুলো ~ করছে, ... wriggling/ moving with the contortions of body.

কিলানো=কিল মারা⇒কিল

কিল্লা=কেল্লা

কিশতি=কিস্তি[2]

কিশমিশ, কিসমিস [P] *n* special kind of dried grape that keeps for a long time, used in the preparation of rich food; currant; raisin.

কিশলয় *n* **1** a shoot from the branch of a tree. **2** tender leaf of a tree: গাছে গাছে ~.

কিশোর *adj* **1** (of boys) of the age group between 11 and 15. ❑*n* a male youth who is advancing to manhood. **কিশোরী** *fem* an adolescent girl.

কিষাণ=কৃষাণ

কিসম [A] *n* a varied assortment; a sort; a kind: হর ~, of all kinds.

কিসমত, কিসমৎ [A] *n* **1** fate which falls to one; lot; luck; destiny: কিসমতের জোর. **2** a part of a revenue settlement unit; division of a *mauza:* ~ কুলকান্দি.

কিসিম=কিসম

কিসে *pron* **1** how; by what means: ~ দু'পয়সা আসে তাই দেখো. **2** in what thing: সুখ ~. **3** in what subject : ~ এম. এ. **4** in what respect: তুমিই বা কম ~. **5** for what reason; from what; why: ~ হলো. **~ আর ~** drawing an improper comparison of a vile thing with a noble one. **~র** *pron* (poss). **1** of what sort; in what respect: ~র গরিব ? what sort of poor is he (implying that he is not at all poor)? **2** of no cause/ point: ~র কষ্ট, ~র লজ্জা.

কিস্তি[1] [P] *n* **1** any one of the parts or instalments in which sth is presented over a period of time: লেখাটি ৩ কিস্তিতে প্রকাশিত হবে, the article will appear in 3 instalments. **2** any of the instalments for paying a debt: ৩ কিস্তিতে আদায়. **~ দেওয়া** *vi* pay an instalment. **~ খেলাপ** *n* default of an instalment. **~বন্দি** *n* agreement to pay by instalments. ~বন্দি করা agree to realize by instalments.

কিস্তি², কিশতি [P] *n* **1** a boat; a ship. **2** (in chess) position when the opponent's king is exposed to direct attack: ঘোড়ার ~. ~মাত *n* complete victory. ~ মাত করা *vt* make a move that prevents the opponent's king from being moved away from a direct attack and thus win the game.

কী¹ *interr pron* **1** what: ~ চাই, ~ বলছো. **2** how: ~ করে, ~ উপায়ে. **3** expressing doubt or reluctance: ~ আর করতে পারলাম, ~ আর বলবো. ❑*adj, adv* how much: ~ কষ্ট, ~ লজ্জা, ~ সুন্দর, ~ জ্বালা. ❑*conj* or, whether: ~ শীত, ~ গ্রীষ্ম. ~ ~ what things. ~ করে how? by what means? ~ নিমিত্ত why ? for what reason? ~ মনে করে on what business ? for what purpose? ~ জ্বালা ! how annoying! how disgusting!

কী² *pron* used in exclamation: কী ভয়ানক, how dreadful !

কীট *n* **1** small arthropod creature, often winged, having three divisions of the body–head, thorax and abdomen set on three pairs of legs, eg an ant, a fly or a wasp; an insect. **2** small creeping animal, eg intestinal worm. ~ঘ্ন *adj* destructive of insects and worms. ❑*n* insecticide. ~জ *adj* produced or grown from a worm or insect. ~তত্ত্ব/বিদ্যা *n* branch of zoology that treats of the structure, habits and classification of insects; entomology. ~তাত্ত্বিক/ বিদ *n* an entomologist. ~দষ্ট *adj* worm-eaten; moth-eaten. ~পতঙ্গ *n* worms and insects. কীটাণু *n* a microscopic worm; a microbe. কীটাণু~ *n* **1** a parasite smaller than a microbe. **2** (fig) a very insignificant person.

কীর্তন *n* **1** narration in praise; glorification; extolment: গুণ~. **2** sort of Hindu religious song in glorification of Radha and Krishna: সং~. **3** a musical mode: কীর্তনের সুর. ~ করা/গাওয়া *vi* sing the glories/ dalliance of Radha and Krishna. কীর্তক *n* **1** one who makes a laudatory speech; a panegyrist; eulogist. **2** one who sings 'Kirton' song. কীর্তনিয়া/ কীর্তনে (colloq) *n* professional singer of 'Kirton' songs; the leader of a professional troupe of 'Kirton' singers. কীর্তনীয় *adj* fit to be celebrated/ eulogized/sung.

কীর্তি *n* **1** (condition of) being widely known and talked about; fame; reputation; renown; celebrity. **2** an act, performance or institution that lives on as one's glorious achievement. **3** (sarcas) a misdeed; an evil action: তোমার ছেলের ~ দেখো. ~কলাপ *n* exploits/glorious deeds (of a hero). ~ধ্বজা *n* standard of fame. ~নাশা *n* name earned by river Padma for destroying the achievements of Raja Rajballava. ~বাস *n* abode of fame; a renowned person. ~মান *adj* illustrious; celebrated: ~মান পুরুষ. ~স্তম্ভ *n* an erection to commemorate a great event or person; a monument.

কীর্তিত (of an event) celebrated; narrated; sung.

কীল, কীলক *n* a bar of a door; a bolt. **2** a sharpened piece of wood or bamboo used to fasten cattle's; a stake; a peg; a wedge. **3** a small spiked length of metal with flat head used for fastening two pieces of wood, etc; a nail. **4** a surgeon's instrument for examining an wound, ulcer or cavity; a probe.

কীলকলিপি *n* wedge-shaped characters in which ancient Babylonian inscriptions were written; cuneiform writing.

কু (opp সু) *adj* bad; evil; wicked; indecent; used as a *pref* in the above senses eg কুকথা, কুশিক্ষা, কুসঙ্গ, কুচিন্তা, কুমন্ত্রণা, etc. কু-আশা *n* an aim that cannot be attained. কুসময় *n* a period full of troubles and difficulties.

কুইনাইন, কুইনিন [E] *n* an alkaline substance obtained from the bark of the cinchona; a medicinal preparation of this used as an antidote for malaria.

কুওত, কুয়ৎ [A] *n* physical strength; vigour; vitality; virility.

কুঁকড়ানো, কোঁকড়ানো *vt, vi* be or cause to become smaller in size; shrivel or cause to shrivel; wrinkle up (as in cold). ❑*adj* shrunk; shrivelled; wrinkled up; contracted.

কুঁচকানো *vi, vt*=কুঁকড়ানো. ভ্রূ ~ *vi* express displeasure by contracting the brow; look stern; frown.

কুঁচকি *n* the part of the human body between the belly and thigh in front; the groin.

কুঁজা¹, কুঁজো *adj* having a crooked back; hunchbacked. ❑*n* a humpbacked person; a hunchback.

কুঁজা², কুজো *n* an earthen pitcher with a long and narrow neck.

কুঁড়া, কুঁড়ো *n* the red powdery coating of rice under the husk. খুদ~ *n* huskings and rice-particles produced in the process of husking. খুদ~ খেয়ে বাঁচা maintain oneself on paltry things. বিদুরের খুদ ~ a poor but hearty present from a poor man.

কুঁড়ি *n* the first shoot of a leaf; a bud.

কুঁড়ে¹ *n* a cottage roofed with straw and dry leaves; a poorman's abode.

কুঁড়ে², কুড়ে *adj* averse to work. ❑*n* a lazy person. কাজে ~ ভোজনে দেড়ে slothful in work, but good in eating. ~ গরু অমাবস্যা খোঁজে (fig) a lazy person is always on the look out for an occasion to spare himself from work. ~মি *n* laziness; indolence; habitual love of ease.

কুঁতা, কুঁথা=কোঁথা ⇒কোঁথ

কুঁদ=কুন্দ[১], কুন্দ[২].

কুঁদরু *n* kind of kitchen vegetable.

কুঁদা[১] *vi* shape an article of wood by turning it on a lathe.

কুঁদা[২] *vt* bluster and talk big (at one) in rage (as if to attack him).

কুঁদা[৩] *n* **1** a stem of a tree; a wooden block; a log of wood. **2** the wooden piece or stock of a gun: বন্দুকের ~.

কুকথা *n* **1** indecent or obscene talk; abusive language. **2** talking unguardedly sth serious that ought not be said (as when a husband says to the wife in a fit of rage 'I divorce thee').

কুকর্ম, কুকার্য *n* a wicked or blamable act; a mischief; a misdeed. **~কারী** *n* an evil-doer; a mischief maker. **কুকর্মাসক্ত** *adj* given to evil ways/ immorality; villainous.

কুকীর্তি *n* a misdeed; a wicked act; a crime.

কুকুর *n* domestic quadruped famous for loyalty to its master; a dog. **কুকুরী** *n fem* a bitch. **কুকুরের ছানা** *n* a puppy. **কুকুরের পাল** *n* a pack of dogs/ hounds. **~-কুণ্ডলী** *n* the manner at lying down in a coil as a dog. **~লেজা** *adj* of the shape of a dog's tail. **~মুখো** *n* an abuse. **কুকুরে ঘুম** short sleep. **কুকুরে দাঁত** *n* (in a human being) two pairs of sharp, pointed teeth between the incisors and the premolars like those of a dog; the canine teeth. **খেঁকি ~** *n* type of rickety and ill-tempered dog that easily gets irritated and snarls at people; (fig) a peevish person without worth. **যেমন ~ তেমনি মুগুর** like dog, like hammer.

কুক্ষণ *n* an inauspicious moment; evil hour.

কুক্ষি *n* **1** the belly; the womb; the abdomen. **2** the inside or hollow of anything; a cave. **~গত** *adj* lying inside the womb or a cave; (fig) seized/ snatched/ grabbed by one; under one's absolute control.

কুখ্যাত *adj* well-known in an unfavourable capacity; publicly known and talked for sth bad; notorious; infamous. **কুখ্যাতি** *n* notoriety; infamy.

কুগ্রহ *n* **1** an unfavourable or evil star (according to Hindu belief). **2** (fig) person who is a source of trouble but is difficult to avoid.

কুঙ্কুম *n* **1** a pollen-tube or stamen of the sweet scented saffron flower of Kashmir. **2** flower.

কুচ[১] *n* either of the breasts of a young woman. **~কুম্ভ** *n* a breast of the shape of a water-jar.

কুচ[২] [P] *n* the march of an army to give battle. **~কাওয়াজ** *n* military drill/ parade.

কুচক্র *n* a gang of bad people; conspiracy; intrigue; a plot. **কুচক্রী** *n* a conspirator; a plotter; an intriguer.

কুজন[১] *n* a wicked or mean person.

কুজন[২] *n* chirping or twittering of birds.

কুজ্ঝটিকা *n* fog; mist. **~ময়** *adj* overspread with mist; filled with fog; misty; foggy.

কুঞ্চন *n* the condition of contraction; shrinking; curling; wrinkling. **ভ্রূ~** frowning; knitting of the brows. কুঞ্চিত *adj*.

কুঞ্চিকা *n* **1** a kind of fruit. **2** a shoot of the bamboo. **3** a key. **4** the index of a book.

কুঞ্চিত *adj* contracted; wrinkled; curled. **~কেশ** curled hair. **~ করা** *vt* to curl; wrinkle; to shrivel; to contract.

কুঞ্জ[১] *n* a shelter in a garden, formed of trees and shrubs; a bower; an arbour. **~বন** *n* a forest having bowers. **~লতা** *n* flowery creepers that make a bower.

কুঞ্জ[২] [P] *n* embroidery work in garments. **~দার** *adj* having decorative embroidery: ~দার শাড়ি.

কুটকুট *int* expressing an itching sensation. **~ করা** *vi* cause to feel itching sensation. **কুটকুটানি** *n*.

কুটন *n* **1** act of cutting fish or vegetables into pieces, or chopping meat for cooking. **2** act of grinding/ pulverizing/ thrashing under a foot-driven molar: চাল ~, চিঁড়া ~. **কুটনা ~** act of dressing fish, meat or vegetables for the kitchen.

কুটনি *n fem* a female who acts as an agent for unlawful union of a man and woman; a procuress; a bawd; a pimp. **~গিরি** *n* the profession of a procuress; bawdry; bawdiness.

কুটা[১], **কুটো** *n* small fragments or shreds of things; pieces of straw, etc: ~কাটি.

কুটা[২] *vt* **1** to dress fish, meat, vegetables for cooking. **2** to grind or pulverize: আটা~.

কুটি=কুটা[১]. **~~** *adj* reduced into fine pieces. **~~ করা** *vt* cut or chop into small shreds. **হেসে ~~ হওয়া** *vi* be beside oneself with laughter.

কুটির *n* **1** a hut; a cottage. **2** (in politeness) humble abode: দরিদ্রের ~. **~বাসী** *n* a cottager. **~ শিল্প** *n* an industry that can be carried on in private houses, eg knitting, pottery, etc; cottage industry.

কুটিল *adj* **1** not straight or level; twined; circuitous; tortuous; zigzag. **2** (of a person or his actions) not straightforward; crooked; hypocritical; deceitful: ~ চরিত্র, ~ স্বভাব. **3** difficult to do, understand or answer; shrewd; complicated: ~ প্রশ্ন. **কুটিলা** *fem*. **~তা** *n* tortuousness; angularity; crookedness; hypocrisy; insincerity.

কুটুম (colloq) *n* a relative by matrimonial connection. **বড়ো ~** wife's brother; brother-in-law (in good-humoured teasing).

কুটুম্ব *n* **1 a** kinsman; a relative : আত্মীয় ~. **2** relatives by marriage (eg son-in-law, son-in-law's parents and relatives, daughter-in-law's parents and relatives). **কুটুম্বিতা** *n* matrimonial alliance. **কুটুম্বিতা করা** *vt* enter into matrimonial relationship. **আত্মীয় ~** *n* kinsmen and relatives by marriage.

কুঠরি *n* a room of a house; an apartment.

কুঠার *n* tool for chopping wood; an axe; a hatchet. **কুঠারিকা** *n* a small axe used in surgical operation.

কুঠি *n* (hist) office and residence of the European indigo-planters in Bengal; official residence of high officials in British India. **~য়াল** *n* indigo planter or trader. **~ওয়ালা** *n* trader in bills of exchange; big businessman.

কুড় *n* **1** medicinal plant. **2** a measure of land. **3** a heap; a pile: আস্তা~.

কুড়ানি *n fem* one who gleans or gathers bits of wood, dry leaves or similar triffles as a means of livelihood: কাঠ ~, ঘুটে ~, পাতা ~.

কুড়ানো *vt* **1** gather together what is lying scattered: আম ~. **2** pick up scraps of things, left-overs of meal, etc to be thrown to the dustbin: এঁটো ~. **3** to sweep the floor: ঘর ~. **4** glean/ collect slowly and assiduously: পাতা ~. ❑*adj* gathered; collected; gleaned; picked up (that which was found by chance): ~ মানিক. **কুড়িয়ে পাওয়া** get (anything) by mere chance.

কুড়াল, কুরালি, কুড়োল=কুঠার

কুড়ি *n, adj* (the number) twenty.

কুনো=কুনো

কুণ্ঠ *adj* **1** (used as *pref*) disinclined, unwilling or reluctant; ungenerous; miserly: ব্যয়~. **2** averse to; viewing with repugnance: শ্রম~. **কুণ্ঠা** *n* hesitation; delicacy; diffidence; want of confidence; bashfulness. **কুণ্ঠিত** *adj* wanting confidence; tending or inclined to hesitate; diffident; bashful. **কুণ্ঠিত হওয়া, কুণ্ঠা বোধ করা** *vi* feel shy/ delicacy; hesitate.

কুণ্ড *n* **1** a hole; a hollow; a cavity: নাভি~. **2** a hollow in the earth; a pit (for fire): অগ্নি~. **3** a receptacle; a pot: ঘৃত~. **4** a pond; a pool; a cistern.

কুণ্ডল *n* **1** a decoration for the ear; an earring. **2** an ornamental ring for the wrist or for the ankle; a bangle. **কুণ্ডলিত** *adj* ring-shaped; twisted or wound like a coil: কুণ্ডলিত নীহারিকা, spiral nebula. **কুণ্ডলী** *n* that which appears like a coil: সাপ কুণ্ডলী পাকিয়ে আছে, the snake has wound itself into a coil. **কুণ্ডলী পাকানো** *vi* to wind into a ring. **কুণ্ডলীকৃত** *adj* wounded into a ring.

কুতুব[1] [A] *n* an appellation of Muslim saints.

কুতুব[2] [A] *n pl* (sing কিতাব) books. **~খানা** *n* a library; a collection of books.

কুতূহল *n* **1** eagerness to see and know; curiosity; inquisitiveness. **2** delight; pleasure; sport. **কুতূহলী** *adj* inquisitive; curious; sportive. **কুতূহলে** *adv* in curiosity; sportively.

কুত্তা [H] *n* the dog. **কুত্তী** *fem* bitch. **~র বাচ্চা** *n* **1** a puppy; a young dog. **2** abuse. **খেঁকি ~**=খেঁকি কুকুর ⇒ কুকুর. **নেড়ি ~** kind of rickety dog lacking hair on the skin. **ডাল ~** *n* kind of dog used in hunting and racing; a hound.

কুত্রাপি *adv* anywhere.

কুৎসা *n* a false and malicious statement about a person, made to damage his character; slander; calumny. **~ করা** *vt* injure by a malicious statement; calumniate; slander; defame. **~কারী** *n* a calumniator; a slanderer; a scandal monger. **~জনক** *adj* calumnious; scandalous; defamatory.

কুৎসিত *adj* **1** ugly to look at; ill-shaped: ~ চেহারা. **2** causing hatred and disgust; abominable; nasty: ~ ব্যবহার. **3** indecent; obscene; filthy.

কুদরত [A] *n* **1** power of doing miracles; glory; majesty: আল্লাহর কুদরতে সবই সম্ভব. **2** creative skill; workmanship; a creditable exploit. **কুদরতি** *adj* natural and not man-made; superhuman.

কুনো *adj* **1** pertaining to a কোণ or corner; home-keeping; domestic: ~ বিড়াল. **2** shy of company; unsocial. **~ ব্যাং** *n* a toad which seldom comes out of its hole; (fig) a shy and timid person.

কুন্তল *n* woman's hair; a tress, a braid, a lock or curl of hair.

কুন্থন *n* act of straining at stool; act of applying one's strength to sth with a groan.

কুন্দ[1] *n* kind of white jasmine.

কুন্দ[2] [P] *n* a machine by which articles of wood are turned and cut into a smooth round form; a turner's lathe.

কুপথ *n* evil way. **কুপথে যাওয়া** *vi* go astray; go to the dogs.

কুপথ্য *n* diet harmful for a patient.

কুপন [E] *n* **1** part of the money order form meant for the payee. **2** a ticket; part of a document, paper, bond, etc, which gives the holder the right to receive sth or do sth; a coupon.

কুপরামর্শ *n* evil counsel; an advice given for sth harmful.

কুপাত্র *n* **1** unfit or undeserving person. **2** unworthy or undesirable bridegroom.

কুপি *n* an oil lamp.

কুপিত *adj* filled with rage; enraged; angered; annoyed. **~ হওয়া** be enraged/annoyed. **কুপিতা** *fem.*

কুপুত্র *n* an unworthy or disobedient son; a son who is wicked or characterless.

কুপুরুষ *n* **1** person without manly qualities. **2** an ugly or characterless person. ❑*adj* devoid of manliness; ugly-looking; cowardly.

কুপো *n* **1** a fat-bellied and narrow-necked earthen or leather vessel. **2** (sarcas) a pot-bellied person. **~কাত** *adj* turned upside down; thoroughly overpowered; knocked down; vanquished.

কুফর [A] *n* **1** act of rejecting Divine message. **2** disbelief in the unity of God. **3** worshipping many gods; polytheism; idolatry. **কুফরি** *adj* of or pertaining to disbelief. **কুফরি ফতোয়া** *n* adjudging one an unbeliever.

কুফল *n* evil consequence; harmful effect; bad result.

কুবলয় *n* blue lotus; blue water-lily.

কুবিচার *n* unfair judgement; miscarriage of justice; wrong verdict.

কুবিন্দু *n* **1** (astron) hypothetical point of the heavens directly beneath an observer; the nadir. **2** (fig) the lowest point; the most depressed stage.

কুবের *n* **1** the Hindu god of wealth. **2** an immensely wealthy person; a millionaire: ধন~. **~তুল্য** *adj* as rich as Kuvera, the god of wealth. **~পুরী** *n* the abode of Kuvera.

কুব্জ=কুঁজো

কুমকুম [A] *n* a kind of cracker filled with red powder and scented water.

কুমড়া, কুমড়ো *n* kind of gourd or vegetable marrow; a pumpkin. **গুড় ~, মিঠা ~, বিলাতি ~** *nn* kind of sweet pumpkin. **চাল ~, দেশী ~** the variety of pumpkin consumed in its green state.

কু-মতলব *n* evil design.

কুমতি *n* evil propensity of mind; sinister motive; evil genius. ❑ *adj* having mischievous propensity.

কুমন্ত্রণা *n* evil counsel; harmful advice.

কুমার[১] *n* **1** a boy (usu between 5 and 10 years). **2** a royal prince; a crown prince. **3** a son. **4** an unmarried man; a bachelor: চির~. **5** Hindu deity Kartikeya. **কুমারাচার** a boy who is undergoing mental and physical discipline to become a good citizen; a boyscout. **~ব্রত** *n* a solemn vow of lifelong celibacy.

কুমার[২], **কুমোর** (dial) *n* **1** one who makes earthenware vessels; a potter; a clay-modeller. **2** professional class among the Hindus. **~শাল** *n* a potter's workshop/ kiln. **কুমারের চাক** *n* a potter's wheel.

কুমারিকা *n* **1** girl aged between ten and twelve. **2** a girl or woman without carnal knowledge of a man; a virgin; a maiden. **3** the southern tip of India extending into the ocean; the Cape Comorin.

কুমারী *n* **1** an unmarried girl of marriageable age; a virgin; a maiden. **2** woman who remains single after the conventional age of marrying; a spinster. **3** a daughter: রাজ~. **~ত্ব** *n* state of being a virgin; virginity. **~-নাম** *n* name derived from that of father or ancestor (in contrast to that derived from husband); maiden name.

কুমির, কুমীর *n* large aquatic reptile of the lizard kind; the crocodile. **জলে ~ ডাঙায় বাঘ** situation when one is faced with a choice between two courses that are equally unfavourable; the horns of a dilemma. **জলে বাস করে কুমিরের সাথে বিবাদ** (fig) quarreling with a powerful person while living within his sphere of influence is like quarreling with the crocodile while staying in water. **মেছো ~** small species of crocodile that lives on fishes.

কুমুদ *n* white or red coloured lotus or water-lily; the stalk of a lotus. **~নাথ** *n* the moon (said to be the নাথ or lord of lotuses). **~বতী** *n* **1** cluster of water lilies. **2** a pond full of water-lilies. ❑*adj* full of water-lilies: ~বতী সরসী. **কুমুদিনী** *n* **1** cluster of water-lilies. **2** a pond beautified with red or white water-lilies.

কুমেরু *n* the southern end of the earth's axis, the south pole. **~ বৃত্ত** *n* the line of latitude 66·5 S; the Antarctic Circle. **~ জ্যোতি, ~প্রভা**=অবাচী উষা⇒উষা.

কুম্ভ *n* **1** a round-shaped jar; a pitcher. **2** (astron) Aquarius, the eleventh sign of the zodiac. **3** the frontal globe at the two sides of an elephant's head.

কুম্ভক *n* Hindu religious or yogic exercise based on the control of one's breath.

কুম্ভকর্ণ *n* **1** (myth) the Ramayana-famous younger brother of Ravana who slept for six months at a stretch. **2** (fig) person who sleeps overmuch. **কুম্ভকর্ণের নিদ্রা** (fig) long and profound sleep (said when it seems difficult to awake one from sleep).

কুম্ভকার=কুমার[২]

কুম্ভমেলা *n* religious gathering of Hindu ascetics at the holy places of Haridwar, Proyaga, etc held every twelve years in the month of Falgun.

কুম্ভিল, কুম্ভিলক *n* **1** person who takes and uses the already published thoughts and words of another as if they were his own; a plagiarist. **2** a thief. **3** a brother-in-law.

কুম্ভীর=কুমির. **কুম্ভীরাশ্রু** *n* literal rendering of the English phrase 'crocodile's tears' which means insincere sympathy.

কুযশ *n* ill-repute; bad name.

কুযাত্রা *n* a journey attended by ill luck; an inauspicious trip.

কুযুক্তি *n* **1** faulty/ fallacious argument or reasoning. **2** evil counsel.

কুয়ত=কুওত

কুয়া, কুয়ো (dial) *n* a shaft hollowed out of the earth with sides supported by bricks or earthenware rings for obtaining water from the underground source; a ring-well; a draw-well.

কুয়াশা=কুজ্ঝটিকা

কুরআন⇒কোরান

কুরঙ্গ *n* the male deer (which has horns). **কুরঙ্গী, কুরঙ্গিণী** *fem* the hind; the doe. **~নয়ন** *adj* having beautiful eyes as a deer's; fawn-eyed; gazelle-eyed. **~নয়না** *fem.*

কুরছিনামা [A+P] *n* a description, diagram or table illustrating the line of descent of a person; a person's pedigree; genealogical table.

কুরণ্ড, কোরণ্ড *n* (med) watery fluid on the testicle; hydrocele. **কুরুণ্ডে** *n* person having hydrocele.

কুরবান, কুরবানি=কোরবান

কুরল *n* a variety of osprey; the eagle.

কুরসি [A] *n* a movable seat; a chair.

কুরা, কোরা *vt* take out sth by rubbing sth smooth with a sharp-edged instrument: নারিকেল ~, scrape out the kernel of a coconut. **নখ ~** *vi* pare nails. **কুরে কুরে খাওয়া** eat into sth bit by bit. **কুরে কুরে প্রশ্ন করা** question searchingly and in detail; probe deep into a question. **~নি** *n* a tool with a notched edge for scraping coconut; a coconut-scraper.

কুরীতি *n* evil usage; bad custom.

কুরুক্ষেত্র *n* **1** the famous battlefield in northern India where the Kauravas and the Pandavas of the Mahabharata fought each other; Kurukshetra. **2** (fig) a noisy disturbance; a row; a brawl: ~ কাণ্ড.

কুরুচি *n* perverted taste; vulgar propensity. **~পূর্ণ** *adj* obscene; indecent. **~সম্পন্ন** *adj* of/ having perverted taste.

কুর্তা [P] *n* upper garment for men; a shirt.

কুর্দন *n* act of blustering; talking boastfully and threateningly.

কুর্নিশ, কুর্নিস [T] *n* manner of paying homage to a sovereign by a deep bow. **~ করা** *vi, vt* salute by bowing/ bending the head and body in obeisance (to a ruler).

কুর্সিকাঁটা=ক্রুশকাঠি

কুল[1] *n* **1** family; line of ancestors; lineage: তিন কুলে কেউ নেই. **2** respectable family: ~জ. **3** honourable descent; aristocracy; high/ noble birth. কুলীন. **4** society; family; domestic life: ~ত্যাগ. **5** faithfulness to one's husband; chastity. **6** race; clan: ক্ষত্র~. **7** a group; a band; a flock: পক্ষি~. **8** a species; a kind; a class: মানব ~ . **~কণ্টক** *n* one who is the cause of disgrace to a family. **~কন্যা, ~কামিনী, ~বধূ, ~বালা ~নারী** *n pl* daughters and daughters-in-law of a household; chaste women. **~কর্ম, ~ক্রিয়া** *n* **1** customs and practices traditional to a family; keeping up the family tradition. **2** marrying a daughter to a *kulin;* matrimonial alliance with a *kulin* family. **~কলঙ্ক**=~কণ্টক. **~কলঙ্কিনী** *n fem* unchaste woman who brings dishonour to a family. **~ক্ষয়** *n* decay of a family due to immature/ untimely death of a large number of members. **~খাকি, ~খাগি** *n* (abuse) woman who has been the cause of many a death in both her father's family and that of her husband. **~গর্ব, ~গৌরব** *n* pride of high birth; reputation of a family. **~গুরু** *n* preceptor (*guru* or *pir*) of a family. **~জ** *adj* high born; born of a noble family. **~জি** *n* history of the descent of a person or family from the earliest ancestor; genealogy; pedigree; lineage. **~জ্ঞ** *adj* versed with the genealogy of a family; a genealogist. ☐*n* a herald. **~টা** *n, adj* an unchaste woman who has forsaken family life for harlotry. **~তন্তু** *n* offspring; progeny; descendants; children. **~তিলক, ~প্রদীপ** *n, adj* the pride of a family; the flower of one's progeny. **~ঙ্কর** *n* descendants. **~পাবন** *n* one who has glorified or sanctified his/ her family. **~বিদ্যা** *n* branch of knowledge or art in which a family has specialized through generations. **~ভঙ্গ** *n* giving a daughter in marriage to a lower family. **~মান** *n* the prestige of a family. **~মিত্র** *n* age old friend and ally of a family. **~লক্ষণ** *n* qualities befitting a person of high birth, eg education, manners, generosity, honesty, integrity, etc. **~স্থান** *adj* highly aristocratic. **~হীন** *adj* born of an obscure family. **অজ্ঞাত~শীল** *adj* coming of an obscure family. ☐*n* one whose antecedents are not known. **~ করা** *vi* enter into matrimonial alliance with a respectable family. **শ্যাম রাখি কি ~ রাখি** whether to pursue one's own inclination or to see to the interests of kith and kin; horns of a dilemma. **কুলে কালি দেওয়া** bring disgrace on one's family; stain the honour of one's family. **কুলে বাতি দেওয়া** keep up the entity of a family (said of one who is the only surviving member of a family). **কুলের বাতি** *n* **1** the pride or flower of a family. **2** the only surviving member of a family. **এ~ ও~ দু~ খাওয়া** be subjected to damage on both sides/ in all respects.

কুল[২] *n* the fruit of a spiny shrub with a hard stone and a mixed taste of sour and sweet; the jujube; the plum. **~কাসুন্দি** *n* pickle made of jujube; the jujube pickle.

কুলকুচা=কুলি[১]

কুলকুল *int* indicating the rippling of running water. **~ করা** *vi* make a rippling sound; ripple.

কুলক্ষণ *n* evil/ inauspicious omen; bad sign. ❑*adj* ominous; inauspicious. **কুলক্ষণা** *adj fem* a woman of ill-omen.

কুলগ্ন *n* (astrol) an unfavourable point of time; an inauspicious moment.

কুলঙ্গি, কুলুঙ্গি *n* a recess in a wall for books or other articles; a niche.

কুলপি, কুলফি [A কুল্‌ফ+ই] *n* a tin-case for freezing ice-cream. **~ বরফ** *n* ice-cream frozen in this tin-case. **~ মালাই** *n* ice-cream made with milk and sugar.

কুলা, কুলো(dial) *n* winnowing fan made of bamboo slips for separating dusts, etc from grains. **ছাই ফেলতে ভাঙ্গা ~** (lit) a broken or damaged winnowing fan has also its use when there is a need to pick up rubbish for the dustbin; (fig) an insignificant or unworthy person may also be useful for some work.

কুলাঙ্গার *n* one who tarnishes the honour of his family. **বংশের ~** black sheep of a family.

কুলানো *vt* **1** be enough/ adequate/ sufficient; suffice: বেতনে না ~, fall or run short of (necessity). **2** serve the purpose.

কুলায় *n* birds nest.

কুলি[১] *n* act of gargling; rinsing one's mouth with water. **~ করা** *vi* gargle.

কুলি[২] *n* a porter; a carrier; a coolie (cooly). **~কামিন** *n pl* male and female labourers. **~ধাওড়া** *n* slum of the working class.

কুলীন *adj* born of a high family. ❑*n* an aristocrat.

কুলুখ [P] *n* a small clod of earth that one uses on easing oneself after the Muslim fashion.

কুল্লে [A] *adv* **1** in all; in total; altogether: ~ তিনজন উপস্থিত. **2** simply; merely; only: ~ পাঁচ টাকা দিয়েছে.

কুশ *n* **1** tall broad-leaved grass growing in marshy places; the reed. **2** the eldest son of Sri Ramchandra and elder brother of Lava. **3** one of seven islands spoken of in Hindu Purana.

কুশণ্ডিকা *n* ritual connected with Hindu marriage by which the bridegroom solemnly undertakes charge of the bride's material and spiritual well-being and the bride avows loyalty to the husband and his family.

কুশপুত্তলি, কুশপুত্তলিকা *n* an effigy of a person made of *kush* grass or other materials. **~ দাহ করা** *vi, vt* **1** burn the effigy of a deadman whose obsequies could not be performed for some reason or other, as a symbolical cremation. **2** burn the effigy of a living person who is undesirable and unwanted by way of expressing dislike and disapproval or severance of connection with him.

কুশল[১] *n* state of being well; well-being; welfare; happiness; weal; prosperity: ~ কামনা করি, wish you a happy life. ❑*adj* being in health; hale and hearty; safe and sound; well. **~ সংবাদ, ~ বিনিময়** *n* exchange of greetings/ compliments. **~ সমাচার** *n* good news; happy tidings. **কুশলী**=কুশল[১] *adj.*

কুশল[২] *adj* having expert resource and ability; skillful with the hands; adroit; dexterous: কর্ম~, রণ~. **~তা** *n* adroitness; skillfulness; ingenuity.

কুশাগ্র *n* the tip of a blade of *kush* grass. ❑*adj* as sharp as the tip of a blade of *kush* grass. **~ধী, ~বুদ্ধি** *adj* possessing very keen intelligence; sharp-witted. **কুশাগ্রীয়** *adj* as sharp as the blade of *kush* grass; very sharp.

কুশাঙ্কুর *n* **1** sharp-pointed young shoot of *kush* grass. **2** a new-grown sharp blade of *kush* grass. ❑*adj* sharp as the tip of a blade of *kush.*

কুশাঙ্গুরী, কুশাঙ্গুরীয় *n* finger-ring made of *kush*-grass worn by Hindus at worship, obsequies and similar sacred occasions.

কুশাসন[১] [কুশ+আসন] *n* a seat made of *kush* grass.

কুশাসন[২] [কু+শাসন] *n* oppressive rule; misrule.

কুশি[১], **কুশী** *n* a spoon-like container made of copper used by Hindus for sprinkling water in worship.

কুশি[২] *n* green and undeveloped mango or other fruit. ❑*adj* raw; green; tender: ~ আম.

কুশিশ=কোশেশ

কুশীদ=কুসীদ

কুশীলব *n* **1** *(pl)* the characters of a play; actors and actresses. **2** *(sing)* an actor; a singer; a dancer, an artiste. **3** Kusha and Laba of the Ramayana.

কুশ্রী *adj* **1** lacking in beauty; ugly; uncouth. **2** exciting disgust; disgusting. abominable; loathsome, detestable.

কুষ্ঠ *n* a foul cuteneous disease, characterized by dusky red or livid tubercles on the face or extremities; leprosy. **~ঘ্ন** *adj* curing leprosy. **কুষ্ঠাশ্রম** *n* hospital or asylum for lepers. **কুষ্ঠী** *n* one affected with leprosy.

কুষ্ঠি *n* (astrol)=কোষ্ঠী

কুষ্মাণ্ড *n* **1** a gourd; a pumpkin. **2** (fig) a worthless person; an idiot (abuse). **অকাল~** ⇒অকাল.

কুসংসর্গ *n* evil company; bad association. **কুসংসর্গী** *adj* keeping evil company; associating with undesirable persons.

কুসংস্কার *n* a popular belief held without reason; agelong practice in social or religious field that goes against common sense; superstition. **~মূলক** *adj* born out of superstition; based on erroneous notion; superstitious. **কুসংস্কারাচ্ছন্ন** *adj* rooted in superstition; engrossed in superstition; superstitious.

কুসীদ, কুশীদ *n* **1** the business of making loans at extortionate rates of interest; usury. **2** interest on loan, usually at very high rate. **~জীবী** *n* one who makes his living by lending out money at exorbitant rates of interest; a usurer. **~ব্যবহার** *n* the practice of usury.

কুসুম[১] *n* a kind of flower used in dying fabrics.

কুসুম[২] *n* **1** flower. **2** women's monthly course; menstruation. **3** a disease of the eye. **4** the yellow part of an egg; the yolk. **~কলি, ~কলিকা, ~কোরক** *n* the first shoot of a flower; a flower bud. **~কানন** *n* garden of flowers; flower-garden. **~কুন্তলা** *adj fem* with flowers stuck in the hair. **~কোমল, ~পেলব** *adj* soft as a flower. **~দাম** *n* **1** a garland; a wreath. **2** a heap of flowers. **~মালিকা** *n* **1** a little wreath of flowers. **2** a poetical metre in Sanskrit. **~শয্যা, ~শয়ন** *n* a soft bed; (fig) ease; comfort. **~স্তবক** *n* a bunch of flowers; a bouquet. **কুসুমাকর** *n* the season of flowers; the spring. **কুসুমাঞ্জলি** *n* handful of flowers. **কুসুমাদপি** *adj* more than a flower: কুসুমাদপি কোমল, softer than a flower. **কুসুমাসব** *n* the sap of flowers, the nectar or honey of a flower. **কুসুমিত** *adj* in blossom; full of blossoms. **কুসুমিতা** *fem.*

কুসুম[৩], **কুসম** *adj* moderately warm; lukewarm; tepid. **~ ~** *adj* in a small degree: ~~ গরম.

কুস্তি [P] *n* **1** the sport of wrestling; the skill of a professional wrestler. **~গির, ~বাজ** *n* a trained wrestler. **2** (fig) struggling with others for doing sth: টিকিট কিনতে রীতিমতো ~ করতে হয়েছে. **~ করা** *vi* engage in a wrestle; wrestle.

কুহক *n* **1** an apparently supernatural power causing wonderful and mysterious happenings; witchcraft; sorcery; magic; enchantment. **2** an artful trick; deception; delusion: কল্পনার ~. **কুহকী** *adj* practising the art of witchcraft, sorcery or magic. ❑*n* a magician; a wizard; a juggler; a sorcerer. **কুহকিনী** *fem.* a witch; a sorceress; a magician; a juggler.

কুহর *n* **1** a hole; a hollow; a cavity: কর্ণ~. **2** articulate human uttering; voice; tone.

কুহু, কুহূ *n* the sweet note or cooing of a cuckoo: **~কণ্ঠ** *n* the cuckoo. **~তান** *n* the melodious note of a cuckoo. **~রব** *n* **1** the soft; gentle call of a cuckoo. **2** the cuckoo.

কুহেলিকা, কুহেলি, কুহেলী *n* fog; mist. **~ময়, ~চ্ছন্ন** *adj* **1** overcast with mist; misty; foggy. **2** (fig) (of ideas) confused; obscure; indistinct.

কূচিকা *n* a painter's brush.

কূজন *n* the soft note or call of a bird; chirping; warbling, cooing. **~ করা** *vi* (of birds) make lively sweet notes; chirp; warble. **কূজিত** *adj* resounding with the chirping of birds.

কূট *adj* **1** sharp-witted; cunning; shrewd; subtle: ~বুদ্ধি. **2** difficult to disentangle; complicated; intricate: ~ প্রশ্ন. **3** false; fabricated: ~ সাক্ষ্য. **4** astute; scheming; crafty; opportune; diplomatic: ~নীতি. **5** full of angularities; delusive; crooked: ~ চরিত্র. **6** mischievous; tricky; deceptive: ~চাল. ❑*n* **1** the unintelligible couplets of the writings of Bedabyasha: ব্যাস~. **2** a peak of a mountain: চিত্র~. **3** the top of anything: প্রাসাদ~. **4** (rhet) a paradox, eg, an assertion or proposition seemingly absurd may yet contain a truth, (eg 'more haste, less speed'). **5** a heap of sth: অন্ন~. **~কচাল** *n* **1** obstacles and hindrances. **2** complication; complexity; intricacy. **3** fallacious reasoning; sophistry; useless argument. **~কচালে** *adj* given to captious reasoning. ❑*n* a captious or fallacious reasoner. **~কর্ম** *n* forgery; fraud; swindling; cheating. **~ঘাত** *n* malicious destruction of public property; sabotage. **~ঘাতী** *adj* of the nature of sabotage. ❑*n* a saboteur. **~তর্ক** *n* hair splitting argument; scholastic reasoning; sophistry. **~তার্কিক** *n* person. given to sophistry; a sophist. **~তুলা** *n* a false scale/balance. **~নীতি** *n* the art of conducting business between nation and nation; the skill in securing advantage in international relations; diplomacy. **~নৈতিক** *adj* pertaining to diplomacy; diplomatic. **~নীতিক** *n* a diplomat. **~প্রশ্ন** *n* an intricate or insoluble question; a puzzle; a riddle. **~বন্ধ** *n* a trap; a snare. **~বুদ্ধি** *n* guile; shrewdness; crookedness; craftiness. ❑*adj* crooked; wily; crafty; guileful. **~যুদ্ধ** *n* **1** diplomatic warfare; manoeuvering and counter manoeuvering in diplomacy. **2** unfair combat/war. **~সাক্ষী** *n* a false witness; a tutored witness. **~সাক্ষ্য** *n* false evidence; perjury.

কূটজ *n* a medicinal plant.

কূটস্থ *adj* **1** (phil) eternally uniform; unchanging (eg, God, soul, the sky). **2** (phil) hidden; invisible; latent: ~ চৈতন্য.

কূটাগার *n* **1** the top room of a building; a garret; an attic. **2** the watch tower of a fortress.

কূটাভাস ⇒ কূট *n* (4)

কূটার্থ *n* **1** a far-fetched or forced meaning. **2** an implied or implicit meaning. **3** a distorted meaning.

কূপ *n* **1** a pit sunk for water; a ring well; a draw-well; a hole; a cavity; a pore: লোম~. **~মণ্ডূক** *n* **1** (lit) a frog that lives in a well. **2** (fig) person of limited knowledge; person living in a narrow circle. **3** (fig) person of confined views and sentiments; a narrow minded person.

কূপি=কুপি

কূপোদক *n* water of a well.

কূয়া=কুয়া

কূর্চ *n* **1** brush made of animal-fur. **2** the space between the eyebrows; the eyelash. **3** bristly hair of one's beard. **4** a tuft of grass.

কূর্চিকা *n* **1** a painter's brush. **2** a needle.

কূর্পর **1** the joint of the arm; the elbow. **2** the joint which connects the foot with the leg; the ankle.

কূর্ম *n* **1** reptile covered with a flattened shell; a tortoise; a turtle. **কূর্মী** *fem.* **~ পুরাণ** *n* one of the eighteen Hindu Purana. **~পৃষ্ঠ** *n* the shell of a tortoise. **কূর্মাবতার** *n* the second incarnation of Vishnu.

কূর্মী[১] ⇒ কূর্ম

কূর্মী[২] *n* a sect among the Hindus.

কূল *n* **1** the edge of a river on either side; a bank: নদীর ~. **2** (fig) a haven; refuge; a shelter; a resort: অকূলে ~পাওয়া. **3** end; limit; termination: দুঃখের ~ নাই. **~ কিনারা** *n* **1** way of solution/settlement/redress. **2** deliverance; rescue; release; remedy. **~কিনারা পাওয়া** find a way out. **~কিনারাহীন** *adj* **1** without limit; unlimited; unbounded; endless. **2** (fig) having no prospect of solution/settlement. **~কিনারা দেখি না** I find no solution. **~ঙ্কষ, ~ঙ্কষা** *n* a river that devastates the riparian lands. **~প্লাবী** *adj* overflowing the banks; inundating the riparian lands. **~বতী** *n* **1** a river. **2** a chaste woman.

কৃকলাস, কৃকলাশ *n* **1** a small long-tongued lizard whose colour changes according to its background; a chameleon. **2** (fig) a showman assuming various forms.

কৃচ্ছ্র *n* **1** strenuous religious practice: ~ সাধনা. **2** severity of manners or life; rigour; austerity. ❑ *adj* stringent; rigid; severe; stern; austere: ~ ব্রত. **~ সাধন** *n* practising austerities; undergoing self-mortification. **~ সাধনা** *n* practice of austerities; act of undergoing a self imposed course of hardship and penance. **~সাধ্য** *adj* requiring strenuous effort/austere practice. **কৃচ্ছ্রাতিকৃচ্ছ্র** *n* an extremely rigid vow.

কৃৎ[১] *n* (gram) a verbal root.

কৃৎ[২] used as *suff* with nouns denoting a doer or performer of a thing, eg, কর্মকৃৎ, পথিকৃৎ, গ্রন্থকৃৎ.

কৃত[১] *n* the first of the four divisions of time or epochs according to Hindu scripture; the age of truth.

কৃত[২] *adj* **1** done; committed: ~ অপরাধ. **2** written; composed: কৃত্তিবাস~ রামায়ণ. **3** received; acquired; learnt: ~বিদ্য. **4** taken; accepted: ~দার. **5** appointed; employed; engaged: ~দাস. **6** constructed; built: শাহজাহান~ তাজমহল. **7** crowned with success; successful: ~কার্য. **~ঋণ** *adj* borrowed from other languages: ~ঋণ শব্দ. **~কর্মা, করিতকর্মা** *adj* **1** competent; adroit; skilful. **2** wise; experienced; accomplished: ~কর্মা ব্যক্তি. **~কাম** *adj* attaining one's end; having had one's desires fulfilled. **~কার্য** *adj* having had completed/finished one's task; successful. **~কার্যতা** *n*. **~নিশ্চয়** *adj* **1** determined; resolute. **2** sure; convinced. **~নিশ্চয় হওয়া** *vt* **1** be determined/resolute. **2** be thoroughly convinced. **~নিশ্চয়তা** *n*. **~পূর্ব** *adj* already done/ accomplished. **~সঙ্কল্প** *adj* resolved; determined. **~সঙ্কল্প হওয়া** *vi, vt* resolve; make up one's mind.

কৃতঘ্ন *adj* not grateful to one's benefactor; harming one's benefactor; ungrateful. **~তা** *n* ingratitude; ungratefulness.

কৃতজ্ঞ *adj* feeling or expressing gratitude to one's benefactor; thankful; grateful. **~তা** *n* emotion of the heart, excited by a favour received; gratitude; gratefulness. **~চিত্ত, ~হৃদয়** *n* a heart full of gratitude to one's benefactor. **~চিত্তে** *adv* with feelings of gratitude.

কৃতাঞ্জলি [কৃত+অঞ্জলি] *n* folded hands. ❑*adj* having one's palms cupped. **~পুটে** *adv* with one's hands folded (in supplication, etc).

কৃতান্ত [কৃত+অন্ত] *n* the angel (or god) who causes the end to human life.

কৃতাপরাধ [কৃত+অপরাধ] *adj* having committed a crime; criminal. ❑*n* a criminal; a convict.

কৃতার্থ [কৃত+অর্থ] *adj* **1** crowned with success; successful. **2** obliged by a kindness; তিনি দয়া করে এসে আমাকে ~ করলেন, he obliged me by his kind visit. **~ হওয়া** *vt* be obliged; be bound by a feeling of gratitude.

কৃতি *n* **1** anything that has been done/ performed; an act; a deed; a work: সু~, a good work. **2** composition; versification: কবি~. **3** effort; endeavour; enterprise: ~সাধ্য. **~স্বত্ব** *n* an official grant securing exclusive right to property in a process or an invention; a patent.

কৃতিত্ব *n* proficiency; skill; achievement.

কৃতী *adj* **1** skilled; proficient; dexterous; adroit. **2** earning fame for some remarkable achievement: ~ ছাত্র. **3** deeply read; learned; erudite.

কৃত্তিবাস *n* the celebrated composer of the Bengali version of the Ramayana. **কৃত্তিবাসী** *adj* composed by Krittibasa: কৃত্তিবাসী রামায়ণ.

কৃত্রিম *adj* **1** made by human art; not natural; artificial: ~ হ্রদ, ~ দাঁত, ~ ফুল. **2** made by human skill/ ingenuity: ~ রেশম. **3** not real or genuine; pretended: ~ অশ্রু, ~ ভালোবাসা. **~তা** *n* artificiality; falseness; pretension.

কৃদন্ত [কৃৎ+অন্ত] *adj* (gram) ending with the inflexion 'কৃৎ' : ~ শব্দ. ❑*n* words formed with the suffix 'কৃৎ' (eg পথিকৃৎ, কর্ম কৃৎ etc).

কৃপণ *adj* **1** miserly; niggardly; parsimonious. **2** mean; base; narrow-minded. **কৃপণা** *fem* . **~তা** *n* miserliness; niggardliness; parsimony. **~স্বভাব** *adj* niggardly by nature. **~স্বভাবা** *fem.*

কৃপা *n* **1** kindness; compassion; benignancy: ~সিন্ধু. **2** mercy; pity; clemency: ~র পাত্র. **3** favour; grace; sympathy: ~দৃষ্টি. **~ করা** *vi, vt* be kind to; pity. **~দৃষ্টি** *n* a kind look; a look of favour. **~দৃষ্টি করা** *vi* look with favour/ compassion; pity. **~দৃষ্টিপূর্বক** *adv* kindly; with sympathy. **~পাত্র** *n* object of pity; one who deserves pity/ sympathy. **~বর্ষণ** *n* a gesture of kindness/ benevolence. **~সিন্ধু** *n* **1** (lit) an ocean of kindness; (fig) a highly benevolent person. ❑*adj* merciful. **~হীন** *adj* unkind; merciless.

কৃপাণ *n* **1** a sword; a scimitar. **2** a short double edged weapon; a dagger. **~পাণি** *adj* wielding a sword in one's hand.

কৃমি *n* **1** an intestinal parasite; a worm. **2** a larva of a fly or other insect; a maggot. **গোল ~** a round worm. **ফিতা ~** a tape-worm. **সুতা ~** a thread-worm. **হুক ~** a hook-worm. **~জ** *adj* produced by worms. **~ল** *adj* full of worms.

কৃশ *adj* **1** emaciated; lean; thin; meagre. **2** weak; feeble. **~কায়** *adj* of a slender frame; lean and thin. **~তা** *n* leanness; thinness.

কৃষক *n* a tiller of soil; a cultivator.

কৃষাণ *n* **1** a peasant; a farmer. **2** one whose profession is rural labour; an agricultural labourer. **কৃষাণী** *fem.*

কৃষাণি *n* **1** agricultural work; cultivation of land. **2** the wages of a farm-hand. ❑*adj* **1** of or pertaining to agriculture. **2** befitting a farmer.

কৃষি *n* tillage of land; cultivation; agriculture; farming. **~কর্ম, ~কার্জ** *n* cultivation; agriculture. **~জ, ~জাত** *adj* produced by agriculture; agricultural. **~জাত দ্রব্য** *n* agricultural produce. **~জীবী** *adj* living by agriculture. ❑*n* a peasant; a cultivator; a farmer. **~বিদ** *adj* expert in the management of the land and the scientific cultivation of crops. ❑*n* an agronomist.

কৃষ্ট *adj* **1** ploughed; tilled; cultivated: ~ জমি. **2** attracted.

কৃষ্টি *n* **1** tilling of the soil; agriculture. **2** the culture of the mind for refinement. **3** state of development among a people as expressed in arts, science, etc.

কৃষ্ণ *n* **1** (myth) an incarnation of Vishnu (according to Hindu scripture). **2** Sri Krishna, the hero of the Mahabharata. ❑*adj* **1** dark complexioned; black or deep blue: ~কায়. **2** dark: ~ রাত্রি. **~কণ্ঠ** *n* god Shiva (according Hindu tradition). **~কলি** *n* kind of flower-plant or its flower. **~কীর্তন** *n* **1** 'Kirtana' song in glorification of Sri Krishna. **2** the lyric composed by Baru Chandidasa on the dalliance of Krishna. **~চন্দন** *n* the white sandal wood; *Santalum album*. **~চূড়া** *n* kind of flowering tree or its red and yellow flower. **~জীরা ~জীরক** *n* the black cumin. **~ তিথি** *n* any of the lunar days of the dark fortnight. **~দ্বৈপায়ন** *n* (myth) Vyasha, son of Parashara and Satyabati. **~পক্ষ** *n* the dark fortnight; the fortnight of the lunar month in which the moon gradually goes out of sight. **~প্রাপ্তি** *n* meeting death (according to Hindu tradition). **~ মুগ** *n* the black variety of pigeon pulse. **~যাত্রা** *n* open-air opera play enacting the life and activities of Sri Krishna. **~সার** *n* a species of deer; the antelope. **~সারথি** *n* the chariot-driver of Sri Krishna, ie, Arjuna (as represented in the Mahabharata). **~সীস** *n* sort of black metal; graphite. **কৃষ্ণা** *adj fem* **1** dark complexioned. **2** appellation of Draupadi (of the Mahabharata). **কৃষ্ণাগুরু** [কৃষ্ণ+অগুরু]= কৃষ্ণ চন্দন. **কৃষ্ণাজিন** *n* the skin of an antelope. **কৃষ্ণাভ** *adj* of a black taint; slightly black; blackish; darkish. **কৃষ্ণাষ্টমী** [কৃষ্ণ+অষ্টমী] *n* **1** the eighth lunar day of the dark fortnight of the month of Bhadra; the birth day of Sri Krishna. **2** the eighth lunar day of the dark fortnight.

কৃষ্য *adj* fit for ploughing; arable; cultivable.

কে *pron* **1** who; which: তোমাদের মধ্যে কে আগে এসেছো, which of you came first ? **2** an unknown person: কে ও, who is that? who goes there ? **3** how related: সে তোমার কে, what is he to you? **4** a certain: কে একজন অপেক্ষা করছে, someone/ a certain person is waiting. **কে কে** who? **কে কে এসেছিল** who are the people that came? **কে জানে,** who knows? there is no knowing. **কে জানে সে কোথায়** who knows where he is. I don't know where he is. **কে না** all; everybody. **কে না জানে একথা ?** who is there that doesn't know this? everybody knows this. কে বা possibly none (কে বা জানে কী তার রূপ?)

কেউ *pron* someone; anyone. ~**কেউ** some. ~-কেটা person of consequence or importance: সে মোটেই ~-কেটা নয়, he is indeed a man of consequence/ a big gun. ~ **না** ~ someone or other.

কেউটে *n* a hooded venomous snake; the cobra.

কেওকেটা=কেউকেটা⇒ কেউ

কেওড়া *n* the screwpine flower or its essence. ~**র পানি** *n* water perfumed with the essence of the screwpine flower.

কেঁচে গণ্ডুষ *n* doing a half done or unfinished work anew.

কেঁচো *n* a long worm that burrows in the soil; the earth-worm.

কেঁদে *infinite verb* participial form of কাঁদা: শিশুটি ~ উঠল, the baby started crying. **ছেলেটি** ~~ **বললো** the boy said weeping.

কেক [E] *n* mixture of flour, eggs, butter, sugar, etc baked; a cake or a piece of it.

কেকা *n* the call of a peacock; a peacock's note.

কেঙ্গারু, ক্যাঙ্গারু [E] *n* an Australian marsupial quadruped that moves forward by leaps and whose young are carried in an external abdominal pouch; the kangaroo.

কেচ্ছা [A] *n* **1** a tale; a story; an episode. **2** a scandal; calumny; malicious gossip : ওর ~ শোনোনি?

কেটলি, কেতলি [E] *n* a metal vessel with a spout and handle, used for boiling water, etc; a kettle.

কেটে participial form of **কাটা:** তাল কেটে গেল.

কেতকী *n* the screwpine flower or its tree.

কেতন *n* a standard of colours; a flag; a banner: ঐ নূতনের ~ ওড়ে.

কেতা[1] [A] *n* a piece; a part; a portion: এক ~ জমি.

কেতা[2] [A] *n* manner; method; custom; fashion; etiquette. ~**দুরস্ত** [A+P] *adj* conforming to all formalities; observant of all etiquette.

কেতাব=কিতাব

কেদার *n* **1** holy place for the Hindus in the Himalyas. **2** an appellation of Shiva.

কেদারা[1] [Pg] *n* a movable seat with or without handles; a chair.

কেদারা[2] *n* a musical mode.

কেন *adv* why; for what reason; wherefore. **যা-ই আসুক না** ~ let come what it may. ~**না** *conj* because; since: সে আসেনি, ~না সে অসুস্থ, he didn't come, because he is ill.

কেনা *vt* buy; purchase; acquire by payment. ❑*adj* bought; purchased. ❑*n* purchase; shopping; buying of. ~**কাটা** *n* purchases. ~**কাটা করা** *vi* make purchases. ~**কাটা করতে যাওয়া** go shopping. ~**দর** *n* cost price; the cost of a commodity. ~**বেচা** *n* buying and selling; trading. ~ **গোলাম** *n* a slave; a bondsman.

কেন্দ্র *n* **1** the middle point; the centre (as of a circle). **2** (geom) the central point of a circle. **3** a place of great activity, esp one to which people are attracted from surrounding places: বাণিজ্য~, শিক্ষা~. **4** (astrol) the fourth, seventh or tenth house from the birth house in the zodiac. **5** (geog) either of the two ends of the earth's axis; North pole; South pole. ~**গত** *adj* being in the centre; central. ~**বিমুখ, কেন্দ্রাতিগ** *adj* tending to fly from the centre; centrifugal. ~**স্থল** *n* the central point. **কেন্দ্রাভিগ, কেন্দ্রাভিমুখ** *adj* tending toward the centre; centripetal. **কেন্দ্রিত** *adj* lying, placed or drawn in the centre; centric. **কেন্দ্রীভূত** *adj* centralized; brought into the centre; placed in a centre. **কেন্দ্রীয়** *adj* pertaining to the centre; central.

কেবল *adj* **1** only; one; nothing else: ~ আপনিই আমার সহায়. **2** unending; continuous: ~ পানি আর পানি. **3** incessant; unceasing; continual: ~ কাঁদছে. ❑*adv* **1** just; just now: ~ এসেছি. **2** instantly: ~ বলেছি, অমনি রেগে আগুন.

কেবলা=কিবলা

কেবিন [E] *n* an apartment in a ship or in a hospital; a cabin.

কেবিনেট [E] *n* the council of ministers; the cabinet.

কেমন *adv* how; of what sort: ~ আছো, how do you do ? ~ **করে** by what means ? ❑*adj* **1** excellent; fine (sarcas): ~ জব্দ, হলো তো! **2** anxious; perturbed; disturbed: মন ~ করছে. ~~ *adj* suspicious; dubious; doubtful; not easy to understand clearly: তার কথাবার্তা ~~ মনে হচ্ছে. ~**তর** *adj* of what sort; queer; strange: ~তর লোক তুমি হে. ~ **যেন** *adj* not appearing all right: ~ যেন অসুস্থ. **কেমনে** *adv* by what means; in which way: তোমাকে কেমনে বুঝাই.

কেমিক্যাল [E] *adj* **1** made through chemical process: ~ বস্ত্র. **2** artificial; imitated: ~ সোনা.

কেয়া[1] *n* the screwpine flower or its tree.

কেয়া[2] [H] *adv* how fine/ excellent!: ~ মজা.

কেয়াম [A] *n* **1** the standing position in prayer. **2** standing in honour of the prophet's memory in a Milad Mahfil.

কেয়ামত [A] the Day of Resurrection; the Day of Judgement.

কেয়ার [E] *n* **1** care; attention; watchful regard: শরীরের প্রতি ~ নিও. **2** regard; fear: আমি তাকে ~ করি না. **3** address: চিঠিটা আমার কেয়ারে পাঠাও.

কেয়ূর *n* ornament for the arm; armlet.

কেরদানি [P] *n* **1** skilfulness; trickery. **2** a boast or brag: আর ~ দেখাতে হবে না.

কেরাত [A] *n* **1** correct recitation of the Holy Qoran. **2** recitation of the Holy Qoran with correct pronunciation and intonation.

কেরানি *n* one who is employed under another as a writer; a clerk. **~গিরি** *n* the profession of a clerk; clerkship. **মাছি মারা ~** (fig) an unintelligent worker who fails to use discretion where necessary.

কেরামত, কেরামতি [A] *n* **1** power; influence; dominance. **2** a supernatural feat; uncommon power of doing miracles; a miraculous act. **~কারী** *n, adj* **1** (one) possessing miraculous power. **2** person possessing power and influence.

কেরোসিন [E] *n* a lamp-oil from petroleum; kerosene.

কেলি *n* **1** the sport of love; love-making; amorous sport. **2** flirting for amusement; recreation; diversion; pastime. **~কদম্ব** *n* (myth) the *kadamba* tree at Mathura, the celebrated scene of dalliance between Radha and Krishna. **~কুঞ্জ** *n* a bower used or suitable for amorous sport. **~গৃহ** *n* a house for pleasure and pastime; a pleasure-house.

কেলেঙ্কার *adj* causing scandal; scandalous; infamous. **কেলেঙ্কারি** *n* **1** public reproach; scandal; shame; disgrace. **2** a scandalous act; a nasty affair.

কেলেন্ডার=ক্যালেন্ডার

কেল্লা [A] *n* a fortified town; a place of security; a stronghold; a fortress. **~দার** [A+P] *n* **1** the commanding officer of a fortress. **2** the governor of a garrison. **~ ফতে** *n* the conquest of a fort. **~ ফতে করা** *vi* capture a fort; (fig) achieve one's goal; realize one's end. **~ মাত করা** (fig) be successful in a hard task.

কেশ *n* the threadlike growths on the human scalp; hair. **~কলাপ, ~গুচ্ছ, ~দাম, ~পাশ** the tuft of hair. **~কীট** *n* a louse; lice. **~তৈল** *n* hair oil; hair tonic. **~প্রসাধন ~বিন্যাস** *n* hair- dressing; the combing and plating of hair. **~প্রসাধন করা** *vi* dress one's hair. **~স্পর্শ, কেশাগ্রস্পর্শ** *n* (fig) act of doing the least harm to: সে আমার কেশাগ্রও স্পর্শ করতে পারবে না, he can't harm me in the least.

কেশব *n* an appellation of Sri Krishna.

কেশর *n* **1** (bot) the pollen-bearing organ of a flower; stamen: পরাগ~, গর্ভ~. **2** the long, thick hair on the back of horses, lions, etc; mane.

কেশরী *n* **1** the lion. **2** animals with mane on the neck. **3** the chief one; the best one: বীর~, the chief among heroes; a lion of heroes.

কেশিয়ার=ক্যাশিয়ার

কেষ্ট *n* corrup of Krishna. **কষ্ট না করলে ~ পাওয়া যায় না** no pains, no gains. **~বিষ্টু** (sarcas) an important person; a big gun.

কেস [E] *n* a lawsuit: ফৌজদারি ~. **2** an affair; an incident: মজার ~. **3** (of a lawsuit or a disease) a patient; a client: ~টা খুব জটিল. **4** an almirah; a box; a covering; a container: শো~, বুক ~, চশমার ~.

কেহ=কেউ

কৈ=কই[1]

কৈকেয়ী *n* step mother of Ramchandra of the Ramayana.

কৈতব *n* **1** trickery; fraud; deceit; chicane; chicanery. **2** the act of gaming for money; gambling. **~বাদ** *n* **1** falsehood; telling lies. **2** flattery; sycophancy; cajolery. **~বাদী** *adj* a liar; a fraud; a gambler.

কৈফিয়ত, কৈফিয়ৎ [A] *n* showing cause or act of explaining (one's conduct, etc); an explanation. **~ চাওয়া** *vi* call to account; take to task; demand an explanation. **~ দেওয়া** *vi* account for; give an explanation.

কৈবর্ত *n* a fisherman by caste; a caste among the Hindus.

কৈবল্য *n* **1** (phil) state of being one and only one; soleness; absoluteness. **2** absolute identity with the divine essence; salvation. **3** release from worldly attraction or the influence of nature (according to Hindu philosophy). **~ দায়িনী** *adj fem* giving eternal salvation(according to Hindu philosophy). ❑*n* an appellation of goddess Durga.

কৈলাস *n* Kailasa mountain on the north of the Himalayas, which is, according to Hindu belief, the abode of Shiva. **~নাথ** *n* the lord of the Kailasa mountain; an appellation of Shiva. **~বাসিনী** *n, adj* (one) residing in the Kailasa mountain. ❑*n* an appellation of goddess Durga.

কৈশিক *adj* **1** resembling a hair. **2** pertaining to hair. ❑*n* one of the minute hair-like blood vessels; capillary: কৈশিকা নাড়ি.

কৈশোর *n* age from the birth to the fifteenth year; early youth; adolescence.

কোঁকড়া *adj* of a twisted or coiled form; curly; wavy.

কোঁচ, কোঁচা *n* kind of harpoon with sharp pointed skewers for catching fish.

কোঁচকানো *vt* cause to contract; shrink; shrivel. ❑*adj* wrinkled. shrivelled; contracted.

কোঁচড় *n* a fold of one's lower garment (as in holding sth): এক ~ ফুল, as many flowers as can be carried in a fold of one's garment. **~ পাতা** *vi* hold out a fold of one's garment to receive sth.

কোঁচা *n* the front tuck of the length of cloth worn by Hindus. **~নো** *vt* fold or plait into a tuck. ❑*adj* folded or plaited into a tuck. **~ দুলিয়ে** বেড়ানো *vi* (fig) pass time idly and in foppishness. **বাইরে ~র পত্তন ভিতরে ছুঁচোর কেত্তন** maintaining elegance in dress while one has no means of maintaining his family.

কোঁত *n* straining effort. **~ দেওয়া/ পাড়া** *vi* strain at voiding stool. **কোঁতানি** *n* straining at sth; hesitation to do sth. **কোঁতানো**=~ দেওয়া/পাড়া.

কোঁথ=কোঁত

কোঁদা=কুঁদা

কোকনদ *n* the red lotus; the red water-lily.

কোকিল *n* migratory bird famous for its sweet note; the cuckoo. **কোকিলা** *fem.* **~কণ্ঠ** *adj* sweet-voiced or melodious like the cuckoo. **~কণ্ঠী** *fem.* **কোকিলাসন** *n* sitting posture in the practice of **~কোকিলেক্ষু** *n* a reddish variety of sugarcane.

কোকেন [E] *n* an alkaloid substance obtained from the coca plant and used as a drug and as a local anaesthetic; cocaine.

কোচ *n* **1** the aborigines of Kochbihar in India. **2** a professional caste of fishermen. **3** a spear with barbs for fishing.

কোচমান [E] *n* person who drives a coach, esp that drawn by horses; a coachman (also কোচওয়ান).

কোজাগর *n* the day of the full moon in the month of Aswin-Kartik; the day on which the Hindus worship goddess Lakshmi. **কোজাগরী** *adj* connected with/ pertaining to this day.

কোট[১] [E] *n* a (sleeved) outer-garment; worn over the shirt; a coat.

কোট[২] *n* **1** a fort; fortress: রাজ~. **2** a garrison town: পাঠান~.

কোটনা,[১] কুটনা *n* act of chopping or cutting vegetables for the kitchen.

কোটনা[২] (*fem* কুটনি) *n* a pander who acts as an agent between an adulterer and adulteress; a male bawd. **~গিরি** *n* the profession or the role played by a pander. **~মি** *n* act of whispering malicious reports against a person.

কোটর *n* **1** a hollow of a tree; a hole: গাছের কোটরে পাখির বাসা. **2** a cavity into which anything is fitted; a socket: চক্ষু~. **~গত চক্ষু** sunken eyes.

কোটা[১]=কুটা

কোটা[২] [E] *n* a share or proportion assigned to each; a quota.

কোটাল[১]=কটাল

কোটাল[২]=কোতোয়াল

কোটি *n* a crore; ten millions: ~পতি, a millionaire.

কোটেশন [E] *n* **1** act of quoting; a passage quoted; an excerpt. **2** the naming of the price of a commodity or cost of a work; a price or cost specified.

কোঠা *n* a room in a building. **~বাড়ি** *n* a brick built house.

কোড [E] *n* **1** a digest of laws; a collection of rules. **2** a system of signals or special symbols for conveying messages rapidly or secretly; a code.

কোডিসিল [E] *n* a writing by way of supplement to a will; a codicil.

কোণ *n* (geom) **1** the inclination of two straight lines which meet in a point but have different directions; an angle: ত্রিভুজের ~. **2** the meeting place of two sides of a thing; a corner: ঘরের ~. **3** the narrow end or point of a thing: আঁখি~. **4** a pointed end: ছুরির ~. **5** the inner apartments of a house meant for women; zenana: বাবুটি সন্ধ্যা হতে না হতেই কোণে ঢোকেন. **~ঠাসা** *adj* **1** driven into a corner; cornered. **2** ignored; neglected. **~ঠাসা করা** *vt, vi* force into a corner; corner. **সন্নিহিত ~** (geom) one of the two adjacent angles formed by the inclination of one line to another which it meets; an adjacent angle. **সম~** *n* (geom) one of the two adjacent angles of 90°; a right angle. **~কোণী** *adj* right-angled. **সরল ~** *n* a straight angle. **সূক্ষ্ম ~** *n* an angle lesser than a right angle; an acute angle. **স্থূল ~** *n* an angle greater than a 90° angle; an obtuse angle.

কোতোয়াল *n* the police chief of the olden days in charge of a city; **কোতোয়ালি** *n* **1** the office of a kotwal. **2** the police headquarters. **কোতোয়ালি থানা** *n* the jurisdiction of the police administration in a town; an urban police station.

কোথা *adv, n* where; which place: ~ থেকে. ❑*adv* where; to which place: ~ যাবে. **~কার** *adj* **1** of which place: ~কার লোক. **2** of a contemptible place: ~কার কোন শয়তান. **3** (reproach) expressive of annoyance: দুষ্ট ~কার. **~য়** *adv* where; in what place. **~ও** *adv* at/in any place; anywhere. **~ও ~ও** at/ in some places. **~ থেকে** from where; whence; wherefrom.

কোদাল, কোদালি *n* a digging hoe; a spade. **কোদলানো** *vi, vt* dig with a spade. **~ দ্বারা খনন** *n* spadework.

কোন, কোন্ *pron, adj* **1** what; which; which one: ~টি ভালো, ~ জন, ~ দিকে. **2** one uncertain or indefinite: ~ দিন হয়তো চলে যাবে. ❑*adv* in what way, in which respect: তুমিই ~ সুবোধ ছেলে.

কোনা=কোণ. **~কুনি, ~কোনি** *adv* in a diagonal direction; from one angle to another of a quadrilateral figure. ❑*adj* lying in an oblique direction; extending from corner to corner; diagonal; slantwise. **~চে** *adj* on slant; aslant. ❑*adv* obliquely; not perpendicularly.

কোনাচ *n* the portion at a corner; the place near the corner.

কোনো *pron, adj* an indefinite person or thing; any; some; certain: ~ একদিন on a certain day; ~ এক লোক, some/ certain person; **~ এক সময়ে,** once upon a time; **~ দিন না ~ দিন,** some day or other. **যে ~ সময়ে** *adv* at anytime. **~ কালে** at any time. ~ কালে না never; at no time. ~ক্রমে/মতে *adv* in any way; any how; some how; by any means ~ক্রমে না by no means. ~খানে *adv* somewhere.

কোন্দল *n* a quarrel; a wrangle; a brawl. ~ করা *vi, vt* quarrel; wrangle, brawl.

কোপ[1] *n* **1** anger; rage; wrath. **2** displeasure; disgust; indignation. কোপে পড়া *vt* incur one's displeasure/ indignation/ wrath. ~কটাক্ষ, ~দৃষ্টি an angry look. ~কটাক্ষ করা cast an angry look. ~ন *adj* **1** easily irritated; irritable; peevish; wrathful. **2** angry; enraged. ~না *fem*. ~স্বভাব *adj* wrathful by nature; ill-tempered; easily irritated; peevish. কোপানল *n* the flame of anger. কোপান্বিত *adj* enraged; flown into a rage; indignant. কোপী *n* one who is angry/ irritable/ ill-tempered.

কোপ[2] [P] *n* a blow with a chopping implement: দা-এর ~. ~ মারা, ~ দেওয়া *vt* deal a blow/ strike with a sharp implement. কোপানো *vt* **1** strike a series of blow with a cutting tool. **2** dig/ turn up earth with a spade: মাটি কোপানো.

কোপ্তা [P] *n* a kind of meat preparation; a chop.

কোবিদ *adj* **1** deeply read; learned; scholarly. **2** skilful; dexterous; adroit.

কোমর [P] *n* part of the human body between the ribs and hips; the waist. ~বন্দ *n* girdle or belt for the waist. ~ বাঁধা *vt* **1** resolve (on doing a thing); fix up one's mind; be determined. **2** be up and doing to achieve one's end; try to do sth in right earnest.

কোমল *adj* **1** soft; tender: ~ শয্যা, ~ হৃদয়. **2** sweet; pleasant; gentle; graceful: ~ কণ্ঠ, ~ গন্ধ. **3** not strong; mild: ~ আলো, ~ পানীয়. ❑*n* (music) a note in the subdued scale: কড়ি ও ~. ~তা *n* softness; gentleness; tenderness; delicacy. ~মতি. ~ স্বভাব, ~প্রাণ, ~ চিত্ত *adj* of a mild disposition ; kind-hearted; soft-natured. কোমলাঙ্গী *adj fem* of a delicate frame. ❑*n* a frail and graceful woman. কোমলায়ন *n* act of tempering glass or metal by heat; annealing. কোমলায়ন করা *vt* anneal. কোমলাস্থি [~ +অস্থি] *n* an elastic substance from which bone is formed; cartilage.

কোম্পানি [E] *n* a group of people associated for business; partners in a firm; a private or a limited company. ~র আমল *n* the period of Indian History during which the country was ruled by the East India Company on behalf of the British crown.

কোয়া *n* the seed-vessel or pod of certain juicy fruits: কাঁঠালের ~, কমলালেবুর ~.

কোয়েল *n* (poet) the cuckoo. কোয়েলা *fem*.

কোরক *n* an unblown flower; a bud.

কোরণ্ড=কুরণ্ড

কোরবান, কুরবান [A] sacrifice made in the way of Allah; self-sacrifice in the struggle for attaining an end.

কোরবানি, কুরবানি [A] *n* the sacrifice of animals on the tenth of Zilhajj in celebration of Eidul Azha according to the Islamic Shariah.

কোরমা=কোর্মা

কোরা[1] [H] *adj* unbleached; brand-new: ~ কাপড়.

কোরা[2] =কুরা

কোরান, কোরআন, কুরআন [A] *n* the Holy Qoran containing the Divine Revelation to Prophet Muhammad(sm). ~ মজিদ *n* the Glorious Qoran. কোরানুল হাকিম *n* the Sagacious Qoran.

কোরেশ [A] *n* the famous Quraish clan of Mecca to which was born prophet Muhammad (sm).

কোর্ট [E] *n* a court of law; a court house.

কোর্টশিপ [E] *n* act of courting a woman in view of marriage; wooing.

কোর্মা [T] *n* sweet-tasting meat or fish curry prepared after the Turkish fashion.

কোল[1] *n* a clan of Indian aborigines.

কোল[2] *n* strip of shallow water in a river formed by the rise of sandy tract above the water level.

কোল[3] *n* the space between the knees and the waist available as a seat or support when one is seated; the lap: শিশুকে কোলে নেওয়া. ~-আকড়া *adj* tied to mother's lap. ~ আঁধার *n* darkness in front caused by one's own image. ~ জুড়ানো (of a child) being a joy to one's mother. কোলে ওঠা *vt, vi* climb up to the lap. কোলে তোলা/ নেওয়া take up in one's arms or on the lap. কোলে পিঠে করে মানুষ করা bring up with care. কোলের শিশু *n* a suckling.

কোল[4] *n* the foot, the bosom, the vicinity or the neighbourhood (of a thing): নদীর কোলে, পাহাড়ের কোলে.

কোলন [E] *n* (gram) a mark of punctuation; a colon.

কোলা *adj* fat; pot-bellied: ~ ব্যাঙ. ❑*n* a large barrel or cask bulging in the middle.

কোলাকুলি *n* embracing as a mode of warm greeting. ~ করা *vi* embrace.

কোলাহল *n* din and bustle; confused noise; uproar; tumult. ~পূর্ণ *adj* full of din and bustle; tumultuous.

কোষ *n* **1** a store; a repertory; a fund; a treasure: রাজ~. **2** a pod or seed-vessel of a fruit: কাঁঠালের ~. **3** a cover or a sack: অণ্ড~. **4** a sheath, a case or a scabbard: ~বদ্ধ অসি. **5** a bladder: পিত্ত~. **6** a dictionary; a lexicography, a glossary: শব্দ~. **7** a germ; a bud: পদ্ম~. ~কাব্য *n* an anthology of poems.

~কার a lexicographer. ~ গঠন (bio) cell formation. ~বদ্ধ *adj* (of a sword) sheathed. ~বদ্ধ করা *vt* sheathe (one's sword). ~মুক্ত *adj* (of a sword) drawn; unsheathed. ~মুক্ত করা *vt* unsheathe or draw ones sword.

কোষাগার *n* place where treasure is laid up; a treasury.

কোষাধ্যক্ষ *n* a treasurer; a cashier.

কোষ্ঠ[১] *n* an apartment of a house.

কোষ্ঠ[২] *n* the bowels; the intestine. ~কাঠিন্য constipation; costiveness. ~ পরিষ্কার হওয়া have a free evacuation of bowels; have a free motion.

কোষ্ঠী *n* (astrol) a figure or scheme of the heavens from which to cast nativities; a horoscope. ~ করা cast one's horoscope or nativity. ~ গণনা করা foretell the future of one's life from one's horoscope. ~গত *adj* horoscopic. ~গণক *n* a horoscopist; an astrologer. ~ গণনা *n* casting of horoscopes; horoscopy.

কোহিনুর [P] *n* **1** the famous diamond of this name. **2** (fig) the most valuable object.

কৌঁসুলি, কৌসুলি *n* advocate of a higher court of law; a counsel; a barrister.

কৌচ [E] *n* a seat for rest and ease; a couch.

কৌটা *n* small container or box with a lid.

কৌটিল্য *n* **1** crookedness; craftiness; double-dealing. **2** hypocrisy; insincerity; guile. **3** Chanakya, the famous minister of Chandragupta, the Maurya emperor.

কৌণিক *adj* pertaining to angle; angular. ~তা *n* angularity.

কৌতুক *n* fun; a joke; a jest. ~ করা *vi* make a fun; crack a joke. ~জনক *adj* funny; amusing; interesting; exciting mirth; curious. ~প্রিয় *adj* fond of fun; jocular; jocose. playful; full of quips and cranks.

কৌতূহল *n* eagerness to know; curiosity; inquisitiveness. ~জনক *adj* exciting curiosity; curious. ~ নিবৃত্তি *n* satisfaction of curiosity. ~ নিবৃত্তি করা satisfy one's curiosity. কৌতূহলী *adj* curious; eager.

কৌন্সিল [E] *n* an assembly for consultation; a body of men designated/ elected to advise the authority; a council.

কৌমার্য *n* the state of bachelorhood or virginity.

কৌমুদী *n* **1** moonlight; moonbeam (also কৌমুদিনী ধন). **2** the full moon of the month of Kartik. ~পতি *n* the lord of moonlight; the moon.

কৌরব *n* **1** the progeny of king Kuru of the Mahabharata. **2** the sons of Dhritarashtra; Durjodhana and his ninty-nine brothers. কৌরব্য, কৌরবেয় *adj* of the dynasty of Kuru.

কৌলিক *adj* pertaining to a family or clan; traditional to a family/ clan: ~ প্রথা.

কৌলিন্য *n* noble descent; aristocracy; nobility of birth.

কৌশল *n* **1** knowledge united with dexterity; skill; dexterity; adroitness: কর্ম~. **2** an artful device; artifice; an expedient means to attain an end; a trick; a stratagem: কৌশলে কার্যসিদ্ধি. **3** an invention; a contrivance: শিল্প~. ~ করা *vt, vi* play a trick; devise (a means) contrive. কৌশলী *adj* tactful; skilful; dexterous; artful; wily; crafty. কৌশলে *adv* tactfully; artfully; by contrivance.

কৌশল্যা *n* mother of Sri Ramchandra of the Ramayana.

কৌশিক[১] *n* Biswamitra, the son of Kushika, the sage.

কৌশিক[২], **কৌষিক** *adj* made of silk; silken.

কৌসুলি⇒কৌঁসুলি

ক্বচিৎ *adv* **1** scarcely; hardly; rarely; seldom. **2** at any place; anywhere.

ক্যাঁক *int* (onom) expressing sudden pain. ~ ~ করা *vi* express annoyance or anger by uttering the word in a harsh voice.

ক্যাঁচ *int* suggesting the sound of chopping. ~~, ~র ~র *int* denoting a repeated creaking sound. ~ক্যাঁচানি *n* creaking noise. ~ ~ করা *vi* make creaking or grating noise. ~র ম্যাচর *int, n* confused noise of talking together: বাচ্চাদের ~র ম্যাচর.

ক্যাঁট ক্যাঁট, ক্যাট ক্যাট *int* word denoting piercing sound; talking sth repeatedly or harshly: বেশি ~ করো না.

ক্যাটালগ [E] *n* a list or register of books or other goods compiled systematically; a catalogue.

ক্যাডেট [E] *n* a member of a school which prepares men to hold commissions in the forces; a cadet.

ক্যানভাস[১] [E] *n* act of soliciting votes for winning an election ; canvass. ❑ *vt, vi* solicit votes from door to door.

ক্যানভাস[২] [E] *n* strong coarse cloth used for tents, sails, bags, etc and by artists for oil-paintings.

ক্যান্সার [E] *n* =কর্কট

ক্যানটিন [E] *n* a refreshment bar, esp in a camp, factory or institution; a canteen.

ক্যামেরা [E] *n* an apparatus for taking photographs; a camera.

ক্যাম্পাস [E] *n* the grounds of a school, college or university; campus.

ক্যাম্বিস, ক্যামবিস [E] *n* a strong coarse cloth made of hemp, etc for making bags, etc and for painting on; canvas.

ক্যারাম, ক্যারোম [E] *n* a kind of game played on a square board with 19 pellets and a striker; caroms.

ক্যারিকেচার [E] *n* ludicrous and exaggerated imitation of someone or sth for amusement; caricature.

ক্যালেন্ডার [E] *n* a list of days and months in a given year with the marking of holidays and days of special interest; a calendar.

ক্যাস্টর অয়েল [E] *n* natural medicinal oil with purgative action obtained from *Ricinas communes*; castor-oil.

ক্রন্দন *n* weeping; sobbing; crying; waiting. ~ **করা** *vi* weep; cry; lament; wail.

ক্রন্দসী *n* **1** heaven and earth; the universe. **2** *fem* a wailing woman.

ক্রম *n* **1** one of a series; a grade: ক্রমে ক্রমে. **2** order; sequence; procedure: নির্মাণ-~. **3** accordance; agreement; conformity: আদেশ-ক্রমে. **4** a step or pace; course: কালক্রমে. **~ণ** *n* act of pacing/ stepping/ going. **~নিম্ন** *adj* sloping downwards; declinations; inclining; slanting. **~নিম্নতা** *n* downward slope; declivity; gradual decrease or inferiority. **~বর্ধমান** *adj* increasing or developing gradually. **~বর্ধিত** *adj* increased or developed gradually. **~বিকাশ** *n* gradual development; evolution. **~বিকাশবাদ** *n* theory of evolution. **~ভঙ্গ** *n* break of continuity. **~শ** *adv* step by step; gradually; by degrees, in succession: ~শ প্রকাশ্য.

ক্রমাগত *adj* **1** continuous; continued : ~ কাজ. **2** coning gradual; successive; serial. ❑*adv* continuously; continually; successively.

ক্রমানুয় *n* **1** a serial order or succession. **2** regular order of a series; continuity. **ক্রমানুয়ে** *adv* in serial order; in due succession by turns; serially; gradually.

ক্রমায়ত *adj* **1** successive; serial; gradual; continuous. ~ **আয়বৃদ্ধি** increasing return. ~ **গুণফল** continued product. ~ **সংখ্যা** serial number.

ক্রমে ক্রমে *adv* gradually ; by degrees; step by step; successively.

ক্রমেল, ক্রমেলক *n* the camel.

ক্রমোৎকর্ষ *n* **1** gradual progress. **2** gradual advance from a rudimentary condition to one of more complex and higher character; evolution.

ক্রমোন্নত [ক্রম+উন্নত] *adj* **1** gradually rising/ ascending. **2** gradually improving. **ক্রমোন্নতি** *n* **1** gradual rise or ascent; acclivity. **2** promotion; advancement. **ক্রমোন্নতিশীল** *adj* **1** gradually improving/ rising/ ascending. **2** making steady progress; progressive.

ক্রয় *n* purchase; buying. ~ **করা** *vtvi* purchase; buy. **~বিক্রয়** *n* buying and selling; trading.

ক্রান্তি *n* **1** transition from one place, state or topic to another; transit. **2** seizure by a disease, attack. **3** act or process of moving; motion. **4** change of state or condition. **5** the apparent path of the sun in the sky; the ecliptic. **~কাল** *n* the period of transition; transitional period. **~পাত** *n* (astron) the two points of intersection of the equator and the ecliptic; the equinoctial points; (geog) the time when the sun passes over the equator, and day and night are of equal length; the equinox. **~বৃত্ত** *n* (geog) line of latitude 23°27′ north (Tropic of Cancer) or south (Tropic of Capricorn) of the equator; the tropics.

ক্রিকেট [E] *n* open-air game played with bats, ball and wickets; cricket.

ক্রিটিক [E] *n* one skilled in judging literary or artistic work; a reviewer; a critic.

ক্রিয়মান *adj* in the state of being done/ made.

ক্রিয়া *n* **1** work; action; act: ভোজন ~. **2** Hindu funeral rite: অন্ত্যেষ্টি~. **3** the part of speech which affirms what a thing is, does or what is becoming of sb or sth: সকর্মক ~, অকর্মক ~, ~বিশেষণ. **~কর্ম** *n pl* performance/ observance of social or religious ceremonies. **~কলাপ, ~কাণ্ড** *n pl* deeds; functions; actions; activities. **~বাচক** *adj* (gram) derived from a verb; verbal. ❑*n* a noun derived from a verb. **~বিশেষণ** (gram) *n* an adverb. **~শীল** *adj* **1** given to work; diligent; active. **2** engaged in work; working; operative. **~সক্ত** *adj* **1** devoted to work; diligent; active. **2** devoted to religious rites. **~সক্তি** *n* devotion to work; diligence. **~সিদ্ধ** *adj* successful by repeated acts.

ক্রীড়ক *adj* playing; showing physical feats; exhibiting shows. ❑a player; a sportsman; a showman.

ক্রীড়ন *n* act of playing; sporting. **~ক** *n* plaything; a toy; a puppet; (fig) a person who is a mere fool; a cats paw. **ক্রীড়নীয়** *adj* fit to be played with; playable.

ক্রীড়া *n* **1** play; sport : জল~. **2** amusement; joke; jest; fun. **3** show of physical feats; acrobatics; wrestling: মল্ল~. ~ **করা** *vi vt* play; sport. **~কন্দুক** *n* playing ball; a ball. **~কৌতুক** *n pl* sports and pastime; amusements and merriment. **~চ্ছলে** *adv* sportingly; playfully; out of fun. **~ভূমি** *n* a play-ground. **~সক্ত** *adj* fond of play or sport; playful; sportive.

ক্রীত *adj* purchased; bought.

ক্রীতদাস *n* person wholly subject to another ; a slave; a bondman. **ক্রীতদাসী** *n fem* a slave woman; a slave-girl. **~ত্ব** *n* slavery. **~বৎ** *adj* slavish.

ক্রীতক *n* a son taken from parents for money.

ক্রুদ্ধ *adj* enraged; indignant; wrathful.

ক্রুশ [E] *n* the cross consisting of two timber pieces placed transversely on which Jesus Christ was crucified; the symbol of Christian religion. **~বিদ্ধ** *adj* crucified.

ক্রূর *adj* **1** crooked-minded; mischievous. **2** hard-hearted; unfeeling; pitiless; cruel. **~তা** *n* crookedness; malice; spite; envy. **~কর্মা** *adj* relentless; unrelenting; merciless; pitiless. **~মতি** *adj* evil-minded; malicious; mischievous.

ক্রেতব্য *adj* worth-buying; purchasable; worthy of purchasing.

ক্রেতা *adj, n* one who purchases; a purchaser; a buyer; a customer.

ক্রেপ [E] *n* a thin, transparent stuff of crisp texture; crape.

ক্রেয় *adj* **1**=ক্রেতব্য. **2** that which is to be or ought to be purchased/ bought.

ক্রোক [A] *n* legal seizure of movable property for debts or arrear of rents; distraint of goods. **মাল~** *n* attachment of movables. **~ করা** *vt* distrain; seize; attach. **ক্রোকি** *adj* **1** that which has been distrained/attached: ক্রোকি সম্পত্তি, property of distraint. **2** pertaining to distraint: ক্রোকি পরওয়ানা, warrant of distraint.

ক্রোটন [E] *n* beautifully foliated hedge-plant; croton.

ক্রোড়=কোল৩

ক্রোধ *n* anger; rage; wrath; fury; passion. **~ উদ্দীপন করা** *vi* incite/ incense/ inflame to anger. **~ করা** *vi* be angry/ incensed. **~ন** *adj* easily provoked to anger; irritable; passionate. **~বহ্নি, ক্রোধানল** *n* flame of anger; rage. **~ভরে** *adv* angrily; indignantly; in a fit of rage. **ক্রোধাগার** *n* (of a Hindu queen) room in which to retire when quarreling with husband. **ক্রোধান্ধ** *adj* blinded with rage. **ক্রোধান্ধ হয়ে** *adv* blind with rage. **ক্রোধান্বিত, ক্রোধাবিষ্ট** *adj* angry; furious; enraged. **ক্রোধিত** *adj* provoked to anger; excited. **ক্রোধী** *adj* wrathful; of violent temper. **ক্রোধোদ্দীপক** *adj* exciting anger. **ক্রোধোদ্দীপন** *n* excitement to anger. **ক্রোধোদ্দীপ্ত** *adj* provoked to anger; enraged; infuriated. **ক্রোধোদ্দীপ্ত হওয়া** *vi* fly into rage; burst into anger. **ক্রোধোন্মত্ত** *adj* maddened or incensed with rage; furious. **ক্রোধোপসম** *n* pacification of anger; appeasement of wrath.

ক্রোর =কোটি

ক্রোশ *n* **1** measure of distance equal to approximately 8000 cubits or a little more than two miles. **2**=আক্রোশ.

ক্রৌঞ্চ *n* a species of stork. **ক্রৌঞ্চী** *fem.* **~মিথুন** *n pl* male and a female stork; a pair of storks.

ক্লান্ত *adj* harassed with toil/ labour; fatigued; tired; wearied.

ক্লান্তি *n* fatigue; weariness. **~কর** *adj* wearisome; tiresome; fatiguing. **~নাশক, ~হর** *adj* allaying fatigue; relieving tiredness/ weariness; refreshing.

ক্লাব [E] *n* an association for some common objects; the meeting place of such association.

ক্লাস [E] *n* **1** a category, a type, kind, sort, a class or a division of things according to some common characteristics, eg a distinction in the style and comfort of accommodation on a train or ship according to the price paid: ফার্স্ট ~, সেকেন্ড ~. **2** a group of students studying the same subject or at the same level: ~ ফোর, ~ ফাইভ. **3** a division of candidates according to their success in an examination: ফার্স্ট ~, সেকেন্ড ~. **4** an economic and social division of society: আপার ~, মিড্‌ল ~. **~ফ্রেন্ড** *n* class-mate; friend reading in the same class. **ক্লাসে ওঠা** *vi* be promoted to a higher class. **ক্লাসে তোলা** *vt* promote (one) to a higher class.

ক্লাসিক [E] *n* **1** a work of art or literature of established excellence and value. **2** a poet, an author or an artist of the highest rank of merit. ❑*adj* of the highest rank of excellence and merit; classic. **ক্লাসিক্যাল** *adj* of the highest excellence: ক্লাসিক্যাল সঙ্গীত.

ক্লিষ্ট *adj* one who is aggrieved/ afflicted/ distressed; troubled or stricken with sorrow. **2** wearied; fatigued; exhausted. **ক্লিষ্টতা, ক্লেশ** *n*.

ক্লীব *n* **1** an asexual being. **2** a sexually impotent person; a man divested of manliness. ❑*adj* cowardly; unmanly; impotent; neuter. **~ত্ব** *n* impotence; absence of virility; timidity; the condition of a eunuch. **~লিঙ্গ** *n* (gram) the neuter gender.

ক্লেদ *n* **1** liquid filthy foul water. **2** filth; discharge from within one's body, eg pus, sweat, saliva, etc. **3** humidity; moisture. **4** (fig) mental pain or discontent excited by another's success/ superiority; envy; malice: মনের ~. **কেদাক্ত** *adj* besmeared with filthy matter; soiled; dirty.

ক্লেশ *n* **1** affliction of the body; pain; trouble: শারীরিক ~. **2** affliction of the mind; anguish grief: মানসিক ~. **ক্লেশিত** *adj* suffering from pain of either body or mind; afflicted; distressed. **~ দেওয়া** *vi* oppress; torture; trouble. **~ পাওয়া** be pained/ distressed/ troubled; suffer. **~কর** *adj* painful; distressing; troublesome. **ক্লেশার্জিত** *adj* acquired with toil and trouble.

ক্লোম *n* **1** (anat) either of the two organs of respiration in animals; lung. **2** (anat) the small pear-shaped membranous sac on the underside of the liver, to receive the bile; gall-bladder. **3** (anat) either of the tow glands which secrete the urine; the kidney. **~-নালিকা** *n* (anat) the passage from lungs to mouth; the trachea; the wind-pipe. **~ শাখা** *n* either of the two forks of the windpipe; bronchus.

ক্ষওয়া, ক্ষয়িত, ক্ষওয়ানো ⇒ খওয়া

ক্ষণ *n* 1 word denoting measure of time; a moment; an instant; a while: ~মাত্র. 2 a period of time: এতো~ কোথায় ছিলে? 3 a particular point of time: শুভ~, an auspicious moment. 4 a short period of time: ~স্থায়ী. **অশুভ ~** *n* an evil hour; an inauspicious moment. **কিছু~** *n* some time; a short while. ❑*adv* for some time; for a while: তিনি এখানে কিছু~ ছিলেন. **কু~**=অশুভ ~. **প্রতি~** *adv* every moment; always; constantly. **বহু~** *n* a long time. ❑*adv* for/ during a long time. **শুভ~** *n* an auspicious moment. **সর্ব~** *adv* at all times; always; continually. **~কাল** *n* a moment; an instant. ❑*adv* for a moment. **~কাল পরে** *adv* shortly after; a little after. **~কাল পূর্বে** *adv* shortly before. **~জন্মা** *adj* 1 born under a lucky star/ in an auspicious moment. 2 highly gifted; exceptionally brilliant; most distinguished. **~দা** *n* the night. **~ধ্বংসী** *adj* perishing in a moment; momentary; transitory; ephemeral; frail. **~ পরে** *adv* shortly after; a little later. **~প্রভ** *adj* flashing/ gleaming only for a moment. **~প্রভা** *n* the lightning. ❑*adj* frail; fragile; perishable. **~মাত্র** *adv* only for a moment; for an instant. **~স্থায়িত্ব** *n* transitoriness; transience. **~স্থায়ী** *adj* lasting for a moment; momentary. **ক্ষণিক** *adj* momentary; transient; instantaneous. ❑*n* a moment : ক্ষণিকের অতিথি.

ক্ষণে *adv* in a moment. **~ ক্ষণে** *adv* every moment; often; every now and then; frequently.

ক্ষণেক *n* one moment; instant. ❑*adv* for a moment: ~ দাঁড়াও, wait a minute; stay a while.

ক্ষত *n* 1 a wound; an ulcer. 2 a part of the body cut or wounded; a cut ; a bruise. 3 a boil; a sore. ❑*adj* hurt; wounded; injured; ulcerated. **~চিহ্ন** *n* mark of a wound or ulcer; a scar. **~জ** *adj* arising from a sore or wound. **~নাশক** *adj* healing up injury/ wound. **~বিক্ষত** *adj* bruised or injured all over. **~যোনি** *adj* (of a woman) one who has lost virginity.

ক্ষতাশৌচ *n* impurity of one's person caused by hemorrhage or discharge of blood from a wound.

ক্ষতি *n* 1 harm; evil; injury. 2 loss; damage; misuse. 3 depreciation; decay. **~ করা** *vt, vi* injure; harm; cause damage or loss. **~ হওয়া** *vi* sustain a loss; suffer an injury/ damage. **~ কি?** what's the harm? **~ নেই** no harm. **~কর, ~কারক** *adj* harmful ; injurious; detrimental; prejudicial. **~গ্রস্ত** *adj* sustaining/ suffering/ incurring a loss. **~গ্রস্ত করা** *vt* cause a loss/ damage to. **~গ্রস্ত হওয়া** *vi* sustain/ suffer a loss or damage. **~পূরণ** *n* compensation: যুদ্ধের ~পূরণ, indemnity/ reparations of war. **~পূরণ করা** *vt,vi* compensate; indemnify. **~পূরণ দেওয়া** *vt* pay damages; pay compensation. **~বৃদ্ধি** *n* loss or gain. **~বৃদ্ধি না হওয়া** have nothing to gain or lose.

ক্ষত্র, ক্ষত্রিয় *n* the second caste amongst Hindus; the Kshatriya or warrior caste. **ক্ষত্রকর্ম** *n* activities becoming a Kshatriya. **~ধর্ম** *n* the Kshatriya's assigned duty of defending the realm. **~ নারী** *fem* a Kshatriya woman (also ক্ষত্রিয়াণী), **ক্ষত্রোচিত; ক্ষত্রিয়োচিত** *adj* becoming a Kshatriya.

ক্ষম *adj* (used as *suff*)able; capable: কর্ম~.

ক্ষমতা *n* 1 power; might; ability; strength; efficiency; proficiency; capacity. 2 influence; control. **~প্রিয়** *adj* power loving. **~প্রিয়তা** *n* love of power. **~বান, ~শালী** *adj* powerful; mighty; strong; influential. **~বতী, ~ শালিনী** *fem*. **~হীন** *adj* powerless; lacking power or influence.

ক্ষমা *n* forgiveness; forbearance. **~ করা** *vt* forgive; pardon; excuse. **~ চাওয়া** *vi* ask for pardon/ forgiveness; apologize. **~ মহতের লক্ষণ** to forgive is divine. **~ প্রার্থনা** *n* begging pardon; asking for forgiveness. **~ প্রার্থনা করা** *vi* beg pardon; ask for forgiveness. **~শীল** *adj* forgiving; forbearing; compassionate.

ক্ষয় *n* 1 gradual loss or decrease; growing lesser and lesser; erosion; waning: চন্দ্রের ~. 2 destruction; death; annihilation: শত্রু~. 3 waste; loss: অর্থ~. 4 defeat: ধর্মের জয় অধর্মের ~. 5 end; termination. 6 tuberculosis; phthisis: ~ রোগ. **~ করা** *vt* waste; destroy; lose. **~ পাওয়া** *vt* wear off/ out; be wasted; corrode; wane. **~কারক** *adj* causing decay/ loss/ waste. **~ক্ষতি** *n* wear and tear. **~প্রাপ্ত** *adj* worn-out; decayed. **ক্ষয়িষ্ণু** *adj* perishable; decaying.

ক্ষরণ *n* secretion; oozing ; exudation; dripping : রক্ত~. **ক্ষরিত** *adj* oozed out; exuded. **ক্ষরিত হওয়া** *vi* ooze out; exude; drip.

ক্ষাত্র *adj* pertaining to Kshatriyas.

ক্ষান্ত *n* ceased; desisted; stopped. **~ করা** *vt* cause to forbear/ desist; stop. **~ দেওয়া** *vi* cease. **~ হওয়া** *vi* desist; cease; stop. **ক্ষান্তি** *n* cessation: desisting; stoppage; forbearance.

ক্ষার *n* a basic salt; alkali. **~ক** *n* 1 a chemical base; alkali. 2 a washerman. **ক্ষারিকা** *fem*. **ক্ষারকীয়** *adj* alkaline. **~ পানি** *n* alkali water; alkaline water; salt water. **~ ধাতু** alkali metal. **~মিতি** *n* alkalimetry. **~ মৃত্তিকা** *n* alkaline earth; fuller's earth.

ক্ষারণ *n* 1 act of causing to ooze out; act of making or becoming liquid. 2 slandering; stigmatization; corruption.

ক্ষারিত *adj* 1 melted; liquefied. 2 slandered; stigmatized.

ক্ষারীয় *adj* of, concerning, or having the nature of an alkali. **~ সন্ধান** *n* alkaline fermentation.

ক্ষালন *n* 1 act of washing: বস্ত্র ~. 2 act of exonerating (one) of a charge or sin: দোষ ~

পাপ ~. ~ **করা** *vt* wash; cleanse; exonerate; purify. **ক্ষালিত** *adj* washed ; cleansed; purified.

ক্ষিতি *n* the earth. ~**জ** *adj* grown on the soil; earth-grown. ~**তল** *n* the surface of the earth; the ground. ~**ধর** *n* a mountain. ~**নাথ**, ~**প**, ~**পতি**, ~**পাল** *n* a ruler; a king. ~**রুহ** *n* a large tree.

ক্ষিপ্ত *adj* **1** (of persons) affected with violent agitation of mind; frenzied; distracted; maddened. **2** (of animals) violently excited; frantic; furious; rabid; mad. **3** thrown over; ejected; scattered. ~ **হওয়া** *vi* go mad; be frenzied/distracted/maddened. ~ **কুকুর** rabid dog. **ক্ষিপ্তা** *fem*. ~**তা** *n* mental distraction; frenzy; madness; derangement.

ক্ষিপ্যমান *adj* in the state of being ejected; being cast away.

ক্ষিপ্র *adj* **1** having the power to move at fast pace; moving with speed; speedy; swift; fleet. **2** acting promptly; prompt; quick. ❑*adv* swiftly; quickly; speedily; promptly; rapidly. ~**কারী** *adj* ready in action; agile; prompt; quick. ~**কারিতা** *n* quickness in action; promptness; agility. ~**গতি** *adj* swift-moving; fast-moving; fast; swift; quick; speedy; agile. ❑*n* swift motion. ~**তা** *n* swiftness; quickness; promptness; rapidity. ~ **বেগে** *adv* swiftly; quickly; rapidly. ~**হস্ত** *adj* swift-handed; neat-handed; nimble. ~**হস্তে** *adv* swift-handedly; swiftly; quickly; promptly.

ক্ষীণ *adj* **1** having relatively little flesh on the body; lean and thin: ~ দেহ. **2** reduced to a slender position; decayed; emaciated; thin: ~ চন্দ্র. **3** narrow in circumference; thin; slim; slender: ~ কটি. **4** very little; negligible: ~আশা. **5** weak; feeble: ~ দৃষ্টি. **6** meagre; faint; indistinct; insufficient: ~ আলো. **7** subdued; low: ~ কণ্ঠ. **ক্ষীণা** *fem*. ~ **করা** *vt* make slender or thin; attenuate; diminish; reduce; enfeeble. ~ **হওয়া** *vi* become lean or thin; wane; weaken; fade. ~ **আশা** *n* faint hope. ~ **আলো** *n* dim light. ~ **কণ্ঠ** *n* feeble or low voice. ~**কণ্ঠ** *adj* feeble-voiced. ~**কণ্ঠে** *adv* in a faint/feeble voice. ~**কায়** *adj* slender-bodied; slim; slender. ~**কায়া** *fem*. ~**চন্দ্র** *n* the waning moon; the moon on the wane. ~**চেতা** *adj* weak-minded; feeble-hearted. ~**জীবী** *adj* having low vitality; frail; week; feeble. ~**তা**, ~**ত্ব** *n* slenderness; leanness; feebleness. ~**দৃষ্টি** *adj* weak-sighted ~**দেহ**=~কায়. ~**প্রাণ**=~জীবী. ~**বল** *adj* enfeebled; weakened. ~**বুদ্ধি** *adj* dull-witted; of weak intellect. ~**মতি** *adj* weak-minded. ~**মধ্য** *adj* of a slender waist. ~**মধ্যা** *fem*. ~**শ্বাস** *adj* with a failing breath. ~**স্বর** *n* faint or feeble voice. **ক্ষীণাঙ্গ**=~কায়.

ক্ষীয়মাণ *adj* in the state of decay; in the waning state; declining; perishing.

ক্ষীর *n* **1** milk condensed by boiling. **2** the milky juice of certain plants; vegetable milk; latex. ~**মোহন** *n* kind of sweet. ~**সমুদ্র/ সাগর** *n* (myth) one of the seven seas; a sea of milk spoken of in Hindu Purana.

ক্ষীরা *n* a small variety of cucumber.

ক্ষীরোদ=ক্ষীরসমুদ্র ⇒ ক্ষীর. ~**তনয়/ নন্দন** *n* the moon. ~**তনয়া** *fem* goddess Lakshmi.

ক্ষুণ্ণ *adj* saddened on account of frustration or for an offence given by sb: ~ মন. **2** lowered; humbled: গৌরব ~ হওয়া. **3** incomplete; mutilated; lacking in perfection: সৌন্দর্য ~. **4** baffled; restricted; stopped: গতি ~. ~ **হওয়া** *vi* be offended/grieved/disappointed. ~**মনা** *adj* disappointed; grieved; offended.

ক্ষুৎ[১] *n* hunger; appetite: ~পিপাসা. ~**কাতর** *adj* stricken with hunger; suffering from hunger. ~**পিপাসা** *n* hunger and thirst. ~**পীড়িত**=~কাতর.

ক্ষুৎ[২] *n* act of sneezing; a sneeze.

ক্ষুদ্র *adj* **1** not tall; dwarf; short: ~কায়. **2** small; petty; tiny: ~ প্রাণী. **3** narrow-minded; mean: ক্ষুদ্রাত্মা. **4** poor; low; insignificant: ~ ব্যক্তি. **5** not spacious; small in size; little: ~ গৃহ. **6** trifling; trivial; trashy; negligible: ~ বিষয়, ~ বস্তু. **ক্ষুদ্রা** *fem*. ~**তম** *adj* the smallest. ~**তর** *adj* smaller. ~**তা**, ~**ত্ব** *n* smallness; narrowness; meanness; insignificance; triviality. ~**চেতা** *adj* mean-minded. ~**প্রাণ** *adj* **1** having short span of life; short-lived. **2** mean-minded. **ক্ষুদ্রান্ত্র** *n* the small intestine. **ক্ষুদ্রাদপি** ~ *adj* the smallest of the small. **ক্ষুদ্রায়তন** *adj* small in size. **ক্ষুদ্রাশয়**=~চেতা.

ক্ষুধা *n* **1** a desire or relish for food; hunger; appetite. **2** carnal appetite; depraved affections; longing desire; lust. ~ **বোধ করা**, ~ **হওয়া** *vi* feel hungry. ~**কর** *adj* causing hunger; appetizing. ~**তুর** *adj* stricken with hunger; famished; hungry. ~**তৃষ্ণা** *n* hunger and thirst. ~**নাশ** *n* loss of appetite. ~ **নাশ করা** *vi* cause loss of appetite. ~**নিবৃত্তি** *n* appeasing of hunger. ~ **নিবৃত্তি করা** *vi* appease/satisfy hunger. ~**বর্ধক**=~কর. ~**মান্দ্য** *n* loss of appetite. ~**র্থ** *adj* hungry.

ক্ষুধিত *adj* **1** hungry. **2** longing or craving for. **ক্ষুধিতা** *fem*.

ক্ষুন্নিবৃত্তি [ক্ষুৎ+নিবৃত্তি] *n* satisfying of hunger.

ক্ষুন্নিবৃত্ত *adj* one whose hunger has been satisfied.

ক্ষুব্ধ *adj* **1** stirred; agitated; distracted; perturbed; aggrieved. **2** pained; afflicted; sorrowful. ~ **করা** *vt* offend; agitate. ~ **হওয়া** *vi* be aggrieved/agitated/troubled.

ক্ষুভিত *adj*=ক্ষুব্ধ

ক্ষুর *n* **1** a sharp instrument for shaving off hair/beard; razor. **2** (of animals) the hoof. **~ধার** *adj* (fig) as sharp as a razor: ~ধার লেখনী.

ক্ষেত, খেত *n* a plot of agricultural land; an agricultural farm. **~মজুর** *n* an agricultural labourer; a farm worker. **~খোলা, ~খামার** agricultural land; crop-land; corn-field. **খেতালি, খেতি** agricultural work; cultivation.

ক্ষেত্র *n* **1** plot of agricultural land; corn-field: কৃষি~. **2** the venue of a meeting/assembly: সভা~. **3** a battle-field: যুদ্ধ~. **4** the sphere of ones activity; a profession: কর্ম~. **5** a place of pilgrimage: তীর্থ~. **7** (geom) a square; a rectangle: বর্গ~, আয়ত~. **8** a particular situation; circumstances: এক্ষেত্রে সকলের সহযোগিতা আবশ্যক. **~কর্ম** *n* agricultural work; cultivation. **~জ** *adj* **1** produced or grown on a field. **2** born of one's wife by a paramour. **~ফল** *n* (math) measurement of an area; area measure. **~মিতি** *n* that part of mathematics which deals with points, lines, surfaces and solids; geometry.

ক্ষেপ[১]=খেপ

ক্ষেপ[২] *n* **1** act of throwing; shooting: শর~. **2** act of intervening: হস্ত~. **3** act of moving; motion; action: পদ~. **4** act of passing or spending: কাল~. **5** act of casting; looking: দৃষ্টি~. **~ক** *adj* that throws.

ক্ষেপণ *n* **1** act of throwing. **2** act of passing (time)/spending: কাল~. **ক্ষেপণাস্ত্র** *n* a weapon or projectile thrown with hostile intention; a missile: দূর পাল্লার ক্ষেপণাস্ত্র. **ক্ষেপণীয়** *adj* to be thrown; fit to be thrown/ hurled down. **~-রকেট** *n* a rocket that launches itself into the air as a self-propelled projectile or missile.

ক্ষেপা=খেপা

ক্ষেপানো *vt* tease (a person); infuriate.

ক্ষোদন *n* the act or art of cutting figures on wood or metal; art of carving or sculpturing figures; carving; engraving. **~ করা** *vt* engrave; carve; sculpture. **ক্ষোদিত** *adj* **1** carved; engraved.

ক্ষোভ *n* **1** mental agitation; distraction; grievance. **2** sorrow; grief; regret: ক্ষোভের বিষয়, matter of regret. **~হীন, ~শূন্য** *adj* unaggrieved; free from agitation; calm; composed.

ক্ষোভিত=ক্ষুব্ধ

ক্ষৌণী, ক্ষৌণি *n* the earth.

ক্ষৌণীশ *n* a king; an emperor (also ক্ষৌণীন্দ্র)

ক্ষৌম *adj* made of silk; silken. ❑*n* silken or linen cloth: ~বস্ত্র.

ক্ষৌর *n* act of shaving: ~কর্ম. **~কার** *n* a barber.

ক্ষৌরি *n* act of shaving. **~ক** a barber.

ক্ষৌরী *n* **1** a razor. **2** act of shaving.

খ

খ[১] *n* the second consonant of the Bengali alphabet. It is pronounced as a velar, unvoiced aspirated plosive sound.

খ[২] *n* **1** the sky. **2** the air; the atmosphere: খগোল.

খই, খৈ *n* toasted paddy or other grain: ধানের ~, ভুট্টার ~. **~ ফোটা** *vi* burst open noisily in the process of being toasted; (fig) talk much and fast: তার মুখে ~ ফোটে. **~ ভাজা** *vi* make ~ by toasting paddy. **~চালা** *n* a sieve for sifting ~ from husks and wastes. ❑*vi* sift ~ from husk with a sieve. **~চুর** *n* globules of sweets made of ~ by boiling in sugar malt. **~ ঢেকুর, ~য়া ঢেকুর** *n* belching with a smell of ~ caused by indigestion. **~য়া ধান** *n* paddy that gives best quality ~.

খইনি [H] *n* dry tobacco leaf twisted with lime for use as a substitute for smoking.

খইল *n* **1** a cake of compressed linseed, rape, or other seed from which oil has been extracted; oil-cake. **2** substance excreted in the ear; ear-wax.

খওয়া *vt* be eaten away gradually; wear away; erode; corrode. ❑*adj* worn away; eroded.

খক *int* denoting the sound of coughing. **~ করে কাশা** *vi* make an effort, with noise, to expel air from the lungs, or to force up phlegm; cough, hawk. **~খক** onomatopoeic word denoting the sound of repeated coughing.

খকখকানি *n* fit of coughing.

খগ *adj* moving in the air/sky. ❑*n* the bird. **~পতি, ~রাজ, খগেন্দ্র** *n* (according to Hindu Purana) the lord of birds; appellations of Garuda, the mount of Vishnu.

খগাবগা *int* word suggesting a clumsy way of doing things just as the unwieldy way of a crane wading in a marsh. ❑*adj* ungainly; uncouth; awkward: হাতের লেখা ~.

খগোল *n* **1** sky or heavens; the region of the air; the firmament. **2** an artificial sphere with a chart of the constellations; a celestial globe. **~বিদ্যা** *n* the scientific study of the heavenly bodies; astronomy. **~বিদ, ~বিৎ** *n* one versed in the science of heavenly bodies; an astronomer.

খচ *int* denoting the sound of cutting or a sensation of pricking. **~খচ** *int* **1** onomatopoeic word denoting a sensation of repeated pricking. **2** word suggestive of a feeling of remorse: টাকাগুলো হারিয়ে মনটা ~~ করছে.

খচমচ *int* indicating a rustling noise (as of straw or dry leaves). **~ করা** *vi, vt* make a rustling noise; rustle. **খচমচানি** *n* rustling; a rustle. **খচমচে** *adj* rustling; making a rustling noise.

খচিত *adj* **1** studded with; inlaid; inset; adorned: রত্ন~, studded with gems. **2** made into a wreath; enwreathed; interwoven; strung (as a garland). **3** pervaded; diffused. **~ করা** *vt* interweave; enwreathe; strung; inlay; inset; embed; bedeck; adorn.

খচ্চর *n* **1** the offspring of an ass and mare, or a horse and she-ass; a mule. **2** an illegitimate son; a bastard. **3** (abuse) a rogue; a scoundrel. **তিলে ~** *n* **1** a mule spotted with mole-like stains. **2** (fig) a criminal; a convict.

খঞ্জ *adj* crippled in a limb or limbs; lame. **খঞ্জা** *fem.* **~তা, ~ত্ব** *n* lameness. **~ করা** *vt* cripple; lame. **~ হওয়া** *vi* be/become lame.

খঞ্জন *n* a small species of agile and restless bird with a long tail which it constantly moves up and down and so is called wagtail. **খঞ্জনা, খঞ্জনিকা** *fem.* **~ আঁখি** *n,adj* one having very agile or quick-moving eyes as those of a wagtail. **~গঞ্জন** *adj* putting the wagtail to shame in agility; more agile than a wagtail.

খঞ্জনি *n* a musical instrument of the drum species played with the hand traditional to Vaishnava singers.

খঞ্জর [A] *n* a kind of double-edged dagger.

খট *int* denoting a low sound as produced by a clash of two pieces of stone or wood. **~~ করে চলা** walk along (with shoes on) with the heels striking the ground.

খটকা *n* **1** a failing of confidence; misgiving; doubt; suspicion: কথাটা শুনে মনে একটা ~ লাগলো, my mind was filled with misgivings to hear the news. **2** hesitation. **3** distrust.

খটমট *int* **1** sound produced by firm steps. **খটমটে** *adj* hard to understand; difficult of comprehension; stiff; abstruse.

খট্টাশ, খট্টাস *n* carnivorous animal, distinguished by its offensive smell, found in Asia and N Africa; a civet-cat; a pole-cat.

খড় *n* **1** the dry stalk of grain, pulse, etc; straw. **2** grass cut and dried for fodder; hay. **~কুটা/কুটো** *n* **1** bits of dry grass; dry leaves or straw. **2** insignificant, trivial or trashy things. **খড়ের আগুন** that which quickly flares up and easily subsides; (fig) person of violent temper. **খড়ের ঘর** a hut roofed with straw; a thatched hut.

খড়খড়ি blind or shutters for doors and windows made of thin slats of wood; Venetian blind.

খড়ম *n* wooden sandal. **~-পেটা** *adj* beaten with wooden sandal.

খড়ি *n* **1** a white calcareous earth or carbonate of lime; chalk. **2** alluvial clay with which pious Hindus mark their forehead. **3** calculation; a character denoting a number; a figure. **4** fire-wood; fuel. **5** dry scales or flakes on the skin; scurf. **~ ওঠা** suffer from scurf or dandruff. **হাতে~** ⇒ হাত.

খড়িমাটি *n*=খড়ি (1)

খড়ো *adj* made of straw. **~ ঘর** *n* a thatched hut.

খড়্গ *n* **1** a short curved sword; a scimitar; a falchion. **2** a sword. **~ হস্ত** *adj* wielding a sword; ready to strike with a sword.

খণ্ড *n* **1** a bit, a slice, or piece of anything solid: মাংস~. **2** a chapter, a section or part (of a book): ২য় ~, second volume. **3** a geographical region; a country: রোহিলা ~. **4** a single object that is an example of a kind or class: এক ~ কেক, এক ~ কাপড়, এক ~ পুস্তক. **5** a portion separated or marked off from a larger or whole body: এক ~ জমি. **~কাব্য** *n* a narrative poem based on a single theme in the style of an epic but not so long and vivid as an epic is; an imperfect epic. **~কাল** *n* a part of the working day. **~কালীন** *adj, adv* for only a part of the working hours: ~কালীন শিক্ষক, a part-time teacher. ❑*n* a part-timer. **~ ~** *adj* broken to pieces; cut to pieces. **~ ~ করা** *vt* cut to pieces; break or divide into pieces. **~ ~ করে** *adv* in pieces; piecemeal. **~গ্রাস** *n* (astron) a partial eclipse of the sun or moon. **~প্রলয়** *n* **1** a tremendous upheaval or revolution causing great social and political change. **2** a brawl; an affray. **~বাক্য** *n* (gram) a clause in a sentence. **~যুদ্ধ** *n* (mil) an irregular short contest in which small numbers are engaged; a skirmish; a pitched battle. **খণ্ডে খণ্ডে** *adv* part by part; in parts.

খণ্ডন *n* **1** act of disproving by argument; refutation; confutation; rebuttal: অভিযোগ ~ করা, refute a charge/complaint; prove a charge to be false. **যুক্তি ~ করা** refute an argument; prove an argument to be wrong/mistaken by counter-argument. **2** act of undoing what had been done; act of removing/dispelling/reversing: বিধিলিপি কে ~ করবে? who can undo the decree of fate? who can reverse what is ordained by fate? **~ করা** *vt* refute; disprove; dispel; reverse; undo. **খণ্ডনীয়** *adj* that can be refuted; refutable.

খণ্ডানো *vt* refute or cause to refute; repel or cause to be repelled; resist; reverse; dispel: অদৃষ্টের লিখন কে খণ্ডাবে?

খণ্ডিত *adj* **1** what has been divided/broken/cut into pieces; divided; fragmented. **2** bisected; bifurcated; cloven: ~ খুর. **~খুর** *adj* having the hoof split up into two parts (as the ox); cloven-hoofed. ❑*n* domestic quadrupeds, eg cows, bulls, oxen; cattle. **3** partial; not complete; incomplete: ~ দৃষ্টি. **খণ্ডিতা** *n fem* a woman offended and jealous at her husband's love-making with another.

খত, খৎ [A] *n* **1** a written message; a letter; hand-writing. **2** a bond containing a promise under the signature of the promissor to pay a specified sum; a promissory note; a note of hand; a bond. **3** a declaration binding oneself under oath to certain condition: দাস~. ~ **দেওয়া** *vi, vt* execute a bond (in one's favour). **নাকে ~ দেওয়া** (fig) admit one's crime and promise not to commit the same offence again. **~-কিতাবত** *n* intercourse by letters; correspondence. **ফার~** *n* letter of divorce. **বন্ধকি ~** *n* a document making a temporary conveyance of property as security for a debt; a mortgage deed.

খতনা, খৎনা [A] *n* cutting off of the foreskin, according to Muslim and Jewish law; circumcision.

খতবা=খোতবা

খতম [A] *n* **1** ending of an act/action/work; termination; conclusion. **2** close of life; death; murder: শত্রু ~. ~ **করা** *vt, vi* **1** put an end to; terminate; finish. **2** remove; kill; destroy. ~ **পড়া** *vi* read or recite the entire Qoranic text. ~ **পড়ানো** *vi* arrange a ceremonial reading of the Holy Qoran for the salvation of a departed soul.

খতরা [A] *n* **1** exposure to injury; danger; jeopardy; risk; difficulty.

খতানো *vt* make up an account; calculate gain and loss; reckon up: এরূপ আচরণের কী পরিণতি হবে তা একবার খতিয়ে দেখো.

খতিব [A] *n* person who delivers *khutba* or Friday sermon.

খতিয়ান [A, H] *n* **1** book containing details of rent-roll, rent realization, etc. **2** book in which debit and credit items are entered in a summary form; ledger book. ~ **করা** *vi* pass into the ledger.

খদ্দর [A] *n* hand woven coarse cloth made of cotton yarn spinned by hand-driven spinning wheel; *khadi*. **~ধারী** *adj* dressed in khadi. ❑*n* one in khadi.

খদ্দের=খরিদ্দার

খনন *n* act of digging; excavation: খাল ~, excavation of a canal. ~ **করা** *vt* dig; excavate. **~কারী** *n* one who digs; a digger; an excavator. **খননীয়** *adj* to be dug/excavated. **খনিত** *adj* dug; excavated.

খনা *n* Khana, the lady of ancient Bengal celebrated for uncommon proficiency in astronomy and mathematics. **~র বচন** *n* any of the numerous rhymed sayings of Khana that have passed through ages as valuable guidance for tillage of the soil, plantation, harvesting, etc.

খনি *n* underground deposit of minerals; a mine. **~জ** of or pertaining to mines; obtained from a mine; mineral. **~জ সম্পদ** *n* mineral resources.

খনি *n* tool with long handle for digging earth; a spud.

খন্তা=খনিত্র

খন্তি=খুন্তি

খন্দ [P] *n* a ditch; a trench. **খানা~** *n pl* ditches and trenches.

খন্দক [A] *n* a long narrow excavation; a trench cut for defence: খন্দকের যুদ্ধ, the battle of the trench.

খন্দকার=খোন্দকার

খপ *int* (onom) indicating quickness, suddenness or haste: ~ করে ধরে ফেললাম ❑*adv* **1** quickly; suddenly. **2** unexpectedly; unawares; surprisingly.

খপোত *n* an aeroplane; an airship.

খপ্পর *n* a plan, scheme, or trick for deceiving one or obtaining an advantage; a conspiracy; an intrigue. **খপ্পরে পড়া** *vi* get into the grips of.

খপ্পা [P] *adj* **1** provoked to anger; angered; enraged. **2** dissatisfied; offended.

খবর [A] *n* **1** report(s) of current events and happenings; news. **2** facts; data; information. ~ **করা** *vi vt* inquire about (one's well-being); communicate with (one) in person or otherwise. ~ **জানা** *vt* get or gather intelligence/information. ~ **পাওয়া** *vt* be informed (of); come to know (of). ~ **রাখা** *vi vt* keep oneself informed of; be in touch with. ~ **হওয়া** *vi* be announced/cause to be known: ঢাকা মেলের ~ হয়েছে. **~গির** *n* **1** a messenger. **2** a detective. **~গিরি** *n* the work or profession of a messenger. **খবরা~** *n pl* **1** exchange of information. **2** all sorts of tidings; news; information. **3** inquiries about sth/sb. **খবরের কাগজ** *n* a newspaper. **খোশ ~** *n* happy tiding; good news.

খবরদার *int* take care ! beware. **খবরদারি** *n* **1** act of taking care/looking after. **2** carefulness; watchfulness.

খবিশ [A] *adj* **1** dirty; nasty; filthy. **2** knavish; malicious; roguish; crooked; dishonest. **3** unholy; impure.

খমক [P] *n* a kind of musical instrument.

খমধ্য *n* the point of the heavens right above a spectator's head; the highest point; the zenith.

খয়রা *n* **1** a species of small fish. **2** a species of bird.

খয়রাত [A] *n* **1** almsgiving; charity: দান ~. **2** charitable gift; donation. ~ **করা** *vt* **1** give in charity. **2** (fig) (sarcas) say sth uncalled for or sth not desirable: উপদেশ ~ করা. **খয়রাতি** *adj* given or received in charity; charitable; gratuitous. **খয়রাতি সাহায্য** *n* test relief.

খয়ের *n* preparation from an astringent vegetable extract used with betel leaves; catechu.

খয়ের-খাঁ *n* a mean flatterer; a servile hanger-on of great people; a sycophant; a parasite.

খয়েরি *adj* of the colour of catechu; dark-brown; dark-tan.

খর[1] *adj* **1** sharp; keen: ~ধার. **2** forceful; fast: ~স্রোতা. **3** severe; fierce: ~রৌদ্র. **4** strong; violent: ~ বায়ু. **5** (of water) saline; salty: ~ পানি, hard water.

খর[2] [P] *n* the ass; the mule. ~ **দরজাল, খরে দজ্জাল** *n* man on the mule who, it is believed, will suddenly appear one day to destroy all good people; (fig) a cruel or oppressive person.

খরগোশ, খরগোস [P] *n* the hare; the rabbit.

খরচ, খরচা [P] *n* **1** expense; expenditure: ~ হওয়া. **2** money for expenses: ~ দেবে কে? **3** cost: মামলার ~, cost of litigation. ~ **করা** *vi, vt* spend; consume; use. ~ **হওয়া** *vi* be spent; be expended; be consumed/used. ~**পত্র** *n pl* expenses. ~**পত্র করা** *vi* bear the expenditure. **খাই** ~ *n* expenses for food; charges for one's board. **পকেট** ~ *n* pocket money. **পথ**~, **রাহা**~ travelling expenses. **বাজে** ~ *n* incidental expenses. **খরচান্ত** *n* having been subjected to heavy expenses: খরচান্ত হওয়া. **খরচে** *adj* lavish in expenditure; extravagant; spendthrift.

খরমুজ *n* fruit akin to watermelon; musk-melon.

খরা[1] *n* **1** sunshine; sunray. **2** want of rain; dry weather; drought. **3** the summer season.

খরা[2] *n* **1** the hare; the rabbit. **2** the ass; the mule.

খরাদ [A] *n* machine by which articles of wood are turned and cut into a smooth round form; lathe.

খরিদ [P] *n* buying; purchase. ~ **করা** *vt, vi* buy; purchase. ~ **বিক্রি** *n* buying and selling. ~**মূল্য** *n* the price at which sth is bought; cost price. **খরিদা** *adj* obtained by purchase; purchased.

খরিদ্দার, খদ্দের (colloq) a buyer; a purchaser; a customer. ~ **খবরদার** (legal usage) buyer beware.

খরিফ [A] the autumnal harvest/crop.

খরোষ্ঠী the ancient language and script of the north-west region of Pakistan; Kharosthi.

খর্জুর *n* the date-palm or its fruit; the date.

খর্পর *n* **1** a piece or fragment of an earthen pot. **2** the hollow of a skull; the skull. **3** a beggar's bowl. **4** a rogue; a cheat.

খর্ব *adj* **1** below the common size; stunted; short: ~কায়. **2** caused to decrease/diminish: শক্তি ~ হওয়া. **3** checked; restrained; curved; foiled: গতি ~ হওয়া. **4** lowered; humbled: গর্ব ~ হওয়া. ❑*n* the number 10 thousand million. ~ **করা** *vt* bring down; reduce; curb; restrain; humiliate; abase. **খর্বাকার, খর্বাকৃতি** *adj* dwarf; dwarfish; short-statured.

খল[1] *adj* **1** deceitful; guileful; cunning; fraudulent. **2** evil in principle or practice; wicked; mean. **3** malicious; spiteful; envious; malignant. **4** low in station; base. ~**কপট** *adj, n* one full of cunning and malice. ~**তা** *n* deceitfulness; wickedness; villainy. ~**স্বভাব** *adj* of a malicious/mischievous nature.

খল[2] *n* a small gallipot, usually boat-shaped, used for pounding medicine. ~**নুড়ি**, ~**নোড়া** *n* gallipot and the compounding pestle.

খলখল *int* (onom) denoting loud laughter or bubbling noise of water. ~ **করে হাসা** *vi* laugh loudly with short catches of the breath; giggle.

খলিফা [A] *n* **1** (lit) a deputy; an agent; a representative. **2** the caliphs who ruled over the Muslim empire after the demise of prophet Muhammad (sm) as the temporal sovereign of the state as well as spiritual chief of Muslim community. **3** a professional maker of garments; a tailor.

খলিশা=খলশে

খলিল [A] *n* a friend; an ally; a well-wisher. **খলিলুল্লাহ্** *n* an appellation of Prophet Ibrahim (ah) meaning 'friend of Allah'.

খসখস[1] *int* (onom) denoting rustling noise. **খসখসে** *adj* not smooth; rough to the touch.

খসখস[2] [P] *n* the fibrous aromatic root of the pearl-millet; cuscus.

খসড়া *n* a rough sketch; a draft. ~ **করা** *vt* make a draft.

খসম [A] *n* the consort of a woman; a husband.

খসরু [P] *n* a king; an emperor.

খসলত [A] *n* the essential qualities of a person; nature; character; habit.

খসা *vt* **1** fall off (as leaves); slough off (as the dead flesh separating from living parts of a wound; come out; slip off. **2** (fig) (of money) be spent: অনেক টাকা খসেছে. ~**নো** *vt* cause to fall, come out or slip off; cause to spend; exact.

খাই[1] *vi, vt* I (or we) eat. ❑*n* eating: ~খরচ. ~**কুঁড়** *adj* given to excessive eating; gluttonous; voracious. ❑*n* a glutton; a voracious eater. ~**কুঁড়ি** *n*. ~**খরচা** *n* expenses for food; boarding expenses. ~**খাই** *n* constant craving for food; ravenous appetite. ~~ **করা** *vi* crave for food off and on. ~**য়ে** *adj* **1** eating to excess; gluttonous; voracious. **2** indulging in good eating; enjoying good dishes. ❑*n* **1**

person cultivating a refined taste in eating; a gourmand; a gourmet. **2** a glutton.

খাই[1] *n* **1** a pit; a ditch; a trench: গড়~. **2** deepness; depth: দশ হাত ~, 10 cubits in depth.

খাই-খালাসি *adj* relating to usufructuary mortgage. **~ সম্পত্তি** *n* property mortgaged for enjoyment of usufruct by way of realization of a debt.

খাওন *n* **1** act of eating. **2** eatables; food: ~ দাওন.

খাওয়া *vt* **1** have (one's) food; eat. **2** take a drink; drink: চা ~. **3** bite: সাপে ~. **4** take (sth) by mouth: ওষুধ ~. **5** take (sth) illegally: ঘুষ ~. **6** smoke: সিগারেট ~. **7** kiss: চুমু ~. **8** cause to loose: চাকুরি ~. **9** suffer (sth): মার ~. **10** spoil or ruin: মাথা ~. ❑*adj* eaten up; corroded: ঘুণে ~. ❑*n* eating. **কুরে ~** *vt* scrape through. **গাল ~** *vi* be rebuked or reprimanded . **চরিত্র ~** *n* character-assassination. **টাকা ~** *vi, vt* receive illegal gratification. **নুন/ নিমক ~** *vi vt* be benefited/patronized. **~ দাওয়া** *n* act of eating and drinking.

খাওয়ানো *vt* **1** give food to; feed. **2** drag one to trouble out of fun; teach one a lesson: মার ~, বকা ~.

খাঁ, খান [P] *n* **1** surname used by the Pathans. **2** family name used with Muslims names. **3** appellation given to Hindus by Muslim kings as a mark of honour: যশোরাজ ~, গুণরাজ ~. **~ সাহেব, ~ বাহাদুর** title of honour given to meritorious Muslims during British rule.

খাঁই [P] *n* eager desire; greediness; avidity; demand: বরের বাপের বেজায় ~. **~ ~ করা** *vi vt* crave for; demand. **~মেটা** *n* satisfaction of greed; fulfilment of demand.

খাঁখাঁ *int* denoting a feeling of dreary emptiness or loneliness: বাড়িটা ~ করছে, the house is gaping empty/looks deserted.

খাঁচা *n* a cage for birds; a coop for poultry. **~র পাখি** a bird in a cage; (fig) one under restraint/in bondage. **~য় ভরা** confine in a cage. **~য় বন্দী** *adj* encaged; confined in a cage.

খাঁজ *n* **1** a slot made in wood or other material; a notch; a groove. **2** a wrinkle or a crease (as on the forehead); a furrow: কপালের ~; a fold: পেটের ~. **~ কাটা** *vt* notch; indent. **~কাটা** *adj* notched; serrated. **~ পড়া** *vi* contract into wrinkles or furrows. **খাঁজে খাঁজে জোড়া** *vi, vt* fit two pieces together by means of dovetailing.

খাঁটি [H] *adj* **1** not contaminated with any base matter; unmixed; unadulterated; pure: ~ সোনা, ~ দুধ. **2** not feigned; sincere; true: ~ ভালোবাসা. **3** honest; truthful; upright, virtuous: ~ লোক. **4** of great worth; precious; valuable: ~ কথা. **5** not forged or faked; genuine; actual; real: ~ অবস্থা.

খাঁড়া *n* a scimitar; a sacrificial falchion. **মরার উপর ~র ঘা** to add insult to injury.

খাঁড়ি *n* the expanding tidal mouth of a river; an estuary.

খাক [P] *n* **1** soil; earth. **2** the dust produced by combustion; ashes: জ্বলে পুড়ে ~. **3** powdery particles of earth; dust. **~ হওয়া** *vi* be reduced to the dust or ashes.

খাকসার, খাকছার [P] *n* **1** (lit) an humble servant. **2** name of a former political party of Indian Muslims founded by Allama Mashrequi. **3** word expressive of modesty, used at the end of a letter above the signature of the writer.

খাকি[1] [P] *adj* **1** of light brown colour; brownish; khaki. **2** (lit) made of earth (ie, man). ❑*n* khaki uniform of the army men.

খাকি[2] *n* **1** *fem* (abuse) one who eats. **2** (suffixed with other words) chiefly used by women as an abuse, eg চোখ~, ভাতার~. **নি~** *fem* woman who eats nothing, or eats less. **খেকো** *mas.*

খাগড়া *n* species of tall grass; reed. **~র কলম** *n* a quill.

খাজনা, খাজানা [A] *n* land-tax; revenue; the annual income of a state. **~-খানা** *n* treasure house; treasury. **~ আদায়** *n* realization of revenue.

খাজা[1] [P] *n* **1** lord; master. **2** an appellation used by certain Muslims: ~ নাজিমউদ্দিন.

খাজা[2] *n* kind of sweet made of flour.

খাজাঞ্চি [T] *n* **1** one who has the charge of a treasury of funds; a treasurer. **2** one in charge of revenue administration. **~খানা** *n* the office of a treasurer.

খাঞ্জাখাঁ *n* **1** Nawab Khan Jahan Khan, famous for luxury and munificence. **2** (fig) person indulging in luxury and floppishness (as if Nawab Khanja Khan).

খাট[1]**, খাটো** *adj* **1** short in size; short-statured: ~ লোক. **2** inferior; lower in place, station, value: সে কিসে ~? in what respect is he lacking? **3** not loud; low: ~ গলা. **4** weak; short: কানে ~, hard of hearing. **5** short in measure: ~ জামা. **~ করা** *vt* **1** reduce; make short; shorten. **2** humble; humiliate abase; lower; undermine. **~ নজর** *n* **1** short sight. **2** narrowness; mean-mindedness. **3** niggardliness. **~ হওয়া** *vi* be humbled; be humiliated; be lowered in the eye of others.

খাট[2] *n* a cot; a bedstead. **~ ভাঙলে ভূমি শয্যা 1** sleep on the floor if the cot is broken. **2** make adjustments in living when on evil days.

খাটা *vi* **1** labour; toil; work: পরীক্ষার জন্য ~. **2** fit or adjust to body: জামাটা ওর গায়ে খাটে না, the shirt doesn't fit to his body. **3** work on hire: ভাড়া ~. **4** be suitable or acceptable: কথা ~.

জেল ~ *vi* serve a term of imprisonment: আমার টাকা ব্যবসায়ে খাটছে, my money is invested in business; ওষুধটা এ রোগে খাটবে না, will not act in this case; এ নিয়ম এ ক্ষেত্রে খাটে না, doesn't apply/hold good in this case; তোমার এ আচরণ খাটে না, such conduct of yours is not appropriate; লালের পাশে কালো খাটে না, black doesn't match with red. **~খাটি, ~খাটনি** *n* hard labour; toil.

খাটানো *vi, vt* **1** set people to work; engage: লোক ~. **2** make an investment; invest: টাকা ~. **3** use; apply: কৌশল ~, বুদ্ধি ~. **4** set up in a marked-out position; pitch: তাবু ~. **5** fix, fasten or secure in position: মশারি ~.

খাটাল=গোয়াল

খাটিয়া *n* an improvised cot.

খাটিয়ে *adj* hard-working; industrious; laborious.

খাটুনি *n* **1** labour with fatigue; toil. **2** effort; endeavour; exertion.

খাটুলি *n* a carriage or frame for conveying a dead body to the grave or crematorium; a bier.

খাটো=খাট[১]

খাড়া[১] [H, U] *adj* **1** standing erect; upright; perpendicular: ~ হয়ে আছে. **2** careful; vigilant: কান ~ আছে. **3** appeared; present: যম শিয়রে ~. **4** full; complete; clear: ~ এক ঘণ্টা. **5** demanding exact observance; strict; stern: ~ হুকুম. **6** rising sharply; steep: ~ পাহাড়. **~ করা** *vt* **1** cause to stand up; set erect. **2** put up; present: মুরুব্বি ~ করা. **3** make a sketch; draw up: খসড়া ~ করা. **4** establish; set up; found: স্কুল ~ করা. **5** bring round; cure: রোগীকে ~ করা. **6** bring forward; place; produce: যুক্তি ~ করা. **~ই** *n* height; altitude; upward slope. **~ ~, ~ক~** *adv* **1** presently; at once; on the spot. **2** without delay; soon; immediately. **~-পাহারা** *n* strict watch; sharp vigilance. **~ ফসল** *n* crop ready for harvesting; standing crop. **খাড়া-হুণ্ডি** *n* bill of exchange payable at sight.

খাড়ু, খাড়ুয়া *n* sort of bangle for the wrist or ankle.

খাত[১] *n* a head of income or expenditure: রাজস্ব ~, উন্নয়ন ~.

খাত[২] *n* **1** a pit; a hole; a ditch; a trench. **2** a tank; a pond. **3** an estuary or mouth of a river. **4** a mine. ❑*adj* what has been dug or excavated.

খাতক *n* one who owes money; a debtor.

খাতা[১] [A+P] *n* **1** a bound book of blank sheets; a book for writing or scribbling; an exercise book. **2** an account-book; a ledger; a register. **~ খোলা** *vi* start transaction. **~পত্র** *n pl* ledgers and registers; books and papers. **~ লেখা** *vi* make entries of daily receipts and payments in the account book; maintain a ledger. **হাল~** *n* ceremonial opening of a fresh account-book on the new year's day; festival connected with the opening of the new ledger and settling of accounts of the previous year.

খাতা[২] [A] *n* flaws and faults; omissions and commissions; lapses and offences: গুনাহ্~ মাফ করবেন, please (be good enough to) excuse my flaws and faults.

খাতির [A] *n* **1** cause; reason, sake: সত্যের খাতিরে স্বীকার করতে হয় যে ... for the sake of truth I must admit that.... **2** cordial reception; careful and respectful treatment (as of a guest). ❑*adv* in honour of; for the sake of: আপনার খাতিরে আমি তাকে ছেড়ে দিয়েছি, I excused him in your honour. ❑*n* cordial or friendly relation: তার সঙ্গে আমার বহুদিনের খাতির, I am on intimate terms with him for a long time. **~ জমানো** *vi* worn into one's affection or confidence.

খাতুন [T] *n* **1** a lady; a woman. **2** a housewife. **3** a surname used with the names of Muslim women. **খাতুনে জান্নাত** *n* (lit) queen of the Paradise; appellation of Hazrat Fatima.

খাদ[১] *n* substance produced by melting together two or more metals; a baser metal mixed with gold or silver; alloy.

খাদ[২] *n* **1** (music) the lowest part in musical harmony; low grave tone; bass note. **2** a ditch; a trench.

খাদক *n* **1** one who eats: নর ~ বাঘ. **2** one who buys for use or consumption; a consumer. **3** person indebted; a debtor. **খাদিকা** *fem.*

খাদা *n* **1** measure of land (= 16 *bighas*). **2** a bowl made of wood or metal.

খাদেম, খাদিম [A] *n* a servant; an attendant. **~দার** *n* one who serves at the dining table. **~দারি** *n* act of serving at the table. **খাদেমা** *fem* **1** a maid-servant. **2** a concubine.

খাদ্য *n* food; eatables. ❑*adj* eatable. **~খাদক সম্বন্ধ** *n* **1** (lit) relation between food and its consumer. **2** (fig) relation of natural antagonism as between the hare and the hunter. **~নালী** *n* (anat) the food canal; easophagus. **~প্রাণ** *n* one of several chemical substances found in natural foods, and essential to life and health; vitamin. **~শস্য** *n* food grains. **খাদ্যাখাদ্য** *n* good food or bad food; edibles and non-edibles. **খাদ্যাভাব** *n* scarcity of food.

খাদ্যাভাব *n* scarcity of food; famine.

খান[১] *n* a place: এখানে, সেখানে, সবখানে.

খান[২], **খানা** *n* **1** a piece; a unit: এক~ কাপড়. **2** number: তিন ~ বই. **~ ~** *adv* into prices: ভেঙ্গে ~ ~, broken to pieces.

খান[৩]=খাঁ

খানকা[১], **খানকাহ্** [A] *n* **1** outer house; drawing room. **2** the seat of a saint.

খানকা[২]=খামকা

খানকি [P] *n* (vulg) harlot; a prostitute. ~**খোর/বাজ** *adj* visiting prostitute. ~**গিরি** *n* prostitution; harlotry. ~**পনা** *n* behaving like a prostitute. ~ **বাড়ি** *n* a brothel.

খানদান, খান্দান [P] *n* line of ancestors/ descent; family. **2** high family; aristocratic descent. **3** descendants; offspring; progeny.

খানদানি *adj* of noble descent; high born; aristocratic. ~ **লোক** *n* an aristocrat.

খানম [T] *n fem* **1** wife of a khan. **2** a woman; a lady. **3** surname suffixed with the names of Muslim women.

খানসামা [P] *n* an orderly. ~**গিরি** *n* the post or occupation of a *khansama*.

খানা[1] [Pg] *n* a hollow place on the ground; a pit; a ditch. ~**খন্দ** *n pl* hollows and pot-holes. ~**খন্দল** *n pl* holes and hollows.

খানা[2] [P] *n* house; abode: গরিব~, দৌলত~. ~**তল্লাস**, ~**তল্লাসি** *n* house-search under a warrant. ~**তল্লাসি পরওয়ানা** *n* a search warrant.

খানা[3] [U] cooked food taken at one time; a meal; a feast; dinner; supper ~**ঘর** *n* dining hall/room. ~**পিনা/দানা** eating and drinking.

খানা,[4] **খানি** *suff* **1** indicating a number: দু~, চার~. **2** used as equivalent to the English definite article 'the': বাড়ি~, the house; বই~, the book.

খানা-এ-কাবা [P+A] *n* the house of Kaaba at Mecca.

খানিক *adv* for a little while; for a moment: ~ অপেক্ষা করো, wait a bit. ~**ক্ষণ** *n* a little while. ❑*adv* for a little while.

খানেক *adj* a little more or less than one: মাইল~.

খান্নাস [A] *n* Satan, the evil spirit; the devil.

খাপ *n* **1** a sheath for a sword; a scabbard: তলোয়ারের ~. **2** a case or cover: চশমার ~. **3** thickness or fineness of texture: মিহিখাপের কাপড়, fine cloth. **4** fitness; consistency; agreement; harmony; adjustment. ~ **খাওয়া** *vi vt* agree with; be consistent with; be in harmony with; suit; adjust. **খাপে রাখা** *vt* sheathe; put in the case. **খাপ থেকে খোলা/খাপমুক্ত করা** *vt* take out of the case; unsheathe. ~-**ছাড়া** *adj* inconsistent; incoherent; odd; queer. ~ **খাওয়ানো** *vt* adapt oneself to; adjust to; accommodate: তার পোশাক তার পদমর্যাদার সাথে খাপ খায় না, his dress is not befitting his position; তার মতো লোকের এমন আচরণ ~ খায় না, such conduct is not becoming of a man of his stature.

খাপরা *n* a piece of a earthen broken pot.

খাপা, খাপ্পা [P] *adj* enraged; angry. ~ **হওয়া** *vi* get angry; be enraged/ indignant.

খাবল, খাবলা *n* **1** a handful (of anything); amount that can be gripped by the palm: এক ~ আটা. ~ **দেওয়া** *vi vt* seize by the palm. **2** a mouthful; a morsel. ~ **মারা** *vt* **1** bite at. **2** (fig) try to appropriate (anything) to oneself forcibly or cunningly. **খাবলানো** *vi,vt* scrape with the hand; handle (anything) roughly: খাবলে খাওয়া.

খাবার *n* **1** that which is eaten to keep oneself living; food; meal. **2** light food; snacks; sweets: ~ জিনিস. ~ **ঘর** *n* dining room. ~ **পানি** *n* drinking water. ~**ওয়ালা** *n* seller of snacks. ~ **দাবার** *n pl* various items of food. **জল~** *n* snack; tiffin.

খাবি *n* short painful catching of the breath; pant; gasp. ~ **খাওয়া** *vi* **1** open the mouth wide to catch breath; labour for breath; be at the last gasp/point of death. **2** (fig) try desperately to freed oneself from oppression or bondage.

খাম[1] [U] *n* wooden or bamboo pillar/post of a Kutchha house. ~ **আলু** *n* a variety of edible tuberous root or yam.

খাম[2] [P] *n* a cover for letter, etc; an envelope.

খামখা, খামকা [P] *adv* **1** suddenly; unexpectedly. **2** without any cause or provocation; unreasonably; for nothing; unnecessarily.

খামখেয়াল[P+A] *n* **1** fickleness; inconsistency. **2** eccentricity; whimsicality. **খামখেয়ালি** *n* fickleness; whimsicality: তোমার এ খামখেয়ালি ছাড়ো. ❑*adj* of abnormal habits and behaviour; eccentric; whimsical; fickle-minded.

খামচা, খামচি *n* act of pinching and twisting with the finger-nails; tweaking. **খামচা-খামচি** *n* mutual tweaking. **খামচানো** *vt* scratch with the nails.

খামার *n* **1** land under cultivation; farm. **2** farmyard used for threshing; threshing-floor. ~ **বাড়ি** *n* a dwelling house with a granary within the precinct of a farm; a farmhouse.

খামোশ [P] *int* an order to keep quiet. ❑*adj* calm; quiet. **খামোশি** *n*.

খাম্বা [U, H] *n* a pillar or column of a building.

খাম্বাজ *n* a musical mode.

খাম্বিরা [A] *n* aromatic tobacco for the hookah.

খায়েশ, খাহেশ [P] *n* **1** wish to achieve aspirations and ideals; ambition; aspiration. **2** strong desire; craving.

খারাপ [A] *adj* **1** not good; bad; harmful: ~ খবর. **2** ominous; portentous, sinister; inauspicious: কপাল ~. **3** obscene; abominable; indecent; filthy; bawdy: ~ কথা. **4** out of order; unserviceable: ~ ঘড়ি. **5** unwholesome; rotten: ~ খাবার. **6** in a bad mood, displeased; out of humour: মেজাজ ~. **7** unwell, indisposed: শরীর ~. **8** contagious; acute; incurable: ~ রোগ. **9** difficult; hard; evil; ominous: ~ দিন. **10** crazy; insane; deranged: মাথা ~. ~ **করা** *vt* cause to become bad or worse; spoil; bungle; pollute; damage. **পেট ~ করা** *vi* be affected with intestinal trouble; suffer from dyspepsia/ diarrohea. মন ~ করা *vi* feel distressed/ disheartened. মাথা ~ করা *vi* be anxious/ worried; get crazy. মুখ ~ করা *vi* use filthy words; talk scurrilous language. মেজাজ ~ করা *vi* go out of humour; lose temper. শরীর ~ করা *vi* be/ feel indisposed.

খারাবি, খারাপি [A] *n* **1** harm; damage; wrong. **2** disaster; utter ruin; sudden misfortune. **3** debauchery; lewdness; wantonness; profligacy. **খুন~** *n* murderous violence; riot.

খারিজ [A] **1** rejected; dismissed; set aside: মামলা ~. **2** substituted; revised: নাম ~. **~ করা** *vt* substitute the name of one tenant in place of another in the rent-roll; cause mutation in the rent-roll. **মামলা ~ করা** dismiss a case.

খাল *n* watercourse cut through land as a means of communication; a canal; a channel. **~ কেটে কুমির আনা** (fig) invite an evil by one's own imprudent act.

খালসা *n* Shikh community who are the followers of Guru Govinda.

খালা *n* mother's sister; maternal aunt.

খালাস [A] *n* **1** release (from jail). **2** acquittal (of an accused). **3** delivery or relief (of a woman in travail). **4** act of taking delivery (of a consignment). **5** unloading of goods, etc: মাল ~. **~ করা** *vi* release (from confinement); relieve (one) (of a pain, duty or responsibility); take delivery (of a consignment etc). **~ দেওয়া** *vt* acquit; relieve; rid one (of). **~ পাওয়া** *vi* be released/relieved/ acquitted. **~পত্র** *n* an order of acquittal/ release.

খালাসি [A] *n* labourer engaged in a ship for loading and unloading of goods.

খালি [A] *adj* **1** empty: ~ পেট. **2** uncovered; bare: ~ মাথা. **3** vacant: পদ ~, situation vacant. **4** open: ~ জায়গা. **5** mere: ~ মিথ্যা কথা. □*adv* only; always: ~ কাজ আর কাজ. **~ হাতে** *adv* empty handed; without anything in hand.

খালু *n* husband of maternal aunt.

খালুই *n* a basket made of bamboo slips for carrying fish; a fish-creel.

খালেস [A] *adj* pure; sincere: ~ নিয়ত.

খাস [A] *adj* **1** pure; unmixed: ~ বাংলায় কথা বলেছি. **2** private; one's personal: ~ কামরা. **3** under direct ownership of the proprietor; belonging to the government: ~ মহল. **4** special; distinctive; having particular scope: ~ দরবার. **~ করা, খাসে আনা** *vt* bring under the actual possession of the owner. **~ খামার** farmyard in the owner's own possession.

খাসলত [A] *n* disposition of a person; habit; behaviour; conduct.

খাসা [A] *adj* of superior quality; excellent; fine; select: ~ দই.

খাসি, খাসী [A] *n* castrated goat or sheep. **~ করা** *vt* castrate.

খাস্তা [P] *adj* spoilt; useless: ~ কাগজ. **সাত নকলে আসল খাস্তা** frequent imitations corrupt the original.

খাস্তগির [P] *n* **1** a candidate; a petitioner. **2** a surname used by certain Muslim/Hindu families.

খিঁচানো *vi* grimace; distort the face; make faces; set the teeth. **দাঁত ~** *vi* show the teeth in scorn; grin (at). **মুখ ~** *vi* make faces at.

খিচুরি, খিচুড়ি *n* a preparation of rice and pulses together; kedgeree; hotchpotch. **~ পাকানো** *vi* **1** cook a hotchpotch. **2** (fig) make a mess of a matter; muddle up ; confuse; complicate.

খিড়কি *n* **1** a window. **2** the backside of a house. **~ দুয়ার** *n* a back door, a private entrance; a postern. **~ পুকুর** *n* a pond at the backside of a house usually reserved for women.

খিদমত=খেদমত

খিল *n* a bar of a door; a bolt. **~ দেওয়া** *vi* bolt; fix the bolt. **~ খোলা** *vi* unbolt. **(পেটে) ~ ধরা/লাগা** be seized with a cramp; have a cramp.

খিলখিল *int* (onom) denoting the sound of laughter/giggling. **~ করে হাসা** *vi* giggle; titter.

খিলাত [A] *n* a robe of honour awarded by a prince.

খিলান *n* (archit) a concave structure of bricks or stones supported by its own curve; a vault; an arch.

খিলাল, খেলাল [A] a tooth-pick.

খিলি *n* betel-leaf creased into a cup with lime, catechu, betel-nut, etc: এক ~ পান.

খিস্তি *n* reviling in obscene language. **~ করা** *vi* use abusive language; scold; inveigh; rail at.

খুঁটি *n* a post of wood or bamboo. **~ গাড়া** *vi* fix a post; (fig) to settle down at a place permanently. **~র জোর** *n* (fig) patronage of an influential person.

খুঁটিনাটি *n pl* the details of a thing, including all trifles and niceties. **2** trifling offences and omissions.

খুঁতখুঁত, খুঁতখুঁতানি *n* discontent over trifles; peevishness; fastidiousness. **খুঁতখুঁত করা** *vi* grumble; murmur with discontent. **খুঁতখুঁতে** *adj* delicate to a fault; difficult to please; peevish; fastidious.

খুকি *n fem* little girl; a daughter. **খোকা** *mas.*

খুকু *n fem* affectionate form of **খুকি**, a girlie.

খুচরা, খুচরো (colloq) *adj* in small quantities; retail. **~ বিক্রয়** *n* retail sale. **~ বিক্রেতা** retail dealer; retailer. **~ করা** *vi, vt* convert a currency note into small coins; change a note for coins. ~ কাজ *n* miscellaneous jobs. ~ খরচ *n* small expenses.

খুড়তুতো *adj* born of a younger brother of one's father: ~ ভাই, ~ বোন, cousin.

খুড়া, খুড়ো *n* younger brother of one's father; an uncle. **খুড়ি** *n* the wife of one's father's younger brother. **~শ্বশুর** *n* younger brother of one's father-in-law. **~শাশুড়ি** *fem.*

খুদ *n* fragment of a grain of rice; broken bits of rice. **~ কুঁড়া/কুঁড়ো** *n* husking mixed with particles of grain; (fig) paltry resources.

খুদি [P] *n* (phil) the 'I' or self; ego; the consciousness of the self and its development.

খুদে *adj* very small; tiny: ~ পিঁপড়ে. **~ রাক্ষস** *n* (fig) a gluttonous person. **~ শয়তান** *n* (fig) an extremely naughty boy.

খুন [P] *n* **1** blood. **2** murder; bloodshed. ❑*adj* troubled; worried: ভেবে ~, কেঁদে কেঁদে ~. **2** beside oneself; at the end of one's self-control: হেসে ~. **3** killed; murdered: লোকটা ~ হলো. **~ করা** *vi, vt* do one to death; murder; kill. **~ চড়া/চাপা** *vi* be blood-thirsty; become possessed with the frenzy of murder; see red. **~খারাপি** *n* bloody deed; murder. **খুনাখুনি, খুনোখুনি** *n* bloodshed. **খুনি** *n* a murderer. **খুনি আসামি** *n* prisoner accused of murder.

খুন্তি *n* cooking tool.

খুপরি *n* a small house; a hovel; a shack.

খুব [P] *adv* **1** very much; too much: ~ চালাক. **2** excellently; nicely: ~ বলেছো. **3** surely; certainly: ~ পারবে. **~ করা** *vt* do much; (sarcas) do nothing.

খুবসুরত [P+ A] *adj* handsome; beautiful.

খুবানি *n* a kind of fruit; apricot.

খুলি *n* **1** the skull; the cranium. **2** earthen vessel resembling a skull.

খুশকি [P] *n* dandruff.

খুশি, খুশী [P] *n* **1** pleasure; happiness; joy; delight: খুশির বিষয়, its a matter of pleasure. **2** will; desire, volition: যা ~ করো, do as you please/wish. ❑*adj* happy; glad; delighted: শুনে ~ হবেন যে, you will be happy to know that.... **খুশিতে বাগবাগ** beside oneself with joy.

খেই *n* **1** an end of a reel of thread. **2** a trail or track to follow sth; a clue to get at sth: ~ পাওয়া. **3** a single thread of a thing made up of many threads; a strand: পাঁচ ~. **~ হারানো** *vi* lose the clue.

খেউরি *n* act of shaving. **~ করা/হওয়া** *vi* shave.

খেঁকশিয়াল *n* a species of carnivorous animal, remarkable for cunning; the fox. **খেঁকশিয়ালি** *fem* vixen.

খেঁকি, খেঁকী *adj* making the snarling sound of a dog or vixen (as one does in anger); peevish; snarling; fretful. **~ কুকুর/কুত্তা** *n* a snarling dog; a mongrel dog; a cur; (fig) a peevish person; a contemptible person.

খেঁচা, খিঁচা *vt* **1** pull tight; pull forcefully and suddenly. **2** have convulsions or spasm; cramp. **খেঁচুনি, খিঁচুনি** *n* convulsion or spasm of the body.

খেকো *adj, suff* **1** who or what eats; eating: মানুষ~ বাঘ. **2** partly eaten; eaten into: পোকা-খেকো, moth-eaten.

খেচর *adj* **1** moving in the air; flying. **2** bird. **খেচরী** *fem.*

খেচরান্ন=খিচুরি

খেচাখেচি *n* **1** pulling at each other; tug of war. **2** mutual abuses; frequent quarrel; constant bickering. **3** mutual ill-will/ ill-feeling.

খেজালত [A] *n* trouble; disturbance; annoyance.

খেজুর *n* small, brown, sweet, oval-shaped fruit of the date-palm; dates. **~ গুড়** *n* date molasses. **~ ছড়ি/ছড়া** *n* cluster of dates. **~ রস** *n* juice of the date-palm. **খেজুরে** *adj* made of dates or of the juice of date-palm. **খেজুরে/খাজুরে আলাপ** *n* idle talk that consumes time but is, nevertheless, attractive.

খেত=ক্ষেত

খেতাব [A] *n* appellation of honour awarded by authority; title. **~ধারী** *adj* having a title of honour. **খেতাবি, খেতাবী** *adj* holding a title of honour.

খেদ *n* **1** sorrow; regret; repentance. **2** lamentation; grief; distress; affliction. **~ করা** *vi* repent; grieve; lament. **~ নিবারণ করা** *vi* assuage grief; alleviate/ relieve sorrow. **~জনক** *adj* lamentable.

খেদমত [A] *n* **1** act of waiting on/ serving; attendance. **2** slavery; servitude; drudgery. **~গার** *n* one who waits on/ attends; servant; attendant. **~গারি** *n* act of serving/attending.

খেদা *n* a kind of trap for catching wild elephants; elephant-trap.

খেদানো *vt* turn out; drive away; chase away; scare away; expel.

খেদোক্তি *n* words of regret; lamentation. **~ করা** *vi* lament; regret; bewail.

খেপ *n* **1** a turn or round of action (as by a rickshaw-puller); a trip: এক ~, দুই ~. **2** carrying of goods by boat; cart, etc: ~ দেওয়া. **~ দেওয়া** *vi* carry goods (to and from) by boat, cart, etc.

খেপা[1] *vt* cast/hurl/throw with violence. ❑*adj* that which has been cast/ hurled.

খেপা[2] *vi* **1** go mad; be in a frenzy. **2** be angry/ excited. **3** become violent: বাতাস খেপেছে. ❑*adj* mad; lunatic; insane; crazy; excited; enraged; violent. **~মি** *n* madness; craziness; insanity.

খেমটা *n* **1** a musical measure. **2** dance in tune with this music. **~ওয়ালী** *n* a professional dancing girl specialized in *khemta*.

খেয়া *n* **1** a ferry-boat. **2** place where boats ply to convey passengers across a river. **~ পারাপার** *n* act of ferrying. **~ পারাপার করা** *vi, vt* ferry; carry across a river in a boat. **~ মাঝি** *n* a ferryman.

খেয়ানত [A] *n* **1** treacherous arrogation of money or other property placed under one's custody; misappropriation. **2** embezzlement of cash; breach of trust. **আমানত ~ করা** *vi* appropriate by breach of trust; embezzle; misappropriate.

খেয়াল [A] *n* **1** a false notion; a fancy; a day-dream: উদ্ভট ~. **2** consciousness; carefulness; attention: তার কিছুই ~ থাকে না, he is forgetful. **3** remembrance; recollection: বিষয়টা ~ ছিল না, I forgot it. **4** inclination; bent of mind; propensity; predisposition: বদ ~. **5** thinking; considering; understanding: wariness: ভবিষ্যতের দিকে খেয়াল রেখো, be wary about the future. **6** a caprice; a whim; a hobby; a vagary: ~ চাপা, প্রকৃতির ~, ~খুশি. **7** a kind of classical music: ~ গাওয়া. **~ করা** *vi* think; consider; remember; be attentive; pay heed to. **~ চাপা** be taken up with a fancy; take a fancy to; be seized with a mania. **~ থাকা** have an eye to; have sth in the mind. **~ না-থাকা** be unmindful of; forget; lose sight of. **~খুশি** *n* a whim; a caprice; a fancy. **~খুশিমতো** *adv* whimsically; capriciously. **খেয়ালি** *adj* whimsical; capricious; fanciful; full of caprice. ❑*n* a singer of 'Khayal'.

খেরাজ [A] *n* land tax; land revenue. **খেরাজি** *adj* (of land) taxable; rent-bearing. **লা~** *adj* rent free; not liable to taxes.

খেলনা *n* a toy; a plaything.

খেলা[1] *n* **1** a game; a sport, a play. **2** toying with; dallying; dalliance: ছেলে~. **3** refreshment of the strength and spirits after toil; recreation; pastime; diversion; amusement. **4** a show or display of an entertaining feat; an exhibition: সাপের ~, জাদু ~. **~ঘর** *n* **1** a stadium for indoor games. **2** house of sand or mud built by children at play. **3** domestic life; earthly life: জীবনের ~ঘর. **~ধুলা** *n pl* games and sports; sports and pastime.

খেলা[2] *vt* **1** play; do things that pass the time pleasantly; have fun. **2** flash; cause lightning: ঝড়ের সাথে সাথে বিদ্যুৎ খেলতে শুরু করে, lightning played across the sky as the storm began. **3** pretend to do sth: সে মেয়েটিকে নিয়ে খেলছে, বিয়ে করবে না, he is only flirting with the girl, but won't marry her. **4** come to the mind; transpire; occur: বুদ্ধি খেলছে না. **খেলানো** *vt* **1** cause to play. **2** make a person do anything one wishes him to do. **3** (in football, hockey, etc) cause one to play by making passes to him. **~র সঙ্গী** *n* a play-mate.

খেলাপ [A] *n* violation (of a rule); breach (of a trust/ promise); infringement; transgression. **~ করা** *vt* infringe; violate; breach. **কথার ~** *n* breach of promise. **কিস্তি ~** *n* non-payment of an installment (of an amount stipulated for payment). **নিয়মের ~** infringement/ breach of a rule. **বিশ্বাসের ~** *n* breach of trust.

খেলাফত, খিলাফত [A] *n* **1** the office or rule of a Khalifa (caliph), successor to prophet Muhammad (sm). **2** (lit) successorship; succession. **3** the period of Islamic history during which the caliphs, as the symbol of unity of the world of Islam, played the dual role of the temporal sovereign and spiritual chief.

খেলো *adj* **1** of inferior quality; tawdry. **2** having no value; hollow; trivial; frolicsome; empty: ~ কথা. **3** base; mean, humiliated: ~ করা. **~ করা** *vt* belittle; cause to seem small or unimportant; debase; humiliate.

খেলোয়াড়, খেলোয়ার *n* **1** one who plays; a player; a sportsman. **2** an expert player/ sportsman. **3** a cunning man; a man clever in tricks, especially for getting what he wants. **4** a fraud; an intriguer; a conspirator; a diplomat.

খেলোয়াড়ি *adj* sportsmanlike. **~ মনোভাব** *n* sporting spirit.

খেশ [P] *adj* one's own. **~-কুটুম** *n* kith and kin; friends an relations. **খেশি** *n* **1** kinship; relationship by blood or matrimonial alliance. **2** kindred; relation; relative.

খেসারত [A] *n* a monetary consideration to make amends for some loss or injury; compensation. **~ দাবি করা** *vi* claim damages. **~ দেওয়া** *vi, vt* recompense for a loss or injury by monetary payment; pay for damages; compensate. **খেসারতি** *n* **1** the amount paid by way of compensation. **2** a suit for damages.

খেসারি *n* a variety of pulse.

খৈ=খই

খৈল=খইল

খোঁচা *n* **1** a puncture by a prick: কাঁটার ~. **2** act of pushing with sth slender: লাঠির ~. **3** (fig) act of hurting one's feelings: কথার ~. **4** a stroke of a pen: কলমের এক ~য় চাকরি খতম, dismissed by a stroke of the pen. ❑*adj* **1** sharp pointed: ~ ~ দাঁড়ি. **2** (fig) (of words) bitter or sarcastic; taunting: ~ ~ কথা. **~ মারা** *vt* **1** push or thrust against with something pointed; poke; pinch; prick. **2** (fig) make a caustic comment/ sarcastic reference.

খোঁচাখুঁচি *n* **1** act of pinching each other; mutual poking. **2** act of poking repeatedly. **3** uncomplimentary remarks against each other made in a meeting or through newspaper columns.

খোঁচানো *vt* 1 poke; pinch; prick. 2 urge on; stir up; provoke; incite. 3 cause annoyance; vex; irritate. 4 pester persistently for (payment of rent, loan, etc); press for or remind repeatedly.

খোঁজ *n* 1 the act of searching/seeking: ~ করা. 2 news; information; tidings: ~ নেওয়া. 3 address; whereabouts: ~ জানা. 4 the act of inquiring about one's welfare; inquiry. **~ করা** *vt* search; inquire about; seek; look for. **~ পাওয়া** *vt* find a trace of; track out; detect; discover. **~ নেওয়া** *vt* make inquiries; inquire about. **~খবর** *n pl* news; information. **~খবর নেওয়া** *vi* make inquiries about one's well-being; seek information about.

খোঁজাখুঁজি *n* looking for in a frantic fashion; hunting up and down. **~ করা** *vi* try frantically to trace out.

খোঁটা[1] *n* a sarcastic or censorious remark; a reflection. **~ দেওয়া** *vi* remind one sarcastically of sth unpleasant; make a cutting remark. **~ শোনা** *vi* be reminded of one's weak point in a sarcastic manner; be the target of a spiteful reference.

খোঁটা[2]=খুঁটা

খোঁড়া[1] *vt* dig in the soil; excavate. ❑*adj* excavated.

খোঁড়া[2] *adj* crippled in a limb or limbs; disabled. **ঘোড়া দেখে ~ হওয়া** be unwilling to walk to to see a conveyance.

খোঁপা *n* a coil of hair done by women at the back of the head; a bun; a chignon. **~ খোলা** *vi* undo/unfasten a bun. **~ বাঁধা** *vi* dress up the hair into a coil or bun. **আলগা ~** *n* a loose bun; a bun not tied with cords.

খোঁয়াড় *n* 1 a place for keeping cattle; cattle shed. 2 a pound where stray cattle are temporarily confined; an enclosure for keeping strayed or distrained cattle; a pen; a pinfold. **খোঁয়াড়ে দেওয়া** *vi vt* put in a pound.

খোকন *n* a child called in endearment; dear child.

খোকা *n* a little boy; a male child.

খোজা [P] *n* a castrated man, formerly employed an officer of state in charge of the *harem,* by Muslim rulers; a eunuch.

খোট্টা *n* (contemp) a man from upper India; an upcountry man. **খোট্টানি** *fem.* ❑*adj* insipid; glum; having no sense of humour: কাঠ~.

খোতবা [A] *n* the Imam's address to the congregation made before the Friday canonical prayer or after the Eid prayers.

খোদ [P] *adj* 1 in person: তিনি ~ উপস্থিত. 2 actual; real: ~ মালিক উপস্থিত. **~-কর্তা** *n* the master himself; the master in person.

খোদকার *n* a cutter of figures on wood or metal; an engraver. ❑*adj* self-acting; automatic. **খোদার উপর খোদকারি** unwarranted interference.

খোদা[1] [P] *n* Allah, the Creator, Nourisher and Sustainer of the universe. **~-ই-খিদমতগার** *n* 1 servant in the way of God. 2 a self-less servant. **~ওন্দ, ~বন্দ** *n* (voc) My Lord; Your Majesty (forms used in addressing sovereigns). **~তায়ালা** *n* Most Gracious Allah. **~ না খাস্তা** *int* God forbid. **~র কসম** *n* swearing by God. **~র খাসি** *n* (joc) *n* a corpulent person; a roly-poly. **~র জীব** *n* creatures made by God; God's creation. **~ই নূর** *n* the lustre of God. **~ হাফেজ** *int* God save you (formula used at parting).

খোদা[2] *vt* 1 cut lines in stone, metal or wood with a graver; cut figures on; engrave. 2 dig (a canal, etc); excavate. ❑*adj* 1 engraved. 2 excavated.

খোনা *adj* nasal; uttered through the nose. ❑*n* one who speaks through the nose. **~ সুর** *n* nasal tune.

খোন্দকার [P] *n* a surname used by some respectable Muslim families.

খোপ, খোপর *n* a hole; a cell for pigeon or poultry.

খোপা=খোঁপা

খোবানি=খুবানি

খোয়া[1] *n* stone chips; brickbats; macadam: ~ দিয়ে বাঁধানো, pave with stone chips; macadamize; cobble; metal. **~ বাঁধানো রাস্তা** *n* cobbled/metalled street.

খোয়া[2] *adj* lost; wasted; decayed; stolen. **~ যাওয়া** *vi* be lost; run to waste. **~নো** *vt* lose; squander away; waste.

খোয়াব [P] *n* 1 a dream. 2 a vain fancy; an illusion.

খোরপোশ [P] *n* 1 means of support or livelihood; maintenance. 2 food and clothing.

খোরমা, খুরমা [P] *n* date; the fruit of the date-palm.

খোরাক [P] *n* 1 that which supplies nourishment; food. 2 portion of food taken at one time; a meal. 3 the type of food or meals habitually eaten; diet. 4 one's capacity for eating: তার ~ বেশি. **খোরাকি** *n* 1 the cost of maintenance; allowance of provisions; ration-money.

খোল *n* 1 a basin-shaped musical instrument of brass, used in pairs; cymbals. 2 a cover or case: বালিশের ~, pillow case. 3 an outside crust or shell (as of a tortoise). 4 a hole; a hollow; a cavity; a socket: চোখের ~.

খোলস *n* the cast-off skin of a serpent, etc; slough: সাপের ~. **~ ছাড়া** *vi* (of snakes) cast off or slough off the skin.

খোলসা [A] *adj* **1** clear; free from ambiguity: ~ করে বলা, speak one's mind. **2** frank; open; candid: ~ মন. ~ হওয়া *vi* **1** clear up (as the sky). **2** (of bowels) have complete evacuation. দিল-~ *adj* open-hearted; frank; above-board.

খোলা[1] *vi, vt* **1** open; start; begin; set up: দোকান ~. **2** reopen: স্কুল খুলেছে, the school has reopened. **3** put off (as shoes or dress). **4** draw; unsheathe (as a sword). **5** unfasten; open: দরজা ~.

খোলা[2] *adj* **1** open; uncovered; bare. **2** unhindered; unrestricted: ~ হাওয়া. ❑*n* **1** a cover; a shell; a skin (of a fruit, etc). **2** a yard; a field; a place: হাট~, ধোপা~. **3** a frying pan.

খোলাখুলি *adv* plainly; openly. ❑*adj* open; frank: ~ আলোচনা, a frank discussion.

খোশ [P] *adj* **1** pleasant; agreeable; delightful: ~ খবর. **2** amusing; entertaining: ~ গল্প. ~ আখলাক *n* good manners; courteous conduct. ❑*adj* well-behaved; polished; refined; elegant. ~ আমদেদ *n* kind reception; welcome. ~ এলহান *n* sweet voice. ~ কবালা *n* (legal) a deed of conveyance willingly executed by the proprietor. ~কেতা *adj* of good physique; handsome. ~খত, ~খৎ *n* good hand-writing. ❑*adj* writing a good hand. ~খবর *n* happy tidings. ~খেয়াল *n* sweet will; fancy; whim; caprice: প্রভুর ~খেয়াল. ~খেয়ালি *adj* self-willed; capricious. ~-খোরাক *n* dainty food; delicious dishes. ~খোরাকি *adj* fond of/used to dainty food. ~গল্প *n* **1** an amusing tale. **2** chit-chat. ~-জবান *adj* well-speaking; eloquent. ~নবিস *n* a good writer; a calligrapher. ~নসিব *adj* lucky; fortunate. ~নসিবি *n* good luck. ~নাম *n* good name; reputation. ~পোশাক *n* fine clothes; good/elegant dress. ~পোশাকি *adj* well-dressed; foppish. ~বু *n* perfume; sweet scent; fragrance. ~বুদার *adj* **1** sweet-smelling; fragrant. **2** having a savoury smell; spicy; balmy; aromatic. ~ মেজাজ *adj* cheerful; gay. ❑*n* good humour. ~ রং *n* agreeable colour; sweet colour. ~রোজ *n* **1** a happy day; a day of rejoicing. **2** new year's day. ~ হাল *n* good condition. ❑*adj* well-to-do; well-off.

খোশামোদ, খোশামোদি [P] *n* servile/obsequious flattery; servility; sycophancy; adulation. ~ করা *vi vt* flatter; adulate. খোসামুদে *adj* flattering; uttering false praise. ❑*n* person who flatters; a flatterer.

খোস *n* a kind of skin disease; itches: ~ পাঁচড়া.

খোসা *n* the skin of a fruit or vegetable: কলার ~. ~ ছাড়ানো *vt* peel off the skin (of a fruit).

খৌরি=খেউরি

খ্যাত *adj* famous; renowned. ~নামা *adj* widely praised; celebrated. খ্যাতি *n* fame; renown; distinction; celebrity. খ্যাতিমান *adj* distinguished; renowned.

খ্যাপা=খেপা

খ্রিষ্ট, খ্রিস্ট *n* Jesus Christ, the founder of Christianity. ~ধর্ম *n* Christianity, the religion founded by Jesus Christ. ~ ধর্মাবলম্বী *n, adj* (one) following Christianity; a Christian. ~পূর্ব *adj* (era) before Christ.

খ্রিষ্টান, খ্রিস্টান *n, adj* Christian.

খ্রিষ্টাব্দ, খ্রিস্টাব্দ *n* Christian era.

খ্রিষ্টীয়, খ্রিস্টীয় *adj* of or relating to Christ/ Christianity; Christian.

গ

গ[1] *n* the third consonant of the Bengali alphabet. It is a velar voiced unaspirated plosive sound.

গ[2] *suff, adj* in the state of moving towards/ upwards/downwards: ঊর্ধ্বগ, নিম্নগ.

গওহর [P] *n* a precious stone; a gem.

গং abbreviation of Arabic গয়রহ, meaning 'and the others': আবদুল করিম গং

গঁদ [U] *n* a sticky and viscous substance exuded from acacia, etc; any sticky substance for use as an adhesive; gum; gum-arabic. ~ লাগানো *vi, vt* stick, join or fasten with gum; smear with gum. গঁদের ~ *n* a relation of a relation; a distant relation.

গগন *n* the sky; the heavens. ~চারী *n* a flying creature; a bird. ❑*adj* moving in the sky. ~চুম্বী *adj* sky-kissing; sky-high; rising to a great height. ~চুম্বী অট্টালিকা *n* a sky-scraper. ~চ্যুত *adj* fallen from the sky. ~তল *n* the region of the air; the firmament. ~মণ্ডল *n* the sky; the heavens; the welkin. ~স্পর্শী *adj* touching the sky; very lofty.

গগলস্ [E] *n* spectacles with or without hoods to protect the eyes from the wind, dust, etc; goggles.

গঙ্গা *n* the Ganges; the river Ganga. ~জলি *n* pouring Ganges water into the mouth of a dying person as an act of piety according to Hindu belief; swearing by the holy water of the Ganges prevalent among the Hindus. ~প্রাপ্ত *adj* one who has attained the Ganges, ie death. ~-যমুনা *n* the Ganges and the Jamuna. ❑*adj* bi-coloured; made of gold and silver.

গঙ্গোপাধ্যায় *n* family name of certain Bengali Brahmins.

গচ্চা *n* penalty or loss suffered for one's folly or carelessness. ~ দেওয়া/খাওয়া *vt* suffer a loss; pay penalty (for).

গচ্ছিত *adj* placed in one's custody; entrusted; deposited. ~ **রাখা** *vt* place sth in the custody of someone; entrust someone with sth for safe custody. ~ **নেওয়া** *vt* receive/keep sth in trust. ~ **অর্থ** *n* trust money. ~ **সম্পদ** *n* trust property.

গছা, গছানো *vt* persuade/cause someone to receive sth.

গজ[১] *n* **1** the elephant. **2** (in chess) a piece which moves diagonally; a bishop. ~**কচ্ছপ** *n* **1** (Hindu myth) two sons of a sage mutually antagonistic and fighting for the paternal wealth were turned into an elephant and a huge tortoise but this couldn't put a stop to their fighting for the coveted inheritance and hence the diction: গজ কচ্ছপের যুদ্ধ, meaning a tug of war between two equals. ~**কপালে** *adj* one having a spacious forehead like the elephant and hence fortunate. ~**কুম্ভ** *n* the frontal globe of an elephant. ~**গতি** *adj* one moving in the slow and majestic pace of an elephant. ❑*n* a metre in Sanskrit verses. ~**গামিনী** *adj fem* **1** riding on an elephant. **2** walking in the stately gait of an elephant. ~**গামী** *mas.* ~**ঘন্টা** *n* a bell tied to the neck of an elephant. ~**চক্ষু** *n* eyes very small and ill-matched to the bulk of the body as those of the elephant. ~**দন্ত** *n* **1** the tusk of an elephant; ivory. **2** tooth overlapping another in humans. ~**পতি** *n* king of elephants; noble elephant. ~**বীথি** *n* an orderly line of elephants. ~**ভুক্ত কপিত্থবৎ** *adj, adv* **1** like the sour wood-apple, eaten up by the microscopic worm গজ, which enters the fruit indiscernibly and eats up the whole kernel without causing any outward injury to the fruit. **2** (fig) utterly hollow and useless though apparently looking sound and intact. ~**মোতি** *n* pearls of a large species fabled to have been shed from an elephant's head. ~**মোতির হার** *n* a necklace strewn with such pearls.

গজ[২] *n* a measure of length equal to two cubits; a yard: তিন ~ কাপড়. ~**কাঠি** *n* a yardstick for measuring cloth.

গজব [A] *n* **1** a punishment from God; an act of God, as the occurrence of a natural calamity. **2** tyranny; oppression; violence; outrage; injustice.

গজল, গযল [A] *n* **1** a musical mode. **2** love-song; love-lyric cultivated by Sufis. **3** religious song.

গজা *n* a variety of dry sweet.

গজানন *n* an appellation of Hindu deity Ganesha.

গজানো *vi* (of seeds) shoot out; sprout. ❑*adj* sprouted; grown.

গজারি *n* a variety of timber tree.

গজাল *n* a large-size nail. ~ **মারা** *vi* drive a nail.

গজেন্দ্র *n* the superb one among elephants; the leader of a herd of wild elephants. ~**গমন** *n* (of a person's movement) like the gait of an elephant.

গঞ্জ *n* a market-place; an entrepot of trade.

গঞ্জন *n* act of scolding/reproaching (a subordinate). **গঞ্জনা** *n* reproach; scolding; upbraiding. **গঞ্জনা দেওয়া** *vt* put (one) to shame by taking to task; reproach; scold; upbraid.

গঞ্জায়িশ [P] *n* capacity to accommodate; accommodation.

গঞ্জিকা *n* ganja, a narcotic drug prepared from the flowering top of hemp plant; an intoxicant. ~ **সেবন করা** *vi,vt* smoke ganja or hemp. ~**সেবী** *adj* given to smoking ganja. ❑*n* a habitual smoker of hemp.

গট গট *int* (onom) suggesting proud footstep that produces sound on the ground. ~ **করে চলা** walk with firm steps that gives an impression of arrogance.

গঠন *n* **1** act of making or forming: দল ~. **2** construction; constitution: দেহের ~. **3** shape; form; appearance: সুন্দর ~. ~ **করা** *vt* form; construct; build; make; create. ~**ভঙ্গি**, ~**শৈলী** *n* the style or the manner of construction. ~**সৌষ্ঠব** *n* the beauty or elegance of a construction. **গঠিত** *adj* formed; shaped; constructed; built.

গড্ডলিকা *n* **1** *fem* the female sheep that walks at the head of a flock. **2** flock of sheep blindly following the ewe at the head. ~ **প্রবাহ** *n* an instance of doing what sb else has done without looking to its merit or demerit just as a flock of sheep blindly follows suit behind the bell-wether.

গড়[১] *n* **1** a fortress; a stronghold. **2** a long ditch usually filled with water around a castle or fort for defence purposes; a trench; a moat. **3** a thrashing hollow for husking grains by a husking pedal. ~**খাই**=গড়[১](2).

গড়[২] *n* an average; an approximate amount. **গড়ে** *adv* on an average. ~**পড়তা** *adj* average; approximate. ❑*adv* approximately; on an average.

গড়গড়া *n* a smoking device in which the smoke is made to come through water by means of a pipe; a hubble-bubble or a hookah.

গড়ন *n* **1** construction; formation; constitution. **2** the beauty or the tidiness of a construction. ~**পিটন**, ~**পেটন** *n* shape; appearance. ~**দার** *n* one who makes things by casting metals; a metal-worker; a moulder.

গড়া *vt* 1 make; mould: পুতুল ~. 2 cause formation of sth; form: দল ~. 3 set up; found: স্কুল ~. 4 bring up; rear: সন্তান ~; cause improvement by hard work; develop: দেশ ~. ❑*adj* built; constructed; made; developed.

গড়াগড়ি *n* 1 rolling about on the ground either in sport or in grief. 2 signs of affluence/ abundance manifest in the careless and negligent handling of things. **টাকা পয়সায় ~ যাওয়া** *vi* roll/wallow in money, riches; be very rich.

গড়ানো *vt* 1 cause to be made: গহনা ~. 2 (of water) roll down; flow on: তারপর পদ্মা মেঘনা দিয়ে বহু জল গড়িয়েছে, much water has rolled down the Padma and Meghna since then; much time has elapsed in the mean time. 3 rest or repose; recline: একটু গড়িয়ে নিই, let me stretch for a while. 4 go forward; advance: ব্যাপারটা অনেক দূর গড়িয়েছে, the matter has run too far.

গড়িমসি *n* wilful delay; procrastination; dilatoriness; shilly-shally. **~ করা** *vi* procrastinate; dilly-dally; shilly-shally.

গণ *n pl* 1 *suff* indicating a number more than one: বালক~, the boys; কৃষক~, the farmers. 2 the common people; the masses: ~ আন্দোলন. 3 a class; a company; a group; a faction; a party. **~ অভ্যুত্থান** *n* an upheaval among the masses; a mass rising; a mass revolt. **~ আন্দোলন** *n* a political movement taking root among the masses; a mass movement. **~ আদালত** *n* people's court. **~তন্ত্র** *n* a form of government in which the supreme power is vested in the elected representatives of all classes of people for the benefit of all classes; democracy. 2 a state run on democratic method; a republic. **~তন্ত্রী, ~তান্ত্রিক** *adj* following the democratic ways and principles; democratic. **~ভোট** *n* a vote of a whole people; plebiscite. **~শক্তি** *n* the united strength of the people; the people collectively; the sovereignty of the people.

গণক *n* 1 one who is versed in the art of foretelling future events from the stars; an astrologer. 2 one who tells fortunes by the hand; a palmist. 3 one who or that which calculates.

গণন, গণনা *n* 1 counting; reckoning; enumeration: সংখ্যা ~. 2 calculation; computation: লাভক্ষতি ~. 3 act of judging (as); judgement; decision: দোষী বলে ~. 4 act of considering/regarding (as): শত্রু বলে ~. 5 (astrol) reading; predicting; foretelling: ভাগ্য ~. **~ করা** *vt* count; compute; regard; calculate. **~কারী** *n* an enumerator. **গণনার্হ** *adj* worthy of being reckoned/counted; worth-considering; to be reckoned with. **গণনীয়** *adj* countable calculable.

গণিকা *n* a prostitute; a harlot. **~লয়** *n* house of ill-fame; a brothel.

গণিত *n* the science of mathematics comprising arithmetic, geometry, algebra, etc (also ~বিদ্যা). **~জ্ঞ** *adj* versed in mathematics. ❑*n* a mathematician. **~ বিষয়ক** *adj* mathematical.

গণিমত [A] *n* spoils of war captured from an enemy; war booty. **মালে ~** *n* goods and chattels captured as booty.

গণেশ *n* Ganesha, the Hindu deity of success and wealth.

গণ্ড *n*1 the side of the face below the eyes on each side; the cheek: ~দেশ. 2 a morbid swelling in any part of the body; a tumour: গল~. 3 any roundish organ in a part of the body secreting some fluid; a gland: ~ মালা. 4 a mound; a mass (as of a rock): ~শৈল. ❑*adj* big; large: ~গ্রাম. **~কূপ** *n* a small natural depression in the cheek or chin; a dimple. **~গ্রাম** *n* 1 a large and populous village. 2 an outlying backward village. **~দেশ** *n* the cheek; the chin. **~মূর্খ** *adj* most foolish/ignorant; grossly stupid. ❑*n* a big fool; an egregious/arrant fool; a blockhead. **~ শৈল** *n* a mass of rock; a hillock. **~স্থল**=~দেশ.

গণ্ডা *n* 1 an aggregate of four: এক ~ বাচ্চা. 2 one's due from someone: পাওনা ~. **~ গণ্ডা** *adv* in large numbers.

গণ্ডার *n* a large heavy-hoofed animal with a thick hide creased into folds, and with one or two horns on the nose; the rhinoceros. **গণ্ডারের চামড়া** *adj* (abusive) thick-skinned.

গণ্ডি *n* 1 a line encircling an area; a boundary line. 2 bounds; limit. 3 an area encircled by a line and immunized by a charm. **~ দেওয়া** *vt* draw a cordon all round.

গণ্ডূষ *n* water of as little amount as one can take on his palm or in his mouth. **~ করা** *vi* (according to Hindu belief) take water on one's palm, utter some sacred incantation and then sip it.

গণ্য *adj* 1 worthy of being reckoned with; deserving consideration. 2 considered or recognized (as): বিদ্বান বলে ~. **~ করা** *vt* reckon; consider; recognize. **~মান্য** *adj* worthy of being honoured; respectable.

গৎ *n* 1 musical note; fixed form of instrumental music. 2 fixed or set form/method of anything: ~ বাঁধা জীবন.

গত *adj* 1 gone by or beyond; past; spent; ended. 2 next before the present; last: ~ বছর. 3 deceased; dead: তিনি ~ হয়েছেন, he is dead/gone. 4 obtained; acquired; gained: পুঁথি~ বিদ্যা. 5 relating to; pertaining to; based on:

বংশ~. **6** in accordance/conformity with; according to: প্রথা~. ~ **হওয়া** *vi, vt* go by; pass away; die. **এক মাস ~ হলো** it is a month since. ~**কল্য,** ~**কাল** *n, adv* yesterday. ~ **পরশু** *n, adv* (the) day before yesterday. ~ **বছর** *n, adv* last year. ~**যৌবন** *adj* past one's prime of life; middle-aged. ~**যৌবনা** *adj fem* past one's youth. ~**শোক** *adj* one who has conquered grief and sorrow. ~**শোচনা** *n* grief for the past.

গতর *n* **1** body; physique. **2** bulkiness of the body. **3** health; the condition of the body. **4** physical strength; ability. ~**খাকি,** ~**খাগি** *adj fem* **1** averse to work despite being physically fit; lazy woman. ~ **খাটানো** *vi* work hard; undergo physical labour. ~**খেকো** *n mas* person who is averse to physical labour.

গতানুগতিক *adj* **1** in accordance with routine; usual; traditional; customary. **2** not admitting new ideas/novelty. **3** having an uninteresting sameness; lacking in variety; monotonous. ~**তা** *n* the tiring or uninteresting sameness; subservience to routine. ~**ভাবে** *adv* in a customary fashion; in the traditional way.

গতি *n* **1** the act or the state of moving; motion; movement. **2** speed; velocity. **3** a method or way (of doing); means: অন্য ~ নেই. **4** a helper; a protector; a refuge or shelter: আপনিই একমাত্র ~. **5** funeral ceremonies; obsequies: মৃতের ~. ~ **করা** *vt* make arrangement for; take necessary action; do the needful. ~**বিদ্যা,** ~**বিজ্ঞান** the science that deals with matter in movement; dynamics. ~**বিধি** *n* one's movement, activity: শত্রুর ~বিধি. ~**রোধ** *n* act of obstructing the motion; obstruction or stoppage of movement. ~**রোধ করা** *vt* check or obstruct the movement. ~**হীন** *adj* **1** motionless; immobile; still.

গতিক *n* **1** state; condition: মনের ~. **2** means of achieving sth; a stratagem: কোনো গতিকে পালাতে হবে. **কার্যগতিকে** *adv* in course of business; on business.

গতিবিধি *n* ⇒গতি

গত্যন্তর *n* an alternative means/course; alternative.

গদগদ *int* **1** suggesting a voice choked with emotion: ~ কণ্ঠ. **2** overwhelmed with emotion; ecstatic: ~ চিত্ত. ~ **কণ্ঠে** *adv* with a voice choked with emotion.

গদা *n* (myth) a wooden hammer used in duels; a mallet; a mace; a club. ~**পাণি** *adj* holding a mallet. ❑*n* an appellation of Vishnu. ~**যুদ্ধ** *n* a duel fought with mallets.

গদাই লস্করি *adj* slow-moving; not very active or quick; sluggish: ~ চাল.

গদি [H] *n* **1** a mattress; a cushion. **2** a mercantile office: মহাজনের ~. **3** power of government; authority to rule: ~ আঁকড়ে থাকা. ~**য়ান** *adj* seated in the position of authority; holding power; ruling.

গদ্য *n, adj* (lit) composition without rhyme; prose: ~ ভাষা. ~ **ছন্দ** *n* prose composition with metrical rhythm. ~ **কবিতা** *n* prose poem.

গনগন *int* (onom) denoting blazing fire. **গনগনে আগুন** *n* blazing fire.

গনৎকার *n* (astrol) one who practises palmistry; a palmist; an astrologer; a foreteller.

গনতি=গুনতি

গনাগোষ্ঠী *n* one's whole family.

গনানো *vt* **1** cause (sth) to be calculated by another. **2** have one's hand/fortune read by a palmist.

গনি [A] *adj* rich; wealthy.

গন্তব্য *adj* the place for which one has set out; the place to which anything is bound; predetermined end; destination; goal (also ~ স্থল). ~ **পথ** *n* the way to be used to reach one's destination.

গন্দম [P] *n* the forbidden fruit of the Heaven spoken of in the Qoran.

গন্ধ *n* **1** that which is perceived by the faculty of smelling; an odour; a scent; a stench. **2** the sense of smell; smelling: ~ নেওয়া. **3** a pleasant smell; a scent; a perfume; fragrance. **4** presence or trace of sth in sth : নাম~ নাই. **5** connection: এ কাজে টাকার কোনো ~ নেই. **6** a hint: বিপদের ~. ~ **ছড়ানো** *vi* emit/give out smell. ~ **পাওয়া** *vi* get the smell of. ~ নেওয়া/শোঁকা *vi* smell. ~**কাষ্ঠ** *n* the fragrant wood of certain trees; the sandal wood. ~**গোকুল** *n* a variety of pole-cat or civet. ~ জল/তৈল *n* perfumed or scented water/oil. ~**দ্রব্য** *n* aromatic substance. ~**পুষ্প** *n* a fragrant flower. ~**বণিক** *n* a Hindu caste dealing in perfumes and spices; a member of this caste. ~**রাজ** *n* the gardenia flower. ~**হীন** *adj* scentless; unscented.

গন্ধক *n* a simple mineral substance of yellow colour which burns with a pale-blue flame; sulphur; brimstone. ~ **চূর্ণ** *n* sulphur powder; gunpowder. ~ **দ্রাবক, গন্ধকাম্ল** *n* sulphuric acid.

গন্ধর্ব *n* **1** heavenly musician (according to Hindu myth). **2** a born musician. ~ **বিদ্যা** *n* the science and art of music. ~ **বিবাহ** *n* love marriage without any formal ceremony. ~ **বেদ** *n* a treatise on music. ~ **লোক** *n* the abode of the heavenly musicians. ~ **ছুটানো** *vi, vt* chase one with severe blows and thrashing.

গপগপ *int* (onom) denoting gulping sound. ~ **করে খাওয়া** *vt* gobble up; gulp.

গবাক্ষ *n* **1** a ventilator; a window.

গবাদি *n* the cow and the domestic animals of the like; the cattle.

গবেষণা *n* a diligent investigation of new facts and additional information; research. ~ **করা** *vi, vt* research; investigate. **গবেষক** *n* one who is engaged in research work; a researcher; research scholar.

গব্য *adj* **1** of or pertaining to cows. **2** produced of the cow or cow milk: ~ ঘৃত.

গভর্নমেন্ট [E] *n* **1** people controlling the administration of public affairs of a state; government. **2** system of polity in a state.

গভর্নর [E] *n* the head of government of a province; a governor.

গভীর *adj* **1** being far below the surface; extending far down; deep: ~ সমুদ্র. **2** intricate; complicated; complex: ~ তত্ত্ব. **3** dense; thick; compact: ~ অরণ্য. **4** intense; absorbing; profound: ~ প্রণয়. **5** far-advanced: ~ রাত্রি. **6** obscure; opaque: ~ অন্ধকার. ~ **রাতে** *adv* at dead of night. ~ **শ্বসন** *n* deep breathing. ~**তা** *n* depth; profundity; intensity; thickness. ~ **পানির মাছ** *n* deep-water fish; (fig) a very cunning and calculating person.

গম *n* a food crop; wheat.

গমক *n* modulation of voice in singing.

গমগম *int* (onom) denoting reverberation or echo: আসর ~ করছে, the assembly is agog/ in a state of eager excitement.

গমন *n* **1** act of going; departure. **2** manner of walking or stepping; gait. **3** motion; movement. **4** amorous sport; love-making: পরদার ~. ~ **করা** *vi, vt* go; move; approach; depart; pass. ~ **পথ** *n* route. **গমনাগমন** *n* coming and going; frequenting. **গমনার্হ, গমনীয়** *adj* fit to be approached; accessible; open to passage; destination. **গমনোদ্যত** *adj* about to go/depart/ move. **গমনোন্মুখ** *adj* ready to go.

গম্বুজ=গুম্বজ

গম্ভীর *adj* **1** grave; thoughtful; weighty: ~ স্বর. **2** having an important or grave air: ~ চাল. **3** serious; momentous: ~ বিষয়. **4** sullen or sad; gloomy; reserved: ~ মুখ.

গম্ভীরা *n* **1** a kind of folk-song connected with the worship of Shiva. **2** the inside of a Hindu temple.

গম্য *adj* **1** fit to be visited; accessible. **2** that may be comprehended; comprehensible; intelligible : বোধ~. **3** fit for sexual union. **গম্যা** *adj fem* fit to be enjoyed : অগম্যা নারী.

গযব=গজব

গযল=গজল

গয়না[1]=গহনা[1]

গয়না[2]=গহনা[2]

গয়বি=গায়েবি

গয়র [A] *adv* without; on the outside of. ~ **ইসলামি** *adj* outside the pale of Islam; anti-Islamic. ~ **হাযির** *adj* absent.

গয়রহ [A] *int* meaning 'and the others'; et cetera.

গয়লা=গোয়ালা

গরজ, গরয [A] *n* **1** interest; exigency; necessity: আপন গরজে, in one's own interest. **2** attention; devotion: পড়াশুনায় ~. ~ **করা** *vi,vt* be earnest; pay attention. **গরজি** *adj* interested; having self-interest. ☐ used as *suff,* eg আপ্তগরজি, self-interested. ~ **বড়ো বালাই** Necessity knows no law.

গরদ *n* a kind of silk fabric.

গরদিশ [P] *n* sudden great misfortune; a disaster; a reverse; an upset: নসিবের ~.

গরবিনী *adj fem* gracious; honoured; proud. **গরবী** *mas.*

গরম [P] *n* **1** heat: খুব ~ পড়েছে. **2** the summer season. **3** arrogance; pride; haughtiness: টাকার ~. ☐*adj* **1** hot: ~ পানি. **2** angry; enraged: মেজাজ ~. **3** producing enough pleasant heat; warm: ~ কাপড়. **4** fresh and exciting: ~ খবর. **5** tasting like spice: ~ মশলা. **6** deer; costly: ~ বাজার. **7** likely to cause people to explode with strong feeling; explosive: ~ পরিস্থিতি. ~ **~, গরমা ~** *adj* **1** (of food) hot and fresh from the oven. **2** (of news, events, etc) fresh and exciting. ~ **মশলা** *n* spices (cardamoms, cinnamon, etc). ~ **মোজা** *n* woolen socks. **কুসুম কুসুম** ~*adj* moderately warm; tepid; lukewarm. **মাথা ~ হওয়া** *vi* (fig) be angry/enraged.

গরমিল [A+U] *n* **1** disunity; discord. **2** discrepancy in the accounts; disagreement between receipts and payment: হিসাবের ~. **3** estrangement; dissension.

গরয=গরজ

গররাজি [A] *adj* not consenting; unwilling; reluctant. ~ **হওয়া** *vi* express one's unwillingness; not to agree; disagree.

গরল *n* **1** poison. **2** a kind of wound; a sore.

গরহাজির [A] *adj* absent. **গরহাজিরা** *n* absence.

গরাদে *n* a bar (of a window).

গরিব [A] *adj* having a low standard of living; poor. ~**খানা** *n* (in polite speech) dwelling house (of the speaker): আমার ~ খানায় আসবেন, Please come to my humble abode. ~ **নওয়াজ** [A+P] *n* the helper or refuge of the poor. **গরিবানা** *adj* **1** of or like a poor; befitting a poor. **2** poverty; indigence. **খাজা ~-নওয়াজ** the famous Sufi saint Khwaja Muinuddin Chisty of Ajmer.

গরীব=গরিব

গরিমা *n* **1** great fame or success; glory; honour. **2** pride; vanity.

গরিলা [E] a large and strong manlike monkey without a tail; a gorilla.

গরিষ্ঠ *adj* most important; largest; greatest; weightiest. **~ সাধারণ গুণনীয়ক, (সং) গ. সা. গু.** **1** (arith) greatest common measure; G. C. M. **2** (in alg) highest common factor; H. C. F. **~ সম্প্রদায়** *n* the majority community.

গরীয়ান *adj* **1** more important; more venerable; larger; richer. **2** full of glory; glorious; honourable; renowned; celebrated; brilliant. **3** most adorable. **গরীয়সী** *fem.*

গরু, গোরু *n* **1** the cow. **2** the ox; the bull: ~র গাড়ি. **3** a cow. **4** (ridi) an illiterate person; an idiot. **~খোঁজা করা** *vt* look for (sth) frantically; move heaven and earth to find out (sth). **~চোর** *n* a cattle-lifter; one who steals/ has stolen a cow. **~ মেরে জুতা দান** the ridiculous idea of making amends for committing a heinous sin with a small gift. **~র গাড়ি** *n* a bullock-cart. **~র পাল** *n* a herd of cows.

গরুড় *n* the prince of birds and mount of Vishnu according to Hindu Purana.

গর্জন[১] *n* **1** loud continued sound; cry of a beast; roar; roaring: মেঘের ~, সিংহের ~. **2** shouting aloud in anger or in reproach; a bawl; a loud scream. **~ করা** *vt* roar; bawl; scream; squall. **গর্জিত** *adj* sounded/ resounded loudly.

গর্জন[২] *n* a kind of tree or its timber. **~ তেল/তৈল** *n* an oily aromatic substance obtained from the ~ tree and used in varnishing, and also as a medicinal oil for rheumatism.

গর্ত *n* **1** a pit; a hole; a burrow; a ditch. **2** a crevice or hollow (as of a tree). **3** a slot; cavity. **4** a cavern; a cave. **~ করা** *vi* make/ dig a hole. **~ ভরাট করা** *vi* fill a hole.

গর্দভ *n* **1** brownish-grey quadruped with long ears, akin to the horse; the ass. **2** (fig) a stupid person; an utter fool. **গর্দভী** *fem.*

গর্দান [P] *n* **1** the shoulder; the neck; the throat. **2** the head with the neck. **~ যাওয়া** *vt* be decapitated (as a legal punishment); be sentenced to death. **~ নেওয়া** *vi* behead; kill; decapitate. **গর্দানি** *n* pushing out by the neck. **গর্দানি দেওয়া** *vt* push by the neck; collar out.

গর্ব *n* **1** inordinate self-esteem; pride; conceit; vanity. **2** boasting; bragging; blustering: ~ খর্ব করা. **3** a cause of pride; glory: শহীদগণ জাতির ~. **~ করা** *vt* pride oneself on; boast; brag. **~ খর্ব করা** humble one's pride; make one kiss the ground; humiliate. **~শূন্য** *adj* free from pride; unpretentious; modest. **গর্বান্ধ** *adj* puffed with pride; haughty; arrogant. **গর্বিত, গর্বী** *adj* proud; conceited; boastful; vainglorious. **গর্বিণী, গর্বিতা** *fem.* **গর্বোজ্জ্বল** *adj* radiant with glory; full of glory; glorious. **গর্বোদ্ধত** *adj* arrogant; vainglorious.

গর্ভ *n* **1** the inside or interior part of a thing: শূন্য~. **2** the ground or bed underneath a mass of water; the bottom: নদী~. **3** any deep cavity; the uterus; the womb: মাতৃ~. **4** the embryo; the fetus or fœtus: ~পাত. **5** the first forming of the embryo in the womb; pregnancy; conception: ~লক্ষণ. **6** a hollow; a pit: খনি~. **~ হওয়া** *vi* become pregnant; be with a child. **~কাল** *n* the carrying of young in the womb from conception to delivery; gestation. **~কেশর** *n* (bot) the female seed bearing part of a flower; the pistil. **~কোষ** *n* (bot) a seed-vessel. **~গৃহ** *n* **1** a lying in room. **2** an ante-chamber. **~চ্যুত** *adj* dropped from the womb; miscarried. **~চ্যুতি** *n* miscarriage. **~জ** *adj* born of the womb. **~ধারণ** *n* impregnation; gestation; conception. **~ ধারণ করা** *vi* conceive; be with a child. **~ধারিণী** *n* mother. **~নাড়ি** *n* the umbilical cord. **~পাত** *n* miscarriage; abortion. **~পাত করা** *vi* cause abortion. **~পাত হওয়া** have abortion; miscarry. **~ফুল** *n* the organ connecting the mother and fœtus; the placenta. **~বতী** *adj* in the family way; with child; pregnant. **~বতী হওয়া** *vt* (of women) conceive; become pregnant; (of beasts) be big with young. **~ বেদনা/ব্যথা** *n* labour pain; travail. **~মোচন** *n* delivery of a child. **~মোচন করা** *vi* be delivered of a child. **~যন্ত্রণা** = ~ব্যথা. **~যন্ত্রণা ভোগ করা** *vi* be in travail; be in labour. **~লক্ষণ** *n* signs of pregnancy. **~সঞ্চার** *n* impregnation; conception. **~ সঞ্চার হওয়া** *vi* be with child; be pregnant. **~স্রাব** *n* abortion; miscarriage. **~স্রাব হওয়া** *vi* miscarry.

গর্হিত *adj* utterly condemned; censured; forbidden; reproachable. **~ কাজ** *n* a heinous act/ reprehensible conduct.

গর্হ্য *adj* abominable; condemnable; blameworthy.

গল *n* **1** the throat; the neck. **~কম্বল** *n* the fold of the skin that hangs from the throat of oxen, etc; dew-lap. **~গণ্ড** *n* a morbid enlargement of the thyroid gland; a goitre. **~গ্রহ** *n* one who is an undesirable burden on another's shoulders; a hanger-on; a parasite. **~দাহ** *n* inflammation of the throat; sore-throat; laryngitis. **~দেশ** *n* the throat; the neck. **~নালী** *n* the wind-pipe; the esophagus; the larynx. **~বস্ত্র** *n* piece of cloth worn round the neck in obeisance or as a mark of humility, according to Indian customs. **~ভঙ্গ** *n* hoarseness of voice; huskiness; sore-throat. **~রন্ধ্র** *n* the cavity of the throat; the larynx. **~রস গ্রন্থি** *n* adenoids. **~হস্ত** *n* act of throttling or collaring (of a person). **~হস্ত দেওয়া** *vi, vt* pushing (one) out by the neck.

গলগল *int* (onom) denoting the sound of liquids flowing profusely. **~ করে** *adv* glibly; by gulps. **~ করে গেলা** *vt* gulp down.

গলতি [A] *n* a mistake; an error; a shortcoming; a defect.

গলদ [A] *n* a failing; fault; an omission. **~ করা** *vt* commit an error/fault; omit (sth) through inadvertence or incapacity. **~ থাকা** *vi* be erroneous or faulty.

গলদা *n* a big-size edible crustacean; The prawn (also ~ চিংড়ি). ❑*adj* fat; bulky: ~ চেহারা.

গলদঘর্ম *adj* weltering in sweat; perspiring copiously. **~ হওয়া** *vi* perspire; sweat.

গলন *n* **1** act of being melted; melting. **2** act of passing through. **3** bursting out (of a boil, etc) and secreting pus, etc. **গলনাঙ্ক** *n* the melting point of heat.

গলা[1] *vi, vt* **1** become liquid through heating; melt: বরফ ~. **2** pass or slip through a hole or crack. **3** (fig) be overwhelmed with emotion: আনন্দে গলে যাওয়া. **4** (of a boil, etc) burst out and secrete morbid substance: ফোঁড়া ~. **5** go into; enter: দরজায় মাথা গলানো. **6** be fully boiled: ভাত/ডাল ~. **7** be sympathetic: মন ~. ❑*adj* melted; burst open; softened.

গলা[2] *n* **1** the front side of the neck; the throat. **2** voice: মোটা ~, মিহি ~. **~ কাটা** *vi* **1** kill (one) by separating the head from the body. **2** (fig) defraud or deceive one. **~ কাটা দর** *n* exorbitant price. **~ খাঁকারি দেওয়া** *vi* clear one's voice by hawking; clear the throat noisily. **গলাধঃকরণ** *n* act of swallowing or gulping. **গলাধঃকরণ করা** *vt* swallow; gulp. **~বাজি** *n* shouting; bragging; bullying. **~বাজি করা** *vi,* talk big; shout; brag. **~বাজি করে জেতা** *vi, vt* shout others down. **ভারী ~** *n* grave voice. **~য় ~য়** *adv* neck to neck; very closely; intimately. ❑*adj* very close; intimate.

গলি [H, U] *n* a narrow street; a lane; an alley. **কানা ~** *n* an alley with an opening on one side only; a blind alley. **~ঘুঁজি** *n pl* lanes and by lanes; nook and corner.

গলিজ [A] *adj* **1** dirty; filthy. **2** decomposed; rotten. **3** full of stench.

গলিত *adj* **1** that which has melted; liquefied. **2** decomposed; rotten. **~ কুষ্ঠ** *n* ulcerous leprosy.

গলুই *n* the tapering parts at the front and at the back of a boat; the prow; the stern.

গল্প *n* **1** a story; a tale; a fable; a novel. **2** talk; conversation; chitchat; gossip. **~ করা** *vt vi* talk; converse; gossip. **~ পড়া** *vi* read a story/novel. **~ ফাঁদা** *vi* invent/ fabricate a story. **~ বলা** *vi* tell a story. **~ লেখা** *vi* write stories or tales. **~ শোনা** *vi* listen to a story. **~ গুজব, ~সল্প** *n pl* gossip; chitchat.

গহনা[1] *n* ornament; jewellery. **~গাঁটি** *n pl* jewellery.

গহনা[2] *n* boat service carrying passengers in between fixed places at fixed times: ~র নৌকা.

গহিন, গহীন *adj* deep; dense: ~ অরণ্য. **2** far advanced: ~ রাত. **~ রাতে** *adv* at dead of night.

গহ্বর *n* a hole; a cavity; a pit.

গা[1] *n* **1** the body; the physique: গায়ের জোর. **2** the surface or outer side of anything: দেয়ালের গা. **3** the natural outer covering of an animal or human body; the skin; the hide: খসখসে গা. **4** sensibility; sensitiveness: অপমান গায়ে লাগে না. **5** attention; willingness; interest: কাজে গা নেই. **গা করা** *vt* be interested (in); set one's mind (to). **গা কাঁপা** *vi* shudder (in fear, etc); shiver (as in cold). **গা কেমন কেমন করা** *vi* **1** have nausea. **2** feel uneasy owing to fear, indisposition, etc. **গা গরম হওয়া** have or run a temperature; become feverish. **~ ঘামানো** *vi* undergo a toilsome job. **গা জুড়ানো** *vi* have rest; refresh. **গা জ্বালা করা** *vi* **1** have a burning sensation in the body. **2** (fig) be irritated at sth; be jealous/ angry. **~ ঝাড়া দেওয়া** *vi* **1** shake up one's body. **2** shake off lethargy/ inertia. **গা ঝিমঝিম করা** *vi* feel dizzy; have an unpleasant feeling. **গা ঢাকা দেওয়া** go into hiding; abscond. **গা তোলা** get up from a sitting or lying position. **গা দেওয়া** = গা করা. **গা মেজমেজ/ম্যাজম্যাজ করা** feel indolent. **গায়ে কাঁটা দেওয়া** have a gooseflesh. **গায়ে দেওয়া** *vt* put on; wear. **গায়ে ফুঁ দিয়ে বেড়ানো** move about shunning all responsibility. **গায়ে মাখা** (fig) be offended; mind. **গায়ে হাতে তোলা** lay hands on; beat. **গায়ের জোরে** by physical/ brute force; unlawfully or unreasonably. **গা সওয়া/সহা** *adj* accustomed; used to. **গায়ে গায়ে** side by side. **গায়ে-পড়া** *adj* too eager to offer advice. **গায়ে হলুদ** *n* ceremony of ritual besmearing of the bride and the groom with turmeric paste held before marriage.

গা[2] *int* used in addressing or in drawing one's attention: কে গা.

গা[3] *n* (music) the third note in the natural scale: সা-রে-গা.

গাই[1], **গাই গরু** *n* the cow. **~ দোহন করা** *vi* milk a cow. **দুধেল ~** *n* a milch cow.

গাই[2] *vi, vt* **1** I sing. **2** I praise: যার খাই তার গাই. **গাইয়ে** *n* one who sings; a singer. **~ বাজিয়ে** *n* a musician. ❑*adj* adept in music.

গাউন [E] *n* **1** outer garment worn by western women; a gown. **2** long loose garment used by men in certain professions: উকিলের ~.

গাওয়া = গব্য

গাওয়া *vi, vt* **1** to sing (a song). **2** to praise: গুণ ~. **গেয়ে বেড়ানো** *vt* spread; circulate; make public.

গাং, গাঙ *n* a river; a stream. **~ চিল** *n* a river gull. **~ শালিক** *n* the horn-bill. **~ পেরুলে কুমিরকে কলা** to laugh at a danger when it is no more.

গাঁ *n* a village; a hamlet. **গাঁয়ে মানে না আপনি মোড়ল 1** fool to others, himself a sage. **2** a self-styled leader.

গাঁইয়া, গেঁয়ো *adj* **1** of rural outlook; unpolished; rustic. **2** living in country. **3** of or pertaining to villages; rural.

গাঁজা[১] *n* an intoxicant made from hemp; ganja. **~ খাওয়া** *vi* smoke ganja. **~খোর** *adj* addicted to smoking ganja. ❑*n* a ganja smoker; a ganja-addict. **~খুরি গল্প** a cock-and-bull story; a foolish story that one shouldn't believe.

গাঁজা[২] (of organic substance) *vi* come up in roth; undergo fermentation. ❑*vt* produce fermentation in (as in grape for conversion into wine). **~নো** *vt* cause sth to ferment / be decomposed for conversion into new compounds.

গাঁট *n* **1** a complication of threads or cords; a tie; a knot. **2** a joint of bones; knuckles: শরীরের ~. **3** a knot on a stem; a node: বাঁশের ~. **4** a large bundle; a bale: কাপড়ের ~. **5** a pouch or pocket in a garment: ~ কাটা. **~কাটা** *n* person who picks pockets; a pick-pocket. **~ছড়া** *n* the custom of tying a knot with the corners of the bride's sari and the groom's garment at wedding; love-knot. **~ছড়া বাঁধা** *vi* tie the ends of garments of the bride and bridegroom as a mark of inseparable union. **গাঁটের কড়ি** *n* one's own money.

গাঁটরি *n* a small bundle; a package.

গাঁট্টাগোট্টা *adj* short statured and robust; thick-set; strong-built: ~-লোক.

গাঁথন *n* **1** act of dressing artistically or composing: বেণী ~. **2** act of stringing together or wreathing: মালা ~. **3** act of laying (bricks) one upon another (as in constructing a building).

গাঁথা *vi* **1** string together; wreathe (as a garland). **2** lay bricks (to construct a building). **3** arrange artistically and in an orderly manner. ছন্দ ~.

গাছ[১] *n* **1** a tree; a plant. **2** a creeper; a herb: শিম ~. **3** a tree-like object (as the grinding tree of an oilman). ❑*adj* tall or getting taller day by day: মেয়েটি দিন দিন গাছ হয়ে উঠছে. **~ গাছড়া, ~ গাছালি** *n pl* **1** trees and plants. **2** shrubs and herbs. **~পালা** *n pl* trees and plants; vegetation.

গাছ[২], **গাছা, গাছি** equivalent to English article 'a', 'an' or 'the': লাঠিগাছ; একগাছা দড়ি; মালাগাছি.

গাছড়া *n* wild shrubs; low bush.

গাজন *n* festival in connection with the worship of Hindu deity Shiva at the end of the month of Chaitra. **অনেক সন্ন্যাসীতে ~ নষ্ট** (fig) too many cooks spoil the broth.

গাজর *n* a kind of vegetable; carrot.

গাজি [A] *n* one who fights in the way of Allah/for the defence of religion.

গাটাপার্চা [E] *n* soft rubber like material used for covering electric wires, etc.

গাড়ওয়ান = গাড়োয়ান

গাড়ল *n* **1** abusive word. **2** a ram; a sheep. **3** a stupid person.

গাড়া *vt* **1** fix or place firmly; drive in: খুঁটি ~. **2** set up; spread firmly; establish: আস্তানা ~. শিকড় ~ *vi* (fig) settle down permanently. হাঁটু ~ *vi* kneel down.

গাড়ি *n* a vehicle; a cart; a coach; a carriage; a car; a cab; a taxi. **~ করা** *vi, vt* **1** hire a taxi or a carriage. **2** purchase a car for one's own use. **~ চাপা পড়া** *vi* be run over by a car. **~ ডাকা** *vi* hail/ get a taxi or a carriage. **~ বারান্দা** *n* a porch in front of a house for parking cars.

গাড়োয়ান *n* person who drives a hackney carriage; a coachman.

গাঢ় *n* **1** (of milk, etc) condensed; thickened; solidified. **2** profound; sound: ~ নিদ্রা. **3** deep; dense; intense: ~ অন্ধকার. **4** (of colour) strong and full but bright: ~ রং. **~ করা** *vi* thicken; condense; solidify ; concentrate. **~ত্ব** *n* thickness; intensity; concentration.

গাণনিক *n* an accountant; a keeper of accounts.

গাণিতিক *adj* **1** versed in mathematics. **2** related to mathematics.

গাণ্ডে পিণ্ডে *adv* up to the throat; to one's fill.

গাত্র *n* **1** the physical structure of a human being; the body. **2** the flank or side of a building or the like: পর্বত~. **~দাহ, ~জ্বালা** *n* **1** burning sensation on the skin/ body. **2** (fig) heart-burning; jealousy; ill-will; malice. spite; grudge. **~ জ্বালা করা** *vi* have burning sensation on the body; (fig) be jealous/ envious of; have grudge against (one). **~বেদনা, ~শূল** *n* pain in the body; muscular pain. **~মার্জনী** *n* that which is used for drying the skin after washing; a towel; a napkin. **~হরিদ্রা** *n* the ceremony connected with wedding when the bride and the groom are besmeared with a paste of green turmeric before the nuptial bath.

গাত্রাবরণ, গাত্রাবরণী *n* **1** a wrapper for the body. **2** clothes; garment. **3** a coat of mail.

গাত্রোত্থান *n* getting up from bed or from a lying or sitting position. **~ করা** *vi* rise/ get up; stand.

গাথক *n* **1** a composer of songs or verses. **2** a singer; a musician.

গাথা *n* **1** a poem; a couplet; a verse. **2** a short narrative poem; a popular song; a ballad. **3** a narration in commendation; eulogy ; panegyric: যশো~.

গাদ *n* **1** that which settles at the bottom of a liquid matter; sediment; lees. **2** impurities which rise to the surface of liquors; scum; refuse.

গাদা[২] *vt* fill methodically with contents; pack; cram load/ ram (as a gun). ~ **বন্দুক** *n* a fire-arm loaded through the muzzle; a muzzle loader.

গাদা[৩] 1*n* a body of matter; a mass; a lump; a heap; a pile; a stack: খড়ের ~. **2** a number of persons or things; a throng; a crowd : এক ~ লোক. ~**গাদা** *adv* in large quantities; in heaps. ❑*adj* heaps of. ~**গাদি** *n* state of being crowded. ~**গাদি করা** *vt* fill by pressing together; fill to excess. ❑*vi* press in numbers; throng.

গাদা[৪] *n* the back portion of a fish: ~র মাছ, a slice from the back of a fish.

গাধ *adj* (of a mass of water) shallow; not deep.

গাধা *n* **1** well-known animal akin to the horse. **2** (fig) a very stupid person. **3** a reproach; a rebuke. ~ **বোট** *n* **1** a boat heavily loaded and slow-moving like an ass. **2** (fig) a sluggish person noted for his dilatoriness. ~ **খাটুনি** *n* very hard labour but requiring no intelligence; drudgery. ~ **পিটুনি** *n* heavy and merciless beating. ~**মি** *n* making an ass of oneself; acting foolishly.

গান *n* **1** a vocal music; a song. **2** a lyric; a poem. **3** a musical play; an open-air opera. **4** the sweet note of a bird: পাখির ~. ~**বাজনা** *n* music. **ওস্তাদি** ~ *n* classical music. **চুটকি** ~ *n* a light tripping song with dancing rhythm, like *khemta*, etc. **গানের দল** *n* an opera party; a party of professional singers.

গান মেটাল [E] *n* a mixture of metals containing copper, tin, lead, and zinc used for making chains, etc; a gunmetal.

গান্দা [P] *adj* **1** smelling bad; ill-smelling; fetid; rotten. **2** impure; unholy.

গান্ধর্ব *adj* **1** of or relating to Gandharvas. **2** system of love marriage recognized in Hindu tradition, in which the willing couple get wedded by exchanging garlands and without observing the customary rites. ~ **বিদ্যা** *n* the science or art of music. ~ **বিধান** *n* the Hindu custom of Gandharva marriage.

গান্ধার *n* **1** (music) the 3rd note in the natural scale. **2** the ancient name of Kandahar in Afghanistan. **3** a musical note. **4** of or made in Gandhara country. **5** a native of Gandhar. **গান্ধারী** *n fem* the princess of Gandhara and mother of Duryodhana and others of the Mahabharata.

গান্ধি, গান্ধিপোকা *n* a kind of cornfly emitting severe odour.

গান্ধী *n* **1** a merchant community of Gujrat in India. **2** the famous Mohandas Karamchand Gandhi, father of modern India.

গাফেল [A] *adj* **1** not attentive; unmindful. **2** unconcerned; disinterested; callous. **3** guilty of neglect; failing in duty; negligent; inactive; indolent. ~**তি** *n* negligence; inaction; laziness; indolence; inattention; failure.

গাব *n* a type of tree bearing a fruit with a thick skin and having juice which is used as a coating matter.

গাভিন *adj* (of beasts) big with young. ~ **হওয়া** *vi* be big with a young.

গাভী = গাই

গামছা *n* a napkin made by handloom. ~ **বাঁধা** *adj* (of curd) very thick and well-formed so much so that it can be tied in a ~: ~ বাঁধা দই. **গলায় ~ দেওয়া** apply humiliating measures to force one to pay off a debt, etc; humiliate one.

গামলা *n* a deep round container for holding water, etc; a bowl.

গামা *n* the famous wrestler of this name. ❑*adj* champion in wrestling.

গামা রশ্মি *n pl* (phys) rays of very short wave-length emitted by radio-active substances; gamma rays.

গামী *suff* indicating movement forwards a destination or the manner of movement: ঢাকাগামী, ধীরগামী, দ্রুতগামী. **গামিনী** *fem*.

গাম্ভীর্য *n* **1** quality of being solemn/ impressive; solemnity ; gravity; impressiveness: ~পূর্ণ পরিবেশ. **2** affected importance; sobriety; reserve.

গায়ক *n* a singer; a songster. **গায়িকা** *fem*.

গায়ত্রী **1** Vedic incantation. **2** Vedic metre of versification.

গায়র মহরম [A] *adj* one with whom marital relation is allowed under the law.

গায়েন *adj* one who sings. ❑*n* a singer. **মূল** ~ *n* the leading person of a party of singers.

গায়েব [A] *adj* **1** hidden; invisible; unseen. **2** misappropriated.

গায়েবি [A] *adj* **1** unseen. **2** queer; fantastic. **3** hidden; concealed. **4** beyond comprehension; mysterious: ~ খুন.

গায়ের মুকাল্লিদ [A] *adj* one who is not a follower of any of the four Imams; not an orthodox Muslim.

গায়ের হাজির [A] *adj* not present; absent.

গারদ [H] *n* **1** sentence of imprisonment. **2** a prison; a jail; a lock-up.

গারো *n* **1** aborigines of Garo Hills in India. **2** tribal people of this name living in northern parts of Bangladesh.

গার্গী *n* daughter of the sage Garga, celebrated as one of the most erudite in ancient India.

গার্জিয়ান [E] *n* **1** one in charge of an orphan or ward. **2** one in whose care children are brought up; a parent; a guardian.

গার্টার [E] *n* a band to hold up a stocking; a garter.

গার্হস্থ্য, গার্হস্থ্ *n* the state or condition of a householder; domestic life. ❑*adj* of domestic life/ the householder; domestic.

গাল[১]=গণ্ড. **~গল্প** *n* idle story; chit-chat. **~গল্প করা** *vi* talk fancies about one's importance; gossip; chit-chat. **~ ফোলানো** *vi* be offended/ dissatisfied. **এক ~ হাসি** *n* a hearty laugh. **গালে চড় দেওয়া** *vi* slap in the face. **গালে হাত দেওয়া** *vi* (fig) be amazed/ surprised.

গাল[২] *n* abuse; reproach; rebuke. **~ খাওয়া** *vi* be reproached. **~ দেওয়া** *vt* reproach; rebuke. **~মন্দ** *n pl* abuses; reproaches.

গালা[১] *n* sealing wax.

গালা[২] *vt* **1** reduce from a solid to a liquid state by heat; melt. **2** cause to flow out: ভাতের ফেন ~, strain off excess water after rice is properly boiled.

গালানো *vt* **1** cause to be melted. **2** strain or squeeze (sth): ফোঁড়া ~.

গালি=গাল[২]. **গালা~, গালাগাল** = গালমন্দ ⇒ গাল[২]. **~গালাজ** *n pl* speaking of (one) in abusive terms; reviling.

গালিচা [P] *n* heavy woven material for covering floors and stairs; carpet.

গাহন *n* bathing by immersion in a pond or river.

গিঁট *n* **1** a joint or node in a plant. **2** a joint of bones in human body; a knuckle.

গিজগিজ *int* (onom) suggesting the presence of many people crowding together: সভায় লোক ~ করছে.

গিধড় [H] *n* the jackal. ❑*adj* (reproaching) dirty; filthy.

গিনি [E] *n* former British gold coin worth one pound one shilling; a guinea. **~ সোনা** *n* gold containing $\frac{1}{12}$th copper alloy; guinea gold.

গিন্নি, গিন্নী, *n* **1** mistress of a house; a housewife; a wife. **~পানা** *n* **1** the experience and adroitness of a housewife. **2** the conduct befitting a housewife. **3** (jocular) the precocious conduct of a young girl.

গিবত=গীবত

গিয়া, গিয়ে, গে infinite form of the verb 'go': বাড়ি গিয়ে পড়তে বোসো. ❑*n* a word of uncertain meaning used in ordinary speech: এটা হলো গিয়ে/ গে....

গিরগিটি *n* a type of lizards that can change their colour to match their surroundings; the chameleon.

গিরা[১] *n* **1** a knot joining two pieces of thread, rope, etc. **2** the joint of bones at the wrist or ankle : পায়ের ~.

গিরা[২] *n* measure of length used esp in tailoring and equal to 2·5 inches.

গিরি *n* **1** a mountain; a hill. **2** an order of Hindu ascetics. **~কন্দর** *n* a mountain cave. **~খাত** *n* a deep narrow valley with steep sides; a gorge; a ravine. **~পথ, ~বর্ত্ম** *n* a way over a range of mountains; a mountain pass. **~রাজ** *n* the king of mountains; an appellation of the Himalayas. **~শৃঙ্গ, ~শিখর** *n* a mountain peak. **~শ্রেণী** *n* a range of mountains; a mountain range. **~সংকট** *n* a gorge; a mountain defile.

গিরি [P] *suff* denoting someone's conduct, profession, etc: কেরানি~, বাবু~, মোল্লা~.

গিরীন্দ্র [গিরি + ইন্দ্র] *n* the king of the mountains; the highest mountain; the Himalayas.

গিরিশ [গিরি + ঈশ] *n* **1** =গিরীন্দ্র. **2** appellation of Hindu deity Shiva.

গির্জা *n* a house consecrated to the worship of God among Christians; a Christian prayer house; a church.

গিলটি[১] *n* the art or practice of overlaying things with gold; a thin coating of gold for a fair superficial show; gilding. **~ করা** *vt* gild. **~-করা** *adj* gilt. **~ সোনা** *n* rolled gold.

গিলটি[২] [E] *adj* chargeable with guilt; guilty; criminal.

গিলন *n* act of swallowing/ devouring; eating.

গিলা[১]=গেলা

গিলা[২] *n* a seed of *Mimosa scandens,* a leguminous plant. **~ করা** *vi* frill the edge of an article of dress by pressing with a seed of *Mimosa scandens;* form into a frill. ❑*vt* decorate with a frill. **~ করা** *adj* frilled or finely creased.

গিলানো *vt* cause (one) to swallow.

গিলিত *adj* swallowed; eaten up; devoured; taken in. **~ চর্বণ** *n* **1** (of animals) chewing the cud; rumination. **2** raising an old topic anew.

গিলোটিন [F] *n* machine used for beheading criminals in France; guillotine.

গিল্লা [P] *n* blame; reproach; complaint.

গিসগিস=গিজগিজ

গীত *n* **1** a song; a hymn; an ode. ❑*adj* **1** what has been sung; chanted. **~ গাওয়া** *vi, vt* sing (a song). **~বাদ্য** *n* vocal and instrumental music.

গীতা *n* the famous Hindu scripture Sreemat Bhagavat Geeta.

গীতি *n* a song; a hymn. **~কবিতা** *n* a lyric poem; a lyric. **~কা** *n* a short lyric poem; a song; a ballad. **~কাব্য** *n* lyric poetry. **~নাট্য** *n* a musical drama.

গীবত [A] *n* speaking ill of others; calumny; slander.

গুজা=গোঁজা

গুঁজামিল⇒গোঁজা

গুঁজি *n* **1** a wedge; a stake. **2** a hair-pin. **~ দেওয়া** plug up a leak in an old thatch by inserting new straw.

গুঁড়া *n* **1** anything in the form of powder. **2** fragments. **3** anything of small size: ~ মাছ. ❑*adj* reduced to powder; powdered; pulverized. **~ করা** *vi* reduce to powder; pulverize; pound.

গুড়াগাঁড়া *n* fragments; crumbs; odds and ends.

গুঁড়ি[1] *n* **1** anything in the form of powder: চালের ~. **2** very small; fine particle: ~ ~ বৃষ্টি. **~ ~ বৃষ্টি** *n* drizzling. **~ ~ বৃষ্টি হওয়া** drizzle.

গুঁড়ি[2] *n* the trunk of stock or a true.

গুঁতা, গুঁতো *n* a sudden thrust or poke; a push with sth sharp in order to move sth or sb. **~গুঁতি** *n* pushing and counter-pushing. **~নো** *vt* strike or push against (sth or sb).

গুচ্ছ *n* a number of things of the same kind growing or being close together; a cluster; a bunch; a bundle.

গুছানো *vt* set in order; arrange neatly. ❑*adj* neatly arranged/ managed: ~ সংসার, a tidy household.

গুজব [P] *n* rumour; hearsay. **~ ছড়ানো/ রটানো** *vi, vt* spread rumour. **~ আছে যে ···** there is a rumour that ····

গুজরতি *n* smaller variety of cardamom grown mostly in Gujrat and hence the name.

গুজরাটি *n* **1** a native of Gujrat in India. **2** language of Gujrat. ❑*adj* of Gujrat.

গুজরান [P] *n* **1** means of keeping alive; living: এই বেতনে ~ চলে না. **2** act of spending/ passing (as time).

গুজরানো *vi, vt* spend or pass: দিন ~.

গুজশতা [P] *adj* **1** of an earlier period; former. **2** next before the present; last. **~ সাল** last year.

গুজার=গুজরান (2)

গুজারেশ [P] *n* polite prayer; representation; submission; petition.

গুঞ্জন *n* **1** a buzzing noise; a humming sound. **2** act of whispering; low murmuring sound.

গুঞ্জরন *n* a low sweet sound; whispering. **গুঞ্জরিত** *adj* resonant with a humming sound.

গুটানো *vt* **1** roll up: মাদুর ~. **2** coil (sth) into a ball: সুতা ~. **3** wind up; close down: কারবার ~. **4** double up or fold: পা ~. **5** pull up; haul up: জাল ~. ❑*adj* rolled up; wound up; folded; hauled up.

গুটি[1], **গুটিকা** *n* **1** a medicine in the form of a little ball; a pill; a tablet. **2** any globular object; a globule; a pilule. **3** (in chess or similar game) a piece; a pawn. **4** a fruit in its early stage of growth: আমের ~. **5** an eruption on the skin; a vesicle; a blister: বসন্তের ~. **6** the covering of the silkworm; a cocoon: ~ পোকা. **~ পোকা** *n* the silkworm.

গুটি[2] *prep* used as an article in referring to a number of things: ~ চারেক আম. **~কত, ~কতক, ~কয়েক** *adj* a small number of; a few.

গুটিগুটি *adv* by slow pace; creeping like snails.

গুটিসুটি *adj* curled up; contracted: ~ মেরে বসা. ❑*adv* with the trunk of the body pressed against the thighs; crouchingly; coweringly. **~ মারা** *vi* creep; crouch.

গুডবাই [E] *n* salutation at parting; farewell; good-bye.

গুড় *n* juice of sugarcane, date-palm, etc in the crystallized form; molasses; treacle: খেজুড়ে ~. **গুড়ে বালি** (fig) circumstance that prevents one to fulfil his hopes; a fly in the ointment.

গুড়গুড়ি *n* a hookah with a long flexible tube.

গুড়ুম *int* denoting sudden loud report of the booming of a gun or rolling of thunder. **~গুড়ুম** *n* roar of artillery.

গুণ *n* **1** special quality that belongs to sth; property; characteristic: দ্রব্য ~. **2** moral goodness; virtue; a merit; an excellence: ~বান. **3** a beneficial effect of sth: শিক্ষার ~, ওষুধের ~. **4** evil influence (of association, etc): সঙ্গগুণে অধঃপতন. **5** (phil) any of the three primordial qualities in living beings: স্বত্ব~, goodness; রজো~, passion; তমো~, darkness. **6** (rhet) any of the qualities that constitute the beauty of a literary composition: ওজঃ~ vigour, মাধুর্য ~ elegance, প্রসাদ ~ lucidity. **7** (math) multiplying or being multiplied; multiplication. **8** (math) one of a number of multiplied instances (2 times, 10 times): চতুর্গুণ, পাঁচ~, শত~. **9** the string of a bow: ধনুর্গুণ. **10** a rope or chain by which a boat is or may be towed; a tow-line; a tow-rope: ~ টানা. **~ করা** *vt* **1** (math) multiply sth by sth. **2** charm (one) by sorcery; bewitch. **~ গাওয়া** *vt* speak in praise of; laud; eulogize. **~ টানা** *vi* pull along (a boat) by a rope or chain; tow. **~ পাওয়া** *vi* be benefited (by the good action or influence) of. **~কীর্তন, ~গান** *n* singing praise of; lauding or praising one. **~কীর্তন/~গান করা** *vi, vt* speak highly of; laud; eulogize. **~গরিমা, ~গৌরব** *n pl* virtues and glories; one's goodness and excellence. **~গ্রহণ** *n* appreciation of one's goodness. **~গ্রহণ করা** *vt* appreciate one's goodness and excellence. **~গ্রাম** *n pl* qualities and virtues. **~গ্রাহিতা** *n* appreciation of goodness and excellence in people. **~গ্রাহী** *adj* appreciating the goodness and excellence in people. **~গ্রাহিণী** *fem.* **গুণজ্ঞ** *adj*=গুণগ্রাহী. **~ধর** *adj* **1** full of good parts; accomplished. **2** (ridi) full of vices; vicious. **~নিধি** *n* person richly endowed with the goodness of head and heart. **~ন** *n* multiplying or being multiplied; multiplication. **~নীয়** *adj* (math) what is to be or may be multiplied (by). **~নীয়ক** *n* (arith) a whole number (except 1) by which a larger number can be divided exactly; a factor. **~পনা** *n pl* attainments; excellences; acomplishment. ~ফল *n* (math) product of multiplication. ~বত্তা *n* possession or presence of good qualities. ~বাচক *adj* **1** expressing or indicating a quality. **2** (gram) adjectival; of or like an adjective; attributive. ~বাদ *n* act of praising; laudation. ~বাদ করা *vt* speak in laudatory terms; praise; eulogize. ~বান *adj* skilled; accomplished. ~বতী *fem*. ~বৃক্ষ *n* the mast of a boat to which a tow-rope is tied. ~বৈষম্য *n* **1** disparity of qualities/ properties. **2** a combination or presence of contrary qualities. ~ময়=~বান. ~মুগ্ধ *adj* having admiration for; admiring. ~মুগ্ধা *fem*. গুণের সাগর *adj* **1**=গুণনিধি. **2** (ridi) known for notorious activities.

গুণাগুণ [গুণ+অগুণ] *n pl* merits and demerits; good and bad qualities; virtues and shortcomings.

গুণাধার [গুণ+আধার] *n* a repository of good qualities; a man of parts.

গুণানুরাগ [গুন+অনুরাগ] *n* love of virtues; admiration for good qualities; appreciation of merit.

গুণান্বিত [গুণ+অন্বিত] *adj* endowed with good qualities; meritorious.

গুণাবলী [গুণ+আবলী] *n pl* sum total of virtues; all the good qualities.

গুণার্ণব [গুণ+অর্ণব] *adj* possessing various good qualities; a sea of virtues.

গুণালঙ্কৃত [গুণ+অলঙ্কৃত] *adj* adorned with many good qualities; accomplished.

গুণিত *adj* (math) multiplied.

গুণিতক *n* a number which contains another an exact number of times; a multiple: ৩৫ ৭-এর ~.

গুণিন=গুনিন

গুণী *adj* well trained or well educated in social arts; talented; meritorious; accomplished.

গুণীভূত *adj* invested with attributes; made secondary or subordinate. ~ ব্যঙ্গ *n* (rhet) an expression, eg a simile or metaphor which is more beautiful than the inner meaning; a figure of speech.

গুণ্ঠন *n* **1** a veil; a screen. **2** a hood; a covering. গুণ্ঠিত *adj* veiled; covered; hooded. গুণ্ঠিতা *fem*.

গুণ্ডা *n* a boisterous/brutal fellow; a ruffian; a hooligan; a gangster. ~মি *n* hooliganism; rowdyism; gangsterism. ~মি করা *vi, vt* practise hooliganism.

গুদাম *n* a storehouse for goods; a ware house; a godown. ~জাত *adj* stored in a warehouse. ~জাত করা *vt* store in a warehouse.

গুদারা [P] *n* **1** a boat for carrying passengers and goods across a river; a ferry-boat. **2** place where boats ply across a river for conveying passengers and goods.

গুনগুন *n* humming sound (as of the bee). ~ করা *vi* hum; buzz.

গুনতি *n* act of counting; computation. ~ করা *vt* count; compute.

গুনা[১], **গুনাহ্** [P] *n* **1** a transgression of the fundamentals of Islamic shariah; a sin. **2** a breach of the law; a crime. ~ খাতা *n pl* flaws and faults; sins and guilt. ~গার *adj* guilty; criminal. ❑*n* a sinner; an offender. ~গারি *n* penalty for a folly or for nonfulfilment of conditions.

গুনা[২] *n* metal string or wire; screw-thread.

গুনিন *n* person having power over the spirits; one who can make spirits obey his biddings. **2** an astrologer. **3** an exorcist professing to have power of healing a snake-bite patient.

গুপ্ত[১] *adj* **1** not revealed; protected . **2** secret; hidden; mysterious; esoteric: ~ রহস্য. **3** invisible; unseen; unknown. ~ কথা *n* confidential or restricted matter; a secret; a mystery. ~ কথা ফাঁস করা divulge/ give out a secret. ~ঘাতক *n* **1** person who commits a secret murder. **2** one who murders a person for political reasons or reward; an assassin. ~চর *n* **1** person employed to obtain secret information; a spy. **2** a policeman on special duty to find out information leading to detection of criminals; a detective. ~চর বৃত্তি *n* the action or profession of a spy; espionage. ~ধন *n* a treasure whose location is not known to any one; a hidden treasure. ~ ভোট *n* a vote by secret ballot. ~ রহস্য *n* a mystery; a secret. ~ হত্যা *n* a murder; an assassination.

গুপ্ত[২] *n* family name among Hindus.

গুবাক *n* the betel-nut or its tree.

গুম [P] *adj* **1** carried off; concealed: লাশ ~ করা. **2** kidnapped; carried away and confined unlawfully and with a motive. **3** speechless and motionless: ~ হয়ে বসে থাকা. ~ করা *vt* carry off; kidnap. ~ হওয়া *vi* be carried off/ kidnapped; go in hiding; abscond; be struck dumb.

গুমট *n* (of weather) lack of air; sultriness.

গুমটি [H] *n* the shed for a watchman; a sentry-box: ~ ঘর.

গুমর [U] *n* **1** self-esteem; pride; vanity. **2** the inner secret which one is unwilling to disclose. ~ করা/ দেখানো *vi* behave in a haughty way in the hope of impressing people; give oneself airs.

গুমরানো *vi* choke down one's sufferings in silence; smoulder in anger. গুমরানি *n* suffering from suppressed grief or pain.

গুমারাহ্ [P] *adj* off the right path; astray; away from the desirable course.

গুম্ফ *n* **1** the hair on the upper lip; moustache. **2** a cluster; a bunch; a bundle.

গুম্বজ [P] *n* a hemispherical roof of a building; a large cupola; a dome.

গুয়া=গুবাক

গুরু *n* **1** a spiritual guide; a preceptor. **2** a teacher; an adviser. **3** an elderly and venerable person. ☐*adj* **1** heavy; weighty. **2** important; momentous: ~ ভার. **3** involving great responsibility: ~ দায়িত্ব. **4** excessive; too much: ~ ভোজন. **5** difficult to digest; rich: ~পাক. **6** (gram) long and accented: ~ স্বর. **~কল্প** *adj* like a preceptor/ spiritual guide. **~কুল** *n* the family or house of one's preceptor. **~গম্ভীর** *adj* grave and solemn. **~গিরি** *n* the profession of a spiritual preceptor. **~গৃহ** *n* the abode of one's preceptor. **~চণ্ডালী** *adj* (of literary composition) containing an undesirable mixture of elegant and inelegant words. **~চণ্ডালী দোষ** *n* use of elegant and inelegant words in the same composition. **~জন** *n* one's superiors or elders. **~তর** *adj* **1** heavier of the two. **2** grave; serious: ~তর বিপদ, grave danger; ~তর অপরাধ, serious crime. **~ত্ব** *n* importance; weight; gravity. **~দক্ষিণা** *n* honorarium paid or payable to a teacher/ religious guide. **~দণ্ড** *n* heavy punishment. **লঘু পাপে ~ দণ্ড** heavy punishment for light offence. **~দেব** *n* spiritual preceptor. **~দ্বার** *n* a temple of the Sikh; Gurudwara. **~নিন্দা** *n* censure of one's teacher/ preceptor. **~পত্নী** *n* the wife of one's teacher/ guide. **~পত্নী গমন** *n* sexual union with the wife of one's teacher/ guide. **~পাক** *adj* (of food) rich; hard to digest. **~পাপ** *n* serious crime. **~বন্ধনী** *n* (math) the third bracket. **~ভক্ত** *adj* devoted to one's teacher. **~ভক্তি** *n* devotion to one's teacher. **~ভাই** *n* a co-disciple; a brother disciple. **~ মারা বিদ্যা** *n* **1** learning in which the disciple excels the preceptor. **2** learning applied against the teacher to discredit him. **~লঘুজ্ঞান** *n* sense of proportion; sense of high and low. **~ স্বর** *n* accented or long vowel. **~ হত্যা** *n* murder of one's preceptor; parricide. **~হন্তা** *n* a parricide.

গুর্খা *n* a hill tribe of Nepal who became famous as soldiers in the British Indian army; Gurkha.

গুর্জর *n* Guzrat, the country in the western region of India; a native of Gujrat. **গুর্জরী** *fem.*

গুল[1] [P] *n* burnt tobacco used as a dentifrice.

গুল[2] *n* a concocted story; a small unimportant lie purposely told to create amusement in course of gossiping; a fib. **~ মারা** *vi* tell fibs; fib.

গুল[3] [P] *n* **1** flower. **2** pattern of flowers on linen; diaper. **~দার** *adj* having floral patterns; diapered. **~জার, ~যার** [P] *adj* **1** full of pomp and grandeur; spectacular; showy. **2** crowded; in full swing; in full glory: সভা ~.

গুলঞ্চ *n* **1** a kind of flower. **2** a kind of creeper.

গুলতানি [P] *n* **1** gossiping; chit-chat. **2** a crowd raising a lot of noise. **~ পাকানো** *vi* assemble in a group and indulge in idle talk.

গুলতি *n* a toy shooter consisting of a Y-shaped stick with a rubber band fastened between the forks for shooting stones at objects; a catapult.

গুলদস্তা [P] *n* a flower bouquet; a flower vase.

গুলদান [P] *n* a flower vase.

গুলদার [P] *adj* having floral designs.

গুলনার *n* **1** the flower of a pomegranate tree. **2** a sari with designs of pomegranate.

গুলপট্টি *n* act of deceiving/playing trick without malice; hoax. **~ মারা** *vt* play mischievous trick on sb for a joke.

গুলফাম [P] *adj* **1** one whose body is like a flower. **2** coloured; rosy.

গুলবদন[1] *adj* one whose face is like a flower. **গুলবদনী** *fem.*

গুলবাগ [P] *n* a garden of flowers; flower-garden (also গুলবাগিচা).

গুলবাহার [P] *n* **1** a sari with floral designs. **2** a well laid flower-garden.

গুলশান [P] *n* a flower-garden.

গুলা[1], গুলি, গুলো, গুলিন, গুলোন *suff* denoting plurality: ফুলগুলিন, বালকগুলা, কলমগুলো, পাখিগুলি.

গুলা[2] *vt* dissolve (in water).

গুলানো (গুলিয়ে ফেলা) *vt* **1** mix (things) without order; muddle; confound; confuse; make a mess of things: মাথা ~, be confused in thought; হিসাব ~, muddle an account. **2** be agitated morbidly: পেট ~. **3** feel/be stricken with nausea: শরীর ~.

গুলাব=গোলাপ

গুলাল *n* **1** a kind of perfumed red powder. **2** an aromatic herb; basil. **3**=গুলতি.

গুলি[1] [U] *n* **1** any small spherical object; a globule; a little ball. **2** a medicine in the form of a little ball; a pill; a pellet. **3** a piece of stone or little ball of mud thrown by children from catapult: গুলতির ~. **4** ammunition for fire-arms; a bullet: বন্দুকের ~. **5** a pill or preparation of opium: ~খোর. **~ করা** *vt* shoot; fire. **~ খাওয়া** *vt* **1** be shot at (with a bullet). **2** smoke opium. **~খোর** *n* an opium-smoker. **~খোরি গল্প** *n* (fig) a cock-and-bull/incredible story. **~ডাণ্ডা** *n* a game in which a spindle-shaped piece of wood is hit into the air and then knocked forward with a stick; tipcat.

গুলি২=গুলা

গুলিকা *n* **1** a globule or pill. **2** a bullet.

গুলিস্তাঁ, গুলিস্তান [P] *n* **1** a flower-garden. **2** title of the famous poetical work of Shaik Saadi. **3** an avenue of this name in Dhaka; Gulistan.

গুলী=গুলি১

গুলফ *n* the ankle or the heel. **~ সন্ধি** *n* the ankle-joint.

গুল্ম *n* a plant with several woody stems from the same root; a woody plant less than a tree; a shrub. **~ রোগ** *n* the morbid enlargement of the spleen.

গুষ্টি, গুষ্ঠি *n* **1** family; line of descent; lineage. **2** an undesirable crowd of people: ~সুদ্ধ এসেছো. **~র পিণ্ডি, ~র মাথা** *n* abusive word expressed in annoyance of an undesirable situation.

গুহ *n* **1** Hindu deity Vishnu. **2** Hindu deity Kartika. **3** family name of certain Bengali Hindus. **~ষষ্ঠী** *n* the sixth day of the lunar fortnight of Agrahayan or the Hindu ritual connected with it.

গুহা *n* **1** a deep natural hole underground with an opening to the surface. **2** a hollow in the side of a cliff or hill; a cave. **~বাসী** *n* **1** a person who lived in a cave in very ancient times; a troglodyte; a caveman. **2** a lion or tiger or similar beasts that sleep in a cave. ❑*adj* dwelling in a cave.

গুহ্য *adj* **1** confidential; private; lonely. **2** secret; hidden; concealed. **3** mysterious; esoteric; occult. ❑*n* the anus: ~দেশ, ~দ্বার.

গূঢ় *adj* **1** (of actions) done secretly, esp for dishonest reasons; surreptitious: ~ অভিসন্ধি. **2** having inner and secret meanings which are understood only by a chosen few; esoteric; mysterious; secret: ~ রহস্য; very deep and difficult; intricate; incomprehensible: ~ তত্ত্ব. **~ত্ব** *n* secrecy; intricacy; incomprehensibility; inaccessibility. **~পাদ** *n* a tortoise. **~ পুরুষ** *n* a spy. **~ বৃক্ষ** *n* the oleander tree. **~ মার্গ** *n* a secret path; a tunnel. **~ সাক্ষী** *n* a witness in possession of the secrets of the opposing party.

গৃধিনী *n fem* a female vulture.

গৃধ্নু *adj* greedy; covetous: অর্থ~.

গৃধ্র *n* a vulture.

গৃহ *n* **1** a house; a home. **2** an abode; a dwelling; a residence. **3** a room; an apartment; a chamber. **4** domestic life; a household: ~ধর্ম. **~কপোত** *n* a tame pigeon. **~কর্তা** *n* the master of a house; the chief of a household. **~কর্ত্রী** *n fem* the mistress of a house; a housewife. **~কর্ম, ~কার্য** *nn* domestic work. **~কলহ, ~বিবাদ** *nn* **1** dissension in a family. **2** civil strife in a state. **~চ্যুত** *adj* ejected/ evicted from one's homestead. **~চ্যুত করা** *vt* evict (one) from one's homestead. **~জাত** *adj* home made; home-grown. **~ত্যাগ** *n* **1** act of quitting one's home/ forsaking one's family. **~ ত্যাগ করা** *vi* forsake one's family; renounce worldly life. **~ত্যাগী** *adj* **1** leading a wandering life. **2** leading the life of an ascetic. ❑*n* **1** a vagabond. **2** a mendicant. **~দাহ** *n* **1** burning of a house, either partly or completely. **2** (fig) a sudden disaster visiting a family. **~দেবতা** *n* a house-hold god worshipped through generations by a Hindu family; a family deity. **~ধর্ম** *n* domestic life; household duties. **~পালিত** *adj* reared in the house; domesticated; domestic; tame. **~প্রবেশ** *n* moving into a newly-built house. **~প্রবেশ করা** *vi* make a formal entry into a newly-built house. **~প্রাঙ্গণ** *n* a courtyard; the premises of a house. **~বাগিচা** *n* a garden within the precincts of a house; a garden-house. **~ বিচ্ছেদ** *n* domestic quarrel; dissension within a family. **~বিবাদ**=~কলহ. **~ভেদী** *adj* sowing dissension in a family. **~ভেদী বিভীষণ** one who betrays the family secrets as did the Ramyana character Bibhisana. **~মণি** *n* light; lamp. **~মার্জন** *n* cleaning a house. **~মার্জন করা** *vi* clean a house. **~মৃগ** *n* a domestic dog. **~যুদ্ধ** *n* war between two sides in a state; a civil war. **~ লক্ষ্মী** *n* a housewife whose gracious management of the household affairs brings prosperity to the family; (facet) a wife. **~শিক্ষক** *n* a house tutor; a private tutor. **~ শত্রু** *n* an enemy within the family. **~সজ্জা** *n pl* furniture and fittings of a house. **~স্থ, গেরস্থ, গেরস্ত** *n* the head of a family; a householder. **~স্থালি, গেরস্থালি** *n* house-keeping; management of household affairs. **~স্থালি করা** *vi* perform household duties; keep a house. **~স্বামী**=~কর্তা. **~স্বামিনী**=~কর্ত্রী.

গৃহাসক্ত *adj* devoted to one's household; very much house-keeping.

গৃহিণী=গিন্নি

গৃহী *n* the chief of a household; a householder. **2** a married person; a family man.

গৃহীত *adj* **1** that which has been admitted/ accepted/ agreed to. **2** received or taken what is offered: প্রস্তাব ~. **3** passed by a resolution: সিদ্ধান্ত ~. **4** obtained; acquired. **5** given shelter to; sheltered.

গেঁজ *n* **1** a shoot of a plant; a sprout. **2** a morbid swelling in some part of the body; a tumour.

গেঁজানো *vi* talk trifling without end; chatter garrulously; gossip endlessly.

গেঁড়া, গ্যাঁড়া *n* act of stealing/ swindling; misappropriation: ~ দেওয়া/ মারা. **~কল** *n* racketeering with a view to entrap people for unlawful gains.

গেঁয়ো *adj* **1** rural; unpolished; uneducated; rustic; vulgar; coarse. **2** of the same village. ~ **যোগী ভিখ পায় না** An anchorite living in the same village with others does not receive due respect.

গেছো *adj* living in trees; climbing trees: ~ ব্যাঙ, ~ সাপ.

গেজেট [E] *n* an official publication, printed by government authority, in which public appointments, promotions and other public notices are recorded; a gazette.

গেঞ্জি *n* an under-garment for the upper portion of the body worn by men; a guernsey.

গেট [E] *n* a large door or entrance; a gate.

গেদা *n* a child. ❑*adj* under-aged. **গেদী** *fem*.

গেন্দা[1] =গেদা

গেন্দা[2], **গাঁদা** *n* marigold flower.

গেরস্ত=গৃহস্ত ⇒গৃহ

গেরিলা [E] *n* a person or a band of fighters not belonging to a regular army and carrying on warfare by secret and sporadic attacks; guerrilla.

গেরুয়া *adj* coloured with red ochre; pale yellow. ❑*n* cloth dyed with red ochre: ~ পরিহিত.

গেরেফতার=গ্রেপ্তার

গেরো *n* **1** a knot; a tie. **2** misfortune; ill luck; evil. ~ **ধরা** *vi* be down on luck.

গের্দ [P] *n* **1** confinement within a circle. **2** a certain area; a region; a jurisdiction.

গেল[1] *vt pt* of go in the 3rd person: সে ~, he went.

গেল[2] *adj* immediately preceding the present: ~ বছর, last year.

গেল[3] *int* expressing surprise, astonishment, etc: এই ~, সর্বনাশ হয়েছে.

গেলা, গিলা *vt* swallow; devour.

গেলাপ, গিলাপ [A] *n* **1** a case (as of a pillow). **2** a piece of cloth for covering sth; a wrap: কাবার ~. **3** a loose upper garment; a wrapper.

গেলাস=গ্লাস

গেলেমান [A] *n* immortal beings employed for the service of the pious in the heavens.

গেহ=গৃহ

গৈরিক *n* **1** clay of brownish red colour used as a pigment by Hindus; red ochre; red chalk. **2** brownish-red colour. **3** gold, the precious metal. **4** cloth dyed with red ochre. ❑*adj* grown in the mountains; hill-born.

গৈরেয় *n* **1**=গৈরিক (1). **2** anything produced or grown in the mountains.

গো[1] *n* **1** a cow. **2** the cow. **3** the ox; the bull. **4** the earth: গোস্বামী. **5** any of the sense organs: গোচর.

গো[2] *int* an exclamation to invite attention: কি গো, হ্যাঁ গো, o you! look here! halloo!

গোঁ *n* strong impulse; ruling passion; obstinacy; stubbornness; dogged perseverance. ~ **ধরা** *vi, vt* hold on obstinately to anything; pursue anything doggedly; stick fast.

গোঁ-গোঁ *int n* groaning or whining sound. ~ **করা** *vi* groan (in pain or sorrow).

গোঁজ *n* a peg; a stake; a wedge. ~ **গাড়া** *vi* drive a wedge.

গোঁজামিল *n* balancing of an account by manipulation. ~ **দেওয়া** *vt* cook up or manipulate an account.

গোঁড় *n* protuberance or swelling of the navel. ~ **নাভি** *n* projecting navel.

গোঁড়া *adj* **1** having blind faith in one's religion; blindly and obstinately following one's religion; orthodox; bigoted; fanatic. **2** extremely conservative. **3** extremely biased. ~**মি** *n* **1** orthodoxy; bigotry; fanaticism. **2** blind faith. **3** conservatism.

গোঁফ=গুম্ফ. **গোঁফে তা দেওয়া** *vi* (lit) trim the ends of one's moustache; (fig) be at ease and without concern; be in a delightful mood.

গোঁয়ার *adj* daring without judgement; foolhardy; headstrong; obstinate; violent; rash. ~ **গোবিন্দ** *n, adj* one who is inclined to act on sudden impulse or with rashness. ~**তুমি** obstinacy; stubbornness; rashness.

গোঁয়ারা [P] *n pl* (*sing* গোর) **1** replica of the coffins of Hazrat Hasan and Hazrat Hussain taken out in procession on the occasion of Muharram. **2** the Muharram festival.

গোঁসাই=গোসাঁই

গোকুল *n* **1** a herd of cows. **2** a cow-shed. **3** a village on the Jamuna near Mathura where Sri Krishna was brought up as a cow-boy. **গোকুলে বাড়া** grow in strength stealthily at an unknown place. **গোকুলের ষাঁড়** (ridi) a person full of troublesome whims; a wayward or wilful person; a self-willed man.

গোক্ষুর *n* **1** (lit) a cow's hoof. **2** a prickly composite plant; the thistle. **3** a hooded venomous snake; the cobra.

গোখরা, গোখরো=গোক্ষুর (3)

গোগ্রাস *n* a large morsel; large swallow (like that of a cow). **গোগ্রাসে খাওয়া/ গেলা** gulp down in haste (without chewing the food well).

গোঙরানো=গোঙানো

গোঙানো *vi* express grief with a whining voice (as by a dumb person); whimper; moan; groan. **গোঙানি** *n* act or noise of moaning/ groaning.

গোচর *n* **1** anything perceptible by the senses. **2** (astrol) jurisdiction or range of influence: শনির ~. **3** knowledge; cognition: গোচরে আনা. **4** direct perception: কর্ণ~, দৃষ্টি~. **গোচরে** *adv* within one's knowledge/ sight/ hearing. **গোচরে আনা** *vt* bring to one's notice; make visible/ manifest. **অগোচর** *adv* beyond knowledge/ perception. □*adj* not perceptible by the senses.

গোচারণ *n* act of tending/ grazing cows; pasturing of cows. ~ **ভূমি** *n* grazing ground; pasture-land.

গোছ *n* **1** a number of small things held or grown together; a bunch; a bundle; a sheaf: পানের ~. **2** a particular kind or class; a type: হালকা গোছের খাবার. **3** the fleshy part at the back of the leg between the knee and the ankle: পায়ের ~.

গোছা *n* a bundle; a bunch: চাবির ~.

গোছানো *vt* =গুছানো

গোট *n* women's ornamental girdle worn at the waist.

গোটা[১] *adj* entire; whole; undivided; unbroken: ~ শরীরে ব্যথা, ~ দেশ দুর্ভিক্ষের কবলে; also used as a particle: এক ~. ~ **কতক,** ~ **কয়েক** *adj* some; a few; a small number of. ~~ *adj adv* in unbroken form.

গোটানো=গুটানো

গোঠ *n* **1** a grazing ground; a pasture-land. **2** a cow-shed.

গোড় *n* the base; the root (as of a tree).

গোড়া *n* **1** the bottom or lowest part of anything; a pedestal: গাছের ~, দাঁতের ~, থামের ~. **2** state of lying or being close or contiguous: দোর ~. **3** the base of an edifice; the groundwork; foundation: ভারতে মুসলিম শাসনের ~পত্তন. **4** the starting point; the beginning; the inception: ~ থেকে. **5** the chief cause; the main reason: নষ্টের ~, root of all evils; the root cause of evil. ~**পত্তন** *n* the groundwork; the foundation. ~**পত্তন করা** *vt* do the groundwork; lay the foundation. ~ **কেটে আগায় পানি ঢালা** (lit) cut a tree to its root and then water the branches to enliven it; (fig) allow a thing to be ruined wilfully or through negligence and then try to mend it when it is too late. **আগা~** *adv* from the beginning to the end. ~**য় গলদ** a flaw at the very inception.

গোড়ালি *n* the back part of the foot; the heel; the ankle.

গোত্র *n* **1** a group of families, all originally descended from one common ancestor; a clan; a tribe. ~**জ** *adj* born of the family; having common descent.

গোদ *n* a disease characterized by chronic inflammation of the limbs, particularly the legs; elephantiasis; a leg swollen in elephantiasis. **গোদের উপর বিষফোড়া** a trouble upon trouble; an extra trouble.

গোদা *adj* **1** suffering from elephantiasis. **2** having a fleshy body; corpulent; very fat. □*n* **1** the leader of a pack of monkeys. **2** (derog) a ring-leader; the chief man of a party: পালের ~.

গো-দান *n* the ceremony of giving away cows in gift.

গোধূলি *n* **1** (lit) cow-dust. **2** the time of sunset; when the herd of cows return home blowing dust in the air; the faint light of the sun reflected after sunset; twilight.

গোপন *n* act of hiding (sth) from others; concealing. □*adj* what is hidden or unrevealed; concealed; secret; confidential. ~ **কথা** *n* confidential talk; secret communication. ~ **করা** *vt* hide; conceal; keep (sth) secret. **সত্য ~ করা** *vi* keep back or suppress truth. ~**তা** *n* secrecy; privacy. **গোপনীয়** *adj* to be kept secret; confidential; private; secret. **গোপনে** *adv* **1** in private; in concealment. **2** secretly; privately; confidentially; surreptitiously.

গোপাল[১] *n* **1** a cow-keeper; a cow boy. **2** a milkman; a dairyman by caste. **3** the boyhood name of Sri Krishna. **4** the name of the first king of the Pal dynasty of Bengal. **আদুরে ~** *n* an over-indulged son. ~**ক** *n* a milkman. ~**ন** *n* act of looking after cows; keeping or feeding cows.

গোপাল[২] *n* a herd of cows.

গোপালভোগ *n* a variety of delicious mango.

গোপিকা, গোপিনী, গোপী *n* a milk-woman; a milk-maid. ~**বল্লভ** *n* appellation given to Sri Krishna in the Purana. **গোপীচন্দন** *n* a kind of yellowish clay found in Brindabana, which is used by Baishnavas as a holy paste for painting their faces and limbs.

গোপীযন্ত্র *n* a kind of one-stringed musical instrument.

গোবৎস *n* the young of a cow; a calf.

গোবর *n* cow-dung; muck. ~**গণেশ** *n, adj* one who is good for nothing; a foolish person; an idiot. ~ **গাদা** *n* a dunghill; a dung-heap. ~**-ভরা** *adj* (ridi) stuffed with cow-dung. ~**-ভরা মাথা** *n* a blockhead; a dunderhead; a dolt. **গোবরে পদ্মফুল** (lit) a lotus on a dunghill; (fig) a gifted child in a rustic family.

গোবরাট, গোবরাঠ *n* the timber which forms the lower horizontal part of a window or door frame; the sill under a door or window.

গোবর্ধন *n* **1** name of a hillock in Brindabana. **2** a big heap (of sth). ~**ধারী** *n* appellation of Sri Krishna in the Purana.

গোবাঘ, গোবাঘা *n* **1** a species of tigers that preys upon cows. **2** the wolf. **3** the leopard. **4** the hyena.

গোবিন্দ *n* appellation of Sri Krishna or Vishnu.

গোবেচারা, গোবেচারি *adj* of a quiet disposition; artless or guileless; harmless. ❑*n* a harmless unaffected person.

গোমক্ষিকা *n* a two-winged fly that bites cattle; the gadfly; the gnat; the horse-fly.

গোমড়া [P] *adj* gloomily angry and silent; silently bad-tempered; sullen; sombre.

গোমতী *n* a river in Bangladesh.

গোময় *n* cow-dung.

গোমরাহি [P] *n* straying from the path of righteousness.

গোমস্তা [P] *n* **1** revenue collector of a landed estate. **2** an agent; a representative.

গোমূর্খ, গোমুখ্যু *n* a grossly illiterate person.

গোমেদ *n* a precious stone of orange colour; sardonyx; onyx.

গোমেধ *n* the Vedic rite of cow sacrifice.

গোযান *n* a carriage drawn by a pair of cows or bulls; a cart.

গোয়াল[1], **গোহাল** *n* a cow-shed.

গোয়াল[2], **গোয়ালা, গয়লা** *n* **1** a milkman (by caste or profession). **2** a cattle farmer. **গোয়ালিনী, গয়লানী** *fem.*

গোয়েন্দা [P] *n* a policeman specially engaged in detecting criminals; a detective. **~গিরি** *n* **1** the profession or action of a detective. **2** espionage.

গোর [P] *n* a grave; a tomb. **~-আজাব** *n* **1** punishment of a dead person after internment in the grave. **~ দেওয়া** *vt* bury (a dead body). **~স্তান** *n* a graveyard.

গোরা *adj* **1** fair-complexioned. **2** European. ❑*n* a native of the western world. **~র বাদ্য** *n* European concert.

গোরাচাঁদ *n* a name of Sri Chaitanya.

গোরু, গরু *n* **1** the cow. **2** the ox; the bull: ~র গাড়ি. **3** a cow. **4** (ridi) an illiterate person; an idiot. **~ খোঁজা করা** *vt* look for (sth) frantically; move heaven and earth to find out (sth). **~ চোর** *n* a cattle-lifter; one who steals/ has stolen a cow. **~ মেরে জুতো দান** the ridiculous idea of making amends for committing a heinous sin with a small gift. **~র গাড়ি** *n* a bullock-cart. **~র পাল** *n* a herd of cows.

গোল[1] *adj* shaped like a ball; round; roundish; globular; circular; spherical. ❑*n* a roundish or spherical thing; a circle. **~ক** *n* a roundish or circular object. **~গাল, গোলাকার** *adj* of the shape of a ball or circle; rounded; circular.

গোল[2] [P] *n* **1** a noisy disturbance; a bustle and clamour; uproar; tumult. **~ করা** *vi* shout; clamour; make an uproar. **2** state of being complex; complication; intricacy; confusion: ~ পাকানো, make a mess of; complicate; confuse. **~মেলে** *adj* **1** confusing; disconcerted. **2** doubtful; suspicious; crooked. **গোলে হরিবোল দেওয়া** take advantage of a noisy crowd to cover one's negligence of duty.

গোল[3] [E] *n* (in football, hockey, etc) **1** the score obtained in such games; a goal. **2** the goal-posts. **~ করা** *vi* score a goal. **~ খাওয়া** be defeated. **~দাতা** *n* a scorer. **~রক্ষক** *n* a goal-keeper; a goalie. **~ দেওয়া** *vt* defeat the opponents; (fig) make a gain by befooling one.

গোলক *n* **1** a round or spherical object: ভূ~. **2** a round object used in play; a ball. **3** a round object on which a map of the earth is painted; a globe.

গোলক ধাঁধা *n* **1** rounded network of narrow twisting passages through which it is difficult to get into the centre and out again; a maze; a labyrinth. **2** something which is very difficult to do or understand because of an intricacy of ideas in it.

গোলদার [H, U+P] *n* an owner of a warehouse; a wholesale trader. **গোলদারি** *n* wholesale trade. ❑*adj* of or pertaining to wholesale trade.

গোলন্দাজ [H,U+P] *n* a soldier of the artillery branch; a gunner; an artilleryman. **~ বাহিনী** *n* branch of the army that manages big guns; the artillery. **গোলন্দাজি, গোলন্দাজী** *n* the profession of an artilleryman; the work of a gunner; gunnery. ❑*adj* relating to the artillery.

গোলপাতা *n* leaves of a small tree, big sized and used in thatching.

গোলমরিচ *n* hot pungent condiment like the seeds of papaw; the black pepper.

গোলমাল [U] *n* **1** a great noise of many confused voices; bustle and clamour. **2** disorder; state of confusion. **3** trouble; difficulty; problem. **4** complexity; complication.

গোলমেলে *adj* **1** noisy; disorderly. **2** perplexing; complex; complicated; intricate. **3** contradictory; inconsistent.

গোলযোগ *n* **1** noisy disturbance; a row; an uproar. **2** state of confusion; disorder. **3** a hitch; a hindrance; an obstacle; an impediment.

গোলা[1] *n* **1** a storehouse for grain; a granary. **2** a storehouse for goods; warehouse: কাঠ~. **3** centre of buying and selling; a central market. **~ঘর** *n* a granary; a warehouse. **~জাত** *adj* stored in a granary/ warehouse. **~জাত করা** *vt* store or stock in a granary/ warehouse. **~-বাড়ি** *n* a farm-house.

গোলা[2] *n* **1** a spherical object; a ball. **2** a cannon-ball. **~গুলি** *n pl* cannon-balls and bullets; ammunition. **~ ছোড়া** *vt* bater with cannon shot; cannonade. **~বারুদ** *n pl* ammunition.

গোলা[3] *vt* make a solution in water; dissolve.

গোলাকার *adj* round; roundish; circular; spherical (also গোলাকৃতি).

গোলাপ, গোলাব, গুলাব [P] *n* the rose plant or flower. **~ পানি/ জল** *n* water tinctured with roses by distillation; rose-water. **~ জাম** *n* a small whitish fruit smelling like the rose; the rose-apple. **~ পাশ** *n* a vessel with a perforated nozzle for spraying rose-water. **গোলাপি, গোলাবি, গুলাবি** *adj* **1** rose-coloured; rosy. **2** smelling like the rose; rose-scented. **3** light; slight; mild, moderate: গোলাপি নেশা.

গোলাম [A] *n* **1** a bond-man; a slave. **2** one who is acting as a tool to another; person most obedient or subservient to another. **3** (of playing cards) the knave. **কেনা ~** *n* one who is purchased as a slave; a bondman (*fem* a slave-girl; a bondswoman). **~খানা** *n* **1** quarters for the slaves; slave quarters. **2** (fig) a manufactory for producing men of slave-mentality. **গোলামি** *n* slavery; servitude; drudgery. **গোলামি করা** *vi* drudge for others.

গোলার্ধ *n* half a sphere; half the earth; a hemisphere: পূর্ব ~, পশ্চিম ~; (geom) a semi-circle.

গোল্লা *n* **1** globular and juicy sweets made of the posset of milk: রস~. **2** cipher; naught; zero: পরীক্ষায় ~ পাওয়া. **~য়** *adv* to the dogs; to the path of ruin. **~য় যাওয়া** *vi* take to the evil way; go to the dogs.

গোশ্‌ত, গোস্ত [P] *n* meat; the flesh of animals used as food. **~খোর** *adj* fond of meat.

গোষ্ঠ *n* **1** a cow-house; a cow-shed. **2** a pasture; a pasturage; a grazing ground. **3** a meeting-place; an assembly. **4** an alliance; an association; a union. **~গৃহ** *n* = গোষ্ঠ (1). **~বিহারী** *n* appellation of Sri Krishna. **~লীলা** *n* pastoral sports of Sri Krishna in Brindabana.

গোষ্ঠী *n* **1** a family; a clan; a tribe. **2** a class; a collection; a group: শিল্প ~, a group of industries. **3** an association; a union; a confederacy: উদয়ন শিল্পী~. **~পতি** *n* the head of a family or clan; a leader; a president. **~বর্গ** *n pl* members of a family; a whole body of kinsfolk. **~ভুক্ত** *adj* included in or belonging to a family/ group. **~সুখ** *n* the pleasure of being with one's kith and kin.

গোষ্পদ *n* a cow's footprint.

গোসল [A] *n* bath; bathing. **~ করা** *vi* take a bath; bathe. **~খানা** *n* room for bathing; bathroom.

গোসা [A] *n* **1** anger; wrath; passion. **2** a sulky fit or mood; a fit of peevishness; sulks; huff. **~ করা** *vi* **1** get angry; be enraged. **2** be in a huff/sulky mood.

গোসাঁই, গোসাই *n* **1** master; lord. **2** God. **3** a title of Vaishnava gurus. **4** word used in referring to husband or elders among the Hindus.

গোসাপ *n* a reptile of the lizard family; the iguana; a terrestrial creature like a small crocodile.

গোসোয়ারা [P] *n* **1** the summary/ salient points of an account. **2** the gist of anything.

গোস্তাকি [P] *n* **1** impudent behaviour; insolence; impertinence; incivility. **2** audacity; offensiveness.

গোস্‌সা=গোসা

গৌড় *n* **1** ancient name of Bangladesh; an ancient country comprising a part of modern Bangladesh. **~সারঙ্গ, ~সারং** *n* a musical mode. **গৌড়ী** *n* **1** a kind of poetical diction. **2** a musical air. **3** a kind of rum distilled from raw sugar or molasses. **গৌড়ীয়** *adj* of or produced in Gaud (গৌড়). ❑*n* an inhabitant of Gaud (গৌড়).

গৌণ *adj* **1** not important; minor; secondary; indirect. **2** delay. **~ করা** *vt* delay; protract. ❑*vi* linger. **~ না করে/ অগৌণে** *adv* without delay; immediately. **~ কর্ম** *n* (gram) indirect object. **গৌণার্থ** *n* (rhet) secondary significance; figurative meaning.

গৌর *adj* fair complexioned; white; beautiful. ❑*n* a name of Sri Chaitanya. **~চন্দ্রিকা** *n* a song in praise of Sri Chaitanya before beginning a lyric song; a preface; a prologue.

গৌরব *n* **1** that of which one may be proud; glory; honour; dignity; importance. **2** majesty; stateliness. **3** excellence; preeminence; superiority. **~ করা** *vi, vt* take pride in; be proud of. **গৌরবের বিষয়** *n* glorious achievement; a prestigious affair; a matter of honour/ prestige. **~রবি** *n* (fig) the sun of glory. **গৌরবান্বিত, ~মণ্ডিত** *adj* crowned with glory; glorious; gloried. **গৌরবান্বিতা** *fem.*

গৌরাঙ্গ *adj* having a fair-complexioned body; fair-skinned. ❑*n* an epithet of Sri Chaitanya. **গৌরাঙ্গী** *fem.*

গৌরী, গৌরি *n fem* **1** a fair-complexioned woman. **2** Hindu goddess Durga. **3** a girl of eight years. **~দান** *n* giving away a Hindu girl of eight in marriage. **~শঙ্কর** *n* **1** a Himalayan peak. **2** goddess Durga and Shiva. **~সেন** *n* a proverbially rich and bounteous person who never cared to keep an account of his money. **~সেনের টাকা** *n* money that can be freely and lavishly spent; (sarcas) public funds.

গ্যাঁট *int* expressing firmness in one's stand: ~ হয়ে বসে থাকা, stick firmly to one's purpose.
গ্যালারি [E] *n* **1** a raised floor with rows of seats gradually sloping to the front. **2** a hall or building for the display of works of art; gallery.
গ্যালি [E] *n* (printing) wooden tray in which types are assembled by the compositors; galley. **~ প্রুফ** *n* a trial copy or proof impressed from the galley; galley proof.
গ্যাস [E] *n* any of the various air-like substances esp the natural one and that obtained from coal and used for lighting and heating; gas.
গ্রথন *n* **1** act of stringing (as flowers in a wreath). **2** act of composing (as a poem or song). **গ্রথিত, গ্রন্থিত** *adj* strung; woven; composed.
গ্রন্থ *n* **1** a printed or written literary work; a book. **2** a holy book; a scripture. **~কার** *n* writer of a book; an author. **~কর্ত্রী** *fem.* **~কীট** *n* **1** (lit) a worm or maggot that eats holes in books. **2** (fig) a person continually reading books; one fond of books; a bookworm. **~না** *n* act of collecting and arranging together. **~স্বত্ব** *n* the exclusive right to print or produce (a book), enjoyed by an author or publisher; copyright.
গ্রন্থাগার *n* **1** a collection of books. **2** an edifice or apartment for holding books; a reading room; a library. **গ্রন্থাগারিক** *n* the keeper of a library; a librarian.
গ্রন্থি *n* **1** a knot; tie. **2** a joint of bones; a knuckle. **3** a sort of knot on a stem where leaves arise; a node; or protuberance. **4** a secreting organ in many parts of the body; a gland. **~কলা** *n* glandular tissue. **~রস** *n* glandular secretion. **~বন্ধন** *n* act of tying the bride and the bridegroom with a knot of the corners of each other's garments at wedding.
গ্রসন *n* act of swallowing/ devouring/ gulping/ eclipsing. **গ্রসমান** *adj* that which is swallowing/ devouring/ eclipsing. **গ্রস্ত** *adj* **1** in the process of being devoured/eclipsed: রাহুগ্রস্ত. **2** devoured; eclipsed. **3** overwhelmed with: ঋণগ্রস্ত.
গ্রহ *n* **1** (astrol) a celestial body which revolves in an orbit around the sun; a planet. **2** an evil planet or star : গ্রহের ফের. **~কোপ** *n* (astrol) the antagonism or evil influence of a star. **~জগৎ** *n* the planetary world; the solar system. **~তত্ত্ব** *n* the science of the heavenly bodies; astronomy. **~বিপাক** = ~কোপ. **~মণ্ডল** = ~জগৎ. **~রাজ** *n* the sun. **~স্ফুট** *n* (astrol) a zodiacal sign indicating the position of a planet. **গ্রহের ফের** evil influence of a star.
গ্রহণ *n* **1** act of receiving/ suffering: শাস্তি ~. **2** act of taking (as a name or title). 3 act of accepting or agreeing to: নিমন্ত্রণ ~. **4** act of adopting or taking to (as a profession). **5** act of appreciating the values in sb or sth: গুণ~. **6** act of eating or taking food: খাদ্য~. **7** act of welcoming one: সাদরে ~. **8** eclipse of the sun or moon: সূর্য~, solar eclipse; চন্দ্র~, lunar eclipse. **গ্রহণীয়, ~যোগ্য** *adj* to be accepted; acceptable.
গ্রহাচার্য *n* one versed in astronomy; an astronomer.
গ্রহীতা *adj* receiving; accepting. ☐*n* a receiver; an acceptor.
গ্রানাইট [E] a rock compound; granite.
গ্রাফাইট [E] *n* a form of carbon, used as pencil lead; graphite.
গ্রাম *n* **1** a village; a rural hamlet. **2** (music) a scale: উচ্চ~. **~কেন্দ্রিক** *adj* rooted in the villages; rural : ~কেন্দ্রিক সমাজ. **~বাসী** *adj* dwelling in a village. ☐*n* a villager.
গ্রামীণ *adj* **1** produced in a village. **2** living in a village. **3** pertaining to villages.
গ্রাম্য of or relating to a village; rural. **~ জীবন** *n* country life; rural life. **~তা** *n* rusticity; simplicity; artlessness.
গ্রাস *n* **1** a mouthful; a morsel. **2** a grip; a handful (as at snatching). **3** act of eating or swallowing. **4** food; provisions; subsistence: গ্রাসাচ্ছাদন. **~ করা** *vt* **1** eat up; swallow. **2** appropriate to oneself. **3** eclipse. **~ হওয়া** *vi* be eclipsed. **গ্রাসাচ্ছাদন** *n* food and clothing; subsistence. **গ্রাসাচ্ছাদন করা** *vi* maintain oneself. **গ্রাসাচ্ছাদন দেওয়া** *vi* provide with food and clothing.
গ্রাহ *n* **1** act of taking/ receiving. **2** seizure; appropriation. **3** knowledge from personal view or experience; cognition; understanding.**4** earnest request; solicitation; entreaty; eagerness. **5** fierce aquatic animals, eg the crocodile, the alligator, the shark, etc. **~ক** *adj* **1** one who receives. **2** one who subscribes (as to a newspaper). ☐*n* a receiver; an acceptor; a customer; a purchaser; a subscriber. **গ্রাহিকা** *fem*. **~ক শ্রেণীভুক্তকরা** *vt* enlist/enroll as a subscriber. **গ্রাহী** *adj n* **1** one who/ that which attracts or captivates: হৃদয়গ্রাহী. **2** one who comprehends or appreciates: গুণগ্রাহী.
গ্রাহ্য *adj* **1** that may be accepted; acceptable; gratifying. **2** that may be perceived/ understood/ appreciated: ইন্দ্রিয়~. **3** worthy of consideration; admissible. **~ করা** *vt* accept; admit; obey; care for. **~ না করা** *vt* reject; dismiss; disobey; pay no heed to. **~ হওয়া** *vi* be accepted/ considered.
গ্রিক, গ্রীক [E] *n* **1** the people of Greece; the Greeks. **2** language of Greece; Greek. ☐*adj* of Greece.

গ্রিনরুম, গ্রীনরুম [E] *n* the waiting and dressing room behind the stage of a theatre for the use of the players.
গ্রীবা *n* **1** the fore part of the neck; the throat. **2** the part of the body connecting the head and the trunk; the neck (also ~দেশ). **~ভঙ্গি** *n* a (beautiful) gesture of the neck.
গ্রীষ্ম *n* the summer season: ~কাল. ❑*adj* hot; torrid: ~মণ্ডল. **~কাল** *n* the summer season comprising the first two months (Baishakh and Jyaistha) of the Bengali calendar. **~কালীন** *adj* of the hot season/ summer. **~নিবাস** *n* a resort at a comparatively colder place for passing the summer; a summer resort. **~পীড়িত** *adj* oppressed/ distressed by the heat of summer. **~প্রধান** *adj* hot; torrid; tropical. **~মণ্ডল** *n* the torrid zone. **গ্রীষ্মাবকাশ** *n* the summer vacation.
গ্রেড [E] *n* **1** a step, stage or degree in rank/ quality/ value; number or class of things of the same kind; grade. **2** a rank; a class; a comparative station.
গ্রেন [E] *n* the smallest measure of weight, as used for medicines (= 0648 gram); a grain.
গ্রেনেড [E] *n* a small bomb which can be thrown by hand or fired from a gun; grenade.
গ্রেপ্তার [P] *n* seizing (a person) in the name of the law and usually put in prison; arrest. ❑*adj* arrested; apprehended. **~ করা** *vt* arrest; apprehend. **গ্রেপ্তারি** *adj* empowering/ directing to arrest: গ্রেপ্তারি পরওয়ানা, warrant of arrest.
গ্লানি *n* **1** tiredness; weariness; fatigue. **2** dirt; filth. **3** shame; disgrace; disrepute: বংশের ~. **4** repentance; repining: মনের
গ্লাস [E] *n* a drinking glass.
গ্লোব [E] *n* a model or spherical chart of the earth; a globe.

ঘ

ঘ *n* The fourth consonant of the Bengali alphabet. It is a velar voiced aspirated plosive sound.
ঘচঘচ *int* (onom) repeated sound of cutting sth soft: ~ করে কাটা.
ঘচাঘচ *int* suggesting continuous cutting of a soft thing. ❑*adv* quickly and noisily.
ঘট *n* **1** a vessel of earthenware; a jar; a pitcher. **2** (sarcas) the head: ঘটে বুদ্ধি থাকলে তো. **ঘটে বুদ্ধি না থাকা** be brainless; have no intelligence.
ঘটক *n, adj* **1** one who causes (an event) to take place. **2** one who makes matches or brings about marriages. ❑*n* a match-maker. **ঘটকালি, ঘটকালী** *n* **1** the role of a match-maker; the art or skill of making matches. **2** the reward or monetary consideration that a match-maker receives for his job. **ঘটকী** *fem.*
ঘটন *n* the act of occurring or taking place. **ঘটিত** *adj* that has happened/ occurred.
ঘটনা *n* an event; an occurrence; an incident. **~ক্রমে, ~চক্রে, ~সূত্রে** *adv* incidentally; by the way; by chance. **~চক্র** *n* the course of events. **~বহুল** *adj* full of important events; eventful. **~বলী** *n pl* (a chain of) events. **~বহ** *adj* that causes an event to occur. **~স্রোত** *n* the course of events. **~স্থল** *n* the place of an occurrence; venue of an event.
ঘটমান *adj* in the process of occurrence; that which is continuing or going on.
ঘটা[1] *n* spectacular array of things; pomp; grandeur: মেঘের ~, সাজের রূপের ~. **~ করে** *adv* with a spectacular display; with pomp and grandeur; ostentatiously.
ঘটা[2] *vi* take place; occur; happen; come about. **~নো** *vt* cause to happen; bring about.
ঘটি *n* a small water-pot used for washing. **~চোর** *n* one who steals small things; a pilferer.
ঘটিকা *n* **1** an hour. **2** an ancient device for measuring time; a water-clock: ~-যন্ত্র. **3** a bell; a gong. **4** a small water-pot. **~য়** *adv* o'clock: দুই ~য়, at 2 o'clock.
ঘটিত *adj* **1** brought about; that which has occurred or taken place. **2** concerning; involving: নারী~. **3** mixed or blended with; containing: পারদ-~.
ঘটিরাম *n* a stupid or worthless person.
ঘড়া *n* a jar; a pitcher.
ঘড়ি *n* a timepiece; a watch; a clock. **~ ঘড়ি** *adv* at every moment; at every hour; frequently. **অ্যালার্ম-~** *n* an alarm-clock. **টেবিল ~** *n* a table-clock; a timepiece. **দেয়াল ~** *n* a wall-clock. **পকেট ~** *n* a pocket watch. **বিরাম ~** *n* (phys) watch that can be started and stopped when desired, used for timing events (such as races) to a fraction of a second; a stop-watch. **হাত ~** *n* a wrist-watch.
ঘড়িয়াল[1] [H] *n* a variety of crocodile with a very long muzzle found in Asian waters; a gavial.
ঘড়িয়াল[2] *n* one who strikes a gong to indicate hours; a gong-striker; a bell-man.
ঘড়িয়াল[3]**, ঘড়েল, ঘোড়েল** *n* a very sly and wily person.
ঘণ্ট *n* a spicy dish of mixed vegetables.
ঘণ্টা *n* **1** a metallic vessel used as a bell; a gong. **2** an hour comprising sixty minutes. **3** (sarcas) nothing; a mare's nest: সে আমার ~ করবে, he can do me little harm. **~ পড়া** *vt* (of

bell) strike an hour: ~ পড়ে, the bell goes. ~ বাজানো *vi* ring a bell. ~য় ~য় *adv* at every hour; frequently.

ঘণ্টাকর্ণ *n* **1** (bot) the bell-shaped flowers of a plant belonging to campanula genus; the bell-flower. **2** a Hindu deity.

ঘণ্টাগার *n* place where a bell is hung; a bell-tower; a belfry.

ঘণ্টাধ্বনি *n* the sound or ringing of a bell.

ঘন *adj* **1** thick; condensed: ~ দুধ. **2** compact; dense: ~ বন. **3** deep; intense: ~ অন্ধকার. **4** close: ~ বুনন. ❑*n* **1** cloud: ~ঘটা, ~ গর্জন. **2** (math) product of a number multiplied by itself twice; cube: ~ফল. **3** (geom) solid body having length, width and height. ~ **করা** *vt* thicken; condense. ~ **হওয়া** *vi* become thick; thicken. ~ **কাল** *n* the rainy season; the rains. ~ **কালো,** ~**কৃষ্ণ** *adj* dark black; dark as a cloud. ~**ঘটা** *n* thick and extensive cumulation of clouds; the cumulus. ~**ঘটাচ্ছন্ন** *adj* overcast with thick clouds. ~ **ঘন** *adv* **1** every now and then; frequently. **2** closely; close to one another: ~ ~গাছ. ~**ঘোর** *adj* overcast/ darkened with thick clouds. ~**ত্ব** *n* **1** density; thickness. **2** solidity; volume. ~**ফল** *n* **1** (math) the product of a number twice multiplied by itself; a cube: ২-এর ~ফল ৮. **2** cubic measure. ~**বর্ত্ম** *n* the path of the cloud across the sky; the sky. ~**বসতি** *n* congested habitation; dense population. ~**বস্তু** *n* (phys) a solid body. ~**বিন্যস্ত** *adj* thickly set; densely packed. ~ **বিন্যাস,** ~**সন্নিবেশ** *n* thick setting; close formation. ~ **বীথি** *n* the region of clouds. ~**মূল** *n* (math) the root of a cube; a cube-root: ৮-এর ~ মূল ২. ~**শ্যাম** *adj* dark like a cloud; of bottle-green complexion. ❑*n* an appellation of Sri Krishna. ~**সন্নিবিষ্ট** *adj* densely set. ~**সিক্ত** *n* anything wet with rain water. ~**সার** *n* camphor; mercury.

ঘনাগম [ঘন+আগম] *n* advent of clouds; the rainy season; the rains.

ঘনাঙ্ক [ঘন+অঙ্ক] *n* (phys) the relation of weight to volume; specific gravity; density.

ঘনাত্যয় [ঘন+অত্যয়], **ঘনান্ত** [ঘন+অন্ত] *n* departure/ end of the rainy season; the autumn.

ঘনানো *vt* **1** draw near; approach; overtake: মৃত্যু ঘনিয়ে আসছে, Death is drawing nigh/ approaching/ impending/ imminent; তার দিন ঘনিয়েছে, His time is up; His days are numbered.

ঘনান্ধকার [ঘন+অন্ধকার] *n* deep darkness. ❑*adj* pitch dark.

ঘনাবৃত [ঘন+আবৃত] *adj* overcast with clouds.

ঘনায়মান *adj* **1** getting dense; thickening. **2** getting closer; approaching.

ঘনিমা *n* closeness of constituent parts; density; thickness; compactness.

ঘনিষ্ঠ *adj* **1** very thick; very close. **2** very near; closely related: ~ আত্মীয়. **3** very intimate: ~ বন্ধু, an intimate friend; a bosom friend. **ঘনিষ্ঠা** *fem.* ~**তা** *n* closeness; nearness; intimacy.

ঘনীকৃত *adj* that has been thickened/ condensed/ solidified/ congealed.

ঘনীভবন *n* condensation; solidification.

ঘনীভূত *adj* become solid or firm: বিপদ ~ হলো.

ঘনোপল [ঘন+উপল] *n* frozen drops of rain; hailstones falling from a cloud; hail.

ঘর *n* **1** an abode; a dwelling; a house; a home. **2** a room; an apartment: পড়ার ~. **3** a Hindu temple : ঠাকুর ~. **4** domestic life; household : ~ করা. **5** family: এক ~ জেলে. **6** a line of ancestors; lineage; pedigree: উচ্চ ~. **7** a column of an account book: জমার ~, খরচের ~. **8** a button-hole: বোতামের ~. **9** an office: ডাক~. **10** a groove; a pocket : ছাপার টাইপের ~. ~ **আলো করা** (fig) bring joy, happiness or pride to a family. ~**কন্না** *n* (of a woman) housekeeping; the duties of a housewife; housewifery. ~**কন্না করা** *vi* keep house ; manage household affairs; run a house. ~ **করা** *vt* **1** build a house. **2** (of a woman) play the part of a housewife or mistress of one's husband's house. ~ **কাটা** *vi* draw columns, squares, etc on a piece of paper. ~-**কাটা** *adj* divided into columns or separate spaces. ~**কুনো** *adj* **1** one who is shy of outdoor activities. **2** not social; not caring to mix with one's fellows. ~**কুনোমি** *n* home-keeping. ~**খরচ** *n* household expenses; maintenance cost of a family. ~ **খোঁজা** *vi* look for a suitable family for matrimonial alliance. ~-**গড়া** *adj* home-made. ~ **গড়া** *vi* **1** construct a house. **2** get married and settle as a householder. **3** equip and embellish a house with all necessaries after one's heart. ~**গুষ্ঠি** *n* all the members of a family. ~ **ঘর** *adv* in every household; from house to house; from door to door. ~**ঘেঁসা** *adj* devoted to one's household. ~ **ছাড়া** *vi* renounce one's hearth and home; abjure worldly life; take to asceticism. ~-**ছাড়া** *adj* one who has renounced worldly life and has taken to asceticism. ~**জামাই** *n* person who puts up with his father-in-law's family. ~**জোড়া** *adj* **1** occupying the whole room/ house: ~জোড়া গালিচা. **2** that which adds to the beauty of the house: ~জোড়া নাতিনাতনী. ~ **জ্বালানো** *vi* **1** set fire to a house. **2** (fig) poison the mutual relationship in a family; make a home unquiet. ~**জ্বালানে** *adj* one who is at the root of unhappiness of a family. ~**জ্বালানী** *fem.* ~ **তোলা** *vi* **1** construct a house. **2** make a knitting design. ~ **নষ্ট করা** *vi* **1** destroy the happiness of a family. **2** do sth that brings dishonour to a family. **3** marry in or give one in marriage to a lower family. ~ পর *n* one's own people and others. ~ পাওয়া *vi* get a suitable bride or bridegroom from a good family. ~ পাতা *vi* be settled in family life. ~-পোড়া *adj* **1** one whose dwelling has been burnt down. **2** one who has gathered experience from the burning of a cowshed: ~-পোড়া গরু. ❑*n* the Ramayana character Hanumana who burnt down houses in Lanka. ~পোড়া গরু সিঁদুরে মেঘ দেখে ডরায় (lit) a cow that has the experience of a conflagration dreads red clouds in the evening sky (prov); once bitten, twice shy; a scolded dog fears cold water; a burnt child dreads the fire. ~পোষা *adj* domesticated; tame. ~বর *n* one's husband and his family. ~ বাঁধা *vi* build a house; settle down (at a place). ~বার করা *vi* go out of doors and come indoors repeatedly in one's anxiety for someone. ~ ভাঙ্গা/ভাঙা *vi* **1** pull down a house. **2** break up a family. **3** cause dissension in a family. ~ভাঙ্গানে *adj* one who causes dissension in a family. ~ভাঙ্গানি *fem*. ~মুখো *adj* **1** eager to go home; home-sick. **2** homeward. ~-সংসার *n* household life/ affairs. ~সংসার করা *vi* live with one's husband/ wife; live the life of a householder/ housewife. ঘরে আগুন দেওয়া = ~ জ্বালানো. ঘরে পরে *adv* **1** everywhere out of doors and within; at home and abroad.**2** irrespective of friend and foe. ঘরের কথা *n* internal secret of a family or party. ঘরেরশত্রু*n* one who betrays his own people; an internal enemy; a fifth columnist; a traitor; a quisling.

ঘরট্ট *n* pair of heavy circular flat stones between which corn is milled; millstones.

ঘরনী, ঘরনি *n* the mistress of a house; a housewife. ❑*adj* skilled and experienced in one's duties and responsibilities as a housewife. ঘরন্তী = ঘরনী *adj*.

ঘরানা *adj* **1** of high status; high born: ~ পরিবার. **2** relating to/ concerning a particular family: ~ ব্যাপার. ❑*n* a typical tradition of music; a particular school of musical tradition: তানসেন ~.

ঘরামি *n* person who is a builder of huts by profession; a thatcher. ~গিরি *n* occupation of a thatcher.

ঘরে পরে ⇒ঘর

ঘরোয়া *adj* **1** concerning a family; pertaining to the internal affairs of a household: ~ ব্যাপার. **2** in close touch; familiar; intimate: ~ লোক. **3** confined within a close circle : ~ অনুষ্ঠান. **4** without ceremony; not in usual form; informal: ~ পরিবেশ.

ঘর্ঘর *int* (onom) denoting a rattling sound as that of a bullock cart in motion. ❑*n* the sound made by a cat when pleased; purr. ~ করা *vi* **1** make a rattling sound; rattle. **2** murmur/ purr (as a cat). ~ শব্দে *adv* with a rattling noise.

ঘর্ম *n* exudation of sweat; perspiration. ~ হওয়া *vi* sweat; perspire; exude. ~সিক্ত, ঘর্মাক্ত, ঘর্মাপ্লুত *adj* drenched with perspiration; sweating profusely. ঘর্মাক্ত কলেবর *adj* one who is sweating all over. ঘর্মাক্ত কলেবরে *adv* with the body sweating all over.

ঘর্ষক *adj* that rubs; rubbing. ~পদী *n* the kind of birds that finds food by purging the ground with their legs (as the chicken).

ঘর্ষণ *n* act of rubbing/ scouring; abrasion. ~ করা *vt* apply friction to the surface of; move sth along the surface (of sth) with pressure; rub; scour; abrade; graze. ঘর্ষিত *adj* that has been rubbed.

ঘষা *vt* move along sth with pressure; rub; graze; scour; abrade. ❑*n* rubbing of; scouring; friction; abrasion. ❑*adj* rubbed; grazed; abraded; scoured: ~ পয়সা. ~-~ *adj* appearing as abraded; slightly grazed. ~ঘষি *n* **1** act of rubbing each other. **2** rubbing repeatedly. **3** (fig) excessive intimacy (with sb). ~-মাজা *n* **1** act of scrubbing or brushing up. **2** (fig) assiduous practice for improvement. ~-মাজা করা *vt* **1** rub hard to make clean or bright. **2** (fig) try assiduously to improve upon. ~-মাজা রূপ *n* beauty with artificial aids; made-up beauty/ glamour.

ঘষ্টানো *vt* **1** scrape off by rubbing continuously. **2** drag along sth hard. **3** (fig) make repeated attempt to master sth. ঘষ্টানি *n*.

ঘা *n* **1** a blow; a stroke; a shock: বেতের ~. **2** a wound; a sore; an ulcer: পচা ~. **3** a sudden disturbing emotion; heart-sore; grief : ~ খাওয়া. **4** damage; waste; loss: কারবারে ~ খাওয়া. **5** knocking: দরজায় ~ দেওয়া. ~ কতক *n* a number of blows. ~ কতক বসিয়ে দেওয়া *vt* deal (one) a good number of blows. ~ খাওয়া *vi* receive a blow; suffer a loss; learn from suffering. ~ খেয়ে বোঝা/ শেখা learn by experience; be wise after the event. ~ দেওয়া *vi* **1** hurt one's feelings; cause shock to one's heart. **2** strike or inflict a blow. ~ মারা = ~ দেওয়া (2). ~ শুকানো *vi* be healed; be cured. ~ শুকিয়েছে the wound is healed. ~ সওয়া *vi* endure a blow/ shock with patience. ❑*adj* one who is capable or in the habit of enduring a blow or insult with calmness. ~ হওয়া *vi* be ulcerated. নালী ~ *n* an ulcer in the form of a cavity and containing pus; a sinus; a fistula. মড়ার উপর খাড়ার ~ (proverb) flogging a dead horse; adding insult to injury. সর্বাঙ্গে ঘা, ওষুধ দেব কোথা When there are sores all over the body, where is the salve to be applied? (fig) An irremediable state.

ঘাই *n* a stroke; a blow; a noisy stroke (as made by a large fish on the surface of water with its tail): ~ মারা.

ঘাঁটা[1] *vt* **1** beat up; stir; agitate. **2** study, review or examine : ফাইলপত্র ~. **~ ঘাঁটি** *n* **1** continuous searching , review or discussion. **2** violent agitation; commotion; bustle. **~ঘাঁটি করা** *vt* beat up; stir; agitate. **~নো** *vt* **1** cause to stir; excite; agitate. **2** disturb; annoy; vex; irritate.

ঘাঁটা[2] *n* a horny excrescence on a toe or foot; a corn.

ঘাঁটি, ঘাটি *n* **1** a watch-post; a police or military outpost. **2** a station; a depot: বিমান ~, an aerodrome; জাহাজ~, a dock. **3** a haunt: a rendezvous: জুয়াড়িদের ~. **~ আগলানো** *vi* guard an outpost. **~য়াল** *n* the chief of an outpost.

ঘাঁত, ঘাত *n* **1** the opportune moment or secret means to fulfil a design. **2** tricks; device; contrivance: also ~ঘোত.

ঘাগরা [H] *n* the lower and loose part of a western woman's garment; a skirt.

ঘাগি, ঘাগী, ঘাগু *adj* **1** experienced by long practice or repeated faults and failures; a veteran. **2** confirmed; obstinate; inveterate; hardened: ~ চোর, ~ বদমাশ.

ঘাঘর *n* a kind of musical instrument; a pair of cymbals.

ঘাট[1] *n* **1** a slope or a flight of steps leading down to the water level of a pond or river; a ghat. **2** a landing stage on a marine route; a quay; a wharf; a moorage: জাহাজ ~. **3** the reed of a harmonium. **4** either of the mountain ranges on the eastern and western side of south India: পশ্চিম ~, পূর্ব ~. **~ কামান** *n* the practice of shaving heads of sons on the expiry of the period of mourning a parent's death as prevalent among Hindus. **ঘাটে এসে নাও ডুবানো** (fig) do a single mistake to spoil a successful process. **ঘাটে ঘাটে** *adv* at every stage; everywhere. **ঘাটের কড়ি** *n* fare or the sum charged for conveying a person across a river. **ঘাটের মড়া** *n* **1** (hit) a corpse for cremation as a Hindu rite. **2** a dying man; an old decrepit person.

ঘাট[2] *n* **1** a fault; an offence; a failure: ~ হওয়া. **2** want; shortage; deficiency: কোনো দিকে ~ নেই. **~ মানা** *vi* admit a fault; apologize. **~ মানানো** *vt* make (one) admit a fault/ apologize. **~ হওয়া** *vi* be at fault: আমার ~ হয়েছে, It's my fault, I apologize.

ঘাটতি [H] *n* the amount short; shortage; deficit. ~ বাজেট, the budget in which expenditure exceeds income; a deficit budget.

ঘাটলা *n* a flight of stairs, built of brick or stone, at the bank of a pond or river.

ঘাটা *n* **1** landing stage on a waterway; a quay; a wharf; a moorage: জাহাজ ~, নৌকা~. **2** a road; a public passage.

ঘাটোয়াল *n* **1** a person who has the charge of a ghat; a superintendent or contractor of a ferryghat; a wharfinger. **2** person in charge of an outpost. **3** a collector of toll from pilgrims. **ঘাটোয়ালী** *fem*. **ঘাটোয়ালি** *n* the profession or post of one in charge of a ghat.

ঘাড় *n* **1** the nape or back of the neck; the neck. **2** the shoulder. **~ ধরা** *vt* hold or seize (one) by the neck. **~ ধরে করানো** *vt* compel (one) to do sth; cause (one) to do sth under compulsion. **~ধাক্কা** *n* pushing by the neck. **~ধাক্কা দেওয়া** *vi, vt* push (one) by the neck. **~ নাড়া** *vi* shrug one's shoulders/ move one's head to indicate assent or dissent. **~ পাতা** *vi* shoulder or agree to shoulder a responsibility. **~ ফুলানো** *vi* show obstinacy. **~ ভাঙ্গা** *vi* cause (one) by cajolery to spend money or pay sth against his will. **ঘাড়ে করা/ লওয়া** *vt* **1** (fig) shoulder a risky charge; admit a responsibility. **ঘাড়ে-গর্দানে** *adj* having a short neck; one whose neck doesn't appear to be separate from the head; short-necked. **ঘাড়ে চাপা, ঘাড়ে পড়া** *vi* fall on (one's) shoulder as a burden. **ঘাড়ে চাপানো** *vt* **1** impute (an evil) to another's account; lay (a charge) to another's door. **2** charge one with a responsibility. **ঘাড়ে দুটো মাথা থাকা** be over-daring; do sth in defiance of authority. **ঘাড়ে ভুত চাপা** be seized with a fancy/ wicked design.

ঘাত *n* **1** a violent striking against; violent onset; a stroke; a shock. **2** beating; chastisement by blows. **3** a wound; a sore; an ulcer. **4** malice; ill-will; rancour. **5** slaughter; killing; murder. **6** (math) the product obtained by multiplying a quantity by itself; power. **~ চিহ্ন** *n* (math) a number placed above and to the right of another number or letter to indicate the power to which it is raised or to denote a root (as a^3); an index. **~-প্রতি~** *n* action and its reaction; blows and counterblows. **~সহ** *adj* (of metals) that can be hammered or pressed into new shapes; capable of being beaten out with a hammer without being broken; malleable.

ঘাতক *n* **1** person guilty of a murder; a murderer; a killer; a slayer. **2** person who executes a sentence of capital punishment; an executioner. □ *adj* one who commits an act of treachery: বিশ্বাস~.

ঘাতন[1] *n* **1** slaying of beasts for market; slaughter. **2** sacrificial slaughter; immolation.

ঘাতন[2] *n* **1** act of causing to slay or slaughter. **2** an implement for beating; a whip or stick. **3** person who beats/ kills.

ঘাতী *adj* (used as *suff)* one who or that which kills: আত্ম~, ভ্রাতৃ~. **ঘাতিনী** *fem.*

ঘাতুক *adj* **1** one who kills or slays; killing; slaying. **2** that destroys; destroying. **3** cruel. **4** ferocious. **5** envious; malicious; crooked.

ঘাত্য *adj* **1** to be killed. **2** capable of being hammered or pressed into new shapes; malleable. **3** to be multiplied; multipliable.

ঘানি, ঘানী *n* hand-mill for expressing oil from oil-seeds; oil-mill (also ~ গাছ). **~ টানা/ঠেলা** *vi* **1** work an oil-mill. **2** (fig) be put to hard labour. **3** suffer rigorous imprisonment. **~তে জোড়া** *vt* **1** yoke to an oil-mill. **2** (fig) put to drudgery.

ঘানিক *adj* **1** (math) pertaining to the cube or third power; cubic. **2** of three dimensions; solid: ~ জ্যামিতি.

ঘাপটি *n* lying in wait in order to surprise; ambush; ambuscade. **~ মারা, ~ মেরে থাকা** *vi* lie in wait; ambush; ambuscade; lurk.

ঘাপলা, ঘাবলা *n* a difficult situation; a tricky turn; a predicament. **~য় পড়া** *vi* be entangled in an intrigue or machination; be in a state of perplexity; get into a predicament or quandary. **~য় ফেলা** *vt* entangle (one) in a tricky situation from which escape seems difficult.

ঘাবড়ানো *vi* be perplexed or puzzled; get nervous. **(কাউকে) ঘাবড়ে দেওয়া** *vt* put (one) out of countenance; perplex or disconcert (one). **ঘাবড়ে যাওয়া** *vi* be non-pulsed/ bewildered; lose nerve. **ঘাবড়ানি** *n* nervousness; panic; fright.

ঘাবলা=ঘাপলা

ঘাম *n* sweat; perspiration. **~ ছোটা** *vi* **1** exude or sweat profusely. **2** undergo hard labour. **~ দিয়ে জ্বর ছাড়া** **1** be relieved of fever with the exudation of sweat. **2** (fig) be relieved of a great anxiety; heave a sigh of relief. **মাথার ~ পায়ে ফেলা** (fig) be under great strain; do hard labour.

ঘামা *vi* perspire; sweat. **~নো** *vt* cause to perspire; employ to weariness; harass with toil; fatigue. **মাথা ~নো** *vi* bring oneself into a certain state by too much thought; think hard to find solution to a difficult problem.

ঘামাচি *n* inflammation of the sweat glands; prickly-heat.

ঘায়েল *adj* **1** wounded; injured. **2** killed. **3** overpowered; discomfited. **~ করা** *vt* defeat heavily; deal a heavy blow. **~ হওয়া** *vi* be routed or discomfited.

ঘাস *n* low-growing green herbage covering the ground; grass. **~ কাটা** *vi* **1** mow grass. **2** (fig) waste time without doing anything worthwhile. **~ খাওয়া** *vi* (fig) prove oneself a blockhead like a grass-eating animal: তুমি কি ~ খাও?

ঘাসিয়াড়া, ঘাসুড়িয়া *n* one who deals in or supplies grass for cattle. **~কাটা কল** *n* a grass cutter; a mowing machine.

ঘাসী *n* a dealer in grass; one who cuts and sells grass for cattle. **~ নৌকা** *n* a long and narrow boat used in carrying grass.

ঘি *n* clarified or melted butter made from the milk of cows or buffaloes; ghee.

ঘিঞ্জি *adj* **1** closely placed; dense; congested; over-crowded. **2** narrow.

ঘিনঘিন *int* suggesting uneasiness caused by detestation of sth: গা ~ করা.

ঘিরা=ঘেরা

ঘিলু *n* **1** the material of which the brain consists; brains. **2** the ability to think; intelligence.

ঘুঁজি, ঘুঞ্জি *n* **1** congested place or narrow lane. **2** dark, narrow and dirty place. **গলি ~** *n* the narrow lanes of a congested and overcrowded area.

ঘুঁটনি, ঘুটনি, ঘুটুনি *n* a pestle for beating up *dal* or split pulse: ডাল ~.

ঘুঁটা=ঘোঁটা

ঘুঁটি, গুটি *n* a piece or pawn in chess or similar other games. **~ চালা** *vi* move a piece from one place to another.

ঘুঁটে *n* cakes made of cowdung and dried for use as fuel; cowdung cakes. **~কুড়ানি, ~কুড়ুনী** *n fem* a woman who makes cowdung cakes to earn her livelihood; (fig) a poor and humble person.

ঘুঘু *n* **1** the dove; the turtle-dove; the famous wild bird of the pigeon family. **2** (fig) a shrewd and designing person. **সেয়ানা ~** (fig) a skilful and experienced person. **~ দেখেছো ফাঁদ দেখোনি** (fig) You have not seen the worst. **~ চরানো** **1** eject (one) from his homestead: ভিটেয় ~ চরানো. **2** cause ruination to one.

ঘুঙুর, ঘুঙ্গুর *n* ornamental ring with bells worn at the ankles; bangle of bells for the ankle.

ঘুচা, ঘোচা *vi* **1** pass away; disappear; be dispelled. **2** come to an end; cease to exist: দুঃখ ~. **~নো** *vt* remove; dispel; relieve: **দুঃখ ~,** alleviate one's sufferings; অন্ধকার ~, dispel darkness; সন্দেহ ~, dispel doubt. **সম্বন্ধ ~** *vi* sever a break off connection.

ঘুটঘুট *int* denoting extreme density of darkness: অন্ধকার ~ করছে. **ঘুটঘুটে** *adj* deep; thick: চারিদিকে ঘুটঘুটে অন্ধকার.

ঘুড়ি, ঘুড্ডি (colloq) *n* a flying toy; a kite.

ঘুণ *n* **1** a small worm that makes holes in wood; wood-worm. **2** (fig) sth that eats into vigour and vitality: ঘুণে ধরা সমাজ. ❑*adj* having ability, cleverness and skill; dexterous; skilful; experienced. **~ পরিমাণ** *adj* of little amount: ~ পরিমাণ তথ্যও আমার জানা নেই. **ঘুণাক্ষর**

n **1** a letter-like mark on a worn-eaten timber. **2** (fig) a slight hint. **ঘুণাক্ষরে** *adv* in the least; to the slightest extent: আমি ঘুণাক্ষরেও জানি না.

ঘুন্টি *n* **1** button made of cloth or thread . **2** a small bell.

ঘুৎকার *n* the cry of an owl.

ঘুনসি *n* thread worn round the waist, esp by woman.

ঘুপচি=ঘুপসি

ঘুপটি *n* act of hiding oneself: ~ মেরে থাকা.

ঘুপসি, ঘুপচি *adj* **1** dark and narrow; like a small closed hole. **2** in a bending state; crouching: ~ মেরে বসা. □ *n* a dark narrow place.

ঘুম *n* **1** natural resting state of unconsciousness; sleep; slumber. **~কাতুরে** *adj* prone to falling asleep quickly; one who enjoys sleeping. **~ঘুম** *adj* inclined to sleep; drowsy; sleepy. **~ঘোর** *n* **1** sound sleep. **2** drowsiness; sleepiness. **ঘুমন্ত** *adj* sleeping; asleep. **~ পাড়ানো** *vi* lull to sleep. **~ ভাঙা** *vi* woke up. **~ ভাঙানো** *vt* rouse (one) from sleep; awake. **ঘুমের ঘোর কাটানো** *vi* shake off sleep or drowsiness. **ঘুমের ঘোরে** *adv* in a state of sleep/ drowsiness. **~ পাড়ানি** *adj* causing sleep; soporific; lulling. **~পাড়ানি গান** *n* a song to lull babies; that which lulls; lullaby. **কাঁচা ~** *n* incomplete sleep.

ঘুমানো *vi* sleep; be asleep.

ঘুর *n* **1** a spell of revolving: ~ দেওয়া. **2** going a long way round instead of in a direct route; a circuitous or indirect way; a deviation from the shortest way of approach; detour: এ পথে অনেক ~ হবে, ~ পথ. **~ঘুর** *int* expressing frequentation to a place. **~~ করা** *vi* visit a place frequently; roam about a place with a motive. **~ঘুরে** *n* a burrowing insect; the mole-cricket. **~পথ** *n* a round-about way; a detour. **~পাক** *n* whirling round; circular motion. **~পাক খাওয়া** *vi* whirl round and round. **~প্যাঁচ** *n* state of being complicated; intricacy; complication; angularity.

ঘুরা, ঘোরা *vi* **1** turn about; turn round; revolve. **2** walk about; travel; journey: দেশ ~. **3** visit a place frequently. **4** trouble the mind continually; haunt: বিষয়টি আমার মাথায় ঘুরছে, the matter is haunting my mind. **~ঘুরি** *n* frequent coming and going with some purpose. **~ঘুরি করা** *vi* visit frequently; pester or annoy by continual visits; haunt. **~নো** *vt* **1** turn round; whirl; cause to revolve or spin. **2** harass (one) with false hopes: সে আমাকে ~চ্ছে, He is putting me off every day. **ঘুরে বেড়ানো** walk about idly; loiter.

ঘুষ, ঘুস *n* a gift to corrupt the conduct or judgement; illegal gratification; bribe. **~ খাওয়া** *vi* take/receive a bribe. **~খোর** *n* person who is in the habit of taking bribes. **~ দেওয়া** *vt* offer bribe; bribe; (idiom) grease sb's palm.

ঘুষঘুষে *adj* **1** secret; subdued; suppressed. **2** not acute; mild; slight. **3** hidden; not manifest; internal: ~ জ্বর.

ঘুষা[1], ঘুষি, ঘুষো *n* a blow with the fist; fisticuff. **~ মারা** *vt* strike (one) with the clenched fist. **~ঘুষি** *n* **1** fighting with the fists for sport; fisticuff; boxing. **2** exchange of blow; striking each other with the fists. **~ঘুষি করা** *vi* exchange blows. **ঘুষি খেলা** *n* a fight between two boxers; boxing-match; the sport of fist-fighting. **~ লড়া** *vt* fight (sb) with the fists for sport; box.

ঘুষা[2] ⇒ ঘুসা

ঘুষি=ঘুষা[1]

ঘুস=ঘুষ

ঘুসা, ঘুসো *n* the smallest variety of shrimp: ~ চিংড়ি.

ঘূর্ণ *n* circular movement; whirling; rotation; revolution. □*adj* rotary; rotatory; turning, as a wheel does on its axis. **~ন** *n* act of turning round; whirling; rolling. **~বাত, ~বায়ু** *n* *n* cyclone; whirlwind. **~মান, ঘূর্ণায়মান, ঘূর্ণ্যমান** *adj* that which is revolving/whirling/rolling/reeling.

ঘূর্ণা *n* whirling motion; eddy.

ঘূর্ণাবর্ত [ঘূর্ণ+আবর্ত] *n* a violent current of water or air moving round in a circle; a whirlpool; a whirlwind; an eddy.

ঘূর্ণায়মান ⇒ ঘূর্ণ

ঘূর্ণি *n* a circular current (eddy) of water or air (also ঘূর্ণিপাক). **~ঝড়** *n* violent wind blowing spirally inwards towards a centre of low barometric pressure; wind-storm; cyclone.

ঘূর্ণিবাত, ঘূর্ণিবায়ু=ঘূর্ণাবাত ⇒ ঘূর্ণ

ঘূর্ণ্যমান ⇒ ঘূর্ণ

ঘৃণা *n* **1** a feeling of dislike, disgust or aversion; repulsion. **2** detestation; abhorrence; hatred; contempt; scorn. **3** feeling of shame/disgrace. **~ করা** *vt* **1** hate; detest, loathe; abhor. **2** look down upon; treat with contempt; despise; disdain. **~র্হ** *adj* despicable; contemptible; abominable; deserving hate.

ঘৃণিত *adj* **1** that has excited hate; hated; despised. **2** arousing hatred; provoking ill-will; detestable; hateful. **3** one who is condemned/ animadverted. **4** blameworthy; reproachable; heinous: ~ আচরণ. **5**. low; vile; base; mean.

ঘৃণ্য=ঘৃণার্হ ⇒ ঘৃণা

ঘৃত *n* clarified butter; ghee. **~পক্ব** *adj* fried or cooked with ghee.

ঘৃতকুমারী *n* small medicinal plant; the aloe.

ঘৃতাক্ত *adj* smeared or anointed with ghee.

ঘৃতান্ন [ঘৃত+অন্ন] *n* rice boiled with ghee; pilau.

ঘৃতাচি, ঘৃতার্চিঃ [ঘৃত+অর্চিঃ] *n* fire.

ঘৃতাহুতি [ঘৃত+আহুতি] *n* libation of sanctified ghee into a Hindu sacred fire. **জ্বলন্ত অগ্নিতে ~ দেওয়া** (fig) add fuel to the fire.

ঘৃষ্ট *adj* **1** what has been rubbed or scoured. **2** trampled; thrashed; pounded: ~ চন্দন. **3** cleansed; brushed. **4** produced by rubbing: ~ ধ্বনি.

ঘেউ *int, n* barking noise; the bark of a dog. **~~ করা** *vi* bark.

ঘেঁচড়া, ঘেচড়া *n* a part of the skin hardened by friction; callosity: ~ পড়া. ❑ *adj* **1** affected with callosity. **2** disobedient; obstinate; refractory: ~ ছেলে. **3** unfeeling; callous.

ঘেঁচু, ঘেচু *n* **1** esculent root of arum: কচু~. **2** (sl) a mere trifle; nothing; fig: ~ হবে. **~ করা** *vi* fail to do anything: ~ করবে. **কচু~** *n* trashy things; trifles.

ঘেঁটু *n* **1** a wild plant or its flower. **2** a Hindu deity.

ঘেঁষ *n* **1** touch; contact. **2** intimacy; close familiarity. **3** indulgence: ~ দেওয়া, admit into familiarity. **~ ঘেঁষ** *adj* very close to each other.

ঘেঁষড়ানো *vt* draw or drag behind. **ঘেঁষড়ানি** *n*.

ঘেঁষা *vt* **1** approach; draw close to; come in contact with. **~ঘেঁষি** *adv* closely; thickly. **~ঘেঁষি করা** *vt* press close to one another; throng together.

ঘেঙানো *vi* express distress by a plaintive drawling cry with a whining voice; whine; whimper. **ঘেঙানি** *n* whining; a whine; a whimper.

ঘেটি (colloq) *n* neck; throat: ~ ধরে বের করে দেওয়া.

ঘেটেল *n* **1** a toll collector at a ferryghat. **2** a ferryman. **ঘেটেলি** *n* the profession or the remuneration of a ferryman.

ঘেনঘেন=ঘ্যান ঘ্যান

ঘেনর-ঘেনর=ঘ্যানর-ঘ্যানর ⇒ ঘ্যান ঘ্যান

ঘেন্না *n* **1** great dislike or aversion; disgust; abhorrence. **2** a sense of guilt or disgrace; shame: এতবার ফেল করেও তোমার ~ হয় না? **~ করা** *vt* **1** feel disgust; be disgusted; abhor. **2** have qualms; be queasy/ squeamish. **~পিত্তি নেই** absence of the feeling of shame or disgrace. **~র কথা** *n* a matter of shame; a shameful affair.

ঘেয়ো *adj* having an ulcer; full of sores and ulcers. **~ কুত্তা** (abuse) used for one who is nasty or shameless.

ঘের *n* **1** the bounding line of a circle; circumference; perimeter. **2** the fencing of a plot of land; enclosure. **3** an open space enclosed by a barrier. **4** a cover; a screen. **~ দেওয়া** *vi, vt* enclose; inclose.

ঘেরা, ঘিরা *vt* **1** shut up or a confine on all sides; enclose; inclose: প্রাচীর দিয়ে ~. **2** encircle; encompass; besiege; surround. **3** wrap up; cover. ❑*n* **1** a fence; a fencing; a railing. **2** act of covering or surrounding. **3** a place surrounded by a fencing. ❑*adj* enclosed; shut in; surrounded; besieged. **~নো** *vt* cause to be covered/surrounded.

ঘেরাও *n* act of surrounding/ besieging; the state of being besieged; besiegement. ❑*adj* enclosed; besieged; surrounded shut in. **~ করা** *vt* besiege; surround: বাড়ি ~ করা, surround a house; শহর ~ করা, besiege a city.

ঘেরাটোপ *n* **1** a cloth-cover for furniture, etc. **2** a hood on a carriage, market stall, etc. **3** veil or purdah worn by Muslim women.

ঘেসো *adj* **1** grassy; grass-like; full of grass: ~ মাঠ. **2** smelling like grass. **3** inferior in quality; unsubstantial: ~ জিনিস. **4** made of grass.

ঘোঁটা, ঘুঁটা *vt* stir up; churn; agitate. **2** mix up; tread on; trample. **3** wander through in search of sth; ransack.

ঘোঁত, ঘোঁৎ *int* denoting the grunting of the boar. **~ করা** *vi* grunt; grumble with anger.

ঘোগ *n* **1** wild animal looking like a dog; a wild dog; a lemur. **2** (in legends) enemy of tiger. **বাঘের ঘরে ঘোগের বাসা** a wolf in the lion's den; cunning beats force.

ঘোটক *n* a horse. **ঘোটকী** *fem* a mare.

ঘোটন, ঘোঁটন *n* stirring; churning; shaking with violence. **ঘোটনা** *n* a pestle or stick for churning.

ঘোড়গাড়ি *n* a carriage drawn by horse(s); a hackney carriage.

ঘোড়দৌড় *n* a race run by horses; horse race. **(কাউকে) ~ করানো** harass (one) by causing him to run like a horse. **ঘোড়দৌড়ের ঘোড়া** *n* a racehorse. **ঘোড়দৌড়ের মাঠ** *n* race-course.

ঘোড়সওয়ার *n* a rider on horseback; a horseman; a cavalier.

ঘোড়া *n* **1** a horse. **2** (in chess) a piece bearing a horse's head; a knight. **3** the cock of a gun; trigger. **(বন্দুকের) ~ টেপা** pull the trigger (of a gun). **~ ডিঙিয়ে ঘাস খাওয়া** bypass the immediate superior/proper channel. **~ দেখে খোঁড়া হওয়া** be unwilling to work when there is sb to help. **~র জিন দিয়ে আসা** be in hot haste. **~র ডিম** (fig) a discovery that amounts to nothing; a hoax; a mare's nest. **~য় চড়া** *vi* ride a horse. **~রোগ** (fig) an extremely expensive hobby; a harmful craze. **~শাল** *n* a house for horses; a stable.

ঘোণা *n* **1** the nose of a horse. **2** (sarcas) the nose.

ঘোনা *n* **1** solitary place; cell for pigeons, etc.

ঘোপ *n* **1** a crevice or hollow. **2** a secret or invisible place. **~ঘাপ** *n* out-of-the-way place.

ঘোমটা *n* a cover for woman's head and forehead with the end of sari; a veil. **~ খোলা** *vi* unveil one's face. **~ টানা** *vi* let down the end of one's sari over one's forehead. **~র ভিতর খেমটা নাচ, ~র মধ্যে সখীসংবাদ** *n* coquetry under the veil of chastity/modesty. **নাচতে এসে ~** sarcastically said of one putting up a false show of modesty.

ঘোর *n* **1** darkness. **2** state of being intoxicated. **3** mental obsession; infatuation; illusion; bewitchment. □*adj* **1** terrible; dreadful; awful: ~ বিপদ. **2** excessive; extreme: ~ পাগল, stark mad; ~ মাতাল, dead drunkard; ~ অন্যায়, gross injustice. **3** deep; intense: ~ অন্ধকার. **4** profound: ~ নিদ্রা. ঘোরা *adj fem:* ঘোরা যামিনী. **~ করা** *vi* darken; become dark. **~ কাটা** *vi* get out of obsession or illusion. **~ ঘোর** *n* **1** darkishness; duskiness. **2** state of being inebriated; inebriety. **~তর** *adj comp* **1** more horrid/awful. **2** very dreadful. **~তরা** *fem.* **~দর্শন** *adj* of frightful appearance; terrible-looking. **~প্যাঁচ, ~পেঁচ** *n* intricacy; complication; crookedness; angularity.

ঘোরালো *adj* **1** overcast with deep darkness; enveloped in thick darkness. **2** deep; dense; thick: ~ অন্ধকার. **3** very complicated; intricate: ~ বিষয়. **4** arousing terror; terrible; dreadful; fearful: ~ বিপদ. **5** thoughtful; sullen; grave; dejected: ~ মুখ.

ঘোরে *adv* under the spell of; because of: জ্বরের ~ বকছে, gone delirious under the spell of high fever.

ঘোল *n* the watery part of milk which remains when butter has been churned; buttermilk; whey. **~ খাওয়া** *vi,vt* (fig) **1** get into a disadvantageous position and suffer harassment. **2** be totally discomfited and involved in great trouble. **~ খাওয়ানো** *vt* (fig) **1** cause (one) to suffer harassment. **2** humiliate (one); chastise (one); teach (one) a lesson. **~মন্থন** *n* churning of butter. **~মন্থনী, ~মউনি** *n* a churning rod. **দুধের সাধ ঘোলে মেটানো** have to be satisfied with an inferior substitute. **মাথায় ~ ঢালা** (fig) humiliate (a person) in public.

ঘোলা *adj* **1** not clear; defiled; turbid; foul: ~ পানি. **2** (of water) containing mud; muddy; dirty. **3** wanting lustre; lack-lustre. **4** dull; dim. **5** frosty: ~ বাল্ব **6** rotten; decomposed: ~ ডিম. **~টে** *adj* rather a bit turbid; somewhat opaque or dull. **~নো**=ঘুলানো.

ঘোষ *n* **1** a sound; a noise; a note. **2** an announcement; a proclamation; a declaration. **3** a milkman by caste. **4** family name of certain Bengali Hindus. **~ক** *adj* one who announces/ proclaims/declares. □*n* an announcer; a proclaimer; a preacher. **~বর্ণ** *n* (gram) a voiced consonant.

ঘোষণা *n* **1** a loud declaration; a proclamation; an announcement. **2** a circular notice; a communiqué; a pamphlet; a handbill. **3** making a declaration with necessary formalities: যুদ্ধ ~. □*vt* proclaim; declare; announce; publish. **~পত্র** *n* a written announcement or proclamation; a communiqué; a bulletin.

ঘোষিত *adj* **1** that which has been announced or proclaimed. **2** that has been sounded/noised.

ঘ্যাগ *n* enlargement of the thyroid gland; goitre.

ঘ্যাচড়া=ঘেঁচড়া

ঘ্যান ঘ্যান *int* suggesting whimpering/whining or continuous complaining about sth. □*n* whining cry. **~ করা** *vi,vt* whine; whimper; solicit sth importunately; complain of sth continuously.

ঘ্যানর ঘ্যানর *int* **1**=ঘ্যান ঘ্যান. **2** continuous grating noise (as of a spinning wheel).

ঘ্রাণ *n* smell; scent. **~ নেওয়া** *vt* smell. **~শক্তি** *n* sense of smell.

ঘ্রাণেন্দ্রিয় [ঘ্রাণ+ইন্দ্রিয়] *n* organ of smell; the nose.

ঙ *n* the fifth consonant of the Bengali alphabet. It is pronounced as 'উঁয়ো'. or 'উমা' It is a voiced velar nasal consonant sound and is not in use as the first letter of a word.

চ

চ *n* the sixth consonant of the Bengali alphabet. It is pronounced as a dorso-alveolar, plato-alveolar voiceless unaspirated plosive sound. Dhaka-Kuttis pronounce it as affricate sound and in some dialects also it is pronounced as affricate sound.

চই, চৈ [চবিকা] *n* kind of creeper with pungent root; *piper chaba.*

চই-চই *int* sound used for calling ducks.

চওড়া *adj* broad; wide. □*n* breadth; width: ~য় একফুট.

চক[1] [E] *n* soft, white, natural substance used for making lime and various writing materials; chalk: ~পেন্সিল.

চক[2] *n* broad open space of the shape of a square or rectangle. **2** a meeting place of streets in a city; a market place in a village: ~বাজার, চাঁদনি~. **3** a square space surrounded by buildings. ~বন্দি, ~বন্দী *n* the settlement of boundary of plots of land. ~মিলান *n* line of buildings round a square: ~-মিলান বাড়ি.

চক চক *int* **1** suggesting the sound of licking water. **2** expressive of brightness, glaze, lustre, etc. ~ **করা** *vt* shine; glitter, sparkle. ~ **করলেই সোনা হয় না** (proverb) All that glitters is not gold. **চকচকে** *adj* bright; lustrous; shining; glittering.

চকমকি [T] *n* fine-textured grey stone that makes small flashes of flame when struck with steel or another piece of stone, used in ancient times for striking fire; a flint. ~ **ঠোকা** *vi* **1** strike fire with the help of flints. **2** (fig) try to incite a quarrel. ~ **বাক্স** *n* **1** a box containing flint-stones and finder (anything highly combustible) for producing a flame. **2** (fig) a very dangerous and uncontrollable state of affairs; a tinder-box.

চকিত *adj* **1** taken aback; quickly surprised; startled. **2** timid; bashful: ~ চাহনি . ☐ *n* an instant; a moment (চকিতের মধ্যে). **চকিতে** *adv* in an instant; in a moment: ~**নয়না** *adj fem* timid-eyed; timorous looking. ~ **নয়নে** *adv* with startled eyes/timorous look.

চকোর *n* kind of bird celebrated in poetry as longing for and highly enjoying moonbeam. *fem* **চকোরী**

চক্কর, চক্কোর *n* **1** anything wheel-shaped or circular. **2** anything in the state of circling/ rotating/. **3** a place or a path in the shape of a circle. **4** act of rotating or circling. **5** dizziness; giddiness: মাথা ~ দেওয়া . **6** a circular mark (as on the hood of a snake). ~ **দেওয়া** *vi, vt* **1** go round; move in a circle; circle. **2** go on an outing.

চক্র *n* **1** circular frame turning on an axis; a wheel (চক্রযান, রথচক্র). **2** a place, a passage or anything in the shape of a wheel or ring: দৌড়ের ~. **3** (fig) anything that recurs in a cycle: কালচক্র, cycle of time; কালের চক্রে একুশ আবার ফিরে এলো, *ekush* is again at our doors in the cycle of time. **4** horizontal revolving disc on which a potter shapes his wares; the potter's wheel. **5** the diagram of the zodiac, used in astrology (রাশি~). **6** array of troops in battle in a circular form (as of ancient times) (~ব্যূহ). **7** a group of people sitting together; a get-together (eg. for tea) : চা-~, a tea party. **8** the hood (or the circular mark on the hood) of a snake. **9** a secret plot or machination of people planning to commit an illegal act; an intrigue; a conspiracy : দশ চক্রে ভগবান ভূত *proverb* (story goes that ten people conspired against a Brahmin named *Bhagwan* and successfully established in the Brahmin's own lifetime that he was not a living being but only a bogey or goblin, thus giving currency to the proverb which means) A widespread conspiracy may be of grave consequences. **10** an extensive kingdom; an empire : চক্রবর্তী, the sovereign of a great kingdom; an emperor. আবর্ত চক্র *n* state of affairs in which cause and effect follow each other until the process results in the first position and the whole process starts again, eg., poverty leads to crime, which leads to prison, which results in unemployment, which again leads to crime; a vicious circle. **চক্রগতি** *n* cyclic motion; rotation; revolution. **চক্রধর** *n* **1** a ruler; a king; **2** the snake. **3** an appellation of Hindu god Vishnu. **চক্রনাভি** *n* the navel or hub at the centre of a wheel in which the spokes are set. ~**নেমি** *n* the circumference or rim of a wheel. ~**পাণি** *n* appellation of Vishnu, the Hindu god. ~**বর্তী** *n* **1** ⇒চক্র (10). **2** family title of certain Bengali Brahmins. ~**বাক** *n* the male bird of a species of wild duck (colloq চখা). ~**বাকী***fem*. ~**বাত** *n* a whirlwind; a cyclone. ~**বাল** *n* the line at which earth and sky seem to meet; the horizon. ~**বৃদ্ধি** *n* (of interest on loan) interest on capital and on accumulated interest; compound interest. ~**যান** *n* vehicle that moves on wheels; a wheeled carriage. ~**বৎ** *adj* wheel-shaped; circular. ☐ *adv* in a circular motion; like a wheel. **পাকচক্রে, পাকেচক্রে** *adv* by the irony of circumstances; as the circumstances have it.

চক্রাকার *adj* wheel-shaped; circular.

চক্রান্ত [চক্র+অন্ত] *n* =চক্র (9). ~ **করা** *vi* conspire; intrigue. ~**কারী** *adj* conspiring; intriguing. ☐*n* a conspirator.

চক্রাবর্ত [চক্র+আবর্ত] *n* **1** act of turning round about an axis. **2** the regular coming round of things or events in succession. **3** a whirlwind.

চক্রিকা *n* **1** the small heart-shaped bone situated at the fore-part of the knee-joint; the knee-pan. **2** the knee.

চক্রী *adj* **1** full of cunning, trickery; crafty; conspiring; crooked. **2** equipped with a circular missile. ☐*n* **1** an appellation of Vishnu. **2** the snake.

চক্ষ *n* =চক্ষু. **চক্ষের পুতলি** *n* **1** the pupil of the eye. **2** (fig) one who is very dear to one's heart.

চক্ষু [চক্ষুঃ] *n* **1** the organ of vision; the eye; **2** the sight of the eye; the power of vision : তার ~ খারাপ, his eyesight is weak. **3** insight or sight into (sth) (দিব্য~, জ্ঞান ~), ~ **কর্ণের বিবাদ ভঞ্জন করা** dispel any doubt that may have been felt about what has been heard by physical verification. ~**ক্ষত** *n* a wound or sore in the eye; eyesore. ~ **খাওয়া** *vi* (fig) fail to see what one ought to see; fail to choose the right thing. ~গোচর *adj* perceptible by the eye; within sight; visible. ~ চড়কগাছ হওয়া be struck with amazement; be extremely astounded. ~ ছানাবড়া হওয়া look with eyes widened in bewilderment. ~দান *n* **1** act of restoring someone's eyesight. **2** act of donating one's eyes on death by a will for the benefit of the sightless. **3** act of educating a person or giving him knowledge/ wisdom. চক্ষুরঞ্জন (also ~রঞ্জন) *adj* pleasing to the sight; pleasant to see. চক্ষুরোগ (also ~রোগ) *n* inflammation of the eye; eye-disease. ~লজ্জা *n* feeling of delicacy in doing sth that appears unseemly to the eye. ~লোম *n* the line of hair that edges the eyelid; eyelashes. ~শূল *adj* that which causes repugnance/ annoyance. ~ষ্মান *adj* **1** possessing the power of vision/ eyesight. **2** capable of perceiving the truth/ the inner truth of sth; possessing insight. ~ষ্মতী*fem.* ~স্থির *n* state of being in a bewilderment.

ট[১] *int* denoting quickness or promptness: ~ করে এসো.

ট[২] *n* coarse cloth made of jute; hessian; gunny. চটের থলি *n* a gunny bag.

টক[১] *n* small brownish-grey bird; the sparrow.

টক[২] *n* a fascinating/ glamourous show. ~দার *adj* having a spectacular appearance; glamorous; attractive.

টকানো *vt* press and squeeze some soft thing with the hands to make a paste of it.

টচট *int* suggesting sth sticky or viscid. চটচটে *adj* that which sticks to anything that touches it; sticky.

টপট *adv* in a quick manner; quickly; promptly: ~ কাজ শেষ করো. চটপটে *adj* full of quick movement.

টা[১] *vi* be irritated/ annoyed; get angry. ~চটি *n* angry exchange of words; quarrel. ~নো *vt* excite the temper of; make angry; irritate. রগ~ *adj* easily annoyed or made angry; tending to get angry at small things; irritable.

টা[২] *vi* break into chinks; crack; split.

টা[৩] *n* thin slip of bamboo used for making mat, etc.

টাস *int* suggesting sound of slapping.

টি[১] *n* kind of slippers open at the heels (also ~ জুতা).

টি[২] *adj* thin, not fat: ~ বই.

টুল *adj* **1** quick, light, and neat in movement; quick-moving; nimble. **2** never quiet; always moving about; restless: ~ স্বভাব. **3** not serious; light: ~ রচনা. **4** fascinating; captivating: ~ নয়না.

চট্টোপাধ্যায় (চট্ট+উপাধ্যায়) *n* title of certain Bengali-speaking Brahmin families (also চাটুয্যে) .

চড় *n* quick blow with the palm; a slap. ~ খাওয়া *vi* be slapped. ~ মারা *vt* slap on the face.

চড়ক *n* Hindu festival on the last day of the Bengali year connected with the worship of Shiva. ~গাছ *n* a tall pole from which a worshipper of Shiva swings as a part of this festival. চক্ষু ~গাছ হওয়া⇒চক্ষু

চড়চড়, চড়চড় *int* onomatopoeic word suggestive of certain sound.

চড়া[১] *vt* **1** get on/ climb/ mount/ ascend: গাড়ীতে ~, গাছে ~, ঘোড়ায় ~. **2** rise in amount or number; go up; increase: দাম ~.

চড়া[২] *adj* **1** haughty, arrogant: ~ মেজাজ. **2** strong; severe: ~ রোদ. **3** excessive; exorbitant: ~ সুদ. **4** rising far upwards, high: ~ সুর, ~ গলা.

চড়া[৩], চরা *n* sandy or silted land mass rising out of a river-bed. ~য় ঠেকা (of a boat/ steamer) be blocked in the shallow waters of a newly arisen island on a river course.

চড়াই[১] [H] *n* **1** a way up; upward slope; altitude. **2** act of ascending/ climbing/ mounting. ~ উৎরাই *n* acclivity and declivity; upward and downward movement.

চড়াই[২], চড়ই/ চড়ুই=চটক[১]

চড়াইভাতি, চড়ুইভাতি *n* pleasure trip by a group of people in which food is taken with or cooked on the spot in the country side.

চড়াও *n* act of violence (on an enemy) intended to harm or defeat; a sudden attack, an assault, a raid; □*adj* one who has fallen upon (an enemy). ~ হওয়া *vt* make an attack upon/ fall upon (an enemy).

চড়াৎ *int* denoting the onomatopoeic sound of cracking, bursting or splitting.

চড়ানো[১] *vt* **1** place sb on sth; cause to mount/ ride/ board. **2** make higher in amount ; raise, increase: দাম ~. **3** make louder: গলা ~. **4** put on, wear: গায়ে জামা ~. **5** (of cooking utensils) place on the oven: হাড়ি ~.

চণ্ড *adj* **1** furious in an uncontrolled way; very angry. **2** fierce; ferocious; severe: ~নীতি. □*n* (myth) name of a furious demon. চণ্ডী, চণ্ডা *fem.*

চণ্ডাল*n* **1** the lowest caste according to Hindu mythology; a member of this caste. **2** (fig) very cruel person. চণ্ডালিনী, চণ্ডালী *fem.*

চণ্ডিকা *n* Hindu goddess Durga.

চণ্ডী*n* **1** a manifestation of goddess Durga. **2** a part of the Hindu Purana (Markandeya) narrating the activities and glory of goddess Chandi. **3** (fig) an irritable or wrathful woman. ~পাঠ *n* recital of the Chandi. ~পাঠ থেকে জুতা সেলাই পর্যন্ত all activities irrespective of high and low, great and small. ~মঙ্গল *n* eulogistic literature about goddess Chandi. ~মণ্ডপ *n* shrine for the worship and glorification of Chandi. উগ্র~ *n fem* a noisy quarrelsome woman. মঙ্গল~ *n* the benignant form of goddess Chandi. রণ~ *n* **1** goddess Chandi in the state of fighting the demons. **2** (fig) a violent and bad-tempered woman.

চণ্ডু [H] a kind of narcotic drug prepared from poppy seeds. ~ সেবন করা *vi* smoke opium. ~খানা *n* place where opium smokers can obtain and use this drug; opium-den.

চতুঃ *n, adj* the number 4. ~শালা *n* a homestead with four houses around the courtyard. ~সীমা *n* outer boundary on four sides of a closed figure.

চতুর *adj* having a quick, effective and able mind; clever; intelligent; cunning; sly. ~তা *n* the quality of being clever; cleverness; artfulness; skill; dexterity. চতুরা *fem.*

চতুরংশ [চতুঃ+অংশ] *n* four shares or parts. ❑*adj* divided into four parts or shares, quadripartite. চতুরংশিত *adj* **1** divided into four parts. **2** (of a sheet of paper) folded twice so as to give four leaves or eight pages; quarto.

চতুরঙ্গ [চতুঃ+অঙ্গ] *adj* **1** (of an ancient army) comprising four parts, namely, elephants, cavalry, chariots and infantry: ~ সেনা. **2** having four limbs/ all the limbs. ❑*n* **1** an army complete in 4 parts. **2** a form of music. **3** the game of chess.

চতুরালি [চতুর+ B আলি] *n* **1** the use of tricks to deceive or cheat; trickery; deception. **2** acting playfully or jokingly; playing tricks for fun; joke; banter. ~ করা *vi, vt.* **1** cause sb to accept as true or good what is false or bad; cheat; deceive. **2** make fun of.

চতুরাশ্রম *n* the four stages of life as prescribed by Vedic theology, eg, the celibate student life (*Brahmacharya*), the life of a house-holder (*garhasthya*), the life of a hermit (*Banaprasthya*) and the life of an ascetic (*sannyasha*).

চতুর্গুণ *adj* four times greater; fourfold. ~ করা *vt* multiply (a number or amount) by 4; quadruple. ~ বাড়া *vi* increase fourfold.

চতুর্থ *n, adj* the last of four; fourth.

চতুর্থী *n* **1** (astrol) the fourth day of a lunar fortnight. **2** (gram) the fourth case-ending. **3** a Hindu rite performed by a married daughter on the fourth day of the death of either of her parents.

চতুর্দশ *n, adj* four and ten; fourteen. ❑*adj* fourteenth. ~পদী *adj* (of a poem) consisting of fourteen lines. ~পদী কবিতা *n* a poem containing 14 lines with formal pattern of rhymes; a sonnet. চতুর্দশী *n fem.* **1** the fourteenth day of a lunar fortnight. **2** a girl of fourteen years. ❑*adj* fourteen years old.

চতুর্দিক [চতুঃ+দিক] the four quarters of a compass, namely, north, south, east and west; all the four sides. চতুর্দিকে *adv* on all sides; in all directions.

চতুর্ধা [চতুঃ+ধা] *adv* in four ways/ parts; on four sides; four times.

চতুর্বর্ণ [চতুঃ+বর্ণ] *n* the four castes or orders of the Hindu society, namely, the Brahmins, the Kshatriyas, the Vaishyas, and the Shudras,

চতুর্বেদ *n* the four Vedas, namely, the Rik, the Yajus, the Sama and the Atharva. চতুর্বেদী *adj* versed in all the four Vedas.

চতুর্ভুজ *adj* having four arms. ❑*n* **1** (geom) a rectilineal or quadrilateral figure. **2** an appellation of Narayan or Vishnu.

চতুষ্ক *n* **1** a square or rectangular courtyard or portico. **2** a platform with four pillars at the four corners.

চতুষ্কোণ *adj* having four corners; having the shape of a quadrangle; quadrangular.

চতুষ্টয় *adj* having four forms/ divisions; of four kinds. ❑*n* an aggregate of four; quartet.

চতুষ্পদ *n* a four-footed animal; a quadruped; a beast. ❑*adj* **1** four-footed. **2** (fig) as foolish as a beast. চতুষ্পদী *adj fem* four-footed. ❑*n* verse of four lines; a quatrain.

চতুষ্পাঠী [চতুঃ+পাঠী] *n* Sanskrit school for teaching the four Vedas, grammar, poetry and philosophy.

চতুষ্পার্শ [চতুঃ+পার্শ্ব] *n* four sides; all sides. চতুষ্পার্শ্বে *adv* on all sides.

চত্বর *n* **1** a space enclosed by walls or buildings; a courtyard. **2** a homestead.

চনচন *int* suggesting a smarting sensation of pain (চনচনে ব্যথা).

চন্দন *n* **1** the famous fragrant wood or its tree; the sandal wood. **2** paste made from sandal wood. ~চর্চিত *adj* smeared/ painted with sandal-paste. ~তিলক *n* mark of sandal paste on the forehead. ~পিঁড়ি *n* the stone mortar on which the sandal wood is reduced to paste by rubbing.

চন্দনা *n* **1** a kind of parrot with red streaks around its neck. **2** a species of hilsa fish.

চন্দ্র *n* **1** the moon. **2** the chief member or the best specimen of anything: কুল~. ❑*n* family title among Bengali Hindus. ~কর *n* the light of the moon; moonlight. ~কলা *n* a digit or phase of the moon. ~কান্ত *n* a precious stone, the moonstone (also ~কান্তমণি). ❑*adj* as beautiful as the moon. ~কান্তা *n fem* **1** the star. **2** the night. **3** moonlight. ~কান্তি *n* the glow or lustre of the moon. ❑*adj* as lustrous as the moon. ~গ্রহণ *n* the disappearance of the moon's light when the earth passes between it and the sun; the lunar eclipse. **~চূড়** *n* one who wears the moon as his crown; an appellation of Hindu deity Shiva. **~পুলি** *n* sweet of coconut kernel made in the shape of a crescent. **~প্রভ** *adj* of pleasing appearance; shining or lustrous like the moon. **~প্রভা** *n* a beam of light from the moon; moonbeam. □*adj fem* as beautiful as the moon. **~বদন** *adj* having a face as beautiful as the moon; moon-faced; (sarcastic) ugly-faced. **~বদনা** *fem.* **~বিন্দু** *n* the nasal sign in Bengali alphabet. **~বোড়া** *n* species of venomous snake. **~ভাগা** *n* the river Chenab in the Punjab. **~মল্লিকা** *n* garden plant with large showy flowers; the Chrysanthemum plant or its flowers. **~লোক** *n* the surface of the moon; the lunar region in space. **~শেখর** = ~চূড়. **~সুধা** *n* moonlight. **~হার** *n* **1** kind of ornamental chain worn round the waist. **2** a necklace. **~হাস** *n* a kind of sword.

ন্দ্রবিন্দু ⇒চন্দ্র

ন্দ্রাতপ *n* **1** a cover of cloth fixed above a bed or seat or fixed on posts in an open space as on ceremonial occasions; a canopy.

ন্দ্রানন *adj* having a face as beautiful as the moon; moon-faced. **চন্দ্রাননা, চন্দ্রাননী** *fem.*

ন্দ্রালোক [চন্দ্র+আলোক] *n* the light of the moon.

ন্দ্রিকা *n* **1** a ray from the moon. **2** the pupil of the eye. **3** kind of silvery-white river-fish. **4** a metre of Sanskrit poetry. **5** a medicinal plant.

ন্দ্রিমা *n* the moon or the moonlight.

ন্দ্রোদয় [চন্দ্র+উদয়] *n* the appearance of the moon; moonrise.

প [E] *n* a preparation of meat fried in a round shape; a chop.

পচপ *int* denoting : **(a)** wetness of sth soft. **(b)** the sound of eating. **চপচপে** *adj* **1** covered with water; wet: চপচপে ভেজা. **2** smeared with oily substance.

পল *adj* **1** never quiet; always moving about; restless. **2** not firm in thoughts and deeds; fickle-minded. **3** liking to talk a lot; talkative. **4** quick-moving; rapid; fast: ~ গতি. **5** quick in action, swift: ~ দৃষ্টির বিনিময়. **~তা, চাপল্য** *n* restlessness; fickleness; quickness, swiftness, talkativeness. **চপলা** *n* **1** flash of light in the sky; lightning. **2** Hindu goddess Lakshmi.

পেটাঘাত *n* a blow with the palm; a slap. **~ করা** *vi* strike with the palm; slap.

প্পল [H] *n* a kind of footwear; sandals.

ব্বিশ *n, adj* twenty-four. **~ ঘণ্টা** *n* twenty four hours. □*adv* all day; always. **চব্বিশে** *n* the 24th day of a month; the twenty-fourth.

মক *n* **1** sudden burst of light; a flash: বিদ্যুতের ~. **2** fear and excitement caused by a possibility of danger; fright; alarm. **3** awareness; consciousness: ~ হওয়া . **4** a feeling of strangeness, surprise or wonder; amazement: ~ লাগা. **~ খাওয়া** *vi* be struck with amazement. **~ দেওয়া** *vi* (of a light) appear or exist for a moment; flash. **~দার** *adj* **1** shining; glowing; lustrous. **2** amazing; wonderful. **~ ভাঙা** *vi* be suddenly aware/ conscious of sth; come to one's senses. **চমকানো** *vi* **1** give out a sudden bright light; flash. **2** be struck with wonder/ amazement/ fear. **চমকানি** *n* a sudden burst of light; a flash. **চমকিত** *adj* one who has been surprised/ amazed/ alarmed; **চমকিতা** *fem.*

চমচম *n* kind of sweet made of posset.

চমৎকার *adj* amazingly nice/ beautiful; excellent. □*adv* in an excellent manner: তিনি ~ পড়ান.

চমৎকারিতা, চমৎকারিত্ব *n* the quality of being excellent; excellence; marvel. **চমৎকৃত** *adj* amazed. **চমৎকৃত করা** *vt* fill with wonder or surprise; amaze. **চমৎকৃত হওয়া** *vi* be; amazed.

চমন, চমনবাগ [P] *n* a garden; a park.

চমর *n* **1** long-tailed ox of Central Asia; the yak. **2** a species of deer. **3** kind of hand-fan made of the hair of a yak's tail. **চমরী** *fem.*

চম্পক **1** *n* a plant or flower belonging to the magnolia family. **2** a variety of plantain. **~দাম** *n* a wreath or garland of *champak* flowers. **~মালা** *n* **1** = ~দাম. **2** a metre of poetry.

চম্পট *n* act of fleeing away; flight; escape. **~ দেওয়া** *vi* take to heels; flee away.

চম্পা=চম্পক

চয় *n* **1** (used as a *suff*) a collection; an assemblage; a heap (অরাতিচয়). **2** act of collecting or gathering.

চয়ন *n* **1** act of plucking or collecting: পুষ্প ~. **2** act of culling or selecting for compilation: কবিতা ~. **~ করা** *vt* collect, gather or select. **চয়নিকা** *n fem* a collection of poems or other literary works; an anthology.

চর[১] a secret emissary; a spy: গুপ্ত ~.

চর[২] *n* strip of sandy land rising out of a river bed.

চর[৩] *adj* one who inhabits/ dwells in/ moves in (a place): জল~, বন~.

চরক *n* an ancient Indian sage who wrote treatises on medicine. **~ সংহিতা** *n* treatise on Ayurvedic medicine written by the Indian sage Charaka.

চরকা *n* a small machine (used esp formerly at home) for spinning thread, in which a foot-driven wheel moves a spindle; a spinning wheel; a spinning jenny. **~ কাটা** *vi* spin wool or cotton into thread; spin thread. **নিজের ~য় তেল দাও** (fig) oil your own machine; mind your own business.

চরকি *n* a type of circular fireworks that is pinned to an upright surface and turns round when set on fire; a rotating fire work; a rotating wheel. **~র মতো ঘোরা** *vi* turn round and round like a wheel; (fig) to have to take unnecessary trouble of visiting this and that place.

চরণ *n* **1** a foot; a leg. **2** a foot or line of a verse. **~কমল, ~পদ্ম** *n* a foot fancied as a lotus out of reverence. **~চারণ** *n* moving on foot; walking. **~চারী** *n* person walking on foot; a pedestrian. **~দাসী** *n* **1** a devoted wife. **2** one belonging to a sect of Vaishnavas founded by Charandas. **3** (sarcas) a female companion of a Vaishnavas. **~ধূলি** *n* the dust of one's feet. **~সেবা** *n* (fig) act of waiting or attending upon one as a devotee; (lit) act of massaging one's legs and feet. **চরণারবিন্দ** = ~কমল.

চরম *n* **1** the highest or ultimate state (of anything); the most critical stage: দুঃখের ~. **2** end; termination: এ বিষয়ের ~ দেখব. ❑*adj* **1** last; ultimate; final: ~পত্র , ~ সিদ্ধান্ত. **2** extreme: ~ জলবায়ু. **3** strong; violent; intense: ~ অসন্তোষ. **~পত্র** *n* **1** letter containing a warning about sth for the last time; an ultimatum. **2** document containing one's advice as to how his property is to be used or inherited; a will. **~পন্থী** *adj* holding extreme views.

চরমোৎকর্ষ [চরম+উৎকর্ষ] *n* the highest state of excellence.

চরস [H] *n* dried hemp leaves made into a drug for smoking; hashish.

চরা *vi* **1** move about (an area) without a fixed course or purpose; wander. **2** (of animal) feed on grass (in); graze. **3** (of fishes) nibble at a bait. **চরে খাওয়া** *vi* go about for food; (sarcas) go about one's business.

চরাচর [চর+অচর] *n* **1** mobile and immobile objects. **2** the world; the universe; the whole creation.

চরানো *vt* **1** tend (cattle); cause (cattle to graze. **2** control or govern a person or persons according to one's wishes.

চরিত *n* **1** character; mental or moral nature of a person. **2** conduct; behaviour; manners. **3** activities or occupation one pursues in life. **4** professional career; biography. **~ ইতিহাস** *n* written account of a person's life; biography. **~কার** *n* a writer of biography; a biographer. **চরিতাবলী** *n pl* collection of biographies. **চরিতাভিধান** *n* biographical dictionary.

চরিতার্থ *adj* one who has attained his end; successful. **~ করা** *vt* fulfil or gratify one's desires. **~তা** *n* fulfilment/ gratification of one's desires; success.

চরিত্র *n* **1** the combination of mental and moral qualities that make a person different from another; character. **2** one's way of behaving; conduct; behaviour; manners. **3** moral strength; honesty; integrity: তার ~ নাই. **4** a person in a book, play, etc. **~ খোয়ানো/হারানো** *vi* lose one's morals; go to the bad. **~ গুণ** *n* the integrity or excellence of one's character. **~-চিত্র** *n* portrait of one's character; a character sketch. **~চিত্রণ** *n* act of portraying a character; character painting. **~ দোষ** *n* **1** vices in one's character; moral corruption. **~বান** *adj* virtuous in word, thought and deed; good-charactered. **~বতী** *fem*. **~ হনন** *n* assassination of one's character. **~ হনন করা** *vi* lead sb to the path of immorality; cause someone go astray. **~হীন** *adj* morally corrupted; dissolute; debauchee; characterless. **কু~, দুশ্চরিত্র** *adj* behaving in a sexually uncontrolled manner; licentious; libertine; profligate.

চরু *n* Hindu religious offering made of sunned rice boiled in milk.

চর্চা *n* **1** practice of mental or physical powers: ব্যায়াম ~. **2** study; discussion; culture; cultivation: কাব্য~. **3** remark, discussion, criticism, etc that finds fault with others' work unwarrantedly: পর~. **4** act of washing, dressing and beautifying oneself: রূপ~. **~ করা** *vt,vi* improve or develop by careful attention, training or study; study; cultivate; practise. **চর্চিত** *adj* studied; cultivated; practised; refined.

চর্বণ *n* act of crushing (food) with the teeth; chewing; mastication. **~ করা** *vt, vi* crush (one's food) between the teeth; chew; masticate. **চর্বণীয়, চর্ব্য** *adj* (food) to be taken by chewing; to be chewed. **চর্বিত** *adj* **1** (of food) what has been swallowed in by chewing. **2** what has been eaten up. **চর্বিত~** *n* **1** (of cattle) act of bringing back food (cud) from the stomach and chewing it again and again; chewing the cud. **2** repetition of discussion on an old topic. **চর্বিত~ করা** *vt, vi* (fig) say or write sth that has already been discussed/ published.

চর্বি [P] *n* oily or greasy substance under the skin of animals and human beings which helps to keep them warm; animal fat.

চর্ব্য=চর্বণীয়⇒চর্বণ.

চর্ব্যচূষ্য, চর্বচোষ্য *adj* **1** (of food) to be taken by chewing and sucking. **~ লেহ্য পেয়** *adj* **1** (of food) to be taken by chewing, sucking, licking and swallowing. **2** (fig) various items of palatable food.

চর্ম *n* **1** natural outer covering of the body of a person or animal, from which hair may grow; skin. **2** animal's skin, esp as an article of commerce and manufacture; hides. **3** animal skin that has been tanned for manufacturing shoes, bags, etc; leather. **4** the outer covering or skin on the trunks and branches of trees; bark. **~কার** *n* person who, by profession, tans hides and skins and/or makes or mends shoes, etc. **~কীল** *n* a small black and often raised mark on a person's skin existing since birth; a mole. **~চক্ষু** *n* the physical eye or eyesight, not the inner or intuitive one. **~চটক** *n* the titmouse; the bat, **~চটিকা** *fem*. **~পেটিকা** *n* leather bag or suitcase. **~সার** *adj* reduced to skin and bone; emaciated.

চর্মাবরণ *n* a cover or jacket made of leather; a leathern cover.

চর্মার *n* a tanner of hides by caste or profession; one who makes or mends shoes; a shoe-maker.

চর্য *adj* that which is to be practised or followed.

চর্যা *n fem* **1** observance of rules and customs; rites and customs to be observed: ধর্ম~, ব্রত ~. **2** looking after; taking care of: রোগী~. **~চর্য** *adj* what is to be practised and what ought to be avoided. **~পদ** *n* collection of lyrical poems composed by Buddhist monks, supposed to be the earliest specimen of Bengali literature.

চল *adj* on the going; not steady; moving; restless. ❑*n* the state of being in common use or general acceptance; currency; a fashion or custom in vogue at a certain time: ~ হওয়া.

চলচিত্ত *adj* **1** mentally unsteady; fickle-minded. **2** restless by nature; never-quiet; always moving/talking.

চলচ্চিত্র a motion picture; a cinema; a movie. **~বিদ্যা** *n* the art of producing moving pictures; cinematography. **~ শিল্প** *n* the cinema industry.

চলৎশক্তি the strength or ability to move. **~হীন** *adj* having no power of motion; unable to move; paralyzed.

চলতি *adj* **1** moving; on the motion: ~ গাড়ি. **2** in vogue; in currency: ~ ফ্যাশন.

চলন *n* act of moving; motion. **~শীল** *adj* going; moving; mobile. **~সই** *adj* not very good ar not very bad to serve a purpose; not good enough; mediocre.

চলন্ত=চলতি

চলমান *adj* **1** in the state of running or moving. **2** that which is flowing.

চলা *vi, vt* **1** go; move; walk: পথ ~. **2** start for (a place) proceed (on a journey). **3** leave (a place); quit: চলে যাওয়া. **4** pass on: দিন ~. **5** run; ply: গাড়ি ~, বাস ~. **6** pass away; elapse: সময় চলে যাওয়া. **7** be enough; suffice: খরচ ~. **8** be operative; work: মেশিন ~, ঘড়ি ~. **9** be allowed or permitted: ফাঁকিবাজি চলবে না. **10** be accepted; be of any worth: ছেঁড়া টাকা চলবে না. ❑*adj* that which is used for coming and going: পায়ে ~ পথ. **~ফেরা** *n* **1** act of walking or moving about: ~ফেরা করা. **2** a way or manner of walking; gait. **চলে আসা** *vt* **1** leave/quit a place. **2** come quickly; come with hasty steps. **কথামতো চলা** act in obedience to; obey; be obedient. **পেট চলা** be able to maintain oneself/make both ends meet. **মুখ ~** *vi* **1** abuse; revile; rebuke; reproach. **2** be in the habit of eating all day. **হাত ~ পা ~** beat or strike (one) with the hands or feet. **তার সংসার চলে না** He can hardly support his family/make both ends meet. **তোমার কেমন চলছে?** How are you getting on? **তুমি ছাড়া আমরা চলে না** I can't do without you. **ঘড়িটি ঠিকমতো চলছে** The watch/clock is giving the right time. **কারবারটি ভালো চলছে না** The business is not thriving. **এখানে অনেক অনিয়ম চলছে** Many irregularities are in practice here. **ভয় করলে চলবে না** Fear must be cast off. **গুলিটি আমার কানের পাশ দিয়ে শনশন করে চলে গেল** The bullet whizzed past my ears. **চল (আমরা) যাই** Let us go. **চলে যাও** *vt* go away.

চলাচল *n* **1** coming and going; movement; passage; traffic: লোক ~, যানবাহন ~. **2** act of being in motion: বায়ু ~, ventilation. **3** diffusion; circulation: রক্ত ~. **~ করা** *vi* move; travel; be circulated.

চলানো *vt* **1** cause to move/walk. **2** bring into practice; introduce; give currency to. **3** give direction; direct. ❑*n* act of causing to move/walk; act of introducing/directing.

চলিত *adj* **1** in common use; commonly accepted; current. **2** (of language) not formal or special to literature; colloquial. ❑*n* (arith) a way of multiplication by means of aliquot parts; practice: ~ নিয়ম. **~ ভাষা, চলতি ভাষা** *n* colloquial language; language used in common parlance.

চলিষ্ণু *adj* **1** moving about; mobile. **2** restless; unsteady. **3** about to depart.

চলুক *vt* let go/continue: গান ~, let music continue.

চলোর্মি *n* dancing waves (of a river or sea). **~চঞ্চল** *adj* agitated with restless waves: ~-চঞ্চল জলধারা.

চল্লিশ *n, adj* the number forty. **চল্লিশা** *n* **1** weakness of the eyesight caused when one attains the age of forty. **2** obsequies of a Muslim deceased performed on the fortieth day after his death.

চশম[1] [P] *n* the eye. **~খোর** [P] *adj* shameless; brazen faced; insolent.

চশম[2] *n* kind of silk thread.

চশমা[1] [P] *n* spectacles; eye-glasses. **~ধারী** *adj* wearing spectacles; spectacled.

চশমা[2] [P] *n* a source; a spring.

চষক *n* **1** wine-cup; drinking-glass. **2** honey. **3** wine.

চষা *vt, vi* plough; cultivate; till. ❑*adj* ploughed; tilled; cultivated. **~নো** *vt,vi* cause to cultivate; cause to be ploughed/tilled. **চষে বেড়ানো** *vi* **1** look for (sth) thoroughly from one place to another; go on ransacking (for sth). **2** travel from place to place; travel a lot.

চা [C] *n* **1** dried and finely cut leaves of the tea-plant; tea-leaves. **2** drink made by infusing tea-leaves in boiling water; tea. **~ খাওয়া** *vi* take tea; drink tea. **চা-খানা** *n* tea-shop; tea-stall. **চা-দানি** *n* **1** tea-pot. **2** tea-tray. **চা বাগান** *n* garden for tea plantation; tea garden. **চায়ের পেটি** *n* large wooden chest in which tea is packed; tea-chest. **চায়ের পেয়ালা** *n* cup in which tea is served; tea cup. **চায়ের পেয়ালা পাতি** *n pl* tea set.

চাই *vt* (in the first person) I/we want

চাইতে, চেয়ে *conj* than (used for introducing the second part of a comparison of inequality): মাছের ~ মাংস সস্তা, Meat is cheaper than fish.

চাইর (colloq)=চার

চাইল=চাল

চানি=চাহনি

চাউল, চা'ল, চাল *n* husked paddy; rice. **আতপ ~** *n* rice obtained from unboiled paddy. **সিদ্ধ ~** *n* rice obtained from boiled and sunned paddy.

চাউল-মুগরা *n* a kind of small plant, whose seeds produce a medicinal oil that cures itches.

চাও *vt* (in second person) you want/wish: তুমি কি ~?

চাওন (colloq) *n* act of wishing/ desiring/ praying/asking for.

চাওয়া[1] *vt* **1** wish for the possession or enjoyment of; desire; covet; aspire: মুক্তি ~. **2** want; ask for; request for: টাকা ~, সময় ~, অনুমতি ~. ❑*n* act of wishing or asking for. **~নো** *vt* cause to want/pray for/request for. **~মাত্র** *adv* for the asking; on demand.

চাওয়া[2] *vi* **1** look at; stare at. **2** open one's eyes; see. ❑*n* act of seeing/looking at. **~-চাওয়ি** *n* meaningful exchange of looks. **মুখ তুলে ~** be fabourably disposed to; bestow favour on.

চাঁই[1] *adj, n* **1** the leader of a circle of persons engaged in an evil course; a ringleader. **2** one who is long experienced; a veteran. **~ চোর** *n* one who is very skilled and artful in theft.

চাঁই[2] *n* **1** a lump of earth; a clod. **2** a trap for fishes, made of bamboo slips.

চাঁচ[1] *n* a coarse mat made of bamboo slips or date-leaves.

চাঁচ[2] *n* piece of a resinous substance (lac) beaten into a leaf; a lac-leaf.

চাঁচর[1] *adj* curled; curly: ~-কেশ.

চাঁচর[2] *n* a ceremony observed on the day before the Hindu festival of 'holi'.

চাঁচা, চাঁছা *vt* **1** remove sth away from a surface by pushing the hard edge of a tool; scrape. **2** shave off: দাড়ি ~. ❑*adj* scraped; shaved; **~ছোলা** *adj* (lit) thoroughly or smoothly cleaned/shaved; (fig) (of speech) rough and plain: লোকটির কথাবার্তা ~ছোলা The man is blunt/outspoken.

চাঁচি, চাঁছি *n* **1** the scrapings of calcined milk: দুধের ~. **2** sticky thing which is scraped off.

চাঁড়াল=চণ্ডাল

চাঁদ *n* **1**=চন্দ্র. **2** an object of endearment; a child: পূর্ণিমার ~ যেন কোলে, as if a full moon in the lap. **3** (sarcas) an ugly person. **~বদন** *adj, n* a face or one having a face as beautiful as the moon. **~বদনী** *fem.* **~মুখ** *n* a face as pretty as the moon. **~ হাতে পাওয়া** come across sth most valued and sth beyond expectation. **চাঁদে কলঙ্ক** an otherwise perfectly beautiful thing containing a slight flaw. **চাঁদেও কলঙ্ক আছে** (proverb) **1** There are lees to every wine. **2** no rose without thorns. **চাঁদের কণা** *n* **1** (lit) a little fragment of the moon. **2** (fig) a highly delightful person. **3** a charming little child. **চাঁদের হাট** *n* **1** a gathering of beautiful young ladies or of lively little children. **2** a household as happy as it is affluent.

চাঁদকুড়া *n* a kind of little fish.

চাঁদনি[1] *n* **1** a covering of cloth over a bed or seat or over an enclosed place on ceremonial occasions; a canopy. **2** a courtyard with a roof supported by pillars; an open portico.

চাঁদনি[2] *n* moonlight

চাঁদনী=চাঁদিনী

চাঁদমারি *n* **1** a round place or board with circles on it for shooting practice; target-practice; target. **2** a person that is made the object of unfavourable remarks or jokes.

চাঁদা[1] *n* **1** (poet) the moon. **2** (geom) instrument in the shape of a half-circle, used for measuring and drawing angles; a protractor. **3** a canopy.

চাঁদা[2] *n* a small silvery-white fish.

চাঁদা[3] [P] *n* **1** money collected from various people for a particular charitable purpose; subscription; contribution: বন্যার্তদের সাহায্যার্থ ~. **2** amount of money given regularly in support of a society: সমিতির ~. **~ দেওয়া** *vi, vt* subscribe; contribute.

চাঁদি[1] *n* pure and bright silver like the moon.

চাঁদি[2] *n* the crown or top of the head. **~-ফাটা** *adj* causing cracks to the crown; extremely hot; very severe: ~-ফাটা রোদ.

চাঁদিনী, চাঁদনী *adj* illuminated by the moon; moonlit: ~ রাত. ❑*n* **1** moonlight. **2** moonlit night.

চাঁদিমা *n* moonbeam; moonlight.

চাঁদোয়া *n*=চাঁদনি[১] (1)

চাঁপা *n* **1** a kind of flower and its tree; the *champak*. **2** a variety of small banana with a soury taste.

চাক *n* **1** a wheel. **2** anything circular in shape. **3** a potter's wheel (which shapes earthenware vessels). **4** beehive: একটি চাকে প্রচুর মধু হয়. **~ চাক** *adv* in round and flat pieces: শশা ~ ~ করে কাটা.

চাকচিক্য *n* **1** brightness; glitter; lustre; glaze; polish. **2** external glamour. **~ময়** *adj* glittering; lustrous; glamorous; glazing; glossy.

চাকতি *n* **1** a small wheel. **2** sth round and flat; a disc. **রূপোর ~** *n* a silver coin.

চাকর [P] *n* **1** a man-servant in a house, receiving wages and usually food and lodgings. **2** a salaried employee engaged in an office or organization. **3** one who attends an officer or master: হুকুমের ~. **চাকরানি** *fem* maid-servant. **~বাকর, ~-নফর, ~-চাকরানি** *n pl* servants or menials collectively.

চাকরান [P] *n* grant of land for the maintenance of a servant in lieu of salary: ~ জমি, rent-free land given to a servant.

চাকরি, চাকুরি [P] *n* **1** working for another for a stated amount of remuneration; employment; a job: তার ~ নেই, he is out of employment/ without a job. **2** the post of an employee: ~ খালি, situation vacant; ~ খালি নেই, (there is) no vacancy. **~ করা** *vi* serve or work (in an office, etc); be in service; hold an appointment: সে সরকারি ~ করে, He is in government service; He works in a government office; He is a government servant/employee. **~ ত্যাগ করা** *vi* resign one's post. **~ থেকে অবসর গ্রহণ করা** *vi* retire from service. **~তে যোগদান করা** *vi* **1** join one's appointment. **2** enter service. **~বাকরি** *n* a profession or source of living.

চাকরে, চাকুরে *adj* in the employ (of a public or business concern); in service; serving: তিনি সরকারি ~, He is in public service/ government employ; ~ মহিলা, a working woman. ❑*n* an employee; a servant.

চাকলা[1] [P] *n* (hist) an administrative unit; a district. **~দার** [P] *n* **1** the administrator of a Chakla or district. **2** a surname or family name.

চাকলা[2] *n* a piece or slice (as of bread).

চাকা[1] *n* **1** a wheel: গাড়ির ~. **2** a piece or slice in the shape of a wheel: মাছের ~. ❑*adj* like a wheel or circle; roundish: ~ দাগ. **~ চাকা** *adj* **1** divided into round pieces: ~~ মাছ. **2** roundish in shape; like circles: ~~ দাগ.

চাকা[2]=চাখা

চাকি *n* **1** anything round and flat. **2** board for rolling dough: ~ বেলুন, rolling pin and board. **3** a grinding-stone; an apparatus for grinding pulses, etc.

চাকু [T] *n* a folding knife with a clasp for fixing the blade when open; a clasp-knife.

চাকুরি=চাকরি

চাকুরে=চাকরে

চাক্কা=চাকা[১]

চাক্কি=চাকি

চাক্তি=চাকতি

চাক্ষুষ *adj* **1** of, for, by, the eyes; seen; visible: ~ প্রমাণ, ocular proof/demonstration. **2** obtained by visual perception: ~ জ্ঞান. **~ সাক্ষী** *n* eye-witness.

চা-খড়ি *n* **1** a kind of soft and white rock, used for making lime and various writing materials; chalk. **2** a white or coloured stick of this material used for writing or drawing; chalk pencil.

চাখন *n* act of tasting (a food item). **~দার** *n, adj* one who tastes.

চাখনাচুর *n* powder; dust. ❑ *adj* reduced to dust; pulverized; destroyed.

চাখা, চাকা *vt* **1** test the taste (of a food or drink). **2** (fig) get pleasure; enjoy: জীবনকে ~. **~নো** *vt* cause to taste or enjoy.

চাখোর [চা C+খোর P] *adj* addicted to tea; habituated to taking tea frequently.

চাগা *vi* become stronger; be more acute. **2** rise; wake up. **3** come into existence; originate. **~নো** *vt* rouse; excite; stimulate; stir up.

চাগাড় *n* act of becoming more acute: ~ দিয়ে ওঠা. **~ দেওয়া** *vi* get agitated; assume high degree.

চাঙ্গ, চাঙ *n* wooden or bamboo platform above the head for keeping things. **চাঙে তুলে রাখা** keep in reserve; not allowing to be used for ordinary purpose.

চাঙ্গড় *n* a large lump; a big clod (of earth).

চাঙ্গা *adj* reinforced; invigorated; refreshed. **~ করা** *vt* give life and energy to; invigorate; enliven. **~ হওয়া** *vi* gain strength; get refreshed.

চাঙ্গাড়ি, চাঙারি *n* a broad basket; a large wicker basket; a creel.

চাচা [H চাচ্চা] *n* father's brother; a paternal uncle. **চাচী** *fem.* an aunt. **~ত** *adj* relating to an uncle; avuncular: ~ত ভাই/ বোন, a cousin.

চাঞ্চল্য *n* **1** the condition of being restless; the state of being unsettled; restlessness; briskness. fickleness. **2** anxiety; uneasiness; agitation; perturbation: মানসিক ~. **3** the glow of enthusiasm or excitement; a thrilling sensation. **~কর** *adj* thrilling; sensational. **~হীন** *adj* unperturbed; calm and quiet; steady.

চাঁট[১], চাট *n* the kick of an animal. **~ খাওয়া** *vi* be kicked (as by a horse). **~ মারা** *vt* hit with the foot; kick.

চাট[২] *n* **1** any tasty food which is taken by licking. **2** a snack taken as a concomitant with alcoholic drink.

চাটনি [H চটনী] *n* any of the various kinds of thick preparation eaten with some kinds of food as a relish; chutney; sauce.

চাটা *vt* move the tongue across in order to take (a food) in; lick: চেটে খাওয়া. ❑*adj* what has been licked. **~চাটি** *n* **1** act of licking each other. **2** repeated or continuous licking. **3** (iron) too much intimacy. **4** (iron) mutual lactation. **চেটে পুটে খাওয়া** eat up every bit; eat clean. **~নো** *vt* cause to lick.

চাটাই *n* a coarse mat made of palm leaves or date leaves or bamboo slips.

চাটি[১] *adj* broken to pieces; destroyed; razed to the ground: ভিটেমাটি ~. **~ বাটি তোলা** *vi* **1** evict one from his homestead. **2** shift one's residence.

চাটি[২], চাঁটি *n* **1** a stroke with the fingers: তবলায় ~ মারা play on a *tabala* (tabour). **2** a blow with the open palm; a slap. **~ মারা** *vt* slap.

চাটিম *n* a kind of banana.

চাটিম চাটিম *int* suggesting the sound of playing on a *tabala.*

চাটু[১] *n* a fry pan.

চাটু[২], চাটু বচন *n* words used to win favour of rich and powerful people; adulatory words; flattery. **~কার, ~বাদী, ~ ভাষী** *adj* one who flatters rich and influential people; flattering. ❑*n* a flatterer; a sycophant. **~বাদিনী** *fem.*

চাটু[৩] *n* the palm of one's hand.

চাটুজ্জে, চাটুজ্যে *n* surname of certain Bengali Brahmins; short form of চট্টোপাধ্যায়.

চাট্টি, চাট্টে *adj* **1** amounting to four. **2** a small quantity: ~খানি/ চাট্টে ভাত দাও.

চাড়, চাঁড়, চাড়া[১] *n* **1** the force applied to lift up sth heavy or the pressure used to force sth open; an upward shoving; a shove; a push; a prop: ~ দেওয়া, push upwards; twist up; prop up. **2** act of urging or pressing (one) repeatedly for: বিয়ের জন্য ~. **3** eagerness; earnestness, enthusiasm; care; interest: লেখাপড়ার ~ নেই, not serious/not in earnest about ones studies. **4** pressure or urgency of work; burden of heavy duty: কাজের ~. **~ করা** *vt* show interest in; be eager to have (sth). **~ থাকা** *vt* have a strong desire for/great interest in. **~ দিয়ে খোলা** *vt* prize up or open (as a box or lid).

চাড়া[২] *n* **1** act of raising or lifting up: ~ দিয়ে তোলা, shove up forcefully. **2** support used to keep sth up; a stick, sake or prop: ~ দিয়ে খাড়া রাখা. ❑*vt* raise or lift up; give an upward shove; prop up. **মাথা ~ দিয়ে উঠা** make an unusual progress; attain a glorious position in the teeth of all opposition and hindrances.

চাড়ি *n* a large earthen manger used for feeding cattle.

চাতক *n* the bird renowned in poetic imagination as taking no other drink except rain-water, and which being always thirsty, longs very much for the rains; the swallow. **চাতকী, চাতকিনী** *fem.*

চাতাল *n* **1** a raised flat area; a terrace. **2** a paved platform for sitting in the open. **3** a corridor or portico of a building.

চাতুরী, চাতুর্য *n* **1** cunning; craftiness; slyness; shrewdness. **2** expert knowledge of any art; skill; artfulness; dexterity; adroitness: শিল্পচাতুর্য. **3** stratagem; trick; artifice; deceit. **~ করা** *vi, vt* play tricks.

চাতুর্বর্ণ্য *n* **1** the hierarchy of the four *varnas* or castes amongst Hindus, namely the Brahmins, the Kshatriyas, the Vaishyas and the Shudras. **2** religious rules and practices prescribed for the *varnas.* ❑*adj* pertaining to the four *varnas.*

চাতুর্য=চাতুরী

চাদর [P] *n* **1** a sheet of cloth used for wrapping the upper part of the body; a wrapper; a scarf: গায়ের ~. **2** a cover for the bed; a bed-sheet; a bed cover: বিছানার ~. **3** a sheet of metal: লোহার ~.

চান[১] (dial) *n* bath; bathing by immersion.

চান[২] (dial) *n* the moon.

চানা *n* a kind of pulse; chick-pea. **~চুর** *n* a salty and spicy crisp snack comprising fried chick-pea, nuts and other things.

চান্দ, চান্দা[১] (poet)=চন্দ্র

চান্দা[২]=চাঁদা

চান্দোয়া=চন্দ্রাতপ

চান্দ্র *adj* **1** of the moon; lunar: ~ মাস. **2** measured by the revolutions of the moon. **~ মাস** *n* the time in which the moon completes a revolution about the earth, from new moon to new moon; a lunar month. **~ বৎসর** *n* a year comprising twelve lunar months or 354·25 days.

চাপ[১] *n* **1** instrument for shooting arrows; a bow. **2** (geom) any part of the circumference of a circle; an arc.

চাপ[2] [P] **1** a load; a burden: কাজের ~. **2** weight or pressing of a thing: পদ~. **3** the force of one body acting on another; pressure: বায়ু-~, রক্ত-~. **4** insistence or importunities or forcing: ~ দিয়ে রাজি করানো. **5** a lump or mass of a thing clod: রক্তের ~. **~ খাওয়া** *vi* be pressed. **~ দেওয়া** *vt* put pressure upon; press. **~দাড়ি** *n* massive beard covering the whole cheek and chin.

চাপকান [P] *n* garment for the upper part of the body from the shoulder to the knee.

চাপড় *n* a slap. **~ মারা** *vi, vt* strike with the flat hand; slap.

চাপড়া *n* a flat lump or mass of a thing: মাটির ~.

চাপড়ানো *vt* strike repeatedly with the flat hand. **কপাল ~** *vi* strike the forehead (in grief, despair, frustration, etc). **বুক ~** *vi* strike the chest in repentance.

চাপরাস, চাপরাশ [P] *n* **1** a badge of office or authority. **2** a piece of metal or other material worn by menials of an office or institution; a badge. **চাপরাসি, চাপরাশি** *n* an orderly with a badge on.

চাপল্য *n* **1** unsteadiness; fickleness; inconsistency. **2** frivolity; flippancy, silliness.

চাপা *vt* **1** weigh on; press by weight: কাঁধে ~. **2** get into; board: নৌকায় ~. **3** ride; mount: ঘোড়ায় ~. **4** burden; fall on the shoulder of: দায়িত্ব কাঁধে ~. **5** suppress; conceal; hide: কথা/ঘটনা ~. ❑*n* **1** act of pressing/weighing on. **2** act of boarding a boat, etc or mounting a horse, etc. **3** act of suppressing; suppression: ~ দেওয়া. **4** act of devolving on. ❑*adj* **1** suppressed; subdued; low: ~ গলা/সুর. **2** secretly circulated: ~ গুজব. **3** reserved; reticent; cautious: ~ লোক. **4** not expressed; hidden: ~ অসন্তোষ. **~ দেওয়া** *vt* **1** suppress; conceal. **2** run over: গাড়ি ~ দেওয়া. **~ পড়া** *vt* **1** be shelved/turned down. **2** be run over: গাড়ি ~ পড়া. **~চাপি** *n* great pressure; continuous pressing. **~চাপি করা** *vi, vt* press hard; request repeatedly. **চেপে ধরা** *vt* hold tight. **চেপে বসা** *vi* sit or settle firmly. **চেপে যাওয়া** *vt* avoid disclosing/mentioning. **চেপে রাখা** *vt* keep concealed; maintain secrecy. **ঘাড়ে ~** *vt* be an undesirable burden on one's shoulders. **ঘাড়ে ভূত ~** *vi* be possessed by a devil.

চাপাটি, চাপাতি [P] *n* paper-like thin bread made by rolling clods of flour by hand; chapati; chapattie; chapatty.

চাপান[1] *n* a problematic charge thrown at the opposite party for answering in song-tournaments like কবিগান or তরজা. ❑*n* sth that has been thrown or placed.

চাপানো, চাপান[2] *vt* **1** load or place sth into/on to sth: গাধার পিঠে মাল ~, উনুনে হাড়ি ~. **2** burden sb(with): ঘাড়ে ~. **3** lay upon; impute; ascribe: দোষ ~, lay the blame upon one/at one's door. **4** place sth in one side: গাড়ি ~.

চাবকানো⇒ চাবুক

চাবি, চাবিকাঠি *n* **1** instrument for shutting or opening a lock; a key. **2** instrument for winding a clock or watch by tightening the spring: ঘড়ির ~. **3** a lever or button for operating a piano, harmonium, typewriter or other instruments. **4** (fig) sth that can provide an answer to a problem: চাবিকাঠি তার হাতেই আছে. **~ তালা** *n* lock and key. **~ দেওয়া** *vi, vt* lock

চাবুক [P] *n* **1** a length of cord or cane or a strip of leather with a handle used for punishing or for urging a horse; a whip; a lash. **2** whipping; lashing: ~ খাওয়া. **3** (fig) a stroke of words; a sarcasm or a rebuke that hits one seriously: কথার ~. **চাবকানো** *vt* whip or flog (one). **চাবকানি** *n* act of whipping/lashing/flogging. **~ সোয়ার** [P] *n* expert horseman or horsebreaker; professional rider in horse-races; jockey.

চাম [চর্ম, P চরম্] *n* =চর্ম(1), চামড়া

চামচ=চামচে[1]

চামচিকা, চামচিকে (colloq) *n* the titmouse; the vampire.

চামচে[1], **চামচ** [P] *n* utensil for taking up food; a spoon.

চামচে[2], **চামচা** [P] *n* a base sycophant; a flatterer. **~গিরি** *n* flattery; adulation; sycophancy.

চামটি=চামাটি

চামড়া *n* **1** human skin. **2** the skin of an animal; hide. **3** dressed or tanned hide; leather. **কাঁচা ~** *n* raw hide. **পাকা ~** *n* leather.

চামর *n* a kind of fan made of the yak's tail and used like the brushing movement of a horse's tail; a fly-whisk. **~ ব্যজন করা** *vi* fan with a fly-whisk. **~ধারিণী, চামরিণী** *adj, fem* one who fans with a fly-whisk. **চামরী** *adj* having a bushy tail. ❑*n* the horse.

চামসা, চামসে *adj* resembling leather or hide: ~ গন্ধ, smelling of hide.

চামাটি *n* a barber's folder for keeping razor, etc.

চামার *n* **1** a shoe-maker or tanner; a cobbler. **2** (fig) an unfeeling or merciless person. **3** a miserly person. **~নী** *fem.*

চামুণ্ডা *n* **1** Hindu goddess Durga in her furious manifestation. **2** (fig) a haughty woman.

চামেলি *n* fragrant shrub bearing small flowers; white jasmine (or jessamine).

চার[1], **চারি** *n, adj* the number 4; four. **~ আনা, ~ আনি** *n* one quarter (of a thing); a fourth part; one-fourth. **~ ইয়ারি** *adj* of or concerning four friends. **~কোনা** *adj* having four angles and four sides; quadrangular. ❑*n* all sides.

~চালা *n, adj* (house) with a roof of four parts on four sides. ~ চোখে দেখা look to one with an eye of favour. ~ চৌকা, ~চৌকো *adj* having four right angles. ~টা, ~টে *n* 4 o'clock; four am or pm ❑*adj* **1** four. **2** of small quantity; some: ~টে ভাত তাও. ~টিখানি, চাট্টি *adj* a little; not much; a small quantity of: আর চাট্টি ভাত দাও. ~তরফ [P] *n* all sides or directions. ~দেওয়ারি [P] *n* a courtyard surrounded by walls. ~পায়া, ~পাই *n* a cot with four legs usually made of coconut-coir. ~ পায়ে (চলা) (crawl) on all fours. ~পেয়ে *adj* four-footed; quadruped. ~ পোয়া four quarters; complete; full; whole; entire. ~ সন্ধ্যা (according to Hindu tradition) four points of the day, namely, the morning, the noon, the evening and the midnight. ~ হাত এক করা arrange the marriage of a couple; give (one) in marriage. ~ হাতে *adv* without discrimination; to excess (of anything). ~ভিত *n* all directions.

চার[২] *n* a secret agent; a detective; a spy.

চার[৩] *n* a bait to entice fish to the hook. **2** a specific area in a pool of water where bait has been placed to attract fishes.

চারক *adj* one who tends or grazes cattle. ❑*n* a grazier: গো~.

চারণ[১] *n* a singer of ballads; a minstrel; a bard. ~ কবি *n* a composer and singer of ballads; a panegyrist.

চারণ[২] *n* **1** act of grazing cattle: গো~. **2** a grazing ground; a pasture (also ~ ভূমি).

চারণ[৩], **চারণা** *n* act of moving or pacing forward: পদ~.

চারা[১] *n* **1** young shoot of a plant or tree; a sapling; a seedling. **2** young fish. ❑*adj* newly grown; new-born: ~ গাছ.

চারা[২], **চার** [P] *n* **1** a means or way of achieving sth: না গিয়ে ~ নেই, There is no way out but to go. **2** a means of reparation or redress; a remedy. **বেচারা, লাচার, নাচার** *adjj* having no means; helpless.

চারা[৩], **চার** *n* **1** a bait for fish. **2** food put in a trap to attract prey.

চারি=চার[১]

-চারিণী⇒ -চারী

চারিত *adj* **1** that which has been tended/grazed. **2** infused or instilled, as principles led; driven; conducted.

চারিত্র, চারিত্র্য *n* **1** character: conduct; behaviour. **2** good conduct; noble qualities. **চারিত্রিক** *adj* relating to character and conduct; characteristic.

চারী *suff* **1** in the state of plying or moving: পথ~, আকাশ~. **2** observing; practising: ব্রহ্ম~, মিথ্যা~. **চারিণী** *fem.*

চারু *adj* **1** giving pleasure or delight to the mind; beautiful; pleasant; charming: ~দর্শন, pleasant to the eyes. **2** elegant; graceful; delicate; polite; fine. ~কলা, ~শিল্প *n* the visual arts that appeal to the sense of beauty, esp painting and sculpture; the fine arts; fine art (cf কারুকলা, crafts). ~নেত্র *adj* having beautiful eyes. ~নেত্রা *fem.* ~শীলা *adj fem* of pleasing manners; virtuous; highly modest. ~হাসিনী *adj fem* of charming smile. ~তা, ~ত্ব *n* charm; grace; elegance; beauty; loveliness.

চার্চ [E] *n* a house of worship among the Christians; a church.

চার্জ [E] *n* **1** work of a person as official duty: বিদায়ী সভাপতি ~ বুঝিয়ে দিয়েছেন, The outgoing president has handed over the charge. **2** a formal accusation of some crime: অর্থ আত্মসাতের ~, charge of misappropriation. **3** the price asked for goods or services: ~ কত? **4** a thing or person entrusted to sb to be taken care of; responsibility; trust: নাবালকের ~. **5** the electricity contained in a battery: ব্যাটারি ~ করা, fill the battery with electricity; charge the battery. **6** sudden and violent attack at high speed (as by a soldier or a football player).

চার্বাক *n* **1** the famous materialistic philosopher of ancient time, Charvaka who denied the immortality of soul and life hereafter. **2** a materialist. **চার্বাকী** *adj* belonging to or befitting the materialist Charvaka: চার্বাকী মতবাদ. ~ দর্শন *n* the philosophy of Charvaka.

চার্ম[১] *adj* pertaining to/consisting of skin; dermal ; cutaneous.

চার্ম[২] [E] *n* charm ; fascination.

চাল[১] = চাউল

চাল[২] *n* **1** a sloping roof or thatch: ঘরের ~. **2** the scenery at the background of a Hindu idol: ~চিত্র. ~ কুমড়া *n* species of the plant of which gourd that grows on a plant usually creeps to a thatched roof. ~ কেটে ওঠানো *vt* evict (one) from his homestead. ~চুলো *n* (fig) food and shelter. ~ নেই চুলো নেই one who has no hearth or home/ means of subsistence.

চাল[৩] *n* **1** the mode or style of living; manners and behaviour: নবাবি ~. **2** manner of waking or stepping; gait: গদাইলস্করি ~. **3** exaggerated ways of behaving in order to impress people; proud airs: ~ মারা. **4** (in chess, etc) act of moving a piece from one position to another; a move; a player's turn to move a piece. **5** a strategic or deceitful move; a trick: ~ চালা, try a stratagem; apply or play a trick. ~ কমানো *vi* **1** cut down cost of living. **2** reduce the standard of living. ~চলন *n* **1** ways or mode of living: সেকেলে ~চলন. **2** conduct; behaviour; habits. **3** bent of mind; inclination; intentions and activities. ~ চালা *vi,vt* make a clever move; play a trick. ~ দেওয়া *vt* **1** make a move (as in chess). **2** give oneself airs; behave with arrogance. **3** make a move to deceive one; play a trick on sb. **~ বদলানো** *vi,vt* **1** change tricks. **2** change one's fashion or style of living. **3** (in chess) change a move. **~বাজ, চালিয়াৎ** [B+P] *adj* **1** one who boasts of one's wealth, power, etc. ❑ a braggart. **2** acting with fraud; deceitful; fraudulent. **3** full of intrigues; scheming; intriguing. **~বাজি** *n* **1** giving oneself airs; snobbery. **2** trickery; fraud. **~ বাড়ানো** *vi,vt* raise one's standard of living. **~ বিগড়ানো** *vi* (of a fraudulent move) get foiled; be unsuccessful.

চাল বাড়ন্ত *n* shortage of rice: আমাদের ~, Our stock of rice has run short.

চালমাৎ *n* **1** an unsatisfactory draw resulting when a player not actually in check has no possible legal move; stalemate. **2** (fig) a move by which someone's plans are brought to an impotent standstill; an inglorious deadlock.

চালক *n, adj* **1** one who commands, controls or guides a leader: রাষ্ট্র~ . **2** one who operates or drives; a driver; an operator.

চালতা, চালতে=চালিতা

চালন, চালনা *n* **1** act of causing movement/setting (sth) in motion: পদ~. **2** act of managing freely in the hands; act of wielding or using (as a sword): অসি ~. **3** application or practice of mental or physical powers; study; exercise: মস্তিষ্ক চালনা, দেহ চালনা. **4** act of ruling or governing: রাজ্য চালনা **5** act of driving: গাড়ি চালনা. **6** act of leading or commanding: সৈন্য চালনা. **7** management or conduct of affairs: সংসার চালনা. **চালনা করা** *vt* **1** conduct; manage; operate or drive; use; exercise. **চালনীয়** *adj* to be used/exercised/d riven/operated/conducted.

চালনি, চালুনি *n* utensil for separating smaller particles, dust or wastes from a loose substance (eg rice, paddy, flour); a sieve. **~ বলে সুঁচ তুমি কেন ছেঁদা** (fig) **1** a man with countless flaws and faults should not laugh at a shortcoming in another. **2** the saucepan calling the kettle black.

চালশে, চালিশা *n* **1** defect in vision occurring at or about the age of forty. **2** defective vision of old age due to inability to focus near objects; presbyopia. **~ ধরা** *vi* have a failing eyesight; be affected with presbyopia.

চালা[1] *vt* **1** move (a piece) from one position to another (as in chess, etc): ঘুঁটি ~ . **2** separate dust or wastes from a loose substance by means of a sieve: আটা ~. **3** apply or use (a trick or stratagem): চাল ~. **4** cause to move by means of occult power: কড়ি ~. **5** spread or circulate: কথা ~. **~চালি** *n* act of circulating about: কথা ~চালি.

চালা[2] *adj* having a thatched roof: ~ ঘর. ❑*n* thatched house; a thatch; a hut. **এক ~** *adj* having a single thatch. ❑*n* a one-roofed hut.

চালাক [P] *adj* **1** endowed with a good intellect; intelligent. **2** clever; sly; shrewd. **~ চতুর** *adj* smart; witty; active; agile.

চালাকি [P] *n* cleverness; slyness; shrewdness. **~ করা** *vt* play a trick; outwit or hoodwink (one).

চালান [P] *n* **1** act of consigning or delivering goods over to another by agreement; the thing consigned; consignment: মাল ~. **2** act of sending up (an accused) for trial: আসামিকে ~ করা/দেওয়া. **3** a written account of the merchandise sent to a person, with the prices annexed; an invoice; a bill of lading: মালের ~. **4** money receipt against deposit of rent, revenue or other changes: ট্রেজারি ~. **~ দেওয়া** *vt* **1** consign or despatch (as goods). **2** commit (an accused)to sessions.

চালানি, চালানী *adj* **1** relating to export. **2** exported; despatched; consigned. **3** ready for export; exportable. **~ কারবার** *n* export trade. **~ মাল** *n* export goods; consignment. **~ শুল্ক** *n* export duty.

চালানো *vt* **1** cause to move/operate; set in motion: মেশিন ~ . **2** organize; manage; administer: প্রতিষ্ঠান ~, run an institution/organization. **3** maintain; look after; defray expenses: খরচ ~, সংসার ~. **4** introduce; give currency: ফ্যাশন ~, নিয়ম ~. **5** cause to be accepted; put (false money, etc) into circulation: অচল টাকা ~, utter a counterfeit coin. **6** find market for: মাল ~. **7** use or apply: ক্ষমতা ~. **8** go on in sth; continue; carry on. **পা ~** *vi* walk with quick steps; quicken one's steps. **মুখ ~** *vi* utter harsh; rude rebuke; scold. **হাত ~** *vi* **1** use one's hands (in anything) more quickly than usual. **2** beat with the hands.

চালিত *vt* (passive) led or guided: বিপথে ~, led or gone astray. **~ হওয়া** *vi* be guided. ❑*adj* **1** moved; driven. **2** led; guided.

চালিতা, চালতা, চালতে *n* a kind of round shaped acid fruit.

চালিয়াৎ, চালিয়াত=চালবাজ⇒ চাল[3]

চালিশা= চালশে

চালু *adj* **1** in common or general use at the present time; current: ~ নিয়ম. **2** that which is currently being done or has acquired popularity; in vogue: ~ ডিজাইন. **3** in operation; working: ~ মেশিন. **4** be in demand in the market: ~ মাল. **5** running well; flourishing: ~ কারবার. **6** smart; witty; lively; capable of managing any situation in one's favour: ~ ছেলে. ~ **করা** *vt* **1** bring (sth) into use for the first time; introduce. **2** set in motion; put (a machinery, etc) in operation. ~ **মাল** *n* **1** goods that are in demand in the market. **2** (iron) a pushing and enterprising person; a go-getter.

চালুনি=চালনি

চাশত [P] *n* early part of the day approximating three hours: চাশতের নামাজ.

চাষ[1] *n* **1** tilling; ploughing; cultivation. **2** production: ফলের ~, মাছের ~ . **3** application of labour for improvement or refinement; culture: বুদ্ধির ~. **~-আবাদ,চাষাবাদ** [B+P] *n* tilling the soil and sowing the seeds; agriculture. ~ **করা** *vt* **1** cultivate; till; plough. **2** grow; produce. **~বাস** *n* tillage of land; living by agriculture.

চাষ[2] *n* a species of the sparrow.

চাষা, চাষি, চাষী *n* **1** one who lives by farming; a farmer; a cultivator; a ploughman. **2** (derog) an ill-mannered or illiterate person; a rustic; a boor. **চাষাড়ে** *adj* **1** like a cultivator. **2** illiterate; ignorant. **3** uncultured; uncivil; rustic; vulgar. **~ভুষা, ~ভুষো** *n* uncultured rural people; uneducated rustic people. **গেঁয়ো** ~ *n* (derog) a heavy-witted farm labourer; a stupid rustic; a clodhopper.

চাহন[1] (old use) *n* **1** act of asking or praying for sth. **2** wish; desire; longing. **চাহা** *vt* (poet) ask/pray for; desire; wish: মরিতে চাহি না আমি সুন্দর ভুবনে.

চাহন[2] *n* **1** act of looking at. **2** act of opening one's eyes.

চাহনি, চাউনি *n* a look; a glance; a gaze.

চাহারম [P] *adj* **1** the ordinal of four; fourth. **2** of or belonging to the class four. ~ **জমি** *n* land of inferior quality.

চাহিদা [H] *n* **1** need; necessity. **2** insufficiency of supply (of commodities) in the market; desire to purchase or possess; demand.

চিংড়ি *n* small aquatic animal known and eaten as fish, but actually belonging to the genus crustacea; shellfish. **কুচো ~, ঘুষা ~,** *n* small edible crustacea; shrimp. **গলদা ~, শলা** ~ *n* large shellfish; prawn; lobster. **বাগদা** ~ *n* edible crustacea of large size with stripes on the body; tiger-shrimp.

চিঁচিঁ *int* indicating **(a)** a feeble cry of anguish; **(b)** a creaking sound as made by a bird .

চিঁড়া, চিঁড়ে *n* **1** a well-known food item prepared by frying wet paddy and then thrashing the grains into flattened size by a husking pedal. **2** (of playing cards) the club. **কথায় ~ ভেজে না** (prov) Mere words do not do anything.

চিঁহি, চিঁহিঁহিঁ *int* the neighing (of a horse). ~ **করা** *vi* neigh.

চিক[1] *n* a tight-filling jewellery for the neck.

চিক[2], **চীক** [T] *n* window screen made of horizontally laced bamboo slips or slats of other material; wicker-screen; Venetian blind.

চিকচিক *int* **1** sound of chirping of the birds. **2** word denoting glossiness, glimmer or lustre. ~ **করা** *vi* shed lustre; shine. **চিকচিকে** *adj* **1** smooth and shining; glossy. **2** glittering; glistening.

চিকন[1], **চিকণ** *adj* **1** bright; glittering; lustrous. **2** smooth; oily; glossy. **3** nice; fine; beautiful; attractive. ~ **কালা** *n* shining black person; appellation of Sri Krishna. ~ **চাকন** *adj* having a well-shaped beautiful body.

চিকন[2] [P] *adj* thin; delicate; fine: ~ চাল. ❑*n* fine sort of embroidery work on cloth.

চিকনাই⇒চেকনাই

চিকা *n* **1** musk-rat; mole-rat. **2** wall-writing.

চিকিচ্ছে corrup of চিকিৎসা.

চিকিৎসক *n* person skilled in the art of healing; a physician; a doctor.

চিকিৎসনীয়, চিকিৎস্য *adj* **1** that which can be treated medically; curable; remediable. **2** one who is to be medically treated.

চিকিৎসা *n* the art of healing a disease; the act of treating medically or/and surgically. ~ **করা** *vt* treat medically; heal a disease. **~ধীন** [~+অধীন] *adj* under medical treatment. **~লয়** [~+আলয়] *n* an institution where medical advice and treatment are given; a hospital; a clinic; a nursing home. **~শাস্ত্র** *n* the science and art of curing diseases. **চিকিৎসিত** *adj* one who has been treated medically and cured of a disease.

চিকীর্ষা *n* desire to do (a thing). **চিকীর্ষিত** *adj* intended to be done. **চিকীর্ষু** *adj* desirous of doing (a thing).

চিকুর *n* **1** hair covering the human scalp; tuft of hair. **2** a discharge of atmospheric electricity; lightning. **~জাল** *n* a tress of hair.

চিচিং-ফাক *n* the secret or magical formula used to open the door of the treasure-cave in the famous play 'Alibaba and the Forty Thieves', which is rendered in English as 'Open sesame'. ❑*adj* (fig) (of sth secret) exposed; revealed; unveiled.

চিচিঙ্গা *n* vegetable in the shape of a tube tapering at both ends and with green and white stripes on.

চিজ[1], **চীজ**[1] [P] *n* **1** a commodity; a thing; an article. **2** a valuable commodity: কী এমন ~টা এনেছো তুমি? What valuable thing is it that you've fetched? **3** (iron) a person not easily classed; a queer fellow: সে একটা ~ বটে.

চিজ[2], **চীজ**[2] [E] *n* a milk-product; cheese.

চিট[1] [E] *n* a short note or letter; a chit; a small piece of paper containing a note for memory or as an evidence.

চিট[2] *n* viscosity; viscidity; adhesiveness. **চিটচিটে** *adj* sticky; viscid; tenacious; adhesive.

চিটা[1], **চিটে**[1] *adj* containing no substance; unsubstantial. ❑*n* a grain of paddy containing no rice.

চিটা[2], **চিটে**[2] *adj* viscid; viscous; sticky. ❑*n* dark black treacle or molasses used in preparing tobacco for the hookah: ~ গুড়.

চিঠা [H] *n* **1** a book for keeping records of receipts and payments; an account book. **2** a small note in writing; a billet. **3** a list of articles. **হাত~** *n* a slip of paper for keeping records of transaction.

চিঠি [H] *n* a written message or communication sent to a person by post or messenger ; a letter. **~পত্র** *n pl* letters and memoranda. **~ পাঠানো** *vi* post or despatch a letter.

চিড় *n* **1** a crack (in a rock, wall, etc); a crevice; a split; a fissure. **2** (fig) disagreement in opinion; dissension; discord; estrangement; strife. **~ খাওয়া/ধরা** *vi, vt* form a fissure in; develop a crack in ; begin to split.

চিড়চিড় *int* **1** suggesting the sound of cracking or splitting. **2** suggesting a feeling of pain: ~ ব্যথা.

চিড়া⇒ চিঁড়া

চিড়িক *n* sudden pinching of a pain; a twinging sensation: ব্যথাটা ~ দিয়ে উঠল, The pain gave a twinge. **~ মারা** *vi, vt* affect with sharp sudden pain; twinge.

চিড়িতন *n* the lowest valued suit in playing cards; marked with trefoils; the club. **চিড়িতনের টেক্কা** *n* the ace of clubs.

চিড়িয়া [H] *n* the bird. **~খানা** *n* a collection of birds and animals in confinement for exhibition; a zoo; a zoological garden.

চিত[1] *adj* **1** lying on the back/in a dorsal position; supine. **2** (fig) killed or discomfitted (as in a battlefield). **~পাত, ~পটাং** *adj* **1** fallen on the back. **2** (fig) be fooled; be discomfitted. **চিতিয়ে পড়া** *vi* fall on the back. **উৎপাতের কড়ি ~ পাতে যায়** ill-got, ill-spent. **~ সাঁতার** *n* swimming stroke done on the back; back-stroke.

চিৎ[1]=চিত[1]

চিৎ[2] *n* **1**(phil) soul (considered as pure knowledge). **2** intellect. **3** heart; mind. **~প্রকর্ষ** *n* culture of the mind.

চিৎকার, চীৎকার *n* a loud piercing outcry; a scream; a yell; a shrill cry. **~ করা** *vi* shout; scream; yell.

চিত[2] *n* (poet) =চিত্ত

চিত[3] *adj* **1** picked out; gathered; collected. **2** compiled.

চিতই *n* a kind of pie made of unsweatened paste of rice: ~ পিঠা.

চিতল *n* a kind of tasteful and big size river fish.

চিতা[1] *n* funeral pyre for the cremation of the dead according to Hindu rite. **~ভস্ম** *n* ashes collected after the cremation of the body on the funeral pyre. **~রোহণ** *n* **1** (of a deceased) ascending the funeral pyre. **2** act of ascending the funeral pyre of one's husband (as a suttee). **রাবণের ~** *n* the funeral pyre of Rabana of the Ramayana, believed to be burning eternally; (fig) an endless pain of mind caused by loss, misfortune, etc.

চিতা,[2] **চিতে** *n* **1** a kind of herb: রাং~. **2** musty spot on clothes caused by damp; mould; mildew; mustiness. **3** black spot or discoloration on the skin, esp on the face; freckles.

চিতা[3] *n* a carnivorous animal with a spotted skin; the leopard; the cheetah.

চিতান, চিতেন *n* that part of the Bengali folksong which is sung in the higher scale: কবিগানের ~.

চিতানো *vi, vt* **1** lie flat on one's back or cause to lie flat on the back. **2** spread out; expand: বুক ~.

চিতি *n* **1** black and round-shaped mark on the skin. **2** a kind of snake with stripes.

চিত্ত *n* **1** the intellectual power in man; the mind. **2** the seat of affections, will, etc; the heart. **~ক্ষোভ** *n* mental depression; lowness of spirits; dejection. **~ গুরু** *n* internal knowledge or judgement of right and wrong; the moral sense; conscience; morality. **~গ্রাহী** *adj* having the power to charm the mind; captivating; fascinating; attractive; charming. **~চমৎকারী** *adj* **1** that fascinates the mind; charming; attractive. **2** causing surprise or wonder; amazing. **~চাঞ্চল্য** *n* mental agitation/perturbation. **~চালন** *n* exercise or exertion of the intellectual faculty. **~জয়, ~দমন** *n n* **1** control of the mind; self-restraint. **2** restraint of the desires and passions; continence; temperance. **~দাহ** *n* extreme pain of the mind; heart-burning; malice. **~দোষ** *n* perversion of the mind. **~দ্রাবক** *adj* that melts the heart; moving; pathetic. **~নিরোধ** *n* withdrawal of the mind from worldly objects; inward concentration of the mind. **~পুত্তলি, ~পুত্তলিকা** *nn* person very dear to one's heart. **~প্রসাদ** *n* contentment of the mind; mental satisfaction. ~বিকার *n* a violent change of mind; a revulsion of feelings. ~বিক্ষেপ *n* **1** distraction of the mind. **2** unsettled state of the mind. **3** want or absence of mental concentration. ~বিনোদন *n* refreshment of the strength and spirits after toil; recreation; amusement. ~ বিনোদন করা *vi* recreate. ~বিপ্লব *n* **1** agitation of the mind. **2** mental derangement. ~বিভ্রম *n* mental derangement. ~বৃত্তি *n* faculties of the mind; feeling; inclination. ~বৈকল্য *n* perplexity of mind; mental bewilderment. ~ভ্রংশ *n* failure of the intellectual faculty; alienation of the mind; aberration. ~রঞ্জন *adj* pleasing to the mind. ❑*n* amusement; recreation. ~রঞ্জনী বৃত্তি *n* the philosophy of taste; aesthetic faculty; aesthetics. ~শুদ্ধি *n* purity or purification of the mind. ~সংযম *n* control of the mind or heart; self-restraint. ~স্থৈর্য *n* mental calmness/ composure; serenity of the mind. ~হারী *adj* that captivates the mind; captivating; fascinating. ~হারিণী *fem.*

চিত্তাকর্ষক [চিত্ত+আকর্ষক] *adj* **1** pleasing to the mind; attractive. **2** exciting interest in; inspiring curiosity. **চিত্তাকর্ষণ** *n.*

চিত্তোন্নতি [চিত্ত+উন্নতি] *n* elevation of the mind; refinement or refined state of mental faculties.

চিত্র *n* **1** a sketch or representation of an object by colours; a picture; a portrait; a painting. **2** an illustrative figure in outline; a diagram. **3** the moving photographs shown in cinematography; the cinema: চলচ্চিত্র. **4** a description or illustration in words; a pen-picture: লেখ~ . **5** decorative paintings on one's person with sandal-paste, etc (as by Vaishnavas). ❑*adj* **1** amazing; wonderful. **2** marked with diverse colours; variegated. ~ক *n* the leopard; the panther; the cheetah. ~কর, ~কার, ~কৃৎ *nn* one whose trade is painting; a painter; an artist. ~কলা *n* the art of painting. ~কাব্য *n* **1** a composition in verse in which words or lines are arranged in the shape of a picture. **2** a poem full of showy and pompous words without figurative or suggested meaning. ~গত *adj* represented in a picture; painted; delineated. ~জগৎ *n* the world of motion picture; cinema world. ~ণ *n* **1** act of painting/ drawing/sketching. **2** act of describing or portraying: চরিত্র ~ণ. ~তারকা *n* well-known cinema actor or actress; a film-star. ~নাট্য *n* cinematic adaptation of a drama or story; scenario. ~নাট্যকার *n* a writer of scenario; a scenarist. ~পট *n* a canvas or plate for painting on; a painter's canvas. ~বৎ *adv* (dumb or motionless) like a statue. ~মৃগ *n* spotted deer. ~লিপি *n* the pictorial symbol of writing in ancient times; pictograph. ~শালা *n* a painter's studio; an art gallery. ~শিল্প *n* the art of painting. ~শিল্পী *n* a painter; an artist. ~সূচি *n* a list of illustrations (as in a book).

চিত্রা *n* **1** the fourteenth of the twenty seven stars of the Indian astronomy. **2** a Sanskrit poetical metre.

চিত্রাঙ্কন *n* act of drawing/painting/sketching (a picture or figure).

চিত্রাঙ্গদা *n* lady-love of Arjuna of the Mahabharata.

চিত্রিত *adj* painted; drawn in picture. **2** described; portrayed; written. **3** decorated; variegated. **4** pointed with a distinctive mark. ~বৎ *adv* (dumb) like a picture.

চিদানন্দ *n* **1** knowledge and delight; cognition and delight of bliss. **2** the Supreme Being.

চিদাভাস *n* **1** the manifestation of spiritual consciousness or knowledge. **2** the individual soul.

চিনা⇒চেনা

চিনি [C] *n* sweet granular substance manufactured from sugar-cane, beet, etc; sugar. ~পাতা দই *n* curd prepared and sweetened with sugar. ~র বলদ one who toils for another's profit without having the right to share it; a drudge.

চিন্তক *adj* one who thinks; thinking.

চিন্তন *n* **1** act of reasoning within the mind; thinking; consideration. **2** act of thinking deeply; reflection; cogitation. **3** the act of looking back on things past; retrospection. **4** serious contemplation; meditation.

চিন্তনীয়⇒চিন্তা

চিন্তা *n* **1** the act or process of thinking; thought; consideration : ~ করা. **2** act of dwelling on anything in thought; meditation; cogitation; reflection: ঈশ্বর~. **3** worry; anxiety: ~ন্বিত, ~কুল. **4** fear; apprehension; concern; suspense: ~ দূর হওয়া. **5** imagination; fancy; caprice; false notion: উদ্ভট ~. ~ করা *vt* have the mind occupied on some subject; think; judge; cogitate; meditate; consider. ❑*vi* be anxious; worry. **চিন্তনীয়, চিন্ত্য** *adj* fit to be thought of/meditated upon; deserving consideration. (কোনো) উপায় ~ করা *vt* devise some means. (কোনো) ~ নেই never mind; don't worry. ~কুল *adj* deeply concerned; anxious; worried. ~ন্বিত *adj* stricken with anxiety; thoughtful; distracted. ~মগ্ন *adj* engrossed in thought. ~শীল *adj* **1** thinking; thoughtful; meditative; pensive. **2** wise; erudite; sagacious.

চিন্তিত *adj* **1** full of thought; thoughtful. **2** worried; anxious.

চিন্ময় [চিৎ+ময়] *adj* full of consciousness or knowledge. ❑*n* epithet of the Supreme Being.

চিপা *vt* press with the hand; squeeze: ভেজা কাপড় ~. ❑*adj* **1** fitting too close; tight: ~ প্যান্ট. **2** not wide; narrow: ~ গলি.

চিবানো *vt* chew and prepare for swallowing; masticate. ❑*adj* chewed; masticated. **কড়মড় করে ~** crush noisily between the teeth; crunch.

চিবুক *n* the lower extremity of the face; the chin. **~ স্পর্শ** *n* touching the chin (in caressing).

চিমটা, চিমটে [H] *n* a metal instrument for taking hold of burning coal, heated metals, etc; tongs; pincers.

চিমটানো *vi vt* catch and compress sharply with the nails; nip; pinch.

চিমটি *n* **1** an instance of pinching; a pinch. **2** very small quantity of anything: এক ~ লবণ. **~ কাটা** *vi* **1** pinch; nip. **2** (fig) make a sarcastic remark; taunt.

চিমড়া, চিমড়ে *adj* **1** hard to tear; like a dried hide: ~ লুচি . **2** (fig) obstinate or disobedient: ~ স্বভাব. **3** lean but strong: ~ গড়ন.

চিমনি [E] *n* the funnel through which the smoke is conveyed; a chimney. **2** a glass funnel for a lamp, etc.

চির[১] *n* **1** a chink or fissure; a crack: দেওয়ালে ~ ধরা. **2** long strips of anything: ~ করে কাটা. **3** a portion or piece of anything: চৌ~ . **~কুট** *n* a small piece of paper; a slip; a chit.

চির[২] *adj* **1** continuing without end; permanent; everlasting; perpetual: ~ নবীন. **2** entire; whole; complete: ~কাল, ~জীবন. ৩ continuing for a long time; existing from time immemorial: চিরাচরিত. **4** for the whole life; till death: ~কুমার. **~ অন্ধকার** *adj* perpetually and profoundly dark. ❑*n* perpetual gloom. **~ অম্লান** *adj* that never fades; unfading; never-fading. **~ঋণী** *adj* indebted for ever. **~কাল** *n* duration without end; eternity; infinite time. ❑*adv* always; for ever; endlessly; perpetually; eternally. **~কালীন, ~কেলে**(dial) *adj* covering all times; lasting for ever. **~কুমার** *adj* one who remains bachelor under a vow or on principle. ❑*n* a confirmed bachelor; a celibate. **~ক্রিয়** *adj* sluggish; slothful; procrastinating; dilatory. **~জীব, ~জীবী** *adjj* undying; immortal. **~জীবী হও** May you live long. **~তরে** *adj* for ever. **~নিদ্রা** *n* eternal sleep; death. **~ন্তন** *adj* of long standing; existing from time immemorial; eternal. **~ন্তনী** *fem.* **~ বিচ্ছেদ** *n* permanent estrangement/ separation. **~বৈরী, ~শত্রু** *n* a perpetual enemy. **~সঙ্গী** *n* constant companion. **~স্মরণীয়** *adj* worthy of being remembered for ever; of everlasting fame; unforgettable.

চিরকুট⇒চির[১]

চিরতা *n* bitter-tasting medicinal herb; *chirata.*

চিরন্তন⇒চির[২]

চিরা⇒চেরা

চিরাগ = চেরাগ

চিরায়ত *adj.* pervading all ages; all-pervading; eternal; universal. **~ সাহিত্য** literary work of established excellence and value; classical literature; classics.

চিরায়ু *adj* living or destined to live for ever; long-lived; undying; immortal (also চিরায়ুষ্মান). **চিরায়ুষ্মতী** *fem.*

চিরুনি, চিরনি *n* instrument for cleaning, adjusting and separating hair; a comb.

চিল *n* a bird of prey of the hawk family with claws; the kite. **চিলের ছোঁ** *n* **1** a swoop or pounce of a kite. **2** (fig) a pouncing that never misses the target.

চিলতা, চিলতে *n* a thin slice of sth: এক ~ মাছ.

চিলমচি, চিলুমচি [T] *n* a moveable wash-basin.

চিলা⇒চিল্লা

চিলাকোঠা⇒চিলেকোঠা

চিলিক *n* a flash of light; a gleam.

চিলা, চিল্লা [P] *n* absorption in religious exercises and meditation in seclusion for forty days at a stress as practised by sages and devout Muslims. **~খানা** *n* venue of such exercises.

চিলেকোঠা, চিলাকোঠা *n* a room on the uppermost floor of a house; a garret; an attic.

চিল্লা = চিলা

চিল্লাচিল্লি *n* hue and cry; clamour; hullabaloo. **~ করা** *vi* raise an uproar; make a hullabaloo.

চিল্লানি *n* an outcry; an uproar.

চিহ্ন *n* **1** a visible sign or impression on sth ; a print; a mark : পদ~. **2** an indication or evidence: ভয়ের ~ . **3** a symptom or characteristic: অনুরাগের ~ . **4** a testimony; a token; a monument: স্মৃতি~. **5** a mark left by anything; a trace: কোথাও গাছ পালার ~ নেই.

চিহ্নিত *adj* marked off; stamped; branded.

চীৎকার ⇒ চিৎকার

চীন *n* the People's Republic of China. **চীনা, চৈনিক** *adj.*

চীনা[১] *n* a native of China. ❑*adj* produced in China; Chinese. **~ংশুক** *n* Chinese silk cloth. **~ ঘাস** *n* fragrant grass produced in China. **~ জোঁক** a species of leech that clings to the body very pertinaciously; (fig) person who is extremely pertinacious in obtaining anything from one. ~ **বাদাম** *n* ground-nut. ~ **মাটি** *n* a fine species of porcelain.

চীনা[2] *n* a kind of grey-coloured food crop like the mustard seeds in shape and size.

চীবর *n* piece of cloth worn by Buddhist monks.

চুঁচড়া *n* fish of exceedingly small size: ~ মাছ.

চুক [H] *n* a fault; a flaw. **ভুল~** *n pl* flaws and faults; omissions and commissions.

চুকা[1], **চুকো** *adj* sour to taste.

চুকা[2] *vi* **1** be finished; come to an end: কাজ ~. **2** be settled or solved: সমস্যা ~. **~নো** *vt* **1** cause to be finished: কাজকর্ম ~. **2** cause to be repaid or settled: দেনাপাওনা ~নো.

চুকচুক *int* (onom) the sound of licking; sipping a liquid.

চুক্তি [H] *n* **1** a stipulation; a bargain: ~তে কাজ করা. **2** an agreement between two or more persons for doing a thing, which is subject to the law of contract; a contract. **~পত্র**, **~নামা** *n* a deed of contract. **~ভঙ্গ** *n* breach of contract.

চুগল, **চুগলখোরি** [P] *n* slandering the reputation of a person who is absent. **~খোর** *adj* one who speaks slanderously about an absent person. ❑*n* a back-biter.

চুঙ্গি [H] *n* **1** a small and narrow tube or pipe. **2** duty levied on goods entering a town; octroi: ~কর.

চুটকি[1] *n* **1** ring with swinging bells worn by women on their toes. **2** snapping with the fingers. **3** small commission for weighmen paid in kind. ❑*adj* short, light and humorous: ~ গান, light song; ~ সাহিত্য light, humorous literature.

চুটকি[2] *n* tuft of hair on the head kept by Brahmins.

চুটানো *vt* exert one's energy to the utmost: চুটিয়ে কাজ করা, চুটিয়ে গালি দেওয়া.

চুড় *n* ornament for the wrist; a bracelet.

চুড়ি *n* thin ornamental ring for the wrist; bangle. **~ওয়ালা** *n* a pedlar or hawker who sells bangles. **~কার** *n* a maker of bangles. **~দাড়** *adj* narrow and filled: ~দাড় পায়জামা.

চুন *n* oxide of calcium obtained by burning limestone; lime. ❑*adj* pale; dim; whitish: বাবাকে দেখে তার মুখ ~ হয়ে গেল. **~কাম** *n* washing or painting walls with lime for whitening; whitewash; limewash. **পাথর ~** *n* lime obtained by burning limestone. **শামুক ~** *n* lime made by burning shells of snails. **চুনের ভাটি** *n* a furnace in which limestone is reduced to lime; lime-kiln.

চুনকালি *n* **1** (lit) lime paste and soot. **2** (fig) disrepute; disgrace; infamy. **মুখে ~ পড়া** be disgraced.

চুনা[1] *adj* of the nature of lime or chalk; containing lime; calcareous; calciferous. **~ পাথর** *n* limestone.

চুনা[2], **চুনো** *n* very small fish. ❑*adj* small and insignificant: ~ পুটি, a small variety of fish. (fig) person of no consequence; an insignificant person.

চুনি *n* precious stone of red colour; ruby.

চুপ *adj* not speaking; making no noise; silent; mute; dumb. ❑ *int* (expressive of a command) silence! hush! hold your tongue! **~ করা** *vi* be silent; keep quiet. **~ থাকা** *vi* remain silent; keep mum; maintain silence. **~ হওয়া** *vi* be quiet/silent. **~চাপ** *adj* not making any noise or movement; speechless; motionless; inactive. ❑*adv* in a silent manner; silently: ~চাপ বসে থাকা. **~টি** *adj* quick silent; absolutely speechless or motionless. **~টি করে/মেরে** *adv* quite silently; stealthily. **~ মারা** *vi* be quiet of one's own accord.

চুপড়ি *n* a wicker-basket: এক ~ মাছ, a basketful of fishes.

চুপসানো ⇒ চোপসা

চুপি *n* silence; quiet; absence of noise. **~চাপি** *adv* without making any noise and beyond the knowledge of others; imperceptibly; surreptitiously; stealthily: ~চাপি সরে পড়া. **~ ~**, **চুপে চুপে** *adv* **1** in a low voice; in a whisper: ~ ~ কথা বলা. **2** without being noticed by others; stealthily; surreptitiously: ~ ~ উকি মারা. **~সারে** *adv* **1** in a silent manner; silently. **2** beyond the knowledge of others; imperceptibly.

চুবানি⇒চুবানো

চুবানো, **চোবানো** *vt* plunge in a liquid; dip: পানিতে ~. **চুবানি**, **চোবানি** *n* act of dipping. **নাকানি-চুবানি/চোবানি** *n* extreme harassment; being harassed with unnecessary troubles.

চুমকি *n* small sparkling object of silvery or golden colour inlaid on garments, etc; a spangle; a foil; a tinsel. **~ বসানো** *adj* spangled; tinselled.

চুমা, **চুমো**, **চুমু** *n* a kiss. **~ খাওয়া/দেওয়া** *vt* kiss.

চুমুক *n* quantity of liquid swallowed once without taking breath; a draught; a sip. **~ দেওয়া** *vi, vt* take a draught/sip. **এক চুমুকে** *adv* in one sip; at a draught.

চুম্বক *n* **1** the loadstone, which has the property of attracting iron; magnet. **2** (fig) sth exercising strong attraction. **3** the summary or gist of a thing; an abstract. **~ত্ব** *n* magnetic power; magnetism. **চুম্বকিত** *adj* magnetized. **~মেরু** *n* the location to which the compass-needle points; magnetic pole. **~ শলাকা** *n* magnetic or compass-needle.

চুম্বন *n* act of kissing; a kiss. **~ করা** *vt* caress by joining lips; kiss. **চুম্বিত** *adj* one who has been kissed. **চুম্বী** *adj* that which kisses or touches; kissing; touching; scraping: গগণচুম্বী অট্টালিকা, a sky scraper.

চুয়াত্তর *n, adj* seventy-four.

চুয়ানো *vi* **1** fall or let fall in drops; exude; ooze out; leak: কলসিটা চোয়াচ্ছে, The pitcher is leaking/exuding. **2** pass or let pass through a filter; percolate: মদ ~. ❑*adj* **1** filtered; percolated: ~ মদ. **2** that which has exuded/oozed out: ~ পানি.

চুয়ান্ন *n, adj* four and fifty; fifty-four.

চুয়াল্লিশ *n, adj* four and forty; forty four.

চুর *n* powder; dust; fragment: লৌহ~. ❑*adj* **1** affected with strong drink; intoxicated; fuddled; tipsy; dead drunk: নেশায় ~. **2** destroyed; razed to the ground. **~মার** *adj* reduced to dust.

চুরট, চুরুট [shurutu (Tamil)] *n* a roll of tobacco with both ends cut square off for smoking; cheroot; cigar.

চুরানব্বই *n, adj* four and ninety; ninety four.

চুরাশি *n, adj* four and eight; eighty four.

চুরি *n* act of stealing; unlawful taking of another's goods; theft. **~ করা** *vi* commit theft; steal. **~ হওয়া** *vi* be lost/stolen. **~ করে/করিয়া** *adv* stealthily; by stealth. **~-চামারি** *n pl* stealing and other small offences; petty theft; pilferage.

চুরুট = চুরট

চুল *n* one or the whole growth of hair covering the scalp of a human being. **চুলাচুলি, চুলোচুলি** *n* **1** a brawl, esp between women, which results in mutual pulling of hair. **2** a very noisy quarrel; an uproar. **~ খোলা** *vi* (of women) undo or undress a braid or tress. **~ বাঁধা** *vi* do up one's hair. **চুলের গোছা** *n* a tuft of hair. **~চেরা** *adj* hair-splitting; very minute. **~চেরা ভাগ** *n* hair-splitting division; minute division. **~দাড়ি পাকানো** *vi* **1** be old enough. **2** (fig) acquire long experience in some matter. **এক ~** *adj* of a little amount/ hair's breadth. ❑*adj* by a hair's breadth.

চুলকানি *n* the skin disease of itching; itches; scabies. **চুলকানো** *vi* scratch with the nails.

চুলবুল [H] *int* suggesting restlessness. **চুলবুলানি** *n* restlessness; fidgetiness. **চুলবুলে** *adj* restless; fickle; fidgety.

চুলা, চুলো, চুল্লি *n* **1** an oven; a furnace. **2** funeral pyre or pile (of the Hindus). **~ জ্বালানো/ধরানো** *vi* make a fire in an oven; ignite an oven or furnace. **চুলোয় যাওয়া** *vt* **1** go to hell; die. **2** be ruined. **চুলোয় যাক** *int* let go to the dogs; let go to rack and ruin.

চুষা, চোষা *vi, vt* draw liquid by sucking; suck milk from the breast. ❑*adj* **1** one who sucks. **2** (fig) one who exploits others: রক্ত চোষা. **3** that which has been sucked: বাদুড়-চোষা.

চুষি *n* **1** an artificial sucker for babies; a sucking toy. **2** a kind of semi-liquid sweet: ~ পিঠা.

চূড়া *n* **1** the top of a mountain ending in a point; a peak: পর্বত~. **2** a badge of royalty worn on the head; a crown; a coronet; a diadem. **3** a tuft or lock of hair left uncut on the head (as among the Hindus). **4** the chief or best man of a race or family: কুল ~মণি.

চূড়ান্ত *n* **1** the top or highest point of excellence; acme. **2** utmost limit; the point that cannot be passed. ❑*adj* final; ultimate; decisive: ~ সিদ্ধান্ত.

চূত *n* **1** the mango tree. **2** the mango fruit. **~ মঞ্জরী** *n* the bud of mango.

চূর্ণ *n* **1** anything reduced to dust; powder. **2** unslaked lime; quicklime. **3** a kind of perfumed powder which the Hindus sprinkle on one another in celebration of the *holi* festival. ❑*adj* **1** reduced to dust; pulverized. **2** broken to pieces; fractured: অস্থি ~ হওয়া. **3** spoiled; crushed; humbled; humiliated: দর্প ~ হওয়া. **~ করা** *vt* **1** break to pieces. **2** reduce to/grind into powder; pulverize. **3** (fig) humble; humiliate: দর্প ~ করা, humble one's pride. **~কার** *n* a manufacturer of lime. **~কুন্তল** *n* a curl or ringlet of hair.

চূর্ণন *n* act of grinding into powder; pulverization; breaking into pieces. **চূর্ণনীয়** *adj* fit to be broken/ pulverized. **চূর্ণিত, চূর্ণীকৃত** *adj* **1** that which has been pulverized. **2** broken; crushed; razed to the ground. **চূর্ণীভূত** *adj* reduced to pieces; pulverized.

চূর্ণিকা *n* pulverized form of pulses or peas.

চূষণীয়, চূষ্য *adj* fit to be sucked.

চূষ্য = চূষণীয়

চেং =চ্যাং

চেংরা = চেঙ্গরা

চেঁচাচেচি, চেঁচামেচি *n* **1** confused outcry of many people at a time. **2** hue and cry; clamour; hullabaloo. **3** noisy opposition to one another; brawling. **~ করা** *vi* clamour; raise a hue and cry; make a hullabaloo.

চেঁচানো *vi* cry out with a piercing noise; scream; yell; utter a shrill cry. **চেঁচানি** *n* loud piercing outcry; yell.

চেচেপুঁছে *adv* **1** without leaving any bit of food in the plate. **2** by wiping and licking every bit of food in the plate.

চেক[১] [E] *n* **1** a design of small squares (on cloth, etc); check: ~ শাড়ি. **2** a piece of checked cloth. **~-কাটা** *adj* checked; checkered; chequered.

চেক[2] [E] *n* a printed form containing an order to a bank to pay a certain amount of money from one's account; a bank cheque. **~ কাটা** *vi* issue or draw a cheque. **~ ভাঙ্গানো/ভাঙানো** *vi* cash a cheque. **চেক অগ্রাহ্য করা** dishonour a cheque. **~ দাখিলা** *n* descriptive rent-receipt containing the particulars about the land and its tenancy. **~ বই** *n* a cheque book (of a bank). **~ মুড়ি** *n* the counterfoil of a descriptive rent-receipt.

চেঙ্গরা, চেঙ্গড়া, চ্যাংড়া *n* an irresponsible young lad; a person speaking confidently without knowledge; a flippant person. ❑*adj* youthful; childish; flippant. **~মি** *n* boyishness; puerile joke; puerility.

চেতন *adj* **1** having life; living; conscious. **2** having knowledge; knowing; enlightened. ❑*n* consciousness; sensibility; knowledge; conscience. **~ পাওয়া** *vi* be awake; be roused from sleep; be aware of. **~ পদার্থ** *n* an animate object.

চেতনা *n* **1** state of being conscious; consciousness; sensibility. **2** perception; conscience: ~রহিত. **~হীন, ~শূন্য** *adj* **1** unconscious; not perceiving; unaware. **2** not animate; inanimate; destitute of life. **~ পাওয়া** *vi* regain consciousness; come back to senses. **~ হারানো** *vi* loose consciousness; swoon; faint.

চেন, চেইন [E] *n* **1** a chain (as of a watch, etc). **2** an ornamental chain for the neck: গলার ~. **3** a device for measuring land, consisting of 100 links, equal to 66 ft: দৈর্ঘে ১ ~.

চেনা *vt, vi* **1** recognize one to be a known person: তাকে চিনি, I know him. **2** know one in his real character: বিপদে প্রকৃত বন্ধু ~ যায়. **3** identify; ascertain to be the same: লাশ ~. **4** take by preference; choose; differentiate: ভালো মন্দ ~. **5** be acquainted with; know; learn: অক্ষর ~. ❑*adj* acquainted; known; familiar: ~ লোক. **~শুনা, ~পরিচয়** *n* familiar knowledge; acquaintance; intimacy.

চেপ্টা = চ্যাপ্টা

চেয়ার [E] a movable seat with or without arms; a chair.

চেয়ারম্যান [E] *n* the presiding officer of an assembly or association; a president.

চেয়ে[1]**, চাইতে** *conj* (indeclinable word used before certain adjectives expressing comparison) than: তোমার ~ ছোট, younger or shorter than you are; এক গজের ~ কম, less than a yard.

চেয়ে[2]**, চাহিয়া** *inf verb* **1** by asking: চেয়ে নাও. **2** with a look: চেয়ে দেখো.

চেরা, চিরা *vt* **1** split, sever or part asunder. **2** cut with a saw: কাঠ চেরা. **3** cut open; operate: পেট চিরে বের করা. **~ই** *n* **1** act of sawing. **2** charge or cost of sawing. **~নো** *vt* cause to be cut/split/cleft. **পটোল~** *adj* like the longitudinal half of the cylinder-like vegetable tapering at both ends called পটোল. **পটোল~ চোখ** *n* wide and very beautiful eyes shaped like the longitudinal half of a পটোল.

চেরাগ, চিরাগ [P] *n* a vessel for containing oil to be burned by means of a wick; a lamp. **চেরাগি, চেরাগিমহাল** *n* a piece of rent-free land granted to the caretaker of the tomb of a Muslim saint for bearing the expenses of burning lamps. **চৌদ্দ পুরুষের ~** (sarcas) the black sheep of a family.

চেলা[1] [H] *n* a disciple or follower of a teacher. **~-চামুণ্ডা** *n pl* disciples and adherents who are insincere and of wicked character. **যেমন গুরু তেমন ~** like master, like man.

চেলা[2] *n* **1** wood prepared as fuel; splinters; firewood. **2** a kind of the spider group with a poisonous sting in its long, jointed tail; a scorpion. **~নো** *vt* came to be chopped; chop wood into splinters.

চেলি *n* silk sari used as wedding dress: বিবাহের লাল চেলি.

চেষ্টা *n* **1** an exertion of strength and will for sth; strenuous; endeavour; struggle. **2** adventurous spirit; enterprise: উন্নতির ~. **3** continued diligence; perseverance. **4** looking for; act of seeking: চাকরির ~. **~ চরিত্র** *n* continuous or careful effort to do or get sth. **~ করা** *vt* make an effort; try; endeavour. **~ন্বিত** *adj* trying; endeavouring. **~হীন** *adj* effortless; unenterprising; inactive.

চেহারা [P] *n* what sth or sb appears to be; one's outward appearance or look; form; shape. **~ দেখানো** *vi* present oneself; show one's appearance; appear in person.

চেহেল সতুন [P] *n* a palace of forty pillars.

চৈ চৈ = চই চই

চৈত *n* the month of Chaitra

চৈতন *n* tuft of uncut hair on the crown of the head maintained by Hindus.

চৈতন্য *n* **1** state of being conscious; consciousness; sensibility; sensation. **2** perception of what passes in one's mind; sense of guilt or innocence; knowledge; good sense. **3** watchfulness; alertness; vigilance. **4** Sri Chaitanya, a religious reformer and founder of Vaishnavism in medieval Bengal. **~ পাওয়া** *vi* come to one's senses. **~ হারানো** *vi* loose consciousness; swoon or faint. **~ময়** *adj* full of sense and knowledge.

চৈতন্যোদয় [চৈতন্য+উদয়] *n* awakening of senses. **~ হওয়া** *vi* come to one's senses.

চৈতালি, চৈতালী *n* **1** crops harvested in the month of Chaitra; green crops; cereals. **2** land revenue payable in the month of Chaitra.

3 the spring time breeze; the vernal breeze. 4 the spring time emotion; the vernal passion. ❑*adj* 1 of or pertaining to Chaitra. 2 growing/harvested in the month of Chaitra.

চৈতি, চৈতী *adj* 1 grown or produced in Chaitra. 2 of Chaitra; of the spring: ~ হাওয়া, ~ ফসল.

চৈত্য[১] *n* 1 a place of worship or sacrifice among Hindus. 2 a Buddhist monastery or shrine.

চৈত্য[২] *adj* relating to চিতা or funeral pyre. ❑*n* a sacred tree at a burning ghat worshipped by Buddhists.

চৈত্র the twelfth or last month of the Bengali calendar; Chaitra.

চৈন, চৈনিক, চৈনেয় *adj* 1 of or pertaining to China. 2 produced in China. ❑*n* a native of China; the language of China; Chinese.

চোঁ *int* denoting the noise of sucking in a quick manner: ~ করে দুধ খাওয়া. **~ করে** *adv* in haste; quickly: ~ করে চলে গেল, ran off at full speed. **খিদেয় পেট ~ ~ করছে,** feeling a wolf in the stomach.

চোখ *n* 1 the organ of vision; the eye. 2 the sight of the eye; view; observation; eyesight. 3 kind disposition; an eye of favour: তার প্রতি আমার ~ আছে. 4 a covetous eye; an avaricious look: পরের জিনিসে ~ দেওয়া. 5 a sort of knot at the root of a bamboo or sugarcane where shoots arise; a node; a protuberance. **~ ওঠা** *vi* be attacked with ophthalmia. ❑*n* inflammation of the eye; ophthalmia. **~ কপালে তোলা** *vi* be amazed/alarmed. **~ কাটানো** *vi* have the cataract of one's eyes removed by ophthalmic surgery. **~-কান খোলা** *adj* careful; watchful; alert. ❑*n* alertness; watchfulness. **~-কান বুজে থাকা** *vi* 1 refuse to be entangled in what one doesn't like. 2 be failing in one's responsibilities. **~ খাওয়া, চোখের মাথা খাওয়া** *vi* 1 fail to choose the right thing. 2 lose one's eyesight. **~ ছলছল করা** *vi* feel like weeping; (of one's eyes) be filled with tears. **~ টাটানো** *vi* be envious or jealous; be apprehensive of rivalry. **~ টেপা, ~ ঠারা** *vt* wink at meaningfully; give a leer or side glance; ogle at (one). **~ দেওয়া** *vt* cast an evil eye (on). **~ পড়া** *vt* feel attraction for; be attracted to. **~ পাকানো** *vi* express anger or displeasure by straining one's eyes; goggle; frown. **~ ফোটা** *vi* 1 (of young birds) have eyes opened for the first time. 2 come to be enlightened about what one was quite in darkness. **~ মিটমিট করা** *vi* shut and open the eyelids rapidly. **~ রাখা** *vt* keep an eye on; be watchful about. **~ রাঙানো** *vt* 1 throw an angry glance/a fierce or piercing look; show temper. 2 give threats; intimidate. **চোখে আঙুল দিয়ে দেখানো** *vi* make one understand sth with positive proof. **চোখে চোখে রাখা** *vt* keep (one) under constant observation/watch. **চোখে ধুলা দেওয়া** *vt* play a trick on; deceive or mislead one; hoodwink. **চোখে মুখে কথা বলা** *vi* talk indiscreetly; display one's gift of the gab. **চোখের আড়ালে** *adv* out of one's sight; behind one's back. **চোখের উপরে** *adv* before one's eyes. **চোখের নেশা** *n* a strong desire just for seeing. **চোখের পরদা** *n* 1 eyelid. 2 a feeling of delicacy in doing sth unseemly. **চোখের বালি** *n* (fig) a detestable person; an eye-sore. **চোখের ভুল** *n* a deceptive appearance; an illusion; a hallucination. **চোখে সরষে ফুল দেখা** be perplexed in a difficult situation; be at a loss what to do.

চোখা [H] *adj* 1 sharp; pointed; piercing. 2 (fig) harsh; rude; severe; strong: ~ কথা, words that cut to the quick; sharp words. 3 smart; intelligent; experienced: ~ লোক. 4 genuine; pure; excellent: ~ মাল.

চোখাচোখি *n* exchange of glances/looks.

চোগা [T] *n* a sort of loose and long outer garment; an overcoat.

চোঙ, চোঙা, চোঙ্গা *n* 1 a short and hollow tube/pipe. 2 a piece of bamboo with a knot on one side used for measuring milk or oil: এক ~ দুধ. 3 the shaft of a chimney through which smoke ascends; a funnel: জাহাজের ~.

চোট [H] *n* 1 a blow; a stroke; a shock: পায়ে ~ লাগা. 2 a wound; bruise or injury caused by a fall or stroke. 3 power exerted: মন্ত্রের চোটে, by dint of/virtue of a charm. 4 fluency; flow (as of words): কথার ~. **কথার/মুখের চোটে** by the art of declamation; by haranguing; by the gift of the gab. **~ খাওয়া/লাগা** *vi* be hurt/wounded; get a bump. **~ মারা** *vt* strike; hurt; hit at. **এক~** *n* one time/course; once. **একচোটে** *adv* at one stroke; at a time.

চোটপাট *n* expression of anger; an instance of bullying/blustering. **~ করা** *vt* talk big and threaten one who is weak; bluster; domineer.

চোট্টা [H] *n* a cheat; a swindler; a thief. **~মি** *n* cheating; deception; fraud; swindling.

চোণা=চোনা

চোদ্দ, চৌদ্দ *n, adj* fourteen. ❑*adj* so many; so much: ~ কথা শুনতে চাই না. **~ই** *n* the fourteenth day of a month. **~ চাকার রথ দেখানো** *vt* put one into various troubles. **~ পুরুষ** *n* one's fourteen generations upwards or downwards. **~ পুরুষ উদ্ধার করা** *vt* vilify one to the fourteenth generation.

চোনা, চোণা *n* urine of cattle: গো~.

চোপরাও [H] *int* hush! silence! be quiet!

চোপসা, চুপসা *adj* 1 pressed down; depressed; sunk; shrunken: ~ গাল. 2 that soaks; soaking; imbibing moisture: ~ কাগজ.

~নো *vi* **1** be depressed; sink-fall: গাল ~নো. **2** be moistened; get wet or damped; soak; blot: এই কাগজ চুপসায়, this paper blots.

চোপা *n* **1** (derog) the face; the mouth. **2** a rude reply; repartee; a retort. **3** scolding; rebuke; calling names. **~ করা** *vi* speak pertly or saucily; call one names.

চোয়াল *n* the bones of the mouth in which the teeth are fixed; the jawbone, the jaw. **~ ধরা** *vi* be affected with the disease that locks the jaw making one unable to masticate; have the lock-jaw.

চোর *n* person who steals or is guilty of theft; a thief. **চুন্নী** (derog) *fem.* **~ ছেঁচড়** *n pl* thieves and swindlers. **~ পালালে বুদ্ধি বাড়ে** (prov) Everybody is wise after the event. **চোরে চোরে মাসতুতো ভাই** All thieves are cousins; Birds of the same feather flock together. **চোরের উপর বাটপাড়ি** to rob the robber. **চোরের ধন বাটপারে খায়** ill-got, ill-spent. **চোরের মার বড়ো গলা** An inveterate thief is the loudest denunciator.

চোরা[১] *n* a thief; a swindler. **~ না শোনে ধর্মের কাহিনী** The devil would not listen to the scriptures.

চোরা[২] *adj* **1** that has been stolen: ~ মাল. **2** secret; unseen; unknown: ~ গর্ত. a pitfall. **3** unlawful; illegal: ~ কারবার. **4** stealthy; sly; furtive: ~ চাহনি, a furtive look/glance. **~গলি** *n* a lane with an opening on one side only; a blind alley. **~গোপ্তা** *adj* secret; surreptitious clandestine: ~গোপ্তা আঘাত. **~ পকেট** *n* a secret pocket in a garment. **~বালি** *n* **1** a movable sandbank under water; sand yielding under the feet; quicksand. **2** (fig) something treacherous.

চোরাই *adj* stolen: ~ মাল, stolen property.

চোল[১] **1** the ancient kingdom of Tanjore in India, the kingdom of the Cholas.

চোল[২], **চোলিকা, চোলী** *n* **1** a woman's close-fitting under-garment for the chest; a bodice. **2** a skirt.

চোলাই *n* the process of purifying a liquid by converting it into vapour and then condensing it again; distillation. **~ করা** *vt* distil.

চোষ *n* suction; drying up. **~ কাগজ** *n* blotting paper.

চোষক *adj* that sucks or blots; sucking; blotting.

চোষণ *n* suction; sucking. **চোষণীয়, চোষ্য** *adj* that can be/is to be sucked.

চোষা *vt* draw (liquid) into the mouth by sucking; suck.

চোস্ত [P] *adj* **1** close-fitting; tight-fitting: ~ পায়জামা. **2** lucid; elegant: তিনি ~ ফারসি বলেন. **3** conspicuous in society; fashionable; well-dressed; smart. **4** having a good, quick brain; showing ingenuity; clever; skilful.

চৌ *adj* (used as *pref*) **1** four: ~কা, ~কো, square, quadrangular. **~কাঠ** *n* a rectilineal door frame; a door-sill. **~কোণ, কোণা** *adj* four-cornered; quadrangular; square. **~খণ্ডি** *n* **1** a four-legged cot/ stool. **2** a house with four sloping roofs on four sides jointed together. ❑*adj* divided into four parts. **~খুপি** *n* square; check. **~গুণ** *adj* four-fold; quadruple. **~চালা** =~খণ্ডি (২). **~চির** *adj* split into four fragments; broken to pieces. **~ঠা** *adj* (of days of a month) fourth. ❑*n* the fourth day of a month. **~তলী** *adj* four-storeyed. ❑ the third floor (of a building). **~ত্রিশ** *n, adj* four and thirty; thirly-four. **~দিক** *n* four sides; all sides. **~দিকে** *adv* on all sides. **~পদী** *n* a variety of four-lined versification. ❑*adj* four-footed (animal). **~মাথা, ~রাস্তা** *n* a junction of four roads; a point where two roads intersect; a cross-road. **~রাশি** *n, adj* four and eighty; eighty-four. **~ষট্টি** *n, adj* four and sixty; sixty-four.

চৌকস [H] *adj* **1** having attention in all directions. **2** experienced and skilful in all fields. **3** having ability in many different ways; all-round.

চৌকা, চৌকো⇒চৌ

চৌকি[১] *n* a four legged bedstead.

চৌকি[২] *n* **1** a guard; a sentinel; a watchman. **2** a beat or jurisdiction of a watchman; a watch-post. **3** an outpost for collecting toll, etc. **4** the act of watching; the duty of a sentinel. **~ দেওয়া** *vi* guard; watch. **~দার** *n* **1** a village watchman; a chowkidar. **2** a collector of taxes in a village. **~দারি** *n* the occupation of a chowkidar. ❑*adj* relating to a chowkidar.

চৌগান [P] *n* a game like hockey, played on horseback; polo.

চৌথ *n* one-fourth; one quarter. **2** one-fourth of the total crop or the value thereof exacted by Marhatta rulers as annual tribute from their subjects or tributary states.

চৌদ্দ=চোদ্দ

চৌধুরী *n* **1** a title of honour. **2** a feudatory prince. **3** a village headman. **4** the chief merchant of a city or entrepot of trade. **চৌধুরানী** *fem.*

চৌবাচ্চা [P] *n* a water reservoir; a storage tank (of water); a cistern.

চৌম্বক *adj* pertaining to the magnet; possessing the properties of the magnet; magnetic.

চৌর *n* a thief.

চৌরস *adj* **1** broad; wide; spacious. **2** level; plain, even; smooth. **3** four-cornered; square; rectangular.

চৌর্য *n* act of stealing; theft. **~বৃত্তি** *n* the practice of stealing.

চৌষট্টি⇒চৌ

চৌহদ্দি, চৌহুদ্দি *n* boundary lines on four sides; the limits of an area. **~ করা** *vi, vt* mark the boundary of; delimit.

চৌহান *n* a branch of the Rajputs.

চ্যাবন *n* a sage of ancient India. **~প্রাশ** *n* a famous Ayurvedic medicine for cough or other bronchial troubles.

চ্যান্সেলার [E] *n* **1** the titular head of a university in some countries. **2** the chief minister of Germany; Chancellor. **ভাইস ~** *n* the administrative chief of a university.

চ্যালেঞ্জ [E] *n* summons to fight; challenge. **~ করা** *vt* summon to fight. **~ দেওয়া** *vt* throw a challenge.

চ্যুত *adj* **1** what has fallen down or dropped: বৃন্ত~ . **2** dismissed; discharged; removed: পদ~ . **3** strayed; deviated: পথ~, কক্ষ ~. **4** ousted; expelled; detached: ধর্ম ~.

চ্যুতি *n* **1** detachment; dislodgement; dismissal; expulsion: পদ~, ধর্ম~. **2** loss; destruction; ruin; disappearance: ধৈর্য~.

ছ

ছ[1] *n* the seventh consonant of the Bengali alphabet. It is a dorso or plato-alveolar aspirated plosive round. Dhaka *kuttis* pronounce it as afficate sound. In some dialects of the eastern part of Bangladesh it is also pronounced as a fricative sound.

ছ[2] ⇒ ছয়

ছই, ছৈ *n* a movable cover made of bamboo slips to shelter the passengers of a cart or boat from the sun; awning.

ছওয়াব=সোয়াব

ছওয়ার=সওয়ার

ছওয়াল=সওয়াল

ছক *n* **1** a check or square in a chess-board; a board with such checks; a checker-board. **2** a diagram or an outline of a plan, etc. **3** a pattern or a prescribed/traditional form: উপন্যাসের ~ . **~ কাগজ** *n* paper with small squares of equal size; graph paper. **~-কাটা** *adj* **1** marked with squares; checkered. **2** circumscribed by fixed and regular way of doing things; monotonous: ~-কাটা জীবন. **~ কাটা** *vi, vt* draw squares; (fig) make a rough sketch/preliminary plan.

ছক্কা[1] *n* a spiced dish of vegetables.

ছক্কা[2] *n* **1** the six of a playing card. **2** (cricket) a hit over the boundary that scores six runs.

ছটফট *int* **1** denoting struggling or tossing about in pain: যন্ত্রণায় ~ করা. **2** suggestive of impatience, anxiety or restlessness. **~ করা** *vi* **1** toss about (in pain). **2** be troubled with anxiety or eagerness. **ছটফটানি** *n* state of being restless; restlessness; impatience; fidgetiness. **ছটফটানো** *vi* toss about; fidget; be troubled with impatience. **ছটফটে** *adj* restless; uneasy; fidgety.

ছটরা, ছড়রা, ছররা *n* quantity of small pellets of lead contained in the cartridge of a gun (instead of a single bullet) used against birds and small animals: ~ গুলি, lead shot, grape-shot.

ছটা *n* **1** reflected light; radiance; lustre; glow; glamour: রূপের ~. **2** beauty; elegance; grace; loveliness: মুখচ্ছটা. **3** serial succession; sequence; a series: শ্লোকের ~.

ছটাক [H] *n* **1** measure of weight ($\frac{1}{16}$ th of a seer) prevalent in the subcontinent before the introduction of metric system. **2** measure of area ($\frac{1}{16}$th of a *katha*).

ছড়[1] *n* **1** a long and slender rod or stick. **2** a bow of a musical instrument; a fiddlestick: বেহালার ~.

ছড়া[1] *n* **1** a skin; a hide. **2** the bark of a tree. **3** a long scratch of abrasion on the body.

ছড়া[2] *n* a loose irregular kind of versification with correspondence of sound in the end of words or verses; a doggerel verse; a rhyme: ছেলে ভোলানো ~, a nursery rhyme; গ্রাম্য ~ , a folk-rhyme. **~ কাটা** *vi* **1** cap verses; compose and recite verses extempore. **2** recite verses composed by others.

ছড়া[3] *n* **1** a number of things threaded together. a set of things threaded together; a string: হার ~. **2** a bunch; a cluster: কলার ~.

ছড়াছড়ি *n* **1** state of being scattered about in a negligent and careless manner; **2** excess; abundance. **3** wastage due to negligence and carelessness.

ছড়ানো *vt* **1** keep or throw in a disorderly manner: আসবাবপত্র ~. **2** stretch oneself: হাত পা ~. **3** scatter over: বীজ ~. **4** spread or extend over larger area: রোগ ~.

ছড়ি *n* **1** a walking stick; a cane: ~ ঘোরানো, brandish one's stick. **2** a young shoot with new leaves. **~বরদার** *n* an attendant; a servant.

ছতর [A] *n* portion of the body from the navel to the knee: ~ ঢাকা ফরজ.

ছত্র[১] *n* an umbrella. **~খান** *adj* spread out like an umbrella; scattered about. **~ দণ্ড** *n* a royal parasol and sceptre. **~ধর/ধরী** *n, adj* one who holds an umbrella over the head of a king; an umbrella-bearer. **~ পতি** *n* **1** a king; an emperor. **2** title of honour used before the name of Shivaji, the Marhatta king.

ছত্র[২] *n* **1** a line of prose writing. **2** a foot of a verse. **3** a row or line (as of soldiers). **~ভঙ্গ** *n* **1** breaking off in disorder; dispersion. **2** flight of an army in disorder and confusion; a rout; a retreat; a debacle. **~ভঙ্গ করা** *vt* put to flight; rout.

ছত্র[৩]=সত্র

ছত্রক, ছত্রাক *n* **1** plant without leaves and flowers growing on decaying matter, eg old wood; fungus. **2** fast-growing fungus of which some kinds are edible; mushroom.

ছত্রাক=ছত্রক

ছত্রাকার *adj* scattered on all sides in a disorderly manner; lying at sixes and sevens. **~ হওয়া** *vi* fall into disorder; be scattered all over.

ছত্রি *n* a cover or awning of a boat or cart. **~ দণ্ড** *n* a pole or rod used for fitting a mosquito net or the awning of a boat.

ছত্রিশ *n* , *adj* six and thirty; thirty-six.

ছত্রী[১] *n* an Indian caste of Kshatriya origin; a member of this caste.

ছত্রী[২] *adj* one with an umbrella on= (ছত্রধারী)

ছদ *n* **1** a leaf (of a tree). **2** a covering; a garment: পোষাক পরিচ্ছদ.

ছদকা=সদকা

ছদর=সদর

ছদ্ম *adj* feigned; simulated; disguised. **~নাম** *n* an assumed name; a pseudonym. **~বেশ** *n* an assumed appearance intended to deceive; a disguise. **~বেশ ধারণ করা** *vi* disguise oneself for the purposes of deception or concealment. **~ বেশী** *adj* appearing in disguise; disguised. **~বেশী লোক** *n* a person in disguise/ incognito. **~বেশে** *adv* in disguise; incognito.

ছন, ছোন *n* a kind of tall grass suitable as a thatching material.

ছনছন *int* (onom) denoting a feeling of physical indisposition. **শরীর ~ করা** *vi* feel indisposed/out of sorts.

ছন্দ[১] *n* **1** a rhythmic arrangement of syllables in verse according to some fixed scheme; poetical metre. **2** the rules of metre or versification; prosody. **~পতন/পাত** *n* a break or defect in the poetical metre; metrical irregularity.

ছন্দ[২] *n* **1** bent of mind; a leaning of the will; inclination; predilection; tendency; liking: ছন্দানুগমন, act of moving or working in one's own way; wilfulness; self-will. **2** act of serving another's will; subservience; subjection: ছন্দানুবর্তন, act of following another's will. **3** method; style; manner: বিভিন্ন ছন্দে, in various ways. **ছন্দানুগামী** *adj* wanton; wilful; not kept in due restraint. **ছন্দানুবর্তী** *adj* one who is at the beck and call of another; serving another's will/whim.

ছন্ন *adj* **1** covered; veiled; overcast. **2** removed; lost; ruined; annihilated. **~ছাড়া** *adj* having no shelter; homeless; vagabond; destitute. **~মতি** *adj* weakened or disordered in intellect; deranged; crazy.

ছফর=সফর

ছফেদ=সফেদ

ছবক=সবক

ছবর= সবর

ছবি[১] *n* **1** a glowing state; a flushed look; lustre: রবিচ্ছবি. **2** beauty; grace; show: মুখচ্ছবি.

ছবি[২] *n* **1** a painting; a picture; a portrait. **2** a figure; a diagram; a sketch; an illustration; a drawing. **3** a cinema show; a motion picture. **~ আঁকা** *vi, vt* draw or paint a picture. **~ তোলা** *vi, vt* take a snapshot/ photograph; photograph.

ছমছম int suggestive of a feeling of fear: ভয়ে গা ~ করছে, having an uncanny feeling of aeriness.

ছয় *n, adj* six.

ছয়লাব [P] *adj* **1** strewn with; partially covered with: নগরী কিনডারগার্টেনে ~ হয়ে গেছে, The city is honeycombed with kindergartens. **2** flooded; overflowing with/ abounding in: বিদেশী জিনিসে বাজার ~, The market is overflowing with foreign goods. **3** squandered; lost; wasted. **~ করা** *vt* **1** fill (sth) to excess. **2** cause (sth) to be wasted. **~ হওয়া** *vt* be overflooded with/abundant in.

ছরফরাজ=সরফরাজ

ছররা= ছটরা

ছরাৎ, সরাৎ, সড়াৎ *int* denoting the sound produced by something going down a glossy surface.

ছল *n* **1** that which deceives or is intended to deceive; an artifice practised (on sb); a deceptive trick; deception; fraud: ছলে বলে, by force or fraud. **2** the course of sth; a context; an occasion: কথাচ্ছলে, in the course of conversation. **3** an ostensible reason or motive; an excuse for doing sth different; a pretext; a plea: স্তুতির ছলে নিন্দা, a censure under the pretext of praising. **4** an assertion with intent to deceive; a pretension: রোগের ~ করা, pretend to be ill. **~চাতুরী** *n pl* tricks and deceptions. **~ছুতা** *n pl* pretexts and pretentious. ❑*adj* practising chicanery; tricky; deceitful.

ছলকানো *vt* (of liquids) flow over. **ছলকানি** *n* overflow. **ছলকে পড়া** *vi* be so full that the contents run over with a little stirring.

ছলচ্ছল *int* denoting the rippling or lapping of waves. ❑*adj* overflowing.

ছলছল *int* denoting the sound of water rippling on the shore. ❑*adj* **1** moist with tears: চক্ষু ~, eyes ready to burst into tears. **2** suffused with tears: ~ আঁখি, eyes filled with tears.

ছলনা *n* **1** a feigning to be what one is not; pretended goodness or sincerity; hypocrisy; insincerity; dissimulation; double-dealing. **2** the act of deceiving; deception; fraud; a fraudulent practice. **~ করা** *vt* put (one) under a delusion causing thereby an injury to (his) interest; practise deceit on; deceive. **ছলিত** *adj* deceived; cheated.

ছলা[১] *n* act of feigning without malice; something done for deception or mockery; a hoax; a practical joke. **~কলা** *n* tricks and artifices used to win one's favour/good-will.

ছলা[২] *vt* beguile (one) into; cheat; deceive; hoodwink.

ছলাৎ *int* denoting the splashing sound of overflowing or the sound of waves dashing against the shore.

ছা, ছাও *n* **1** the young of a bird or animal: পাখির ~. **2** an infant; a child. **~-পোষা** *adj* one burdened with the responsibility of rearing a good number of children on a small income: ~পোষা কেরানি.

ছাই *n* **1** powder that remains after the burning of firewood; ash. **2** a negligible or trashy thing; rubbish. **3** a meaningless affair; nothing: সে আমার ~ করবে, He can do no harm to me. **~ করা** *vt* **1** render (sth) fruitless; spoil; damage; mar. **2** do nothing. **~-চাপা আগুন** *n* **1** (lit) fire smouldering under ashes. **2** a suppressed feeling. **~পাঁশ, ~ভস্ম** *nn pl* rubbish; nonsense; triviality. **~ ফেলতে ভাঙা কুলো** ⇒ কুলো. **দূর হোক না ~** *int* expression of annoyance wishing to get rid of a trouble. **শত্রুর মুখে ~** a wish that the design of an enemy may remain unfulfilled.

ছাউনি[১] *n* **1** a permanent military station; a cantonment. **2** an observation post for defensive purposes; a military base; an outpost. **~ ফেলা** *vi* pitch a tent; encamp.

ছাউনি[২] *n* **1** a cover; a roofing; a thatch: খড়ের ~ **2** a canopy. **3** an awning for a boat or cart.

ছাও=ছা

ছাওয়া *vt* **1** cover a house or hut with a thatch; repair the thatch of a hut: ঘর ~. **2** spread or expand; be diffused through; pervade; overcast; overspread: আকাশ মেঘে ছেয়ে গেল, the sky is overcast with clouds. ❑*adj* covered. **~নো** *vt* cause to be covered: ঘর ~নো.

ছাওয়াল, ছাবাল *n* **1** an offspring; a son. **2** a child; an infant. ❑*adj* under-aged; very young.

ছাঁকনা, ছাঁকনি *n* a tool for filtration; a strainer: চায়ের ~, a tea strainer.

ছাঁকা *vt* separate waste or hard substance from a liquid with the help of a strainer; strain; filtrate: চা ~.

ছাঁচ *n* **1** form in which a thing is cast; a model; a mould; a casting matrix: পুতুলের ~. **2** a food item shaped in a mould: ক্ষীরের ~. **3** likeness; resemblance; similarity: একই ছাঁচে গড়া, made of the same mould.

ছাঁচি *adj* indigenous; genuine; pure; fresh. **~ কুমড়া** *n* the evergreen variety of the pumpkin. **~ পান** *n* a kind of fragrant betel leaves.

ছাঁট *n* **1** scraps of anything; cuttings; clippings; loppings. **2** a style of cutting: জামার ~. **~কাপড়** *n* small scraps of cloth; cut pieces.

ছাঁটা *vt* **1** cut with scissors; make short by cutting off the unnecessary portion: চুল ~. **2** remove the powdery portion from rice: চাউল ~. **~ই** *n* act of cutting off; act of excluding/removing: দল থেকে ~ই. **~ই করা** *vt* exclude; remove; retrench: চাকরি থেকে ~ই করা. **~ই প্রস্তাব** *n* a cut motion (as in the parliament). **~নো** *vt* cause to be but off; cause to be cleaned of the wastes or unnecessary portion.

ছাঁৎ *int* denoting a sudden sense of alarm or sth shocking or disturbing: বুকের ভিতর ~ করে ওঠা.

ছাগ, ছাগল *n* a he-goat; a male goat. **ছাগি, ছাগলি** *fem* a she-goat. **ছাগল দাড়ি** *n* a sparse beard, not dense or thick. **ছাগলাদ্য ঘৃত** *n* Ayurvedic medicine prepared from the fat of a castrated goat. **রামছাগল** *n* a big variety of goat with long ears, (fig) a fool.

ছাড় *n* **1** omission; exclusion: ~ পড়া. **2** act of allowing or permitting; consent: ~পত্র. **3** release (as from jail). **4** permit for unloading a ship. ~পত্র *n* a permit. ~ দেওয়া *vi, vt* release; let off; have a discount on; allow a discount on; discount. ~ পাওয়া *vi* be released; be set free.

ছাড়া *vt* **1** go away from; depart from; leave; quit: বাড়ি ~. **2** take off sth and put sth else on; change: কাপড় ~. **3** give up (a post, etc); resign; desert: দল ~. **4** drop (letters, etc) into a postbox; post: চিঠি ~. **5** have a respite or remission: জ্বর ~. **6** start moving: গাড়ি ছেড়েছে, The train has started; প্লেন ছেড়েছে, the plain has taken off. ~নো *vt* **1** cause to give up: নেশা ~নো. **2** take the skin off; peel off: খোসা ~নো. **3** drive away; cause to quit: ভূত ~নো. **4** obtain release: আসামি ~নো.

ছাতা[1], **ছাতি** *n* an umbrella.

ছাতা[2] *n* **1** a fungus; a mushroom. **2** spongy growth appearing upon moist surfaces; mould. **দাঁতের ~** *n* chalk-like substance deposited on the teeth; tartar. **ব্যাঙের ~** *n* a mashroom; a toadstool. ~ ধরা/পড়া *vi* get mouldy or musty. ❑*adj* mouldy; musty.

ছাতি[1] =ছাতা[1]

ছাতি[2] *n* **1** the chest; the width of the chest: বুকের ~. **2** (fig) courage; spirit; vivacity. ~ ফাটা *vi* be overwhelmed with thirst or sorrow. ~ ফোলানো *vi* **1** make a vain display of one's strength. **2** talk big; brag; bluster.

ছাতিম *n* a kind of tree branching into divisions like fingers; a seven-leaf tree.

ছাতু *n* ground barley or maize; flour made of barley, maize or pigeon-pea; meal. ~খোর *n* **1** one mainly living on barley-meal. **2** (derog) an upcountry Indian whose staple food is barley or maize.

ছাত্র one who is studying at an institution; a student; a pupil; a scholar. **ছাত্রী** *fem*. ~জীবন *n* the period during which one receives formal education; student life. **ছাত্রাবাস** *n* a boarding-house or residential hall for male students; a hostel. **ছাত্রীনিবাস** *n* a hostel or hall for the female students of an institution.

ছাদ *n* the roof or top covering of a building.

ছানা[1] *n* a milk-product gathered as a conglomerated mass by separating water by means of acid; posset: ~র মিষ্টি, sweets made of posset. ~র জল *n* whey. ~ কাটা *vi* turn milk into posset in the above-mentioned process.

ছানা[2] *vt* reduce (sth boiled or soft) into a paste by working with the hands; knead.

ছানা[3] *n* the young one of a bird or beast. ~পোনা *n pl* young ones. **কুকুর ~** *n* a pup; a puppy. **ছাগল~** *n* a kid. **বিড়াল~** *n* a kitten. **মুরগির ~** *n* a chick. **শৃগাল~** *n* a cub. **শূকর ~** *n* a pig. **সিংহের ~** *n* a whelp; a cub. **হরিণ~** *n* a fawn. **হাঁসের ~** *n* a duckling. **রাজহাঁসের ~** *n* a gosling.

ছানাবড়া *n* a kind of sweet made of posset. ❑*adj* large as the sweet of this name: চোখ ~ হওয়া, have one's eyes wide open with wonder; be struck with awe; be dumbfounded.

ছানি[1] *n* disease of the eye, in which the chrystalline lens is gradually shrouded obscuring the eyesight; cataract. ~ কাটানো *vi* have the cataract removed by a surgical operation. ~ পড়া *vi* be affected with cataract formation.

ছানি[2] [A] *n* prayer for the revision of a law case: ~ করা.

ছানি[3] *n* a sign with the hand or head; a beck.

ছানি[4] [U] *n* fodder for cattle.

ছাপ *n* **1** a mark; a print: পায়ের ~, a foot print. **2** a seal; a stamp: সিলমোহরের ~. ~ মারা *vt* seal; stamp.

ছাপরা, ছাপড়া *n* a thatched house; a hut.

ছাপা[1] *vt* publish sth in printed form; print (as a book) ❑*adj* printed. ❑*n* print; impression. ~খানা *n* a printing press; a publishing house. ~নো *vt* get sth printed.

ছাপা[2] *adj* suppressed; concealed; covered. ~নো *vt* conceal; hide.

ছাব্বিশ *n, adj* six and twenty. **ছাব্বিশে** *n* the twenty sixth day of a month.

ছায়া *n* **1** shade produced by the interception of light. **2** shadow of a person or object. **3** similarity; semblance; resemblance; image. **4** a haven; a refuge; a shelter: ছত্র~. ~ মাড়ানো *vt* give company to one. ~ না মাড়ানো *vt* shun one's company. ~র ন্যায় like a shadow or inseparable companion. ~চিত্র *n* a cinema film. ~চ্ছন্ন *adj* abounding in shade; affording shade; shady; shadowy. ~তরু *n* **1** a large tree affording abundant shade. **2** a banyan tree. ~দেহ *n* an incorporeal figure; a phantom; a ghost. ~নট *n* a musical mode. ~পথ *n* the long luminous track in the heavens, formed by a multitude of stars; the Milky Way; the Galaxy. ~ মণ্ডপ *n* a place in the open covered by a canopy.

ছার *n* **1** the remains of firewood after burning; ashes. **2** an insignificant or contemptible person: তুমি কোন ~. **3** a trashy thing; rubbish. **4** ruin; destruction. ❑*adj* vile; hateful; contemptible; abominable. ~কপাল *n* bad luck; misfortune. ~কপালে *adj* unlucky; unfortunate. ~কপালী *fem*.

ছারখার, ছারেখার *adj* laid waste; destroyed; desolated. ❑*n* ruin; destruction; desolation. **ছারখার করা** *vt* reduce to ashes; raze to the ground. **ছারেখারে যাওয়া** *vi* go to rack and ruin.

ছাল *n* **1** the natural outer coating of animals; skin; hide. **2** the outer rind of a tree; bark. **3** the skin of a fruit; peel.

ছালন, ছালুন *n* spiced preparation of fish or meat with or without vegetables; curry.

ছালা *n* a sack; a gunny bag.

ছি, ছিঃ *int* fie! for shame. **ছি ছি করা** *vi vt* cry shame on; condemn.

ছিঁচকা[১], **ছিঁচকে**[১] *n* a pin of metal for cleansing the wooden pipe of a hookah; a skewer.

ছিঁচকা[২], **ছিঁচকে**[২] *adj* one who steals petty things: ~ চোর, a pilferer.

ছিচকাঁদুনে *adj* in the habit of weeping; prone to weeping at triffles; maudlin. **ছিচকাঁদুনি** *fem*.

ছিঁড়া=ছেঁড়া

ছিট[১] *n* **1** a drop of liquid; a spot of colour; a blob: কালির ~. **2** cotton cloth with designs of colour; chintz: ~ কাপড়. **3** a bit of craziness: তার মাথায় ~ আছে. **4** a sign; a symptom: পাগলামির ~.

ছিট[২] *n* a fragment; a piece; a portion. ❑*adj* detached; separate: ~মহল, a holding lying detached from the parent estate; an enclave.

ছিটকানো *vi vt* **1** (of liquids) be dashed about as a result of being struck, or violently shaken: ছিটকে পড়া, splash up or about. **2** sprinkle a liquid (on); throw or scatter liquid in small particles: রাস্তায় পানি ~, sprinkle water on the road.

ছিটকিনি *n* a bar (of a door) or anything which fastens or secures; a bolt; a hook.

ছিটা, ছিটে *n* **1** a globule of liquid or a solid particle; a very small quantity: এক ~ নুন, a pinch of salt. **2** a splash or sprinklings from the rains: বৃষ্টির ~.**3** a spot of dirt; a patch of colour: কাদার/কালির ~.**4** a hail of shot made by firing a cluster of small iron balls from a gun: ~ গুলি, grape-shot. ~ **ছিটি** *n* act of sprinkling (water, etc) at one another. ~ **পাড়া** *vt* sprinkle the body with water sanctified by means of uttering an incantation. ~ **ফোঁটা** *n* very small quantity; tit-bits. ~ **বেড়া** *n* wall or fence made of bamboo laths plastered with mud. ~ **বোনা** *vt* scatter seeds without tilling the soil. **কাটা ঘায়ে নুনের ছিটা** ⇒ কাটা.

ছিটানো *vt* **1** throw a shower of liquid (on a surface); sprinkle; spray: গোলাপ পানি ~. **2** throw (solid particles) in different directions; scatter; spread: বীজ ~.

ছিতম, সিতম *n* oppression; tyranny; coercion.

ছিদর *adj* crafty; cunning; sly.

ছিদ্যমান *adj* in the process of being cut up or dissected.

ছিদ্র **1** a narrow opening in a solid body; a hole; a pore; a perforation; a slot; a slit; a cavity. **2** a fault; a failure; a shortcoming: পরের ~ অন্বেষণ. ~ **করা** *vt* make a hole; bore; perforate. ~ **খুঁজে বেড়ানো** *vt* try to find fault (with). ~**দর্শী** *adj* making unnecessary complaints against; finding fault with others. **ছিদ্রানুসন্ধান, ছিদ্রান্বেষণ** *n* act of looking for others' weak points/faults. **ছিদ্রানুসন্ধানী, ছিদ্রান্বেষী** *adj* picking holes in another's coat; making unwarranted criticisms. **ছিদ্রানুসন্ধান/ছিদ্রান্বেষণ করা** *vt* try to find fault (with).

ছিদ্রিত *adj* bored or penetrated through; pierced with a pointed instrument; perforated.

ছিনতাই [H] *n* **1** act of snatching away goods or valuables from a person on way or on board a vehicle. **2** use of force or threat of force by a person or persons against the crew on board an aircraft to change the direction/ destination or to achieve some other ends; hijacking: বিমান ~. ~ **করা** *vt* hijack. ~**কারী** *n* a hijacker.

ছিনা[১] [P] *n* the chest; the width of the chest. ~-ব-~ *adv* (of oral transmission of some message or maxim) from person to person; from one generation to the next.

ছিনা[২], **ছিনে** *adj* slender; lean; thin: ~ গড়ন. ~ **জোঁক** *n* a thin species of leech which is a very obstinate sticker. (fig) a very pertinacious person.

ছিনানো *vt* snatch away; seize hastily or abruptly. **ছিনিয়ে নেওয়া** *vt* take away or seize forcibly. ❑*adj* appropriated by forcible seizure.

ছিনাল *n* **1** a woman openly given to lewdness; a prostitute; a harlot; a whore. **2** a woman who flirts with many people; a vain triffling woman; a flirt; a coquette. **ছিনালিপনা** *n* the arts of a coquette; coquetry. **ছিনালি** *n* coquetry; flirtation. ~ **করা** *n* triffle in love; flirt; coquet.

ছিনিমিনি *n* **1** a children's game in which flat stones are made to skip along water; the game of ducks and drakes. **2** (fig) act of spending one's money lavishly and wastefully. ~ **খেলা** *vt* play ducks and drakes with one's money; squander; waste.

ছিন্ন *adj* **1** torn apart; split up; rent: ~ বস্ত্র. **2** cut off; lopped off; severed: ~ মস্তক. **3** pulled up; uprooted: ~মূল. **4** disconnected; detached; separated; removed; freed: শৃঙ্খল ~. ~ **করা** *vt* tear; cut off; sever; uproot; remove: সম্পর্ক ~ করা, sever one's connection with. ~**দ্বৈধ** *adj* freed from doubt or hesitation; confirmed; convinced. ~**পক্ষ** *adj* (of a bird) having the wings cut off. ~**প্রায়** *adj* almost torn apart. ~**বিচ্ছিন্ন** *adj* scattered about. ~**ভিন্ন** *adj* **1** in a mess; in disorder and confusion. **2** scattered about. ~**মস্তক** *adj* having the head cut off; beheaded; decapitated. ~**মস্তা** *n* a truncated manifestation of Hindu Goddess Durga. ~**মূল**

adj uprooted; displaced: ~মূল মানুষ, displaced people; floating poputation. ছিন্না *adj fem* of ~. ❑*n* a prostitute; a harlot.

ছিপ[১], সিপ *n* a kind of long and narrow-bodied boat that moves very fast.

ছিপ[২] *n* a fishing rod.

ছিপছিপে *adj* of a tall slender stature. ~ **গড়ন** *n* slim figure.

ছিপি *n* a stopple of a bottle, etc usually made of the bark of a species of oak tree; a cork. ~ **আঁটা** *vt* stopple; cork.

ছিবড়া, ছিবড়ে *n* the rough fibres of a fruit, etc, that remain after being sucked; the remainder of anything after being chewed out.

ছিম=শিম

ছিমছাম *adj* **1** neat in dress; trim; spruce. **2** neat and clean; orderly; tidy: ~ সংসার.

ছিয়াত্তর *n, adj* six and seventy; seventy-six.

ছিয়ানব্বই *n, adj* six and ninety; ninety-six.

ছিয়াশি *n, adj* six and eighty; eighty-six.

ছিরি *n* **1** beauty; grace; elegance. **2** form; appearance. **3** (sarcas) ugliness: আহা কি ~. **4** mode or way (of living): সংসারের ~ ফিরে আসবে. ~**ছাঁদ** *n* beauty and gracefulness.

ছিলকা, ছিলকে *n* **1** a piece; a fragment. **2** the bark of a tree. **3** the skin of a fruit. **4** the skin of animals.

ছিলা *n* the string of a bow; a bow-string.

ছিলাম, ছিলেম *vi pt* of 'am' and 'are' in the 1st person: আমি ~. I was; আমরা ~, we were.

ছিলিম, ছিলুম [H] *n* **1** the bowl of a hookah that contains and burns the tobacco; a chillum. **2** the quantity of tobacco or hemp that may be smoked at one time: এক ~ তামাক, a chillumful of tobacco. ~**চি** *n* the top portion of the wooden rod of a hookah (hubble-bubble) where the bowl or chillum is placed; chillum-holder.

ছিলে, ছিলা *vi pt* of 'are' in the 2nd person: তুমি/তোমরা ~, you were.

ছিষ্টি=সৃষ্টি

ছুঁই ছুঁই *int* indicating the state of a thing about to touch or reach sth: বয়স ১৬ ~ করছে, age is nearing 16.

ছুঁচ, সুচ *n* a sewing needle. ~ **ফুটানো** *vi* **1** bore with a needle. **2** (fig) make a cutting remark.

ছুঁচা, ছুঁচো **1** a small, dark-grey, fur-covered burrowing animal; the mole; the musk-rat. **2** (fig) a greedy person. **3** a mean and detestable person. ~**মি** *n* meanness; greediness; baseness; mischievousness. ~ **মেরে হাত গন্ধ করা** (fig) sue a beggar and get a louse. ~**র কেত্তন** (fig) a disgusting noise (as that made by a musk-rat).

ছুঁচালো *adj* sharp-pointed like needle; tapering to a sharp point.

ছুঁড়ি *n fem* (derog) a girl; a lass. **ওঠ ~ তোর বিয়ে** (fig) a call for an important action in haste or without elaborate preparation. ছোঁড়া *mas.*

ছুঁৎ, ছুঁত *n* **1** impurity caused by physical contact (according to Hindu belief). **2** touch; physical contact. **3** a defect; a fault. ~ **বাই** *n* extreme obedience to the cult of untouchability; a sort of mania caused by such obedience: ~বাই রোগ. ~**মার্গ** *n* the Hindu system of untouchability.

ছুকরি *n fem* (in contempt) an under-aged girl; a lass. **ছোকড়া** *mas.*

ছুছুন্দরী *n, fem* a female musk-rat; a she-mole. *mas* চুন্দর.

ছুট[১] *n* **1** what has been discarded/cast off. **2** omission; that which is omitted. ❑*adj* discarded; discharged; cast off.

ছুট[২] *n* **1** a string or ribbon for dressing hair. **2** a wearing cloth; a sari.

ছুট[৩] temporary intermission; recess; respite; leisure; relief; exemption: ~ পাওয়া.

ছুট[৪] *n* act of running; a run: ~ দেওয়া. ~ **দেওয়া,** ~ **মারা** *vi* run off. **এক ছুটে** *adv* in a run; in a breath.

ছুটকা/ছুটকো *adj* **1** having strayed; stray. **2** small and paltry: ~ কাজ. ~**-ছাটকা** *adj* lying here and there not important; not countable.

ছুটকি, ছুটকী [H] (colloq) *adj* the younger or youngest (cf বড়কি).

ছুটকো⇒ছুটকা

ছুটা[১]=ছোটা[১]

ছুটা[২] (colloq) ❑*adj* **1** not permanent; temporary: ছুটা কাজ. **2** (also *adv*) for only a part of the working day; part-time.

ছুটি *n* **1** time during which work or business is suspended; recess; leisure; vacant time. **2** termination or break-up of a day's routine work: পাঁচটায় ~. **3** suspension of routine work on account of solemn occasions or festivals; holiday; vacation: ঈদের ~; রোজার ~. **4**. number of days during which an employer enjoys leave as per rules: নৈমিত্তিক ~, casual leave: অর্জিত ~, earned leave. ~ **পাওয়া** *vi* get a leave of absence from duty. ~ **লওয়া** *vi* take leave of absence.

ছুড়া=ছোড়া

ছুড়ি=ছুড়ি

ছুত=ছুঁৎ

ছুতা, ছুতো *n* **1** an ostensible reason or motive; a pretext; a plea; an excuse. **2** a fault or failure; an omission: ~ ধরা. **3** a triffling cause; a shallow pretext. **~নাতা, ছল~** *n* a lame excuse.

ছুতার, ছুতোর *n* **1** one who works in timber; a carpenter. **2** a surname among Hindus.

ছুতো=ছুতা

ছুতোর=ছুতার

ছুরত, ছুরৎ=সুরত

ছুরি, ছুরিকা, ছুরী *n* a cutting instrument consisting of blade attached to a handle; a knife; a pen-knife. **2** a pointed and usually two-edged knife used as a weapon; a dagger. **~ মারা** *vi, vt* aim a blow (at sb) with a knife; pierce or wound (one) with a knife; stab (one) to death. **গলায় ~ দেওয়া** *vt* **1** cut one's throat. **2** (fig) cause a great harm to (one) by deception. **মিছরির ~** *n* person with a honeyed totgue and a mischievous mind.

ছুলা, ছোলা *vt* **1** strip off (as bark or rind); peel off (as a banana). **2** rub with sth hard; clean by a sharp edge; scrape: জিভ ~. ❑*adj* stripped off; peeled off; scraped. ❑*n* act of stripping/peeling/scraping. **~নো** *vt* cause to peel.

ছুলি *n* a kind of skin disease; an irritable eruption upon the skin, resembling a nettle sting; nettle-rash; urticaria.

ছে *n* **1** a slice or cutting of sth : কাঠের ~, a chip of wood. **2** recess; interval; leisure; rest. **~ দেওয়া** *vt* cut into pieces.

ছেইছেই *int* suggestive of slighting, neglecting or treating with contempt: দূর দূর ~ করা.

ছেও=ছে

ছেঁক[১]=সেক

ছেঁক[২], ছ্যাঁকা *int* suggesting the sound produced by the fall of sth into hot oil.

ছেঁকা[১] *n* a burning or searing by a hot iron; cauterization. **~ দেওয়া** *vt* burn with a hot iron; cauterize.

ছেঁকা[২] *vt* singe lightly in oil or ghee.

ছেঁকে ধরা⇒ছাঁকা

ছেঁচড়, ছ্যাঁচড়, ছ্যাঁচড়া *adj* **1** void of honesty; having no scruples; dishonest; knavish; fraudulent; perfidious. **2** unwilling to pay one's dues. ❑*n a* base or unscrupulous person; a loafer; a knave; a cheat. **ছেঁচড়ামি** *n* unscrupulousness; knavery; cheating.

ছেঁচড়ানো *vt* drag or draw along the ground; haul along with considerable effort. **ছেঁচড়ানি** *n* act of dragging.

ছেঁচা *vt* pound or thrash: পান ~. **~নো** *vt* cause to be pounded or thrashed.

ছেঁড়া, ছিঁড়া *vt* **1** pull apart; tear; rend: জামা ~.**2** pick or gather; pluck: ফুল ~. **3** pull up; tear off: চুল ~. **4** cut off; detach: মুণ্ড ~. ❑*adj* torn; rent; plucked; pulled up; cut off: ~ কাপড়, torn cloth.

ছেঁদা *n* a hole; an opening; a perforation; an eyelet. **~ করা** *vi, vt* bore a hole; perforate.

ছেকড়া, ছ্যাকড়া, ছ্যাকরা *n* a horse-drawn coach or carriage that may be hired; a hackney carriage.

ছেচল্লিশ *n, adj* six and forty; forty-six.

ছেদ *n* **1** act of cutting off or severing: মুণ্ডচ্ছেদ. **2** a stop; a pause; a punctuation mark. **3** cessation; termination; stoppage. **4** a part; a chapter: পরিচ্ছেদ. **~ পড়া** *vi* cease; come to an end; be stopped. **~ক** *adj* one who or that which cuts or severs. ❑*n* a cutter; a divider. **~ন** *n* act of cutting/severing. **~নী** *n* a tool for cutting; a cutter. **~নীয়, ছেদ্য** *adj* to be cut or cleaved. **ছেদিত** *adj* cut; cleft; severed.

ছেনি *n* **1** a tool for cutting stone or metal; a chisel. **2** a sickle or scythe used in harvesting.

ছেপারা ⇒ সিপারা

ছেব [P] *n* the fruit of the apple-tree; apple.

ছেবলা ⇒ ছ্যাবলা

ছেমড়া *n* **1** an orphan. **2** (derog) a boy. **ছেমড়ি** *fem.*

ছেরেফ⇒সেরেফ

ছেলে *n* **1** a boy; a lad; a male child or baby. **2** a son: রাজার ~. **3** a person: বেটা ~, মেয়ে ~. **~খেলা** *n* **1** an irresponsible frolic; a jolly joking action. **2** something as easy as a child's play. **~খেলা করা** *vi, vt* triffle with (sth). **~-ছোকরা** [A সোগরা=ছোট] *n pl* children and young people. **~ধরা** *n* a child-lifter. **~পিলে, ~পেলে** *n pl* **1** children. **2** sons and daughters. **~বেলা** *n* childhood; infancy. **~ মানুষ** *adj* **1** tender-aged; minor. **2** inexperienced. **~মানুষি,** *n* unbecoming levity; frivolousness; childishness. **~মেয়ে** *n pl* **1** boys and girls; children. **2** sons and daughters. **বেটা~** *n* men. **মেয়ে~** *n* women.

ছেষট্টি *n, adj* six and sixty; sixty-six.

ছৈ ⇒ ছই

ছোঁ *n* (of a bird of prey) a sudden downward swoop with intent to seize; pounce. **~ মারা** *vt* pounce upon.

ছোঁচা *adj* ravenously selfish and immodest in eating; ludicrously eager for eating. **~মি** *n* ludicrous greed for food.

ছোঁচানো *vt* cause to clean after defecation.

ছোঁড়া *n* (derog) *n* a boy; a chap; a young fellow.

ছোঁয়া *vt* touch with the hand. ❑*n* act of touching; touch: ~ লাগা. ❑*adj* **1** touched; contacted: ~ খাবার. **2** touching; going to meet: আকাশ-~ দালান. **~চ** *n* **1** a touch or contact or the influence of a touch/contact: আধুনিকতার ~চ

লেগেছে. 2 harmful contagion; poisonous emanation; infection. ~চে *adj* catching, affecting others by contact; contagious: ~চে রোগ, contagious disease. ~ছুয়ি *n* 1 repeated touching. 2 touching each other; mutual touching. 3 impurity caused by the touch of the untouchable (according to the cult of untouchability). ~লেপা *n* 1 contact of the untouchable. 2 contactile impurity.

ছোকরা [A] *n* 1 (derog) a young man. 2 a boy-servant. ❑*adj* underage; immature; inexperienced.

ছোট, ছোটো *adj* 1 younger; youngest: ~ ভাই. 2 comparatively young: সে আমার ~. 3 short; small; tiny: ~ আকার. 4 base; mean; low: ~ মন. 5 lowly; socially depressed: ~ জাত. 6 lower in status or power: ~ বউ, ~ আদালত. **~খাটো** *adj* 1 trivial; insignificant; triffling: ছোটখাটো ব্যাপার. ২ not very elaborate/detailed/ long: ছোটখাটো বক্তৃতা. 3 small, not spacious: ছোটখাটো ঘর. 4 short-statured: ছোটখাটো মানুষটি. **~ মুখে বড়ো কথা** (prov) too big a talk for a child. **~ লোক** *n* 1 a bulgar or mean fellow. 2 a rough or uncivil person. 3 person belonging to a depressed class. **~লোকি** *n* contemptible conduct; meanness. ❑*adj* befitting a mean fellow.

ছোটা[1]**, ছুটা** *vi* 1 run fast; take part in a race: ঘোড়া ~. 2 begin to blow; go on blowing: হাওয়া ~. 3 pass out; issue forth; ooze: রক্ত ~. 4 cease; terminate: ঘুম ~, be awake; নেশা ~ get over the intoxication. 5 emit the moisture of the body through skin; perspire; sweat: ঘাম ~. **~ছুটি** *n* 1 run about from one place to another. 2 the state of being busy. **~নো** *vt* cause to run or flow with speed; emit; discharge; cause to cease or terminate. **মন ~** *vi* feel a strong desire to visit sb/sth. **মুখ ~** *vi* go on talking at a stretch.

ছোটা[2] *n* sheathing stalks of a plaintain tree or anything of the kind used as a string.

ছোটো=ছোট

ছোট্ট *adj* 1 very small; little; tiny: ~ মেয়ে. 2 very humble; very modest: ~ একটা অনুরোধ.

ছোড়া, ছুড়া *vt* 1 strike with sth thrown; pelt; hurl; throw: ঢিল ~. 2 discharge (firearms); throw missiles; fire; shoot: গুলি ~, তীর ~, বন্দুক ~. 3 stretch out; spread: হাত-পা ~. **ছুঁড়ে মারা** *vt* pelt (one) with; hurl (sth) at.

ছোপ *n* 1 a stain; a spot: ~ লাগা, take stains; become stained. 2 a coating or smearing; a tint; a tinge; a point. **ছোপানো** *vi* stain, dye (as a piece of cloth. ❑*adj* stained; dyed.

ছোবড়া *n* 1 the shell or outside covering of some fruits (as a coconut). 2 fibre of the dried shells of coconut, used for making ropes, matting, etc; coconut fibre; coir.

ছোবল *n* 1 act of snapping (at) (sth); a sudden attempt to snatch with the teeth; a snap. 2 a sudden downward swoop to seize sth; a pounce. **~ মারা** *vt* snap (at); pounce (upon). সাপের ~ a snap.

ছোবা *n* coconut fibre; coir.

ছোরা *n* a sharp-pointed double-edged knife; a dagger. **~ মারা** *vt, vi* stab.

ছোলা[1]= ছুলা

ছোলা[2] *n* gram; chick-pea.

ছ্যাঁক=ছেঁক

ছ্যাঁচড়=ছেঁচড়

ছ্যাকড়া=ছেকড়া

ছ্যাপ *n* the moist matter ejected from the mouth; saliva; spittle. **~ ফেলা** *vi* spit.

ছ্যাবলা *adj* 1 having a puerile character; frivolous; boyish; childish. 2 given to much talking; garrulous; talkative. **~মি** *n* lightness of character; frivolous act or utterance. **~মি করা** *vi* behave in a frivolous manner; indulge in frivolities.

জ[1] *n* the eighth consonant of the Bengali alphabet. It is a palato-alveolar unaspirated voiced plosive sound. In the eastern parts of Bangladesh it is sometimes pronounced as a fricative sound. The local people of Dhaka also pronounce it as an affricate sound.

জ[2] *n* a measure of length equel to $\frac{1}{4}$ inch prevalent in ancient India.

জ[3] *adj* (used as suff) born of; produced in or by: দেশজ, জলজ, শিল্পজ.

জই *n* a kind of cereal; oat.

জইফ [A] *adj* weak; feeble; infirm; frail.

জউ *n* a resinous substance produced by insects on trees; lac. **~ ঘর** *n* house built with lac.

জও *n* a species of grain used specially for making malt; barley.

জওজ, যওজ [A] *n* the consort of a woman; a husband. **জওজিয়ত** *n* the status of being one's husband.

জওয়ান [P] *n* 1 a young man. 2 a strong and stout person. ❑*adj* 1 grown to manhood/ youthful. 2 strong; stout; robust. **জওয়ানি** *n* 1 youth; youthful age. 2 state or quality of being young. 3 the spirit and vigour befitting a young man.

জওয়াব=জবাব

জওহর [A] *n* precious stone or jewel (*pl* জওহেরাত).

জং [P] *n* reddish-brown coating or fungus formed on iron exposed to moisture; rust. ~ **ধরা** *vi* rust; become rusty. ~-**ধরা** *adj* rusty; rusted: ~-ধরা লোহা, rusty iron.

জংলা, জঙ্গলা *adj* **1** full of bushes; bushy. **2** born in state of nature; wild: ~ কচু. **3** having a wild nature; uncivilized; rude.

জংলি, জঙ্গলী [P] *adj* **1** living in a state of nature; dwelling in a forest; wild; uncivil; ill-mannered: ~ জাতি, a wild/aboriginal race.

জখম [P] *n* **1** a wound; a sore; an ulcer. **2** a hurt or damage done to a man's person; an injury. ~ **করা** *vi, vt* wound; injure; hurt. **জখমি** *adj* **1** wounded; injured. **2** relating to wounds.

জগ– *n* (in compounds) the world; the universe: ~জন the people of the world. ~**জীবন** *adj* life to the world. □*n* the air which we breathe.

জগ [E] *n* a vessel for water usually with a handle; a jug.

জগজ্জননী *n* the mother of the world; an appellation of goddess Durga.

জগজ্জয়ী *adj* world-conquering.

জগঝম্প *n* **1** a kettle-drum. **2** a war-drum of ancient time.

জগৎ *n* **1** the earth; the universe; the world. **2** a human society: সভ্য~. **3** a sphere or field of activity: কাব্য~. **4** one's own immediate or familiar environs: মনো~. ~-**কর্তা** *n* the Lord of the universe; Allah. ~-**কারণ** *n* the cause or source of the universe; the Creator. ~**পিতা**, ~**পতি** *n* the Creator, Nourisher and Sustainer of the universe; Allah. ~-**সংসার** *n* the whole world. ~**স্রষ্টা** *n* Creator of the universe.

জগতি *n* a throne.

জগতী *n* **1** *fem* the earth. **2** *pl* the whole creation on earth. ~-**তল** *n* the surface of the earth.

জগদম্বা [জগৎ+অম্বা] *n* **1** the mother of the world, an appellation of Hindu goddess Durga.

জগদীশ, জগদীশ্বর [জগৎ+ঈশ, ঈশ্বর] *n* the Lord of the world; God.

জগদ্গুরু [জগৎ+গুরু] *n* the teacher of the world; God.

জগদ্দল *adj* **1** (lit) weighing heavily on the universe. **2** extremely heavy; too heavy to be displaced. **3** most oppressive: ~ পাথর, an extremely heavy burden.

জগদ্ধাত্রী *n* one who nourishes the earth, an appellation of Durga.

জগদ্বন্ধু, জগবন্ধু *n* **1** the friend and benefactor of the whole world. **2** God. **3** the sun.

জগদ্বাসী [জগৎ+বাসী] *adj, n* dwelling on earth; people inhabiting the earth.

জগদ্বিখ্যাত [জগৎ+বিখ্যাত] *adj* celebrated throughout the world.

জগদ্ব্যাপী *adj* spread over the world; world-wide.

জগন্নাথ [জগৎ+নাথ] *n* **1** the Lord of the universe; God. **2** Hindu god Vishnu or his avatar. **3** the presiding deity of the famous temple at Puri in India; Juggernaut. ~ **ক্ষেত্র** *n* site of the famous temple of Juggernaut at Puri in India.

জগন্নিবাস [জগৎ+নিবাস] *n* **1** one who is the receptacle or container of the universe. **2** the Supreme Soul/Being. **3** Hindu god Vishnu.

জগন্মণ্ডল [জগৎ+মণ্ডল] *n* **1** the earth; the world. **2** the universe.

জগন্ময় [জগৎ+ময়] *adj* pervading the whole universe; existing everywhere at the same time; ubiquitous. **জগন্ময়ী** *fem*.

জগন্মাতা [জগৎ+মাতা] *n fem* the Supreme Being viewed as Mother of the world according to Hindu philosophy.

জগন্মোহন, জগমোহন [জগৎ+মোহন] *adj n* one who captivates or charms the whole world. **জগন্মোহিনী** *fem*.

জগাই–মাধাই *n* **1** Jogai and Madhai, the two notorious sons of a Brahmin of Nabadwip. **2** (fig) one who, having gone astray, at last returns to the path of righteousness.

জগাখিচুড়ি *n* **1** a food item of rice cooked with various kinds of vegetables; a hodge-podge; a hotch-potch. **2** a medley of various odd things; a mess.

জগাতি [A] *n* **1** a collector of tolls and taxes. **2** dangers and difficulties; hindrances.

জঘন *n* **1** the lower part of a woman's abdomen. **2** the waist. **3** the back side of a woman's hip; the loins.

জঘন্য *adj* **1** abounding in filth; filthy; dirty; foul; nasty; obscene. **2** abominable; loathsome; detestable; hateful. **3** vile; base; mean; contemptible. ~**তা** *n*.

জঙ, জঙ্গ=জং

জঙ্গ[1]**, জংগ** [P] *n* **1** a contest between nations or parties carried on by force of arms; a battle; a war. **2** a tumultuous brawl; a noisy quarrel. ~ **ডিঙা** *n* a battle ship; warship. ~-**নামা** *n* **1** an account of a battle. **2** a book on warfare and bravery in Bengali. ~**বাজ** *adj, n* skilled in fighting; a brave warrior; a war-lord. ~ **বাহাদুর** *adj* skilled in warfare; warlike; martial. ~ **বাহাদুরি** *n* military tactics; art of warfare; strategies.

জঙ্গ[2]=জং

জঙ্গম *adj* **1** having the power of locomotion; mobile; movable; dynamic. **2** living; lively;

animate. ~তা *n* **1** state of being mobile; susceptibility of motion; mobility. **2** changeable; fickle.

জঙ্গল [P] *n* **1** an extensive wood; a forest; a jungle. **2** uncultivated land with plants and herbs. **3** weeds; bushes; shrubs. **~ বাড়ি, ~বুরি তালুক** *n* forest estate let out to tenants for clearing and cultivation. **জঙ্গলা** *adj* full of bushes and shrubs; bushy; wild.

জঙ্গাল, জাঙ্গাল *n* **1** a dam; an embankment. **2** a bridge over a river or canal. **3** ridges of earth marking the boundaries of agricultural plots. **4** a way; a path.

জঙ্গি, জঙ্গী [P] *adj* **1** of or concerning an army or war; military: ~ তৎপরতা, military activities. **2** skilled in warfare; warlike: ~ লোক. ❑*n* a soldier; a warrior. **~ জাহাজ** *n* a battle ship; a man-of-war. **~ বিমান** *n* a fighter-plane; a fighter. **~ লাট** [~+Lord] *n* the Commander-in-Chief of British India.

জঙ্ঘা *n* part of the leg between the knee and the ankle; shin-bone; shank.

জজ [E] *n* a civil officer who hears and decides cases in a law court; a judge; a justice. **জজিয়তি, ~গিরি** *n* the office or function of a judge; judgeship.

জজবা, জযবা [A] *n* in the exalted state of feeling; excessive joy; extreme delight; a state of ecstasy: পীর সাহেবের ~ এলো.

জজিরা [A] *n* a landmass bound by water on three sides; a peninsula. **~তুল আরব** *n* the Arabian peninsula.

জঞ্জাল [H] *n* **1** refuse; rubbish, debris; trash. **2** wild plant that hinders the growth of cultivated plants; weeds. **3** (fig) a condition of difficulty; a trouble; a fix. **4** (fig) an unwanted and troublesome person. **জঞ্জালে** *adj* complex; intricate; confused.

জট *n* **1** matted or clotted hair. **2** a confused knot of threads, etc; a tangle. **3** aerial root of a banyan tree. **4** a confused state of mind; an intricate state of a problem. **~ বাঁধা** *vi* get matted/clotted/tangled. **~ পাকানো/বাঁধানো** *vi* get matted/ tangled; become complicated/complex.

জটলা *n* **1** a gathering of a number of people talking and discussing in a leisurely way. **2** a crowd; a throng. **~ করা**. *vi* **1** throng together. **2** make a clique.

জটা *n* **1** matted or clotted hair: **~জাল**. **2** the long thick hair on the neck of a lion or horse; mane; an aerial or hanging root of a tree: বটগাছের ~. **~জাল, ~জুট** *n* mass of matted locks. **~ধর, ~ধারী** *adj* having matted hair. ❑*n* an appellation of Shiva. **~ধরা, ~ধারিণী** *fem*. **~বল্কল** *n pl* matted hair and the bark of a tree (as worn by ascetics). **~মাংসী** *n* **1** an aromatic plant; spikenard. **~ল** *adj* **1** having matted hair. **2** having aerial or hanging roots. **3** the banyan tree. **4** the lion.

জটায়ু *n* kind of bird spoken of in the Ramayana.

জটিল *adj* **1** hard to understand; abstruse; unintelligible: ~ তত্ত্ব. **2** difficult to disentangle; intricate; complicated: ~ প্রশ্ন. **3** mixed together; muddled; confused: ~ ব্যাপার. **4** composed of two or more ingredients; compound: ~ সংখ্যা, a complex number. **জটিলা** *adj fem* **1** mischievously shrewd. **2** ever ready in finding faults with daughters-in-law; quarrelsome. **3** name of the mother-in-law of Radhika. **~তা** *n* complexity; intricacy; state of confusion.

জটী *adj* **1** having matted hair or mane. **2** having aerial roots. ❑*n* **1** one with matted hair. **2** the banyan tree. **3** the lion.

জটুল *n* natural mark on the body; a birth-mark; a naevus; a mole.

জটে, জটিয়া *adj* covered with matted or clotted hair. **জটেবুড়ি** *n* **1** old woman with clotted hair. **2** (fig) something real or imaginary that causes terror; bugbear (also জুজু বুড়ি).

জঠর *n* **1** the belly; the abdomen. **2** the stomach. **3** the womb; the uterus. **~ জ্বালা** *n* pangs of hunger. **~বাস** *n* stay in the mother's womb; embryonic stage. **~ যন্ত্রণা** *n* travail or anguish of travail in childbirth. **~স্থ** *adj* existing in the womb. **জঠরাগ্নি, জঠরানল** *n* **1** (fig) digestive fluid; gastric juice. **2** hunger. **জঠরানল নিবৃত্তি করা** *vi* satisfy one's hunger.

জড়[1] *adj* **1** unable to move itself or resist motion; inanimate; inert; lifeless: ~ পদার্থ, inanimate object. **2** produced by elements; elemental; material; physical; natural: ~ জগৎ, material world. **3** inactive; effortless. **4** destitute of sense; insensate; stupid; irrational. **5** affected with an illusion; stupefied; bewitched. ❑*n* **1** an extremely foolish and weak-minded person. **2** an illiterate and ignorant person. **3** substance or material of which physical objects are made; matter: জড়ের তিন অবস্থা. **~ক্রিয়** *adj* not quick; sluggish; lazy; slothful; inert. **~ জগৎ** *n* the inanimate/material/physical world. **~তা, ~ত্ব** *n* **1** absence of life or animation; the state of being inanimate; inanimateness. **2** inactivity; inertia; lethargy; indolence. **3** the condition of being numb or torpid; numbness; torpidity. **4** foolishness; dullness; idiocy. **~ পদার্থ** *n* inanimate object; matter. **~পিণ্ড** *n* **1** a conglomerated mass of matter. **2** (fig) an inactive or indolent person. **~ পুত্তলি** *n* **1** a lifeless doll. **2** (fig) an inactive person. **3** (fig) a person without freedom of action. **~ প্রকৃতি** *n*

1 the material world; the inanimate nature. 2 the quality of being inanimate; inaction; inactivity. ❑*adj* having the nature of an inanimate object. **~বাদ** *n* the theory that admits only material things as valid and important and dismisses the spiritual and supernatural as imaginary; materialism. 2 tendency to value material progress and physical comforts too much in disregard of the spiritual life and/or intellectual pursuits. **~বাদী** *adj* advocating the doctrine of materialism; materialistic. ❑*n* a materialist. **~বিজ্ঞান** *n* 1 the natural science, eg botany, zoology. 2 the physical sciences, eg physics, chemistry. **~সড়** *adj* 1 shrunk back from fear or shame; cowered. 2 curled up; contracted. **~সড় হওয়া** *vi* shrink (as through fear).

জড়[২], **জড়ো** *adj* 1 assembled; collected; crowded: লোক ~ হলো. 2 amassed; heaped together; rolled up. **~ করা** *vt* collect; heap together; amass; roll up. **~ হওয়া** *vi* be collected/assembled.

জড়[৩] [H] *n* 1 the roots (of a tree). 2 the root cause of anything: নষ্টের ~. **~ মারা** *vi* remove/uproot/eradicate the root cause.

জড়বফ্‌ত [P] *n* fine fabric woven of golden and silvery fibre.

জড়া *adj* clasped together; clotted: ~ ভাত. **~জড়ি** *n* 1 mutual hugging; intertwining; interlocking. **~জড়ি করা** *vi* hug together; infertwine; interlock. **~জড়িভাবে** *adj* hugging together; clasped in arms; locked in an embrace.

জড়ানো *vt* 1 press close in an embrace; hold fast with open arms; hug. 2 shut in on all sides; surround; hem in; encompass; encircle. 3 enclose or enfold (in an outer covering); wrap up; envelop: কাগজ ~, কম্বল ~. 4 roll up (as the thread of a kite on its spool). 5 involve (one) or be involved in sth: মামলায় ~. 6 be deprived of sensation; become stupefied or numb: হাত পা ~. 7 be indistinct or fumbled: কথা ~. 8 form into a tangle: চুল ~, সুতা ~. ❑*adj* hugged; surrounded; wrapped; rolled up; benumbed; tangled; indistinct.

জড়ি *n* kind of herbal roots used as an empiric medicine. **~বুটি** *n* 1 tablet of medicine prepared from this herbal root. 2 empiric medicine.

জড়িত *adj* 1 concerned; connected; related; attached. 2 engaged in; involved or implicated in. 3 studded with; inlaid. 4 mixed with: ভয়~, কান্না~. 5 deeply engrossed: ঋণে ~. 6 indistinct or numbling: ~ স্বর. **~ করা** *vt* involve; implicate. **~ হওয়া** *vi* be involved/implicated.

জড়িবুটি⇒**জড়ি**

জড়িমা *n* 1 inertia; lethargy; languor of body or mind; lassitude. 2 indistinctness; obscurity; haziness.

জড়ীভূত *adj* 1 rendered insensate; stupefied; benumbed. 2 effortless; unenterprising affectedly pensive; lackadaisical. 3 beset with; affected with; engrossed in: ঋণজালে ~.

জড়ুল, জড়ুর *n* a birth-mark; a mole.

জড়ো=**জড়**[২]

জড়োপাসক [জড়+উপাসক] *adj* worshipping inanimate/natural object; animistic. ❑*n* a nature-worshipper; an animist. **জড়োপাসনা** *n* worship of inanimate objects; nature-worship; animism.

জড়োয়া *adj* studded with gems and jewels; bejewelled. ❑*n* a piece of bejewelled ornament.

জতু *n* 1 lac-dye. 2 sealing wax. **~গৃহ** *n* 1 a house built with lac (spoken of in the Mahabharata). 2 (fig) an extremely dangerous abode. **~রস, ~রাগ** *n* lac-dye.

জত্রু *n* each of the two bones of the neck; the collar-bone; the clavicle.

জদ্দজেহাদ [A] *n* 1 a tough or terrible fighting. 2 utmost effort; uttermost endeavour.

জন *n* 1 a person; an individual: অন্ধজনে দেহ আলো. 2 a labourer; a worker: ~ খাটানো. 3 the common people; the masses: ~কল্যাণ. 4 a suffix used to indicate plurality: গোপী~. ❑*adj* indicative of the number of people: দশ~ কর্মচারী. **~কল্যাণ** *n* people's welfare; welfare of the masses. **~কল্যাণকর** *adj* beneficial to the people/public. **~গণ, ~সাধারণ** *n* the masses; the multitude; the common people; the public. **~তন্ত্র** *n* a state in which the supreme power is vested in elected representatives; a republic. **~তা** *n* 1 a mob; a crowd; a number of people; an assembly. 2 the lower or the poor classes; the proletariat. **~নেতা, ~নায়ক** *n* 1 a leader of the people; a public leader. 2 a factious orator; a demagogue. **~পদ, ~পাদ** *n* a human habitation; a settlement; a village; a township. **~প্রবাদ** *n* common talk; hearsay; rumour. **~প্রাণী, ~মানব** *nn* a single person or creature: কোথাও কোনো ~প্রাণী নেই, not a single creature anywhere. **~প্রিয়** *adj* liked by people in general; popular. **~বহুল** *adj* abounding in people; full of habitants; populous. **~বিরল** *adj* sparsely populated. **~মজুর** *n* a labourer; a person who earns his bread by manual labour. **~মত** *n* what the majority of people think; public opinion. **~মানব**=**~প্রাণী**. **~যুদ্ধ** *n* a war supported and backed by the people; a people's war. **~রব**=**~ প্রবাদ**. **~শিক্ষা** *n* instructions imparted for the education of the masses; public instruction. ~শূন্য *n* destitute of habitants; desolate. ~শ্রুত *adj* well-known; famous. ~শ্রুতি *n* **1** stories or anecdotes handed down by tradition. **2** hearsay; rumour. ~সংখ্যা *n* number of people in a country; population. ~সঙ্ঘ *n* a society founded for public welfare or social service; a social welfare institution. ~সভা *n* a public meeting. ~সমাজ *n* the human society. ~সমাবেশ *n* an assemblage or gathering of people. ~সমুদ্র *n* a vast concourse of people. ~সেবা *n* service to the welfare of the people. ~স্বাস্থ্য *n* health-care for the public; public health. ~স্রোত a stream or wave of moving people. ~হিত *n* public welfare. ~হিতকর *adj*=~কল্যাণকর. ~হীন=~শূন্য.

জনক *n* **1** the first ancestor; the male parent; father. **2** Janak, the king of Mithila and father of Sita of The Ramayana. ❑*adj* producing; causing: আনন্দ ~. জনিকা *fem.* ~-জননী *n* father and mother; parents. ~-জননী-জননী *n* **1** the earth. **2** the motherland.

জনতা *n* **1** a mob; a crowd; an assemblage of people. **2** the people: ~র সংগ্রাম.

জনন *n* **1** the act procreating/begetting. **2** birth; origination; production; reproduction. ~কোষ *n* a reproductive cell; a germ-cell. ~যন্ত্র *n* the reproductive organ. ~রস *n* the fecundating fluid of male animals; semen; sperm. ~শক্তি *n* generative or procreative power. ~শক্তিহীন *adj* destitute of the power of begetting children; impotent.

জননাশৌচ [জনন+অশৌচ] *n* the unholy state consequent on the birth of a child as enjoined by Hindu scriptures.

জননী *n fem* **1** mother; female parent. **2** a female producer.

জননীয় *adj* to be produced/begotten; producible.

জননেন্দ্রিয় *n* reproductive organs in males and females.

জনম *n* (poet)=জন্ম

জনয়িতা=জনক. জনয়িত্রী *fem.*

জনা *n* **1**= জন (1). **2** prefix for counting heads. ~পাঁচেক. ~কতক *adj* a few people. ~-জনা *n* everybody; everyone.

জনাকীর্ণ *adj* overcrowded; populous; teeming with people: ~ শহর.

জনাজা=জানাজা

জনানা=জানানা

জনান্তিক *n* **1** presence or proximity of people. **2** words spoken (in a drama) which other persons (on the stage) are supposed not to hear. জনান্তিকে *adv* on or to one side; aside or from behind (the stage) or to oneself.

জনাপবাদ *n* public reproach; public censure or reproof; scandal; slander.

জনাব [A] *n* **1** respectful form of address to a man, which is equivalent to 'sir' in English. **2** title equivalent to Mr, Miss or Ms, prefixed to the name of a person (man or woman). জনাবে আলী, জনাবে আলা *n* your excellency; gentleman; sir.

জনার *n* a kind of maize; mealies.

জনারণ্য [জন+অরণ্য] *n* people crowded together in great numbers like a dense forest.

জনার্দন *n* one who vanquished the mythical demon Jana (জন), an appellation of Vishnu.

জনি, জণি *conj, adv* (archaic) if; perhaps; let not; by no means; not in any manner; nowise.

জনিকা⇒জনক

জনিত *adj* **1** born of; begotten by. **2** caused or produced by; resulting from: প্রেম ~ দুর্বলতা. জনিতা *fem.*

জনিতা[1] *n* father; producer. জনিত্রী *fem.*

জনিতা[2]⇒জনিত

জনিত্র *n* machinery used in manufacturing process; an industrial plant.

জনী=জনি

জনীন *adj* **1** of mankind; concerning man: বিশ্ব~. **2** beneficial to the people. **3** good for or suitable to humanity: সর্ব~.

জনু[1] *adv* (archaic) as if; perhaps.

জনু[2] *n* birth; origination.

জনৈক *adj* a certain; one: ~ শিক্ষক, a certain teacher; ~ করিম সাহেব, one Mr. Karim.

জন্তু *n* **1** an animal; a creature. **2** lower animal; a beast.

জন্ম *n* **1** the process of being born; act of coming into life; birth. **2** origin; descent; lineage. **3** duration of life; lifetime: জন্মের মতো বিদায়, separation for (the whole) life. **4** reanimation or re-birth (according to Hindu philosophy). ~ দেওয়া *vt* **1** beget; procreate; produce. **2** give birth to; bring forth. ~ নেওয়া *vi* take birth; be born. ~ এয়োতি, ~ এয়ো *n, adj fem* one who is outlived by one's husband; a married woman who lives her life without being a widow. ~ কুঁড়ে *adj* indolent throughout one's life; habitually slothful. ~ কুণ্ডলী, ~ কোষ্ঠী *n* (astrol) a diagram or scheme based on the observation of the position of stars and planets at the moment of a child's birth from which to foretell its future; a horoscope. ~ক্ষেত্র *n* place of birth; birthplace. ~গত *adj* pertaining to an individual from his birth; congenital; innate; inborn; inherent; hereditary. ~গ্রহণ *n* act of being born or coming into existence. ~ গ্রহণ করা *vi* be born; come into life. ~ঘটিত *adj* pertaining to birth; dating from one's birth. ~ ~, জন্মে জন্মে *adv* (belief according to certain religions) in every birth; every time one is born. ~ **জন্মান্তর** *n* (in certain philosophy) this life and the next; birth and rebirth. ~ **জন্মান্তরে** *adv* (according to certain religious beliefs) in every succeeding life; from one birth to the next; eternally. ~ **জরা মরণ** *n* birth, decrepitude and death. ~**তিথি** *n* **1** the lunar day on which (one) is born; anniversary of (one's) birth. ~**দ**, ~**দাতা** *n* one who begets; a begetter; a father. ~**দা**, ~**দাত্রী***n fem* the female parent; mother. ~**দান** *n* act of procreating or begetting; act of giving birth to. ~ **দান করা** *vt* **1** procreate; beget. **2** give birth to; bring birth. ~**দিন**, ~**দিবস** *n* the day on which one is born, or its anniversary. ~ **নক্ষত্র** *n* the ascendant star under which one is born; the natal star. ~**পত্র**, ~**পত্রিকা**=~কুণ্ডলী ~ **পরিগ্রহ** *n* taking birth; coming into life. ~**বাসর** *n* birthday. ~**বৃত্তান্ত** *n* an account of one's birth. ~**ভূমি** *n* fatherland; the country of one's origin. ~**মাস** *n* the month in which one is born; the month of one's birth. ~**মৃত্যু** in birth and death; origin and decay. ~**রহস্য** *n* the secrets about one's birth/origin. ~**রাশি** *n* (astrol) the zodiacal sign of nativity. ~**রোগী** *n* a lifelong patient. ~**শোধ**, **জন্মের মতো** *adv* for the whole life; once for all. ~**হেতু** *n* **1** the cause of birth. **2** the begetter. **জন্মে** *adv* **1** since birth. **2** within one's lifetime.

জন্মা *vi* **1** be born: সন্তান জন্মিল, a child is born. **2** grow; be produced: পাট জন্মে.

জন্মাধিকার *n* any right to which a person is entitled by birth; birthright.

জন্মানো **1** *vt* produce; grow or cause to grow : চাষি ফসল জন্মায়, The farmer grows crops. **2** *vi* be born; come into the world by birth. **3** be produced; grow: গ্রীষ্মপ্রধান অঞ্চলে ধান জন্মায়, Rice grows in warm climates.

জন্মান্তর [জন্ম+অন্তর] *n* (according to certain religious faiths) another birth; re-birth; a previous birth; a future or next birth. ~**বাদ** *n* the doctrine that after death every person takes a new birth in a new form and that his soul repeatedly/ continuously assumes an incarnate body in various forms; the doctrine of re-birth.

জন্মান্তরে *adv* in another birth/life; in the life to come (according to the doctrine of re-birth).

জন্মান্ধ [জন্ম+অন্ধ] *adj* born as blind; born blind.

জন্মাবচ্ছিন্ন [জন্ম+অবচ্ছিন্ন] *adv* throughout life; in (one's) whole life.

জন্মাবধি *adv* since one's birth; throughout life.

জন্মাষ্টমী *n* birthday of Sri Krishna; the eighth lunar day of the dark fortnight of the month of Bhadra.

জন্মিত *adj* **1** born (of); begotten. **2** produced; generated.

জন্মোৎসব *n* festivity in celebration of a birthday.

জন্য[1], **জন্যে** *prep* **1** owing to; because of; for: অসুস্থতার ~ অনুপস্থিত, absent for illness. **2** in consequence of ; as the result of : রোগভোগের ~ দুর্বল, weak in consequence of illness. **3** for the purpose of: চড়ুইভাতির ~ সমবেত, gathered for the purpose of a picnic. ❑*conj* for; because: অসুস্থতার ~ আসতে পারেনি, could not come, for/because he is ill.

জন্য[2] *adj* **1** originating/ resulting from; caused or produced by: অতিবৃষ্টির ~ বন্যা. **2** that produces. ~**জনক সম্বন্ধ** *n* the relation between the producer and the produced or between cause and effect.

জপ *n* repeated reading or reciting of (sth) silently or in a low voice while telling the beads of a rosary. ~ **করা**, **জপা** *vi* **1** recite prayers silently and repeatedly while telling one's beads. **2** (fig) think or remember sth constantly. **জপের মন্ত্র** *n* esoteric words which a devotee counts over the beads. ~**মালা**, **জপের মালা** *n* a string of beads on which a devotee numbers his/her prayers; a rosary. ~**তপ** *n* prayers and meditation.

জপা=জপকরা⇒ জপ

জবজব *int* suggesting a state of thorough wetness: তেলে ~, saturated in oil. **জবজবে** *adj* thoroughly wet; saturated; soaked with moisture.

জবড়জং *adj* **1** indecorously showy or pompous; ill-matched; unbecoming; un-fitting; clumsy and heavy. **2** disorderly; untidy; wild.

জবর [A] *adj* **1** such as may cause fear; formidable; tremendous; terrible: ~ ভুল করেছি, terrible/great mistake. **2** ostentatiously fine; pompous; splendid; showy: ~ আয়োজন. **3** of high quality; highly finished; excellent; exquisite: দইটা ~ হয়েছে, The curd is excellent. **4** having great strength, skill; strong; skilful: ~ পালোয়ান, ~ খেলোয়াড়. **5** serving to thrill; thrilling; exciting: ~ খবর. **6** severe; utmost; extreme: এ কাজে ~ কষ্ট, This job exacts very hard labour. ~ **জুলুম** [A] *n* severe oppression; extreme tyranny. ~ **দখল** *n* occupation by physical force; forcible occupation. ~**দস্ত** [P] *adj* **1** very powerful; irresistible: ~ সেনাবাহিনী. **2** of a very strong built, stout; robust: ~ গড়ন. **3** (sarcas) of great erudition; talented; scholarly: ~ আলেম. **4** (fig) having the power of attracting; attractive. ~**দস্তি** [P] *n* application of force; coercion. **2** oppression; tyranny.

জবহ=জবাই

জবা *n* the red species of china-rose. ~**কুসুমসঙ্কাশ** *adj* deep-red as the china-rose.

জবাই, **জবেহ্**, **জবে** *n* **1** slaughter of animals in the Muslim method. **2** (fig) ruin; destruction. **জবাইঘর** *n* slaughter-house. **জবাই হওয়া** *vi* (fig) be ruined root and branch.

জবান, যবান [P] *n* **1** human speech peculiar to a nation; language: উর্দু ~. **2** sth said binding the person saying; a promise; an assurance; a word of honour: ~ দেওয়া. **3** the organ of taste, speech, etc; the tongue. **জবানবন্দি** *n* **1** a legal statement; witness; testimony. **2** a written statement to an investigator or inquiry commission; a deposition. **~বন্দি দেওয়া** *vi* bear witness; give testimony in writing; depose. **~বন্দি নবিশ** *n* a writer of a testimony or deposition. **জবানি** *n* a statement. ❑*adj* oral; verbal; spoken. ❑*adv* from another person's lips: চাকরের জবানি.

জবাব, জওয়াব [A] *n* **1** an answer; a reply. **2** a reason or cause shown by way of accounting for sth; an explanation. **3** dismissal or resignation: চাকরিতে ~ হওয়া/দেওয়া. **4** a physician's declaration of the hopelessness of a case: ডাক্তারের ~. **~ চাওয়া** *vi* **1** ask for a reply. **2** call for an explanation. **~ দেওয়া** *vi* **1** respond; answer to; reply. **2** answer back; retort. **3** submit an explanation. **~দিহি** [A+P] *n* **1** an explanation of one's conduct. **2** liability to explain one's conduct. ❑ *adj* answerable for consequences; liable; responsible. **সওয়াল ~** *n* **1** question and answer; query and reply. **2** argument and counter argument.

জবুথবু *adj* broken down with age; being in the last stage of decay; decrepit. **2** deprived of sensation; be numbed; stupefied: বেদনায় ~. **3** not tidy; untidy; slovenly: ~ পোশাক.

জবুর [A] *n* Divine Scripture sent down to prophet David, father of Solomon.

জবে=জবাই

জব্দ *adj* **1** outwitted; insulted; disgraced; humiliated. **2** brought under control; overpowered; subdued: শত্রু ~. **3** forfeited to the public treasury; confiscated; foreclosed: ভিটেমাটি ~. **~ করা** *vi* **1** put (one) out of countenance; outwit; humiliate. **2** control; subdue; overpower. **3** forfeit; confiscate; foreclose. **~ হওয়া** *vi* outwitted; befooled.

জব্বার [A] *n* the Almighty Allah.

জমক *n* **1** pomp; grandeur; ostentation; show (chiefly prefixed by জাঁক) : জাঁক~. **2** lustre; brightness; brilliancy.

জমকানো *vi* **1** be glowing or blaring. **2** grow or cause to grow in prosperity; become vigorous or strong; thrive flourish. ❑*adj* in a flourishing condition; thriving : ~ অবস্থা.

জমকালো, যমকালো *adj* displaying pomp; pompous; ostentatious; showy; high-flown.

জমজ=যমজ

জমজম[1] *int* suggesting a crowded state or a state of enthusiasm and excitement.

জমজম[2] [A] *n* the well-known holy well at Mecca: জমজমের পানি.

জমজমা *adj*=জমকালো. ❑*n* a crowded state.

জমজমাট *adj* **1** well arranged and attractive: ~ জলসা. **2** full of high spirits; full of excitement and enthusiasm: ~ আড্ডা.

জমরুদ, জমররুদ [A] *n* precious stone of green colour; emerald. **জমরুদি, জমররুদি** *adj* **1** inlaid or studded with emeralds. **2** of the colour of emerald. **জমহুরিয়াত** [A] *n* democratic rule; a republic.

জমা[1] *vi* **1** collect; accumulate; gather: টাকা ~, মেঘ ~. **2** heap up; pile up: জঞ্জাল ~. **3** change from a fluid into a fixed state; freeze; congeal; coagulate: দই ~. **4** come together; assemble: লোক ~. **5** be stagnant; stop flowing; stagnate: পানি জমে আছে, Water is stagnating. **6** come as a natural growth or development; accrue (interest) from (one's deposit): সুদ ~. **7** (of a drama, musical soiree, etc) put the audience in good humour; prove grand and enjoyable: নাটক ~, গান ~. ❑*adj* collected; accumulated; gathered; accrued; frozen; coagulated; stagnated.

জমা[2] *n* **1** money used in starting and carrying on a business; capital. **2** sums accumulated by economy; savings. **3** receipts regularly coming in from property or employment; income: ~ খরচ. **4** land revenue or the rate of revenue: বার্ষিক ~ পাঁচ টাকা, annual rate of revenue is Tk 5/00. **~ করা** *vt* **1** enter on the credit side of an account; credit. **2** deposit money in a bank or an appropriate office. **~ দেওয়া** *vt* deposit. **~র দিক** *n* (in a book of account) the credit side. **~-ওয়াসিল** [A] *n* amount payable and the amount actually paid. **~ ওয়াসিল করা** *vi* balance an account. **~ ওয়াসিল বাকি** *n* statement showing the sums due including the arrears and the amount received and outstanding. **~ খরচ** *n* income and expenditure; credit and debit. **~ খারিজ** [A] *n* an arrangement for paying the revenue of a joint property separately by the co-sharers. **~বন্দি** [A+P] in descriptive rent-roll containing the particulars of land, the annual revenue and realization and dues thereof.

জমাট *adj* **1** condensed into a fixed state; coagulated; frozen: ~ দই. **2** thickly set; compact: ~ গাথনি, ~ বুননি. **3** very close; inseparable; most intimate: ~বন্ধুত্ব. **4** very dense: ~ অন্ধকার. **5** most interesting and absorbing: ~ গান. **~ বাঁধা** *vi* freeze; coagulate; thicken; crystallize; congeal. **~-বাঁধা** *adj* hardened; frozen; congealed; coagulated.

জমাত=জামাত

জমাদার [A+P] *n* **1** a head sweeper. **2** a head constable. **3** a non-commissioned army officer below the rank of subedar. **~নী** *fem*.

জমানত=জামানত

জমানা,জামানা [A] *n* an age; an era; an epoch.

জমানো *vt* **1** lay up; save; accumulate; hoard: টাকা ~. **2** cause to assemble or gather: লোক ~. **3** heap up; pile up. **4** congeal; coagulate; freeze: বরফ ~. **5** cause to be of absorbing interest: গান ~. ❑ *adj* saved up; hoarded; accumulated; coagulated; frozen; congealed.

জমায়েত [A] *n* an assemblage; a gathering. ~ **হওয়া** *vi* come together; assemble; gather. **অবৈধ** ~ *n* an unlawful assembly.

জমি, জমিন [P] *n* **1** the upper stratum of the earth; soil; land. **2** an agricultural plot. **3** landed property. **4** texture of a cloth: কাপড়ের জমিন. **জমিজমা** *n* landed property; real estate. **জমিজিরাত, জমিজিরেত** (colloq) *n* agricultural land. **জমিদার, জমিনদার** *n* (hist) one who, as the owner of land, receives revenue from tenants; a zemindar; a landlord. **জমিদারি** *n* **1** the jurisdiction of the estate of a zemindar. **2** a real estate. **3** work or office of a zemindar. ❑*adj* pertaining to a zemindary or zemindar.

জম্বির *n* **1** a large species of lemon; citron. **2** the citron tree.

জম্মু *n* **1** the rose-apple or its tree.

জম্বুক *n* the jackal. **জম্বুকী** *fem.* ❑*adj* as sly as a jackal; (fig) one who is clever and knavish as a jackal.

জম্বুরা[1] *n* **1** instrument for gripping anything; pincers. **2** the wasp; the hornet.

জম্বুরা[2] **জাম্বুরা** *n* the citron.

জয় *n* **1** act of bringing under control; repression; subjugation: ইন্দ্রিয় ~, শত্রু ~. **2** defeat of an enemy; victory or triumph over the opponent: যুদ্ধ ~. **3** act of conquering; that which is conquered: রাজ্য ~. **4** favourable result; success: বুদ্ধির ~. **5** a shout of joy or applause: ~গুরু. ~ **করা** *vt* win (a battle); conquer (a country) ; defeat or vanquish (an enemy); succeed (in the struggle for life): জীবন যুদ্ধে ~লাভ করা. ~ **হওয়া** *vi* be crowned with success. ~ ~ *n* a shout of victory. ~ **~কার** *n* **1** a triumphal reception; public marks of ovation. **2** all-round triumph or success. ~ **~কার করা** *vt* accord reception to a hero by shouts of applause; celebrate a victory. ~ **~কার হওয়া** *vi* be received with shouts of joy and applause. **~জয়ন্তী** *n* a musical mode. **~ডঙ্কা, ~ঢাক** *n* drum beaten to announce a victory; a war-drum. **~তু** vt let victory attend you; may you be victorious; glory be to you. **~ধ্বজা** *n* the banner or standard of victory. **~ধ্বনি** *n* shouts of victory. **~ধ্বনি করা** *vi* receive (a hero) with shouts of ovation; accord public marks of respect (to a hero). **~পতাকা** *n* the flag which. is flown to symbolize a victory. **~পত্র** *n* **1** a written certificate of success or victory. **2** a letter of decree issued by a judge to a winner party on the conclusion of a trial. **~পত্রী** *n* letter from an opponent accepting/admitting defeat. ~ **পরাজয়** *n* victory and defeat; success and failure. **~ভেরী** *n* **1** *n* the sound of a drum announcing victory. **2** a war-drum. **~মালা/মাল্য** *n* a wreath or laurel of victory. **~যুক্ত** *adj* victorious; triumphant; successful. **~লক্ষ্মী, ~শ্রী** *n* the presiding goddess of victory (according to Hindu scriptures). **~শীল** *n* one who attains victory everywhere and every time. **~স্তম্ভ** *n* a monument erected to commemorate a victory.

জয়তুন [A] *n* the olive tree or its fruit, from which a valuable oil is extracted. **জয়তুনি** *adj* relating to olive or its evergreen colour.

জয়ত্রী, জয়িত্রী *n* the dried covering of the nutmeg, used as a spice; mace.

জয়দেব *n* the famous Bengali poet and author of 'Geeta Gobinda'.

জয়ন্ত *n* **1** son of Indra of the Hindu Purana. **2** god Shiva. **জয়ন্তী** *fem.*

জয়ন্তিকা *n* turmeric.

জয়ন্তী *n* **1** Hindu goddess Durga. **2** the daughter of Indra. **3** a flag; symbolizing the aspirations of a nation; a banner; a standard. **4** a day on which some event is annually celebrated, eg a birth day, an anniversary: নজরুল ~. **5** a kind of tree. **রজত/রৌপ্য** ~ *n* a celebration of an event after it has lasted or completed twenty five years; a silver jubilee. **সুবর্ণ** ~ *n* celebration of a special anniversary of an event on its fiftieth year; golden jubilee. **হীরক** ~ *n* celebration of a special anniversary of an event on its sixtieth year; diamond jubilee.

জয়পাল *n* a kind of tree whose seeds are used as medicine.

জয়া *n* **1** name of goddess Parbati. **2** an attendant of Parbati. **3** myrobalan. **4** an intoxicant made from the leaves and shoots of hemp; bhang.

জয়িত্রী=জয়ত্রী

জয়িষ্ণু *adj* one who always proves victorious; ever successful.

জয়ী *adj* one who has attained victory; victorious; successful.

জয়ীফ=জইফ

জয়েন [E] *n* act of joining one's duty; join.

জয়োৎসব [জয়+উৎসব] *n* celebration of victory or triumph.

জয়োন্মত্ত *adj* maddened or intoxicated with victory.

জয়োল্লাস *n* rejoicings in celebration of victory.

জয়োস্তু=জয়তু

জর, যর [P] *n* **1** gold. **2** money; riches. **~কশি, ~দোজি** *n* embroidery work with gold and silver thread.

জরজর=জর্জর

জরতারি [P] *n* fine cloth made with a mixture of gold thread.

জরতী *adj fem* **1** very old; decrepit; decaying. **2** ancient; antique; not having any novelty: ~ ধরণী. **জরৎ** *mas.*

জরৎকারু *n* Husband of the Hindu deity Manasa.

জরথুস্ত্র *n* Zoroaster, the founder of Zoroastrianism, the ancient Persian religion.

জরদ *n* **1** yellow colour. **2** cloth with embroidery designs in gold and silver thread.

জরদা, জর্দা, যরদা [P] *n* **1** sweet pilau coloured with saffron. **2** scented tobacco preparation taken with betel leaves.

জরদ্গব, জরদ্দাব *adj* a decrepit old fellow; a stupid and indolent person. ❑ *n* **1** a decrepit bull. **2** the vulture. **জরদ্গবী, জরদ্দাবী** *n* a decrepit cow.

জরা *n* the state of being worn out, broken down and weakened by age; the crazy state of the body produced by decay or age; decrepitude. **~গ্রস্ত** *adj* broken down with age; being in the last stage of decay; decrepit. **~জীর্ণ** *adj* worn out and decayed through age.

জরা[২] *vt* **1** wear out or cause to wear out. **2** be digested. **জারিত, জীর্ণ** *adj* worn out. **~নো** *v t* smear with sth (as salt) or saturate (in oil, etc) for the purpose of preservation. ❑*adj* that has been preserved in this way.

জরায়ু *n* the uterus; the womb.

জরায়ুজ *adj* animal that is born of a uterus (not from eggs); viviparous (cf অন্ডজ).

জরাসন্ধ *n* an ancient king of Magadha in India.

জরি, জরী [P] *n* gold or silver thread; an ornamental cord or braid. **~দার** *adj* embroidered with gold or silver thread.

জরিপ, জরীপ [A] *n* measurement and mapping of the position, size, boundaries, etc of an area of land; land survey: ~ দল, cadastral surveying party. **~ করা** *vt* survey; measure and value (land). **~-আমিন** *n* a land surveyor. **জরিপি** *adj* concerning survey of land.

জরিমানা *n* payment of money imposed as a punishment; a.fine. **~ করা** *vt* impose a fine; fine.

জরিষ্ণু *adj* in a state of decay; decaying.

জরু, জরূ, জোরু [U] *n* the consort of a man; wife. **~জাত** *n pl* children; offspring.

জরুড় =জটুল

জরুর [A] *adv* surely; certainly; of necessity; by all means. **~ত, ~ৎ, জরুরিয়ত** [A] *n* what is absolutely requisite; need; necessity. **জরুরি** [A] *adj* **1** absolutely necessary; very important; essential. **2** immediately necessary; urgent; pressing. **3** relating to a crisis; critical; momentous; emergent. **জরুরি অবস্থা** *n* an emergent situation needing prompt action; emergency.

জরূ =জরু

জরে-নেগার *adj* inlaid with gold; decorated embellished with gold; golden.

জর্জর, জরজর *adj* **1** deeply stricken with: শোকে ~. **2** thoroughly engrossed in: প্রেমে ~, ঋণে ~. **3** worn-out; shattered; tottering: ঘুণে খেয়ে ~ করা.

জর্জরিত *adj* **1** one who is afflicted/stricken with: শোকে ~, stricken with sorrow. **2** seriously affected with: আঘাতে ~. **জর্জরীকৃত** *adj* one who has been seriously hurt/injured/wounded. **জর্জরীভূত** *adj* that which has worn out or is distressed or oppressed. **জর্জরীভূতা** *fem.*

জর্ডন [A] *n* river flowing through Palestine, whose water is reckoned by Christians as holy and is used in baptizing.

জর্দা=জরদা

জল *n* **1** transparent fluid consisting of hydrogen and oxygen; water; aqua. **2** shower of rain; downpour. **3** a light meal; refreshment; snack: ~খাবার . **4** strained; overtasked; overtaxed: রক্ত ~ হওয়া. **5** something easy like water : অঙ্কটা একেবারেই ~. **খর~** *n* water containing mineral salts that prevent lathering of soap; hard water. **চক্ষের ~** *n* tears. **নারিকেলের ~** *n* milk of coconut. **বৃষ্টির ~** *n* rain-water. **ভারী ~** *n* (phys) water where molecules consist of two heavy hydrogen atoms and one ordinary oxygen atom; heavy water. **মিঠে ~** *n* water of the rivers, not of the sea; fresh water. **মৃদু ~** *n* water free of mineral salts; soft water. **~ ওঠা** *vi* **1** bubble up (as water) from a fountain; gush out (from beneath the soil). **2** enter through a leakage (as into a boat). **3** overflow; submerge: উঠানে ~ ওঠা. **~কণ্টক** *n* **1** an aquatic fruit; cress. **2** crocodile. **~কবন্ধ** *n* **1** coconut. **2** couch-shell. **3** the lotus; the water-lily. **4** the cloud. **~কর** *n* water-rate; tax imposed on fisheries. **~ করা** *vt* make (sth) easy to understand. **2** assuage one's rage; cause one's arger to calm down. **3** suffer a loss: টাকা ~ করা. **4** make torpid; benumb (as in cold). **~কল্লোল** *n* **1** the murmur of stream. **2** roaring waves of water. **~কষ্ট** *n* inconvenience caused by restricted water supply; scarcity of water. **~কাক, ~পারাবত, ~বায়স** *n* a species of diving bird. **~কাদা** *n* holes of water and soft mud on the road caused by rains. **~কুক্কুট** *n* =গাংচিল. **~কুক্কুটী** *fem.* **~কুন্তল** *n* cryptogramous plant growing on marshy ground; moss. **~কে** *adv* to fetch water: ~কে চল. **~কেলি, ~ক্রীড়া** *n* bathing by immersion, swimming, etc in sport. **~ খরচ করা** *vi* clean after defecation. **~ খাওয়া** *vi* **1** drink water. **2** have a snack. **~খাবার** *n* **1** a light repast; a snack; tiffin; refreshment. **2** sweets. **~গণ্ডূষ** *n* a handful of water; quantity of water that may be held on one's palm. **~গর্ভ** *adj* containing water within; full of water. **~গর্ভা** *fem.* **~ গালা** *vi* **1** cause to drip (as water from boiled rice). **2** press and squeeze out (as water from cloth). **~ গ্রহণ করা** *vi* **1** (lit) drink water. **2** take any food. **~গ্রাহী** *adj* taking in moisture from the atmosphere; hygroscopic. **~চর** *adj* living in water; aquatic. ❑*n* an aquatic animal. **~চরী** *fem.* **~চল** *adj* (among Hindus) belonging to a caste whose contact does not pollute water for the high-caste people. **~চারী** *adj* moving in water; aquatic. **~চারিণী** *fem.* **~চৌকি** *n* wooden stool of square or rectangular size. **~ছত্র, ~সত্র** *n* place by the side of a high way for supplying drinking water to thirsty travellers. **~ছবি** *n* kind of picture which, after dipping in water, can be reproduced by pressing against another sheet of paper; transfer-picture. **~ছাপ** *n* a mark or design made in some kinds of paper during manufacture, which may be seen by holding the paper against light; water mark. **~জ** *adj* born in or of water; aquatic: ~জ পাদপ, aquatic plant. ❑*n* **1** the water-lily; the lotus. **2** the conch-shell. **~জন্তু** *n* animals that are born in and live in water; aquatic animal. **~জান** *n* the gaseous elementary substance (symbol H) which combines with oxygen to form water; hydrogen. **~জিয়ন্ত, ~জীয়ন্ত, ~জ্যান্ত** *adj* **1** fresh; not faded; in good condition. **2** very clear; direct: ~জ্যান্ত দৃষ্টান্ত, direct instance. **3** alive; hale and hearty: এমন ~জ্যান্ত মানুষটাকে তোমরা কিভাবে গুম করলে? how could you vanish such a perfectly living person like him? **4** plain; utter; quite obvious; arrant; downright: ~জ্যান্ত মিথ্যা. **~ঝড়** *n* rain and storm; a rainstorm. **~টুঙি** *n* a house built on a raised platform in the middle of a water pool. **~ঢোঁড়া** *n* a species of non-venomous water snake. **~তরঙ্গ** *n* **1** a swell or ridge on moving water; a wave. **2** a kind of musical instrument consisting of seven bowls which are struck with two sticks to produce ripples of sound. **~তরঙ্গ চুড়ি** *n* bangles of wavy design for the wrist. **~ত্রাস**জলাতঙ্ক. **~দস্যু** *n* a robber on the high seas; a pirate; a buccaneer. **~দস্যুতা** *n* piracy; buccaneering. **~দস্যুতা করা** *vi* engage in piracy/ buccaneering. **~দুর্গ** *n* fortress surrounded by a protective trench; a citadel with a moat around it for defence. **~দেবতা** *n* (according to Hindu belief) a deity inhabiting waters; water-god; Varuna (বরুণ). **~দোষ** *n* **1** (med) an unnatural collection of water in any part of the body; dropsy. **2** (med) dropsy of the testicle; water on the testicle; hydrocele. **~দ্রোণী** *n* a trough used to free a boat from water; a bailing bucket. **~ধর** *adj* containing water; full of water. ❑*n* **1** the cloud. **2** the sea. **~ধারা** *n* **1** a stream or flow of water. **2** rainfall. **~নকুল, ~বিড়াল** *nn* an aquatic carnivorous animal; the otter. **~নালী, ~প্রণালী** *n* a drain or a system of pipes and drains for carrying away sewage and waste-water from buildings; a sewer; a system of sewers; sewerage. **~নিকাশ** *n* outlet of water; draining out of water; drainage. **~ নিকাশ করা** *vi* drain out water. **~ নিকাশের পথ** *n* outlet of water; a drain. **~নিধি** *n* a sea; an ocean. **~নির্গম** *n* outflow of water; passage of water; drainage. **~নির্গম প্রণালী** *n* channel to convey waste-water or to drain off filth; drainage system; a conduit. **~পট্টি** *n* strip of cloth with several folds and soaked in water for the relief of pain or temperature. **~-পড়া** *n* a quality of water with supernatural power (belived to be) infused into it by means of incantation or holy words for the relief/ cure of some disease. **~পথ** *n* **1** a navigable river or canal or the part of the sea through which vessels sail; waterway. **2** an outlet for water. **~পথে** *adv* by water; across the sea. **~পথে ভ্রমণ** *n* a journey by water, esp between countries; a voyage. **~পাত্র** *n* a water-vessel; a water-pot; a drinking cup/glass. **~পান** *n* **1** act of drinking water. **2** a light repast; snacks. **~পান করা** *vi* take tiffin/light repast; eat some snacks; refresh (oneself) with some snacks. **~পানি** *n* **1** a student's stipend; a scholarship; a studentship. **2** pocket-money for snacks. **~-পিঁড়ি** *n* water for washing and a stool for sitting. **~-পুলিশ** *n* police for the protection of waterway; marine police. **~প্রপাত** *n* a waterfall; a cataract; a cascade. **~প্রবাহ** *n* a flow of water. **~প্লাবন** *n* a flood; an inundation; a deluge. **~বৎ** *adj* (fig) clear as water; easy to understand; perspicuous. **~বসন্ত** *n* an eruptive contagious disease generally appearing in children; chicken-pox. **~বায়ু** *n* the condition of a country or region in respect of temperature; dryness, wind, etc; climate. **~বাহ** *n* **1** the cloud. **2** a water carrier. **~বাহিত** *adj* **1** contacted or infected through water; water borne: ~বাহিত রোগ. **2** (of goods) water-borne. **~বিছুটি** *n* a weed with stinging hairs; nettle. **~বিজ্ঞান** *n* the science which treats of the weight pressure and equilibrium of water, when in a state of rest; hydrostatics. **~বিদ্যুৎ** *n* electricity generated by water-power; hydel power; hydro-electricity. **~বিন্দু** *n* a drop of water. **~বিম্ব** *n* a bubble of water. **~ বিভাজিকা** *n* a line of high land separating river systems; watershed; water-shield. **~বিয়োজন** *n* the act or process of freeing a compound from water; dehydration. **~ বিয়োজন করা** *vt* dehydrate. **~বিষুব** *n* the time of the month of Kartik when the day and night are of equal length; the autumnal equinox. ~বিহার *n* =~কেলি. ~বুদ্বুদ =~বিম্ব. ~ভ্রমি *n* a place in a river or sea where there are whirling currents; circular eddies in the river or sea; whirlpool. ~মগ্ন *adj* immersed in water; flooded or submerged. ~মগ্না *fem.* ~মগ্ন হওয়া *vi* go down into water; be submerged; sink; drown. ~ময় *adj* full of water; flooded with water; watery. ~ময়ী *fem.* ~মার্জার =~নকুল. ~মুহরি *n* mouth of an outlet for water. ~যন্ত্র *n* **1** a revolving cylinder on which a rope is wound, used for lifting water from a well by hand or other power; a windlass. **2** a water-clock. **3** a spraying instrument. ~যান *n* a vessel for travelling by water; a ship; a boat. ~যুদ্ধ *n* a naval battle; sea-warfare. ~যোগ=~পান (২). ~রাশি *n* a mass of water; a sea. ~রোধক *adj* adapted in such a way as to retain, or not to admit water; free from leaks; water-tight; waterproof. ~শূকর *n* a crocodile. ~শৌচ *n* act of cleaning after defecation. ~সত্র *n* a place for charitable distribution of water and refreshments to the passers-by in hot season. ~সম *adj* level with water. ~ সমতল *n* water-level; water-surface. ~সেক *n* **1** hot compress applied to a part of the body with a wet pad or piece of cloth after water is squeezed off. **2** act of sprinkling water. ~সিঞ্চন, ~সেচন *n n* act watering (trees, etc); irrigation. ~ সিঞ্চন/~ সেচন করা *vt* sprinkle (sth) with water; irrigate. ~স্তম্ভ *n* a whirling column of water drawn up from the sea by a violent whirlwind; a water-spout. ~স্ফীতি *n* the rise of the sea-level caused by the attraction of the moon; high tide. ~ হওয়া *vi* **1** to rain. **2** (of anger) be calmed down. **3** (of snow, etc) melt; liquefy; become liquid. **4** (fig) be easy to understand. ~হস্তী *n* elephant-like aquatic animal inhabiting the Nile and other African rivers; the hippopotamus. ~হস্তিনী *fem.* জলে পড়া *vi* **1** (fig) get into a disadvantageous/ dangerous position. **2** (fig) be bestowed on an undeserving person; be misused. জলে ফেলা/দেওয়া *vt* **1** (fig) bestow (sth) on an undeserving person. **2** (fig) make unnecessary expenditure; waste or misuse money. জলে যাওয়া *vi* be lost; suffer or incur a loss; be misused/wasted. জলের আলপনা *n* a transient or transitory thing. জলের দাম *n* a very cheap rate or price. জলের দামে *adv* at a throwaway price. জলের মতো *adj* (fig) very easy. ❑*adv* easily; without any difficulty; without strain or effort; readily. ডুবে ডুবে ~ খাওয়া indulge in forbidden or immoral acts by hoodwinking other people. সাত ঘাটে ~ খাওয়ানো subject one to unnecessary harassment.

জলই=জলুই

জলওয়া, জলোয়া [A] *n* lustre; brightness.

জলংগা, জলঙ্গা *adj* (of a colour) like water.

জলদ[1] *adj* that gives water. ❑*n* the cloud. জলদা *fem.* ~কাল *n* the rainy season. ~ক্ষয় *n* the autumn. ~গম্ভীর *adj* deep and grave like the rumbling of clouds. ~গম্ভীর স্বরে *adv* in a voice as deep and grave as the rumbling of clouds; in an extremely loud voice. জলদাগম [~+আগম] *n* the advent of the monsoon; the rainy season; the rains. ~জাল *n* a series of clouds. ~মন্দ্র *n* the grave sound of clouds. জলদোদয় [~+উদয়] *n* the appearance of clouds.

জলদ[2] [A] *adj* quick; rapid; swift.

জলদি [A] *adv* quickly, hurriedly; hastily. ~ করা *vt* make haste.

জলধর *n* **1** the cloud. **2** the sea.

জলধি *n* the sea.

জলনিধি *n* the sea.

জলনীলিকা, জলনীলী *n* cryptogameous plant growing on marshy ground; moss.

জলপতি *n* **1** Hindu deity Varuna. **2** the sea.

জলপাই *n* olive tree and its fruit. ~-বর্ণ *adj* olive-green. ~য়ের তেল *n* olive-oil.

জলসা [A] *n* **1** a sitting or assembly of people; a meeting; a majlis. **2** a musical soiree.

জলা *adj* low-lying; watery; marshy: ~ভূমি, marshy land. ❑*n* a marsh; a swamp; a bog.

জলাচরণীয় *adj* of a Hindu caste whose contact does not render water unfit for higher castes.

জলাঞ্জলি [জল+অঞ্জলি] *n* **1** quantity of water that can be held on one's cupped palms; a handful of water. **2** a handful of water for offering to a deceased after the cremation is over. **3** (fig) act of abandoning or severing connection; bidding farewell: লেখাপড়ায় ~. **4** act of wasting; waste; misuse: টাকা পয়সা ~. ~ দেওয়া *vt* **1** wash one's hands off; relinquish; bid farewell; give up; abandon. **2** waste; misuse; squander.

জলাতঙ্ক *n* morbid dread of water caused by the bite of a mad animal, esp a dog; hydrophobia.

জলাধার [জল+আধার] *n* **1** a receptacle of water; a water-vessel . **2** a reservoir of water; a tank; a lake. **3** a river or sea.

জলাধিপ, জলাধিপতি [জল+অধিপ/অধিপতি] *n* **1** Hindu god of water; Varuna (বরুণ). **2** the sea.

জলার্দ্র [জল+আর্দ্র] *adj* moist with water.

জলাশয় [জল+আশয়] *n* a place containing water; a pond; a lake; a river; a sea.

জলাসার [জল+আসার] *n* downpour of rain; torrential rain.

জলি *n* variety of paddy grown in water.

জলীয় *adj* **1** of or like water; watery; aqueous. **2** produced from water: ~ বাষ্প, aqueous vapour or water vapour.

জলুই, জলই *n* **1** kind of nail pointed on both ends used for joining pieces of wood (as in a boat). **2** a large and thick nail; a spike.

জলুস, জৌলুস [A] *n* **1** lustre; radiance; brightness. **2** magnificence; pomp; grandeur; splendour. ~ দেওয়া *vi* shed lustre; shine; glare; glaze; gleam; glimmer.

জলেশ, জলেশ্বর =জলাধিপ

জলো *adj* mixed with water: ~ দুধ. **2** full of water; watery; tearful: ~ চোখ. **3** watery in taste; insipid. **4** moist or damp: ~ হাওয়া, air with moisture/humidity; damp air.

জলোকা=জলৌকা

জলোচ্ছ্বাস [জল+উচ্ছ্বাস] *n* **1** a sudden flood, esp of a river after rain; spate. **2** high tidal wave, often many feet high and destructive of life and property, eg one caused by cyclone or earthquake; a tidal bore. **3** high tide; flow-tide.

জলোৎকা *n* a variety of fish.

জলোদ্ভব [জল+উদ্ভব] *adj* sprung from water; aquatic.

জলোয়া=জলওয়া

জলৌকা, জলোকা *n* the leech.

জলৌষধি [জল+ঔষধি] *n* medicinal plant produced in water, esp the kind with hot-tasting leaves; water-cresses.

জল্প *n* **1** (logic) establishing one's opinion by successfully refuting that of the opposition. **2** trifling talk; idle talk; garrulity; babbling.

জল্পক *adj* given to long prosy talk; talkative; garrulous; loquacious. ❑*n* a garrulous fellow; a babbler, a prattler; a chatterer.

জল্পন, জল্পনা *n* idle talk; gossip; speculation; garrulity; prating; babbling. ~ করা *vi* talk much; chatter; prate; babble.

জল্পিত *adj* uttered; discussed; speculated; proposed.

জল্লাদ [A] *n* **1** person who executes a sentence of capital punishment; a public executioner; a hangman. **2** (fig) an extremely merciless and hard-hearted person. ~পনা *n* the cruelty befitting an executioner; mercilessness; hard-heartedness. জল্লাদীয় *adj* of or pertaining to an executioner.

জশন [P] *n* festivity; merriment.

জশম =জওসম

জসদ *n* a metal of bluish-white colour, used in alloys and in coating iron sheets for protection against rust; zinc (symbol zn).

জসম= জওসম

জহমত [A] *n* hardship; misery; suffering; distress.

জহর[1] [P] *n* substance capable of producing a morbid effect on anything endowed with life; poison. ~ আলুদা [P] *adj* poisonous.

জহর[2] [A জওহর] *n* precious stone; a gem; a jewel.

জহরত [A] *n pl* pearls and gems; jewellery.

জহরব্রত *n* (hist) the practice prevalent among Rajput women of medieval India of burning themselves alive in order to uphold their honour.

জহরি=জহুরি

জহান=জাহান

জহিন, জহীন [A] *adj* endowed with good parts; meritorious; intelligent; gifted.

জহুদ [P] *n* a jew; a heretic; an infidel. ❑*adj* quarrelsome; obstinate; headstrong.

জহুর [A] *n* divine grace; greatness; nobility; sublimity. জহুরা *fem.*

জহুরি [A] *n* **1** dealer in precious stones; a jeweller. **2** a lapidary who knows and understands the quality of jewels: ~ জহর চেনে, a shepherd knows his ewe. **3** a judge of any art; a connoisseur: ~ সাহিত্যিক.

জহ্নু *n* the sage of Hindu mythology who drunk up the Ganges and passed it through his knees. ~কন্যা, ~তনয়া, জাহ্নবী *n* the Ganges.

জা, জাল *n fem* wife of one's husband's brother; a sister-in-law.

-জা *n* (used as *suff*) offspring : দত্তজা, ঘোষজা.

জাইগির=জায়গির

জাউ *n* a thick broth prepared by boiling rice; gruel; porridge. ক্ষুদের ~ *n* gruel prepared of ground rice.

জাওয়া *n* a variety of bamboo: ~ বাঁশ.

জাওর=জাবর

জাং, জাঙ *n* the thick part of the leg above the knee; the thigh.

জাংগাল=জাঙ্গাল

জাংগিয়া=জাঙ্গিয়া

জাংলা *n* a platform for creeping plants to shoot up and spread.

জাঁক *n* **1** inordinate self-esteem; pride; brag; boasting. **2** ambitious display; ostentation; splendour; pomp; parade; vain show. ~ করা *vi* boast of; brag; vaunt. ~ দেখানো *vi* make a vain display of; show off; parade one's importance. ~জমক *n* pomp and grandeur; splendour; ostentation. ~জমক করা *vi* display grandeur; make an ostentatious show of.

জাঁকড় [H] *n* purchase of a commodity on condition that, in case it is not approved, it is to be returned; a conditional purchase. জাঁকড়ি *adj* pertaining to conditional purchase. ~ বই/খাতা *n* **1** a register containing record of the articles of conditional purchase. **জাঁকড়ে কেনা** *vt* purchase an article on condition of its being of acceptable quality.

জাঁকা *vi* **1** be splendid or showy. **2** press or fasten tightly. **3** sit firmly upon. **জেঁকে (জাঁকিয়া) ওঠা** *vi* grow brisk/vigorous; thrive; prosper; flourish. **জেঁকে (জাকিয়া) বসা** *vi* sit tight/firmly.

জাঁকানো *vi* grow splendid; become showy.

জাঁকালো *adj* **1** full of pomp and grandeur; ostentatious. **2** that thrives; thriving: ~ ব্যবসায়, roaring trade. **3** weighty; thoughtful, not gay; serious; grave.

জাঁত *n* press; pressure; compressor : জাঁতে পাকা, ripened through heat generated by compressor.

জাঁতা[১], **যাঁতা** *n* **1** pair of heavy circular flat stones for grinding wheat, pulses, etc; millstone; grindstone. **2** an instrument for blowing fires (as that of blacksmith); bellows. **~ ভাঙ্গা, ~ পেষা** *adj* that has been ground by millstones: ~-ভাঙ্গা আটা.

জাঁতা[২] *vt* press down; compress; massage; squeeze: পা ~. **~ দেওয়া** *vt* put pressure upon.

জাঁতানো *vt* **1** charge with a crammed load; stuff or pack heavily. **2** eat to excess.

জাঁতি, যাঁতি *n* instrument for cutting betel nuts; a nut-cracker. **~কল** *n* a contrivance in the shape of a nut-cracker for entrapping rats; a rat-trap. **~কলে পড়া** (fig) be in tight corner.

জাঁদরেল [E]*n* general; a commander; a hero. ❑*adj* **1** having reputation; widely known; renowned: ~ উকিল. **2** huge; colossal; immense; gigantic. **3** grand; pompous; ostentatious. **4** very strong and powerful: ~ গভর্নর.

জাঁহাপনা, জাহাঁপনা, জাহানপানা [P] *n* form of address to a sovereign ruler, literally meaning "the refuge or shelter of the world," and corresponding to the English form 'Your Majesty'.

জাঁহাবাজ, জাহাঁবাজ [P] *adj* **1** full of troublesome whims; perverse; wicked; wayward. **2** shrewd; crooked; deceitful. **3** having seen much; having varied experience; well-experienced.

জাকাত, যাকাত [A] *n* **1** (lit) purification. **2** tax on savings (not income) and hoarded wealth at 2·5% payable by way of purifying the mind and for the benefit of the poor and the destitute, as prescribed by Islam.

জাগ *n* **1** act of generating artificial warmth by the compression of straw, dry leaves, etc and thereby causing green fruits to ripen. **2** act of causing stalks of flax, jute, etc to decompose by steeping in water: পাট ~ দেওয়া. **~ দেওয়া** *vi* **t 1** subject sth to artificial warmth (for ripening). **2** rot (flax, jute, etc) by soaking or exposing to moisture; ret. **~ দিয়ে পাকানো** cause to ripen artificially; (fig) try to adapt sth to immediate needs by short-cut means. **জাগে পাকা** *adj* ripened by artificial means.

জাগ-গান *n* night-long winter folk-song sung esp in northern part of Bangladesh; the festivity connected with it.

জাগন্ত *adj* awake; not sleeping; wakeful.

জাগর *n* awakened state; wakefulness. ❑*adj* awake; wakeful. **~ স্বপ্ন** *n* a loose train of thoughts; a day-dream; reverie.

জাগরণ *n* **1** break of sleep; awakening; waking. **2** wakefulness; watchfulness; awakened state. **3** sleeplessness; insomnia. **4** (fig) regaining vigour and vitality ; coming back to activity: জাতির ~, national awakening.

জাগরণী *n* **1** a song for awakening or rousing; an awakening song. **2** the period of waking. ❑*adj* relating to waking.

জাগরিত *adj* **1** risen from sleep; awakened. **2** awake; not sleeping. **3** brought back/come back to one's senses. **জাগরিতা** *fem.* **~ করা** *vt* **1** rouse from sleep; awaken. **2** (fig) bring one to one's senses. **~ হওয়া** *vi* **1** wake up; rise from sleep. **2** (fig) regain one's consciousness.

জাগরী *adj* **1** keeping awake; wakeful. **2** sleepless; watchful; vigilant.

জাগরূক *adj* **1** waking; awake; wakeful. **2** watchful; heedful; vigilant; careful. **3** fresh in memory: তোমার স্মৃতি হৃদয়ে ~.

জাগা *vi* **1** rise from sleep; wake up; awake: ভোরে ~. **2** keep or remain awake: রাত ~. **3** become conscious; be inspired with: প্রেম ~. **4** come to the mind; occur; strike: মনে ~. **5** feel a desire/longing: সাধ ~.

জাগানো *vt* **1** rouse from sleep; awaken. **2** warn; caution against; inform previously. **3** cause (one) to remember; remind.

জাগুয়ার *n* a large carnivorous animal with a spotted fur, found in central and south America; the American tiger; the jaguar.

জাগ্রত *adj* **1** awake; wakeful. **2** vigilant; watchful. **3** having supernatural power. **~ দেবতা** *n* a live deity.

জাঙ= **জাং** made of bamboo.

জাঙলা=জাংলা

জাঙ্গল *adj* **1** of jungles; abounding in woods; woody. **2** living in a jungle; wild. **3** produced in forests; forest-grown.

জাঙ্গাল *n* a bank to confine water; a dam; an embankment: ~ ভাঙা স্রোত. **2** a bridge. **3** an elevated and wide path; a ridge. **4** the rust of copper or iron; verdigris. **5** a retinue or train of anything: পিঁপড়ার ~. **6** fallow land.

জাঙ্গি *n* a kind of myrobalan fruit.

জাঙ্গিয়া *n* drawers reaching down to the thigh; briefs.

জাজা, জাযা [A] *n* what is given in return for good done; recompense; reward. **জাজাকাল্লাহ্/জাযাকাল্লাহ্** may God recompense you for what you have done.

জাজিম [P] *n* **1** a stuffed contrivance used as a support for a bed; a mattress. **2** a decorated cloth-sheet to cover a bed or seat.

জাজ্বল্যমান *adj* casting a bright light; refulgent; blazing; shining; vivid: ~ প্রমাণ. **2** clear; manifest; evident; obvious : কথাটা ~ হবে তার কাছে.

জাট[1], **জাঠ**[1] *n* a Hindu community inhabiting the Punjab and Rajasthan; a member of this community.

জাট[2], **জাঠ**[2] *n* a long slender piece of wood; a wooden rod or wand; a staff. **2** the block of wood used in the oilman's grinding tree.

জাট[3] =জেঠ

জাঠ=জেঠ

জাঠর *adj* relating to the belly or womb; abdominal.

জাঠা *n* iron cudgel used as a weapon of war in ancient times.

জাড্য *n* **1** inertia; inactivity; slothfulness. **2** stupidity; idiocy. **3** frigidity; coldness. **4** the property of matter by which it tends to retain its state of rest.

জাড় *n* **1** a spell of cold weather; cold; chill. **2** numbness caused by cold.

জাড়ি *n* a herbal medicine for fever.

জাড়ুল=জারুল

জাত[1] *adj* **1** born: সদ্যো~. **2** grown; produced: ক্ষেত্র~. **3** resulted from; caused by: শ্রম~. **4** made of; manufactured from: দুগ্ধ~. ❑*n* **1** the process of being born; birth: ~কৃত্য. **2** a group; a collection: দ্রব্য~. **~ক** *adj* taking birth; born begotten. ❑ *n* **1** a new-born child. **2** astrological calculation of nativity; a horoscope. **3** religious ceremony connected with child-birth. **4** a book in Pali narrating the incidents of the former lives of Gautama Buddha. **5** a Buddhist monk. **~কর্ম/কৃত্য/ক্রিয়া** *n* rites at child-birth. **~কোপ, ~ক্রোধ** *n* smouldering anger; spirit of revenge; burning indignation. ❑*adj* burning with a spirit of revenge; furious with rage. **~ক্রোধ হওয়া** get into a towering rage; work oneself up into fury. **~চক্ষু/নেত্র** *adj* having eyes opened for the first time. **~পক্ষ** *adj* newly fledged; fledgeling. ❑*n* a bird just fledged. **~পত্র** *n* a horoscope. **~পুত্র** *adj* one to whom a son is born. **~পুত্রা** *fem.* **~প্রত্যয়** *adj* having confidence; confident; convinced. **~প্রত্যয়া** *fem.* **~ব্যবহার** *adj* one who has come of age/attained majority. ❑*n* an adult. **~মাত্র** *adv* as soon as one is born. ❑*adj* just born. **~শত্রু** *adj* one who has many enemies. ❑*n* a born enemy. **~শ্মশ্রু** *adj* one whose beard has appeared/ grown. **~স্পৃহ** *adj* one who has felt a desire; desirous.

জাত[2] *n* **1** one of the hereditary social classes among the Hindus; a caste: ছোট জাতের মেয়ে. **2** a religious community: ইহুদি ~. **3** a class or kind of anything: নানা জাতের ফুল, flowers of various kinds. **4** a racial variety; a group possessing common qualities; breed : ভালো জাতের ঘোড়া, horse of good breed. ❑*adj* **1** by or since birth: ~ শয়তান, a born devil. **2** belonging to the same class: ~ ভাই, fellow-man. **3** descending by inheritance; hereditary : ~ ব্যবসায়. **~ মারা/খাওয়া** *vt* **1** make (one) contemptible to one's own people by defiling one's caste. **2** outcaste; declassify; expel (one) from one's caste. **~ খোয়ানো/হারানো** *vi* be outcasted; loose one's caste. **জাতজন্ম, জাতজন্ম** *n* **1** birth and descent. **2** family status. **~ দেওয়া** *vi* marry a person of a different caste and consequently loose one's own caste. **~ ব্যবসায়/ব্যবসা** *n* hereditary trade. **~ভাই, জাতিভাই** *n* fellow man. ❑*adj* belonging to the same class/ caste. **জাতে ওঠা** *vi* **1** be reclaimed/restored to caste. **2** be uplifted to a higher status in Hindu society. **জাতে তোলা** *vt* **1** admit one to a status of equality in Hindu society. **2** reinstate an outcaste.

জাত[3] *adj* real; best; chief: ~ লেখক. **~ বোষ্টম, ~ বৈষ্ণব** *n* Vaishnava by birth or by caste; real Vaishnava. **~ সাপ** *n* a venomous snake; a cobra; the king cobra.

জাত[4] *adj suff* that which has been collected or stored: গোলা~, গুদাম~.

জাতক ⇒ জাত[1]

জাতাঙ্কুর [জাত+অঙ্কুর] *adj* sprouted. ❑*n* a new sprout.

জাতান্ধ [জাত+অন্ধ] *adj* born blind.

জাতাপত্য [জাত+অপত্য] *adj fem* one who has borne children. ❑*n* a mother.

জাতাশৌচ [জাত+অশৌচ] *n* state of personal impurity consequent on the birth of a child.

জাতি[1] *n* **1** (biol) a group having common characteristics; a genus or species : মানব ~ the human race; পশু ~, the species of beasts.

2 a religious community : মুসলিম ~, হিন্দু ~. 3 a group of people having a common nationality, culture and political affiliation; a nation : বাঙালি ~, ফরাসি ~, জর্মন ~. 4 a class of people following hereditary trade or profession; a caste: জাতিতে মুচি, a cobbler by caste. 5 one of the main racial divisions of mankind: আর্য ~, সেমিটিক ~, মঙ্গোলীয় ~. 6 a division among the Hindu society according to caste distinction : কায়স্থ ~, নমঃশূদ্র ~. 7 a kind, sort or variety: সাহিত্যের নানা ~. 8 birth; origin : জাতিতে ইহুদি, a Jew by birth. **~কুল** *n* 1 caste and family. 2 birth and descent. **~ খাওয়া/লওয়া** *vt* expel one from one's caste. **~ খোয়ানো** *vi* lose one's caste. **~গত** *adj* pertaining to the race, class, caste or nationality; racial; national; communal : ~গত দাঙ্গা, communal riot. **~চ্যুত** *adj* expelled from one's caste; outcasted; fallen from one's caste for violating a scriptural law or for an unsocial act. **~চ্যুতা** *fem.* **~চ্যুতি** *n.* **~তত্ত্ব** *n* that branch of science which treats of the different races of mankind; ethnology. **~ত্ব** *n* entity of a nation. **~ধর্ম** *n* 1 the characteristics peculiar to a people; racial character. 2 beliefs and practices of a caste. **~ধর্ম নির্বিশেষে** *adv* without distinction of caste and creed. **~বাচক** *adj* 1 pertaining to a genus; generic. 2 (gram) denoting or suggesting a class; common (as a noun). **~বাচক শব্দ** *n* a generic name. **~বিদ্বেষ** *n* prejudice against a race or nation; mutual antagonism between nations; racial antagonism. **~বৈর** *n* instinctive hostility between nations. **~ ব্যবসায়/ব্যবসা** *n* hereditary trade or occupation. **~ভেদ** *n* caste-distinction (among the Hindu society). **~ভেদ প্রথা** *n* hereditary social division among the Hindus; caste-system. **~ভ্রংশ** *n* expulsion from one's caste; loss of caste. **~ভ্রষ্ট**=জাতিচ্যুত. **~ভ্রষ্টা** *fem.* **~সঙ্কর** *n* an animal or plant produced from the mixture of two species or varieties; a hybrid; a mongrel. **~সঙ্ঘ** the United Nations Organization (UNO) with its Hqs in New York. **~স্মর** *adj* one who can remember the incidents of one's former lives (according to the Hindu theory of rebirth).

জাতি[২], **জাতী** *n* 1 jasmine flower or plant. 2 fruit with aromatic kernel; nutmeg; the tree bearing this fruit, grown mostly in Malaysia. **জাতিকোশ, জাতিফল, জাতীফল** *n* the nutmeg. **জাতিপত্র, জাতিপত্রী, জাতীপত্র, জাতীপত্রী** *n* the dried covering of the seed of the nutmeg, used as spice; mace.

জাতী=জাতি[২]

জাতীয় *adj* 1 of or pertaining to a/the nation; national: ~ সঙ্গীত. 2 common to a/ the whole nation: ~ বৈশিষ্ট্য. 3 belonging to a class or variety: নানা ~ ফুল. 4 characteristic of a/ the nation: ~ ভাব 5 concerning a/ the nation as a whole: ~ সংসদ. 6 similar; resembling; like; identical with: চর্বি~. **জাতীয়া** *fem.*

জাতীয়তা *n* being a member of a nation; the official status of membership of a particular nation; nationality. **~বাদ** *n* devotion to one's own nation and strong sense of duty to uphold national interests against competing forces; nationalism. **~বাদী** *n* person who places the interests of his own country before all others; a believer in nationalism; a nationalist.

জাতেষ্টি [জাত+ইষ্টি] *n* Hindu religious rites connected with child-birth.

জাত্যে *adj* 1 high-born; aristocratic; of noble descent. 2 noblest; best. 3 graceful; beautiful; elegant.

জাত্যংশ [জাতি+অংশ] *n* 1 a part or relation of a caste. 2 family; descent; lineage. **জাত্যংশে** *adv* by caste : জাত্যংশে কায়স্থ.

জাত্যভিমান [জাতি+অভিমান] *n* pride in one's lineage; pride of noble birth. **জাত্যভিমানী** *adj* proud of one's lineage. **জাত্যভিমানিনী** *fem.*

জাত্যর্থ [জাতি+অর্থ] *n* that which constitutes the meaning of a word; connotation.

জাদ *n* a narrow band of silk, satin, etc for binding or fastening hair; a ribbon.

জাদা [P] *n suff* a son; a male offspring: শাহ~, the son of a king. **জাদী** *fem* daughter.

জাদু[১] *n* word used (a) to address a child in endearment: ~আমার, my darling; (b) as a taunt : কিহে~. **~মণি** *n* dear; darling.

জাদু[২], **যাদু** [P] *n* 1 the art of producing effects by apparently superhuman means; magic; sorcery; enchantment; witchcraft: ~বিদ্যা. 2 act of bringing sb under one's control by means of some occult power: ~ করা. **জাদু/যাদু করা** *vi vt* enchant; bewitch; charm. **~কর/গর** *n* 1 one skilled in magic; a magician; a sorcerer; an enchanter. 2 one who can exercise influence over the will of others by means of mesmerism or hypnotism; a mesmerist; a hypnotist. **জাদুকরী, যাদুকরী** *adj* that enchants; magical. ❑ *n fem* a female magician; a sorceress; a witch; an enchantress. **জাদুঘর, যাদুঘর** *n* a repository of specimens and objects of cultural, historical and scientific interest; a museum. **জাদুবিদ্যা, যাদুবিদ্যা** *n* magic; jugglery; sorcery.

জান[১] *n* 1 one who can foretell future events; an astrologer; a soothsayer; a diviner. 2 person possessing occult power to predict future.

জান[২] [P] *n* the living condition of man; life. **~ কবুল** *int* expressing firm determination to do (sth) or die: ~ কবুল করে যুদ্ধ করা. **~মান** *n* life and honour. **~মাল** *n* life and property. **জানি দুশমন** *n* an arch-enemy; an enemy posing a threat to one's life. **জানি দোস্ত** *n* a bosom friend.

জান[3] [P] *suff* used in addressing parents and near relations to show respects: আব্বা ~, আম্মা~, ভাই~, বুবু~.

জানকী *n* the daughter of king Janaka of Hindu mythology; appellation of Sita of the Ramayana.

জানত *adv* knowingly; consciously.

জানপদ *adj* **1** pertaining to human habitation. **2** rural population. **3** produced in human habitation.

জানলা=জানালা

জানা *vi* **1** have knowledge of; know: আমি তার অবস্থা জানি. **2** be aware of; be informed : কেউ জানে না, nobody knows. **3** form an opinion without certain means of knowledge; guess; conjecture; surmise: আমি জানি তোমার হয়তো অসুবিধা ছিল, I could guess your difficulty/problem. **4** feel; perceive; realize : মরম না জানে ধরম বাখানে. **5** have acquaintance/ speaking term with: তাকে জানি. **6** have ability to do sth: কাজ ~. **7** have education or ability to read and write : লেখাপড়া ~. ❑*adj* in the knowledge of; known: ~ কথা. **~জানি** *adj* made public: কথা ~জানি হয়েছে. **~নো** *vt* make known; inform. **~শুনা/শোনা** *adj* known; acquainted with: তার সাথে ~শুনা নেই, not acquainted with him. ❑ *n* acquaintance; familiarity.

জানাজা, জনাজা [A] *n* prayer for salvation of a departed soul before burial of the body.

জানানা, জেনানা [P] *n* **1** an adult female; a woman. **2** a wife. **3** a woman living in seclusion. **4** zenana or inner apartments of a house meant for isolation of women. **5** seclusion; purdah system.

জানালা *n* a window.

জানু *n* the joint connecting the two principal parts of the leg; the knee. **~ কাপালিক** *n* the movable bone covering the knee-joint in front; the knee-cap. **~ত্রাণ** *n* protective covering for the knee; knee-cap or knee-plate. **~সন্ধি** *n* the knee-joint.

জানুয়ারি [E] *n* the first month of the Christian calendar; January.

জানোয়ার [P] *n* **1** living being; animal. **2** a four footed animal; a beast. ❑ *adj* lacking common sense; inhuman; brutal; beastly.

জান্তব *adj* **1** of or relating to animals. **2** like a beast or its ways; beastly. **3** produced from animals: ~ চর্বি, animal fat.

জান্তা *adj* one who knows; knowing; experienced: সব~.

জান্নাত, জন্নাত [A] *n* paradise; the garden of Eden. **~বাসী** *adj* **1** living in the abode of bliss or paradise. **2** dead; deceased. **~বাসিনী** *fem.* **জান্নাতুল বাকি** *n* **1** graveyard in the eastern part of Medina. **2** the greatest paradise.

জাপ [E] *adj* of Japan; Japanese : ~ নৌবহর.

জাপক *n adj* one who tells one's beads silently and repeatedly.

জাপটানো *vt* embrace closely; clasp; grapple. **জাপটে ধরা** *vt* seize (one) by throwing the arms around; clasp in the arms. **জাপটা জাপটি করা** *vi vt* clasp one another; grasp each other.

জাপানি *adj* of Japan; Japanese. ❑*n* a native of Japan; the language of Japan; Japanese.

জাফরান [A] *n* **1** the orange-yellow colouring and flavouring powder obtained from the flowers of the crocus plant; saffron. **2** the bright orange-yellow colour of this. **জাফরানি**=জাফরান (২).

জাফরি [A] *n* a framework of wood, metal or bamboo strips set obliquely, used as screen, fence or as a support for climbing plants; a lattice; a trellis. **~ কাটা** *adj* latticed; trellised.

জাব, জাবনা *n* fodder for cattle made of chopped straw, oil cake, chaff, salt, etc mixed with water. **জাবনাভাণ্ড, জাব-পাত্র** *n* a manger.

জাবড়া *adj* wet or drenched like জাব. **~নো** *vt* **1** wet or drench thoroughly. **2** make mess of sth. **3** grapple; hug; clasp in the arms. ❑*adj* drenched; messy; hugged.

জাবদা, জাবেদা [A] *n* **1** a rule; an act; a law. **2** book of daily accounts. **~ আপিল** *n* prayer for retrial of a case by a higher court as per law. **~ নকল** a certified copy; copy from the original draft.

জাবনা⇒জাব

জাবর, জাওর *n* the food which ruminating animals bring up from the first stomach to chew at leisure; the cud. **~ কাটা** *vi* **1** chew the cud; ruminate. **2** (fig) bring up an old topic to discuss anew.

জাবেদা = জাবদা

জাম[1] [P] *n* a cup; a bowl. **~বাটি** *n* a large cup or bowl made of bell-metal; a big goblet.

জাম[2] *n* blackberry. **2** (also **কালো ~**) a variety of sweet.

জাম[3] [E] *n* state of being squeezed together; tight; tense; jam: জানালাটা ~ হয়ে আছে. ❑*adj* overcrowded; forcibly compact; jammed : সভাগৃহ ~.

জামড়া *n* part of the skin hardened by friction; horny hardness; callosity.

জামদানি [P] *n* a variety of muslin woven in floral designs; jamdani. ❑*adj* woven in floral designs.

জামরুদ[1] [A] *n* precious stone of bright greenish colour; emerald.

জামরুদ[২] *n* an old fortress near the Khaibar Pass.

জামরুল *n* a kind of small greenish-white juicy fruit.

জামা [P] *n* garment for the upper body; eg shirt, blouse, jacket, etc. **~জোড়া** *n pl* a suit of garments.

জামাই *n* husband of one's daughter; a son-in-law. **~ আদর** *n* **1** cordial entertaining with good food. **2** reception with care and attention befitting a son-in-law. **~ষষ্ঠী** *n* **1** the sixth day of the bright fortnight in the month of Joistha when a son-in-law is received and blessed by his parents-in-law, according to Hindu tradition. **2** rite connected with this. **ঘর~** *n* a son-in-law who puts up with his parents-in-law.

জামাত=জামায়েত

জামাতা=জামাই

জামানত [A] *n* **1** money or anything valuable given as a pledge for the repayment of a loan or the fulfilment of a promise or undertaking; security. **2** person who stands surety/ makes himself responsible for the conduct or debt(s) of another; a surety; a bail. **~নামা** *n* document containing the terms of security.

জামানা [A] *n* a period of time; an epoch; an age; an era.

জামাল [A] *n* beauty; elegance; grace.

জামিউল আজহার [A] *n* the oldest university of the world situated in Cairo.

জামিন [A] *n* a person standing monetary security for a defendant's appearance in court. **2** a sum of money paid or pledged on behalf of an accused awaiting trial to secure his release on condition that he will present himself for trial when required; bail. **~দার** *n* the surety of a defendant on bail. **~নামা** *n* document containing the terms of the bail; bail-bond. **~ দেওয়া** grant bail. **~ নেওয়া** accept a surety/bail. **জামিনে খালাস** release on bail. **জামিনে খালাস করা** bail out. **~ হওয়া** stand surety/ bail. **জামিনের অযোগ্য** non-bailable. **জামিনের যোগ্য** bailable.

জামিয়ার [P] *n* costly Kashmiri shawl embroidered with floral designs.

জামির *n* a large species of lemon; citron.

জামে মসজিদ [A] *n* a mosque big enough for Friday congregational prayers.

জাম্বীর *n* citron. ❑*adj* **1** of citron; citric. **2** produced from citron.

জাম্বু=জাম

জাম্বুরা=বাতাবি লেবু

জাযা=জাজা

জায় [P] *n* **1** a list; a catalogue; an inventory. **2** a detailed statement of accounts. **3** exchange: টাকার জায়ে জিনিস খরিদ. **~বাকি, বাকি~** *n* a statement of amounts standing due. **~ সুদী** *n* usufruct of a mortgaged agricultural land, enjoyed by a mortgagee.

জায়গা [P] *n* **1** space; room: তিল ধারণের ~ নেই, no room left for even an iota. **2** landed property : বহু ~র মালিক. **3** situation; circumstances: এমন ~য় কী করার আছে? what can you do under such circumstances/in such a situation. **4** stead; post; position : করিমের ~য় রহিম, Rahim in place/stead of Karim. **5** a receptacle; a container: চাল রাখার ~. **6** shelter; refuge: তার কোথাও ~ নেই. **7** habitation; abode : সুন্দরবন বাঘের ~. **8** a plot of land for building on; site: বাড়ি করার ~. **~ করা/দেওয়া** *vt* make room for.

জায়গির, জায়গীর [P] *n* **1** (hist) rent-free landed estate granted by a king to one in return for his meritorious services; a fief. **2** food and accommodation in exchange normally of tuition to children. **~দার** [P] *n* the recipient of a free-hold; a fief-holder. ❑*adj* enjoying or possessing a freehold. **~দারি** *n* possession and enjoyment of a jaghir.

জায়দাদ *n* [P] **1** landed property. **2** right to a landed property by virtue of occupation; occupancy right.

জায়নামাজ [P] *n* a mat or carpet on which one says one's prayer.

জায়ফল *n* the aromatic kernel of the nutmeg fruit used as spice.

জায়বদলি [P+A] act of exchanging; interchange; barter.

জায়বেজায় [P] *adj* right or wrong, just or unjust whatever one pleases: ~ গালি-গালাজ.

জায়মান *adj* springing up; coming into being; arising.

জায়া *n fem* the consort of a man; wife.

জায়াজীব, জায়াজীবী *n* **1** a man who lives on the income of his wife. **2** the husband of a professional actress or dancing-girl.

জায়াপতি *n* a man and his wife; couple.

জায়ু *n* a medicine; a drug. **~জব্যাধি** *n* a disease caused by/ resulting from the continuous use of a medicine; drug disease.

জায়েজ [A] *adj* allowed by Islamic *shariah*; lawful in Islam; in vogue; current.

জার *n* the paramour of a married woman; a man who wrongfully holds the place of a spouse. **~জাত**=জারজ.

জার, যার [P] *suff* suggesting abundance: গুল~, a garden of flowers.

জারক *adj* promoting or aiding digestion; digestive: ~ লেবু, pickled lemon.

জারজ *adj* unlawfully begotten; misbegotten; illegitimate; bastard. **~ সন্তান** *n* a bastard.

জারজার=জারেজার

জারণ *n* **1** the process of digestion. **2** (of metal) the process of heating (as ore) to extract metal; reducing metal: লৌহ ~. **জারিত** *adj* **1** dissolved in the stomach; digested. **2** (of metals) reduced for medicinal purposes: জারিত লোহা.

জাররা=জেরা[৩]

জারা[১]=জেরা[৩]

জারা[২] *vi* vt **1** cause to waste or decay; dissolve; digest. **2** make or be made into powder or ashes by burning; calcine or oxidize (metals). ❑*adj* dissolved; calcined; reduced: ~ লোহা, calcined iron.

জারানো *vt* b **1** cause to decay or dissolve. **2** change to another form; reduce to another state. ❑*adj* dissolved; reduced; calcined.

জারি[১], **জারী** [A] *n* **1** enforcing or being enforced; enforcement; introduction : আইন ~ করা/হওয়া. **2** announcement; circulation; publicity; propaganda. **3** display; boast; vaunt. **~ করা** *vt* **1** introduce; enforce; bring into force: আইন ~ করা, bring a law into force. **2** (legal) serve with a court summons. **শমন ~ করা** issue a summons; summon sb (to sth/to do sth). **3** announce; circulate; publicize; proclaim. **4** make a vain display of; boast; brag. ❑*adj* introduced; enforced; served; issued.

জারি[২] [P] *n* a kind of folk-song composed and sung in memory of the tragedy of Karbala.

জারিজুরি *n* **1** display of power and influence. **2** tricks and tactics; expedients; skill. **3** boast; bragging.

জারী⇒জারি

জারুল *n* a kind of tree or its timber which is used in making furniture.

জারেজার, জারজার [P] *adv* in an incessant stream; in a continuous flow. ❑*adj* flowing or trickling in drops; melting with tears: কান্দে ~.

জার্নাল [E] *n* **1** an account of daily transactions, or the book containing such an account. **2** a diary. **3** a daily newspaper. **4** any periodical magazine; journal.

জার্নি [E] *n* a travel from one place to another; a tour ; a journey.

জাল[১] *n* **1** a texture of twine, cord, silk, etc with meshes, commonly used to catch fish; a fishing net. **2** a piece of such open-work fabric used to scare birds or to protect fruits. **3** an oblong strip of such material used to divide a tennis court or a ping-pong table. **4** an implement for dressing woman's hair: খোপার ~. **5** the threads which a spider spins; a cobweb: মাকড়সার ~. **6** (fig) anything having power to allure or fascinate: রূপের ~. **7** a fine lattice-work: ~ঘেরা জানালা. **8** evil influence: কুহক ~. **9** love; attachment: মায়া~. **~ পাতা** *vi* lay or set a trap. **~ ফেলা** *vi* cast a net. **খেপলা-~** *n* a cast-net. **ছাঁকি~** *n* a scoop-net; a dripping net. **টানা-~** *n* a draw-net. **~ গুটানো** *vi* haul up the net. **~জীবী** *n* one whose occupation is to catch fish; a fisherman. **~ ছেঁড়া** *vi* (fig) get rid of a danger/trouble. **~পাদ** *adj* having the toes united by a membrane; web-footed. ❑*n* animals whose toes are united by a membrane (as a duck).

জাল[২] [A] *adj* **1** made in skilful imitation; spurious; counterfeit; fake: ~ টাকা. **2** forged in order to deceive; not genuine or original : ~ দলিল. **3** one who has disguised his identity for the purpose of deception; dissembling; dissimulating; false; hypocritical : ~ সাধু. **~ করা** *vt* **1** forge; commit forgery; counterfeit: টাকা বা দলিল ~ করা. **2** hide under a false appearance; disguise; dissemble; dissimulate; impersonate. **~-সাজ** *n* a forger. **~সাজি** *n* forgery.

জাল[৩] =জা[১]

জালক *n* **1** a flower bud. **2** a net used to protect fruits, vegetables, etc from birds. **3** a net fixed at the end of a pole used in plucking fruits.

জালতি *n* **1** a small net. **2** a long stuff with a net fixed to its end used for plucking fruits.

জালসাজ, জালসাজি ⇒ জাল[২]

জালা[১] *n* large fat-bellied earthen jar; an earthen barrel.

জালা[২] *n* young plant of paddy for transplantation: ধানের ~. **~নো** *vr* sprout; grow.

জালাতন=জ্বালাতন

জালি[১] *n* **1** a small net. **2** anything woven like a net. ❑*adj* woven like a net; reticular: ~ গেঞ্জি.

জালি[২] *n* the immature state of a gourd or pumpkin: কুমড়ার ~. ❑*adj* very young and tender: ~ লাউ.

জালিক *adj* **1** fraudulent; deceitful. **2** practising forgery. ❑*n* **1** a fisherman. **2** a hunter. **3** a spider. **জালিকী** *fem.*

জালিবোট *n* a ship's boat; a jolly-boat.

জালিম [A] *n* oppressive; tyrannical. ❑*n* one who oppresses; an oppressor; a tyrant.

জালিয়া *n* **1** a fisherman. **2** a hunter.

জালিয়াত [A] **1** *n, adj* practicing fraud/forgery; a fraud; cheat; forger.

জালিয়াতি *n* **1** act of forging; forgery. **2** act of manufacturing spurious or fake things. **3** cheating; deception; deceit; swindle; fraud. **~ করা** practise forgery; fraud.

জালুয়া *n* a fisherman.

জালোম=জালিম

জাল্ম *adj* **1** vulgar; vile; mean; base. **2** illiterate; ignorant. **3** injudicious; inconsiderate; indiscreet; imprudent; thoughtless; rash. **4** wicked; roguish; depraved; villainous. **5** cruel; hard-hearted. **6** crooked; deceitful; fraudulent.

জাসু, জাসুস [A] *adj* **1** (derog) topmost; foremost; first: কৃপণের ~. **2** clever; guileful; deceitful; knavish. **3** (derog) experienced; expert; veteran: চোরের ~, an expert thief. ❑*n* an emissary; a spy.

জাস্তি *n* excess; abundance; plenty. ❑*adj* excessive.

জাহাপনা=জাঁহাপনা

জাহাজ [A] *n* a large ocean-going vessel; a ship; a steamship; a steamer. **উড়ো~** *n* an airship; an aeroplane. **ডুবো~** *n* a submarine. **বিদ্যার ~** *n* (fig) a vastly erudite person. **যুদ্ধ ~** *n* a naval vessel fitted with armaments; a warship; a man-of-war. **সওদাগরি ~** *n* a merchantman; a merchant ship. **জাহাজে ওঠা** *vi* board a ship; get on board a ship; embark. **~ থেকে নামা** *vi* disembark. **~ঘাটা** *n* a dock; a wharf; a jetty. **~ডুবি** *n* shipwreck. **জাহাজি** *adj* **1** relating to a ship/ships. **2** borne by a ship; imported by ship. **3** working on board a ship. **জাহাজি মাল** *n* cargo. **এক ~ মাল** a shipload of goods.

জাহান [P] *n* the world: মুসলিম ~, the Muslim world.

জাহান্নাম [A] *n* the place or state of punishment for the wicked after death; hell; perdition. **জাহান্নামি** *n, adj* one deserving to be condemned to hell; a sinner; a wrong-doer. **জাহান্নামে দেওয়া** *vt* (fig) lead (one) to utter ruin. **জাহান্নামে যাওয়া** *vi* **1** go to perdition. **2** go to the dogs. **3** take the path of evil. **জাহান্নামের পথ** *n* the path of ruin.

জাহাঁবাজ=জাঁহাবাজ

জাহির [A] *adj* ostentatiously manifest; displayed; demonstrated. ❑*n* demonstration; display; exhibition. **~ করা** *vt* make a show; display; demonstrate: বিদ্যা ~ করা. **~ হওয়া** *vi* be disclosed/demonstrated/paraded; come to light; make a mark.

জাহিল, জাহেল [A] *adj* illiterate; unlettered; ignorant.

জাহিলিয়া, জাহিলিয়াত [A] *n* (lit) the age of ignorance; the age of chaos and confusion immediately preceding the rise of Islam.

জাহের=জাহির

জাহেল=জাহিল

জাহ্নবী *n* **1** the daughter of Hindu mythological sage **জহ্নু**. **2** an appellation of the Ganges.

জি = জী

জিওল, জিয়ল *n* **1** a kind of tree that lives long and is famous for exuding good gum, popularly called জিকা. **2** kinds of fresh water fish that can be kept alive in a vessel a long time. ❑*adj* that lives long; long-lived: ~ মাছ, live fish.

জিংগো, জিঙ্গো [E] *n* anyone who advocates a warlike policy or brags of his country's readiness to fight; a jingo. **~পনা** *n* jingoism.

জিকির, জিগির [A] *n* **1** reciting or repeating the name of Allah. **2** a watchword; a slogan; a clamorous shout. **3** an emphatic assertion. **4** repeated outcry. **5** a shout of triumph. **6** hue and cry; uproar; huge clamour. **~ দিয়ে বলা** *vi* cry aloud; assert with all emphasis.

জিগমিষা *n* willingness or eagerness to go. **জিগমিষু** *adj* willing or eager to go.

জিগর, যিগর [P] *n* **1** heart; liver. **2** courage; boldness; bravery. **~ পস্তানি** *adj* heart-rending; very much painful.

জিগা=জিওল

জিগির, জিগী=জিকির

জিগীষা *n* desire for conquest. **জিগীষু** *adj* desirous of conquest.

জিঘাংসক *adj* revengeful; malicious; blood-thirsty.

জিঘাংসা *n* desire to kill or injure. **~ বৃত্তি** *n* propensity to murder; murderous instinct; blood-thirstiness.

জিঘাংসু *adj* seeking to kill or injure; spiteful; resentful; revengeful.

জিজিয়া [A] *n* **1** (hist) tax in lieu of military service levied by the Muslim states on non-Muslim subjects (who were not required to render military service to the state as the Muslims were). **2** a tax levied by the poll or head; a poll-tax; a capitation-tax.

জিজীবিষা *n* desire to live on; love of life. **জিজীবিষু** *adj* desirous of a long life.

জিজ্ঞাসা *n* **1** desire to know; curiosity; inquisitiveness. **2** question; act of asking; an interrogation; inquiry; subject of inquiry. **~ করা** *vi* ask a question. ❑*vt* question; interrogate; inquire of. **জিজ্ঞাসক** *adj* one who questions or inquires. **জিজ্ঞাসন** *n* act of asking a question. **জিজ্ঞাসনীয়** *adj* fit to be asked; proper to be questioned about. **~বাদ** *n* inquiry and discussion. **~বাদ করা**= ~ করা. **জিজ্ঞাসিত** *adj* one who has been questioned; that which has been asked. **জিজ্ঞাসু** *adj* desirous to know; inquiring; inquisitive. **জিজ্ঞাস্য** *adj* fit to be inquired of; proper to ask about; the subject to ask or know: এখন জিজ্ঞাস্য এই ..., now the question is . . . .

জিঞ্জির [P] *n* **1** a chain; shackles; fetters. **2** (fig) love; affection; attachment: হৃদয়ের ~. **3** imprisonment; confinement; captivity.

-জিৎ *adj* (used as *suff*) one who wins victory or conquers sb/sth: ইন্দ্র~, বিশ্ব~, রণ~.

জিত *adj* **1** that has been conquered/ overpowered; vanquished; subdued; subjugated. **2** made obedient; tamed; controlled. ❑ *n* conquest; triumph; victory: তার ~ হয়েছে, he has won.

জিতা=জেতা

জিতেন্দ্রিয় [জিত+ইন্দ্রিয়] *adj* one who has mastered all sorts of passions; self-restrained; continent. **~তা** *n* self-restraint; self-control; continence; temperance.

জিদ, জেদ [A] *n* **1** obstinate resolution to do or not to do sth; dogged perseverance : কথাটা শুনে আমার মনে ~ হলো যে ..., when I heard this, I was recklessly determined that .... **2** a violent passion excited by real or supposed injury; anger; resentment : সব যুদ্ধই জেদের ফল, every war is the outcome of insane passion/anger. **~ ধরা** *vt* insist importunately on sb's doing sth; urge (one) persistently on; press hard. **~ হওয়া** *vi* be possessed with an inflexible resolution : তার ~ হয়েছে, এবার সে পরীক্ষায় পাশ করবেই, he is hell-bent on passing the exam this time by any means.

জিদালো, জেদালো *adj* fixed firmly in opinion or resolution; obstinate; stubborn; inflexible.

জিদি, জেদি *adj* under the influence of self-will; wilful; wayward. **জিদাজেদি, জেদাজেদি** *n* importunity; being importunate.

জিন[১] [A] *n* a supernatural being or spirit; a demon.

জিন[২] *adj* having gained the victory; victorious.

জিন[৩], **জীন** [P] *n* a leathern seat for a rider on a horse's back; a saddle.

জিন[৪] [E] *n* a twilled cotton cloth; jean.

জিনা[১] *vt* **1** (poet) defeat; conquer; vanquish; win. **2** (poet) surpass; excel; outdo; transcend.

জিনা[২] =জেনা

জিনিস, জিনিষ [A] *n* **1** a thing; an article; a commodity. **2** substantiality; substance; essence; worth : এতে ~ কিছু নেই, it contains no substance. **3** household fittings and furnishings: ঘরে অনেক ~. **4** subject; affair; business: সব জিনিসে মাথা গলানো. **5** matter: বাপের বাড়ি আর শ্বশুর বাড়ি এক ~ নয়. **~পত্র** *n pl* goods; merchandise; personal belongings; household articles; various kinds of things.

জিন্দা, জেন্দা [P] *adj* **1** living; alive. **2** having spiritual power: ~ পীর. **~ দিল** *adj* full of vitality and animation; lively; vivacious. **~ পীর** *n* **1** a living saint. **2** a saint who has attained spiritual success. **~বাদ** *int, n* slogan wishing long life: ইনকিলাব ~বাদ, long live the revolution.

জিন্দান [P] *n* **1** a jail; a prison (also ~খানা). **2** (fig) a tie; a bondage: দুনিয়ার ~খানা. **~বাসী** *n* the inmates of a prison.

জিন্দিগি, জিন্দেগি [P] *n* **1** the span of one's life; lifetime. **2** life; longevity. **~ ভর/ভোর** *adv* throughout one's life.

জিন্দেগানি [P] *n* life; lifetime.

জিপ [E] *n* small, high-powered utility motor vehicle, specially useful on rough ground; jeep.

জিব= জিভ

জিবরাইল, জিবরীল [A] *n* heavenly messenger/ angel who communicates Divine messages to the prophets.

জিভ, জিব *n* the organ of taste, speech, etc; the tongue. **~- আলগা** *adj* one who cannot keep a secret. **~ কাটা** *vi* press the tongue between the teeth in abasement. **~ ছোলা** *vi* scrape the tongue. **~-ছোলা** *n* tongue-scraper. **~ বের হওয়া** *vi* be overworked; feel exhaustion through overwork. **জিভে** *adj* shaped like a tongue; tongue shaped: জিভে গজা. **জিভে জল/ পানি আসা** make mouth water: সুন্দর আঙুরগুলো দেখে আমার জিভে জল এলো, the sight of the grapes made my mouth water.

জিমনাস্টিক [E] *n pl* the art of performing athletic exercises; gymnastics.

জিম্মা [A] *n* **1** responsibility for looking after; custody; guardianship; care : বাক্সটি দারোয়ানের ~য় আছে. **2** make hostage of sth/sb in the care/ custody of.... ❑*adj* committed to the custody/ care of. **~ করা, ~য় দেওয়া** *vt* commit to the custody/ charge of; put under care of. **~দার** *n* a custodian. **~ দারি** *n* custodianship.

জিম্মি [A]*n* **1** hostage. **2** (hist) the non-Muslim subjects of a Muslim state, whose security is the charge of the state; protected people; person (or thing) given or taken as a pledge/ security to ensure that demands will be fulfilled.

জিয়ন্ত=জীবন্ত

জিয়ল=জিওল

জিয়াদতি [A] *n* **1** excess; abundance. **2** oppression; tyranny.

জিয়াদা=জেয়াদা

জিয়ানো *vt* keep alive (as fish in a small reservoir). ❑ *adj* kept alive. **জিইয়ে (জিয়াইয়া) রাখা** *vt* keep in a sound state; preserve. (fig) keep in force.

জিয়াপুতি *n, adj fem* a woman who dies leaving all her children alive and who has not experienced any shock due to the death of any of her children in her life.

জিয়াফ=জেয়াফত

জিয়ারত=জেয়ারত

জিরগা, জির্গা *n* Afghan tribal assembly.

জিরা *n* carminative seeds of *Cuminium cyminum* plant, used as spice; cumin; cummin.

জিরাত, জেরাত [A] *n* **1** cultivation. **2** land for homestead or agricultural use: জমি ~. **জিরাতি** *adj* cultivable. **জিরাতি জমি** *n* cultivable land.

জিরান [A, P] *n* **1** ease; comfort; relaxation; rest. **2** temporary intermission; respite; leisure. ~ **কাট** *n* the first day of the renewed incision into a date-tree for its juice after a respite of three days.

জিরানো *vi* lay at rest; repose; refresh oneself.

জিরাফ [E] *n* the tallest of animals, with long neck and a small, narrow head; the camelopard; the giraffe.

জিরে=জিরা

জিল=জিলদ

জিলদ, জেলদ [A] *n* **1** a copy of a book or a volume of a set of books. **2** a leathern cover or jacket of a book. **3** leather. ~**গর** [A+P] *n* a book-binder.

জিলা, জেলা [A] *n* the largest administrative unit; a district.

জিলাপি, জিলিপি [H] *n* a coil-like juicy sweet. ~**র প্যাঁচ** *n* **1** (lit) the tortuous bends of this sweet. **2** (fig) duplicity; angularity; trickery; crookedness.

জিল্লত=জেল্লত

জিল্লা=জেল্লা

জিষ্ণু *adj* victorious; triumphant; winning; successful. ❑*n* **1** Hindu deity Vishnu. **2** Hindu deity Indra. **3** Arjuna of the Mahabharata.

জিহাদ=জেহাদ

জিহীর্ষা *n* a desire to steal. **জিহীর্ষু** *adj* desirous of stealing.

জিহ্বা *n* the organ of taste in animals, and more especially of speech in man; the tongue. ~**গ্র** *n* the tip of one's tongue. ~**গ্রবর্তী** *adj* about to be uttered; ready to be expressed. **জিহ্বাগ্রে** *adj* at the tip of one's tongue; in readiness to be uttered. ~**মূল** *n* the root of the tongue. ~**মূলীয়** *adj* **1** pertaining to the root of the tongue. **2** pronounced from the root of the tongue: ~মূলীয় বর্ণ, velar or guttural letter. ❑*n* the letters pronounced from the root of the tongue; the sound of the ক group of letters. ~**স্তম্ভ** *n* paralysis of the tongue.

জী[১], জি[১] *n mas fem* title of courtesy used at the end of a person's name or surname, current in the Hindu society: নেতাজী, গান্ধীজী, মাতাজী, পিতাজী.

জী[২], জি[২] *int* word used in responding to a call or in expressing one's consent to sth: জী আসছি, জী হ্যাঁ.

জীউ[১] [H] title of honour used with the names of Hindu deities: বাসুদেব ~.

জীউ[২]=জিউ

জীন=জিন[৩]

জীব *n* **1** an animal; a creature. **2** life; soul; spirit: জীব হত্যা মহাপাপ. ❑*adj* জৈব. ~**জগৎ** *n* the animal kingdom; the animate world. ~**জন্তু** *n pl* living creatures. ~**তত্ত্ব** *n* the science of life; biology. ~**তত্ত্বীয়** *adj* biological. ~**তাত্ত্বিক** *adj* pertaining to biology; biological. ❑*n* a biologist. ~**ধন** *n* cattle, sheep, etc; livestock. ~**ধর্ম** *n* natural faculties in animals, eg hunger, thirst, etc. ~**ধাত্রী** *n* the nourisher of living creatures; the earth. ~**বলি** *n* animal sacrifice. ~**বিদ্যা** *n* the science of life; biology. ~**রহস্য** *n* the secret of animal life; zoology; biology. ~**লোক** *n* the animate world; the animal kingdom; the earth. ~**হত্যা** *n* killing of an animal; murder; slaughter. **কৃষ্ণের** ~ *n* harmless, meek or gentle animals; animals deserving compassion and kind treatment.

জীবক *n* a money-lender who charges exorbitant rates of interest; a usurer. **2** an orderly; a servant. **3** a snake-charmer. **4** a beggar.

জীবৎ *adj* alive; living; lively. ~**কাল, জীবদ্দশা** *n* *n* duration of life; lifetime. ~**মানে** *adv* during (one's) lifetime.

জীবদ্দশা ⇒জীবৎ

জীবন *n* **1** the condition of an animal or plant organism in which it is capable of performing its natural functions; life; vitality. **2** the time from birth to death; period of existence: ~ কাটানো. **3** the length of one's life; longevity: ~ ফুরালো. **4** livelihood: জীবনোপায়. **5** water. **6** air. **7** person as dear as (one's life): তুমি আমার ~. ~ **উৎসর্গ করা** sacrifice one's life for; dedicate oneself to. ~ **যাওয়া** lose one's life; die. ~ **নেওয়া** take one's life; kill. ~**কথা,** ~ **কাহিনী** *n* a written account of the events and affairs of a person's life; biography; memoirs. ~**কীর্তি** *n* achievements of one's life. ~**চরিত** =~কথা. ~**চরিতকার** *n* a writer of biography; biographer. ~**দর্শন** *n* the guiding principles or practical wisdom of one's life; philosophy of life. ~**ধারণ** *n* act of leading or maintaining one's life. ~ **ধারণ করা** *vi* live on; lead one's life. ~ **নাট্যশালা** *n* domestic life or earthly attachment and interests compared with an amphitheater; amphitheater of life. ~**বল্লভ** *adj* dear as life. ❑*n* husband. ~**বিমা** *n* a system of securing, by making certain payments, a certain sum of money in case of accident or death; life insurance. ~**বিমা করা** *vi* insure one's life. ~বেদ *n* philosophy treating of the world as a whole; *weltanschauung*. ~যাত্রা *n* livelihood. ~যৌবন *n* life and youth. ~সংগ্রাম *n* struggle for earning livelihood; struggle for life. ~-সঙ্গিনী *n fem* life partner; wife. ~সঙ্গী *n mas* life companion; a husband. ~ সঞ্চার *n* infusion of life; restoration to life; resuscitation. ~স্বত্ব *n* right to enjoy for life. ~স্মৃতি *n* **1** recollection and reminiscences of one's life. **2** an autobiographical memoir.

জীবনাধিক [জীবন+অধিক] *adj* dearer than one's life.

জীবনান্ত [জীবন+অন্ত] *n* end of life; death. **জীবনান্তে** *adv* at the end of life; after death.

জীবনান্তকর *adj* that which contaminates life; fatal.

জীবনান্তকাল *n* time of death.

জীবনাবধি [জীবন+অবধি] *adv* during/ throughout one's life.

জীবনাবসান [জীবন+অবসান] *n* death; demise.

জীবনালেখ্য [জীবন+আলেখ্য] *n* the picture of one's life.

জীবনাহুতি [জীবন+আহুতি] *n* dedication of life. ~ দেওয়া *vi* sacrifice life.

জীবনী *adj* that gives strength and energy; life-giving; animating: ~শক্তি, vital power. ❑*n* a biography. ~কার *n* biographer.

জীবনেতিবৃত্ত [জীবন+ইতিবৃত্ত] *n* a life-history; a biography.

জীবনোচ্ছ্বাস [জীবন+উচ্ছ্বাস] *n* swollen state of life; life full of vitality.

জীবনোপায় [জীবন+উপায়] *n* means of livelihood/sustenance.

জীবন্ত *adj* **1** in a live state; alive; living. **2** clear; obvious; vivid; bright : ~ সত্য. **3** full of life; active: ~ আগ্নেয়গিরি, active volcano.

জীবন্তিকা *n* **1** (bot) a parasitic plant. **2** a hanger-on; a parasite; a sycophant. **3** a short drama or play; a playlet.

জীবন্মুক্ত [জীবৎ+মুক্ত] *adj* freed from earthly attachment while living on earth; spiritually enlightened. **জীবন্মুক্তি** *n* liberation from physical bondage; other worldliness.

জীবন্মৃত [জীবৎ+মৃত] *adj* almost dead although living; dispirited; disabled.

জীবাণু [জীব+অণু] *n* a microscopic organism, eg a bacillus or bacterium; a microbe. **রোগ~** *n* a microscopic organism which causes disease; a bacillus.

জীবাত্মা [জীব+আত্মা] *n* **1** the sentient or embodied soul. **2** the Supreme Soul as existent in individual creatures.

জীবান্তক [জীব+অন্তক] *adj* that destroys life; life-taking; killing. ❑ *n* a hunter.

জীবাবশেষ [জীব+অবশেষ] *n* the fossilized remains of a living being dug out of the earth.

জীবাশ্ম [জীব+অশ্ম] *n* (geol) the form of the body of a plant or animal petrified and preserved in the strata of the earth's surface; a fossil.

জীবিকা *n* means of living; livelihood; a trade; a profession; a calling. ~ নির্বাহ *n* act of maintaining; act of supporting (oneself or family); maintenance. ~ অর্জন *n* act of earning one's bread; earning of livelihood. ~ অর্জন করা *vi* earn a living.

জীবিত *adj* living; alive; existent: ~ প্রাণী. ❑*n* existence; life: জীবিতেশ্বর. **জীবিতা** *fem*. ~ কাল *n* period/duration of life; lifetime. ~নাথ, জীবিতেশ, জীবিতেশ্বর *n* **1** husband. **2** lord of one's heart. **3** lord of one's life; god.

-জীবী *adj suff* **1** having life; living; existing: দীর্ঘ~. **2** working for livelihood: মসী~, ব্যবহার ~.

জীমূত *n* **1** the cloud. **2** the mountain. ~ নাদ, ~মন্দ্র *nn* the roar or rumbling of the cloud. ~বাহন *n* (Hindu myth) one who is borne by clouds, an appellation of Indra.

জীয়ন, জিয়ন *n* act of living; life. ~কাঠি *n* (fig) the wand that infuses life. **জীয়ন্ত** *adj* living. **জীয়ন্তে** *adv* in a state of living; while living. **জীয়ন্তে মরা** *adj* dead while yet alive.

জীয়ল=জিওল

জীয়ানো=জিয়ানো

জীরক, জীরা=জিরা

জীর্ণ *adj* **1** emaciated; become lean: রোগ~. **2** decayed; dilapidated: ~ অট্টালিকা. **3** worn-out: ~ গ্রন্থ. **4** digested; dissolved in the stomach: ~ খাদ্য. **5** eaten away; corroded: ~ গরাদে. **6** decrepit; infirm; senile: ~ দেহ. ~তা *n*. **জীর্ণা** *fem*. ~ জ্বর *n* chronic fever. ~ বসন *n* old and tattered raiment ~-বসন *adj* in tattered clothes. ~শীর্ণ *adj* emaciated and shrivelled; lean and thin. ~ সংস্কার *n* repairing; mending. ~ সংস্কার করা *vt* repair; recondition; renovate; overhaul.

জুঁই, যুঁই *n* a sort of jasmine.

জুখা=জোঁকা

জুগুপ্সা *n* **1** upbraiding sb for doing sth; a chiding; a reproof. **2** scorn; hatred; disgust; aversion. **জুগুপ্সক** *adj*. **জুগুপ্সন** *vt* abuse; upbraid; scold reproach. **জুগুপ্সিত** *adj* upbraided; reproached; censured; abused.

জুচ্চুরি⇒ জুয়া

জুজ [A] *n* (book-binding) a forme of a book. ~বন্দি *n* act of book-binding. ❑*adj* bound with each forme sewn separately. ~ সেলাই *n* method of book binding in which each forme is sewn separately.

জুজু *n* sth imaginary that causes terror; an alarming apparition; a bogey; an evil spirit; a bugbear; a ghost; a hobgoblin: ~র ভয় দেখানো.

~বুড়ি, ~বুড়ী *n* imaginary witch spoken of to control or rectify children. **~র ভয়** *n* extreme terror about an imaginary danger.

জুজুৎসু [Jap] *n* the Japanese art of wrestling; jujutsu.

জুঝা, জুঝাজুঝি=জোঝা

জুটন *n* fabric produced from jute; jute-fabric.

জুটা, জুটানো ⇒জোটা

জুঠা [H[*n, adj* (of food) partially eaten; left over of one's meal.

জুডো [Jap] *n* an advanced form of jujutsu in which an opponents own weight and strength are used against him; judo.

জুড়ন, জুড়া=জোড়া[২]

জুড়ানো, জুড়নো *vi* **1** make cold; become cool: খাবার ~. **2** allay or be allayed; soothe, calm or relieve; be soothed/ calmed/relieved: জ্বালা ~. **3** satisfy or be satisfied; console or be consoled: প্রাণ ~ . ❑*adj* allayed; cooled; calmed; consoled; satisfied.

জুড়ি *n* **1** a pair of two equals; a couple: ~ বাঁধা; a match; an equal; a parallel; second man: এর ~ মেলা ভার. **3** an associate; a helper; a companion. **4** a carriage drawn by a pair of horses: ~ গাড়ি. **5** a pair of singers in an opera. **6** the two additional strings of a সেতার. ❑*adj* of equal power or ability: ~ লোক. **~দার** *n* an associate; a companion; a match.

জুত[১], জুৎ[১] *n* comfort after one's heart; perfect fitness (for a purpose); complete ease or contentment: ঠাণ্ডায় জমে গেছি, এক কাপ চা পেলে বেশ ~ হবে. **2** suitability; convenience; advantage; fitness. **~সই** *adj* to one's heart; filling; advantageous; convenient; suitable.

জুত[২], জুৎ[২] *n* **1** brightness, esp of reflected light; lustre; shine: চোখের ~. **2** strength; energy; vigour; fitness: দেহের ~. **3** habit of talking much; garrulity; long-tongue; sharp-tongue: মুখের ~.

জুতা, জুতো [U] *n* a covering for the foot, usually of leather; foot-wear; shoe(or a pair of shoes). **~ খাওয়া** *vi* be beaten with a shoe. **2** be insulted. **3** (fig) be fooled. **~জুতি** *n* beating one another with shoes. **~ ছাড়া** *vi* put off shoes. **~নো** *vt* **1** beat with a shoe. **2** (fig) insult (one) grossly. **~ মারা**=জুতানো. **~ সেলাই থেকে চণ্ডীপাঠ** ⇒চণ্ডী.

জুৎ⇒জুত[১], জুত[২]

জুদা [P] *adj* gone apart; separated; detached; disjoined. **~ করা** *vt, vi* separate; set apart. **~ হওয়া** *vi* be separated; part asunder. **~ ~** *adv* separately. **~ই** [P] *n* **1** separation or estrangement from one's lover. **2** difference.

জুন [E] *n* the sixth month of the Christian calendar; coinciding the period covering the later half of Jaistha and first half of Ashar of the Bengali calendar; the month of June.

জুনিয়র [E] *adj* **1** younger. **2** later or lower in office/ rank; junior.

জুবা= জোব্বা

জুবিলি, জুবিলী [E] *n* a jubilee or great festive occasion to celebrate the anniversary of a notable event after it has completed its twenty fifth, fiftieth and sixtieth year, called silver jubilee, golden jubilee and diamond jubilee respectively.

জুম *n* method of cultivation among hill tribes, carried on by digging holes and putting seeds of various crops together in a single hole: ~ চাষ.

জুম্মা, জুমা [A] *n* **1** weekly congregational prayer on Friday. **2** Friday. **~ ঘর** *n* a mosque in which weekly congregational prayer as well as five canonical prayers are hold regularly. **~বার** *n* Friday. **~ মসজিদ** *n* **1** a mosque spacious enough to accommodate weekly congregational prayers. **2** the famous congregational mosque at old Delhi built by emperor Shahjahan.

জুয়া, জুয়ো [H] *n* game of chance; the practice of gaming for money; the act of gambling; gamble. **~ খেলা** *vi* play games of chance for money; gamble. **~র আড্ডা** *n* a gambling house; a gambling-den. **~ড়ি, ~রি** *n* one who gambles habitually; a gambler.

জুয়াচুরি, জুচ্চুরি, জোচ্চুরি *n* fraud practiced in gambling; deception; swindling. **~ করা** *vi* have recourse to fraud; defraud; deceive; swindle.

জুয়াচোর, জোচ্চোর *n* **1** one who plays deceitful tricks in gambling. **2** one who lives by sharp practices; a tricky fellow; a cheat; a sharper. **জোচ্চোরিপনা** *n* behaving like cheat; cheating.

জুরি, জুরী [E] *n* a sworn body of persons who must pronounce a verdict on the facts of a case in a court of justice after direction by a judge; the jury.

জুলফি, জুলফি, জুলফ [A] *n* hair allowed to grow on the sides of a man's face; side-burns; whiskers.

জুলফিকার [A] *n* the famous sword of Caliph Ali.

জুলমাত [A] *n* **1** perpetration of tyranny and injustice and consequent disorder, chaos and confusion. **2** indication of a great upheaval.

জুলাই [E] *n* the seventh month of the Christian calendar; July.

জুলাপ = জোলাপ

জুলি *n* a narrow drain for waste water.

জুলু [E]*n* the Zulu tribe of South Africa or their language.

জুলুম [A] *n* **1** torture; oppression; tyranny. **2** application of force; pressure; violence; intimidation. ~**বাজ** *adj* one who uses violent and unjust means to achieve his ends. ~**বাজি** *n* taking recourse to oppressive and violent means.

জুষ, জুস [P] *n* the liquid portion of a curry; soup; juice; broth.

জুস=জুজ

জেওর [P] *n* **1** jewellery. **2** dress and decoration. **জেওরাত** *pl.*

জেটি [E] *n* a structure built out into a body of water as a landing place for ships; a jetty.

জেঠ, জাঠ *adj* related through the elder brother brother of one's father or father-in-law: ~শ্বশুর, elder brother of one's father-in-law.

জেঠতুত, জেঠতুতো, জেঠাত *adj* related as being the children of the elder brother of one's father. ~ **ভাই/বোন** *n* cousin.

জেঠা *n* father's elder brother; an uncle. ❑*adj* (derog) acting like ripe before the natural time; talkative; impertinent. ~**মি** ~**মো** *n* precocity; impertinence.

জেঠাইমা=জেঠি

জেঠাত⇒জেঠতুত

জেঠি *n* tiny reptile found in dwelling horses; the lizard.

জেঠী, জেঠীমা, জেঠাইমা *n* wife of one's father's elder brother; an aunt.

জেতা[১] *adj* one who has won victory; victorious.

জেতা[২], **জিতা** *vi* **1** achieve victory; be victorious. **2** get as profit or advantage; gain. **3** win; get or acquire by winning (as a stake). ~**নো** *vt* **1** cause or help to win; make victorious. **2** cause to gain sth.

জেদ=জিদ

জেনা, জিনা [A] *n* **1** voluntary sexual intercourse between a man and a woman married to another person; adultery. **2** voluntary sexual intercourse between unmarried persons; fornication. **3** sexual intercourse with a woman or girl against her will; rape. ~ **করা** *vi,vt* commit adultery or fornication; rape. ~**কার** *adj* guilty of adultery/fornication or violating a woman against her will. ❑*n* an adulterer/ adulteress; a fornicator/fornicatress; a rapist.

জেনানা=জানানা

জেনারেল [E] *n* an army general; a commander.

জেন্দ [P] *n* **1** the language of ancient Persia. **2** the language of the scripture of Zoroaster, the Persian religious teacher. **জেন্দাবেস্তা, জেন্দা আবেস্তা** *n* the Zoroastrian scripture Avesta and its language Zend.

জেন্দা=জিন্দা

জেব [A, P] *n* **1** a small bag or pouch in a garment; a pocket. **2** a small bag for money; a purse. ~ **ঘড়ি** *n* a pocket watch.

জেব্রা [E] *n* a striped South African animal allied to the horse and ass; a zebra.

জেম্মা–=জিম্মা

জেয় *adj* fit to be won/ conquered; worth winning/ conquering; conquerable (opp অজেয়).

জেয়াদা, জিয়াদা [A] adj **1** many; much, more; more than; exceeding. **2** very much; excessive; abundant; plentiful. ❑*adv* in an excessive manner; beyond the limit: এটা খুব ~ হচ্ছে.

জেয়াফত, জিয়াফত [A] *n* bidding to an entertainment; invitation to a feast, etc.

জেয়ারত, জিয়ারত [A] *n* **1** visiting a grave or graveyard and praying for the salvation of the departed soul(s). **2** visiting a holy place.

জের [P] *adj* **1** humbled; overpowered. **2** weakened; enfeebled: ~দস্ত. ❑ *n* **1** defeat; discomfiture. **2** that which is left; remnant. **3** that which remains unpaid; arrears. **4** (accounts) the totals of the credit and debit side to be carried over or brought forward to the next page. ~ **টানা** *vi* **1** (accounts) bring forward or carry over the totals of the credit and debit sides. **2** suffer the consequences of one's deeds and misdeeds. ~**দস্ত** *adj* weak (opp জবরদস্ত). ~ **মেটানো** *vi* **1** balance the accounts; pay up the arrears. **2** finish the remaining or arrear work.

জেরবার [P] *adj* **1** much troubled and afflicted; wounded; overwhelmed; harassed. **2** weakened; exhausted; reduced to poverty. **3** humble; humiliated. ~ **করা** *vt vi* overwhelm; humble; harass; ruin. ~ **হওয়া** *vi* be reduced to poverty; be ruined.

জেরা[১] [A] *n* (legal) subjecting a witness of the opposite party to close questioning by the counsel of the other party; cross-examination. ~ **করা** *vt* cross-examine.

জেরা[২] *n* a piece of metal armour for the protection of the upper part of the body in war; a coat of mail.

জেরা[৩], **জারা, জার্‌রা** [U,H] *adj* a bit; a little; slight; small in size or extent; short in duration: ~ অপেক্ষা করো.

জেরাত=জিরাত

জেল [E] *n* **1** a place of confinement; a jail; a prison. **2** imprisonment : তার ~ হয়েছে, has been sentenced to imprisonment. ~**খানা** *n* a prison; a jail. ~ **খাটা** *vi* serve or undergo a term of imprisonment. ~ **হওয়া** *vi* be jailed/sentenced to imprisonment. **জেলে দেওয়া/পাঠানো** *vt* commit to prison. **জেলে যাওয়া** *vi* be jailed/imprisoned.

জেলদ=জিলদ

জেলা=জিলা

জেলার [E] *n* superintendent of a jail; a jailer.

জেলি [E] *n* soft, semi-solid food substance made of fruit juice and sugar; jelly.

জেলে *n* **1** one whose occupation is to catch fish; a fisherman. **2** a fisher by caste. ~**নী** *fem.* ~ **ডিঙ্গি** *n* a longish and open boat for fishing; a fishing-boat. ~ **পাড়া** *n* fishermen's quarters in a village or town.

জেল্লৎ, জেল্লত, জিল্লত [A] *n* dishonour; disgrace.

জেল্লা, জিল্লা [A] *n* **1** brightness; brilliance; radiance; shine. **2** glaze; glossiness, polish; glamour. ~ **ই** *n* splendour; grandeur; magnificence. ~ **দেওয়া** *vi* shine; glitter. ~ **ধরানো** *vt* put a shine on; cause to be shining. ~**দার** *adj* shining; glittering; bright; splendid.

জেহাদ, জিহাদ [A] *n* **1** Muslim religious war against infidels. **2** war in defence of religion; a holy war. **3** struggle against falsehood and injustice and for upholding truth and justice. **জেহাদি, জেহাদী** *adj* concerning and pertaining to holy war.

জেহেন [A] *n* **1** intellect; good memory. **2** creative or inventive capacity; genius.

জৈতুন [A] *n* the olive tree or its fruits. **জৈতুনি** *adj* produced or manufactured from olive.

জৈত্র *adj* victorious; triumphant; successful. ❑*n* quicksilver; mercury. **জৈত্রী** *fem.*

জৈত্রি=জয়ত্রী

জৈন *n* **1** Indian religious community adhering to Jainism, founded by Mahavira. **2** Jainism.

জৈব *adj* pertaining to the animal and vegetable worlds; organic (opp অজৈব). ~ **রসায়ন** *n* branch of chemistry dealing with carbon compounds; organic chemistry. ~ **সার** *n* a mixture of soil and various manure; compost.

জো *n* **1** scope; opportunity; chance: অস্বীকার করার ~ নেই. **2** the favorable condition of soil for psloughing or proper time for sowing. **3** advantageous circumstances for doing sth which is otherwise improper or difficult: ~ পেয়ে গেছে. **4** an untoward situation occurring un-expectedly: উৎসব মাটি হবার ~. ~ **কাল** *n* proper time for sowing. ~-**বৃষ্টি** *n* favourable rain for sowing. ~ **পাওয়া** find an opportunity. ~ **পেলে** given favou'able circumstances.

জোঁক *n* blood-suckirg worm living in water and wet places; the leech. **জোঁকের মুখে নুন** (fig) a fitting punishment for a wicked person; a fitting retort that effectively silences a braggart.

জোক, জোখ *n* act of measuring; measurement: মাপ~ করা. মাপ ~ *adj* measured; conforming to the schedule of measurement.

জোকা, জোখা, *vt* measure sth with sth ~ দেওয়া লেখা~ *n* written statement of expenses.

জোকার[1] *n* sound made by Hindu women with their tongues on festive occasions. ~ **দেওয়া** *vi* make this sound.

জোকার[2] [E] *n* **1** one who jokes; a joker; a jester. **2** the fifty-third card in a pack used in some games as highest trump.

জোখ=জোক

জোগাড়=যোগাড়

জোগান=যোগান

জোচ্চুরি=জুয়া

জোছনা *n* (poet) moonlight.

জোঝা, জুঝা *vt* fight with; struggle for. ~**জুঝি** *n* fighting with each other.

জোট *n* **1** union; confederacy: ~ বাঁধা. **2** assemblage; collection. ~ **করা** *vt* collect; assemble; unite. ~ **পাকানো** *vi* unite together; combine in a body; form a pact. ~ **বেঁধে, এক জোটে** *adv* in a body; all together; unitedly.

জোটা *vt* be available/ collected/earned: অন্ন ~. **2** come or gather together; assemble; collect: ছেলেরা জুটেছে **3** be present; appear: এসে ~.**4** get; gain; obtain: একটা চাকরি জুটে গেল. ~**নো** *vt* cause to come together/assemble; make (sth) available

জোড়, যোড় *n* **1** joining of two or more things; a joint: জোড়ের মুখ. **2** a couple; a pair: মানিক ~. **3** a pair of upper and lower garments; a piece of sari and scarf: বেনারসি ~. ❑*adj* **1** clasped; folded: ~ হাত. **2** even: ~ সংখ্যা. ~ **করা** *vt* join; clasp; fold (as one's hands). ~ **বাঁধা** *vt* unite or join in pairs. ~ **বাঁধানো** *vi* cause to unite. ~ **ভাঙা** *vt* sever; separate; disunite. ~ **মেলানো** *vt* find one to pair with; pair . ~**কলম** *n* a horticultural graft. ~ **হাতে, করজোড়ে** *adv* with folded hands. **জোড়ে জোড়ে** *adv* by/in pairs. **জোড়ের পায়রা** constant companion; bosom friend.

জোড়া[1] *adj* two in number: ~ গরু. ❑*n* **1** a pair; a couple: এক ~ গরু. **2** a match; an equal: ~ পাওয়া ভার, hard to find an equal. **3** a joint: ~ **খুলে যাওয়া** be disjointed. ~ **দেওয়া** join (piees or parts of sth).

জোড়া[2]**, জুড়া** *vt* **1** fasten; affix; yoke: গাড়িতে ঘোড়া ~. **2** begin; commence: গল্প ~. **3** overspread; occupy : জায়গা জুড়ে থাকা, occupy space; মন জুড়ে থাকা; fill or penetrate into the whole mind.

জোড়াতালি *n* patchwork. ~ **দেওয়া** *vt* patch up; (fig) make up sth temporarily. ~ **দিয়ে** *adv* somehow; perfunctorily or haphazardly. ~

দিয়ে কাজ চালানো manage to do with whatever is available.

জোত[1] [A] *n* **1** landed estate held on proprietary basis. **2** landed property used for agricultural purpose. **~জমা** *n* landed property; real estate. ~জমি *n* (hist) landed estate held by a tenure-holder under a zemindar. **~দার** [A+P] *n* (hist) the owner of a proprietary agricultural farm; a tenure-holder under a zemindar.

জোত[2] *n* ropes or straps that fasten a bullock or a draught animal to the yoke ; rope-reins.

জোতা, জুতা *vt* yoke or harness an animal to a cart or plough or a grinding tree.

জোত্র/জোত্তর *n* **1** an opportunity; means: রোজগারের ~, means of earning. **2** provision; preparation: খাওয়ার ~.

জোনাকি, জুনি পোকা *n* the firefly; the glow-worm.

জোন্দা, জোঁদা *adj* **1** extremely sour. **2** very powerful.

জোব্বা, জুব্বা [A] *n* long-skirted loose outer garment.

জোয়ান [P] *n* **1** a person grown to manhood; adult. **2** (mil) a soldier. ❑*adj* full of youth; strong and stout: ~ লোক. **~কি** *n* youth. ❑*adj* youthful. **জোয়ানি** *n* youthfulness; youth; calf-time.

জোয়ার[1] *n* high tide; flow tide. **~-ভাটা** *n* the rising and falling of the sea; high and low tides; ebb and flow.

জোয়ার[2] *n* a kind of food grain; millet. **জোয়ারি** *adj* made of millet.

জোয়াল *n* the wooden crosspiece put over the shoulders of cattle used for draught; yoke. **জোয়ালে বাঁধা** *vt* put a yoke on; yoke.

জোর [P] *n* **1** strength; power; might. **2** force; pressure; violence: ~ করে নেওয়া, take forcibly. **3** loudness: গলার ~. **4** firmness: মনের ~. **5** integrity; probity: চরিত্রের ~. **6** stress of the voice on a syllable; accent: উচ্চারণে ~. ❑*adj* **1** loud; harsh; high: ~ গলা. **2** strict; urgent: ~ তলব. **3** unexpectedly good: ~ বরাত. **4** quick; swift: ~ কদম. **5** turbulent; violent; tumultuous: ~ আন্দোলন. **~ করা** *vt* force; coerce; compel; put pressure. **~ করে, জোরে** *adv* perforce; forcibly; by force; by means of coercion. **~ দেওয়া** *vt* emphasize; place emphasis on. **~ কলম** *adj* (of literary style) forceful and vigorous. **~ গলায়** *adv* at the top of one's voice; boldly; emphatically. **~ তলব** *n* **1** urgent summons (for personal attendance). **2** pressing demand (of taxes, etc). **~ বরাত** *n* very good luck. **~ হুকুম** *n* strict order. **~ জবরদস্তি** *n* coercion; application of force; pressure. **~ জবরদস্তি করা** *vt* coerce; put pressure on; force. **~ জুলুম** *n* oppression; violence; tyranny. **~ জুলুম করা** *vt* oppress; tyrannize; use violence. **~ যার মুলুক তার** a mighty person has his sway over everything; (prov) might is right. **জোরে জোরে** *adv* **1** quickly (as in walking). **2** loudly (as in speaking). **জোরে শোরে** *adv* severely; fiercely; violently. **~সে** *adv* with force; with pressure; with severity.

জোরাজুরি *n* **1** insistence; persistency. **2** use of force; coercion. **3** application of force against each other; mutual display of force.

জোরালো *adj* **1** forceful; emphatic; appealing: ~ আহবান. **2** strong; firm; forcible; convincing; earnest: ~ দাবি. **~ ভাবে** *adv* firmly; emphatically; strongly.

জোরু=জরু

জোলা[1], **জোল** *n* a narrow canal or ditch. **জোলান** *n* marshy land.

জোলা[2] [A] *n* **1** a Muslim weaver. **2** (fig) a fool; an idiot. **~নী** *fem.*

জোলাপ, জোলার, জুলার [A] *n* medicine having the power of purging; cathartic medicine; purgative. **~ নেওয়া** *vi* take a purgative.

জোলায়খা, জোলেখা *n* wife of ancient Egyptian minister Aziz Meser, and famous in romantic literature as the love-lady of Yusuf: ইউসুফ ~.

জোশ [P] *n* **1** heat; warmth. **2** strength; energy. **3** ardent zeal; enthusiasm: ইসলামি ~. **4** an ecstasy of mind, as if from spiritual influence; elevation of fancy.

জোহর, যোহর [A] *n* **1** afternoon. **2** afternoon prayers.

জোহরা[1], **যোহরা**[1] [A] morning star; Venus (seen in the eastern sky); evening star; Vesper (seen the western sky).

জোহরা[2], **যোহরা**[2] [A] *adj* **1** bright; far complexioned. **2** surname of the celebrated daughter of the prophet of Islam, Fatimah: ফাতিমাতুয যোহরা.

জো হুকুম [U+A] *n* an obedient servant. ❑*adj* one who obeys one's master unquestioningly.

জৌ *n* resinous substance produced by insects on trees; lac.

জৌলুশ, জৌলুস=জলুস

-জ্ঞ *adj* (used as *suff*) **1** one who knows; knowing. **2** learned; erudite: বিশেষজ্ঞ, গণিতজ্ঞ, শাস্ত্রজ্ঞ.

জ্ঞাত *adj* **1** that which is known; understood; familiar: ~বিষয়. **2** celebrated; renowned; famed. **3** one who knows; knowing; aware; informed; versed; acquainted with. **~ সিদ্ধান্ত** *adj* one who knows the injunction of the *shastras* or scriptural law; conversant with the *shastras*.

জ্ঞাতব্য *adj* **1** that which is to be learnt. **2** worth-knowing.

জ্ঞাতসারে *adv* **1** to one's knowledge; knowingly. **2** within one's knowledge/ cognizance.

জ্ঞাতা *adj* **1** one who knows; aware; informed. **2** experienced; conversant; wise. **জ্ঞাত্রী** *fem.*

জ্ঞাতি *n* **1** man or woman of the same kin; person related by blood or birth; kinsman; kinswoman. **~কুটুম্ব** *n pl* kinsfolk and other relations. **~ গোষ্ঠী** *n pl* kith and kin. **~ত্ব** *n* kinship. **~ ভাই** *n* a kinsman; a cousin.

জ্ঞান *n* **1** knowledge from personal view; cognition; understanding; perception: ইন্দ্রিয়লব্ধ ~. **2** the faculty of receiving impressions; consciousness; sense: রোগীর ~ ফেরেনি. **3** ability of understanding, appreciating or good judgement: রস~. **4** consideration: পুত্রজ্ঞানে স্নেহ করা. **5** knowledge; information: সজ্ঞানে এমনটি করা যায় না. **6** knowledge gained by study; erudition; learning; scholarship: শাস্ত্র~. **7** knowledge gained through experience and training: বিষয়কর্মের ~. **8** the inner enlightenment; spiritual knowledge ; wisdom: ~চক্ষু, ~যোগ্য. **9** common sense; discretion: ভালমন্দ ~. **~ করা** *vt* regard; consider; think; count: আমি তাকে আমার পরম মিত্র ~ করি, I consider him as a good friend of mine. **~ দান করা** *vt* impart knowledge; give lessons; teach; enlighten; make (one) wise. **~ লাভ করা** *vi* acquire knowledge; take lessons; learn. **~ হওয়া** *vi* **1** be restored to consciousness; regain one's consciousness. **2** grow in wisdom; be wise. **~ হারানো** *vi* **1** faint; swoon. **2** be beside oneself (as in anger). **~কাণ্ড** *n* **1** the philosophical portion of the Vedas. **2** intelligence; common sense; discretion. **~কৃত** *adj* done knowingly or intentionally; committed consciously or wilfully. **~কৃত পাপ** *n* wilful wrong-doing; deliberate sin. **~গত** *adj* relating to perception or knowledge; conscious. **~গম্য** *adj* attainable by knowledge and understanding; knowable; comprehensible. **~গম্যি** (colloq) *n* common sense; intelligence. **~গর্ভ** *adj* full of wisdom; enlightening; instructive. **~গোচর** *adj* within the range of knowledge; knowable; cognizable. **~গোচর করা** *vt* bring to one's notice/knowledge. **~গোচর হওয়া** *vi* come to one's notice/knowledge. **~গোচরে** *adv* within one's knowledge. **2** knowingly. **~গৌরব** *n* **1** the honour that one receives for knowledge and erudition. **2** the superiority of knowledge over everything. **~চক্ষু** *n* the mind's eye; the light of knowledge intellect; enlightenment. **~চক্ষু উন্মীলন করা** give one the light of knowledge. **~জগৎ** *n* the realm of knowledge and learning. **~তৃষ্ণা** *n* thirst for knowledge. **~দান** *n* imparting of knowledge. **~পাপী** *n adj* one who commits sins wilfully and consciously; a wilful sinner. **~পিপাসা** = ~তৃষ্ণা. **~পিপাসু** *adj* thirting or questing for knowledge. **~বাদ** *n* the theory that knowledge in the *summum bonum* of life; the theory of knowledge. **~বাদী** *n, adj* one who believes in knowledge as the end of life. **~বান** *adj* wise; larned; erudite. **~বিজ্ঞান** *n* knowledge and wisdom; arts and crafts. **~বিরুদ্ধ** *adj* contrary to knowledge and reason. **~বৃদ্ধ** *adj* veteran in knowledge and wisdom; venerable for one's profound wisdom. **~ব্রত** *n* pursuit of knowledge. **~ব্রতী** *adj* devoted to the pursuit of knowledge. **~ব্রতিনী** *fem.* **~ভাণ্ডার** *n* repertory of knowledge and wisdom. **~ময়** *adj* full of knowledge. ❑*n* the all-knowing; the supreme being. **~মার্গ** *n* knowledge considered as the way to salvation. **~যোগ** *n* knowledge as a means of salvation. **~লিপ্সা** *n* passion for knowledge; intellectual yearning; inquisitiveness. **~লিপ্সু** *adj* ardently desirous of acquiring knowledge; inquisitive. **~রহিত** *adj* void of knowledge; ignorant; foolish. **~সঞ্চার** *n* **1** regaining of consciousness; bringing back to sense. **2** infusion of knowledge. **~হীন** =রহিত.

জ্ঞানাঙ্কুর [জ্ঞান+অঙ্কুর] *n* (lit) the sprout or the beginning of knowledge; the rudiments of knowledge.

জ্ঞানানুশীলন [জ্ঞান+অনুশীলন] *n* cultivation of knowledge; study; culture. **~ করা** *vi* pursue or cultivate knowledge.

জ্ঞানার্জন [জ্ঞান+অর্জন] *n* acquisition of knowledge. **~ করা** *vi* acquire knowledge.

জ্ঞানী adj wise, learned; erudite.

জ্ঞানেন্দ্রিয় [জ্ঞান+ইন্দ্রিয়] *n* organs of perception; sense organs (ie the eyes, the nose, the tongue and the skin).

জ্ঞানোদয় [জ্ঞান+উদয়] *n* beginning or dawning of knowledge.

জ্ঞাপক *adj* **1** one who or that which forms. **2** indicative; expressive.

জ্ঞাপন *n* act of informing/ apprising/intimating; information; intimation; communication; indication; expression. **~ করা** *v t* inform; intimate; indicate; communicate; circulate. **~কারী** *n* one who informs. **~কারিণী** *fem.* **~পত্র** *n* an official statement of news; a bulletin.

জ্ঞাপনীয় *adj* to be announced/notified; fit to be circulated/made known.

জ্ঞাপয়িতা *n*, *adj* one who informs. **জ্ঞাপয়িত্রী** *fem.*

জ্ঞাপিত *adj* made known.

জ্ঞেয় *adj* **1** that should be known; worth-knowing. **2** knowable; congnizable.

জ্বর *n* disease characterised by a rise in temperature; fever. ~ **হওয়া** *vi* be ill with fever; run temperature. ~ **ছাড়া** *vi* have a remission of fever. ~ ~ **ভাব** *n* feverishness. ~ ~ **বোধ করা** *vi* feel feverish. **জ্বরে ভোগা** *vi* suffer from fever. **জ্বরের প্রকোপ** *n* rage of fever. **জ্বরে শয্যাগত** *adj* laid up with fever. ~**ঘ্ন** *adj* destroying/dispelling fever; febrifugal. ❑*n* febrifuge. ~**জনক** *adj* febrific; febrile. ~ **জ্বালা** *n* fever and attendant symptoms. ~**ঠুঁটো** *n* fever-blister. ~**বিকার** *n* high fever attended with delirium.

জ্বরাতিসার *n* fever attended with diarrhoea or dysentery.

জ্বরিত *adj* attacked with fever; suffering from fever.

জ্বলজ্বল *int* suggesting a glaring or sparkling state. ~ **করা** *vi* shine; glare; glitter; sparkle. **জ্বলজ্বলে** *adj* very bright; shining; glaring; sparkling; glittering.

জ্বলৎ *adj* burning; flaming; blazing.

জ্বলদগ্নি *n* blazing fire.

জ্বলন *n* burning; blazing; ignition.

জ্বলনাঙ্ক *n* temperature at which vapour from oil may be ignited; flash-point; ignition temperature.

জ্বলন্ত *adj* burning; flaming; blazing. ~ **অক্ষরে** *adv* in glowing letters. ~ **অগ্নি** *n* blazing fire.

জ্বলা *vi* **1** be enkindled: আগুন ~. **2** burn; be burning: লাকড়ি ~. **3** give a burning sensation: চোখ ~. **জ্বলে ওঠা** *vi* flare up. **ক্রোধে জ্বলে ওঠা** *vi* fly into rage; flare up.

জ্বলানো *vt* **1** enkindle; kindle; light. **2** set on fire; burn.

জ্বাল *n* heat of lire; burning heat; the process of boiling or burning on fire. ~ **দেওয়া** *vt* **1** apply heat; boil or burn (sth) on fire. **2** put fuel into a burning oven.

জ্বালা[1] *n* **1** a fire; a flame. **2** burning sensation; smarting pain: চোখ ~ করা. **3** mental torment or worry due to separation: বিরহ ~. **4** vexation; annoyance: কি ~!.

জ্বালা[2] *vt* **1** set fire; ignite; kindle: আগুন ~, বাতি~.

জ্বালাতন =জালাতন

জ্বালানি[1] *adj* fit for use as a fuel: ~ কাঠ. ❑*n* fuel; firewood.

জ্বালানি[2] *n* sensation of burning; irritation.

জ্বালানী *fem* of জ্বালানে.

জ্বালানে *adj* **1** one who burns or sets fire to: ঘর ~ লোক. **2** one who is too much exacting; demanding authoritative: ~ মহাজন.

জ্বালানো *vt* **1** kindle; light: চুলা ~, বাতি ~. **2** set fire to; set on fire: ঘর ~. **3** consume with fire; burn: মরা ~. **4** cause vexation/ annoyance/ disturbance to: ছেলেটা মাকে জ্বালায়.

জ্বালামুখ *n* the circular cavity or mouth of a volcano; a crater.

জ্বালাযন্ত্রণা *n* **1** burning sensation; pain. **2** worries; troubles; distress; tribulations of life: সংসারের ~.

জ্যা *n* **1** the string of a bow; a bow-string. **2** (geom) a straight line joining the ends of the arc of a circle or curve; a chord. **3** the earth.

জ্যাকেট [E] *n* **1** a short sleeved coat; a jacket. **2** the loose paper cover of a hardback book.

জ্যাঠা =জেঠা

জ্যান্ত *adj* **1** having life; living; alive.

জ্যামিতি *n* that branch of mathematics which treats of the properties and relations of lines, angles, surfaces and solids; geometry. ~**ক** *adj* geometrical. ~**বিদ** *adj* versed in geometry. ❑*n* a geometrician.

জ্যেষ্ঠ *adj* **1** eldest: ~ পুত্র. **2** elder: ~ ভ্রাতা. **3** older; senior: বয়ো~. ~**তাত** *n* elder brother of one's father. ~ **বর্ণ** *n* the highest caste among Hindus; the Brahmins. **জ্যেষ্ঠা** *fem.* **জ্যেষ্ঠাধিকার** *n* the right by which the eldest son succeeds to his father's real estate (as prevalent among certain people); primogeniture.

জ্যেষ্ঠী *n* the common lizard found in dwelling houses.

জ্যৈষ্ঠ *n* the second month of the Bengali calendar corresponding to the period between the middle of May and middle of June.

জ্যোতি,জ্যোতিঃ *n* **1** light; lustre; glow. **2** a star or planet. **3** eyesight: চোখের ~.

জ্যোতিঃশাস্ত্র *n* the art of foretelling future events from the positions of the stars at a given moment; astrology.

জ্যোতির্বিদ্যা *n* the science of the heavenly bodies; astronomy. **জ্যোতির্বিদ, জ্যোতির্বিৎ, জ্যোতির্বেত্তা** *n, adj* **1** one versed in astronomy; an astronomer. **2** versed in astrology; an astrologer.

জ্যোতির্মণ্ডল *n* the sphere of heavenly bodies; the celestial sphere.

জ্যোতির্ময় *adj* giving light; luminous; radiant; lustrous; brilliant. **জ্যোতির্ময়ী** *fem.*

জ্যোতিষ *n* the science of heavenly bodies; astronomy; astrology. **জ্যোতিষিক** *adj* astronomical; astrological. জ্যোতিষী *n* an astrologer.

জ্যোতিষ্ক *n* any light-giving body in the sky; a luminary; the sun or moon; a star. ~মণ্ডল=জ্যোতির্মণ্ডল.

জ্যোতিষ্মতী *adj fem* of জ্যোতিষ্মান

জ্যোতিষ্মত্তা *n* brightness; luminosity.

জ্যোতিষ্মান *adj* luminous; lustrous; shining.

জ্যোৎস্না *n* moonlight. ~ময় *adj* full of moonlight; gleaming in moonlight. ~ময়ী *fem.* ~ রাত্রি *n* a moonlit night.

ঝ

ঝ *n* the ninth consonant of the Bengali alphabet. It is a dorso or palato-alveolar voiced aspirated plosive sound. In some parts of Bangladesh, it is pronounced as a fricative sound. The local people of Dhaka pronounce it mostly as an africate sound.

ঝংকার, ঝঙ্কার *n* **1** a jingling sound (as of the strings of a musical instrument). **2** buzzing sound (as of bees). **3** a clattering or clanging sound (as of an armour). **4** a jesture/sound expressing anger: ~ দিয়ে ওঠা. ~ দেওয়া=ঝংকারা.

ঝংকারা, ঝঙ্কারা (poet) *vi* make clinking sound; jangle; hum, buzz.

ঝংকৃত, ঝঙ্কৃত *adj* jangled; clattered; hummed, humming; sounded in rhymes. **ঝংকৃতি, ঝঙ্কৃতি** *n*=ঝংকার.

ঝকঝক, ঝকমক *int* denoting brightness/ lustre/glare/splendour. ~ **করা** *vi* glitter; shine, glare; sparkle. **ঝকঝকানি, ঝকমকানি** *n* glare; lustre; splendour. **ঝকঝকে, ঝকমকে** *adj* luminous; glittering; shining. **ঝকঝকে তকতকে** *adj* neat and tidy.

ঝকমারি *n* **1** fault; failing; short-coming. **2** foolishness; folly; idiocy. **3** trouble; disturbance; affliction; distress; harassment. ~ করা *vi* act foolishly; commit a blunder; make a mistake: এমন কাজ করাটা ~, It is foolish enough to do such things. ~**র মাশুল** *n* penalty for a wrong; wages of sin.

ঝক্কি *n* **1** responsibility involving trouble and risk; charge; burden. **2** trouble; botheration. ~ পোয়ানো *vi* face trouble; be in a troublous/disquieting situation.

ঝগড়া [H] *n* **1** quarrel; an altercation. **2** a noisy disturbance; a brawl; an uproar; a row. **3** a dispute; a controversy; a strife; a contest. ~ করা *vi* quarrel; altercate; wrangle. ~ **বাঁধানো** *vi* set by the ears; stir up a quarrel; set at strife. ~ মেটানো *vi* make up a quarrel; settle a dispute ~**ঝাঁটি**, ~**ফসাদ** *n* (usu *pl)* quarrel; strife; dispute; dissension.

ঝগড়াটে *adj* quarrelsome; contentious; cantankerous.

ঝঙ্কার = ঝংকার

ঝঙ্কারা = ঝংকারা

ঝঙ্কৃত = ঝংকৃত

ঝঙ্কৃতি⇒ঝংকৃত

ঝঞ্ঝনা *n* **1** clattering sound: অস্ত্রের ~. **2** sound made by the collision of metallic bodies; clank. **3** the clap of a thunder; thunder.

ঝঞ্ঝা *n* high wind and rain; rainstorm; thunderstorm; gale; hurricane; tempest. ~**ক্ষুব্ধ** *adj* affected by a rainstorm. **তাড়িত** *adj* driven by a gale. ~**বর্ত** *n* a cyclone. ~**বাত/বায়ু** *n* a strong gale.

ঝঞ্ঝাট *n* **1** botheration; annoyance; vexation: ~ পোহানো. **2** a condition of difficulty; troubles; complexities; dilemma: ঝঞ্ঝাটে পড়া. ~ **করা/বাঁধানো** *vi* create trouble; put (one) to embarassing position. **ঝঞ্ঝাটে পড়া** *vi* get into an awkward predicament; be in a troublesome/trying state. ~ **পোহানো** *vi* undergo the stress and strain of a crisis. ঝঞ্ঝাটে *adj* full of troubles; bothersome; annoying.

ঝট *int* denoting speed, quickness or haste. ~ করে *adv* instantly; quickly, hastily.

ঝটকা, ঝটকানি *n* a sudden and forceful pull or jerk. ~ **মারা** *vt* pull or snatch away suddenly and forcefully. **ঝটকা বাতাস** *n* gust of wind; blast; squall.

ঝটপট[১] *adv* quickly; hastily: ~ কাজ সেরে নাও.

ঝটপট[২] *int* denoting the act or the sound of moving some broad flat object up and down or to and fro (as a bird's wings). ~ **করা** *vi vt* flap. **ঝটপটানি** *n* the act or noise of flapping.

ঝটিকা *n* high wind; storm; tempest; hurricane; gale.

ঝড় *n* a violent and usually destructive commotion in the atmosphere; a rainstorm; tempest; nor'wester. ~**ঝাপটা** *n* **1** storm; tempest. **2** (fig) dangers and difficulties; trials and tribulations. ~**তুফান** *n* violent storm accompanied by high waves.

ঝড়ো *adj* **1** like a storm; of or pertaining to a storm; stormy; tempestuous: ~ বাতাস. **2** storm-beaten: ~ আম, ~ কাক.

ঝণ্ডা [H] *n* a flag; a banner; a standard.

ঝনকাঠ *n* the horizontal part of the door or window frame; lintel.

ঝনঝন *int* **1** denoting a jingling or clattering sound; clanking: অস্ত্রের ~. **2** suggesting aching pain: মাথা ~ করছে. ~ **করা** *vi* **1** make a sharp sound, as by striking metallic substances; clank. **2** be in continued pain; ache. ~ করে বাজানো *vt* jangle.

ঝনঝনানো *vi* make a clattering or clanking sound. **ঝনঝনায়মান** *adj* clattering; clanking.

ঝনাৎ *int* denoting a sudden and violent clanging sound or banging: ~ করে দরজা বন্ধ করা, shut the door with a bang.

ঝপ *int* **1** denoting a splash, ie a noise from water dashed about. **2** denoting quickness or suddenness. **~ করে** *adv* **1** with a splash. **2** suddenly; sharply; abruptly: ~ করে ঝাপ দেওয়া. **~ ~** *int* **1** denoting a continuous splashing sound. **2** the sound produced by continuous rainfall.

ঝপাৎ *int* denoting the sound of diving or of falling sth heavy into water. **~ করে** *adv* with a splash.

ঝমঝম *int* denoting the pattering sound of heavy rainfall. **~ করে বৃষ্টি পড়া** rain cats and dogs; rain heavily.

ঝমর *int* denoting the jingle of bells in an anklet: ~ ~ মল বাজে, the anklets ringing rhythmically.

ঝম্প *n* act of jumping; a jump; a leap; a spring; a plunge (into water). **~ দেওয়া** *vi* **1** pass over by a leap; jump; skip; spring. **2** plunge (as into water).

ঝরকা, ঝরোকা *n* a window with cross bars forming small openings like network; a lattice window.

ঝরঝর *int* **1** indicating a continuous downpour: ~ বারিধারা. **2** a soft flow; a oozing (as of blood): ~ করে রক্ত ঝরছে. **3** neatness. □*adv* in a continuous shower.

ঝরঝরানি *n* **1** incessant flow or downpour. **2** oozing (as of blood).

ঝরঝরে *adj* **1** neat and clean: ঘরদোর ~ **2** refreshed; sound; hale: শরীরটা ~ লাগছে. **3** free of moisture: ~ ভাত. **4** clean and clear: ~ লেখা. **5** cracked; worn-out; out of repair: বাড়িটার অবস্থা ~. **6** spoilt; hopeless: আখের ~ হওয়া.

ঝরতি *n* the portion of the bulk of corn, etc that falls off the bags in transit. **~ পড়তি** *n* the portion which is wasted in storage or transit.

ঝরনা, ঝর্না *n* **1** a fountain; a spring. **2** a waterfall; a cascade; a cataract. **~ কলম** *n* a fountain pen.

ঝরা *vi, vt* **1** fall in drops: অশ্রু ~. **2** issue forth gently; percolate; ooze: রক্ত ~. **3** be shed: গাছের পাতা ~. **4** let ooze out; exude: ঘাম ~. **5** cast off; moult: পাখির পালক ~. **~নো** *vt* cause to fall in drops/shed/ooze/exude/moult; shake or cause to fall off.

ঝরিত *adj* fallen in drops; oozed; exuded; cast off; withered; moulted.

ঝরোকা, ঝরোখা =ঝরকা

ঝর্ঝর *n* **1** sound produced by running stream of water. **2** a strainer; a sieve; a colander. **3** a kind of musical instrument; a cymbal.

ঝর্ঝরিত *adj* **1** full of the babbling noise of a stream. **2** pierced in several places; perforated.

ঝর্ঝরী *n* a strainer with a handle used for sifting frys from oil.

ঝলক *n* **1** a flash of fire or light: আলোর ~. আগুনের ~. **2** a sudden and violent issue of a fluid; a gush: রক্তের ~. **3** a dazzling flash: রূপের ~. **4** a captivating spell of music: সুরের ~. **ঝলকানো** *vt* flash (as lightning). **ঝলকানি** *n* flashing. **ঝলকে ঝলকে** *adv* in gushes. **ঝলকিত** *adj* flashed.

ঝলঝল *int* denoting a dangling state or flapping motion. **~ করা** *vi* hang loose; swing; dangle; flap. **ঝলঝলে** *adj* dangling loosely; flapping.

ঝলমল *int* denoting a glittering or gleaming state. **~ করা** *vi* glitter; dazzle; sparkle. **ঝলমলে** *adj* shining; dazzling; sparkling; glittering.

ঝলসানো *vt* **1** overpower with light or splendour; dazzle: চোখ ঝলসে দেওয়া. **2** roast; singe: আগুনে মাংস ~. **3** be half-burnt. □*adj* **1** half-burnt: ~ রুটি. **2** that dazzles; dazzling. □ *n* act of scorching or singing; scorched or singed state; browned state; daze; dazing. **ঝলসিত** *adj* dazed; dazzled; scorched; singed; browned.

ঝল্লক, ঝল্লরী *n* dish-shaped gong rung at the worship of a Hindu deity; a cymbal.

ঝল্লকণ্ঠ *n* the pigeon; the dove.

ঝল্লিকা *n* the glow of sunrays.

ঝাউ *n* tamarisk tree; *Tamarica Indica*.

ঝাঁ *int* denoting quickness, haste, etc. **~ করে** *adv* quickly; instantly; without delay. **~ ~ করা** *vi* **1** make haste. **2** burn in the sun: রোদে ~ ~ করে.

ঝাঁক *n* **1** a flock: পাখির ~. **2** a swarm: মৌমাছির ~. **3** a shoal: মাছের ~. **~ বাঁধা** *vi* assemble; swarm; congregate. **ঝাঁকে ঝাঁকে** *adv* in flocks; in swarms; in shoals.

ঝাঁকড়া *adj* like a bush; bushy; shaggy: ~ চুল.

ঝাঁকা[১] [H] *n* large basket for carrying goods. **~-মুটে** *n* a porter who carries goods in a large basket.

ঝাঁকা[২] *vt* shake sth up to mix well (as a medicine). **~নো** *vt* cause to move from side to side, up and down: বোতল ~নো.

ঝাঁকুনি *n* shake; act of shaking.

ঝাঁজ[১] *n* **1** heat, flame: আগুনের/রৌদ্রের ~. **2** strong pungent taste: ওষুধের ~. **3** harshness; taunt: কথার ~.

ঝাঁজ[২] *n* a gong for ringing at a Hindu worship.

ঝাঁজর *adj* full of holes; porous; perforated.

ঝাঁজরা, ঝাঁঝরা *adj* **1** having little cells resembling honey-combs; full of holes. **2** very old; worn out : বুকের ভিতরটা যেন ~ হয়ে গেছে.

ঝাঁজালো, ঝাঁঝালো *adj* **1** pungently aromatic; strong to the taste. **2** (fig) harsh; severe: ~ কথা.

ঝাঁট *n* act of sweeping with a broom: ঘর ~ দেওয়া.

ঝাঁটা *n* handled implement for sweeping floors, etc; a broom. **~ খাওয়া** *vi* be insulted; be beaten with a broom. **~পেটা করা** *vt* give a good beating with a broom. **~র বাড়ি** *n* a stroke of broom. **~খেকো** *n* term of abuse. ❑ *adj* one who is beaten with a broom; contemptible.

ঝাঁপ[১] *n* act of jumping; a jump; a spring. **~ দেওয়া** *vi* spring suddenly from the ground; jump; leap; skip.

ঝাঁপ[২] *n* a hanging door or lid; a mat-door.

ঝাঁপানো = ঝাঁপ দেওয়া ⇒ ঝাঁপ

ঝাট *adv* quickly; at once: ~ করে এসে.

ঝাড়[১] *n* **1** a bush; a thicket: বাঁশের ~. **1** a cluster; a clump; a bunch. **3** a pedigree; a stock: ঝাড়ের দোষ. **4** a chandelier: বেলোয়ারির ~. **~বংশ** *n* all the members of a family. **ঝাড়েবংশে, ঝাড়েমূলে** *adv* root and branch; one and all.

ঝাড়[২] *n* act of sweeping floors, etc. **~ফুঁক** *n* the expulsion of a evil spirit or curing a disease by charms or religious rite; exorcism. **~ফুঁক করা** *vi* expel an evil spirit or cure a disease by means of exorcism.

ঝাড়ন *n* **1** sweeping and dusting. **2** a duster. **3** = ঝাড়ফুঁক ⇒ ঝাড়[২].

ঝাড়া *vt* **1** dust off; brush off; remove dust or dirt with a duster. **2** separate the chaff from corn; winnow: চাল ~. **3** show temper; vent one's spleen: গায়ের ঝাল ~. **4** exorcise: ভূত ~. ❑ *adj* **1** winnowed or cleaned: ~ চাল. **2** full; complete: ~ দুই ঘণ্টা অপেক্ষা করেছি, waited for full two hours. **~নো** *vt* **1** cause to be threshed/ winnowed. **2** cause to exorcise: ভূত ~নো. **~ হাত-পা** *adj* having no liability or burden of responsibility; free to pursue one's inclination.

ঝাড়ু *n* a broom. **~ দেওয়া** *vt* sweep; clean. **~দার** *n* a sweeper.

ঝাণ্ডা = ঝাগুা

ঝানু *adj* **1** having been long experienced; veteran. **2** clever; shrewd; sly.

ঝাপটা *n* **1** a sudden stroke; a gust (as of wind). **2** flapping (as of the wings of a bird). **ঝড়-~** *n* (fig) dangers and difficulties; trials and tribulations.

ঝাপসা *adj* not distinct; obscure; hazy; dim. **~ দেখা** *vi, vt* see dimly. **~ দৃষ্টি** *n* dim sight.

ঝামটা *n* chiding; scolding; snubbing: মুখ ~. **মুখ ~ খাওয়া** *vi* be snubbed. **মুখ ~ দেওয়া** *vi* t give a snubbing; snub.

ঝামর *adj* **1** overcast with rainy clouds. **2** pale; not bright. **ঝামরানো** *vi* become heavy with fluid; become browned or pale.

ঝামা *n* a piece of over-burnt brick; vitrified brick.

ঝামেলা *n* trouble; botheration; disturbance. **~ করা** *vi* create a disturbance, kick up a row. **~ পোহানো** *vi* bear a disturbance or botheration. **ঝামেলায় পড়া** *vi* get into a trouble; be in a fix.

ঝারা *n* water-pot with a porous device to sprinkle water on a plant.

ঝারি *n* water-can with a porous spout.

ঝাল[১] *adj* **1** hot or biting to the taste; pungent; acrid. ❑ *n* **1** secret enmity; acrimony; grudge: গায়ের ~. **2** acrid quality; acridity; pungency: লঙ্কার ~. **~ ঝাড়া** *vi* give vent to feelings of anger; satisfy a grudge. **~ চচ্চড়ি** *n* a variety of hot curry. **ঝালে-ঝোলে-অম্বলে** *adv* in every respect; in all affairs; everywhere.

ঝাল[২] *n* a metallic cement; solder. **~ দেওয়া** *vi* unite metals by solder; solder.

ঝালর *n* an ornamental fringe; a frill. **~দার** *adj* furnished with a fringe; fringed.

ঝালা[১] *vt* (music) twist up a sharp and loud sound on the string of an instrument; blaze up. ❑*n* a spell of blazing up.

ঝালা[২] *vt* **1** unite or join metal pieces with solder; solder. **2** dredge a river or pond. **ঝালানো** *vt* **1** cause to be soldered; get sth mended. **2** have a river, etc re-exacted/ dredged.

ঝালাপালা *int, n* word denoting an unpleasant feeling produced by the repeated sound of sth. **কান ~ হওয়া** *vi* be deafened; be annoyed.

ঝি *n* **1** a daughter: রাজার ~. **2** a maid servant. **ঝিকে মেরে বৌকে শেখানো** punish one's innocent daughter to correct the faults of one's daughter-in-law.

ঝিউড়ি *n* **1** daughter. **2** an unmarried daughter.

ঝিক *n* earthen proper support over an oven; any device to serve the purpose.

ঝিঁকা, ঝিঁকে *n* a jerk. **~ দেওয়া** *vi* give a jerk; jerk; push about.

ঝিঁঝি[১] *n* an insect that makes a creaking sound; the cricket. **~ শব্দ** *n* drone of the cricket.

ঝিঁঝি[২] *n, int* indicating a twinging or tinging sensation; pins and needles. **~ ধরা** *vi* have pins and needles.

ঝিকমিক, ঝিকিমিকি *int* suggesting a sparkling or glittering state. **~ করা** *vi* glitter; glisten; gleam; glimmer.

ঝিঙা, ঝিঙে, ঝিঙ্গা *n* cucurbetaceous plant or its vegetable fruit.

ঝিঙ্গুর, ঝিঙুর =ঝিঁঝি

ঝিনিঝিনি, ঝিনিকিঝিনি *int* indicating musical jingling of a dancer's anklets.

ঝিনুক *n* **1** a bivalve mollusc; the cockle; the oyster. **2** ear shaped valve of the cockle; an abalone. **3** metallic spoon in the shape of an abalone.

ঝিনঝিন=ঝিঁঝি[২]

ঝিম *n* a listless and dreamy state; languidness; lassitude: ~ হয়ে বসে থাকা.

ঝিমঝিম *int* indicating dizziness. **গা ~ করা** *vi* feel dizziness.

ঝিমনি, ঝিমুনি *n* drowsiness; nodding in slumber; dozing.

ঝিমানো *vi* nod in slumber; drowse; doze.

ঝিরঝির *int* suggesting a gentle current of air: ~ করে বাতাস বইছে, A gentle breeze is blowing. **ঝিরঝিরে বাতাস** *n* a gentle breeze. **~ করে বৃষ্টি পড়ছে** It is drizzling.

ঝিল *n* a long pool of water.

ঝিলমিল[১] [H] *n* a shutter; a Venetian blind.

ঝিলমিল[২] *int* denoting a glittering or flashing or quick vibration of light. **~ করা** *vi* sparkle finely. **ঝিলমিলে** *adj* that which is sparkling.

ঝিলিক *n* a flash; a glitter; a lustre. **~ দেওয়া** *vi* sparkle with light; be showy or striking; glitter.

ঝিল্লি, ঝিল্লিকা *n* **1** = ঝিঁঝি. **2** a thin flexible texture in animal bodies; membrane.

ঝুঁকা=ঝোঁকা

ঝুঁকি *n* a responsibility that involves risk; hazard; peril; jeopardy. **~ লওয়া** *vi* dare to risk. **~ সামলানো** *vi* accomplish a risky job successfully.

ঝুঁটি *n* **1** tuft of hair on the crown of the head tied in a bun. **2** crash on the head of a bird: কাকাতুয়ার ~. **3** the hump of a bull. **~ বাঁধা** *vi* tie up hair into a knot.

ঝুটা, ঝুটো [H] *adj* false; feigned; faked. **2** (of a meal) partly eaten.

ঝুড়ি *n* a basket; a scuttle. **~ ঝুড়ি** *adv* basketfuls of: ~ ~ আম.

ঝুনা, ঝুনো *adj* **1** mature and hardened: ~নারকেল. **2** experienced; veteran: ~ লোক.

ঝুপ *int* denoting the sound of a plunge into water or the sound of a dive or dip. **~ করে** *adv* with a plunge/dive/dip.

ঝুপড়ি *n* a small cottage made of tree-leaves, wicker, bamboo, etc.

ঝুমকা *n* **1** passion flower; passiflora. **2** earring with pendants.

ঝুমঝুম *int* denoting soft jingling of anklets/ornaments.

ঝুমঝুমি *n* a rattle for children that makes a clattering sound.

ঝুমরি *n* (music) a musical note.

ঝুমুর *n* a kind of love-song accompanied with dance.

ঝুরঝুর *adv* by small bits; in loose grains. **ঝুরঝুরে** *adj* having minute particles; granular.

ঝুরি [H] *n* **1** hanging or aerial root of a tree: বটের ~. **2** a kind of crisp snack (also ~ভাজা).

ঝুল *n* **1** black substance caught in cobweb; soot: ~কালি. **2** vertical or downward length (of a garment, etc).

ঝুলন *n* act of swinging; oscillation; the Hindu festival of this name (also ~যাত্রা).

ঝুলা *vi* **1** oscillate; be suspended; hang. **2** (hum) be hanged. **3** incline towards; lean to; be partial or biased to. **4** in action; in the process: মামলা ঝুলছে. **~নো** *vt* **1** hang; suspend. **2** (hum) hang by the neck: ফাঁসিতে ~নো.

ঝুলি *n* a cloth-bag that can be carried by suspending from the shoulder. **~ ঝাড়া** *adj* available on unloading a bag or wallet. **~ লওয়া** *vi* take to begging.

ঝোঁক *n* **1** bent of mind; inclination: পড়াশুনার ~. **2** a favourite object of pursuit; hobby: ভ্রমণের ~. **3** overwhelming influence; addiction: নেশার ~. **4** bias; leaving: একদিকে ~.

ঝোঁকা, ঝুঁকা *vi* **1** bend the body forward and downward; stoop. **2** be partial or biased. **3** be attracted; have interest for.

ঝোঁটন *n* a crest on the head (as of a bird). ❑*adj* having a crest; crested: ~ বুলবুলি.

ঝোড়া *vt* lop off the unwanted portion; trim (a tree).

ঝোপ *n* a small wood; a thicket of small trees and undergrowth; a bush; a copse. **~ঝাড়** *n* underwood: coppice.

ঝোরা[১] *n* **1** a fountain: পাগলা ~. **2** a water course.

ঝোরা[২] *n* rice plant bearing no corn.

ঝোল *n* the fluid of a curry; soup. **~ ভাত** *n* rice and soup. **~ ভাত খাওয়ানো** (fig) teach one a lesson; subject one to discipline.

ঝোলা[১] *vi* **1** hang loosely; dangle: গাছের ডাল থেকে ~. **2** swing; oscillate. ❑ *adj* swinging; pendent; hanging; oscillatory.

ঝোলা[২] *n* a large-size cloth bag.

ঝোলাগুড় *n* liquid treacle; molasses.

ঝোলাঝুলি *n pl* one's luggage and belongings collectively; baggage. **~সহ** *adv* bag and baggage.

ঞ

ঞ *n* the tenth consonant of the Bengali alphabet. It is pronounced as dorso-alveolar or palato-alveolar nasal voiced unaspirated sound. ঞ is not in use as the first letter of word but it forms compound letters with other letters. It is used in nasal pronunciation of 'চ' group of letters, such as, মঞ্চ, লাঞ্ছিত, ব্যঞ্জন, ঝঞ্ঝা.

ট

ট *n* the eleventh consonant and first letter of the 'ট' -group of Bengali alphabet. It is pronounced as alveolo-retroflex unvoiced unaspirated plosive sound.

টইটম্বুর *adj* full to the brim; brimful; overfull; overflowing.

টং[1] *int* denoting the sound made by a clock, a gong, a stringed musical instrument, etc: ~ করে ঘণ্টা বাজলো, Ding-dong went the bell.

টং[2] *adj* very angry: রেগে ~ হওয়া, be in a white heat; be inflamed with rage.

টং[3] *n* a high platform used as a watch-tower or for shooting purposes.

টংকার, টঙ্কার *n* the sound made by a bow-string when stretched and suddenly pulled; twang.

টক *adj* sour; acid. ❑*n* sour taste; acidity; a sour tasting pickle. ~ **লাগা** *vi* taste sour.

টকটক *int* denoting bright red colour: লাল ~. **টকটকে** *adj* brilliant red; purple: টকটকে লাল, blood-red; deep red.

টকা *vi* turn sour; be acidified: দাঁত ~.

টকো *adj* sour to taste; acidulous; sourish.

টক্কর *n* **1** a knock; a stumble: ~**খাওয়া,** stumble (against); collide (with). **2** friction; competition; vying: ~ দিয়ে চলা. ~ **দেওয়া** *vi* compete (with); be in competition/strife with; vie with.

টগবগ *int* denoting **(a)** the bubbling noise of liquids in a boiling state; **(b)** the sound of the galloping of horses. ~ **করে ছোটা** (of horses) gallop fast. ~ **করে ফোটা** *vi* boil and bubble. **রাগে** ~ **করা** *vi* seethe in anger; boil with indignation.

টগর *n* a kind of small white flower.

টঙ =টং[3]

টঙ্ক[1] *n* a native salt; borax.

টঙ্ক[2] *n* hatchet; a spade; hoc.

টন[1] *n, int* denoting the sound made metallic substance when hit by sth hard.

টন[2] [E] *n* **1** measure of weight (1000 Kg in metric system, 2240 lbs in FPS system). **2** measure of the internal capacity (100 cft). **3** measure of carrying capacity of a ship (40 cft); a ton.

টনক *n* the seat of memory. ~ **নড়া** *vi* occur to the mind; flash suddenly through the mind; come to one's senses; be alerted.

টনটন *int* denoting twinging sensation: ফোড়া ~ করা. ~ **করা** *vi* twinge; shoot; ache; .throb. **টনটনানি** *n* twinging sensation throbbing pain.

টনটনে *adj* **1** throbbing or twinging (as a pain). **2** thorough; complete: ~ **জ্ঞান,** thorough knowledge; ~ **বুদ্ধি,** sharp intellect.

টনিক [E] *n* a medicine that gives tone to the system or restores healthy functions; a tonic.

টপ *int* denoting **(a)** the sound of falling drops; **(b)** quickness or promptness of doing sth: ~ করে গিলে ফেলা. ~ **করে** *adv* all at once. ~ **টপ** *int* denoting repetition of the sound of dropping: ~ ~ করে বৃষ্টি পড়ে. ~ ~ **করে পড়া** *vi* drip.

টপকানো *vt* leap over; cross by leaping over; scale (as a wall).

টপটপ *int* denoting repeated sound of the dropping of liquid matter.

টপাটপ *int, adv* in quick succession: ~ গেলা, gulp fast; gobble up.

টপ্পর *n* the herd of a bullock cart.

টপ্পা *n* a form of light classical sub-continental music. ~**বাজ** *n* a gossip. ~ **মারা** *vi* pass time in gossip and merriment.

টব [E] *n* **1** a wooden or metallic vessel for water or for use as a bath; a tub. **2** an earthen pot for a flower plant: ফুলের ~.

ট-বর্গ *n* letters of the ট-group of Bengali alphabet.

টমটম *n* a wheeled carriage drawn by a single horse; a tandem.

টমেটো [E] *n* small, roundish vegetable of the brinjal family; tomato.

টর্চ [E] *n* a light to be carried in the hand; a torch.

টলটল *int* denoting translucence (as of water) or a slow stir or movement of liquid. ❑*adj* stirred; agitated. ❑*n* under a staggering/tottering condition.

টলটলানি *n* the state of being in a tottering condition. **টলটলায়মান** *adj* on the verge of crashing or falling down. **টলটলে** *adj* (of water) very clear; translucent.

টলটলানো *vi* stagger; totter; waver; tremble.

টলমল *int* denoting an unsteady state. ~ **করা** *vi* tremble; stagger; reel; be in a tottering condition. **টলমলে** *adj* unsteady; tremulous; timorous; trembling.

টলা *vi* **1** be agitated/perturbed/tremulous. **2** waver; vacillate: মন ~. **3** stagger; totter: পা ~. **4** be displayed/dislocated. **5** go back from; flinch. ~**নো** *vt* **1** cause to waver or vacillate. **2** cause to flinch or retract. **3** cause to displace or dislocate.

টস *int* denoting sound of the dropping of a liquid or of trickling (as tears). ~ **টস** *int* denoting the state of being full of juice: পেকে ~ ~ করছে. **টসটসে** *adj* full of juice; juicy; fished.

টহল *n* going round by a guard to secure the safety of an area; patrol. ~ **দেওয়া** *vi* go one's rounds; patrol. ~**দার** *n* policemen on rounds; a watchman; an ambulator. ~**দারি** *n* act of keeping watch by ambulation.

টহলানো *vt* cause (a horse) to go backwards and forwards/walk up and down (to recover from exhaustion of running long distance).

টা *suff* used **(a)** to indicate a definite person or thing: বাড়িটা, কাজটা, লোকটা;; **(b)** in contempt: চাকরটা, চোরটা; **(c)** in endearment: মেয়েটা বড়ো কষ্টে পড়েছে.

টাইট [E] *adj* fitting close or too close; compact; tight.

টাইপ [E] *n* **1** letter used in printing. **2** a representative; member of a class or kind; modal; type: ঐ টাইপের ছেলেরা ভালো হয় না. **3** the kind, variety or general class of a thing: ~ চরিত্রের অভিনয়ে তিনি অদ্বিতীয়. ~ **করা** *vt, vi* typewrite; type. ~ **রাইটার** *n* machine used as a substitute for the pen, producing letters by inked types; a typewriter. **টাইপিস্ট** *n* one who types; a typist.

টাইফয়েড [E] *n* a fever characterized by abdominal pains and diarrhoea; typhoid.

টাইফুন [E] *n* a violent hurricane on the coasts of China and Japan; typhoon.

টাইম [E] *n* **1** a measure of duration; age; epoch; era; time. **2** occasion; opportunity; leisure. ~**টেবল** *n* a list of times at which certain tasks have to be done or certain events are due to happen; a schedule. ~**পিস** *n* a clock.

টাইল [E] *n* a slab of beaked clay for roofing; tile.

টাউন [E] *n* a populous place larger than village; a town.

টাঁক[১] *n* **1** aim; a fixed gaze; a covetous look. **2** act of waiting with a hope.

টাঁক[২], **টাক** [E] *n* a stitched fold in a garment for shortening or for ornament; a tuck.

টাঁকশাল *n* the place where money is coined; a mint.

টাঁকা[১] *vt* stitch; put a tuck in; tuck.

টাঁকা[২] *vt* aim at; anticipate.

টাক *n* **1** want of hair on the head; baldness. **2** hairless head. ☐*adj* wanting hair; bald. **টেকো** *adj* bald. ~ **পড়া** *vi* be bald.

টাকা *n* unit of money in Bangladesh; Taka. ~**র মানুষ** *n* wealthy person. ~ **ওড়ানো** *vi* squander money. ~ **করা** *vi* make/earn money; amass wealth. ~ **খাওয়া** *vi* accept bribe; receive unlawful gratification. ~ **ভাঙানো** *vi* change a currency note. ~ **মারা** *vi* misappropriate; embezzle. ~**ওয়ালা** *adj* rich; wealthy; moneyed. ~**কড়ি** *n pl* money; riches. ~**র গরম** *n* pride of wealth. ~**র শ্রাদ্ধ** *n* misuse of money.

টাকু *n* a pin carrying a bobbin in a spinning machine; a spindle.

টাগ *n* the knee.

টাঙ্গা *n* a light one-horse carriage with one pair of wheels; a gig; a tonga.

টাঙ্গানো *vt* **1** suspend; hang up: ছবি ~. **2** stretch; pitch: তাবু ~. **3** rig up: মশারি ~. **4** hoist; hang up: পাল ~.

টাঙ্গি *n* a hatchet; an axe.

টাট *n* a copper plate used in worship by Hindus.

টাটকা *adj* **1** not faded; in good condition; fresh: ~ সবজি. **2** not stale: ~ **খাবার**. **3** new; latest: ~ খবর. **4** newly grown/plucked: ~ ফুল.

টা-টা *int, n* a familiar form of salutation at parting; good-bye.

টাটানো *vi* be acutely painful; course to feel sharp pain; smart: ফোঁড়াটা টাটাচ্ছে. **টাটানি** *n* smarting pain. **চোখ** ~ be envious of sb's good fortune.

টাটি[১] *n* course mat made of bamboo slips.

টাটি[২] *n* small earthen cup.

টাটি[৩] [H] *n* **1** latrine; lavatory. **2** a discharge from the bowels; stool.

টাট্টী =টাটি[৩]

টাটু [H] *n* a small horse; a pony.

টান *n* **1** act of drawing towards one; a pull; a tug: জোর ~. **2** attachment; affection: ছেলের প্রতি ~. **3** attraction: স্নেহের ~. **4** a puff (of cigarette, etc) **5** insufficiency; shortage: টাকার ~, জিনিসের ~. **6** an increase in demand: বাজারে মালের ~. **7** a tone or modulation of certain dialects: কুমিল্লার ~. **8** force of a stream: স্রোতের ~. **9** difficult breathing; spasm: হাঁপানির ~. **10** the stroke of a pen: কলমের ~. **11** dry land: ~ জায়গা. ~ **দেওয়া** *vt* **1** draw towards one; pull. **2** have a puff of a cigarette, etc: সিগারেটে ~ দেওয়া. ~ **ধরা** *vi* begin to dry; have a sensation of cramp: ফোঁড়ায় ~ ধরা. ~ **পড়া** *vi* fall short; be insufficient. ~-**টান** *adj* **1** very tight; tense. **2**

full of vanity and arrogance. ❑*adv* with the body fully stretched out: ~-~ হয়ে শোওয়া. **~টোন** *n pl* ornamental strokes and flourishes (as in calligraphy and painting). **এক টানে** *adv* at a stretch.

টানা[১] *n* **1** (in weaving) the threads extended lengthwise in a loom; warp. **2** a drawer (in a chest, etc). **~-পোড়ন/ পড়েন** *n* **1** the threads extended both lengthwise and breadthwise in a loom; warp and woof. **2** the tiresome frequentation to a place.

টানা[২] *vt* **1** pull along or towards; drag; draw: দড়ি ~. **2** represent by lines drawn on a surface: লাইন ~. **3** carry; convey; transport: মাল ~. **4** drink; smoke: গাঁজা ~, মদ ~. **5** draw out; extract: রস ~. **6** be partial to: আত্মীয়তার টান ~. **7** get dried: ঝোল ~. **8** cut down expenditure: টেনে চলা. ❑*adj* **1** pulled; drawn: ঘোড়ায় ~ গাড়ি. **2** operated by pulling: ~ পাখা. **3** unbroken; continuous: ~ দুই ঘণ্টা. **4** long and straight: ~ পথ. **5** large; big; wide: ~ চোখ. **গুণ ~** *vi* drag (a boat) by a rope; tow. **দাঁড় ~** *vi* row, scull. **~-জাল** *n* a drag-net. **~-টানা** *adj* wide; large: ~-~চোখ. **~টানি** *n* **1** pulling in opposite directions; tugging. **2** continuous pulling. **3** want; shortage; deficiency; insufficiency; hardship: ~টানির সংসার. **~-হেঁচড়া** *n* act of dragging forcibly. **~হেঁচড়া করা** *vt* drag and pull. **এক~** *adj* continuous. ❑*adv* at a stretch. **দো~** *n* fluctuation of mind; vacillation; wavering.

টাপুর-টুপুর *int, adv* continuous pattering of rains: বৃষ্টি পড়ে ~.

টায়টায় *adv* barely enough to do; not more.

টায়রা *n* an ornament worn on the head; a tiara.

টাল[১] *n* **1** the state of being curved; curvature: লোহার কড়ির ~. **2** slant; slope; inclination: চাকার ~. **3** state of being unsteady; staggering movement: ~ খেয়ে পড়া. **4** danger; difficulty; risk: ~ সামলানো. **~ খাওয়া** *vi* **1** incline; bend. **2** walk unsteadily; stagger. **3** be faced with a crisis. **~ দেওয়া** *vi* act or speak evasively; misrepresent (sth) by giving evasive evidence; prevaricate. **~বাহানা** *n* dilly-dallying; shilly-shallying. **~বাহানা করা** *vi* make pretexts; prevaricate. **~মাটাল** *n* **1** precarious state; crises; turmoil. **2** restlessness; uneasiness; anxiety. **3** procrastination. **~ সামলানো** *vi* get over a crisis.

টাল[২] *n* a heap; a pile. **~ দেওয়া** *vi* heap; pile up.

টালি *n* thin glazed or unglazed clay brick for roofing; tile.

-টি=-টা

টিউটর *n* [E] a teacher; a private instructor; tutor.

টিউশনি=টুইশনি

টিক *n* [E] **1** a light tapping sound as made by a watch or clock; tick. **~ টিক** *n* ticking sound of a watch/clock; tick-tick; tick-tock: ঘড়িটি ~~ করছে, tick-tick goes the clock. **2** a mark (√) used to indicate approval or correctness: ~ দেওয়া, put a tick-mark; tick.

টিকটিকি *n* **1** small reptile living in dwelling houses; house-lizard. **2** (sarcas) a police officer whose duty is to detect criminals; a detective. **~ পড়া** *n* ticking of a house-lizard, commonly believed to be an ill-omen, specially, if it occurs on the eve of one's going out or starting a work.

টিকলি *n* **1** a thin slice; a small piece: আখের ~. **2** a jewellery worn on the forehead; a tiara.

টিকা[১] *n* small cake of charcoal dust used as fuel for the hookah.

টিকা[২] *n* inoculation with vaccine in order to ward off small-pox; vaccination. **~ দেওয়া** *vi* inoculate; vaccinate. **~ নেওয়া** *vi* be vaccinated/inoculated. **~দার** *n* a vaccinator.

টিকা[৩]=টেকা

টিকি *n* tuft of uncut hair kept on the head by Hindus. **~ দেখতে না পাওয়া** get no trace of: তার ~টিও দেখা যাচ্ছে না, He is hardly to be seen. He has made himself scarce.

টিকিট, টিকেট [E] *n* a card or paper issued as a proof that the holder has paid for and is entitled to certain privilege: সিনেমার ~, রেলের ~. **ডাক~** *n* a postage-stamp. **~ কেনা** *vi* buy a ticket; book. **~-ঘর** *n* booking office. **~ মাস্টার** *n* booking-clerk. **~ পরীক্ষক** *n* ticket checker. **~ সংগ্রাহক** *n* ticket collector.

টিকিন [E] *n* a kind of coarse cloth for making mattress, etc; ticking.

টিটকারি *n* a jeer; a scof; a biting jest; sneer. **~ দেওয়া** *vi* utter sarcastic reflections; mock; jeer; sneer; scof.

টিন [E] *n* **1** a malleable metal of white colour used in alloys; tin. **2** thin pliable sheets of tin used for wrapping and packing; tinfoil. **3** corrugated iron-sheet used for roofing, etc. **4** boxes or containers made of tin; canister.

টিপ *n* **1** small round paint put by women on their forehead. **2** the mark or stain made by a thumb; thumb-mark; thumb-impression. **3** a piece of tinsel worn on the forehead as a decoration. **4** a small quantity as can be held by the fore-finger and the thumb: এক ~ নস্য, a pinch of snuff. **~ পড়া** *vi* paint the forehead with the tip of a finger; wear a bit of tinsel on the forehead. **~-কল** *n* a machine that can be operated by pressure. **~বোতাম** *n* pair of buttons that may be fixed to one another by the pressure of finger tips; press-button.

টিপটপ [E] *adj* **1** well-arranged; neat and tidy. **2** excellent; the best imaginable; superlative; tip-top.

টিপটিপ *int* denoting (a) dropping, drizzling, throbbing, etc: ~ করে বৃষ্টি পড়ছে; (b) dimness of light: ~ করে প্রদীপ জ্বলছে. **3** palpitation of heart caused by fear: বুকটা ~ করতে লাগলো. **4** slow pace of movement: ~ করে হাঁটা.

টিপটিপানি *n* dripping; drizzling; twinge; throb.

টিপয় *n* three-legged small table; tripod.

টিপা=টেপা. **টিপে দেওয়া** *vt* massage.

টিপ্পনি *n* **1** a sarcastic comment; a reflection. **2** commentary; annotation; note.

টিফিন [E] *n* **1** light repast; snack; tiffin. **2** a recess during working hours for tiffin.

টিমটিম *int* suggesting flickering of a lamp or depressed state of existence of sth. **~ করা** *vi* **1** (of a lamp) sheet a dim light. **2** (of an institution) be at the fag-end of its glory. **টিমটিমে** *adj* flickering; blinking; dim.

টিয়া *n* a species of parrot; the parakeet.

টিলা *n* a small hill; a hillock.

-টী =টি

টীকা *n* a comment on some passage of a book; commentary; annotation; note. **~ করা** *vi* comment; annotate. **~কার** *n* commentator; annotator. **~কারে** *adv* in the form of an annotation/ commentary.

টু = টু

-টু *suff* used to indicate smallness of quantity or volume: একটু, আধটু.

টুইল [E] *n* textile fabric with a kind of diagonal ribbed surface; twill.

টুইশনি *n* the profession of a private tutor; tuition. **~ করা** *vi* teach a student as a private tutor.

টুঁ *int* denoting the least noise or feeblest objection. **~ শব্দ না করা** raise no objection/make no protest of any kind.

টুঁটি *n* the passage by which food enters the stomach; gullet; throat.. **~ চেপে ধরা** *vi* seize by the throat. **~ টিপে মারা** *vt* throttle. **~-কাটা** *n* a murderer; an assassin; a cut-throat.

টুকটাক *adj* **1** of small quantity; paltry: ~ জিনিস. **2** brief and casual: ~ কাজ. ❑*adv* in small quantity. **~ করে** *adv* by small bits of work or income: ~ করে সংসার চলছে.

টুকটুক *int* denoting glow, glare or ruddiness. **~ করা** *vi* shine with a glare; appear ruddy; glow. **টুকটুকে** *adj* of a lively flesh colour; reddish. **টুকটুকে লাল** *adj* deep red.

টুকরা, টুকরো *n* a piece; a fragment; a scrap; a bit: ~ কাপড়, cut-piece. **~ করা** *vt* cut to/divide into pieces. **~ টুকরা** in pieces; in small bits; piecemeal.

টুকরা-টাকরা *n* odds and ends; small fragments.

টুকরি *n* basket for carrying goods on the head

টুকরো ⇒ টুকরা

টুকা=টোকা

টুকিটাকি *n* trivial or trashy things. ❑*adj* **1** paltry: ~ কাজ. **2** negligible; of little value: ~ দান.

টুঙি, টঙ্গি, টঙ্গ *n* hut built on a high platform. **জল ~** *n* a house built in a pool of water.

টুটা *vi* **1** be broken or torn. **2** be dispelled: ঘুম ~, স্বপ্ন ~. ❑*adj* broken; torn; dispelled. **~নো** *vt* cause to be broken/torn/removed/dispelled.

টুনটুন *nt* denoting a clinking sound. **~ করা** *vi* clink; tinkle.

টুনটুনি *n* a species of tiny warbling bird; the tailor-bird.

টুপি *n* a covering for the head; a cap; a hat.

টুল *n* a wooden seat without a back for one person; a stool.

টুলি, টুলী [U] *n* (used as *suff*) a locality: মোগল~.

টুসি, টুসকি= তুড়ি

টেংরা *n* a variety of small fish without scales.

টেংরি [H] *n* the shin-bone of a sheep or goat: ~র সুপ, bone-marrow soup.

টেঁক, ট্যাক *n* **1** the waist. **2** the fold of one's cloth at waist. **3** (fig) money; purse: ~ খালি, out of pocket. **টেঁকে গোঁজা** keep in the fold of one's cloth; (fig) appropriate to oneself; misappropriate.

টেকসই *adj* durable; long lasting.

টেকা, টিকা *vi* **1** be durable; last long. **2** stand a test; endure: ধোপে ~.

টেকো *adj* bald; without hair on the head.

টেক্কা *n* **1** ace (in cards). **2** competition. ❑*adj* superiority; excellence; triumph. **~ দেওয়া/মারা** *vi* **1** complete with. **2** excel; surpass; get the better of; score.

টেটা *n* a fishing-spear; a harpoon.

টেড়া, ট্যাড়া *adj* **1** looking obliquely; squint-eyed. **2** haughty; peevish: ~ মেজাজ. **~ চাউনি** *n* oblique glance. **~বাঁকা** *adj* not straight; distorted; sinuous; zigzag.

টেড়ি *n* parting of hair of the head. **~ কাটা** *vi* dress the hair; have parting of the hair.

টেপ [E] *n* **1** a strip of thin flexible metal or hard cloth graduated for measuring things with; a tape-measure; a tape. **2** a strip of plastic material magnetized to record sound or vision; magnetic tape; tape. **~ করা** *vt* record songs, talks, etc on a magnetized tape for playing back on a tape-recorder.

টেপা, টিপা *vt* 1 press with the hands to relieve (one) of pain, etc; massage; squeeze: শরীর ~. 2 give a hint by the eyelids; wink: চোখ ~. 3 put or place lightly and noiselessly: পা টিপে হাঁটা. ~নো *vt* cause to press or massage.

টেপারি *n* a shrub or its fruit; gooseberry.

টেবিল [E] *n* a piece of furniture with a flat surface and usually four supports or legs at the corners; a table.

টের *n* feeling; sensation; awareness. ~ পাওয়া *vt* 1 feel; perceive; have the sense of: ব্যথা ~ পাওয়া. 2 come to know; be aware; sense; apprehend: বিপদ ~ পাওয়া. 3 (fig) pay the penalty for; be made to suffer: এবার ~ পাবে কত ধানে কত চাল. ~ পাওয়ানো *vt* cause one to have a lesson; teach one a lesson; give one a taste of (a penalty, etc).

টেরচা, টেরছা ⇒ তেরছা

টেরা=টেড়া

টেরি= টেড়ি

টেলিগ্রাফ [E] *n* an apparatus for transmitting messages along a wire by electricity, but now also wireless; telegraph.

টেলিগ্রাম [E] *n* a communication sent by telegraph; telegram.

টেলিফোন [E] *n* an instrument transmitting sound to a distance by means of electricity and telegraph wires; telephone.

টেলিস্কোপ [E] *n* an optical instrument for viewing distant objects; telescope.

টেলিভিশন [E] *n* transmission of scenes or pictures and sound so that they can be received at a distance by a receiving set operated by electricity; television.

টোকা[1], টুকা *vt* 1 note down; write down. 2 copy; make a copy of written matter. 3 write answers in examination script by unfair means. 4 paint out a mistake or fault. 5 pick up and collect what is lying scattered.

টোকা[2] *n* a stroke with a finger; a tap. ~ দেওয়া *vi, vt* strike with the finger; tap; fillip.

টোকানো *vt* procure by picking up from here and there; collect bits of things by picking.

টোটকা *n* quack remedy; an empiric medicine/cure. ❑*adj* empiric; empirical. ~-টাটকি *n pl* quack or empirical remedies/cure.

টোটা *n* a case containing the charge of a firearm; cartridge.

টো-টো *int* denoting aimless wandering or strolling about. ~ করে বেড়ানো *vi* ramble here and there without an aim, as a vagabond does. ~ কোম্পানি a group of vagabonds or gadabouts. ~ কোম্পানির ম্যানেজার an inveterate vagabond.

টোপ[1] *n* 1 substance used by anglers to allure fish; a bait. 2 (fig) anything used as allurement: ~ গেলা. 3 an artful device; an artifice; a stratagem. ~ গেলা *vi* gulp a bait. ~ ঠোকরানো *vi* nibble at the bait. ~ ফেলা *vi* hold out some bait or allurement; set a trap.

টোপ[2] *n* 1 diapered fancy-work on ornaments. 2 linen fabric with diamond pattern. 3 a cap; a hat. 4 button made of cloth.

টোপর *n* a conical hat worn by a Hindu bridegroom at wedding.

টোপা *adj* 1 inflated; swollen. 2 round; roundish. ❑*n* a variety of plum.

টোপানো *vt* fall or let fall in drops/drop by drop; distil.

টোল[1] *n* tax paid for using roads, bridges, etc or for selling goods in a market; a toll.

টোল[2] *n* school for teaching Sanskrit.

টোল[3] *n* a small hollow forming esp on the cheek; a dimple; a depression. ~-খাওয়া/পড়া *adj* dimpled; dented. ~ খাওয়া/পড়া *vi* be dented; have a dimple.

টোলা *n* a quarter or locality: আরমানি ~, মালি~.

ট্যাঁ, ট্যাঁ-ট্যাঁ *int* denoting the cry of a baby.

ট্যাঁক=টেক

ট্যাঁপারি=টেপারি

ট্যাঁস *adj* of mixed origin; hybrid; Indo-European; Eurasian: ~ ফিরিঙ্গি.

ট্যাক্স [E] *n* a rate, duty or impost charged by authority on income or property; a tax.

ট্যাক্সি [E] *n* a hackney motor car; taxi; taxicab.

ট্যারা=টেরা

ট্রাক [E] *n* an open railway wagon or motor vehicle for carrying goods; a truck.

ট্রাফিক, ট্র্যাফিক [E] *n* goods and persons passing along a road, railway, etc; traffic. ~ পুলিশ *n* policemen controlling movement of vehicles on the street.

ট্রে [E] *n* a flat object with a rim, made of wood or metal, used for carrying dishes, etc; a tray.

ট্রেজারি [E] *n* 1 place where treasure is laid up; treasury. 2 department of government which controls revenue.

ট্রেন *n* [E] a line of carriages on a railway caused to run by an engine; a train.

ট্র্যাজেডি *n* [E] play of a solemn kind with a sad ending; a tragedy.

ট্র্যাফিক=ট্রাফিক

ঠ

ঠ *n* the twelfth consonant of the Bengali alphabet. It is pronounced as alveolo-retroflex unvoiced aspirated plosive sound.

ঠং *int* denoting the sound of a metallic object when struck with sth hard. **ঠং ঠং** *int* sound of the repeated concussion of a metallic object. ~-~ করে ঘণ্টা বাজলো Ding-dong went the bell.

ঠক[১], **ঠগ** *n* a dishonest person who defrauds people grossly; a swindler; a cheat; a knave; a rogue; a rascal. ☐*adj* deceitful; roguish; knavish (also ~বাজ). ~**বাজি** *n* cheating; swindling; knavery.

ঠক[২], **ঠকঠক** *int* denoting **(a)** the sound made by the knocking of a stuff on the floor; **(b)** shivering or quivering with cold: শীতে ঠকঠক করে কাঁপা, have shivers all over in cold.

ঠকঠকানো *vi* shiver violently in cold, fear or anger. **ঠকঠকানি** *n* a spell of violent shiver.

ঠকা *vi* **1** be cheated/swindled/defrauded. **2** be deluded/ outwitted: তিন টাকা ঠকিয়েছে. ~**নো** *vt* deceive cheat; swindle; outwit; beguile. ~**নে** *adj* deceitful; puzzling; misleading: ~নে প্রশ্ন, catch question; quiz. ~**মি** *n* cheating; deception; fraud; swindling.

ঠক্কর, ঠোক্কর *n* collision; act of striking together.

ঠগ *n* **1** one who imposes on others; an imposter. **2** a member of a bond of highway robbers; a thug. **ঠগি** *n* (hist) a band of murderous/ robbers infesting the highways of medieval India.

ঠন *int* denoting a ringing sound or ding-dong of a bell. ~~ **করা** *vi* **1** ring; clank; clatter. **2** (fig) be empty or sound as an empty vessel: পকেট ~.

ঠমক[১] *n* affected or artful gait; show; pomp; parade: ~ দেখানো. ~**চাল** *n* proud airs.

ঠমক[২] *n* the arts of coquette; coquetry; dalliance; flirtation.

ঠাওর, ঠাহর *n* **1** a careful gaze. **2** attention. **3** perception. ~ **করা** *vt* perceive; recognize; notice. **ঠাওরানো** *vt* **1** consider; ascertain; determine. **2** guess; surmise; conjecture; form an opinion without certain means of knowledge.

ঠাঁই *n* space; place; room; accommodation. ~**ঠাঁই** *adj* separated; disunited; levying apart from one another: ভাইভাই ~ ~.

ঠাকঠমক *n* ambitious display; ostentation; vain show; parade; pomp.

ঠাকরুন *n fem* respectable woman (among Hindus); mistress. ~**দিদি** grandmother.

ঠাকুর *n* **1** a Hindu god or deity. **2** an idol. **3** God : ~, রক্ষা করো. **4** person deserving respect and reverence: পিতা~. **5** a preceptor: গুরু~. **6** a Brahmin. **7** a Brahmin cook: ঠাকুরের রান্না. **8** a priest: ~ পূজা করেন. **9** the father-in-law of a woman: ~পো. **10** title of the Brahmins: রবীন্দ্রনাথ ~. **ঠাকুরানী, ঠাকরুন** *fem.* ~-**ঘর** *n* room for an idol. ~-**জামাই** *n* husband of husband's sister. ~-**ঝি** *n* husband's sister. ~**দাদা** *n* grandfather. ~**দালান** *n* a hall or building containing an idol attached to a dwelling house. ~**পুত্র** *n* son of a spiritual preceptor. ~**পো** *n* husband's younger brother. ~**বাড়ি** *n* temple; shrine. ~**মা** *n* paternal grandmother. **ঠাকুরালি** *n* **1** jest; joke; fun: ছাড়ো তোমার ঠাকুরালি. **2** authority; supremacy; predominance.

ঠাট *n* **1** outward show; appearance: ~ বজায় রাখা, keep up appearance. **2** structure or fabric for supporting anything; a framework: প্রতিমার ~. ~ **বদল করা** *vi* change one's style of living.

ঠাটা *n* thunderbolt; thunder.

ঠাট্টা *n* good humoured tearing; joke; jest; fun; banter; waggery. ~ **করা** *vt* make fun; cut jokes; attack with jocularity; banter; tease in a playful way. ~ **করে বলা** say (sth) playfully/ by way of joke. ~**বাজ** *n* a waggish fellow; a wag; a humorist. ~**বাজি** *n* witticism; waggishness; mockery.

ঠাড় *adj* erect; standing upright. ~ **করা** *vt* erect; set up. ~ **হওয়া** *vi* stand erect; set upright.

ঠাণ্ডা *adj* **1** cold; cool: ~ পানি. **2** gentle; agreeable; comfortable: ~ স্বভাব ☐*n* chill: ~ পড়েছে. ~ **করা** *vt* **1** cool; cool down. **2** comfort; pacify; console; appease: রাগ ~ করা . **3** put down; put to silence; quell: বিদ্রোহ ~ করা. ~ **লাগা** *vi* catch cold. ~ **হওয়া** *vi* become cold; cool down; be pacified. ~-**লড়াই** *n* struggle for supremacy carried by hostile propaganda, etc without actual fighting; cold war.

ঠান *n* (among Hindus) a respectable woman: মাঠান, বউঠান. ~**দিদি**, ~**দি** *n* grandmother.

ঠায়[১] *n* place: ~ দাঁড়িয়ে/বসে থাকা, stay or wait at a place.

ঠায়[২] *adv* at a stretch; continually; steadily: ~ দাঁড়িয়ে থাকা, stand at a stretch without moving.

ঠার *n* a hint; a gesticulation; a beckoning **ঠারা** *vt* make a sign with; gesticulate; beckon. **ঠারে ঠোরে** *adv* by hints and signs; by beckoning; by gestures and postures.

ঠাস[১] *int* denoting the sound of slapping: ~ করে চড় মারা, give a tight slap.

ঠাস[২] *adj* closely united; compact; thick; close: ~বুননি, compact knitting.

ঠাসা *vt* thrust in by force; cram; staff; ram down; load or charge (as a gun); work into a mass; knead (as dough). ☐*adj* compressed:

staffed; kneaded. ~ঠাসি *n* overcrowding; overfulness. ~ঠাসি করে *adv* huddling together; pressing hard.

ঠাহর=ঠাওর

ঠিক *adj* **1** fixed; settled: তারিখ ~ হওয়া. **2** proper; appropriate: ~ কাজটিই করেছে. **3** right; correct: অঙ্কের ফল ~. **4** not more, nor less; exact: ~ দুদিন পরে. **5** in order; orderly; neat: চুল ~ করো. **6** fit; fitting; accurate: জামা ~ হয়েছে. **7** true; fact: ~ কথা বলবে. **8** appointed; specified: ~ সময়ে এসেছো. **9** rectified; correct: ছেলেকে মেরে ~ করেছে. **10** suitable; deserving; worthy: এ কাজের জন্য ~ লোক. ❑*n* **1** fixity; firmness: কথার ~ নেই. **2** normal state of anything: মাথার ~ নেই. ❑*adv* **1** certainly; surely: ~ যাবো. **2** exactly; precisely: ~ বলেছো. ~ **করা** *vt* fix; settle; correct; cure; repair; set right/in order. ~ **খাটা** *vi* fit exactly; hold good. ~ **দেওয়া** *vi* cast up a sum; add. ~ **যেন** as if. ~ **যেমন** the same as. **কথা ~ রাখা** *vi* be true to one's word; keep one's word/promise. ~ **লাগা** *vi* fit in. ~ **হওয়া** be repaired/ corrected; be exact/precise. ~**ঠাক** *adj* correct, exact; accurate. ~**ঠাক করা** *vt* arrange properly; settle: বিবাহ ~ করা. ~**ঠাক করে রাখা** *vi* keep things tidy/ in order. ~**ঠিকানা** *n* **1** fixity; surety. **2** trace; whereabouts.

ঠিকরা *n* a small clay ball used in the bowl of a hookah.

ঠিকরানো *vi* **1** scatter; disperse; spatter. **2** emit rays of light; radiate: আলো ~. **3** stupefy; stun; daze: আলোতে চোখ ঠিকরাচ্ছে.

ঠিকা, ঠিকে *adj* **1** employed on part-time basis: ~ ঝি. **2** holding temporary possession for a fixed period: ~ প্রজা. **3** that which is done under contract as a piece work: ~ কাজ, ~ গাড়ি. ❑*n* job done on contract: ~ পাওয়া. ~ **কাজ** *n* a part-time job; a job work; a piece work. ~ **গাড়ি** *n* a hackney carriage. ~ **চাকর/ঝি** *n* a hired servant/ maidservant. ~ **দেওয়া** *vt* let or lease out: জমি ~ দেওয়া.

ঠিকাদার *n* one who contracts to perform any work or service; a contractor. **ঠিকাদারি** *n* contractorship. ❑*adj* relating to contract work.

ঠিকানা *n* one's place of residence; whereabouts; address.

ঠিকুজি, ঠিকুজি-কোষ্ঠী *n* one's horoscope from which astrologers can foretell future events of one's life.

ঠিং *int* denoting a simple light clink. ~**ঠিং** repeated clinking sound.

ঠুংরি *n* mode and measure of the Lucknow school of Indian classical music.

ঠুঁটা, ঠুঁটো[1] *adj* mutilated; maimed; disabled. ~ **করা** *vi* **1** mutilate; maim; disable. **2** (fig) make powerless. ~ **জগন্নাথ** *n* **1** (lit) Juggernaut, the handless Hindu deity at Puri. **2** (fig) one in high position but with no power; a figurative head; a puppet.

ঠুঁটো[2] *adj* **1** having wide lips. **2** having a long beak.

ঠুক *int* denoting a gentle stroke or a mild sound by a knock. ~**ঠুক** repetition of this sound. ~ ~ **করে** *adv* by mild strokes.

ঠুকরানো=ঠোকরানো

ঠুকা=ঠোকা

ঠুঙি =ঠুংগি

ঠুটা =ঠুঁটা

ঠুন *int* denoting a low ringing sound.

ঠুনকা[1], **ঠুনকো**[1] *adj* **1** not tough or tenacious; apt to break; brittle; fragile. **2** (fig) worthless; trashy; useless.

ঠুনকা[2], **ঠুনকো**[2] *n* a kind of breast-disease occurring in parturient weman.

ঠুমকি *n* a mode or posture of dancing.

ঠুলি *n* a flap to prevent an animal from seeing; a blinker; a blind. ~ **দেওয়া** *vi* hoodwink.

ঠুস *int* denoting a light sound: ~ করে পড়া, fall with a sound; ~ করে ভেঙ্গে যাওয়া, break easily. ~**ঠাস** *int* denoting the sound of beating: ~ঠাস করে মারা.

ঠুসা, ঠোসা *vt* **1** thrust in forcibly; cram; stuff. **2** eat overmuch. **3** beat profusely.

ঠুসি *n* pustule or bladder-like protuberance on the skin containing watery matter; a blister.

ঠেং=ঠ্যাং

ঠেক, ঠেকনা *n* a pole or post used as a saluting support to prevent a thing from falling; a stanchion; a prop; a lean-to. ~ **দেওয়া** *vt* **1** support by a slanting; prop. **2** (fig) give a temporary support for living.

ঠেকা[1] *n* want; need; difficulty: ~য় পড়া. ~**ঠেকি** *n* hardship; financial stringency.

ঠেকা[2] *vi,vt* **1** come in contact with; touch: পায়ে ~. **2** reach and stop at: তীরে গিয়ে ঠেকলো. **3** have the sense of; feel: খারাপ ~. **4** come down; diminish: আয় শূন্যের কোঠায় ঠেকেছে. **5** dash against: পিঠ দেয়ালে ঠেকে গেল. **6** be entangled/involved: বিপদে ~. **দায়ে ~** *vi* get into a serape. **ঠেকে শেখা** learn by experience. **চোখে ~** *vi* look unseemly. ~**নো** *vt* **1** cause to reach/touch. **2** prevent; check. ~**নো দায়** It is difficult to counter/ check/ stop.

ঠেঙ্গা, ঠেঙা *n* a staff; a stave; a heavy stick or club; a wooden or bamboo pole: লাঠি ~. ~ **মারা** *vi* belabour or thump with a staff. ~**নো** =~ মারা. ~**নি** *n* striking or beating with a club. ~**ঠেঙ্গি** *n* fighting with staves. ~**ঠেঙ্গি করা** *vi* strike one another with clubs.

ঠেলা, ঠ্যালা *n* **1** a push; a thrust; a shove: ~ মারা. **2** a difficult task; a crisis; a danger: ~য়

পড়া. **3** a hand-barrow; a push cart: ~গাড়ি. ☐*vt* **1** push; thrust; shove. ~ দেওয়া/মারা give a push. ~ **সামলানো** *vi* cope with a difficult situation; grapple in a tough situation. ~**র নাম বাবাজি** (fig) A cat in a mesh calls the mouse its brother. ~**ঠেলি** pushing and shoving of a crowd; jostling each other. ~**ঠেলি করা** *vi* push and shove.

ঠেস *n* **1** act of leaning against; a reclining position; recumbence: দেয়ালে ~ দেওয়া. **2** anything to lean against: চেয়ারের ~. **3** an insinuating remark; a reflection: ~ দিয়ে কথা বলা.

ঠোঁট *n* **1** the lips. **2** the beak (of a bird). ~ **ওলটানো /বাঁকানো** *vi* thrust out the lips in derision. ~ **ফোলানো** *vi* pout lips in displeasure. ~**কাটা** *adj* bold in speech; outspoken; hare-lipped. **ঠোঁটে ঠোঁটে** *adv* lip to lip; from mouth to mouth.

ঠোকর *n* **1** act of pecking or nibbling (as by a bird). **2** a poke or knock with the tip of one's toes or shoe: জুতার ~. **3** act of interposing a speaker with a cutting remark. ~ **খাওয়া** *vi* stumble (against). ~ **মারা** *vi* peck; poke; carp at. ~ **লাগানো** *vi* cause to stumble; give a knock.

ঠোকরানো *vi* **1** peck at; nibble at. **2** bite (at a bait). ☐*adj* pecked.

ঠোকাঠুকি *n* mutual bantering; repeated collision.

ঠোঙ্গা *n* a cone-shaped container made of tree-leaves or paper.

ঠোসা= ঠুসা

ঠ্যাং, ঠ্যাঙ *n* the leg; shank.

ঠ্যাঙ্গানো =ঠেঙ্গানো

ড *n* the thirteenth consonant of the Bengali alphabet. It is pronounced as alveolo-retroflex voiced unaspirated plosive sound.

ডক [E] *n* area on the side of a harbour or bank of a river where ships are loaded, unloaded and repaired; a dock.

ডগ, ডগা *n* **1** a tip or extremity: আঙ্গুলের ডগা. **2** a sprout or young shoot of a creeper: লাউয়ের ডগা.

ডগডগ *int* denoting glow or brightness. **ডগডগে** *adj* very deep; glowing: ডগডগে লাল, deep red.

ডগমগ *adj* flushed (with); gushing; effusive; overflowing with: খুশিতে ~. ~ **করা** *vi* overflow (with); be overwhelmed (with).

ডঙ্কা *n* a large kettle-drum; a trumpet; a drum. ~ **দিয়ে জানানো** proclaim by beat of a drum; announce by drum- beat.

ডজন [E] *n* a set of twelve; a dozen.

ডন *n* physical exercise done by waving the diaphragm on fours.

ডবকা *adj* of budding youth; blooming; adolescent: ~ ছেলে, ~ মেয়ে. ~ **বয়স** *n* blooming youth.

ডবডব *int* denoting wetness or swelling. ~ **করা** *vi* be suffused (with). **ডবডবে** *adj* tearful; swelled: ডবডবে চোখ.

ডবল [E] *adj* twofold; double. ~ **ডেকার** *n* a bus or a ship having two decks or floors; a double-decker. ~ **প্রমোশন** (of a school student) promotion to the class above the next higher one for doing exceptionally brilliant results in an examination; double promotion. ~ **ব্যারেল** *adj* having two barrels; double barreled.

ডবি *adj* ripe before the natural time; precocious.

ডমর *n* **1** a quarrel; a dispute. **2** a brawl; an uproar; a riot. **3** rebellion; an insurrection; an uprising.

ডমরু, ডম্বরু *n* a small drum shaped like an hour-glass, which is played by moving it with one hand; a tabo(u)r. ~**-মধ্য** *adj* having a slender waist just as that of a tabor. ☐*n* **1** a slender waist like that of a tabor. **2** a neck of land connecting two much larger portions; an isthmus.

ডম্ফ[1] *n* a kind of musical instrument of the ancient times.

ডম্ফ[2] *n* boast; vaunting. ~ **করা** *vi* boast; vaunt.

ডম্বর *n* an ostentatious show; a splendid array of things.

ডম্বুরু = ডমরু

ডম্বল, ডাম্বেল [E] *n* a pair of weights used for exercise; dumb-bells.

ডর *n* apprehension of danger; fear; fright; dread; panic. ~ **করা** *vi* feel fear; fear. ~ **লাগা** *vi* be alarmed/frightened/afraid of; take fright.

ডরানো *vi* fear; dread; be panicky.

ডলন *n* act of rubbing/ massaging/ pressing/ kneading.

ডলা *vt* **1** massage or rub (as parts of a person's body to effect a cure). **2** press or squeeze: হাত-পা ~. **3** knead or work into amass with the hands (a dough for bread). ~**নো** *vt* cause to rub in (as an ointment); massage one's body or knead flour into a dough.

ডলার [E] *n* unit of money in the US, Canada, Australia and some other countries.

ডহর *adj* having great depth; deep. ❑*n* **1** a hollow in the earth; a ditch; a pit. **2** a watercourse; a channel. **3** a marshy land. **4** a waste land; pasturage. **ডহরা** *n* the hold of a ship or boat. **ডহরা-জমি** *n* low land.

ডাইন, ডান *adj* belonging to the right side; right. ❑*n* the side opposite to the left; right side. **~দিকে** *adv* to the right. ❑*adj* on the right side. **~ হাত** *n* **1** (lit) the right hand. **2** (fig) an unfailing and dependable aid. **ডান-হাত বাঁ-হাত করা** misappropriate; commit a breach of trust. **~ হাতের কাজ** *n* act of eating. **ডানে আনতে বাঁয়ে কুলায় না** fail to make both ends meet; live from hand to mouth.

ডাইনি *n* a witch. **~পনা** *n* witchcraft.

ডাইরি = ডায়েরি

ডাইল = ডাল

ডাংগুলি *n* a game in which a small piece of wood or bamboo slip is hit into the air and then knocked forward with a stick; tipcat.

ডাঁট[1] *n* that part of an instrument which is taken into the hand; a handle; a haft.

ডাঁট[2] *n* **1** firmness; the condition of being firm; steadfast; resolute or strong. **2** vanity; conceit; arrogance. **~ দেখানো** display arrogance; assume an air of superiority.

ডাঁটা *n* the stalk or stem of a plant; a slender branch of a free.

ডাঁটি *n* the handle of a spoon, etc.

ডাঁশ *n* a fly which bites cattle; the gadfly; the gnat.

ডাঁসা *adj* not fully ripened; half-ripe. ❑*n* wooden crossbar of a frame which supports the deck (as in a boat or wooden cot).

ডাক[1] *n* **1** asking one to come; call; summons: যদি তোর ~ শুনে.... **2** the cry or call of a bird or animal: পাখির ~, গাভীর ~. **3** loud cry; shout: ~ ছাড়া. **4** the rumbling noise or row of a cloud: মেঘের ~. **5** fame; glory; reputation; renown: নাম~. **6** an offer or bid at a sale: নিলামের ~. **7** ornaments of sola, tinsel, etc used to decorate a Hindu idol: ডাকের সাজ. ❑*adj* a short and convenient for use. **~ ছাড়া** *vi* cry out; shout. **~ দেওয়া** *vt* ask to come; call. **~নাম** *n* a nickname. **~ পাড়া** *vt* call (one) repeatedly. **~ বাড়া** *vi* (of auction bid) rise or increase gradually. **~-সাইটে** *adj* **1** famous and formidable: ~সাইটে লাঠিয়াল. **2** (hum) renowned: ~-সাইটে কবি. **~হাঁক, হাঁক~** *n* bustle; tumult; hue and cry. **ডাকের সুন্দরী** *n fem* one widely known for beauty; paragon of beauty. **একডাকে চেনা** know and recognize one at the first mention (because of one's wide acquaintance). **এক ডাকের পথ** *n* calling distance; distance of a stone's throw. **নাম-~** *n* fame; reputation; celebrity. **অশ্বের ~** neighing. **ইঁদুরের ~** squeaking. **কাকের ~** cawing. **কুকুরের ~** barking. **গরুর ~** lowing. **গর্দভের ~** braying. **ঘুঘুর ~** cooing. **পাখির ~** chirping. **পেঁচকের ~** hooting; screeching. **বাঘের ~** howling. **ভল্লুকের ~** growling. **বাঁদরের ~** chattering; gibbering. **বিড়ালের ~** mewing. **ভেকের ~** croaking. **মৌমাছির ~** humming. **মাছির ~** buzzing. **মেষের ~** bleating. **মোরগের ~** crowing. **শকুন/শকুনির ~** screaming. **শূকরের ~** grunting. **শৃগালের ~** yelping; howling. **ষাঁড়ের ~** bellowing. **সাপের ~** hissing. **সিংহের ~** roaring. **হাঁসের ~** cackling. **হস্তীর ~** trumpeting.

ডাক[2] [H]*n* **1** the postal system of collecting; carrying and delivering letters and parcels: ~ বিভাগ. **2** a postal collection or delivery; one collection/delivery of letters, etc; post; mail: আজকের ডাকে যাবে. **3** a batch or bag of letters, parcels, etc carried or conveyed by post: বিলাতের ~. **~ খরচা/ মাসুল** *n* postal charge; postage. **~গাড়ি** *n* a mail-coach; a mail-van; a mail train. **~ঘর** *n* office where postal business is carried on; a post office. **ডাকের থলি** *n* bag in which mails are carried; mail-bag. **~টিকিট** *n* postage. **~পিয়ন** *n* person who collects and delivers postal packages; a postman. **~বাক্স** *n* **1** box into which letters are dropped for collection; a letter box. **2** a numbered box in a post office for mails addressed to an individual or company; post office (PO) box. **~বিভাগ** *n* the postal department. **~মাসুল** = ~ খরচা. **~হরকরা** *n* a postman; a mail-runner. **ডাকে, ~যোগে** *adv* by post. **ফেরত ~** next/return mail. **ফেরত ডাকে** by return of post; by return mail.

ডাক[3] *n* a kind of aquatic bird; the water-bowl.

ডাক[4] **1** a milkman of ancient India who was famous for his wisdom: ডাকের বচন. **2** wise sayings; proverbs.

ডাকবাংলা, ডাকবাংলো [H] *n* a rest house for officers and travellers; a dak bungalow.

ডাকসাইটে ⇒ ডাক[1]

ডাকা *vt* **1** ask (one) to come: চাকরকে ~. **2** summon: আদালতে ~. **3** ask to an entertainment; invite: ভোজ উৎসবে ~. **4** (at an auction sale) bid for; offer certain price: নিলাম ~. **5** (cards, bridge) make a bid. **6** address in prayer; summon aid from; invoke: ঈশ্বরকে ~. **7** make an undesirable or morbid sound: নাক ~, পেট ~. **8** roar or rumble: মেঘ ~, সমুদ্র ~. **9** call one; address one: নাম ধরে ~. **~ডাকি 1** calling one repeatedly. **2** sending for one frequently. **3** asking people in a loud voice to come and gather together. **~নো** *vt* send for (one). **ডেকে আনা** *vt* fetch (one). **ডেকে আনানো** *vt* summon (one) (by a messenger). **ডেকে পাঠানো** *vt* send for. পাখি ~ *adj* resounding with the chirping of birds. বিপদ ডেকে আনা be the cause of a mishap by one's own imprudence.

ডাকাত, ডাকাইত [H] *n* member of a gang of armed robbers; a dacoit; a brigand; a bandit. ~ **পড়া** be raided by a gang of robbers. **ডাকাতি** *n* dacoity; robbery; banditry brigandage. **ডাকাতি করা** *vi* commit robbery. **ডাকাতে কালী** *n* goddess Kali as worshipped by dacoits. **দিনে ডাকাতি** *n* (fig) act of open corruption.

ডাকাবুকা *adj* uncommonly daring; dare-devil.

ডাকিনী = ডাইনি

ডাকু = ডাকাত

ডাক্তার *n* **1** a practitioner in medicine; a physician; a doctor. **2** person who has received the highest university degree 'Doctor of Philosophy (abbr Ph D)'. ~**খানা** *n* **1** medical establishment where sick and injured persons are received and treated; a hospital; a clinic. **2** place where medicines are dispensed as per doctor's advice; a dispensary; a pharmacy. ~ **দেখানো** *vi* **1** (of a disease) cause to be examined by a doctor for medical advice and treatment. **2** be under the treatment of a doctor. **ডাক্তারি** *n* **1** the science of medicine and surgery. **2** medical treatment. **3** the profession of a physician. **ডাক্তারি** *adj* pertaining to physicians.

ডাগর *adj* large; big, prominent: ~ চোখ. **2** grown up; aged; adult: ~ মেয়ে. ~ **হওয়া** *vi* grow big; develop. ~**ডাগর** *adj* very big and prominent. ~**ডোগর** *adj* appearing prominent.

ডাঙর, ডাঙ্গর *adj* big; large; fat.

ডাঙ্গশ, ডাঙ্গস *n* a pointed stick for driving an elephant; a good.

ডাঙ্গা *n* **1** dry land; up land: ~ জমি. **2** the bank of a river: ~য় নামা. ~**পথ** *n* overland route. ~**য় বাঘ জলে কুমির** (fig) between the devil and the deep sea; between the horns of a dilemma.

ডাণ্ডা *n* a thick wooden rod; a short bamboo staff. ~ **মারা** *vt* strike or hit with a rod. ~**গুলি** = ডাংগুলি.

ডান = ডাইন

ডানপিটে *adj* daring without judgment; foolhardy; dare-devil; reckless; obstinate. ~**গিরি** *n* dare-devil activities. ~**র মরণ গাছের আগায়** a reckless person comes by a violent death.

ডানা *n* a wing (as of birds); a fin (as of fishes). ~**কাটা** *adj* having the wings cut off. ~**কাটা পরী** *n* **1** fairy with the wings cut off. **2** a girl as beautiful as a fairy.

ডাব *n* green coconut.

ডাবর *n* **1** vessel for betel leaves. **2** a small metal basin.

ডাবা, ডাব্বা *n* **1** large earthen trough or tub. **2** a hookah with a water container made of coconut shell.

ডামাডোল *n* tumultuous confusion; wild uproar; widespread disorder; hurly-burly: যুদ্ধের ~.

ডাম্বেল = ডম্বল

ডায়মন [E]*n* **1** diamond. **2** level-work as is done on a piece of diamond. ~-**কাটা** *adj* having decorative works of bevelled pattern: ~-কাটা বালা.

ডায়েরি [E] *n* book for daily record of events, thoughts, etc; a diary.

ডাল[1] *n* **1** pigeon pea; pulse. **2** soup of pigeon pea.

ডাল[2] *n* a bough; a branch (of a tree); a twig.

ডালকুত্তা *n* tall, slender, fast-running dog kept for the chase; a greyhound. ~ **লেলিয়ে দেওয়া** set a greyhound on.

ডালনা *n* a kind of curry.

ডালা *n* **1** flat basket with a high rim; a high-rimmed tray. **2** a tray containing offerings.

ডালি *n* a basket full of articles or offerings to a deity: পুজোর ~.

ডালিম *n* the pomegranate.

ডাহা *adj* pure; unmixed. ~ **মিথ্যা** downright falsehood; arrant lie.

ডিক্রি, ডিক্রী [E] *n* a judicial decision; judgment of a court; decree. ~**দার** *n* one in whose favour a decree is issued; a decree-holder. ~ **জারি করা** *vi* execute a decree. ~ **পাওয়া** *vi* obtain a decree.

ডিগবাজি *n* a leap in which the heels turn over the head; a turn of the body in the air; a tumble; a somersault. ~ **খাওয়া** *vi* **1** play a somersault. **2** (fig) change one's views for convenience: রাজনৈতিক ~.

ডিগ্রি [E] *n* **1** a grade or a step; a graduation on a scale; 360th part of a revolution. **2** a mark of distinction conferred by universities; degree.

ডিঙ্গা *n* a boat; a canoe.

ডিঙ্গানো *vt* cross by leaping; leap over: বেড়া ~.

ডিঙ্গি *n* a small boat.

ডিপো [E] *n* **1** a place for deposit of sth; a depot. **2** a birth-place or breeding ground: রোগের ~.

ডিবা, ডিবে *n* **1** a small box or container: পানের ~. **2** a lamp without a chimney: কেরোসিনের ~.

ডিম *n* **1** eggs of hens or ducks (used as human food). **2** eggs of birds; reptiles or insects. **3** eggs of fish and certain water animals, frogs; spawn. ~ **ছাড়া** *vi* spawn. ~

পাড়া *vi* lay an egg. ডিমে তা দেওয়া *vi* hatch eggs. ডিমের কুসুম *n* the yolk. ডিমের শ্বেতাংশ *n* the white of an egg; glair. ডিমের খোলা *n* an egg-shell. ঘোড়ার ~ *n* sth absurd; a mare's nest.

ডিমাই [E] *n* a particular size of paper, generally 22·5 x 17·5 inches (23" x 18" in Bangladesh); demy.

ডিম্ব = ডিম. **~ক** *n* a small ovum; a germinal vesicle of animals; ovule. **~ক ত্বক** *n* a covering, esp a skin, membrane or shell; integument. **~ক নাড়ি** *n* (bot) a little stack by which the seed is joined to the placenta; funiculus. **~কোষ** *n* (bot) egg-cell; ovary; ovum. **~জ** *adj* born of an egg; oviparous. **ডিম্বাকার** *adj* egg-shaped; oval. **ডিম্বাণু** *n* an egg-cell; ovum. **ডিম্বাশয়** the female organ in which ova are formed; the ovary.

ডুগডুগি *n* a small tabor played by moving it with one hand. **~ বাজানো** (fig) express a feeling of joy and satisfaction at the defect and humiliation of one's opponent.

ডুগি *n* the smaller one of the pair of instruments played as musical accompaniment: ডুগি–তবলা.

ডুণ্ডুভ *n* species of non-venomous snakes; the water-snake.

ডুব *n* immersion in water; bathing by immersion; dive; dip. ❑*adj* a depth of water as will sink one standing on his feet: ~-জল. **~ দেওয়া/মারা** *vi vt* **1** dip into water; dive. **2** (sarcas) go into hiding. **~ পাড়া** *vi* dive or dip repeatedly. **~ন্ত** *adj* that which is sinking/ in the state of setting: ~ন্ত সূর্য. **ডুবে ডুবে পানি/জল খাওয়া** (fig) act surreptitiously. **ডুবে মরা** *vi* drown.

ডুবা, ডোবা *vt* **1** be submerged/ inundated; sink: রাস্তা–ঘাট ~. **2** give a dive; have a dip. **3** be drowned; die by drowning. **4** (fig) be ruined. **5** disappear below the horizon; set: সূর্য ~. **6** be absorbed in: ভাবরসে ~. **~নো** *vt* **1** cause to sink; submerge. **2** (fig) lead (one) to the path of ruin. **দেনায় ~** be over head and ears in debt. **নাম ~** harm one's reputation; earn disrepute.

ডুবি *n* an instance of sinking or capsizing: নৌকা ~.

ডুবুডুবু *adj* in the state of being sunk/ submerged/drowned.

ডুবুরি *n* person who works under water in a diving suit; a diver.

ডুমা, ডুমো *n* a piece or slice. ❑*adj* that has been cut into pieces: ~ সুপারি. **~-~** *adj* cut into pieces.

ডুলি *n* a kind of small litter much in use in former times; doolie.

ডেঁপো *adj* acting like an adult though not grown up; precocious. **~মি** *n* precocity; pertness; sauciness.

ডেক[1] *n* a large cooking utensil; cauldron.

ডেক[2] [E] *n* the platform or floor of a ship or bus; deck.

ডেকচি *n* metallic cooking utensil; a small cauldron.

ডেবরা *adj* (of a person) using the left hand more easily and frequently than the right; left-handed. ❑*n* a left-hander.

ডেমি [E] *n* prescribed paper used in writing legal deeds, etc; demy.

ডেরা [H] *n* a temporary abode; an improvised or tented accommodation; a camp. **~ গাড়া/ বাঁধা** *vi* build a hut for one's lodging; pitch a tent. **~ তোলা** *vi* wind up one's affairs and strike the tent. **~-ডাণ্ডা** camp and its gear; tent and its equipage.

ডেলা *n* a clotted mass; a clod or lump: মাটির ~. **~ পাকানো** *vt, vi* work into a lump; lump; clot.

ডেস্ক [E] *n* an inclining table to write or read upon; a portable case for the same purpose; a desk.

ডোঙ্গা *n* **1** a small and narrow boat. **2** a boat made of the trunk of a fanpalm or palmyra. **3** a dug-out or hollowed-out canoe from a trunk of tree used for irrigation purpose; a bail; a bale.

ডোজ [E] *n* the quantity of medicine given at one time; a dose.

ডোবা[1] *n* a ditch filled with water.

ডোবা[2] = ডুবা

ডোম *n* **1** a Hindu caste having the assigned duty of burning the dead and looking after the crematorium. **2** a member of this caste.

ডোর *n* thread; a string (of a garland); a rope. **2** (fig) a tie; a bond; an attraction: মায়া~. **3** the outer garment of the Vaishnavas: ~ কৌপীন.

ডোরা *n* a stripe; a streak. **~-কাটা, ~-~** *adj* having stripes of different colours; striped; streaky.

ডোল[1] *n* **1** large hollow basket made of bamboo slips, etc used for keeping grain, etc. **2** a bucket for drawing water from a well.

ডোল[2]**, ডোলা** *n* large litter; a palanquin.

ডোল[3] [E] *n* gratuity awarded to the poor and destitute; dole.

ডৌল [H] *n* the make or form of anything; external appearance: সু~. **~ করা** *vt* give shape to; mould; adapt; adjust; fashion. **সু~** *adj* beautiful shape; symmetrical; graceful.

ঢ

ঢ *n* the fourteenth consonant of the Bengali alphabet and fourth letter of ট group. It is pronounced as an alveolo retroflex voiced aspirated plosive sound.

ঢং[1], ঢঙ *n* **1** the mode in which anything is done; style; manner; method; fashion: গাইবার ~. **2** false pretension; dissimulation; artifice; hypocrisy: ~ করা. **3** manner of speaking: কথার ~. **ঢংগি, ঢঙি** *adj fem* one who dissimulates; dissimulating; coquettish: ঢংগি মেয়ে. **~ করা** *vi* feign; affect; flirt; dissimulate.

ঢং, ঢন *int* (onom) denoting the hollow sound of a metallic vessel or the ringing of a bell: ঢং ঢং করে ঘন্টা বেজে গেল, Ding-dong goes the bell. **ঢন ঢন** *int* suggesting absolute emptiness: পকেট ঢন ঢন.

ঢক,[1] ঢক ঢক *int* denoting the sound of gulping water. **~ করে গেলা** *vt* gulp down quickly.

ঢক[2] *n* shape; form; appearance; cut: বে–~.

ঢন ⇒ঢং

ঢপ[1] *int* denoting the hollow sound of a flatulent belly. **~~ করা** *vi* sound hollow.

ঢপ[2] *n* **1** shape; form; appearance. **2** a kind of কীর্তন song.

ঢল *n* **1** a slope; a declivity; an oblique direction; an incline. **2** part of a river where a steep slope causes the water to flow fast; a rapid: ~ নামা. **3** the sudden swell of a river due to flood or heavy rainfall: নদীতে ~ নেমেছে, The river is in spate. **~কানো** *vi* spurt over; swell forth; bubble over; get loose.

ঢলঢল *int* denoting excessive looseness: হাতে চুড়ি ~ করছে. **~ করা** *vt* move loosely. **ঢলঢলে** *adj* loose; slack.

ঢলা *vi* bend or hang downwards (through tiredness or weakness); droop. **ঢলে পড়া** *vi* collapse or breakdown (from loss of muscular strength, mental powers).

ঢলাঢলি *n* amorous sports; interchange of cuddling and caressing; dalliance. **~ করা** *vi* hug; embrace; fondle; cuddle; behave lasciviously.

ঢাক *n* large instrument of percussion; a drum. **~ পেটা/ বাজানো** *vi* **1** beat a drum. **2** (fig) make (sth) public; announce publicly. **ঢাকের কাঠি** *n* **1** drum-stick. **2** (fig) a constant companion but very insignificant in comparison. **ঢাকের বাঁয়া** some thing having no use except as a decoration; useless appurtenances. **ঢাকের বাদ্য** drum-beat. **ঢাকের দায়ে মনসা বিকানো** (fig) excessive expense for a useless thing; (prov) to sell one's homestead to grease one's car. **ধর্মের ~ আপনি বাজে** (prov) Virtue proclaims itself. **~-~ গুড়-গুড়** *n* an attempt to conceal or hush up.

ঢাকনা, ঢাকনি *n* a cover; a lid.

ঢাকা[1] *vt* cover; veil; hide; conceal. ❑*adj* covered. **~ দেওয়া** *vt* cover; conceal.

ঢাকা[2] *n* Dhaka, the capital of Bangladesh.

ঢাকাই *adj* made or manufactured in Dhaka.

ঢাকি *n* a drum beater; a drummer. **~শুদ্ধ বিসর্জন** to make wholesale sacrifice; to throw the rope after the bucket.

ঢাল[1] *n* a protective plate used by warriors to ward off weapons; a shield; a buckler.

ঢাল[2] a slope; a declivity; an incline.

ঢালা *vt* **1** pour out (as tea, etc) from one pot to another. **2** cast or mould (as in a matrix). **3** make lavish expenditure: ছেলের পেছনে টাকা ~. **4** invest huge capital: ব্যবসায়ে টাকা ~. ❑*adj* that which has been moulded: ~ কড়াই. **2** extensively spread out: ~ বিছানা. **3** general; permanent; standing: ~ হুকুম. **~ও** *adj* **1** extensive: ~ও ফরাস. **2** without exception; general: ~ও হুকুম, tall order. **3** abundant; plenty; sufficient; ample: ~ও খাবার. **~ঢালি** *n* pouring out from one vessel to another repeatedly; repeated pouring and re-pouring. **~ লোহা** *n* cast iron. **ঢেলে সাজা** *vt* change lock, stock and barrel and recast anew; do sth afresh.

ঢালাই *n* act of casting or moulding; melting and pouring. **~ করা** *vt* cast; mould. **~কর** *n* a caster. **~ কারখানা** *n* an iron-foundry; a foundry.

ঢালি, ঢালী *adj* wearing a shield; armed with a shield. ❑*n* a soldier bearing a shield.

ঢালু *adj* slanting downwards; sloping; declining.

ঢিট *adj* **1** wanting shame or modesty; brazen-faced; impudent; insolent. **2** chastised; subdued; corrected; controlled. **~ করা** *vt* teach one a lesson; chastise; bring under control. **~ হওয়া** *vi* be put in one's place; get a snubbing; be subdued. **~-পনা** *n* impudence; brazen-facedness; shamelessness.

ঢিঢি *n* (of a scandal, etc) wide circulation; widespread rumour; extensive publicity: ~ পড়ে গেছে. ❑*adj* circulated; declared; given a bad name; defamed; slandered. **~ করা** *vt* proclaim in public; circulate (a bad name).

ঢিপ *int* denoting the sound of sth falling from a height. **~ করে** *adv* with a thump or thud. **~ ~** *int* denoting palpitation of heart (as in fear). **বুক ~~ করা** *vi* (of heart) thud; pound.

ঢিপি *n* a mound; a hillock; a pile; a heap: উইয়ের ~, an ant-hill.

ঢিপুনি *n* heavy blow given with the fist; striking with the fist; thumping; drubbing. **~ খাওয়া** *vi* receive a drubbing; be thumped. ~ দেওয়া *vt* give a thumping.

ঢিবি = ঢিপি

ঢিমা, ঢিমে *adj* 1 mild; low; gentle: ~ আওয়াজ. 2 slow; slothful; dilatory. ~ তেতালা *n* 1 a protracted musical measure. 2 procrastination; dilatoriness; sluggishness.

ঢিল *n* a clod of earth; a stone; a brickbat. ~ ছোড়া, ~ মারা *vi*, *vt* throw stones at; pelt (one) with stones. ঢিল দেওয়া *vi* be sluggish; be lazy. ~ মারলে পাটকেল পড়ে (prov) Tit for tat.

ঢিলা, ঢিলে *adj* 1 loose; slack: ~ জামা. 2 slow; sluggish; slothful: ~ মানুষ. 3 not strict, lax: ~ প্রশাসন. ~ দেওয়া *vi* slacken; loosen; relax. ঢিলেঢালা *adj* slothful; careless; sloppy: ঢিলেঢালা রকমের মানুষ. ~মি *n* slothfulness; laziness; sluggishness; laxity. ~মি করা *vi* be lax; procrastinate.

ঢু, ঢুঁ *n* act of pushing with the head or butt. ~ মারা *vi* 1 strike with the head or butt. 2 pay a casual visit to a place: ফেরার পথে একবার ~ মেরে যেও, Please pop in and see me on your way back. 3 move from door to door in search of sth: চাকুরির জন্য ~ মারা.

ঢুঁড়া *vi* look for; search; seek; haunt about; traverse: দেশে দেশে ~.

ঢুকা, ঢোকা *vt* 1 get in; go in; enter: ঘরে ~. 2 be admitted into: দলে ~. 3 be appointed/ employed: চাকুরিতে ~. 4 occur to; strike (one): মাথায় ~. ~নো *vt* cause to enter; push in; drive in: পেরেক ~নো; fix or fit: আংটি ~নো; make one understand/ comprehend: মাথায় ~নো.

ঢুঢু *int* denoting nothingness. ❑*adj* empty; hollow; good-for-nothing. ~ করা *vi* be empty; sound empty.

ঢুল *n* nodding or stooping in drowsiness/ intoxication: চোখে ~ নামা, feel drowsy; be dozing. ~ঢুলে, ঢুলুঢুলু *adj* heavy with drowsiness/ intoxication; drowsy; dull.

ঢুলা *vi* nod with sleep/ intoxication; be drowsy; doze. ~নো *vt* move; shake; agitate; wave: মা শিশুকে ঢুলাচ্ছেন.

ঢুলি *n* person who plays on the drum; a drummer.

ঢুসানো *vt* but with the head (as by a goat). ঢুসাঢুসি *n* act of butting one another.

ঢেউ *n* wave; billow; surge. ~ ওঠা *vt* rise in waves; wave; surge; ripple. ~ কাটানো dodge waves (in steering a boat). ~ খেলা *vt* move in waves or ripples. ~ তোলা *vt* cause to rise in waves; swell up in waves; surge up. ~-খেলানো, ~-তোলা *adj* wavy; undulating; waving; corrugated. ~টিন, ~-খেলানো টিন *n* corrugated iron sheet.

ঢেঁকি *n* husking pedal consisting of solid wooden body with a rod or fulcrum fixed to its mouth, worked usu by women with their feet. ~-অবতার *n* a foolish and lazy person. ~ গেলা *vi* 1 (lit) swallow a husking pedal. 2 (fig) agree to shoulder a heavy responsibility against one's will only to keep up appearances. ~র আঁকশলি *n* the fulcrum of the husking pedal. ~র কচকচি *n* a noisy quarrel like the unpleasant sound of a husking pedal. ~শাক *n* an edible fern. ~শাল *n* the shed in which a husking pedal is fixed. ~তে পাড় দেওয়া *vi* work a husking pedal by the foot. বুকে ~র পাড় পড়া (fig) (of one's heart) throb; palpitate. ~ স্বর্গে গেলেও ধান ভানে (prov) A drudge will drudge even in heaven. বুদ্ধির ~ (fig) a big fool.

ঢেঁকুর *n* a noisy expulsion of wind upwards from the stomach; a belch; an eructation. ~ তোলা *vi, vt* make a belch; belch; eructate. চোঁয়া ~ *n* soury eructation caused by over-eating or indigestion.

ঢেঁড়স *n* a kind of vegetable; the lady's finger.

ঢেঁঢরা = ঢেঁড়া

ঢেঁড়া, ঢ্যাঁড়া *n* a kind of drum which is beaten under authority to make a public announcement. ~ পেটা *vi* make a proclamation by drum-beat.

ঢেঁড়ি *n* 1 a kind of earring. 2 a pod or seed-vessel of poppy; a poppy-seed. 3 = ঢেঁড়া.

ঢেকুর = ঢেঁকুর

ঢেঙ্গা = ঢ্যাংগা

ঢেপসা, ঢ্যাপসা *adj* looking like a mound; bulky and odd shaped; ugly to see.

ঢেমনা[১] *adj* 1 lewd; libertine; profligate. 2 bastard.

ঢেমনা[২] *n* a species of non-venomous snake.

ঢেমনি *n fem* a concubine; a kept woman.

ঢের *adj* abundant; profuse; lavish; plentiful; enough; sufficient.

ঢেরা, ঢ্যারা *n* 1 a cross 'x' mark. 2 wooden cylinder on which thread, wire, etc is wound; a bobbin. ~সই *n* a cross mark put by an illiterate to have his name signed by another at that place.

ঢেরি *n* a heap; a pile; a stack. ~ করা *vt* heap; pile.

ঢেলা *n* a lump (of earth); a clod; a brickbat. ~ মারা *vi* throw stones at; pelt.

ঢোঁক, ঢোক *n* act of taking a swallow; a gulp. ~ গেলা/গিলা *vi* gulp; swallow. ~ গিলে কথা বলা falter in speaking; stammer; hesitate; hum and haw.

ঢোঁড়ন *n* act of seeking/ searching.

ঢোঁড়া *n* a non-venomous snake. ❑*adj* lacking in vigour but full of boasts; worthless.

ঢোক = ঢোঁক

ঢোকা = ঢুকা

ঢোল *n* instrument of percussion which is not so fat as a drum but longer in size; a tomtom. ❑*adj* hollow; swelled: ফুলে ~ হওয়া. **~ক** *n* narrow kind of tomtom beaten with the hands. **~ দেওয়া** *vi* **1** announce by beating a tomtom. **2** proclaim; circulate. **~ পেটা, ঢোলে কাঠি দেওয়া** *vi* **1** beat a tomtom. **2** announce or circulate. **~-শহরত** *n* announcement of sth by the beat of a tomtom. **নিজের ~ নিজে বাজানো** blow one's own trumpet; (fig) praise oneself.

ঢোলা *adj* loose; not tight: ~ পায়জামা.

ঢৌকন *n* gift; presentation; illegal gratification; bribe: উপ~.

ঢৌল *n* **1** tomtom. **2** humiliation; harassment. ❑ *adj* humiliated; harassed; insulted.

ঢ্যাংগা, ঢেঙ্গা *adj* tall and slender; lean and thin.

ঢ্যাঁড়স = ঢেঁরস

ঢ্যাঙা = ঢ্যাংগা

ঢ্যামনা = ঢেমনা

ঢ্যারা = ঢেরা

ণ

ণ *n* the fifteenth letter of the Bengali alphabet and fifth letter of the ট group. ণ stands for nasal sound of the ট group of letters, eg কন্টক, কণ্ঠ, দণ্ড.

ণই (archaic) *n* a river.

ণত্ববিধান, ণত্ববিধি *n* (gram) Sanskrit grammatical rules for changing the dental ন into the cerebral ণ, used for Sanskrit words in Bengali.

ণ-ফলা *n* the joining of 'ণ' with other letters.

ণালিকা *n* a weapon having a cylinder or barrel; a gun.

ণিচ্ *n* (gram) a causative inflection of verbs (eg √জন্, produce +ণিচ্+অন *(suff)* = জনন, act of reproducing).

ণিজন্ত *adj* (gram) *adj* inflected with ণিচ্: ~ ধাতু.

তᐟ *n* the sixteenth consonant and first of the ত group of letters. It is a dental, unvoiced, unaspirated, plosive sound.

তᐟᐟ, তো *int* (presently 'তো' is preferred to 'ত') **1** denoting an inquiry: যাবে ~? You are going, isn't it? **2** indicating an assurance or certainty: এই~ টাকা এসে গেছে, Here comes the money. **3** expressing a request: একটু দেখুন ~. Would you please look to it. **4** meaning an assertion or positive declaration: আমি ~ এমন কথা বলিনি, Why, I haven't said such things! **5** in the sense of 'though', 'in spite', etc: সে ~ যাবে না, তবু বলে দেখো. **6** indicating uncertainty: যাই ~, তারপর বোঝা যাবে. **7** expressing doubt: হয়~. **8** indicating certainty: তিনি ~ জানেন, He knows it already. **9** meaning 'if', 'in case': বাঁচতে চাও ~. **10** indicating a reflection: সে কেরানি বই ~ নয়, He is but a clerk. **11** pointing to some fact: সে ~ ছেলেমানুষ, He is but a child. **12** suggesting possibility of some event: পারো ~ একবার এসো, বলো ~ যাব.

তই *n* frying pan without rims.

তইখন *adv*, *conj* (poet, archaic) by that time; then; at once; at that time.

তওবা [A] *n* **1** a confession of sin and begging pardon of God. **2** a declaration or avowal of faith.

তওয়াক্কুল [A] *n* faith; reliance: আল্লাহ্‌র উপর ~ রাখা. **~ করা** *vt* have faith in; rely on.

তওয়াক্কা, তোয়াক্কা [A] *n* heedfulness; care; dependence; deference; fear. **~ করা/রাখা** *vt* be afraid of; depend upon; treat with deference. **~ না করা** *vi* not to care.

তওয়াজা, তওজা [A] *n* respect; courtesy.

তওয়াফ [A] *n* act of going round on foot with reverence from right to left; clockwise circumambulation around an object of reverence: কাবা শরিফ ~ করা. **~ করা** *vt* circumambulate in a clockwise manner around a holy object.

তওয়ারিখ, তায়ারীখ [A] *n* history.

তওরাত, তৌরাত [A] *n* the Holy Book revealed to Prophet Moses; the Torah.

তওহিদ, তৌহিদ [A] *n* the doctrine that there is only one God; monotheism. **~বাদ** *n* the basic doctrine of Islam that there is no object of adoration except Allah, the Creator, Nourisher and Sustainer of the universe.

তক *prep* (used chiefly as *suff*) until; up to; till: শেষ~. **কাঁহা~** *adv* how far? how long? to what extent?

তকছির=তকসির

তকতক *int* **1** denoting tidiness: ঘরখানা ~ করছে. **2** indicating a dazzling effect of a sheet of water. **3** suggesting brightness or freshness. **~ করা** *vi* glare; shine; dazzle. **তকতকে** *adj* tidy; neat and clean; bright and fresh; transparent.

তকদির [A] *n* that which happens to a person; fate; luck; fortune; destiny.

তকবির [A] *n* **1** the shout of "Allahu Akbar" meaning 'Allah is Great'. **2** proclamation of the greatness of Allah. **3** shout; noise.

তকব্বরি [A] *n* pride; self-esteem; conceit; vanity; arrogance. ❑ *adj* proud; self-conceited; arrogant; vainglorious. ~ **করা** *vi* give oneself airs.

তকমা=তমগা

তকরার [A] *n* **1** argument; altercation; recapitulation; debate .**2** decision; judgment; adjudication. ~ **করা** *vi* make a row; bandy words. **তকরারি** *adj* **1** one that argues/ altercates; quarrelsome. **2** under judicial consideration; subjudice.

তকলি *n* a pin carrying a bobbin in a spinning machine; spindle; distaff. ~ **কাটা** *vi* spin yarn.

তকলিফ [A] *n* hardship; suffering ; trouble; difficulty. ~ **দেওয়া** *vt* put into trouble; harass; cause hardship or suffering to.

তকল্লুফ [A] *n* forms of ceremony or decorum; social observances; etiquette.

তকসিম [A] *n* **1** administrative division in Mughal India. **2** partition; division; distribution.

তকসির [A] *n* a flaw; a fault; a slight offence.

তক্ত=তখত

তক্তপোশ [P] *n* a plain rectangular bedstead.

তক্তা [P] *n* **1** a plank of wood; a piece of board. **2** a flat sheet of anything: ~~ কাগজ. **মেরে ~ বানানো** (sl) flatten by beating/thrashing.

তক্তি [P] *n* **1** a small plank of wood. **2** a small piece of board to write on (for children); a wooden slate. **3** a hard and flat sweet in the shape of a tablet. **4** a medal-like jewel for the neck.

তক্র *n* the thin, watery part of milk which remains after removing the curds; whey. **~পিণ্ড, ~কুচিকা** *n* lump of curdled milk made after separating the watery part; posset. ~ **মাংস** *n* meat curry cooked with curd/whey.

তক্ষক *n* **1** a carpenter skilled in carving wood; one who carves; a carver. **2** a kind of venomous snake. **3** a kind of venomous lizard with sucker on its feet; gecko. **4** the manager of an opera party. **তক্ষণ** *n* act of abrading/ planing/ carving. **তক্ষণী** *n* a carpenter's tool for planing, shaping or trimming wood; a chisel; a plane.

তক্ষণ, তক্ষণী ⇒ তক্ষক

তক্ষনি, তক্ষুনি *adv* immediately; instantly; without delay.

তক্ষশীলা *n* **1** the city that was carved out of rocks. **2** Taxila, the ancient city in the Punjab, famous as a centre of learning.

তখত [P] *n* **1** a royal throne. **2** a wooden board. **~তাউস** *n* the famous peacock throne of Shahjahan, the magnificent emperor of India. **~নসীন** *n* seated on the throne; enthroned. **~নামা** *n* a kind of conveyance carried by men, formerly used in marriage processions.

তখন *adv* (also *conj*) **1** at that time; in those days: ~ টাকায় আট মণ চাল পাওয়া যেত. **2** then; in that case: যদি আসে, ~ ব্যবস্থা করা যাবে. **3** so; after that; and then: দাওয়াত পেলাম, ~ গেলাম. **4** that time: ~ থেকে, since then/that time. **~ই, তখনি** *adv* just then; forthwith; immediately; at once. **~কার** *adj* of that time/age.

তখমা ⇒ তমগা

তখল্লুস [A] *n* an assumed name, esp one assumed for the publication of literary works; a pseudonym.

তচনচ=তছনছ

তছনছ, তচনচ [A] *adj* utterly spoiled/messed up; upset; thrown about; destroyed.

তছরুপ, তছরুফ [A] *n* act of fraudulently appropriating money, etc entrusted to one's care; embezzlement. ~ **করা** *vt* embezzle; appropriate by breach of trust. **তহবিল ~** *n* defalcation; embezzlement.

তছু *pron* (poet, archaic) his, her.

তজকিরা [A] *n* description; discussion; biography: তজকিরাত–উল আম্বিয়া, biography of saints.

তজদিগ [A] *n* proof, evidence.

তজল্লি [A] *n* light; lustre; brightness.

তজ্জনিত [তৎ+জনিত] *adj* arising out of that; caused by that.

তজ্জন্য [তৎ+জন্য] *adj* because of that; for that reason; owing to/due to/ in consequence of that; hence; therefore; so.

তজ্জাত [তৎ+জাত] *adj* born of him/her/that; growing out of that; caused by that.

তঞ্চ *n* deception; fraud; artifice; double-dealing.

তঞ্চক[1] *adj* one who cheats/deceives/swindles. ❑ *n* misrepresentation of fact; perversion/ distortion of truth; prevarication. **~তা** *n* cheating; deception; swindling; trickery.

তঞ্চক[2] *n* **1** contraction; shrinking. **2** (chem) change of a fluid into a fixed state; coagulation.

তঞ্চন *n* the process or state of coagulating/ clotting: দুধ থেকে ~ প্রক্রিয়ায় দই হয়. **তঞ্চিত** *adj* clotted; coagulated; congealed.

তট *n* **1** the shore of the sea, the bank of a river; beach; shore; coast; bank: সমুদ্র~, নদী~. **2** land ; soil: ~ভাগ. **3** high land: কটি~. **4** tract of level ground on the top of a mountain: গিরি~. **~পথ** *n* land route. **~ভূমি** *n* coast land. **~রেখা** *n* coast line.

তটস্থ[1] *adj* very much perturbed; worried and bustling; extremely busy.

তটস্থ[2] *adj* **1** lying on the shore/bank; coastal; littoral. **2** impartial; unbiased; disinterested; neutral. **তটস্থা** *fem.*

তটিনী *n* a river; a stream.
তটী *n* **1** bank; shore. **2** a region; a country.
তড়কা[1] *n* disease causing spasmodic fit or convulsion in children; tetanus.
তড়কা[2] *n* leaping; jumping; rushing with violence: নদীর ~. **ব্যাঙ–~** *n* a jump like that of a frog.
তড়তড় *int* denoting **(a)** the sound of rainfall; **(b)** hasty steps: ~ করে চলে গেল.
তড়পানো *n* **1** vaunt and be refractory; brag; jump; boast. **2** spring or turn with sudden effort; flounce (as fish). **3** move violently; agitate; be restless: দিল তড়পাচ্ছে. **তড়পানি** *n* act of jumping and bragging; act of fretting and fussing; violent movement; restlessness.
তড়বড় *int* denoting haste and hurry. **তড়বড়ানো** *vi* move or speak in excessive hurry. **~ করে** *adv* quickly; hastily; hurry-scurry. **তড়বড়ানি** *n* haste and hurry. **তড়বড়ে** *adj* hasty; quick; hurry-scurry.
তড়াক[1] *int* expressing suddenness or quickness: ~ করে লাফ দিলো.
তড়াক[2], **তড়াগ** *n* a large pool of water.
তড়িঘড়ি *adv* hurriedly; instantly; promptly; at once; forth with; immediately.
তড়িচ্চালক [তড়িৎ+চালক] *adj* producing motion by means of electricity; electro-motive. **~ বল** *n* electro-motive force.
তড়িচ্চুম্বক [তড়িৎ + চুম্বক] *n* a magnet energized by a coil of wire carrying an electric current round it; electro-magnet.
তড়িচ্চুম্বকীয় *adj* relating to, producing, derived from electro-magnetism; electro-magnetic.
তড়িৎ *n* lightning; electricity. **~ শিখা** *n* a flash of lightning.
তড়িত্বান, তড়িদ্গর্ভ *n* a cloud; a thunder-cloud.
তড়িদ্দ্বার [তড়িৎ+দ্বার] *n* one of the points which an electric current passes from a conducting or producing circuit into another conducting medium; an electrode.
তড়িদ্বিশ্লেষণ *n* chemical change or decomposition produced by electric energy; electrolysis.
তড়িদ্বীক্ষণ [তড়িৎ + বীক্ষণ] *n* an instrument which tests the presence, nature and intensity of electricity; an electroscope.
তড়িন্ময় [তড়িৎ+ ময়] *adj* charged with electricity.
তড়িল্লতা [তড়িৎ + লতা] *n* a streak of lightning; a wave of electricity
তণ্ডুল *n* husked rice. **~কণা** *n* grain of rice. **~চূর্ণ** *n* rice reduced to powder; rice-powder.
তৎ (তদ্) *pron* **1** he; she. **2** it; that. **~কর্তৃক** *adv* by him/her/it. **~কাল** *n* that time/ age; those days. **~কালিক/ কালীন** *adj* of/for/during that time or age; occurring/ prevalent at that time or in those days. **~কালে** *adv* at that time; then; in those days. **~কালোচিত** *adj* suitable to the occasion; befitting the age. **~কৃত** *adj* done by him/her. **~ক্ষণাৎ** *adv* at that moment; at once; immediately. **~ক্ষণে** *adv* at the moment; by that time. **~পর** *adv* after that; thereafter. ❑*adj* **1** skilful; adroit; expert. **2** enterprising; earnest; zealous; endeavouring. **~পরতা** *n* skilfulness; adroitness; zeal; earnestness; enterprise; endeavour. **~পরায়ণ** *adj* sincerely attached to that; zealously engaged in that; absorbed in that. **~পরে**=তৎপর (adv). **~পশ্চাৎ** *adv* behind him/her. **~পুরুষ** *n* **1** the Supreme Being; God. **2** (gram) a system of compounding two words into one in which the preceding word loses its inflexion giving prominence to the succeeding word (eg গাছে পাকা=গাছপাকা). **~পূর্বে** *adv* before that; prior to that. **~ সংক্রান্ত/ সম্বন্ধীয়** *adj* relating to/ concerning that. **~সদৃশ** *adj* similar to that; resembling/ like that. **~সম** *adj* same as that. **~সম শব্দ** (gram) Sanskrit word used in Bengali without any change. **~স্থলাভিষিক্ত** *adj* installed in his/her/its place. **~স্বরূপ** *adj* resembling that.
তত[1] *adj* outspread; expanded; stretched out; extended; diffused. ❑*n* a stringed musical instrument (also ~যন্ত্র).
তত[2] *adv*, *conj* **1** to that extent/ amount/ number/ proportion: যত হাসি ~ কান্না (prov). **2** so much (as might have been expected); enough; up to the expectation: ছবিটা ~ ভালো নয়. **~ক্ষণ** *adv* up to/ during that time: যতক্ষণ না আসি ~ক্ষণ অপেক্ষা করো. **~ক্ষণে** *adv* by that time; in the meantime: ~ক্ষণে আমি এসে যাবো. **~দিন** *adv* for those days; during so many days. **~দিনে**=~ক্ষণে. **~হি, ~হিঁ** *adj* at that.
ততোধিক [ততঃ+ অধিক] *adj* more than that.
ততঃ *adv* thereafter; then. **~কিম** then what? what next?
তত্তুল্য [তৎ + তুল্য] like him/her; similar/equal to that.
তত্ত্ব *n* **1** (fundamental) truth; essence; reality: ~দর্শী. **2** one's own nature; disposition; form; identity. **3** the twenty four principal constituting elements according to the Sankhya philosophy, eg the sense organs, the limbs, the mind, intellect, the earth, the sky; air, etc. **4** information; data. **5** matter. **6** news; welfare: ~ লওয়া. **7** investigation; search; inquiry. **8** wedding gift: বিয়ের ~. **9** God. **10** spiritual knowledge: ~ কথা. **11** presentation on Hindu religious occasion: পূজার ~. **12** theory: মাধ্যাকর্ষণ ~. **13** philosophy; science and knowledge in these fields: পরলোক ~, কৃষি ~. **~ করা** *vt* inquire about; search after; send presents to. **~ কহা** *vt* declare the truth. **~ জানা** *vi* be acquainted with a fact. **~ নির্ণয় করা** *vt* ascertain the truth. **~**

লওয়া *vt* superintend; look after; inquire about. ~চিন্তা *n* meditation on the Creator and the creation. ~জিজ্ঞাসা *n* inquisitiveness about truth; search after knowledge. ~জিজ্ঞাসু *adj* desirous of knowing the truth. ~জ্ঞ *adj* having knowledge of the truth. ❑ *n* a spiritualist; a theologian; a philosopher; a metaphysician. ~জ্ঞান *n* knowledge of the first principle or the fundamental truth; knowledge about reality and truth. ~জ্ঞানী *adj* knowing the true nature of a thing. ❑ *n* a philosopher; a theologist; a metaphysician. তত্ত্বত *adv* in truth; truly; accurately; philosophically. ~তালাশ *n* exchange of news and greetings and presents. ~তাবাশ *n* inquiry about welfare. ~দর্শিতা *n* acquaintance with the true state of things; wisdom. ~দর্শী *adj* having spiritual and philosophical knowledge; wise; judicious. ~বিদ, ~বিৎ *adj* wise; sagacious; experienced. ~বিদ্যা *n* the doctrine of being; that part of metaphysics which treats of things or existences; ontology. ~বোধ *n* perception of truth.

তত্ত্বানুসন্ধান [তত্ত্ব + অনুসন্ধান] *n* **1** search for information; research; investigation. **2** search for knowledge about the Creator. **3** search for the truth of anything. ~ করা *vt* search or inquire after truth. তত্ত্বানুসন্ধানী *n*, *adj* one who seeks after truth.

তত্ত্বাবধান [তত্ত্ব + অবধান] *n* **1** superintendence; guidance. **2** taking care of; looking after; guardianship or custody. ~ করা *vt* look after; take care of; manage; superintend; inspect. তত্ত্বাবধানে রাখা *vt* put or keep under care/ guardianship/ custody of.

তত্ত্বাবধায়ক [তত্ত্ব + অধায়ক] *n*, *adj* one who takes care of/looks after; caretaker; guardian; custodian.

তত্ত্বাবধারক *adj* one who ascertains the truth/ reality/ actual state of a thing.

তত্ত্বাবধারণ *n* ascertainment of truth or reality.

তত্ত্বাববোধ [তত্ত্ব + অববোধ] *n* perception of truth/ reality; knowledge of the fundamental truth.

তত্ত্বার্থ [তত্ত্ব + অর্থ] *n* the highest truth; reality; God.

তত্ত্বালোচনা [তত্ত্ব + আলোচনা] *n* discussion about truth or reality; ontological discourse.

তত্ত্বীয় *adj* **1** relating to truth/ reality. **2** pertaining to theory; theoretical.

তত্র *adv* there; at that place. ❑ *conj* so: যত্র আয় ~ ব্যয়. ~ত্য *adj* of that place; belonging to that place; lying or situated there. যত্র~ *adv* everywhere.

তত্রাচ [তত্র + চ] *conj* still then; nonetheless; nevertheless; notwithstanding; in spite of that.

তত্রাপি [তত্র + অপি] *adv* even then; yet; nevertheless; notwithstanding.

তথা *n* that place: ~ হইতে. ❑ *adv* at/in/to that place; there. ❑ *conj*, *adv* **1** so; like: যথা আয় ~ ব্যয়. **2** and also; for the matter of that: বাংলাদেশ ~ দক্ষিণ এশিয়া. **3** for example/ instance: তথা বাৎস্যায়নে. ~কথিত *adj* so named; having certain pretensions to being; so-called: ~কথিত সভ্যসমাজে. ~কার *adj* of that place. ~গত *adj* come and gone in that manner. ❑ *n* **1** one who has attained nirvana according to Buddhism. **2** an appellation of Gautama Buddha. ~চ, তত্রাপি *adv* even then; in spite of that; notwithstanding; nevertheless; still. ~বিধ *adj* of that kind/ nature; similar; such. ~ভূত *adj* of/in that state; born/ produced/ grown in that way. ~য় *adv* at or in that place; there. ~স্তু *int* so be it; be it so; amen. যথা~ *adv* everywhere; anywhere.

তথৈব [তথা + এব] *adv* even thus; just so. ❑*adj* of that manner/way. ❑ *n* that manner/ way.

তথৈবচ [তথা + এবচ] *adv* (sarcas) just the same; just so; of a similar nature: তুমি যেমন ভোলানাথ, তোমার বন্ধুটিও ~.

তথ্য *n* **1** genuineness; authenticity; reality; truth; justness; actual state of affairs: তথ্যানুসন্ধান. **2** facts; data: বৈজ্ঞানিক ~. **3** information. ❑ *adj* undisputed; real; true; unanimous; universal: ~ বচন. ~জ্ঞান *n* knowledge of truth/facts; true or accurate knowledge. ~ নিরূপণ/নির্ণয় *n* determination of truth; ascertainment of facts. ~বাদী/ভাষী *adj* truthful. ~বাহী *adj* informative.

তথ্যানুসন্ধান [তথ্য + অনুসন্ধান] *n* search after accurate knowledge/ correct information.

তদ্‌ (rare), তৎ *pron* he; she. **2** (according to Hindu idea) Brahma.

তদতিরিক্ত [তৎ + অতিরিক্ত] *adj* more than/beyond that; besides that.

তদনন্তর [তৎ + অনন্তর] *adv* after that; thereafter.

তদনুগ [তৎ + অনুগ] *adj* following him/her/that.

তদনুগামী=তদনুগ

তদনুপাতে [তৎ + অনুপাতে] *adv* in proportion to that; proportionately.

তদনুবর্তী=তদনুগ

তদনুযায়ী [তৎ + অনুযায়ী] *adj* following or like that. ❑ *adv* according to that; accordingly.

তদনুরূপ [তৎ + অনুরূপ] *adj* similar to that; such; like.

তদনুসারী [তৎ + অনুসারী] *adj* following/like that.

তদনুসারে [তৎ + অনুসারে] *adv* according to that; accordingly; agreeably.

তদন্ত [তৎ + অন্ত] *n* careful and thorough inquiry; investigation. ~ করা *vt* investigate. ~কারী *n* one who investigates; an investigator.

তদন্য [তদ্ + অন্য] *adj* other than that; different/ apart from that.

তদবধি [তদ্ + অবধি] *adv* **1** since then; ever since; from then onwards. **2** till then.

তদবস্থ [তদ্ + অবস্থা] *adj* in that condition/ state/ position. **তদবস্থা** *n* that state; the former or previous condition. **তদবস্থায়** *adv* in that condition/state.

তদবির [A] *n* **1** act of taking necessary action; act of doing the needful to achieve an end; effort; endeavour: মামলার ~. **2** remedy; redress; prevention; counteraction. **3** management; supervision; looking after. **4** effort; endeavour: চাকুরির ~. **~ করা** *vt* take necessary steps for; look after; strive after; endeavour. **~কারক** *adj* one who takes necessary steps/ makes necessary efforts.

তদর্থ [তৎ + অর্থ] *adv* for that; for the sake of that. ❑ *n* the meaning of that. **~ক** *adj, adv* ad hoc arranged for that purpose; informal. **তদর্থে** *adv* in that meaning/sense; for that purpose; for the sake of that.

তদা *adv, conj* at that time; in that age; then.

তদাকার [তৎ + আকার] *adj* of that shape/ form.

তদাত্মা [তদ্ + আত্মা] *adj* having the same soul as his or her; identical with him/her.

তদানীং *adv* at that time; in that age/those days; then.

তদানীন্তন *adj* of that time/age; the then: ~ সরকার.

তদারক [A] *n* **1** investigation; inquiry. **2** supervision; superintendence; looking after; management: সম্পত্তির ~, স্বাস্থ্যের ~. **~ করা** *vi ,vt* investigate; look after; take care, supervise. **তদারকি** *n* investigation; taking care; supervision.

তদীয় *adj* of him/her/it/that.

তদুত্তরে [তদ্ + উত্তরে] *adv* in reply to that.

তদুপযুক্ত, তদুপযোগী [তদ্ + উপযুক্ত, উপযোগী] *adj* befitting that; proportionate/ suitable to that.

তদুপরি [তদ্ + উপরি] *adv* upon this/that; over and above that; besides that; in addition.

তদুপলক্ষে, তদুপলক্ষ্যে [তদ্ + উপলক্ষে] *adv* on that occasion; on account of that.

তদূর্ধ্বে [তদ্ + উর্ধ্বে] *adv* high over that; on the top of it; beyond; over and above that.

তদেক [তদ্ + এক] *adj* **1** one identical with him/her: ~ চিত্ত. **2** no other: ~ শরণ.

তদ্‌গত [তৎ + গত] *adj* absorbed or engrossed in him/her/it; inseparable or inalienable from him/ her/ that. **~চিত্ত** *adj* rapt in attention; very attentive; engrossed. **~চিত্তে** *adv* with highly concentrated mind; with rapt attention; with intent and undivided mind.

তদ্দণ্ডে [তৎ + দণ্ডে] *adv* at that very moment; immediately; at once; forthwith.

তদ্দরুন [তৎ + দরুন] *adv* because of that; on account of that; on that account.

তদ্দিন [তৎ + দিন] *adv* for those days.

তদ্দ্বারা [তদ্ + দ্বারা] *pron, adv* by him/ her/ it.

তদ্ধিত [তৎ + হিত] *n* (gram) any of the inflexions or suffixes added to nouns, pronouns and objectives; secondary suffix; nominal inflexion: কাঠ + উরিয়া=কাঠুরিয়া. **তদ্ধিতান্ত পদ** *n* derivative from a noun, pronoun or adjective.

তদ্বৎ [তৎ + বৎ] *adj, adv* like/ similar/ comparable to him, her or that.

তদ্বাচক [তদ্ + বাচক] *adj* signifying or indicating that.

তদ্বিধ [তৎ + বিধ] *adj* of that sort/kind.

তদ্বিধায় [তদ্ + বিধায়] *adv* owing to/on account of that; because of it.

তদ্বির=তদবির

তদ্বিষয়ক [তদ্ + বিষয়ক] *adj* relating to that; concerning that subject. **তদ্বিষয়ে** *adv* regarding/ as regards that subject.

তদ্ব্যতিরিক্ত, তদ্ব্যতীত [তদ্ + বি + অতিরিক্ত, অতীত] *adj, adv* with the exception of that; over and above that; besides or in addition to that.

তদ্ভব [তদ্ + ভব] *adj* **1** born of that. **2** descended or derived from Aryan. **~ শব্দ** (gram) Bengali word derived from Aryan language.

তদ্ভাব [তদ্+ভাব] *n* **1** the nature/ state/ condition/ sentiment of his or her own. **2** thought or feeling about that. **3** that state/condition. **তদ্ভাবাপন্ন** *adj* having that feeling or sentiment. **তদ্ভাবে** *adv* in that state or condition; in that way/manner.

তদ্ভিন্ন=তদ্ব্যতীত

তদ্রূপ [তৎ+রূপ] *adj* of that form/ kind/ description; like that; such. ❑ *adv* so; similarly; in that manner: ~ কিছু, anything like that. **তদ্রূপে**=তদ্রূপ (adv).

-তন *suff* inflection indicating time: অধুনাতন, তদানীন্তন.

তনকা, তনখা [P] *n* **1** money. **2** salary; wage; remuneration.

তনয় *n* a son; a male offspring. **~বৎসল** *adj* affectionate to sons. **~ বাৎসল্য** *n* fondness for one's children; filial affection. **তনয়া** *n fem* daughter.

তনিমা *n* graceful slimness (of the body); subtlety.

তনু, তনূ *n* the body. ❑ *adj* delicately slim; graceful; lovely: ~দেহ. **~চ্ছদ** *n* an armour; a mail. **~জ** *n* a son. **~জা** *n* daughter. **~তা** *n* **1** graceful slimness; fineness. **2** leanness; delicacy; slimness. **~ত্যাগ** *n* ending of life; death; demise. **~ ত্যাগ করা** *vi* die. **~ত্র, ~ত্রাণ**= ~চ্ছদ. **~মধ্যা** *adj* of a slender waist. ❑ *n* a woman with a slender waist. ~রুচি *n* physical beauty or grace. ~রুহ *n* 1 hair (of the body and not of the head). 2 a feather (of a bird). 3 offspring; children. ~ল *adj* spread out; outspread. ~ভব *n* that which/one who is born or produced from the body; son. ~ভবা daughter. ~নপাৎ *n* fire.

তন্তু *n* 1 thread. 2 fibre. 3 handloom. ~কীট *n* the silk worm; the caterpillar. ~নাভ *n* the spider. ~বায় *n* a weaver. ~মূল *n* a fibrous root. ~শালা *n* a weaver's workshop. ~সার *n* a tree with fibrous root; a betel-nut tree. ❑*adj* reduced to skin and bone; very lean and thin.

তন্ত্র *n* 1 a scripture containing Tantras or rules of austere religious practices as that of the Shaktas (শাক্ত).2 a section or branch of the Vedas. 3 a system of government: প্রজা~, শাসন~. 4 a branch of science: চিকিৎসা~. 5 opinion; belief; doctrine: বস্তু~, জড়~. 6 esoteric and mystical charms and incantation: মন্ত্র ~. 7 a handloom: ~বায়. 8 intestines of animals: পশুর ~. 9 the string of a musical instrument: বীণা~. 10 a section; a chapter: পঞ্চ~. ~ধার, ~ধারক *n* an assistant priest who recites from the scriptures at a Hindu religious service. ~বাপ *n* a weaver. ~মন্ত্র *n* charms and incantations; text of the Tantra. ~সার *n* digest of religious service or Tantras.

তন্ত্রী[1] *n* 1 the string of a musical instrument: মনের বীণার সহস্র তন্ত্রীতে সুরের স্পন্দন জাগছে. 2 a stringed musical instrument.

তন্ত্রী[2] *adj* 1 fitted with strings; stringed: ~ বাদ্যযন্ত্র. 2 belonging to a religious order: শৈব~.

তন্দুর [P] *n* a baking oven; a covered furnace.

তন্দুরস্ত [P] *adj* free from disease or illness; hale; healthy.

তন্দুরস্তি [P] *n* soundness of body; healthiness; freedom from disease.

তন্দ্রা *n* drowsiness; sleepiness; stupor. ~গত, ~ভিভূত *adj* slumbering; overcome with sleep. ~গত/ ~ভিভূত হওয়া slumber; drowse; be asleep. ~বেশ *n* drowsiness; sleepiness; cat-nap. ~লু *adj* drowsy; sleepy. ~লু হওয়া *vi* feel sleepy; drowse. তন্দ্রিত *adj* slumbering; drowsing.

তন্নতন্ন [তৎ+ন,তৎ+ন] *adj* thorough; minute: ~ করে খোঁজা, search thoroughly; ransack; rummage; comb.

তন্নিবন্ধন [তৎ+নিবন্ধন] *adv* on account of that; for that reason.

তন্মধ্যে [তৎ+মধ্যে] *adv* within that; in the midst of that; among them.

তন্মন *adj* in an absorbed state of mind; single-minded.

তন্মনা, তন্মনাঃ, তন্মনস্ক *adj* having the mind set on that; intent on that; preoccupied.

তন্ময় *adj* quite lost/absorbed in that. ~ হয়ে *adv* being quite absorbed in that. ~তা *n* rapt attention; absorption.

তন্মাত্র [তৎ + মাত্র] *pron* that much; only that: ~ বস্তু. ❑*adv* only to that extent/degree: ~ দেখেছি.

তপ[1] *n* 1 sun. 2 the summer season. ❑*adj* that gives heat.

তপ[2], **তপঃ** (in compounds) *n* practice of ascetic austerities; religious austerity; meditation; austere devotion. ~কর *adj* one who practises ascetic austerities. ~ক্লেশ *n* physical suffering caused by the practice of religious austerities. ~প্রভাব *n* power derived from meditation; spiritual force acquired by austere devotion. ~সাধ্য *adj* attainable by austere devotion; obtainable only through religious austerities and meditation. ~সিদ্ধ *adj* accomplished by religious austerities and mediation; one having attained spiritual success through austerities and meditation.

তপতী *n* 1 (myth) wife of the sungod; shadow (personified). 2 (myth) the daughter of the sungod. 3 the Tapti river in India.

তপন *n* 1 the sun. 2 flint-glass; burning glass; sun-stone. 3 the summer season. ~ তনয় *n* (myth) Yama, the Hindu god of death. ~তনয়া *n* 1 the river Jamuna. 2 the *Acacia suma* tree. ~তপ্ত *adj* heated by the sun-rays. ~তাপন *n* the sun rays. ~মণি *n* 1 the sun-stone. 2 the flint-glass.

তপনীয় *adj* requiring to be heated; that which is to be heated. ❑*n* gold.

তপসি *n* a kind of sweet-tasting little fish; the mango fish.

তপসিল=তফসিল

তপস্যা *n* divine contemplation; deep meditation; religious austerities. ~ করা *vi* meditate; be absorbed in divine contemplation; practise religious austerities as a penance for a sin or to attain religious merit. ~জনিত *adj* produced by austere devotion; proceeding from deep meditation.

তপস্বী *adj* engaged in meditation and religious devotion; one who has forsaken domestic life and has taken to ascetism. বিড়াল~ *adj* maintaining a show of righteousness, but in reality an unscrupulous opportunist.

তপাত্যয় [তপ + অত্যয়] *n* the rainy season.

তপাস *n act* of seeking/searching/looking for.

তপোধন *n* one who values religious austerity more than riches; a hermit; an ascetic.

তপোবন *n* the grove of an ascetic; the forest where a hermit lives.

তপোভঙ্গ *n* interruption of religious devotion; break in divine contemplation.

তপ্ত *adj* **1** heated; hot; warm. **2** angry; enraged; agitated: ~ বাক্য. **3** reddened with rage: ~ আঁখি. **4** bright as molten gold: ~ কাঞ্চন. **~কাঞ্চনসন্নিভ** *adj* as bright and fair as burnt gold.

তফসির [A] *n* annotation; explanation; elucidation; interpretation. **~ করা** *vt* annotate; explain; elucidate; interpret. **~কারী** *n* one who annotates the passages of books, etc; an annotator.

তফসিল, তপসিল [A] *n* a paper containing a list or statement of details, and annexed to a larger writing, as to will, deed, etc; a schedule. **তফসিলি** *adj* included in the schedule; scheduled; listed. **তফসিলি সম্প্রদায়** *n* backward Hindu communities listed in the government schedule; scheduled caste.

তফাত, তফাৎ [P] *n* **1** intervening space; distance: উভয় স্থানের মধ্যে এক মাইল ~, the two places are a mile apart; there is a distance of one mile between the two places. **2** discrimination; distinction; difference: মানুষে মানুষে ~ নেই, There ought not be any discrimination among men. ❑*adj* separate; different: যতনের খাটুনি অযতনের খাটুনি দুয়ের ফল ~. **~ করা** *vt* remove to a distance; separate; discriminate; make a distinction. **~ হওয়া** *vi* get away; part; be separated. **তফাতে থাকা** *vi* keep aloof; keep one's distance; remain at a distance. **~ হও** *int* be off! away with you! go hence! get you gone! go away! begone! **~ তফাত** *adv* at a distance. **~ দিয়ে যাওয়া** give wide birth to; give one the slip; evade (one).

তব[1] *pron* (poet) your; yours; thy; thine.

তব[2] *adv, conj* then.

তবক[1] [A] *n* a stratum; a layer: তবকে তবকে ভাসন্ত মেঘ. **তবকে তবকে** *adv* in layers; in strata.

তবক[2] [A] *n* a leaf or foil of gold or silver.

তবক[3], **তপক** [P] *n* a gun: তবকের গুলি.

তবকী *n* a soldier armed with a gun; a gunman.

তবররক [A] *n* food sanctified by the touch of a holy man.

তবল[1] [P তবর] *n* an axe. **~দার** *n* a wood-cutter.

তবল[2]=তবলা

তবলা, তবল [A]*n* a pair of small drums played on by both hands as musical accompaniment; a pair of tabors (or tabours). **~-বাঁয়া** *n* both the units of tabor, the one played with the right hand as well as the one played with the left. **~ সঙ্গত করা** *vi* play on the tabor as musical accompaniment.

তবলচি [A তবল + T চি] *n* one who plays on a tabor (or tabour) as musical accompaniment.

তবলিগ [A] *n* preaching; the preaching of religion. **~ জামাত** *n* organization for the preaching of Islam.

তবিব [A] *n* a practitioner in the Muslim system of medicine; one who is versed in that science.

তবিয়ত, তবিয়ৎ [A] *n* **1** state of one's health: আপনার ~ ভালো তো? **2** mental state; mood; humour: অনুষ্ঠানে এসে তার ~ খোশ হয়ে গেল. **বহাল তবিয়তে** *adv* in good health and humour: তিনি বহাল তবিয়তে আছেন.

তবীব=তবিব

তবীয়ত=তবিয়ত

তবু, তবুও *adv, conj* yet; still; notwithstanding; nevertheless; in spite of that.

তবে *conj, adv* **1** (used in expressing a condition) then; in that case: যদি তুমি না আসো ~ আমিও তোমার বাড়ি যাবো না. **2** so; now; well: ~ আসি, Well, let me rise now. **3** thereafter; only then; then alone: আগে অভাবে পড়ো ~ পয়সা চিনবে. **4** but: করতে বলি না ~ যদি করো বাধা দেবো না. ❑ *int* well ! : ~রে পাজি, Well ! let me have it out, you naughty one! **~ই হয়েছে** nothing doing ! it's all up ! **~ কিনা** but; except that.

তম *n* **1** darkness. **2** the third and the lowest element of human nature marked by ignorance and termed as তমোগুণ, the other two being সত্ত্বগুণ and রজোগুণ.

-তম[1] *suff* forming ordinal numerals: অশীতি~, the eightieth.

-তম[2] *suff* forming superlative adjectives: বৃহত্তম, মহত্তম, নীচতম, প্রিয়তম.

তমঃ *n* **1** darkness. **2** the gloom of ignorance: তমোগুণ (~ + গুণ) ⇒ তম (2). **3** vanity; arrogance. **4** sin; vice. **5** sorrow; grief.

তমগা, তমঘা [T] *n* **1** a small piece of metal disc containing a device of inscription, etc issued as a reward, prize or distinction; a medal. **2** a title of honour awarded in recognition of some meritorious service. **~-তাবিজ** [T+A] *n* a certificate.

তমদ্দুন [A] *n* **1** urban civilization; civilization; culture. **তামাদ্দুনিক** *adj.*

তমস *n* darkness. **তামস** *adj.*

তমসা *n* **1** darkness. **2** (fig) the gloom of ignorance. **3** a river of this name. **~চ্ছন্ন, ~বৃত** *adj* **1** covered with darkness. **2** (fig) enwrapped in the gloom of ignorance.

তমসুক [A] *n* a bond executed in security for money; a note of hand. **বন্ধকী ~** *n* a mortgage deed.

তমস্বিনী *adj fem* overcast with darkness. ❑*n fem* a dark night.

তমস্বী *adj* full of darkness; dark; gloomy.

তমা *n fem* the night.

-তমা *fem* of -তম[2]

তমাদি=তামাদি

তমাম=তামাম

তমাল *n* a dark-coloured tree akin to mangosteen.

তমালক *n* a kind of vegetable fern.

তমালিকা, তমালিনী *n fem* a grove of trees of the mangosteen kind.

তমিজ, তমীজ [A] *n* civility; courtesy; good manners.

তমিস্র *n* darkness; gloom. ❑*adj* dark; gloomy. **তমিস্রা** *adj* overcast with darkness; dark. ❑*n* a night of deep darkness. **~ পক্ষ** *n* the dark fortnight.

তমীয=তমিজ

তমোগুণ=তম (2)

তমোঘ্ন *adj* dispelling darkness; removing ignorance. ❑*n* **1** the noon. **2** the sun. **3** fire. **4** lamp. **5** knowledge.

তমোজ্যোতি *n* winged insect which emits a brilliant light at night; the fire-fly; the glow-worm.

তমোমণি=তমোজ্যোতি

তমোময় *adj* full of darkness; dark ; gloomy.

তমোরাশি *n* mass of darkness.

তমোহর=তমোঘ্ন

তমোহা=তমোঘ্ন

তম্বি, তম্বী [A] *n* **1** blustering; bullying; reproof. **2** oppression; intimidation; threat; pressure. **~ করা** *vi* speak in extravagant language; bluster; rant; breathe fire; threaten. **~তম্বা, ~তাম্বি** *n pl*.

তম্বু=তাঁবু

তম্বুর, তম্বুরা [P] *n* stringed musical instrument; mandoline.

তম্বুরিন [A]=তম্বুর

তয় [P] *n* **1** final settlement; conclusion; end. **2** doubling or folding of cloth, etc; plait: কাপড় ~ করে রাখা.

তয়খানা, তহখানা [P] *n* underground cellar or shelter, esp one used in hot summer days.

তয়ফা [A] *n* a party of professional dancing girls. ❑*adj* befitting a ballerina or dancing girl. **~ওয়ালী** *n* a dancing girl.

তয়ম্মুম [A] *n* an alternative method of purifying oneself for prayer, instead of obligatory ablution, under condition of illness or when water is not available.

তর[১] [P] *adj* **1** besotted; stupefied: শরাব খেয়ে ~ হওয়া, be stupefied under the effect of drunkenness. **2** covered or soaked with water; wet: ভিজে ~ হওয়া .

তর[২]**, তরো** [A] *adj* (used as *suff*) of or pertaining to a kind or sort: কেমন~ মানুষ তুমি ! What sort of man you are! এমন~ তো আর দেখিনি. **তরো-বেতরো** *adj* of different sorts/ kinds. **বেতর** *adj* of a bad sort; wicked; naughty.

তর[৩] *n* delay: তোমার কি ~ সইছে না, Can't you brook any delay? Can't you wait?

তর[৪] *n* act of crossing (as a river or desert). **তরানো** *vi* move across; cross: বিপদে তরানো, get over a crisis.

-তর [P] *suff* forming comparative adjectives: মহত্তর, বৃহত্তর, অধিকতর.

তরক [A] *n* violation; infringement; transgression; breaking; missing: ফরজ ~ করা.

তরকশ [P তীরকশ] *n* a case or sheath for arrows; a quiver.

তরকারি *n* **1** kitchen vegetables. **2** juicy and spicy dish cooked with or without vegetables; curry. **~ কোটা** *vi* chop vegetables.

তরক্কি, তরক্কী [A] *n* progress; upliftment; advancement.

তরক্ষু *n* the wolf; the hyaena.

তরঙ্গ *n* **1** a rolling swell of water; a surge; a wave; a billow. **2** anything rolling like a succession of waves: চিন্তা~, বিদ্যুৎ~. **~ক্ষুব্ধ** *adj* agitated with rolling waves; billowy. **~ভঙ্গ** *n* the breaking or dancing of waves. **~মালা** *n* succession of waves or billows. **~সঙ্কুল** *adj* swelling into high waves; lashed into fury by rolling waves; billowy.

তরঙ্গাকুল [তরঙ্গ+আকুল] *adj* restless on account of rolling waves.

তরঙ্গাভিঘাত [তরঙ্গ+অভিঘাত] *n* the push of waves.

তরঙ্গায়িত *adj* undulating; wavy.

তরঙ্গিণী *n* a river; a stream.

তরঙ্গিত *adj* full of waves; undulatory; rough; boisterous. **~ করা** *vi* lash into waves; undulate. **~ হওয়া** *vi* rise in waves; undulate; swell.

তরঙ্গোচ্ছ্বাস [তরঙ্গ+উচ্ছ্বাস] *n* rise and fall of waves.

তরজমা, তর্জমা [A] rendering (a passage, a book, etc) from one language to another; translation. **~ করা** *vt* translate; render into another language. **~কারক** *n* a translator.

তরণ *n* **1** act of crossing over (a river, etc). **2** getting over a trial or difficulty. **3** that which carries one across (a river); a boat; a raft.

তরণি, তরণী *n* a vessel carrying one over a river, etc; a boat; a ship.

তরতর *int* denoting the running or swiftness of a stream: নদী ~ করে বয়ে যাচ্ছে, the river runs swiftly away.

তরতাজা [P] *adj* fresh; lively.

তরতিব [A] *n* **1** an order of succession; serial order. **2** a rule; a system. **2** a tradition.

তরফ [A] *n* **1** a side: আগের তরফের বিবি. **2** a direction: খোদার ~ থেকে. **3** either of the two contesting parties: উভয় ~. **4** behalf: বাদীর তরফের উকিল. **5** a revenue area ; a *tahsil* : ~ ইসলামপুর. **6** a share or a sharer of a zemindary: বড়ো ~. **~ সানি** *n* the second wife.

তরফদার [A তরফ+ P দার] *n* **1** the revenue collector of a তরফ. **2** an adherent of a party or faction; a partisan. **3** a surname or family name among Bengalis.

তরফা *adj* relating to/affecting a party: এক ~ রায়, ex-parte judgment. **এক ~** *adj* biased to one party; partial. ❑*n* that which comes from one side/direction only. **দো-~** *n* deposition from both sides. ❑*adj* come from both sides.

তরবার, তরবারি *n* a sword; a scimitar.

তরমুজ, তরবুয [P]*n* the water-melon.

তরল *adj* **1** liquid; fluid; watery: ~ পদার্থ. **2** melted; softened: স্নেহে ~ হওয়া. **3** light; not serious: ~ আলাপ. **~ করা** *vt* dissolve by heat; liquefy. **~ হওয়া** *vi* melt; liquefy; become liquefied. **~ত্ব** *n* liquidity; fluidity. **~নয়না** *adj fem* having wanton eyes; wanton-eyed. **~মতি** *adj* fickle-minded; irresolute; weak in intellect.

তরলাবস্থা [তরল+অবস্থা] *n* liquid state; fluidity.

তরলিত *adj* liquefied; dilute; melted.

তরলীকরণ *n* liquefaction; dilution; melting.

তরলীকৃত *adj* liquefied; diluted; dissolved.

তরলীভবন *n* act of being liquefied/ diluted/ melted.

তরলীভূত *adj* liquefied; diluted; melted.

তরশু *adv* **1** three days ago. **2** three days hence.

তরসা *adv* quickly; promptly; soon.

তরস্থান *n* a landing place; a ferry-station; a wharf.

তরস্বান, তরস্বী *adj* **1** speedy; swift; quick. **2** strong; powerful.

-তরা *fem* of -তর

তরা *vt* **1** go across; cross; pass over. **2** escape or get over (a crisis).

তরাই [H] *n* a marshy tract covered with jungles at the foot of a hill.

তরাজু [P] *n* a pair of scales; a balance.

তরানা [P] *n* tune; music; an opening song or poem.

তরানো *vt* take across; rescue.

তরাস=ত্রাস

তরি, তরী *n* a boat.

তরিক *n* a ferryman.

তরিকা, তরীকা [A]*n* a system; a way: ইসলামে চার ~.

তরি-তরকারি *n pl* kitchen vegetables.

তরিবত, তরিবৎ [A] *n* **1** education; training; instruction. **2** good manners; discipline; etiquette. **3** advice.

তরী⇒তরি

তরু *n* a tree; a plant. **~কোটর** *n* a hollow of a tree. **~ক্ষীর** *n* the milky juice of certain plants; vegetable milk; latex. **~তল, ~মূল** *nn* the foot of a tree. **~নখ** *n* thorns; spines; prickles. **~বর, ~রাজ** *nn* a large tree (eg banyan, palm). **~রুহা** *n* a parasitic plant. **~শির** *n* the top of a tree. **~সার** *n* camphor; a whitish volatile substance used in medicine.

তরুণ *adj* **1** adolescent; juvenile. **2** one who has newly attained majority. **3** new: ~ জ্বর. **4** newly risen: ~ রবি. **5** immature young: ~ বয়স. ❑*n* a young man; a youth; a lad. **তরুণী** *fem*. **~ত্ব** *n* youth; juvenility; adolescence; tenderness. **~ বয়স্ক** *adj* tender-aged; youth.

তরুণাস্থি [তরুণ+অস্থি]*n* an elastic substance from which bone is formed; cartilage; gristle.

তরুণিমা *n*= তরুণত্ব ⇒ তরুণ

তরে *prep* on account of; because of; for the sake of.

তর্ক *n* **1** altercation; heated dispute; wrangle. **2** contention in words or arguments; discussion; controversy; debate. **3** the art of reasoning; logic: ~শাস্ত্র. **4** doubt; suspicion; uncertainty: মনে মনে ~ জাগছে কাজটা ঠিক হলো কিনা. **5** cause; reason. **~ করা** *vi* argue; debate; discuss; dispute; wrangle; bandy words. **~ক, ~কারী** *adj ,n* one who debates, argues, reasons or altercates; an arguer; a debater; a logician; a disputant. **~জাল** *n* array of arguments; (derog) cobweb of arguments. **~বিদ্যা, ~শাস্ত্র** *n* the science of reasons; logic. **~বিতর্ক** *n* argumentation; discussion; bandying of words. **~ বিতর্ক করা** *vi* argue; debate; discuss. **~যুদ্ধ** *n* battle of words; debate. **~যোগ্য** *adj* arguable; debatable; controversial. **~স্থলে** *adv* by way of argument; in the course of argument. **~চ্ছলে স্বীকার করা** admit for the sake of argument; concede in an argument. **তর্কে নামা** *vi* enter into an argument. **তর্কে তর্কে** *adv* in the course of argument.

তর্কাতর্কি *n* altercation; debate.

তর্কাভাস *n* fallacious argument; sophistry; a sophism; a fallacy.

তর্কিত *adj* argued; debated; discussed.

তর্কু *n* a spindle; a distaff. **~পিণ্ড** *n* the ball at the lower end of the spindle.

তর্কে তর্কে ⇒ তর্ক

তর্জন *n* angry roar; storming (in rage); severe scolding; bullying; boasting. **~ করা** *vi* bully; shout angrily; bluster; brag angrily. **~গর্জন** *n* threats and roars; raging and storming. **~গর্জন**

করা *vi* rage and storm; scold severely; bully; bluster; threaten angrily. **~গর্জনকারী** *adj* blustering; one who roars and threats.

তর্জনী *n* the fore-finger; the index finger. **~ হেলনে** *adv* by waving one's index-finger.

তর্জমা=তরজমা

তর্পণ *n* offering of water to the manes or deities; oblations of water. **~ করা** *vi* make oblations of water (to the manes or deities).

তর্পিত *adj* satisfied; pleased; satiated; appeased; pacified; placated.

তল *n* **1** lower part; bottom: পদ~. **2** the root; the foot: বৃক্ষ~. **3** the depth; bottom or bed of a pond; river or sea: সমুদ্র~. **4** the surface: ধরা~. **5** a plane: সম~. **6** the palm of the hand: কর~. **~দেশ** *n* bottom; base; foot. **~পেট** *n* the lower part of the belly; the abdomen. **~প্রহার** *n* a stroke with the palm. **~প্রহার করা** *vt* slap. **তলে তলে** *adv* **1** at bottom; at heart. **2** from behind the curtain; unobservedly; secretly; clandestinely; surreptitiously. **~স্থিত** *adj* lying at the bottom.

তলওয়ার=তলোয়ার

তলতল *int* indicating oversoftness or flabbiness. **~ করা** *vi* feel exceedingly soft. **তলতলে** *adj* oversoft.

তলপি=তল্পি

তলব [A] *n* **1** a call; a summons; a demand. **2** salary; remuneration. **~ করা** *vt* send for; summon. **~ চিঠি** *n* writ of summons; process. **~ বাকি** *n* instalment of rent overdue.

তলবানা *n* the fee of a peon for serving a summons from the court; process fee.

তলা *n* **1** the part of anything which is situated beneath the rest; underneath: পায়ের ~. **2** the foot or base of anything: গাছ~. **3** bottom; bed: সমুদ্রের ~. **4** area; locality: কল~, জাম~. **5** the bottom of a shoe, sole: জুতার ~. **6** (of a building, etc) a storey; a floor: চার ~. **~গুছি** *n* favour or patronage in secret. **~-চোঁয়া** *adj* **1** singed to the bottom causing water to leak out. **2** indigent; destitute; penniless. **~য়** *adv* at the bottom. **~য় ~য়** *adv* in secret; secretly. **~শূন্য** *adj* **1** having no bottom; bottomless: **~শূন্য ঝুড়ি,** an institution that cannot utilize its resources properly and misuses most of it.

তলানি *n* that which settles at the bottom of a liquid; sediment; dregs; lees.

তলানো *vi* **1** be drowned. **2** sink down: নৌকা ~. **তলিয়ে দেখা** *vi* look beyond the surface; see closely or think minutely; go deep into a matter; probe; scrutinize. **তলিয়ে যাওয়া** *vi* sink or settle down to the bottom.

তলাশ,তালাশ, তল্লাশ [P] *n* search; inquiry; quest; seeking after/for. **~ করা** *vt* search; trace; investigate. **তল্লাশি** *n* seeking; searching. **তল্লাশি-পরওয়ানা** *n* written order giving official authority for searching; search warrant. **তল্লাশি ফি** *n* search fee. **খানা তল্লাশ** *n* act of searching a house under authority for a person suspected of a criminal offence or for a stolen property.

তলি *n* the bottom: জুতার ~.

-তলি *suff* denoting end, outskirt or vicinity: শহর~, suburb.

তলোয়ার *n* the sword.

তল্পি, তলপি *n* **1** a bundle or packet of anything. **2** luggage; baggage. **~তল্পা** *n* articles and effects that one brings with to put up at a place; luggage. **~তল্পা নিয়ে** *adv* bag and baggage. **~বাহক** *n* servant carrying one's luggage; a porter.

তল্লাট *n* a region; a locality: এ তল্লাটে, in the neighbourhood/vicinity.

তল্লাবাঁশ *n* a variety of bamboo.

তল্লাশ=তলাশ

তশতরি [P] *n* a small plate; a quarter plate; a half plate.

তশরিফ, তশরীফ [A]*n* **1** (one's personal) dignity. **2** presence; being present: ~ আনুন, Please come in; Please be good enough to come; ~ রাখুন, Please be seated.

তশাহুদ= তসহদ

তসদিক=তজদিগ

তসনস, তছনছ [A] *n* a mess of things; chaos; disorder; destruction. ❑*adj* ruined; destroyed; confused. **~ করা** *vt* make a mess of sth; turn upside down; rain; destroy.

তসনিফ [A] *n* act of compiling (as a book); compilation.

তসবি, তসবীহ্ [A] *n* rosary of 100 beads used by Muslims. **~ পড়া** *vi* recite holy words silently to a certain number counting on the rosary.

তসবির [A] *n* a portrait; a picture.

তসর *n* fawn coloured thread made from the cocoons of silkworms; a coarse variety of silk cloth made of this thread; tusser. **তসরে** *adj* made of tusser: তসরে শাড়ি.

তসরুফ=তছরুপ

তসলিম [A] *n* (*pl* তসলিমাত) **1** greeting or obeisance in the Muslim fashion. **2** (hist) method of making obeisance to a sovereign king by bowing to the ground.

তসল্লি [A] *n* alleviation of messy; what helps to cheer/gives comfort; a solace or consolation.

তসহদ, তশাহুদ [A] *n* witness—I do bear witness that there is no God except Allah and that Muhammad (sm) is His Messenger.

তস্কর *n* one who steals; a thief. **~তা** *n* act of stealing; theft.

তস্য *pron* his.

তহ [P] *n* expenses; rent payable to a lease holder of a market for selling one's merchandise. **~খরচ, তখরচ** *n* extra or incidental expenses.

তহখানা [P] *n* a subterranean room; an underground cellar.

তহফা, তোহ্ফা [A] *n* **1** a presentation; a gift. **2** an excellent choice for a gift. ❑*adj* excellent; superb.

তহবন্দ [P] *n* a loose indoor lower garment for man; a *lungi*.

তহবিল [A] *n* cash in hand; treasury fund; capital of a business. **~দার** *n* treasurer; cashier; one in charge of cash. **~দারি** *n* office of a cashier. **~ তসরুফ** *n* defalcation; embezzlement. **~ ভাঙ্গা** *vi* defalcate.

তহমত, তোহ্‌মৎ [A] *n* slander; calumny; defamation; bad name.

তহরি, তহুরি [A] *n* **1** fee of a deed-writer or copyist of a legal document. **2** customary extra payment made by tenants to the officers of a land owner. **3** discount given to an agent of purchase or for the personal appropriation of a servant making purchases for his master.

তহরিমা, তহরীমা [A] *n* joining of the two hands, the right over the left, while uttering the formula 'Allahu Akbar' to start saying one's prayer.

তহসিল [A] *n* **1** collected revenue. **2** collection of revenue. **3** the office of a revenue collector. **4** a revenue circle; a *tahsil*. **~দার** [A+P] *n* officer in charge of collection of revenue of a circle; a *tahsilder*. **~দারি** *n* the post or the work of revenue collector.

তহুরা-শরাব [A শরাবান্‌-তহুরা] *n* the holy drink of the paradise.

তহুরি=তহরি

তা[1] *n* act of hatching an egg; incubation: ডিমে ~ দেওয়া, incubate.

তা[2] [P] a twist, trimming: গোঁফে ~ দেওয়া. **গোঁফে ~ দেওয়া** *vi* **1** twist the ends of one's moustache. **2** express one's feeling of satisfaction at the good prospect of a plan. **3** express satisfaction at having successfully done away with a rival.

তা[3] [P] *n* a full sheet or 24th part of a quire of paper: এক ~ কাগজ.

তা[4] *int* an expletive having no meaning but often inserted in speech: ~ তোমার কি ধারণা ? ❑*conj* but; still: রোজই যাবো যাবো করি, ~ যাওয়া আর হয়ে ওঠে না.

তা[5] *pron* that.

-তা *suff* indicating state, quality, nature, etc: মূর্খতা, জটিলতা, নীরবতা, নির্জনতা.

তাই[1] *pron* (short form of তাহাই) the same thing: যা চাও ~ পাবে, You will get what you want. **~ বলে** for that reason: ~ বলে এ কাজ হবে না?

তাই[2] *conj* that is why; so; because: জানে না ~ বলে. **~ত, ~তো** *adv, conj* and so; because: মূর্খ, ~তো এমন কথা বলে. ❑*int* expressing certainty, wonder, amazement, etc: ~তো, ঠিক বলেছ. **~তে** *adv* in that; at that; for that; therefore: ব্যস্ত ছিলাম, ~তে যেতে পারিনি. **~ নাকি** *int* Is it so? **~না** *int* Isn't it so?

তাই[3] *n* a striking of hands with joy or in applause; clap; clapping: ~ ~~, মামা বাড়ি যাই. **~ দেওয়া** *vi* clap.

তাইরে-নাইরে *int* **1** the noise of a song. **2** whiling away one's time; idling: ~ করে দিন কাটানো.

তাউই, তালই, তালুই *n* father-in-law of brother or sister.

তাওয়া [P] *n* baking pan: রুটি সেঁকার ~.

তাওয়ানো *vt* **1** heat; warm. **2** make red-hot by burning. **3** (fig) provoke one to anger. **4** (fig) move one to action by impulse or influence; instigate; incite.

তাং *n* short form of তারিখ

তাঁকে *pron* **1** colloquial form of 'তাঁহাকে'.

তাঁত *n* a weaving machine; loom. **~ঘর/শালা** *n* a weaver's workshop. **~ বোনা** *vi* work a loom; weave. **তাঁতি** *n* a weaver. **তাঁতিনী** *fem*. **অতিলোভে তাঁতি নষ্ট** (prov) Grasp all, lose all.

তাঁবু, তাম্বু [P] *n* a portable shelter consisting of a flexible covering; a tent. **~ খাটানো** *vi* pitch a tent. **~ তোলা** *vi* strike a tent.

তাবে [A] *n* control; authority; command. **~ থাকা** be under one's control, command or authority. **~দার** *n* one who carries out another's orders; a henchman; a servant; a servile person.

তাক[1] *n* **1** that which is aimed at; aim; target. **2** guess; conjecture; surmise: অন্ধকারে ~ করা. **3** act of lying in wait; ambush; ambuscade: বিড়ালটা ইঁদুরের জন্যে ~ করে আছে. **4** wonder; amazement: বক্তৃতা দিয়ে ~ লাগানো. **~ করা** *vt* aim at; make an aim. **~ লাগা** *vi* be struck with wonder; be amazed/dumb-founded. **~ লাগানো** *vi* strike with wonder. **তাকে তাকে** *adv* in waiting. **তাকে তাকে থাকা** *vi, vt* lie in wait; be on the lookout; wait for a chance/ opportunity.

তাক[2] [P] *n* a board fixed along a wall or an almirah to support articles; a shelf.

তাকওয়া [A] *n* **1** firm faith in or great devotion to religion; piety; religiosity. **2** devotion to duty; dutifulness.

তাকত, তাকৎ [A] *n* physical strength.

তাকানো *vt* look at; see; behold; gaze. **তাকিয়ে থাকা** *vi* stare at; gaze on. **তাকিয়ে দেখা** *vi, vt* gaze; see with open eyes; look attentively. ❑*n* gaze; look.

তাকাব্বরি=তকব্বরি

তাকিদ=তাগিদ

তাকিয়া [P] *n* large pillow used to lean against; a dumpy bolster.

তাগড়া [H] *adj* of massive built; tall and robust; stalwart; stout; gigantic: ~ জোয়ান.

তাগা *n* **1** ornament for the arm; armlet. **2** a sacred thread worn round the arm or waist. **3** a band or bandage put tightly on a part of the body to stop blood circulation (as in the case of snake-bite).

তাগাড় [P] *n* **1** mixture of lime, sand and water used to hold bricks together in building; mortar. **2** a pan for mortar; mortar pit. **3** clay made by watering on a piece of ploughed land for the germination of seeds.

তাগাদা [A তা'কাদা] *n* **1** a reminder (for payment, etc); dunning: বাড়ি-ভাড়ার ~. **2** repeated demand: লেখার জন্য ~. **3** repeated urging: পড়াশুনার জন্য ~. **~ করা** *vi, vt* give reminder for payment; demand a debt/house rent, etc from; press repeatedly for; urge repeatedly.

তাগারি *n* a large trough; a vat.

তাগিদ [A তা'কিদ] *n* urging forward; reminder. **~ করা** *vi, vt* press; urge; look sharp. **~ দেওয়া** *vt* remind; buck up; press; urge. **~-চিঠি** *n* letter of injunction; reminder. **~দার** *n* one who demands or urges on for sth. **তাগিদে** *adv* under pressure of; on one's insistence/repeated request.

তাচ্ছিল্য, তাচ্ছল্য *n* **1** slight; contempt; disregard. **2** lack of attention/cordiality; neglect. **~ করা** *vi* treat with contempt; slight; scorn; triffle with; overlook; ignore; neglect. **~পূর্ণ** *adj* contemptuous; scornful; manifesting contempt and disregard; neglectful.

তাছির, তাসির [A] *n* power serving to affect; effect produced on the mind; influence; impression. **~ করা** *vt* exercise influence on; impress: বাবা-মার গুণাবলী সন্তানের দেহমনে ~ করে.

তাজ [A] *n* **1** head dress; a cap. **2** a crown; a coronet; a diadem.

তাজমহল [A] *n* the monumental sepulchre in marble built by emperor Shahjahan in memory of his queen Mamtazmahal at Agra, deemed as one of the wonders of the world.

তাজা [P] *adj* **1** full of health; fresh; in good condition: ~ তরকারি. **2** new; not before known; not second-hand: ~ খবর. **3** living; alive: ~ মাছ. **4** lively; spirited: ~ প্রাণ. **~-ব-~** *adj* new; fresh; lively; invigorated.

তাজি, তাজী [P] *n* **1** a horse of good breed; an Arabian horse. **2** a horse of high mettle; a steed.

তাজিম, তাজীম [A] *n* **1** regard; respect; veneration; esteem. **2** cordial reception; welcome. **3** courtesy; civility.

তাজিয়া, তাযিয়া [A] *n* **1** imitation of the graves of Imam Hasan and Hussain carried in the Muharram procession by Shia Muslims. **2** mourning; affliction; sorrow; grief; woe. **3** consolation; solace; comfort.

তাজ্জব [A] *n* amazement; wonder; perplexity: তাজ্জবের বিষয়. ❑*adj* **1** amazing: ~ ব্যাপার, a marvellous affair. **2** amazed: সে ~ হয়ে গেল.

তাঞ্জাম [H] *n* **1** a palanquin. **2** an ornamented sedan-chair.

তাড় *n* a kind of ornament for the arm; armlet.

তাড়ক *n* one who drives; a task-master; a chastiser.

তাড়কা *n* **1** a female Rakshasa mentioned in the Ramayana. **2** (fig) a vicious woman of monstrous appearance.

তাড়ন, তাড়না *n* **1** guiding rule or control. **2** beating; flogging; lashing; chastisement. **3** rebuke; scolding; reprimand. **4** oppression; tyranny. **তাড়না করা** *vt* drive; threaten; chastise; press; urge; reprimand. **ক্ষুধার তাড়নায়** *adv* being goaded/driven by hunger.

তাড়নী *n* whip; lash; scourge; goad.

তাড়নীয় *adj* chastisable; punishable.

তাড়স *n* inflammation; inflammatory pain; brunt: ব্যথার ~; stupor: জ্বরের ~. **তাড়সের জ্বর** sympathetic fever; fever caused by the effect of pain, shock;, injury or fright.

তাড়া[1] *n* a sheaf; a bundle: এক ~ নোট.

তাড়া[2] *vt, vi* pursue in order to catch or kill; chase: তেড়ে ধরা. ❑*n* **1** act of chasing; a chase: পুলিশের ~. **2** reprimand; rebuke; censure; reproof; reprehension: গুরুজনের ~. **3** act of striking with terror/ frightening/ scaring away; a sudden fright: ~ পেয়ে বাঘটা পালিয়েছে. **~ করা** *vt* run at; pursue; chase. **~ খাওয়া** *vi* be chased. **~ দেওয়া** *vt* **1** reprimand; chide; snub: পড়াশুনার জন্য ~ দেওয়া. **2** frighten away; scare away.

তাড়া[3] *n* **1** urgency; pressure of necessity: কাজের ~. **2** act of hurrying; hurry: আমার কোনো ~ নেই, I am not in a hurry. **3** pressure for hurrying/ doing sth in haste.

তাড়াতাড়ি *n adv* quickly; hurriedly; hastily: ~ করো, Make haste, Hurry up. ❑*n* hurry. **~তে** *adv* being in haste; hurry-scurry.

তাড়ানো *vt* **1** chase away ; drive away/out: ~ কুকুর. **2** turn out; expel; banish: দেশ থেকে ~. ❑*adj* chased/driven away; expelled or banished. **তাড়িয়ে দেওয়া** *vt* drive away; turn out.

তাড়াহুড়া *n* excessive hurry/ haste/ bustle: সে তার ব্যাগটি নিয়েই ~ করে চলে গেল, He picked up his bag and hurried off.

তাড়ি[1] *n* a small bundle; a sheaf: এক ~ খড়.

তাড়ি[2] *n* liquor from the palm or date juice; arrack; toddy. **~খানা** *n* grog-shop; tavern; toddy-shop; arrack-shop.

তাড়িত[1] *adj* **1** beaten; flogged; reprimanded; reproved; rebuked. **2** driven or chastised away; expelled or banished.

তাড়িত[2] *adj* **1** of electricity; electric. **2** produced from electricity. **3** containing or conveying electricity. **4** run or worked by electricity. ❑*n* electricity. **~চুম্বক** *n* an electric magnet. **~প্রবাহ** *n* electric current. **~ বার্তা** *n* message sent by the use of electric current along wires or by wireless; telegraphic message. **~ বিজ্ঞান** *n* the science of electricity. **~ বিজ্ঞানী** *n* an electrical scientist.

তাড়িতালোক [তাড়িত+আলোক] *n* electric light.

তাড়িতী *n* an electrician.

তাড়ু *n* a metal ladle with a broad perforated blade used in making sweets.

তাড্যমান *adj* **1** in the state of being beaten. **2** (of a musical instrument) in the state of being played upon.

তাণ্ডব *n* **1** a noisy and drunken revel; a frenzied dance of annihilation; a bacchanal dance. **2** (fig) a dreadful and destructive affair: অগ্নির ~লীলা, the fury of the fire. **~লীলা** *n* a destructive event/ incident.

তাত[1] *n* **1** father. **2** uncle: খুল্ল~. **3** respectable elderly person. **4** a form of address in endearment to a son or one like a son.

তাত[2] *n* **1** heat; warmth: ~ সয় বাত সয় না (prov), Hot weather is bad indeed, but foul weather is worse still. **2** (fig) anger; bad temper. **3** (sarcas) the fire of hunger: পেটে ~ লেগেছে বুঝি.

তাতা *vi* **1** be heated; warm up. **2** (fig) get angry/excited.

তাতা-থৈ *n* symbolical words denoting a musical time or measure.

তাতানো *vt,vi* **1** make hot; heat; warm up. **2** (fig) make angry; excite; provoke to anger. ❑*adj* heated; warmed up; provoked; excited.

তাতার *n* a native of Tartary in central Asia, a Tartar. **তাতারি** *adj* of or pertaining to Tartary.

তাতারসি, তাতরসি *n* boiled juice of sugarcane; treacle.

তাতারা *n* a kind of bird.

তাতাল *n* tool used to join pieces of metal with solder; soldering iron.

তাৎকলিক *adj* **1** of or relating to that time; (the) then. **2** living or occurring at the same time; contemporary. ❑*n* one who lives at the same time with another.

তাত্ত্বিক *adj* **1** pertaining to theory; theoretical; speculative; not practical. **2** versed in theory; acquainted with the ultimate truth. ❑*n* one versed in the knowledge of an art: প্রত্ন~.

তাৎপর্য *n* sense; purport; meaning; intent. **~গ্রহণ** *n* comprehension of meaning or purport; appreciation of the sense or import. **তাৎপর্যার্থ** *n* plain meaning; purport; gist.

তাথ্যিক *adj* relating to/ concerned with facts: factual; real.

তাদাত্ম্য *n* identity; unity; sameness with sth.

তাদৃশ *adj* like that; similar; such. **তাদৃশী** *fem.*

তাধিয়া=তাতা-থৈ

তান *n* **1** musical note; strain; melody; key-note; tune. **~ ছাড়া** *vi* (of music) open out one's voice; flourish a tune. **~ তোলা** *vi* (music) open out one's voice gradually. **~ ধরা** *vt* (music) hum a tune; begin to sing a particular melody. **~পুরা** *n* a musical instrument of four or six strings; tambourine.

তানা-না-না *n* **1** prefatory airs of music. **2** (fig) wasting time on useless preliminaries. **~ করা** *vi* **1** hum a tune. **2** waste time by dilatoriness.

তান্তব *adj* **1** made of thread. **2** cotton cloth.

তান্ত্রিক[1] *adj* pursuing the rites prescribed in the Tantras of Shaktas; of the Tantras. ❑*n* a follower of the doctrines taught by the Tantras; one versed in the Tantras.

তান্ত্রিক[2] *suff* used with nouns to form adjectives: গণ~, বস্তু~.

তাপ *n* **1** heat; warmth. **2** temperature; fever. **3** anger. **4** sorrow; grief; affliction; suffering; mental agony. **~ক** *n* one who/that which heats, excites or afflicts. **~ক্লিষ্ট** *adj* afflicted with heat. **~-গতি বিদ্যা** *n* science of the relations between heat and mechanical work; thermo-dynamics. **~গ্রহণ** *n* (phys) absorption of heat. **~গ্রাহিতা** *n* (phys) number of units of heat needed to raise the temperature of a body by one degree; thermal capacity. **~জনক** *adj* causing or producing heat; calorific. **~ত্রয়** *n* (according to Hindu philosophy) the three kinds of affliction—spiritual, supernatural, material. **~মান** *n* measurement/degree of heat; temperature. **~মান যন্ত্র** *n* thermometer. **~হরণ** *n* absorption of heat. **~হারী** *adj* relieving heat; consoling; alleviating distress; soothing.

তাপন *n* **1** generation of heat. **2** application of heat. **3** the sun.

তাপনীয় *adj* fit to be heated; inflammable.

তাপস *n* an ascetic; a hermit; a devotee. **তাপসী** *fem.*

তাপা *vi* get heated; warm up: আগুন ~নো. **~নো** *vt* heat; warm up.

তাপিত *adj* **1** heated. **2** afflicted; mortified; sorrow-stricken. **তাপিতা** *fem.*

তাপী[1] *adj* **1** heated; hot. **2** afflicted; remorseful.

তাপী[2] *adj* **1** producing heat; calorific. **2** causing affliction or mortification.

তাফতা [P] *n* a mixed fabric of silk and wool; taffeta.

তাবৎ *adj, pron* **1** all; all that; all those: পৃথিবীর ~ লোক. **2** to that number/quantity/extent: যাবৎ আনিবে ~ নষ্ট হইবে. **3** till; till then: যাবৎ আমি না আসি ~.

তাবা, তাবাহ্ [P] *n* ruin; destruction.

তাবিজ [A] *n* an amulet containing holy words or a charm against evils, usually worn on the arm.

তাবেঈন [A] *n pl* **1** followers; adherents; disciples; attendants. **2** adherents or attendants of the companions of Prophet Muhammad (sm); adherents of the second generation.

তামড়ি *n* a precious stone, generally of the colour of copper; a garnet.

তামরস *n* **1** the lotus. **2** copper. **3** gold. **4** a Sanskrit poetical measure.

তামস *adj* enwrapped in deep darkness. **2** enslaved by all vile passions; full of ignorance and vice. **তামসী** *fem*. **~তপ** *n* religious devotion and worship with the aim of causing harm to one; austere and harmful practices undertaken through ignorance. **~দান** *n* charity to an undeserving person. **~প্রকৃতি** *adj* having the vilest elements of human nature. **~যজ্ঞ** *n* ritual performed with pomp but without conforming to the scripture. **~ দর্শন** *n* the philosophy of atheism or nihilism.

তামসিক *adj* **1** of or pertaining to the lowest elements of human nature. **2** full of vice and ignorance; vicious; grossly vile. **3** overcast with clouds; cloud-ridden.

তামা *n* a malleable metal, reddish-brown in colour, and a good conductor; copper. **~-তুলসী** *n* copper and basil; the twain matters considered holy by Hindus. **~টে** *adj* of the colour of copper; copper-coloured.

তামাক, তামাকু *n* narcotic plant, the leaves of which when dried are used for smoking and chewing, and in snuff; tobacco. **~ খাওয়া/টানা** *vt* smoke a hookah or a pipe. **~ সাজা** *vt* prepare the bowl of a hookah or fill a pipe with tobacco for smoking. **তামাকুসেবী, তামাকখোর** *n* a smoker; a tobacco-smoker; a tobaccanalian. **~ বিক্রেতা** *n* a tobacconist. **অম্বরী ~** *n* sweet and fragrant tobacco blended with ambergris. **গুড়ক ~** *n* tobacco mixed with molasses. **বড়ো ~** *n* hemp; ganja. **সুরভি ~** *n* fragrant preparation of tobacco taken with betel-leaves.

তামাদি [A] *n* lapse of the scheduled time; the state of being time-barred. ❑*adj* barred by limitation; time-barred. **~ হওয়া** *vi* be barred by limitation.

তামান্না [A] *n* hope; ambition; aspiration.

তামাম [A] *adj* all; entire; whole; complete. ❑*n* end; termination; completion. **সালতামামি** *n* completion of the year; ceremony connected with it.

তামাশা [A] *n* **1** an entertaining and amusing performance; a joke; a jest; a fun; a sport. **2** a display of interesting and instructive things; an exhibition; a public show. **~ করা** *vi* make fun (of); joke; jest. **~ দেখা** *vi* enjoy a show; find fun in. **~ দেখানো** *vi* give a show; arrange an entertaining performance. **এ ~ নয়** It's no joke.

তামিল[1] [A] act of carrying out (an instruction); compliance: **হুকুম ~ করা** *vt* carry out/execute an order.

তামিল[2] *n* an Indian language spoken in Madras.

তাম্বু=তাঁবু

তাম্বুল *n* **1** betel-leaf. **2** betel-leaf wrapped round bits of areca-nut, lime, catechu, etc, which is chewed as a quid. **~-করঙ্ক** *n* a betel box. **~ বল্লি** *n* a betel creeper. **~রাগ** *n* ruddy tint on the lips caused by the chewing of betels. **তাম্বুলাকার** [~+আকার] *adj* shaped like belet-leaf; heart-shaped; cordate.

তাম্বুলিক, তাম্বুলী *n* betel-dealer; betel-seller.

তাম্র *n*=তামা *adj* **1** copper-coloured; reddish-brown: ~কেশ. **2** made of copper: ~পাত্র. **~কার** *n* a craftsman who works in copper; a coppersmith; a brazier. **~কুণ্ড** *n* a copper basin; copper pot used in Hindu religious service. **~গর্ভ** *n* **1** a vessel made of copper. **2** green vitriol or sulphate of iron; copperas. **~চূড়** *n* the male of the domestic fowl; a cock. **~পট্ট, ~পত্র, ~ফলক** *n* **1** a plate or sheet of polished copper with an engraving or etching upon it. **2** (hist) copper plate on which royal edicts, etc used to be engraved; a copper plate inscription. **~পাত্র** *n* a copper vessel. **~বর্ণ** *adj* copper-coloured. ❑*n* copper-colour; pale and dark red colour. **~লিপি**= ~পট্ট. **~শাসন** *n* (hist) royal edict inscribed on copper plate. **~সার** *n* red sandal wood.

তাম্রকূট *n* tobacco. **~ সেবন** *n* act of smoking tobacco. **~সেবী** *n* a tobacco smoker; a smoker.

তাম্রাভ *adj* copper-coloured; reddish brown.

তাম্রাশ্ম [তাম্র+অশ্ম] *n* a gem or precious stone of various shades of red; a ruby.

তায় *pron* (poet) him or her; in him or her. ❑*adv, conj* over and above; and moreover; on the top of: একে অমাবস্যা ~ মেঘাচ্ছন্ন.

তায়দাদ [A] *n* **1** number; amount. **2** boundary. **3** document containing description of the boundary of a plot of land.

তার[১] [P] *n* **1** metal string; wire: টেলিগ্রাফের ~, সেতারের ~. **2** a telegram or communication sent by telegraph. ~ **করা** *vi* telegraph; wire; cable. ~ **পাওয়া** *vi* receive a telegram. ~ **পাঠানো** *vi* send a telegram; telegraph. **তারের কাজ** *n* filigree work. **তারের জাল** *n* wire netting.

তার[২] *n* loud voice; high note or tone in music. ❑*adj* loud (as voice); high (as a note). ~**স্বর** *n* very loud voice.

তার[৩] *n* act of crossing/going across: বিপদ সাগর ~ হওয়া.

তার[৪] *n* taste; savour; savouriness: ব্যঞ্জনের ~.

তার[৫] *pron* his; her.

তারক *adj* one who rescues or saves or delivers. ❑*n* **1** a rescuer; a deliverer; a saviour. **2** a helmsman; a pilot. **3** a boat; a raft. **4** the pupil of the eye. **5** a star. ~**নাথ** *n* Hindu god Shiva.

তারকা *n* **1** the star. **2** the pupil of the eye. **3** the star-mark; an asterisk. **4** a famous actor or actress of the film; a film-star: চিত্র~. ~**খচিত**, ~**মণ্ডিত** *adj* bedecked/studded with stars; starry; star-spangled. ~**চিহ্নিত** *adj* marked with an asterisk.

তারতম্য *n* state of being more or less; difference; distinction; discrimination; disparity. ~ **করা** *vt* discriminate; make out a difference; draw a distinction; differentiate.

তারপর *adv* after that; thereafter; then.

তারপলিন *n* canvas covered with tar; tarpaulin.

তারল্য *n* **1** liquid state; fluidity; wateriness. **2** lack of concentration; inconsistency; fickleness. **3** restlessness; unsteadiness.

তারস্বর⇒তার[২]

তারা *n fem* **1** one who rescues or delivers from sufferings; a manifestation or appellation of Hindu goddess Durga. **2** the pupil of the eye. **3** (music) the major E-scale: উদারা মুদারা ~. **4** the star. **5** an asterisk. ~**পতি** *n* the lord of the stellar world; an appellation of the moon. ~**পতন** *n* the fall of a meteor. ~**পথ** *n* the stellar course; the sky; the welkin. ~ **মণ্ডল** *n* the stellar region or orbit; a constellation. ~ **মাছ** *n* star-shaped sea-animal; the star fish.

তারাকারা [তারা+আকারা] *adj* having the shape of a star; starlike.

তারাবি, তারাবী [A] *n* special prayer prescribed for the month of Ramadan which is said after the night prayer. **খতম** ~ *n* the *tarabi* prayer in which the recital of the Holy Qoran is completed in thirty days.

তারিখ[১] *n* the numerical designation of a day; a date. ~ **দেওয়া** *vi* give a date. **আগামী মাসের দশ তারিখে** on the 10th of the coming month; on the 10th proximo. **গত মাসের ১০ তারিখে** on the 10th of the last month; on the 10th ultimo. **বর্তমান/চলতি মাসের ১০ তারিখে** on the 10th of the current month; on the 10th instant. ~**বিহীন** *adj* undated.

তারিখ[২] [A] *n* history; the narrative of events recorded chronologically.

তারিফ [A] *n* **1** praise; applause; approbation; commendation. **2** a laudatory speech; panegyric; eulogy; laudation. ~ **করা** *vi* praise; appreciate; laud; admire; applaud.

তারুণ্য *n* youth; juvenility; freshness; newness.

তারে *prep* (poet) him, her.

তার্কিক *adj* versed or skilled in logic; fond of arguing; logical; argumentative; polemical. ❑*n* a logician; a sophist; an arguer.

তার্কিকতা *n* sophism; sophistry; casuistry.

তার্পিন *n* resinous substance flowing from trees like pine, larch, fir, etc; turpentine. ~ **তেল** *n* the oil distilled from turpentine.

তাল[১] *n* the fanpalm or palmyra tree; its fruit. ~**কাঁড়ি** *n* the juice of the palmyra fruit. ~**ক্ষীর** *n* the juice of the palmyra fruit boiled and thickened into a semi-solid state. ~**চঞ্চু**, ~**চোঁচ** *n* the weaver bird. ~**নবমী** *n* the ninth day of the waxing moon of the month of Bhadra. ~ **পড়া** *vi* **1** (of palmyra fruit) fall from the tree. ❑*n* (facet) the fall of heavy fisticuffs (on a person). ~**পাখা** *n* a hand fan made of the palmyra-leaf. ~**পাতার সেপাই** (facet) a cowardly and thin-built person who introduces himself as a soldier. ~**শাঁস** *n* the edible kernel of the stone of a palmyra-fruit.

তাল[২] *n* a clod; a ball; a lump: এক ~ কাদা, a lump of clay. ~ **করা** *vt* heap up; amass; collect into a lump. ~**গোল পাকানো**, ~ **পাকানো** *vt* form a confused mass of; make mess of; do sth clumsily; muddle; bungle. ~**গোল** *n* a confused round mass; confusion. ~ ~ *adj* large amounts of; lumps of.

তাল[৩] *n* **1** a musical time or measure: গানের ~. **2** beating of time (by means of clapping the hands): ~ দেওয়া. ~ **কাটা** *vi* loose musical time; fail to maintain musical measure. ~**কানা** *adj* having no musical ear; ignorant of musical measure; devoid of rhythmic sense. ~**জ্ঞান** *n* sense of time and measure in music; sense of proportion. ~ **রাখা** *vi* maintain musical time. ~ **রেখে চলা** *vi* step to measure; keep pace with. **তালে তালে** *adv* keeping time; agreeably to musical measure; in harmony with. ~**মান** *n* musical measure and pitch. ~**মাফিক** *adv* at the right moment; in tune with circumstances. **সময়ের সাথে** ~ **রেখে চলা** keep abreast of the times.

তাল[৪] *n* a push; a sudden stock; a risk; a danger. ~ **সামলানো** balance oneself with difficulty; get through a difficult situation; tide over a crisis.

তালই=তালুই

তালবাহানা *n* a plea; a pretext; a lame excuse. ~ করা *vi* procrastinate: dilly-dally.

তালব্য *adj* uttered by the aid of the palate; palatal. ~ বর্ণ *n* a palatal letter.

তালা[1] *n* a padlock; a lock. ~ দেওয়া/ লাগানো *vt* lock; put a lock (on).

তালা[2] *n* **1** a storey or floor (of a building). **2** a deck or tier (of a ship or omnibus).

তালা[3] *n* sensation of being stunned or deafened. (কানে) ~ লাগা *vi* be stunned/ deafened.

তালাক [A] *n* repudiation of marriage tie; legal dissolution of marriage; divorce. ~ দেওয়া *vt* dissolve the marriage contract; divorce. ~নামা [A+P] *n* deed of divorcement (executed by either party).

তালাফি [A] *n* **1** looking after; taking care of; care; attention. তত্ত্ব~ করা *vt* look after/ take care with earnest attendance. **2** act of compensating; recompense; compensation.

তালাশ=তলাশ

তালি[1] *n* act of clapping; striking of the palms together. ~ দেওয়া *vi* clap.

তালি[2] *n* a patch (as on a torn cloth). ~ দেওয়া *vt* patch; mend by sewing on a patch.

তালি[3]=তালা[3]

তালি[4] *n* the palmyra tree. ~বন *n* palmyra grove.

তালি[5] *n* a small lock.

তালিকা [A]*n* a roll of entries; a list; a catalogue; an inventory.

তালিব [A] *n* a seeker; an inquirer; a questioner. ~-উল-এল্‌ম *n* a seeker after knowledge; a student.

তালিম, তালীম *n* **1** act of instructing of giving useful lesson; act of imparting education or training; instruction; advice; lesson. **2** education; training. **3** the application of labour for improvement; culture; exercise. দেওয়া*vi,vt* teach; instruct; educate; train.

তালিমি [A] *adj* of or concerning education.

তালু *n* the roof of the mouth; palate.

তালুক [A] *n* **1** (hist) landed estate held under a zeminder or directly under the government; a taluk. **2** landed property. ~দার *n* the owner of a taluk or landed estate. ~দারি *n* the estate or the privileges of a talukdar. ❑*adj* relating to a taluk or talukdar.

তালেব এল্‌ম=তালিব-উল-এল্‌ম ⇒ তালিব

তালেবর [A তালি + P বর] *adj* **1** fortunate; influential; respectable. **2** rich; wealthy.

তাস [H] *n* one of the fifty-two pieces of thin pasteboard marked with figures used in games; playing card(s). ~ কাটা *vi* cut cards. ~-খেলা *n* card-game. ~ খেলা/পেটা *vi* play cards. ~ বাঁটা *vi* deal out cards. ~ ভাঁজা *vi* shuffle cards. তাসের ঘর (lit) house of cards: (fig) very dangerous or uncertain condition. ~ খেলার পিঠ বা মার *n* a trick. তাসের রং *n* trump.

তাসা[1] *vi* shuffle cards. ❑*adj* shuffled.

তাসা[2] *vt* rebuke; reprimand.

তাসাওফ, তাসাওওফ [A] *n* Muslim mysticism; Sufism.

তাস্কর্য *n* act of stealing; theft.

তাহজিব [A] *n* courtesy; civility; good manners; etiquette.

তাহা *pron* that (thing). ~কে, ~রে (poet) *prom* him. ~দিগকে, ~দেরকে *pron pl* them. ~তে, তাতে *pron* **1** in that; in him/her. **2** for that reason: তাতে কি আসে যায়? **3** hearing that; as a result of that; after that: তাতে সে চটে গেল. **4** with him: ~তে আমাতে সম্ভাব নাই. **5** for that reason: তাতে কিছুই হয় না. **6** even then: যদি না পারো তাতে বিপদ নাই. **7** on the other hand; over and above that: একে রাত তাতে বৃষ্টি. ~র, তার *pron* of that person/ thing; pertaining to that thing.

তাহাজ্জত, তাহাজ্জদ [A] *n* optional prayer prescribed for the small hours of the night.

তাহে, তায় *conj, adv* over and above; more over; on the top of it: একে মূর্খ ~ নির্বোধ. ❑*pron* (poet) in him/her/that; him; her; it.

তাহেরি, তিহারি *n* snack prepared with a mixture of rice, pulses and meat.

-তি *suff* giving a different meaning to words: কমতি, চলতি, etc.

তিক্ত *adj* **1** of bitter taste; bitter. **2** (fig) unpleasant; distressing: ~ অভিজ্ঞতা, bitter experience. ~তা *n* **1** bitterness. **2** (fig) unpleasantness.

তিজারত=তেজারত

তিড়বিড় *int* denoting restlessness, uneasiness or fidgetiness. তিড়বিড়ানি *n* restlessness; irritation; fidgets. তিড়বিড়ে *adj* restless; fidgety.

তিড়িং-বিড়িং *int* denoting sudden jump or frisk in a fit of wanton gaity: ~ করে বেড়ানো, dance, skip and gambol in frolic and gaity like a grasshopper or a cricket.

তিত, তিতা=তিক্ত

তিতকুটে *adj* slightly bitter.

তিতিক্ষা *n* holding oneself in check; forbearance; patience; forgiveness. তিতিক্ষিত *adj* that has been endured with patience or forgiven. তিতিক্ষু *adj* showing forbearance and forgiveness.

তিতির *n* a bird somewhat like a partridge; sand-piper; lapwing.

তিতীর্ষা *n* desire to cross/get over. **তিতীর্ষু** *adj* desirous of going across or being rescued.

তিথি *n* (astrol) a lunar day. **~কৃত** *n* rituals (according to Hindu tradition) to be performed on a particular lunar day. **~ক্ষয়** *n* the conjunction of three lunar days occurring on one lunar day. **তিথ্যমৃতযোগ** *n* an auspicious moment according to Hindu astrology.

তিন *n, adj* three. **~কাল** *n* 1 three stages of life—childhood, youth and manhood. 2 three tenses—past, present and future. **~কুল** *n* the three lineages to which one is connected—that of the father, mother and father-in-law. **~গুণ** *n pl* the three primary elements of human nature according to Indian philosophy —সত্ত্ব, রজঃ and তমঃ —the first being the highest one is marked by knowledge and virtue, the second characterised by activeness and spiritedness, and the lowest one marked by ignorance and vice. ❑*adj, adv* threefold; three times. **~ তালাক** *n* the final dissolution of the marriage tie of a Muslim couple; an irrevocable divorce. **~ সন্ধ্যা** *n* three parts of the day—morning, midday and evening.

তিনি *pron* he (used in reverence in place of সে).

তিন্তিড়ি, তিন্তিড়ী *n* the tamarind tree or its fruit.

তিন্দু, তিন্দুক *n* the mangosteen tree, its fruits.

তিপ্পান্ন, তেপ্পান্ন *n, adj* three and fifty; fifty-three.

তিব্বতী, তিব্বতীয় *adj* of Tibet; Tibetan. ❑*n* a Tibetan; the language of Tibet ; Tibetan.

তিমি *n* the whale, the largest of sea animals, a mammal. (*mas* the bull-whale, *fem* the cow-whale). **~ শাবক** *n* a whale-calf; a calf whale. **~শিকার** *n* whale-fishing; whaling; whalery. **~শিকারি** *n* (person or ship) whaler; whale-fisher. **~ তৈল** *n* train-oil; whale-oil.

তিমিত *adj* 1 wet; drenched; moist; damp. 2 dim; faint.

তিমির *n* 1 darkness. 2 a disease of the eye affecting the crystalline lens; cataract. **~নাশক** *n* the sun. **~ নাশ করা** *vi* dispel darkness. **~-গর্ভ** *n* the dark bowels or interior; abyss of darkness. **তিমিরাবগুণ্ঠিত** [~+অবগুণ্ঠিত] *n* enveloped in darkness.

তিয়াত্তর *n, adj* three and seventy; seventy-three.

তিরস্কার *n* 1 rebuke; reproof; reprimand. 2 neglect; slight. 3 censure; blame; reproach. **~ করা** *vi* take to task; reprove; reprimand; censure; reproach; neglect; slight. **তিরস্কৃত** *adj* 1 reproved; reprimanded. 2 censured; reproached. 3 slighted; neglected. **তিরস্কৃতা** *fem.*

তিরানব্বই, তিরানব্বুই *n,adj* three and ninety; ninety-three.

তিরাশি *n, adj* three and eighty; eighty-three.

তিরিক্ষি, তিরিক্ষে *adj* 1 angry; wrathful. 2 readily made angry; easily provoked; irritable; peevish; irascible: ~ মেজাজ.

তিরিশ *n adj* thirty.

তিরোধান, তিরোভাব *n* 1 disappearance; passing away; departure. 2 death of a great personality. **তিরোধান করা** *vi* 1 disappear; depart; vanish. 2 die.

তিরোহিত, তিরোভূত *adj* 1 disappeared; vanished; passed away. 2 dead. **তিরোহিতা, তিরোভূতা** *fem.*

তির্যক *adj* 1 neither perpendicular nor parallel; oblique ; slanting: ~ রেখা. 2 tortuous; circuitous; roundabout: ~ পথ. 3 lower than human beings; sub-human: ~ প্রাণী. **~ কম্পন** *n* transverse vibration. **~ কিরণ** *n* slanting rays. **~দৃষ্টি** *adj* squint-eyed. **~পাতন** *n* the process of distilling; distillation. **~ভাবে** *adv* obliquely. **~ সংঘাত** *n* (mech) oblique impact.

তিল *n* 1 an annual herbaceous plant, the seeds of which yield a fine oil; sesame; sesamum. 2 a small, black or dark-brown protuberance like a grain of sesame on the human body; a mole. 3 eightieth part of a cowry (shell). 4 a small fraction of a thing: আমি এ ঘটনার ~মাত্র জানি না. 5 a minute portion of time; a moment: ~ বিলম্ব না করে. 6 a very little space: ~ ঠাঁই আর নাহিরে. **~কে তাল করা** *vt* exaggerate beyond measure; make a mountain of a mole-hill. **~মাত্র** *n* even an iota. ❑*adj* even an iota of; slightest. ❑*adv* 1 even to the slightest amount/ measure/ degree; at all. 2 even for a moment: আমার ~মাত্র সময় নেই, I cannot spare an instant. **তিলে তিলে** *adv* little by little; by very slow degrees. **তিলে তিলে মরা** die by inches.

তিলক *n* 1 mark of sandal-paste on the forehead or upon the bridge of the nose (as painted by Vaishnavas). 2=তিল (2). ❑*adj* like an ornament or jewel; pre-eminent: কুল~. **~ কাটা / পড়া** *vi* wear marks of sandal-paste. **~ মৃত্তিকা** *n* clay of holy places with which sectarian marks are painted. **~সেবা** *n* daily painting of sectarian marks on the eight places of the body by Vaishnavas.

তিলকা *n* a mark of sandal-paste on the body resembling a sesame blossom: অলকা ~.

তিলাওত, তেলাওত [A] *n* the reading or reciting of the Holy Qoran with due reverence.

তিলাঞ্জলি *n* offering of water and sesamum as a part of obsequial rites by Hindus; farewell.

তিলেক *adj* 1 of the slightest amount: ~ সুখ. 2 of the slightest duration. ❑*adv* 1 even to the slightest amount: ~ ভালোবাসা. 2 even for the fraction of a moment: ~ ফুরসত.

তিলে খচ্চর *adj* of wicked nature: ~ লোক.

তিলোত্তমা *n* **1** Hindu mythological nymph of incomparable beauty. **2** (fig) a woman who is a paragon of beauty.

তিষ্ঠনো, তিষ্ঠানো *vi* **1** continue to stay: তাদের অত্যাচারে দেশে ~ গেল না. **2** stay; pause; wait: তিষ্ঠ ক্ষণকাল, stay a little.

তিষ্য *n* (astron) the name of a star.

তিসি, তিষী *n* linseed. **~র তেল** *n* linseed oil.

তিহারি=তাহেরী

তীক্ষ্ণ *adj* **1** sharp; keen; penetrating: ~ দৃষ্টি. **2** sharp-pointed: ~ কণ্টক. **3** extreme in degree; severe; intense: ~ তাপ. **4** piercing in sound; shrill: ~ স্বর. **5** poignant; acute: ~ যন্ত্রণা. **6** rude; bitter: ~ কথা. **7** strong: ~ বিষ. **তীক্ষ্ণা** *fem*. **~তা, ~ত্ব** *n* sharpness; keenness; intensity; shrillness; acuteness. **~দংষ্ট্রা/দ্রংষ্ট্রা** *adj* sharp toothed; rodent. **~দৃষ্টি** *adj* keen-sighted. **~ধার** *adj* sharp-edged. **~ধী** *adj* sharp-witted. **~লৌহ** *n* steel. **তীক্ষ্ণাগ্র** (~+অগ্র) sharp-pointed.

তীব্র *adj* **1** severe; intense: ~ রোদ. **2** unbearable; intolerable: ~ জ্বালা. **3** implacable; fatal; deadly: ~ বিষ. **4** strong; violent: ~ বাতাস. **5** dazzling; overpowering: ~ আলো. **6** harsh; rough; rude: ~ ভাষা. **7** severe; keen; acute: ~ ব্যথা. **8** pungent; acrid; caustic: ~ গন্ধ. **~তা** *n*.

তীর[1] *n* the bank of a river, etc.

তীর[2] [P] *n* an arrow; a dart. **~ ছোড়া/মারা** *vi* shoot an arrow; shoot with an arrow. **তীরের ফলা** *n* an arrow-head. **~ ধনুক** *n* bow and arrow. **~ন্দাজ** *n* an archer; a bowman. **~বেগে** *adv* with the speed of an arrow; dartingly.

তীর্থ *n* **1** a place of pilgrimage. **2** absolution from sin: মক্কা~. **3** a river or lake revered by Hindus as containing holy waters: পঞ্চ~. **4** a landing place on the bank of a river believed to be containing holy waters: সাগর~. **5** a preceptor; a teacher; alma mater : সতীর্থ. **6** a title awarded for scholarship in Sanskrit : কাব্য~. **~ করা** *vi* go on a pilgrimage. **তীর্থের কাক** (fig) *n* a servile fellow who, like a crow in a holy place, looks expectantly to others for charity. **~ক্ষেত্র/স্থান** *n* a place of pilgrimage. **~যাত্রা** *n* going on pilgrimage. **~যাত্রী** *n* a pilgrim.

তীর্থঙ্কর, তীর্থংকর *n* **1** a Jaina or Buddhist monk who has attained spiritual perfection. **2** a Jaina lawgiver.

তু *int* sound used to call a dog.

তুই *pron* you; thou (used in familiar, affectionate, contemptuous or solemn address): ইয়া আল্লাহ্ ~ রক্ষা কর. **~ তোকারি** *n* use of ~, তোর and তোকে in talking to one to show disrespect or contempt. **~ তোকারি করা** *vt* show contempt to one by using ~, in place of তুমি or আপনি.

তুঁত [A] *n* the berry of a tree, and the tree itself, cultivated to supply food for silk-worms; mulberry. **~পোকা** *n* silk-worm which feeds on mulberry leaves and spins silk to form a cocoon to protect itself.

তুঁতিয়া, তুঁতে *n* a metal produced from copper mixed with the salt of suphuric acid; sulphate of copper; copper sulphate.

তুক *n* **1** esoteric means used with a view to enchant one: স্বামীকে ~ করা. **~তাক** *n* magical incantations or underhand means of enchantment. **~তাক করা** *vt* cast a spell over a person with a view to harming him.

তুখড়, তুখোড় *adj* sharp-witted; ready-witted; resourceful; artful; adroit; smart; brisk: ~ রাজনীতিক.

তুঙ্গ *adj* high; tall; lofty; elevated. **~শেখর** *n* **1** a mountain. **2** a lofty peak. **তুঙ্গী** *adj* **1** situated on a lofty place. **2** (astrol) occupying an ascending position in the zodiac; ascendant; elevated: তুঙ্গী গ্রহ. **~তা** *n* height; altitude; loftiness.

তুচ্ছ *adj* **1** very little; insufficient; scanty. **2** insignificant; trivial; triffling. **3** unsubstantial; worthless; trashy. **4** despicable; contemptible; low; vile; mean: ~ ব্যক্তি. **~ জ্ঞান করা** *vt* treat with contempt; slight; despise; consider as worthless or insignificant. **~ বিষয়** *n* trivial matter; triffle. **~তাচ্ছিল্য** *n* contemptuous or neglectful treatment. **~তাচ্ছিল্য করা** *vt* disregard; ignore; undervalue; make light or little of. **~তা** *n* insignificance; triviality; worthlessness.

তুড়ি *n* act or sound of snapping; a snap. **~ দিয়ে/মেরে উড়ানো** *vi* defeat one easily; smash the opposition without toil or trouble or in a carefree manner. **~ মারা** *vi* **1** snap the fingers. **2** ignore or triffle one. **~ লাফ** *n* a sudden skip in delight. **এক তুড়িতে** *adv* in an instant; without strain or effort; playfully.

তুড়ুক=তুরুপ

তুণ *n* a case for carrying arrows; a quiver.

তুত=তুঁত

তুন্দিভ, তুন্দিল *adj* having a large belly; pot-bellied; corpulent; fat.

তুফান [A] *n* **1** a violent storm; a tempest; a hurricane; a nor'wester. **2** a violent brawl: চায়ের কাপে ~, tempest in the tea pot.

তুবড়ানো *vi* have a dent or depression: গাল ~; shrink; contract; wrinkle. ❑*adj* shrivelled; shrunken. **তুবড়ে যাওয়া** *vi* be depressed or dented; be shrivelled or shrunken; be hollow.

তুবড়ি *n* **1** a kind of firework. **2** a snake-charmer's flute. **কথার ~** *n* (facet) profusion or volubility of speech; highly fluent and voluble talk. **কথার তুবড়ি ছোটানো** (facet) give a fluent and voluble speech.

তুমি *pron* of the second person used in the case of affectionate and intimate persons.

তুমুল *adj* **1** tumultuous; terrible; fierce: ~ যুদ্ধ. **2** grand; grandiose: ~ কাণ্ড. ❑*n* a tumultuous brawl; a noisy affair.

তুম্ব, তুম্বক, তুম্বি *n* **1** gourd. **2** the hollow shell of a dry gourd. **3** a one-stringed musical instrument made of the hollow shell of a dry gourd.

তুরগ, তুরঙ্গ *n* the horse. **তুরগী, তুরঙ্গমী** *n* the mare. **তুরঙ্গী** *n* a horseman.

তুরন্ত [H] *adv* quickly, swiftly; hastily.

তুরপুন [U] *n* a carpenter's drill; an auger; a gimlet; a fiddle-drill. **তুরপানো** *vt* bore a hole; drill.

তুরি *n* **1** a weaver's shuttle. **2** a horn sounded in war, etc; a bugle-horn.

তুরীয় *n* **1** spiritual trance. **2** the supreme Being. ❑*adj* fourth: ~ বর্ণ (the fourth caste). ~ **অবস্থা** *n* a state of supreme bliss when one is in communion with the divine spirit; spiritual trance. **তুরীয়ানন্দ** *n* **1** transcendental happiness found in the most engrossing state of spiritual trance. **2** (sarcas) state of being beside oneself with joy.

তুরুক *adj* immediate; prompt: ~ জবাব. ❑*adv* immediately; promptly; readily. ~**-সওয়ার** *n* a Turkish horseman/ cavalier.

তুরুপ, তুরুফ *n* **1** winning card; trump card; one of a suit for the time being superior to the others. **2** act of trumping at cards; a trump. ~ **করা** *vt* trump instead of following suit at cards; take with a trump card; trump; ruff.

তুর্ক, তুর্কি [T] *n* **1** a native of Turkey; a Turk. **2** the Turks. **3** the Turkish language. ~ **নাচন** *n* **1** wild dance by turning round and round; a whirling dance. **2** (fig) state of affairs putting one into great stress and strain.

তুলক *n* (phys) a balancer.

তুলকালাম [A] *n* a noisy quarrel; tumultuous brawl; an uproar.

তুলট *adj* made of cotton pulp: ~ কাগজ, stained (yellow) paper.

তুলতুল *int* denoting over-softness. ~ **করা** *vt* feel flabby or very soft; yield to touch. **তুলতুলে** *adj* soft and puffy; over-soft.

তুলনা *n* **1** similarity; likeness; resemblance: ~ মেলে না. **2** a similar thing or person: সে সুন্দর মুখের ~ একমাত্র পূর্ণচন্দ্র. **3** act of comparing sth with another; comparison. **4** an instance; an example. ~ **করা** *vi* compare; liken. ~**য়** *adv* in comparison with; compared to (sth). ~**মূলক** *adj* comparative: ~মূলক সাহিত্য, comparative literature. ~**হীন** *adj* matchless, peerless, incomparable

তুলনীয় *adj* worth-comparing; comparable.

তুলসী *n* a basil plant; its leaves.

তুলা[1] *n* **1** a weighing machine; a pair of scales; a balance. **2** the seventh sign of the zodiac, ie the Libra: ~ রাশি. **3** a measure of weight of gold and silver (=400 tola or 145 ounces). ~**দণ্ড** *n* the beam of a balance; a pair of scales. ~ **দান** *n* gift of gold, silver or money equal to the weight of the donor. ~**ধারী** *n* **1** person trading in commodities that are sold by weights. **2** one who gives weights; a weighman. ~**মান** *n* a measure of weight; act of weighing in the balance. ~**যন্ত্র** *n* a weighing machine.

তুলা[2], **তুলো** *n* soft, white fibrous substance obtained from the pods of several plants and used for making thread, cloth, etc; cotton. ~**ধোনা করা** *vt, vi* **1** shred cotton in a cotton-gin. **2** give a sound drubbing.

তুলা[3] *vt* (poet) compare with.

তুলা[4]=তোলা

তুলি, তুলিকা *n* brush for applying paint; a paint-brush.

তুলিত *adj* that has been compared; weighed.

তুলো=তুলা[2]

তুল্য *adj* **1** having like parts and relations but not of the same magnitude; similar; comparable; identical. **2** (math and phys) equivalent. ~**কৌণিক** *adj* consisting of or having equal angles; equiangular. ~**প্রতিযোগিতা** *n* a contest between equals; an evenly balanced contest. ~**বল** *adj* equal in strength; equally strong. ~**মান** *adj* of equal measure or weight. ❑*n* an equal measure or weight. ~**মূল্য** *adj* of equal value or worth; equivalent; at par. ~**রূপ** *adj* of the same class or kind; of the equal form; analogous. ~**রূপে** *adv* equally; as well as; no less than. **তুল্যাকৃতি** [~+আকৃতি] *adj* similar in shape or form. ❑*n* similar appearance or shape. **তুল্যাঙ্ক** [~+অঙ্ক] *adj* equivalent. ~**তা** *n* comparability; similarity; likeness; identity.

তুষ *n* husk of grains; chaff; bran. ~ **ঝাড়া** *vi* winnow the husk; separate the husk from grain.

তুষানল *n* **1** fire of husk or chaff that burns and smokes without flame and is not easily extinguished; smouldering fire. **2** heart-rending affliction that exists for long in a suppressed state like a smouldering fire.

তুষার *n* snow; ice; frost: ~পাত. ❑*adj* cold as ice; ice-cold. ~ **পড়া** *vi* (of snow) come down from the sky; snow. ~**কণা** *n* particle of snow; icicle; hoarfrost. ~**কর** *n* the moon. ~**কাল** *n*

the winter season. ~গিরি, তুষারাদ্রি *n* the Himalayas. ~ঝটিকা *n* snow-storm; blizzard. ~ধবল *adj* white as snow; snow-white. ~পাত *n* snow-fall; frost. ~পিণ্ড *n* conglomerated mass of snow; a snow-ball or snow-flake. ~বর্ষ *n* hail or snow mingled with rain; sleet. ~ভূমি *n* snow-field.

তুষ্ট *adj* contented; satisfied; gratified; appeased; propitiated. ~ করা *vt* appease; satisfy (one); propitiate; gratify.

তুষ্টি *n* gratification; satisfaction; contentment; pleasure; satiety; appeasement; propitiation. ~কর, ~জনক *adj* gratifying; pleasing; satisfactory; appeasing. ~বিধান, ~সাধন *n* act of gratifying/ satisfying/ pleasing/ propitiating. ~সাধন/ বিধান করা *vt* gratify; satisfy; appease; propitiate; please.

তুস *n* a kind of soft woolen cloth.

তুহিন *n* snow; frost; ice; hoar-frost. ❑*adj* cold as snow; ice-cold: ~ শীতল.

তূণ, তূণীর *n* a case for arrows; a quiver.

তূণক *n* a Sanskrit poetical metre.

তূরন্ত *adj* violent; forceful; impetuous: ~ দুরন্ত গতি.

তূরী *n* a horn blown in ancient wars; a bugle-horn.

তূর্ণ *adv* quickly; swiftly; hastily. ❑*adj* swift; expeditious; quick: ~পত্র, express letter.

তূর্য *n* **1**=তূরী. **2** a metal wind-instrument of music; a trumpet. ~ধ্বনি, ~নাদ *n* the sound of a trumpet. তূর্যাচার্য [~+আচার্য] *n* a trainer in the art of blowing a trumpet.

তূলি, তূলিকা, তূলী= তুলি

তৃণ *n* **1** herbage of the family to which belong the grain-yielding and pasture plants; grass; straw. **2** a trashy thing; a triffle: ~জ্ঞানে অবহেলা করা. ~ জ্ঞান করা *vt* treat with absolute contempt; take (one) as worthless as a straw; not to care a straw for one. ~কান্তার *n* a pasture-land. ~কুটির *n* a hut of straw; a thatched cottage; a mean hovel. ~গুল্ম *n* grass and shrubs. ~জীবী *adj* subsisting on herbaceous plants; herbivorous. ~ভোজী *adj* feeding on grass; graminivorous. ~ময় *adj* abounding in grass grassy. ~শূন্য/হীন *adj* devoid of plants or vegetation.

তৃণাদ *adj* herbivorous; eating herbs.

তৃণাসন *n* seat of grass.

তৃতীয় *adj* the next after the second; third being one of three equal parts. ❑*n* the third part of anything. তৃতীয়া *fem adj* third. ❑*n* the third lunar day of either fortnight; the third day of the waxing or waning moon. ~ প্রকৃতি *n* an asexual or neuter human being; a eunuch. তৃতীয়া বিভক্তি *n* (gram) third or instrumental case-ending. ~ ব্যক্তি *n* a third party; third person; a neutral person. ~ মূল (arith) cube root.

তৃপ্ত *adj* satisfied; satiated; gratified; pleased; delighted. ~ করা *vt* satisfy; satiate; gratify; please. ~ হওয়া *vi* be satisfied/ gratified/ satiated.

তৃপ্তি *n* satisfaction; satiety; delight; gratification. ~ লাভ/ বোধ করা *vi* feel satisfied; have satisfaction; be satiated. ~কর/দায়ক *adj* giving satisfaction; pleasing; gratifying; satisfactory; delightful. ~পূর্বক *adv* with satisfaction; contentedly.

তৃষা, তৃষ্ণা *n* feeling caused by a desire or need to drink; the suffering caused by this desire; thirst. ~ পাওয়া *vi* be thirsty. ~ বোধ করা *vi* feel thirsty. ~ মেটানো *vi* allay or quench one's thirst. ~তুর *adj* thirsty; suffering from thirst.

তৃষিত=তৃষাতুর ⇒ তৃষা

তে[১] *adj* (used as *pref*) three; tri, triple: তেতালা, তেকাঠা. ~এঁটে *adj* (of fruits) **1** three-stoned. **2** triple-veined; three-veined. **3** ugly-looking. **4** rougish; knavish. তেকাঁটা *n* a kind of three-veined plant. তেকাঠা *n* a triangular frame made of three pieces of wood. তেতলা, তেতালা[১] *n* **1** (of a building) the second floor. **2** (of a vessel) the third deck. ❑*adj* three-storeyed; three-decked. তেতালা[২] *n* a mode of musical measure. তেপায়া *adj* three legged. ❑*n* a tripod; a teapoy. তেমাথা *n* a meeting-place/junction of three roads. তেমোহনা *n* a junction of the mouths of three streams.

তে[২] *suff* (used as *prep*): বাড়িতে, ঘড়িতে, আমার ঘড়িতে এখন ছ'টা বাজে, It is six by my watch now.

তেইশ *n*, *adj* three and twenty; twenty-three. তেইশে *n* the twenty-third day of a month. ❑*adj* (of the days of a month) twenty-third.

তেউড় *n* a sapling from the root of a banana tree; a sucker.

তেওড় *adj* crooked; curved. তেওড়ানো *vi* be crooked/bent; lend; warp.

তেঁতুল *n* the tamarind tree or its leguminous sour fruit. তেঁতুলে *adj* **1** shaped like a pod of tamarind: তেঁতুলে বিছে. **2** as dark-coloured as a tamarind seed.

তেঁদড় *adj* obstinate; impertinent; disobedient; wicked; headstrong; brazen-faced; shameless. তেঁদড়ামি *n* obstinacy; impertinence; disobedience. তেঁদড়ামি করা *vi* show impertinence; be obstinate/disobedient; behave shamelessly.

তেজ, তেজঃ *n* **1** light; lustre; glow; radiation. **2** strength; power; influence; might; force; energy; vigour; valour; prowess; spirit. **3** manliness; semen; virility. **4** haughtiness. insolence; pride; vanity; arrogance. ~ করা *vi* show strength and spirit; be defiant; have a defiant look; display haughtiness; carry oneself with a lofty air. ~ কমানো *vt* humble one's position; humble sb's pride; humiliate one. ~ দেখানো *vi* show haughtiness; carry things with a high hand.

তেজাই ⇒ তেজা

তেজপত্র *n* leaf of cassia tree; cassia-leaf.

তেজপুঞ্জ, তেজপুঞ্জঃ *adj* spirited; lustrous; with an air of glory and power.

তেজবর *n* a man who has married for the third time. তেজবরে *adj* one who has taken two wives before the present one.

তেজস্কর *adj* invigorating; stimulating; that gives vigour and energy.

তেজস্ক্রিয় *adj* having the quality of spontaneously and continuously emitting electronic energy, as radium, thorium, etc; radio-active. ~তা *n* radio-activity.

তেজস্বান, তেজস্বী *adj* **1** rich and impressive to the eye; brilliant; lustrous; splendid. **2** spirited; vigorous; mighty; energetic; strong; powerful. তেজস্বী, তেজস্বিনী *fem.*

তেজা *vt* (poet) give up; forsake; abandon; forgo; relinquish. তেজই (he) forsakes. তেজব (I) will forsake. তেজলি (he) forsook. তেজলু (I) forsake/ forsook.

তেজারত [A] *n* **1** trade; business. **2** money-lending business; usury. তেজারতি *n* the practice of making loans at very high rates of interest; usury. ❑*adj* **1** of or pertaining to trade and commerce. **2** of usury.

তেজালো *adj* **1** severe; intense; tremendous: ~ রোদ. **2** spirited; vigorous; strong. **3** haughty; arrogant. **4** bitterly pungent; acrid.

তেজি-মন্দি *n* (commerce) fluctuation in prices of commodities in the market; rise and fall in prices; boom and slump.

তেজী *adj* **1** spirited; vigorous: ~ লোক. **2** strong; powerful: ~ ওষুধ.

তেজীয়ান *adj* highly spirited; valorous. তেজীয়সী *fem.*

তেজোগর্ভ *adj* full of spirit or energy; fiery.

তেজোময় *adj* **1** vigorous; energetic; spirited. **2** lustrous; luminous; shining; radiating. তেজোময়ী *fem.*

তেজোমূর্তি, তেজোরূপ *n* man with a lustrous appearance ❑*adj* having a lustrous appearance.

তেজোহীন *adj* void of fire; spiritless; lacking in vigour and energy.

তেড়ছা *adj* crooked; oblique; slanting.

তেড়ে *adv* in a challenging mood; chasing wrathfully. ~ফুড়ে *adv* running behind threateningly and offensively; chasing and threatening.

তেতাল্লিশ *n, adj* three and forty; forty-three.

তেতো *adj* bitter; pungent.

তেত্রিশ *n, adj* three and thirty; thirty-three.

তেপান্তর [ত্রি+প্রান্তর] *n* an extensive plain; a vast stretch of wilderness. তেপান্তরের মাঠ *n* (generally used in folktales and legends) a boundless stretch of wilderness.

তেপায়া ⇒ তে

তেমাথা=তিমাথা

তেমন *adj* like that; similar to that; such. ~ করে *adv* in that way; in that manner. ~ই, তেমনি *adj* just like that. ❑*adv* in the same manner; in that way; similarly.

তেমাথা ⇒ তে

তেমোহনা ⇒ তে

তের *n, adj* thirteen. ~ই *n* the thirteenth day of a month.

তেরছা=তেড়ছা

তেরপল, তেরপাল=ত্রিপল

তেরাত্তির=ত্রিরাত্রি

তেরেট *n* a kind of tree-leaf formerly used as a writing material like the palm-leaf, but more durable than palm-leaf.

তেল *n* **1** inflammable liquid drawn from vegetable, animal and mineral sources; oil. **2** (sarcas) pride; vanity; audacity: তার ~ হয়েছে. **3** (sarcas) servile flattery; adulation; sycophancy: কর্তার পায়ে ~ মেখে কাজ উদ্ধার করো. ~ দেওয়া *vi,vt* **1** smear or rub over with oil; lubricate; oil. **2** give or pour oil. **3** flatter; butter up. নিজের চরকায় ~ দেওয়া mind one's own business; oil one's own machine. ~ মাখা *vi* rub one's body with oil. ~ মাখানো *vi* **1** massage another's body with oil. **2** praise one falsely; flatter; adulate. তেলে বেগুনে জ্বলে ওঠা be whipped into fury; be flared up in anger. ~-কল *n* an oil mill. ~-কুচকুচে, ~-চুকচুকে *adj* well-oiled; glossy. ~চিট, ~চিটে *adj* so thickly soiled as to look greasy. ~-পড়া *n* charmed oil. ~ হওয়া (fig) be arrogant/ vainglorious.

তেলা *adj* oily; greasy; glossy; smooth; slippery. ~ মাথায় তেল দেওয়া (fig) bestow favours on an affluent person; (idiom) carry coal to Newcastle.

তেলাকুচা *n* a small cylinder-like inedible fruit of a creeping plant, which becomes red when ripe.

তেলানো *vt* **1** besmear or anoint with oil; make oily or greasy. **2** (sarcas) pay-artful compliments; praise excessively or servilely; flatter. তেলানি *n* servile flattery; adulation.

তেলাপোকা *n* large, dark-brown insect frequenting kitchen and places where food is kept; cockroach.

তেলি *n* an oilman; a member of the Hindu caste manufacturing and selling oil.

তেলেগু *n* South Indian language spoken in Andhra and Telingana region.

তেলেনা *n* (music) a set of meaningless words, eg 'তেরে নে তেরে' which one hums before tuning up an instrument or setting to music. ~ **ভাঁজা** *vt vi* (fig) dwell on irrelevant talk as a prelude to the topic in hand.

তেলেভাজা *n* snacks prepared by frying in oil. ❑*adj* fried in oil; (fig) turned dark brown as copper as a result of continuous or frequent exposure to the sun; sun-burnt.

তেলেসমাত [A] *n* **1** magic; enchantment. **2** something very strange; a prodigy or marvel; wonder: এ যে দেখি ~ কাণ্ড. **তেলেসমাতি** *adj* magical; enchanting: তেলেসমাতি কারবার.

তেলো[১] *n* the crown of the head: মাথার ~.

তেলো[২] *n* the palm (of the hand) : হাতের ~.

তেশিরা ⇒ তে

তেষট্টি *n,adj* three and sixty; sixty-three.

তেসরা *n* the third day of a month (৩রা): ~ জুলাই

তেহাই[১] *n* (music) tri-fold stroke on the drum before finishing the measure.

তেহাই[২] *n* one-third part.

তেহারা *adj* three-fold; having three strands; three-stranded.

তৈজস *adj* **1** relating to light or radiation. **2** made of metal. ❑*n* household utensils made of metal eg brass, copper, aluminium: ~পত্র.

তৈয়ব [A] the name of the basic article of faith in Islam, affirming that "there is no God but Allah and that Muhammad (sm) is His messenger."

তৈয়ম্মুম=তয়ম্মুম

তৈরি, তৈরী [A] *adj* made; manufactured; built; constructed: সে তার নতুন ~ বাড়িতে উঠেছে. **2** ready for use; fit for work: ~ আম, ripe mango; ~ জামা, ready-made garment. **3** educated; trained; experienced: কাজ করার মতো লোক ~ হচ্ছে. **4** (sarcas) prematurely developed; ripe before the natural time; precocious: ~ ছেলে. ❑*n* act of making/ manufacturing/ constructing. ~ **করা** *vt* **1** make; build; construct: ঘরবাড়ি ~ করা. **2** produce; create; manufacture: শিল্পদ্রব্য ~ করা. **3** write; compose: ছড়া ~ করা. **4** draw up; paint: ছবি/নকশা ~ করা. **5** prepare: পড়া ~ করা. **6** train up; educate: কর্মী ~ করা.

তৈল=তেল. ~**কল্ক, ~কিট্ট** *n* oil-cake. ~-**কার** *n* an oilman; a oil-manufacturer. ~**চক্র** *n* an oilman's grinding tree. ~**চিত্র** *n* picture painted in oil-colours. ~**দান** *n* (sarcas) mean flattery. ~**দ্রোণী** *n* a oil-can; an oil-tub. ~**প, ~পা, ~পায়িকা** *n* the cockroach. ~ **পক্ব** *adj* **1** fried in oil. **2** cooked with oil. **3** hardened and glazed with oil: ~পক্ব লাঠি. ~**বীজ** *n* oil-seeds; mustard, linseed, etc. ~**যন্ত্র** *n* an oil-mill. ~**রঙ** *n* paints made by mixing colouring matter in oil.

তৈলঙ্গ *n* **1** a region in South India comprising modern Andhra and Telingana. **2** natives of Andhra and Telingana.

তৈলাক্ত [তৈল+অক্ত] *adj* smeared or anointed with oil, oily; greasy; unctuous.

তো[১] [P তহ্] *n* a fold: শাড়ি ~ করা. ~ **করা** *vt* lay in plaits; fold up.

তো[২]=ত[২]

তোকমা, তোকমারি [P তুখম-ই-রয়হান] *n* the seed of the holly-hock used in poultices. ~ **দেওয়া** *vi* poultice with the seed of the holly-hock.

তোকে *pron* thee; to thee; you; to you: ~ দিব না.

তোখড়=তুখড়

তোগরা, তুগরা [T] *n* ornamented Arabic characters; royal signature or seal.

তোটক *n* a Sanskrit poetical metre.

তোড় *n* **1** the rush of a stream; the impact of a strong current. **2** speed. **3** fluency of speech; the current of words: মুখের ~.

তোড়জোর *n* hectic preparations or preliminary arrangement for sth. ~ **করা** *vt* make preparations for sth in a hectic manner.

তোড়া [A] *n* **1** a bag of money; a purse: টাকার ~. **2** a bunch of anything: চাবির ~, ফুলের ~. **3** a bundle: নোটের ~. **4** a kind of jingling ornament for the ankles. ~ **বাঁধা** *vt* tie in a bundle; string in a bunch; fasten in a bag.

তোতলা, তোৎলা *adj* one who suffers from a defect of speech marked by involuntary repetitions of a syllable or sound; one who stammers; with a stammer; stammering. ❑*n* a stammerer; a stutterer. **তোতলামি** *n* act or the defect of stammering. **তোতলানো, তোতলামি করা** *vi,vt* speak with a stammer; stammer; stutter.

তোতা [P তুতী] *n* a bird which can imitate the human voice; the parrot.

তোৎলা=তোতলা

তোপ [T] *n* **1** a great gun; a cannon. **2** a gun. **3** the sound or shot of a cannon. ~**খানা** *n* a public establishment where firearms and ammunition are manufactured and stored; arsenal. ~ **দাগা** *vi* fire a cannon. **তোপের মুখে উড়িয়ে দেওয়া** *vt* cannonade or batter with cannon-shot. **তোপের গোলা** *n* a cannonball; cannon-shot. **তোপের পাল্লা** *n* the range of a cannon. ~**চি** *n* cannoneer; cannonier.

তোপচিনি *n* the tuberous root of a creeper in China and Japan; China root.

তোফা, তোহ্‌ফা [A] *adj* excellent; highly delicious; uncommon; wonderful. ❑*n* a gift; a presentation; a good news; a rare thing.

তোফাঙ্গা [P] *n* a pistol.

তোবড়া [P] *adj* having a depression or dent; sunken: ~ গাল, ~ বাসন. ~নো *vi* have a dent or depression; shrink; contract; wrinkle. ❑*adj* shrivelled; shrunken. **তুবড়ে যাওয়া** be depressed or dented; become shrivelled or shrunken.

তোমরা *pron pl* of তুমি

তোমা *pron*1 (poet) you: ~ হতে. **2** to you; you. --

তোমাকে, তোমায় *pron* you; to you.

তোমার *pron* your, yours.

তোয়াক্কা=তওয়াক্কা

তোয়াজ [A]*n* act of persuading by fondling and flattering; cajolery. ~ **করা** *vt* coax; cajole; fondle; flatter humour.

তোয়ালে *n* a towel.

তোর *pron* of you; your; thine; thy.

তোরঙ্গ, তোরঙ্গ *n* a steel box with a hinged lid, for clothes, etc; a trunk.

তোরণ *n* ornamented gateway/arch; outer door; portal. ~-**দ্বার** *n* grand outer gateway/ archway.

তোঁরা *pron pl* you.

তোলপাড় *n* violent agitation; tossing and moving; rise and fall; commotion. ~ **করা** *vi,vt* revolve or weigh in the mind; toss and move; ponder.

তোলা[1] *n* measure of weight (=160 grains).

তোলা[2] *n* **1** tax in kind paid to the owner of a market; rate in kind levied in markets. ❑*adj* **1** set apart (for special purpose): ~ খাবার, ~ পোশাক. **2** raised, lifted; hoisted. **3** constructed; built: নতুন ~ বাড়ি. **4** lifted and carried from a river: ~ পানি. **5** plucked; culled: ~ ফুল. **6** churned: মাখন ~ দুধ. **7** painted; engraved; moulded: পল-~.

তোলা[3] *vt* **1** raise; lift; introduce for consideration: প্রসঙ্গ ~. **2** rouse; wake: ঘুম থেকে ~. **3** take a deep involuntary breath from drowsiness, etc; yawn: হাই ~. **4** pluck; cull: ফুল ~, শাক ~. **5** pull up; extract: দাঁত ~. **6** uproot; remove: পাকা চুল ~. **7** collect; raise: চাঁদা ~. **8** wash away; obliterate: দাগ ~. **9** tune up: গানের সুর ~. **10** take: ফটো ~, snap. **11** evict; eject: ভাড়াটে ~. **12** set up; fix: পাল ~. **চাম** ~ *vt* take the skin off; hide off; flay. **ছবি** ~ *vi vt* take a photograph; make a motion picture; film. **হাই** ~ *vi* yawn. **গায়ে হাত** ~ *vt* assault.

তোশক [P] *n* a mattress.

তোশা [P]*n* valuable things or belongings. ~**খানা** *n* a room/house in which household valuables are stored; wardrobe; vestry; store-house.

তোষণ *n* act of pleasing or propitiating; act of flattering/adulating; act of appeasing. ~ **করা** *vt* try to appease or conciliate. ~**নীতি** *n* policy of conciliation or appeasement.

তোষামুদে *adj* hanging on obsequiously; full of flattery; flattering; adulating.

তোষামোদ *n* act of hanging on obsequiously; flattery; adulation; sycophancy. ~ **করা** *vi.vt* flatter; adulate; cringe (on). ~-**প্রিয়** *adj* fond of flattery/adulation.

তোষিত *adj* one who has been conciliated; gratified; appeased.

তৌজি [A] *n* a descriptive inventory containing the names of tenants, the amounts of their holding and rents thereof; rent-collector's roll; rent-roll.

তৌফিক [A] *n* strength; ability .

তৌরাত =তওরাত

তৌল *n* **1** act of weighing; weighment; measurement. **2** a weighing machine; a balance. **3** (fig) act of comparing; comparison. ~ **করা** *vt* weigh; compare. ~**ন** *n* act of weighing/comparing. ~**নিক** *adj* comparative. ~**মান** *n* (mech) weight. ~**যন্ত্র** *n* a weighing machine.

তৌলিক[1] *n* a painter.

তৌলিক[2] *n* a weighman.

তৌহিদ=তওহিদ

ত্যক্ত *adj* **1** given up; relinquished; abandoned: পরি~. **2** annoyed; vexed. ~ **করা** *vt* annoy; vex. ~**বিরক্ত** *adj* extremely annoyed/vexed; exceedingly disgusted; exasperated.

ত্যজন *n* act of forsaking/giving up; abandonment; relinquishment.

ত্যজ্যমান *adj* that which/one who is being abandoned/forsaken.

ত্যাঁদড়=তেঁদড়

ত্যাগ *n* **1** act of giving up: দাবি ~, প্রাণ ~. **2** act of forsaking; abandonment; act of leaving; desertion: দেশ ~. **3** resignation; relinquishment: পদ~, কর্ম~. ~ **করা** *vt* give up; abandon; forsake; relinquish; desert. ~**স্বীকার** *n* self-sacrifice; self-denial; self-abnegation. ~**স্বীকার করা** *vi* , *vt* forgo one's claims; renounce one's interests; make sacrifice; deny oneself. **ত্যাগী** *adj* self-denying; self-abnegating; selfless. ❑*n* a self-denier; a self-abnegator; a renouncer of self-interests.

ত্যাজ্য *adj* (fig) to be relinquished/ abandoned/ disowned/ given up. ~**পুত্র** *n* a son disowned and disinherited by his father. ~**পুত্র করা** *vt* disown or disinherit a son.

ত্রপমান *adj* in the state of being abashed.

ত্রপা *n* modesty; bashfulness. ~**ন্বিত** *adj* struck with bashfulness.

ত্রপিত *adj* abashed.

ত্রপু *n* **1** lead. **2** zinc. **3** tin.

ত্রয় *n* three united; trio; a union of three; a triad; trinity: ব্যক্তি~. ❑*adj* consisting of three; triple;

threefold. ~ঃপঞ্চাশ *adj* fifty-third. ~ঃপঞ্চাশৎ *n,adj* fifty-three. ~ঃপঞ্চাশত্তম *adj* fifty-third. ~ঃষষ্টি *n,adj* sixty-three ~ ষষ্টিতম *adj* sixty-third. ~ঃসপ্ততি *n,adj* seventy-three. ~ঃসপ্ততিতম *adj* seventy-third. ~শ্চত্বারিংশ, ~শ্চত্বারিংশতম forty three. ~শ্চত্বারিংশৎ *n,adj* forty-three. ~শ্চত্বারিংশতী *fem.* ~শ্চত্বারিংশত্তম *adj* forty-third. ~শ্চত্বারিংশত্তমী *fem.* ~স্ত্রিংশ *adj* thirty-three. ~স্ত্রিংশৎ *n adj* thirty-three. ~স্ত্রিংশতী *fem.* ~স্ত্রিংশত্তম *adj* thirty-third. ~স্ত্রিংশত্তমী *fem.*

ত্রয়ী *adj fem* of ত্রয়. ❑*n* (according to Hindu idea)**1** three godheads---Brahma, Vishnu and Shiva. **2** three Vedas collectively.

ত্রয়োদশ *n,adj* thirteen. ❑*adj* thirteenth. **ত্রয়োদশী** *adj fem* **1** thirteenth; thirteen years old. ❑*n fem* **1** a girl of thirteen. **2** the thirteenth day of a lunar fortnight.

ত্রয়োবিংশ *adj* twenty third; twenty-three. ত্রয়োবিংশতি *n,adj* twenty-three. ত্রয়োবিংশতিতম *adj* twenty-third. ত্রয়োবিংশতিতমী *fem.*

ত্রসন *n* **1** state of being frightened/alarmed. **2** fright; alarm; panic. **3** anxiety; concern.

ত্রসরেণু *n* **1** (phys) particles of dust seen to be floating on sunbeam. **2** a minute body containing six atoms.

ত্রস্ত *adj***1** frightened; alarmed; terror-stricken; fearful. **2** trembled; startled; shaken; timorous. **3** hurried. ~ হয়ে *adv* in a hurry; in a state of hurly-burly; in a panic.

ত্রাণ *n* rescue; deliverance; relief; salvation. ~ করা *vt* save; protect; deliver; rescue. ~কর্তা *n* a saviour; a deliverer; a protector.

ত্রাত *adj* saved; delivered; rescued; relieved.

ত্রাতা=ত্রাণকর্তা ⇒ ত্রাণ

ত্রাস *n* terror; panic; fright; alarm. ~কর *adj* terrifying; alarming; frightful; dreadful. **ত্রাসিত** *adj* terrified; frightened; alarmed; terror-stricken; panicky.

ত্রাহি *vt* please save/ rescue/ deliver/ protect. ~~ *int* save! save! ~~ করা *vi* cry for help or mercy. ~ মধুসূদন O God, save me.

ত্রি *n,adj* three. ~কাল *n* three ages—past, present and future. ~কালজ্ঞ *adj* acquainted with all the three ages---past, present and future; all-knowing. ~কালদর্শী *adj* one who or that which sees all the three ages---past, present and future; omniscient; all-seeing. ~কালবেত্তা=~কালজ্ঞ. ~কুল *n* three family lines with which one is connected through one's father, mother and father-in-law. ~কূট *n* the three-peaked mountain of Southern India. ~কেশর *adj* (bot) with three stamens; triandrous. ~কোণ *adj* triangular. ❑*n* a triangle. ~কোণমিতি *n* trigonometry. ~কোণী *n* a set square. ~কোষ্ঠ *adj* (bot) three-celled; trilocular. ~খণ্ড *adj* trisected; cut into three equal parts. ~খণ্ডন *n* trisection. ~গঙ্গ *n* the confluence of three streams—the Ganges, the Jumuna and the Saraswati at Allahabad in India. ~গামী *adj* (phys) three-way. ~গুণ *n* the three basic elements of human nature, namely সত্ত্ব, রজঃ and তমঃ. ❑*adj* **1** having the aforesaid qualities. **2** three times; trebled; multiplied by three. ~গুণা *n fem* an appellation of goddess Durga. ~গুণাত্মক *adj* having the three basic elements of human character, namely. সত্ত্ব, রজঃ and তমঃ according to Indian philosophy. ~গুণাত্মিকা *fem.* ~গুণিত *adj* multiplied three times over; threefold; trebled. ~ঘাত *adj* **1** (arith and alg) having the form or properties of a cube; cubic. **2** (geom) having three dimensions; solid. ~চক্রযান *n* a three-wheel carriage; tricycle. ~চত্বারিংশ *adj* forty-third. ~চত্বারিংশৎ *n,adj* forty-three. ~চত্বারিংশতী *fem.* ~ চত্বারিংশত্তম *adj* forty-third. ~চত্বারিংশত্তমী *fem.* ~জগৎ *n* the three worlds, namely, heaven, earth and underworld; the universe. ~তন্ত্রী *n* a three-stringed harp. ~তয় *n* triad; triplet; three. ~তল *adj* (of buildings) three-storeyed; (of ships, buses, etc) three-decked. ❑*n* the second floor; the third deck. ~তাপ *n* the three kinds of affliction—spiritual, material and supernatural. ~দণ্ডী *adj* three-stringed: ~দণ্ডী পইতা. ~দোষ *n* disorder of the three humours of the body----bile, blood and phlegm. ~দোষজ *adj* caused by the disorder of the three humours of the body. ~ধা *adv* in or from three ways; of three kinds; threefold. ~ধার *adj* triangular. ~ধারা *n* river with three streams. ~নবতি *n,adj* ninety-three. ~নবতিতম *adj* ninety-third. ~নবতিতমী *fem.* ~নয়ন *adj* three-eyed. ❑*n* an appellation of Shiva. ~নয়না, ~নয়নী *nn adj fem* of ~নয়ন. ❑*n* an appellation of goddess Durga. ~পক্ষ, ~পক্ষীয়, ~পাক্ষিক *adjj* divided into three parts; made between three parties; tripartite. ~পঞ্চাশৎ *n,adj* fifty-three. ~পঞ্চাশতী *fem.* ~পঞ্চাশত্তম *adj* fifty-third. ~পঞ্চাশত্তমী *fem.* ~পত্র *adj* three-leafed; trifoliate. ❑*n* a trefoil. ~পদ *n* a three-legged stool, table, etc; a tripod. ~পদী *n* Bengali or sanskrit poetical metre. ~পাদ *adj* three-legged; three-footed. ❑*n* an incarnation of Vishnu. ~পিটক *n* the Buddhist scripture. ~পুণ্ড্রক *n* trident-shaped sectarian mark on the forehead. ~ফলক *adj* arranged in threes; ternate (leaf). ~ফলা *n* three kinds of myrobalans collectively. ~বর্ণ *n* the three higher castes of Hindus collectively. ❑*adj* tri-coloured. ~বলি, ~বলী *nn* the three muscular folds or wrinkles on the belly or throat. ~বার্ষিক *adj* continuing three years; happening every three years; triennial. ~বিধ *n* of three kinds; three-fold. ~বেণী *n* the confluence of the Ganges, Jumuna and Saraswati at Allahabad. ত্রিবেদী *n* a Brahmin conversant with the three Vedas, namely, the Rik, the Sama and the Yajus. ~ভঙ্গ, ~ভঙ্গিম *adj* bent or crooked in three parts of the body. ~ভঙ্গ মুরারি *n* **1** (sarcas) an ugly and decrepit person who cannot keep his body erect. **2** Sri Krishna posing with a twist head, waist and legs. ~ভুজ *n* (geom) a triangle. ~ভুবন *n* heaven, earth and the underworld collectively; the universe. ~মাত্রিক *adj* **1** (geom) having three dimensions; solid. **2** (arith, alg) cubic. ~মূর্তি *n* the Hindu trinity consisting of Brahma, Vishnu and Shiva. ~শূল *n* a three-pronged spear; a trident used by Hindu ascetics. ~শূলী, ~শূলধারী *adj* holding a trident. ❑ *n* an appellation of Shiva. ~শূলিন, ~শূলধারিণী *fem.* ~সংসার=~ভুবন. ~সন্ধ্যা *n* three parts of the day taken collectively—morning, midday and afternoon. ~সপ্ততি *n, adj* seventy three. ~সপ্ততিতম *adj* seventy-third. ~সপ্ততিতমী *fem.* ~সীমা, ~সীমানা *n* three boundaries; approach; proximity. ~সীমা না মাড়ানো keep aloof from; not to approach; avoid; shun.

ত্রিদিব *n* heaven; the sky. ত্রিদিবেশ *n* the lord of heaven, an appellation of Indra.

ত্রিপল *n* canvas covered with tar; tarpaulin.

ত্রিশ *n,adj* thirty.

ত্রিশঙ্কু *n* Trishanku, a king of ancient India. ~ অবস্থা *n* situation when one finds himself between two fires/on the horns of a dilemma.

ত্রুটি *n* a shortcoming; a deficiency; a flaw; a failing; a lapse. ~বিচ্যুতি *n* faults and failures; omissions and commissions. ~হীন *adj.*

ত্রেতা *n* the second age of the world according to Hindus: ~ যুগ.

ত্রৈকালিক *adj* of or relating to three ages—past, present and future; eternal.

ত্রৈগুণ্য *n* an aggregate of the three basic elements of human nature according to Hindu philosophy—namely, সত্ত্ব or knowledge, রজঃ or action and তমঃ or ignorance.

ত্রৈবার্ষিক *adj* occurring every third year; continuing for three years; triennial.

ত্রৈমাসিক *adj* happening once in three months. ❑*n* a periodical published every third month; a quarterly.

ত্র্যংশ *n* the third part or share; three parts or shares.

ত্র্যঙ্ক *adj* consisting of three acts; three-act: ~ নাটক.

ত্র্যঙ্গু *adj* measuring three fingers.

ত্র্যম্বক *n* an appellation Shiva.

ত্র্যস্র *adj* triangular.

ত্র্যহস্পর্শ *n* a conjunction of three lunar days on one calendar day.

–ত্ব *suff* indicating nature, quality, state, propensity, etc: রাজত্ব, মহত্ব, লঘুত্ব.

ত্বক *n* **1** skin; hide. **2** the bark (of a tree) . **3** peel or rind of a fruit or vegetable. **4** the sense of touch. ~চ্ছেদ *n* circumcision. ~চ্ছেদন *n* act of cutting the foreskin. ~চ্ছেদন করা *v i* circumcise.

ত্বদীয় *adj* relating to you; of you; thy; thine.

ত্বর *n* delay: ~ সয় না.

ত্বরণ *n* act of accelerating; increase of velocity; acceleration.

ত্বরমাণ *adj* hurrying; hastening.

ত্বরা *n* haste; hurry; quickness. ~ করা *vt* make haste; hasten; hurry; expedite. ~ন্বিত *adj* hurried; quickened; hastened. ~ন্বিত করা *vt* expedite; hasten. ~য় *adv* hastily; hurriedly; quickly.

ত্বরিত[১] *adj* accelerated; hastened; quickened; hurried.

ত্বরিত[২] *adj* quick; swift; hasty; speedy; prompt. ~গতি, ~গামী *adjj* quick-moving; fast-going; swift.

ত্বষ্টা *n* **1** a carpenter. **2** Hindu god Vishwakarma.

ত্বষ্টি *n* carpentry.

ত্বাচ *adj* **1** relating to the skin; dermal. **2** derived by touch: ~ প্রত্যক্ষণ, tactual perception.

ত্বাদৃশ *adj* like thee; similar to you.

ত্বিষ, ত্বিষা *n* glow; lustre; radiation. ত্বিষাম্পতি *n* the sun (personified).

থ

থ[১] *n* the seventeenth letter of the Bengali alphabet and second one of the ত group of letters. It is an unvoiced, aspirated, dental, plosive sound.

থ[২] *adj* **1** struck dumb with amazement/dismay; bewildered; flabbergasted; confounded; motionless: তার অবস্থা দেখে আমি ~. ~ বানানো *vt* make one a fool. ~ হওয়া *vi* be at a standstill; be non-plussed; be struck with amazement.

থই, থৈ, থা, থাই *n* **1** bottom (as of a water-pool). **2** depth (as of water). ~ পাওয়া *vi* reach the bottom; feel the depth. ~ না পাওয়া *vt* be out of depth.

থই থই, থৈ থৈ *int* indicating expanse or vastness of sth: পানি ~ করছে

থক *int* denoting **(a)** the sound of a thick juice or a sticky substance dropping down on hard surface; **(b)** the sound of spitting.

থক থক *int* denoting sth muddy and thick. ~ **করা** *vi* appear sticky or thick. ~**থকে** *adj* soft and thick; turbid.

থতমত *int* denoting a state of perplexity or embarrassment. ~ **খাওয়া** *vi* be perplexed or confounded; be taken aback.

থপ *int* denoting a thudding or thumping sound. ~ **করে** *adv* with a heavy thump. ~ **করে বসে পড়া** plump down. ~~ *int* denoting repeated thumps or thuds ~~ **করে** *adv* in a clumsy manner. ~~ **করে চলা** walk with heavy, unsteady footsteps; walk clumsily. ~**থপে** *adj* giving a thudding noise; heavy; clumsy.

থমক *n* sudden halting while one is on a walk. **থমকে দাঁড়ানো/থমকানো** *vi* stop suddenly; halt abruptly; be startled.

থমথম *int* denoting heaviness, darkness or silence: রাত ~ করছে, the night is dead silent; it is an erie night.

থমথমে *adj* dreadfully still and dark, filled with suspense.

থর *n* a layer; a stratum; a tier. **থরে থরে, থরে বিথরে** *adv* in rows; in layers; arranged in rows/layers.

থরথর *int* denoting trembling or palpitation. ~ **করে** *adv* with a trembling or quaking motion. ~ **করে কাঁপা** *vi* shiver; tremble violently.

থরথরানি *n* violent agitation; shivering; palpitation.

থরথরানো *vi* tremble; shiver;

থলথল *int* denoting flabbiness, looseness, laxity, etc. ~ **করা** *vi* appear flabby; hang loosely. **থলথলে** *adj* fleshy; flabby; lax; plump.

থলি, থলে *n* a bag; a sack; a purse; a pocket; a bladder.

থলো *n* a cluster; a bunch. ~~ *adv* in bunches/clusters.

থসথস *int* denoting moistness/ looseness/ puffiness/ elasticity. ~ **করা** *vi* be flabby. **থসথসে** *adj* moist; wet; flabby; oversoft; loose.

থাক *n* a tier; a layer; row; shelf; stack; group. ~ **দিয়ে রাখা** *vi* set up in stacks/ piles/ rows/layers. ~ **দিয়ে সাজানো** *adj* arranged in layers/ rows/ stocks/ piles. **থাকে থাকে** *adj* in tiers/rows/layers.

থাকা *vi vt* **1** live; dwell: সে ঢাকায় থাকে. **2** stay; remain: পালিয়ে ~. **3** pass time: কষ্টে ~. **4** be in possession of: টাকা ~. **5** exist; continue; last: রং ~. **6** be alive: বেঁচে ~.**7** remember: মনে ~. **8** be observed or kept: কথা ~. **থেকে থেকে** *adv* at intervals; by fits and starts; every now and then.

থান *adj* whole; entire; unbroken: ~ ইট, ~ কাপড়. ☐*n* a piece (of cloth, etc). ~ **কাপড়** *n* an entire sheet of woven fabric.

থানকুনি *n* a variety of edible pungent herb.

থানা *n* a police station or outpost.

থাপ্পড় *n* a slap; a pat. ~ **মারা** *vt* slap; pat.

থাবড়ানো *vt* strike with the palm; slap; pats.

থাবা *n* a paw or claw (of an animal). ~ **দেওয়া/মারা** *vt* **1** seize or snatch with the paw; paw. **2** (facet) seize or snatch with the palm of the hand.

থামা[1] *n* a pillar; a column; a post.

থামা[2] *vi* **1** stop; come to a stop; half; pause; stop in the midst of talking or doing sth. **2** cease; discontinue: বৃষ্টি ~.

থামানো *vt* **1** cause to stop; stop sb from doing or talking sth. **2** calm down; console; conciliate: কান্না ~. **3** prevent (one) from doing sth; check.

থাম্বা=থাম

থার্মোমিটার [E] *n* instrument for measuring temperature; thermometer.

থাল, থালা *n* metallic or porcelain dish; a plate.

থালি *n* a small plate or salver.

থিতানো *vi* **1** sink down to the bottom; settle down (as sediment of liquid). **2** (fig) tranquillize; become quiet; be calmed or quietened: আন্দোলন ~.

থিয়েটার [E] *n* building or arena for the performance of plays, for dramatic spectacles, etc; theatre. ~ **করা** *vi* act on the stage. ~**ওয়ালা** *n* proprietor or manager of a theatre. **থিয়েটারি, থিয়েটারী** *adj* relating to thetre; theatrical.

থু, থুঃ *int* **1** denoting the noise/sound of spitting. **2** used to express contempt or hatred; fie. ~**কদানি** *n* a spittoon.

থুড়থুড় *int* denoting decrepitude. **থুড়থুড়ে** *adj* old and decrepit: থুড়থুড়ে বুড়ো.

থুড়ি *int* indicating withdrawal of sth spoken.

থুতনি, থুঁতনি *n* the front of the tower jaw; the .chin.

থুতু, থুথু *n* spittle; saliva. ~ **দেওয়া** *vi* spit (at, upon). ~ **ফেলা** *vi* spit.

থুৎকার *n* **1** act or the sound of spitting. **2** expressing contempt/hatred.

থুথু ⇒ থুতু

থুপ[1] *n* (colloq) stack; a heap; a pile. ~ **করা** *vt* heap; pile; stack.

থুপ[2] (onom) *int* expressing a thudding noise. ~ **করে** *adv* suddenly; all on a sudden: ছেলেটি কাদার মধ্যে ~ করে পড়ে গেল.

থুবড়া *adj* **1** elderly and unmarried. **2** very old; decrepit. **থুবড়ি** *fem.* **থুবড়ি মেয়ে** an old maid; spinster.

থুবড়ানো *vi* fall with one's face downward; fall flat on one's face: মুখ থুবড়ে পড়া.

থুয়ে *vt* keeping; leaving; putting off; placing: বইটি ওখানে ~ দাও.

থেঁতলানো, থেঁতানো *vt* **1** smash; pound; bruise; maul. **2** make soft and shapeless by repeated pounding: কুমোরের মাটি ~. ❑*adj* smashed; pounded; bruised; mauled.

থেঁতো *adj* smashed; bruised; pounded. ~ **করা** *vt* pound; maul; bruise; smash: আঙুল ~ হয়ে গেছে.

থেকে *prep* **1** from: বাড়ি ~ কবে এসেছ? **2** since: সেই কখন ~ বসে আছি! **3** than: ঘোড়া ~ হাতি বড়ো.

থেবড়া, থ্যাবড়া *adj* flat; snub. ~ **নাক** *n* snub nose. ~ **করা** *vt* flatten. **থেবড়ানো** *vt* depress; flatten. ❑*adj* depressed; snub; flattened: থেবড়ানো নাক.

থৈ থৈ=থই থই

থোওয়া, থোয়া (colloq)*vt* keep; put; place; lay down; deposit: বইটি থোও. ❑*adj* deposited; laid down; placed; put; kept: তুলে ~ জিনিস.

থোঁতা[1] *adj* rendered toothless or blunt. ~ **মুখ ভোতা করা** (fig) put an end to one's tall talk; humble one's pride.

থোঁতা[2]=থুতনি

থোক *n* **1** net amount; an aggregate; total; a lump. **2** an installment; an item: থোকে থোকে সাজানো. **3** a bundle; a bunch. ❑*adj* total; net; lump: ~ লাভ ৫০০ টাকা.

থোকা *n* a bundle; a cluster; a bunch. ~ **বাঁধা** *vt* gather/collect together in a bundle. ~**য় ~য়** *adv* in bunches/clusters/bundles: থোকায় থোকায় ফুল ফোটে.

থোড় *n* **1** spathe of plantain tree. **2** (fig, vulg) mere trifle; nothing. **থোড়-বড়ি-খাড়া খাড়া-বড়ি-থোড়** (idiom) monotonous repetition; lack of variety.

থোড়া *adj* little; few.

থোড়াই *adv* not much; but little. ~ **কেয়ার করা** (sl) not to care a straw/ damn.

থ্যাতলানো=থেঁতলানো

থ্যাবড়া=থেবড়া

দ

দ[1] *n* the eighteenth consonant of the Bengali alphabet. It is pronounced as a voiced unaspirated dental plosive sound.

দ[2] *n* (colloq)= দহ. ~ **পড়া** *vi* (of land) subside. **দয়ে পড়া/মজা** *vi* (fig) be in a precarious position; be put in jeopardy; be utterly ruined. **দয়ে মজানো** *vt* jeopardize; ruin utterly.

-দ *adj* (used as a *suff*) giving; granting; offering; effecting; producing: ধন~; mhn~.

দই *n* yoghurt, yogurt, yoghourt; curd; coagulated milk. ~ **পাতা** *vt* make yoghurt. **চিনিপাতা** ~ *n* sugared yoghurt. **টক** ~ *n* sour yoghurt. **সাজো** ~ *n* fresh yoghurt. ~**বড়া** n kind of balls made of yoghurt and different kinds of pulses. **পান্তাভাতে টক** ~⇒ পান্তা. **যার ধন তার নয় নেপোয় মারে** ~⇒ নেপো.

দং abbr of দরুন; on account of.

দংশ *n* **1** gnat; gad-fly. **2** bite; sting. **3** tooth. **4** pincers. ~**ক** *n* gnat; gad-fly. ❑*adj* biting. ~**ন** *n* (the act of) biting; bite; sting. ~**ন করা** *vt* bite; sting. **দংশা** *vi* (poet)=~ন করা. **দংশানো** *vt* cause to bite.

দংশিত *adj* bitten; stung. **দংশী** *n fem* small gad-fly (⇒ দংশ).

দংষ্ট্র *n* (large) tooth; tusk; fang. **দংষ্ট্রা** *n* **1** large tooth. **2** claw; prong; fang. **3** sting (eg of a gad-fly). **দংষ্ট্রাকরাল** *adj* having terrible tusks. **দংষ্ট্রাঘাত** *n* bite; sting. **দংষ্ট্রায়ুধ** *adj* using tusks as weapons. ❑*n* wild boar. **দংষ্ট্রাল** *adj* tusked; having large teeth; clawed; pronged; fanged; stinged.

দংষ্ট্রী *adj* =দংষ্ট্রাল (⇒দংষ্ট্র)

দঃ abbr of দরুদ.

দক, দঁক *n* muddy water; mire; mudhole; muck; quagmire; slough. **দকে পড়া** *vi* (fig) get involved in great difficulties; run into trouble; be in a predicament.

দপ্তি [P] *n* **1** paste-board. **2** weaver's reed; sley.

দক্ষ *adj* adroit; expert; clever; fit; able; dexterous; intelligent; skilful; competent; skilled. ❑*n* (myth) name of one of the Projapatis, born from Brahma's right thumb—he is the father of Sati and father-in-law of Shiva. ~**কন্যা** *n fem* daughter of Daksha; goddess Durga. ~**তা** *n* dexterity; ability; skill; adroitness; competence; expertness. ~**যজ্ঞ** *n* **1** Daksha's sacrifice, in which Shiva was not invited and was publicly abused. The sacrifice was spoiled and Daksha was killed by Shiva. **2** (fig) chaotic scene;

pandemonium; topsy-turvydom; bedlam; maelstrom; madhouse.

দক্ষিণ *n* **1** the south. **2** right hand (side). **3** the south. ❑*adj* **1** southern; south. **2** candid; sincere; straightforward; pleasing. **3** right: ~ হস্ত. **4** able; clever; dexterous. **5** favourable; graceful; pleased: দেবতার ~মুখ. **~-অয়নান্ত** *n* winter solstice. **~কালিকা, ~কালী** *nn fem* form of Durga, worshipped by the Tantrikas. ~ কেন্দ্র ⇒ ~ মেরু. **~পবন** *n* southerly breezes. **~-পশ্চিম** *n* south-west. ❑*adj* south-western. **~-পূর্ব** *n* south-east. ❑*adj* south-eastern. **~মেরু** *n* the south pole. **~মেরু অঞ্চল** *n* the Antarctic. **~হস্ত** *n* **1** right hand. **2** right-hand man. **~ হস্তের ব্যাপার** *n* (fig) eating; affair/business of taking one's meal. **দক্ষিণে** *adv* on the right side/south; on the right side of/southward from.

দক্ষিণরায় *n* (myth) name of the presiding tiger-deity of the Sundarbans.

দক্ষিণা[১] *n* **1** gift; donation. **2** fees/present to the officiating priest; donation to the priest. **3** reward. **4** (rhet) a mistress who loves to be cajoled by her lover. **~ন্ত** *n* a payment of the sacrificial fee. **~ন্ত করা** *vi* conclude/terminate a religious function by paying the priest his fees.

দক্ষিণা[২] *adj* southern; south; southerly: ~ বাতাস. **~গ্র** *adj* having the points turned to the south. **~চল** *n* **1** (myth) the Malaya range. **2** the Antarctic Mountain. **~চার** *n* a system of Tantrik rituals. **~চারী** *adj, n* (one) who follows the above rituals. **~নিল** *n* southerly breezes. **~পথ** *n* the southern region; the Deccan. **~প্রবণ** *adj* sloping south-wards. **~ভিমুখ** *adj* having the face turned southwards; flowing southwards. **~মুখ** *adj* standing with the face to the south/right. **~য়ন** *n* the winter half year; southward way; winter solstice. **~য়নবৃত্ত** *n* (astron) the Tropic of Cancer. **~রণ্য**=দণ্ডকারণ্য. **~বর্ত** *adj* turning (from the left) to the right; (moving/winding) clockwise; dextral. ❑*n* the Deccan. **~বহ**=~নিল.

দক্ষিণী *adj* southern.

দক্ষিণে *adj* (colloq) southern.

দখল [A] *n* **1** possession; occupation; access; (right to) hold; control; entrance; admission; reach. **2** proficiency; knowledge; skill; mastery: তার ইংরেজিতে ~ আছে. **~ করা** *vt* **1** occupy: জমি ~ করা. **2** grab; get one's hand on; corner; take possession of: বইটা সে ~ করেছে. **3** monopolize; take under control: রাস্তাটা ফেরিওয়ালাদের দখলে. **~ থাকা** *vt* **1** have possession: জমিতে ~ থাকা. **2** have knowledge/ proficiency/ mastery; be skilful/ proficient in: অঙ্কে/দাবায় ~ থাকা. **3** have hold/control; have possession: ছাত্রদের উপর তার কোনো ~ নেই. **দখলে থাকা** *vt* be in possession/ control/ occupation. **~ দেওয়া** *vt* give possession; **~ নেওয়া** *vt* come into possession; take possession of (sth). **~ পাওয়া** *vt* **1** obtain possession. **2** get admission; have access. **~কার** *adj* one who is in possession/occupation; occupying. ❑*n* occupant; occupier; possessor. **~কারী** *n* taking/ obtaining possession; occupancy. **~চ্যুত** *adj* dispossessed. **~দার**=~কার. **~দার বাহিনী** *n* army of occupation. **~নামা** *n* writ of possession of lands; document giving the right of occupancy.

দখলি *adj* relating to possession/occupancy; hold; occupied. **~কার, ~দার**=দখলকার. **~স্বত্ব** *n* right by possession; possessorship; possessory right.

দখিন *n, adj* (colloq, poet)= দক্ষিণ

দখিনা *adj*=দক্ষিণা

দগড় *n* kind of war-drum/kettle-drum.

দগড়া *n* **1** rope-like mark. **2** raised streak on the skin left by a blow with a lash, etc; wale. **3** track (left by a moving vehicle). **~ পড়া** *vi* be marked with wale. **~ ফেলা** *vt* wale.

দগদগ *n* (onom) expressing burning sensation; sore; inflammation; festering. **~ করা** *vi* burn; fester. **দগদগানি** *n* burning sensation; festering; inflammation.

দগদগে *adj* fervid; glowing; burning; inflamed, festering: ~ ঘা.

দগ্ধ *adj* **1** burnt; scorched; consumed by fire; roasted; parched. **2** red hot: ~ লৌহ. **3** tormented; pained; consumed by grief/hunger; distressed: ~ হৃদয়. **3** inauspicious; miserable ill: ~ কপাল, ~ বিধাতা. **4** disgraced; humiliated: ~ বদন. **দগ্ধা** *vi,vt* (poet) **1** burn; parch; scorch; roast. **2** afflict; distress; torment; pain; badger. ❑*n* certain inauspicious days: দিনদগ্ধা, মাসদগ্ধা. **দগ্ধানো** *vt* =দগ্ধা. **~হৃদয়** *adj* having a distressed/ disconsolate/ grief-stricken heart; heart-broken. **দগ্ধাবশেষ** *n* residue after burning. ❑*adj* remaining as residue after burning.

দঙ্গল *n* **1** tumultuous assembly; crowd; swarm. **2** wrestling arena. **3** wrestling bout. **4** (hunting) party. **~ বাঁধা** *vi* (form into a) crowd; swarm. **~ লড়া** *vi* wrestle; have a wrestling bout.

দজ্জাল [A] *n* **1** one-eyed man; liar; great deceiver. **2** imposter. **3** (of women) spiteful woman; shrew; virago; termagant; furious. ❑*adj* wicked; refractory; devilish; hell-born; fiendish; bad-tempered; ill-tempered; spiteful; shrewish.

দড় *adj* **1** firm; strong; hard; steady; strong; stiff. **2** skilled; competent; adroit; adept; expert:

কাজে ~. 3 stronger; harder; stiffer: বাঁশের চেয়ে কঞ্চি ~. 4 sharp: কথায় ~.

ড়দড় *n* (onom) expressing; sound of quick footsteps.

ড়বড় *n* (onom) expressing; sound of galloping horses. ~ **করে** *adv* quickly; swiftly; hastily at a gallop; posthaste; chop-chop; on the double. **দড়বড়ানি** *n* quick motion; hurry; rush; haste. **দড়বড়ানে** *adj* galloping; hurried; quick-footed. ~**নো** *vi* hurry; gallop; fly; rush about; bound.

ড়মা=দরমা

ড়া *n* rope; thick cord/wire; hawser. ~**দড়ি** *n pl* ropes and cables; rigging (of a ship); cordage. ~**বাজি** *n* rope-dancing; rope-walking; acrobatics; funambulation. ~**বাজিকর** *n* rope-walker; rope-dancer; funambulist; acrobat. ~**বাজি করা** *vi* funambulate; perform rope-walking.

ড়াম *n* (onom) expressing banging/slamming sound; bang; thud; slam; thump; crash. ~ **করে** **চাপড় মারা** *vi* thump; give a thump. ~ **করে পড়ে** **যাওয়া** *vi* fall with a thud/crash/bump. ~ **করে** **বন্ধ করা** *vi* shut with a bang; slam. ~ **দড়াম** *n* repeated thump/ thud/ bang/ crash.

ড়ি *n* 1 cord; string; tether; rope; twine. 2 fillet; lace: চুল বাঁধার ~. 3 noose; halter: ফাঁসির ~. ~ **ছেঁড়া** *v* snap a string; break loose (from sb/sth); run amok; escape confinement/ restriction. ~ **পাকানো** *v* make ropes/cords; twist a cord/rope out of sth; twist sth into a rope. ~-**কলসি** *n pl* piece of cord and a pitcher (as equipment for committing suicide). তোমার ~-**কলসি জোটে না** (as a curse or in scolding) go, get yourself drowned. **তোমার গলায়** ~ (as a curse or in scolding) go, hang yourself. **ভেবে ভেবে** ~ **হওয়া** (fig) be reduced to a skeleton through worries and anxieties. ~-**ছেঁড়া** *adj* broken loose of (sth); unrestrained; refractory; frenzied . ~দড়া=দড়া~.

ণ্ড[1] *n* 1 stick; staff; rod; pole; cudgel; club; mace. 2 handle (of a ladle, sauce-pan, fly-flap, parasol, etc). 3 a pole as a measure of length (=4 cubits). 4 churning-stick. 5 wallet; pestle. 6 stalk/stem (of a tree). 7 staff of banner. 8 beam of a plough. 9 staff/sceptre (as a symbol of power of sovereignty). 10 control; restraint. 11 embodied power; army; column. 12 the rod as a symbol of judicial authority and punishment; punishment; fine; reprimand; penalty; chastisement; sentence. 13 loss: কে জানত, ব্যবসায়ে এত ~ দিতে হবে? 14 a ramrod. 15 maulstick. 16 anything resembling a rod. ~**ক** *n* 1 handle (of a parasol). 2 staff of a banner. 3 beam of a plough. ~**কর্তা** *n* punisher; judge; governor. ~**কর্ত্রী** *fem*. ~**গ্রহণ** *n* 1 acceptance of/submission to punishment. 2 becoming an ascetic. ~ **গ্রহণ করা** *v* 1 accept punishment; submit to punishment; kiss the rod. 2 become an ascetic; renounce the world. ~**চুম্বক** *n* bar magnet. ~**দাতা** *n* inflicter of punishment; punisher; judge; avenger. ~**দাত্রী** *fem*. ~**দান** *n* infliction of punishment; award of a sentence of punishment. ~**দান করা,** ~ **দেওয়া** *vi, vt* punish; sentence to punishment; award a sentence of punishment; fine. ~**ধর** *adj* armed with/bearing a staff; staff-bearings; sceptred. ❑*n* 1 punisher; king; judge; ruler; governor. 2 name of Yama, the god of death and punisher of sinners. ~**ধার,** ~**ধারী** *adj* =~ধর. ~**ন** *n* beating; chastising; punishing; (infliction of) punishment. ~**নায়ক** *n* 1 judge; punisher; king. 2 commander of an army. ~**নীতি** *n* administration of justice; judicature; penal system. ~**নীয়** *adj* to be punished; punishable. ~**নীয়া** *fem*. ~**পাণি** *n* policeman; judge; punisher. ~**পাল,** ~**পালক** *nn* 1 gatekeeper; porter. 2 superintendent of judicature. ~**প্রণাম** *n* prostration of the body at full length (like a stick). ~**প্রণালী** *n* criminal procedure. ~**প্রণেতা** *n* judge; punisher. ~**প্রদান**=~দান. ~**বৎ** *adj* 1 like a stick. 2 (with prostrating the body) in a straight line. ❑*n* lying prostrate in worship/respect. ~**বৎ করা** *vi* prostrate oneself in worship/respect (to/before). ~**বৎ হওয়া** *vi* lie prostrate in worship/rest. **খুরে খুরে** ~**বৎ** (iron) bow down to your/his/her hoofs (calling the person a beast and get rid of him/her). ~**বিধাতা** =~ দাতা. ~**বিধাত্রী** *fem*. ~**বিধান** *n* award/ determination of punishment; penal code. ~**বিধি** *n* penal code; criminal/penal law or code or procedure. ~**ব্যূহ** *n* arraying army in columns. ~**মুখ** *n* leader of a column; captain; general. ~**মুণ্ড** *n* all sorts of punishment (ranging from the most lenient ones to capital punishment). ~**মুণ্ডের কর্তা** *n* one who has the absolute power of punishing; king; judge. ~**মূলক** *adj* penal. ~**যোগ্য** *adj* punishable. ~**স্বরূপ** *adv* by way of punishment; as a penalty. **দণ্ডা** *vi* 1 beat; strike with a rod. 2 punish; inflict punishment. **দণ্ডাঘাত** *n* blow with a stick; beating up with a rod. **দণ্ডাদণ্ডি** *n* fighting with sticks/staffs; serious quarrel. **দণ্ডাধিকরণ** *n* criminal court. **দণ্ডাধীন** *adj* 1 subject to punishment; liable to be punished. 2 sentenced to punishment. 3 subject to government/rule. **দণ্ডার্হ** *adj* penal. **দণ্ডার্হ** *adj* deserving punishment; punishable. **দণ্ডাহত** *adj* struck with stick.

দণ্ড[2] *n* a measure of time (=24 minutes). ~**ঢক্কা** *n* a drum or gong on which the hours are struck. **এক দণ্ডে** *adv* in a trice/moment/jiffy; in a short time. **দণ্ডে দণ্ডে** *adv* every now and then; frequently; oftentimes; at every moment; repeatedly; incessantly.

দণ্ডকারণ্য *n* the Dandaka forest in the Deccan India.

দণ্ডায়মান *adj* standing (up); in the standing posture. ~ **হওয়া** *vi* stand up.

দণ্ডি *n* sacred thread of the Hindus measuring four cubits in length.

দণ্ডিক *adj* carrying a stick.

দণ্ডিত *adj* sentenced to a punishment; penalized; subjected to financial loss/fine. **2** punished.

দণ্ডী *adj* carrying/armed with a stick/staff; sceptered. ❑*n* **1** king; judge. **2** door-keeper; policeman. **3** Yama, the god of death and punishment. **4** a Brahmin at the 4th stage of his life.

দণ্ড্য *adj* punishable.

দত্ত *adj* **1** given. **2** granted; awarded; conferred; bestowed. **3** presented; extended. **4** placed. **5** paid. **দত্তা** *fem.* ❑*n* given away in marriage; betrothed. ~**ক (পুত্র)** *n* adopted son. ~**হারী, দত্তাপহারক, দত্তাপহারী** *adjj* (committing the offence of) taking back what has been given away by oneself. **দত্তাপহরণ** *n* (offence of) taking back what has been given by oneself. **দত্তাপহৃত** *adj* given and taken back again **দত্তাবধান** *adj* attentive.

দদ্রু *n* ringworm. ~**ঘ্ন**, ~**নাশন** *adjj, nn* curative (medicine) of ringworm.

দধি *n*=দই. ~**জ** *n* fresh butter. ~**ভাণ্ড** *n* vessel for holding yoghurt. ~**মঙ্গল** *n* ritual of feeding a Hindu bride in the small hours peivious to the wedding day. ~**মণ্ড** *n* whey. ~**মন্থ** *n* beverage obtained by churning yoghurt; buttermilk. ~**মন্থন** *n* churning yoghurt into buttermilk. ~**সার** *n* butter.

দধীচি *n* (myth) name of a saint who devoted himself to death that Indra might slay the demon Vritra with the thunderbolt fabricated out of bones; Dadhici.

দধ্যম্ল *n* rennet.

দনা *n* kind of tree; *Artemisia indica.*

দনু *n* (myth) name of a daughter of Dhaksha (দক্ষ). ~**জ** *n* son/descendant of Danu; a demon. ~**জা** *fem.* ~**জদলনী** *n fem* destroyer of demons; Durga.

দন্ত *n* **1** tooth. **2** tusk; ivory: হস্তী~. **3** fang: সর্প~. **4** pin used in playing a lute. **5** point of an arrow. ~**কাষ্ঠ** *n* small piece of wood used for cleaning the teeth. ~**কিড়(ড়ি)মিড়ি** *n* gnashing the teeth. ~**ঘর্ষ** *n* chattering of the teeth. **দন্তাঘাত** n bite. ~**চিকিৎসক** *n* dentist. ~**চিকিৎসা** *n* dentistry. ~**ধাব(ন)** *n* cleaning the teeth. ~**ধাবনী** *n* tooth brush; piece of wood for cleaning the teeth. ~**পঙ্‌ক্তি**, ~**পাটি**, ~**পাতি** *n* row of teeth. ~**পাবন**, ~**প্রক্ষালন**=~ধাবন. ~**পেশি** *n* gums. ~**বল্ক** *n* enamel of the teeth. ~**বিকাশ** *n* showing the teeth; (derog) smile; simper. ~**বিকাশ করা** *vi* (derog, facet) smile; simper; show the teeth; bare one's teeth. ~**বীজ** *n* pomegranate. ~**বেষ্ট(ক)** *n* gums. ~**ভঙ্গ** *n* fracture of the teeth. ~**মঞ্জন** *n* **1** cleaning/brushing the teeth. **2** tooth-powder; toothpaste; dentifrice. ~**মল** *n* impurity/tartar of the teeth. ~**মাংস** *n* gums. ~**মার্জন**=~মঞ্জন (2). ~**মূল** *n* root of the tooth. ~**মূলীয়** *adj* belonging to the root of the tooth; (phon) alveolar. ~**রুচি** *n* brilliance/brightness of the teeth. ~**রোগ** *n* dental disease. ~**শর্করা** *n* tartar of the teeth. ~**শুদ্ধি**=~ধাবন. ~**শূল** *n* tooth-ache; odontalgia. ~**শোধন**=~ধাবন. ~**সংঘর্ষ** *n* gnashing the teeth. ~**স্ফুট** *n* **1** piercing with teeth; biting. **2** (fig) comprehension; grasp. ~**স্ফুট করা** *vt* **1** bite. **2** comprehend; penetrate; fathom. ~**স্ফুট করতে না পারা** make nothing of; not make head or tail of; be beyond one; be baffled/puzzled. ~**হীন** *adj* toothless; edentate. ~**হীন প্রাণী** *n* an edentate. ~**হীন প্রাণীবর্গ** *n* the Edentata. **দন্তাগ্র** top/point of a tooth. **দন্তাঘাত** *n* bite. **দন্তাদন্তি** *n* fighting with the teeth. **দন্তাবল** *n* elephant. **দন্তায়ুধ** *adj* tusked. ❑*n* boar; hog. **দন্তাল** *adj* having large teeth/tusks.

দন্তক *n* **1** projection in a rock. **2** a pin projecting from the wall; hook.

দন্তালিকা *n* horse's bridle.

দন্তী *adj* toothed; tusked; rodent. ❑*n* elephant.

দন্তুর *adj* toothed; tusked; dentate; having large/dreadful teeth. ~ **প্রাণী** *n* rodent. ~ **প্রাণীবর্গ** *n* the Rodentia.

দন্তোদ্‌গম, দন্তোদ্‌ভেদ *n* appearance of the teeth; dentition; teething. ~ **হওয়া** *v* **1** teethe; cut a tooth. **2** (of teeth) push out through the gum.

দন্তৌষ্ঠ্য *adj* (phon) labio-dental. ~ **ধ্বনি** *n* labio-dental sound.

দন্ত্য *adj* (phon) dental.

দপ expressing a sudden blaze/flare/burst. ~ **করে জ্বলে ওঠা** *vi* flare; blaze up; burst into flames. ~ **করে নিবে যাওয়া** *vi* go suddenly. ~ **দপ** expressing (a) blazing up tremulously; (b) palpitation; throbbing; smarting, burning. ~ **করা** *vi* **1** blaze. **2** throb; smart. **দপদপা**=দবদবা. ~**দপানি** *n* palpitation; blazing; throbbing. ~**দপানো** *vi*=~দপ করা.

দপাদপ *n* (onom) expressing; repeated kicking. ~ **লাথি মারা** keep on/begin kicking violently.

দপ্তর=দপ্তর

দফ [A] *n* tambourine.

দফতর, দপ্তর [P] *n* **1** office; secretariat; department; **2** official papers; register; roll; record; file; large volume; account-book. **3** portfolio; charge: খাদ্যমন্ত্রীর ~; record-room. **~হীন** *adj* without portfolio.

দফতরি, দপ্তরি *n* **1** office keeper; one who has charge of office stationery, etc; office-boy. **2** book binder. ❑*adj* official.

দফা[1] [A] *n* **1** time; moment; turn. **2** section; article; clause; paragraph; division; item; class. **3** instalment. **~ওয়ারি** *adj, adv* item by item; itemwise; by instalments; section by section. **~য় ~য়** *adv* by instalments; again and again; frequently.

দফা[2] [A] *n* repulsion; prevention; avoiding; remedy; cure; warding off. **~ করা** *vt* repel; ward off; prevent; dispel; avert; ward off; settle; deal with. **~রফা** *n* end; ruin; undoing; destruction. **~ রফা/নিকেশ/শেষ করা** *vt* finish off; ruin; undo; deal a deadly blow; make an end of (sth); dispose of. **~দার** *n* **1** an officer commanding a small body of cavalry. **2** chief of village guards.

দফে=দফা[1]

দবকানো *vi* **1** press down; suppress; squeeze; suppress; keep under; crush; subdue; curb. **2** awe; intimidate.

দবদব=দপদপ (⇒ দপ)

দবদবা [P] *n* splendour; majesty; power; pomp and show; state; parade .

দবা [A] *n* medicine; remedy; cure.

দবজ [P] *adj* thick; coated; strong.

দম[1] *n* (onom) expressing a thudding/thumping sound; thump; thud; bang; report of a gun. **~ করে** *adv* with a thump/ bang/ thud. **দমাদম** *adv* thumping/ banging repeatedly.

দম[2] [P] *n* **1** breath; breathing: ~ বন্ধ হওয়া. **2** vitality; life; energy; spirit: তার আর ~ নেই, একেবারে হাঁপিয়ে পড়েছে. **3** moment; instant: এক দমে পৌঁছা. **4** long pull (at); whiff: গাঁজার কল্কিতে ~ দেওয়া. **5** breath of life: ~ বের হয়ে যাওয়া. **6** deceit; tick; bluff; fib; hoax; wheedling: তার কথা বিশ্বাস কোরো না, ওসব তার ~. **7** winding a machine: ঘড়িতে ~ দেওয়া. **8** spring: ঘড়ির ~, দমের গদি. **9** mild heat: খাবার দমে রাখা. **10** a kind of highly seasoned curry: বাঁধাকপির ~. **11** edge (of a sword); point (of a spear). **12** puff of steam; steam-power. **~ আটকানো** *vi, vt* **1** gasp; be choked/suffocated; catch one's breath; be confused. **2** suffocate; choke. **~ খিঁচানো** *vi* remain breathless; hold one's breath; suspend breath; remain silent. **~ ছাড়া** *vi* get one's breath again/back; (be able to) breathe again; exhale; heave a sigh of relief; take/have a breath. **~ ছাড়ার অবকাশ** *n* breather; breathing-space; breathing-time. **~ টানা** *vi* draw breath; puff (at/on sth); puff away at/on; take a long pull at. **~ দেওয়া** *vt, vi* **1** wind (a watch). **2** deceive; coax; wheedle; inveigle; bamboozle. **3** take/have a spell at smoking: গাঁজায় ~ দেওয়া. **~ নেওয়া** *vi* rest oneself; take breath; have a breather/respite. **~ ফাটা** *vi* suffocate; choke. **~ ফুরানো** *vi* **1** be breathless; be dying; die; be at one's last gasp; be cut of breath. **2** (of clocks, etc) require fresh winding. **~ ফেলা** *vi* pant; gasp; breathe short; be exhausted. **~ বন্ধ করা** *vi* catch/ hold one's breath. **~ বন্ধ করানো** *vt* suffocate; choke; cause to catch one's breath. **~ বন্ধ করে মারা** *vt* suffocate; strangulate; stifle; smothered; strangle; choke the life out of sb. **~ বন্ধ করা** *adj* suffocating; stifling. **~ বন্ধ হওয়া** *vi* be choked/ suffocated; suffocate; stifle. **~ বের করা** *vt* suffocate; smother; choke the life out of sb. **~ রাখা** *vi* hold one's breath. **~ লাগানো** = ~ দেওয়া. **~ সাধা** *vi* hold one's breath (like yogis). **~বাজ** *adj* **1** artful; treacherous; bragging; boastful; pompous; inflated; swollen. ❑*n* **1** deceiver; wheedler. **2** gasbag; windbag; brag; braggart; bluffer; fibber. **~বাজি** *n* bragging; bombast; tall talk; hoaxing; fib. **~বেদম** *adv* every moment; continually; constantly; breath by breath . **একদমে** *adv* **1** instantly; forthwith; at a gallop; immediately. **2** in the same breath. **পুরাদমে** *adv* in full swing; at full speed; headlong.

দম[3] [P] *n* tail; end.

দম[4] *n* control; continence; self-command; self-control; self-restrainted.

দমক[1] *adj* taming; restraining; subduing. ❑*n* tamer one who restrains/subdues.

দমক[2] *n* sudden blast/burst; flash; gust; spell: বাতাসের ~.

দমকল *n* **1** fire-engine; fire-brigade. **2** water-pump. **~ বাহিনী** *n* fire-brigade.

দমকা *adj* **1** gusty: ~ হাওয়া. **২** unforeseen; unexpected: ~ খরচ. ❑*n* gusty wind; fitful; gusts of wind.

দমদম *n* (onom) **1** repeated thud/thump bang. **2** boom (of the guns).

দমদমা [P]*n* **1** mound. **2** raised battery; entrenchment. **3** raised mound of earth or target practice.

দমন *n* **1** taming; subduing; overpowering; quelling: বিদ্রোহ ~. **2** suppression; coercion. **3** restraint; repression: ইন্দ্রিয় ~. **4** punishing; check. **5** removal; abatement: রোগ ~. **~ করা** *vt* tame; subdue; quell; restrain; repress; supress; bring under control; punish; overpower; check; remove; abate. **~নীতি** *n* policy of repression/coercion.

দমনীয়, দম্য *adj* to be restrained; tamable; restrainable; suppressible; repressible; mitigable; removable; controllable.

দময়িতা *adj* one who subdues/ controls/ restrains/ represses/ suppresses/ tames/ removes/ checks/ coerces; ruler; tamer. **দময়িত্রী** *fem.*

দমসম *n* suffocation caused by overeating.

দমা *vi* **1** be tamed/ subdued/ restrained; be submissive; be repressed/ chastened/ suppressed/ disciplined/ broken in. **2** become dejected/ downcast/ depressed/ disheartened/ low-spirited/ down-hearted/ gloomy: যুবক ছেলেটার মৃত্যুতে সে বড়ো দমে গেছে. **3** (of land, etc) sink; sub-side; fall slowly, downwards: জল বসে দেয়াল দমে গেছে. **4** (of diseases, etc) be mitigated; abate; subside; be mitigated. **~নো** *vt* **1** tame; subdue; restrain; chasten; repress; bring under control; suppress; subjugate; break in; discipline. **2** depress; cast down; dishearten; dampen; dispirit. **3** mitigate; abate; allay; alleviate; remove. ❑*adj* depressed; dejected; sunk.

দমিত *adj* **1** tamed; subdued; restrained; repressed; disciplined; broken in; subjugated; chastened. **2** depressed; dejected; downcast; discouraged; mitigated; alleviated; brought under control; abated; allayed. **4** subsided; depressed; sunk.

দমী *adj* **1** = দময়িতা. **2** self-controlled; having subjugated one's senses.

দমের গাড়ি *n* (colloq) motor car.

দম্পতি *n* **1** husband and wife; couple. **2** a couple of male and female creatures.

দম্বল *n* rennet.

দম্ভ *n* arrogance; vaunt; tall talk; boast(ing); conceit; pride; brag. **~ করা** *vi* boast; vaunt; talk tall/big; brag; blow one's own trumpet; give oneself airs; swank.

দম্ভী *adj* boastful; bragging; swaggering; arrogant; conceited; vainglorious; braggart; haughty; proud; pompous. ❑*n* brag; braggart; boaster.

দম্ভোক্তি *n* boastful talk; brag.

দয়া *n* **1** compassion; pity(for); sympathy; kindliness; kindness; sympathy; mercy; tender-heartedness; commiseration; leniency. **2** benignancy; favour; grace; generosity; good nature; benevolence. **~ করা** *vi* be kind to; have mercy on; have/take pity on; have mercy on; treat mercifully; relent; be merciful; be gracious towards; be good to. **~ করে** *adv* kindly. **~দাক্ষিণ্য** *n* kindness and generosity. **~ধর্ম** *n* kindness and virtue; compassionate nature. **~নিধি** *n* treasure of mercy; a very compassionate person. **~ন্বিত, ~পরবশ, ~পরতন্ত্র** *adjj* full of pity; compassionate; merciful; kind-hearted. **~বান, ~ময়** *adjj* pitiful; taking pity on; compassionate; tender-hearted; merciful; benevolent; gracious. **~বতী, ~ময়ী** *fem.* **~বীর** *n* a hero in compassion; very merciful man. **~মায়া** *n* compassion and affection; kindness and love; kindheartedness. **~র পাত্র** *n* object of pity; miserable/ despicable man. **~র সাগর** *n* ocean of kindness/ compassion; extremely kind/ compassionate man. **~র্দ্র** *adj* melted/ softened with kindness/ mercy/ compassion. **~র্দ্রা** *fem.* **~র্দ্রচিত্ত** *adj* kind-hearted; having one's heart softened with compassion/kindness. **~র্দ্রচিত্তা** *fem.* **~ল, ~লু** = **~**বান. **~শীল** *adj* kind/ compassionate/gracious/bountiful by nature; kind-hearted; tender-hearted. **~শীলা** *fem.* **~শূন্য, ~হীন** *adjj* unkind; merciless; pitiless; uncompassionate; uncharitable; unsensitive; unfeeling. **~শূন্যা, ~হীনা** *fem.* **~ হওয়া** *vi* feel pity/compassion for; have mercy on; commiserate.

দয়িত *adj* cherished; beloved; dear. ❑*n* lover; husband. **দয়িতা** *n* wife; beloved woman; lady-love.

দয়েল = দোয়েল

দর[১] *n* **1** price; rate; value; worth; quotation; price quoted. **2** (fig) quality; status; dignity: উঁচু দরের লোকসাহিত্য. **3** esteem. **~ করা** *vi* bargain; discuss prices; negotiate; haggle. **~ দেওয়া** *vi* quote (a price). **~ কষাকষি** *n* bargaining; haggling. **~ কষাকষি করা** *vi* haggle; bargain. **~দস্তুর** *n* bargain; terms and prices in transactive business. **~দাম** *n* rate and price. **~পত্র** *n* tender; quotation. **দরে বনা** *vi* agree about terms.

দর[২] *n* **1** hole (in the ground); pet; cave; crevice (of a mountain). **2** quake; shake; terror; fear. **3** stream. **4** exudation. ❑ *adv* a little; slightly. **~বিগলিত** *adj* slightly streaming; (modern) flowing (freely in a stream). **~বিগলিত ধারায়/ধারে** *adv* slightly streaming; flowing freely. **~বিগলিত ধারায়/ধারে কাঁদা** weep profusely; shed/weep bitter tears.

দর-ইজারা [P] *n* sub-lease; under-lease; subleased holding. **~দার** *n* sub-lessee; under-lessee.

দরওয়াজা [P] = দরজা (1)

দরওয়ান = দারোয়ান

দরকচা, দরকাঁচা *adj* **1** partly ripe; not mellow. **2** (of vegetables, meat, etc) not to be easily boiled. **3** (of skin) callous. ❑*n* **1** unripe part (of a fruit); unboiled part of vegetables, meat, etc: ~টা বাদ দিয়ে যাও. **2** callus. **~ পড়া/মারা** *vi* be calloused.

দর-কষাকষি ⇒ দর[১]

দরকার *adj* [P] necessary; needful. ❑*n* necessity; need; requirement; use: তোমার ~ কতো? How much do you need? তোমার ~ কী? What do you want ? What is your business? তাতে তোমার কী ~ ? That is none of your business/is no business of yours ? How does it concern you? তাকে তোমার কী ~ ? What do you want him for? Why do you want him? তোমার ~ নেই, It is none of your business/ concern? **~মতো** *adv* according to necessity; as and when necessary; if need be/necessary.

দরকারি *adj* [P] necessary; useful; important.

দরখাস্ত [P] *n* application; request; petition; appeal; entreaty; proposal. **~ করা** *vi* apply (for); put in/submit an application/a petition; entreat; request. **~কারী** *adj* applying; petitioning. ❑*n* applicant; petitioner. **~কারিণী** *fem*.

দরগুজ(া)র [P] *n* pardon; forgiveness; disregard. **~ করা** *vt* pardon; forgive; pass over; overlook; neglect.

দরজা [A] *n* **1** (in Bengali) = door; gate; entrance, doorway. **~ দেওয়া** *vi* shut/ close the door. 2 (original meaning) grade; class; degree; rank; step; gradation; dignity.

দরজি [P] *n* tailor, seamster; outfitter. **মেয়ে ~** *n fem* sempstress; seamstress.

দরদ[১] *n* bank. **2** mountain. **3** precipice. **4** an ancient Indian race. ❑*adj* dreadful; frightful.

দরদ[২] [P] *n* **1** pain; ache; affliction. **2** sympathy; affection; compassion; attachment. **~ করা** *vi* feel the pain/ compassion; ache; pain. **~ লাগা** *vi* feel sympathy (for); be deeply affected. **~ হওয়া** *vi* pain; ache. **~মন্দ** *adj* compassionate; sympathetic; pitiful. **~মন্দি** *n* compassion; sympathy; affliction.

দরদর *n* (onom) expressing continuous and rapid flow/oozing. **~ করে** *adj* flowing freely; streaming.

দরদস্তুর , দরদাম *nn* ⇒ দর[১]

দরদালান *n* corridor; large verandah.

দরদি, দরদী *adj* **1** sympathetic; compassionate; full of affection/attachment; affectionate; understanding. **2** (of criticism) appreciative. ❑*n* sympathizer; intimate; well-wisher; soul mate.

দরপত্তন *n* sub-lease; under-lease. **~ দেওয়া** *vt* sub-lease; under-lease. **দরপত্তনি** *n* sub-leased/underleased holding. **দরপত্তনিদার** *n* sub-lessee; under-lessee.

দরপরদা *adv* [P] behind the curtains.

দরপেশ [P] *adj* submitted to the court; under trial; subjudice.

দরবার [P] *n* **1** court; hall of royal audience; audience-chamber. **2** holding of a court; durbar; levee. **3** seeking; solicitation: plead: দাবি আদায়ের জন্যে ~ করা. **~ করা** *vi* **1** hold a court/levee. **2** seek; solicit; canvass; plead for. **~ বসা** *vi* (of the court) sit. **~ ভাঙা** *vi* (of the court) rise. **দরবারে বসা** *vi* sit at court.

দরবারি *adj* [P] **1** courtly. **2** elegant; elegant and polished: ~ ভাষা. **3** of the court; frequenting a royal court: ~ লোক. **4** befitting a court; according to the regulations and customs of a court: ~ রীতিনীতি. **~ কানাড়া** *n* an Indian musical mode. **~ চালচলন** *n* court-manners. **~ পোশাক** *n* court-dress. **~ ব্যাপার** *n* court-affair. **~ ভাষা** *n* court-language. **~ রীতিনীতি** *n* court-regulations; protocol. **~ লোক** *n* courtier; court gentleman; people at court.

দরবিগলিত ⇒ দর[২]

দরবেশ [P] *n* dervish; beggar; mendicant.

দরবেশি *adj* dervish-like. ❑*n* doctrine/office of a dervish; poverty; mendicancy.

দরমা *n* mat (made of bamboo slips, etc and used in walling up buildings, etc)

দরশ(ন) *n* (poet) = দর্শন

দরহাম [P] *n* kind of silver coin.

দরাজ *adj* [P] **1** long; tall. **2** extended; stretched out. **3** liberal; generous: ~ হাত/দিল. **4** unrestrained: ~ মুখ. **~ গলা** *n* loud/ resonant/ sonorous/ deep/full voice; stentorian voice. **~দস্ত** *adj* open-handed giving freely; generous; liberal. **~দিল** *adj* large-hearted; open handed; magnanimous. **~ মুখ** *n* outspokenness; outspoken/ straightforward words/ talk; straight forwardness; plain talk; blunt talk. **~ হাত** = ~দস্ত.

দরাদরি = দর-কাষাকষি (⇒ দর[১])

দরানি *n* oozing; exudation.

দরানো *vt* **1** dissolve. **2** melt; soften; move (to) pity.

দরি *n* cave; gorge; ravine; glen.

দরিদ্র *adj* **1** poor; needy; wretched; impecunious; penurious; indigent. **2** lacking; deprived/destitute of; deficient in. **দরিদ্রা** *fem*. **~তা** *n* poverty; penury; indigence; lack; poorness; deficiency; wretchedness; impoverishment; adversity; pauperism. **~নারায়ণ** *n* the poor (conceived as God personified); poor people. **~নিবাস** *n* poorhouse; workhouse. **দরিদ্রিত** *adj* impoverished; reduced to poverty.

দরিয়া [P]*n* **1** sea; ocean. **2** large river. **3** waters. **মাঝ ~য় তরী ডোবা** (fig) be completely ruined.

দরী[১] = দরি

দরী[২] *n* durrie; small carpet.

দরুদ [A] *n* benediction; blessing; salutation (esp of Prophet Muhammad (sm)).

দরুন *prep* [P] for; because of; on account of; due to; owing to; for the sake of.

দরুদ = দরুদ

দরেগ, দেরেগ [P]*nn* sigh; sorrow; grief; regret.

দরোজা = দরজা

দরোয়ান *n* **1** door-keeper; gate-keeper; gateman; porter; doorman. **2** janitor.

দরোয়ানের ঘর *n* porter's lodge. **দারোয়ানি** *n* duty/post of a gatekeeper/doorman.

দর্গা = দরগা

দর্জা = দরজা

দর্জি = দরজি

দর্দুর *n* frog.

দর্প *n* pride; arrogance; haughtiness; insolence; conceit; vanity; vaunt; boast. ~ **করা** *vi* boast; vaunt; be arrogant/ extravagant/ proud/wild; take pride in. ~ **চূর্ণ করা/ভাঙা** *vi* destroy/humble sb's pride; humiliate. **দর্পাধ্মাত** *adj* puffed up with pride. ~**নাশ** *n* ruin/ destruction of pride. ~**হর,** ~**হারী** *adjj* humbling/ destroying pride or vanity.

দর্পণ *n* mirror; looking-glass.

দর্পিত, দর্পী *adjj* proud; arrogant; haughty; insolent; overbearing; puffed up; vainglorious; conceited. **দর্পিণী** *fem.*

দর্বি, দর্বী *nn* ladle. **দর্বিকা** *n* small ladle; spoon.

দর্ভ *n* a tuft of/bunch of grass (esp *kush* grass). ~**ময়** *adj* made of grass. **দর্ভাসন** *n* grass mat for sitting upon.

দর্শক *adj* **1** seeing; looking at/for. **2** showing; pointing out. ❑*n* **1** spectator; onlooker; observer. **2** member of an audience. **3** guide; demonstrator; displayer.

দর্শন *n* **1** view; philosophical system; philosophy; doctrine. **2** seeing; observing; looking; noticing; observation; viewing. **3** perception. **4** ocular perception. **5** eye-sight. **6** inspection; examination. **7** visiting; meeting interview; audience: তীর্থ~, রাজ~. **8** discernment; understanding; intellect. **9** appearance (before the judge). **10** vision; dream: অতীন্দ্রিয় ~. **11** eye. **12** becoming visible presence. **13** knowledge; experience: ভুয়ো~. ~ **করা** *vt* **1** see; look at; regard; behold; consider. **2** see, ie wait on; visit: তীর্থ~ করা. **3** see with the mind; understand; learn. **4** notice; observe; look into; try; examine. **5** see by divine intuition; think; find out. **6** meet; interview; drop in; pay a visit. **7** experience; perceive. ~ **দেওয়া** *vi* **1** put in an appearance; come into view; come in sight; appear; turn up; show up; make an entrance. **2** grant an interview; give an audience; meet. ~ **পাওয়া** *vt* able to meet/see; be granted an audience; catch sight of; clap eyes on. ~**ক্ষম** *adj* capable of seeing. ~**গোচর** *n* range of sight. ~**ডালি,** ~**দারি,** ~**দারী,** ~**ভারি,** ~**ভারী** *n* consideration of outward show/beauty. ❑*adj* good-looking. ~**প্রতিভূ** *n* bail for appearance. ~**শাস্ত্র** *n* philosophy. **দর্শনার্থ** *adj* intending to see sb; to visit. **দর্শনার্থী** *adj* come to visit. ❑*n*, visitor; caller. **প্রথম দর্শনে** at first sight.

দর্শনী *n* **1** fee/contribution paid on visiting a shrine, etc. **2** physician's fee. **3** entrance fee (for exhibition, etc). ~ **হুণ্ডি** *n* (commerce) bill at sight.

দর্শনীয় *adj* **1** visible; conspicuous. **2** worth seeing; good-looking; beautiful.

দর্শনেচ্ছু, দর্শনেপ্সু *adjj* desirous of visiting/beholding.

দর্শনেন্দ্রিয় *n* sense of sight; eye; visual organ.

দর্শয়িতা *adj* showing; exhibiting. ❑*n* shower; guide; exhibitor; displayer. **দর্শয়িত্রী** *fem.*

দর্শা *vt* show (result, etc); be seen/visible: সুফল দর্শে. ~**নো** *vi* show; cause; exhibit: কারণ ~নো.

দর্শিত *adj* shown; displayed; exposed to view; exhibited.

-দর্শী *adj* (used as a *suff)* **1** seeing; looking at; observing; finding; exhibiting. **2** understanding; knowing; experiencing perceiving. **3** conversant with; versed in: তত্ত্ব~.

দল[1] *n* **1** petal; leaf; small shoot; blade: ফুল~, তৃণ~. **2** piece torn off or split off; fragment: মেঘ~. **3** party; group; company; body; band; team; gang. **4** flock; swarm; herd: ভেড়ার ~. **5** side; party: মোকদ্দমার দুই ~. **6** (derog) evil company: দলে ভিড়ে বখে যাওয়া. **7** faction; clique: ~ পাকানো. **8** union: ~ বাধা. ~ **ছাড়া** *vi* **1** leave/quit/desert one's party. **2** give up evil company. ~ **পাকানো/বাঁধা** *vi* unite into a body; team up; band together; gang up; form a faction/clique. ~ **বেঁধে** *adv* in a body. ~ **ভাঙা** *vi* **1** disrupt/disintegrate/breakup a party; disperse. **2** demobilize a troop. ~ **ভেঙে বের হয়ে আসা** break away from a party; defect; cross the floor. ~**কচু** *n* kind of edible arum. ~**কমল** *n* lotus. ~**চ্যুত** *adj* separated/expelled from one's party/flock. ~**চ্যুতি** *n* separation/ expulsion from one's party/flock. ~**ছুট** *adj* separated from one's party; breakaway. ❑*n* oddity; odd/queer fish; odd man/one out. ~**ছাড়** *adj* separated from the party/flock; solitary; queer; odd; singular; moving alone. ~**ত্যাগ** *n* act of leaving/deserting one's party/flock. ~ **ত্যাগ করা** *vi* leave/desert one's party/flock ~**ত্যাগী** *adj* leaving/deserting one's party or flock. ~**ত্যাগী ব্যক্তি** *n* one who has left his party; defector; deserter of one's party renegade; apostate; turncoat. ~**পতি** *n* leader; chief; headman; chieftain; ringleader gangster; bellwether. ~ **পরিবর্তন** *n* change of party/side; transfer from one club/team to another. ~বদ্ধ *adj* 1 united; united into a body; combined banded together; flocked/herded together. 2 gregarious: ~বদ্ধ জীবন. ~বদ্ধভাবে *adj* in a body; unitedly; in a block; en masse; gregariously. ~বদ্ধ হওয়া *vi* unite (in a group); band/league together; team up. ~বল *n* one's followers and forces. ~ভুক্ত *adj* included in/belonging to a party. ~ভ্রষ্ট = ~ছাড়া. ~মণ্ডল *n* (bot) corolla. ~লগ্ন *adj* (bot) epipetalous. ~হীন *adj* 1 unattached to any party; non-party; independent. 2 (bot) apetalous. দলাদলি *n* 1 partisanship; party-spirit; factionalism; grouping; formation of factions/ cliques. 2 dissension; dissidence. ~দলি করা *vi* 1 indulge in factionalism/ partisanship/ infighting. 2 form factions/ cliques. দলে দলে *adv* 1 in (different) groups/flocks; in large numbers: দলে দলে যোগ দিন. 2 between/amongst parties or factions: দলে দলে মারামারি. দলে ভারী enjoying a majority; large/greater in number; having a numerical superiority. দলে ভেড়া *vi* join a party/group; associate oneself with a body of like-minded people; join forces. দলে হালকা *n* small/ smaller in number; numerically inferior. খেলোয়াড়ের ~ *n* team (of players). দস্যু~ *n* band/gang of robbers. নর্তকের ~ *n* group/band of dancers; dance troupe. নাচের ~ *n* dancing party; dance troupe. নাবিক~ *n* party/band of sailors; crew. পশুর ~ *n* herd of beasts. পাখির ~ *n* flock of bird. বদমাসের ~*n* gang of ruffians. যাত্রার ~ *n* opera party. রাজনীতিক/ রাজনৈতিক~ *n* political party. সৈন্য~ *n* army of soldiers; troops.

দলন *n* 1 kneading; pressing; crushing; grinding. 2 trampling under foot; splitting; destruction; chastisement; repression; subdual. 3 breaking (of a heart); tormenting. ❑*n* one who chastises/represses/subdues; subduer: destroyer; spoiler. দলনী *adj fem.* ~ করা *vt* knead; press; crush; grind; mash; chastise; repress; destroy; subdue; break; torment; trample under foot; tread over. ~মলন =দলাই-মলাই.

দলনীয় *adj* to be crushed/trampled under foot/ subdued/ repressed/ destroyed.

দলা[১] *vt*=দলন করা (⇒ দলন). পায়ে ~ *vt* trample under foot; tread over. ~নো cause to trample under foot; cause to crush.

দলা[২] *n* *n* handful; clamp; heap; clod: এক ~ মাটি.

দলাই-মলাই *n* 1 currying (a horse). 2 massaging (a human being). 3 (fig) strenuous and continuous effort. ~ করা *vt* 1 curry. 2 massage. 3 make strenuous and continuous effort.

দলাদলি *n* ⇒ দল

দলান=দালান

দলিজ=দহলিজ

দলিত *adj* 1 kneaded; pressed; ground; mashed. 2 crushed; trampled under foot; trodden; chastised; repressed; subdued; broken; tormented : ~ হৃদয়, tormented/broken heart.

দলিল *n* [A] 1 deed; document; evidential document; piece of evidence. 2 proof. ~ করা *vi* draw up/sign a deed/contract. ~ দেখানো *vi* adduce proofs. ~ পেশ করা *vi* bring forward. proof; submit documents. ~গ্রহীতা *n* recipient of the deed/document; lessee; buyer. ~-দস্তাবেজ *n* (collect) deeds and documents; papers. ~দাতা *n* seller; lessor. দলিলি প্রমাণ *n* documentary proof.

দলীয় *adj* relating/belonging to a party/ group/ community; (attirb) party: ~ কোন্দল, party infighting;

দলুয়া, দলো *nn* kind of reddish sugar made of dried molasses.

দশ *n* 1 ten. 2 public; people; দশের কাজ. 3 several persons united into a body. ❑*adj* 1 ten. 2 many; several: ~ কথা শোনানো. ~ই *n adj* (the) tenth (day of the month). ~ক *n* 1 number ten. 2 place of tens. 3 decade. ❑*adj* consisting of ten; having ten parts. ~কণ্ঠ *n* ten-necked; Ravana. ~কথা *n* many words; lot of talking; much scolding; many rude words; tongue-lashing; lecture; admonition; taking-to. ~ কথা শোনানো give sb a lecture; scold; give a tongue-lashing. ~কর্ম *n* ten sacraments of the Hindus. ~কর্মান্বিত *adj* taking the ten Hindu sacraments. ~কাহন *n* ten *kahans* (কাহন); much talking; many rude words; exaggeration ❑*adj* a great deal of; a lot of; a(steady) stream of: ~ কাহন কথা. ~কিয়া *n* table of numeration by multiple of ten. ~কোশী, ~কুশী *n* a measure of *kirtan* (কীর্তন). ~গুণ *adj, adv* tenfold; ten times. ~গুণিত *adj* multiplied by ten. ~ চক্র *n* plot/intrigue by ten/many persons. ~চক্রে ভগবান ভূত(⇒ চক্র). ~ জনের একজন *n* one of the ten; somebody; notable. ~তলক *n* decahedron. ~ দশা *n* the ten forms of devotion/charity according to Vaishnavas. ~দিক, ~দিশ *nn* the ten regions (including that overhead and underneath). ~ধা *adj* in ten parts; tenfold. ~পঁচিশ *n* an indoor game like dice played with *cowries* (কড়ি). ~প্রহরণধারিণী *adj fem* holding ten weapons. ❑*n* goddess Durga. ~বল *n* possessing ten powers; Buddha. ~বিধ *adj* of ten kinds/varieties; tenfold. ~ভুক্ত (~কোণী) ক্ষেত্র *n* decagon. ~ভুজা *adj fem* ten-handed. ❑*n* goddess Durga. ~ম *adj* tenth. ~মহাবিদ্যা *n* 'one who possesses the ten great sciences'; Durga. ~মাংশ *n* tenth (part). ~মাবতার *n* Kalki, the tenth and the last incarnation of Vishnu. ~মিক *adj* decimal. ❑*n* decimal fraction. ~মিক পদ্ধতি *n* decimal system. ~মিক-মুদ্রা প্রথা decimal system of coinage. ~মিক-মুদ্রা প্রথা চালু করা/হওয়া go decimal. ~মী *n* the tenth day of the lunar fortnight. ~মী দশা *n* last stage of life. ~মূল *n* a tonic medicine prepared from ten roots. ~ শত *n, adj* ten thousand. ~সনা, ~সমা *adjj* ten years old. ~ সহস্র *n*, *adj* ten thousand; myriad. ~সালা *adj* decennial. ~সালা বন্দোবস্ত (hist) the decennial settlement (of land). ~স্কন্ধ=~কণ্ঠ. ~হরা *n fem* **1** Hindu goddess who take away the ten sins; Ganga. **2** the last day festival of Durga Puja. ~হাত *n* ten cubits; fifteen feet. ❑*adj* **1** measuring ten cubits. **2** (fig) very much expanded/puffed up: বুক ফুলে ~হাত. ~হাতি *adj* measuring ten cubits; (of a sari) having the standard length (of ten cubits). দশাংশ=~মাংশ. দশাক্ষর *adj* containing ten syllables; decasyllabic. দশানন *adj, n* ten-headed (being); Ravana. দশাবতার *n* ten incarnations of Vishnu. দশাশ্ব *adj, n* having ten horses; the moon. দশাহ *n* (ceremony lasting) ten days.

দশন *n* **1** tooth. **2** bite. ~চ্ছদ *n* lips. ~পঙ্ক্তি *n* set/row of teeth.

দশা[1] *n* **1** fringe of a garment; loose ends of any piece of cloth; skirt; hem. **2** wick. **3** state/condition (of life). **4** period of life (youth, manhood, etc). **5** condition. circumstances; state: দুর্দশা. **6** fate of man as depending on the position of the planets: পোড়া ~. **7** aspect/position of the planets: শনির ~. **8** phase (of the moon). **9** disposition: মনের ~. **10** phase; stage: জীবনের শেষ ~. **11** one of the ten stages of human life (eg staying in the womb, birth, of infancy, etc). **12** one of the ten erotic states (eg desire, thought, memory, etc). **13** a Hindu obsequial rite observed on the tenth day of death. **14** (religious) ecstasy; trance; reverie: ~য় পড়া. **15** one of the ten forms of devotion according to Vaishnavas (eg audition, glorification, recollection, etc). ~ক্ষয় *n* end of the influence of a planet. ~র শেষ, শেষ~ *nn* last stage (of life); at death's door. ~য় পড়া **1** fall into a state. **2** get oneself into a state. **3** go into/be thrown into ecstasy; go/fall into a trance; fall into a reverie. ~ বিপর্যয় *n* reversal of fortune; set-back misfortune .

দশা[2] *n* a festival lasting ten days.

দশাসই *adj* hefty; gigantic; imposing; colossal; gargantuan: ~ চেহারা.

দশি, দশী *nn* thin strip/shred of cloth; tatting; fringe of a garment; wick.

দষ্ট *adj* **1** bitten; stung. **2** eaten: কীট~.

দস্ত [P] *n* hand. ~খত *n* signature. ~খত করা *vt* sign; endorse. ~খতি *adj* signed; endorsed; written with one's own hand. ~গির *n* one who holds the hand (of); helper; protector; saint. ~গিরি *n* assistance; support; patronage; bossing. ~দরাজ *n* oppressor; extortioner. ❑*adj* openhanded; generous. ~বদস্ত *adj* hand to hand. ~বরদার *adj* renouncing; abstaining. ~বরদারি *n* renunciation; withdrawal. ~বস্তু *adj, adv* with folded hands; humbly; respectfully. ~মুবারক *n* blessed/hold hands.

দস্তক [P] *n* summons; warrant (of arrest); commission.

দস্তর [P] *n* turban. ~খান *n* table cloth; piece of cloth spread on the ground on which meal dishes are placed.

দস্তা[1] *n* zinc. ~র চাদর *n* zinc sheet.

দস্তা[2] [P] *n* handle; pestle.

দস্তানা [P] *n* glove; gauntlet. ~পরা *adj* gloved.

দস্তাবেজ, দস্তাবিজ [P] *nn* bond; instrument; note of hand; title deed; document; deed; certificate.

দস্তার=দস্তর

দস্তুর [P] *n* **1** custom; usage; practice; convention. **2** fashion; manner; mode. **3** rule; regulation. ~মতো, ~মাফিক *adj* customary; conventional; in keeping with custom/convention; according to usage. ❑*adv* thoroughly; quite.

দস্তুরি [P] *n* perquisites; fees; commission (of a broker); discount; brokerage.

দস্যি *n* (affectionately) little rogue/imp/ villain/ rascal. ❑*adj* cheeky; impish; extremely naughty and dare-devil; mischievous. ~পনা *n* impishness; michievousness; cheekiness; roguery; naughtiness.

দস্যু *n* **1** robber; highwayman; bandit; brigand; dacoit; pirate. **2** (affectionately)=দস্যি. **3** (old) any outcast/Hindu who has become so by neglect of the essential rites. ~তা, ~বৃত্তি *nn* robbery; banditry; dacoity; plunder; rape. ~তা করা *vi,vt* commit robbery/hold-up; plunder; rob; pillage; hold up. ~দল *n* band/ gang of robbers/ highwayman/ gangsters. ~পনা *n* **1** =~তা. **2** dare-devilry. ~ভয় *n* fear of robbers. জল~ *n* pirate; buccaneer; corsair; filibuster; privateer.

দহ[1] *n* **1** deep water(s). **2** whirlpool; eddy. **3** lake. **4** abyss; deep pit. **5** (fig) terrible danger; deep water(s).

দহ[2] [P] *n* village.

দহন *n***1** burning; consuming by fire; scorching; **2** (phy) combustion. **3** inflammation. **4** fire. **5** anguish; affliction. **6** cremation. **7** cauterization. ❑*adj* burning; scorching; destroying; consuming; reducing to ashes;

tormenting; causing a conflagration. ~ **করা** *vt* **1** burn; consume (by fire); scorch; roast; inflame. **2** destroy completely; consume. **3** cauterize. **4** torment; torture; pain; distress; disturb; grieve. **5** cremate. ~ **ক্রিয়া** *n* combustion.

দহনীয় *adj* to be burnt; combustible; inflammable. ~**তা** *n* combustibility.

দহনোপল *n* sun-gem.

দহরম, দহরম-মহরম [P]*n* intimate friendship; intimacy; hob-nob; intimate association; familiarity. ~ **করা** *vi* cultivate (the friendship of); hob-nob; make free with; befriend; ingratiate oneself with.

দহলা *n* the ten of playing cards. ~ **নহলা করা** *vi* be in two minds; hesitate; vacillate; shilly-shally.

দহলিজ [P] *n* **1** portico; threshold. **2** drawing-room; parlour; lounge. **3** court.

দহা *vt, vi* **1**=দহন করা. **2** burn; be consumed by internal heat/grief; suffer pain; be distressed/vexed; be in flames; be brunt.

দহি=দই

দহিয়াল=দোয়েল

দহ্যমান *adj* burning; blazing; aflame; ablaze; flaming; being afflicted/tormented.

দা[1] *n* a heavy knife with a haft; chopper. ~**কাটা** *adj* (chiefly of tobacco) minced/chopped fine with a chopper. ~**কুমড়া সম্পর্ক** *n* relationship as between a chopper and a pumpkin; (fig) implacable antagonism; inveterate hatred; deadly enmity.

-দা[2] *n* (colloq)=দাদা

-দা[3] *adj fem*=-দ[3]

দাই *n*(popular)=ধাই

দাউ *n*(onom) expressing sudden burst of fire. ~ **দাউ** *n* expressing furious burning. ~ **করে জ্বলে ওঠা** *vi* flare up; burst into flames; blaze up. ~ **দাউ করে জ্বলা** *vi* blaze; burn fiercely; be in flames; flame.

দাও *n* (dial)=দা[1]

দাওয়া[1] *n* verandah; terrace; gallery.

দাওয়া[2] *n* [A] claim; demand; pretension; law-suit; accusation; dues; right: দাবি~. ~**দার** *n* plaintiff; claimant; pretender.

দাওয়া[3] *vt* harvest; reap. ~**নো** *vt* get harvested/reaped.

দাওয়া(ই)[8] *n* [A] medicine; remedy; cure. ~ **দেওয়া** *vi* give/administer medicine; treat a patient; (fig) take action for correction/to remedy a wrong. ~**খানা** *n* dispensary; apothecary's shop; pharmacy; drug-store.

দাওয়াত [A] **1** invitation; convocation. **2** feast; banquet; entertainment. ~ **করা/ দেওয়া** *vt* invite; send out invitations; give a feast. ~ **খাওয়া** *vi* have an invitation; feast (on sth); enjoy a feast; be invited to a party.

দাওয়াল, দাওয়ালে *nn* harvester; reaper.

দাঁ, দাঁও *nn* **1** opportunity; chance: ~ পাওয়া. **2** fluke; lucky stroke. ~ **মারা** *vi* score a hit; hit the jackpot; make a fat bargain; make good use of an opportunity.

দাঁড় *n* **1** oar (of a boat). **2** bar/rod for a bird to sit on; perch. **3** standing (position). ~ **করানো** *vt* **1** set erect/upright; cause to stand; make stand erect: পড়ে যাওয়া খুঁটিটা সে আবার ~ করালো. **2** establish (firmly); build up: ব্যবসাটা/ছেলেকে সে ভালোই ~ করিয়েছে. **3** keep waiting: তুমি আমাদের আর কতক্ষণ ~ করিয়ে রাখবে. **4** bring in; present: সাক্ষী ~ করানো. **5** halt: পুলিশ গাড়িটা ~ করালো. **6** make up: মামলাটা ~ করানো. **7** bring/reduce to: অবস্থাটা যা ~ করিয়েছে, তাতে . . . . ~ **টানা/বাওয়া** *vi* row; ply the oars. ~ **হওয়া** *vi* stand up; stand erect; upright. **দাঁড়ে বসা** *vi* perch; roost.

দাঁড়কাক *n* raven; jackdaw; rook.

দাঁড়া[1]**,দাড়া** *n* **1** backbone; spine. **2** pincer/claw (of crabs/lobsters, etc).

দাঁড়া[2] *n* custom; practice; usage; go; manner: উল্টা ~.

দাঁড়ানো *vi* **1** stand (up). **2** wait (for); await; stay: এক মিনিট দাঁড়াও. **3** linger; delay; tarry (archaic); stand still: সময় তো আর দাঁড়িয়ে থাকবে না. **4** stop; halt: গাড়িটা সামনের স্টেশনে দাঁড়াবে. **5** settle: এক স্থানে মন ~. **6** collect; accumulate: নাবাল জমিতে জল দাঁড়ায়. **7** stand up to (sb); be match for sb/sb's match; match; be equal to; bear/stand comparison with sb/sth; compete: তোমার বিদ্যাবুদ্ধির সামনে সে কি দাঁড়াতে পারে? **8** endup; terminate: ব্যাপারটা এখন কোথায় গিয়ে দাঁড়ায় দেখো. **9** become; come to be; turn out (to be sb/sth): সে এখন মহা শত্রু দাঁড়িয়ে গেল. **10** mean: come to: কথাটা তাহলে এই দাঁড়াচ্ছে. **11** stand up for: তুমি কি তোমার বন্ধুর পক্ষে দাঁড়াবে না? **12** be firmly established; flourish; thrive; come off: ব্যাবসাটা দাঁড়ালো না. ❑ *n* **1** standing/upright position. **2** manner/posture of standing. ❑*adj* standing; erect; upright: ~ অবস্থা.

দাঁড়াশ *n* a species of large snake.

দাঁড়ি[1] *n* oarsman; oarswoman; rower.

দাঁড়ি[2] *n* beam of a balance; (pair of) scales. ~**পাল্লা**, ~**বাটখাড়া** *n* scales and weights.

দাঁড়ি[3] *n* Bengali punctuation mark corresponding to a full stop (।).

দাঁড়ী=দাঁড়ি[1]

দাঁত *n* tooth; tusk; fang (⇒ also দন্ত). ~ **ওঠা** *vi* teethe; cut a tooth. ~ **ওঠানো** *vi* extract a tooth; have a tooth extracted. ~ **কনকন(ানি)** *n* toothache. ~ **কনকন করা** *vi* (of a tooth) ache;

have toothache. ~কপাটি *n* lockjaw; trismus. ~কপাটি লাগা *vi* have lockjaw/the jaws rigidly closed. ~ কিড়মিড় করা *vi* grind/gnash one's teeth (esp in anger). ~খামাটি *n* biting the lower lip with the upper row of teeth. ~ খিঁচানো *vi* show one's teeth; jaw at; abuse; give hell to. ~খিঁচুনি *n* jawing; abuse; dressing down. ~ছোলা *vi* **1** brush/cleanse one's teeth. **2** have one's teeth blackened with a dentifrice made of green vitriol, roasted tobacco, etc. ~ তোলা *vi* extract a tooth. ~ তোলানো *vi* have a tooth extracted. ~ থাকতে দাঁতের মর্যাদা না জানা/বোঝা (fig) not to value blessings till they are gone. ~ দেখানো *vi* **1**= ~ খিচানো. **2** make faces (at); grin (at); grimace. ~ নড়া *vi* have a tooth loosened. ~ পড়া *vi* have a tooth fallen away. ~ পড়ে যাওয়া *vi* grow old; age. ~ ফেলা =~ ওঠানো. ~ ফোটানো *vi* **1** bite; pierce with teeth. **2** (fig) comprehend; penetrate; fathom; catch on (to sth). ~ বাঁধানো *vi* make/have artifical tooth/teeth. ~ বের করা *vi* **1**=~ খিচানো. **2** simper; grin (at). ~ বিঁধানো =~ ফোটানো. ~ ভাঙা *vi* (fig) humble sb's pride; draw sb's teeth/fangs. ~ ভাঙা *adj* **1** sharp; befitting; crushing; cutting: ~ভাঙা জবাব. **2** difficult to understand/pronounce; breakjaw. ~ মাজা *vi*=~ ছোলা. ~-মাজা *n* tooth-powder; tooth-paste; dentifrice. ~শূল *n* toothache. দাঁতে কুটা করা (fig) eat humble pie; be on bended knee; swallow one's pride; lick sb's boots. দাঁতে দড়ি দিয়ে পড়ে থাকা (fig) keep one's bed without food or drink; fast. দাঁতে দাঁতে লাগা *v*=~কপাটি লাগা. দাঁতের গোড়া *n* root of the teeth; gum. দাঁতের পাথরি *n* tartar. দাঁতের পোকা *n* caries. দাঁতের মাজন *n* dentifrice. আক্কেল ~ *n* wisdom tooth. কুকুরে ~ *n* canine tooth; incisor. গজ~ *n* an additional/extra tooth growing out of the root of another tooth; subsidiary teeth. দুধে দাঁত *n* milk-tooth; baby tooth. পোকা ~ *n* carious tooth. মাঢ়ির ~ *n* molar (tooth). শূকরের ~ *n* tusk. সাপের ~ *n* fang. হাতির ~ *n* tusk.

দাঁতন (also ~ কাঠি) piece of wood for cleaning the teeth.

দাঁতাল *adj* having large/dreadful teeth/tusk; toothed; tusked.

দাক্ষায়ণী *n fem* daughter of Daksha (দক্ষ); goddess Durga in her previous birth.

দাক্ষিণাত্য *adj* southern; southerly; of the Deccan. □*n* the Deccan.

দাক্ষিণ্য *n* **1** kindness; piety; liberality; generosity; benevolence; charity; favour; consideration. **2** cordiality; simplicity; gracefulness; amiability. **3** dexterity; skill; gallantry.

দাখিল [A] *adj* **1** entering; penetrating; arriving. **2** filed; registered; produced; submitted; included; inserted: কাগজপত্র ~. **3** paid; brought (in/before): খাজনা ~. **4** admitted; allowed entrance. **5** as good as rendered/reduced almost to: মরার ~, corpselike; at the point of death. ~ করা *vt* **1** file; lodge: মামলা/দলিল ~ করা. **2** present; produce; bring in/before: আসামিকে আদালতে ~ করা. **3** deposit; submit; send in: দরখাস্ত/ফি ~ করা. **4** present; submit: তথ্য ~ করা. **5** admit; enter; place/fix in; include; register; enroll: নাম ~ করা. **6** render/reduce almost to: মরার ~ করা. ~ হওয়া *vi* enter; arrive; penetrate; be inserted; be filed; be included; be deposited; be enrolled/registered. ~কার *n* occupant. ~কারী *n* hereditary occupancy. ~খারিজ *n* mutation; registration; proceedings of the transfer of property to the new proprietor. দাখিলে যাওয়া *vi* die; give up the ghost; croak.

দাখিলা [A] *n* **1** payment of money; receipt of payment. **2** admission; entrance.

দাখিলি [A] *adj* **1** submitted; paid; filed; presented; relating to presentation/filing/ payment/ submission. contained; included; inclusive; internal; interior. ~ মৌজা *n* newly formed village; attached to/included in the older village.

দাগ [P] *n* **1** mark; spot; scratch; speck; stain; smudge: কাপড়ের ~. **2** scar: পোড়া ~. **2** blemish; stigma; slur; blot; taint; aspersion: কলঙ্কের ~. **3** dark spot in printing; mackle. **4** grief; calamity; misfortune; loss; injury; damage; morbid/unfavourable impression: মনের ~. **5** rust: লোহায় ~ ধরা. **6** brand; distinctive mark; earmark: পশুর গায়ে ~ দেওয়া. **7** line; tick: ~ কাটা/দেওয়া. **8** bounded plot of land bearing an official number: ~ নম্বর. ~ করা *vt* mark; scratch. ~ কাটা *vi* **1** tick off; draw a line. **2** mark (off); determine (a share/ the boundary, etc). **3** leave a good/bad impression on; impress upon: মনে ~ কাটা. ~ ছুটানো/তোলা *vi* **1** remove/ erase/a mark/ spot/ stain. **2** remove an unfavourable/a morbid impression. ~ দেওয়া/লাগানো *vt* **1** brand; mark by burning with a hot iron; scar; earmark. **2** draw a line; tick/off mark (off); determine. **3** cause grief/depression (to); produce an unfavourable impression. **4** slur; blacken; cast aspersion. blemish; mar; stain; taint; stigmatize; tarnish. ~ মোছা=~ ছুটানো. ~ ধরা/ পড়া/ লাগা *vi* **1** be stained/ soiled/ tainted/ blemished/ discoloured/ blotted; be covered in blotches. **2** be stigmatized/ tarnished/ besmeared/ tainted/ slurred; get a bad name. **3** be affected with an unfavourable/a morbid impression; be left with a bad impression. **4** accept/bear a mark: জলে ~ পড়ে না. ~নী *n* branding-iron; brand. ~বিলি *n* account/ description of a landholding and its tenants. ~রাজি *n* repair work (of a building etc).

দাগড়া=দগড়া

দাগা[1] [P] *n* 1 deceit; treachery; cheating; fraud; deception; artifice; delusion. 2 affliction; emotional shock/ distress; heartbreak: মনে ~ পাওয়া. ~ **দেওয়া** *vt* deceive; cheat; act deceitfully/ treacherously. **~দার, ~বাজ** *adjj* deceitful; fraudulent; treacherous. ❑*nn* cheat; imposter; betrayer; traitor; swindler. **~দারি, ~বাজি** *nn* cheating; imposture; trickery; treachery; deceitfulness; villainy; fraudulence; deception; fraud. **~বাজি করা** *vi* practise deception/fraud/treachery.

দাগা[2] [P] *n* (⇒ দাগ) 1 specimen script for tracing to practise handwriting. ~ **বোলানো** *vi* practise handwriting by tracing on a specimen script.

দাগা[3] *vt, vi* 1 mark; tick: পড়া ~. 2 brand. 3 paint: গায়ে হরিনাম ~. **~নো** *vi, vt* (cause to) mark/tick/paint/brand.

দাগা(নো)[8] *vt* fire (of a gun); shoot (a bullet) (with a gun).

দাগি, দাগী *adj* 1 spoiled; stained. 2 spoilt; spoiled: ~ আম. 3 branded: ~ লোক. 4 previously convicted. ~ **আসামি** *n* convict. ~ **চোর** *n* convicted thief.

দাঙ্গা *n* riot; row; fracas; affray. ~ **করা** *vi* riot; be engaged in rioting/affray/fracas; riot; disturb/violate/shatter the peace. **~ফেসাদ, ~হাঙ্গামা** *nn* continuous riot; rioting; disturbance of the peace; outbreak of rioting disturbances; convulsions. **~বাজ** *adj* riotous; rowdy; violent; tumultuous. ❑*n* rioter. **~বাজি** *n* rioting.

দাড়া=দাঁড়া[1]

দাড়ি *n* 1 beard. 2 chin. ~ **কামানো/চাঁছা** *vi, vt* shave. **~ওয়ালা** *adj* bearded. **চাপ~** *n* thick-set beard. **ছাগল~** *n* goatee. **বুকে বসে ~ ওপড়ানো** (fig) bite the hand that feeds one.

দাড়িম, দাড়িম্ব *n* pomegranate.

দাতব্য *adj* 1 to be given; to be paid/ restored; to be communicated. 2 charitable: ~ প্রতিষ্ঠান charitable institution; ~ বিদ্যালয়, free school. ❑*n* (colloq) munificence; charity: তোমার যে বড়ো ~! ~ করা *vt* (colloq) give (away) in charity.

দাতা *adj* 1 liberal; munificent; charitable; benevolent; magnanimous; generous. 2 (used as a *suff*) giving; permitting; granting: অন্ন~, আশ্রয়~. ❑*n* 1 giver; donor; one who offers; payer; creditor; contributor. 2 father/brother who gives a daughter/sister in marriage. 3 munificent giver; benefactor; benevolent/ generous person. **দাত্রী** *fem.* **~কর্ণ** *n* (fig) person of boundless generosity like Karna of the Mahabharata.

দাতৃ (used as a *suff*)=দাতা. **~ত্ব** *n* liberality; munificence; generosity.

দাত্যূহ *n* the gallinule.

দাত্রী ⇒ দাতা

দাত্র *n* a heavy knife/chopper with a haft.

দাদ[1] *n* ringworm.

দাদ[2] [P] *n* revenge; grudge; appeal; complaint. ~ **তোলা/নেওয়া** *vi* (take/ have/ get one's) revenge; pay off old scores; avenge oneself on sb/sth; take vengeance (on/upon sb). **~ফরিয়াদ** *n* application/cry for justice/redress.

দাদখানি *n* a variety of superfine rice.

দাদন [P] *n* advance; earnest money; loan. **~দার** *n* one who pays an advance; person doing business on advance payment.

দাদনি, দাদনী *adjj* done/obtained on advance payment. ❑*n* advance payment.

দাদরা *n* an Indian musical measure.

দাদা *n* 1 grandfather. 2 elder brother/cousin brother. 3 (in address) older/senior man. 4 (in affectionate address) younger brother/cousin; grandson; younger/junior man. **~বাবু** *n* 1 husband of an elder sister/cousin. 2 employer/master as respectable as one's elder brother. **~মহাশয়** *n* 1 maternal grandfather. 2 (in respectful address) eldest brother.

দাদী *n fem* paternal grandmother.

দাদু *n* (term of endearment)=দাদা

দাদুপন্থী *adj, n* following/follower of the religious sect founded by Dadu (16th century).

দাদুর *n* frog. **দাদুরী** *fem.*

দান[1] *n* 1 giving (up away) act of giving. 2 grant; bestowal; award. 3 distribution: অন্ন~. 4 imparting; communicating; teaching: বিদ্যা~. 5 giving in marriage: কন্যা~. 6 offering; sacrifice; dedication. 7 throw(ing); score; cast: পাশাখেলার ~. 8 levy; tax; duty: ঘাটের ~. 9 gift; donation: মূল্যবান ~. 10 contribution: সাহিত্যে তাঁর ~ স্মরণীয়. 11 turn (for doing sth): এবার কার ~? 12 paying back; restoring. ~ **করা** *vi* 1 give (away/up). 2 bestow; grant; award; confer. 3 impart; communicate; yield; present; offer (to). 4 give (a daughter) in marriage. 5 hand over; give back. 6 cede; give up. 7 pay. 8 sacrifice; dedicate: জীবন ~ করা. 9 donate; contribute. 10 give/distribute (in charity). 11 utter; give: উত্তর ~ করা. **~কর্ম, ~কার্য** *n* (practice of) charity; liberality; largess(e). **~কাতর, ~কুণ্ঠ** *adjj* uncharitable; parsimonious; stingy; niggardly; closefisted; miserly; tightfisted; illiberal. **~ধর্ম, ~ধ্যান** *nn* duty of liberality. **~পতি** *n* munificent man. **~পত্র** *n* deed of gift. **~বীর**=~পতি. **~যোগ্য** *adj* worthy of a gift. **~শালা** *n* hall for almsgiving. **~শীল** *adj* bountiful; generous; liberally disposed; munificent; charitable;

magnanimous. ~শীলতা *n* bounty; generosity; munificence; magnanimity. ~শৌণ্ড *adj* very liberal. ~সজ্জা *n* (in a wedding) display of gifts given to the bride and the bridegroom. ~সত্র *n* charitable institution; almshouse. ~সাগর *n* sixteen sets of gifts given in a sraddha (শ্রাদ্ধ) ceremony. ~সামগ্রী *n* article of gift; gifts. যেমন ~ তেমনি দক্ষিণা 1 the amount of fee will commensurate with the amount of gift. 2 (fig) A niggardly master will have a niggardly servant.

-দান [P] *n* (used as a *suff*) pot; holder; vase; case; receptacle; container: কলম~, আতর~.

দানব *n* (a class of) demons; monster; evil spirit; devil; Titan; giant. দানবী *fem* giantess; demoness. ~দলনী *n fem* conqueror of the Danavas; goddess Durga. দানবারি *n* enemy of the Danavas; Indra (ইন্দ্র).

দানবীয় *adj* monstrous; gigantic; demoniac(al); diabolical; devilish.

দানা[1] *n* (colloq)=দানব. ~য় পাওয়া *vi* be possessed by a devil/an evil spirit.

দানা[2] [P] *n* 1 grain; corn. 2 seed; stone; pip: ডালিমের ~. 3 food: ~পানি, food and drink; victuals; subsistence. 4 necklace of pea-shaped beads. 5 granule. ~ বাঁধা *vi* form into grains; gr anulate. ~দার *adj* granulated; granular

দানি[2] *n* receiver (of stolen goods).

দানিশবন্দ, দানিশমন্দ [P] *adjj* wise; learned; sagacious. দানিশমন্দি *n* learning; wisdom; sagacity.

দানী[1] *adj* liberal; bountiful; generous; munificent.

দানী[2] *n* tollman at a ferry.

-দানী *nn*=-দান

দানীয় *adj* worthy of gifts/offerings; worth giving; to be given. ❑*n* gift.

দানেশবন্দ=দানিশবন্দ

দানো *n* (colloq)=দানব

দান্ত[1] *adj* 1 continent; self-restrained; self-disciplined; self-controlled; ascetic. 2 tamed; restrained; broken; subdued. 3 mild; patient.

দান্ত[2] *adj* dental; made of ivory.

দান্তি *n* continence; self-control; self-restraint; temperance.

দাপ *n* 1 pride; haughtiness; vanity. 2 tyranny; repression; oppression. 3 power; authority; might; prowess. 4 passion; rage.

দাপক *adj* obliging/forcing to give/pay. ❑*n* one who forces/obliges to give/pay.

দাপট *n* power; mightiness; immense/terrible authority/influence/might; sway; dominance; omnipotence; ascendancy; brute force.

দাপদুপ=দুপদাপ

দাপন[1] *n* act of obliging/forcing to pay/give.

দাপন[2] *n* pressure; pressing; trampling.

দাপনা=দাবনা

দাপনি *n* 1=দাপাদাপি. 2 pressure; pressing.

দাপাদাপি *n* 1 agitation; stamping; restlessness; restiveness; the fidgets; the jitters; huff; trepidation; romp. 2 vaunting; bragging; bullying with a show of authority; presumption. 3 fuss; turbulence; excitement. ~ করা *vi* 1 agitate; be agitated/ restless/ restive; fidget; stamp; get the fidgets; jitter; romp have/get the jitters; fret. 2 vaunt; brag; swagger; strut. 3 fuss (about); make/kick up a fuss (about/over sth); rampage; rage; fulminate; romp noisily; stampede.

দাপানি *n* 1=দাপাদাপি. 2 burning (sensation); heat.

দাপানো *vi*=দাপাদাপি করা

দাপিত *adj* caused to give; caused to be given; got; procured; obtained; condemned to pay; fined.

দাব[1] *n* 1 pressure; weight; force; control; check; restraint: দাবে রাখা *vt* keep under control; exercise authority over; hold sway over. 2 scolding; rebuke; reprimand.

দাব[2] *n* 1 conflagration; forest conflagration; fire; heat; distress. 2 forest. ~দগ্ধ *adj* burnt down in a forest conflagration; (fig) extremely distressed; tormented; anguished. ~দাহ *n* heat of a forest conflagration. দাবাগ্নি, দাবানল *n* forest conflagration; wildfire.

দাবড়, দাবড়া *n* 1 threats; threatening; menace; bullying; intimidation; thundering. 2 scolding; tonguelashing; stern reproof; revilement; rebuke. 3 chase; pursuit. দাবড়ানো *vi* 1 threat; menace; bully; intimidate; thunder. 2 scold; tonguelash; revile; rebuke; reprove. 3 chase; give chase; pursue. 4 ride (at a gallop); ride (a horse/horseback): ঘোড়া দাবড়ানো.

দাবড়ানি, দাবড়ি=দাবড়

দাবনা *n* (the fleshy part of the) thigh.

দাবা[1] *vi, vt* 1 sink; subside: মেঝেটা দেবে গেছে 2 =~নো. ~নো *vt* 1 press down; compress; squeeze: দাবিয়ে ধরা. 2 suppress; restrain; hold/keep in check; curb; stifle; quash; dominate; subjugate; repress; suppress; keep down: কাউকে দাবিয়ে রাখা. 3 dig in: পা ~নো.

দাবা[2] *n* 1 (the game of) chess. 2 the queen (of chess). ~ খেলা *vi* play chess. ~খেলা *n* chess. ~বড়ে, ~বোড়ে *nn* chessboard and chessmen. ~ড়ু, ~ড়ে *nn* chess-player.

দাবা[3]=দাওয়া[1]

দাবাই=দাওয়া[4]

দাবাগ্নি, দাবানল ⇒ দাব[2]

দাবাড়ু, দাবাড়ে, দাবাবড়ে ⇒ দাবা[2]

দাবি, দাবী [A] *nn* 1 claim; right; title; pretension: জমির ~ সে ছাড়েনি. 2 demand; claim: তোমার কী ~ বলো? 3 law-suit; charge;

accusation; charge: বাদীপক্ষের ~. **4** complaint; prayer. ~ **করা** *vi* **1** claim; demand; press for; urge upon; require. **2** pray; complain. ~ **খারিজ করা** *vi* dismiss a suit/claim. ~**দাওয়া** *n* rights and claims. ~**দার** *n* **1** claimant; plaintiff; pretender. **2** successor; inheritor.

দাম[1] *n* price; value; cost. ~ **দেওয়া** *vi* **1** pay. **2** (fig) pay for sth; pay a/the price (for sth). ~ **পড়া/লাগা** *vi* cost. **চাওয়া-~** *n* asking price.

দাম[2] *n* **1** thread; cord; rope; fetter. **2** wreath; garland; string; chaplet; girdle: কুসুম-~. **3** lock; cluster; bunch: কেশ~. **4** kind of duck-weed or green moss-like grass growing in pools.

দামড়া *n* (also ~**গরু**) castrated bull; bullock. ~ **ঘোড়া** *n* gelding. ~ **বাছুর** *n* castrated calf.

দামন [P] *n* skirt (of a garment); sheet (of a sail). ~ **ধরা** *vi* become a follower (of).

দামাদ [P] *n* (dial) son-in-law.

দামামা [P] *n* drum; kettle-drum; war-drum. ~**ধ্বনি** *n* drumbeat; fanfare.

দামাল *adj* (chiefly of a child) indomitable; spirited; sparkling; gallant; vigorous; lively; zippy; dauntless; plucky; brave. ~**পনা** *n* liveliness; spirit; vitality; vivacity; get-up-and-go; restiveness; turbulence.

দামী=দামি

দামিনী *n fem* lightning.

দামোদর *n* "having a rope round the waist"; name of Sri Krishna.

দাম্পত্য *n* state of husband and wife; conjugal/matrimonial relationship. ❑*adj* conjugal; nuptial. ~ **প্রণয়**, ~ **প্রেম** *nn* conjugal love.

দাম্ভিক *adj* conceited; vainglorious; arrogant; swollen; self-important; egotistical; bloated; cocky. ~**তা** *n* hauteur; vaingloriousness; presumption; self-importance; pretensions; pretentiousness; pompousness; airs.

দায় *n* **1** patrimony; inheritance; heritage. **2** wealth; property. **3** danger; difficulty; encumbrance; problem: দায়ে পড়ে এখানে আসা. **4** harm; loss. **5** necessity; need: তার কী ~ পড়েছে? **6** important duty/responsibility/ obligation: কন্যা~, মাতৃ~. **7** mortgage; debt; hypothecation: ~বদ্ধ. **8** (criminal) charge: চুরির দায়ে ধরা পড়া. **9** risk; risky charge; responsibility: পরের ~ ঘাড়ে নেওয়া. **10** sake; account: প্রাণের দায়ে. **11** legacy. **দায়ে ঠেকা/পড়া** *vi* be in an awkward predicament; run into troubles; be in difficulty; get into scrape; get into difficulties; be in trouble; have a hard/thin time (of it); come to a (pretty) pass; be in/get into a fix. **কী ~ পড়েছে** what necessity is there? **তাকে বলার জন্যে আমার ~ পড়েছে** I have no business to tell him. **তোমার কী দায় পড়েছে** why on earth should you... **প্রাণের দায়ে** for dear life/one's life; for the sake of one's life. **প্রাণের দায়ে দৌড়ানো** run for one's life.

দায়ক *adj* (also used as a *suff*) giving; granting; bestowing; imparting; communicating; uttering; telling; causing; fulfiling; effecting: স্বস্তি~, আনন্দ~, শিক্ষা~.

দায়গ্রস্ত *adj* **1** bound by obligation/ duty/ responsibility; encumbered; burdened with. **2** endangered; faced with/exposed to danger. **3** indebted; mortgaged.

দায়গ্রহণ *n* underwriting.

দায়ভাগ *n* **1** division of patrimony. **2** name of an ancient book on inheritance written by Jimutabahana.

দায়মাল *n* stolen goods.

দায়রা [A] *adj* pending; under consideration; in process. ❑*n* (law) sessions. ~**-আদালত** *n* sessions-court. ~ **জজ** *n* sessions-judge. ~**য় সোপর্দ করা** *vi* commit to sessions.

দায়াদ *n* **1** claimant to an inheritance; heir; sharer of one's patrimony. **2** son. **3** kinsman.

দায়াদি *n fem* **1**=দায়াদ (1). **2** daughter. **3** kinswoman. ❑*adj* inherited; obtained by inheritance.

দায়িক=দায়ী

-দায়িকা *adj fem*=-দায়ক

দায়িতা *n* liability.

দায়িত্ব *n* responsibility; liability; risk; charge; duty. ~**জ্ঞান**, ~**বোধ** *nn* sense of responsibility/ duty.

দায়িনী ⇒ দায়ী

দায়ী *adj* **1** responsible; liable. **2** (used as a *suff*) giving; granting; communicating; yielding; ceding; allowing; permitting; causing; effecting; producing; performing. **দায়িনী** *fem*.

দায়েম [A] *adj* perpetual; permanent; continual; always. **দায়েমুল হবস** *adj* imprisoned for life.

দায়ের [A] *adj* submitted/filed for consideration; lodged. ~ **করা** *vt* file; institute; submit; lodge: মামলা ~ করা.

দার[1] *n* wife. ~**কর্ম**, ~**গ্রহণ**, ~**পরিগ্রহ** *n* taking a wife; marriage; wedding. ~**গ্রহণ**/~**পরিগ্রহ করা** *vi* take a wife; marry.

-দার[2] [P] *adj* (used as a *suff*) **1** having; furnished/ embroidered with: বুটি~. **2** holder: হিসসা~. **3** causing; producing: মজা~. **4** employed in; taking to: বাজনা~. **5** owning; possessing; having: পাওনা~. **6** superintending; controllring: থানা~. **-দারি** *n* (used as a *suff*) implying -ship: হিসসাদারি, জমিদারি.

দারওয়ান=দরোয়ান

দারক *adj* cleaving; splitting. ❑*n* son; boy; child.

দারকর্ম ⇒ দার[1]

দারগা=দারোগা

দারগ্রহণ ⇒ দার[১]
দারচিনি=দারুচিনি (⇒ দারু[১])
দারণ *n* tearing; splitting; rending; bursting; flying open.
দারপরিগ্রহ⇒ দার[১]
দারা *n* wife.
দারাজ=দরাজ
-দারি ⇒ দার[২]
দারিকা *n fem* daughter. ❑*adj fem* cleaving; splitting.
দারিত *adj* torn; rent; divided; cleft.
দারিদ্র্য, দারিদ্র *nn* poverty; penury; lack; want; indigence; poorness. **~ব্যঞ্জক, ~সূচক** *adjj* betraying/indicating poverty. **~মোচন** *n* alleviation/ removal/ elimination/ eradication of poverty.
দারু[১] *n* (piece of) wood; timber. **~চিনি** *n* cinnamon. **~জ** *adj* made of wood; wooden. **~পাত্র** *n* wooden vessel. **~ভূত** *adj* transformed/ changed into a wooden entity; (fig) numb; inert. **~ময়**=~জ.
দারু[২] [P] *n* **1** liquor; wine. **2** medicine; remedy.
দারুকা *n* chain; iron rod.
দারুণ *adj* **1** very; great; excessive: ~ সুখ, ~ বুড়ো. **2** terrible; dreadful; frightful: ~ মূর্তি. **3** severe: ~ শীত. **4** cruel; pitiless; violent: ~ নির্যাতন. **5** very high: ~ জ্বর. **6** sharp; unbearable; severe: ~ যন্ত্রণা. **7** cutting to the quick; unkind; cruel: ~ বাক্য. **8** strong; firm; steely: ~ সঙ্কল্প/প্রতিজ্ঞা. **9** heart-rending; poignant; heart-breaking: ~ শোক.
দারুল ইসলাম [A] *n* Islamic state.
দারুল উলুম [A] *n* college; university.
দারোগা [P] *n* inspector/sub-inspector/assistant sub-inspector (of police); overseer; superintendent. **~গিরি** *n* office/duty of a police officer. **বড় ~** *n* officer-in-charge of a police station. **ছোট ~** *n* sub-inspector (or an assistant sub-inspector of police) who is the second in command of a police station; second officer.
দারোয়ান=দরোয়ান
দার্ঢ্য *n* hardness; firmness; strength; steadiness; stiffness; stability; strictness; stubbornness.
দার্শনিক *adj* philosophical; metaphysical; thoughtful. ❑*n* philosopher; metaphysician. **~তা** *n* philosophical character/ quality/ attitude; philosophical thought; philosophizing. **~তত্ত্ব** *n* philosophical principles/doctrines.
দার্ষ্টান্তিক *adj* exemplary; exemplified.
দাল, ডাল *n* pulse; dal; lentils. **~ভাত** *n* **1** pulse and rice. **2** (fig) poor sustenance; child's play; easy meat; piece of cake; cinch.
দালচিনি *n* (dial)=দারুচিনি (⇒ দারু)
দালনা, ডালনা *n* kind of rich curry.
দালপুরি, ডালপুরি *nn* kind of thin bread fried in butter or oil and stuffed with a paste of pulses.
দালমুট *n* snack prepared with fried and spiced chick-peas (and often with other ingredients).
দালান [P] *n* **1** (brick-built or stone-built) building. **2** platform; hall; room. **3** corridor (of a building). **~-কোঠা** *n* buildings.
দালাল [A] *n* **1** broker; agent; commission-agent; go-between. **2** (derog) tout; a go-between **3** supporter; helper.
দালালি *n* **1** business of a broker; brokery; commission agency. **2** act/business of a tout/go-between. **3** brokerage (an agent's); commission. **4** (derog) support; help.
দালিম *n* pomegranate.
দাশ *n* **1** a title of the Bangali Baidya caste: জীবনানন্দ দাশ. **2** fisherman; one belonging to the caste of fisherman.
দাশরথি, দাশরথ *adjj* belonging to/coming from Dasharatha. ❑*n* descendant of Dasharatha; Ramchandra.
দাশী *n fem* of দাশ.
দাস *n* **1** slave; servant; bondsman; serf attendant. **2** savage; barbarian; infidel. **3** fisherman. **4** Sudra. **5** humble man; dependent; servant: আপনার অনুগত ~. **6** victim; minion: অবস্থান ~. **দাসী** *fem* female servant/slave; bondwoman. **~খত** *n* written bond of slavery. **~ত্ব** *n* slavery; servitude; bondage; enslavement; chains; state of being a victim; dependence. **~ত্ব করা** *vi* be a slave of; serve; obey; submit to; be at the mercy of; fall prey to; depend upon. **~ত্ব প্রথা** *n* slavery; practice of having slaves. **~ত্ব বন্ধন, ~ত্ব শৃঙ্খল** *nn* bonds of slavery. **~ত্ব শৃঙ্খল মোচন** *n* emancipation/freedom from bondage/slavery. **~ত্ব বৃত্তি** *n* slavery. **~ত্বে আবদ্ধ** *adj* enslaved; held in bondage. **~দাসী** *n pl* servants/slaves (male and female); man-servants and maid-servants. **~প্রথা**=~ত্বপ্রথা. **~ ব্যবসায়** *n* slave-trade. **~ মনোবৃত্তি, ~মনোভাব** *nn* slave mentality; servility; slavishness. **দাসানুদাস** *n* slave of one's slave; very humble servant/dependent.
দাসী *n fem* (of দাস) female servant/slave. **~গিরি, ~পনা, ~বৃত্তি, ~ত্ব** *n* condition profession/service of a maid-servant/female slave; slavery. **~পুত্র** *n* son of a female slave; low wretch/miscreant (as an abusive term). **~ভাব**=~গিরি.
দাসেয় *adj* born of a slave girl. ❑*n* son of a female slave.
দাস্ত[১] [P] *n* purge; evacuation; lose motion; diarrhoea; faeces.
দাস্ত[২] [P] *n* desert; arid plain: দাস্তে কারবালা.
দাস্য *n* **1** servitude; slavery; service; servility; state of being a servant. **2** considering

oneself as the servant of one's god. **~বৃত্তি** *n* slavery; servility; service.

দাহ *n* **1** burning; conflagration; setting on fire; combustion; heat; fire: গৃহ~. **2** internal heat; fever. **3** severe/scorching heat: গ্রীষ্মের ~. **4** inflammation: রোগের ~. **5** cremation: শব~. **6** affliction; agony; anguish; torment: মনের ~. **~কর, ~জনক** *adjj* burning. **~ক্রিয়া** *n* cremation. **~জ্বর** *n* inflammatory fever. **~ভূমি** *n* burning/cremation ground. **~ময়** *adj* consisting of heat; burning; inflamed.

দাহক *adj* burning; scorching; reducing to ashes; inflammatory; afflicting; distressing; tormenting; cremating. **দাহিকা** *fem.*

দাহন *n* (act of) burning; scorching; inflammation; affliction. ❑*adj*=দাহক.

দাহ্য *adj* combustible; inflammable; to be burnt; fit to be burnt. **~ পদার্থ** *n* combustible substance.

দি *n* (colloq)=দিদি

দিওয়ান [P] *n* book of poetical pieces in which rhymes of different poems end successively with a particular letter of the alphabet.

দিওয়ানা=দেওয়ানা

দিক[1], দিক্[1] *n* **1** quarter/region (pointed at); direction; cardinal point; point of the compass: দক্ষিণ দিক. **2** share; portion: কোন ~ তোমার আর কোন ~ তোমার ভাইয়ের? **3** party; side: এ মামলায় সে কোন দিকে থাকবে? **4** way; place; part: এদিকে কাউকে দেখেছ? **5** part; side: আমার ~ থেকে বলতে পারি ... . **6** part; portion: ভিতরের ~. **7** extremity; end; side; frontier: এদেশের দক্ষিণ দিকে সমুদ্র. **~কন্যা**=দিগাঙ্গনা. **~চক্র(বাল)** *n* horizon. **~পতি, ~পাল** *nn* **1** regent/guardian of a quarter of the sky. **2** (fig) very powerful and prominent man; giant. **~শূল** *n* any inauspicious planetary conjunction. **~স্থিতি** *n* (bot) orientation. **দিকে দিকে** *adv* in all directions; everywhere; hither and thither. **দশ~** *n* ten quarters of the globe.

দিক্[2], দিক[2] *n* annoyance; vexation; irritation; teasing; torment; trouble. **~দারি**=~. **~দারি করা** *vt* tease; torment; plague; annoy; vex; irritate.

দিগ *n* (in compounds)=দিক্[1]. **~ংশ** *n* azimuth. **~ঙ্গনা** *n* any one of the ten quarters of the sky deified as a young virgin. **~ঞ্চল** *n* all quarters. **~ন্ত** *n* (end of) the horizon; remote distance. **~প্রসারী, ~বিস্তৃত, ~ব্যাপী** *adj* extending/stretching to or as far as the horizon; extending/stretching endlessly. **~ন্তর** *n* **1** another region; foreign country; another direction. **2** distance/space between two points of the compass/two directions. **~ন্তরে** *adv* to/in another direction/point of the compass; beyond the horizon; in/to another country/region. **~ন্তরাল** *n* space/distance between two quarters of the globe; sky. **~ন্তরালে** *adv* beyond/below the horizon. **~ম্বর** *adj* **1** (lit) "sky-clad"; quite naked. ❑*n* naked mendicant; name of Shiva. **~ম্বরী** *adj fem.* ❑*n* goddess Kali.

দিগ্ *n* (in compounds)=দিক্. **~গজ** *n* one of the eight mythical elephants which stand in the quarters of the sky and support the earth. ❑*adj* (often iron) very erudite/ prominent/ capable; vastly learned: **~গজ পণ্ডিত/ উকিল/** ছেলে. **~জ্ঞান** *n* **1** sense of direction; knowledge of the quarters of the globe. **2** (fig) minimum knowledge; common sense. **~জয়** *n* conquest of the various countries in all directions; world-conquest. **~ দর্শন** *n* act of looking to every quarter; general survey. **~দর্শন করা** *vi* make a general survey. **~দর্শন-যন্ত্র** *n* (mariner's) compass. **~দর্শী** *adj* looking round on all sides; having a general view; experienced. **~দিগন্ত** *n* all quarters/directions of the globe; all regions/places. **~দিগন্তর** *n* different quarters/directions of the globe; different regions/places. **~দিগন্তে, ~দিগন্তরে** *advv* far and near/wide; everywhere. **~বধূ**=**দিগঙ্গনা** (⇒ দিগ). **~বলয়** *n* the horizon. **~বসন**=~ম্বর. **~বসনা** *fem.* **~বালা, ~বালিকা**= দিগঙ্গনা. **~বিজয়, দিগ্বিজয়**=~জয়. **~বিজয়, দিগ্বিজয় করা** *vi* conquer the whole world. **~বিজয়ী, দিগ্বিজয়ী** *adj* world conquering. ❑*n* world-conqueror. **~বিদিক** *n* **1** all quarters/regions/ places. **2** what is good and what is evil; what is right and what is wrong. **~বিদিকজ্ঞান** *n* power of discrimination between right and wrong; mental balance; senses; sanity; common sense; composure/calmness of mind. **~বিদিকজ্ঞানশূন্য** *adj* bewildered; completely confounded; disoriented. **~বিদিকজ্ঞানশূন্য হয়ে** *adv* in bewilderment; taking leave of one's senses; hell for leather; helter skelter; in disarray. **~বিন্দু** *n* (geog) cardinal point. **~বিভ্রম, ~ভ্রম, ~ভ্রান্ত** *n n* perplexity about points of the compass; mistaking the way/directions. **~ভ্রান্ত** *adj* mistaking the way/directions; gone astray; disorientated; puzzled; perplexed; bewildered.

দিগর [P] *adj* other; another; again. ❑*n* and others; and such others; et al; et cetera.

দিগ্ধ *adj* anointed (with); smeared; steeped (in); mixed (with); soiled; defiled; poisoned. **দিগ্ধা** *fem.*

দিঘ *n* (dial) length: আড়েদিঘে. **~ল** *adj* (chiefly poet) long; large; tall.

দিঘি *n* large (oblong) pond/lake.

দিঙ্ *n* (in compounds)=দিক্[1]. **~নাগ** *n*= দিগ্গজ. **~নিরূপণ, ~নির্ণয়** *n* ascertainment of the points of the compass; ascertainment of a particular/ the right direction. **~নিরূপণ/ ~নির্ণয় করা** *vi* ascertain the points of the compass;

ascertain the direction. **~নির্ণয় যন্ত্র** *n* (mariner's) compass. **~মণ্ডল** *n* horizon. **~মাত্র** *n* mere direction/indication. **~মুখ** *adj* facing any point/quarter. **~মূঢ়** *adj* **1** confused about the quarter of the compass. **2** =দিগ্‌ভ্রান্ত.

দিঠি *n* (poet, colloq) **1** look; glance. **2** eye.

দিতি *n* (myth) name of the mother of *Daityas*. **~জ ~সুত** *nn* son of Diti; any of the mythological demons hostile to gods.

দিৎসা *n* desire/intention to give.

দিৎসু *adj* wishing to give/grant/contribute.

দিদা *n fem* (as a term of endearment) grand-mother; grand-daughter.

দিদার *n* [P] sight; interview; meeting.

দিদি *n fem* **1** elder sister/ cousin. **2** (in affectionate or courteous address) lady; woman; girl. **3** (as a term of endearment) grand-mother; grand- daughter. **~ঠাকুরানী** *n* (facet) lady; woman; girl. **~মা** *n* grand-mother; grand-aunt.

দিদৃক্ষমাণ *adj* wishing to see/examine.

দিদৃক্ষা *n* desire of seeing.

দিদৃক্ষু=দিদৃক্ষমাণ

দিধিষু *n* second husband of a woman twice married.

দিন[১] *n* **1** day; daytime. **2** twenty-four hours. **3** length of time; period: দীর্ঘ~. **4** time of existence; duration of life; days: তার ~ ফুরিয়েছে, His days are numbered. **5** daily working hours/period. **6** time: তোমার ~ কেমন করে কাটে? **7** age; days: সে~ কি আর আছে? **8** favourable/ auspicious time: যদি কখনো ~ আসে. **~ আনা ~ খাওয়া** live from hand to mouth. **~ কাটানো** *vi* spend one's days; pass one's time; spend a day; lead a life. **~ গনা** *vi* count the days; look forward to eagerly. **~কর** *n* the sun. **~ গুজরানো**=~কাটানো. **~ ঘনিয়ে আসা/ ফুরানো** *vi* sb's/sth's days are numbered. **~কাল** *n* times; present time. **~কৃতি** *n* daily duties; ceremonies to be performed daily. **~ক্ষণ** *n* (astrol) auspicious day and moment (for doing sth). **~ক্ষয়** *n* **1** evening; decline of the day. **2** conjunction of three lunations with one solar day. **~ক্ষেপ(ণ)**=~যাপন. **~গত পাপক্ষয়** *n* **1** daily religious purification for purging sins. **2** routine drudgery; monotonous toil of daily life. **~দগ্ধ** *n* (astrol) inauspicious day for doing sth. **~ দিন** *adv* day by day; everyday; day after day; day in day out; daily. **~দুপুরে** *adv* in broad daylight. **~দুপুরে দিনের নাগাল পাওয়া** be in sight of better days. **~নাথ, ~পতি** *nn* the sun. **~পঞ্জি** *n* day-to-day record of events; diary; calendar. **~পঞ্জিকার** *n* diarist. **~পত্রী** *n* daily journal. **~পাত**=~যাপন. **~বন্ধু** *n* the sun. **~ভর** *adj* the whole day long. **~মজুর** *n* day-labourer. **~মণি** *n* the sun. **~মান** *n* daytime; daylight hours. **~মাহিনা** *n* daily wage. **~মুখ** *n* **1** daybreak. **2** the sun. **~মুখরবি** *n* the morning sun. **~যাপন** *n* act of passing a day. **~যাপন করা**=~ কাটানো. **~যামিনী, ~রজনী, ~রাত** *nn* day and night. ❑*adv* at all hours of the day and night; day and night; continuously. **~শেষ** *n* close of a day; evening; sunset. **দিনাত্যয়, দিনান্ত, দিনাবসান** *nn*= ~শেষ. **দিনান্তক** *n* darkness; night. **দিনান্তে** *adv* at the close/end of the day; in the evening. **দিনান্ধ** *adj* unable to see in daylight; day-blind. **~কে রাত করা 1** exaggerate beyond recognition; make mountains out of molehills. **2** tell a downright lie. **দিনে-ডাকাতি** *n* **1** robbery in broad daylight. **2** daring villainy/ misdeed. **দিনে দিনে** *adv* day by day; every day. **দিনেদুপুরে**=~দুপুরে.

দিন[২], **দ্বীন** [A] *n* religion; faith. **~-আখেরি** *n* religion and the hereafter. **~-দার** *adj* religious; pious; virtuous. **~দারি** *n* piety; religiousness; religiosity. **~দুনিয়া** *n* religion and worldly goods. **~দুনিয়ার মালিক** *n* lord of this world and the hereafter.

দিনার [A] *n* a coin; ducat.

দিনি [A] *adj* religious; spiritual. **~ ইলম** *n* religious/spiritual knowledge/learning.

দিনেমার *n* native of Denmark; Dane. ❑*adj* of Denmark; Danish. **~ জাতি** *n* Danes.

দিনেশ *n* lord of the day; the sun.

দিবস *n*=দিন[১] (1), (2). **দিবসাত্যয়, দিবসাবসন**= দিনাত্যয় and দিনাবসান respectively (⇒ দিন[১]). **দিবসালোক** *n* daylight.

দিবা *adj* by day: ~ দ্বিপ্রহরের সময়. ❑*n* day time; day. **~কর** *n* the sun. **~চর** *adj* active during daytime. **~তন** *adj* of the day; diurnal. **~নিদ্রা** *n* sleeping by day; siesta. **~নিশ, ~নিশি** *adv* day and night; all the time; always. **~ন্ধ** *adj* blind by day. ❑*n* owl. **~বসান** *n* close of the day; sunset. **~বসু** *n* the sun. **~বিহার** *n* **1** rest-by day; nap. **2** sexual enjoyment in daytime. **~ভাগ** *n* daytime. **~ভীত** *adj* timid by day. ❑ *n* thief; owl. **~মণি** *n* the sun. **~মধ্য** *n* noon. **~রাত্র, ~রাত্রি** *adv*=~নিশ. **~লোক** *n* day light. **স্পষ্ট/প্রকাশ্য দিবালোক** broad daylight. **~শয়** *adj* sleeping by day. **~সঙ্কেত** *n* appointment (of lovers) by day. **~স্বপ্ন** *n* **1** day-dream; reverie; waking dream; fantasy. **2** castle in the air; pipedream. **~স্বপ্ন দেখা** *vi* day-dream; be lost in day-dreams/ reverie; build castles in Spain.

দিব্ব, দিব্বি *nn* (colloq)=দিব্যি

দিব্য *adj* **1** divine; heavenly; celestial. **2** wonderful; supernatural; miraculous; magical. **3** charming; fine; beautiful; excellent; agreeable; pleasant; delightful. ❑*n* oath; pledge. **~ করা** *vi, vt* swear (to); affirm solemnly; swear to god; take one's oath; vow; give one's (sacred) word/word of honour/one's pledge/one's promise. ~ দেওয়া *vt* adjure. ~ কানন *n* celestial grove. ~গন্ধ *n* **1** divine odour. **2** cloves. ❑*adj* sweet-scented; having a divine odour. ~চক্ষু *n* divine eye; supernatural vision; insight; beautiful/fair eye. ❑*adj* having a divine eye/ supernatural vision/ insight; fair-eyed. দিব্যচক্ষুতে দেখা *vi* foresee; envisage; see in (a divine) vision. ~জ্ঞান *n* divine/ transcendental/ spiritual/ supernatural knowledge/ wisdom. ~তা *n* divinity; divine nature. ~দর্শন *adj* of a divine aspect. ~দর্শী *adj* having a divine vision/insight. ~দৃষ্টি *n*=~চক্ষু. ❑*adj*=~দর্শী. ~দেহ *n* divine/celestial body/form. ❑*adj* having a divine/celestial body/form. ~ধাম *n* celestial abode; heaven. ~নদী *n* divine stream. ~নারী *n* divine female; nymph. ~নেত্র=~চক্ষু. ~মন্ত্র *n* divine syllable, Om. ~রথ *n* divine car; vehicle of the gods. ~লোক *n* divine/celestial region; heaven. দিব্যাঙ্গনা= ~নারী. দিব্যাস্ত্র *n* divine weapon; a god's weapon.

দিব্যি *adj, n* (colloq)=দিব্য

দিব্যোদক *n* divine water; rainwater; dew.

দিয়া[১], দিয়ে *prep* **1** by; with; by means of; through; by the instrumentality of: হাত ~ ধরা. **2** in: তেল ~ ভাজা. **3** through: পাখি জানালা ~ পালিয়েছে. **4** from: ছাদ ~ জল গড়ানো. **5** along: সে কোন রাস্তা ~ গেল? **6** adding; mixing with; together with: দুধ ~ জ্বাল দাও.

দিয়া[২] (colloq) *n* lamp; light. ~ **কাঠি** *n* match-stick; wick (of a lamp).

দিয়ালা=দেয়ালা

দিয়ালি=দেয়ালি

দিয়াশলাই *n* match(es); safety matches; match-box. ~ **কাঠি** *n* match-stick. ~ **বাক্স** *n* match-box.

দিয়ে *prep* (colloq)=দিয়া[১]

দিল [P] *n* **1** heart; mind; soul. **2** courage. **3** conscience. **4** generosity. **5** wish. **6** inclination. ~ **ওঠা** *vi* feel inclined; feel like. ~ **ভাঙা** *vt* dishearten; disappoint; mortify. ~**ওয়ার** *adj* intrepid; brave; bold; valiant; courageous. ~**কোঠা** *n* heart of heart; innermost heart. ~**খোলসা**, ~**খোলা** *adjj* frank; candid; sincere; free and frank; straightforward. ~**খুশ**, ~**খোশ** *adj* enchanted; pleased; heartened; delighted. ~ **খুশি করা** *vi, vt* gladden the heart (of); please; enjoy. ~**গির** *adj* oppressed in mind; sad; melancholy; low-spirited; melancholy. ~ **জাগানো/মাতানো** *vi* enchant; enthuse; charm; captivate. ~ **তড়পানো** *vi* be anxiously eager/ dying for. ~**দরাজ** *adj* large-hearted; generous; lavish. ~-**দরাজি** *n* large-heartedness; generosity; magnanimity. ~**দারিয়া** *adj* magnanimous; free-handed; princely; bountiful; free-hearted. ~**দাগা** *adj* heart-ravishing; alluring; seductive. ~**দার** *adj* possessing/ delighting the heart; charming; beloved; sweetheart. ❑ *n* lover; sweetheart. ~ দেওয়া *vi* lose one's heart; fall in love (with). ~ **ভরে যাওয়া** *vi* be satiated/ satisfied. ~**পিয়ারা** *n* intimate; best friend; sweetheart; ladylove. ~**মাতানো** *adj* enchanting; captivating; winsome; joyous; joyful. ~**মোহর** *n* impression of the heart; kiss. ~**রুবা** *adj* fascinating; bewitching; alluring; heart-ravishing. ❑*n* sweetheart. ~**লগি** *n* **1** amusement; merriment; jollying; jocularity; diversion. **2** attachment; inclination.

দিলাবর, দিলাবার=দিলওয়ার (⇒ দিল)

দিলির [P] *adj* bold; daring; intrepid; courageous; valiant.

দিল্লগি, দিল্লাগি=দিললগি (⇒ দিল)

দিল্লিকা লাড্ডু *n* **1** (lit) a ball-shaped sweet-meat made in Delhi. **2** (fig) sth which causes unhappiness when not obtained and disappointment when obtained.

দিশ *n*=দিক্[১]. ~**দিশ**, ~**বিদিশ**=দিকবিদিক (⇒ দিক[১]). ~**পাশ** *n* **1** estimate; reckoning. **2** limit; end:. কাজের ~পাশ নেই, have work without end; have to drudge endlessly; work in a disorderly manner.

দিশা *n* **1** direction; region; quarter/ point of the compass. **2** trace; direction. **3** composure; collectedness of mind; self-possession: ~ হারানো. **4** way; manner; method: ~ দেখানো. **5** puzzle; uncertainty: "পথে লাগে ~". ~ **না পাওয়া** *vi* be at a loss; be/ get lost; be perplexed/ puzzled; be bewildered. ~ **হারানো** = ~ না পাওয়া. ~**হারা** *adj* lost; puzzled; perplexed; bewildered; confused. ~**হীন** *adj* **1**=~হারা. **2** endless; boundless: ~হীন সাগর.

দিশি[১] *n* **1** day: নিশি~. **2** country; region; side; quarter; direction: সকল ~র দিশারী. ~-**দিশি** *n* all quarters/ sides/ directions. ❑ *adv* to/towards/ in all sides/ quarters; all around; everywhere.

দিশি[২], দিশী *adjj* (dial)=দেশী

দিশে *n* (colloq)=দিশা

দিষ্ট *adj* shown; pointed out; appointed; assigned; directed; bidden.

দিষ্টি *n* (colloq)=দৃষ্টি

দিস্তা, দিস্তে [P] (colloq) *nn* **1** quire (of paper). **2** pestle: হামান~. **3** skein of thread. **4** bundle of 24 arrows.

দীওয়ান=দিওয়ান

দীক্ষক *adj* initiating (to a religious teacher). ❑*n* initiator; spiritual guide; preceptor.

দীক্ষণ *n* initiation; consecration.

দীক্ষণীয় *adj* to be initiated (into); worthy of being initiated (into); fit for initiation.

দীক্ষা *n* **1** initiation (into); dedication; preparation/ consecration for a religious ceremony. **2** instruction; teaching; inspiration; sacrament. **3** (derog) instigation. ~ **দেওয়া** *vt* initiate (into); convert (to); baptize; imbibe/ inspire (with); indoctrinate (with); instigate; teach. ~ **নেওয়া/পাওয়া** *vi* be initiated (into); be converted to/ baptized; be indoctrinated (with); be imbibed/ inspired (with); be taught; learn; be instigated (with). **~গুরু** *n* teacher; initiator; preceptor; guru. **~গ্রহণ** *n* act of receiving initiation. ~ **গ্রহণ করা**=~ নেওয়া. **~মন্ত্র** *n* a mysterious formula that a person is taught at initiation; motto.

দীক্ষিত *adj* initiated into; converted to; baptized; imbued with; indoctrinated (with). ~ **করা** *vt*= দীক্ষা দেওয়া (⇒ দীক্ষা). ~ **হওয়া** *vi*= দীক্ষা নেওয়া (⇒ দীক্ষা).

দীগর=দিগর

দীঘল=দিঘল

দীঘি=দিঘি

দীধিতি *n* brightness; splendour; light.

দীন[১]=দিন[২]

দীন[২] *adj* **1** extremely poor; indigent; needy; destitute; wretched; miserable. **2** humble; lowly; modest; submissive; docile; meek. **3** afflicted; painful; sad: ~ নয়ন. **4** dejected; depressed; downcast; cast down. **দীনা** *fem*. **~চিত্ত** *adj* distressed in mind; dejected; in low spirits. **~চিত্তে** *adv* humbly; on bended knees; modestly; dejectedly. **~তা** *n* extreme poverty; indigence; destitution ; distress; affliction; wretchedness; weakness; misery; humbleness; modesty; humility. **~দয়াময়** *adj* kind to the poor. **~দরিদ্র** *adj* very wretched/ miserable; extremely humble and poor; downtrodden. **~দুঃখী** *adj* indigent and distressed. ❑*n* the poor. **~নাথ** *n* protector/ patron/ refuge of the poor. **~বৎসল** *adj* sympathetic/ kind/ friendly to the poor. **~বন্ধু** *n* friend of the poor; God. **~ভাব** *n* humbleness; modesty; humility; poverty; affectation of humility/ poverty. **~ভাবাপন্ন** *adj* modest; humble; humble-minded; servile; meek; unpretentious. **~মুখ** *adj* looking melancholy. **~রূপ** *adj* of melancholy aspect; dejected. **~সরণ** *n* refuge of the poor; God. **~সত্ত্ব, ~চিত্ত, ~হীন** *adj* extremely poor/indigent; beggarly; destitute; poor and lowly.

দীনার=দিনার

দীনি=দিনি

দীনেশ =দীননাথ (⇒ দীন[২])

দীপ *n* light; lamp; lantern. **~কিট্ট** *n* lamp-black; soot. **~কূপী** *n* wick of a lamp. **~গাছ, ~গাছা, ~ঝাড়** *nn* **1** chandelier. **2** lamp-stand; candle-stick. **~গৃহ** *n* light house. **~ধ্বজ** *n* flame; wick; soot. **~নির্বাণ** *n* extinction of a light; lights out; black-out. **~নির্বাণ করা** *vi* put out a lamp; extinguish lights. **~পুঞ্জ** *n* multitude of lamps. **~বতী**=দীপান্বিতা. **~প্রজ্বালন** *n* lighting a lamp. **~প্রজ্বালন করা** *vi* light a lamp. **~বর্তিকা** *n* wick of a lamp. **~বৃক্ষ** *n* lamp-stand; candle-stick. **~মালা** *n* row/ set of lights. **~শক্তি** *n* candle power. **~শলাকা** *n* match-stick; match. **~শিখা** *n* flame of a lamp. **দীপাগার** *n* lighthouse. **দীপাধার** *n* lamp stand. **দীপান্বিতা** *adj* furnished with lights; illuminated; radiating. ❑*n* = দীপালি. **দীপাবলী, দীপালি, দীপালী** *nn* **1** row of lights. **2** a Hindu festival with illuminations on the day of new moon in the month of Aswin or Kartik, when the goddess Kali is worshipped. **দীপালোক** *n* lamplight. **দীপালোকিত** *adj* illuminated with lamplight. **দীপালোচনা** *n* lantern lecture.

দীপক *adj* **1** illuminating; kindling; radiating; enlightening; illuminating; setting on fire. **2** inflaming. **3** exciting; stimulating; rousing. **4** beautifying; embellishing. **5** revealing; exhibiting; displaying. **দীপিকা** *fem*. ❑*n* **1** light; lamp; lantern. **2** name of a musical mode. **3** saffron; safflower. **4** a rhetorical figure (identity of action and agent). **5** bird of prey.

দীপন *adj* = দীপক. ❑*n* **1** illumination; enlightenment; radiation; act of illuminating/ kindling. **2** inflammation. **3** act of inspiring/ rousing; excitation. **4** beautification; embellishment. **5** display; exhibition; revelation. **~মাত্রা** *n* (phys) intensity of illumination. **~শক্তি***n* (phys)illuminating power.

দীপনীয় *adj* to be lighted/ kindled/ illuminated/ excited/ stimulated; excitable; to be embellished/ beautified; appetizing; helping digestion.

দীপা *vi* (poet) shine; blaze; flare; be luminous/ illustrious; glow; burn.

দীপাবলী, দীপালি⇒দীপ

দীপিকা *n* **1** *fem* commentary/ glossary (of a text). **2** moonlight. **3** lamp. name of a musical mode. ❑*adj*=দীপক.

দীপিত *adj* set on fire; inflamed; illuminated; brought to light; lighted; enkindled; manifested; displayed; revealed; excited; roused. **দীপিতা** *fem.*

দীপ্ত *adj* **1** burning; blazing; flaming; hot. **2** shining; bright; brilliant; splendid; luminous; lustrous; dozzling; glaring. **3** manifested; revealed; brought to light. **~কিরণ** *n* "hot-rayed"; the sun. **~কীর্তি** *adj* widely famous/ renowned; of brilliant/ immortal fame; most illustrious. **~কেতু** *adj* "bright-bannered"; carrying a brilliant flag. **~তপ** *adj* fervent in devotion; of glowing piety. **~তেজ** *adj* radiant with glory. **~দৃষ্টি, ~নয়ন** *adjj* having glittering eyes. **~দেহ, ~মূর্তি** *adjj* having a radiant figure. **~হুতাশন** *n* blazing fire. **দীপ্তাক্ষ** *adj* having bright/glittering/ blazing eyes. ❑*n* cat. **দীপ্তাগ্নি** *n* blazing fire. **দীপ্তাঙ্গ** *adj* having a brilliant body. ❑*n* peacock.

দীপ্তি *n* brightness; splendour; light; beauty; radiance; glow; lustre; shine; brilliance. **~পাওয়া** *vi* shine; glow; radiate; blaze; flare. **~ময়, ~মান** *adjj* brilliant; bright; splendid; lustrous; luminous; shining; glowing; sparkling; radiant; glowing with high spirit; conspicuous; resplendent. **~মতী, ~ময়ী** *fem.* **~মাপক** *n* (phys) photometer. **~মিতি** *n* photometry. **~শীল**=~ময়.

দীপ্তোজ্জ্বল *adj* gloriously bright; refulgent; resplendent.

দীপ্তোপল *n* sun gem.

দীপ্য=দীপনীয়. **~মান** *adj*=দীপ্তিময়.

দীপ্র *adj* flaming; shining; radiant; glowing.

দীয়মান *adj* in the state of being given/ distributed.

দীর্ঘ *adj* **1** long: ~ যষ্টি. **2** much; long: ~ সময়. **3** tall; high; lofty: ~ দেহ. **4** lengthy: ~ রচনা. **5** deep: ~শ্বাস. **6** large: ~ নয়ন. **7** prolonged; long: ~ জীবন. **8** (phonetics) long: ~ স্বর. **~ করা** *vt* lengthen; elongate. **~কণ্ঠ** *adj* long-necked. ❑*n* heron; crane. **~কাণ্ড** *adj* having long joints tall. ❑*n* **1** kind of radish. **2** lengthy affair. **~কায়** *adj* tall. **~কায়া** *fem.* **~কাল** *n* long time. **~কালব্যাপী** *adj* continuing for a long time. **~কেশ** *adj* long-haired. ❑*n* bear. **~কেশা, ~কেশী** *fem.* **~গতি** *adj* walking with long steps; striding. **~চ্ছেদ** *n* (geom) longitudinal section. **~জঙ্ঘ** *adj* long-legged. ❑*n* camel. **~জিহ্ব** *adj* long-tongued. ❑*n* snake. **~জীবন** *n* long life. **~জীবিতা** *n* longevity. **~জীবী** *adj* long-lived. **~জীবিনী** *fem.* **~তনু** *adj* having a long body; tall. **~তপা** *adj* having meditated for a long time. **~তম** *adj* longest; tallest. **~তমা** *fem.* **~তর** *adj* longer; taller. **~তরা** *fem.* **~তা, ~ত্ব** *nn* length; lengthiness. **~ত্রিপদী** *n* (prosody) a verse containing 26 syllables. **~দর্শন, ~দর্শী** *adjj* far-sighted; provident; far-seeing; sagacious; wise. **~দর্শিনী** *fem.* **~ দিন, ~ দিবস** *nn* long day; long time. **~ দৃষ্টি**=~দর্শন. **~নখ** *adj* having long nails. **~নাদ** *adj* long-sounding; loud. ❑*n* dog; conch-shell. **~নাস** *adj* long-nosed. **~নিদ্রা** *n* long sleep; death. **~নিঃশ্বাস, ~নিশ্বাস** *nn* long/deep-drawn sigh. **~নিঃশ্বাস নেওয়া** *vi* take a deep breath. **~নিঃশ্বাস ফেলা** *vi* (heave a) sigh. **~পক্ষ** *n* long wing. ❑*adj* long-winged; fork-tailed. **~পথ** *n* long way. **~পদ** *adj* long-legged. ❑*n* lengthy word. **~পাদ** *adj* long-legged. ❑*n* crane; heron; camel. **~বাহু** *adj* long-armed. **~বিলম্বিত** *adj* **1** long delayed. **2** hung low. **~ভুজ**=~বাহু. **~মাত্রা** *n* **1** (prosody) long syllable. **2** bracket. **3** large amount/dose. **4** great deal: ~মাত্রায় নিদ্রা যাওয়া. **~মুখ** *adj* long-faced; long-mouthed; long-beaked. **~যাত্রা** *n* long journey. **~রাত্র, ~রাত্রি** *nn* long night. **~রোগী** *adj* long ill/sick. **~রোমা** *adj* long-haired; shaggy. ❑*n* bear. **~রোষ** *adj* bearing a grudge. **~লোচন** *adj* long-eyed. **~শাখ** *adj* having long branches. **~শ্বাস**=~নিঃশ্বাস. **~সূত্র, ~সূত্রী** *adjj* "spinning a long yarn"; slow; procrastinating; dilatory; sluggish; slothful. **~সূত্রতা** *n* procrastination; dilatoriness; sluggishness; sloth. **~সূত্রতা করা** *vi* procrastinate. **~স্বর** *n* **1** (phonetics) long vowel. **2** (music) long note. ❑*adj* having a long note. **দীর্ঘাকার, দীর্ঘাকৃতি** *adjj* tall; long-formed; oblong; large. **দীর্ঘায়ত** *adj* large. **দীর্ঘায়ু(ঃ)** *adj* long-lived.

দীর্ঘিকা *n* (oblong) pond/lake.

দীর্ণ *adj* **1** torn; rent; sundered; split; cleft; broken. **2** scattered; dispersed.

দু- *adj* (used as a *pref*) two. **দু-আনি**=দুয়ানি. **দু-এক**=দুয়েক. **দুকথা** *n* **1** few words. **2** harsh words; rebuke:দুকথা শুনিয়ে দেওয়া. **3** altercation; argument: তার সঙ্গে অনর্থক দুকথা হয়ে গেল. **4** conversation; exchange of words: দুকথা না হলে বুঝবে কিরূপে? **দুকলম লেখা** write a few lines. **দুকান করা** *vi* give out (a secret). **দুকানকাটা** *adj* (fig) utterly shameless; brazen-faced; bare-faced; unblushing. **দুকাঠি বাজানো** (fig) set sb against sb. **দুকুল** *n* **1** the paternal and maternal lines (of any person). **2** the father's family and the father-in-law's family (of a woman). **3** (fig) both alternatives/ options. **দুকুল খাওয়া** *vi* (fig) lose all means of aid/ support; burn one's boats/ bridges. **দুকূল** *n* **1** both the banks (of a river). **2** this world and the next; both worlds. **3** (fig) both alternatives. **দুখানা, দুখানি, দুখান** (colloq) *n* two pieces; two. ❑*adj* two pieces of; two; split/ torn/ broken into two. **দুগুণ** *adj* twice; double. **দুঘড়ি** *n* **1** two hours. **2** noon; midnight. **দুচালা, দোচালা** *adj* having two (thatched) roofs. ❑*n* house with two (thatched) roofs. **দুচোখ** *n* two eyes. **দুচোখের দেখা** *n* brief meeting. **দুচোখের বিষ** (fig) anathema; bête noire; eyesore. **দুচোখের মিলন** *n* exchange of glances. **দুচোখ যেদিকে যায়** wherever (my) eyes lead (me) to. **দুচোখো** *adj* biased; one-sided; squint-eyed; unfair; jaundiced; partisan. **দুজন** *n* two (persons). ❑*adj* two. **দুজনই** *pron, adj* both. **দুটা, দুটো** *adjj* two (objects/things). ❑*n* two o'clock. **দুটি** *adj*=দুটা. **দুটানা, দোটানা** *n* simultaneous pulls in two opposite directions; dilemma; fix; oscillation; hesitation. **দুটানায়/দোটানায় পড়া** *vi* be in a dilemma/ fix/ quandary; not to know which way to turn; have misgivings. **~তরফা** *adj* pertaining to/ shared by/ contested by both the opposite sides; bipartite. **দুতলা, দোতলা** *adj* two-storied; double-decked. ❑*n* first floor; upper deck. **দুতারা, দোতারা** *adj* two-stringed. ❑*n* a double-stringed musical instrument. **দুধার** *n* both/two sides. **দুধারী** *adj* pertaining/ inclined to both the sides; two-sided; double-handled; double-edged: দুধারী তলোয়ার. **দুনলা, দোনলা** *adjj, nn* double-barrelled (gun). **দুনা, দুনো** *adjj* double; two-fold; twice as much. **দু-নৌকায় পা দেওয়া** (fig) fall between two stools; serve God and Mammon simultaneously. **~পহর**=দ্বিপ্রহর. **~-পাক** *n* **1** act/instance of twisting/ enfolding/ taking round twice. **2** two coils. **3** short stroll/ leisurely walk. **~-পাটি** *n* two rows of. **~পেয়ে** *adj* two-legged; biped. **দু-ফলা** *adj* **1** (of a knife) having two blades. **2** (of a tree) bearing fruit twice yearly. **দুফাঁক** *adj* split asunder into two. **দু-ফালি** *n* two slices. ❑*adj* sliced/ parted into two. **দুবার** *n* two times. ❑*adv* twice. **দুভাষী**=দোভাষী (⇒ দো). **দু-মনা** *adj* hesitating; of two minds; wavering; vacillating; shilly-shallying. **দুমুখো** *adj* **1** double-faced; two-faced. **2** two-way: দুমুখো রাস্তা. **দুমুখো আচরণ** *n* double-dealing; double-crossing; duplicity. **দুমুখো লোক** *n* double-dealer; hypocrite. **দু-মুঠী, দুমুঠো** *adj* two handfuls of. **দু-মেটে** *adj* (of clay images, etc) doubly plastered. **দুয়ানি** *n* two-*annas* bit/ piece. **দুরঙা** *adj* bi-coloured. **দু-সন্ধ্যা** *adj, adv* both in the day-time and evening; twice a day. **দুসুতি** *adj, n* (coarse cloth) woven in double thread. **দুহাত এক করা** *vi* **1** unite (a bride and bridegroom) in marriage. **2** cup one's palms. **দু-হাত এক হওয়া** *vi* be united in marriage. **দু-হাতি** *adj* measuring two cubits. **দুহাতিয়া** *adj* (of a stroke) dealt with both hands. ❑*adv* with both hands.

দুই *n, adj* two. ❑*adj, pron* both: ও ~ই এক কথা. **~-এক** *adj* one or two; a few.

দুও=দুয়ো

দুঃ- *pref* implying, evil, vile, wicked, bad, difficult, hard, prohibited; inauspicious, distressing, sorrowful, badly, slight;inferior, etc.

দুঃখ *n* **1** sorrow; uneasiness; trouble, difficulty; grief; distress; unhappiness; misery; suffering; woe; tribulation: তার দুঃখের শেষ নেই. **2** pain; inflammation. **3** regret; remorse; repentance. **4** apology: আসতে না পেরে তিনি ~ প্রকাশ করলেন. **~ করা** *vi* **1** regret; remorse (for sth). **2** grieve (for sb); grieve (over/ about sb/ sth); sorrow (at/for/over sth); be/ feel sorry for. **3** repent; rue: তোমাকে এজন্যে ~ করতে হবে, You will live to rue it. **4** suffer (pain); take trouble: ছেলেটাকে মানুষ করতে তার মা অনেক ~ করছে. **~ দেওয়া** *vi* pain; grieve; distress; hurt; (give) trouble; anguish; gall; cause pain/ trouble/ distress. **~ পাওয়া/ ভোগ করা** *vi* suffer (pain); be stricken with sorrow/ grief/ misery; be in pain/ trouble; be afflicted/ distressed/ pained. **~ সওয়া** *vi* suffer pain/ torture; bear one's sorrow/ sufferings; pass through trouble. **দুঃখে পড়া** *vi* run into trouble/ distress; fall upon evil days. **~কর, ~জনক, ~দ** *adjj* causing pain; painful; afflicting; grievous; woeful; sad; agonizing; distressing. **~দগ্ধ** *adj* pained; distressed. **~দায়ক, ~দায়ী**=~কর. **~দায়িনী** *fem.* **~দারিদ্র্য** *n* sorrows and poverty; miseries. **~ধান্দা** *n* painful manual labour; drudgery. **~প্রদ**=~কর. **~বহুল** *adj* full of trouble and pain. **~বাদ** *n* pessimism. **~বাদী** *n* pessimist. ❑*adj* pessimistic. **~বেগ** *n* violent grief. **~বোধ** *n* feeling of sorrow/grief. **~বোধ করা** *vi* feel sorry/ pity; be sorry. **~ভাগী** *adj* sharing the sorrow of another; having pain as one's portion; unhappy. **~ভাগিনী** *fem.* **~ভোগ** *n* act of suffering pain/ undergoing distress. **~ময়** *adj* full of/ abounding in sorrow/ suffering. **~মোচন** *n* deliverance from pain; allaying/ alleviation/ mitigation of sorrow/suffering; relieving pain/ distress. **~লভ্য** *adj* attainable through sorrow/ suffering. **~শোক** *n* pain and sorrow. **~সহিষ্ণু** *adj* patiently enduring sorrow/ suffering. **~সাগর** *n* ocean of pain; great sorrow; sea of distress; endless sorrow/ suffering. **~হর, ~হারী** *adjj* removing pain; relieving pain/ sorrow/ suffering. **~হরা, ~হারিণী** *fem.* **দুঃখাকুল** *adj* filled with sorrow. **দুঃখাতীত** *adj* freed/ escaped from pain; past all sorrow/ suffering; immune to sorrow/ suffering. **দুঃখান্ত** *n* end of pain/ trouble. **দুঃখান্বিত** *adj* accompanied with pain; filled with grief; distressed. **দুঃখান্বিতা** *fem.* **দুঃখার্ত** *adj* visited by pain; distressed; rueful; suffering. **দুঃখের কাহিনী** *n* pathetic/ woeful tale. **~বিষয়** *n* matter of regret; pity; painful affair. **দুঃখের সাগর**=~সাগর.

দুঃখিত *adj* pained; sorry; distressed; afflicted; unhappy; rueful; grieved; sad; sorrowful; suffering; regretful; stricken with sorrow. **দুঃখিতা** *fem.* **~চিত্ত, ~হৃদয়** *adj* pained at heart; having a sorrowing/ regretful mind/ heart; grief laden; heavy-hearted; sore at heart; broken hearted.

দুঃখী *adj* **1**=দুঃখিত. **2** poor; destitute; poverty-stricken; needy. □*n* poor person; destitute; pauper; wretch. **দুঃখিনী** *fem.* **দুঃখের ~** *n* sympathizer.

দুঃখোক্তি *n* regrets; lament; rueful/ woeful utterance/ remark.

দুঃশাসন *adj* **1** difficult to be controlled; unruly; indomitable; intractable; refractory. **2** misgoverning; tyrannous. □*n* misgovernment; tyranny.

দুঃশীল *adj* badly disposed; ill-behaved; wicked; depraved; vicious. **দুঃশীলা** *fem.* **~তা** *n* misbehaviour; wickedness; depravity; bad nature; viciousness.

দুঃশ্রব *adj* unpleasant to be heard. **~ত্ব** *n* cacophony.

দুঃসংবাদ *n* bad/evil news.

দুঃসম *adj* unequal; uneven; unfit; perverse.

দুঃসময় *n* evil days; hard days.

দুঃসহ *adj* unbearable; intolerable; insufferable; severe; insupportable.

দুঃসাধ্য *adj* difficult; arduous; uphill; difficult to be performed/ accomplished; difficult to be cured. **~ কার্য** *n* arduous/ uphill task. **~তা** *n* state of being hard to accomplish; difficulty; formidability.

দুঃসাহস *n* audacity; intrepidity; daring; overmuch boldness; foolhardiness; bravado; temerity. **দুঃসাহসিক, দুঃসাহসী** *adjj* audacious; intrepid; daring; daredevil; adventuresome; impetuous; foolhardy; excessively bold. **দুঃসাহসিকতা**=~.

দুঃস্থ *adj* **1** poor; miserable; indigent; needy; wretched. **2** distressed; desolate; afflicted; woebegone. **~তা** *n* poverty; indigence; wretchedness; misery; ill condition.

দুঃস্থিত=দুঃস্থ. **দুঃস্থিতি**=দুঃস্থিতি

দুঃস্পর্শ *adj* difficult to be touched; unpleasant to the touch.

দুঃস্মৃতি *n* unpleasant memory.

দুঃস্বপ্ন *n* bad/distressing/ inauspicious/ terrifying dream; nightmare.

দুঁদে *adj* **1** terrible; difficult to cope/contend with; roguish; terribly wicked; turbulent; unruly; riotous; wild; wilful; rowdy; headstrong. **2** quarrelsome; litigious; wrangling; contentious; bellicose; pugnacious; factious; disruptive.

দুকান=দু–

দুকুল[১]⇒দু–

দুকুল[২] *n* very fine cloth; silk-cloth; linen; white cloth. **~ধারী** *adj* wearing a garment of fine cloth/ silk-cloth. **~ধারিণী** *fem.* **~বাস**=~.

দুখ, দুখী, দুখিনী (poet, dial)=দুঃখ, দুঃখী and দুঃখিনী respectively.

দুগুণ ⇒ দু–

দুগ্ধ *n* milk; milky juice of plants; sap; latex. **~কৃপিকা** *n* a cake made of ground rice and filled with coagulated milk. **~জ, ~জাত** *adjj* produced from milk. **~জাত দ্রব্য** *n* milk-product. **~দোহন** *n* milking. **~ধবল** *adj* milky white. **~পাত্র** *n* milk-pan; milk-pail. **~পান** *n* drinking of milk. **~পায়ী** *adj* suckling (baby). **~পোষ্য** *adj* suckling; living on one's mother's milk; breast-fed. □*n* suckling. **~পোষ্য শিশু** *n* suckling; a child at the breast. **~ফেন** *n* froth of milk. **~ফেননিভ** *adj* milky white; as white and soft as the froth of milk. **~বতী** *adj* giving milk; milch. **~বতী গাভী** *n* milch-cow. **~বৎ** *adj* milk-like; milky. **~বিক্রেতা** *n* milkman; milk-seller. **~ভাণ্ড**=~পাত্র. **~মুখ** *adj* having milk in the mouth; very young. **~শর্করা** *n* lactose. **দুগ্ধাল**=~বতী.

দুঘড়ি, দুচালা, দু–চুচকো, দুটানা ⇒ দু

দুড়দাড়, দুড়দুড় *nn* (onom) expressing **(a)** noise of (heavy and) hurried footsteps; **(b)** rumbling of clouds; rumble; **(c)** rapid and audible of palpitation; throb. 4 noise of beating or boxing; knock; rap.

দুড়ুম n (onom) milder form of দড়াম; crash; bang-bang.

দুৎ *int* hang ! dash ! blow !

দুত্তোর *int* go to blaze ! brat it ! confound it ! bother !

দুদ্দাড়=দুড়দাড়

দুধ=দুগ্ধ. **~ কেটে যাওয়া** (of milk) turn sour; curdle. **~ খাওয়া** *vi* drink milk; suck (one's mother's breast). **~ খাওয়ানো** *vt* suckle; give suck (to). **~ ছাড়ানো** *vt* wean (a baby). **~ ছানা হয়ে যাওয়া/ছিঁড়ে যাওয়া**=~ কেটে যাওয়া. **~ তোলা** *vi* (of babies) vomit/spew milk. **~ দেওয়া** *ui* give/yield milk. **~ দোওয়া** *vi* milk. **~ কলা দিয়ে সাপ পোষা** (fig) nourish a viper in one's breast; fatten one's mortal enemy. **~কুসুম্ভা** *n* kind of milkshake mixed with a paste of hemp-leaves. **~-ক্ষীর** *n* milk condensed by boiling (taken as a sweet-meat). **~রুটি** *n* milksop. **~স্রোত** *n* stream of milk. **~ নামা, ~ ভর করা** *vv* (of breasts) swell (during pregnancy). **দুধে-আলতা** *adj* (of complexion) rosy; deep pink. **দুধে-জলে মেশা** get mixed/blended completely; (fig) be compromised thoroughly. **দুধে(র) দাঁত** *n* milk-tooth. **দুধে-ভাতে থাকা** *vi* live in affluence; never have had it so good; have one's bread buttered on both sides. **দুধের ছেলে** *n* infant boy; suckling. **দুধের মেয়ে** *n* infant girl; suckling. **দুধের মাছি** *n* **1** kind of house-fly that feeds on milk. **2** (fig) fair-weather friend. **দুধের সর** *n* cream. **দুধের স্বাদ ঘোলে মেটানো** to have to be satisfied with an inferior alternative.

দুধাল, দুগ্ধাল=দুগ্ধাল (⇒ দুগ্ধ)

দুন *n* (music) kind of quick time; act of playing a musical instrument or singing in quick temp.

দুনা ⇒দু–

দুনি *n* bucket; vessel; trough.

দুনিয়া [A] *n* the world; life or people of this world; worldly goods; good things of this life; wealth; earth. **~দার** *adj* worldly; self-seeking; worldly-minded. **~দারি** *n* worldly affairs; goods; worldliness; attention to worldly concerns; intercourse; the (whole) world. **~বি** *adj* worldly; belonging to the world.

দুনো ⇒দু–

দুন্দুভি *n* sort of large kettle-drum.

দুপ *n* (onom) thud; plonk. **~ করে** *adv* with a thud/plonk; plonk. **~দাপ, ~দুপ** *n* express repeated thuds/romping.

দুপুর, দুপর *n* midday; noon. **~ রাত, রাত ~** *nn* midnight.

দুপুস *n* (onom) thud. **~দাপুস** *n* throbs.

দুম *n*=দুপ. **~ করে** *adv* **1** with a thud; plonk. **2** all on a sudden; abruptly. **~দুম, ~দাম, দুমাদুম** *n* repeated banging/booming/thumping noise.

দুমচি [P] *n* crupper; lower part of he back.

দুমড়ন *n* crumpling; twisting.

দুমড়া *adj* turned; crumpled; twisted. **~নো** *vi, vt* bend/turn the edge; crumple; twist. ❑*adj* =~.

দুমাদুম ⇒ দুম

দুম্বা [P] *n* kind of sheep with a thick fatty tail.

দুয়া *adj* (archaic)=দুয়ো

দুয়া[2] *n*=দোয়া[2]

দুয়ার *n* door; gate. **দুয়ারি, দুয়ারী** *n* door-keeper; gateman. **দুয়ারে কাঁটা দেওয়া** (fig) bar sb's entrance. **দুয়ারে বাঁধা হাতি** (fig) rolling in wealth; exceptionally affluent; booming; opulent.

দুয়েম [P] *adj* second (class); inferior: ~ জমি.

দুয়ো *adj* unfortunate; miserable; forlorn; wretched; neglected by one's husband. **~রানী** *n* a queen neglected by her royal husband who is misguided by his other wife/wives.

দুরক্ষর *n* evil word; abuse; rebuke.

দুরতিক্রম *adj* hard/difficult to overcome/go across/through; insurmountable; inevitable. **দুরতিক্রমা** *fem.* **দুরতিক্রমণ** *n* difficult passage. **~নীয়, দুরতিক্রম্য** *adjj*=~. **~নীয়া, দুরতিক্রম্যা** *fem.*

দুরত্যয় *adj* **1**=দুরতিক্রম. **2** inaccessible. **3** unfathomable; inscrutable.

দুরদুর *n* (onom) throb; palpitation; tremble; tremor. ❑*adj* palpitating; throbbing; tremulous; trembling; fearful; frightful. **~ করা** *vi* throb; palpitate; tremble.

দুরদৃষ্ট *n* ill luck/fate/fortune/misfortune. ❑*adj* unfortunate; unlucky; unhappy; luckless. **~ক্রমে, ~বশত** *adv* unluckily; as ill luck would have it; unfortunately.

দুরধিগম(্য) *adj* **1** difficult to be obtained; not easily available. **2** not easily accessible; inaccessible; difficult to access. **3** unfathomable; incomprehensible; inscrutable; abstruse. **দুরধিগম্যা** *fem.*

দুরধ্যয় *adj* difficult/hard to read; hard-reading.

দুরন্ত *adj* **1** unmanageably restless/naughty; turbulent; wild; unruly; mischievous; romping: ~ শিশু. **2** severe; harsh; rigorous: ~ শীত. **3** relentless; fierce; ferocious; implacable; unrelenting: ~ শত্রু. **4** awful; terrible; violent: ~ লোভ. **5** very strong; fierce; violent: ~ ঝড়. **6** hard to cure; relentless; persistent: ~ রোগ. **7** devilish/intolerably hot: ~ দিন. **8** billowy; turbulent; stormy: ~ সমুদ্র. **9** difficult to go through/across; steep; difficult to be passed along: ~ পথ. **10** indomitable: ~ সাহস. **~পনা** *n* turbulence; naughtiness; romping and mischievous behaviour/conduct; pranks; restlessness.

দুরপনেয় *adj* difficult to remove/efface; not easily delible. **~ কলঙ্ক** *n* indelible stain/ blot/ blemish.

দুরবগাহ *adj* difficult to bathe in; difficult to access; difficult to be fathomed/found out; inaccessible.

দুরবস্থ *adj* **1** badly situated. **2** wretched; miserable; fallen into a bad state; poverty-stricken; indigent; in strained circumstances. **দুরবস্থা** *n* bad situation; bad/low state; distress; poverty; indigence; wretchedness; misery.

দুরবিন [P] *n* telescope.

দুরভিগ্রহ *adj* difficult to be laid hold of; difficult to comprehend/know; difficult to accept/take/ apprehend; abstruse.

দুরভিসন্ধি *n* evil design/motive; bad intention; sinister motive. **~মূলক** *adj* ill-motivated; stemming from a sinister motive.

দুরমুশ *n* **1** rammer; act of beating down with a rammer. **2** (iron) sound drubbing/thrashing. **~ করা** *vt* **1** beat down with a rammer. **2** drub soundly.

দুরস্ত [P] *adj* **1** right; fit; proper; correct ; true. **2** corrected; amended; rectified: ভুল ~ হওয়া. **3** orderly; tidy; well-arranged; will-kept; spruce; clean; prim; কাপড়চোপড় ~ থাকা. **4** levelled: রাস্তা ~ থাকা. **5** chastened; chastised: চোর ~ হওয়া.

❑*adv* in keeping with: কেতা–~, লেফাফা–~. ~করা *vt* correct; amend; fit; arrange; adjust; put in order; repair; rectify; mend; restore; level; chasten; chastise.

দুরাকাঙ্ক্ষ *adj* inordinately/audaciously ambitious; insatiable. **দুরাকাঙ্ক্ষা** *n* inordinate/audacious ambition; aspiration; yearning; unrealizable longing; cry for the moon. **দুরাকাঙ্ক্ষী**=~ দুরাকাঙ্ক্ষিণী *fem.*

দুরাক্রম(্য) *adj* difficult to be ascended/ approached; unassailable.

দুরাগ্রহ *n* wicked/difficult venture; desire for/interest in evil/difficult things; wicked obstinacy. ❑*adj* indulging/engaged in wicked/difficult venture; desirous of/interested in evil/difficult things; evil-minded.

দুরাচর *adj* difficult to be practised/performed; difficult to be treated/cured; incurable.

দুরাচার *n* bad behaviour; ill conduct; wickedness; depravity; infamy; evildoing; vile/abominable/nasty practice. ❑*adj* wicked; infamous; depraved; sinful; nefarious; sinful; perverted; corrupt; monstrous. **দুরাচারিণী** *fem.*

দুরাত্মা *adj* 1 evil-natured; wicked; bad; sinful; depraved. 2 roguish; villainous; oppressive; tyrannous.

দুরাধর্ষ *adj* difficult to attack/approach; dangerous; invincible; irresistible; indomitable.

দুরারাধ্য *adj* difficult to be propitiated/ won/ overcome; obstinate.

দুরারোগ্য *adj* difficult to cure; incurable; irremediable.

দুরারোহ *adj* difficult to climb/ascend/scale; very steep; precipitous.

দুরালাপ *n* curse; imprecation; abuse.

দুরাশয় *adj* evil-minded; malicious; wicked. ❑*n* evil design/purpose.

দুরাশা *n* vain hope; despair.

দুরাসদ *adj* 1 difficult/dangerous to be approached; difficult to be accomplished; difficult to be found/met with; unparalleled; unheard of; difficult to obtain/procure; not easily available/attainable. 2 hard to bear/suffer; unbearable; intolerable. 3 wicked; villainous; indomitable; fierce. 4 difficult to comprehend; inscrutable.

দুরি *n* the two of playing cards/dice; deuce.

দুরিত *n* evil; sin; danger; discomfort. ❑*adj* wicked; sinful; bad; difficult.

দুরী=দুরি

দুরুক্ত *adj* harsh; injurious; harshly addressed. ❑*n* harsh/bad word.

দুরুক্তি *n* harsh/injurious speech; revilement; rude words; abuse.

দুরুচ্চার, দুরুচ্চার্য *adjj* 1 difficult to pronounce/ utter; break-jaw. 2 obscene; filthy.

দুরুত্তর *adj* 1 unanswerable. 2 difficult to cross/overcome. ❑*n* inappropriate answer.

দুরুদুরু *n* (onom)=দুরদুর

দুরূহ *adj* difficult to be inferred/understood; difficult; hard; stiff; abstruse; tough; arduous; intricate; knotty. ~তা *n* difficulty; complexity; intricacy; abstruseness.

দুর্গ *n* 1 citadel; stronghold; fort; fortress; castle; fortification. 2 difficult/narrow passage. ~পতি *n* commandant/governor of a fortress. ~প্রাকার *n* rampart. ~সঞ্চর *n* difficult passage; defile.

দুর্গত *adj* fairing ill; unfortunate; miserable; destitute; wreched; indigent; poverty-stricken; distressed; affected; afflicted; in adverse circumstances.

দুর্গতি *n* 1 misfortune; distress; adversity; misery; wretchedness; poverty; indigence; danger; calamity; affliction. 2 hell. ~নাশিনী *adj fem* removing distress. ❑*n* goddess Durga.

দুর্গন্ধ *n* bad/offensive smell; stink. ❑*adj* ill-smelling; stinking; offensive; fetid. **দুর্গন্ধী** *adj*=~.

দুর্গম *adj* 1 difficult to be traversed/travelled over; impassable; inaccessible; difficult to access/approach. 2 unattainable.

দুর্গা *n fem* goddess Durga, wife of Shiva. ~পূজা *n* worship of goddess Durga; chief festival in honour of Durga, held in autumn.

দুর্গাধিকারী, দুর্গাধ্যক্ষ=দুর্গপতি (⇒ দুর্গ)

দুর্গেশ=দুর্গপতি (⇒ দুর্গ). ~নন্দিনী *n fem* castellan's daughter.

দুর্গোৎসব=দুর্গাপূজা (⇒দুর্গা)

দুর্গ্রহ১ *adj* difficult to take/seize/catch/ capture/ comprehend/understand/win/attain; unfathomable; inscrutable.

দুর্গ্রহ২ *n* (astrol) malicious/ill-boding star.

দর্গ্রাহ্য=দুর্গ্রহ১

দুর্ঘট *adj* hard to be accomplished; difficult; unlikely to happen; of rare occurrence.

দুর্ঘটনা *n* accident; mishap; calamity.

দুর্ঘোষ *adj* harsh-sounding. ❑*n* bear.

দুর্জন *adj* wicked; malicious; villainous; roguish. ❑*n* bad man; villain; scoundrel; rogue. ~তা *n* wickedness; villainy; roguery.

দুর্জয় *adj* difficult to be conquered/won; invincible; irresistible.

দুর্জাত *adj* badly born; ill-starred; miserable; wretched.

দুর্জেয়=দুর্জয়

দুর্জ্ঞেয় *adj* difficult to understand/know/find/ comprehend; abstruse; impenetrable; recondite; obscure; inscrutable.

দুর্ণয় *n* bad/imprudent conduct.

দুর্দম, দুর্দমনীয়, দুর্দম্য *adjj* hard/difficult to subdue; indomitable; obstinate; unruly.

দুর্দশা *n* adversity; hard times; misfortune; ill/evil/adverse/hard fortune/luck; hardship; downfall; evil day. **~গ্রস্ত, ~পন্ন** *adjj* in adverse circumstances; stricken with adversity; disastrous; miserable; wretched; fallen into bad state; dilapidated; fallen upon evil days.

দুর্দর্শ *adj* difficult to be seen/met with.

দুর্দান্ত *adj* badly tamed; untamable; uncontrollable unruly; violent.

দুর্দিন *n* **1** rainy/cloudy day; bad/foul weather. **2** evil days; difficult time; hard times; time of adversity/distress. **দুর্দিনের বন্ধু/সহায়** *n* friend in adversity/need.

দুর্দৈব *n* bad/ill-luck; misfortune; mishap.

দুর্ধর্ষ *adj* difficult to capture/conquer/vanquish; unconquerable; invincible; dangerous; dreadful; fearful; awful; inviolable; inaccessible.

দুর্নাম *n* bad name; ill fame; disrepute; notoriety; discredit, odium; ill repute.

দুর্নিবার, দুর্নিবার্য *adjj* difficult to be kept back; irresistible; unrestrainable; irrepressible.

দুর্নিমিত্ত *n* bad/ill omen.

দুর্নিরীক্ষ্য *adj* difficult to be looked at/seen; invisible; undiscernible; indistinct; imperceptible.

দুর্নীত *adj* ill-conducted; wrong; morally degenerated corrupt; depraved; wicked; perverted. ❑*n* misconduct; folly; moral degeneration; malpractice; wickedness; corruption; malpractice; maladministration.

দুর্নীতি *n* =দুর্নীত. **~গ্রস্ত, ~পরায়ণ** *adj* =দুর্নীত

দুর্বচন *n* rude/bad/hard language/words; revilement; discourteous language/words; invective; swearword. ❑*adj* using bad/harsh language; given to speaking rude/bad/harsh words; foul-mouthed; vituperative; venomous; rudely outspoken; harsh-tongued.

দুর্বচনীয়=দুর্বাচ্য

দুর্বৎসর *n* bad/troublesome/inauspicious year; year of scarcity/hardship/famine.

দুর্বল *adj* **1** weak; feeble; infirm; fragile; unwell; delicate; sick; debilitated; frail; faint; weakened: ~ শক্তি/স্বাস্থ্য/দৃষ্টি. **2** spineless; nerveless; weak: ~ চরিত্র. **3** powerless; impotent: ~ দেশ. **দুর্বলা** *fem.* **~ করা** *vt* weaken; enfeeble; impair; debilitate; disable; unman; sap; devitalize; cripple. **~ হওয়া** *vi* become weak; weaken; sag; decline; dwindle; flag. **~চিত্ত** *adj* weak-minded; chicken hearted; faint hearted; unmanly. **~তা** *n* weakness; infirmity; feebleness debility; impotence; enfeeblement; exhaustion; frailty; fragility.

দুর্বহ *adj* hard to bear/carry; heavy; hard to endure/suffer; unbearable; intolerable.

দুর্বাক *adj*=দুর্বচন

দুর্বাক্য *n*=দুর্বচন

দুর্বাচ্য *adj* hard to be uttered; unutterable; unspeakable; vile; obscene. ❑*n* harsh word; revilement.

দুর্বার(ণ) *adj* hard to be checked/prevented/ resisted; restrained; irrepressible; irresistible.

দুর্বাসনা *n* bad inclination; evil desire; vain longing.

দুর্বাসা *n* badly clad; naked. ❑ (myth) name of a Hindu saint.

দুর্বিনীত *adj* badly educated; ill-bred; ill-conducted; undisciplined; mean; wicked; obstinate; rude; restive; impolite; discourteous; ill-mannered; arrogant; haughty; insolent. **দুর্বিনীতা** *fem.*

দুর্বিনেয় *adj* untamable; rebellious; defiant; refractory.

দুর্বিপাক *n* trouble; predicament; difficult straits; entanglement; impasse; danger; disaster; difficulty; fix. **দুর্বিপাকে পড়া** *vi* be in a predicament; meet with difficulty; run into trouble; get into difficulties .

দুর্বিমোচন *adj* difficult to set free.

দুর্বিষহ *adj* difficult to bear/suffer/endure; intolerable; unendurable; insufferable; unbearable.

দুর্বুদ্ধি *n* **1** folly; evil/mischivous thought/design; foolishness; bad disposition of the minds; bad/evil idea; imprudence. **2** villain; scoundrel fool; blockhead. ❑*adj* evil-minded; foolish; mindless; malicious; ignorant; silly.

দুর্বৃত্ত *adj* vile; behaving badly; mean; vicious wicked; villainous; roguish; depraved. ❑*n* **1** rogue; villain; scoundrel; wicked person; mischief-monger; miscreant. **2** bad conduct; meanness. **~তা, দুর্বৃত্তি** *nn* vice; crime; bad conduct; villainy; wickedness; roguery; depravity.

দুর্বোধ(্য) *adj* difficult to understand; not easily intelligible; unfathomable; obscure; inscrutable; incomprehensible; unintelligible.

দুর্ব্যবহার *n* misbehaviour; harsh treatment; rude behaviour/demeanour; ill-treatment. **~ করা** *vi* misbehave (with); treat sb rudely/ harshly; ill-treat; treat sb unkindly.

দুর্ভক্ষ্য *adj* hard/difficult to eat; unfit for eating; inedible.

দুর্ভগ *adj* unfortunate; unlucky. **দুর্ভগা** *fem.*

দুর্ভর *adj* difficult to be borne/ supported/ maintained; heavily laden with; heavy; hard to sustain/endure. **দুর্ভাগা** *adj* unfortunate; unlucky; ill-fated; miserable; wretched. **দুর্ভাগিনী** *fem.*

দুর্ভাগ্য *n* ill/bad luck; misfortune; sinister fate. □*adj* =দুর্ভাগা. **দুর্ভাগ্যা** *fem.* **~ক্রমে, ~বশত** *adv* unluckily; unfortunately; as ill luck would have it .

দুর্ভাবনা *n* worry; anxiety; troublesome thought; apprehension; misgiving; concern; care; solicitude. **~ করা** *vi* worry; trouble oneself; be anxious; have misgivings. **~গ্রস্ত, ~পীড়িত** *adjj* worried; anxious; apprehensive; troubled; care-worn; perturbed; bothered; disturbed.

দুর্ভিক্ষ *n* famine; (time of) scarcity; extreme want/shortage. **~পীড়িত** *adj* famine-stricken.

দুর্ভেদ(্য) *adj* **1** difficult to be broken/torn asunder; difficult to penetrate/enter/force one's way into; impenetrable; impervious; impregnable. **2** unfathomable; obscure; unintelligible; unscrutable. **দুর্ভেদ্যতা** *n* impenetrability; obscurity; imperviousness; inscrutability; density; opaqueness. **~প্রকোষ্ঠ** *n* strong room.

দুর্ভোগ *n* suffering; distress; harassment; misery; trouble; anguish.

দুর্মতি=দুর্বুদ্ধি

দুর্মদ *adj* terribly drunken/intoxicated; mad; fierce; infatuated by; frenzied; difficult to subdue/resist; indomitable; irresistible.

দুর্মনা *adj* **1** sad; melancholy; in bad/low spirits. **2** anxious; worried. **~য়মান** worrying; worried; anxious.

দুর্মর *adj* dying hard; die-hard; tenacious of life; inflexible; obstinate; stubborn; rigid.

দুর্মুখ *adj* ugly-faced; foul-mouthed; abusive; scurrilous.

দুর্মূল্য *adj* dear in price; very costly; highly expensive. **~তা** *n* excessive costliness/ dearness.

দুর্মেধা *adj* dull-witted; stupid; ignorant; foolish; evil-minded.

দুর্মোচ্য *adj* hard to unloose; indelible.

দুর্যোগ *n* **1** inclement/foul weather. **2** difficult time; hard times; (time of) danger; gathering clouds; evil days. **~পূর্ণ** *adj* foul; inclement; stormy; dangerous; fateful; ugly; treacherous; perilous.

দুর্যোধন *adj* difficult to be conquered. □*n* name of the eldest son of Dhritarashtra of the Mahabharata.

দুর্লক্ষণ *n* ill/inauspicious omen; bad sign/symptom. □*adj* having an inauspicious omen/sign; sinister; unlucky; ill-fated; bearing on one's person an inauspicious mark; badly marked. **দুর্লক্ষণা** *fem.*

দুর্লঙ্ঘ(্য) *adj* difficult to be surmounted/ overcome; insurmountable; impassable. **~বাধা** *n* insuperable barriers.

দুর্লভ *adj* difficult to be obtained/found; hard; scarce; rare; extremely costly/dear; extraordinary; eminent . **দুর্লভা** *fem.*. **~তা** *adj* scarceness; rarity.

দুর্ললিত *adj* ill-mannered; wayward; spoilt.

দুর্লেখ্য *n* illegible writing; forged document.

দুর্হৃদ(য়) *adj* bad-hearted; wicked. □*n* enemy.

দুল *n* earring; ear-drop.

দুলকি *n* trot. **~ চালে চলা** *vi* **1** trot. **2** (of a person) move slowly with an air of self-importance; saunter; strut.

দুলহা= দুলা[২]

দুলা[১], দোলা *vi* swing; dangle; rock; oscillate; shake to and fro. **দোলানো** *vt* swing; rock; dangle; oscillate; shake to and fro.

দুলা[২] *n* bridegroom. **দুলহিন** *fem* bride.

দুলাল *adj* dear; beloved; darling. □*n* sweet-heart; darling; dear; apple of the eye; minion. **দুলালী** *fem.*

দুলিচা *n* piece of small carpet; rug.

দুলুনি *n* **1** rocking; swinging; swing. **2** sth/sb which swings/rocks.

দুলে *n* one of a backward caste amongst the Hindus (usually employed as palanquin bearers). **~নী** *fem.*

দুশমন [P] *n* enemy; foe; adversary.

দুশমনি [P] *n* enmity; hostility; hatred; detestation. **~ করা** *vi* be hostile/unfriendly; show ill will; bear malice; begrudge; bear a grudge.

দুশ্চর *adj* **1** difficult to traverse: ~ কান্তার. **2** difficult to be performed; extremely austere: ~ তপস্যা.

দুশ্চরিত্র, দুশ্চরিত্রা *adj* wicked; characterless; vile; having a vitiated character; corrupt; depraved. □*n* wickedness; ill-conduct; misbehaviour; vileness; vitiated/depraved character. **দুশ্চরিত্রতা** *n* wickedness; vileness; depravation; corruption. **দুশ্চিকিৎস্য** *adj* difficult to cure; without remedy.

দুশ্চিন্তা=দুর্ভাবনা

দুশ্চেষ্টা *n* **1** misconduct; error; wickedness; wrongdoing; misdeeds; misdoing. **2** attempt to accomplish an impossible task; desperate/futile attempt.

দুশ্চেষ্টিত *adj* **1** doing evil; wicked; villainous; maleficent. **2** attempting to accomplish an impossible task; making a desperate/futile/ impossible attempt.

দুশ্ছেদ্য *adj* difficult to cut (off)/sever/destroy; difficult to separate/tear off.

দুষমন=দুশমন

দুষা *vt* blame; accuse; hold responsible for; reproach.

দুষ্কর *adj* difficult; arduous; uphill; difficult to do/accomplish/execute/perform. **~তা** *n* difficulty.

দুষ্কর্ম *n* wickedness; sin; misdeed; mischief; crime; wicked act. **দুষ্কর্মা** *adj* acting wickedly; criminal; evil-doing; mischievous; sinful; vicious; maleficent. □*n* evildoer; criminal; malefactor; miscreant; mischief-maker.

দুষ্কার্য=দুষ্কর্ম

দুষ্কাল *n* evil time; unpropitious/inauspicious time.

দুষ্কুল *n* low family/race. □*adj* of a low family; low-born.

দুষ্কৃত *n* evil action; sin; guilt; wicked act; crime; misdeed; mischief. □*adj* wrongly/ mischievously/wickedly done; badly arranged/ organized/applied. **~কারী**=দুষ্কর্মা.

দুষ্কৃতি *n*=দুষ্কৃত

দুষ্কৃতী *adj*=দুষ্কর্মা

দুষ্ক্রিয় *adj*=দুষ্কর্মা. **দুষ্ক্রিয়া** *n*=দুষ্কর্ম. **দুষ্ক্রিয়ান্বিত** *adj*=দুষ্কর্মা

দুষ্ক্রীত *adj* badly/dearly bought.

দুষ্ট *adj* **1** spoilt; defective; faulty; wrong; false: ~ প্রকাশভঙ্গি. **2** bad; wicked; vile; vicious; depraved: ~ লোক. **3** naughty; mischievous: ~ ছেলে. **4** malignant; dangerous; fatal; septic; morbid: ~ ব্যাধি. **5** inimical; offensive: ~ গন্ধ. **6** evil; bad: ~ সঙ্গী. **7** guilty; culpable: ~ মন. **8** malicious: ~ গ্রহ. **9** sinning through; defiled with: কর্ম~, বাগ~. **দুষ্টা** *n fem* bad/unchaste woman. **~কর্মা** *adj*=দুষ্কর্মা. **~ ক্ষত** *n* ulcer; septic wound. **~ ক্ষুধা** *n* morbid/unwholesome appetite; false/abnormal hunger. **~গ্রহ** *n* (astrol) malicious/evil planet. **~চরিত্র, ~চারী** *adjj* ill-conducted; evil-minded; vicious. **~চেতা** *adj* evil-minded; mischievous; malevolent. **~তা, ~ত্ব** *nn* badness; wickedness; falsehood; defilement; violation. **~প্রকৃতি** *adj* ill-natured; wicked; mischievous; reprobate; depraved; evil-natured; vicious. **~বুদ্ধি, ~মতি**=~চেতা. **~ ব্রণ** *n* malignant tumour; morbid boil; carbuncle. **দুষ্টামি** *n* naughtiness; mischievousness; mischief; prank. **দুষ্টাশয়** *adj* wicked; vicious; roguish.

দুষ্টু *adj* mischievous; naughty; roguish. **~মি** *n* mischievousness; naughtiness; prank. **~মি করা** *vi* be naughty; make a mischief; play a mischievous trick; play a prank.

দুষ্পরাজেয় *adj* difficult to conquer.

দুষ্পরিহর, দুষ্পরিহার্য *adjj* **1** difficult to avoid; unavoidable. **2** indelible.

দুষ্পাচ্য *adj* difficult to be digested; hard to digest.

দুষ্পাঠ্য *adj* hard to read.

দুষ্পূরণীয় *adj* difficult to be filled/satisfied.

দুষ্প্রবৃত্তি *n* evil/wicked desire/ inclination/ disposition.

দুষ্প্রবেশ(্য) *adj* difficult to enter/penetrate; impenetrable; abstruse.

দুষ্প্রমেয় *adj* difficult to be measured; immense; immeasurable.

দুষ্প্রসহ *adj* difficult to be borne/supported/ suffered; unbearable; intolerable.

দুষ্প্রাপণীয়, দুষ্প্রাপ্য *adj* hard to obtain/attain; rare; scarce; inaccessible.

দুসুতি ⇒দু–

দুস্তর *adj* difficult to go across/pass/overcome; endless.

দুহা *vt* **1** milk (a cow, etc). **2** (iron) extort (money, etc). **~নো** *vt* (cause to) milk.

দুহাকার *adj* of the two; of both.

দুহিতা *n fem* daughter.

দুহ্য *adj* (fit) to be milked; milkable. **~মানা** *adj fem* being milked.

দূত *n* **1** messenger; envoy. **2** courier. **3** ambassador; emissary. **4** harbinger; forerunner: বসন্তের ~. **5** negotiator; go-between. **6** pander; procurer; pimp. **7** spy. **দূতী, দূতি** *adj* (esp in the sense of) procuress or go-between. **দূতাবাস** *n* ambassador's residence (and office); embassy. **দূতালি** *n* office of a messenger/ envoy/ambassador; mediation; good offices; intervention.

দূতীগিরি, দূতিগিরি, দূতিয়ালি, দূতীয়ালি *adj* office of a procuress/female go-between.

দূর *n* distance; remoteness; long way. □*adj* **1** far; remote; distant; far from; long way off; long period back. **2** far-reaching: ~দৃষ্টি. **3** long; extensive: ~ পথ. **4** removed; expelled; driven away/out: দুঃখ ~ হওয়া. □*int* hang it; fie; drat it; dash ! go to blazes ! **~ করা** *vt* **1** turn out; expel; banish; drive away/out; dispel; eject. **2** relieve; eliminate: ব্যথা ~ করা. **3** put away; take away: এই বাসনাগুলি ~ করো. **~ হওয়া** *vi* **1** go away; pass out of sight; be off; leave. **2** be removed/expelled; be eliminated/relieved. **~ হও !** off with you ! **~ হোক (ছাই)** *int* hang it ! damn it ! chuck it ! **~ক** *n* (astron) radius vector. **~ক ক্ষেত্র** *n* (astron) sectional area. **~গ, ~গামী** *adj* **1** going /travelling far; remote; far-going; long-distance. **2** far-reaching; long; extensive. **~গা, ~গামিনী** *fem*. **~গত** *adj* gone far away. **~গমন** *n* travelling far. **~ছাই করা** *vi* treat contemptuously; pooh-pooh; slight;

sneer at; scorn. ~ত *adv* from afar; at a distance; from a remote place. ~তম *adj* remotest; farthest; longest. ~তা, ~ত্ব *n n* distance; remoteness; length; (amount of) difference. ~ত্ব রক্ষা করা keep one's distance. ~দর্শন *n* 1 long-sightedness; foresight; far-sight; far-sightedness; prudence. 2 television. □*adj* far-seeing; visible only from afar. ~দর্শী *adj* far-seeing; long-sighted; farsighted; prudence. □*n* seer; prophet. ~দর্শিনী *fem.* ~দর্শিতা *n*=~দর্শন. ~-দূর ! *int* fie ! blast it ! hang it ! damn ! ~দূর করা=~ছাই করা. ~-দূরান্তর *n* very distant/remote places. ~-দূরান্তর থেকে from afar. ~-দূরান্তরে *adv* far and wide. ~দৃষ্টি *n*=~দর্শন. ~দৃষ্টিসম্পন্ন=~দর্শী. ~পাল্লা *n* long-range/distance. ~পাল্লার ক্ষেপণাস্ত্র *n* long-range missiles. ~প্রসারিত, ~প্রসারী *adj* reaching far; far-reaching; far-extending; very long. ~বর্তিতা *n* state of being/lying at a distance; remoteness; (fig) separation by a large margin/great distance. ~বর্তী *adj* being in the distance; distant; far-removed; far-off; remote; lying/staying at a distance; (fig) separated by a large margin; differing to a great extent. ~বর্তিনী *fem.* ~বীক্ষণ *n* telescope. ~বেধী *adj* piercing from afar. ~ব্যাপী *adj* far-extending; far-reaching. ~স্থ, ~স্থিত *adj* being in the distance; remote; distant, situated/lying/ located/staying at a distance. দূরে *adv* at/to a distance; far; afar. দূরে থাকা keep aloof. দূরের কথা 1 an affair of distant future. 2 far from doing sth; not to speak of: আপ্যায়ন দূরের কথা, সে ভালো করে কথাই বললো না.

দূরাগত *adj* come from afar; distant.

দূরান্ত *n* remote/distant/far-off place.

দূরান্তর *n* wide space; long distance.

দূরীকরণ *n* removing; removal; expulsion; elimination; banishment; relief; act of driving out/turning out.

দূরীকৃত *adj* expelled; repelled; remove; driven out/away; turned out; banished.

দূরীভবন *n* act of being turned out/driven away; removal; expulsion; elimination; dislodgment.

দূরীভূত *adj* removed; expelled; turned out; dislodged; ejected; driven away/out.

দূরেক্ষণ *n* television.

দূর্বা *n* (bent/panic) grass. ~দল *n* blade of grass. ~দলশ্যাম *n, adj* grass-green.

দূষক *adj* 1 corrupting; spoiling; disgracing; seducing. 2 fault-finding; disparaging; distracting; carping; caviling; vitiating; wicked; sinful. 3 polluting; defiling; vitiating; violating. 4 sinful; wicked. □*n* seducer; disparager. দূষিকা *fem.*

দূষণ *adj* (used as a *suff*)=দূষক. □*n* 1 pollution; polluting; seduction; corruption; defilement; violation. 2 fault-finding; blaming; disparaging; disparagement.

দূষণীয় *adj* 1 blamable; reprehensible; condemnable; vile; bad. 2 corruptible; liable to be soiled/defiled/disgraced.

দূষয়িতা *adj*=দূষক. দূষয়িত্রী *fem.*

দূষিত *adj* polluted; corrupt; defiled; soiled; contaminated; vitiated; impure; blemished. ~ করা *vt* pollute; corrupt; defile; soil; contaminate; vitiate; violate.

দূষ্য=দূষণীয়

দৃক্ *n* (in compounds) eye; sight; vision. ~কোণ *n* visual angle. ~পাত *n* casting a glance; look. ~পাত করা *vi* look at; cast a glance (at); take (any) notice of; pay (any) heed to. ~শক্তি *n* sight; eyesight.

দৃগ্ *n* (in compounds)=দৃক্. দৃগক্ষ *n* visual axis. ~বিজ্ঞান n optics.

দৃঢ় *adj* 1 firm; fixed; steady; strong; sound; solid; massive: ~ পদ. 2 firmly fastened; shut fast; tight; taut; close. ~ মুষ্টি. 3 durable; sound; strong: ~ ভিত্তি. 4 resolute; persevering; steady; steadfast; constant; firm: ~সঙ্কল্প. 5 confirmed; established; certain; sure: ~ অভিমত. 6 categorical; firm: ~ উত্তর. 7 strict; mighty; intense; violent; severe: ~ শাসন. 8 deep; profound; unswerving; unflinching; unwavering: ~ আনুগত্য/ ভক্তি. 9 unfaltering; firm; steady: ~ কণ্ঠ. ~ করা *vt* make firm/strong; make stronger/more firm; strengthen; consolidate; brace; fortify; prop up; harden; steel; buttress; tone up; intensify. ~কায় *adj* having a well-built/strong body; robust; vigorous; able-bodied. ~চিত্ত *adj* firm-minded; strong-willed; resolute; firm in mind; determined; unswerving; strong-willed; single-minded. ~জ্ঞান *n* certain/positive knowledge; firm conviction/belief. ~তা *n* firmness; hardness; solidity; strength; steadiness; perseverance; soundness; severity; constancy; strictness; durability. ~তাসহকারে *adv* firmly; categorically. ~নিশ্চয় *adj* certain; undoubted; convinced; firmly resolved; confident. ~পদ *adj* firm-footed . ~পদে *adv* with steady steps. ~প্রতিজ্ঞ *adj* firm in keeping a pledge/promise/agreement; firmly resolved; resolute; determined; firm in determination. ~প্রত্যয়, ~বিশ্বাস *n* firm conviction/belief; strong faith. ~বদ্ধ *adj* firmly bound/fastened; tied tightly; taut; tightened. ~বন্ধন strong tie/bondage; close ties/bonds. ~বর্মী *adj* crustacean. ~বুদ্ধি *adj* firm-minded. ~ভূমি *n* firm ground. ~ভাবে=~তাসহকারে. ~মতি=~চেতা. ~মুষ্টি *n* strong fist. □*adj* 1 strong-fisted (whose grasp is difficult to unloose). 2 close-fisted; niggardly. 3 determined; resolved. ~মূল

adj firmly rooted; deep-rooted; deep-seated. ~সঙ্কল্প *adj* firmly resolved/ determined; resolute. ~সন্ধ *adj* firm in one's promise/vow; faithful to one's engagements; firmly resolved. ~সন্ধি *adj* firmly united; closely joined; strong-knit; thick set; close; compact. ~স্বরে *adv* in a firm tone; in an unfaltering voice.

দৃঢ়ীকরণ *n* strengthening; tightening; confirmation; corroboration; congelation; consolidation.

দৃঢ়ীকৃত *adj* made strong/firm; strengthened; tightened; firmly established; confirmed; congealed; consolidated.

দৃঢ়ীভবন *n* act of becoming strong/firm; act of being tightened/confirmed/firmly established; confirmation; consolidation; hardening.

দৃঢ়ীভূত *adj* strengthened; become strong(er); become firm(er); confirmed; congealed; become firmly established; consolidated.

দৃপ্ত *adj* **1** proud; arrogant; vain; haughty. **2** spirited: ~ পদক্ষেপ. **3** flaming; blazing; scorching; glaring.

দৃশ্য *adj* **1** visible; conspicuous; obvious; apparent. **2** worth seeing. □*n* **1** scenery; sight; scene; view; spectacle. **2** (drama) scene. ~কাব্য *n* drama; play. ~ত *adj* apparently; obviously; visibly; manifestly; prima facie. ~তা *n* visibility; vision; sight. ~দিগন্ত *n* (astron) visible horizon. ~পট *n* (stage) scene; scenery. ~মান *adj* visible; present in view. ~সঙ্গীত *n* dance. দৃশ্যাদৃশ্য *adj* visible and invisible.

দৃষ্ট *adj* **1** seen; looked at; perceived; beheld; noticed; observed. **2** visible; apparent; manifest. **3** considered; regarded; treated. ~চর, ~পূর্ব *adjj* seen/noticed before; not quite unknown. ~ত *adj* apparently; obviously; visibly; manifestly. ~বৎ *adj* (as if) seen. ~বাদ *n* (phil) positivism. ~বাদী *n* positivist. □*adj* positivistic. ~মাত্র *adj* just/merely seen. দৃষ্টাদৃষ্ট *adj* visible and invisible; relating to the present and future life.

দৃষ্টান্ত *n* **1** example; instance; illustration; exemplification; type; specimen; paragon; standard. **2** precedent. **3** (rhet) parallel. ~ দেওয়া *vi* cite an example; show a precedent; exemplify; illustrate. ~ রাখা/ স্থাপন করা *vi* set an example; make a precedent; show/quote a precedent; cite an example. ~প্রদর্শন *n* act of showing a precedent/citing an example; act of setting an example; illustration; exemplification. ~ প্রদর্শন করা=~ দেওয়া. ~মূলক, ~স্থানীয় *adj* exemplary. ~স্থল *n* exemplary person/thing; model. ~স্বরূপ *adv* for instance/example. □*adj* fit to be cited as an example.

দৃষ্টি *n* **1** seeing; viewing; beholding. **2** faculty of seeing; sight. **3** organ of sight/vision; eye; eyesight. **4** vision; observation; perception. **5** mind's eye; wisdom; knowledge; cognition; foresight. **6** careful attention/observation; regard; consideration: স্বাস্থ্যের দিকে ~ রেখো. **7** view; notion; opinion: তার ~তে .... **8** aim: নিশানার দিকে ~ ঠিক করা. **9** look; glance; sinister/malicious look; covetous/evil glance: তোমার বাড়িটার উপর তার ~ পড়েছে. **10** pupil of the eye. **11** (astrol) (esp sinister) aspect of stars: শনির ~. ~ করা *vi* look at; cast a glance; notice; aim (at); keep one's eye on; keep an eye on. ~ দেওয়া *vi* cast a glance; look at; behold; regard; consider; notice; take care of; care for; look into; keep an eye on; pay heed to; cast a covetous glance; look at covetously; (astrol) influence (unfavourably). ~ পড়া *vi* look at (sth) with longing eye. ~কৃপণ *adj* niggardly; small-minded. ~কোণ *n* view-point; angle of vision. ~ক্ষুধা *n* morbid hunger which is roused as soon as one sees an article of food. ~ক্ষেত্র *n* (phys) field of vision/view. ~ক্ষেপ *n* casting glances. ~গোচর *n* range of sight. □*adj* visible. ~গোচর হওয়া *vi* come into sight/view; be visible. ~দোষ *n* evil influence of the human eye. ~নিপাত *n* look; glance. ~নিবন্ধ *n* (phys) persistence of vision. ~পথ *n* path/range of vision. ~পথবর্তী *adj* lying in the range of vision. ~পথবর্তী হওয়া *vi* come into view; appear in sight; become visible. ~পাত *n* (casting a) glance; look; notice; observation. ~পাত করা *vi* cast a glance; look at; notice; pay heed to; fix the eyes upon. ~বিক্ষেপ=~ক্ষেপ. ~বিক্ষেপ করা *vi* cast glances; cast a side-glance; leer. ~বিজ্ঞান *n* optics. ~বিনিময় *n* exchange of glances; attitude. ~বিভ্রম *n* optical illusion. ~ভঙ্গি *n* attitude; view-point. ~মণ্ডল *n* pupil of the eye. ~শক্তি *n* power of seeing; eye-sight; sight; vision; perception. ~শক্তিহীন *adj* sightless; blind; lacking in/deprived of perception/foresight. ~শূন্য, ~হীন *adjj* sightless; blind; careless; indifferent; paying no heed to; heedless; lacking in perception/foresight. ~হীনতা *n* sightlessness; blindness. দৃষ্টে *adv* (used chiefly as a *suff*).**1** at the sight of; as soon as seen. **2** in view of; seeing: অবস্থাদৃষ্টে. **3** looking: একদৃষ্টে.

দে[১] *n* title of Bengali Hindu Kayastha.

দে[২] *prep* (colloq, dial)=দিয়া[১]

দেউটি *n* lamp; light.

দেউড়ি *n* main gate; porch; portico; vestibule.

দেউল *n* temple; shrine.

দেউলিয়া, দেউলে (colloq) *adj* bankrupt; insolvent; beggared.

দেও [P] *n* giant; spirit; devil; monster; demon.

দেওদার=দেবদারু (⇒ দেব)

দেওন *n* giving; distribution.

দেওয়া[1]=দেয়া[1]

দেওয়া[2] *vt* **1** give. **2** award: পুরস্কার ~. **3** confer; bestow: খেতাব ~. **4** give up; sacrifice; lay down: দেশের জন্য প্রাণ ~. **5** provide; supply; give: ভাত-কাপড় ~. **6** distribute; apportion: বেটে ~. **7** give out of charity: ভিক্ষা ~. **8** establish; found; set up: মসজিদ ~. **9** pay: দাম/ পরীক্ষার ফি ~. **10** repay: দেনা ~. **11** render; extend; give: ধন্যবাদ ~. **12** build; construct: পাঁচিল/ বেড়া ~. **13** impose; inflict; administer: শাস্তি ~. **14** administer; apply: ঔষধ ~. **15** cite; give: দৃষ্টান্ত ~. **16** write (down): ঠিকানা/ তারিখ ~. **17** put on; wear: টুপি মাথায় ~, বালা হাতে ~. **18** hold over: মাথায় ছাতা ~. **19** throw into: জলে ~. **20** deal; inflict: আঘাত ~. **21** insert; thrust into: গলায় আঙুল ~. **22** marry; wed; given in marriage: মেয়ে ~. **23** perform: বিবাহ/ পূজা ~. **24** donate: চাঁদা ~. **25** ascribe; give: নাম ~. **26** spare: সময় ~. **27** furnish with: ঠেকনো ~. **28** lean against: ভর/ ঠেক ~. **29** entrust with; give; hand over: ভার ~. **30** touch with; set to: হাত/ পা/ মুখ ~. **31** impart; give: উপদেশ ~. **32** sprinkle: গাছে পানি ~. **33** spray; sprinkle: গায়ে রং ~. **34** send: ছেলেকে স্কুলে ~. **35** add; mix: দুধে জল ~. **36** utter: ডাক/ চিৎকার ~. **37** take: লম্ফ ~. **38** sell (for); give in exchange: মাছটা এক শ টাকায় ~. **39** allow: ভাববার সময় ~. **40** place: কাপড় রোদে ~. **41** offer; dedicate; মসজিদে শিরনি ~. **42** draw: গণ্ডি ~. **43** yield; produce: গরুর দুধ ~. **44** set: কাজে হাত ~. **45** execute: ফাঁকি ~. **46** employ in ; give: চাকরি ~. **47** put to: লজ্জা ~. **48** fasten: খিল ~. **49** shut; close; bolt: দরজা ~. **50** keep; leave; ফাঁক ~. **51** paint; put: ফোঁটা ~. **52** post: চিঠি ডাকে ~. **53** take to; দৌড় ~. **54** serve: টেবিলে খাবার ~. **55** sew; stitch: কাপড়ে তালি ~. **56** keep out: বাদ ~. **57** affix: চিঠিতে টিকিট ~. **58** pronounce: মামলার রায় ~. **59** pass: মতামত ~. **60** lend: ঋণ/ ধার ~. **61** cast: দৃষ্টি ~. **62** inform; apprise; intimate to: খবর ~. **63** sharpen; whet: ছুরিতে ধার ~. **64** grant; sanction: ছুটি ~. **65** keep time; strike in unison. **66** let; permit; allow: যেতে ~. **67** pierce with; thrust at sb (with sth): বুকে ছুরি ~. **68** accord; give: অনুমোদন ~. **69** sow; scatter: জমিতে বীজ/ সার ~. **70** give out: ধোঁয়া ~. **71** light: উনানে আগুন ~. **72** set to: গানে সুর ~. **73** used after certain verbs to indicate completion of an action, eg: ফেলে ~, দিয়ে ~, জ্বালিয়ে/ পুড়িয়ে ~. ☐*adj* given; offered; conferred; awarded; bestowed. **~-নেওয়া** *n* give and take. **~নো** *vt* cause to give/award/put (⇒ the meanings of দেওয়া above).

দেওয়ান [P] *n* **1** royal court. **2** tribunal. **3** chief officer of a state; secretary; minister; finance secretary; steward; dewan. **~-ই-আম** *n* public hall of audience. **~-ই-খাস** *n* privy council chamber; cabinet. **~খানা** *n* hall of audience; court.

দেওয়ানা [P] *adj* mad; frenzied; inspired; obsessed. ☐*n* madman; lunatic; God-intoxicated person; lover.

দেওয়ানি, দেওয়ানী [P] *n* **1** office/jurisdiction of a dewan (⇒ দেওয়ান[3]). **2** civil court. **~ আদালত** *n* civil court. **~ মামলা** *n* civil suit.

দেওয়াল *n*=দেয়াল

দেওয়ালি, দেওয়ালী=দীপালি ⇒ (দীপ). **~-পোকা** *n* kind of lepidopters that are found in late autumn nights; moth.

দেওর *n* younger brother of one's husband; brother-in-law. **~ঝি** *n* daughter of one's husband's younger brother. **~পো** *n* son of one's husband's younger brother.

দেঁতো *adj* **1** large-toothed; tusked. **2** displaying one's teeth. **3** (fig) insincere; forced: ~ হাসি.

দেক=দিক[2]

দেখতা *adj* seen; occurring before one's eyes. ☐*adv* before one's eyes; contemporaneously: তার যা কিছু সবই আমার ~.

দেখন *n* act of seeing/looking/beholding/ viewing. **~হাসি** *adj* **1** who smiles at first sight. **2** who makes one smile (in delight) at first sight. **3** (derog) who always greets with a smile. ☐*n fem* boon companion.

দেখা *vt* **1** see; look (at); view; behold; notice; espy. **2** glance at; look on. **3** gaze at/on/upon. **4** consider; judge:দেখো, এখনও সময় আছে. **5** examine: পরীক্ষার খাতা ~. **6** try: আমি যথেষ্ট দেখলাম, কিছু হলো না. **7** visit: যাদুঘর ~. **8** observe: দেখো, ঘটনা কোন দিকে মোড় নেয়. **9** (in drawing attention) listen: দেখো, কাজটা কিন্তু তুমি ভালো করছো না. **10** inspect: এই হিসাবটা একটু দেখবে? **11** be careful/aware: দেখো যেন পড়ে যেয়ো না. **12** feel: নাড়ি ~. **13** wait: আরেকটু দেখি, সে আসতেও পারে. **14** attend on; nurse: এই রোগীকে কে দেখবে? **15** attend to; look after: তোমরা না দেখলে তাকে আর কে দেখবে? বিষয়সম্পত্তি ~. **16** treat: তাকে কি কোনো ডাক্তার দেখছেন? **17** watch: টেলিভিশন ~. **18** witness: খেলা ~, দুর্ঘটনা ~. **19** look for: একজন লোক দেখো. **20** cast a favourable glance; এই অভাগাকে কি তিনি দেখবেন? **21** experience directly; learn from experience: দেখে শেখা. **22** think over: কথাটা ভেবে দেখবো. **23** come across; meet: ফেরার পথে

এক বুড়োকে দেখলাম. **24** follow; take to; go (one's way): নিজের পথ দেখো. **25** think: তার সঙ্গে আর দেখাই হবে না দেখছি. **26** not to spare: সে পালাবে কোথায়, তাকে আমি দেখে নেব. ❑*n* **1** seeing; looking; viewing. **2** meeting: তার সঙ্গে ~ হওয়াই ভার. ❑*adj* seen; beheld; viewed; noticed; espied; visited; examined; experienced; read; inspected. ~ **করা** *vt* drop/call in/on; see; visit with; drop by. ~ **দেওয়া** *vi* appear; show up; present to the view; come in sight; become manifest: স্বপ্নে ~ দিয়ে তিনি বললেন ... . ~ **যাক** let me/us see/try; let us wait. ~**দেখি** *n* **1** mutual seeing/meeting/visits; visiting terms; friendly terms: তাদের মুখ-দেখাদেখি নেই, there's little/no love lost between them. **2** copying from another's paper by adoption of unfair means (as in an examination). ❑*adj* in imitation of; following the example of: তোমার ~দেখি সে-ও নাচ শিখতে শুরু করেছে. ~নে, ~নো *adjj* (used as a *suff*) ostentatious; ostentatiously; formal; affected; pretended; showy: লোক-~. ~নো *vt* **1** show; point out; display; exhibit; expose; demonstrate; indicate. **2** consult: ডাক্তার ~নো. **3** bear the expenses of; take (to): সিনেমা ~নো. **4** teach; teach sb a lesson: তোমার এতো বড়ো ধৃষ্টতা, দাঁড়াও, দেখাচ্ছি! **5** get examined/inspected/reviewed: লেখাটা তাকে দেখিয়ে নিয়ো. ~**শোনা** *n* **1** meeting: আমাদের অনেক দিন ~শোনা নেই. **2** visit (esp for examination or negotiation): ~শোনার একটা দিন ঠিক করো. **3** act of looking after; attendance; supervision; custody; care: ছেলেটার ~শোনার ভার মামা নিয়েছে. **4** experience: জীবনে ~শোনা তো আর কম হলো না. **5** examination; inspection: অনেক ~শোনার পর একটা বাড়ি তার পছন্দ হলো. ~**শোনা করা** *vt* **1** visit (esp for examination or negotiation). **2** meet/visit mutually. **3** look after; attend to/on; take care of; supervise; keep an eye on; superintend; look/see to; care for. **4** examine; inspect. ~-**সাক্ষাৎ** *n* **1** meeting; visit. **2** intercourse. **3** rendezvous. **দেখতে কুৎসিত** *adj* ugly to look at; ugly-looking. **দেখতে সুন্দর** *adj* beautiful to look at; good-looking. **দেখতে দেখতে** *adv* soon; ere/before long; shortly; in a twinkle; in an instant; before one's eyes.

দেড় *adj* one and a half (of). ~**গুণ** *adj* one and a half times (of). **দেড়া**= ~ গুণ.

দেড়কো *n* lamp-stand.

দেদার [P] *adj* lot of; plentiful; abundant; profuse; plenty of; innumerable; immeasurable.

দেদীপ্যমান *adj* resplendent; shining intensely; glowing; blazing; brilliant.

দেদো (colloq)*adj* stricken with ring-worm.

দেনদার=দেনাদার (⇒ দেনা)

দেনমোহর [A] *n* amount of money pledged to be paid to the bride by the bridegroom in a Muslim marriage. (⇒কাবিন).

দেনা *n* debt; loan; outstanding bill/payment; dues; liability. ~ **করা** *vt, vi* borrow; incur a debt; take a loan; run into a debt. ~ **থাকা** *vi* be indebted; owe. ~ **দেওয়া/শোধ করা** *vi* repay/pay off a debt; discharge a debt; acquit oneself of debts. ~**য় ডুবুডুবু** over head and ears in debt. ~**য় মাথার চুল বিকানো** (fig) be on one's last legs to pay off one's debts. ~**দার** *adj* indebted; in debt; loaded down with debts. ❑*n* debtor; borrower; defaulter. ~-**পাওনা** *n* assets and liabilities; pecuniary transaction/interest; dealings.

দেব *n* **1** a Hindu deity; a god. **2** God. **3** image of a god; idol. **4** god on earth/among men; a Brahmin according to Hindu notion. **5** (in respectful address or reference) king; prince; master; father; husband; preceptor; any person commanding respect. **6** chief/best man: নর~. ~**কণ্ঠ** *adj* having a god-like voice. ~**কণ্ঠী** *fem.* ~**কন্যা** *n* celestial maiden; nymph. ~**কল্প** *adj* godlike; godly. ~**কর্ম** ~**কার্য** *nn* religious act/rite; worship of the gods; religious mission. ~**কাষ্ঠ**=~দারু. ~**কুল** *n* race of gods; temple; shrine. ~**কুলপ্রিয়** *adj* favoured of the gods. ~**কুসুম** *n* cloves. ~**কৃত** *adj* made/done by the gods. ~**খাত** *n* natural lake. ~**গণ** *n* troop/class of gods. ~**গায়ন** *n* celestial songster; Gandharva. ~**গুরু** *n* preceptor of the gods; Brihaspati. ~**গৃহ** *n* house of the worship; temple. ~**চরিত্র** *adj, n* (having) a divinely pure/saintly character. ~**চর্যা** *n* service of the gods. ~**চ্ছন্দ** *n* necklace of pearls (composed of 100 strings). ~**জন** *n* godlike person. ~**তরু** *n* divine tree. ~**তুল্য** *adj* godlike; godly. ~**ত্ব** *n* godhead; divinity; godliness. ~**ত্বারোপ** *n* apotheosis. ~**ত্র** *n* property endowed for defraying the cost of worshipping a deity. ~**দত্ত** *adj* god-given. ~**দর্শন** *n* visit to pay homage to an idol; pilgrimage to a seat/temple of a god. ~**দারু** *n* *Pinus devadaru*; deodar. ~**দাসী** *n fem* woman dedicated to the service of an idol of a particular temple. ~**দুর্লভ** *adj* even difficult for gods to obtain; rare even amongst gods. ~**দূত** *n* divine messenger; angel. ~**দূতী** *fem.* ~**দেব** *n* the god of gods; name of Brahma, Vishnu and Shiva. ~**দ্বিজ** *n* gods and Brahmins. ~**দ্বেষী** *adj* hostile/inimical to the gods; godless; atheistic; anti-god. ~**দ্বেষিণী** *fem.* ❑*n* any of the mythological demons hostile to gods. ~**ধান্য** *n* sorghum. ~**ধূপ** *n* bdellium. ~নাগরী *n* Devanagari (character in which Sanskrit is usually written). ~নিষ্ঠ *adj* devoted to gods; religious; godly. ~নিষ্ঠা *n* devotion to gods. ~পতি *n* lord of gods; Indra. ~পথ *n* gods' path; heaven; the Milky Way. ~পশু *n* any animal consecrated to a deity. ~পুরী *n* Indra's residence; paradise. ~পূজক *n* worshipper of the gods. ~পূজা *n* worship of the gods. ~পূজ্য *adj* to be honoured by the gods. ❑*n* planet Brihaspati. ~প্রতিম=~তুল্য. ~প্রতিমা *n* image of a deity; idol. ~প্রতিষ্ঠা *n* ceremony of establishing an idol at a particular place. ~প্রসাদ *n* divine favour. ~প্রিয় *adj* dear to the gods; beloved of gods. ~বাক্য *n* divine voice; oracle. ~বাণী *n* **1**=~বাক্য. **2** the Sanskrit language. ~বাহন *n* fire. ~ভক্ত *adj* devoted to gods; pious. ~ভক্তি *n* devotion to/service of gods. ~ভাষা *n* the Sanskrit language. ~ভাষিত *n* =~বাক্য. ~ভীতি *n* fear of the gods. ~ভূমি *n* heaven; the Himalayas; holy place. ~ভোগ *n* pleasure of the gods; heavenly joy. ~ভোগ্য *adj* fit to be enjoyed by the gods. ~মন্দির *n* temple; shrine. ~মহিমা *n* divine greatness/grandeur/splendour/glory. ~মাতা *n* Aditi, the first mother of gods. ~মাতৃক *adj* moistened only by rain-water. ~যজী, ~যাজি, ~যাজী *adj* sacrificing to the gods. ~যাত্রা *n* idol procession; pilgrimage. ~যান *n* vehicle of a god; celestial chariot; way leading to the gods. ~যুগ *n* the first age of the world. ~যোনি *n* demi-god; demon. ❑*adj* of divine origin. ~রক্ষিত *adj* protected by the gods. ~রথ *n* celestial chariot/car. ~রহস্য *n* divine mystery. ~রাজ=~পতি. ~র্ষি *n* saint of the celestial class. ~ল *n* priestly Brahmin. ❑*adj* employed in priestly service. ~লোক *n* abode of the gods; heaven; paradise. ~শিল্পী *n* Vishwakarma, the celestial artisan and designer. ~সভা *n* assembly of gods; court of Indra. ~সেনা *n* host of celestials; wife of Kartikeya. ~সেনাপতি *n* Kartikeya, the commander of the army of gods. ~স্ব *n* divine property(⇒ also ~ত্র). দেবাক্রীড় *n* playing-place of the gods. দেবাগার *n* temple. দেবাঙ্গনা *n* celestial female. দেবাত্মজ *n* son of a god. দেবাত্মা *n* divine soul. ❑*adj* being of divine nature; godlike; holy. দেবাদিদেব *n* supreme god; name of Brahma, Vishnu and Shiva. দেবাদেশ *n* divine command/inspiration; commandment. দেবায়তন *n* dwelling of a god; temple. দেবায়ুধ *n* weapon of the gods; divine celestial weapon; rainbow. দেবারাধনা *n* worship of the gods; religious service/worship. দেবারি *n* enemy of gods; Asura. দেবার্চন(া)= দেবারাধনা. দেবালয় *n* temple. দেবাশ্রিত *adj* protected by god(s); under a god's protection/care; in a god's favour/care. দেবাসুর *n* gods and Asuras.

দেবতা *n* godhead; divinity; image of a deity; idol. ~গার, ~গৃহ *nn* temple.

দেবন *n* die; dice for gambling; sport; pastime; gaming; game of dice.

দেবর *n*=দেওর

দেবা *n* (derog, iron) god; man. যেমন ~ তেমনি দেবী like man like wife.

দেবী *n fem* (of দেব) **1** goddess; female deity. **2** goddess Durga or Chandi. **3** (as a form of address) lady: মাতৃ~, সরলা~.

দেবেন্দ্র *n* chief of the gods; Indra.

দেবেশ *n* chief/god of gods; Shiva.

দেবোচিত *adj* befitting a god; right and proper for a god; godlike; godly.

দেবোত্তর *n* (colloq)=দেবত্র (⇒ দেব)

দেবোদ্যান *n* heavenly garden.

দেবোপম *adj* godlike; godly.

দেবোপাসক=দেবপূজক (⇒ দেব)

দেবোপাসনা=দেবপূজা (⇒ দেব)

দেমাক, দেমাগ [A] *nn* pride; haughtiness; airs; conceit; intoxication. ~ করা *vi* be proud/haughty; be vain; put on airs; be insolent; give oneself airs. ~ দেখানো *vi* express anger/haughtiness; get/go into a huff; give oneself airs; be in a fit of pique. ~ হওয়া *vi* be vain/proud/haughty; be puffed up with pride.

দেমাকি, দেমাকে, দেমাগি, দেমাগী *adjj* haughty; arrogant; proud; disdainful; vain; conceited.

দেয় *adj* to be given/granted; worth-giving; fit/proper for a gift; to be paid/returned; due; payable.

দেয়ক *n* fee.

দেয়া[1] *n* **1** sky. **2** cloud. ~র ডাক/ গর্জন *n* roar/rumble of clouds.

দেয়া[2] *vi* =দেওয়া[2]

দেয়ান *n* (colloq)=দেওয়ান[1]

দেয়াল *n* wall. ~ তোলা/ দেওয়া *vi* raise/build a wall. ~ দিয়ে ঘেরা/ বন্ধ করা *vt* wall up. ~গিরি *n* tapestry/cloth to adorn a wall. ~-পঞ্জি *n* wall calendar. দেয়ালেরও কান আছে walls have ears.

দেয়ালা *n* smile and cry of a dreaming baby.

দেয়ালি, দেয়ালী *nn*=দীপালি (⇒ দীপ)

দেয়াসিনী *n fem* votaress; female worshipper; nun; woman versed in mystic incantations.

দেয়াসী *n* votary (of certain goddesses).

দেরকো *n* wooden lamp-stand.

দেরাজ [A] *n* drawers (of a cabinet, desk, etc).

দেরি, দেরী [P] *nn* delay; tardiness; slowness. ~ করা *vi, vt* be late; delay. ~ করানো *vt* (cause to) delay; procrastinate; defer. ~ হওয়া *vi* be late/delayed.

দেরেগ [P] *n* sigh; sorrow; grief.

দেরেঙ্গ [P] *n* delay.

দেল *n*=দিল

দেশ *n* **1** country; land; state; province; kingdom. **2** motherland; native land: আমার দেশের মাটি. **3** native village; country: ছুটিতে সে দেশের বাড়িতে গিয়েছিল. **4** part; portion: মধ্য~. **5** point; spot; place: গল~. **6** region: মরু~. **7** direction; quarter: ঊর্ধ্ব~. **8** an Indian musical mode. ~কাল *n* place and time; particular circumstances. ~কালজ্ঞ, ~কালবিদ *adj* conversant with the nature of a particular place and time. ~কালপাত্র *n* a particular place and a point of time and a person or their nature/condition. ~কাল ব্যতীত *adj* regardless of place and time. ~কালসন্ততি *n* space-time continuum. ~কালাতীত *adj* transcending space and time. ~কালোচিত *adj* befitting/serving the needs of a particular place and time; befitting the circumstances. ~খ্যাত *adj* famous all over the country. ~গৌরব *n* pride of a/one's country. ~জ, ~জাত *adjj* indigenous. ~জোড়া *adj* country-wide. ~ত্যাগ *n* leaving a/one's own country; emigration/migration from one's own country. ~ত্যাগ করা *vi* leave a/one's own country; emigrate; migrate. ~ত্যাগী *n, adj* migrant; emigrant. ~ত্যাগিনী *fem.* ~দেশান্তর *n* countries far and near; one's native land and other countries; different countries. ~দ্রোহ *n* treason; treachery to one's country/state. ~দ্রোহমূলক *adj* treasonable. ~দ্রোহী *adj* committing treason. ☐*n* traitor; quisling. ~ধর্ম *n* law/usage of a country. ~পতি *n* ruler of a country; king. ~পর্যটন *n* travel (in different lands or in different parts of a country); travelling; journeying from country to country; wandering about a country; touring. ~ পর্যটন করা *vi* travel (in different countries or in different parts of a country); tour in a country. ~প্রথা *n* customs and practices peculiar to a country. ~প্রসিদ্ধ=~খ্যাত. ~প্রিয় *adj* beloved of one's countrymen. ~প্রেম *n* attachment to/love for one's motherland; patriotism. ~প্রেমিক *n* lover of one's motherland; patriot. ~বন্ধু *n* friend of one's country. ~বিখ্যাত*n* =~খ্যাত. ~বিদেশ *n* home and abroad. ~বিধান *n* customs and conventions peculiar to a country. ~বিভাগ *n* partition of a country. ~বিশ্রুত=~খ্যাত. ~ব্যাপী=~জোড়া. ~ভাষা *n* language/dialect of a country. ~ভেদে *adv* in different countries. ~ভ্রমণ=~পর্যটন. ~ময় *adj* country-wide. ☐*adv* all over the country. ~মাতৃকা *n fem* country personified as the mother of its inhabitants; motherland. ~মুখ *n* **1** leader of a country. **2** king. ~রক্ষা *n* defence of a country. ~রক্ষী *n* protector of a country. ~সেবক *n* servant of one's motherland. ~সেবা *n* service to one's motherland. ~স্থ *adj* situated/living in a country; indigenous. ~হিত *n* welfare of a country. ~হিতকর *adj* beneficial to a country; conducive to a country's welfare. ~হিতব্রত *n* mission of doing good to one's country. ~হিতব্রতী *adj* avowedly devoted to the welfare of one's country. ~হিতৈষণা, ~হিতৈষিতা *nn* desire of doing good to one's country. ~হিতৈষী *adj* desirous of doing good to one's country. দেশাচার *n* local usage/custom. দেশাত্মবোধ *n* act of identification with one's country; patriotism; nationalism. দেশাধিপতি=~পতি. দেশান্তর *n* **1** another country; different land/country; abroad. **2** (geog) longitude. দেশান্তরগমন *n* going abroad; travelling. দেশান্তরিত *adj* **1** living in a foreign land. **2** gone to another/a different country; gone to a distant/foreign land. **3** expelled from a/one's country. দেশান্তরী *adj*=দেশান্তরিত (1, 2).

দেশনা *n* direction; instruction.

দেশলাই=দিয়াশলাই

দেশিক *adj* local. ☐*n* **1** native. **2** guide. **3** spiritual teacher; preceptor. **4** traveller.

দেশী, দেশি *adjj* native; indigenous. ☐*n* an Indian musical mode. ~ জিনিস/ পণ্য *nn* home product; indigenous goods.

দেশীয় *adj* peculiar / belonging to or inhabiting a country; native; indigenous. ~করণ *n* nationalization. ~ কলহ *n* internal strife. ~ জন *n* native. ~ বাণিজ্য *n* inland trade. ~ ব্যাপার *n* home affairs. ~ হানাহানি *n* civil war.

দেশোয়ালি *n* countryman; co-villager; rustic. ~ ভাই *n* country cousin.

দেশ্য=দেশীয়. ~ভূত *adj* naturalized.

দেহ *n* body; physique; form; shape; corpse. ~ মাটি করা *vi* (fig) ruin one's health. ~ রাখা=~রক্ষা করা. ~ক্ষয় *n* waste/ decay of the body; disease; sickness; death. ~ক্ষয় করা *vi* ruin one's health (by hard work); die. ~চর্যা *n* care of the body; physical exercise. ~জ *adj* bodily: ~জ মল. ☐ *n* son. ~জা *n adj* daughter. ~ত *adv* bodily; physically. ~তত্ত্ব *n* **1** physiology; anatomy. **2** the doctrine that the body is the seat of all truths. ~তত্ত্বজ্ঞ *n* versed in physiology/ anatomy/ the aforesaid doctrine. ~ত্যাগ *n* relinquishing the body; death. ~ত্যাগ করা *vi* die; give up the ghost. ~ধারণ *n* assuming a body/ visible form; incarnation; birth; living; life; existence;

subsistence. ~ **ধারণ করা** *v* assume a body/ visible form; take one's birth; live; exist; subsist. ~**ধারী** *adj* having a body; living; corporeal; bodied; incarnate. ~**পতন**, ~পাত=~ক্ষয়. ~**পিঞ্জর** *n* the body conceived as a cage for the spirit. ~ **পুষ্টি** *n* nourishment of the body. ~**ভার** *n* body weight; burden of the body. ~**ভৃৎ** *n* living creature. ~**যষ্টি** *n* the body conceived as an upright stick; body; figure: ~ 2*n* supporting the body; subsistence. ~ **রক্ষা** *n* **1** care of the body. **2** death. ~ **রক্ষা করা** *vi* die. ~ **রক্ষী** *n* bodyguard. ~**সার** *n* marrow.
দেহাতিরিক্ত, দেহাতীত *adjj* beyond (the reach of) the body; transcending the body; transcendental; unembodied; incorporeal. **দেহাত্মপ্রত্যয়** *n* the belief that the body is the soul; materialistic belief; ❑ *adj* materialistic. **দেহাত্মবাদ** *n* the belief in the identity of the body and the soul; materialism. **দেহাত্মবাদী** *adj* materialistic. ❑ *n* materialist. **দেহান্ত** *n* end of the body; death. **দেহান্ত হওয়া** *vi* die; pass away. **দেহান্তর** *n* another body; rebirth; transmigration; **দেহান্তরপ্রাপ্তি** *n* transmigration; rebirth; death. **দেহান্তর লাভ করা** *vi* pass into another body; be reborn; die. **দেহাবসান**=দেহান্ত.

দেহালা *n* (archaic)=দেয়ালা

দেহী *adj* having a body; corporeal; material. ❑ *n* **1** living creature; man. **2** spirit; soul.

দৈ=দই

দৈত্য *n* **1** (myth) son of Diti; demon. **2** giant; monster; ogre. **3** gigantic man; colossus. ~**কুল** *n* race of demons. ~**কুলে প্রহ্লাদ** (fig) a saint born in the race of sinners; a Christ amongst Jews. ~**গুরু** *n* (myth) Shukracharya, the preceptor of the Daityas. ~**নিসূদন** *n* destroyer of Daityas; Vishnu. ~**পতি** *n* king of the demons. ~**মাতা** *n* mother of the Daityas; Diti. **দৈত্যারি** *n* foe of the Daityas; Vishnu.

দৈনন্দিন *adj* (happening) daily; routine: ~ ব্যাপার.

দৈনিক *adj* daily; diurnal. ❑*n* daily (newspaper).

দৈন্য *n* wretchedness; miserable state; utter poverty; indigence; misery; distress; affliction. ~**দশা** *n* miserable/ humble/ wretched state; straited circumstances; utter poverty; destitution. ~**দশাগ্রস্ত**, ~**দশাপন্ন**, ~**দশাপীড়িত** *adjj* poverty-stricken; in straited circumstances; impoverished; miserable; wretched; indigent; destitute. **দৈন্যাবস্থা**=~দশা.

দৈব *adj* **1** belonging to/ coming from the gods; divine; celestial; heavenly. **2** depending on fate; fatal; providential. **3** miraculous. **4** accidental. ❑ *n* **1** divine power/ will; fate; destiny; chance; luck; providence. **2** chance occurrence. ~**কর্ম** *n* oblation to the gods; religious rite. ~**ক্রমে** *adv* by chance/ providence; accidentally; luckily; miraculously. ~**গতি** *n* course of destiny; fortune. ~**গতিকে**=~ক্রমে. ~ **ঘটনা** *n* chance occurrence; accident; providential/ miraculous incident; ~**চয়ন** *n* random selection. ~**চিন্তক** *adj* reflecting on fate. ❑*n* astrologer; soothsayer; fortuneteller; diviner. ~**চিন্তা** *n* fatalism; astrology. ~**জ্ঞ** *adj* knowing fate/ men's destiny. ❑*n*=~চিন্তক. ~**দুর্ঘটনা** *n* accident; mishap. ~**দুর্বিপাক** *n* unforeseen calamity/ adversity; misfortune. ~**দোষ** evil fate; ill fate/ luck; misfortune. ~**দোষে** *adv* through ill luck. ~**ধন** *n* heaven-sent treasure; treasure found by chance; windfall; hidden treasure. ~**নির্দিষ্ট**, ~**নির্ধারিত** *adjj* foreordained; predestined; ordained by God. ~**বল** *n* divine power; God-gifted power. ~**বশত**, ~**বশে** *advv*=~ক্রমে. ~**বাণী** *n* voice from heaven; oracle; word of God; revelation; prophecy ~**বিড়ম্বনা** *n* irony of fate; misfortune. ~**যোগ** *n* juncture of fate; fortune; chance. ~**যোগে** *adv*=~ক্রমে. ~**লব্ধ** *adj* obtained by chance; God-gifted. ~**লেখক**=~জ্ঞ. ~**শক্তি**=বল. ~**শক্তিসম্পন্ন** *adj* endowed with divine/ God-gifted power. ~**হত** *adj* stricken by destiny. **দৈব্যাৎ** *adv* by chance; by a stroke of luck; luckily; accidentally; suddenly. **দৈবাগত** *adj* come by chance. **দৈবাদেশ** *n* divine command/ inspiration; commandment; oracle. **দৈবাধীন** *adj* subject to/ dependent on fate; fateful; controlled by destiny. **দৈবানুগ্রহীত** *adj* favoured by destiny/ the gods. **দৈবানুকূল্য, দৈবানুগ্রহ** *n* grace of God; divine favour. **দৈবানুগ্রহে** *adj* through the grace of God. **দৈবায়ত্ত**=~ধীন.

দৈবিক *adj*=দৈব

দৈবী *adj fem* of দৈব

দৈবোপহত *adj* struck by fate.

দৈব্য *adj* divine.

দৈর্ঘ্য *n* length. ~-**প্রসারণ** *n* linear extension.

দৈশিক *adj* **1** relating to space; spatial. **2** relating to any place/ country/ province/ region/ locality; local; regional; national. **3** relating to a part; partial. **4** native; indigenous; home (attrib).

দৈহিক *adj* bodily; physical; corporal; corporeal.

দো *adj* (used as a *perf*) two; two-fold; twice. **দোয়ানি**=দুয়ানি. **দোয়াব** *n* tract of land lying between two rivers. **দোআঁশ** *adj* loamy. **দোআঁশ মাটি** *n* loamy soil; loam. **দোআঁশলা** *adj* hybrid; crossbred; mongrel; loamy. ❑*n* hybrid; crossbred; mongrel. **দোকর** *adj* two times of; double. ❑*adv* two times; twice; doubly. **দোকলা, দোকা** *adj, adv* in pair; having a second/ companion; only two together. **দোকাটি** *n* two sticks; two sticks striking against each other (⇒ also দুকাঠি). দোচালা=দুচালা (⇒ দু). দোচুঙ্গী *adj* double-barrelled. দোছুট, দোছোট *nn* piece of large scarf worn loosely on the upper part of the body. দোটানা=দুটানা (⇒ দু-). দোতরফা=দুতরফা (⇒ দু). দোতলা=দুতলা (⇒ দু-). দোতারা=দুতারা (⇒ দু-). দোধারী=দুধারী (⇒ দু-). দোনলা=দুনলা (⇒ দু-). দোপাট্টা *adj* arranged into two folds; folded in two parts; double-folded. ❑ *n* wrapper; a cloth thrown loosely over the head and shoulders by women. দোপেয়াজা, দোপেঁয়াজা, দোপিয়াজি, দোপিঁয়াজি *n* kind of dish in which a double quantity of onion is used, and which has little or no gravy. ~পেয়ে=দুপেয়ে (⇒ দু-). দোফরকা, দোফাঁকড়া *adjj* bifurcated; two-forked. দোফলা=দুফলা (দু-). দোবরা *adj* doubly refined and granular. ❑ *n* doubly refined and granular sugar. ❑ *adj* twice over: দোবরা কাজ করা. দোবারা *adj* twice; doubly; a second time; again. ~ভাঁজ *adj* doubly folded; doubled; folded in two plaits. দোভাপা *adj* twice boiled. দোভাষী *adj* bilingual. ❑*n* interpreter. দোমনা=দুমনা (⇒ দু-). দোমুখো=দুমুখো (⇒ দু-). দোমেটে=দুমেটে (⇒ দু-). দোয়ানি=দুয়ানি (⇒ দু-). দোয়াব=দোআব. দ্যোরকা, দোরোকা, দোরখা, দোরোখা *adj* double-faced; facing both sides; the same on both sides; embroidered on both sides. দোরঙা *adj* of two colours; bi-coloured. দোরসা *adj* **1** (of tobacco) mixed; medium. **2** (of fish etc) partly decomposed/ rotten; not quite fresh. **3** (of soil) loamy. দোশালা *n* doubly plaited shawl; shawl woven in double plaits; pair of shawls. দোসুতি, দোসূতি=দুসুতি (⇒ দু-). দোহাতিয়া=দুহাতিয়া (⇒দু-).

দোকলা *adj* two; second.

দোকা *adj* two. ❑ *adv* together.

দোকান [P] *n* **1** shop. **2** goods for sale; merchandise. ~ করা *vi* **1** start/ open/ keep/ run a shop. **2** open a shop for the day's work. **3** go to a shop to buy things; shop. ~ খোলা *vi*=~করা (1, 2). ~ চলা *vi* have a good sale. ~ চালানো *vi* run a shop. ~ তোলা *vi* **1** close down/ wind up a shop; shut the shop. **2** close a shop for the day; shut the shop. ~ দেওয়া *vi* set up/ open a shop; arrange goods for sale. ~ বন্ধ করা=~ তোলা. ~ সাজানো *vi* display goods for sale; furnish a shop. ~-কর্মচারী *n* shop-assistant; salesclerk. ~দার *n* shopkeeper. ~দারি *n* shopkeeping; business-dealing; haggling; selfish behaviour. ~দারি করা *vi* keep/ run a shop; (fig) haggle; behave like a shopkeeper. ~দারি কথাবার্তা *n* shoppy talk. ~দারি কথাবার্তা বলা *vi* talk shop. ~পাট *n* shop and its commodities; shops. ~-হাট করা *vi* do one's shopping.

দোকানি, দোকানী *n* shopkeeper; tradesman.

দোকতা, দোক্তা *n* dried tobacco-leaf which is taken with betel-leaf.

দোজখ [P] *n* hell; inferno. দোজখি *adj* hellish; infernal; damned. ❑*n* dweller in hell; sinner.

দোজবর, দোজবরে *adjj* married/ marrying for a second time.

দোদুল *adj* swinging; moving to and fro; dangling; oscillating; wavering. দোদুল্যমান *adj* swinging/ being swung repeatedly/ violently; constantly swinging/ oscillating/ wavering. দোদুল্যমান হওয়া *vi* swing/ oscillate/ waver constantly.

দোনা[১] *n* a pouch for holding a roll of betel-leaf.

দোনা[২] *n* canoe; dug-out; tub.

দোনি *n* small dug-out.

দোপাটি *n* balsam.

দোবজা *n* kind of large silk scarf.

দোমড়ানো *vt*=দুমড়ানো (⇒ দুমড়া)

দোমালা *adj* (of coconut) half-ripe.

দোয়জ *adj* second.

দোয়া[১] *vt* **1** milk (a cow etc.). **2** extort; exploit. ~নো *vt* cause to milk etc.

দোয়া[২] [A] *n* blessing; benediction; prayer; salutation; wish; invocation; supplication. ~ করা/ দেওয়া *vi* give a blessing; bless; pray for. ~ চাওয়া/ মাগা *vi* invoke blessings; pray; ask for sb's blessings. ~ (এ) খায়ের *n* prayer for sb's well-being. ~গো *n* one who blesses/ prays for. আল্লাহর ~য়, by the grace of God. বদ~ *n* curse; imprecation.

দোয়াজ *adj* second. ~ দহম *adj* twelfth.

দোয়াত [A] *n* ink-pot.

দোয়ার=দোহার. ~কি *n* **1** singing the burden of a chorus sung after the leader. **2** sycophancy.

দোয়েম=দুয়েম

দোয়েল *n* kind of small bird; magpie robin of Bangaldesh.

দোর=দ্বার. ~গোড়া *n* doorstep; threshold.

দোরমা=দোলমা

দোরকা ⇒ দো

দোররা [P] *n* scourge made of twisted thongs; sort of whip to punish offenders with.

দোরস্ত=দুরস্ত

দোর্দণ্ড *n* long arm. ❑*adj* **1** terrible; fierce; fiery: ~ তাপ, ~ ক্রোধ. **2** mighty; powerful; iron-handed. ~প্রতাপ *adj* terribly mighty/ powerful; strong; iron-handed ❑ *n* terrible might.

দোর্মা=দোলমা

ধীরোদাত্ত *adj* (rhet) brave and noble-minded.
ধীরোদ্ধত *adj* (rhet) brave but haughty.
ধীশক্তি *n* ⇒ ধী
ধু *n* shaking; trembling.
ধুঁকনি *n* heaving; panting; palpitation; throbbing.
ধুঁকা *vi* pant; gasp for breath; palpitate; throb.
ধুঁকুনি=ধুঁকনি
ধুঁদুল=ধুন্দুল
ধুয়া=ধোঁয়া
ধুকড়ি *n* coarse bag.
ধুকধুক, ধুকপুক *nn* (onom) *n* imitating a feeble breathing/palpitating, when in a dying state; also a palpitation with hard running/excessive fear; pant; throb; wheeze. ~ **করা** *vi* palpitate; throb. **ধুকপুকানি** *n* palpitation; throbbing.
ধুকধুকি *n* pendant from a necklace; locket.
ধুকপুকুনি *n* throbbing; palpitation; restlessness; restiveness; uneasiness; panting; agitation.
ধুকা=ধুঁকা.
ধুচনি, ধুচুনি *nn* kind of basket for washing rice. ~ **টুপি** *n* straw-hat shaped like a wicker-basket.
ধুৎ, ~**ধুৎ** *int* hang! dash! blow! bother; confound it !
ধুত *adj* shaken; agitated; shaken off; removed; abandoned.
ধুতরা *n* (colloq)=ধুতুরা
ধুতি *n* loin-cloth (about five cubits long worn by Hindus about the loins); dhoti. **থান** ~ *n* dhoti without coloured border/edge.
ধুতুরা *n* thorn-apple. ~**রস,** ~**নির্যাস** *n* daturine.
ধুত্তোর *int*=ধুৎ
ধু-ধু *n* (onom) expressing: **(a)** blazing up of fire; **(b)** vast expanse: ~মাঠ; **(c)** excessive heat: ~ রোদ; **(d)** desolateness; emptiness. ~ **মাঠ** *n* endless expanse of arid land; fields stretching as far as the eye can see. ~ **করে জ্বলা** *vi* blaze; burn fiercely. **মন** ~ **করা** *vi* feel desolate/empty/miserable; eat one's heart out.
ধুনকার *n* carder; comber (of cotton).
ধুনকারা *n* bow for cleaning cotton; cotton-gin.
ধুনচি, ধুনাচি, ধুনুচি *nn* incense-burner; incenser; censer.
ধুনন, ধূনন *n* **1** shaking; fluttering; agitation. **2** sounding/playing (on a stringed instrument). **3** cleaning/combing cotton with a bow/cotton-gin; ginning; carding; combing.
ধুনরি *n*=ধুনারি
ধুনা[১] *n* incense; resin.
ধুনা[২] *vt* **1** shake; agitate; flutter. **2** clean/comb/card cotton with a bow. **3** beat; thrash; pound. ~**নি** *n* combing; carding; beating; pounding.
ধুনচি *n* ⇒ ধুনচি
ধুনারি, ধুনারী *nn*=ধুনকার
ধুনি[১], **ধুনী** *nn* stream; river: সুরধুনী.
ধুনি[২] *n* a fire lighted by Hindu ascetics.
ধুনুচি *n* ⇒ ধুনচি
ধুনুরী=ধুনকার
ধুন্দুল *n* a courgette-like vegetable.
ধুন্ধুকার *adj* hazy; misty; nebulous.
ধুন্ধুমার *n* **1** smoke of a house. **2** uproar; tumult; tumultuous affair; hurly-burly; hullabaloo. ❑*adj* uproarious; tumultuous; terrible.
ধুপ[১] *n* sunlight; the sun.
ধুপ[২], **ধুপ ধুপ, ধুপধাপ, ধুপুসধাপুস** *nn* (onom) lighter variants of ধপ.
ধুপচি *n*=ধুনচি
ধুপছায়া *n* **1** sunshine and shade. **2** peacock-blue. **3** kind of variegated cloth. ❑ *adj* peacock-blue; chiaroscuro.
ধুপুচি=ধুনচি
ধুম *n* (onom) **1** thud; slap. **2** ardour; zeal; fervour; excess; surfeit: বক্তৃতার ~, কেনাকাটার ~. **3** éclat; pomp and show; pageant; splendour; bustle; tumult: উৎসবের ~. ❑*adj* heavy; thick; hard; gross; terrible: ~ ঝগড়াঝাটি. ~**ধড়াক্কা,** ~**ধাম** *nn* great/tremendous pomp/éclat; grand pageantry; pomp and ceremony/circumstance.
ধুমড়ী *n fem* fat vagabond woman; concubine; slut; strumpet.
ধুমসা, ধুমসো *adj* extremely dark and corpulent; hideous. ❑*n* very dark and corpulent adult. **ধুমসী** *fem.*
ধুমসানো=ধামসানো
ধুম্বৰ(া) *adj*=ধুমসা. **ধুম্বী** *fem.*
ধুয়া, ধুয়ো (colloq) *nn* **1** burden (of a song); refrain. **2** chorus (also ~ গান). **3** (fig) hackneyed talk/ comment; cliché; platitude; commonplace: ওদের ওই একই ~. **4** pretext; excuse. **5** insistent demand/claim; slogan; cry. ~ **ওঠা** *vi* be the current talk/demand; be the cry; be in vogue; be the demand. ~ **তোলা** *vi* demand insistently; demour for; make loud demands. ~ **ধরা** *vi* **1** repeat/ follow up the burden (of a song); join in the chorus. **2** (fig) clamour for; cry in chorus/ unison.
ধুর *n* **1** pole/shaft of a carriage (esp their forepart). **2** axle; axle-tree. **3** yoke. **4** burden; load. **5** top; summit; front; place of honour. ~**ন্ধর** *adj* **1** bearing a yoke/burden. **2** helping another out of need. **3** very efficient/adroit;

clever; efficient; skilful. **4** cunning; sly. **5** chief; leading. ❑*n* chief; leader.

ধুরী=ধুর

ধুরীণ=ধুরন্ধর (⇒ ধুর)

ধুরীয় *adj* fit for a burden; charged with important duties.

ধুল[১] *n* a measure of land (=০.৫ কাঠা).

ধুল[২] *n* (poet, dial) dust. **~ট** *n* wallowing in the dust in ecstasy during a session of devotional song.

ধুলা, ধুলো=ধূলি

ধুস্তর, ধস্তুর *nn* thorn-apple.

ধূত=ধুত

ধূধূ=ধুধু

ধূনন ⇒ ধুনন

ধূনা=ধুনা

ধূপ *n* incense; perfume; aromatic vapour/ smoke (proceeding from gum/resin); gum; resin. **~চি** *n*=ধুনচি. **~দান** *n* censer. **~দীপ, ~ধুনা** *nn* incense and lamp (as part of an offering to a god). **ধূপিত** *adj* made fragrant/ fumigated with incense, perfumed; incensed. **~ন** *n* incensing; fumigation; perfume; incense. **~পাত্র** *n* vessel for incense; censer. **~যন্ত্র** *n* fumigating apparatus.

ধূপায়িত *adjj*=ধূপিত (⇒ ধূপ).

ধূম *n* smoke; vapour; mist; fume; gas; steam; fog. **~কুণ্ডলী** *n* ring/coil of smoke. **~কেতন, ~কেতু** *nn* comet. **~জাল** *n* mass of smoke/cloud. **~ধড়াক্কা**=ধুমধড়াক্কা (⇒ ধুম). **~ধূম্র** *adj* dark like smoke; fumigation . **~নালী** *n* pipe/conduit for escape of smoke, vapour; etc; chimney. **~নির্গম(ন)** *n* escape of smoke, vapour etc; smoke-outlet. **~পথ** *n* =~নালী. **~পান** *n* (tobacco-)smoking; smoke. **~পান করা** *vi* smoke. **~পায়ী** *adj* addicted to smoking. ❑*n* smoker. **~বারণ** *n* prevention of smoke. **~বর্ণ** *adj* smoke-coloured. **~বিহীন** *adj* free from smoke/vapour; smokeless: **~ময়** *adj* full/made of smoke; smoke-filled; smoky; vapoury; misty; foggy; funny; gaseous. **~যোনি** *n* cloud. **~রাজি** *n* column of smoke. **~ল** *adj* smoke-coloured; purple. ❑*n* colour compounded of black and red. **~হীন** =~বিহীন. **~হীনতা** *n* smokelessness.

ধূমা *adj* = ধূমাকার. **~কার** *adj* having the form of smoke; smoky. **ধূমাকীর্ণ, ধূমাচ্ছন্ন** *adjj* covered with/enveloped in smoke, vapour, etc. **ধূমাক্ষ** *adj* dim-eyed. **ধূমাভ**=~ল. **ধূমায়মান** *adj* emitting smoke; smoking; steaming; fuming; smouldering. **ধূমায়িত** *adj* **1** =~য়মান. **2** fumigated; full of smoke.

ধূমিত *adj* tasting of smoke; obscured; darkened; fumigated.

ধূমোৎপাত *n* smoke nuisance.

ধূমোদ্‌গম *n* ascending/ issuing/ discharge/ emission of smoke, vapour, etc.

ধূমোদ্‌গার, ধূমোদ্‌গিরণ=ধূমোদ্‌গম. **~ করা** *vi* emit smoke/vapour; smoke.

ধূম্র *adj* **1** smoke-coloured; smoky; dark-coloured; grey; dark-red; purple. **2** dim; obscured. **~ক** *n* camel. **~কেশ** *n* dark hair. ❑*adj* dark-haired. **~কেশী** *adj* dark-haired. **~কেশিনী** *fem.* **~বর্ণ** *adj* smoke-coloured; grey; dark. **~ল**=ধূমল. **~লোচন** *adj* **1** dark-eyed. **2** (derog)=ধুমসা. **~লোহিত** *adj* deep purple; dark-red. **ধূম্রাক্ষ** *adj* grey-eyed. **ধূম্রালোক** *n* light and shade.

ধূয়মান *adj* trembling; quivering; fluttering.

ধূর্জটি *n* name of Shiva.

ধূর্ত *adj* sly; cunning; crafty; shrewd; fraudulent; subtle; mischievous; knavish: deceitful. ❑*n* cheat; rogue; deceiver; swindler; sharper; trickster; knave. **~তা, ধুর্তামি** *nn* slyness; cunning; craftiness; knavery; roguery; deceitfulness; shrewdness.

ধূল=ধূলি

ধূলট=ধুলট

ধূলা=ধূলি. **~ ওড়া** *vi* (of dust) blow in the wind. **~ ওড়ানো** *vi* raise a cloud of dust. **~খেলা** *n* child's play; beer and skittles. **~গুঁড়া** *n* speck of dust. **~ঘর** *n* doll's house. **~বালি** *n* sand and dust. **~য় লুটানো** *vi, vt* trail along; drag through the mud/mire. **~ মুঠা ধরলে সোনা মুঠা হয়** (fig) (said of a very fortunate person) Whatever he touches turns into gold.

ধূলি, ধূলী *nn* **1** dust. **2** powder. **3** pollen. **~ ঝাড়া** *v* shake/brush off dust; dust. **গায়ে ~ দেওয়া** *vi* **1** fling/throw dust at. **2** (fig) fling/sling/throw mud (at sb); scoft. **চোখে ~ দেওয়া** (fig) throw dust in sb's eyes; hoodwink; deceive. **~কণা** *n* particle of dust. **~ঝড়** *n* dust-cloud. **~ধূসর, ~ধূসরিক** *adj* covered with dust; dusty; made grey with dust. **~পটল** *n* cloud of dust. **~ময়** *adj* full of dust; dusty; covered with dust. **~মলিন** *adj* soiled with dust. **~মাখা** *adj* covered with dust; dusty. **~মুষ্টি স্বর্ণমুষ্টি হওয়া** (lit) common dust becomes gold-dust; (fig) (of a person) whatever he touches turns-into gold. **~লুণ্ঠিত** *adj* wallowing/ lying in dust; fallen/knocked to the ground. **~শয্যা** *n* making the ground one's bed; bed of bare ground. **~শায়ী** *adj* lying on the bare ground; fallen/knocked to the ground. **~সাৎ** *adj* reduced to dust; razed to the ground; ruined; destroyed; annihilated. **~সাৎ হওয়া** *vi* be reduced to dust/ruined/destroyed; be razed to the ground; bite the dust.

ধূল্যবলুণ্ঠিত=ধূলিলুণ্ঠিত (⇒ ধূলি)

ধূসর *adj* dust-coloured; grey; ashy grey; ashen. ❑*n* grey; ashy grey. **ধূসরাভ** *adj* greyish.

ধূসরিত *adj* made grey; greyish.

ধূসরিমা *n* grey; dusty-white; greyness.

ধৃত *adj* caught; held; arrested; worn (as clothes, etc); detained; taken; supported; maintained; borne; kept; possessed; drawn light (reins). ~ **করা** *vt* catch; arrest; detain; take. ~**ব্রত** *adj* firmly resolute; devoted; attached. **ধৃতাত্মা** *adj* firm-minded; steady; calm; self-possessed. **ধৃতাস্ত্র** *adj* armed; in arms.

ধৃতি *n* **1** holding; seizing; keeping; containing supporting. **2** firmness; constancy; will; resolution; command. **3** satisfaction; content; joy. **4** conception; notion; idea; impression. **5** perseverance; persistence. ~**বিন্দু** *n* point of support. ~**মান** *adj* steadfast; calm; resolute; patient; content; satisfied; persevering. ~**মতী** *fem.* ~**হোম** *n* a sacramental sacrifice done at a Hindu wedding.

ধৃষ্ট *adj* **1** audacious; impudent; arrogant; insolent; impertinent; haughty; pert; saucy; cheeky. **2** bold; daring; confident. **2** profligate; abandoned; shameless; lewd; lascivious. **ধৃষ্টা** *fem.* ~**তা** *n* **1** impudence; insolence; audacity; arrogance; sauciness; impertinence; cheek. **2** shamelessness; lewdness; profligacy. **3** boldness. **ধৃষ্টামি** *n*=ধৃষ্টতা (1, 2) (⇒ ধৃষ্ট).

ধৃষ্য *adj* assailable; to be attacked.

ধেইধেই *n* (onom) **1** (dancing) frantic/ wild/ frenzied dance. **2** style or cue-words of the above dance. ~ **করে বেড়ানো** *vi* gad about/around; roam around.

ধেড়ানো *vi, vt* **1** soil clothes by failing to retain motion of stool/urine. **2** bungle; make a mess of.

ধেড়ে *n* otter. ❑*adj* full grown; overgrown.

ধেৎ=ধুৎ

ধেনু *n* (milch) cow; a cow that has recently calved.

ধেনো *adj* **1** produced from rice: ~ মদ. **2** yielding rice: ~ জমি. **3** rice-growing: ~ চাষা. **4** paddy-like: ~ গন্ধ. **5** resembling a rice-growing peasant; rustic; boorish. ❑*n* wine produced from rice.

ধেবড়া=ধাবড়া

ধেয় *adj* **1** to be held/taken; worth holding/ taking; acceptable. **2** knowable; cognizable; comprehensible.

ধেয়ান *n* (poet, dial)=ধ্যান. **ধেয়ানী**=ধ্যানী

ধেয়ানো *v* (poet, colloq)=ধ্যান করা

ধৈবত *n* the sixth note of the gamut.

ধৈয়জ *n* (poet, archaic)=ধৈর্য

ধৈর্য *n* **1** patience; fortitude; calmness; endurance; forbearance. **2** firmness; constancy; courage; composure. ~ **ধরা** *vi* have patience; be patient; forbear; bide one's time; bear with; keep calm. ~ **রক্ষা করা** *vi* have patience; keep calm; endure; forbear; contain oneself. ~**চ্যুত** *adj* impatient; out of patience; weary of; failing to contain oneself; chafing. ~**চ্যুতি** *n* loss of patience; impatience. ~**ধারণ** *n* forbearance; keeping patient; containing oneself. ~ **ধারণ করা**=ধরা. ~**বান,** ~**শালী,** ~**শীল** *adjj* possessed of patience/firmness/fortitude; firm; steady; patient; enduring; forbearing. ~**বতী,** ~**শালিনী,** ~**শীলা** *fem.* ~**শীলতা** *n* patience; forbearance; calmness; composure. ~ **রহিত**=~ হীন. ~**হীরা**=~চ্যুত. ~**হীন** *adj* devoid of/lacking patience; impatient; restless; fretting. ~**হীনা** *fem.* ~**হীনতা** *n* impatience; lack of patience; restlessness; impetuosity. **ধৈর্যাবলম্বন**=~ধারণ. **অসীম** ~, endless patience; patience of job.

ধোওয়া=ধোয়া

ধোঁকা[1] *vi*=ধুকা

ধোঁকা[2] *n* **1** doubt; suspicion; misgiving: ~য় পড়া. **2** deception; hoax; fraud; dodge; bluff. **3** puzzle; bewilderment; perplexity. ~ **খাওয়া** *vi* be the dupe of; be deceived/ cheated/ duped/ butted/ bamboozled/ beguiled. ~ **দেওয়া** *vt* deceive; cheat; dupe; bamboozle; bluff; beguile; mystify; hoax; hoodwink; dodge. ~ **লাগা** *v* **1** be puzzled/ bewildered/ bamboozled/ dazed. **2** have doubt; feel hesitation; be in a fix. ~**য় পড়া** *vi* be in doubt/suspicion; feel uncertain; not known which way to treat; be in a fix/dilemma; be non-plussed/perplexed; be mystified. ~**বাজ** *adj* given to deceiving/ hoaxing/ hoodwinking/dodging. ❑*n* deceiver; cheat; crook; fraud; dodger. ~**বাজি** *n* practice of cheating/ hoaxing/ hoodwinking; deception; deceit; sharp practices; hanky-panky; hocus-pocus; duplicity; double dealing. ~**বাজি করা** *vi* practise deception/ hoaxing/ trickery/ dodging; deceive; cheat; bamboozle; hoodwink; dodge.

ধোঁয়া *n* **1** smoke; vapour; steam; fume. **2** sth obscure/unclear; mists. ~ **ওঠানো/ছাড়া** *vi* **1** emit smoke; smoke. **2** (hum) puff (at/on cigarette); smoke. **3** puff smoke: কারো মুখে ~ ছাড়া. ~ **করা/দেওয়া** *vi* emit smoke; smoke. **বুদ্ধির গোড়ায়** ~ **দেওয়া** *vi* (try to) awaken one's dormant intelligence by means of smoking tobacco; sit puffing one's pipe and cogitate/ think hard. ~**টে** *adj* **1** smoke-like; smoky; vaporous. **2** (fig) foggy; vague; indistinct; misty; confused; obscure; woolly. ~**পথ** *n* chimney.

ধোকড় *n* coarse cloth; sack; rag. **কথার ~** *n* windbag; chatter-box. **মাকড় মারলে ~ হয়** (fig) what is a mortal sin for others is a vernal offence for one's own self.

ধোচনা *n* a kind of trap for catching fish.

ধোনা=ধুনা[২]

ধোপ, ধোব (dial) *n* washing and bleaching of clothes. ❑*adj* washed and bleached. **~ দেওয়া** *vi* put to washing; launder. **~ লাগা** *vi* whiten. **ধোপে টেকা** *vi* **1** stand wear and tear. **2** (fig) stand to reason; stand a test/trial; hold good. **~দুরস্ত, ~দস্ত** *adjj* **1** properly washed and bleached; neat and clean/tidy. **2** (fig) elegant; refined; polished; suave; civilized; graceful: ~দুরস্ত ব্যবহার.

ধোপা, ধোবা (dial) *n* washerman. **ধোপানি, ধোপানী, ধোবানি, ধোবানী** *fem* washerwoman. **~র বাড়ি দেওয়া** *vt* send clothes to be laundered; send (one's washing) laundry. **~র ঘাট** *n* place for washing clothes. **~র পাট** *n* a washerman's stone/ board on which he beats clothes for washing. **~-নাপিত বন্ধ করা** *vi* boycott socially by depriving sb of the services of the washerman and the barber; ostracize.

ধোব *n* wash.

ধোবা *n* ⇒ ধোপা

ধোয়া *n* wash; clean; cleanse; rinse; purify; polish; make bright; wash and bleach; scrub; scour. ❑*adj* washed; cleansed/scrubbed scoured with water; rinsed; washed and bleached. **~নো** *vt* cause to wash/ cleanse/ scrub; get sth washed. **~নি** *n* water/ liquid with which sth has been washed; waste/ dirty water; slops; effluent; sewage. **~পাকলা** *n* washing.

ধোয়াট *n* **1** rolling waves. **2** silt; deposits.

ধোলাই *n* **1** washing. **2** sound beating; thrashing. ❑*adj* washed and bleached.

ধোসা[১] *n* course woolen cloth.

ধোসা[২] *n* kind of South Indian dish.

ধৌত *adj* washed; cleansed; purified; rinsed; scrubbed; scoured with water. **~ করা** *vt* wash; cleanse; clean; rinse.

ধৌতি *n* **1** washing and cleaning. **2** method of cleaning entrails by swallowing a strip of white cloth and then drawing it out of the mouth.

ধৌরিতক *n* trot.

ধ্মাত *adj* blown; blown up/into; inflamed; excited.

ধ্মাপন *n* act of reducing to (powder, etc); fusion.

ধ্মাপিত *adj* fused.

ধ্যাত *adj* meditated on; thought of. **~ব্য** *adj* to be thought of/reflected up.

ধ্যান *n* **1** meditation; thought; reflection; contemplation; profound and abstract religious meditation. **2** recollection. **~ করা** *vi* meditate on; contemplate; think of; imagine; call to mind; recollect; be absorbed in religious meditation; be thoughtful/meditative. **~গম্ভীর** *adj* motionless/solemnly absorbed in meditation. **~গম্য, ~গোচর** *adj* attainable by meditation. **~চক্ষু** *n* eye of meditation. **~জ্ঞান** *n* **1** thought and feeling. **2** sole occupation; only preoccupation; obsession. **~দৃষ্টি** *n*=~চক্ষু *adj* seeing with the mind's eye. **~তৎপর, ~ধীর, ~নিরত, ~নিষ্ঠ, ~পর** *adjj* engaged/absorbed in meditation/contemplation; thoughtful; meditative. **~ধারণা** *adj* thoughts; thinking; way of thinking. **~পারিমতা** *n* perfection of meditation. **~ভঙ্গ** *n* interruption of meditation/thought. **~মগ্ন** *adj* engrossed in meditation. **~রত, ~স্থ**=~তৎপর.

ধ্যানী *adj* engaged in (religious) meditation; contemplative. ❑*n* one who meditates/ contemplates.

ধ্যাবড়া=ধাবড়া

ধ্যেয় *adj* to be meditated on; fit for meditation; to be pondered/imagined.

ধ্রিয়মাণ *adj* **1** being held/ sustained/ worn/ assumed/ caught. **2** alive; existing.

ধ্রুপদ *n* classical music.

ধ্রুপদী *adj* **1** classical; aristocratic; elevated; excellent. **2** versed in *dhrupada/* classical music or songs.

ধ্রুব *adj* fixed; firm; immovable; unchangeable; constant; permanent; lasting; eternal; sure; certain; deep-seated. ❑*adv* for sure/certain. ❑*n* **1** the polar star; polestar; North Star. **2** celestial pole. **3** unchangeable longitude of fixed stars; constant arc. **4** North Pole. **5** post; stake. **~ক** *n* **1** (math) constant (quantity). **2** (music)=~পদ. **~তা, ~ত্ব** *nn* constancy; certainty; permanence; surety; firmness. **~তারা, ~নক্ষত্র** *nn* =~ (1). **~পদ** *n* (music) introductory verse of a song; refrain; constant note; leit-motiv. **~ বিশ্বাস** *n* firm faith/belief/conviction. **~রেখা** *n* (geog) equator. **~লোক** *n* paradise.

ধ্রুবা=ধ্রুবপদ (⇒ ধ্রুব)

ধ্রুবাক্ষ *n* (astron) polar axis.

ধ্রুবাঙ্ক *n*=ধ্রুবক (⇒ ধ্রুব)

ধ্বংস *n* **1** destruction; ruin; falling down; perishing; disintegration; fall; demolition; devastation; loss. **2** annihilation; ravage; dilapidation; havoc; wreck; wreckage; decimation; slaughter; killing. **3** waste; squandering; dissipation: সম্পত্তি ~. **4** undeserving consumption: অন্ন~. **5** corruption; depravation: চরিত্র ~. **~ করা** *vt* **1** destroy; ruin; demolish; devastate; annihilate; ravage; play havoc with; obliterate; overthrow; shatter; desolate; exterminate; lay waste. **2** waste; squander; dissipate. **3** corrupt; deprave. ~ **হওয়া** *vi* **1** be destroyed/ ruined/ annihilated/ obliterated/ exterminated/ decimated/ dashed/ shattered; be demolished/devastated. **2** be dissipated/ wasted/ squandered; go down the drain. **3** be depraved/ corrupted. **~ক** *adj* destroying; ruining; devastating. (⇒ the meanings of the verb ~ করা). **~কর** *adj*=ধ্বংসাত্মক. **~কারী**=~ক. **~কারিণী** *fem.* **~ন** *n*=~. **~নীয়** *adj* destructible; perishable. **~প্রাপ্ত** *adj* destroyed; ruined; demolished; devastated; annihilated; ravaged; laid waste; fallen; dead; gone to one's death; wasted; depraved (⇒ the meanings of the verb ~ হওয়া). **~প্রাপ্ত হওয়া**=~ হওয়া. **~মুখ** *n* verge/ jaws of destruction/ ruin/ annihilation (see the meanings of ~). **~মুখে পতিত হওয়া** *vi* be on the verge of destruction/ ruin; reduced to a state of ruin. **~যজ্ঞ, ~লীলা** *nn* havoc; vandalism; destructive; frenzy; mass-slaughter; destructiveness; massacre. **~স্তূপ** *n* (heap/pile of) ruins; wreckage; debris. **স্মৃতি~** *n* loss of memory; amnesia. **ধ্বংসা** (poet), **ধ্বংসানো**=~ করা. **ধ্বংসাত্মক** *adj* destructive; ruinous; vandalistic; baneful; pernicious; slaughterous; nihilistic; predatory. **ধ্বংসাবশেষ** *n* remains; ruins; wreckage; relics; debris.

ধ্বংসী *adj* destroying; ruining; devastating; annihilating; wrecking; squandering; corrupting; perishing; perishable; decaying. (⇒ the meanings of the verb ধ্বংস করা above).

ধ্বংসোন্মুখ *adj* on the verge of ruin; on the point of destruction; about to go to rack and ruin; collapsing; crumbling; ramshackle; tottering.

ধ্বজ *n* **1** flag; banner; standard; flag-stand. **2** mark; emblem; ensign; sign. **2** male organ; penis. **~ক** *n* flag; standard. ❑*n* (bot) vexillary. **~দণ্ড** *n* flag-staff; flag-pole. **~পট** *n* bunting of a flag; flag. **~বাহক** *n* standard-bearer. **~বাহী** *adj* carrying a standard/flag. **~ভঙ্গ** *n* loss of sexual power of males; impotence. **ধ্বজা** *n* **1**=ধ্বজ. **2** simulacrum. **3** pretender: বিদ্যার ~. **3** (bot) vexilum. **ধ্বজাধারী** *adj* **1** bearing a standard. **2** (iron) keeping a tuft of hair uncut on one's crown as a mark of one's holiness/piety. **3** (iron) hypocritically defending/ upholding. ❑*n* defender; upholder; champion; standard-bearer: ধর্মের ~ধারী.

ধ্বজী *adj* ধ্বজাধারী (⇒ধ্বজ)

ধ্বনন *n* **1** sounding; ringing, humming; singing. **2** hinting at; allusion; suggestion.

ধ্বনি *n* **1** sound; noise; echo; voice; tone; tune; report. **2** (rhet) allusion; hint; suggestion; implied meaning. **~কাব্য** *n* (rhet) suggestive poetry. **~গ্রহ** *n* ear. **~ত** *adj* **1** caused to sound; sounded; voiced; rung; played. **2** (rhet) suggested; implied; alluded to. **~ত করা** *vt* sound; ring; place; voice. **~ত হওয়া** *vi* be sounded; give out a sound; sound; ring. **~ত প্রতিধ্বনিত হওয়া** *vi* reverberate. **~তত্ত্ব** *n* **1** phonology. **2** (rhet) theory of poetic suggestion. ❑ **~তাত্ত্বিক** *adj* phonological. *n* phonologist. **~বাদ** *n* (rhet) name of a theory of poetry which maintains that poetry consists essentially in suggestive meaning. **~বিজ্ঞান** *n* phonetics. **~বিদ্যা** *n* phonetics; phonology. **~বৃত্তি** *n* (rhet) suggestive power. **~রেখা** *n* sound-line; mark of sound-wave; line of vibration.

ধ্বন্যাত্মক *adj* onomatopoeic. **~শব্দ** *n* onomatopoeia.

ধ্বস=ধস. **ধ্বসা** *vi* fall; come down; crumble down; collapse; slide; sink; subside; cave in; flounder; tumble down.

ধ্বস্ত *adj* destroyed; ruined; ravaged; laid waste; wrecked; perished; devastated; vanquished; demolished; run down; fallen.

ধ্বস্তাধ্বস্তি=ধস্তাধস্তি

ধ্বান্ত *n* darkness; night; gloom. **ধ্বান্তারি** *n* the sun, enemy of darkness.

ন

ন[1] *n* the twentieth letter of the Bengali alphabet. It is pronounced as voiced unaspirated alveolo-nasal consonant sound.

ন[2] *n, adj* (colloq)=নয়

ন[3] *adj* **1** new: ন বউ. **2** fourth in order of seniority: ন কাকা.

ন[4] *pref* indicating: negation, opposition, etc: নইলে, নগণ্য.

নই[1] *adj* female. **~-বাছুর** *n* calf-cow.

নই[2] *adj* new.

নইচা, নইচে[1] (colloq) [P] *nn* tubepipe of a hookah.

নইচে[2] *n* **1** young fish (also ~মাছ); fingerling. **2** sapling.

নইলে *conj* or; else; otherwise: ~ মুশকিল হবে. ❑*pref* except; other than; but; without: তুমি ~ কাজটা হবার নয়.

নউই *adj* (of the days of the month) ninth: ~ ভাদ্র. ❑*n* the ninth day of the month.

নও [P] *adj* new; young; fresh; raw. **~আবাদ** *adj* newly settled/ peopled/ colonized /cultivated. **~জোয়ান** *adj* in the bloom of youth; in the prime of life; fresh and young.

❑*n* youth; young man; law. ~জোয়ানি *n* youth; prime of life. bloom/ flower of youth. ~বাহার *n* dawn of spring; early spring in full bloom/ splendour. ~মুসলিম *n* new convert to Islam. ~রোজ *n* new year's day (according to Persian calendar). নওশা *n* bridegroom; young monarch.

নওকর [P] *n* servant; dependent; retainer. নওকর চাকরি *n* domestics in general; servants.

নওকরি *n* service; employment; post.

নওবত [A] *n* (sounding of) kettle-drum (at the residence of a great man at certain intervals). ~-খানা *n* house where kettle-drums are beaten; guard house.

নওয়াব= নবাব

নওয়াবি=নবাবি

নওয়ালা [P] *n* **1** morsel; mouthful. **2** gift; presents.

নওয়ালি *adj* new.

নওরাতি *n* night of festivities.

নওল *adj* (poet) young; tender-aged.

নওলা= নহলা

নং *n* abbr of নম্বর (cf no).

নকড়া *n* **1** nine cowries. **2** dregs; scum; trash; raff. ~ছকড়া *n* **1** slight; neglect. disorder; confusion. **2** squandering. ~-ছকড়া করা *vt* **1** slight; neglect; scorn; disdain; trifle with; pooh-pooh; sneeze at. **2** make a mess of; mess up; muddle; throw at sixes and sevens. **3** squander; play ducks and drakes with. ~ছকড়া হওয়া *vi* **1** be slighted/ neglected. **2** be messed up/ in a mess; be at sixes and sevens. **3** be squandered.

নকর=নওকর

নকরি=নওকরি

নকল [A] *n* **1** copying. **2** copy; transcript; reproduction. **3** imitation. **4** copying by unfair means. **5** mimicking; mimicry; aping. **6** forgery; counterfeiting; plagiarism. ❑*adj* **1** artificial; imitation; sham; spurious: ~ সোনা. **2** forged: ~ দলিল. **3** counterfeit: ~ টাকা. ~ করা *vt* **1** copy; make a copy of; transcript. **2** copy by unfair means. **3** imitate. **4** mimic; ape. **5** forge; counterfeit; plagiarize. ~নবিস, ~নবীস *n* (professional) copyist/ transcriber. ~নবিসি *n* professional copying/ transcribing; profession of a copyist. ~বয়ান *n* reading of a copy. ~বাজ *n* **1** copyist; imitator; plagiarist. **2** forger. ~বাজি *n* copying; plagiarism; forgery; imitation. পাঁচ নকলে আসল খাস্ত, সাত নকলে আসল ভেস্ত (fig) the original has got lost in a multitude of imitations.

নকশা [A] *n* **1** design; sketch; rough sketch/ cast. **2** map; plan; chart; outline map; drawing; design in outlines. **3** diagram; pattern; table. **4** portrait. **5** embroidered design; engraving. ~ আঁকা/করা *vi* draw a map/plan/ sketch (in outlines); sketch; make a design; plan; work out a plan of; make a plan. ~-আঁকা, ~-কাটা, ~দার *adjj*=নকশি. ~কার, ~-নবিস *nn* draughts man. ~-পাড় *adj* having an artistically designed border: ~-পাড় শাড়ি.

নকশি, নকসী [A] *adjj* ornamented with designs; embroidered; engraved: ~ কাঁথা.

নকাশি, নকাশী [A] *nn* painting; drawing; embroidery; engraving.

নকিঞ্চন *adj* poor; destitute; unfortunate; wretched.

নকিব, নকীব [A] *nn* herald; proclaimer.

নকুল *n* **1** mongoose; ichneumon. **2** Shiva.

নকুলদানা *n* kind of roundish white toffee.

নকুলে *adj* given to/expert in copying/mimicry; mimicking; imitating; copying.

নক্ত *n* night. ~চর, ~চারী, ~ঞ্চর *adjj* walking at night; active/ wandering by night; night faring. ❑*n* owl; *rakshas;* thief; burglar; bat; night-bird; person active by night. নক্তান্ধ *adj* blind at night. নক্তান্ধতা *n* nyctalopia; night-blindness.

নক্র *n* crocodile; alligator. ~নক্রা *fem.* ~রাজ *n* shark.

নক্ষত্র *n* **1** (fixed) star; heavenly body. **2** an asterism/ constellation through which the moon passes; lunar mansion. ~খচিত *adj* studded with stars; star-spangled; starry. ~গতি *n* meteoric/ tremendous speed; lightning speed. ❑*adj* having meteoric/ lightning speed. ~গতিতে *adv* with lightning speed. ~দর্শক *n* astronomer; sky-gazer. ~দর্শন *n* sky-gazing. ~নাথ, ~নেমী, ~পতি *nn* the moon. ~পতন. ~পাত *nn* **1** fall of a meteor/ meteorite. **2** (fig) death/ downfall of a great man. ~পথ *n* starry sky. ~পুঞ্জ *n* group/ multitude of stars; constellation. ~বিজ্ঞান *n* astronomy. ~বিজ্ঞানী *n* astronomer. ~বিদ্যা *n* astronomy. ~বৃষ্টি *n* shooting star. ~বেগ =~গতি. ~মণ্ডল *n* stellar/ starry region; firmament. ~মণ্ডিত=~খচিত. ~মালা *n* star-group; stars (collectively). ~লোক=~মণ্ডল. নক্ষত্রালোক *n* star-light. নক্ষত্রালোকিত *adj* star-lit.

নক্সা=নকশা

নখ *n* **1** finger-nail; toe-nail; nail. **2** talon. **3** claw. ~ কাটা *vi* cut/pare nails. ~কাটা ছুরি/কাঁচি/নরুন *nn* nail-cutter. ~ বসানো *vi* make marks with the nails. ~কোনি *n* painful ingrowing nail; whitlow. ~ক্ষত *n* scratch. ~দর্পণ *n* (lit) mirror of one's nails; (lit) finger tips: কোনো কিছু ~দর্পণে থাকা, have sth at one's fingertips. ~ব্রণ=~ক্ষত. নখভিন্ন *adj* scratched/ torn off with a nail. ~র *n*=~. ❑*adj* shaped like a claw; curved; crooked. ~রঞ্জনী *n* nail-polish. ~রাগ্র *n* tip of the claw. ~রাঘাত *n* clawing. ~রাঘাত করা *vt* claw. ~রেখা, ~লেখা

nn scratch with the nail. **~মূল** *n* whitlow. **নখাগ্র** *n* tip of a nail; nail-point; tip of the claw. কোনো কিছু **নখাগ্রে থাকা** =কোনোকিছু ~ দর্পণে থাকা. **নখঘাত**=~ক্ষত. **নখাঙ্ক** *n* nail-mark. **নখানখি** *n* close fighting (with mutual scratching). **নখায়ুধ** *adj* armed with claws. ❑*n*, tiger; lion.

নখরা [A] *n* trickery; pretense; coquetry.

নখী[1] *adj* haring claws/ nails; armed with claws. ❑*n* clawed beast/ bird.

নখী[2] *n* an aromatic substance which gives out a sweet smell when fried.

নগ *n* **1** mountain. **2** tree; plant. **~জ** *n* elephant. **~নদী** *n* mountain stream. **~নন্দিনী** *n* daughter of a mountain; Durga. **~পতি, ~রাজ** *nn* the Himalayas.

নগণ্য *adj* insignificant; negligible; contemptible; paltry; worthless; of no importance; unimportant. **~ লোক** *n* an insignificant man; nobody; man of straw.

নগদ *n* ready money/cash; cash: আমার হাতে ~ কিছুই নেই. ❑*adj* **1** cash: ~ দাম/টাকা. **2** (fig) ready; prompt; immediate: ~ জবাব. **~ কারবার** *n* cash transaction. **~ বিক্রয়** *n* cash sale; sale for prompt payment. **~ বিদায়** *n* **1** ready payment in cash (of wages, charges, fees, etc on execution of the job undertaken); payment in ready money. **2** prompt/ ready dismissal. **নগদা** *adj* **1** cash: নগদা দাম. **2** ready: নগদা কারবার. **3** working for ready payment in cash: নগদা মজুর. **নগদানগদি** *adj, adv* promt(ly); (in) cash; with immediate payment of cash; cash down.

নগদি, নগদী *nn* **1** armed footman of a landlord, etc. collecting rents, issuing summons, etc. **2** ready money. ❑*adj*=নগদা.

নগর *n* city; town; metropolis. **নগরী** *fem.* **~কাক** *n* town-crow (a term of contempt). **~কীর্তন** *n* singing religious songs in procession through a city/village; a song sung thus. **~ঘণ্ট** *n* hodgepodge. **~চত্বর** *n* market-place of a city. **~জন** *n* townsfolk; townsman; townspeople. **~জীবন** *n* city-life; town-life; urban life. **~দালান** *n* town-hall. **~দ্বার** *n* gate of a town/city; city-gate. **~ পরিকল্পনা** *n* town planning. **~পাল** *n* police chief of a city; commissioner of police; city father; city-magistrate; town-chief. **~প্রান্ত** *n* outskirts/ suburbs of a city/town. **~বাসী** *adj* living in a city/town; urban. ❑*n*=~জন. **~বাসিনী** *n* townswoman. **~বিজ্ঞান, ~বিদ্যা** *nn* town planning. **~রক্ষক, ~রক্ষী** *nn* town-watchman; city-guard; metropolis. **~বৃদ্ধ** *n* townelder. **~রাষ্ট্র** *n* city state. **~ সঙ্কীর্তন**=~ কীর্তন. **~স্থ** *adj* of town/city; situated/ living in a city/ town. **~স্থাপনা** *n* building/ founding a city/ town. **নগরধ্যক্ষ** *n* governor/ mayor of a city/ town; head police-officer.

নগরিয়া=নগুরে

নগরীয় *adj* belonging to a town; civic; urban.

নগরোপান্ত=নগরপ্রান্ত (⇒ নগর)

নগাধিপ, নগাধিরাজ=নগপতি (⇒ নগ)

নগুরে *adj* =নগরবাসী (⇒ নগর)

নগ্ন *adj* **1** without clothe; naked; in one's birthday suit; unclad; stripped; nude; bare-skinned. **2** uncovered; bare: ~বাহু. **3** without ornaments; bare. **4** without spectacles; naked: ~ চক্ষু. **5** denuded; exposed: ~ প্রান্তর. **6** unsheathed; naked: ~ তরবারি. **7** clear; cloudless: ~ আকাশ. **8** dry; matter-of-fact; plain; naked; obvious; simple; unvarnished: ~ সত্য/বাস্তব. **নগ্না** *fem.* ❑*n* naked/wanton woman; a girl before menstruation; prostitute. **~ করা** *vt* undress; unclothe; divest sb of his/her clothes; strip, bare; denude; uncover; lay bare; make naked. **~ হওয়া** *vi* take off one's clothes; undress. **~ক** *adj*=~. ❑*n* naked mendicant. **~ ক্ষপণক** *n*=~ক. **~তা** *n* nakedness; nudity; bareness; obviousness; denudation; bare skin. **নগ্নাট** *n* wanderer; Buddhist or Jaina mendicant. **~ সত্য** *n* naked truth; stark reality.

নগ্নিকা *adj fem* of নগ্নক (⇒ নগ্ন). ❑*n* naked/ wanton woman; a girl before menstruation; nude.

নগ্নী *adj* (in compounds)=নগ্ন. **~করণ** *n* stripping; undressing; denudation; uncovering; making naked. **~কৃত** *adj* made naked; undressed; unclothed; stripped; denuded; exposed. **~ভবন** *n* becoming naked; undressing; denudation.

নঙর, নঙ্গর=নোঙর

নচেৎ *con* otherwise; else.

নচ্ছার *adj* **1** despicable; detestable; hateful; abominable; abhorrent. **2** good for nothing; worthless.

নছিব=নসিব

নজগজ *n* (onom) expressing stagger, shakiness, unsteadiness, tottering. **~ করা** *vi* totter; stagger; falter. **নজগজে** *adj* tottering; unsteady; shaky; wavery; irresolute; careless; unfirm.

নজদিক [P] *adj* near; close; contiguous; neighbouring.

নজর[1] [A] *n* **1** look; glance: ~ দেওয়া. eye; vision; sight: চোখের ~ খারাপ হওয়া. **2** favour; consideration; regard; (good) opinion: সুনজরে থাকা. **3** point of view; viewpoint; view; opinion: নেক~. **4** supervision; care: সে আমার নজরে আছে. **5** notice; inspection; observation; watch; surveillance: পুলিশের নজরে থাকা. **6** influence of an evil eye; greedy/evil eye; malicious/evil look: ওর ওপর শত্রুর ~ পড়েছে. **7** attention; care: কাজের প্রতি ~ থাকা. **8** view: এখন জাহাজটা নজরে আসছে. **9** ambition; aim: উঁচু ~. **10** outlook; mentality: নিচু ~. **~ করা** *vt* look; behold;

observe/mark (closely); fix the eye on; gaze; notice; catch sight of; espy; strain one's eyes to see: ~ করে দেখা. ~ দেওয়া *vi* **1** fix the gaze on; give an eye to; take care of; be attentive to; attend to: স্বাস্থ্যের দিকে ~ দাও. **2** keep an eye on; watch: ছেলের দিকে ~ দিয়ো. **3** look maliciously at; give sb the evil eye: ডাইনিটা বাছার উপর ~ দিয়েছে. **4** look covetously: কুকুরটা খাবারের উপর ~ দিচ্ছে. **~ থাকা** *vi* have an eye to; be attentive to: উন্নতির দিকে তার সব সময়ে ~ আছে. **~ পড়া** *vi* have one's glance directed towards; take a fancy to sb/sth: মেয়েটার উপর তার ~ পড়েছে. **~ বাঁচানো** *vi* avoid the looks/sight (of). **~ বোলানো** *vi* cast an eye/one's eye(s) over sb/sth. **~ রাখা** *vi* keep an eye on sb/sth; watch; look after sb/sth: এই বাক্সোটার দিকে একটু ~ রেখো. **~ খোলা রাখা** *vi* keep an eye open/ out (for sb/ sth); keep one's eyes open: আমি একটি আংটি হারিয়েছি, ঘর ঝাড় দেবার সময়ে একটু ~ খোলা রেখো. **~ লাগা** *v* be under the influence of an evil eye. **~ লাগানো** *vi* give sb the evil eye; cast a malignant look (on); regard sb with evil intent. **নজরে আসা** *vi* come into view; come to sb's view. **নজরে থাকা** *vi* be under observation/ watch; be in view; be aware/ cognizant of: বিষয়টা আমাদের নজরে আছে. **নজরে পড়া** *vi* catch sight of; attract notice of; come to sb's notice; find favour with sb. **নজরে রাখা** *vi* keep under observation/ control; keep in view; keep an eye on; watch. **নজরে লাগা** *vi* catch/take sb's fancy; attract sb. **~বন্দ** *adj* strictly watched; under surveillance. **~বন্দি** *n* confinement; arrest; house arrest. **~বন্দি করা** *vt* keep under house arrest. **~বন্দি থাকা** *vi* be under house arrest. **~বাজ** *n* ogler; juggler. **~বাজি** *n* ogling; casting amorous glances. **নজরের দোষ** *n* **1** defect of vision. **2** evil eye; malicious look. **উঁচু ~** *n* noble outlook; lofty aim; high-mindedness. **কু~** *n* evil eye; malicious/lustful look; disfavour; base motif. **কুনজরে পড়া** *vi* be out of sb's favour; lose favour with sb/in sb's eye; be in sb's bad books; incur the displeasure of sb. **ছোট /নিচু ~** *n* pettiness; meanness; lowness; pusillanimity. **নেক ~**=সুনজর. **বড় ~**=উঁচু ~. **বদ ~**=কু~. **সু~** *n* favour; good graces; favourable/ kindly look/ glance. **সুনজরে থাকা** be in sb's good graces; be/ stand high in sb's favour; be in sb's good books. **সুনজরে পড়া** *vi* find favour with sb/ in sb's eyes.

নজর[2] [A] *n* **1** tribute; present; gift. **2** (iron) bribe: পুলিশকে ~ দেওয়া. **~ নিয়াজ, ~সেলামি** *nn* respectful present. **নজরানা**=~.

নজাত=**নাজাত**

নজির [A] *n* example; instance; precedent. **~ দেওয়া** quote an instance/ precedent. **~ দেখানো** *vi* cite a case law/precedent. **~ রাখা** *vi* set an example. **~স্বরূপ** *adj* precedental.

নজুল [A] *n* descent: শানে~.

নজ্জুম [A] *n* astrologer.

নঞ্ *pref* name of the negative particle ন; negation. **~ তৎপুরুষ** *n* class of compounds in which the last member is qualified by the first without losing its grammatical independence. **নঞর্থক** *adj* negative.

নট *n* **1** actor; dancer; mime. **2** name of a particular caste. **3** name of an Indian musical mode. ❑*n* lewd; licentious; wicked; profligate; vile; depraved. **নটী** *fem* dancing-girl; ballerina; actress; courtesan. **~চর্যা** *n* an actor's performance. **~ন** *n* dancing; dance; pantomime. **~নারায়ণ** *n* name of an Indian musical mode. **~বর** *n* **1** chief actor/dancer. **2** Sri Krishna. ❑*adj* unparalleled in amorous intrigues/gallantry. **~ভবন, ~মন্দির** *nn* dancing hall; theatre; opera house. **~রাজ** *n* **1** best dancer. **2** Shiva.

নটক *adj*=নট

নটকনা, নটকান *nn* **1** anatto. **2** light orange colour.

নটখট, নটখটি *nn* **1** light trouble; hitch; snag. **2** discord; quarrel; variance; disagreement. **নটখটে** *adj* bothersome; troublesome; ticklish.

নটঘট, নটঘটি *nn* petty love affair; affair; philandering; flirtation; amour. **নটঘটে** *adj* consisting of an amour/ scandalous affair; flirtations; philandering.

নটিনী *n fem* of নট=নটী (⇒ নট)

নটিয়া, নটে (colloq) *nn* kind of pot-herb; amaranthus.

নটুয়া *adj* dancing; acting; theatre-loving.

নটে ⇒ নটিয়া

নড়চড় *n* **1** movement; motion; stirring; moving. **2** change; deviation; reversion; retreat; backout; modification; violation. **কথার ~** *n* breach/ nonfulfilment of promise/ pledge; backing out of a pledge. **কথার ~ হওয়া** go back on one's word.

নড়ন *n* **1** movement; stirring; shaking. **2**=নড়চড়: কথার ~. **~চড়ন**=নড়চড়.

নড়নড় *n* dangling motion of sth which only hangs by a fibre or bit of skin; loose/shaky motion. **~ করা** *vi* hang loose; dangle. **নড়নড়ে** *adj* dangling; flabby; hanging loose; limp.

নড়বড় *n*=নড়নড়. **~ করা** *vi* crumble; dangle; totter; teeter; heavy loose; be unsteady/ unstable. **নড়বড়ে** *adj* dangling; hanging loose; tottering; ramshackle; crumbling; shaking; unsteady; unstable, teetering.

নড়া[1] *vi* **1** move; stir; shake; budge; move/ sway about. **2** get loose: দাঁত ~. **3** shift; deviate; become otherwise; be altered; change: হাকিম নড়ে তো হুকুম নড়ে না. **~চড়া** *n* (casual) movement; stir(ring); moving about/around; mobility; stroll; walking/ pacing up and down. **~চড়া করা** *vi* move; move about/ around; stir; walk/ pace up and down. **~নো** *vt* cause to stir/move; displace; shift; shake; loosen; alter; remove; dislodge.

নড়া² *n* (derog) arm; hand.

নড়ি *n* **1** stick. **2** (fig) support; prop.

নত *adj* **1** bent; bowed; curved; inclined; inclining. **2** bowing to; saluting. **3** low; depressed; sunk: ~ জমি. **4** deep; hanging down. **5** bent down by; turned towards; directed downwards: ~ দৃষ্টি. **6** humble; meek; low: ~কণ্ঠ. **7** lowered; humbled: উচ্চশির ~ হওয়া. **8** submissive; yielding; meek: শক্তিমানের সামনে ~. **~ করা** *vt* **1** bend; lower; incline; direct downwards; flex. **2** humble; bring sb to his knees; humiliate. **~ হওয়া** *vi* stoop; bend; bow (to); submit/ subject one's self; yield; give way; genuflect; bend the knee. **~জানু** *adj* **1** knelt down; on bended knee(s); genuflected. **2** (fig) submissive; subservient. **~তল** *n* (geom) plane of inclination. **~দৃষ্টি, ~নয়ন** *nn* lowered eyes. ❑*adjj* with lowered eyes. **~নাস, ~নাসিক** *adjj* flat-nosed; snub-nosed. **~মস্তক** *adj* **1** stooping (forward); bending/ hanging down the head; having the head hanging down. **2** downcast; submissive; defeated; humiliated; meek. **~মস্তকে** *adv* hanging one's head (in shame, etc). **~মুখ** *adj* having one's face bent downwards; looking down; abashed. **~মুখী** *adj.* **~শির**=~মস্তক.

নতাংশ *n* (astron) zenith distance. **নতাঙ্গ** *adj* bent; curved; bowed; stoopedy. **নতাঙ্গী** *fem.* ❑*n* smooth-/round-limbed woman.

নতি *n* **1** bending; bowing; stooping. **2** modesty; humbleness; meekness; humility. **3** submission; humbling; yielding. **4** genuflexion. **5** (astron) inclination; parallax in latitude; dip of the horizon. **6** curvature; crookedness. **7** (mech) slope. **~মাত্রা** *n* (math, mech) gradient. **~মান** *adj*=নত. **~ স্বীকার করা** *vi* yield; submit; concede defeat.

নতুন *adj* **1** new; novel. **2** young; at the first blush/ onset; youthful: ~ যৌবন. **3** tender; youthful: ~ বয়স. **4** modern; recent. **5** unknown; strange; new: ~ মানুষ. **6** newly born/ grown; new-fledged; newborn: ~ শাবক. **7** fresh; early; first: ~ ফল/শাকসব্জি. **8** original; fresh; new-fangled: ~ ধারণা. **9** changed: সে এখন ~ লোক. **10** fourth in order of seniority: ~দা. **~ করে** *adv* anew; afresh; over again. **~ত্ব** *n* newness; novelty; originality; freshness; modernity. **~ব্রতী** *adj* newly ordained/ initiated; neophyte.

নতুবা *con* otherwise; else; or.

নতোদর *adj* **1** 'deep-naveled'; slim; thin. **2** concave.

নতোন্নত *adj* depressed and elevated; undulating.

নত্তা *n* Hindu sacrament observed on the ninth day from birth of a baby.

নথ *n* nose-ring. **~ নাড়া দেওয়া** *vi* (of a wife) pull a wry face; get into a huff; scold/ rebuke (one's husband); flare up.

নথি *n* **1** file; record; dossier; list; roll; papers. **2** (law) documents; plains; brief. **~পট্ট** *n* file-board. **~পত্র** *n pl* records and papers (collectively). **~ভুক্ত** *adj* filed; recorded; on the record. **~ভুক্ত করা** *vt* file, place on record. **~নিবন্ধ** *n* file-register. **~নিবন্ধক** *n* file-registrar. **~নিষ্পত্তিপত্রী** *n* file disposal slip. **~প্রাপক** *n* record-finder. **~রক্ষক** *n* record-keeper. **~শামিল**=~ভুক্ত

নদ *n* large river. **~নদী** *n pl* rivers (collectively).

নদারৎ [P] (phrase) have no. **খাতির ~** no favour.

নদী *n* river; stream. **~কূল** *n* bank of a river; riverside. **~গর্ভ** *n* bottom of a river; riverbed. **~তট, ~তীর**=~কূল. **~তীরবর্তী, ~তীরস্থ** *adj* situated on the bank of a river; riparian; riverside. **~তীরবাসী** *adj, n* dwelling on the riverside; riverside dweller; riverain. **~তীরবাসিনী** *fem.* **~পথ** *n* waterway; riverway; course of a river. **~পথে** *adv* by river. **~প্রবাহ** *n* current/ tide of a river. **~বক্ষ** *n* bosom/surface of a river. **~বক্ষে** *adv* on/ upon river. **~বহুল** *adj* abounding in rivers; rivery. **~মাতৃক** *adj* irrigated/ watered by rivers; well watered. **~মুখ** *n* mouth of a river; estuary. **~সৈকত**=~কূল. **~স্রোত**=~প্রবাহ.

নদ্ধ *adj* **1** bound; tied; fastened; bound on/ around. **2** put on; worn. **3** joined; connected; wound; inlaid; interwoven.

নধর *adj* **1** succulent; luscious; savoury; mellow; juicy; delicious, sweet; plump: ~ অধর; লাউয়ের ~ ডগা. **2** buxom; bonny; plump; rotund; shapely; ravishing; voluptuous; luscious; well-proportioned; fleshy: ~ তনু. **~ কান্তি** *adj* luscious; bonny; lovely; exquisite; beauteous.

ননদ *n fem* sister of one's husband; sister-in-law. **ননদাই** *n* husband of one's husband sister; brother-in-law.

ননদিনী, ননদী *nn fem* (poet)=ননদ

ননাস *n fem* eldest sister of one's husband.

ননী, ননি *nn* cream (of milk). **~র পুতুল** *n* **1** (lit) doll made of cream ;of jelly baby. **2** (fiq) (iron) one who is physically too delicate to undertake any strenuous work; sissy; weakling.

নন্দদুলাল *n* **1** beloved son of Nanda; Sri Krishna. **2** (derog) worthless son of doting parents.

নন্দন *adj* rejoicing; gladdening; pleasing: দৃষ্টি~. ❑*n* **1** son. **2** divine garden; Indra's paradise. ~কানন *n* paradise; Eden.

নন্দনন্দন *n* son of Nanda; Sri Krishna.

নন্দলাল=নন্দদুলাল

নন্দা[১]=ননদ

নন্দা[২] *n* **1** goddess Durga. **2** the three auspicious lunar days (1st, 6th and 11th).

নন্দাই=ননদাই.

নন্দি *n* **1** joy; happiness; welfare. **2** name of the chief attendant of Shiva. **3** Shiva. ❑*adj* delightful; pleasant; joyous. ~ভৃঙ্গি *n* **1** Nandi and Bhringi, the two chief attendants of Shiva. **2** (iron) undesirable associates/ lieutenants; accomplices; mischievous attendants/ entourage.

নন্দিত *adj* **1** delighted; pleased; gladdened. **2** congratulated; felicitated; honoured; glorified; celebrated. নন্দিতা *fem.*

নন্দিনী *n fem* **1** daughter. **2** name of a fabulous cow. **3** goddess Durga.

নন্দী *n*=নন্দি (2). ❑*adj* delighted.

নন্দ্য *adj* worth rejoicing; to be felicitated/ honoured.

নন্নড়ে *adj* (colloq)=নড়নড়ে

নপুংসক *n* eunuch; hermaphrodite; castrated man/ animal. ❑*adj* **1** hermaphroditic; castrated; impotent. **2** (fig) impotent; futile: ~ ক্রোধ.

নফর [A] *n* groom; servant; menial. নফরানি *n* office/state of a groom/servant.

নফরৎ [A] *n* abomination; abhorrence; disgust; aversion.

নফল [A] *n* voluntary act of religion, the observance of which is not prescribed; work of supererogation. ❑*adj* additional; secondary.

নফ্‌স [A] *n* soul; self; spirit; person; body; animal life; essence; lust; concupiscence; sensuality. ~ আম্মারা *n* inordinate appetites; concupiscence; evil propensity. নফসানিয়াত *n* sensuality; egotism; carnality; luxury; pride.

নফসি [A] *adj* of / relating to the soul; psychic; carnal; sensual. ইয়া ~ each one for himself.

নফিস [A] *adj* choice; exquisite; delicate; precious.

নব[১] *adj* new; fresh; recent; young; modern; new-born; early; novel; newly grown: ~কলিকা *n*=~মুকুল. ~কারিকা *n* newly-married woman. ~কার্তিক *n* **1** new-born Kartika. **2** (iron) very ugly man; paragon of beauty. **3** (hum) foppish gallant. ~কুমার *n* new-born son. ~কোরক =~মুকুল. ~জলধর *n* newly formed/fresh cloud. ~জলধরপটল *n* heap of fresh clouds; cumulus. ~জলধরশ্যাম *adj* as charmingly dark as a fresh rain-bearing cloud. ~জাত *adj* new-born; newly grown/produced; fresh. ~জাতক *n* newborn baby. ~জীবন *n* **1** new life; young life. **2** fresh lease of life; rejuvenation. ~ডঙ্কা *n* (hum) nothing; zero; cipher; nil. ~তর *adj* newer; fresher; younger. ~তা, ~ত্ব *n n* newness; freshness; novelty; modernity. ~দম্পতি *n* newly married couple. ~দল *n* fresh/ tender leaf (of a lotus); young leaf. ~নব *adj* ever/always new; most various/ manifold. ~নিযুক্ত *adj* newly appointed. ~নীরদ=~জলধর. ~পরিণীত *adj* newly married. ~পল্লব *n* new shoot; young sprout. ~প্রসূতী *adj fem* who has lately brought forth. ~বধূ *n* newly married woman/ bride. ~বর্ষ *n* new year. ~বর্ষা *n* early rains. ~বসন্ত *n* early/new spring. ~বিধান *n* **1** new system/law/order. **2** the New Testament. ~মল্লিকা *n* name of a variety of jasmine; *Jasminum arborescens.* ~মুকুল *n* new/early bud/ blossom. ~যুগ *n* new age. ~যুবক *n* (fool-blooded) young man. ~যুবতী *n* young woman. ~যৌবন *n* **1** early/fresh youth; bloom/ first flush/ prime of youth. **2** fresh lease of youth; rejuvenation: ~যৌবন লাভ. ~যৌবনসম্পন্ন *adj* in the prime of youth; in the first/full flush of youth. ~যৌবনসম্পন্না, ~যৌবনা *fem.* নবাগত *adj* justcome; newly arrived. ❑*n* new-comer. নবাগতা *fem.*

নব[২] *n, adj* nine. ❑*adj* ninth. ~গুণ *n* nine marks (of high birth). ~গুণিত *adj* multiplied by nine. ~গ্রহ *n* nine planets (collectively). ~চত্বারিংশ *adj* forty-nine. ~চত্বারিংশৎ *n, adj* forty-nine. ~চত্বারিংশত্তম *adj* forty-ninth. ~চত্বারিংশত্তমী *fem.* ~তি *n, adj* ninety. নবতিতম *adj* ninetieth. ~তিতমী *fem.* ~দুর্গা *n* goddess Durga in her nine forms. ~দ্বার *n* nine-doors/apertures of the body. ~ধা *adj* nine parts/ways/times; of nine kinds. ❑*adv* in nine ways/parts; by nine times. ~নবতি *n, adj* ninety-nine. ~নবতিতম *adj* ninety-ninth. ~নবতিতমী *fem.* ~বিংশতি *n, adj* twenty-nine. ~বিংশতিতম *adj* twenty-ninth. ~বিংশতিতমী *fem.* ~ম *adj* ninth. ~মী *n* ninth day of a lunar fortnight. ~মুখ *adj* having nine aperturer/ openings. ~রত্ন *n* **1** nine precious gems (pearl, ruby, topaz, etc). **2** nine jewels (ie, nine men of letters at the court of Vikramaditya). ~রত্নসভা *n* court of Vikramaditya adorned with nine men of letters. ~রস *n* (rhet) nine sentiments/ passions (love, heroism, anger, etc). ~লক্ষণ=~গুণ. ~শাখ, ~শায়ক *nn* name given to any of the nine inferior castes (cowherd, gardener, oilman, weaver, confectioner, water-carrier, potter, blacksmith and barber). ~সম্পর্কিত *adj* newly allied.

নবৎ, নবত=নওবত

নবতন *adj* new; fresh.

নবনী, নবনীত *n* fresh butter. ~তুল্য *adj* soft and white like cream; cream-like.

নবাংশ *n* (astrol) ninth part.

নবাঙ্কুর *n* 1 new shoot/bud. 2 (fig) inception; germination: ভালোবাসার ~.

নবান্ন *n* new rice/ grain; ceremony observed on first eating new rice in the month of Agrahayan (অগ্রহায়ণ).

নবাব [A] *n* 1 nabob; nawab; ruler of a territory; governor of a district/ town; viceroy. 2 arrogant, ease-loving, luxurious man. ~জাদা *n* nawab's son. ~জাদি *fem* nawab's daughter. ~-নাজিম *n* provincial governor and judge. ~পুত্তুর *n* (iron)=~ (2). ~পুত্র=~জাদা. ~পুত্রী =~জাদি.

নবাবি, নবাবী *adj* 1 relating to a nawab. 2 extravagant; lavish; luxurious: ~ চাল. ❑*n* 1 office/ state of a nawab. 2 deportment/ bearing like that of a nawab. 3 extravagant/ luxurious way of life.

নবারুণ *n* newly risen sun; first light of the day; daybreak; dawn.

নবার্জিত *adj* newly earned/ acquired.

নবি=নবী .

নবিস[1] [E] *n* novice; probationer. নবিসি *n* probation; noviciate; novitiate.

-নবিস[2], -নবিশ [P] *n* writing. ❑*suff* writer; scribe; clerk. খাস~*n* private secretary.

নবিসিন্দা [P] *n* scribe; correspondent.

নবী[1] [A] *n* prophet.

নবী[2] *adj* (in compounds)=নব[1]. ~করণ *n* making new; renewing; renewal; renovation; repair; mending. ~কৃত *adj* renewed; renovated; revived; mended; rapaired. ~ভবন *n* becoming new; state of being renewed; renewal; renovation. ~ভাব *n* becoming new; renovation; renewed state. ~ভূত *adj* become new; renewed; renovated.

নবীন *adj* fresh; new; young; tender-aged; modern; novel. নবীনা *fem*. ~তা, ~ত্ব *nn* freshness; newness; youthfulness; novelty; modernity.

নবীয়সী *adj fem*=নবীনা

নবুয়ত [A] *n* office of a prophet; prophethood.

নবেতর *adj* other than new; old.

নবোঢ়া *adj fem* newly/ recently married; newlywed. ❑*n* newly-married woman.

নবোৎসাহ *n* new/renewed/ fresh enthusiasm/ zeal/ vigour.

নবোদয় *n* new/recent rise; new appearance/ revelation.

নবোদিত *adj* newly/recently risen; newly appeared/ revealed.

নবোদ্গত *adj* 1 newly sprouted/ grown: ~ পাতা. 2 cut; appeared: ~ দাঁত. 3 arisen: ~ সমস্যা.

নবোদ্গম *n* new sprouting/ shooting forth/ appearance.

নবোদ্ধৃত *adj* newly quoted/ cited. ❑*n* fresh butter

নবোদ্ভাবিত *adj* newly intended/ devised/ designed/ contrived; newfangled.

নবোদ্ভিন্ন=নবোদ্গত

নবোদ্যম *n* 1 new initiative/ undertaking. 2=নবোৎসাহ.

নবোন্মেষ *n* new opening/blossoming.

নবোন্মেষিত, নবোন্মিষিত *adj* newly opened/ blossomed/ appeared.

নবোপলীয় *adj* neolithic.

নব্বই, নব্বুই (colloq) *n, adj* ninety.

নব্য *adj* new; modern; recent; novel; young. নব্যা *fem*. ❑*n* newly-married woman. ~তন্ত্র *n* new system; modernism. ~বঙ্গ *n* young/ modern Bengal. ~ সম্প্রদায় *n* the youth (collectively).

নভ *n* sky; atmosphere; firmament; heavens. ~গ *adj* flying (in the sky). ~চিত্র, ~দৃশ্য *nn* skyscape. ~শ্চক্ষু *n* the sun. ~শ্চর *adj* aerial; celestial; heavenly. ❑*n* 1 bird. 2 wind. 3 cloud. ~শ্চ্যুত *adj* fallen from the sky. ~স্তল *nn* 'surface of the sky'; firmament; skyey region/ expanse.

নভঃ *n*=নভ. ~সরিৎ *n* Milky Way. ~স্থ, ~স্থিত *adjj* aerial; celestial; heavenly. ~স্থল=নভস্তল (⇒ নভ). ~স্পর্শী, ~স্পৃক *adj* touching/ kissing/ reaching the sky; sky-high; lofty. ~স্বান *n* wind.

নভেম্বর [E] *n* November.

নভেল [E] *n* novel. ~-লেখক *n* novelist. নভেলিয়ানা *n* behaving like a character of a novel.

নভো *n* (in compounds)=নভ. ~গতি *n* flying; soaring. ~নীল *adj* sky-blue; azure. ~বস্তুবিদ্যা *n* astrophysics. ~বীক্ষণ *n* astronomical telescope. ~যোগ্য *adj* sky-worthy. ~যোগ্যতা *n* air-worthiness ~যোগ্যতা-পত্র *n* certificate of air-worthiness. ~মণ্ডল *n* firmament; atmosphere.

নম *nn* bow; obeisance; reverential salutation; adoration; glorification. ~ করা *vi* bow; salute; make an obeisance; genuflect. ~-নম করে সারা hurry through; deal with summarily; gloss over; scratch the surface. ~শূদ্র, নমঃশূদ্র *n* name of a Hindu caste. ~স্কর্তা *adj* bowing; saluting; worshipping; making an obeisance. ❑*n* one bows/ salutes/ makes an obeisance; worshipper. ~কর্ত্রী *fem*. ~স্কার *n* bow; salute; obeisance; homage; genuflexion. ~স্কার করা *vi* bow; salute; make a bow/ obeisance; genuflect. ~স্কারী *n* a present given in obeisance to respected relatives by a bride/ bridegroom at a Hindu wedding. ~স্কার্য =~স্কৃত *adj* greeted with a bow; saluted. ~ক্রিয়া=~স্কার. ~স্য *adj* worthy of being saluted; deserving homage; worthy of respect; venerable; adorable. ~স্যা *fem*.

নমঃ=নম

নমঃশূদ্র⇒নম

নমন *n* bending; bowing; flexion. ~ **বল** *n* (phys) bending force. **নমনাঙ্ক** *n* (phys) bending moment.

নমনীয় *adj* **1** pliable; flexible; yielding; submission; supple; soft; pliant; malleable; ductile; plastic. **2** amiable; benign; mild; tender. ~**তা** *n* **1** pliability; flexibility; malleability; ductility; plasticity; pliancy; softness. **2** amiability; mildness; tender-heartedness.

নমা *vi* (poet) bow; salute; make obeisance; genuflect.

নমাজ *n* =নামাজ

নমাসে-ছমাসে *adv* once in a blue moon; seldom; rarely; hardly ever.

নমিত *adj* bowed; bent down (in obeisance); subdued; arched. **নমিতা** *fem.*

নমুনা [P] *n* sample; specimen; model; type; pattern; example; form; case.

নম্বর *n* **1** number; serial number. **2** (in examination) marks. ~ **দেওয়া** *vi* **1** give a number to (sth); number. **2** give marks; mark. **নম্বরী** *adj* **1** bearing a number; numbered. **2** marked (as of one under suspicion).

নম্য *adj* **1**=নমনীয়. **2** to be bowed down. **3** venerable.

নম্র *adj* **1** polite; gentle; mild; modest; suave; bland; meek, humble; kindly; submissive; reverential. **2** bowing; bent down; cast/ turned downwards: ~ মুখ. **3** soft; gentle; faint; low; feeble: ~ কণ্ঠ. **4** flexible; pliable. ~**কণ্ঠ** *adj* soft-spoken; mild-spoken. ~ **কণ্ঠে** *adj* in a gentle voice; softly. ~**তা** *n* **1** gentleness; politeness; modesty; affability; good manners; meekness; humbleness. **2** softness; tenderness; suavity; blandness. **3** flexibility; pliability. ~**নয়ন**, ~**নেত্র** *adjj* having downcast eyes. ~**নয়নে** *adj* with downcast eyes; looking down. ~**প্রকৃতি** *adj* of a gentle/ submissive disposition; gentle-natured; benign; unassuming. ~**ভাব** *n*=~তা. ~**ভাবে** adv gently; politely; softly; modestly; meekly; humbly. ~**মুখ** *adj* having the face bent down; looking down; stooping. ~**স্বভাব**=~-প্রকৃতি.

নয়[১] *n, adj* nine. ~-**ছয়** *adj* 1 scattered at sixes and sevens. 2 squandered away; wasted. ~-**ছয় করা** vt 1 scatter over/ about. **2** squander; scatter around.

নয়[২] *n* **1** (prudent) conduct/ behaviour; good management; polity; civil and military government. **2** wisdom; prudence; reason-leading thought; principle; system; method; doctrine; method. ~**কোবিদ**, ~**জ্ঞ**, ~**চিৎ** *adj* skilled in policy; prudent. ❑*n* person skilled in policy. ~**জ্ঞান** *n* political wisdom. ~**শাস্ত্র** *n* doctrines of political wisdom.

নয়[৩] 3rd pers form of the verb নহা. ❑*n* not-being; impossibility; no. ❑*conj* or; nor; else; otherwise: তুমি ~ আমি, হয় এটা ~ ওটা. ~**ক**, ~**কো** *vii* is/are nor. ~**ত**, ~**তো** *conj* or; else; otherwise.

নয়ন *n* **1** eye. **2** glance; sight. **3** leading; directing. **4** carrying; bringing. ~**কোণ** *n* corner of an eye. ~**গোচর** *n* being within the range of vision; visible. ~**গোচর হওয়া** *vi* come into view; become visible; be perceived. ~**জল** *n* tears. ~**ঠার** *n* (meaningful) wink. ~**তারা** *n* pupil of the eye; apple of the eye. ~**নন্দন** *adj* pleasing/ agreeable to the eye; lovely; handsome; beautiful. ~**নীর** *n* tears. ~**পথ** *n* range/ field of sight. ~**পল্লব** *n* eyelid conceived as a new shoot or sprout. ~**পুট** *n* eyelid. ~**প্রীতি** *n* lovely sight. ~**প্রীতিকর**, ~**রঞ্জন**=~ নন্দন. ~**বাণ** *n* amorous darting glance; sidelong glance; leer. ~**বারি** *n* tears. ~**বুদ্বুদ** *n* eyeball. ~**মণি**=~তারা. ~**যুগল** *n* pair of eyes. ~**সলিল** *n* tears. **নয়নাঞ্জন** *n* eye-ointment. **নয়নানন্দ** *n* lovely sight/ object; delight of the eye. ❑*adj* delightful to the eye. **নয়নাভিরাম**=~ নন্দন. **নয়নাসার** *n* tears.

নয়নজুলি *n* gutter; drain; ditch.

নয়নসুখ *n* cambric.

নয়না *n* (poet) eye; side-long glance.

নয়নী *adj fem* having (particular kind of) eyes: তরল~. ❑*n* pupil of the eye.

নয়নোৎসব *n*=নয়নানন্দ (⇒ নয়ন)

নয়নোন্মীলন *n* opening of one's eyes.

নয়নোপান্ত *n* corner of the eye.

নয়া *adj* new; fresh; recent; modern. ~ **আবাদি** *n* new settlement.

নয়ান *n* (poet)=নয়ন

নয়ানছুলি=নয়নজুলি

নর[১] *n* man; human being; male; person. ❑*adj* male: ~ ও মাদি. ~**কঙ্কাল** *n* human skeleton. ~**কপাল** *n* skull of a dead person. ~**কেশরী** *n* a lion amongst men; man of great prowess. ~**করোটি**=~কপাল. ~**ঘাতক** *n* homicide. ~**ঘাতী** *n* homicidal. ~**ত্ব** *n* manhood; humanity. **নরারোপ** *n* anthropomorphism. ~**দেব** *n* king. ~**দ্বেষ** *n* misanthropy. ~**দ্বেষী** *n* misanthropist. ~**নারায়ণ** *n* (myth) name of two sages who were born as Arjuna and Sri Krishna. ~**নারী** *n* men and women. ~**পতি** *n* king. ~**পশু** *n*/beast in human form; brute. ~**পাল** *n* king. ~**পিশাচ** *n* fiend/ ogre/ demon in human form; devilish/ malevolent being. ~**পুঙ্গব** *n* (lit) 'man-bull'; (fig) excellent/ great hero. ~**বর** *n* best/ excellent man. ~**বলি** *n* human sacrifice. ~**ব্যাঘ্র** *n* tiger of a man; eminent/ excellent man; man of great prowess. ~**ভুক** *adj* man-eating; cannibal; anthropophagous. ~**ভুক প্রাণী** *n* man-eater;

anthropophagite. ~ভুক মানুষ *n* cannibal. ~মাংস *n* human flesh. ~মাংস ভোজন *n* cannibalism. ~মাংসভোজ্য *adj* cannibalistic. ❑*n* cannibal. ~মালা *n* string/ girdle of human skulls. ~মালিনী *n fem* woman wearing a string/ girdle of human skulls. ❑*n* goddess Kali. ~মুণ্ড *n* human skull. ~মুণ্ডমালিনী=~মালিনী. ~মেধ=~বলি. ~রূপ *n* human form. ~রূপী *adj* having the form of a human being. ~রূপে *adv* in the form/ shape of a human being. ~লীলা *n* activities (of a god) in a human existence. ~লোক *n* 'men's world; the earth; mortals; men. ~শার্দূল *n*=~ব্যাঘ্র. ~শ্রেষ্ঠ *n* the best of men. ~সিংহ *n* **1**=~কেশরী. **2** name of Vishnu in his fourth incarnation (when he was half man half lion). ~হত্যা *n* homicide; murder. ~হত্যা করা *vi* commit murder/ homicide; murder. ~হত্যাকারী *n* murderer; homicide. ~হত্যাঘটিত *adj* homicidal. ~হন্তা=~হত্যাকারী. ~হন্ত্রী *n fem* murderess. ~হরি=~সিংহ (2). **নরাকার, নরাকৃতি** *adj* having a human shape/ form; human shaped. **নরাকার পশু**=~পশু. **নরাধম** *n* vile/ low man; wretch; mean; rascal. **নরাধিপ** *n* king. **নরান্তক** *adj* killing; murdering. ❑*n* murderer; Yama, the god of death.

নর[2] *n* string; row; line: এক~, দু~.

নরক *n* hell; inferno; place of torment; hellish/ abominable place. ~কুণ্ড *n* **1** pit in hell for tormenting the wicked. **2** (fig) hellish/ vicious/ filthy/ abominable/ extremely disorderly place. ~গামী *adj* condemned to hell; damned; wicked. ~গুলজার *n* pandemonium; babel. ~গুলজার করা *vi* kick up no end of a racket; racket (about/ around). ~বাস, ~ভোগ *nn* **1** abode in hell; condemnation to hell; damnation. **2** (fig) torment; extreme suffering. ~যন্ত্রণা *n* hellish torment; hell. ~যন্ত্রণা ভোগ করা *vi* suffer hell. ~স্থ *adj* living/ being in hell; damned; condemned to hell. **নরকাগ্নি** *n* hell-fire.

নরদমা=নর্দমা

নরম [P] *adj* **1** soft: ~ শরীর. **2** low; gentle; soft: ~ সুর. **3** tender; delicate: ~ ঘাস. **4** moist; cool: ~ হাওয়া. **5** mild; gentle: ~ মেজাজ. **6** loose; slack: ~ বাঁধন. **7** mellowed; slightly rotten: আমগুলি ~ হয়ে গেছে. **8** softened/ appeased/ moved with pity: মন ~ হওয়া. **9** tender; soft; delicate; kindly: ~ মন. **10** deprived of crispiness: মুড়ি ~ হলে খেতে ভালো লাগে না. **11** weak; feeble; week: তাকে ~ পেয়ে সবাই তার উপর উপদ্রব করে. **12** tender; tender-hearted; soft; kind: ~ মন. **13** dull; slack: বাজার ~. **14** moderate: ~ দর. **15** smooth; sleek: ~ চুল. **16** slow: ~ গতি/ পা. **17** loosened; slackened: বাঁধন ~ হওয়া. **18** pleasant; cool; soft: ~ আলো. **19** not hardened: নরম পাকের সন্দেশ. **20** abated; low: জ্বর ~ হওয়া. ~ করা *vt* soften; mollify; melt; appease; mellow; mash; knead. ~ হওয়া *vi* soften; be appeased; slacken; loosen; relent; abate; loose crispiness; weaken; come down; slump. ~দিল *adj* tender-hearted; soft-hearted; gentle. ~-গরম *adj* lukewarm; angry and soft at the same time. ❑*n* the carrot and the stick; harsh words spoken in a bland voice.

নরী *adj*=নর[2]

নরুন *n* a small chisel-shaped nail-cutter. ~-পেড়ে *adj* (of loin-cloths) having a thin coloured border.

নরেন্দ্র, নরেশ, নরেশ্বর *nn* lord of men; greatest/ best of men; king.

নরোত্তম *n* best of men; Vishnu.

নর্তক *adj* dancing. ❑*n* dancer. **নর্তকী** *n, adj fem* dancing-girl; female dancer.

নর্তন *n* dancing; dance. ~কুর্দন *n* **1** dancing and romping; frolicking. **2** bragging and vaunting; bravado. ~প্রিয় *adj* fond of dancing. ❑*n* peacock. ~-শালা *n* dancing-room; dance-hall. ~-শিক্ষক *n* dancing-master.

নর্তিত *adj* made to dance; dancing; dandled.

নর্দন *n* sounding; roaring; roar.

নর্দমা *n* drain; gutter; sewer.

নর্দিত *adj* sounding; bellowed; roared.

নর্ম *n* sport; play; amusement; pleasure; pastime; pleasantry; dalliance; jest; joke; merry-making; diversion; fun; luxury; pleasure. ~দ *adj* delightful. ~সখা, ~সচিব, ~সহচর *nn* promoter of the amusement of a prince; playmate; jester; clown; courtier. ~সখী, ~সহচরী *nn fem* girl playmate; partner in merry-making; mistress; concubine.

নল *n* **1** species of reed. **2** tube; cylinder; pipe; barrel; rod. **3** a measure of length. **4** measuring rod. ~ক *n* any long bone of the body; to be/ tubular organ of the body. ~কূপ *n* tube-well. ~কূপ বসানো *vi* sink a tube-well. ~খাগড়া *n* reed. ~-চালা *n* trick of setting a rod on move, presumably by occult incantation, to detect a thief. ~ চালা *vi* set a rod on move to detect a thief by means of occult incantation. ~বন *n* thicket of reed. **নলাকার** *adj* tubular; cylindrical.

নলচে=নলিচা

নলপত *n* **1** procrastination. **2** coaxing. ~ করা *vi, vt* **1** procrastinate. **2** coax.

নলা[1] *n* tubular bone; (esp) tibia or shinbone. ~মাছ *n* species of fresh-water fish.

-নলা[2] *adj* (used as a *suff*) having a certain number of tubes/ barrels: দো~, double-barrelled.

নলানো *vi*=নল চালা (⇒ নল)

নলি *n* **1** small tube/ pipe/ cylinder. **2** tubular bone: পায়ের ~, shinbone. **3** narrow drain.

নলিকা *n* 1 small pipe/ tube. 2 stem/stalk (of a plant). 3 artery.
নলিতা *n* pipe of a hookah.
নলিন *n* lotus; water-lily. **নলিনাক্ষ** *adj* lotus-eyed.
নলিনী *n fem* (of নলিন) 1 lotus; assemblage of lotus flowers; lotus point. 2=পদ্মিনী. **~দল** *n* leaf of the lotus plant. **~রুহ** *n* (fibres of a) lotus-stalk.
নলী=নলি and নলি.
নলেন *adj* new. **~ গুড়** *n* molasses prepared from new date-juice.
নশ্বর *n* perishable; transitory; transient; mortal. **~তা** *n* transitoriness; perishableness; transience; frailty; mortality.
নষ্ট *adj* 1 lost; perished; disappeared. 2 destroyed; ruined: ~ রাজ্য. 3 spoiled; damaged; wasted: ~ বিষয়সম্পত্তি. 4 fruitless; unsuccessful; futile: ~ চেষ্টা. 5 misspent; dissipated: ~ যৌবন. 6 lost; gone: ~ চেতনা. 7 rotten; turned; putrefied; deteriorated; decomposed: ~ দুধ/মাংস. 8 corrupted; depraved: ~ চরিত্র. 9 unchaste; wayward; loose; lewd; shameless; wanton: ~ মেয়েলোক. 10 wicked; mischievous; vile; vicious: ~ বুদ্ধি. **~ করা** *vt* 1 destroy; ruin; lay waste; wreck. 2 spoil; squander; damage; waste; scatter around. 3 dissipate; misspend. 4 render futile/ fruitless/ useless; mar; foil; undo; spoil. 5 pervert; demoralize; corrupt; deprave; debauch. 6 deface; disfigure: চেহারা ~ করা. 7 indulge; pamper; spoil; coddle: ছেলে ~ করা. 8 blunt. **~ হওয়া** *vi* 1 perish; be destroyed/ ruined. 2 be spoiled/ undone. 3 be worse; lose quality; deteriorate; decay; rot; turn; decompose. 4 be depraved/ corrupted/ perverted; go astray; fall. 5 be wasted/ squandered. 6 be dissipated/ misspent. **~কোষ্ঠী** *n* lost/ missing horoscope. **~কোষ্ঠী উদ্ধার করা** *vi* recast one's nativity from assumed data. **~চন্দ্র** *n* the fourth day in both halves of Bhadra. **~চেতন** *adj* unconscious; insensible. **~চেষ্ট** *adj* 1 who has lost his power of motion; rigid; fainted; insensible. 2 inactive; lethargic. **~দৃষ্টি** *adj* sightless; blind. **~ধী** *adj* unmindful; forgetful. **~নিদ্র** *adj* sleepless. **~মতি** *adj* who has lost his senses; depraved; evil-minded; wicked; unchaste; (endearment) mischievous. **~স্মৃতি** *adj* who has lost his memory; forgetful. **নষ্টা** *adj fem* unchaste; wicked; vile; vicious; wanton; wayward; shameless; whorish. ❑*n* woman of easy virtue; strumpet; jade; shut; trollop. **নষ্টামি, নষ্টামো** *nn* 1 mischievousness; pranks; roguery; rascality; villainy; knavery; delinquency; devilry. 2 debauchery; depravity; promiscuous behaviour. **নষ্টামি/ নষ্টামো করা** *vi* 1 make mischief; play tricks; be up to mischievous tricks. 2 spend time in idle dalliance; dally with sb; womanize; philander; gallivant (about).
নষ্টেন্দুকলা *n* night in which the moon is invisible; night of a new moon.
নষ্টোদ্ধার *n* reclamation/ recovery of the sth lost.
নসিব, নসীব [A] *nn* lot; luck; destiny; fate; fortune. **~ খুলে যাওয়া** *vi* be greatly favoured by fortune; be in the ascendant; have a turn of luck. **~ বিগড়ানো** *n* be unlucky/ unfortunate. **~ হওয়া** *vi* gain; fall to the lot of; be lucky. **নসিবের গর্দিশ/ দোষ/ ফের** *n* ill-luck; frowns of fortune; reversal of fortune. **নসিবের দোষে/ফেরে** *adv* through ill-luck; as ill-luck would have it; through reversal of fortune. **নসিবের লেখা** *n* what is destined; fate; destiny.
নসিহত *n* advice; counsel; admonition; precept; sermon. **~ করা/ দেওয়া** *vt* advise; admonish; counsel; exhort; (derog) sermonize.
নস্য *n* 1 snuff. 2 (hum) iota; trifle. **~ করা** *vt* (fig) destroy; pulverize. **~ নেওয়া** *vi* take (a pinch of) snuff. **~দান, ~দানি, নস্যের কৌটা/ ডিবা** *nn* snuff-box.
নস্যাৎ *adj* perishing; being destroyed; lost. **~ করা** *vt* 1 destroy; annihilate; pulverize; dash; nullify; shatter; spoil; undo. 2 refute; reject; rebut; disprove; explode.
নস্যি *n* (colloq)=নস্য
নহবত=নওবত
নহর [A] *n* stream; brook; canal (of running water); rivulet.
নহলা *n* nine of playing-cards.
নহলী *adj* (poet) new; young; early.
নহিলে (old use)=নইলে
না[1] *n* (colloq) boat; canoe; dug-out.
না[2] *neg adv* 1 no; not. ❑*int* 1 no: বৃষ্টি পড়ছে? ~, পড়ছে না. 2 request: একটা গল্প বলো ~. 3 refusal: এ বিষয়ে ~ কোরো না. 4 permission: দিতে চাও—দাও ~. 5 uncertainty: যাবে কি যাবে ~. 6 sorrow; complaint; huff; annoyance: ~ হয় ~ই হবে. 7 indeed; nay: মনুষ্য কে? ~ যে হৃদয়বান. 8 contempt; taunt; ridicule: কি বলেছিলাম ~? 9 want; excess; what a: তার কত ~ দুঃখ! 10 ironical: ঘোড়া ~ হাতি. 11 certainty: সেই যে একটা গাছ আছে না? তার বাপ তাই ~ শুনে, when/ as soon as his/her father heard it. 12 amazement: মারলেও সে কাঁদে ~, ~? ❑*prep* without: ~ জেনে তোমার মনে কষ্ট দিয়েছি ❑*conj* or; nor: ~ আমি, ~ তুমি. **~ কেন** even though; whether or not; however much: তারা অন্য পাখির মতো উড়তে সমর্থ না হোক ~ কেন, সে যতো চেষ্টা করুক ~ কেন. **না ... না** neither ... nor: ~মাছ ~ মাংস. **~ রাম ~ গঙ্গা** (fig) neither fish nor fowl.
না[3] *pref* expressing negation, opposition, absence, refusal, etc: ~কবুল, ~রাজ.

নাই[১] *adv* used with other verbs to express negation: সে এখনো ফেরে ~, কাজটা করা হয় ~. ❑*adj* **1** non-existent: ~মাথা. **2** indigent: ~ ঘরে খাই. **~-আঁকড়া** *adj* obstinate: tenacious; dogged; persistent; obdurate; unrelenting; adamant. **~ ঘরে খাই** (fig) the lesser the supply, the greater the hunger. **~ মামার চেয়ে কানা মামা ভালো** (prov) Something is better than nothing. Half a loaf is better than no loaf.

নাই[২] *vi* am/is/are: তিনি বাড়িতে ~.

নাই[৩] *n* (colloq of লাই) indulgence; pampering. **~ দেওয়া** *vi* indulge; pamper; treat with too much indulgence; spoil. **কুকুর ~ পেলে মাথায় চড়ে** (fig) A saucy scamp scandalizes his patron.

নাই[৪] *n* (colloq) navel; nave/ hub (of a wheel).

নাইট্রোজেন [E] *n* nitrogen.

নাইয়র *n* father's house of a married woman.

নাইয়া *n* (old use) boatman; sailor.

নাইলন [E] *n* nylon.

নাউজুবিল্লাহ [A] *n* We seek refuge of God; Heaven preserve us? God forbid!

না-উম্মেদ [P] *adj* hopeless; despairing; despondent.

নাএব=নায়েব

নাও=না[২]

নাওন *n* bathing.

নাওয়া *vi* bathe; have/ take a bath; bath. ❑*n* bathing; washing. **~নো** *vt* **1** bathe; bath; **2** dip (idol, etc) in water; immerse.

নাঃ, নাহ্ emphatic form of না[২].

নাক *n* **1** nose. **2** olfactory organ; nose. **3** sense of smell; nose. **~ উঁচু হওয়া** *vi* be exalted/ putted up. **~ উঁচানো/ কোঁচকানো** *vi* (fig) turn one's nose up at sth; look down one's nose at sb/sth; spurn; scorn. **~ কাটা** *vt* put sb to shame; humiliate; disgrace; discountenance. **~ কাটা যাওয়া** *vi* be put to shame/ disgraced/ humiliated. **নিজের ~ কেটে পরের যাত্রা ভঙ্গ করা** cut off one's nose to spite one's face. **~ খোঁটা** *vi* pick one's nose. **~ গলানো** *vi* poke/ stick one's nose into sth. **~ ঝরা** *vi* (of the nose) run; have a running at the nose. **~-ঝরা** *n* flowing of mucus from the nose. **~ ঝাঁঝানো** *vi* smell pungent. **~ ঝাড়া** *vi* blow one's nose. **~ টেপা** *vi* **1** press one's nose (in disgust). **2** (iron) pretend to say one's prayers (silently). **~ ডাকা** *vi* snore. **~ ফোঁড়া/ বেঁধানো** *vi* bore/ perforate the nose (for wearing ornaments). **~ বন্ধ হওয়া** *vi* catch cold; suffocate owing to an attack of catarrh. **~ বাঁকানো**=~ উঁচানো. **~ মলা** *vi* admit one's fault and promise to refrain from repeating it; do penance (for one's sins). **~ সিঁটকানো**=~ উঁচানো. **~কড়াই** *n* a small ring worn in the nose. **~কাটা** *adj* **1** having one's nose cut off. **2** brazen-faced; shameless. **~কান-কাটা** *adj* **1** one who has his/her nose and ear cut off. **2**= ~কাটা (2). **~খত** *n*=নাকে খত. **~-খাঁদা** *adj* snub-nosed. **~ছাবি** *n* an ornament for the nose; nose-pin. **~ঝামটা**=মুখ-ঝামটা (⇒ মুখ). **~-তোলা** *n* contempt; scorn. **~-ফোঁড়া** *adj* having one's nose perforated. **~সাট** *n* snoring. **নাকা** *adj* **1** spoken through the nose; nasal: ~ স্বর. **2** given to speaking through the nose. **3** having a prominent/ fine nose. **~ বরাবর/সিধা** *adv* just in front; in a straight line. **~ বরাবর/ সিধা যাওয়া** *vi* follow one's (own) nose. **নাকানি-চুবানি, নাকানি-চোবানি** *n* **1** frantic efforts to save oneself from drowning. **2** persistent harassment; torment; vexation. **নাকানি-চুবানি খাওয়া** *vi* **1** make frantic efforts to save one-self from drowning. **2** be harassed/ bothered/ distressed/ tormented persistently. **নাকানি-চুবানি খাওয়ানো** *vt* **1** duck sb. **2** harass/ torment/ distress sb persistently. **নাকি**=নাকা. **নাকি-কান্না** *n* **1** whimper; blubber. **2** (iron) crocodile tears. **নাকে-কাঁদুনে** *adj* blubbering; whimpering. **নাকে-কান্না**=নাকি-কান্না. **নাকে খত** *n* rubbing one's nose on the ground as a penance. **নাকে খত দেওয়া** *vi* rub one's nose on the ground as a penance; do penance for one's sins. **নাকে-চোখে কথা বলা** *vi* talk through one's hat; talk nineteen to the dozen; talk the hind leg oft a donkey. **নাকে দড়ি দিয়ে ঘোরানো** *vi* lead sb by the nose. **নাকে দম আসা/ ওঠা** *vi* be greatly worried/ harassed; be exasperated. **নাকে দম ওঠানো** *vi* worry; harass; exasperate. **নাকে-মুখে গোঁজা** *vi* gulp (down); gobble (up/ down); have a bite to eat. **নাকে (সর্ষের) তেল দিয়ে ঘুমানো** *vi* sleep tight; let the grass grow under one's feet. **নাকের ছেঁদা** *n* nostril; a perforation in the nose. **নাকের জলে চোখের জলে হওয়া** **1** cry one's eyes out; weep in inconsolably/ abundantly/ copiously; dissolve in tears. **2** (fig) be in deep waters/ quagmire. **নাকের ওগা** *n* tip of the nose. **নাকের ডাঁটি/ দাঁড়া** *n* bridge. **নাকের ফ্যাটা** *n* large nostril.

নাকচ [A] *adj* unsound; vicious; cancelled; set aside; rejected; repealed. **~ করা** *vt* set aside; reject; annul; rescind; repeal; cancel.

নাকড়া=নাকারা. **~খানা** *n* porch of a palace where the drums are beaten at stated interval.

নাকা ⇒ নাক

নাকাড়া=নাকারা

নাকানি-চুবানি ⇒ নাক

নাকারচি [P] *n* drummer.

নাকারা [P] *n* kettle-drum.

নাকাল [A] *adj* **1** tired; fatigued; wearied; exhausted. **2** put to shame; put out of countenance; harassed; embarrassed; humiliated; discomfited; discountenanced. ❑*n* **1** fatigue; exhaustion; weariness. **2** sound/

adequate punishment; discomfiture; humiliation; embarrassment; harassment. ~ করা *vt* **1** exhaust; weary. **2** harass; embarrass; put to shame; give sb trouble; discomfit; humiliate; punish adequately/ soundly; teach sb a lesson. ~ হওয়া *vi* be discomfited/ embarrassed/ humiliated/ put out of countenance; be taught a lesson.

নাকি[১], নাকী *adj*=নাকা (⇒ নাক). ~ **সুর, ~ স্বর** *nn* nasal sound. ~ **সুরে কথা বলা** *vi* speak through the nose.

নাকি[২] *particle* expressing **(a)** an opinion/ alternative; or not/ no/ what: তুমি যাবে ~? **(b)** doubt; supposition: সে ~ আসবে? **(c)** impossibility: এমন লোকের সঙ্গে ~ ঘর করা যায়.

নাকু, নাকুয়া *adjj*=নাকা (⇒ নাক)

নাকিস, নাকেস [A] *adjj* deficient; wanting. ~ **আকেল** *adj* deficient in understanding; of unsound mind; foolish; stupid; silly; ignorant.

নাক্ষত্র *adj* starry; sidereal; astral; stellar. ~ **কাল** *n* sidereal time. ~ **দিবস** *n* sidereal day. ~ **বৎসর** *n* sidereal year. ~ **মাস** *n* sidereal/ stellar month. ~ **লম্বন** *n* (astron) secular parallax.

নাক্ষত্রিক=নাক্ষত্র. **নাক্ষত্রিকী** *fem.*

নাখুদা, নাখোদা [P] *nn* **1** master/ commander of a ship; captain; seaman. **2** name of a Muslim community.

নাখুশ, নাখোশ *adjj* displeased; unhappy; disgusted; dissatisfied. **নাখুশি** *n* displeasure; fretting; unhappiness.

নাগ *n* **1** snake; serpent. **2** (myth) serpent-demon. **3** elephant. **4** cloud. **নাগিনী, নাগী** *fem.* ~**কন্যা** *n* (myth) serpent-virgin. ~**কর্ণ** *n* the plant red ricinus. ~**কেশর** *n* name of a flowering plant; *Mesua roxburghii.* ~**গর্ভ** *n* red lead. ~**চূড়** *n* 'serpent-crested' one; Shiva. ~**দন্ত** *n* **1** elephant's task; ivory. **2** a peg on the wall to hang things upon. ~**দন্তিকা** *n* nettle; *Tragia involucrata.* ~**পঞ্চমী** *n* the fifth day in the light half of month Sravan or in the dark half of month Ashar (a day on which the serpents are worshipped). ~**পাশ** *n* **1** (myth) sort of magical noose (used in battles). **2** (fig) fetters. ~**ফণী**=ফণীমনসা. ~**মাতা** *n* (myth) **1** serpent-mother; Kadru. **2** goddess Manasa. ~**রাজ** *n* **1** serpent-king; Ananta or Vasuki. **2** large/ noble elephant. ~**লোক** *n* the world of serpents/ serpent-demons (called Patal and thought to be under the earth). **অষ্ট~** *n* (myth) eight of chief serpent-demons (born of Kadru and inhabiting the waters or the city Bhagavati under the earth, they are supposed to have a human face with serpent-like lower extremities).

নাগর *adj* **1** town-born; town-bred; civic; spoken in a town. **2** polite; civil. **3** clever; dexterous; cunning. ❑*n* philanderer; gallant; paramour; libertine; illicit lover. ~**পনা** *n*=নাগরালি.

নাগরঙ্গ *n* orange.

নাগরদোলা *n* merry-go-round; roundabout; whirligig; carousel; swing.

নাগরা[১] *n* kind of shoe.

নাগরা[২] *n*=নাকারা

নাগরালি, নাগরালী *nn* **1** philandering gallantry; dalliance; flirting; flirtation. **2** lewdness; sensuality; lust; lasciviousness. **3** witticism.

নাগরি *n* earthen pitcher.

নাগরিক *adj* civic; urban; polite; courtly; born/ living in a town. **নাগরিকী** *fem.* ❑*n* citizen; national; town-dweller; inhabitant of a town. **নাগরিকা** *fem.* ~**তা** *n* citizenship; nationality; urbanity.

নাগরী *n* **1** the Devanagari script. **2** clever/ intriguing/ witty woman; coquette; flirt; lewd women. ❑*adj* নাগর (1, 2).

নাগা *n* **1** naked ascetic. **2** one of the aboriginal tribe of Naga hills.

নাগাইদ *prep* (archaic)=নাগাদ

নাগাড় *n* order; continuity; stretch. **নাগাড়ে** *adv* ceaselessly; incessantly; continuously. **একনাগাড়ে** *adv* at a stretch; non-stop.

নাগাদ, নাগাত [A] *prep* **1** to the end of; upto; inclusive: ২৫শে জানুয়ারি ~. **2** by: কাল ~. **3** till; until: শেষ ~. **4** nearly; about: দশটাকা ~.

নাগারা *n*=নাকারা

নাগাল *n* **1** nearness-range: হাতের ~. **2** reach: ~ পাওয়া. **3** overtaking; contact: ~ ধরা. **4** access; approach; understanding; comprehension: মনের ~ পাওয়া. ~ **ধরা** *vi* overtake; catch up with; catch sb up; contact; reach (for); touch. ~ **পাওয়া** *vi* reach; overtake; attain; catch up with; have an access to: মনের ~ পাওয়া. **নাগালে থাকা** *vi* be within the range/ reach of. **নাগালে পড়া** *vi* come within the reach/ range of.

নাগেন্দ্র, নাগেশ *nn* **1** Airavata, the king of elephant. **2** Ananta/ Vasuki, the king of serpents.

নাগেশ্বর *n* kind of plant.

নাঙ, নাঙ্গ *nn* (vulg) (illicit) lover; paramour.

নাঙ্গা *n* naked; bare; unclad; uncovered; nude.

নাচ *n* **1** dance; dancing. **2** gesticulation; gyration. **3** caper; capering. **4** acting. **5** frisking about. ~**উলী, ~ওয়ালী** *nn fem* professional female dancer; dancing-girl. ~**ঘর** *n* dancing hall; ball room; play house; theatre. ~**ন, ~নি** *nn* dancing; ludicrous gesticulation; antics. ~ **নাচা** *vi* dance a dance. ~ **নাচানো** *vt* make sb dance; dance; tease; harass; worry; lead sb a (merry) dance. **নাচুনি** *n fem*=~উলি. ❑*adj* **1** dancing; adept/ expert/ engaged in dancing: নাচুনি মেয়ে. **2** rhythmic(al); lilting; dancing: নাচুনি ছন্দ.

দোল *n* **1** swing(ing); oscillating; oscillation; dangling movement. **2** Hindu festival (in the month of Phalgun) when images of the boy Krishna are swung); the Holi festival. **~ খাওয়া** *vi* swing; oscillate; dangle; ride on the swing; have a swing; rock. **~ খাওয়ানো/ দেওয়া** *vt* cause to swing; give sb a swing; rock; dangle; oscillate. **~-দুর্গোৎসব** *n* the principal festivals of Hindus (such as the Holi and the worship of Durga); expensive festivals. **~ন** *n* **1** swinging; dangling; oscillation. **2** swing. **~ন-কাল** *n* period of oscillation. **~ন-তল** *n* plane of oscillation. **~না** *n* swing; rocking cradle. **~নায় চড়া** *vi* ride a swing. **~পিঁড়ি** *n* seat of a swing. **~মঞ্চ** *n* the alter on which the rocking cradle of Krishna and Radha is set up. **~যাত্রা** *n*=~ (2).

দোলক *n* pendulum (of a clock, etc).

দোলমা *n* food item prepared by stuffing *patol* (পটোল) with minced meat/ fish.

দোলা[1]=দুলা[1]. **~নো**=দুলানো

দোলা[2] *n* **1** litter. **2** rocking cradle. **3** improvised cot to carry a corpse to the crematorium. **4** দোলাই.

দোলাই *n* quilt; double sheet.

দোলায়মান *adj* **1** swinging; oscillating; dangling; rocking. **2** wavering; vacillating; hesitating. **~চিত্ত, ~-মতি** *adj* doubtful in mind; wavering; irresolute; diffident.

দোলায়িত *adj* **1** caused to swing/ oscillate/ dangle; swing; oscillated; hung. **2** caused to waver/ vacillate/ hesitate; wavering; hesitating. **~চিত্ত** *adj* দোলায়মানচিত্ত. ❑*n* vacillating mind.

দোলিকা, দোলী *nn* small litter.

দোষ *n* sin; vice; guilt; offence; crime; transgression; bad practice/ tendency: এটা তার একটা দোষ বলতেই হবে. **2** fault; deficiency; flaw; blemish; want; lapse; inconvenience; disadvantage; weak point; demerit; defect: পরের ~ খোঁজা. **3** badness; sinfulness; wickedness. **4** accusation; reproach; blame: দোষের ভাগী হওয়া. **5** alteration; affection; morbid element; disease (esp of the 3 humours of the body): চোখের/ মাথার ~. **6** damage; harm; bad consequence; detrimental effect: এতে কোনো ~ নেই. **7** sinister influence: গ্রহের ~. **8** inauspiciousness: যাওয়ার সময়ে পিছু ডাকা দোষের. **~ করা** *vi* be at fault; do wrong; offend; commit a sin/ offence/ crime. **~ খণ্ডানো** *vi* **1** free from/ refute/ rebut a charge; disprove a charge; give the lie to. **2** (astrol) counteract/ undo the sinister influence of a planet. **~ক্ষালন** *n* exculpation; vindication, exoneration; absolution. **~ ক্ষালন করা** *vi* **1** exculpate; exonerate; clear of charges; absolve; vindicate. **2** rectify an error/ fault. **~ খোঁজা** *vi* try to find fault with; look for mistakes. **~ ঘোচানো**=~ খণ্ডানো. **~ দেওয়া** *vi* accuse; blame; censure; hold responsible for; lay/ put the blame (for sth) on sb; recriminate against; find fault with; impute a fault to. **~ দেখা/ ধরা** *vi* notice a fault/ an error/ a mistake/ a defect; find fault with; pick holes; put the finger at. **~গুণ** *n* bad and good qualities. **~গ্রস্ত** *adj* involved in guilt; guilty. **~গ্রহণ** *n* fault-finding. **~গ্রহী** *adj* fault-finding; censorious; captious; quibbling. **~ঘ্ন** *adj* removing the bad humours/ detrimental effect of. **~জ্ঞ** *adj* knowing the faults of; knowing what is evil/ to be avoided; prudent; discerning. ❑ *n* discerning man; physician; erudite person. **~ণ** *n* imputation of crime; accusation. **~দর্শন** *n* fault-finding. **~দর্শী**=~গ্রাহী. **~স্বীকার** *n* admission of guilt; confession. **~ স্বীকার করা** *vi* plead guilty to a crime; admit/ acknowledge one's guilt; confess a crime/ sin/ fault/ guilt. **দোষা** *vt*=দুষা.

দোষাকর *n* mine/ heap of faults. **দোষাক্রান্ত** *adj* defective; faulty; flawed; vicious; morbid. **দোষাদোষ** *n* merits and demerits; vices and virtues. **দোষান্বেষণ** *n* search for a defect/ fault (in); fault-finding **দোষান্বেষণ করা** *vi*=~ খোঁজা. **দোষান্বেষী**=~গ্রাহী. **দোষাবহ** *adj* **1**=দোষাক্রান্ত. **2** harmful; noxious; blamable. **দোষারোপ** *n* imputation of a fault; finding fault with; accusation; recrimination. **দোষারোপ করা**=~ দেওয়া. **দোষাশ্রিত** *adj* **1**= দোষাক্রান্ত. **2** given to vices; vicious.

দোষী *adj* guilty of an offence; be to blame (for sth); sinning; offending. **~ (সাব্যস্ত) করা** *vt* find sb guilty (of a crime etc.); adjudge guilty; hold responsible for; blame. **~ সাব্যস্ত হওয়া** *vi* found/ adjudged guilty.

দোসর *adj* second; next; equal; accompanying; seconding; associating. ❑*n* second; companion; associate; accomplice; match; equal; comrade. **দোসরা** *adj* **1** second; another; next. **2** (of the days of a month) second. ❑*n* the second day: বৈশাখের দোসরা.

দোস্ত [P] *n* friend; chum; (derog) crony.

দোস্তি *n* friendship.

দোহ *n* **1** milking. **2** milk-pail. ❑*adj* dairy *n* **~ক** *adj* milking. ❑ *n* milker; extortionist. **~দ** *n* **1** pregnancy. **2** peculiar longing of a pregnant woman. **~দদান** *n* ceremony of giving an expectant mother delicacies she longs to eat. **~দবতী** *n* pregnant woman longing to have peculiar delicacies. **~দলক্ষণ** *n* signs/ symptoms of pregnancy. **~ন** *n* **1** milking. **2** extortion; exaction; exploitation. **~ন করা**=দোয়া[1]. **~নী** *n* milk-pail. **~নীয়** *adj* to be milked. **~শালা** *n* dairy (farm). **দোহা** *vt*=দোয়া[2]. **দোহানো**=দোয়ানো. **দোহাল** *n* milker.

দোহা[1], **দোঁহা**[1] *n* Hindi couplet; distich.

দোহা^২, দোঁহা^২ *pron* (poet) two; both. **~কার** *poss pron* (of two/ both).

দোহাই *n* **1** cry for help and mercy. **2** oath. **3** pretext; plea; excuse: অসুখের ~. **4** appeal for justice. **5** imprecation. **~ দেওয়া/ পাড়া** *vi* **1** appeal to (for justice/ support); cry for (justice etc); adjure. **2** put forward as a pretext/ plea. **3** swear by sb/sth. **~ খোদার** by God. **~ তোমার** please, I entreat you.

দোহার *n* **1** member of a chorus who repeats the leitmotif/ each line after the leader of the group; chorister. **2** (derog) yes-man; henchman; sycophant; toady.

দোহারা *adj* **1** double; twice. **2** woven in double threads/ plaits; doubly woven; doubled: ~ কাপড়/ সুতা. **3** of midium/ middling built; well-proportioned: ~ গড়ন/ চেহারা.

দোহাল ⇒ **দোহ**

দোহ্য=দোহনীয় (⇒ দোহ)

দৌড় *n* **1** running; run. **2** race: ঘোড়~. **2** fleeing; flight: পড়ি মরি করে ~. **3** (iron) extent; limit: range: বিদ্যার ~. **4** ability; strength: তোমার ~ আমার জানা আছে. **~ করানো** *vt* **1** cause to run/ race; run; rush. **2** harass by causing to move about repeatedly/ constantly; vex. **~ দেওয়া/ মারা** *vi* start running; run off; take to one's heels; bolt; rush; spurt; flee; dart; gallop; run hell for leather. **~ঝাঁপ, ~ধাপ** *nn* **1** running and jumping; romping; romp; gambol; boisterous movement; frolicking. **2** great effort; exertions. **~ঝাঁপ করা** *vi* **1** romp (around); gambol (about/ around); frolic. **2** make every effort; exert oneself; go from pillar to post. **দৌড়ানো** *vi, vt* **1** run; race; dash. **2** cause to run; run. **~বাজ** *n* runner; racer. **দৌড়াদৌড়ি** *n* **1** running about. **2** gadding. **3**=~ঝাঁপ. **দৌড়াদৌড়ি করা** *vi* **1** run about. **2** gad about. **3**=~ঝাঁপ করা. **এক দৌড়ে** *adj* at a hasty run; double-quick.

দৌত্য=দূতালি (⇒ দূত)

দৌবারিক *n* door-keeper; janitor; porter; gateman.

দৌরাত্ম্য *n* **1** oppression; tyranny; heartlessness; cruel treatment. **2** naughtiness; boisterousness; roguery; devilry. **~ করা** *vi, vt* oppress; tyrannize; treat cruelly. **2** be naughty; be up to some devilry; play tricks; make mischief.

দৌর্গত্য *n* distress; misery; poverty; wretchedness.

দৌলত [A] *n* **1** riches; wealth; felicity; fortune; prosperity. **2** empire; state; country. **3** cause; means; favour; grace. **~খানা** *n* mansion; palace; house (in a polite sense. **~দার, ~মান্দ** *adj* wealthy; rich; opulent. ❑ *n* wealthy person. **~দারি, ~মান্দি** *nn* wealth; prosperity; opulence; riches. **~শালা** *n* treasure. **দৌলতে, ব~** *adv* by means of; by the favour/ grace of; by the good fortune of.

দৌহিত্র *n* daughter's son; grandson. **দৌহিত্রী** *fem* daughter's daughter; grand-daughter.

দ্যু *n* sky; heaven.

দ্যুতি *n* **1** brightness; lustre; glow; shine; splendour; refulgence. **2** majesty; dignity. **3** ray. **~কর** *adj* producing splendour; illuminating; bright. **~ময়, ~মান্** *adj* resplendent; bright; radiating; refulgent; shining; glowing; lustrous; splendid; majestic; dignified. **~মতী, ~ময়ী** *fem.*

দ্যুতিত *adj* enlightened; illuminated; shining.

দ্যুলোক *n* region of heaven.

দ্যূত *n* gaming; gambling (esp with dice); playing with dice. **~কর, ~কার** *n* gambler. **~ক্রীড়া** *n* playing with dice.

দ্যোতক *adj* shining; illuminating; expressing; indicating; explaining; expressive/ suggestive (of); meaning; illustrating; signifying; enlightening; making clear.

দ্যোতন *n* illumination; enlightenment; expression; act of indicating/ illuminating/ signifying/ expressing/ indicating; indication; inspiration. **দ্যোতনা** *n* implication; suggestion; figurative expression; significance; connotation.

দ্যোতিত *adj* **1** illustrated; bright; resplendent. **2** suggested; signified; connoted; indicated.

দ্রঢ়িমা *n* hardness; firmness; toughness; stiffness; steadiness. (⇒ also দার্ঢ্য).

দ্রব *adj* **1** liquid; fluid; flowing; dropping; dripping; trickling. **2** liquefied; melted; fused. ❑ *n* (chem) (liquid) solution. **~ করা** *vt* liquefy; melt; dissolve; solve. **~ হওয়া** *vi* be liquefied/ melted; melt; liquefy; be dissolved/ solved; dissolve; flow; trickle; drip. **~ণ** *n* liquefaction; melting; (chem) solution; dissolution. **~তা** *n* fluidity. **~ণশীল** *adj* liquefiable; (chem) soluble; flowing; overflowing. **দ্রবাঙ্ক** *n* melting-point.

দ্রবণীয়=দ্রবণশীল (⇒ দ্রব). **~তা** *n* solubility.

দ্রবীকরণ=দ্রবণ (⇒ দ্রব)

দ্রবীকৃত *adj* liquefied; melted; (chem) dissolved, solved.

দ্রবীভবন *n* becoming liquid; liquefaction; melting.

দ্রবীভূত=দ্রবীকৃত

দ্রব্য *n* **1** thing; object; article; substance; ingredients/ materials of anything. **2** medical substance; drug. **3** (phil) elementary substance; matter. **~গুণ** *n* property present in a thing/ substance; medicinal property of a thing/ plant. **~জাত** *adj* produced of a material thing. ❑ *n* collection of things; all kinds of things. **~জাত বস্তু** *n* product. **~ত্ব** *n* substantiality. **~বাচক** *adj* (gram) material. **~ময়**

adj material; substantial. ~শুদ্ধি cleansing of soiled articles. ~সামগ্রী *n pl* things (collection).

দ্রষ্টব্য *adj* **1** to be seen. **2** worth seeing/ visiting: ~ স্থান. **3** to be examined/ investigated. **4** worthy of note; warranting attention/ consideration; remarkable: ~ পৃ. ৫, see/ vide p. 5.

দ্রষ্টা *adj* who sees/ observes/ witnesses. ☐ *n* seer; observer; onlooker; witness; philosopher; judge.

দ্রাক্ষা *n* grape; vine. ~কুঞ্জ, ~ক্ষেত্র *nn* vineyard. ~ফল *n* grape. ~ রস *n* grape-juice; wine. ~রিষ্ট *n* a medicinal liquor prepared from grape-juice. ~লতা *n* vine; vine-tendril. ~শর্করা *n* grape sugar.

দ্রাঘিমা *n* **1** length. **2** (geog) (degree of) longitude. দ্রাঘিমান্তর *n* longitudinal distance; distance east or west from the prime meridian.

দ্রাঘিষ্ঠ *adj* longest; extremely long.

দ্রাঘীয়ান্ *adj* longer. দ্রাঘীয়সী *fem.*

দ্রাব *n* liquefacting; melting; fusing; solution; dissolution. ~ক *adj* **1** solvent; corrosive; melting. **2** captivating. enchanting. ☐ *n* solvent; acid. ~ণ *n* liquefaction; melting; solution; dissolution.

দ্রাবিড় *n* Dravidian; Dravidian language; country of the Dravidians. ☐ *adj* Dravidian. দ্রাবিড়ী *n fem.* Dravidian woman/ language.

দ্রাবিত *adj* liquefied; melted; dissolved; solved.

দ্রাব্য *adj* liquefiable; soluble; dissolvable; fusible. ~তা *n* solubility.

দ্রুত *adj* quick; speedy; swift; rapid; expeditious; fast. ☐ *adv* quickly; speedily; expeditiously; prompt; swiftly; fast. ~ক্রিয় *n* prompt; agile; quick in action; nimble. ~গতি *adj* going quickly; swift-moving; fast; swift; rapid; speedy; quick-paced. ☐ *adv* moving quickly; swiftly; quickly; fleetingly; speedily; with quick pace; in full career; rapidly. ~গামী *adj*=~গতি. ~তা *n* swiftness; alacrity; speed; speediness; nimbleness; fastness; quickness; celerity; rapidity; agility. ~পদ *n* quick pace/ step. ~পদে *adv* at a brisk pace; apace; swiftly; at full speed; in a hurry; in haste. ~বিলম্বিত *n* name of a Sanskrit metre. ~বেগ *n* great speed; rapidity; celerity. ~বেগে *adv* speedily; quickly; fast; rapidly; briskly.

দ্রুতি *n* (mech) speed; quickness; swiftness; celerity; fastness; speediness; velocity. ~গণক, ~মাপক *nn* speedometer; speed-counter. ~জ্ঞাপক, ~সূচক *n* speed-indicator. ~লিখ্ *n* speed-recorder.

দ্রুম *n* tree; plant.

দ্রোণ *n* **1** wooden vessel; bucket; **2** dry measure (= 32 seers). **3** measuring vessel with a capacity of 32 seers. **4** raven; crow. ~কলস *n* large wooden vessel for the (সোম). ~কাক *n* raven.

দ্রোণি, দ্রোণী *n* **1** dug-out; small boat; canoe. **2** bailing bucket. **3** wooden vessel; trough; pitcher. **4** gorge; pass.

দ্রোহ *n* **1** enmity; hostility; harm; injury; perfidy; treachery; offence; malice; mischief. **2** revolt; rebellion. রাষ্ট্র~ *n* treason; sedition.

দ্রোহিতা=দ্রোহ

দ্রোহী *adj* **1** hostile; perfidious; malicious; malevolent. **2** rebellious; opposing; revolting. রাষ্ট্র~ *adj* guilty of treason; seditious. ☐*n* traitor.

দ্রৌপদী *n* name of the heroine of the Mahabharata. রন্ধনে~ a female cook of incomparable excellence.

দ্বন্দ্ব *n* **1** strife; quarrel; fight; contest; dispute; duel; competition; rivalry. **2** pair; couple; male and female. **3** pair of opposites (eg শীতগ্রীষ্ম, আনন্দবেদনা). **4** (gram) copulative compound (in which the members if uncompounded could be in the same case and connected by the conjunction "and"). ~ করা *vi* quarrel/ fight with; contend with; compete/ rival/ vie (with). ~প্রিয় *adj* pugnacious; quarrelsome; factious; cantankerous; fond of fighting duels; bellicose; combative; disputatious. ~প্রিয়তা *n* quarrelsomeness; pugnacity; bellicosity. ~যুদ্ধ *n* single combat; duel. ~যোদ্ধা *n* duellist. দ্বন্দ্বাতীত *adj* **1** (philo) gone beyond/ freed from opposites; transcending all feelings of conflict/ opposition. **2** beyond controversy; indisputable incontrovertible; incontestable.

দ্বন্দ্বী *adj* opposed to one another; contradictory; antagonistic; conflicting; quarrelling; competing; vying; rivalling; duelling; fighting (with/ against).

দ্বয় *adj* two; both; two/ both of a pair/ couple. দ্বয়ী *n* couple; pair; দ্বয়ী শিক্ষা *n* co-education.

দ্বাচত্বারিংশ *adj* forty-two. ~ৎ *n, adj* forty-two. ~ত্তম *adj* forty-second. ~ত্তমী *fem.*

দ্বাত্রিংশ *adj* thirty-two. ~ৎ *n, adj* thirty-two. ~ত্তম *adj* thirty-second. ~ত্তমী *fem.*

দ্বাদশ *n, adj* twelve. ☐ *adj* twelfth. ~বার্ষিক *adj* duodecennial. দ্বাদশাক্ষর *adj* containing twelve syllables.

দ্বাদশিক *adj* (math) duodecimal.

দ্বাদশী *adj fem* twelfth; twelve years old. ☐ *n* the twelfth day (of a lunar fortnight).

দ্বাপর *n* the third of the four yugas or ages of the world according to Hindu mythology.

দ্বাবিংশ *adj* twenty-two. ~তি *adj, n* twenty-two. ~তিতম *adj* twenty-second. ~তিতমী *fem.*

দ্বার *n* door; gate; passage; entrance; doorway; gateway; portico. ~দেশ, ~প্রান্ত *n* proximity of a gate/ door; doorstep; doorway; portal; gateway. ~দেশে, ~প্রান্তে *adv* at the door/

doorstep/ gate. ~পাল(ক), ~বান, ~রক্ষক, ~রক্ষী *n* doorkeeper; janitor; gateman. porter; ~স্থ *adj* standing/ lying/ situated at the door/ gate; waiting/ begging at another's door; seeking help/ alms from another. ~স্থ হওয়া *vi* seek help/ alms from another; supplicate; woo; turn to sb for help; have recourse to sb. দ্বারে দ্বারে *adv* from door to door.

দ্বারা *prep* by, with, through, by means of.

দ্বারাদেয় *adj* to be levied at the gate/ point of entry. ~ শুল্ক *n* octroi duty.

দ্বারিক, দ্বারী *n*=দ্বারপাল (⇒ দ্বারা)

দ্বারোদ্‌ঘাটন *n* opening the gate/ door; inauguration; inaugural/ opening ceremony (of an establishment).

দ্বাষষ্টি *n, adj* sixty-two. ~তম *adj* sixty-second. ~তমী *fem.*

দ্বাসপ্ততি *n, adj* seventy-two. ~তম *adj* seventy-second. ~তমী *fem.*

দ্বি *n* two. ❑ *adj* two; double; two-fold; bi-; di. দ্বি-অংশক *adj* (bot) bimerous. দ্বি-আর্ক *adj* (bot) di-arch. দ্বিকক্ষ *adj* bicameral. দ্বিকর্মক *adj* (gram) having two/ double objects. দ্বিকেশর *adj* (bot) diandrous. দ্বিকোষ *adj* (biol) bivalve; bivalvular. দ্বিকোষ্ঠ *adj* (bot) bilocular. দ্বিখণ্ড, দ্বিখণ্ডিত *adj* cut/ divided into two pieces; bisected; bifurcated. দ্বিখণ্ড করা *vt* cut/ divide into two pieces; bisect; bifurcate. দ্বিখণ্ডক *n* (geom) bisector. দ্বিখণ্ডন *n* (geom) bisection; bifurcation; dichotomy. দ্বিগর্ভ *adj* (zoo) marsupial; (bot) bicarellate. দ্বিগর্ভ পশু/ প্রাণী *n* marsupial animal. দ্বিগুচ্ছ *adj* (bot) diadelphous. দ্বিগুণ *adj* multiplied by two; double; two-fold; doubled; twice as large/ as much as. দ্বিগুণিত, দ্বিগুণীকৃত *adj* doubled; multiplied by two. দ্বিঘাত *adj* (alg) quadratic. দ্বিঘাত সমীকরণ *n* quadratic equation. আমিশ্র দ্বিঘাত *adj* pure quadratic. দ্বিচারিণী *adj fem* attached to two men; unfaithful to one's husband; adulterous; unchaste. দ্বিজ *adj* twice-born. ❑ a Brahmin. দ্বিজাত *adj* twice-born; regenerated. দ্বিজাতিতত্ত্ব *n* two-nation theory. ~জিহ্ব *adj* 1 double-tongued; having a bifurcated/ double-pronged tongue. 2 (fig) given to lying/insincere talk; double-talking; hypocritical. ❑*n* snake; liar. দ্বিতয় *adj* consisting of two; twofold; double. ❑*n* aggregate of two; pair; couple. দ্বিতল *adj* 1 (of ship, bus, etc) double-decked. 2 (science) dihedral. ❑*n* first floor; upper deck. দ্বিতলকোণ *n* (geom) dihedral angle. দ্বিত্ব *n* duality; duplication; repetition. দ্বিদল *adj* (bot) bipetalous. ❑*n* pulses. দ্বিদৃক *adj* binocular. দ্বিধাতুক *adj* bi-metallic. দ্বিধাতুমান *n* bimetallism. দ্বিধার *adj* forming two streams. দ্বিনবতি *n, adj* ninety-two. দ্বিনবতিতম *adj* ninety-second. দ্বিনবতিতমী *fam* দ্বিনেত্র *adj* two-eyed; binocular. দ্বিনেত্র দৃষ্টি *n* binocular vision. দ্বিপক্ষ *adj* two-winged; bipartite. ❑*n* two lunar fortnighter. দ্বিপঞ্চাশৎ *n, adj* fifty-two. দ্বিপঞ্চাশত্তম *adj* fifty-second. দ্বিপঞ্চাশত্তমী *fem.* দ্বিপত্নীক *adj* having two wives. দ্বিপথ *n* crossways. ❑*adj* two-way. দ্বিপদ *adj* 1 two-footed; biped; bipedal; two-legged. 2 (alg) binomial. ❑*n* biped. দ্বিপদ সমীকরণ *n* (alg) binomial equation. দ্বিপদী *n* couplet. দ্বিপরমাণুক *adj* (phys) diatomic. দ্বিপর্ণ *adj* two-leafed. দ্বিপাক্ষিক *adj* bipartite; bipartisan. দ্বিপাদ =দ্বিপদ. দ্বিপার্শ্ব, দ্বিপার্শ্বীয় *adj* bilateral; biparous. দ্বিবচন *n* (gram) dual number. দ্বিবন্ধ *n* (chem) double bond. দ্বিবর্ণ *n* bicolour. দ্বিবর্ষ, দ্বিবর্ষক, দ্বিবর্ষী *adj* two years old. দ্বিবর্ষজীবী *adj* (bot) biennial. দ্বিবার্ষিক *adj* two years old; biennial; second annual. দ্বিবাহিক *n* litter carried by two. দ্বিবাহু *adj* two-armed; two-sided; bilateral; double-handed; having two branches; bifurcate. দ্বিবিধ *adj* two-fold; of two kinds/sorts. দ্বিবীজপত্রী *adj* (bot) dicotyledon. দ্বিবেদী *adj* versed in two Vedas. দ্বিভাব *n* 1 double nature; duplicity; deceit; insincerity; hypocrisy; double-mindedness. 2 hesitation; wavering. 3 two ways/ attitudes. 4 division/ separation into two. ❑*adj* 1 hypocritical; deceitful; insincere; double-minded. 2 wavering; hesitant. 3 two-way; having two attitudes. দ্বিভাষিক, দ্বিভাষী *adjj* speaking two languages; bilingual. ❑*n* bilingual person; interpreter. দ্বিভুজ *adj* two-armed; two-handed; bimerous; two-sided. দ্বিভুজা *fem.* দ্বিমার্গ *n* cross-way. দ্বিমাসিক *adj* bi-monthly. দ্বিমুখ *adj* 1 having two mouths/ faces; two-mouthed; double-faced. 2 branching into two directions; bifurcate. দ্বিমুখ টেলিগ্রাফ *n* duplex telegraph. দ্বিমূল *adj* (phys) binary. দ্বিমূল যৌগিক *n* binary compound. দ্বিমেরু *adj* bipolar. দ্বিরদ *adj* two-tusked. ❑*n* elephant. দ্বিরাত্র *adj* lasting two nights. দ্বিরূপ *adj* biform; bicolour; twofold; (bot) bimorphic; spelt/ written in two ways. দ্বিরূপতা *n* (bot) bimorphism. দ্বিরেফ *n* a large black bee; bumble-bee. দ্বিলিঙ্গ *adj* bisexual. দ্বিশত *n, adj* two-hundred. দ্বিশততম *adj* two-hundredth. দ্বিশততমী *fem.* দ্বিশফ *adj* cloven-footed. দ্বিশাখ *adj* two-branched; forked. দ্বিশির(স্ক), দ্বিশিরা, দ্বিশীর্ষ(ক) *adjj* two-headed; bicephalous. দ্বিশৃঙ্গ *adj* having two horns/points; two-horned. দ্বিষষ্ঠ *adj* sixty second. দ্বিষষ্টি= দ্বাষষ্টি. দ্বিসপ্ততি= দ্বাসপ্ততি. দ্বিসমত্রিভুজ *n* (geom) isosceles triangle. দ্বিসূত্র, দ্বিসূত্রী *adj* (bot) bifilar.

দ্বিগু *n* (gram) a compound in which the first number is a numeral.

দ্বিজ *adj* twice-born; regenerated. ❑*n* 1 man of any one of the first three Hindu castes. 2 Brahmin. 3 any oviparous animal; bird. দ্বিজা *fem.* দ্বিজত্ব *n* condition/ rank of a Brahmin or any one of the first three castes. ~পতি, ~বর,

~রাজ, দ্বিজাগ্র, দ্বিজেন্দ্র, দ্বিজোত্তম *nn* excellent Brahmin.

দ্বিতীয় *adj* second; another. দ্বিতীয়া *fem* of দ্বিতীয়. ❑ *n* second day of a lunar fortnight. দ্বিতীয়ত *adj* secondly; in the second place. দ্বিতীয়াশ্রম *n* domestic/ married life (the second of the four stages of the life of a Brahmin).

দ্বিধ *adj* divided in two; split asunder; forked.

দ্বিধা *adj* in two ways/ parts; twofold; divided; partitioned. ❑*adv* in two ways/ directions. ❑*n* hesitation; wavering; suspicion; misgiving; doubt. দ্বিধা করা *vi, vt* 1 hesitate; waver; have misgivings; not know which way to turn. 2 divide into two; partition. দ্বিধাকরণ *n* 1 dividing into two; making two-fold; arranging in two ways. 2 hesitation. দ্বিধাকৃত *adj* divided into two; partitioned. দ্বিধাবিভক্ত *adj* divided/ split into two.

দ্বিপ *n* elephant.

দ্বিরাগমন *n* the ceremony of the second entrance of the bride into her husband's house after a visit to that of her father.

দ্বিরুক্ত *adj* twice said; repeated; doubled; reduplicated.

দ্বিরুক্তি *n* 1 repetition; tautology; telling anything in two or various ways. 2 word/ saying repeated; objection; demur; hesitation. ~ না করে without demur.

দ্বিষৎ *n* enemy; foe; malicious/unfriendly person.

দ্বিষ্ট *adj* 1 envied; disliked. 2 unfriendly; hostile; odious.

দ্বীপ *n* island. ~পুঞ্জ *n* group of islands; archipelago. ~বাসী *adj* an islander. ~ময় *adj* abounding in islands. দ্বীপান্তর *n* 1 another/ a different island. 2 banishment of offenders beyond the seas; deportation; exile. দ্বীপান্তর হওয়া *vi* be deported exiled. দ্বীপান্তরিত *adj* deported; exiled. দ্বীপান্তরিত করা, দ্বীপান্তরে পাঠানো *vt* deport; exile. দ্বীপান্তরিত হওয়া *vi* = দ্বীপান্তর হওয়া. ক্ষুদ্র ~ *n* islet; small island. ব্রিটিশ ~পুঞ্জ *n* the British Isles.

দ্বীপী *adj* having spots like islands. ❑*n* tiger; panther; leopard.

দ্বেষ *n* malice; envy; aversion; dislike; hostility; hatred; antipathy; grudge; enmity. ~ করা *vt* hate; show hatred against; bear malice; envy; grudge; be hostile/ unfriendly; dislike; be averse/ antipathetic. ~ণ *n* hating; disliking; bearing malice; envying; grudge; hatred. দ্বেষ্য *adj* to be hated/ disliked; odious; detestable.

দ্বেষী, দেষ্টা *adjj* envying; malicious; hating; hostile; spiteful; grudging; antipathetic; inimical; averse. দ্বেষিণী *fem*.

দ্বৈগুণ্য *n* possession of two out of the three qualities; duality.

দ্বৈত *n* duality; duplicity; dualism; dyad. ~বাদ *n* (phil) dualism. ~বাদী *adj* dualistic. ❑*n* duelist. ~শাসন *n* diarchy. ~সঙ্গীত *n* duet (song); antiphony. দ্বৈতাদ্বৈত *n* (phil) simultaneous diversity and unity of God and the soul.

দ্বৈতী *adj* = দ্বৈতবাদী (⇒দ্বৈত)

দ্বৈধ *adj* two-fold; double. ❑*n* twofold form/ state; duality; duplicity; division; separate into two parts; dispute; contest; doubt; uncertainty hesitation.

দ্বৈধী *n* (in compounds) = দ্বৈধ. ~করণ *n* making into two; separating. ~কৃত *adj* separated; made twofold. ~ভাব *n* duality; double nature; doubt; dilemma; uncertainty; hesitation; duplicity; double-dealing.

দ্বৈপ *adj* being/ living/ happening on an island; relating to an island; belonging to a tiger/ panther. ❑*n* islander. দ্বৈপায়ন *n* 'island born'; name of Vyasa (author or compiler of the Mahabharata). দ্বৈপ্য = দ্বৈপ.

দ্বৈবার্ষিক, দ্বৈবর্ষিক *adjj* biennial.

দ্বৈবিধ্য *n* twofold nature/ state/ character; duality; variance; duplicity.

দ্বৈভাষিকী *adj* bilingual.

দ্বৈমাতৃক *adj* (of countries/ lands) nourished by rain and rivers.

দ্বৈমাসিক *adj* bimonthly.

দ্বৈরথ *n*. single combat in chariots. ❑*adj* involving chariot-duels.

দ্বৈরাজ্য *n* diarchy.

দ্বৈরাত্রিক *adj* of/ relating to a period of two nights.

দ্ব্যক্ষ *adj* (phys) biaxial.

দ্ব্যক্ষর *adj* two-syllabled; two-lettered. ❑*n* two-syllabled word/ incantation.

দ্ব্যঙ্গুল *n* two finger's breadth. ❑*adj* measuring two fingers.

দ্ব্যণুক *n* combination of two atoms (the first step in the formation of substance when they become visible).

দ্ব্যর্থ *adj* having two senses; ambiguous senses; ambiguous; equivocal. ❑*n* double meaning; double entendre. দ্ব্যর্থক *adj* =~. দ্ব্যর্থক কথা *n* quibble; equivocation. দ্ব্যর্থক শব্দ *n* double entendre. দ্ব্যর্থকতা, দ্ব্যর্থতা *n* ambiguity; equivocation.

দ্ব্যশীতি *adj* eighty-two. ~তম *adj* eighty-second. ~তমী *fem*.

দ্ব্যহ *n* period of two days; couple of days.

দ্ব্যাত্মবাদী *adj* (phys) dualistic. ❑*n* duelist.

দ্ব্যাহিক *adj* recurring every other day; occurring after an interval of two days; continuing for two days.

ধ

ধ *n* the nineteenth letter of the Bengali alphabet. It is pronounced as voiced aspirated dental plosive sound.

ধক *n* (onom) expressing: **(a)** sudden flare/ blaze/ glowing (of fire); **(b)** violent throb/ jerk/ thumped: আগুনটা ~ করে জ্বলে উঠল, the fire flared up; আমার বুকটা ~ করে উঠল. My heart thumped violently. **~ধক** *n* **1** continuous flare; blazing up. **2** pulsation; palpitation; throbbing up. **~ ~ করা** *vi* **1** burn fiercely; blaze by flashes. **2** throb; thump; palpitate. **3** sparkle; glitter. **~ধকানি** *n* **1** blazing up; glowing; flare-up. **2** throbbing; thumping; palpitating. **~ধকাস** *n* = ~ধক.

ধকল *n* **1** stress; pressure of work; strain; hard labour: তার ওপর দিয়ে কী ধকলটাই না গেল. **2** rough use; manhandling: অত ফিনফিনে কাপড় ~ সইবে না. **3** troublesome/ disturbing charge; mischievous behaviour; roguery: ছেলেদের ধকল সইতে পারো তো থাকো.

ধঞ্চে *n* (colloq) = ধনিচা

ধটি, ধটিকা, ধটী *nn* loin-cloth; piece of cloth worn over the privities; old cloth/raiment; rag.

ধড় *n* body (apart from the head and limbs); trunk; torso; truncated body. **ধড়ে প্রাণ আসা** (fig) heave a sigh of relief; feel relief; take comfort; breathe again; take heart; thank one's lucky stars; see light at the end of the tunnel.

ধড়ধড় *n* (onom) expressing palpitation of the heart; throbbing. **~ করা** *vi* beat rapidly; palpitate; throb. **ধড়ধড়ানি** *n* palpitation; throbbing. **ধড়ধড়ানে** *adj* palpitating; throbbing; beating rapidly. **ধড়ধড়ানো** *vi* = ~করা.

ধড়ফড় *n* (onom) expressing **(a)** palpitation; **(b)** restlessness; **(c)** flutter of wings. **~ করা** *vi* **1** palpitate; throb; pulsate. **2** be restless; be impatient with eagerness; long: ঘরে ফিরে যাওয়ার জন্যে সে ~ করছে. **ধড়পড়ানি** *n* = ~. **ধড়পড়ানো** *vi* = ~ করা. **ধড়ফড়ে** *adj* **1** palpitating; throbbing; pulsating. **2** restless; fidgety; fretful. **3** fluttering.

ধড়মড় *n* (onom) expressing sudden/hurry/ bustle/ flutter. **~ করে** *adv* in a hurry; hurriedly; precipitately. **ধড়মড়ানি** *n* hurry; hasty. **ধড়মড়ে** *adj* restive; rash; impatient.

ধড়া *n* = ধটি. **~চূড়া** *n* **1** loin-cloth and head-dress; (as worn by Sri Krishna). **2** outfit; attire. **3** (iron) official dress; formal attire.

ধড়াম *n* (onom) expressing a heavy fall; thud. **~ করে** *adv* with a thud.

ধড়াস *n* (onom) **1** thud. **2** throb; throbbing. **3** bang: বুকটা ভয়ে ~ করে উঠল, It gave me the shudders. **~-ধড়াস** *n* repeated thuds/ throbs/ bangs. **~-ধড়াস করা** *vi* thud/ throb/ bang continuously/ repeatedly; throb/ palpitate impetuously.

ধড়িবাজ *adj* crafty; waggish; guileful; roguish; full of ruses; deceitful; cunning; tricky; deceptive. **ধড়িবাজি** *n* craftiness; guilefulness; deceitfulness; roguishness; guile; cunning; deceit; trickery. **~ লোক** *n* trickster; fraud; rogue; humbug.

ধন *n* **1** money. **2** property; wealth; riches. **3** treasure: গুপ্ত~. **4** any valued object; wealth: বিদ্যা পরম ~. **5** darling; treasure: আদরের ~. **~কষ্ট** *n* suffering from lack of money; impecuniousness. **~কাম** *adj* desirous of wealth; covetous. **~কুবের** *n* fabulously wealthy man (as the god of wealth); as rich as Croesus; plutocrat. **~কোষ** *n* treasure of wealth/ money. **~ক্ষয়** *n* loss/ waste of wealth/ money; impoverishment. **~ক্ষয়কর, ~ক্ষয়কারী** wasteful. **~গর্ব, ~গৌরব** *nn* pride of wealth. **~গর্বিত, ~গর্বী** *adj* proud of money; purse-proud. **~গর্বিতা** *fem.* **~চিন্তা** *n* concern for acquisition of wealth; acquisitiveness. **~চিহ্ন** *n* (math) plus sign. **~চ্যুত** *adj* fallen from wealth; impoverished. **~জন** *n* men and money. **~তন্ত্র(বাদ), ~তান্ত্রিকতা** *nn* capitalism. **~তন্ত্রবাদী, ~তান্ত্রিক** *adjj* capitalist; capitalistic. ❑*nn* capitalist. **~তৃষা, ~তৃষ্ণা** *nn* thirst for money; covetousness; cupidity. **~দ** *adj* wealth-giving; liberal. ❑*n* appellation of Kuvera, the god of wealth. **~দা** *fem.* Lakshmi, the goddess of wealth. **~দণ্ড** *n* fine. **~দর্প** = ~গর্ব. **~দাতা** *n* giving wealth/ money. **~দাত্রী** *fem.* **~দৃপ্ত** = গর্বিত. **~দেবতা** *n* Kuvera, the god of wealth; Mammon. **~দৌলত** *n* wealth and property; riches. **~ধান্য** *n* money and grain; affluence; abundant wealth. **~ধান্যপূর্ণ** *adj* full of milk and honey; affluent; prosperous. **~নাশ** *n* loss of wealth/ property. **~নিয়োগ** *n* investment (of money). **~পতি** *n* **1** lord of wealth; Kuvera. **2** rich/ wealthy man. **~পাল** *n* guardian of treasure; treasurer. **~পিপাসা** = ~তৃষ্ণা. **~পিশাচ** *n* scrooge; money-grubber. **~পিশাচিকা, ~পিশাচী** *fem.* **~পূর্ণ** *adj* replete with wealth. **~প্রাণ** *n* one's total possessions; everything. **~প্রিয়** *adj* fond of wealth. **~বণ্টন** *n* distribution of wealth. **~বত্তা** *n* opulence. **~বর্জিত** *adj* destitute of wealth; poor. **~বান** *adj* wealthy; rich; opulent. **~বতী** *fem.* **~বিজ্ঞান** *n* economics; political economy. **~-বিধেয়ক** *n* money bill. **~বিনিয়োগ** = ~নিয়োগ. **~ বিনিয়োগ করা** *vi* invest (money). **~বিভাগ** = ~বণ্টন. **~বৃদ্ধি** *n* increase of property; growth of wealth. **~ব্যয়** *n* spending of money; expenditure; extravagance. **~ভাগ্য** *n* luck for earning money. **~ভাণ্ডার** *n* treasury; fund. **~মত্ত** *adj* intoxicated by wealth. ~মদ *n* intoxication of wealth. ~মান *n* wealth and honour. ~মূল *n* principal; capital. ~যৌবনশালী *adj* endowed with wealth and youth. ~যৌবনশালিনী *fem.* ~রক্ষা *n* safe-keeping/preservation of wealth. ~রাশি *n* **1** riches. **2** (math) positive quantity. ~লক্ষ্মী *n* goddess of wealth. ~লালসা, ~লিপ্সা, ~লোভ *nn* desire of wealth; greed for wealth; covetousness; avarice. ~লিপ্সু, ~লুব্ধ, ~লোভী *adjj* greedy of wealth; avaricious; covetous. ~শালিতা *n* wealthiness; affluence. ~শালী *adj* wealthy; rich; opulent; affluent; moneyed. ~সঞ্চয় *n* accumulation/ saving of wealth. ~সঞ্চয়ী *n* one who accumulates wealth. ~সম্পত্তি, ~সম্পদ = ~দৌলত. ~সাধনা *n* acquisition of money/wealth. ~স্থান *n* treasury; (astrol) the second mansion. ~স্থানী *n* owner of money; capitalist. ~হর, ~হর্তা *nn* thief. ~হীন = ~বর্জিত. ~হীনা *fem.* ধনাকাঙ্ক্ষা = ~তৃষ্ণা. ধনাগম *n* income; accession of wealth; gain; earning. ধনাগমতৃষা, ধনাগমতৃষ্ণা *nn* desire for earning money; thirst for wealth. ধনাগার = ধনভাণ্ডার. ধনাঢ্য = ধনশালী. ধনাত্মক *adj* (math, phys) positive. ধনাধার *n* treasury; treasure-chest. ধনাধিকার *n* right/ title to property. ধনাধিকারী *adj* possessing wealth; wealthy. ❑*n* treasures. ধনাধিকারিণী *fem.* ধনাধিপ(তি) = ধনপতি. ধনাধ্যক্ষ *n* treasurer; cashier; Chancellor of the Exchequer. ধনাধ্যক্ষতা *n* treasurership. ধনাপহরণ *n* stealing/ misappropriation of money; embezzlement; defalcation. ধনাপহরণ করা *vi* steal/ misappropriate money; embezzle; defalcate; rob sb of his money. ধনাপহারক, ধনাপহারী *adjj* stealing/ misappropriating money. ❑*nn* thief; embezzler; robber. ধনাপহারিকা, ধনাপহারিণী *fem.* ধনার্চিত *n* rich; opulent. ধনার্জন *n* acquisition of wealth/ properly. ধনার্জন করা *vi* acquire wealth/ property. ধনার্জনস্পৃহা, ধনার্জনানুরাগ *nn* = ধনাগমতৃষ্ণা. ধনার্থী *adj* seeking money; desirous of earning money; covetous. ধনার্থিনী *fem.* ধনাশা *n* longing for wealth; desire for riches.

ধনাশ্রী *n* name of an Indian musical mode.

ধনি *n* (poet) (in addressing a young woman) O there beautiful/ blessed one. ❑*adj* beautiful and young.

ধনিক *adj* **1** wealthy; opulent; rich; moneyed. **2** capitalist; capitalistic. ❑*n* rich man; owner; creditor; capitalist; rich merchant; merchant prince; investor; money-lender. ধনিকা *fem* **1** young and beautiful woman. **2** rich man's wife. ~গোষ্ঠী, ~শ্রেণী, ~সমাজ, ~সম্প্রদায় *nn* moneyed class; capitalist group/ world. ~তন্ত্র *n* capitalism.

ধনিচা *n* a jute-like fibrous plant; *Sesbania cannabina.*

ধনিয়া *n* coriander; coriander-seed.

ধনিষ্ঠ *adj* very rich; opulent. ধনিষ্ঠা *n* (astrol) the twenty-third lunar mansion.

ধনী *adj* **1** rich; wealthy; well off; moneyed; opulent. **2** *(fem)* young and beautiful. ❑*n* rich man. ধনিনী *fem.*

ধনু *n* **1** bow. **2** measure of length (=4 cubits). **3** (geom) arc; part of a circle. **4** (astron) arc/ quadrant for ascertaining the sun's altitude and Zenith-distance. **5** fiddle-stick. **6** (astrol) the Sagittarius. ~ক *n* **1** bow. **2** fiddle-stick. **3** bow-like device for carding and cleaning cotton. ~কধারী *n* archer; bowman. ~রাশি *n* (astrol) the Sagittarius. ধনুকাকার, ধনুকাকৃতি *adj* bow-shaped; arched. ধনুকাসন *n* name of a yoga posture. ~র্গুণ *n* bow-string. ~র্গুণ আরোপণ করা, string a bow. ~র্ধর *n* **1** archer; bowman. **2** very efficient/ expert person; wizard; whiz-ked: ব্যাকরণে ~. ❑*adj* expert; adept; brilliant: ~ পণ্ডিত. ~র্ধারী *n* = ~র্ধর. ❑*ad j* wielding a bow. ~র্বন্ধনী *n* second bracket; braces. ~র্বাণ *n* bow and arrow. ~র্বিদ্যা *n* (science of) archery. ~র্বেদ *n* science of archery, an ancient treatise written by Vishwamitra. ~র্বেদী *adj* versed in archery. ~র্ভঙ্গ *n* splitting a bow into two. ~র্ভঙ্গ-পণ *n* (fig) a solemn vow; grim/ inflexible resolution/ resolve. ~র্মধ্য *n* middle part of a bow. ~ষ্কর *adj* armed with a bow. ~ষ্কোটি *n* the curved end of a bow. ~ষ্টঙ্কার *n* **1** twang of a bow. **2** (med) tetanus; spasm; convulsion. ~ষ্পাণি *adj* bow in hand. ~ষ্মান = ~র্ধারী.

ধনুঃ = ধনু

ধনে *n* (colloq) = ধনিয়া

ধনেশ *n* Kuvera, the god of wealth. ❑*adj* very rich; opulent.

ধনোপার্জন = ধনার্জন (⇒ ধন)

ধন্দ, ধন্দা, ধন্ধ *nn* **1** (archaic) doubt; labyrinth; puzzle; confusion; suspicion; misgiving; uncertainty. **2** wonder; marvel; miracle. **3** worldly affairs; worries of everyday life. ~লাগা *vi* be confused/ puzzled/ dazzled.

ধন্না *n* colloq of ধরনা

ধন্য *adj* **1** fortunate; auspicious; happy: ~ রাজার পুণ্য দেশ. **2** gratified; blessed: আমার জীবন আজ ~. **3** admirable; praiseworthy; laudable; glorious; commendable: ~ ছেলে তুমি. **4** virtuous; holy; good. **5** thanks; thanks giving. ধন্যা *fem.* ~ করা *vt* gratify; oblige. ~বাদ *n* thanks; thanksgiving. ~বাদ দেওয়া *vi* thank; give thanks.

ধন্যা = ধনে

ধন্ব(1) *n* = ধনুক

ধন্বন্তরি *n* **1** (myth) name of the physician of the gods. **2** a superb physician.

-ধন্বা *adj* carrying/ bearing/ armed with a bow: গাণ্ডীব-~.

ধন্বী *adj* = -ধন্ব

ধপ *n* (onom) expressing the sound arising from the fall of a heavy body upon the ground; thud; thump. ~ **করে** *adv* with a thud/ thump.

ধপধপ *n* (onom) expressing sensation produced by clearness or brightness. ~ **করা** *vi* appear dazzling/ immaculately white/ clean; appear silvery white; shimmer: জ্যোৎস্না ~ করছে. **ধপধপে** *adj* **1** brilliantly/ dazzling/ immaculately white; snowy/ milky white: ধপধপে কাপড়. **2** immaculate; brilliant; dazzling; snowy: ধপধপে সাদা. **3** shimmering; brilliant; dazzling: ধপধপে জ্যোৎস্না. **4** immaculately clean/ tidy: ধপধপে মেঝে.

ধপাৎ = ধপ

ধপাধপ *n* (onom) expressing repeated thuds. ~ **করে** *adv* with thuds.

ধপাস = ধপ

ধবধব = ধপধপ

ধবল *adj* (dazzling) white. ❑*n* **1** white (the colour). **2** white leprosy; leucoderma. **ধবলা** *fem* white cow. ~**কুষ্ঠ** *n* = ~(2). **ধবলাকার, ধবলাকৃতি** *adj* (looking) white. ~**গিরি** *n* name of one of the highest peaks of the Himalayas. ~**মৃত্তিকা** *n* chalk.

ধবলিত *adj* whitened; made white; burned white/ grey: ~ কেশ.

ধবলিমা *n* whiteness; whitishness.

ধবলী[1] *n fem* white cow.

ধবলী[2] *adj* (in compounds) = ধবল. ~**কৃত** *adj* made white; whitened. ~**ভূত** *adj* made/ turned white/ grey.

ধবলোৎপল *n* white esculent water-lily.

ধমক *n* **1** reproof; reprimand; scolding; rebuke; dressing down: বড়ো সাহেবের ~. **2** intimidation; threat: তোমার ধমকে আমি ভয় পাই না. ~ **দেওয়া** *vt* **1** administer a reproof; reprove; reprimand; chide; rebuke; scold. **2** threaten; intimidate; make a threat/ threats. ~-**ধামক** *n* mild reproof; admonition; talking-to; rebuke. **ধমকানি** = ~. **ধমকানো** ~ দেওয়া.

ধমনি, ধমনী *nn* **1** (anat) canal of the human body; artery. **2** throat; neck. ~**ঘাত,** ~**স্পন্দন** *n* pulse; pulse-beat; arterial throbbing.

ধম্মিল *n* woman's braided and ornamented hair wound round the head; bun.

-**ধর** *adj* (used as a *suff*) holding; bearing; possessing; having; carrying; wearing; keeping; sustaining; preserving; observing: শক্তি~, শ্রুতি~.

ধরণী *n* earth; world. ~**তল** *n* surface of the earth. ~**ধর,** ~**পতি,** ~**পাল** *nn* king. ~**ধাম** *n* earthly abode. ~**মণ্ডল** *n* the whole earth; terrestrial globe.

ধরতা *n* **1** consideration: ওটা আমাদের ~র মধ্যেই নয়. **2** = ধরতি. **3** burden (of a song); cue. **ধরতাই** *adj* fixed. **ধরতাই বুলি** *n* commonplace; cliche´.

ধরতি *n* (commerce) extra amount given by the seller to the buyer to guard against any possible shortage during weighing; compensation.

ধরন *n* **1** manner; way; mode; method: কাজের ~. **2** kind; sort: নানা ধরনের জিনিস. **3** appearance; look; cut: মুখের ~. **4** bearing; deportment: ছেলেটার ~ ভালো মনে হচ্ছে না. **5** condition; state: রোগের ~. **6** course; workings. **7** fashion; style; mode: পোশাকের ~. ~**ধারন** *n* **1** behaviour; comportment: তার ~ধারন উচ্ছৃঙ্খল. **2** = ~ in the plural.

ধরনা *n* act of lying obstinately at sb's door or at the temple of a deity begging for sth; supplication. ~ **দেওয়া/ ধরে বসে থাকা/ পাতা** *vi* lie obstinately at sb's door or at the temple of a deity begging for sth; supplicate; lie in supplication.

ধরপাকড় *n* **1** large-scale/ collective arrests (by the police); round-up. **2** insistent solicitation. ~ **করা** *vt* **1** make large-scale arrests. **2** solicit insistently: চাকরির জন্যে ~ করা.

ধরম *n* (poet) = ধর্ম

ধরা[1] =ধরণী. ~**তল 1** surface of the earth. **2** ground: ~তলে পতন. ~**পতি** *n* king. ~**পৃষ্ঠ** = ~তল. ~**ভৃৎ** *n* mountain. ~**শয়ন,** ~**শয্যা** *nn* the bed of the earth/ ground; eternal rest. ~**শায়ী** *adj* lying prostrate on the ground; knocked down; floored. ~**শায়ী করা** *vt* knock down; floor; bowl sb over. ~**শায়ী হওয়া** *vi* lie prostrate; be toppled over; be knocked down; collapse; fall to the ground.

ধরা[2] *vt* **1** hold (with the hand): ছাতাটা ধরো. **2** catch; catch hold of; grab/ seize/ take hold of: বলটা সে ধরতে পারলো না. **3** grasp: দড়িটা শক্ত করে ধরো. **4** grab: কলার চেপে ~. **5** seize: সে আমার হাত ধরলো. He seized me by the hand. **6** clasp: ছুরিটা সে শক্ত করে ধরেছিল. **7** clutch: পয়সাটা সে খপ করে ধরল. **8** grip: ভয় পেয়ে সে আমার হাত ধরলো. **9** take: এটা তোমার পাওনা—ধরো. **10** touch: গরম হাড়িটা ধরো না. **11** arrest; apprehend; nab; capture: চোর ~. **12** reach: হাত দিয়ে চোর ~. **13** support; give support to: ছেলেটা পড়ে গেল, ধরো. **14** overtake: আগের গাড়িটাকে ধরতে পারো কিনা দেখো. **15** wear; put on: কী বেশই না ধরেছো. **16.** board; embark; catch: জাহাজ/ট্রেন ~. **17** catch; entrap: মাছ/বাঘ ~. **18** assume: মূর্তি ~. **19** keep to: সে ঐ এক খেয়াল ধরেই আছে. **20** lean on: সে লাঠি ধরে চলছে. **21** be choked with: কান্নায় গলা ধরে গেছে. **22** become hoarse; crack: চিৎকার করতে করতে গলা ধরে গেছে. **23** restrain; check keep back: পাগলটাকে ধরো, নইলে নদীতে ঝাঁপ দেবে. **24** accommodate; hold; contain; take in; admit: ঘরে লোক ~; কলসিতে ~ ধরা. **25** bear: গাছে ফল ~. **26** carry: গর্ভে ~. **27** bud; be in bud; produce buds: গাছে কুঁড়ি ~. **28** be affected with: দেওয়ালে লোনা ~. **29** be smeared with: কালির/

কলঙ্কের দাগ ~. **30** be infested with: আমে পোকা ধরেছে. **31** work; act upon successfully; be effective; take (effect): ওষুধ ধরা. **32** cherish: মনে উচ্চাশা ~. **33** take up: অস্ত্র ~. **34** attack: রোগে ~, ডাকাতে ~. **35** have the desired effect; take: কাঠে রং ~. **36** be affected with: মরিচায় ~, rust (away). **37** woo; persuade; curry favour with: বড়ো সাহেবকে ধরতে পারলে কাজ হবে. **38** be a disciple/ follower of; find: মুরব্বি ~, পীর ~. **39** supplicate; implore; lie obstinately at: দেবতার কত দোর ধরে তার রোগ ভালো হয়েছে. **40** resort to; take to: লাঠি ~. **41** follow; go: এই পথ ধরে চলে যাও. **42** persist: গোঁ/ আবদার/ জেদ ~. **43** be affected/ infected with; catch: চোখে চালসে ~, ম্যালেরিয়ায় ~. **44** ache: মাথা ~. **45** be benumbed: এক ঠায় দাঁড়িয়ে পা ধরে গেছে. **46** be dazed: চোখ ~. **47** be addicted/ accustomed to; take to: নেশা ~, জুয়া খেলা ~. **48** be under the influence of: নেশায় ~, ভূতে ~. **49** cease; stop: বৃষ্টি ধরলে যাবো. **50** charge; fix; decide; ascertain: তুমিই এর একটা দর ধরো. **51** impose; assess: ট্যাক্স ~. **52** find out; detect, show: ভুল ~. **53** see through: ছল ~. **54** compare; count; regard; consider: পাঁচ জনের সঙ্গে তাকে ~ যায়. **55** suppose; consider: ধরো যদি তাই হয়. **56** be stricken/ affected with: শীতে/ ভয়ে ~. **57** catch: কাপড়ে আগুন ~. **58** hear (sth); understand; grasp; catch: তোমার কথাটা ঠিক ধরতে পারলাম না. **59** catch/ take. sb's fancy: শাড়িটা তার মনে ধরেছে. **60** begin; commence; start; turn: চুলে পাক ~, গান ~.**61** take fire; ignite; catch: উনানে আগুন ধরেছে. **62** stick: হাড়ির তলায় ভাত একটু ধরে গেছে. **63** stop at; touch: ডাক গাড়ি এত ছোট স্টেশনে ধরে না. **64** catch up; reach: তুমি আগে যাও, আমি তোমাকে পথে ধরবো. **65** diagnose; find out; discover: ডাক্তার রোগ পারেননি, তার উদ্দেশ্য যে কী তা ~ শক্ত. **66** pay heed to; listen: আমার কথা ~. **67** appeal; touch; be pleasing/ acceptable: তোমার কথাটা আমার মনে ধরেছে. **68** kidnap: ছেলে~. **69** pronounce; utter: আল্লাহর নাম ধরো. **70** adopt: বাদশাহ হয়ে তিনি শাহজাহান নাম ধরলেন. **71** discern; determine: এটা কার হাতের লেখা ~ শক্ত. **72** be overdone/ overfried; stick: তরকারিটা ধরে গেছে. **73** bid; risk (money): বাজি ~, bet. **74** buy a ticket of: লটারি ~. **75** go into: পেশিতে টান ধরেছে, the muscles went into spasm. **76** insist upon; implore; beseech; entreat: তাকে কত করে ধরলাম, সে কিছুতেই রাজি হলো না. **77** reveal/ disclose oneself: ছদ্মবেশী রাজা নিজেকে ~ দিলেন. **78** make use of; resort to: এ নামের ব্যাখ্যা সংস্কৃত ধরে হবে না. **79** be overjoyed: তার মুখে হাসি আর ধরে না, He grinned in delight/from ear to ear. **80** have (the heart, etc) to; bring oneself to: কৃপণ প্রাণ ধরে একটা পয়সা খরচ করতে পারে না. **81** preserve; sustain; maintain: সে কোনোমতে প্রাণ ধরে আছে. **82** take on: ফল থাকলে রং ধরবে. **83** be inflamed or irritated: মুখে ওল ধরেছে. **84** fold; hang on to: গলা ধরা, fold in one's arms; hug; embrace. ❑*adj* **1** caught; held; kept; possessed; arrested; seized; choked: ~ গলা (⇒ also the meanings of the verb). **~ দেওয়া** *vi* **1** surrender; give oneself up. **2** disclose/ reveal oneself. **~নো** *vi* cause to catch/ hold/ seize (⇒ the meanings of ~ above). **~ পড়া** *vi* **1** be caught/ seized. **2** be found out/ discovered/ disclosed/ detected. **~ধরি** *n* **1** scuffle; tussle; fray. **2** entreaty; solicitation; begging; pleading: অনেক ~ধরির পর সে রাজি হয়েছে. **~বাঁধা** *adj* hard and fast; rigid. **ধরি মাছ না ছুঁই পানি** (fig) reap the fruits without making any effort. **ধরে আসা** *vi* cease: বৃষ্টি ধরে এসেছে. **ধরে পড়া/বসা** *vi* implore; beseech; entreat; beg earnestly. **ধরে রাখা** keep/hold back; hold on to.

ধরাট *n* (commerce) discount; ransom.

ধরিত্রী *n* earth; world.

ধরিয়া *prep* = ধরে

ধরিয়ে *adj, n* (one) who holds/ catches/ captures.

ধর্তব্য *adj* to be upheld/ supported; worthy of being taken into consideration/ account; counted. **ধর্তব্যের মধ্যে নয়** not worth considering/troubling about.

ধর্ম *n* **1** virtue; piety; morality; holiness; religion. **2** God. **3** law/ justice personified; divine Judge: ধর্ম জানেন, তিনিই এর বিচার করবেন. **4** steadfast decree; statute; ordinance; law. **5** good works; religious merit. **6** nature; propensity; character; disposition: খলের/সাধুর ~. **7** form of worship: তান্ত্রিক ~. **8** peculiar condition; essential quality; property; mark; function; peculiarity: ওষুধের ~. **9** usage; practice; spirit: কালের ~. **10** duty; customary observance; prescribed conduct: এটা তুমি ~ ভেবেই করবে. **11** right; justice. **12** ethical precepts. **13** religious abstraction; devotion. **14** chastity: স্ত্রীলোকের ~নাশ. **15** (astrol) ninth mansion. **16** theology: ~গ্রন্থ. **17** Yama, the Hindu god of piety and death. **18** name of a popular god of Bengladesh. ~ঠাকুর. **19** law/ doctrine of Buddhism. **~-অর্থ-কাম-মোক্ষ** *n* piety, wealth, fulfilment of desire and salvation of the soul (the four principal aim of human life). **~কন্যা** *n fem* one solemnly accepted as a daughter by a person other than her parents; god-daughter. **~কথা** *n* discourse upon law/religion; sermon; pious admonition. **~কর্ম, ~কার্য, ~ক্রিয়া** *nn* act/work of duty; pious action; act of religion; good work; virtuous conduct; religious practices; observance of duties; pious work; righteous conduct of attaining virtue through religious practices. **~কৃত্য** *n* virtue; moral/ religious observance. **~ক্ষেত্র** *n* holy/ consecrated place;

place of pilgrimage. ~গত *adj* concerning/ pertaining to religion; religious; pious; virtuous. ~গতপ্রাণ *adj* profoundly/ deeply religious/ pious; very religious minded. ~গ্রন্থ *n* holy book/ scripture. ~ঘট *n* strike. ~ঘট করা *vi* (go on) strike. ~ঘটকালীন ভাতা *n* strike-pay. ~ঘটী *adj* striking. ❑*n* striker. ~চক্র *n* wheel/ range of the law (according to Buddhism). ~চক্ষু *n* eye of law/ religion/ justice. ~চর্চা *n* religious discussion/ practice. ~চর্যা *n* observance of religious rules and rites; practice of religion/ virtue; performance of duty; observance of the law. ~চারী *adj* observant of the religious rules and rites; fulfilling one's duties; virtuous; pious; dutiful; moral; devoted to religious practices. ~চারিণী *fem* ~চিন্তক *adj* meditating on religion; virtuous. ~চিন্তন, ~চিন্তা *nn* religious/ theological/ spiritual meditation; reflection on religion. ~চ্যুত *adj* gone astray from the religious/ righteous course; renegade; apostate. ~ছেলে *n* one who is solemnly accepted as a son by a person other than his parents; god-son. ~জ *adj* **1** legitimately born. **2** produced by a sense of duty. ~জায়া = ~পত্নী. ~জিজ্ঞাসা *n* inquiry into religion; religious/ spiritual inquiry. ~জিজ্ঞাসু *adj* seeking after/ inquisitive about religious/ spiritual truths. ~জীবন *n* religious/ spiritual/ pious/ virtuous life; ecclesiastical life. ~জ্ঞ *adj* knowing the law/ what is right; conversant with religion/ religious rules and rites; pious; virtuous. ~জ্ঞান *n* knowledge of religion/ duty/ law; religious knowledge; deep sense of piety. ~ঠাকুর = ~ (17). ~ত *adj* according to law/ rule; rightly; justly. ~তত্ত্ব *n* essence of religion; theology; religious doctrine. ~তত্ত্ববিৎ, ~তত্ত্ববিদ *nn* one conversant with the mysteries of religion; theologian. ~তত্ত্বীয় *adj* religious; theological. ~ত্যাগ *n* abandonment of one's religion; apostasy; recantation. ~ত্যাগ করা *vi* renounce/ abandon one's religion; apostatize. ~ত্যাগী *adj* abandoning one's religion; renegade; apostate. ❑*n* apostate; renegade. ~দ্রোহ, ~দ্বেষ *nn* revolt against religion; hostility to religion; ungodliness; godlessness; irreligion; blasphemy; impiety. ~দ্রোহী, ~দ্বেষী *adjj* hostile to/ revolting against religion; godless; irreligious; blasphemous. ❑*nn* enemy of religion; blasphemer; atheist; infidel. ~দ্রোহিণী, ~দ্বেষিণী *fem.* ~দ্রোহিতা = ~দ্রোহ. ~ধ্বজী *adj* simulating piety/ virtuousness; feigning virtue; hypocritical; self-righteous; sanctimonious. ❑*n* religions imposter; hypocrite. ~নাশ *n* **1** defilement/ destruction/ profanation of religion; sacrilege. **2** rape; sexual assault. ~নাশ করা *vi* **1** profane/ defile sb's religion/ idol. **2** rape; ravish. ~নিন্দা *n* disparagement of religion; blasphemy. ~নিরপেক্ষ *adj* irrespective of creed; secular. ~নির্দিষ্ট *adj* enjoined by religion/ scriptures; scriptural; canonical. ~নিষ্ঠ *adj* devoted to religion/ religious practices/ virtue; devout; pious; virtuous; righteous. ~নিষ্ঠা *n* devotion to religion/ virtue/ religious practices; piety; virtuousness; righteousness. ~নীতি *n* principles of religion; religious/ moral principles; ethics. ~পত্নী *n* lawful wife; lawfully married wife. ~পথ *n* path/ way virtue/ piety. ~পথে থাকা *vi* follow the path of virtue/ piety; lead a virtuous life; practise virtue/ piety; walk in the presence of God. ~পর, ~পরায়ণ *adjj* = ~নিষ্ঠ. ~পাল *n* defender of religion/ faith. ~পালক *n* **1** = ~পাল. **2** one who observes religious rites and practices; one who practises his religion. ~পালন *n* defence of faith/ religious observance of religious rites and practices. ~ পালন করা *vi* practise one's religion. ~পিতা *n* one solemnly accepted as father by a person other than his children; godfather. ~পুতুর (colloq), ~পুত্র *nn* **1** adopted son; godson. **2** name of Judhishthir of the Mahabharata. **3** (iron) profoundly pious/ truthful man; inveterate liar. ~পুত্র যুধিষ্ঠির *n* = ~পুত্র (3). ~পুস্তক = ~গ্রন্থ. ~প্রচার *n* preaching of religion; propagation of faith; religious preaching/ propaganda; evangelism. ~প্রচার করা *vi* preach religion; propagate faith; evangelize. ~প্রচারক *adj* preaching/ propagating religion; evangelizing. ❑*n* preacher/ propagator of religion; evangelist. ~প্রধান *adj* chiefly guided by religion/ religious principles; religious. minded; devout. ~প্রবক্তা *n* expounder of religion/ faith; preacher; prophet; religious teacher. ~প্রবণ *n* having propensity towards religion; devout; deeply religious; religious minded. ~প্রবণতা *n* leaning towards religion; religious mindedness; religious bent. ~প্রবৃত্তি *n* religious impulse; inclination towards virtue. ~প্রাণ *adj* profoundly religious/ devout. ~প্রাণতা *n* profound religiousness/ devoutness. ~বৎসল *adj* tenderly alive to duty; loving piety. ~বন্ধন *n* bond of religion; religious fraternity; sacred/ solemn tie/bond. ~বন্ধু *n* friend/ servant of religion; sworn friend. ~বল *n* force of piety; power of faith. ~বাণী *n* holy/ sacred word; message/ teaching of religion. ~বাসর *n* day of full moon. ~বাহ্য *adj* contrary to what is right; extra-religious. ~বিচার *n* discussion on religion; religions argument/ debate. ~বিজয় *n* victory of justice/ virtue. ~বিদ = ~জ্ঞ. ~বিদ্যা = ~তত্ত্ব. ~বিধান, ~বিধি *nn* religious/ sacred law/ rule; scriptural/ religious precept/ injunction.

~বিপ্লব *n* religious revolution. ~বিবেচনা *n* religious consideration. ~বিরুদ্ধ, ~বিরোধী *adj* **1** hostile to religion/ piety; irreligious; ungodly; impious. **2** contrary to religion; unjust; unfair; opposed to law; illegal; immoral. ~বিরোধ *n* religious conflict/ strife. ~বিশ্বাস *n* faith (in religion; creed. ~বিশ্বাসী *adj* having religious faith; pious; virtuous. ❑*n* believer. ~বুদ্ধি *n* sense of piety; pious/ virtuous/ just thought/ intention; virtuous disposition; good faith; rectitude. ❑*adj* having a virtuous mind; pious-minded. ~বৃদ্ধ *adj* advanced in virtue. ❑*n* religious/ ecclesiastical elder. ~ব্যবসা(য়) *n* trade on religion; religion-mongering. ~ব্যবসায়ী *adj* trading on religion; religion-mongerer. ~ভয় *n* fear of God; religious qualms/ scruples. ~ভগিনী *n* **1** sister in respect of religion. **2** one solemnly accepted as a sister by a person other than her brother or sister; member of a sisterhood; nun; sister. ~ভাই = ~ভ্রাতা. ~ভিক্ষুক *n* mendicant from virtuous motives; religious mendicant. ~ভীরু *adj* God-fearing. ~ভ্রষ্ট = ~চ্যুত. ~ভ্রাতা *n* **1** brother in (respect of) religion/ piety. **2** one solemnly accepted as a brother by a person other than his brother or sister; member of a brotherhood/ sect/ faith; brother. ~মঙ্গল *n* long poem narrating the glory of Dharmathakur (⇒ ধর্ম 16). ~মত *n* religious tenet/ doctrine. ~মতি = ~বুদ্ধি. ~মন্দির *n* house of worship; sanctuary; holy place; temple; shrine. ~ময় *n* full of piety; virtuous; moral; righteous; devout; pious. ~মাতা *n* godmother. ~মার্গ = ~পথ. ~ মূল *n* foundation of religion/piety. ~মূলক *n* concerning religion; religious. ~যাজক *n* priest; ecclesiastic. ~যুক্ত *adj* righteous. ~যুদ্ধ *n* war for the cause of religion; religious war; religious strife; holy war; crusade. ~যোদ্ধা *n* warrior in the defence of true faith; crusader. ~রক্ষা *n* **1** defence of faith; preservation of one's religion/ piety. **2** preservation of one's chastity. ~ রক্ষা করা *vi* **1** defend/ preserve one's faith/ religion/ piety. **2** preserve one's chastity. ~রত *adj* virtuous; pious; attached to one's faith. ~রাজ *n* **1** lord of justice; just/ righteous king. **2** an appellation of Yama; an appellation of Yudhishthira of the Mahabharata. ~রাজ্য *n* holy state; realm of justice. ~রাষ্ট্র *n* theocratic state. ~লক্ষণ *n* any one of the ten (self-control, honesty, etc) characteristic signs/ essential marks of piety/ virtuousness. ~লোপ *n* **1** violation of law; neglect of duty; irreligion. **2** destruction/ extinction of religion/ piety/ faith; profanation of sb's faith. **3** ravishment of a woman's chastity. ~ লোপ করা = ~নাশ করা. ~শালা *n* **1** court of justice; tribunal. **2** charitable/ religious asylum. ~শাসন *n* **1** code of laws; religious edict/ precept; administration of justice; lawful rule. **2** theocracy. ~শাস্ত্র *n* scriptures; holy writings. ~শাস্ত্রব্যবসায়ী *n* **1** dealer in religious books and scriptures. **2** expounder and teacher of scriptures; scribe. ~শাস্ত্রানুমত *adj* conforming to/ as prescribed by scriptures; scriptural. ~শাস্ত্রী *n* theologian; one learned in the scriptures. ~শিক্ষক *n* religious teacher/ preceptor. ~শিক্ষা *n* religious teaching/ education. ~শীল *adj* of a virtuous disposition; pious; virtuous; just. ~সংস্কার *n* **1** religious reformation. **2** holy sacrament. ~সংস্কারক *n* religious reformer. ~সংস্থাপন *n* introduction/ firm establishment/ foundation of a religion; restoration/ rejuvenation/ reinforce of religion. ~সংহিতা *n* code/ collection of laws. ~সঙ্কর *n* mixing of different religions. ~সঙ্গত *adj* conform to the rules and prescriptions of religion/ piety; just; lawful; virtuous; pious. ~সঙ্গীত *n* devotional song; hymn; psalm. ~সত্যব্রত *adj* devoted to truth and virtue. ~সভা *n* **1** religious gathering/ congress/ convention/ society; congregation. **2** court of justice; tribunal. ~সম্প্রদায় *n* religious community/sect/ group. ~সম্মত = ~সঙ্গত. ~সহায় *n* companion in religion. ❑*adj* conducive to piety. ~সাক্ষী *n* oath in the name of the god of piety. ❑*adj* having/ claiming the god of piety as witness. ~সাক্ষী করে বলা take a solemn oath; swear by almighty God; take an oath in the name of God; promise solemnly; take a solemn oath. ~সাধন *n* fulfilment of duties; practice of virtue/ religion; means of the fulfilment of duty; practice of virtue/ religion. ~স্ব *n* endowment. ~হানি = ~লোপ. ~হীন *adj* irreligious; godless; ungodly; impious. ~হীনতা *n* irreligion; impiety; ungodliness. ধর্মাখ্যান *n* explanation of religion/ duties. ধর্মাচরণ = ~ চর্যা. ধর্মাতিক্রম *n* transgression of duties/ moral or religious precepts or principles. ধর্মাত্মা *adj* religious-minded; profoundly virtuous/ pious. ধর্মাধর্ম *n* right and wrong; justice and injustice; virtue and vice. ধর্মাধর্মবিচারশূন্য *adj* not discriminating between/ regardless of right and wrong; unscrupulous; wanton; conscienceless. ধর্মাধিকরণ *n* **1** administration/ court of justice. **2** judge. ধর্মাধিকার *n* administration of justice; office/ jurisdiction of judge; judgeship. ধর্মাধিকারিক *adj* relating to law/ justice; judicial. ❑*n* judge. ধর্মাধিকারী *n* administrator of law; chief officer of justice; judge; magistrate. ধর্মাধ্যক্ষ *n* superintendent of religious affairs; religious head; judge; magistrate. ধর্মানুষ্ঠান *n* fulfilment of duty; virtuous/ moral conduct; performance of a religious/ scriptural rites; rituals; act of piety; practice of virtue.

ধর্মানুষ্ঠাতা *n* performer of a rite; ritualist; virtuous/ pious man. **ধর্মানুষ্ঠাত্রী** *fem.* **ধর্মানুসারে** *adj* according to/ following precepts of religion/ morality. **ধর্মান্তর** *n* another religion. **ধর্মান্তরগ্রহণ** *n* adoption of/ conversion to a different religion. **ধর্মান্তর গ্রহণ করা** *vi* adopt a different religion; be converted (to a different religion). **ধর্মান্তরিত** *adj* converted (to a different religion). **ধর্মান্তরিতা** *fem.* **ধর্মান্তরিত ব্যক্তি** *n* convert. **ধর্মান্তরীকরণ** *n* conversion; proslytism. **ধর্মান্দোলন** *n* religious/ theological movement/ discussion; religious/ theological dispute/ agitation. **ধর্মান্ধ** *adj* fanatic; fanatical; bigoted. **ধর্মান্ধতা** *n* fanaticism; zealotry; bigotry. **ধর্মান্ধ ব্যক্তি** *n* fanatic; zealot; bigot. **ধর্মাবতার** *n* justice/ piety/ virtue incarnate; (in addressing a judge) my lord. **ধর্মালম্বন** *n* practice of a religion; adoption of a religion. **ধর্মালম্বন করা** *vi* practise/ follow a religion/ creed; adopt a religion. **ধর্মাবলম্বী** *adj* following/ practising a religion: ইসলাম ধর্মাবলম্বী, follower of Islam. **ধর্মাবলম্বিনী** *fem.* **ধর্মারণ্য** *n* sacred grove/ wood. **ধর্মার্জন** *n* acquisition of virtue/ piety. **ধর্মার্জন করা** *vi* acquire virtue/ piety. **ধর্মার্থ** *n* religious merit and wealth. ❑*adv* for religious purpose; for the sake of religion/ faith; according to precepts of religion. **ধর্মার্থে** *adj* = ধর্মার্থ. **ধর্মাশ্রিত** *adj* seeking virtue; just; pious. **ধর্মাসন** *n* throne of justice; judgement-seat; bench; seat of justice. **ধর্মের কল বাতাসে নড়ে, ধর্মের ঢাক আপনি বাজে** (fig) Truth must come out. The voice of justice will make itself heard. **ধর্মের ষাঁড়** *n* (fig) a wildly bullheaded person; rake; bullhead. **ধর্মের ঘর/সংসার** *n* virtuous/ pious family. **ধর্মে সওয়া** *vi* (of sins, misdeeds) be tolerated by God/ the Divine judge.

ধর্মিষ্ঠ *adj* **1** profoundly religious/ virtuous/ righteous/ pious. **2** completely lawful/ legal. **ধর্মিষ্ঠা** *fem.*

ধর্মী *adj* (used as a *suff)* endowed with a characteristic mark/ peculiar property; haring the rights/ attributes/ peculiarities/ property/ quality: নিরীক্ষা~. **~য়** *adj* religious.

ধর্মেন্দ্র *n* lord of justice; appellation of Yama. ❑*adj* most pious/virtuous.

ধর্মোত্তর *adj* entirely devoted to justice/virtue.

ধর্মোদ্দেশে *adj*=ধর্মার্থে (⇒ ধর্ম)

ধর্মোন্নত্ত *n* advancement of religion.

ধর্মোন্মাদ *adj* fanatical; having a religious craze.❑*n* =ধর্মান্ধ (⇒ ধর্ম)

ধর্মোপদেশ *n* religious/moral instruction; sermon. **~ দেওয়া** *vi* impart religious/moral instruction; (derog) sermonize. **~ক** *adj* imparting religious instruction; (derog) sermonizing. ❑*n* spiritual preceptor; religious instructor. **ধর্মোপদোশিকা** *fem.*

ধর্মোপদেষ্টা=ধর্মোপদেশক (⇒ ধর্মোপদেশ). **ধর্মোপদেষ্টী** *fem.*

ধর্মোপাসক *adj* devoted to/following a religion. ❑*n* devotee (of a religion). **ধর্মোপাসিকা** *fem.*

ধর্মোপাসনা *n* (religious) worship; devotions; prayer. **~ করা** *n* observe religious rites; practise religion; say one's prayers.

ধর্মোপেত *adj* endowed with virtue.

ধর্ম্য *adj* **1** just; virtuous; righteous. **2** legal; legitimate.

ধর্ষ, ধর্ষণ *nn* **1** rape; ravishment; outrage; violation: নারী~. **2** assault(ing); oppression; overpowering; defeating; subdue: প্রজা~. **ধর্ষণ করা** *vt* **1** violate (a woman); rape; outrage; ravish. **2** oppress; assault; overpower; overcome; defeat; subdue. **~ক** *adj* raping; assaulting; assailing; violating. ❑*n* rapist; oppressor; assailant; violator. **~নীয়** *adj* liable to be raped/outraged/ravished; liable to be attacked/assaulted; violable; conquerable. **~নীয়া** *fem.*

ধর্ষিত *adj* overpowered; violated; ill-treated; abused; outraged; raped; subdued; defeated; ravished. **ধর্ষিতা** *fem.*

ধলা *adj* (dial) white; fair; fair-complexioned. **ধলী** *fem.*

ধস *n* (onom) **1** noise of a landslide; crash. **2** landslide; landslip. **3** chunk. **~ করে** *adv* with a crash. (⇒ also **ধ্বস**).

ধসকা *adj* **1** (hanging) loose; crumbly; crumbling: ~ মাটি. **2** flabby; flaccid: ~ শরীর. ❑*vi* become/hang loose; crumble; decay; waste away; be failing (in health). **~নো** *vi*=~.

ধসধস *n* (onom) expressing noise of sth falling off. **ধসধসে** *adj* loose; crumbly.

ধসা *vi* **1** collapse: বাড়িটা ধসে পড়েছে. **2** crumble: কত বড়ো বড়ো সাম্রাজ্য ধসে গেল. **3** (of health) collapse. **4** cave in: ছাদ ~. **5** come off and fall down; crumble: নদীর পাড় ~. ❑*adj* collapsing; crumbling; crumbly; deteriorating; decaying; declining. **~নো** *vt* cause to crumble/collapse; ruin; demolish; raze; dilapidate.

ধস্কা=ধসকা

ধস্তাধস্তি *n* scuffle; tussle; fray; rough-and-tumble; struggle. **~ করা** *vi, vt* scuffle; tussle; grapple (with); struggle; wrestle with.

ধা *n* (music) the sixth note of the gamut.

-ধা *suff* meaning: ways; means; -fold: দ্বিধা, ত্রিধা, বহুধা.

ধাই(-মা) *n fem* nurse; wet-nurse; foster-mother; midwife. **~তেলা** *adj* excessively ointed with oil.

ধাউড় *n* cheat; swindler; crook.

ধাউড়ে *n* fast messenger; errand-boy.

ধাউস *adj* very large/big; huge; enormous.

ধাওড়া[১]=ধাউস

ধাওড়া[২] *n* mud-built huts for day-labourers.

ধাওন *n* race; running; galloping; pursuit.

ধাওয়া *vi* run (after); chase hotly; gallop. **~ করা** *vt* chase; give chase. **ধাওয়ানো** *vt* cause to run/chase; run; chase away; give a hot chase; pursue.

ধাঁ *n* (onom) expressing: sound of brisk motion; quickness; noise of burning; noisy abruptness: ধাঁ করে কিছু বলা, say sth abruptly; ধাঁ করে জ্বলে ওঠা, flare up; ধাঁ করে কাজ শেষ করা, finish a job promptly/ straightway; ধাঁ করে চলে যাওয়া, go off abruptly; ধাঁ করে চলে আসা, come back in a trice; ধাঁ করে ছড়িয়ে পড়া, spread like wildfire; ধাঁ করে ঝাঁপ ফেলা, shut the hatchway with a bang, bang/slam the hatchway; ধাঁ করে চড় মারা, give sb a loud slap.

ধাঁচ(া), ধাজ *n* **1** shape; form; cut. **2** mould; model. **3** manner; type; pattern; fashion; kind: এ কোন ধাঁচের ব্যবহার ?

ধাঁধা *n* **1** dazzle; optical illusion; sleight; hoodwinking. **2** puzzle; enigma; riddle; maze. **3** confusion; bewilderment; daze. **4** intricate/ puzzling/ tricky question; poser. **5** suspicion; doubt; misgiving: আমার মনে একটা ~ থেকে গেল. **6** goad; urge; compulsion; constraint: পেটের ~. **7** search; hunt; quest; pursuit: চাকরির ~. ❑*vt* dazzle; daze. **~ দেওয়া** *vt* hoodwink: bamboozle; confound. **~নো** *vt* dazzle; blind; daze. ❑*adj* dazzling: চোখ ~নো. **~ লাগা** *vi* be dazzled; be dazed; be puzzled/ confused; be struck with wonder; be wonder-struck. **~ লাগানো** *vt* dazzle; daze; hoodwink; confuse; puzzle; hoodwink; strike with wonder.

ধাকড়া *adj* hefty; robust; sturdy; strapping.

ধাক্কা *n* **1** push; thrust; shove; jolt; jerk. **2** collision; shock; impact: গাড়িতে গাড়িতে ধাক্কা. **3** lashing; blow; impact: বাতাসের ~. **4** pressure; strain: কাজের ~. **5** attack: রোগের ~. **6** (mental) shock. **~ খাওয়া** *vi* **1** collide; bump/dash against; hit; smash into: দেয়ালে ~ খাওয়া. **2** be pushed/shoved. **3** be shocked: মনে ~ খাওয়া. **4** be driven onto; hit (against); be knocked about. **5** suffer/receive a set-back: রাজনীতিতে নেমে প্রথমেই সে একটা ~ খেলো. **~ দেওয়া** *vt* push; shove; dash; give a push; jostle (against); jab; press. **ধাক্কা দিয়ে সরানো** *vt* push back/ aside/ away; shore; repulse; thrust back. **~ লাগা**=~ খাওয়া. **~ধাক্কি** *n* pushing on shoving; jostling; mêlée. **~নো**=~ দেওয়া.

ধাঙড়, ধাঙ্গড় *nn* a sweeper (by caste or trade).

ধাড়ি, ধাড়ী *nn* **1** dam (of beasts). **2** (hum) mother of many children. **3** leader; ringleader: চোরের ~. **4** grown-up/ robust person/ child: এত বড়ো ~, তার আবার ছেলেমানুষি. ❑*adj* **1** grown-up; full grown; husky ~ মেয়ে. **2** inveterate; hardened: ~ বদমাস.

ধাত *n* **1** metal: অষ্টধাতের আংটি. **2** temperament; disposition; nature; mettle; spirit: এত দিন তার সঙ্গে বাস করেও তার ~ বুঝলে না ? **3** pulse: ~ছেড়ে যাওয়া. **4** humour: শ্লেষ্মার ~. **5** semen; seed; blood: ধাতের রোগ. **~ ছেড়ে যাওয়া** (of a patient) collapse; be in a state of collapse; sink. **~সহ** *adj* in agreement with bodily condition/ constitution/ temperament/ nature. **~সহ হওয়া** *vi* agree with the constitution/ temperament (of); be compatible/ consistent/ consonant with the temperament, etc (of). **~স্থ** *adj* **1** in a state of composure; collected; composed; at peace. **2** accustomed; acclimatized. **~স্থ হওয়া** *vi* **1** regain mental calm/ composure/ poise/ aplomb. **2** accustom oneself to; be accustomed to; acclimatize oneself to.

ধাতকী *n* name of a beautiful flowering shrub; *Griselea tomentosa.*

ধাতব *adj* metallic; mineral. **~ দ্যুতি** *n* metallic lustre. **~ প্রস্রবণ** *n* mineral spring. **~ ব্যাধি** *n* disease/disorder of semen; spermatorrhoea.

ধাতসহ, ধাতস্থ ⇒ ধাত

ধাতা *adj* regulating; creating. ❑*n* Creator; Providence; Brahma; God.

ধাতানি *n* tongue-lashing; sound scolding; upbraiding; reprimand; jawing. **ধাতানো** *vi* scold soundly; jaw at; upbraid; reprimand; rail at.

ধাতু *n* **1** metal; metallic ore; mineral. **2** principle/humour of the body (phlegm, wind and bile). **3** constituent part of the body (as blood, flesh, etc). **4** primary/elementary substance (earth, water, etc). **5** mettle: সে বড়ো শক্ত ধাতুতে গড়া. **6** temperament; disposition: তার ~ তো আমি জানি. **7** semen; virile. **8** property of matter (odour, flavour, etc). **9** pulse. **10** (gram) element/root of a word. **~কল্প** *n* metalloid. **~কুশল** *adj* skilled in metals. ❑*n* metallurgist. **~ক্ষয়** *n* **1** decay of one or more of the constituent principles of the body; loss of seminal fluid; seminal emission; waste of the humours; consumption. **2** abrasion of metal. **~-ক্ষয়কারক, ~ক্ষয়কারী** *adjj* causing decay of the vitals; producing mortal disease. **~ক্ষয়জনিত** *adj* produced by/arising from a decay of the vital functions. **~গত** *adj* **1** temperamental; constitutional; characteristic. **2** seminal. **~গর্ভ** *adj* metalliferous. **~ঘটিত** *adj* **1** metallic; mineral; (med) haring metal as a constituent. **2** occurring in/occasioned by the constituent parts of the body; concerning semen. **~চূর্ণ** *n* mineral powder. **~দৌর্বল্য** *n* spermatorrhoea. **~দ্রাবক** *n* borax. **~নাশন** *n* sour gruel. **~নিঃস্রব** *n* flowing out of molten metal; lava; flowing out of semen. **~পাত্র** *n* metal vessel. **~পুষ্টিকর, ~পোষক** *adjj* nutritive; nourishing. **~বল্লভ** *n* borax. **~বিকার** *n* **1**=~ক্ষয়. **2** gonorrhea. **~বিজ্ঞান, ~বিদ্যা** *nn* metallurgy.

~বিদ্ *n* metallurgist. ~ময় *adj* metallic. ~মল *n* rust. ~মাক্ষিক *n* pyrite. ~রূপ *n* conjugation. ~লেপন *n* plating. অবর~ base metal. বর~ *n* noble metal.

ধাত্রী *n fem* **1** mother; progenitress. **2** midwife. **3** nurse; wet-nurse; foster-mother. **4** earth. ❑*adj* bearing (like a mother); nourishing. ~পুত্র *n* son of a nurse-mother/wet-nurse. ~বিদ্যা *n* obstetrics; midwifery. ~বিদ্যা-বিশারদ *n* obstetrician; midwife.

ধাত্রেয়ী *n fem*=ধাত্রী (2, 3).

ধান *n* **1** paddy; rice. **2** grain (as a measure of weight). ~ কাঁড়া/ কোটা *vi* husk paddy. ~ কাড়ানো *v* plough a paddy-field in order to remove weeds. ~ দিয়ে লেখাপড়া করা (fig) **1** spend little for one's education. **2** receive scant/indifferent education. ~ নেড়ে দেওয়া *vi* **1** stir paddy while it is being dried in the sun; stir paddy when it is being husked by a husking pedal. **2** re-sow/replant paddy-shoots in well-arranged lines. ~ পালা দেওয়া *vi* stack paddy. ~ বোনা *vi* sow paddy-seeds. ~ ভাঙা/ভানা *vi* husk paddy. ~ মাড়ানো *vi* thresh paddy; separate paddy from straw (by making cows walk upon it). ~ রোয়া *vi* transplant paddy-shoots. ~ শুকানো *vi* dry paddy in the sun. ~-কাটা *n* harvest of paddy. ~কুটুনি *n* charges for husking paddy. ~ক্ষেত *n* paddy-field; paddy-land. ~চারা *n* paddy-shoot. ~দাম *n* paddy land. ~দূর্বা *n* paddy-grains and grass/used as auspicious articles in blessing. ~বাড়ি *n* loan of paddy on interest. husking machine; rice-mills. ধানের আঁটি *n* bundle of paddy. ধানের পালা *n* paddy-stack; rick of paddy. ধানের শিষ *n* ear of corn. ~ ভানতে শিবের গীত (fig) irrelevant talk/ digression. ~ ভানতে শিবের গীত গাওয়া (fig) digress; talk off the subject; get side-tracked; miss the point. কত ধানে কত চাল (fig) **1** actual state of affairs; correct position. **2** consequence; backlash. পাকা ধানে মই দেওয়া (fig) blast one's hopes when they are about to be realized; play havoc with; do sb an irreparable loss. আউস ~ *n* autumn rice. আমন ~ *n* winter rice. বীজ~ *n* paddy-seed.

ধানবাড়ি ⇒ ধান

ধানসী, ধানসি *nn* name of an Indian musical mode.

ধানাই-পানাই *n* irrelevant talk/ excuse; poppycock. ~ করা/কথা বলা *vi* talk through one's hat; talk nonsense.

ধানী[1] *adj* **1** paddy-green: ~ রং. **2** suitable for cultivation of paddy: ~ জমি. **3** very small; puny: ~ লঙ্কা. ~মদ *n* wine distilled from rice. ~ লঙ্কা *n* kind of tiny/ small capsicum.

-ধানী[2] *n* (used as a *suff*) place; residence; seat: রাজ~.

ধানুকী, ধানুষ্ক *nn* bowman; archer. ❑*adj* armed with bow and arrow; versed in archery.

ধান্দা, ধান্ধা *nn* **1**=ধাঁধা. **2** trouble; worry: দুঃখ~.

ধান্য *n* paddy; rice. ~কর্তন, ~চ্ছেদন *n* reaping/harvesting of paddy-crop. ~ক্ষেত্র *n* paddy-field; land. ~বপন *n* sowing of paddy-seeds. ~বীজ *n* paddy-seed. ~রোপণ *n* planting of rice/paddy-seeds. ~শূক *n* awn/beard of paddy.

ধান্যক, ধান্যাক *nn* coriander.

ধান্যাম্ল *n* sour gruel.

ধান্যেশ্বরী *n* (hum)=ধানী মদ (⇒ ধানী[1])

ধাপ *n* **1** step (of a staircase, etc). **2** leap; jump. **3** stratum. ধাপে ধাপে *adv* step by step; by degrees; gradually; at every step.

ধাপধারা-গোবিন্দপুর *n* (facet) an obscure, contemptible and remote place; a god-forsaken/out-of-the-way place.

ধাপা, ধাপাড় *nn* low and usually marshy land where rubbish is dumped; dumping ground. ~র মাঠ=~.

ধাপুস *n* (onom) imitating the sound of a gentle fall. ~ করে *adv* gently; highly.

ধাপ্পা *n* bluff; hoax. ~ দেওয়া *vt* bluff; hoax; fob; dupe. ~বাজ *adj* deceitful; given to bluffing/hoaxing. ❑*n* hoaxer; bluffer; fraud; humbug. ~বাজি *n* (practice of) hoaxing/bluffing. ~বাজি করা *vi* practice bluffing/hoaxing; bluff; hoax; defraud.

ধাবক[1] *adj* running. ❑*n* runner; flier; messenger; courier.

ধাবক[2] *adj* washing; cleansing: ~ পদার্থ. ❑*n* washerman.

ধাবড়া *adj* patchy and ugly; blotchy: ~ দানা. ❑*n* ugly patch; blotch; splotch: কালির ~. ~নো *vi* scatter in patches; splatter; smudge. ❑*adj* smudgy; splotched; splotchy.

ধাবন[1] *n* running; galloping; race; flight. ~ করা *vi* run; fly. ~-পথ *n* air-strip.

ধাবন[2] *n* washing; cleansing. ~ করা *vt* wash; cleanse.

ধাবমান *adj* running; flying; fleeting.

ধাবিত[1] *adj* running; having begun to run; flying; fleeting; in flight. ~ করা *vt* cause to run/fly; run. ~ হওয়া *vi* run; fly; to take to one's heels.

ধাবিত[2] *adj* washed; cleansed. ~ করা *vt* wash. ~ হওয়া *vi* be washed; wash.

ধাম *n* (used chiefly as a *suff)* **1** dwelling-place; house; abode; domain; residence: নিজ ~. **2** address: নাম-~. **3** seat; site; place; holy place: আনন্দ~, বৃন্দাবন ~. **4** repository; receptacle: গুণধাম.

ধামনিক *adj* arterial; venous; nervous.

ধামসানো *vt* **1** trample sb (down). **2** smite; give sb a good thrashing; smack/ punch repeatedly.

ধামা *n* scuttle/basket of rattan. **~চাপা** *adj* concealed; hushed-up; shelved. **~চাপা দেওয়া** *vt* conceal; hush up; shelve. **~ধরা** *v* fawn on; cringe to/before sb; truckle to sb; ingratiate oneself with. **~ধরা** *adj* cringing; fawning; obsequious; ingratiating. ❑*n* toady; sycophant; hanger on; servile flatterer. **~ধামা** *adv* baskets of.

ধামার *n* name of an Indian musical mode.

ধামী *n* small basket.

-ধার[১] *adj* (used as a subject) holding; gripping; supporting; containing: বর্ণ~.

ধার[২] *n* stream; flow.

ধার[৩] *n* **1** edge; end; boundary; border; brim; brink; brow: নদীর ~, পথের ~, পাহাড়ের ~, brow of a hill. **2** side; face: এ ধার; ওধার. **3** nearness; proximity; vicinity; contiguity; approach: বাজারের ধারে. **4** sharpness; edge: তরবারির ~. **5** keenness; sharpness; acuity: বুদ্ধির ~. **6** intelligence; acumen; wit. **~ করা/ দেওয়া** *vt* sharpen; whet; put an edge on. **হয় ধারে কাটা নয় ভারে কাটা** (fig) pass/be counted highly by virtue either of merit/worth or of position/ weight/ importance.

ধার[৪] *n* debt; loan; credit. **~ করা** *vt* borrow; have the loan of (sth); get sth loan. **~ চাওয়া** *v* ask for a loan. **~ চুকানো** *vt* repay/settle a loan. **~ দেওয়া** *vt* lend; loan. **~ ধারা** *vi* **1** fig) care for; have any concern with; pay heed to. **~ না ধারা** (fig) not care (for); who cares? not care/give a damn (about sb). **~ পড়া** *vi* owe; be outstanding: পাঁচ শ টাকা ~ পড়েছে. **~ হওয়া** *vi* be in debt. **ধারে কেনা/বেচা** *vi* buy/sell on credit. **ধারে কেনা-বেচা** *n* buying and selling on credit. **ধারে খাটানো** *vt* lend/loan on interest. **ধারে ডোবা** *vi* be over head and ears in debt; be deeply involved in debt; run into debt. **~কর্জ, ~ধোর** *nn* loans.

ধারক *adj* keeping; holding; containing; possessing; carrying; bearing; preserving; supporting; upholding. ❑*n* container; receptacle; repository; upholder; champion: সংস্কৃতির ~. **~তা** *nn* capacity.

ধারণ *n* **1** preserving; protecting; maintaining; possessing; having: যিনি এই বিশ্বলোককে ~ করছেন. **2** putting on; wearing: পোশাক ~. **3** assuming: মূর্তি~. **4** carrying; carriage: গর্ভে ~. **5** retaining in memory: চঞ্চলমতির জন্যে কোনো বিষয়ই সে ~ করতে পারে না. **6** bearing: ভার/মোট ~. **7** keeping; wearing: বাতের জন্য কটিতে মাদুলি ~. **8** retaining; retention: প্রস্রাবের বেগ ~. **9** holding; containing: এই পাত্রটি কত জল ~ করতে পারবে? **10** accepting; acceptance: আপনার আদেশ/উপদেশ আমি শিরে ~ করে নিচ্ছি. **~ করা** *vt* **1** maintain; keep; preserve; possess; have. **2** put on; wear. **3** assume. **4** carry in the womb. **5** retain in memory; remember. **6** bear. **7** wear; keep. **8** retain. **9** hold; contain. **10** accept. **~কারী** *adj.* keeping; bearing; holding; maintaining; wearing; assuming; carrying. (⟹ the meanings of ~ above). **~কারিণী** *fem.* **~শক্তি** *n* capacity; powers of retention.

ধারণা *n* **1** conception; concept. **2** notion; idea; faith; belief. **3** realization; comprehension; understanding. **4** (retentive) memory; remembrance. **5** feeling; impression. **6** supposition; assumption; surmise. **7** collection/ concentration of the mind; rapt attention. **8** conclusion. **~ করা** *vt* **1** conceive. **2** realize; understand; comprehend; grasp. **3** suppose; assume; guess; form/have an idea (of). **4** feel; have an impression (of); believe; think. **~তীত** *adj* inconceivable; incomprehensible; unimaginable. **~বান** *adj* intelligent. **~শক্তি** *n* ability to conceive an idea; comprehension; retentive capacity/ power; mental ability; intelligence.

ধারণীয় *adj* to be held/ borne/ sustained; capable of being held/ borne/ retained; conceivable (⟹ meanings of ধারণ above).

ধারয়িতা=ধারক (⟹ ধারণ). **ধারয়িত্রী** *fem* (as a *n*) the earth.

ধারয়িষ্ণু *adj* capable of bearing; accustomed to bear.

ধারা[১] *vi* **1** owe. **2** have any connection or concern with: ধার ~. (⟹ ধার[৩]).

ধারা[২] *n* **1** stream; current of water; flow: শোণিত~. **2** flood; gush; jet; drop (of any liquid). **3** shower; rain (also fig of arrows, flowers, etc). **4** spring; fountain; water fall; cascade. **5** system; method; way: কাজের ~? **6** fashion; manner: এ কেমন ~? **7** succession; continuous line/ series; serial order; train: চিন্তা~. **8** line of a family: বংশ~. **9** rule; go; way: সংসারের ধারাই এ রকম. **10** (law) clause; paragraph; section. **11** pace of a horse. **12** custom; usage; practice. **~কদম্ব** *n* name of a tree bearing beautiful globular flowers in the rainy season; *Nauclea cordifolia*. **~কারে** *adv* in/like a stream; streamingly; profusely; in a continuous stream; ceaselessly. **~ক্রমে** *adv* according to system/method; methodically; systematically; serially; successively. **~গৃহ** *n* bath-room with flowing water; shower-bath. **~স্কুর** *n* rain-drop. **~ট** name of a bird (=চাতক). **~ধর** *n* 'water-bearer'; cloud. **ধারানি** *n* **1** flow of tears. **2** torrent of rain. **~নিবদ্ধ** *adj* systematic; methodical. **~বর্ত** *n* whirlpool. **~বর্ষ(ণ)** *n* torrent of rain; heavy/incessant rain/ downpour. **~বাহিক, ~বাহী** *adjj* continuous; serial; successive. **~বাহিকতা** *n* sequence; continuity; succession; seriality. **~বাহিকভাবে** *adv* continuously serially; successively. **~যন্ত্র** *n* fountain; shower; shower-bath; syringe;

spraying apparatus. ~শ্রাবণ *n* month of Shravan when it rains incessantly; rainy Shravan. ~শ্রু *n* flood of tears. ~সম্পাত, ~সার *nn*=~পাত (1) (⇒ below).

ধারা[৩] *n* sharp edge; rim; blade (of a sword, etc). ~গ্র *n* broad-edged head of an arrow. ~বিষ ⇒ below.

ধারাপাত *n* **1** rain-shower; torrential rain/ downpour. **2** arithmetical tables.

ধারাবিষ *n* having a poisoned edge; sword; scimitar.

ধারালো , ধারাল *adjj* sharp; sharp-edged; incisive; trenchant; keen.

ধারি, ধারী[১] *nn* **1** narrow verandah/gallery of a mud-built house. **2** edge.

ধারিণী *adj fem* of ধারী[২]. ❑*n* the earth.

ধারী[২] *adj* (used as a *suff)*=ধারণকারী (⇒ ধারণ).

ধারোষ্ণ *adj* (of milk) warm from the cow.

ধার্তরাষ্ট্র *n* son of king Dhritarashtra.

ধার্মিক *adj* righteous; pious; virtuous; just; righteous-minded; religious; godly. ❑*n* pious/righteous/religious person. **ধার্মিকা** *fem.* ~তা, ~ত্ব *nn* piety; righteousness godliness; virtuousness; justice; religiosity.

ধার্য *adj* **1** to be upheld/maintained. **2** to be observed/followed: শিরো~. **3** to be inflicted/ imposed on. **4** to be borne/ worn/ carried. **5** to be fixed/ settled. ~ করা *vt* **1** impose; inflict: জরিমানা/ কর ~ করা. **2** fix: দিন ~ করা. ~মান *adj* being held/ maintained/ fixed/ imposed/ settled.

ধার্ষ্টামি, ধার্ষ্টামো, ধার্ষ্ট্য *nn* impertinence; audacity; sauciness; insolence; boldness; pertness; knavery. ~ করা *vi* be impertinent/ saucy; behave impertinently.

ধিক *n, int* fie! shame! out upon! what a pity! pooh! **ধিককার, ধিক্‌ক্রিয়া** reproach; contempt; scooting; crying fie upon.**ধিক্‌কার দেওয়া** *v* reproach; reprimand; curse; cry fie upon; hoot. pooh-pooh ! **ধিককৃত** *adj* cursed; hooted; mocked; derided; reproached. ❑ *n* reproach; contempt. ~ জীবন *n* cursed life. হা ~! Woe me! Woe betide sb!

ধিকধিক *n* (onom) expressing: quivering; burning slowly as if about to go out; flicker; gentle glow. ~ (করে) জ্বলা *vi* flicker; shimmer; glimmer; smoulder; burn slowly.

ধিকিধিকি *n* (onom)=ধিকধিক. ❑*adj* flickering; shimmering; glimmering; smouldering; quivering; glowing: ~ আগুন.

ধিক্কার=ধিককার(⇒ ধিক)

ধিক্কৃত=ধিককৃত(⇒ ধিক)

ধিঙ্গি, ধিঙ্গী *adj* **1** husky. **2** romping; unruly; wayward; immodest; unseemly; brazen; brassy; shameless; wanton; impudent. ❑*n* **1** leader/chief (of a gang). **2** *fem*=~ মেয়ে. ~পনা *n* immodest/ unseemly/ shameless behaviour; antics, high jinks; romping and revelries. ~ মেয়ে *n* brazen; hussy; shameless/ immodest girl; tomboy; wench; slut.

ধিন ধিন, ধিন–তা–ধিন *nn* (onom) imitating sound produced by some musical instruments; keywords indicating the measure of a dance.

ধিমা *adj* slow; mild; low; sluggish; lazy. (⇒ ঢিমা).

ধিষণ *n* intelligence; intellect.

ধী *n* intelligence; intellect; understanding; cognition; reflection; meditation; wisdom; knowledge. ~দীপ্ত *adj* brilliant; bright; intelligent; keen-minded. ~মান *adj* intelligent; sensible; talented; clever; quick-witted; smart; agile. ~মতী *fem.* ~শক্তি *n* mental/intellectual faculty. ~শক্তিসম্পন্ন=~মান.

ধীবর *n* fisherman. **ধীবরী** *fem* fisher-woman.

ধীমতি,ধীমান ⇒ ধী

ধীর *adj* **1** steady; constant; firm; resolute; self-possessed; unperturbed; composed; calm; grave; energetic: ~চিত্ত. **2** unhurried; slow; gentle; tardy: ~গতি. **3** deep; low; dull; saft: ~ কণ্ঠ. **4** gentle; mild; well-bred; modest; cool: ~ স্বভাব, ~ বায়ু. **5** judicious; considerate; prudent: ~ মানুষ. ~চিত্ত *adj* strong-minded; self-possessed; self-composed. ~তা, ~ত্ব *nn* **1** slowness; gentleness; mildness; modesty. **2** calm; coolness; calmness; fortitude; firmness; courage; composure; unperturbedness; steadiness; gravity; judiciousness; considerateness. ~প্রকৃতি *adj* gentle/modest by nature. ~প্রশান্ত *adj* deep and calm: ~ প্রশান্ত স্বর; constant and calm: ~ প্রশান্ত নায়ক. ~ভাব *n* constancy; firmness. ~ভাবে *adj* slowly; mildly; gently; calmly; firmly. ~ললিত *n* (rhet) firm and brave, but reckless and sportive (as a hero). ~ললিতা *fem.* ~ স্বভাব=~ প্রকৃতি. ~ স্থির *adj* calm and composed.

ধীরা *adj fem* of ধীর. ❑*n* (rhet) woman who keeps down of expression of resentment/ jealousy. ~ধীরা *n* (rhet) a jealous woman who alternately expresses and suppresses her jealousy.

ধীরি, ~ধীরি *adv* (poet)=ধীরে.

ধীরে, ~ ধীরে *advv* slowly; gently; softly; leisurely; by degrees; tardily; by fits and bounds; gradually; little by little. ~সুস্থে *adv* in a leisurely manner; sluggishly; ponderously; in due course; with deliberation; (undue) haste.

নাচা *vi, vt* **1** dance. **2** leap (in joy): হৃদয় নেচে ওঠে. **3** dance to sb's tune: পরের কথায় ~. **4** twinkle; sparkle; vibrate; shake: চোখ ~. **5** caper: ছাগল ~. ☐*n* =নাচ. **নাচতে না জানলে উঠান বাঁকা** (prov) A bad workman quarrels with his tools. **নাচতে নেমে ঘোমটা দেওয়া** (fig) sham/ feigned/ hypocritical modesty. **~কোঁদা** *n*=নর্তন-কুর্দন (⇒ নর্তন). **~নাচি** *n* dancing; frolicking; merriment; excitement. **~নো** *vt* **1** (cause to) dance. **2** work up; make sb dance to one's tune; excite; lead sb by the nose.

নাচার *adj* constrained; helpless; destitute.

নাচি *n* rivet. **~ করা** *vt* rivet.

নাচিয়ে *n* dancer. ☐*adj*=নাচনী (⇒ নাচ).

নাচুনি *n*=নাচনি (⇒ নাচ)

নাচুনী *n, adj*= নাচুনি (⇒ নাচ)

নাচুনে *n , adj*=নাচনি (⇒ নাচ)

নাছ [A] *n* road; path; way. **~-দুয়ার** *n* **1** front door. **2** back door.

নাছোড় *adj* unyielding; obstinate; pertinacious; stubborn; unrelenting; unbending; refusing to give up: ~বান্দা.

নাজাত [A] *n* freedom; salvation; liberation; deliverance; escape; absolution.

নাজায়েজ, নাজায়িজ *adjj* unlawful; contraband.

নাজিম [A] *n* administrator; governor; ruler; manager; director; controller.

নাজির [A] *n* sheriff in a civil court; supervisor; bailiff; superintendent; inspector. **নাজিরি** *n* office of a nazir.

নাজিল *adj* descending; alighting; arriving at. **~ হওয়া** *vi* descend; fall/ come down; alight.

নাজুক [P] *adj* delicate; fragile; brittle; gracious; subtle; elegant; nice.

নাজেল=নাজিল

নাজেহাল [P] *n* delicate situation. ☐*adj* harassed; pestered; tormented; persecuted; molested. **~ করা** *vt* harass; torment; molest; abuse; ill-treat; persecute; heckle.

নাট *n* **1** dance. **2** acting; dramatic performance. **3** fun; joke. **4** stage. **~মন্দির, ~শালা** *nn* hall within/ in front of a temple for devotional dancing and musical performances; theatre; opera-house; ball-room; dancing-hall. **নাটের গুরু** *n* **1** director of a performance. **2** (iron) ringleader; mastermind; instigator; wire-pulled.

নাটক *n* drama; play; mime.

নাটকিত *adj* dramatized.

নাটকীয় *adj* dramatic; theatrical; histrionic.

নাটা[1] *adj* **1** dwarfish; short. **2** round; globular: ~ চোখ.

নাটা[2] *n* name of a climbing thorny shrub; *Caesalpinia bonducella.*

নাটা[3] *n* reel for silk.

নাটাই *n* reel; spool; bobbin.

নাটা-দুরবিন *n* opera-glass.

নাটানো *vi, vt* **1** reel (silk/ thread): wind up/ ravel in. **2** roll.

নাটিকা *n* short play/ drama; playlet.

নাটুকে *adj* **1** dramatic; theatrical; histrionic: ~ চালচলন. **2** theatre-loving; writing drama. ~ রামনারায়ণ. **~পনা** *n* theatrical behaviour/ manners; histrionics; dramatics.

নাটুয়া *adj* performing; acting; dancing. ☐*n* dancer; actor.

নাট্য *n* **1** dramatic art; theatre; dramatics. **2** dancing; mimic representation. **3** play; drama. **4** dances, songs and music; performing arts. **~কলা** *n* dramatics; theatre. **~কার** *n* playwright; dramatist. **~গৃহ** *n* theatre; dancing-hall; opera-house; music-hall. **~দুরবিন** *n* opera-glass. **~মন্দির, ~শালা** =~গৃহ. **~রসিক** *adj* theatergoing. ☐*n* connoisseur of drama. **~-সমিতি** *n* dramatic society. **নাট্যাচার্য** *n* dancing-master; great actor. **নাট্যাভিনয়** *n* dramatic performance. **নাট্যালয়**=~গৃহ.

নাট্যোক্তি *n* dramatic phraseology/ dialogue.

নাট্যোল্লিখিত *adj* mentioned in a drama. **~ ব্যক্তিবর্গ** *n* dramatis personae.

নাড়ন *n* stirring; moving.

নাড়া[1] *vt* **1** move; put in motion; oscillate. **2** shake; stir: দুধটা ভালো করে নেড়ে দাও. **3** shift; remove; transfer; move: খাটটা এখন ~ যাবে না. **4** give a jerk; push; jolt; give a jolt: ঘটনাটা তাকে খুব ~ দিয়েছে. **5** wave: হাত ~. **6** wag: লেজ ~. **7** ring; sound: ঘণ্টা ~. **8** handle: টাকা-পয়সা ~. **9** mix up; muddle; rummage through: কাগজপত্রগুলি কে নেড়েছে? **10** flutter: পাখা ~. **11** study; pore over: শাস্ত্র ~. **12** loosen: গোড়ার মাটিটা নেড়ে দিতে হবে. **13** sound sb out: লোকটা কে? একটু নেড়ে দেখলে হতো না? **~ খাওয়া** *vi* be shaken/ stirred/ jolted; jerk. **~ দেওয়া** *vt* stir; shake; jolt; give a jolt; jerk; push. **~চাড়া, ~নাড়ি** *nn* **1** moving; stirring; shifting; rummaging; rummage; displacing. **2** casual study; browsing: শাস্ত্র ~চাড়া. **3** handling: টাকা-পয়সা ~চাড়া. **4** dealing with; deliberation; examination; debate: তথ্য নিয়ে ~চাড়া. **5** tittle-tattle; petty gossip: পরের কলঙ্ক নিয়ে ~চাড়া. **6** sounding; testing. **~চাড়া করা** *vt* **1** stir; shift; rummage through; displace; move. **2** pore over; browse; study casually. **3** handle. **4** deal with; deliberate about/ on; examine; debate. **5** gossip (about sth); tittle-tattle. **6** sound sb out. **~নো** *vt* **1** move; put in action; oscillate. **2** shake; stir. **3** remove; shift; move; displace. **4** shake; stir; wave; twinkle; dangle: জিহ্বা ~নো. **5** push; give a jerk/ jolt.

নাড়া[2] *n* stubble. **~বুনে** *n* **1** cultivator; peasant; farmer. **2** rustic; clodhopper; dunce.

নাড়ি, নাড়ী *nn* **1** any tubular organ (as a vein or artery of the body). **2** pulse: ~ দেখা. **3** umbilical cord: ~-ছেঁড়া ধন. **4** intestines: ~ জ্বলা.

~ কাটা *vi* cut the umbilical cord. ~ ছেঁড়া/জ্বলা *vi* have agonizing pain in the stomach. ক্ষুধায় ~ জ্বলা *vi* be famished; starve. ~ টেপা/দেখা *vi* feel sb's pulse. ~ মরা *vi* lose appetite; suffer from anorexia. ~ঘাত *n* pulse-beat. ~ঘাতের হার (প্রতি মিনিটে) *n* pulse-rate. ~চক্র *n* (occult) navel-circle (combination of sixteen tubular organs). ~জ্ঞান *n* **1** ability to feel a patient's pulse; diagnostic skill. **2** ability to see at a glance the state of a thing; discernment; judgement; acumen. ~নক্ষত্র *n* **1** planet of a person's nativity. **2** thorough knowledge; ins and outs; details. ~ব্রণ=নালীব্রণ (⇒ নালি). ~ভুঁড়ি *n* entrails; intestines. ~ছেঁড়া ধন *n* one's flesh and blood (said of a child). ~টেপা (ডাক্তার) *adj, n* (iron) quack; charlatan. ~মরা *adj* having little appetite; anorexic; anorectic.

নাড়ু *n* a sweet drop.

নাত[1] [A] *n* praise (especially of the Holy Prophet); a song in praise of the Holy Prophet.

নাত[2] *n* (in compounds)=নাতি. ~জামাই *n* husband of a grand-daughter. ~বউ, ~বৌ *nn* wife of a grandson.

নাতনি=নাতিনী (⇒ নাতি[1])

নাতি[1] *n* grandson. ~নী *fem* grand-daughter. ~পুতি *n* grand-children.

নাতি[2] *adv* (used as a *pref*) not very/ much; not too; moderately. ~খর্ব *adj* not very short/ dwarfish; moderately tall; of moderately tall; of medium height. ~দীর্ঘ *adj* not too long. ~বিলম্ব, ~বিলম্বিত *adjj* not too late. ~শীতল *adj* not too/moderately cold. ~শীতোষ্ণ *adj* neither too cold nor too hot; temperate. ~শীতোষ্ণমণ্ডল *n* (geog) temperate zone. ~স্থূল *adj* not very fat/ bulky. ~হ্রস্ব=~খর্ব.

নাৎসি [G] *n* Naji.

নাথ[1] *n* protector; master; patron; lord; owner; possessor; husband; custodian; guardian. ~বতী *adj fem* having a husband.

নাথ[2] *n* rope attached to a bull's nosering.

নাদ[1] *n* loud sound; roar(ing); bellowing; any sound/ tone; crying. নাদা *vi* (poet) roar; bellow.

নাদ[2] *n* droppings (of cattle); dung. নাদা *vi* **1** (of cattle) excrete; defecate. **2** (derog) make dirty work of.

নাদ[3], নাদা *nn* large earthen trough; vat; tun. নাদা-পেটা *adj* pot-bellied; abdominous; tun-bellied.

নাদন[1] *n* excretion (of cattle).

নাদন[2], নাদনা *nn* heavy stick.

নাদান [P] *adj* ignorant; silly; foolish; innocent. নাদানি *n* ignorance; foolishness.

নাদারৎ=নদারৎ

নাদিত *adj* made to resound; sounding (with); reverberant.

নাদী *adj* (often used as a *suff*) sounding; resonant; howling; roaring. নাদিনী *fem.*

না-দুরস্ত (দোরস্ত) *adj* not right; incorrect; wrong; false; untrue; crooked; improper; imperfect.

নাদুসনুদুস *adj* portly; roly-poly; plump; buxom; fleshy; rotund;

নাদেয়, নাদ্য *adj* coming from/ belonging to a river; fluvial; aquatic; riverine.

না-ধর্মী *adj* negative.

নানকপন্থী, নানকশাহী *adj, n* following Guru Nanak (founder of Sikhism); Sikh.

নানা[1] *n* maternal grandfather.

নানা[2] *adj* different; various; diverse. ~কার *adj* manifold; various. ~ কারণ *n* various reasons. ~ জাতি *n* different races/ nations. ~জাতীয় *adj* of many and/ diverse kinds; of various kinds. ~ত্ব *n* diversity; variety. ~ দেশ *n* different regions/ countries. ~দেশীয় *adj* of/coming from different/ various countries. ~ প্রকার *adj* of various kinds/ descriptions; manifold. ~ প্রকারে *adv* in various ways/ means. ~বর্ণ *n* various colours. ❑*adj* many-coloured; variegated; dappled; pied. ~বিধ, ~বিধি *adjj* of various sorts; manifold; multiform. ~মত *n* different opinions/ views. ~মতে *adv*=~প্রকারে. ~রূপ *nn* various forms/ shapes. ❑*adj* of various forms/ descriptions/ kinds; multiform; manifold; various. ~রূপে *adv* **1** in different forms/ shapes. **2**=~ প্রকারে. ~র্থ *adj* having different meaning; homonymous. ~র্থ বোধকতা *n* homonym. ~র্থ শব্দ *n* homonym. ~র্থক *adj* multipurpose. ~স্থানী *adj* abiding in different places; without any fixed abode; vagrant; roving; wandering. ~স্থানী হওয়া *vi* abide in different places; rove about.

নানী *n fem* (of নানা[1]) maternal grandmother.

নান্দী *n* eulogism/ praise of a deity; kind of blessing pronounced as a prologue in a drama; invocation. ~কর *n* speaker of the prologue/ invocation. ~পট *n* lid of a well. ~পাঠ *n* recital of the prologue/ invitation (at the opening of a drama). ~মুখ *n* obsequial rite performed at the start of a happy ceremony.

নাপছন্দ [P] *adj* disliked; unacceptable; disapproved; disagreeable. ~ করা *vt* disapprove; dislike; reject.

নাপতিনী *n* (colloq)=নাপিতানী (⇒ নাপিত)

নাপতে *n* (colloq)=নাপিত

নাপাক [P] *adj* polluted; dirty; unclean; filthy; impure; defiled; lewd. নাপাকি *n* impurity; uncleanliness; defilement; pollution; lewdness.

নাপিত *n* barber. নাপিতানী *fem.*

নাফরমান [P] *adj* disobedient. **নাফরমানি** *n* disobedience.

নাফা [A] *n* profit; gain; advantage; interest; good; benefit.

নাবা *vi* (colloq)=নামা. ~নো=নামানো.

নাবাল *adj* low: ~ জমি.

নাবালক, নাবালগ, নাবলিগ, নাবালেগ [P] *adj* underage; immature; inexperienced. ❑*n* minor. **নাবালিকা** *fem.*

নাবি *adj* (of agricultural produce) late (in growing)

নাবিক *adj* belonging to a boat/ ship; nautical. ❑*n* boatman, sailor; navigator. ~**বিদ্যা** *n* navigation.

নাবী=নাবি

নাবুদ [P] *adj* non-existent; annihilated; destroyed; vanished; extinct.

নাব্য *adj* navigable. ~**তা** *n* navigability.

নাভি *n* **1** navel; umbilicus. **2** nave (of a wheel); hub. **3** navel-like cavity. **4** centre; central point. **5** (phys) focus. ~**কমল** *n* lotus-like navel. ~**কুণ্ডল**, ~**কূপ** *nn* umbilical cavity; deep navel; depression in the middle of a navel. ~**চ্ছেদন** *n* cutting off of the umbilical cord. ~**দেশ** *n* region of the navel. ~**পদ্ম**=~কমল. ~**লম্ব** *n* (glom) lotus rectum. ~**শ্বাস** *n* last gasp; death-rattle; pangs of death. ~**শ্বাস ওঠা** *vi* be at one's last gasp; gasp for air/ breath; drop with fatigue; be totally exhausted; be worn out; pant for breath.

নাম *n* **1** name; appellation; personal name; designation; title. **2** good/ great name; renown; fame; reputation. **3** mention; name: একটা ফুলের ~ করো. **4** remembrance: সে কি আমার ~ করে? **5** identity: কিছুতেই সে ~ বলতে চায় না. **6** plea; pretext; pretense: কাজের ~ করে অফিস ফাঁকি. **7** roll (call): ~ ডাকা. **8** small amount; trace; iota: ~মাত্র কালির দাগ. **9** mere words; empty talk: কেবল ~মাত্র কাজের কিছুই নয়. **10** nominal existence/ possession: নামেই বড়ো সাহেব কাজে নয়, in name only. **11** name (in calling sb/ sth to witness): আল্লাহর নামে, in Allah's name. **12** (gram) noun; substantic. ~ **করা** *vi* **1** mention (sb's name); name; utter the name of. **2** become famous; make a name for oneself/ make one's name; cut a figure. **3** recite/ invoke the name of one's idol: সাধুরা ~ জপছে. **4** name a child. ~ **করে** *adv* **1** on/ under the pretext of: কাজের ~ করে সিনেমায় যাওয়া. **2** in the name of: খোদার ~ করে বলছি. ~ **করে যাওয়া** *vi* leave a good name behind. ~ **কাটা** *vi* strike off sb/ sb's name; remove sb's name (from a register, roll, etc); expel; rusticate. ~**কাটা** *adj* dismissed; expelled: ~-কাটা সিপাই. ~ **খারাপ করা** *vi* defame; dishonour; disgrace. ~ **গাওয়া** *vi* celebrate sb's name; repeat the name of (devotionally); praise; laud. ~ **জপা** *vi* tell one's beads. ~ **ডাকা** *n* call sb by his name; call the name; summon sb loudly by name. ~ **ডোবানো** *vi* bring disgrace upon; drag sb/ sb's name through the mire/ mud. ~ **দেওয়া** *vi* **1** give a name; name; christen; baptize. **2** propose (sb's name). **3** blame; accuse; put/lay the blame (for sth) on sb. ~ **ধরা** *vi* **1** pronounce/ utter/ tell the name of. **2** assume a name/ designation. ~ **ধরে ডাকা** *vi* call/ summon by sb's name. ~ **নেওয়া** *vi* utter/ pronounce the name of; remember; worship; recite the name of (God, a deity, etc). ~ **বলা** *vi* tell one's name; name; mention. ~ **রটা** *vi* become famous/ notorious; make one's name; make one's mark; make a splash; build/establish/make up/ gain a reputation for oneself; achieve fame; win one's spurs: ~ **রটানো** *vi* make famous/ notorious; glorify; publicize; acclaim; lionize. ~ **রাখা** *vi* **1** give a name to; name; christen; baptize; designate. **2** live up to the reputation of; be on honour to: বংশের ~ রাখা. **3** leave behind a lasting name; go down in history. ~ **লওয়া**=~ নেওয়া. ~ **লাগানো** *vt* accuse; charge. ~ **লেখা** *vi* write one's name; register; record; enter sth (up) (in sth); sign; enroll. ~ **লেখানো** *vi* enter one's name/ put one's name down; apply to enter (a course, school, etc); have oneself enlisted/ enrolled/ registered; become a member of; enter. ~ **শোনানো** *vi* sing the name of (a deity) to sb. ~ **হওয়া** *vi* be famous/ renowned; gain a reputation for oneself. (⇒ ~ রটা). ~ **হারানো** *vi* suffer in reputation; get a bad name. ~**ক** *adj* by name; called; named; designated. ~**করণ** *n* **1** naming; name-giving; nomenclature. **2** ceremony of naming a child after birth. ~**করণ করা** *vi* give a name to; name; christen; baptize; designate. ~**করা** *adj* reputed; famous; illustrious; celebrated; notorious; renowned; noted. ~**কীর্তন** *n* mentioning the name of; incessant reputation of the name of God/ a god; praising; celebration of a name. ~**কীর্তন করা** *vi* repeat incessantly the name of God/ a god; sing the praises of; celebrate/ glorify the name of. ~**গন্ধ** *n* slightest trace/ mention/ sign. ~**গান**=~কীর্তন. ~**গোত্র** *n* personal and family name. ~**গোত্রহীন** *adj* (fig) having no established position/ credentials; nondescript; undistinctive; baseborn. ~**গ্রহণ** *n* calling by name; naming. ~**চিহ্নিত** *adj* marked with a name. ~**জপ** *n* incessant reputation of the name of God/ a god. ~ **জপ করা/ জপা** *vii* repeat incessantly the name of God/ a god. ~**জাদা**=~করা. ~**জারি** *n* **1** mutation/ substitution of a name in an official register (esp in lands records). **2** publication/ upholding of one's name. ~ জারি করা *vi* **1** alter/ substitute a name in an official register. **2** publicize/ uphold a name. ~ডাক *n* fame; celebrity; name and fame; prominence. prestige; reputation. ~ডাকওয়ালা *adj* prominent (in public life); notable; of note; pre-eminent. ~ত *adj* by name; namely; in name only; nominally. ❑*adj* nominal; titular. ~ধর *adj* bearing the name; being called. ~ধাতু *n* (gram) verbal noun. ~ধাম *n* name and address. ~ধারক, ~ধারী *adjj*=~ধর. ~ধারণ *n* assuming/ bearing a name/ designation. ~ ধারণ করা *vi* assume/ bear a name/ designation. ~ধেয় *adj* named; called; designated. ❑*n* name; title; appellation; designation. ~নিশান(া) *n* **1** name and address/ particulars; trade mark. **2**=~গন্ধ. ~পদ *n* (gram) noun. ~-প্রত্যাহার *n* withdrawal of one's name/ candidature. ~বর্জিত *adj* nameless. ~বাচক *adj* (gram) expressing/ denoting a name; proper. ~বাচক বিশেষ্য *n* proper noun. ~বিহীন *adj* nameless; anonymous; obscure; unknown. ~ভূমিকা *n* title-role; name-part. ~মাত্র *adj* nominal; only a little/ few; titular. ❑*adv* nominally; merely; in name only; only a little/ few. ❑*n* mere name; slightest hint/ mention; slightest amount. ~মালা *n* list of names; nomenclature. ~মুদ্রা *n* seal (-ring) with a name (engraved on it). ~মুদ্রাঙ্কিত *adj* sealed with a seal bearing a name. ~যশ *n* fame; renown. ~লোপ *n* extinction of a person's name; loss/ decay of reputation. ~শরণ *adj* taking refuge in sb's name. ~সঙ্কীর্তন=~কীর্তন. ~সর্বস্ব *adj* existing merely in name. ❑*n* mere name. ~স্মরণ *n* remembrance of sb's name (esp of God/ a god). ~হারা, ~হীন=~বিহীন. নামাঙ্ক *n* mark of a name. নামাঙ্কন *n* marking with a name. নামাঙ্কশোভিত *adj* adorned with the mark of the name/ name and cipher. নামাঙ্কিত *adj* marked with a name; bearing a signature; signed; carved/ engraved with a name; with a name carved/ engraved. নামান্তর *n* another/ different name; difference only in name and not in any other respect. নামাবলি, নামাবলী *n* **1** piece of scarf with names of a deity printed on it. **2** list of names; nomenclature. নামামৃত *n* a name as sweet as nactar. নামাশ্রিত *adj* secured/ protected by a name. নামে *adj* by name; named; called; designated; in name only; nominal; titular. ❑*adv* in name only. নামে নামে *adv* separately by/ in/ under individual names. নামে গোয়ালা কাঁজি ভক্ষণ a milkman in name only, not in his way of life; (fig) a person whose way of life is not in accordance with his profession. ছদ্ম~ *n* pseudonym. ডাক-~ *n* nickname. ভালো-~ *n* name by which one is known to the public; formal name. ভুল ~ *n* misnomer.

নামঞ্জুর [P] *adj* disallowed; refused; rejected; disapproved; inadmissible; turned down. ~ করা *vt* turn down; not allow; disallow; reject; disapprove. নামঞ্জুরি *n* disapproval; rejection.

নামতা *n* (arith) multiplication table.

নামা[1] *adj* (used as a *suff)* named; by name; called; bearing a particular name; designated. অজ্ঞাত~ *adj* nameless; unknown.

নামা[2] [P] *n* (used as a *suff)* **1** letter; writing; deed: চুক্তি~. **2** written authorization: ওকালত~. **3** history; chronicle; narrative: জঙ্গ~.

নামা[3] *vi* **1** descend; come/ go/ get down; alight; get off; dismount; climb down: গাছ থেকে ~. **2** get out of; disembark: জাহাজ থেকে ~. **3** go down into; descend into: জলে ~. **4** enter into; get down to; get in on sth; join: তর্কে/ ব্যবসায়ে ~. **5** stoop; slope; sink; incline; cave in; become lower/ depressed: বাড়ির ছাদ ~, পথটা এখানে নেমে গেছে. **6** ebb; go out: জোয়ারের পানি নামছে. **7** go down: তাপমাত্রা তিন ডিগ্রি নেমেছে. **8** land; go on shore; come down, উড়োজাহাজ নেমেছে, তীরে ~. **9** stoop (low): এতো নীচে সে নামল কী করে? **10** decrease; fall; come down; abate: জ্বর ~. **11** go down; come down; fall; plummet: বাজারদর নেমে যাওয়া. **12** set; go down: সূর্য পাটে নেমেছে. **13** set in; begin; come down: বৃষ্টি বুঝি নামলো. **14** come out in; set out: পথে ~. **15** flow out; stream (down): চোখের জল ~. **16** appear in; present oneself; take (the floor, etc): আসরে ~. **17** degrade: তার চরিত্র অনেক নেমে গেছে. **18** be downgraded/ degraded: উচ্চপদ/ ক্লাস থেকে ~. **19** have loose motion/ diarrhoea: পেট ~. **20** come down to sth: তার চুল পিঠ পর্যন্ত নেমেছে. **21** cool/ calm down: তার সে রাগ আর নেই, সে এখন অনেক নেমে এসেছে. **22** become milder; bend; relent; budge: তার ধনুক-ভাঙা পণ আর নেই, এখন দর নেমে এসেছে. **23** quote a lower price/ easier terms: আমি আর নামতে পারব না, নিলে এই দামেই নিতে হবে. **24** go into: রাজনীতিতে ~. ~-ওঠা *n* descending and ascending. ❑*adj* sunk; depressed: ~ জমি.

নামাজ [P] *n* prayer (esp as prescribed by Islam); divine service; adoration.

নামানো *vt* **1** bring/ reach down: মালপত্র ~. **2** lower; let sth down: চোখ/ বোঝা/ পাল/ পতাকা/ দাম ~. **3** unload: জাহাজ থেকে মাল ~. **4** degrade; demote; downgrade: নীচের পদে ~. **5** deprave; corrupt: ছেলেটাকে সে অনেক নীচে নামিয়েছে. **6** cause to come down/ set in: বৃষ্টি ~. **7** cause to appear in; bring: আসরে ~. **8** encourage/ induce sb to get involved in sth: ব্যবসায়/ রাজনীতিতে ~. **9** bring down: জ্বর/ দর ~. **10** purge; evacuate; cause loose motions: পেট ~. **11** cause to come out in: পথে ~. **12** bring:

চোখের জল ~. **13** topple; bring down: ক্ষমতা থেকে ~.

নামাল *adj* (of land) low; low-lying. ❑*n* lowland.

নামাশ্ব শক্তি *n* nominal horse-power.

নামিতক *n* nominee.

নামী *adj*=নাম-করা (⇒ নাম). ~**দামি** *adj* important; eminent. ~**দামি লোক** *n* notable; elite.

নামোচ্চারণ *n* utterance/ mention of a name; (slightest) mention. ~ **করা** *vi* utter the name of; mention (slightly).

নামোল্লেখ *n* mention of a name. ~ **করা** *vi* mention the name; refer/allude to sb.

-**নাম্নী** *adj* fem (of-নামা[১]).

নাযাকৎ [P] *n* delicacy; neatness; elegance; softness; politeness.

নায়ক *n* **1** leader; chief; guide; commander; general; lord. **2** hero (of a drama, novel, etc). **3** lover; gallant. ❑*adj* leading; guiding; commanding; principal; chief.

নায়কী *n* the main string of a stringed instrument.

নায়কীয় *adj* of a hero; heroic.

নায়র *n*=নাইয়র

নায়িকা *n fem* (of নায়ক) **1** heroine (of a drama, novel, etc). **2** noble lady; mistress; courtesan. **3** any one of the eight manifestations of goddess Durga.

নায়েক *n* soldier holding the lowest non-commissioned rank in the armies of the sub-continent; naik. **ল্যান্স**-~ *n* brevet naik.

নায়েব [A] *n* deputy; delegate; vicegerent; attorney; assistant; administrator and rent-collector of a landlord's state.

নায়েবি, নায়েবী *nn* post/ position of a deputy. ❑*adjj* relating to a deputy.

নার [A] *n* fire.

নারক *adj* hellish; infernal. **নারকী** *fem.* ❑*n* hell; infernal.

নারকল, নারকেল, নারকোল *nn* (colloq) = নারিকেল

নারকী *adj*=নারক. ~**য়** *adj* hellish; diabolical; devilish; fiendish; infernal.

নারকুলে, নারকেলি *adj* (colloq)=নারিকেলী-

নারগিস=নার্গিস

নারঙ্গ, নারঙ্গি, নারাঙ্গ *n* orange; orange-tree.

নারদ *n* (myth) name of a sage given to fomenting discord among gods and men. ~ **নারদ** *inter* let them/ may they engage in a quarrel.

নারদীয় *adj* relating to/ composed by Narada.

নারা[১] *vi* (poet) cannot; be unable to; fail to.

নারা[২] [A] *n* slogan; spouting; clamour; crying. ~**য়ে তকবির** *n* the slogan "God is great".

নারাচ *n* iron-shaft; iron arrow.

নারাজ [P] *adjj* displeased; unwilling; dissatisfied; discontented; offended. **নারাজি** *adj* discontent; displeasure.

নারায়ণ *n* an appellation of Vishnu. **নারায়ণী** *fem* goddess Lakshmi the wife of Narayana. ❑*adj* relating to/ evolved from Narayana. ~**ক্ষেত্র** *n* plot of land on the bank of the Ganges stretching four cubits from the watermark; bank of the Ganges. **নারায়ণী সেনা** *n* band of unrelenting warriors said to be born out of the parson of Narayan or Krishna.

নারিকেল *n* coconut; coco; coconut palm. ~-**কুঞ্জ** *n* coconut-grove. ~**কুরি** *n* shredded coco. ~-**ছোবড়া** *n* coir. ~ **তেল** *n* coconut-oil. ~ **দড়ি** *n* coir-rope. ~-**বাগান** *n* coconut-grove. ~**বৃক্ষ** *n* coconut tree; coconut palm. ~**ভস্ম** *n* medicine prepared from the coconut. ~-**মালা** *n* coconut-shell. ~**মুড়ি** *n* broom made of stalks of the coco-leaf. **নারিকেলের জল** *n* coconut-milk; coconut-water. **নারিকেলের দুধ/ রস** *n* coco-juice. **নারিকেলের শাঁস** *n* kernel of a coconut; coconut. **নারিকেলের শুষ্ক শাঁস** *n* copra.

নারিকেলী *adj* coconut-shaped tasting like coconut; containing kernel like a coconut.

নারী *n* woman; wife; female; womankind. ~**জন্ম** *n* birth as a woman; woman's life; womanhood. ~ **জাতি** *n* womankind. ~**জীবন** *n* life of a woman; womanhood. ~**ত্ব** *n* womanhood; femininity. ~**দূষণ** *n* any of the six vices of a woman (drinking spirits, keeping bad company; sleeping and dwelling in a strange house, etc). ~**ধর্ম** *n* duties of a woman; womanly qualities/ virtues; womanliness. ~**ধর্ষণ** *n* rape. ~**নিগ্রহ**, ~**নির্যাতন** *nn* molestation/ persecution of a woman; rape. ~**প্রকৃতি**=~**স্বভাব**. ~**বেশ** *n* woman's apparel. ~**মুক্তি** *n* Women's Lib(eration). ~**রত্ন** *n* jewel of a woman; excellent woman. ~**সমাজ** *n* community of women. ~**সুলভ**=~**স্বভাবসুলভ**. ~**স্থান** *n* women's land. ~**স্বভাব** *n* womanliness; womanly nature; femininity. ❑*adj* (of a man) womanish; effeminate. ~**স্বভাবসুলভ** *adj* **1** womanly; feminine. **2** (of a man) womanish; effeminate.

নার্গিস [P] *n* narcissus.

নার্ভ [E] *n* nerve. ~**তন্ত্র** *n* nervous system.

নার্স [E] *n* nurse.

নার্সারি [E] *n* nursery.

নাল[১] *n* **1** hollow stalk; lotus-stalk. **2** any tube/ tubular vessel/ vein of the body. **3** reed.

নাল[২] [A] *n* **1** horseshoe; shoe. **2** ferrule. ~ **পরানো/ বাঁধানো** *vt* shoe (a horse). ~**বন্দ** *n* farrier; blacksmith (who makes and fits horseshoes). ~**বন্দি** *n* shoeing; giving a horse new shoes. ~-**পরা**, ~**বাঁধা(নো)** *adj* shod.

নাল[৩] *n* saliva; slaver. ~ **ঝরা/পড়া** *vi* water; slaver over sth; drool: মাংস দেখে তার মুখ থেকে ~

ঝরছে, He is slavering over the plate of meat. ~ ঝরানো/ ফেলা *vi* slaver; drool; dribble.

নালতা, নালতে *nn* (colloq)=নালিতা

নালফুল *n* white water-lily; lotus.

নালা *n* **1** drain; duct. **2** cannel; channel; wayside gutter. ~ **কেটে জল আনা** (fig) tempt fate; ask for trouble.

নালায়েক [P] *adj* **1** unworthy; unfit; inconvenient; improper; unsuitable; incapable; incompetent. **2** under-age; minor.

নালি *n* **1** any tubular vessel, vein, etc. of the body. **2** small drain/ duct. **3** pipe; tube. **4** fissure. **5** sinus. **~-ঘা, ~ব্রণ** *nn* sinus. **~কা** *n* small tube/ pipe/ vein. **~কা-বান্ডিল** *n* (anat) vascular bundle.

নালিক *n* **1** kind of arrow/ spear. **2** gun.

নালিতা *n* edible leaves of a jute-plant.

নালিশ, নালিস *nn* **1** complaint; charge; accusation; plaint; (legal) action; (law) suit; appeal/ prayer for redress. **2** lamentation; groan; complaint. ~ **করা** *vi* complain against; bring an action; prosecute; sue; bring/ file a lawsuit. **~বন্দ** *adj* bringing a legal action. **নালিশি** *adj* concerning a lawsuit/ complaint; in suit.

নালী=নালি.

নাশ *n* **1** destruction; annihilation; extinction; disappearance. **2** elimination; extermination: কীটের বংশ~. **3** removal; elimination: দারিদ্র্য~. **4** ruin; impairment: স্বাস্থ্য~. **5** loss; waste: সম্পত্তি ~. **6** spoiling; loss; spoilage: শস্য~, কর্ম~. **7** death. ~ **করা** *vt* **1** destroy; annihilate; **2** eliminate; exterminate. **3** remove; relieve. **4** ruin; impair. **5** squander; waste. **6** spoil; mar. **7** kill. ~ **হওয়া** *vi* **1** be destroyed/ annihilated; disappear; become extinct. **2** be eliminated/ exterminated. **3** be removed/ relieved. **4** be ruined/ impaired. **5** be lost/ squandered; go down the drain. **6** die; be killed. **~ক** *adj* destroying; annihilating; eliminating; destructive; wasting; prodigal; removing; exterminating; causing ruin; killing. **~কতা** *n* destructiveness; sabotage. **~কতামূলক** *adj* destructive. **~কতামূলক তৎপরতা** *n* sabotage. **~ন** *n* destroying; destruction; removal; exterminating; extermination; ruining; wasting; spoiling; impairing; killing. ❑*adj* (used as a *suff*)=~ক. **নাশা** *vt* (poet)=~ করা. ❑*adj* (used as a *suff*)=~ক: সর্ব~. **নাশী** *fem.*

নাশতা [P] *n* breakfast; repast.

নাশিত *adj* destroyed; ruined; wrecked; perished; lost; exterminated; eliminated; removed; wasted; spoiled; killed.

নাশী *adj* (used as a *suff*) perishing; perishable; destroying; destructive; wasting; ruining; removing; spoiling; killing. **নাশিনী** *fem.*

নাশ্য *adj* liable to be destroyed/ removed/ eliminated.

নাস[১] *n* **1** snuff. **2** sth inhaled/ taken in like snuff: জলের ~. ~ **নেওয়া** *vi* take snuff; inhale; take/ draw in.

নাস[২]=নাসা

নাসা *n* **1** nose. **2** polypus of the nose. **~গ্র** *n* point of the nose. **~ছিদ্র** *n* nostril. **~জ্বর** *n* kind of disease of the nose. **~দারু** *n* piece of wood projecting like a nose over a door. **~পথ** *n* nasal passage. **~পান** *n* drinking water through the nose. **~পুট** *n* wing of the nose; nostril. **~ভেদ** *n* perforation of the nose. **~মূল** *n* root of the nose. **~রন্ধ্র** *n* nostril. **~শোষ** *n* parchedness of the nostrils.

নাসারা [A] *n* a Christian.

নাসিকা *n* nose. **~গ্র** *n* point of the nose. **~বুদ** *n* nasal polypus.

নাসিক্য *adj* nasal. **~ধ্বনি** *n* nasal sound.

নাস্তা=নাশতা

নাস্তানাবুদ [P] *adj* annihilated; totally destroyed; extinct; routed; discomfited. ~ **করা** *vt* **1** annihilate; demolish; obliterate; pulverize; nullify. **2** subject to extreme harassment; exasperate; heckle; torment.

নাস্তি *vi* is/ are not. ❑*n* non-existence. **~বান** *n* (one of the) have-nots.

নাস্তিক *adj* atheistic. ❑*n* atheist; infidel. **~তা, নাস্তিক্য** *nn* atheism; infidelity.

নাহক *adj* unjust; illegal; untrue; false. ❑*adv* unjustly; falsely; improperly; wrongly; in vain; for nothing: ~ কয়েদ, ~ কষ্ট দেওয়া.

নাহয় *adv* **1** better: ~ তুমিই যাও. **2** what if: ~ টাকাটা তোমাকে দিলাম. **3** at best; at the worst: তাতে ~ কিছু খরচাপাতি হবে. **4** all right: কথাটা আমিই ~ পাড়বো. ❑*conj* **1** or: হয় যাবে ~ যাবে না. **2** or else: হয় চিকিৎসা করাও ~ ভোগো.

নাহা *vi* (old use)=নাওয়া

নাহি *vi* (old use)=নাই[২]

নি[১] *pref* indicating proximity, certainty, want, completeness, etc: নিক্ষেপ, নিখুঁত, নিবেশ.

নি[২] *n* (music) the seventh note of the octave.

নি[৩] *adv* (colloq)=নাই[১]

নিউক্লিয়াস [E] *n* nucleus.

নিউমোনিয়া [E] *n* pneumonia.

নিংড়ানো *vt* **1** squeeze (out); wring out: কাপড় ~, জল ~. **3** (fig) extort; squeeze. ❑*adj* squeezed/ wrung (out); extorted.

নিঃ *pref* indicating out forth, away, etc. **~ক্ষত্র, ~ক্ষত্রিয়** *adjj* devoid of kshatriyas (ক্ষত্রিয়). **~শঙ্ক** *adj* fearless; undaunted; intrepid. **~শঙ্কচিত্ত** *adj* having a dauntless/ fearless heart. **~শঙ্কচিত্তে** *adv* with a dauntless heart; fearlessly. **~শত্রু** *adj* free from enemies. **~শব্দ** *adj* noiseless; silent; still. **~শব্দ পদসঞ্চারে** *adv* with soundless steps; stepping silently/ noiselessly/ with stealthy footsteps; stealthily

~শব্দে *adv* silently; noiselessly. ~শরণ *adj* defenceless; unprotected. ~শর্ত *adj* unconditional. ~শস্ত্র *adj* unarmed. ~শস্ত্র প্রতিরোধ *n* unarmed/ passive resistance. ~শাখ *adj* branchless. ~শূন্য *adj* quite empty. ~শেষ *adj* **1** leaving no remains: সব তহবিল ~শেষ. **2** utterly ruined; finished: মেয়ের বিয়েতে সে ~শেষ. **3** complete; whole; entire; full; thorough: ~শেষ অধিকার. **4** thoroughly exhausted: সারাদিন হাঁটাহাঁটি করে ~শেষ হয়ে গেলাম. ~শেষ করা *vt* finish; exhaust; consume. ~শেষিত *adj* totally consumed/ finished/ destroyed/ exhausted/ spent up. ~শেষে *adv* thoroughly; completely; fully. ~শোক *adj* free from sorrow/ care. ~শ্রীক *adj* ugly. ~শ্রয়ণী, ~শ্রেণী *nn* ladder. ~শ্রেয়স *adj* best; most excellent. ~শ্বসন *n* breathing; respiration; exhalation. ~শ্বসিত *adj* breathed in/ out; exhaled. ~শ্বাস ছাড়া/ ফেলা *vi* breathe; exhale; sigh. ~শ্বাস টানা/ নেওয়া *vi* breathe (in); draw breath; inhale; respire. ~শ্বাস ফেলার অবকাশ *n* breathing space; breather; (least) respite; time to breathe. ~শ্বাস বন্ধ/ রোধ করা *vi* catch hold one's breathe. ~শ্বাস রোধ করে হত্যা করা *vi* strangle/ throttle to death. ~শ্বাস বন্ধ/ রোধ হওয়া *vi* **1** be suffocated: বদ্ধ ঘরে ~শ্বাস বন্ধ হয়ে আসে. **2** be out of breath: ভারী বোঝা টেনে ~শ্বাস বন্ধ হওয়া. **3** cease to breathe; die; draw one's last breath. ~শ্বাসপ্রশ্বাস *n* respiration. এক ~শ্বাসে *adv* **1** without pausing for breath. **2** in the same breath. ~ষ্যন্দন *n* trickling; flowing down; streaming. ~সংজ্ঞ *adj* unconscious; fainted; swooned. ~সংশয় *adj* undoubting; unhesitating; undoubted; certain; convinced; doubtless; sure; positive. ~সংশয়ে *adv* undoubtedly; certainly; surely; positively; without doubt/ hesitation; unhesitatingly. ~সঙ্কোচ *adj* straightforward; unhesitating; free and frank; candid; self-assured. ~সঙ্কোচে *adv* without hesitation/ fear; candidly; frankly; unhesitatingly. ~সঙ্গ *adj* lonely; companionless; unattended; solitary; detached; unrelated; disinterested. ~সঙ্গতা *n* loneliness; solitude. ~সত্ত্ব *adj* unsubstantial; inexistence; lifeless; inanimate; impotent; feeble; weak; wretched. ~সন্তান *adj* childless. ~সন্দিগ্ধ, ~সন্দেহ *adj* free from doubt; certain; sure; doubtless; convinced; undoubting; unsuspecting; positive. ~সন্দেহে *adv* without doubt; undoubtedly; surely; certainly; doubtlessly; positively. ~সপত্ন *adj* having no rival; unrivalled; unparalleled; having no enemy/ adversary. ~সম্পর্ক, ~সম্বন্ধ *adj* without relatives; unrelated; not related by blood; unconnected; detached. ~সম্বল *adj* resourceless; broke; destitute; indigent; penniless. ~সরণ *n* going out/ forth; issue; egress; flowing out; emission; oozing; exudation; escape. ~সহ *adj* unbearable; intolerable. ~সহায় *adj* helpless; unassisted. ~সাড় *adj* insensible; unconscious; motionless; silent; noiseless. ~সার *adj* sapless; pathless; worthless; vain; unsubstantial. ~সারক *adj* causing to flow/go out/go forth; discharging; emitting ejecting; expelling; purging. ~সারণ *n* turning out; egress; discharge; emission; ejection; expulsion; purgation; issue; escape. ~সারিত *adj* turned out; expelled; emitted; issued; exuded; ejected. ~সীম *adj* unbounded; immeasurable; infinite; boundless; endless. ~সুপ্ত *adj* profoundly asleep. ~সৃত= ~সারিতা. ~সৃত হওয়া *vi* go out; come forth; depart; flow out; exude; ooze; issue; escape. ~স্নেহ *adj* **1** not unctuous/ greasy. **2** insensible; cold; unfeeling. ~স্পন্দ *adj* motionless. ~স্পৃহ *adj* free from desire; disinterested; unattached; abstaining from; callous; indifferent. ~স্পৃহতা *n* absence of desire/ liking; disinterestedness; callousness; indifference. ~স্রব *n* **1**=~সরণ. **2** scum. ~স্ব *adj* destitute; poor; indigent. ~স্বতা *n* indigence; utter poverty; destitution. ~স্বত্ব *adj* having no title/ right; dispossessed. ~স্বন *adj* soundless. ~স্বর *adj* voiceless; silent. ~স্বামিকা *adj* having no lord/ husband. ~স্বীকৃত, ~স্বীভূত *adjj* impoverished.

নিঁদ *n* (poet)=নিদ্রা

নিকট *n* nearness; proximity. ❑*adj* **1** approaching; imminent: ~ মৃত্যু. **2** close: ~ আত্মীয়. **3** intimate; bosom: ~ বন্ধু. ❑*prep* **1** near; proximate to; about: বাজারের ~. **2** to; towards; by: বড়ো সাহেবের ~ গিয়েছিলাম. **3** from: কার ~ শুনেছ? **4** in possession/ in the custody of; with: কামালের ~ বইটা আছে. ~বর্তী, ~স্থ *adjj* **1** near-by; near; close to; neighbouring; proximate. **2** approaching; impending; imminent: বিপদ ~বর্তী. ~বর্তিনী, ~স্থা *fem*. ~বর্তী হওয়া *vi* draw near; approach; close upon. ~বর্তিতা *n* nearness; proximity; closeness; approach. নিকটে *adv* drawing near; approaching; closing upon: বিপদ ~. ❑prep=~.

নিকড়িয়া, নিকড়ে (colloq) *adj* **1** penniless; indigent. **2** without pay: ~ ছুটি.

নিকন, নিকনো=নিকানো

নিকপিক *n* (onom) expressing: slight motion; swaying. ~ করা *vi* sway: ~ করে ক্ষীণ কাঁকাল.

নিকর *n* heap; pile; flock; multitude; mass; collection; assemblage: মধুকর~.

নিকষ *n* **1** touchstone. **2** testing streak of gold. ~ণ *n* rubbing / testing (gold) on a touchstone. নিকষিত *adj* **1** rubbed/ tested on a touchstone. **2** found to be genuine by testing on a touchstone; sterling; pure. **3** polished. **4** whetted.

নিকা [A] *n* **1** matrimony; marriage; nuptials. **2** any marriage other than the first one. ~ **করা** *vi* marry for the second (third, etc) time; re-marry. ~ **বসা** *vi* (of women)=~ করা.

নিকানো *vt* **1** rub with a swab/ mop drenched in a solution of cow-dung. **2** swab; clean; mop; sweep. ❑*adj* swabbed with a solution of cow-dung; swabbed; mopped; swept.

নিকামাইয়ে *adj* having no earning; unemployed.

নিকায় *n* **1** collection; group; class; assemblage. **2** association; brotherhood; congregation; school; body. **3** habitation; dwelling. **4** Supreme Being.

নিকাল *int* get out ! avaunt ! go off !

নিকাশ, নিকাস *nn* **1** outlet; discharge; issue; vent; drainage: পানি~. **2** completion; finalization. **3** adjustments of accounts; balance-sheet; final accounts. ~ **করা** *vi* **1** drain/ let out. **2** complete; finalize. **3** settle up/adjust (accounts). **4** put an end to; destroy: দফা ~ করা. ~ **দেওয়া** *vi* render/ submit (final) accounts/ a balance-sheet. ~ **হওয়া** *vi* **1** (of water) come/ go out. **2** be completed/ finalized. **3** be settled up. **4** come to an end; be destroyed. **নিকাশী** *adj* relating to final accounts/ balance-sheet. ~-**পত্র** *n* balance-sheet.

নিকাহ=নিকা

নিকি *n* young/ egg of a louse; nit.

নিকুচি *n*(vulg) ruin; destruction. ~ **করা** *vt* destroy; ruin; damn.

নিকুঞ্জ *n* arbour; bower; thicket. ~**কানন**, ~**বন**=~.

নিকুম্ভিলা *n* (myth) a grove at the western gate of Lanka for the performance off sacrificial rites.

নিকৃত *adj* **1** reprimanded; scolded; taken to task. **2** defeated; humiliated; insulted; oppressed. **নিকৃতি** *n* reprimand; scolding; humiliation; oppression.

নিকৃন্তন *n* cutting down/ off; destroying; destruction.

নিকৃষ্ট *adj* inferior; of poor quality; bad; debased; vile; low; despised; mean; hateful. ~**তা** *n* inferiority; lowness; vileness; meanness; poor quality.

নিকেত, নিকেতন *nn* house; habitation; abode; home; dwelling house.

নিকোচন=সঙ্কোচন

নিক্তি *n* pair of small scales.

নিক্বণ *n* (musical) sound; note; sweet jingle; tinkling: কিঙ্কিণী-~.

নিক্ষিপ্ত *adj* **1** thrown (away/ down); hurled; abandoned; cast; flung; scattered; shot. **2** placed; deposited. **3** given away; conferred; imputed.

নিক্ষেপ *n* **1** throwing/ sending away; abandoning; removing; casting; hurling; flinging; scattering; shooting; ejection. **2** deposit; pledge; placing; depositing. **3** imputing; conferring; giving. ~ **করা** *vt* throw (down/ away): put/ lay (down); pour in; lay aside; abandon; leave; give up; cast (off); hurl; fling; shoot; scatter; confer; place; deposit; pledge. ~**ক** *adj* **1** throwing; casting; hurling; depositing (⇒ ~ করা). **2** launching device. ~**ণ** =~.

নিখরচ(া) [P] *adv* free of cost/ charges; gratis; without expense. **নিখরচে** *adj* niggardly; stingy; parsimonious.

নিখর্ব *adj* dwarfish. ❑*n* **1** thousand millions; billion. **2** dwarf.

নিখাকি *adj fem* (sl) eating nothing/ little; having little appetite. ❑*n* woman eating nothing/ little.

নিখাত *adj* **1** dug in; buried; fixed in the ground. **2** dug up; excavated. ~-**নিধি** *n* treasure-trove.

নিখাদ[১] *n* (music) the seventh note of the octave.

নিখাদ[২] *adj* unalloyed; unadulterated; pure; genuine: ~ সোনা.

নিখিল *adj* complete; all; whole; entire: ~ বিশ্ব ❑*n* the whole universe: নিখিলের অধিপতি.

নিখুঁত *adj* flawless; faultless; perfect; spotless; immaculate; impeccable; unblemished.

নিগড় *n* iron chain for the feet; heel chains for an elephant; fetter; shackle. ~**বদ্ধ** *adj* chained; fettered; enchained.

নিগড়িত *adj*=নিগড়বদ্ধ (⇒ নিগড়)

নিগদ *n* reciting; audible recitation; discourse; utterance; speech. **নিগদিত** *adj* recited; told; uttered; spoken.

নিগম *n* **1** insertion. **2** place/passage (esp of the Vedas). **3** (gram) root; derived form. **4** Veda; Vedic text; any work auxiliary to and explanatory of the Vedas. **5** sacred precept; words of a god/holy man; doctrine; instruction. **6** market-place; town; city. **7** road; path; exit; way; corporation; municipality; commercial guild; chamber of commerce. ~-**কর** *n* corporation tax. ~**ন** *n* **1** insertion; quotation of words; deduction. **2** going in/into. **3** going out; issue; exit; outflow. ~**বদ্ধ** *adj* incorporated. ~**বন্ধন** *n* incorporation.

নিগমিত *adj* =নিগমবদ্ধ (⇒ নিগম)

নিগর(ণ) *n* **1** eating; swallowing; gulping down. **2** throat.

নিগাবান=নিগাহবান

নিগার [E] *n* (vulg) nigger; negro; blackie.

নিগাহবান [P] *n* watchman; guard; keeper; protector. **নিগাহবানি** *n* watching; guarding; custody; care.

নিগীর্ণ *adj* swallowed; devoured; gulped down; eaten up.

নিগূঢ় *adj* **1** concealed; hidden. **2** obscure; mysterious; mystical; occult; secret. **3** abstruse; intricate. **4** very profound/deep. ~ অর্থ *n* hidden/underlying/mysterious meaning/sense/implication. ~চারী *adj* walking concealed/in disguise; moving secretly. ~চ্ছদ *n* secret cover. ~তা *n* concealment; secrecy; mysteriousness; intricacy; obscurity; abstruseness; profundity; depth; mystery. নিগূঢ়ার্থ *n* = ~ অর্থ. ❑ *adj* having a hidden/underlying/mysterious meaning/ sense; occult; abstruse. নিগূঢ়ার্থক *adj*=নিগূঢ়ার্থ.

নিগৃহীত *adj* **1** harassed; assailed; attacked; harried; persecuted. **2** held down/back; caught; checked; seized. **3** coerced; oppressed; subjected to torture; afflicted. ~ করা *vt* **1** harass; assail; attack; harry; humiliate; persecute. **2** keep/hold back; seize; catch; hold; hold fast; stop; restrain; check; curb; tame. **4** punish; repress; subject to torture; harrow; coerce; persecute.

নিগ্রহ *n* **1** punishment; chastisement; severe treatment. **2** seizing; catching; arresting; holding fast. **3** oppression; persecution; harassment; repression:পুলিশের ~. **4** affliction; misery:দারিদ্র্যজনিত ~. **5** keeping down/back; restraining; coercion; subjugation; suppression; quelling: শূদ্র ~. **6** defeat; overthrow; destruction. **7** humiliation; ignominy; discomfiture. **8** scolding; reprimand; reproof; lashing. ~ করা=নিগৃহীত করা. ~ ভোগ করা *vi* be subjected to harassment/ humiliation/ repression/ ignominy/ torture; suffer harassment/ humiliation/ ignominy; be humiliated/ persecuted/ oppressed/ coerced/ harassed/ afflicted/ harried.

নিগ্রাহক *n, adj* (one) who keeps back/ prevents/ oppresses/ coerces/ harasses/ humiliates/ persecutes/ represses/ afflicts; assailant; oppressor; persecutor.

নির্ঘণ্ট *n* glossary; index; table of contents.

নিচ=নিচু

নিচয় *n* **1** mass; heap; quantity; collection; multitude; assemblage. **2** increase; development; accretion.

নিচু *adj* **1** low:~ ছাদ. **2** low-lying:~ জমি. **3** depressed; low: ~ জায়গা, ~ অবস্থা. **4** stooping; bent down: মাথা ~ করা. **5** inferior; low-class; low-grade, low-paid:~ পদ. **6** sloping: রাস্তা ~ হয়ে গেছে. **7** low; soft:~ গলা. ❑ *n* **1** place/position below/underneath:~ থেকে. **2** low/depressed position/state: সে ~ থেকে বড়ো হয়েছে. ~ করা *vt* lower; bend; drop; strike (a sail); reduce. ~ হওয়া *vi* stoop; be/the low; crouch; cower; bend one's head.

নিচুল *n* **1** rattan-plant. **2** upper garment. **3** lower lip.

নিচে, নীচে *adv, prep* **1** below; under; beneath; underneath. **2** in the bottom of; under:সাগরের ~. **3** at the foot of: পাহাড়ের ~.

নিচেতন=নিশ্চেতন

নিচোল *n* **1** upper garment; scarf; wrapper; modesty-vest. **2** skirt. **3** armour.

নিশ্চিন্দি *adj* (colloq, dial)=নিশ্চিন্ত

নিচ্ছিদ্র =নিশ্ছিদ্র

নিছক *adj* mere; sheer; absolute; undiluted: ~ সন্দেহ ❑*adv* merely; sheer; absolutely; only: simply: ~ মিথ্যাচার.

নিছনি, নিছুনি (dial) *n* **1** beauty; physical grace; embellishment (of the body); toilet. **2** gift; presentation; offering; worship. **3** evil; harm. **4** a rite performed at a wedding ceremony to guard the couple from evils. **5** comparison. **6** sweeping; wiping.

নিছল *adj* artless; unaffected; ingenuous; frank.

নিজ *adj* own; innate; native. ~কীয় *adj* one's own. ❑*n* one's self. ~ত্ব *n* individuality; originality: ~ নিজ *adj* respective. ~স্ব *adj* **1** one's own property. **2** belonging to/devised by one's ownself; personal; own; proper; individual; particular; original. ~স্ব করা *vt* appropriate to oneself; make one's own.

নিজাম [A] *n* **1** arrangement; order; disposition; administrator. **2** (hist) ruler of Hyderabad; Nizam. ~ৎ, ~ত *adj* **1** government; administration; office of an administrator; department. **2** office/rule of a Nizam.

নিজামতি, নিজামতী *n*=নিজামৎ (⇒ নিজাম). ❑*adj* administrative; of a Nizam.

নিজে *refl pron* by one's self: আমি/তুমি/ সে/ এটা/ আমরা/ তোমরা/ তারা/ এরা নিজে, myself, yourself, himself or herself, itself, ourselves yourselves, themselves respectively. ~ নিজে by one's own(self); without external help. ~র *adj* own. ~র কোলে ঝোল টানা (fig) put oneself first; look after number one. ~র চরকায় তেল দেওয়া (fig) mind one's own business. ~র পায়ে কুড়ুল মারা (fig) dig one's own grave.

নিঝর *n* (poet)=নির্ঝর

নিঝুম, নিঝঝুম (colloq) *adjj* still; calm; silent; motionless.

নিট[1] *adj* genuine; fair; just.

নিট[2] [E] *adj* net: ~ মুনাফা.

নিটুট *adj* sound; robust; flawless; in full bloom: ~ যৌবন/ স্বাস্থ্য.

নিটোল *adj* **1** perfect; flawless; immaculate; faultless: ~ সৌন্দর্য. **2** perfect; robust; sound; blooming with:~ স্বাস্থ্য. **3** plump; stout:~ শরীর.

নিঠুর *adj* (poet)=নিষ্ঠুর

নিড়বিড় *n* (onom) procrastination; dilly-dallying; dilatoriness; dallying; excessive slowness. **নিড়বিড়ে** *adj* procrastinating; dilatory; sluggish; dilly-dallying; dawdling.

নিড়ানি, নিড়েন *n* 1 weeding tool; hoe. 2 act of weeding out; weeding.

নিড়ানো *vt* weed (out). ☐*adj* weeded.

নিতকনে *n fem* bridesmaid.

নিতবর *n* best man.

নিতম্ব *n* 1 buttocks/hinder parts (esp of a woman); hips; posterior. 2 ridge/swell/side (of a mountain); sloping bank/shore (of a river). **~বিম্ব** *n* disk-like round hips. **~বতী** *adj fem* having beautiful hips/buttocks. ☐*n*=নিতম্বিনী. **~দেশ, ~স্থল, ~স্থলী** *nn* region of the buttocks/hips. **নিতম্বিনী, নিতম্বী** *adj* 1 having beautiful hips. 2 having beautiful sides (as a mountain). ☐*n* woman with large and handsome hips.

নিতল *n* (myth) one of the seven divisions of the lower regions.

নিতা *n* (dial) invitation (to dinner or lunch).

নিতান্ত *adj* 1 extreme; excessive; very much:~ দায়ে পড়ে আসা. 2 out-and-out; thorough; downright; inveterate: ~ বদমাস. 3 very close; intimate:~ আত্মীয়/ বন্ধু. ☐*adj* 1 extremely; to the extreme; excessively: ~ নিষ্ঠুর লোক. 2 thoroughly; downright; out-and-out; very:~ সৎ/ ভালো মানুষ. 3 very closely; intimately:~ ঘনিষ্ঠ. 4 if at all; if:~ই যদি বইটা নিতে চাও, if you insist ... . 5 perforce; of necessity; still; even then:চাকরিটা যদি ~ই পেতে চাও: **~পক্ষে** *adv* at least; leastwise. **~কর্তব্য** *adj* indispensable.

নিতি, নিতুই *advv*=নিত্য and নিত্যই respectively.

নিত্য *adv* always; constantly; regularly; ever; for ever; daily; every day:সে ওখানে ~ যাওয়া-আসা করে. ☐*adj* 1 daily: ~কর্ম. 2 diurnal:সূর্যের ~গতি. 3 eternal; perpetual; immortal; everlasting: ~মুক্তি. 4 constant; invariable; fixed. 5 (phy) constant. **~কর্ম, ~কার্য** *nn* daily rites/duties. **~কাল** *n* infinite time; eternity. **~কাল ধরে** *adv* for ever; always; eternally; constantly; perpetually. **~কালীন** *adj* eternal; constant; perpetual; everlasting. **~কৃত্য, ~ক্রিয়া**=~কর্ম. **~গতি** *adj* moving constantly. ☐*n* wind. **~তা** *n* perpetuity; eternity; immortality; continuance; constancy; imperishability; endless/infinite time: **~দান** *n* daily alms-giving. **~নৈমিত্তিক** *adj* daily/regular and occasional; constant; usual:~নৈমিত্তিক অভ্যাস. **~পদার্থ** *adj* indestructible. **~প্রলয়** *n* sound sleep. **~বৃত্ত** *n* (gram) indefinite:~বৃত্ত অতীত. **~বৃন্দাবন** *n* the paradise of the Vaishnavas; Elysium; eternal heaven. **~ব্রত** *n* perpetual observance. **~মুক্ত** *adj* emancipated for ever; ever disinterested. **~যুক্ত** *adj* always busy/intent upon. **~যৌবন** *n* eternal/ unfading/ perpetual youth. ☐*adj* always/ ever young. **~লীলা** *n* daily sports/ activities. **~শঃ** *adv* always; constantly; eternally. **~শ্রী** *adj* of lasting beauty. **~সঙ্গী** *n* constant companion. **~সত্য** *n* eternal truth. **~সহচর**=সঙ্গী. **~সমাস** *n* (gram) a compound which cannot be expounded. **~সেবক** *adj* always serving others. **~সেবা** *n* constant service; daily worship. **~স্থ** *adj* always abiding (in). **নিত্যানন্দ** *n* eternal happiness/bliss. ☐*adj* eternally happy/blissful. **নিত্যানিত্য** *adj* eternal and perishable/transitory; permanent and temporary; perpetual and transient. **নিত্যানিত্য-বিচার** *n* discrimination of/discernment between what is eternal and what is perishable.

নিথর *n* motionless; still; calm; tranquil.

নিদ *n* (poet)=নিদ্রা

নিদয় *adj* (poet)=নির্দয়

নিদর্শ *n* (printed or typed) form.

নিদর্শন *n* 1 instance; example; illustration; precedence. 2 proof; evidence; testimony. 3 prognostic; mark; sign; token; omen; keepsake; memento. **~পত্র** *n* certificate; testimonial; identity card; introduction. **~স্তম্ভ** *n* pillar to fix/mark a boundary. **নিদর্শনা** *n* (rhet) transference of attributes.

নিদর্শনী *n* index; table of contents.

নিদাঘ *n* 1 hot season; summer. 2 (intense oppressive) heat. 3 sweat; perspiration. **~কাল** *n* summer-time. **~ক্লিষ্ট, ~তপ্ত, ~তাপিত, ~দগ্ধ, ~পীড়িত, নিদাঘার্ত** *adjj* suffering from/afflicted with summer heat; oppressed with intense heat.

নিদান *n* 1 first/primary cause. 2 cause of existence; any cause/motive; root cause. 3 cause of a disease and inquiry into it; pathology; actiology. 4 diagnosis. 5 cessation; end. 6 purification; correctness. 7 symptoms of imminent death. **~কাল** *n* time of death; last hour; dying day. **~তত্ত্ব, ~বিদ্যা** *nn* pathology; actiology; diagnostics. **~পক্ষে** *adv* at least; at the lowest; perforce; still. **~ভূত** *adj* become a primary/remote cause (of a disease); causative; causal. **~শালা** *n* clinic. **~শাস্ত্র**=~তত্ত্ব.

নিদানিক *adj* actiological; clinical.

নিদানীভূত *adj*=নিদানভূত (⇒ নিদান)

নিদারুণ *adj* 1 extremely severe; terrible. 2 extremely cruel; merciless; relentless:~ দুর্ভাগ্য. 3 unbearable; intolerable:~ গরম.

নিদালি *n* handful of dust rendered soporific by occult charm.

নিদিগ্ধ *adj* smeared; plastered; clinging to. ☐*n* cardamoms.

নিদিধ্যাস(ন) *n* profound and repeated meditation.

নিদিষ্ট *adj* ordered; commanded; directed; instructed.

নিদুটি, নিদুলি *nn* (colloq)=নিদালি

নিদেন *n* (colloq)=নিদান

নিদেশ *n* **1** order; command; directive; instruction; direction; advice. **2** talk; conversation. **3** vicinity; neighbourhood. **~কর্তা** *n* one who directs/commands/gives an order; director. **~পত্র** *n* directive; letter containing instructions/order. **~বর্তী** *adj* obedient; at sb's command/beck and call; subordinate.

নিদেষ্টা *adj* commanding; pointing out; ordering; instructing; prescribing; explaining; advising. ❑*n* নিদেশকর্তা (⇒ নিদেশ).

নিদ্রা *n* sleep; slumber; sleepiness; sloth. **~ আসা** *vi* feel sleepy; fall asleep. **~ টুটা**=~ ভাঙা. **~ দেওয়া** *vi* (go to) sleep. **~ পাওয়া** *vi* feel sleepy. **~ ভাঙা** *vi* **1** wake up; awake; get up. **2** (fig) shake off inactivity/sloth/blind faith; awake. **~ ভাঙানো** *vt* **1** wake sb up; awake sb; awaken; rouse. **2** (fig) cause sb to become active; rouse; awaken; arouse sb from (apathy, inaction, etc). **~ যাওয়া**=~ দেওয়া. **~ হওয়া** *vi* have sleep. **~কর** *adj* making sleepy; producing sleep; soporific; narcotic; somniferous. **~কর্ষণ** *n* inducement of sleep; drowsiness; somnolence; sleepiness. **~কর্ষণ হওয়া**=~ আসা. **~ক্ষণ, ~কাল** *nn* hour/time of sleep; bedtime. **~গত**=নিদ্রিত. **~ ঘোর** *n* drowsiness; sleeping spell. **~জনক**=~কর. **~তুর** *adj* sleepy; drowsy. **~প্রিয়** *adj* fond of sleeping. **~বস্থা** *n* state of sleep. **~বিষ্ট** *adj* dozing; asleep. **~বিহীন** *adj* sleepless. **~বেশ**=~ঘোর. **~বেশে** *adv* somnolently; sleepily; in a sleepy state. **~ব্যাকুল** *adj* overcome with sleep. **~ভঙ্গ** *n* interruption of sleep. **~ভঙ্গ করা** *vi* rouse from sleep; awake; disturb sb's sleep/slumber. **~ভঙ্গ হওয়া** *vi* awake; rouse from sleep; be awakened (by). **~ভাব** *n* **1** want of sleep; sleeplessness; insomnia. **2** sleepiness; drowsiness. **~ভিভূত** *adj* overcome with sleep; fast asleep. **~ভিভূত করা** *vi* overcome with sleep; cause to sleep soundly. **~ভিভূত থাকা** *vi* be sleeping soundly. **~ভিভূত হওয়া** *vi* be overcome with sleep; sleep soundly. **~মগ্ন** *adj* **1** fast asleep; sleeping. **2** (fig) fallen into a deep slumber; completely unconscious; slumbering. **~মগ্ন থাকা** *vi* be sleeping/slumbering; be fast asleep. **~মগ্ন হওয়া** *vi* fall asleep; fall into a deep slumber; slumber. **~য়মাণ** *adj* sleeping; slumbering. **~লস** *n* slothful/indolent from drowsiness; drowsy; sleepy; indolent. **~লসা** *fem.* **~লস্য** *n* sleepiness; long sleeping. **~লু** *adj* sleeping; sleepy; slumberous; somnolent; drowsy; lethargic. **~লুতা** *n* sleepiness; drowsiness; somnolence. **~হীন** *adj* sleepless; wakeful. **গভীর/ ঘোর ~** *n* sound/ profound/ deep sleep. **মহা~** *n* everlasting/ eternal sleep; death. **সুখ~** *n* peaceful sleep. **সু~** *n* good sleep.

নিদ্রিত *adj* asleep; sleeping; slumbering. **নিদ্রিতা** *fem.* **~ থাকা** *vi* be sleeping/slumbering; slumberous; be insensitive/ indifferent/ heedless/listless. **~ হওয়া** *vi* fall asleep.

নিদ্রোত্থান *n* getting up from sleep.

নিদ্রোত্থিত *adj* risen from sleep; awakened; be roused from impassivity/listlessness. **নিদ্রোত্থিতা** *fem.* **~ হওয়া** *vi* wake; awake; awaken; get up from sleep.

নিদ্রোপক্রম *n* readiness for sleep.

নিধন *adj* having no property; resourceless; poor. ❑*n* death; destruction; annihilation; loss; killing. **~ করা** *vt* destroy; kill. **~তা** *n* poverty. **~ প্রাপ্ত হওয়া** *vi* perish; be destroyed/killed; die. **~প্রাপ্তি** *n* perishing; destruction; disappearance; death.

নিধান *n* **1** putting/laying down; depositing; keeping; preserving. **2** receptacle; treasure-house; store; repertory; house; abode: বিদ্যার ~. **3** treasure; fund; store; hoard; deposit. **4** (logarithm) base. **নিধানীয়** *adj* (logarithm) natural.

নিধার[১] *adj* blunt; edgeless; dull.

নিধার[২] *adj* out of debt.

নিধি *n* **1** receptacle; store; treasure; wealth-hoard. **2** fund. **3** (myth) Kuvera's treasure. **4** ocean; sea. **5** deposit; pledge. **~-আবণ্টন** *r* allotment of funds.

নিধুবন *n* **1** shaking; trembling; agitation; fluttering. **2** sexual intercourse/union; copulation. **3** sports; amusements.

নিধেয় *adj* to be placed in/on; to be deposited/ kept/ preserved.

নিনাদ *n* sound; noise; crying; roar; report; humming. **~ করা** *vi* sound; cry out; roar; resound. **নিনাদিত** *adj* filled with noise; resonant with; sounded; blown; played; rung; beaten; resounding.

নিনু *adj* (dial) **1** submissive; obsequious; cringing. **2** low.

নিন্দ *n* (poet)=নিদ্রা

নিন্দক *adj* reviling; reproaching; censuring; slandering; slanderous; blaming; censorious; vilifying. ❑*n* one who reviles/ reproaches/ censures; slanderer; detractor; backbiter; scoffer.

নিন্দন *n* reproach; censure; blame; slandering; reproaching; reviling; animadversion; vilification; blaming; condemnation; calumny; reflection.

নিন্দনীয় *adj* blamable; reprehensible; condemnable; discreditable; censurable; disreputable.

নিন্দা *n* **1**=নিন্দন. **2** disrepute; discredit. ❑*vi* (poet)=~ করা. ~ **করা** *vi* **1** blame; censure; revile; despise; ridicule; animadvert; reflect upon; condemn; vilify; slander; calumniate; speak ill of. **2** (poet) put to shame; bring discredit upon. ~**কর** *adj* disgraceful; discreditable; shameful; reprehensible; scandalous; slanderous. ~**কারী** *adj*=নিন্দক. ~**কারিণী** *fem*. ~**জনক** *adj*=~কর. ~**বাদ** *n* censure; condemnation; censorious comments/utterance. ~**ভাজন** *adj* (of a person) deserving censure/reproach; blameworthy; censurable. ~**যোগ্য**, ~**র্হ**=নিন্দনীয়. ~**সূচক** *adj* slanderous; calumnious; denunciatory; disparaging; derogatory; scornful; derisive. ~**সূচক প্রস্তাব** *n* censure motion. ~**স্তুতি** *n* censure and praise.

নিন্দিত *adj* **1** reproached; reviled; blamed; censured; defamed; abused; condemned; animadverted; calumniated; vilified; discredited; disgraced; hated; despicable; despised; looked down upon; derided. **2** (in compounds) (used as a *suff*) putting to shame; excelling: কোকিল ~. **নিন্দিতা** *fem*.

নিন্দুক *n, adj* (colloq)=নিন্দক

নিন্দ্য=নিন্দনীয়

নিপট[১] *adj* **1** real; true; absolute; genuine:~ সত্য. **2** complete; downright:~ মিথ্যা. **3** extreme; complete; excessive; intense; utter; unmitigated:~ দারিদ্র্য, ~ অন্ধকার.

নিপট[২] *adj* lewd; licentious; dissolute; rakish.

নিপতন *n* fall; falling; descending; downfall.

নিপতিত *adj* **1** fallen down; descended. **2** decayed; sunk; withered; crumbled. ~ **হওয়া** *vi* **1** fall down; descend on. **2** rush upon; attack; assail. **3** fall into ruin/decay; crumble. **4** befall; happen; take place; occur; fall to the share of.

নিপাত *n* **1** falling down; descending; rushing upon. **2** decay; destruction; ruin; death. ~ **যাওয়া** *vi* be killed/ruined/destroyed; die; go to rack and ruin; be damned. ~ **যাও** (as an exclamation) To hell with you ! Oh go to hell ! ~ **যাক** *inter* down with ! ~**ন** *n* **1** throwing down; killing; destroying; knocking out; overthrowing; destruction. **2** causing to descend/fall; throwing down; letting drop/sink; felling (as of a tree). **3** (gram) irregular form; exception. ~**নে সিদ্ধ** *adj* (gram) irregular but accepted. ~**নীয়** *adj* to be felled/ destroyed.

নিপাতিত *adj* **1** overthrown; destroyed; killed; knocked down/out; made to fall/descend on. **2** (gram) irregular; exceptional. ~ **করা** *vt* destroy; kill; knock out/down; fell; overthrow; throw down.

নিপান *n* **1** place/trough for watering cattle; well; pool; tank. **2** milk-pail.

নিপিস্তে *adj* (colloq) shameless; brazen-faced; unblushing.

নিপীড়ক *adj* oppressing; afflicting; repressive; persecuting. ❑*n* oppressor; tormentor.

নিপীড়ন *n* **1** squeezing; pressing. **2** hurting; oppression; repression; persecution; torture; harrying; torment. ~ **করা** *vt* **1** squeeze; press together. **2** oppress; repress; trouble; torment; afflict; plague; persecute; tyrannize over; harry.

নিপীড়িত *adj* **1** squeezed; pressed; embraced. **2** oppressed; repressed; persecuted; tormented; afflicted; harried; plagued. ~ **করা**=নিপীড়ন করা (⇒ নিপীড়ন).

নিপীত *adj* drunk in/up/off; drunk to the dregs; drained to the lees; absorbed; imbibed.

নিপুণ *adj* skilful; adroit; clever; dexterous; skilled; sharp; acute; adept; deft; expert; efficient. **নিপুণা** *fem*. ~**তা** *n* skilfulness; adroitness; dexterity; deftness; skill; efficiency; expertness.

নিফলা *adj* (of a tree) barren.

নিব [E] *n* nib.

নিবদ্ধ *adj* **1** bound; fettered; chained; fastened/tied to; fixed, attached; adhering to; affixed. **2** worn; put on. **3** inserted; entered; written down; composed. **4** covered with; veiled in. **5** adorned/inlaid with; consisting of; accompanied by; furnished with. **6** steadfast; fixed; firm and unchanging: দৃষ্টি ~ করা. **7** registered. **8** arranged; arrayed; strung: ব্যূহ~. **9** planted. ~ **করা** *vt* **1** bind (on); tie; fasten (to); enchain; fetter. **2** unite; join; attach. **3** compose; draw up; write down. **4** put/fix upon. **5** arrange; array. **6** register; insert. **7** plant. ~**করণ**, **নিবদ্ধীকরণ** *nn* registration; fixation; planting.

নিবনিব=নিবুনিবু

নিবস্ত *adj* **1** (of a light, etc) about to go out; flickering; faint. **2** (fig) dying. **3** exhausted; worn out; dropping. **4** flagging; diminishing; drooping: ~ উৎসাহ.

নিবন্ধ *n* **1** essay; dissertation; (literary) composition; thesis; treatise; book. **2** means; device. **3** rule; system. **4** fastening; tying; fixation; determination. **5** bondage; tie; bond. ~**ক** *n* registrar. ~**ন** *n* **1** binding; tying; fastening; fettering; ligation. **2** bond; fetter; stay; support. **3** registration. **4** fixation. **5** literary composition; treatise. **6** cause; origin; basis; foundation. ❑*adj* (in compounds) (used as a *suff*) due/ owing to; because of: তার অনুরোধ ~ন. ~**নভুক্ত** *adj* registered; entered in a register. ~**নভুক্ত করা** *vt* register. ~**ন-সংখ্যা** *n* registration number. **নিবন্ধিত** *adj* **1** bound;

fastened; tied. **2** written; composed. **3** strung. **4** registered.

নিবর্ত *n* desisted; refrained; stopped; turning back. ❑*n* prohibition. **~ক** *adj* causing to cease; abolishing; removing; preventing; desisting from; ceasing; stopping; opposed to; dissuasive; preventive; deterrent. ❑*n* opponent; antagonist. **~ন** *n* **1** turning back; ceasing; desisting; giving up; refraining; cessation; stopping. **2** prevention; suppression; deterrence; discouragement. **~নমূলক** *adj* preventive; deterrent. **~নীয়** *adj* to be brought back; to be prevented/ hindered/ averted/ suppressed. **নিবর্তিত** *adj* turned/ brought back; caused to give up/ desist from; suppressed; prevented; averted; abandoned.

নিবসতি, নিবসন *nn* dwelling; habitation; abode; residing.

নিবহ *n* multitude; quantity; neap; collection.

নিবা *vi* (of light, fire, etc) go out; be extinguished/ quenched/ blown out. ❑*adj* extinguished; quenched; put out. **~নো** *vt* put out; extinguish; quench; blow out. ❑*adj*=~.

নিবাত *adj* **1** sheltered from the wind; calm; still; steady: ~ নিষ্কম্প. **2** airless; stuffy. **3** not flickering; burning steadily: ~ দীপের মতো.

নিবাপ *n* oblation/offering (esp to deceased relatives).

নিবার=নিবারণ. **~ক** *adj* keeping off; preventing; stopping mitigating; allaying; hindering; preventive. ❑*n* one who prevents/ prohibits/ stops/wards off; allaying agent.

নিবারণ *n* prevention; keeping off; hindering; warding off; stopping; hindrance; mitigation; allaying; restraining. **~ করা** *vt* prevent; prohibit; restrain; hold back from; stop; ward off; hinder; suppress; remove; mitigate; allay; put off. **~ হওয়া** *vi* stop; desist from; refrain from; be mitigated/allayed/removed; be prevented/warded off. **নিবারণা** *vt* (poet)=~ করা.

নিবারণীয় *adj* to be kept off/ prevented/ mitigated/ allayed/ restrained/ warded off; preventable; resistible; mitigable; capable of being warded off/ allayed.

নিবারিত *adj* kept off; prevented; restrained; hindered; forbidden; warded off; mitigated; allayed. **~ করা**=নিবারণ করা (⇒ নিবারণ).

নিবার্য=নিবারণীয়

নিবাস *n* living; dwelling; residing; dwelling-place; abode; house; habitation; residence; dwelling-house. **~ করা** *vi* dwell; live in; sojourn; inhabit; reside. **~ন** *n* living; residing; sojourn; abode. **নিবাসী** *adj* dewelling/living/ residing in; inhabiting. ❑*n* inhabitant. **নিবাসিনী** *fem.*

নিবিড় *adj* **1** close; intimate: ~ বন্ধুত্ব. **2** compact; think; dense; deep; intense: ~ অরণ্য/ অন্ধকার. **3** tight; close: ~ আলিঙ্গন. **4** full of; abounding in: ছায়া~. **5** thick-set; large; heavy; plump: ~ নিতম্ব. **~তা** *n* closeness; intimacy; compactness; density; thickness; tightness; heaviness; largeness; amplitude; depth; intensity.

নিবিদ *n* instruction; information.

নিবিষ্ট *adj* **1** absorbed; intent on; engrossed; deeply engaged; concentrated; occupied with; taken up with; rapt; enrapt. **2** placed; located; settled down; encamped; seated/sitting on/in; situated; arrayed; entered. **নিবিষ্টা** *fem.* **~ করা** *vt* **1** engage deeply; absorb; engross; interest deeply. **2** concentrate. **3** array; place in an orderly manner; enter. **~চিত্ত** *adj* having one's mind deeply absorbed/ engrossed/ engaged; intently attentive. **~চিত্ততা** *n* intense concentration. **~চিত্তে** *adv* with undivided/ rapt/ close attention. **~তা** *n* concentration; absorption; rapt; attention; great application; intense concentration.

নিবীত *n* **1** wrapper; veil; mantle. **2** the Brahminical thread worn round the neck.

নিবুনিবু *adj* about to go out; flickering; about to be extinguished. **~ হওয়া** *vi* be on the point of going out/be extinguished; flicker.

নিবৃত *adj* surrounded; enclosed; wrapped. ❑*n* veil; mantle; wrapper.

নিবৃত্ত *adj* desisted; restrained; prevented; stopped; turned back; averted; receded; warded off; ceased. **~ করা** *vt* turn back; stop; dissuade; restrain; thwart; deter. **~ হওয়া** *vi* desist/refrain from; cease; stop; abstain from; leave off; give up; recede.

নিবৃত্তি *n* abstaining/desisting from; cessation; ceasing; stoppage; renunciation; renouncement. **~-বেতন** *n* pension. **~মার্গ** *n* path of renunciation.

নিবেদক *adj* communicating; informing; relating; narrating; petitioning; representing; submitting humbly; dedicating. ❑*n* one who communicates/informs/petitions/submits humbly; petitioner; narrator; applicant; deponent.

নিবেদন *n* announcement; declaration; communication; submission; presentation; humble/ polite narration; petition; representation; dedication; offering; statement; deposition. **~ করা** *vt* communicate; submit; present; narrate/ state/ represent/ petition humbly/ politely; make an statement; depose; make a deposition; dedicate; offer; deliver. **~-পত্র** *n* petition; representation; memorandum.

নিবেদনীয় *adj* to be communicated/ presented/ submitted/ delivered/ offered. (⇒ নিবেদন).

নিবেদিত *adj* made known; communicated; told; presented; submitted; delivered; offered; petitioned; represented.

নিবেদ্য=নিবেদনীয়

নিবেশ *n* **1** entering; sitting; settling in a place; encampment; camp: সেনা~. **2** putting in order; arrangement; deposition; arraying: ব্যূহ~. **3** insertion; placing; emplacement. **4** application; concentration: মনো~. **5** interpolation. ~ক *adj* encamping; arraying; inserting; interpolating; recording; placing; applying. ❑*n* one who encamps/ arrays/ arranges/ inserts/ records/ places/ applies/ interpolates/ concentrates. ~ন *n* **1** entering; entrance; settling; placing; emplacement; array; fixing; insertion. **2** dwelling-place; camp; house; home; lair; rest. **3** interpolation. ~-প্রদর্শ *n* recorder's guide book.

নিবেশিত *adj* made to enter; placed in/upon; fixed/intent upon; engaged in; encamped; arrayed; inserted; interpolated; entered; recorded; domiciled; seated; put; applied.

নিবেশী *adj* resting in; lying on/in/near; domiciled. ❑*n* domiciled person.

-নিভ *adj* (used as a *suff*) resembling; like; similar: দুগ্ধফেন~.

নিভন্ত=নিবন্ত

নিভা=নিবা. ~নো=নিবানো

নিভাঁজ *adj* free from folds/wrinkled; fresh; plane; smooth; genuine; unadulterated; unalloyed; pure.

নিভৃত *adj* **1** secret; private: ~ আলাপ. **2** quiet; silent; lonely; solitary; hidden: ~ স্থান. ~ কক্ষ *n* private room; closet. ~ চিন্তা *n* meditations in solitude. ~ স্থান *n* lonely/solitary place; lonely retreat; solitude. নিভৃতার্থ *n* secret meaning. নিভৃতে *adv* secretly; privately; silently; quietly; in solitude.

নিম[1] [P] *adj* (used as a *pref*) half; middle.

নিম[2] *n* margosa tree.

নিমক [P] *n* salt. ~ খাওয়া *vi* eat sb's salt; (fig) be indebted to/benefited by; be under an obligation to. ~দান *n* salt-cellar; salt-shaker. ~মহল *n* estate consisting of salt-yielding land/salt-pit/salt-marsh. ~হারাম *adj* disloyal; perfidious; ungrateful; disobedient; vile; wicked; evil. ~হারামি *n* disloyalty; perfidy; ingratitude; treason; treachery. ~হারামি করা *vi* act/behave perfidiously/ treacherously; bite the hand that feeds one. ~হালাল *adj* grateful; loyal; true; dutiful. ~হালালি *n* gratitude; fidelity; loyalty. ~ হালাল করা, নিমকের হক আদায় করা discharge one's obligations.

নিমকি [P] *adj* saltish; salted. ❑*n* name of a salted and crisp snack.

নিমখুন *adj* half-killed; almost murdered. ❑*n* grievous hurt amounting to murder.

নিমগন *adj* (poet)=নিমগ্ন

নিমগ্ন *adj* **1** submerged/ plunged/ immersed in; overwhelmed; engrossed: চিন্তা~. **2** over heads and ears; plunged into: ঋণ~. নিমগ্না *fem.* ~ হওয়া *vi* sink; plunge; be absorbed in.

নিমচা [P] *n* scimitar.

নিমজ্জন *n* **1** submersion; immersion; diving; bathing; sinking; drowning; dip; plunge. **2** absorption; engrossment.

নিমজ্জমান *adj* sinking; drowning; being absorbed/engrossed/overwhelmed. নিমজ্জমানা *fem.*

নিমজ্জিত *adj* plunged (into the water); sunken; drowned; submerged; immersed; absorbed; overwhelmed; engrossed. নিমজ্জিতা *fem.*

নিমন্ত্রক *n* inviter.

নিমন্ত্রণ *n* **1** invitation. **2** call(ing); summon. ~ করা *vt* invite; call to; summon. ~ গ্রহণ করা *vi* accept an invitation. ~ প্রত্যাখ্যান করা *vi* refuse/decline an invitation. ~ রক্ষা করা *vi* pay a visit to the host in response to an invitation. ~পত্র *n* letter of invitation; invitation-card. বিনা নিমন্ত্রণে without invitation; uninvitedly; unasked.

নিমন্ত্রয়িতা *n* host; inviter. নিমন্ত্রয়িত্রী *fem* hostess.

নিমন্ত্রাতা *n* host.

নিমন্ত্রিত *adj* invited; summoned; called; convoked. নিমন্ত্রিতা *fem.* ~ ব্যক্তি *n* guest; invitee.

নিমরাজি [P] *adj* half-willing; half-inclined; reluctantly consenting.

নিমহাকিম [P] *n* quack; charlatan.

নিমা [P] *n* short under-garment; half-sleeved shirt/jacket.

নিমিখ *n* (colloq)=নিমিষ

নিমিত্ত *n* **1** cause; motive; ground; reason. **2** end in view; object; aim; necessity. **3** agent; tool; instrument. ❑*prep* because of; on account of; for; due/owing to. ~ কারণ *n* instrumental/ efficient cause. ~কাল *n* period/ moment of time which may be regarded as causing any event. ~জ্ঞ *adj* acquainted with omens. ❑*n* diviner; augur; soothsayer. ~তা, ~ত্ব *adj* causality; instrumentality. ~বিদ=~জ্ঞ. ~মাত্র *n* mere instrument/efficient cause. নিমিত্তার্থ *n* (gram) infinitive mood. নিমিত্তের ভাগী *adj* involved in sth by mere accident. নিমিত্তের ভাগী হওয়া *vi* get involved in sth by mere accident.

নিমিষ *n* **1** twinkling; shutting the eye; wink. **2** moment; twinkling of an eye; instant. ~ ফেলা *vi* shut the eyelids; wink. ~রহিত, ~শূন্য, ~হারা, ~হীনা *adjj* (of eyes/glance) unwinking; fixed; steadfast. ~হারা চোখে চাওয়া/ তাকানো *vi* stare without blinking; gaze; look steadfastly. (এক) নিমিষে *adv* in the twinkling of an eye; in a jiffy/trice.

নিমীলন *n* 1 shutting the eyes. 2 closing of a flower. ~ করা *vt* shut; close.

নিমীলিকা *n* fraud; trick.

নিমীলিত *adj* closed; shut. ~ করা=নিমীলন করা (⇒ নিমীলন). ~চক্ষে *adv* with eyes closed/shut. ~দৃষ্টি, নিমীলিতাক্ষ *adjj* having the eyes closed/shut.

নিমেষ=নিমিষ

নি-মোরাদ *adj* unmanly; impotent.

নিম্ন *adj* 1 low; deep; low-lying; inclined towards; sunk; depressed: ~ভূমি. 2 downcast: ~দৃষ্টি. 3 subordinate; junior: ~পদ. 4 base; mean; low: ~রুচি. 5 socially lower/depressed: ~ জাতি. 6 lower: ~ আদালত. ☐*n* depth; low ground; depression: ~ থেকে, from below. ~ অক্ষাংশ *n* (geog) low latitude. ~গ *adj* 1 going downwards; declining; descending. 2 going astray; going to the bad. ☐*n* river. ~গা *fem*. ~গামী *adj*=~গ. ~গামিনী *fem*. ~চাপ *n* 1 (meteo) depression; low pressure. 2 (med) low pressure. 3 (geog) downward pressure. ~তর *adj* lower. ~তর কক্ষ *n* (of a legislature) lower house/chamber. ~তম *adj* lowest; minimum. ~তা, ~ত্ব *adjj* lowness; depth; depression; baseness; degeneration; meanness; shortage; scarcity. ~তাপ *n* (abnormally) low temperature. ~দৃষ্টি *n* 1 downcast eyes/look. 2 mean inclination/outlook. ~দৃষ্টিতে *adj* looking downwards; with downcast eyes. ~দেশ *n* lower part; region underneath. ~দেশে *adv* below; under; in/to a lower part; beneath; underneath. ~ধৃত *adj* under mentioned. ~পদ *n* lower/junior/subordinate position/post. ~পাত *n* descending node. ~প্রদেশ *n* lower region/part; lowlands; part of the body under the waist; posterior. ~প্রবণ *adj* flowing downwards; sloping. ~প্রাথমিক *adj* lower primary. ~ভাগ = ~দেশ. ~ভূমি *n* lowlands; low/ depressed land. ~মুখ *adj* (bot) reclinate. ~লিখিত *adj* undermentioned; written below. ~সীমা *n* lowest limit. নিম্নাকর্ষণ downward attraction. নিম্নাভিমুখ *adj* tending/ flowing downwards; downwards.

নিম্নীভূত *adj* depressed; sunk. ~ সমভূমি *n* (geog) sunk plain.

নিম্নোক্ত *adj* undermentioned.

নিম্নোদ্ধৃত *adj* quoted below; undermentioned.

নিম্নোন্নত *adj* low and high; depressed and elevated; uneven; undulating.

নিম্ব(কে) *n* margosa (tree/seed).

নিম্বু, নিম্বুক *nn* lemon; common lime. ~পানি *n* lemonade.

নিযুত *n*, *adj* a million.

নিযুক্ত *adj* appointed; employed; engaged; placed in authority; devoted. ~ করা *vt* appoint; employ; engage; install; trust/ charge with; devote. ~ হওয়া *vi* be appointed/ employed/ engaged in; devote oneself to. ~ক *n* (commerce) agent. ~ক স্থান *n* agency.

নিযোক্তা *n* employer; master; appointing/ employing authority.

নিযোজ্য *adj* to be appointed/ employed/ engaged/ directed/ commanded/ applied.

নিয়ত[1], **নিয়ৎ** [A] *nn* intention; will; purpose; design; aim; wish. ~ করা/ বাঁধা *vi* 1 repeat the prayer formula. 2 intend; be determined; resolve (on/ upon).

নিয়ত[2] *adj* 1 fixed; established; settled; sure; regular; invariable; positive; definite. 2 constant; steady; unchanging; continuous; perpetual: ~ চিন্তা, ~ বায়ু, constant wind. 3 restrained; checked; controlled; curbed; suppressed; restricted. 4 disciplined; self governed; abstemious; temperate. ☐*adv* always; ever; constantly; continuously; often. ~বৃত্ত *n* (conics) director cirle. ~ব্রত *adj* constant in the observance of vows; regular in observances; pious; religious. নিয়তাচার = ~ব্রত. নিয়তাত্মা *adj* self-controlled; self-restrained; abstemious; self-disciplined; continent. নিয়তাশন, নিয়তাহার *adjj* abstemious in food; temperate. ☐*n* abstemiousness; temperance.

নিয়তি *n* 1 fixed order of things; necessity. 2 destiny; fate; predestination; luck. 3 inevitable occurrence. 4 self-command; self-restraint. 5 regulation; control. ~নির্দিষ্ট *adj* foreordained; predestined; foredoomed; ordained by fate; fated; decreed by providence. ~নির্দেশ *n* providence; God's will; fate.

নিয়তেন্দ্রিয় *adj* self-controlled; abstemious.

নিয়ন্তা *adj* who or what holds in/ restrains/ governs/ controls/ tames/ destines/ directs/ determines. ☐*n* controller; tamer; deciding factor; decision maker. নিয়ন্ত্রী *fem*.

নিয়ন্ত্রক *adj* controlling; regulating; deciding. ☐*n* controlled; regulator.

নিয়ন্ত্রণ *n* control; restraint; regulation; rule; determination; restraining; governing; checking; restricting. ~ করা *vt* control; restrain; regulate; govern; check; restrict; determine. ~-ব্যবস্থা *n* control system. নিয়ন্ত্রণাধীন *adj* controlled; under control; regulated.

নিয়ন্ত্রিত *adj* 1 restrained; checked; fettered. 2 controlled; regulated; determined. 3 governed by; depending on.

নিয়ম *n* 1 (fixed) rule; law; regulation; ruling. 2 necessity; obligation. 2 precept; prescription; direction: শাস্ত্রীয় ~. 3 system; method;

discipline: কাজের ~. 4 stipulation; condition; convention; contract; promise; vow. 5 custom; convention; practice: এটা আমাদের পারিবারিক ~. 6 routine duty; regular practice: ছেলেকে বকাবকি করা তার একটা ~ হয়ে দাঁড়িয়েছে. 7 act of voluntary penance/ meritorious piety: ~ পালন. 8 self-discipline; restraint of the mind; self-control; abstemiousness; temperance. 9 restraining; checking; holding back; controlling. 10 limitation; restriction. ~ করা *vi* 1 lay down a rule; make a law; stipulate. 2 make (it) a rule give judicial/ authoritative decision; rule. ~তন্ত্র *n* set/code of laws; constitution; system; regularity; constitutionalism. ~তান্ত্রিক *adj* systematic; regular; constitutional. ~ন *n* 1 restraining; checking; controlling; regulating. 2 regularization. 3 laying down rules; issuing laws. 4 precept; fixed practice/ rule. 5 restriction; limitation. 6 stipulating. 7 issuing a ruling. ~নিষ্ঠ *adj* zealously observing prescribed rites; ardently obedient to rules and systems; regular; disciplined; methodical; well-regulated; scrupulous; ceremonious; rigid; regular in one's habits. ~নিষ্ঠা *n* rigid observance of prescribed rites; strict obedience to rules and regulations; discipline; regular habits; regularity; methodicalness. ~পত্র *n* agreement; covenant. ~পর(তন্ত্র), ~পরায়ণ *adjj* observing fixed rules. ~পালন *n* observance of rules and regulations/ prescribed rites/ stipulations; regularity in practice. ~ পালন করা *vi* observe/ abide by rules and regulations; practice religious observances; go by the rule; abide by stipulations and conditions. ~পূর্বক *adv* according to rules (and regulations); regularly; methodically; systematically; routinely; as a matter of course; invariable; in keeping with (fixed) rules. ~বর্জিত, ~বহির্ভূত, ~বিরুদ্ধ *adj* contrary to rules; irregular; flouting rules/ stipulations; ultra vires; unmethodical; anomalous; illegal. ~ভঙ্গ *n* 1 breach of a stipulation/ contract. 2 breach/ violation/ infringement of a rule. 3 completion/ termination/ breach of a religious rite/ vow. ~ভঙ্গ করা *vi* 1 break/ violate/ infringe a rule/ stipulation. 2 complete/ terminate/ break/ interrupt a religious rite/ vow. ~মর্তো, ~মাফিক = নিয়মানুযায়ী. ~-রক্ষা *n* compliance with/ observance of rules/ rites; adherence to customs/ practices. ~ রক্ষা করা *vi* observe rules/ rites; keep up/ up hold customs/ practices; comply with rules (and regulations). ~ রক্ষা করে *adv* in conformity with the rules/ customs. ~লঙ্ঘন *n* transgression/ violation of a fixed rule/ obligation/ customs/ practices.

নিয়মাধীন *adj* subject to/bound by rules; regulated; regular; well-regulated. **নিয়মানুগ** *adj* regular. **নিয়মানুবর্তন, নিয়মানুবর্তিতা** = ~নিষ্ঠা. **নিয়মানুবর্তী** = ~নিষ্ঠ. **নিয়মানুযায়ী** *adj* regular; regulated; methodical; systematic; disciplined. ❑*adj* according to fixed/ fixed rules; in accordance/ conformity with the rules/ practices. **নিয়মানুসারে** *adv* = নিয়মানুযায়ী. **নিয়মাবলী** *n pl* set/code of rules; rules; regulations.

নিয়মিত *adj* 1 regular; regulated. 2 prescribed; stipulated. 3 checked; restrained; bound by; controlled. ❑*adv* in a regular manner; regularly. ~ করা *vt* regulate; regularize. ~ সময়ে at the appointed/ stipulated time.

নিয়মী *adj* 1 = নিয়মানুবর্তী (⇒ নিয়ম). 2 self-disciplined; abstemious; temperate.

নিয়ম্য *adj* to be restrained/ controlled/ checked; controllable.

নিয়াই *n* (dial) = নেহাই

নিয়ামক *adj* controlling; regulating; governing; checking; restraining; directing; guiding; regularizing. ❑*n* 1 regulator; director; controller; registrar. 2 factor. 3 (geom) directrix. 4 guide; pilot; ruler.

নিয়ামন = নিয়মন (⇒ নিয়ম)

নিয়ামত, নিয়ামৎ [A] *nn* blessings/ favours of heaven; good things/ comforts of life; delight; joy; wealth. ~খানা *n* home/ abode of affluence; palace; meat safe.

নিয়োগ *n* 1 employment; appointment; election. 2 use; application. 3 commission; charge; appointed task/ duty; business; order. ~ করা *vt* 1 appoint; employ; engage; nominate; elect, install use; employ; apply; make use of: সর্বশক্তি ~ করা. ~-অধিকর্তা *n* director of employment. ~কর্তা = নিয়োক্তা. ~কর্ত্রী *fem.* ~পত্র *n* appointment letter.

নিয়োগী *adj* appointed; employed; engaged. ❑*n* functionary; employee; official; minister.

নিয়োজক = নিয়োক্তা

নিয়োজন = নিয়োগ

নিয়োজয়িতা = নিয়োক্তা. **নিয়োজয়িত্রী** *fem.*

নিয়োজিত = নিযুক্ত

নিরংশ *n* (astrol) the first and the last day of the ascendance of a sign of the zodiac; passage of a sun or a planet from one sign/ position in the heaven into another. ❑*adj* receiving no share. ~ক *adj* = ~. **নিরংশী** *adj fem.*

নিরংশু *adj* rayless; lustreless; dark.

নিরক্ষ, নিরক্ষদেশ *nn* equator; equatorial region. ~ দূরবীক্ষণ *n* equatorial telescope. ~বৃত্ত, ~রেখা *nn* equator.

নিরক্ষর *adj* illiterate. ~তা *n* illiteracy. ~তা দূরীকরণ *n* removal of illiteracy.

নিরক্ষীয় *adj* equatorial. ~ তাপরেখা *n* heat equator. ~ শান্তবলয় *n* doldrums.

নিরখা *vi* (poet) see; look at; notice; observe.

নিরগ্নি *adj* having no (consecrated) fire.

নিরঙ্কুশ *adj* 1 unchecked; uncontrolled; unbridled; extravagant. 2 independent. 3 inevitable; unpreventable. 4 absolute. ~ **সংখ্যাগরিষ্ঠতা** *n* absolute majority.

নিরঙ্গ *adj* having no limbs; maimed.

নিরঞ্জন *adj* spotless; pure; simple; clean; immaculate. ❑*n* 1 the Supreme Being. 2 Shiva. 3 absolute non-existence (with Buddhists).

নিরত *adj* attached/ devoted to; quite intent upon; deeply engaged in/ occupied with; delighting in; engrossed; absorbed.

নিরতি *adj* deep attachment to; taking delight in.

নিরতিশয় *adj* very much; excessive; unparalleled; too much; extreme. ❑*adv* excessively; extremely; exceedingly; too/ very much.

নিরত্যয় *adj* 1 free from danger; secure; safe. 2 unblamable; faultless. 3 imperishable; deathless; everlasting.

নিরধিকার *adj* having no right/ title; dispossessed.

নিরন্তর *adj* 1 close; compact; having no interval; dense; thick. 2 uninterrupted; ceaseless; constant; perpetual; continuous. ❑*adv* 1 closely; tightly. 2 constantly; continually; ceaselessly; without break; always. ~ **পরিবৃত্তি** *n* continuous variation. **নিরন্তরাল** *adj* without an intervening space; close; narrow.

নিরন্ন *adj* wanting food; starving.

নিরন্বয় *adj* 1 unrelated; unconnected. 2 childless.

নিরপত্য *adj* having no offspring; childless.

নিরপরাধ *adj* guiltless; blameless; innocent. ❑*n* faultlessness; innocence. **নিরপরাধী, নিরপরাধিনী** *adjj*. **নিরাপরাধে** *adv* unjustly; wrongfully.

নিরপবাদ *adj* blameless.

নিরপেক্ষ *adj* 1 impartial; unprejudiced; unbiased; fair: ~ মতামত. 2 independent of; disinterested (in); indifferent: ধর্ম~. 3 regardless of. 4 (phil) categorical. ~**তা** *n* impartiality; independence; fairness; freedom from bias/ prejudice; disinterestedness; (phil) categoricalness. ~**ভাবে** *adv* impartially; without prejudice/ bias; regardlessly; independently; regardless of; with fairness. ~ **রাষ্ট্র** *n* neutral/ non-aligned state. ~ **সাহায্য** *n* unconditional/ gratuitous aid.

নিরপেক্ষে *adv* = নিরপেক্ষভাবে (⇒ নিরপেক্ষ)

নিরবকাশ *adj* 1 wanting room; crowded. 2 incessant; leisureless; continuous; ceaseless.

নিরবগ্রহ *adj* unrestrained; independent; free.

নিরবচ্ছিন্ন *adj* 1 close; compact; dense; thick: ~ সৌধশ্রেণী. 2 incessant; ceaseless; continuous; uninterrupted: ~ বৃষ্টিধারা, ~ সুখ. ~**তা** *n* continuity endlessness; compactness; interminability ~**ভাবে** *adv* ceaselessly; continuously; without interruption; incessantly.

নিরবদ্য *adj* faultless; flawless; unblamable; unobjectionable; excellent. ~**তা** *n* blamelessness; excellence; perfection; faultlessness.

নিরবধি *adj* 1 unlimited; endless; infinite; boundless; eternal: কাল ~. 2 ceaseless; continuous; perpetual: ~ যন্ত্রণা. ❑*adv* continuously; endlessly; without end; always.

নিরবয়ব *adj* having no limbs/ members; formless; incorporeal; unembodied.

নিরবলম্ব, নিরলম্বন *n* supportless; helpless; having no prop/support; destitute; helpless; homeless.

নিরবশেষ *adj* without a residue; complete; thorough; whole. **নিরবশেষে** *adv* completely; totally; thoroughly; fully.

নিরবশেষিত *adj* completed; exhausted.

নিরবসাদ *adj* not cast down; cheerful; untiring.

নিরভিমান, নিরভিমানী *adj* unassuming; modest; unpretentious. **নিরভিমানিনী** *fem*.

নিরভ্র *adj* cloudless.

নিরম্বু *adj* abstaining from water; waterless. ~ **উপবাস** *n* fasting in which drinking of water is not permitted.

নিরয় *n* the underworld; hell. ~**গামী** *adj* condemned to hell. ~**ভোগ** *n* suffering in hell.

নিরর্গল *adj* unbarred; unimpeded; free; irresistible.

নিরর্থ *adj* useless; vain; meaningless; pointless; unnecessary; nonsensical; purposeless; unsuccessfull. ~**ক** *adj* = ~. ❑*adv* in vain; uselessly; without purpose; unnecessarily; meaninglessly. ~**কতা** *n* meaninglessness; futility; nonsense; pointlessness.

নিরলঙ্কার *adv* unornamented; unadorned; inelaborate; plain; simple; unrhetorical.

নিরলস *adj* untiring; tireless; indefatigable; ceaseless; diligent.

নিরস = নীরস

নিরসন[১] *adj* abstaining from food; fasting.

নিরসন[২] *n* 1 casting out; driving away; removing; removal: দুঃখ ~. 2 alleviation; mitigation: দারিদ্র্য ~, যন্ত্রণা ~. 3 rejection; refutation: যুক্তি ~. 4 protection from; covering: লজ্জা ~. 5 destruction; extermination. ~ **করা** *vt* cast out; drive away; peal; removing; alleviate; mitigate; reject; refute; hide; conceal; expel; destroy; annihilate. ~ **হওয়া** *vi* be removed/ alleviated/ mitigated.

নিরসনীয় *adj* to be driven out/ expelled/ removed/ alleviated/ mitigated/ rejected/ refuted.

নিরস্ত *adj* desisted; refrained; repelled; stopped. ~ **করা** *vt* restrain; stop; keep back; deter; hold back; check; prevent; contain; repel. ~ **হওয়া** *vi* desist from; stop; refrain from; keep from; forgo; abstain from; forbear. ~**পাদপ** *adj* treeless; denuded of trees.

নিরস্ত্র *adj* disarmed; unarmed. ~ **করা** *vt* disarm. **নিরস্ত্রীকরণ** *n* disarmament.

নিরহঙ্কার, নিরহঙ্কারী *adj* free from egotism; unassuming; humble; modest; unselfish; unpretentious; affable. **নিরহঙ্কারা** *fem.* ~**তা** *n* modesty; humility; affability.

নিরাকরণ *n* **1** driving out; turning out; expelling; removing; removal; repulsion. **2** refutation; repudiation; rejection. **3** mitigation; alleviation. **4** prevention. **5** determination; ascertainment. ~ **করা** *vt* drive away; turn/ keep off; remove; repudiate; refute; reject; expel; eliminate; mitigate; alleviate; prevent; ward off; determine; ascertain. ~ **হওয়া** *vi* be driven away/ turned off/ kept off/ removed/ repudiated/ rejected/ refuted/ expelled/ eliminated/ determined/ ascertained.

নিরাকাঙ্ক্ষ *adj* expecting/ wishing nothing; desireless; unambitious; disinterested; contented. **নিরাকাঙ্ক্ষা** *n* absence of desire; contentment; contentedness.

নিরাকার *adj* formless; shapeless; incorporeal. ❑*n* **1** sky. **2** universal spirit.

নিরাকুল *adj* **1** extremely agitated/ perturbed/ worried/ anxious. **2** not too much beset; unperturbed; calm. **3** abundant: ~ ফুলভার.

নিরাকৃত *adj* pushed/ driven away; removed; eliminated; mitigated; allayed; refuted; rejected; repudiated; warded off; repulsed; determined; ascertained. ~ **করা** = নিরাকরণ করা (⇒ নিরাকরণ).

নিরাকৃতি[১] *n* = নিরাকরণ

নিরাকৃতি[২] *adj* = নিরাকার

নিরাতঙ্ক *adj* free from fear; fearless; unafraid.

নিরাতপ *adj* shady.

নিরাধার *adj* without a receptacle/ support/ shelter; homeless; destitute; helpless.

নিরানন্দ *adj* joyless; cheerless; dreary; dismal; gloomy. ❑*n* cheerlessness; gloominess; sadness; unhappiness; bleakness; dismalness. ~**কর** *adj* causing no pleasure; distressing; dismal; afflicting; cheerless. **নিরানন্দী** *adj* = ~.

নিরানব্বই, নিরানব্বুই (colloq) *n, adj* ninety-nine.

নিরাপত্তা *n* safety; security. ~ **আইন** *n* security act. ~-**পরিষদ** *n* the Security Council (of the UNO).

নিরাপদ, নিরাপৎ *adj* secure; safe. **নিরাপদেষু, নিরাপৎসু** (in addressing sb in a letter) to one who is safe from dangers. **নিরাপদে** *adv* safely; securely; safe and sound; unharmed.

নিরাবরণ *adj* uncovered; bare; unveiled; manifest; evident.

নিরাবাধ *adj* undisturbed; unmolested; secure; free.

নিরাভরণ *adj* unornamented; unadorned; bare; plain. **নিরাভরণা** *fem.*

নিরাময় *adj* **1** free from illness; healthy; well. **2** recovered from/ cured of illness. **3** wholesome. ❑*n* freedom from illness; health; welfare; cure; recovery from illness. ~ **করা** *vt* cure; bring round; heal. ~ **হওয়া** *vi* be cured; come round; recover from illness.

নিরামিষ *adj* fleshless; vegetarian. ~ **ভোজন** *n* vegetarianism. ~**ভোজী, নিরামিষাশী** *adj, n* vegetarian.

নিরায়ত *adj* unextended; contracted; compact.

নিরায়াস *adj* easy.

নিরায়ুধ *adj* weaponless; unarmed.

নিরালম্ব(ন) *adj* supportless; self-supported; not resting on another; without support/ prop; free; unaided; helpless; shelterless; homeless.

নিরালয় *adj* homeless; shelterless.

নিরালস্য *adj* not slothful; energetic.

নিরালা *adj* lonely; solitary; secluded; secret; private. ❑*n* lonely retreat. ~**য়** *adj* in solitude; privately; tite a tite. **

নিরালোক *adj* deprived of light; dark; blind.

নিরাশ *adj* without any hope; hopeless; disappointed; despondent; dejected; despairing. ~ **করা** *vt* disappoint. ~ **হওয়া** *vi* be disappointed/dejected; lose hope; dispair. **নিরাশা** *n* loss of hope; despair; dejection; despondency; disappointment; forlorn hope. **নিরাশার আশা** *n* hoping against hope; last hope.

নিরাশ্রয় *adj* shelterless; homeless; supportless; destitute; alone; helpless. **নিরাশ্রয়া** *fem.*

নিরাশ্বাস *adj* despairing; dejected; sunk in despair; despondent.

নিরাস্বাদ *adj* tasteless; insipid; unsavoury.

নিরাহার *n* want of food; starvation; fasting. ❑*adj* having no food; starving; fasting. **নিরাহারে** *adj* going without food; of starvation; fasting.

নিরিখ [P] *n* market rate; current price; tariff; assize. ~**বন্দি** *n* fixation of rates.

নিরিন্দ্রিয় *adj* destitute of sense-organ; deprived/ destitute of sense-perception.

নিরিবিলি *adj* lonely; solitary; secluded; forlorn. ❑*n* lonely/ solitary place. ❑*adv* **1** privately ~ আলাপ করা. **2** in/at a lonely place: ~ বসা.

নিরীক্ষক *adj* observing; seeing; viewing; scrutinizing; auditing. ❑*n* observer; viewer; onlooker; scrutinizer; auditor.

নিরীক্ষণ *n* looking at; regarding; observing; observation; seeing; scrutiny; auditing; audit. ~ **করা** *vt* look at/ toward; behold; see; regard; observe; perceive; scrutinize; audit.

নিরীক্ষমাণ *adj* = নিরীক্ষক. **নিরীক্ষমাণা** *fem.*

নিরীক্ষা *n* = নিরীক্ষণ. ~**সার** *n* audit manual.

নিরীক্ষিত *adj* seen; observed; scrutinized; audited.

নিরীক্ষ্যমাণ *adj* being seen/ observed/ scrutinized/ audited.

নিরীশ্বর *adj* godless; atheistic. ~**বাদ** *n* atheism. ~**বাদী** *adj* atheistic(al). ❑atheist.

নিরীহ *adj* **1** innocent; gentle; week; mild; harmless; inoffensive; unoffending. **2** inactive; indifferent. ~**তা** *adj* mildness; innocence; harmlessness; gentleness; weekness; indifference.

নিরুক্ত *n* explanation/ etymological interpretation of a word; etymology. ❑*adj* uttered; pronounced; defined; explained; expressed; explicitly enjoined/ mentioned; interpreted. ~**বিদ্যা** *n* etymology.

নিরুক্তি *n* etymological interpretation of a word; etymology; categorical statement; assertion.

নিরুৎকণ্ঠ *adj* free from longing/ desire/ anxiety.

নিরুত্তর *adj* answerless; silenced; silent; unprotesting; unanswering.

নিরুৎসাহ *adj* without enthusiasm/ courage/ zeal; dejected; lackadaisical; disinterested; indifferent; indolent; listless; disheartened. ❑*n* lack/ loss of enthusiasm/ zeal; discouragement; indolence; dejection; despair; downheartedness; dismay. ~ **করা** *vt* discourage; dishearten; dismay; depress.

নিরুৎসাহী *adj* = নিরুৎসাহ

নিরুদ্দিষ্ট *adj* missing; traceless. ~ **হওয়া** *vi* vanish; run away; decamp; make off; be absconding; abscond; disappear; vanish into thin air; get lost: সে ~, we have lost all trace of him.

নিরুদ্দেশ *adj* **1** having no destination. **2** = নিরুদ্দিষ্ট. ~ **যাত্রা** a journey into the unknown.

নিরুদ্ধ *adj* **1** held back; restrained; checked; stopped; halted: ~ গতি. **2** shut; closed; confined; held fast; besieged; bolt: ~ গৃহ, ~ দ্বার. **3** obstructed; barred: ~ পথ. **4** choked: ~ কণ্ঠ. **5** besieged. ~ **করা** *vt* = নিরোধ করা (⇒ নিরোধ).

নিরুদ্যম *adj* inactive; lazy; lethargic; slothful; unenterprising; callous; indolent; shiftless; lackadaisical; nonchalant; insouciant.

নিরুদ্যোগ *adj* = নিরুদ্যম

নিরুদ্বিগ্ন *adj* unperturbed; calm; unruffled; imperturble; unworried; sedate; undisturbed; unexcited. ~**চিত্ত** *adj* undisturbed in mind.

নিরুদ্বেগ *adj* = নিরুদ্বিগ্ন. ❑*n* unperturbedness; imperturbability; calm; calmness; nonchalange; insouciant; placidity; phlegm; aplomb. **নিরুদ্বেগে** *adv* without worries and anxieties; calmly; nonchalantly; imperturbably.

নিরুপদ্রব *adj* free from affliction/ danger; untroubled; undisturbed; secure; unharmed; untrammelled; safe; peaceful; harmless. **নিরুপদ্রবে** *adv* without troubles/ dangers; in peace and safety; peacefully; safety; free from troubles/ disturbance.

নিরুপম *adj* peerless; unequalled; incomparable; unparalleled; matchless; unrivalled; nonpareil; unique.

নিরুপহত *adj* unhurt; uninjured.

নিরুপাখ্য *adj* **1** indescribable; inexpressible. **2** immaterial; unreal; false; non-existent.

নিরুপাধি(ক) *adj* **1** having no title/ surname. **2** without attributes/ qualities; absolute.

নিরুপায় *adj* without expedients; helpless; resourceless; destitute; powerless.

নিরূপ *adj* = নিরাকার

নিরূপক *adj* stating; determining; defining; ascertaining; fixing. ❑*n* one who determines/ defines/ ascertains. **নিরূপিকা** *fem.*

নিরূপণ *n* defining; determining; ascertaining; fixing; ascertainment; fixation; determination; investigation; realization; examination. ~ **করা** *vt* notice; find out; ascertain; fix; define; determine; examine; investigate; realize; choose; search.

নিরূপণীয় *adj* to be looked into/ investigated/ defined/ ascertained/ fixed/ determined/ realized; definable; ascertainable; determinable.

নিরূপিত *adj* fixed; appointed; ascertained; determined; weighed; considered; defined; discovered. ~ **মূল্যে** at fixed/ settled price. ~ **সময়ে** at the appointed time/ hour.

নিরেট *adj* **1** solid; hard; not hollow; compact; dense; tight. **2** dull-headed; stupid; silly. **3** downright; utter; thorough: ~ গর্দভ. ❑*n* dullard; dunce; blockhead.

নিরেস *adj* inferior; of poor quality; low.

নিরোধ *n* **1** confinement; locking up; imprisonment. **2** restraint; control; repression; check; suppression. **3** siege. **4** obstruction; hindrance: পথ ~ করা. **5** opposition; counteraction. **6** checking. ~ **করা** *vt* **1** shut up; confine; imprisonment. **2** restrain; check; suppress; control. **3** besiege; surround; invest. **4** obstruct; hinder; bar; stop. **5** keep away; ward off; remove. **6** oppose; counteract.

7 choke. ~ক *adj* obstructing; confining; hindering; restraining; repressing; opposing; besieging; preventing; controlling; choking. ~-কুণ্ডলী *n* (phy) choking coil. ~ন *n* **1** = ~. **2** quarantine.

নির্গত *adj* come forth; gone out; issued; emerged; appeared; ejected; become visible; flowed out. ~ করা *vt* bring/ send out; issue; give out; cause to flow; emit; throw off; spout; eject; discharge. ~ হওয়া *vi* go out; come forth; depart from; set out; come out; appear; flow out; emerge; emanate; escape; issue; stream; spurt.

নির্গন্ধ *adj* void of smell; inodorous; odourless; scentless.

নির্গম *n* **1** going forth; setting out; departure; outflow; emergence; exit; escape; egress; escaping from; issue; outlet. **2** door. **3** export. ~ কোণ *n* (science) angle of emergence. ~ন *n* = ~. ~-নিবন্ধ *n* outward register. ~-পথ *n* outlet. ~-বাণিজ্য *n* export trade. ~-শুল্ক *n* export duty.

নির্গলন *n* **1** melting; dissolving; flowing out; exudation; oozing. **2** (chem) filtration.

নির্গলিত *adj* melted; dissolved; flowed out; exuded; oozing; filtered. ~ করা *vt* melt; dissolve; fuse; cause to exude; filter. ~ হওয়া *vi* flow out; melt; dissolve; thaw; exude; be filtered; ooze. **নির্গলিতার্থ** *adj* real import; sum and substance; gist; burden; essence.

নির্গুণ *adj* **1** having no good qualities/ virtues; bad; worthless; vicious; incompetent; unworthy. **2** devoid of all qualities/ properties; having no epithet (said of the supreme Being). **3** having no cord/ string. ~তা, ~ত্ব *nn* absence of qualities/ properties; want of good qualities; wickedness; viciousness; worthlessness.

নির্গূঢ় *adj* extremely obscure/ mysterious/ secret/ hidden/ abstruse/ intricated/ secluded.

নির্গৃহ *adj* houseless; homeless; shelterless.

নির্গ্রন্থ *adj* **1** free from all ties/ hindrances; unattached; without possessions. **2** naked. ❑*n* saint who has withdrawn from the world and lives either as a hermit or a religious mendicant wandering about naked. ~ন *n* killing; slaughter.

নির্গ্রন্থক, নির্গ্রন্থিক = নির্গ্রন্থ

নির্ঘণ্ট *n* table of contents; index; programme; bill of fare.

নির্ঘাত *n* **1** roar of whirlwind, hurricane, etc. **2** thunderclap. **3** stroke; blow. ❑*adj* **1** violent; terrible; fierce. **2** unfailing; certain; sure; inevitable: ~ বিপদ, ~ মিথ্যা. ❑*adv* surely; certainly; of certain/ inevitably: সে ~ আসবে, এ ওষুধে ~ কাজ হবে.

নির্ঘৃণ *adj* having no feeling of disgust towards filthy things; shameless; immodest.

নির্ঘোষ *n* deep sound; loud noise; rattling; tramping; report.

নির্জন *adj* lonely; desolate; secluded; solitary. ❑*n* lonely place; solitude. ~তা *n* loneliness; solitude; desolateness; seclusion; desolation; void.

নির্জর *adj* not subject to old age/ decay; ever young/ fresh; ageless; imperishable; immortal. ❑god; immortal. **নির্জরা** *adj fem.*

নির্জল, নির্জলা *adj* **1** waterless; dry. **2** undiluted; not mixed with water; raw: ~ হুইস্কি. **3** having no permission to drink water: ~ উপবাস. **4** dehydrated. **5** absolute; unmixed; genuine; downright: ~ মিথ্যা কথা, ~ আনন্দ. ~ কোহল *n* absolute alcohol. **নির্জলা একাদশী** *n* the eleventh day in the light half of the month Jaishtha on which even the drinking of water is forbidden.

নির্জিত *adj* conquered; subdued; vanquished; defeated; crushed; subjugated.

নির্জীব *adj* **1** lifeless; dead. **2** inanimate; inert: ~ পদার্থ. **3** languid; disheartened; dejected; effete; listless; enervated; exhausted, supine; sluggish; torpid; languorous. ~তা *n* **1** lifelessness; inertness. **2** lethargy; lassitude; inertia; torpor; sloth; listlessness; effeteness; languor; debility; enervation; exhaustion; feebleness; fatigue.

নির্জ্ঞান *adj* ignorant; stupid; silly. ❑*n* (psych) the unconscious.

নির্জ্যোতি *adj* lightless; dark.

নির্ঝঞ্ঝাট *n* untroubled; untrammelled; unencumbered; unhindered; carefree; undisturbed; peaceful; quiet; smooth. **নির্ঝঞ্ঝাটে** *adv* without hindrance/ trouble/ impediment/ encumbrance; smoothly; without a hitch; peacefully.

নির্ঝর *n* waterfall; cataract; mountain torrent; cascade; fountain; spring; rivulet.

নির্ঝরিণী *n fem* torrent; river.

নির্ণয় *n* **1** ascertainment; determination; settlement; discernment. **2** deduction; inference; conclusion. **3** decision; verdict; sentence; decree; resolution. ~ করা *vi* find out; ascertain; investigate; settle; decide; discern; conclude; determine; verify; resolve. ~ন = ~.

নির্ণায়ক *adj* conclusive; decisive; determinative; ascertaining; discerning; deciding. ❑*n* determinant; criterion. ~-মত,~-ভোট *nn* casting vote. ~-সভা *n* jury. ~-সভ্য *n* member of a jury; juror.

নির্ণীত *adj* traced out; ascertained; settled; decided; determined; resolved; discerned.

নির্ণেতা *adj* = নির্ণায়ক. ❑*n* one who determines/ decides/ ascertains/ settles/ resolves; guide; judge; assessor. নির্ণেত্রী *fem.*

নির্ণেয় *adj* to be ascertained/ determined/ decided/ discerned/ resolved/ settled; ascertainable; discernible.

নির্দন্ত *adj* toothless.

নির্দয় *adj* **1** pitiless; unkind; cruel; merciless; hard-hearted. **2** hard; severe; excessive; rigorous. **3** violent; fierce; ferocious. **~তা** *n* cruelty; mercilessness; hard-heartedness; savagery; brutality; ruthlessness; severity; rigour.

নির্দহন *adj* not burning.

নির্দানি *adj* unclaimed.

নির্দায় *adj* having no liability/ responsibility; free from liabilities/ responsibilities; without responsibilities; carefree.

নির্দিষ্ট *adj* **1** determined; appointed; fixed; stated; settled. **2** pointed out; shown; demonstrated; indicated. **3** enjoined; announced; foretold; ordered; directed. **4** particular. **5** definite; defined; ascertained. **~ করা** *vt* **1** point to/ out; show. **2** define; state; specify; indicate; name; fix; decide; settle. **3** particularize. announce; order; enjoin; recommend; suggest; advice; instruct; direct.

নির্দেশ *n* **1** pointing out; indicating; directing; indication. **2** order; instruction; direction; directive; command. **3** specification; details; particulars; description; special mention. **4** reference. **5** fixation; appointment; definition. **~ করা/ দেওয়া** *vi* indicate; point out; determine; direct; instruct; command; enjoin; designate; specify; denote; suggest. **~ক** *adj* pointing out; showing; indicating; suggesting; describing; defining; instructing; direction. ❑*n* instructor; director; adviser; counsellor. **~ন, নির্দেশনা** *nn* = ~. **~নামা, ~পত্র** *nn* directive; written order.

নির্দেষ্টা *n* = নির্দেশক (⇒ নির্দেশ)

নির্দোষ *adj* **1** faultless; guiltless; immaculate; spotless; clean: ~ চরিত্র. **2** not guilty; innocent; unreproachable: আসামি ~. **3** flawless; impeccable; unblemished: ~ শিল্পকর্ম. **4** harmless; inoffensive; innocuous; innocent: ~ আমোদ, ~ পানীয়. ❑*adv* completely: দীর্ঘদিন রোগে ভুগে এখন সে ~ আরোগ্য লাভ করেছে. **~ আমোদ-প্রমোদ** *n* innocent amusements/ pastime/ diversion.

নির্দোষী *adj* (dial) = নির্দোষ. ❑*n* innocent person.

নির্দ্বন্দ্ব *adj* **1** indifferent to the alternatives/ opposite pairs (of feelings, as pleasure and pain); free from envy/ jealousy. **2** not contested; indisputable. **3** free from doubt; at peace; definite; certain: আমি এ বিষয়ে ~. **4** peace-loving; amicable.

নির্ধন *adj* without property; poor; indigent; resourceless; impecunious. **~তা** *n* poverty; indigence; lack of wealth; impecuniousness.

নির্ধর্ম *adj* irreligious; impious; unrighteous; lawless.

নির্ধার *n* **1** = নির্ধারণ. **2** assessment. **~ক** *adj* ascertaining; defining; specifying; determining. ❑*n* one who ascertains/ defines/ determines/ specifics; decision-maker.

নির্ধারণ *n* ascertainment; defining; particularizing; specifying; specification; assessment; determination; decision-making. **~ করা** *vt* settle; ascertain; take/ pick out; determine; particularize; specify; fix; define; decide; appoint; assess. **নির্ধারণী** *adj* = নির্ধারক (⇒ নির্ধার). **নির্ধারণীয়** = নির্ধার্য.

নির্ধারিত *adj* determined; specified; fixed; ascertained; settled; appointed; (accurately) stated/ told; assessed; decided. **~ করা** = নির্ধারণ করা (⇒ নির্ধারণ).

নির্ধারী *n* assessor.

নির্ধার্য *adj* to be ascertained/ determined/ fixed/ settled/ decided/ assessed/ specified; ascertainable.

নির্ধূত *adj* shaken; agitated.

নির্ধূম *adj* smokeless.

নির্নিমিখ *adj, adv* (poet) = নির্নিমেষ

নির্নিমিত্ত *adj* without reason/ motive; causeless. ❑*adv* without cause; for nothing.

নির্নিমেষ *adj* **1** not twinkling/ winking/ blinking: ~ চোখ. **2** fixed; steadfast: ~ দৃষ্টি. ❑*adv* with the eyes wide open; steadily; in a fixed gaze; without blinking. **~ আঁখি, ~ চক্ষু, ~ নয়ন, ~ দৃষ্টি** *adjj* with fixed gaze; with the eyes wide open (in a fixed gaze). **~ দৃষ্টিতে তাকানো** *vi* stare (without blinking); look steadily; look at sth/ sb with the eyes wide open in a fixed gaze; gaze/ store at; gaze at sth/ sb with staring eyes.

নির্বংশ *adj* having no descendants/ family/ inheritors. **~ করা** *vt* eliminate/ exertiminate sb with all his kith and kin; wipe out; obliterate.

নির্বংশে *adj* (colloq) = নির্বংশ. ❑*n* one who has no descendants; one whose descendants have all perished.

নির্বচন *n* **1** saying; proverb; maxim. **2** categorical statement. **3** interpretation; explanation; etymology. **4** (geom) enunciation. ❑*adj* not speaking; silent.

নির্বন্ধ *n* **1** insisting upon; insistence; pertinacity; obstinacy; entreaty; plea; appeal; persistent request; solicitude. **2** foreordaining; predestination; decree; law: দেবের ~. **3** importunity. **4** discipline; arrangement. **5** concatenation of (adverse) circumstances; occurrence; happening. **6** contact;

communication: নির্বন্ধাভাব. নির্বন্ধাতিশয়, নির্বন্ধাতিশয্য *adjj* excessive insistence; great importunity; persistent request/ demand.

নির্বন্ধিত *adj* **1** insistent; persistent. **2** intent upon. **3** disposed; arranged.

নির্বর্তক *adj* accomplishing; performing; finishing. ❑*n* one who accomplishes/ performs/ finishes/ executes.

নির্বর্তন *n* accomplishment; execution; finishing/ performance.

নির্বল *adj* powerless; weak; debilitated; weakened.

নির্বর্ষ *adj* rainless; affected by drought.

নির্বস্ত্র *adj* having no clothes; naked; unclad; unclothed.

নির্বহণ *n* end; issue; completion; enforcement. ~-শাখা *n* enforcement branch.

নির্বাক *adj* speechless; dumbfounded; silent. ~ করা *vt* render speechless; silence; dumbfound; astound.

নির্বাক্য *adj* speechless.

নির্বাচক *adj* elective; selective; voting; electing; selecting. ❑*n* elector; voter; selector. ~মণ্ডলী *n* electors (collectively); electorate.

নির্বাচন *n* election; voting; polling; suffrage; selection. ~ করা *vi, vt* **1** hold an election. **2** elect; return; select. ~-কেন্দ্র *n* polling station; polling-booth. ~-ক্ষেত্র *n* constituency. ~-নিযুক্তক *n* polling agent. ~প্রার্থী *adj* seeking election. ❑*n* candidate for election. ~যোগ্য *adj* eligible for election; worthy of selection/ choice.

নির্বাচনী *adj* of election; electoral. ~ এলাকা *n* constituency. ~ বক্তৃতা *n* election speech.

নির্বাচিত *adj* elected; returned; selected. নির্বাচিতা *fem.* ~ করা *vt* elect; return; select.

নির্বাচ্য *adj* **1** to be said; worth saying. **2** to be explained.

নির্বাণ *n* **1** blowing out; extinction: দীপ~. **2** cessation; setting; vanishing; disappearance. **3** extinction of the flame of life; dissolution; death; final emancipation from matter and re-union with the supreme spirit. **4** (with Buddhists and Jainas) absolute extinction/ annihilation of individual existence or of all desires and passions. **5** perfect calm/ repose/ happiness; highest bliss; beatitude. ❑*adj* **1** blown/ put out; extinguished (as a lamp/ fire). **2** set (as the sun). **3** calmed; quieted; tamed. **4** dead; deceased; lost; disappeared. **5** immersed; plunged.

নির্বাণোন্মুখ *adj* about to go out/ be extinguished; dying.

নির্বাত *adj* free from wind; windless; sheltered; still; motionless; airless; stuffy.

নির্বাধ *adj* free from vexation/ annoyance; unhindered; unopposed; free; unrestricted; unhampered; unobstructed; unencumbered. নির্বাধে *adv* without hindrance; freely; with no restraint; at will.

নির্বাপক *adj* **1** putting out; extinguishing. **2** allaying; alleviating; mitigating; quenching; cooling. ❑*n* sth that extinguishes/ mitigates/ quenches; extinguisher. অগ্নি~ যন্ত্র *n* fire-extinguisher.

নির্বাপণ *n* extinguishing; putting out; extinction; quenching; allaying; mitigation; cooling; annihilation. ~ করা *vt* put out; extinguish; allay; cool; mitigate; quench.

নির্বাপিত *adj* put out; extinguished; quenched; allayed; cooled; mitigated; extinct.

নির্বাসন *n* **1** exile; banishment; deportation; expatriation. **2** (fig) expulsion; eviction; ouster; removal. ~ দেওয়া *n* **1** exile; send into exile; banish; expatriate; deport. **2** expel; evict; dislodge. ~দণ্ড *n* banishment; exile. নির্বাসনে পাঠানো = ~ দেওয়া.

নির্বাসিত *adj* **1** exiled; banished; deported; expatriate. **2** (fig) expelled; ousted; evicted; removed. নির্বাসিতা *fem.* ~ করা = নির্বাসন দেওয়া (⇒নির্বাসন).

নির্বাহ *n* **1** carrying out; accomplishing; performing; completion; execution; কার্য~. **2** carrying on: জীবিকা~. **3** leading; passing; spending: জীবন~; defraying: ব্যয় ~. **5** conclusion; accomplishment: দায়িত্ব ~. ~ করা *vt* **1** carry out; accomplish; perform; complete; execute; finish. **2** carry on. **3** lead; pass; spend. **4** defray. **5** conclude. ~ হওয়া *vi* be carried out/ accomplished/ performed/ executed/ completed/ defrayed. ~ক *adj* carrying out; accomplishing; executing; effecting; performing; carrying on; passing; spending; leading; defraying; concluding. ❑*n* one who carries out, accomplishes, executes, etc; accomplisher.

নির্বাহিত *adj* carried out; accomplished; executed; carried on; spent; passed; led; defrayed; concluded; completed; performed.

নির্বাহী *adj* executing; leading; carrying out; executive.

নির্বিকল্প(ক) *adj* **1** not admitting an alternative; free from change/ differences; absolute. **2** admitting no doubt; unerring; unwavering; unhesitating; sure. **3** having no distinction between the knower and the knowable. **4** completely identified with/absorbed into the infinite. ❑*n* knowledge not depending upon/ derived from the senses; absolute knowledge. ~ সমাধি *n* a trance in which one is completely identified with the infinite.

নির্বিকার *adj* **1** unchanged; unchangeable; immutable; uniform. **2** not offended at anything; unperturbed; unruffled; unmoved; indifferent; callous; steady; disinterested; impassive; insensitive; untouched; stoical. ❑*adv* impassively: সে ~ তাকিয়ে রইলো. **~চিত্তে, নির্বিকারে** *advv* showing no sign of emotion/ feeling; impassively; stoically; at ease; calmly; placidly; imperturbably; unconcernedly; with unruffled calm; unfeelingly.

নির্বিঘ্ন *adj* uninterrupted; unhindered; undisturbed; safe; secure; free from dangers. **নির্বিঘ্নে** *adv* safely; without any obstacle/ a hitch/ any obstacle/ any disturbance; freely; smoothly.

নির্বিচার *adj* indiscriminate; not reflecting/ considering; inconsiderate; thoughtless; promiscuous. **নির্বিচারে** *adv* indiscriminately; without careful judgement/ reflection; inconsiderately; promiscuously.

নির্বিণ্ণ *adj* despondent; depressed; sorrowful; regretful; penitent.

নির্বিবাদ *adj* free from strife/ quarrel; undisputed; incontestable; unopposed; peaceful; peaceable; not quarrelsome. **নির্বিবাদে** *adv* without strife/ opposition/ quarrel/ difficulty; peacefully; smoothly; amicably; peaceably.

নির্বিবাদী *adj* of peaceful/ quiet/ amicable disposition; guileless; peaceable; not quarrelsome.

নির্বিবেক *adj* having no conscience; conscienceless; unscrupulous; undiscriminating; inconsiderate.

নিবিরোধ=নির্বিবাদ. **নির্বিরোধে**=নির্বিবাদে

নির্বিশঙ্ক *adj* fearless; confident; dauntless; brave; bold.

নির্বিশেষ *adj* showing/ making no difference; undiscriminating; without distinction; irrespective; not different from; same; like; equal. **নির্বিশেষে** *adv* irrespective of; equally; alike; the same as; regardless of: ধনীদরিদ্র ~.

নির্বিষ *adj* **1** non-venomous; non-poisonous: ~ সাপ, ~ ঔষধ. **2** free/freed from poison; delivered from/ divested of poison. **3** (fig) divested of ability to harm; rendered harmless; neutralize; incapacitated; have one's teeth/ fangs drawn. **~ করা** *vt* free/deliver from poison; neutralize; render harmless; incapacitate; draw sth/ sb's teeth/ fangs.

নির্বিষয় *adj* not attached to sensual objects; imperceptible.

নির্বীজ *adj* **1** seedless. **2** impotent. **3** sterile; aseptic; disinfected. **~ করা** *vt* **1** remove the seeds from sth; seed. **2** make/ render impotent; sterilize. **3** (surgically) sterilize; disinfect. **~ন** *n* sterilization; disinfection. **নির্বীজিত** *adj* sterilized; disinfected.

নির্বীর্য *adj* powerless; unmanly; impotent; cowardly; pusillanimous; faint-hearted.

নির্বুদ্ধি *adj* ignorant; stupid; foolish. **~তা** *n* stupidity; foolishness; ignorance; senselessness.

নির্বৃত *adj* satisfied; happy; at rest/ ease. **নিবৃতি** *n* complete satisfaction/ happiness; bliss; pleasure; delight.

নির্বৃত্ত *adj* **1** sprung forth; originated; grown out (of). **2** accomplished; finished. **নিবৃত্তি** *n* **1** originating; development. **2** completion; termination.

নির্বেদ *n* **1** complete indifference; disregard of worldly objects. **2** despondency; dejection. **3** repentance; remorse.

নির্বেদন *adj* free from pain; painless.

নির্বৈর *n* absence of enmity. ❑*adj* free from enmity; having no enemy; peaceable; amicable.

নির্বোধ *adj* dull; stupid; foolish. ❑*n* blockhead; dullard.

নির্ব্যথন *adj* free from pain. ❑*n* torture; affliction.

নির্ব্যলীক *adj* harmless; easy; hearty; willing; ready; sincere.

নির্ব্যাজ *adj* free from deceit/ ambiguity; honest; sincere; frank; candid.

নির্ব্যূঢ় *adj* **1** sure; proven; proved; conclusive; positive. **2** finished; completed. **3** absolute; complete; full: ~ অধিকার.

নির্ভয় *adj* fearless; dauntless; free from danger; secure. ❑*n* fearlessness; security. **~চিত্ত, ~হৃদয়** *adv* having no fear at heart; having a fearless heart. **নির্ভয়ে** *adv* fearlessly; boldly without fear/ misgivings.

নির্ভর *n* **1** prop; support. **2** refuge; recourse. **3** dependence; confidence; reliance. **~ করা** *vi* depend upon; rely on. **~ রাখা** *vi* have confidence/ firm trust in. **~পত্র** *n* warranty. **~তা** *n* dependence; reliance; confidence.

নির্ভরসা *adj* bereft of hope; in despair; disheartened; helpless; desolate.

নির্ভর্ৎসন *n* reproach; reprimand; blame; condemnation; censure. **নির্ভর্ৎসিত** *adj* reproached; reprimanded; condemned; censured; reviled; abused.

নির্ভাগ্য *adj* unfortunate; unlucky.

নির্ভাবনা *n* freedom from worries and anxieties; insouciance; nonchalance. ❑*adj* carefree; free from worries and anxieties/ responsibilities; insouciant.

নির্ভার *adj* not heavy; light; handy; light-weight.

নির্ভিন্ন *adj* **1** indistinguished; equal; like. **2** separated; cleft. **3** opened; blossomed budded.

নির্ভীক *adj* fearless; dauntless; undaunted; bold. **~তা** *n* fearlessness; boldness; courage.

নির্ভুল *adj* free from mistake/ error; correct; accurate; right; just; unerring. **~তা** *n* correctness; accuracy.

নির্ভেজাল *adj* unadulterated; undiluted; pure; genuine.

নির্মক্ষিক *adj* **1** free from flies. **2** desolate; lonely; solitary.

নির্মঞ্ছন *n* ceremony of lustration; waving lights before an idol as an act of adoration; articles placed before an idol in adoration.

নির্মৎসর *adj* free from envy/ jealousy; without envy; unselfish.

নির্মথন=নির্মন্থন

নির্মদ *adj* unintoxicated; sober; quiet; humble; modest.

নির্মনস্ক *adj* mindless.

নির্মনুষ্য *adj* depopulated; desolate; forlorn.

নির্মন্থ(ন) *n* churning; friction.

নির্মম *adj* **1** merciless; ruthless; heartless; pitiless; cruel; brutal; unfeeling; relentless; hard-hearted. **2** disinterested; indifferent. **~তা** *n* mercilessness; ruthlessness; cruelty; hard-heartedness; brutality.

নির্মল *adj* **1** spotless; unsullied; clean; neat; immaculate: ~ পরিচ্ছদ. **2** clear; cloudless; bright; fair: ~ আকাশ. **3** clear; transparent; pellucid; pure: ~ জল. **4** shining; bright; resplendent: ~ আলো. **5** sinless; virtuous; guiltless; unblemished; spotless; holy; chaste: ~ চরিত্র. **6** candid; immaculate; honest; innocent; open; frank; ingenuous: ~ হাসি. **7** unmixed; unadulterated; pure; complete: ~ আনন্দ/সুখ. **8** fresh: ~ বায়ু. **9** untainted; unblemished; perfect: ~ যশ. **নির্মলা** *fem.* **~তা** *n* cleanness; purity; cleanliness; freshness; brightness; resplendence; virtuousness; chastity; honesty; innocence; transparence; clearness; pellucidity; immaculateness; integrity; shine; perfection.

নির্মলা, নির্মলি, নির্মলী *nn* kind of fruit that cleanses water; cleaning nut; *Strychnos potalorum.*

নির্মা *vt* (poet)=নির্মাণ করা (⇒ নির্মাণ)

নির্মাণ *n* **1** forming; making; building; composing; creating; formation; composition; creation; construction; manufacture. **2** organizing; organization: দল ~. **3** setting up; establishment; foundation: হাসপাতাল ~, রাজ্য ~. **~ করা** *vt* build; make (out); construct; form; compose; create; manufacture; organize; set up; establish; found. **~ কাজ** *n* construction work. **~কারক, ~কারী**=নির্মাতা.

নির্মাতা *adj* making; composing; constructing; building; manufacturing; creating; organizing; setting up; founding; establishing. ❑*n* maker; builder; creator; author; manufacturer; architect; founder; composer; organizer; constructor.

নির্মাল্য *n* **1** flowers left at a sacrificial ceremony. **2** remains of an offering to a deity. **3** garland made of flowers left at a sacrifice.

নির্মিত *adj* constructed; built; made; formed; created; manufactured; fashioned; composed; organized; established; founded; set up.

নির্মিতি *n* **1**=নির্মাণ. **2** structure. **~বাদ** *n* structuralism. **~বাদী** *adj, n* structuralist.

নির্মিৎসা, নির্মিমিৎসা *nn* desire of creating.

নির্মিৎসু *adj* wishing to create.

নির্মীয়মাণ *adj* in the process of being made/ built/ constructed/ created (⇒ নির্মাণ); under construction.

নির্মুকুল *adj* (of trees) stripped/ destitute of buds/ flowers/ blossoms.

নির্মুক্ত *adj* **1** liberated/ saved/escaped/ free from. **2** loosed; separated; sundered. **3** uncovered; unsheathed; released. **4** deprived of. **5** free from every attachment. **6** flung; hurled: জ্যা~ বাণ. **নির্মুক্তি** *n* liberation; deliverance.

নির্মূল *adj* **1** rootless; uprooted; eradicated; extirpated; exterminated; annihilated. **2** unfounded; baseless; groundless. **~ করা** *vt* uproot; eradicate; extirpate; exterminate; annihilate; destroy/ expel completely. **~তা** *n* rootlessness; baselessness. **~ন** *n* uprooting; extirpating; extirpation; eradication; annihilation; extermination; total destruction/ expulsion.

নির্মূলিত *adj*=নির্মূল

নির্মোক *n* **1** setting free; liberating. **2** cast-off skin (of a snake); slough. **3** armour; mail. **4** sky; atmosphere.

নির্মোচক *adj* setting free; liberating.

নির্মোচন *n* **1** removing; taking off; putting off. **2** deliverance. **3** thorough peeling. **4** moult; moulting.

নির্মোচ্য *adj* which is to be/ can be removed/ taken off/ put off completely; removable.

নির্মোহ *adj* free from illusion; disillusioned; dispassionate.

নির্যাতক *adj* oppressing; torturing; tormenting; afflicting; persecuting. ❑*n* oppressor; tormentor; torturer; persecutor.

নির্যাতন *n* oppression; torture; affliction; persecution; tormenting. **~ করা** *vt* oppress; torture; afflict; torment; persecute. **~কারী**=নির্যাতক. **~কারিণী** *fem.*

নির্যাতিত *adj* oppressed; tortured; afflicted; persecuted; torment. **নির্যাতিতা** *fem*

নির্যাস *n* essence; extract; exudation (of trees/plants); juice; resin; any thick fluid/ substance; decoction.

নির্লক্ষ্য *adj* inobservable; invisible.

নির্লজ্জ *adj* shameless; brazen; impudent barefaced; unblushing; brazen-faced. নির্লজ্জা *fem.* ~তা *n* shamelessness; impudence; immodesty.

নির্লিপ্ত *adj* disinterested; unconcerned; keeping aloof; having no attachment for; detached; indifferent; callous; apathetic; free from all earthly attachment. ~তা *n* disinterestedness; indifference; callousness; aloofness; freedom from all earthly attachment. ~ থাকা *vt* keep aloof; be indifferent/ disinterested; take no interest in.

নির্লিখন *n* **1** scraping. **2** scraper.

নির্লেপ *adj* unsmeared.

নির্লোভ *adj* free from greed/desire; unavaricious; not greedy.

নির্লোম *adj* hairless; smooth.

নিলম্বন *n* **1** adjournment (of a decision). **2** suspension (as of an employee).

নিলম্বিত *adj* **1** adjourned. **2** suspended. ~ করা *vt* adjourn; suspend. ~ রাখা *vt* adjourn.

নিলয় *n* **1** resting-place; house; abode; residence; home; dwelling-house; place of refuge; hiding place; den; lair; nest. **2** receptacle; store. **3** (anat) ventricle. **4** complete annihilation.

নিলাজ *adj* (colloq, poet)=নির্লজ্জ

নিলাম *n* (Pg) auction; auction sale. ~ করা/ করানো *vt* sell sth by auction; put sth up to auction; auction sth up. ~ কেনা *vt* purchase sth at auction. ~ ডাকা *n* bid at an auction. ~কারক, ~দার *nn* auctioneer. ~ক্রেতা *n* auction purchaser. ~খরিদ *n* purchase at an auction. নিলামে কেনা=~ কেনা. নিলামে চড়া *vi* be up for auction. নিলামে তোলা *vt* auction; put up for/to auction. নিলামে বেচা *vt* sell sth by auction; auction (off). নিলামের দোকান *n* auction-house.

নিলামি, নিলামী *adj* sold by auction; up for auction; purchased at an auction; auctioned; to be auctioned; as cheap as an article sold by auction; cut-price; cut-rate; dirt-cheap: ~ মাল.

নিলীন *adj* **1** fused into; invoved; encompassed; warped up. **2** completely sunk/ drowned (in). **3** clinging to; hidden in. **4** quite intent upon/ devoted to; completely lost/ absorbed (in). **5** destroyed; perished.

নিলীয়মান *adj* disappearing; vanishing; sinking; being fused into; hiding.

নিশঙ্ক=নিঃশঙ্ক (⇒ নিঃ-)

নিশপিশ *n* (onom) expressing, itching, irritation; agitation. ~ করা *vi* itch (for/to).

নিশা *n* night. ~কর, ~কান্ত *nn* the moon. ~কাল *n* night-time. ~গম *n* nightfall. ~গমে *adv* at the nightfall. ~চর *adj* moving about by night; nocturnal. ❑*n* *rakshasa*; fiend; owl; jackal; burglar. ~চরী *fem.* ~জল *n* dew. নিশাতিক্রম *n* passing away of night. ~ত্যয় *n* daybreak; close of night. ~নাথ *n* the moon. ~ন্ত=~ত্যয়. ~পতি *n* the moon. ~বসান=~ত্যয়. ~বিহার=~চর. ~মুখ *n* beginning of night; evening. ~র্ধ *n* first part of the night; midnight. ~সমাগম *n* nightfall.

নিশাদল *n* [P] ammonium chloride; salammoniac.

নিশান *n* [P] **1** flag; standard. **2** mark; sign; signal. **3** trace. **4** coat of arms; badge; ensign. ~ গাড়া *vi* set a mark; mark off. ~দার *n* identifier. ~দিহি *n* identification; marking off. ~দিহি করা *vt* identify; mark off. ~বরদার *n* standard-bearer.

নিশানা [P] *n* mark; target; butt; aim. ~ করা *vi* take aim; target.

নিশানি [P] *n* mark; sign; token; souvenir; keepsake; identity.

নিশাস *n* (poet)=নিঃশ্বাস (⇒ নিঃ-)

নিশি *n* **1** night. **2** an evil spirit which calls a sleeping person out of his bed; somnambulism. ~তে পাওয়া *vi* be hypnotized by the above-mentioned evil spirit; be afflicted with somnambulism. ~দিন, ~দিশি *advv* day and night; constantly; always. ~পালন *n* religious fasting/ diet-control on a full/ new moon night. ~পালন করা *vi* fast or control one's diet on a full/ new moon night. ~ভোরে *adv* at daybreak. ~যাপন *n* passing/ spending the night; staying for a night. ~ যাপন করা *vi* stay/ put up for a night; stay/ spend the night; stay over night.

নিশিত *adj* sharpened; whetted; keen; sharp; stimulated; excited.

নিশীথ *n* night; midnight. ~ সূর্য *n* midnight sun.

নিশীথিনী *n fem* night.

নিশুতি *n* late night; still of the night; night far advanced. ❑*adj* late; far advanced. ~ রাতে *adv* in the/ at dead of night; in the still of the night.

নিশ্চয় *n* **1** conviction; certainty; positiveness. **2** firm/ sure knowledge. **3** inquiry; ascertainment. **4** decision; resolution; resolve. ❑*adj* **1** certain; convinced; sure; ensured: আগে ~ হও, তারপর কিছু করো. **2** firm; sure; positive: ~ বাক্য. ❑*adv* without doubt; for certain; certainly; surely; positively; definitely; of course: আসবে বৈকি, ~ আসবে. ~ করা *vt* make sure/ certain (that); ensure; ascertain; determine; resolve; settle. ~ করে *adv* firmly; with conviction; for certain. ~তা *n* certainty; sureness; surety; assurance; guarantee.

নিশ্চল *adj* motionless; immovable; fixed; steady; stationary; immobile; invariable. নিশ্চলা *fem.* ~তা *n* motionlessness; immobility; steadiness; fixate.

নিশ্চায়ক *adj* who/what ascertains and determines; decisive; determining; convincing. ❑*n* one who ascertains/ determines/ ensures/ decides.

নিশ্চিত *adj* **1** convinced; certain; sure; definite; positive: আমি ~যে সে কোনো অন্যায় করেনি. **2** certain; sure; unfailing; determined; decisive: ~ পদক্ষেপ. ❑*adv*=নিশ্চয়. ~ করা=নিশ্চয় করা (⇒ নিশ্চয়) . ~ জানা *vi* know for certain. ~ভাবে, ~রূপে *adv* certainly; definitely; for certain.

নিশ্চিন্ত *adj* **1** not worried/ anxious; untroubled; unperturbed. **2** carefree; unconcerned; thoughtless; insouciant; easy; unruffled. ~ করা *vt* put/ set sb's mind at ease/ rest; relieve anxiety; still the fears; remove sb's fears/ doubts/ worries; relieve the mind of; reassure sb (about sth). ~ হওয়া *vi* be/ feel relieved; be reassured; be/ feel at one's ease; be/ feel completely relaxed. ~তা *n* freedom from care; unconcern; carefreeness; nonchalance; peace of mind; tranquillity.

নিশ্চেতন *adj* unconscious; insensitive; ignorant; thoughtless; unfeeling. নিশ্চেতনা *n* unconsciousness; lack of consciousness/ awareness; insensitivity.

নিশ্চেষ্ট *adj* **1** inactive; lethargic; lazy; unenterprising; indolent; vegetative. **2** incapable of motion; motionless; immobile. ~তা *n* inaction; lethargy; indolence; laziness; lack of enterprise; inertia.

নিশ্ছিদ্র *adj* having no rents/holes; without weak points/ defects; solid; flawless; compact.

নিশ্বসন, নিশ্বসিত, নিশ্বাস=নিঃশ্বসন, নিঃশ্বসিত, নিঃশ্বাস respectively (⇒ নিঃ-)

নিষক্ত *adj* hung/ hanging on; fixed in; fastened to.

নিষঙ্গ *n* case for carrying arrows; quiver. নিষঙ্গী *adj* having a quiver. ❑*n* bowman; archer.

নিষণ্ণ *adj* **1** sitting; seated; lying; located. **2** sunk down; afflicted; distressed.

নিষদ *n* syndicate.

নিষাদ[১] *n* name of a wild non-Aryan tribe in India (described as hunters, fisherman, robbers, etc); man of any degraded tribe; out-caste. নিষাদী[১] *fem.*

নিষাদ[২] *n* (music) the last or seventh note of the gamut.

নিষাদী *n* elephant-keeper/driver.

নিষিক্ত *adj* sprinkled; infused; thoroughly wet/ drenched/ soaked (in); soppy. ~ করা *vt* moisten; wet; drench; soak; pour upon/ into.

নিষিদ্ধ *adj* **1** forbidden; prohibited; outlawed: ~ ঔষধ. **2** outlawed; interdicted: ~ লোক. **3** banned; proscribed: ~ গ্রন্থ. **4** out of bounds: ~ এলাকা/পল্লী. **5** unlawful: ~ কার্যকলাপ. ❑*n* taboo. ~ করা *vi* forbid; prohibit; outlaw; interdict; ban; proscribe; place (a locality, etc) out of bounds. ~করণ *n* prohibition; interdiction; proscription; banning; exclusion excommunication. ~ ব্যক্তি *n* outlaw.

নিষুতি *adj* **1** fast asleep; sleeping soundly: নগরী. **2** hushed; still; drowned in silence: রাত্রি.

নিষুপ্ত *adj* fast asleep; slumbering; sleeping soundly. নিষুপ্তি *adj* profound sleep; slumber(s).

নিষূদন=নিসূদন

নিষেক *n* **1** sprinkling; infusion; dripping; showering. **2** exudation. **3** seminal infusion; fertilization; impregnation. পর~ *n* cross-fertilization. স্ব~ *n* self-fertilization.

নিষেধ *n* prohibition; forbidding; interdiction; hindering; prevention. ~ করা *vt* forbid; prohibit; interdict; object to. ~ক *adj* prohibiting; prohibitory; prohibitive; forbidding; proscriptive.

নিষেবক *adj* **1** visiting; frequenting. **2** using; enjoying. **3** serving; attending on.

নিষেবণ *n* **1** visiting; frequenting. **2** adherence/ devotion to; worship; service; attendance. **3** use.

নিষেবিত *adj* **1** visited; frequented. **2** honoured; worshipped; attended; served; obeyed. **3** resorted to; used.

নিষ্ক *n* gold; gold coin; measure for weighing gold; golden ornament for the neck or breast.

নিষ্কণ্টক *adj* free from thorns/enemies; untroubled; secure; free from troubles/ dangers; safe; undisturbed. নিষ্কণ্টকে *adj* without trouble/ obstacle/ opposition/ danger; freely; peacefully; safely.

নিষ্কপট *adj* free from deceit/ fraud; guileless; frank; candid; honest.

নিষ্কম্প *adj* not shaking/ tremulous/ trembling/ vibrating; motionless; still; immovable.

নিষ্কর *adj* free from taxes; rent-free; tax-free; freehold. ~ সম্পত্তি *n* freehold.

নিষ্করুণ *adj* pitiless; merciless; cruel; hard-hearted; relentless.

নিষ্কর্মা *adj* **1** inactive; lazy; averse to work; good-for-nothing; worthless. **2** unemployed; unoccupied.

নিষ্কর্ষ *n* **1** drawing out; extracting; extract; essence; gist; substance; chief/main point. **2** abstraction. নিষ্কর্ষণ *n* **1** drawing out; extracting; abstraction; extraction. **3** removal; elimination; squeezing. ~ করা *vt* remove; eliminate; draw out; extract; abstract.

নিষ্কল *adj* **1** without parts; undivided; whole; indivisible; compact. **2** seedless; impotent; waned; diminished; decayed; infirm. নিষ্কলা *fem.*

নিষ্কলঙ্ক *adj* stainless; immaculate; unblemished.

নিষ্কলুষ, নিষ্কল্মষ *adjj* stainless; sinless; pure; free from vice; clean; free from dirt.

নিষ্কাণ্ড *adj* (bot) acaulescent.

নিষ্কাম *adj* **1** desireless; disinterested; unselfish; dispassionate; not actuated by any desire/ gainful motive: ~ কর্ম. **2** close and deep but not sexual; platonic: ~ প্রেম.

নিষ্কাশ *n* issue; egress; exist; outflow; drain; emergence; drainage. **~ন** *n* driving away; extraction; drawing out/ unsheathing (of a sword). **নিষ্কাশন করা** *vt* drive/turn out; expel; remove; extract; drain away/off; draw out/ unsheathe (a sword).

নিষ্কাশিত *adj* expelled; turned out; extracted; removed; drained away/off; drawn out/unsheathed (like a sword).

নিষ্কাসন, নিষ্কাসিত=নিষ্কাশন, নিষ্কাসিত

নিষ্কৃত *adj* **1** removed; expelled. **2** rescued; delivered; set free; atoned; exempted; freed; released.

নিষ্কৃতি *n* **1** acquittance; requital; release; deliverance; rescue. **2** exemption; remission. **3** atonement; expiation. **4** removal; doing away. **~ দেওয়া** *vt* deliver; set free; rescue; release; relieve; discharge; exempt; excuse. **~ পাওয়া** *vi* be delivered/ freed/ rescued/ released/ relieved/ discharged/ exempted/ excused/ absolved.

নিষ্কোষণ *n* **1** drawing out; unsheathing. **2** tearing off/ out; husking; shelling; extracting. **~ করা**=নিষ্কোষিত করা (⇒ নিষ্কোষিত)

নিষ্কোষিত *adj* **1** drawn; unsheathed. **2** torn/stripped off; forced out; extracted. **~ করা** *vt* **1** draw out; unsheathe. **2** pull out; strip off; husk; shell; extract.

নিষ্ক্রম *n*=নিষ্ক্রমণ

নিষ্ক্রমণ *n* going out; coming forth; exit; emergence; departing (from); departure; going away; leaving. **~ করা** *vi* go out; come forth; depart; (take) leave; make an exit; quit; emerge; go away; set out. **~পত্র** *n* passport.

নিষ্ক্রয় *n* **1** price; reward; hire; wages; exchange; charge/ fee. **2** redemption; ransom; compensation. **3** selling; sale. **~ণ** *n* redeeming; buying off; redemption; ransoming; commutation.

নিষ্ক্রান্ত *adj* gone out; come forth; departed; emerged. **~ হওয়া**=নিষ্ক্রমণ করা (⇒ নিষ্ক্রমণ).

নিষ্ক্রিয় *adj* **1** inactive; idle; lethargic; indolent; inert. **2** inoperative: ~ আইন. **3** out of order; broken down. **4** offering no opposition; passive: ~ প্রতিরোধ. **5** dormant: ~ শক্তি. **6** unemployed; unoccupied. **~তা** *n* inaction; idleness; inactivity; laziness; lethargy; indolence; inoperativeness; passiveness; passivity; unemployment; inertness.

নিষ্ঠ *adj* (used also as a *suff*) **1** intent on: devoted to: কর্ম~, ধর্ম~, কর্তব্য~. **2** being in/ on; situated on; grounded/ resting on; fixed; firm. **নিষ্ঠা** *n* **1** attachment; devotion; application. **2** devoutness; strict observance of religious rites. **3** firmness; steadiness. **4** position; state; condition. **~বান** *adj* **1** devoted; attentive to; dedicated; devout; orthodox; traditional. **~বতী** *fem.* **~ভরে** *adv* devoutly; devotedly; loyally; religiously.

নিষ্ঠিত *adj* attached/ devoted to.

নিষ্ঠীব(ন) *n* spittle; saliva. **~ ত্যাগ করা** *vi* spit.

নিষ্ঠুর *adj* cruel; heartless; merciless; hard; severe; harsh; rough; savage; brutal; biting; ruthless; fell; remorseless. **নিষ্ঠুরা** *fem.* **~তা, ~ত্ব** *nn* cruelty; ruthlessness; mercilessness; heartlessness; hard-heartedness; severity; harshness; brutality; coarseness. **~ বাক্য** *n* cruel words; acerbic/ biting/ cutting remarks. **~ভাষী** *adj* speaking harshly; sharp-tongued. **~ হৃদয়** *adj* cruel-minded. **নিষ্ঠুরাচরণ** *n* cruel behabiour; cruelty; barbarity; savagery; brutality.

নিষ্ঠ্যূত *adj* spit out; ejected from the mouth; vomited; ejected; belched out.

নিষ্পক্ব *adj* well-cooked; well ripened.

নিষ্পঙ্ক *adj* free from mud; clear; pure.

নিষ্পতন *n* rushing out; issuing quickly.

নিষ্পত্তি *n* **1** settlement; decision: মামলার ~. **2** solution; resolution: সমস্যার ~. **3** completion; consummation; execution; accomplishment: কার্য ~. **4** going forth/out; utterance: বাঙ~. **5** compromise; settlement: বিবাদের ~. **~ করা** *vt* settle; decide; solve; resolve; complete; execute; carry out; accomplish; come to terms/ a settlement; reach/ make a compromise; compromise. **~ হওয়া** *vi* be settled/ decided/solved/ resolved/ completed/ accomplished/ carried out/ executed/ compromised.

নিষ্পত্র *adj* leafless.

নিষ্পন্ন *adj* **1** brought about; effected; completed; attained; finished; executed; realized; performed; accomplished: অনুষ্ঠান ~ হয়েছে. **2** gone forth; sprung up; arisen; descended from. **3** (gram) derived from. **~ করা** *vt* bring about; effect; complete; attain; finish; execute; realize; carry out; perform; accomplish; derive. **~ হওয়া** *vi* come forth; issue; arise; be accomplished/ performed/ completed/ executed/ carried out/ realized; derive.

নিষ্পাদক *adj* accomplishing; performing; carrying out. ☐*n* one who accomplishes/ performs/ executes/ carries out.

নিষ্পাদন *n* effecting; execution; carrying out; completion; accomplishment. ~ করা=নিষ্পন্ন করা (⇒ নিষ্পন্ন).

নিষ্পাদনীয় *adj* to be accomplished/ effected/brought about/ carried out/ performed.

নিষ্পাদপ *adj* denuded of trees; treeless. ~ প্রান্তর *n* wilderness.

নিষ্পাদিত *adj* done; effected; carried out; accomplished; completed; achieved; performed; executed. ~ করা=নিষ্পন্ন করা (⇒ নিষ্পন্ন). ~ হওয়া=নিষ্পন্ন ~.

নিষ্পাদ্য=নিষ্পাদনীয়

নিষ্পাপ *adj* sinless; guiltless; innocent; pure; holy; virtuous.

নিষ্পিষ্ট *adj* 1 grounded; pounded; crushed; kneaded. 2 stamped; trampled on; heavily trodden. 3 beaten; oppressed; hard-pressed; severely thrashed; routed. ~ করা *vt* grind; pulverize; pound; crush; knead; beat to powder; stamp; beat; rub; trample on; tread heavily on; thrash severely; oppress; rout; press hard; squeeze.

নিষ্পেষ *n*=নিষ্পেষণ. ~ক *adj* grinding; crushing; pounding; oppressing; thrashing; trampling. ❑*n* one who or that which grinds or crushes/ beats to powder/ pounds/ thrashes/ tramples. (⇒ নিষ্পিষ্ট করা). ~ণ *n* grinding; striking; beating to powder; pulverization; squeezing; crushing; kneading; stamping; trampling on; treading heavily on; pressing; stamped; thrashing; oppressing; oppression; routing.

নিষ্পেষিত *adj*=নিষ্পিষ্ট

নিষ্প্রতিভ *adj* lacking brightness; lustreless; gloomy; dull; obscure; unimaginative; dull-witted.

নিষ্প্রত্যাশ *adj* hopeless; despondent.

নিষ্প্রদীপ *adj* having no lamp burning; blacked out; dark. ❑*n* black-out; lights out.

নিষ্প্রভ *adj* deprived of light/ radiance; lustreless; dim; dull; lacklustre; gloomy; dark; wan; pallid. ~ করা *vt* (fig) outshine; eclipse; put in the shade. ~ হওয়া *vi* (fig) lose colour; fade; pale (before, beside, etc sth). ~তা *n* lack of brightness/ lustre; dimness; dullness; paleness; pallor; pallidness.

নিষ্প্রয়োজন *adj* unnecessary; useless; needless; purposeless. নিষ্প্রয়োজনে *adv* unnecessarily; uselessly; needlessly; to no purpose.

নিষ্প্রাণ *adj* 1 lifeless; breathless; dead; dying; inanimate. 2 dull; insipid; prosy; stale; vapid; colourless; flat; inane; spiritless. 3 heartless; vacuous; empty; stupid: ~ দৃষ্টি.

নিষ্ফল *adj* 1 bearing no fruit; fruitless: ~ বৃক্ষ. 2 useless; vain; ineffectual; futile; of no avail; fruitless; abortive; unproductive; unsuccessful: ~ আলোচনা, ~ চেষ্টা. 3 seedless; barren; impotent. নিষ্ফলা *fem* barren. ~ করা *vt* frustrate; baffle; foil; thwart. ~ হওয়া *vi* fail; come to naught/ nothing; be futile/ in vain; miss the mark; go to the wall; fall through; turn out badly. ~তা *n* fruitlessness; ineffectiveness; uselessness; futility; barrenness; failure; impotence; miscarriage.

নিষ্যন্দ=নিস্যন্দ

নিষ্যুত *adj* sewn in; embroidered.

নিসকড়ি *adj* uncooked; raw.

নিসপিস=নিশপিশ

নিসর্গ *n* 1 natural state/ condition/ form/ character; nature. 2 creation; cosmos. ~জ *adj* innate; natural; inborn. ~বিদ্যা *n* natural science. ~বাদী *n* naturalist. ~শোভা *n* scenic beauty; beauty; beauty of nature.

নিসর্গী *n* naturalist.

নিসাড় *adj* 1 benumbed; unconscious; senseless; insensitive. 2 insensate. 3 stealthy; noiseless; still: ~ রীতি, নিসাড়া *adj*=~ (3).

নিসাদল=নিশাদল

নিসান=নিশান

নিসিন্দা *n* a herbal plant; *Vitex negundo.*

নিসূদক *n* killer; slayer; destroyer. ❑*ad*=নিসূদন.

নিসূদন *n* killing; destroying; slaughter. ❑*adj* (used as a *suff)* killing; slaying; destroying: মধু~; killer of Madhu.

নিসৃষ্ট *adj* 1 entrusted; committed. 2 granted: bestowed. 3 despatched; accredited; sent forth; authorized; allowed. 4 being in the middle; being between/ among; mediating. নিসৃষ্টার্থ *adj* entrusted with sth; authorized. ❑*n* charge´ d´ affaires; agent; messenger.

নিসৃষ্টিপত্র *n* credentials.

নিস্তন্দ্র *adj* awake; fresh; healthy; active.

নিস্তব্ধ *adj* 1 paralyzed; fixed; motionless; still. 2 silent; speechless; noiseless. ~তা *n* motionlessness; immobility; stillness; calmness; complete silence: রাত্রির নিস্তব্ধতা, the still of the night.

নিস্তম্ভিত *adj*=নিস্তব্ধ

নিস্তরঙ্গ *adj* having no waves; still; motionless; calm.

নিস্তরণ *n* 1 passing over; crossing. 2 release; rescue; deliverance. 3 going forth; coming out; emergence. নিস্তরণীয় *adj* to be passed over/overcome/ conquered.

নিস্তল *adj* 1 bottomless; fathomless. 2 not flat; round; globular.

নিস্তার *n* 1 crossing; passing over. 2 rescue; deliverance; release; final liberation; salvation. 3 acquittal: অভিযোগ থেকে ~. 4 exemption; discharge of a debt: ঋণের দায় থেকে ~. ~ করা *vt* rescue; deliver (from); save; succour. ~ দেওয়া *vt* spare; save; deliver; rescue; exempt; set free; acquit. ~ পাওয়া *vi* be rescued/ delivered/ saved/ released/ set free/ acquitted/ exempted; escape; save one's hide/ skin; be spared. **~ কর্তা** *n* saviour; rescuer; deliverer.

নিস্তারিণী *adj fem* one who delivers. ❑*n* goddess Durga.

নিস্তীর্ণ *adj* crossed; passed over; gone through; rescued; saved; delivered; escaped.

নিস্তুষ *adj* freed from husk/ chaff; husked.

নিস্তেজ *adj* **1** destitute of fire/ energy; weak; feeble; listless; droopy; debilitated. **2** depressed; down in the mouth. **3** lacking brightness/ lustre; dim; dull; faint; feeble. **4** insipid; flat; dull: ~ সুরা. **~ হওয়া** *vi* droop; flag; languish; weaken; decline; fail; wane; fade; rebate; relent; become weak; wither; lessen.

নিস্পন্দ *adj* **1** (of the pulse and the heart) not beating/ throbbing. **2** motionless; immovable; still; steady: ~ দৃষ্টি. **3** benumbed; numb: ~ বাহু.

নিস্পৃহ=নিঃস্পৃহ (⇒ নিঃ -)

নিস্যন্দ(ন) *n* flowing/dripping down; trickling down/ forth; issuing; stream; gush; discharge; exudation; oozing; essence.

নিস্যন্দিত *adj* trickled; exuded; issued; discharged; oozed.

নিস্যন্দী *adj* flowing/ dripping down; trickling down/ forth; streaming; flowing with; oozing; issuing; exuding.

নিস্রব, নিস্রাব *adj* **1** flowing down/ out. **2** stream; torrent; exudation; oozing; discharge. **3** scum of boiled rice.

নিস্রুত *adj* flowed down/ out; exuded; discharged.

নিস্বন, নিস্বান *n* sound; noise; voice; note; murmur.

নিহত *adj* struck down; killed; smitten; slain. **~ করা** *vt* strike/ hew down; kill; slay; smite; destroy.

নিহন্তা *adj* killing; slaying. ❑*n* slayer; killer; destroyer.

নিহাই *n* anvil.

নিহারণ *n* (poet) seeing; looking at; watching.

নিহারা *vt* (poet) look at; see; watch; observe.

নিহারি [P]*n* **1** breakfast. **2** kind of soup taken with leavened bread.

নিহিত *adj* **1** placed; deposited; fixed/kept in; laid. **2** entrusted; bestowed; given; delivered. **3** residing in; rested in; lying hidden: অন্তরে নিহিত. **4** thrown; flung. **5** intrinsic. **~ ঋণ** *n* funded debt.

নিহিলিস্ট [E]*n* nihilist.

নিহ্নব *n* **1** denial; concealment; secrecy; lie; perjury; contradiction. **2** suspicion; mistrust. **3** atonement; expiation; amends for. **~বাদী** *adj* lying; prevaricating. ❑*n* liar; perjurer; prevaricator.

নীচ *adj* **1** low; not high; short; dwarfish. **2** deep; depressed: ~ নাভি. **3** deep; lowered: ~ গলায়. **4** low; vile; inferior (socially or morally); base; mean. **~ কুল** *n* low (-caste) family. **~কুলজাত, ~কুলোদ্ভব** *adjj* descended from a low family; low-born; base-born; of low birth. **~কুলজাতা, ~ কুলোদ্ভবা** *fem.* **~ গ** *adj* going low; descending. **~গামী** *adj* **1** (of a river) going towards low ground. **2** indulging in vile activities; following low courses; wanton; fallen; way-ward; depraved. **3** frequenting women of bad repute/ low birth. **~গামিনী** *fem.* **~চেতা**=~মনা. **~জাত, ~জাতীয়**=~কুলজাত. **~জাতি** *n* low caste/ race. **~তা, ~ত্ব** *nn* lowness; social inferiority; meanness; baseness; vileness. **~প্রকৃতি** *n* mean nature; meanness. ❑*n* mean by nature; vicious; beastly; essentially mean. **~প্রবৃত্তি** *n* base instinct/ inclination. ❑*adj* having base instincts/ propensities/ tendencies; mean-minded; evil-minded; wicked; vile. **~ ভাষা** *n* vulgar tongue/ language; slang. **~মনা** *adj* mean-minded; small minded. **~যোনি** *n* creature of an inferior order (esp non-human); birth in an inferior order of creatures. ❑*adj* born as/of an inferior creature; of low origin. **~স্বভাব**=~প্রকৃতি. **~স্বভাবা** *fem.* **~ হৃদয়, ~ন্তঃকরণ**=~মনা. **নীচাশয়**=~প্রবৃত্তি. **~শয়া** *fem.* **নীচাসক্ত**=~গামী. **নীচাসক্তা** *fem.*

নীচু, নীচে=নিচু, নিচে respectively.

নীট=নিট[২]

নীড় *n* nest; resting-place; abode.

নীত[১] *adj* guided; led; conducted; brought; carried; conveyed; gained; obtained; accepted; received. **নীতার্থ** *n* plain/clear meaning.

নীত[২] *n* (colloq)=নীতি

নীতি *n* **1** policy; politics; political wisdom/ science: রাষ্ট্রীয় ~. **2** moral philosophy/ precept; morality; morals; moral; ethics; moral teaching: ~-বিরুদ্ধ কাজ. **3** principle: শত্রুকে ক্ষমা করা তাঁর ~. **4** right/ wise/ moral conduct/ behaviour; prudence. **5** custom; practice: সমাজের ~. **6** prescription; precept: ধর্মীয় ~. **7** justice. **8** branch of learning; science: রাষ্ট্র~. **9** leading; bringing; guidance; management. **~কথা** *n* moral (saying/advice); maxim; aphorism; didactic/ moral story/ tale; fable. **~কুশল, ~জ্ঞ** *adjj* conversant with policy/ political science/ diplomacy; diplomatic; worldly-wise; judicious; astute; sagacious. **~কুশলা** *fem.* **~কুশলতা, ~জ্ঞান** *nn* political knowledge; knowledge of politics/ diplomacy/ ethics; political/ diplomat acumen; moral sense. **~জ্ঞানবর্জিত, ~জ্ঞানশূন্য, ~জ্ঞানহীন** *adjj* devoid of moral principles/ scruples; unscrupulous; immoral; unethical. **~বচন, ~বাক্য** *nn* moral saying/advice; aphorism;

maxim; words of wisdom. **~বাগীশ** *adj* priggish; self-righteous; sanctimonious; puritanical. ❑*n* sanctimonious person; prig; puritan; prude. **~বিজ্ঞান, ~বিদ্যা** *nn* moral philosophy/ science; ethics. **~বিদ**=~জ্ঞ. **~বিরুদ্ধ, ~বিরোধী** *adjj* contrary to moral principles; contrary to one's principles; unjust; immoral; unrighteous. **~মান্** *adj* moral; scrupulous; righteous; just; virtuous; upright. **~মূলক** *adj* moral; ethical; didactic; concerning a particular principle or principles. **~শাস্ত্র** =~বিজ্ঞান. **~শাস্ত্রবিদ, ~শাস্ত্রবেত্তা** *adjj* versed in moral science/philosophy. ❑*n* moral philosopher. **~শিক্ষা** *n* moral education/ instruction. **~সঙ্গত, ~সম্মত** *adjj* conforming to morality/moral principles/ justice; righteous; just; conforming to a particular principle/ principles; moral; conscientious.

নীধ্র *n* **1** eaves of a roof. **2** circumference of a wheel.

নীপ *n* the *kadamba* (কদম্ব) tree and its flower; *Nauclea cadamba.*

নীবার *n* wild rice.

নীবি, নীবী *n* **1** piece of cloth wrapped round the waist (esp as worn by women); kind of skirt/ petticoat. **2** capital; principal stock. **~বন্ধ(ন)** *vi* band/ cord tying the above-mentioned piece of cloth.

নীয়মান *adj* being carried (off)/ borne/ conducted/ led. **নীয়মানা** *fem.*

নীর *n* water; juice; liquid. **নীরজ** *adj* water-born; aquatic. ❑*n* lotus. **নীরজা** *fem.* **~জাত** *adj*=নীরজ. **~ময়** *adj* watery; aqueous; full of water.

নীরক্ত *adj* bloodless; anæmic; colourless; pale; faded.

নীরজ[1] ⇒ নীর

নীরজ[2] *adj* free from dust. **2** having no pollen. **নীরজা** *adj* (of girls) whose menstruation has not yet begun to function.

নীরদ *n* cloud. **~বরণ** *adj* dark as a cloud; blue-black; dark-grey.

নীরন্ধ্র *adj* having no holes/openings; close; thick; dense; compact; uninterrupted; firmly closed; closely woven; closed on all sides.

নীরব *adj* soundless; noiseless; silent; quiet; hushed; speechless; mute. **~ করা** *vt* silence; hush; quiet; gag; muzzle. **~ থাকা** *vi* remain silent; tongue-tied. **~ হওয়া** *vi* be silent; hold one's tongue; quiet down; hush; be hushed; fall silent. **~তা** *n* silence; noiselessness; quiet; hush; taciturnity; calm; stillness. **নীরবে** *adv* silently; noiselessly; quietly; stealthily. **নীরবে সহ্য করা** *vt* bear/tolerate silently/ patiently; bear without complaint.

নীরস *adj* **1** without juice; sapless; dry; dried up; withered. **2** flavourless; tasteless; insipid: ~ পানীয়. **3** dull; inane; jejune; uninteresting; tedious; dreary; insipid: ~ আলোচনা. **4** humourless; boring; tiresome: ~ লোক/সমালোচক. **5** prosaic; dull; vapid; colourless; drab; arid; stereotyped; lifeless; stale; threadbare: ~ সমালোচনা. **6** cheerless; unexciting; dull; monotonous; prosaic; humdrum: ~ জীবন. **7** gloomy; cheerless; dreary; bleak; dismal: ~ আবহাওয়া. **8** glum; mirthless; sullen; dour; joyless: ~ হাসি/মুখ. **~তা** *n* lack of juice/sap; dullness; unsavouriness; insipidity; vapidity; tediousness; boredom; tedium; monotony; prosiness; cheerlessness; gloom; gloominess; sullenness; inanity; dreariness; flatness.

নীরাজন(া) **1** lustration of arms (a ceremony performed by kings before taking the field); waving lights before an idol as an act of adoration.

নীরোগ *adj* free from disease/ illness; healthy; well; in health.

নীল *adj* **1** dark-blue; blue; azure. **2** dyed with indigo. ❑*n* **1** deep-blue colour; blue; azure. **2** indigo (plant). **3** sapphire. **4** the mountain Nila. **5** peacock. **6** blue-necked jay. **~কণ্ঠ** *adj* blue-necked. ❑*n* **1** name of Shiva (as having a blue throat from swallowing the poison produced at the churning of the ocean). **2** peacock. **3** species of gallinule/water-hen. **~কমল** *n* blue lotus/ water-lily. **~কর** *n* indigo planter. **~কান্ত(মণি)** *n* sapphire. **~কান্তি** *n* azure. **~কুঠি** *n* indigo-factory. **~গাই** *n* large Indian antelope; nilgai; nilgau. **~পদ্ম**=~কমল. **নীল~** *n* worship of Shiva on the penultimate or the last day of the Bengali year. **~প্রভ** *adj* having a blue lustre/ radiance. **~বর্ণ** *n, adj* blue; azure. **~বসন** *adj* dressed in blue/ dark-blue clothes. **~বসনা** *fem.* **~মক্ষিক** *n* kind of blue fly/ bee. **~মণি** *n* sapphire. **~লোহিত** *n* **1** dark blue and red; purple; dark-red. **2** Shiva. ❑*adj* purple; dark-red. **~ষষ্ঠী** *n*=~পূজা. **নীলা** *n* sapphire. **নীলাংশুক** *n* blue garment. **নীলাকাশ** *n* blue sky. **নীলাচল** *n*=~ (3). **নীলাঞ্চল** *n* blue end/ border of a sari/garment. **নীলাঞ্জন** *n* blue antimony. **নীলাব্জ**=~কমল. **নীলাভ** *adj* bluish. **নীলাভা** *n* bluishness; blue tinge/ tint. **নীলাভ্র** *n* dark cloud. **নীলাম্বর** *n* **1** piece of blue cloth. **2** blue sky. ❑*adj* dressed in a blue garment/ sari. **নীলাম্বরী** *n* blue sari. **নীলাম্বু, নীলাম্বুধি** *nn* ocean; sea; high seas; expanse of blue water. **নীলাম্বুবিস্তার** *n* wide expanses of the ocean.

নীলডাউন *adj* knelt down. **~ হওয়া** *vi* kneel down.

নীলাম=নিলাম

নীলিকা *n* **1** indigo plant. **2** kind of eye-disease.

নীলিমময় *adj* blue; azure. **নীলিমময়ী** *fem.*

নীলিমা *n* blueness; azure.
নীলী *n* **1** indigo plant/ dye. **2** blue.
নীলোৎপল *n* blue lotus/ water-lily.
নীলোপল *n* sapphire.
নীহার *n* snow; ice; dew; fog; mist. **~স্ফোট** *n* avalanche.
নীহারিকা *n* nebula. **~বাদ** *n* nebular theory.
নুটি *n* ball/ wisp (of string, wool, etc). **~ পাকানো** *vi* roll into a ball.
নুড়নুড়ি *n* **1** uvula; epiglottis. **2** clapper (of a bell).
নুড়া *n* **1** bundle of grass; faggot. **2** bundle.
নুড়ি *n* pebble; stone-chip.
নুড়ো *n* (colloq)=নুড়া
নুদি *n* pot-belly.
নুদো *n*=নুদি. ❑*adj* pot-bellied.
নুন *n* salt. **~ খাওয়া**=নিমক খাওয়া (⇒ নিমক). **~ আনতে পান্তা ফুরায়** (fig) live from hand to mouth. **~ খাই যার গুণ গাই তার** (fig) I must be loud in praises of my benefactor. **~ শোধা** *vi* discharge one's obligations.
নুনিয়া *n* salt-manufacturer by caste; salter.
নুন্নড়ি *n* (colloq)=নুড়নড়ি
নুয়া *vi* (old style)=নত হওয়া. **~নো**=নত করা.
নুর=নূর
নুলা *n* **1** paw (of a cat, etc). **2** (iron) hand (of a man). ❑*adj* having no hands; crippled. **~ লেংড়া** *adj* lame and crippled.
নুলো *n, adj* (colloq)=নুলা
নুসকা, নুসখা [A] *n* prescription; recipe.
নূতন=নতুন
নূপুর *n* anklet; an ornament for the toes/ ankles/ feet. **~নিক্বণ** *n* jingle of anklet.
নূর [A] *n* light; splendour. **~জাহান** *n* light of the world. **~নবী** *n* the prophet of the Light; the Holy Prophet Muhammad (sm). **নূরানি, নূরানী** *adj* of/ relating to light; composed of light; luminous; resplendent.
নৃ *n* (chiefly used as a *pref*) man; mankind; people; hero; person. **~কপাল** *n* human skull. **~কলবিদ, ~কুলবিৎ** *n* ethnologist. **~কুলবিদ্যা** *n* ethnology. **~কেশরী** *n* lion of a man; Vishnu in his fourth Avatara. **~তত্ত্ব, ~বিদ্যা** *nn* anthropology. **~তাত্ত্বিক** *adj* anthropological. ❑*n* anthropologist. **~দেব** *n* 'man-god'; king. **~মণি** *n* jewel of a man; excellent man; king. **~মুণ্ড** *n* human head/ skull. **~মুণ্ডমালা** *n* garland/ wreath of human heads. **~মুণ্ডমালী** *adj* wearing a garland of human heads. **~মুণ্ডমালিনী** *adj fem* of নৃমুণ্ডমালী. ❑*n* goddess Kali. **~মেধ** *n* human-sacrifice. **~যজ্ঞ** *n* hospitality. **~লোক** *n* world of men; earth; world.
নৃত্য *n* **1** dance; dancing. **2** gesticulation; gyration. **3** caper; capering. **4** acting. **5** frisking; skipping. **6** leap. **~ করা** *vi* dance; leap; dance about; frisk; skip. **~কলা** *n* art of dancing. **~কারী** *adj* dancing; leaping. **~কারিণী** *fem.* **~গীত** *n* dancing and singing. **~গুরু** *n* dancing-master. **~পটু** *adj* adept in dancing. **~পটীয়সী** *fem.* **~পর** *adj* dancing. **~পরা** *fem* fond of dancing. **~পরায়ণ** *adj* dancing; fond of dancing. **~পরায়ণা** *fem.* **~প্রিয়** *adj* fond of dancing. **~প্রিয়া** *fem.* **~বিদ্যা** *n* art/ science of dancing. **~শালা** *n* dancing-room.
নৃপ *n* protection of men; prince; king; sovereign. **~গৃহ** *n* palace. **~বর, ~মণি** *nn* great king. **নৃপাসন** *n* royal seat; throne.
নৃপতি *n* lord of men; prince; king; sovereign.
নৃপেন্দ্র *n* great king; king of kings.
নৃপোচিত *adj* befitting a king; kingly; princely.
নৃশংস *adj* cruel; barbarous; savage; atrocious; ferocious; heinous. **~তা** *n* cruelty; barbarity; savagery; atrocity; ferocity; ferociousness; heinousness.
নৃসিংহ *n* **1** 'man-lion'; great/ illustrious man. **2** (also **নৃসিংহাবতার**) the fourth incarnation of Vishnu.
নে *neg adv* (colloq)=না[১]
নেই *adv* (colloq)=নাই[২]
নেই-আঁকড়া *adj*=নাই-আঁকড়া (⇒ নাই)
নেউল *n* mongoose; ichneumon.
নেওটা *adj* (of a child) extremely attached to/fond of; clinging; clingy: মা-~ ছেলে.
নেওয়া *vt* (colloq)=লওয়া
নেং *n* (colloq)=ল্যাং
নেংচানো *vi* (colloq)=লেংচানো (⇒ লেংচা)
নেংটা, নেংটো (colloq) *adj* **1** naked; unclad. **2** destitute; penniless; miserable. **3** shameless; brazen. **~পনা** *n* shameless conduct/ behaviour; obscenity; indecency.
নেংটি[১] *n* (colloq)=লেংটি
নেংটি[২] *adj* small; tiny. ❑*n* (also **~ ইঁদুর**) mouse.
নেংড়া=লেংড়া
নেক [P] *adj* good; lucky; virtuous; pious; mannerly. **~ খাসলাত** *n* good conduct/ habits. ❑*adj* of good dispositions/ habits; good-natured. **~ নজর** *n* favourable look; fancy. **~ নজরে পড়া** *vi* find favour with sb/ in sb's eyes; catch/ take sb's fancy. **~নাম** *n* good repute; renown. ❑*adj* reputed; famous; renowned. **~নামি** *n*=~নাম. **~নিয়ত** *n* good intention. **~বখত** *adj* lucky; well-behaved; of good disposition; dutiful. **~বখতি** *n* good fortune; happiness.
নেকড়া *n* rag; rags; tatters. **~পরা** *adj* dressed in rags and tatters.
নেকড়ে *n* wolf.
নেকরা *n*=নখরা
নেকা=ন্যাকা
নেকাব [A] *n* veil.
নেকার *n* (dial)=ন্যাক্কার
নেকি [P] *n* goodness; virtue; piety; good. **~বদি** *n* good and evil; weal or woe.

নেগা(হ) [P] look; sight; glance; view; watching; attention; care;, custody. ~বান ⇒নিগাহবান.

নেঙ, নেঙচানো, নেঙড়া=ল্যাং, ল্যাংচানো and ন্যাংড়া respectively.

নেছার=নেসার

নেজ *n* (dial)=লেজ

নেজা *n* (dial)=লেজা

নেজামত=নিজামত (⇒নিজাম)

নেজুর *n* (dial)=লেজুড়

নেট [E] *n* net: নেটের মশারি.

নেটা *adj* left-handed.

নেড়া *adj* **1** shaven; tonsured; shorn: ~ মাথা. **2** having a shaven head; tonsured: ~ লোক. **3** bald: চুল পড়ে মাথা ~ হয়ে যাচ্ছে. **4** leafless; bare: ~গাছ. **5** denuded; bald; bare: ~ মাঠ. **6** having no ornaments; bare: ~ হাত. **7** undecorated; scantily decorated: বইয়ের ~ মলাট. **8** bare of furniture: ~ ঘর. **9** not surrounded by walls: ~ ছাদ. **10** hornless: ~ গরু. ❑*n* (derog) **1** tonsured boy/man. **2** Vaishnava friar/ mendicant. **3** (also নেড়ে) (vulg) a Muslim. নেড়ী *fem.* ~ **করা** *vt* shave (a head). ~**বোঁচা** *adj* plain; naked; bare; bald. ~**মুড়া** *adj* **1** having the head shaven. **2** (of trees) bare. **3** (fig) drastically pruned.

নেড়িকুত্তা *n* cur; tyke.

নেত *n* kind of fine muslin.

নেতা[১] *adj* leading; guiding; commanding; pioneering; directing. ❑*n* leader; guide; conductor; director; headman; chief; commander; pioneer. নেত্রী *fem.*

নেতা[২] *n* **1** rag; tattered cloth. **2** mop (made of rag). ~ **দেওয়া** *vt* mop; sweep. ~ **হওয়া** *vi* **1** droop; flay. **2** cower (in fear). **3** be exhausted; languish: গরমে ~ হওয়া. **4** lose crispiness. ~নো *vt*=~ দেওয়া. ❑*vi*=~ হওয়া.

নেতিবাচক *adj* negative.

নেতৃ *adj*, *n*=নেতা[১]. নেত্রী *n fem.* ~**ত্ব** *n* leadership; guidance; command; lead. ~**ত্ব করা/দেওয়া** *vt* lead; guide; direct; command; head; pioneer.

নেত্র *n* eye. ~**গোচর** *adj* within the range of the eye; visible. ~**গোচর করা** *vt* see; look at. ~**গোচর হওয়া** *vt* come into view; become visible. ~**গোলক** *n* eyeball. ~**চ্ছদ** *n* eyelid. ~**জল** *n* tears. ~**পত্র** *n* eye-brows. ~**পল্লব** *n* eyelid; eyelash. ~**পাত** *n* glance; looking (at). ~**পাত করা** *vi* glance (at); cast glance (at); look at; see. ~**পীড়া**, ~**রোগ** *nn* eye-disease; ~**বর্ত্মকলা** *n* conjunctiva. ~**বর্ত্মকলা-প্রদাহ** *n* conjunctivitis. ~**মল** *n* sticky matter (in eye). ~**রঞ্জন** *n* collyrium.

নেত্রী *n fem* of নেতা[১]

নেপথ্য *n* **1** (theatre) place behind the stage; dressing room. **2** make-up (used by actors and actresses). **3** ornaments; decoration; costume. ~**বিধান** *n* dressing and make-up of actors and actresses. নেপথ্যে *adv* behind the scenes.

নেপা *vt* (dial)=লেপা

নেপালি *adj* Nepalese. ❑*n* Nepalese; Napalese language.

নেপো *n* (dial) king. **যার ধন তার নয় ~য় মারে দই** (prov) The idle knave get the better of the honest toiler.

নেবা[১] *vi* (colloq)=নিবা

নেবা[২] *n* jaundice.

নেবু *n* (dial)=লেবু

নেভা *vi* (colloq)=নিবা

নেমক *n* (dial)=নিমক

নেমন্তন্ন *n* (colloq)=নিমন্ত্রণ

নেমি, নেমী *n* **1** circumference (of a wheel); rim; edge. **2** windlass/ framework for the rope of a well.

নেয়া *vt* (dial)=লওয়া

নেয়াই=নিহাই

নেয়াপতি *adj* having very thinly grown kernel: ~ ডাব.

নেয়াড়, নেয়ার *nn* kind of broad tape.

নেয়ে *n* boatman.

নেলোখেপা *n* madcap; loony; crackpot.

নেশা [A] *n* **1** intoxication; stupefaction; inebriation: ~র ঘোর. **2** intoxicating drug/ liquor; narcotics. **3** addiction: মদের ~. **4** (fig) strong interest; addiction; fascination; intoxication: ক্ষমতার ~, প্রেমের ~. **5** (fig) enthusiasm; hobby; fad; craze: ছবি আঁকার ~. ~ **করা** *vi* **1** be addicted to intoxicants/ drinking; be a drug-addict. **2** take/ use drugs/ liquor; tipple; imbibe; booze; be on drugs; be on the booze. ~ **কেটে যাওয়া** *vi* come to one's senses. ~**খোর** *adj* addicted to intoxicating drinks/ drugs/ intoxicants. ❑*n* drunkard; drug-addict. ~**গ্রস্ত** *adj* intoxicated; inebriated; stupefied with drink. ~**গ্রস্ত করা** *vt* intoxicate; stupefy. ~**য় চুর/বুঁদ** *adj* dead drunk; under the influence; befuddled by dunk. ~**র ঘোরে** *adv* in a state of intoxication; under the influence of alcohol/ drug etc; being intoxicated with sth: ক্ষমতার ~র ঘোরে

নেশারি, নেশারী *adj* intoxicating; enchanting; captivating: ~ রূপ.

নেস্ত–নাবুঁদ=নাস্তানাবুদ

নেহাই *n* anvil.

নেহাত, নেহায়ত, নেহায়েত [A] *adv* **1** very; extremely; exceedingly; quite; thoroughly: ~ ছোট্ট, ~ দুর্নীতিবাজ. **2** at all; to any extent; in any way; must; necessarily; perforce: তোমাকে যদি ~ এখানে আসতেই হয়. **3** at the utmost: ~ একদিনের ব্যাপার বই তো নয়.

নেহারণ=নিহারণ
নেহারা=নিহারা
নৈ=নই
নৈঃশব্দ(্য) *n* noiselessness; silence; stillness.
নৈঃস্ব *n* absence of property; destitution; poverty.
নৈকট্য *n* nearness; proximity; neighbourhood; closeness; intimacy; imminence.
নৈকতলীয় *n* (geom) skew.
নৈকষেয় *n* son of Nikasha (a Rakshasa in the Ramayana).
নৈকষ্য *adj* **1** tested on a streak-plate. **2** pure-blooded; blue-blooded: ~ কুলীন. **3** pure-bred; pedigree; thorough-bred.
নৈচা, নেচে=নইচা
নৈতিক *adj* moral; ethical. **~চরিত্র** *n* moral character.
নৈত্যিক *adj* to be always/ regularly done; constantly repeated; invariable; obligatory; routine.
নৈদাঘ *adj* relating to the hot season; summerlike; summer; scorching: ~ ঝটিকা, northwester. নৈদাঘী *fem.*
নৈপুণ্য *n* dexterity; skill; adroitness; expertness; experience; efficiency.
নৈবচ *adv* not such/so; unlike this. **~ নৈবচ, নৈব ~** will never be; ought not to.
নৈবিড়্য=নিবিড়তা (⇒ নিবিড়)
নৈবেদ্য *n* offering (presented to a deity/idol).
নৈমিত্তিক *adj* **1** occasional; special; accidental; irregular, casual; contingent; adventitious. **2** versed in augury. **~ কর্ম, ~ ক্রিয়া** *nn* occasional/ periodic ceremony/rite. **~ ছুটি** *n* casual leave.
নৈমিষ *adj* momentary; transient. ❑*n* (also ~কানন, নৈমিষারণ্য) (myth) name of a forest.
নৈয়মিক *adj* regular; settled; prescribed; enjoined.
নৈয়ায়িক *adj* **1** versed in the Naya (ন্যায়) philosophy. **2** logical. ❑*n* **1** follower of the Naya system. **2** logician; dialectician; sophist.
নৈরপেক্ষ(্য) *n*=নিরপেক্ষতা (⇒ নিরপেক্ষ)
নৈরাকার *adj* (dial)=নিরাকার
নৈরাজ্য *n* lawlessness; anarchy; disorder; mob rule. **~বাদ** *n* anarchism. **~বাদী** *adj* anarchic(al). ❑*n* anarchist.
নৈরাশ্য *n* hopelessness; despair; pessimism. **~বাদ** *n* pessimism. **~বাদী** *adj* pessimistic. ❑*n* pessimist.
নৈঋত *n* south-west.
নৈর্গুণ্য=নির্গুণতা
নৈর্ব্যক্তিক *adj* **1** impersonal. **2** divine.
নৈলে=নইলে
নৈশ *adj* relating to/ happening at night; nightly; nocturnal; night. **~ ক্লাব** *n* night-club. **~ জীবন** *n* night-life. **~ বিদ্যালয়** *n* night-school.
নৈশ্চিত্য=নিশ্চয়তা (⇒ নিশ্চয়)
নৈষধ *adj* relating to Nishadha (নিষধ), an ancient Indian state. ❑*n* prince of the Nishadhas (people of Nishadha).
নৈষ্কর্ম্য *n* **1** inactivity; inaction; unemployment **2** laziness; aversion to work; lassitude; idleness; cessation of work. **3** solemn abstention from all work. **4** salvation.
নৈষ্ঠিক *adj* **1** =নিষ্ঠাবান (⇒ নিষ্ঠা). **2** devotional; ritual; ritualistic.
নৈসর্গিক, নৈসর্গিকা *adjj* innate; natural; inborn; physical.
নোংরা *adj* **1** dirty; filthy; unclean; soiled; shabby; dingy; messy; squalid. ~ হাত/কাপড়/ঘর. **2** base; mean; vile; abject; nesty; shameful: ~ কাজ/ মন. **3** vulgar; obscene; indecent; foul; bawdy; squalid; coarse: ~ ভাষা/আলাপ. **4** impure; unholy; unclean; contaminated; unhygienic; polluted: ~পানি/খাবার. **5** slovenly; sloppy; untidy; frowzy: ~ চালচলন, ~ লোক. ❑*n* dirt; filth; squalor; smut. **~ করা** *vt* dirty; soil; mess up; litter sth up. **~মি, ~মো** *nn* **1** dirtiness; filthiness. **2** obscenity; vulgarity; lasciviousness; dirty tricks; foul play; bad habits; baseness; villainy; meanness; vileness; depravity; ribaldry; indecent behaviour.
নোকর *n* = নওকর. **নোকরি** *n* service; employment; pay; reward; post. **নোকরি করা** *vi* serve; be in the employment (of).
নোকসান=লোকসান
নোক্তা [A] *n* point; subtle/quaint conceit. **~ করা** *vi* be conceited. **~র আঁচড়** *n* stroke of the pen.
নোঙর [P] *n* anchor. **~ উঠানো/ তোলা** *vi* weigh anchor. **~ করা/ফেলা** *vi* anchor; let go the anchor; cast anchor; lay at anchor; bring (a ship) come to anchor; drop/lower (the)an anchor.
নোট [E] *n* **1** currency note; banknote; bill. **2** short letter; note; short comment. **~ করা** *vi* take notes; make a note of sth; note/jot sth down. **~ করা** *adj* noted down. **~ দেওয়া** *vi* dictate sth (to sb). **~ ভাঙানো** *vi* cash a banknote; exchange a banknote of high denomination for notes of lower value. **~খাতা** *n* notebook. **~বই** *n* note-book; commentary; note; key.
নোটিস [E] *n* notice. **~ দেওয়া** *vi* serve a notice; notify.
নোড়া *n* pestle (esp one made of stone).
নোতুন *adj* (colloq)=নতুন
নোনতা *adj* **1** saline; salt: ~ পানি. **2** salty: ~ স্বাদ. ❑*n* salty snacks.
নোনা[1] *adj* **1** saline; salted: ~ মাছ, **~ জল** *n* saline/salt water. **~ মাংস** *n* salt/salted meat.
নোনা[2] *n* custard-apple.

নোয়া[1] *vi* =(colloq)=নত হওয়া (⇒ নত). **~নো** *vt*=নত করা (⇒ নত)

নোয়া[2] *n* (dial) **1** iron. **2** iron wristlet (worn by Hindu women whose husbands are alive). **হাতের ~ অক্ষয় হওয়া** have one's husband alive till one's death.

নোলক *n* nose-ring set with a pendant.

নোলা *n* (hum) **1** tongue. **2** greediness. **~ বড়ো হওয়া** *vi* become audaciously greedy. **~য় জল আসা** *vi* have one's mouth watering; become greedy.

নৌ *n* (used chiefly as a *pref)* boat; ship; vessel. ❑*adj* nautical. **~কর্ম** *n* helm of a ship. **~কর্ণধার** *n* helmsman. **~ঘাঁটি** *n* naval base. **~চালন(1)** *n* rowing; navigation. **~চালনা করা** *vi* row; navigate. **~চালনাবিদ্যা** *n* navigation. **~জীবিকা** *n* sailor; boatman. **~দিগ্‌দর্শী** *n* mariner's compass. **~পথ** *n* waterway. **~পথে** *adv* by water; by boat. **~পরিমাপক** *n* nautical surveyor. **~বল** *n* navy; naval force; seapower. **~বহর** *n* fleet (of ships/warships). **~বাহ** *n* **1** navigation. **2** boatman; oarsman. **~বাহিনী** *n* navy. **~বাহী, ~বাহ্য** *adjj* navigability. **~বিদ্যা** *n* **1** navigation. **2** ship-building. **~বিভাগ** *n* navy; marine department. **~বিমান** *n* seaplane. **~বিহার** *n* pleasure-trip in a boat; pleasure cruising; boat journey. **~বিহার করা** *vi* go on/for a cruise; have a pleasure-trip in a boat; journey by boat. **~যান** *n* **1** ship; vessel. **2** going in a ship; navigation. **~যায়ী** *adj* going in a boat. ❑*n* passenger. **~যুদ্ধ** *n* naval battle; naval warfare. **~সম্বন্ধীয়** *adj* naval; nautical. **~সারণী** *n* nautical almanac. **~সেনা, ~সৈন্য** *nn* seaman. **~সেনাপতি** *n* admiral. **~সেনাবিভাগ** *n* admiralty; navy.

নৌকতা *n* **1** (dial) social formality; etiquette; ceremony; civilities; suavities. **2** gift/ present given for the sake of formality. **~ করা** *vi* observe social formalities; stand on ceremony.

নৌকা *n* boat (esp one plying on a river). **~জীবী** *n* boatman. **~ডুবি** *n* shipwreck. **~পথ**=নৌপথ (⇒ নৌ). **~বাহক** *n* boatman. **~বাহিত** *adj* borne/ carried by boat. **~বিহার**=নৌবিহার. **~বিলাস** *n* pleasure-trip in a boat; rowing (as a sport); boating. **~যাত্রা** *n* journey by boat. **~যাত্রী** *n* passenger of a boat. **~যোগে** *adv* by boat. **~যোগে ভ্রমণ** *n* journey by boat. **~রোহণ** *n* going on board a ship/ boat; embarkation. **~রোহণ করা** *vi* go on board a boat; embark. **~রোহণে** *adv* by boat. **~রোহী** *adj* aboard a boat; going by a boat. ❑*n* passenger of a boat. **~রোহিণী** *fem.* **~সংক্রান্ত, ~সম্বন্ধী** *adjj* naval. **দুই ~য় পা দেওয়া** *vi* have/want it/things both ways; satisfy two demands.

নৌজোয়ান=নওজোয়ান (⇒ নও)

নৌবত=নওবত

ন্যক্কার *n* **1** humiliation; contempt; disgust; abhorrent. **2** vomiting; nausea. **~জনক** *adj* disgusting; nauseating; abominable; abhorrent; loathsome.

ন্যগ্রোধ *n* banyan; banian-tree; Indian fig-tree. **~ পরিমণ্ডলী** *adj fem* buxom. ❑*n* elegant woman.

ন্যস্ত *adj* **1** thrown/ cast/ laid down; flung; put; placed. **2** deposited; committed; put in the custody (of); confided/entrusted to. **3** stretched out; lying: শয্যায় ~. **4** inserted; applied; fixed. **5** arrayed; arranged in order. **6** committed to: লেখায়/চিত্রে **~. ন্যস্তা** *fem.* **~ করা** *vt* **1** throw/ cast/ lay down; place; fling. **2** deposit; commit; put in the custody of; confide/ entrust to. **3** stretch out; lie. **4** insert; apply; fix. **5** array; arranged in order. **6** commit to. **~ধন** *n* trust money.

ন্যাওটা=নেওটা

ন্যাংটা *adj* (colloq)=ল্যাংটা

ন্যাকড়া=নেকড়া

ন্যাকরা=নখরা

ন্যাকা *adj* **1** foolish; silly; feigning. **2** affected; feigned. ❑*n* **1** fool; booby; dolt; dissembler; fibber. **~. সাজা**=~মি করা. **~মি, ~মো** *nn* affectation (of ignorance/honest); silliness; sham; make-believe. **~মি করা** *vi* affect in ignorance; sham; feign.

ন্যাকার *n* (colloq)=ন্যক্কার

ন্যাটা=নেটা

ন্যাতন্যাতে *adj* loose; sluggish; slothful; slack.

ন্যাবা=নেবা[2]

ন্যায় *n* **1** reasoning; logic; argument. **2** logical/syllogistic argument/ inference. **3** science of reasoning; logic; dialectic. **4** system of philosophy delivered by Gautama. **5** (universal/ general) rule; principle; axiom; system. **6** justice; equity; truth; fitness; propriety. **7** honesty; righteousness. **~ অন্যায় যেভাবেই হোক** by fair means or foul. **~কর্তা** *n* judge; logician. **~কর্ত্রী** *fem.* **ন্যায়ত** *adv* according to/ in keeping with justly; justly; properly; rightly; according to right. **~তীর্থ** *n* a title given to graduates in Indian logic and philosophy. **~-নির্ণয়** *n* adjudication. **~-নির্ণয় করা** *vi* adjudicate. **~-নির্ণায়ক** *n* adjudicator. **~নিষ্ঠ** *adj* righteous; upright; virtuous. **~নিষ্ঠতা, ~নিষ্ঠা** *nn* righteousness; uprightness; justness; integrity. **~পথ** *n* path of justice/ righteousness/ uprightness/ rectitude/ right/ rightful way; path of reasoning. **~পথাবলম্বন করা** *vi* follow the path of justice/ righteousness; act justly/ uprightly; lead a life of virtue. **~পথাবলম্বী, ~পথাশ্রয়ী** *adjj* righteous; virtuous; upright. **~পথাবলম্বিনী, ~পথাশ্রয়িণী** *fem.* **~পর, ~পরায়ণ, ~বান**=~নিষ্ঠ. **~পরায়ণা** *fem.* **~পরতা, ~পরায়ণতা, ~বত্তা**=~নিষ্ঠতা. **~পীঠ**

n tribunal. ~বিচার *n* justice; equity. ~বাদী *adj* speaking reasonably/ properly; reasonable. ~বিচার করা *vi* do justice; administer/dispense justice; judge impartially/ uprightly/ fairly. ~বিচারক *n* even handed/ impartial/ upright. ~বিরোধী *adj* contrary/ prejudicial to justice; unjust; unfair; wrongful; inequitable; improper; unreasonable; illogical. ~বিচারশূন্য *adj* incapable of judging correctly; devoid of a sense of justice; unjust; unfair. ~বিরুদ্ধ=~বিরোধী. ~বুদ্ধি *n* sense of justice; discernment; conscience; conscientiousness. ~বুদ্ধিপরায়ণ, ~বুদ্ধিসম্পন্ন *adjj* endowed with sense of justice; discerning; conscientious; righteous. ~বুদ্ধিপরায়ণা, ~বুদ্ধিসম্পন্না *fem.* ~বুদ্ধিহীন *adj* devoid of the sense of justice/conscience; unscrupulous. ~বুদ্ধিহীনা *fem.* ~বোধ *n* sense of justice. ~মার্গ=~পথ. ~রত্ন *n* 'jewel of a logician/philosopher'; title awarded to some Sanskrit scholars. ~শাসন *n* administration/ dispensation of justice; good/just administration/ government. ~শাস্ত্র *n* logic. ~শৃঙ্খলা *n* reasoning; sorites. ~সংহিতা *n* civil code. ~সঙ্গত, ~সম্মত, ~সম্বন্ধ *adj* logical; reasonable; just; proper; equitable. ~সঙ্গতি *n* logicality; logic; (chain of) reasoning. ~সিদ্ধ *adj* logical. ~সূত্র *n* aphorisms of the Naya philosophy of Gautama. ন্যায়াচার *n* just/righteous/virtuous conduct. ন্যায়াধার *n* example of virtue/propriety. ন্যায়াধিকরণ *n* court of justice; law-court. ন্যায়াধীশ *n* judge; justice. ন্যায়ান্যায় *n* right and wrong. ন্যায়ান্বেষণ *n* seeking for justice. ন্যায়াভাস *n* semblance of a reason; sophism. ন্যায়ালঙ্কার *n* 'ornament of logic'; title awarded to certain Sanskrit scholars. ন্যায়ালয়, ন্যায়াধিকরণ. ন্যায়াসন *n* (law) bench. ন্যায়ের তর্ক/বিচার *n* logical discussion; (derog) sophistry. ন্যায়ের ফাঁকি *n* logical fallacy. ন্যায়ের ভাষ্য *n* explanation of a logical point.

ন্যায়িক *adj* logical; judicial.

ন্যায়ী *adj* =ন্যায়নিষ্ঠ (⇒ ন্যায়)

ন্যায়োপেত=ন্যায়নিষ্ঠ (⇒ ন্যায়)

ন্যায্য *adj* 1 correct; right; just; fit; proper. 2 reasonable; logical; logically admissible. 3 rightful; lawful; legitimate: ~ দাবি. 4 equitable; upright; just: ~ ভাগ. ~তা *n* fitness; propriety; correctness; justness; reasonableness; logicality; logic; equity; rightfulness; legitimacy. ন্যায্যান্যায্য *n* right and wrong.

ন্যালনেলে *adj* 1 slavering. 2 greedy; avid. 3 slender; lean; wispy.

ন্যালাখ্যাপা=নেলাখেপা

ন্যাস *n* 1 deposit; pledge; depositing; entrusting; trust. 2 custody; guardianship. 3 putting down/in; placing; fixing; inserting. 4 laying aside; putting away; taking off. 5 (in yoga) breathing-control. ~ধারক *n* holder of a deposit. ~ধারণ *n* holding in deposit. ~পাল, ~রক্ষক *nn* trustee. ~ সমিতি *n* trust board.

ন্যুব্জ *adj* 1 hump-backed; hunch-backed; crooked-backed. 2 looking downward; bent (forward); stooping; curved; bent/turned downwards; hunched up. 3 convex. ~ হওয়া *vi* bend (down/forward); stoop; double up; curve; turn upside down; become convex. ~খড়গ *n* crooked sword; sabre. ~তা *n* 1 hump; abnormal curvature of the back. 2 bending (forward); stooping; stoop; curvature; curving; bend. 3 convexity. ~ দেহ *adj* hunch-backed; stooping forward; stooped. ~ পৃষ্ঠ *adjj* 1 convex; bent forward. 2 (derog) weak-kneed; spineless.

ন্যূন *adj* less (than) ; short (of); deficient (in); inferior (to). ~ হওয়া *vi* be less (than); be deficient (in); be inferior (to); fall short (of). ~কল্প *adj* least. ~কল্পে *adv* at least. ~তর *adj* less/lower (than). ~তা *n* want; deficiency; inferiority; lack; scarcity; shortage. ~পক্ষে =কল্পে. ~ সংখ্যায় *adv* in the least number; at least. ন্যূনাতিরেক=ন্যূনাধিক্য. ন্যূনাধিক *adj* more or less. ন্যূনাধিক্য *n* shortage or/and excess; disparity; difference. ~ পরিমাণে *adv* to some extent; a little; in small quantity.

ন্যূনী *adj* (in compounds)=ন্যূন. ~করণ *n* reduction; lessening. ~কৃত *adj* reduced; lessened; diminished.

প

প[১] *n* the twenty-first consonant of the Bengali alphabet. ~-বর্গ *n* the প series (the labial series of consonants).

প[২] *adj* (used as a *suff*) 1 drinking: মধু~, মদ্য~, পাদ~. 2 guarding; possessing; protecting; ruling: গো~, ভূমি~, ভূ~.

পইছা *n* kind of bangle/ bracelet.

পইঠা *n* step/flight of stairs.

পইতা *n* 1 sacred thread/cord (worn by the first three classes of Hindus). 2 sacrament of wearing the sacred thread for the first time. ~ কাটা *vi* spin the sacred thread (from cotton/ ordinary thread). ~ নেওয়া/পরা *vi* put on/ wear the sacred thread (sacramental). ~ ফেলে দেওয়া *vi* discard the sacred thread. ~ হওয়া *vi* be invested with the sacred thread. ~ধারী *adj* wearing a sacred thread; belonging to any of the Hindu upper castes, esp the Brahmin community. চেনা বামুনের ~র দরকার নেই (fig) A well-known person needs no credentials.

পইপই করে *adv* repeatedly; again and again.

পউষ=পৌষ

পঁইছা=পইছা

পঁইত্রিশ *n, adj* (colloq)=পঁয়ত্রিশ

পঁচাত্তর *n, adj* seventy-five.

পঁচানব্বই, পঁচানব্বুই *n, adj* ninety-five.

পঁচাশি *n, adj* eighty-five.

পঁচিশ *n, adv* twenty-five. **পঁচিশে** *adj* (of the days of a month) twenty-fifth. ❑*n* twenty-fifth day of a month; the twenty-fifth.

পঁয়তাল্লিশ *n, adj* forty-five.

পঁয়ত্রিশ *n, adj* thirty-five.

পঁয়ষট্টি *n, adj* sixty-five.

পকেট [E] *n* pocket. ~ **কাটা/ মারা** *vi* pick sb's pocket. ~ **ভরা, পকেটে পোরা** *vt* pocket; misappropriate. ~ **ঘড়ি** *n* pocket-watch. ~ **বই** *n* pocket book. **~মার** *n* pick-pocket. **ঝুল-~** *n* side-pocket . **পিছনের ~** *n* hip-pocket. **বুক-~** *n* breast-pocket. **ভিতরে ~** *n* inside pocket. **পকেটে হাত পড়া** (fig) be pinched for money; feel the pinch; (of one's interests) be at stake.

পক্ব *adj* 1 ripe; mature: ~ কাঁঠাল. 2 cooked; roasted; baked; boiled; dried; burnt: ~ অন্ন, আতপ ~. 3 grey; hoary: ~ কেশ. 4 accomplished; fully developed; perfect; mature; experienced: ~ বুদ্ধি. 5 concentrated; thick: ~ মধু. 6 seasoned: ~ বংশদণ্ড. 7 digested: উদরে খাদ্য ~ হচ্ছে. **~কেশ** *n* grey hair. ❑*adj* grey-haired; old; hoary-headed; aged. **~তা** *n* ripeness; maturity; greyness; experience; condensation; seasoning; digestion. **পক্বান্ন** *n* cooked/ dressed food. **পক্বাশয়** *n* stomach.

পক্ষ *n* 1 wing; pinion. 2 feather. 3 feathers (on both sides of an arrow). 3 fin of a fish. 4 name of the number two. 5 shoulder. 6 flank/ side/half of anything. 7 side/wing of a building; aisle. 8 wing/flank of an army. 9 half of a lunar month; fortnight. 10 side; team; faction; party: তিনি কোনো পক্ষেই নেই. 11 partisan; adherent; follower; friend: শত্রু~, enemy's side. 12 position; place; stead; side; behalf: আমার ~ হয়ে কিছু বলুন. 13 one of two cases/ one side of an argument; alternative. 14 point/matter under discussion; thesis; particular theory; position advanced; argument to be maintained: আত্ম~ সমর্থন করা. 15 action; law-suit. 16 (logic) proposition to be proved (in syllogism). 17 supposition; view; notion; idea; opinion. 18 question; answer: পূর্ব~, উত্তর~. 19 marriage: প্রথম পক্ষের সংসার. 20 wife: তার দ্বিতীয় ~. 21 multitude; number; troop; set; class of being. 22 (alg) primary division; side of an equation in a primary division. 23 wall (of a house). 24 army. 25 favour. 26 contradiction; rejoinder. 27 limb/ member of the body: পক্ষাঘাত. 28 direction; side; hand: অপর পক্ষে. 29 care: পারতপক্ষে. 30 royal elephant. 31 half of a couplet. 32 ash-pit of a fire-place/ an oven. **~ক** *n* 1 partisan. 2 side door. 3 side. 4 (bot) pinule. ~ **করা** *vi* marry. **~ক্ষয়** *n* end of a half month. **~ক্ষেপ** *n* stroke/beat of a wing. **~গ্রহণ** *n* taking the side of; supporting; backing; championship; partisanship; bias towards; playing for a particular team. ~ **গ্রহণ করা** *vi* side with; adhere to; support; plead for; defend; back (up); make common cause with; come to the defense of; tilt in favour of; be biased in favour of; stand for; follow; adhere to; defend; champion; advocate; ally/align oneself with; subscribe to; play for. **~চ্ছেদ(ন)** *n* 1 cutting off/ clipping of the wings. 2 (fig) making powerless; disablement; refutation of sb's arguments. **~চ্ছেদ(ন) করা** *vi* cut off/clip the wings of); (fig) render powerless; disable; incapacitate. **~তা, ~ত্ব** *nn* 1 partisanship; adherence to a party; support; partiality. 2 (phil) taking up a side/ argument; maintaining/ defending a thesis. 3 being a part of. **~দ্বয়** *n* 1 two wings. 2 both sides of an argument. **~দ্বার** *n* side/inner/ back door; private entrance. **~ধর** *adj* 1 having wings; winged. 2 taking the side of; clinging to. ❑*n* bird. **~পাত, ~পাতিতা, ~পাতিত্ব** *nn* 1 siding with; partiality; favouritism; unfairness; preference; bias; inclination for. **~পাতদুষ্ট** *adj* partial; biased; prejudiced; one-sided; unfair. **~পাতশূন্য** *adj* impartial; unbiased; fair; neutral; even-handed; fair-minded; unprejudiced. **~পাতিত্ব করা** *vi* be partial/ biased; prejudiced; have a bias; favour; discriminate. **~পাতী** *adj* 1 partial; prejudiced; prejudicial; biased; predisposed. 2 favourable; favouring; siding with; in favour of; having a preference for; inclined towards; prone/leaning to; preferring. **~পাতিনী** *fem.* **~পুট** *n* inner part/ inside of a wing. **~পোষণ** *n* partisanship. **~বল** *n* 1 strength of wing (of a bird). 2 strength of a party/side/ team; party-strength; allies. **~বান** *adj* winged. **~ভুক্ত** *adj* included in a side/ team. **~ভেদ** *n* 1 distinction between two sides of an argument. 2 distinguishing one side from another. **~মূল** *n* root/articulation of a wing. **~ল** *adj* winged. **~শিরাবিন্যাস** *n* (bot) pinnate venation. **~শিরিত** *adj* (bot) pinnately veined. **~সঞ্চালন** *n* flutter/flapping of wings. **~ সঞ্চালন করা** *vi* (of a bird) flutter/ flap (its) wings. **~সমর্থক** *adj* siding with; supporting; standing for; adhering to; defending; championing; advocating. ❑*n* supporter; partisan; adherent; party-man; champion; advocate; follower; defender. **~ সমর্থন**=~ গ্রহণ. ~ **সমর্থন করা**=~ গ্রহণ করা. ~

সমর্থনকারী=~ সমর্থক. ~ **সমর্থনকারিণী** *fem.* ~**হীন** *adj* wingless. **পক্ষাকার, পক্ষাকৃতি** *adj* wing-shaped; fin-shaped; pinnate. **পক্ষাঘাত** *n* paralysis (of one side); palsy. **পক্ষাঘাতগ্রস্ত** *adj* paralyzed; palsied. **পক্ষান্ত** *n* **1** full/ new moon. **2** end/termination of a fortnight: পক্ষান্তকাল মধ্যে. **পক্ষান্তর** *n* other side/ view (of an argument). **পক্ষান্তরকরণ** *n* (alg) transposition. **পক্ষান্তরে** *adv* on the other hand/ side; on the contrary. **পক্ষাপক্ষ** *n* one's friends and foes/ adversaries; supporters and antagonists. **পক্ষাপক্ষবিচার** *n* distinction/ discrimination between one's friends and foes. **পক্ষাপক্ষবিচারহীন** *adj* **1** impartial; nonpartisan; equitable; objective: পক্ষাপক্ষবিচারহীন মনোভাব. **2** indiscriminate: পক্ষাপক্ষবিচারহীন অত্যাচার. **পক্ষাবলম্বন**=~ গ্রহণ. **পক্ষাবলম্বী**=~ সমর্থক. **পক্ষাবলম্বিনী** *fem.*

পক্ষি *n* (in compounds)=পক্ষী. ~**নীড়** *n* nest. ~**পালক** *adj* employed in aviculture/bird-rearing. ❑*n* bird-fancier. ~**পালন** *n* bird-rearing; aviculture. ~**পালন করা** *vi* rear birds. ~**পালনশালা** *n* aviary. ~**বিদ্যা** *n* ornithology. ~**রাজ** *n* **1** (myth) kind of birds; name of Garuda (গরুড়). **2** (in fairy tales) winged horse. ~**শাবক** *n* young bird; young of a bird. ~**শালা** *n* aviary. ~**শিকার** *n* fowling.

পক্ষী *n* bird. ~**মার** *n* fouler.

পক্ষীয় *adj* of/concerning a party; belonging to a party; siding with; taking the side/ party of.

পক্ষোদ্‌গম, পক্ষোদ্‌ভেদ *n* fledging. **পক্ষোদ্‌গম/ পক্ষোদ্‌ভেদ হওয়া** *vi* be fledged.

পক্ষ্ম *n* **1** eyelash. **2** feather. ~**মণ্ডল** *n* circle of the eyelashes. ~**সম্পাত** *n* closing of the eyes; instant. ~**স্পন্দ** *n* quivering of the eyelashes.

পগার *n* ditch/drain (marking the boundary of a tract of land). ~ **পার হওয়া** *vi* **1** leap over/cross a ditch. **2** (fig) make good one's escape; get away; run away beyond reach.

পঙ্ক *n* **1** mud; mire; clay; dirt. **2** ointment; unguent; paste. **3** moral impurity; vice. **4** (biol) protoplasm. **5** (geog) silt. **6** (arch) finial. ~**জ** *adj* mud-born. ❑*n* lotus. ~**জা** *fem.* ~**জন্ম** *n* 'lotus-born'; Brahma. ~**জ নয়ন,** ~**জ নেত্র,** ~**জাক্ষি** *adjj* lotus-eyed. ~**নয়না,** ~**নেত্রা** *fem.* ~**জাত** *adj* born/grown in mud. ~**জিনী** *n* **1** lotus-pond. **2** lotus plant; clump/ cluster of lotuses; lotus-stalk. ~**তা** *n* muddiness. ~**রুহ** *n* lotus.

পঙ্কিল *adj* muddy; covered with mud; miry; turbid; dirty; nasty; vicious; filthy. ~**তা** *n* muddiness; turbidity; sloppy; filthiness; viciousness.

পঙ্কোদ্ধার *n* **1** dredging (of a river). **2** cleansing; purification; correction; rectification. **3** clearing up a mess. **4** reclamation from vice. ~ **করা** *vi* **1** dredge. **2** clear up the mess. **3** cleanse; purify. **4** reclaim from vice.

পঙ্‌ক্তি *n* row; set; series; line; group. ~**দূষক** *n, adj* (any person) improper to associate with. ~**ভোজন** *n* community-dining; community dinner. ~**মালা** *n* lines; verses.

পঙ্খী *n* **1** (dial) bird. **2** (sl) ganja-smoker and teller of cock-and-bull stories.

পঙ্গ *n* locust. ~**পাল** *n* **1** swarm of locusts. **2** (fig) huge crowd.

পঙ্গু *adj* lame; crippled in the legs; disabled; rendered powerless. ❑*n* cripple. ~**তা** *n* lameness; motionless; invalidity; incapacity; disablement.

পচ *n* rotting; putrefaction; decay; decomposition. ~ **ধরা** *vi* begin to rot/ decay/ putrefy/ decompose/ spoil; fester; become septic.

পচন *n* **1**=পচ. **2** sepsis. **3** cooking. ~ **ধরা**=পচ ধরা (⇒পচ). ~**নিবারক** *adj* antiseptic. ~**শীল** *adj* **1** likely to go bad/decay quickly; perishable. **2** rotting; decaying; decomposing; putrescent. **3** (getting) septic.

পচপচ *n* (onom) expressing the sound of walking on mud.

পচা *vi* **1** rot; putrefy; decay; decompose; go bad; spoil. **2** become septic; fester. **3** become hackneyed. ❑*adj* **1** rotten; putrid; putrefied; decayed; decomposed; spoiled; gone bad. **2** addled: ~ ডিম. **3** septic; festering. **4** (fig) hackneyed; stale: ~ খবর. **5** ugly; bad; shabby: ~ চেহারা, ~ কাপড়-চোপড়. ~ **কাল** *vi* vile/ putrefying weather; rainy season. ~**গলা** *adj* putrefied; decomposed. ~ **ভাদ্র/ভাদ্দর** *n* humid and sweltering month of Bhadra. ~**ই** *n* a liquor distilled from rice; arrack. ~**নি** *n* putrefaction; morbid discharge; purulence; sepsis; festering. ~**নো** *vt* **1** rot; putrefy; decompose; spoil. **2** make septic. **পচ্য** *adj* to be cooked; digestible.

পচাল *n* volubility; blabber; blather; idle talk; tittle-tattle; prattle; ramble. ~ **পাড়া** *vi* be voluble; blabber (on); blather (on); tittle-tattle; talk nineteen to the dozen; talk the hind leg off a donkey; ramble on; prattle on.

পচ্চীকারী *n* mosaic.

পছন্দ choice; preference; approval; selection; approbation; liking. ❑*adj* chosen; liked; favourite; approved; selected. ~ **করা** *vt* like; choose; select; prefer; approve. ~**মাফিক,** ~**সই** *adj* to one's liking; choice; select; pleasing; desirable.

পঞ্চ *n, adj* five. ~**ক** *adj* relating to/made of five. ❑*n* set/collection/aggregate of five; pentad; quintet; five percent. ~**কর্ম** *n* five kinds of treatment in medicine. ~ **কর্মেন্দ্রিয়** *n* five organs to work with (tongue, hands, feet, rectum and genitals). ~কষায় *n* a decoction from the astringent bark of five different trees. ~কোণ *adj* pentangular; pentagonal. ❑*n* pentagon. ~কোণী *adj*=~ কোণ. ~কোষ *n* five souls supped to invest the soul. ~গব্য *n* five products of the cow (milk, coagulated milk, butter, liquid and solid excreta). ~গুণ *adj* five times; fivefold. ❑*n* five attributes/qualities (form, taste, smell, touch, sound). ~গৌড় *n* collective name of Gaud, Mithila, Utkal, Kanauj and the region situated on the bank of the river Saraswati. ~চত্বারিংশ *adj* forty-fifth. ~চত্বারিংশৎ *n, adj* forty-five. ~চত্বারিংশত্তম *adj* forty-fifth. ~চত্বারিংশত্তমী *fem.* ~চূড় *adj* having five tufts of hair. ~জন *n* **1** five elements. **2** man; mankind. ~জনীন *n* actor; buffoon. ~জ্ঞানেন্দ্রিয় *n* five-sense-organs. ~তপা *adj* (of an ascetic) sitting between the five fires (in self-mortification). ~তা=~ত্ব. ~তিক্ত *n* five bitter things. ~ত্রিংশ *adj* thirty-fifth. ~ত্রিংশৎ *n, adj* thirty-five. ~ত্রিংশত্তম *adj* thirty-fifth. ~ত্রিংশত্তমী *fem.* ~ত্ব *n* **1** fivefoldness; fivefold state/ amount; aggregate/collection of five things. **2** five elements. **3** dissolution in the elements; death. ~ত্ব ঘটা *vi* give up the ghost; die. ~ত্ব প্রাপ্ত *adj* dead. ~ত্ব প্রাপ্ত হওয়া=~ত্ব ঘটা. ~ত্ব প্রাপ্তি *n* death; demise. ~দল *adj* having five petals; quinquepetalous; pentamerous. ~দল পুষ্প *n* cinque-foil. ~দলীয় *adj* pentameral; pertaining to/consisting of five parties; five-party; quinquepartite. ~দশ *n, adj* fifteen. ❑*adj* fifteenth. ~দশী *adj fem* fifteenth; fifteen years old. ❑*n* fifteenth day of a half month; day of full or new moon. ~দেবতা *n* five deities/gods. ~নখ *n* five-clawed animal. ~নদ *n* the Punjab, country of five rivers. ~নবত *adj* ninety-fifth. ~নবতি *n, adj* ninety-five. ~নবতিতম *adj* ninety-fifth. ~নবতিতমী *fem.* ~পাণ্ডব *n* five Pandava, brothers of the Mahabharata. ~পাত্র *n* five vessels used in Hindu religious service; five ancestors to whom oblations are made. ~-পিতা *n* one's five fathers (viz progenitor, deliverer from fear, father-in-law, preceptor and provider). ~পুরুষ *n* five generations. ~প্রদীপ *n* metal lamp with five wicks. ~প্রাণ *n* five vital airs (supposed to be in the body). ~প্রেত=~ভূত. ~বট *n* five fig-trees. ~বর্গ *n* class group/series of five. ~বর্ণ *adj* five-coloured. ~বর্ষ *adj* five years old. ~বান *n* five arrow of Kama (কাম), the love god; Kama, the god of love. ~বায়ু=~প্রাণ. ~বার্ষিক *adj* five years old; recurring every five years; five-years: ~বার্ষিক পরিকল্পনা. ~বিংশ *adj* twenty-five. ~বিংশতি *n, adj* twenty-five. ~বিংশতিতম *adj* twenty-fifth. ~বিংশতিতমী *fem.* ~বিধ *adj* of five kinds; fivefold. ~ভুজ *adj* five-armed; pentagonal. ❑*n* pentagon. ~ভূত *n* five elements (viz earth, air, fire, water and atmosphere). ~ভূতে মেশা *vi* be dissolved into the five basic elements according to Hindu mythology; die. ~ভূতময়, ~ভূতাত্মক *adj* consisting of the five elements (as the human body). ~ভূতাত্মিকা *fem.* ~ম *adj* fifth. ❑*n* **1** the fifth note of the gamut. **2** name of an Indian musical mode. ~ মকার *n* five essentials of *tantra* rituals (viz wine, meat, fish, intertwining of the fingers and sexual union—মদ্য, মাংস, মৎস্য, মুদ্রা, মৈথুন). ~ম স্বর *n*=~ম. ~ মহাপাতক *n* five mortal sins/ crimes according to Hindu scriptures (viz killing a Brahmin, drinking alcohol, theft, committing adultery with the wife of a preceptor and associating with anyone guilty of these crimes). ~মী *adj fem* fifth. ❑*n* fifth day of the lunar fortnight. ~মুখ *n* **1** five faces/mouths. **2** an appellation of Shiva. ❑*adj* **1** five-faced; five-headed. **2** eloquent; profuse in: ~মুখে প্রশংসা. ~মুখী *adj fem* **1** five-faced. **2** pentapetalous. **2** having five surfaces: ~মুখী হীরা. **3** having five parts/sections; five-pronged; pentamerous. **4** having five bores/holes: ~মুখী রুদ্রাক্ষ. ~মুখী পুষ্প *n* cinque-foil. ~মূল *n* group of five roots/ plants with tuberous roots; a decoction made of these roots. ~রং, ~রঙ্গ *nn* (in chess) one of the systems of checkmating. ~রত্ন *n* collection of five jewels/precious stones (viz gold, diamond, sapphire, ruby, pearl or coral). ~রসা *n* embic myrobalan. ~রাত্র(ক) *n* period of five rights (days). ❑*n* lasting five days. ~রাশিক *n* (arith) rule of 5; rule of proportion with 5 terms. ~শর=~বাণ. ~শস্য *n* five species of grain (viz paddy, kidney-bean/ oat, barley, sesame and pigeon-pea). ~শাখ *adj* five-branched; five-fingered. ~শিখ=~চূড়. ~ সুগন্ধ *n* collection of five kinds of aromatic vegetable substances (viz cloves, nutmeg, camphor, aloe wood and kakkol (কক্কোল). পঞ্চাক্ষর *n* five syllables. ❑*adj* pentasyllabic. পঞ্চাগ্নি *n* **1** five sacred fires. **2** five mystic fires supposed to be present in the body. পঞ্চাঙ্ক *adj* consisting of five acts; five-act. পঞ্চাঙ্গ *n* five members of the body; five parts of a tree; five modes of devotion; aggregate of five parts. ❑*adj* five limbed; five-part. পঞ্চাঙ্গপ্রণাম *n* obeisance made with five members of the body (viz arms, knees, head, voice and look). পঞ্চাঙ্গুল *n* five fingers. ❑*adj* measuring five fingers. পঞ্চাতপা=~তপা. পঞ্চাত্মক *adj* consisting of five elements; fivefold. পঞ্চানন *n* **1**=মুখ. **2** lion. পঞ্চানন্দ *n* **1** variety of pleasures. **2** fun; amusement; pleasantry. পঞ্চান্ন *n, adj* fifty-five. পঞ্চামৃত *n* **1** five kinds of divine food (viz milk, coagulated/sour milk, butter, honey and sugar). **2** custom of feeding Hindu women

with the above-mentioned food items. **পঞ্চাম্ল** *n* aggregate of five acid plants (viz jujube, pomegranate, sorrel, spondias and citron).
পঞ্চাশ (ৃ) *n, adj* fifty. **পঞ্চাশত্তম** *adj* fiftieth. **~শত্তমী** *fem.* **পঞ্চাশবার** *adv* **1** fifty times. **2** (fig) many times; time without number. **পঞ্চাশীতি** *n, adj* eighty-five. **পঞ্চাশীতিতম** *adj* eighty-fifth. **পঞ্চাশীতিতমী** *fem.* **পঞ্চাস্র** *adj* five-handed. ❑*n* pentagon.

পঞ্চায়েত, পঞ্চায়ত *nn* court of arbitration consisting of five or more members; village council; jury. **পঞ্চায়েতি, পঞ্চায়তি** *nn* work/ arbitration of a *panchayet*/village council; councillorship (of a *panchayet). **পঞ্চায়েতি, পঞ্চায়তি** *adjj* relating to a village *panchayet*/village council.

পঞ্চালিকা, পঞ্চালী[১] *nn* doll; puppet.

পঞ্চালী[২] *n* a style of singing.

পঞ্চেন্দ্রিয় *n* five sense-organs.

পঞ্চোপচার *n* five oblations.

পঞ্জর *n* **1** cage; aviary; dove-cot; net. **2** ribs; skeleton; thorax; flank. **3** body. **পঞ্জরাস্থি** *n* rib-bone; rib.

পঞ্জা *n* **1** five of playing-cards/dice. **2**=পাঞ্জ.

পঞ্জাবি=পাঞ্জাবি

পঞ্জি, পঞ্জিকা, পঞ্জী *nn* almanac; calendar; register; journal; diary. **পঞ্জিকর, পঞ্জিকাকার** *nn* maker of almanac.

পঞ্জেরি=পাঞ্জেরি

পট[১] *n* (onom) expressing sudden sharp sound; snap; crack. **~ করে** *adv* **1** with a snap/ cracking sound: ~ করে খোলা, crack (open). **2** quickly; suddenly. **~পট, পটাপট** *nn* crackle; crackling: আতশবাজির ~পট. ❑*adj* (crackling/ snapping) in quick succession; quickly.

পট[২] *n* **1** cloth; screen; veil; canvas; garment. **2** painting; canvas; painted piece of cloth; picture. **3** scene; curtain: দৃশ্য~. **~কার** *n* painter; weaver. **~বাস** *n* tent. **~ভূমিকা** *n* background; backdrop. **~মঞ্জরী** *n* name of an Indian musical mode. **~মণ্ডপ** *n* tent; canopied pavilion.

পটকনো=পটকানো

পটকা *adj* sickly; frail; delicate; fragile; rickety; slightly-built. ❑*n* **1** cracker; squib; fire works. **2** bladder of a fish.

পটকানি *n* throw(ing) to the ground; violent throw. **~ খাওয়া** *vi* thrown down. **~ দেওয়া**= পটকানো.

পটকানো *vt, vi* **1** fling/dash to the ground; knock down; defeat; vanquish; overpower. **2** be overpowered. **3** be down/laid up in bed; go down with. **4** die; kick the bucket. **পটকে দেওয়া** *vt*=~(1)

পটপটানো *vi* babble; chatter; prattle (away).

পটপটি[১] *n* **1** mania for cleanliness/purity; fastidiousness; faddiness; fad. **2** exaggeration; tall talk; bragging: থামাও তো তোমার যত ~!

পটপটি[২], **পটপটী** *n* (onom) **1** tiny fire-work; small cracker. **2** kind of crackling toy; cracker. **3** crackling sound; crackle. **4** bladder (of a fish). **5** kind of small creeper. **6** a swish (of a whip).

পটপটি[৩], **পটপটী** *n* an Ayurvedic medicine.

পটল *n* **1** heap; mass; multitude: জলধর~. **2** veil; cover. **3** membrane (esp of the eyes). **4** section; chapter. **5** roof; thatch. basket; box; chest. **6**=পটোল. **~ তোলা** *vi* die; kick the bucket; croak. **~প্রান্ত** *n* edge of a roof.

পটহ *n* **1** kettle-drum; war-drum; drum; tabor. **2** ear-drum. **~ধ্বনি, ~নিনাদ** *nn* sound of a drum.

পটা *vi* **1** get along; get on well; hit it off; be with the same wave-length; see eye to eye: বউয়ের সঙ্গে তার একেবারেই পটে না. **2** fall in love with sb; fall for sb; be taken with sb: মেয়েটা শেষ পর্যন্ত ঐ বখাটে ছেলেটার সঙ্গে পটলো. **3** give in; come to terms; agree: অনেক তর্কাতর্কির পর সে পটেছে. **~নো** *vt* **1** seduce; wood; entice sb (away) (from sth); entice sb (into sth/ doing sth): মেয়েটাকে সে পটিয়ে বিয়ে করেছে. **2** persuade; win over; cajole sb (into/out of sth); cajole sb (into/out of doing sth); coax sb (into/out of (doing) sth); inveigle sb into sth/ doing sth: বড়ো সাহেবকে পটিয়ে চাকরিটা সে নিজের ছেলেকে দিয়েছে.

পটাপট ⇒ পট

পটাশ [E] *n* potash.

পটাস *n* (onom) loud crack/crackle/snap.

পটি *n* **1** narrow piece of cloth; strip/band of cloth; fillet; bandage: মাথায় ~ দেওয়া. **2** hem/edge of a garment. **3** tuck; pleat. **4** puttee (as part of an army uniform). **5** parish; quarters; township; locality: শাখারি ~. **6** (section of a) market; row. সুতা~. **~ দেওয়া/লাগানো** *vi* **1** put in a tuck (in a dress); make pleats in. **2** apply a moistened strip of cloth; wind a bandage round; dress; (apply a) bandage. **~ পরা** *vi* put on a puttee. **~ মারা** *vi* cover with a patch.

পটিকা *n* পটি

পটীয়সী *adj fem* (of পটীয়ান)

পটীয়ান *adj* very/more expert/adroit/skilful.

পটু *adj* smart; clever; expert; sharp; skilful; adroit; efficient; proficient; able. **~তা, ~ত্ব** *nn* smartness; cleverness; expertness; skill; adroitness; dexterity; efficiency; proficiency; ability; experience; sharpness; acuteness.

পটুয়া, পটো (colloq) *n* painter.

পটোল *n* kind of vegetable; *Trichosanthes roxburgii.* **~-চেরা** *adj* (of eyes) shaped like the longitudinal half of the aforesaid vegetable; very large and beautiful.

পট্ট *n* **1** slab; tablet (for painting/writing upon); plate: তাম্র~. **2** flat/ level surface of anything. **3** seat; throne: রাজ~. **4** frontlet; turban: ~দেবী. **5** bandage; ligature; strip; fillet(of cloth, leather, etc). **6** coloured/fine cloth; woven silk. **7** upper/outer garment. **8** town; city. **9** jute; silk. **~ক** *n* counter. **~দেবী** *n* turbaned queen; principal wife of a king. **~ন** *n* port; city; town. **~বস্ত্র, ~বাস** *nn* silk-cloth; linen. **~মহিষী, ~রাজ্ঞী**=দেবী.

পট্টি[১]=পটি

পট্টি[২] *n* fib; deception. **~ দেওয়া/মারা** *vi* fib; deceive; cheat; put sb upto some trick. **~ পড়ানো** *vt* advise; counsel; coax; seduce. **~বাজ** *n* deceiver; fibber; cheat.

পট্টিকা *n* **1** small slab/plate. **2** silk band. **3** strip/band of cloth.

পট্টী *n* horse's girth; strap and badge.

পট্টু *n* kind of coarse woolen cloth.

পঠন *n* reading; reciting; study(ing); perusal; recitation.

পঠনীয় *adj* fit to be read/studied; worth reading; prescribed for reading/study; readable; legible.

পঠিত *adj* read; studied; recited; perused. **~ব্য**=পঠনীয়.

পঠ্যমান *adj* being read/studied/recited.

পড়তা *n* **1** continuous succession of winning/ lucky throws (as of dice). **2** favourable time; opportunity; fortune: ~র সময়. **3** (commerce) cost of production/procurement: ~য় পোষাবে না. **4** approximation: গড়~. **~ পড়া** *vi* **1** (at dice, etc) be able to make winning/lucky throws in a row. **2** have a favourable/ fortunate period. **3** (commerce) meet the cost of production/ procurement. **~ পোষানো** *vi* (commerce) cover/meet the cost of production/ procurement. **গড়~** *adj* average. ❑*adv* on (the) average.

পড়তি *n* **1** fall; decline. **2** (commerce) fall in prices, business, etc; slump; depression; recession. **3** wastage (in transport, production, etc). **~ বাজার** *n*=~(2).

পড়ন[১] *n* reading; recitation; perusal; study.

পড়ন[২] *n* falling; fall; decline.

পড়ন্ত *adj* about to fall; declining; setting: ~ দিন, ~ রোদ.

পড়পড়[১] *adj* about to fall/collapse/cave in; crumbling; almost collapsing; ramshackle: ~ বাড়ি.

পড়পড়[২] *n* (onom) imitating the noise of tearing cloth, etc.

পড়শি, পড়সী *nn* neighbour.

পড়া[১] *vi* **1** read; recite (aloud); read to oneself; peruse; study. **2** swear; take: হলফ ~ ❑ *n* = পড়ন. ❑ *adj* = পঠিত. **~ করা** *vi* learn/prepare one's lessons. **~ দেওয়া** *vi* say one's lessons. **~ ধরা/নেওয়া** *vi* test whether one can say one's, lessons. **~ বলা**=~ দেওয়া. **(কারো) কাছে ~** *vi* read with; take lessons from. **~নো** *vi* **1** teach; instruct; give instruction to; give lessons. **2** cause to read/study/recite; send to school, college, etc. **3** prime: সাক্ষী ~নো. **~শোনা** *n* study; schooling; academic education. **~শোনা করা** *vi* study; learn one's lessons; have one's schooling. **~শোনায় মন থাকা** *vi* take care of one's lessons/studies; be mindful of one's lessons/studies. **পড়ে শোনানো** *vi* read to.

পড়া[২] *vi* **1** fall (down/off); come down; drop (down): গাছের পাতা পড়ে, ছাদ থেকে ~, বৃষ্টি পড়ছে. **2** get stuck; stick in: চাকা কাদায় পড়েছে. **3** descend; alight: পাখিটা গাছের ডালে পড়েছে. **4** fall (to a person's share): তোমার ভাগে কত পড়লো? **5** fall on: দুরবস্থায় পড়া, fall on evil days. **6** hang down; fall over; come down to: তার চুল কাঁধে পড়েছে. **7** decrease in number/ amount/ intensity), fall; come down: মাছের দাম কিছুটা পড়েছে. **8** be shot; fall: তার গুলিতে তিনটা পাখি পড়ল. **9** take the position/direction specified; fall: কোন অক্ষরে ঝোঁক পড়বে; হঠাৎ বইটার উপর তার চোখ পড়লো, ছায়া ~. **10** pass into a specified state; fall (into sth); come down with sth: ঘুমিয়ে ~, রোগে ~. **11** happen; occur; fall: সোমবার ঈদ পড়বে. **12** be overtaken (by sb/sth); fail to keep level (with sb/sth); fall behind (sb/sth): পিছিয়ে ~. **13** be attracted to sb; fall in love; fall for sb: সে তার প্রেমে পড়েছে. **14** collapse; fall in: ছাদটা পড়ে গেছে. **15** become involved with sb/sth; fall in with sth: অসৎ সংসর্গে ~. **16** be trapped by sth; fall into sth: ফাঁদে ~. **17** decrease in quantity/ quality; fall off: লেখাপড়ার মান পড়ে যাওয়া. **18** attack sb/sth fiercely; fall on/upon sb/sth: গ্রামে ডাকাত পড়েছে. **19** be borne/incurred by sb; fall on/upon sb: বিয়ের সব খরচ আমার উপর পড়েছে. **20** become the duty/responsibility of sb; fall to sb (to sth): খবরটা জানাবার ভার আমার উপর পড়লো. **21** be classified among sth; fall under: এই প্রবন্ধটা কোন ভাগে পড়বে? **22** set in; begin: শীত ~, আকাল পড়া. **23** infest: পোকা ~. **24** be caught (in): জালে মাছ পড়া. **25** come/spring to: মনে ~. **26** be affected with: মরচে পড়া, rust. **27** become: মাথায় টাক ~, be balding. **28** come across/on/upon: পথে একটা মাঠ পড়লো. **29** get: ঠাণ্ডা ~, (of weather) getting colder. **30** require; involve; entail: এতে কিন্তু খরচ পড়বে অনেক. **31** flow out; exude; ooze: রক্ত/ঘাম/রস ~. **32** let run down: লালা ~, salivate; slaver (over sth). **33** be placed: পাত ~. **34** be served; fall: তার পাতে প্রায় কিছুই পড়েনি. **35** decline; come to a close: বেলা ~. **36** be undertaken/be touched: হাত ~. **37** abate; subside: বাতাস পড়লে নৌকা

ছাড়বে. **38** lessen; be appeased: রাগ ~. **39** decrease; cool down/off: তেজ ~. **40** be attracted; be taken with: মন ~. **41** be married: মেয়েটা বড়ো ঘরে পড়েছে. **42** go into; take in: সারা সকাল পেটে কিছু পড়েনি, I haven't had a bite (to eat) all morning. **43** lean to: গায়ে ~. **44** used as a complimentary verb to indicate the completion of an action: ঘুমিয়ে ~, fall asleep; নুয়ে ~, bend down. **পড়ে থাকা** *vi* **1** lie (idle): সে বিছানায় পড়ে আছে. **2** lie vacant/unoccupied: বাড়িটা শুধু শুধু পড়ে আছে. **3** be unrealized/ unpaid/outstanding; remain unpaid: অনেক টাকা পড়ে আছে. **4** be outstanding; be in arrears: কাজটা অনেক দিন ধরে পড়ে আছে. **5** lie fallow/idle: জমিটা পড়ে আছে, চাষ করা দরকার. **পড়ে পাওয়া** *vi* chance on sth; find by chance. **পড়ে পড়ে ঢিল/মার খাওয়া** take sth lying down. **ঝুলে পড়া** *vi* **1** hang loose: চামড়া ঝুলে পড়া. **2** embark on sth; take sth on; jump at sth: আর দেরি নয়, এখনই ঝুলে পড়ো. **বাজারে পড়তে না পাওয়া** go/sell like hot cakes; have a ready market. ❑*n* fall: এমন ~ পড়েছে যে কিছু দিন আর উঠতে পারবে না. ❑*adj* **1** fallen; dropped; fallen/dropped down. **2** vacant; fallow; desolate; deserted; unoccupied: ~ জমি/বাড়ি. **3** abandoned: ~ মাল. **4** found by chance; lying unclaimed: ~ টাকা. **5** hanging loose: ঝুলে-~ চামড়া. **6** laid down; ridden: বিছানায় ~ লোক. **~নো** *vt* (rare) cause to fall/drop/involve.

পড়াং *n* (onom) swish (of a lash, scythe, etc). ~ **করে** *adv* with a swish.

পড়িয়ান *n* (old use)=পড়েন

পড়ুয়া *adj* **1** studious; scholarly; bookish: ~ ছেলে. **2** studying; being a student: ~ অবস্থা. ❑*n* pupil; learner; student; scholar.

পড়েন[1] *n* weight.

পড়েন[2] *n* woof; weft.

পড়ো[1] *n, adj* (colloq)=পড়ুয়া

পড়ো[2] *adj* **1** fallow; uncultivated: ~ জমি. **2** deserted; desolate; vacant; unoccupied; abandoned: ~ বাড়ি.

পণ *n* **1** promise; resolve; vow: ধনুক-ভাঙা ~. **2** wager; bet; stake: ~ রেখে খেলা. **3** compact; stipulation; agreement; treaty. **4** compulsory dowry (esp one paid by a Hindu father to his son-in-law); marriage-money. **5** price. **6** commodity for sale. **7** a measure of counting (20 *ganda*=80). **8** play; game; playing for a stake; bet; wager. **9** wages; hire; reward. ~ **করা** *vi* resolve; make a solemn vow. ~ **দেওয়া** *vi* pay the bridegroom (the bride) compulsory dowry/ marriage money. ~ **ধরা/রাখা** *vi* bet; stake; lay a wager. ~ **নেওয়া** *vi* exact compulsory dowry/marriage money. **কন্যা~** *n* compulsory dowry/ marriage money given to the bride. **বর~** *n* compulsory dowry/ marriage money given to the bridegroom. **ধনুক-ভাঙা** ~ *n* (fig) solemn/ unflinching vow. ~ **কর** *n* betting tax. **~কিয়া** *n* table of reckoning by *panas* (⇒ পণ 7). **~ন** *n* exchange; barter; selling; sale. **~প্রথা** *n* system of exacting marriage-money; dowry system. **~বদ্ধ** *adj* bound by a promise; pledge-bound; under a vow.

পণব *n* small drum; cymbal.

পণায়িত, পণিত *adjj* **1** transacted at business. **2** betted; staked.

পণ্ড *adj* foiled; spoiled; abortive; futile; unavailing; fruitless; vain; marred; useless. ~ **করা** *vt* spoil; mar; foil; baffle; dash; thwart; defeat; blight. **~শ্রম** *n* fruitless toil; vain/ useless/ futile/ abortive efforts.

পণ্ডিত *adj* **1** learned; scholarly; erudite. **2** conversant with; versed in. **3** wise; shrewd; clever. **4** expert; skilled in: রণ~. ❑*n* scholar; learned man; teacher; Sanskrit scholar; pundit. ~ **চূড়ামণি** *n* the most precious jewel amongst the learned; the most learned scholar. **~প্রবর, ~বর** *adjj* most learned. ❑*nn* the most learned scholar; great scholar. **~মণ্ডলী** *n* assembly of learned men; learned community; community of scholars; learned men (collectively). **~মানী**=~ম্মন্য. **~মূর্খ** *adj* learned but foolish. ❑*n* learned fool; wiseacre; know-all. **~শ্রেষ্ঠ**=~প্রবর. **~ম্মন্য, পণ্ডিতাভিমানী** *adj* fancying one's self learned/clever. **~ম্মন্যা, পণ্ডিতাভিমানিনী** *fem*. **~ম্মন্যতা** *n* pretentious to learning. **~ম্মন্য ব্যক্তি** *n* ignorant and conceited person; wiseacre; know-all.

পণ্ডিতি *adj* **1** relating to/like a pundit/ (Sanskrit) scholar: ~ বেশভূষা. **2** (of Bengali language style) sanskritized; full of bombast; high-falutin. ❑*n* **1** post/job of a pundit/ Sanskrit teacher. **2** (iron) learning; wisdom: ~ ফলানো.

পণ্য *n* **1** commodity; article of trade; ware; merchandise. **2** price; charge; cost; fee. ❑*adj* to be bought/sold; saleable; salable; marketable. **~জীবী** *adj* living on/engaged in trade/business. ❑*n* trader; merchant; businessman; tradesman; dealer. **~দ্রব্য** *n* commodity; wares; merchandise. **~পত্তন** *n* port town. **~বিপণী, ~বীথি, ~বীথী, ~বীথিকা** *nn* place of sale; market. **~মূল্য** *n* price of a commodity. **~শালা** *n* shop; bazaar; department store; market. **~স্ত্রী** *n* venal woman; courtesan; whore; prostitute. **পণ্যাগার** *n* warehouse. **পণ্যাঙ্গনা**=~স্ত্রী. **পণ্যাজীব**=~জীবী. **পণ্যার্হ** *adj* fit for sale.

পণ্যোপচার *n* merchandise; commodities.

পতগ *n* bird.

পতঙ্গ *n* **1** any flying insect; butterfly; moth; bee; grasshopper. **2** bird. **3** arrow. **4** sun. **~নাশক**

adj insecticidal. **~নাশক পদার্থ** *n* insecticide. **~পরাগণ** *n* (bot) entomophily. **~পরাগিত** *adj* (bot) insect-pollinated. **~পরাগী** *adj* (bot) entomophilous. **~বিজ্ঞান, ~বিদ্যা** *n n* entomology. **~বিজ্ঞানী, ~ বিদ** *nn* entomologist. **~বৃত্ত** *adj* having a moth-like instinct to kill oneself in the fire of one's depravity. **~বৃত্তি** *n* moth-like instinct to kill oneself in the fire of one's depravity. **~ভুক** *adj* insectivorous. **~ভুক প্রাণী** *n* insectivore. **~ম** = ~. **~ময়** *adj* infested with insects.

পতত্র *n* wing (of a bird).

পতত্রি, পতত্রী *n* bird.

পতন *n* **1** fall; decline; rain; downfall: সাম্রাজ্যের ~. **2** coming down; alighting; descending; fall; falling. **3** slaughter; death ;overthrow; defeat: শত্রুর ~. **4** destruction : শরীরের ~. **5** loss of caste; apostasy. **6** corruption; depravation: দেবতুল্য চরিত্রের ~. **7** failing; omission: স্খলন–পতন–ত্রুটি. **8** hanging down; becoming flaccid (said of the breasts). **9** defect; flaw: ছন্দ~. **~ ঘটা** *vi* **1** fall; have a fall; drop. **2** decline; have a downfall. **3** be overthrown/ defeated/ destroyed/ captured. **4** be flawed: ছন্দ~ ঘটা. **~ ঘটানো** *vt* **1** cause to fall; fell; drop. **2** overthrow; defeat; capture. **3** deprave; corrupt. **~শীল** *adj* falling; dropping; being shed; declining ;perishable.

পতনোন্মুখ *adj* about to fall/ drop; tottering; crumbling.

পতপত *n* (onom) flutter. **~ করে ওড়া** *vi* flutter.

পতর *n* metal hoop. **~ আঁটা** *vi* fasten a metal hoop.

পতাকা *n* **1** flag; pennon; banner; standard. **2** sign; emblem. **~ অর্ধনমিত/ অবনমিত করা** *vi* fly a flag at half-mast. **~ উত্তোলন করা** *vi* hoist a flag. **~ ঊর্ধ্বে তুলে ধরা** (fig) keep the flag flying. **~ নামিয়ে ফেলা** *vi* take down/ lower/ strike a flag. **~ দণ্ড** *n* flag-staff; flag-pole. **~ধারী, ~বাহী** *adjj* carrying/ bearing a flag/ standard; adored with flags; ensign. ❑*n* standard-bearer; flag-carrier; flag-bearer.

পতি *n* **1** husband. **2** master; lord; boss. **3** owner. **4** ruler; overlord; chief; king. **পতিংবরা** *adj, n* (woman) who chooses her husband. **~ঘাতিনী** *adj* murdering her husband. ❑*n* murderess of her husband; cause of her husband's death. **~ঘ্ন** *n* murderer of one's master. **~ঘ্নী** *fem.* **~ত্ব** *n* state of being a husband/ master; ownership; rule; overlordship; mastery; office/ post of a chief. **~ত্বে বরণ করা** *vt* accept/ take as one's husband. **~ ত্যাগ করা** *vt* desert/ divorce one's husband. **~দেব(তা)** *n* one's husband regarded as a divinity; venerable husband. **~ধর্ম** *n* duty towards a husband. **~পরায়ণা** *adj* extremely devoted to one's husband. **~-পত্নী** *n* husband and wife. **~-পুত্র** husband and son(s). **~পুত্রহীনা** *adj* deprived of one's husband and son. **~প্রাণা** *adj* extremely devoted to/ doting on her husband. **~বত্নী** *adj* having a husband; married. **~বিয়োগ** *n* death of one's husband. **~বিরহ** *n* separation from one's husband. **~বিরহিণী** *adj* separated from one's husband. **~ব্রত** *n* loyalty/ fidelity to a husband. **~ব্রতা** *adj* = ~পরায়ণা. **~ মতী** *adj* **1** = ~বত্নী. **2** having a master/ ruler: **~শোক** *n* grief for a husband. **পতিশোকাতুর** *adj* overwhelmed with grief for a husband. **~সেবা** *n* devotion to a husband. **~হীনা** *adj* widowed. **~হীনা নারী** *n* widow.

পতিত *n* **1** fallen; dropped. **2** descended; alighted. **3** shed; showered. **4** wicked; degraded; depraved. **5** out-caste; depressed: ~ জাতি. **6** fallen into/ upon: দুর্দশায় ~. **7** overthrown; defeated; killed; slain: যুদ্ধক্ষেত্রে ~. **8** declined. **9** uncultivated; fallow: ~ জমি. **10** abandoned; deserted: ~ বাড়ি. **11** appeared; emerged: নয়ন পথে ~. **~ করা** *vt* expel from the society/ a caste; excommunicate. **~ হওয়া** *vi* **1** = পড়া. **2** be an outcast/ out-caste; be guilty of a failing/ lapse; be excommunicated; degrade oneself. **~পাবন** *adj* redeeming/ delivering the sinners from damnation. ❑*n* deliverer/ saviour of the sinners. **পতিতাবাদ** [পতিত+আবাদ] *n* redemption of fallow/ waste land.

পতিতা *adj fem* (of পতিত) unchaste; wanton; whorish; wayward. ❑*n* fallen woman; prostitute; whore; woman of easy virtue. **~বৃত্তি** *n* prostitution.

পতিতোদ্ধার *n* redemption of the sinful.

পত্তন *n* **1** town; city; port. **2** colony; settlement. **3** lease; settlement; tenure: তালুকের ~. **4** foundation; setting up: establishment; institution; base; construction; groundwork. **5** beginning; commencement; onset. **6** length: কোঁচার ~. **~ করা** *vt* **1** found; set up ;lay the foundation of; establish; construct; institute; inaugurate. **2** begin; commence. **~ দেওয়া** *vt* settle; lease out. **~ নেওয়া** *vt* come into possession by dint of a lease/ settlement. **~দার** *n* (middle class) tenure-holder; lease-holder. **~ পাল, পত্তনাধ্যক্ষ** *nn* port-commissioner.

পত্তনি *n* piece of land leased out; leasehold; settlement. **~দার** = পত্তনদার (⇒ পত্তন). ❑*adj* leased out; held by dint of a settled tenure.

পত্তর *n* (colloq) = পত্র

পত্তি *n* foot-soldier; infantryman.

পত্নী *n* wife. **~ ত্যাগ করা** *vi* desert/ divorce one's wife. **~বিয়োগ** *n* death/ loss of one's wife.

পত্র *n* **1** leaf (of a tree). **2** leaf (of a book); page. **3** letter; missive; note. **4** piece of paper; order. **5** document; deed: বায়না~. **6** plate; foil; leaf: তাম্র~. **7** written marriage-contract. **8** wing (of a bird); feather. **9** collection and similar things; et cetera: কাগজ~, মাল~. **10** feather of an arrow. **~ করা** *vi* make a marriage-contract in writing. **~ দেওয়া** *vi* write a letter to; send sb a letter; write to sb. **~ক** *n* leaf; (bot) pinna. **~কণ্টক** *n* (bot) leaf-spine. **~ক্ষত** *n* (bot) leaf-scar. **~দারক** *n* saw. **~ধারা** *n* edge of a leaf. **~নবিস** *n* correspondence clerk. **~পত্রিকা** *n* newspapers. **~পাঠ** *n* perusal of a letter. ❑*adv* as soon as a letter is read; immediately; forthwith; promptly. **~পুট** *n* cup made of a leaf (folded or doubled). **~পুষ্প** *n* leaves and flowers; holy basil with small leaves. **~বন্ধু** *n* adorning with leaves/ flowers. **~বন্ধু** *n* pen-friend. **~বল্লী** *n* decoration consisting in lines/ streaks drawn on the face and body with musk and other fragrant substances. **~বাহ(ক)** *n* carrier/ bearer of a letter; messenger; postman; courier. **~বাহী** *adj* mail-carrying; mail. **~বিনিময়** *n* exchange of letters; correspondence. **~ বিনিময় করা** *vi* write letters to one another; correspond with. **~বিন্যাস** *n* (bot) phyllotaxy. **~ব্যবহার** *n* writing a letter to. **~ ব্যবহার করা** *vi* write a letter to; correspond with. **~মঞ্জরী** *n* **1** tip of a leaf. **2** (bot) leafstalk; petiole. **~মুকুল** *n* (bot) leaf-bud. **~মুদ্রা** *n* currency note; paper-money. **~মূল** *n* (bot) leaf-base. **~মোচন** *n* (bot) leaf-fall; defoliation. **~যোগে** *adv* by letter. **~রচনা** *n* **1** writing a letter. **2** (bot) foliation; foliage. **~রন্ধ্র** *n* stoma. **~রেখা** = ~বল্লী. **~ল** *adj* thin. **~লেখা** *n* **1** writing a letter. **2** = ~বল্লী. **~সূচি** *n* **1** thorn. **2** index; table of contents. **~হরিৎ** *n* (bot) chlorophyl. **পত্রাঙ্ক** *n* page-number; page-mark. **পত্রাঙ্কন** *n* pagination. **পত্রাঙ্কিত** *adj* paginated. **পত্রাঙ্ক দেওয়া, পত্রাঙ্কিত করা** *vt* page; paginate. **পত্রাবলি, পত্রাবলী** *n* **1** letters (collectively); correspondence. **2** leaves; foliage. **3** = ~বল্লী. **পত্রালিকা** *n* = ~বল্লী. **পত্রাশ্রয়ী** *n* (bot) epiphyllous.

পত্রিকা *n* **1** newspaper; periodical; magazine. **2** leaf (for writing upon); letter; document; deed. **3** horoscope: জন্ম ~. **4** leaf; young shoot: নব~.

পত্রী *adj* having leaves/ wings/ feathers; leafed; winged; foliaceous. ❑*n* **1** tree. **2** arrow. **3** bird. **4** letter; epistle. **5** newspaper; periodical.

পত্রোদ্গম *n* (bot) foliation.

পত্রোল্লাস *n* bud/ eye of a plant.

পথ *n* **1** path; road; course; way; street; passage. **2** doorway; entrance. **3** mode; manner; way: সৎ~; কু~. **4** range; reach: দৃষ্টি~. **5** means; expedient; path: মুক্তির ~. **~ আগলানো/ আটকানো** = ~ জোড়া. **~ করা** *vi* make (one's) way. **~ করে দেওয়া** *vi* pave the way for sth. **~ খুঁজে পাওয়া** *vi* find one's way (to). **~ চলা** *vi* walk; travel (on foot); go plodding on; jog on; go one's way; amble along. **~ চাওয়া** *vi* looking forward to the coming of; watch for sb; wait/ expect eagerly the coming of. **~ ছাড়া** *vi* **1** make way for; get out of the way; let one pass; give way to sb. **2** get out of the way of (doing sth); give up a practice/ way: অসৎ ~ ছাড়ো. **~ জোড়া** *vi* block a/ sb's way/ a road/ a passage; be/ get in the way of (sb/ sth); obstruct sth (with sth). **~ দেওয়া** *vi* = ~ ছাড়া(1). **~ দেখা** *vi* **1** find one's way (to)/ a way out; devise ways and means; see one's way. **2** (iron) go one's way; clear off; part company. **~ দেখানো** *vi* **1** show sb the way; lead the way; point the way; take the lead. **2** (iron) turn out; show the door. **~ ধরা** *vi* **1** set off/ out; depart; leave. **2** follow a (particular) path; adopt a (particular) method/ practice; follow suit; take to. **~ ফেলা** *vi* tread/ make a path. **~ ভোলা** *vi* lose one's way; get lost. **~ মাড়ানো** *vi* **1** go/ come by a particular way. **2** (fig) set foot in/ on; associate oneself with; deal with sb. **~ হারানো** = ~ ভোলা. **পথে আসা** *vi* **1** reform; return one's ways/ habits; change one's way; change for the better; mend one's ways. **2** made to see reason; be prevailed upon; yield; come round/ around to (sb's way of thinking, etc). **পথে কাঁটা দেওয়া** *vi* (fig) block/ obstruct sb's progress; hinder. **পথে দেখা হওয়া** *vi* cross sb's path. **পথে পড়া** *vi* come one's way. **পথে বসা** *vi* (fig) be utterly ruined; go bankrupt; be undone; be completely broken. **পথে বসানো** *vt* ruin utterly. **পথের কুকুর** *n* **1** stray (dog). **2** (fig) street beggar; bum. **পথের কাঁটা** *n* a thorn in one's flesh/ side. **পথের কাঁটা হওয়া** (fig) stand in sb's way. **পথের পথিক** *n* wanderer; homeless person; wayfarer. **এক পথের পথিক** *n* fellow-traveller; (fig) one who is in the same boat. **~কর** *n* road cess. **~খরচ(া)** *n* **1** travelling expenses; cost of travel; travelling expenses. **2** viaticum. **~চলতি** *adj* **1** passing; wayfaring; ambulant: ~চলতি লোক. **2** happening/ experienced on one's way/ the way: ~চলতি ঘটনা. ❑*adv* on one's/ the way: ~চলতি তার সঙ্গে দেখা. **~চলতি লোক** *n* = ~চারী. **~চারী** *adj* wayfaring; travelling. ❑*n* pedestrian; traveller; passer-by; wayfarer. **~চারিণী** *fem.* **~চ্যুত** = ~ভ্রষ্ট. **~দেশক** *n* pilot. **~পার্শ্ব** *n* road side; wayside. **~পার্শ্বস্থ** *adj* standing on the road way; roadside; wayside. **~-প্রদর্শক** *adj* showing/ leading the way; guiding; leading. ❑*n* guide; conductor; leader; pioneer. **~-প্রদর্শন** *n* showing the way; guidance; leadership. **~-প্রদর্শন করা** = ~ দেখানো. **~-প্রান্ত** *n* **1** = ~-পার্শ্ব. **2** end of a road. **পথে-প্রান্তরে** *adv* on roads and in the fields; in the open fields. **~ভোলা, ~ভ্রষ্ট, ~ভ্রান্ত** *adjj* **1** strayed; lost. **2** wayward; aberrant; errant; erring. **~ভ্রান্তি** *n* waywardness; aberration. **~রোধ** *n* obstruction of sb's way; road-blocking. **~রোধ করা** = ~জোড়া. **~শ্রান্ত** *adj* worn-out after a long journey; weary; way worn. **~হারা** = ~ভোলা. **অর্ধপথে মিলিত হওয়া** meet half way; compromise.

পথি *n* (in compounds) = পথ. **~কৃৎ** *adj* making a way/ road; preparing the way. ❑*n* pioneer. **~পার্শ্বস্থ** = পথপার্শ্বস্থ (⇒ পথ). **~পার্শ্বে** *adj* by the roadside. **~মধ্যে** *adv* in the middle of the road; on the road; on one's/ the way; on route.

পথিক *adj* going on a road; wayfaring. ❑*n* traveller; wayfarer; pedestrian; passer-by.

পথে–ঘাটে *adv* anywhere and everywhere; here and there; in the open fields; at all places; in all parts.

পথ্য *adj* (of diet) wholesome; salutary; suitable; fit; proper. ❑*n* diet. **~ করা** *vi* (of a convalescent) take diet for the first time after an illness. **~বিচার** *n* dietetics. **পথ্যাপথ্য** *adj* wholesome and unwholesome; beneficial or harmful. ❑*n* good and harmful/ wholesome and unwholesome diet.

পদ *n* **1** foot; leg. **2** step; footstep; pace; stride. **3** footprint; vestige; mark; trace. **4** portion of a verse; quarter/ line of a stanza. **5** song; lyric: বৈষ্ণব পদাবলী. **6** (logic) term. **7** position; post; rank; station; footing: ~মর্যাদা. **8** office; employment; post: ~প্রার্থী. **9** site; abode; home; habitation: জন~. **10** part; portion; division. **11** (gram) (inflected) word; part of speech. **12** favour; grace; shelter; refuge: 'তব পদে দিয়ো ঠাঁই'. **13** item; dish: কয় ~ রান্না হয়েছে? **14** foot as a measure of length. **~ অধিকার করা** occupy/ hold a post. **~কমল** *n* lotus-like foot. **~কর্তা, ~কার** *n* composer/ author (esp) of a Vaishnava song/ lyric; poet. **~ক্রম** *n* **1** series of steps; pace; walking. **2** (gram) syntax. **~ক্রমবিদ্যা** *n* syntactic. **~ক্ষেপ** *n* pace; step; stride; stepping; pacing. **~ক্ষেপ করা** *vt* step (into); set foot/ come; tread. **~ক্ষেপ নেওয়া** *n* take measures/ steps/ action. **প্রতি ~ক্ষেপে** *adv* at every step. **~গর্ব, ~গৌরব** *nn* dignity of office; high rank; high office/ position; official status. **~গৌরবান্বিত** *adj* high-ranking. **~চারণ** *n* strolling; pacing; walking. **~চারণ করা** *vi* stroll; pace; walk. **~চারী** *adj* going on foot; walking. **~চারিণী** *fem.* **~চালনা** *n* **1** walking; strolling; pacing. **2** kicking. **3** (football) footwork. **~চালনা করা** *vi* pace; stroll; walk; amble; saunter; kick; foot. **~চালিত** *adj* (of a lever, treadle, etc). driven/ operated/ propelled by foot. **~চিহ্ন** *n* footprint; footmark; vestige. **~ছায়া** *n* shelter at one's feet; grace; favour; gracious protection. **~চ্ছেদ** *n* separation of words; parsing. **~চ্যুত** *adj* fallen from a position; dismissed/ removed from office; sacked; cashiered. **~চ্যুত করা** *vt* dismiss; (give sb the) sack; fire; cashier. **~চ্যুতি** *n* dismissal; the sack. **~তল** *n* sole (of the foot). **~তলে** *adv* **1** under foot: ~তলে পিষ্ট. **2** at sb's foot: ~তলে আশ্রয় নেওয়া. **~তলে পড়া/ পতিত হওয়া** fall at the feet of sb (to beg for mercy, help, etc); fell on one's knees; prostrate oneself at the feet of. **~ত্যাগ** *n* resignation/ relinquishment of post/ office/ position. **~ত্যাগ করা** *vi* resign; submit resignation; relinquish; abdicate. **~ত্যাগপত্র** *n* letter of resignation. **~দলন** *n* **1** trample; trampling. **2** (fig) utter disregard; blatant violation/ disobedience; trampling; infringement. **3** (fig) oppression. **~দলন করা** *vt* **1** trample sth/ sb down. **2** (fig) trample on (sb's rights, feelings, etc); disregard utterly; disobey/ disrespect/ infringe on/ violate blatantly. **3** oppress. **~দলিত** *adj* trampled; disregarded/ violated/ disobeyed/ infringed on blatantly; oppressed. **~দলিতা** *fem.* **~দলিত করা**=~দলন করা. **~ধূলি** *n* dust of sb's feet (touched as a mark of reverence). **~ধূলি দেওয়া** *vi* **1** allow sb to touch the dust of one's feet; allow sb to show reverence. **2** honour with one's presence/ visit. **~ধ্বনি** *n* footfall. **~ন্যাস** *n* **1** putting down the feet; step; footmark; position of the feet (in a particular attitude. **2** syntax. **3** writing down (quarters of) verses. **~পঙ্কজ**=~কমল. **~পরিচয়** *n* parsing. **~পল্লব** *n* foot as tender as buds. **~পাত** *n* footfall; tread; step. **~পূরণ** *n* filling out/ completing a verse. **~পৃষ্ঠ** *n* instep. **~প্রান্ত** *n* **1** corner of a foot. **2** sole of a foot **~প্রান্তে** *adv* at sb's feet. **~প্রার্থী** *adj* offering one's candidature for a post/ employment/ job; applying for a job/ post/ employment. ❑ *n* applicant; candidate. **~প্রার্থিনী** *fem.* **~বিক্ষেপ** *n* step; pace; walking; gait. **~বিচ্ছেদ** *n* separation of words. **~বিন্যাস** *n* **1** step; gait. **2** syntax. **~বিরাম** *n* pause after a quarter of a verse. **~বৃদ্ধি** *n* advancement in office/ rank; promotion. **~ব্রজ** *n* walking; going on foot. **~ব্রজে** *adv* on foot. **~ভরে** *adv* under the weight of one's feet (when walking proudly or haughtily) **~-ভস্ত্রা** *n* (phy) foot-blower. **~ভূষণ** *n* ornament for the feet. **~ভ্রষ্ট**=~চ্যুত. **~মদমত্ত** *adj* intoxicated with high-office; proud of one's rank/ status. **~মর্যাদা**=~গর্ব. **~স্তর** *n* weight of one's feet. **~যুগল** *n* pair of feet/ legs. **~যোজন(1)** *n* arrangement of words; wording. **~রচনা** *n* **1**=~যোজন. **2** literary composition. **~রজ, ~রেণু** =~ধূলি. **~লেহন** *n* licking sb's feet; bootlicking; abject flattery; servility; obsequiousness. **~লেহন করা** *vi* lick sb's boots; cringe to; ingratiate oneself with. **~লেহী** *adj* licking sb's feet/ boot; cringing; servile; obsequious; bootlicking. **~লেহী ব্যক্তি** *n* bootlicker; footlicker; vile flatterer; sycophant. **~শব্দ** *n* noise of footsteps; footfall. ~সেবা *n* 1 massaging sb's feet. 2 devoted service; worship. 3 (derog) cringing; bootlicking; abject flattery. ~স্খলন *n* 1 false step; slip; stumbling. 2 (fig) moral lapse/ slip/ aberration; degradation. ~স্খলন হওয়া *vi* 1 stumble; slip. 2 (fig) go astray; (of women) fall; stoop to folly. ~স্খলিত *adj* 1 stumbled; slipped. 2 (fig) fallen; loose; erring; wayward; lost. পদা *fem.* ~স্থ *adj* 1 high-ranking; in high office. 2 placed in a post/ station/ office. ~স্থিত *adj* being in a station/ office. ~হেতু *adv* ex officio. পদাংশ *n* syllable. পদাগ্র *n* tip of a foot. পদাঘাত *n* kick. পদাঙ্ক *n* footmark; footprint; vestige. পদাঙ্গুল *n* toe. পদাঙ্গুলাকার *adj* (bot) pedate. পদাতি(ক) *n* footsoldier; infantryman; footman; armed messenger. পদাধিকার *n* holding of an office/ a post. পদাধিকার বলে, পদাধিকারে *adv* by virtue of one's office/ position; ex officio. পদানত *adj* trampled; prostrate at sb's feet; thoroughly subdued/ dominated; brought to one's knees; submissive; dependent. পদানতা *fem.* পদানত করা *vt* bring to one's knees; trample; subdue/ dominate thoroughly; trounce; crush; subjugate. পদানুগ *adj* following at sb's heels/ footprints. পদানুগমন *n* following at sb heels/ footprints. পদানুগমন করা *vi* to follow at sb's heels/ footprints; follow; succeed; shadow; dog the footsteps of; trail. পদানুগামী *adj* following at sb's heels/ footprints; succeeding. ❑ *n* follower; disciple; camp-follower; hanger-on; attendant; adherent. পদানুবর্তী=পদানুগামী. পদানুবর্তী হওয়া=পদানুগমন করা. পদান্ত *n* end of a line in a stanza; end of a word. পদান্তর *n* 1 interval of one step. 2 another word. পদান্বয় *n* syntax; parsing. পদান্বয়ী *adj* prepositional. পদান্বয়ী অব্যয় *n* preposition. পদাবনত *adj* 1= পদানত. 2 demoted; degraded in rank/ office. পদাবনতা *fem.* পদাবনতি *n* demotion; degradation in rank/ office. পদাবলি, পদাবলী *n* series of verses; collection/ anthology of songs/ lyrics/ verses. পদাভিলাষী *adj* wishing for/ desirous of holding a post/ office. পদাভিলাষিণী *fem.* পদাম্বুজ, পদারবিন্দ=~কমল. পদার্পণ *n* setting one's feet in/ on; stepping in; coming; reaching; attaining. পদার্পণ করা *vi* set one's foot in/ on; step in; reach; attain: চল্লিশ বৎসরে পদার্পণ করা. পদাশ্রয় *n* shelter at one's feet; favour; grace; indulgence; gracious protection. পদাশ্রয় দেওয়া *vi* give shelter at one's feet; treat with favour/ grace; give refuge to. পদাশ্রয়ী, পদাশ্রিত *adjj* sheltered at one's/ sb's feet; enjoying favour/ grace of; protected by; favoured; under the wing of. পদাসন *n* footstool. পদাহত *adj* 1 kicked; spurned. 2 insulted; humiliated; despised. পদাহতা *fem.* পদে থাকা *vi* 1 hold a post/ an office. 2 continue (somehow) in a (particular) post/ station. 3 be in a tolerable condition; be so-so. পদে পদে, প্রতি পদে *adv* at every step; everywhere; on every occasion.

পদক *n* medal; locket. ~প্রাপ্ত *adj* decorated with/ obtaining a medal; medalled. ~প্রাপ্ত ব্যক্তি *n* medallist.

পদবি, পদবী *n* 1 title; appellation. 2 surname; family name. 3 nickname.

পদার্থ *n* 1 meaning of a word. 2 thing; article; material; object. 3 substance; intrinsic worth. 4 matter. 5 (logic) category; predicament. 6 (science) element. ~বিজ্ঞান, ~বিদ্যা *n* physics; natural science/ philosophy. ~বিজ্ঞানী, ~বিদ, ~বিদ্যাবিদ *adjj* versed in physics. ❑ *nn* physicist; natural philosopher.

পদালী *n* cadre.

পদোদক=পাদোদক

পদোন্নতি=পদবৃদ্ধি (⇒ পদ)

পদোপহত=পদাহিত (⇒ পদ)

পদ্ধতি *n* 1 way; path; course; line; road. 2 method; mode; manner; procedure; system; rule. 3 custom; practice. 4 stretch; row; series. 5 current. ~ অনুসারে *adv* methodically; systematically. ~-প্রণালী *n* methodology. ~-প্রণালীগত *adj* methodological; procedural.

পদ্ম *n* lotus. ❑ *n, adj* one thousand millions/ billions. ~-আঁখি *n* lotus-eye. ❑ *adj* lotus-eyed. ~কর *n* lotus-like hand. ~কাঁটা *n* thorn on the stem of a lotus; Lichen papilaris. ~কর্ণিক(া) *n* pericarp of a lotus. ~কলি *n* lotus-bud. ~কেশর *n* filament of a lotus. ~কোষ *n* calyx of a lotus. ~গন্ধ *adj* smelling like a lotus. ~গর্ভ *n* interior/ calyx of a lotus; name of Brahma. ~তন্তু *n* fibre of a lotus-stalk. ~দিঘি *n* large pond full of lotus; lotus-pond. ~নাভ *n* 'lotus-naveled'; name of Vishnu. ~নাল *n* lotus-stalk. ~নেত্র *adj* lotus-eyed. ~পত্র *n* lotus-leaf. ~পলাশ *n* lotus-leaf; lotus-petal. ~পলাশলোচন *adj* having eyes as large as lotus-leaves. ~পাণি *adj* holding a lotus in the hand; lotus-handed. ❑ *n* Brahma; Vishnu; sun. ~বৎ *adj* lotus-like. ~বন *n* clump of lotus. ~বর্ণ *adj* lotus-hued. ~বীজ *n* lotus-seed. ~মধু *n* nectar of the lotus. ~মুখ *adj* having a face as sweet/ beautiful as a lotus. ~মুখী *fem.* ~মূল *n* lotus-root. ~যোনি *n* 'lotus-born'; name of Brahma. ~রাগ *adj* lotus-hued. ❑ *n* ruby. ~লোচন *adj* lotus-eyed. ~শ্রী *adj* beautiful as a lotus flower. পদ্মাকর *n* lotus-pool; assemblage of lotuses. পদ্মাক্ষ *adj* lotus-eyed. পদ্মালয় *n* 'dwelling in a lotus'; Brahma. পদ্মালয়া *n* goddess Lakshmi. পদ্মাসন *n* lotus as a seat; a particular posture of yoga; name of Brahma. ❑ *adj* sitting in a lotus/ in the position called 'padmasan'. পদ্মাসনা *adj fem.* ❑ *n* goddess Lakshmi. পদ্মাসীন=পদ্মাসন. পদ্মাসীনা *fem.*

পদ্মা *n fem* the lotus-hued one; goddess Lakshmi; Manasa, the snake-goddess; the river Padma. **~পুরাণ** *n* a legend in verse narrating the glory of Padma or Manasa. **~বতী** *n* name of Lakshmi or Manasa.

পদ্মিনী *n fem* **1** lotus; multitude of lotuses; lotus-pool. **2** a woman belonging to the first of the four classes into which the female sex is classified; an excellent woman. **~কান্ত, ~বল্লভ** *nn* the sun.

পদ্য *n* verse; metre; poetry.

পনর *n, adj* fifteen. **~ই** *adj, n* (the) fifteenth (day of a month).

পনস, পণশ *n* **1** commodity; article of sale/ commerce. **2** jack fruit.

পনা *suff* denoting quality, state or character: গৃহিণী~, ন্যাকা~.

পনাহ=পানাহ

পনি [E] *n* Pony; tattoo.

পনির, পনীর [P] *n* cheese.

পনের=পনর

পন্থ *n* (dial, poet) path; road; way.

পন্থা *n* **1** way; path; road. **2** means; expedient; way-out: এখান থেকে বেরোবার ~ কী? **3** system (of religious practice): সাধন~. **4** mode; school; manner; style: আধুনিক শিল্পীদের ~. **~নুসরণ** *n* following a particular path/mode/ system/ school. **~নুসারী** *adj* following/ obeying a particular path/ mode/ system/ school.

পন্থী *adj* (often used as a *suff)* **1** belonging to a particular school/ religious community: কর্তাভজা-~. **2** following a particular style/ mode: ক্লাসিক~. **3** following a particular doctrine: আধুনিক~. **4** -ist.

পন্নগ *n* snake; serpent; serpent-demon. **পন্নগী** *fem.*

পবন *n* **1** wind; air; breeze. **2** god of wind. **3** purification. **4** winnowing of corn. **~গতি** *n* speed of the wind. ❑ *adj* swift as wind. **~গামী** *adj* going as fast as the wind. **~নন্দন, পবনাত্মজ** *nn* (myth) Hanuman, the son of the god of the wind. **~বেগে** *adv* with the speed of the wind; as swiftly as the wind. **~হিল্লোল** *n* gust of wind; breeze.

পবিত্র *adj* **1** purified; purifying; pure; holy; sanctified; sacred. **2** sinless; beneficent; virtuous; clean. **পবিত্রা** *fem.* **~তা** *n* purity; cleanness; holiness; sanctity; sacredness; virtuousness. **~ মহিমা** *n* unction. **পবিত্রাত্মা** *adj* pure-hearted; holy.

পবিত্রিত *adj* purified; cleansed; sanctified; consecrated; made holy/ sacred.

পবিত্রী *adj* (in compounds)=পবিত্র. **~করণ** *n* purification; sanctification; cleansing. **~কৃত**=পবিত্রিত.

পমেটম [E] *n* pomatum; pomade.

পয় *n* auspiciousness; luck; good fortune. **~মন্ত, পয়া** *adj* **1** luck; auspicious. **2** having an auspicious/ lucky aspect: ~মন্ত চেহারা. **3** bringing in good fortune: ~মন্ত মেয়ে.

পয়ঃ *n* **1** water. **2** milk. **~প্রণালী** *n* drain; gutter; watercourse; sewerage.

পয়গম্বর, পয়গাম্বর [P] *n* messenger; envoy; prophet. **পয়গম্বরি** *n* mission; office of a messenger; carrying a message.

পয়গাম [P] *n* message; mission; news.

পয়জার [P] *n* slipper; shoe. **~ মারা** *vi* **1** beat with a slipper. **2** (fig) humiliate; insult.

পয়দল *adj* on foot. ❑ *n* infantry; foot-soldier.

পয়দা [P] *adj* born; produced; invented. ❑ *n* birth; production; creation. **~ করা** *vt* bring into being; produce; create; breed; beget. **~ হওয়া** *vi* be born/ created/ produced. **~য়েশ** *n* birth; creation; production.

পদনালা, পয়নালী=পয়ঃপ্রণালী (⇒ পয়ঃ)

পয়মন্ত ⇒ পয়

পয়মাল [P] *adj* trodden under foot; ruined; annihilated; destroyed; spoiled.

পয়রা *adj* thin; watery: ~ গুড়.

পয়লা *adj, n* (colloq)=পহেলা

পয়সা *n* **1** paisa (=0·01 taka or rupee); pice. **2** money; wealth; substance. **~ করা** *vi* make/ amass money; earn/ require wealth; heap up riches. **~ওয়ালা** *adj* moneyed; of substance; wealthy; rich. **~-কড়ি** *n* cash money; wealth; substance. **~র কাজ** *n* profitable work. **আধ-~** *n* **1** half a pice. **2** (fig) insignificant amount; paltry sum. **সিকি ~** *n* quarter pice.

পয়স্তি [P] *n* alluvial land.

পয়স্য *adj* made of milk. ❑*n* coagulated milk; curds. **~ দ্রব্য** *n* milk-curd.

পয়স্বিনী *adj fem* **1** yielding milk; milch. **2** full of water; containing water. ❑ *n* **1** milch-cow. **2** river.

পয়া *adj* ⇒ পয়

পয়ার *n* name of a Bengali metre in which each line consists of fourteen syllables.

পয়ো *n* (in compounds)=পয়ঃ. **~দ** *n* cloud. **~ধর** *n* **1** cloud. **2** woman's breast; udder. **~ধরা** *adj* having a specified kind of breasts: পীন ~ধরা, having swelling/ full breasts. **~ধি** *n* ocean; sea. **~নালী**=পয়ঃপ্রণালী (⇒ পয়ঃ). **~নিধি** *n* sea; ocean. **পয়োভার** *n* weight of one's breasts. **~মুক** *n* cloud. **~মুখ** *adj* milk-faced; sweet-tongued.

পর[1] [P] *n* feather.

পর[2] *prep* (colloq)=উপর

পর[3] *n* (colloq)=প্রহর

পর[4] *n* **1** stranger; alien; foreigner; outsider: সে কি আমাদের ~? **2** foe; enemy; adversary: ~ন্তপ. **3** universal soul; Supreme/ Absolute Being. ❑ *adj* **1** other than; different from; another; unrelated: ~জন **2** future; later; next: ~জীবন,

~কাল. **3** highest; supreme; chief ; best; absolute: ~ব্রহ্ম. **4** following; succeeding; subsequent; final. ❑*prep* other (s): পরের কথায় কান দিয়ো না. ❑ *adv* then; after; later: ~বর্তী, তার~. **পরের ধনে পোদ্দারি করা** (fig) be proud of other people's money. **পরের মাথায় কাঁঠাল ভাঙা** (fig) get a rise out of somebody. **পরের মাথায় হাত বোলানো** (fig) swindle others. **পরের মুখে ঝাল খাওয়া** (fig) criticize sth on the basis of second-hand gossip/ knowledge.

পর[৫] *adj* (used as a *suff)* meaning of the nature of; resembling; devoted to; -ish; -ly; -ous: তৎ~, পরার্থ~. **পরা** *adj.*

পরওয়া=পরোয়া

পরওয়ানা [P] *n* written order; warrant; writ; licence; permit; pass; permission; command; summons. ~ **জারি করা** *vi* serve/ issue a warrant/ writ/ order. **গ্রেপ্তারি** ~ *n* warrant of arrest. **তল্লাশি** ~ *n* search warrant.

পরওয়ার [P] *adj* nourisher; cherisher; protector. ~**দিগর,** ~**দেগার** *n* the Cherisher; the Providence; an epithet of the deity.

পরওয়ারিশ [P] *n* fostering; rearing; support; sustenance.

পরক *adj* alien.

পরকলা [P] *n* lens; mirror; pane of glass.

পরকার্য *adj* another's business/ affair.

পরকাল *n* life after death; the hereafter; the future; afterlife; the eternal life. ~ **খাওয়া/ ঝরঝরে করা/ নষ্ট করা** (fig) **1** ruin one's future. **2** deprave; lead astray; spoil. **পরকালের কাজ** *n* act of piety. **পরকালের চিন্তা** *n* spiritual meditation; meditations on the life after death.

পরকীকরণ *n* alienation.

পরকীয় *adj* belonging to another/ a stranger; foreign; alien; not one's own. **পরকীয়া** *adj fem.* ❑ *n fem* **1** another's wife; woman dependent on others. **2** lady-love who is unmarried or married to somebody else; mistress. **পরকীয়াবাদ** *n* a doctrine of the Vaishnava; philosophy of love.

পরক্ষণ *n* next moment. **পরক্ষণে** *adv* at the next moment.

পরক্ষেত্র *n* another's field/ wife.

পরখ *n* test; trial; examination; experiment. ~ **করা, পরখা** (poet) *vt* test; try; experiment; examine. **পরখাই** *n* (dial)=~.

পরগনা [P] *n* an administrative unit; subdivision of a district; pargana.

পরগাছা *n* **1** parasite; parasitic plant. **2** (fig) parasite; hanger-on; sycophant.

পরগৃহ *n* another's house. **পরগৃহবাস** *n* residence at another person's house.

পরগ্রন্থি *n* articulation; joint.

পরগ্লানি *n* slander(ing); scandal; backbiting.

পরঘরী *adj* living in the house of another; dependent on/ sheltered by others. ❑ *n* dependent; poor relation.

পরচর্চা *n* discussion about others; backbiting; slandering; gossip; scandal-mongering. ~ **করা** *vi* backbite; gossip about others; slander. ~**কারী** *n* backbiter; gossip-monger.

পরচা [P] *n* slip of paper; settlement record.

পরচালা *n* small roof over a door.

পরচুল, পরচুলা *n* false hair; wig. ~ **পরা** *vi* put on a wig. ~**পরা** *adj* wigged.

পরচ্ছিদ্র *n* another's fault/ defect. **পরচ্ছিদ্রান্বেষণ** *n* fault-finding; captiousness. **পরচ্ছিদ্রান্বেষণ করা** *vi* find fault with others; carp; pick holes in sth. **পরচ্ছিদ্রান্বেষী** *adj* fault-finding; captious. **পরচ্ছিদ্রান্বেষিণী** *fem.*

পরজ *n* name of an Indian musical mode.

পরজন *n* another person; stranger.

পরজাতি *n* another/ a different people/ race/ nation.

পরজিত *adj* vanquished by one's enemy.

পরজীবিতা *n* parasitism.

পরজীবী *adj* parasitic(al). ❑ *n* parasitic plant/ animal; parasite. ~**য়** *adj* parasitic.

পরটা *n* kind of thin bread fried in oil or butter.

পরত[১] *n* fold; layer; plait; flake. **পরতে পরতে** *adv n* every layer; layer by layer.

পরত[২] *adv* by/ in/ from another.

পরতন্ত্র *adj* dependent on/ subject to (another); subservient; obedient; affected with; overcome by; given to: ইন্দ্রিয়~.

পরতা **1** highest degree; absoluteness. **2** being quite devoted to/ intent upon/ overcome by.

পরতাল *n* **1** examination; verification; test; trial. **2** (land-survey) second measurement (to check the accuracy of the first one). ~ **করা** *vi* examine; reexamine; verify; test; try; check/ revise a measurement.

পরত্র *adj* elsewhere; in a future state/ world; hereafter.

পরদার *n* another's wife. ~**গমন** *n* adultery. ~**গমন করা** *vi* commit adultery. ~**গামী, পরদারিক** *adjj* cohabiting with another's wife; committing adultery. ❑ *n* adulterer.

পরদিন *n, adv* next/ the following day.

পরদুঃখ *n* another's pain/ sorrow/ distress. ~**কাতর** *adj* compassionate; commiserative. ~**কাতরা** *fem.* ~**কাতরতা** *n* compassion; commiseration.

পরদেশ *n* another/ foreign country/ land.

পরদেশী *adj* foreign; exotic; inhabiting/ living in a foreign land. ❑ *n* foreigner. **পরদেশিনী** *fem.*

পরদ্রব্য *n* another's property/ goods.

পরদ্বেষ *n* hatred for another; malice; spite; ill-will. **পরদ্বেষী, পরদ্বেষ্টা** *adjj adj* hating another; inimical to; malicious; spiteful. পরদ্বেষিণী *fem.*

পরধন *n* another's wealth/ money/ property. ~ হরণ করা *vi* rob/ misappropriate another's wealth/ money/ property; defalcate; rob; steal. ~লুব্ধ, ~লোভী *adjj* greedy for another's wealth/ property. ~স্পৃহা *n* greed for another's wealth/ property.

পরধর্ম *n* another's duty/ business/ religion; calling/ profession/ job which is not one's own. ~ গ্রহণ *n* embracing another faith/ religion; apostasy.~ দ্বেষ *n* hostility to other religion/ faith; religious intolerance. ~দ্বেষী *adj* hostile to other's religion/ creed; intolerant of other's religion/ faith.

পরন *n* wearing; putting on.

পরনারী = পরদার. ~ হরণ *n* abduction of another's wife.

পরনিন্দা *n* reviling other's slander; vilification; gossip; animadversion. ~ করা *vi* revile others; slander; animadvert (on sb/sth); gossip.

পরনিন্দুক *adj* given to reviling/ vilifying other's. ❑*n* slanderer; gossip.

পরনিষেক *n* cross-impregnation; cross-fertilization.

পরন্তপ *adj* destroying the foes; victorious.

পরন্তু *con.* but; on the otherhand. ❑*adv* still; moreover; notwithstanding.

পরপতি *n* **1** another's husband; lover; paramour. **2** Supreme Being.

পরপত্নী = পরদার

পরপদ *n* **1** highest position. **2** final emancipation.

পরপর *adj* successively; one after another; consecutively; side by side.

পরপার *n* **1** other/opposite shore/ bank. **2** the next world; the hereafter; the world to come.

পরপীড়ক *adj* oppressing others; tyrannous. ❑*n* oppressor; tyrant; bully.

পরপীড়ন *n* oppression; tyranny. ~ করা *vt* oppress others; tyrannize; bully.

পরপুরুষ *n* **1** husband of another; man other than one's husband. **2** the Supreme Spirit. **3** next/ future generation. ~গামিনী *adj fem* committing adultery; adulterous; whorish; sluttish.

পরপুষ্ট *adj* nourished/ fostered/ brought up by another/ a stranger. ❑*n* cuckoo. পরপুষ্টা *adj fem.* ❑*n* prostitute; whore.

পরপূর্বা *adj fem* who has had a former husband.

পরব *n* festival; festivities; feast.

পরবর্তী *adj* next; subsequent; following; ensuing; succeeding. পরবর্তিনী *fem.*

পরবশ = পরতন্ত্র. ~তা, ~ত্ব *n* subjection (to another); dependence; subservience; dominance; sway; rule.

পরবাদ *n* **1** talk of others; popular rumour/ report; slander. **2** objection; controversy; retort.

পরবাস *n* (poet) = প্রবাস

পরবাসী = প্রবাসী

পরবী *adj* festive. ❑*n* gift offered on a festive occasion.

পরব্রহ্ম *n* Supreme Spirit/ Being; God.

পরভাগ *n* **1** the best part. **2** next/ last part; remainder. **3** excellence; supremacy.

পরভাগ্য *n* another's wealth/ fortune. পরভাগ্যোপজীবী *adj* living on another's fortune/ earning. পরভাগ্যোপজীবিনী *fem.*

পরভাষা *n* foreign language.

পরভূমি *n* foreign/ hostile country.

পরভৃৎ *adj* nourishing another. ❑*n* crow.

পরভৃত = পরপুষ্ট

পরভোজী *adj* parasitical; heterotrophic.

পরম *adj* **1** chief; principal; prime; highest; primary; most prominent/ conspicuous. **2** absolute. **3** first; primordial; supreme. **4** of the highest degree; best; most excellent; worst; extreme: ~ আনন্দ, ~ দুঃখ. **5** real; true. ~ আপ্যায়িত *adj* highly pleased/ gratified. ~ উষ্ণতা/ উষ্মা *n* (phys) absolute temperature. ~ একক *n* (phys) absolute unit. ~ কারণ *n* final/ ultimate cause; God. ~ কারুণিক *adj* most merciful/ kind/ gracious. ~ ক্রম *n* (phys) absolute scale. ~ ক্রুদ্ধ *adj* extremely angry. ~ গতি *n* **1** final beatitude; salvation. **2** chief resource/ refuge (as a god or preceptor). ~ গুরু *n* most venerable/ supreme/ greatest preceptor; absolute lord. ~ ঘনত্ব/ ঘনাঙ্ক *nn* (phys) absolute density. ~ জ্যোতি *n* greatest light; Supreme Being. ~ তত্ত্ব *n* **1** highest truth/knowledge. **2** Absolute Being; God. **3** prime character; intrinsic nature. **4** reality. **5** secrets; mystery. ~ পদ = ~ গতি. ~ পদার্থ *n* highest good; Supreme Being. ~ পিতা *n* Heavenly Father; God. ~ পুরুষ *n* the Supreme Spirit. ~ প্রসার(ণ) (phys) absolute expansion. ~ প্রীত *adj* exceedingly rejoiced. ~ বিত্ত *n* greatest treasure; object of great joy and hope. ~ বিস্মিত *adj* greatly surprised/ amazed. ~ ব্রহ্ম *n* the Supreme Spirit. ~ মান *n* (phys) absolute measurement. ~ মুক্তি/ মোক্ষ *n* final emancipation. ~ রহস্য *n* deepest mystery. ~ শূন্য *n* (phys) absolute zero. ~ শোভন *adj* exceedingly brilliant/ beautiful. ~ সুন্দর *adj* most/ exceedingly beautiful. ~ সুন্দরী *fem.* ~স্পন্দসংখ্যা *n* (phys) absolute frequency of vibration. ~হংস *n* an ascetic of the highest order; religious man who has subdued all his senses by abstract meditation.

পরমত *n* different opinion/ doctrine; another's/ other's view/ opinion. **পরমতাবলম্বী** *adj* guided by/ adopting another's view; hearing no opinion of one's own. **পরমতাবলম্বিনী** *fem.* **~সহিষ্ণু** *adj* tolerant of other's views/ opinions. **~সহিষ্ণুতা** *n* tolerance/ toleration of others views/ opinions.

পরমা *adj fem* = পরম. ~ **গতি** = পরম গতি. ~ **প্রকৃতি** *n* primeval power; goddess Durga.

পরমাকৃতি *n* beautiful form/ figure/ shape. ❑*adj* beautiful; lovely.

পরমাণব, পরমাণবিক *adj* atomic.

পরমাণু *n* atom. **~-সংখ্যা** *n* atomic number. **~তত্ত্ব, ~বাদ** *nn* atomic theory; atomism. **~তাত্ত্বিক, ~বাদী** *adjj* atomistic. ❑*n* atomist. **~-তাপ** *n* atomic heat. **~ওজন** *n* atomic weight.

পরমাত্মা *n* Supreme Spirit/ Soul/ Being; God.

পরমাত্মীয় *adj* closely related; intimate. ❑*n* close relative; intimate/ great/ best friend. **পরমাত্মীয়া** *fem.* **~তা** *n* close relationship; intimate friendship.

পরমাদর *n* great attachment/ love; great cordiality; great care/ attention; very cordial reception. **পরমাদরে** *adv* with great love/ care/ cordiality; cordially.

পরমাদৃত *adj* highly treasured; greatly loved; received with great cordiality. **পরমাদৃতা** *fem.*

পরমদ্বৈত *n* highest being without a second; pure being; Supreme Being.

পরমানন্দ *n* supreme felicity; beatitude; ecstasy; heavenly bliss; soul of the universe.

পরমানন্দিত *adj* greatly/ extremely delighted; blissful; ecstatic.

পরমান্ন *n* best food; rice boiled in milk with sugar (offered to gods or deceased ancestors).

পরমাপদ *n* greatest misfortune.

পরমাবধি *n* utmost term/ limit.

পরমায়ু(ঃ) *n* longevity; period of a person's life. ❑*adj* reaching to a very advanced age. ~ **ক্ষয় হওয়া** *n* have one's longevity/ life cut down; have one's life-blood running out; approach one's death: to be on the decline; have one's period of life diminished. ~ **ক্ষয়কর** *adj* diminishing/ wearing away the period of life. ~ **বর্ধিত** *adj* increasing/ contributing to longevity.

পরমারাধ্য *adj* most venerable/ adorable. **পরমারাধ্যা** *fem.*

পরমার্থ *n* **1** the highest/ whole truth; highest good; spiritual knowledge; reality; God; religion. **2** excellent/ important object. **3** best kind of wealth. ~ **চিন্তা** *n* meditation about God/ reality; spiritual meditation. ~ **তত্ত্ব** *n* highest truth; reality; spiritual truth. **~বিদ** *adj* who knows the highest truth. ❑*n* philosopher.

পরমুখ *n* another's favour/ help. **পরমুখাপেক্ষা, পরমুখাপেক্ষিতা** *n* dependence on another/ others. **পরমুখাপেক্ষী** *adj* dependent on another/ others. **পরমুখাপেক্ষিণী** *fem.*

পরমেশ, পরমেশ্বর *n* the Supreme Lord; Supreme Being; God. **পরমেশ্বরী** =পরমা প্রকৃতি (⇒ পরমা).

পরমৈশ্বর্য *n* greatest wealth; most valuable treasure/ acquisition; great fortune; pomp and grandeur.

পরমোৎকর্ষ *n* highest excellence; perfection.

পরমোৎকৃষ্ট *adj* most excellent; perfect.

পরমোৎসব *n* great festival/ festivities.

পরমোন্নত *adj* developed/ advanced/ elevated/ uplifted to the highest degree; lofty; exalted.

পরমোন্নতি *n* towering; sublime; highest elevation; highest attitude; loftiness; highest development; culmination; highest point; sublimity; eminence; exaltation.

পরম্পর *adj* one following the other; successive; serial; proceeding from one to another. **পরম্পরা** *n* **1** order; series; succession; continuation. **2** tradition. **3** lineage; progeny. **~ক্রমে, পরম্পরায়** *adv* successively; uninterruptedly; serially; one after another; in regular succession; by tradition; traditionally. **পরম্পরাগত** *adj* received by tradition; traditional; hereditary.

পরম্পরিত *adj* forming an uninterrupted series; continuous.

পরম্পরীণ *adj* successive; serial; traditional; hereditary.

পররশ্মি *n* (phys) positive ray.

পররাষ্ট্র *n* foreign state/ country. ~ **দপ্তর** *n* foreign office. ~ **নীতি** *n* foreign policy. ~ **মন্ত্রণালয়** *n* ministry of foreign/ external affairs. ~ **মন্ত্রী** *n* minister of foreign/external affairs; foreign minister. ~ **সচিব** *n* foreign secretary.

পরলোক *n* the other/ future world; next world; death. **~গত, ~প্রাপ্ত** *adjj* gone to heaven/the next world; dead; deceased. **~গমন, ~প্রাপ্তি** *nn* dying; passing away; death. ~ **গমন করা** *vi* pass away; die. **~যাত্রা** = **~গমন**.

পরশ *n* (poet) = স্পর্শ. **~ন** =স্পর্শন. **~পাথর, ~মণি** *nn* philosopher's stone.

পরশু[১] *n* hatchet; axe; battle-axe.

পরশু[২] *n, adv* day after tomorrow; day before tomorrow.

পরশ্রমজীবী *adj* living on the labour of others; parasiting; living by exploitation.

পরশ্রী *n* another's good fortune. **~কাতর** *adj* envious (of others good fortune): jealous; distressed at another's glory/prosperity. **~কাতরা** *fem.* **~কাতরতা** *n* envy; jealousy.

পরশ্ব = পরশু[২]

পরস্ত্রী = পরদার

পরস্পর *adj* mutual; reciprocal; one another's; each other's. ❑*adv* mutually; reciprocally; each other; one another; with/ from one another. ❑*pron* one another; each other. ~ প্রীতি *n* mutual delight/ content. ~-বিরুদ্ধ, ~বিরোধী *adj* opposed to each other/ one another; mutually opposite/ contradictory; antagonistic. ~ বিরোধ, ~ বিরোধিতা *n* mutual opposition; contradiction; antagonism.

পরস্মৈপদ *n* **1** (Sanskrit gram) transitive/ active verb and its terminations. **2** (hum) another's money/ wealth/ property. **পরস্মৈপদী** *adj* **1** (Sanskrit gram) taking the terminations of the transitive/ active verb. **2** (hum) done for another; belonging to another.

পরস্ব *n* another property/ money/ wealth. ~**হরণ**, **পরস্বাপহরণ** *nn* taking/ robbing another's property; misappropriation of another's property/ money. ~**হারী**, **পরস্বাপহারী** *adjj* taking/ robbing another's property; guilty of misappropriation.

পরহস্তগত *adj* in the possession of another; paved into another's possession; in the hand of another.

পরহিংসক *adj* malicious; spiteful; envious; rancorous; full of rancour.

পরহিংসা *n* malice; rancour; spite; envy.

পরহিত *n* another's welfare; good of others; philanthropy; public welfare; benevolence. ~**কামী** *adj* wishing/ doing good to others; benevolent; philanthropic. ~ **ব্রত** *n* public spirit; philanthropy. ❑*adjj* devoted to doing good to others; working for public welfare; altruistic; philanthropic; public spirited. ~**ব্রতী** *adj* = ~ ব্রত. ~ **সাধন** *n* doing good to others; philanthropy; benevolence; social service. **পরহিতাকাঙ্ক্ষা** *n* desire to do good to others; benevolence; philanthropic motives. **পরহিতাকাঙ্ক্ষী** *adj* = ~কামী. **পরিহতাকাঙ্ক্ষিণী** *fem.* **পরহিতানুষ্ঠান** *n* benevolent activities; public welfare; social service.

পরহিতৈষণা *n* = পরহিতাকাঙ্ক্ষা (⇒ পরহিত)

পরহিতৈষী *adj* = পরহিতকামী (⇒ পরহিত)

পরা[1] *pref* denoting **(a)** away; off; aside; along; **(b)** excessiveness; **(c)** opposition; **(d)** contrariety.

পরা[2] *adj fem* supreme; highest; chief; best; final primordial: ~ প্রকৃতি.

পরা[3] *fem* of পর[3], -পর[4].

পরা[4] *vt* **1** put on; wear: কাপড় ~. **2** paint; put: টিপ ~, কাজল ~. ❑*adj* worn; wearing; dressed in; painted with; bearing. ~**নো** *vt* dress; harness; put; paint.

পরাকরণ *n* setting aside; disdaining; contempt; slight.

পরাকাষ্ঠা *n* climax; highest excellence; zenith; acme; culmination.

পরাকৃত *adj* set aside; disdained; despised; slighted.

পরাক্রম *n* bold advance; attack; heroism; courage; power; strength; energy; exertion; might; valour; prowess. ~**শালী** *adj* bold; valorous; strong; mighty; energetic; powerful; heroic.

পরাক্রমী, **পরাক্রান্ত** *adjj* = পরাক্রমশালী (⇒ পরাক্রম)

পরাক্ষ *n* (phys) major axis.

পরাগ *n* **1** pollen (of a flower). **2** fragrant powder used after bathing . **3** sandal. ~ **কেশর** *n* stamen. ~**কোষ**, ~**ধানী** *nn* anther. ~ **মিলন**, ~**যোগ** *nn* pollination. ~**স্থালী** *n* pollen-sac. **পরাগিত** *adj* pollinated. **পরাগিত করা** *vt* pollinate. **ইতর** ~**যোগ** *n* cross pollination. **স্ব~যোগ** *n* self-pollination.

পরাগত *adj* **1** gone; deceased. **2** come; returned; arrived. **3** regressive .

পরাঙ্মুখ *adj* **1** turning away (from); averse (to); disinclined; hostile; opposed (to); shunning; avoiding; unfavourable. **2** falling back; flinching from; desisting from. ~ **হওয়া** *vt* **1** turn away (the face) from; be averse/ disinclined/ unfavourable to; shun; avoid; oppose; disfavour. **2** fall back; flinch from; desist from; take to flight; retreat.

পরাজয় *n* defeat. ~ **বরণ করা** *n* court/ suffer defeat; be defeated. ~ **স্বীকার করা** *n* acknowledge/own defeat; give in; yield; concede defeat. **পরাজয়ের গ্লানি** *n* disgrace/ ignominy/ stigma/ anguish of defeat.

পরাজিত *adj* defeated; vanquished; conquered; overthrown; trounced. **পরাজিতা** *fem.* ~ **করা** *vt* defeat; vanquish; conquer; overthrow; trounce.

পরাজেয় *adj* conquerable; vulnerable.

পরাণ *n* (poet, dial) = প্রাণ

পরাণি, **পরাণী** *nn* (poet, dial) = প্রাণী

পরাণুবীক্ষণ *n* ultra microscope.

পরাত [Pg] *n* large tray/ saucer.

পরাৎপর *adj* highest than the highest; greatest than the greatest; supreme. ❑*n* Supreme Being; God.

পরাধিকার *n* **1** another's right/ jurisdiction/ property. **2** another's domain/ jurisdiction/ domination; foreign domination/ rule. ~ **চর্চা** *n* interference/ meddling (in other's affairs); intrusion.

পরাধীন *adj* dominated by another; subject; dependent; subjugated; subordinate; subservient. **পরাধীনা** *fem.* ~**তা** *n* dependence upon another; subjection; subjugation; domination by another; bondage; subordination; subservience; foreign rule.

পরান *n* (poet, dial) = প্রাণ

পরানি *n* (poet, dial) = প্রাণী

পরানো *vt* ⇒ পরা[৪]

পরান্ন *n* food given in charity by another; unearned/ unpaid-for food. ~**জীবী** *adj* living on food given by another; parasitic. ❑*n* parasite. ~**পালিত**, ~**পুষ্ট** *adjj* nourished by food given by another. ~**ভোজী** *adj* eating another's food; eating at another's table. ❑*n* servant.

পরান্নোপজীবী *adj* = পরান্নজীবী (⇒ পরান্ন)

পরাবর্ত *n* turning back/ round; exchange; barter; interchange; restoration; return; retreat; transposition. ~**ক** *n* reflector. ~**ক চুল্লি** *n* reverberation furnace. ~**ন** *n* turning back/ round; return; reflection. ~**মাপক** *n* eflectometer.

পরাবর্তিত *adj* turned back; returned; sent back; reflected.

পরাবৃত্ত[১] *adj* turned; returned; averted from; retreated; receded; fled.

পরাবৃত্ত[২] *n* (geom) hyperbola.

পরাবৃত্তি *n* turning back/ round; returning; revolving; retreat; flight.

পরাভব *n* defeat; overthrow; humiliation; ruin.

পরাভূত *adj* defeated; overthrown; humbled; vanquished; overcome. **পরাভূতা** *fem.*

পরামর্শ *n* counsel; consultation; conference; advice. ~ **করা** *vi* consult (sb); hold/ take counsel with sb; take counsel together; confer with sb. ~ **দেওয়া** *vi* advise; counsel; give a piece of advice. ~ **নেওয়া** *vi* take sb's advice; take/ hold counsel with sb; consult sb. ~**দাতা** *n* **1** adviser; counsellor. **2** (legal) counsel. ~**সভা** *n* council; conference.

পরামর্ষ *n* endurance; toleration; tolerance; forbearance.

পরামানিক *n* barber.

পরায়ণ *adj* (used as a *suff*) making anything one's chief object; wholly devoted/ destined to; engaged in; intent upon; filled/ occupied with; affected/ possessed by; attached/ addicted to; -ous: ন্যায়~, সেবা~. ❑*n* final end/ aim; last resort/ refuge. **পরায়ণা** *fem.* ~**তা** *n* quality/ state of being intent on.

পরায়ত্ত *adj* in possession/ under control of another; dependent on another; wholly subdued/ overwhelmed.

পরার্থ *n* **1** another's interest/ advantage; good/ need of others. **2** highest advantage/ interest; important object. ~**পর**, ~**পরায়ণ** *adj* intent upon/ devoted to another's welfare/ doing good to others; devoted to serving the interest/ need of others; unselfish; altruistic. ~**পরায়ণা** *fem.* ~**পরতা** *n* care for another's welfare; unselfishness; benevolence; altruism. ~**বাদ**, **পরার্থিতা** *nn* altruism. **পরার্থে** *adv* for (the sake of) others/ another.

পরার্ধ *n* the highest number (hundred thousand billions).

পরাশ্রয় *n* dependence on others; house/ refuge/ shelter other than one's own. ❑*adj* = পরাশ্রয়ী.

পরাশ্রয়ী *adj* clinging to/ dependent on others; parasite; living off others; parasitic(al). ~ **উদ্ভিদ** *n* parasite; epiphyte.

পরাশ্রিত *adj* sheltered/ protected by others; dependent on others. ❑*n* dependent; servant; slave. **পরাশ্রিতা** *fem.*

পরাস্ত *adj* thrown away; defeated; vanquished; overcome. ~ **করা** *vt* defeat; vanquish; conquer; overcome. ~ **হওয়া** *vi* be defeated/ vanquished/ overcome.

পরাহ *n* the next day.

পরাহত *adj* **1** defeated; overcome; vanquished. **2** assailed; attacked. **3** resisted; frustrated; baffled; prevented; obstructed

পরাহ্ন *n* afternoon.

পরি *(pref)* denoting **(a)** round; around; about; round about; **(b)** fully; abundantly; richly; **(c)** against; opposite to; in the direction of; towards; to; **(d)** beyond; more than; successively; severally; from; away from; out of; **(e)** outside of, except, etc.

পরিকথা *n* religious tale/ narrative.

পরিকর *n* **1** attendants; followers; entourage; retinue; train; companion; assistant . **2** multitude; abundance: মধুকর ~. **3** girth; waist-band; zone; girdle: বদ্ধ~.

পরিকর্ম *n* **1** dressing; painting/ perfuming the body; cleansing; purification. **2** attendance; worship; adoration. **3** servant; assistant. **পরিকর্মা**, **পরিকর্মী** *adjj* **1** adorning; decorating. **2** servant; assistant; attendant.

পরিকর্ষ *n* dragging about; strong attraction.

পরিকল্পক *n* planner; designer; deviser; planning officer.

পরিকল্পন, **পরিকল্পনা** *n* planning; devising; inventing; contriving; designing; plan; design; scheme. ~ **করা** *vt* plan; design; devise; invent; contrive.

পরিকল্পয়িতা *n* designer. **পরিকল্পয়িত্রী** *fem.*

পরিকল্পিত *adj* planned; untended; devised; designed; contrived.

পরিকাম্য *adj* highly desirable.

পরিকীর্ণ *adj* spread; scattered around; diffused; widely strewn; pervaded. surrounded; crowded.

পরিকীর্তন *n* proclaiming; announcing; glorifying; praising aloud.

পরিকীর্তিত *adj* announced; proclaimed; said; sung; praised; glorified.

পরিকৃশ *adj* very thin; emaciated; wasted; slender.

পরিকেন্দ্র *n* circumcentre.

পরিকেন্দ্রিক, পরিকেন্দ্রী *adjj* circumcentric.

পরিক্রম *n* 1 roaming about; walking (through); circumambulation; strolling; travelling; traversing; going round; peregrination. 2 (astron) circuit. ~ **কাল** *n* periodic time. ~**ণ** *n* 1 = ~ (1). 2 (mech) revolution. ~**ণ করা** *vi* walk round/ about; circumambulate; walk through; stroll; pace; travel; traverse; go round/ past; peregrinate; roam over. **পরিক্রমা** *n* 1 going round; circumambulation. 2 (astron) revolution; rotation. 3 journey; peregrination; visit: তীর্থ পরিক্রমা. 4 critical survey: সাহিত্য পরিক্রমা.

পরিক্রয় *n* buying off; redemption.

পরিক্রান্ত *adj* walked round; traversed; trod; stepped upon.

পরিক্রিয়া *n* 1 surrounding; enclosing; entrenching. 2 exercise; practice. 3 operation.

পরিক্লান্ত *adj* very tired; tired out; exhausted.

পরিক্লিষ্ট *adj* much vexed/ troubled; pained; harassed; afflicted; distressed; exhausted.

পরিক্লেশ *n* hardship; pain; trouble; fatigue.

পরিক্ষত *adj* wounded; hurt; injured.

পরিক্ষয় *n* decay; destruction; dissolution; loss; ruin.

পরিক্ষিপ্ত *adj* 1 thrown (about); scattered. 2 overspread; surrounded. 3 abandoned; left.

পরিক্ষীণ *adj* wasted; exhausted; diminished; ruined; lost; emaciated.

পরিক্ষেপ *n* 1 throwing about; scattering. 2 surrounding; encircling. 3 railing . 4 abandoning; abandonment.

পরিখা *n* moat; trench (round a tourn or fort); ditch.

পরিখেদ *n* lassitude; weariness; exhaustion.

পরিখ্যাত *adj* 1 celebrated; famous. 2 regarded as; passing for.

পরিগণক *n* enumerator; reckoner; computer.

পরিগণন *n* 1 complete enumeration; accurate calculation/ statement; computation. 2 consideration. **পরিগণনা** *n* = ~. **পরিগণনা করা** *vt* 1 count over; reckon up completely; ascertain by calculation; compute; enumerate. 2 consider/ regard (as).

পরিগণিত *adj* 1 enumerated; calculated; reckoned; computed. 2 considered/ regarded/ esteemed as. **পরিগণিতা** *fem.*

পরিগণ্য *adj* 1 to be enumerated completely/ stated accurately. 2 to be considered/ regarded/ esteemed as.

পরিগত *adj* 1 experienced; known; learnt. 2 obtained. 3 surrounded; encompassed. **পরিগতা** *fem.*

পরিগমিত *adj* brought; conducted; driven.

পরিগম্য *adj* accessible.

পরিগীত *adj* sung; celebrated; proclaimed; declared.

পরিগৃহীত *adj* 1 taken hold of. 2 accepted; adopted; admitted. 3 assumed; put on; worn. 4 seized; grasped; taken; received; embraced; obtained. **পরিগৃহীতা** *fem.*

পরিগৃহ্য *adj* to be taken/ accepted/ regarded/ accepted/admitted.

পরিগ্রহ *n* 1 laying hold of (on all sides). 2 wrapping round; putting on; assuming; wearing: রূপ ~. 3 taking; accepting: দার ~. ~ **করা** *vt* 1 take hold of; embrace; enfold; surround. 2 put on; wear; assume. 3 take; accept; receive.

পরিগ্রাহক *n* 1 one who takes/ accepts. 2 one who puts on/ wears/ assumes. **পরিগ্রাহিকা** *fem.*

পরিঘ *n* 1 iron bar/ beam used for locking/ shutting a gate. 2 iron bludgeon; club studded with iron.

পরিঘট্টিত *adj* stirred about; touched/ rubbed repeatedly.

পরিঘাতন *n* blow; killing; destroying.

পরিচয় *n* 1 acquaintance; familiarity. 2 introduction; presentation. 3 identity. 4 knowledge; experience; acquaintance: বাংলা ভাষার সঙ্গে ~. 5 taken; sign: ভালোবাসার ~. 6 mark: সর্বত্র পাশবিক নির্যাতনের ~. 7 reputation; fame: শিল্পী হিসেবে ~. ~ **করা** *vi* get to know sb; make sb's acquaintance; make the acquaintance of sb. ~ **করানো** *vt* introduce/ present sb (to sb). ~ **থাকা** *n* be acquainted with (sth/ sb); be on familiar terms with; know sb/sth. **সামান্য ~ থাকা** *vi* have a nodding acquaintance with sb/ sth. ~ **দেওয়া** *vi* 1 introduce (oneself); reveal one's/ sb's identity. 2 show; prove (one self): সুবুদ্ধির ~ দেওয়া. ~ **নেওয়া** *vi* ask for sb's identity/ particulars; get acquainted with sth; learn particulars/ details (of). ~ **পাওয়া** *vi* (fig) get/ take the measure of sb; appreciate: শক্তির ~ পাওয়া. ~ **পত্র** *n* identity card; letter of introduction; credentials.

পরিচর *n* 1 attendant; servant; follower. 2 bodyguard; patrol.

পরিচর্যা *n* attendance; service; nursing; worship; treatment; waiting upon.

পরিচলন *n* (phys) convection.

পরিচায়ক *adj* indicative/ suggestive; showing; introductory; introducing; informing; prefatory; testifying to; denoting. **পরিচায়িকা** *fem.*

পরিচারক *n* servant; man-servant; attendant; valet; assistant. **পরিচারিকা** *fem* female attendant; waiting maid; maidservant.

পরিচারণ *n* attendance.

পরিচালক *adj* managing; directing; conducting; leading; guiding; administrating.

❑*n* director; manager; conductor; driver; leader; chief; administrator. **পরিচালিকা** *fem.* **~তা** *n* **1** management; direction. **2** (phys) conductivity. **~ সমিতি** *n* managing committee.

পরিচালন *n* conducting; directing; direction; management; administration; lead; guiding; driving. **পরিচালনা** = ~. **পরিচালনা করা** *vt* direct; conduct; drive; manage; run; administer; lead; guide.

পরিচালিত *adj* directed; conducted; managed; guided; led; run; driven; administered. **~ করা** *vt* lead; conduct.

পরিচিত *adj* **1** known; acquainted; familiar; well-known: ~ দৃশ্য. **2** aware; abreast; familiar; informed; acquainted with; alive to: সমস্যার সঙ্গে ~. **~ ব্যক্তি** *n* acquaintance.

পরিচিতি *n* = পরিচয়

পরিচিন্তন *n* careful thinking; planning; design; deliberation.

পরিচিন্তিত *adj* designed; well-planned; deeply/ carefully thought out; deliberated.

পরিচ্ছদ *n* cover; covering; garment; dress; clothing; paraphernalia.

পরিচ্ছন্ন *adj* **1** neat; tidy; clean; spruce; neat and tidy; trim; orderly; smug. **2** hygienic: ~পরিবেশ. **3** honest; virtuous; pure; clean; good; innocent; candid; straightforward: ~ মন, ~ আচরণ. **4** not unfair; clean: ~ খেলা. **5** covered; clad; veiled. **~তা** *n* neatness; cleanness; tidiness; purity; innocence; honesty; candidness.

পরিচ্ছিত্ত *n* accurate definition; limitation; limit; partition; separation.

পরিচ্ছিন্ন *adj* **1** (sharply/ clearly) defined; determined. **2** cut off; divided; detached; confined; limited; circumscribed. **~ করা** *vt* **1** cut off; separate; limit; divide; part. **2** define/ fix accurately; determine; discriminate.

পরিচ্ছেদ *n* **1** cutting; severing; division; separation. **2** chapter; section. **3** accurate definition; exact discrimination. **4** limit; boundary.

পরিচ্যুত *adj* fallen/ descended from; streaming (with).

পরিজন *n* **1** attendant; surrounding company of people; members of a family; dependents; kinsmen. **2** servants; attendants. **3** train; retinue; followers; suite.

পরিজ্ঞাত *adj* **1** thoroughly known; recognized; ascertained; learnt; familiar. **2** well aquainted with; cognizant/ aware of sth. **~ থাকা** *vi* be fully aware of; be familiar of/ alive to.

পরিজ্ঞান *n* thorough knowledge; perception; experience; ascertainment; discrimination; finding.

পরিণত *adj* **1** changed/ transformed into; reduced to: ধ্বংসস্তূপে ~. **2** developed; ripened; mature; full-grown; perfect: ~ বুদ্ধি. **3** advanced; ripe: ~ বয়স. **4** turned/ rendered into; resulting in; converted to. **পরিণতা** *fem.* **~ করা** *vi* change/ turn/ transform/ render into; reduce to; convert into. **~ হওয়া** *vi* turn/ change into; become; be reduced to; develop into; result in. **~ বয়স** *n* advanced age; ripe years; ripe old age. **~ বয়স্ক** *adj* advanced in age/ years; mature; grown-up.

পরিণতি *n* **1** ripeness; maturity. **2** end; consequence; result; issue; term; termination. **3** change; transformation; (natural) development. **4** mature/ old age. **~লাভ করা** *vi* mature; result in; develop into; grow into; evolve.

পরিণদ্ধ *adj* **1** bound/ wrapped round; attached; connected. **2** embraced; surrounded; encircled; girt; girdled.

পরিণয় *n* **1** marriage; wedding. **~ন** *n* marrying; marriage. **~ হওয়া** *vi* be married/ wedded to. **~ বন্ধন, ~ সূত্র** *nn* wedlock.

পরিণাম *n* **1** change; alteration; transformation (into). **2** development; evolution. **3** result; consequence; issue; end. **4** ripeness; maturity. **~দর্শিতা** *n* foresightedness; foresight; prudence. **~দর্শী** *adj* foresighted; prudent; far-sighted; provident. **~দর্শিনী** *fem.* **পরিণামে** *adv* in the end; at last; finally; ultimately; in the long run.

পরিণাহ *n* circumference; width; breadth; extent; compass; periphery. **পরিণাহী** *adj* large; wide; expansive.

পরিণীত *adj* married; wedded. **পরিণীতা** *fem.*

পরিণেতা *n* husband.

পরিণেয় *adj* to be married; marriageable; fit for marrying. **পরিণেয়া** *fem.*

পরিতপ্ত *adj* **1** heated; burnt. **2** afflicted; tormented; distressed.

পরিতাপ *n* **1** heat; glow. **2** pain; agony; grief; sorrow. **3** deep regret; remorse; repentance; compunction. **~ করা** *vi* regret deeply; lament; grieve; deplore; repent. **পরিতাপের বিষয়** *n* matter of deep regret; lamentable affair. ❑*adj* unfortunately; regretably.

পরিতুষ্ট *adj* completely satisfied; delighted; very glad; gratified; very pleased. **পরিতুষ্টা** *fem.* **~ করা** *vt* satisfy completely; delight; gratify; appease; flatter.

পরিতুষ্টি = পরিতোষ

পরিতৃপ্ত = পরিতুষ্ট

পরিতৃপ্তি =পরিতোষ

পরিতোষ *n* complete satisfaction; delight (in); gratification; contentment; deep pleasure . **~ক** *adj* satisfying; pleasing. **~জনক** *adj* highly satisfactory/ gratifying; delightful. **~ন** *n* satisfaction; gratification. **~পূর্বক** *adv* to one's heart's content; with great/ thorough satisfaction; with great pleasure.

পরিত্যক্ত *adj* left (off); quitted; abandoned; given up; deserted; relinquished; renounced; forsaken; rejected. **পরিত্যক্তা** *fem.*

পরিত্যজন = পরিত্যাগ

পরিত্যাগ *n* leaving; abandoning; deserting; quitting; giving up; renouncing; desertion; abandonment; relinquishment; renunciation; renouncement. ~ **করা** *vt* leave; quit; abandon; give up; reject; desert; forsake; relinquish; renounce.

পরিত্যাজ্য *adj* to be left/ abandoned/ deserted/ relinquished/ renounced/ given up/ forsaken. **পরিত্যাজ্যা** *fem.*

পরিত্রাণ *n* rescue; deliverance; (means of) protection; salvation; relief; exemption; preservation; refuge; reprieve; respite. ~ **করা** *vt* rescue; save; protect; spare; defend; deliver; relieve; liberate. ~ **দেওয়া** *vt* spare; exempt; relieve; liberate; show mercy; reprieve. ~ **পাওয়া** *vi* be rescued/ saved/ spared; get rid of; be relieved/ liberated/ exempted. ~ **কর্তা** *n* saviour; protector; deliverer; defender; liberator; rescuer. **পরিত্রাণের উপায়/ পথ** *n* path of salvation; way out; way of escape.

পরিত্রাতা *n* = পরিত্রাণকর্তা (⇒ পরিত্রাণ)

পরিত্রাহি *vi* (imperative) help! to the rescue! ~ **ডাক ছাড়া** call out/ cry for help; ask for mercy; ask quarter.

পরিদর্শ = পরিদর্শন

পরিদর্শক *n* inspector; observer; beholder; visitor; supervisor; spectator.

পরিদর্শন *n* inspection; supervision; visit; (careful) observation. ~ **করা** *vt* inspect; visit; supervise; observe (carefully); behold.

পরিদর্শী *adj* observing; inspecting; visiting; supervising.

পরিদান *n* exchange; restitution of a deposit.

পরিদৃশ্যমান *adj* visible (all around); conspicuous; manifest; apparent; in (full) view; exposed to view; in sight.

পরিদৃষ্ট *adj* seen; observed; beheld; perceived; noticed; inspected.

পরিদেবন(া) *n* lamentation; bewailing; complaint; repentance; wailing.

পরিদোলক *n* pendulum.

পরিধান *n* putting on; wearing; wrapping round; dressing; clothing; garment; dress; clothes. ~ **করা** *vi* put on; wear. ~ **বস্ত্র** *n* garment; clothes.

পরিধারণ *n* bearing; supporting; enduring.

পরিধি *n* circumference; circle; periphery;.girth. ~**মাপক** *n* perimeter.

পরিধৃত *n* borne; supported.

পরিধেয় *adj* (fit) to be worn/ put on. ❑*n* garment; clothes; attire.

পরিনির্বাণ *n* complete extinction of individuality entire cessation of re-births; nirvana.

পরিপক্ব *adj* **1** quite ripe; mature. **2** complete cooked/ dressed. **3** accomplished; perfect; highly cultivated; very sharp/ shrewd; seasoned; well experienced; practised; astute. **4** fully digested. ~**তা** *n* maturity; ripeness; perfection; shrewdness.

পরিপণ *n* capital; stock.

পরিপণিত *adj* pledged; wagered; promised.

পরিপত্র *n* circular.

পরিপন্থক *n* one who obstructs the way; antagonist; adversary; enemy.

পরিপন্থী *adj* standing in the way; hindering; hostile/ inimical to; contrary to; adverse; opposing; unfavourable; adverse.

পরিপাক *n* digestion; assimilation. ~ **করা** *vt* digest; assimilate. ~-**দোষ** *n* digestive trouble. ~ **যন্ত্র** *n* digestive organ; stomach. ~ **শক্তি** *n* digestive power; power of assimilation.

পরিপাটি, পরিপাটী *nn* succession; order; method; arrangement; orderliness; trim. ❑*adjj* orderly; neat and tidy; in good/ excellent trim; spruce; well-kept; prim.

পরিপার্শ্ব *n* surroundings; environment; entourage. ~**চর** *adj* going at/ by sb's side.

পরিপালক *adj* guarding; keeping; maintaining. ❑*n* one who brings up; rearer; administrator.

পরিপালন *n* fostering; nourishing; bringing up; rearing; protection; care; nurture; administration. ~ **করা** *vi* bring up; nourish; nurture; foster; rear; support; maintain; guard.

পরিপালনীয় *adj* to be brought up/ nurtured/ nourished/ reared/ fostered/ guarded/ maintained/ kept preserved.

পরিপালিত *adj* brought up; reared; fostered; nourished; nurtured; maintained.

পরিপুষ্ট *adj* **1** nourished; cherished; well-fed; amply provided with. **2** well-developed; plump; full-grown; full-blown; stout; well-rounded. **পরিপুষ্টা** *fem.* ~**তা** *n* good development; nourishment; plumpness; rotundity; stoutness. full growth.

পরিপুষ্টি=পুরপুষ্টতা (⇒ পরিপুষ্ট)

পরিপূত *adj* purified.

পরিপূরক *adj* filling; fulfilling; completing; complimentary.

পরিপূরণ *n* filling; completing; accomplishing; perfecting; fulfilment; completion; implementing; repletion. ~ **করা** *vi* fill; make full; fulfil; accomplish; replete; complement; complete.

পরিপূরণীয় *adj* to be fill/ fulfilled/ completed/ complemented.

পরিপূরিত *adj*=পরিপূর্ণ. **পরিপূরিতা** *fem.*

পরিপূর্ণ *adj* filled; occupied by; completely filled/ covered with; accomplished; perfect; whole; complete; fully satisfied; content; fulfilled; replete/ teeming (with); complemented. ~ **করা**=পরিপূরণ করা. ~**তা** *n* completeness; perfection; accomplishment; attainment; fulfilment; repleteness; repletion; consummation; culmination.

পরিপূর্তি *n*=পরিপূর্ণতা (⇒ পরিপূর্ণ)

পরিপৃক্ত *adj* saturate. ~ **করা** *vt* saturate. ~**তা**=পরিপৃক্তি. ~ **দ্রব** *n* saturated solution.

পরিপৃক্তি *n* saturation.

পরিপৃচ্ছা *n* question; inquiry.

পরিপোষক *adj* nourishing; fostering; supporting; cherishing; promoting; protecting; protective.

পরিপোষণ *n* cherishing; nourishing; fostering; nourishment; support; protection; furthering; promoting; furtherance; promotion; rearing. ~ **করা** *vt* nourish; foster; cherish; support; further; promote; protect; rear.

পরিপ্রেক্ষণ *n*=পরিদর্শন. **পরিপ্রেক্ষণা** *n* perspective.

পরিপ্রেক্ষিত *n* perspective.

পরিপ্লব(ন) *n* flooding; flood; inundation; submersion; drenching.

পরিপ্লুত *adj* flooded; inundated; bathed; immersed; submersed; soaked; saturated; drenched; overwhelmed/ visited by. **পরিপ্লুতা** *fem.* ~ **করা** *vt* flood; inundate; submerge; drench; saturate; overwhelm; visit.

পরিপ্লুতি *n*=পরিপ্লব

পরিবর্জন *n* avoidance; avoiding; abstaining from; giving up; renouncement; boycott; abstention; abstinence. ~ **করা** *vt* avoid; eschew; abstain from; boycott; give up; renounce; shun.

পরিবর্জিত *adj* shunned; avoided; eschewed; abandoned; renounced; rejected; devoid/ deprived of.

পরিবর্ত *n* **1** change; exchange; barter. **2** revolving; revolution. **3** substitute. ~ **বিবাহ** *n* inter-marriage. ~**ক** *n* one who or that exchanges/ barters/ alters/ changes/ modifies/ converts/ metamorphoses/ rotates/ revolves/ returns. ❑*adj* changing; bartering; exchanging; modifying; converting; transforming; totaling; revolving; alternating. ~**ন** *n* change; exchange; barter; alteration; transformation; modification; metamorphosis; change in circumstances; rotation; revolution; conversion. ~**ন করা** *vt* change; exchange; barter; alter; alternate; transform; metamorphose; modify; bring about a change in circumstances; rotate. ~**নীয়** *adj* to be changed/ exchanged; bartered; exchangeable; convertible; alterable/ modifiable; variable; changeable; transformable. ~**নশীল** *adj* changing; changeful; varying; fluctuating; unstable; inconstant.

পরিবর্তিত *adj* changed; modified; altered; transformed; metamorphosed; converted; rotated; exchanged; bartered.

পরিবর্তী *adj* **1** changeful; changing; variable. **2** (phys) alternating. ~ **মোক্ষণ** *n* oscillatory discharge.

পরিবর্তে *advi* in place of; instead of; in lieu of; in exchange for.

পরিবর্ধক *adj* developing; magnifying; enlarging; amplifying; promoting; furthering; improving; extending. ❑*n* magnifier; amplifier; enlarger; promoter. ~ **কাচ** *n* magnifying glass.

পরিবর্ধন *n* development; developing; multiplying; augmenting; magnification; enlargement; amplification; swelling; increasing; improvement.

পরিবর্ধিত *adj* grown; increased; augmented; swollen; magnified; amplified; enlarged; developed. ~ **করা** *vt* increase; augment; multiply; enlarge; magnify; amplify; develop.

পরিবলন *n* (bot) circumnutation.

পরিবহণ, পরিবহন *n* **1** transportation; transport; conveyance; carriage. **2** (elec) conduction. ~ **করা** *vt* transport; convey; carry; conduct.

পরিবাদ *n* blame; censure; reproach; charge; accusation; slander; calumny. ~**ক** *adj* blaming; reproaching; slandering; calumniating. ❑*n* accuser; slanderer; calumniator; complainant.

পরিবাদী=পরিবাদক (⇒ পরিবাদ). **পরিবাদিনী** *fem.* **1**=পরিবাদী. **2** a seven-stringed musical instrument.

পরিবার *n* **1** family; family circle. **2** (dial) wife. ~-**পরিকল্পনা** *n* family-planning.

পরিবাহ *n* **1** overflowing of a tank; inundation. **2** watercourse; drain. ~ **ক্ষেত্র** *n* (geog) basin; catchment area. ~**ক** *n* drainage.

পরিবাহন *n* (phys) conduction.

পরিবাহিত *adj* conducted. **পরিবাহিতা** *fem.*

পরিবাহিতা *n* conductivity.

পরিবাহী *adj* conducting. ❑*n* conductor.

পরিবীত *adj* surrounded; encompassed by; covered; overspread; veiled.

পরিবৃত *adj* surrounded by; covered with; veiled; encircled; beset. **পরিবৃতা** *fem.*

পরিবৃতি *n* surrounding; encirclement; covering.

পরিবৃত্ত *n* (geom) circumcircle.

পরিবৃত্তি *n* change; alteration; transition; exchange; barter; transfer. ~ **কাল** *n* (phys) transition period.

পরিবেদন(া) *n* **1** great pain; anguish; distress; sorrow. **2** shrewdness; wit; prudence.

পরিবেশ *n* environment; surroundings; circle; circumference; entourage.

পরিবেশক, পরিবেষক *nn* **1** one who serves up needs; waiter; servant. **2** dealer; distributor.

পরিবেশন, পরিবেষণ *n* **1** serving up meals; distributing food; attendance; waiting. **2** dispensation. **~ করা** *vt* serve (food at table); wait on; distribute; deal out.

পরিবেষ্টক *adj* surrounding; enclosing; going round; encircling. ☐*n* one who/ that which surrounds/ enclose/ goes round/ encircles.

পরিবেষ্টন *n* surrounding; encompassing; enclosing; enclosure; cover; covering; encirclement. **~ করা** *vi* surround; encompass; enclose; wrap up; cover; clothe; embrace; go round; encircle.

পরিবেষ্টনী *n* surroundings; enclosure; fencing; railings; entourage.

পরিবেষ্টিত *adj* surrounded; enclosed; beset; covered; veiled; swathed; encircled; encompassed. **পরিবেষ্টিতা** *fem.*

পরিব্যক্ত *adj* expressed; very clear/ distinct.

পরিব্যক্তি *n* **1** (clear) expression; manifestation. **2** mutation.

পরিব্যয় *n* cost. **~ মূল্য** *n* cost price.

পরিব্রজ্যা *n* strolling; wandering from place to place; (esp) leading the life of a religious mendicant; abandonment of the world; pilgrimage.

পরিব্রাজক *n* traveller; wandering religious mendicant. **পরিব্রাজিকা** *fem.*

পরিব্রাজন *n* wandering; travel(ling); religious mendicancy.

পরিভব *n* **1** defeat; discomfiture; humiliation. **2** insult; injury; contempt; disgrace.

পরিভাবী *adj* **1** defeating; vanquishing; overpowering; subduing. **2** despising; insulting; slighting; mocking; defying; injuring.

পরিভাষণ *n* **1** speaking; discourse; talking. **2** admonition; reproof; reprimand.

পরিভাষা *n* technical word/ term; technical terminology. **পরিভাষিত** *adj* defined.

পরিভুক্ত *adj* eaten; enjoyed; possessed.

পরিভূত *adj* overpowered; conquered; vanquished; defeated; discomfited.

পরিভৃতি *n* emolument; wages; pay; salary.

পরিভোগ *n* enjoyment; sexual intercourse.

পরিভ্রম *n* **1** flying round/ about; wandering; going about; travelling; roaming; peregrination; walking; strolling. **2** rotation; revolving. **3** circumlocution; confusion; rambling discourse. **~ণ** *n*=~(1,2). **~ণ করা** *vi* go round/ about; rove; ramble; wander about/ through; travel; stroll; walk; perigrinate; rotate; whirl round; revolve; describe a circle round.

পরিভ্রষ্ট *adj* fallen (from); dropped (off); deprived (of); lost; ruined; sunk; shed; detached. **পরিভ্রষ্টা** *fem.* **~ হওয়া** *vi* fall (from); drop (off); be deprived (of); be lost/ ruined; be shed/ detached.

পরিভ্রূণ *n* perisperm.

পরিমণ্ডল *n* **1** globe; sphere; orbit; circumference; circle. **2** (fig) society; sphere; environment. ☐*adj* round; circular; globular. **পরিমণ্ডলাকার, পরিমণ্ডলাকৃতি** *adj*=~.

পরিমণ্ডলিত *adj* rounded; made round/ circular.

পরিমণ্ডিত *adj* adorned/ decorated all around; well ornamented; endowed (with).

পরিমল *n* **1** fragrance; fragrant substance; perfume (esp arising from the trituration of fragrant substances). **2** copulation; connubial pleasure. **3** nectar of flowers. **~জ** *adj* (enjoyment) arising from copulation.

পরিমাণ *n* **1** measuring; meting out; measure; measurement; weight; length; size; number; value; duration; degree; quantity; amount; extent. **2** (math) magnitude. **~ করা** *vt* measure; weigh; count; survey; assess; estimate; determine. **~ত** *adv* by measure; in weight. **~ফল** *n* result of measurement/ counting; area; square-measure. **পরিমাণে হওয়া** *vi* measure; weigh; be adequate in proportion to. **পরিমাণাত্মক** *adj* quantitative.

পরিমাত্রা *n* (mech) intensity.

পরিমাপ=পরিমাণ. **~ক** *adj* measuring; weighing; counting; surveying assessing. ☐*n* one who measures/ weighs/ counts/ surveys/ assesses; surveyor; assessor; counter; measuring/ weighing/ surveying/ counting machine. **~ন** *n* measuring; weighing; counting; surveying; assessing.

পরিমার্জন(া) *n* wiping off; cleaning; polishing; refining; cleansing; refinement; polish; elegance.

পরিমার্জিত *adj* cleaned; polished; scoured; refined. **~ করা** *vt* cleanse; purify; scour; clean; polish; refine.

পরিমিত *adj* **1** measured; limited; regulated; moderate; sparing; abstemious; temperate. **2** measuring; amounting to: দুই হস্ত ~. **3** finite. **~বাক্** *adj* speaking little; taciturn. **~-ব্যয়ী** *adj* frugal; thrifty; economical; sparing with. **~ভোজন** *n* moderation in eating; abstemiousness. **~ভোজী** *adj* eating sparingly; abstemious. **পরিমিতাচার** *n* moderation; temperance. ☐*adj*=পরিমিতাচারী. **~চারী** *adj* abstemious; temperate; eating sparingly. **পরিমিতাভরণ** *adj* moderately adorned. **পরিমিতাহার** *adj*=~ভোজী.

পরিমিতি *n* measure; measurement; quantity; limitation; mensuration; temperance; moderation; proportion. **~-বোধ** *n* sense of proportion.

পরিমুক্ত *adj* released; emancipated; liberated from. ~ **বন্ধন** *adj* released from bonds; unfettered; emancipated. ~ **সঙ্গ** *adj* liberated from worldly desires.

পরিমুক্তি *n* liberation.

পরিমেয় *adj* **1** measurable; limited; finite. **2** (arith) commensurable.

পরিমেল *n* association. ~-**নিয়মাবলী** *n* articles of association. ~**বন্ধ** *n* memorandum of association.

পরিমোক্ষ *n* setting free; liberation; deliverance.

পরিমোচিত *adj* liberated; emancipated; discharged.

পরিম্লান *adj* faded; withered; jaded; worn-out; exhausted; languid; emaciated.

পরিযান *n* traffic; migration.

পরিযায়ী *adj* trafficking; migratory; itinerant.

পরিরক্ষক *n* guardian; protector; keeper.

পরিরক্ষণ *n* guarding; protecting; defending; preserving; preservation; keeping; maintaining; protection; custodianship.

পরিরক্ষিত *adj* well guarded/ preserved/ kept/ maintained; protected.

পরিরম্ভ(ণ) *n* embrace; embracing.

পরিলক্ষিত *adj* noticed.

পরিলিখন *n* circumscribing; drawing lines round about.

পরিলিখিত *adj* circumscribed; enclosed in a circle.

পরিলেখ *n* outline; delineation; picture. ~**ন** *n*=পরিলিখন.

পরিশঙ্কনীয় *adj* to be feared/ apprehended/ distrusted/ doubted.

পরিশঙ্কা *n* suspicion; distrust; apprehension.

পরিশঙ্ক্য=পরিশঙ্কনীয়

পরিশিষ্ট *adj* left; remaining. ❑*n* appendix; supplement.

পরিশীলন *n* **1** practice; study; constant occupation; pursuit of; cultivation; refinement; sophistication. **2** contact; embrace.

পরিশীলিত *adj* **1** practised; studied; pursued; cultivated; refined; sophisticated. **2** embraced.

পরিশুদ্ধ *adj* cleaned; purified; pure; refined; sanctified; polished. ~ **করা** *vt* purify; clean; refine; polish; sanctify.

পরিশুদ্ধি *n* complete purification; refinement; purity; sanctity; polishing.

পরিশুষ্ক *adj* very dry; thoroughly dried/ parched up; withered; shrivelled; shrunk; hollow (as the cheats). **পরিশুষ্কা** *fem.* ~-**তালু** *adj* having the palate dried up.

পরিশেষ *n* remnant; remains; remainder; residue; end; conclusion; last stage; concluding part; termination. **পরিশেষে** *adv* at last; in the end; finally; ultimately; in the long run; at long last.

পরিশোধ *n* **1** discharging; paying off; repayment. **2** revenge; retaliation. ~ **করা** *vt* **1** repay; pay back; restore; clear off. **2** (fig)/ avenge; retaliate. ~**ন** *n* cleaning/ purification; refining; polishing; correction; refinement. ~**নীয়, পরিশোধ্য** *adjj* which can be/ is to be repaid; repayable; outstanding.

পরিশোষ *n* complete dryness; desiccation; evaporation. ~**ণ** *n* drying; parching; emaciation.

পরিশোষিত=পরিশুষ্ক

পরিশ্রম *n* labour; toil; exertion; fatigue; trouble; pain; industry; effort; endeavour; diligent. ~ **করা** *vi* work hard; exert/ fatigue oneself; toil; labour; work diligently; take (great) pains (with/ over/ to do sth). ~**কাতর**, ~**বিমুখ** *adj* averse to hard work; lazy; indolent; slothful.

পরিশ্রমী *adj* hardworking; laborious; diligent; industrious.

পরিশ্রান্ত *adj* thoroughly fatigued/ worn out; exhausted; tired; wearied.

পরিশ্রান্তি *n* fatigue; exhaustion; tiredness; weariness.

পরিশ্লেষ *n* embrace.

পরিষদ, পরিষৎ *n* association; assembly; society; academy; (legislative) council. ~**পাল** *n* chairman of a legislative council. ~-**সচিব** *n* parliamentary secretary. **ব্যবস্থা**-~ *n* legislative council.

পরিষিক্ত *adj* sprinkled about; moistened; diffused.

পরিষেক, পরিষেচন *nn* sprinkling over; moistening; pouring over.

পরিষেবক *n* nurse; sicknurse. **পরিষেবিকা** *fem.*

পরিষেবা *n* nursing; care of the sick.

পরিস্করণ *n* cleansing; refining; purification.

পরিস্কার *adj* **1** clean; pure; cleansed; neat; tidy; clear; orderly; spruce; transparent; limpid. **2** legible; clean; clear: ~ হাতের লেখা. **3** clear-cut; out-spoken; unequivocal; frank; lucid; candid; plain: ~ কথা. **4** cloudless; clear: ~ আকাশ. **5** fair; bright; beautiful; clear: ~ রং. **6** free from confusion; clear: ~ মাথা. **7** keen; discerning; clear: ~ দৃষ্টি. **8** distinct; easy to hear; clear: ~ গলা. **9** free from morbidity; clear: ~ বুক. **10** straight forward; candid; frank; open; guileless. ~ মন. **11** free from guilt; clear: ~ বিবেক. ❑*n* cleanliness; tidiness; neatness; clarity. ~ **করা** *vt* **1** cleanse; clean; tidy. **2** clear (sth) up; clear sth out; remove. **3** wash: কাপড় ~ করা. ~**ক** *adj* cleansing; detergent. ❑*n* cleansing agent; detergent. ~**পরিচ্ছন্ন** *adj* neat and clean; clean and tidy; speck and span.

পরিস্কৃত *adj* cleaned; cleansed; cleared; purified; tidied; washed; refined.

পরিস্কৃতি, পরিষ্ক্রিয়া *nn* cleaning; cleansing; purification.

পরিসংখ্যা *n* enumeration; computation; sum; total; exhaustive enumeration; special mention; exhaustive specification. **~ত** *adj* enumerated; reckoned up; tabulated; specified exclusively. **~ন** *n* **1** statistics. **2** =~.

পরিসমাপন=পরিসমাপ্তি

পরিসমাপ্ত *adj* finished ended; completed; concluded.

পরিসমাপ্তি *n* completion; end; ending; conclusion; termination.

পরিসম্পৎ *n* assets.

পরিসর *n* **1** extent; width; area; limit; breadth. **2** proximity; neighbourhood; environs; border. **~ণ** *n* running/ moving about.

পরিসীমা *n* boundary; extreme term/ limit; bound; perimeter; end.

পরিস্থিতি *n* circumstances; situation.

পরিস্পন্দ(ন) *n* throbbing; vibration; stirring; starting.

পরিস্ফুট *adj* very clear; manifest; obvious; clearly expressed; well-developed; (clearly) visible. **~ন** *n* development (of film).

পরিস্ফুটিত *adj* developed.

পরিস্ফুরণ *n* **1** throbbing; vibration. **2** effervescence. **3** manifestation. **4** shooting; budding.

পরিস্ফুরিত *adj* **1** quivering; palpitating. **2** opened; expanded.

পরিস্রব *n* placenta.

পরিস্রাবণ *n* filtration; distillation.

পরিস্রাবী *adj* flowing.

পরিস্রুত *adj* filtered; distilled.

পরিস্রুতি=পরিস্রাবণ

পরিহরণ =পরিহার

পরিহরণীয়=পরিহার্য

পরিহরা *vt* (poet)=পরিহার করা

পরিহর্তব্য=পরিহার্য

পরিহসনীয় *adj* laughable; ridiculous; fit to be derided/ mocked.

পরিহার *n* **1** shunning; avoiding; avoidance; abandoning; giving up; resigning. **2** contempt; disregard; slight; neglect. **3** leaving out; omission; casting off. **~ করা** *vt* **1** give up; shun; avoid; abandon; cost off. **2** leave; quit; desert. **3** leave out; omit; abstain from; keep away from. **4** neglect; not heed; disregard; slight.

পরিহার্য *adj* **1** to be shunned/ avoided/ omitted/ escaped from/ abandoned/ given up. **2** avoidable.

পরিহাস *n* jesting; joking; jest; joke; mirth; merriment; derision; mockery. **~ করা** *vi* jest; joke; laugh at; ridicule; deride; make fun of sb/ sth; poke fun at sb/ sth. **~ছলে, ~ভরে** *advv* as a joke; (just) in fun; (just) for fun/ for the fun of it/ jokingly; mockingly. **~প্রিয়** *adj* full of fun; fond of joking/ jesting; humorous; witty; jocular; playful.

পরিহিত *adj* **1** clothed; clad in; dressed (in); wearing. **2** put on; worn: ~ পরিচ্ছদ. **পরিহিতা** *fem.*

পরিহৃত *adj* shunned; avoided; abandoned; quitted.

পরী [P] *n* fairy. **~দেশ, ~রাজ্য** *nn* fairy-land. **~র গল্প** *n* fairy tale; fairy story. **ডানাকাটা ~** *n* paragon of beauty; nymph.

পরীক্ষক *n* examiner; prover; experimenter; investigator. **ভাগ্য-~** *n* **1** fortune-teller. **2** adventurer.

পরীক্ষণ *n* trying; testing; experiment; investigation; examining; examination; reading.

পরীক্ষণীয় *adj* to be tried/ tested/ examined/ investigated/ experimented upon.

পরীক্ষা *n* **1** examination; test; investigation; probe; experiment. **2** trial; ordeal: অগ্নি~. **3** (cross-) examination: উকিল সাক্ষীকে ~ করলেন. **4** scrutiny; inspections. **5** reading: হস্তরেখা ~. **~ করা** *vt* examine; test; try; test by an ordeal; put to a test; inspect; scrutinize; investigate; verify; study; experiment; read. **~ দেওয়া** *vi* **1** sit for/ take an examination; take a test. **2** undergo a trial; go through an ordeal. **~ নেওয়া** *vt* examine; give a test to sb; test (on sth); hold an examination. **~য় টেকা** *vi* stand a test/ scrutiny. **~গার, ~গৃহ, ~ভবন, ~লয়, ~শালা** *nn* **1** examination hall. **2** laboratory. **~ধীন** *adj* under/ subject to examination/ trial/ investigation/ experiment/ test. **~মূলক** *adj* experimental. **~মূলকভাবে** *adv* experimentally. **~র্থী** *adj* taking an examination. ❑ *n* candidate; examinee. **~র্থিনী** *fem.* **অদৃষ্ট-~** *n* fortune-telling; seeking one's fortune. **অদৃষ্ট ~ করা** *vi* **1** tell sb's fortune. **2** seek one's fortune; try one's luck.

পরীক্ষিত *adj* examined; tested; tried; experimented; investigated; proven.

পরীক্ষোত্তীর্ণ *adj* successful/ passed at an examination; come through a test/ ordeal successfully; found suitable on trial/ test; qualified. **পরীক্ষোত্তীর্ণা** *fem.* **~ হওয়া** *vi* pass an examination/ ordeal; stand a test/ ordeal; qualify; be found suitable/ good on test/ trial.

পরীণাহ=পরিণাহ

পরুষ *adj* **1** hard; stiff; rugged; rough; uneven; shaggy. **2** piercing; keen; sharp; harsh; rude; violent; severe; unkind. **3** cruel: ~ হৃদয়; arrogant; haughty. **~কণ্ঠ** *n* harsh voice. ❑*adj* having a harsh voice; sharp-tongued; gruff voiced. **~কণ্ঠে** *adj* in a rough/ husky voice; rudely. **~তা, ~ত্ব** *nn* roughness; harshness; rudeness; arrogance; haughtiness; cruelty

~বচন, ~বাক্য *nn* harsh speech/ words; contumely; cutting/ unkind/ rude words/ remarks. ~বাদী, ~ভাষী *adjj* harsh-spoken; speaking unkindly; sharp-tongued.

পরুষোক্তি *n* harsh/ abusing language.

পরে১ *adv* **1** after; later; afterwards: সে তার ~ গেছে. **2** then; after this/ that; thereafter; thereupon; next: ~ সে হাসপাতালে চলে গেল. **3** in future; later; next: দেখো ~ কী হয়. ❑*prep* after; next to; following; beside: মালার ~ নীলা বসেছে, তুমি অফিস হওয়ার ~ এসেছো. **~ পরে** *adv* one after another; gradually; in succession; in course of time.

পরে২ *pron* others: ~ এ কথা শুনবে কেন?

'পরে *prep* in; on: তোমার ~ আমার বিশ্বাস আছে.

পরেশ *n* the highest lord; Brahma; Vishnu; God.

পরোক্ষ *adj* **1** beyond the range of sight; invisible; absent; unknown; unintelligible: ~ আর সমক্ষের ভেদ বিচার. **2** indirect: ~ উক্তি. **3** circumstantial: ~ প্রমাণ. **~ জ্ঞান** *n* **1** indirect knowledge. **2** transcendental knowledge. **~তা, ~ত্ব** *nn* **1** invisibility; imperceptibility. **2** indirectness. **~ প্রমাণ** *n* circumstantial evidence. **~ ভোগ** *n* enjoyment/ possession of sth in the proprietor/ absence. **পরোক্ষে** *adv* out of sight; behind one's back; in the absence/ without the knowledge of; secretly; indirectly.

পরোটা=পরটা

পরোপকার *n* assisting others; doing good to others; benevolence; charity; philanthroply; public welfare. **~ করা** *vi* do good to others; help others; do sb a good turn. **~ক** *adj* doing good to/ assisting others; benevolent; charitable; beneficient.

পরোপকারিতা *n*=পরোপকার

পরোপকারী=পরোপকারক (⇒ পরোপকার). **পরোপকারিণী** *fem.*

পরোপচিকীর্ষা *n* desire to do good to others; benevolence.

পরোপজীবী, পরোপজীব্য *adjj* living/ depending/ hanging on another for subsistence; parasitic.

পরোয়া [P] *n* care; concern; anxiety; want; fear; terror. **~ করা** *vi* care; pay heed to; be afraid of; fear. **কুছ ~ নেই** don't care; no fear; no matter; never mind.

পরোয়ানা= পরওয়ানা

পর্চা=পরচা

পর্জন্য *n* rain-cloud; cloud; rain; Indra, the god of rain.

পর্জারি [E] *n* perjury.

পর্ণ *n* **1** leaf of a tree. **2** betel-leaf. **3** feather; wing; plume. **~কার** *n* vender of betel. **~কুটির** *n* hut made of leaves; hut. **~পুট** *n* leaf rolled into the shape of a funnel. **~ভোজী** *adj* feeding on leaves. **~মোচী** *adj* deciduous. **~শয্যা** *n* couch of leaves. **~শালা**=~কুটির.

পর্ণাঙ্গ *n* (bot) fern.

পর্ণী *adj* leaf; leaved; leafed. ❑*n* tree.

পর্দা [P] *n* **1** curtain; screen; veil; cover; purdah; zenana: ~নশিন. **2** secrecy; privacy; modesty: মেয়েটার ~ নেই. **3** thin skin; membrane; film: চোখের ~. **4** drum of the ear. **5** covering; layer; strip; flake: চামড়ার ~. **6** (of voice) scale. **7** (of musical instruments) fret. **~ ওঠানো** *vi* lift/ raise the curtain/ a veil; expose; reveal. **~ করা** *vi* sit behind a curtain; live in purduh; maintain privacy; put on a veil. **~ দেওয়া** *vi* hung a curtain; draw the curtains. **~ রাখা** *vi* maintain privacy; hide things (from); relate a matter in such a way that it may be understood in part only. **~নশিন, ~নশীন** *adj* living in purdah; veiled. **~-প্রথা** *n* purduh-system. **চোখের ~** *n* (fig) sense of shame/ modesty.

পর্পট *n* **1** species of medicinal plant. **2**=পাঁপর.

পর্পটিকা, পর্পটী *nn* an Ayurvedic drug; *Aethiops mineral.*

পর্ব *n* **1** joint; knot; knuckle. **2** the period of a change of the moon. **3** break; pause; division; section (esp of a book); canto; chapter. **4** (bot) node. **5** holiday; festival; feast; fiesta. **6** step of a staircase; member of a compound. **7** phase. **~দিন**=~(5). **~মধ্য** *n* (bot) internode.

পর্বত *n* mountain; mountain-range; hill; hillock; rock; mount. **~কন্দর** *n* mountain-cave. **~চূড়া** *n* peak of a mountain; hill-top. **~নিবাসী**=~বাসী. **~পার্শ্ব** *n* mountain-side; hillside. **~প্রমাণ** *adj* mountain-high; high as a mountain; mountainous; gigantic; huge. **~বাসী** *adj* living in mountains; highland. ❑*n* mountain dweller; highlander. **~বাসিনী** *fem.* **~মালা**=~শ্রেণী. **~শিখর, ~শৃঙ্গ**=~চূড়া. **~শ্রেণী** *n* mountain-range. **~স্থ** *adj* situated on a mountain/ hill. **পর্বতাকার** *adj* mountain-shaped; formed like a mountain; mountainous; huge.

পর্বতীয় *adj* belonging to/ produced in mountains; highland; mountains.

পর্বাস্ফোট *n* cracking the fingers.

পর্বাহ=পর্ব (5)

পর্যঙ্ক *n* costly bedstead; couch; sofa; divan.

পর্যটক *n* traveller; tourist; perigrinator.

পর্যটন *n* travel; travelling; tour; perigrination; tourism. **~ করা** *vt* tour; travel; wander about; perigrinate. **~শীল** *adj* travelling; wandering.

পর্যন্ত *n* **1** limit; edge; border; end; extremity. **2** side; flank. ❑*prep* **1** to; to the end of; as far as; up to: রাস্তার মোড় ~. **2** till; until: তুমি না যাওয়া ~. ❑*adv* even; too; also: তার বাবা ~ তাকে দুচোখে দেখতে পারে না.

পর্যবসান *n* end; termination; close; conclusion; result; issue. **~ হওয়া** *vi* end in; amount to:

terminate; result in; perish; be lost; decline; conclude; be reduced to.

পর্যবসিত *adj* finished; ended; concluded; terminated; resolved (into); reduced to; resulting in. ~ **হওয়া**=পর্যবসান হওয়া.

পর্যবস্থা(ন) *n* opposition; contradiction.

পর্যবস্থিত *adj* standing; stationed; omnipresent.

পর্যবেক্ষক *adj* watching; observing. ❑*n* watcher; observer.

পর্যবেক্ষণ *n* observation; watching. ~ **করা** *vt* observe; watch.

পর্যবেক্ষণিকা *n* observatory.

পর্যবেক্ষিত *adj* watched; observed.

পর্যশ্রু *adj* bathed in tears; shedding tears; tearful.

পর্যসন *n* putting off/ away; removal; throwing/ tossing about; casting.

পর্যস্ত *adj* **1** thrown/ cast about; spread; scattered; diffused. **2** removed; thrown away. **3** overturned; upset; inverted; changed. **4** struck; killed; dismissed; laid aside.

পর্যাস্তিকা *n* bed.

পর্যাকুল *adj* full of; filled with; disordered; confused; excited; bewildered.

পর্যাটক=পর্যটক

পর্যাণ *n* saddle; circuit.

পর্যাপ্ত *adj* **1** adequate; equal to; sufficient; enough. **2** abundant; copious; many. **3** extensive; spacious; large; ample. **4** moderate; temperate. **5** competent; capable; a match to. **6** obtained; gained. **7** finished; completed; full. ❑*adj* fully; completely; enough; one's fill: সে ~ খেয়েছে.

পর্যাপ্তি *n* **1** sufficiency; fullness; entireness; plenty; amplitude. **2** adequacy; competency; fitness for; capability; competence. **3** obtaining; acquisition; gain.

পর্যাবর্তক *adj* periodic.

পর্যাবৃত্ত *adj* periodic.

পর্যাবৃত্তি *n* periodicity.

পর্যায় *n* **1** regular recurrence; repetition; alternation; succession; turn. **2** going/ turning/ winding round; revolving; revolution: ঋতু~. **3** course; lapse; expiration of time. **4** convertible term; synonym: ~-শব্দ. **5** way; manner; method of proceeding. **6** opportunity; occasion. **7** serial order; state; condition; shape; form; series: নব~. **8** phase; grade. **9** generation. **10** period. ~**কাল** *n* period. ~**ক্রম** *n* order of succession; regular rotation/ turn. ~**ক্রমে** *adv* in turn; successively; alternately; (consecutively) by turns; serially. ~**শব্দ** *n* synonym. ~**শয়ন** *n* alternate to sleeping and watching. ~**সম** *n* alternate rhyme. ~**সারণী** *n* (chem) periodic table.

পর্যায়িক *adj* periodic; composed in strophes.

পর্যায়ী *adj* periodical.

পর্যায়োক্ত *adj* said successively. ❑*n* (rhet) a figure of speech in which the fact to be intimated is expressed by a turn of speech or periphrasis.

পর্যালোচন(া) *n* consideration; reflection; thorough study/ discussion/ review. ~ **করা** *vt* consider; ponder; study/ discuss/ review thoroughly.

পর্যালোচিত *adj* considered; pondered; studied/ discussed/ reviewed thoroughly.

পর্যাস *n* **1** inverted order/ position; disorder; confusion; reversal; great change. **2** rotation; revolution. **3** end; conclusion.

পর্যাসিত *adj* upset; topsyturvy; inverted; reverse.

পর্যাহার *n* carrying; conveying; transfer.

পর্যুৎসুক *adj* very restless; much excited; eagerly desirous; longing for.

পর্যুদস্ত *adj* **1** utterly defeated; crushed; routed. **2** prevented; repulsed; foiled; marred; completely baffled; totally forbidden. ~ **করা** *vt* defeat utterly; crush; rout; prevent; repulse; baffle; mar; foil; forbid totally.

পর্যুদাস *n* utter/ crushing defeat; rout; prevention; repulsion; complete frustration; bafflement.

পর্যুষিত *adj* having passed the night; not fresh; stale; insipid.

পর্যেষণ(া) *n* search; inquiry; study; investigation; research.

পর্শু *n*=পরশু

পর্শুকা *n* rib; vertebra.

পর্ষৎ, পর্ষদ (=পরিষদ) *nn* assembly; council; board; society; company; audience.

পল[১] *n* **1** a measure of time (=24 seconds); moment; instant; a while. **2** a measure of weight (=46·8 gr).

পল[২] [P] *n* bevel; side; edge. ~**-তোলা** *adj* bevelled.

পলক *n* **1** eyelashes. **2** wink (of eyes); twinkling of an eye. **3** moment; instant. ~ **খোলা** *vi* open one's eyes. ~ **পড়া** *vi* (of eyes) close; wink. ~ **ফেলা** *vi* blink; wink; close the eyelids. ~**পাত** *n* closing of eyelids. ~**মধ্যে**=পলকে. ~**রহিত, ~শূন্য, ~হীন** *adjj* **1** (of eyes) unblinking; unwinking. **2** (of look) steady; fixed. ~**হীনভাবে** *adv* unblinkingly; without blinking; steadily. **(এক) পলকে** *adv* in the twinkling of an eye; in an instant; in a moment; instantaneously. **পলকে পলকে** *adv* every moment; in very quick succession. **পলকে প্রলয়** *n* instant disaster.

পলকা *adj* **1** fragile; brittle; friable; flimsy. **2** frail; delicate; slight. **3** worthless; insubstantial; paltry; trifling; trashy.

পলটন [E] *n* platoon; armed force. **পলটনি** *adj* of a platoon; military.
পলটি *vi* (imperfect) turning back.
পলতা *n* the creeper bearing 'patol' (পটোল); its leaves.
পলতে *n* (colloq)=পলিতা
পলল *n* **1** meat. **2** silt; slime; mud; mire. **3** kind of sweetmeat made of ground sesame seeds. **~-ভূমি** *n* alluvial soil.
পলস্তারা [E] *n* plaster. **~ দেওয়া/ লাগানো** *vt* plaster (a wall, etc).
পলা *n* **1** coral. **2** kind of iron ladle.
পলাগ্নি *n* bile; bilious humour.
পলাণ্ডু *n* onion.
পলাতক *adj* fled; fugitive; fleeing; taking to flight; absconding; run away. ❑*n* fugitive; absconder; runaway. **পলাতকা** *fem.* **~ হওয়া** *vi* abscond; flee; run away.
পলানে *adi*=পালানো
পলানো *vi*=পালানো
পলান্ন *n* rice with meat.
পলায়ন *n* flight; fleeing; escape; running away. **~ করা**=পালানো. **~পর** *adj* fleeing; fugitive; absconding; escaping; retreating.
পলায়নোদ্যত *adj* about to run away; on the point of fleeing/ running away/ making one's escape; attempting to flee/ escape.
পলায়মান=পলায়নপর (⇒ পলায়ন)
পলায়িত *adj* fled; absconded escaped; runaway. **পলায়িতা** *fem.*
পলাশ *n* **1** the tree frondosa. **2** leaf; petal; foliage.
পলি *n* silt; alluvium. **~ পড়া** *vi* silt (up); collect alluvial deposits. **~-পড়া** *adj* silted. **~জ** *adj* alluvial.
পলিত *adj* prey; hoary; old; aged. ❑*n* greyness; hoariness. **~ কেশ** *adj* hoary-headed; grey-haird; old; ayed.
পলিতা [P] *n* wick (of a lamp); match (of gun). **~ ধরা** *vi* **1** (of a lamp/ wick) be lighted/ ignited. **2** (fig) be excited/ enthusiastic (about/ over); enthuse (about/ over).
পলিদ [P] *adj* unclean; polluted; defiled.
পলিসি [E] *n* policy. **~বাজ** *adj* self-seeking; scheming.
পলীয় *n* protein.
পলু *n* species of silk-worm living on the mulberry tree.
পলেস্তারা=পলস্তারা
পলো *n* a basket of wicker-work for catching fish.
পল্টন=পলটন
পল্যঙ্ক=পর্যঙ্ক
পল্যয়ন *n* saddle; caparison.
পল্লব *n* **1** sprout; shoot; twig; spray. **2** bud; blossom. **3** lid: অক্ষি~. **~গ্রাহিতা** *n* superficial knowledge; eclecticism. **~গ্রাহী** *adj* superficial (as knowledge); eclectic; diffusive; dilettantish. **~গ্রাহিণী, ~গ্রাহী লোক** *n* dilettante; jack-of-all-trades; dabbler. **পল্লবাধার** *n* branch.
পল্লবিত *adj* **1** sprouted; having young shoots; leafy; lush; luxuriant. **2** (fig) diffuse; prolix; exaggerated.
পল্লি, পল্লী *n* **1** small village; hamlet; locality. **2** municipal division; ward; quarter; district. **~-অঞ্চল** *n* rural areas; country-side. **~উন্নয়ন** *n* village development; rural uplift. **~গীত, ~গীতি** *n* folk-song. **~গ্রাম** *vi* village; countryside; rural areas. **~গ্রামবাসী** *adj* living in a village; rural. ❑*n* villager; countryman; countrywoman; rural people; country folk. **~জীবন** *n* rural/ country life. **~নৃত্য** *n* country dance; folk-dance. **~বধূ** *n* country woman; country-wife. **~বালা, ~বালিকা** *nn* country-girl; country-maid; village girl. **~বাস** *n* living in the country; country-house; village home; country residence. **~বাসী**=~গ্রামবাসী. **~বাসিনী** *fem.* **~ভবন** *n* country-house; country-seat. **~মঙ্গল** *vi* village welfare. **~সংগঠন** *n* rural organization. **~সংস্কার** *n* rural reconstruction. **~সঙ্ঘ** *n* rural association/ organization. **~ সমিতি** *n* village society; rural association.
পল্বল *n* pool; small tank; pond.
পশতু, পশতো *n* Pashto (the language of the Pathans).
পশম [P] *n* wool; fur; hair. **~ পরিষ্কার করা** *vi* card/ comb wool.
পশমি, পশমী *adj* woollen; hairy.
পশমিনা *n* a kind of woollen cloth.
পশরা=পসরা
পশলা *n* short spell; brief fall; shower: এক ~ বৃষ্টি.
পশা *vi* (poet) enter; penetrate.
পশার, পশরা, পশারী=পসার, পসারা and পসারী respectively.
পশু *n* **1** quadruped animal; beast. **2** brute; brutal/ beastly man. **~চর্ম** *n* animal's skin; hide; pelt. **~চারণ** *n* grazing cattle. **~ চারণ করা** *vi* graze/pasture cattle. **~চারণ ক্ষেত্র** *n* pasture; pasturage. **~চারণযোগ্য** *adj* pasturable. **~চিকিৎসক** *n* veterinary surgeon. **~ত্ব** *n* bestiality; animality; brutality. **~ধর্ম** *n* law of animals; manner of beasts; copulation; animal desires; bestiality. **~ধর্মী** *adj* bestial; beastly; brutal; given to excessive sexual intercourse. **~পতি** *n* lord of animals; Shiva. **~পাল** *n* **1** herd/ flock of animals/ cattle. **2** keeper of herds; herdsman; cowherd; shepherd. **~পালক**=~পাল (2). **~পালন** *n* tending/ rearing of cattle; cattle breeding; animal husbandry/ farming. **~পালন-বিশারদ** *n* livestock expert. **~বৎ** *adj* like an animal; as in an animal; beastlike; beastly; brutal; bestial. **~বৎ আচরণ** *n* bestiality; brutality. **~ভাব**

n=~ধর্ম. ~রজ্জু *n* rope for tethering cattle. ~রাজ *n* king of beasts; lion. ~লোম *n* wool; fur. ~শক্তি *n* brute force. ~শালা *n* stable; cattleshed; zoo. ~শিকার *n* hunting (of animals). ~শিকারি *n* hunter (of animals). ~সুলভ=~বৎ. কোরবানির ~ *n* sacrificial animal. গবাদি পশু *n* cattle. গৃহপালিত পশু *n* domestic animal; livestock. বলির পশু *n* sacrificial animal; victim. ভারবাহী ~ *n* beast of burden; pack animal; draught animal. শিকারি ~ *n* beast of prey. শিকারের পশু *n* game.

পশুরি=পসুরি

পশ্চাৎ *prep* (from) behind; in the rear; backwards; at/ to the back of; after. ❑*adv* afterwards; later; at last; there after; from/ in the west; westwards; after. ❑*adj* back; reverse: পশ্চাদ্দ্বার. ❑*n* back; rear; backside; hindquarters; buttocks; behind; future. **পশ্চাতে** *adv, prep* behind. ~পদ *adj* lagging behind; retreated; turned back; withdrawn. ~পদ হওয়া *vi* lag behind; retreat; turn back; withdraw.

পশ্চাত্তাপ *n* regret; repentance; remorse; sorrow.

পশ্চাদ্‌ (in compounds)=পশ্চাৎ. ~গতি *n* regression; retrograde motion. ~গমন *n* going after; following. ~গমন করা *vi* go after; follow. ~গামী *adj* going after; in pursuit; following; in the wake of; coming after/ next; succeeding; trailing. ~গামিনী *fem.* ~গামী হওয়া *vi* go/ come after; follow; pursue; come/ go next; succeed; trail. ~দ্বার *n* back door. ~ধাবন *n* running after; pursuing; chasing; chase; pursuit; hunt. ~ধাবন করা *vt* run after; chase; pursue; give chase; track; trail; dog the footsteps of. ~ধাবিত *adj* running after; chasing; pursuing; trailing. ~বর্তী *adj* remaining/ lagging behind; following after; trailing along (behind sb/ sth). ~বর্তিনী *fem.* ~বর্তী হওয়া *vi* remain/ lag behind; follow after; trail along (behind sb/ sth). ~ভাগ *n* backside; rear; back; behind. ~ভাগে *adv* in the rear; behind. ~ভূমি *n* rear; hinterland; background.

পশ্চাদনুসরণ *n*=পশ্চাদ্‌গমন (⇒ পশ্চাদ্‌). ~কারী = পশ্চাদ্‌গামী. ~কারিণী *fem.*

পশ্চাদপসরণ *n* retreat; withdrawal. ~ করা *vi* retreat; withdraw; turn/ move/ fall back.

পশ্চার্ধ *n* lower half (of the human body); latter/ other half.

পশ্চিম *adj* west; western; westerly; final; last; ultimate; subsequent. ❑*n* the west; the Occident; western world/ hemisphere. ~দেশীয় *adj* western; of a western country; up-country. ~বঙ্গ *n* West Bengal. ~ বায়ুপ্রবাহ *n* west wind; westerly winds. ~ ভারতীয় দ্বীপপুঞ্জ *n* the West Indies. **পাশ্চিমা** *adj* western; up-country. ❑*n* up-country man. **পশ্চিমাঞ্চল** *n* western region/ part. **পশ্চিমার্ধ** *n* hind-part; later half. **পশ্চিমাস্য** *adj* facing westward.

পশ্চিমী *adj* western; Occidental.

পশ্চিমোত্তরা *adj* north-western.

পশ্বাচার *n* **1** particular form of Tantrik worship. **2** beastly conduct; bestiality.

পশ্বাচারী *n* **1** practising পশ্বাচার. **2** bestial; brutal.

পশ্বাধম *adj* even worse than a beast/ brute.

পষ্ট *adj* (colloq)=স্পষ্ট

পষ্টাপষ্টি=স্পষ্টাস্পষ্টি

পসন্দ=(পছন্দ) [P] *n* choice; liking; approval; preference; approbation; selection. ❑*adj* chosen; fovourite; liked; approved; desirable; selected. ~ করা *vt* choose; like; select; approve; prefer. ~মাফিক, ~সই *adjj* to one's liking; choice; select.

পসরা *n* **1** commodity; articles for sale; merchandise; wares; goods: ~ সাজানো. **2** load/ heap of articles for sale. **3** basket containing articles for sale; basket of wares. **4** (fig) load; heap; basket: কলঙ্কের ~. ~ সাজানো *vi* display one's wares.

পসলা=পশলা

পসার[১] *n* **1** shop; bazaar; market-place. **2** wares; articles of traffic; basket of wares.

পসার[২] *n* **1** (good) practice; professional man's business; good reputation; fame; influence. **2** extension; width.

পসারা *vt* (poet) extend; stretch out; spread; display.

পসারি, পসারী *n* shopkeeper; seller; pedlar; dealer. **পসারিণী** *fem.*

পসুরি, পসুরী *n* a measure of weight (= five seers).

পস্তানি *n* regret; repentance.

পস্তানো *vi* repent; regret; rue.

পস্তু=পশতু

পহর *n* (colloq)=প্রহর

পহলবি [P] *n* Pahlavi.

পহেলা *adj* (esp of days of a month) first: ~ বৈশাখ, ~ নম্বর. ❑*adv* first; at first. ❑*n* the first (day of a month).

পা[১] *n* **1** leg; foot; paw. **2** leg of a piece of furniture. ~ ওঠা *vi* (of a foot) be raised to kick. ~ চলা *vi* (of a person) be quick-footed. ~ চাটা *vi* lick sb's boots; toady. ~-চাটা *adj* bootlicking; servile; obsequious. ❑*n* toady; bootlicker; truckler. ~ চালানো *vi* **1** quicken one's steps; step out. **2** kick; hoof. ~ জড়িয়ে পড়া *vi* falter (because of weakness, fear, modesty, etc); waver; feel faint and tottery. ~ টেপা *vi* massage sb's feet. ~ তোলা *vi* raise one's foot (to kick); set out. ~ দেওয়া *vi* set foot in/ on sth; step in; arrive. ~ ধরা=পায়ে ধরা. ~ ধুতেও না আসা *vt* avoid visiting/ using a place out of sheer contempt/ abomination; deign to visit/ set one s foot in/ on. ~ না ওঠা *vi* dare not proceed/ set out; not have the heart to; feel diffident (about sth). ~ ফেলা *vi*, step (in); tread; set one's foot in/ on; set one's foot down. ~ বাড়ানো *vi* **1** set out; be on the point of setting out/ going/ departing; turn one's back on; take off. **2** step out; go out; leave. ~ ভারী হওয়া *vi* have swollen feet. ~ টিপে (টিপে) *adv* on tiptoe; stealthily. ~-পা (করে) *adv* step by step. **পায়ে ঠেলা** *vi* spurn; reject/ refuse (sb/ sth) scornfully or contemptuously. **পায়ে তেল দেওয়া** *vi* toady (to sb); soft-soap; curry favour (with sb). **পায়ে দলা** *vi* trample sth/ sb (down); trample on sth/ sb; tread sth (in/ down/ out); crush sth with feet. **পায়ে ধরা** *vi* supplicate/ implore/ entreat humbly. **পায়ে পড়া** *vi* fall at sb's feet in supplication. **পায়ে-পায়ে, পায়-পায়** *adv* **1** at every step: পায়ে-পায়ে বাধা. **2** pursuing; dogging sb's footsteps; following closely: পুলিশ তাদের পায়ে-পায়ে অনুসরণ করছে. **3** with slow but steady steps: পায়ে-পায়ে এগিয়ে যাওয়া. **4** having legs tied together; having one another's legs tied together. **পায়ের উপর পা দিয়ে থাকা** *vt* lead a care-free life/ life of ease; be rolling (in money). **পায়ের ধূলি** *n* dust of sb's feet. **পায়ের পাতা** *n* instep; foot. **পাঁয়ে রাখা** *vt* treat/ shelter graciously. **পায়ে হাত দেওয়া** *vi* touch sb's feet in obeisance. **ধূলা পায়ে** *adv* **1** without washing one's feet. **2** directly; immediately; at once.

পা[২] *n* the fifth note of the gamut.

পাই *n* an obsolete Indian coin (1 rupee=16 annas=192 pie) pie.

পাইক [P] *n* foot soldier; footman; infantry-man. **2** courier; messenger; runner. ~-**বরকন্দাজ** *n* footmen and other followers.

পাইকা [E] *n* pica.

পাইকার, পাইকের (colloq) *n* wholesale buyer/ trader; wholesaler; pedlar.

পাইকারি, পাইকারী *adj* **1** wholesale. **2** collective: ~ জরিমানা.

পাইখানা=পায়খানা

পাইন=পান[২]

পাইন্ট [E] *n* pint.

পাইপ [E] *n* pipe.

পাইলট [E] *n* pilot.

পাউডার [E] *n* powder. ~ **বোলানো/ মাখা** *vi* daub/ dust with powder; powder. **পাউডারের কৌটা** *n* powder-box; powder-case.

পাউন্ড [E] *n* pound.

পাউরুটি, পাঁউরুটি *n* bread (baked in the European fashion).

পাওন *n* act of getting/ obtaining/ attaining; receiving.

পাওনা *n* **1** due; arrears; money due to sb: তার কাছে আমার পাঁচ হাজার টাকা ~, He owes me five thousand takas. **2** earnings; income: উপরি ~. **3** assets; outstanding bills: দেনা-~. ❑*adj* that which ought to be paid/ done to sb; due. ~ **আদায় করা** *vi* realize what is due; realize a bill. ~ **দেওয়া/ মেটানো** *vi* pay what is due; make payment; foot the bill. ~-**গণ্ডা**, ~-**থোওনা** *nn* dues; earnings; income. ~**দার** *n* creditor.

পাওয়া *vt, vi* **1** get; receive; obtain; take in: খবর ~, আশীর্বাদ ~. **2** attain; achieve; realize: সিদ্ধি ~. **3** earn; gain; acquire; win: টাকা ~. **4** find: চাকরি ~. **5** inherit: সে তার মায়ের চেহারা পেয়েছে. **6** be able to: শুনতে ~. **7** feel; be stricken with: ক্ষুধা/তৃষ্ণা ~. **8** sustain: আঘাত ~. **9** come/ happen to; come upon: দেখতে ~. **10** feel like: কান্না ~. **11** enjoy: আরাম ~. **12** be possessed by: ভূতে ~. **13** sense; be aware of; get scent: টের ~. ❑*adj* **1** obtained; earned: ~ জিনিস. **2** possessed: ভূতে ~ লোক. **পড়ে ~** *vt* get by chance; come upon. **প্রকাশ ~** *vi* appear; be revealed. **যো ~** *vt* get an opportunity.

পাওয়ানো *vt* cause to get/ obtain/ find/ gain/ attain; procure.

পাওয়ার [E] *n* power.

পাংশন *adj* defiling; vitiating; disgracing; spoiling: কুল~.

পাংশু *adj* **1** dusty; sandy; ashy. **2** livid; pale: ~ মুখ. ❑*n* **1** dust; sand; crumbling soil. **2** dung; manure. ~ **বর্ণ** *adj* ash-coloured; ashen; ashy (grey); livid. ❑*n* ash-colour. ~**ল** *adj* **1** dusty; sandy; ashy; grey. **2** sullied; defiled; disgraced by. ~**লা** *fem.* ❑*n* **1** the earth. **2** licentious woman.

পাংসন =পাংশন

পাঁইজ *n* (archaic) =পাঁজ

পাঁইজর=পাঁয়জোর

পাঁইট [E] *n* pint.

পাঁউরুটি =পাউরুটি

পাঁক *n* slime; mud; silt.

পাঁকাটি=পাকাটি

পাঁকাল *n* **1** kind of eel. **2**=পান্তাভাত. ❑*adj* muddy; miry; slimy.

পাঁকুই *n* foot-sore caused by mud; chilblain.

পাঁচ *n, adj* five. ~**ই** *adj* (of the days of a month) fifth. ❑*n* the fifth day of the month; the fifth. ~ **কথা** *n* lot of talking; many and varied topics; harsh words; reproof; rebuke; talking-to. ~ **জন** *n* **1** (lit) five persons. **2** (fig) people at large; they; others. ~**নর** *n* five-stringed necklace. ~**নরী** *n*=~নর. ❑*adj* five-stringed. ~-**ফোড়ন** *n* five kinds of spices collectively (namely, cumin-seed, black cumin-seed, aniseed, fenugreek seed and parsley). ~**মিশালি** *adj* assorted. ~**হাতি** *adj* five cubits long: ~হাতি চাদর.

পাঁচড়া *n* scabies; itches.

পাঁচন *n* medicinal preparation/ decoction (prepared by boiling five different herbs).
পাঁচনবাড়ি, পাঁচনি=পাচনবাড়ি
পাঁচাপাঁচি *n* altercation; argumentation; affray; quibble.
পাঁচালি, পাঁচালী *n* **1** kind of Bengali dramatic poem often set to music. **2** (fig) long-winding; narrative.
পাঁচিল *n* fence; wall.
পাঁচুই *n adj* (colloq) পাঁচই (⇒ পাঁচ)
পাঁজ *n* **1** skein/roll/wisp of carded cotton. **2** thick wick.
পাঁজর, পাঁজরা *nn* rib; the ribs; rib-bone; thorax.
পাঁজা[1] *n* kiln; brick-kiln.
পাঁজা[2] *n* bundle; faggot; heap; pile. **~ করা** *vt* pile; bundle; heap.
পাঁজা[3] [P] *n* **1** the hand with fingers extended. **2** outspread hands in the form of a stretcher. **~কোলা** *adj* lifted upon hands outspread in the shape of a stretcher. **~কোলা করা** *vt* lift on hands outspread in the shape of a stretcher.
পাঁজি, পাঁজী *n* almanac; calendar. **~পুঁথি** *n* books (collectively); papers; books and manuscripts. **হাতে ~ মঙ্গলবার** (fig) unnecessary anxiety for a solution which is already there.
পাঁট [E] *n* pint.
পাঁঠা *n* **1** he-goat. **2** (derog) fool; ass; body. **পাঁঠী** *fem.*
পাঁড় *adj* **1** ripe: ~ শশা. **2** inveterate: ~ মাতাল.
পাঁতি *n* **1** row; line; range: দাঁতের ~. **2** scriptural prescription; citation from scriptures: ~ দেওয়া. **3** list. **4** style; manner: কথার ~. **5** particulars; information about identity: জাতির ~. **6** letter. **~পত্র** *n* solemn marriage contract drawn up in black and white. **~পত্র করা** *vi* draw up a solemn marriage contract in black and white. **~পাঁতি করে** *adv* thoroughly.
পাঁদাড় *n* dump/rubbish-heap (at the back of a house; backside of the house).
পাঁপড়, পাঁপর[1] *n* thin crisp cake made of pulse mixed with spices. **~ বেলা** *vi* roll out thin crisp cakes.
পাঁপর[2] [E] *n* pauper.
পাঁয়জোর *n* anklet fitted with small jingling bells.
পাঁয়তারা [A] *n* **1** act of pacing to find an opportunity to attack/grapple (as in wrestling). **2** preliminary preparations; getting ready. **~ কষা** *vt* **1** pace up and down to find a suitable moment to attack/grapple. **2** prepare oneself; get ready.
পাঁশ *n* **1** ashes; ashes of cow-dung. **2** worthless thing; rubbish. **~কুড়** *n* rubbish-heap; heap of ashes.
পাঁশুটে *adj* ash-coloured; ashen; livid; pale.
পাক[1] *n* **1** cooking; baking; roasting; boiling. **2** condensing by heat: সন্দেশের ~. **3** digestion; assimilation of food. **4** development of consequences; result: বিপাক. **~ করা** *vt* cook; bake; roast; boil. **~ ধরা** *vi* be condensed by heat. **~ হওয়া** *vi* be cooked/boiled; be ready to be served. **~কর্ম, ~ক্রিয়া** *n* **1** act of cooking. **2** digestion. **~জ** *adj* produced by cooking/ roasting. **~তৈল** *n* medicinal oil. **~পাত্র** *n* cooking utensil; boiler. **~মণ্ড** *n* chyme. **~যন্ত্র** *n* digestive organ; stomach. **~যন্ত্র প্রদাহ** *n* inflammation of the stomach; gastritis. **~শাক** *n* cookery and other kitchen service. **~শালা** *n* cooking-room; kitchen. **~স্থলী** *n* stomach. **~স্থালী**=~পাত্র.
পাক[2] *n* ripening; greyness. **~ ধরা** *vi* begin to (turn) grey.
পাক[3] *n* **1** going round; winding; spin; twist; whirl; circumambulation; revolution: rotation; circular movement; gyration. **2** ring; coil: জিলাপির ~. **3** twisting (of a rope). **4** providential/ chance occurrence: পাকেচক্রে. **5** intrigue; conspiracy; plot; trap; tangle. **6** course: ~চক্রে. **~ খাওয়া** *vi* **1** go round; wind; spin; twirl; rotate; revolve; turn round; gyrate; pivot; swivel. **2** twist; twine; tangle; ravel. **~ দেওয়া** *vt, vi* **1** go round; rotate; gyrate; whirl; revolve; writhe; turn round. **2** twist; twirl; coil; twine; ravel. **~ ধরা** *vi* twine: এ সুতায় কিছুতেই ~ ধরে না. **~ পড়া/লাগা** *vi* become twisted/ tangled; get tangled up. **~ লাগানো**=~ দেওয়া. **পাকে পড়া** *vi* get/become entangled (with); get into difficulty/ trouble; be in a predicament; be in a (tight) corner; fell in a trap. **পাকে ফেলা** *vt* get sb into trouble; trap sb (into sth). **~দণ্ডী** *n* circuitous/ spiral route leading to the top of a mountain. **পাকেচক্রে, পাকে-প্রকারে** *adv* by this trick or other; somehow; by hook or by crook; through cunning devices; cunningly.
পাক[4] [P] *adj* pare; clean; holy; spotless; immaculate; sacred; chaste; innocent. **~ সাফ** *adj* pure; chaste; clean; undefiled; unpolluted. **~ সাফ করা** *vt* purify; clean; wash.
পাকচক্র *n* **1** intrigue; cunning device; machination; scheme. **2** complexity; intricacy; mystery: সে ~ ভেদ করা সহজ নয়. **পাকচক্রে**=পাকেচক্রে (⇒ পাক[3]).
পাকজল *n* whirlpool; eddy; vortex; maelstrom.
পাকড় *n* act of seizing; seizing; arrest; capture; hold; grip; wrestling; grasp; clutch. **পাকড়াও** *n* arrest; seizure; capture. **পাকড়াও করা** *vt* catch; arrest; lay hold of; seize; apprehend; overtake. **পাকড়ানো**=পাকড়াও করা.
পাকতেড়ে *adj* lean; tangy; skinny; scraggy; scrawny; gangling.

পাকন *n* **1** ripening; ripeness; maturing. **2** turning grey; greying. **3** suppuration. **4** being seasoned/experienced. **5** (derog) becoming precocious/depraved.

পাকনা *n* (colloq) **1** =পাখনা. **2** shoulder blades. **3** fins. **4** eddy.

পাকনাড়া *n* rotation; whirl; spin.

পাকপুটি *n* kiln.

পাকমোড়া *n* **1** fastening with a twisted rope. **2** fastening (the arms) behind the back.

পাকল[১] *adj* red; crimson. ❑*n* name of a fragrant medicinal herb; *Cansurea ceuriculata.*

পাকল[২], **পাকলো** *adj* ripening; (almost) ripe; mellow; mature.

পাকলা *adj* =পাকল[২]

পাকলানো[১] =পাখলানো (⇒ পাখলা)

পাকলানো[২] *vt* (archaic, poet) redden: ~ চোখ, bloodshot eyes.

পাকসাঁড়াশি *n* turn-screw; vice; pair of pincers/tongs.

পাকসাট=পাখসাট

পাকা *n vi* **1** ripen; mellow: ফল ~. **2** mature; attain maturity; ripen: বুদ্ধি ~. **3** grey; turn grey: চুল ~. **4** suppurate: ফোঁড়া ~. ⇒ become seasoned; ripen; mature: লোকটা আজন্মকাল দেখে দেখে পেকে গেছে. **5** be hardened: শয়তানিতে ~. **6** be skilled/ experienced/ seasoned: রাজনীতিতে সে বেশ পেকেছে. **7** be precocious/ forward; become spoilt/depraved: এই বয়সেই ছোঁড়াটা খুব পেকেছে. ❑*adj* **1** ripe; mature; mellow: ~ আম. **2** grey: ~ চুল. **3** grey haired; hoary; grizzled: ~ মাথা. **4** glib; slick: কথায় ~. **5** skilled; expert; experienced; seasoned: পরীক্ষায় বোঝা গেল সে বেশ ~ লোক. **6** sound; solid. **7** consummate; skillful; adroit: ~ শিল্পী/ রাঁধুনি. **8** baked; burnt: ~ ইট. **9** brick-built; made of brick: ~ বাড়ি. **10** metalled: ~ রাস্তা. **11** concrete: ~ ছাদ. **12** inveterate; hardened; consummate: ~ বদমাশ. **13** permanent: ~ চাকরি. **14** standard; full; net: ~ ওজন, ~ পাঁচ সের. **15** fast; lasting; durable: ~ রং. **16** final; firm; fixed; settled : ~ কথা/ তারিখ. **17** downright; thorough: ~ বদমাশি. **18** set: তার ~ হাতের লেখা, He writes a good/legible hand. **19** precocious; forward; spoilt; depraved: ছেলেটি এই বয়সেই বেশ ~. **20** pure; genuine; unalloyed: ~ সোনা. **21** perfect; consummate; impeccable; of a high standard: ~ লেখা. **22** seasoned: ~ কাঠ. **23** tanned: ~ চামড়া. **24** legally/formally drawn up: ~ দলিল. **25** consisting of pieces of লুচি and sweet-meat; substantial: ~ ফলার. **26** (of a সের) consisting of 80 or more tolas (তোলা): ~ সের. ~ **ওজন** *n* standard measure, esp in which one seer (সের) is equal to 80 tolas or more. ~ **কথা** *n* (final) word; promise. ~ **করা** *vt* confirm; finalize. ~ **কলা পাওয়া** (fig) get sth without toil/hardship; achieve without undergoing much trouble. ~ **খাতা** *n* finalized book of accounts. ~ **গাঁথনি/গাঁথুনি** *n* mortar. ~ **ঘর** *n* house made of brick. ~ **ঘুঁটি** *n* (in dice and similar games) an advanced piece. ~ **ঘুঁটি কেঁচে যাওয়া** (fig) be undone what is almost done; come to nothing; come unstuck. ~ **চামড়া** *n* leather. ~ **তাল** *n* (fig) heavy blow. ~ **দেখা** *vi* visit formally a prospective bride's house in order to arrange a marriage. ~**-দেখা** *n* formal visit to a prospective bride's house in order to arrange a marriage; final view of a girl by the bridegroom's party before she is accepted in marriage. ~ **ধানে মই দেওয়া** (fig) undo an accomplished piece of work; wreck sb's good prospects; do incalculable harm to. ~**পনা** =পাকামি. ~**পাকি** *adj* settled; confirmed; fixed; finalized; sure; firm. ~**পাকি করা** *vt* settle; finalize; confirm; fix; make sure. ~**পোক্ত** *adj* **1** permanent; finalized; confirmed; settled; fixed. **2** seasoned; experienced; veteran: ~পোক্ত রাজনীতিক. ~ **বয়স** *n* ripe years; ripe old age. ~ **বাড়ি** *n* house made of brick; building. ~ **বুদ্ধি** *n* mature/careful thought; sharp/acute intelligence. ~ **মাছ** *n* full/fully grown fish. ~ **মাটি** *n* baked clay; hard/burnt soil. ~ **মাথা** *n* mature brain. ~ **মাথায় সিঁদুর পরা** (of a woman) have one's husband living even in ripe old age. ~ **রাস্তা** *n* metalled road. ~ **লোহা** *n* steel. ~ **হাড়ে ভেলকি দেখানো** show amazing power/proficiency even in one's old age. ~ **হাত** *n* set/good hand; skilled/old hand; experienced person; veteran; expert; adept. ~ **হিসাব** *n* final accounts.

পাকাটি *n* **1** stalks of hemp, jute, etc when the fibres have been stripped off. **2** (fig) lean rickety person.

পাকাটে *adj* skinny; rickety; wizened.

পাকানে *adj* **1** cooking. **2** causing to ripen. **3** twisting; screwing.

পাকানো *vt* **1** cook. **2** (cause to) ripen; mature. **3** twist; screw; twirl. **4** cause to turn grey; grey. **5** cause to suppurate. **6** wring; writhe: শরীর ~. **7** organize; form; brew sth (up): দল ~. **8** complicate: তুমি পুরো ব্যাপারটাকে পাকিয়ে তুলেছ. **9** wizen; shrivel; emaciate. **10** season. **11** make experienced/skilled; hardened. **12** make precocious; sproil; deprave. ❑*adj* **1** cooked. **2** ripened. **3** twisted; twirled; ravelled; screwed. **4** muscular: ~ শরীর.

পাকামি, পাকামো *nn* precocity; forwardness; depravity. ~ **করা** *vi* be precocious; behave precociously.

পাকাশয় *n* stomach. ~ **প্রদাহ** *n* inflammation of the stomach; gastritis.

পাকাশয়িক *adj* stomachal; stomachic; gastric.

পাকি[১] [P] *n* cleanliness; purity.

পাকি[২] *adj* measured by the standard weight in which one seer is equal to 80 tolas or more; standard.

পাকিস্তান *n* Pakistan. **পাকিস্তানি** *n adj* Pakistani.

পাকুড় *n* kind of fig-tree; *Ficus infectoria.*

পাকোয়ান *n* cooked/dressed food; victuals fried in butter or oil; cakes; pastry.

পাক্কা *adj* (emphatic) =পাকা

পাক্ষিক *adj* **1** fortnightly. **2** partisan; biased. ❑*n* fortnightly journal.

পাখ *n* =পাখনা. ~ **পাখালি** *n* birds of various kinds.

পাখওয়াজ=পাখোয়াজ

পাখনা *n* **1** wing; feather. **2** fin.

পাখলা *n* rubbing and washing; scouring; rinsing. ~**নো** *vt* rub and wash; scour; rinse.

পাখসাট *n* flow/flap of wings; flapping of wings. ~ **মারা** *vi* (of birds) flap one's wings.

পাখা *n* **1** wing; feather. **2** fin. **3** fan. **4** propeller. **5** vane/sail (of a windmill). ~ **ওঠা** *vi* grow wings. ~ **করা** *vt* fan. ~ **গজানো** =~ ওঠা. ~ **ঘোরানো** *vi* set a propeller/ vane moving/in motion; switch on an electric fan. ~ **ঝাপটানো** *vi* (of a bird) flutter/flap one's wings. ~ **টানা** *vi* pull a punkah. **টানা** ~ *n* large fan suspended from a pole and moved by pulling; punkah; panka. **বিজলি/ বৈদ্যুতিক** ~ *n* electric fan. **হাত** ~ *n* fan.

পাখাওয়ালা *adj* **1** winged; feathered. **2** finned. **3** having a propeller/ vane/ sail. ❑*n* **1** punkah puller. **2** dealer/ pedlar of fans. **3** repairer of electric fans.

পাখি, পাখী *n* **1** bird. **2** blind (of a window). **3** spoke (of a wheel). **4** step/rung (of a ladder). **5** a measure of land. ~ **পড়ানো** *vi* cram (pupils); teach by rote. ~**র প্রাণ** *n* very feeble vitality; frailty. ~**র বাসা** *n* nest.

পাখোয়াজ [P] *n* a percussion instrument shaped almost like a tom-tom. **পাখোয়াজি** *n* person who plays the Pakhwaj.

পাগড়ি, পাগড়ী *n* turban: headgear. ~**ধারী** *adj* turbaned.

পাগল *adj* **1** mad; lunatic; insane; crazy; deranged; frenzied; cracked; out of one's mind; demented. **2** intoxicated: মদ খেয়ে ~. **3** (of elephant) must. **4** (of dogs) rabid. **5** beside oneself; delicious; mad with: আনন্দে ~. **6** very excited; wild; frenzied; beside oneself; raving: ক্রোধে ~. **7** craving; crazy; crazed; mad: সে গাড়িটা কেনার জন্যে ~. **8** gusty; squally; turbulent; wild; stormy: ~ হাওয়া. **9** (in affection) foolish; simple; ignorant; crazy: ~ ছেলে. ❑*n* **1** madman; lunatic; madcap; crazy fellow; eccentric; maniac; crackpot; mental patient. **2** (in affection) naughty/ unreasonable/ crazy child. **পাগলিনী, পাগলী** *fem.* ❑*n* madwoman; crazy woman. ~ **করা** *vt* **1** drive sb crazy; make sb go crazy; make sb mad; madden. **2** intoxicate: excite; make sb wild; enrage. ~-**করা** *adj* intoxicating; exciting; breath-taking; maddening; soul-stirring. ~ **হওয়া** *vi* **1** go mad; be/ become insane; loose one's senses/mind; go out of one's mind; rave; run amok; be crazed with; be crazy. **2** go crazy (about sth/sb); be crazy/mad; be intoxicated by/with; be delirious (with); be wildly excited/agitated; be enraged. **পাগলা** =~.

পাগলা-গারদ *n* lunatic asylum; insane asylum; bedlam; mad-house; mental hospital. **পাগলা-ঝোরা** *n* cataract; cascade; waterfall. **পাগলাটে** *adj* crazy; crack-brained; eccentric; cracked; loony; nutty. **পাগলাটে লোক** *n* eccentric; crackpot; loony; nut; crank; crack-brain. **পাগলামি, পাগলামো** (colloq) **1** *n* madness; craziness; craze; insanity; eccentricity. **2** foolishness: folly.

পা-গাড়ি *n* bicycle.

পাঙাশ=পাঙ্গাশ

পাঙক্তেয় *adj* fit to be associated with; admissible into the row of caste-fellows at meals.

পাঙ্গাশ[১] *n* a large silver-coloured fish.

পাঙ্গাশ[২] *adj* ash-coloured; ashy; ashen; livid; pale.

পাচক *adj* **1** cooking; baking; roasting. **2** digestive; gastric. ❑*n* cook. **পাচিকা** *n* female cook. ~**রস** *n* digestive fluid; gastric juice.

পাচকতন্ত্র *n* digestive system.

পাচন[১] *adj* digestive; gastric; softening. ❑*n* medicinal preparation/decoction. ~-**যন্ত্র** *n* digestive/gastric organ.

পাচন[২], ~**বাড়ি** *nn* goad.

পাচনি=পাচন[২]

পাচার *n* **1** act of finishing/ consuming; slaughter; murder; killing; dispatch. **2** kidnapping. **3** smuggling. **4** secret removal and doing away. ~ **করা** *vt* **1** finish; slay; consume; knock sb off; murder; do sb in. **2** kidnap. **3** smuggle. **4** remove secretly and do away with; help oneself to; walk off with; swipe; knock sth off.

পাচালি=পাঁচালি

পাচিকা⇒পাচক

পাচিত *adj* roasted; cooked.

পাচ্য *adj* **1** capable of being cooked; to be cooked. **2** to be digested; digestible.

পাছ *n* back; back part. ~**দুয়ার** *n* back-door. ~**তলা** *n* lower half of the body; back part of a dwelling-house; backyard.

পাছড়ানো *vt* =পাছড়ানো

পাছড়া-পাছড়ি *n* mutual grappling; scuffle; wrestling. ~ **করা** *vt* grapple with each other; scuffle with; wrestling with.

পাছা *n* **1** hip; buttocks; posteriors; behind; bottom. **2** rump. **3** stern. **~পেড়ে** *adj* (of a sari) having a broad length-wise furbelow in the middle.

পাছাড় *n* =আছাড়

পাছু *n* back: ~ তাকানো, look/glare behind. ❑*adj* flinching; retreated. ❑*adv* **1** back; towards one's back; behind: ~ ফেরা. **2** from behind: ~ ডাকা. **3** later on; afterwards: আমার কথা ~ বলব. ❑*prep* behind; after: সে আমার ~ আসছে. ❑*conj* lest; for fear that: ~ কেউ শুনে ফেলে. **~ লাগা** *vt* pursue; chase; follow (sb) closely; be on sb's back; tease; hound; dog the footsteps of; shadow; tail. **~ হওয়া** *vi* retreat; shrink back; flinch; fall back. **~পাছু** *prep, adv* close behind; after.

পাছে *prep, adv*=পিছে. ❑*conj* lest; for fear that. **~ পাছে** =পিছে-পিছে

পাজামা=পায়জামা

পাজি, পাজী [P] *adj* mean; low; base; vile; wicked; mischievous. ❑*n* rascal; scoundrel; rogue; knave; villain. **~পনা** *n* meanness; vileness; rascality. **~র পা-ঝাড়া/হদ্দ** *adj* extremely mean/low/base/vile. ❑*n* downright scoundrel/rascal/rogue. **~ লোক** *n* =~.

পাজেন [P] *n* ornament worn on the feet/ankles.

পাঞ্চ *n adj* (archaic) five. **~জন্য** *n* (myth) Krishna's couch taken from the demon Panchajan. **~দশ** *adj* fifteenth; relating to the fifteenth day of a month. **~বার্ষিক** *adj* five years old; quinquennial. **~ভৌতিক** *adj* composed of/containing the five elements.

পাঞ্চাল *adj* relating/belonging to the Panchalas (পঞ্চাল). ❑*n* country of the Panchalas.

পাঞ্চালিকা *n* doll; puppet.

পাঞ্চালী *n fem* princess of the Panchalas; Draupadi of the Mahabharata.

পাঞ্জতন (also **পাক~**) *n* five holy persons (Profhet Muhammad sm , Ali, Fatima, Hassan and Hossain).

পাঞ্জর=পাঁজর

পাঞ্জা=পঞ্জা

পাঞ্জাব=পাঞ্জাব

পাঞ্জাবি[১]=পঞ্জাবি

পাঞ্জাবি[২] =*n* kind of loose shirt.

পাঞ্জী =পাঁজি

পাঞ্জেগানা [P] *adj* (of Muslim prayer) five times.

পাঞ্জেরি [P] *n* night-watch on a ship.

পাট[১] *n* **1** jute. **2** coloured/ fine cloth; woven silk. **3** jute bag. **4** bandage; ligature; strip; fillet (cloth or leather). **5** frontlet; turban (of 5 kinds, viz those of kings, queens, princes, generals and the turban of honour). **~খড়ি** *n* jute-stalk. **~নেত** *n* fine silk cloth. **~রানী** *n* turbaned queen; principal wife of a king.

পাট[২] *n* **1** flat/level surface of anything. **2** slab; tablet; copper plate for inscribing royal grants/orders. **3** plank; board: ধোপার ~. **4** seat; throne; tool; official seat: রাজ~. **5** capital (city): **6** holy place: শ্রী~ নবদ্বীপ. **7** the western mountain (behind which the sun is supposed to set). **8** domicile; residence; routine duties of a house-hold; household duties; household/ domestic chores. **9** fold; folding; plait; laying in order: শাড়ির ~. **10** tradition; business; practice: বাপের ~ বজায় রাখা. **11** leaf/fold of a door. **12** one of a pair: এক ~ চটি. ❑*adj* royal: ~ হাতি. **~ ওঠানো** *vi* complete household duties; call it a day; close down; wind sth up. **~ করা** *vt* fold; plait; pleat. **~ চুকানো** *vi* finish with sth; be finished with sth; sever one's connection with. **~ তোলা** =~ ওঠানো. **~ খোলা/ভাঙা** *vt* unfold; spread out. **~ মারা** *vi* complete household duties/chores; be through with sth. **পাটে নামা** *vi* (of the sun) set; go down. **পাটে বসা** *vi* **1** sit on a throne; be seated on the official seat. **2** (of the sun) set. **পাটে-পাটে** *adv* in every fold; by/in folds.

পাট[৩] *n* well-curb; earthen hoop/brace used to make walls for wells.

পাট[৪] [E] *n* (theatre) part. **~ করা** *vi* take/play the part of.

পাটক *n* (municipal) ward.

পাটকাটি *n* =পাকাটি

পাটকিলে *adj* =পাটল

পাটকেল *n* brickbat. **ঢিল মারলে ~ খাওয়া** tit for tat.

পাটন *n* **1** city; settlement; habitation: সিংহল ~. **2** trade and commerce; sea-trade. **পাটনে যাওয়া** *vi* set out on sea-trade.

পাটনাই *adj* of Patna; grown in/produced/ coming from Patna.

পাটনি *n* ferryman.

পাটব =পটুতা

পাটল *adj* pale red; pink; pallid. ❑*n* **1** pale red hue; rose colour. **2** trumpet-flower. **3** species of rice ripening in the rains.

পাটলা, পাটলি, পাটলী *n* trumpet-flower or its plant.

পাটশাক *n* leaves of jute-plant used as a vegetable.

পাটা *n* **1** plank; board. **2** plate (of metals). **3** stone slab for grinding spices. **4** face; surface; expanse; breadth: বুকের ~. **5** (fig) courage; daring: কার এত বড়ো বুকের পাটা? **6** document of purchase/ lease hold of land. **~তন** *n* flooring of planks; wooden deck. **~পুতা** =শিলনোড়া.

পাটালি, পাটালী *n* rectangular solid tablet of molasses.

পাটি[১], পাটী[১] *n* mat made of an aquatic plant.

পাটি[২], পাটি[২] *n* **1** (regular) order; orderliness; series; succession; method; system. **2** row; line: দাঁতের ~. **3** one of a pair: জুতার ~. **4**

household duties: সংসারের ~. **5** hair-do: পাড়ে মোহন ~. **6** (alg) column. **7** quarters; locality. **~গণিত** *n* arithmetic. **~সাপটা** *n* kind of sweet roll.

পাটী *n* sac; bag.

পাটুনী=পাটনি

পাটেশ্বরী =পাটরানী (⇒ পাট[১])

পাটোয়ার *adj* **1** skilful; astute; shrewd. **2** calculating. ❑*n* **1** one who strings beads, etc for necklace or other things. **2** officer employed in collecting rents.

পাটোয়ারি *n* =পাটোয়ার. ❑*adj* **1** relating to a patwar. **2** calculating. **~ বুদ্ধি** *n* keen/shrewd practical sense; cunning; discernment; craftiness.

পাট্টা *n* **1** lease of land; patent; deed of lease. **2** fold; plait; pleat: দো~. **3** thick layer. **~ দেওয়া** *vt* sell/lease out (land). **~ নেওয়া** *vt* purchase/take on lease (as land). **~গ্রহীতা** *n* lease-holder; lessee. **~দাতা** *n* lessor. **~দার** *n* =~ গ্রহীতা.

পাঠ *n* **1** reading; study; perusal. **2** recitation; recital. **3** text (of a book). **4** reading of a book. **5** text-book. **6** lesson. **~ করা** *vt* read; study; peruse; recite. **~ তৈরি করা** *n* learn/prepare one's lesson. **~ দেওয়া** *vi* give lessons. **~ নেওয়া** *vi* take lessons (from a teacher). **~ক** *n* **1** reader. **2** reciter. **3** public reciter of the Puranas. **4** student; pupil. **5** scholar; lecturer; preceptor; teacher. **~কক্ষ** *n* study; reading-room; class-room. **~কারী** *adj* reading; repeating. **~ক্রম** *n* curriculum. **~গৃহ** *n* study; library; reading-room. **~গ্রহণ** *n* taking lessons; apprenticeship. **~ন, ~না** *n* teaching; lecturing. **~নিবিষ্ট, ~মগ্ন** *adjj* absorbed in reading/study. **~ভবন, ~মন্দির** *nn* =**1** ~গৃহ. **2** school. **~যোগ্য** *adj* worth reading; readable. **~রত** *adj* engaged in reading/study. **~রতি** *n* studiousness. **~শালা** *n* primary school. **পাঠানুরাগ** *adj* devotion to study; love of reading. **পাঠানুরাগী** *adj* fond of reading; devoted to study; studious. **পাঠান্তর** *n* another text/version; variant; variation of a text. **পাঠাভ্যাস করা** *vi* learn one's lessons; study. **পাঠার্থী** *adj* desirous of reading/studying. ❑*n* student; pupil; learner. **পাঠার্থিনী** *fem.*

পাঠান *n* Pathan; Afgan.

পাঠানো *vt* send; despatch; transmit; forward. **ডেকে ~** *vt* send for; summon; call sb out. **বলে ~** *vi* send intimation to sb through a messenger; intimate; let; know.

পাঠিকা *n fem* of পাঠক (⇒পাঠ)

পাঠিনী *n fem* of পাঠী

পাঠেচ্ছা *n* desire to read/ study. **পাঠেচ্ছু** *adj* desirous of reading; eager to read.

পাঠোদ্ধার *n* deciphering an obscure piece of writing/passage.

পাঠ্য *adj* to be read/ recited; prescribed for reading; readable. **~ক্রম** *n* syllabus. **~তালিকা** *n* syllabus; book-list. **~পুস্তক** *n* text-book. **~সূচি, ~সূচী** *n* syllabus. **পাঠ্যাবস্থা** *n* student life.

পাড়[১] *n* **1** bank; shore; margin: পুকুর~. **2** mound of earth raised round a piece of arable land. **3** well-curb. **4** fur-below; flounce; coloured/ decorated border (of a cloth). **~ লাগানো** *vi* furbelow; flounce; border with a lace, etc.

পাড়[২] *n* a beam laid on pillars to support other beams; cross-beam.

পাড়[৩] *n* act of pedalling a husking-pestle. **~ দেওয়া** *vt* pedal in an up-and-down manner.

পাড়ন *n* **1** laying down of a carpet/mat on a floor. **2** causing a thing to fall down; collecting of fruits/flowers.

পাড়া[১] *vt* **1** lay a thing down; spread (a carpet on a floor); spread out (a mat). **2** cast/throw down. **3** gather (fruits/flowers); bring down. **4** make: বিছানা ~. **5** knock down: অত বড়ো পালোয়ানকে সে পেড়ে ফেলল. **6** cause to take to one's bed; be prostrated by; be prostrate with (an illness). **7** lay: ডিম ~. **8** utter; shout: গালি ~, hurl (a stream of) abuse at sb. **9** invoke; call upon; appeal to: দোহাই ~. **10** remove; clear: এটো~, clear the table.

পাড়া[২] *n* **1** village; hamlet. **2** locality; quarters/ district (of a town); neighbourhood; canton. **~-কুঁদুলি** *adj fem* given to constant and boisterous brawling with neighbours; cantankerous; quarrelsome; vixenish; shrewish. ❑*n fem* cantankerous woman; termagant; virago; vixen; shrew. **~-গাঁ** *n* rural area; countryside; village. **~-গেঁয়ে** *adj* rural; rustic. **~-পড়শি** *n* neighbour. **~বেড়ানি** *n fem* woman wandering constantly through her neigbourhood or roaming through the neighbourhood for hours on end. **~ বেড়ানো** *vi* wander constantly through one's neighbourhood; roam around in the neighbourhood. **~ মাত করা** *vi* win/ captivate the neighbourhood; take neighbourhood by storm. **~ মাথায় করা** *vi* raise Cain/hell/the roof; make the rafters ring.

পাড়ানি(য়া) *adj* **1** inducing/inductive to: ঘুম ~ গান, lullaby. **2** collecting fruits or flowers (esp from tall trees).

পাড়ানো *vt* **1** cause to bring down/gather: আম ~. **2** cause to pluck; pick/pluck: ফুল ~. **3** induce to sleep. ঘুম ~ lull to sleep.

পাড়ি *n* **1** crossing (a river, etc); passing to the opposite side/shore. **2** width/expanse (of a river, etc). **~ জমানো/দেওয়া** *vt* pass over/cross (a river, etc); turn a boat's head in order to cross over.

পাণি *n* hand. **~গ্রহ(ণ)** *n* taking (the bride) by the hand; marriage. **~গ্রহণ করা** *vt* marry. **~তল** *n* palm of the hand. **~পীড়ন** *n* pressing the hand (of a bride); marriage. **~পীড়ন করা** *vt* marry.

পাণ্ডব *n* son/race/descendants of king Pandu of the Mahabharata. **~বর্জিত** *adj* **1** (of places) not habitable/worth visiting because avoided even by the Pandavas. **2** (fig) god-forsaken; dismal. **~-সখা** *n* friend of the Pandavas; Krishna.

পাণ্ডবেয় =পাণ্ডব

পাণ্ডা *n* **1** Brahmin priest acting as a guide to pilgrims at holy places; stationary priest at a particular temple. **2** lender. **3** ring-leader.

পাণ্ডিত্য *n* **1** scholarship; erudition; learning; cleverness. **2** (derog) pedantry. **~ প্রকাশ** *n* display/parade of one's learning.

পাণ্ডু *adj* (yellowish) white; pale; wan; jaundiced; etiolated; whitish-yellow. ❑*n* **1** pale/yellowish white colour. **2** jaundice. **~ বর্ণ** =~. **~র**=~. **~রাগ** *n* whiteness; pallor. **~রোগ** *n* jaundice. **~লিপি, ~লেখ(্য)** *adj* **1** hand-written sheet/copy; manuscript. **2** outline; sketch; rough sketch; draft. **3** (parliamentary) bill.

পাত[1] *n* **1** fall; downfall: নক্ষত্র~, বৃষ্টি~. **2** decay (of the body); death: দেহ~. **3** rain; destruction: শত্রুকে ~ করা. **4** shedding; dropping: রক্ত~. **5** casting/throwing upon; cast; ball; shot: বজ্র~. **6** casting; directing; throwing: দৃষ্টি~. **7** stroke (of a sword). **8** application (of ointment). **9** fall of the fetus; miscarriage: **গর্ভ~**. **10** happening; occurrence; appearance; incidence: অনর্থ~. **11** attack; incursion. **12** node in a planet's orbit. **উচ্চ~** *n* ascending node. **নিম্ন~** *n* descending node. **~ করা** *vt* ruin; destroy; impair; waste; wreck.

পাত[2] *n* **1** leaf (of a tree or book). **2** sheet; foil; leaf: সোনার ~, gold-leaf; gold foil. **3** leaf of banana or *sal* (শাল) on which food is eaten. ❑*adj* thin. **~ করা** *vi* **1** flatten into a sheet; hammer into a very thin flexible sheet. **2** lay the table; serve food on leaves of banana or *sal*. **~চাটা** *vi* eat off another's table like beggar; fawn on; lick the boots of; cadge meals from others; bum sth (from sb). **~চাটা** *adj* cringing; fawning; cadging. **~চাটা লোক** *n* bum; cadge. **~পাড়া** *vi* (derog) enjoy another's hospitality (without being invited); sponge on/off sb.

পাতক *n* sin; crime; guilt. **~যুক্ত** *adj* sinful; guilty. **~রহিত, ~শূন্য** *adjj* free from sin; sinless; innocent; guileless.

পাতকী *adj* sinful; guilty of a crime; wicked. ❑*n* sinner. **পাতকিনী** *fem.*

পাতকুয়া, পাতকুয়ো (colloq) *n* well; draw-well.

পাতখোলা *n* piece of incompletely burnt potsherd.

পাতড়া *n* **1** leaf. **2** food left on a leaf of banana or *sal*. **3** quantity of food which is dealt out; ration of food. **4** dish of vegetables or fish fried on a banana leaf· **~চাটা**=পাত-চাটা (⇒ পাত[2]).

পাততাড়ি *n* (hist) bundle of palm-leaves used in writing by a pupil; bundle of papers. **~ গোটানো** *vi* **1** (lit) put away the bundle of palm-leaves when the lesson is over. **2** (fig) leave bag and baggage; decamp; close down/wind up (a business, etc.); slip away; skip off; make off.

পাতন *n* **1** causing to fall; felling; laying low. **2** throwing; hurling down; striking off/down. **3** casting (as dice/a glance of the eyes. **4** overthrowing; killing. **5** writing; arrangement: অঙ্ক~. **6** (chem) distillation. **7** extraction. **~যন্ত্র** *n* retort.

পাতনামা *n* beginning; inception; preface.

পাতলা, পাতল (dial) *adj* **1** lean; thin; delicate; slim; slight: ~ শরীর. **2** sparse; thin: ~ চুল/ঝোপ. **3** slender: ~ বেত. **4** fine: ~ কাগজ/কাপড়. **5** light: ~ ঘুম. **6** loose: ~ দাস্ত. **7** diluted; thin; watery: ~ দুধ. **8** thin: ~ কুয়াশা/সোনার পাত. **~ করা** *vt* **1** thin sth down: রং ~ করা. **2** thin (sth) (out): ধানের চারা ~ করে লাগাও. **~ হওয়া** *vi* **1** get thin: চুল ~ হওয়া. **2** thin out: কুয়াশা/ভিড় ~ হওয়া. **3** thin down: না খেয়ে ~ হওয়া. **~ করে** *adv* thinly.

পাতলুন [E] *n* pantaloon; trousers.

পাতশা(হ) [P]*n*=বাদশাহ. **পাতশাহী**=বাদশাহী

পাতা[1] *n* **1** leaf: গাছের/বইয়ের ~. **2** page: বইয়ের ~. **3** lid: চোখের ~. **4** flat surface: পায়ের ~. **5** leaf of banana and *sal* (শাল) on which food is served. **6** pleat; plait; braid. **~ করা** *vi*=পাত করা (⇒ পাত[2]). **~ কাটা** *vi* **1** plait/ braid (hair). **2** cut banana leaves to be used as dinner-plates. **~ চাটা**=পাত চাটা (⇒ পাত[2]). **~ পাতা** =পাত করা/পাড়া (⇒ পাত[2]). **~-পা** *adj* flat-footed; web-footed. **~কুড়ানি, ~কুড়ানী** (colloq) *adj fem* earning one's livelihood by gathering dried leaves. ❑ *n* such a woman. **চোখের ~** *n* eyelid. **পায়ের ~** *n* instep; foot.

পাতা[2] *vt* **1** spread; lay out; make: বিছানা ~. **2** set: টেবিল ~. **3** place ready for use: পাত ~. **4** set up; establish: সংসার/দোকান ~. **5** lay: ফাঁদ ~. **6** instal: পূজার ঘট ~. **7** stretch out: হাত ~. **8** bend down submissively: পিঠ ~. **9** set; give: কান ~. **10** make: দই ~.

পাতা[3] *adj* (used as a *suff*) protecting; preserving; defending. ❑*n* protector; preserver; defender: বিশ্ব~.

পাতা[4] *adj* one who drinks. ❑*n* drinker.

পাতানো *vt* **1** cause to spread/lay out/set up/ install, etc (⇒ পাতা[2]). **2** form an alliance, relation, etc; establish; make: সম্বন্ধ ~, বন্ধুত্ব ~

form a friendship; make friends with. ❑*adj* in all the senses of the verb, esp formed by mutual consent only: ~ মামা.

পাতাবাহার *n* a tropical hedge-plant of the croton genus; *Codiacum variegatum.*

পাতাল *n* **1** (myth) one of the seven regions under the earth and the abode of the Nagas (নাগ) or serpents and demons. **2** lower regions; underworld; Hades; hell. **~তল** *n* bottom of the underworld/hell. **~পুরী** *n* capital city of the netherworld; Hades; underworld. **~বাসী** *adj* inhabiting the underworld. ❑*n* inhabitant of the underworld. **~বাসিনী** *fem.*

পাতালিক *adj* (geog) sedimentary; plutonic: ~ শিলা.

পাতি[১] *adj* (used as a *suff*) small; inferior; little; diminutive; petty. **~ কাক** *n* common crow. **~ চোর** *n* petty thief; pilferer. **~ লেবু** *n* a small variety of lime/lemon. **~শিয়াল** *n* fox. **~শিয়ালী** *n* vixen. **~হাঁস** *n* common duck.

পাতি[২] *n* leaf: চায়ের ~, তামাকের ~.

পাতি[৩] *n* address; whereabouts.

পাতি[৪] *n* row; line; order: জাতির ~.

পাতিত *adj* **1** made to fall; felled; struck down; knocked down; flung down. **2** lowered; humbled; brought down. **3** distilled.

পাতিত্য *n* state of being socially cast down; degeneration; depravity; degradation.

পাতিপাতি *adv* in the most minute manner; line by line; minutely; thoroughly. **~ করা/করে খোঁজা** *vt* search (a place) thoroughly; ransack.

পাতিব্রত্য *n* devotedness to a husband conjugal fidelity.

পাতিল *n* (earthen) pot (used for cooking).

পাতী *adj* **1** falling; sinking. **2** deciduous: ~ অরণ্য. **3** causing to fall; emitting; throwing down. **4** included: অন্তঃ~.

পাতুক *adj* **1** disposed/tending to fall; (repeatedly/habitually) falling; falling down. **2** losing caste; going to the lower regions. ❑*n* precipice.

পাত্তা *n* **1** address (to which a letter is directed). **2** news; information. **3** trace; where-abouts. **4** hint; clue; sign. **~ দেওয়া** *vi* attach importance: treat as important. **~ না দেওয়া** *vt* treat as of little/no importance; take a dim view of; make light of; dismiss scornfully; pooh-pooh. **~ পাওয়া** *vt* **1** find trace/whereabouts of; obtain a clue; trace; discover; locate; search out. **2** be considered of some value; be of some account; be considered as somebody **~ না পাওয়া** *vt* loose trace of. **2** be of small account; be considered of little value. **~ মেলা** *v* =~ পাওয়া(1).

পাত্তাড়ি=পাততাড়ি

পাত্র *n* **1** drinking-vessel; goblet; bowl; cup; dish; pot; plate; utensil; any vessel/ receptacle; container. **2** capable/competent person; deserving man; any one worthy of /fit for; object of: শ্রদ্ধার ~. **3** king's counsellor; minister: মহা~. **4** male character (in a play). **5** (prospective) bridegroom. **6** man; fellow: সে ভোলার ~ নয়. **~তা** *n* worthiness; eligibility. **~ দেখা** *vi* interview a prospective bridegroom for selection; choose a bridegroom. **~পক্ষ** *n* bridegroom's party/ people. **~মিত্র** *n pl* (a monarch's) courtiers and friends; entourage. **~স্থ** *adj* **1** being in a receptacle/dish. **2** (of a girl) married; wedded. **~স্থ করা** *vt* give (a girl) in marriage; marry. **পাত্রাপাত্র** *n* deserving and undeserving/worthy and unworthy persons. **পাত্রাপাত্রবিচার** *n* discrimination between deserving and undeserving persons. **যোগ্য ~, সৎ ~** *nn* **1** deserving person. **2** worthy groom.

পাত্রী *n fem* (of পাত্র) **1** deserving/worthy woman or female object. **2** female character (in a play). **3** prospective bride. **~ দেখা** *vi* interview a prospective bride for selection; choose a bride. **~পক্ষ** *n* bride's party/people. **যোগ্য ~** *n* worthy bride.

পাথর *n* **1** stone. **2** stone-made dinner-plate. **3** precious-stone; gem. **4** (fig) stone-hearted/ heartless person. **~ ভাঙা** *vi* crush (up) stones. **~ হয়ে যাওয়া** *vi* become as hard as stone; be unfeeling/unmerciful. **~কুচি** *n* **1** stone-chips; rubble. **2** an aromatic medical herb; *Coleus aromaticus.* **3** stonework. **~ চাপা** *adj* (fig) incapable of thriving. **~চুন** *n* lime (obtained by heating limestone); quicklime. **~-বাটি** *n* stone-cup. **পাথরে পাঁচ কিল** (fig) the most formidable good fortune; the devil's own luck.

পাথরি *n* (med) stone; calculus; concretion. **দাঁতের ~** *n* tartar.

পাথার *n* ocean; sea; vast expanse of water.

পাথুরে, পাথুরিয়া *adj* (colloq) **1** (made) of stone: **~বাটি. 2** full of/ covered in/having stones; stony. ~ পথ/মাটি. **3** (fig;) stony: ~ দৃষ্টি/মন. **~ কয়লা** *n* coal.

পাথেয় *n* provender/ provisions for a journey; viaticum.

পাদ[১] *n* **1** foot; leg; step; pace. **2** column; pillar. **3** foot as a measure. **4** foot / roof of a tree. **5** foot /hill at the foot of a mountain: পর্বতের ~দেশ. **6** bottom. **7** ray/beam of light. **8** quarter; fourth part; (alg, astron) quadrant. **9** verse/line (as the fourth part of a stanza). **10** caesura of a verse. **11** a title added in token of respect; majesty: পিতৃ~, the venerable father; দেব ~, the king's majesty. **~কটক** *n* foot-ring; anklet. **~ক্ষেপ**=পদক্ষেপ (⇒ পদ). **~গণ্ডিব** *n* swelling of the legs and foot. **~গম্য** *adj* walkable. **~গ্রহণ** *n* laying hold of/clasping the foot (as a mark of respectful *salutation*). **~চাপল্য** *n* carelessness in placing the feet. **~চার, ~চারণ(1)** *nn* going/walking on foot. ~চারী *adj* going on foot; walking. ~চারে *adv* on foot. ~চিহ্ন *n* foot-mark; foot-print. ~চ্ছেদ *n* comma. ~জল *n* water for (washing) the feet. ~টীকা *n* footnote. ~তল *n* sole of a foot. ~ত্রাণ *n* shoe. ~ত্রিভুজ *n* (geom) pedal triangle. ~দাহ *n* burning sensation in the foot. ~দেশ *n* region at the foot/root/bottom; foot. ~নখ *n* toe-nail. ~ন্যাস *n* putting down/ placing the feet. ~পতন *n* falling/bowing to another's feet. ~পতিত *adj* fallen at another's feet. ~পদ্ম *n* a feet as beautiful as a lotus; feet reverentially conceived as a pair of lotuses. ~পীঠ *n* foot-stool. ~পূরণ *n* filling out (a verse, etc.); expletive. ~পূরণ করা *vt* supply the missing line; fill out a line/measure of a verse. ~পৃষ্ঠ *n* instep. ~প্রক্ষালন *n* washing the feet. ~প্রণাম *n* bowing to the feet; prostration. ~প্রসারণ *n* stretching out the feet. ~প্রহার *n* kick. ~প্রহার করা *vt* kick. ~বদ্ধ *adj* **1** bound/held together by feet. **2** consisting of verses. ~বন্দন(া) *n* respectful salutation; respect shown to revered person by touching his feet. ~বন্ধ *n* tie/fetter for the feet. ~বন্ধন *n* stock of cattle. ~বিধান *n* arrangement of verses. ~বিক্ষেপ *n*=পদবিক্ষেপ (⇒ পদ). ~মূল *n* sole; heel. ~রজ্জু *n* rope/tether for the foot. ~লেহন *n*=পদলেহন (⇒ পদ). ~শৈল *n* hill at the foot of a mountain. ~সংস্থান *n* (astron) quadrature. ~সেবন *n* service; duty. ~স্ফোট *n* sore/ulcer on the foot.

পাদ[২] *n* (vulg) fart. ~ পাদা *vi* (vulg) fart.

পাদক=পাদোদক

পাদকা *n* tree; plant.

পাদবিক *adj* travelling on foot; pedestrian. ❑*n* traveller; pedestrian.

পাদরি, পাদরী [Pg] *n* christian clergyman; priest; padre.

পাদাগ্র *n* point/extremity of the foot.

পাদাঙ্গদ *n* anklet.

পাদাঙ্গুলি *n* toe.

পাদাতি *n* foot soldier.

পাদান, পাদানি *n* footboard.

পাদুকা *n* shoe; slipper. ~-পরিহিত *adj* wearing shoes; shod; booted.

পাদোদক *n* **1** water with which the feet of a revered person is washed. **2** water used for washing the feet.

পাদ্য *adj* relating/belonging to the feet. ❑*n* = পাদোদক (2).

পাদ্রি, পাদ্রী *n*=পাদরি

পান[১] *n* **1** drinking (spirituous liquors); draught. **2** (fig) thorough enjoyment; drinking in. ~ করা *vt* **1** drink (spirituous liquors); take alcohol. **2** (fig) drink in: সৌন্দর্য ~ করা. ~ক *n* draught; drink; beverage; potion. ~গোষ্ঠী *n* drinking party. ~দোষ *n* vice of drinking; drunkenness. ~পর *adj* addicted to drinking. ~পাত্র *n* drinking-vessel; cup; goblet. ~ভোজন *n* eating and drinking. ~মত্ত *adj* intoxicated. ~শৌণ্ড, পানাসক্ত *adjj*=~পর. পানাগার *n* drinking-house; tavern. পানাহার=~ভোজন.

পান[২] *n* betel-leaf. ~ খাওয়া *vi* chew betel-leaf (with betel-nut, lime, etc).~ সাজা *vi* prepare betel-leaf (with other ingredients for chewing). ~দান *n* box in which betel-leaf and its accessories are kept. ~ থেকে চুন খসা (fig) commit a very trivial/ negligible offence/ lapse/ mistake. পানের খিলি/ঠিলি *n* betel-leaf rolled into a small conical cup.

পান[৩] *n* **1** (of iron and baser metals) temper; annealing. **2** (of gold and noble metals) alloy. ~ দেওয়া *vt* **1** temper; anneal. **2** alloy.

পান[৪] *n* dose: ওষুধের ~.

পানই *n* (wooden) slipper

পানকৌড়ি *n* species of a diver bird akin to the cormorant.

পানতি *n* high-rimmed metal dish.

পানতুয়া *n* kind of bale-shaped sweet-meat.

পানফল=পানিফল (⇒ পানি)

পান-সরা *n* (of gold and noble metals) loss in weight owing to alloying.

পানসি, পানসী [E] *n* pinnace.

পানসে *adj* **1** tasting like water; watery; thin; insipid; flat; vapid: ~ দুধ/ঘোল. **2** dull; trivial; frivolous; insipid; inane: ~ কথাবার্তা; milk and water: ~ লেখা. **3** lachrymose; mournful: ~ মেজাজ.

পানা[১] *n* beverage; drink; sherbet.

পানা[২] *n* width; breadth: কাপড়ের ~

পানা[৩] [P] *n* protection; asylum; refuge; shade; shelter. ~ চাওয়া *vi* seek protection/ refuge. ~ দেওয়া *vt* shelter; protect; give shelter; harbour.

পানা[৪] *n* kind of aquatic plant; water-hyacinth. ~ পুকুর *n* pond covered with water-hyacinth.

পানা[৫] *suff* like; resembling; seeming to be: চাঁদ~ মুখ.

পানাকাঙ্ক্ষা *n* desire of drinking; thirst. **পানাকাঙ্ক্ষী** *adj* desirous of drinking; thirsty.

পানানো *vt* **1** cause a calf to suck in order to induce the cow give her milk freely. **2** temper alloy (⇒পান[৩]).

পানাভিলাষ *n*= পানাকাঙ্ক্ষা. **পানাভিলাষী** *adj*=পানাকাঙ্ক্ষী

পানার্থী *adj*=পানাকাঙ্ক্ষী

পানাসক্ত *adj* পানপর (⇒পান[১]). **পানাসক্তা** *fem.* ~ ব্যক্তি *n* drunkard. **পানাসক্তি** *n* addiction to drinking.

পানি *n* water. ~ডুবি *n* harrier. ~ফল *n* an aquatic fruit; water chestnut. ~বসন্ত *n* chicken pox. ~ ভাঙা *vi* (of a pregnant woman) have membrane rupture.

পানীয় *adj* to be drunk; drinkable; potable. ❑*n*

drink; beverage; water. ~ জল *n* drinking water.

পানে *prep* to, towards; in the direction of: আকাশ ~.

পান্তা *adj* **1** (of boiled rice) put in fresh water and preserved for a future meal. **2** (fig) stale: ~ খবর. ❑*n* boiled rice which is put in fresh water and preserved for a future meal. ~ **ভাতে ঘি** (fig) unnecessary expenditure. ~ **ভাতে টোকো দই** (fig) an unpalatable meal.

পান্তি=পানতি

পান্তুয়া=পানতুয়া

পান্থ *n* wander; traveller; wayfarer. ~**তরু**, ~**পাদপ** *nn* traveller's tree/palm; *Ravenala madagascariensis*. ~**নিবাস**, ~**শালা** *nn* caravansarai; inn; hotel; tavern; wayside boarding-house.

পান্না *n* emerald.

পান্সি, পান্সী=পানসি

পাপ *n* **1** sin; vice; crime; guilt. **2** evil; misfortune; ill-luck; trouble; mischief; harm; wickedness. **3** wicked man; wretch; villain; pest; troublesome person: ~ বিদায় করো. ❑*dj* **1** bad; vicious; wicked; evil; wretched; vile; low . **2** (astron) boding evil; inauspicious. ~ **করা** *v* commit a sin/crime; sin. **কী** ~! what a plague/pest! ~**কর** *adj* wicked; sinful. ~**কর্ম** *n* wicked/sinful deed or act; crime. ~**কর্মা**, ~**কৃৎ** *adjj* wicked; committing crimes/ sins; sinful; given to vice/ wickedness. ❑*nn* villain; sinner; criminal; ill-doer. ~**কারক**. ~**কারী** *adj*=~কর্মা. ~**ক্ষয়** *n* gradual destruction/ mortification of sin. ~**ক্ষয়-কারক**, ~**ক্ষয়কারী** *adj* causing the mortification of sin; mortifying. ~**ক্ষালন** *n* rescue from/ remission of sins; absolution; purification. ~**ক্ষালন করা** *vt* rescue from sin/vice; absolve; free/save from sin; purify. ~**গ্রহ** *n* **1** (astrol) inauspicious planet. **2** (fig) unavoidable evil person. ~**ঘ্ন** *adj* destroying sin/evil; freeing/ rescuing from sin. ~**জ** *adj* springing from evil. ~**জনক** *adj* sinful; vicious; wicked. ~**জীব**, ~**জীবী** *adjj* leading an evil life. ❑*nn* villain. ~**তিমির** *adj* sin-bedarkened; blinded by sin. ~**দৃষ্টি** *adj* evil-eyed. ~**ধী** *adj* evil-minded. ~**নাশন**=~ঘ্ন. ~**নাশী** *adj* sin-destroying; purifying. ~**নিষ্কৃতি** *n* atonement for sin. ~**পঙ্ক** *n* mire of sin/vice. ~**পতি** *n* paramour. ~**পুণ্য** *n* vice and virtue. ~**প্রবণ** *adj* of sinful/wicked disposition; evil-minded. ~**বুদ্ধি** *n* evil intent. ❑*adj* evil-minded; wicked; vicious. ~**ভাগী** *adj* partaking of sin; guilty; sharing in sin/guilt. ~**মতি**=~বুদ্ধি. ~**ময়** *adj* consisting of evil; sinful; vicious; wicked. ~**মুক্ত** *adj* freed from sin; purified; absolved from sin. ~**মুক্তি**, ~**মোচন** *nn* liberating/ absolution from sin/vice ~**যোগ** *n* (astrol) inauspicious/unholy planetary conjunction. ~**রহিত** *adj* free from guilt/sin; harmless; innocent. ~**লোক** *n* evil world; place of suffering. ~**শীল** *adj* of evil character; wicked. ~**স্রোত** *n* current of sinful/vicious life. ~**হর**, ~**হারক**, ~**হারী** *adjj* expiating crimes/sin; taking away guilt/crime. ~**হীন**=~রহিত. ~**হেতুক** *adj* caused by/arising from sin/guilt. **পাপাকাঙ্ক্ষা** *n* wicked desire; criminal inclination. **পাপাকাঙ্ক্ষী** *adj* inclined to wickedness. **পাপাচরণ**, **পাপাচার** *nn* wicked practice/conduct; sinful/wicked act. **পাপাচারী** *adj* practising sin; living in wickedness. **পাপাচারিণী** *fem*. **পাপাত্মা** *adj* sinful; wicked. **পাপানুষ্ঠান** *n* commission of sin; practice of vice. **পাপাভিলাষ**=পাপাকাঙ্ক্ষা. **পাপাশয়** *adj* wicked; intending evil/crime; evil-intentioned. **পাপাসক্ত** *adj* addicted to sin/vice; sinful; wicked. **পাপাসক্তি** *n* addiction to sin/vice. **পাপের ধন** *n* dishonest earnings; ill-gotten gains. **পাপের ধন প্রায়শ্চিত্তে যায়** (prov) Ill-gotten goods/gains seldom prosper; Ill gotten ill spent. **পাপের ফল** *n* consequences of sin.

পাপড়ি *n* petal (of a flower).

পাপর [E] *n* pauper.

পাপান্তঃকরণ=পাপাত্মা (⇒পাপ)

পাপিয়া *n* the Indian cuckoo/ nightingale; hawk cuckoo.

পাপিষ্ঠ *adj* most wicked/ bad/ sinful. ❑*n* extremely wicked/ vicious person. **পাপিষ্ঠা** *fem*.

পাপী *adj* wicked; sinful; bad; depraved; criminal ❑*n* sinner,; criminal; wicked/ depraved/ vicious person. **পাপিনী** *fem*. **পুরাণ** ~ *n* old/ hardened/ inveterate offender/ criminal/ sinner.

পাপীয়সী *adj fem* most wicked; sinful; criminal; adulterous. ❑*n* sinful/wicked woman; female criminal; adulteress.

পাপেচ্ছা *n* sinful desire; criminal inclination.

পাপেচ্ছু *adj* inclined to sin; desirous of committing wickedness.

পাপোশ *n* door-mat.

পাব *n* **1** joint (of a reed/bamboo). **2** knuckle (of a finger). **3** (bot) node. **4** space between two nodes (as of the bamboo).

পাবক *n* fire. ❑*adj* purifying; cleansing; sanctifying.

পাবড়া *n* frond.

পাবদা *n* name of a particular species of fish; *Callichrus pabda*.

পাবন *adj* **1** purifying; purificatory; sanctifying. **2** rescuing; saving: পতিত~. ❑*n* **1** cleansing; purification; sanctification. **2** penance; atonement. **পাবনী** *adj fem*. ❑*n* the Ganges.

পাবন্দ [P] *adj* obedient to; observant of: শরিয়তের ~. ~ **থাকা** *vi* adhere to. ~ **হওয়া** *vi* conform to; observe; follow.

পাবলিক [E] *n* , *adj* public.

পামর *adj* wicked; vile; low; base; sinful. ❑*n* **1** man of lowest extraction; wretch; villain. **2** idiot; fool. **পামরী** *fem.*

পামসু [E] *n* kind of shoe; pump.

পাম্প [E] *n* pump. **~ করা** *vt* pump.

পায়খানা [P] *n* **1** latrine; lavatory; toilet; loo, privy. **2** stool; faeces; motion. **~করা** *vi* relieve oneself; go to the bathroom; defecate; excrete; move the bowels.

পায়চারি *n* walking about; stroll; perambulation. **~ করা** *vi* walk about; perambulate; stroll (around); go for/have a stroll; pace up and down.

পায়জামা [P] *n* trousers; long drawers; pyjamas; slacks.

পায়দল *adv* (walking) on foot.

পায়পড়া *adj* sycophant; servile.

পায়-পায় *adv* ⇒ পা২

পায়রা *n* pigeon; dove. **পায়রী** *fem.* **~র খাঁচা/বাসা** *n* pigeon-house; dove-cot. **~র খোপ** *n* pigeon-hole.

পায়স, পায়সান্ন *nn* sort of food made of rice, milk and sugar; frumenty.

পায়া [P]*n* **1** leg/foot of a piece of furniture; support. **2** leg/foot of an animal. **3** (derog) position; rank; dignity. **~ভারী** *n* vanity (for holding a high post); vainglory; self-importance; conceit. ❑*adj* vainglorious; full of vainglory; conceited and boastful; self-important. **উঁচু ~** *n* high post/rank.

পায়ী *adj* **1** (used as a *suff)* drinking; sucking; sipping: স্তন্য~. **2** drawing: ধূম~.

পায়ু *n* anus. **~কাম** *n* sodomy.

পায়েল *n* anklet of gold or silver.

পায়েস=পায়স

পার *n* **1** the further bank/shore/boundary. **2** bank; shore; coast; opposite side. **3** end; limit; utmost reach; bounds; fullest extent. **4** crossing (over); passing beyond. **5** deliverance; rescue. **~ করা** *vt* **1** take a person over a river; ferry/carry sb/sth across (a river, a sea, etc.); take sb to the opposite/other bank. **2** get a person through a difficulty; take sb over an obstacle; conduct sb through; let pass. **3** deliver; rescue. **~ হওয়া** *vt* **1** pass over (river, etc); cross (over to the opposite/other bank). **2** pass through; get through/over (a difficulty). **পারের কড়ি** *n* **1** fare paid for ferrying; ferriage. **2** provision for ferrying; ferriage. **~গ** *adj* **1** going to the opposite shore; crossing over. **2** one who has gone through/ accomplished/ mastered; knowing thoroughly; fully conversant/familiar with; profoundly learned. **~গত** *adj* **1** one who has reached the opposite shore of; passed over in safety. **2** pure; holy. **~গতা** *n* ability; skill; capability. **~গমন** *n* reaching the opposite shore; crossing; going to the end of. **~গামী** *adj* passing over; crossing; landing. **~ঘাট** *n* place where a ferry service operates; ferry: ~ঘাটে অপেক্ষা করা, wait at the ferry.

পারক *adj* **1** carrying over; saving; delivering; **2** capable; able; competent; skilful; dexterous. **~তা** *n* ability; capability; competence; dexterity; skill.

পারক্য *n* alienage. **~যোগ্য** *adj* alienable.

পারগ ⇒ পার. **~পক্ষে**=পারতপক্ষে

পারগ্রামিক *adj* **1** belonging to another village. **2** hostile; inimical.

পারঙ্গম *adj* =পারগ (⇒পার)

পারজায়িক *n* one who intrigues with another's wife; adulterer.

পারণ, পারণা *nn* **1** bringing over; delivering. **2** conclusion (esp of a fast); eating and drinking after a fast; breakfast. **3** satisfaction; pleasure; enjoyment. **4** passage.

পারতন্ত্র্য *n* dependence on others; subservience.

পারতপক্ষে *adv* if (it is) possible; if it can be avoided; as far as possible; possibly.

পারত্রিক *adj* relating to/advantageous in another world; spiritual; other-worldly.

পারদ *n* mercury; quicksilver. **~মিশ্র** *n* amalgam. **~জারণ** *n* killing of mercury.

পারদর্শক *adj* showing the opposite shore.

পারদর্শন *n* beholding the opposite shore; surveying all things.

পারদর্শী *adj* **1** far-seeing; far-sighted; wise. **2** completely familiar with/ versed in; expert; adept; competent; experienced; judicious. **পারদর্শিনী** *fem.* **পারদর্শিতা** *n* **1** foresight; farsightedness; wisdom. **2** expertise; competence; experience; skill.

পারদারিক *n*=পারজায়িক. ❑*adj* adulterous. **~তা** *n* adultery.

পারদার্য *n* adultery.

পারদেশিক, পারদেশ্য *adjj* outlandish; foreign. ❑*n* foreigner; traveller.

পারপত্র *n* passport.

পারবশ্য *n* dependence (on another); subservience; subjection to other.

পারভিন [P] *n* pleiads.

পারমাণব, পারমাণবিক *adjj* atomic.

পারমার্থিক *adj* relating/belonging to or coming from the supreme God; spiritual; theological.

পারমিট [E] *n* permit.

পারম্পর্য *n* **1** uninterrupted series/succession; continuity; sequence. **2** tradition. **3** intermediation.

পারম্পর্যোপদেশ *n* traditional instruction.

পারলৌকিক *adj* **1** relating to the next world; other-worldly; spiritual. **2** obsequial. ~ **ক্রিয়া** *n* obsequies.

পারশী=পারসিক

পারশে *n* a species of small fish; mugil lotus.

পারসিক *adj* Persian; Iranian. ❑*n* Persian; Iranian.

পারসি *adj* Persian; of the Parsees. ❑*n* Persian; Parsee; Parsi.

পারস্য *n* Persia; Iran.

পারস্ত্রৈণেয় *n* son by other's wife; illegitimate son.

পারা[১] *modal vi, vt* **1** can; may; be able to; সে গান গাইতে পারে. **2** do; perform; manage; execute: কাজটা কি তুমি পারবে? **3** compete/vie with; be sb's match; be match for sb: সে তোমার সঙ্গে পারবে না.

পারা[২] *n* mercury; quicksilver. ~ **ঘটিত** *adj* containing mercury; mercurial.

পারা[৩] *adj* (poet) like; as; resembling: পাগল-~.

পারা[৪] [P] *n* fragment; volume; division: কোরান শরিফের এক ~.

পারা[৫] *n* step: পায়ের ~.

পারানি *n* =পারের কড়ি (⇒পার)

পারানো[১] *vt, vi* **1**=পার করা (⇒ পার). **2** =পার হওয়া (⇒পার)

পারানো[২] *vt* cause to be able; enable.

পারাপার *n* **1** the two banks/shores of a river, sea, etc. **2** crossing a river, sea, etc; ferrying across. ~ **করা** *vt* **1**=পার করা (⇒পার). **2** (of boats) ply. ~ **হওয়া** *vi*=পার হওয়া (⇒পার).

পারাবত *n* turtle-dove; pigeon. **বার্তাবাহী** ~ *n* carrier-pigeon.

পারাবার *n* **1** sea; ocean. **2** the further and nearer shore; the two banks.

পারায়ণ *n* **1** whole; totality; completeness; thoroughness; completion. **2** going over; reading through; perusing; shudying.

পারিজাত *n* **1** coral tree; *Erythrina indica.* **2** (myth) one of the five trees of paradise.

পারিণয্য *n* property/paraphernalia received by a woman at the time of marriage.

পারিতোষিক *n* reward; gratuity; prize.

পারিপাট্য *n* orderliness; neatness; regularity; methodicalness; tidiness.

পারিপার্শ্বিক *adj* surrounding; neighbouring. ❑*n* **1** retinue; attendants; bystanders. **2** assistant of the manager of a play. ~ **অবস্থা** *n* surroundings; environment.

পারিপাল্য *n* governorship.

পারিপ্রেক্ষিক *adj* perspective.

পারিপ্লব *adj* moving to and fro; agitated; tremulous; unsteady; wavering; irresolute. ❑*n* swimming.

পারিবারিক *adj* pertaining/restricted to a family; characteristic of a family; familial; family: ~ কোন্দল, family feud. ~ **ব্যাপার** *n* family affair/matter.

পারিব্রজ্য *n* life of a religious mendicant. ❑*adj* intended for a religious mendicant.

পারিভাষিক *adj* technical; terminological. ~ **শব্দ** *n* technical term.

পারিমুখিক *adj* being before the eyes; present; near.

পারিমুখ্য *n* nearness; presence; state of being towards.

পারিশা *n*=পারশে

পারিশ্রমিক *n* remuneration; fee.

পারিষদ *adj* fit for an assembly; decent. ❑*n* **1** member of an assembly; assessor at a council; courtier; councillor. **2** (derog) toady; (cringing) companion; flatterer.

পারিসাংখ্যিক *adj* statistical.

পারিহাস্য *n* jest; joke; fun. ❑*adj* in jest/ fun.

পারুল *n* a species of trumpet-flower.

পারুষ্য *n* roughness; rudeness; harshness; shagginess; dishevelled state; insult.

পার্ট [E] *n* part/role (in a play or film).

পার্টি [E] *n* party.

পার্টিশন [E] *n* partition.

পার্থ *n* Arjuna (অর্জুন) of the Mahabharata.

পার্থক্য *n* difference; severalty; dissimilarity; differentia.

পার্থিব *adj* worldly; earthly; earthy; terrestrial; material; mundane.

পার্বণ *n* **1** festival; fast; festive days: পৌষ ~. **2** oblations offered at new and full moon. ❑*adj* belonging/relating to a division of time or to the changes of the moon.

পার্বণী *n* gift given on account of certain festivals.

পার্বত, পার্বতীয় *adjj*=পার্বত্য

পার্বতী *n fem* goddess Durga, the daughter of the Himalayas.

পার্বত্য *adj* being in/growing on/coming from/consisting of mountains or hills; mountainous; hilly; highland. ~ **অঞ্চল/ প্রদেশ** *nn* hill-district; hilly region/ country; mountainous country. ~ **উদ্ভিদ** *n* mountain vegetation. ~ **জাতি** *n* hill-tribe. ~ **জাতির লোক** *n* hill-man; highlander; hill-folk (*pl*).

পার্লামেন্ট (E) *n* parliament.

পার্শী *n* Parsee; Parsi.

পার্শে = পারশে

পার্শ্ব *n* **1** side; flank: পূর্ব ~. **2** region of the ribs; side. **3** end; border; side: নগর ~ . **4** brink; brim; margin; edge: পুকুর ~. **5** bank; shore: সমুদ্রের ~. **6** nearness; proximity: বিপদে বন্ধুর পার্শ্বে থাকা. **7** vicinity; adjacent space: বাড়ির ~. **8** curve/ circumference of wheel. ~**গ** *adj* going at a person's side; accompanying; being in close proximity to. ~**গত** *adj* being close to/beside; being at the side; attending; accompanying:

very near; adjacent. ~গ্রাবরেখা *n* (geog) lateral moraine. ~চর *n* attendant; companion; follower; servant; retinue (*pl*); sycophant; toady. ~চরী, ~চারিণী *fem*. ~চিত্র *n* profile. ~ত *adv* by/from the side; at the side; sideways; near; edgeways; edgewise; sidelong. ~দেশ *n* flank; side; the ribs. ~পরিবর্তন *n* **1** turning round; turning in bed from one side to the other. **2** name of a festival on the eleventh day of the light half the month Bhadra (ভাদ্র) (on which Vishnu is supposed to turn upon the other side in sleep). ~ পরিবর্তন করা *vi* turn round; turn upon the other side. ~বর্তী *adj* standing by the side; adjacent; neihgbouring; proximate; staying/situated along side/at the side. ~বর্তিনী *fem*. ~ভাগ=~ দেশ. ~ শূল *n* shooting pain in the side. ~স্থ=~বর্তী. ~স্থা *fem*. পার্শ্বানুচর *adj* attendant. পার্শ্বাভিমুখ *adj* sidewise; sidelong. পার্শ্বাস্থি *n* rib. পার্শ্বে *adv* **1** at the side of; sidewise; alongside; by the side of; beside; in company/presence of. **2** in comparison to: রুমানার পার্শ্বে তার বান্ধবীরা ম্লান.

পার্শ্বিক *adj* lateral. ~ উৎক্রম *n* (phys) lateral inversion.

পার্শ্বীয় *adj* lateral.

পার্ষদ, পারিষদ *n* **1** courtier; associate; councillor; companion; attendant. **2**(derog) toady; flatterer.

পার্ষ্ণিক *n* **1** heel. **2** rear of an army. **3** extremity of the fore-axle to which the outside horses of a four-horse chariot is attached. ~গ্রাহ *n* attack from the rear; enemy in the rear of an army.

পার্সী= পারসি

পার্সেল [E] *n* parcel.

পাল[১] *n* flock; herd; drove. **পালের গোদা** *n* **1** leader of a herd. **2** (derog) ringleader. **এক ~ উট** *n* a drove of camels. **এক ~ কুকুর ছানা** *n* a litter of puppies. **এক ~ গরু/মহিষ** *n* a herd of cattle. **এক ~ নেকড়ে** *n* a pack of wolves. **এক ~ ভেড়া** *n* a flock of sheep. **এক ~ মুরগির ছানা** *n* a brood of chicken. **এক ~ হরিণ** *n* a herd of deer.

পাল[২] *n* sail. **~ খাটানো/ তোলা** *v* hoist the sail(s). **~ নামানো** *vi* lower the sail(s). **~-তোলা** *adj* under sail; sailing. **~তোলা জাহাজ/নৌকা** *nn* sailing-ship; sailing-boat. **সমস্ত ~ তুলে** in full sail.

পাল[৩] *n* copulation of beasts; mating; coupling. ~ দেওয়া/ধরানো *vi* mate; couple.

পাল[৪] (used as a *suff*) protector; guard; keeper; herdsman: গো~, ধর্ম~.

পালই=পালুই

পালওয়ান=পালোয়ান

পালং=পালঙ

পালক[১] *n* feather; wing: পাখির ~.

পালক[২] *adj* **1** guarding; protecting; nourishing; preserving; cherishing; supporting; bringing up; maintaining; rearing; breeding; fostering; nursing; defending. **2** observing: নিয়ম ~. ❑*n* guardian; protector; preserver; defender. **2** foster-father. **3** maintainer; nurse; breeder; groom; keeper. **4** ruler; sovereign; prince. **5** observer. ~ ছেলে *n* adopted son. ~-পিতা *n* foster-father.

পালকি *n* palanquin. ~ বেহারা *n* palanquin-bearer.

পালখ=পালক[১]

পালঙ[১] *n* spinach.

পালঙ[২] = পর্যঙ্ক. ~পোষ *n* **1** bed-cover; bed-spread; counterpane; cover for a divan. **2** divan (and a bed).

পালট *n* return; reversal; recession.

পালটা[১] *adj* counter; counteracting; contrary; return; opposing; exchanging; revoking. **~ অভিযোগ** *n* counter-charge; counter-complaint. **~ আক্রমণ** *n* counter-attack. **~ আঘাত** *n* counter blow. **~ আমন্ত্রণ** *n* return invitation. **~ জবাব** *n* retort. **~ নালিশ**=~ অভিযোগ. **~ বিবৃতি** *n* counter-statement. **~ মামলা** *n* counter-claim; counter-case. **~ হুকুম** *n* countermand. **~নো** *vt* change; alter; revoke; exchange; interchange. **~পালটি** *n* exchange; changing for/with another. **~পালটি করা** *vt* exchange; change for/with another; swap.

পালটা[২] *vi* change (for); change hands; alter.

পালটি *adj* **1** (of a family) being on equal social footing with another making matrimonial alliance permissible. **2** mutual; reciprocal.

পালন *n* **1** upbringing; rearing: শিশু~. **2** fostering; nursing: দুঃস্থ শিশু ~. **3** keeping; breeding; tending: পশু~. **4** guarding; protecting; defending; protection; defence; preservation: রাজ্য~. **5** maintenance: পোষ্য~. **6** observing; observation; compliance (with): ধর্ম~, আদেশ ~, নিয়ম ~. **7** nourishment; care: শরীর ~. **8** redemption; fulfilment: প্রতিশ্রুতি ~. **~ করা** *vt* **1** bring up; rear. **2** foster; nurse. **3** keep; breed; tend. **4** guard; protect; defend; preserve. **5** maintain. **6** observe; comply with; practise. **7** nourish; take care of. **8** redeem; fulfil. **~কর্তা** *n* = পালক[২]. **~কর্ত্রী** *fem*.

পালনীয় *adj* to be guarded/ protected/ maintained/ observed/ redeemed/ brought up/ reared (⇒ পালন করা).

পালপার্বণ *n* different festivals-religious and secular; festivities; festive events.

পালম *n* spinach.

পালয়িতা=পালক[২]. **পালয়িত্রী** *fem*.

পাললিক *adj* alluvial.

পালা[১] *vt*=পালন করা (⇒ পালন). ❑*adj* pet domestic: ~ কুকুর.

পালা[২] *n* **1** turn; time in rotation: ~ করে এগিয়ে যাওয়া. **2** story/plot of a drama/narrative:

বেহুলার ~. **3** period; spell. **~ক্রমে** *adv* by turns. **~গান** *n* narrative opera. **~জ্বর** *n* periodic/ remittent fever.

পালা[3] *n* branch; twig; offshoot; branchlet: গাছ~.

পালা[4] *n* rick of corn; pile; stack. **~ দেওয়া** *vt* stack (sth into piles); build up a rick.

পালান[1] [P] *n* **1** packsaddle. **2** girth (of a horse); cinch.

পালান[2] *n* cow's udder/teat.

পালান[3] *n* escape; flight; prank; bolting: এমন ~ পালাবে যে তাকে আর ধরা যাবে না.

পালান[4] *n* courtyard; kitchen garden: পালানের তরকারি.

পালানে *adj* fleeing; fugitive; escaping; absconding; runaway. **ঘর~ ছেলে** *n* runaway child. **স্কুল ~ ছেলে** *n* truant.

পালানো *vi* **1** flee; run away; fly/run away; evade; bolt; show a clean pair of heels. **2** play truant; have a lark: স্কুল ~. ❑*adj*=পালানে.

পালি[1] *n* **1** row; line; range. **2** boundary; limit; margin; edge. **3** a dry measure of grains (= 2.5 seers).

পালি[2] *n* Pali (language).

পালিকা *n fem* of পালক[2]

পালিটামান্দার *n* Indian coral tree.

পালিত *adj* **1** pet; tamed; kept; domestic: ~ পশুপাখি. **2** brought up; reared; nourished; cherished; bred. **3** protected; preserved; defended. **4** complied with; carried out: আদেশ ~ হয়েছে. **5** redeemed; fulfilled: প্রতিশ্রুতি ~. **6** observed: নিয়ম/আনুষ্ঠানিকতা ~. **পালিতা** *fem*. **~ কন্যা** *n fem* foster-daughter. **~-পুত্র** *n* foster-son. **~-সন্তান** *n* foster-child.

পালিনী *adj fem* (used as a *suff*)=পালিকা: জগৎ~.

পালিশ [E] *n* polish. **~ করা** *vt* polish. **~-করা** *adj* polished.

পালী=পালি[1]

পালুই *n* stack of paddy/hay; rick.

পালো *n* starch obtained from zedoary or shathi (শঠি).

পালোয়ান [P] *n* strong man; wrestler; champion; hero; athlete; stout and sturdy fellow.

পালোয়ানি [P] *n* heroism; athletic exercise; wrestling; gymnastics; brute force; prowess. ❑*adj* of a wrestler/wrestling; gymnastic; heroic; mighty; titanic; burly; athletic.

পাল্কি, পাল্কী=পালকি

পাল্টা=পালটা

পাল্টানো=পালটানো

পাল্য *adj* **1**=পালনীয়. **2** being under one's protection/guardianship.

পাল্লা *n* **1** thin layer; strip: এক ~ চামড়া. **2** scale (of a pair of balance); pan; balance. **3** leaf (of a door). **4** lid/shutter moving on a hinge. **5** distance: দূর ~. **6** range; reach: বন্দুকের ~. **7** competition: দৌড়ের ~. **8** speed: পায়ের ~. **9** snares; clutches; grasp; hold; trap; toils. **10** company; association: অসৎ সঙ্গীর ~. **~ চাপানো** *vi* put a weight (on a scale). **~ দেওয়া** *vi* compete/vie with; rival; race (with/against). **~ ভারী করা** *vt* tip the scale/balance. **~য় পড়া** *vi* fall into the clutches of sb/sth; be in sb's clutches; get into the company of.

পাশ[1] *n* **1** snare; trap; noose: মায়া~. **2** tie; bond; cord; chain; fetter; bondage: ভুজ~. **3** abundance; quantity: কেশ~. **4** rope; string. **5** die; dice. **6** selvage; edge; border (of anything woven). **~ক্রীড়া** *n* dice-play, gambling.

পাশ[2] *n* (myth) a missile by throwing which adversary can be fastened.

পাশ[3] [P] *n* apparatus for spraying; spray: গোলাপ~.

পাশ[4] *n*=পার্শ্ব. **~ কাটানো** *vi* turn/move aside; step aside and avoid; dodge; evade; shun; steer/keep/shy clear of; by-pass; parry; side-step; walk off without a glance in sb's direction. **~ দেওয়া** *vi* step aside to let sb pass; make way for. **~ ফেরা** *vi* turn in bed from one side to the other; turn on the side. **~ মোড়া** *n* turning from one side to the other (while lying in bed). **~মোড়া দেওয়া** *vi* =~ ফেরা.

পাশক *n* die; dice.

পাশব *adj* derived from/relating to/belonging to cattle/animals; beastly; bestial; inhuman; brutal. **~তা** *n* beastliness; bestiality; brutality; inhumanity. **~ প্রবৃত্তি** *n* beastly propensity/inclination; bestiality. **~ বল/শক্তি** *n* brute force.

পাশবদ্ধ *adj* entrapped; ensnared.

পাশবালিশ *n* bolster (at the side of a bed).

পাশবিক *adj*=পাশব. **~ অত্যাচার** *n* rape; inhuman torture. **~ অত্যাচার করা** *vi* rape; violate.

পাশা[1] *n* dice (for play). **~খেলা** *n* play at dice. **~ খেলা** *vi* play at dice; cast/throw dice.

পাশা[2] *n* small ornament for the ear.

পাশা[3] [T] *n* title of Turkish nobles/officers; lord; Pasha.

পাশাপাশি *adv* lying/situated side by side; contiguous; adjacent; adjoining; neighbouring: ~ বাড়ি/গ্রাম. ❑*adj* side by side; near; alongside.

পাশী *adj* having a net/noose; laying snares. ❑*n* **1** name of Varuna (বরুণ) or Yama (যম). **2** bird-catcher.

পাশুপত *adj* relating/sacred to/coming from Shiva Pashupati. ❑*n* **1** follower/worshipper of Shiva. **2** a celebrated weapon given by Shiva to Arjuna.

পাশে *adv*=পার্শ্বে (⇒ পার্শ্ব)

পাশ্চাত্য, পাশ্চাত্ত্য *adjj* **1** of the west/western world; western; Occidental. **2** hinder; posterior. ❑*n* the western world; the west; the Occident.

পাষণ্ড, পাষণ্ডী *adj* **1** heretical; impious; godless; atheistic; blasphemous. **2** extremely wicked and hard-hearted; sinful; vile; pernicious; accursed. ❑*n* **1** heretic; hypocrite; impostor; atheist. **2** inveterate sinner; villain; rogue; wicked and hard-hearted person. **~তা** *n* **1** heresy; heterodoxy; hypocrisy; blasphemy. **2** impiety; wickedness; hard-heartedness; brutality; villainy; deviltry; infamy; atrocity. **~দলন** *n* repression/ destruction of the wicked.

পাষাণ *n* **1** stone; rock. **2** small stone used as a weight. **3**(fig) stone-hearted man. ❑*adj* (used mostly as a *suff*) **1** (made) of stone; stonelike; stony. **2** unfeeling; pitiless; stony-hearted; hard-hearted; stony: ~ হৃদয়. **3** callous; indifferent: অতিশোকে ~. **~তুল্য** *adj* stone-like; stony; unfeeling; unmoved. **~-প্রাচীর** *n* stone-wall. **~বিদারক, ~বিদারী** *adj* able to pierce even stone; heart-rending. ❑*n* a species of plant; *Coleuns amboinicus*. **~ভার** *n* weight as heavy as a stone. **~ভেদী**=~বিদারক. **~ময়** *adj* made/full/consisting of stone; stony. **~হৃদয়** *n* a heart of stone. ❑*adj* stony-hearted. **পাষাণী** *fem*.

পাস [E] *n* **1** passing (an examination); success in an examination; pass. **2** permission; pass: গেট~. **3** free/complementary ticket; pass. **4** (football) pass. **5** gap in a range of mountains; pass: খাইবার ~. **6** (card-games) pass. **7** (in conjuring) pass: হাতের ~. ❑*adj* pass: ~ কোর্স, ~ গ্রাজুয়েট. **~ করা** *vi, vt* pass. **~ হওয়া** *vi* pass (an examination); be passed/sanctioned; be allowed to pass through.

পাসরণ, পাসরন *n* (poet) forgetting; oblivion.

পাসরা *vt* (poet) forget.

পাহলবী, পাহলভী [P] *n, adj* Pahlavi.

পাহাড় *n* **1** hill; mountain; rock. **2** dune; mound: বালুর ~. **3** upland. **4** heap: টাকার ~. **~তলি** *n* valley; dale; foot of a hill.

পাহাড়ি *adj*=পাহাড়িয়া. ❑*n* hill-man; high-lander; hill-tribe.

পাহাড়ে, পাহাড়িয়া (colloq) *adjj* **1** of hills and mountains; hilly; mountainous; highland; growing/lying/dwelling on hills/mountains. **2** huge; terrible: ~ শরীর.

পাহারা *n* **1** watch; watching; guarding. **2** watchman; guard; sentinel; watcher; sentry; guardsman. **~ দেওয়া** *vt* watch; guard; patrol; keep a watch. **~ বসানো** *vi* place a guard over; post sentries. **~ওয়ালা** *n* constable; policeman; sentry.

পিউলি, পিউরি *nn* **1** kind of light yellow flower. **2** a yellow pigment made from the cow's urine.

পিউ পিউ *n* (onom) note/cooing of a nightingale.

পিওন *n*=পিয়ন

পিচুঁটি *n* excretion/discharge concrete rheum/sordes of the eyes.

পিঁজর(া) *n* cage. **পিঁজরা পোল** *n* an establishment for keeping disabled cattle; veterinary asylum.

পিঁজা *vt ,vi* **1** clean cotton from the seeds; comb (cotton, wool, etc); pick into separate threads; tease; card. **2** (of cloth, clothing, etc) become threadbare: কাপড়টা পিজে গেছে. ❑*adj* worn thin; threadbare; shabby.

পিড়াঁ *n* **1** raised floor of a house; terrace; portico. **2** veranda. **3** (dial)=পিড়ি.

পিঁড়ি, পিঁড়ে (dial) *n* **1** a low wooden seat. **2** pedestal of an idol; stand.

পিঁপড়া, পিঁপড়ে (colloq) *n* ant.

পিঁপীড়া *n* (old use)=পিপড়া

পিঁপুল *n*=পিপ্পল

পিঁয়াজ *n*=পিয়াজ

পিক[১] *n* (Indian) cuckoo. **~তান, ~ধ্বনি, ~রব** *nn* note/call of the cuckoo. **~বধূ** *n* female cuckoo.

পিক[২] *n* spittle (coloured red by chewing betel-leaf). **~ ফেলা** *vi* spit (after chewing betel). **~দান, ~দানি** *n* spitting pot; spittoon.

পিকনিক [E] *n* picnic.

পিকেটিং [E] *n* picketing. **~ করা** *vi* picket. **~কারী** *n* picketer.

পিগমি [E] *n* pigmy.

পিঙ্ক [E] *n* pink; Dianthus. ❑*adj* pink.

পিঙ্গল *adj* reddish-brown; tawny; brownish yellow; gold-coloured. ❑*n* reddish-brown/ yellow colour. **পিঙ্গলা** *adj fem*.

পিঙ্গলা *n* a particular vessel of the body (the right of 3 tubular vessels which according to the yoga philosophy are the chief passages of breath and air).

পিচ[১] *n*=পিক[২]

পিচ[২] [E] *n* (cricket) pitch.

পিচ[৩] [E] *n* black substance made from coal tar; pitch. **~ঢালা** *adj* tarred. **~ ঢালা/দেওয়া** *vi* cover (sth) with tar; tar.

পিচ[৪] [E] *n* peach.

পিচকারি *n* **1** syringe; spray. **2** squirt. **~র মতো বেরনো** *vi* squirt.

পিচবোর্ড [E] *n* pasteboard; cardboard.

পিচাশ *n* (colloq)=পিশাচ

পিচুটি=পিচুটি

পিচ্ছল, পিচ্ছিল *adj* **1** slippery; slick; slithery; greasy; very smooth. **~তা** *n* slipperiness; greasiness.

পিছ *n* **1** back; backside; rear. **2** past; back. **~টান** *n* pull (from the back); (fig) attachment to one's family/near one's. **~পা** *n* desisting; receding; falling back; reluctant. **~পা হওয়া** *vi* fall back; be reluctant; shy at; fight shy of; shrink; hesitate; go back (on sth). **~মোড়া** *adj* held with one's arms pinioned together behind one's back. **~মোড়া করে বাঁধা** *vi* **1** (of a person) bind/hold sb with his arms pinioned together behind his back. **2** (of arms) pinion together behind sb's back. **পিছে** *adv* behind; at the back of; backwards; following behind; after: ~ হাঁটা. ❑*prep* (in/to a position) at the back of; behind; on/in the back of: বাড়িটা পার্কের ~. **~পিছে** *adv* **1**=~. **2** closely following; hard on sb's heels; hot on sb's heel; hot on the trail (of sth).

পিছন *n*=পিছ. **~ ফেরা** *vi* **1** turn back; fall back: এখন আর ~ ফেরার উপায় নেই. **2** glance behind oneself; look behind. **3** look back (on sth): একটু ~ ফিরে যদি ছেলে বেলার কথা ভাবো ... . **পিছনে চলা** *vi* go/move back-wards; back; draw back; move back; back out. **পিছনে চাওয়া/ তাকানো/ দেখা** *vi* **1** look at one's won back. **2**=পিছনে ফেরা. **পিছনে থাকা** *vi* be supportive of; be behind: তার বন্ধুরা তার পিছনে আছে. **~টান** *n*=পিছটান (⇒ পিছ). **~পিছন, পিছনে পিছনে** *adv*= পিছে পিছে (⇒ পিছ). **পিছনে** *adv, prep*=পিছে (⇒পিছ).

পিছলা *adj* (colloq)=পিচ্ছল. **~ খাওয়া**=পিছলানো.

পিছলানো *vi* slip; slide; glide.

পিছা *n* broomstick.

পিছানো *vi, vt* **1** draw back; move back; go backwards; retreat; recoil. **2** fall back; back out; shrink; flinch. **3** put off; delay; postpone; defer; be put off/ delayed/ postponed/ deferred. **পিছিয়ে আসা** *vi* retreat; back out. **পিছিয়ে থাকা**/পড়া *vi* lag (behind sb/sth); fail to keep pace with; be behind; be behind schedule. **পিছিয়ে যাওয়া** *vi* be deferred/ postponed: পরীক্ষা পিছিয়ে যাওয়া.

পিছু=পাছু and পিছ

পিজবোর্ড [E] *n* pasteboard.

পিঞ্জট *n*=পিচুটি

পিঞ্জন *n* **1**=bow/bow-shaped instrument used for cleaning cotton. **2** cleaning of cotton with a bow; teasing.

পিঞ্জর *n* **1** bird-cage; aviary; cage. **2** ribs; thorax. **পিঞ্জরাবদ্ধ** *adj* in a cage; caged; captive. **পিঞ্জরাবদ্ধ করা** *vt* put in a cage; cage; shut up in a cage; encage.

পিঞ্জিকা *n* roll of cotton from which threads are spun.

পিট[1] *n* (colloq)=পিঠ

পিট[2] *n* basket; box.

পিটটান *n* fleeing; flight; beating a retreat; drawing back; qualm; diffidence. **~ দেওয়া** *vi* flee; depart quietly; take to one's heels; draw back; beat a retreat; feel/have qualms about sth; flinch; waver.

পিটন *n* beating; thrashing; hammering; striking.

পিটনা *n* rammer/beater (used to beat down the roof or floor and make them compact).

পিটনি *n* **1** name of a large tree; *Trevia nudiflora*. **2** pulp of rice prepared by grinding it with water.

পিটপিট *n* (onom) expressing **(a)** twitching (as of the eye); wink; **(b)** itching; tingling; **(c)** (of a light) wink; blink; flickering; **(d)** fastidiousness; mania for cleanliness; peevishness. **~ করা, পিটপিটানো** *vi* **1** twitch; wink (at sb); blink; squint (at sth). **2** itch; tingle. **3** blink; wink; flicker; twinkle. **4** show a mania for cleanliness; behave fastidiously/ peevishly. **পিটপিটানি** *n* = ~. **পিটপিটে** *adj* **1** winking. **2** fastidious; peevish; having a mania for fastidiousness.

পিটা[1] *vt* **1** strike; beat: লোহা ~. **2** batter; pound; ram: ছাদ ~. **3** hit; beat; thrash; give a (good) beating; lash sb with a stick. ❑*adj* beaten; thrashed; wrought.

পিটা[2] *n* (colloq) =পিঠা

পিটাই, পিটানি *nn* beating; striking; thrashing; ramming; hammering. **~ দেওয়া** *vi* give a (good) beating/thrashing.

পিটানো *vi* cause to beat/ hammer/ thrash; give a (good) beating: গুণ্ডা দিয়ে ~.

পিটাপিটি *n* reciprocal beating; brawl; free-for-all.

পিটালি=পিটলা

পিটিশন [E] *n* petition. **~ করা** *vi* petition. **~কারী** *n* petitioner.

পিটুনি *n* (colloq)=পিটাই. **~ পুলিশ** *n* punitive police. **~ কর/জরিমানা** *n* punitive tax/fine.

পিটুলি=পিটলি

পিট্টান=পিটটান

পিঠ *n* **1** back; rear. **2** face; surface; side: এপিঠ, obverse; ওপিঠ, reverse. **3** (in game of cards) trick. **~ চাপড়ানো** *vi* **1** pat sb on the back; give sb a pat on the back. **2** (fig) congratulate sb; pat sb on the back. **~ ভাঙা** *vi* break sb's/one's back (to do sth). **~ভাঙা** *adj* back-breaking. **~দাঁড়া** *n* spine. **পিঠের চামড়া তোলা** *vi* beat sb black and blue; flog severely. **পিঠে পিঠে** *adj ,adv* **1** back to back; with back against back; on the back of. **2** born next; immediately succeeding in birth.

পিঠা, পিঠে (colloq) *nn* sort of cake.

পিঠা-পিঠি=পিঠে পিঠে (⇒ পিঠ)

পিঠালি=পিটলি

পিড়পিড় *n* (onom) expressing pricking, itching, tingling. **~ করা** *vi* tingle; prick; itch. **পিড়পিড়ে** *adj* tingling; pricking; itching.

পিড়া, পিড়ি, পিড়ে *nn*=পিড়ি

পিড়াপিড়ি *n* insistence; entreaty; importunity; plea; solicitation. **~ করা** *vi* insist; entreat; importune; nag; beseech; press for; pester.

পিড়িং *n* (onom) twang. **~ করা** *vi* make a twang; twang.

পিণ্ড *n* **1** any round/roundish mass/heap; lump; ball; clod; piece. **2** roundish lump of food; bite; morsel; mouthful. **3** ball of rice, flour, etc offered to the deceased ancestors; oblation. **4** food; daily bread; livelihood; subsistence. **5** solid mass; material object; body; bodily frame. **6** calf of the leg. **7** the two projections of an elephant's frontal sinus. **8** fleshy parts of the shoulder situated above the collar-bone. **9** quantity; collection. ~ **গেলা** *vi* (derog) have one's daily food; fall to eating with great gusto. ~ **চটকানো** *vi* **1** crush lump of food offered to the deceased ancestors. **2** (fig) revile; inveigh against; backbite. **3** (fig) give a sound thrashing; castigate; make an example of; trounce; punish severely; teach a lesson to. ~**তা** *n* being a lump/ball; density; condensation. ~ **দেওয়া** *vi* offer oblations to deceased ancestors. ~**খর্জুর** *n* a kind of dates. ~**দ,** ~**দাতা** *adj* offering/qualified to offer oblations to deceased ancestors. ~**দা,** ~**দাত্রী** *fem.* ~**দান,** ~**ন** *nn* offering of balls of rice, etc to deceased ancestors. ~ **রোগী** *n* valetudinarian. ~**লোপ** *n* **1** neglect/cessation of offering oblations to deceased ancestors. **2** extinction of one's line of descent. **পিণ্ডাকার, পিণ্ডাকৃতি** *adj* lumpy; shaped like a lamp; roundish.

পিণ্ডতাপত্তি *n* coagulation.

পিণ্ডারি, পিণ্ডারী *nn* **1** band of mercenary free-booters under Shivajee; Pindaris. **2** portmanteau. ~ **শব্দ** *n* portmanteau-word.

পিণ্ডালু *n* a kind of potato; *Dioscova globosa.*

পিণ্ডি *n* (colloq)=পিণ্ড

পিণ্ডিত *adj* rolled into a ball/lamp; thick; massy; densified. **2** mixed; mingled. **3** heaped; collected.

পিণ্ডী *n* (in compounds) =পিণ্ড. ~**কৃত** made into a lump/ball; heaped; collected. ~**ভূত** *adj* lumped; heaped; conglomerate; coagulated. ~**ভূত দানা** *n* conglomerate crystal. ~**শূর** *n* cowardly boaster; poltroon.

পিতঃ *int* o father!

পিতল *n* brass; bell-metal.

পিতা *n* father. ~**পুত্র** *n* father and son. ~**মহ** *n* paternal grandfather. ~**মহী** *n fem* paternal grandmother.

পিতুঃস্বসা=পিতৃষ্বসা (⇒ পিতৃ).

পিতৃ *n* (in compounds) father. ~**আজ্ঞা** *n* father's command. ~-**ঋণ** *n* **1** one's obligations to one's father; filial piety/duty. **2** debt incurred by one's father (and to be paid by children. ~**কর্ম** *n* rite performed in honour of deceased ancestors; obsequial rites. ~**কল্প** *adj* father-like; fatherly. ❑*n* precepts relating to the sites in honour of deceased ancestors. ~**কানন** *n* place of the departed. ~-**কার্য**=~কর্ম. ~**কুল** *n* one's father's line; paternal race/family. ~**কৃত্য,**~**ক্রিয়া**=~কর্ম. ~**গণ** *n* (myth) group/ class of sages from whom the gods, demons, Yakshas and men are said to have evolved. ~**গৃহ** *n* paternal house; father's house. ~**গোত্র** *n* paternal race/family. ~**ঘাতক,** ~**ঘ্ন** *n* parricide. ❑*adj* parricidal. ~**ঘাতী** *adj* parricidal. ~ **তর্পণ** *n* (according to Hindu belief) refreshing of the deceased ancestors (with water thrown from the right hand); offering water, etc to deceased ancestors. ~**তুল্য** *adj* = ~কল্প. ~**ত্ব** *n* fatherhood; paternity. ~**দত্ত** *adj* given by a father (as a woman's peculiar property). ~**দান** *n* oblation to deceased ancestors. ~**দায়** *n* **1** solemn obligation of performing the obsequies rites of one's deceased father. **2** property inherited from a father; patrimony, ~**দায়গ্রস্ত** *adj* under the obligation of performing the obsequial rites of one's father. ~**দেব** *n* father looked upon as a deity (used as a term of suspect). ~**দ্রোহ** *n* plotting/rebellion against one's father; ill-treatment of one's father. ~**দ্রোহক,** ~**দ্রোহী** *adjj* plotting/ rebellions against one's father. ~**দ্বেষ** *n* malice/ spite towards one's father. ~**দ্বেষী** *adj* malicious/ spiteful to one's father. ~**ধন** *n* paternal wealth; hereditary property; patrimony. ~**ধনসংক্রান্ত** *adj* patrimonial. ~**পক্ষ** *n* **1** relations on the father's side; paternal relationship. **2** dark half in the Aswin (আশ্বিন) (particularly dedicated to the performance of oblations). ~**পতি** *n* Yama, the regent of death. ~**পদ** *n* **1** office/station held by a father. **2** feet of one's father. ~**পিতামহাদি** *n* paternal ancestry; progenitors. ~**পুরুষ** *n* line of paternal ancestors; fore-father; paternal ancestor. ~**প্রতিম** *adj* =~কল্প. ~**বংশ** *n* paternal family/ race. ~**বৎ**= ~কল্প. ~**বন্ধু** *n* father's friend. ~**বিয়োগ** *n* death/ decease of one's father. ~**ব্রত** *n* worship of ancestors. ~**ব্য** *n* paternal uncle. ~**ব্যপুত্র** *n* son of a paternal uncle; cousin. ~**ব্যপুত্রী** *n fem* daughter of a paternal uncle; cousin sister. ~**ভক্ত** *adj* devoted to/loyal to/fond of one's father. ~**ভক্তি** *n* devotion to/fondness of one's father; filial piety. ~**মাতৃদায়** *n* solemn obligation of performing the obsequial rites of one's deceased parents. ~**মাতৃহীন** *adj* bereft of parents; orphan. ~**মেধ,** ~**যজ্ঞ** *nn* oblation made to the deceased ancestors. ~**বান** *n* trodden by/ leading to the deceased ancestors. ~**রিষ্টি** *n* (astrol) location of the zodiacal signs in one's horoscope indicating loss of one's father. ~-**লোক** *n* world/sphere of the deceased ancestors. ~**শাসন** *n* paternal discipline/ authority. ~**শোক** *n* grief/ mourning for one's deceased father. ~**শ্রাদ্ধ** *n* obsequies of one's deceased father. ~**ষ্বসা** *n fem* paternal aunt;

father's sister. ~সদৃশ, ~সম *adjj*=~কল্প. ~সম্বন্ধীয়, ~সম্পর্কীয় *adjj* paternal. ~সেবা *n* attendance one's father; serving one's father devotedly. ~স্থানীয় *adj* deserving to be respected as one's father. ~হত্যা *n* parricide. patricidal. ~হত্যামূলক *adj* parricidal. ~হন্তা *n* patricide; parricide. ❑*adj* guilty of parricide. ~হন্ত্রী *fem.* ~হীন *adj* fatherless. ~হীনা *fem.*

পিত্ত *n* bile; gall. ~ জ্বলা *vi* got sb's/one's dander up; become infuriated; be enraged. ~ পড়া *vi* lose appetite because of abstinence from food when hungry. ~কোষ *n* gall-bladder. ~ঘ্ন *adj* antibilious. ~জ্বর *n* bilious fever. ~নালী *n* biliary duct. ~নাশ *n* destruction/ cure of bilious diseases. ~নাশক *adj* antibilious; good for curing bilious diseases. ~-পাথরি *n* gall-stone. ~বিকার *n* biliary/ bilious disorder/ trouble. ~রক্ত *n* plethora. ~রক্ষা *n* appeasement of hunger by taking a small quantity of food. ~শূল *n* biliay colic. পিত্তাতিসার *n* bilious form of dysentery. পিত্তাশয় *n* gall-bladder.

পিত্তল *n* brass; bell-metal. ~নির্মিত *adj* made of brass; brazen. ~-ফলক *n* brass-plate.

পিত্তি *n* (colloq)=পিত্ত. ~কাটা=পিত্ত জ্বলা.

পিত্যেশ, পিত্যেস *nn* (colloq)=প্রত্যাশা

পিত্রালয় *n* father's/parental house (esp of a married woman).

পিদিম *n* (colloq)=প্রদীপ

পিধান *n* 1 covering; stopping; shuttling; closing. 2 cover; lid; sheath.

পিন *n* [E] pin. ~/পিনে আটকানো *vt* pin (up)

পিনদ্ধ *adj* fastened; covered; wrapped; dressed; put on; worn; armed.

পিনাক *n* bow of Shiva. ~পাণি, পিনাকী *nn* Shiva.

পিনাফোর *n* [E] pinafore.

পিনাল কোড *n* [E] penal code.

পিনাস, পিনেস (colloq) *nn* nasal catarrh; atrophic rhinitis.

পিন্ধন *n* (archaic) wearing; putting on or clothed.

পিন্ধা *vt* (archaic) wear; put on; dress.

পিপা *n* [Pg] barrel; cask; coop.

পিপাসা *n* 1 thirst. 2 (fig) strong desire; craving. ~ পাওয়া *vi* fell thirsty. ~ দূর করা/মেটানো *vi* 1 quench/slake one's thirst. 2 (fig) satisfy one's desire; slake one's lust; quench sb's ardent passion. ~কর, ~কারক *adj* causing/exciting thirst. ~ নিবারক *adj* preventing thirst. ~ নিবারণ, ~নিবৃত্তি *nn* preventing/ quenching of thirst. ~বর্ধক *adj* increasing thirst.

পিপাসার্ত, পিপাসিত, পিপাসী, পিপাসু *adj* 1 thirsty. 2 eagerly desirous of; craving for. পিপাসার্তা, পিপাসিতা, পিপাসিনী *fem.*

পিপীড়া, পিপীলিকা *n* ant.

পিপুল *n*=পিপুল

পিপে *n* (colloq)=পিপা

পিপ্পল *n* the sacred fig-tree of the Hindus; *Ficus religiosa.*

পিপ্পলি, পিপ্পলী *nn* long pepper; *Piper longum.*

পিয় *n* (poet)=প্রিয়

পিয়ন [F] *n* peon; postman; footman; liveried messenger.

পিয়া *n* (poet)=প্রিয়া

পিয়াজ [P] *n* onion.

পিয়াজি *n* 1 kind of snack made of minced onion and pulses. 2 sauciness; effrontery; waggishness. 3 light purple colour. ❑*adj* of light purple colour; crimson; pink.

পিয়াদা [P] *n* 1 footman; foot-soldier; liveried messenger. 2 (chess) pawn.

পিয়ানো[1] *vt* (poet) make one drink; cause to drink; suckle.

পিয়ানো[2] [E] *n* piano.

পিয়ার *n* love; affection; attachment; fondness; expression of love by kissing; friendship; kindness. ~ করা *vt* love; caress; fondle.

পিয়ারা *adj* beloved; dear; favourite; charming; lovable; pleasing. ❑*n* sweet-heart.

পিয়াল *n* kind of nut-tree; its nut or seed; *Bucanania latifolia.*

পিয়ালা [P] *n* cup; goblet.

পিয়াস, পিয়াসা *n* (poet)=পিপাসা

পিয়াসী, পিয়াসু *adj* (poet)=পিপাসী

পিরান [P] *n* long robe; long shirt.

পিরামিড [E] *n* pyramid.

পিরিচ *n* [Pg] saucer.

পিরিত, পিরিতি, পিরীত, পিরীতি *n* (poet, archaic, sl) love; affection; attachment; secret/ illicit love; liaison; love-affair; intimacy. ~ করা *vi* have an affair with; in love (with sb).

পিল[1] [E] *n* pill.

পিল[2] [P] *n* 1 elephant. 2 (chess) bishop. ~খানা *n* stable for housing elephants. ~বান *n* elephant keeper.

পিল করা *vt* (in certain games) send (a ball/marble) into the pocket; pocket.

পিলপা, পিলপে, পিল্পা *nn* [P] pillar; column. ~ গাড়ি *n* building/ fixing/ planting a pillar.

পিলপিল *n* (onom) expressing swarming. ~ করা *vi* swarm. ~ করে *adv* by swarms/ multitudes. ~ করে বেরনো *vi* swarm out.

পিলপে ⇒ পিলপা

পিলসুজ *n* [P] candlestick; brass/tin lamp.

পিলা *n* spleen; disease/ enlargement of the spleen.

পিলু[1] *n* an Indian musical mode.

পিলু[2] *n* name of a tree; walnut.

পিলে=পিলা

পিল্লা ⇒ পিলপা

পিশাচ *n* 1 name of a class of demons; fiend; ogre; demon; imp; ghoul. 2 malevolent/ devilish being. পিশাচী *fem.* ~তত্ত্ব *n* demonology. ~চর্যা, ~পদ্ধতি *nn* practice of demons; demonic/ demoniac/ diabolic/ ghoulish/fiendish practice/ways. ~প্রকৃতি *n* demoniac/fiendish nature. ~সিদ্ধ *adj* who has made a demon his slave by means of rigorous ascetic practices. ~সিদ্ধা *fem.*

পিশিত *n* flesh; meat.

পিশুন *adj* backbiting; slanderous; calumnious; malicious; malignant; base; treacherous ; wicked; scandal-mongering. ~তা *n* slander; scandal; detraction.

পিষণ *n* grinding; pounding; crushing; squeezing; kneading; pulping; pulverization.

পিষা *vt* **1** grind; crush; knead; pound; crush to powder; pulp; pulverize; press. **2** bruise; injure; oppress; squeeze. পিষাই *n* **1**=পিষণ. **2** cost/charge of grinding. পিষাই করা = ~. ~নো *vt* cause to grind/ pound/ knead; get sth ground.

পিষ্ট *adj* crashed; ground; pulverized; kneaded; pulped; pressed; squeezed.

পিষ্টক *n* cake made of (rice) flour; pastry.

পিষ্টিক *n* **1** (cake made of) rice flour. **2** paste.

পিষ্টোদক *n* water mixed with rice flour.

পিসতুত, পিসতুতো *adj* born of a sister of one's father. ~ ভাই/বোন *nn* cousin.

পিস বোর্ড [E] *n* pasteboard.

পিসশাশুড়ি *n fem* sister of one's father-in-law.

পিসশ্বশুর *n* husband of a sister of one's father-in-law.

পিসা *n* father's sister's husband. ~ত *adj* = পিসতুত

পিসি, পিসী *nn fem* father's sister.

পিসে *n* (colloq)=পিসা

পিস্তন *n* [E] piston.

পিস্তল *n* [Pg] pistol. ~ ছোঁড়া *vi* fire a pistol.

পিহিত *adj* covered with; sheathed; encased; shut; hidden.

পী *n* (onom) expressing; the note of the pied cuckoo.

পীড়াঁ =পিড়াঁ.

পীচ[1] [E] *n* peach.

পীচ[2] [E] *n* pitch.

পীঠ[1] *n* **1** religious student's seat. **2** alter; case; pedestal; seat. **3** royal seat; throne. **4** place; office. **5** (myth) any of the fifty-one holy places (where the limbs of Parvati fell after she had been cut to pieces). ~স্থান *n* seat

পীঠ[2] *n* (much) base.

পীড্যমান *adj* being afflicted/ distressed/ troubled/ hurt/ squeezed; suffering pain.

পীড়ক *adj* oppressing; persecuting; tormenting; forcing; vexatious. ❑*n* oppressor; tormentor; persecutor.

পীড়কা *n* (ms) eruptions.

পীড়ন *n* **1** oppression; torment; persecution. **2** pressing; afflicting; molesting. **3** insistence; pressure. **4** squeezing. **5** accepting in marriage. ~ করা *vt* **1** oppress; torment; hurt; persecute; force. **2** press; squeeze: হস্ত ~ করা. **3** accept in marriage: পাণি~ করা.

পীড়া *n* **1** disease; ailment; afflictions: মনঃ~. **2** suffering; vexation; trouble; annoyance; harm; injury; pain; distress; torture. ~ দেওয়া *vt* afflict; pain; annoy; distress; trouble; vex; hurt. ~কর *adj* tormenting; distressing; painful; vexatious; afflicting. ~গ্রস্ত *adj* ill; sick; ailing; deceased. ~জনক, ~দায়ক *adjj*=~কর.

পীড়াপীড়ি=পিড়াপিড়ি

পীড়িত *adj* **1** ill; sick; ailing; diseased; suffering (from). **2** afflicted (with); distressed; troubled; injured; hurt; oppressed. **3** squeezed; pressed. পীড়িতা *fem.*

পীত[1] *adj* yellow. ❑*n* yellow colour. ~কদলী *n* a species of banana. ~কন্দ *n* carrot. ~করবী *n* oleander with yellow flowers. ~কাষ্ঠ = ~চন্দন. ~গন্ধক *n* yellow sulphur. ~চন্দন *n* yellow sandal. ~চম্পক *n* yellow *champaka*. ~জ্বর *n* yellow fever. ~ধড়া *n* yellow loin-cloth. ~পর্ণী *n* a species of nettle. ~পুষ্প *n*=~চম্পক. ~বাস, পীতাম্বর *nn* **1**=~ ধড়া. **2** Sri Krishna. ❑*adj* wearing a yellow loin-cloth. ~মণি, ~রক্ত *nn* topaz. ~বাস *n* yellowness. ❑*adj* of a yellow colour.

পীত[2] *adj* sipped; sucked; drunk; imbibed.

পীন *adj* swelling; swollen; full; round; thick; large; fat; fleshy; plump; corpulent. ~তা *n* fatness; corpulency; plumpness; compactness; tenseness. ~নিতম্বা *adj fem* having full/large hips. ~ পয়োধরা *adj* having full/large breast; full-breasted. ~বক্ষ *adj* full-breasted; large-chested. ~শ্রোণী *adj fem* having swelling hips.

পীনস *n* nasal catarrh; coryza.

পীনোত্তুঙ্গ=পীনোন্নত

পীনোন্নত *n adj* large and prominent. ~ পয়োধরা, ~স্তনী *adj fem* having large and prominent breasts.

পীবর *adj* fat; stout; large; plump; thick; dense; corpulent; barley; well-developed. পীবরা, পীবরী *fem.* ~ত্ব *adj* thickness; denseness. ~স্তনী *n*, *adj* (woman) with large breasts; (cow) with large udder.

পীযূষ *adj* **1** nectar (drink of immortality). ambrosia. **2** milk of a cow during the first seven days after calving; beestings. ~ধারা *n* stream of nectar. ~পূর্ণ *adj* full of nectar. ~বর্ষ *n* shower of nectar. ~বর্ষী *adj* showering nectar; mellifluent; mellifluous.

পীর [P] *n* saint; holy man; spiritual guide. ~ ধরা *vi* be disciple of a saint. ~জাদা *n* son of a saint. ~ভাই *n* fellow disciple. পীরের দরগা *n* shrine of a saint.

পীরি [P] *n* status of a saint.

পীরিত, পীরিতি *nn* ⇒ পিরিত

পীল *n*=পিল[২]

পীলসুজ *n*=পিলসুজ

পুং[১] abbr of পুনশ্চ

পুং[২] *n* (in compounds) man. ☐*adj* male; masculine; he. ~কেশর *n* (bot) stamen. ~গব=পুঙ্গব. ~ জননকোষ *n* (bot) male gamete. ~দণ্ড *n* (bot) filament. ~বৎ *adj* like a man; manly; like/in the masculine gender. ~বৎস *n* bull-calf. ~বাচক *adj* (gram) masculine. ~বৃষ *n* 1 bull. 2 musk rat. ~বেশ *adj* wearily male attire; dressed like a man. ~ভাব *n* masculinity; virility; manliness. ~ভাবাপন্ন *adj* masculine type; mannish; manly. ~যোগ *n* connection /with/relation to a man. ~রত্ন *n* jewel of a man. ~লক্ষণ *n* mark of man; manliness. ~লিঙ্গ *n* 1 male organ. 2 (gram) masculine gender. ☐*adj* (gram) masculine. ~শ্চলী *adj fem* running after men. ☐*n* whore; harlot; courtesan. ~শ্চিহ্ন *n* membrum virile. ~সবন *n* Hindu sacrament performed in the third month of gestation and before the period of quickening. ~স্কামা *n,adj* (woman) desirous of a lover/husband. ~স্কোকিল *n* male of the Indian cuckoo. ~স্তবক *n* (bot) androecium ~স্ত্ব *n* being a man; manhood; virility; semen virile.

পুঁই *n* a creeper used as a vegetable; *Basella alba.* ~ডাঁটা *n* stem of this creeper.

পুঁইয়া=পুঁয়ে

পুঁচকে *adj* tiny; wee; teeny; midget.

পুঁইন *n* wiping (off); rubbing (off); mopping.

পুঁছা[১] *vt* mop; swab; rub off; wipe (away). পুঁছানো *vt* cause a person to mop/wipe (away)/ swab/rub off.

পুঁছা[২] *vt* 1 (poet) ask; inquire (after); question. 2 care about; value; invite; attach importance to; pay heed to.

পুঁজি *n* capital (money); savings; resources; possessions; belongings; accumulation. ~পাটরা *n* one's movable and immovable possessions; property; assets; savings; wealth; substance.

পুঁটকি *n* (vulg) anus.

পুঁটলি *n* small bundle/ packet.

পুঁটি[১] *n* a tiny fresh-water fish. ~ মাছের প্রাণ *n* (fig) 1 short-lived/frail person; weakling; 2 mean-minded/niggardly person. ~ মাছের ফরফরানি *n* bragging of a man of a little/no substance.

পুঁটি[২] *n* a little girl; girlie; lass. (⇒ পোঁটা[২]).

পুঁটে[১] *adj* tiny; minuscule. 2 mean; mingy; stingy.

পুঁটে[২] *n* 1 ends/joint of bangles, etc. 2 button made of cloth.

পুঁঠি=পুঁটি

পুঁড়া *n* large straw-basket for preserving grains.

পোঁতা *vt* 1 plant: গাছ ~. 2 sow: বীজ ~. 3 drive in: পেরেক ~. 4 dig. 5 bury; inter. 6 set; fix; sink: খুঁটি ~. ~নো *vt* cause to plant/sow/fix.

পুঁতি *n* glass-beads. ~র মালা *n* string of glass-beads.

পুঁথি *n* 1 book. 2 manuscript. ~ বাড়ানো *vi* lengthen; prolong a discussion; spin yarns. ~গত *adj* bookish; learnt from books. ~গত বিদ্যা *n* bookish knowledge; book-learning. ~পত্র *n* books and papers. ~শালা *n* library; archive.

পুকুর *n* pond; pool. ~ কাটা *vi* excavate a pond. ~ ঝালানো *vi* dredge a pond. ~ প্রতিষ্ঠা করা *vi* perform solemn rites before putting a newly excavated pond to use. ~-চুরি *n* monstrous fraud/swindle. ~পাড় *n* bank of a pond.

পুঙ্খ *n* shaft of an arrow.

পুঙ্খানুপুঙ্খ *adj* thorough; thorough-going; minute; detailed; minutely searching/ scrutinizing. ~রূপে *adj* thoroughly; minutely; in detail.

পুঙ্গব *n* 1 bull. 2 hero; eminent person; chief.

পুচ্ছ *n* tail; hinder part; last/ extreme end; posteriors. ~হীন *adj* tailess.

পুছ(ন) *n* asking; interrogation; questioning; inquiry. পুছ করা=পুঁছা.

পুছা=পুঁছা

পুঞ্জ *n* heap; mass; quantity; multitude; accumulation; collection; pile; crowd. ~মেঘ *n* cumulus.

পুঞ্জি *n*=পুঁজি

পুঞ্জিত *adj* heaped; pressed/put together; accumulated; piled up; collected together; crowded; amassed; gathered/ pressed together.

পুঞ্জী *n*=পুঞ্জ. ~কৃত, ~ভূত *adjj*=পুঞ্জিত. ~ গণিতক *n* capital accounts.

পুট[১] *n* 1 fold; pocket; hollow space; slit; concavity: অক্ষি~. 2 cup; basket; vessel; container. 3 cloth worn to cover the privities. 4 cup made of leaves. 5 casket. 6 horse's hoof. 7 eyelid. 8 enveloping/wrapping of any substance (esp for baking or heating it). 9 sheath. ~কুণ্ড, ~গর্ত *nn* roasting pit. ~গ্রীব *n* churn. ~পাক *n* a particular method of preparing drugs (the various substances being wrapped up in leaves covered with clay and heated in fire).

পুট[২] *n* part of the body lying between the nape and the shoulder-joint; the length of this part.

~-আস্তিন, ~হাতা *nn* measurement of length from the nape to the wrist.

পুটক *n* **1** fold; pocket; slit; cavity. **2** bag/vessel made of a leaf doubled over in funnel-shape.

পুটকিত *adj* covered; cropped; closed in.

পুটলি=পুঁটলি

পুটিং [E] *n* putty. ~ করা/দেওয়া/ মারা *vt* putty (sth up).

পুটিত *adj* **1** sewn; stitched. **2** kneaded; rubbed; ground. **3** covered. **4** strung (as a garland). **5** roasted; boiled in a crucible.

পুটুলি, পুটুলী *nn* =পুঁটলি

পুড়ন, পোড়ানি *n* **1** barring; scorching; scalding; calculation; incineration. **2** inflammation; state of becoming very hot; affliction.

পুড়া=পোড়া

পুড়ানি *n* affliction; distress; pangs of separation; longing.

পুড়ানে *adj* burning; distressing; afflicting; incendiary; bringing unhappiness and strife. পুড়ানী *fem.*

পড়ুনি=পুড়ানি

পুডিং [E] *n* pudding.

পুণ্ডরীক *n* white lotus. **পুণ্ডরীকাক্ষ** *n* lotus-eyed; Vishnu; Sri Krishna.

পুণ্ড্র(ক) *n* **1** sugar-cane (or a red variety of it). **2** a sectarian mark on the forehead. **3** name of an ancient people and their country (Bengal and Bihar).

পুণ্য *n* the good/right; virtue; purity; good work; meritorious act; moral/religious merit; piety. ❑*adj* good; right; virtuous; meritorious; pure; holy; sacred; pious; auspicious; propitious; fair; pleasant. পুণ্যা *adj.* ~কর্ম *n* act of piety/ virtue; meritorious act. ~কর্মা *adj* doing right; pious; virtuous; performing meritorious actions; practising holy/virtuous actions. ~কাল *n* auspicious time; holy tide. ~কীর্তি *adj* bearing a good name; famous; celebrated. ~কৃৎ=~কর্মা. ~ক্ষয় *n* decay/ waning of one's religious merits. ~ক্ষেত্র *n* holy place; place of pilgrimage. ~গন্ধ *adj* sweet-scented; fragrant. ~গৃহ *n* a house, ie, a place/seat of virtue. ~জন *n* good/honest man; good people. ~জল *adj* having good/holy water. ~তর *adj* purer; holier. ~তা, ~ত্ব *n* purity; holiness. ~তীর্থ=~ক্ষেত্র. ~তোয়া=~জল. ~দ *adj* conferring purity/ holiness/ bestowing religious merits; sanctifying; virtue; holy; virtuous. ~দা *fem.* ~দর্শন *adj* of holy/beautiful appearance. ~ধ্বংস, ~নাশ *nn* destruction of purity/ holiness/religious merits. ~ধ্বংসী, ~নাশক *adjj* destructive of purity/holiness/religious merits. ~ফল *n* fruits of purity/holiness/religious merits; fruit/reward of good works. ~ফলে *adv* by virtue of one's religious merits. ~বল *n* strength/ force of one's virtue/ piety. ~বান *adj* holy; pure; virtuous; religious; pious. ~বতী *fem.* ~ভাক *adj* partaking/ sharing in bliss/ holiness/ purity/ religious merits. ~ভূমি *n* holy land. ~ভোগ *n* enjoyment of the fruits of one's good works. ~যোগ *n* **1** effect of one's virtuous actions in former life; (astrol) auspicious time/ conjunction of stars for performing solemn rites. ~রাত্র *n* holy/auspicious night. ~লব্ধ *n* attained by good works. ~লাভ *n* attainment of religious merit. ~লোভ *n* earnest desire/ craving for religious merit. ~লোভী *adj* greedy for religious merit. ~শালী *adj* virtuous; pious; holy; righteous. ~শালিনী *fem.* ~শীল *adj* of a virtuous disposition; virtuous; pious; righteous. ~শীলা *fem.* ~শ্লোক *adj* well spoken of; of good fame/reputation; celebrated for virtue/piety; holy. ~সঞ্চয় *n* accumulation of religious merits. ~সঞ্চয়ী *adj* accumulating religious merits. ~হীন *adj* destitute of religious merits/holiness. **পুণ্যাকাঙ্ক্ষা** *n* desire for holiness/purity/religious merits. **পুণ্যাকাঙ্ক্ষী** *adj* desirous of holiness/religious merits. **পুণ্যাচরণ, পুণ্যাচার** *nn* pure/holy conduct; holy life; practice of religion. **পুণ্যাচারী** *adj* practising religious actions; leading a holy/ pure life. **পুণ্যাত্মা** *adj* holy; pure; virtuous; righteous; pious. **পুণ্যাপনা** *n* holiness and the want of it; purity and its absence; holiness and sin; virtue and vice. **পুণ্যাভিলাষ** = পুণ্যাকাঙ্ক্ষা. **পুণ্যাভিলাষী** = পুণ্যাকাঙ্ক্ষী. **পুণ্যার্থী** = পুণ্যাকাঙ্ক্ষী. **পুণ্যার্থে** *adv* for the sake of purity/ holiness/ religious merits. **পুণ্যাহ** *n* **1** happy/ auspicious day. **2** (hist) day on which the tenants pay the first payment of their rents to the land lord.

পুণ্যি *n adj* (colloq) =পুণ্য. ~পুকুর *n* **1** sacred pond. **2** a vow observed by young unmarried Hindu girls.

পুণ্যোদক *adj* having sacred waters.

পুণ্যোদয় *n* occurrence of good fortune (result from virtuous acts done in a former life).

পুত *n* (dial)=পুত্র

পুতলি *n* **1** doll; puppet; marionette; image. **2** pet; favourite ; idol; apple of sb's eye. **3** pupil of the eye.

পুতা *n*=নোড়া

পুতি *n* (dial) =পুত্রী

পুতুপুতু *n* (onom) expressing: excessive carefulness/attention/fondling; doting. ~ করা *vi* worry excessively about; dote on; take excessive care of.

পুতুল *n* **1** doll; puppet; marionette. **2** small statue; effigy; image; idol. **3** (fig) puppet. ~খেলা *n* **1** playing with dolls. **2** (fig) meaningless action; childish play. ~ ঘর *n* doll's house. ~নাচ *n* puppet-show; puppet-play. ~ নাচিয়ে *n* puppet-player. ~ পূজা *n* idolatry; idol-worship. (পরের) হাতের ~ *n* puppet (in another's hand).

পুত্তল *n* পুতুল

পুত্তলি[1], **পুত্তলিকা** *nn* =পুতলি

পুত্তলি[2] *n* pupa.

পুত্তিকা *n* **1** white ant. **2** bee. **3** chrysolite.

পুত্র *n* son; child. ~কন্যা *n* son and daughter. ~ কলত্র *n* son and wife; wife and children. ~কাম *adj* desirous of sons/children. ~কামী *fem.* ~পৌত্র *n* sons and grandsons. ~পৌত্রাদি *n* sons and daughters; posterity; future generation. ~পৌত্রাদিক্রমে *adv* from generation to generation. ~বৎ *adj* like a son; as with a son. ~বৎসল *adj* fond of/affectionate towards sons. ~বধূ *n* son's wife; daughter-in-law. ~বাৎসল্য *n* love/affection for sons. ~বান *adj* having son/sons, children. ~বতী *fem.* ~রত্ন *n* jewel of a son. ~লাভ *n* obtaining/ begetting a son/ sons. ~ শোক *n* grief caused by the death of a son; bereavement at the loss of a son. ~সন্তান *n* male child/posterity. ~সম=~বৎ ~হীন *adj* sonless; childless. পুত্রাকাঙ্ক্ষা *n* desire for a son. পুত্রাকাঙ্ক্ষী, পুত্রার্থী *adj* desirous of a son. পুত্রার্থে *adv* with a view to getting a son.

পুত্রিকা *n fem* **1** daughter. **2** foster-daughter. **3** doll; puppet.

পুত্রী *n fem* daughter.

পুত্রীয় *adj* of/for a son.

পুত্রেচ্ছা=পুত্রাকাঙ্ক্ষা (⇒পুত্র). **পুত্রেচ্ছু**=পুত্রাকাঙ্ক্ষী

পুত্রেষ্টি(কা) *n* a sacrifice made for the purpose of obtaining a son.

পুথি=পুঁথি

পুদিনা *n* spearmint; mint.

পুন, পুনঃ (in compounds) *adv* again; once more; over again. □*conj* further; besides; moreover. পুনঃপুনঃ, পুনঃপুন *adv* again and again; repeatedly; over and over again. ~প্রয়োগ *n* repetition. ~প্রাপ্ত *adj* regained; recovered. ~প্রাপ্ত হওয়া *vt* regain; recover. ~প্রাপ্তি *n* regaining; recovery. ~প্রাপ্য *adj* to be obtained again; recoverable. ~প্রেরণ *n* sending back/again. ~প্রেরিত *adj* sent again/back. ~শিলীভবন *n* regulation. ~সংস্কার *n* renovation; renewed investiture. ~সংস্কার করা *vt* renovate; restore to good condition. ~স্থাপন *n* re-installation. ~স্থাপন করা *vt* re-install. ~স্থাপিত *adj* re-installed.

পুনরধিকার *n* recapture; reoccupation. ~ করা *vt* recapture; retake; reoccupy.

পুনরধিকৃত *adj* recaptured; retaken.

পুনরপি *adv* again; once again; once more; also.

পুনরর্পণ *n* giving again/back; restitution; return; restoration. ~ করা *vt* give again/back; destitute; return; restore.

পুনরাগত *adj* come back; returned.

পুনরাগমন *n* return; coming back. ~ করা *vi* come back; return.

পুনরাবর্ত(ন) *n* **1** return. **2** rebirth. **3** revolution; revolving. পুনরাবর্তন করা *vi* **1** return. **2** be born again. **3** revolve.

পুনরাবর্তী *adj* returning (to mundane existence); revolving.

পুনরাবৃত্ত *adj* **1** repeated; read again and again; recited. **2** returned. **3** born again. **4** revolved.

পুনরাবৃত্তি *n* **1** repetition; recital; second reading. **2** revolving; revolution. **3** return. **4** rebirth. ~ করা *vt* repeat; read again; recite; revolve; return.

পুনরায়=পুনরপি

পুনরাহূত *adj* called again; recalled.

পুনরাহ্বান *n* calling again; recall. ~ করা *vt* call again; call back; recall.

পুনরীক্ষণ *n* review. ~ করা *vt* review.

পুনরুক্ত *adj* said again; repeated; reiterated; uttered again; superfluous. ~ বদাভাস *n* (rhet) seeming tautology.

পুনরুক্তি *n* **1** repetition; reiteration. **2** (rhet) tautological. ~ করা *vt* say/utter again; repeat; reiterate. ~ দোষ *n* (rhet) tautology.

পুনরুজ্জীবন *n* reanimation; resuscitation; revival.

পুনরুজ্জীবিত *adj* reanimated; resuscitated; revived; brought back to life. ~ করা *vt* reanimate; resuscitate; revive; bring back to life.

পুনরুত্থান *n* rising again; resurrection; reawakening. ~ করা *vi* rise again; be resurrected; reawaken.

পুনরুত্থিত *adj* risen again; resurrected; reawakened.

পুনরুৎপত্তি *n* re-appearance; rebirth; recurrence; regeneration.

পুনরুৎপন্ন *adj* reappeared; reborn; regenerated.

পুনরুৎপাদন *n* reproduction. ~ করা *vt* reproduce.

পুনরুৎপাদিত *adj* reproduced.

পুনরুদ্দীপন *n* re-awakening; re-animation; revival; rejuvenation; rekindling.

পুনরুদ্দীপ্ত *adj* re-awakened; re-animated; revived; rejuvenated; rekindled. ~ করা *vt* re-awaken; re-animate; revive; rejuvenate; rekindle.

পুনরুদ্ভব=পুনরুৎপত্তি

পুনরুদ্ভূত=পুনরুৎপন্ন

পুনরুপলব্ধি *n* realizing again. ~ করা *vt* realize again.

পুনরুল্লিখিত *adj* said/mentioned again; repeated; recapitulated; restated.
পুনরুল্লেখ *n* repetition; restatement; recapitulation. ~ **করা** *vt* say/mention again; repeat; recapitulate; restate.
পুনর্গমন *n* going/setting out again; return.
পুনর্গঠন *n* reconstruction; reorganization. ~ **করা** *vt* reconstruct; reorganize.
পুনর্গঠিত *adj* reconstructed; reorganized.
পুনর্জন্ম *n* rebirth; reanimation; metamorphosis; new lease of life.
পুনর্জাত *adj* reborn; regenerated.
পুনর্জীবন *n* new (lease of) life; restoration to life.
পুনর্জীবিত *adj* restored to life; re-animated; having a new (lease of) life.
পুনর্নব *adj* becoming new/young again; renewed. ❑*n* finger-nail.
পুনর্নবা *n* a kind of medicinal herb; hogweed; *Boerhavia procumbens.*
পুনর্নির্ণয় *n* redefinition; recount; re-evaluation; revision. ~ **করা** *vt* redefine; recount; revise; re-evaluate, re-examine.
পুনর্নির্ণীত *adj* redefined; recounted; revised; re-evaluated; re-examined.
পুনর্নির্বাচন *n* re-election. ~ **করা** *vt* re-elect; hold reelections.
পুনর্নির্বাচিত *adj* re-elected.
পুনর্নির্মাণ *n* reconstruction; rebuild. ~ **করা** *vt* reconstruct; rebuild.
পুনর্নির্মিত *adj* reconstructed; rebuilt.
পুনর্নিযুক্ত *adj* reappointed. ~ **করা** *vt* reappoint.
পুনর্নিয়োগ, পুনর্নিয়োজন *nn* reappointment.
পুনর্বক্তব্য *adj* to be repeated.
পুনর্বচন *n* saying again; repetition.
পুনর্বসতি *n* rehabilitation.
পুনর্বসু *n* (astrol) the fifth or the seventh lunar mansion.
পুনর্বার=পুনরপি
পুনর্বাসন *n* rehabilitation.
পুনর্বাসিত *adj* rehabilitated. ~ **করা** *vt* rehabilitate.
পুনর্বিচার *n* retrial; reconsideration; review; reappraisal; rehearing. ~ **করা** *vt* review; reconsider; re-examine; re-evaluate. ~**প্রার্থী** *n* appellant.
পুনর্বিবাহ *n* remarriage; second marriage. ~ **করা** *vi* remarry; marry again.
পুনর্বিলোচন *n* review.
পুনর্ভব *adj* reborn. ❑*n* rebirth; transmigration.
পুনর্ভূ *adj* (virgin) widow remarried.
পুনর্মিলন *n* re-union; reconciliation.
পুনর্মিলনী *n* re-union.
পুনর্মিলিত *adj* reunited; reconciled.
পুনর্মূষিকভব (phrase) (fig) reverted to a former (very inferior) state.
পুনর্যাত্রা *n* **1** setting out on a journey for the second time; second march; return journey. **2** (myth) return journey of Juggernaut (জগন্নাথ) in his chariot. ~ **করা** *vi* set out on a journey for the second time; set out again.
পুনর্যৌবন *n* rejuvenation. ~**প্রাপ্ত** *adj* rejuvenated. ~ **লাভ করা** *vt* be rejuvenated).
পুনর্লাভ *n* obtaining again; recovery.
পুনর্লিখন, পুনর্লেখন *n* writing down again; rewriting.
পুনশ্চ *adv* once again; once more. ❑*n* postscript.
পুন্নরক *n* (myth) (a particular) hell (to which the childless are condemned).
পুন্নাগ *n* **1** white elephant. **2** white lotus; nutmeg. **3** elephant among men; a distinguished man.
পুন্নামনরক =পুন্নরক
পুব *n*, *adj* (colloq) =পূর্ব
পুবাল, পুবালি, পুবে *adj* coming/ blowing from the east; eastern.
পুয়া, পুয়ারা *nn* a kind of cake.
পুর[১] *n* stuffing; dressing. ~ **দেওয়া** *vt* stuff sth (with sth).
পুর[২] *n* **1** stronghold; fortress; castle. **2** house; dwelling-house; abode; residence. **3** city; town. **4** female apartments; gynaeceum. ~**জন** *n* townsfolk; citizens; inmates (of a house). ~**তোরণ** *n* outer gate of a city. ~**দ্বার** *n* city gate. ~**নারী** *n fem* womenfolk of a city; townswoman; women usually keeping to the zenana; housewife; female member of a family. ~**পাল** *n* governor of a city. ~**প্রান্ত** *n* edge of a town; outskirts. ~**বধূ** =~নারী. ~**বাসী** *adj* dwelling in a town. ❑*n* citizen; towndweller; inmate of a house. ~**বাসিনী** *fem.* ~**মহিলা** = ~নারী. ~**রক্ষক**, ~**রক্ষী** *nn* watchman of a town; constable. ~**লক্ষ্মী** *n* **1** guardian goddess of a city. **2** women in the harem; female inmate of a house. ~**ললনা**=~নারী. ~**শাসক** *n* =~পাল. **2** presidency magistrate. ~**স্ত্রী**=~নারী.
পুরঃসর *adj* going before/in advance. ❑*adv* having first made/done: প্রণাম ~.
পুরঞ্জন *n* living principle; life; soul.
পুরঞ্জয় *n* **1** conqueror of a city. **2** enemy.
পুরতঃ *adv* before; in front/presence of.
পুরনো *adj* (colloq)=পুরানো
পুরন্ত *adj* **1** full; perfect; complete: ~ সুখ. **2** plump; round; chubby; well-developed; full-grown. ~ মুখ.
পুরন্দর *n* destroyer of stronghold; name of Indra.
পুরন্ধি, পুরন্ধ্রী *n* wife; women (esp a married woman having or able to bear children); matron; housewife.

পুরব (poet)= পূর্ব
পুরশ্চরণ *n* preparatory/ introductory rite.
পুরস্করণ *n* =পুরস্ক্রিয়া
পুরস্কার *n* **1** reward; prize; remuneration. **2** honouring; preference; distinction; honour; advancement; promotion. **3** royal gift. ~ **দেওয়া** *v* reward.
পুরস্কার্য *adj* to be rewarded/ honoured/ remunerated/ distinguished.
পুরস্কৃত *adj* rewarded; remunerated; felicitated; honoured. ~ **করা** *vt* reward.
পুরা[1] *adj* full; entire; whole; complete; replete. ❑*adv* fully; entirely; wholly; thoroughly; full: ~ দশ হাত. ~ **করা** = পূর্ণ করা. ~ **হওয়া** = পূর্ণ হওয়া.
পুরা[2] *adj* before; formerly; of old; in the past; in ancient times. ~ **কথা** *n* story of the past; old legend. ~**কল্প** *n* former age; olden time. ~**কাল** *n* ancient times. ~**কীর্তি** *n* monuments. ~**কৃত** *adj* done formerly/long ago. ~**গত** *adj* gone before; former; of old. ~**তত্ত্ব** *n* ancient history; antiquities; archaeology. ~**তত্ত্বজ্ঞ**, ~**তত্ত্ববিদ** *adj* knowing the events of former times; versed in ancient history/ archaeology/ antiquities. ❑*n* archaeologist; antiquarian; antiquary; one versed in ancient history. ~**দ্রব্যাগার**, ~**দ্রব্যালয়** *nn* museum. ~**বিদ** *n*=~তত্ত্বজ্ঞ. ~**বৃত্ত** *n*=~তত্ত্ব.
পুরা[3]=পোরা
পুরাঙ্গনা=পুরনারী (⇒পুর[2])
পুরাণ *adj* belonging to ancient/ olden times; ancient; old. ❑*n* name of a class of Hindu sacred works; myth; mythology. ~**কর্তা**, ~**কার** *n* author of mythology. ~**পুরুষ** *n* primeval male; Vishnu. ~**প্রসিদ্ধ** *adj* celebrated in the Puranas. ~**প্রসিদ্ধি** *n* mention in the Puranas/ mythology; long-standing fame.
পুরানা *adj* (colloq) =পুরাতন
পুরাতন *adj* **1** belonging to the past: former; old; ancient. **2** used-up; worn out: ~ কাপড়. **3** experienced; old: ~ কর্মচারী, old hand. **4** inveterate: ~ পাপী. **5** long-standing: ~ প্রথা. **6** chronic: ~ রোগ. **পুরাতনী** *fem.*
পুরাদস্তুর *adj* complete; thorough; downright; thorough-going; out-and-out. ❑*adv* completely; thoroughly; to the fullest extent; in downright manner.
পুরাধ্যক্ষ *n* =পুরপাল (⇒ পুর[2])
পুরানো[1] =পুরাতন
পুরানো[2]=পূর্ণ করা (⇒পূর্ণ)
পুরাপুরি *adj* complete; full; entire; downright; thorough. ❑*adv* completely; fully; entirely; in a downright manner; wholly.
পুরি *n* a kind of thin saucer-shaped bread stuffed with pulses, mashed potatoes, etc and fried in oil or butter.
পুরিয়া *n* **1** tiny packet. **2** dose of medicine or other articles in a tiny packet.
পুরী[1] =পুরি
পুরী *n* **1**=পুর[2]. **2** title of certain Hindu ascetics.
পুরীষ *n* **1** faeces; excrement; stool. **2** ordure; rubbish; dung.
পুরু *adj* **1** thick; fat: ~ তক্তা. **2** coarse: ~ কাপড়. **3** having a specific number of folds/layers: বারো ~ বসন.
পুরুত, পুরুৎ *n* (colloq) =পুরোহিত
পুরুভুজ *n* polyp; hydra.
পুরুষ *n* **1** (a) man; male; human being; (male) person; male creature. **2** manly man; he-man: একজন সত্যিকার ~. **3** officer; functionary: রাজ~. **4** the primeval man as the soul and original source of the universe. **5** the personal and animating principle in men and other beings ; soul; spirit. **6** the Supreme Being; soul of the universe; Brahma. **7** the spirit as passive and the spectator of the Prakriti (প্রকৃতি) or creative force. **8** (gram) person: উত্তম/মধ্যম/প্রথম ~. **9** generation: সাত পুরুষের বসতবাটি. **10** husband. ❑*attrib adj* male; he: ~-হাতি. ~**কার** *n* human effort (opposed to fate); prowess; manly act; virility; heroism. ~**কেশরী** *n* eminent man; hero; lion of a man. ~**জন** *n* men; people. ~**জাতীয়** *adj* male; masculine. ~**তন্ত্র** *n* patriarchy. ~**ত্ব** *n* manliness; manhood; masculinity; vigour; virility; sexual potency (of men). ~**ত্ববর্জিত**, ~**ত্ববিহীন**, ~**ত্বরহিত**, ~**ত্বশূন্য**, ~**ত্বহীন** *adjj* lacking in sexual potency; impotent; unmanly; effeminate; faint hearted. ~**ত্বহানি** *n* loss of sexual potency; impotence. ~**ধর্ম**=~ত্ব. ~ **পরম্পরা** *n* succession of generations; lineal succession; heredity; tradition. ~ **পরম্পরাক্রমে** *adv* from generation to generation; in successive generations; hereditarily. ~ **পরম্পরাগত** *adj* coming from generation to generation; hereditary; traditional; inherited. ~**পুঙ্গব** *n* a bull of men; eminent/ excellent man. ~**প্রধান** *n* chief amongst man; Supreme Being. ❑*adj* male-dominated. ~ **প্রকৃতি** *n* **1** the passive spirit and the creative force. **2** male nature. ~ **ব্যাঘ্র** *n* tiger of a man. ~ **মানুষ** *n* man; male; manly man. ~ **শার্দূল** =~-ব্যাঘ্র. ~**শ্রেষ্ঠ** *n* chief amongst men; eminent man. ~**সিংহ**= ~কেশরী. ~**সুলভ** *adj* befitting a man; masculine; manly. **পুরুষাঙ্গ** *n* male organ of generation; penis. **পুরুষাধম** *n* lowest/vilest of men; outcast; rascal; rogue; dirty fellow; extremely cowardly man. **পুরুষানুক্রম** =~ পরম্পরা. **পুরুষানুক্রমিক**=~ পরম্পরাগত. **পুরুষানুক্রমে** =~ পরম্পরাক্রমে. **পুরুষার্থ** *n* **1** any object of human pursuit; any one of the four objects/aims of existence (viz gratification of desire, acquirement of wealth, discharge of duty and final emancipation).

পুরুষালি *n* **1** manliness; virility; masculinity. **2** (of women) mannishness. ❑*adj* **1** manly; virile; masculine. **2** (of women) mannish; manly.

পুরুষোচিত *adj* becoming/befitting a man; manly; virile; proper for a man.

পুরুষোত্তম *n* **1** the best of men; excellent/ supreme man; superman. **2** the highest being; Supreme Spirit. **3** Vishnu.

পুরুষ্টু *adj* thick; well-developed; plump; full; fleshy.

পুরো =পুরা[১]

পুরোগ, পুরোগামী *adj* going before; leading; preceding; pioneering.

পুরোগত *adj* **1** gone before. **2** standing/being in front/before a person's eyes.

পুরোডাশ *n* mass of ground rice rounded into a kind of cake.

পুরোধা *n* **1** priest. **2** pioneer; leader; standard-bearer; vanguard.

পুরোপুরি *adj adv* (colloq) =পুরাপুরি

পুরোবর্তী *adj* being before a person's eyes; lying in front; advanced; forward; obtrusive; preceding.

পুরোভাগ *n* front; front part; facade. **সৈন্যবাহিনীর ~** *n* vanguard.

পুরোভূমি *n* foreground.

পুরোযায়ী *adj* preceding; leading; pioneering. ❑*n* pioneer.

পুরোহিত *n* priest; domestic chaplain; family priest.

পুল [P] *n* bridge (as on a river).

পুলক *n* erection/bristling of the hair of the body (considered to be occasioned by delight or rapture); thrill; delight; rapture; joy; horripilation. **~ কন্টকিত**=পুলকিত.

পুলকিত *adj* thrilled with delight/joy; ecstatic; enraptured; rapturous.

পুলকোচ্ছ্বাস *n* thrill of joy; outburst of delight.

পুলটিস [E] *n* poultice.

পুলি[১] (also **~ পিঠা**) *n* a kind of sweet roll.

পুলি[২] *n* Port Blair in the Andamans. **~ পোলাও** *n* deportation to the Andamans.

পুলি[৩] [E]*n* pulley.

পুলিন *n* sandy beach; sand-bank; bank of a river.

পুলিন্দা [P] *n* packet; bundle; parcel.

পুলিস [E] *n* police; policeman; police constable.

পুশিদা =পুসিদা

পুষণ *n*=পোষণ

পুষা *vt*=পোষা

পুষ্কর *n* **1** blue lotus. **2** water. **3** sky; heaven.

পুষ্করাবর্তক *n* name of a particular class of clouds.

পুষ্করিণী *n* pool; pond; lotus pool.

পুষ্ট *adj* **1** nourished; brought-up; bred; cherished; well-fed. **2** grown up; plump; mature; ripe; fattened; fat; full; complete; perfect; ample. **3** thriving; strong; rich; great; abundant. **4** (as a *suff*) rich in; blessed with. **~তাড়িত** *n* (phys) positive electricity. **পুষ্টাঙ্গ** *adj* well-developed; fat; fattened.

পুষ্টি *n* **1** nourishment; nutrition. **2** upbringing; breeding; development; growth; increase; thriving; prosperity. **3** well-nourished condition; fatness; plumpness; maturity; ripeness. **~কর, ~জনক, ~সাধক** *adjj* nutritious; nourishing; nutrient. **~কর উপাদান** *n* nutrient. **~সাধন** *n* nutrition; nourishment. **~ সাধন করা** *vi* nourish.

পুষ্প *n* **1** flower; blossom. **2** menstrual flux. **~করণ্ডক** *n* flower-basket. **~কীট** *n* large bee. **~কেতন, ~কেতু** *nn* characterized by flowers; Madana, the god of love. **~গুচ্ছ** *n* bunch of flowers. **~গৃহ** *n* conservatory; flower-house. **~চয়ন** *n* flower-gathering. **~ চয়ন করা** *vt* gather/pluck flowers. **~জ** *adj* derived/coming from flowers. ❑*n* honey. **~জীবী** *n* florist; gardener. **~দণ্ড** *n* (bot) penducle. **~দল** *n* petal. **~দাম** *n* wreath of flowers; garland. **~ধনু** *adj* armed with a bow of flowers. ❑*n* **1** bow of flowers. **2** Madana, the god of love. **~ধন্বা** *adj*=~ধনু. ❑*n* Madana, the god of love. **~ধ্বজ**=~কেতন. **~নির্যাস** *n* essence of flower. **~পত্র** *n* petal; flowers and petals. **~পত্রবিন্যাস** *n* (bot) prefloration. **~পল্লব** *n* flowers and foliage. **~পাত্র** *n* vase; saucer for holding flowers. **~পুট** *n* **1** cup/bag filled with flowers. **2** (bot) calyx. **3** the hands arranged in the shape of a calyx. **~প্রতীক** *n* floral diagram. **~বৎ** *n* like a flower. **~বন** *n* flower-garden. **~বতী** *adj fem* **1** having the menses. **2** decorated with flowers; flowering; blooming. **~বর্ষ(ণ)** *n* shower of flowers; flowers showered on sb. **~বাটিকা, ~বাটী** *nn* flower-garden; garden-house. **~বাণ** *n* arrow made of flowers; Madana, the god of love. **~বিন্যাস** *n* (bot) inflorescence. **~বৃন্ত** *n* flower-stalk. **~বৃন্তিকা** *n* (bot) pedicel. **~বৃষ্টি** =~বর্ষ. **~ভূষণ** *n* ornament of flowers. **~ভূষিত** *adj* adorned with flowers. **~মঞ্জরি** *n* flower-bud; spike of flowers. **~মধু** = ~রস. **~ময়** *adj* covered with flowers; flowery. **~মালা, ~মাল্য** *n* garland of flowers. **~মাস** *n* spring. **~মুকুট** *n* chaplet/ crown of flowers. **~মুকুল** *n* flower-bud. **~মেঘ** *n* a cloud raining flowers. **~রক্ত** *adj* red as a flower. **~রচনা** *n* making flowers into a garland. **~রজ** *n* flower-dust; pollen. **~রথ** *n* a car for travelling/ pleasure. **~রস** *n* nectar/ honey of flowers. **~রাগ** *n* topaz. **~রেণু** = ~রজ. **~লাবী** *n fem* flower-gatherer; garland-maker; florist. **~লিহ** *n* large black bee. **~শয্যা** *n* bed/couch of flowers. **~শর** = ~বাণ. **~শরাসন** = ~ধনু. **~শূন্য**

adj flowerless. ~সঙ্কেত *n* (bot) floral formula. ~সায়ক=~বান. ~সার *n* nectar/essence of flowers. ~সৌরভ *n* fragrance of a flower. ~হীন *adj* flowerless; not flowering. পুষ্পাকর *adj* rich in flowers; flowery. পুষ্পাগম *n* florescence or its season; spring. পুষ্পাগম-কাল *n* time of florescence; season of flowers; spring. পুষ্পাগ্র *n* pistil. পুষ্পাজীব *adj* dealing in flowers and flower-wreaths. ❑*n* florist; garland-maker; gardener. পুষ্পাঞ্জলি *n* two handfuls of flowers; offering of a handful of flowers. পুষ্পাঞ্জলি দেওয়া *vi* offer a handful of flowers in devotion. পুষ্পাধার *n* flower-vase; flower-pot. পুষ্পানন *adj* flower-faced. পুষ্পাবকীর্ণ=পুষ্পাভিকীর্ণ. পুষ্পাবচায়ী = পুষ্পাজীব. পুষ্পাভরণ=~ভূষণ. পুষ্পাভিকীর্ণ *adj* strewed with flowers. পুষ্পায়ুধ *n* 'flower-armed'; Madana, the god of love. পুষ্পালঙ্কার = ~ভূষণ. পুষ্পাসব = ~রস. পুষ্পাস্তীর্ণ = ~ভিকীর্ণ.

পুষ্পক *n* **1** air ship. **2** name of the self-moving aerial car of Kubera (কুবের).

পুষ্পিকা *n* **1** the last word of a chapter (which state the subject treated therein). **2** tartar of the teeth; mucus of the tongue.

পুষ্পিত *adj* **1** flowered; bearing flowers; blooming; in bloom. **2** having marks like flowers; variegated; spotted. **3** florid; flowery (as speech). পুষ্পিতা *fem*. ❑*n* menstruous woman.

পুষ্পী *adj* (used as a *suff*) bearing flowers; flowering; blossoming.

পুষ্পেষু=পুষ্পবাণ (⇒ পুষ্প)

পুষ্পোদ্‌গম=পুষ্পাগম (⇒ পুষ্প)

পুষ্পোদ্যান *n* flower-garden. ~বিদ্যা *n* floriculture.

পুষ্যা *n* (astrol) the eighth of the lunar asterism. ~স্নান *n* a ceremony of purification performed while the moon is passing through the eighth asterism.

পুষ্যি *n* (colloq)=পোষ্য

পুসিদা [P] *n* concealment; covering; securing. ❑*n* concealed; hidden; covered. ~করা *vi* **1** hide; conceal; keep secret. **2** wear a veil.

পুস্ত [P] *n* generation: পুস্তের পর ~.

পুস্তক *n* book; manuscript; booklet. ~ বিক্রেতা *n* book-seller. ~ বিপণি *n* book-shop. ~ ব্যবসায়/ব্যবসা *n* book-trade. ~ ব্যবসায়ী *n* book-trader. ~স্থ *adj* contained/written in a book. পুস্তকাগার *n* library. পুস্তকালয় *n* book-shop. পুস্তকের দোকান *n* book-shop.

পুস্তনি, পুস্তনী *n* flying leaf (of a book).

পুস্তবিকলন *n* book debit.

পুস্তা(ন)=পোস্তা

পুস্তিকা, পুস্তি *nn* booklet; pamphlet.

পূগ *n* **1** betel-nut. **2** assemblage/ combination/ body of persons.

পূজক *adj* honouring; worshipping; adoring; respecting. ❑*n* worshipper; priest; devotee; votary.

পূজন *n* worship; honouring,; respect; reverencing; attention; hospitable reception.

পূজনীয় *adj* to be revered/ worshipped; venerable; honourable; worthy of reverence/ worship/ honour. পূজনীয়া *fem*.

পূজয়িতা=পূজক. পূজয়িত্রী *fem*.

পূজা *n* worship; ceremony of Hindu religious worship; service; devotion, honour; respect; reverence; veneration; homage (to superiors); adoration (of the gods); idol worship; glorification; offering. ~ করা *vi* worship; honour; revere; respect; regard; adore; welcome; glorify; accord cordial reception to. ~ দেওয়া *vi* offer religious worship (to a deity); offer presents in homage. ~ পাওয়া *vi* be worshipped/ adored/ revered/ venerated; be received cordially; receive offerings from devotees. ~অর্চনা, ~অর্চা *nn* religious worship and prayers. ~গৃহ *n* house of worship; temple. ~পার্বণ *n* religious worship and festivities. ~মণ্ডপ *n* pavilion for the worship of a god; temple. ~বকাশ, ~বসর, ~র ছুটি *n* vacation during a holy season; puja holidays/vacation. ~বাড়ি *n* a house in which worship is offered to a deity. ~র দালান=~মণ্ডপ. ~রী=পূজক. ~রিণী *fem*. ~র্হ=পূজনীয়. ~হ্নিক *n* daily religious service.

পূজিত *adj* worshipper revered; adored; glorified; received/treated with honour/respectfully. পূজিতা *fem*.

পূজিতব্য=পূজনীয়

পূজোৎসব *n* puja (পূজা) festivities.

পূজোপহার *n* gift/present offered during the puja festival; puja gift/present.

পূজ্য *adj* = পূজনীয়. পূজ্যা *fem*. ~তা *n* venerableness; honourableness; entitlement to worship/honour. ~পাদ *n* one whose feet are worthy of worship. ❑*adj* most reverend/ venerable/ adorable. ~মান *adj* being worshipped/ adored/ honoured/ revered.

পূত *adj* cleaned; purified; pure; clear; holy; sacred; sanctified. পূতাত্মা pure-souled; pure-hearted; holy; virtuous; pious.

পূতি[১] *n* purity; purification.

পূতি[২] *n* **1** stench; stink; pus. **2** (chem) putrefaction. ~গন্ধ *n* stink; fetid smell; stench. ~গন্ধময় *adj* stinking; putrid; foul-smelling; fetid; ill-smelling. ~মাংস *n* rotten/ putrid meat.

পূতোদক *n* holy water.

পূপ *n* cake; sort of bread. ~কার *n* bakes. ~শালা *n* baker's shop.

পূব (poet)=পূর্ব

পূয *n* purulent matter; pus; suppuration; discharge from an ulcer/wound. ~ জমা/হওয়া

vi suppurate. ~ ঝরা *vi* discharge/secrete pus.

পূর *n* 1 filling; making full; fulfilling. 2 swelling/ rising of a river/the sea; large quantity of water; flood; stream.

পূরক *adj* 1 filling; completing; fulfilling; satisfying. 2 (arith, alg) multiplying. 3 (geom) complementary. ❑*n* 1 (arith, alg) multiplier. 2 closing the right nostril with forefinger and then drawing up air through the left and then closing the left nostril and drawing up air through the right (as a religious exercise). ~ কুম্ভক-রেচক *n* inhaling and then staining and then exhaling air. ~ কোণ *n* complementary angle.

পূরণ *n* 1 filling; stuffing: উদর ~. 2 fulfilling; satisfying; fulfilment: ইচ্ছা ~. 3 causing; effecting; completing. 4 completion: মেয়াদ ~. 5 compensation: ক্ষতি ~. 6 repletion. 7 increase. 8 (arith, alg) multiplication. 9 solution: সমস্যা ~. ~ করা *vt* 1 fill; stuff. 2 fulfil; satisfy; gratify; meet: দাবি ~ করা. 3 solve. 4 complete; fill in/out/ up: শূন্যস্থান/ফর্ম ~ করা. 5 fill in (for sb): কারো শূন্যস্থান ~ করা. 6 make up; replace: অভাব ~ করা. 7 compensate; make sth good: ক্ষতি ~ করা. 8 increase; (arith, alg) multiply. ~বাচক *n* ordinal.

পূরণীয় *adj* to be filled (in/out/up)/supplied/ completed/ solved/ made up/ fulfilled/ satisfied/ met/ multiplied.

পূরণ (poet)=পূর্ণ

পূরবী *n* an Indian musical mode.

পূরা=পূরা[১], পুরা[২]

পূরিকা=পুরি

পূরিত *adj* filled; completed; replete; fulfilled; solved; met; multiplied.

পূরী=পুরি

পূর্ণ *adj* 1 filled (with); full (of). 2 whole; total; complete; all; entire. 3 perfect: ~ আনন্দ. 4 replete with; abundant; rich in. 5 concluded; finished; accomplished; completed. 6 gratified; fulfilled; satisfied; realized; contented. 7 mature; fully grown. পূর্ণা *fem.* ~ করা *vt* 1 fill; load; make full to the brim; stuff; crowd. 2 complete; fill in/out; conclude; finish; accomplish; carry/ through. 3 fulfil; satisfy; gratify. 4 redeem; keep: প্রতিশ্রুতি ~ করা. 5 fill with air; blow into: বায়ু ~ করা. ~ হওয়া *vi* 1 be filled with; become full (of). 2 become complete; be fulfilled; be redeemed. ~কাম *adj* one whose wishes are fulfilled; satisfied; content. ~কাল *adj* full-time. ~কাল কর্মী *n* full-time/whole-time worker; full-timer. ~কুম্ভ *n* full jar/pitcher. ~গর্ভা *adj* ready to bring forth; in the advanced/last stage of pregnancy. ~গ্রাস *n* total eclipse. ~চন্দ্র *n* full moon. ~চ্ছেদ *n* (gram) full stop. ~চ্ছেদ পড়া *vi* (fig) come to a stand/ close/full stop; be terminated; cease to exist. ~তা, ~ত্ব *nn* fulness; completeness; perfection; fulfilment; repletion; accomplishment; full growth; maturity. ~পাত্র *n* full vessel/ cup/ plate. ~বয়স *n* adulthood; maturity. ~বয়স্ক *adj* grown up; adult; full-blown; full-grown. ~বয়স্কা *fem.* ~বয়স্ক হওয়া *vi* be/come of age; attain one's majority. ~বিকশিত *adj* full-blown; fully developed. ~ বিকাশ *n* full bloom; full development; full manifestation. ~বেগ *n* full speed/tilt/pelt. ~বেগে *adv* at full speed; full tilt/pelt. ~ব্রহ্ম *n* Absolute Being. ~মাত্রা *n* 1 fullest measure/extent. 2 (of drugs) full dose. ~মাত্রায় *adv* fully; to the fullest measure/ extent; entirely; wholly; thoroughly. ~মাসী=পৌর্ণমাসী. ~যুবক *n* full-grown young man. ~যুবতী *fem.* ~যৌবন *n* full flush of youth. ❑*adj* full of youth; in the full flush of youth. ~শক্তি *n* full energy/ vigour/ force. ~সংখ্যা *n* (arith) integer; whole number. পূর্ণাঙ্গ *adj* having all the limbs; complete in all parts; fully grown/ developed; thorough; perfect. পূর্ণাঙ্গতা *n* completeness in all parts; full growth/ development; perfection; thoroughness. পূর্ণানন্দ *n* 1 full joy/delight. 2 Supreme Being. পূর্ণাবতার *n* perfect incarnation; name of the fourth, seventh and the eighth incarnations of Vishnu. পূর্ণাভিলাষ=~কাম. পূর্ণায়ত *adj* fully wide/ widened/ expanded. পূর্ণায়ু *adj* enjoying full longevity; long-lived; living to a great age. পূর্ণাহুতি *n* 1 complete oblation; concluding (burnt) offering; final offering. 2 completion; self-sacrifice. পূর্ণাহুতি দেওয়া *vi* 1 offer the concluding (burnt) offering. 2 (fig) sacrifice oneself; complete.

পূর্ণক *n* characteristic (of logarithm).

পূর্ণিমা *n* day/night of full moon. ~ নিশি, ~ নিশীথ, ~ রজনী, ~ রাত্র *nn* night of full moon. ~র চাঁদ *n* full moon.

পূর্ণেন্দু *n* full moon.

পূর্ণোপমা *n* complete comparison; sustained simile.

পূর্ত *n* public works. ~কর্ম=~. ~বিভাগ *n* Public Works Department.

পূর্তি *n* 1 filling; completion; repletion. 2 ending; coming to an end. 3 satiety; satisfaction: উদর ~. 4 granting: বাসনা ~. 5 compensation. ~ভাতা *n* compensatory allowance.

পূর্ব *n* 1 the east. 2 precedence in time/ place. 3 past. ❑*adj* 1 being before/in front of; fore; first. 2 eastern; to the east of. 3 former; prior; preceding; previous to; earlier than. 4 (esp after past part) done before: কৃত~. 5 ancient; old; traditional. 6 first (in a series); initial. 7 foregoing; aforesaid; mentioned before. 8 senior in age; first. ~ক *adj* (used as a *suff*) 1 having in advance; preceded/ accompanied by; having first made/ done: প্রণাম ~ক. 2 after; with: প্রীতি ~ক. 3 in the specified manner; by: অনুগ্রহ ~ক. **~কথিত** *adj* aforesaid. **~কর্ম** *n* former work/action; preparation. **~কায়** *n* fore (part of the) body (of animals); upper (part of the) body (of men). **~কাল** *n* former/previous time ; past; ancient/former times. **~কালিক, ~কালীন** *adj* belonging to former times; ancient; past; of the past; former; of ancient times. **~কৃত** *adj* done formerly/in a prior existence; previous; done beforehand/in anticipation. **~গ** *adj* going before; preceding. **~গত** *adj* gone before; previous. **~গামী** *adj* 1 going before; foregoing; preceding; previous; antecedent; former. 2 going east(wards). ❑*n* predecessor; pioneer. **~গামিনী** *fem.* ছায়া ~গামিনী coming events cast their shadows before. **~গামিত্ব** *n* precedence. **~জ** *adj* born/produced before/formerly; former; ancient; primeval; first-born; elder; the eldest; born in the east; eastern; antecedent. ❑*n* 1 elder-brother; the eldest born. 2 ancestor; forefather. 3 eldest son. **~জা** *fem* (esp) elder sister. **~জন্ম** *n* former birth; former state of existence/life; previous/former birth. **~জন্মা** *fem.* **~জন্মলব্ধ, ~জন্মার্জিত** *adjj* acquired in some former state of existence. **~জীবন** *n* 1 past/ early life. 2 previous/former state of existence. **~জ্ঞান** *n* 1 past experiences. 2 foreknowledge; anticipation. 3 knowledge of a former life. **~তন** *adj* former; earlier. **~তর** *adj* earlier; previous; prior; anterior. **~তা, ~ত্ব** *nn* precedence; priority; former state/condition. **~দক্ষিণ** *n* the southeast. ❑*adj* south-eastern. **~দত্ত** *adj* given before. **~দিক** *n* the east; east quarter; eastern region. **~দিন** *n* the day before; the earlier part of the day; forenoon. **~দীক্ষা** *n* former consecration. **~দুস্কৃতভোগ** *n* pain/ penalty consequent on sins committed earlier/ in a former birth. **~দৃষ্ট** *adj* seen before; appeared in former times; previously seen; anticipated. **~দৃষ্টান্ত** *n* precedent. **~দৃষ্টি** *n* former view/sight; foresight. **~দেশ** *n* eastern country/ region; the east/orient. **~দেশীয়** *adj* of an eastern country/region; eastern; oriental. **~দেশীয়া** *fem.* **~দেহ** *n* former body. **~নিপাত** *n* (gram) irregular priority of a word in a compound. **~নিবাস** *n* former residence/ existence. **~নির্ধারণ** *n* predetermination; prearrangement. **~নির্ধারিত** *adj* predetermined; prearranged. **~নিরীক্ষিত** *adj* pre-audited. **~নিরূপণ** *n* 1= ~নির্ধারণ. 2 predestination; foreordainment. **~নিরূপিত** *adj* 1=~নির্ধারিত. 2 predestined; foreordained. **~নির্ণয়**=~নির্ধারণ. **~নির্ণীত**=~নির্ধারিত. **~পক্ষ** *n* 1 the forepart/ side. 2 the first part of a lunar month; the fortnight of the working moon. 3 action at law; the first statement of the plaintiff; first step in a lawsuit. 4 the first objection to an assertion in any discussion; prima facie view/argument in any question. **~পরিচয়** *n* previous acquaintance. **~পরিচিত** *adj* known for a long time; familiar; formerly/already known. **~পরিচিতা** *fem.* **~পরিচিত লোক** *n* old acquaintance. **~পরিচিতি** *n* previous acquaintance; familiarity. **~পশ্চিম** *n* the east and the west. **~পুরুষ** *n* forefather; ancestor; former generation. **~প্রচলিত** *adj* previously in vogue; formerly current/ prevalent; current/ prevalent in the past. **~ফল্গুনী** *n* (astrol) name of the eleventh lunar asterism. **~বঙ্গ** *n* East/ Eastern Bengal. **~বৎ** *adv* 1 as before/ hitherto/ heretofore/ aforesaid; according to sth previous. 2 (logic) (an argument) in which a conclusion is drawn from a previous cause to an effect. **~বর্ণিত** *adj* described/ narrated/ mentioned before; aforesaid; aforementioned. **~বর্তিতা** *n* precedence. **~বর্তী** *adj* preceding; antecedent; prior; previous; former; senior; existing before. **~বর্তিনী** *fem.* **~বাদ** *n* the first plea/plaint in an action at law. **~বাদী** *n* complainant; plaintiff. **~বাদিনী** *fem.* **~ভাগ** *n* fore part; upper part; front; eastern part; earlier part of the day; forenoon. **~ভাদ্রপদ** *n* (astrol) the twenty-fifth lunar asterism. **~ভাব** *n* former/original state/ condition. **~ভাষ** *n* foreword; preface. **~মত** *n* former opinion. **~মীমাংসা** *n* name of the system of philosophy attributed to Jaimini. **~মুখ** *adj* having the face turned towards the east; east-facing. **~রঙ্গ** *n* commencement/prelude of a drama. **~রাগ** *n* earlier/ incipient affection; courtship. **~রাত্র** *n* 1 the first part of the night; the time from dusk to midnight. 2 previous/ last night. **~রাত্রি** *n* previous/ last night. **~রাশি** *n* (math) antecedent. **~রীতি** *n* former practice. **~রূপ** *n* 1 indication of sth approaching; omen; sth antecedent/ prior to. 2 previous state/form. **~লক্ষণ** *n* indication of anything about to occur; presage; symptom; foreboding. **~লক্ষণ প্রকাশ করা** *vi* presage; forebode. **~লেখ** *n* draft. **~শৈল**=পূর্বাচল. **~সংস্কার** *adj* 1 notion/ idea/ habit/ impression formed in a former birth or in the past. 2 predisposition; prejudice. 3 outdated notion/idea. **~সূরি** *n* predecessor. **~স্বত্ব** *n* lien. **পূর্বাচরিত**=পূর্বানুষ্ঠিত. **পূর্বাচল, পূর্বাদ্রি** *nn* the eastern mountain (from behind which the sun is supposed to rise). **পূর্বাদেশ** *n* previous order. **পূর্বাধিকার** *n* 1 possession/right obtained earlier; priority. 2 right/ claim of the first-born; primogeniture. 3 former right/claim. **পূর্বাধিকারী** *adj* prior owner; former proprietary. **পূর্বানুরাগ** *n* 1 first love; nascent affection. 2 old love. **পূর্বানুবৃত্তি** *n* continuation (of sth already begun).

পূর্বানুভূত *adj* formerly felt/enjoyed. পূর্বানুষ্ঠিত *adj* observed/ performed before. পূর্বাপর *adj*, *adv* first and last; preceding and following; directed forward and backward; prior and subsequent; following one another; connected with one another; from beginning to end; alpha and omega; thorough; one after another. ❑*n* that which is before and behind; connection. **পূর্বাপর বিবেচনা করা** look before and after; consider the pros and cons of a proposal. **পূর্বাপর-বিরোধ** *n* opposition of prior and subsequent; inconsistency. **পূর্বাপরবৃত্ত** *n* (astron) prime vertical. **পূর্বাপেক্ষা** *adv* than before. **পূর্বাবধি** *adv* from former times/ antiquities. **পূর্বাবস্থা** *n* past/ previous/ former state/ condition. **পূর্বাভাষ** *n* **1** presage; foreboding. **2** preface; foreword. **3** forecast (also পূর্বাভাস) (of weather). **পূর্বাভাষ দেওয়া** *vi* **1** presage; forebode. **2** forecast. **পূর্বাবিমুখ** *adj* turned/ flowing towards the east. **পূর্বাভ্যাস** *n* **1** previous/ former/ old habit/ practice. **পূর্বার্জিত** *adj* attained/ gained formerly. **পূর্বার্ধ** *n* **1** the first half; the eastern half; the fore half; front/upper part. **2** (geog) the eastern hemisphere. **পূর্বাশা** *n* the east. **পূর্বাষাঢ়া** *n* (astrol) the first of the two constellations called Ashadha (আষাঢ়) (the twentieth lunar asterism). **পূর্বাহ্ণ** *n* the earlier part of the day; forenoon. **পূর্বাহ্ণিক** *adj* of the forenoon; to be done in the forenoon.

পূর্বিতা *n* priority; precedence.

পূর্বে *adv* **1** before; formerly; previously; in the past. **2** in the front. **3** in the east.

পূর্বোক্ত *adj* aforesaid; mentioned before/above; said before.

পূর্বোক্তি *n* previous statement; prefatory remark/ utterance.

পূর্বোত্তর *n* the north-east. ❑*adj* north-eastern.

পূর্বোদ্ধৃত *adj* quoted before/above.

পূর্বোল্লিখিত *adj* mentioned before; above-mentioned.

পূর্বোল্লেখ *n* prior indication/ mentioning.

পূষা *n* the sun.

পৃক্ত *adj* mixed/mingled with; full of; brought into contact with; touching; adjoining; contiguous; attached; related; connected; concerned; associated; saturated; incorporated.

পৃক্তি *n* (geom) contact.

পৃচ্ছা *n* asking; questioning; question; inquiry.

পৃথক, পৃথক্ (in compound) *adj* **1** separate; different; separated; differentiated; segregated; moved/lying aside. **2** estranged; alienated. **3** segregated. ❑*adj* apart; separately; differently; singly; severally; individually one by one. **~ করা** *vt* separate; differentiate; dissociate; remove apart; alienate; estrange; segregate. **~করণ** *n* separating; separation; setting apart; differentiation; dissociation; estrangement; alienation; segregation. **~কৃত** *adj* separated; sundered; cut off; differentiated; set apart; dissociated; alienated; estranged; segregated. **~চার** *n* (psycho) dissociation. **~ত্ব** *n* separateness; singleness; severalty; individuality. **~পৃথক** *adv*=~.

পৃথকীকরণ=পৃথককরণ (⇒ পৃথক)

পৃথকীকৃত=পৃথককৃত

পৃথগ্‌ *adj*, *adv* (in compounds)=পৃথক. **~গুণ** *n* distinct property. **~জন** *n* man of lower caste/ character/profession. **~বিধ** *adj* of different kinds; manifold; various. **~ভাব** *n* separate state/condition; difference; distinctness; individuality. **~ভাবে** *adv*=পৃথকভাবে. **~ভূত** *adj* separated; differentiated; differented; alienated; estranged; segregated.

পৃথগন্ন *adj* (of a family) having separate messing arrangements; separated; split up.

পৃথগাত্মা *adj* separate; distinct; individual; having a separate nature/essence.

পৃথিবী *n* the earth/wide world. **~তল** surface of the earth; ground; terrestrial regions. **~পতি, ~পাল** *nn* prince; king; emperor. **~ব্যাপী, ~ময়** *adjj* extending all over the world; world-wide. **~মণ্ডল** *n* orb of the world; the whole world.

পৃথু *adj* **1** broad; wide; expansive; extensive; spacious; large. **2** great; important. **3** ample; abundant. **4** bulky; heavy; fat; robust; muscular. **~গ্রীব** *adj* broad-necked. **~জঘন, ~নিতম্ব** *adj* large-hipped. **~জঘনা, ~নিতম্বা** *fem.* **~ল** *adj* broad; large; great. **~ললোচন** *adj* large-eyed. **~বক্ষ** *adj* broad-breasted. **~লাক্ষ**= ~ললোচন.

পৃথ্বী *n* the earth; the world. **~তল** *n* surface of the earth; ground. **~ধর** *n* mountain. **~পতি** *n* king; prince;

পৃষ্ট *adj* asked; inquired; questioned; interrogated.

পৃষ্ঠ *n* **1** the back; the hinder part/ rear of anything; the region of the back; back/ rear part. **2** upper side; face; surface; top; height. **3** (bot) dorsal surface. **~গ্রন্থি** *n* hump on the back. **~টান** *n* (phys) surface tension. **~তল** *n* surface. **~দান** *n* fleeing; taking to one's heels; flight. **~দান করা** *vi* flee, run away; take to one's heels. **~দেশ**=~ (1,2). **~পোষক** *n* supporter; patron; upholder; customer; client. **~পোষকতা** *n* support; patronization. **~পোষকতা করা** *vi* patronize; support; uphold. **~পোষণ** *n* supporting; patronization; patronizing. **~প্রদর্শন** =~দান. **~প্রবাহ** *n* (geog) surface drift. **~ফল** *n* (alg) superficial contents of a figure. **~বংশ** *n**

backbone; spine; spinal/vertebral column. ~ব্রণ *n* dorsal carbuncle. ~ভঙ্গ = ~দান. ~ভাগ *n* hinder part; back; rear. ~মধ্য *n* middle of the back. ~মাংস *n* flesh on the back. ~রক্ষক *n* body-guard. ~রক্ষণ *n* protection/defence of the back. ~রক্ষা করা *vi* guard/ protect the rear; act as a bodyguard to. ~লগ্ন *adj* hanging about a person's back; following. ~লেখ *n* endorsement. পৃষ্ঠে আরোহণ করা *vi* ride on. পৃষ্ঠে বহন করা *vi* carry on the back. ঘূর্ণ~ *n* surface of revolution. পৃষ্ঠাঙ্কন *n* endorsement.

পৃষ্ঠা *n* page (of a book). ~ঙ্ক *n* page-number.

পৃষ্ঠোপরি *adv* on the back (of).

পেঁকাটি=পাকাটি

পেঁকো *adj* full of slime/mire; slimy; miry; silty.

পেঁচ [P] *n* **1** screw; thread (of a screw). **2** spiral bend; coil; twist. **3** perplexity; intricate/ perplexing situation; false position; difficulty; complication; trouble; predicament; intricacy. **4** machination; deceit; intrigue; stratagem intricate scheme. **5** entanglement; mutual entwining: ঘুড়ির ~. **6** tricky/shrewd turn; involution: কথার ~. **7** a trick in wrestling. **8** tangle: সুতার ~. **9** spiral motion. ~ আঁটা/কষা *vi* **1** tighten (a screw); give (a nut, etc) another screw. **2** (in wrestling) seize. **3** (fig) put the screw(s) on (sb); tighten one's grip on; twist. ~ খাওয়া *vi* **1** get in tangle; coil; be tangled up. **2** (fig) get entangled; become complicated; become embroiled; be in a tangle. ~ খেলা *vi* play a trick on sb. ~ খোলা *vt, vi* loosen; open; unscrew; slacken; disentangle; untwist; unravel; unscrew; be unscrewed/ disentangled/ untwisted/ unravelled (as a mystery). ~ দেওয়া *vt* **1** twist; twine. **2** (fig) throw obstacles in the way; entangle; be up to one's (old) tricks; complicate matters; make difficulties for. **3** (wrestling) seize. ~ পড়া/ লাগা = ~খাওয়া. ~ লড়া *vi* entangle the string of an adversary's kite. ~ লাগানো *vi* raise difficulties; complete; bungle. পেঁচে পড়া *vi* be (caught) in a the cleft stick; fall into sb's trap; be tricked; be the dupe of; be entrapped; swallow the bait; be in trouble/a predicament; be in a false position/ quandary; be enmeshed in sth. পেঁচে ফেলা *vt* entrap; trick; trap sb (into sth/doing sth).

পেঁচা *n* owl . পেঁচী *fem.* ~র ডাক *n* hooting; hoot. পেঁচাও *adj* twisted; coiled; spiral; winding; crooked; intricate; devious. ~র বাচ্চা *n* owlet. কাল~ *n* hawk owl. কুটুরে ~ *n* spotty owl. লক্ষ্মী ~ *n* barn owl. হুতুম ~ *n* brown fish owl.

পেঁচানো *vt* **1** twist; twine; wring; screw. **2** make intricate; complicate; entangle. **3** involve; implicate: আমাকে আবার এর মধ্যে ~ কেন? **4** twist; avoid the issue; ramble about: কথা ~. ☐*adj* **1** twisted; wrung; entangled; enmeshed. **2** involved; involute; tricky; tortuous; convoluted; devious: ~ কথাবার্তা. **3** zigzag; tortuous; twisty; snaky; devious: ~ রাস্তা. **4** complicated; complex; confused; crooked: ~ মন.

পেঁচাপেঁচি *n* reciprocal intricacy; disputation; contention; controversy; feud.

পেঁচাল *n*=প্যাচাল

পেঁচালো *adj*=পেঁচানো

পেঁচো *n* hysterics; involuntary distortion of the body; post-natal tetanus. ~য় পাওয়া *n* be affected with tetanus.

পেঁচোয়া *adj*=পেঁচানো

পেঁজন *n* cleaning/carding of cotton.

পেঁজা=পিঁজা

পেঁটরা=পেটরা

পেঁড়া=পেড়া

পেঁদানি *n* (sl) drubbing; beating; belabouring; thrashing.

পেঁদানো *vt* (sl) **1** beat up; give sb a good drubbing; beat soundly; belabour. **2** dress sb down.

পেঁপে *n* papaya; papaw; pawpaw.

পেঁয়াজ=পিঁয়াজ

পেঁয়াজি=পিঁয়াজি

পেখম *n* tail feathers (of a peacock). ~ ধরা/ ফোলানো *n* **1** (of a peacock) spread out/expand tail feathers. **2** (fig) be beside oneself with joy; bubble (over) with enthusiasm/joy/ excitement. **3** (fig) be foppish; be dressed like a dog's dinner; be dressed (up) to kill.

পেচ=পেঁচ

পেচক *n* owl. পেচকী *fem.* ~শাবক *n* owlet.

পেচ্ছাব *n* (colloq) = প্রস্রাব

পেছন *n*=পিছ

পেছপা=পিছপা (⇒ পিছ)

পেছু=পাছু

পেছুনো=পিছানো

পেজমি, পেজমো *nn*=পাজিপনা. ~ করা *vi* make a mischief; play tricks; be mischievous; commit an act of roguery; do the dirty on sb; be up to some mischief.

পেজি *adj* (used as a *suff)* having a specific number of pages: ষোল-ফর্মা.

পেট *n* **1** belly; stomach; abdomen; bowel. **2** foetus; pregnancy. **3** womb. **4** inside; hold; belly; bowels: জাহাজের ~. **5** the inmost part of one's heart; secret: পেটের কথা. **6** loins: পেটে কাপড় থাকে না. **7** livelihood; subsistence; body and soul: ~ চালানো. ~ আঁটা *vi* be constipated. ~ ওঠা *vi* (of the stomach) bulge (after a hearty meal). ~ ওলটানো *vi* (of the stomach) be ready to burst (due to overeating). ~ কনকন করা *n* have bellyache/a gnawing pain in the stomach. ~ করা *vi* (sl) make pregnant; put sb in the family way. ~ কলকল করা *vi* (of the stomach) rumble. ~ কাটা *vi* cut the abdomen; perform a Caesarean (section). ~ কামড়ানো *vi* **1** (of the stomach) gripe; have a griping pain in the stomach. **2** have a bowel movement. ~খসা *vi* (sl) miscarry; have an abortion; abort. ~ খসানো *vi* (sl) abort (an expectant mother/a foetus); terminate a pregnancy; perform an abortion. ~ খোঁচানো *vi* (of the stomach) gripe; have the gripes. ~ গড়গড়/গুড়গুড় করা *vi* (of the stomach) rumble (due to hunger). ~ চড়চড় করা *vi* (of the stomach) be about to burst. ~ চনচন করা=~ চিনচিন করা. ~ চলা *vi* **1** make (both) ends meet; live from hand to mouth; just manage to subsist. **2** have loose bowels; have an attack of diarrhoea. ~ চালানো *vi* earn one's living/ a subsistence wage; make a meagre living; live from hand to mouth; keep the wolf from the door. ~ চিন চিন করা *vi* feel an aching feeling in (the pit of) one's stomach (due to hungry); be hungry/ famished. ~ চুঁই চুঁই করা *vi* feel the gnawing pains of hunger; be awfully hungry. ~ চেরা=~ কাটা. ~ জ্বলা/জ্বলে যাওয়া *vi* have a burning sensation in the stomach (caused by hunger). ~ টাঁই টাঁই করা *vi* (of the stomach) be ready to burst (due to overeating). ~ ঠাসা *vi* have one's fill. ~ ডাকা *vi* have collywobbles; (of the stomach) rumble. ~ ধরা *vi* stop having loose bowels; be cured of diarrhoea/ loose bowels. ~ ধুয়ে বের হওয়া *vi* empty the belly of a person; purge sb. ~ নরম করা *vi* cause loose motions. ~ নামা (sl) *vi* have loose bowels/ diarrhoea. ~ নামানো *vi* (sl) purge sb's bowels. ~ পালা/পোষা *vi*=~ চালানো. ~ পোরা *vi* have one's fill; devour. ~ ফাঁপা, ~ ফুটফাট/ ফুটফুট করা *vi* suffer from flatulence. ~ ফেলা=~ খসানো. ~ ফোলা *vi* **1**=~ ফাঁপা. **2** be pregnant; be with child; be in the family way; conceive. ~ বড়ো হওয়া *vi* **1** (of the stomach) bulge; have a pot-belly; develop a corporation; get stout. **2**=~ ফোলা (2). পেট বসা *vi* (of a stomach) shrink (because of starvation). ~ বাঁধা *vi* **1** bind the abdomen after deliver. **2** stint oneself of food. ~ বাঁধানো *vi* be pregnant; conceive. ~ বাজানো *vi* feel very happy. ~ ভরা *vi* have one's fill; fill one's belly; be satisfied; feel full to satiety. ~ ভরে খাওয়া *vt* have one's fill. ~ ভরে খাওয়ানো *vi* give sb a square meal. ~ ভাঙা *vi* have an attack of diarrhoea. ~ ভারী হওয়া *vi* suffer from indigestion; be pregnant. ~ মরা *vi* lose appetite; suffer from anorexia. ~ সামলানো/ সামলে খাওয়া *vi* eat moderately. ~ হওয়া *vi*=~ ফোলা (2). ~ হড় হড়/গড় গড়/হড় হড় করা *vi*=~ গড়গড় করা. পেটে অন্ন থাকা/না থাকা *vi* (not) have a means of living; have to do without food. পেটে আসা *vi* be conceived. পেটে জ্বালা ধরা *vi*=~ জ্বলা. পেটে কালির আঁচড় না থাকা be utterly illiterate. পেটে তলানো *vi* be accepted in one's stomach; be stomached. পেটে থাকা *vi* **1**=পেটে তলানো. **2** (of a person) be able to keep a secret: তাঁর পেটে কথা থাকে না. **3** be in the innermost recesses of the mind; be kept secret; have in oneself: এত সুসংবাদ তোমার পেটে ছিল. পেটে দড়ি দিয়ে (পড়ে) থাকা *vi* go hungry; suffer starvation; starve oneself. পেটে ধরা *vi* conceive; bear; carry in one's womb. পেটে পোরা *vi* gulp sth (down); swallow; devour. পেটে বিদ্যা থাকা *vi* be learned; have learning; be clever. পেটে বোমা মারলেও কিছু বের না হওয়া be utterly illiterate/ignorant. পেটে মারা *vi* starve sb; deprive sb of his/her means of living/subsistence/livelihood. পেটে যাওয়া *vi* be devoured/ swallowed. পেটে রাখা *vi* **1**=পেটে ধরা. **2** keep sth secret. পেটের অন্ন থাকা *vi* have a means of living. পেটে সওয়া *vi* (of a person)suit one's stomach; be able to digest. পেটের ভাত চাল হওয়া be unnerved/ over strung/extremely distressed. পেটের ভিতর হাত-পা সেঁধুনো feel one's blood run cold/one's knees knock/ one's hair stand on end; break out in a cold sweat; take fright; lose one's nerve; get/have the wind up (about sth). পেটে সওয়া *vi* be accepted in one's stomach; suit one's stomach. ~ওয়ালী *adj* pregnant. ~কাপড় *n* food and clothing. ~কামড়ানি *n* the gripes; gnawing pain in the stomach; bellyache. ~ ঢক ঢক *n* rumble in an empty stomach. ~পাতলা, ~হালকা *adj* unable to keep a secret. ~ফাটা হাসি *n* belly-laugh. ~ব্যথা *n* bellyache; stomach-pain; gripes. ~ভাতা *n* personal subsistence; food given in lieu of wages. □*adv* for personal subsistence; for food in lieu of wages. ~মরা *adj* incapable of eating much; anorexic. ~মোটা *adj* pot-bellied; big-bellied. পেটের কথা *n* secret of one's heart; secret intention; innermost feelings. পেটের গোলমাল *n* stomach trouble; bowel complaint/ disorder. পেটের চিন্তা *n* worries about one's livelihood. পেটের ছেলে *n* one's (ie, a mother's) own son. পেটের জ্বালা/দায় *n* pangs of hunger; hunger pangs. পেটের জ্বালায় *adv* goaded/impelled by the pangs of hunger. পেটের বাছা = পেটের ছেলে. পেটের বোঝা *n* foetus; pregnancy. পেটের শত্রু *n* child who causes grief to its mother. ~রোগা *adj* dyspeptic. ~সওয়া *adj* tolerable for the stomach; easily digestible. ~সর্বস্ব *adj* gluttonous; hoggish. ~সর্বস্ব ব্যক্তি *n* glutton. পেটে এক মুখে আর হওয়া be double faced/ insincere/ hypocritical; lie through one's teeth; say one thing and mean another. পেটে খিদে মুখে লাজ too modest to express one's desire. পেটে খেলে পিঠে সয় (fig) one can put up with all kinds of indignities if it is paying. পেটে পেটে *adv* beneath one's innocent surface; kept to oneself; kept concealed. উপর~ *n* belly. এক পেটের *adj* born of the same mother; uterine. খালি ~ *n* empty stomach. জালা-~ *n* pot-belly. ❑*n* pot-bellied; big-bellied. তল~ *n* abdomen. নাদা-~=জালা-~. ভরা ~ *n* full stomach. হাঁদা ~ *adj* big-bellied.

পেটক *n* little basket; casket; box; wicker-basket; portmanteau; chest.

পেটন, পেটনি=পিটাই

পেটরা *n* portmanteau; suitcase; box.

পেটা=পিটা[১]

পেটাই, পেটাও=পিটাই

পেটানো=পিটানো

পেটি *n* **1** waist-band; belt: girdle. **2** casket; box; portmanteau; chest, iron safe; breast/ middle part of a fish: ~র মাছ

পেটিকা, পেটী=পেটক

পেটুক *adj* gluttonous; voracious; greedy. ❑*n* glutton; voracious eater.

পেটেন্ট [E] *n,adj* patent.

পেটুনি=পিটাই

পেটে পেটে *adv* ⇒ পেট

পেটো[১] *adj* made of jute; related to/ trading in jute.

পেটো[২] *n* integument/ outer covering of a banana tree. ~ **পাড়া** *vi* dress the hair of a woman by parting it on the forehead towards the temples.

পেটোয়া *n* obedient; faithful; dependent; cringing. ~ **তালুকদার** *n* tenant of a holding subordinate to a *taluk* (তালুক). ~ **বাহিনী** *n* henchmen; lackeys; musclemen; hangers-on.

পেট্রল [E] *n* petrol.

পেড়া[১]=পেটক

পেড়া[২] *n* kind of sweetmeat made of condensed milk.

পেড়াপীড়ি *n* (dail)=পিড়াপিড়ি

পেন্ট,পেন্টুলুন, পেন্টালুন [E] *n* pantaloons; trousers.

পেন্ডাল [E] *n* pandal.

পেন্ডুলাম [E] *n* pendulum.

পেতনি, পেত্নী *n fem* **1** female spirit; apparition; spectre. **2** extremely ugly/dirty woman; hag; slut.

পেতল *n* (dial)=পিতল

পেন[১] [E] *n* fountain-pen.

পেন[২] [E] *n* pain; labour-pain.

পেনশন, পেনসন [E] *n* pension. ~ **নেওয়া, পেনশনে যাওয়া** *vi* retire on a pension. ~**ভোগী** *adj* living on a pension. ❑*n* pensioner.

পেনসিল [E] *n* pencil.

পেনা *n* peg of wood; pin.

পেনাল কোড [E] *n* penel code.

পেনেট *n* circular pedestal of the sacred phallic sign of the Hindus.

পেন্নাম *n* (dial)=প্রণাম

পেন্সন=পেনশন

পেন্সিল=পেনসিল

পেপারমেন্ট [E] *n* pepperment.

পেয় *adj* to be drunk; drinkable. ❑*n* drink.

পেয়াজ [P] *n* onion.

পেয়াদা=পিয়াদা

পেয়ার=পিয়ার. **পেয়ারের দোস্ত/ বন্ধু** *n* close/ bosom friend; chum.

পেয়ারা [Pg] *n* guava.

পিয়ারি=পিয়ারা

পেয়ালা = পেয়ালা

পেয়ে *adj* (used as a *suff*) legged; footed; ped চার~ four-legged; four-footed; quadruped.

পেরনো=পেরোনো

পেরু *n* [Pg] turkey (cock).

পেরুভীয় *adj* Peruvian.

পেরেক *n* [Pg] nail; wire-nail; spike. ~ **ঠোকা** *v* drive a nail into.

পেরেশান *adj* [P] tired; worn out; troubled; distressed. ~ **করা** *vt* trouble; distress; harass confuse; perplex.

পেরেশানি [P]*n* distress; trouble; perturbation tiredness.

পেরোনো *vi* (colloq)=পার হওয়া (⇒ পার)

পেলব *adj* **1** delicate; fine; tender; soft; graceful; gentle. **2** slender; slim; frail. **3** ligh ~**তা** *n* **1** delicateness; softness; gentleness grace; delicacy, tenderness. **2** slenderness slimness; frailty. **3** lightness.

পেলা[১] gift/reward given to an artist at a function.

পেলা[২] *n* prop.

পেল্লয়, পেল্লায় *adjj* huge; gigantic; enormous monstrous; tremendous.

পেশ [P]*n* front; fore-part. ❑*adj* advanced promoted; presented; submitted. ❑*pre* before; in front of. ~ **করা** *vt* present; submi put up; produce. ~ **ইমাম** *n* one who lead congregational prayers. ~**কার** *n* manage reader (to a magistrate); agent; deputy. ~**কা** *n* office/profession of a manager/reader. ~**ক** *n* present; tribute. ~**কৃত** *adj* presente submitted; put up; produced. ~**গি** *n* earne money; advance of money.

পেশওয়া=পেশোয়া

পেশওয়াজ=পেশোয়াজ

পেশল *adj* 1 adorned; decorated. 2 beautiful; charming; graceful; lovely; pleasant. 3 soft; tender; delicate. 4 expert; skilful; clever. ~তা *n* dexterity; skill.

পেশা [P] *n* 1 trade; profession; calling; office; occupation. 2 practice; habit. ~দার *adj* professional. ~দারি *n* professionalism. ❑*adj* professional.

পেশানি *n* forehead; brow.

পেশি, পেশী *nn* 1 muscle; tendon. 2 sheath of sword: scabbard. ~বহুল *adj* muscular; brawny; robust. পেশীয় *adj* relating to muscles; muscular. ~সঞ্চালন *n* movement/ flexing of muscles.

পেশোয়া [P]*n* leader; priest; guide; title of a Marhatta minister; peshwa.

পেশোয়াজ *n* [P] a gown worn by dancing-girls.

পেষক *n, adj* (one) who pounds (grinds).

পেষণ *n*=পিষণ. ~দন্ত *n* molar tooth; grinder. ~যন্ত্র *n* grinding stone; handmill.

পেষণি, পেষণী *nn* grind-stone; mill-stone.

পেষল=পেশল

পেষা=পিষা

পেস্তা [P] *n* pistachio.

পৈছা=পইছা

পৈঠা=পইঠা

পৈতা=পইতা

পৈতামহ *adj* relating to a paternal grand-father.

পৈতৃক *adj* 1 paternal; ancestral: ~ সম্পত্তি/বাড়ি. 2 hereditary: ~ রোগ.

পৈত্ত, পৈত্তিক *adjj* biliary; bilious.

পৈত্র, পৈত্র্য=পৈতৃক

পৈশাচ *adj* relating/belonging to the Pisachas (পিশাচ); demon-like; infernal; ghoulish; monstrous; fiendish. পৈশাচী *fem.* ❑*n* the eighth or lowest from of Hindu marriage (when a lover secretly embraces a damsel either sleeping or intoxicated or disordered in her intellect).

পৈশাচিক=পৈশাচ. পৈশাচিকী *fem.* ~তা *n* monstrosity; deviltry; atrocity; ghoulishness.

পৈশুন, পৈশুন্য *nn* malice; malignity; tale bearing; backbiting; wickedness. পৈষ্টিক *adj* made of meal/flour. ❑*n* quantity of cakes.

পো¹ *n* (dial) son; male descendant: তালকদারের পো.

পো²=পোয়া

পোঁ *n* (onom) imitating many of the sounds in music; wail. পোঁ করে *adv* 1 wailing. 2 in a trice/ jifty; instantly; very quickly. পোঁ দৌড় *n* running heel for leather. পোঁ ধরা *vi* fawn/upon; cringe to; dance attendance to; today to. পোঁ-ধরা *adj* fawning; cringing. পোঁ-পোঁ *n* swish (of swishly moving canes, sticks, etc). ❑*adj* very swift. ❑*adv* very swiftly.

পোঁচ *n* coating; coat (of paint). ~দেওয়া *vi* apply a coating/a coat of paint. ~ড়া, ~লা *n* 1 coating. 2 brush for whitewashing made of jute fibres.

পোঁছ *n* mopping; wiping; swabbing.

পোঁছা¹=পুঁছা¹. ~নো=পুঁছানো

পোঁছা²=পুঁছা²

পোঁছা³ *n* 1 tail of a fish. 2 part of the hand from the wrist to the finger-tips.

পোঁটলা *n* bundle; baggage.

পোঁটা¹ *n* 1 entails; intestines; gut: মাছের ~. 2 drop of nasal catarrh/mucus; shot.

পোঁটা² *n* little boy; kiddy.

পোঁত *n* length of the part of anything buried or implanted underground.

পোঁতা¹=পুঁতা. ~নো=পুঁতানো

পোঁতা² *n* plinth (of a house).

পোঁদ *n* 1 (sl) anus. 2 (sl) posteriors; hips; buttocks.

পোক *n* (dial)=পোকা

পোকা *n* worm; insect; vermin; moth; beetle. ~-ধরা, ~য়-খাওয়া *adjj* worm-eaten; moth-eaten. ~-মাকড় *n* worms and insects. ~য় ধরা *vi* 1 be infested with vermin/worms. 2 (of teeth) be affected with caries; become carious.

পোক্ত *adj* [P] 1 strong; firm; solid. 2 durable; lasting. 3 mature; expert; experienced; accustomed; seasoned. 4 (of wood) seasoned. 5 ripe. 6 well made; matured. ~ করা *vi* 1 make strong; reinforce. 2 ripen. ~ হওয়া 1 be strong/reinforced. 2 be definite. 3 ripen; mature. পাকা~ *adj* 1 strong; firm. 2 definite; definitive; permanent.

পোখরাজ [P] *n* topaz.

পোগণ্ড *adj* 1 deformed. 2 not full-grown/adult; young. ❑*n* 1 cripple. 2 a child between the age of five and fifteen.

পোঙ্গা *n* 1 hollow bamboo. 2 (sl) anus.

পোছা *vi* পুঁছা²

পোট *n* 1 contact; union. 2 agreement; friendly terms; love; affection. ~খাওয়া *vi* be on friendly terms (with); concur/agree with (sb); be in love with; get along/on with.

পোটলা *n* bundle; packet.

পোটা *n* hermaphrodite; woman with a beard.

পোড় *n* 1 burning; scalding; singeing. 2 affliction; severe ordeal; distress. ~-খাওয়া *adj* 1 burnt; baked; scalded; singed. 2 passed through an off affliction/ ordeal/ distressed; hard-bitten.

পোড়ন=পুড়ন

পোড়া *vi* 1 burn. 2 be burnt/ scalded/ scorched/ parched/ charred/ roasted/ calcined. 3 be inflamed; burn: জ্বরে কপাল পুড়ে যাচ্ছে. **4** be afflicted/ distressed; burning with desire/ longing: মন~. ❑*adj* **1** burnt (down); scalded; charred; scorched; calcined. **2** (fig) cursed; unhappy; tormented: ~ মন. **~ কপাল** *n* hard luck; ill fortune; bad luck. ❑*int* woe is me! ah me! **~কপালী** *adj* unfortunate; wretched; abandoned; unlucky. ❑*n* accursed/ hateful one; accursed/ wretched creature. **~কপালে** *adj* =~কপালী. **~রমুখী** *n*=~কপালী.

পোড়ানি=পুড়ানি

পোড়ানে=পুড়ানে

পোড়ানো *vt* **1** burn; scorch; parch; char; roast; calcine; singe; heat; scald; incinerate; destroy by fire. **2** distress; afflict; agonize.

পোড়েন *n* woof.

পোড়ো[1] *n*=পড়ুয়া

পোড়ো[2] *adj* **1** unoccupied; deserted; vacant: ~ বাড়ি. **2** fallow; uncultivated: ~ জমি. **3** confined to bed; deprived of the power of movement; bed-ridden: ~ লোক. **4** fallen; crumbling.

পোড়ো[3] *n* placenta.

পোণা=পোনা

পোত *n* boat; ship; vessel. **~ চালানো** *vi* pilot a ship. **~চালক** *n* captain/pilot of a ship; master of a vessel; steersman. **~ধ্বংস, ~ভঙ্গ** *nn* shipwreck. **~নায়ক**=~চালক. **~নিয়ামক** *n* boatman; steersman. **পোতাধিপাল, পোতাধ্যক্ষ** *nn* captain/ master of a ship. **পোতারোহী** *adj* sailing in a ship. ❑*n* passenger of a ship. **পোতাশ্রয়** *n* harbour; haven.

পোতা[1] *n* plinth (of a house).

পোতা[2] *n* (dial) son's son; grandson.

পোত্রী *n* placenta.

পোদ্দার [P]*n* **1** professional examiner of the genuineness of coins. **2** treasurer; cashier; banker; money-changer; pawn-broker; money-lender. **পোদ্দারি** *n* **1** profession of a coin examiner/ treasurer/ money-changer/ pawn-broker/ banker. **2** (derog) display of false authority/ power.

পোনা *n* young of fish; fry. **~ মাছ** *n* a fish of the species of *rui* (রুই), *katla* (কাতলা) *mrigel* (মৃগেল), etc.

পোনি [E]*n* pony; tattoo.

পোয়া *n* **1** fourth part; quarter. **2** one-fourth of a seer (সের). **~বারো** *vi* **1** a particular throw at dice. **2** success/fortune in everything; run of luck: তোমার তো ~বারো, you are lucky in every respect. **চার~** *adj* complete; full.

পোয়াতি, পোয়াতী *nn* **1** pregnant woman; would-be mother. **2** woman recently delivered of a child; mother. ❑*adj* pregnant. **2** recently delivered of a child. **~ হওয়া** *vi* conceive; be in the family way.

পোয়ানো=পোহানো

পোয়াল *n* straw.

পোরা *vt, vi* **1** fill; load: বোতলে মদ ~. **2** stuff; cram: বালিশে তুলা ~. **3** thrust in; insert; put in/into: মুখে আঙুল ~. **4** confine; put in: জেলে ~. **5** be filled with; be swarm with: কৌতূহলী জনতায় রাস্তা পুরেছে. **6** blow/sound (as a wind-instrument); play: বাঁশিতে সুর ~. **7** be completed/ accomplished: কাজ পুরেছে. **8** satisfied/ attained/ realized: তার আশা পুরেছে. **পকেটে ~** *vt* pocket. ❑*adj* filled.

পোর্টফোলিয়ো [E]*n* portfolio.

পোর্টম্যানটো [E]*n* portmanteau.

পোল [P]*n* bridge; cause-way. **~সিরাত** *n* according to Muslims; the bridge over which the righteous will pass into paradise.

পোলা *n* (dial) son. **~পান** *n* children; kids.

পোলাও [P] *n* a dish made of rice boiled in soup with spices; pilau.

পোলো[1] [E]*n* polo.

পোলো[2]=পলো

পোশ [P] *adj* (used as a *suff*) wearing; dressed in; covered in: বোরখা~. ❑*n* covering; clothing: সর~, বালা ~, ঘোর ~.

পোশাক [P]*n* dress; garment; clothes; attire; raiment; accoutrement; covering. **~ খোলা/ ছাড়া** *vi* undress (oneself). **~ খোলানো/ ছাড়ানো** *vt* undress sb. **~ পরা** *vi* put clothes on; dress; get dressed; dress up. **~-পরা** *adj* dressed. **~ পরানো** *vt* dress (sb).

পোশাকি, পোশাকী *adj* **1** relating to clothes/ dress; fashionable: ~ কথাবার্তা. **2** elegant or elaborate, to be worn on special occasions; dressy: ~ জামাকাপড়. **3** refined; elegant: ~ ভাষা. **4** merely formal; insincere; hypocritical: ~ ভদ্রতা. **খোশ~** *adj* dressy; modish; fashionable foppish.

পোষ[1] *n*=পউষ

পোষ[2]=পোশ

পোষ[3] *n* **1** taming; domestication. **2** subdual. **~ মানা** *vi* **1** become tame/domesticated; be tameable. **2** be subdued/disciplined/broken. **3** (of a horse) be broken. **~ মানানো** *vt* **1** tame domesticate. **2** bring under one's control subdue;, discipline; break in. **3** (of a horse) break. **~মানা** *adj* **1** tame; domesticated. **2** brought under control; subdued; disciplined docile; meek; submissive. **3** (of a horse) broken.

পোষক *adj* **1** feeding; nourishing; cherishing. **2** supporting; aiding; upholding; abetting. ❑*n* nourishes; breeder; keeper. **2** supporter upholder; abettor. **~তা** *n* aiding; supporting support; upholding; abetment; backing; help **~তা করা** *vt* aid; help; support; uphold; back countenance; abet. **~ স্তর** *n* (bot) tapetum.

পোষড়া = পৌষপার্বণ

পোষণ *n* **1** upbringing; fostering; nourishing; feeding; cherishing; keeping; nourishment; supporting. **2** maintaining; maintenance; cherishment. **~ করা** *vt* **1** nourish; foster; bring up; feed; keep; further; promote. **2** maintain; support; uphold: মত ~ করা, আশা ~ করা.

পোষণীয় *adj*=পোষ্য

পোষা *vt* **1** bring up; rear; keep; breed; fancy: পাখি ~. **2** nourish; feed; care for maintain; support: ছেলেমেয়ে ~. **3** cherish: মনে আশা ~. ❑*adj* **1** tame; pet; domesticated: ~ বিড়াল. **2** meek; docile; subservient; obediently following. **~ কুকুর** *n* **1** pet dog. **2** obedient/ servile follower.

পোষাক =পোশাক

পোষানো *vi* **1** be sufficient for; suffice; serve the purpose; do; be adequate: এই অল্প খাবারে এত মানুষের কি পোষাবে? **2** get on/along with sb; go along with: এমন লোকের সঙ্গে আমার পোষায় না. **3** able to bear/tolerate; put up with; cope with: এত ঝামেলা তার পোষাবে না. **4** cause to bring up/ rear. **5** compensate for; pay for; make up for; give satisfaction; recompense for; make sth good: লোকসান ~. **পুষিয়ে নেওয়া** *vi* make do with sth; make (sth) do.

পোষানি *n* **1** money for the maintenance. **2** handing over cattle to others in exchange for milk, etc.

পোষিত *adj* brought up; nourished; fostered; cherished; supported; maintained.

পোষ্ট=পোস্ট

পোষ্টা=পোষক

পোষ্টাই *adj* nutritious; nourishing. ❑*n* **1** nourishment; nutrition. **2** nutritious food. **3** a diet made by boiling coarse flour in milk.

পোষ্য *adj* **1** to be fed/ nourished/ brought up/taken care of/ maintained/ supported. **2** dependent (for maintenance). ❑*n* dependent. **~ পুত্র** *n* adopted son. **~বর্গ** *n pl* one's dependents.

পোস্ট[১] [E] *n* **1** the postal system; post. **2** mail. **~ করা** *vt* send sth by post; mail sth. **~-অফিস** *n* post-office. **~-কার্ড** *n* post-card. **~-মার্কা** *n* post-mark. **~-মাস্টার** *n* post-master.

পোস্ট[২] [E] *n* office; appointment; post.

পোস্ট[৩] [E]*n* pillar; post: গোল-~.

পোস্ট-গ্রাজুয়েট *adj* [E] post-graduate.

পোস্ত [P]*n* poppy; poppy head; capsule of poppy. **~ দানা** *n* poppy seed.

পোস্তা [P] *n* **1** prop; tie-beam; buttress. **2** bulwark; dyke; embankment. **3** (central/wholesale) market. **মেরে ~ ওড়ানো** *vi* beat/knock the (living) daylight out of sb.

পোহানো[১] *vi* **1** warm oneself (by fire); bask. **2** suffer; undergo; take: ঝামেলা ~. **আগুন ~** *vi* warm oneself by the fire; bask by the fire. **রোদ ~** *vi* bask in the sunshine.

পোহানো[২] *vi* become light; dawn; break: রাত পোহাচ্ছে, the dawn/day is breaking; It is dawning; the day is dawning.

পৌঁছ *n* **1** reach: ছুটে গিয়ে তার ~ পাওয়া গেল না. **2** arrival: ~-সংবাদ. **~ পাওয়া** *vi* reach; catch up with (sb).

পৌঁছনো=পৌঁছা

পৌঁছা *vi* **1** arrive at; get to; reach: কর্মস্থলে ~. **2** come to hand; reach. **3** extend to sth; be able to stretch out/up etc and touch sth; reach: হাত ~. **~নো** *vi* **1** convey/carry (to); deliver; transmit: খবর ~. **2** dead to; escort (to); accompany sb to: তাকে স্টেশনে পৌঁছে দিয়ো.

পৌগণ্ড *adj* relating to a boy; boyish. ❑*n* boyhood; a period lasting from the fifth to the sixteenth year.

পৌণ্ড্র=পুণ্ড্র

পৌত্তলিক *adj* idolatrous. ❑*n* idolater. **~তা** *n* worship of idols; idolatry.

পৌত্র *n* son's son; grandson. **পৌত্রী** *fem.* son's daughter; granddaughter.

পৌনঃপুনিক *adj* frequently repeated; repeated again and again; frequent; recurring. **~ দশমিক** *n* recurring decimal. **~তা** *n*=পৌনঃপুন্য.

পৌনঃপুন্য *n* frequent repetition; frequency; recurrence.

পৌনরুক্ত *n* repetition; tautology.

পৌনে *adj* **1** three quarters of; three-fourths of: ~ একসের. **2** a quarter to: ~ ন'টা.

পৌর *adj* **1** belonging to a town/city; urban; civic; municipal; public. **2** relating to a house; indoor. **~-অধিকার** *n* civic rights. **~কন্যা** *n* maiden of the city. **~কার্য** *n* public business. **~ ক্রীড়া** *n* indoor game. **~ চিকিৎসক** *n* civil surgeon. **~জন** = পুরজন (⇒পুর[২]). **~ জনাধিকার** *n* citizenship. **~নিগম** *n* municipal corporation. **~পদ** *n* citizenship. **~পিতা** *n* city father; mayor. **~-প্রতিষ্ঠান** *n* municipality. **~বর্গ**=পুরজন (⇒পুর[২]) **~বিজ্ঞান** *n* civics. **~বৃদ্ধ, ~মুখ্য** *n* chief man of the city; alderman (of a municipal corporation). **~-সঙ্ঘ** = ~-প্রতিষ্ঠান. **~সভা** *n* municipality; municipal corporation. **~ স্ত্রী**=পুরনারী (⇒ পুর[২]). **পৌরব** *adj* descended from king Puru (পুরু). ❑*n* descendant of king Puru.

পৌরাঙ্গনা=পুরনারী (⇒ পুর[২])

পৌরাণিক *adj* relating to/versed in Hindu Puranas (পুরাণ)/ancient legends and stories; mythical; mythological; ancient; primeval **পৌরাণিকী** *fem.* **~ কাহিনী** *n* mythological tale/episode; legend. **~ নাটক** *n* mythological drama.

পৌরুষ=পুরুষত্ব (⇒ পুরুষ)

পৌরুষেয় *adj* relating to/derived from/made by man; human; man-made; masculine.

পৌরোহিত্য *n* **1** office/position of a priest; priesthood. **2** presidentship; chairmanship; presidency: সভার ~. **3** leadership: মিছিলের ~. ~ করা *vi* **1** act as a priest. **2** preside over/chair (a meeting). **3** lead.

পৌর্ণমাসী *n* a day/night of full moon.

পৌর্ব *adj* **1** relating/belonging to the past; past. **2** relating to the east; eastern. পৌর্বী *fem*. ~দেহিক, ~দৈহিক *adjj* belonging to/derived from a former body/existence; done in a former life.

পৌর্বাধিক *adj* living/situated on the eastern side of.

পৌর্বাপর্য *n* priority and posteriority; the relation of prior and posterior; succession; continuity; sequence.

পৌর্বাহিক *adj* relating to the previous day.

পৌর্বাহ্নিক *adj* relating to the morning; produced in the forenoon; matutinal.

পৌর্বিক *adj* former; past; prior; ancient; old; ancestral. পৌর্বিকী *fem*.

পৌষ *n* the ninth month of the Bengali calendar; Paush.

পৌষালি *adj* relating to/grown in/ produced in the month of Paush (পৌষ).

পৌষ্টিক *adj* **1** relating to growth/ welfare/ nutrition; nutritional. **2** nutritive; nutritious; nourishing; invigorating. **3** alimentary. **4** furthering; promotion. ~ নালী *n* alimentary canal.

প্যাঁক *n* (onom) quack (of a duck). ~ প্যাঁক *n*, *int* quack! quack.

প্যাঁকাটি=পাকাটি

প্যাঁচ=পেঁচ

প্যাঁচা=পেঁচা

প্যাঁচাল *n* endless talk; verbal diarrhoea; hot air; claptrap; long-winded speech; prattle. ~ পাড়া *vi* talk endlessly; rattle on; prattle on (about sth), prate (on about sth); talk the hind legs off a donkey; talk nineteen to the dozens.

প্যাঁচালো *adj*=পেঁচানো

প্যাঁটরা=পেটরা

প্যাঁড়া=পেটক

প্যাকবন্ধি *adj* packed (in a box, etc); packed up.

প্যাকিং [E]*n* packing; package.

প্যাক্ট [E]*n* = pact.

প্যাচপ্যাচ *n* (onom) expressing: the noise of walking through a slimy/miry place; squelch; squelching sound. ~ করে চলা *vi* squelch across. প্যাচপ্যাচে *adj* squelching; sticky.

প্যাটরা=পেটরা

প্যাটার্ন [E]*n* pattern.

প্যাডেল [E]*n* paddle; paddling. ~ করা *vi* paddle.

প্যানপ্যান *n* (onom) expressing: whimper; whine. ~ করা *vi* say sth in a pleading/ complaining voice; whine (about). প্যানপ্যানানি *n* whining; whimper. প্যানপ্যানে *adj* whining; whimpering. প্যানপ্যানানো=~ করা.

প্যানেল [E]*n* panel.

প্যান্ট *n* trousers; pantaloons; shorts. হাফ ~ *n* shorts.

প্যান্টোমাইম *n* [E] pantomime.

প্যামফ্লেট [E] *n* pamphlet.

প্যারা [E]*n* paragraph.

প্যারী=পিয়ারা[১]

প্যালা=পেলা[২]

প্যাসেঞ্জার [E]*n* passenger. ❑*attrib* carrying passengers; passenger: ~ ট্রেন.

প্র- *pref* indicating **(a)** before, forward, in front, on, forth; **(b)** excessively, very, much, great.

প্রকট *adj* evident; clear; manifest; open; plain; public; obvious. ~ন *n* bringing to light; manifesting; manifestation; clear exposition/ revelation. ~ভাবে *adv* clearly; evidently; manifestly; visibly; openly; in public.

প্রকটিত *adj* manifested; unfolded; revealed; clearly exposed/explained; proclaimed. ~ করা *vt* manifest; reveal; bring to light; expose/ explain clearly; unfold; unveil.

প্রকটীকৃত=প্রকটিত

প্রকম্প *n* trembling; violent motion; quake; severe tremor; thrill. ~ন *n* great trembling; violent/excessive motion.

প্রকম্পিত *adj* trembling; quacking; shaking violently. ~ করা *vt* cause to tremble; swing; shake violently; reverberate. ~ হওয়া *vi* tremble/quake violently; shake violently; be shaken; reverberate with.

প্রকর *n* (scattered) heap; multitude; quantity; plenty.

প্রকরণ *n* **1** subject; topic; question; matter; item. **2** chapter (of a book). **3** context. **4** production; creation. **5** treatment; discussion; explanation. **6** treatise; monograph; book. **7** (biol) variation. **8** process; procedure; technique; method.

প্রকর্মী *n* technician.

প্রকর্ষ *n* **1** excellence; pre-eminence; superiority. **2** development; amelioration; cultivation; advancement.

প্রকর্ষণ *n* **1**=প্রকর্ষ. **2** attraction.

প্রকর্ষিত *adj* **1** cultivated. **2** attracted.

প্রকল্প *n* **1** project; plan; design. **2** hypotheses. ~ন *n* projection.

প্রকল্পিত *adj* **1** projected; contemplated; planned. **2** hypothetical; imagined.

প্রকাণ্ড *n* stem/trunk of a tree. ❑*adj* huge; gigantic; colossal; enormous; monstrous;

stupendous. ~কায় *adj* enormous in size; colossal; bulky; massive; monstrous.

প্রকাম *adj* sufficient; enough; abundant.

প্রকার *n* **1** kind; class; type; sort. **2** variety; species; genes: নানা ~ গাছপালা. **3** mode; manner; way; method. **4** process; procedure; manner. **কী/কোন প্রকারে** in what way? by which means? **কোনো না কোনো প্রকারে** by some means of or other; somehow; by hook or by crook. **~ভেদ** *n* variety; variation; a particular sort. **প্রকারাত্মক** *adj* modal. **প্রকারান্তর** *n* another/a different kind/ sort/ mode/ way/ method. **প্রকারান্তরে** adv **1** in/by another/a different manner/ way/method. **2** in other words. **3** indirectly; by insinuation.

প্রকারণ *n* variation.

প্রকাশ *n* **1** appearance; display; manifestation; expansion; diffusion: আলোর ~. **2** clearness; brightness; splendour; lustre; light. **3** revelation; exposition: রহস্য ~. **4** elucidation; explanation: অর্থ ~. **5** expression: মনোভাব ~. **6** demonstration; expression: দুঃখ ~. **7** suggestion. **8** blooming; efflorescence: পুষ্প~; disclosure; divulging; divulgation: গোপন কথা ~. **9** publication: পুস্তক ~. **10** announcement; notification; declaration: আদেশ ~. ❑*adj* **1** visible; shining; bright; clear; manifest. **2** open; public. **3** revealed; transpired; stated: খবরে ~, It is stated that. **~ করা** *vt* make visible; reveal; manifest; cause to appear/shine; illumine; irradiate; evince; show; display; express; expose; explain; indicate: demonstrate; suggest; declare; announce; pronounce; disclose; divulge; betray publish. **~ পাওয়া/ হওয়া** *vt* be visible/ revealed/ manifest/ exposed/ divulged/ published/ expressed; appear; shine; come to light; transpire; be demonstrated.

প্রকাশক *adj* revealing; exposing; manifesting; expressive of; suggesting; illustrating; explaining; demonstrating; showing; indicating; displaying; announcing; betraying; disclosing; divulging; publishing. ❑*n* **1** publisher. **2** revealed; demonstrator; betrayer; one who/ that which suggests/ expresses; announcer. **প্রকাশিকা** *fem.* **~ সঙ্ঘ** *n* publishers association/ guild.

প্রকাশন *n* **1** publication. **2** expression. **প্রকাশনা** *n* publication.

প্রকাশনীয় *adj* **1** to be published; worth publishing; fit for/worthy of publication. **2** to be displayed/ shown/ manifested/ expressed/ disclosed/ revealed/ demonstrated.

প্রকাশমান *adj* **1** rising; appearing; shining; resplendent; brilliant. **2** in the state of being published/revealed.

প্রকাশিত *adj* **1** become visible; brought to light; clear; manifest; evident; displayed; unfolded; discovered; illumined. **2** declared; announced. **3** disclosed; divulged; exposed. **4** published.

প্রকাশিতব্য=প্রকাশনীয়

প্রকাশ্য *adj* **1**=প্রকাশনীয়. **2** under publication. **3** open to the public: ~ অধিবেশন. **4** open; public: ~ আলোচনা/স্থান. **~ দিবালোকে** *adv* in broad daylight. **~ত, প্রকাশ্যে** *adv* openly; publicly; before the world; before the eyes of all. **ক্রমশ ~** to be continued.

প্রকীর্ণ *adj* **1** scattered; thrown about; dispersed; spread/strewn over. **2** disordered; disheveled. **3** mixed; miscellaneous; various.

প্রকীর্ণক *n* **1** tuft of hair used as an ornament for horses. **2** section/division of a book. **3** extent; length. **4** horse.

প্রকীর্তন *n* announcing; proclaiming; encomium; extolling; celebrating; praising; publicity.

প্রকীর্তি *n* celebration; great fame; wide celebrity. **~ত** *adj* **1** announced; proclaimed; mentioned; said; revealed. **2** praised; extolled; (widely) celebrated; famed.

প্রকুপিত *adj* agitated; shaken; very angry; incensed; enraged; angered; infuriated; excited. **প্রকুপিতা** *fem.*

প্রকৃত *adj* **1** genuine; real; true; pure; actual: ~ সত্য/ঘটনা. **2** right; correct. **3** veritable: ~ শয়তান. **~তা, ~ত্ব** *nn* genuineness; truth; correctness. **~পক্ষে, ~ প্রস্তাবে** *adv* in fact; actually; indeed; truly; in truth. **~রূপে** *adv* rightly; really; correctly; properly.

প্রকৃতার্থ *adj* true significance; real meaning; inner significance.

প্রকৃতি *n* **1** nature; character; constitution; disposition; temper; temperament. **2** material world; nature: বস্তু~. **3** fundamental form; pattern; standard; model; rule. **4** Nature (distinguished from Purusha). **5** Shakti or personified energy/ wife of a deity. **6** people; subjects. **7** (gram) crude/elementary form of a ward; root; base; uninflicted word. **~গত** *adj* pertaining to one's nature; natural; instinctive; habitual. **~জ, ~জাত** *adj* springing from nature; natural; inborn; innate; instinctive; native; inherent. **~দত্ত** *adj* given by nature; natural; innate. **~পুঞ্জ** *n* creatures. **~পুজক** *adj* worshipping nature; animistic. ❑*n* animist. **~পূজা** *n* **1** nature-worship; animism. **2** phallism. **~বাদ** *n* **1** naturalism; materialism. **2** (gram) consideration of the root-meaning only. **~বাদী** *adj* naturalistic; materialistic. **~বিজ্ঞান** *n* natural science/philosophy; physics. **~বিজ্ঞানবিদ, ~বিজ্ঞানী** *n* physicist. **~বিরুদ্ধ** *adj* contrary to nature. **~ভূত** *adj* natural; original. **~সিদ্ধ** *adj*=~জ. **~স্থ** *adj* **1** in one's natural/

normal state; normal; well; healthy; in/come to one's senses; in one's right mind. **2** genuine; unaltered; unimpaired. **~স্থ হওয়া** *vi* come to one's senses; recover; regain one's mental balance/equilibrium.

প্রকৃষ্ট *adj* **1** excellent; best: ~ নিদর্শন. **2** distinguished; eminent; superior. **3** most auspicious/suitable: ~ সময়. **প্রকৃষ্টা** *fem.* **~তা** *n* **1** excellence; superiority; pre-eminence. **2** suspiciousness; suitability.

প্রকোপ *n* **1** raging; virulence; severity; violent outbreak: জ্বরের/উদরাময়ের ~. **2** excess; superabundance; vitiation: পিত্তের ~. **3** violent anger; rage; fury; wrath; ire; great excitement. **~ন** *n* excitement; excitation; provocation; exasperation; irritating; irritation; incensing.

প্রকোপিত *adj* **1** enraged; incensed; angered; roused; provoked; excited. **2** (of a disease) aggravated; grown virulent. **3** (of an epidemic) violently broken out. **~ হওয়া** *vi* **1** be enraged/ excited/ provoked; flare up; lose one's temper; fly into a rage; blow one's temper; blow one's top; fly off the handle. **2** aggravate; grow virulent; break out violently.

প্রকোষ্ঠ *n* **1** fore-arm. **2** room; compartment; cabin; room near the gate. **3** court in a house; quadrangle/square surrounded by buildings. **4** part of a door-frame.

প্রক্রম *n* **1** commencement; beginning. **2** stepping; proceeding. **3** step; stride; pace. **4** course; procedure. **5** method; order; regularity.

প্রক্রান্ত *adj* **1** proceeded; gone. **2** commenced; begun.

প্রক্রিয়া *n* process; procedure; way; manner; method.

প্রক্বণ *n* sound of a vina/lute.

প্রক্লিন্ন *adj* moist; humid; putrefied.

প্রক্ষালন *n* washing; cleaning; cleansing; purifying. **~ করা** *vt* wash; bathe; rinse; cleanse.

প্রক্ষালিত *adj* washed; cleansed; purified; bathed; expatiated.

প্রক্ষিপ্ত *adj* **1** thrown/cast at; hurled; thrown forth. **2** projected. **3** inserted; interpolated. **প্রক্ষিপ্তাংশ** *n* interpolated part; interpolation.

প্রক্ষেপ *n* **1** throwing; casting; flinging; hurling; throw. **2** projection. **3** interpolation. **~ করা** *vt* **1** throw/cast (at); hurl; fling; launch. **2** place in; insert; interpolate. **~ক** *adj* **1** throwing; casting; flinging; hurling. **2** inserting; interpolating. ❑*n* thrower; interpolation. **~ণ**=~. **~ণীয়** *adj* to be thrown/cast forth; to be thrown away.

প্রক্ষেপাক্ষ *n* (geom) axis of projection.

প্রক্ষোভ *n* agitation; emotion; excitement.

প্রক্ষ্বেড়ন *n* iron arrow.

প্রখর *adj* **1** very sharp/cutting; very acute/keen: ~ বুদ্ধি. **2** very hot/acrid; severe: ~ রোদ. **3** very hard/rough; harsh: ~ বাক্য, rigorous. **4** very strict: ~ শাসন. **প্রখরা** *fem.* **~তা, ~ত্ব** *n* sharpness; keenness; harshness; severity; rigour; strictness.

প্রখ্যাত *adj* celebrated; acknowledged; renowned; famous. **প্রখ্যাতা** *fem.* **~কীর্তি** *adj* of celebrated exploits; famous; illustrious. **~নামক** *adj* of celebrated name; renowned. **~নাম্নী** *fem.*

প্রখ্যাতি *n* celebrity; fame; renown.

প্রখ্যাপক *adj* announcing; proclaiming; making known. ❑*n* announcer; proclamation.

প্রখ্যাপন *n* **1** making known; proclamation; acclaimation; report. **2** promulgation. **~ করা** *vt* make known; celebrate; acclaim; proclaim; announce; promulgate.

প্রগণ্ড *n* upper part of the arm.

প্রগত *adj* **1** gone forward; started. **2** gone. **3** separate; apart. **4** dead. **~-জানু** *adj* having the knees far apart; bandy-legged; bowlegged.

প্রগতি *n* **1** progress; advancement. **2** (arith) progression. **~বাদ** *n* theory favouring rapid progress/reform. **~পন্থী**. **~বাদী** *adj n* progressive. **~শীল** *n* progressive. **~শীলতা** *n* progressiveness.

প্রগমন *n* **1** advance; progress. **2** going away; parting; exit; leaving.

প্রগল্‌ভ *adj* **1** proud; arrogant; boastful; bragging. **2** impudent; saucy; shameless; impertinent. **3** bold; smart; resolute; confident; brave. **4** voluble; glib; having the gift of the gab. **প্রগল্‌ভা** *adj fem.* ❑*n* (esp in drama) a bold and confident woman. **~তা** *n* **1** arrogance; bragging; boastfulness. **2** impudence; impertinence; sauciness. **3** boldness; wilfulness; intrepidity; confidence. **4** volubility; gift of the gab; smart talk; glibness.

প্রগাঢ় *adj* **1** very deep; profound; fathomless; unfathomable. **2** much; excessive; exceeding. **3** very dense/thick. **4** intense; intensive. **~তা** *n* **1** great depth; profundity. **2** great thickness; density. **3** excessiveness. **4** intensity.

প্রগাতা *adj* singing; celebrating; glorifying; acclaiming. ❑*n* singer; proclaimer; glorifier.

প্রগ্রহ, প্রগ্রাহ *nn* **1** seizing; clutching; holding. **2** rein; bridle. **3** rope.

প্রগ্রাহ্য *adj* (law) cognizable.

প্রঘাত *n* blow; stroke.

প্রঘূর্ণ *n* turning round/rolling violently.

প্রঘূর্ণিত *adj* revolving violently.

প্রঘোষক *adj* proclaiming; announcing. ❑*n* proclaimer; announcer.

প্রঘোষিত *adj* proclaimed; announced; sounding forth.

প্রচণ্ড *adj* excessively violent; impetuous; furious; fierce; passionate; terrible; severe; formidable; wrathful indomitable; burning; sharp. **~তা** *n* great violence/passion; fierceness; furiousness; terribleness; severity; fearfulness; fury; vehemence; ferocity; savagery; brutality. **~ মূর্তি** *adj* having a terrible fare/aspect; fierce-looking; fearful.

প্রচয়, প্রচয়ন *n* **1** collecting; gathering. **2** accumulation; heap; mass; quantity; multitude. **প্রচয়ন করা** *vt* gather; collect.

প্রচর *n* usage; custom; currency. **~রূপ** *adj* current; in common/general use.

প্রচল *adj* current; circulating; customary. ❑*n* convention. **~ন** *n* **1** bringing into practice; introduction. **2** practice; introduction; usage; currency. **~ন করা** *vt* bring into practice/currency; introduce. **~ন হওয়া** *vi* gain currency; become current; be introduced/practised; be in/come into rogue; become popular.

প্রচলিত *adj* **1** current; customary; usual; circulating; in vogue; prevailing. **2** conventional.

প্রচায় =প্রচয়

প্রচার *n* **1** currency; prevalence; custom; usage. **2** proclamation; announcement. **3** publicity; propaganda; ballyhoo. **4** circulation; propagation; dissemination. **5** preaching. **6** disclosure; publication. **7** renown; fame; notoriety. **~ করা** *vi* **1** give currency to. **2** proclaim; announce. **3** propagate; give publicity to; disseminate; spread sth by propaganda; propagandize; trumpet. **4** circulate. **5** preach. **6** disclose; publish; make public; publicize; advertise; make known. **7** broadcast; air; put on the air. **~ হওয়া** *vi* **1** gain currency. **2** be announced/ proclaimed. **3** be publicized; attract publicity. **4** be circulated/propagated/disseminated. **5** be disclosed/ divulged/published; become public. **6** come to light; leak out; be known. **~ক** *adj* **1** giving currency to. **2** proclaiming; announcing. **3** giving publicity to; publicizing; propagating; circulating. **4** preaching; disseminating; propagating. **5** disclosing. **6** spreading; advertising. ❑*n* **1** proclaimer; announcer. **2** preacher; missionary. **3** propagandist; publicist. **4** propagator; promoter. **~ণ, ~ণা** *nn*=~.

প্রচারা *vt* (poet, archaic)=প্রচার করা (⇒ প্রচার)

প্রচার্য *adj* to be proclaimed/ publicized/ advertised/ circulated.

প্রচারিত *adj* **1** prevalent; become current. **2** announced; proclaimed. **3** publicized; advertised; circulated; propagated; disseminated. **4** disclosed; published. **5** preached.

প্রচিত *adj* gathered; collected; heaped; accumulated.

প্রচীয়মান *adj* accumulating; increasing.

প্রচুর *adj* **1** abundant; plenteous; plentiful; profuse; ample; a lot of; a great deal of; numerous. **2** enough; sufficient. **~তা**=প্রাচুর্য. **~ পরিমাণে** *adv* in abundance; in a large quantity; in plenty.

প্রচেতা *adj* wise; clever; attentive; observant; mindful. ❑*n* name of Varuna, the sea-god.

প্রচেতন *adj*=প্রচেতা

প্রচেতিত *adj* noticed; observed.

প্রচেয় *adj* to be gathered/ collected/ increased.

প্রচেষ্টা *n* effort; endeavour; application; struggle; (persistent) attempt; assiduity; perseverance; exertion. **~ করা** *vi* make an effort; apply one's mind/energies to; endeavour; exert oneself; strive; struggle.

প্রচোদনা *n* instigating; instigation; exciting.

প্রচোদিত *adj* driven on; urged; impelled.

প্রচ্ছদ, প্রচ্ছদ-পট *n* cover; covering; jacket of a book.

প্রচ্ছন্ন *adj* **1** covered; enveloped; shut up. **2** hidden; concealed; unobserved; secret; invisible; latent; covert; clandestine; disguised; furtive. **~চারী** *adj* moving furtively/clandestinely/stealthily; acting secretly. **~তা** *n* covertness; concealment; secrecy; hiding; cover; disguise; dissimulation; invisibility; latency. **~ বেশে** *adv* in disguise; incognito. **~ভাবে** *adv* secretly; clandestinely; covertly; furtively; stealthily; surreptiously; under cover; underhand.

প্রচ্ছাদন *n* **1** cover; upper or outer garment. **2** concealing; hiding. **3** covering; concealment.

প্রচ্ছাদিত *adj* **1** covered; wrapped; clothed. **2** hidden; concealed.

প্রচ্ছায় *n* dense/deep shade; shadowy place.

প্রচ্ছায়া *n* (phys) umbra.

প্রজ *adj* (used as a *suff*) bringing forth; bearing forth; bearing; producing: বহু~, prolific. ❑*n* husband. **~ন** *n* begetting; impregnation; breeding (of cattle); bringing forth; generation; bearing. **~নন** *n* begetting; generation; procreation; production; breeding; birth. **~নন করা** *vi* generate; produce; beget; bring forth; bread. **~নন ক্ষমতা, ~নন শক্তি** *nn* generative energy. **অতিপ্রজনন** *n* over-production.

প্রজনিকা *n* mother.

প্রজনিষ্ণু *adj* generative; procreative; productive; producing.

প্রজল্প(ন) *n* prattle; gossip; heedless/ frivolous words.

প্রজা *n* **1** people; subjects (of a prince); tenant. **2** creature; animal. **3** man; mankind. offspring; children; family race; descendants; posterity. **~ই** *adj* relating to subjects/tenants: ~ করা. ❑*n* duty of a subject/tenant. **~তন্ত্র** *n* republic. **~তন্ত্রী, ~তান্ত্রিক** *adjj* republican. **~পতি** *n* **1** 'lord of creatures'; creator; Brahma; any one of the ten sons of Brahma. **2** divinity presiding over procreation; protector of life. **3** butterfly. **~পতির নির্বন্ধ** *n* the will of the lord of creation; (fig) predestination in marriage. **~পালক** *adj* who protects his subjects. ❑*n* king; ruler. **~পালন** *n* protection of subjects. **~ পালন করা** *vi* protect one's subjects; rule over and look after the people. **~পীড়ক** *adj* tyrannical; oppressive. **~পীড়ন** *n* oppression of subjects; tyranny. **~বতী** *adj fem* having children/offspring; fruitful; prolific. **~বর্গ** *n* **1** the whole body of subjects/citizens; people. **2** tenantry; peasantry. **~বিলি** *n* act/ system of leasing out land on fixed terms and rents. **~বৃদ্ধি** *n* increase/ abundance of offspring; growth of population. **~রঞ্জক** *adj*=~রঞ্জন. **~রঞ্জন** *n* disposition to please the people/ subjects; preserving/ defending/ protecting of the subjects. ❑*adj* disposed to please the people/ subjects. **~শক্তি** *n* power of the people of a state; popular power. **~সৃষ্টি** *n* **1** creation of living beings. **2** leasing of land to tenants. **~হিত** *n* welfare of the subjects/people.

প্রজাত *adj* born; produced; grown. **প্রজাতা** *fem.*

প্রজাতি *n* species.

প্রজায়িনী *n* mother.

প্রজ্ঞ *adj* wire; prudent.

প্রজ্ঞপ্তি *n* communication; notice.

প্রজ্ঞা *n* **1** wisdom; intelligence; knowledge; discrimination; understanding. **2** reason. **~চক্ষু** *n* eye of understanding. ❑*adj* wise; intelligent. **~পারমিতা** *n* perfection in knowledge. **~বান** *adj* endowed with wisdom; wise.

প্রজ্ঞাত *adj* **1** known; understood; found out; discerned; known as. **2** public; common; well-known; widely known; famous.

প্রজ্ঞান *n* **1** wisdom; intelligence; (superior) knowledge. **2** sign; token; hint.

প্রজ্ঞাপক *n* publicity man/officer; propagandist.

প্রজ্ঞাপন *n* **1** notification. **2** communiqué. **3** publicity; propaganda.

প্রজ্বলন *n* **1** blazing; flaring; burning; flare-up. **2** enkindling; lighting; ignition; (fig) excitation; rousing.

প্রজ্বলিত *adj* **1** flaming; blazing; burning. **2** enkindled; lighted; ignited. **3** excited; flared up; roused. **~ হওয়া** *vi* **1** flare up; blaze; be enkindled/ ignited; be aflame/ ablaze. **2** be roused/ excited. **~ হুতাশন** *n* blazing fire.

প্রজ্বালন *n* **1** kindling; setting on fire; ignition; enkindling; lighting. **2** exciting; rousing.

প্রজ্বালিত *adj* **1** enkindled; ignited; lighted; inflamed. **2** excited; roused. **~ করা** *vt* **1** set on fire; light; kindle; inflame; ignite. **2** excite; rouse.

প্রণত *adj* bent forwards; bowed; inclined; stooping; bowed to. **2** humble; submissive to. **প্রণতা** *fem.* **~ হওয়া** *vi* bend/bow down before; make obeisance to; stoop; inching; prostrate oneself; humble oneself.

প্রণতি *n* bending; bowing; inclination; respectful salutation; reverence; obeisance; prostration. stooping. **~পূর্বক** = প্রণামপূর্বক (⇒ প্রণাম).

প্রণব *n* the mystical/sacred syllable *Om* (ওঁ).

প্রণমন *n* bowing before; salutation; reverence.

প্রণমা *vt* (poet)=প্রণাম করা

প্রণয় *n* **1** love; attachment; affection. **2** friendship; good terms; intimacy; familiarity; concord. **~ আলাপ** *n* amorous conversation. **~ কথা** *n* affectionate/ loving words/ conversation; love-story. **~কলহ** *n* quarrel of lovers; playful/ amorous quarrel. **~কুপিত** *adj* angry through love. **~কোপ** *n* (feigned) anger of a coquette towards her lover; feigning anger. **~গর্ভ** *adj* full of love; amorous; loving; affectionate. **~গাথা** *n* romantic ballad; love-lyric. **~গীতি** *n* love-song; love-lyric. **~ঘটিত** *adj* amorous; amatory. **~দৃষ্টি** *n* amorous look. **~পত্র** *n* loveletter; billet-doux. **~পতি** *n* object of love/affection; lover. **~পাশ** *n* noose/bond of love. **~পীড়িত** *adj* love-sick; lovelorn. **~প্রকর্ষ** *n* excess of affection; extraordinary attachment. **~বচন** *n* declaration of love/affection. **~বন্ধন** *n* ties/ bond of love. **~বিমুখ** *adj* averse to love/ friendship. **~ভঙ্গ** *n* breach of confidence; faithlessness; breach in an affair of love. **~ভাজন** *adj* worthy of being loved; beloved; favourite. ❑*n*=~পাত্র. **~মগ্ন** *adj* head over; heels in love; very much in love with. **~ময়**=~শালী. **~ময়ী** *fem.* **~মুগ্ধ** *adj* filled with an intense love; infatuated with/by. **~লিপি**=~পত্র. **~লীলা** *n* **1** amorous play; love making. **2** courtship; romance; love affair. **~শর** *n* shaft of love. **~শালী** *adj* loving; affectionate; full of love. **~শালিনী** *fem.* **~সঙ্গীত**=~গীতি. **~সঞ্চার** *n* dawn of love. **~সম্পর্ক** *n* amorous relationship. **~সম্ভাষণ** *n* amorous/affectionate words; advances; wooing; courting. **প্রণয়াকর্ষণ** *n* bonds of love. **প্রণয়াকাঙ্ক্ষা** *n* longing/ desire/ hunger for love. **প্রণয়াকাঙ্ক্ষী** *adj* longing for/ hungry for/ desirous of love. **প্রণয়াকাঙ্ক্ষা** *n* hunger for love. **প্রণয়াদর** *n* loving caresses. **প্রণয়ানল** *n* flame of passion/ love. **প্রণয়ানুরাগ** *n* passion; passionate love. **প্রণয়ানুরাগী**=~মুগ্ধ. **প্রণয়ানুরাগিণী** *fem.* **প্রণয়াভিমান** *n* jealousy of love. **প্রণয়ালাপ** *n* amorous tittle-tattle.

প্রণয়াসক্ত=~মুগ্ধ. প্রণয়াসক্তি *n* passionate love; infatuation. প্রণয়াস্পদ = ~ভাজন. প্রণয়াহ্বান = ~বচন.

প্রণয়ন *n* **1** composing; writing; composition; compilation; drawing up (of a deed, etc). **2** making; creation. ~ করা *vt* **1** write (out); compose; draw up; author. **3** make; create.

প্রণয়ী *n* lover; beloved; gallant. ❑*adj* having affection for; attached to; beloved; dear; intimate; feeling attracted towards; longing for; affectionate; loving; desirous of; clinging to. প্রণয়িনী *n fem* beloved female; sweet-heart; lady-love; mistress. ❑*adj*=~.

প্রণাম *n* **1** respectful salutation; reverence; prostration; obeisance. **2** bending; bow; bowing. ~ করা *vi* bow; incline; make obeisance to; prostrate oneself (as a sign of reverence/worship); salute. ~পূর্বক *adj* humbly; submissively.

প্রণামী *n* money/present given at the time of making obeisance.

প্রণালী *n* **1** water-course; drain; aqueduct. **2** (geog) channel; method; procedure; system; way; mode. ~বদ্ধ *adj* systematic; methodical. ~বদ্ধ করা *vi* systematize.

প্রণাশ *n* **1** destruction; annihilation; extinction; death. **2** loss; disappearance; vanishing.

প্রণিধান *n* **1** attention (paid to); close attention. **2** profound meditation; abstract contemplation. **3** serious consideration; earnest application. **4** exertion; endeavour. ~ করা *vi* give the whole attention to; consider; turn/ direct one's thoughts; give heed to; pay close attention to; bend one's mind to; give one's mind to sth. ~যোগ্য *adj* deserving close attention/ serious consideration.

প্রণিধি *n* **1** secret agent; spy; emissary; guide. **2** care; close attention. **3** attendant.

প্রণিপাত=প্রণাম

প্রণিয়ম *n* regulation.

প্রণিহিত *adj* **1** laid on; imposed; applied; put down; deposited. **2** directed towards; fixed upon. **3** contained in. **4** intent upon. **5** obtained; acquired.

প্রণীত *adj* **1** written; composed; compiled; drawn up; authored. **2** made; created. **3** performed; executed; finished; done. **4** led towards; conveyed to.

প্রণেতা *n* **1** author; writer; compiler; one who alarms out. **2** promulgator of a doctrine. **3** maker; creator. **4** leader; guide. প্রণেত্রী *fem.*

প্রণোদন *n* driving; encouragement; urging; goading; instigation; incitement; inducement.

প্রণোদিত *adj* driven; urged; goaded; encouraged; instigated; induced; incited. ~ করা *vi* drive (on); urge; goad; encourage; instigate; induce; incite.

প্রতাত *n* spreading; extension.

প্রতন *adj* ancient; old.

প্রতনু *adj* very thin/fine; delicate; minute; slender; small; insignificant.

প্রতপ্ত *adj* **1** very hot; glowing; shining; overheated; subjected to great heat; heated; annealed. **2** very much angered/excited.

প্রতর্ক *n* **1** doubt; hesitation. **2** conjecture; supposition. **3** anticipation.

প্রতান *n* **1** branching out; ramification. **2** diffuseness; prolixity. **3** tendril; shoot. **4** (astron) elongation.

প্রতানিনী *n* spreading creeper; climbing plant.

প্রতাপ *n* **1** power; strength; might; prowess; domineering influence; majesty; splendour; energy; glory; authority; sway; mightiness; supremacy; preponderance. **2** (glowing) heat; warmth. ~শালী, প্রতাপান্বিত, প্রতাপী *adj* full of splendour; majestic; mighty; powerful; glorious; predominant; influential; preponderating. ~শালিনী *fem.*

প্রতাপন *n* making hot; heating; paining; tormenting.

প্রতারক *adj* cheating; deceitful; deceiving. ❑*n* cheat; deceiver; imposter; swindler; fraud; knave; sneak.

প্রতারণ, প্রতারণা *n* deceiving; cheating; deception; swindle; fraud; beguilement; fraudulence; chicanery; bluff; sharp practices; trickery; treachery; imposture; hoodwinking. প্রতারণা করা *vi* deceive; beguile; fool; cheat; bamboozle; hoodwink; swindle; trick/delude/ dupe sb (into doing sth). প্রতারণাকারী *adj* practising deceit/ imposture; deceitful; fraudulent. ❑*n*=প্রতারক. প্রতারণাজনিত, প্রতারণাপ্রযুক্ত *adj* caused by/because of fraud/ deceit. প্রতারণাত্মক *adj* deceitful; fraudulent; delusive; treacherous; artful; underhand. প্রতারণার্থক *adv* for the purpose of deceit/ fraud. প্রতারণামূলক = প্রতারণাত্মক.

প্রতারিত *adj* deceived; cheated; swindled; be guiled; hoodwinked; fooled; bamboozled. ~ হওয়া *vi* be deceived/ swindled/ cheated/ hoodwinked; be the dupe of; swallow the bait. প্রতারিতা *fem.*

প্রতি[১] *prep* to; towards.

প্রতি[২] *pref* indicating: **(a)** towards; near to; **(b)** against; in opposition to; **(c)** back again; in return; **(d)** down upon; upon; on; **(e)** in the direction of; **(f)** opposite; before; in the presence of; **(g)** like; similar; resembling; exact; **(h)** every; each; **(i)** contrary to; anti **(j)** equal to; **(k)** deputizing; vice; counter; **(l)** re.

প্রতি-আক্রমণ *n* counter-attack.

প্রতিকরণীয়=প্রতিকার্য

প্রতিকর্তব্য *adj* to be requited/ returned/ repaid; to be counteracted/ resisted.
প্রতিকর্তা *adj* redressing; remedying; avenging; counteracting; preventing. ❑*n* redresser; avenger; recompenser.
প্রতিকর্ম *n* **1** requital; retaliation; counteraction; redress; remedying; prevention; reaction. **2** dressing; toilet.
প্রতিকর্ষ *n* attraction.
প্রতিকল্প *n* **1** substitute; counter-part. **~ন** *n* substitution.
প্রতিকায় *n* **1** effigy; likeness; picture. **2** adversary; enemy.
প্রতিকার *n* **1** remedy; redress. **2** revenge; requital; retaliation; retribution; counteraction. **~ করা** *vi* remedy; redress; requite; counteract; resist; repair; amend; avenge; prevent.
প্রতিকার্য *adj* **1** to be remedied/redressed; remediable; redressable; preventible. **2** to be revenged.
প্রতিকূল *adj* contrary; adverse; opposite; inimical; disagreeable; opposed; hostile; unfavourable; malignant. **~তা** *n* opposition; hostility; antagonism; contrariety; adverseness; disfavour; contumacy. **~তা করা** *vi* oppose; be hostile/inimical to; be ill disposed towards. **প্রতিকূলাচরণ** *n* opposition; hostility; antagonism. **প্রতিকূলে** *prep* against.
প্রতিকৃত *adj*. remedied; redressed; requited; avenged; prevented; counteracted.
প্রতিকৃতি *n* **1** portrait; image; likeness; model; reflection. **2** counterpart; substitute.
প্রতিকৃষ্ট *adj* bad; vile; abominable; atrocious; worthless; nasty.
প্রতিক্রম *n* reverse/inverse/ inverted order.
প্রতিক্রিয়া *n* **1** reaction; responsive; a reactionary activity; surging-back. **2** counteraction; retaliation; retribution. **3** remedy. **~শীল** *adj* **1** (pol) reactionary. **2** (rare) responsive; reactive. **~শীল হওয়া** *vi* be a reactionary; react. **~শীল ব্যক্তি** *n* reactionary.
প্রতিক্ষণ *adv* (at) every moment; continually; always.
প্রতিক্ষিপ্ত *adj* thrown into; rebounded; sent; dispatched. **~ হওয়া** *vi* rebound.
প্রতিক্ষেপ *n* **1** throwing back; rebounding. **2** objection; contradiction; repudiation; contest. **~ণ**=~. **~ণ করা** *vi* **1** throw back; rebound; throw into. **2** reject; oppose; repudiate; contradict.
প্রতিগত=প্রত্যাগত
প্রতিগমন *vi* return. **~ করা** *vi* go back; return; recede.
প্রতিগর্জন *n* thundering/roaring against/ in return; answering roar.
প্রতিগামী *adj* returning; receding.
প্রতিগৃহীত *adj* taken; received; accepted. **প্রতিগৃহীতা** *fem.*
প্রতিগ্রহ *n* **1** acceptance; accepting; receiving gift; present. **2 ~ণ**=~. **~ণ করা** *vi* accept/ receive (as a gift); seize; appropriate. **~ণীয়** *adj* to be taken/accepted acceptable (as a gift).
প্রতিগ্রাহ *n* accepting gifts. **প্রতিগ্রাহিত** *adj* caused to accept a gift. **প্রতিগ্রাহী** *adj* accepting/ receiving (a gift). **প্রতিগ্রাহ্য** *adj*=প্রতিগ্রহণীয় (⇒প্রতিগ্রহ).
প্রতিঘ *n* hindrance; obstruction; resistance; opposition.
প্রতিঘাত *n* counter-stroke; counter-blow; resistance; prevention; warding off. **~ হানা** *vi* deal (sb) a counterblow; resist; offer resistance; ward off. **~ন** *vi* **1** killing; warding off. **2** killing; slaughter. **প্রতিঘাতী** *adj* keeping off; repulsing; injuring; killing. **প্রতিঘাতিনী** *fem.*
প্রতিচিত্র *n* blue-print. **~ মুদ্রক** *n* blue-printer.
প্রতিচ্ছন্ন *adj* covered; enveloped; hidden; concealed; disguised.
প্রতিচ্ছায়া *n* reflection; likeness; image; shadow; phantom; resemblance.
প্রতিচ্ছেদ, প্রতিচ্ছেদন *n* cutting off; intersection.
প্রতিজঙ্ঘা *n* shin-bone.
প্রতিজন *n* **1** every person. **2** adversary. ❑*pron* everybody; everyone.
প্রতিজিহ্বা *n* uvula.
প্রতিজীবন *n* resuscitation; rebirth.
প্রতিজ্ঞা *n* promise; vow; pledge. **2** solemn resolve. **3** solemn declaration. **4** proposition; assertion/proposition to be proved. **5** (geom) theorem; problem; proposition. **~ করা** *vi* make a resolve/ vow; take a vow to; promise; engage oneself; commit oneself; swear; pledge; pledge oneself; give a pledge; give one's (sacred) word/word of honour; covenant; give one's pledge; be on/under oath. **~ করানো** *vt* pledge; bind sb; put/ place sb on/ upon oath. **~ত** *adj* **1** promised; resolved; accepted. **2** proposed. **~তব্য** *adj* to be promised/ pledged/assented. **~ন** *n* promise; pledge; admission; assent; assertion; agreement. **~ন্তর** *vi* reviewed pledge. **~পত্র** *n* written promise/declaration; bond; written contract; promissory note. **~ পালন** *n* keeping a promise/ one's word/ a solemn vow; redemption/ fulfil pledges; fulfilment of a promise/ pledges. **~ পালন করা** *vi* keep a promise/a solemn vow/one's word; fulfil a promise; redeem one's pledges. **~পূর্বক** *adj* on one's oath/ honour; solemnly. **~বদ্ধ** *adj* **1** bound by a promise/ pledge; pledge bound. **2** resolved; resolute; determined. **~বাক্য**=~. **~বিরোধ** *n* contradiction between logical proposition and the agreement. **~বিবাহিত** *adj* promised in marriage; betrothed. **~ভঙ্গ** *n* break of a promise. **~ভঙ্গ করা** *vi* break a promise/ (a solemn) vow; break one's word. **~ভঙ্গকারী** *adj*,

n (one) who breaks a promise/one's word. **~ভঙ্গকারিণী** *fem.* **~ রক্ষা**=~পালন.

প্রতিজ্ঞেয় *adj* to be promised/ assented to.

প্রতিদত্ত *adj* given in return/ exchange; returned; requited.

প্রতিদান *n* **1** giving/gift in return; exchange. **2** requital; restitution; restoration; retribution; repayment. **3** revenge. **~ দেওয়া** *vi* give in return/exchange. **2** give back; return; restore; retribute; repay. **3** requite: প্রেমের ~. **4** take revenge upon. **~হীন** *adj* unrequited.

প্রতিদিকে *adv* in every direction/ quarter; all around.

প্রতিদিন *adj* daily; every day; day by day; per diem.

প্রতিদিষ্ট *adj* overruled.

প্রতিদেয় *adj* to be given back/ returned; to be given in return/ exchange.

প্রতিদ্বন্দ্ব *n* rivalry; opposition; hostility; competition.

প্রতিদ্বন্দ্বিতা=প্রতিদ্বন্দ্ব. **~ করা** *vi* fight/contend with; compete with; contest; vie with sb (for sth/to do sth); vie for sth; rival sb for sth. **~মূলক** *adj* competitive.

প্রতিদ্বন্দ্বী *adj* contesting; competing; contending; rivalling. ❑*n* competitor; contender; rival; adversary. **প্রতিদ্বন্দ্বিনী** *fem.*

প্রতিধ্বনি *n* echo; reverberation. **~ করা** *vt* echo; reverberate; resound (through). **~ত** *adj* echoed; reverberated; resounded. **~ত হওয়া** *vi* echo; resound (with sth); reverberate.

প্রতিনাদ *n*=প্রতিধ্বনি. **প্রতিনাদী** *adj* echoing.

প্রতিনিধি *n* representative; substitute; agent; proxy; deputy; delegate. **~ দ্বারা** *adv* by proxy. **~ত্ব** *n* representation; agency; office of a deputy; proxy. **~ত্ব করা** *vi* represent; act as an agent of; deputize; act as a delegate/ as sb's proxy. **~ত্বমূলক** *adj* representative. **~বর্গ** *n* delegation; deputation; body of representation. **~ সভা** *n* meeting of delegates/ representatives/ deputies; house of deputies. **রাজ ~** *n* viceroy.

প্রতিনিনাদ=প্রতিধ্বনি

প্রতিনিবর্তন *n* return; coming back; refraining; desisting.

প্রতিনিবৃত্ত *adj* returned; come back; turned back; refrained/ desisted from. **~ হওয়া** *vi* return; come back; desist/refrain from.

প্রতিনিবৃত্তি=প্রতিনিবর্তন

প্রতিনিয়ত *adj* every moment; constantly; always; for ever; ever; perpetually.

প্রতিনির্দেশ *n* cross-reference.

প্রতিন্যাস *n* attitude.

প্রতিপক্ষ *n* **1** opposite side; hostile party. **2** adversary; opponent; foe. **3** opposition. **4** rival in; match for; equal; similar. **5** (law) respondent; defendant.

প্রতিপণ *n* barter.

প্রতিপত্তি *n* **1** good standing; dignity; influence; power; sway; high rank; honour; fame. **2** proof; ascertainment. **~শালী, ~শীল, ~সম্পন্ন** *adjj* influential; powerful; well-established; enjoying high standing.

প্রতিপত্র *n* counterfoil.

প্রতিপদ *n* the first day of a lunar fortnight.

প্রতিপদে *adv* at every step; constantly.

প্রতিপন্ন *adj* ascertained; confirmed; demonstrated; proved; substantiated; corroborated; verified. **~ করা** *vt* prove; demonstrate; substantiate; establish; vindicate; show.

প্রতিপরীক্ষা *n* cross-examination.

প্রতিপাদ *adj* (geog) antipodal. **~ স্থান** *n* antipodes.

প্রতিপাদক *adj* ascertaining; proving; demonstrating; establishing; stating; verifying; substantiating; performing; corroborating. **প্রতিপাদিকা** *fem.*

প্রতিপাদন *n* ascertainment; proof; proving; establishment; demonstration; confirmation; verification; performance; accomplishment. **~ করা** *vt* **1**= প্রতিপন্ন করা. **2** accomplish; perform.

প্রতিপাদনীয় *adj* =প্রতিপাদ্য

প্রতিপাদিত *adj* **1**=প্রতিপন্ন. **2** accomplished; performed.

প্রতিপাদ্য *adj* **1** to be ascertained/proved/ demonstrated/ established/ confirmed/ substantiated/ justified/ verified; demonstrable; attestable; conformable; verifiable. **2** to be treated/ discussed; to be explained/ propounded. **3** to be performed/ accomplished.

প্রতিপালক *adj* rearing; providing for; fostering; bringing up; maintaining; keeping; feeding; protecting; preserving. ❑*n* preserver; protector; provider; cherisher; sustainer; guardian; maintainer. **প্রতিপালিকা** *fem.*

প্রতিপালন *n* **1** upbringing; rearing; fostering: সন্তান-~. **2** maintenance; feeding; supporting: পরিবার-~. **3** obeying; compliance with: আদেশ-~. **4** keeping; fulfilment; observance: প্রতিশ্রুতি-~. **5** sustaining; cherishing; protection; looking after the well-being of; preserving; providing for a person; succouring. **~ করা** *vt* **1** bring up; rear; foster. **2** maintain; feed; support. **3** obey; comply with. **4** keep; fulfill. **5** sustain; cherish; provide for; preserve; protect; look after the well-being of; succour.

প্রতিপালনীয় *adj* **1** to be brought up/ reared/ fostered. **2** to be maintained/ fed/ supported. **3** to be obeyed/ complied with. **4** to be kept/

fulfilled. **5** to be sustained/ provided for/ preserved/ cherished/ protected/ looked after.

প্রতিপালিত *adj* **1** brought up; reared; fostered. **2** maintained; fed; supported. **3** obeyed; complied with. **4** kept; fulfilled. **5** sustained; preserved; provided for; protected; cherished; looked after. প্রতিপালিতা *fem.*

প্রতিপাল্য *adj*=প্রতিপালনীয়. ❑*n* ward.

প্রতিপুরুষ=প্রতিনিধি

প্রতিপোষক *adj* **1** corroborative; bearing out; supportive; aiding. **2**=প্রতিপালক.

প্রতিপোষণ *n* corroboration; validation; confirmation; support; assistance. ~ **করা** *vt* corroborate; bear out; support; confirm; validate; assist.

প্রতিপ্রভ *adj* (phys) fluorescent. **প্রতিপ্রভা** *n* fluorescence.

প্রতিফল *n* retribution; retributory punishment; requital; reward; remuneration; retaliation; punishment; revenge. ~ **দেওয়া** *vi* mete out retributory punishment; punish; take revenge upon; pay sb back (for sth); be/get even (with sb). ~ **পাওয়া** *vi* suffer the consequences (of); be punished; be paid back (for sth); get what one deserves.

প্রতিফলন *n* reflection. ~-**কোণ** *n* (phys) angle of reflection.

প্রতিফলিত *adj* reflected. ~ **করা** *vt* reflect. ~ **হওয়া** *vi* reflect; be reflected.

প্রতিবচন *n*=প্রতিবাক্য

প্রতিবদ্ধ *adj* hindered; excluded; cut off; impeded; obstructed.

প্রতিবন্ধ *n* obstacle; hindrance; impediment; frustration; opposition; resistance. ~**ক** *n*=~. ❑*adj* obstructing; hindering; opposing; impeding; frustrating.

প্রতিবন্ধী *adj* impeded; hindered; obstructing; handicapped. ❑*n* handicapped.

প্রতিবর্ণীকরণ *n* transliteration. **প্রতিবর্ণীকৃত** *adj* transliterated.

প্রতিবর্তন *n* obversion.

প্রতিবল *adj* equally strong/ powerful; a match for; equally matched. ❑*n* enemy forces.

প্রতিবস্তূপমা *n* (rhet) parallel simile.

প্রতিবাক্য *n* **1** answer; reply. **2** retort. **3** adverse comment.

প্রতিবাত *n* contrary wind. ❑*adv* against the wind.

প্রতিবাদ *n* contradiction; counter-argument; counter-plea; protest; rejoinder. ~ **করা** *vi* protest; contradict; send a rejoinder; put forward a counter-argument/counter-plea; make/ stage a protest. ~ **বিক্ষোভ** *n* protest demonstration. ~ **সভা** *n* protest meeting.

প্রতিবাদী *adj* protesting; contradicting; contending; dissenting; pleading against; pleading in reply. ❑*n* **1** protester. **2**(law) respondent; defendant. **প্রতিবাদিনী** *fem.*

প্রতিবার্তা *n* account; information; reply by return.

প্রতিবাসী=প্রতিবেশী. **প্রতিবাসিনী** *fem.*

প্রতিবিধান *n* arrangement against; prevention; precaution; redress; remedy; counter measure. ~ **করা** *vi* counteract; act against; take measures against; remedy; redress; right; put/set sth right; avenge.

প্রতিবিধিৎসা *n* desire/intention to counteract/remedy/redress; revengefulness.

প্রতিবিধিৎসু *adj* desirous of counteracting/ of taking measures against/redressing/ remedying; revengeful; avenging.

প্রতিবিধেয় *adj* to be counteracted/ remedied/ redressed; remediable; redressable.

প্রতিবিম্ব *n* reflection; reflected image; mirrored form. ~**ন** *n* reflection.

প্রতিবিম্বিত *adj* reflected.

প্রতিবিষ *n* anti-toxin; antidote.

প্রতিবিহিত *adj* counteracted; remedied; redressed; righted; guarded against; avenged.

প্রতিবেদক *n* reporter.

প্রতিবেদন *n* report; petition of complaint.

প্রতিবেদিত *adj* reported.

প্রতিবেশ *n* environment; environs; surroundings; neighbourhood; neighbouring houses. ~-**প্রভাব** *n* environmental influence. ~-**দূষণ** *n* pollution of the environment; environmental pollution.

প্রতিবেশী *adj* neighbouring; living/residing in the neighbourhood. ❑*n* neighbour. **প্রতিবেশিনী** *fem.*

প্রতিবোধ **1** *n* awaking; waking. **2** perception; knowledge. **3** awakening. ~**ক** *adj* awakening. ~**ন** *n* awakening; expanding; spreading; manifestation; revelation; recovering consciousness.

প্রতিবোধিত *adj* awakened.

প্রতিভা *n* genius; keen intelligence; intellect; presence of mind; brilliance; innovative/ creative faculty; glow; splendour. ~**ধর**, ~**ন্বিত**, ~ **শালী**, ~ **সম্পন্ন** *adjj* endowed with genius/presence of mind/ creative faculty; keenly intelligent; brilliant. ~**ধর ব্যক্তি** *n* man of genius; genius.

প্রতিভাত *adj* manifest; clearly revealed/known/ visible; evident.

প্রতিভার *n* counter-balance.

প্রতিভাষ *n* answer; reply; rejoinder.

প্রতিভাস *n* **1** appearance; look. **2** illumination; radiance; splendour; manifestation; revelation. **3** illusion.

প্রতিভাসিত *adj* manifested; revealed; radiant.

প্রতিভূ *n* representative; agent; deputy; substitute; hostage.

প্রতিভূতি *n* bail. **~পত্র** *n* bail-bond.

প্রতিম *adj* (used as a *suff*) like; resembling; equal to: সোদর ~.

প্রতিমা *n* image; idol; icon; figure; symbol; likeness. **~ চূর্ণকারী** *adj*=~ভঞ্জক. **~চূর্ণন**=~ভঞ্জন. **~তত্ত্ব** *n* iconology. **~ নিরঞ্জন** =~ বিসর্জন. **~পূজক** *adj* idolatrous. ❑*n* idolater; image-worshipper. **~ পূজা** *n* idolatry; image-worship. **~ পূজাবিরোধী** *adj* opposed to idolatry/image-worship; iconoclastic. **~ বিসর্জন** *n* ceremonial immersion of an idol. **~ভঞ্জক** *adj* iconoclastic. ❑*n* iconoclast. **~ভঞ্জন** *n* iconoclasm.

প্রতিমান *n* **1** image; model; pattern; idol. **2** comparison; likeness; similarity; resemblance. **3** standard. **4** balancing; weight. **~ করা** *vi* (phys) balance.

প্রতিমাননা *n* honour; homage; reverence.

প্রতিমাসে *adv* every month; monthly.

প্রতিমুখ *n* **1** direction towards; front; face. **2** (mech) representation. ❑*adj* **1** facing; standing before the face. **2** (mech) unlike. **3** (bot) opposite.

প্রতিমুখাগত *adj* coming towards/ in front of.

প্রতিমুখে *adv* towards; in front of; before; in the direction of.

প্রতিমুহূর্ত *adv* every moment/instant; constantly; always.

প্রতিমূর্তি *n* image; model; portrait; icon; likeness; exactly similar figure.

প্রতিযত্ন *n* effort; endeavour; exertion.

প্রতিযাতনা *n* retaliation.

প্রতিযুদ্ধ *n* battle in return; counter attack.

প্রতিযোগ *n* opposition; contradiction; quarrel; rivalry; enmity.

প্রতিযোগিতা *n* competition; contest; rivalry; vying; contention; bout; tussle; match; tournament. **~ করা** *vi* compete; contest; vie with. **~পূর্ণ, ~মূলক** *adjj* competitive.

প্রতিযোগী *adj* **1** competing; contesting; vying; rivalling; contending. **2** (geom) conjugate. ❑*n* competitor; contestant; rival; contender. **প্রতিযোগিনী** *fem.*

প্রতিযোজন *n* **1** (bot) adaptation **2** (plil) accommodation.

প্রতিযোজয়িতব্য *adj* to be adapted/ accommodated.

প্রতিযোদ্ধা *n* antagonist; well-matched opponent; rival; adversary.

প্রতিরক্ষণ *n* act of protecting; preserving.

প্রতিরক্ষা *n* defence; safety.

প্রতিরুদ্ধ *adj* **1** kept away; shut off; withdrawn. **2** checked; prevented; stopped; interrupted; disturbed; resisted; obstructed; blockaded; opposed. **~ করা** *vi* check; prevent; stop interrupt; disturb; resist; obstruct; block; oppose.

প্রতিরূপ *n* image; likeness; representation; exactly similar figure/appearance; reflection; reflected image; resemblance. **2** duplicate. **3** counterpart. ❑*adj* like; exactly similar/resembling. **~ক** *n* **1**= ~. **2** counterpart. **3** (rhet) synecdoche.

প্রতিরোধ *n* opposition; resistance; impediment; obstruction; hindrance; prevention; check; stoppage; blockade. **~ করা**= প্রতিরুদ্ধ করা (⇒ প্রতিরুদ্ধ). **~ক** *adj* preventing; opposing; resistant; obstructing; hindering; obstructive; stopping; blockading; preventive. ❑*n* **1** opposer; preventer; obstacle. **2** (med) preventive; preventative. **~মূলক** *adj* preventive. **~ শক্তি** *n* power/capacity for resistance. **রোগ ~ক শক্তি** *n* body's natural resistance to diseases; resistance to infection.

প্রতিরোধী *adj*=প্রতিরোধক (⇒প্রতিরোধ)

প্রতিরোধিত=প্রতিরুদ্ধ

প্রতিলিপি *n* facsimile; copy; transcript; replica.

প্রতিলেখ *n* copy; transcription; copying; transcript. **~ক** *n* copyist. **~ন** *n* copying.

প্রতিলোম *adj* **1** contrary to natural course/ order; reverse; inverse; inverted. **2** adverse; hostile; disagreeable. **3** contrary to caste. **~জ** *adj* born in the inverse order of castes (as a Kshatriya father and a Brahmin mother). **~ বিবাহ** *n* marriage of a high-caste bride with a low-caste bridegroom.

প্রতিশঙ্কনীয় *adj* to be doubted about/feared.

প্রতিশঙ্কা *n* constant fear/doubt.

প্রতিশব্দ *n* **1** echo. **2** synonym.

প্রতিশয়, প্রতিশয়ন *n* persistent supplication at a temple for divine favour/boon. **প্রতিশয়িত** *adj* lying persistently in supplication (at a temple for divine grace).

প্রতিশোধ *n* revenge; retaliation; vengeance; reprisal; requital. **~ দেওয়া/ নেওয়া** *vi* take/ have/ get revenge for; revenge; avenge oneself on sb for sth; revenge oneself on sb; take revenge (on sb). **~ কামনা, ~স্পৃহা** *nn* desire for revenge. **~কামী, ~পরায়ণ** *adjj* revengeful; vindictive.

প্রতিশ্রুত *adj* promised; pledged; covenanted; committed; engaged by promise. **~ হওয়া** *vi* pledge oneself; be pledged to sth; be under pledge of sth.

প্রতিশ্রুতি *n* promise; pledge; (sacred) word; word of honour. **~ দেওয়া** *vi* promise; give one's (sacred) word/word of honour; give one's pledge. **~-ভঙ্গ** *n* breach of a promise/pledge/contract. **~ ভঙ্গ করা** *vi* break a promise/pledge; break one's word. **~শীল** *adj* promising. **~শীলা** *fem.*

প্রতিষঙ্গ *n* correspondence.

প্রতিষিদ্ধ *adj* **1** prohibited; forbidden; denied; disallowed; interdicted. **2** driven back; kept off. **~ করা** *vt* prohibit; forbid; interdict; disallow; deny.

প্রতিষেধ *n* **1** prohibition; interdiction; denial. **2** prevention. **3** antidote; prophylactic; therapeutics. **~ক** *adj* **1** forbidding; prohibiting; prohibitive. **2** antidotal; preventive; prophylactic. ❑*n* prophylactic; preventive.

প্রতিষ্ঠ *adj* standing firmly; established; steadfast.

প্রতিষ্ঠা *n* **1** establishment; setting up; foundation: হাসপাতাল ~. **2** pre-eminence; high rank/position; fame; celebrity; superiority; reputation; footing; standing: জীবনে ~ পাওয়া. **3** establishment on/accession to (the throne). **4** performance of any ceremony/solemn act; consecration; dedication: বিগ্রহ ~. **5** completion of a vow. **6** installation. **7** settling down; habitation. **8** standpoint; resting-place; ground; foundation; stay; prop; base; support. **~ করা** *vt* **1** fix; found; prop. **2** set up; institute; establish; lay the foundations of. **3** consecrate; dedicate. **4** install. **5** prove; establish. **~ পাওয়া** *vi* gain a firm foothold; be firmly established (in); earn fame/ celebrity/ (good) reputation. **~কামী** *adj* desirous of a fixed abode/high position/fame/celebrity. **~তা** *n* founder. **প্রতিষ্ঠাত্রী** *fem.* **~ধিকার** *n* good will. **~ন** *n* establishment; institution; institute. **~ন্বিত** *adj* renowned; celebrated; famous; illustrious; well-established; reputed. **~পক** = ~তা. **~পন**=~ (except 2). **~পয়িতা**=~তা. **~পয়িত্রী** *fem.* **~পিত** *adj* **1** rested/dependent on; fixed; firm. **2** founded; set up; established. **3** secure; thriving; well off. **4** consecrated; dedicated. **5** settled down; established in life. **6** famous; celebrated; of a good standing. **7** installed. **~বান, ~শালী**=~ন্বিত. **~বতী, ~শালিনী** *fem.* **~ভিলাষ** *n* desire for fame/celebrity/high position. **~ভিলাষী** *adj* desirous of fame/ celebrity.

প্রতিষ্ঠিত *adj* = প্রতিষ্ঠাপিত (⇒প্রতিষ্ঠা). **~ করা** *vt* **1** = প্রতিষ্ঠা করা. **2** set sb up: ব্যবসায়ে ~ করা.

প্রতিসংহার *n* drawing in; withdrawing; withholding; warding off; keeping away; abstention from. **~ করা** *vi* **1** draw/keep back; withdraw; withhold; shrink. **2** absorb; annihilate; destroy. **3** check; stop; repress.

প্রতিসংহৃত *adj* kept back; checked; restrained; withdrawn; withheld; held up; warded off.

প্রতিসন্ধান *n* **1** putting together again; joining together. **2** search; inquest.

প্রতিসম *adj* symmetrical. **প্রতিসাম্য** *n* symmetry.

প্রতিসমাধান =প্রতিবিধান. **প্রতিসমাধেয়**=প্রতিবিধেয়

প্রতিসর *n* a cord/ribbon used as an amulet worn round the neck or wrist at nuptials, etc.

প্রতিসরণ *n* (phys) refraction. **~ করা** *vt* refract. **~ কোণ** *n* angle of refraction. **প্রতিসরণীয়** *adj* refrangible. **প্রতিসরণাঙ্ক, প্রতিসরাঙ্ক** *nn* refracting index.

প্রতিসর্গ *n* secondary/ continued creation out of primitive matter.

প্রতিসারণ *n* **1** removal; expulsion. **2** dressing and anointing the edges of a wound. **~ করা** *vi* remove; expel; draw/lead away; repel.

প্রতিসারিত *adj* repelled; removed; led away.

প্রতিসারী *adj* **1** going round/from one to the other. **2** (phys) refracting.

প্রতিসৃত *adj* (phy) refracted.

প্রতিস্পর্ধা *n* emulation; rivalry; rebellion. **প্রতিস্পর্ধিত, প্রতিস্পর্ধী** *adjj* emulous; coping with; rebellious. **প্রতিস্পর্ধিনী** *fem.*

প্রতিস্রোত *n* contrary current/ stream. প্রতিস্রোতে *adv* up/ against the stream; against the current.

প্রতিস্বাক্ষর *n* counter signature. **প্রতিস্বাক্ষরিত** *adj* counter signed.

প্রতিহত *adj* **1** repelled; warded off; resisted; checked; impeded; obstructed; prevented; staved off. **2** struck against; hurt; smitten in return. **~ করা** *vt* repel; prevent; ward off; check; impede; obstruct; stave off; repulse; beat back; throw back; resist.

প্রতিহনন *n* killing a slayer; returning of a blow; resistance; back stroke.

প্রতিহন্তা *n* one who kills a slayer; one who wards off. **প্রতিহন্ত্রী** *fem.*

প্রতিহরণ *n* throwing back; repelling.

প্রতিহর্তা *n* one who strikes back; destroyer.

প্রতিহার *n* **1** door; gate. **2** door-keeper; porter. **3** juggler. **~ক** *n* **1** juggler. **2** swindler; cheat.

প্রতিহারী *n* armed guard stationed at a gate; door-keeper; gateman. **প্রতিহারিণী** *fem.*

প্রতিহার্য *adj* to be pushed back/ repelled; resistible; to be abandoned/ avoided.

প্রতিহিংসা *n* revenge; retaliation. **~ গ্রহণ করা** *vi* = প্রতিশোধ দেওয়া (⇒প্রতিশোধ). **~ পরায়ণ** *adj* revengeful; vindictive.

প্রতিহিংসিত *adj* on whom revenge has been taken.

প্রতীক *n* symbol; sign; token; image. **~তা, ~বাদ** *nn* symbolism. **~বাদী** *n, adj* symbolist. **~ ধর্মঘট** *n* token strike.

প্রতীকার =প্রতিকার

প্রতীক্ষণ *n* looking to/at; considering; regard; attention.

প্রতীক্ষমাণ *adj* waiting for; awaiting; expecting; expectant. **প্রতীক্ষমাণা** *fem.*

প্রতীক্ষা *n* waiting; awaiting; expectation; attention. **~ করা** *vt* wait for; await; expect; look forward to.

প্রতীক্ষিত *adj* awaited; expected; contemplated; hoped.

প্রতীক্ষ্য *adj* to be awaited/ waited for; to be expected.

প্রতীচী *n* the west; the western world/hemisphere; the Occident. **~ন, প্রতীচ্য** *adj* western; Occidental.

প্রতীত *adj* **1** known; realized; apprehended; understood. **2** recognized; acknowledged. **3** convinced of; satisfied.

প্রতীতি *n* clear apprehension/ insight (into); complete understanding/ ascertainment; conviction; faith; belief; notion; impression; cognition; realization. **~সমুৎপাদ** *n* **1** chain of causation. **2** conviction. **~সমুৎপাদী** *adj* convincing.

প্রতীপ *adj* going in an opposite direction; meeting; encountering. **1** contrary; adverse; opposite; reverse; negative. **2** inverted. **3** (geom) vertically opposite. **4** resisting; refractory; cross; obstinate. **5** backward; retrograde; turned away. **6** displeasing; disagreeable. **~ কোণ** *n* (geom) vertically opposite angle. **~ গতি** *n* (astron) retrograde motion; retrogression. **~গমন** *n* retrograde movement. **~গামী** *adj* going against; retrograde. **~ চাপ** *n* (phys) negative pressure. **~ স্রোত** *n* (geog) anti-current.

প্রতীয়মান *adj* **1** apparent; seeming; clear; distinct; visible; suggested. **~ হওয়া** *vi* appear; seem; become visible; look; come in sight **~ত** *adv* apparently; visibly; in appearance; seemingly; visibly.

প্রতুল *adj* abundant; bountiful; plentiful; profuse; lavish. ❑*n* abundance; plenty; profusion; lavishness; deluge. **~তা** *n* = ~.

প্রতোলী *n* broad way; avenue; boulevard.

প্রত্ন *adj* ancient; old. **~ জীববিদ্যা** *n pt* palaeontology. **~তত্ত্ব** *n* archaeology. **~তত্ত্বজ্ঞ, ~তত্ত্ববিদ, ~তত্ত্ববেত্তা** *nn* archaeologist; antiquary; antiquarian. **~ প্রাণিবিদ্যা** *n* palaeo-zoology. **~বিদ্যা** = ~তত্ত্ব. **~বিদ** = ~তত্ত্বজ্ঞ.

প্রত্নতত্ত্বীয়, প্রত্নতাত্ত্বিক *adjj* archaeological; antiquarian.

প্রত্নোদ্ভিদ্‌বিদ্যা *n* palaeo-botany.

প্রত্যক *adj* **1** inward; inner; interior; sub. **2** western; westward; occidental. **3** subjective. **~ চৈতন্য** *n* subconscious; subconsciousness.

প্রত্যক্ষ *adj* **1** present before the eyes; visible; perceptible. **2** clear; distinct; manifest; evident. **3** direct; immediate. **4** actual; real. ❑*n* perception; sense-perception. **~ করা** *vt* see, view; witness; perceive (by senses) ; see with one's own eyes. **~ উক্তি** (gram) direct speech; narration. **~কারী** *adj* seeing with one's eyes; one who has seen with his own eyes; directly perceiving. ❑*n* eye-witness. **~কারিণী** *fem.* **~গোচর** *adj* perceptible by the senses; visible; directly perceptible. **~ জ্ঞান** *n* immediate perception; direct knowledge. **~ত** *adj* before the eyes; visibly; perceptibly; apparently. **~তা** *n* directness; being visible; visibility; explicitness. **~ দর্শন** *n* seeing with one's own eyes; direct perception. **~দর্শী** = ~কারী. **~ দর্শিনী** *fem.* **~ দিগন্ত** *n* visible/ apparent horizon. **~ প্রমাণ** *n* ocular/ visible proof; ocular evidence. **~ ফল** *n* direct/ visible consequence. **~বাদ** *n* positivism. **~বাদী** *adj* materialistic. ❑*n* positivist. **~ ভোগ** *n* immediate suffering of consequences **~ রূপ** *n* visible form. **~ লাভ** *n* direct benefit/ gain. **~ সাক্ষ্য** *n* direct/ ocular evidence. **~ সিদ্ধ** *adj* determined by evidence of the eyes.

প্রত্যক্ষী *n* =~কারী (⇒প্রত্যক্ষ). **~করণ** *n* **1** looking at; viewing. perception. **2** making manifest/apparent. **3 ~কৃত** *adj* **1** seen with the eyes; witnessed; viewed. **2** perceived (by senses). **3** made present/visible; manifested. **~ভূত** *adj* seen; visible; perceived.

প্রত্যগাত্মা *n* universal permeation of spirit. **2** individual soul.

প্রত্যংশ *n* portion; share.

প্রত্যঙ্গ *n* **1** minor/secondary member of the body; appendage. **2** organ. **3** small component; supplementary part.

প্রত্যনুমান *n* contrary deduction; opposite conclusion.

প্রত্যন্ত *adj* **1** bordering on; adjacent/continuous to; skirting; neighbouring. **2** far-flung; far-away; distant; remote. ❑*n* border; frontier (region). **~ অঞ্চল** *n* far-flung/ remote areas. **~ জনপদ ~, দেশ** *nn* bordering country. **~ পর্বত** *n* adjacent (small) hill. **~বাসী** *adj* dwelling on the outskirts of a town/village/country.

প্রত্যবয়ব *n* every part of the body.

প্রত্যবসান *n* eating; consuming. **প্রত্যবসিত** *adj* **1** eaten; consumed. **2** relapsed into the old (bad) way of life.

প্রত্যবস্থাতা *n* opponent; adversary.

প্রত্যবস্থান *n* **1** opposition; hostility. **2** former state/place.

প্রত্যবহার *n* drawing back; withdrawal.

প্রত্যবায় *n* **1** offence; sin; sinfulness. **2** decrease; diminution. **3** contrary course; opposite conduct; annoyance. **প্রত্যবায়ী** *adj* **1** offending; committing sin. **2** opposing.

প্রত্যবেক্ষণ, প্রত্যবেক্ষা *nn* looking after; care; attention; supervision.

প্রত্যবেক্ষ্য *adj* to be regarded/paid attention to; to be looked after/searched for/investigated.

প্রত্যভিজ্ঞা, প্রত্যভিজ্ঞান *n* regaining knowledge; recognition. **প্রত্যভিজ্ঞাত** *adj* recognized.

প্রত্যভিবাদ, প্রত্যভিবাদন *n* return salutation. **~ করা** *vi* salute in return; return a salute.

প্রত্যভিযুক্ত *adj* counter-charged; accused in return/by a counter plaint.

প্রত্যভিযোগ *n* counter charge/plaint/suit; recrimination. ~ **করা** *vi* bring a counter charge.

প্রত্যভিলেখ *n* document brought forward by the opposite party; counter document.

প্রত্যয় *n* **1** belief; firm conviction; trust; faith; confidence; assurance; certainty. **2** conception; assumption; notion; idea. **3** (gram) affix (suffix to roots forming verbs, substantives, adjectives and all derivatives). ~ **করা** *vi* belief; trust; have confidence/faith in. ~ **কর**, ~ **কারক**, ~ **জনক**, ~ **যোগ্য** *adj* trustworthy; convincing; worthy of belief; credible; plausible; believable. ~ **ন** *n* believing; trusting.

প্রত্যয়াতীত *adj* unbelievable; incredible; implausible; beyond belief.

প্রত্যয়ান্বিত = ~কর (⇒প্রত্যয়)

প্রত্যয়ার্হ= ~কর

প্রত্যয়িত *adj* **1** proved; attested. **2** trustworthy; trusty.

প্রত্যয়ী *adj* **1** trusting; believing; confident. **2** deserving confidence; trustworthy; credible.

প্রত্যর্থপত্র *n* promissory note.

প্রত্যর্থী *n* defendant; contestant; opposite party; opponent; accused. □*adj* opposing; rivalling; hostile; inimical.

প্রত্যর্পণ *n* giving back; return; restoration; repayment. ~ **করা** *vt* give back; return; restore; repay.

প্রত্যর্পিত *adj* given back; returned; repaid; restored.

প্রত্যহ *adv* daily; every day; day by day; par diem.

প্রত্যাকর্ষণ *n* counter-attraction.

প্রত্যাখ্যাত *adj* **1** rejected; refused; disallowed; denied; set aside; discarded. **2** slighted; neglected; repudiated.

প্রত্যাখ্যান *n* **1** rejection; non-admission; refutation; refusal; denial; disallowance; repulse. **2** slight; neglect; repudiation. ~ **করা** *vt* reject; decline; refuse; repudiate; deny; refute; disallow; refuse to accept/ entertain; discard; slight; neglect.

প্রত্যাখ্যেয় *adj* to be declined/ rejected/ refused.

প্রত্যাগত *adj* **1** come back; returned; arrived. **2** (mech) recoiled. **প্রত্যাগতা** *fem.*

প্রত্যাগতি *n* **1** coming back; return; arrival. **2** (mech) recoil.

প্রত্যাগমন *n* =প্রত্যাগতি (1). ~ **করা** *vi* **1** come back; return. **2** (mech) return.

প্রত্যাঘাত *n* counterblow. ~ **করা** *vi* deal a counterblow; strike/hit back.

প্রত্যাদিষ্ট *adj* **1** divinely commanded/ enjoined/ inspired. **2** repealed; made void; voided; nullified.

প্রত্যাদেশ *n* **1** divine command/ inspiration; commandment; oracle; divine order/ announcement. **2** nullification; repeal.

প্রত্যাদেষ্টা *n* one who commands/ warns/ cautions/ repeals/ inspires.

প্রত্যানয়ন *n* leading/ bringing back; recovery; restoration. ~ **করা** *vt* lead/ bring back; restore.

প্রত্যাবর্তন *n* coming back; returning; return. ~ **করা** *vi* come back; return.

প্রত্যাবাসন *n* repatriation. **প্রত্যাবাসিত** *adj* repatriated. **প্রত্যাবৃত্ত** *adj* come/gone back; returned; repeated. ~ **হওয়া** *vi* come/go back; return.

প্রত্যাবৃত্তি *n* **1** coming back; return. **2** (astron) regression.

প্রত্যাভূতি *n* guarantee.

প্রত্যায়ক *adj* convincing; credible; attesting. □*n* one who attests.

প্রত্যায়ন *n* **1** convincing; persuasion. **2** attestation. ~ **করা** *vt* attest.

প্রত্যায়িত *adj* **1** convinced of; trusting. **2** attested.

প্রত্যালীঢ় *n* a particular attitude in shooting (the left foot advanced and right drawn back).

প্রত্যাশা *n* hope; expectation; trust; longing; awaiting; prospect. ~ **করা** *vi* hope/long for; expect; await; trust.

প্রত্যাশিত *adj* expected; hoped/longed for; awaited; prospective.

প্রত্যাশী *adj* hoping/longing for; awaiting; expecting; expectant. **প্রত্যাশিনী** *fem.* **প্রত্যাশ্বাস** *n* **1** breathing again; respiration; recovery. **2** consolation. ~**ন** *n* consolation.

প্রত্যাসত্তি *n* immediate proximity (in space, time, etc).

প্রত্যাসন্ন *adj* near at hand; close to; proximate; neighbouring; imminent; impending; closely connected/related.

প্রত্যাহত *adj* driven back; repelled; repulsed; rejected; beaten back; prevented; resisted; foiled; frustrated.

প্রত্যাহরণ *n* bringing/drawing back; withdrawing; withdrawal; recovery; revocation; retraction; repeal;

প্রত্যাহরণী=প্রত্যাহার্য

প্রত্যাহার *n* **1** =প্রত্যাহরণ. **2** (phil) abstraction. ~ **করা** *vt* bring/draw back; withdraw; revoke; retract; repeal; recover; rescind.

প্রত্যাহার্য *adj* to be taken back/ withheld/repealed/revoked/rescinded.

প্রত্যাহৃত *adj* withheld; rescinded; repealed; retracted.

প্রত্যুক্ত *adj* answered.

প্রত্যুক্তি *n* answer; reply; retort.

প্রত্যুজীবন *n* returning to life; restoring to life; revivifying.

প্রত্যুত *con, adv* on the contrary; rather; even.

প্রত্যুৎকর্ষ *n* outdoing; surpassing.

প্রত্যুৎক্রম, প্রত্যুৎক্রান্তি *nn* setting out to assail an enemy; declaration of war.

প্রত্যুত্তর *n* reply to an answer; rejoinder; answer.

প্রত্যুত্থান *n* rising from a seat to welcome a visitor; respectful salutation/reception.

প্রত্যুৎপন্ন *adj* existing in the present moment; present; prompt; ready; extemporaneous; produced on the spur of the moment. ~মতি *adj* ready-minded; sharp; sharp-witted; ready-witted. ~মতিত্ব *n* presence of mind.

প্রত্যুদাহরণ *n* counter-example/ illustration/ precedent.

প্রত্যুদগত *adj* gone to meet (a friend or an enemy); encountered.

প্রত্যুদগম, প্রত্যুদগমন *n* going forth towards; rising from a seat (as a mark of respect/and going out to meet (esp a guest). প্রত্যুদগমন করা *vi* go out towards; advance to meet (a friend or an enemy).

প্রত্যুদ্ঘাত *n* **1** =প্রত্যপক্রম. **2** counter-initiative; counter-blow.

প্রত্যুদ্ধরণ, প্রত্যুদ্ধার *nn* recovery; restoration.

প্রত্যুদ্ধৃত *adj* recovered; restored.

প্রত্যুপকর্তা=প্রত্যুপকারী

প্রত্যুপকার *n* requiting a favour/ service; good turn in return; gratitude. ~ করা *vi* do a service/good turn in return; requite a favour.

প্রত্যুপকারী *adj* requiting a favour; grateful. ☐*n* one who requites a favour/does a good turn in return.

প্রত্যুপকৃত *adj* benefited in return.

প্রত্যুপদিষ্ট *adj* advised/cautioned in return.

প্রত্যুপদেশ *n* advice/instruction in return. ~ক *adj* advising/ instructing in return. প্রত্যুপদেশিকা *fem.*

প্রত্যুপ্ত *adj* fixed into; set with.

প্রত্যুষ, প্রত্যূষ *n* dawn; daybreak; morning. প্রত্যুষে *adj* early in the morning; at dawn/daybreak.

প্রত্যেক *adj* each; every: ~ দিকে, ~ মানুষ. প্রত্যেকে *adv* each of; everyone; everybody; each: প্রত্যেকে যাবে.

প্রথম *adj* **1** first: ~ দিন. **2** foremost; chief; principal; best: এক্ষেত্রে তিনিই সকলের ~. **3** of the beginning; initial; early; inceptive: ~ অবস্থা. **4** earliest; original; former; prior; primitive: ~ যুগ. **5** eldest; first-born: ~ পুত্র. **6** best; excellent; first: ~ শ্রেণী. ☐*n* the first: ~ থেকে শেষ পর্যন্ত. ☐*adv* for the first time: তাকে এই ~ দেখলাম. প্রথমা *fem.* (পরীক্ষায়) ~ হওয়া *vi* stand first; top the list. ~জ *adj* first-born. ☐*n* firstling. ~জা *fem.* ~জাত *adj* first-born .~ত *adj* first; at first; firstly; in the first place. ~ দর্শন *n* first sight. ~ দর্শনে প্রণয় love at first sight. ~ পাদ *n* first quarter. ~ পুরুষ *n* (gram) the third person. ~ বয়স *n* early age; early youth. ~ বয়সী *adj* young. ~ বিরহ *n* first separation. ~ যৌবন *n* early youth. ~ রাত্রি *n* beginning of night. প্রথমে *adv* **1** at first; first; in the first place; in the beginning; earlier; previously. **2** in front; before all.

প্রথমাঙ্গুলি *n* thumb.

প্রথা *n* usage; custom; practice; customary way; system; method; way. ~গত *adj* usual; customary. ~নুসারে, ~মতো *adv* according to custom/ practice/ usage; customarily; assorting to general practice; following usual practice.

প্রথিত *adj* spread; extended; published; known; celebrated. ~নামা *adj* having a well-known name/established reputation; widely known; famous; renowned; of great renown. ~যশা *adj* of wide renown.

প্রথিমা *n* extension; width; greatness.

প্রথীয়ান *adj* very great; huge; enormous.

প্রদ *adj* (used as a *suff)* giving; yielding; offering; granting; bestowing; causing: দুঃখ~. প্রদা *fem.*

প্রদক্ষিণ *n* **1** going round sth; revolving; rotating; revolution; rotation. **2** circumambulation from left to the right of a person/ object (as a kind of worship). ~ করা *vi* **1** go round sth; revolve round/ around sth. **2** go round/ circumambulate from left to the right (as a mark of respect/ kind of worship).

প্রদত্ত *adj* given; presented; granted; bestowed; offered; given away (also in marriage) conferred.

প্রদমিত *adj* subdued; vanquished; suppressed; restrained; crushed; broken; tamed; brought down; humbled.

প্রদর *n* moenorrhagia.

প্রদর্শক *adj* showing; indicating; exhibiting; displaying; demonstrating; foretelling. ☐*n* one who shows; one who shows sb round; guide; displayer; demonstrator; exhibitor. প্রদর্শিকা *fem.*

প্রদর্শন *n* **1** showing; pointing out; exhibiting; displaying; demonstrating; demonstration; indication. **2** seeing/observing carefully/ thoroughly/ minutely. ~ করা *vi* **1** see/observe carefully/thoroughly/minutely. **2** show; demonstrate; display; indicate; exhibit; make visible; point out. ~ করানো *vt* **1** = ~ (1).**2** show sb round.

প্রদর্শনী *n* (public) show; display; exhibition.

প্রদর্শশালা *n* museum.

প্রদর্শিত adj pointed out; shown; shown round; displayed; demonstrated; exhibited; indicated.

প্রদাতা *adj* giving; bestowing; offering; conferring; yielding; imparting; granting. ❑*n* giver; bestower; donor. প্রদাত্রী *fem.*

প্রদান *n* giving; bestowing; bestowal; presentation; conferring; conferment; yielding; imparting; delivery. ~ করা *vt* give; bestow; confer; award; grant; yield; impart; mete out; accord; donate; assign; give away; hand out; deliver; hand (over); endow; favour with; render; deal; give/deal out.

প্রদায়ক, প্রদায়ী =প্রদাতা. প্রদায়িকা, প্রদায়িনী *fem.*

প্রদাহ *n* **1** burning; heating; consuming by fire. **2** inflammation; burning pain. **3** distress; affliction: মর্ম~.

প্রদিগ্ধ *adj* smeared over; anointed; stained/ covered with.

প্রদিষ্ট *adj* pointed out; indicated; fixed; ordained.

প্রদীপ *n* **1** light; lamp; lantern. **2** the light, ie the glory/ ornament of: বংশ~. ~ক *adj* illuminating; brightening; lighting up; irradiating. ~ন *n* **1** illuminating; lighting = (of lamps). **2** exciting; inflaming.

প্রদীপ্ত *adj* **1** kindled; enkindled; shining; blazing; glowing; radiant; resplendent. **2** excited; inflamed; burning; brilliant; illuminating; ~ বক্তৃতা. ~ করা *vt* illuminate; enkindle; kindle; light; inflame; excite.

প্রদীপ্তি *n* light; lustre; brilliance; illumination; glow; glitter; brightness; splendour.

প্রদুষ্ট *adj* wicked; bad; corrupt; sinful.

প্রদূষ্য *adj* reprehensible; abominable; despicable.

প্রদৃপ্ত *adj* **1** very proud/arrogant/haughty; insolent. **2** very energetic, vigorous; brisk; animated.

প্রদেয় *adj* to be given/ presented/ granted/ offered/ imparted/ accorded/ given away/ delivered/ endowed/ rendered/ handed over/ awarded/ conferred.

প্রদেশ *n* **1** province; district; region; country; state. **2** spot; place.

প্রদেহ *n* medicated plaster.

প্রদোষ *n* the first part of the night; evening; nightfall; evening twilight. ~কাল =~. ~তিমির, ~তমঃ *nn* evening darkness; dusk of early night; gloom of the evening. ~ বেলা =~. প্রদোষান্ধকার= ~তিমির.

প্রদ্যুতিত *adj* beginning to shine; illuminated.

প্রদ্যোত *n* radiance; light; glow; shine.

প্রধান *adj* **1** chief; principal; main; prime; leading; foremost; pre-eminent; predominant; most important; key; primary; capital; top; pivotal; staple; cardinal; vital. **2** dominated/chiefly characterized by: গ্রীষ্ম~ দেশ. ❑*n* chief (thing/person); most important/ essential part; head (of); leader; headman; royal counsellor. ~ অক্ষ *n* principal axis. ~ খাদ্য *n* staple diet. ~ত *adv* chiefly; mainly; principally; predominantly; pre-eminently; importantly; in the main; above all; in the first place. ~তা *n* pre-eminence; excellence; superiority; predominance; supremacy. ~মন্ত্রী prime minister. ~ মূল *n* (bot) tap-root. ~ শিক্ষক *n* headmaster. ~ শিক্ষিকা/ শিক্ষয়িত্রী *fem* headmistress. ~ সেনাপতি *n* commander-in-chief.

প্রধাবন *n* act of running rapidly; quick run/race.

প্রধাবিত *adj* running away; running rapidly/fast; racing; careering; galloping; started; set out. ~ করা *vt* set in motion; race. ~ হওয়া *vi* run fast/rapidly; race; career; dart; run forth; set out; run forward.

প্রধূপিত *adj* **1** fumigated; perfumed; heated; burnt. **2** lighted; inflamed; excited; afflicted. প্রধূপিতা *fem.*

প্রধূমিত *adj* smothered with smoke; giving out smoke; smouldering. প্রধূমিতা *fem.* ~ করা *vt* cause to give out smoke; fume; fumigate. ~ হওয়া *vt* emit smoke; fume.

প্রধৃষ্ট *adj* proud; arrogant; insolent.

প্রধ্বংস *n* destruction; annihilation; perishing; disappearance. প্রধ্বংসী *adj* destructive; annihilating; destroying.

প্রনষ্ট *adj* utterly destroyed/ ruined/ lost.

প্রপঞ্চ *n* **1** expansion; development; manifestation. **2** amplification; prolixity; diffuseness; copiousness. **3** appearance; phenomenon; phenomenal reality; expansion of the universe; the visible world. **4** deceit; trick; fraud. **5** error; untruth; falsehood. **6** illusion; delusion. **7** multitude; collection. ~ময় *adj* full of illusions; illusory; phenomenal.

প্রপঞ্চিত *adj* amplified; extended; extensive; illusory; erroneous.

প্রপতন *n* **1** falling/ flying down; falling from; downfall. **2** death; destruction.

প্রপন্ন *adj* fallen at a person's feet; poor; distressed. প্রপন্নাধিকার *n* court of wards.

প্রপা, প্রপান *n* place for supplying water; place for watering cattle; shed on the road-side containing a reservoir of water for travellers; fountain; cistern.

প্রপাত *n* **1** falling down/from/into. **2** discharge; emission. **3** fall; waterfall; cataract; cascade. **4** steep bank/shore; precipice; cliff. ~ রেখা *n* fall line.

প্রপিতামহ *n* great-grand-father (on one's father's side). প্রপিতামহী *fem* great-grand-mother (on one's father's side).

প্রপূরণ *n* filling (up); putting in; inserting; injecting; satiating.

প্রপূরিত *adj* filled up; completed; satiated.

প্রপেলার [E]*n* propeller.

প্রপৌত্র *n* grandson of one's son or nephew; great-grandson. **প্রপৌত্রী** *fem* great-granddaughter.

প্রফুল্ল *adj* **1** blooming forth; blown; fully blossomed; full-blown: ~ পদ্মমালা. **2** covered with blossoms/flowers. **3** expanded; opened wide (like a full-blown flower); shining: ~ নয়ন. **4** smiling; cheerful; pleased; blithe; gay; happy; bright. **~চিত্ত** *adj* having a cheerful/ happy heart; hearty; cheerful. **~চিত্ততা** *n* cheerfulness; heartiness. **~চিত্তে** *adv* with a happy/cheerful heart; heartily; cheerfully; lightheartedly; with good grace. **~তা** *n* cheerfulness; gaiety; lightheartedness; cheeriness; sunny nature. **~নয়ন, ~নেত্র** *adjj* having fully opened/sparkling eyes; having eyes expanded with joy. **~বদন** *adj* having the face expanded with joy; looking gay/happy. **~ভাবে** *adv* cheerfully; with good grace; lightheartedly; gladly. **~হৃদয়** =~চিত্ত.

প্রফেসর [E] *n* professor. **প্রফেসরি** *n* professorship. **প্রফেসরি করা** *vi* work as a professor.

প্রবংশ *n* race. **~ রক্ষা** *n* preservation of race.

প্রবক্তা *n* **1** good speaker; expounder. **2** exponent; advocate: নারী স্বাধীনতার ~. **প্রবক্ত্রী** *fem.*

প্রবচন *n* **1** proverb; adage; maxim. **2** exposition; expounding; interpretation.

প্রবচনীয় *adj* to be expounded; to be well/elegantly spoken.

প্রবঞ্চক *n* cheat; swindler; deceiver; knave; fraud; crook; impostor.

প্রবঞ্চনা *n* cheating; swindle; fraud; deception; deceit; fraudulence; bluff; trickery; knavery. **~ করা** *vi* deceive; cheat; swindle; defraud sb (of sth); beguile sb (into doing sth); hoodwink sb (into sth); trick; dupe sb (into doing sth.

প্রবঞ্চিত *adj* deceived; cheated; swindled; beguiled; defrauded; hoodwinked; deluded.

প্রবণ *adj* **1** declining; bent; sloping; down; inclined: ~ভূমি. **2** inclined/disposed/directed to; intent upon; tending to; prone to: স্নেহ~. **3** attached/given/addicted to: মিথ্যাচার~. **4** ready to; eager to; proficient in. **~তা** *n* tendency; inclination; propensity; proneness to; declivity; disposition; addiction; attachment; readiness; eagerness. **~ভূমি** *n* declivity; escarpment.

প্রবন্ধ *n* **1** essay; article; paper; dissertation; treatise. **2** connection; continuance; sequence. **3** trick; stratagem: 'যতেক ~ করে নিশাচরগণে'. **~কার** *n* essayist; writer of an article/paper.

প্রবর[১] *adj* (used as a *suff)* most excellent; chief; principal; best; great: পণ্ডিত~.

প্রবর[২] *n* (series of) ancestors, family, race.

প্রবর্তক *adj* introducing; initiating; starting; setting in motion; advancing; promoting; forwarding; bringing into use/currency; founding; establishing; inaugurating. ❑*n* originator; author; founder; initiator; pioneer.

প্রবর্তন *n* incitement to activity; bringing into action; introduction; introducing; initiation; starting; start; inception; employment; beginning; inauguration. **~ করা** *vi* introduce; initiate; originate; begin; start; bring into use/currency; inaugurate; found; establish.

প্রবর্তনা *n* **1** initiation. **2** inducement; inspiration; impulsion; motivation; encouragement. **~ দেওয়া** *vi* incite; induce; motivate; inspire; drive; goad; instigate.

প্রবর্তয়িতা *n* originator; founder; initiator; instigator. **প্রবর্তয়িত্রী** *fem.*

প্রবর্তিত *adj* introduced; started; set in motion; commenced; originated; inaugurated; brought into use; initiated; established; founded; stimulated; incited; instigated; kindled; employed; motivated.

প্রবর্ধক *adj* augmenting; increasing; causing growth/ increase; enhancing. ❑*n* one who/that which augment/increases/enhances.

প্রবর্ধন *n* augmenting; augmentation; increasing; increase; enhancement; growth; boost. **~ করা** *vt* augment; increase; enhance; boost; magnify; multiply.

প্রবল *adj* **1** very strong/powerful; mighty; irresistible; great: ~ পরাক্রম. **2** violent; intense; severe; acute; sharp; extreme; excessive: ~ যন্ত্রণা. **3** vigorous; forceful; vehement: ~ আক্রমণ/ প্রতিবাদ. **4** important (as a word). **~ ঝড়** *n* violent/ mighty storm. **~তা** *n* great strength/ power/ might; violence; severity; intensity; acuteness; vehemence; sharpness; extremity. **~ পরাক্রম, ~ পরাক্রান্ত, ~ প্রতাপ** *adj* extremely powerful/strong; mighty; irresistible; overpowering; all-powerful; overwhelming; formidable. **~ বারিপাত** *n* heavy shower/ downpour.

প্রবসিত *adj* emigrated; emigrant. ❑*n* emigrant.

প্রবহ *n* current; flow; flowing/streaming forth. **~ণ** *n* =প্রবাহ. **~ণশীল, ~মাণ** *adj* flowing; blowing; streaming; running.

প্রবাক *n* orator. ❑*adj* eloquent.

প্রবাচক *adj* speaking well; eloquent.

প্রবাচ্য *adj* to be proclaimed aloud; praiseworthy; glorious.

প্রবাদ *n* **1** popular saying/belief; proverb; adage. **2** hearsay: জন~. **~ আছে যে** it is said that ; as the saying goes. ~ বচন, ~বাক্য *nn* proverb.

প্রবারণ *n* fulfilment of a wish.

প্রবাল *n* **1** coral. **2** young shoot; sprout; new leaf/branch. ~ **কীট** *n* polyp. ~ **দ্বীপ** *n* coral island. ~ **পদ্ম** *n* red lotus-flower. ~ **প্রাচীর** *n* coral reef; barrier reef. ~ **ফল** *n* red sandalwood. ~ **ভস্ম** *n* calyx of coral. ~ **বর্ণ** *adj* coral-coloured; coral; red.

প্রবাস *n* **1** dwelling abroad; foreign residence; absence from home. **2** foreign country/land. ~ **গমন** *n* act of going abroad; travelling abroad. ~**গামী** *adj* going abroad; travelling abroad. ~**ন** *n* sending away from home; exile; banishment; deportation.

প্রবাসাজ্ঞা *n* visa.

প্রবাসিত *adj* sent abroad; exiled; banished; deported. **প্রবাসিতা** *fem.*

প্রবাসী *adj* dwelling/living abroad; absent from home. ❑*n* one who is dwelling/living abroad/absent from home. **প্রবাসিনী** *fem.*

প্রবাহ *n* **1** stream; current; flow; running water: বায়ু~, জল~. **2** continuous flow/passage; unbroken series/succession; continuity. **3** train/sequence (of); current: জীবন~, current of life; চিন্তা~, train/stream of thought; ঘটনা ~, course of events.

প্রবাহক *adj* carrying forwards; bearing/carrying well.

প্রবাহিণী *adj fem* streaming; flowing. ❑*n* stream; river.

প্রবাহিত *adj* **1** flowing; streaming; running. **2** blowing: ~ বায়ু. **3** (fig) moving continuously onward: ~ জীবনধারা. **প্রবাহিতা** *fem.* ~ **হওয়া** *vi* **1** flow; stream; run. **2** roll on: সময় ~ . **3** blow: বায়ু ~ হচ্ছে.

প্রবাহী *adj* flowing; running; streaming; blowing. ~ **ঋণ** *n* floating debt. ~ **পরিসম্পদ** *n* floating assets. ~ **পুঁজি** *n* floating capital.

প্রবাহু *n* fore-arm.

প্রবিধান *n* regulation.

প্রবিষ্ট *adj* **1** entered; one who has entered/gone into/come into. **2** initiated into. **3** engaged in. **প্রবিষ্টা** *fem.* ~ **হওয়া** *vi* **1** enter (into); go/come into: কর্ণে ~ হওয়া, be heard. **2** take possession of: হৃদয়ে ~ হওয়া. **3** pierce; penetrate. **প্রবিষ্টা** *fem.*

প্রবীণ *adj* **1** elderly; old; aged. **2** wise; experienced; judicious; skilful. **প্রবীণা** *fem.* ~**তা**, ~**ত্ব** *nn* **1** (old) age. **2** experience; skill; proficiency; judiciousness; wisdom.

প্রবীর *n* hero; prince.

প্রবুদ্ধ *adj* awakened; enlightened; clear-sighted; wise.

প্রবৃত্ত *adj* **1** engaged in; occupied with. **2** commenced; begun; having set about/commenced to. ~ **করা** *vt* induce; set sb to; impel sb (to sth); incline sb towards sth; actuate; motivate; prompt; incite. ~ **হওয়া** *vi* set about sth; set to; commence; begin; enter upon; embark on; undertake; make a start; engage in.

প্রবৃত্তি *n* **1** inclination/predilection for; bent; course/ tendency towards; desire; taste (for); instinct (for); appetite (for). **2** giving/devoting one's self to; engagement; occupation; initiation. ~ **দেওয়া** *vi* induce; incite; prompt; instigate. ~ **মার্গ** *n* active/worldly life; preoccupation with the business and pleasures of the world.

প্রবৃদ্ধ *adj* **1** very old. **2** grown up; fully developed. **3** increased; augmented; intense; swollen; heaving. ~ **কোণ** *n* (geom) reflex angle.

প্রবৃদ্ধি *n* growth; increase; augmentation.

প্রবেট [E]*n* probate.

প্রবেশ *n* **1** entrance; entry. **2** penetration; intrusion. **3** access; admission; admittance. ~ **করা** *vi* enter; go into; come into; pass into; flow in; penetrate; pierce; permeate; infiltrate. ~ **করানো** *vt* admit into; usher; enter; drive/thrust into. ~**ক** *adj* entering. ❑*n* **1** one who enter; entrant. **2** introduction. **প্রবেশিকা**[1] *fem.* ~ **দ্বার** *n* entrance; gate. ~**ন** *n* entering; entrance/penetration into; admission. ~**পত্র** *n* admit card. ~ **পথ** *n* entrance; gateway. ~**মান** *adj* entering. ~ **মূল্য** *n* admission fee. ~ **লাভ করা** *vi* be admitted to; get access to; be able to enter. ~ **নেই** no entry. ~ **নিষেধ** no entrance; entrance prohibited; no admission/entry/admittance.

প্রবেশা *vi* (poet) =প্রবেশ করা (⇒প্রবেশ)

প্রবেশাধিকার *n* right/freedom of entrance; access; entry; right of entry; admittance.

প্রবেশানুমতি *n* permission to enter; admittance.

প্রবেশিকা[2] *n* **1** introductory/elementary text-book. **2** (also ~ **পরীক্ষা**) entrance/matriculation examination.

প্রবেশিত *adj* caused to enter; brought/sent in; introduced; ushered in; admitted into.

প্রবেশী *n* recruit.

প্রবেশ্য *adj* to be entered; accessible; open; permeable. ❑*n* preamble. ~ **শিলা** *n* permeable rock.

প্রবেষ্টা *n* one who enters/goes into.

প্রবোধ *n* **1** consolation; comfort; solace; words of consolation. **2** knowledge; understanding; intelligence. **3** opening; blowing (of flowers). ~ **দেওয়া** *vt* console; solace; comfort; soothe. ~ **পাওয়া** *vi* get consolation; be comforted; solaced. ~ **মানা** *vi* be comforted; be amenable to consolation. ~ **না মানা** *vi* refuse to be comforted; be disconsolate.

প্রবোধন *n* 1 consoling; comforting. 2 awaking; arousing. 3 enlightening.

প্রবোধিত *adj* 1 consoled; solaced; comforted; soothed. 2 enlightened; awakened.

প্রব্যক্ত *adj* apparent; manifest.

প্রব্রজন *n* migration.

প্রব্রজিত *n* religious mendicant; monk. **প্রব্রজিতা** *fem* female ascetic; nun.

প্রব্রজ্যা *n* order of a religious mendicant. **~ নেওয়া** *vi* take order of a religious mendicant.

প্রব্রাজন *n* banishment.

প্রব্রাজিত *adj* banished.

প্রভ *adj* (used as a *suff)* glowing/shining like; as bright/glorious as: হেম~, বিদ্যুৎ~.

প্রভঞ্জন *n* wind; god of wind; storm; tempest; hurricane.

প্রভব *n* 1 origin; source; production; cause of existence (as father or mother); birth-place. 2 influence; might; power. ❑*adj* producing; generating.

প্রভবিষ্ণু *adj* powerful; potent; influential; prominent; predominant; distinguished; excelling. **~তা** *n* power; potency; influence; prominence; predominance; distinction; excellence.

প্রভা *n* light; splendour; radiance; beautiful appearance; glow; brightness; lustre. **~কর** *n* 1 the sun. 2 the moon. **~কীট** *n* fire-fly; glow-worm. **~বান** *adj* luminous; radiant; splendid; glowing; shining. **~বতী** *fem.* **~মণ্ডল** *n* circle/crown of rays. **~ময়** *adj* consisting of light; radiant; luminous; splendid. **~ময়ী** *fem.*

প্রভাত *n* daybreak; dawn; morning; sunrise. **~ হওয়া** *vi* dawn; (of day/dawn) break: ~ হয়েছে. It is already day. **~কাল** *n* morning; rack of dawn; break of day; time of daybreak. **~চারণ, ~ফেরি** *nn* morning procession of people singing awakening songs. **~তপন** *n* morning sun; newly risen sun. **~রাগ** *n* morning glow.

প্রভাতি, প্রভাতী *adj* of the morning; (attrib) morning: ~ অনুষ্ঠান, morning ceremony/ programme. ❑*n* morning song.

প্রভাব *n* influence; authority; sway; might; power; strength; dignity; majesty; splendour; dominance; weight; prestige. **~ খাটানো/ বিস্তার করা** *vi* influence; exert one's influence/ authority; extend (the sphere of) one's influence; use one's influence with. **~ক, ~শালী, ~সম্পন্ন** *adjj* influential; having power/influence; prominent. **~শালিনী, ~সম্পন্না** *fem.* **~বলয়** *n* sphere of influence. **~মণ্ডল** *n* 1 surrounding influence. 2=~ বলয়. **প্রভাবে** *adv* by means/in consequence of; through.

প্রভাবান্বিত *adj* influenced; (rare) influential.

প্রভাবিত *adj* influenced. **~ করা** *vt* influence.

প্রভিন্ন *adj* split asunder; cleft; broken; pierced; opened; blown (as flowers).

প্রভু *n* 1 master; lord; overlord. 2 king. 3 God. 4 holy/revered man. 5 owner; employer. 6 husband. 7 boss; chief; leader. **~তা, ~ত্ব** *nn* lordship; dominion; supremacy; mastery; overlordship; authority; sovereignty; rule; might; power over. **~ত্ব করা** *vi* lord it over; dominate; hold sway over; rule(over); control the affairs of; be in charge of; govern; reign; have authority over. **~ত্বকারী** *adj* domineering; masterful; dictatorial; bullying; browbeating. **~ত্বব্যঞ্জক, ~সূচক** *adjj* authoritative; domineering; imperious; bossy; peremptory; masterful; dominating. **~পত্নী** *n, fem* master's wife; mistress. **~পরায়ণ, ~ভক্ত** *adjj* devoted/ faithful to one's master; loyal. **~ভক্তি** *n* devotion/faithfulness to one's master; loyalty. **~শক্তি** *n* dominance; ruling power; dominion; authority to rule; effective control.

প্রভূত *adj* ascendant; much; profuse; numerous; considerable; great; high; plentiful.

প্রভৃতি *pron* and other similar things; et cetera; etc; and the rest; and so on.

প্রভেদ *n*1 difference; distinction; discrimination. 2 variety; division; subdivision; species. **~ করা** *vi* differentiate; distinguish; discriminate; separate. **~ক** *adj* differential.

প্রভ্রষ্ট *adj* fallen down.

প্রমগ্ন *adj* immersed; dipped; drowned.

প্রমত্ত *adj* 1 excited; wanton; lascivious; rutting: ~ হস্তী. 2 drunken; intoxicated; inebriate; tipsy; besotted. 3 passionate; inflamed; headstrong; furious; turbulent; mad; insane; frenzied. 4 inattentive; careless; heedless; negligent; forgetful of; blundering; reckless. violent; stormy; raging; ferocious: ~ নদী. **প্রমত্তা** *fem.* **~চিত্ত** *adj* careless; heedless; inattentive; negligent. **~তা** *n* 1 excitement; wantonness; lasciviousness. 2 drunkenness; intoxication; inebriety; inebriation; tipsiness. 3 madness; insanity; frenzy; passion; vehemence. 4 carelessness; negligence; inattentiveness; forgetfulness. 5 recklessness; blunder. 6 violence; fury; turbulence; vehemence: নদীর/ঝড়ের ~তা. 7 infatuation.

প্রমথ *n* (myth) name of a class of demons attending on Shiva (শিব); trampling; routing;

প্রমথন *n* 1 harassing; tormenting; destroying; killing. 2 agitating; churning.

প্রমথিত *adj* 1 well churned. 2 harassed; injured; tormented; trampled; routed; killed.

প্রমথেশ *n* lord of the Pramathas (প্রমথ); Shiva.

প্রমদ *n* joy; pleasure; delight. ❑*adj* 1 wanton; dissolute. 2 mad; intoxicated. **প্রমদা** *n, fem* young and wanton woman; woman.

প্রমা *n* true knowledge; correct notion; truth.

প্রমাই *n* (dial)=পরমায়ু

প্রমাণ *n* **1** proof; evidence; testimony; witness. **2** authority. **3** right measure; standard: ~ সাইজ. **4** conviction. **5** precedent. **6** (mech) experiment. **7** (arith) test. ❑*adj* **1** of the standard size; standard: ~ সাইজ চাদর. **2** (phys) normal: ~ প্রেষ. **3** as big as: পর্বত~, colossal; gigantic: পর্বত~ ভুল, tremendous bloomer. ~ **করা** *vt* prove; establish; vindicate; substantiate; demonstrate; afford proof/ authority. ~ **দেওয়া** *vi* give evidence/ proof of; produce evidence; demonstrate; testify to; document; attest; put forward as proof. ~ **হওয়া** *vi* be proved/ established/ demonstrated/ vindicated/ justified/ conformed. ~**ক** *n* voucher. ~**গ্রন্থ** *n* authoritative book. ~**ত** *adv* according to proof/evidence/authority. ~ **দৃষ্টে** *adv* on the evidence of. ~**পঞ্জি** *n* bibliography. ~**পত্র** *n* **1** documents; written evidence; papers; documentation. **2** testimony; certificate; credentials. **3** voucher; receipt. **4** written warrant; affidavit. ~**বাক্য** *n* authoritative statement/ saying; authority. ~**সই**, ~**সহি** *adjj* of normal/ standard size; middling. ~**সাপেক্ষ** *adj* subject to proof; yet to be proved. ~**সিদ্ধ** *adj* established; authoritative; proved.

প্রমাণাভাব *n* want of evidence/proof.

প্রমাণিত *adj* proved; established; vindicated; shown clearly; demonstrated; substantiated. ~ **হওয়া**=প্রমাণ হওয়া (⇒ প্রমাণ).

প্রমাণীকরণ *n* proving; vindication; establishing; substantiation; demonstration. **প্রমাণীকৃত** *adj* **1**=প্রমাণিত. **2** authenticated.

প্রমাতা *adj* proving; vindicating; demonstrating. ❑*n* one who proves/ vindicates/ demonstrates.

প্রমাতামহ *n* grandfather/ grand uncle of one's mother.; maternal great-grandfather. **প্রমাতামহী** *fem* maternal great-grandmother.

প্রমাথ *n* trampling; racking; tormenting; paining.

প্রমাথী *adj* trampling; routing; harassing; destroying. **প্রমাথিনী** *fem.*

প্রমাদ *n* **1** negligence; carelessness; inadvertance; oblivion. **2** error; mistake; blunder; bloomer. **3** madness; frenzy; insanity. **4** intoxication. **5** calamity; terrible danger/distress. ~**কৃত** *adj* inadvertent; done by mistake. ~**যুক্ত** *adj* mistaken; erroneous; wrongheaded. ~**শূন্য** *adj* free of error; accurate; unimpeachable.

প্রমাদিকা *n fem* deflowered girl; impudent/ careless woman.

প্রমাদী *adj* **1** negligent; careless; incautious. **2** drunken; intoxicated. **3** insane; mad.

প্রমারা *n* [Pg] a card game; primero.

প্রমিত *adj* **1** meted out; measured. **2** limited; moderate; little. **3** established; proved; ascertained. **4** standardized; standard: ~ ভাষা. **5** measuring: চারি হস্ত ~. ~ **করা** *vt* **1** standardize. **2** prove; ascertained. ~**করণ** *n* standardization. ~ **দ্রব** *n* standard solution.

প্রমিতি *n* **1** measure; moderation. **2** proof. **3** knowledge gained/ established by proof; true knowledge; correct notion. 4 conviction.

প্রমীত *adj* deceased; dead; immolated.

প্রমীলন *n* shutting the eyes; lassitude.

প্রমীলা *n* **1** drowsiness; lassitude; enervation. **2** name of a female character in the Ramayana.

প্রমীলিত *adj* one who has closed his eyes; closed.

প্রমুক্ত *adj* loosened; untied; released.

প্রমুখ *adj* **1** first; foremost; chief; principal; most excellent. **3** (used as a *suff*) having as foremost/ chief; headed/ preceded by; accompanied by/with; beginning with. ❑*n* commencement of a chapter.

প্রমুখাৎ *adj* from the mouth of; verbally from; by word of sb's mouth.

প্রমুদিত *adj* delighted; pleased; glad. **2** expanded; blown. ~**হৃদয়** *adj* delighted in heart.

প্রমুদ্রা *n* stamp.

প্রমূর্ত *adj* manifest; evident; embodied; incarnate.

প্রমৃষ্ট *adj* rubbed off; cleaned; polished.

প্রমেয় *adj* **1** to be measured; measurable. **2** to be ascertained/proved; provable. **3** insignificant; limited; small. **4** commensurable.

প্রমেহ *n* urinary disease; gonorrhoea; diabetes.

প্রমোচন *n* liberating from; release.

প্রমোদ *n* excessive joy; delight; gladness; merriment; pleasure; enjoyment; hilarity; frolic; entertainment; recreation. ~ **উদ্যান** *n* pleasure-garden. ~**ক** *adj* gladdening; pleasing; exhilarating. ~-**কানন** *n*=~-উদ্যান. ~**গৃহ** *n* pleasure house; recreation-room ~**তরী** *n* pleasure-craft. yacht; cruiser. ~**ন** *n* act of gladdening/ pleasing/ exhilarating/ entertaining/ delighting: চিত্ত~ন. ~ **নৃত্য** *n* joyous dancing; joyful dance. ~ **বন**=~ কানন. ~ **বাজার** *n* carnival. ~ **ভবন** *n* pleasure-place. ~**ভূমি** *n* playground; recreation ground; pleasure-ground. ~**ভ্রমণ** *n* pleasure-trip; cruise; pleasure cruising; promenade. ~**ভ্রমণ করা** *vi* go on a pleasure-trip; go on/for a cruise; promenade. ~**মত্ত** *adj* revelling; intoxicated with sensuous pleasure. ~**মদিরা** *n* rapturous merry-making/ pleasure/ amusements.

প্রমোদাগার=প্রমোদগৃহ (⇒ প্রমোদ)

প্রমোদিত *adj* delighted; rejoiced; pleased; entertained; amused; enchanted.

প্রমোদোদ্যান=প্রমোদ–উদ্যান (⇒ প্রমোদ)

প্রমোদী *adj* delighting; delightful; joyous; entertaining. প্রমোদিনী *fem.*

প্রমোহ, প্রমোহন *n* bewilderment; infatuation.

প্রমোহিত *adj* bewildered; infatuated.

প্রযত *adj* **1** piously disposed; intent on devotion; self-subdued; dutiful; careful; prudent. **2** ritually pure; holy; pious. **~মানস, প্রযতাত্মা** *adj* pious-minded; devout; ascetic.

প্রযত্ন *n* **1** persevering effort; continued exertion/ endeavour. **2** activity; action; act; active efforts. **3** great care; caution. **~ করা** *vi* strive; endeavour; exert oneself; devote/apply oneself to. **~শীল, ~বান** *adjj* assiduous; diligent; persevering. **~শীল হওয়া** *vi*=~ করা. **~ সহকারে** *adj* with special effort; zealously; diligently; carefully; perseveringly.

প্রযুক্ত *adj* **1** used; employed; practised; applied. **2** yoked; harnessed; attached. **3** uttered; pronounced; recited. **4** performed; done. **5** (used as a *suff)* due to; because of; caused by; for the sake of; actuated by; owing to: ভক্তি ~.

প্রযুক্তি *n* **1** setting in motion; employment; application. **2** technique. **3** impulse; motive. **~ বিদ্যা** *n* technology. **~ বিদ্যাগত** *adj* technological.

প্রযুজ্যমান *adj* being applied.

প্রযুত *adj* mingled with; confused. ❑*n* million.

প্রযোক্তা *n* employer; applier; performer; undertaker.

প্রযোজক *adj*=প্রয়োজক. ❑*n* **1** producer; film-producer. **2** instigator; promoter.

প্রযোজ্য *adj* applicable; practical. **~তা** *n* applicability; practicality.

প্রয়াণ *n* **1** setting out; starting; advancing; progress; journey; march; invasion. **2** departure; death. **~ করা** *vi* **1** set out; go forth; advance towards/against; progress; proceed; go; repair. **2** pass away; vanish; die; depart. **~কাল** *n* time of departure; death.

প্রয়াত *adj* **1** set out; gone; advanced. **2** gone/passed away; deceased; dead; departed; vanished.

প্রয়াম *n* **1** checking; restraining. **2** extension; length. **3** scarcity; dearth.

প্রয়াস *n* exertion; effort; endeavour; pains; trouble; toil. **~ করা / পাওয়া** *vi* endeavour; labour; strive for/after; exert oneself; apply oneself; take (great) pains (to do sth); take trouble (to do sth).

প্রয়াসী *adj* **1** desirous of. **2** endeavouring; toiling hard; taking great pains. প্রয়াসিনী *fem.*

প্রয়োগ *n* **1** application; employment; use. **2** practice; experiment. **3** example; precedent; usage; mention; usual form. **~ করা** *vt* employ; use; apply. **~ত** *adj* according to usage/ practice. **~দোষ** *n* misapplication; wrong/unjust use. **~বাদ** *n* pragmatism. **~বাদী** *adj* pragmatic. ❑*n* pragmatist. **~বিন্দু** *n* (phys) point of application. **~যোগ্য** *adj* applicable. **~শালা** *n* laboratory. **~শালা সহায়ক** *n* laboratory assistant. প্রয়োগে *adv* by means of.

প্রয়োগিক *adj* **1** empirical. **2** practical; (attrib) utility: ~ মূল্য, utility value.

প্রয়োজক *adj* employing; causing; applying; using; effecting; introducing; prompting; instigating. **~ ক্রিয়া** *n* causative verb.

প্রয়োজন *n* **1** need; necessity; requirement. **2** purpose; aim; end; object; motive; cause; occasion; use. **~ থাকা** *vi* need; require; be necessary. **প্রয়োজনাতিরিক্ত, প্রয়োজনাতীত** *adjj* more than what is necessary; more than enough; unnecessary; redundant; superfluous. **প্রয়োজনানুরূপ** *adj* satisfying needs; adequate; sufficient; just enough to meet (one's) requirement. **কী ~** what is the need/use of.

প্রয়োজনীয় *adj* necessary; needful; useful; serviceable. **~তা** *n* **1**=প্রয়োজন. **2** usefulness; serviceability.

প্ররূঢ় *adj* grown up; full-grown.

প্ররোচক *adj* inciting; exciting; inducing; instigating; persuading; seductive. ❑*n* inducer; instigator; provoker; abettor.

প্ররোচন *n* act of exciting/ inciting/ inducing. instigation.

প্ররোচনা *n* instigation; inducement; incitement; motivation; provocation; encouragement; stimulation; seduction. **~ দেওয়া** *vt* instigate; induce; incite; motivate; provoke; encourage; excite; stimulate; seduce. **~দায়ক** *adj*=প্ররোচক. **~মূলক** *adj* provocative; seductive.

প্ররোচিত *adj* instigated; incited; induced; motivated; provoked; encouraged; excited; persuaded. **~ করা**=প্ররোচনা দেওয়া (⇒ প্ররোচনা).

প্ররোহ *n* **1** shoot; bud; sprout; twig. **2** excrescence. **3** sprouting; germinating; growing/ shooting forth.

প্ররোহী *adj* growing/shooting up.

প্রলপন *n* prattling; talking; delirium; babbling; raving.

প্রলপিত *adj* **1** prattling. **2** spoken; uttered; said; spoken dolefully; uttered incoherently. **3** babbled. ❑*n*=প্রলাপ.

প্রলম্ব *n* **1** branch/aerial root of a tree. **2** shoot of the vine-palm. **3** anything hanging/ creeping pendant. **~তা** *n* hanging down; being pendulous. **~ন** *n* **1** hanging down; depending. **2** prolongation. **3** projection. **~ বাহু** *adj* having hanging arms.

প্রলম্বিত *adj* **1** hanging down; pendulous; pendent; suspended. **2** creeping. **3** prolonged. **4** projected. **~ করা** *vt* hang; suspend; prolong; project.

প্রলম্বী *adj* hanging down.

প্রলয় *n* **1** (universal) dissolution/annihilation; destruction; reabsorption; holocaust; upheaval. **2** terrible disturbance; commotion; death and destruction; cataclysm; apocalypse. **~কাণ্ড**= ~. **~কাল** *n* time of universal dissolution/ annihilation. **~ক্রীড়া**=~. **প্রলয়ংকর, ~ঙ্কর** *adj* causing (universal) destruction; destructive; ruinous; tumultuous; uproarious; cataclysmic; disastrous; catastrophic. **প্রলয়ংকরী** *fem*. **~ পবন** *n* cataclysmic storm. **~ পয়োধী** *n* the ocean of universal annihilation/ cataclysm. **~ মেঘ** *n* cataclysmic cloud; cloud which causes the destruction of the world. **~ লক্ষণ** *n* portents of disaster/ coming upheavals. **~লীলা**=~.

প্রলয়াঙ্ককার *n* gloom of universal dissolution/ destruction.

প্রলাপ *n* incoherent/delirious speech; raving; delirium; stuff and nonsense; rubbish; twaddle; claptrap; poppycock. **~ বকা** *vi* rave; be delirious; blather on.

প্রলাপী *adj* raving; delirious; blathering. **প্রলাপিনী** *fem*.

প্রলিপ্ত *adj* **1** cleaving/ sticking to; coated/ smeared with. **2** engaged/ employed in. **3** implicated/ involved in.

প্রলীন *adj* **1** dissolved; disappeared; lost; dead. **2** fainted; unconscious; insensible.

প্রলুব্ধ *adj* seduced; allured; tempted; enticed; covetous; very greedy. **~তা** *n* greediness covetousness; cupidity; greed; temptation; allurement. **~ হওয়া** *vi* be tempted/ allured; lust after; be lustful; follow one's lusts.

প্রলেপ *n* **1** anointing; coating; smearing. **2** ointment; unguent; salve; plaster. **~ দেওয়া** *vi* smear on/over sth/sb; apply a coating/ ointment (to); coat; plaster. **~ক** *adj* coating; anointing; smearing; plastering. **~ন**=~ (1). **~ন করা** *vi* smear on/ over; coat with.

প্রলোভ *n* strong greed; covetousness; allurement; seduction. **~ন** *n* **1** temptation; allurement; enticement; seduction. **2** tempting object; temptation; inducement; lure; bait. **~ন দেখানো** *vi* try to allure/ tempt/ seduce/ allure; attempt to seduce; entice.

প্রলোভিত *adj* allured; enticed; tempted; seduced. **~ করা** *vt* allure; entice; seduce; tempt. **~ করে নিয়ে যাওয়া** *vi* entice away; seduce.

প্রশংসক *n* one who speaks highly of; praiser; extoller; acclaimer; admirer.

প্রশংসন *n* praising; commending; extolling; acclaiming.

প্রশংসনীয় *adj* to be praised; praiseworthy; laudable; commendable; admirable.

প্রশংসা *n* praise; commendation; acclamation; acclaim; applause; compliment; admiration; glorification; eulogy; celebration; extolment; fame. **~ করা** *vt* praise; commend; acclaim; compliment; admire; glorify; extol; laud; celebrate. **~পত্র** *n* certificate of merit commendation; (written) address of honour/ felicitation. **~বাক্য, ~বাদ** *nn* compliment; eulogy; commendation. **~ব্যঞ্জক**=~সূচক. **~ভাজন** *adj*=~ই ❑*n* object of praise; praiseworthy/ admirable person. **~মুখর** *adj* loud with praise; praising loudly; admiring; acclaiming; extolling. **~মূলক**=~সূচক. **~ই** *adj* praiseworthy; laudable; commendable. **~সূচক** *adj* laudatory; commending; eulogistic; flattering; admiring.

প্রশংসিত *adj* praised; commended; extolled; applauded; acclaimed; glorified; celebrated. **প্রশংসিতা** *fem*.

প্রশম *n* **1** calmness; tranquillity; quiet; rest. **2** cessation; extinction; abatement; alleviation; **3** mitigation; pacification. **~ক** *adj* allaying; quenching; mitigating; tranquillizing; pacifying; alleviating. ❑*n* one who brings to rest; pacifier; tranquillizer. **~ন** *n* **1** act of tranquillizing/ pacifying/ curing/ healing/ alleviating/ allaying/ mitigating/ soothing. **2** act of restraining/ quelling/ quenching/ dissuasion. **3** neutralization. **~ন করা** *vt* **1** pacify; soothe; allay; alleviate; tranquillize; mitigate; calm; appease; stop. **2** restrain; dissuade; check; quell; subdue. **3** neutralize. **~ লবণ** *n* (chem) neutral salt.

প্রশমিত *adj* **1** tranquillized; calmed; relieved; quelled; soothed; quenched; allayed; alleviated; mitigated. **2** pacified; dissuaded; checked; stopped; restrained; resisted; subdued. **3** neutralized. **~ করা**=প্রশমন করা.

প্রশস্ত *adj* **1** extensive; wide; broad: ~ রাস্তা. **2** spacious; capacious; roomy; large; commodious: ~ কামরা. **3** magnanimous; liberal; broad; open; large; generous; big: ~ হৃদয়. **4** auspicious: ~ ক্ষণ. **5** most suitable; fittest; most convenient/ appropriate; right: ~ উপায়. **6** commendable; happy; praiseworthy; best; excellent. **7** praised; commended. **~চিত্ত, ~মনা, ~হৃদয়, প্রশস্তান্তঃকরণ** *adjj* large-hearted; broad-minded; generous; magnanimous; big-hearted; open-hearted. **~তা** *n* **1** width; breadth; spaciousness; capacity; extent; capaciousness; spaciousness; roominess; largeness. **2** fitness; propriety; suitability. **3** auspiciousness. **4** broadness; magnanimity; excellence; goodness/generosity; liberality; largeness.

প্রশস্তি *n* **1** praise; glorification; fame; encomium; panegyric; eulogy; benediction; homage; accolade; plaudit; exaltation. **2** hymn of praise. ~ **করা** *vi* sing sb's praises; glorify; eulogize; bestow praise upon; extol; laud; pay tribute to; applaud.

প্রশস্য *adj* very praiseworthy/ commendable/ laudable.

প্রশাখা *n* small branch; offshoot.

প্রশান্ত *adj* tranquil; very calm/ quiet; composed; serene; unperturbed; unruffled; tranquilized; peaceful; at rest/ place; self-collected; sedate; equanimous. ~ **চিত্ত** *n* peaceful/ serene mind/ heart. ❑*adj* peaceful; enjoying peace/ composed in mind; tranquillity at heart; calm; self-composed; sedate; serene. ~**তা**=প্রশান্তি. ~ **দৃষ্টি** *n* serene look. ❑*adj* having a serene look. ~ **বদন** *n* serene/calm face. ❑*adj* having a serene/ tranquil face/ appearance; of tranquil/ serene/ composed appearance. ~ **মহাসাগর** *n* the Pacific (Ocean). ~ **মূর্তি**= ~ বদন. ~ **স্বর** *n* quiet / gentle/ serene voice. ~ **স্বরে** *adv* in a quiet/ gentle/ serene voice. ~ **হৃদয়**=~চিত্ত . ~ **হৃদয়ে** *adv* calmly; peacefully; serenely; tranquilly; with unruffled calm.

প্রশাসক *n* administrator.

প্রশাসন *n* administration; government; rule.

প্রশাসিত *adj* administered; governed; ruled.

প্রশিষ্য *n* pupil of a pupil; disciple of a disciple. **প্রশিষ্যা** *fem.*

প্রশ্ন *n* **1** question; interrogation; query; inquiry (after). **2** subject of inquiry; point at issue; problem; disputed issue; controversy; controverted point. **3** task. ~ **করা** *vi* **1** ask; question; interrogate; inquire (about); ask (after); demand. **2** set questions/ paper: ইতিহাসের প্রশ্ন কে করেছেন? who set the history paper? ~**কর্তা** *n* **1** questioner; inquirer; interrogator. **2** one who sets questions/ paper; paper-setter; setter of an examination paper. ~**কর্ত্রী** *fem.* ~**পত্র** *n* set of examination questions; (examination) paper. ~**পূর্বক** *adv* questioningly. ~ **বাণ** *n* a volley of (embarrassing/ troublesome) questions. ~ **বাণে জর্জরিত করা** *vt* badger sb with (embarrassing/ troublesome) questions; heckle. ~ **মালা** *n* **1** set of questions. **2** exercise.

প্রশ্নোত্তর *n* question and answer.

প্রশ্নোত্তরী *n* catechism.

প্রশ্রয় *n* **1** indulgence; permissiveness; pamper; too much latitude. **2** affection respect. ~ **দেওয়া** *vi* indulge; pamper; allow sb too much latitude; humour; cosset; kill sb with kindness; pander to; spoil. ~ **পাওয়া** *vi* be indulged/ pampered; find favour with sb; be treated with kindness/ affection; find a great support in sb; be supported by. ~**দাতা** *adj* indulgent; pampering. ❑*n* one who indulges; indulger. ~**দান** *n* pampering; indulging; indulgence. ~**প্রাপ্ত** *adj* **1** indulged; pampered; spoilt. **2** enjoying the favour/ support of.

প্রশ্রিত *adj*=প্রশ্রয়প্রাপ্ত (⇒ প্রশ্রয়)

প্রশ্বাস *n* breathing; inhaling.

প্রষ্টব্য *adj* to be asked.

প্রসক্ত *adj* **1** attached to; enamoured of/with; being in love; devoted to; strongly addicted to. **2** cleaving/adhering to; attached to. **3** fixed/intent on; engaged on; occupied with. ~ **চিত্ত**, ~ **হৃদয়** *adj* with heart/mind intent on/occupied with; being in love.

প্রসক্তি *n* attachment; devotion/addiction to; indulgence/perseverance in; occupation with; adherence.

প্রসঙ্গ *n* **1** context. **2** subject for/under discussion; topic for discussion. **3** occasion; circumstance; conjuncture. **4** connection; relevance. ~ **উল্লেখপূর্বক** *adv* with reference to the context. ~**কথা** *n* subject-matter; foreword. ~ **ক্রমে**, ~**ত** *adv* by the by; by the way; incidentally; in course of discussion; in this context/connection. **প্রসঙ্গান্তর** *n* another/a different topic. **প্রসঙ্গে** *adv* in connection with.

প্রসঞ্জন *n* **1** attaching; uniting; combining; connecting. **2** mention; mentioning; reference.

প্রসত্তি=প্রসন্নতা (⇒ প্রসন্ন)

প্রসন্ন *adj* **1** pleased; gracious; soothed; kind; kindly disposed towards; propitious; propitiated; favourable. **2** delighted; satisfied; glad; happy; pleasing. **3** clear; bright; pure; limpid; transparent: ~ আকাশ, ~ সলিল. **4** calm; complacent. **প্রসন্না** *fem.* ~ **করা** *vt* placate; appease; propitiate; pacify; mollify; please; pander to. ~ **হওয়া** *vi* **1** grow clear and bright; become placid and tranquil: আকাশ/ সাগর ~ হয়েছে. **2** become satisfied/pleased/ glad; be gracious/kind; be appeased/ pacified/ placated/ propitiated/ mollified. **3** smile on: ভাগ্য ~ হয়েছে. ~ **চিত্ত** *n* contented/ cheerful mind; serene/ peaceful mind. ❑*adj* cheerful; at peace (with oneself); unperturbed; composed. ~**চিত্তে** *adv* gladly; readily; with (a) good grace; willingly; freely; cheerfully. ~**তা** *n* **1** brightness; clearness; purity; clarity; limpidity. **2** serenity; complacence; good humour; graciousness; calmness; composure. **3** clearness of expression; perspicacity. **4** suspiciousness; propitiousness; favourableness. ~ **মুখ** *n* serene/smiling face. ❑*adj* smiling; looking pleased; glad. ~ **মুখে** *adv* smilingly; with (a) good grace; cheerfully. ~ **সলিল** *n* clear/limpid water. ❑*adj* containing clear/limpid water.

প্রসব *n* **1** childbirth; childbearing; parturition; bringing forth; confinement; delivery. **2** creation; production; birth. **3** procreation. **4** offspring. ~ **করা** *vi* **1** give birth (to); bring forth; bear (a child); be delivered of (a child). **2** (of a cow) calve. **3** (facet) produce. ~ **করানো** *vi* help a mother to give birth to (a child); deliver a woman. ~ **হওয়া** *vi* be delivered of a child/young. ~**কাল** *n* time of delivery; confinement; labour. ~**বেদনা,** ~**ব্যথা** *nn* pangs of childbirth; throes of labour. ~**বেদনা ওঠা** *vi* begin/go into / be in labour. ~**মাস** *n* last month of pregnancy.

প্রসবিতা *adj* bringing forth; producing; begetting. ❑*n* father; progenitor; begetter; producer. **প্রসবিত্রী** *fem n* mother; progenitress; (female) producer.

প্রসবিনী=প্রসবিনী (⇒ প্রসবিতা)

প্রসবী=প্রসবিতা

প্রসভ *adj* forcibly; violently. ~**হরণ** *n* carrying of by force; violent seizure.

প্রসর *n* **1** going forwards; advance; progress; free course. **2** spreading; extension; diffusion; range; expanse. **3** speed. **4** prevalence; influence. ~**ণ** *n* **1** going forth; running away; escaping. **2** strolling. **3** spreading over the country to forage. **4**=প্রসারণ (⇒ প্রসার). **উষ্ণতার** ~*,n* (geog) range of temperature.

প্রসর্পণ *n* **1** going forwards; entering. **2** strolling. **3**=প্রসারণ.

প্রসর্পিত *adj* **1** crawling along. **2**=প্রসারিত.

প্রসর্পী *adj* coming forth; issuing from.

প্রসহ *adj* enduring; withstanding. ❑*n* bird/beast of prey. ~**ন** *n* resistance; endurance.

প্রসাদ *n* **1** favour; graciousness; kindness; kind behaviour; aid; mediation. **2** serenity of disposition; good humour. **3** calmness; tranquillity; absence of excitement. **4** (also ~**গুণ**) clearness of style; perspicacity; lucidity. **5** free gift; gratuity: রাজার ~. **6** propitiatory offering/gift; food presented to an idol; remnants of food left by a spiritual teacher. ~ **দেওয়া** *vt* **1** give sb one's blessing; favour sb with sth; bestow as a mark of favour; bestow graciously; present (with). **2** give sb a portion of the propitiatory offering/remands of food left by a spiritual teacher. ~ **নেওয়া** *vi*=~ পাওয়া (2). ~ **পাওয়া** *vi* **1** find favour with sb; win sb's favour; be in sb's good graces. **2** partake of the food offered to an idol/the remnants of food left by a spiritual teacher. ~**দান** *n* propitiatory offering; gift in token of favour; gift of food by a superior. ~**ন** *n* **1** clearing; rendering clear. **2** calming; soothing; cheering; pleasing; gratifying; rendering gracious; propitiating; propitiation. ~**পত্র** *n* deed of gift. ~**পাত্র** *n* object of favour; favourite. ~ **প্রার্থনা** *n* **1** seeking/ asking a favour of sb. **2** asking for partaking of the food offered to an idol/remnants of food left by a superior. ~**প্রার্থী** *n, adj* **1** (one) who asks for/seek a favour. **2** (one) desirous of partaking of the food offered to an idol/remnants of food left by a superior. **প্রসাদপ্রার্থিনী** *fem.* ~**ভাজন**=~**পাত্র.** ~**ভোজী** *adj* **1** living on the food offered to an idol/remnants of food left by a superior. **2** (fig) living on charity. ❑*n* hanger-on.

প্রসাদাৎ *adv* thanks to; by the favour of; because of sb/sth.

প্রসাদিত *adj* **1** pleased; conciliated; propitiated. **2** cleared; rendered clear.

প্রসাদী *adj* **1** (of food, etc) offered to an idol. **2** left by a superior.

প্রসাধক *adj* adorning; beautifying; embellishing. ❑*n* beautician; dresser; decorator. **প্রসাধিকা** *fem.*

প্রসাধন *n* embellishment; decoration; beautification. **2** make-up; toilet; dressing. ~ **করা** *vi* **1** make up; wear make-up; paint one's face; make oneself up; dress up. **2** embellish; decorate; adorn; beautify.

প্রসাধনী *n* cosmetics; toiletries; toilet articles; make-up.

প্রসাধিত *adj* dressed up; painted; decorated; embellished; adorned

প্রসার *n* **1** spreading/stretching out. **2** extension; extent; expanse; width. **3** spread; diffusion: শিক্ষার ~. ~**ণ** *n* **1**= ~. **2** extending; expansion; spreading. **3** displaying. **4** increase; development; augmentation. **5** (phys) dilatation; dilation. ~ **করা**=প্রসারিত করা. **প্রসারাঙ্ক** (phys) co-efficient of expansion/ dilation.

প্রসারিত *adj* **1** held forth; stretched out; extended: ~ হস্ত. **2** expanded; spread (out); diffused. **3** displayed; exposed; laid out; exhibited. ~ **করা** *vt* **1** extend; stretch (out); spread (out). **2** diffuse; circulate; spread. **3** display; exhibit; lay out; expose. **4** be wide open. **5** (phys) dilate. ~ **হওয়া** *vi* **1** spread; extend; stretch. **2** be spread/ diffused. **3** be displayed/ exposed.

প্রসারী *adj* extending (over); expanding; stretching; extensive; expansive; wide. **প্রসারিণী** *fem.* **সুদূর~** *adj* far-reaching; far-flung; widely extended.

প্রসার্য *adj* to be extended/ stretched out; extensible; stretchy; expansive. ~**মাণ** *adj* expanding; stretching; extending.

প্রসিক্ত *adj* sprinkled with; moistened; thoroughly wet.

প্রসিদ্ধ *adj* famous; well-known; celebrated; renowned; reputed; notorious. **প্রসিদ্ধা** *fem.*

প্রসিদ্ধি *n* **1** fame; celebrity; renown; reputation; notoriety. **2** general opinion; rumour.

প্রসীদ *vt imp* be pleased: ~ নগনন্দিনী.

প্রসুপ্ত *adj* **1** fallen into sleep; fast asleep; sleeping; slumbering. **2** quiet; inactive; latent. **3** (of flowers) closed. ~ **থাকা** *vi* **1** be fast/sound asleep; slumber. **2** be latent.

প্রসুপ্তি *n* sound sleeping; sleepiness; slumber.

প্রসূ *adj* (used chiefly as a *suff)* bringing forth; bearing; giving birth to; productive (of); producing; fruitful. □*n* mother; progenitress. ~**ত** *adj* **1** procreated; brought forth; begotten; born. **2** produced (of); resulted (from); born (of); evolved (out of). ~**তা** *fem.*

প্রসূতি *n fem* **1** mother; progenitress. **3** woman recently delivered of her child. **3** woman in confinement. ~**তন্ত্র** *n* midwifery. ~ **সদন** *n* maternity ward/ hospital.

প্রসূন *n* flower; blossom. □*adj* born; produced.

প্রসৃত *adj* **1** come forth; issued from; emerged from. **2** held/stretched out. **3** widened; expanded; extended; extending over. **4** wide-spreading. ~ **হওয়া** *vi* emerge (from); widen; expand; stretch out.

প্রসৃতি *n* **1** act of streaming/ flowing; emergence; issuing. **2** extension; diffusion; spreading. **3** width.

প্রসেক *n* sprinkling; wetting.

প্রস্ত *n* **1** set: এক ~ চায়ের কাপ. **2** suit: এক ~ পোশাক. **3** wad: এক ~ নোট. **4** copy. **5** spell: এক ~ তর্কাতর্কি.

প্রস্তর *n* **1** rock; stone; pebble; boulder. **2** fossil. **3** gem; jewel; stone. ~**খণ্ড** *n* piece of stone. ~ **তত্ত্ব** *n* paleontology. ~**তত্ত্বজ্ঞ**, ~**তত্ত্ববেত্তা** *nn* paleontologist. ~**তুল্য** *adj* stone-like; stony; unfeeling; motionless. ~**নির্মিত** *adj* built/made of stone; stony. ~**ফলক** *n* stone slab; slab of rock. ~ **বেদিকা** *n* stone altar. ~**ময়** *adj* stony; rocky; made of stone. ~ **মূর্তি** *n* stone statue. ~ **মূর্তিবৎ** *adj* like a stone statue; statuesque; maintaining a stony silence. ~ **যুগ** *n* stone age.

প্রস্তরীভবন *n* fossilization; petrifaction.

প্রস্তরীভূত *adj* transformed into stone; petrified; fossilized.

প্রস্তাব *n* **1** proposal; suggestion. **2** motion. **3** subject for/under discussion; topic. **4** context; discourse. **5** (of a book) chapter; section. ~ **করা** *vi* **1** propose; put forward for consideration; suggest; put forward a proposal. **2** propose sb for sth; propose sb as sth: সভাপতির পদে নাম ~ করা. **3** propose/move a motion. ~ **তোলা** *vi* raise a topic; propose; propose/move a motion. ~**ক** *n* proposer; mover (of a motion). ~**না** *n* **1** proposal. **2** introduction; beginning; commencement; preface. **3** dramatic prologue.

প্রস্তাবিকা *n* prospectus.

প্রস্তাবিত *adj* proposed; mentioned; suggested; under discussion; in question; raised/moved (as a topic).

প্রস্তুত *adj* **1** made; ready; prepared; manufactured; formed. 2 proposed; propounded; introduced as a topic/subject; under discussion; commenced; begun. ~ **করা** *vt* make; prepare; form; manufacture; make ready; groom. ~ **হওয়া** *vi* be made/ manufactured/ prepared/ formed; be ready; get ready. ~-**প্রণালী** *n* recipe (for sth); instructions for preparing sth; formula.

প্রস্তুতি *n* **1** preparation; readiness. **2** making; manufacture; formation.

প্রস্তৃত *adj* spread out; extended.

প্রস্থ[1] *n* **1** width; breadth. **2** expanse; extent. **3** table-land on the top of a mountain; plateau. **4** level expanse; plain: ইন্দ্র~. ~**চ্ছেদ** *n* (math) cross-section.

প্রস্থ[2]=প্রস্ত

প্রস্থান *n* **1** going out; departure. **2** exit. **2** march; journey. **3** course; method; system; school (of thought). ~ **করা** *vi* set out; go off; depart (from); proceed/march to; leave; quit; go out; withdraw; make one's departure; take leave.

প্রস্থানোদ্যত *adj* on the point of going out/ departing; ready to go/leave; departing.

প্রস্থানোদ্যোগ *n* preparation/readiness for departure.

প্রস্থানোন্মুখ *adj* eager to leave/depart.

প্রস্থাপন *n* causing to depart; sending away; dismissing; dispatching.

প্রস্থাপিত *adj* sent away; dismissed; dispatched.

প্রস্থায়ী *adj* setting forth; departing; marching; outgoing.

প্রস্থিত *adj* **1** set forth; gone off; set out; departed. **2** standing forth; prominent.

প্রস্ফুট *adj* **1** cleft open; burst; expanded; blown; full-blown; in (full) bloom. **2** open; evident; clear; fully revealed/manifested/ unfolded. ~**ন** *n* splitting; bursting; opening; expanding; blossoming; blowing.

প্রস্ফুটিত=প্রস্ফুট. **প্রস্ফুটিতা** *fem.* ~ **হওয়া** *vi* burst open; open fully; blow; split.

প্রস্ফুরণ *n* **1** slight vibration/tremor; quiver; vibration; throb. **2** sparkle; glitter; flash; phosphorescence; effervescence. ~**শীল** *adj* **1** quivering; tremulous; slightly vibrating/ trembling; throbbing. **2** sparkling; glittering; flashing; effervescent.

প্রস্ফুরিত *adj* **1** become tremulous; quivering; vibrating; tremulous. **2** trembled; vibrated. **3** glittering; sparkling. ~ **হওয়া** *vi* **1** become tremulous; quiver; palpitate; tremble/vibrate slightly; throb. **2** glitter; flash; sparkle; shine forth; effervesce. স্ফুরিতাধর *adj* one whose lower lip quivers.

প্রস্ফোটন=প্রস্ফুটন (⇒ প্রস্ফুট)

প্রস্রব *n* flowing forth; stream; flow; gush; oozing; trickling.

প্রস্রবণ *n* **1**=প্রস্রব. **2** fountain; spring. অন্ত ~ *n* underground spring. উপরি ~ *n* surface spring. উষ্ণ ~ *n* geyser; hot spring. গর্ভোত্থ-~ *n* deep-seated spring. ধাতব ~ *n* mineral spring. সবিরাম ~ *n* intermittent spring.

প্রস্রাব *n* urine; urination; (sl) piss. ~ করা *vi* urinate; pass urine; make/pass water; (sl) piss; have/ go for a piss. প্রস্রাবের পীড়া *n* urinary disease.

প্রস্রুত *adj* flowed forth; oozed out; issued; trickled; dripped. ~ হওয়া *vi* flow forth/from; ooze; trickle; drip.

প্রস্বাপন *adj* opiate; soporific.

প্রস্বেদ *n* great/ excessive perspiration; sweat.

প্রহত *adj* **1** struck; beaten; injured ; hurt; wounded. **2** slain; killed.

প্রহর *n* division of time (about 3 hours); the eighth part of a day; watch. ~ গোনা *vi* **1** idle away the hours. **2** bear one's sufferings patiently. **3** bide one's time. প্রহরার্ধ *n* one and half hours.

প্রহরণ *n* **1** weapon. **2** striking; beating; pecking; attack; combat.

প্রহরা *n* **1** watching; guarding; watch. **2** watchman; guard; sentry; watch; watcher; sentinel; guardsman. **3** custody; escort: পুলিশ ~. ~ দেওয়া *vi* guard; watch (over) sb/sth; protect sb/sth; keep watch (for sb/sth); stand guard (over sb/sth). ~রত *adj* engaged in guarding/ watching; on watch; watchful; keeping guard; on guard. প্রহারাধীন *adj* under (close) guard.

প্রহরী *n* guard; watchman; watcher; bellman; sentry; guardsman. প্রহরিণী *fem.*

প্রহর্তা *n* assailant; combatant; warrior.

প্রহর্ষণ *adj* causing erection of the hair of the body; enrapturing; delighting; thrilling.

প্রহসন *n* **1** laughter; mirth; mockery; derision. **2** farce; joke; banter. কিছু/কাউকে নিয়ে ~ করা make a farce of; make fun of; make sport of.

প্রহসিত *adj* laughing; cheerful.

প্রহার *n* striking; hitting; beating; blow; stroke; thump; knock. ~ করা *vt* strike; beat; thrash; hit; attack; assail; hurt. ~ দেওয়া *vi* give sb a thrashing/beating/ licking; beat; knock out.

প্রহারী *adj* striking; beating; hitting; smiting; attacking; assailing.

প্রহাস *n* (loud) laughter; derision; irony.

প্রহীন *adj* left; cast off; standing alone; worn out.

প্রহৃত *adj* struck; beaten; hit; wounded; hurt; smitten.

প্রহৃষ্ট *adj* erect; bristling (as the hair of the body); thrilled with delight; exceedingly pleased; delighted. ~চিত্ত, ~হৃদয় *adjj* delighted at heart; exceedingly glad. ~মুখ *adj* having a cheerful face; looking pleased.

প্রহেলিকা *n* enigma; riddle; puzzle; puzzling question; mystery. ~ময় *adj* enigmatic; puzzling; mysterious.

প্রহ্লাদ *n* **1** joyful excitement; delight; joy; happiness. **2** (myth) name of a pious demon. দৈত্যকুলে ~ (fig) a saint amongst infidels.

প্রাইজ [E] *n* prize.

প্রাইভেট [E] *adj* private. ~ টিউটর *n* private tutor.

প্রাইমারি [E] *adj* primary.

প্রাংশু *adj* **1** tall; towering; high; lofty: ~ বৃক্ষ. **2** long: ~ ভুজ. **3** strong; stout: ~ দেহ. ~লভ্য *adj* obtainable by a tall/great man; to be reached by a tall person.

প্রাক্‌ (in compound) *pref* denoting: directed towards/ forwards; being in front; facing opposite. ~কলন *n* estimate. ~কলনিক *n* estimator. ~কলিত *adj* estimated. ~কাল *n* former age/time; previous/preceding time; immediately preceding time; eve. ~কালিক, ~কালীন *adj* previous; former; ancient. ~কালে *adv* **1** on the eve of; before. **2** formerly.

প্রাকরণিক *adj* **1** belonging to the matter in question/a chapter. **2** technical.

প্রাকাম্য *n* freedom of will; wilfulness; irresistible will; fiat (one of the supernatural powers).

প্রাকার *n* wall; fence; rampart; surrounding wall; bulwark; enclosure; parapet. ~বেষ্টিত *adj* surrounded by a wall.

প্রাকৃত *adj* **1** original; natural; artless; normal; ordinary; usual; commonplace; general. **2** low; vulgar; unrefined; base; mean. **3** provincial; vernacular. **4** plebeian; popular. ❑*n* the Prakrit language (also ~ ভাষা). ~জন *n* the vulgar. ~ জ্বর *n* common fever. ~তত্ত্ব *n* natural philosophy. ~তত্ত্ব দর্শন *n* natural theology. ~ভূগোল *n* physical geography.

প্রাকৃতিক *adj* natural; physical; material; common; vulgar; elemental. ~ ইতিবৃত্ত *n* natural history. ~ দর্শন *n* natural philosophy. ~ দৃশ্য *n* natural scenery. ~ নিয়ম *n* law of nature; physical/natural law. ~ নির্বাচন *n* natural selection. ~ বিজ্ঞান *n* natural science. ~ বিপর্যয় *n* natural calamity. ~ ভূগোল *n* physical geography. ~ মানচিত্র *n* physical map.

প্রাক্কাল=প্রাককাল (⇒ প্রাক)

প্রাক্তন *adj* **1** prior; previous; preceding; former; old; ancient. **2** earned/ acquired/done in a previous birth; of a previous birth. ❑*n* (also ~ কর্ম) any act formerly done/ done in a former state of existence; fate; destiny. ~ জন্ম *n* former birth.

প্রাক্‌পরিচয় *n* **1** previous acquaintance. **2** antecedents.

প্রাক্‌প্রস্তর *adj* eolithic. ~ **যুগ** *n* eolithic age.

প্রাখর্য *n*=প্রখরতা (⇒ প্রখর)

প্রাগ্‌ *pref* (in compounds)=প্রাক্‌. ~-**জ্যোতিষ** *n* ancient name of Kamrup (কামরূপ). ~**দৃষ্ট** *adj* seen before.

প্রাগল্‌ভ্য=প্রগল্‌ভতা (⇒ প্রগল্‌ভ)

প্রাগাধুনিক *adj* eocene.

প্রাগাহ্নিক *adj* relating to the forenoon.

প্রাগুক্ত *adj* aforesaid; aforementioned.

প্রাগুদীচী *n* the north-east.

প্রাগৈতিহাসিক *adj* pre-historic.

প্রাগ্‌ভাব *n* non-existence of anything which may yet be; be not yet existing.

প্রাগ্র্য *adj* advanced; leading; chief.

প্রাগ্রসর *adj* advanced.

প্রাঙ্‌ *pref* (in compounds)=প্রাক্‌. ~**ন্যায়** *n* (in law) former trial of a cause. ~**মানব** *n* Neanderthal man. ~**মুখ** *adj* having the tip/face turned forward/eastward; facing east.

প্রাঙ্গণ *n* courtyard; yard; court; compound.

প্রাচী *n* the East; the Orient; the Eastern World. **দূর**~ *n* the Far East. **নিকট**~ *n* the Near East.

প্রাচীন *adj* **1** ancient; old; aged; antique; former; prior; preceding. **2** out-of-date; dated; old-fashioned; outmoded; antiquated; obsolete. **প্রাচীনা** *fem*. ~**তা**, ~**ত্ব** *n* oldness; antiquity; agedness; obsoleteness.

প্রাচীর *n* wall; enclosure; hedge; rampart; fence. ~ **চিত্রণ**, **প্রাচীরাঙ্কন** *n* wall painting. ~**বেষ্টিত** *adj* walled; enclosed with a wall.

প্রাচুর্য *n* abundance; plenty; affluence; profusion; multitude; numerousness; opulence; milk and honey.

প্রাচ্য *n* =প্রাচী. ❑*adj* eastern; easterly; oriental. ~ **দেশ** *n* eastern country; the East; the Orient. ~ **দেশীয়** *adj*=~. ~ **দেশবাসী** *adj* living in the East. ❑*n* inhabitant of the East; Oriental. ~ **দেশবাসিনী** *fem*. ~**বিদ্যা** *n* oriental learning; orientalism. ~**বিদ্যাবিশারদ** *n* orientalist. ~ **ভাষা** *n* oriental language. ~ **ভাষাবিদ** *n* orientalist.

প্রাচ্যামি *n* oriental chauvinism.

প্রাজন *n* goad.

প্রাজিতা *n* driver; coachman.

প্রাজাপত্য *adj* coming/derived from Prajapati (⇒ প্রজাপতি); sacred/related to Prajapati. ❑*n* a form of marriage (in which the father gives his daughter to the bridegroom without receiving a gift from him).

প্রাজ্ঞ *adj* wise; learned; prudent. **প্রাজ্ঞা**, **প্রাজ্ঞী** *fem*. ~**তা** *n* wisdom; learning; intelligence; prudence.

প্রাঞ্জল *n* lucid; plain; perspicuous; clear; transparent; limpid. ~**তা** *n* lucidity; perspicuity; clarity; transparency; limpidity.

প্রাণ *n* **1** life. **2** breath of life; breath; respiration. **3** spirit; life and soul: তিনিই এই সংগঠনের ~. **4** heart; mind; essence of sth; earnest desire: ~ কী চায়. **5** vitality; energy; vigour; vivacity; liveliness: ছেলের ~ আছে. **6** vital air; vital organ. **7** (as a term of endearment) extremely beloved person; dear; precious; sweetheart; beloved. ~ **আইঢাই/কেমন করা** *vi* feel extremely uneasy. ~ **ওষ্ঠাগত করা** *vt* lead sb a dog's life; make sb's life wretched/ a misery; play hell with sb; give sb hell. ~ **ওষ্ঠাগত হওয়া** *vi* **1** be at the last grasp/point of death; feel like dying. **2** be extremely tired/ harassed/ troubled; be exhausted/dead beat/dog-beat; pant for breath. **3** have one's heart in one's mouth; slog/ sweat one's guts out; sweat blood. ~ **কাঁদা** *vi* pine for sth/sb; pine to; one's heart goes out to sb; one's; heart bleeds for sb. ~ **খোলা** *vi* open one's heart/mind to sb; bare one's heart/soul; speak one's mind; be frank; speak freely. ~ **চাওয়া** *vi* (of the heart) desire; long for. ~ **ছাড়া** *vi* give up the ghost; breath; one's last; die. ~ **জুড়ানো** *vi* soothe; comport; bring comfort to ~ **টানা** *vi* attract; interest; fascinate; appeal to; stir the soul. ~ **থাকা** *vi* remain/be alive. ~ **দেওয়া** *vi* **1** lay down one's life (for sb/ sth); make the supreme sacrifice; sacrifice one's life; die for. **2** infuse life (into); give life (to); enliven; put more heart into; bring sb/sth to life; animate; resuscitate; revive invigorate; restore to life; bring back to life; give back sb's life save sb's life. ~ **ধরা** *vi* **1** be alive; keep body and soul together. **2** have the heart to do sth; find it in one's heart/oneself to do sth: ~ ধরে কী করে তাকে কথাটা বলি. ~ **নেওয়া** *vi* take sb's life; kill; slay; deprive sb of life. **নিজের হাতে নিজের ~ নেওয়া** put an end to one's life/oneself; take one's (own) life; die by one's own hand. ~ **পড়ে থাকা** *vi* long/pine/languish for. ~ **পাওয়া** *vi* come to life (again); revive; have a new lease of life; spring to life; be enlivened; become vibrant/full of life. ~ **ফিরে পাওয়া** *vi* be revived/ refreshed; be reassured/ relieved/comforted; heave a sigh of relief; come to life again. ~ **বাঁচা** *vi* be saved (from death); save one's (one) hide/skin; save one's neck. ~ **বাঁচানো** *vi* save (sb's) life; rescue; sustain; support; keep sb alive. ~ **বের করা** *vi* exhaust sb's patience; exasperate; beyond endurance; plague; give sb hell; tire out; wear sb out; finish off. ~ **বের হওয়া** *vi* breathe one's last; depart (from) this life; give up the ghost; die; expire; gasp for air/breath; be utterly exhausted/ worn out; be weary/dying; pant for breath. ~ **ভরা/ভরে যাওয়া** *vi* be satiated/highly pleased; be overflowing with happiness; joy; be fully satisfied. ~ ভরিয়ে দেওয়া *vi* fill the heart with joy; gladden sb's heart. ~ মাতানো *vi* gladden sb's heart; enthrall; exhilarate; enchant; charm; delight; enrapture; thrill; elate; ravish. ~ মানা *vi* be consoled; yield to consolation; be comforted; console oneself. ~ না মানা *vi* be disconsolate; be unable to console oneself. ~ হারানো *vi* loose one's life; die; be killed. ~কর *adj* life-giving; invigorating; refreshing. ~কান্ত *n* lord of one's life; husband; lover. ~খোলা *adj* frank; candid; hearty. ~গত *adj* lying in one's heart of hearts; inmost; sincere. ~গতিক *adj* concerning one's life/living; bodily; physical. ~গ্রাহী, ~ঘাতক, ~ঘাতী, ~ঘ্ন *adj* life-destroying; killing; killer; mortal; murderous; fatal; dearly. ~গ্রাহিকা, ~ঘাতিকা *fem.* ~ঘাতন = ~বধ. ~ছাড়া *adj*=~হীন. ~চ্ছেদ *n* destruction of life; murder. ~তুল্য *adj* as dear as life. ~ত্যাগ *n* abandonment of life; death; suicide. ~ ত্যাগ করা *vi* die. ~ত্রাণ *n* saving of life. ~দ *adj* life-giving; saving/ preserving life; invigorating. ~দা *fem.* ~দণ্ড *n* punishment of death; capital punishment; death sentence. ~দণ্ড দেওয়া *vi* sentence sb to death; award capital punishment. ~দাতা *adj* one who saves another's life; giver of life; saviour. ~দাত্রী *fem.* ~দান *n* gift of life; saving a person's life; infusion of life; invigoration; resuscitation; reviving; sacrifice of one's life; supreme sacrifice. ~ দান করা = ~ দেওয়া. ~দায়ক=~দ. ~দায়িকা *fem.* ~ দিয়ে *adj* with all one's heart/one's whole heart; with might and main; desperately; whole heartedly. ~ধন *adj* very precious. ~ধারণ *n* support/ maintenance/ prolongation of life; living. ~ ধারণ করা *vi* live; stay alive; sustain oneself; keep body and soul together; subsist (on). ~নাথ=~কান্ত. ~নাশ destruction of life; murder. ~ নাশের চেষ্টা *n* attempt to murder. ~ নাশ করা *vt* kill; murder. ~নাশক=~গ্রাহী. ~পঙ্ক *n* protoplasm. ~পণ *n* resolve of doing sth even at the cost of one's life. ❑*adj* desperate; obstinate; stubborn; vigorous; vehement; utmost. ~পণ চেষ্টা করেও for the life of one. ~পণে *adj* for dear life; vigorously; desperately; with might and main; with all one's might; even at the cost of one's life; for one's life; hell for leather. ~পণ যত্নে *adv* with almost care; with might and main; with all one's might. ~পরিগ্রহ *n* possession of breath/life; existence. ~পাখি *n* bird of life imprisoned in the cage of the body; breath of life. ~পাত= ~ত্যাগ. ~পাত করা *vi* apply/devote all one's energies (to a task); strain every nerve (to do sth); wreck/lay down/sacrifice one's life. ~পুরুষ *n* life and soul of sth; leading spirit. ~পূর্ণ *adj* lively; full of the joys of spring; full of beans/ life vivacious; sprightly; living; alive; animate; full of vital power; genial; cordial; active; animated; vital; spirited; vivid; bustling; vibrant. ~প্রতিম= ~তুল্য. ~প্রতিমা *n* idol of one's life; a woman as dear as one's life. ~প্রতিষ্ঠা *n* breathing life into; consecration of an idol; rite of investing an idol with life; infusion of life (into); revitalization. ~ প্রতিষ্ঠা করা *vt* invest (an idol) with life; consecrate; infuse/breathe (fresh) life into; revitalize. ~প্রদ=~দ. ~প্রদা *fem.* ~প্রদায়ক=~দ. ~প্রাণ *n* life of life. ~প্রিয় *adj* as dear as life; dearer than life; most favourite. ~প্রিয়া *fem.* ~বঁধু *n* a lover as dear as one's life; sweetheart; beloved. ~বধ *n* killing; slaying; man-slaughter. ~ বধ করা *vt* kill; slay; take sb's life. ~বন্ত=~পূর্ণ. ~বন্ততা *n* liveliness; vivacity; cordiality; geniality; animation; animal spirits; ebullience; verve; vigour. ~বল্লভ=~কান্ত. ~বল্লভা *n* a mistress/wife as dear as life. ~বান *adj* 1=~বন্ত. 2 kind; kind-hearted; sympathetic; sensitive. ~বায়ু *n* life-breath; vital air. ~বায়ু নির্গত/বাহির হওয়া *vi* breathe one's last; die; give up the ghost. ~বিনাশ=~নাশ. ~বিয়োগ *n* separation from life; death. ~ বিয়োগ হওয়া *vi* die; pass away. ~বিসর্জন *n* sacrifice of one's life. ~ বিসর্জন দেওয়া *vi* sacrifice one's life. ~ভয় *n* fear of one's life; peril of death. ~ভয়ে *adv* for dear life/one's life; for fear of life. ~ ভরে যাওয়া *vi* be satiated/highly pleased; be overflowing with happiness/joy. ~ভিক্ষা দেওয়া *vi* spare sb's life. ~ভূত *adj* being the breath of life. ~ময় *adj*=~পূর্ণ. ~ময়ী *fem.* ~ময় কোষ *n* (Indian phil) vital case (one of the cases/investitures of the soul). ~মাতানো *adj* exhilarating; thrilling; captivating; exciting; enchanting; delightful. ~যাত্রা *n* support of life; subsistence; living one's life. ~যুক্ত *adj* endowed with life. ~রক্ষণ, ~রক্ষা *nn* preservation/ saving of life. ~ রক্ষা করা= ~ বাঁচানো. ~রসায়ন *n* biochemistry. ~রোধ *n* suppression/ suspension of breath. ~লাভ *n* coming (back) to life; resuscitation; revival; new lease of life; resurgence; regeneration. ~ লাভ করা=~ পাওয়া. ~শক্তি *n* vitality; vivacity; stamina; life force; vital spark/ flame; energy. ~শূন্য *adj* lifeless; inanimate; dull; cold; spiritless; insipid; torpid; vapid; sluggish; inert; tedious; colourless; tame; wooden; slothful; supine; without (a) soul. ~শূন্যা *fem.* ~সংযম=~রোধ. ~সংশয় *n* danger to life; peril of one's life; life at risk; risk to one's/sb's life. ~সংহার=~বধ. ~সংহারক, ~সংহারী *adj* fatal; mortal; deadly; lethal. ~সংহারিকা, ~সংহারিণী *adjj fem.* ~সখা *n* dear/ bosom friend. ~সঙ্কট=~সংশয়. ~সঞ্চার=~দান. ~সঞ্চার করা *vt* breathe life into; infuse new life into; resuscitate; revive; revitalize. ~সম,

~সমান *adjj* equal to/as dear as life. ~সমা *fem.* ~স্নিগ্ধকর *adj* soothing; balmy. ~ স্পর্শ করা *vt* touch one's heart; touch the right cord. ~হন্তা, ~হর, ~হারক, ~হারী *adjj*=~গ্রাহী. ~হন্ত্রী, ~হরা, ~হারিকা, ~হারিণী *fem.* ~হিংসা=~বধ. ~হীন = ~শূন্য. ~হীনতা *n* lifelessness; dullness; insipidity; sluggishness; listlessness; tediousness; vapidity; lethargy. প্রাণে জাগা *vi* come/ spring to mind; haunt one's mind/ thoughts; brood (on/over sth); return repeatedly/ continuously to the mind; be haunted by the memory of sth. প্রাণে থাকা *vi* have sth at heart. প্রাণে বাঁচা/ বেঁচে যাওয়া *vi* 1 have a narrow escape; be spared (one's life); save one's (own) neck survive. 2 thank one's luck stars that; be/feel especially fortunate: ঐ অনুষ্ঠানে যেতে হয়নি বলে প্রাণে বেঁচেছি. প্রাণে বাঁচানো *vi* spare sb/sb's life; spare a person his life; keep sb alive/in existence. প্রাণে বেঁচে থাকা *vi* be/stay alive; keep body and soul together; (joc) be in the land of the living. প্রাণে বাজা/লাগা *vi* take sth to heart; take offence; be cut to the quick; be offended/ deeply hurt; be touched. প্রাণে মারা *vt* kill; take sb's life; ruin; finish sb off. ~ সওয়া *vi* bear; put up with; tolerate; endure; suffer. প্রাণের অন্তঃস্থল *n* one's heart of hearts; the bottom of one's heart. প্রাণের আশা না থাকা have no hope of life; be on the point of death. প্রাণের কথা *n* one's inmost/innermost feelings/ thoughts. প্রাণের ঝুঁকি *n* risk of life. প্রাণের ঝুঁকি থাকা *vi* be in danger of one's life. প্রাণের ঝুঁকি নেওয়া *vt* take one's life in one's hand; risk one's; neck; endanger one's life. প্রাণের দুঃখ/কষ্ট *nn* mental sufferings; anguish. প্রাণের শত্রু *n* mortal enemy.

প্রাণাঙ্কুর *n* protoplasm.

প্রাণাত্যয় *n* destruction/ loss of life; death; one's last/ dying breath.

প্রাণাধিক *adj* dearer than (one's) life. প্রাণাধিকা *fem.*

প্রাণান্ত *n* end/termination of life; death. ~কর *adj* 1 destructive/dangerous to life; fatal; mortal. 2 beak-breaking; gruelling; arduous; exhausting. ~কর পরিশ্রম *n* hard labour; uphill grind; hard work; great application. ~কর পরিশ্রম করা *vt* break one's neck (to do sth); slog/sweat one's guts out; spare no effort; do one's utmost. ~ পরিচ্ছেদ *n* 1 that which ends in/ extends up to death. 2 extreme toil/suffering; agony.

প্রাণান্তিক=প্রাণান্তকর (⇒ প্রাণান্ত)

প্রাণাপান *n* air inhaled and exhaled; respiration and expiration.

প্রাণায়াম *n* name of three breath-exercises prescribed in yoga.

প্রাণি *n* (in compounds)=প্রাণী. ~কুল *n* fauna. ~জগত *n* animal kingdom/ world. ~তত্ত্ব, ~বিজ্ঞান, ~বিদ্যা *nn* zoology. ~তত্ত্বজ্ঞ, ~বিজ্ঞানী, ~বিদ্যাবিদ *nn* zoologist. ~তত্ত্বীয় *adj* zoological. ~ত্ব *n* state of a living being; life. ~পরাগিত *adj* zoophilous. ~হত্যা *n* slaughter of living beings. ~হিংসা *n* injuring/killing an animal; cruelty to animals.

প্রাণিত *adj* animated; inspired.

প্রাণী *n* 1 living/sentient being; (living) creature; animal. 2 human being; man; person: এখানে আমরা দুটি মাত্র ~.

প্রাণেশ, প্রাণেশ্বর *nn*=প্রাণকান্ত (⇒ প্রাণ). প্রাণেশ্বরী *fem* mistress of one's life; wife; sweetheart; beloved (woman).

প্রাণোৎসর্গ *n* sacrifice of one's life; dedication. ~ করা *vt* sacrifice one's life; dedicate oneself (to).

প্রাত *n* (in compounds)=প্রাতঃ. ~রাশ, ~র্ভোজন *n* morning meal; breakfast. ~রাশ আহার করা, ~র্ভোজন করা *vt* take the morning meal; breakfast. ~র্বাক্য *n* the first words uttered on waking in the morning. প্রাতে *adv* in the early morning; at dawn/daybreak.

প্রাতঃ *n* 1 (early) morning; daybreak; dawn. 2 (fig) beginning; inception. ~কর্ম=~কৃত্য. ~কাল *n* (early) morning; morning time. ~কালীন *adj* of/for/in the morning; morning. ~কালীন সঙ্গীত *n* morning song. ~কৃত্য, ~ক্রিয়া *nn* morning business/ceremony; routine morning duties of evacuation of bowels; personal washing; religious prayers, etc. ~নমস্কার *n* morning salutation; good morning. ~প্রণাম *n* morning obeisance. ~সন্ধ্যা *n* morning twilight; morning meditation/devotion/prayers. ~সমীর/সমীরণ *n* morning breeze. ~স্নান *n* morning ablution/ bath. ~স্মরণীয় *adj* to be remembered every morning; (fig) ever memorable; of immortal fame.

প্রাতিকূল্য *n*=প্রতিকূলতা (⇒ প্রতিকূল)

প্রাতিজনিক *adj* personal. ~ খতিয়ান *n* personal ledger account.

প্রাতিপদিক *adj* (gram) uninflected. ❑*n* uninflected noun or adjective.

প্রাতিভাসিক *adj* existing only in appearance; phenomenal; apparent.

প্রাতিষঙ্গিক *adj* corresponding.

প্রাতিস্বিক *adj* own; individual; characteristic; personal. ~তা *n* individuality.

প্রাত্যহিক *adj* daily; diurnal. প্রাত্যহিকী *fem.*

প্রাথমিক *adj* primary; initial; early; primitive. ~তা *n* priority; precedence; primitiveness; initial state. ~ পুস্তক *n* primer. ~ বিদ্যালয় *n* primary school. ~ শিক্ষা *n* primary education.

প্রাদি *n* collective name of twenty Sanskrit prefixes. ~ সমাস *n* (gram) system of forming compounds by adding any one of the Sanskrit prefixes.

প্রাদুর্ভাব *n* **1** manifestation; appearance; occurrence. **2** outbreak: কলেরার ~. **3** extensive and terrible prevalence; invasion: মশার ~. **4** (iron) rise to power/eminence.

প্রাদুর্ভূত *adj* **1** come to life; become manifest/ evident; appeared; revealed. **2** broken out. **3** prevalent; invading. **4** (iron) risen to power/eminence. **~ হওয়া** *vi* **1** become manifest; appear; arise; occur; be visible. **2** break out. **3** become/ be prevalent; invade. **4** rise to power/eminence.

প্রাদেশিক *adj* provincial; regional. **~তা** *n* provincialism; regionalism; parochialism.

প্রাধান্য *n* predominance; supremacy; ascendancy; prevalence; preeminence; supremacy; privilege. prominence; priority. **~ করা** *vi* predominate; dominate; domineer; lord it over; reign supreme; have the upper hand; prevail; preponderate (over). **~ দেওয়া** *vi* attach more importance to; give reference to; prefer. **~ পাওয়া** *vi* become predominant; gain the ascendancy (over); gain supremacy/ prominence; assume greater importance; take/get priority.

প্রাধিকার *n* authority; privilege. **~প্রাপ্ত** *adj* authorized; privileged.

প্রাধিকারী *n* authority.

প্রাধিকৃত *adj* authorized.

প্রান্ত *n* edge; border; margin; verge; extremity; end; tip; brim; rim; outskirts; fringe. **~গ্রাবরেখা** *n* (geog) terminal moraine. **~বর্তী, ~স্থ, ~স্থিত** *adjj* lying/situated at/in/on the border; terminal; bordering; marginal. **~স্পর্শী** *adj* **1** bordering on. **2** (bot) valvate.

প্রান্তর *n* prairie; vast expanse of arid land; large tract of grassland; desolate field; wilderness; waste.

প্রান্তিক *adj* lying/situated at /in/on the border; bordering; marginal; terminal; (attrib) fringe. **~ উপযোগিতা** *n* marginal utility. **~ চাষি** *n* marginal farmer. **~ সুযোগসুবিধা** *n* fringe benefits.

প্রান্তীয় *adj* **1** =প্রান্তিক. **2** (with) extreme. **বহু~** *adj* parietal.

প্রান্ত্য=প্রান্তিক

প্রাপক *n* receiver; recipient; delivery-man.

প্রাপণ *n* receiving; obtaining; attaining.

প্রাপণীয় *adj* obtainable; attainable; available; acquirable.

প্রাপিত *adj* got; procured; obtained; received; attained.

প্রাপ্ত *adj* **1** obtained; got; received; attained to; reached; arrived at; met with; found; acquired; gained; incurred. **2** who has attained to/reached; come to mature. **3** informed of: সংবাদ ~. **~ হওয়া** *vt* **1** obtain; attain; reach; arrive at; meet with; get; receive; be given; find; come across; acquire; gain; be informed of. **2** incur; suffer: শাস্তি ~. **3** pass/change into. **~কাল** *n* fit time; proper season. ❑*adj* **1** whose time has come; seasonable; suitable; opportune. **2** whose time/last hour has come; on the point of death; dying; hearing attained the fullness of age. **~বয়স্ক** *adj* adult; grown-up; come of age; who has attained majority. ❑*n* adult; grown-up. **~ব্য** *adj*=প্রাপণীয়. **~ ব্যবহার** =~বয়স্ক. **~যৌবন** *adj* who has reached the age of puberty; in the bloom of youth. **~যৌবনা** *fem.*

প্রাপ্তা *n* payee.

প্রাপ্তি *n* **1** obtaining; getting; receiving. **2** receipt; income; earnings; gain. **3** acquisition; acquirement. **4** finding; meeting; attainment; reaching. **5** (joc) project; benefit. **~যোগ** *n* (hum) occasion for some gain; unexpected gain. **~যোগ্য**=প্রাপণীয়. **~স্থান** *n* place from which sth may be had.

প্রাপ্য *adj* **1** =প্রাপণীয়. **2** to be paid; due: ~ অর্থ. ❑*n* due.

প্রাবর *n* enclosure; fence; wall.

প্রাবরণ *n* **1** covering; veiling. **2** cover; outer garment; cloak; mantle.

প্রাবল্য *n*=প্রবলতা (⇒ প্রবল)

প্রাবাদিক *adj* proverbial; legendary.

প্রাবার=প্রাবরণ

প্রাবাসিক=প্রবাসী

প্রাবীণ্য=প্রবীণতা (⇒ প্রবীণ)

প্রাবৃট *n* rainy season; wet seasons; rains. **~কাল**=~.

প্রাবৃত *adj* covered; enclosed; screened; hid in.

প্রাবৃষিক, প্রাবৃষ্য *adjj* relating to/ born in the rainy season.

প্রাবেশন *n* workshop.

প্রাবেশিক *adj* relating to entrance/admission. **~ পরীক্ষা** *n* admission test.

প্রাভাতিক *adj* relating to morning; morning.

প্রামাণিক *adj* authentic; authenticated; authoritative; credible. **~তা** *n* authenticity; authoritativeness; credibility; authority; trustworthiness .

প্রামাণ্য *adj*=প্রামাণিক. ❑*n* =প্রামাণিকতা

প্রামাদিক *adj* arising from carelessness; erroneous; faulty; wrong.

প্রাযুক্তিক *n* technologist.

প্রায়[1] *adv* **1** often; every now than; frequently; from time to time: সে ~ বেড়াতে যায়. **2** about; nearly; around; almost; nearing about; little less than: ~ পাঁচ শ টাকা. **3** generally; usually: এ রকম তো ~ দেখা যায়. **~ই** *adv* usually; often; frequently; generally; usually. **~শ** *adv* usually; frequently; generally; often.

প্রায়[2] *adj* (often used as a *suff*) like; resembling; near: মৃত~.

প্রায়[৩] *n* seeking death by fasting (as a religious or penitentiary act or to enforce compliance with a demand).

প্রায়শ ⇒ প্রায়[১]

প্রায়শ্চিত্ত *n* 1 atonement; expiation; penance. 2 amends; satisfaction. ~ করা *vi* atone for; do penance for (one's sins); expiate (one's sin/crime/one's guilt); make amends (to sb) (for sth), give satisfaction. ~মূলক *adj* expiatory.

প্রায়শ্চিত্তি *n* (colloq)=প্রায়শ্চিত্ত

প্রায়িক *adj* 1 common; usual; frequent. 2 approximate.

প্রায়োগিক *adjj* pragmatic; empirical; technical.

প্রায়োদ্বীপ *n* peninsula.

প্রায়োপবিষ্ট *adj* seated fasting till death.

প্রায়োপবেশন *n* abstaining from food and awaiting in a sitting posture the approach of death.

প্রারব্ধ *adj* commenced; begun; undertaken; taken up; started; embarked on. ❑*n* 1 consequences of the activities of a previous birth which have begun to take effect. 2 fate; destiny.

প্রারম্ভ *n* 1 beginning; commencement; inception; outset. 2 enterprise; undertaking.

প্রারম্ভিক *adj* initial; first; early; maiden.

প্রার্থক=প্রার্থী

প্রার্থন=প্রার্থনা

প্রার্থনা *n* prayer; petition; asking for; solicitation; request; supplication; application; entreaty. ~ করা *vi* pray; say one's prayer; ask for; solicit; beg for; request; petition; apply (for); supplicate; woo; demand in marriage. ~পূর্ণ করা *vi* grant a prayer/ request. ~ সিদ্ধি *n* accomplishment of a desire; fulfilment of a prayer.

প্রার্থনীয়, প্রার্থয়িতব্য *adjj* to be asked/ begged/ prayed for; to be applied for; worth praying/ asking/ applying for; desirable.

প্রার্থয়িতা=প্রার্থী. প্রার্থয়িত্রী *fem*

প্রার্থিত *adj* prayed/asked/ applied/ requested for; desired; wished for; wanted; solicited.

প্রার্থিতা *n* candidature.

প্রার্থী *adj* praying/asking for; begging/ applying for; wishing for; desirous of; soliciting; courting. ❑*n* one who prays/ asks for; candidate; applicant; solicitor; wooer; suitor.

প্রাশ, প্রাশন *n* 1 eating; feeding upon; feeding (esp the first feeding of a child). 2 food; victuals.

প্রাশ্নিক *n*=প্রশ্নকর্তা (⇒ প্রশ্ন). ❑*adj* containing questions.

প্রাস *n* (myth) a barbed missile/dart.

প্রাসঙ্গিক *adj* relevant; pertinent; contextual; incidental.

প্রাসঙ্গিকী *n* book of reference.

প্রাসাদ *n* palace; lofty palatial mansion; edifice; royal residence. ~-কুক্কুট domestic pigeon. ~চূড়া, ~শিখর, ~শীর্ষ *nn* spire/ pinnacle of a palace; turret. ~বাসী *adj* dwelling in a palace. ~বাসিনী *fem.* ~প্রহরী *n* palace-guard.

প্রাস্থানিক *adj* relating/favorable to departure.

প্রাহ্ন *n* early part of the day; forenoon; morning.

প্রিজম *n* [E] prism.

প্রিন্টার *n* [E] printer.

প্রিন্সিপাল *n* [E] Principal.

প্রিভি কাউন্সিল *n* [E] the Privy Council (of Great Britain).

প্রিমিয়াম *n* [E] premium.

প্রিয় *adj* dear; beloved; favorite; liked; pleasant. ❑*n* beloved person; lover; darling; friend; dear. প্রিয়ংবদ *adj* speaking kindly; sweet-tongued; soft-spoken. প্রিয়ংবদী *fem.* ~কর *adj* giving/ causing pleasure; pleasant. ~কারক *adj* doing a kindness to causing pleasure/ gladness; agreeable. ~কারী *adj* doing a kindness/ favour to; showing kindness to. ~কারিণী *fem.* ~চিকীর্ষা *n* desire of doing a kindness to; benevolence. ~চিকীর্ষু *adj* wishing to do a kindness to benevolent. ~জন *n* dear person; dear; beloved one; favourite; friend; kinsman; relative. ~তনয় *n* loving son. ~তম *adj* most beloved; dearest; most favourite. ❑*n* most beloved person; lover; darling; husband. ~তমা *fem.* ❑*n* mistress; sweetheart; beloved woman; darling; wife. ~তর *adj* dearer. ~তা, ~ত্ব *nn* the being dear/ beloved; charm; amiability. ~দর্শন *adj* pleasant/ graceful to the sight; good-looking; handsome; attractive. ~দর্শী *adj* 1 looking with kindness (upon everything). 2=~দর্শন. ~দর্শিনী *fem.* ~পাত্র *adj* favourite; beloved. ❑*n* favourite; beloved person. ~পাত্রী *fem.* ~বচন, ~বাক্য, ~বাদ *nn* kind pleasant/ flattering/ sweet words; agreeable speech. ~বয়স্য *n* dear friend; chum; confidant; bosom friend. ~বাদী *adj* speaking agreeably/kindly; flattering. ~বাদিনী *fem.* ~বিয়োগ *n* loss/ death of a dear one; bereavement. ~বিয়োগবিধুর *adj* mourning/ grieving over the loss of a dear one. ~বিয়োগবিধুরা *fem.* ~বিয়োগবিধুরতা *n* grief over the loss of a dear one. ~বিরহ *n* separation from one's lover/a dear one/ one's beloved. ~বিরহিত *adj* separated from one's lover/one's beloved/a dear one. ~বিরহিতা *fem.* ~বিরহী=~ বিরহিত. ~বিরহিণী *fem.* ~ভাষণ *n* kind/ friendly speech; flattering words. ~ভাষী=~বাদী. ~ভাষিণী *fem.* ~সখা=~বয়স্য. ~সখী *fem* dear female friend/ companion. ~সমাগম *n* union/re-union with a dear one/ dear one's /

beloved object. ~সহচর= ~বয়স্য. ~ সহচরী *fem*=~সখী.

প্রিয়ঙ্কর *adj*=প্রিয়কারক (⇒প্রিয়)

প্রিয়ঙ্গু *n* a kind of sweet-swelling creeper; *Agalia roxburghiana.*

প্রিয়ম্বদ=প্রিয়ংবদ (⇒ প্রিয়). **প্রিয়ম্বদা** *fem*

প্রিয়া *adj fem*=প্রিয়. ❑*n* mistress; beloved (woman); ladylove; sweetheart; darling; wife.

প্রীণ *adj* pleased; satisfied; delighted. ~ন *n* pleasing; citifying; delighting; satisfying. **প্রীণিক** *adj*=~.

প্রীত *adj* pleased; delighted; satisfied; glad.

প্রীতি *n* **1** pleasure; pleasurable sensation; joy; gladness; satisfaction; delight. **2** love; affection; fondness; attachment. **3** friendly disposition; friendliness; kindness; favour; grace; amity; amicability; amiability. ~ **অর্জন করা** *vi* earn favour of. ~ **লাভ করা** *vi* be pleased/delighted/ satisfied. ~-**উপহার** *n* gift/ token of life; complementary gift/present. ~**কর**, ~**দ**, ~**দায়ক** *adjj* pleasing; pleasant; delightful; agreeable. ~**দ**, ~**দায়িকা** *fem.* ~**দত্ত** *adj* given through love/ affection. ~ **দান**= ~ উপহার. ~**নিলয়** *n* = ~পাত্র. ~**পরায়ণ** *adj* **1** delighted; very pleased. **2** affectionate; loving; full of love/kindness. ~**পরায়ণা** *fem.* ~**পাত্র** *n* repository of affection and confidence; object of affection; beloved person or thing; favourite. ~**পূর্ণ** *adj* loving; affectionate; friendly; cordial; amiable; amicable. ~**পূর্বক** *adv* with the accompaniment of kindness; kindly; affectionately; friendly. ~**প্রদ**=~কর. ~**প্রফুল্ল** *adj* bubbling with joy; excited; thrilled. ~**বর্ধক** *adj* increasing promoting love/ friendliness/ affection/joy. ~**বর্ধন** *n* increasing love/joy. ~**ভরে** *adv* lovingly; affectionately; kindly; cordially; amiably; in a friendly spirit; with pleasure/ delight. ~**ভাজন**=~পাত্র. ~**ভোজ(ন)** *n* feast; feasting. ~**মান** *adj* **1** having pleasurable sensations; pleased; glad; gratified; satisfied. **2** having love/affection for; affectionate; favourable; loving. ~**মতী** *fem.* ~**সম্ভাষণ** *n* cordial/friendly greeting. ~**সূচক** *adj* expressing pleasure/delight; friendly; cordial. ~**স্নিগ্ধ** *adj* (of the eyes) moist through love; charming through affection.

প্রীয়মাণ *adj* delighted; pleased.

প্রুষ্ট *adj* burnt; roasted; roasted.

প্রেক=পেরেক

প্রুফ [E] *n* (printing) proof; proof copy; proof-sheet. ~ **তোলা** *vi* pull a proof. ~ **দেখা/সংশোধন করা** *vi* read/correct/ check the proofs (of); proof-read. ~-**রিডার** *n* proof-reader. ~**রিডিং**, ~**সংশোধন** *n* proof-reading. ~-**সংশোধক** *n* proof-reader.

প্রেক্ষক *adj* looking at; viewing; considering; judging. ❑*n* spectator; member of an audience; onlooker. **প্রেক্ষিকা** *fem.*

প্রেক্ষণ *n* **1** viewing; looking at; view; look; sight. **2** eye. ~ **করা** *vi* view; look at; observe; behold.

প্রেক্ষণা *n* view; viewing; observation.

প্রেক্ষণিক=প্রেক্ষক. **প্রেক্ষণিকা** *fem* exhibition.

প্রেক্ষণীয় *adj* to be seen/watched/viewed; worth seeing/watching; slightly; beautiful to the view; visible.

প্রেক্ষা *n* **1** seeing; viewing; be holding; regarding; looking on; observation; watching. **2** (esp a beautiful) sight/view. **3** public show/entertainment. ~**গার**, ~**গৃহ** *n* **1** play-house; theatre; music-hall; opera-house; gallery; auditorium. **2** observatory. ~**বান** *adj* circumspect; prudent; deliberate; judicious; rational; wise.

প্রেক্ষিত *adj* looked at; seen; viewed; watched; observed. ❑*n* look; glance.

প্রেঙ্খন *n* trembling; rocking; swaying.

প্রেঙ্খা *n* swing; hammock; swinging-cot.

প্রেঙ্খিত *adj* swing; shaken; set in motion.

প্রেত *n* **1** spirit of a dead person (esp before obsequial rites are performed). **2** ghost; evil spirit; ghoul; apparition; spectre; evil being; goblin. **3** dead person. ❑*adj* deported; deceased. ~**কর্ম**, ~**কার্য**, ~**কৃত্য**, ~**ক্রিয়া** *nn* obsequial rite; funeral rites. ~**গৃহ** *n* burning-place. ~**চারী** *adj* roaming among the dead. ❑*n* name of Shiva (শিব). ~**তত্ত্ব** *n* separation; spiritualism. ~**তর্পণ** *n* offering of water to the spirit of a deceased person. ~**দেহ** *n* ghost of a dead person. ~**নদী** *n* river of the dead; Baitarani (⇒ বৈতরণী). ~**পক্ষ** *n* dark half in the month of Aswin (আশ্বিন). ~**পটহ** *n* drum beaten at the burning of the dead. ~**পতি** *n* lord of the dead; Yama (যম). ~**পিণ্ড** *n* lump of food offered to the spirit of a deceased person. ~**পুর**, ~**পুরী** *n* city of the dead; Yama's abode. ~**বৎ** *adj* as if dead; ghostly; ghoulish. ~**বাহিত** *adj* possessed by an evil spirit. ~**ভূমি** *n* 'place of the dead'; burning-ground. ~**ভোগ্য** *adj* (fit) to be devoured by ghosts. ~**মূর্তি** *n*=~দেহ. ~**যোনি** *n* ghost; evil spirit; ghoul. ~**রাজ**=~পতি. ~**লোক** *n* world of the dead. ~**শরীর** *n* the body with which a departed spirit is invested. ~**শুদ্ধি**, ~**শৌচ** *n* purification after the death of a kinsman. ~**শ্রাদ্ধ** *n* obsequial ceremonies performed for a relative at death.

প্রেতাত্মা *n*=প্রেত

প্রেতান্ন *n* food offered to a dead person.

প্রেতাশৌচ *n* impurity of one's body caused by carrying a dead person.

প্রেতিনী *n fem* (of প্রেত); ghost of a dead woman; female evil spirit; extremely ugly woman; hag; witch; ogress.

প্রেপ্সু *adj* wishing to attain; desirous of attaining; seeking; longing for; covetous.

প্রেম *n* love; tenderness; affection; attachment; tender regard; predilection; fondness; amour; friendliness; devotion. **~ করা** *vi* love; be (very much) in love (with each other); court; woo. **~ দেওয়া** *vi* love; treat with love/affection. **~কথা** *n* love-story. **~ডোর** *n* bond of love. **~দৃষ্টি** *n* amorous look/glance; fond/ loving look. **~দৃষ্টিতে তাকানো** *vi* look lovingly at; look sweet at; ogle. **~ধারা** *n* tears of love. **~পত্র** *n* love-letter; billet-doux. **~পাত্র** *n* object of affection/ love; beloved person. **~পীড়িত** *n* love-sick; lovelorn. **~পূর্ণ** *adj* full of love; loving; full of affection; amorous; fond; full of devotion. **~প্রতিমা** *n* idol/image/embodiment of love. **~বন্ধন** *n* ties of love; love; affection. **~বাণ** *n* amorous glances; shafts of love. **~বারি**=~ধারা. **~বিরহিত, ~বিহীন** *adjj* loveless; heartless; unkind. **~ভক্তি** *n* loving devotion. **~ভিক্ষা** *n* begging for love; courting; wooing. **~ ভিক্ষা করা** *vi* beg for (the) love (of); court; woo. **~মদ** *n* intoxication of love; passion. **~ মধু** *n* nectar/ambrosia of love. **~ময়**=~পূর্ণ. **~ময়ী** *fem.* **~মাধুরী** *n* fascination/charm of love. **~মুগ্ধ** *adj* intoxicated with love; fascinated by love; enamoured or infatuated with; amorous; loving; taken up with. **~রহিত, ~শূন্য, ~হীন** *adj*=~বিরহিত. **~লীলা**=প্রণয়লীলা (⇒ প্রণয়). **~শর**=~বাণ. **~সঙ্গীত** *n* love-song. **~সাগর** *n* ocean of love. **প্রেমে পড়া** *vi* fall in love with; be in love with; lose one's heart to; fall for; be taken up with; be enamoured of.

প্রেমাকাঙ্ক্ষা *n* longing for love.

প্রেমাকাঙ্ক্ষী *adj* longing/yearning for love; love-starved. **প্রেমাকাঙ্ক্ষিণী** *fem.*

প্রেমানন্দ *n* joy/ delight of love.

প্রেমানল *n* fire of love; burning passion.

প্রেমানুরঞ্জন, প্রেমার্চন *nn* courtship.

প্রেমাবতার *n* embodiment/ incarnation of love.

প্রেমাবেগ *n* emotion/passion of love; surge of love.

প্রেমামৃত=প্রেমমধু (⇒ প্রেম)

প্রেমারা= প্রমারা

প্রেমার্দ্র *adj* softened with love.

প্রেমালাপ *n* lovers' tête-à-tête/ conversation/ tittle-tattle. **~ করা** *vi* be engaged in amorous conversation; chat amorously; chat up.

প্রেমালিঙ্গন *n* fond/amorous embrace.

প্রেমাশ্রু *n*=প্রেমধারা (⇒ প্রেম)

প্রেমাসক্ত *adj* fallen in love with; deeply attached; enamoured of; infatuated with.

প্রেমাসক্তি *n* deep attachment; passion for sb; intense love; infatuation; tender feelings.

প্রেমিক *adj* loving; affectionate; amorous; adoring. ❑*n* lover; suitor; sweetheart; devotee; beloved; darling; amateur: শিল্প ~. **প্রেমিকা** *fem.* ❑*n* mistress; sweetheart; darling; beloved; devotee; amateur

প্রেমী *adj*=প্রেমিক

প্রেয় *adj*=প্রিয়

প্রেয়ান *adj* dearer; more desired; more agreeable; dearest; most extremely favourite/ beloved. **প্রেয়সী** *n fem* =প্রেমিকা (⇒ প্রেমিকা).

প্রেরক *adj* sending; despatching; setting in motion; urging; transmitting; remitting. ❑*n* sender; despatcher; transmitter; remitter

প্রেরণ *n* sending; dispatch; urging; transmission; remittance; direction; setting in motion. **~ করা** *vt* send; despatch; set in motion; transmit; remit; direct.

প্রেরণা *n* urge; inspiration; incitement; impulse. **~ দেওয়া** *vi* inspire; urge; impel; incite; push on; drive forward; stimulate; excite. **~প্রাপ্ত** *adj* inspired; impelled; urged; incited; stimulated.

প্রেরণীয় *adj* to be sent/ dispatched/ transmitted.

প্রেরয়িতা=প্রেরক. **প্রেরয়িত্রী** *fem.*

প্রেরিত *adj* sent; dispatched; forwarded; transmitted; remitted; impelled; directed. **~পুরুষ** *n* (divine) messenger; apostle.

প্রেষ *n* pressing; pressure. **~ক্রম, ~নতি** *n* pressure gradient. **~বর্ধক** *n* booster. **~বেদন** *n* pressure-sensation.

প্রেষক=প্রেরক

প্রেষণ *n* **1**=প্রেরণ. **2** deputation. **~ অধিদেয় / ভাতা** *n* deputation allowance. **প্রেষণে যোগ দেওয়া** *vi* join on deputation.

প্রেষণা *n* **1**=প্রেরণা. **2** inspiration; urge; impulse. **3** motivation. **~প্রণোদিত** *adj* motivated.

প্রেষণী *n fem* maid-servant; female go-between in a love-affair.

প্রেষণীয়=প্রেরণীয়

প্রেষিত *adj* **1**=প্রেরিত. **2** dependent. **3** commanded. **প্রেষিতা** *fem.*

প্রেষ্ঠ *adj* most beloved/favourite; dearest. **প্রেষ্ঠা** *fem.*

প্রেষ্য *adj* **1**= প্রেরণীয়. **2** fit to be dispatched/ sent/ remitted. ❑*n* servant; menial. **প্রেষ্যা** *fem.*

প্রেস [E] *n* press; printing-press.

প্রেসক্রিপশন [E] *n* prescription.

প্রেসিডেন্ট [E] *n* president.

প্রেসিডেন্সি [E] *n* presidency.

প্রৈতিশক্তি *n* (mech) kinetic energy.

প্রৈষ *n* sending; direction; summons; call. ❑*adj* of dispatch/ transmission; of postal transmission; postal.

প্রোক্ত *adj* announced; told; taught; said.

প্রোগ্রাম [E] *n* programme.

প্রোঞ্ছন *n* wiping out; cleaning; effacing.

প্রোজ্জ্বল *adj* shining brilliantly; flashing; brilliant; resplendent; splendid ; radiant.

প্রোটিন *n* protein.

প্রোত *adj* **1** sewed. **2** tugged up; fixed on/ in. **3** set; inlaid. **4** contained; pervaded by.

প্রোৎফুল্ল *adj* fully blown; widely expanded. **~ নয়ন** *adj* having the eyes wide open.

প্রোৎসাদন *n* destroying; elimination. **প্রোৎসাদিত** *adj* eliminated; destroyed; perished.

প্রোৎসারণ *n* sending away; removing; expelling; removal; expulsion; elimination; ejection.

প্রোৎসারিত *adj* ejected; expelled; removed; eliminated; leaping; gushing (out).

প্রোৎসাহ *n* **1** zeal; ardour; great exertion. **2** stimulus; incitement; encouragement; incentive. **~ক** *n* inciter; instigator. **~ন** *n* inspiration; inciting; instigation; invitation to.

প্রোৎসাহিত *adj* encouraged; stimulated; inspired; incited; instigated.

প্রোথ *n* **1** nostrils of a horse. **2** snout of a hog. **3** loins; hip. **4** petticoat. **5** womb.

প্রোথিত *adj* **1** planted; driven into; set. **2** sown. **3** buried; interred. **~ করা**=পোঁতা.

প্রোদ্গত *adj* projecting; prominent.

প্রোদ্দীপ্ত *adj* blazing up; glaring; ardent.

প্রোদ্যত *adj* **1** uplifted: ~ যষ্টি.

প্রোন্নত, প্রোন্নমিত *adjj* raised up; elevated; erected; lofty; high; superior.

প্রফেসর, প্রোফেসর [E] *n* professor.

প্রোবেট [E] *n* probate.

প্রোষিত *adj* one who has set on a journey; absent from home; gone abroad. **~পত্নীক** *adj* whose wife is abroad. **~ভর্তৃকা** *adj fem* whose husband is abroad. **~ভার্যা**=~পত্নীক.

প্রৌঢ় *adj* middle-aged; elderly; mature. **প্রৌঢ়া** *fem.* **~তা, ~ত্ব** *nn* age between youth and old age; elderliness; middle age. **~বয়স্ক** *adj* middle-aged. **~বয়স্কা** *fem.*

প্রৌঢ়ি *n* maturity; energy; capacity; boldness; zeal; exertion.

প্র্যাকটিস [E] *n* practice. **~ করা** *vi* practise: উকিল হিসেবে ~ করা, পিয়ানো ~ করা.

প্লব *n* **1** swimming; floating. **2** leaping; hopping. **3** float; raft; boat. flood; swelling of a river. **~ক** *adj* leaping; galloping. ❑*n* leaper (by profession); rope-dancer. **~কেন্দ্র** *n* centre of buoyancy. **~গ** *n* frog. **~ঙ্গম** flickering. ❑*n* deer; monkey. **~তা, ~ত্ব** *n* buoyancy; floating; swimming; going by leaps/plunges; hopping. **~ন শক্তি** *n* buoyancy. **~মান** *adj* buoyant; bloating.

প্লাগ [E] *n* plug.

প্লাকার্ড=প্ল্যাকার্ড

প্লাটিনাম [E] *n* platinum.

প্লাটফর্ম=প্ল্যাটফর্ম

প্লানচেট =প্ল্যানচেট

প্লাবক *adj* flooding; inundating; submerging. ❑*n* one who/that which floods/inundates/ submerges.

প্লাবন *n* flood; inundation; deluge. **~ পীড়িত** *adj* flood-stricken.

প্লাবিত *adj* **1** flooded; inundated; submerged; deluged; overflowed. **2** soaked; moistened/ covered with; streaming with; drenched/ steeped in: ~ চোখ, tearful eyes. **~ করা** *vt* flood; inundate; wash; submerge; overwhelm; bathe; overflow; drench/steep (in). **প্লাবিতা**[1] *fem.*

প্লাবিতা[2] *n* buoyance.

প্লাবী *adj* flooding; overflowing; inundating; submerging; drenching/steeping in. **প্লাবিনী** *fem.*

প্লাব্য *adj* to be jumped/leaped.

প্লাস[1] [E] *n* (math) plus.

প্লাসটার *n* plaster; plastering. **~ করা** *vt* plaster.

প্লিডার [E] *n* pleader; advocate. **প্লিডারি** *n* profession of a pleader/advocate.

প্লীহা *n* **1** spleen. **2** (also) **~ বৃদ্ধি** enlargement of the spleen. **~ রোগ** =~ (2).

প্লুত *adj* **1** floated; swimming; over-flowing; bathed; submerged.. **2** probated/ lengthenned (as a vowel). ❑*n* **1** leap; hop. **2** gallop (of a horse); capering. **~ গতি** *n* gallop; capering. ❑*adj* galloping; moving by leaps.

প্লুষ্ট *n* burnt; scorched; roasted; singed.

প্লেগ [E] *n* plague.

প্লেট[1] [E] *n* plate.

প্লেট[2] [E] *n* plait.

প্লেন[1] [E] *adj* plain; simple; ordinary.

প্লেন[2] [E] *adj* plane; flat; plain. **~ করা** *vt* plane.

প্লেন[3] [E] *n* aeroplane; plane.

প্ল্যাকার্ড [E] *n* placard.

প্ল্যাটফর্ম [E] *n* platform; dais.

প্ল্যান [E] *n* plan; scheme; design. **~ করা** *vi* plan; scheme; draw an outline sketch of.

প্ল্যানচেট [E] *n* planchette.

প্ল্যাসটার= প্লাসটার

ফ

ফ *n* The twenty-second consonant of the Bengali alphabet. It is an unvoiced aspirated bilabial plosive sound. In dialect it is pronounced as unvoiced aspirated fricative sound.

ফইজত, ফইজৎ [A] *n* **1** reproach; reprimand. **2** quarrel; squabble; wrangle. **3** bad repute; bad name; disrepute; stigma. **~ করা** *vi* reproach; rebuke; quarrel; kick up/make a row.

ফক *n* (onom) (only in) **ফক করে** *adv* **1** suddenly; on the spur of the moment: ~ করে কিছু বলে ফেলা. **2** seizing upon an opportunity.

ফকফক *n* **1** (onom) imitating the sound of passing of breath through toothless gums. **2** bright: ফকফকে জ্যোৎস্না.

ফকির [A] *n* pauper; mendicant; beggar. **2** a (Muslim) ascetic or saint; fakir. **আমির ও ~** the rich and the poor. **~ হওয়া** become poor/a pauper; be reduced to poverty. **~ ফোকরা** *n* saints and ascetics; dervishes; holy men; men of god. **~নী** *fem.*

ফকিরি *n* **1** beggary; mendicancy; destitution; indigence. **2** saintliness; the state of a fakir/ ascetic. ❑*adj* poor; beggarly.

ফক্কড়, ফক্কর [A] *n* **1** deceiver; cheat. **2** swindler; trickster. **3** jester; buffoon; joker; clown. ❑*adj* hollow; empty; saucy; impudent; impertinent.

ফক্কা *adj* empty; insubstantial; hollow; false.

ফক্কিকা *n* fallacy; hoax; empty talk; quibble; riddle. **~র** *n* hoaxing; hoodwinking. ❑*adj* empty; hollow.

ফক্কুড়ি, ফুক্কুড়ি *n* (colloq) loquacity; talkativeness. **2** buffoonery; waggery; jesting tomfoolery. **~ করা** *vi* wag; waggle; jest; indulge in buffoonery.

ফক্কুড়ে *adj* fond of jesting or buffoonery; waggish; flippant.

ফচ *n* (onom) imitating the sound of thrusting sth hard (eg a piece of wood or metal) into sth soft. **~ করে** *adv* (thrust) with such a sound.

ফচকামি, ফচকুমি *n* (colloq) frivolity; precocious behaviour; pertness; impertinence; impudence; flippancy; sauciness. **~ করা** *vi* be frivolous or saucy; behave impertiniently or saucily.

ফচকে *adj* (colloq)**1** garrulous; talkative. **2** flippant; waggish; frivolous. **ফচকেমি** *n* **1** garrulity. **2** frivolity; flippancy; light-heartedness; buffoonery.

ফচফচ, ফেচফেচ *n* (colloq) continuous vexatious prattle; chatter; waffle. **~ করা** *vi* prate; drone on; prattle; chatter.

ফচাং *n* (onom) = ফচ; indicates a sound more extensive than ফচ.

ফজর [A] *n* **1** early morning; dawn. **2** (Muslim) morning prayer.

ফজল [A] *n* grace; favour. **খোদার ফজলে** by the grace of God.

ফজলি (আম) [A] *n* a large variety of delicious mango (grown in Rajshahi and Maldah).

ফজিলত, ফজিলহ [A] *n* (moral) excellence; virtue; merit; advantage; exquisiteness; prosperity.

ফজিহত *n* = ফইজত

ফজুল [A] *adj* **1** excessive; abundant. **2** unnecessary; superfluous.

ফট *n* (onom) **1** a popping sound; pop: ছিপিটা ~ করে খুলে গেল. **2** suddenness. **~ করে** *adv* hurriedly; promptly. **~ ফট** *n* **1** repeated pops, **ফটাফট** *adv* pronto; quickly. **ফটফটে** *adj* **1** making popping sounds. **2** clear.

ফটক *n* **1** main gate; portal; entrance. **2** prison.

ফটকা, ফাটকা *n* speculation (in the share market or in business). **~বাজ** *n* speculator. **~ বাজার** *n* share market; speculative business. **~বাজি** *n* speculation.

ফটকি *n* fun; joking; jest; badinage; banter. **~নাটকি** *n* jest; banter; leg-pulling.

ফটকিরি, ফিটকিরি *n* alum.

ফটিক *n* crystal; quartz. ❑*adj* crystal clear; transparent. **~ চাঁদ** *n* **1** the spotless moon. **2** an elegant young man; a dandy. **~ জল** *n* **1** clear/ crystalline water. **2** pied-crested cuckoo.

ফটো [E] *n* photo. **~গ্রাফ** *n* photograph. **~গ্রাফার** *n* photographer. **~গ্রাফি** *n* photography.

ফড় *n* long piece of bamboo or wood attached to the two sides of a bullock-cart.

ফড়ফড় *n* (onom) **1** sound of drilling or of tearing a piece of cloth apart. **2** buzzing or fluttering of wings (as of insects). **3** voluble or wordy display of one's importance. **4** ostensible bustling or fussing. **5** sound of having an ant or other insects in the ear. **~ করা** *vi* prattle; rattle on; ramble.

ফড়া *n* **1** (colloq) branch of a tree; offshoot. **2** limb. **3** leg. **~ ছেঁড়া** *vt* have one's limbs scratched or torn off.

ফড়িং *n* **1** insect. **2** grasshopper.

ফড়িঙ্গা *n* **1** cricket. **2** insect.

ফড়ে, ফড়িয়া *n* **1** one of a class of traders purchasing commodities (esp agricultural products) form the original producers and selling them to the wholesalers; middleman. **2** hawker; vendor.

ফণ *n* extended hood of a serpent; hood. **ফণা** *fem* = ফণ. **~কর, ফণাকর** *n* serpent; snake. **~ধর, ~বান, ফণাভৃত, ফণাধর, ফণাবান, ফণাভৃৎ** *n* serpent; hooded snake. **~মণি** *n* snake-gem (said to be found on snake's head).

ফণি = **ফণী** (in compounds). **~ভুক** *n* serpent-eater; peacock. **~ভূষণ** *n* a bracelet/ armlet in the form of a serpent. **~মণ্ডল** *n* a ring in the form of a serpent. **~রাজ** *n* the king/ lord of snakes.

ফণী *n* snake; serpent. **ফণিনী** *fem.* **~ন্দ্র, ~শ্বর** *nn* the king/ lord of snakes.

ফতুই, ফতুয়া [A] *n* a kind of sleeveless waistcoat.

ফতুয়া *n* = ফতোয়া

ফতুর [A] *adj* stony/ flat broke; hard up; penniless; pauperized. **~ করা** *vt* impoverish;

ruin; beggar. ~ হওয়া *vt* go broke/ bust; fall on hard times; be penniless or pauperized.

ফতে [A] *n* **1** conquest; victory; triumph. **2** accomplishment; success: কাজ ~ হয়েছে. কেল্লা ~ conquest of a fort; (fig) the goal has been reached. ~ **করা** *vt* conquer; win; accomplish; succeed in.

ফতো [A] *adj* **1** parasitic; without means; impecunious; foppish. **2** worthless; trashy. ~ **নবাব, ~ বাবু, ~ কাপ্তান** *nn* a resourceless parasitical dandy; hollow man; poseur; fop. ~ **নবাবি** *n* hollow ostentatiousness; braggadocio.

ফতোয়া [A] *n* (judicial) decree (esp one conforming to Islamic laws); sentence delivered by a kadi; judgement; decision; award. ~ **দেওয়া** *vi* give a verdict; pass judgement. ~**বাজ** *adj* fond of issuing decrees.

ফনোগ্রাফ,ফোনোগ্রাফ [E] *n* phonograph.

ফন্দি [P] *n* intrigue; scheme; stratagem; ruse; trick; plot; deception; secret intention; ulterior motive. ~ **আঁটা, ~ করা** *vi* plot; intrigue; devise a scheme/ plan/ stratagem. ~ **খাটানো** *vi* apply a scheme/ stratagem. ~**ফিকির** *n* tricks and subterfuges. ~**বাজ** *adj* intriguing; scheming; full of intrigues. ❑*n* schemer; plotter; snake in the grass.

ফপরদালাল, ফফড়দালাল *n* uncalled-for meddler; busybody. ~**দালালি** *n* uncalled-for meddling/ interference; officiousness. ~**দালালি করা** *vi* meddle; interfere.

ফয়তা[1] *n* =ফতোয়া

ফয়তা[2] [A] *n* **1** (Muslim) solemn prayers for the dead. **2** offerings to saints with prayers. ~ **পড়া** *vi* pray for the dead.

ফয়দা, ফায়দা [A] *n* **1** result; yield; gain; profit. **2** benefit; advantage; importance. **3** use; utility; necessity.

ফয়সালা [A] *n* **1** settlement; adjudication; adjudgement: মালিকানা স্বত্বের ~. **2** decree; decision; judgement: আদালতের ~. ~ **করা** *vt* settle; decide; to pronounce or pass judgement.

ফরকান, ফরকানি *n* bragging; boasting; swanking; insolence.

ফরকানো *vi* **1** sparkle; glitter. **2** fret; fume; rage; run amok; rush out; brag menacingly.

ফরজ [A] *n* (Muslim) Divine command; duty; responsibility; moral obligation; compulsory duty. ❑*adj* compulsory; obligatory.

ফরজন্দ [P] *n* **1** child. **2** descendant.

ফরফর *n* (onom) **1** rustle. **2** bustle. **3** restlessness; fidgetiness. **4** babble. ~ **করা** *vi* rustle: পাতা ~ করছে; bustle: মেয়েটা ~ করছে; rattle on: তুমি বাপু বেশি ~ করো না. **ফরফরানি** *n* (colloq) rustle; bustle; restlessness. **ফরফরে** *adj* (colloq) rustling; bustling; voluble; chatty; effusive.

ফরম, ফর্ম [E] *n* form; printed paper with space to be filled in.

ফরমা, ফর্মা [E] *n* **1** number of pages (of books) to be printed at a time. **2** forme; format.

ফরমান [P] *n* royal decree or patent; mandate; order; edict; grant; charter; firman. ~**বরদার** *adj* obedient; subject to orders; charged with orders; complying. ~**বরদারি** *n* obedience; execution of orders. **ফরমানো** *vt* command; order; declare; affirm; grant.

ফরমানি [P] *n* carrier of an order; commander. ❑*adj* commanding.

ফরমাশ, ফরমায়েশ, ফরমাইশ [P] *n* **1** order; command. **2** order for supply; requisition; commission for goods. **3** demand; wish: আমার ছেলের ~. ~ **করা/ দেওয়া** *vt* order; place an order (with). ~ **খাটা** *vi* carry out orders (as by a servant). **ফরমায়েশি, ফরমাশি** *adj* ordered for; as ordered; as desired; made to order; requisitioned.

ফরসা, ফরশা, ফর্সা *adj* **1** fair complexioned; bright; fair: ~ মেয়ে/ রং. **2** brightened with daylight: ভোরের আকাশ ~ হয়েছে. **3** clean/ washed: ~ কাপড়. **4** clear/ cloudless: মেঘ কেটে আকাশ ~ হয়েছে. **5** exhausted: ভাঁড়ার ~. **6** desolate: কলেরায় গ্রাম ~. **7** plain; precise: যা বলার ~ করে বলো. **8** blank; not promising or auspicious: ভবিষ্যৎ ~. **9** accomplished; executed: কাজ ~. **10** lost: আশা-ভরসা ~. **11** gone; melted into thin air: হেডমাস্টারকে আসতে দেখে ছেলের দল এক মুহূর্তে ফরসা.

ফরসি [A]*n* flat-bottomed hubble-bubble; hookah.

ফরাকত, ফরাগত [A] *n* **1** an open space. **2** separation; divorce; divorcement; seclusion. ~ **করে দেওয়া** *vt* separate/ divorce. **3** leisure or interval.

ফরায়েজ, ফরাজ [A] *n* Muslim law of inheritance and patrimony; division of inheritances according to law. ~ **করা** *vt* divide inheritances according to Islamic law.

ফরাশ, ফরাস [A] *n* **1** Any covering for the floor or bed, eg a carpet or a bed-cover. **2** a bed-maker; chamberlain; a servant whose business is to spread the carpets and prepare the lamps, etc.

ফরাসি (Pg) *n* a French; the French language; French. ❑*adj* French.

ফরিয়াদ [P] *n* complaint; charge and suit; legal complaint; a suit; crying out for help. **ফরিয়াদি** *n* complainant; plaintiff.

ফরোখত [P] *n* sale; disposal.

ফর্দ [A] *n* list; roll; inventory; catalogue; estimate of expenditure; piece; a sheet of paper; fragment.

ফর্দা [A] *adj* **1** open; cleared; uncovered: ~ জায়গা. **2** extensive; wide; spacious: ~ মাঠ. ❑*n* open space. **~ফাঁই** *adj* tattered; torn asunder; in tatters; ragged.

ফর্ম ⇒ ফরম

ফর্মা ⇒ ফরমা

ফর্সা ⇒ ফরসা

ফল *n* **1** fruit; yield. **2** issue; children. **3** result of a calculation; product or quotient: গুণ~. **4** consequence; effect; result: পরীক্ষার ~; issue or end of an action. **5** judgement; verdict: মোকদ্দমার ~. **6** retribution; gain or loss; reward or punishment; advantage or disadvantage. **7** benefit; enjoyment. **8** findings: ভাগ্যগণনার ~. **~ওয়ালা** *n* fruit-dealer; fruit-seller; fruiterer. **~ওয়ালী** *fem*. **~কথা** *n* the long and short (of it); the sum and substance; gist. ❑*adv* on the whole; roughly; in fact; indeed. **~কর** *adj* yielding/ bearing fruits; fruitful; productive; rewarding; effectual; efficacious; effective. ❑*n* fruit-tax; a fruit-garden. **~ত, ফলে** = ~কথা; consequently; as a result. **~দ, ~দায়ক, ~প্রদ** *adjj* = ~কর. **~দর্শিতা** *n* foresight; prudence. **~দর্শী** *adj* having foresight; foreseeing; prudent. **~ন্ত** *adj* fruit-bearing. **~পাকান্ত** *adj* that which dies when its fruits ripen. **~প্রসূ** *adj* = ~কর. **~প্রাপ্তি** *n* obtaining (the desired) fruit or result; success. **~বান, ~বতী** *adj* = ~ন্ত. **~বিক্রেতা, ~বিক্রেত্রী** *n fem* = ~ওয়ালা, ~ওয়ালী. **~ভাগী** *adj* sharing in profit/ advantage/ consequences. **~ভাগিনী** *fem*. **~ভুক** *adj* enjoying fruit; fruit-eater. **~ভোগ** *n* enjoyment/ suffering of consequences. **~ভোগী** *adj* suffering or taking the consequences; enjoying the fruits; receiving profits. **~মূল** *n* fruits and roots/ vegetables. **~মূলাহারী** *adj* living on fruits and roots; vegetarian. **~শর্করা** *n* fructose; fruit-sugar. **~শালী, ~শালিনী** *adj* = ~কর. **~শূন্য** *adj* fruitless; unproductive; useless; unprofitable; sterile; vain; abortive. **~শ্রুতি** *n* **1** narration of the effect of an act of piety or act of hearing this narration. **2** effect on the mind caused by reading a particular class of literature; results; consequences. **~শ্রেষ্ঠ** *n* the best of fruits; mango (tree). **~ দেওয়া , ~ দান করা** *vt* yield fruits; to be effective; give a fruit offering to a deity. **~ ধরা** *vi* fructify; fructuate. **~ পাওয়া** *vt* get fruits; get good results; suffer or take the consequences; profit. **~ ভোগা, ~ ভোগ করা** *vt* suffer or take the consequences; enjoy the fruits. **~সিদ্ধি** *n* realizing an object; success; a prosperous issue. **~হীন** *adj* = ~শূন্য. **ফলের বাগান** *n* orchard.

ফলই, ফলি *n* a species of small fresh water fish having silvery colour.

ফলক *n* **1** tapering flat end or head; point: তীরের ~. **2** plank; board: ধোপার ~. **3** lath; bench; slab; wooden bench. **4** any flat surface. **5** shield. **6** gaming-board. **7** a slab at the base (of a pedestal). **~পাণি** *n* soldier armed with a shield. **~-লিপি** *n* name-plate. **ফলকাকার** *adj* (bot) foliaceous.

ফলকী *n* **1** = ফলই. **2** soldier armed with a shield.

ফলন *n* **1** yield; production; output; harvest; crop. **2** origin; birth; source.

ফলনা [A] *n* so-and-so.

ফলন্ত ⇒ ফল

ফলশি *n* dried slices of green mango (preserved in salt or in salt and mustard).

ফলসা, ফালসা [P] *n* a kind of purple berries having a sweet and sour taste; *Grewia asiatica*.

ফলা[১] *n* **1** blade. **2** point (of an arrow/ sword); edge. **3** shield. **4** system of forming conjunct letters of two or more consonants: য ~, র ~; any of the consonantal symbols added to another consonant to from a conjunct letter (eg ্য, ্র).

ফলা[২] *adj* fruit-bearing: দো~, bearing fruits twice a year.

ফলা[৩] = ফলন

ফলা[৪] *vi* fructify; bear fruits: গাছটা এ বছর ফলবে; grow: ধান ভালো ফলেছে; to come true: তোমার কথা ফলেছে; follow as a consequence: কর্মের ফল ~.

ফলাও *adj* **1** extensive; profuse; wide; ample: ~ কারবার/ বুদ্ধি. **2** exaggerated; magnified: ~ প্রচার. **3** abundant. **~ করা** *vt* exaggerate; make much of; blow up; overstate; inflate.

ফলাকাঙ্ক্ষা *n* hope or expectation of success/ favourable consequences. **~ করা** *vt* desire success. **ফলাকাঙ্ক্ষী** *adj* desirous of success/ results.

ফলাগম *n* fructification; production of fruits; the fruit season; (fig) attainment of success. **~ হওয়া** *vt* fructify.

ফলানুসন্ধান, ফলান্বেষণ *nn* looking for results; search for results/ reward; desire of success. **~ করা** *vt* search/ look for results; desire/ seek success. **ফলান্বেষী** *adj* seeking results/ reward/ fruits/ success.

ফলানো *vt* **1** fructify; grow: আম ~. **2** exaggerate; overexpose: ফলিয়ে বলা. **3** assert oneself; show off; put on airs. **রং ~** *vi* exaggerate; embellish; embroider; dress up.

ফলাপেক্ষা *n* regard to results; expectation of consequences/ success.

ফলাফল *n* good or bad effect or outcome of an action; consequences; results; upshot, outcome.

ফলার *n* **1** a meal consisting of vegetarian food other than rice. **2** act of eating such a meal. ~ **করা** *vi* take such a meal. **ফলারে** *adj* given to eating such meals.

ফলার্থী = ফলান্বেষী

ফলাশী *adj* feeding or living on fruits; frugivorous.

ফলাস্বাদন *n* enjoyment of fruits/ consequences.

ফলাহার *n* = ফলার; act of eating fruits. **ফলাহারী** *adj* subsisting on fruits only.

ফলি ⇒ ফলই

ফলিত *adj* bearing or yielding fruit; resulting as a consequence; applied. ~ **জ্যোতিষ** *n* astrology. ~ **বিজ্ঞান** *n* applied science.

ফলিতার্থ *n* purport; gist; substance; import.

ফলুই ⇒ ফলই

ফলে = ফলত

ফলোৎপত্তি *n* **1** production of fruits; fructuation. **2** profit; gain; advantage; attainment of success.

ফলোৎপাদক *adj* **1** = ফলকর. **2** profitable; useful. **3** pleasant. **ফলোৎপাদন** *n* act of producing/ growing/bearing fruits. **ফলোৎপাদন করা** *vi, vt* grow or bear fruits.

ফলোদয় *n* fructification; appearance of consequences or results; reward or punishment; getting proper results.

ফলোন্মুখ *adj* on the point of fructification; about to give fruits.

ফলোপজীবী *n* fruit-seller; fruiterer.

ফলোপলব্ধি *n* realization of consequences; attainment of desired result.

ফল্গু *n* a subterranean river at Gaya. ~**ধারা**, ~**প্রবাহ** (fig) an undercurrent of any feeling.

ফল্গুনী *n* name of the twin stars according to Indian astronomy: পূর্ব~, উত্তর~.

ফল্গূৎসব *n* the vernal festival commonly called Holi.

ফষ্টি-নষ্টি *n* **1** flirtation. **2** badinage; drollery; flippant witticism. ~ **করা** *vi* **1** flirt. **2** indulge in badinage/ light banter; frolic.

ফস *adj* (onom) **1** loose; slack. **2** quick. **3** sudden; abrupt. ~ **করে** *adv* abruptly; on the spur of the moment; in a flash; off the cuff; all of a sudden; impertinently.

ফসকা, ফস্কা *adj* loose; slack. ~ **গেরো** loose knot.

ফসকানো, ফস্কানো *vi, vt* **1** slip: পা ~. **2** miss: শিকার/ সুযোগ ~.

ফসফরাস [E] *n* phosphorus.

ফসল [A] *n* **1** harvest; crop. **2** effect; benefit; advantage; result: গবেষণার ~. **ফসলের সময়** *n* harvesting season or time. **ফসলি** *adj* relative to harvest or crops: এক ফসলি ক্ষেত; calculated from the harvest-time. **ফসলি সন** *n* an era introduced by Akbar, the Mughal emperor.

ফাইন [E] *n* fine. ~ **করা** *vt* fine. ~ **দেওয়া** *n* to pay a fine.

ফাই-ফরমাশ *n* odd jobs; errands. ~ **খাটা** *vi* to carry out odd jobs; to run errands; to go on errands for sb.

ফাইল [E] *n* file. ~ **করা** *vi* file; to put (papers) in a file.

ফাউন্টেন পেন [E]*n* fountain-pen.

ফাও *n* an extra or anything obtained gratis. ❑*adj* **1** extra. **2** trivial; insignificant.

ফাওড়া *n* spade with a long handle.

ফাঁক *n* **1** gap; intervening space; interval; difference; breach: দুটোর মধ্যে খানিকটা ~ রয়েছে. **2** fissure; break; crevice; crack; rupture; rift: দেয়ালের ~. **3** respite; leisure; relief; breather: কাজের ফাঁকে. **4** open space: হিমের সময়ে ফাঁকে এতক্ষণ বসে থেকো না. **5** isolated/ desolate/ deserted; solitary place: একটু ~ পেয়ে সেখানে বসে পড়লাম. **6** opportunity; chance: একবার ফাঁকে পেলে সে শোধ নেবে. **7** loop-hole: আইনের ~. **8** vacuum: বোতলটায় আর ~ নেই. **9** fault; shortcoming; failing: শুধু ~ খোঁজা. **10** void; room: ঘরে আর ~নেই. **11** omission: নেমন্তন্ন থেকে ফাঁকে পড়লাম. **12** hiding; aloofness: ফাঁকে-ফাঁকে থাকা. **13** exception; exclusion: এক দিনও ~ যায় না. **14** deception; hoax: ফাঁকে পড়া. **15** off-beat in an Indian musical measure: তিন তাল এক ~. ❑*adj* empty: পকেট ~. ~ **করা** *vt* **1** open: দরজা ~ করা. **2** cleave; tear asunder; split. **3** part: ঠোঁট ~ করা. **4** exhaust; defalcate; misappropriate: তহবিল ~ করা. **5** widen the gap: পা ~ করা. **6** perforate; bore; rend. ~ **দেওয়া** *vt* omit; skip. ~ **ধরা** *vt* find fault with; looking out for faults or flaws. ~ **পড়া** *vi* fall short; be missing; get omitted. ~ **পাওয়া** *vt* **1** get respite/ breather/ leisure. **2** get an opportunity/ chance. **3** find empty/ vacant. ~ **হওয়া** *vi* open; move apart; part; be misappropriated/ defalcated; be exhausted/ consumed. **ফাঁক ফাঁক** *adj* sparse; few and far between; scattered; dotted about. ~ **বের করা** *vt* find fault with. ~ **যাওয়া** *vi* get omitted; be left off; be counted out; be missed out. **ফাঁকে পড়া** *vi be* cheated/ swindled out. **ফাঁকে ফাঁকে** *adv* **1** during leisure hours. **2** keeping aloof or apart; in hiding. **দো**~ *n* two sections. ~ **ফাঁক করা** *vt* to divide into two.

ফাঁকতাল *n* a measure in Indian music. **ফাঁকতালে** *adv* by an accidental piece of luck; unobservedly; stealthily: ফাঁকতালে পালিয়ে এসেছি.

ফাঁকা *adj* **1** uncovered; open: ~ জায়গা. **2** empty; desolate; vacant: ~ বাড়ি. **3** lonely; solitary. **4** vain; hollow; worthless; futile: ~ কথা. **5** blank: বন্দুকের ~ আওয়াজ. **6** extra: কিছু ~ রোজগারের সুযোগ. ~-~ **ঠেকা** *vi* seem almost empty or desolate. ~ **কথা** *n* vain talk; futility. **ফাঁকায়**

ফাঁকায় *adv* 1 at every pore. 2 unobservedly. 3 keeping aloof; unconcernedly.

ফাঁকি *n* 1 deception; trickery; evasion; eye wash. 2 fallacy; sophistry. 3 fraud; hoax; quibble; dodge; trick. 4 loss; damage; harm. **~জুঁখি, ~জুঁকি** *n* cheating; fraud; deception; trickery; sharp practice; hanky-panky; ruse; neglect; perfunctoriness. **~বাজ** *adj* deceitful; evasive; slyly neglectful. ❑*n* shirker; crook; trickster; deceiver. **~বাজি** *n* 1 shirking; sly neglectfulness. 2 practice of deception; trickery; swindle. **~ দেওয়া, ~বাজি করা** *vi, vt* deceive; cheat; hoax; quibble; hoodwink; swindle; shirk; dodge; skate over. **~তে পড়া** *vi, vt* be deceived/ cheated/ swindled; suffer losses.

ফাঁট *n* 1 infusion; decoction. 2 churned paste of lentils. **ফাঁটানো** *vt* stir; churn.

ফাঁড় *n* (colloq) 1 stomach; belly. 2 middle section of a pot, vase, etc. 3 breadth.

ফাঁড়া *n* bad luck; probability of some danger or even death according to astrology; injury; damage. **~ উতরানো/ কাটানো** *vi* get out of danger or a risk of death.

ফাঁড়ি *n* outpost; police outpost; watch-post. **~দার** *n* watchman; sentinel. **~দারি** *n* the office of a watchman.

ফাঁদ *n* 1 trap; snare; pitfall. 2 (fig) plot; intrigue; deception; ploy. 3 (of bangles, nose-rings, etc) diameter. **~ পাতা** *vt* set or lay a trap; (fig) hatch a plot/ intrigue. **ফাঁদে পড়া** *vi* get into a trap or pitfall; be ensnared; get involved in an intrigue. **ফাঁদে ফেলা** *vt* trap; ensnare; get one into a trap or pitfall; (fig) involve one in an intrigue; take in a trap. **ফাঁদে পা দেওয়া** = ফাঁদে পড়া.

ফাঁদা *vi, vt* 1 start; lay the foundation of; set up: বাড়ি/ ব্যবসা ~. 2 expand: দোকানখানা বেশ ফেঁদে বসেছে. 3 settle down firmly; put down roots: এ তল্লাটে সে ফেঁদে বসেছে. 4 lay: ফাঁদ ~. 5 hatch; devise: মতলব ~. **ফাঁদাল** *adj* large; having a large diameter or opening: ফাঁদাল হাঁড়ি.

ফাঁদি *adj* large; wide; broad. **~ কথা** *n* tall talk/ story; hot air; cock and bull story; claptrap; waffle.

ফাঁপ *n* swelling; inflation; distention; flatulence: পেটের ~. **~ ধরা** *vi* swell; inflate; distend; become flatulent.

ফাঁপর *n* 1 embarrassment; perplexing difficulty; scrape; vexation; trouble. 2 perplexity; bafflement. 3 emptiness: বুকের ~. **ফাঁপরে পড়া** *vi* be perplexed; be in/ get oneself into a fix; get into an embarrassing situation/ a light corner.

ফাঁপা *vi* 1 swell; inflate; distend. 2 increase; grow. 3 prosper; flourish; thrive: লোকটা ফেঁপে উঠেছে. ❑*adj* 1 swelled; inflated; distended; flatulent. 2 hollow; empty. **ফাঁপন** *n* swelling. **~ ঢেঁকির শব্দ বড়ো** (prov) An empty vessel sounds much. **ফেঁপে ওঠা** *vi* prosper; make a fortune. **পেট ~** *vi* 1 have flatulence. 2 be unable to keep sth secret. **~নো** *vt* 1 inflate; cause to swell. 2 extol; puff up.

ফাঁফর ⇒ ফাঁপর

ফাঁস[১] *n* 1 rope; cord; string; line. 2 trap; snare. 3 noose; slip-knot; loop; a rope for hanging criminals; halter. 4 strangling; death by hanging. **~ দেওয়া** *vt* strangle. **ফাঁসে যাওয়া** *vt* die by hanging; be hanged.

ফাঁস[২] *n* divulgence (of secrets). ❑*adj* 1 loose; slack. 2 disclosed; divulged. **~ করা** *vt* 1 baffle; spoil; mar. 2 divulge; reveal inadvertently; leak; give the game away; let the cat out of the bag.

ফাঁসা[১] *vt* 1 be torn: কাপড়টা ফেঁসে গেল. 2 get detached; crack; come away: হাঁড়ির তলা ফেঁসেছে. 3 miscarry; fail; come to nothing; flop: সব পরিকল্পনা ফেঁসে গেল. 4 be divulged; come to light.

ফাঁসা[২] ivi (derog) be trapped; get into a scrape/ trap. **ফেঁসে যাওয়া** *vi* 1 get involved. 2 be torn; crack.

ফাঁসানো, ফাঁসান *vt* 1 tear; rend; detach; cause to come away. 2 let down; foil. 3 implicate in; get one into a scrape. 4 divulge; bring to light.

ফাঁসি *n* 1 noose; rope; cord; halter. 2 hanging; death or killing or suicide by hanging; sentence to death by hanging. **~কাঠ** *n* gallows. **~ দেওয়া** *vt* hang; strangle; sentenced to death by hanging. **~ যাওয়া** *vi* be hanged. **~র আসামি** *n* convict sentenced to death by hanging. **~র দড়ি** *n* rope for hanging; halter.

ফাঁসুড়ে *n* highwayman who strangles travellers and robs them; thug.

ফাক্কা *n* foam; froth; scum.

ফাগ, ফাগু *n* (poet) red powder (usually of the root of wild ginger coloured with sappan wood) which Hindus throw at one another during the Holi (হোলি) festival.

ফাগুন (poet) = ফাল্গুন

ফাজলামি, ফাজলামো [A] *n* extreme talkativeness; impudence; impertinence; sauciness; pertness; flippancy; frivolity; waggery.

ফাজিল [A] *n* 1 scholar. 2 stage in Islamic theological education. ❑*adj* 1 impudent; impertinent; flippant; priggish. 2 overmuch; excessive. **~চালাক** *adj* over-forward.

ফাট *n* crack; chink; fissure. **~ ধরা** *vi* crack; form a crack; crack up.

ফাটক *n* 1 main gate; portal; entrance. 2 gaol; jail; prison. **~ হওয়া** *vi* be sentenced to imprisonment; imprisoned; be jailed. ~বন্দী *adj* jailed; imprisoned.

ফাটকি[1] = ফটকি

ফাটকি[2] *adj* **1** tiny; minuscule; paltry; puny; petty. **2** false; fake; make-believe; bogus; sham; illusory. ~-নাটকি *n* **1** knick-knack; sundries; trifles. **2** trifling matter; triviality; small beer.

ফাটন *n* breaking; splitting; cleaving; piercing; rending; cracking; bursting; explosion; fission.

ফাটল *n* fissure; crack; crevice; interstice.

ফাটা *vi* crack; split; go to pieces; fall apart; chap: চামড়া ~; burst; explode; burst open: ফোঁড়া ~. ❑*adj* cracked; split; rent; fractured; chapped; exploded; bad: ~ কপাল bad luck. ~নো *vt* crack; spit; rend; burst (open); explode; smash. ~ফাটি *n* violent scuffle; melee; brawl; stiff affray; a rowdy quarrel.

ফাড়া *vt* cleave; tear; rend; halve. ~নো *vt* cause to cleave etc.

ফাৎ *n* (onom) **1** sound of fire suddenly flaring up. **2** whiff; puff.

ফাতনা, ফাৎনা *n* float (used on a fishing line).

ফাতরা *n* withered spathe of banana-palm with frond.

ফাতেহা [A] *n* **1** the opening chapter of the Holy Qoran. **2** (Muslim) obsequies with prayers and distribution of food among the poor.

ফানা [A] *n* dissolution; destruction. ❑*adj* lost in sth or sb; absorbed/ engaged wholly; engrossed; rapt. ~ হওয়া *vi* perish; be destroyed; be lost/ absorbed/ engrossed.

ফানুশ, ফানুস [P] *n* **1** paper-balloon. **2** lamp-shade (made of paper). **3** lantern.

ফানেল [E] *n* funnel.

ফান্ট *n* **1** substance used in tempering metals. **2** solder; decoction. **3** sth easily obtained.

ফান্ড [E] *n* fund.

ফান্দ = ফাঁদ

ফায়দা = ফয়দা

ফার[1] *n* splitting; cleaving. ❑*adj* split; cleft.

ফারখত, ফারখতি [A] *n* **1** deed of release or discharge; deed of dissolution of partnership. **2** deed of divorcement. **3** receipt; acquittance.

ফারফোর *adj* full of holes; porous; honeycombed.

ফারসি *n* Persian language. ❑*adj* of or pertaining to Persia.

ফারাক [A] *n* **1** differences; contrast; incongruity. **2** distance; separation. ❑*adj* different; distinct; separated.

ফার্ন [E] *n* fern.

ফার্স [E] *n* farce.

ফার্সী *n*= ফারসি

ফার্নিচার [E] *n* furniture.

ফাল[1] *n* ploughshare; coulter.

ফাল[2] *n* jump. ~ দেওয়া, ~ মারা *adj* jump; brag; vaunt; bluster; swagger; swank.

ফাল[3] = ফালা

ফালতু, ফালতো *adj* **1** additional; extra; surplus. **2** unnecessary; useless. **3** pointless; superfluous; senseless.

ফালা *n* long slice or strip. ~ দেওয়া *vt* cut in strips; slice. ~-ফালা *adj* cut in long strips or slices; sliced; torn into strips; tattered. ~-ফালা করা *vt* cut or tear into long slices; tear to shreds; tatter.

ফালি *n* long slice or strip. ~ করা, ~ দেওয়া *vt* cut/ tear into long; small slices/ strips. ~-ফালি *adj* cut into small pieces; torn into small strips; sliced. ❑*adv* strip by strip.

ফালুদা [P] *n* kind of flummery pressed through a sieve and mixed with sugar and milk.

ফাল্গুন *n* the eleventh month of the Bengali calendar (from the middle of February to the middle of March). **ফাল্গুনী** *adj* of or pertaining to Phalgoon; relating to Phalgooni Nakshatra; the full moon day of Phalgoon.

ফি[1] *adj* each; every; per: ~বছর. ~-রোজ every day.

ফি[2], **ফিস** [E]*n* fee.

ফিক[1] *n* (onom) **1** spasm caused by sudden contraction of muscles; neuralgia; stitch. ~ ব্যথা *n* spasm; stitch; spasmodic pain in one's sides; twinge. ~ ধরা *vi* have a stitch/ spasmodic pain in one's sides.

ফিক[2] *n* (onom) (devoting) giggle; titter; snigger. **ফিক-ফিক** *n* the giggles; titters. **ফিক-ফিক করা** *vt* giggle; titter; snigger.

ফিকা, ফিকে (colloq) *adj* **1** light; pale; wan; dull; washed out; discoloured. **2** insipid; thin; diluted; wishy-washy; watery; tasteless. **3** trifling; paltry; airy; uninteresting; vapid; flat.

ফিকির [A] *n* **1** reflection; consideration; imagination. **2** intrigue; plot; care; ruse; stratagem; deception. **3** device; contrivance; artifice. ~ করা *vi, vt* consider; reflect; care; contrive; plot against; intrigue. **ফিকিরে ফকির** *n* hypocritical ascetic; hypocrite; impostor.

ফিঙা, ফিঙে, ফিঙ্গা *n* **1** black drongo. **2** small Y-shaped piece of wood. **3** sling; catapult.

ফিচাল, ফিচেল (rare) *adj* **1** sly; knavish; tricksy; crafty; wily; shifty. **2** flippant; pert; impudently talkative. **ফিচলেমি** *n* trickery; craftiness; sharp practice.

ফিট[1] [E] *n* fainting fit.

ফিট[2] [E] *adj* fit; ready; fitted; pieced together; well-dressed; thorough: ~ বাবু. ~ হওয়া *vi* get ready; be fit. ~ করা *vt* fit; make ready; fit out; to piece together; adjust; arrange.

ফিট[3] *adj* **1** bright. **2** neat and clean; tidy. ~ফাট *adj* neat and tidy; well-dressed; well-decorated; well-furnished; spruce: ~ফাট লোক.

~ফাট করা *vt* furnish; embellish; make neat and tidy.

ফিতরা, ফেতরা [A] *n* alms given on the Id-ul-fitr day (festival following the month of Ramadan).

ফিতা, ফিতে (colloq) *n* **1** tape. **2** lace. **3** ribbon; riband. **4** frill. **চুলের ~** *n* ribbon. **লাল ~** *n* red tape; (fig) excessive use of formalities in public business. **লাল ~র কারবার** red-tapism. **~ওয়ালা, ~ বিক্রেতা** *n* haberdasher. **~-কৃমি** *n* tapeworm.

ফিনকি *n* spark (as of fire); a thin jet or spray (as of any fluid). **~ দিয়ে বের হওয়া** (of blood, etc) spurt out; gush; spout; come out in a sudden spurt.

ফিনফিনে *adj* (of clothes, etc) very fine; flimsy.

ফিনাইল [E] *n* phenyl.

ফিনিক *n* glow; shine; shimmer: জ্যোৎস্নায় ~ ফুটেছে. **~ ফোটা** *vt* glow; shine; shimmer.

ফিরকা ⇒ ফেরকা

ফিরকি *n* a bolt (of a window) which can rotate round its axis; a rotating bolt.

ফিরঙ্গ *n* syphilis. **~ রোগ, ~ ব্যাধি** *n* syphilis. **~ রুটি** *n* bread baked in the European fashion.

ফিরত ⇒ ফেরত

ফিরতি *adj* returning; return: ~ ডাক, return mail. ❑*n* what has been returned or saved; balance; surplus: সাত টাকার ~. **~ পথ** *n* return journey again.

ফিরনি [P] *n* A sort of a pudding of ground rice and milk.

ফিরা[১]**,ফিরানো** ⇒ ফেরা[১]

ফিরা[২] *adv* again. **~ফিরতি** *adv* again; over again.

ফিরানো ⇒ ফেরা[১]

ফিরিঙ্গি *n, adj* **1** Indo-Portuguese; Anglo-Indian; Eurasian. **2** European; Christian. **~-খোঁপা** *n* bun or chignon in the European style. **ফিরিঙ্গিনী** *fem*.

ফিরিস্তি, ফিরিস্তা (rare) [P] *n* **1** list; inventory; catalogue. **2** table of contents; index. **3** a description. **কাজের ~ দেওয়া** render an account of jobs done.

ফিরে *adj* next. ❑*adv* again; afresh: ~ বসা.

ফিরোজা [P] *n* turquoise. ❑*adj* turquoise blue: আকাশের ~ পর্দা. **ফিরোজি** *adj* turquoise blue.

ফিল, পিল [A] *n* **1** elephant. **2** (chess) bishop. **~খানা** *n* elephant-stable.

ফিলটার [E] *n* filter. **~ করা** *vi* filter.

ফিলসফি, ফিলজফি [E]*n* philosophy. **ফিলসফার, ফিলজফর** *n* philosopher.

ফিলহাল [A] *adv* recently (more usu হালফিল).

ফিল্ডমার্শাল [E] *n* Field Marshal.

ফিল্ম, ফিলম [E] *n* **1** motion-picture; film. **2** (photographic) film.

ফিস = ফি

ফিসফিস *n* (onom) whisper; mutter. **~ করা** *vi* whisper; mutter. **ফিসফিসানি** *n* whisper; whispering noise.

ফিসাবিলিল্লাহ [A] (phrase) In the way of God.

ফী[১] ⇒ ফি[১]

ফী[২]**, ফি, ফিস** *n* fee.

ফুঁ, ফু *n* puff; whiff; puffing; blowing. **এক ~য়ে** *adv* easily; with ease; blindfold. **এক ~য়ে উড়ানো** *vt* foil/ baffle an adversary easily (in his plans); trounce; beat hollow; make mince meat of; crush at one (a single) blow. **~ দেওয়া/ মারা** *vt* blow; play: বাঁশিতে ~ দেওয়া. **~ লাগা** *vi* have a puff of air. **~ লাগানো** *vt* = ~ দেওয়া.

ফুঁক, ফুক *n* **1** uttering charms and incantations and blowing (as a remedy or a means of exorcising). **2** blow: শাঁখে ফুঁক পাড়া. **ঝাড়-~ করা** *vt* exorcise evil or cure an illness by uttering charms and incantations.

ফুঁকা, ফোঁকা, ফুকা *vt* **1** puff; huff. **2** blow; play: বাঁশি ~. **3** squander; waste; blow: সম্পত্তি ফুঁকে দেওয়া. **4** smoke with puffs; puff. **5** shape by blowing. **শিঙা/ শিঙ্গা ~** *vi* (fig) die; kick the bucket. ❑*adj* shaped by slowing: ~ শিশি.

ফুঁড়া ⇒ ফোঁড়া

ফুঁপানো ⇒ ফোঁপানো

ফুঁপি, ফুপি *n* the corner of a piece of cloth.

ফুঁসা, ফোঁসা *vt* hiss; growl in suppressed anger; fume; seethe with anger. **ফুঁসে উঠা** *vi* explode (with rage).

ফুক *vt* puff; whiff. **~ করে** *adv* with a puff. **2** in a trice; in an instant; in a jiffy.

ফুকন *n* puffing; whiffing; blowing. **~ নল** *n* goldsmith's or silversmith's blowpipe. **ফুকনি** *n* bladder.

ফুকচি, ফুচকি *n* peep.

ফুকর, ফোকর *n* **1** hole; crevice. **2** cell; niche; recess.

ফুকরানো *vi, vt* **1** call/ proclaim aloud; shout. **2** cry in a loud voice; wail; lament. **ফুকরে কাঁদা** *vi* cry out; wail.

ফুকা[১] ⇒ ফুঁকা

ফুকা[২]**, ফুকো** *n* the practice of blowing in air through the vagina of a milch cow. **~ দেওয়া** *vi* blow air through the vagina of milch cow. ❑*adj* hollow.

ফুকার *n* **1** shout; scream; yell. **2** call; invitation. **3** wail.

ফুঙ্গি *n* Buddhist friar or priest (esp of Myanmar).

ফুচকে = পুচকে

ফুট[১] *n* a foot (= 12 inches).

ফুট[২] *n* bubble or bubbles of liquid caused by boiling; effervescence caused by boiling; boiling state; frying and bursting open as a result of frying. **~ ধরা** *vi* effervesce or rise in bubbles as a result of boiling; burst open as a result of frying. **~ফাট** *n* (onom) **1** crack. **2** grumbling noise in the abdomen; flatulence.

ফুটকলাই, ~কড়াই *n* a kind of peas which burst open when fried.

ফুটকি *n* minute speckle; dot.

ফুটন *n* **1** blooming; blowing; blossoming. **2** expression. **3** piercing; opening. **4** boiling; effervescence or rising in bubbles by being boiled; bursting open as a result of frying.

ফুটনোট [E]*n* footnote.

ফুটন্ত *adj* **1** blown; blossomed; blooming; blossoming. **2** boiling; effervescent; rising in bubbles as a result of boiling.

ফুটপাথ, ফুটপাত [E]*n* footpath.

ফুট–ফরমাশ = ফাই–ফরমাস

ফুটফুট, ফুটফাট *n* (onom) **1** bubbling noise. **2** cracking (sound of gunpowder explosion, etc). **3** growling noise in the abdomen (due to indigestion): পেট ~ করা, have rumbling sounds in the bowels.

ফুটফুটে *adj* **1** very bright; silvery white; glittery; dazzling: ~ জ্যোৎস্না. **2** very fair complexioned and good-looking; fair skinned; lovely little: ~ মেয়ে. **3** cheerful; gay.

ফুটবল [E] *n* football.

ফুটা[১] *n* **1** hole; crack; crevice; pore; leak ❑*adj* **1** porous; leaky; cracked; containing a hole or holes; punctured. **2** pierced.

ফুটা[২]**, ফোটা** *vi, vt* **1** bloom; blossom; flower: ফুল ~. **2** become visible; rise; emerge; loom; go up: আকাশে তারা ফুটেছে. **3** be uttered/ expressed: মুখ ফুটে কিছু বলা. **4** open: চোখ ~, (fig) become clever; be able to look to one's own interests. **5** bubble up/ burble (when boiling): ভাত ~. **6** parch; puff out: খই ফুটছে. **7** prick; be pricked: কাঁটা ~. **8** begin to speak: বাচ্চার মুখে কথা ফুটেছে. **9** be expressed: ভাব ফুটে ওঠা. **10** become cracked: হাড়ির তলা ফুটে গেল. **11** ooze out: রক্ত ফুটে বের হওয়া. **12** make sound: তার তুড়ি ফোটে না. **13** be unfolded; become distinct or manifest: চরিত্র ~. **14** = ফাটা. ❑*adj* full-blown; in (full) bloom; blooming. **কথা ~** *vt* **1** (of children) begin to make use of speech; babble. **2** (fig) find one's tongue. **দাঁত ~** *vi* **1** be pierced with teeth; be bitten. **2** (fig) be accessible/ comprehensible. **ফিনিক ~** sparkle/ glow (in the moonlight). **বিয়ের ফুল ~** *vi* to be married soon. **মুখে খই ~** *vi* become voluble/ eloquent; talk nineteen to the dozen. **(মুখে) হাসি ~** (of smile) light up.

ফুটানো, ফোটানো *vt* (causative of ফুটা) **1** cause to / make bloom; blossom or blow: ফুল ~. **2** cause to appear; rise. **3** cause to stand out: রং ~. **4** prick; pierce: হুল ~. **দাঁত ~** *vi* **1** pierce with teeth; bite. **2** (fig) able to understand/ comprehend; interfere; meddle in: ওখানে দাঁত ফোটাবার জো নেই. **5** improve; ameliorate. **6** cause to effervesce or rise in bubbles as a result of boiling; boil or cook: চাল ~. **7** cause to puff out/ parch: খই ~. **8** express; cause to express intelligibly. **9** unfold; make distinct/ manifest. **10** puncture; prick: বেলুন ~.

ফুটানি *n* **1** ostentation; extravagance; pretentiousness; airs; pomposity; ostentatiousness; vanity. **2** biting words. **দাঁত~** *n* access to a subject; interference.

ফুটি *n* a variety of melon. **~ফাটা** *adj* thoroughly frayed/ rent asunder/ burst asunder. **আহ্লাদে ~-ফাটা** (phrase) bubbling over with joy.

ফুটুস *adj* (sl) absent; out; nonexistent; gone.

ফুটোন্মুখ *adj* about to burst open/ bloom.

ফুড়া, ফোড়া *vt* **1** pierce; prick; rend asunder. **2** gin and card (cotton, etc.): তুলা ~.

ফুড়ুক, ফুড়ুৎ *n* **1** (onom) sound denoting sudden flying away; whirr. **~ করে** *adv* in a flash; in a trice. **2** sound denoting puffing (away) at a hookah. **ফুড়ুক-ফুড়ুক, ফুড়ুৎ-ফুড়ুৎ** *n* (onom) sound denoting continual comings and goings (of a bird) or puffing at a hubble-bubble.

ফুৎকার *n* puffing; blowing; whiff; puff. **~ দেওয়া** *vi* puff; whiff; blow. **ফুৎকারে** *adv* with ease; handily.

ফুফা *n* husband of one's father's sister. **ফুফু** *n fem* sister of one's father. **ফুফাত** *adj* descended from one's father's sister. **ফুফাত ভাই/ বোন** *n* cousin (related as above).

ফুরকান, ফোরকান [A] *n* the Qoran(distinguising truth from falsehood).

ফুরন *n* (archaic) piecework.

ফুরফুর *n* **1** (onom) sound denoting gentle blowing of wind; fluttering of cloth, hair, etc; rustle. **2** sound denoting fluttering of the wings of a fledgling. **ফুরফুরানো** *vi* **1** rustle; flutter; try to fly. **2** (fig) get/ be fresh with; behave insolently with one's elders. **ফুরফুরে** *adj* gently blowing; fluttering; rustling. **~ হাওয়া** *n* gentle/ pleasant breeze.

ফুরসত [A] *n* leisure; respite; relief; rest; opportunity; leave. **~মাফিক** at one's leisure.

ফুরসি = ফরসি

ফুরানো *vi, vt* **1** end; come to an end; finish; terminate; conclude; close: আয়ু/ দিন/ পথ ~, গল্প ~. **2** be spent/ exhausted/ consumed: টাকা/ খাবার/ শক্তি ~. **3** be completed/ accomplished: কাজ ফুরিয়েছে. **4** settle; enter into/ make a contract. **5** cease to exist; be lost/ gone: আশা ~.

ফুর্তি *n* joy; delight; merriment; amusement; thrill; fun; good time; agility: শরীরে ফুর্তি নেই. **~ করা** *vi* have fun/ good time; amuse oneself. **~বাজ** *adj* jovial; jolly; cheerful; light-hearted; out to enjoy oneself.

ফুল[১] *n* **1** flower; blossom. **2** floral design of ornaments; floral designs of embroidery. **~ওয়ালী** *n fem* florist; flower-girl. **~কপি** *n* cauliflower. **~কাটা** *adj* embroidered with floral designs; floriated; floreated. **~কারি** *n* ornamental or decorated needlework; embroidery with floral designs. **~কোঁচা** *adj* frilled (like a flower); frilly. **~খড়ি** *n* (writing) chalk. **~খেলা** *n* playing with flowers. **~চন্দন** *n* flowers and sandal-paste (offered to receive or felicitate sb with respect or affection). **মুখে ~চন্দন পড়ুক** (phrase) God bless you. **~ছড়ি** *n* stick decorated with floral designs or shaped like a flowery bough. **~ঝাঁপা** *n* kind of earring in the form of a flower. **~ঝুরি** *n* firework emitting starry sparks. **~টুকি** *n* honeysucker. **~টুসি** *n* a very thin-skinned/ sensitive girl or woman, who is easily hurt. **~তৈল** *n* scented or perfumed oil. **~-তোলা** *n* flower-gathering. ❑*adj* embroidered with floral designs; floriated; floreated. **~দান, ~দানি** *n* flower-vase. **~দোল** *n* a festival held in honour of Sri Krishna on the full moon day of Baishakh. **~ধনু** *n* Madana, the god of love; a bow made of flowers. **~স্ত** *adj* in flowers; blossomed. **~বড়ি** *n* small conical ball made of the foamy paste of pigeon-pea and dried in the sun (⇒ বড়ি). **~বাগান** *n* flower-garden. **~বাণ, ~শর** *n* Madana, the god of love; Madana's shaft (cf Cupid). **~বাবু** *n* a thorough dandy; a beau; fop; a playboy; a coxcomb. **~মালা** *n* garland of flowers. **~শয্যা** *n* (lit) a bed of flowers; the ceremony after marriage when the bride and the bridegroom are to sleep on a bed of flowers. **~তোলা** *vi, vt* **1** pick/ pluck/ cull flowers. **2** embroider a floral design. **~ দেওয়া** *vt* (according to Hindu rite) offer flowers (to a God). **~ ধরা** *vi* flower; be in blossom. **~ পাড়া** *vt* = ~ তোলা. **ফুলের সাজি** *n* flower-basket. **ফুলের ঘায়ে মূর্ছা যাওয়া** (phrase) one who is hurt by trifles; be thin-skinned; display over-sensitiveness.

ফুল[২] *n* (zoo) placenta. **~ পড়া** *vi* (of placenta) be expelled.

ফুল[৩] [E]*adj* full; complete; large; standard: ~শার্ট, ~টিকিট.

ফুল[৪] [E] *n* fool.

ফুলক:প *n* cauliflower.

ফুলকা *n* **1** gill (of a fish). **2** pouch-like formation under the eyes of a lock. ❑*adj* thin; hollow and inflated; puffed up: ~ লুচি.

ফুলকি *n* spark.

ফুলল *adj* **1** full of flowers; flowery. **2** scented (with flowers).

ফুলস্ক্যাপ, ফুলস্কেপ *adj* foolscap.

ফুলা, ফোলা *vi* **1** swell (up); distend; balloon; be inflated; bulge out. **2** grow fat; put on weight or flesh. **3** be puffed up; be filled with pride. **4** have (inflammatory) swelling. **5** flourish; thrive; prosper. **6** be elated or exalted. **7** bloom. **8** heave; well up; surge; smile upon: কপাল ফোলা. ❑*n* swelling. ❑*adj* swelled up; swollen; inflamed; bulgy; puffy; bumpy; flatulent. **ফুলে ওঠা** *vi,vt* **1** prosper; flourish; make a fortune; come into money. **2** be puffed up; be filled/ bloated with pride. **3** put on weight/ fat; grow fat. **ফুলে পড়া** *vi* be affected with dropsy; have swelling. **পেট ~** *vi* have one's belly distended owing to the accumulation of gas in the alimentary canal; be affected with flatulence.

ফুলানো, ফোলানো *vt* **1** inflate; blow up; cause to swell; bloat. **2** raise blisters: মশা কামড়িয়ে মুখ ফুলিয়ে দিয়েছে. **3** pout: ঠোঁট ~. **4** provoke. **5** flatter; puff; butter (up). **গা ~** *vi* have one's hackles up. ❑*adj* swelled; bloated; puffy; blubbery; lumpy.

ফুলুরি, ফুলরি *n* a kind of chop made of powdered pigeon-peas or gram.

ফুলেল *adj* **1** full of flowers; flowery; bearing flowers; flowered; bloomed. **2** sweet-smelling; fragrant; balmy. **3** lovely/ delightful like a flower. **4** mixed with the essence of flowers: ~-তেল.

ফুল্ল *adj* **1** blooming; blown; in full bloom; full-blown. **2** highly delighted; beaming; cheerful; happy: ~ নয়ন. **3** thoroughly manifest; dazzling: ~ জ্যোৎস্না. ❑*n* flower; blossom. **~কুসুমদাম** *n* a garland of full-blown flowers. **~দাম** *n* wreath of flowers. **ফুল্লাধর** *n* smiling face lips.

ফুস *n* **1** a kind of grass. **2** trifle; bagatelle.

ফুসকুড়ি, ফুস্কুড়ি *n* rash; pimple; boil; eruption; pustule; vesicle.

ফুসফাস *n* (onom) **1** whisper; murmur. **2** gossip; rumour.

ফুসফুস *n* the lung. **ফুসফুসীয় ধমনি** (anat) *n* the pulmonary artery. **~ প্রদাহ** *n* inflammation of the lungs; pneumonia. **ফুসফুসীয় ধমনি ও শিরা** *n* the pulmonary artery and vein. **ফুসফসীয়** *adj* pulmonary. **ফুসফুসীয় সংবহন** *n* pulmonary circulation.

ফুস মন্তর *n* **1** an imaginary esoteric incantation endowing one with supernatural power; (magic) spell; charm. **2** instigation; incitement; enticement; secret counsel; an imaginary secret incantation to entice or evade. **~ দেওয়া** *vt* instigate; incite; inveigle; seduce. **ফুসমন্তরে, ফুসমন্তরের চোটে** in a jiffy; in the twinkling of an eye; in a trice.

ফুসলানো, ফুসলান *vt* seduce; instigate; entice; prompt; cajole; wheedle; get sb round one's little finger; induce. **ফুসলিয়ে নিয়ে যাওয়া** *vt* entice sb away; tempt; seduce. **ফুসলানি** *n* instigation; enticement; seduction; cajolery; coaxing.

ফুসুরফুসুর, ফুসুরফাসুর *n* (sl) continual whispering; secret counselling or consulltation; continual secret palaver.

ফেঁউ *n* **1** jackal. **2** a mad or rabid jackal. **3** a kind of jackal which follows tigers howlingly. **4** person who torments sb with irritating questions or prayers. **5** trouble; bother. ~ **তোলা** *vi* begin howling/ yowling. ~ ~ **করা** *vi* **1** yowl; howl. **2** rattle on; prate; talk nineteen to the dozen; maunder. ~ **লাগা** *vt* **1** (of a tiger) be pursued by howling jackals. **2** (fig) dog sb's footsteps; shadow; tail; be doggedly pursued by a sleuth or a detective; be pestered by pursuers.

ফেঁকড়া, ফ্যাঁকড়া *n* **1** twig; spring. **2** (fig) branch; offshoot. **3** incidental trouble/ hindrance; inconvenience; bother; tangle; knot; snag. **ফেঁকড়ি** *n* a small twig. ~ **তোলা** *vt* raise an objection. ~ **বাধানো** *vt* cause an incidental trouble; make difficulties for. ~ **বের হওয়া** *vt* branch out/ off.

ফেঁশো *n* **1** beard of corn; awn. **2** fibre.

ফেকা, ফেকো *n* frothy spittle that comes out of the mouth whilst talking caused usually by fasting or talking too long. ~ **পাড়া** *vi* talk continually so that frothy spittle comes out of the mouth; talk the hind leg off a donkey; jabber. ~ **পাড়ানো** *adj* loquacious; voluble; gabby.

ফেচফেচ, ফ্যাচফ্যাচ *n* (onom) (colloq) **1** sound of sneezing. **2** irritating talkativeness; logorrhoea; verbal diarrhoea. ~ **করা** *vi* indulge in logorrhoea.

ফেচাং, ফ্যাচাং *n* (colloq) trouble; troublesome burden; hitch; difficulty; disorder. ~ **তোলা** *vi* raise an objection. ~ **বাধানো** *vt* create trouble.

ফেজ [T] *n* fez.

ফেটা, ফ্যাটা *n* **1** (large) band or strip of cloth. **2** turban made of a long band of cloth. ❑*adj* flat: ~ নাক.

ফেটানো, ফেটান *n* beat upto froth; whisk; whip.

ফেটি *n* **1** puttee; bandage; skein or reel of thread. **2** a small turban made of a long strip of cloth. **3** a kind of triangular fishing net. ~ **জাল** *n* = ফেটি.

ফেণী *n* a cluster of banana.

ফেতনা, ফেৎনা [A] *n* **1** mischief; harm. **2** sedition; disorder; disturbance.

ফেতরা, ফিৎরা = ফিতরা

ফেন *n* **1** foam; froth; scum; spume. **2** water strained off from boiled rice: ভাতের ~. **3** bubble. ~ **দিয়ে ভাত খায় গল্পে মারে দই** (prov) (lit) Eats rice without straining off (liquefied) starch but brags of eating yogurt (said about a poor man pretending to be wealthy). **ফেনে ফেনে** *adj* without straining off water. ~ **গালা** *vt* strain off water from boiled rice. **সমুদ্র~** *n* sea-foam; the bone of the cattle-fish. ~**নিভ** *adj* foam-like; foamy.

ফেনক *n* **1** foam; froth. **2** soap. **3** a peacock's tail or plumage. **4** a kind of cake.

ফেনল[১] *n* phenol.

ফেনল[২] *adj* foamy; frothy.

ফেনা *n* **1** = ফেন (১). **2** lather: সাবানের ~. **মুখে ~ কাটা** (phrase) slobber (due to continual talking). **ফেনানো** *vt* **1** stir up into foam or froth; whisk; whip. **2** (fig) exaggerate; colour; inflate; magnify; blow up. ❑*adj* exaggerated; inflated; over-wrought; highly coloured; extravagant; over-blown. ❑exaggeration; overstatement; magnification. **ফেনায়মান** *adj* rising in foam; foaming; effervescent. **ফেনায়িত** *adj* = ফেনানো.

ফেনি (also ~**বাতাসা**) *n* a hollow sweet drop made of treacle or sugar.

ফেনিকা *n* a kind of crisp sweetmeat made of flour and sugar.

ফেনিল *adj* **1** foamy; frothy; spumy. **2** stirred up into foam or froth; whipped.

ফেব্রুয়ারি, ফেব্রুআরি *n* February.

ফের[১] *n* **1** trouble; hindrance; obstacle; peril; difficulty; danger: ফেরে পড়া. **2** tight corner; critical situation. **3** disturbance; disorder. **4** intricacy; mystery: এ-~ বোঝা দায়. **5** obligation; risk: টাকার ~. **6** confusion: নামের ~. **7** change. **8** reverse: অবস্থার ~. **9** witty turn; artful language: কথার ~. **10** consequence: কর্মের ~. **11** purpose; course: কাজের ~. **12** girth; a circuitous fold; circumference. **13** difference between the scales when there is a tilt on either side. ~**ঘোর** *n* **1** intricacy; complication; crookedness; deception; deceptive trick; trickery. **2** confusion; chaos. ~**ফার** *n* **1** interchange; alternation. **2** deception; trickery; jugglery; subterfuge. **3** harassment; persecution. ~**বদল,** ~**ভাঙা** *vt* adjusting the scales to secure correct weight or measure. **অদৃষ্টের** ~ *n* reverses of fortune; reversal of fortune. **ওজনের** ~ *n* uneven scales (in weighing). **কথার** ~ *n* artful language. **কপালের** ~ *n* caprice of fate. **গ্রহের** ~ evil influence of a planet. **হের~** *n* **1** = ~ঘোর. **2** interchange; alternation; modification. ❑*adv* again: ~এসো. ❑*prep* for; for the sake of: নামের ফেরে মানুষ ফেরে.

ফের[২], **ফেরু** = ফেউ

ফেরকা, ফিরকা [A] *n* sect. ~ **বন্দি** *n* classification.

ফেরত, ফেরৎ *n* **1** giving or sending back; return; coming/ going/ putting back. ~ **আনা** *vt* bring back. ~ **আসা** *vi* come back; come back unaccepted; be returned to sender. ~ **দেওয়া** *vt* give/ send back; return; repay; refuse to accept; refuse; redirect. ~ **নেওয়া** *vt* take back; withdraw; retract. ~ **পাঠানো** *vt* send back; return; refuse to accept; refuse; return. ❑*adj* **1** returning. **2** given/ sent back; returned; returned as unaccepted; refused; redirected: ~ চিঠি; immediately coming back; return: ~ ডাক; returning from: অফিস ~; returned from: বিলাত-~. **ফেরতা** *adj* **1** returned or returning from: অফিস-ফেরতা, বিলাত-ফেরতা. **2** return; counter: ~ ডাক. **3** transferred: হাত ফেরতা. **4** double-folded: ফেরতা দিয়ে কাপড় পড়া. **ফেরতা ডাক** *n* return mail. **তাল ফেরতা** *n* (music) switching over to another measure and then playing the former again. **রাগ ফেরতা** in (music) changing from one raga to another in the above manner. **হাত ফেরতা** *adj* transferred. ❑*n* transfer; swap; change of hands.

ফেরদৌস, ফিরদৌস [A] *n* garden; paradise. **~-আলা** *n* the highest heaven.

ফেরফার ⇒ ফের[১]

ফেরফের *n* (onom) used about very light material which quivers at the slightest touch of wind. **ফেরফেরে** *adj* coarse; thin; net-like: ফেরফেরে কাপড়. ~ **করা** *vi* quiver like a thin piece of cloth.

ফেরা, ফিরা *vi* **1** come back; return. **2** be returned; saved as balance: দশ টাকা থেকে কতো ফিরেছে? **3** turn: বাড়ির দিকে ~. **অবস্থা ~** improve; take a good turn. **ফিরে তাকানো** turn back or round. **মন ~** become apathetic to; turn away from. **পথে পথে ~** wander; roam; loiter. **দ্বার থেকে ~** return disappointed.

ফেরানো, ফিরানো *vt* **1** bring or send back; cause to return. **2** cause to turn; turn: তাকে সৎপথে ফেরাও. **3** turn one back or round. **4** cause to take a good turn; improve. **5** turn one from: মন ~. **6** send back disappointed. **7** apply; apply anew; wash: কলি ~. **8** exchange. **9** change. **10** comb: চুল ~. **11** retract; withdraw: কথা ~; word off; fend off; parry: আঘাত ~. **ফিরিয়ে আনা** *vt* same as balance; bring back. ~ **দেওয়া** *vt* return; send back; change: বইটা দোকানদারকে ফিরিয়ে দেওয়া. **কলি ~** *vi* whitewash; limewash.

ফেরার [A] *adj* absconding; runaway; absconded. **ফেরারি** *n* absconder; fugitive; runaway. ~ **হওয়া** *vi* abscond; runaway; flee: **ফেরারি আসামি/ লোক** *n* absconder; escaped convict.

ফেরি[১] *n* **1** huckstery; pedlary; peddling. ~ **করা** *vi* hawk (about/ around); peddle; huckster. **~ওয়ালা** *n* pedlar; hawker; huckster; peddler. **~ওয়ালী** *fem* hucksteress; huckstress. **~র মাল, ~ওয়ালার মাল** *n* pedlary; the wares of a pedlar. **2** act of singing awakening songs in procession through the streets of a town or village (⇒ প্রভাত~). **3** gift or reward given to an artiste.

ফেরি[২] [E] *n* ferry. **~ঘাট** *n* ferry station. **~নৌকা** *n* = ~.

ফেরু *n* jackal. **~পাল** *n* a pack of jackals.

ফেরেব, ফেরেবি, ফেরেববাজি [P]*nn* deception; deceit; trick; fraud; cheating; swindling. **~বাজ** *adj, n* deceitful; fraudulent; dishonest; swindler; cheat; humbug; fraud; impostor. **~বাজি করা** *vt* cheat; swindle; deceive; defraud; beguile.

ফেরেশতা, ফিরিশতা [P] *n* angel.

ফেরেশতা ⇒ ফিরিশতা

ফেল [E] *adj* **1** failed; unsuccessful. **2** stopping to function: হার্ট ~. **3** gone bankrupt; run insolvent: ব্যাংক ~. **4** missed (because of lateness): ট্রেন ~. ~ **করা** *vi* fail; be unsuccessful; cease working; stop functioning; miss; break down; go bankrupt; crush; go bust. ~ **করানো** *vt* fail (a candidate); pronounce (one) unsuccessful. ~ **পড়া** *vi* go bankrupt; become insolvent; be exhausted. ~ **ফেলানো** *vt* cause to run insolvent; exhaust. ~ **হওয়া** *vi* = ~ করা.

ফেলজামিন [A] *n* surety for good conduct.

ফেলন *n* **1** throwing away. **2** abandonment.

ফেলনা *adj* fit to be cast away; insignificant; negligible; contemptible; unworthy of attention.

ফেলসানি [A] *n* **1** adultery. **2** abortion (following illicit conception).

ফেলা[১] *vt* **1** throw; throw away; fling; cast: যেখানে-সেখানে ময়লা ফেলবেন না. **2** place; put: বিপদে ~, মাটিতে পা ~. **3** drop; let fall: চোখের পাতা ~, ফোঁটা ~. **4** reject: তার কথাটা ফেলবেন না. **5** invest: কারবারে টাকা ~. **6** dissipate; waste: শুধু শুধু টাকা ~. **7** spend: সৎকাজে টাকা ~. **8** leave; leave unused: মিষ্টিটা ফেলো না, খাও. **9** involve: মামলায় ~. **10** fix: তারিখ ~. **11** disregard; disobey: গুরুজনের কথা ~. **12** write; put down: অঙ্ক ~. **13** propose: বিয়ের কথা ~. **14** desert; abandon: বাপ-মাকে সে ফেলবে না. **15** used to complete an incomplete verb: বলে ~, করে ~. **দীর্ঘনিঃশ্বাস ~** *vt* heave a sigh. **ফেলে যাওয়া** *vt* abandon; desert. **ফেলো কড়ি মাখো তেল** (phrase) You shall have to pay before you take away the goods. Do your work and have your remuneration. **~ছড়া** *n* **1** scattering away wastefully or negligently; disarray; welter; mess. **2** dissipation; squandering. **3** making large discount or allowance: ~ছড়া করে ধরলেও. **~ফেলি** *n* = ~ছড়ি (1,2).

ফেলা[২] *adj* **1** rejected; thrown away. **2** put in; invested: ব্যবসায়ে ~ টাকা. **3** that which has come in contact with cooked food: ~ হাঁড়ি.

ফেলো [E] *n* fellow.

ফেসাদ, ফ্যাসাদ [A] *n* mischief; wickedness; brawl; disturbance; trouble; violence; quarrel. **ফেসাদে** *adj* quarrelsome; quarrelling; troublemaker; mischievous; factious. **ফেসাদি** *adj* **1** = ফেসাদে. **2** troublesome. **ফেসাদে পড়া** be in trouble; get into a scrape or trouble; be in a predicament or difficulty. **~ করা/ বানানো** create or excite disturbance; raise a tumult; create difficulty or trouble.

ফৈজৎ, ফৈজত ⇒ ফইজত

ফোঁকল *n* = ফুকর (1)

ফোঁকা ⇒ ফুঁকা

ফোঁটা *n* **1** a small roundish mark on the forehead (made with coloured earth, sandalwood or unguents; either as an ornament or a sectarian distinction). **2** a drop; a blob: এক ~ ওষুধ. **3** a globular mark; a point. **4** pip on playing-cards. **5** point obtained in some card-games. **এক-~** *adj* very small; a little; tiny; meagre; puny; scanty. **অনভ্যাসের ~** (phrase) luxury or pleasure one is not used to. **এক ~ মেয়ে** a (mere) slip of a girl.

ফোঁড় *n* bore; perforation; stitch. **আস্ত খেয়েছ ফোঁড় তো গোনোনি** (phrase) You've relished the fruit, but are unaware of the consequences. **এ-~-ও-~** pierced all through. **~ন** *n* boring; perforation; stitching.

ফোঁড়া, ফোড়া, ফুড়া *vt* pierce; penetrate; probe; bore; prick a hole; break or burst through: মাটি ফুঁড়ে বের হওয়া. **~-ফুঁড়ি** *n* piercing at numerous places; repeated piercing or pricking; (facet) medical injection.

ফোঁৎ *n* (onom) sound of sneezing or of blowing one's nose.

ফোঁপরা, ফোপরা, ফোঁপর *adj* **1** hollow; empty. **2** full of holes; porous; honeycombed. ❑*n* kernel within a mature coconut which is likely to become a seedling.

ফোঁপর-দালাল, ফোঁপল-দালাল = ফপরদালাল

ফোঁপানো, ফোঁফানো, ফুঁপানো *vi* (onom) **1** sob; snivel; whimper. **2** growl in suppressed anger; fume; boil with rage. **3** hiss. **ফোঁপানি, ফুঁপানি** *n* sob; whimper; growl; hissing; hiss.

ফোঁস *n* (onom) **1** (sound denoting) a sudden deep sigh of suppressed grief; anger or disappointment. **2** hiss of a snake. **3** sudden angry growl. **4** expanded hood of a snake. **~ করা** *vi* **1** hiss; growl. **2** protest. **3** hiss threateningly. **4** come/ go at threateningly to bite. **~চক্র** *n* expanded hood of a snake about to bite. **~ডঙ্কা** *n* expanded hood of an attacking snake. **ফোঁসফোঁস, ফোঁসর~** (iron) *nn* **1** (repeated) hissing/ angry growls or snarl. **2** (repeated) deep sighs of suppressed grief, etc. **ফোঁসফোঁস করা, ফোঁসফোঁসানো** *vi* **1** hiss (repeatedly). **2** growl; make angry growls continually. **3** have repeated sighs of suppressed anger, grief, etc. **4** grumble: প্রতিশোধ নিতে না পেরে ফোঁস-ফোঁস করছে. **5** make angry; growl continuously. **6** blubber; sob. **ফোঁসানি, ফোঁসফোঁসানি** *n* hissing; continuous growls; blubbering; repeated deep sighs of suppressed grief, etc. **হাঁস~ করা** *vi* wheeze.

ফোঁসা ⇒ ফুঁসা

ফোঁসানো = ফোঁসফোঁস করা

ফোকট *n* fluke. **ফোকটে** by a fluke.

ফোকর ⇒ ফুকর

ফোকলা, ফোগলা *adj* without teeth; toothless (eg a child, an old man, gums). ❑*n* **1** toothless person: ফোকলা আবার হাসছে. **2** toothless gums.

ফোকাস [E]*n* (phys) focus. **অসৎ ~** virtual focus. **সৎ~** real focus.

ফোটা ⇒ ফুটা

ফোটা ⇒ ফোঁটা

ফোটানো ⇒ ফুটানো

ফোটো, ফোটোগ্রাফ ⇒ ফটো

ফোড়[1] *n* weeding tool; hoe.

ফোড়[2] ⇒ ফোঁড়

ফোড়ন, ফোড়ং *n* **1** spices (chillies, bay leaves, cumin, cloves, cardamom, cinnamon, mustard seeds, fenugreek seeds, aniseeds, black cumin, parsley, etc) singed or fried and then mixed with any cooked (hot) dish for flavouring. **2** (fig, facet) a (sharp) remark thrown in. **~ কাটা** *vi* throw in a (sharp) remark or comment. **~ দেওয়া** *vi* **1** = ~ কাটা. **2** mix singed or fried spices for flavouring.

ফোড়া[1] ⇒ ফোঁড়া

ফোড়া[2] *n* abscess; boil; furuncle. **বয়স ~** *n* acne. **বিষ ~** *n* septic or sore. **লোম ~** *n* a boil bursting through a pore. **~ পাকা** *vi* suppurate; form pus; come to a head. **~ ফাটা** *vi* open; burst open. **~ বসে যাওয়া** *vi* subside.

ফোতো= ফতো

ফোন [E] *n* phone; telephone.

ফোনোগ্রাফ[E] *n* phonograph; record-player.

ফোপরদলাল ⇒ ফপরদালাল

ফোপরা ⇒ ফোঁপরা

ফোয়ারা [A] *n* fountain; spring; jet.

ফোরম্যান [E]*n* foreman.

ফোরাত [A] *n* the river Euphrates.

ফোলন, ফুলন *n* **1** swelling; inflation; distension. **2** (fig) state of being puffed up. **3** prosperity; opulence.

ফোলা ⇒ ফুলা

ফোলানো ⇒ ফুলানো

ফোস্কা, ফোসকা *n* **1** blister. **2** vesicle. **~ পড়া** *vi* blister; develop a blister. **~ ফাটা** *vi* (of a blister) burst open. **~ ফেলা** *vi* blister.

ফৌজ [A] *n* **1** an army. **2** a host; a multitude. **~দার** *n* commandant of the military force in a district. **2** magistrate. **3** an office of the police; commissioner of police. **~দারি** *n* **1** office or duty of a commandant/ magistrate/ police commissioner. **2** criminal case/ law-suit. ❑*adj* **1** related to a ~. **2** administrative. **3** criminal. **~দারি আদালত** *n* criminal court. **~দারি মামলা** *n* criminal case. **~দারি সোপর্দ** *adj* subjudice in a magistrate's court. **ফৌজি** *adj* military.

ফৌত, ফোত [A] *n* death; failure. ❑*adj* **1** dead; deceased; killed. **2** dead intestate. **3** insolvent. **~ ফেরার** *adj* dead or absconded.

ফৌতি [A]*adj* related to a deceased person. **~ মাল** *n* a dead man's property.

ফ্যাঁকড়া ⇒ ফেঁকড়া

ফ্যাকাশে, ফ্যাকাশে *adj* **1** pale; pallid; ashen; ashy. **2** dim; faint: ~ আলো.

ফ্যাচাং ⇒ ফেচাং

ফ্যাটা ⇒ ফেটা

ফ্যা-ফ্যা *n* (onom) **1** (denoting) continuous prating. **2** continuous useless wandering (in search of something). **3** continuous useless solicitation.

ফ্যানসা *adj* (colloq) **1** (of rice) not properly strained after boiling; sticky. **2** foamy; frothy.

ফ্যাকাতুড়া= ফেকাতুড়া

ফ্যারফ্যার = ফেরফের

ফ্যালফ্যাল *adj* (onom) vacant; bewildered; blank. **~ করে** *adv* in bewilderment; confusedly. dumbfounded; flabbergasted: ~ করে তাকানো.

ফ্যাশন, ফ্যাশান [E] *n* fashion; fashionableness.

ফ্যাসাদ ⇒ ফেসাদ

ফ্রক [E] *n* frock (esp for girls). **~কোট** *n* frock-coat.

ফ্রি [E]*adj* free. **~তে পাওয়া** obtain free of cost.

ফ্রেম [E] *n* frame.

ফ্লানেল, ফ্ল্যানেল [E]*n* flannel.

ফ্লাশ [E] *n* a kind of card-game; flush.

ফ্লাস্ক [E] *n* flask; thermos; thermos flask.

ফ্লু [E] *n* flu; influenza.

ফ্ল্যাট [E] *n* **1** flat; apartment. **2** flatboat. ❑*adj* **1** lying or laid fully on one's back: ~ হয়ে শুয়ে পড়ল. **2** (iron) utterly dejected: জুয়ো খেলে টাকা হেরে ~ হয়ে পড়েছে.

ব

ব[1] *n* the twenty-third letter of the Bengali alphabet. It is a voiced unspirated bilibial plosive sound.

ব[2] [P] *prep* with; by: বমাল, বতদ্বির; according to: বতারিখ, বদস্তর.

বই[1]**, বহি** *n* **1** book. **2** register; ledger. **~পত্র** *n* books and similar other things. **~য়ের পোকা** *n* (lit, fig) bookworm. **~ বের করা** *vt* publish (a book). **~ বের হওয়া** *vi* be published/on the market.

বই[2] *n* the creeping root of a kind of arum.

বই[3]**, বৈ** *prep n* without; except; other than; nothing else than: তুমি ~ আর কেউ জানে না. **~কি** *adv* of course; surely: যাব ~কি; (iron) (in question) denoting denial, disbelief, etc: বলব ~কি ? I'm not going to tell you. **~ নয়, ~ তো নয়** only: দুদিন ~ তো নয়. **তা ~কি 1** that's it. **2** It's doubtful.

বইঠা, বৈঠা *n* scull.

বউ *n* **1** wife. **2** daughter-in-law. **3** brother's wife; sister-in-law. **4** a married woman: ঘরের ~. **5** bride. **6** housewife. **7** someone as bashful as a newly married woman: তার এতো লজ্জা, যেন ঘরের ~টি. **~-ঝি, ~-বেটি** *nn* daughters and daughters-in-law; women-folk. **~-মানুষ** *n* **1** family woman. **2** child-wife. **কলা~** *n* a young banana-plant dressed as a married lady and conceived as a female deity worshipped by Hindus; a wife with a long veil; a awkwardly bashful woman. **কুলের ~** *n*=~-মানুষ. **বউ-কথা-কও** *n* the Indian nightingale. **~-কাটকি** *n* a woman given to torturing her daughter-in-law. **~ড়ি** *n* a young wife; child-wife. **~দিদি, ~দি** (colloq) *n* an elder brother's wife; sister-in-law. **~-ভাত** *n* the ceremony of a bride's serving out food for the first time to her husband's kinsfolk; a marriage feast in honour of the bride. **~মা** *n* son's wife; daughter-in-law; a younger brother's wife; sister-in-law. **~গড়া** *n* a ceremony to welcome the bride to her father-in-law's house.

বউনি[1] *n* (cost) of carrying goods; carriage.

বউনি[2] *n* the first (cash) sale or earning of the day.

বউল *n* bud; blossom. **~ ধরা** *vi* bud; be in blossom; put forth buds.

বউলি, বউলী *n* an earning or eardrop.

বওয়া *vt vi* (colloq form of বহা) **1** convey; endure; suffer; carry; bear. **2** flow; run: শীতল বাতাস বইছে. **3** keep up/active: এ শরীর আর বয় না. **4** have an interest in; feel like: কোনো বিষয়ে তার আর গা বয় না. **5** elapse; pass: সময় বয়ে গেল. **6** go to the bad; go to the dogs: কুসঙ্গে মিলে ছেলেটা বয়ে গেল. ❑*adj* spoiled by bad association; dissolute. **~টে** *adj* dissipated; dissolute. **আমার বয়ে গেছে** (phrase) I don't care a damn/hang. **বয়ে-যাওয়া ছেলে** a spoiled/ dissipated boy. **বওয়ানো, বওয়ান** *vt* (causative of বওয়া) cause to bear/carry/endure/ convey/ suffer; cause to flow/run.

বংশ[1] *n* **1** offspring; children. **2** family; clan house. **3** lineage; pedigree. **4** posterity. **~ক্ষয়**

n destruction or decay of a family. **~গত** *adj* hereditary. **~গতি** *n* heredity. **~গৌরব** *n* family prestige or pride; pride of birth; dignity of a family. **~চরিত্র** *n* **1** biography of men or women born of a particular family. **2** family history; history of a dynasty or race. **3** hereditary characteristic and behaviour. **~জ** *n* **1** born of a particular family. **2** of good lineage. **3** born of *kulin* (কুলীন) family which has been socially lowered by matrimonial alliance with an inferior family. **~তালিকা** *n* genealogical table; family tree. **~ধর** *n* descendant; scion. **~নাশ** *n* destruction of a family. **~পরম্পরা** *n* a regular line of descent or succession; heredity. **~পরম্পরায়** *adv* from generation to generation; hereditarily. **~বর্ধন** *n* **1** prosperity of a family. **2** increase or multiplication of a race or family; growth in family size; breeding; procreation. **~বৃদ্ধি**=~বর্ধন (2). **~ বৃদ্ধি করা** *vi* increase or multiply one's race or family: procreate; breed. **~বিস্তার** *n*=~বৃদ্ধি. **~বৈশিষ্ট্য** *n* family trait or characteristic. **~মর্যাদা** *n* family prestige; aristocracy. **~রক্ষা** *n* preservation of one's family or race. **~ রক্ষা করা** *vt* preserve one's lineage. **~লতা** *n*=~তালিকা. **~লোপ** *n*=~ক্ষয়. **~ লোপ করা** *vt* destroy a family or race. **~স্থিতি** *n* continuation/continuity of a line of descent. **~হীন** *adj* destitute of family or descendahts; having none to succeed or continue the line.

বংশ[2] *n* **1** bamboo. **2** backbone; spine. **~কর্পূর** *n* manna of the bamboo; tabasheer. **~দণ্ড** *n* bamboo-staff; bamboo-stick. **~পত্র** *n* bamboo-leaf. **~লোচন**=~কর্পূর. **~শলাকা** *n* slender (often short) slip of bamboo; bamboo-slip.

বংশাগ্র *n* tip of a bamboo.

বংশাঙ্কুর *n* bamboo-shoot.

বংশানুক্রম *n* a regular line of descent or succession; family succession; lineal inheritance; heredity. **বংশানুক্রমিক** *adj* hereditary. **বংশানুক্রমে** *adv* from generation to generation; hereditarily.

বংশানুচরিত *n* history of a family or dynasty; genealogy; genealogical register.

বংশাবতংশ *n* (fig) ornament or glory of one's family.

বংশাবলী, বংশাবলি *n* genealogy; family tree; genealogical table.

বংশিকা *n* =বংশী

বংশী *n* flute or pipe made of bamboo; flute; pipe; reed. **~ধর, ~ধারী** *adj* holding a flute. ❑*n* flutist; piper; Sri Krishna. **~তট** *n* the bank of the Jamuna at Brindaban where Sri Krishna played his flute. **~ধ্বনি, ~রব** *nn* sound/note of a flute. **~বট** *n* a banyan tree at Brindaban under which Sri Krishna played his flute. **~বদন**=~ধর. **~বাদক** *n* flutist. **~বাদন** *n* playing a flute.

বংশীয় *adj* **1** born of a particular (or good) family; pertaining to a family or race.

বঁইচি *n* kind of wild juicy berry.

বঁটানো *vt* ⇒ বঁটি

বঁটি *n* kind of large knife fixed almost at a right angle in a piece of wood on which one sits while chopping fish, vegetables, etc. **~ কাটা** *n* cut or chopped with a ~. **~ঝাঁপ** *n* the practice of throwing oneself upon aforesaid knives during the feast of charak (চড়ক).

বঁড়শি, বঁড়শী ⇒ বড়শি

বঁদিয়া, বঁদে ⇒ বুঁদিয়া

বঁধু, বঁধুয়া *n* (poet) friend; lover; love; sweetheart; darling; truelove.

বক *n* **1** a kind of heron or crane. **2** kind of heron-shaped flower. **3** a hypocrite; a cheat. **~ দেখানো** *vi* taunt by cupping one's palms almost in the shape of a heron. **বকী** *fem* of ~. **~ঠুঁটো** *n* a species of sweet-water fish with a long slender beak. **~ধার্মিক** *adj* feigning or simulating piety or virtuousness; hypocritical; sanctimonious. ❑*n* hypocrite; a cheat; a false devotee. **~ধ্যান** *n* sanctimonious/hypocritical meditation. **~বৃত্তি** *n* feigned piety or virtuosity; sanctimony; hypocrisy. **~ব্রত** *n* crane-like conduct; hypocrisy. **~ব্রতী** *adj* **1**=~ধার্মিক. **2** given to false play; deceitful. **~যন্ত্র** *n* (chem) retort; still.

বকন[1] *n* **1** chattering; prating. **2** reproof; rebuke; reproach; talking to.

বকন[2] *n* **1**=বকনা. **2 ~ বাছুর** *n*=বৎসতরী

বকনা *n* a young cow that has not yet had a calf; heifer.

বকনি ⇒ বকুনি

বকবক *n* **1** (onom) suggesting water entering into a pitcher; gurgle. **2** chatter; tittle-tattle; blabber; prattle; prating. **~ করা** *vi* chatter continuously; prattle; drone on; rabbit on.

বকবকম ⇒ বকম

বকবকানো *vi* = বকবক করা. **বকবকানি** *n* intolerable prattling; prating; tittle-tattle.

বকভাণ্ড *n* (chem) flask.

বকম[1], **বকমবকম, বকবকম** *n* (onom) suggesting cooing of the pigeon or any similar noise. **~ করা** *vi* coo.

বকম[2], **বকম কাঠ** *n* a kind of tree or its timber which gives a red dye-stuff.

বকরি, বকরী [A] *n* she-goat; nanny-goat; goat.

বকরী ঈদ, বকরীদ [A] *n* the Muslim festival of sacrifice on the 10th of the month of Zilhaj, in commemoration of Abraham's offering to sacrifice his son Ismail.

বকলম [A] *n* **1** person signing for an illiterate person. **2** act of signing for an illiterate person. ❑*adj* an alphabet; illiterate.

বকলম [E] *n* buckle. **~ আঁটা** *vi, vt* buckle.

বকশি, বক্সী [P] *n* **1** (hist) general; commander-in-chief; paymaster; disbursing officer; collector of taxes. **2** title of some rural and urban eminent persons.

বকশিশ, বকশিস, বকসিস, বখশিশ=বখশিশ

বকা[1] *vt,vi* **1** prattle; prate; talk overmuch; chatter; ramble. **2** scold; chide; castigate. বাজে ~ *vi* talk nonsense.

বকা[2], **বকাট, বকাটে** ⇒ বখা

বকা[3] *n* (derog)=বকা. ❑*adj* **1** of or like a heron. **2** (fig) hypocritical: ~ ধার্মিক.

বকাঝকা *n* scolding; chiding; upbraiding. ~ করা *vi,vt* scold; chide; upbraid; reprove; tongue-lash.

বকাণ্ডপ্রত্যাশা(ন্যায়) *n* a hope as vain as the expectation of a heron to obtain the scrotum of bull; vain hope.

বকানো, বকান *vt* **1** cause to talk overmuch. **2** prolong a discussion by raising objections.

বকাবকি *n* **1** debate; argumentation; altercation; dispute. **2** scolding; chiding; reproof. ~ করা *vi,vt* **1** debate; argue; altercate. **2** scold; chide; upbraid.

বকামি ⇒ বখা

বকাল [A] *n* **1**=বক্কাল (1). **2** bark (of a tree). **3** medicinal herbs. **3** spices.

বকালি *n* druggist.

বকুনি *n* **1** scolding; chiding. **2** garrulity; prating. ~ খাওয়া *vt* be scolded/rebuked/chided. ~ দেওয়া *vt* scold; chide; rebuke.

বকুল *n* a large evergreen tree; its sweet scented white flower.

বকেয়া [A] *adj* still unpaid or undone; remaining; outstanding. ❑*n* arrears; arrearage; dues; balances. ~ খাজনা *n* arrears of rent; outstanding rent. ~ বাকি *n* arrears or arrearage of the last year.

বক্কাল [A] *n* **1** grocer. **2** a medicinal herb. বেনে~ *n* (derog) traders (as a class).

বক্কেশ্বর *n* fool; tomfool; idiot.

বক্ত, বখত [P] *n* good fortune; luck; lot; portion. কম~ *adj* unfortunate; unlucky; wretched; cursed. কমবক্তি *fem.*

বক্তব্য *n* one's say; a subject or context of discussion. ❑*adj* to be said; under discussion; worth saying; fit to be said or spoken.

বক্তা *n* speaker; lecturer; orator. ❑*adj* eloquent; having the gift of the gab.

বক্তার *n* **1** made eloquent by divine aspiration. **2** garrulous person; wind box.

বক্তৃতা *n* **1** speech; lecture; (derog) prattling; rigmarole; harangue; tirade. ~ করা/দেওয়া *vi* deliver a speech; speak; lecture; (derog) indulge in a rigmarole; harangue; prattle. ~ থামাও, ~ রাখো (phrase) stop talking; stop your harangue. ~কার *n* (derog)=বক্তা.

বক্ত্র *n* mouth.

বক্র *adj* **1** curved; bent; tortuous; oblique; squint. **2** curving; crooked; fraudulent; dishonest. evasive; ambiguous. **3** (geom) curved. **4** (astrol) antipathetic. **5** retrograde. ❑*n* bent; turn. ~কীট *n* hookworm. ~গতি *adj* having a curved, tortuous or sinuous motion; crooked; dishonest. ~গামী *adj* moving curvedly, sinuously or tortuously; fraudulent; crooked. ~গ্রীব *adj* having a curved neck. ❑*n* camel. ~চঞ্চু *n* parrot. ~চ্ছেদ *n* (geom) an oblique section. ~ণ *n* bending; curving. ~তা *n* curvedness; curvature; crookedness; sinuosity; tortuousness; ambiguity; (astron) retrograde motion; (astrol) antipathy. ~তা কেন্দ্র *n* (phys) centre of curvature. ~তুণ্ড *n*=~চঞ্চু. ~দংষ্ট্র *adj n* having curved tusks; hog boar. ~দৃষ্টি *adj* squint-eyed; cock-eyed; looking askance; squinting; jealous; envious. ~দৃষ্টি oblique look; hostile view; malignant regard. ~নাস, ~নাসিক *adj* having curved or aquiline nose. ❑*n* owl. ~পুচ্ছ *n* dog. ~পৃষ্ঠ *adj* convex; arch-backed. ~রেখা *n* curved line; a curve. ~শিরাল *adj* (bot) curvi-veined. ~ সংঘাত *n* (eng) oblique impact. বক্রাংশু রেখা *n* (phy) caustic curve. বক্রাংশুস্পর্শ *n* (phy) causticity.

বক্রিমা=বক্রতা (⇒ বক্র)

বক্রী[1] falsely sanskritized form of বাকি.

বক্রী[2] *adj* curved; tortuous; sinuous; (astrol) antipathetic. ~করণ *n* curving; bending; distortion; curvation. ~কৃত *adj* curved; bent. ~ভাব *n* curvature; curve. ~ভূত *adj* curved; bent; inauspicious; hostile; dishonest.

বক্রোক্তি *n* **1** indirect mode of expression; sarcasm; sarcastic utterance; equivoke; quibble; irony. **2** (rhet) figure of speech consisting in the use of evasive speech or reply (either by means of pun or by an affected change of tone). **3** insinuation.

বক্রোষ্ঠিকা *n* smile.

বক্ষ *n* **1** breast; chest; bosom. **2** (fig) heart. ~কোষ্ঠক *n* inner apartment. ~পঞ্জর *n* thorax; skeletal frame of the chest. ~পট *n* chest. ~পীড়া *n* chest disease. **বক্ষঃস্থল, ~স্থল,** *n* region of the chest. **~স্পন্দন, বক্ষঃস্পন্দন** *adj* lying on the breast/chest or in the heart. ❑*n* palpitation or throbbing of the heart; heart-beat.

বক্ষোজ, বক্ষোরুহ *nn* breast.

বক্ষ্যমাণ *adj* to be spoken of or mentioned hereafter; under discussion.

বক্সী ⇒ বকশি

বখৎ=বক্ত

বখরা *n* share; sharing. ~ করা *vi* share; apportion; divide into shares. ~ দেওয়া *vt* give a share; share. ~ পাওয়া *vt* get a share;

share. ~ লওয়া *vt* take a share; share. ~দান *n* sharer; shareholder; partner. ~দারি *n* sharing; apportioning; partnership; joint-ownership.

বখশ [P] *n* giving; imparting; bestowing. বখশে দেওয়া *vt* give; bestow: কোরান তেলাওয়াত করে দোয়া বখশে দেওয়া.

বখশিশ, বকশিশ [P] *n* reward; gift; tip. ~ দেওয়া *vi vt* reward; give a tip.

বখা *vi* be spoilt by bad association; go to the bad; sow one's wild oats. ❑*adj* **1** spoilt by bad association; gone to the bad; errant; dissolute; immoral; debauched; rakish. **2** saucy; pert; impudent. **3** impertinent. ~ট *adj n* thoroughly spoilt or depraved. ~টে *adj*=~. ~নো *vt* deprave; pervert; debauch; corrupt. ~মো, ~মি *n* dissipation; depravity; sauciness; impertinence. বখে যাওয়া *vi*=বখা. বখিয়ে দেওয়া *vt*=~নো.

বখিল [A] *n adj* miser; niggard; miserly; close-fisted; stingy; niggardly. বখিলি *n* niggardliness; stinginess.

বখেড়া *n* **1** hindrance; obstacle. **2** trouble; disturbance. **3** dispute; brawl; quarrel.

বখেয়া [P] *n* kind of strong and fine stitching.

বগ *n* (colloq)=বক. ~ দেখানো=বক দেখানো. ~চর *n* sloping banks of a pond.

বগয়রহ [A] (phrase) et cetera; and so forth; and others.

বগল [P] *n* **1** armpit; flank. **2** proximity; neighbourhood; side. ~দাবা করা *vt* **1** carry or conceal under one's armpit. **3** (fig) appropriate secretly to oneself; take possession of or bring under control. ~ বাজানো *vi* **1** rap one's armpit by putting a palm in it as a mark of mad delight; (fig) be highly pleased; rejoice madly. **2** rejoice over another's downfall. **3** mock. বগলে *adv* near; beside.

বগলি [P] *n* **1** a handbag; a beggar's sack. **2** trick in wrestling.

বগা *n* (joc, derog)=বক. ❑*adj* **1** white. **2** crane-like: ~ ঠোঁট.

বগি[1], **বগী** [E] *n* (hooded) buggy.

বগি[2], **বগী** [E] *n* railway carriage; bogie.

বগি[3], **বগী** *adj* crane-like; crane-necked. ❑*n* high-rimmed metal dish (also ~ থালা).

বঙ্ক *adj* (poet, archaic) **1** bent; curved. **2** oblique; squint. ❑ **1** kind of twisted bangle for the ankle. **2** turn/bend of a river.

বঙ্কিম *adj* bent; curved; slightly bent: squint; oblique. ~বিহারী *n* Sri Krishna.

বঙ্কু *adj*=বঙ্কু. বেঁটে ~ stubby and crooked.

বঙ্গ[1] *n* solder; read lead; tin.

বঙ্গ[2] *n* **1** Bengal, the old name of Bangladesh. **2** Bengali people. ~জ *adj* born or produced in Bengal. ❑*n* section of Kayasthas (কায়স্থ) of Bengal. ~দেশ *n* Bengal. ~দেশীয় *adj*=বঙ্গীয়. ~বিভাগ, ~ভঙ্গ *n* partition of Bengal. বঙ্গাধিপ, বঙ্গেশ্বর *nn* king of Bengal. বঙ্গানুবাদ *n* translation or rendering into Bengali. বঙ্গাব্দ *n* the Bengali era. বঙ্গীয় *adj* of Bengal; born or produced in Bengal; Bengali.

বচ *n* sweet-flag.

বচন *n* **1** speech; utterance; speaking. **2** saying; adage; maxim. **3** statement; declaration. **4** (gram) number. এক~ singular number. দ্বি~ dual number. বহু~ plural number. ~বাগীশ *adj, n* garrulous; gassy; having gift of the gab; windbag; all talk. ~বিন্যাস *n* art or mode of speaking; arrangement of words or speech; disposition of words. ~সর্বস্ব ব্যক্তি *n* person of mere words; windbag. বচনীয় *adj* **1** to be spoken of or uttered; mentionable. **2** censurable; blamable. বচনীয়তা *n* **1** blamableness. **2** utterableness.

বচসা *n* altercation; wrangle; brawl; dispute; war of words. ~ করা *vi* altercate; wrangle; bandy words; cross words; brawl.

বছর, বচ্ছর *n* (colloq) year. ~ বছর *adv* every year. বচ্ছুরে *adj* being so many years old: একশ বচ্ছুরে বুড়ি.

বজনিশ, বজনিস [A] *adj* identical; exactly similar; true: ~ নকল.

বজবজ *adj* **1** putrid; putrefied: পচা ~. **2** *n* (onom) suggesting bubbling sound of putrefaction.

বজরা[1] *n* large please or state boat; barge.

বজরা[2] *n*=বাজরা

বজা [P] *adj* in place; fit; proper; right; suitable. ~ আনা *vt* perform; execute; accomplish; comply with; obey.

বজায় [P] (phrase)**1** instead of; in place of. **2** in force; intact; in position. ~ থাকা be in force/intact/in position. ~ রাখা keep in force/intact/in force; keep up; maintain.

বজ্জাত [P] *adj* low-born; base; ill-bred; wicked; vicious; evil-minded; mischievous. ❑*n* low-born/wicked/ person. বজ্জাত *n* wickedness; mischievousness; naughtiness; viciousness; mischief-making.

বজ্র *n* **1** thunderbolt; thunder. **2** (by extension) lightning. **3** weapon of Indra, the king of gods. **4** severe blow; cruel affliction. **5** sharp remark or reproach. **6** diamond. **7** (astrol) cross-sign (×) on the palm. ❑*adj* cruel; sharp; severe; hard; unbearable. ~কঠিন, ~কঠোর *adjj* extremely hard or severe; adamantine; rock-like; steely; resolute; stubborn; stiff; firm. ~কীট *n* kind of insect; woodworm; termite. ~গম্ভীর *adj* deep and loud as thunderclap. ~গম্ভীর স্বরে in a thunderous voice. ~গুণন *n* (math) cross-multiplication. ~চিহ্ন *n* cross-sign (×). ~জ্বালা *n* lightning. ~তুল্য *adj, n* adamantine; thunderous; lapis lazuli. **~ধর** *adj, n* one holding a thunderbolt; one whose weapon is thunderbolt; Indra. **~ধ্বনি, ~নাদ, ~নির্ঘোষ** *nn* thunderclap; thunder-peal; (fig) a voice or noise as deep and loud as a thunderclap. **~পাণি**=~ধর. **~পাত** *n* thunderbolt; crush of thunder. **~বহ** *n* (phys) lightning conductor. **~ধারক** *n* (phys) lightning arrester. **~লেপ** *n* (Ayu) kind of hard mortar or cement used as a coating of vessels for heating mercury, etc; adamantine cement. **~শলাকা** *n*=~বহ. **~সার** *adj* having the essence or nature of a diamond; adamantine. **বজ্রাগ্নি** *n* lightning. **বজ্রাঘাত** *n* thunder-stroke; (fig) sudden shock or calamity. **বজ্রাঙ্গ** *adj* having an adamantine frame or a very hardy body. **বজ্রাভ** *adj* diamond-like; as dazzling bright as a flash of lightning. **বজ্রাসন** *n* a particular posture of sitting in yogic meditation. **বজ্রাস্ত্র** *n* electric weapon; fire-arm. **বজ্রাহত** *adj* thunder-struck.

বঞ্চক *adj, n* deceitful; crafty; fraudulent; swindler; deceiver; fraud; cheat; one who deprives (another).

বঞ্চনা, বঞ্চন *n* **1** deception; deceit; fraud; cheating. **2** deprivation. **~ করা** *vt* deceive; defraud; cheat; deprive (of). **~পূর্বক** *adv* deceitfully; fraudulently; craftily. **~ময়** *adj* deceptive; illusory.

বঞ্চা *vt, vi* **1** (poet)=বঞ্চনা করা. **2** (poet) spend/pass (time): সখে বঞ্চিল না জানি কোথা কার সনে. **3** (poet) live; lead one's life: আমি বঞ্চি একাকিনী. **4** enjoy.

বঞ্চিত *adj* deceived; beguiled; defrauded; deprived (from). **বঞ্চিতা** *fem.*

বঞ্চুক *n*=বঞ্চক

বঞ্জুল *n* **1** a kind of flower and its tree; commonly called অশোক. **2** cane-plant; rattan-plant.

বট *n* the banyan tree. **~পত্র** *n* banyan-leaf.

বটকিরি, বটখিরি *adj* suitable for an assembly or party. ❑*n* banter/badinage suitable for a party.

বটকেরা, বটখেরা *n* banter/badinage (in a party).

বটা *vi* (poet, archaic) to be: কে ~ কামিনী মোরে দেহ পরিচয়.

বটিকা, বটী *n* pile; globule.

বটু, বটুক *n* (archaic) a Brahmin lad.

বটুয়া *n* a small bag made of cloth.

বটে *pres t 3rd pers* of the verb বটা; is; are: সে কে বটে ? (idiomatic use) **তা ~** that's true. **তাই ~** just so. **~ই তো** exactly. **~ এমন কথা ?** is it ? **কী বলছ ~** well. **~ রে** (threateningly) take care. **~~** oh yes, just so; there you are. **সে সাহসী বটে** (iron) He is no doubt a brave fellow.

বটের *n* a species of small partridge akin to the quail.

বটঠাকুর *n* an elder brother of one's husband.

বড্ড (colloq)=বড়

বড্ডবার, বড়বার *n* (euphem) Saturday.

বড়[1], বড়ো *adj* **1** big; large; sizeable; massive: ~ বাড়ি. **2** long; lengthy; high; tall; lofty: মাথায় ~. **3** (emph) excessive; severe: সে ~ বাড় বেড়েছে. **4** older; elder; eldest: ~ দাদা. **5** senior in position; most important; principal; chief; eminent; leading: **~ সাহেব,** সবচেয়ে ~ কথা. **6** great; magnanimous; noble; respectable: ~ প্রাণ/মন/হৃদয়. **7** rich: ~ মানুষের বাড়ি. **8** (emph) at all (generally negative): **~ হাসির কথা নয়,** not a matter of joke; ~ ফেলনা নয়. **9** (iron or derog) ~ তো বিয়ে তার দুপায়ে আলতা. **10** (iron or derog) used in a negative sense: বিপদের সময় ~ তো দেখলে, ie you did not attend. **11** (used to express surprise): তুমি যে ~ এসেছ ? ❑*n* the rich: ~র পিরীতি বালির বাঁধ. ❑*adv* very; very much; too much; excessively: ~ লেগেছে, ~ই দুঃখিত. **~ করা** *vt* **1** bring up: ছেলে ~ করা. **2** make one flourish. **3** extol; exalt. **4** lengthen: লেখাটা আর ~ কোরো না. **5** increase: নামযশ ~ করা. **6** enlarge: ফটো ~ করা. **7** expand: রাজ্য ~ করা. **8** magnify; exaggerate: ~ করে দেখা বা বলা. **9** lionize. **10** liberalize: মন বা হাত ~ করা. **11** make louder; raise: গলা ~ করা. **12** dilate: চোখ ~ করা. **13** edify; elevate: চরিত্র ~ করা. **14** heighten; raise: আশা ~ করা. **~ দেখানো** *vi, vt* look large/big; loom large; magnify. **~ হওয়া** *vi* grow; come of age; flourish; be expanded; be liberalized; be glorified; be edified, etc: **~ উকিল** *n* senior advocate; eminent/leading advocate/pleader: **~-একটা না** not much; not at all; rarely; hardly; scarcely; seldom; infrequently; once in a blue moon: ~-একটা যাওয়া-আসা নেই. **~ কথা 1** the most important words; important thing. **2** hyperbole; bragging; hot air; bombast. **~ কর্তা** *n* master or head of a family; chief or boss of an office. **~ কাণ্ড, ~ কারখানা** *n* a grand event or assembly. **~ কুটুম্ব, ~ কুটুম** *n* a wife's brother; brother-in-law. **~ গলা** *n* loud voice; proud/arrogant tone. **~ গল্প** *n* long story. **~ গাছে নৌকা বাঁধা** (phrase) resort to a great patron. **~ ঘর** *n* **1** a large or spacious room; a hall. **2** (fig) high/noble/aristocratic family. **~ চাল** *n* expensive/aristocratic mode of living or manners; high life. **~ চিংড়ি** *n* large crustaceans; such as lobster; crayfish; prawn. **~ ছেলে** *n* eldest son. **~ছোট** *n* big and small; high and low; rich and poor. **~ জোর** at most; at the very most; at best. **~ জ্বালা** *n* great or severe affliction. **~ ঝড়** great/violent storm. **~ ঠাকুর**=বটঠাকুর. **~ দরের** of high standing/status. **~ দাদা, ~দা** (colloq) *n* the eldest brother. **~**

দিদি, ~দি (colloq) *n fem* the eldest sister. ~ দিন *n* the Christmas Day; (astron) winter solstice. ~ দুঃখ *n* deep/intense grief or sorrow. ~ দুর্দিন *n* terribly hard times. ~ পেট *n* large belly; voracious appetite; (fig) exorbitant demand; excessive greed. ~ বই *n* a fat volume; an enormous book. ~ বংশ *n* high/respectable/noble family. ~ ~ বানরের ~ ~ পেট/লেজ (prov) The more one has, the more one demands; The wealthier a man; the greater is his demand. ~ বাপ *n* great-grandfather (on one's father's side). ~ বাবু *n* head clerk; senior-most male member of a Hindu family. ~ বার ⇒ বড্ডবার. ~ বোন *n fem* elder sister; eldest sister; big sister. ~ ব্যাপার a great affair. ~ ভাই *n* elder brother; big brother; eldest brother. ~ মকদ্দমা/মামলা big/leading case. ~ মজা great fun. ~ মন large/magnanimous heart; master mind; optimistic outlook. ~ মা great-grandmother (on one's father's side). ~ মানুষ *n* rich man; great man. ~ মানুষি, ~মানষি *n* ostentatious display of wealthiness/riches; ostentation; ostentatiousness. ~ মুখ1 delight; gladness. 2 boast; pride; bragging. ~ মুখে বলা boast; be proud to say. ~ মুখ নিয়ে আসা come nourishing a great hope. ~ মুখ ছোট হওয়া feel disgraced; be put out of countenance; be disappointed. ~ রাজা great king. ~ রানী the first or consecrated wife of a king; chief queen. ~ লড়াই hard fight; great battle. ~লাট viceroy. ~লোক=~ মানুষ. ~লোকি=~ মানুষি. ~ শরিক senior partner of an estate. ~ শিকার big game; big game hunting. ~ শীত severe cold. ~ সাহেব boss of an office; senior partner of a firm. ~ হাজরি dinner.

বড়[২] *n* 1 kind of thick rope of straw (which is used in wrapping a large corn-bin). বড় জড়িয়ে, জড় বড়িয়ে বেড়ানো (phrase) move awkwardly in a bundle of clothes. 2 banyan tree. ~ নামা (of aerial roots of a banyan) come down; descend; (of flesh) hang loosely (due to obesity).

বড়বড় *n* (onom) suggesting muttering; prattle. বড়বড়ানি *n* prattling; blether; gibber. বড়বড়ে *adj* 1 raving; chattering; gabbling. 2 all talk; big-mouthed; garrulous. ~ করা, বড়বড়ানো *vi* 1 prattle; jabber; prate. 2 rave; gabble; ramble. 3 grumble.

বড়বা *n* (myth) a sea-horse vomiting fire constantly; mare. ~গ্নি, ~নল *n* fire vomited by the aforesaid sea-horse.

বড়শি *n* fish-hook; hook for angling.

বড়া *n* 1 kind of chop fried in oil: চিংড়ির ~. 2 chop-like sweet-meat: তালের ~.

বড়াই[১] *n* boasting; bragging; brag. ~ করা brag; boast; vaunt; swank.

বড়াই[২], বড়ায়ি *n* an old woman who acted as a go-between Radha and Krishna.

বড়াইবুড়ি *n* 1 great grand-mother. 2 decrepit old woman.

বড়াশ *n* (naut) stem (of a boat).

বড়ি *n* 1 pill; globule: কবরেজি ~. 2 tablet; ball: কালির ~. 3 small conical ball made of the paste of pigeon-pea with spices and dried in the sun (to be eaten after being fried or cooked).

বড়ু *n* 1 (archaic) son of a Brahmin. 2 a respectable title: ~ চণ্ডীদাস.

বড়ুয়া *n* a surname (common among the Bengali Buddhists and Asamese Brahmin).

বড়ে *n* (chess) pawn. ~ টেপা 1 play chess; move a pawn. 2 move with circumspection; play a trick. ~র চাল move of a pawn; a very unassuming and yet danger-spelling move.

বণিক *n* merchant; trader; banian; trader by caste. বণিকিনী *fem*. ~ সভা, ~ সমিতি *n n* chamber of commerce; association of traders or merchants. বণিগ্‌বৃত্তি *n* trade; trading; business; trafiq; commerce; commercialism.

বণ্টক *n* distributor; one who apportions or divides; apportioner.

বণ্টন *n* distribution; apportionment; apportioning; dividing into shares; division. ~ করা *vt* distribute; apportion; divide (into shares). বণ্টিত *adj* distributed; apportioned; divided (into shares). বণ্টিত *adj* distributed; apportioned; divided.

বণ্ড, বণ্ডা *n* (vulg) penis. ❑ tailless.

বৎ *suff* -like: মাতৃ~, জল~.

বতর, বতোর (agri) proper/right/due time: জমিতে চাষ দেবার ~ হয়েছে.

বতারিখ [P] *adj* according to date; with date; dated.

বতী (suff) *fem* of বান.

বত্রিশ *adj, n* thirty-two.

বৎস *n* 1 (as a term of endearment) my dear child; my darling. 2 calf; the young of any animal; offspring; child. ~কামা *adj* longing for child/calf. ~তর *n* more than a calf; a weaved calf; bull-calf. ~তরী *fem* cow-calf; heifer. ~নাভ *n* Indian aconite.

বৎসর, বছর, বচ্ছর (colloq) *n* year; era. বৎসরান্তে *adj* at the end of a year; at year-ending. ~খানেক about a year.

বৎসল *adj* (usu *suff*) affectionate (towards offspring); loving: সন্তান~. বৎসলা *fem*. ~তা *n* affectionateness; affection; love.

বৎসা *n* 1 (affectionate address) dear girl. 2 = বকনা.

বদ [P] *adj* bad; evil; wicked; naughty; mischievous; offensive. ~ ইন্তিজাম *n* mismanagement; misrule. ~কাম *n* misdeed; mischief; crime; wicked act; sinful act;

fornication. ~কার *adj* evil-doer; malefactor; wicked; sinful; bad character. ~খত, ~খৎ *adj* **1** bad or illegibe writer. scrawler. **2** troublesome; mischievous; self-willed; violent; naughty: ~খত ছেলে. ~খেয়াল *n* wicked inclination or desire; perverse propensity; evil intention or design. ~খেয়ালি *adj* having wicked inclination, etc. ~খোব *adj* of evil disposition; having bad habits; evil-minded. ~খাসলত *adj* having bad habits; wicked; vicious. ~ জবান *n* abusive; indecent; foul or filthy language; abuse. ❑*adj* indecent (speaker); abusive; reveller. ~ জবান করা *vi vt* abuse; revile; use abusive or filthy language. ~জাত=বজ্জাত. ~দোয়া *n* curse; malediction; imprecation. ~ নসিব *n* ill luck; misfortune. ❑*adj* unfortunate; unlucky. ~নাম *n* bad name/reputation; discredit; ignominy; dishonour; calumny. ❑*adj* disreputable; infamous; notorious. ~নাম করা *vt* speak ill of; defame; vilify; calumniate. ~নামি *n*=~নাম. ~নিয়ত *n* evil intention; ill-will; malice. ~ ফাল *n* adultery; misdeed; wickedness. ~বক্ত *adj* unlucky; unfortunate; wretched. ~ ব্যক্তি *n* misfortune; adversity; wretchedness. ~বু, ~বো *n* bad/foul smell; stink. ~ মতলব *n* evil intention. ~মাশ, ~মাস, ~মাইশ, ~মাইস, ~মায়েস *adj* wicked; roguish; mischievous; immoral; having an evil profession; having a bad way of life; (affectionately) naughty. ❑*n* bad character; rascal; blackguard; vagabond. ~মাশি, ~মাশী, ~মাসী, ~মাইশি, ~মাইসি *n* wickedness; profligacy; roguishness; immorality; naughtiness. ~মাশি/ ~মাসি করা *vi* indulge in wickedness/ mischief/ roguery/ profligacy; be naughty. ~ মেজাজ *adj* ill-tempered; ill-natured; peevish. ❑*n* ill-humour; ill-temper; peevishness. ~মেজাজি *n, adj*=~মেজাজ. ~ রং, ~ রঙ *n* bad colour; another colour; dull/faded colour; a playing-card of a different suit or a playing-card which is not a suit. ~ রক্ত *n* infected/contaminated blood. ❑*adj* of low birth; low-born. ~রসিক *adj* having no sense of humour; bad connoisseur. ~রাগ *n* peevishness; ill-temper; petulance; bad temper; hot-headedness. ~রাগি, ~রাগী *n* short-tempered; ill-tempered; hotheaded; choleric. ~রাহ *adj* wicked sinful; on the wrong path. ~ রীতি *n* bad manners. ~রুচি *n* bad taste. ❑*adj* in bad taste; indecent. ~রোখা, ~রোকা *adj* peevish; irritable; sharp-tempered. ~সলা *n* bad or evil counsel. ~সুরত, ~ছুরত *adj* ugly; ill-shaped; repulsive; hideous. ~ হজম *n* indigestion; dyspepsia. ~হজমি=~হজম. ~ হাওয়া *n* polluted air. ~ হাল *n* evil plight; bad circumstance; wretchedness; poverty; bad/low state; misery.

বদন *n* face; countenance; appearance; mouth. ~-ইন্দু *n* moonface; moon-like face. ~ কমল lotus-like face. ~চন্দ্র = ~-ইন্দু. ~ ভরে *adv* with full-throated ease. ~মণ্ডল *n* face; countenance. বদনা, বদনী *fem* suffixed to another word to form a compound, eg, ইন্দুবদনী, চাঁদবদনী.

বদনা *n* a kind of small pitcher with a slender spout.

বদভ্যাস *n* bad habit.

বদমাশ ⇒ বদ

বদনামৃত *n* saliva; spittle.

বদনারবিন্দ = বদন-কমল

বদমান *adj* speaking. ❑*n* speaker.

বদর[1] [A] *n* **1** full moon. **2** a Muslim saint (whose name is uttered by boatmen to ensure a safe voyage).

বদর[2], **বদরিকা, বদরী** *n* jujube tree; jujube.

বদল [A] *n* exchange; change; substitution; barter; alteration; transfer. ~ করা *vt* exchange; change; vary; alter; transfer; barter; substitute. ~ হওয়া *vi* be changed. বদলানো=~ করা. বদলে যাওয়া *vi* change: দিন বদলে গেছে. বদলে নেওয়া *vt* exchange. বদলাবদলি *n* exchange; change; mutual transfer. বদলি, বদলী *n* **1** change. **2** exchange. **3** substitution; transfer. **4** substitute. ❑*adj* given or taken in exchange; substituting; bartered; substituted; transferred. বদলে *adv* in exchange of; in lieu of; in place of; instead; instead of.

বদলা [A] *n* revenge; retaliation; compensation; requital; substitution; thing or person seized or killed in retaliation. ~ দেওয়া *vt* compensate; indemnify; requite. ~ নেওয়া *vi* seize or kill in retaliation; take revenge; avenge; retaliate; wreak vengeance on.

বদস্ত [P] *adv* by hand; from hand to hand; readily; promptly; red-handed.

বদস্তুর [P] *adv* as usual; according to custom; in the usual manner; customarily.

বদান্য *adj* generous; liberal; munificent; bountiful; charitable. ~তা *n* generosity; liberality; munificence; bounty; charity.

বদি [P] *n* wickedness; badness; evil; vice; mischief. ❑*n* bad; wicked; evil.

বদিয়তি, বদিয়তী *n* mischief; pranks.

বদৌলত, বদৌলতে *adv* by the kindness/grace of; by the bounty (of); by means of.

বদ্ধ *adj* **1** tied; bound; fastened. **2** shut; closed: দরজা~. **3** entrapped; ensnared. **4** confined; imprisoned; encaged: খাঁচায় ~ পাখি. **5** bound by an obligation: প্রতিজ্ঞা~. **6** caught in: ফাঁদে ~. **7** dressed; put up; interwoven: গুচ্ছ~. **8** joined together: একতা~, বদ্ধাঞ্জলি. **9** clasped: আলিঙ্গনাবদ্ধ. **10** stagnant: ~ পানি. **11** restrained; arrested: ~ স্রোত. **12** deep-rooted; deep-seated: ~ ধারণা. **13** firm: ~মূল. **14** downright;

thorough; confirmed; stark: ~ কালা/পাগল. **15** placed; arranged; put; well-ordered: শ্রেণী~. **16** (math) concrete: ~সংখ্যা. **~চিত্ত** *adj* intent on (sth), having the thoughts fixed upon. **~জীব** *adj* attached to mundane existence. **~দৃষ্টি** *adj* having one's gaze fixed on. **~পরিকর** firmly resolved; ready for anything. **~ পাগল** stark mad. **~ পাজি** downright scoundrel/villain. **~ বখা/ বখাটে** downright rogue; thoroughly spoilt/debauched. **~বৈর** *n* perpetual or long-lasting enemy or feud. **~মুষ্টি** *adj* having closed or clenched one's palm/fist; (fig) close-fisted; niggardly; miserly. **~মূল** *adj* firmly rooted; deep-rooted; deep-seated. **~লক্ষ্য** *adj*=~দৃষ্টি.

বদ্ধাঞ্জলি *adj* having joined the hollowed palms of the hands. **~ হওয়া** *vt* join or fold one's palms.

বদ্ধাধান *n* (phys) a bounded charge.

বদ্বীপ *n* delta. **~শীর্ষ** *n* head of the delta.

বধ *n* killing; slaughter. **~ করা** *vt* kill; slay; slaughter. **~কর্তা** *n* killer; slaughterer; slayer; executioner. **~কর্ত্রী** *fem*. **~দণ্ড** *n* capital punishment. **~স্থলী, ~স্থান** *nn* place of execution or slaughter; slaughty-house. **বধার্থ** *adv* for killing/slaughter. **বধোদ্যত** *adj* prepared or ready to kill; murderous. **বধার্হ** *n* to be slain or killed; to be capitally punished; deserving death.

বধা *vt* (poet, archaic)=বধ করা

বধাজ্ঞা *n* order of execution.

বধির *adj* deaf; (fig) refusing to listen. **~ করা** *vt* deafen. **~ হওয়া** *vi* become deaf; (fig) turn a deaf ear (to). **~তা, ~ত্ব** *n* deafness.

বধী *n, adj* killer; assassin; killing.

বধূ *n* **1** bride; newly-married woman. **2** young wife; spouse. **3** wife; woman. **4** daughter-in-law (usu ~মাতা). **5** a family woman. **~জন** *n* married woman esp one whose husband is alive; (collect) women. **~টী** *n* child-wife. **~ৎসব** *n* feast on the first appearance of a bride's menses. **~মাতা** *n* daughter-in-law. **~ত্ব** *n* condition of a bride.

বধোদ্যত ⇒ বধ

বধোপায় *n* **1** instrument or means of putting to death. **2** killing; execution.

বধ্য *adj* to be slain or killed; to be capitally punished. **~পাল** *n* guardian of criminals; jailor. **~ভূমি** *n*=বধস্থলী.

বন *n* **1** forest; wood; jungle; grove; thicket; arbour; bower. **2** (prefixed to other words to form compounds) wild; sylvan: ~মানুষ, ~মল্লিকা, ~পুষ্প. **~কদলী** *n* wild banana or plantain. **~কপোত** *n* wood-pigeon; cushat. **~কর** *n* forest revenue or cess. **~-কর্মী** *n* worker in the forest department; forester. **~কুক্কুট** *n* wild-fowl; jungle fowl; woodcock. **~কুসুম** *n* wild flower. **~কৃত্যক** *n* forest service. **~গহন** *n* the depth or the thick part of a forest. **~গো** *n* wild cow. **~গোচর** *adj, n* dwelling in a forest; denizen or inhabitant of forests. **~গোলাপ** *n* briar; briar-rose; sweet briar. **~চর, ~চারী** *adj n* living in a forest or woods; woodman. **~জ** *adj* forest-grown/-born. **~জঙ্গল** *n* thickets; underwood; woodlands. **~দেবতা** *n* wood-god; silvan. **~দেবী** *fem*. **~পথ** *n* forest/jungle path. **~পরী** *n* wood-nymph; dryad. **~পাল** *n* conservator of forests. **~ফল** *n* wild fruit. **~ফুল** *n* wild flower. **~বাদাড়/~বাঁদড়া** *n*=~জঙ্গল. **~বাঁদড়া গাছ** *n* orchid. **~বাস** *n* dwelling or residence in a forest; banishment to the forest. **~বাসে দেওয়া/পাঠানো** *vt* banish or exile (one) to the forest. **~বাসে যাওয়া** *vi* be exiled to the forest; go to live in a forest as a punishment. **~বাসী** *adj, n* living in a forest; forest-dweller; a hermit; an anchorite. **~বাসিনী** *fem*. **~বিড়াল** *n* a kind of wild cat. **~বিড়ালী** *fem*. **~বিহার** *n* roving or wandering in a forest (esp for pleasure). **~বিহারী** *adj* **1** roving/wandering in forests and groves (esp for pleasure). **2** ❑*n* Sri Krishna. **~বৃক্ষ** *n* forest-tree. **~ভোজ, ~ভোজন** *n* picnic; outing. **~মক্ষিকা** *n* gad-fly. **~মধু** *n* wild-honey. **~মল্লিকা** *n* wild jasmine. **~মানুষ** *n* any anthropoid ape such as the gorilla; the chimpanzee, etc. **~মালা** *n* a garland of wild flowers. **~মালী** *n* one wearing a garland of wild flowers; Sri Krishna. **~মালিনী** *fem*. **~রক্ষক** *n* forest-ranger. **~রক্ষী** *n* forest-keeper; forest-guard. **~রাজি, ~রাজী** *n pl* a long track of forest or a path in a forest. **~শূকর** *n* wild hog. **~স্থ, ~স্থিত** *adjj* of a forest; situated in a forest; forest-grown; wild; sylvan. **~স্থলী** *n* forest-region; wood. **~স্পতি** *n* a forest-tree (esp a large tree bearing fruit apparently without blossoms, as several species of the fig, the jack tree, etc, but also applied to any tree). **~হংসী** *n* wild-duck; wild-duck.

বনবন[১] *n* (onom) suggesting sound of sth whirling swiftly eg a toy; whirr. **~ করে ঘোরা** *vt* rotate/whirl swiftly.

বনবন[২] [E] *n* bonbon; sweetmeat.

বনস্পতি ⇒ বন

বনা *vi* **1** get on together; agree; be on good terms; get along: তার সঙ্গে একদণ্ডও বনে না. **2** assume as false dress or appearance; pretend to be: সাধু ~. **3** be reduced to; be proved to; become: ভেড়া ~.

বনাত *n* broad-cloth; baize.

বনানো, বনান *vt* cause to get along; cause to agree. **বনিয়ে থাকা** manage to get along.

বনানী *n* great/extensive forest.

বনান্ত *n* **1** outskirts/edge of a forest. **2** forest-region.

বনান্তর *n* interior of a forest; another forest.

বনাবনি, বনাবস্তি *n* agreement; concord; entente; harmony; adjustment.

বনাম [P] *prep* **1** in the name of. **2** versus.

বনায়ন *n* afforestation.

বনাশ্রম *n* abode in the forest.

বনাশ্রয় *n* forest as a refuge. ❑*adj* living in a forest.

বনাশ্রিত *adj* dwelling in a forest; taking refuge in a forest. ❑*n* anchorite.

বনিতা *n* **1** woman. **2** wife. **3** sweetheart; darling.

বনিবনা, বনিবনাও, বনিবনাত *nn*=বনাবনি.

বনিয়াদ, বনেদ [P] *n* foundation; base; basis; groundwork. **বনিয়াদি** *adj* **1** fundamental; basic. **2** traditional; (traditionally) aristocratic or noble: বনিয়াদি পরিবার.

বনীকরণ *n* afforestation.

বনেচর *n adj*=বনচর

বনেট [E] *n* bonnet

বনেদ ⇒ বনিয়াদ.

বনেদি=বনিয়াদি. **বনেদিআনা** *n* aristocratic manners. **বনেদিপনা** *n* aristocratic pride/ bearing.

বনোয়ারি *n* **1** one wearing a garland of wild flowers. **2** (an appellation of) Sri Krishna.

বন্ত *suff* denoting possession or endowment: প্রাণ~, জ্ঞান~.

বন্দ *n* [P] **1** (measurement in determining the size of a house) total of length and breadth: পঁচিশের বন্দের ঘর (eg 16+9=25). **2** a piece; a plot; a lot: এক ~ জমি.

বন্দক *adj* singing in adoration; praising; adoring; worshiping. ❑*n* one who sings in praise; one who salutes; worshipper; votary; one employed to glorify (esp a prince) in songs; glorifier; adorer; hymner.

বন্দন, বন্দনা *n* praise; worship; adoration; singing in adoration; song of praise; hymn; salutation; salute; hymning; glorification; magnification. **বন্দনা করা** *vt* sing praises; sing in adoration; hymn; worship; adore; salute; extol; glorify; prostrate oneself before; celebrate; invoke. **বন্দনীয়** *adj* worthy of being praised/ glorified in songs; deserving obeisance; venerable; adorable. **বন্দনীয়া** *fem.*

বন্দর [P] *n* port; harbour; sea-port; trading-town. **~পাল** *n* port commissioner. **মুক্ত ~** free port.

বন্দা[1]=বান্দা

বন্দা[2]=বন্দনা করা

বন্দারু *adj* praising; celebrating. ❑*n* worshipper; idolater; adorer; glorifier; flatterer; adulator.

বন্দি [P]=বন্দী[2]

বন্দিগৃহ, বন্দিখানা, বন্দিঘর=বন্দিশালা

বন্দিত *adj* glorified in songs; praised; lauded; extolled; celebrated; worshipped; adored; revered; venerated. **বন্দিতা** *fem.*

বন্দিত্ব, বন্দিদশা *n* imprisonment; confinement; captivity; duress.

বন্দিনী *n fem* of বন্দী[2]

বন্দিপাল *n* jailor; gaoler; jailer.

বন্দিশালা *n* prison; jail; gaol; guard-room; guardhouse.

বন্দী[1]=বন্দক

বন্দী[2] [P] *n* prisoner; captive. ❑*adj* imprisoned; confined; captive. **~ প্রদর্শন** (law) habeas corpus. **~ করা** *vt* imprison; capture; take (one) prisoner.

বন্দুক [T] *n* gun; musket; rifle. **~ধারী** *adj* armed with or carrying a gun/rifle. **~ধারী লোক** *n* gunman; musketeer; rifleman.

বন্দে *vt* I salute you.

বন্দেগি, বন্দেগী, বন্দগি [P] *n* (old use) **1** (mode of) humble salutation. **~জনাব** (phrase) I humbly salute you, sir; I bow to thee, sir. **2** service; devotion; servitude. **3** worship: এবাদত-~.

বন্দেজ [P] *n* **1** composition; arrangement; elegance of style: কাজের ~. **2** plan; settlement. **3** contrivance; artifice. **4** discipline. **5** act or state of tying/binding. **~ করা** *vt* arrange; dispose; plan.

বন্দে মাতরম (phrase) **1** I salute thee mother. **2** the first two words of the national anthem of India.

বন্দেশ [P] *n*=বন্দেজ

বন্দোবস্ত, বন্দবস্ত *n* **1** arrangement; preparation; provision; organization. **2** method; order; system; regulation. **3** settlement; land settlement; tenure. **~ করা** *vi, vt* arrange; make arrangements; provide for; make preparations (for); make contract (with). **~ দেওয়া** *vt* settle tenure (of land, etc) on a person or party. **~ নেওয়া** *vt* have tenure (of land, etc) settled on oneself. **চিরস্থায়ী ~** the permanent settlement. **~ মহাল, বন্দোবস্তি ~** *n* a landed estate or district brought under settlement.

বন্দ্য *adj*=বন্দনীয় (⇒ বন্দনীয়). **বন্দ্যা** *fem.*

বন্দ্যবংশ *n* (lit) an adorable or noble family; Bandyopadhyay or Banarji family.

বন্দ্যোপাধ্যায় *n* hereditary title of a class of Bengali Brahmins.

বন্ধ *n* **1** any device for binding or fastening. **2** binding; fastening; tying. **3** tie; bond; bandage; knot; joint; knuckle. **4** band; belt; string; chain; filters. **5** clasp; embrace: বাহু~. **6** obstacle; obstruction; stoppage; blockage: স্রোতো~. **7** dike; dam; embankment; building; construction: সেতু~. **8** composition; arrangement of words; construction: বাক্য~.

ছন্দো~. **9** putting together; uniting; combining; forming; joining. producing: মাল্য~. **10** restraint; repression: ইন্দ্রিয়~. **11** enclosure; circle. **11** capture; arrest; imprisonment; custody. **12** mundane bondage; attachment to this world. **13** any configuration or position of the body. **14** knitting (the brows). **15** fixing; directing (mind, eyes, etc). **16** vacation; holidays; recess; closure. ❑*adj* **1** shut; closed: ঘরের দরজা ~. **2** fastened; tied; bound: হাত-পা ~. **3** discontinued; barred; stopped: আসা-যাওয়া ~. **4** obstructed; checked; arrested: নর্দমার জল/রক্ত ~. **5** confined; shut in: ঘরে ~. **6** prevented; checked; restrained: আস্ফালন ~, চলাচল ~. **~ করা** *vt* shut; close: দরজা জানালা ~ করা; stop; discontinue: কথাবার্তা ~ করা; confine; shut in: ঘরে ~; obstruct; bar: পথ ~ করা. **~ হওয়া** *vi* cease; be stopped/ discontinued; be obstructed, etc. **~করণ** *n* binding; stopping; obstructing. গ্রীষ্মের ~ the summer vacation.

বন্ধক *n* **1** pawning; mortgage; hypothecation. **2** pawn; pledge. **~ দেওয়া** *vt* pawn; pledge; mortgage; hypothecate; raise a mortgage (eg on one's) house. **~ রাখা** *vi* lend money taking sth in pawn or mortgage. **~গ্রহীতা** *n* pawnbroker; pawnee, mortgagor. **~পত্র** *n* bond; pledge; mortgage deed. **বন্ধকী** *adj* of pawning/ mortgage/hypothecation; pawned; mortgaged; hypothecated. **বন্ধকী দলিল** *n* = ~পত্র. **বন্ধকী দোকান** *n* pawnshop. **বন্ধকী কারবার** *n* pawnbroker's business.

বন্ধন *n* **1** binding; tying; fastening; fathering; tethering. **2** tie; bondage; bond; rope; cord; tether. **3** binding on or round; clasping: বাহু~. **4** (med) binding up; bandaging; bandage. **5** embanking; embankment; bridging over: সেতু~. **6** building; construction. **7** joining; junction; connection; coherence; unification: হৃদয়ের ~. **8** checking; suppressing; obstruction; obstacle: স্রোতো~. **9** restraint; stoppage. **10** (chem) alloying (of metals). **11** catching; capturing; confining; detention; custody; imprisonment; confinement: কারা~. **12** composition: কবরী~. **13** (anat) sinew; muscle. **14** (phil) mundane bondage: ভব~. **15** style; manner; fashion. **16** compactness. **17** fixation. **~ক্রিয়া** *n* bandage. **~গ্রন্থি** *n* knot. **~দশা** *n* captivity; imprisonment; incarceration. **~মুক্তি** *n* freedom from bondage or captivity. **~রজ্জু** *n* rope for tying or fastening; tether. **~শালা** *n* gaol; prison. **~স্তম্ভ** *n* tying post. **~হীন** *adj* free

বন্ধনাগার, বন্ধনালয় *n* gaol; prison.

বন্ধনী *n* **1** any device to bind or fasten; tie; band; ligament. **2** (math) bracket. **~ভুক্ত** *adj* bracketed. **3** (med) ligature. **~য়** *adj* to be tied or bound.

বন্ধু *n* friend; crony; well-wisher; intimate; confidant; comrade; mate; chum; pal; patron; ally; associate; lover. **~নী** *fem*. **~তা, ~ত্ব** *n* friendship; amity; alliance; intimacy; camaraoderie. **~জন** *n* **1**=~. **2** friends. **~ত্ব করা** *vi* make friends with; be friends; cultivate/gain the friendship of. **~পূর্ণ** *adj* friendly; amiable; affable; amicable; congenial. **~বর** *n* my great friend. **~বান্ধব** *n pl* friends and relations. **~বিচ্ছেদ** *n* estrangement or separation of friends/from a friend. **~য়া** *n* (poet)=বন্ধু. **~সুলভ** friendly. **~হীন** *adj* friendless. **~তাসূত্রে** *adv* through/due to friendship.

বন্ধুক *n* a tree with crimson flowers. **~ পুষ্প** *n* flower of this tree.

বন্ধুর *adj* **1** uneven; wavy; rugged; rough; bumpy. **2** (geog) relief. **~তা** *n* ruggedness; unevenness; roughness; relief.

বন্ধুল, বন্ধুলি *n*=বন্ধুক

বন্ধ্য *adj* **1** unproductive; sterile; barren; childless; fruitless. **2** to be bound/ fettered/ imprisoned. **বন্ধ্যা** *fem* barren or childless woman. **~তা** *n* **1** fitness for being bound or tied. **2** barrenness; sterility; unproductivity.

বন্য *adj* growing; produced or existing in a forest; being; existing; roving or dwelling in woods; wild; savage; sylvan churlish; unfit for civilized society; uncivilized; aboriginal. ❑*n* aboriginal (people); bushman. **বন্যা** *fem.*

বন্যা *n* flood; inundation; deluge. **~র জল** *n* flood water. **~উপদ্রুত, ~পীড়িত** *adjj* flood-affected, flood-stricken. **~প্লাবিত** *adj* flood inundated.

বপক *n* sower; planter.

বপন *n* sowing; planting; plantation. **~ করা** *vt* sow; plant. **~যন্ত্র** *n* sowing-machine.

বপা *vt* (poet)=বপন করা

বপু *vt* body; figure; form; physique; a bulky body. **~মান** *adj* bulky; corpulent; burly; hefty; heavy-bodied. **~মতী** *fem.*

বপ্তা *n*=বপক. **বপ্ত্রী** *fem.*

বপ্র *n* **1** ground; field. **2** (high) river-bank; any shore or bank. **3** hillock; slope or declivity of a hill; table-land on a mountain. **4** wall; mud wall. **5** rampart. **~কেলি, ~ক্রিয়া, ~ক্রীড়া** *n* playful butting of an elephant or a bull against a bank or a mound of any kind.

বব-কাট [E] *n* bob cut.

বম *n* (onom) **1** denoting firing of a shell; roll; boom; thunder. **2** a peculiar sound produced by striking one's inflated cheeks with fingers. **3** rub-a-dub (of a drum).

বমন *n* vomiting; belching or ejecting (as by a volcano). **~দ্রব্য** *n* emetics. **~ করা** *vi, vt* vomit; spew; spue; belch; eject violently. **বমনোদ্রেক** *n*

nausea; retching. **বমনোদ্রেককর** *adj* nauseous; nauseating. **বমনোদ্রেককর ঔষধ** *n* emetic.

বমবম[1], **ববমবম** *n* (onom)=বম

বমবম[2] *n* (onom) cannonade; rumbling; roll.

বমাল [A,P] *adv* together with the stolen or looted thing; red-handed.

বমি *n* vomiting; vomited matter; vomit; spue; spew. **~ করা** *vi, vt*=বমন করা. **গা ~-~ করা** *vi* have nausea; have qualms or qualmishness; feel qualmish. **~ত** *adj* violently ejected.

বম্বেটে=বোম্বেটে

বয় [E] *n* waiter; shop-boy.

বয়ঃ (in compounds) *n* age; period of life; longevity; lifetime; youth; prime of life. **~ক্রম** *n* age. **~প্রাপ্ত, ~স্থ** *adj* being in the bloom of age; grown-up; bull-grown; of age; adult; of marriageable age. **~প্রাপ্তা, ~স্থা** *fem*. **~প্রাপ্ত পুরুষ বা নারী** *n* adult; major. **~প্রাপ্তি** *n* coming of age. **~স্থ-ভোটাধিকার** adult suffrage. **~সন্ধি** *n* puberty; adolescence. **~সীমা** *n* age-limit.

বয়কট *n* boycott. **~ করা** *vt* boycott.

বয়ড়া *n*=বহেড়া

বয়ন *n* weaving; knitting. **~ করা** *vi, vt* weave; knit. **~প্রদর্শক** *n* weaving demonstrator. **~বিদ্যা** *n* art of weaving. **~শিল্প** *n* weaving industry. **~শিল্পী** *n* weaver.

বয়না weaver. ⇒ বায়না

বয়নাক্কা=বায়নাক্কা

বয়নামা [A, P] *n* sale-deed.

বয়রা *adj* (dial) deaf.

বয়লার [E] *n* boiler.

বয়স *n* age; agedness; youth; majority. **~ হওয়া** *vi* come of age; grow old; become aged. **~কাল** *n* youth; majority; prime of youth. **~কালে** *adv* in one's youth. **~ফোঁড়া** *n* acne. **বয়সা** *n* breaking or cracking of voice on attaining adolescence. **বয়সা ধরা** *vi* (of voice) crack on attaining adolescence. **বয়সী** *adj* **1** of a particular age: আধাবয়সী, middle-aged; সে আমার ছেলের বয়সী. **2** advanced in age; aged; old. **বয়সিনী** *fem*. **বয়সোচিত** *adj* right and proper for one's age; befitting one's age; natural to a particular age. **বয়সের গাছ-পাথর নেই** (phrase) hoary with age.

বয়স্ক *adj* **1**=বয়ঃস্থ. **2** aged.

বয়স্থ=বয়ঃস্থ

বয়স্য *n* one of the same age; boon companion; intimate associate; attendant or flatterer. **বয়স্যা** *fem*.

বয়া [E] buoy; life-buoy.

বয়াটে=বখাটে (⇒ বখা)

বয়ান[1] *n* (poet) face; countenance.

বয়ান[2] [A] *n* narration; description; account; statement.

বয়াম, বয়েম [Pg] *n* jar (usu with a detachable lid and made of porcelain or glass).

বয়ার *n* **1** buffalo. **2** boar. ❑*adj* **1** thoroughly spoilt or dissolute. **2** indomitable; unruly.

বয়েত, বয়েৎ [A] *n* **1** couplet; verse (esp one in Arabic, Persian or urdu). **~বাজি** *n* contest of poets. **2** act of receiving initiation; accepting discipleship; fealty; homagge. **~ হওয়া** *vi* become a disciple; take the oath of allegiance.

বয়োগুণ *n* tendencies or propensities natural to a particular age.

বয়োজীর্ণ *adj* worn out/decayed (as a result of aging).

বয়োজ্যেষ্ঠ *adj* older in age; elder.

বয়োতীত *adj* past youth advanced in age; exceedingly old or decrepit.

বয়োদোষ *n* vices natural to a particular age.

বয়োধর্ম=বয়োগুণ

বয়োধিক *adj* older; elder; superior in years.

বয়োবৃদ্ধ *adj* older in age; advanced in age. **বয়োবৃদ্ধা** *fem*. **বয়োবৃদ্ধ** *n* increase of years.

বর *n* **1** act or object of choosing; choice; election; wish; request: ~ চাওয়া. **2** boon; gift; reward; benefit; blessing; favour: ~ দেওয়া. **3** bridegroom. **4** husband. ❑*adj* **1** desired. **2** select; choicest; valuable; precious; best; most excellent or eminent; fine: পণ্ডিত~, তরু~, ~নারী. **~ চাওয়া** *vt* ask a boon. **~ দেওয়া** *vi* grant a boon. **~ নেওয়া** *vt* choose a boon. **~ পাওয়া** *vt* obtain a boon. **~কনে** *n pl* the bride and the bridegroom. **~বধূ** *n pl*=~কনে. **~কর্তা** *n* head of the bridegrooms party. **~দ** *adj* granting wishes; conferring a boon; ready to fulfil request or prayers. **বরদা** **1** *fem* of ~দ. **2** goddess Durga. **~দাতা** *n* one who confers a boon. **~দাত্রী** *fem*. **~দান** *n* granting a boon or request. **~দান করা** *vt* grant a boon or wish. **~ধাতু** *n* noble metal. **~পক্ষ** *n* bridegroom's party or side. **~পণ** *n* a dowry in cash paid by the bride's parents or party to the bridegroom. **~পত্র** *n* a minion (esp of a deity); a darling; a favourite. **~প্রদ** *adj*=~দ. **~প্রদা** *fem*. **~বর্ণিনী** *n* a woman with a beautiful complexion; an excellent or handsome woman; any woman. **~মাল্য** *n* a garland of flower which the bride puts ceremonially round the neck of the bridegroom whilst accepting him as her husband; a garland of highest honour. **~যাত্রা** *n* procession of a bridegroom (to the bride's house). **~যাত্রী, ~যাত্র** *n* one who accompanies a bridegroom to a wedding. **বরের ঘরের মাসি কনের ঘরের পিসি** (phrase) one who hunts with the hound and runs with the hare.

বরই *n* jujube.

বরওক্ত, বরবক্ত [P] *adv* in time; at the proper/right/suitable/due time.

বরং *adv* rather; in preference.

বরক *adj, n* receiving; welcoming; choosing; electing selecting; one who receives/ welcomes etc; elector.

বরকত [A] *n* abundance; prosperity; auspiciousness; good fortune; blessing.

বরকন্দাজ [P] *n* footman or follower carrying a firearm; an armed guard; body-guard. **বরকন্দাজি, বরকন্দাজী** *n* profession of a footman or body-guard.

বরখাস্ত [P] *n* recall or removal from office; discharge; dismissal. ❑*adj* removed from office; discharged; dismissed. ~ **করা** *vt* remove from office; discharge; dismiss. ~ **হওয়া** *vi* be removed from office; be discharged/dismissed. **বরখাস্তি** *adj*/removed from office; abandoned; set aside: বরখাস্তি জমি.

বরখেলাপ, বরখেলাফ [P] *adj, adv* unnecessary; against; contrary to; opposite; unnecessarily; for nothing; unwarrantedly: হুকুমের ~, contrary to orders. ~ **করা** *vt* disobey; oppose; break (one's word or promise). **কানুন** ~ against law; unlowful.

বরগা[1] [Pg] *n* rafter (কড়ি-~). ~ **গণা** *vt* (iron) undergo a term of imprisonment; serve term.

বরগা[2]=বর্গা

বরচন্দন *n* **1** deodar. **2** fragrant aloe wood and tree.

বরজ *n* plantation of betel-leaves.

বরঞ্চ *adv* rather; by preference; preferably.

বরণ[1]=বরন

বরণ[2] *n* **1** the act of choosing; wishing; wooing. **2** devotional/respectful/ cordial/ ceremonial reception or acceptance or nomination; welcome: বধূ~, প্রতিমা~. **3** appointment; election: সভাপতি পদে ~. **4** submissive/ deliberate acceptance: দুঃখ~. ~ **করা** *vt* **1** receive/ accept/nominate/elect respectfully; devotionally; cordially or ceremonially; welcome; appoint; employ; accept submissively or voluntarily; (fig) embrace; submit oneself to. ~**ডালা** *n* a wicker-tray holding articles with which one is received ceremonially. ~**পত্র** *n* warrant (giving authority). ~**মালা** *n* garland placed by a maiden round the neck of a selected suitor; a similar garland to welcome sb respectfully or cordially. **বরণীয়** *adj* fit to be received/ accepted/ nominated/elected respectfully; devotionally; cordially or ceremonially; fit to be welcomed; adorable; acceptable; venerable. **বরণীয়া** *fem*.

বরতরফ [P] *adj* dismissed; discharged. **বরতরফি** *n* dismissal; discharge.

বরদ ⇒ বর

বরদার, বরদার [P] bearer; carrier (used as *suff* as in নিশান-~ , flag-bearer; হুকুম~, obedient; আসা~, mace-bearer).

বরদাস্ত, বরদাশ্‌ত [P] *n* endurance; patience; tolerance; resignation. ~ **করা** *vt* tolerate; bear (with); endure; brook; suffer. ~ **হওয়া** *vi* be tolerable; be endured.

বরন *n* (poet) colour; complexion.

বরনারী *n fem* best woman; most excellent woman.

বরন্তী *adj fem* **1** (girl) yearning or longing madly for marriage. **2** well-educated about her conjugal duties (before marriage).

বরফ [P] *n* ice; snow. ~ **পড়া** *vi* snow. ~**জল** *n* ice-water. ~**তুল্য** *adj* icy.

বরফট্টাই *n*=বড়াই[1]

বরফি *n* a kind of sweetmeat made of condensed cowmilk.

বরবটি, বরবটী *n* a kind of kidney bean; *Dolichos catjong.*

বরবর্ণিনী ⇒ বর

বরবাদ [P] *adj* desolated; ruined; laid waste; wasted; destroyed; squandered; cast away; thrown to the wind. ~ **করা** *vt* ruin; destroy; ravage; waste; squander; throw away; throw to the winds. ~ **হওয়া** *vi* be ruined/ destroyed/squandered.

বরমাল্য, বরযাত্র, বরযাত্রী *nn* ⇒ বর

বরয়িতা *n* one who accepts, receives, elects or selects (respectfully, cordially, devotionally or ceremoniously); welcomer. **2** one who accepts voluntarily or submissively. **3** welcomer. **4** chooser; elector. **বরয়িত্রী** *n fem* maiden who herself chooses her husband.

বরযুবতী *n fem*=বরনারী

বররুচি *adj* **1** having excellent taste or inclination. **2** lustrous; glowing brilliantly; radiant; luminous. **3** a famous poet, grammarian and lexicographer; reputed to be one of the nine gems of the court of Vikramaditya.

বরলব্ধ *adj* **1** received as a boon. **2** having received a boon.

বরলাভ *n* receiving a boon. ~ **করা** *vt* receive a boon.

বরষ, বরষণ, বরষা, বরা[1] poet forms of বর্ষ, বর্ষণ, বর্ষা, বরণ করা respectively.

বরা[2] *n* boar; hog. ~**খুরে** *adj* having hoofs like a boar.

বরাঙ্গ *n* **1** best part of the body; head. **2** an elegant form or body. **3** female pudenda. ❑*adj* having an excellent form; excellent or beautiful in all parts. **বরাঙ্গী** *fem* fine-limbed (woman).

বরাঙ্গনা *n fem* excellent/beautiful woman.

বরাত [A] *n* **1** fate; luck; fortune; good luck. **2** charge; commission; assignment; warrant; order: কাজের ~ দেওয়া. **3** necessity; business: সেখানে একটু ~ ছিল. **4** warrant of authority; authority to represent: নিজে না গিয়ে তাকে ~ দিয়ে

দাও. 5 representative. 6 letter. 7 bill of exchange. ~ দেওয়া *vi* entrust a charge; authorize; assign; commission. ~গুণে *adv* by virtue of luck. ~জোরে *adv* through good/a stroke of luck. ~চিঠি *n* letter of authority or assignment; bill of exchange. **বরাতি** *adj* 1 lucky. 2 commissioned; representing; entrusted: বরাতি কাজ হওয়া. 3 necessary. ❑*n* messenger; courier; emissary; go-between. **বরাতে** *adj* lucky. ❑*prep* in front of; in sb's presence; before: কথাটা তার বরাতেই বলো.

বরাতি[2] *n* (old use)=বরযাত্রী

বরাদ্দ [P] *n* allotment; fixation; allocation; estimate; budget; ration. ❑*adj* allotted; fixed; allocated; apportioned. ~ করা *vt* allocate; allot; fix; estimate; apportion.

বরানুগমন *n* act of accompanying a bridegroom to a wedding. **বরানুগামী** *n*=বরযাত্রী.

বরাবর [P] *adv* 1 always; ever; each time: সে ~ আমার কাছে আছে. 2 straight; straightway: ~ পশ্চিমে যাও. 3 all along; all through: আমরা ~ মাঠের ভিতর দিয়ে এসেছি. 4 all the way: সে ~ তার সঙ্গে গেল. ❑*adj* like; alike; on a par: সুধা বিষে ~. ❑*prep* to; towards; near; along: অধ্যক্ষের ~ লেখো, রাস্তা ~ চলো. **বরাবরেষু** *prep* (used in letter-writing) to; addressed to.

বরাবরি *prep* (archaic) to; in sb's presence.

বরাভয় *n* 1 a particular sign made with the right hand stretching downward and the left hand stretching upward indicating grant of desire and assurance of safety. 2 fulfilment of one's desire and assurance of safety. ~দাতা *n* one who grants desire and the assurance of safety. ~দাত্রী *fem.*

বরাভরণ *n* dress and ornaments given as gifts to a bridegroom by the bride's party.

বরামদ [P] *n* coming up; recovery of stolen property: মাল ~ করা recover stolen property through search.

বরারোহা *adj fem* having well-shaped and well-developed hips; a beautiful woman.

বরাসন *n* 1 highest/best seat. 2 seat of honour. 3 seat for the bridegroom.

বরাহ *n* 1 boar; hog. 2 the third incarnation of Vishnu when he slew the demon called Baraha. বন্য ~ wild boar. **বরাহী** *fem* sow.

বরিখ, বরিখন, বরিখা, বরিষ, বরিষণ, বরিষা *nn* old poetical forms of বর্ষ, বর্ষণ, বর্ষা, বর্ষ, বর্ষণ, বর্ষা respectively.

বরিষ্ঠ *adj* best; greatest; most excellent; most preferable among; better than; chief; high. ~ আদালত *n* High Court.

বরীয়ান *adj* better; more or most excellent of; chief of; more honourable; senior; venerable to all. **বরীয়সী** *fem.*

বরুণ *n* 1 (myth) the Hindu seagod. 2 ocean. **বরুণাত্মজা** *fem* Varuna's daughter, Varuni. **বরুণানী** *fem* Varuna's wife. **বরুণালয়** *n* Varuna's abode, the sea.

বরেণ্য *adj* 1 to be wished for; desirable. 2 excellent; best among. 3 venerable; most honourable; deserving honourable or cordial reception.

বরেন্দ্র, বরেন্দ্রভূমি *n* ancient Gauda or North Bengal.

বরোন্মুখ *adj* ready/about to grant a boon.

বর্গ *n* 1 a separate division; class; set; multitude of similar things; group; company; genus; aggregate; collection: প্রাণি~. 2 (gram) any one of the five groups (ক-~, চ-~, ট-~, ত-~, প-~) into which Bengali consonantal stops are classified. 3 chapter or section of a book; sub-division. 4 any of the four principal pursuits of life (⇒ চতুর্বর্গ). 5 (arith) square (of a number). 6 (used as a *pl suff*): বন্ধু~, আত্মীয়~. ~ক্ষেত্র *n* (geom) square. ~ঘন *n* (geom) square of a cube. ~ফল *n* (math) square. ~মূল *n* (arith) square root. ~মূল নির্ণয়/বের করা find out the square root of.

বর্গা[1]=বরগা[1]

বর্গা[2] *n* a temporary lease of land on the basis of sharing the crop between the cultivator and the land-owner; share cropping; land under share-cropping. ~দার, ~ইত *nn* a cultivator cultivating land on the above basis; share-cropper. ~ দেওয়া *vt* lease land to a sharecropper. ~ভাগ *n* share of crop received from a piece of land leased to a sharecropper.

বর্গাকার *adj* square.

বর্গি, বর্গী *n* (hist) the Mahratha cavalry notorious for their sudden attacks and ruthless plundering. ~র হাঙ্গামা frequent inroads of the Mahratha cavalry in the 18th century Bengal.

বর্গীয় *adj* 1 of a class; generic; specific. 2 (math) relating to square. 3 (gram) of or classified into the groups of the Bengali stops. ~ বর্ণ *n* (gram) any of the twenty-five stops of the Bengali alphabet.

বর্গ্য=বর্গীয়

বর্চঃ *n* 1 vigour; energy. 2 brilliance; lustre; splendour; glory. 3 form; figure; shape; physical grace.

বর্জক *adj* abandoning; shuning; leaving. ❑*n* one who abandons/shuns; leaves.

বর্জন *n* abandoning; excluding; exclusion; omission; abandonment; disownment; desertion: স্ত্রীপুত্র ~; boycott: বিদেশী দ্রব্য ~. ~ করা *vt* abandon; exclude; desert; disown; boycott. **বর্জনীয়** *adj* to be avoided/shunned/abandoned/excluded/boycotted/given up/disowned. **বর্জনীয়া** *fem.*

বর্জাইস *n* (printing) bourgeois.

বর্জিত *adj* abandoned; excluded; omitted; deserted; boycotted; given up; left out; devoid of; deprived of; without: কাণ্ডজ্ঞান-~. **বর্জিতা** *fem.*

বর্জ্য *adj* **1**=বর্জনীয়. **2** waste: ~ পদার্থ, waste product.

বর্ডার [E] *n* border; edge; frontier.

বর্ণ *n* **1** colour; tint; dye; pigment. **2** colour of the face; complexion. **3** class of men; caste; race. **4** letter of the alphabet. **~চোরা** *adj* (chiefly of mangoes) ripe and sweet; though apparently green and unripe; deceptive of colour; (fig) hypocritical; two-faced. **~চোরা আম** a variety of mango that looks green even when ripe; (fig) a person concealing his/her merits. **~জ্ঞান** *n* knowledge of the alphabet. **~জ্ঞানশূন্য, ~জ্ঞানহীন** *adj* illiterate. **~জ্যেষ্ঠ** *n* highest in caste; a Brahmin. **~জ্যেষ্ঠা** *n fem*. **~তুলি** *n* painting brush. **~দাসী** *n* prostitute. **~দৃক** *n* chromoscope. **~ধর্ম** *n* particular duty of any caste or tribe. **~পরিচয়** *n*=~জ্ঞান. **~পাত্র** *n* colour-vessel; paint-box. **~বিপর্যয়** *n* metathesis. **~বিশ্লেষণ** *n* analysis or separation of the letters of a word. **~বিশ্লেষণ করা** *vi* analyse/separate the letters of a word. **~মণ্ডল** *n* (phys) the chromosphere. **~মাপক** *n* colourimeter. **~মালা** *n* the alphabet. **~রেখচ্ছটা** *n* (phys) line of spectrum. **~রেখা** *n* chalk. **~শ্রেষ্ঠ** *n* one belonging to the best of castes; Brahmin. **~শ্রেষ্ঠা** *n fem*. **~সঙ্কর** *adj* halfbred; crossbred; hybrid; mongrel. ❑*n* a half-caste; hybrid; half-breed; cross-breed; mongrel; mixture or confusion of castes through intermarriage. **~সঙ্করত্ব** *n* hybridity; cross-breeding. **~সাম্য** *n* resemblance or symmetry in colour. **~হীন** *n* colourless; pale; out-caste.

বর্ণক *n* **1** an encomiast; acclaimer; strolling player or singer. **2** fragrant ointment; anything for swearing on the body; unguent. **3** yellow ochre; colour; pigment.

বর্ণন *n* **1** act of praising; commendation. **2** painting; colouring. **3** embellishment; decoration. **বর্ণনা** *n* **1** description; narration; delineation; depiction. **2** explanation. **3** statement. **4** colouration. **বর্ণনা করা** *vt* describe; narrate; depict; delineate; paint; colour. **বর্ণনা দেওয়া** *vt* give an account (of); narrate. **বর্ণনাকুশল** *adj* adept/skilful in describing or delineating or depicting or narrating or painting. **বর্ণনাতীত** *adj* indescribable; ineffable. **বর্ণনাপত্র** *n* written statement; representation.

বর্ণনীয়, বর্ণয়িতব্য *adj* to be described/ narrated/ painted/ delineated; describable.

বর্ণা *vt* (poet)=বর্ণনা করা

বর্ণাত্মকতা *n* nationalism; racialism.

বর্ণানো *vt* (poet)=বর্ণনা করা

বর্ণানুক্রম *n* alphabetical order. **বর্ণানুক্রমিক** *adj* arranged alphabetically. **বর্ণানুক্রমে** *adv* alphabetically; in the alphabetical order.

বর্ণানুভাবকতা *n* sense of colour.

বর্ণানুভূতি *n*=বর্ণানুভাবকতা

বর্ণান্ধ *adj* colour-blind. **~তা** *n* colour-blindness.

বর্ণাপেরণ *n* (phys) chromatic aberration.

বর্ণালি, বর্ণালী *n* (phys) spectrum. **শুদ্ধ ~** pure spectrum. **শোষণ ~** spectrum absorption. **সৌর ~** solar spectrum. **~গত, ~বিষয়ক** *adj* spectroscopic. **~বিশ্লেষণ** *n* spectrum analysis. **~বীক্ষণ** *n* spectroscope. **সমক্ষ ~বীক্ষণ** *n* direct vision spectroscope. **~মাপক** *n* spectrometer. **~-লিখন** *n* spectrography. **~-লেখ** *n* spectrograph. **~-লেখী** *adj* spectrographic.

বর্ণাশুদ্ধি *n* misspelling; spelling mistake.

বর্ণাশ্রম *n* duties of the four Hindu castes; as enjoined by scriptures. **~ ধর্ম** *n* duties or rites of the four castes in each of the four stages of life as enjoined in the Vedas (⇒ চতুরাশ্রম).

বর্ণিক *n* **1** painter. **2** writer.

বর্ণিত *adj* described; narrated; delineated; stated; depicted; painted; portrayed; explained.

বর্ণিনী *n* woman.

বর্ণী *n* **1** painter. **2** writer.

বর্ণ্য *adj*=বর্ণনীয়

বর্তন *n* **1** livelihood; occupation. **2** utensil; vessel. **3** road; path. **4** crushing; grinding; kneading; turning into paste. **5** paste. **বর্তনী** *n* **1** road. **2** (phys) circuit. **খণ্ডিত বর্তনী** *n* open circuit. **সংহত বর্তনী** *n* closed circuit. **বর্তনী-ছেদক** *n* circuit-breaker. **বর্তনী-প্রবাহ** *n* circuit-current.

বর্তমান *adj* **1** present. **2** of the present; present-day; current; modern. **3** alive; living; existing. ❑*n* **1** the present time; the present; current/modern times. **2** (gram) present tense. **~ থাকা** *vi* be present; be existing/ alive/living. **~ কাল** *n*=~ (১). **~কালীন** *adj* present-day; current; occurring or being done when one is present or alive. **~তা, ~ত্ব** *n* presence; existence; state of being alive. **বর্তমানে** *adv* at present; when one is alive/living/present: পিতা বর্তমানে পুত্র দায়িত্ব পেয়েছে.

বর্তা, বর্তান, বর্তানো *vi* **1** keep going: বেঁচে বর্তে আছি. **2** devolve on; সব সম্পত্তি তাকেই বর্তেছে. **3** be gratified; be kept going; come back to life: তোমার দেখা পেলেই বর্তে যাই.

বর্তি *n* **1** lamp. **2** wick of a lamp. **3** light. **4** painter's brush. **5** varnish.

বর্তিক, বর্তিকা *n* lamp; a light.

বর্তিত *adj* brought about; accomplished; prepared.

বর্তিষ্ণু *adj* stable; durable; lasting.

বর্তিষ্যমান *adj* about to be/ take place; future.

বর্তী *adj* (used as a *suff*) present; a sperical solid located: নিকট~; amenable to: বশ~.

বর্তুল *n* **1** ball. **2** (geom) sphere. **3** iron projectile used in games; a shot. **~ নিক্ষেপ** *n* putting the shot. ❑*adj* round; circular; spherical.

বর্তুলাকার *adj*=বর্তুল

বর্ত্ম *n* **1** road; way, path; course. **2** a set of rules of conduct or moral practice. **~নি** *n*=~ (1).

বর্ধক *adj* **1** causing to increase/ grow/ thrive/ prosper/expand/augment/improve; strengthening; granting prosperity; animating. **2** used as a *suff* in the senses mentioned above: শক্তি~.

বর্ধন *n* increasing; growing; thriving; augmenting; increase; growth; development; expansion; multiplication; augmentation. ❑*adj*=বর্ধক. **~ করা** *vt* increase; grow; augment; enhance; expand; develop; multiply. **~ক্ষম** *adj* capable of being increased/ augmented/developed/expanded. **~শীল** *adj* growing; developing; expanding; increasing; thriving; prosperous. **বর্ধনাঙ্ক** *n* (phys) power (of a lens).

বর্ধমান *adj*=বর্ধনশীল (⇒ বর্ধন)

বর্ধিত *adj* increased; grown; expanded; augmented; strengthened; promoted.

বর্ধিষ্ণু *adj*=বর্ধনশীল (⇒ বর্ধন)

বর্বর *n* barbarian; a low fellow; savage; brute; blockhead; fool; rogue; villain. ❑*adj* uncivilized; barbarous; barbaric; savage; brutal; rude; beastly; atrocious; heinous; stupid; ignorant. **~তা** *n* barbarianism; barbarism; savagery; barbarousness; boorishness; rudeness; stupidety; beastliness; brutality; ignorance; atrocity; heinousness.

বর্ম **1** coat of mail; armour; envelop; mail. **2** (zoo) carapace. **বর্মিত** *adj* clad in armour; mailed. **বর্মী** *adj*=বর্মিত.

বর্মা *n* **1** Burma. **2** Burmese cigar.

বর্মি *n, adj* Burmese.

বর্শা *n* spear; lance; pike. **~দণ্ড** *n* shaft of a spear; pikestaff. **তিমি ধরার ~** *n* harpoon. **~ধারী** *adj* armed with a spear/lance/pike. ❑*n* spearman; pikeman. **~ফলক** *n* spearhead. **~বিদ্ধ** *adj* pierced with a speared; speared; harpooned.

বর্ষ *n* **1** year. **2** rain. **3** cloud. **4** shower or fall: তুষার ~. **~কাল** *n* a period of one year; a full calendar year. **~জীবী** *adj* lasting or living for a year only; (bot) annual. **~প্রবেশ** *n* New Year's Day. **~বরণ** *n* welcoming the New Year; New Year's Day. **~বৃদ্ধি** *n* **1** increase in years. **2** anniversary; birth-day. **3** excessive rain. **~বলয়** *n* (bot) annual ring. **~ভোগ্য** *adj* to be enjoyed for one year. **~মান** *adj* raining; pouring; showering. **~মান** *n* rain-gauge.

বর্ষণ *n* **1** raining. **2** rain; rainfall. **3** falling or pouring like rain; pouring out; shedding out; sprinkling/ scattering/ dispersing upon: গোলাপজল ~; (লাক্ষ.) gracious bestowal: আশীর্বাদ ~. **~ করা** *vt* rain upon; shower/ scatter/ sprinkle) disperse upon; bestow graciously (upon). **~বিধৌত** *adj* washed by rain. **~মুখর** *adj* vibrant/reverberant with palter of rain. **~শীল** *adj* raining; pouring out; showering.

বর্ষপ্রবেশ, বর্ষবলয় *nn* ⇒ বর্ষ

বর্ষা[1] *n* **1** rain; rainfall. **2** the rains; rainy season; monsoon. **~কাল** *n*=~ (2). **~গম** *n* beginning of the rainy season; break of the monsoon. **~তি** *n* rain-coat; mackintosh; waterproof umbrella. **2** mushroom. ❑*adj* grown in the rainy season; mushroom. **~ত্যয়** *n* cessation of rain; termination of the rainy season; autumn. **~ধৌত** *adj* washed by/ submerged in rain. **~পোকা** *n* scarlet mite. **~প্লাবিত** *adj* flooded by rainstorms. **~বসান** *n*= ~ত্যয়. **~বাদল** *n* rain; rain and shower. **~ম্লান** *adj* darkened by rain. **~স্নাত** *adj*=~ধৌত.

বর্ষা[2] *vi* (poet)=বর্ষণ করা (⇒ বর্ষণ)

বর্ষিক *adj* **1** growing in the rainy season. **2** annual; yearly. **3** rainy; relating/ belonging to the rains. **4** shedding; showering; pouring.

বর্ষিত *adj* poured; showered.

বর্ষিষ্ঠ *adj* **1** very old; burdened with age; hoary. **2** oldest; eldest; older.

বর্ষী[1] (used as a *suff*) raining; pouring out; showering down; distributing; scattering; dispersing: অনল-~, emitting fire.

বর্ষী[2], **বর্ষীয়** (used as *suff*) of the age of; aged: অষ্টাদশ~. **বর্ষীয়া** *fem.*

বর্ষীয়ান *adj* very old; elderly; older; elder. **বর্ষীয়সী** *fem.*

বর্ষুক *adj*=বর্ষণশীল (⇒ বর্ষণ)

বর্ষোপল *n* hail-stone.

বর্হ *n* peacock's tail or feather. **~ভরা** *n* burden of feathers; peacock's tail.

বর্হী *n* the peacock.

বল[1] *n* **1** power; strength; might; vigour; force, energy. **2** (mech) force. **3** man or piece in chess. **4** an armed force. **5** support; help; supporter; helper: তুমিই আমার ~. **~ করা** *vi* force; apply force; insist. **~কর, ~কারক, ~কৃৎ** *adj* strengthening; invigorating; (med) tonic. **~কৃত** *adj* done by force or against free will. **~ক্ষয়** *n* loss/decay of strength; loss/decrease of soldiers or men; loss of pieces (in chess). **~ক্ষয়কর** *n* debilitating; weakening. **~গর্ব** *n* pride of strength or power. **~গর্বিত** *adj* proud of strength or power. **~ত্রিভুজ** *n* triangle of forces. **~দ** *adj* giving strength. **~দর্প** *n*=~গর্ব. **~দর্পিত, ~দৃপ্ত** *adjj*=~গর্বিত. **~পূর্বক** *adv* by force/violence. ~প্রদ *adj*=~কর. ~ প্রদান করা *vt* strengthen; invigorate. ~প্রয়োগ *n* application/ exercise/use of force or violence. ~প্রয়োগে *adv* by force/violence. ~বৎ *adj* prevailing; operative; in force; intact. ~বৎ করা *vt,* give effect to; put (a law, etc) into force. ~বত্তর *adj* stronger; more powerful. ~বত্তা *n* strength; powerfulness; mightiness; preponderance. ~বন্ত *adj* strong; powerful; mighty; robust; sturdy. ~বর্জিত *adj* destitute of strength; weak; infirm. ~বর্ধক *adj* strengthening; invigorating; (med) tonic. ~বর্ধন *n* increase of strength or power; invigoration; strengthening. ❑*adj* causing increase of power/strength; strengthening; increasing power/ strength; invigoration; (med) tonic; accelerating the force of. ~ বর্ধন করা *vi* increase strength/power; invigorate; strengthen; fortify; (med) tone up. ~বান *n*= ~বন্ত. ~বতী *fem* of ~বান. ~বিদ্যা *n* mechanics. ~বিন্যাস *n* arrangement of forces; array of troops; arraying of pieces in chess. ~বীর্য *n* strength and heroism. ~শালিতা *n*= ~বত্তা. ~শালী *adj*= ~বান. ~শূন্য *adj* destitute of strength; weak. ~শ্রেণী *n* (phys) system of forces. ~সামন্তরিক *n* (mech) parallelogram of forces. ~সাম্য, ~স্থিতি *nn* (phys) equilibrium of force. ~হীন *adj*= ~শূন্য. ~হীনা *fem.*

বল[2] [E] *n* ball; football; playing ball. ~ করা, ~ দেওয়া *vi* (cricket) bowl. ~ খেলা *vt* play football. ~ খেলা *n* game of football. ~ ছোড়া *vt* throw a ball. ~ মারা *vi* (cricket) bat. ~বেয়ারিং *n* ball-bearings.

বল[3], **বল-নাচ** [E] *n* ball; ball-dance.

বলক *n* swelling up of milk, etc by boiling. ~ আসা *vi* swell up by boiling. **বলকা** *adj* swelled up by boiling: এক বলকা দুধ, milk swelled up but once by boiling.

বলদ *n* bull; bullock; ox. **কলুর ~** ⇒ কলু. **চিনির ~** ⇒ চিনি.

বলন[1] *n* growth; increase; plumpness; bulk.

বলন[2] *n* speaking; narrating; telling; narration.

বলন[3] *n* **1** hope like a ring; rotundity; curvedness; contour. **2** shape; build.

বলনী *n*=বলন[3]

বলভি, বলভী *n* **1** ridge of a roof. **2** top or pinnacle of a house. **3** turret or temporary building on the roof of a house; upper room.

বলয় *n* **1** (an ornament for the wrist eg) bracelet, armlet, ring, bangle. **2** zone; circle; girdle; round; enclosure; circumference. ~গ্রাম *n* (astron) annular eclipse. **বলয়াকার, বলয়াঙ্কিত** *adj* ring-shaped; circular; annular. **বলয়িত** *adj* encircled; surrounded; encompassed; enclosed; forming a circle; ring-shaped; annular; curling: সাগর-বলয়িত, sea-girt. **বলয়ী** *adj* (bot) annulated.

বলশেভিক *n adj* Bolshevik. ~বাদ *n* Bolshevism.

বলা *vt, vi* **1** say: তুমি কী বলো ? **2** tell: গল্প ~. **3** speak: কিছু বলো. **4** advise; counsel: তাকে বলো সাবধান হতে. **5** inform: আমাকে না বললে জানবো কী করে? **6** get permission: মাকে বলে সে খেলতে গেছে. **7** express; reveal; speak out: কথাটা বলোই না, লুকোচ্ছ কেন? **8** mention: তার কথা আর বোলো না, বড়ো ফাঁকিবাজ. **9** narrate; relate: কাহিনীটা আমিই বলবো. **10** permit; allow; command: তিনি বললে আমি সব করতে পারি; বলোতো আমি নিজেই যাই. **11** use (a word, etc) about: তাঁর মতো লোককে অমন কথা বলা উচিত নয়. **12** decide; determine: "তাহলে আপনি কবে যাবেন"? "যখন বলবেন". **13** reproach; rebuke; censure; put to shame: আমায় কেন বলবে ? আর বোলো না, ঢের হয়েছে. **14** request; ask: আমার হয়ে ওকে আসতে বলো. **15** invite; call: বিয়েতে কাকে কাকে বলেছ? **16** agree: যদি বলো তো, এখনই যাই. **17** make one hear; sing for sb: একটা গান বলো না, শুনি. **18** whether ... or; be it: ধন বলো জন বলো সম্পদ বলো সবই অসার. ❑*adj* said/ told/ narrated/ mentioned/ spoken of before: ~ কথা. **বলো কি?** (expressing amazement or doubt) Is it so? How amazing? **বলো না** (request or insistence) please tell me. **বলোই না** (more insistent) You must tell me, I insist. **আহা ! বলোই না !** (request with irritation). **আহা ! বলোই না ছাই !** (impatient with anger and irritation). (In a softer tone: বলোতো? বলো দেখি!) **বোলো না, আর বোলো না 1** That's enough! I've had enough! stop it! **2** (expresses regret and pessimism at the mention of sth to be lamented) How unfortunate! **~-কওয়া, ~-কহা** *vt, vi* **1** advise; admonish; counsel. **2** discuss. ❑*n* **1** earnest solicitation; entreaty; begging: অনেক ~-কওয়ার পর সে রাজি হয়েছে. **2** mention; hint: তো কিছু ~-কওয়া নেই, হুট করে এসে হাজির. **~বলি** *n* conversation; discussion; repeated request. **~বলি করা** *vt, vi* discuss; talk about; talk together; request repeatedly. **বলতে কি** so to say; to tell the truth. **লোকে বলে** It is said. They/People say.

বলা[2] *vi* increase; grow. **বলে যাওয়া, বুক বলে যাওয়া** be more audacious.

বলাক *n* kind of crane. **বলাকা** *fem* **1** crane. **2** flight of cranes.

বলাৎকার *n* **1** rape; ravishment; violation. **2** applying force; violence; oppression; outrage. ~ করা *vt* force; outrage; violate; defile; rape; abuse; ravish. **বলাৎকৃত** *adj* raped; treated violently; forced; abuse; violated.

বলাত্মক *adj* strong; powerful; forceful, strengthful. **বলাত্মিকা** *fem.*

বলাধান *n* infusion of strength; invigoration; stimulation; rejuvenation. ~ করা *vt* infuse strength into; invigorate; stimulate; rejuvenate; energize.

বলাধিক্য *n* excess/abundance/increase of strength or forces; superiority in strength.

বলাধীন *adj* amenable to force.

বলাধ্যক্ষ *n* commander of an army; general; minister of war.

বলানো, বলান *vt* make one say/ speak/ tell/confess/ divulge.

বলান্বিত *adj* **1** powerful, strong; invigorated. **2** having armed forces or soldiers.

বলাবল *n* strength and weakness; ability and disability; state of one's strength/abilities/ resources.

বলাসান, বেলসান [A] *n* belsam.

বলাহক *n* **1** rain or thunder-cloud; cloud. **2** mountain.

বলি[১] *n* **1** sacrifice; sacrificing; immolation. **2** sacrificial animal; victim. **3** offering; gift; oblation; any offering or propitiatory; oblation. **4** (fig) victim. **~ দেওয়া** *vt* immolate; sacrifice; victimize. **~দান** *n* presentation of an offering to a deity. **~দান দেওয়া** *vt*=বলি দেওয়া.

বলি[২] *n* **1** fold of the skin; wrinkle; line of folding of the skin; the three folds over the navel or of the throat. **2** (geog) fold. **~রেখাঙ্কিত** *adj* marked with folds or wrinkles; wrinkled.

বলিত *adj* **1** wrinkled; worked with wrinkles or lines of folding; furrowed. **2** dangling; flabby; flaccid; slack. **~ পর্বত** fold mountain.

বলিভুক *n* crow; sparrow (or any bird subsisting on orts of a meal). ❑*adj* devouring oblations.

বলিয়া (old lit)=বলে

বলিয়ে *adj* having good speaking power; eloquent; having the gift of the gab; articulate; ❑*n* good talker.

বলিষ্ঠ *adj* robust, very strong, stout, sturdy; vigorous; hefty; mighty. **~কায়** *adj* having a strong body; hefty; burly.

বলিহারি *adj, int* (often iron) excellent; how excellent; How amazing! bravo: ~ তোমার সাহস! **~ যাওয়া** *vi* fail to describe; words fail me.

বলী *adj* powerful; mighty; stout; strong; stalwart; robust; full of strength; valorous. ❑*n* strong man; wrestler; hero. **~ খেলা** *n* wrestling. **~শ্রেষ্ঠ** *n* strongest man; greatest of heroes.

বলীবর্দ *n* ox; bull.

বলীয়ান *adj* very strong or powerful. **বলীয়সী** *fem.*

বলুনি *n* saying; word; rebuke; telling-off: তাকে এমন ~ বলেছে যে সে তা আর ভুলতে পারবে না।

বলে (*pres part* of বলা) saying: এই কথা বলে তিনি হাসলেন. **~কয়ে** by request; through persuasion: অনেক ~-কয়ে তাকে রাজি করেছি.

বলে[২] *adv* **1** shortly: presently: একটু বসুন, সে এলো ~. **2** by name: আপনাকে কী ~ ডাকব? **3** not only: আমি ~ নয়, কথাটা সবাই জানে. **4** so that: হাওয়া আসবে ~ জানলাটা খোলা হয়েছে. **5** promising: আসি ~ সেই যে গেল,.... **6** with information: সে কি কাউকে ~ গেছে? **7** how; on pretext: এতো কাণ্ডের পর ওখানে যাই কী ~? ❑*conj* **1** as: তোমাকে বন্ধু ~ জানতাম. **2** because, as: অসুখ ~ সে আসতে পারেনি. **3** lest: লোকে নানা কথা বলবে ~ চুপ করে আছি. **তা ~, তাই ~ 1** for that; on account of that; because of that. **2** but: এখন না হয় দিলাম, আর তা ~ দিচ্ছি না.

বল্কল *n* bark of a tree; garment made of bark. **~ধারী** *adj* wearing bark; clad in bark. **~ধারিণী** *fem.*

বল্কা, বলকা=বলক

বল্গ *n* galloping; jumping; bounding.

বল্গমান *adj* galloping; bounding.

বলগা, বল্গা *n* bridle; rein. **~ আঁটা** (lit, fig) bridle; rein (in) **~ হরিণ** *n* reindeer. **~হীন** *adj* reinless.

বলগিত *n* gallop of a horse; jump.

বলটু=বোলটু

বল্মীক, বল্মিক *n* ant-hill; mole-hill.

বল্লকী *n* kind of lute (often mentioned with *vina*); *vina.*

বল্লব *n* milkman; cook. **বল্লবী** *fem* milkmaid.

বল্লভ *n* **1** a favourite; lover; friend; husband; sweetheart. **2** courtier. **বল্লভা** *fem* mistress; wife; a beloved female.

বল্লম *n* a kind of missile with a pointed edge; spear.

বল্লরী, বল্লরি *n* **1** spike; sprout. **2** creeper; any climbing or creeping plant.

বল্লা *n* (dial) wasp.

বল্লালী *adj* relating to king Ballal Sen of Bengal. **~ প্রথা** the order of nobility of certain families as introduced by Ballal Sen.

বল্লি, বল্লী *n* creeper. **~তনু** *adj* slender-bodied; slim; having a creeper-like body. **~বিতান** a retreat shaded with creepers; bower; arbour.

বশ *n* control; power; command; dominion; domination; will; authority; influence: তার প্রবৃত্তি তার বশে নেই. ❑*adj* subject to another's will or command; subjugated; controlled; willing; submissive; obedient; subject to or dependent on; influenced; charmed; docile; sensible to: মিষ্টি কথার ~, জাদুর ~, শক্তির ~. **~ করা, বশে আনা** *vt* reduce to subjection; subdue; bring under control; tame; break (as a horse); win over; charm; influence. **~ মানা, ~ হওয়া, বশে আসা** *vi* fall into a person's power; become subject; give way to; be brought under control; be tamed/ won over/influenced/charmed. **~ক্রিয়া** *n*=বশীকরণ. **~গ, ~গত** *adj*=বশংবদ. **বশংবদ** *adj* obedient;

obsequious; compliant; submissive; docile; at one's beck and call; being in the power of. ~ত, ~তঃ *adv* on account of; owing to; because of; by force of. **~তা** *n* subjection; dependence on; subjection to another's will or command; subordination; obedience; submission; submissiveness; state of being controlled/charmed/influenced. **~তাপন্ন** *adj*=~বর্তী. **~বর্তী** *adj* being under the control of; acting obediently to the will of; obedient; subject; obsequious; attached/addicted (to); influenced by. **~বর্তিনী** *fem*. **~বর্তিতা**=~তা.

বশা=বসা[1]

বশানুগ *adj*=~বর্তী (⇒ বশ)

বশিতা *n* **1** the supernatural power of subjugating all to one's will; unbounded power (of); the power to control/ charm everybody. **2** perfect continence (one of the eight divine graces of Shiva).

বশিত্ব *n* **1**=বশিতা (1). **2** obedience; submissiveness. **3** freedom of will; continence; mastery of one's self; self-command. **4**=বশিতা (2). **5** subduing by magical means; fascinating.

বশিনী *n fem* **1** woman brought under control or made obedient; woman under charm. **2** parasite.

বশী *adj* **1** perfectly continent; master of one's self; having the mastery of one's passions. **2** one who subdues or charms. **~করণ** *n* **1** act of making subject; bewitching (by means of spells, etc); enchantment; hypnotization; enslavement by enchantment or mesmerism or incantation. **2** a weird process to bring sb under one's control. **~করণ করা** *vt* reduce to subjugation; subdue; bring sb under one's control (esp by means of some magical or weird process). **~করণ মন্ত্র** *n* incantation believed to possess occult power of bringing others under control. **~কৃত** *adj* brought under control/into subjugation; tamed; enchanted; fascinated; made obedient. **~কৃতা** *fem*. **~ভূত** *adj* become subjugated/obedient; attached or addicted to; enchanted; brought under control; fond of and obedient. **~ভূতা** *fem*.

বশ্য *adj* **1** to be subjected; easy to control/tame/subjugate; controllable; tamable; subduable; obedient to another's will; docile; dutiful; humble; tame. **2**=বশবর্তী (⇒ বশ). **বশ্যা** *fem*. **~কা** *n* an obedient and docile wife. **~তা** *n* obedience; humility; dependence; submissiveness; attachment or addiction; loyalty; being under the control of. **~তা স্বীকার করা** *vi* surrender; give in; yield (to).

বস[1], **বাস, ব্যস, ব্যাস** [P] *int* **1** enough! no more! all right ! **2** that will do! hold! stay! ❑*adv* at once; instantly; presently: ~ শুরু হলো হাতাহাতি.

বস[2] [E] *n* boss.

বসত, বসতি *n* residing; dwelling; residence; habitation; dwelling-house; colony; locality. **বসতকার** *n* resident. **বসতবাটি, বসতবাড়ি** *nn* dwelling-house; homestead. **বসতি করা** *vt* dwell; reside; set up/build one's dwelling-house or residence; settle; colonize. **বসতি স্থাপন করা** *vt* set up one's residence; settle; colonize.

বসন *n* cloth; cloths; garment; raiment; dress; cover. **~প্রান্ত, বসনাঞ্চল** *n* end or hem of a garment. **অশন-~** *n* food and clothing. **~ভূষণ** *n* clothing and ornaments.

বসন্ত *n* **1** spring; springtime; season of spring; springtide. **2** pox; small pox. **3** a *raga* or musical mode. **~কাল** *n* springtime; vernal season. **~কালীন** *adj* of spring; vernal. **~ঘোষ, ~দূত** *nn* the cuckoo. **~দূতী** *fem*. **~পঞ্চমী** the fifth lunar day of the light-fortnight of the month Magh when goddess Saraswati is worshipped. **~বায়ু** *n* vernal breeze; south wind. **~সখ** *n* friend of spring; Kama (god of love); the cuckoo. **বসন্তোৎসব** *n* spring festival; the *holi* festival.

বসবাস *n* act of residing or dwelling permanently; act of settling down. **~ করা** *vi* reside/dwell permanently; settle down.

বসা[1] *n* marrow-fat; muscle-fat; lard.

বসা[2] *vi* **1** sit; take one's seat; be seated. **2** be installed; settle down: গদিতে/আরাম করে ~. **3** wait: একটু বসো, আমি এখনি আসছি. **4** fit: জোড়ের মুখ বসছে না. **4** settle: খাটের একটা পায়া ঠিক বসছে না. **5** coagulate; solidify; thicken: দইটা এখনো ভালো বসেনি. **6** sink down to the bottom; settle; subside: তেলের কাইট ~. **7** be set up/ founded/ established: এখানে একটা বাজার বসেছে. **8** come to stay or reside; set up one's residence/ dwelling; settle: এ জমিতে এখনো প্রজা বসেনি. **9** start; commence: স্কুল কটায় বসে. **10** gather (as in a market): এখানে প্রতি শনিবার হাট বসে: There is a market here every Saturday. **11** be employed/engaged: সে একটা ভালো চাকরিতে বসেছে. **12** stay: আমি এখানে বসতে আসিনি. **13** be imposed/levied: ট্যাক্স ~. **14** accumulate; settle: বুকে সর্দি ~. **15** enter; go into: পেরেকটা ঠিক বসেনি. **16** stick; get stuck: কাদায় চাকা বসতে পারে. **17** engaged in: আমরা এখানে বিচার করতে বসিনি. **18** pierce; go into/through: ছুরি/দাঁত ~. **19** be soaked in: গায়ে জল বসে সর্দি হয়েছে. **20** stick: সে কোথাও স্থির হয়ে বসতে পারছে না. **21** be imprinted: কাপড়ে দাগ বসেছে. **22** be soaked (in): গায়ে জল বসে সর্দি হয়েছে. **23** (used as a complementary verb to express suddenness of an action): do/commit sth suddenly or all on a sudden: কেঁদে ~, ধরে ~, বলে ~, করে ~. ❑*adj* **1** seated.

2 frozen; congealed; solidified. **3** unemployed: ওরা সব ভাইই ~. **4** hoarse: ~ গলা. **5** haggard; drawn; wan: ~ চোখমুখ. **6** sunken, depressed: ~ জমি. **7** requiring much sitting, sedentary: ~ কাজ. ❑*n* sitting: শালগ্রামের শোয়া ~. **বসে খাওয়া** *vi* eat and drink; doing no work; consume one's fortune idly; live in idleness; sponge on/upon sb; live on others as parasite. **বসে থাকা** *vi* **1** be/remain sitting. **2** wait for. **3** be unemployed. **4** be without work. **5** pass time in laziness. **বসে পড়া** *vi* **1** sit down. **2** be utterly disappointed. **3** be completely exhausted. **4** be ruined utterly: ব্যবসায় ফেল মেরে সে বসে গেল. **বসে বসে** *adj* **1** doing nothing; in a state of unemployment. **2** by waiting for a long time: বসে বসে দুপুর গড়িয়ে গেল. **বসে বসে খাওয়া** *vi*=বসে খাওয়া. **বসে যাওয়া** *vi* sink; become depressed: জমিটা/ছাদ বসে গেছে. **2** become hoarse: বরফ খেয়ে গলা বসে গেছে. **3** sink in/into: অতিরিক্ত পরিশ্রমে তার চোখদুটি বসে গেছে, চাকা কাদায় বসে গেছে. **4** be ruined: ব্যবসায়ে লোকসান দিয়ে সে একেবারেই বসে গেছে. **5** get stuck: হাতির পা কাদায় বসে গেছে. **6** desist; rest: আর খেলো না, এবার বসে যাও. **7** be/become flat: গাড়ির একটা চাকা বসে গেছে. **8** stop: বাধাই যখন পড়ল এগিয়ো না, বসে যাও. **9** be disappointed: খেলায় হেরে সে বসে গেছে. **উবু হয়ে ~** *vi* sit on one's heels; squat. **একটু ~** *vi* wait a bit; stay for a moment. **কোপ ~, চোপ ~, ঘা ~** *vi* (of a blow, etc) go into/deep/through; pierce; hit. **চেপে ~** *vi* sit firmly (with all the weight of the body). **টাকা ~** *vi* (of money) get lost/wasted. **থাবড়ে বসা** *vi* sit on the hips spread out. **দাঁত ~** *vi* **1** (of a loose tooth) become set. **2** grip; seize firmly. **3** bite; be penetrated. **4** (fig) be intelligible. **5** be brought under control. **6** be able to exert one's influence; be able to bear upon. **দানা ~** be imprinted. **মাথায় হাত দিয়ে ~** *vi* become utterly disappointed; be frustrated/let down. **যেতে ~** *vi* **1** about to get out of possession; about to be ruined; be on the point of destruction; about to go to rack and ruin: তার বিষয়আশয় তো যেতে বসেছে. **2** be dying; about to breathe one's last. **কাজে মন ~** ⇒ মন.

বসানো, বসান *vt* (causative of বসা) **1** cause to sit; seat; place; put. **2** settle: প্রজা ~. **3** set up; establish; found: কারখানা ~. **4** give (a blow, etc) implant; deal: ছেলেটার পিঠে ঘা কতক বসিয়ে দিয়েছে. **5** congeal; freeze: দইটা বসাও. **6** put; place: উনুনে হাঁড়ি বসিয়ে দাও. **7** set/stud with; inlay: আংটিতে পাথর ~. **8** allow to be soaked (in): গায়ে জল বসানো. **9** plant; fix; drive into: খুঁটিটা এখানে বসাও. **10** impose levy: কর ~. **11** imprint: দাগ ~. **12** apply closely: কাজে মন ~. **13** drive into; enter: পেরেক ~. **14** pierce with: ছুরি ~. **15** organize: সভা ~. **16** cause to stay/settle: ভাড়াটে ~. **17** engage: কাজে ~.

একেবারে বাপের/মায়ের মুখ ~ be the image of one's father/mother.

বসু *n* **1** one of a particular class of gods (whose number is eight). **2** wealth; riches. **3** ray; beam. **~দেব** *n* **1** Kubera, the Hindu god of wealth. **2** the father of Sri Krishna. **~ধা** *n* the earth. **~ধারা** *n* an auspicious symbol painted on the inner wall of a room by Hindus at wedding, etc. **~ন্ধরা, ~মতী** *n* the earth.

বস্তব্য *adj* fit to be lived in; habitable.

বস্তা [P]*n* **1** sack; large bag; bale. **2** loads of: এক ~ ঝাঁকড়া চুল. **~নি, ~নী** *n* case for musical instruments; satchel; portmanteau; kitbag. **~পচা** *adj* **1** rotted or spoilt by being packed in a sack for a long time. **2** (fig) hackneyed; stale; trite; banal; moth-eaten. **~বন্দি, ~বন্দী** *adj* packed in a bale or sack.

বস্তান [P] *n* **1** garden. **2** tomb.

বস্তি[1] *n* **1** a settlement. **2** quarters for the poor people; slum. **~বাসী** *n, adj* slum-dweller; dwelling in a slum.

বস্তি[2], **বস্তী** *n* **1** the lower belly; abdomen. **2** bladder. **~কর্ম, ~ক্রিয়া** *nn* application of an enema or injection. **~যন্ত্র** *n* injection-syringe. **~শোধন** *n* **1** (cleaning of the rectum and the colon by) application of an enema. **2** a purgative. **3** a diuretic.

বস্তু *n* **1** thing; object; article; material. **2** the real; truth. **3** essence; substance. **4** (phys) mass. **5** (mech) body. **6** (phil) matter. **7** (mech) substance. **8** the right thing; a valuable or worth object; object. **9** subject; subject-matter; contents; theme; plot (of a drama, etc). **10** goods; wealth; property. **11** the thing in question; matter; affair; circumstances. **~গত** *adj* relating to a thing or matter; material; objective. **~গত মান** *n* intrinsic value. **~চিত্র** *n* pictograph. **~জগৎ** *n* the material world. **বস্তুত, বস্তুতঃ** *adv* in fact; indeed; in reality; actually; verily; essentially; really. **~তত্ত্ব** *n* physics. **~তত্ত্ববিদ** *n* physicist **~তন্ত্র** *n* realism. ❑*adj* **1** real. **2** (phil) objective. **3** (law) immovable. **~তন্ত্রী, ~তন্ত্রীয়, ~তান্ত্রিক** *adj* realistic; materialistic. **~তন্ত্রবাদ, ~তন্ত্রতা, ~তান্ত্রিকতা, ~স্বাতন্ত্র্যবাদ** *n n* materialism; realism; naturalism. **~রতি** *n* fetishism. **~সংক্ষেপ** *n* summary; substance.

বস্ত্র *n* cloth; clothes; garment; raiment; dress; cover. **~কুট্টিম, ~গৃহ** *nn* tent. **~গ্রন্থি** *n* the knot which fastens the lower garments above the hips. **~পুত্রিকা** *n* doll or puppet made of cloth. **~বিলাস** *n* foppery in dress. **~ভূষণ** *n* clothing and ornaments. **~মণ্ডিত** *adj* clad in clothes. **~হরণ** *n* stealing of (another's) clothes; act of making naked; uncovering; stripping. **~হীন** *adj* having no cloth/clothing to cover the body; naked; bare-skinned. **বস্ত্রাঞ্চল** *n* end or hem of a garment. **বস্ত্রাবরণ** *n* covering of cloth. **বস্ত্রাবাস** *n* tent; pavilion. **বস্ত্রালঙ্কার** = ~ভূষণ. **বস্ত্রালয়** *n* cloth shop.

বহ *n* (used as *suff*) carrier/bearer/conveyer of: বার্তা~, শব্দ~.

বহতা *adj* **1** flowing: ~ নদী. **2** current: ~ খাজনা.

বহন *n* **1** carrying; bearing; conveying; bringing: বার্তা ~, যাত্রী ~. **2** enduring; suffering; bearing: শোক ~. **3** shouldering: দায়িত্ব ~. **4** vehicle; carriage. **~পত্র** *n* bill of lading. **বহনীয়** *adj* to be carried/borne/drawn/conducted; bearable; conveyable; portable.

বহমান *adj* **1** flowing; running. **2** carrying; bearing; conveying.

বহর [A] *n* **1** fleet; navy. **2** multitude; collection of; array; fleet of: গাড়ির ~. **3** breadth; width: কাপড়ের ~. **4** glamour; display; ostentatious show: রূপের ~.

বহলপ [A] *adv* on oath.

বহস, বহাস [A] *n* debate; dispute; controversy; discussion; altercation; argument. **~ করা** *vi vt* debate; dispute; argue.

বহা *vi* (older form of বওয়া)=বওয়া

বহানো *vi, vt* (older from of বওয়ানো) ⇒ বওয়া

বহাল [A] *adj* **1** appointed, employed: চাকরিতে ~. **2** reinstated in office/work; continuing in: পদে ~. **3** (still) in force; effective: আগের হুকুম ~ আছে. **4** in the usual state/condition; unaltered. **5** restored to (health); refreshed; healthy; hale; flourishing: ~ তবিয়ত. **~ করা** *vt* appoint; employ; install; reinstate; re-establish; restore; confirm; bring in force; make effective. **~ রাখা** *vt* keep in the same condition; uphold a decision; maintain; keep in force: ঠাট ~ রাখা. **~ হওয়া** *vi* be reinstated; return to a former state; begin to flourish again. **~ তবিয়তে** *adv* in good/sound/perfect health.

বহাস=বাহাস

বহি (archaic)=বই

বহিঃ (used as a *pref*) out; outwards; outside; outer; exterior; external. **~কঙ্কাল** *n* (zoo) exoskeleton. **~কর্ণ** *n* (anat) external ear; auricle. **~কেন্দ্র** *n* (mech) eccentric. **~কোণ** *n* (geom) external angle. **~প্রকোষ্ঠ** *n* room at the side of a house. **~প্রকোষ্ঠাস্থি** *n* (anat) radius. **~প্রকোষ্ঠগত** *adj* radial. **~শুল্ক** *n* customs duty. **~শুল্ক-সমার্হতা** *n* collector of customs. **~সংসার** *n* external world. **~সমর্পণ** *n* extradition. **~সমুদ্র** *n* high sea. **~স্থ** *adj* external; outer; exterior. **~স্থিত**=~স্থ.

বহিত্র *n* **1** ship; boat; vessel. **2** scull; oar.

বহিন *n* sister; cousin (sister). **~-ঝি** *n* sister's daughter; niece. **~-পো** *n* sister's son; nephew.

বহিরঙ্গ *adj* external; outer; superficial; unrelated. ❑*n* external limb.

বহিরাগত *adj* coming from outside; emerged, issued out; foreign; outsider.

বহিরাগমন *n* act of issuing out/forth; emergence.

বহিরাবরণ *n* outer covering; outside coating; wrapping; wrapper; envelope; crust; coat; shell; slough; rind.

বহিরায়ণ *n* compelling (a person) to live outside certain limits (opposite of অন্তরায়ণ); driving out; exclusion.

বহিরিন্দ্রিয় *n* outer organ; organ of sense or perception.

বহির্গত *adj* gone or come out/forth; issued forth; emerged; externally manifested. **বহির্গতা** *fem.* **~ হওয়া** *vi* go/come out; issue (forth); emerge.

বহির্গমন *n* act or going out/forth; act of issuing forth; emergence; disembarkation. **~ করা** *vi* go out; issue forth; emerge.

বহির্গামী *adj* going out/forth; issuing forth; emerging.

বহির্গ্রহ *n* (astron) superior planet.

বহির্জগৎ *n* outer/external world; material world; visible/phenomenal world.

বহির্জনিষ্ণু *adj* (biol) endogenous.

বহির্দেশ *n* **1** outer/external/exterior part or portion. **2** outskirts (of a village or town).

বহির্দ্বার *n* front-door (of a building); space outside a door or gate; gate; main gate; portico; covered terrace in front of the door of a house.

বহির্দ্বিখণ্ডক *n* (geom) external bisector.

বহির্বর্তী *adj* being on the outside; exterior.

বহির্বাটি *n* outhouse; parlour or drawing-room.

বহির্বাণিজ্য *n* foreign trade; external trade.

বহির্বাস *n* outer or upper garment.

বহির্বৃত্ত *n* (geom) ex-circle.

বহির্ভাগ *n* outer side or part; exterior.

বহির্ভূত *adj* being out; expelled or excluded from; issued forth; emerged; lying outside/beyond: এলাকা ~; beyond the range of: দৃষ্টি~; contravening: বিধি~.

বহির্মুখ *adj* facing outwards; having one's mind directed to external things; worldly-minded; (physiol) efferent; (bot) extrose; extrovert. **বহির্মুখী** *fem.* **~ নার্ভ** *n* efferent nerve. **~ ব্যক্তি** *n* extrovert; worldly-minded man. **~তা** *n* state of facing outside; extroversion; worldly-mindedness; state of being efferent.

বহির্লিখিত *adj* (geom) escribed.

বহিশ্চর *n* one who moves outside his village.

বহিশ্চর্ম *n*=বহিস্ত্বক

বহিস্করণ, বহিস্কার *n* expulsion; exclusion from; removal; banishment; ejectment; extraction; drainage. **~ করা** *vt* expel; exclude; drive out; remove; banish; eject; extract; drain; draw out; turn out.

বহিস্কৃত *adj* expelled; excluded; removed; turned out; driven out; banished; ejected, extracted; drained.
বহিষ্ক্রান্ত *adj* gone/come out; issued forth.
বহিস্ত্বক *n* epidermis; cuticle.
বহিস্থ=বহিঃস্থ (⇒ বহিঃ)
বহু[১] *adj* many; numerous; great or considerable in quantity; much; abundant; profuse; diverse; manifold; long; several; poly-; multi-. **~কষ্টে** *adj* with great difficulty. **~কাল** *n* a long time. ❑*adv* for a long time. **~কাল ধরে, ~কালাবধি** for a long time; for long. **~কাল পরে** after a long time. **~কাল পূর্বে** long ago. **~কালব্যাপী** *adj* long-lasting; long-continued; very old. **~কালাশ্রিত** *adj* sheltered/ supported for a long time. **~কালাশ্রিতা** *fem.* **~কালীন, ~কেলে** *adj* long-standing; old; ancient; antique. **~কেশর** *adj* (bot) polyandrous. **~কোষ্ঠ** *adj* (bot) multicellular. **~ক্ষণ** *n, adv* (for) a long while/ time. **~ক্ষম** *adj* enduring much; long suffering. **~গর্ভপত্রী** *adj* (bot) polycarpellary. **~গুচ্ছ** (bot) polyadelphous. **~গুণ** *adj* multiplied many time; many times over; many more; much more; many fold; multifarious. **~গ্রন্থি** *adj* having many knots. **~জ্ঞ** *adj, n* possessed of great knowledge; having varied or vast experience; polymath. **~জ্ঞ ব্যক্তি** *n* polymath; man of varied/ vast experience. **~ত** *adj* much; many. **~তঃ** *adv* in many ways; from many sides. **~তন্ত্রী, ~তন্ত্রীক** *adj* many-fibred; having many strings. **~তম** *adj superl* very many; most; most numerous; remotest; farthest. **~তর** *adj comp* many more; too many; more abundant/ numerous; greater or very great; more; very; too much; various; diverse; manifold; profuse. **~তলক** *n* (geom) polyhedron. **~তা** *n* muchness; numerousness; abundance; multitude; plurality; profusion; excessiveness; diversity. **~ত্র** *adv* in many ways or places; at many diverse places; amongst many. **~দ** *adj* liberal; munificent. **~দর্শন, ~দর্শী** *adjj* seeing much; having varied/ vast experience; prudence; circumspect. **~দর্শিতা** *n* varied/ vast/ wide experience; circumspection; prudence. **~দর্শিনী** *fem* of **~দর্শী**. **~দুগ্ধা** *adj* having/giving much milk. **~দূর** *adj* very far; far-away; far-off; distant. ❑*adv* very far; far off; far away; at a great distance. **~দূরবর্তী** *adj* far-off; remote; faraway. **~দূরবর্তিতা** *n* remoteness; farness. **~দূরবর্তিনী** *adj fem* of **~দূরবর্তী**. **~দূরস্থ** *adj*=**~দূরবর্তী**. **~দূরস্থা** *fem.* **~দৃষ্ট**= **~দর্শী**. **~দেশদর্শী** *adj* one who has seen many countries; great traveller. **~দেশদর্শিনী** *fem.* **~দেশদর্শিতা** *n* experience of visiting many countries. **~দোষ** *n* great harm/ disadvantage. ❑*adj* very wicked/bad. **~ধন** *adj* possessing much wealth; wealthy. **~ধা** *adv* in many and diverse modes/ methods/ ways/ directions/ parts; diversely; many times. **~ধারা** *adj* many-edged. **~পতিত্ব** *n* polyandry. **~-পত্নীক** *adj* having many wives; polygamous. **~পদ** *adj* (alg) polynomial. **~পদ প্রাণী** *n* polypod; multiped. **~পুত্র** *adj masc* having many sons. **~পুত্রী** *adj fem* having many children. **~পার্শ্বিক** *adj* (bot) multiparous; multilateral. **~প্রদ** *adj* having a numerous progeny. **~প্রদ** *adj* liberal; munificent; bountiful. **~প্রবাহ** *adj* flowing in many streams. **~প্রবাহী** *adj* having many streams. **~প্রসবিনী** *adj fem* bearing many children; prolific; fertile. **~প্রসূ** *adj fem* = **~প্রসবিনী**. **~প্রান্তীয়** *adj* parietal. **~ফলক** *n* (geom) polyhedron. **~ফলকপত্র** *n* (bot) compound leaf. **~ফলী** *adj* bearing many fruits. **~বচন** *n (gram)* plural number. **~বর্ষজীবী** *adj* long-lived; (bot) perennial. **~বল** *adj* very strong; mighty. **~বল্লভ** adj one beloved of many women; Sri Krishna. **~বল্লভা** *fem* a woman beloved of many men; flirt; prostitute. **~বাদী** *adj* garrulous; babbling. **~বার** *adv* many times. **~বিদ** *adj* much knowing; very learned. **~বিধ** *adj* of many sorts/ kinds; manifold; various. **~বিবাহ** *n* polygamy. **~বিবাহকারী** *adj, n* polygamous; polygamist. **~বিস্তীর্ণ** *adj* wide-spread; widely diffused; far-flung. **~বীজপত্রী** *adj* (bot) polycotyledon. **~বেত্তা** *adj, n* = **~জ্ঞ**. **~ব্যয়সাধ্য** *adj* very expensive or costly. **~ব্যয়ী** *adj* prodigal. **~ ব্যয়ে** *adv* at a great cost or expense. **~ব্রীহি** *adj* possessing much rice. ❑*n* mode of forming compound words (in which the last member loses its character of a substantive and together with the first member serves to qualify a noun). **~ভর্তৃক** *adj* having many husbands. **~ভঙ্গিম** *adj* having many expressions or styles. **~ভাগ, ~ভাগী, ~ভাগ্য** *adjj* very fortunate; of great fortune. ❑*n* a great fortune **~ভাগা, ~ভাগিনী, ~ভাগ্যা** *fem.* **~ভাষিতা** *n* act of speaking many languages; garrulity; talkativeness. **~ভাষী** *adj* speaking many languages; polyglot; garrulous; talkative. ❑*n* a polyglot. **~ভাষিণী** *fem.* **~ভাষী ব্যক্তি** *n* a polyglot; garrulous/ talkative person. **~ভুজ** *n* (geom) polygon; (bio) polyp. ❑*adj* polygonal; polyporous. **~ভুজক্ষেত্র** *n* (geom) polygon. **~ভ্রূণবীজতা** *n* (bot) polyembryony. **~ভ্রূণবীজী** *adj* (bot) polyembryony. **~মত** *adj* highly esteemed; valued. **~মান** *n* high esteem/ estimation; great respect/ regard for. **~মানাস্পদ, ~মানী** *adjj* thought much of; highly esteemed; revered. **~মান্য** *adj* to be thought much of; to

be highly esteemed; estimable. ~মুখ *adj* multifaceted; multifarious; multiplex; multilateral: ~মুখ টেলিগ্রাম, ~মুখ বিদ্যালয়. ~মুখী = ~মুখ. ~মূত্র *n* diabetes. ~মূত্রগত *adj* diabetic. ~মূত্রপীড়িত *adj* diabetic. ~মূর্তি *adj* multiform. ~মূল, ~মূলক *adj* many-rooted. ~মূল্য *adj* very costly; precious; high-priced; valuable. ~যৌগিক *adj* (bot) decompound. ~রত্ন *adj* rich in gems or jewels; very wealthy. ~রন্ধ্র *adj* porous; full of holes. ~রাশিক *n* (arith) the double rule of three. ~রূপ *adj* multiform; variegated; checkered; diverse; multifarious; manifold. ❑*n* **1** an itinerant showman who amuses people by assuming various forms. **2** various forms. ~রূপা *n* chameleon. ~রূপী *adj* multiform; manifold; assuming different forms; polymorphic. ❑*n* = ~রূপ (1). ~রূপিণী *fem.* ~রূপতা *n* polymorphism; variegation; diversity. ~রেখ, ~রেখা *adj* having many lines or wrinkles; wrinkled. ~রোখা *adj* having much hair or wool. ❑*n* sheep. ~শ, ~শ: *adv* many (times); in a great measure; to a great extent; repeatedly; oft; manifoldly; much. ~শত্রু *adj* having many enemies. ~শাখা *adj* having many branches or ramifications; multifarious; manifold. ~শাস্ত্রজ্ঞ *n, adj* acquainted with many sciences; polymath. ~শিখ, ~শিখা *adj* having many flames or points. ~শিরাল *adj* (bot) multicostate. ~শ্রুত *adj* profoundly/ vastly learned; erudite; well versed in the Vedas. ~শ্রেয়াস *adj* endowed with many qualities; by far the best. ~শ্রেয়সী *fem* ~সংখ্যক *adj* numerous; many. ~স্ত্রীক = ~পত্নীক. ~স্বামিক *adj* having to serve many masters; having many owners.

বহু[২] *n* (poet, archaic)=বউ

বহুড়ি *n fem* (archaic) childwife; newly-married wife.

বহুত *adj* ⇒ বহু. ~ আচ্ছা *int* very good; okay; excellent.

বহুল *adj* much; many; numerous; abundant; profuse; plentiful. ~তা, ~ত্ব *n* muchness; abundance; multiplicity; numerousness. ~পরিমাণে *adv* in a great/ large measure; abundantly; profusely. **বহুলীকরণ** *n* multiplying; magnifying; multiplication; winnowing **বহুলীকৃত** *adj* multiplied; magnified; aggrandized; augmented; increased; extended.

বহেড়া, বয়ড়া *n* a medicinal fruit; *Balearica myrobalan.*

বহ্নি *n* fire. ~গর্ভ *adj* having fire in the womb. ❑*n* bamboo. ~জ্বালা *n* flame; glow/ heat of fire. ~বিবিক্ষু *adj* wishing to enter into the fire. ~মান *adj* flaming; blazing. ~শিখ *n* safflower. ~শিখা *n* flame; tongue of fire. ~সংস্কার *n* cremation of a dead body.

বহ্বর্থ *adj* having multiple meanings; polysemantic.

বহ্বাড়ম্বর *n* excessive pomp of éclat; great fuss.

বহ্বারম্ভ *n* a grand/ grandiose/ fussy/ pompous beginning or preparation. **বহ্বারম্ভে লঘুক্রিয়া** much cry, little wool.

বহ্বাস্ফোট *n* excessive vaunting or boasting; bragging.

বা[১] *conj* or. বা . . .বা whether . . . or: তুমি থাকলেই বা কি, গেলেই বা কি. ❑*adv* **1** possibly; perhaps: তা হবেও বা. **2** (expresses doubt): সেই বা এসব কাণ্ড করে বসেছে. **3** alternatively; instead: তুমিই বা গেলে. **4** (expressing comparison): এই-ই বা মন্দ কিসে হলো, ওই বা ভালো কিসে হলো? **5** (used to emphasize a question): কে বা গেছে তদ্দূর?

বা[২]=বাঃ

বাই[১] *n* **1** neurosis; madness; dementia. **2** mania; craze; strong hobby; crotchet: শুচি~, ফুটবলের ~.

বাই[২], **বাঈ** *n fem* a title affixed to the names of Rajput, Gujrati, Maratha, etc women; lady. **2** professional dancing-girl and songstress. ~ওয়ালী=বাই

বাইক [E] *n* bike.

বাইচ, বাইচ খেলা *n* boat-race; regatta.

বাইজী=বাই[২] (2)

বাইদ *n* (dial) low land.

বাইন[১] *n* capricious demand.

বাইন[২] *n* **1** place where juice of sugar-cane, exudation from date-palm, etc is boiled to produce molasses. **2** boiling juice of sugar-cane, etc to produce molasses.

বাইন[৩] *n* **1** (agri) a kind of disease affecting paddy. **2** the insect causing the above disease.

বাইন[৪]=বান[২]

বাইন[৫] *n* (naut) **1** small flat metal staples for fastening planks in the keel. **2** joints in the keel of a boat.

বাইনাচ *n* dance of a professional dancing-girl.

বাইবেল *n* the Bible.

বাইর *n* (colloq) outside; exterior. **বাইরে** *adv* outside; abroad; away from home. ❑*prep* other than; more than; outside; beyond: এর বাইরে কিছুই জানি না, শহরের বাইরে, নাগালের বাইরে. **বাইরেকার** *adj* external; outer; exterior.

বাইল *n* **1** stalked leaf of the coconut-palms, date-palms, etc **2** leaf of a door.

বাইশ[১] *n, adj* twenty-two. **বাইশে** *n* the twenty-second day of the month; the twenty-second. ❑*adj* (of the days of a month) twenty-second.

বাইশ[২], **বাইস** *n* **1** (carpenter's) adze; adz. vice.

বাইশকোপ [E] *n* bioscope.

বাইস [E] *n* vice. ~মান, ~ম্যান [E] *n* viceman.

বাইসিকল, বাইসাইকেল, বাইসিকল [E]*n* bicycle.

বাইসিকলে চড়া *vi* ride a bicycle. **বাইসিকলে চড়ে যাওয়া** *vt* cycle. ~ **আরোহী** *n* cyclist.

বাঙ্গী=বাই[২]

বাউ=বাউটি

বাউটি *n* kind of bracelet.

বাউন্ডারি [E] *n* boundary.

বাউণ্ডুলে, বাইণ্ডুলা *adj* mad-like; vagrant. ❑*n* vagabond; tramp; Bohemian. **বাউণ্ডুলি** *fem.*

বাউনে *adj* dwarfish; puny. ❑*n* dwarf; midget.

বাউরা *n* madman; lunatic. **বাউরি** *fem.*

বাউরি *n* a Hindu caste; a member of this caste.

বাউল *n* **1** a class of unorthodox religious devotees singing devotional songs in a special mode. **2** a mendicant of the above class of devotees. **3** their songs or mode of singing. **4** madman; lunatic. ~ **গান** *n* Baul song.

বাউলি, বাউলী *adj* **1** belonging to the Baul sect. **2** mad; distracted; deranged.

বাও[১] *n* wind. ~**বাতাস** *n* touch of the airy body of a ghost or as evil supernatural being which is supposed to cause illness.

বাও[২] *n* bubo.

বাওন[১] *n* dwarf; midget. ❑*adj* dwarfish; stunted; scrubby.

বাওন[২] *n* rowing.

বাওয়া[১] *vt* **1** row; steer; scull; ply (the oar). **2** cover; pass over: অনেক পথ বেয়ে আসতে হয়েছে. **3** climbs up or down: সিঁড়ি বেয়ে ওঠা-নামা করা.

বাওয়া[২] *adj* containing no embryo; barren; sterile; addle; addled: ~ ডিম.

বাওয়ালি *n* a class of people engaged in extracting wood, timber and honey from the Sundarbans.

বাওরা *adj* mad; insane; deranged.

বাংলা *n* **1** Bengal. **2** Bangla; Bengali language. **3** bungalow. ❑*adj* Bengali: ~ সাবান, country-made soap.

বাঃ, বাহ্ *int* (an exclamation in praise, wonder, disgust, taunt) **1** well; good; excellent; bravo: বাঃ বেশ লিখেছ তো! **2** expressing surprise: বাঃ আমি কখন বললাম! **3** ironical: বাঃ ভালো কথাই বলেছ! **4** protesting: বাঃ তা-ও কি কখনো হয়!

বাঁ *adj, n* left. **বাঁ দিক** *n* left side. **বাঁ-হাতি** *adj* lying on the left. **বাঁ-হাতের ব্যাপার** (iron) act of accepting bribes.

বাঁও *n* measure of depth of water; 5 feet 3 inches.

বাঁওড় *n* **1** bend of a river where current is obstructed. **2** water accumulated in a depressed land.

বাঁওয়া *adj* (dial) left-handed.

বাঁক[১] *n* **1** curve; curvature; bend; turn. **2** piece of long and bent pole brone on one's shoulder for carrying loads fastened to its ends. ~ **ফেরা**, ~ **নেওয়া** *vi* turn . ~**নল** *n* blowpipe; U-tube; (bot) bent tube. ~**মল** *n* kind of twisted bangle for the ankle; twisted anklet.

বাঁক[২] *n* **1** (naut) strong plank used in building the keel of a boat. **2** bend of a river.

বাঁকড়া *n* crookedness.

বাঁকল *n* ⇒ বাকা[২]

বাঁকা[১] *adj* **1** bent; curved; oblique; tortuous: ~ বাঁশ ~ পথ. **2** uneven; rugged; rough. **নাচতে না জানলে উঠান** ~ (prov) A bad workman quarrels with his tools. **3** crooked; insincere; deceitful: ~ মন, ~ লোক. **4** unfavourable: ভাগ্য ~. **5** slanting; aslant: থামটা ~. **6** furtive, oblique; furtive: ~ চাহনি. **7** stooping; hunched: ~ পিঠ. **8** cynical; unfriendly: ~ মনোভাব. **9** tortuous; winding; round-about; special; sinuous: ~ পথ/ সিঁড়ি. **10** insinuating; sly: ~ মন্তব্য **11** rude; harsh: ~ কথা. **12** reluctant; antipathetic. ❑*n* **1** anything bent; curved; tortuous etc: ~র কোলে সোজা. **2** curve; curvature: ~-টা কোথায়, তুমি তোমার ~ নিয়েই থাক. ~**চোরা** *adj* bent and invisible; having many curves and twists; sinuous; zigzag: ~ চোরা পথ, ~ চোরা কথা. ~ **পথ** *n* **1** tortuous/round-about way. **2** evil way; falsehood. বাঁকাবাঁকা *adj* tortuous; slightly winding. ~**সোজা** *adj* partly tortuous, etc; partly; straight or straight forward; being a mixture fo candour and crookedness. ~ **সিঁথি/সিঁতে** a slanting parting of the hair. **আঁকা~** *adj* tortuous; sinuous; winding. ~ **করা** *vt* =বাঁকানো.

বাঁকা[২] *vi* **1** bend; curve; lean; incline; tilt; stoop. **2** turn swing swerve; veer; deflect: রাস্তা এখানে ডানে বেঁকেছে. **3** become unfavourable/ reluctant/ averse; be loath/ opposed to; jib; back out; hang back; backtrack; be dead against: বড়ো সাহেব বেঁকে বসেছেন. **বেঁকে বসা** *vi* **1** sit in slanting position; lean back. **2**=~ (3). **বাঁকন** *n* **1** bending; turning; twisting; hold; curvature. **2** (fig) retraction; backout; backsliding; volte-face; reluctance. **3** aversion; opposition; antagonism; hostility; ill feeling.

বাঁকানো, বাঁকান *vt* **1** bend; turn; twist; divert. **2** make reluctant/ unfavourable; cause to swerve/ waver/ deviate; deflect; divert; dissuade. **3** turn on side: ঘাড় ~.

বাঁখারি *n*=বাখারি

বাঁচন *n* **1** act of living/ keeping alive; subsisting; life. **2** survival; relief; relaxation; escape; deliverance; rescue; safety. **3** resuscitation; revival. **4** freedom from involvement; state of being unharmed/ unimpaired. ~**কাঠি মরণ**-~ **1** (in fairy tales) two magic wands; one causing death; the other giving life. **2** a person on whose words or advice depend sb's life and death. ~**মরণ, মরণ** ~ *nn* life and death.

বাঁচা *vi* **1** live; keep alive; subsist. **2** get back life; be resuscitated; revive: ওষুধ খেলে রোগী বাঁচবে. **3** be saved/ relieved/ rescued/ released: তুমি এসেছ, আমি বাঁচলাম! **4** be protected/ preserved/ maintained/ kept up; remain unharmed/ unimpaired: মান ~, স্বাস্থ্য ~. **5** be spared; escape; avoid: পরিশ্রম/খরচ/লোকসান বাঁচবে. **6** become surplus; be left: সবাইকে দেওয়ার পর এখানে থেকে কিছু মিষ্টি বাঁচবে. **কারো পরে বেঁচে থাকা** outlive/ survive sb. **কিছুর পরে/ কিছু এড়িয়ে বেঁচে থাকা** survive/ outlast sth. **বেঁচে থাকা** live; be alive; continue in life. **বেঁচে বর্তে থাকা** be alive; live long. **~-মরা, মরা ~** life and death.

বাঁচানো *vt* **1** give back life; revive; resuscitate; bring to life. **2** save; rescue; relieve: তুমি আমাকে বাঁচালে. **3** carry on; maintain; save: ব্যবসা/চাকরি ~. **4** spare; exempt; save. **5** escape; cut; curtail: খরচ ~. **6** keep up/ protect; maintain: এই অসহায় ছেলেটিকে কে বাঁচাবে? **7** avoid: ঝুঁকি ~. **8** cover up (mistake, etc). **9** hide; conceal: কাপড়ের ছেঁড়া বাঁচিয়ে ঘুরিয়ে পরা.

বাঁচোয়া= বাঁচন

বাঁজা, বাঁঝা *adj* barren; sterile; unproductive. **বাঁঝি** *n* barren woman.

বাঁট *n* **1** handle; haft; hilt. **2** teat (of cattle). **3** (vulg) penis.

বাঁটওয়ারা=বাঁটোয়ারা

বাঁটন *n* =বণ্টন

বাঁটা *vt* distribute; divide; apportion; share out; allot. **বাঁটানো, বাঁটান** *vt* cause to distribute, etc. **~বাটি** *n* sharing out; apportionment/ partition/ allotment (among partners).

বাঁটুল *n* **1** small ball (uses of iron and used as a missile). **2** shot. **3** (facet) short and fat man; dumpy fellow. **বাঁটুল ~** *n* a children's game played with a ball and a stick.

বাঁটোয়ারা *n* partition; division; apportionment.

বাঁদর *n* **1** monkey; ape. **2** barbarian; stupid fellow. **3** mischievous person. **বাঁদরী** *fem.* **বাঁদুরে** *adj* of or like a monkey. **বাঁদুরে বুদ্ধি** *n* monkey trick; mischievousness. **~মুখা, ~মুখো** *adj* having a face as ugly as that of a monkey. **~মুখী** *fem.* **বাঁদরামি, বাঁদরামো** *n* mischievousness; monkey trick; monkey-like behaviour; monkeyism.

বাঁদি [P] *n* **1** maid-servant; hand-maid. **2** female slave. **3** mistress; concubine.

বাঁদিপোতা *n* chequered cloth with multi-coloured stop stripes used in making quilts.

বাঁধ *n* **1** dam; breakwater; embanking; embankment. **2** bar; obstruction; hindrance: তার এখানে আসতে কোনো ~ নেই. **3**=বাঁধনি: শিল্পের ছাদ~. **~ দেওয়া** *vt* dam; build a dam/a dike/ an embankment; (fig) restraint; check; hold back. **~ নির্মাণ করা, ~বাঁধা** *vi* build a dam/dike/ embankment.

বাঁধন *n*=বন্ধন. **গান ~** composition of a song. **ঘর ~** construction of a house; getting married. **সুর ~** tuning; attuning; composition of a tune. **কথার ~** compactness of speech; rhetoric. **দানা ~** granulation; crystallization. **~হারা** *adj* free; unbridled; unbound; foot-loose (and fancy-free). **বাঁধনি** *n* binding; fastening; tie; knot; rigour; compactness; punctiliousness; methodicalness; terseness: কাজের ~.

বাঁধা[1] *n* **1**=বন্ধন. **2** bar; hindrance; obstruction. **3** detention; confinement; restraint. **~ পড়া** *vi* become confined/ detained/ obstructed. ☐*adj* **1** bound; tied; fastened: কার সঙ্গে তোমার মন ~? **2** composed; done: ~ চুল. **3** tuned: ~ তার. **4** fixed: ~ মাইনে. **5** regular: ~ খদ্দের. **6** rigid; hand and fast: ~ নিয়ম. **7** routine: ~ কাজ. **8** appropriate; precise; accurate; proper: ~ গৎ. **8** brick-built; stone-built: ~ ঘাট. **9** attached/ addicted to under control. **~ আলো** *n* rows of light illuminating a street for ceremonial purpose. **~ ঔষধ** *n* medicine to be taken at fixed times. **~কপি** *n* cabbage. **~ খরিদ্দার** *n* regular customer. **~গৎ, বাঁধিগৎ** *n* **1** appropriate/ precise tune or mode. **2** stock phrase; same old story; cliché; set phrase; rigid rule or system. **~ছাদা** *n* packing. **~ছাদা করা** *vt* pack (up) things. **~ধরা, ধরা~** *adj* rigid; fixed; routine; monotonous; strict; strait-laced; stifle; static; systematic. **~বুলি** *n* cliché; commonplace; catchword; slogan. **~ রোশনাই** *n*=~ আলো. **~ শরীর** *n* stout/ well-built body.

বাঁধা[2] *vt* **1** bind; tie; fasten; felter knot; chain. **2** check obstruct: স্রোত ~. **3** embank; dam: খাল ~. **4** join: হাতে হাত ~. **5** compose: গান ~. **6** tune: সুর ~. **7** form; do: খোপা ~. **8** set up; build: ঘর ~. **9** restrain; appease; control: মন ~. **10** unite: প্রাণে প্রাণে ~. **11** turn into; reduced to; rendered into: দানা ~, জমাট ~. **কোমর ~** *vi* (fig) gird up one's loins. **কোমর বেঁধে লাগা** *vi* set about resolutely. **খোঁপা ~** *vi* dress/put up hair in a bun. **গাছ~** *vi* fix a small pitcher at the top of a date-palm or fan palm to collect its exudation. **চুল/মাথা ~** dress hair; do hair. **ঘর ~** *vi* construct a house; get married. **জোট ~** *vi* group together. **বই ~** *vi* bind a book. **বুক ~** take/ pluck up/ muster up/ summon up courage; dare.

বাঁধা[3] *n* **1** pawning; mortgaging; pledge. **2** article left with a pawn-broker; pledge. ☐*adj* pawned; pledged; mortgaged. **~ দেওয়া** *vi* pawn; pledge; mortgage. **~ রাখা** *vi* put/hold sth in pledge.

বাঁধাই *n* act or cost of binding (a book); act or cost of enframing (a picture).

বাঁধানো, বাঁধান *n* **1** bind (as a book). **2** enframe (as a picture). **3** pave; macadamize. **4** inlay (in/into/ with); plate: হীরা/সোনা দিয়ে ~. **5** cause to build or set up: ঘর ~. **6** fix artificial ones: দাঁড় ~. **7** build with stone or brick: ঘাট ~. **8** reduce to; render into: জমাট ~. **10** dam (up): খাল ~. **11** cause to tune (up): তার ~. **12** cause to compose: গান ~. ❑*adj* **1** bound. **2** enframed. **3** paved; macadamized. **4** inlaid (in/ into/with). **5** artificial. ~ **দাঁত** set of artificial teeth; denture. **6** brick-built or stone-built. **7** plated. **8** dammed. **9** built; set up.

বাঁধাবাঁধি *n* rigid/ hard and fast rule; strictness; rigidity; rigid system.

বাঁধাল *n* dam; dyke.

বাঁধিগৎ=বাঁধাগৎ (⇒ বাঁধা[১])

বাঁধুনি=বাঁধনি (⇒ বাঁধন)

বাঁয়া *n* small semicircular percussion instrument played with the left hand along with the table (⇒ তবলা). **ঢাকের** ~ (fig, derog) useless accompaniment; cipher.

বাঁশ *n* bamboo. **(পোঁদে)** ~ **দেওয়া 1** drive in a bamboo-stick into the anus. **2** (fig) torture; inflict severe bodily or mental suffering; ruin. **বুকে ~ডলা দেওয়া 1** make a person lie at full length in between two bamboo-poles and then roll the poles oppressively as a punishment. **2** (fig) torment severely. **~বন** *n* forest of bamboo. **~বনে ডোম কানা** have too many alternatives. **বাঁশের চেয়ে কঞ্চি দড়** the chip is tougher than the old block. **~গাড়ি** *n* (law) act of planting a bamboo-pole in the ground of an estate as a sign of taking possession of it. **~ঝাড়** *n* bamboo-clump. **~বাগান** *n*=~ঝাড়. **~বাজি** *n* acrobatic feats performed on a bamboo-pole.

বাঁশড়া *n* forest of bamboo.

বাঁশরি, বাঁশরী *n* (poet) flute made of bamboo; pipe; reed.

বাঁশি, বাঁশী *n*=বাঁশরি. ~ **বাজানো** *vi* play on a flute; pipe. **~ওয়ালা, বাঁশুরিয়া** (poet) *n* flutist; fluter; piper.

বাঁসমতি, বাসমতী *n* =বাসমতি

বাক, বাক্ (in compounds) *n* speech; language; voice; talk; sound; word; saying; phrase; statement; sentence. **~কলহ** *n* altercation; quarrel; dispute. **~কৌশল, ~চাতুরী, ~চাতুর্য** *n* cleverness of speech; gift of the gab; quibble; eloquence; rhetoric. **~চাপল্য** *n* flippancy in speech; idle talk. **~ছল** *n* untruthful talk; equivocation; quibble . **~পটু** *adj* skilled in speech; eloquent; having the gift of the gab. **~পটুতা, ~পটুত্ব** *n* cleverness of speech; eloquence; gift of the gab. **~পতি** *n* master of speech/ language; orator. **~পারুষ্য** *n* harshness of speech; abusive words; insulting/ scurrilous language; defamation. **~প্রণালী** *n* mode of speech; syntactical rules; idiom. **~প্রপঞ্চ** *n* elaborate speech; loquaciousness; grandiloquence; verbosity. **~শক্তি** *n* power of speaking; faculty of speech. **~শক্তিরহিত, ~শক্তিহীন** *adjj* rendered speechless; dumb founded; struck dumb; speechless; dumb struck. **~সংযম** *n* (exercise of) restraint or control speech; reticence; discretion; taciturnity. **~সর্বস্ব** *adj* excelling only in words and incapable of action; all talk. **~সর্বস্ব ব্যক্তি** *n* person of mere words; windbag. **~সিদ্ধ** *adj* having supernatural power to utter infallible words. **~সিদ্ধা** *fem.* **~সিদ্ধি** *n* supernatural power to utter in fallible words. **~সূত্র** *n* beginning of a conversation. **~স্ফূর্তি** *n* fluency in speech; eloquence; utterance of words.

বাকম, বাক বাকম *n*=বকবকম

বাকল, বাকলা *n* **1** rind of a tree; bark. **2** skin (of fruits).

বাকি [A] *adj* **1** remaining; the rest of: ~ জীবন. **2** outstanding; the rest of: ~ কাজ. **3** unrealized; unpaid; overdue; outstanding; unsettled: ~ পাওনা. ❑*n* **1** (with) remainder. **2** balance. **3** arrears: ~ শোধ. **4** residue; remains; residuum; rest; remnant; carry-over; surplus. ~ **অংশ** *n* call money. ~ **কাটা** *vt* deduct the arrears. ~ **খাজনা** *n* arrears of rent. **~জায়** *n* list of unrealized rent or revenue; arrears of rent collected from tenants. **~তে** *adv* on credit. **~দার** *n* defaulters. ~ **পড়া** *vi* fall into arrears; be overdue. **~বকেয়া, বকেয়া~** *n* dues. **~য়াত** *n* **1** (law) pending cases. **2** arrears. **বিলাত~** ⇒ বিলাত[২].

বাকুল *n* mud-built house.

বাক্য *n* **1** (gram) sentence. **2** speech; words; statement; saying; assertion; command; expression; pledge. **~জ্বালা** *n* abrasive language; roasting. **~দান করা,** ~ **দেওয়া** *vi* give one's word; promise. **~নবাব, ~বীর** *n* person of mere words; windbag. **~নিঃসরণ** *n* flow of words. **~পরম্পরা** *n* succession of words/ sentences. **~প্রয়োগ** *n* use of (particular) words/ language. **~বাগীশ** *adj* **1** having the gift of the gab; glib; voluble; excelling in words but incapable of action; all talk. ❑*n* glib talker; windbag. **~বাণ** *n* (lit) shaft of words; piercing/ cruel words. **~বিন্যাস** *n* arrangement or order of sentences; (gram) syntax; skilful use of words. **~বিশারদ, ~বীর** *n*=~বাগীশ. **~ব্যয়** *n* talking/ speaking (uselessly); waste of breath. **~ব্যয় করা** *vi* speak/ talk (two much/ uselessly). **~স্খলন** *n* stammering; slip of the tongue. **~স্থ** *adj* **1** faithful to one's promise. **2**

obsequious. ~স্ফূর্তি *n* utterance/ flow of words. ~হীন *adj*=বাকশক্তিরহিত (⇒ বাক).

বাক্যাড়ম্বর *n* boastful bombastic language; bombast; pomposity; turgidity; verbosity; fustian; hot air; bluster; grandiloquence; rhetoric. ~প্রিয় *adj* fond of bombast; blustering; grandiloquent.

বাক্যার্থ *n* meaning or contents of a sentence.

বাক্যালাপ *n* conversation; speaking terms. ~ করা *vi* converse; talk together; speak with; have a talk with;

বাক্স, বাক্‌স [E] *n* box; case. ~জাত, ~বন্দি *adj* kept into a box. ~জাত/~বন্দি করা *vi* put into a box; box.

বাখড়, বাখড়া *n* frond (of palms).

বাখর *n* ferment; leaven.

বাখান *n* **1** explanation; commentary. **2** praise; eulogy. **3** description. **4** (iron) unpleasant description.

বাখানা *vt* (poet, archaic) **1** explain. **2** praise; eulogize; extol. **3** describe; narrate. **4** grow. **5** exaggerate.

বাখানি *n* (poet, archaic) praise; eulogy. ❑*adj* grown; expanded.

বাখারি *n* piece of split bamboo; bamboo-slip. ~চুন *n* lime obtained by burning shells of oysters, shell-fish, etc.

বাগ[1] [P] *n* garden. ~বাগিচা *n* small and large gardens. ~বান *n* gardener. ~বানি *n* gardening.

বাগ[2] *n* **1** direction; route; way. **2** device; technique; system; mode: ~ করে কাজ করা. **3** opportunity; advantage: ~ পাওয়া. ~ করা *vt* **1** bring under control; master; dominate; tame; subjugate. **2** devise cleverly or artfully; play a trick (on/with). **3** make arrangements; put in due order. বাগে আসা *vi* be subjugated/ dominated; come under control. ~ মানানো, বাগে আনা *vt* bring under control. বাগে পাওয়া *vi* get under one's control. বাগে বাগে *adv* in all directions; every where. তাগ~ *n* aim and stratagem.

বাগড়, বাগড়া *n* (colloq) obstacle; hindrance; hitch; impediment. ~ দেওয়া create a hitch; take the wind out of sb's sail; make difficulties for; complicate matter's; impede.

বাগডোর *n* rein.

বাগদা, বাগদা চিংড়ি *n* kind of prawn.

বাগদি, বাগদী *n* a Hindu caste; a member of this caste. বাগদিনী *fem.*

বাগাড়ম্বর *n*=বাক্যাড়ম্বর (⇒ বাক্য). ~ করা *vi* talk big; bluster; brag; speak verbosely; indulge in verbosity.

বাগান [P] *n* garden; grove; pleasure-ground. আম~ *n* mango-grove. কলা~ *n* orchard of banana-trees. নারিকেল ~ *n* coconut-grove. ফল~ *n* orchard. ফুল~ *n* garden; flower-garden. সবজি~ *n* kitchen garden; market garden. ~বাগিচা *n* gardens and orchards. ~বাড়ি *n* pleasure-garden; garden-house. ~বিলাস *n* bougainvillea. ~ করা *vi* garden. বাগানে কাজ করা *vi* garden. বাগানের কাজ *n* gardening.

বাগানো, বাগান *vt* **1** bring under control; dominate; master. **2** tame; break (as a horse). **3** manage to obtain: ভালো চাকরি বাগিয়েছ. **4** wangle: এক সপ্তাহ ছুটি ~. **5** defalcate; misappropriate: তহবিল থেকে টাকা ~. **6** manage to have sth performed/ executed; make arrangements for: কাজ ~. **7** turn (in a different direction). **8** do hair in a particular style: টেরি ~.

বাগার *adj n* breaking promise/ faith; deceiver.

বাগি, বাগী, বাঘী *n* bubo.

বাগিচা [P] *n* small garden; grove.

বাগিন্দ্রিয় *n* organ of speech.

বাগীশ *n* **1** loquacious person. **2** orator.

বাগীশ্বর=বাগীশ. **বাগীশ্বরী** *fem* Saraswati, goddess of speech.

বাগুড়া *n* **1** stalked leaf of the banana-tree. **2** stalked leaf of the betel-nut tree.

বাগুরা *n* (obs) net or snare. ~বদ্ধ *adj* caught in a trap or snare

বাগেবাগ *adj* overflowing with (only in) খুশিতে ~ হওয়া bubble over with joy.

বাগ্‌জাল *n* confused mess or multitude of words; web/ mesh/ trap of words; verbiage. ~ বিস্তার করা *vi* weave a web/ set a trap of words; indulge in circumlocution; expatiate upon; ramble.

বাগ্‌দণ্ড *n* verbal rebuke/ reprimand; reproof; admonition.

বাগ্‌দত্ত *adj* given by word of mouth; promised. বাগ্‌দত্তা *fem adj* betrothed; affianced. ❑*n* betrothed virgin/ girl; fiancee.

বাগ্‌দরিদ্র *adj* **1** poor in speech; of few words. **2** speaking measuredly or little/ reserved; reticent; discreet.

বাগ্‌দান *n* promise or betrothment of a maiden in marriage; betrothal; engagement. ~ করা *vt* betroth; engage (a woman by word of month).

বাগ্‌দুষ্ট *adj* vitiated through use of corrupt language; speaking badly or ill.

বাগ্‌দেবতা, বাগ্‌দেবী, বাগ্‌বাদিনী *nn* goddess of speech; Saraswati.

বাগ্‌ধারা *n* manner/ mode of using words in speech; idiom. ~গত *adj* idiomatic.

বাগ্‌বহুল *adj* wordy; prolix; verbose; diffuse.

বাগ্‌বাহুল্য *n* wordiness; prolixity; verbosity; diffuseness; long-windedness.

বাগ্‌বিতণ্ডা *n* altercation; wragling; hot dispute, war of words.

বাগ্‌বিদগ্ধ *adj* clever in speech; eloquent; silver-tongued. বাগ্‌বিদগ্ধা *fem.*

বাগ্বৈদগ্ধ, বাগ্বৈদগ্ধ্য, বাগবৈদগ্ধী *n n* cleverness of speech; art of speaking; eloquence; gift of the gab.
বাগ্মী *adj*=বাগ্বিদগ্ধ. ❑*n* orator; good/ eloquent speaker. **বাগ্মিতা** *n* eloquence; oratory.
বাগ্যত *adj* observing silence; silent; taciturn.
বাগ্যন্ত্র *n* larynx.
বাগ্যুদ্ধ *n* war of words; controversy; vehement debate/ discussion; wrangle; altercation. ~ **করা** *vi* debate; dispute hotly; bandy words (with); wrangle (with).
বাগ্রোধ *n* loss of speech/ speaking power; obstruction/ suppression of speech. ~ **করা** *vi* strike dumb; silence; stifle. ~ **হওয়া** *vi* become speechless; be struck dumb; be stifled.
বাঘ *n* **1** tiger. **2** (colloq) panther; leopard; cheetah; wolf. **বাঘী, বাঘিনী** *fem.* ~ **আচড়া** *n* **1** black stripes on a tiger's skin. **2** scratched by a tiger. ~**ছড়ি**, ~**ছাল**, ~**ছালা** *n* tiger's skin. ~**জাল** *n* snare for catching tigers. ~ **থাবা** *n* tiger's claw. ~**নখ**[১] *n* **1** tiger's nail. **2** (hist) nail-like weapon worn by Shivaji as handgloves. **3** gold ornament (medal or locket) with a tiger's claw. ~**নখ**[২], ~**নখী** *n* kind of perfume; unguis odoratus. ~**বন্দী** *n* **1**=~জাল. **2** an indoor game akin to fox and geese. ~**হাখা** *n* **1** leather band in the form of a tiger's claw fastened round a prisoner's wrists. **2**=~ নখ (2), (3). **বাঘের আড়ি** *n* (fig) enmity of an unrelenting adversary. **বাঘের মাসি** *n* cat. ❑*adj* fearless; dauntless. **বাঘের মাসি হওয়া** become dauntless. **বাঘে-গরুতে এক ঘাটে জল খাওয়া** (fig) a very powerful administration forcing even inveterate antagonists behave as friends. **বাঘে ছুঁলে আঠারো ঘা** (prov) **1** (lit) The tiger's teeth and nails are so poisonous that its mere touch inflicts numerous wounds. **2** (fig) an involvement entailing endless troubles. **বাঘের ঘরে ঘোগের বাসা 1** (lit) a tiger-wolf taking up its abode in a tiger's den. **2** (fig) a weakling settling in the den of its deadly enemy and continue to harass him **বাঘাম্বর** *n* piece of tiger's skin worn as loin-cloth.
বাঘা *n* tiger. ❑*adj* big; large. great. ~**হামা** *n* crawling on all fours. ~**টে** *adj* like a tiger; tigerish; strong; powerful.
বাঙলা *n*=বাংলা
বাঙাল, বাঙ্গাল *n* (pejorative) a native of former East Bengal; (iron) an unrefined rustic. ❑*adj* of East Bengal; born in East Bengal; obstinate; obdurate. ~**নী, বাঙালিনী, বাঙ্গালিনী** *fem*
বাঙালি *n* Bengali; a native of Bangladesh. ❑*adj* of Bengalis/ Bengali; Bengali: ~ সংস্কৃতি.
বাঙালে, বাঙ্গালে *adj* (pejorative) pertaining to former East Bengal or its people.
বাঙ্খুর *adj* dwarfish; stunted. বেটে ~=~. **বাঙ্খুরী** *fem.*
বাঙ্গলা *n* **1**=বাংলা. **2** bungalow.
বাঙ্গালা=বাংলা.
বাঙ্গালি, বাঙ্গালী=বাঙালি
বাঙ্গি, বাঙ্গী *n* (dial) kind of melon.
বাঙ্নিষ্ঠ *adj* true to one's word. **বাঙ্নিষ্ঠা** *n* faithful to one's promise; faithfulness; punctuality in fulfilling one's promise.
বাঙ্নিষ্পত্তি *n* utterance of words. ~ **করা** *vi* speak; talk.
বাঙ্ময় *adj* consisted of speech; depending on speech; relating to speech; composed of words; eloquent; expressive. ❑*n* rhetoric; eloquence. **বাঙ্ময়ী** *adj fem.*
বাঙ্মাত্র *adj* mere words.
বাঙ্মুখ *n* opening of a speech; exordium.
বাচ[১]=বাইচ
বাচ[২] *n* **1** selection; choosing. **2** what remains after the better ones have been selected; residue: ভালোগুলি সব বেছে নিয়েছে, এখন সব ~ পড়ে গেছে.
বাচক *adj* expressive of; signifying; denoting; speaking of. ❑*n* speaker; reciter.
বাচন *n* **1** speaking; reading; recitation; a saying. **2** causing to speak. ~**ভঙ্গি** *n* manner of speaking; delivery. **বাচনিক** *adv* verbal; oral; mentioned expressly; in word.
বাচনক *n* enigma.
বাচনা *n* **1** reading. **2** explanation; expounding.
বাচবিচার, বাছবিচার *n* discrimination (between good and bad); choice; diffentiate (between). ~ **করা** *vi, vt* discriminate. **বিনা বাচবিচারে** *adv* indiscriminately.
বাচস্পতি *n* **1** master of speech; orator; linguist; learned man. **2** Brihaspati; the preceptor of gods. **3**=বাক্পটু (⇒ বাক).
বাচস্পত্য *n* eloquence; eloquent speech; harangue; erudition.
বাচা *n* kind of small sweet-water fish.
বাচাই =বাছাই
বাচাল *adj* talkative; garrulous; voluble; loquacious. ❑*n* chatterer; chatterbox; gasbag; ~**তা** *n* talkativeness; garrulity; volubility.
বাচিক *adj* communicated by speech; oral. ~**পত্র** *n* written agreement/ contract.
বাচ্চা, বাচ্ছা *n* **1** young child; infant; kid; brat; toddler; tot; baby. **2** offspring; child: আমি যদি মানুষের ~ হই. **3** the young of a beast: শুয়োরের ~. ❑*adj* **1** young; infant: ~ মেয়ে/ছেলে. **2** ignorant; immature: এ বিষয়ে সে নিতান্ত ~. ~**কাচ্চা** *n pl* **1** young/infant children; kiddies; little ones; the young of any animal.
বাচ্য *adj* **1** to be spoken/ said/told/ announced/ stated/ communicated/ named/ enumerated/ spoken of; speakable; utterable. **2** fit to be

regarded as; namable: সে মনুষ্যপদ ~ নয়. ❑*n* **1** what may be said. **2** (gram) voice. **~তা** *n* the being to be said or spoken; the being predicated of. **~মান** *adj* **1** under discussion. **2** in the state of being revealed.

বাচ্যার্থ *n* directly expressed meaning; actual/ simple meaning or sense of a word or sentence; primary/ original meaning. **~ত্ব** *n* direct expression of meaning.

বাছ=বাচ

বাছন *n* **1** = বাচ (1). **2** sorting; sifting. **3** choice. **~দার** *n* one who chooses; chooser; elector. **~দারি** *n* choosing; sorting.

বাছনি[১]=বাছন

বাছনি[২] *n* (archaic, poet)=বাছা

বাছবিচার=বাচবিচার

বাছা[১] *n* **1** (as a term of endearment) my dear child; my darling. **2** child. **3** (archaic) calf. **~ধন** *n*=~ (often iron): এবার ~ধন বুঝবে মজা.

বাছা[২] *vt* **1** select; choose; pick and choose. **2** sort out; separate; sift: খুদ/ কাঁকর ~. **3** eliminate unwanted elements; clean; purge; cleanse; expurgate: ঢাল ~. **4** eliminate; kill; pick up: উকুন ~. ❑*adj* chosen; selected; select; choice; freed from unwanted elements; sifted: ~ আম, ~ চাল. **বাছা-বাছা** *adj* select; best; top-notch choicest: ~-~ লোক. **বাছের বাছ** *adj* choicest; top-notch; unexcelled.

বাছাই *n* **1** choosing; selection; choice. **2** sorting; separating; sifting; elimination of unwanted elements. ❑*adj*=বাছা[২]. ~ **করা** *vt*=বাছা[২].

বাছাধন ⇒ বাছা[১]

বাছানো *vt* cause to choose/ select/ sort/ sift.

বাছুনি[১] *n* (archaic, poet)=বাছা[১]

বাছুনি *n*=বাছাই

বাছুর *n* young of the cow; calf. **বাছুরি** *fem.* **~ বিয়ানো** *vi* calf. **বাছুরের মাংস** *n* veal.

বাজ[১] *n* thunderbolt; thunder; (colloq) lightning.

বাজ[২] *n* hawk; falcon.

বাজ[৩] [P] *suff* denoting: skilled, given to, full of, etc: ধড়ি~, ফুর্তি~, জাহাঁ~.

বাজখাঁই *adj* (of voice) very harsh and loud; raspy; strident.

বাজন *n* state of being played/ beaten/ sounded/ rung (as a musical instrument, bell, coin, etc); sound of playing on/ beating a musical instrument, bell, etc; sounding; playing; sound; music. **~দার, বাজনাদার, বাজনাওয়ালা** *nn* player on any musical instrument; instrumentalist (esp a professional one); musician. **বাজনা** *n* **1** act/ sound of playing on a musical instrument; music; instrumental music. **2** musical instrument.

বাজবহরী, বাজবেরী *n* variety of large falcons.

বাজরা[১] *n* **1** millet.

বাজরা[২] *n* large wicker-basket.

বাজরা[৩] *n* barge; large pleasure or state boat.

বাজা *vi* **1** be played on: বাঁশি বাজছে. **2** sound; be sounded: মোটরের হর্ন বাজে. **3** strike: ঘড়িতে পাঁচটা বাজে. **4** ring; toll; be rung: স্কুলের ঘণ্টা বাজল. **5** be announced by a sound: প্রহর ~. **6** jar on: শব্দটা কানে বাজে. **7** be felt: হাতে কী যেন বাজছে. **8** get entangled; be/get obstructed: গাছের ডালে ঘুড়ি বেজেছে (বেধেছে is more usual). **9** cause pain; hurt; touch; smart: কথাটা তাকে খুব বেজেছে. ঘড়ি/ঘণ্টা বাজে: the clock/ bell chimes. **ঘড়িতে . . . . .টা বাজে** the clock strikes . . . . **স্কুলের ঘণ্টা বাজে** The school-bell goes. **কারো/কোনো কিছুর বারোটা** ~ be kaput/ ruined/done for; go to pot.

বাজানো, বাজান *vt* **1** play (on): সেতার/বাঁশি ~. **2** beat: ঢাক ~ **3** blow: শাঁখ ~. **4** sound; ring; toll: ঘণ্টা ~. **5** clink: পয়সা ~. **6** try to discover the inclinations, thoughts, etc of; feel sb out; sound sth (out) (about/on sth); put out/ feelers/ a feeler; give sb a trial: লোকটাকে বাজিয়ে দেখো. **7** (old use) complete; accomplished: **কাজ** ~. **গাল** ~ produce a peculiar sound by inflating cheeks and striking them with fingers. **ঢাক** ~ (fig) make public; trumpet out; ballyhoo; blaze (abroad); blazon; noise it round. **নিজের ঢাক নিজে** ~ blow one's own trumpet.

বাজার *n* **1** market; bazaar. **2** fair: মিনা~. **3** goods/ stores esp for cooking purchased from the market; provisions: ~টা রেখেই চলে এসো. ❑*adj* cheap: ~ সংস্করণ. **~ করা** *vi* visit a market for buying things (esp daily necessities or stores); shop; do one's shopping; go to market. **~ খরচ** *n* expenditure on daily necessities. **~ গরম** prices are high/ prohibitive; the market is lively/up; a seller's market. **~ চড়া** prices are rising/ soaring/ spiraling. **~ দর** market price. **~ নরম, ~ মন্দ** prices are low; the market is dull/ sluggish/ down/ depressed; a buyer's market. **~ বসেছে** the market has opened for the day; a new market has opened; a fair is held (⇒ বসা). **বাজারিক, বাজারে** *adj* **1** relating to market. **2** selling or dealing at a market: ~ লোক marketer; marketman; rabble; mob; dregs. **3** market-going. **4** cheap; shoddy; trashy. **বাজারে মেয়েলোক** prostitute; street-girl; street-walker; trollop.

বাজি[১] *n* **1** magic; jugglery; conjuring trick; legerdemain. **2** play; game; **3** fireworks; pastime; amusement; pyrotechnics: আতস~. **4** turn; spell; bout: এক ~ তাস/দাবা. **5** stake; wager; bet. **6** feat: দড়া ~ মুখ ~. **7** one's existence and activities in the world: এবার ~ ভোর হলো. **~কর, ~কার, ~গর** *n* **1** magician; juggler; conjurer. **2** pyrotechnist; maker of fireworks. **3** puppet-player. **~জেতা** *vi* win a stake. ~ ধরা *vi* lay a wager; stake. ~ পোড়ানো *vi* make a display of fire-works. ~ ভোর *n* end of the game; (fig) end of life; death. ~মাৎ *n* (chess) checkmate; victory; triumph. ~মাৎ করা *vi* (chess) checkmate; win; triumph over; carry the day; be victorious; prevail; come out on top. ~ হারা *vt* lose a stake.

বাজি[২] [P] *suff* denoting: practice; propensity etc; full of: ধান্ধা ~, ফন্দি ~.

বাজিয়ে *adj* skilled in playing on a musical instrument. ❑*n* instrumentalist; musician.

বাজী[১]=বাজি[১]

বাজী[২] *n* (archaic) horse.

বাজীকরণ *n* an aphrodisiac process or drug; aphrodisiac.

বাজু [P] *n* **1** arm. **2** an ornament for the arm; armlet; bracelet. **3** fold of door. **4** side of a bedstead. ~বন্দ, ~বন্ধ *n*=~ (2).

বাজে *adj* **1** trashy; cheap; paltry; useless trifling; shoddy: ~ জিনিস/মাল. **2** worthless; good-for-nothing; vulgar; despicable; contemptible; unimportant; insignificant; inconsequential: ~ লোক. **3** vain; idle; futile; pointless: ~ কথা. **4** undesirable; unwanted; bothersome: ~ ঝামেলা. **5** useless; senseless; pointless: ~ খাটুনি. **7** extra; unnecessary; wasteful; extravagant: ~ খরচ. ~ আদায় *n* extra/incidental collection (of money, etc). ~ কথা *n* **1** unnecessary/useless talk or words. **2** vain/idle talk; gossip. **3** lie; cock and bull story; old wives' tale. ~ জিনিস *n* unnecessary/useless articles/things; sundries; trash; rubbish. ~ জমা *n* income from incidental sources; extra income. ~ জমি *nn* barren land. ~ মার্কা *adj, n* of inferior make/brands; substandard/poor or low-quality/low-grade/ shoddy(goods); trashy/ spurious (goods/articles); trash. ~ মাল *n*=~ মার্কা. ~ লোক *n* outsider (⇒ also (2) above).

বাজেট [E] *n* budget.

বাজেয়াপ্ত, বাজেয়াপ্তি *adj* confiscated; forfeited; foreclosed. ~করণ, বাজেয়াপ্তি *n* confiscation; forfeiture; foreclosure. ~ করা *vt* confiscate; forfeit; foreclose.

বাঞ্চোৎ, বাঞ্চোৎ *adj n* (taboo) (abusive term) having illicit intercourse with a sister; incestuous; lecher; rake.

বাঞ্ছন (used as *suff* in *comp*) desired (by); longed for: কামিনী ~. ❑*n* desire; wish; longing for; wishing; desiring.

বাঞ্ছনীয় *adj* to be wished for; desirable; agreeable.

বাঞ্ছা *n* desire; longing for; wish. ~ করা *vt* desire; long for; wish (for). ~কল্পতরু *n* **1** mythical tree which satisfies all desires. **2** a tutelary god granting all desires of supplicants.

বাঞ্ছিত *adj* desired; longed for; wished; beloved. বাঞ্ছিতা *fem.*

বাট[১] *n* path; road. ~দান *n* road tax/cess. ~পাড় *n* highwayman; bandit; robber; swindler. ~পাড়ি *n* highway robbery; robbery. চোরের উপর ~পাড়ি (fig) a highwayman robs a thief.

বাট[২] *n* (archaic) house; building; temple.

বাট[৩] *n* bullion; ingot.

বাটখারা *n* weight (used in scales of weighing things).

বাটন *n* grinding; crushing; act of turning into paste by rolling on a flat mortar with a pestle. বাটনা *n* spices turned thus into paste; quantity of spices to be rolled thus.

বাটা[১] *n* metal case (esp one for holding betel-leaves).

বাটা[২] variety of small silvery-white fresh-water fish.

বাটা[৩] *n* **1** tax; profit. **2** (commerce) discount. আসল ~ true discount.

বাটা[৪] *n* Hindu rite of offering dishes and gifts to a son-in-law.

বাটা[৫]=বাঁটা

বাটা[৬] *vt* turn into paste by rolling (spices, etc) on a flat mortar with a pestle; crush; grind. ❑*adj* (of spices, etc) thus reduced to or turned into paste: ~ মশলা.

বাটালি *n* chisel. এককোণে ~ *n* angular chisel. কোর ~ *n* small gouge. গেবে ~ *n* large gouge.

বাটি *n* cup; hemispherical cup without handles; bowl. এক ~ a cup/bowl (of). ~ চালা *vi* set a cup/bowl chasing a suspected offender by means of occult incantations. জামবাটি *n* a large bowl of bell metal or glass; goblet.

বাটিকা *n* glass; goblet.

বাটিকা *n* small house.

বাটী=বাড়ি

বাটুল=বাঁটুল

বাটোয়ারা=বাঁটোয়ারা

বাট্টা=বাটা[৩]

বাড় *n* **1** growth; development: শরীরের ~. **2** augmentation; increase; rise; advancement: বেতনের ~. **3** aggravation: রোগের ~. **4** audacity; effrontery; cheek. **5** edge. **6** circumference. **7** (naut) gunwale. ~ বাড়া grow audacious; become intolerably haughty; be high and mighty. ~বাড়ন্ত *n* prosperity; affluence; opulence; great/growing prosperity.

বাড়ই, বাড়ুই *n* carpenter; joiner.

বাড়তি *n* growth; development; increase; rise: জ্বরটা এখন ~র দিকে. ❑*adj* surplus; extra; in excess; excessive: ~ রোজগার/ মাল/ লাভ/ পাওয়া. কমতি~, খাটতি~ *nn* shortage and or excess; rise and fall.

বাড়ন[১] *n*=বাড় (1), (2), (3), (4).

বাড়ন[২], **বাড়নি** *n* broomstick.

বাড়ন্ত *adj* **1** growing; inclined to grow/develop: ~ গড়ন/শরীর. **2** flourishing; booming: ~ অবস্থা. **3** (euphem) exhausted; wanting; scanty: ঘরে চাল ~.

বাড়ব *n* **1** submarine fire. **2** *pl* of বড়বা. **3** relating to বড়বা. **4** stallion; stud-horse. **বাড়বাগ্নি, বাড়বানল** *nn*=~ (1).

বাড়া[1] *vi* **1** grow; grow up. develop; burgeon: চারাগুলি বাড়ছে. **2** increase; swell; surge; rise: ভিড়/ নদীর জল বাড়ছে. **3** proliferate; multiply: সংখ্যা ~. **4** rise; climb; spiral; rocket: দাম ~. **5** expand; be expanded; thrive; prosper; flourish: রাজ্য ~, ব্যবসা ~. **6** accumulate: শরীরে মেদ ~. **7** become worse/more serious; be aggravated: রোগ ~, বিপদ ~. **8** grow audacious/haughty: লোকটা বড়ো বেড়েছে. **9** be filled/extended; become longer/ stronger/ larger; be heightened/ strengthened. ☐*adj* **1** more/than: দেশের মাটি মায়ের ~. **2** excessive.

বাড়া[2] *vi* proceed; go. **আগে ~** go forward/ ahead; advance.

বাড়া[3] *vt* serve (on a dinner-plate): ভাত ~. ☐*adj* served on a dinner-plate **~ ভাতে ছাই** (fig) a hindrance or an obstacle to attaining the final success; a fly in the ointment.

বাড়ানো, বাড়ান *vt* **1** increase; augment; enhance; cause to grow/prosper: বেতন/ আয় ~. **2** multiply: জনসংখ্যা ~. **3** enlarge; expand: ব্যবসা ~. **4** cause to swell: ভিড় ~. **5** strengthen; bolster; boost: ক্ষমতা/খ্যাতি/ প্রতিপত্তি ~. **6** cause to prosper/thrive: অন্যের সহায় সম্পদ ~. **7** accelerate: গতি ~. **8** aggravate; worsen; exacerbate; heighten; intensify; sharpen: রোগ/বিপদ/দুঃখ/ যন্ত্রণা ~. **9** exaggerate; magnify: বাড়িয়ে বলা. **10** embolden; boost; bolster (up): সাহস ~. **11** exalt/extol unduly; give undue importance; aggrandize; glorify: অযোগ্য লোককে ~. **12** intensify; step up: যত্ন ~. **13** mend; sharpen: পেনসিল ~. **14** stretch; extend; crane: হাত/গলা ~. **15** over-indulge; pamper: ছেলেমেয়েদের অতো বাড়াতে নেই. **16** enhance falsely: বয়স বাড়িয়ে বলা. **17** cause to serve on a dinner-plate: ভাত/মাংস ~. **18** promote; further; cause to go forward; put/help forward; advance: ছেলেটাকে সামনে বাড়াও. **নোলা ~** pamper sb's greed. **পা ~** move the foot forward; set off/out; be on the point setting out/departing. **পেট ~** *vi* grow fat.

বাড়াবাড়ি *n* **1** excess; extremes; immoderation; intemperance; too much. **2** exacerbation; aggravation: রোগের ~. ☐*adv* excessively; too much: ডুব দিয়ো না ~. **~ করা** *vi* go beyond the limit; work oneself up; get excited: এ নিয়ে এখানে ~র দরকার নেই. **~ হওয়া** *vi* be aggravated/ exacerbated; be in excess.

বাড়ি[1], বাড়ী *n* home; house; residence; building; dwelling-house; living quarters; abode; homestead; household; family. **~ওয়ালা** *n* owner of a house (esp of a tenanted one); landlord. **~ওয়ালী, ~উলি** *n* (colloq) *fem.* **~ঘর, ঘর~** *n pl* houses and buildings; habitations; dwellings; homestead. **~শুদ্ধ** including all the members of the household/family. **কাঁচা~** *n* a house built with mud, wood, bamboo, straw, etc (not with stone or brick); cutcha house; shanty. **মেটে ~** mud-built house. **কাছারি ~** office building; court; outhouse. **কোঠা ~, পাকা ~** brick-/stone-built house; mansion; building. **গোয়াল ~** cowshed. **গোলা ~, চাষ ~** *nn* farmyard; barn. **বাহির বার ~, সদর ~,** *nn* outer portion/ apartment of a residential building. **ভাড়া ~** *n* tenanted/rented house. **যমের ~** *n* the world of the dead; death; death's door. **শ্বশুর ~** *n* **1** father-in-law's house. **2** any place when one is lavishly entertained. **3** (iron) any unpleasant place; gaol.

বাড়ি[2] *n* **1** staff; stick. **2** cudgel: পাচন ~. **3** whip. **4** blow; stroke: লাঠির ~. **~ দেওয়া, ~ মারা** *vt* deal/strike (one) a blow; strike; hit.

বাণ *n* arrow; shaft. **~ ছোড়া** *vt* shoot an arrow. **~-বিদ্ধ** *adj* pierced with an arrow.

বাণিজ্য *n* commerce; trade; traffic; merchandise. **~ করা** *vi* trade; traffic. **~-অধ্যক্ষ** *n* commercial manager. **~ উদ্বৃত্ত** *n* balance of trade. **~ কর** *n* commercial tax. **~কেন্দ্র** *n* trade centre. **~তরী** *n* merchant ship. **~দূত** *n* consul. **~দূতাবাস** *n* consulate. **~নাবী** *n* merchant navy. **~পোত**=~তরী. **~বায়ু** *n* trade winds. **~বিবরণী** *n* trade report. **~মন্ত্রী** *n* Minister of Commerce. **~শালা** *n* trading house; shop. **~সামগ্রী** *n* merchandise; stock-in-trade; ware; commodity.

বাণিজ্যালয়, বাণিজ্যাগার *nn* trading house; trading post; shop.

বাণী *n* **1** words; language; speech. **2** messages; maxim; apophthegm. **3** Saraswati, the goddess of speech. **~বহ** *n* scholar; man of letters/learning.

বাত[1], বাৎ *n* word; speech; saying; discourse; information; news; talk; tale; story; gossip.

বাত[2] *n* **1** wind; air. **2** different kinds of painful conditions, eg rheumatism, arthritis, osteo-arthrosis; gout. **~কর্ম** *n* farting; breaking wind. **~কুম্ভ** *n* the part of an elephant's forehead, below the frontal sinuses. **~গহ্বর** *n* air-pocket. **~গ্রস্ত** *n* rheumatic epileptic. **~ঘ্ন** *adj* removing/curing diseases of the wind (rheumatism, etc). **~চক্র** *n* circular markings of a compass. **~জ, ~জনিত** *adj* produced caused by wind; rheumatic **~জ্বর** *n* rheumatic fever. **~তৈল** *n* essential oil. **~পিত্ত** *n* a form of rheumatism. **~পৈত্তিক** *adj* rheumatic and biliary. **~বেদনা** *n* rheumatic pain. **~ব্যাধি** *n* any disease supposed to arise from a diseased state of the wind in the body (eg gout, rheumatism, paralysis); (pop) paralysis. **~ব্যাধি, ~গ্রস্ত** *adj* paralytic. **~মৃগ** *n* kind of antelope. **~যন্ত্র** *n* wind-driven machine. **~রক্ত** *n* acute gout or rheumatism (ascribed to vitiated state of wind and blood). **~রোগ**=~ব্যাধি. **~রোগগ্রস্ত**=~ব্যাধিগ্রস্ত. **~শূল** *n* colic with flatulence. **~শোষক** *n* (bot) aspirator. **~সহ** *adj* **1** bearing/enduring the wind (as a ship). **2** suffering from gout or rheumatism.

বাতলানো, বাতলান *vt* tell; explain; point out; instruct; impart; suggest; show: পথ ~. ❑*adj* suggested; showed.

বাতা *n* **1** slip of bamboo or wood used crosswise in thatching; slat; lath. **2** (naut) timber; rib.

বাতানুকূল *adj* air-conditioned. **~তা** *n* air-conditioning.

বাতানো *vt*=বাতলানো

বাতান্দোলিত *adj* agitated/moved/tossed by wind.

বাতান্বিত *adj* aerated. **~ পানীয়** aerated water; mineral water.

বাতাবকাশ *n* air space.

বাতাবরণ *n* environment; surroundings; atmosphere.

বাতাবর্ত *n* whirl wind; cyclone.

বাতাবি *n* (also ~লেবু) shaddock; pomelo.

বাতায়ন *n* window; air-hole; ventilator. **বাতায়িত** *adj* ventilated.

বাতাস *n* **1** air; wind. **2** gust of wind; fanning. **3** (fig) (evil) influence; association; company; touch: বখাটে ছেলেটার ~ লেগেছে. **~ করা** *vt* fan. **~ খাওয়া** *vi* **1** cool oneself with fanning; enjoy fanning. **2** take the air; have some fresh air. **~ চলা** *vi* (of wind) flow. **~ দেওয়া** *vt* **1** fan. **2** (fig) kindle; encourage; fan: দুপক্ষের বিবাদে ~ দেওয়া. **~ পাওয়া** *vt* **1** get air; (of boats) get favourable wind. **2** (fig) (derog) be influenced by. **~ বওয়া** *vi* (of wind) blow; be windy. **~ লাগা** *vi* **1**=~ পাওয়া (1). **2** be influenced by; be possessed by an evil spirit. **বাতাসে ওড়া** *vi* fly in air; (fig) move light heartedly/airily. **বাতাসে ভর করে চলা** *vi* (fig) **1** move as swiftly as the wind. **2** move very lightly. **3** move light-heartedly. **বাতাসের সঙ্গে লড়াই করা** fight imaginary enemies; fight/tilt at windmills.

বাতাসা *n* kind of convex sweet drop of sugar or molasses. **ফেনি ~** ⇒ ফেণি. **~ কাটা** *vt* fashion the above sweets.

বাতাহত *adj* stirred/shaken/tossed by wind; wind-beaten; wind-stricken.

বাতি[1] *n* lamp; light; candle; a stick or rod: গ্লিসারিন ~. **~দান** *n* candlestick. **বংশে ~ দেওয়া 1** suspend a light from the top of pole set up every evening by the Hindus during the month of Kartik in reverence to their deceased fore fathers. **2** (fig) continue the line of descent. **মোম~** *n* candle. **সাঁঝের ~**=সন্ধ্যাদীপ.

বাতি[2] *n* bamboo-slip.

বাতিক *n* **1** disease supposed to arise from a diseased state of the wind in the body. **2** neurosis. **3** mania. **4** strong hobby; crotchet; craze; obsession. **~গ্রস্ত** *adj* maniacal; crotchety; neurotic; obsessed. **~গ্রস্ত ব্যক্তি** *n* maniac; crazy fellow; neurotic.

বাতিল [A] *adj* **1** cancelled; rejected; false; useless; forsaken; disowned; spurious. **2** (law) null and void; set aside; rescinded; annulled; void; cancelled. ❑*n* falsehood. **~ করা** *vt* **1** cancel; reject; abolish; refute. **2** (law) void; set aside; rescind; revoke; annul.

বাতুল *adj* mad; insane; crazy; deranged; berserk; frenzied; neurotic; lunatic. ❑*n* madman; lunatic; maniac; psychotic. **~তা** *n* madness; insanity; neurosis; craziness; lunacy;

বাতেন [A] *n* the innermost part; the inside; the internal. **বাতেনি** *adj* hidden; concealed; secret; internal: বাতেনি কথা.

বাতোন্মূলিত *adj* uprooted by wind.

বাত্তি *n* bamboo-split.

বাত্যা *n* strong wind; gale; storm; hurricane. **~কুল** *adj* stormy; tempestuous; turbulent; rough; rugged. **~চক্র** *n* whirlwind. **~পীড়িত** *adj* storm-beaten; storm-stricken. **~বিক্ষুব্ধ** *adj* storm-tossed; tempestuous; turbulent. **~বিধ্বস্ত** *adj* destroyed by wind/stormed; storm-stricken.

বাৎসরিক *adj* yearly; annual.

বাৎসল্য *n* **1** affection/tenderness (esp towards offspring); fondness/love for; parental love. **2** (Vaishnava phil) sentiment of parental love or act of regarding God as one's child; parental devotion towards God. **3** the tender sentiment in a poem.

বাথরুম [E] *n* bathroom.

বাথান *n* **1** cattle-shed; cow-house; cow-shed. **2** pasture; grazing ground. **3** (of cows) heat. **বাথানে** *adj* (of cows) in/on/at heat.

বাথুয়া, বেথো *n* a variety of spinach; *Chenopodium album.*

বাদ[1] *n* **1** utterance; speech; discourse; talk. **2** debate. **3** (used after certain *preff* or words like লোক) reproach: লোক~, পরি~. **4** protest; complain. **5** hitch; controversy; hostility. **5** (phil) doctrine; ism; theory. **~ করা** *vi* oppose; be hostile to; quarrel. **~প্রতিবাদ** *n* a set disputation; assertion and counter-assertion; statement and contradiction; controversy; argument; debate. **~প্রতিবাদ করা** *vi* assert and counter-assert; issue statements and contradictions; dispute; debate; argue; wrangle (about/over/with). ~বিতণ্ডা, ~বিবাদ, ~বিসংবাদ *nn* hot dispute; argument and disputation; wrangling; altercation; quarrel; brawl. ~বিতণ্ডা করা *vi* dispute; quarrel; brawl.

বাদ[2] *n* obstacle; hindrance; impediment opposition. ~ সাধা *vt* hinder; obstruct; get in the way of; oppose; impede; block; interfere with; foil; baffle; balk.

বাদ[3] [A] *n* **1** exception; exclusion; omission; deduction; exemption; subtraction. **2** (commerce) deduction. **3** remainder; rest; residue: কোনো কিছুর ~ রাখা ভালো নয়. ❑*prep*= বাদে: এক ঘণ্টা ~ এসো. ~ দেওয়া *vt* exclude; except; omit; deduct; subtract; exempt; discount. ~ পড়া/ যাওয়া/হওয়া *vi* be excluded/ excepted/ omitted/ deducted/ subtracted/ discounted. ~বাকি *adj* remaining. ❑*n* the rest. ~সাদ, ~সাধ *n* partial discount/ deduction/ allowance; deductions; omissions. ~সাদ দিয়ে after (necessary) deductions/ discount/ omissions. বাদে *prep* **1** after; except, excepting, excluding, without: তিন দিন বাদে, মিনু বাদে সবাই এসেছে. **2** (archaic) for: কার বাদে জল নিয়ে যাও. ❑*adv* **1** later; afterwards; late: এত বাদে এলে যে বড়ো? আজ বাদে কাল very soon: আজ বাদে কাল বিয়ে....

বাদক *n* instrumentalist; player; musician; performer. ~ সম্প্রদায় *n* musical band.

বাদন *n* playing on a musical instrument; music.

বাদর *n* (poet)=বাদল

বাদল *n* **1** rain; rainy day. **2** cloud. ~ পোকা=বর্ষাপোকা. ~ মেঘ *n* nimbus. বর্ষা~, বৃষ্টি~ ⇒ বর্ষা and বৃষ্টি respectively.

বাদলা[1] *n* rain; rainy day. ❑*adj* rainy; cloudy of rain; of the rainy season; rain-soaked; growing in the rainy season. ~ দিন *n* rainy day.

বাদলা[2] *n* gold-thread; silver-thread. ~র কাজ *n* embroidery with gold-or silver-thread.

বাদশা, বাদশাহ [P] *n* **1** king; sovereign; emperor. **2** the king of playing-cards. ~জাদা *n* prince. ~জাদী *n* princess. বাদশাহি, বাদশাহী *n* empire; reign; rule; sovereignty. ❑*adj* royal; regal; imperial; princely; majestic.

বাদা [A] *n* **1** an (extensive) marsh; fen. **2** jungle; woodland. ~ড় *n* jungle; woodland area. বন-বাদাড় *n*=বনজঙ্গল (⇒ বন).

বাদানুবাদ=বাদপ্রতিবাদ (⇒ বাদ)

বাদাম[1] *n* sail.

বাদাম[2] [P] *n* **1** (any) nut. **2** almond. কাগজি ~, কাবুলি ~ *nn* almond. চীনা ~ ⇒ চীনা. পাত~ *n* an indigenous variety of nut; almond-fruit. হিজলি ~ *n* kind of large nut with a hard shell. বাদামি *adj* almond-coloured; light red; brown; almond-shaped; almond-like. বাদামের খোলা/ খোসা *n* nutshell.

বাদার্থ *n* syntax; syntactic.

বাদিত *adj* (of musical instruments) made to sound; sounded; played.

বাদিতা *suff* denoting; habit of speaking: obedience to/practice of an ism: সত্য~ আদর্শ~, বাস্তব~.

বাদিত্র *n* musical instrument; music; musical choir; musical performance.

বাদিয়া, বেদে ⇒ বেদিয়া

বাদী[1] (also ~সুর) *n* principal note of a musical mode.

বাদী[2] *n* **1** plaintiff; accuser; complainant. **2** speaker; asserter. **3** opponent; antagonist; adversary. বাদিনী *fem.* ~প্রতিবাদী *n* complainant and defender.

বাদী[3] *suff* denoting speaking/accustomed to speak; obedient to/practising an ism; -ist; -istic: আদর্শ~, সত্য~, মার্ক্স~.

বাদীয় *adj* theoretical⇒বাদ[1] (5).

বাদুড় *n* bat; flying-fox.

বাদুলে ⇒ বাদলা

বাদে ⇒ বাদ[3]

বাদ্য *n* **1** musical instrument. **2** instrumental music. ❑*adj* to be sounded/played (as a musical instrument) ~কর *n* instrumentalist; musician. ~করদল *n pl* musical band; concert-party. ~ধ্বনি *n* sound of (instrumental) music. ~ভাণ্ড *n* musical instruments; a set of musical instruments; percussion instruments. ~যন্ত্র *n* musical instrument.

বাধ *n* **1**=বাদ[2] **2** (psych) inhibition.

বাধক *adj* obstructive; hindering. ❑*n* **1** obstacle; hindrance. **2** dysmenorrhoea.

বাধন *n* obstruction; hindrance; hindering.

বাধবাধ, বাধোবাধো *adj* **1** uneasy; hesitating; diffident; faltering; wavering; self-conscious: ~ গলায়. **2** tight; ill-fitted; tense: জুতোটা কেমন ~ লাগছে. ~ ঠেকা feel ill-at case/shy; be embarrassed; be hesitant; be in two minds; feel tense/tight; be uneasy.

বাধা[1] *n* **1** obstacle; hindrance; impediment; obstruction. **2** trouble; distress. **3** (mech) resistance. **4** ill omen: যাওয়ার পথে একটা ~ পড়ল. ~ দেওয়া *vt* obstruct; hinder; oppose; impede; prevent; resist; hamper. ~ পাওয়া *vi* be hindered/opposed/prevented. ~ জনক, ~দায়ক *adj* obstructive; hindering; preventive; unhelpful. ~দান *n* obstructing; hindering; preventing; obstruction; prevention. ~দান করা *vt*=~ দেওয়া. ~প্রাপ্ত *adj* obstructed; hindered; frustrated; impeded; thwarted; baffled; resisted; prevented. ~বন্ধ, ~বিঘ্ন *n* obstructions; impediments; obstacles; fetters; snags; barriers; hurdles; encumbrances.

বাধা[2] *vi* **1** be obstructed; opposed (to); be contrary/revolting to; clash with; jar with: ধর্মে

~, চক্ষুলজ্জায় ~. **2** stick: শাড়ির আঁচল কাঁটায় বেধেছে. **3** break out; start/begin suddenly: যুদ্ধ/ ঝগড়া ~. **4** find it difficult/impossible: তার কথা বুঝতে বাধে. **~নো, ~ন** *vt* **1** cause to stick: ঘুড়িটা গাছে বাধালে. **2** bring about; initiate; start (suddenly); provoke; cause: লড়াই/ঝগড়া/মারামারি বাধানো.

বাধিত *adj* **1** obstructed; impeded; hindered; prevented; blocked; throttled. **2** thankful; grateful; beholden to; obliged. **~ করা** *vt* oblige. **~ থাকা/হওয়া** *vi* remain/be thankful/ grateful/ obliged; be beholden to.

বাধ্য *adj* **1** obedient; dutiful; docile; meek; well-behaved; submissive; tame; subservient; servile; obsequious; law-abiding; amenable; obliged: পিতার ~ পুত্র, যুক্তির ~. obliged to; compelled/sure (to): তারা আমার কথা শুনতে ~, এ যুদ্ধে হার মানতে তোমরা ~. **~ করা** *vt* compel; force; make. **~তা** *n* obedience; dutifulness; docility; servility; meekness; obligation; compulsion; amenability. **~তাজনক, ~তামূলক** *adj* compulsory; obligatory; imperative; binding; compelling; compulsive; coercive. **~বাধকতা** *n* mutual obligations; compulsion; strictness; rigidity; coercion; constraint.

বান[১] *n* **1** flood; deluge; tidal wave; bore; eagre. **2** (fig) surge flood. **বান ডাকা 1** (of a river) rise in flood; be in flood; to rise/surge in bore or eagre. **2** (fig) surge; well up: আনন্দের ~ ডেকেছে. **বানের জলে ভেসে আসা 1** come floating on flood-water. **2** (fig) be insignificant/less important; consequential; come without being invited; be the scum (of). **বানে ভেসে যাওয়া** *vi* to be swept/carried off in a flood; be overflooded. **~ভাসি** *n, adj* flooding; (objects) carried ashore by flood-water.

বান[২] *n* eel.

বান[৩] *suff* denoting, endowed with; possessing: গুণ~, ধন~, বেগ~. **বতী** *fem.*

বান[৪] *suff* [P] signifying; keeper; guardian: দর~, বাগ~.

বান[৫] *n* (naut) groove cut in a piece of wood for joining.

বানচাল *n* **1** (naut) getting the bottom ripped open. **2** frustrating: thwarting; foiling: পরিকল্পনা ~ করা. **~ করা** *vt* rip the bottom open; frustrate; foil; thwart. **~ হওয়া** *vi* have the bottom ripped open; fail; miscarry; collapse; abort; fall through; flop; end in a fiasco.

বানপুটি, বানকুচলি *nn* rope made of straw or hay.

বানপ্রস্থ *n* **1** the third stage of life according to Hindu scriptures when a Brahmin should abandon his house and family for an ascetic life in the woods. **2** a Brahmin in the third stage of his life.

বানর *n* monkey; ape. **বানরী** *fem.* **~তুল্য** *n* monkeyish; apish. **বানরের গলায় মুক্তার হার** casting pearls before swine. **বানরের ভূষণ** a monkey's ornament; used in the sense of the above phrase. **বানুরে** *adj* monkey-like; monkeyish; apish. **বানুরে বুদ্ধি** *n* mischieviousness; mischief.

বানা *n* weaving; knitting.

বানান *n* spelling; orthography. **~ করা** *vt* spell. **~ সমস্যা** *n* problem of orthography.

বানানো, বানান *vt* **1** make; create; construct; build: বাড়ি/কল/ রাস্তা ~. **2** manufacture; fabricate; produce: জামা/ঘড়ি ~. **3** found; set up: স্কুল/হাসপাতাল ~. **4** coin; mint; make: টাকা/পয়সা ~. **5** beget; produce: বাচ্চা ~. **6** synthesize: সুগন্ধি/ রাসায়নিক দ্রব্য ~. **7** compose: গান/কবিতা ~. **8** draw up: দলিল ~. **9** coin; form: শব্দ ~. **10** devise; conceive; contrive; design: কৌশল/ নকশা ~. **11** organize: দল ~. **12** concoct; fabricate; invent; devise; frame: অজুহাত/মামলা/ মিথ্যা ~. **13** cause to appear as: কাউকে ভেড়া ~. **14** chop: মাংস ~. **15** dress: সালাদ ~. **16** cook; bake: কোর্মা/পিঠা ~. **17** prepare; prime; call on: সাক্ষী ~. **18** shape; form; fashion; throw: হাড়ি/পুতুল ~. **19** pluck: মুরগি ~. **20** drive: পাগল ~. ❑*adj* **1** artificial: ~ পাহাড়. **2** faked; counterfeit; forged: ~ দলিল. **3** concocted: ~ গল্প. **4** primed: ~ সাক্ষী.

বানারসী=বেনারসি

বানি, বানী *n* making charge (esp for ornaments and dress).

বানিয়া *n* trader; tradesman; merchant; (derog) niggard; petty minded person.

বানু *n fem* princess; gentle-woman.

বান্ডিল, বানডিল [E] *n* bundle.

বান্ত *adj* vomitted.

বান্দর *n* (dial)=বানর

বান্দা *n* [P] **1** slave; bondsman. **2** individual; man: এই ~ই কি সবকিছুর জন্য দায়ী? **3** created being. **4** servant. **5** obedient person. **বান্দি, বাঁদি** *fem* slave-woman; maid-servant; obedient/ devoted woman.

বান্ধব *n* **1** friend. **2** kinsman; relation. **3** ally. ❑**বান্ধবী** *fem.*

বান্ধা (dial)=বাঁধা

বান্ধুলি=বন্ধুক

বাপ *int* expressing surprise, pain, fear, regret, etc; good God ! my goodness!

বাপ[২] *n* **1** sowing. **2** fertilization.

বাপ[৩] *n* **1** father. **2** (as a term of endearment) my son: একটু সবুর করো বাপ, এখনই তোমার মা আসবে. **~কা বেটা, বাপের বেটা** like father, like son; a chip of the old block. **~কা বেটা সেপাইকা ঘোড়া কুছ নেহি তো থোড়া থোড়া** (prov) a son must inherit some qualities at least of his father. **~কেলে** *adj* paternal; ancestral; obsolescent; antediluvian. **~-তোলা** *vi* abuse one by calling name of one's father. **~দাদা** *n* ancestors; forefathers; pedigree. **~দাদার আমলে** in the time of one's forefathers. **~ধন**=~ (2). **~পো** *n* father and son. **~ বলা** *vi* (fig) flatter; curry favour (with sb) butter up; surrender. **~বাপ, ~রে ~** (exclamation of surprise, fear, etc; cry for help/mercy) O father ! **~ ~ করা** *vi* (being punished) cry for help. **~বেটা**=~পো. **~মা** *n* father and mother; (fig) only defender; last refuge. **বাপের জন্মে, বাপের কালে, বাপের জম্মে** in one's father's lifetime; (fig) at any time; ever; in a month of Saturdays **বাপের ঠাকুর** *n* highly revered; venerable; august. **(কারো) বাপের সাধ্য (নেই), কার বাপের সাধ্য** (fig) there is no power on earth...; not within anybody's capacity. **বাপের নাম ভুলিয়ে দেওয়া** make one forget one's father's name (indicating the severity of punishment/chastisement); curse the day he was born. **আপনি বাঁচলে বাপের নাম** (prov) self-preservation is one's foremost duty. **বাপান্ত করা** *v*=~ তোলা.

বাপক *n*=sower.

বাপকেলে ⇒ বাপ৩

বাপঠাকুরদাদা =বাপদাদা (⇒ বাপ৩)

বাপধন ⇒ **বাপ**৩

বাপন *n* causing to sow.

বাপরে বাপ ⇒ বাপ৩

বাপস্=বাপ্১

বাপা=বাপ৩

বাপান্ত ⇒ বাপ৩

বাপি, বাপী *n* pond; large pond; lake.

বাপিত *adj* **1** swon. **2** shaved.

বাপু *n* **1** (term of endearment) my dear; my darling. **2** (form of address to one's inferiors or juniors) my boy; my girl; man! ❑*int* used in emphasizing disgust, amazement, interrogation, etc: একটু চুপ করো তো ~! ভারী বিপদে পড়া গেল ~! **4** father; daddy.

বাফতা [P] *n* a silk and cotton material; taffeta.

বাব১ [A] *n* chapter/section (of a book).

বাব২ [A] *n* **1** tax; rent. **2** excuse: একটা ~ করে বসে রইল.

বাবই=বাবুই

বাবদ, বাবত [A] *prep* as regards; in the matter of; on account of; for. ❑*n* head; account; item. **এই ~** on this account. **কিসের ~** on what account. **কোন ~** in which account; on what account.

বাবদূক *adj* garrulous; loquacious.

বাবরি, বাবরী *n* mass of long curling hair flowing down to a person's neck; man; tresses. **~কাটা** *adj* curling; wavy.

বাবর্চি ⇒ বাবুর্চি

বাবলা *n* sort of thorny tree from which gum is obtained; bablah; babul; *Acacia arabica*. **~আঠা** *n* gum acacia.

বাবা [T] *n* **1** father. **2** (term of endearment) my child; my son. **3** (form of address) reverend; venerable: ~ নানক. **4** old man. **5** (iron form of address) my good sir/man friend: যাওনা ~ আর কথা বাড়াও কেন? ❑*int*=বাপু. **~রে, ~রে ~**=বাপরে, বাপরে বাপ. **~জান** *n* dear father. **~জীবন** *n* (form of address to a son/son-in-law/junior person) my dear son.

বাবাজি, বাবাজী *n* **1** (title applied to saints and holy men) reverend father. **2** (form of address) my dear son.

বাবাঃ, বাবাহ্ *int* expressing fright, amazement, etc; goodness me! thank goodness! good God!

বাবু *n* **1** title affixed to the name of a Hindu gentleman; Mr. **2**=বাপু (1). **3** proprietor; owner. **4** master; employer; landlord: ~ বাড়িতে নেই. **5** gentleman: একজন ~ এসেছিলেন দেখা করতে. **6** male member of a family: বাড়ির ~রা সব মেলায় গেছেন. **7** clerk; officer: অফিসের ~রা ধর্মঘট করেছেন. **8** Baboo; babu: কলকাতার ~সম্প্রদায়. **9** a fashionable youngman; a fop; a dandy; coxcomb: লোকটা ~ হয়ে পড়েছে. **10** (derog) man; guy: ~র ঘরে ছুচোর কেত্তন, বাইরে কোঁচার পত্তন. **11** form of address to a father or husband. **~গিরি, ~য়ানা**, *n* indulgence in luxury; life of luxury; extravagance; fashionableness; foppishness; foppery; elegance; daintiness; fastidiousness; dandyism. **~ চাকর** *n* a dandy of servant; lazy servant. **~জি, ~জী, ~মশাই** *nn* respectful term for addressing a man. **বড়ো ~** *n* **1** eldest male member of a family. **2** head of an office/establishment. **~ বাছা করা** *vt* treat a young person affectionately. **~ বাছা বলা** *vi* address a young person affectionately.

বাবুই *n* weaver-bird. **~তুলসী** *n* kind of wild basil.

বাবুর্চি *n* [T] cook; chef. **~খানা** *n* kitchen; cookhouse.

বাম *n*=বাঁ. ❑*adj* **1** reverse; contrary; opposite. **2** unfavourable; adverse: বিধি হল ~. **3** crooked; oblique. **4** lovely; dear; pleasant; agreeable; fair; beautiful; noble; splendid. **5** vile; wicked; base; low. **~পথী** *adj fem* always disagreeing with one's husband; antagonistic to one's husband. **~পন্থী** *adj* leftist. **~পার্শ্ব** *n* left side.

বামন[১] *n* **1** Brahmin. **2** Brahmin priest or cook. **বামনা** *n* derog term for a Brahmin. **বামনী** *fem*. ~ **গেল ঘর তো লাঙ্গল তুলে ধর** (fig) when the master is away, servants neglect their work. **বামনের গরু** (fig) a sb/sth that yields maximum benefit at the minimum cost. ~**ঠাকুর** *n* Brahmin priest or cook. ~**ঠাকরুন** *n fem* female Brahmin cook. **বামনাই** *n* (pejo) **1** rank and condition of a Brahmin. **2** pride of being a Brahmin.

বামন[২] *n* **1** dwarf. **2** the fifth incarnation of Vishnu in the form of a dwarf. ❑*adj* dwarfish; midget (attrib); stunted. ~ **হয়ে চাঁদে হাত** (fig) demand sth impossible; cry for the moon.

বামলোচনা *n* **1** fair-eyed woman. **2** beautiful woman. **3** woman.

বামা *n* **1** beautiful woman. **2** woman.

বামাক্ষী *n* fair-eyed woman.

বামাঙ্গ *n* left side of the body. **বামাঙ্গী** *fem adj* fair-bodied. ❑*n* lovely woman.

বামাচার *n* religious practices or doctrines of the Tantras. **বামাচারী** *n* follower of those practices.

বামাবর্তী *adj* winding/wound/turned towards the left or west; anti-clockwise; sinistral.

বামাল=বমাল

বামাস্বর *n* a woman's voice.

বামী *n fem* mare.

বামুন (colloq)=বামন

বামেতর *adj* right.

বামোরূ *n* a handsome-thighed woman.

বায় (poet)=বায়ু, বায়ুতে: "গা ঢেলে দাও মধুর মলয় বায়."

বায়তুলমাল [A] *n* public exchequer/treasury.

বায়তুল্লাহ [A]*n* the House of Allah; the Holy Kaaba.

বায়না[১] [P] *n* **1** insistent and unreasonable/ capricious demand. **2** pretext; excuse; pretense; evasion.

বায়না[২] [P]*n* earnest money. ~ **করা** *vi* deposit/advance earnest money. ~**পত্র** *n* conditional agreement of bargain drawn up on payment of earnest money.

বায়নাক্কা *n* **1** detailed description; details. **2** fastidiousness; capriciousness; unreasonable insistence about details. **3** excuse; pretext.

বায়নামা, বয়নামা [P] *n*=বায়না-পত্র (⇒ বায়না).

বায়ব *adj* relating/belonging to wind or air; windy; airy; aerial; atmospheric; ethereal; pneumatic; air-like; gaseous; aerobic; aerological; unsubstantial; vaporous; rarefied. ~ **অবরোহ/মূল** *n* (bot) aerial root. ~ **প্রতিসরণ** *n* (astron) atmospheric refraction.

বায়বীয়=বায়ব

বায়বাকার *adj* aeriform

বায়ব্য=বায়ব. ~ **মূল্য**=বায়ব অবরোহ. **বায়ব্যাস্ত্র** *n* air-gun.

বায়স *n* crow.

বায়স্কোপ [E] *n* bioscope.

বায়া [A] *n* **1** (law) one who sells his rights. **2** a tabour used by the left hand.

বায়াত=বয়েত

বায়ু *n* **1** air; wind; breeze; atmosphere. **2** (Hindu phil) the wind of the body; vital air (of which five are reckoned). **3** (Ayu) the windy humour. **4** any morbid affectation of the windy humours. **5** wind as a kind of demon producing madness. **6** flatulence; neurosis. **অধিগ্রাহ্য** ~ *n* complemental air. **অধিত্যাজ্য** ~ *n* supplemental air. **অশুদ্ধ** ~ *n* impure air. **আদ্য** ~ *n* supplemental air. **আয়ন** ~ *n* trade-wind. **দূষিত** ~ *n* vitiated/polluted air. **নিয়ত** ~ *n* constant wind. **প্রত্যায়ন** ~ *n* anti-trade wind. **প্রবাহী** ~*n* tidal air. **প্রেক্ষগ্রাহ্য** ~ *n* complemental air. **বিদ্ধ** ~ *n* fresh air. **মুক্ত** ~ *n* open air. **শিষ্ট**~ *n* residual air. ~**কেতু** *n* dust. ~**কোণ** *n* north-west quarter. ~**কোষ** *n* air-cell. ~**গতি** *adj* swift as wind; fleet. ~**গতিবিদ্যা** *n* aerodynamics. ~**গর্ভ** *n* air-core. ~**গহ্বর** *n* air-pocket. ~**গ্রস্ত** *adj* affected by wind; mad; neurotic; flatulent; gouty. ~**খরচ** *n* windmill. ~**চলন,** ~**চলাচল** *nn* ventilation. ~**চাপ** *n* (phys) atmospheric pressure. ~**চোষক** *n* (phys) aspirator. ~**চ্ছেদ** *n* air-gap. ~**জীবী** *adj* (bot) aerobic. ~**তত্ত্ব** *n* pneumatics. ~**তনয়,** ~**নন্দন** *n* Hanumana. ~**তরঙ্গ** *n* wind-wave; current of air. ~**তাড়িত** *adj* wind-driven. ~**দেবতা** *n* the wind-god. ~**ধারকত্ব** *n* (chem) vital capacity. ~**নিয়ন্ত্রিত** *adj* air-conditioned. ~**নিস্কাশন-যন্ত্র** *n* air-pump. ~**পথ** *n* airway. ~**পরিবর্তন** *n* change of air. ~ **পরিবর্তন করা** *vi* go (to a new place) to have a change of air. ~**প্রবাহ** *n* air current; stream of air; gust of wind. ~**প্রেস**=~চাপ. ~**প্রেষক** *n* air-compressor. ~**প্রেষদৃক** *n* baroscope. ~**প্রেষলিক** *n* biograph. ~**বাহ** *n* smoke; vapour; cloud. ~**বেগ** *n* velocity/speed of wind. ~**বেগে** *adv* as speedily/swiftly as the wind. ~**বেগমাপক** *n* anemometer. ~**ভক্ষ** *adj* eating (only) air; living on air. ❑ *n* ascetic. ~**ভক্ষণ** *n* act of eating/living on air; fasting. ~**ভুক** *adj* feeding only on air. ❑*n* snake. ~**মণ্ডল** *n* atmosphere. ~**মণ্ডলীয়** *adj* atmospheric. ~**ময়** *adj* having the nature of wind or air; full of air. ~**মান,** ~**মানযন্ত্র** *nn* aerometer; barometer. ~**মানবিদ্যা** *n* aerometry. ~**মার্গ** *n* path/track of the wind; atmosphere. ~**যান** *n* aircraft. ~**বন্ধ্র** *n* air-pore; air-space. ~**রোগ** *n* neurosis; madness; flatulence. ~**রোগী** *n* neurotic; madman; maniac; patient of flatulence. ~**রোধী** *adj* airtight. ~**শকুন** *n* weather-cock. ~**সখ,** ~**সখা** *n* fire. ~**সঞ্চালন** *n* ventilation. ~**সম** *adj* swift as wind. ~ **সেবন করা** *vt* have (some) fresh air; go for an airing. ~ সেবনার্থ *adv* for an airing. ~স্তর *n* a layer of air. ~স্থলী *n* air-bladder. ~স্নান *n* air-bath. ~হীন *adj* destitute of wind.

বায়েত=বয়েত

বায়েন *n* **1** percussionist. **2** leading tomtom-player (of a band).

বায়োস্কোপ [E] *n* bioscope.

বার[১] (old use **বাহির,** often **বের**) *n* **1** outside; exterior: সে কেবল ভিতর ~ করছে. **2** presence: দেমাগে প্রায় তাঁর ~ পাওয়া যায় না, he is not available for a meeting. **3** interviewed: কবে থেকে খবর দিচ্ছি, তা তার আর ~ হয় না. ❑*adj* outer; external; exterior: ~ দিক থেকে দেখ, ~ বাড়ি. ❑*prep* outside; beyond (the limits of): সে এখন শাসনের ~ হয়ে পড়েছে. **~ করা** *vt* **1** bring out; draw out: চিঠিটা দেরাজ থেকে ~ করো. **2** expose; show; uncover: হাতটা ~ করো তো. **3** bare; lay bare. **4** reveal; express. **5** publish; bring out: বই ~ করা. **6** find out: ভুলটা ~ করতে পারো? **7** cause to elope with oneself: পরের বউ ~ করে আনা. **8** expel: দল থেকে ~ করা. **9** extract; press: রস ~ করা. **10** squeeze/wring out: নিংড়ে জল ~ করা. **11** drain out: ময়লা জল ~ করা. **12** unsheathe: তলোয়ার ~ করা. **13** let out; cause to flow out; bleed: রক্ত ~ করা. **14** expose; put an end to; punish for; exorcise (sth from)/(sb of); drive out: দোষ/ অপরাধ/ অন্যায়/ ন্যাকামো/ দুষ্টামি/ নষ্টামি/ পাগলামি/ ভূত ইত্যাদি ~ করা. **15** invent; devise: উপায়/ যন্ত্র/ ফ্যাশন/ অজুহাত ~ করা. **16** make famous: নাম ~ করা. **~ হওয়া** *vi* **1** come/go out: বইটা কোত্থেকে ~ হলো. **2** be exposed/uncovered. **3** bared; laid bare. **4** be revealed/expressed. **5** be published; be brought out. **6** be found out/detected/exposed. **7** elope; leave one's home (and take to prostitution). **8** be expelled/thrown out. **9** be extracted/ pressed. **10** be squeezed/wrung out. **11** be drained out. **12** be unsheathed/ drawn out. **13** ooze; sprout; flow out; come out; gush; squirt: রক্ত ~ হয়েছে. **14** germinate; sprout: অঙ্কুর ~ হওয়া. **15** be invented/devised. **16** be famous: নাম ~হয়েছে. **~দরিয়া** *n* high seas; the open seas. **~ফটকা**=~ মুখো. **~ফট্টাই**=বড়াই. **~ফট্টাই করা**=বড়াই করা. **~বাগে** *adv* **1** outside. **2** outside the house. **3** to a man/woman other than one's husband/wife. **~মুখ** *adj* facing outwards; external; outer. **~মুখো** *adj* (of a married man) given up to dissipated merrymaking away from one's dwelling-place; leading life of debauchery.

বার[২] [P] *n* royal court; court; hall of royal audience; holding of a court; appearance before applicants/visitors or in public. **~ দেওয়া** *vi* hold a court: রাজা আজ ~ দেবেন.

বার[৩] *n* **1** day (of the week). **2** fixed or allotted day: হাট ~, market-day. **3** daily religious rites. **4** turn: আমার বারেই যতো গণ্ডগোল. **5** time: একবার, দুবার. **6** occasion/opportunity for doing sth; time: এবারের মতো ক্ষান্ত হও. **~ করা** *vt* observed certain religious rites on Sunday, Monday or Tuesday. **~বার**=বারবার (⇒) **~বার তিন~** three times consecutively. **বারে বারে** each/every time.

বার[৪] [E] *n* bar. **~লাইব্রেরি** *n* bar-library.

বার[৫] *n* [P] burden; load. **~বরদার** *n* porter; traveller's luggage-carrying attendant. carrier; beast of burden. **~বরদারি** *n* **1** job of porter; service of a traveller's luggage attendant. **2** cost of conveyance; carriage; transport; porterage.

বার[৬], **বারো** *n adj* twelve. **~ই** *n* the twelfth day of a month; twelfth. ❑*adj* (of the days of a month) twelfth. **~ইয়ারি**=বারোয়ারি. **~দুয়ারি, ~দ্বারী** *adj* **1** having twelve gates/doors. **2** begging at many gates; seeking alms from many people. **~ভুঁইয়া, ~ভূঞা** *n* (hist) group of twelve feudal princes or landlords of Bengal who fought against the Mughal army for the independence. **~মাস** *n* twelve consecutive months; a year. ❑*adj* throughout the year; always ever. **~মাস ত্রিশ দিন** every day; daily; always. **~ মাসে তের পার্বণ** (lit) thirteen religious festivities in twelve months; (fig) too many (religious) festivities. **~ মতের** *n* various details; numerous minor articles. **~ হাত কাঁকুড়ের তের হাত বিচি** (Prov) (iron) (said of) sth disproportionately/excessively lengthy; oddity; monstrosity; instance of ungainly extravagance. **বারর মধ্যে তের** (iron) excessively numerous; more often than not; always; তিনি তো বার মাসের মধ্যে তের মাসই থাকেন অসুস্থ.

বারই *n* **1** person engaged in growing and selling betel-leaves. **2** Hindu caste occupied in growing and selling betel-leaves.

বারইয়ারি, বারইয়ারী=বারোয়ারি

বারংবার *adv* again and again; time and again; repeatedly.

বারক *n, adj* restrainer; opposer; obstacle; resistive; prohibitive.

বারকস *n* large wooden tray.

বারণ[১] *n* prohibition; prevention; resistance; restraining; warding off; resisting. **~ করা** *vt* prohibit; prevent; check; resist; restraint; ward off. **বারণীয়** *adj* to be checked/restrained/ prohibited; preventable; resistible. **বারণোপায়** *n* preventive measure.

বারণ[২] *n* elephant.

বারতা *n* (poet)=বার্তা

বারদরিয়া ⇒ বার[১]

বারদিগর *adv* (law) another/second time; again

বারদুয়ারি ⇒ বার[৬]

বারনারী=বারাঙ্গনা

বারফটকা=বারমুখো (⇒ বার[১])

বারফট্টাই=বড়াই[১]

বারবধূ, বারবনিতা=বারাঙ্গনা

বারবরদার ⇒ বার[৫]

বারবাণ *n* armour; suit of armour.

বারবার *adv* **1** many times. **2** time and again; again and again; repeatedly; often.

বারবিলাসিনী=বারাঙ্গনা

বারবেলা *n* (astron) **1** hours regarded as inauspicious for any work. **2** certain hours of the day regarded as inauspicious for undertaking any important work.

বারব্রত *n* prescribed holy rites for each day.

বারভুঁইয়া ⇒ বার[৬]

বারমাস ⇒ বার[৬]

বারমাসি, বারমাস্যা *n* (poet) a heroine's own account of her weal and woe described month by month. ❑*adj* existing/lasting all (the) year round.

বারমুখী, বারমুখ্যা *n fem* chief of a number of harlots.

বারমুখো ⇒ বার[১]

বারমেসে *adj*=grown/occurring throughout the year: ~ তাল, ~ দুঃখ/ ব্যাপার.

বারযোষিৎ=বারাঙ্গনা

বারয়িতা *n* prohibitor; prohibiter; preventer. বারয়িত্রী *fem.*

বারশিঙা, বারশিঙ্গা *adj* having twelve horns. ❑*n* kind of deer having six branches in either of its two horns.

বারস্ত্রী=বারাঙ্গনা

বারা *vt* (poet) prevent; prohibit; resist; ward off.

বারাঙ্গনা *n* prostitute; whore; courtesan; woman of easy virtue; street walker; trollop; slut; woman of the town; white slave.

বারাণ্ডা=বারান্দা

বারান্তর *n* another time; different occasion. বারান্তরে *adv* another time; on a different occasion.

বারান্দা [P] *n* verandah; balcony; gallery.

বারাহ *adj* relating to/coming from/belonging to a boar.

বারাষে, বারাসিয়া, বারাসে⇒বারমাসি

বারি[১] *n* water; rain; fluid; fluidity. ~চর *adj* living in or near water; aquatic. ❑*n* aquatic animal. ~জ *adj* born/produced in or by water. ❑*n* lotus. ~তস্কর *n* pirate. ~দ *adj* giving water or rain. ❑*n* rain-cloud. ~ধি, ~নাথ, ~বিধি *nn* sea; ocean. ~পথ *n* water-way. ~পর্ণী *n* kind of algae; *Pistia stratiotes*. ~পাত *n* rainfall; shower of rain. ~প্রবাহ *n* **1** waterfall; cascade. **2** stream/current of water. ~বাহ *n* rain-cloud. ~বিহঙ্গ *n* aquatic bird. ~মণ্ডল *n* hydrosphere. ~রাশি *n* great mass of water.

বারি[২] *n* **1** place for tying/catching an elephant. **2** rope for tying an elephant. **3** (archaic) captive; prisoner. **4** water-pot; pitcher; jar.

বারিক[১] [E] *n* barrack.

বারিক[২] [P] *n* fine; thin; slender; beautiful.

বারিত *adj* prohibited; warded off; prevented; hindered; impeded; restrained.

বারীন্দ্র, বারীশ *nn* ocean.

বারুই *n* (colloq)=বারই

বারুজীবী *n*=বারই

বারুণ *adj* **1** relating to/belonging to Varuna. **2** relating to sea or water; marine; aquatic; oceanic. **3** western. **4** water. **5** broom-stick.

বারুণি *n* **1** son of Varuna, eg Agastya. **2** spirituous liquor.

বারুণী *n fem* **1** particular kind of spirit (prepared from hogweed mixed with the juice of date or palm and distilled); any spirituous liquor. **2** the goddess of spirituous liquor Varuna's female energy. **3** (astron) Uranus. **4** the western quarter region.

বারুদ [T] *n* gun-powder. ~খানা *n* powder magazine.

বারেক *adv* (chiefly poet) once; only once; but for once.

বারেন্দ্র *n* **1** a native of ancient Gauda or North Bengal. **2** one of a class of Bengali Brahmin.

বারো=বার[৬]

বারোয়াঁ, বারোঁয়া *n* an Indian musical mode.

বারোয়ারি *adj* **1** (lit) done/organized collectively by twelve friends. **2** performed by the public for the public; joint; combined; collective; public. ~তলা/খোলা *n* place where a public/collective worship is organized.

বার্ণিক *n* **1** writer; scribe. **2** painter. ❑*n* **1** relating to a sound or letter. **2** literal.

বার্তা *n* **1** an account of anything that has happened; report; story of/about; tidings. **2** message; news; intelligence; information; dispatch. **3** exchange of words; discussion: তার সঙ্গে বার্তালাপ কিছুই হয়নি. **4** livelihood; business; profession. ~জীবী *n* journalist. ~নীতি=~শাস্ত্র. ~বহ *n* **1** messenger; courier; emissary; spy. **2** reporter; correspondent. বার্তায়ন *n* **1**=~বহ (1),(2). **2** economics. বার্তায়নশাস্ত্র *n* economics.

বার্তাকু, বার্তাকী, বার্তাক *n* brinjal; aubergine.

বার্তিক *n* **1** relating to news, report, message, etc. **2** journalist. **3** relating to profession; professional. **4** critical gloss or annotation.

বার্ধক *n* super-annuation.

বার্ধক্য *n* old age; declining years. ~গ্রস্ত *n* old; decrepit; senile.

বার্ধুষি, বার্ধুষিক *n* usurer.

বার্ধুষ্য *n* usury.

বার্নিশ [E] *n* varnish. ~ করা *vt* varnish.

বার্য *adj* preventable; to be prohibited. **~মান** *adj* being prevented/prohibited.

বার্লি [E] *n* barley.

বার্ষিক[1] *adj* annual; yearly. ❑*n* **1** annual salary or rent; annuity. **2** annual grant/pension. **3** annual publication/issue (of a periodical). **4** anniversary. **~ গতি** *n* annual motion. **~ লম্বন** *n* annual parallax. **~ বৃত্তি** *n* annuity.

বার্ষিক[2] *adj* **1** relating/belonging to rainy season. **2** to be given or received in the rainy season.

বার্ষিকী *n* **1** a ceremony to be held annually; annual. **2** annual publication or issue (of a periodical).

বার্ষুক *adj* raining.

বাল[1] *n* male child; boy. ❑*adj* (in compounds) **1** young; childish; infantile; not full grown or developed. **2** newly risen; early; new; waxing. **3** puerile; ignorant; simple; foolish. **4** pure. **~কাণ্ড** *n* the first book of the Ramayana. **~ক্রীড়া** *n* a child's play/amusement; boyish sport. **~গর্ভিণী** *n* cow with calf for the first time. **~গোপাল** *n* a youthful herdsman. **~গ্রহ** *n* kind of demon (said to cause possessions) **~চর্য** *n* behaviour of a child. **~চর্যা** *n* act of bringing up children; childcare. **~চাপল্য** *n* childish frivolities. **~তৃণ** *n* young grass. **~ধন** *n* property of a minor/infant. **~বাচ্চা** *n* young/infant children; kiddies; little ones. **~বাহ্য** *adj* portable by a child; light. **~বিধবা** *n* child-widow. **~বৈধব্য** *n* widowhood at a very early age. **~ভাষিত** *n* baby-talk; childlike talk; prattle; (fig) utterance of no importance; babble. **~ভোগ** *n* (facet) breakfast. **~ভোজ্য** *n* children's food; pease. ❑*adj* fit for children's consumption. **~মূষিক** *n* small rat. **~রাজ** *n* **1** child-king. **2** lapis lazuli. **~রোগ** *n* children's disease. **~শশী** *n* the moon of the second lunar night of a light fortnight. **~সুলভ** *adj* childish; childlike. **~সূর্য** *n* **1** the newly risen sun. **2** lapis lazuli.

বাল[2] *n* **1** (vulg) pubic hair. **2** hair of any animal's tail. **3** any hair or tail. **~কৃমি** *n* louse.

বালক *n* **1** boy; male child; child. **2** tyro; greenhorn. ❑*adj* ignorant; inexperienced; silly. **বালিকা** *fem.* **~কাল** *n* boyhood; childhood days. **~তা, ~ত্ব** *nn* **1** boyhood. **2** immaturity; inexperience. **~ভৃত্য** *n* boy-servant; page. **~সুলভ** *adj* boyish; childish.

বালকীয় *adj* childish; infantile; puerile.

বালকোচিত *adj* boyish; childish; silly; foolish.

বালতি [Pg] *n* pail; bucket.

বালদো *n* frond.

বালব [E] *n* (electric) bulb.

বালসা, বালশা *n* children's disease (fever, diarrhoea, etc). **~নো, ~ন** *vi* (of a child) become ill; catch cold; have fever.

বালা[1] *n fem* **1** young girl; maiden; female child; girl. **2** woman. **3** wife under 16 years of age. **4** young woman of a delicate frame. **5** full-grown young woman. **6** a beauty; belle. **7** daughter.

বালা[2] *n* ring/armlet/bracelet (worn on the wrist).

বালা[3] [A]*n*=বালাই. **~মসিবত** *n* misfortunes and difficulties.

বালাই [A] *n* **1** calamity; misfortune; distress; danger; harm; an awful and terrible thing: এতো বড়ো ~ তোমার উপর! **2** evil; ill; vice; enormity: ছেলেমেয়ে মানুষ হলো না, এমন ~ কি আর আছে? **3** obstacle; hindrance: আর সবাইকে ঠিক করেছি, কিন্তু আমার স্ত্রীই হয়েছে বড়ো ~. **~ নিয়ে মরা** die taking away with oneself all harm that may happen to another. **আপদ~** *n* **1** misfortunes; calamities; great obstacles. **2** person or thing causing extreme distress and anxieties; plague; pest; a thorn in one's flesh/side. **রোগ~** *n* afflictions and calamities. **~ ষাট** *int* (expressing extreme affection and concern for a dear one) God forbid.

বালাখানা [P] *n* **1** upper room; upper storey. **2** (high-rise) building; palace.

বালাকি=বালামচি

বালাপোশ, বালাপোষ [P] *n* kind of light wrapper stuffed with cotton.

বালাভোলা *adj* **1** disorderly; ruffled. **2** not disciplined; wayward; dissolute. **3** simple; artless; innocent; ingenuous. **4** old.

বালাম *n* **1** a large boat used in carrying rice in Barisal district. **2** boat for carrying a fine variety of rice (called balam). **3** a fine variety of rice.

বালাম[2] [E] *n* volume.

বালামচি *n* hair of a cow's or horse's tail (esp horse's tail).

বালার্ক *n* newly risen sun.

বালি[1] *n* sand; gravel. **~চর** *n* sand-bed; shoal of sand. **~ ধরানো** *vt* (in building construction) plaster. **~র বাঁধ** *n* **1** (lit) dike made of sand. **2** (fig) ineffectual action/measure; transitory object; deceptive foundation; gossamer; cobweb; empty promise; pie in the sky; hot air; house of cards: এই প্রবল আক্রমণ কি ~র বাঁধ দিয়ে ঠেকাবে ভেবেছ? বড়োর পীরিতি ~র বাঁধ. **গুড়ে ~** (fig) disappointment; a fly in the ointment. **চোখের ~** object of hatred or dislike; anathema; bite noire; rotter; an abomination.

বালি[2] *n* (poet; archaic)=বালিকা

বালিকা *n* **1** female child. **2** girl; maiden. **3** virgin; young woman. **4** ignorant/inexperienced woman. **~বধূ** *n* child-wife. **~বয়স** *n* girlhood; youthhood; teens. **~সুলভ** *adj* girlish; maidenly; girly; maidenlike.

বালিগ [A] *adj* having attained puberty/ reached the age of maturity.

বালিঘট *n* jar (full) of sand. ❑*n* adult.

বালিঘড়ি *n* sand-glass.

বালিয়াড়ি *n* dune; sand-hill.

বালিশ[১] [P] *n* pillow; cushion; bolster. **কোল~, পাশ~** *n* side-pillow.

বালিশ[২] young; ignorant; childish; puerile.

বালু *n*=বালি. **~চর**=বালিচর. **~ঝড়** *n* sand-storm. **~প্রস্তর, ~শিলা** *nn* sandstone.

বালুকা *n*=বালি. **~কৃষি** *n* sand-culture. **~তট** *n* sandy shore. **~ময়** *adj* consisting or made of sand; full of sand; sandy.

বালুশাই *n* kind of sweet made of curd and sugar.

বালেগ=বালিগ

বালেন্দু *n* **1** the moon of second lunar night of the light fortnight. **2** crescent. **~ শৃঙ্গ** *n* horns of the crescent.

বাল্য *n* childhood; infancy; boyhood or girlhood. **~কাল** *n* period/ age of childhood; babyhood. **~চাপল্য** *n* childish frivolities/ whims/ frivolity/ flippancy. **~প্রণয়, ~ প্রেম** *nn* calf-love; childhood friend-ship. **~বন্ধু** *n* friend of one's childhood days. **~বিবাহ** *n* child-marriage; early marriage. **~শিক্ষা** *n* primary education. **~সখা, ~সঙ্গী, ~সহচর, ~মহৎ** *nn*=~বন্ধু. **বাল্যাবস্থা** *n* childhood.

বাশ *n*=বাইশ[২]

বাষট্টি *n, adj* sixty-two.

বাষ্প *n* **1** vapour; steam. **2** tear; tears. **3** anger; rage; excitement. **4** (fig) faintest knowledge/ appearance; an inkling of; ghost; shadow; slightest idea: এ বিষয়ে বাষ্পমাত্র জানি না. **~ হওয়া** *vi* be vaporized; evaporate. **~গদগদ** *adj* choked with tears. **~গাহ** *n* vapour-bath. **~চালিত** *adj* steam-driven. **~টান** *n* (phys) steam-tension. **~তরী** *n* steam-vessel; steamer; steam-ship. **~দাহ** *n* scald. **~পর্যাকুল** *adj* suffused with tears. **~পোত** *n*=~তরী. **~বিন্দু** *n* tear-drop. **~বৃষ্টি** *n* shower of tears. **~মান** *n* hygrometer; gasometer. **~মোচন** *n* shedding of tears. **~মান, ~রথ, ~শকট** *nn* steam-driven vehicle; railway train. **~স্নান** *n* vapour-bath **বাষ্পাকার** *adj* in the form of vapour; vaporous. **বাষ্পাকুল, বাষ্পাপুত** *adjj* dimmed/ interrupted by tear; tearful. **বাষ্পীকরণ, বাষ্পীভবন** *nn* vaporization; evaporation. **বাষ্পীকৃত, বাষ্পীভূত** *adj* vaporized; evaporated.

বাষ্পীয় *adj* relating to vapour/ steam; steam-driven; vaporous; vapoury. **~ পোত** *n*=বাষ্পপোত. **~ যন্ত্র** *n* steam engine. **~যান, ~রথ, ~শকট**=বাষ্পযান.

বাস=বস[১]

বাস[১] [E] *n* bus; omnibus.

বাস[২] *n* **1** habitation; settlement: যেখানে কোনো মানুষের ~ নেই. **2** house; dwelling; home; abode: এখানেই আমাদের ~. **3** stay; staying; residence: remaining: বিদেশ ~. **4** refuge; haven. **~ করা** *vi* live; dwell ; abide; settle; reside; stay. **~গৃহ** *n* dwelling-house. **~ তোলা** *vi,vt* move; move house; change residence. **~ বাঁধা** *vi* settle (down); abide; be permanent. **~যোগ্য** *adj* habitable; livable (in).

বাস[৩] *n* cloth; clothing; garment; raiment; habiliments; attire; garb; covering.

বাস[৪] *n* **1** perfume; scent; fragrance. **2** smell; odour. **3** (fig) trail; clue; hint; smell: সে এখানে টাকাপয়সার ~ পেয়েছে. **~যোগ** *n* powder formed of various fragrant substances.

বাসক[১] *n* a medicinal plant; *Gendarussa vulgaris.*

বাসক[২] *adj* perfuming; fumigating.

বাসক[৩] *n* sleeping-room; bed-chamber. **~শয়ন** *n* lying in the bedchamber. **~সজ্জা, ~সজ্জিকা** *nn* woman who embellishes herself and her bedchamber to receive her lovers/ husband.

বাসকক্ষ *n* bedroom; bedchamber.

বাসগৃহ ⇒ বাস[২]

বাসঘর=বাসগৃহ

বাসন[১] *n* **1** vessel; container. **2** utensil. **3** plate; dish; platter. **~কোশন** *n pl* crockery; utensils.

বাসন[২] *n* act of perfuming or fumigating.

বাসন[৩] *n* **1** habitating; dwelling. **2** causing to abide/ dwell.

বাসন[৪] *n* covering; garment; dress; clothing.

বাসনা[১] *n* **1** longing for; desire; inclination. **2** expectation. **3** wish; intention. **4** (psych) impression of anything remaining unconsciously in the mind; present consciousness of past perceptions; knowledge derived from memory. **5** imagination; fancy. **6** liking; respectful regard; inclination; trust. **~কুল** *adj* filled/ agitated with passion/ desire.

বাসনা[২] *n* **1** dried leaf or spathe of the banana and similar plants. **2** (colloq) perfume; scent.

বাসন্ত *adj* **1** relating to or produced in the spring season; vernal. **2** being in the spring of life; youthful. **3** south wind; vernal breeze. **4** cuckoo.

বাসন্তি *adj* vernal.

বাসন্তিক *adj* **1** relating to spring; vernal. **2** actor; dancer; the buffoon in a drama.

বাসন্তী *adj fem* **1** vernal. **2** light orange-coloured; light yellow-coloured. ❑*n* **1** name of various plants; a kind of jasmine; *Biganonia suaveolens* . **2** light-orange colour. **3** goddess Durga. **~ পূজা** *n* spring festival when goddess Durga is worshipped.

বাসব *n* Indra, the king of gods. **বাসবী** *n fem* Indra's wife, Indrani.

বাসভবন *n* dwelling-house; residence (esp an official one).

বাসমতি=variety of fragrant rice.

বাসর[১] *n* day; week-day; gathering on a particular day: জন্ম~, রবি~. **বাসরীয়** *adj* pertaining to (particular) day: রবিবাসরীয়.

বাসর, বাসরঘর *n* nuptial chamber; bride-chamber. **~জাগানি** *n* money obtained from the bridegroom or his party for keeping vigil in the nuptial chamber. **~শয্যা** *n* nuptial/ bridal bed. **~সজ্জা** *n*=বাসকশয্যা.

বাসা[১] *n* **1** house; dwelling; residence; home; dwelling-place. **2** rented or temporary residence; lodging-house. **3** nest; habitat. **4** den; lair. **5** (derog) haunt; den; hotbed: দুর্নীতির ~, চোরডাকাতের ~. **~ড়ে** *n* lodge. **~বাটি, ~বাড়ি** *n* lodging-house.

বাসা[২]=বাসক[১]. **~রিষ্ট** (Ayu) Ayurvedic tonic containing essence of Vasak.

বাসা[৩] *vi,vt* **1** (poet) love: "আমি নিশিদিন তোমায় ভালোবাসি, তুমি অবসর মতো বাসিয়ো". **2** (old use) like; long for; desire: যুবতী বুড়ায় নাঞি বাসে". **3** (old use) consider; deem; "কেমনে বাসিবে পর". **4** (old use): বাসি ভয়/দুঃখ/লাজ.

বাসি[১], **বাসী** *adj* **1** stale; not fresh; having passed the night; vapid/ tasteless: ~ দুধ/মাংস/ভাত. **2** used/ made/ collected. overnight: ~ কাপড়. **3** withered; faded: ~ ফুল. **~কাপড়** *n* cloth used overnight. **~ঘর** *n* a room which has not tidied up in the morning. **~জল** *n* water collected overnight; water left in the open overnight. **~দুগ্ধ** *n* milk which was collected earlier. **~ফুল** *n* **1** flower picked a day or long before. **2** flower used overnight. **~বিবাহ** *n* solemnities to be performed on the morning following the wedding night. **~ভাত** *n* stale rice. **~মড়া** *n* deadbody which has not been buried or cremated in due course. **~মুখ** *n* a person's face and mouth before washing and taking his breakfast. **~মুখে জল দেওয়া** wash oneself and have breakfast after fasting overnight. **~হাত** *n* hand which has not been washed after eating.

বাসি[২] *adj* **1** (of clothing) washed. **2** (old use) washed and scented. **~ করা** *vt* wash. **~করা** *adj* washed.

বাসি[৩] *n*=বাইশ

বাসিত[১] *adj* perfumed; scented.

বাসিত[২] *adj* clothed; dressed. **বাসিতা** *fem* of বাসী.

বাসিন্দা [P] *n* inhabitant; resident.

বাসী[১] ⇒ বাসি[১]

বাসী[২] (used as a *suff*) inhabiting; dwelling; residing. **বাসিনী** *fem.*

বাসুকি *n* (myth) the snake-king.

বাসুদেব *n* Sri Krishna.

বাসোপযোগী *adj* habitable; inhabitable; livable.

বাস্তব *adj* **1** true; real, genuine; substantial; actual. **2** (phil) real; material; objectives. **3** (math) real. ❑*n* **1** truth; reality. **2** (phys) objective. **~ তথ্য** *n* facts and figures. **~তা** *n* reality; substantiality; genuineness; objectivity; factuality; actuality. **~বাদ** *n* realism; objectivism; materialism. **~বাদী** *adj* realistic; objectivistic; materialistic. ❑*n* realist; objectivist; materialist.

বাস্তবিক *adj* real; true; actual; sure. ❑*adv* really; indeed. **~তা** *n* reality; genuineness; substantiality; truth. **~পক্ষে** *adv* as a matter of fact; indeed.

বাস্তব্য *adj* habitable; livable. **~বিদ্যা** *n* (biol) ecology.

বাস্তু *n* **1** site or foundation of a house; site; ground. **2** dwelling-place; building; habitation; homestead; house. **3** ancestral homestead. **4** buildings and works. **5** (iron) person living in a place or a community or being given shelter in a family for a long time; pupil who fails to pass examinations and remains in the same school for a long time; fixture. **6**=বাস্তুক. **~কর্ম** *n* house-building; public works. **~কার** *n* architect; civil engineer. **~কৃত্যক** *n* engineering service. **~গৃহ** *n* permanent and ancestral home-stead. **~ঘুঘু** *n* **1** kind of dove which builds its nest in a homestead and goes about for food all around. **2** (fig) wicked person taking up his abode with a family and bringing about its ruin; snake in the grass. **~দেবতা, ~পুরুষ** *n* deity presiding over a house; guardian/ titular deity of a homestead or family. **~বিদ্যা** *n* architecture. **~ভিটা** *n* ancestral homestead. **~যাগ** *n* sacrifice performed before the construction of a house. **~সংস্থান** *n* provision for dwelling. **~সাপ** *n* snake that lives permanently in a homestead and becomes harmless. **বাস্তুক** *n* the pot-herb *Chenopodium album.*

-বাহ *suff* denoting: bearing, carrying, conveying.

বাহক *n* **1** carrier; bearer; conveyer; porter. **2** charioteer. ❑*adj* carrying; bearing; conveying.

বাহন *n* **1** any vehicle/ conveyance/ draught-animal; carriage; chariot; horse; elephant; any animal. **2** medium; vehicle: শিক্ষার ~.**2** (the act of) carrying; bearing; conveying; drawing. ❑*suff* denoting riding/ mounting on: বৃষ ~.

বাহবা, বাহা *int* **1** (expressing surprise) oh. **2** (expresses encouragement)=বাঃ (1). ❑*n* praise; applause: acclaim: লোকের ~র লোভে কাজ করলে চলবে না.

বাহা *vi, vt* (liter; old style)=বাওয়া[১].

বাহাত্তর *n* , *adj* seventy-two. **বাহাত্তুরে** *adj* **1** (pejor) aged seventy-two years. **2** senile; very old; dotard. **বাহাত্তুরে ধরা** *vi* be in one's dotage.

বাহাদুর [P] *adj* **1** brave; bold; valiant; courageous; high-spirited. **2** skilled; skilful;

adroit; adept. ☐*n* **1** hero. **2** a title equivalent to 'Honorable': খান~; রাজা~.

বাহাদুরি [P] *n* **1** bravery; heroism; valour. **2** skill; adroitness; credit; praiseworthiness. **3** great feat/ achievement. **4** (derog) bravado; swashbuckling. **~ করা** *vi* make a display of skill/ bravery; brag; vaunt. **~ দেওয়া** *vt* give credit; applaud; acclaim; commend. **~ দেখানো** *vi* make a show of skill/ courage; swank; swagger. **~কাঠ, ~কাষ্ঠ** *n* hard wood; timber. **~ কাঠের আবাদ** *n* arboriculture.

বাহানা [P] *n* **1** excuse; pretent; pretense; evasion; contrivance; affectation. **2** insistent and capricious demand. **3** cause; reason. **4** deceit; feint. **~বাজ** *adj* deceitful; pretender; adept in making excuses. **~ করা** *vi* make an excuse; pretend; evade; seek an excuse.

বাহান্ন *n adj* fifty-two. **যাহা ~ তাহা তিপান্ন** (fig) the difference is too small to merit serious attention; it makes little difference.

বাহার [P] *n* **1** beauty; glory; bloom elegance; glamour; flourishing state; beautiful show/ exhibition; ostentatious display. **2** an Indian musical mode. **3** delight; enjoyment. **4** spring. **~ দেওয়া** *vt* decorate/ embellish elegantly or ostentatiously. **গুল~** *n* piece of delicately embroidered/ diapered cloth.

বাহারি [P] *adj* beautiful; showy; flashy; ostentatious; glamourous; flamboyant; dashing.

বাহাল ⇒ **বহাল**

বাহাস [A] *n* disputation; dispute; debate; argument.

বাহিক *n* **1** car/ vehicle drawn by oxen. **2** large drum. ☐*adj* carrying/drawing.

বাহিত *adj* **1** carried; borne; conveyed; transported. **2** driven; rowed; paddled; propelled; steered.

বাহিনী[1] *n* **1** division of an army consisting of 81 elephants, 81 chariots, 243 horses and 405 foot. **2** army; host; body of forces. **3** river.

বাহিনী[2] *fem* (used as *suff* denoting) conveying/ driving along; drawing; flowing; streaming; causing to flow; shedding; bearing along; wafting; bringing; causing; producing; effecting; carrying; bearing; wearing; having; possessing; undergoing; performing; practising.

বাহির=বার[2]. **~ করা**=বের করা. **~ হওয়া**=বের হওয়া. **~সমুদ্র** *n* high seas. **বাহিরান** *vi* (poet)=বের হওয়া. **বাহিরে**=বাইরে. **বাহিরে/বাইরে যাওয়া** *vi* **1** go out. **2** go on an excursion or for a stroll. **3** go abroad. **4** go out to relieve oneself. **5** go beyond control.

বাহী=বাহ

বাহু *n* **1** arm; fore-arm. **2** (mech) arm (of a couple). **3** (geom) arm; side. **~গর্ব** *n* pride in one's physical strength. **~গর্বী** *adj* proud of one's physical strength. **~ত্র, ~ত্রাণ** *n* armour for the arms; gauntlet. **~দর্পিত, ~দর্পী. ~দৃপ্ত** *adjj*=~গর্বী. **~বন্ধ** *n* armlet; bracelet. **~ভঙ্গি** *n* bending/ twisting the arms. **~বল** *n* strength of arm; power; might. **~বলদৃপ্ত** *adj* proud of physical strength/ prowess. **~ভূষণ, ~ভূষা** *nn* ornament for arm; armlet. **~মূল** *n* armpit. **~যুগল** *n pl* pair of arms. **~যুদ্ধ** *n* close fight; wrestling; scuffle. **~শালী** *adj* possessing strong arms.

বাহুল্য *n* abundance; plenty; multitude; variety; superfluity; excess; redundancy. **(এ কথা) বলা ~ (যে)** it is needless to say (that); it goes without saying (that). **~বোধে** *adv* considering it superfluous/ unnecessary.

বাহ্বাস্ফোট *n* slapping of one's arms as a show of one's strength or abilities (eg in wrestling); vaunt; bragging; swank.

বাহ্য[1] *adj* to be (or being) drawn/ driven/ ridden/ carried; borne; portable; bearable. ☐*n* any vehicle or a beast of burden. **~মান** *adj* **1** carrying; drawing; bearing. **2** being carried/ drawn/ borne.

বাহ্য[2] *adj* being outside (a door, house, etc); outward; situated without; outer; exterior; superficial; external. ☐*n* outside; exterior: কেবল বাহ্যটা দেখলেই চলে না. **~ কৃত্য** *n* evacuation/ defecation in the morning. **~জগৎ** *n* external world; material world. **~জ্ঞান** *n* knowledge of the external world; sense-perception; consciousness; worldly wisdom. **~জ্ঞানবাহিত, ~জ্ঞানশূন্য** *adjj* deprived of consciousness of one's surroundings (in a state of rage, in a daze, etc); stupefied; beside oneself; astounded; rapt; bewildered; frenzied; hysterical; frantic; incensed. **~ত, ~তঃ** *adv* externally; outwardly; superficially; apparently. enraged. **~তা, ~ত্ব** *nn* the state of being outside; exclusion; exteriority; outwardness; externality. **~দৃষ্টি** *n* outward/ external view; materialistic point of view. **~দৃশ্য** *n* external/ outward view or form. **~বস্তু** *n* material object; external wealth/ riches. **বাহ্যে যাওয়া** *vi* go out for defecation.

বাহ্য[3]=বাহ্যে

বাহ্যিক=*adj* external; outward; material; extrinsic; superficial.

বাহ্যে *n* **1** excreta; faeces; excrement; stool. **2** defecation; evacuation; bowels movement. **~ করা** *vi* defecate; evacuate (the bowels); relieve oneself; (of infants) soil. **~ করানো** *vt* purge another's bowels; relieve. **~পাওয়া** *vi* have a bowel movement. **~ যাওয়া** ⇒ বাহ্য.

বাহ্যেন্দ্রিয় *n* outer organ of sense (eye. ear. etc).

বি- *pref* expresses: division, distinction, distribution, arrangement, order, opposition, deliberation, absence, badness.

বিউগ্‌ল [E] *n* bugle.

বিউনি, বিউনী *n* (dial)=বিনুনি

বিউনি, বিউনী *n* **1** frond of the fanpalm. **2** fan.

বিউলি, বিউলী *n* variety of husked pigeon-pea.

বি এ, বি. এ. [E] B. A.

বি. এল. [E] B. L.

বি. এস-সি [E] B. Sc.

বিংশ *adj* twenty; score; twentieth: ~ শতাব্দী. **~ক** *adj* accompanied/ increased by twenty; twenty. ❑*n* number twenty. **~তি** *n, adj*=~. **~তিতম** *adj* twentieth. **~তিতমী** *fem.*

বিঁড়া=বিড়া

বিঁদ *n* small hole; dot; point; prick **~কি** minute dot.

বিঁধ *n* hole; bore; perforation. **~ করা** *vt* make a hole; bore; perforate. **~ন** *n* **1** boring; perforation. **2** pricking.

বিঁধা *vt* **1** be pierced/ pricked. **2** pierce; prick. **3** perforate; bore. **~নো, ~ন** *vt* **1** pierce; prick. **2** perforate; bore. **3** cause to be pierced/ pricked/ bored.

বিকচ[1] *adj* (poet) opened; blown; blooming. **2** shining; resplendent; radiant with; having radiant beauty; with a radiant face: বিকচাননা, ~ পুষ্পদল.

বিকচ[2] *adj* hairless; bald.

বিকচোন্মুখ *adj* about to burst/ open out.

বিকচ্ছ *adj* not having the part of the cloth which the weaver tucks behind him between his legs; having that part of the cloth unfastened.

বিকট *adj* **1** huge; large; great. **2** monstrous; horrible, dreadful. **3** large-toothed. **4** deformed; disfigured. **~দর্শন** *n* monstrous-looking; of a frightful shape. **~মূর্তি, বিকটাকার, বিকটাকৃতি** *adjj* having a hideous/ distorted shape; of dreadful appearance; **বিকটানন, ~বদন** *adjj* ugly-faced; hideous.

বিকত্থন *n* **1** boasting; bragging. **2** boaster; braggart.

বি. কম. [E] B. Com.

বিকম্প *n* trembling; heaving. **~ন** *n*=~.

বিকম্পিত *adj* trembling; tremulous; shaking; agitated; unsteady; rudely shaken.

বিকরাল *adj* dreadful; hideous; monstrous.

বিকরুণ *adj* cruel; brutal; atrocious; hard-hearted; merciless.

বিকর্ণ *adj* earless; deaf.

বিকর্ণিক *adj* (of flowers) having no pollen-tube.

বিকর্তন *n* sun.

বিকর্ষণ *n* **1** pull in the opposite direction. **2** attraction. **3** (mech) repulsion. **~ করা** *vt* repulse.

বিকল *adj* **1** deprived of a limb/part/ member; mutilated; maimed; lamed; crippled: বিকলাঙ্গ. **2** impaired; ruined: ~ স্বাস্থ্য. **3** exhausted; disabled: ~ দেহ. **4** agitated; confused; depressed; sorrowful; exhausted: ~ মন. **5** harried; despondent; distraught; anguished; hart-broken; dejected: ~ প্রাণ. **6** out of order/service: যন্ত্রটা ~. **~ করা** *vt* maim; mutilate; impair; ruin; disable; exhaust; depress ; harry; harrow; make distraught/ distraught/ dejected; anguish; deject; confuse; overwhelm; put out of order. **~ হওয়া** *vi* be crippled/ maimed/ confused; be out of order etc. **~চিত্ত** *adj* dejected; distraught; distracted. **~তা, ~ত্ব** *nn* mutilation; exhaustion; impairment; ruin; infirmity, agitation; confusion; distraction; dejection; despondency; unserviceable/ disordered state; break-down. **বিকলা** *fem.*

বিকলন *n* debit.

বিকলা *n* second; the 60th part of minute of time.

বিকলাঙ্গ *adj* crippled; having defective limbs; deformed; disabled; lame. ❑*n* cripple.

বিকলি *n*=বিকলতা (⇒ বিকল)

বিকলেন্দ্রিয় *adj* having impaired/ defective organs of sense; deformed; crippled.

বিকল্প *n* **1** alternative; substitute. **2** option. **3** alternative concept; difference of perception. **4** doubt; hesitation. **5** collateral form. **6** dilemma. **7** (gram) variant; doublet. **8** (phil) antithesis of opposites; fancy. **9** false notion. **~ প্রমাণ** *n* alternative proof. **~ন** *n* substitution; allowing an option/ alternative; use of a collateral form. **বিকল্পিত** *adj* prepared; arranged; substituted; doubtful.

বিকশন *n*=বিকাশ

বিকশিত, বিকসিত *adj* **1** opened; open; budded; blown: ~ ফুল. **2** displayed; exhibited: ~ দন্তপঙ্‌ক্তি. **3** developed: ~ বুদ্ধি. **4** expanded:~ ব্যবসা-বাণিজ্য. **5** manifested: ~ মহিমা. **6** opened; widened: ~ চক্ষু. **~ করা** *vt* open; blow; display; exhibit; develop; expand; manifest; widen. **~ হওয়া** *vi* be opened; develop; bloom; arise; widen.

বিকানো, বিকান *vi* **1** sell; be sold. **2** (fig) capitulates; give away; bow to; yield: আত্মসম্মান ~. **3** be accepted/ received; gain currency; sell. **নামে ~** (of worthless goods or persons) sell/ find buyers or admirers by virtue of its/ one's name or title.

বিকার *n* **1** change of form or nature; alternation or deviation from any natural state.. **2** perversion; perversity; depravity; aberration:

চরিত্র~, বুদ্ধি~, রুচি~. **3** change (esp for the worse) of bodily/ mental condition; disease; sickness; morbidity; perturbation; agitation; passion; derangement: মস্তিস্ক~. **4** delirium: জ্বর~. **5** decomposition; decay. **6** corruption. **7** transformation. **8** apparition; spectre. **9** darkness. **বিকারী** *adj* **1** altered/ changed for the words; spoiled; corrupted; perverted. **2** corrupting; producing a change for the worse. **3** liable to change ; changeable; variable. **~ক** *n* (chem) reagent. **~করশ্মি** *n* (phys) actinic ray. **~গ্রস্ত** *adj* perverted; perverse; depraved; aberrant; morbid; delirious. **~তত্ত্ব** *n* pathology. **~তাত্ত্বিক** *adj* pathological. ❑*n* pathologist. **~প্রাপ্ত** *adj* changed; converted; altered; transformed.

বিকার্য *adj* to be changed; prone/ liable to change; changeable.

বিকাল, বিকালবেলা *n* afternoon.

বিকাশ, বিকাশন *nn* **1** manifestation; appearance, display: বুদ্ধির ~. **2** expansion; extension; development: শিক্ষার ~. **3** uncovering; opening; display; widening; দন্তনেত্র ~. **4** blooming. **~ পাওয়া**=বিকশিত হওয়া (⇒ বিকশিত).

বিকাশা, বিকাসা *vt* (poet)=বিকশিত করা (⇒ বিকশিত)

বিকাশোন্মুখ *adj* on the point of being manifested/ displayed/exhibited; on the point of development; on the point of opening/ widening/ blooming.

বিকি *n* sale. **~কিনি** *n* buying and selling trade.

বিকিরণ *n* **1** scattering; strewing. **2** diffusion; dissemination; dispersal; dispersion. **3** radiation. **4** ray. **~ করা** *vt* diffuse; disperse; scatter; radiate; disseminate.

বিকীর্ণ *adj* scattered; diffused; thrown about; full of; filled with. **~ করা**=বিকিরণ করা. **~ তাপ** *n* radiated/ diffused heat.

বিকীর্ণমান *adj* being diffused/ radiated.

বিকুণ্ঠ *adj* unhesitating.

বিকুণ্ঠিত *n* **1** blunted. **2** very blunt.

বিকুলি *n* bewilderness; perplexity; utter confusion. **আকুলি-~** *n* extreme anxiety/ impatience.

বিকৃত *adj* **1** perverted; corrupted; depraved; vitiated: ~ রুচি. **2** deformed; disfigured; mutilated; mained; ugly: ~ মুখ. **3** decomposed. **4** changed; transformed; altered. **5** heinous; monstrous; revolting: ~ মূর্তি. **6** faded; discoloured: ~ বর্ণ. **7** unnatural; affected: ~ কণ্ঠ. **8** out of order: ঘড়ির যন্ত্র ~ হয়েছে. **~ করা** *vt* **1** pervert; corrupt; distort; deprave; vitiate. **2** deform; disfigure; mutilate; main. **3** decompose. **4** change; transform; alter. **5** discolour. **6** affected; raucous; hoarse. **~কণ্ঠ** *adj* speaking in an affected/ unnatural voice; speaking in a hoarse/ raucous voice. ❑*n* affected/ unnatural voice; hoarse/ raucous/ gruff voice. **~কণ্ঠে** *adv* in an affected/ hoarse. voice. **~চরিত্র** *adj* depraved; debauched; perverted; vitiated in character. **~বদন** *adj* having a distorted face; ugly faced. **~বুদ্ধি** *adj* perverted in thoughts; vicious; evil-minded; wrong-headed. **~মস্তিষ্ক** *adj* mentally deranged; demented; crackbrained; crazy; crazed; out of one's mind/ head. **~মুখ**=~বদন. **~রুচি** *adj* perverted/depraved in taste. ❑*n* perverted/ depraved taste. **~লোচন** *n* having troubled eyes. **~স্বভাব** *adj* perverted in nature; vicious; vile; degenerate; degraded. **~স্বর**=~কণ্ঠ. **বিকৃতাকার** *adj* change in shape/ appearance; misshaped; distorted in form. **বিকৃতাকৃতি** *adj* having a deformed shape/ aspect. **বিকৃতাঙ্গ** *adj* changed in form; having misshaped limbs; deformed. **বিকৃতাবস্থ** *adj* **1** fallen into a different state. **2** distressed; fallen into a bad state; poverty-stricken.

বিকৃতি *n* **1** perversion; corruption; depravity. **2** change; alteration; changed condition; modification. **3** disease; sickness; derangement; morbidity. **4** deformity; disfigurement; decomposition.

বিকৃষ্ট *adj* **1** violently attracted. **2** drawn apart/ asunder; separated; isolated.

বিকেন্দ্রণ *n* decentralization.

বিকেন্দ্রিত *adj* decentralized. **~ করা** *vt* decentralize.

বিকোষ *adj* **1** uncovered. **2** unsheathed; drawn.

বিক্রম *n* **1** physical strength; power; might; force. **2** valour; prowess; heroism; bravery; gallantry; intrepidity; temerity. **3** attack; assault; offensive; onslaught. **4** stride; pace; step; gait; proceeding; motion; course; way; manner. **~শালী, বিক্রমী** *adjj* courageous; bold; valourous; brave; heroic; intrepid; strong; mighty; powerful; dauntless; manly.

বিক্রয় *n* selling; sale. **~ করা** *vt* sell. **~কর্তা** *n* seller. **~কর্ত্রী** *fem*. **~কারী** *n, adj* seller; selling. **~মূল্য** *n* selling price. **~যোগ্য** *adj* salable; saleable; marketable. **~লব্ধ** *adj* received/ obtained from sale. **~সাধ্য**=~যোগ্য.

বিক্রয়িক *n* seller.

বিক্রয়ী *n* seller.

বিক্রান্ত=বিক্রমশালী (⇒ বিক্রম)

বিক্রান্তি=বিক্রম

বিক্রি *n* (colloq)=বিক্রয়

বিক্রিয়া *n* **1** (chem) reaction. **2** transformation; change; **3** deterioration; disfiguration. **4** ailment; affection; indisposition; **5** perturbation; agitation; perplexity. **6** hostile feeling; rebellion; defection; morbid reaction: চিত্ত ~.

বিক্রীড়িত *n* various sports and games; child's play; gambol. ❑*adj* played; played with; made a plaything.

বিক্রীত *n* sold.

বিক্রুষ্ট *adj* rancorous; spiteful; malicious; vindictive; vengeful; acrimonious; grudging; resentful; bitter.

বিক্রেতা *n* seller; salesman; vendor; vender. বিক্রেত্রী *fem.*

বিক্রেয় *adj* to be sold; salable; on/for sale. ~ **দ্রব্য** *n* goods for sale.

বিক্লব *n* **1** anxiety; phobia; fear; alarm; trepidation; horror; consternation. **2** agitation; bewilderment; perplexity; confusion. **3** sluggishness; inertia. **4** indifference; irresolution; despondency; dejection. **5** delusion; stupefaction; shock.

বিক্লিন্ন *adj* **1** dissolved; saturated; wet; doused. **2** worn out; decayed. ~ **হৃদয়** *adj* soft-hearted.

বিক্লিষ্ট *adj* hurt; harassed; destroyed; troubled.

বিক্ষত *adj* **1** severely hurt/ wounded. **2** split; rent. **3** divided.

বিক্ষিপ্ত *adj* **1** thrown asunder/ away/ about; scattered; dispersed; strewn. **2** agitated; distraught; bewildered; distracted. **3** cast/ moved hither and thither. **4** distorted; frenzied; maddened. **5** sent; dispatched. ~**চিত্ত** *adj* distraught in mind. ~**ভ্রু** *adj* having contracted eyebrows. **বিক্ষিপ্তি** *n*=বিক্ষেপ.

বিক্ষুব্ধ *n* agitated; disturbed; offended; mortified; aggrieved; perturbed.

বিক্ষেপ *n* **1** act of throwing asunder/ away/ about; scattering; dispersion. **2** moving about/ to and fro; waving; shaking; casting; tossing. **3** projection; throwing; discharging; drawing (a bow-string): শর ~. **4** inattention; distraction; confusion; perplexity: চিত্ত ~. **5** polar extent; extension; width. **6** (astron) celestial/ polar latitude. **7** (phys) deflection. ~**গতি** *n* motion that a body gains from throwing. ~ **শক্তি** *n* **1** power of objects to be transfered from one place to another. **2** the power of regarding falsehood as truth; maya. ~**ণ** *n* scattering.

বিক্ষোভ *n* **1** agitation; shaking; motion; commotion. **2** offended state; sorrow; grief; pain; distress. **3** mental agitation; discontent; distraction; perturbation; **4** alarm. **5** bewilderment. **6** (pol) unrest: গণ~, popular unrest. ~ **প্রদর্শন করা** *vi* agitate; demonstrate; organize demonstration.

বিখণ্ডিত *adj* cut into pieces; divided; torn asunder; cleft in two; refuted.

বিখাউজ *n* eczema.

বিখ্যাত *adj* famous; renowned; celebrated; famed; eminent; illustrious. **বিখ্যাতা** *fem.*

বিখ্যাতি *n* fame; renown; repute; eminence.

বিখ্যাপন *n* announcing; publishing; commendation; glorification; exaltation; publicity.

বিগড়ন *n* **1**=বিকৃতি. **2** degradation.

বিগড়ানো, বিগড়ান *vt, vi* **1** go/put out of order; break down: ইঞ্জিন ~. **2** corrupt; spoil; deprave; debanch: কচি ছেলেটাকে আর কেন বিগড়াচ্ছ? **3** be depraved/ spoiled; go to the bad. **4** confuse; fuddle; bewilder; confound: বুদ্ধি ~. **5** be confused/ fuddled/ befogged. **6** make/ become disloyal/ unfriendly/ refractory/ disaffected; fall out; balk; dig one's heels; fight shy of; not pull one's weight: বন্ধু/ দলের লোক/ বড়ো সাহেব বিগড়েছে. **7** upset; be upset; sour: মন/ মেজাজ ~. **মত** ~ *vt* change one's mind. **বিগড়ে দেওয়া** *vt* spoil; corrupt; put out of order; fuddle etc. **বিগড়ে যাওয়া** *vi* be depraved/ spoiled/ fuddled; go out of order.

বিগণন *n* **1** enumeration; reckoning; computing. **2** paying off; discharge of a debt.

বিগণিত *adj* enumerated; reckoned; calculated; considered; weighed.

বিগত *adj* **1** gone; gone away; departed; disappeared; ceased. **2** past. **3** dead; deceased. **4** (as the first term of a compound) free from; destitute of. ~**ক্লম** *adj* relieved from fatigue. ~**জ্বর** *adj* cured of fever; freed from feverishness. ~**দৃষ্টি** *adj* blind. ~**প্রাণ** *adj* dead . ~**যৌবন** *adj* past one's prime/ youth. ~**যৌবনা** *fem* passée. ~**রাগ** *adj* devoid of passion/ affection. ~**শ্রী** *adj* passed one's/fallen from one's glory/ splendour; destitute of fortune/ splendour; a mere wreck of one's former glory. ~**স্পৃহ**, ~**স্পৃহা** *adjj* devoid of wish/ desire; indifferent; rendered apathetic; free from desire; dispassionate; desireless; calm; tranquil.

বিগতার্তবা *n fem* woman in whom the menstrual excretion has ceased.

বিগতাসু *adj* lifeless; dead.

বিগতি, বিগতিক *n* adverse/ unfavourable condition or circumstance; crisis; mortal danger; danger.

বিগম *n* **1** departure; going away. **2** cessation. **3** end; absence; destruction.

বিগর্হন *n* censure; reproach; calumny; slander; scandal.

বিগর্হিত *adj* **1** reprehensible; bad; wicked. **2** discreditable; abominable; detestable. **3** forbidden; prohibited. **4** corrupted; polluted; vitiated.

বিগলন *n* **1** melting; dissolving; flow; flowing; falling; dripping; oozing. **2** (chem) smelting.

বিগলিত *adj* **1** melted away; dissolved. **2** flowed away; drained off. **3** slackened; untied; dishevelled: ~ কেশ. **4** fallen down/ out;

slipped out of. **5** decomposed; putrefied: ~ শব. **~ বন্ধন** *adj* having the band loosened. **~ বসন** *adj* unclothed. **~ লজ্জা** *adj* free from shame; bold. **বিগলিতা** *fem.* **~ করা** *vt* melt; dissolve; smelt; decompose; (fig) soften; move: করুণায় ~ করা.

বিগাঢ় *adj* **1** plunged into; bathed; submerged. **2** excessive; deep; profound.

বিগীত *adj* **1** blamed; reproached; defamed; disparaged; abused; cried down. **2**=বিগর্হিত.

বিগুণ *adj* **1** void of qualities; destitute of merits; wicked; bad. **2** disordered; corrupted. **3** hostile; adverse. ❑*n* adversity; malignity: কপালের বিগুণে.

বিগূঢ় *adj* concealed; hidden.

বিগ্রহ *n* **1** body; form; figure. **2** an image of a deity; idol. **3** (gram) resolution of a compound word into its constituent parts. **4** war; battle; strife. **5** quarrel; discord. **~প্রতিষ্ঠা** *n* installation/ consecration of an idol. **~বাক্য** (gram) words by which a compund word is expounded. **~সেবা** *n* worship and daily services to an idol.

বিগ্রাম *n* **1** another village. **2** unknown village.

বিঘটন *n* **1** misfortune; mishap. **2** separation into different component parts; analysis; dissolution. **3** harm. **4** friction. **5** obstacle; hindrance.

বিঘটিত *adj* **1** separated into different component parts; analyzed; dissolved. **2** built; constructed. **3** developed. **4** opposite.

বিঘট্টন *n* **1** striking against; friction; hewing to pieces; rubbing. **2** shaking; stirring. **3** assemblage; occurrence. **4** loosening; untying; analysis; separation.

বিঘট্টিত *adj* **1** stirred; shaken. **2** analyzed; separated. **3** blended; whipped; thrashed. **4** moved; set in motion.

বিঘৎ, বিঘত *n* span (=9 inches). **~প্রমাণ** *adj* equal to a span; nine inches in length.

বিঘা *n* measure of land (=6400 sq cubits=0.33 acre approx). **~কালি** *n* (arith) square-measure in terms of bighas.

বিঘাত *n* **1** destruction; ruin. **2** stroke; blow. **3** obstacle; impediment; hindrance; opposition. ❑*adj* struck; beaten; smitten. **বিঘাতী** *adj* **1** opposing; hindering; preventing; interrupting. **2** hindered; impeded; opposed. **3** destroyed; ruined. **4** slaying; fighting. ❑*n* fighter; slayer. **~ক** *n* destroyer; killer; slayer.

বিঘূর্ণন *n* swaying to and fro; thorough revolution; rotation; wild/ dreadful rolling: অক্ষি ~; reeling: মস্তক ~.

বিঘূর্ণিত *adj* thoroughly rotated/ revolved; rotating; wildly/ dreadfully rolling: ~ ক্ষেত্র; reeling: ~ মস্তক; rolled about; shaken; agitated. **~ করা** *vt* roll; revolve; rotate. **~ হওয়া** *vi* roll; whirl about; be agitated; rotate. **মস্তক ~ করা** *vt* make one giddy; turn one's head; make one's head swim; dizzy; make swollen-headed.

বিঘোর=বেঘোর

বিঘোষণ *n* act of proclaiming about; proclamation. **বিঘোষিত** *adj* proclaimed loudly; cried; widely publicized. **~ করা** *vt* proclaim; announce extensively; publicized widely.

বিঘ্ন *n* obstacle; impediment; hindrance; difficulty; trouble; hitch. **~কর** *adj* causing any obstacle/ interruption; impeding; obstructing. **~কারক, ~কারী** *adj, n*=~কর; impediment; obstacle. **~নাশক, ~নাশন, ~বিনাশন** *adjj* who/what removes obstacles or difficulties. **~নাশন** *n* removal of obstacles/ difficulties. **~ময়, ~সঙ্কুল** *adjj* full of/ beset with obstacles/ difficulties. **~হর, ~হারী**=~নাশক.

বিঘ্নিত *adj* impeded; hindered; obstructed; prevented.

বিচ, বীচ *prep* (dial) in; inside; within.

বিচক্ষণ *adj* clever; wise; experienced/ versed (in); clever-sighted; sagacious; judicious; discreet; expert; adroit. **~তা** *n* cleverness; wisdom; discreetness; clear-sightedness; farsightedness; judiciousness; adroitness.

বিচক্ষু *adj* eyeless; blind.

বিচঞ্চল *adj* greatly agitated; tremulous; trembling; glittering. restless; fitful; high-strung; fidgety; perturbed; troubled; worried.

বিচয়, বিচয়ন *n* gathering; putting together; arrangement.

বিচরণ *n* wandering; roaming; walking; strolling; rambling; loitering. **~ করা** *vi* **1** wander; roam; ramble; loiter. **2** follow; lead (a way of life); take to; practise; abide by; faithful to: ধর্মের/ ন্যায়ের পথে ~ করা. **~ক্ষেত্র, ~ভূমি, ~স্থান** *nn* ground/place for walking or strolling; (fig) hunting ground.

বিচরা *vi* (poet) roam; wander; stroll; walk.

বিচর্চিকা *n* form of cutaneous eruption; skin disease (eg herpes, scabies, itch, eczema).

বিচল *adj* restless; restive. ❑*n* deviation; violation. **চল~** *n* deviation; violation; failing: কথার চল~ হবে না. **~ন** *n* **1** agitation; restlessness; unsteadiness. **2** deviation; departure; straying; swerving; wavering; falling off/ down.

বিচলিত *adj* **1** agitated; perturbed; exited; nervous; jelleny; troubled. **2** deviated; swerving; deviating; strayed; departed: সত্যের পথ থেকে ~. **3** motionless. **বিচলিতা** *fem.* **~ করা** *vt* **1** agitate; excite; perturb; shake; stir up; trouble. **2** lead astray; cause to swerve/ deviate/ stray. **~ হওয়া** *vi* **1** be excited/ agitated/ perturbed/ troubled/ disturbed/ nervous/ jelleny. **2** move away; depart;

deviate; fail; swerve; desist from; go astray; fall off / down.

বিচার *n* 1 ascertainment/ determination of truth; verification. 2 judgement; decision; verdict. 3 deliberation; consideration; pondering; reflection. 4 examination; investigation; discussion. 5 (judicial) trial; finding; adjudication; settlement. 6 justice: আমি চাই. **~আচার** *n* law; justice; authority: দেশে কি কোনো ~ আচার নেই ? **~ করা** *iv vt* consider; deliberate; reflect; ascertain; verify; decide; judge; adjudicate; argue; discuss; examine; infer; try (judicially); put sb on trial; conduct trial; bring sb to trial; bring sb up for trial; settle. **~ক** *n* judge; Justice; magistrate. **~কর্তা** *n* judge; investigator. **~কর্ত্রী** *fem.* **~করণিক** *n* judicial clerk. **~ক্ষম** *adj* able/ authorized to judge; discerning; acute. **~ক্ষমতা** *n* ability to judge; competence/ authority to judge; judgement. **~জ্ঞ** *adj* knowing how to discriminate/ judge; able to decide on the merits of case. ❑*n* judge; jurist. **~নীয়** *adj*=বিচার্য. **~দেয়ক** *n* court-fee. **~পতি** *n* judge; justice. **~পতিমণ্ডলী, ~পীঠ** *n* the bench **~ফল** *n* verdict; judgement; finding. **~-বিভাগ** *n* judiciary. **~-বিভ্রাট** *n* miscarriage of justice; travesty of justice. **~বিহীন** *adj* lacking in judgement; unjust; indiscriminate; inconsiderate. **~মল্ল** *n* a great debater/ dialectician/ polemist/ logician. **~শীল** *adj* disposed to deliberation/ reflection; considerate; deliberative; discriminating; judicious. **~শূন্য**=~বিহীন. **~স্থল, ~স্থান** *nn* place for discussion/ investigation; tribunal; court. **বিচারাজ্ঞা** *n* order for trial/ adjudication/ consideration/ deliberation. **বিচারাধীন** *adj* on trial; under (judicial) consideration; sub judice; under investigation. **বিচারালয়** *n* court; law-court; court of justice. **বিচারালয়-রক্ষক** *n* court-overseer. **বিচারাসন** *n* seat of judgement; bench.

বিচারণ *n* 1=বিচার. 2 debate; argument .

বিচারণা *n* 1=বিচার. 2 conception; notion; impression. 3 criticism.

বিচারিক *adj* judicial.

বিচারিত *adj* considered; deliberated; judged; discussed; decided; ascertained; settled; adjudged; (judically) tried; adjudicated.

বিচারী *adj* deliberating; judging; discussing; one who considers/ judges/ settles/ adjudicates.

বিচার্য *adj* 1 to be deliberated/ discussed/ judged/ tried/ considered/ settled/ adjudicated/ examined. 2 under discussion/ consideration/ trial.

বিচাল[1] *adj* 1 with seed. 2 seedy.

বিচাল[2]=বেচাল

বিচালি *n* straw (of rice).

বিচালিত *adj* set in motion; moved; circulated; agitated; stirred; excited; transferred.

বিচি *n* 1 seed; stone (of a fruit). 2 scrotum. **~বিচি** *adj* 1 hard; gritty. 2 full of seeds. **~গজগজে** *adj* full of seeds; seedy.

বিচিকিচ্চি, বিচিকিচ্ছি *adj* 1 past treatment/ reform. 2 extremely ugly; hideous; repulsive; unsightly; very unpleasant/ troublesome/ unpalatable: ~ কাজ/ ব্যাপার / অবস্থা. **~ অবস্থায় ফেলা** put (one) in a false position/ embarrassing situation.

বিচিকিৎসা *n* doubt; suspicion; uncertainty.

বিচিত[1] *adj* 1 gathered; collected. 2 searched (through).

বিচিত[2] *adj*=বিচিত্র

বিচিত্র *adj* 1 variegated; many-coloured; motley; multi-coloured; brilliant. 2 variedly painted: ~চিত্র 3 queer; strange; wonderful; surprising; full of variety/ diversity / vicissitudes: কী ~ এই জীবন/ জগৎ! 4 charming; lovely; beautiful. 5 amusing; entertaining: ~ গল্প. 6 various; manifold; diverse: ~ মানুষের আনাগোনা. 7 multifarious: ~ কার্যকলাপ. **বিচিত্রা** *fem.* **~ক** *adj* wonderful; surprising. ❑*n* the tree *Betula bhojpatra* (ভূর্জবৃক্ষ). **~চরিত্র** *adj* behaving in a wonderful manner. **~তা** *n* variegation; variety; wonderfulness; strangeness. **~দেহ** *adj* having a painted body. **~বর্ণ** *adj* multicoloured; variegated. **~বীর্য** *adj* of marvellous heroism. **বিচিত্রাঙ্গ** *adj n* having variegated limbs or a spotted body; peacock. **~ নয় যে** it is no wonder (that).

বিচিত্রিত *adj* variegated; coloured; painted; spotted; variously painted; embellished by; adorned/ decorated with; wonderful. **বিচিত্রিতা** *fem.*

বিচিন্তন *n* thinking; thought.

বিচিন্তা *n* thought; reflection; care for anything.

বিচিন্তিত *adj* thought of; considered, imagined.

বিচিন্ত্য *adj* to be considered/ thought of/ cared for. **~মান** *adj* under consideration; being deliberated on.

বিচূর্ণ *adj* 1 pounded; pulverized; powdered; triturated; ground to powder. 2 completely broken; fractured; smashed. ❑*n* (fine) powder. **~ করা** *vt* grind to pieces; pound; pulverize; smash; fracture; shatter; fragment. **~ হওয়া** *vi* be ground to pieces/ pounded/ fractured/ smashed; fall to pieces; disintegrate; give way; crumble; crackle. **~ন** *n* grinding to pieces; pulverizing; pulverization; fragmenting; fracture; breakage; pounding, trituration.

বিচূর্ণিত *adj*=বিচূর্ণ

বিচূর্ণীভবন *n* 1 pulverization; trituration. 2 (geog) weathering.

বিচেতন *adj* 1 unconscious; senseless; insensate. 2 lacking in conscientiousness; unscrupulous; insensible; undiscriminating. 3 discerning; wise; conscious; alert.

বিচেতা *adj* 1 anxious; worried; impassive. 2 unhappy; cheerless; joyless; sad; melancholic. 3 ignorant; thoughtless.

বিচেয় *adj* to be searched (through); worth collecting.

বিচেষ্ট *adj* making no effort; passive; inactive; vegetative; lazy; lethargic. ~ **হওয়া** *vi* give up efforts; desist from.

বিচেষ্টা *n* acting; proceeding; conduct; behaviour.

বিচেষ্টিত *adj*=বিচেষ্ট. ❑*n* exertion; action; endeavour. ~ **হওয়া** *vi* endeavour; make efforts; exert oneself; strive.

বিচ্ছায় *n* absence of shadow. ❑*adj* shadowless.

বিচ্ছিত্তি *n* 1 separation. 2 destruction . 3 variety.

বিচ্ছিন্ন *adj* separated; cut/ torn/ cleft/ split/ broken asunder; interrupted; disconnected; detached; isolated; estranged; stray; sporadic. **বিচ্ছিন্না** *fem.* ~ **করা** *vt* separate; cut/ tear/ cleave/ spilt/ break asunder; cut off; divide; detach; disconnect; interrupt; isolate; estrange; alienate. ~**তা** *n* separation; detachment; disconnection; isolation; interruption; estrangement; alienation; isolatedness.

বিচ্ছিরি *adj* (colloq)=বিশ্রী

বিচ্ছু *n* 1 scorpion. 2 sharp mischievous person; devil. ❑*adj* 1 very restless; mischievous; naughty: ~ ছেলে. 2 malicious; rancorous; vicious; savage; ferocious.

বিচ্ছুরণ *n* 1 dispersion; radiation; emanation. 2 besprinkling; bestrewing; powdering. 3 smearing; painting.

বিচ্ছুরিত *adj* 1 dispersed; radiated; scattered. 2 bestrewed/ covered/ powdered/ with. ~ **করা** *vt* disperse; radiate; scatter; cause to emanate.

বিচ্ছেদ *n* 1 separation; estrangement. 2 discord; dissension; difference; division. 3 interval; intermission. 4 disintegration. 5 cleaving; piercing; cutting asunder; breaking. ~**কাতর** *adj* pained by separation. ~**বেদন,** ~**বেদনা** *n* anguish of separation. ~**শূন্য** *adj* unseparated; ever united.

বিচ্যুত *adj* 1 fallen asunder/ to pieces; shed. 2 fallen/ departed; strayed; swerved/ deviated from. 3 detached/ separated from. 4 oozed; exuded. **বিচ্যুতা** *fem.* ~ **হওয়া** *vi* to be detached/ separated; to be shed; deviate; depart; turn away; stray; fail to observe/ execute; fall. **বিচ্যুতি** *n* falling from; separation; detachment; deviation; straying; dereliction; shedding; failure; miscarriage (গর্ভবিচ্যুতি).

বিছা *n* 1 scorpion. 2 (astrol) scorpion. 3 kind of broad necklace in the form of a scorpion (also called ~**হার**). 4 an ornament worn round the waist. **কাঁকড়া~** scorpion. **গুবরে~** sort of beetle found in cow-dung. **তেতুঁলে~** kind of caterpillar covered with bristles.

বিছাতি,বিছাটী=বিছুটি

বিছানা *n* bed. ~ **করা/পাতা** *vi* make a bed.

বিছানো, বিছান *vt* 1 spread: শয্যা ~. 2 lay; strew; scatter: ফুল/নুড়ি ~.

বিছুটি *n* a kind of nettle. **জল** ~ *n* nettle soaked in water (which increases its virulence).

বিজকুড়ি *n* 1 very small letters. 2 small bubbles; drops. 3 rash; eruption. ~-**বিজকুড়ি** *adj* like small dots or seeds.

বিজড়িত *adj* 1 intertwined; interlaced; enmeshed; entangled; combined; fused; interspersed; interwoven; criss-crossed; tangled: **শাখা-প্রশাখা** ~. 2 involved; embroiled: ষড়যন্ত্রে ~ হওয়া. 3 beset with; full of; begone: দুঃখ~, woe-begone; আনন্দ ~, মেঘ~, 4 encumbered/ burdened/ saddled/ fettered (with): দেনায় ~. ~ **করা** *vt* 1 intertwine; interlace; entangle; interweave. 2 involve; embroil. 3 beset with. 4 encumber/ burden/ saddle. with.

বিজন *adj* solitary; lonely; deserted; desolate.

বিজনন *n* birth; origin; delivery.

বিজন্মা *adj* bastard; illegitimate. ❑*n* bastard; illegitimate child.

বিজবিজ *n* multitude; swarming; crawling. ~ **করা** *vi* swarm; crawl: পোকা ~ করছে. **বিজবিজে** *adj* swarming; crawling.

বিজয় *n* 1 victory; triumph; conquest: রাজ্য~. 2 subjugation; mastery: শত্রু~. 3 success; superiority. 4 (archaic) departure; parting. ~**কেতন** *n* banner of victory. ~**গর্ব** *n* pride of victory. ~**গৌরব** *n* glory of victory. ~**তোরণ** *n* triumphal arch. ~**দুন্দুভি** *n* triumphal drum. ~**দৃপ্ত** *adj* triumphant; proud of/flushed with victory. ~**পতাকা** *n* triumphal flag. ~**ফল** *n* victory for a result. ~**লক্ষ্মী** *n fem* the goddess of victory. ~**লাভ** *n* winning victory: ~**লাভ করা** *vi* gain/ win victory; conquer. ~**স্তম্ভ** *n* monument commemorating a victory; victory column.

বিজয়া *n fem* 1 goddess Durga. 2 a female companion of Durga. 3=~ দশমী. ~**দশমী** *n* the tenth day of the light half of the month of Ashwin on which the image of Durga is immersed. ~**সঙ্গীত** *n* mournful songs about Durga's going to her husband's home. ~**সপ্তমী** *n* the seventh day of the light half of a month falling on a Sunday.

বিজয়ী *adj* victorious; triumphant; conquering; vanquishing. ❑*n* victor; conqueror; subduer; vanquisher. বিজয়িনী *fem.*

বিজয়োৎসব *n* celebration of victory; triumph. ~ করা *vi* celebrate a victory; triumph (over).

বিজয়োন্মত্ত *adj* intoxicated by victory/ success.

বিজয়োল্লসিত *adj* triumphant; exultant.

বিজয়োল্লাস *n* exultation/ rejoicing over a victory/ at a success; triumph.

বিজর *adj* not growing old; ageless.

বিজল *adj* sticky; mucous; slimy. ❑*n* sticky/ slimy substance.

বিজলি, বিজলী *n* lightning; electricity. ~ তার *n* electric wire. ~ পাখা *n* electric fan. ~ বাতি *n* electric light/ lamp.

বিজল্প *n* nonsense; ravings; mumbo jumbo; balderdash.

বিজাত *adj, n*=বিজন্মা

বিজাতি *n* 1 different race/cast; hostile race. 2 inferior race. জাতি-~ *n* obscene/ abusive/ filthy language.

বিজাতীয় *adj* 1 pertaining to a different race; outlandish; queer; barbaric: ~ চালচলন. 2 heterogeneous; opposite; contrary; converse: ~ পদ্ধতি. 3 deadly; terrible; virulent; violent: ~ ক্রোধ. ~তা *n* differnece of caste or race; outlandishness; queerness; heterogeneous; diverseness. ~ ভেদ *n* racial difference/ diversity.

বিজামাতা *n* defective son-in-law (who pays marriage-money to his father-in-law).

বিজারক *n* (chem) reducing agent.

বিজারণ *n* (chem) reduction.

বিজিগীষা *n* desire for victory; desire to conquer/ subdue/ overcome.

বিজিগীষু *adj* desirous of victory/ conquest; emulous; ambitious.

বিজিঘৃক্ষু *adj* bellicose.

বিজিত *adj* conquered; subdued; defeated; vanquished; won; gained. বিজিতা *fem.*

বিজিতেন্দ্রিয় *adj, n* (one) who has subdued his passions/ desires.

বিজুরি, বিজুরী, বিজুলি, বিজুলী *nn* (poet)=বিজলি

বিজৃম্ভণ *n* 1 yawning; yawn; gape. 2 expansion; extension; budding; blossoming. বিজৃম্ভমাণ *adj* 1 gaping; yawning; 2 expanding; blossoming.

বিজৃম্ভিত *adj* 1 yawned; gaped. 2 opened; expanded; blown. ❑*n* yawn.

বিজেতা *adj, n*=বিজয়ী. বিজেত্রী *fem.*

বিজেয় *adj* to be vanquished/ overcome; conquerable; defeatable; capable of being vanquished.

বিজোড় *adj* 1 odd; uneven. 2 separated; unpaired. uncoupled. 3 disjointed. ~ অঙ্ক *n* odd number.

বিজ্ঞ *adj* learned; erudite; wise; experienced; clever; expert; prudent; judicious. বিজ্ঞা *fem.* ~তা, ~ত্ব *n* learning; erudition; wisdom; experience; expertise; judiciousness; prudence; cleverness.

বিজ্ঞপ্তি, বিজ্ঞাপ্তি *n* notice; announcement; advertisement; information; report; circular; bill; placard; bulletin.

বিজ্ঞাত *adj* 1 discerned; understood; known. 2 well-known. famous.

বিজ্ঞান *n* science; knowledge; doctrine. ~চর্চা *n* cultivation of science. ~বিদ, ~বিশারদ, ~বেত্তা, বিজ্ঞানী *n, adj* scientist; man of science; versed in science. ~শাস্ত্র *n* scientific knowledge/ discipline. বিজ্ঞানাগার *n* laboratory. বিজ্ঞানাচার্য, বিজ্ঞানাধ্যাপক *nn* professor of science. বিজ্ঞানানুশীলন *n*=~চর্চা.

বিজ্ঞানিক=বৈজ্ঞানিক

বিজ্ঞানী⇒ বিজ্ঞান

বিজ্ঞাপক *n* advertiser; informant.

বিজ্ঞাপন *n* advertisement; notification; announcement; information; communication; notice; circular; placard; bill; petition. ~ করা/দেওয়া *vt* advertise; announce; notify; bill. ~দাতা *n* advertiser. ~দাত্রী *fem.*

বিজ্ঞাপনী *n* notice; circular; handbill; announcement; bulletin. ~ ডিক্রি *n* (law) declaratory decree. ~য় *adj* to be made known/ communicated/ advertised/ notified/ announced.

বিজ্ঞাপিত *adj* advertised; notified; announced; billed; circulated.

বিজ্ঞাপ্তি⇒ বিজ্ঞপ্তি

বিজ্ঞাপ্য=বিজ্ঞাপনীয় (⇒ বিজ্ঞাপনী)

বিজ্ঞেয় *adj* to be known/ perceived; knowable; cognisable; worth knowing; to be learned thoroughly/ particularly.

বিজ্বর *adj* free from fever.

বিট[1] 1 libertine; debauchee; profligate; sensualist; roué; rake. 2 hypocrite; trickster. 3 orange tree. 4 mouse. 5 black variety of salt. ~ খদির *n Acacia catechu* (having very hard wood, the resin of which is used in medicine) ~নুন=~(5).

বিট[2] *n* (bot) beet.

বিটকেল, বিটকাল *adj* 1 hideous; monstrous; dreadful; ghastly; fearful: ~ চেহারা. 2

abominable; repulsive; atrocious; horrid; offensive: ~ গন্ধ. **3** ugly; scandalous; odious; shocking; revolting; obnoxious; indecent; vulgar: ~ চালচলন, ~ খাওয়াদাওয়া. **4** queer; strange; absurd: ~ ব্যাপার. **5** cranky; of a queer sort; puckish; impish; waggish. **~ লোক** *n* wag; prankster; practical joker. **~মি** *n* prank; practical jokes; waggish tricks/ remarks. **~মি করা** *vi* play pranks on sb; play waggish tricks; play a practical joke.

বিটঙ্ক *n* **1** trap for catching birds; snare; fowling-net. **2** dove-cote; aviary.

বিটপ *n* young branch of a tree; twig; bough; sprout; shoot.

বিটপালং, বিটপালম *n* variety of beet used as a vegetable; beet.

বিটপী *n* tree.

বিটলবণ=বিটনুন (⇒ বিট[১])

বিটলে, বিটল, বিটলা *adj* roguish; deceitful; knavish; sly; impish. ❑*n* rogue; crook; scamp; rascal. **~মি** *n* roguery; knavery; crookedness; waggery; trickery; mischief.

বিটা [E] *n* (phys) beta. **~ কণা** *n* beta-particles. **~ রশ্মি** *n* beta-rays.

বিটী=বেটি

বিড়ঙ্গ *n* a medicinal plant or its fruit, *Embelia ribes* (a vermifuge). ❑*adj* able; skilful; experienced.

বিড়বিড় *n* (onom) **1** muttering; grumbling; mumbling; mutter; mumble; murmur. **বিড়ির বিড়ির** *n* continuous muttering, etc. **বড়বড়** *n* excessive muttering, etc. **ব্যাড় ব্যাড়** *n* disgusting muttering, etc. **ব্যাড়র ব্যাড়র** *n* prolonged disgusting muttering, etc. **2** sensation of disgust and disgusting. nausea; shudders. **~ করা, বিড়বিড়ানো, বিড়বিড়ান** *vi* mutter/ mumble to oneself; grumble; murmur. **গা ~ করা** make one's flesh ~. **বিড়বিড়ানি** *n*=বিড়বিড়. **ব্যাড়ব্যাড়ানি** *n*=ব্যাড়ব্যাড়.

বিড়ম্বন, বিড়ম্বনা *n* **1** deception; deprivation. **2** mockery; derision; irony: ভাগ্যের **~**. **3** affliction; trouble; curse; annoyance; harassment, vexation; disappointment; anguish: তার সঙ্গে কথা বলাটাই ~.

বিড়ম্বিত *adj* **1** deceived; disappointed. **2** mocked; held in derision; treated unkindly/ badly: ভাগ্য **~**. **3** troubled; harassed; vexed; afflicted.

বিড়া, বিড়ে *n* **1** (of betel-leaves, etc) bundle (of 40 usually). **2** coil of cloth or straw used as a cushion on the head of a porter. **3** similar coil used as a stand for cooking-urns, pitchers, etc; wad.

বিড়াল *n* cat. **বিড়ালি** *fem.* **~ছানা, ~ছাগ, ~শাবক** *nn* kitten; kitty; catling. **~জাতীয়** *adj* felive. **~তপস্বী** *n* hypocrite; whited sepulcher; impostor. **~তুল্য** *adj* cat-like; feline. **বিড়ালাক্ষি** *adj* cat-eyed. **বিড়ালের আড়াই পা** (fig) (said about) a person who quickly forgets his promises; ill will; resolve. **বিড়ালের ভাগ্যে শিকা ছেঁড়া** (fig) unexpected piece of good fortune; windfall; lucky stroke.

বিড়ি *n* kind of slender cigarette with tree-leaf as enclosing material.

বিড়ে=বিড়া

বিৎ, বিদ *suff* knowing; knower; versed: সঙ্গীত~, ইতিহাস~.

বিতং *n* details; specification; detailed account. **~ দিয়ে** *adv* specifying; in detail; dwelling on. **~ করা/** দেওয়া *vt* specify; give details; detail.

বিতংস, বীতংস *n* net/chain/ apparatus for catching and confining beasts or birds.

বিতণ্ডা *n* perverse/ frivolous argument; captious objection; fallacious controversy; quibble; idle carping at the argument of another; without attempting to prove the opposite side of the question; altercation; sophistry.

বিতত *adj* **1** spread out; expanded; extended; diffused; pervaded; outstreched; broad; wide. ❑*n* any stringed instrument.

বিততি *n* **1** extent; length; expanse; expansion; extension; diffusion; spreading. **2** row; cluster; series; succession. **3** collection.

বিতথ *adj* **1** untrue; false; unreal; incorrect **2** futile; vain. **3** deception; trickery.

বিতথা *n* (archaic) calamity; blow; misfortune.

বিতথ্য *adj*=বিতথ (1)

বিতনু *adj* **1** extremely thin/ slender; slim; lean; slight. **2** fine; delicate; lovely; sweet; graceful.

বিতরণ *n* bestowal; granting; donation; distribution; giving away. **~ করা** *vt* give away; grant; bestow; distribute. **~ কেন্দ্র** *n* distributing centre.

বিতরা *vt* (poet)=বিতরণ করা

বিতরিত *adj* given away; granted; bestowed; distributed.

বিতর্ক *n* **1** debate; deliberation; discussion; reasoning. **2** altercation; wrangling; dispute; controversy; contention; polemic; affray. **3** doubt; uncertainty. **4** conjecture; guess; supposition. **~নীয়** *adj* debatable; contestable; arguable; moot; questionable; controversial.

বিতর্কিকা *n* debate; polemics; debating forum.

বিতর্কিত *adj* debated; argued; reasoned; deliberated upon; disputed; controversial; moot; questionable; contestable.

বিতর্দি *n* altar; dais; platform.

বিতল *n* (myth) the second of the seven underworlds.

বিতস্তা *n* the river Jhelum.

বিতস্তি *n* measure of length; span (=9 inches).

বিতান *n* **1** open hall or temporary shed; pavilion; temple; arbour; bower: লতা~. **2** tent. **3** awning; canopy. **4** great extent/ quantity. **5** stretch. **6** leisure; opportunity. **~ক** *n* tent.

বিতানীকৃত *adj* **1** spread/ extended over; stretched. **2** covered; overshadowed.

বিতায়মান *n* awning; canopy. ❑*adj*=বিতত.

বিতারিখ=বতারিখ

বিতিকিচ্ছি=বিচিকিচ্ছি

বিতীর্ণ *adj* **1** covered; enveloped; extended/ spread over; pervaded; diffused. **2** crossed/ passed/ gone over or through; overcome. **3** granted; bestowed; given.

বিতুষ্ট *adj* displeased; dissatisfied. **বিতুষ্টি** *n* dissatisfaction; displeasure.

বিতৃষ্ণ *adj* **1** free from thirst; not thirsty. **2** free from desire. **3** indifferent; disinterested; apathetic; callous; averse to, disgusted (with). **বিতৃষ্ণা** *n* **1** indifference; disinterestedness; callousness; apathy; disgust; aversion. **2** freedom from thirst; saliety.

বিত্ত *n* wealth; property; riches; substance; assets; resources; fortune; affluence. **~দ** *n* benefactor. **~বান, ~শালী** *adjj* wealthy; rich; well-to-do; moneyed; affluent; opulent; rolling in wealth; substantial. **~বানরা, ~শালীরা ~শালিনী** *n pl fem* the haves. **~ সঞ্চয় করা** *vt* amass/accumulate wealth/ riches; make money; get rich; fill one's pockets **~সমাগম** *n* accumulation of wealth; income. **~হীন** *adj* poor; indigent; destitute; moneyless. **~হীনরা** *n pl* the have-nots.

বিত্রপ *adj* shameless.

বিত্রস্ত *adj* frightened; terrified; alarmed.

বিত্রাস *n* fear; terror; alarm. ❑*adj* freed from terror. **~ন** *adj* terrifying. **বিত্রাসিত**= বিত্রস্ত.

বিথর (*adj*) (archaic)=বিস্তর. ❑*n* (only in **থরে-বিথরে**) ⇒ থর.

বিথার *n* (archaic; poet)=বিস্তার=বিথারিত=বিস্তারিত

বিথারা *vt* (archaic, poet)=বিস্তার করা

বিদ ⇒ বিং

বিদ'আত *n* (A) heresy; schism. **বিদ'আতি** *adj* heretic.

বিদংশ *n* **1** biting. **2** any pungent food which excites thirst.

বিদকুটে=বিদঘুটে

বিদগ্ধ *adj* **1** learned; perceptive; subtle; sensitive **2** skilled; skilful; adroit; astute. **3** shrewd; crafty; clever; sharp. **4** witty; having excellent taste/ the qualification of a connoisseur; cultured; refined; cultivated; scholarly. ❑*n* scholar; connoisseur. **বিদগ্ধা** *n fem* **1** a witty woman; a refined/ cultivated woman; **2** witty/ sharp ladylove. **~জন** *n*=~. **~তা** *n* wit; excellence in taste; discernment; acute sensitivity; skill; sharpness. **~ সভা, ~ সমাজ** *n* intelligentsia; assembly/ company of connoisseur; learned society.

বিদগ্ধাজীর্ণ *n* acid dyspepsia.

বিদঘুটে *adj* **1** ugly; hideous; monstrous; horrid; grotesque; bizarre; strange; queer; awkward; quaint. **2** complicated; knotty; tricky; troublesome; ticklish; puzzling: ~ প্রশ্ন.

বিদরা *vi* (poet)=বিদীর্ণ করা/হওয়া

বিদরী *n* inlaid work.

বিদল *n* **1** split pea; pigeon-pea. **2** opposite party; adversary; rival. ❑*adj* leafless; blown; rent asunder; split.

বিদলন *n* trampling; crushing; grinding; pounding; thrashing, laying waste; rout; devastation; destruction; extreme oppression.

বিদলিত *adj* **1** trampled; crushed; pounded; thrashed; laid waste; devastated; routed. **2** split; burst/ rent asunder. **3** expanded; blown. **4** oppressed. **~ করা** *vt* trample; crush; rout.

বিদলীকরণ *n* **1**=বিদলন. **2** rending asunder; splitting; dividing. **3** separating; separation. **বিদলীকৃত** *adj*=বিদলিত.

বিদশা *n* adversity; hard times; hardship; evil day.

বিদা *n* harrow; rake (agri) harrow; rake. **~ দেওয়া** *vt*.

বিদাই *n* recompense; due; reward.

বিদায়[১] *n* [A] **1** farewell; adieu; bidding farewell; parting; leave-taking. **2** permission to leave: এবার আমাকে ~ দিন . **3** departure; exit; retreat; withdrawal; retirement. ❑*int* good-by; adieu; bye-bye. **~ অভিভাষণ/ সম্ভাষণ** *n* farewell address; valedictory speech. **~কাল** *n* time of parting/ departure; time of retirement. **~কালীন** *adj* relating to the time of parting/ farewell; valedictory; farewell: ~কালীন উপদেশ. **~ গ্রহণ** *n* leave-taking; retirement. **~ চাওয়া/ মাগা** *vi* ask leave for departure; ask for leave of absence. **~দৃশ্য** *n* farewell-scene. **~ দেওয়া** *vi* bid farewell to; see/ send sb off; give one leave to depart. **~ নেওয়া** *vi* depart; leave; take/ make one's departure; make one's farewell; take leave; part; say good-bye; withdraw; go away. **~ ভোজ** *n* farewell dinner/ banquet. **~ভোগী** *adj* (of a person) on leave. **~ সঙ্গীত** *n* farewell/ valedictory song. **~ সংবর্ধনা** *n* farewell reception. **~ সম্ভাষণ** *n* farewell greetings. **~সূচক** *adj* valedictory; farewell.

বিদায়[২] *n* **1** gift; grant; present; presentation; tip: ব্রাহ্মণ ~, কাঙ্গালি ~. **2** reward; recompense; prize: ভারী ~. **3** departure; exit; withdrawl;

retirement; dismissal; resignation; abdication; retreat. **4** immersion: আনন্দ~. ~ **করা** *vt* **1** dismiss; fire; retire; discharge; give one notice; remove; expel; throw/ drive/ turnout; oust; pack sb off; send sb packing. **2** give leave of absence. **3** allow to leave with gifts; pay off: পাল্কিবহারা ~ করা. ~**কাল** *n* time of dismissal/ removal/ retirement. ~ দেওয়া=~ করা. **পেনসনসহ ~ দেওয়া** *vt* pension sb off. ~ **হওয়া** *vi* go away; leave; take/ make one's departure; say good-bye; depart; quit; turn one's back on; decamp; bolt; past company; be off; clear off.

বিদায়ী[১] *n* farewell gift; perquisite; parting gift.

বিদায়ী[২] *adj* departing; outgoing; retiring; parting; valedictory; farewell: ~ সভাপতি, ~ উপদেশ.

বিদার *n* **1** rending/ tearing asunder; cutting; lacerating; splitting. **2** war; battle. **3** inundation. ❑*adj*=বিদীর্ণ. ~**ক** *adj* rending; splitting; piercing; cleaving; causing to burst. **হৃদয় ~ক** *adj* heart-rending. ~**ণ** *n*=বিদার. ~**ণ রেখা** *n* cleavage.

বিদারা *vt, vi* (poet) বিদীর্ণ করা.

বিদারিত=বিদীর্ণ

বিদারী *n* (Ayu) phlegmonous pharyngitis. ❑*adj*=বিদারক: গগন~.

বিদিক *n* an intermediate point of the compass (as south-east). ❑*adj* going into different quarters or regions: দিগ্~ **2** (dial) confounded; bewildered: লোকটা কি ~ হয়ে গেল?

বিদিত *adj* **1** known (as) understood; learnt; perceived: ~ বিষয়. **2** informed; apprised; acquainted/ familiar with: তিনি এ বিষয়ে ~. **3** famed; celebrated; renowned: ভুবন~.

বিদিশ=বিদিক

বিদীর্ণ *adj* rent (asunder); torn; split; pierced; broken; cleft; burst open; ripped up; opened. ~ **করা** *vt* rend (asunder); tear; split; break; cleave; pierce; burst open. ~ **মুখ** *adj* open-mouthed. ~ **হৃদয়** *adj* broken-hearted.

বিদুর *adj* knowing; wise; intelligent. ❑*n* **1** learned/clever man. **2** younger brother of Dhritarashtra and Pandu (in the Mahabharata). **বিদুরের খুদ** an extremely small offering given in deep devotion.

বিদুষী *n fem* learned/ erudite woman; bluestocking.

বিদূর[১] *adj* **1** very remote/ distant: "তোমায় আমায় সম্বন্ধ ~". **2** long: পক্ষ ~. ❑*n* remote place: দূরে-বিদূরে. ~**গ** *adj* going far away; far-spreading (as scent). ~**গমন** *n* going far away. ~**ত্ব** *n* great distance.

বিদূর[২], **বিদূরজ** *n* cat's eye.

বিদূরিত *adj* driven away; removed; expelled.

বিদূরে *adv* far distant; far away.

বিদূষক *n* **1** jester; wag. **2** (in dramas) the jocose companion and confidential friend of the hero; buffoon; jester; clown. **3** slanderer, scandal-monger, ❑*adj* disgracing; scandalous; defiling.

বিদূষণ *n* slander; scandal; calumny; defiling; reviling; detracting; satire.

বিদে=বিদা

বিদেশ *n* foreign country/ land. ~**গত** *adj* gone abroad; living/ dwelling abroad. ~**গমন** *n* act of going abroad. ~**গামী** *adj* going abroad. ~**জ**, ~**জাত** *adj* born/ produced abroad; foreign; exotic. ~**বাস** *n* dwelling/ living/ stay abroad. ~**বাসী** *adj* dwelling/ living abroad; foreign. ❑*n* inhabitant of a foreign country; foreigner. ~**যাত্রা** *n* starting on a journey abroad. ~**স্থ** *adj* living in a foreign country; remaining abroad; of a foreign land; foreign. **বিদেশাগত** *adj* coming from/ imported from a foreign land. **বিদেশে** *adv* in/to a foreign country; abroad. **বিদেশী, বিদেশি** *adj* belonging to another country; foreign; exotic; alien. ❑*n* foreigner; alien; stranger. **বিদেশিনী** *fem*. **বিদেশীয়**=~.

বিদেহ *adj* bodiless; incorporeal. **বিদেহী** *fem*. **বিদেহী আত্মা** departed soul. ❑*n* modern Mithila or Bihar.

বিদ্ধ *adj* **1** pierced; impaled; perforated; bored; pricked; cleft; split; burst asunder. **2** wounded; injured; penetrated; stabbed; stung; struck; torn; beaten; hurt. **3** thrown; sent. **4** filled/ affected/ provided/ joined/ mixed with. ~ **করা** *vt* pierce; impale; perforate; prick; split; injure; fill; affect. ~**পত্র** *n* (bot) perfoliated leaf. ~**ব্রণ** *n* (Ayu) punctured wound.

বিদ্বজ্জন *n* wise/ learned/erudite man; scholar.

বিদ্বৎকল্প *n* a little learned; slightly learned; just short of being learned.

বিদ্বৎকুল, বিদ্বৎসমাজ *nn pl* learned people; learned society; intelligentsia. ~**তিলক** *n* great scholar/ savant; prince of learned men.

বিদ্বত্তম *adj* wisest; most learned. **বিদ্বত্তমা** *fem*.

বিদ্বত্তর *adj* wiser; more/ very learned. **বিদ্বত্তরা** *fem*.

বিদ্বদ্গণ, বিদ্বদ্গোষ্ঠী *nn*=বিদ্বৎকুল

বিদ্বদ্দেশীয় *adj*=বিদ্বৎকল্প

বিদ্বান *adj* learned; erudite. ❑*n*=বিদ্বজ্জন.

বিদ্বিষ্ট *adj* **1** hated; disliked; odious; maligned; grudged; envied. **2** hostile to.

বিদ্বেষ *n* **1** malice; envy; spite; grudge; gall; enmity; hostility; virulence; animosity; hatred; dislike; contempt; aversion. ~ **করা** *vt* bear malice (against); envy; show hostility towards; grudge; malign; hate; loathe; show ill will. ~**কষায়িত** *adj* tinged with malice/ spite; malicious; rancorous; despiteful; spiteful; malevolent; malignant. ~**পরায়ণ**=বিদ্বেষী. ~**পূর্ণ** *adj* full of malice. ~**বুদ্ধি** *n* malicious/ spiteful/

envious disposition; malignancy; malignity ~বুদ্ধি প্রণোদিত, ~বুদ্ধিপ্রসূত *adj* actuated by malicious/ spiteful/ malignant/ envious disposition; motivated by malice/ spite/ animosity/ envy. ~ভাজন *n* object of malice/ animosity/ envy. বিদ্বেষানল *n* fire of malice/ animosity; gall; wrath; rancor.

বিদ্বেষী, বিদ্বেষ্টা *adj* malicious; malignant; virulent; hating; grudging; hostile; inimical; envious; full of animosity; spiteful; malevolent; rancorous; spleenful; squint-eyed; venomous; vicious; viperous.

বিদ্যমান *adj* **1** existing; existent; present; alive; living. **2** (old use) near; close to. ~তা *n* **1** existence; presence; state of being alive. **2** proximity; nearness. বিদ্যমানে *adv* whilst one is existent/ alive; in one's presence.

বিদ্যা *n* **1** learning; scholarship; erudition; knowledge; education: তার পেটে ~ নেই. **2** philosophy. **3** knowledge of soul/ spiritual truth. **4** practical arts, eg, agriculture. commerce, medicine. **5** science: উদ্ভিদ ~. **6** subject of study: তুমি কোন বিদ্যায় পারদর্শী? **7** an art; a skill: চুরি~, জাদু~. **8** discipline; branch of knowledge ~কর *n* mine of learning; great scholar/ man of learning. ❑*adj* giving knowledge; causing wisdom. ~করী *fem.* ~.গম *n* acquirement of knowledge/ learning. ~গুরু *n* teacher; instructor in science. ~চুঞ্চু *adj* famous for learning. ❑*n* renowned scholar. ~তীর্থ *n* knowledge compared to a sacred bathing-place. ~দাতা *n* teacher; preceptor. ~দাত্রী *fem.* ~দান *n* imparting of knowledge; instruction. ~ দান করা *vt* teach; instruct; impart knowledge (gratuitously). ~দায়ী *adj* instructive; edifying; educative; enlightening. ~দায়িনী *fem.* ~দিগ্গজ *adj. n* **1** vastly learned (man). **2** (iron) ignoramus; blockhead; thick-head. ~দেবী *n fem* Saraswati, the goddess of learning. ~ধন *n* treasure of knowledge; wealth consisting in learning. ~ধর *n* a kind of supernatural being said to possess great personal beauty and skill in music. ~ধরী *fem.* ~নিকেতন *n*=~পীঠ. ~নিধি *n* ocean of learning; title conferred on a scholar ~নুরাগ *n* love of learning; attachment to learning. ~নুরাগী *adj* fond of/ attached to learning. ~নুরাগিণী *fem.* ~নুশীলন *n* cultivation of learning; study. ~নুশীলন করা *vi* cultivate learning/ science; study; read. ~পীঠ *n* centre of learning; educational establishment/ academy; school. ~ফল *n* fruit of learning. ~বংশ *n* chronological list of teacher's in any branch of knowledge; school (of thought, etc.) ~বতী *fem.* of ~বান. ~বত্তা *n* possession of learning; scholarship; erudition. ~বল *n* power/ force of learning. ~বয়োবৃদ্ধ *adj* advanced in learning and years. ~বাগীশ *n* master in science and speech. ~বান *adj* learned; knowledgeable. ~বিক্রয় *n* sale of knowledge; instruction in return for payment. ~বিনোদ *n* delight of goddess Saraswati; title conferred on a scholar. ~বিরুদ্ধ *adj* conflicting with science/ knowledge. ~বিশারদ *adj* vastly learned; pundit; man of learning; walking encyclopedia. ❑*n* title conferred on a scholar. ~বিশিষ্ট *adj* possessed of learning; distinguished for learning ~বিষয়ক *adj* academic ~বিস্তার *n* spread of education/ learning/ knowledge. ~বিহীন *adj* destitute of knowledge; ignorant; unlearned; uninstructed. ~ব্যবসায় *n* pursuit of learning. ~ব্যবসায়ী *adj, n* teaching professionally/ in return for payment; professional teacher. ~ব্রত *n* duty of acquiring learning. ~ভিমান *n* fancy/idea that one is learned. ~ভিমানী *adj, n* imagining oneself learned; wiseacre. ~ভূষণ *n* an ornament of learning; title conferred on a scholar. ~ভ্যাস *n* practice/ pursuit of learning; application to books; study. ~ভ্যাস করা *vt* pursue one's studies; study; learn one's lessons; apply oneself to learning. ~মঠ *n* school; college; monastic school. ~মদ *n* pride in one's learning. ~মন্দির *n* temple of learning; school; college. ~ময় *adj* consisting of/ absorbed in knowledge. ~ম্বুধি=~নিধি. ~রত্ন *n* jewel of learning; valuable knowledge; title conferred on a scholar. ~রম্ভ *n* beginning of study; initiation into one's study. ~রম্ভকাল *n* appropriate age for beginning one's studies. ~রম্ভ করা *vt* commence one's studies. ~র্জন *n* acquirement/ acquisition of knowledge/ learning. ~র্জিত *adj* acquired/ gained by knowledge. ~র্ণব *n*= ~নিধি. ~র্থবৃত্তি *n* scholarship. ~র্থী *adj* desirous of knowledge; engaged in studies. ❑*n* student; pupil. scholar. ~র্থিনী *fem.* ~লঙ্কার=~ভূষণ. ~লব্ধ *adj*=~র্জিত. ~লয় *n* school; abode/ seat of learning; institution; academy; seminary. ~লয়ের ছুটির দিন school holiday. ~লয়ের ছুটির সময় closing time of a school; school vacation. ~লয়ের সময় school hours; school time. ~লাপ *n* learned discussion. ~লাভ *n*=~র্জন. ~লাভ করা *vt* acquire learning/ knowledge; receive education; become a student; take courses; have one's education. ~শিক্ষা *n* learning; acquisition of learning/ knowledge; pursuit of knowledge; schooling; education. ~শিক্ষা করা *vt* learn; receive education; pursue one's studies; go to school; acquire/ gain knowledge/ learning. ~শূন্য *adj*=~বিহীন. ~সাগর=~নিধি. ~সাধ্য *n* **1** education. **2** learning and ability. **3** (physical and mental) powers. ❑*adj* attainable/ obtainable by learning. ~স্নাতক *n* one who has finished his studentship and completed his study (of the Vedas); graduate. ~হীন *adj*=~বিহীন. ~হীনা *fem*. ~য় বৃহস্পতি *n* man of unbounded learning (like Brihaspati, the preceptor of gods; Brishaspati in learning; know-all. ~র জাহাজ *n* a prodigy of learning; a walking encyclopedia. ~র বহর *n* (iron) sb's range of knowledge/ extent of learning (ie very limited).

বিদ্যুচ্চমক *n* flash of lightning.

বিদ্যুৎজিহ্ব *adj* having a lightning-like tongue.

বিদ্যুজ্জ্বালা *n* the flashing of lightning.

বিদ্যুৎ *n* **1** lightning. **2** electricity. **3** flashing thunderbolt. **4** flashing; shining; glittering. ~কম্প *n* quivering/ flashing of lightning. ~কোষ *n* electric battery. ~পতাকা *adj* having lightning for its banner. ~পাত *n* stroke of lightning. ~প্রপতন=~পাত. ~প্রবাহ *n* electric current. ~প্রভ *adj* flashing like lightning; dazzlingly bright. ~প্রভা *fem*. also *n* flash of lightning. ~স্পন্দন, ~স্ফুরণ *nn* electric vibration; flashing/ quivering of electricity. ~স্পৃষ্ট *adj* struck by lightning; electrocuted. ~স্ফুলিঙ্গ *n* electric spark.

বিদ্যুতালোক *n* electric light; flash of lightning.

বিদ্যুদ্গর্ভ *adj* impregnated/ charged with electricity; electric.

বিদ্যুদ্দাম *n* garland/ mass of lightning; flash/ streak of forked lightning. ~বর্ষা *adj* showering flashes of lightning. ~বর্ষিণী *fem*.

বিদ্যুদ্দীপ্ত *adj* **1** illuminated by flashes of lightning; lighted/ illuminated by electricity. **2** as dazzlingly bright as electric light/ flash of lightning. বিদ্যুদ্দীপ্তি *n* flash of lightning; brightness of lightning.

বিদ্যুদ্বর্ষী *adj* discharging electricity.

বিদ্যুদ্বিকাশ *n* flash of lightning/electric light; electric spark.

বিদ্যুদ্বিজ্ঞান *n* science of electricity.

বিদ্যুদ্বেগ *n* lightning speed; speed of electricity. বিদ্যুদ্বেগে *adv* with lightning speed; in a flash.

বিদ্যুদ্ব্যজন *n* electric fan.

বিদ্যুন্মালা *n* **1** garland/ wreath of lightning; streak of forked lightning. **2** kind of Sanskrit metre consisting of 8 long syllables. বিদ্যুন্মালী *adj* wreathed with lightning; wearing a lightning-like dazzling wreath.

বিদ্যুল্লতা *n* forked lightning; streak of lightning.

বিদ্যুল্লেখা *n* **1** streak of lightning. **2** kind of Sanskrit metre.

বিদ্যোত *n* flashing; glittering; flash of light. ~ক *adj* irradiating; illuminating; illustrating. ~মান *adj* bright; dazzling; shining.

বিদ্যোৎসাহী *adj, n* encouraging/ patronizing promotion of learning or spread of education; lover of learning; patron of learning. বিদ্যোৎসাহিনী *fem*. বিদ্যোৎসাহিনীসভা *n* society for promotion/ spread of education or learning.

বিদ্যোদ্বোধন সভা *n* convocation.

বিদ্যোপার্জন *n* acquisition of knowledge. বিদ্যোপার্জিত *adj* acquired by learning.

বিদ্রধি *n* (internal) abscess. ~কা *n* carbuncle.

বিদ্রব *n* **1** running away; fleeing; flight; retreat; panic. **2** flowing out; oozing; liquefaction; melting; dissolving; thaw. **3** intellect. **4** censure; reproach. **5** taunt; ridicule.

বিদ্রাবণ *n* **1** putting to flight; fleeing; flight. **2** dissolving. ❑*adj* **1** putting to flight; agitating. **2** (Ayu) inducing discharge.

বিদ্রাবিত *adj* **1** dissolved; melted; thawed. **2** liquefied; fused. **3** caused to disperse; driven away; defeated; routed.

বিদ্রুত *adj* **1** liquefied; fluid (as an oily or metallic substance when heated). **2** run away/ asunder; running to and fro; flown; fled. **3** destroyed; routed. **4** agitated; perplexed; distraught.

বিদ্রুম *n* **1** coral; red coral. **2** young sprout/ shoot. ❑*adj* treeless.

বিদ্রূপ *n* jesting; joking; ridicule; deriding; jest; taunt; sarcasm; derision; mockery; teasing; persiflage; irony; raillery. ~ করা *vt* taunt; deride; mock at; ridicule; tease; laugh at; poke fun at; make fun of; jeer; scoft at. ~প্রিয় *adj* fond of jesting/ deriding/ poking/ fun at. ~প্রিয় লোক *n* tease; mocker; taunter; scoffer; derider. ~বিদ্রূপাত্মক *adj* derisive; ironic; sardonic; mordant; sarcastic.

বিদ্রোহ *n* **1** revolt; rebellion; uprising; insurrection; insurgence; insurgency. **2** coup; coup d'état; muting; treason. **3** harm; offence; wrong; treachery; perfidy; mischief. ~ করা *vi* revolt; rebel; rise in rebellion; mutiny. বিদ্রোহাচরণ *n* **1** hostility; rebelliousness; recalcitrancy; recalcitrance; hostility; insurgency; treason; sedition. **2** mischief-making. wrongdoing; malefaction; misdoing. বিদ্রোহাচরণ করা *vi* revolt; become hostile/ disloyal; bear malice; be hostile. বিদ্রোহী *adj* rebellious; insurgent; mutinous; recalcitrant; seditious; defiant; hostile; disloyal. ❑*n* rebel; insurgent; insurrectionist; disloyal person; mutineer; maverick; recalcitrant; traitor. বিদ্রোহিণী *fem*.

বিধ *suff* sort; form; kind; type. নানা~ of various kinds. বহু~ of many kinds.

বিধবা *n fem* widow. ~ করা *vt* bereave (a woman) of her husband. ~বিবাহ *n* widow marriage.

বিধর্মা, বিধর্মী *adj* Professing a different religion/ creed. ❑*n* devotee of another religion; infidel.

বিধা *n* **1** sort; kind; type; variety. **2** manner; form; mode; arrangement.

বিধাতা *n* **1** God; Providence; Brahma. **2** distributor; disposer; arranger; accomplisher; maker; author; creator; granter; giver; bestower: ভাগ্য~, disposer of men's fate. ❑*adj* distributing; arranging; disposing; ordering: ~ পুরুষ providence personified. **বিধাত্রী** *fem.*

বিধাতৃ=বিধাতা

বিধান *n* **1** scriptural prescript/ ruling; prescription: ধর্মের ~. **2** provision; arrangement: সুখ ~. **3** order; measure; disposition; arrangement; regulation; rule; law; legislation; precept; method; manner: আইনের ~. **4** medical prescription/ regulation; diet. **5** fate; destiny. **6** creating; creation: বিশ্ব~. **7** means; expedient. **8** performance (esp of prescribed acts or rites); execution; making; doing; accomplishing. **9** enumeration; statement of particulars. **10** system: নব~. **11** (gram) affixing; prefixing; taking as an affix. **12** (anat) structure (of body) ~ **করা** *vi, vt* provide for; prescribe; dispose; order; decide; execute; accomplish. ~ **দেওয়া** *vi, vt* prescribe; issue a ruling; rule. ~**কর্তা** *n* disposer; provider; regulator; controller; director; law-giver; legislator; one who knows how to arrange. ~**কর্ত্রী** *fem.* ~**জ্ঞ** *n, adj* (one) who knows rules or precepts; teacher. ~**ত** *adv* according to rule/ precept; de jure. ~**তন্তু** *n* (anat) tissue. ~**তন্ত্র** *n* code of laws; system of legislation. ~**পরিষদ** *n* legislative council. ~**বিদ** *adj* versed in rules/ precepts. ~**মণ্ডল** *n* legislature. ~**শাস্ত্র** *n* jurisprudence; law. ~**সংসদ** *n* parliament. ~**সংহিতা** *n* a treatise on jurisprudence; a law-book. ~**সভা** *n* legislative assembly

বিধানিক *adj* legislative. ~**ক্ষমতা** *n* legislative power. ~ **প্রণালী** *n* legislative procedure. ~ **বিবাহ** *n* civil marriage.

বিধায় *prep* on account of; owing to; because of; for; due to: স্থানের অসঙ্কুলান ~.

বিধায়ক *adj* legislating; enacting; enjoining; performing; controlling; regulating; directing; prescribing; issuing a rule; making provision/ arrangements for; providing for; causing; occasioning; bringing about; securing. ❑*n* legislator; provider; disposer. **বিধায়িকা** *fem.*

বিধায়ী *adj*=বিধায়ক. **বিধায়িনী** *fem.*

বিধি *n* **1** rule; formula; injunction; ordinance; regulation; statute; precept; law; **2** direction (esp for performance of a rite). **3** (gram) grammatical rule/ precept. **4** any prescribed act/ rite/ ceremony. **5** use ' employment; application. **6** system; method/ manner/ a way of acting; procedure; mode of life; conduct. **7** means; expedient. **8** creation. **9** fate; destiny; **10** The Creator. **11** any act/ action; performance; accomplishment; contrivance; work; business. ~**আধিকারিক** *n* law officer. ~**জ্ঞ** *adj* one who knows the prescribed mode/ form; learned in ritual; conversant with the laws/ rules. ~**ত** *adv* according to rule. ~**দর্শী** *n* a priest who sees that a sacrifice is conducted according to prescribed rules and corrects any deviation from them. ~**দর্শিনী** *fem.* ~**দৃষ্ট** prescribed by rule. ~**দেশক**, ~**নির্দেশক** *n* legal remembrances. ~**নিষেধ** *n* commandment and prohibition. ~**পূর্বক** *adj* according to rule. ~**প্রয়োগ** *n* application of a rule/ law. ~**বৎ**=~পূর্বক. ~**বদ্ধ** *adj* regulated; codified; formal; enacted; in keeping with form/ established mode. ~**বদ্ধ করা** *vt* codify; enact. ~**বশাত** *adv* through the power of fate/ destiny. ~**বিড়ম্বনা** *n* deception by fate; irony of fate. ~**বিড়ম্বিত** *adj* beguiled by fate; ill-fated. ~**বিদ্** *adj*=~জ্ঞ. ~**বিরুদ্ধ** *adj* contrary to law/ rule; unlawful; irregular. ~**বিহিত** *adj* established by rule; lawful; regular. ~**বেত্তা**=~জ্ঞ. ~**বোধিত** = ~বিহিত. ~**মতো** *adj* in keeping with scriptural prescripts/ edicts/ rules/laws; rightful; lawful; formal; adequate. ~**মতে**, ~**মোতাবেক**=~পূর্বক ~**লিপি** *n* prescripts of providence; destiny; lot; fate. ~ **শাস্ত্র** *n* jurisprudence. ~**সঙ্গত**, ~**সম্মত**=~মত. ~**হীন** *adj* destitute of rule; unauthorized; unlawful; irregular; contrary to rule/ law.

বিধিৎসা *n* intention to do; intention/ design/ purpose/ desire for; desire to provide for. **বিধিৎসু** *adj* wishing to do/ make; proposing to perform; desirous of making provision/ arrangement for.

বিধু *n* the moon. ~**বদন** *n* moon-like face. **বিধুবদনী, বিধুবদনী** *adj fem* moon-faced. ❑*n* lovely woman. ~**মুখ**=~বদন. ~**মুখী**=~বদনী.

বিধুত, বিধূত *adj* **1** shaken/ tossed about; vibrated; fluttered; trembling; tremulous. **2** shaken off; dispelled; removed. **3** abandoned; relinquished. ~ **করা** *vt* shake; set trembling; flutter; shake off; dispel; remove.

বিধুনন, বিধূনন *n* **1** trembling; shaking; vibration; fluttering; agitation; waving. **2** shaking off; removal; repulsion. **3** abandonment.

বিধুনিত, বিধূনিত *adj* **1** shaken; fluttered; trembling; set to tremble; shivering. **2** abandoned; relinquished. **3** overwhelmed; agitated. **4** frightened; alarmed.

বিধুবন *n* trembling; tremor.

বিধুর *adj* **1** bereft; bereaved (esp of any loved person); alone; solitary; separated from; suffering from want; destitute of; wanting: বিরহ

~. **2** miserable; distressed; afflicted. **3** frightened; troubled; alarmed. **4** helpless; powerless. **5** overwhelmed; perplexed; dejected; depressed. **6** redolent of; surcharged with: গন্ধ~. **বিধুরা** *fem.* **~তা, ~ত্ব** *nn* loveliness; solitariness; want; distress; trouble; affliction; bewilderment.

বিধূয়মান *adj* set to tremble; trembling; fluttering; vibrating; quivering; tremulous.

বিধৃত *adj* **1** held fast; firmly caught; seized, arrested; laid hold of; grasped. **2** maintained; held; borne; supported; possessed; saved; preserved; taken one of.

বিধেয় *adj* **1** lawful; rightful; proper. **2** to be (or being) enjoined (as a rule); to be performed/ practised/ done; to be stated/ settled/ established. **3** docile; compliant; submissive. □*n* **1** what is to be done; duty; necessity. **2** (gram) predicate. **3** (phil) predicable. **~ পদ** *n* predicate. **~তা** *n* propriety; fitness; applicability; usefulness; necessity. **~মার্গ** *n* path of righteousness/ rectitude; right/ rightful way.

বিধেয়ক *n* draft of a proposed law; bill.

বিধৌত *adj* washed; cleansed; washed off; purified; removed. **বিধৌতি** *n* washing; cleaning; purifying; purification; cleansing.

বিধ্বংস *n* **1** ruin; destruction; devastation; annihilation; demolition; ravage; dilapidation. **2** hurt; injury; offence. **বিধ্বংসিত** *adj* ruined; distorted; devastated; fallen to pieces. **বিধ্বংসী** *adj* **1** falling to pieces; perishing. **2** causing to fall; ruining; destroying; devastating. **বিধ্বংসিনী** *fem.*

বিধ্বস্ত *adj* ruined; destroyed; demolished; fallen to pieces; annihilated. **~ করা** *vt* ruin; devastate; destroy; rout; demolish.

বিনত *adj* **1** bent; bent down; curved; bowed; stooping; inclined; sunk down; deepened. **2** modest; humble; meek; polite; submissive. **বিনতা** *fem.* **বিনতানন** one who has his face bent/ cast down; dejected; dispirited.

বিনতা¹ ⇒ বিনত

বিনতা² *n* one of Kashyap's wives (in the Mahabharata). **~নন্দন** *n* son of Vinata; Aruna; Garuda.

বিনতি *n* **1** bowing; obeisance; stooping. **2** modesty; decency; good conduct; politeness. **3** good breeding; discipline. **4** entreaty; solicitation; earnest request; supplication; begging. **5** submissiveness; meekness. **6** (phys) dip.

বিননি, বিননী=বিনুনি

বিননিয়া=বিনানিয়া

বিননো=বিনানো

বিনমন *n* **1** act of bending down. **2** inclination. **3** flexibility; pliability; gentleness; humility.

বিনমিত *adj* **1** bent down; inclined. **2** gentle; tender; polite; humble. **বিনমিতা** *fem.*

বিনম্র *adj* **1** very humble/ modest/ submissive; reverential; bowing to; obeisant. **2** gentle; soft; polite; feeble; low suave; mild; tender; pliant. **বিনম্রিতা** *fem.* **~তা** *n* **1** humbleness; meekness; great humility/ modesty; submissiveness; politeness; affability; bow/ stooping in submission or politeness. **2** gentleness; suavity; softness; mildness; tenderness.

বিনয় *n* **1** modesty; mildness; humility; decency; meekness; submissiveness; solicitation. **2** gentleness; softness; politeness; suavity. **3** good breeding; propriety of conduct; education; good conduct; discipline. **বিনয়া** *fem.* **~গ্রাহী** *adj* conforming to rules of discipline; compliant; tractable; modest. **~ন** *n* **1**=বিনয়. **2** act of taming/ training; disciplining. **3** education; training. **4** taking away; removing. **~পূর্বক** *adv* with humble submission. **~বচন** *n* modest speech; profession of modesty; salutation. **~বধির** *adj* deaf to solicitation; insensible to modesty/ politeness.

বিনয়াবনত *adj* bending down modestly; bowing low with modesty. **বিনয়াবনতা** *fem.*

বিনয়ী *adj* modest; humble; meek; polite; gentle; unassuming; demure; submissive; obeisant; disciplined. **বিনয়িনী** *fem.*

বিনশ্বর *adj* perishable; transitory; destructible.

বিনষ্ট *adj* **1** utterly lost/ ruined; destroyed; perished: ~ নগরী. **2** disappeared; past. **3** lost; wasted: ~ তেজ, ~ দৃষ্টি. **4** spoilt; corrupted; depraved: ~ ধর্ম, ~ চরিত্র. **5** killed; dead. **6** wrecked: ~ তরণী.

বিনা *prep* without; except; save; but; excluding.

বিনানো *vt* **1** plait (hair in a pigtail); intertwine into the shape of; braid; form into plait; arrange in braids. **2** narrate (eg one's misfortunes) at great length; expatiate; snivel; moan about; wail over: বিনিয়ে বিনিয়ে বলা, narrate with wails and whines.

বিনামা¹ *adj* **1** under a different name. =বেনামা. **2** nameless.

বিনামা² *n* shoe; slipper; boot.

বিনায়ক *n* **1** leader; guide. **2** Ganesha; the god of the people. **3** Guru or spiritual preceptor. **4** Lord Buddha.

বিনাশ *n* **1** utter loss; annihilation; perdition; destruction; decay; removal; ruin; wreck; extermination. **2** extinction; death. **3** perversion; degradation; corruption; depravation: চরিত্র ~. **4** violation: সতীত্ব ~. **~ করা** *vi* annihilate; destroy; exterminate; ruin;

demolish; shatter; wreck; kill. ~ক *adj* destructive; annihilating; ruinous; wasting; pernicious; sinister; depraving; degrading; corrupting; violating. ❑*n* destroyer; killer; spoiler; wrecker. ~ন *n*=~. ~সাধন *n*=~ন. ~প্রাপ্ত, বিনাশিত *adjj*=বিনষ্ট.

বিনাশী *adj* **1** perishable; perishing; mortal; destructible. **2**=বিনাশক. বিনাশিনী *fem.*

বিনাশোন্মুখ *adj* **1** dying; moribund; on death-bed; at the point of death; at death's door. **2** about to perish; about to be destroyed/ ruined; on the brink/ verge of destruction/ ruin.

বিনি, বিনে (colloq)=বিনা

বিনিঃশেষ *adj* completely exhausted; finished; thoroughly spent up/ consumed/ depleted.

বিনিঃসরণ *n* act of going out/forth; issuing forth/ out; emergence; exudation; outflow; discharge; effusion. বিনিঃসৃত *adj* gone forth/ out; issued forth/ out; sprung from; escaped; trickled; exuded; spouted; discharged.

বিনিক্ষিপ্ত *adj* thrown/ put down; placed in/ under. বিনিক্ষেপ *n* tossing; throwing; sending.

বিনিগ্রহ *n* restraining; subduing; checking; stopping; controlling.

বিনিদ্র *adj* sleepless; awake; wakeful; occurring in the waking condition.

বিনিন্দিত *adj* (used chiefly as the last term of a compound) reproached; reviled; abused; mocked: কোকিল ~ কণ্ঠ, a voice which puts even the cuckoo to shame.

বিনিপাত *n* **1** great fall; ruin; loss. **2** disgrace; ignominy; odium; infamy. **3** family decay. **4** distress; calamity. **5** death. বিনিপাতিত *adj* thrown down; killed; destroyed.

বিনিবর্তিত *adj* come back; returned.

বিনিময় *n* **1** exchange; barter. **2** return. **3** pledge; deposit; security. **4** substitution. ~ **করা** *vt* exchange; barter; give in return; substitute. **বিনিময়ে দেওয়া** *vt* give in return (for); give in exchange (for)/ lieu (of); recompense. ~**নিয়ম** *n* (alg) commutative law. ~**লব্ধ** *adj* received/ obtained in exchange/ return. ~ **হার** *n* rate of exchange.

বিনিমিত *adj* exchanged; bartered.

বিনিমেয় *adj* to be exchanged; exchangeable; (of coins) convertible.

বিনিযুক্ত *adj* **1** appointed to; employed. **2** sent; commissioned; entrusted with; destined for. **3** (of money) invested. ~**ক** *n* minister in charge of appointment; employer.

বিনিযোক্তব্য *adj* **1** to be appointed/ employed. **2** to be sent/ commissioned. **3** to be enjoined/ commanded. **4** to be invested.

বিনিযোক্তা *n* employer; appointer.

বিনিয়ত *adj* restrained; controlled; regulated; checked.

বিনিয়ন্ত্রণ *n* decontrol. ~ **করা** *vt* decontrol. বিনিয়ন্ত্রিত *adj* decontrolled.

বিনিয়ম *n* **1** special rule. **2** limitation; restriction; restraint; prohibition. **3** disorder; irregularity.

বিনিয়োগ *n* **1** investment. **2** appointment; commission; employment. **3** charge; duty; sending; task. **4** application; use; employment. ~ **করা** *vt* invest; lay out; appoint; commission; employ; entrust/ charge with; send; make use of.

বিনীত *adj* **1** modest; humble; well behaved; meek; polite; submissive. **2** led/ taken away; removed. **3** trained; disciplined; tamed; educated. **4** one who has subdued his passions. বিনীতা *fem.* ~**ভাবে** *adv* humbly; politely.

বিনু (archaic, poet)=বিনা

বিনুনি *n* plaiting of hair; arranging (hair) in braids; forming into plait; braid of hair; pigtail.

বিনে ⇒ বিনা

বিনোদ *n* **1** satisfaction; pleasure. **2** diversion; sport; pastime; playing/ amusing one's self with. **3** eagerness; vehemence. ❑*adj* pleasant; pleasurable; charming; good-looking; pretty; exquisite; graceful; elegant; fair; comely; pleasing; entertaining; gratifying. বিনোদী, বিনোদিনী *fem.* বিনোদন *n* **1** amusement; pastime; recreation; diversion; entertainment; gratification; act of making/ giving pleasure; relaxation: চিত্ত~. **2** removal; driving away: শ্রম~. ~**বেণী** *n* kind of gold necklace. ~**রসিক** *adj* given/ addicted to pleasure. ~**শালা** *n* house for pleasure/ entertainment. ~**স্থান** *n* pleasure-ground; ground for entertainment.

বিনোদা *vt* (archaic, poet) divert; amuse; entertain; give pleasure; please; delight.

বিনোদিত *adj* diverted; amused; delighted.

বিনোদা, বিনোদিয়া *adj* (archaic)=বিনোদ, বিনোদী.

বিন্তি [Pg] *n* **1** a kind of card-game. **2** (in some card-games) tierce.

বিন্দু *n* **1** a detached particle; globule. **2** drop: এক ~ জল. **3** dot; spot: দশমিক ~. **4** coloured mark made on the forehead between the eyebrows: কপালের সিন্দুর ~. **5** zero; cypher. **6** (geom) point. **7** a whit; an iota; a particle: মনে এক ~ সুখ নেই. **8** Anusvar (ং) (⇒ বিন্দু-বিসর্গ). **9** semen. ~**ক** *n* small mark. ~ **চিত্রক** *n* spotted antelope. ~**জাল**, ~**জালক** *n* collection/ mass of dots or spots. ~**পাত** *n* falling in drops; dripping. ~ **বিন্দু** *adv* drop by drop; in drops. ~**বিসর্গ** *n* (lit) the alphabetical letters ং and ঃ; (fig) a particle; whit; an idea; the faintest hint; an inkling; তার এ বিষয়ে ~মাত্র ধারণা নেই. ~**বিসর্গ জানা** have the faintest knowledge/ idea (of). ~**মাত্র** even an iota/ bit/ faintest trace/ shadow of. ~মাত্র না not in the least; not at all; not a whit/ jot/ tittle.

বিন্ধ্য *n* the Vindhyas. ~বাসিনী *n* goddess Durga.

বিন্ধ্যাচল *n* the Vindhya mountains.

বিন্যস্ত *adj* **1** placed (down); put: পর পর ~. **2** placed in an orderly manner; disposed; arranged. **3** tidied up; dressed; composed; neatly arranged: ~ কেশদাম. **4** arranged; spread out. ~ করা *vt* put/ place (down); dispose; arrange; tidy up; compose; place/ lay on; array.

বিন্যাস *n* **1** arrangement; disposition; order; act of placing in an orderly manner. **2** putting on (ornaments). **3** composition (of literary works, etc). **4** establishment; foundation. **5** array; arraying (of troops). **6** elaboration; narration at great length. **7** (alg) permutation.

বিপক্ব *adj* completely matured/ ripened/ developed.

বিপক্ষ *n* opponent; rival; adversary; enemy; disputant; opposite party; antagonist. ❑*adj* deprived of wings; wingless. ~তা *n* rivalry; hostility; enmity; opposition; antagonism. ~দল *n* rival/ opposite party; enemy forces. ~পাত *adj* impartial; unbiased. ~পাতী *adj* opposed/ hostile to; against. ~ভাব *n* hostile disposition. বিপক্ষীয় *adj* of a rival party/ the enemy forces. বিপক্ষে *prep* against.

বিপজ্জনক *adj* dangerous; risky; unsafe; perilous; hazardous; insecure.

বিপণন *n* marketing; selling.

বিপণি, বিপণী *n* shop; stall; fair; market-place; sales emporium. বিপণী *n* trader; shopkeeper; merchant.

বিপৎ *n*=বিপদ. ~কাল *n* **1** time of misfortune/ calamity. **2** adversity. ~পূর্ণ *n* fraught with dangers. ~পাত *n* misfortune; calamity. ~সঙ্কুল *adj* full of dangers and difficulties. ~সাগর *n* ocean of misfortune; heavy calamity.

বিপত্তারিণী *n fem* any Hindu goddess who keeps/ saves from trouble or danger.

বিপত্তি *n* **1** going wrongly; adversity; misfortune; agony; torment; mishap; danger; failure; disaster. **2** destruction; ruin; death. **3** unfavourableness (of time); sharp turn in one's affair. ~কর *adj* causing misfortune/ calamity/ danger/ adversity/ trouble; calamitous. ~কাল *n* season of adversity/ misfortune. ~খণ্ডন *n* removal of adversity. ~নাশন, ~ভঞ্জন *adjj, nn* removing/ remedying misfortune/ adversity. ~রহিত *adj* free from misfortune.

বিপত্নীক *adj* one whose wife is dead. ❑*n* widower.

বিপথ *n* wrong road; bad road; evil way; evil course; bad conduct. ~গামী *adj* **1** going in a wrong way/ evil course; gone astray; gone to the bad. **2** (astron) aberrated. ~গামিনী *fem*. বিপথে যাওয়া *vi* go astray; go to the bad; pursue evil courses; (astron) aberrate; be on the wrong track.

বিপদ (in compounds) *n* misfortune; adversity; calamity; mishap; failure; ruin; danger; risk; hazard; difficulty; disaster; trouble. ~গর্ভ *adj* dangerous; fraught with dangers and diffculties. ~গ্রস্ত *adj* fallen into misfortune; afflicted; endangered; imperilled ~দশা *n* state of misfortune; calamitous position. ~বহুল *adj* fraught with dangers and difficulties; perilous. ~ভঞ্জন *adj* =বিপত্তিনাশন. ~যুক্ত *adj* attended with misfortune; dangerous. ~রহিত *adj* free from danger/ misfortune. বিপদে পড়া *vt* run/ fall into a danger; be involved in a danger. বিপদে ফেলা *vt* endanger; imperil; put/ bring into danger; put at risk.

বিপদাত্মক *adj* dangerous; risky; perilous.

বিপদাপদ *n pl* dangers and difficulties.

বিপদাপন্ন=বিপন্ন

বিপদুদ্ধার *n* rescue/ release/ deliverance from danger. ~ করা *vt* rescue/ release/ free/ deliver/ save from danger.

বিপন্ন *adj* involved in danger/ difficulty; afflicted; distressed; endangered; imperilled; fallen on evil days. বিপন্না *fem*. ~তা *n* misfortune; adversity; bad/ evil/ adverse fortune; affliction; hardship; trouble; ill fortune.

বিপন্মুক্ত *adj* free/ freed/ rescued/ delivered from danger or difficulty; out of danger. ~ করা *vt* free/ rescue/ deliver from danger or difficulty. বিপন্মুক্তি *n*=বিপদুদ্ধার.

বিপরিণাম *n* **1** change; reverse; upsetting. **2** death; destruction. বিপরিণামী *adj* undergoing a change of state/ form; reversed; upset.

বিপরীত *adj* **1** opposite; contrary; contradictory; opposing; contending; counteracting. **2** unusual; odd; strange: ~ কর্ম. **3** unfavourable; adverse; inauspicious: ~ বিধি/ ভাগ্য. **4** hideous; monstrous; terrific: ~ মূর্তি. **5** turned round; reversed; inverted. **6** perverse; wrong; contrary to rule. **7** (arith) reciprocal. **8** (geom) converse; opposite: ~ কোণ. ❑*n* (logic) contrary proposition. ~কারী *adj* acting in a contrary manner; perverse; hostile; disobedient. ~ ক্রিয়া (alg) invertendo. ~ গতি *n* course against the current. ~ প্রতিজ্ঞা (geom) converse proposition. ~ প্রতিবিম্ব (phys) inverted image. ~ বুদ্ধি *adj* wrong-headed. ~ শব্দ *n* antonym. ~ শ্রেণী (alg) harmonic series. ~ভাবে *adv* in reverse order; in the opposite manner; conversely.

বিপর্যয় *n* **1** disaster; upset; reverse; reverse of fortune; change for the worse; calamity; misfortune; loss; ruin; overthrow; destruction

2 turning round; transposition; change; alteration; inverted order/ succession; opposite; inversion; disorder. ~ ঘটানো *vi* cause/ bring about disaster/ destruction/ ruin; cause serious disruption. ~ কাণ্ড *n* a monstrous/ disastrous/ affair/ thing; a catastrophe.

বিপর্যস্ত *adj* 1 turned over; overturned; upturned; reversed; contrary; inverted; topsy-turvy; thrown into confusion; disorderly. 2 upset; routed; destroyed; shattered; undone; demolished; utterly embarrassed; confounded. ~ করা *vt* 1 turn over; overturn; turn round; reverse; invert; put into disorder; thrown into confusion; disrupt. 2 destroy; demolish; upset; confound; disrupt; rout; embarrass utterly; convulse.

বিপর্যাস=বিপর্যয়

বিপল *n* a measure of time; moment; instant.

বিপশ্চিৎ *n* learned man; savant; scholar.

বিপাক *n* 1 cooking; dressing. 2 effect; result; consequence. 3 bad/ ugly consequences: কর্ম ~. 4 calamity; distress; misfortune; trouble. 5 metabolism; digestion. বিপাকে পড়া *vi* be in a predicament; fall/ run into a trouble or danger; get into scrapes. বিপাকীয় *adj* metabolic.

বিপাশা *n* the Beas (river in the Punjab).

বিপিতা *n* step-father.

বিপিন *n* forest; grove; wood; thicket. ~বিহারী *adj* wandering in woods for pleasure. ❑*n* Sri Krishna.

বিপুল *adj* 1 large; big; huge: ~ শরীর. 2 extensive; wide; vast: ~ সমুদ্র. 3 abundant; numerous; important: ~ ফলসম্ভার. 4 loud: ~ শব্দ. 5 noble; magnanimous: ~ হৃদয়. 6 very deep; profound; greet: ~ স্নেহরাশি. 7 long: ~ সময়. 8 thick: ~ কান্তার. বিপুলা *fem.* ~তা *n* largeness; greatness; extent; width; magnitude; vastness; loudness; abundance; profundity; magnanimity. ~কায় *adj* having a large/ huge body.

বিপ্র *n* learned Brahmin.

বিপ্রকর্ষ *n* 1 distance; remoteness; difference; contrast. 2 (gram) separation of two consonants by the insertion a vowel; vowel insertion. ~ণ *n* dragging/ driving away; carrying off; repelling; repulsion.

বিপ্রতীপ *adj* vertically opposite. ~ কোণ *n* (geom) vertically opposite angle.

বিপ্রযুক্ত *adj* separated; removed; absent from; free from; destitute of; severed; disunited; detached.

বিপ্রয়াণ *n* departure; flight.

বিপ্রয়োগ *n* 1 disjunction; dissociation; separation (from). 2 quarrel; disagreement.

বিপ্রলব্ধ *adj* deceived; disappointed. বিপ্রলব্ধা *n fem* a female disappointed by her lover's breaking his appointment.

বিপ্রলম্ভ *n* 1 quarrel; disagreement. 2 deception; deceit. 3 separation of lovers. 4 disunion; disjunction.

বিপ্রলাপ *n* 1 talking idly; prattle; prattling. 2 altercation; mutual contradiction.

বিপ্লব *n* 1 revolution; revolt; tumult; affray; rebellion; mutiny. 2 confusion; trouble; disaster; evil; calamity; misery; distress. 3 destruction; ruin. 4 loss; damage. বিপ্লবী *adj* revolutionary. ❑*n* revolutionary; revolutionist. অন্তর্বিপ্লব *n* internal strife; civil war. প্রতি~ *n* counter revolution. ~ ঘটানো *vt* cause/ bring about a revolution; revolutionize.

বিপ্লুত *adj* 1 upset; inundated; immersed. 2 disturbed; troubled; pestered. 3 thrown into confusion; routed; raided; confused; disordered; lost; perished. 4 agitated; excited; overwhelmed; troubled (as speech or reason); bewildered: আবেগ~. 5 broken; violated (as chastity, vow, etc). 6 vicious; immoral. ~নেত্র, ~লোচন *adj* having the eyes suffused/ bathed (with tears, joy, etc). ~ভাষী *adj* speaking confusedly; smattering.

বিফল *adj* fruitless; useless; ineffectual; vain; futile; idle. ~ করা *vt* make fruitless; frustrate; foil; defeat; baffle. ~ হওয়া *vi* be fruitless/ useless; be of no avail; abort; fail; be frustrated/ baffled. ~তা, ~ত্ব *nn* fruitlessness; uselessness; futility; unprofitableness; failure. ~প্রযত্ন *adj* failed in one's attempt; thwarted; baffled. ~শ্রম *adj* exerting oneself in vain. বিফলীকরণ *n* making fruitless; frustrating; foiling; defeating. বিফলীকৃত *adj* made fruitless; foiled; frustrated; baffled. বিফলীভবন *n* becoming fruitless. বিফলীভূত *adj* become fruitless/ useless; baffled; foiled; frustrated. বিফলে *adv* in vain.

বিবদমান *adj* quarrelling; disputing; contending.

বিবমিষা *n* vomiting tendency; nausea; qualm. বিবমিষু *adj* feeling nausea.

বিবর *n* 1 hole; chasm; slit; cleft; hollow; vacuity; interstice; cave; cavity; crevice; fissure.

বিবরণ *n* 1 explanation; exposition; interpretation; gloss; comment. 2 account; description; narration; statement; recounting; narrative. 3 laying open/ bare; act of uncovering; spreading out. ~ দেওয়া *vt* give an account; narrate; describe. বিবরণী *n* written account; report; communication; message; statement. বিবরণীয় *adj* to be described/ narrated; worth publishing/ describing.

বিবর্জক *adj* avoiding; shunning; leaving. বিবর্জন *n* act of avoiding/shunning/leaving. বিবর্জনীয় *adj* to be avoided/ left/ abandoned. বিবর্জনীয়া *fem.*

বিবর্জিত *adj* 1 avoided; left; abandoned. 2 destitute/ deprived of; free/ exempt from: বিবেক~. বিবর্জিতা *fem.*

বিবর্ণ *adj* discoloured; pale; wan; faded; washed-out; bloodless; sallow; pale-faced; waxen.

বিবর্ত *n* 1 change; alteration; transformation. 2 turning round; rolling onwards; moving about; rotation; revolution. 3 consequence. 4 altered/ changed form or state. 5 dance. 6 (phil) error; illusion; apparent/ illusory form; unreality. 7 presence/ existence in a particular state. 8 collection; multitude. 9 travelling. ~বাদ, ~নবাদ *n* 1 theory of evolution. 2 (phil) illusionism; the doctrine affirming the world to be illusion.

বিবর্তন *n* 1 evolution. 2 change; transformation; turning round; revolving; rotation; revolution. 3 moving/ wandering to and fro. 4 turning; turn; return. ~বাদ ⇒ বিবর্ত. ~শীল *adj* changing; rotating; evolving; turning round; rolling.

বিবর্তিত *adj* 1 turned round; rotated; revolved. 2 returned; turned back. 3 evolved; changed; transformed. 4 averted; removed. ~ সন্ধিভঙ্গ *n* complete dislocation.

বিবর্ধক *adj* magnifying; amplifying. ~ কাচ *n* magnifying lens. ধ্বনি~ যন্ত্র *n* amplifier.

বিবর্ধন *n* 1 augmenting; increasing; promoting; furthering. 2 augmentation; growth; increase; prosperity. 3 (phy) amplification; magnification. 4 enlargement.

বিবর্ধিত *adj* 1 fully developed; grown; increased; enhanced; augmented; furthered; promoted; enlarged. 2 (phys) magnified; amplified. ~ করা *vi* 1 develop/ augment/ enlarge fully. 2 amplify; magnify.

বিবশ *adj* 1 benumbed; stupefied; overwhelmed; deprived/ destitute of will. 2 fatigued; utterly helpless; powerless; inconsolable; beside oneself with. 3 unrestrained; independent. বিবশা *fem.*

বিবসন *adj* unclothed; naked; without clothes. বিবসনা *fem.*

বিবস্ত্র=বিবসন. বিবস্ত্রা *fem.*

বিবস্বান *n* 1 god. 2 sun; sungod.

বিবাগী *adj* 1 indifferent to worldly interests or pleasures; self-renouncing; self-abnegating. 2 leaving one's home or country; outcast. ❑*n* one who has renounced domestic ties or has left one's home for good; wanderer.

বিবাদ *n* 1 quarrel; dispute; contest; brawl; controversy; conflict; strife; altercation; hostility; fight. 2 contest at law; legal dispute; litigation; lawsuit. ~ করা *vi* quarrel; dispute; contest; altercate; dispute; brawl; fight; fight at law. ~পদ *n* subject to a dispute; lawsuit. ~প্রিয় *adj* quarrelsome; contentious. ~শূন্য *adj* harmonious; strifeless. ~সূচি *n* cause list.

বিবাদার্থী *adj* 1=বিবাদপ্রিয় (⇒ বিবাদ). 2 seeking for litigation. ❑*n* litigant; plaintiff.

বিবাদী *adj* 1 disputing; contending; contesting. 2 under dispute: ~ সম্পত্তি. 3 opposite; hostile. ❑*n* 1 litigant; party in a lawsuit; defendant. 2 contestant; opponent; opposite party. 3 (music) a note which is seldom used or altogether discarded in a particular musical mode. বিবাদিনী *fem.*

বিবাস, বিবাসন *nn* banishment; separation. বিবাসিত *adj* banished; exiled.

বিবাসী *adj* 1 banished; exiled. 2 living/ dwelling abroad. বিবাসিনী *fem.*

বিবাহ *n* marriage; taking a wife; wedding; matrimony; wedlock; alliance; nuptial tie; union; consortium. ~ করা *vt* marry; get married; take sb in marriage; take a wife; wed. ~ দেওয়া *vt* unite in marriage; give sb in marriage; marry; wed; unite. ~কাল *n* the (right) time for marriage. ~বিচ্ছেদ *n* divorce; legal dissolution of marriage. ~বিচ্ছেদ করা *vt* divorce; dissolve a marriage. ~বিচ্ছেদকারী *n* divorcee. ~ভোজ *n* wedding-feast; bridal. ~যোগ্য *adj* marriageable. ~যোগ্যা *fem.* ~সভা *n* place/ venue for a marriage-ceremony. ~সম্বন্ধ *n* relation/ connection by marriage.

বিবাহার্য=বিবাহযোগ্য (⇒ বিবাহ)

বিবাহিত *adj* married. বিবাহিতা *fem.*

বিবি [P] *n fem* 1 lady; respectable woman. 2 European/ Muslim lady. 3 wife. 4 mistress of the house. 5 foppish and ease-loving woman. 6 (cards) the queen. ❑*adj* foppish and ease-loving; elegant: ~বউ. ~য়ানা, ~আনি *n* style of living in ease and foppishness; imitation of aristocratic or Eurpean ladies. ~জান *n fem* 1 (term of endearment for one's wife) dear lady; my treasure/ darling/ dear. 2 European lady; foppish and ease-loving woman. ~জি *n fem* Mrs; Madame.

বিবিক্ত *adj* 1 separated; kept apart; detached; distinguished. 2 solitary; alone; isolated. 3 intent upon. 4 clear; distinct. বিবিক্তা *fem.*

বিবিক্ষা *n* wish to enter. বিবিক্ষু *adj* wishing/ intending to enter.

বিবিধ *adj* of various sorts; manifold; diverse; miscellaneous; various. ~পত্রী *adj* (bot) heterophillous.

বিবীত *n* enclosed spot or ground (esp pasture ground); paddock.

বিবুধ *n* 1 learned man; scholar. 2 a god.

বিবৃত *adj* 1 narrated; described; stated. 2 explained; exposed; revealed; manifest;

known. **3** uncovered; unconcealed; divulged; opened. **4** extensive; wide; large. ~ **করা** *vt* state; explain; narrate; reveal; uncover: expose; open.

বিবৃতি *n* **1** statement; narration. **2** explanation; exposition. **3** annotation. **4** expansion.

বিবৃত্ত *adj* turned/ twisted round; revolved; returned. **বিবৃত্তি** *n* turning round; revolution; expansion; opening; development.

বিবৃদ্ধ *adj* grown; increased; enhanced; augmented; enlarged; fully developed; large; abundant; mighty. **বিবৃদ্ধি** *n* growth; increase; augmentation; enlargement; furthering; promotion.

বিবেক *n* **1** conscience. **2** true knowledge. **3** discretion; right judgement; faculty of distinguishing between good and evil. **4** discrimination; distinction. **5** consideration; sense of duty. ~**চালিত,** ~**তাড়িত** *adj* goaded/ impelled by conscience. ~**জ্ঞান** *n* faculty of discretion. ~**দংশন** *n* prick of conscience. ~**দর্শী,** ~**বান** *adjj* conscientious; judicious; discerning; scrupulous. ~**পীড়িত** *adj* conscience-stricken. ~**বুদ্ধি** *n* faculty of discriminating between good and evil; conscientiousness; conscience. ~**বুদ্ধিসম্পন্ন** *adj* conscientious; judicious. ~**বিহীন,** ~**রহিত,** ~**শূন্য,** ~**হীন** *adj* wanting discernment; lacking in conscience; unscrupulous; conscienceless; wanton; devoid of judgement/ discriminatory power.

বিবেকী *adj* **1** discriminating; judicious; prudent; considerate; discrete. **2** conscientious. **3** having no attachment; disinterested. **বিবেকিনী** *fem*. **বিবেকিতা** *n* discriminativeness; discernment; judgement; scrupulousness.

বিবেচক *adj* discriminating; considerate; judicious; thoughtful; prudent; wise; discrete. ~**তা** *n* discernment; correct judgement; consideration; thoughtfulness.

বিবেচন *n* debate; investigation; consideration; judging; treating critically. **বিবেচনীয়** *adj* to be considered/ debated/ discussed.

বিবেচনা *n* **1** consideration; discrimination; examination; critical treatment; investigation; right judgement; considerateness; deliberation; judiciousness; right judgement; prudence. **2** idea; opinion; view. ~ **করা** *vt* consider; judge; reflect; think; deliberate. ~**ধীন** *adj* under consideration. ~**শক্তি** *n* power of discernment/ judgement; discretion. ~**সাপেক্ষ** *adj* subject to/ under consideration.

বিবেচিত *adj* deliberated; considered; judged; discussed; investigated; thought.

বিবেচ্য *adj* to be considered/ judged/ investigated; worthy of consideration; under consideration.

বিব্রত *adj* **1** embarrassed; uneasy; disconcerted; shamefaced; abashed; confused. **2** refractory; reluctant. ~ **করা** *vt* embarrass; disconcert; confuse; abash; put out of countenance.

বিভক্ত *adj* divided; distributed; parted; separated; secluded; partitioned. ~ **করা** *vt* divide; distribute; partition; apportion; separate; part.

বিভক্তি *n* **1** division; partition; separation. **2** (gram) inflection of nouns; declension; an affix of declension; case-ending; a termination or inflection either of a case or of the persons of a verb.

বিভঙ্গ *n* **1** arrangement; composition. **2** division; part; fracture; bending; contraction: ভ্রূ~.

বিভব *n* **1** being everywhere; omnipresence; omnipotence. **2** emancipation; liberation; release from worldly existence; final/ eternal emancipation. **3** magnanimity; lofty-mindedness; generosity. **4** power; might; greatness; exalted position; dignity; majesty; dominion; wealth; riches; fortune; property. **5** godliness; godhead; divinity; unction; sanctifying grace. **6** (phys) (electric) potential; potentia. ~**ক্ষয়** *n* loss of fortune/ property. ~**শালী** *adj* possessed of power; wealthy; great; magnanimous; unctuous. ~**শালিনী** *fem.*

বিভা *n* **1** lustre; splendour; ray; glow; beam. **2** light; **3** revelation; manifestation. **4** beauty. ~**কর** *n* **1** sun. **2** fire. ❑*adj* shining; bright.

বিভাগ *n* **1** division; distribution; partition; apportionment. **2** partition of patrimony; law of inheritance. **3** share; portion; section; part; constituent part of anything. **4** department: ইংরেজি ~. **5** partition/ division of a country etc. ~ **করা** *vt* divide; distribute; partition; apportion. ~**পত্র** *n* deed of partition. ~**রেখা** *n* partition-line; boundary between. ~**ত** *adv* according to a part/ share; proportionately. **বিভাগী** *adj* fissile. **বিভাগী-ছত্রাক** *n* fissile fungus. **বিভাগী-শৈবাল** *n* fissile alga. **বিভাগীয়** *adj* divisional; departmental.

বিভাজক *adj* dividing: ~ শৈলমালা; distributing; apportioning; partitioning. ❑*n* divider; distributor; (math) divisor. **বিভাজিকা** *fem.*

বিভাজন *n* **1** division; partition; distribution; apportionment; parting. **2** (mech) resolution of velocity. **পরমাণু** ~ *n* splitting of atoms.

বিভাজ্য *adj* **1** to be divided/ apportioned/ distributed/ partitioned. **2** (arith) divisible. ❑*n* (math) dividend. ~**তা** *n* divisibility.

বিভাব *n* **1** feeling. **2** reflection. **3** expression. **4** act of producing a particular emotion by a work of art. **বিভাবনীয়** *adj* to be clearly perceived/ ascertained.

বিভাবন *n* **1** (rhet) any cause of aesthetic emotion (eg the persons and circumstances representated in a drama as opposed to অনুভাব or external signs or effects of emotion). **2** enthusiasm; excitement.

বিভাবনা *n* **1** (rhet) description of effects the causes of which are left to be conjectured. **2** deliberation; reflection; clear ascertainment.

বিভাবরী *n* night.

বিভাবসু *n* **1** sun; fire. **2** moon. **3** kind of necklace.

বিভাবিত *adj* **1** felt; considered; deliberated; perceived. **2** absorbed in a feeling. **3** established. **4** famous; famed.

বিভাব্য *adj* **1** to be clearly perceived/ observed. **2** thinkable; comprehensible. **3** to be considered; to be attended to/ heeded.

বিভাষা *n* **1** foreign language. **2** alternative; option.

বিভাস[১] *n* an Indian musical mode.

বিভাস[২] *n* brightness; splendour. **বিভাসিত** *adj* made bright; illuminated; lighted; revealed; embellished; adorned.

বিভিন্ন *adj* **1** split/ broken into two or more. **2** various; manifold; diverse; of different kinds; different; of a different kind. **3** separated; disunited; living at variance; contradictory. **4** opened; blown. **5** cleft. **~তা** *n* state of being broken/ split asunder; difference; diversity; variety. **~ধর্মা** *adj* following a different religion. **~ পথে যাওয়া** *vi* go severally.

বিভীষণ *adj* fearful; terrifying; horrific. ❑*n* **1** name of a brother of Ravana (in the Ramayana). **2** (fig) a traitor to one's family/ country; a quisling; a fifth-columnist. **~বাহিনী** *n* the fifth column.

বিভীষিকা *n* terror; dread; panic; threat; intimidation; horror; frightful/ horrifying sight; frightful hallucination; dismay; trepidation. **~ময়** *adj* terrific; terrifying; horrifying; ghoulish; horrendous; gruesome; full of frightful sights/ hallucinations; horrific; grisly.

বিভু *n* **1** god. **2** lord; ruler; sovereign; king. ❑*adj* **1** all-pervading; omnipresent; eternal. **2** mighty; powerful; great; strong. **~তা, ~ত্ব** *n* power; supremacy; omnipotence; omnipresence; sovereignty. **~প্রেম** *n* love of/ devotion to god.

বিভূঁই *n* foreign land.

বিভূতি *n* **1** prosperity; plenty; abundance; riches; wealth. **2** manifestation of might; great power; superhuman power. **3** splendour; glory; magnificence. **4** ashes (of cow-dung). **5** godhead; divinity. **~ভূষণ** *n* one who smears his body with ashes; Shiva.

বিভূষণ *n* ornament; adornment; decoration; adorning; splendour. ❑*adj* unadorned; unembellished; naked; plain; simple. **বিভূষণা** *fem.*

বিভূক্ষা *n* ornament; beauty; splendour.

বিভূষিত *adj* adorned; decorated; embellished **বিভূষিতা** *fem.*

বিভৃত *adj* supported; maintained; upheld.

বিভেদ *n* **1** breaking asunder; splitting; piercing; division; separation. **2** difference; discrimination; distinction. **3** (also biol) differentiation. **~ করা** *vi* differentiate; discriminate; separate; split/ break in pieces; pierce; cleave asunder. **~ সৃষ্টি করা** *vi* create dissension/ disunity. **কলা~** *n* (bot) differentiation of tissues. **~ক** *adj* **1** differentiating; separating. **2** splitting. ❑*n* (mech) differential (of pulley). **~ন** *n*=**~** (1).

বিভোর, বিভোল (poet, colloq)=বিহ্বল

বিভ্রম *n* **1** illusion; illusive appearance; delusion; mere semblance of anything. **2** error; mistake; blunder; doubt. **3** feminine coquetry; amorous gestures/ actions of any kind (esp play of the eyes). **4** perturbation; flurry (as when a woman in her confusion puts her ornaments in wrong places). **5** caprice; whim; sport; enjoyment (esp amorous). **6** beauty; grace. **7** restlessness; unsteadiness. **8** hurry; agitation; rapture; disturbance; perturbation; confusion.

বিভ্রষ্ট *adj* fallen; sunk; strayed from; disappeared; vanished; gone; unsuccessful; destroyed.

বিভ্রাজ *adj* shining; splendid; luminous.

বিভ্রাট *n* crisis; danger; trouble; difficulty; confusion; turmoil; disorder. **বিচার ~** *n* miscarriage of justice.

বিভ্রান্ত *adj* **1** confused; bewildered; erroneous; blundering; erring; wrong; mistaken; wrongheaded; misguided. **2** wandered or wandering about; rolling/ ogling (as the eyes). **~ করা** *vt* confuse; bewilder; delude; mislead; blur with illusion; distract; cause to blunder; nonplus; fill with doubt.

বিভ্রান্তি *n* **1** error; blunder; mistake. **2** hurry; agitation; delusion; illusion; distraction; doubt. **3** whirling; going round.

বিমজ্জিম [P] *prep* according to.

বিমত *adj* **1** of a different mind/ opinion/ disposition. **2** undesirable; unwanted. **3** disagreed; hostile. **বিমতি** *n* **1** disapproval; dissent; disagreement. **2** doubt; uncertainty. **3** different opinion; hostility. **4** wicked/ harmful inclination or thought or design; evil propensity.

বিমৎসর *adj* free from envy/ jealousy; unenvious; unselfish.

বিমথিত *adj* crushed; dashed to pieces; destroyed.

বিমন *n* distracted; worried; annoyed; disturbed; anxious.

বিমনা *adj* dejected; downcast; discomposed; perplexed; out of one's mind/ senses; distracted; restless; jittery; absent-minded; inattentive.

বিমর্দন=বিমর্দ. ~ করা *vt* crush; pound; grind; press; rub; churn; stir; agitate; trample; destroy; rout. ❑*adj* pressing; squeezing; crushing; destroying: কংস~.

বিমর্দিত *adj* crushed; pounded; ground; pressed; rubbed; churned; stirred; trampled; destroyed; routed.

বিমর্শ *n* **1** special consideration; deliberation. **2** critical test; examination; trial. **3** reasoning; discussion; debate. **4** impatience; fidgetiness. dissatisfaction; displeasure; discontent.

বিমর্শন *n* sadness; unhappiness; melancholy; sorrow.

বিমর্ষ[১], বিমর্ষণ *n* **1** impatience; **2** discontent; dissatisfaction; irritation; displeasure.

বিমর্ষ[২] *adj* sad; melancholy; unhappy; glum; morose. ~তা *n* sadness; glumness; unhappiness; moroseness; melancholy.

বিমল *adj* **1** clear; transparent; pristine. **2** innocent; pure; impeccable; guileless; holy; immaculate. **3** stainless; spotless; untarnished bright; unblemished; unsullied; untainted; faultless. **4** white. বিমলা *fem.* ~চরিত্র *adj* having an immaculate character. ~চরিত্রা *fem.* ~হৃদয় *adj* pure-hearted; pure-minded; pure in heart. বিমলাত্মা *adj* pure-souled. বিমলানন্দ *n* immaculate/ unadulterated joy or delight.

বিমা, বীমা [P] *n* insurance; assurance. ~ করা *vt* insure. ~র কিস্তি *n* insurance premium. ~র দালাল *n* insurance agent. অগ্নি ~ *n* fire insurance. জাহাজি ~ *n* marine insurance. জীবন~ *n* life insurance. বিবাহ ~ *n* marriage insurance. ~কারী *n* the insured; the insurer. ❑*adj* insuring. ~পত্র *n* insurance policy.

বিমাতা *n fem* step-mother.

বিমাতৃজ *n* step-brother. বিমাতৃজা *fem* step-sister.

বিমান *n* **1** aircraft; aeroplane; balloon. **2** car/ chariot of the gods. **3** high-rise (esp with 7 storeyed) building; palace of an emperor or supreme monarch. **4** (mod use) sky. ~ আক্রমণ, ~ হামলা *nn* air-raid. ~ঘাটি *n* aerodrome; airfield. ~চলন *n* aviation. ~চারী *adj* travelling by air/ in a celestial car; moving in the sky/ air; aerial; ethereal. ❑*n* one capable of flying; flyer; airman; aviator. ~চারিণী *fem.* ~চালক *n* pilot; aviator. ~ ডাক *n* air-mail. ~ধ্বংসী *adj* anti-aircraft. ~পত্তন, ~বন্দর *nn* air-port. ~পথ *n* airway. ~পরিবহন *n* air-transport. ~বালা *n fem* air-hostess. ~বাহিনী *n* Air Force. ~বিদ্যা *n* aeronautics. বিমানাঙ্গন *n* airfield.

বিমাননা *n* reproach; rebuke; insult. বিমানিত *adj* rebuked; reproached; insulted.

বিমার *adj* [P] ill-sick; indisposed. বিমারি *n* illness; disease; ailment. বিমারিস্তান *n* hospital.

বিমার্গ *n* wrong road; evil course; abominable/ loathsome habits or practice.

বিমিশ্র *adj* **1** mixed; mingled; miscellaneous; attended/ accompanied by. **2** (bot) polygamous. ~ প্রক্রিয়া *n* (math) allegation.

বিমুক্ত *adj* **1** unloosed; freed; unharnessed; untied; set free; disengaged. **2** liberated (esp from, mundane existence); redeemed; emancipated; delivered; escaped from; saved. **3** given up; abandoned; relinquished; deserted. **4** released; emitted; discharged; hurled; thrown; launched; shed; bestowed on; flowing from; disengaged. **5** cured; relieved: জ্বর~. ~কণ্ঠ *adj* raising a loud cry. ~কেশ *adj* having flowing/ dishevelled hair. ~তা *n* loss of. ~ শাপ *adj* released from the (consequences of) of a curse.

বিমুক্তি *n* disjunction; release; giving up; deliverance; liberation; release from the bonds of existence; final emancipation. ~ পথ *n* the way of final emancipation.

বিমুখ *adj* **1** having the face averted; averse; opposed to; adverse; hostile; indifferent to; disinclined; apathetic; disinterested; unfavourable; displeased: কর্ম~, ভাগ্য~. **2** abstaining/ desisting from. ~ করা *vt* render averse to; make one apathetic/ disinclined; make sb adverse/ unfavourable; avert; ward off; refuse; disappoint; displease; cause to turn away; displease. ~তা *n* aversion; disinclination; apathy; displeasure; hostility; lack of interest; disappointment; adverseness.

বিমুখী *adj* averse from; hostile; having the face averted. বিমুখিতা *n* turning away; aversion; hostility. বিমুখীকরণ *n* the rendering averse to. বিমুখীভাব *n* aversion. বিমুখে *adv* having the face averted.

বিমুগ্ধ *adj* **1** extremely fascinated; magnetized; charmed; enthralled; spellbound; enchanted; captivated; seduced; infatuated; bewitched; enamoured. **2** bewildered; confused; confounded; perplexed as to; uncertain about. **3** foolish; stupid. বিমুগ্ধা *fem adj* foolish-minded; simple. ~তা *n* **1** fascination; enchantment; enthrallment; stupefaction; infatuation; seduction. **2** bewilderment; utter confusion; perplexity. ~ভাব *n* bewildered state; confusion; fascination; enchantment.

বিমূঢ় *adj* **1** incapable of discriminating between good and evil; irresponsible; light-hearted. **2** foolish; utterly stupid; ignorant;

silly; idiotic; light-headed; soft in the head. 3 infatuated; fascinated; bewitched. 4 perplexed; bewildered; stupefied; confounded. ~তা *n* 1 incapability of discriminating; indiscretion. 2 foolishness; utter stupidity; ignorance; thick-headedness; light-headedness; imbecility; obtuseness; folly. 3 infatuation; fascination; bewitchment. 4 stupefaction; bewilderment; perplexity; confusion. ~মতি *adj* foolish-minded; thick-headed; obtuse. ~সংজ্ঞ *adj* bewildered in mind; senseless; unconscious.

বিমূর্ছন *n* modulation; melody.

বিমূর্ছিত *adj* swooned; fainted.

বিমূর্ত *adj* abstract; formless; unbodied.

বিমৃষ্ট *adj* reflected on; considered.

বিমৃষ্যকারী, বিমৃশ্যকারী *adj* prudent; heedful; calculating; cautious; discreet; careful. বিমৃষ্যকারিতা, বিমৃশ্যকারিতা *n* prudence; caution; foresight; discretion; carefulness; precaution.

বিমোক্ষ *n* release; deliverance; liberation of the soul; final emancipation. ~ণ *n*=বিমুক্তি.

বিমোচন=বিমোক্ষ

বিমোচিত *adj* let loose; loosened; liberated; delivered; released; freed; discharged; relieved; removed; cured; dispelled.

বিমোহ *n* fascination; enchantment; bewilderment; perplexity; confusion of the mind; infatuation; inertia. ~ন *n* act of confusing/ bewildering; act of fascinating/ infatuating. ❑*adj* fascinating; enchanting; infatuating; charming; bewitching: রমণী~ন. বিমোহিত *adj* 1 fascinated; enchanted; charmed. 2 bewildered; perplexed; confounded; infatuated; 3 fainted. বিমোহিত করা *vt* 1 fascinate; enchant; charm. infatuate; 2 bewilder; confound; perplex.

বিম্ব *n* 1 bubble. 2 image; reflection; shadow; reflected/ represented form; picture; type. 3 dive of the sun or moon; any disc; sphere; orb. 4 (rhet) the object compared (as opposed to প্রতিবিম্ব, the counterpart to which it is compared). 5 the fruit *Momordica monadelpha* (a plant bearing a bright-red gourd). বিম্বাধর, বিম্বোষ্ঠ, বিম্বৌষ্ঠ *nn* a lip as red as the *bimba* fruit; red lip. ❑*adj* having lips like the *bimba* fruit; red-lipped. বিম্বাধরা, বিম্বোষ্ঠা, বিম্বোষ্ঠী *fem.*

বিম্বক *n* 1 disc of the sun or moon. 2 the fruit *Momordica monadelpha.*

বিম্বকি, বিম্বকী *n* locket; pendant; medal.

বিম্বাগত *adj* reflected.

বিম্বিত *adj* reflected; mirrored back.

বিম্বু *n* betel-nut (tree).

বিম্লনি *adj* unfaded; unblemished; fresh. বিম্লানা *fem.*

বিয়ন্ত *adj* recently delivered of a child or young: ~ বউ, ~ বাঘিনী.

বিয়া *n* (dial)=বিবাহ

বিয়াকুল *adj* (archaic; poet)=ব্যাকুল

বিয়ান[1] *n* (dial)=বিহান

বিয়ান[2] *n fem* mother-in-law of one's son or daughter.

বিয়ান[3] *n* act/instance of bringing forth; delivery; giving birth; parturition. এক ~ *adj* having calved once.

বিয়ানো, বিয়ান *vi* give birth to; bring forth (a child. a young); deliver; calve.

বিয়াবান [P] *n* desert; wilderness; desolate place.

বিয়ারিং=বেয়ারিং

বিয়াল্লিশ *n, adj* forty-two.

বিযুক্ত *adj* 1 disjoined; detached; separated/ delivered from; not being in conjunction with; deprived/ destitute of; that from which sth has been subtracted. 2 deserted; abandoned. 3 (math) subtracted. ❑*prep* minus. ~ করা *vt* detach; separate; disjoin; disconnect; deprive of; exclude from.

বিযুত *adj*=বিযুক্ত (1, 2)

বিয়ে *n* (colloq) marriage (⇒ বিবাহ). ~র ফুল ফোটা ⇒ ফুটা[২]. ~ করা/ দেওয়া=বিবাহ করা/ দেওয়া. ~পাগলা *adj* crazy about mad for marriage.

বিয়েন *n* (colloq)=বিয়ান[3]

বিয়োগ *n* 1 separation; estrangement: বন্ধু~. 2 loss; absence; want; bereavement; death: পিতৃ~. 3 (arith) subtraction. ~ করা *vt* subtract. ~কাতর, ~বিধুর *adjj* suffering from/ afflicted by separation/ bereavement/ loss. ~কাতরা, ~বিধুরা *fem.* ~ফল *n* (arith) result of subtraction; difference. বিয়োগান্ত *adj* ending unhappily or in separation of lovers; tragic; ending in death/ disaster etc; disastrous; lamentable; grievous. বিয়োগান্ত ঘটনা, বিয়োগান্ত নাটক *n* tragedy.

বিয়োগী *adj* separated/ absent from; separated from one's lover. বিয়োগিনী *fem.*

বিযোড়=বিজোড়

বিয়োজন *n* detaching; absence; separation; loss; bereavement; disconnection; decomposition; subtraction.

বিয়োজিত *adj* detached; separated; disjoined; disunited; disconnected.

বিয়োজ্য *adj* to be separated/ detached/ subtracted.

বিয়োনো=বিয়ানো

বিরক্ত *adj* 1 annoyed; irritated; vexed; irked; offended; displeased; bothered; disturbed; tormented. 2 having no interest in; averse; disinterested; indifferent; apathetic. 3 disaffected; estranged. বিরক্তা *fem.* ~ করা *vt* 1 annoy; irritate; vex; disgust; irk; offend; displease; bother; disturb; torment; get on the nerves of; tread on the toes of; badger; importune. **2** make indifferent/ apathetic. **3** estrange; antagonize; alienate; disaffect. **~চিত্ত** *adj* disaffected at heart.

বিরক্তি *n* **1** annoyance; irritation; vexation; exasperation; displeasure. **2** indifference; apathy; want of interest; disinterest. **3** disaffection; estrangement. **~কর, ~জনক** *adjj* annoying; irritating; vexatious; irksome; nettlesome, bothersome; troublesome; importunate; disgusting; exasperating.

বিরঙ্গ *n* various colours. রঙ্গ~ ⇒ রঙ্গ.

বিরচন *n* **1** writing; composing. **2** composition; fashioning; forming; making; arrangement. **3** construction; building.

বিরচিত *n* **1** written; composed. **2** formed; fashioned; arranged; made; put together; **3** constructed; built.

বিরজা[১] *n* **1** Puri in Orissa (which is a holy place for Hindus). **2** (Vaishnaba myth) a river which the soul has to cross in order to reach the blissful abode of Vishnu. **~ধাম** *n* =~.

বিরজা[২] *adj* **1** free from the menstrual excretion. **2** free from dust; clean; pure. **3** free from passion. ❑*n* a woman who has ceased to menstruate.

বিরঞ্জন *n* bleaching; decolourization.

বিরত *adj* **1** stopped; ceased; ended; discontinued; dissuaded; desisted; resigned; prevented; desisting/ abstaining from. **বিরতা** *fem.* **~ করা** *vt* stop; dissuade; turn sb away; deter; cause to leave off/ abstain; prevent. **~ হওয়া** *vi* stop; desist/ abstain from; cease; discontinue; give up; resign; abandon; pause; come to an end.

বিরতি *n* **1** desistance; abstention (from); resignation. **2** pause; cessation; recess; interval; stop; end; termination. **3** dislike; indifference; aversion. **4** peace; serenity; calm; quiet; tranquillity. **5** dash (—).

বিরল *adj* **1** rare; scarcely found; unfrequent; scanty; few. **2** sparse; wide apart; having interstices; separated by intervals; not thick/ compact. **3** loose; thin. **4** desolate; solitary; secluded; lonely: ~ স্থান. **5** secret; confidential: ~ কথন. ❑*n* **1** solitary/ lonely/ secluded place. **~কেশ** *adj* thin-haired; bald-headed. **~জানুক** *adj, n* having knees wide apart; bandy-legged (man). **~তা** *n* rarity; rareness; scarcity; sparseness; sparsity. **~ বসতি** *adj* thinly/ sparsely. populated. **বিরলে** *adv* in seclusion; in private; in solitude; solitarily.

বিরস *adj* **1** juiceless; sapless; dry. **2** flavourless; dull; unseasoned; tasteless; flat; insipid. **3** unpleasant; unsavoury; disagreeable; painful. **4** melancholic; gloomy; sad; sullen; glum; dispirited; displeased. ❑*n* **1** melancholy; sadness; gloom. **2** interruption of enjoyment. **~তা** *n* **1** want of juice/ sap; dullness; unsavouriness; insipidity; vapidity; bad taste. **2** gloom; sadness; melancholy; sullenness; dispiritedness. **~মৃত্তিকা** *n* (chem) rare earth.

বিরহ *n* **1** parting (esp of lovers); separation; abandonment; desertion. **2** absence (from); lack; want; lacking; with the exception of. **~কাতর** *adj* distressed by separation. **~কাতরা** *fem.* **~ জ, ~ জনিত** *adjj* arising from separation. **~জ্বর** *n* anguish of separation. **~বিধুর** *adj*=~কাতর. **~বিরস** *adj* painful through separation. **~ব্যথা** *n* pang of separation. **~ব্যাকুল** *adj*=~কাতর. **~শয়ন** *n* solitary bed/ couch. **বিরহানল** *n* fire of separation. **বিরহার্ত** *adj* pained by separation. **বিরহাবস্থা** *n* state of separation. **বিরহে** *adv* in the absence of; away from.

বিরহিত *adj* **1** free from; deprived of; devoid/ destitute of; wanting in; with the exception of; separated from. **2** abandoned; deserted; solitary; lonely. **3** detached; disjoined; freed from: বন্ধন~. **বিরহিতা** *fem.*

বিরহী *adj* separated; parted (esp from a beloved person); lonely; solitary. ❑*n* a man separated from his wife or sweetheart. **বিরহিণী** *fem.*

বিরহোৎকণ্ঠ *adj* longing after one's absent lover. **বিরহোৎকণ্ঠা** *n* longing after one's absent beloved. **বিরহোৎকণ্ঠিত** *n* (in drama) woman who longs after her absent lover/ husband. **বিরহোৎকণ্ঠিতা** *fem* of ~.

বিরহোৎসুক *adj* suffering from separation.

বিরাগ *n* **1** indifference to external things or worldly objects; want of attachment; apathy; lack of interest; unconcern; disinterest; stoicism. **2** aversion; repugnance; dislike; disaffection; resentment; dissatisfaction; discontent; distaste. **3** displeasure; disinclination; antipathy; loathing. **4** freedom from all worldly desires; asceticism. **~ভাজন** *adj* causing displeasure; loathesome; repugnant; disagreeable. ❑*n* object of displeasure. **~ ভাজন হাওয়া** *vi* incur displeasure.

বিরাগী *adj* indifferent; having no attachment; disinterested; unconcerned; displeased; apathetic. **বিরাগিণী** *fem.*

বিরাজ *n* the supreme Being. **~ করা** *vi* shine forth/ out; reign; rule; govern; exist; be present; be illustrious/ eminent; excel; appear. **~মান** *adj* **1** eminent; brilliant; illustrious; splendid; glorious. **2** existing; existent; present. **~মানা** *fem.*

বিরাজিত *adj* **1** = বিরাজমান (⇒ বিরাজ). **2** manifest; conspicuous; revealed. **বিরাজিতা** *fem.*

বিরাট *adj* vast; great; enormous; gigantic; huge, immense. ❑*n* **1** North Bengal. **2** king of North Bengal. **3** (phil) the Supreme Intellect located in a supposed aggregate of gross bodies. **~ত্ব** *n* vastness; immensity; enormity.

বিরাদর, বিরাদার=বেরাদার

বিরান [P] *adj* desolate; laid waste; depopulated; ruined. **~ করা** *vt* ruin; lay waste; depopulate.

বিরানব্বই, বিরানব্বুই (colloq) *n, adj* ninety-two.

বিরানা [P] *adj* stranger; not related; unrelated: ~ মানুষ.

বিরাব *n* clamour; noise; sound; buzzing; humming. ❑*adj* noiseless; silent; soundless; quiet; hushed. **বিরাবী** *adj*=~.

বিরাবান [P] *n* desolate place.

বিরাম *n* **1** abstention. **2**=বিরাগ (4). **3** cessation; termination; end. **4** pause; intermission; stop; respite; leisure; interval; rest. **5** (gram) end of a word or sentence; the stop. **~ চিহ্ন** *n* punctuation mark. **~হীন** *adj* incessant; ceaseless; unending; interminable; unremitting; continuous; never-ending; non-stop.

বিরাশি *n, adj* eighty-two. **~ সিক্কার ওজন** **1** unit of mass equalling the weight of eighty-two one-rupee silver coins; standard weight. **2** very heavy; costly; sumptuous. **~ সিক্কা ওজনের চাপড়** hard smack.

বিরিঞ্চি *n* Brahma.

বিরিঞ্জি [P] *n* small iron nail.

বিরিয়ানি [P] *n* a dish of meat and rice cooked together in clarified butter.

বিরুত *n* indistinct sound; humming; chirping; shrieking; ❑*adj* filled with the cries/ chirping of.

বিরুদ্ধ *adj* **1** opposed; adverse; unfavourable; hostile; at variance/ enmity with; inimical; antipathetic. **2** opposite; contrary; unpleasant; hateful; odious; repugnant; disagreeable; reverse; inconsistent/ incompatible with. **~তা** *n* opposition; hostility; repugnance; enmity; contrariety; incompatibility; adverseness; antipathy. **~-তড়িচ্চালক বল** (phy) back electromotive force. **~বচন** *n* malignant/ abusive language; hostile words; adverse/ contradictory speech. **~বাদী** *adj* making adverse/ contradictory speech or remarks. ❑*n* adversary; opponent. **~বাদিনী** *fem.* **~ সমালোচনা** *n* hostile/ unfavourable criticism; animadversion. **~ সমালোচনা করা** *vi* make hostile/ adverse criticism; censure; criticize unfavourably; animadvert. **বিরুদ্ধাচরণ** *n* **1** opposition; hostility. **2** wrong/ improper course of conduct. **বিরুদ্ধাচারণ করা** *vt* oppose; be inimical/ hostile to; be against. **বিরুদ্ধাচার** *n* opposition; antagonism. **বিরুদ্ধাচারী** *adj* indulging in practices in opposition to usage; opposing; hostile; adverse; inimical. **বিরুদ্ধাচারিণী** *fem.* **বিরুদ্ধাবর্তন** *n* (logic) conversion by contraposition. **বিরুদ্ধে** *adv* against; in the teeth of; in opposition to; counter to; in defiance of; in the face of.

বিরূপ *adj* **1** unfavourable; adverse; unfriendly; averse. **2** displeased; grudging; cross; resentful; disgruntled; opposed; bitter. **3** ugly; deformed; monstrous; misshapen. **বিরূপা** *fem.* **~ প্রণালী** *n* (logic) method of difference. **~তা** *n* **1** opposition; contrariety; disfavour; hostility; antagonism; inimicality. **2** displeasure; resentment; disgruntlement; umbrage; animosity. **3** ugliness; deformity.

বিরূপাক্ষ *n* Shiva. ❑*adj* having deformed eyes.

বিরূপানুমান *n* (logic) inference by opposition.

বিরূপিকা *adj fem* ugly; hideous; deformed.

বিরেক *n* purging; evacuation of the bowels.

বিরেচক *adj* purgative; aperient; laxative. ❑*n* purgative; laxative.

বিরেচন *n* purging; purgation; evacuation of the bowels.

বিরোচন *n* **1** sun; sun-god. **2** moon. **3** fire, **4** (myth) name of an Asura (son of Prahlada)

বিরোধ *n* **1** enmity; hostility; opposition; difference; antipathy; disagreement. **2** quarrel; dispute; conflicts; strife; contention; **3** contradiction; contrariety; antithesis; inconsistency; incompatibility; incongruity; dissimilarity. **4** adversity; calamity; misfortune. **5** hindrance; prevention; obstacle. **6** (old use) siege; blockade. **7** (rhet) an apparent contradiction. **~ করা** *vi* quarrel; dispute; oppose; contend; clash; pick a quarrel; wrangle. **~ন** *n* =~. ❑*n*=*adj* opposing; fighting; checking. **~ নিয়ম** *n* (logic) law of contradiction. **~ পরিহার** *n* removal of incompatibility; reconciliation.

বিরোধানল *n* conflagration of conflict.

বিরোধাভাস *n* (rhet) a figure of speech involving an apparent contradiction; semblance of opposite qualities.

বিরোধিত *adj* opposed; contended against; fought with; obstructed; hindered.

বিরোধিতা *n* opposition; antagonism; hostility; enmity; antipathy; disagreement; hindrance; rivalry. **~ করা** *vt* oppose; be hostile/ inimical/ antipathic to; disagree; fight.

বিরোধী *adj* **1** opposing; hindering; preventing; obstructing; disturbing; opposed; contradictory; inconsistent. **2** adverse; hostile; inimical. **বিরোধিনী** *fem.* **~ পক্ষ** *n* **1**

opposite/hostile/ rival party. **2** (in parliament) the opposition.

বিরোধোক্তি **1**=বিরুদ্ধবচন (⇒ বিরুদ্ধ). **2** (rhet) apparent contraction.

বিল[1] *n* marsh; marshland; swamp; swampland; fen; slough.

বিল[2] *n* hole; cave; cavity; pit; opening.

বিল[3] [E] *n* bill; promissory note; draft. ~ **করা** *vi* make out/ draw a bill. ~ **পাস করা** pass a bill. ~ **মেটানো** foot the bill; pay off/ settle a bill.

বিলকুল [A] *adj* complete; thorough; positive; outright; clear: ~ মিথ্যা কথা. ❑*adv* completely; thoroughly; outright; positively; entirely; wholly; unreservedly; altogether.

বিলক্ষ *adj* **1** having no fixed aim. **2** having no characteristic mark/ property.

বিলক্ষণ *adj* **1** uncommon; extraordinary; unusual; much; great; considerable; enormous. **2** different. ❑*adv* very well; of course; thoroughly; surely; to a great extent; certainly; fine; excellent: আমি তাকে ~ চিনি.

বিলক্ষিত *adj* observed; perceived; noticed; distinguished; marked by.

বিলগ্ন *adj* attached/ fastened/ clung to; connected with; resting/ hanging on.

বিলঙ্ঘন *n* leaping over; crossing; surmounting; overcoming; passing beyond. **বিলঙ্ঘনীয়, বিলঙ্ঘ্য** *adj* to be overstepped/ passed over/ transgressed/ surmounted: **বিলঙ্ঘিত** *adj* overleaped; overcome; surmounted; surpassed; baffled; defied.

বিলজ্জ *n* shameless. ~**মান** *adj* blushing; abashed; ashamed.

বিলম্ব *n* **1** delay; lateness; procrastination; slowness. **2** hanging/ falling down; pendulousness. ~ **করা** *vi, vt* delay; be late; procrastinate; linger; tarry. ~ **করানো** *vt* delay; retard. ~**ন** *n* **1** delaying; procrastination; slowness; lingering. **2** hanging down; suspension. ~ **শুল্ক** *n* demurrage. **বিলম্বে** *adv* late. **অতি বিলম্বে** *adv* very late; a day after the fair.

বিলম্বিত *adj* **1** retarded; delayed; late; tardy; slow. **2** hanging down; pendulous; suspended. ~ **লয়** (music) slow measure (opp to দ্রুতলয়).

বিলম্বী *adj* **1** delaying; making late; procrastinating; tarrying; slow; lingering. **2** hanging down; pendulous; hanging to/ from; leaning against; suspended.

বিলয় *n* **1** destruction (esp of the world). **2** dissolution; liquefaction; annihilation; disappearance; death. ❑*adj* (music) unmeasured. ~**ন** *n* dissolving; liquefying.

বিলসা *vi* (poet) gleam; flush; shine forth; glitter; play; sport; dally; vibrate. **বিলসন** *n* gleaming; flashing; play; sport.

বিলসিত *adj* **1** gleaming; flashing; glittering; shining forth; beautified; adorned. **2** enjoyed; played; amused; sported; delighted.

বিলাই *n* (dial)=বিড়াল

বিলাত[1], **বিলেত** [A] *n* **1** England. **2** Europe. **3** foreign country. **4** kingdom; domain. ~ **ফেরত**, ~**ফেরতা** *adj* returned from England/ Europe.

বিলাত[2] *n* (of bills, etc) non-realization; non-recovery. ~ **পড়া** *v* fall into arrears; be overdue; become a bad debt. ~**বাকি** *n* bad debt; arrears; outstanding; unrealized dues, bills, etc.

বিলাতি, বিলেতি *adj* English; European; foreign; produced in/ imported from England/ Europe/ a foreign country. ~ **আমড়া** *n* hog-plum. ~ **কাপড়** *n* English/ foreign textile material. ~ **কুমড়া** *n* gourd. ~ **বেগুন** *n* tomato. ~**য়ানা** *n* **1** (derog) adoption/ initiation of English or European way of life; anglomania. **2** anglicism; Europeanism.

বিলানো *vt* give away; distribute: ~ অর্থ.

বিলাপ *n* wailing; lamenting; lamentation; lament. ~ **করা** *vi, vt* wail; lament; bewail; utter moaning sounds. ~**ন** *n*=~. ~**বচন** *n* lamentation. **বিলাপী** *adj* lamenting; wailing; uttering/ moaning/ inarticulate sounds. ~ **বিলাপিনী** *fem.*

বিলাস *n* **1** luxury; indulgence; self-indulgence; bed of roses; extravagance; overindulgence; wastefulness; high living; daintiness; foppery; enjoyment of milk and honey. **2** sport; play; pastime; pleasure; diversion (esp with women, etc). **3** fun; merriment; jollily; liveliness; good time. **4** pleasure; delight; enjoyment; kick (colloq); joviality. **5** amorous sport; dalliance; voluptuousness; dissoluteness; dissipation. **6** coquetry; affectation of coyness; wantonness; any playful action or gesture. **7** a form of feminine gesture considered as indicative of amorous sentiments. **8** grace; charm; beauty. **9** expression; manifestation. **10** display; flash; sparkle; fireworks: বুদ্ধির ~. ~**কানন** *n* pleasure-grove; pleasure-garden. ~**কুঞ্জ** *n*=~কানন. ~**গৃহ** *n* pleasure-house. ~**তরণী** *n* pleasure-boat. ~**তৃষ্ণা** *n* thirst/ lust for pleasure. ~**পর**, ~**পরায়ণ**, ~**প্রিয়** *adjj*=বিলাসী. ~**পরায়ণা** *fem.* ~**পরতা**, ~**পরায়ণতা**, ~**প্রিয়তা** *nn*=বিলাসিতা. ~**বাসনা** *n* pleasure seeking; lust for pleasure; sensualism; sensuality. ~**বিভ্রম** *n* amorous gestures; coquetry. ~**বিহার** *n* pleasure-walk; promenading. ~**ব্যসন** *n* dissipation; self-indulgence; sybaritism; life of pleasure; (all) beer and skittles; gay life. ~**ভবন**, ~**মন্দির** *nn*=~গৃহ. ~**মত্ত** *adj* lost in luxury; mad with wanton frolics; rollicking. ~**ময়** *adj* full of grace; charming. ~**শয্যা** *n* pleasure-couch.

বিলাসিতা *n* **1** luxury; foppishness; high living; stylishness; fashionableness. **2** love of pleasure; self-indulgence; wantonness; dissipation; playfulness; sensualism; life of pleasure; amusement; entertainment; self-gratification.

বিলাসী *adj* **1** luxurious; fond of luxuries; self-indulgent; pleasure-seeking; sybaritic; voluptuous; sensual; dissolute. **2** wanton; sportive; playful; dallying with; fond of. ❑*n* lover; husband: উর্মিলা~. **বিলাসিনী** *fem, adj* **1**=~ (1, 2). **2** coquettish. ❑*n* **1** woman. **2** whore; lively/ coquettish/ wanton woman. **3** mistress; wife.

বিলি[1] *n* **1** distribution; dealing/ giving out; dispensation; handing out: টাকা/ খাবার ~. **2** settlement: জমি ~. **3** delivery: চিঠি ~. **4** assignment; allotment: কাজ ~. **~ করা** *vt* distribute; give/ deal out; hand out; dispense; settle (land); deliver; assign; allot. **~বন্দোবস্ত, ~ব্যবস্থা, ~বন্দেজ** *n* settlement; assignment; disbursement; orderly arrangement and distribution. **~ব্যবস্থাপক** *n* manager; supervisor.

বিলি[2] *n* removing lice from hair. **চুলে ~ দেওয়া** pick lice from hair.

বিলিখা, বিলেখন *n* **1** writing. **2** scratching; scraping. **3** dividing; splitting. **4** digging; delving; rooting up.

বিলিপ্ত *adj* smeared over; anointed.

বিলীন *adj* **1** dissolved; vanished; destroyed. disappeared; melted; faded. **2** absorbed; engrossed; lost. **3** mixed; blended. **4** sunk; plunged; immersed in. **~ হওয়া** *vi* dissolve; vanish; disappear; fade away; melt; be absorbed/ engrossed/ lost; be mixed/ blended; be sunk/ plunged/ immersed; sink.

বিলীয়মান *adj* vanishing; dissolving; fading; melting; evanescent; in the state of being absorbed/ destroyed.

বিলুণ্ঠন *n* robbing; plundering.

বিলুণ্ঠিত *adj* **1** rolling; wallowing. **2** robbed; plundered. **বিলুণ্ঠিতা** *fem.* **~ হওয়া** *vi* **1** roll about; wallow. **2** be robbed/ plundered.

বিলুপ্ত *adj* destroyed; ruined; extinct; vanished; abolished; annihilated; faded away; dead; defunct; perished; gone lost.

বিলুলিত *adj* shaken; agitated; disarranged; disordered.

বিলেখন ⇒ বিলিখন

বিলেপ, বিলেপন *n* **1** anointing; plastering; smearing. **2** ointment; unguent; perfume for the person (as saffron, camphor etc); balm; salve; plaster. **বিলেপন করা** *vt* anoint; smear; plaster; spread over.

বিলোকন *n* act of looking/ seeing; looking at; regarding; observing; contemplating; observation; staring; look; glance; stare. **বিলোকনীয়** *adj* to be looked at/ observed: worthy to be looked at; beautiful; lovely.

বিলোকিত *adj* looked at; seen; beheld: observed; noticed.

বিলোচন *n* **1** seeing; viewing . **2** eye; sight.

বিলোড়ন *n* stirring up; churning; splashing (in water); agitating; agitation. **বিলোড়িত** *adj* stirred up; churned; splashed; agitated.

বিলোপ, বিলোপন *n* **1** extinction; death. **2** destruction; abolish; ruin; annihilation. **3** disappearance; passing away. **বিলোপ/ বিলোপসাধন করা** *vt* destroy; nullify; render null; ruin; blot out; abolish; abrogate; obliterate; annihilate. **বিলোপপ্রাপ্ত হওয়া** *vi* cease to exist; be/ become extinct; die out; disappear; vanish; fade; dissolve; pass away; perish; be abolished / abrogated/ destroyed.

বিলোভন *n* beguiling; seduction; temptation; tempting. ❑*adj* very tempting; enticing; alluring.

বিলোম *adj* turned in the opposite direction; turned the wrong way; inverted; contrary to the usual/ proper course; opposed; reversed; inverse; produced in reverse order; refractory. ❑*n* **1** reverse order; opposite course; reverse. **2** water-wheel/ machine for raising water from a well. **3** (music) descending from a higher tone to a lower one. **~কেন্দ্র** *n* (geom) centre of inversion. **~ ক্রিয়া** *n* **1** (geom) inversion. **2** reverse action; doing anything in reverse order or backwards. **~জ, ~জাত** *adjj* born of a mother belonging to a higher caste than the father. **~তা** *n* perverseness. **~বিধি** *n* (arith) rule of inversion. **2** inverted rite; reversed ceremony. **~ব্যাসার্ধ** *n* (geom) radius of inversion.

বিলোমাঙ্ক *n* (geom) constant of inversion.

বিলোল *adj* **1** moving to and fro from side to side; unsteady; rolling; waving; quivering; flickering: ~ কটাক্ষ. **2** very greedy; covetous; wistful; lustful; yearning; hungry: ~ দৃষ্টি. **3** dishevelled; rumpled; disarranged: ~ বসনভূষণ. **~তা** *n* tremulousness; unsteadiness; rolling (of the eyes). **~কটাক্ষ** *adj* with tremulous glance. **~তারক** *adj* with rolling (pupils of the) eyes. **~দৃষ্টি, ~লোচন** *adjj* with rolling/ tremulous/ covetous/ leering eyes. **বিলোলিত** *adj* moved hither and thither; shaken; agitated; tossed about.

বিল্টি [E] *n* bill of lading; bill of fare.

বিল্ব *n* wood-apple (tree); *Aegle marmelos.*

বিল্লি *n* (facet) cat.

বিশ *n, adj* twenty. **~ বাঁও পানি** great trouble.

বিশঙ্ক *adj* **1** fearless; confident. **2** apprehensive; alarmed; fearful. **~মান** *adj* apprehensive; suspicious.

বিশদ *adj* **1** clear; evident; manifest; intelligible; lucid: ~ আলোচনা. **2** white: ~ বস্ত্র. **3** clean; spotless; pure; brilliant; shining; splendid. ❑*n* white (the colour). **~ করা** *vt* elucidate; elaborate; explain clearly; clarity. **~তা** *n* clearness; lucidity. **~ভাবে** *adj* clearly; lucidly; elaborately. **বিশদিত** *adj* purified; elaborated; clarified; explained clearly; elucidated.

বিশল্য *adj* freed from an arrow-head; healed of an arrow-wound; freed from pain; without trouble/ care/ pain. **~করণী** *n* a particular herb with wonder-working properties.

বিশা *adj* (dial)=বিশে

বিশাই *n* (dial)=বিশ্বকর্মা

বিশাখ *adj* branchless; handless. ❑*n* name of the Hindu god Kartikeya.

বিশাখা *n* the sixteenth of the twenty-seven stars according to Hindu astronomy.

বিশারদ *adj* **1** experienced/ skilled/ proficient in; conversant with. **2** learned; wise; erudite. **3** famous; celebrated. **4** clever; expert. **বিশারদা** *fem.*

বিশাল *adj* **1** huge; enormous; immense; gigantic; colossal; monumental. **2** spacious; extensive; broad; wide; vast. **3** excessive: পশ্চাতে ঢোলের বাদ্য বাজায় ~. **4** magnanimous; lion-hearted; generous. **5** great; important; powerful; mighty; illustrious; eminent. **~তা** *n* hugeness; vastness; enormity; immensity; great extent; spaciousness; greatness; eminence; majesty; distinction. **~নয়না, ~লোচনা** *adjj fem* having large eyes. **~হৃদয়** *adj* large-hearted; magnanimous.

বিশালাক্ষ *adj* large-eyed. ❑*n* **1** the Hindu god Shiva. **2** Garuda. **বিশালাক্ষী** *adj fem* of ~. ❑*n* goddess Durga.

বিশিখ *n* **1** arrow; shaft. **2** spear; javelin. **3** iron crow. ❑*adj* **1** flameless. **2** devoid of the top-knot/ tuft of hair (left on the hair after tonsure). **বিশিখা** *fem* **1** bald. **2** unfeathered (as an arrow).

বিশিষ্ট *adj* **1** distinguished; pre-eminent; prominent; excellent; excelling in: ~ লেখক/ লোক. **2** educated; cultured; remarkable: ~ ভদ্রলোক. **3** distinct; particular; especial: ~ স্থান. **4** peculiar; specific; characteristic: ~ লক্ষণ. **5** (used as the later member of a compound word) characterized by; possessing; containing: গুণ~, দন্ত~. **বিশিষ্টা** *fem.* **বিশিষ্টতা** *adj* distinction; excellence; superiority; specialty; peculiarity; characteristic; prominence; remarkability; conspicuousness.

বিশিষ্টাদ্বৈতবাদ *n* (phil) the doctrine that the spirits of men have a qualified identity with the one spirit; doctrine of qualified non-duality.

বিশীর্ণ *adj* withered; shrivelled; wizened; thin; slender; skinny; emaciated; lean; haggard; wasted; worn out. **বিশীর্ণা** *fem.* **~তা** *n* state of being extremely withered/ shrivelled/ wasted etc; thinness; emaciation; skinniness; slenderness; leanness.

বিশীর্ণমান *adj* withering; shrivelling; emaciating; drying.

বিশুদ্ধ *adj* **1** pure; holy; sacred; saintly; godly: ~ চরিত্র. **2** uncontaminated; unalloyed; unblended; unmixed; unadulterated; genuine; pure: ~ তেল, ~ শান্তি. **3** free from vice; virtuous; honest; righteous. **4** completely cleaned/ purified; clean; clear; refined: ~ স্বর্ণ. **5** raw: ~ কোহল. **6** innocent: ~ আমোদ-প্রমোদ. **7** perfectly faultless; unblemished; immaculate. **8** correct; accurate: ~ যোগফল. **~ গণিত** *n* pure mathematics. **~ চরিত্র** *adj* of virtuous conduct/ character. **~তা, ~ত্ব** *n* purity; genuineness; holiness; innocence; clearness; immaculateness; correctness; accuracy. **~ প্রকৃতি** *adj* of pure/ virtuous disposition. **~ ভাব, ~ মানস** *adj* pure-minded. **~ সত্ত্ব** *adj* of a pure character. **বিশুদ্ধাত্মা** *adj* of a pure nature/ character; pure souled.

বিশুদ্ধি *n* purification; purity; holiness; virtue; rectification; removal of error/ doubt.

বিশুষ্ক *adj* **1** completely dried up/ withered stale; faded; desiccated: ~ পাতা/ফুল/ ফল. **2** parched; scorched; arid; thirsty: ~ গলা. **3** sapless; juiceless; moistureless. **4**=বিশীর্ণ. **~তা** *n* dryness; aridness; aridity; drought; parchedness; desiccation; state of being wizened; wanness; pallor; emaciation; moroseness; glumness.

বিশৃঙ্খল *adj* **1** disorderly; wild; tumultuous; unruly; riotous; noisy; confused; unsystematic; chaotic; unmethodical; haphazard; disorganized. **2** undisciplined; lawless; disobedient; wayward; dissolute. **3** uncontrolled; unfettered; unrestrained; unbounded; uncontrollable; irregular. **~ করা** *vt* throw into confusion; disorder; disarrange; disorganize; mess up; embroil; upset; throw into disarray; muddle; rumple; ruffle; dishevel. **~তা, বিশৃঙ্খলা** *nn* disorder; disorderliness; tumult; turbulence; lawlessness; disarray; disarrangement; disorganization; untidiness; confusion; muddle; jumble; welter; mess; uproar; pandemonium; disturbance; anarchy; hullabaloo; dissoluteness; irregularity.

বিশে *n* the twentieth (day of a month). ❑*adj* (of the days of a month) twentieth.

বিশেষ *adj* **1** particular; special: ~ কাজ, ~ ব্যবস্থা. **2** urgent: ~ প্রয়োজন. **3** peculiar; characteristic: ~ লক্ষণ, ~ গুণ. **4** excellent; superior; choice; distinguished; extraordinary: ~ বিধি, ~ তারা, ~

ঘটনা, ~ ব্যক্তি. 5 specific: ~ দর. 6 remarkable: ~ আগ্রহ. 7 (phil) individual. 8 (logic) particular. ❑*adv* particularly; especially; peculiarly; very; exceedingly: ~ আকর্ষণীয়, ~ আনন্দিত. ❑*n* 1 difference; distinction. 2 characteristic difference; peculiar mark; special property; speciality; peculiarity. 3 kind; species; type; individual; sort: বৃক্ষ~. 4 excellence; distinction; peculiar merit; superiority: ইতর~. 5 variety; novelty. 6 (phil) individuality; particularity; essential difference; individual essence. 7 (rhet) statement of difference/ distinction; individualization; variation. ~ করা *vt* specify; particularize; differentiate; distinguish; make distinct/ different; define. ~ গুণ *n* special/ distinct quality; (phil) a substance of a distinct kind (eg soul, time, space). ~জ্ঞ *adj* having special knowledge; knowing distinctions; expert; specialized; judicious. ❑*n* expert; specialist. ~ত *adj* especially; particularly; above all. ~তা, ত্ব *nn* distinction; peculiarity; particularity; speciality; excellence; superiority; difference. ~ ধর্ম *n* special quality/ nature/ law. ~ প্রমাণ *n* special authority. ~ বিধি *n* special rule/ observance. ~ লক্ষণ *n* any specific/ characteristic mark or sign. ~ভাবে, ~রূপে *advv* especially; particularly; specifically. বিশেষার্থ *n* sense/ essence of distinction; special meaning.

বিশেষক *adj* distinguishing; qualifying; specifying; differentiating; discriminative. ❑*n* 1 a mark on the forehead. 2 (gram) attribute; predicate.

বিশেষণ *n* 1 (gram) a word which particularizes or defines; adjective; attribute; adverb; apposition; predicate. 2 distinguishing; specifying; qualifying; discrimination; particularization. 3 distinguishing mark; attribute. বিশেষণীয় *adj* 1 to be distinguished discriminated; to be particularized; to be marked as different/ distinct; distinguishable; attributable. 2 adjectival. ক্রিয়া~ *n* adverb. বিশেষণের ~ *n* adjective.

বিশেষাধিকার *n* privilege.

বিশেষাভিধান *n* denotation.

বিশেষিত *adj* distinguished; defined; characterized; specified; predicated; attributed.

বিশেষোক্তি *n* (rhet) a figure of speech in which the cause is stated as not producing the usual result.

বিশেষ্য *n* 1 (gram) noun; substantive; object or subject of a predicate. 2 to be distinguished/ qualified/ particularized. ~তা *n* the being defined/ qualified; substantial nature.

বিশোক *adj* free from sorrow. ❑*n* 1 cessation of sorrow. 2 the tree of *Jonesia asoka.*

বিশোধক *adj* purifying; cleaning; clearing; rectifying; corrective; correcting; amending. ❑*n* purifier; cleanser; detergent.

বিশোধন *n* 1 cleaning; purging; cleansing; washing away; purification; rectification; refinement. 2 correction; amendment. বিশোধনীয় *adj* to be purified/ cleaned/ rectified; to be corrected/ amended.

বিশোধিত *adj* purified; cleaned; freed from soil/ taint; rectified; refined; corrected; amended.

বিশোধী *adj*=বিশোধক

বিশোধ্য *adj* to be cleansed/ purified; purifiable; rectifiable; correctible; corrigible; amendable.

বিশোষণ *n* (the act of) drying up; desiccation; healing (a wound); absorption; absorbing. বিশোষিত *adj* completely dried up/ withered; desiccated; absorbed.

বিশ্ব *n* world; universe; earth. ❑*adj* 1 all; every; every one. 2 whole; entire; universal. 3 all-pervading; all-containing; omnipresent. ~কর্তা *n* creator of the world. ~কর্মা *n* all-maker; (myth) the divine creative architect/ artist. ~কৃৎ *n* the creator of all things. ~কোষ, ~কোশ *n* encyclopedia. ~গত *adj* omnipresent. ~গুরু *n* father of the universe. ~চক্র *n* revolving universe; a wheel made of gold representing the universe. ~চরাচর *n* the whole/ entire universe (containing everything mobile and immobile). ~জন *n* all men; mankind. ~জননী *n fem* mother of the world; Durga. ~জনীন *adj* containing all kinds of people; good for/ benefiting all men; ruling all people; universal; altruistic. ~জনীনতা *n* universality; altruism; universal benefit. ~জনীয় *adj* suitable for/ benefiting all men; universal. ~জন্য *adj* containing all men; existing everywhere; universal; dear to all men. ~জয়ী *adj* conquering the universe. ~জিৎ *adj* all-conquering; all-pervading. ❑*n* conqueror of the universe/ world. ~ত *adv* from/ on all sides; everywhere; all around; universally. ~ধাত্রী *n fem* all-sustainer; earth. ~ধারিণী *n fem* earth. ~নন্দিত *adj* world-acclaimed; universally acclaimed. ~নাথ *n* lord of the universe; Shiva. ~নিখিল *n* the whole universe. ~নিন্দক, ~নিন্দুক *adj* (given to) decrying the whole world/ everything and everybody in the world; cynical. ❑*n* mudslinger; slanderer; scandalmonger; muckraker; cynic; scoffer. ~পতি *n*=~নাথ. ~পা, ~পাতা, ~পালক *adj* all-protecting. ❑*n* preserver of the world; God. ~পিতা *n* father of the world; God. ~পূজিত *adj* universally honoured/ revered. ~পূজ্য *adj* all-venerable. ~প্রীতি, ~প্রেম *nn* universal love. ~প্রেমিক *adj* loving the whole world. ❑*n* one who loves the whole world; lover of the whole world. ~বখাটে

n thorough rake. ~বঞ্চক *n* perfect cheat/ swindler. ~বন্ধু *n* friend of the whole world. ~বাসী *adj* inhabiting the world; cosmopolitan. ❑*n* people of the world; mankind. ~বিখ্যাত *adj* known in the whole world; world-famous. ~বিজয়ী *adj* all-conquering. ~বিদ্যালয় *n* university. ~বিধাতা *n* all-maker; creator of the world; God; providence. ~বিধায়ী *n*=~বিধাতা. ~বিধায়িনী *fem.* ~বিধাতৃ *n* creator; deity. ~বিমোহন, ~বিমোহী *adj* charming/ bewitching the whole world. ~বিমোহিনী *fem.* ~বিশ্রুত *adj* = ~বিখ্যাত. ~বোধ *n* universal consciousness. ~ব্যাপক, ~ব্যাপী *adj* all-pervading; world-wide; filling the universe; all diffused. ~ব্যাপিনী *fem.* ~ব্যাপ্তি universal diffusion/ permeation. ~ব্রহ্মাণ্ড *n* the whole universe. ~ভূত *adj* being everywhere; all-pervading. ~ভ্রাতৃত্ব *n* universal brotherhood; internationalism. ~ময় *adj* = ~ব্যাপী. ~মণ্ডল *n*=~ব্রহ্মাণ্ড. ~মাতা *n fem* = ~জননী. ~মানবতা *n* humanitarianism; universal friendship. ~মৈত্রী *n* universal/ international amity or friendship. ~ম্ভর *adj* all-bearing; all sustaining. ❑*n* God; Vishnu. ~ম্ভরা, ~ম্ভরী mother earth. ~যোনি *n* source/ Creator of the universe. ~রাজ *n* universal Sovereign. ~রূপ *n* one who wears all forms; Vishnu. ~শ্রী *n* grace of the universe; fire. ~সংসার *n* the whole universe. ~সংহার *n* general/ universal destruction/ cataclysm. ~সখা *n* universal friend. ~সার *n* essence of the universe. ~সাহিত্য *n* world literature. ~সৃক, ~স্রষ্টা *n* creator of the universe. ~সৃষ্টি *n* creation of the universe. ~হিত *n* universal welfare; welfare of the humanity. বিশ্বাতীত *adj* all-surpassing. বিশ্বাত্মা *n* soul of the universe; universal spirit; supreme Being. বিশ্বামিত্র *n* "friend of all"; a celebrated sage. বিশ্বেশ, বিশ্বেশ্বর *n* Lord of the universe; a form of Shiva (esp worshipped in Benaras). বিশ্বেশ্বরী *fem* goddess Durga.

বিশ্বতোমুখ *adj* facing all sides; one whose face is turned everywhere.

বিশ্বসিত *adj* **1** trusted; believed/ confided in. **2** full of confidence; fearless; unsuspecting.

বিশ্বস্ত *adj* **1** trusted; faithful; trustworthy; loyal; true; truthful; dependable; constant; reliable; unfailing; confided in. **2** full of confidence; trustful; trusting; confident; unsuspecting; fearless; bold; **3** bona fide বিশ্বস্তা *fem.* ~তা *n* trustworthiness; reliability; dependability; bona fides; fidelity; constancy; loyalty; faithfulness. ~সূত্র *n* reliable source. ~সূত্রে *adv* from a reliable source.

বিশ্বাস *n* **1** trust; faith; belief; reliance; confidence; religious faith; notion; credence; credit; opinion; impression; assumption. **2** conviction; confidence; self-assurance; self-confidence; assurance. **3** respect; regard. **4** a family title. ~ করা *vt* believe (in); trust; confide in; put one's trust in; have faith in; place reliance on; rely upon; count on; depend on; give faith/ credit/ credence; presume; deem; have/ hold/ cherish/ entertain a belief; think. ~ করে বলা *vi* confide in. ~ঘাতক, ~ঘাতী *adj* treacherous; betraying; traitorous; insidious; shifty; perfidious; seditious. ❑*n* traitor (*fem* traitress); betrayer; quisling. ~ঘাতিকা, ~ঘাতিনী *fem.* ~ঘাতকতা *n* treachery; perfidy; perfidiousness; betrayal; infidelity. ~ঘাতকতা করা *vi* betray; treason against; play false; go back on; go over/ sell out to the enemy. ~ঘাতকতা করে ধরিয়ে দেওয়া *vt* betray. ~জনক *adj* convincing. ~পাত্র *n* reliable/ trustworthy person; confidant. ~পাত্রী *fem.* ~প্রদ *adj* inspiring confidence. ~ভঙ্গ *n* violation of confidence; breach of faith/ trust; perfidy. ~ভাগী, ~ভাজন *adj* trustworthy. ❑*n*=~পাত্র. ~যোগ্য *adj* reliable; believable; credible; dependable; creditable; trustworthy. ~হন্তা traitor; betrayer. ~হন্ত্রী *fem* traitress.

বিশ্বাসী *adj* **1** trustworthy; reliable; honest; faithful; loyal. **2** trustful; confiding.

বিশ্বাস্য *adj*=বিশ্বাসযোগ্য (⇒ বিশ্বাস)

বিশ্রব্ধ *adj* **1** trusted; intimate; trustworthy: ~ সুহৃদ confidant; crony. **2** fearless; confident; firm. **3** tranquil; calm. **4** reposed; rested; relaxed. **5** confidential; secret: ~ আলাপ. **6** profound: ~ তান.

বিশ্রম্ভ *n* **1** lovers' quarrel; quarrel in jest/ joke. **2** love; amour; romance; love affair; free love; intimacy; familiarity. trust; confidence. **3** unrestrained enjoyment; absence of restraint. ~ কথা *n* confidential talk; affectionate conversation. ~তা *n* trust; confidence. ~ ভৃত্য *n* confidential servant. বিশ্রম্ভালাপ *n* (lovers) te^te-a`-te^te; confidential talk. বিশ্রম্ভী *adj* trusting in; relying on; enjoying trust; confidential.

বিশ্রান্ত *adj* **1** reposed; rested; refreshed; relaxed. **2** fatigued; tired. **3** ceased (from); abated; stopped; coming to rest/ an end. বিশ্রান্তি *n* rest; repose; abatement; cessation.

বিশ্রাম *n* **1** rest; repose; relaxation; calm; tranquillity. **2** cessation; abatement; pause; caesura; interval. ~ করা, ~ নেওয়া *vi* rest; repose; relax; take rest; pause for breath; rest from labour; take one's time; take a break; cease; stop; desist. ~ দেওয়া *vt* give rest; release from/ relieve of work/ labour; let off; grant remission; give a respite. ~কাল *n* time for rest/ repose; interval.

বিশ্রী *adj* **1** ugly; hideous; monstrous; ill-shaped; repulsive; unsightly. **2** disgraceful; scandalous; inglorious; shameful: ~ পরাজয়. **3**

indecent; obscene; dirty: ~ কথাবার্তা, ~ আলাপ. **4** nasty; vile; filthy; detestable; foul: ~ ব্যাপার/ ঘটনা, ~ লোক. **5** bad; awful; abominable; atrocious: ~ খাবার. **6** naughty; uncivil; rude; wicked; obnoxious: ~ আচরণ, ~ চালচলন. **7** cumbersome; unwieldy; awkward: ~ বোঝা. **8** deplorable; lamentable; regrettable; unfortunate: ~ দুর্ঘটনা. **9** embarrassing; awkward; uncomfortable; disconcerting: ~ অবস্থা. **~ অবস্থায় পড়া** *vi* be in/ get into a false position/ an embarrassing situation; get into scrapes; be in a predicament. **~ অবস্থায় ফেলা** *vt* put sb in a false position; put to trouble.

বিশ্রুত *adj* famous; celebrated; noted. **বিশ্রুতি** *n* great fame/ celebrity.

বিশ্লথ *adj* loose; relaxed; languid.

বিশ্লিষ্ট *adj* **1** disunited; disjoined; separated; loosened; detached; disconnected; severed from; dislocated (as limbs). **2** analyzed. **~ করা** *vt* disunite; disjoin; separate; loosen; detach; disconnect; analyze.

বিশ্লেষ *n* **1** loosening; separation; dissolution; disjunction; falling asunder. **2** (arith) subtraction. **3** analysis. **4** division. **~ণ** *n* **1** separation; dissolving; dissolution. **2** analysis. **~ণ করা** *vt* analyze. **~ণাত্মক** *adj* analytical. **বিশ্লেষিত** *adj* **1** analyzed. **2** separated; torn/ rent asunder; dissolved; severed.

বিষ *n* **1** poison; venom; bane. **2** anything actively pernicious; extremely detestable person/ thing; abhorrence; abomination; bite noire: দুচোখের ~. **3** envy; malice; suspicion; canker: মনের ~. **4** fibres attached to the stalk of the lotus. **~ খাওয়া** *vi* take/ swallow poison (esp in order to commit suicide). **~ খাওয়ানো** *vt* poison; administer poison (esp to kill). **~ ঝাড়া** *vi* remove poison by charms. **~ ঢোকা** *vi* **1** become poisoned; be infected with poison. **2** (fig) become malicious/ envious. **~ ঢোকানো** *vt* **1** poison; infuse/ infect with poison. **2** make malicious/ envious. **~ তোলা** *vt* remove poison. **~ দেওয়া** *vt* administer poison; poison (esp to kill). **~ মারা** *vt* take out the poison of; (fig) render powerless; make harmless; incapacitate. **~কণ্ঠ** *n* poisoned-necked; Shiva. **~কন্যা** *n fem* a girl supposed to cause the death of a man who has had intercourse with her. **~কাঁটালি** *n* belladonna. **~কুম্ভ** *n* jar of poison; (fig) malicious heart. **~কুম্ভ পয়োমুখ** (fig) very sweet-tongued but venomous at heart; snake in the grass. **~কৃমি** *n* 'poison-worm'; worm bred in poison. **~কোষ** *n* poison-gland. **~ক্রিয়া** *n* act of poisoning; (fig) very harmful/ perverse reaction. **~ঘটিত** *adj* of/ caused by poison; toxic; poisonous. **~ঘাতক** *n* one who kills with poison. **~ঘাতী** *adj* antidotal. ❑ *n* antidote. **~ঘ্ন** *adj* destroying/ counteracting poison; disinfectant; antidotal. ❑*n* antidote. **~ঘ্ন ঔষধ/ পদার্থ** *n* antidote. **~চক্ষে** *adv* maliciously; spitefully; with rancour; with an evil eye. **~চিকিৎসক** = ~বৈদ্য. **~জ** *adj* produced by poison. **~জ্বর** *n* septic fever. **বিষণা** *n* poisoning; inflammation. **~তন্ত্র** *n* toxicology. **~তা, ~ত্ব** *nn* poisonousness. **~তুল্য** *adj* venom-like; fatal; deadly; (fig) unbearable; insufferable. **~দ** *adj* yielding poison; poisonous. **~দশন, ~দন্ত, ~দাঁত** *nn* fang; poison-tooth (of a snake). **~দাঁত ভাঙা** *vt* **1** extract the fangs. **2** (fig) render harmless/ powerless; put out of action. **~দংশন** *n* venomous bite. **~দায়ক, ~দায়ী** *adj, n* giving poison; poisoning; poisoner. **~দিগ্ধ** *adj* **1** smeared with poison; empoisoned; poisoned. **2** (fig) spiteful; heart-rending; venomous. **~দুষ্ট** *adj* infected with poison; poisonous; venomous. **~দূষণ** *n* corrupting by admixture of poison; poisoning. **~দৃষ্টি** *n* **1** spiteful/ malicious glance; evil eye. **2** (fig) animosity; intense hatred/ dislike. **~দৃষ্টিতে পড়া** *vi* incur sb's hatred/ displeasure/ animosity. **~দোষহর** *adj* taking away the ill effects of poison. **~ধর** *adj, n* venomous; snake. **~নখ** *n* poisonous nails/ claws. **~নয়ন**=~দৃষ্টি. **~নাশক, ~নাশন**=~ঘ্ন. **~নাশী** *adj* removing/ curing/ destroying poison. **~পান** *n* drinking poison. **~প্রয়োগ** *n* use/ employment of poison; administering poison (as a medicine); poisoning. **~ফল** *n* poisonous fruit; (fig) evil consequences. **~ফোঁড়া** *n* septic boil/sore; malignant tumour; carbuncle. **~বৎ** *adj* poisonous; like poison, **~বল্লরী, ~বল্লী** *nn* poisonous creeper. **~বিজ্ঞান, ~বিদ্যা** *nn* administration of antidotes; cure of poisons by drugs or charms; toxicology. **~বিদ্যাগত** *adj* toxicological. **~বিজ্ঞানী, ~বিদ্যাবিদ** *adjj* versed in toxicology. ❑*nn* toxicologist. **~বিধান** *n* administering poison judicially or by way of ordeal. **~বৃক্ষ** *n* **1** poison-tree. **2** (fig) an abject which sb nourishes to kill/ ruin himself. **~বৈদ্য** *n* 'poison-doctor'; dealer in antidotes; one professing to cure the bites of snakes. **~ভক্ষণ** *n* act of eating poison; taking poison. **~ভুজঙ্গ** *n* poisonous snake. **~মন্ত্র** *n* **1** charm for curing snake-bites. **2** snake-charmer. **~ময়** *adj* **1** poisonous; venomous; consisting of poison. **2** agonizing; tormenting; cruel; distressing; bitter. **~মিশ্রিত** *adj* mixed with poison; poisoned. **~মুখ** *adj* **1** discharging poison; venomous (as speech). **2** serpent. **~রস** *n* poison- juice; poisoned. draught/ potion. **~রোগ** *n* sickness arising from being poisoned. **~লতা**=~বল্লরী. **~লক্ষ্য** *adj* having a poisoned tip. **~লাড়ু** *n* poisoned sweetball. **~হর** *adj* removing poison; antidotal. **~হরা**

fem. ~হরী *n fem* the goddess who protects from the venom of snakes. ~হীন *adj* free from poison (as a serpent). ~হৃদয় *adj* poison-hearted; cherishing hatred/ hostility; malicious; malignant. জঙ্গম~ *n* venom. স্থাবর~ *v* poison like arsenic, nux vomica, etc. **বিষাক্ত** *adj* **1** smeared with poison; poisoned; poisonous; venomous. **2** malignant; septic: বিষাক্ত ঘা, বিষাক্ত ফোড়া. **3** spiteful; acrimonious; bitter: বিষাক্ত বচন; বিষাক্ত সম্পর্ক. **বিষাক্ত করা** *vt* poison; cause sepsis; make malignant/ septic; embitter: সম্পর্ক বিষাক্ত করা. **বিষাঙ্গনা** *n fem*=~কন্যা. **বিষানল** *n* fire of poison; burning poison. **বিষান্তক** *adj* antidotal. **বিষাপহরণ** *n* removing/ destroying poison. **বিষামৃত** *n* poison and nectar. **বিষের পুঁটলি, বিষের হাঁড়ি** *n n* venomous/ spiteful/ malignant heart.

বিষজ্ঞা *adj* dissociated.

বিষণ্ণ *adj* **1** sad; dejected; despondent; sorrowful; downcast; out of spirits; depressed; morose; melancholy. **2** darkened; gloomy: ~ আকাশ. বিষণ্ণা *fem.* ~চিত্ত *adj* dejected in mind; low spirited; dejected; sad at heart; down-hearted. ~চিত্তা *fem.* ~তা *n* dejection; sadness; languor; lassitude; melancholy; depression; gloominess; gloom; darkness. ~দৃষ্টি *adj* having sorrowful glance; having sad/ sullen look. ~ দৃষ্টিতে *adj* looking sadly; with a mournful glance. ~নয়ন, ~নেত্র *adjj* with mournful/ sorrowful eyes. ~প্রকৃতি *adj* of a melancholy temperament; hypochondriac. ~বদন, ~মুখ *adjj* dejected in countenance; looking sad/ dejected. ~বদনা, ~মুখী *fem.* ~ভাব=~তা. ~মানস=~চিত্ত. ~রূপ *adj* having a sorrowful aspect; being in a dejected mood.

বিষম *adj* **1** severe; unbearable; deadly; insufferable; terrible: ~ প্রহার, ~ বিপদ/ যন্ত্রণা. **2** hard to traverse; difficult; inconvenient; painful; dangerous; adverse; vexatious; disagreeable; bad; wicked; violent: ~ ঝামেলা, ~ মারামারি, ~ বিবাদ. **3** reckless; headstrong; desperate; heedless; over: ~ সাহস. **4** acute; serious: রোগের ~ অবস্থা. **5** extraordinary; tumultuous; riotous; uproarious: ~ কাণ্ড. **6** uneven; rugged; rough; undulating: ~ পথ/ক্ষেত্র. **7** unequal; irregular; dissimilar; different; inconstant: ~ কোণ, দুটি ~ বস্তু. **8** (arith) odd; not even. **9** hard to be understood; obtuse: ~ প্রশ্ন. **10** unsuitable; wrong. **11** unfair; dishonest; partial. **12** rough; coarse; rude; cross: ~ মেজাজ. **13** odd; unequalled; unusual. ❑*n* sudden choking and hiccups whilst eating/ drinking. ~কর্ণ *adj* having unequal diagonals. ~কর্ম *n* an odd/ unequalled act. ~কাল *n* unfavourable time; inauspicious season. ~কোণ *n* (geom) acute/ obtuse angle. ~কোণী *adj* acute-/ obtuse-angled. ~ গতি *n* (phys, astron) variable motion. ~ চতুর্ভুজ, ~ চতুষ্কোণ *nn* unequal four-sided figure; trapezium. ~চ্ছায়া *n* shadow of the gnomon at noon when the sun is on the equinotical line. ~ জ্বর *n* irregular (chronic) fever. ~তা, ~ত্ব *n n* inequality; difference; dangerousness; terribleness. ~ ত্রিভুজ *n* (geom) scalene triangle. ~দৃক *adj* (phys) astigmatic. ~ দৃষ্টি *n* looking obliquely; squint-eyed; (phys) astigmatism. ~ধাতু *adj* having the body humours unequally proportioned; unhealthy. ~নয়ন, ~নেত্র *adjj, nn* three-eyed; Shiva. ~পদ *adj* having unequal steps. ~ পরিণতি *n* (bot) dichogamy. ~পৃষ্ঠ *adj* (bot) bifacial; (geol) having an uneven/ undulating surface. ~ বিভাগ *n* unequal division of property. ~ বেগ *n* (phys) variable velocity; terrible speed. ~ ভুজ *n* (geom) scalene. ~ ভুজ তুলা *n* steelyard. ~ ভোজন *n* eating at irregular hours. ~ রাশি *n* (arith) odd number. ~শর *adj, n* 'five-arrowed'; the god of love. ~শায়ী *adj* sleeping; irregularly. ~সপ্তম *n* (astrol) inauspicious matching of bride and bridegroom (having incompatible horoscopes; eg the Aries and the Libra, the Gemini and the Sagittarius, the Leo and the Aquarius). **বিষমাক্ষ** *n* Shiva. **বিষমায়ুধ** *n* god of love.

বিষয় *n* **1** object (of sense-perception); anything perceptible by the senses. **2** any object of affection/ concern/ attention. **3** any special worldly object/ aim/matter/ business. **4** sensual enjoyments; sensuality. **5** any subject or topic; subject-matter; theme; matter; substance. **6** an object (as opposed to subject). **7** fit/suitable object (for). **8** (phil) subject of an argument; category; general head. **9** sphere (of influence/ activity). **10** dominion; kingdom; territory; region; district; county. **11** scope; compass; horizon; range; reach (of eyes, ears, mind, etc). **12** special sphere/ department; peculiar province/ field of action; peculiar element; concern (⇒ বিষয়ে). **13** lands; possessions. **14** space/ room (for). ❑prep=বিষয়ে. ~আশয় *n* worldly possessions; property; substance. ~ক *suff* having anything for subject/ an object; concerning; in the sphere of; relating to; with regard/ reference to. ~কর্ম *n* worldly business/ act; management of one's affairs. ~কাম *n* desire of worldly goods/ pleasures. ~জ্ঞ one who has a particular domain of knowledge; specialist. ~জ্ঞান *n* acquaintance with worldly affairs. ~তা, ~ত্ব *nn* character/ condition of being an object; having anything for an object; relation between an object and the knowledge of it. ~তৃষ্ণা *n* thirst for property and riches/ worldly pleasures and enjoyments. ~নিরতি *n* attachment to sensual objects. ~নির্ধারণ *n* determination of subject/ topic ~পরাঙ্মুখ *adj* averted/ averse from mundane affairs. ~পরায়ণ *adj* attached to sensual pleasures/ worldly possessions. ~পরায়ণা *fem*. ~প্রবণ *adj* attached to objects of sense. ~বর্তী *adj* directed to anything as an object. ~বস্তু *n* subject-matter. ~বাসনা *n*=~কাম. ~বিতৃষ্ণ, ~বিমুখ *adj* = ~পরান্মুখ. ~বিতৃষ্ণা, ~বিমুখতা *n* aversion to mundane affairs/ worldly possessions/ worldly pleasures. ~বিষয়ী *n* object and subject. ~বুদ্ধি *n* worldly wisdom; business acumen. ~বৈরাগ্য *n*=~বিতৃষ্ণা. ~ভেদ *n* different subject/object; difference of object. ~ভোগ *n* enjoyment of worldly riches/ pleasures. ~লালসা *n* greed for sensual objects/ worldly possessions or riches. ~লোলুপ *adj* eager for sensual enjoyment. ~সঙ্গ *n* addiction to sensual objects. ~সুখ *n* pleasure of sense. ~সূচি, ~সূচী *n* (table of) contents; agenda. ~স্পৃহা *n* desire for sensual objects. বিষয়াত্মক *adj* consisting of/ identified with worldly objects; sensual; carnal. বিষয়ানুরাগ *n* attachment to sensual pleasures/ worldly possessions. বিষয়ানুরাগী *adj* attached to sensual pleasured, etc. বিষয়ান্তর *n* another/ a different subject/ object/ topic. বিষয়াসক্ত *adj*=বিষয়ানুরাগী. বিষয়াসক্তি *n*=বিষয়ানুরাগ. বিষয়ী *adj* relating to/ attached to worldly objects; wealthy; sensual; carnal; possessing property/ an estate. ❑*n* subject; materialist; sensualist; voluptuary. বিষয়ীভূত *adj* become the domain/ object of; included in the domain/ jurisdiction/ agenda of: সমালোচনার বিষয়ীভূত. বিষয়ে *prep* concerning; relating to; regarding; with regard/ reference to; about.

বিষাণ *n* **1** horn (of any animal). **2** tusk (of an elephant/ boar). **3** horn (wind-instrument). বিষাণী *adj* having horns/ tusks; horned. ❑*n* elephant.

বিষাদ *n* **1** languor; drooping state; lassitude. **2** dejection; depression; despondency; low spirits. **3** sorrow; sadness; grief. **4** disappointment; despair. ~গ্রস্ত, বিষাদিত, বিষাদী *adjj* caused to sink down; made sorrowful; dejected; low-spirited; sad; sick at heart; sorrowful; down-hearted; melancholy; despondent; downcast; gloomy; depressed; dispirited. ~গ্রস্তা, বিষাদিতা, বিষাদিনী *fem*. ~জনক *adj* causing grief/ depression; distressing. ~ময় *adj* full of sorrow; sorrow-laden; sorry; distressful; sorrow-worn; grief-stricken; woeful. ~মাখা *adj*=~ময়. ~সাগর *n* sea of sorrow/ grief; profound/ unbounded grief/ sadness.

বিষানো *vt* **1** make poisonous; poison. **2** become poisonous/ poisoned. **3** be inflamed (as a wound/ boil); suppurate; turn septic; fester. **4** cause to suppurate; make septic. **5** (fig) embitter; poison; sour; exacerbate; rankle; fester.

বিষুব *n* equinox. ~ দিন *n* day of the equinox. ~বৃত্ত *n* equinoctial circle; equator; celestial equator; equinoctial. ~ রেখা *n* equinoctial line; equator; equinoctial. ~ লম্ব *n* (astron) declination. ~ সংক্রান্তি *n* the sun's equinoctial passage; passing of the sun into the next sign at either equinox. বিষুবাংশ *n* (astron) right ascension. বিষুবীয় *adj* equinoctial. খ-~ বৃত্ত *n* (astron) celestial equinoctial. খ-~ রেখা *n* (astron) celestial equator. ভূ-~ রেখা *n* (astron) terrestrial equator. মহা~ *n* (astron) vernal equinox. জল~ *n* (astron) autumnal equinox.

বিষ্টম্ভ *n* **1** checking; stopping; restraint; impediment. **2** obstruction of the urine/faeces; ischury; constipation. বিষ্টম্ভী *adj* causing ischury.

বিষ্টি *n* (colloq)=বৃষ্টি

বিষ্টু *n* (colloq)=বিষ্ণু

বিষ্ঠা *n* faeces; excrement; stool; dung. ~কীট ~কৃমি *nn* a worm living in ordure. ~কুন্ড *n* **1** hole/pit for receiving excrement; muck-heap. **2** a sordid/squalid/filthy place.

বিষ্ণু *n* name of one of the principal Hindu deities (regarded as the 'preserver'). ~প্রিয়া *n fem* goddess Lakshmi; the wife of Vishnu.

বিসংবাদ *n* **1** contradiction; disagreement; discord. **2** strife; dispute; quarrel. **3** breaking one's word; disappointing; deception. বিসংবাদিত *adj* not generally proved; disputed; opposed; contested. বিসংবাদী *adj* contradicting; disputing; contesting; opposing; discordant; deceiving.

বিসঙ্কুল *adj* crowded together; disordered; confused; mixed/mingled with.

বিসদৃশ *adj* unlike; dissimilar; different; not corresponding; unequal; incompatible; contrary; unbecoming; irrelevant; grotesque; odd. ~তা *n* dissimilarily; irrelevance; incompatibility; oddity.

বিসমিল্লাহ [A] (phrase) **1** In the name of God (a formula generally pronounced by Muslims at the beginning of any work or action). **2** beginning; commencement. ~ করা *vt* begin; commence; start. ~য় গলদ a mistake at the very beginning; a false/ erroneous start.

বিসরণ[1] *n* **1** spreading; extension. **2** (phys)deviation. ~ কোণ *n* angle of deviation. গরিষ্ঠ/বরিষ্ঠ ~ কোণ *n* angle of maximum deviation. লঘিষ্ঠ ~ কোণ *n* angle of minimum deviation.

বিসরণ[2] *n* (archaic, poet)=বিস্মরণ

বিসরা *vt* (archaic, poet) forget.

বিসর্গ *n* name of a symbol in grammar (marked by two perpendicular dots [ঃ] representing a hard and distinctly audible aspiration. **~ সন্ধি** ⇒ সন্ধি. বিন্দু ~⇒ বিন্দু.

বিসর্জন *n* **1** giving up; renouncing; abandoning; deserting; abandonment; renunciation; relinquishment. **2** shedding; sacrifice: অশ্রু~, জীবন~. **3** throwing (the image of a deity into holy water as the concluding rite of a festival). **~ করা/ দেওয়া** *vt* give up; abandon; desert; relinquish; renounce; sacrifice; shed; pour forth; throw/cast off. **বিসর্জনা** *vt* (poet)=~ করা/ দেওয়া. **বিসর্জনীয়** *adj* to be given up/ renounced/ abandoned/ sacrificed/ relinquished/ thrown off/ cast off. **বিসর্জিত** *adj* given up; abandoned; renounced; relinquished; deserted; sacrificed; shed; thrown/ cast off. **বিসর্জিতা** *fem.*

বিসর্প *n* **1** erysipelas. **2** creeping about/ along. **3** diffusion; spreading. **4** (mech) sliding friction. ❑*adj* (mech) sliding. **~ণ** *n* **1**= ~ (2-3). **2** (mech) sliding. **3** shifting. **বিসর্পিত** *adj* spread; diffused; scattered; dispersed. **বিসর্পী** *adj* **1** suffering from erysipelas. **2** creeping/ gliding/ roaming/ swimming/ winding about; spreading; sneaking. **বিসর্পিণী** *fem.*

বিসার *n* **1** extent; expanse; range; stretch. **2** motion. **~ণ** *n* spreading; extension; dispersion; diffusion. **বিসারিত** *adj* spread; extended; dispersed; diffused. **বিসারী** *adj* stretching over/ through; spreading; diffusing; extending to.

বিসূচি, বিসূচী, বিসূচিকা *nn* a kind of cholera.

বিসৃত *adj* stretched out; spread; extended; dispersed; gone in various directions.

বিসৃষ্ট *adj* **1** discharged; emitted; thrown; hurled; shed; cast. **2** abandoned; deserted; renounced; given up. **3** sent (away); sent/ poured forth.

বিসৃষ্টি *n* creation; production.

বিস্কুট [E] *n* biscuit.

বিস্তর *adj* many; much; extensive; long; a lot/ multitude of; enough; too many/ much. ❑*n* multitude; number quantity; long; large company; assemblage. **~শঃ** *adv* diffusely; at length.

বিস্তার *n* **1** spreading; extent; expansion; stretching; stretch; expanse; spread. **2** width; breadth; amplitude. **3** specification; detailed description/ enumeration. **~ করা** *vt* spread out; stretch; expand; extend; enlarge; expatiate upon; propagate; peak diffusely about. **~ন** (biol) distribution. **বিস্তারিত** *adj* spread; extended; detailed; fully stated; elaborated; amplified. **বিস্তারী** *adj* stretching over/ through; spreading; diffusing; extending; large.

বিস্তার্য *adj* to be expanded/ spread/ extended/ scattered; capable of being spread (out)/ extended/ amplified/widened; tensile; tensible; extensible. **~তা** *n* tensility; tensibility; extensibility.

বিস্তীর্ণ *adj* **1** spread out; expanded; outstreched; opened wide; scattered/ strewn/ covered/ studded with; displayed; extended. **2** broad; large; ample; copious; great; numerous; expansive; pervasive; wide; vast. **~জানু** *adj, n* bandy-legged (girl). **~তা** *adj* width; breadth. diffusion; vastness; largeness; amplitude. **~ললাট** *adj* having a large forehead.

বিস্তৃত *adj* = বিস্তারিত. **~ করা** *vt* widen; expand; stretch out; open wide; display; extend; spread; amplify; elaborate. **বিস্তৃতি** *n* **1**=বিস্তার. **2** (math) expansion.

বিস্ফার, বিস্ফারণ *n* **1** opening wide. **2**= বিস্তার. **3** discharging a bow; twang of a bow; string. **বিস্ফারিত** *adj* **1** opened wide. **2**=বিস্তারিত. **3** torn/ rent asunder. **4** sounded; clanking. **5** trembling; shaken; trembled. **বিস্ফারিত নেত্রে** *adv* with wide eyes; with eyes opened wide.

বিস্ফুরণ *n* **1** quivering; trembling; quiver; tremor. **2** sparkle; flash; glitter; flicker. **বিস্ফুরিত** *adj* **1** trembling; quivering; tremulous; vibrating; shaken; trembled. **2** flashing; glittering; flickering; sparkling. **বিস্ফুরিতাধর** *adj* having quivering lips. **বিস্ফুরিতেক্ষণ** *adj* having trembling eyes.

বিস্ফুলিঙ্গ *n* spark of fire.

বিস্ফোট, বিস্ফোটক *n* blister; boil.

বিস্ফোরক *adj* explosive. ❑*n* explosive; combustible. **বিস্ফোরণ** *n* explosion; detonation. **বিস্ফোরণ হওয়া** *vi* explode; detonate.

বিস্বন *n* roar; yell.

বিস্বাদ *adj* tasteless; distasteful; unsavoury; flat; insipid; vapid; unpalatable.

বিস্ময় *n* wonder; surprise; amazement; astonishment; marvel. **~কর, ~জনক** *adjj* causing astonishment/ admiration; wonderful; astonishing; marvellous; amazing; surprising. **~চিহ্ন** *n* (gram) note of admiration/ exclamation (!). **~বিস্ফারিত** *adj* wide open/ staring with astonishment. **~বিহ্বল** *adj* beside oneself with wonder; astounded. **~মগ্ন** *adj* lost in wonder/ amazement. **~স্তিমিত** *adj* stupefied with amazement; stunned. **বিস্ময়াকুল, বিস্ময়ান্বিত, বিস্ময়াপন্ন, বিস্ময়াভিভূত, বিস্ময়াবিষ্ট** *adjj* filled with astonishment/ wonder. **বিস্ময়াবহ** *adj* =~কর. **বিস্ময়োৎপাদক, বিস্ময়োৎপাদী** *adjj* producing wonder/ amazement; amazing; wonderful. **বিস্ময়োৎপাদন করা** *vi* arouse wonder; strike with wonder; astonish;

astound; stun. **বিস্ময়োৎফুল্ল** *adj* elated with wonder.

বিস্মরণ *n* act of forgetting; oblivion. **বিস্মরণা** *vt* (poet) forget. **~হওয়া** *vt* forget. **~শীল** *adj* forgetful; oblivious. **~শীলতা** *n* forgetfulness. **বিস্মরণীয়** *adj* to be forgotten; forgettable.

বিস্মিত *adj* astonished; surprised; amazed; perplexed. **বিস্মিতা** *fem.* **~ করা** *vt* astonish; surprise; amaze; startle; astound. **~ হওয়া** *vi* be surprised/ amazed/ astonished; feel surprise; wonder; marvel (at). **~ভাবে** *adv* with astonishment; to one's great surprise; wonderingly.

বিস্মৃত *adj* **1** one who has forgotten anything; forgetful (of); unmindful. **2** forgotten; unremembered. **বিস্মৃতা** *fem.* **~ হওয়া** *vi* forget; be unmindful of. **বিস্মৃতি** *n* forgetting; forgetfulness; loss of memory; oblivion. **বিস্মৃতিশীল** *adj* forgetful **বিস্মৃতিশীলতা** *n* forgetfulness.

বিস্যুৎবার *n* (colloq)=বৃহস্পতিবার

বিস্রংস *n* falling asunder; dropping down; weakness. **বিস্রংসন** *n* causing to fall down/away; casting off; falling down; slackening; loosening; relaxation; unfastening; casting off. **বিস্রংসিত** *adj* caused to fall down/as under; dropped; loosened; untied. **বিস্রংসিত কেশবন্ধন** *adj* one whose hair-band has become loose. **বিস্রংসিতাংশুক** *adj* one whose white garment has slipped down. **বিস্রংসী** *adj* falling/slipping down.

বিস্রস্ত *adj* fallen asunder/down; unfastened; untied; loosened; detached; dishevelled (as hair); slackened; relaxed **~চিত্ত** *adj* one whose spirit is dejected. **~বন্ধন** *adj* having bonds/ fetters unfastened. **~বসন** *adj* having loosened garment. **~হার** *adj* one whose necklace has slipped off. **বিস্রংসাঙ্গ** *adj* having a languid body/relaxed limbs.

বিস্রাব *n* flowing; forth; issuing; discharge. **~ণ** *n* causing to flow (blood, matter etc); bleeding; draining; flushing. **বিস্রাবিত** *adj* wasted away; caused to flow out; flushed; drained; bled. **বিস্রুত** *adj* **1** flowed forth; dropped; flowing. **2** oozed; exuded. **3** spread; diffused; stretched. **বিস্রুতি** *n* **1** flowing forth; issuing from. **2** oozing; trickle; exudation; scapage.

বিহগ, বিহঙ্গ, বিহঙ্গম *nn* (lit) bird. **বিহগী, বিহঙ্গী, বিহঙ্গিনী, বিহঙ্গমী** *fem.* **বিহঙ্গমা** *n* an imaginary bird mentioned in folk-tales.

বিহত *adj* **1** torn up; struck/beaten away; dashed out; struck/touched/visited by. **2** warded off; repulled; impeded. **বিহতি** *n* **1** stroke; blow; striking; killing. **2** prevention; removal.

বিহনে *prep* (archaic, poetic) without; in absence of.

বিহরণ *n* **1** going about for pleasure/exercise; roaming; strolling. **2** (amorous) frolicking; sporting. **3** act of taking away/removing; robbing.

বিহরা *vi* (archaic, poet)=বিহার করা

বিহসন *n* gentle laughter; smiling. **বিহসিত** *adj* smiling; laughing; smiled/ laughed at. ❑*n* laughter; laughing; smiling.

বিহস্ত *adj* **1** without a hand/trunk; handless. **2** unhandy; inexperienced. **3** confounded; perplexed; helpless. **4** completely absorbed in. **5** adroit; killed; experienced; learned.

বিহা *n* (dial)=বিবাহ

বিহান[১] *n* (dial; poet) morning; dawn; daybreak.

বিহান[২] *n* (dial)=বেয়ান

বিহায়স *n* (myth) a flying chariot.

বিহার[১] *n* **1** walking for pleasure or amusement; wandering; roaming; strolling; promenade; pleasure-trip. **2** sport; play; pastime; diversion; pleasure; enjoyment. **3** pleasure-ground; plan of recreation. **4** (with Buddhists and Jainas) monastery; temple. **~ করা** *vi* **1** move on; walk; roam; wander through; walk/roam about for pleasure; promenade. **2** spend/ pass (time); divert oneself; sport; indulge in amorous frolics. **বিহারী** *adj* **1** wandering about for pleasure; roaming; strolling; sporting; dallying. **2** enjoing one's self with; delighting in; fond of; given/ addicted to. **3** going as far as; extending to; depending on. **বিহারিণী** *fem.*

বিহার[২] *n* the state of Bihar in India. **বিহারি** *adj* of Bihar. ❑*vi* native of Bihar. **বিহারা** (poet; archaic) = বিহার করা.

বিহি [P] *n* quince. **~দানা** *n* quince seed.

বিহিত *adj* **1** conforming to the established/prescribed mode or form; formal; prescribed; enjoined; decreed. **2** performed; made; accomplished; contrived; done. **3** supplied; endowed; furnished (with). **4** put in order; arranged; determined; fined; ordained; ordered. **5** distributed; divided; apportioned; bestowed. **6** destined/ meant for. **7** proper; just; appropriate. ❑*n* **1** order; command; decree. **2** remedy redress; reparation. **~ করা** *vt* **1** prescribe; enjoin; decree; enact. **2** perform; accomplish; execute. **3** supply/provide with; endow; make arrangements for; arrange for. **4** remedy; redress; right; repair. **~ অর্থ** *n* legal tender. **~ক** *n* legislative enactment; act.

বিহীন *adj* destitute/deprived of; free from; wanting; missing; absent; separated from. **বিহীনা** *fem.* **~তা** *n* absence/want of.

বিহ্বল *adj* overwhelmed; agitated; perturbed; beside oneself; distressed; bewildered; dazzled; dazed; stunned; nonplussed;

flustered; staggered. বিহ্বলা *fem*. ~ করা *vt* overwhelm; dazzle; daze; stagger; confuse; stun; nonplus; fluster; daze. ~তা *n* bewilderment; daze; perturbation; agitation; consternation; fluster.

বীক্ষণ *n* looking at; seeing; inspection; investigation; observation; glance; gaze. বীক্ষণীয় *adj* to be looked at/regarded/ considered; visible; observable. বীক্ষ্যমাণ *adj* observing; seeing.

বীক্ষমাণ *adj* under observation; being investigated.

বীক্ষিত *adj* looked at; seen; beheld; regarded; observed.

বীচ *n* **1**=বীজ. **2** seedling (of paddy, etc). ~তলা *n* seed-bed.

বীচালি=বিচালি

বীচি[১]= বিচি

বীচি[২] *n* **1** wave; ripple; billow. **2** ray; beam. ~ক্ষোভ, ~বিক্ষোভ *nn* agitation/ roughness of waves. ~ক্ষুব্ধ, ~বিক্ষুব্ধ *adj* agitated with waves; turbulent; rugged; surging choppy; rolling; billowy. ~তরঙ্গন্যায় *n* wave-undulation method (or the rule by which sound reaches the ear, a term used to denote successive operation). ~বিক্ষেপ *n* curling and falling of waves. ~ভঙ্গ *n* breaking of waves (over/on/against); breaker. ~মালা *n* string/series of waves. ~মালী *adj* 'wave-garlanded'. ☐*n* **1** ocean. **2** sun.

বীজ *n* **1** seed (of plants). **2** seed-corn; grain. **3** semen (of men and animals). **4** any germ; element; primary cause/ principle; source; origin. **5** mystical letter/syllable which forms the essential part of the *mantra* of any deity. **6** sacred formula (addressed to any individual deity; *mantra*. **7** germ/origin of any composition (as of a poem of the plot of a drama, of a magical formula, etc). **8** anything serving as a receptacle/ support. **9** calculation of original/ primary germs; analysis; algebra. ~ক *n* short statement of account; chit; tab. ~অন্তস্ত্বক *n* (bot) tegmen. ~কোষ *n* seed-vessel; ovary of a flower. ~কোষধারী *adj* leguminous. ~ক্রিয়া *n* (math) operation of analysis; algebraic solution. ~গণিত *n* algebra. ~গাণিতিক *adj* algebraic; algebraical. ~গুটি *n* (bot) spare. ~গুপ্তি *n* pod. ~ঘ্ন *adj* disinfectant. ~ঘ্ন পদার্থ *n* disinfectant. ~তলা *n* seed-bed; seed-plot. ~তঃ *adv* according to/from seed. ~ত্ব *n* being an origin/a cause; causality. ~ত্বক *n* (bot) seed-coat. ~দূষণ *n* sepsis. ~দূষিত *adj* septic. ~ধান *n* seed-corn; seed-paddy. ~পত্র *n* (bot) cotyledon. ~পুর, ~পূর *n* citron; citrus medica. ~পুরুষ *n* progenitor of a tribal family. ~ বপন *n* sowing seeds. ~ বপন করা *vt* sow seeds. ~বহিস্ত্বক *n* (bot) testa. ~বারক *adj* antiseptic. ~বারক পদার্থ *n* antiseptic. ~বোকা *n* large billy-goat. ~মন্ত্র *n* mystical syllable of a mantra (⇒ 5 & 6 above). ~মাতৃকা *n* seed-vessel of the lotus. ~ল *adj* seedy. ~হীন *adj* seedless; (bot) aspermous. বীজাঙ্কুর *n* **1** seedling; seed-shot. **2** seed and sprout. বীজাঙ্কুর-ন্যায় *n* rule of seed and sprout (where two things stand to each other in the relation of cause and effect). বীজাণু *n* germ. বীজিত *adj* sown with seed; having for seed. বীজ্য *adj* bearing seed; seedy. ☐*n* real progenitor.

বীজন *n* fanning; wafting. ~ করা *vt* fan; waft. বীজিত *adj* fanned; cooled.

বীট[১], বীট পালং=বিট[২]

বীট[২] [E] *n* beat (as of a postman, sentinel, etc).

বীটল [E] *n* (zoo) beetle.

বীটি, বীটী, বীড়া=বিড়া

বীণ=বীণা

বীণা *n* Indian lute; usually having seven strings raised upon nineteen frets fixed on a long rounded board; towards the ends of which are two large gourds. ~দণ্ড *n* neck or long rounded board of a vina. ~ধ্বনি *n* sound of a vina. ~নিন্দিত, ~বিনিন্দিত *adj* (of a voice) putting to shame even the sound of a lute; surpassing/ sweeter than the sound of a lute. ~নিন্দিতা, ~বিনিন্দিতা *fem*. ~পাণি *n fem*. goddess Saraswati. ~বাদক *n* vina player; lutanist. ~বাদন *n* act of playing on a vina. ~বাদ্য *n* music of a vina. ~মন্ত্র *n*=~রব *n*= ~ধ্বনি.

বীত *adj* gone away; departed; vanished; free/ exempt from; without; less. ~কাম *adj* free from desire. ~কৃষ্ণ *adj* free from all passions/desires. ~নিদ্র *adj* sleepless; wakeful; awake. ~ভয় *adj* fearless; undaunted. ~মল *adj* free from obscurity/darkness; clear; pure. ~মোহ *adj* free from illusion. ~রাগ *adj* free from passions/affections; dispassionate; desireless; calm, tranquil; disaffected; disgusted. ~শঙ্ক *adj*=~ভয়. ~শোক *adj* free from sorrow; past of all grief. ~শ্রদ্ধ *adj* having lost one's faith (in)/respect for; disaffected; displeased; disgusted. ~স্পৃহ *adj* free from wish/desire; indifferent.

বীতংস ⇒ বিতংস

বীথি, বীথিকা, বীথী *n* **1** row; line. **2** avenue; vista; road street. **3** row of pictures; gallery. বীথীকৃত *adj* placed/ arranged in rows.

বীন[১], ফরম (ফরাম) ~ [E] *n* bean.

বীন[২]=বীণা

বীপ্সা *n* desire of pervading; several/ successive order or series; distribution; repetition; frequency. ~ব্যঞ্জক, ~সূচক *adj*, (gram) frequentative. ~সূচক শব্দ *n* frequentative.

বীবর [E] *n* beaver.
বীভৎস *n* **1** loathsome; disgusting; revolting; abominable hideous. **2** perverted; grotesque; monstrous. **3** cruel; brutal; grim; atrocious; inhuman; savage. **4** wicked; heinous; villainous; pernicious. ❑*n* (rhet) sentiment of disgust. **~তা** *n* loathsome detestableness; abominableness; atrocity; grotesqueness; monstrosity. **~ রস** *n*=~. **বীভৎসু** *adj* loathing; detesting; feeling disgust/repugnance.
বীম [E] *n* (archit) beam.
বীমা *n* ⇒ বিমা
বীর *adj* heroic; valiant; brave; powerful; strong; valorous; soldierly; spirited. ❑*n* **1** hero; brave man; valiant person. **2** skilled warrior. **3** eminent/ great man or person. **~কালী** *n* kind of military musical instrument; large drum. **~কুঞ্জর** *n* matchless hero. **~কুলগর্ব** *adj n* ' pride of the family of heroes'; greatest of heroes. **~কুলগ্লানি** *n* shame to the family of heroes; despicable coward; sneak. **~কুলতিলক** *n* greatest of heroes. **~কুলর্ষভ** *n*=~কুলতিলক. **~কেশরী** *adj* most valiant hero. **~চূড়ামণি** *n* greatest of heroes; supreme hero. **~চরিত্র** n exploits of the hero. **~জননী** *n fem* mother of a hero. **~জয়ন্তিকা** *n fem* kind of dance performed by soldiers after a victory or on going to battle. **~জায়া** *n fem* wife of a hero. **~তম** *n* eminent hero. **~তর** *adj* stronger; bolder. ❑*n* greater hero. **~তা, ~ত্ব** *n* heroism; marliness. **~ত্বপূর্ণ** *adj* heroic; valorous. **~ত্বব্যঞ্জক** *adj* indicating heroism/valour; valiant; heroic. **~দর্প** *n* hero's challenge; brag. **~ধটী, ~ধড়া** *nn* a hero's attire. **~নারী** *n fem* heroic woman; wife of a hero. **~পনা** *n* (derog) heroism; bravado; heroics. **~পত্নী**=~জায়া. **~পুত্রধাত্রী** *n fem*=~প্রসবা. **~পুরুষ** *n* heroic man; hero. **~প্রসবা, ~প্রসবিনী, ~প্রসূ, ~সূ** *fem* mother of a hero. **~প্রসূন** *n* heroic son. **~বৎসা**= ~প্রসবা. **~বর** *n* best of heroes. **~বল** *n* heroic strength; prowess. **~বাক্য** *n* heroic word. **~বাহু** *adj* strong-armed. **~বৌলী** *n* a earring worn by a hero or men in general. **~ব্যূহ** *n* heroic/ bold military army. **~ব্রত** *adj* acting like a hero/man; adhering to one's purpose. **~ভার্যা**=~ জায়া. **~ভোগ্যা** *adj fem* to be enjoyed by heroes. **~ভোগ্যা বসুন্ধরা** the earth belongs to the brave. **~মর্দল** *n* war-drum. **~মাতা** = ~প্রসবা. **~মার্গ** *n* course/ career of a hero. **~রস** *n* (rhet) *rasa* of heroism; heroic sentiment. **~সিংহ** *n*=~কেশরী. **বীরা** *n fem* **1** wife/matron whose husband and sons are still alive. **2** an intoxicating beverage. **বীরাঙ্গনা** *n fem* heroic woman; wife of a hero. **বীরাচার** *n* rites performed according to Tantrism. **বীরাসন** *n* a particular posture practised by ascetics (squatting on the thighs, the lower legs being crossed over each other). **বীরেন্দ্র, বীরেশ, বীরেশ্বর** *nn* chief of heroes.
বীর্য *n* **1** heroism; heroic deed; manly. vigour; manliness; valour. **2** strength; power; energy; spirit; potency. **3** semen; virility. **~বত্তা** *n* heroism; prowess; vigour; virility; vigorousness. **~বন্ত, ~বান, ~শালী** *adj* possessing vigour/heroism; strong; heroic; mighty; vigorous; spirited; powerful. **~বতী, ~শালিনী** *fem.* **~বিরহিত** *adj* devoid of prowess/ vigour. **~বিশিষ্ট** *adj* distinguished by courage/ vigour. **~বৃদ্ধিকর** *adj,n* causing in increase of virile energy; aphrodisiac. **~মত্ত** *adj* intoxicated by power. **~হানি** *n* loss of vigour/ virile energy; impotence. **~হীন** *adj* deprived of valour; cowardly; seedless. **বীর্যান্বিত** *adj* possessed of strength; powerful.
বু *n fem* (colloq)=বুবু
বুচকি [T] *n* a small bundle; package; parcel.
বুঁদ *adj* **1** (dead) drunk; besotted; intoxicated; boozy; fuddled. **~ হওয়া** *vi* be in a fuddled state; be on the booze. **2** absorbed; engrossed; lost; rapt: চিন্তায় ~. **3** dot-like; almost invisible: ঘুড়িখানা আকাশে ~ হয়ে গেছে.
বুঁদি *n* small dot. **~য়া** *n* kind of small globular sweetmeat made of powdered pigeon-pea dipped in liquefied sugar.
বুক[১] *n* **1** chest; breast. **2** bosom: ছেলেটিকে বুকে তুলে নাও. **3** heart: ~ভরা ভালোবাসা. **4** physical and mental strength: বিপদে-আপদে ~ দিয়ে পড়া. **5** courage: তার বড়ো ~ বেড়েছে. **~ কনকন করা** feel pricking pain in the chest. **~ কাঁপা** be frightened; have one's heart in one's mouth. **~ গুরগুর/গুরুগুরু করা** tremble (for fear or cold). **~ গেল, ~ যায়** have a heart torn by grief, pain, etc. **~ চচ্চড় করা** be envious; have heart burning. **~ চাপড়ানো** beat one's breast. **~চাপা** *adj* oppressive; stifling; crushing. **~জল** *n* chest-high water. **~জ্বালা** *n* hurt-burn. **~ ঠোকা** *vi* strike one's breast lightly (while giving sb encouragement, assurance, etc or to parade one's courage). **~ ঠুকে বলা** *vi* dare say; have the courage to assert. **~ ঠুকে লাগা** *vi* begin sth in right earnest /impetuously. **~ ঢিপ ঢিপ করা** *vi* (of heart) palpitate; throb. **~ দশ হাত হওয়া** *vi* be elated/exultant; feel encouraged. **~ দিয়ে পড়া** *vi* come to help with might and main; put one's heart and soul (into the work). **~ দুড় দুড় করা** *vi* have palpitation; feel nervous. **~ ধড় ধড় করা** *vi* (of heart) throb/pound (with terror, from great efforts, etc). **~ ধড়ফড় করা** *vi* (of heart) palpitate /throb (with anxiety, eagerness, etc). **~-ফাটা** *adj* heart-rending; piercing. **~ফাটা আর্তনাদ** *n* scream; yelp. **~ ফাটা আর্তনাদ করা** *vi* scream; yelp. **~ ফাটা** *vi* (of heart) bleed (with grief, regret, etc). **~ ফাটে তো মুখ ফোটে না** unable to

give vent to one's feelings though the heart is full. ~ ফুলিয়ে *adv* proudly; boldly; resolutely; unflinchingly. ~ ফুলে ওঠা *vi* be proud; pride oneself on. ~ বাধা *vi* **1** take (fresh) heart (at sth). **2** be patient and courageous in danger/ difficult; brace oneself; screw up one's courage; put a brave face on. **3** be reassured. ~ বাজানো *vi* beat one's own breast. ~ বাড়া *vi* grow audacious; be emboldened. ~ ভাঙা *vi* loose heart; have one's heart in one's boots; break a person's heart; be broken-hearted. ~-ভাঙা *adj* heart breaking; poignant; piteous. ~ শুকানো *vi* have one's heart in one's mouth; be badly frightened; be discouraged; loose heart. ~শূল *n* pain in the chest. বুকে ঢেঁকির পাড় পড়া/পাড়া (of heart) throb violently on account of fear, jealousy, etc. বুকে বসে দাড়ি ওপড়ানো bite the hand that feeds. বুকে বাঁশ দেওয়া ⇒ বাঁশ. বুকে ভাতের হাঁড়ি নামানো put sb to the torture; break on the wheel; do great harm. বুকে লাগা take sth to heart; be affected by. বুকে সাহস নেই মুখে সাহস mere bravado; swashbuckling. বুকে সুর তোলা call up/bring back sweet memories; ring a bell. বুকের ছাতি/পাটা **1** expanse/measure of one's chest. **2** (fig) audacity; pluck; courage. বুকের রক্ত চুষে খাওয়া/চোষা (fig) bleed sb to death. বুকের রক্ত দেওয়া shed one's own blood; sacrifice one's life. বুকের রক্ত দিয়ে with all one's heart; heart and soul; at the cost of one's life. বুকে হাঁটা *vi* crawl. বুকে হাত দিয়ে বলা say/utter in all conscience/ sincerity or courageously. ভাঙা~ *n* broken heart; pessimism; hopelessness.

বুক[2] [E] *n* booking. ~ করা *vt* book (seats etc); book (goods). বুকিং অফিস *n* booking office. বুকিং ক্লার্ক *n* booking clerk.

বুক[3] [E] *n* book. ~কিপার *n* book-keeper. ~ডিপো *n* book depot. ~পোস্ট *n* book-post. ~পোস্ট করা *vt* send by book-post. ~বাইণ্ডার *n* book-binder. ~বাইন্ডিং *n* book-binding. ~স্টল *n* book-stall. ~শেলফ *n* book-shelf.

বুকড়ি *adj* **1** large and ill-formed: ~ দাঁত. **2** coarse: ~ কাল.

বুকনি *n* **1** ready-made phrase; quotations; cliché; mixture of foreign words; catch phrase; platitude; witty remarks/talks. **2** powder. **3** particles of sugar-loaf. **4** mixture. ~ ঝাড়া/দেওয়া *vi* put/throw in quotations/cliché/ piquant remarks; indulge in witticisms; throw in foreign words/ phrases in one's conversation.

বুকি *n* (term of endearment for children) little one; chick; (tiny) tot; bairn; cherub.

বুক্কার *n* bark whine (of a dog); roar of a lion.

বুক্কাস্থি *n* (anat) true rib.

বুক্কুশী *n fem* female evil spirit/ ghost// ghoul.

বুচকি *n*=বুঁচকি. ~দানা *n* seed of *Vermonia anthelminthia* (a herb like black cumin).

বুজকড়ি *n* bubble; effervescence. ~ দেওয়া *vi* rise in bubbles; bubble (up); effervesce; ferment; fizz; foam; froth.

বুজদিল [P] *n adj* coward; faint-hearted (person).

বুজন *n* shutting (the eyes); closing.

বুজরুক [P] *adj* pretentious; showy; fake; tricky; crafty; duplicitous. ☐*n* charlatan; impostor; fake; quack; poseur; humbug. বুজরুকি, বুজরুগি *n* charlatantism; pretension; imposture; quackery; show; deception.

বুজা, বুজানো, =বোজা

বুজি[1] *n adj* (form of address to) an elder sister.

বুজি[2] *n* plug.

বুঝ *n* **1** understanding; gumption. **2** consolation; solace; comfort. **3** mutual understanding; agreement. **4** explanation; manipulation: হিসাবের ~. ~ থাকা *vi* have (mutual) understanding. ~ দেওয়া *vt* **1** console; comfort; give solace. **2** manipulate; explain apparently; persuade sb to believe what one says. ~ মানা *vi* be consoled/ comforted/ /solaced. ~সুঝ *n* gumption; understanding; discernment; percipience.

বুঝা, বোঝা *vi, vt* **1** understand; comprehend; grasp; realize: সে আগে বোঝেনি. **2** know; divine: আমি তার মন বুঝি. **3** test; sound: তার মন বোঝার চেষ্টা করো. **4** get; follow; figure out; make head or tail of; fathom: তুমি কি তার কথা কিছু বুঝলে? **5** deliberate: বুঝে জবাব দেওয়া. ~নো *vt* **1** make one understand/ comprehend/ realize. **2** console; solace; comfort: তাকে কতো বোঝালাম, কিন্তু সে কেবলই কাঁদছে. **3** explain; expound: সমস্যা/হিসাব ~. **4** admonish; advise; persuade; exhort. **5** বোঝাপড়া, বোঝাবুঝি *n* (mutual) understanding; accord; agreement; confrontation; fight; struggle. বোঝাপড়া করা *vi* settle one's account (with); come to terms; arrive at a mutual understanding (with); compromise; confront; fight.

বুঝি, বুঝিবা *adv* perhaps; may be; probably; possibly: তাই ~ তুমি উঠে গেলে? ~বা সে চলে গেছে, তাই ~ ? Is it so ? তুমি ~ আবার আসবে? You're coming back, I suppose. বুঝে *adv* knowingly; consciously; deliberately.

বুট[1] *n* chick-pea; gram.

বুট[2] [E] *n* boot.

বুটা, বুটি *n* flower/flowery pattern worked on cloth; embroidery. বুটি তোলা *vt* work flowers/flowery pattern on cloth; embroider. বুটিদার *adj* embroidered; flowered.

বুড়ন[1] *n* growing old; aging.

বুড়ন[2] *n* submersion; going under water.

বুড়বাক *n* old fool; blockhead.

বুড়া[১] *adj* **1** old; aged; elderly; decrepit: ~ লোক. **2** precocious; forward; impertinent: ~ কথা. **3** very old; ancient: ~ বট. **4** puerile; childish: ~ খোকা. ❑*n* old man. **~নো, ~ হওয়া** *vi* grow old; become old; ripen; age; wither; decay; mature; become a veteran: মাস্টারিতে ~ হওয়া. **~ আঙুল** *n* thumb. **~টে** *adj* oldish. **~ ঠাকুরদাদা** *n* great grandfather (on one's father's side). **~ থুড়থুড়া** *n* very old; decrepit; hoary. **~পনা** *n* precocity; precocious behaviour (of a child); forwardness; impertinence. **~ বাঁদর** *n* old fool. **~ বুড়া** *adj* oldish; ludicrously elderly; precocious: ~ বুড়া কথাবার্তা. **~মি** *n*=~পনা. **~ হাবড়া** *n* dotard; greybeard.

বুড়া[২], বোড়া *vi* sink; be submerged; go under water; be immersed; be covered up: ক্ষেতটা আগাছায় বুড়েছে. **~নো, ~ন** *vt* submerge; sink; dip; immerse; cover up.

বুড়ি[১], বুড়ী *n fem* (of বুড়া) old; aged; grown-up: ~ মেয়ে ❑*n* **1** old woman. **2** a female child imitating an old woman. **3** (term of endearment for a) female child. **4** precocious little girl. **~র দাঁত** *n* seed/stone as large and hard as an old woman's teeth. **পাকা ~** *n* (facet) a little girl behaving like a grown-up/an elderly woman.

বুড়ি[২] *n* unit of counting by twenties. **~কিয়া** *n* table of enumeration by twenties. **~তে চতুর কাহনে কানা** (fig) penny wise pound foolish. **~ ছুঁয়ে থাকা** (fig) observe the ruler nominally.

বুড়ো *adj* (colloq)=বুড়া. বুড়ুটে =বুড়াটে. **~বুড়ি** *n* old man and wife. **~ মেরে খুনের দায়** (fig) heavy punishment for a light offence. **~ শালিকের ঘাড়ে রোঁ** (fig) boyish / youthlike conduct in old age.

বুঢ়া *adj, n* (colloq) =বুড়া

বুত [P] *n* idol; image. **~পরস্ত** *adj, n* idol-worshipping; idol-worshipper; idolator.

বুদ্দু *adj n* fool; devoid of sense.

বুদ্ধ *adj* enlightened; awakened; wise. ❑*n* Gautama Buddha, the founder of the Buddhist religion. **~ত্ব** *n* condition/ rank of a Buddha; supreme enlightenment/wisdom.

বুদ্ধি *n* **1** intelligence; intellect; reason; understanding; discernment; judgement; perception. **2** mind; talent; gumption. **3** counsel; advice. **4** device; scheme. **5** propensity; tendency: দুষ্ট ~. **~ করা** *vt,vi* plan; scheme; contrive; consult/confer with. **~ খাটানো** *vi* apply one's mind (to sth/to doing sth); have recourse to a contrivance; make use of one's intelligence. **~ দেওয়া** *vt* advise; counsel; show the ropes; show sb the way; instigate; encourage. **~ নেওয়া** *vi* seek/take advice; call in; consult; take one's use from; confer with; be advised by; take counsel with. **~ হারানো** *vi* be at one's wit's end; loose one's senses; be confused/ perturbed/ blustered. **~কৃত** *adj* acted wisely. **~কৌশল** *n* brilliance; mental agility. **~গম্য, ~গ্রাহ্য** *adj* to be apprehended by the intellect; intelligible; conceivable. **~চাতুর্য** *n* cleverness; wits; sagacity. **~জীবী** *adj* subsisting by intelligence; intelligent. ❑*n* intellectual. **~জীবী সম্প্রদায়** *n* intelligentsia. **~দাতা** *n* adviser; counsellor. **~দাত্রী** *fem.* **~নাশ** *n* loss of understanding; folly; deficiency of intellect/ intelligence. **~পূর্ব** *adj* premeditated; intentional; wilful. **~বল** *n* strength of intelligence. **~বিলাস** *n* play of the mind /fancy. **~বৃত্তি** *n* faculty of understanding; intellect; reasoning; sense; discernment. **~বৃত্তিমূলক** *adj* intellectual; rational. **~বৃদ্ধি, ~বিকাশ** *n* growth/ development of intellect; growth of understanding/wisdom. **~বৈভব** *n* strength/force of understanding. **~ভ্রংশ** *n* = ~নাশ. **~ভ্রম** *n* disturbance/aberration of mind. **~ভ্রষ্ট** *adj* mentally deranged/ unhinged; out of one's senses/mind/head; of unsound mind; stupid; foolish; bewildered. **~মত্তা** *n* intelligence; wisdom; understanding. **~মান** *adj* intelligent; learned; wise; shrewd; clever; sagacious. **~মতী** *fem.* **~মোহ** *n* confusion of mind. **~যুক্ত** *adj* endowed with understanding; intelligent. **~যোগ** *n* intellectual union with the Supreme Spirit. **~লাঘব** *n* lightness/levity of judgment. **~লোপ** *n* =~নাশ. **~শক্তি** *n* intellectual faculty. **~শুদ্ধি** *n* purification of the mind; good sense. **~সম্পন্ন** *adj*=~যুক্ত. **~স্থ** *adj* fixed in/ present to the mind. **~হত, ~হারা** *adjj* =~ভ্রষ্ট. **~হীন** *adj* destitute of understanding; foolish; ignorant; stupid. **~হীনা** *fem.* **~হীনতা** *n* stupidity; foolishness; folly. **~র অতীত** beyond the reach of the understanding. **~র ঢেঁকি** *n* (fig) thickhead; addlehead; thickwit; dunderhead; blockhead. **বুদ্ধীন্দ্রিয়** *n* organ of sense /perception.

বুদ্বুদ *n* bubble. **~ ওঠা** *vi* effervesce; rise in bubbles; send up bubbles; bubble. **~ন** *n* effervescence.

বুধ *n* **1** the planet Mercury. **2** wise/ learned man. **~বার** *n*=Wednesday (1).

বুনন *n* **1** sowing. **2** weaving; knitting. বুননি *n* =বুনানি.

বুনা *vi, vt* **1** sow. **2** weave; knit. ❑*adj* sown; woven; knitted. **~ট, ~নি** *n* **1** sowing. **2** weaving; knitting. **3** charger for sowing or weaving/knitting. **4** texture.

বুনিয়াদ=বনিয়াদ. বুনিয়াদি=বনিয়াদি

বুনুনি *n* (colloq)=বুনানি (⇒ বুনা)

বুনো *adj*=বন্য

বুবু *n fem* an elder sister.

বুভুক্ষা *n* desire of enjoying anything; hunger; appetite. বুভুক্ষিত, বুভুক্ষু *adjj* hungry;

starving; ravenous; desirous of worldly enjoyment.

বুরুচ [E] *n* broach.

বুরুজ [A] *n* **1** bastion; turret; tower. **2** kind of card-game.

বুরুশ [E] *n* brush. ~ করা, ~ দিয়ে ঝাড়া, ~ লাগানো *vt* brush.

বুর্জোয়া [F] *n, adj* bourgeois.

বুলক, বুলাক [A] *n* an ornament worn in nose.

বুলন্দ [P] *adj* high; lofty; elevated; sublime; raised; exalted; tall; loud. ~ আওয়াজ *n* loud sound/voice. ~ করা *vt* lift; elevate; exalt; raise up. ~নসিব *adj* lucky; fortunate; privileged.

বুলবুল, বুলবুলি *n* nightingale; bulbul.

বুলা *vt* (archaic; poet) roam; stroll; walk.

বুলানো, বুলান *vt* pass (one's hand, a brush, a pen, etc) lightly across/over/through sth. চোখ ~ pass one's eye; glance. তুলি ~ touch lightly with a brush.

বুলি *n* **1** word; speech; language; idiom; phrase; parlance. **2** lingo; jargon. **3** dialect; patois: দেহাতি ~. **4** animal cry; prattle; babble: পাখির/ শিশুর ~. **5** stereotyped phrase; slogan; catch phrase; crammed speech; cant; cliché. **6** maxim; motto; principle. ~ আওড়ানো/ঝাড়া *vi* prattle; babble; blather; rant; use clichés; talk jargon; utter a stereotyped phrase/ maxim/slogan. বাঁধা-~ *n* stereotyped/ hackneyed phrase; cant; cliché.

বুলেট [E] *n* bullet.

বুসা [P] *n* kiss.

বুস্তান [P] *n* garden.

বুহিত *n* (archaic) merchant ship.

বৃংহন *adj* nourishing; restorative; fattening. ❑*n* **1** roar of an elephant. **2** restorative tonic.

বৃংহিত *n* roar of an elephant. ❑*adj* strengthened; nourished.

বৃক *n* **1** wolf. **2** jackal. **3** crow. **4** hunger. ~দংশ *n* dog. ~ধূর্ত *n* jackal.

বৃকোদর *n* Bhima, the second son of Pandu (in the Mahabharata).

বৃক্ক *n* the kidneys. বৃক্কাকার *adj* kidney-shaped; reniform.

বৃক্ষ *n* tree; plant. ~ক *n* small tree; under-shrub. ~কাণ্ড *n* tree-trunk. ~কুক্কুট *n* wild cock. ~গুল্ম *n pl*/trees and shrubs. ~চর *n* monkey. ~চ্ছায় *n* shade of many trees; grove. ~চ্ছায়া *n* shade of a tree. ~জাতীয় *adj* belonging to the genus tree. ~তল *n* foot of a tree. ~তুল *adv* underneath the tree. ~দেবতা *n* tree-divinity; dryad. ~নির্যাস *n* exudation of trees; resin; gum. ~পাল *n* wood-keeper. ~বাটি, ~বাটিকা *n* garden house; grove of trees/ garden near a house. ~ময় *adj* abounding in trees; woody; wooden. ~মূল *n* root of a tree. ~রূহ *n* parasitical plant. ~ রোপক *n* planter of trees. ~রোপণ *n* tree-planting. ~রোপণ করা *vt* plant tree(s). ~শূন্য *adj* destitute of trees. ~সেচন *n* watering of trees. ~স্থ, ~স্থিত *adj* staying on/in a tree. ~হীন *adj* treeless. বৃক্ষাগ্র *n* top of a tree. বৃক্ষান্তরাল *n* place screened from the view by a tree/trees. বৃক্ষারূঢ় *adj* perched/ mounted on a tree. বৃক্ষারোহণ *n* climbing on a tree. বৃক্ষাশ্রয়ী *adj n* dwelling on/in a tree; tree-dweller. বৃক্ষোপাসনা *n* tree-worship.

বৃত *adj* **1** respectfully or honourably received/ chosen/ appointed; selected; preferred. **2** ordained: যাজক পদে ~. **3** solicited. **4** concealed; hidden; enveloped; surrounded by; covered with; screened. ~বিশোষণ, ~শোষণ *n* (phys, bot) selective absorption.

বৃতি *n* **1** respectful/ honourable reception/ appointment; selection; choosing; choice; ordainment. **2** solicitation; covering; surrounding. **3** hedge; fence; enclosure; enclosed piece of ground/ place enclosed for particular cultivation. **4** (bot) calyx. ~নল *n* (bot) calyx tube. ~সদৃশ *adj* (bot) sepaloid.

বৃত্ত *n* **1** (geom) circle. **2** sphere; field; domain; arena; orbit; circuit. **3** mode of life; practice; conduct; behaviour; action: সু~, দুর্বৃত্ত. **4** system of versification: অক্ষর~. ❑*adj* **1** round; rounded; circular. **2** past; elapsed; gone. **3** born. ~কলা *n* (geom) sector. ~খণ্ড *n* (geom) portion/ segment of a circle. ~পাদ *n* (astron) quadrature. অধি~ *n* (geom) parabola. অর্ধ~ *n* (geom) semi-circle. উপ~ *n* (geom) ellipse. ক্রান্তি~ *adj* (astron) ecliptic. গুরু~ *n* (astron) great circle. লঘু~ *n* (astron) small circle. ~সমবর্তিত আলোক *n* circularly polarized light. ~স্থ *adj* **1** situated within a circle. **2** (geom) cyclic. **3** of good moral conduct; virtuous. বৃত্তাংশ *n* (geom) segment of a circle. বৃত্তাকার *adj* rotund; circular. বৃত্তার্ধ *n* semi-circle.

বৃত্তান্ত *n* **1** tidings; report; information; account; tale; story; news; history; facts; details. **2** occurrence; incident; event; topic; subject.

বৃত্তাভাস *n* **1** semi-circle. **2** poetic prose.

বৃত্তি *n* **1** faculty; mood; disposition: চিত্ত~. **2** mode of life; conduct; course of action; behaviour; moral conduct: নীচ~, হীন~, বক~.**3** mode of being; nature; character. **4** profession; occupation; vocation; calling; practice; livelihood; trade business; devotion/ addiction to. **5** function; working. **6** use/ occurrence of a word in a particular sense; its function/ force. **7** commentary; elucidation; comment; gloss; explanation. **8** (rhet) alliteration; frequent repetition of the same consonant. **9** stipend; scholarship; regular allowance; subsistence; maintenance. ~ দান করা *vi* give/ award/ endow a stipend or scholarship. ~ প্রশিক্ষণ *n* vocational training. ~প্রাপ্ত *adj* recipient of a scholarship. ~প্রাপ্ত

ছাত্র *n* scholar; scholarship-holder. ~মূলক *adj* vocational. ~শিক্ষা *n* vocational education.

বৃত্তীয় *adj* circular; spherical. ~ মান *n* (trigo) circular measure.

বৃত্য *adj* deserving/ honourable/ cordial reception; to be received honourably/ cordially; most honourable.

বৃত্যংশ *n* (bot) sepal).

বৃথা *adj* futile; useless; vain; fruitless; abortive; ineffectual. ❑*adv* in vain; vainly; uselessly; fruitlessly; to no purpose. ~ কথা *n* idle talk; nonsense. ~ কর্ম *n* useless action. ~ শ্রম *n* vain exertion; useless labour.

বৃদ্ধ *adj* 1 old; aged; ancient; advanced in years; senior; distinguished; grown up; full-grown. 2 experienced; wise; learned: জ্ঞান~, বয়ো~. 3 grown; become larger/ longer/ stronger; increased; augmented. ❑*n* old man. বৃদ্ধা *fem.* ~তা, ~ত্ব *nn* oldness; agedness; pre-eminence (in). ~ প্রপিতামহ *n* paternal great-great-grandfather ~ প্রপিতামহী *fem.* ~ প্রমাতামহ *n* maternal great-great-grandfather. ~ প্রমাতামহী *fem.*

বৃদ্ধাঙ্গুলি *n* thumb; big toe. ~ দেখানো (fig) defy; mock; flout; laugh in the face of. বৃদ্ধাবস্থা *n* condition/ period of old age; senility.

বৃদ্ধি *n* 1 growth; increase; development; augmentation. 2 rise; advancement; extension; welfare; prosperity; success; fortune; happiness. 3 prolongation (of life). 4 swelling (eg of the body). 5 enlargement (as of the scrotum). 6 swelling/ rising (of the sea). 7 waxing (of the moon). 8 profit from lending money, etc; usury; interest. 9 gain; profit. 10 excess; plethora; over abundance; audacity. 11 (gram) the second modification/ increase of vowels (to which they are subject under certain conditions). 12 (bot) accescence. ~ পাওয়া *vi* grow; grow up; thrive; prosper; succeed; advance; rise; ascend; accrete. ~কর *adj* yielding/ causing increase; promoting growth/ prosperity; augmenting. ~করী *fem.* ~ কাল *n* period of growth. মুখ্য ~কাল *n* (bot) grand period of growth movement. ~জীবিকা *n* livelihood gained by usury. ~জীবী *adj* living by usury. ❑*n* usurer. ~জীবিনী *fem.* ~দশা *n* (bot) phase of growth. ~বিস্তার *n* (bot) distribution of growth. ~মান *adj* having increase; growing; increasing; flourishing; thriving. ~মতী *fem.* ~শীল *adj* = ~মান. ~শ্রাদ্ধ *n* obsequial offerings to progenitors on any prosperous occasion (as on the eve of a marriage ceremony). ~ হার *n* rate of growth.

বৃন্ত *n* 1 footstalk of a leaf/ flower/ fruit; any stalk. 2 nipple. 3 stand of a water-jar. ~চ্যুত *adj* detached/ nipped from the stalk. ~মধ্যক *adj* (bot) interpetiolar.

বৃন্দ *n* 1 a heap; multitude; host; flock; swarm; number; quantity; aggregation. 2 thousand million. 3 chorus of singers and musicians. ❑*suff* use to form the *pl* of certain *nn*: দর্শক~, ভক্ত~.

বৃন্দাবন *n* a wood near the town of Gokula in the district of Mathura.

বৃন্দার *adj* most beautiful; pleasant; lovely.

বৃশ্চিক *n* 1 scorpion. 2 (astrol). Scorpio. 3 centipede. ~দংশন *n* sting of a scorpion; (fig) utter mortification.

বৃষ *n* 1 bull; ox. 2 (astrol) Taurus. 3 strong/ potent man (according to erotic works). 4 chief of a class of anything; the most excellent or preeminent or best of its kind. 5 justice or virtue personified as a bull. ~কর্ণী *n* (bot) *Cocculus tomantosus.* ~গন্ধা *n* (bot)*Convolulus argentous.* ~ণ *n* scrotum; testicles. ~ণ কচ্ছু ulceration of the scrotum. ~ধ্বজ, ~কেতন *nn* 'having the bull for a sign'; Shiva. ~ভ *n* 1 bull. 2 chief; most excellent/ eminent; lord/ best among. ~ভধ্বজ *n* Shiva. ~ রাশি *n* = ~ (2). ~স্কন্ধ *n* bull's neck. ❑*adj* having shouiders like a bull; broad shouldered.

বৃষল *n* a Shudra. ❑*adj* low; mean; wicked; sinful.

বৃষোৎসর্গ *n* letting loose a bull and four heifers (as a work of merit, esp as part of a obsequial ceremony).

বৃষ্টি *n* rain; shower; rain-water. ~ পড়া/হওয়া *vi* rain. ~ পড়ে It rains. বৃষ্ট *adj* fallen/ dropped as rain. ~ছায় *n* (geog) rain-shadow. ~জল *n* rain-water. ~পাত *n* rainfall; shower of rain. ~বিন্দু *n* rain drop. ~মান, ~মানযন্ত্র, ~মাপক *nn* rain-gauge; pluviometer. ~সম্বন্ধীয় *adj* pluvial. ~স্নাত *adj* drenched/ soaked in rain. ~হীন *adj* rainless.

বৃষ্য *adj* 1 productive of sexual vigour; stimulating. 2 invigorating. 3 aphrodisiac.

বৃহৎ *adj* huge; big; large; wide; vast; lofty; tall; great; high; abundant; solid; massy; strong; mighty; complicated; magnanimous; extensive; pompous. বৃহতী *fem.* ~কায় *adj* 'large bodied'; colossal; gigantic; bulky; huge. বৃহত্তম *superl* of ~. বৃহত্তর comp of~.

বৃহতিকা *n* 1 upper garment; mantle; wrapper. 2 kind of aubergine.

বৃহদন্ত্র *n* (anat) large intestine.

বৃহদাকার *adj* large in shape/size; huge; colossal; enormous.

বৃহস্পতি *n* 1 (myth) the preceptor of the gods and the god of wisdom and eloquence. 2 (astron) the Jupiter. 3 Thursday. 4 a great scholar/ savant: বিদ্যায় ~. ~ বার *n* =~. ~র বারবেলা *n* (astrol) a part of Thursday considered utterly inauspicious for any work. ~র দশা *n* (astrol) planetary influence of the Jupiter. একাদশ ~*n* (astrol) a very auspicious conjunction of stars in one's life.

বে[২] [P] *pre* denoting: absence, lack, negation, perversion, etc. (it forms compound words corresponding to the English words beginning with *in, im, un, ir,* etc, or ending in-*less*). ~আক্কেল *adj* stupid; unwise; senseless. ~য়াকুফ *adj* foolish; stupid; dolt. ❑*n* fool; stupid. ~য়াকুফ বানানো *vt* make a fool (of); make fun (of); ridicule. ~য়াকুফি *n n* foolishness; stupidity; want of understanding. ~আইন, ~আইনি, *adjj* unlawful; illegal; lawless; outlawed; proscribed; banned. ~আইনি করা *vt* prohibit by law; interdict; outlaw; prescribe; ban; do sth unlawful. ~আইনি জনতা *n* unlawful assembly. ~ত্যাড়া = বেয়াড়া. ~আদব *adj* rude; brazen-faced; unmannerly; impudent; disrespectful. ❑*n* rude person; boor; lout; brute. ~আদবি *n* discourtesy; bad/poor manners; ill breeding; insolence; disrespect; impudence. ~আদবি করা *vi* be discourteous/insolent, etc. ~আন্দাজ, ~আন্দাজি *adjj* unlimited; beyond estimate; extravagant; excessive; endless. ~আবরু, ~ আব্রু *adj* **1** (of a woman) not keeping to the inner appartments; having one's modesty outraged. **2** shameless; dishonourable; disreputable; disgraced. **3** shamefully/ indecorously exposed to public view. ~আবাদ *adj* uncultivated; unpopulated. ~আরাম, ব্যারাম *n* illness; disease; ailment. ব্যারামে পড়া be ill; ail; waste away. ~ইজ্জত, ~ইজ্জৎ *adj* without honour/ respect; disgraceful; disgraced; put out of countenance; insulted; (of a woman) having one's modestly/ chastity outraged. ❑*n* disgrace; insult; dishonour; ignominy; indignity; odium; (of a woman) outrage of modesty/ chastity. ~ইজ্জত করা *vt* disgrace; defile; dishonour; outrage the modesty (of); bring disgrace upon; put to shame; expose to disgrace. ~ইজ্জতি *n* = ~ইজ্জত. ~ইনসাফ *adj* unjust; unfair; iniquitous. ~ইনসাফি *n* injustice; unfairness; inequity. ~ইমান, ~ঈমান *adj* **1** perfidious; unfaithful; false; dishonest; liar; cheat. **2** infidel; faithless; unbeliever; godless; irreligious. ❑*n* traitor; infidel. ~ইমানি, ~ঈমানি *nn* perfidy; treachery; faithlessness; perfidiousness; falseness; infidelity; ungodliness; impiety. ~এক্তিয়ার = *adj* beyond jurisdiction; ultra vires; out of one's control; helpless; want of power; want of choice. ~একরার *n* **1** unconditionality. **2** disavowal; denial. ~একরারি *adj* unconditional. ~এলাকাদার *adj, n* unconcerned (person). ~ওআকিফ, ~ওয়াকিফ *adj* uninformed. ~ওকুফ = ~অকুফ. ~ওক্ত *n* inopportune/ unsuitable time. ❑*adj* untimely; out of season; ill-timed. ~ওজন *adj* unmeasured; immeasurable; extravagant; excessive. ~ওজনী *n* excess; extravagance. ~ওজর *adj* admitting no excuse/ protest. ❑*adv* without excuse/ protest. ~ওতন *n* without country; homeless. ~ওফা *adj* faithless; perfidious; treacherous; ungrateful. ~ওয়া *n* childless widow. ~ওয়ারিশ *adj* unclaimed; ownerless; heirless; derelict. ~কবুল *adj* denied; repudiated. ~করার *adj* without contract; unsettled; uneasy; restless; variable; impatient. ~কসুর *adj* innocent; faultless; not guilty; guiltless. ~কসুর খালাস acquitted on account of being found not guilty; clean acquittal. ~কানুন *adj* illegal. ~কানুনি *adj* contrary to land. ~কার *adj* not brought under control; out of ones power/ reach; uncontrollable; having no control/ restraint over; uncontained; unbridled; not subdued. ~কায়দা *adj* unwieldy; disadvantageous; driven into a corner; awkward; against rules/ regulations. ❑*n* tight corner; awkward situation. ~কার *adj* unemployed; unoccupied; idle; useless; unserviceable. ~কারত্ব, ~কারি *nn* unemployment; idleness. ~কার সমস্যা *n* unemployment problem. ~কুফ, ~কুব = ~ওকুফ. ~কুফি, ~কুবি = ~অকুফি. ~খবর *adj* uninformed; ignorant; stupid; negligent; neglectful; careless. ~খরচ, ~খরচা *adj* **1** gratuitous; free of costs; for nothing. **2** penniless; indigent. ~খাপ, ~খাপ্পা *adj* unfitting; unsuited; awkward; uncouth; infelicitous; inapt; ill-befitting; unsuitable; inappropriate; irrelevant; inconsistent; disproportionate; incompatible. ~গতিক *adj* helpless; unfavourable; critical; difficult; awkward. ❑*n* awkward/ unfavourable/ helpless situation; tight corner; danger; difficulty. ~গর *prep* without ~গরজ, ~গরজি *adj* disinterested; selfless; indifferent; unnecessary. ~গানা *adj* not related; alien; outsider. ~গানা পুরুষ/ লোক *n* stranger; foreigner; outsider. ~গার *n* forced labour; compulsory labour with or without payment; drudgery ~গার খাটা *vi* work without payment; render service gratis under pressure; slave; drudge. ~গার ঠেলা *vi* work in a perfunctory manner/ carelessly. ~গারে *adj* available for rendering corvée or gratuitous service. ~গুনাহ *adj* innocent; guiltless. ~গোছ *adj* disorderly; untidy; sloppy; disarrayed; disadvantageous. ❑*n* disorder; disadvantage; inconvenience; trouble; awkward situation;

tight corner. ~গোড় *adj* baseless; flimsy; having no foundation. ~ঘুম *n* sleeplessness; insomnia. ~চইন *adj* restless; uneasy. ~চারা, ~চারি *adj* helpless; poor; miserable; unfortunate. ❑*n* helpless/ wretched/ pitiable person; harmless/ innocent person. ~চাল *adj* misbehaving; unmannerly; ill-mannered, dissolute; depraved. ❑*n* misbehaviour; misdemeanour; bad manners; dissoluteness; refractoriness; depravity; difficulty. ~ছপ্পর *adj* homeless; outcast. ~জন্মা *adj* bastard; illegitimate. ~জবাব *adj* unanswering; unresponsive; silent. ~জয় *adj* unjust; improper unreasonable. ~জাত *adj* degenerated in caste; degraded; illegitimate. ❑*n* degenerated caste; bastard; rake; degenerate. ~জান *adj* lifeless; dead; inanimate; dying. ~জায় *adj* much; many; excessive; tremendous; extreme; enormous. ❑*adv* tremendously; greatly; exceedingly; infinitely. ~জার *adj* disgusted; displeased; saddened; sulky. ~জার হয়ে *adv* with a bad grace. ~জারি *n* non-execution (of orders). ~জুত *n* tight corner; disadvantage; indisposition. ❑*adj* disadvantageous; adverse; indisposed. ~জোড় = বিজোড়. ~জোর *adj* weak; impotent; powerless. ~টাইম *n* unsuitable/ improper/ inopportune time. ❑*adj* untimely; inopportune; ill-timed. ~ঠিক *adj* incorrect; wrong; mistaken. ~ঠিকানা *adj*, *n* having no abode/ domicile; vagabond; wanderer. ~ভাড়া *adj* spineless; contrary to custom and usage; anomalous. ~ডৌল *adj* ill-shaped; misshapen; shapeless; ungainly; disproportionate; less.; ugly. ~ঢপ *adj* ill-shaped; ugly; unmannerly; awkward; unfitting. ~তদবির *adj* **1** lethargic; indolent; shiftless; without any plan. **2** unopposed; unresisted; not remedied. ❑*n* absence or lack of redress/ solicitude/ supervision/ management. ~তমিজ *adj* **1** rude; uncultured; incivil; ill-bred; unmannerly. **2** lacking discrimination; indiscreet; unwise; inexperienced. ~তর *adj* indisposed; besotted; fuddled; tipsy; off one's guard; embarrassed; dissimilar: ~তর শরীর, নেশায় ~তর, উকিলের জেরায় ~তর. ~তরিবত *adj* ill-bred ; unmannerly; ill-behaved; unrefined; uneducated. ~তাক, ~তাগ *adj* missing the mark; beside the mark. ~তাকত, ~তাগৎ *adj* weak; powerless; feeble; infirm; frail. ~তার[১] *adj* tasteless; insipid; distasteful; flat; dull; uninteresting. ~তার[২] *adj* wireless. ❑*n* radio; wireless telegraphy. ~ঘোষণা *n* radio announcement; broadcast. ~ঘোষণা করা *vt* broadcast. ~তার বার্তা *n* radio news; wireless telegrams/ message. ~যন্ত্র *n* radio(-set). ~তাল *adj* **1** (music) failing in measure; failing to maintain measure out of tune. **2** (fig) ill-timed; confused; upset; confusing; wayward; bizarre; queer; whimsical; curious. ❑*n* breach of measure; inappropriate/ wrong measure. ~তালা *adj* = ~তাল. ~থাক *adj* disarrayed; disordered; out of time; disarranged; upset; inappropriate; unfitting; unbecoming; infelicitous; unsuited. ~দখল *adj* **1** (of a person) dispossessed; ousted; ejected. **2** (of lands) put out of possession; not taken possession of; taken possession of unlawfully (and forcibly). **2** not brought under control; beyond one's reach/ power; not mastered; unconquered. ~দখল করা *vt* eject; evict; dispossess; take possession of unlawfully. ~দখল হওয়া *vi* be dispossessed/ evicted; be taken possession of unlawfully; pass out of possession. ~দখলি *n* ejectment; eviction. ❑*adj* taken possession of unlawfully. ~দম *adj* breathless; lifeless; out of breath; giving or taking no respite even to breathe; ruthless; relentless: ~দম ছুট/ মার. ❑*adv* severely; ruthlessly; relentlessly; out of breath; breathlessly. ~দম পেটানো *vt* thrash the living daylights out of; give a good hiding. ~দরকারি *adj* unnecessary. ~দরদ, ~দরদি *adj* feelingless; void of compassion; heartless; pitiless; merciless. ~দল *adj* separated from one's flock/ party; solitary; singular; queer. ~দলিল, ~দলিলি *adj* having no documentary proof; ungrounded; causeless; baseless; without foundation. ~দস্তুর *adj* contrary to rule/ practice; unusual; unconventional; anomalous; atypical; irregular. ~দাগ *adj* spotless; without blemish; faultless; innocent. ~দানা *adj* seedless. ❑*n* pomegranate. ~দার *adj* not disciplined; ungoverned; insolent; haughty; headstrong. ~দাবা, ~দাবি *adj* **1** having no liability/ responsibility. **2** of peaceful/ quiet disposition; peace loving. **3** without rightful owner. ~দাম, ~দামি *adj* valueless; priceless; invaluable. ~দিল *adj* dejected; sad; melancholic; dispirited; dissatisfied; heartless. ~দিশা, ~দিশে *nn* error in ascertainment of right direction; bewilderment; perplexity; missing the target; confusion. ❑*adj* confounded; perplexed; stunned; staggered. ~দীন *adj* irreligious; faithless. ~দেরেগ *adj, adv* without regret/ hesitation; rashly. ~ধড়ক *adj* **1** measureless; abundant; excessive; bountiful. **2** fearless; bold. ❑*adv* excessively; bountifully; abundantly; readily; fearlessly; rashly. ~ধারা *adj* bad manners; harmful customs/ usage; disorder. ~নজির *adj* matchless; incomparable; unique; peerless; unequalled. ~নসিব *adj* unfortunate; deprived; frustrated.

~নসিবি *n* misfortune; bad luck. ~নাম *adj* **1** nameless. **2** anonymous; pseudonymous. ❑*n* one's name used by another; false name; pen name; nom de plume; pseudonym. ~নাম করা *vt* transfer (a property) to another only nominally (chiefly in order to evade liabilities). বেনামে (কিছু) করা do (sth) under another's name. বেনামে লেখা *vt* write under a pseudonym. ~নামদার *adj* pseudonymous; anonymous; unnamed; unknown; incognito. বেনামা, বেনামি *adj* **1** anonymous; pseudonymous; with an assumed name; incognito; nameless. **2** transferred to another only nominally. ~নামিদার *n* ostensible holder. ~নোটিস *adj* without information/ notification. ~পছন্দ, ~পসন্দ *adj* not to one's liking; disfavoured; disliked; dislikeable; in the bad graces of; out of favour. ~পরওয়া, ~পরোয়া *adj* heedless; careless; thoughtless; reckless desperate; rash; dauntless; devil-may-care; headstrong. ~পরোয়া লোক *n* absolutely heedless/ dauntless/ reckless man; daredevil; desperado. ~পরোয়াই *n* carelessness; unconcern; indifference; recklessness; heedlessness; desperation. ~পর্দা *adj* **1** having no covering/ veil; exposed; using no covering; bare faced; unveiled; immodest; not keeping to the inner apartments. **2** shameless; brazen; brazen faced. **3** disreputable; dishonourable; disgraced; shameful. ~ফজুল *adj* useless; superfluous; needless; profuse: ~ফজুল খরচ. ~ফয়দা, ~ফায়দা *adj* unprofitable; of no consequence; futile; purposeless; vain; useless. ~ফাঁস *adj* **1** uttered off guard / indiscreetly; indiscreet: ~ফাঁস কথা. **2** unrestrained; loose; free: ~ফাঁস মুখ. **3** divulged. ~বদল *n* invariability; constancy. ❑*adj* unchanging; changeless; invariable. ~বন্দেজ *adj* disorderly; not properly managed; extravagant; unplanned. ❑*n* disorder; mismanagement. ~বন্দোবস্ত *adj* **1** disorderly; unsystematic; disorganized; messed up; messy; muddled; not properly managed; mismanaged; (of lands) not settled on. ❑*n* disorderliness; disorder; mismanagement; disarray; muddle; mix-up; chaos; tangle; jumble. ~বন্দোবস্তি *adj* (of lands) not settled on. ~বহা *adj* invaluable; very precious; wonderful; excellent. ~বাক *adj* all; whole; entire. ❑*adv* entirely; wholly. ~বুনিয়াদ *adj* groundless; baseless; without foundation. ~মওকা, ~মক্কা *adj* out of place; untimely; improper; inopportune; inconvenient; inappropriate; sudden. ~মজলিসি *adj* not fit for a party/ assembly; unsocial; reserved. ~মতলব *adj* **1** purposeless; aimless. **2** selfless; unselfish; uncalculating. ~মনাসিব, ~মোনাসিব *adj* **1** improper ; inappropriate; uncalled for; unseemly; inapropos; malapropos; unseasonable. **2** after one's own heart; to one's liking. ~মানান *adj* unfitting; unbecoming; unbefitting; unsuitable; inappropriate; unseemly; unpresentable; unreasonable; inapt; in congruous; ill-matched; awkward; incompatible ~মালুম *adj*. unperceived; unknown to; stealthy; secret. ❑*adj* imperceptibly; stealthily; silently; unknowingly; un-consciously; surreptitiously. ~মালেক *adj* dispossessed; not entitled; having no right. ~মেরামত *adj* unrepaired; in a bad state of repair; derelict; dilapidated. ❑*n* disrepair; unrepair; negligence. ~মেল *adj* dissimilar; incompatible; unlike; disparate; incomparable; incommensurable. ❑*n* dissimilarity; disparity; incommensurability; unlikeness; disharmony; discord; dissonance. ~মৌসুম *adj* out of season; unseasonable. ~য়াড়া *adj* **1** self willed; obstinate; stubborn; headstrong; refractory: ~য়াড়া ছেলে **2** ungainly; ill-shaped; ugly; unmannerly; odd-looking; awkward: ~য়াড়া পরিস্থিতি. **3** queer; odd; strange; difficult; outlandish; bizarre: ~য়াড়া প্রশ্ন. ~য়ারাম, ব্যায়রাম, ব্যায়ারাম, ব্যারাম *n* disease; illness; ailment; malady; infirmity; malaise. ~রং, ~রঙ, ~রঙ্গ *n* **1** spoilt/faded colour unsuitable/different colour. **2** (card-game) a suit other than the trump. ❑*adj* discoloured, faded. ~রসিক *adj* **1** devoid of sense of humour/taste/appreciative power; dull; blunt. **2** prosaic; colourless; dry; tedious; stodgy. ~রহম *adj* merciless; pitiless; cruel. ~রেয়া, ~রিয়া *adj* **1** guileless; candid; sincere; without any show/formality. **2** taking no bribes. ~রোজগারি *adj* having no income; not earning. ~লয় *adj* (music) out of time. **2** irrelevant; impertinent; inapropos; pointless. ~লাগাম *adj* unbridled; licentious; intemperate. ~লিহাজ, ~লেহাজ *adj* shameless; indiscreet; unmannerly; impertinent. ~লেল্লা *adj* **1** way-ward; dissolute; profligate; rakish; lascivious; lecherous. **2** shameless. ill-bred; boorish; rowdy. ~লেল্লাগিরি, ~লেল্লাপনা *nn* **1** way wardness; profligacy; debauchery; moral turpitude; lasciviousness; lechery. **2** shamelessness; boorishness; bad manness; rowdyism. ~শক, ~সক *adv* surely; certainly; positively; of course. ~শরম *adj* shameless; immodest; impudent; brazen-faced. ~শরা *adj* acting against the law of Islam; heretical; unorthodox: ~শরা ফকির. ~শুমার, ~সুমার *adj* countless; innumerable; numberless. ~সবর, ~সবুর *adj* devoid of patience; impatient restless. **~সরকারি** *adj* unofficial; non-official;; not belonging to the government; non-governmental; private; personal. **~সামাল** *adj* **1** unable to check/restrain; divested of self-control; beside oneself with. **2** unguarded; careless; inadvertent; indiscreet; thoughtless: ~সামাল উক্তি. **3** powerless; helpless; impotent. **~সুদি** *adj* bearing no interest; interest-free. **~সুর, ~সুরা, ~সুরো** *adj* out of tune; not keeping with the tune; unmelodious; unmusical; incapable of maintaining the tune: ~সুরো বাজনা/ গলা/ গায়ক. ❑*n* discordant; disharmonious; cacophonous; grating; jarring: ~সুরো কথাবার্তা, ~সুরো আলাপ. **~হক** *adj* **1** unjust; unfair; wrongful; inequitable; unseasonable; immoderate; unjustifiable. **2** having no right; not rightful. **~হদ, ~হদ্দ** *adj* boundless; endless; excessive; out-and-out; thorough; extreme: ~হদ্দ বদমাশ, ~হদ্দ লোভ. **~হাত** *adj* (passed) out of one's hand/ possession/ control; gone into another hand/ possession/ control. **~হায়া** *adj* shameless; immodest; impudent; brazen-faced. **~হায়াপনা** *n* shameless conduct; immodesty. **~হাল** *adj* out of condition; ill-circumstanced; weary; miserable; worn out: impecunious; destitute. **~হিসাব** *adj* **1** countless; beyond calculation; unlimited; excessive. **2** extravagant; uneconomical; incautious; improvident; unrestrained; incautious imprudent. **3** without challenge; unchallenged. ❑*n* absence of estimate; extravagance; improvidence; lack of caution; imprudence. **~হিসাবি** *adj*=~হিসাব. **~হুশ, ~হোশ, ~হোস** *adj* **1** senseless; fainted; insensible. **2** heedless; careless; unmindful; not in one's proper senses. **~হুঁশিয়ার** *adj* **1** ignorant; insensate; negligent; uninformed. **2** guileless; naive, artless; simple minded. **3** incautious; unheeding, unwary; thought-less. **~হুকুম** *adj adv* against/ without orders; contrary to orders/instructions. **~হুদা** *adj* unjust; improper; without reason; unnecessary; useless; superfluous; uncalled for; gratuitous. ❑*adv* unjustly; unnecessarily; for nothing. **~হেড** *adj* **1** deranged; having one's head turned; frenzied; crazy; out of one's mind; unbalanced; unhinged; wild; zany. **2** besotted; sotted; dead-drunk; blind-drunk. **3** thoughtless; wrong-headed; perverse.

বে[২]**, বে'** *n*=(colloq)=বিবাহ

বেউড়-বাঁশ *n* a thorny variety of bamboo.

বেওয়া ⇒ বে[১]

বেং=ব্যাঙ

বেঁকা *adj* (colloq)=বাঁকা

বেঁজি, বেঁজী=বেজি

বেঁটে *adj* dwarfish; short. statured stunted. **~খাটো, ~খেটে** *adj* dumpy; pudgy; stumpy; diminutive.

বেঁড়ে *adj* tailless; dock-tailed.

বেঁধা *vi* (colloq)=বিঁধা

বেঁয়ে *adj* left-handed.

বেগ[১] *n* **1** speed; rapidly; quickness; swiftness; velocity; vehemence; haste; impetuosity; **2** rush; dash; impetus; momentum; onset. **3** outburst *outburst (of passion); emotion; excitement; emotion; **4** virulence; attack; paroxysm (of a disease); violent agitation; shock; jerk. **5** stream; current (of water, tears etc); flood. **6** desire to evacuate bowels/ urinate; expulsion of the faeces. **7** trouble: ~ দেওয়া. **8** (mech); velocity. **অসম ~** *n* variable velocity. **কৌণিক ~** *n* angular velocity. **কৌণিক ভর~** *n* momentum. **সম~** *n* uniform velocity. **~গামী** *adj* going/streaming fast; swiftly moving. **~ত্রিভুজ** *n* (mech) triangle of velocities. **~নাশক** *adj* preventing speed. **~নিয়ামক** *n* speed-governor. **~বন্ত, ~বান** *adj* fast-moving; speedy; swift; impetuous; rapid; hasty; having a strong current; rushing; flowing rapidly; torrential; irresistible; violent; emotional: ~বান হৃদয়. **~বতী** *fem.* **~বাহী** *adj* going/flowing/flying swiftly. **~বৃদ্ধি** *n* acceleration of speed; speed-up. **~মাপক** *adj* measuring speed. **~মাপকযন্ত্র** speedometer. **~শালী, ~সম্পন্ন** *adjj* endowed with swiftness; swift. **~শালিনী** *fem.* **~বিতরণ** *n* swift descent. **বেগার্ত** *adj* extremely speedy; (fig) utterly irresistible, violent: বেগার্ত হৃদয়. **বেগিত, বেগী** *adj* **1** impetuous; swift; rapid; hasty; fleet. **2** agitated; rough (as the) sea. **বেগে** *adv* swiftly; hastily.

বেগ[২] *n* **1** Mughal title corresponding to English "Lord"; master. **বেগম** *fem* **1** title of Mughal ladies. **2** lady; wife; queen;

বেগুন *n* aubergine; egg-plant. **বেগুনিত, বেগুনি, বেগনি** *adj* violet; purple. ❑*n* **1** violet/purple colour; **2** kind of fried snack prepared by dipping slices of aubergine in a thin paste of powdered pulse. **~ গাছে আঁকষি দেওয়া** (facet) requiring a crooked stick to pull down aubergines; (fig) midget; diminutive. **তেলে-বেগুনে জ্বলে/ নেচে ওঠা** flare up in anger/ excitement; fly into a rage/passion/temper.

বেগো *adj* of tiger; tiger-like; tigerish: ~ দাঁত/গন্ধ.

বেঘোর *n* **1** utterly helpless situation: বেঘোরে মরা. **2** insensibility: torpor: বেঘোরে ঘুমানো: sleep like a log/top.

বেঙ, বেঙ্গ=ব্যাঙ. **ব্যাঙাচি** *n* tadpole. **বেঙ্গাপিতল** *n* kind of brass/bell-metal.

বেঙ্গমা=বিহঙ্গমা (⇒ বিহগ). **বেঙ্গমী** *fem.*

বেচন *n* selling. **~দার** *n* seller.

বেচা *vt* sell. ❑*adj* sold. **~কেনা, কেনা~** *nn* buying and selling; trade; traffic; commerce. **~কেনা**

করা *vt* buy and sell; trade; traffic (in). ~নো *vt* cause to sell. ~বেচি *n* trading; selling; swop.

বেজি, বেজী *n* weasel; mongoose.

বেজিত *adj* agitated; frightened; worried; anxious.

বেঞ্চ [E] *n* **1** bench. **2** (law) bench.

বেঞ্চি *n*=বেঞ্চ (1). ~ গরম করা (ironic) sit idly. ~ দখল করা (facet) occupy a seat.

বেটন[1], বেটম *n* [E] batten.

বেটন[2] *n* [E] baton.

বেটা *n* **1** son. **2** male: মেয়ে না ~. **3** (endearing term) infant boy; younger man; son; my son; sonny. **4** (derog) fellow; chap; wretch. বেটি, বেটী *fem* **1** daughter. **2** female. **3** infant girl; younger women. **3** jade; hussy; wench. ~কাটা *vt* curse sb calling for the death/destruction of his/her son. ~ছেলে, ~চ্ছেলে *n* male person; male; man. ~র বেটা, ~চ্ছেলে *n* (term of abuse) bloke; bugger. ~বেটি *n pl* contemptible men and women; the scum (of): ~বেটিদের জ্বালায় অতিষ্ঠ।

বেটে, বেটো *adj* twisted; lanky; skinny; scraggy: ~ কুকুর. ❑*n* **1** twisted rope. **2** worn out horse.

বেড় *n* **1** circumference; girth. **2** encirclement; enclosure; hedge. ~ দেওয়া *vt* surround; enclose; encircle.

বেড়া[1] *n* fence; hedge; enclosure; wall. ❑*adj* enclosing; encircling; surrounding; encircled; surrounded; enclosed. ~ আগুন *n* encircling fire. ~ নেড়ে গৃহস্থের মন জানা **1** (of a thief) test the vigilance of the householder by shaking the wall. **2** sound sb (out) (about/on sth); throw out a feeler to feel the pulse; see how the land lies.

বেড়া[2] *vt*=বেড় দেওয়া

বেড়ানো *vt* **1** walk (for pleasure or exercise); go for a walk/stroll; promenade. rove; roam; travel; go on an excursion/tour/a trip; visit; go on a visit. বেড়িয়ে বেড়ানো *vi* go roaming; roam about; have a stroll. বেড়ানে *adj* fond of travelling; wandering; fond of visiting friends/ places etc. বেড়ানি *n fem* woman who is very fond of visiting her neighbours/ relatives etc.

বেড়ি, বেড়ী *n* **1** shackle; chain; fetters; manacle; bonds; handcuff: কোমরের/হাতের ~. **2** kind of tongs for gripping cooking utensils. ~ দেওয়া/ পরানো *vt* fetter; shackle; chain; strait-jacket. ~ পড়া *vi* be shackled/fettered/chained: হাতে পায়ে ~ পড়েছে. ~ পরা *vi* put shackles on; be shackled. ~ ভাঙা *vi* break up/smash the shackles. পায়ের ~ fetters.

বেড়ে *adj, adv* **1** excellent; fine; superb. **2** right; appropriate. ~ হয়েছে it serves him right. ❑*int* bravo!

বেড়েন *n* cudgelling; flagellation; whipping; drubbing.

বেড়েলা *n* kind of shrub; *Sida cordifolia.*

বেণা=বেনা

বেণি, বেণী *n* **1** hair twisted into a single unornamented braid and allowed to fall on the neck; braided hair; braid of hair. **2**=বিনুনি. **3** water of a river (compared to a braid of hair.); confluence/meeting of two or more rivers/ streams in a common point of union; cascade. ~ করা/বাঁধা *vt* twist (hair) into a braid. ~বদ্ধ *adj* braided; a braid. ~সংহার *n* binding up braided hair.

বেণিয়া =বেনে

বেণীর *n* soup nut; *Sapindus detergens.*

বেণু *n* **1** bamboo; reed. ~কার *n* flute-maker. **2** flute made of bamboo. ~কুঞ্জ *n* bamboo-thicket. ~দন্ড *n* bamboo staff. ~ধ্বনি, ~রব *nn* note of a bamboo-flute. ~বন *n* forest of bamboo. ~বাদক *n* flute-player. ~বাদন *n* playing on the flute.

বেণে=বেনে

বেত *n* **1** cane; ratan, rattan; reed, **2** rod; stick; ferule; cane. ~ খাওয়া *vt* get the cane. ~ বোনা *vi* weave cane into furniture, basket etc. ~ মারা, বেতানো *vt* cane. ~ লাগানো *vt* **1** punish with a cane; cane. **2** (chair, etc) fit/mend with cane or stipes of cane. ~তোলানি *n fem* woman expert in wicker-work. বেতের চেয়ার *n* wicker chair. বেতের ছড়ি *n* ratan; cane. বেতের ঝুড়ি *n* wicker-basket.

বেতন *n* wages; salary; subsistence, livelihood. ~ক্রম *n* pay-scale. ~গ্রাহী *adj* accepting wages; subsisting by wages; wage-earning. ~দান *n* paying of wages; hiring. ~দেয়ক *n* pay-bill; acquittance roll. ~ভুক, ~ভোগী *adj* earning wages; paid; salaried. বেতনী *adj* receiving wages.

বেতস *n* **1** ratan-plant; cane-plant; cane; ratan. **2** abounding in canes. ~গৃহ *n* arbour formed of reeds. ~পত্র *n* leaf of the ratan. ~পুষ্প *n* blossom of the ratan. ~বৃত্তি *adj, n* pliant as a reed; obsequiousness.

বেতাগ *n* cane shoot.

বেতার ⇒ বে[1]

বেতাল[1] ⇒ বে[2]

বেতাল[2] *n* kind of demon; ghost; spirit: goblin; vampire (esp one occupying a dead body). ~সিদ্ধ *adj* having absolute domination over Vetal.

বেতি, বেতী *n* strip of cane or bamboo as used for basket-work, furniture, etc. ~খাল *n* narrow canal.

বে-তে (আবে-তাবে) *n* (only in ~ করা) *vt* talk with sb with haughty contempt.

বেতো *adj* rheumatic. ~ ঘোড়া *n* sorry horse; jade.

বেত্তা *adj* (used as a *suff*) versed in: ধর্ম~, ইতিহাস~.

বেত্র *n*=বেত. **~দণ্ড** *n* **1** cane; ferule; staff; rod/mace of an officer; staff of a door-keeper. **2** sentence of/punishment by caning/ whipping. **~ধর** *adj n* staff bearer; door keeper. **~ধারী** *adj n* staff-bearer; servant of a great man. **~ধারিণী** *fem*. **~পাণি** *adj* mace bearer. **~বতী** *adj, n fem* carrying a cane/ratan staff; name of a river. **~হস্ত** *adj*=~পাণি. **বেত্রাঘাত** *n* blow with a cane; caning; flogging. **বেত্রাঘাত করা** *vt* cane; whip. **বেত্রাসন** *n* cane seat; small oblong low couch of cane-work. **বেত্রাহত** *adj* caned; whipped; flogged. **বেত্রাহত কুকুরের মতো** like a dog which has been whipped; (fig) with the tail between the legs.

বেথুয়া, বেথো *n* variety of spinach; *Chenopodium album.*

বেদ *n* **1** any of the four Vedas. **2** knowledge; knowledge of ritual; true/sacred knowledge/ lore. **~গর্ভ** *n* **1** Brahma. **2** Brahmin. **~গুপ্তি** *n* preservation of the Veda. **~চতুষ্টয়** *n pl* the four Vedas. **~জ্ঞ, ~বিদ** *adjj* knowing/ versed in the Veda. **~জ্ঞান** *n* knowledge of the Vedas. **~তত্ত্ব** *n* true doctrine of the Veda. **~নিন্দুক** *n* anyone who disbelieve in the Veda; unbeliever; atheist; Buddhist; Jaina. **~নিন্দা** *n* denying the Veda; unbelief; heresy. **~পরায়ণ** *adj* devoted to the Veda. **~পারগ** *n* a Brahmin skilled in the Veda. **~ফল** *n* meritorious fruit/result of (reciting/ repeating) the Veda. **~ভাষ্য** *n* commentary on the Veda. **~বাক্য** *n* **1** text/ statement of the Veda; an absolute/ inviolable truth or command. **~বিদ** *adj* =~জ্ঞ. **~বেদাঙ্গ** *n* the Vedas and other branches/ subsidiary parts. **~ব্যাস** *n* arranger of the Veda; name of Vyasa or Badarayan. **~মন্ত্র** *n* mantra/ verse of the Veda. **~মাত্রা** *n* mother of the Veda; Gayatri. **~সম্মত, ~সম্মিত** *adj* conformable to the Veda. **বেদাদি** *n* beginning of the Veda; the sacred syllable Om. **বেদাঙ্গ** *n* certain works or classes of works regarded as auxiliary to and even some sense as part of the Veda (six are usually enumerated). **বেদাধ্যাপন, বেদাধ্যাপনা** *n* act of teaching the Veda; repetition/ recitation of the Veda. **বেদান্ত** *n* end of the Veda; the second and most important part of the Minansa or third of the three great divisions of Hindu philosophy. **~ত্তবাদ** *n* (assertion of) the Vedanta doctrine. **~ত্তবাদী** *n, adi* one who asserts the Vedanta doctrine. **~ত্তবাদিনী** *fem* = ব্রহ্মবাদিনী. **বেদান্তী** *n* follower of the Vedanta philosophy. **বেদাভ্যাস** *n* study of the Veda; constant repetition of the Veda; repetition of the mystical syllable Om. **~পুরাণে/ ~কোরানে নেই** contrary to/not included in scriptures; unscriptural. **বেদের গোচর** within the range of the Veda. **বেদোক্ত** *adj* mentioned in/conformable to the Veda. **বেদোক্তি**=~ বাক্য.

বেদ'আত, বেদাত [A] innovation in religion; heresy. **বেদ'আতি, বেদাতি** *adj* heretical.

বেদক *adj* proclaiming; announcing; making known.

বেদড়া *adj*=বেয়াড়া (⇒ বে[১])

বেদন *n* **1** perception; sensation; feeling; knowledge. **2** (poet) pain. **3** marriage. **4** gift. **5** announcing; proclaiming.

বেদনা *n* **1** pain; ache; twinge; pang. **2** sorrow; grief; affliction; anguish; agony; torment **3** feeling. **~ করা** *vi* ache; hurt; pain: পায়ে ~ করছে. **~ দেওয়া** *vt* pain; cause pain; hurt; agonize; torture; inflict pain on; sting; torment. **~ পাওয়া** *vi* be in pain; be pained; suffer; feel pain; agonize; anguish; writhe. **~কর, ~জনক, ~দায়ক** *adj* painful; hurtful; aching; agonizing; tormenting racking; grievous anguishing afflicting; pitiable; cruel; sad. **~বোধ** *n* feeling of pain. **বেদনী** *adj* sympathetic.

বেদনীয় *adj* to be felt/known; capable of being felt; perceivable; cognizable.

বেদয়িতব্য *adj* to be communicated/made known.

বেদাত=বেদ'আত

বেদানা ⇒ বে[১]

বেদি[১] *n* wise man; teacher; Pandit. ❑*adj* versed in the Veda. **~ত** *adj* announced; proclaimed; reported; represented for information. **~তব্য** *adj* to be learnt/ known/understood; to be taken for. **~তা, ~ত্ব** *n* acquaintance/ familiarity with.

বেদি[২], বেদিকা, বেদী *n* **1** elevated piece of ground serving for a sacrificial alter. **2** pulpit; stand; basis; pedestal; dais; platform; bench

বেদিয়া, বেদে, বাদিয়া [A] *n* one of the gypsy tribes of the Indian sub-continent. **বেদিয়ানি, বেদেনী** *fem.*

বেদী *adj* **1** (used as a sult) knowing; acquainted with; versed in. **2** feeling; perceiving.

বেদুইন, বেদুঈন, বেদুয়িন [A] *n* bedouin.

বেদুয়া, বেধুয়া *adj* **1** illegitimate; bastard. **2** lecherous.

বেদ্য *adj* to be learnt/known/understood; knowable; intelligible. **~তা** *n* knowableness; intelligibility.

বেধ *n* **1** thickness; depth. **2** penetration; piercing; perforation; bore; hole. **~ক** *n* piercer; perforator. **~ধন** *n* piercing; puncturing; perforating; wounding; pricking; perforation. **বেধনীয়** *adj* capable of being pierced; penetrable; vulnerable. **বেধা** *vi*=বিঁধা. **বেধিত** *adj* pierced; perforated; penetrated. **বেধী** *adj* piercing; perforating; hitting. **বেধিনী** *fem*. **বেধ্য** *adj* to be pierced/penetrated/cut open/ punctured; ❑*n* target.

বেধনিকা, বেধনী *nn* **1** sharp-pointed perforating instrument (esp for piercing jewels/shell). **2** augur; awl; gimlet. **3** probe; skewer. **4** needle.

বেধস *n* part of the hand under the root of the thumb.

বেনা[1] *n* a fragrant grass; *Andropogon muricatus*. **~মূল** *n* root of the above grass. **~বনে মুক্তা ছড়ানো** (fig) cast pearls before swine.

বেনা[2] *n* bow with which cotton is combed or cleaned.

বেনারসি, বেনারসী *adj* made in Benaras made of Benaras silk. ❑*n* a particular variety of silk sari (originally made of Benaras silk).

বেনিয়া=বানিয়া

বেনিয়ান *n* **1** broker; financier; banian; banyan. **2** Guernsey.

বেনে *n*=বানিয়া. **বেনেনী, বেন্যানী, বেনিনী** *fem*. **~খোঁপা** *n* braided hair worn in a bun. **~র কাছে মেকি চালানো** sell spurious coins/metal to a jweller (which is an impossibility) **~গয়না, ~গহনা** *n* meretricious jewellery; trinket. **~পুতুল** *n* small puppets made of clay. **~বউ** *n* **1** traders wife. **2** kind of small bird with yellow feathers.

বেনো *adj* of flood; produced/borne by flood. **~জল** *n* floodwater.

বেপথু *n* quivering; trembling; tremor. ❑*adj* trembling; quivering; scintillating.

বেপন *n* quivering; scintillation.

বেপমান *adj* trembling; quivering; scintillating.

বেপার *n* **1** trade; commerce; traffic. **2** affair; incident. **বেপারি** *n* trader; wholesaler.

বেপালট *n* disaster; trouble; tight corner; catastrophe.

বেয়াই *n* father-in-law or uncle-in-law of a son/daughter. **বেয়ান** *fem*.

বেয়াকুল *adj* (poet, archaic)=ব্যাকুল

বেয়াধি *n* (poet, archaic)=ব্যাধি

বেয়ান *n fem* mother-in-law or aunt-in-law of a son/daughter.

বেয়ারা, বেহারা *n* [E] bearer; carrier; messenger; orderly.

বেয়ারাম=বেআরাম (⇒ বে[1])

বেয়ারিং [E] *adj* sent by post with postage unpaid or underpaid; bearing. **~ পোস্ট** *n* bearing post.

বেয়াল্লিশ (colloq)=বিয়াল্লিশ

বেয়ে participle of বাওয়া. **~চেয়ে** *adv* with continuous/great efforts.

বের=বার[1]

বেরন[1] *adj* [P] fried: বেগুন ~.

বেরন[2], **বেরুনো, বেরোনো** *vi*=বের হওয়া. **বেরিয়ে পড়া** *vi* set out on a journey; get out (of); come to light. **বেরিয়ে যাওয়া** *vi* **1** get out (of); set out, on a journey; leave one's home for good (and take to prostitution); elope with a man; to be exposed; to be adequately punished: তোমার জারিজুরি বেরিয়ে যাবে.

বেরাদর, বেরাদার [P] *n* **1** brother. **2** kinsman; cousin; relative. 3 friend. **ভাই~** *n* brothers and sisters; near and dear ones **বেরাদারি** *n* **1** brotherhood; fraternity. **2** relationship.

বেরাল=বিড়াল

বেরিবেরি *n* [E] beriberi.

বেরুণ [P] *n* **1** wages of a labourer. **2** salary; payment.

বেল[1] (**বেলফুল**) *n* a species or jasmine; *Jasminum zambac*.

বেল[2] *n* wood-apple; *Aegle marmelos*. **~ পাকলে কাকের কী?** (fig) it makes no difference for the blind when a circus-party come to the city. **~শুঁঠা, ~সুঁট** *nn* pieces of dried unripe wood-apple. **বেলের মোরব্বা** *n* wood-apple jam. **নেড়া ~তলা কবার যায়?** (fig) one does not commit the same mistake twice.

বেল[3] *n* [E] bell. **~ দেওয়া** *vi* ring the bell. **~ পড়া/বাজা** *vi* (of a bell) go: ~ পড়েছে, the bell goes. **~ বাজানো** *vi* ring the bell.

বেল[4] *n* [E] bail. **~ দেওয়া** *vi* accept/allow/admit bail (as by a magistrate); bail sb out. **~ পাওয়া** *vi* be out on ~; be allowed bail. **~ হওয়া** *vi* go/put in/stand bail (for sb). **বেলে খালাস করা** *vt* bail sb out. **বেলে থাকা** *vi* be on bail.

বেল[5] *n* ornamental lace; braid. **~ দেওয়া/ বসানো** *vt* lace (up); braid. **~ দেওয়া, ~বসানো** *adj* trimmed with lace. **~দার** *adj*=~ দেওয়া; laced.

বেল[6] [E] *n* bale; large bundle.

বেলওয়ারি=বেলোয়ারি

বেলচা *n* shovel; spade; hoe; mattock.

বেলদার *n* **1** digger; roadman. **2** workman who fixes chandeliers, lights etc. **~নী** *fem*.

বেলন, বেলনা *n* **1** act of rolling the flour into a flat cake. **2** rolling pin. **3** cylinder. **~পিঁড়ি, চাকি~** *n* rolling pin and the board. **~নাকার** *adj* cylindrical.

বেলফুল ⇒ বেল[1]

বেলমুক্তা, বেলমোক্তা [A] *adv* in the aggregate; in the lump; all told; in all.

বেলা[1]=বেল[1]

বেলা[2] *n* coast; shore; sea-shore; coast-line, sea-beach. **~কূল** *n* ancient post of Tamralipti. **~তট** *n* sea-shore. **~তিগ** *adj* overflowing the shore (as the ocean). **~নিল** *n* sea-breeze; coast wind. **~বাসী** *adj* (bio) littoral. **~বীচি** *n* shore-wave; breaker. **~ভূমি** *n* sea-beach; coast land. **~মুখ** *n* beach-head.

বেলা[3] *n* **1** limit of time; time of day; hour; o'clock: ~ দশটা. **2** day; daytime: ~ অবসান প্রায়. **3** case; matter: ক্ষতি করার ~তেও তার জুড়ি নেই. **4** turn; case; regard: তার ~ কোনো দোষ নেই. **5** opportunity; occasion; advantageous point of time; interval; leisure: নিজের বিয়ের ~ কোনো কথা বলতে নেই. **6** moment; right moment/season; the moment when the matter is under consideration: এই ~ ভবিষ্যতের ভাবনা ভাবো. **7**

delay (esp made in the morning): তার স্কুলে যেতে প্রত্যহই ~ হয়. **8** round: একেক ~ পাঁচটি করে পাখি ধরা পড়েছে. **9** age: ছেলে~, এইটুক ~য় বিয়ে. **10** time; specified time; meal-time: খাওয়ার ~. **11** advance of the morning: ~ বাড়ছে. **12** length; duration; period; last hour; hour of death: জীবনের ~, ~শেষের গান. ~ **অবেলা** *n* proper and improper time; auspicious and inauspicious moment. **এই ~** right now; now that there is time; while this opportunity lasts; meanwhile. **কাল~** *n* ⇒ কাল. **কুলিক ~** *n* certain portions of each day on which it is improper to begin any good business. **তার ~** in his case. **দিনের ~** by day; in daylight. **দুপুর ~** (at) midday/noon. **~ গেল** the day is closing/over; the sun has/is set; it's getting late. **~তিক্রম** *n* overstepping the (right) time; tardiness. **~বসান** *n* close of the day; evening; (late) afternoon. **~বেলি** *adv* when there is still daylight. **~ হওয়া** *vi* (of morning) advance; be late. **ভোর~** *n* morning. ❑*adv* in the morning **রাত্রি~, রাতের ~** *n* nighttime. ❑*adv* by/at night. **সকাল~** =ভোর~. **সন্ধ্যা~** *n* evening; nightfall. ❑*adv* in the evening; by nightfall. **সারা~***adv* the whole day; all the time.

বেলা[4] *vt* roll the flour into a flat cake. ❑*adj* rolled. **~নো** *vt* cause to roll (flour).

বেলাওল, বেলাবল *n* a particular mode of Indian music.

বেলি[1] **বেলী** *n*=বেল[1]

বেলি[2] *n* (poet, archaic)=বেলা[3]

বেলিফ *n* [E] bailiff.

বেলুন[1] *n* rolling-pin.

বেলুন[2] *n* [E] balloon.

বেলে *adj* **1** sandy. **2** not sticky. **~ পাথর** *n* sandstone. **~ মাছ** *n* kind of small fresh-water fish.

বেলেস্তারা *n* [E] blister.

বেলোয়ারি, বেলোয়ারী [A] *adj* **1** made of crystal/glass/ cut glass: ~ ঝাড়/চুড়ি. **2** clear and shining; transparent.

বেলোর্মি *n* tidal wave; breaker.

বেল্ট [E] *n* belt.

বেল্লিক *adj* **1** lascivious; licentious; lecherous; rakish. **2** shameless; brazen faced; depraved; debauched. ❑*n* **1** lecher; libertine; debaucher; rake; roue; profligate. **2** boor; cad; squirt; brazen face; hussy (*fem*). **3** clown. **~পনা** *n* lasciviousness; lechery; debauchery; rakishness; profligacy licentiousness; bad manners; incivility; churlish behaviour.

বেশ[1] *n* **1** dress; apparel; garment; habit; attire; garb; outfit; ornament. **2** artificial exterior; assumed appearance; guise. **3** house of ill fame; brothel. **~কার** *n* one who helps sb in dressing and toilet; one who decorates an idol; dresser; decorator. **~ ধারণ করা** *vi* **1** get dressed; dress (oneself); put on; wear; don. **2** put on an appearance/guise. **~ধারী** *adj* wearing the dress of; dressed/guised as. ❑*n* hypocrite. **~ধারিণী** *fem.* **~বিন্যাস** *n* dressing; toilet. **~ভূষা** *n* clothing and ornaments; finery. **~ভূষাপরায়ণ** *adj* fond of fine dress, ornaments and toilet; foppish; dandified; fashionable. **~ভূষাপরায়ণা** *fem.*

বেশ[2] [P] *adj* excellent; good; nice, fine; better; superior: ~ বাড়িঘর/চেহারা. **2** more; thorough; large in amount/measure/degree: ~ টাকা/ পরিশ্রম/ পিটুনি. ❑*adv* much; fairly; too much; nicely, excellently; greatly; very; great deal: ~ সুন্দর, ~ মেরেছে, ~ যেতে পারে. **~করা** do as one wishes. **~ কম** *adj* considerably less. **~কম** *n* slight difference. ❑*adv* more or less. **~ কিছু, ~ কিঞ্চিৎ** *adv* a little more; fairly/pretty large/good/considerable: ~ কিছু টাকা, ~ কিঞ্চিৎ উপরি.

বেশক *n* who or what enters.

বেশবার, বেসবার *n* a particular condiment/kind of seasoning. (consisting of ground coriander, mustard, pepper, ginger, asafoetida; cumin).

বেশর[1]=বেশবার

বেশর[2] *n* a particular ornament for the nose.

বেশাত, বেসাত [A] *n* **1** capital; stock; property: ~ ভেঙে যাওয়া. **2** wares; merchandise; goods. **3** trade; trading; shopping; business. **বেসাতি, বেসাতী** *n* **1** vender of small wares; peddler; haberdasher, shopkeeper; trader; trafficker. **2** wares; merchandise; commodities. **3** buying and selling; trading. trafficking. **4** provisions; necessaries. ❑*adj* of trading/business; of commodity price. **বেসাতি করা** *vi, vt* trade/traffic/deal in; go shopping/ marketing.

বেশি, বেশী *adj* [P] more; excessive; many; much; in excess: ~ টাকা/সম্মান. ❑*adv* excessively; much; too. much: ~ যেয়ো না. ❑*n* excess; surplus. **~র ভাগ** *n* the greater part/portion/number (of) for the most part; the majority of; most (of): ~র ভাগ লোক.

বেশী *adj* (used as a *suff)* wearing the dress of; dressed/ guised as; as in the garb of. **বেশিনী** *fem.*

বেশোআর *n* (archaic) =বেশবার

বেশ্ম *n* house; dwelling; mansion; abode; apartment. **~ভূ** *n* building-ground; site of a habitation.

বেশ্যা *n fem* prostitute; whore; trollop; slut. **~গমন** *n* going after/ visiting prostitutes. **~গামী** *adj* visiting prostitutes; licentious. **~গিরি, ~বৃত্তি** *nn* prostitution; whoredom; street-walking. **~গৃহ, ~লয়** *n* house of prostitution/ ill-fame; brothel; whorehouse. **~সক্ত** *adj* given to visiting prostitutes; licentious. **~সক্ত ব্যক্তি** *n* whore-monger; lecher.

বেষ্ট *n* **1** enclosing; enclosure; fence. **2** circumference. **3** band; noose. **4** turpentine. **~ক** *adj* enclosing ; surrounding; encircling. ❑*n* fence; wall. **~ন** *n* **1** act of surrounding/ encompassing/ enclosing/ encircling. **2** enclosure; wall; fence. **3** girth; circumference; span. **4** bandage; band; girdle. **5** head-band; tiara; diadem. **~ন করা** *vi* enclose; surround; wind/ twist/ wrap round; wrap up; envelop; cover; hem in. **~নী** *n* anything that encloses; cordon; fence; enclosure; wall; girth; circumference. **~নীয়** *adj* to be surrounded/ enclosed. **বেষ্টিত** *adj* surrounded; enclosed; cordonned; hemmed in; encompassed; wrapped up; enveloped; bound round; covered with; veiled in; twisted (as a rope).

বেসন *n* particular flour made of peas or chick-peas.

বেসর *n* =বেশবার

বেসাত=বেশাত

বেসাতি ⇒ বেসাত

বেসালি *n* [Pg] bucket or vessel (esp for milk); pail.

বেসেড়া[১] *adj* stale.

বেসেড়া[২] *adj* dwelling temporarily. ❑*n* temporary dweller.

বেসো *adj* fragrant.

বেহাই=বেয়াই

বেহাগ *n* an Indian musical mode.

বেহান=বেয়ান

বেহার=বিহার[২]. **বেহারী**=বিহারী (⇒বিহার[২])

বেহালা *n* [Pg] violin; fiddle. **~র ছড়** *n* violin bow; fiddlestick. **~বাদক** *n* violinist; fiddler.

বেহেশত, বেহেস্ত [P] *n* heaven.

বৈ=বই[২] and বই[৩]

বৈঁচি=বঁইচি

বৈকল্পিক *adj* alternative; optional; variant (⇒ বিকল্প). **~ প্রমাণ** *n* (geom) alternative proof.

বৈকল্য *n* (=বিকলতা). **1** imperfection; weakness: defectiveness; defect; frailty. **2** despondency; confusion; flurry. **3** incompetence; insufficiency.

বৈকারিক *adj* based on/ subject to modification; modifying; modified.

বৈকার্য *n* change; transformation; modification.

বৈকাল(=বিকাল) *n* afternoon; evening. **বৈকালী, বৈকালিক, বৈকালীন** *adj* occurring in/ belonging to the evening; afternoon; evening. ❑*n* evening devotion; evening meal. **বৈকালিকী** *fem.*

বৈকি =বই কি (⇒ বই)

বৈকুণ্ঠ *n* **1** Vishnu's abode. **2** Vishnu. **3** heaven. **~ গতি** *n* going to heaven. **~ ধাম, ~ পুরী** *n* (Vishnu's) heaven. **~নাথ, ~পতি** *n* Vishnu. **~বাসী** *adj* residing in heaven. ❑inhabitant of heaven. **~বাসিনী** *fem.*

বৈক্লব্য *n* bewilderment; despondency ; mental weakness; distress; frailty; dejection.

বৈগুণ্য *n* **1** difference/ contrariety of properties; absence of/ freedom from qualities; absence of attributes. **2**=বৈকল্য. 3 imperfection; defectiveness; faultiness. **4** hostility; unfavourableness: অবস্থা~, গ্রহ~.

বৈচিত্ত্য *n* mental confusion; loss of mental powers; absence of mind; swoon.

বৈচিত্র্য *n* **1** variety; diversity; manifoldness; variegation; multifariousness; multi-colouredness; vicissitude. **2** strangeness; queerness. **3** wonderfulness; beauty. **~ময়** *adj* full of variety/ diversity; multifarious; diverse. **~ময়ী** *fem.*

বৈজয়ন্ত *n* **1** place/ banner/ necklace of Indra. **2** banner; flag. **3** kind of garland prognosticating victory. **4** ensign. **~ধাম** *n* place/ capital of Indra.

বৈজয়ন্তিক *adj* bearing a flag. ❑*n* flag-bearer; flag. **বৈজয়ন্তিকা** *fem.* **1** banner; flag. **2** the tree *Premna seratifolia*. **3** the tree *Sesbania aegyptiaca*. **4** kind of pearl necklace.

বৈজয়ন্তী *n fem* **1** flag; banner. **2** staircase; flight of stairs. **3** kind of five-coloured garland reaching down to the knee. **বিজয় ~** *n* banner of victory.

বৈজাত্য *n* **1** diverseness; heterogeneousness. **2** strangeness; looseness; wantonness. **3** exclusion from caste; difference of cast/ nature.

বৈজিক *adj* **1** of seed; seminal; paternal; maternal. **2** algebraical: ~ রাশি.

বৈজ্ঞানিক *adj* scientific; versed in science. ❑*n* scientist. **বৈজ্ঞানিকী** *n* **1** scientific work/ achievement. **2** (collection of) scientific papers/ essays/ articles.

বৈঠক *n* **1** sitting; meeting. **2** conference; session. **3** hookah-stand. **4** form of physical exercise by repeated sitting down and standing up alternately. **~খানা** *n* **1** drawing-room; salon; lounge. **2**=~ (1). **বৈঠকি, বৈঠকী** *adj* suitable for an assembly/ a party: বৈঠকী গল্প/ গান. **বৈঠকী ঘর** *n*=~(1).

বৈঠন *n* sitting.

বৈঠা=বইঠা

বৈড়াল *adj* feline. **~ব্রত** *n* putting on a show of virtue/ piety to conceal malice and evil design; simulated holiness; sanctimoniousness. **~ব্রতী** *adj* acting like a cat; hypocritical; sanctimonious. ❑*n* one who leads a chaste/ continent life merely from the absence of women or temptation; religious impostor; hypocrite.

বৈতনিক *adj* living on/ serving for wages; salaried; wage earning; stipendiary. ❑*n* hireling; labourer; wage-earner.

বৈতরণী *n* (myth) a river that flows between the earth and the lower regions or abode of departed souls presided over by Yama.

বৈতান, বৈতানিক *adj* **1** relating to sacred fire; sacrificial; sacred. **2** relating to a summer house/ canopy. ❑*n* **1** burnt-offering. **2** oblation with fire. **3** sacred fire.

বৈতাল, বৈতালিক *nn* **1** panegyrist of a king (whose duty also is to proclaim the hour of the day); bard herald.

বৈতালিকী *n* **1** song of praise sung in the morning. **2** solemn song sung (esp) to wake a prince.

বৈদগ্ধ, বৈদগ্ধ্য *n* **1** wit; witticism; connoisseurship.**2** culture; erudition; learning. **3** dexterity; acuteness; intelligence; cunning.

বৈদগ্ধী =বৈদগ্ধ

বৈদর্ভ *adj* **1** relating to Vidarbha/ the Vidarbhas. **2** produced in Vidarbha. **3** a king of the Vidarbhas. **4** witticism. **বৈদর্ভী** *fem.* **বৈদর্ভী রীতি** *n* the Vidarbha style of composition.

বৈদান্তিক *adj* Vedantic. ❑*n* one who is learned in the Vedanta; believer in the Vendanta doctrine; Vedantist.

বৈদিক *adj* Vedic. ❑*n* a class of Bengali Brahmins; Vedist.

বৈদূর্য *n* cat's eye; lapis-lazuli. **~কান্তি** *adj* having the colour of a cat's eye gem. **~ মণি** *n*=~.

বৈদেশিক, বৈদেশী *adjj* foreign; exotic; alien; external. ❑ foreigner; stranger; alien. **~ত্ব** *n* foreignness.

বৈদেহ *adj* **1** belonging to the country of Videha. ❑*n* **1** a king of Videha. **2** trader. **বৈদেহী** *fem* a princess of Videha, esp Sita of the Ramayana.

বৈদ্য *n* **1** physician; healer. **2** an upper-class Hindu caste (accounted a mixed caste). **3** expert; learned man. ❑*adj* **1 relating**/ belonging to the Veda. **2** learned; skilled in the art of healing. **3** medical; medicinal. **~ক** *adj* relating to a physician. ❑*n* **1** physician practising Ayurveda. **2** Ayurvedic system/ science of medicine. **~কোষ** *n* medical dictionary and glossary. **~নাথ** *n* lord of physicians; Shiva. **~শালা** *n* hospital; clinic. **~শাস্ত্র** *n* Ayurvedic system/ science of medicine; textbook for physicians. **~সঙ্কট** *n* miscarriage of treatment on account of being treated by numerous physicians simultaneously.

বৈদ্যুতিক *adj* **1** electric; electrical. **2** flashing; brilliant. **~ যান, ~ শকট** *nn* electric vehicle. **~ বার্তাবহ** *n* telegraph. **~ আলোক** *n* electric light.

বৈধ *adj* lawful; enjoined by rule/ precept; just; prescribed; formal. **~ ক্রিয়া** *n* lawful act/ rite. **~তা, ~ত্ব** *nn* lawfulness; legality.

বৈধব্য *n* widowhood. **~বাস** *n* widow's clothes.

বৈধর্ম্য *n* **1** difference in religious creed; religious difference; heresy; heterodoxy; atheism. **2** difference; heterogeneity. **3** difference of duty/ obligation. **4** unlawfulness; injustice.

বৈধাত্র *adj* derived from Brahma/ fate.

বৈধিক *adj* in accordance with rule; perceptive; ritual;

বৈধেয় *adj* relating to rule/ precept; prescribed.

বৈনতেয় *n* =বিনতা-নন্দন (⇒ বিনতা)

বৈনায়িক *adj, n* Buddhist.

বৈনাশিক *adj* **1** perishable. **2** destructive; causing destruction/ ruin; ruinous. **3** believing in complete annihilation.

বৈপরীত্য *n* **1** contrast; oppositeness; contrariety; opposition . **2** reverse; adversity; upset. **3** inconsistency.

বৈপিত্র, বৈপিত্রেয় *adj* **1** born of the same mother and of a step-father: ~ ভ্রাতা, half-brother. **2** of a step father: ~ সম্পত্তি. **বৈপিত্রী, বৈপিত্রেয়ী** *adjj.*

বৈপ্লবিক *adj* revolutionary; causing/ effecting a radical change.

বৈবর্ণ=বিবর্ণতা

বৈবস্বত *adj* coming from/ belonging to the sun; solar. ❑*n* name of one of the Rudras. **বৈবস্বতী** *fem* the south.

বৈবাহিক *adj* matrimonial; nuptial. ❑*n*=বেয়াই

বৈভব *n* **1** great wealth; riches; opulence. **2** godhead; divinity. **3** might; power; superhuman power/might. **4** grandeur; glory; magnificence; greatness. **~শালী** *adj* **1** wealthy; rich; opulent. **2** endowed with divinity/glory/unction.

বৈভাষিক *adj* alternative; optional; variant.

বৈমাত্র, বৈমাত্রেয় *adj, n* born of a step-mother; step-mother's son; step-brother. **~ ভ্রাতা** *n* step-brother. **বৈমাত্রী, বৈমাত্রেয়ী** *fem* step-sister.

বৈমানিক *adj* aeronautical. ❑*n* airman; aeronaut; aviator; pilot.

বৈমুখ *adj* (old use)=বিমুখ. **বৈমুখ্য** *n* =বিমুখতা

বৈয়াকরণ *n* grammarian. ❑*adj* grammatical; versed in grammar. **বৈয়াকরণিক** *n* grammarian.

বৈয়াঘ্র *adj* relating to the tiger; made of / covered with a tiger-skin.

বৈয়াম=বয়েম

বৈর *n* enmity; hostility; animosity; grudge; quarrel/ feud with. **~কার** *n* enemy; foe. **~ নির্যাতন** *n* requital of enmity; revenge. **~নির্যাতন করা** *vi,vt* take revenge on sb; be revenged on sb ; revenge oneself on sb. **~প্রতিকার** *n*=~নির্যাতন. **~ভাব** *n* =~. **~সাধন** *n* act of hostility; malicious mischief; disservice; retaliation.

বৈরক্ত্য *n* freedom from affections/ passions; absence of affection; indifference; aversion.

বৈরাগী *adj* freed from all worldly desires. ❑*n* a particular class of religious devotees/ mendicants (generally Vaisnavas) who have freed themselves from all worldly desires.

বৈরাগ্য, বৈরাগ *nn* **1** absence of worldly passion; freedom from all desires; indifference to worldly objects and to life; spirit of renunciation; asceticism. **2** disgust; aversion; distaste for; loathing of. **3** Vaishnava religion. **4** philosophical/ spiritual consciousness. বৈরাগ্যোদয় *n* awakening of the spirit of renunciation; awakening of philosophical/ spiritual consciousness.

বৈরী *adj* hostile; inimical; malicious; adverse; unfavourable. ❑*n* enemy; foe; adversary. বৈরিতা *n* enmity; hostility; malice.

বৈরূপ্য *n* deformity; ugliness.

বৈলক্ষণ্য *n* difference; disparity; diverseness; indeterminateness; strangeness.

বৈলক্ষ্য *n* **1** feeling of shame; embarrassment. **2** surprise. **3** unnaturalness; reverse; contrariety.

বৈশদ্য *n* clearness; purity; brightness; freshness; distinctness; intelligibleness; whiteness.

বৈশাখ *n* the first month of the Bengali calendar (from the middle of April to the middle of May). বৈশাখী *adj* of/ relating to Baishakh. বৈশাখী (ঝড়) *n* nor'-wester.

বৈশিষ্ট্য *n* characteristic; distinction; difference; speciality; peculiarity. ~ রেখা *n* (phy) characteristic curve.

বৈশেষিক *n* the later of the two great divisions of the Naya school of philosophy (it was founded by Kanada). ❑*n* relating/ belonging to/ based on/ dealing with the Vaisheshika doctrine.

বৈশ্য *n* man of the third Hindu caste (whose business was trade as well as agriculture); trader. বৈশ্যা *fem.* ~ভাব *n* state or mentality of a Vaishya; commercialism.

বৈশ্বানর *n* fire; the god of fire.

বৈষম্য *n* **1** inequality; discrimination; disparity; disproportion; injustice; harshness; unkindness. **2** unevenness (of ground); oddness; diversity . **3** incorrectness; impropriety; error; mistake in/ about. ~ জ্ঞান *n* sense of inequality/ difference. ~মূলক *adj* discriminatory; differential. ~মূলক আচরণ *n* differential/ unfair treatment.

বৈষয়িক *adj* relating to an object of sense/ property/ wealth/ earthly possessions; mundane; sensual; material; worldly. ❑*n* (also ~ লোক) one addicted/ attached to the pleasures of the sense or absorbed in worldly objects: wordly (-minded) man.

বৈষ্ণব *adj* **1** relating/ belonging/ devoted/ consecrated to Vishnu. **2** relating to one of the sects of modern Hinduism (বৈষ্ণব ধর্ম). ❑*n* **1** worshipper of Vishnu. **2** follower of Sri Chaitanya; Vaishnava mendicant. বৈষ্ণবী *fem.*

বৈসা (archaic, dial)=বসা; বাস করা.

বৈসাদৃশ্য *n* dissimilarity; difference; inequality; disparity.

বৈহাসিক *n* comic actor; buffoon; playfellow.

বোঁ, বোঁ–বোঁ *n* (onom) whirr. ~ করে *adv* with a whirr; whirringly; dartingly. ~ করে উড়ে যাওয়া whirr past.

বোঁচকা [T] *n* bundle tied up in a piece of cloth; package. ~বুঁচকি *n* luggage. ~বুঁচকি সমেত *adv* bag and baggage.

বোঁচা, বোচা *adj* **1** snub-nosed; pug-nosed. **2** (of a nose) squat; snub; flat; depressed. **3** noseless; mutilated; defaced. **4** shameless; brazen faced. **5** (of a person's features) flat and broad.

বোঁটা *n*=বৃন্ত

বোঁদে (colloq) *n* =বুঁদিয়া (⇒) বুঁদি

বোকনো, বোখনো, বোগনা *nn* kind of metal vessel with a curved spout.

বোকা *adj* stupid; foolish; silly; witless. ❑*n* **1** fool; idiot; dunce; simpleton; donkey; half-wit; blockhead. **2** goat; he-goat. ~কান্ত, ~চণ্ডী, ~রাম *adj* utterly stupid. ~ছাগল *n* billy-goat. ~টে *adj* fool-like; silly. ~পাঁঠা *n* **1** over-grown billy-goat. **2** utter fool; tomfool. ~বোকা *adj* having the repulsive odour of a billy goat; goatish. ~মি, ~মো *n* foolishness; silliness; stupidity; folly. ~মি, করা *vi* act like a fool.

বোচকা =বোঁচকা. বুচকি *fem.*

বোজা *vt,vi* **1** close; shut: চোখ ~. **2** be filled up: গর্ত ~. ❑*adj* closed; shut; filled up. চোখ ~ *vi* **1** close one's eyes. **2** ignore; disregard; turn a deaf ear to. নাক ~ *vi* (of a nose) be stuffed up. মুখ বোঁজা *vi* shut one's mouth; be tight-lipped. ~নো *vt* (cause to) shut or close; fill up.

বোঝা[১]=বুঝা

বোঝা[২] *n* burden; load; freight; cargo; goods; weight; charge. ~ই *n* loading; lading; stuffing; filling; repleting; repletion. ❑*adj* loaded; laden ; charged; loaded to the full; filled/ replate (with); burdened (with); crammed; encumbered (with): পানিতে/ পুঁজে ~ই, দুঃখে ~ই, ~ই করা *vt* load (to the full); fill (with); charge; lade; cram; overload; stuff; overstuff; replete (with). ~-করা *adj*=~ই. ~টানা *adj* load-carrying ~টানা ঘোড়া *n* pack-horse. ~টানা জানোয়ার *n* beast of burden; pack-animal. ~ দেওয়া =~ই করা. ~ নামানো, ~ খালাস করা *vi* **1** unload; discharge. **2** unburden; load off one's mind disencumber; get rid of. ~ই নেওয়া *vi* take load/ cargo.

বোঝানো =বুঝানো (⇒ বুঝা)

বোঝাপড়া=বুঝাপড়া (⇒ বুঝা)

বোট [E] *n* boat. জালি~ *n* jolly boat. লং~, ল্যাং ~ *nn* long boat. লাইফ ~*n* life-boat.

বোটকা *adj* resembling the body odour of a billy-goat; goatish. ~ গন্ধ *n* horrid smell; stink.

বোটে *n* (colloq) scull.

বোঠান *n* (colloq)=বৌঠান

বোঠি *n* (colloq) =বঁটি. ~র পাট *n* the piece of wood in which the knife is fixed in a বঁটি.

বোড়া[1] *n* boa constrictor.

বোড়া[2]=বুড়া[1]. ~নো=বুড়ানো

বোড়ে=বড়ে

বোতল [E] *n* bottle. বোতলে পোরা/ ভরা *vt* bottle (up). ~ধারক *n* bottle washer.

বোতাম [Pg] *n* button. ~পরানো/লাগানো *vi* button (up/down); sew a button on; fit with buttons. বোতামের ঘর/ পাট *n* button-hole.

বোদমাটি *n* humus; peat.

বোদা *adj* **1** insipid; distasteful; tasteless; stale. **2** rather offensive; stinking: ~ গন্ধ. **3** flat; dull; uninteresting; boring; jejune: ~ লেখা/ লোক.

বোদ্ধা *adj* knowing; knowledgeable; able to understand/ appreciate/ comprehend; versed in. ❑*n* connoisseur; an expert.

বোধ *n* **1** knowing; understanding; knowledge; intellect; intelligence; notion; idea; thought. **2** feeling; perception; consciousness; apprehension; comprehension. **3** consolation. **4** awakening; arousing. ~ করা *vi* feel; perceive; have a notion; apprehend; deem; regard as; observe; notice. ~ থাকা *vt* have feeling/ understanding/ sense/ consciousness/ intelligence/ perception. ~ দেওয়া *vt* console. ~ মানা *vi* be consoled/ amenable to consolation: ~ হওয়া *vi* seem; appear (to be). ~ হয় *adv* perhaps. ~ক *adj* denoting; indicating; signifying; arousing; awakening; explaining. ~কর *adj* arousing. ~গম্য *adj* intelligible; understandable; comprehensible; perceivable; knowable. ~ন *n* arousing; exciting; awakening; enlightening; instructing; teaching; waking; inspiration; causing to perceive/ understanding; ceremonial awakening of goddess Durga on the sixth lunar day immediately preceding the tide of her autumnal worship. ~নীয় *adj* to be known/ understood; to be made known/ understood; to be admonished. ~য়িতা *n* awakener; teacher; preceptor. ~য়িত্রী *fem.* ~শক্তি *n* power of understanding/ feeling; power of intellect/ appreciation; sensation; consciousness; comprehension. ~শক্তিহীন *adj* devoid of understanding/ feeling/ perception; stupid; dull; insensible. ~শক্তিহীনতা *n* lack of the power of understanding; insensibility. ~শোধ *n* common sense. ~হীন *adj* incapable of understanding/ feeling/ perceiving/ appreciating; dull; stupid; insensate. বোধাতীত *adj* beyond comprehension/ understanding; unintelligible; incomprehensible; unknowable; imperceptible. বোধিত *adj* made known; apprised; informed; explained; instructed; admonished বোধিতব্য *adj* to be made known; to be imparted/ communicated. বোধ্য *adj* to be known/ understood; intelligible; comprehensible; knowable; perceivable.

বোধি *n* **1** perfect knowledge/ wisdom; illuminated/ enlightened intellect. **2** intuition. **3** knowledge; intellect. **4** enlightenment achieved through sustained meditation. **5**=~দ্রুম. ~তরু, ~দ্রুম, ~বৃক্ষ *nn* the tree at Gaya under which Gautama is said to have attained absolute enlightenment; peepul tree. ~সত্ত্ব *n* according to Buddhist theology one who is on the way to the attainment of perfect knowledge.

বোধিকা *adj fem* of বোধক

বোধোদয় *n* enlightenment; awakening.

বোন *n fem* sister. ~ঝি *n fem* sister's daughter; niece. ~পো *n* sister's son; nephew.

বোনা = বুনা

বোনাই *n* a sister's husband; brother-in-law.

বোবা *adj* dumb; speechless; mute; mum; inarticulate. ❑*n* dumb person. ~কালা *adj* deaf and mute.

বোমা [E] *n* bomb; shell; grenade. ~ ছোড়া/ ছুড়ে মারা *vi* throw a bomb/ grenade; bomb. ~প্রতিরোধী *adj* bombproof. ~বর্ষণ *n* bombing. ~বর্ষণ করা *vi* bomb. ~রু *adj* employed in bombing. ~রু বিমান *n* bomber.

বোম্বাই *n* Bombay. ❑*adj* grown or produced in Bombay; large-shaped; of a superior quality: ~ মরিচ/আম.

বোম্বেটে, বোম্বেটিয়া *n* pirate; corsair; buccaneer; sea-rover; dare-devil. ~গিরি *n* piracy; plagiarism; indulgence in dare-devil activities.

বোয়াল *n* kind of large fish; catfish. রাঘব ~⇒ রাঘব.

বোর *n* kind of ornament (worn by children around the waist) consisting of oval beads made of gold or silver.

বোরকা, বোরখা [A] *n* veil, kind of mantle/ veil covering the whole body from head to foot; yashmak.

বোরহান [A] *n* proof; evidence; demonstration.

বোরা *n* sack; gunny-bag; bag made of ropes; sackful.

বোরাক, বোররাক, বুররাক [A] *n* the horse-like animal on which the Holy Prophet ascended the heaven.

বোরো *n* kind of paddy which is harvested in April.

বোর্ড [E] *n* **1** board: ব্ল্যাক~, পিচ~. **2** board: রাজস্ব ~.

বোল[১] = বউল

বোল[২] = *n* **1** speech; language; word. **2** advice. **3** note/ call (as of birds). **4** sound; babbling noise; babble: শিশুর ~. **5** witty remark; witticism. **6** symbolic sound; musical notation: তবলার ~. ~**চাল** *n* **1** speech and conduct. **2** impertinence; impudence; effrontery; precocity; precocious talk. **3** trick; subterfuge; artifice. **4** affected speech and air; affected manners/ comportment. **5** conversation.

বোল[৩] *n* **1** gum-myrrh. **2** soap-suds.

বোলটু [E] *n* bolt. ~ **পরানো/লাগানো** *vt* fit with a bolt.

বোলতা *n* wasp; hornet. ~**র চাকে খোঁচা দেওয়া/ঢিল ছোড়া** (fig) stir up a hornet's nest; bring a hornet's nest about one's ears.

বোলানো[১] *vt* = বুলোনো

বোলানো[২] *vt* (dial) **1** call; call for sb. **2** answer back. **3** cause to speak.

বোলাবুলি *n* **1** altercation; dispute. **2** tumult; uproar.

বোল্টু = বোলটু

বৌ =বউ

বৌদ্ধ *adj* relating/ belonging to Buddha; Buddhist; Buddhistic. ❑*n* Buddhist. ~**চক্র** *n* the Buddhist cross/ wheel. ~ **দর্শন**, ~ **মত** *nn* Buddhist doctrine. ~ **ধর্ম** *n* Buddhism. ~ **ধর্মাবলম্বী** *adj* practising Buddhism. ❑*n* Buddhist.

বৌলি = বউলি

ব্যক্ত *adj* manifested; revealed; expressed; exposed; said; disclosed; divulged; uttered. **2** apparent; visible; manifest; evident; known; specific; individual. ~ **করা** *vt* manifest; reveal; express; expose; utter; say; disclose; divulge. ~ **হওয়া** *vi* be manifested/ revealed/ expressed. ~**দৃষ্টার্থ** *adj* perceiving or witnessing a transaction with one's own eyes. ❑*n* witness. ~**বীজী** *adj* (bot) gymnosperm. ~**রাশি** *n* (arith) known/ absolute quantity. ~**রূপ** *adj* having a manifested form. ❑*n* Vishnu. ~**লক্ষ্মণ** *n* having evidence/signs/ marks; clearly characterized. **ব্যক্তার্থ** *n* denotation.

ব্যক্তি *n* **1** individual; individuality. **2** person; man. **3** manifestation; specific appearance; distinctness. ~**ক**, ~**গত** *adj* personal; individual; private. ~**জনি** *n* (biol) ontogeny. ~**গত জামিন** *n* personal security. ~**তন্ত্র**, ~**তন্ত্রতা**, ~**বাদ** *nn* individualism. ~**তা**, ~**ত্ব** *n* **1** individualism; personality. **2** distinctness. ~**তান্ত্রিক** *adj* individualistic. ~**বাদী** *adj* individualistic. ❑*n* individualist. ~**মুদ্রাদোষ** *n* idiosyncrasy . ~**স্বাতন্ত্র্য** *n* individualism.

ব্যক্তীকরণ *n* act of making manifest/ clear/ distinct.

ব্যক্তীকৃত *adj* manifested; revealed; expressed.

ব্যগ্র *adj* **1** eager; anxious; earnest; intent on. **2** agitated; excited; alarmed. **3** inquisitive; curious. ~**তা** *n* eagerness; anxiousness; earnestness; agitation; excitement; anxiety; curiosity.

ব্যঙ্গ *n* **1** mockery; irony; sarcasm; taunt; raillery; ridicule. **2** suggested sense/ meaning. ~ **করা** *vt* mock; ridicule; taunt; jeer at; make fun of; deride; scoff at. ~ **কবিতা**, ~**কাব্য** *nn* satire; lampoon. ~**চিত্র** *n* cartoon. ~**প্রিয়** *adj* fond of/ given to mockery/ taunting; fond of sardonic merriment; jocular; jocose. ~**বাণী** *n* taunting remark; raillery; gibe; taunt; persiflage; insinuation. **ব্যঙ্গোক্তি** *n* **1** = ~বাণী. **2** (rhet) suggested/implied meaning; allusion.

ব্যঙ্গ্য *adj* indicated by allusion/ insinuation; implied; suggestive. **ব্যঙ্গ্যোক্তি** *n* covert language; insinuation.

ব্যজন *n* **1** fanning. **2** palm-leaf or other article used for fanning; fan; whisk. ~ **করা** *vi* fan.

ব্যজনী *n* = ~ (2).

ব্যঞ্জক *adj* indicating; denoting; suggesting; signifying; implying; expressing; indicative (of).

ব্যঞ্জন[১] *n* **1** anything used in cooking or preparing food; seasoning; sauce; condiment. **2** cooked dish (of vegetables, fish or meat); any spicy dish of cooked food.

ব্যঞ্জন[২] **1** (gram) consonant. **2** mark; badge; spot; sign; token; insignia. **3** (rhet) allusion; suggestion; figurative expression; irony. ~ **বর্ণ** *n* consonant (letter). ~ **সন্ধি** *n* (gram) junction of two consonants or of a consonant and a vowel. **ব্যঞ্জনান্ত** *adj* (gram) ending in a consonant or a consonantal sound.

ব্যঞ্জনা *n* (rhet) suggestion; implied indication; allusion. ~ **বৃত্তি** *n* figurative style; suggestive power. **ব্যঞ্জিত** *adj* suggested; alluded; clearly manifested.

ব্যতিকর *adj* acting reciprocally; reciprocal.

ব্যতিক্রম *n* **1** exception. **2** overstepping; transgressing; violation; lapse (of time); disregard of; non-performance; violation of established order; inverted order; infringement. **3** anomaly; transgression. ~ **করা** *vt* violate; transgress; step over/beyond; neglect; omit. ~**ণ** *n* transgression; making exception; infringement. **ব্যতিক্রমী** *adj* exceptional; overstepping; violating; transgressing. **ব্যতিক্রান্ত** *adj* passed over;

transgressed; violated; anomalous. **ব্যতিক্রান্তি** *n* = ~.

ব্যতিব্যস্ত *adj* **1** awfully busy; astir; anxious; worried; excited. **2** harassed; hurried; plagued; bothered: পাওনাদারদের তাগাদায় ~. **3** embarrassed; badgered: সাংবাদিকদের প্রশ্নে ~. **4** very much irritated; disturbed, exasperated: গোলমালে ~. **~ করা** *vt* bother; trouble; badger; plague; embarrass; get on the nerves of; torment; irritate; disturb; pester.

ব্যতিরিক্ত *adj* **1** other than; different/ distinct from; separate; with the exception of; excepting. **2** excessive; reaching beyond; immoderate.

ব্যতিরেক *n* **1** difference; distinction; separateness. **2** absence; lack; omission; exclusion; separation; negation; contrariety. **3** overstepping; transgression. **4** (rhet) a figure of speech in which the qualities of the subject excel those of the object. **ব্যতিরেকী** *adj* distinctive; excluding; excepting; different; reverse; negative. **ব্যতিরেকীভাবে বলা** *vt* affirm negatively. **ব্যতিরেকে** *adv* with exception of; without; excluding; in addition to.

ব্যতিষক্ত *adj* mutually connected/ joined/ related; intertwined; mixed together; intermarried.

ব্যতিষঙ্গ *n* **1** mutual connection; entanglement. **2** absorption; strong addiction/ attachment.

ব্যতিহার, ব্যতীহার *n* **1** exchange; barter; interchange; reciprocity; alternation. **2** exchange of blows or abuse.

ব্যতীত *adj* passed (away); gone. ❑*prep* without; save; except; excluding.

ব্যতীপাত *n* **1** great calamity (eg earthquake, appearance of a comet, etc); disaster. **2** an unauspicious conjunction of planets according to astrology. **3** disrespect.

ব্যত্যয় *n* =ব্যতিক্রম. **ব্যত্যস্ত** *adj* **1** reversed; inverted. **2** = ব্যতিক্রান্ত (⇒ ব্যতিক্রম). **3** placed across/ crosswise; crossed (as the hands).

ব্যথা *n* **1** pain; ache; pang; throe; twinge; twitch; sting; smart. **2** distress; affliction; agony; uneasiness; anguish. **3** mourning; grief. **4** labour pains; childbirth pains; travail. **~ ওঠা** *vi* be in labour ; have labour pains. **~ করা** *vi* pain; ache; smart; twinge; burn. **~ দেওয়া** *vt* give/ cause pain; pain; afflict; torment; trouble; distress; gall; offend; hurt. **মনে ~ দেওয়া** hurt/ pain sb's feelings; tread on sb's corns. **~ পাওয়া** *vi* get/ be hurt; hurt oneself; feel pain; be pained/ afflicted/ distressed/ offended. **~ লাগা** *vi* be hurt/ pained; feel; take offense. **~কর** *adj* causing pain; painful. **~কুল, ~তুর** *adj* agitated by fear; anguished; distressed; afflicted; agonized; tormented; writhing . **~কুলা, ~তুরা** *fem* . **~নিবারক** *n* painkiller; analgesic drug. **~ভরা** *adj* pained; agonized; distressed.

ব্যথিত *adj* pained; afflicted; distressed; agitated; disquieted; perturbed; troubled; hurt; offended. **ব্যথিতা** *fem*. **ব্যথী** *adj* feeling pain/ sympathy: ব্যথার ব্যথী.

ব্যধ্য *adj* to be pierced/ perforated.

ব্যপদেশ *n* **1** pretext; excuse; stratagem; pretence; plea; fraud. **2** hint; suggestion. **3** name; title; designation. **4** (mod use) necessity; exigency. **কার্যব্যপদেশে** in course of work. **ব্যপদিষ্ট** *adj* pleaded as an excused; tricked. **ব্যপদেষ্টা** *n* **1** pretender; cheat; impostor. **2** one who represents/ shows/ names. **ব্যপদেষ্ট্রী** *fem.*

ব্যপনয়ন *n* **1** denial. **2** refusal. **3** removing; removal. **ব্যপনীত** *adj* denied; refused; removed.

ব্যপবর্তিত *adj* called back; returned. **ব্যপবর্তিতা** *fem.*

ব্যপহরণ *n* defalcation.

ব্যবকলন *n* **1** separation. **2** (arith) subtraction; deduction. **~ করা** *vt* subtract; deduct.

ব্যবচ্ছিন্ন *adj* **1** (anat) dissected. **2** cut off; separated; interrupted.

ব্যবচ্ছেদ *n* **1** (anat) dissection. **2** separation; interruption; exclusion. **~ করা** *vt* dissect; cut off; separate; tear asunder. **~ বিদ্যা** *n* science of anatomy. **ব্যবচ্ছেদাগার** *n* dissection room.

ব্যবধান, ব্যবধি *n* **1** distance; intervening distance; interval; space. **2** covering; cover; screen. **3** estrangement: স্বামীস্ত্রীর মধ্যে সৃষ্ট ~. **4** aloofness. **ব্যবধায়ক** *adj* intervening; interposing; separating; interrupting; concealing; covering; hiding; screening.

ব্যবসা, ব্যবসায় *n* **1** business; trade; commerce. **2** act; work; action; pursuit. **3** profession; vocation; livelihood; occupation; calling; line. **4** (strenuous) effort; exertion. **~ করা** *vi,vt* **1** be engaged in commerce/ trade; do business; be in business; go into business; trade/ deal (in). **2** follow a particular calling/ profession. **3** make/ gain profit. **ব্যবসায়ী, ব্যবসাদার** *n* **1** businessman; trader; tradesman; man in business; merchant; dealer. **2** one who follows a particular calling/profession. **3** one who is commercial in spirit/ temperament; one who is keenly alive to one's interests; one skilled in worldly affairs. ❑*adj* **1** engaged in business/ trade/ commerce; trading/ dealing in; commercial; mercantile; commercial in spirit/ temperament; businesslike. **2** following a particular calling/ profession; professional. **~বাণিজ্য** *n* trade and commerce. **~প্রতিষ্ঠান, ব্যবসায়ী প্রতিষ্ঠান** *nn* business house/ concern; enterprise; firm. **ব্যবসায়ী সঙ্ঘ** *n* traders' guild;

chamber of commerce. **ব্যবসাত্মক** *adj* **1** vocational; professional; business; commercial; mercantile. **2** full of resolve/ energy; resolute; energetic; laborious.

ব্যবসিক = ব্যবসায়ী (⇒ ব্যবসা)

ব্যবসিত *adj* **1** planned; projected. **2** intended; desired; aimed. **3** settled; ascertained; known. **4** finished; ended; done. **5** energetic; persevering; endeavouring; making effort/ exertion.

ব্যবস্থা *n* **1** arrangement; preparation: টাকাপয়সার ~. **2** provision: খাবারের ~. **3** procurement: পুঁজির ~. **4** statute; rule; law; legislation; decision; legal decision/ opinion. **5** settlement: জমিজমার ~. **6** prescription; direction: শাস্ত্রীয় ~. **7** establishment. **8** engagement; agreement; contract. **9** order; system: এ বাড়িতে কোনো ~ নেই. **10** fixity; perseverance; constancy; fixed limit. ~ **করা** *vt* arrange (for); provide (for); make arrangements/ preparations (for); manage; settle; prescribe; direct determine; procure. ~ **দেওয়া** *vi* prescribe; enjoin; direct. ~ **হওয়া** *vi* be arranged/ prepared/ provided for; be procured; be prescribed/ directed; be settled; be managed. ~**জাল** *n* (tangle of) rules and regulations. ~**দাতা** *n* prescriber; law-giver. ~**দাত্রী** *fem.* ~**পক** *n* legislator; law-giver regulator; controller; prescriber; director; manager; procurer; founder; one who settles/ determines. ❑*adj* legislative; law-giving; regulating; settling; arranging; deciding; establishing; prescribing; directing; prescriptive; founding; instituting; preparative. **ব্যবস্থাপিকা** *fem.* ~**পক পরিষদ** *n* legislative council. ~**পক সভা** *n* legislative assembly. ~**পত্র** *n* prescription; directive; prescript. ~**পদ্ধতি** *n* rules and regulations. ~**পন** *n* legislation; enactment; law-making; regulation; preparation; management; arrangement; prescription; direction; fixing; settlement; deciding; institution; founding; decision. ~**পনীয়** *adj* to be settled/ established/ decided. ~**-পরিষদ** *n* legislative council. ~**প্য** *adj* to be established/ arranged/ settled. ~**পিত** *adj* legislated; enacted; regulated; arranged; settled; managed; prescribed; directed; founded; instituted; established. ~**শাস্ত্র** *n* law; jurisprudence; law-book; the code of ancient Hindu laws (স্মৃতি). ~**সংহিতা** *n* the code of ancient Hindu laws (স্মৃতি). ~**সঙ্গত,** ~**সম্মত** *adj* lawful; legitimate; according to rule; regular; customary; consistent with law. ~**-সভা** *n* legislative assembly.

ব্যবস্থিত *adj* **1** placed in order; drawn up (in battle); placed; laid; put; stationed. situated; settled; established; fixed; exactly determined. **2** constant; unchanging; permanent. ~**চিত্ত** *adj* of settled mind; calm and composed; of unruffled temperament; determined; cool-headed; self-possessed; even-tempered; level-headed; equanimous; unflustered; imperturbable. **ব্যবস্থিতি** *n* **1** fixed rule/ statute; decision; fixity. **2** determination. **3** constancy; steadfastness.

ব্যবহর্তব্য *adj* to be used/ employed/ managed.

ব্যবহর্তা *n* user; engaged in; occupied with; manager of any business; conductor of any judicial procedure; secretary.

ব্যবহার *n* **1** behaviour; conduct; demeanour; action; practice; comportment. **2** treatment of others: প্রতিবেশীদের সঙ্গে ~. **3** law; jurisprudence. **4** law-suit; legal procedure; contest at law; litigation; legal process; practices of law. **5** usage; custom; wont; common practice; ordinary life. **6** use; application: ওষুধের ~. **7** mercantile transaction; trade; dealing; traffic. **8** work for earning one's living; occupation/ business with; activity; action; practice (of). **9** commerce/ intercourse with. **10** gift; present; token (also ব্যাভার). **11** consumption. ~ **করা** *vi*, *vt* behave; treat (a person); behave towards; use; employ; make use of; apply; have intercourse with; deal with. ~ **থাকা** *vi* be in use. ~ **হওয়া** *vi* be used / applied/ employed; be in use. ~**ক** *n* consumer; user; trader; dealer. ~**-করণিক** *n* bench-clerk. ~**গত** *adj* pertaining to one's behaviour; regarding use. ~**জীব,** ~**জীবী** *n* lawyer; advocate; pleader; barrister; attorney; solicitor. ~**জ্ঞ** *adj* **1** knowing the ways of world; acquainted with practice/ legal procedure; versed in law/ jurisprudence. **2** one competent to manage one's affairs (ie one who has passed his 16th year and legally arrived at his maturity). ~**ত** *adv* according to established practice; practically; conventionally. ~**দর্শন** *n* law; jurisprudence; judicial investigation; trial. ~**দর্শী** *n* judge; jurist; juror. ~**দেশক** *n* attorney-at-law; attorney; solicitor. ~**প্রাপ্ত** *adj* = ~**জ্ঞ** (২). ~**বিদ** *n* jurist. ~**বিধি** *n* **1** code of laws; jurisprudence. **2** direction/ rules for use. ~**যোগ্য** *adj* fit to be used/ applied; serviceable; useful. ~**শাস্ত্র** *n* jurisprudence. ~**শাস্ত্রজ্ঞ** *adj* versed in jurisprudence. ❑*n* jurist. ~**সংহিতা** *n* compendium / collection/code of laws.

ব্যবহারিক *adj* **1** practical ; functional; applied; experimental: ~ বিজ্ঞান. **2** legal; judicial. **3** behavioural. **4** pertaining to daily routine duties for earning one's livelihood. **5** (phil) materialistic; pragmatic. ❑*n* jurist; judge; lawyer.

ব্যবহার্য *adj* (lit) to be used/ applied/ employed; serviceable; useful; usual; customary.

ব্যবহিত *adj* **1** placed apart/asunder; lying at a distance; drawn apart. **2** screened from view; concealed; covered. **3** remote; distant. **4** removed; gone.

ব্যবহৃত *adj* used; employed; applied; practised.

ব্যভিচার *n* **1** unlawful sexual intercourse; adultery; fornication; infidelity; incest; sexual immorality. **2** deviating; deviation. **3** contrary/ unlawful conduct or action; transgression; vice; sin; violation; crime. **4** (logic) wandering from an argument; erroneous/ fallacious reasoning. **5** (gram) deviation from/ exception to a rule. ~ **করা** *vi* **1** commit adultery; fornicate; indulge in unlawful sexual intercourse. **2** deviate from; go beyond; transgress. **3** sin against; offend; injure. **4** behave/ act contrarily or unlawfully. ~**স্থল** *n* example of transgression/ adultery/ deviation. **ব্যভিচারী** *adj* going astray; straying/ deviating/ diverging from; following bad courses; doing what is improper/ profligate/ unchaste; adulterous; indulging in adultery/ unlawful sexual intercourse; transgressing; inconstant; changeable; violating; irregular; anomalous; (of feelings, etc) transitory. ❑*n* one who goes astray; transgressor; adulterer; fornicator. **ব্যভিচারিণী** *fem* wanton woman; unchaste woman; adulteress. **ব্যভিচারিতা**=ব্যভিচার.

ব্যয় *n* **1** expenditure; spending; expense; outlay; disbursement; charge; cost. **2** disappearance; decay; ruin; loss: পুঁজি ~. **3** waste; prodigality: সময় ~. **4** use; application: ~ করা. ~ **করা** *vt* spend; expend; waste; consume; use; apply; pass: সময় ~ করা. ~ **পড়া** *vt* cost. ~ **হওয়া** *vi* be spent/ expended/ wasted/ dissipated/ consumed/ used/ applied/ passed. ~**করণ** *n* payment. ~**-কুণ্ঠ** *adj* miserly; stingy; parsimonious; niggardly; close-fisted. ~**কুণ্ঠ ব্যক্তি** *n* niggard; miser; skinflint. ~**কুণ্ঠতা** *n* stinginess; parsimoniousness; niggardliness; miserliness; parsimony; closefistedness. ~**ন** *n* disbursement. ~**নাধিকারিক** *n* disbursing officer. ~**বহুল** *adj* expensive; costly; high-priced. ~**বহুলতা**, ~**বাহুল্য** *nn* expensiveness; costliness. ~**বিহীন** *adj* involving no expenditure; inexpensive; free of cost. ~**শীল** *adj* disposed to prodigality; extravagant; spendthrift; lavish; wasteful. ~**শীলতা** *n* prodigality; extravagance; lavishness; wastefulness. ~**শীল ব্যক্তি** *n* prodigal; spendthrift; dissipater. ~**শূন্য**=~বিহীন. ~**সাধ্য**, ~**সাপেক্ষ** *adjj* expensive; costly; extravagant; sumptuous. **ব্যয়াধিক্য** *n* excessive/ prohibitive/ exorbitant cost or expenditure.

ব্যয়িত *adj* spent; expended; dissipated; dispersed; used up; disbursed.

ব্যয়ী *adj*=ব্যয়শীল (⇒ ব্যয়)

ব্যর্থ *adj* futile; vain; useless; unavailing; abortive; unprofitable; unsuccessful. ~ **করা** *vt* baffle; foil; thwart; frustrate; balk. ~ **হওয়া** *vi* fail; be of no avail; abort; be foiled; flop; flounder; collapse; come to naught; fall through; run aground. ~**কাম** *adj* foiled; frustrated; unsuccessful; thwarted in one's attempt. ~ **চেষ্টা** *n* futile/ unsuccessful/ vain/ abortive efforts or endeavour or attempt. ~**তা** *n* failure; futility; uselessness; debacle; fiasco. ~ **মনোরথ** =~কাম. ~**যত্ন** *adj* useless in its efforts.

ব্যলীক *adj* **1** lascivious; licentious; debauched; profligate. **2** uncivil; impolite; impertinent; false; untruthful. ❑*n* **1** libertine; profligate; debauchee. **2** boor; end; churl.

ব্যষ্টি *n* singleness; individuality; separated aggregate (such as man, viewed as a part of a whole while himself composed of individual parts).

ব্যস ⇒ বস[1]

ব্যসন *n* **1** attachment/ devotion/ addiction (to); passion; evil passion; vice; sin; crime; dissipation. **2** favourite pursuit/ occupation; hobby. **3** evil predicament/ plight; disaster; accident; calamity; misfortune; ill-luck; distress. **4** destruction; defeat; fall; ruin. **ব্যসনাসক্ত** *adj* addicted to vices; dissolute; pleasure-loving. **ব্যসনী** *n* **1** addicted to any kind of vice/ evil practice; vicious; dissolute; passionately addicted to; fond of. **2** calamitous; unfortunate; unlucky.

ব্যস্ত *adj* **1** agitated; anxious; impatient; worried; eager. **2** occupied; busy; employed; engaged. **3** hurried; hasty **4** distracted; confused; bewildered. **5** disordered; disarranged; scattered; dispersed: ~ কেশ, having dishevelled hair. **6** (arith) inverse. ~ **অনুপাত** *n* inverse ratio. ~ **অনুরূপ** *n* inversely similar. ~ **করা** *vt* worry; hurry; make sb eager/ impatient/ anxious; perplex; hustle. ~ **থাকা** *vi* be engaged (in)/ busy (with); be preoccupied (with); occupy oneself; employ oneself in. ~ **রাখা** *vt* keep one engaged (in)/ busy (with). ~**তা** *n* **1** preoccupation; engrossment; eagerness; anxiety; impatience; excitement; worry; agitation. **2** hurry; hustle. **3** perplexity; scattered state. **4** inversion. ~ **ত্রৈরাশিক** *n* (arith) inverse rule of three. ~**বাগীশ** *adj* fussy; busy for nothing. ~**সমস্ত** *adj* flurried; flustered; very busy; bustling; overwrought. ~**সমস্ত হয়ে** *adv* helter-skelter; in a hurry; hurriedly in flurry (of excitement etc). ব্যস্তালোক *n* (phys) diffused light.

ব্যা *n* (onom) cry of lamb, kid, etc; bleat.

ব্যাং, ব্যাঙ *n* frog; toad.

ব্যাংক [E] *n* bank. ~ করণিক *n* bank clerk. ~ নোট bank note. ব্যাংকের পাসবই *n* bank-book.

ব্যাকটেরিয়া [E] *n* bacterium; bacteria.

ব্যাকরণ *n* grammar; etymology; grammatical analysis. ~গত *adj* grammatical. ~বিদ, ~শাস্ত্রজ্ঞ *adjj* versed in grammar. ❑*n* grammarian.

ব্যাকুল, ব্যাকুলিত *adjj* extremely anxious/ agitated; bewildered; perplexed; confounded; troubled; confused; eager; intent on; curious; inquisitive. ব্যাকুলা, ব্যাকুলিতা *fem*. ~চিত্ত *adj* agitated/ perplexed in mind. ব্যাকুলতা *n* perturbation; agitation; perplexity; bewilderment; alarm; anxiousness; eagerness. ~মনা, ~মানস, ব্যাকুলাত্মা *adj*=~চিত্ত.

ব্যাকৃতি *n* 1 deformity. 2 detailed description; explanation.

ব্যাক্রোশ *n* 1 abuse; abusive language; invective; reviling. 2 reprimand; reproach.

ব্যাখ্যা, ব্যাখ্যান *n* 1 explanation; elucidation; annotation; exposition; expounding; gloss; commentary; interpretation. 2 detailed description/ narration. 3 lecture. ~ করা *vt* explain; elucidate; annotate; expose; discuss; interpret; expound; narrate; describe in detail; account for; relate. ~কর্তা, ~কারী *n* commentator; annotater; expounder; author of a commentary; interpreter. ~গ্রন্থ *n* commentary; annotation; critique; gloss. ~ত *adj* explained; elucidated; interpreted; accounted for; annotated; expounded; narrated; described in detail. ~তা *n*=~কর্তা. ~মূলক *adj* explanatory; expository; explicative; interpretative; exegetical.

ব্যাখ্যানা *n* (iron)=ব্যাখ্যা

ব্যাখ্যেয় *adj* to be explained/ expounded/ commented upon; explainable; explicable; accountable.

ব্যাগ [E] *n* bag.

ব্যাঘাত *n* 1 obstacle; impediment; hindrance; interruption. 2 striking against; beating; stroke; blow. ~ করা *vt* hinder; obstruct; interrupt. ~ক *adj* hindering; thwarting; opposing; obstructive; interruptive; resisting.

ব্যাঘ্র *n* tiger. ব্যাঘ্রী *fem* tigress. ~তুল্য *adj* tiger-like; tigerish. ~নখ *n* tiger's claw. ~ শাবক, ~ শিশু *nn* whelp/ cub of a tiger.

ব্যাঙ ⇒ ব্যাং

ব্যাঙ্ক=ব্যাংক

ব্যাঙ্গমা=বিহঙ্গমা

ব্যাচ [E] *n* batch.

ব্যাজ *n* 1 pretext; pretence; disguise; deceit; fraud; deception; semblance; appearance; artifice; conceit; contrivance. 2 delay; dalliance; delaying. ~স্তুতি *n* 1 false/ deceitful praise. 2 (rhet) praise or censure conveyed in language that expresses the contrary; indirect eulogy; ironical commendation; praise or reproach in disguise;

ব্যাজার=বেজার (⇒ বে[১])

ব্যাজোক্তি *n* (rhet) a figure of speech in which the effect of one cause is ascribed to another, or where a feeling is dissembled by being attributed to a different cause; dissimulating statement.

ব্যাট [E] *n* bat; cricket-bat; racket. ~ করা *vi vt* bat. ~বল *n* bat and ball; cricket. ~সম্যান *n* batsman.

ব্যাটা=বেটা

ব্যাটারি [E] *n* battery.

ব্যাটালিয়ন [E] *n* battalion.

ব্যাডমিন্টন [E] *n* badminton.

ব্যাদান *n* 1 opening wide; opening: মুখ ~. 2 disclosing. ~ করা *vt* gape; open; expand. ব্যাদিত *adj* opened; open-mouthed; gaping.

ব্যাধ *n* hunter (by caste or profession); one who lives by hunting. ~বৃত্তি *n* hunting; fowling. ব্যাধিনী *fem* hunter's wife; huntress.

ব্যাধন *n* (med) puncturing; opening a vein.

ব্যাধি *n* disease; ailment; disorder; sickness; illness; malady; morbidity. ~কল্পনারোগ *n* hypochondria. ~গ্রস্ত *adj* seized/ afflicted with disease; diseased; sick; ill; ailing. ~ত =*adj* 1 ~গ্রস্ত. 2 morbid. ~ নিগ্রহ *n* suppression of disease. ~পীড়িত=~গ্রস্ত. ~ভয় *n* fear of disease. ~মন্দির *n* temple of disease; body. ~মুক্ত *adj* free from disease; cured of a disease; healthy. ~ মুক্ত করা *vt* cure sb of a disease. ~মুক্তি *n* recovery from illness; cure of a disease. ~যুক্ত *adj* suffering from a disease; diseased; sick. ~রহিত, ~শূন্য, ~হীন *adjj* free from disease; convalescent; healthy. ~স্থান *n* station of disease; (fig) body.

ব্যান *n* one of the five vital airs (that circulates or is diffused through the body).

ব্যান্ড[১] *n* 1 musical band; band music; band. 2 strap for fastening; band. ~মাস্টার *n* bandmaster.

ব্যান্ড[২] *adj* opened; expanded; gaping.

ব্যান্ডেজ [E] *n* bandage.

ব্যাপক *n* 1 extensive; pervading; widespread; far-reaching; diffusive; comprehensive; rife; pervasive; prevalent. 2 (logic) invariably pervading/ inherent/ concomitant (as an attribute which is always found (as smoke) where some other (fire) is found. (রোগাদি) ~ আকারে দেখা দেওয়া break out in an epidemic form. ~তা, ~ত্ব *nn* extensiveness; pervasiveness; pervasion; diffusion; comprehensiveness; prevalence. ব্যাপন *n* spreading through; pervading; penetration; covering; filling; extending far and wide; pervasion; (bot) diffusion. ব্যাপা *vt* reach/ spread through; pervade; permeate; cover; fill; spread far and wide. ব্যাপানো *vt* cause to reach/ spread through; cause to pervade/ permeate.

ব্যাপার *n* 1 doing; performance; action; operation; happening; occurrence; incident; transaction; exertion; concern: এটা তোমার ~. 2 business; trade; commerce; profession; occupation; employment; function. 3 affair ; matter: কী ~. 4 ceremony; function: বিবাহ ~. 5 phenomenon. ~ নির্বাহক *n* commercial manager. ~মহাধ্যক্ষ *n* trade commissioner. ~স্থিতি *n* trade-balance. ব্যাপারিক *adj* concerning trade; commercial. ব্যাপারিক-অচ্ছার *n* trade discount. ~সংভার *n* stock-in-trade. ব্যাপারী *adj* busy; engaged in. ❑*n* trader; dealer; agent; merchant.

ব্যাপিকা *n fem* a woman who shows herself everywhere; pert/ saucy woman; hussy; jade.

ব্যাপিনী ⇒ ব্যাপী

ব্যাপী *adj* (used as a *suff*) pervading; extending over; covering; reaching through; spread over; filling up; containing. ব্যাপিনী *fem.* ব্যাপিতা *n* immanence.

ব্যাপৃত *adj* occupied/ busy/ engaged/ employed/ concerned in or with. বাপৃতা *fem.*

ব্যাপ্ত *adj* pervaded; spread through; extended; covered/ filled with; thoroughly occupied/ penetrated by; filled up; diffused; beset with. ~ করা=ব্যাপা (⇒ ব্যাপক). ব্যাপ্তি *adj* extension; extent; extensiveness; pervasion; pervasiveness; diffusion; covering. ব্যাপ্তিগ্রহ *n* apprehension of a general proposition; induction. ~নির্ণয় *n* generalization. ব্যাপ্তিশীল *adj* expansive; pervasive; diffusive.

ব্যাপ্য *adj* 1 permeable; penetrable. 2 extendible; extensible; stretchable; extensile. ❑*n* reason; proof; inference. ~তা *n* permeableness; pervasiveness. ~মান *adj* being permeated/ pervaded/ comprehended/ included.

ব্যাবর্তন, ব্যাবর্ত *n* 1 rotation; torsion; turning round; revolving. 2 averting; removing. 3 coming/ bringing back; return. ব্যাবর্ত-তুলা *n* torsion-balance. ব্যাবর্ত-শির *n* torsion-head. ব্যাবর্তিত *adj* rotated; twisted; rotating; made to turn away; returned.

ব্যাবহারিক=ব্যবহারিক

ব্যাবৃত্ত *adj* 1 averted; ceased; disappeared. 2 turned away from; freed from; rid of. 3 split asunder; opened. 4 covered. ব্যাবৃত্তি *n* 1 turning away; turning the back; retreat. 2 removal. 3 getting rid of; deliverance from.

ব্যাভার=ব্যবহার (10)

ব্যাম *n* fathom.

ব্যামিশ্র *adj* mixed together; blended. 2 (bot) polygamous.

ব্যামো *n* (colloq) illness; disease; ailment.

ব্যামোহ *n* 1 loss of consciousness; mental confusion; bewilderment; perplexity; embarrassment; ignorance; delusion. 2 infatuation. 3 disease. 4 stupor. ব্যামোহিত *adj* bewildered; infatuated. ব্যামোহী *adj* perplexing; bewildering.

ব্যায়ত *adj* wide; long; distant; expanded.

ব্যায়রাম, ব্যারাম=বেআরাম (⇒ বে[১]). ব্যায়ারামি *adj* sick; diseased; ailing.

ব্যায়াম *n* physical exercise; exercise; gymnastics; exertion; manly effort. ~ করা *vi* take (physical) exercise; exercise. ~কুশল *adj* skilled in gymnastics. ~কুশলী *n* gymnast; skilled gymnast. ~ ক্রীড়া *n* gymnastics. ~ বীর *n* gymnast; body-builder. ~ শালা *n* gymnasium. ~ শিক্ষক *n* physical instructor. ~ শিক্ষা *n* physical training. ~ সংক্রান্ত *adj* relating to physical exercise; gymnastic; gymnastical. ব্যায়ামাগার=~শালা.

ব্যারাক [E] *n* barrack.

ব্যারাম ⇒ ব্যায়রাম

ব্যারিস্টার [E] *n* barrister. ব্যারিস্টারি *n* profession/ work of a barrister. ব্যারিস্টারি করা *vi* proactive as a barrister/ counsel.

ব্যালট (also ~ পেপার) [E] *n* ballot; ballot paper.

ব্যালোল *adj* rolling about; quivering; tremulous; shaking; waving; eager; restless.

ব্যাস[১]=বস[১]

ব্যাস[২] *n* (geom) diameter (of a circle) or its measure. 2 width; breadth; expanse. 3 Vyasa, the celabrated mythical sage and compiler. 4 division. ~কলন *n* differential calculus. ~কূট *n* puzzle; an obscure composition or passage. ~বাক্য *n* (gram) formal words used in expounding a compound word. ব্যাসার্ধ *n* radius.

ব্যাসক্ত *adj* 1 excessively addicted/ attached. 2 attached; adhering/ clinging to; joined.

ব্যাসঙ্গ *n* excessive attachment/ addiction.

ব্যাসিলি, ব্যাসিলাস [E] *n* bacilli; bacillus. ~ ঘটিত, ~ সংক্রান্ত *adj* bacillary.

ব্যাহত *adj* obstructed; impeded; repelled; frustrated; foiled; prevented. ~ করা *vt* obstruct; impede; repel; frustrate; foil; prevent; thwart.

ব্যাহৃতি *n* 1 utterance; statement; speech; declaration. 2 the mystical utterance of the names of the seven worlds.

ব্যুৎক্রম *n* inverted order; transgression; offence; exception; irregularity. ব্যুৎক্রাম *adv* in an inverted order. ব্যুৎক্রান্ত *adj* gone apart/ in different directions; transgressed; disregarded.

ব্যুৎপত্তি *n* **1** proficiency; comprehensive learning/ scholarship; perfection. **2** production; origin. **3** (gram) derivation; etymology. ~গত *adj* derivational; etymological.

ব্যুৎপন্ন *adj* **1** learned; erudite; versed in; accomplished. **2** derived; originated; arisen.

ব্যুৎপাদক *adj* **1** giving rise to; producing; productive. **2** (gram) tracing back (a word to its roots, etc); explaining etymologically. ব্যুৎপাদিকা *fem*. ~ শব্দ *n* (gram) root-word.

ব্যুৎপাদন *n* **1** (gram) etymological explanation; derivation from. **2** teaching; instruction.

ব্যুৎপাদিত =ব্যুৎপন্ন

ব্যূঢ় *adj* **1** carried/ taken away. **2** married. **3** wide; expanded; developed: ~ বক্ষঃস্থল. **4** arranged; transposed. **5** compact; firm; solid; thick. ব্যূঢ়ি *n* orderly arrangement/ disposition; array. ব্যূঢ়োরস্ক *adj* broad-chested.

ব্যূহ *n* **1** military array; battle formation; line of battle. **2** array; host; squadron. **3** arrangement; orderly arrangement of the parts of a whole; disposition. **4** aggregate; multitude; flock. ~ন *n* arrangement; array (of an array). ~ নির্মাণ, ~ রচনা, ~ স্থাপন *nn* arrangement/ alignment of troops. ~পতি *n* commander of an array. ~ভঙ্গ, ~ভেদ *nn* breaking of an array; throwing into disorder. ~ ভেদ করা *vt* break an array; break through a line of battle. ~ রচনা করা *vt* array/ form a line of battle; form into columns/ line. ব্যূহিত *adj* arranged in order of battle.

ব্যোম *n* **1** sky; space; heaven. **2** atmosphere; ether; wind; air. **3** water. ~কেশ *n* Shiva. ~চর, ~চারী *adjj* moving through the air; flying; ethereal; playing in the air. ❑*n* a being that moves in the air; god; planet; bird; astronaut. ~চারিণী *fem*. ~মণ্ডল *n* sky; firmament; atmosphere. ~যাত্রা *n* aerial navigation; aviation; flight. ~যাত্রী *n* aviator; astronaut; airman; air-passenger; balloonist. ~যান *n* celestial car; chariot of the gods; aeroplane; balloon.

ব্রঙ্কাইটিস [E] *n* bronchitis.

ব্রজ[১] *n* **1** wandering; roaming; going; moving; motion. **2** way; road. **3** fold; stall; cow-pen; cattle-shed; enclosure/ station for herdsmen; pasture (esp for cows).

ব্রজ[২] *n* a district around Agra and Mathura; scene of Sri Krishna's juvenile adventures. ~কামিনী, ~গোপী, ~নারী, ~বধূ, ~বালা, ~যুবতী, ~রমণী *nn fem* young cowherdess/ shepherdess (of Vraja). ~কিশোর *n* young lad of Vraja; Sri Krishna. ~কিশোরী *fem* young maiden of Vraja; Radha/ sweetheart of Sri Krishna. ~গোপাল *n* cowherd of Vraja; Sri Krishna. ~দুলাল darling of Vraja; Sri Krishna. ~মোহন *n* fascinator of Vraja; Sri Krishna. ~লাল = ~দুলাল. ~রমণ = ~বিলাসী. ~রাজ *n* king of Vraja. ~ধাম *n* =বৃন্দাবন. ~নাথ *n* lord of the herd/Vraja; Sri Krishna. ~প্রেম *n* love of God as preached by Vaishnavas (ie loving God as one's own child, friend, etc). ~বল্লভ *n* beloved in Vraja; Sri Krishna. ~বাসী *n adj* residing in Vraja. ❑*n* inhabitant of Vraja. ~বাসিনী *fem*. ~বিনোদ *n* enchanter of Vraja; Sri Krishna. ~বিনোদিনী *n fem* enchantress of Vraja; Radha. ~বিলাসী *n* merrymaker of Vraja; Sri Krishna. ~বিলাসিনী *n fem* Radha. ~বিহারী *n* rover of Vraja; Sri Krishna. ~বিহারিণী *n fem* Radha. ~বুলি *n* kind of mixed language used in Vaishnava literature. ~ভাষা *n* language current around Agra and Mathura. ~মণ্ডল *n* district of Vraja. ~মোহন *n* fascinator of Vraja; Sri Krishna. ~রমণ = ~বিলাসী. ~রাজ = ~নাথ. ~লাল = ~দুলাল. ~লীলা *n* juvenile adventures of Sri Krishna in Vraja. ~সুন্দর *n* the handsome youngman of Vraja; Sri Krishna. ~সুন্দরী *n fem* shepherdess of Vraja; Radha. ব্রজাঙ্গনা *n fem* cowherdess/ milkmaid of Vraja. ব্রজেন্দ্র, ব্রজেশ্বর *nn* = ~নাথ. ব্রজেশ্বরী *n fem* Radha.

ব্রজন *n* going; travelling; travel. ~শীল *adj* travelling; roaming; wandering.

ব্রজ্যা *n* = ব্রজন

ব্রণ *n* **1** boil; abscess; tumour. **2** ulcer; sore; cancer. **3** anthrax; malignant pustule. **4** wound; scar; cicatrix. **5** flaw; blemish. ~গ্রন্থি *n* sore. ~ধূপন *n* fumigation of an ulcer. ~পট্ট, ~পট্টিকা *n* bandage on a wound. ~বেদনা *n* pain of sore. ~যুক্ত *adj* wounded; sore. ~রহিত *adj* unscarred; sound; unhurt. ~রোপক *adj* healing sores. ~শোধন *n* cleaning/ cicatrizing a sore. ~শোথ *n* abscess. ব্রণিত, ব্রণী *adj* wounded; sore; ulcerated.

ব্রত *n* **1** religious vow/ practice; any pious observance; meritorious act of devotion/ austerity; penance; solemn vow; rule; holy practice (as fasting, continence, etc). **2** any vow/ firm purpose; resolve to. **3** conduct; manner; usage; custom. **4** obedience; service. **5** sphere of action; function; mode/ manner of life. **6** dominion; realm; command; law; ordinance. ❑*adj* undertaking/ observing a vow: পুণ্য.~ ব্যক্তি. ~ আচরণ/ পালন করা *vt* observe/be under a vow. ~ উদ্‌যাপন করা *vt* fulfil a vow. ~ গ্রহণ/ধারণ করা, ~ নেওয়া *vt* take a vow; start practising certain religious rites. ~গ্রহণ *n* taking upon oneself a religious vow; becoming a monk. ~চর্যা *n* practice of any religious observance/ vow. ~চারী *adj* observing a vow; engaged in any religious observance/ practice. ❑*n* a kind of folk-dance. ~**চারিণী** *fem.* ~**দেশ** *n* investiture with the sacred cord. ~**ধারণ** *n* fulfilling of a religious observance/ vow. ~**ধারী** *adj* fulfilling a religious observance/ vow. ~**ধারিণী** *fem.* ~**প্রতিষ্ঠা** *n* performance of a voluntary religious act. ~**ভঙ্গ** *n* breaking of a vow. ~**ভিক্ষা** *n* soliciting alms (as one of the ceremonies at investiture with the sacred thread). ~ **সমাপন** *n* concluding a religious observance. ~ **সম্পাদন** *n* fulfilling a religious obligation/ vow. ~**স্থ**, ~**স্থিত** *adjj* engaged in a vow/ religious observance. ~**স্নাত** *adj* one who has bathed after completing a religious vow. ~**স্নান** *n* bathing after the completion of a religious vow. **ব্রতামৃত** *n* a variety of banana. **ব্রতী** *adj* observing a vow; engaged in a religious observance, etc; engaged in; worshipping; behaving like. ~**বালক** *n* boy scout. **ব্রতিনী** *fem.* **ব্রতোপবাস** *n* fasting as a religious obligation.

ব্রততি, ব্রততী *n* **1** a creeping plant; creeper. **2** expansion; extension; spreading.

ব্রহ্ম *n* **1** the one self-existing spirit; the Absolute; the Eternal; the Self-existent. **2** (myth) Brahma (ব্রহ্মা) or one self-existent impersonal spirit; the one universal soul. 3 Providence. 4 superhuman power obtained through one's knowledge; Brahma. **5** the Vedas. **6** Vedic spell• **7** knowledge of the Vedas; religious/ spiritual knowledge. **8** holy life. **9** prayer. **10** the class of men who are the repositories and communicators of sacred knowledge; the Brahminical caste as a body. **11** one who prays; devout/ religious man; a Brahmin who is a knower of Vedic texts/ spells; one versed in sacred knowledge. **12** final emancipation. ~**ঘাতক**, ~**ঘ্ন** *nn* killer/ murderer of a Brahmin. ~**ঘাতী** *adj* one who kills a Brahmin. ~**ঘাতিনী** *fem.* ~**ঘোষ** *n* murmur (arising from the recital) of the Vedas. ~**চর্য** *n* study of the Veda; state of an unmarried religious student; state of continence and chastity. ~**চর্যত্ব** *n* the unmarried state; continence; chastity. ~**চর্যব্রত** *n* vow of chastity. ~**চর্যাশ্রম** *n* period of unmarried religious studentship. ~**চারী** *adj* practising sacred study as an unmarried student; observing chastity. ❑*n* young Brahmin who is a student of the Veda (under a preceptor) or who practises chastity; young Brahimin before marriage (in the first period of his life); one practising obstinence from sexual or other pleasures (and preparing to join an order of hermits). ~**চারিণী** *fem.* ~**জিজ্ঞাসা** *n* desire of knowing Brahma. ~**জীবী** *adj* subsisting by sacred learning. ❑*n* **1** a mercenary Brahmin (who converts his religious duties into a trade). **2** degraded Brahmin. ~**জ্ঞ** *adj* possessing sacred knowledge; knowing the sacred text; spiritually wise; holy. ❑*n* an inspired sage; a saint. ~**জ্ঞান** *n* divine/ sacred knowledge; spiritual wisdom. ~**জ্ঞানী** = **1**=~জ্ঞ. **2** a Brahmo. ~**জ্যোতি** *n* splendour of Brahmin/ the Supreme Being. ~**ডাঙ্গা** *n* barren tract of high land. ~**ডিম্ব** *n* = ব্রহ্মাণ্ড. ~**ণ্য** *adj* relating to Brahma or Brahmins. ❑*n* **1**= ~তেজ. **2** Narayana (also ব্রহ্মণ্যদেব). **3** planet Saturn. ~**তত্ত্ব** *n* true knowledge of Brahma. ~**তন্ত্র** *n* all that is taught of in the Veda. ~**তাল** *n* (music) a kind of measure. ~**তালু** *n* crown of the head; palate. ~**তীর্থ** *n* a place of pilgrimage on the Reva. ~**তেজঃ** ~**তেজ** *n* power and glory of Brahma; glory and lustre supposed to surround Brahma. ~**ত্ব** *n* state/ condition of a Brahmin; state/ nature of Brahma; divine nature; identification with Brahma. ~**ত্র** *n* piece of rent-free land given away to a Brahmin. ~**দণ্ড** *n* curse of a Brahmin. ~**দান** *n* gift of the Veda/ sacred knowledge. ~**দৈত্য** *n* a Brahmin changed into a Daitya; demoniac ghost of a Brahmin. ~**ন** *n* =~. ~**নাভ** *n* one proceeding out of the navel of Brahma; Vishnu. ~**নির্বাণ** *n* extinction in Brahma; absorption into the one self-existent spirit. ~**নিষ্ঠ** *adj* absorbed in contemplating Brahma. ~**পাদপ** *n* the tree *Butea frondosa.* ~**পিশাচ** *n* necro-phagous ghost of a Brahmin; of Brahmin ghoul. ~**পুত্র** *n* a famous river of Bengal. ~**পুর, পুরী** *nn* world/ heaven of Brahma. ~**বন্ধু** *n* an unworthy/ merely nominal Brahmin. ~**বাদ** *n* discourse on/ explanation of sacred texts. ~**বাদী** *adj* discoursing on sacred texts; having knowledge about Brahma; versed in/ following Vedantic philosophy. ❑*n* defender/ expounder of the Veda; one who asserts that all things are to be identified wih Brahma. ~**বাদিনী** *fem.* ~**বিদ** = ~জ্ঞ. ~**বিদ্যা** =~জ্ঞান. ~**বৈবর্ত** *n* one of the eighteen Puranas. ~**ময়** *adj* formed/ consisting of/ identified with Brahma. ~**ময়ী** *fem.* ~**মীমাংসা** *n* investigation into Brahma/ spiritual doctrine of the Veda; the Vedanta philosophy treating of the self-existing spirit. ~**রন্ধ্র** *n* an aperture in the crown of head (through which the soul is said to escape on death). ~**রস** *n* savour of Brahma. ~**রাক্ষস** *n* kind of evil demon; ghost of a Brahmin who led an unholy life. ~**রাত্র** *n* **1** Brahma's night. **2** =ব্রাহ্ম মুহূর্ত. ~**রাত্রি** *n* night of Brahma. ~**রূপ** *n* nature of the Supreme Being; the Supreme Being. ~**র্ষি** *n* a particular class of sages supposed to belong to the Brahmin caste. ~**লোক** = ~পুর. ~**শাপ** = ~দণ্ড. ~**শিরঃ**, ~**শিরা** *n* a mythical weapon. ~**সংহিতা** *n* collection of prayers. ~সঙ্গীত *n* song of devotion to God. ~সমাজ = ব্রাহ্মসমাজ. ~সাযুজ্য =~ত্ব. ~সূত্র *n* the sacred thread worn by Brahmins. ~স্ব *n* property/ possessions of a Brahmin. ব্রহ্মাপহরণ করা *vt* rob/misappropriate the property of a Brahmin. ~স্বরূপ = ~রূপ. ~হত্যা *n* murder of a Brahmin. ব্রহ্মোত্তর = ~ত্র.

ব্রহ্ম[2], ব্রহ্মদেশ *n* Burmah; Myanmar. ~বাসী *adj*, Burmese. ❑*n* Burmese; Burman. ~বাসিনী *fem*.

ব্রহ্মা *n* the one impersonal universal spirit manifested as a personal creator and as the first of the triad of personal gods. ~নী *fem* wife of Brahma; the Shakti or personified female energy of Brahma.

ব্রহ্মাণ্ড *n* the universe; the world; the creation.

ব্রহ্মাস্ত্র *n* 'Braham's missile'; a mythical weapon (which deals infallible destruction).

ব্রাত্য *n* a man of the mendicant or vagrant class; tramps; outcaste; low/vile person. ❑*adj* degenerated; fallen; failed in observing one's vows/ religious rites; outcaste.

ব্রান্ডি *n* brandy.

ব্রাশ [E] *n* brush. ~ করা *vt* brush.

ব্রাহ্ম *adj* **1** relating to Brahma; holy; sacred; divine. **2** relating to sacred knowledge prescribed by the Veda; sacred to the Veda; scriptural. **3** relating/ belonging to the Brahmins or the sacerdotal class; peculiar/ favourable to or consisting of Brahmins; Brahminicals. ❑*n* **1** inspired sage; saint. **2** worshipper of Brahma; a monotheistic religious community founded by Raja Rammohan Roy; a Brahmo. **3** a form of marriage (in which the bride is bestowed on the bridegroom without requiring anything from him). ~ধর্ম *n* Brahmoism (⇒ 2 above). ~ধর্মবীজ *n* principles of Brahmoism. ~বিধান *n* **1** Brahmo marriage (⇒ ~(3) above). **2** religious rites of Brahmoism. ~বিবাহ *n* **1** = ~(3). **2** marriage (by registration) in accordance with the rules of the Brahmo Samaj. ~মন্দির *n* temple of the Brahmos. ~ মুহূর্ত *n* the period of forty-eight minutes immediately preceding sunrise; dawn. ~সমাজ *n* monotheistic religious community founded by Rammohan Roy; Brahmo Samaj; assembly of the Brahmos. ~সমাজী *adj* belonging to the Brahmo Samaj. ❑*n* member of the Brahmo community/ society.

ব্রাহ্মণ *n* **1** one who has divine knowledge. **2** a man belonging to the first divisions of the Hindu body; Brahmin. **3** portion of the Veda containing rules for the employment of Mantras or hymns at various sacrifices. **4** Brahmin priest. **5** a Brahmin cook. **6** poor fellow: এখন ~ করে কী , যায় বা কোথায়? ব্রাহ্মণী *fem* **1** female Brahmin. **2** wife of a Brahmin. **3** female Brahmin cook. ~কুল *n* family of a Brahmin. ~চাণ্ডাল *n* 'Chandal among Brahmin'; degraded/ outcaste Brahmin. ~ জাতি *n* Brahminical caste/ race. ~তা, ~ত্ব *n* rank/ condition/ powers/ characteristics of a Brahmin. ~ পণ্ডিত *n* Brahmin scholar. ~ শাসন *n* rent-free land possessed by a Brahmin. ~সমাজ *n* the community of the Brahmins.

ব্রাহ্মণায়ন *n* a Brahmin sprung from learned and holy progenitors; good Brahmin.

ব্রাহ্মণ্য *n* **1** state/ rank/ powers/ characteristics of a Brahmin. **2** functions and duties of a Brahmin. **3** community of Brahmins. ~ ধর্ম *n* **1** = ~ (2). **2** religion based on the superiority of the Brahminical caste; Hindu caste system. ~বাদ *n* ideology based on the superiority of the Brahminical caste; Brahminism. ~শ্রী *n* splendour arising from superhuman power of a Brahmin.

ব্রাহ্মিকা *n fem* female Brahmo.

ব্রাহ্মী *n* **1** the Sakti or personified energy of Brahma. **2** speech or the goddess of speech. **3** wife of a Brahmin. **4** kind of medicinal plant aiding memory. **5** an ancient script/ alphabet. ~লিপি *n* Brahmi script.

ব্রিজ [E] *n* **1** bridge. **2** (card-game) bridge.

ব্রিটিশ [E] *n* Britisher. ❑*adj* British.

ব্রীড়া *n* bashfulness; shyness; modesty; coyness; shame. ~নত, ~বনত *adj* bowed down in coyness/ with shame. ~ন্বিত, ব্রীড়িত *adj* bashful; ashamed; modest; abashed; embarrassed.

ব্রীহি *n* **1** paddy; rice. **2** rice ripening in the rainy season. ~শ্রেষ্ঠ *n* rice of the best quality; *aman* paddy.

ব্রুচ =ব্রোচ

ব্রুস = বুরুশ

ব্রেক [E] *n* brake (of vehicle/ machine). ~ কষা *vi* brake; put on the brake; slow down.

ব্র্যাকেট [E] *n* **1** parenthesis; bracket. **2** bracket (fastened to a wall).

ব্র্যানডি, ব্র্যান্ডি [E] *n* brandy.

ব্লক [E] *n* **1** piece of wood or metal with designs etc cut on it for printing; block. **2** mass of buildings etc; block.

ব্লটিং (also ~ কাগজ, ~ পেপার) [E] *n* blotting paper.

ব্লাউজ, ব্লাউস [E] *nn* blouse.

ব্ল্যাকবোর্ড [E] *n* blackboard.

ভ *n* the twenty-fourth consonant of the Bengali alphabet. Voiced aspirated bilibial plosive sound. In dialect it is pronounced as voiced aspirated libiodental fricative sound.

ভইষ, ভইস *n* buffalo. **ভইষা** *adj* made of buffalo-milk; drawn by the buffalo: ভইষা ঘি/গাড়ি.

ভক *n* (onom) denoting sudden emission of noise; smoke and (esp offensive) smell; spurt; burst; gust. **~ করে** (বমি করা, ধোঁয়া ছাড়া ইত্যাদি) *adv* suddenly; in profusion; (appropriate verb); come out in a sudden burst. **~ ভক** *n* denoting repetition and prolongation of the above phenomenon: ~ ভক করে ধোঁয়া বেরোচ্ছে Smoke is spurting (out).

ভকত *adj* **1** (poet)=ভক্ত. **2** (derog) hypocrite; bigot; impostor.

ভকতি *n* (poet)=ভক্তি

ভক্ত[1] *adj* **1** devoted/attached to; adoring; worshipping; honouring; serving; reverent; devout: ~ বৈষ্ণব. **2** faithful; loyal; obedient: প্রভু~. **3** faithfully following/pursuing: সুনীতির ~. **4** having profound admiration for; lover of: রবীন্দ্র~. **5** fond of; admiring; enamored: গানের ~. **6** submissive; docile; yielding to the control/authority of: শক্তের ~ ❑*n* devotee; votary; idolater; worshipper; lover; devout person; fan; faithful follower/observer; admirer; adorer. **~প্রাণ** *adj* having a devout heart. **~বৎসল** *n* kind to worshippers/ faithful attendants; graciously affectionate to votaries/admirers. **~বিটল, ~বিটেল** *n* hypocrite; sanctimonious person; impostor; false devotee. **~শ্রেষ্ঠ, ভক্তাগ্রগণ্য** *adjj* best/foremost among votaries or worshippers. **ভক্তাধীন** *adj* graciously obedient to one's votaries (fulfilling their desires).

ভক্ত[2] *n* food; meal; boiled rice; any eatable grain boiled with water.

ভক্তি *n* **1** devotion; worship; piety; devoutness; faith/love (as a religious principle or means of salvation); devotion to; fondness for; trust; reliance; homage; strong attachment; addiction; profound admiration; obedience. **2** predisposition; inclination; appetite; relish: আহারে ~. **3** division; share; portion. **~ করা** *vt* be devoted to; worship; love; admire profoundly; be fond of; be attached/addicted to; follow faithfully; have faith/trust in; serve; honour; revere; adore; venerate; respect; rely on; have inclination/appetite/relish (for). **~গম্য** *adj* accessible by devotion. **~গ্রন্থ** *n* devotional book. **~চিহ্ন** *n* mark/sign of devotion. **~জ্ঞ** *n* knowing faith/devotion. **~তত্ত্ব** *n* doctrine/cult of or a treatise on devotion or piety. **~নম্র** *n* bent down in devotion; making a humble obeisance. **~নম্রভাবে** *adv* devoutly. **~পথ**=~মার্গ. **~পরায়ণ, ~প্রবণ** *adj* devout; faithfully devoted (to); pietist; strongly attached/ addicted (to); reverent; respectful; obeisant; deferential; having inclination/relish/appetite for. **~পরায়ণা** *fem*. **~পরায়ণতা** *adj* devoutness; devotion; piety; pietism; profound admiration; strong attachment/ addiction. **পূর্বক** *adv* devoutly; reverentially; with devotion/respect/ reverence; with pleasure. **~পুত** *adj* full of piety/ reverence; steeped in piety. **~পুতচিত্তে** *adv* with mind steeped in piety; reverentially. **~বস্তু** *n* (psych) fetish. **~বাদ** *n* the doctrine holding that salvation is attainable by means of devotion only (without knowledge and practice); devotionalism. **~বাদী** *adj* devotionalistic; devotionistic. ❑*n* devotionist; devotionalist. **~বিহ্বল** *adj* overwhelmed with devotion. **~ভরে** *adv*=~পূর্বক. **~ভাজন** *adj* worthy of reverence/veneration; venerable; adorable; revered; respectable. ❑*n* venerable /reverend/ adorable person. **~ভাব** *n* sense/feeling of devotion; deep respect; devout/ reverential disposition of mind. **~ভাবে** *adv*=~পূর্বক. **~মান**=~পরায়ণ. **~মতী** *fem*. **~মার্গ** *n* 'the way of devotion' (regarded as a means of salvation and opposed to *karma*-and *jnana-marga*); path of devotionalism. **~মূলক** *adj* devotional. **~যোগ** *n* worship of God or effort to attain beatitude by means of devotion only; loving devotion . **~যোগে** *adv* through devotion. **~রস** *n* sense of devotion; feeling of loving faith. **~রাগ** *n* affection/predilection for. **~শীল**=~পরায়ণ. **~শীলা** *fem*. **~শূন্য, ~হীন** *adj* destitute of devotion; irreverent; undevout; impious; having no attachment (to); having no faith/ trust (in). **~সাধন**=~যোগ. **~স্রোত** *n* surge of devotion.

ভক্ষ *n* **1** food; eating. **~ক** *adj* eating; feeding on; voracious; gluttonous. ❑*n* **1** one who eats; eater; enjoyer; one who feeds/lives upon. **2** (fig) spoiler; vitiator; killer; grabber. এতিমের সম্পত্তি ~. **~ণ** *n* eating; consuming; feeding. **~ণ করা** *vi, vt* eat; consume; devour; feed on; use up; waste; destroy. **~ণীয়** *adj* to be eaten; edible; eatable; fit for food. ❑*n* that which is to be eaten; an edible/eatable; food; dish. **ভক্ষ্য**=~ণীয়. **~বস্তু** *n* edible matter; victuals; viands. **ভক্ষক** *n* food and the eater. **ভক্ষ্যাবশেষ** *n* leavings of food after eating; orts; remnants of food. **ভক্ষ্যাভক্ষ্য** *n* what may and may not be eaten; food allowed and prohibited.

ভক্ষিত *adj* eaten; consumed; devoured; eaten up. **~ব্য** *adj* to be eaten; edible. **~শেষ** *n*=ভক্ষ্যাবশেষ (⇒ ভক্ষ).

ভগ *n* **1** the six divine graces collectively, ie, riches, vigour, fame, fortune, knowledge and renunciation. **2** good fortune ; happiness; welfare; prosperity. **3** glory; dignity; majesty; distinction; excellence. **4** beauty; loveliness. **5** love; affection; sexual passion; amorous pleasure; dalliance. **6** female organ; vagina. **7** anus. **8** one of twelve Adityas (bestowing wealth and presiding over love and marriage). **9** the sun. **10** the moon. **11** godhead; divinity. **12** salvation. **~ণ** *n* (astron) revolution. **~ন্দর** *n* fistula in the anus. **~পক্ষ** *n* (anat) labia minora.

ভগবতী *adj fem* **1** endowed with six divine graces (⇒ভগ). **2** reverend; venerable; holy. ❑*n* **1** goddess Durga. **2** term of address for a reverend lady.

ভগবদর্চনা, ভগবদারাধনা *n* worship of God; propitiation of God.

ভগবদ্‌গীতা *n* the celebrated mystical poem (interpolated in the Mahabharata); the Holy Gita.

ভগবদ্ভক্ত *adj* devoted to God; God-fearing; pious.

ভগবদ্ভক্তি *n* devotion to God; devoutness; piety.

ভগবন্‌ *n* (vocative) Your Holiness; o God; Reverend Sir.

ভগবান *adj* **1** glorious; illustrious; divine; holy; adorable; venerable. **2** endowed with six divine graces (⇒ভগ). ❑*n* God; the divine or holy one.

ভগাঙ্কুর *n* (anat) clitoris.

ভগিনী, ভগ্নি *n* **1** *fem* sister; cousin. **2** (term of address) any woman. **~পতি** *n* sister's husband; brother-in-law.

ভগীরথ *n* mythical king who brought down the sacred Ganga from heaven to earth and then conducted it to the ocean in order to purify the ashes of his ancestors.

ভগোল *n* the zodiac.

ভগৌষ্ঠ *n* (anat) labia majora.

ভগ্ন *adj* **1** broken; shattered; split. **2** torn; severed; detached; fractured. ~অস্থি, ~ শাখা. **3** ground; pounded; pulverized: ~শস্য. **4** defeated; routed; checked; frustrated. ~ আশা/বাহিনী. **5** curved; hunched; stooping: ~পৃষ্ঠ. **6** interrupted; disturbed: ~ নিদ্রা. **7** disappointed ; ungratified: ~ মনোরথ. **8** dilapidated; ruined: ~ অট্টালিকা. **9** hoarse; husky. ~ কণ্ঠ. **10** impaired; shattered: ~ স্বাস্থ্য. **11** fractional: ~ সংখ্যা. **12** depressed: dejected: ~ হৃদয়. **~কণ্ঠ** *adj* hoarse; husky. **~কণ্ঠে** *adv* in a cracked/broken/husky voice; huskily; hoarsely. **~ক্রম** *n* breaking (ie violating) of grammatical order/ construction. **~গৃহ** *n* a dilapidated house; (fig) a house in utter disorder/confusion. **~চিত্ত** *adj* broken-hearted; discouraged; disappointed; dejected. **~চেষ্ট** *adj* broken in effort; disappointed. **~জানু** *adj* having a broken knee or leg. **~তা** *n* condition of being broken. **~তাল** *n* (music) a kind of measure. **~দর্প** *adj* one whose pride is broken; humiliated. **~দশা** *n* = ভগ্নাবস্থা. **~দূত** *n* messenger/soldier bringing the news of defeat from the battle field. **~দেহ** *adj* having one's health ruined/impaired/shattered. **~নিদ্র** *adj* one whose sleep is broken or interrupted. **~পরিণাম** *adj* prevented from finishing (anything). **~পাইক**=~দূত. **~পৃষ্ঠ** *adj* 'broken-backed'; hunchbacked. **~প্রক্রম** *n* 'broken arrangement'; (rhet) use of a word which does not correspond to one used before. **~প্রতিজ্ঞ** *adj* one who has broken a promise; faithless. **~প্রায়** *adj* crumbling; threatening to fall; tottering; almost falling; about to collapse. **~ব্রত** *adj* one who has broken a vow. **~বাহু** *adj* broken-armed. **~মনাঃ**=~চিত্ত. **~মনোরথ** *adj* frustrated; balked; disappointed. **~মান**=~দর্প. **~শক্তি** *adj* one whose strength is broken. **~শ্রী** *adj* one whose prosperity is blighted; deprived of one's beauty/grace. **~সন্ধি** *adj* one whose joints are broken. **~স্তূপ** *n* (heap of) ruins; wreckage; desolate place. **~হৃদয়**=~চিত্ত. **ভগ্নাংশ** *n* **1** (arith) fraction. **2** broken-away past; fraction. **ভগ্নাঙ্ক** *n* (arith) fraction. **ভগ্নাত্মা** *n* the moon (cut in two by the trident of Shiva). **~বিশিষ্ট** *adj* lying/remaining in or as ruins. **~বিশেষ** *n* broken-down remains; ruins; relics; wreckage. **ভগ্নাবস্থ** *adj* dilapidated; in ruins; desolate; decayed. **ভগ্নাবস্থা** *n* broken-down/dilapidated/ ruined state; state of decay. **ভগ্নাশ, ভগ্নাশা** *adj* one whose hopes are broken; disappointed in expectation. **ভগ্নাস্থি** *adj* one whose bones are broken. **ভগ্নোৎসাহ, ভগ্নোদ্যম** *adjj* one whose efforts have been frustrated; disheartened; disappointed; discouraged.

ভগ্নি ⇒ ভগিনী

ভঙ্গ *n* **1** breaking; bursting; splitting; dividing; shattering; breaking down/up. **2** break; breach: বাধ~. **3** rupture; fracture: অস্থি ~. **4** overthrow; rout; defeat: শত্রুব্যূহ ~. **5** breach: বিশ্বাস ~. **6** discontinuance; break: অনশন ~. **7** bending; bowing; stretching out: গ্রীবা~. **8** knitting; contraction: ভূ~. **9** violation; infringement: আইন~. **10** suspension; break; postponement; interruption: যাত্রা~. **11** non-observance; non-compliance; breach: প্রতিশ্রুতি ~. **12** dissolution: সভা ~. **13** severance: সম্পর্ক ~. **14** loss: আশা~. **15** estrangement: বন্ধুত্ব ~. **16** disturbance; frustration ; humiliation. **17** abatement; decay; ruin; destruction. **18** impairment: স্বাস্থ্য ~. **19** disbandment; break-up: দল ~. **20** act of fleeing away ; flight; retreat: রণে ~. **21** dispersal: জনতা ~. **22**

interruption; break: নিদ্রা~. **23** toilet; fashion; style: কবরী~. **24** disintegration. **25** discouragement: মনো~. **26** bend; fold; contraction: ত্রি~. **27** obstruction; drawback; obstacle. **28** termination; close. **29** crack: স্বর~. **30** pain: পার্শ্ব~. **31** piece broken off; morsel; fragment. **32** wave. **33** act/manner of rolling or dancing: তরঙ্গ~. **34** removal; refutation; rejection; refusal: সন্দেহ~. **~ করা** *vt* break; split; divide; shatter ; break up/down; fracture; rupture; overthrow; rout; defeat; discontinue; violate; infringe; stretch; knit; contract; suspend; postpone; interrupt; dissolve; disturb; frustrate; impair; disband; disperse; flee away; retreat; obstruct; terminate; close; crack, remove; refute; sever; discourage; fail/refuse to observe or maintain or keep; cause the loss of; disintegrate. **ভঙ্গ দেওয়া** *vi* take to flight; beat a retreat; flee/withdraw defeated ; take to one's heels; pull out; strike camp; bow out: রণে/তর্কযুদ্ধে ~ দেওয়া. **~ হওয়া** *vi* be broken/split/fractured/ impaired/ discontinued. **~কুলীন** *n* a *kulin* family (ie a Brahmin family of the highest class in Bengal) or a member of it failing to observe the social (esp matrimonial) restrictions enjoined on them. **~দ** *adj* brittle; fragile; frail; delicate. **~পয়ার** *n* a kind of metre in which the second line of each of the four-line stanzas is merely the repetition of the first and the first three lines consist of eight syllables each, while the fourth consists of six syllables only. **~প্রবণ** *adj*=~দ. **~প্রবণতা** *n* brittleness; fragility; breakableness.

ভঙ্গ[২] *n* (phys) diffraction.

ভঙ্গন *n* breaking; collapse; collapsing.

ভঙ্গা *n* hemp; *Cannabis sativa;* an intoxicating beverage (or narcotic drug commonly called 'bhang') prepared from the hemp plant.

ভঙ্গি, ভঙ্গী *n* **1** pose; posture; figure. বসার/নাচের ~. **2** gesture. **3** beauty; charm; elegance; grace. **4** bent; curve: গ্রীবা~. **5** mode; manner; style; way: কথা বলার ~. **6** roundabout mode of acting/speaking. **7** way of dressing; fashion; toilet. **8** distinction of style: রচনা ~. **9** shape; form: গঠন~. **10** mere appearance/ semblance of. **11** iron; wit; repartee. **12** attitude; attitudinization; affectation: তার এই ~ আমার ভালো লাগে না. **13** fraud; deception. **14** wave. **15** jesting; joke: কতো ~ তুমি জানো. **~ করা** *vi* strike attitudes; attitudinize. **~মা** *n*=~. **~মান** *adj* wavy; curled; undulated.

ভঙ্গিয়ান *adj* fleeing/running away (from the battlefield).

ভঙ্গিল *adj* **1** fragile; brittle. **2** having folds; produced by folding processes. **~ পর্বত** *n* (geog) fold mountain.

ভঙ্গীভূত, ভঙ্গিভূত *adj* **1** having the appearance of. **2** mannered.

ভঙ্গুর *adj* **1** apt to break; fragile. **2** (phys) brittle. **3** transitory; perishable: ~ জীবন. **4** bent; curled; crisped; wrinkled. **5** bent/reach of a river. **~তা** *n* fragility; brittleness; transitoriness; transience.

ভচকানি, ভোচকানি=ভোকছানি (⇒ ভোক)

ভচক্র *n* the whole multitude of stars/asterisms. **~নাভি** *n* centre of the zodiac.

ভচাৎ *n* (onom) sound used to express the sinking of the foot or anything in mud/other soft substances; splashing.

ভজকট *n* **1** obstacle; hitch; trouble; stumbling block; snag; bottleneck; encumbrance; hurdle. **2** difficult enterprise; uphill struggle; no picnic; scrape.

ভজন *n* **1** glorification of a deity. **2** worship; adoration; reverence. **3** serving; service; attendance. **4** taking sb's shelter. **5** kind of devotional songs; hymn; canticle. **6** (rare) act of sharing. **~পূজন** *n* prayer and worship; singing and chanting. **~ভাজন** *n* (fig) coaxing and cajoling; cajolery; wheedling; persuasion; persuading by flattery. **ভজনা** *n* **1** worship; adoration; glorification; veneration; homage; supplication. **2** serving; waiting upon; service; attendance. **3** coaxing and cajoling; adulation; cajolery; wheedling; flattery. **ভজনা করা** *vt* **1** worship; adore; glorify; venerate; supplicate. **2** serve; wait/attend upon. **3** coax; cajole; wheedle; adulate; flatter. **ভজনালয়** *n* place/house of worship; house of God; temple. **ভজনীয়** *adj* to be loved/ revered/ worshipped/ waited upon; venerable.

ভজমান *adj* **1** apportioning. **2** worshipping; adoring.

ভজা *vt*=ভজনা করা (⇒ ভজন). ❑*adj* worshipping; devoted to; devotee/votary of: কর্তা~. **~নো** *vt* **1** cause to worship/adore; cause to serve. **2** convince. **3** persuade; win over; wheedle; cajole; wax.

ভজ্যমান *adj* **1** being worshipped/ adored/ glorified. **2** being apportioned.

ভঞ্জক *adj* breaking; splitting; dividing; dispelling; destroying; removing. ❑*n* breaker; destroyer; dispeller.

ভঞ্জন *n* breaking; splitting; shattering; crushing; annihilating removing ; dispelling; destroying. ❑*adj* (used as a *suff*)=ভঞ্জক: বিপদ~. **~ করা** *vt* break; split; shatter; crush; annihilate; frustrate; remove; dispel; destroy.

ভঞ্জা *vt* (poet)=ভঞ্জন করা

ভটচায্যি *n* (colloq)=ভট্টাচার্য (⇒ ভট্ট)

ভটভট *n* (onom) indicating a sound like that of water entering an empty pitcher, etc; gurgle; gabble. ভটভটানি *n* gurgling (noise); rattle:

স্কুটারের ভটভটানি. ভটভটি *n* (fact) scooter; autocycle; motor-scooter. ভটভটে *adj* gurgling; rattling.

ভটাভট *n* (onom) thump. ☐*adv* again and again: ~ ঘুষি মারা.

ভট্ট *n* **1** a particular mixed caste of hereditary panegyrics; bard; encomiast. **2** learned man; scholar; learned Brahmin. **3** one has learnt by heart one of the Vedas. **4** teacher; master. **5** philosopher; doctor. **6** title of a class of Brahmins. **~পল্লী** *n* a village/locality inhabited by a large number of pundits. **ভট্টাচার্য** *n* **1** title given to a learned Brahmin or any great teacher or doctor. **2** teacher. **3** title of a class of Brahmins. **ভট্টারক** *n* **1** great lord; venerable/worshipful person (esp of gods and of great/learned men). **2** sage; saint. **3** the sun. **4** God. ☐*adj* venerable. **ভট্টারিকা** *fem.* **পরমভট্টারক** *n* His/Your Majesty.

ভট্টিনী *n fem* noble lady (applied to queens not crowned or consecrated like the Devi, to the wife of a Brahmin and any woman of high rank).

ভড় *n* **1** large freight boat (used in transporting elephants, canons, etc); barge.**2** a particular mixed caste.

ভড়ং, ভড়ঙ *n* **1** a kind of ancient war-trumpet. **2**=ভড়ক.

ভড়ক, ভড়ং *n* ostentation; show; display; pretension; swank; airs; show-off. **~ করা** *vi* give oneself/put on airs; show off; swank; splurge; make a splurge; swagger; flaunt oneself. **~দার, ভড়কালো** *adj* ostentatious; swanky; showy; grandiose; pretentious; pompous; flashy; gaudy; tawdry; glittery; flamboyant.

ভড়কানো *vi* **1** start (up) (from fear, etc); balk/baulk (at); be startled. **2** take fright/alarm; be scared/afraid; cower; be startled. **ভড়কে দেওয়া** *vt* startle; scare (away); scare and confuse; scare sb out of his wits. **ভড়কে যাওয়া** *vi* be scared; stop dead; be startled out one's wits.

ভড়ভড় *n* (onom) **1** denoting: the noise of rapid emission of sth loose e.g rapid or hasty discharge of the faeces; shuffling sound in the nose occasioned by a cold; signify the speedy rising of water when hole are made in the mud of a pond . **2** gabbling. **ভড়ভড়া** *vi* babble.

ভড়রভড়র *n* (onom) babbling; nonsensical/ useless talk.

ভড়াৎ *n* (onom) expressing a quick discharge of the faeces.

ভণা *vt* (poet; archaic) say; tell; narrate.

ভণিত *adj* said; told; narrated; composed. ☐*n* saying; telling. **ভণিতা** *n* **1** mention of the name of the author in the opening or concluding lines of a poem. **2** (iron) long-winded introductory remark (before coming to the point); circumlocution: আর ভণিতা কোরো না, আসল কথায় এসো.

ভণ্ড *n* **1** hypocrite; deceiver; cheat; impostor; bluffer; humbug; sham; charlatan; quack; pretender; sanctimonious person . **2** jester; buffoon; mime. ☐*adj* feigning; pretentious; deceptive; deceitful; artful; beguiling; fraudulent; hypocritical; sanctimonious; crafty; wily. **~ তপস্বী** *n* hypocritical ascetic; impostor. **~ তপস্বিনী** *fem.* **~তা, ~ত্ব** *n n* hypocrisy; imposture; deceit; sanctimony; humbug; fraud; quackery ; pretension; feigning; duplicity. **~হাসিনী** *n fem* prostitute; whore. **~নো** *vt* deceive; beguile; cheat; bamboozle; hoodwink. **ভণ্ডামি, ভণ্ডামো** *nn*=~তা.

ভণ্ডুল, ভণ্ডুর *adj* spoiled; foiled; frustrated; thwarted; balked; baffled; fruitless; futile; lost. **~ করা** *vi* spoil; bungle; frustrate; thwart; balk; baffle; render fruitless. **~ হওয়া** *vi* fail; miscarry; abort; flounder; flop; feezle out; collapse; come to naught; misfire.

ভদন্ত *n* term of respect applied to a Buddhist (mendicant).

ভদরকুঁড়ে *adj* extremely lazy; slothful; indolent.

ভদ্দর *adj* (colloq)=ভদ্র

ভদ্র *adj* **1** gentle; gracious; courteous; civilized; civil mannerly; well behaved; well mannered; polished/elegant in demeanor or taste; amiable; gentlemanly; mild; genial; kind; kindly; suave; pleasant; graceful: ~ আচরণ. **2** refined; urbane; bland. **3** belonging to polished/high society; noble. **4** blessed; auspicious fortunate; propitious; salutary. ☐*n* **1** (term of address) my good sir/lady; my dear (good people). **2** prosperity; happiness; health; weal; welfare; good fortune. **~ আচরণ** *n* good manners; courtesy; civility; politeness. **~তা, ~ত্ব** *adjj* **1** courtesy; politeness; (good) manners; civility; suavity; refinement; urbanity; civilities; formality. **2** honesty; probity; salutariness. **~তা করা** *vi, vt* treat sb courteously; be formal/ceremonious with; be suave/ polite/ attentive/ civil. **~তার অনুরোধে/ খাতিরে** for courtesy's sake; for the sake of formalities. **~তাচরণ, ~ ব্যবহার** *nn* courteous behaviour; suave manners; courtesy; politeness; gracious deportment. **~তাবিরুদ্ধ** *adj* discourteous; impolite; mannerless; uncivil. **~তামূলক** *adj* pertaining to courtesy; formal; ceremonious. **~ মহিলা** *n fem* gentlewoman; lady. **~লোক** *n* gentleman; courteous/ amiable man; honest man. **~লোকের এক কথা** (phrase) A gentleman/an honest man is always true to his word/ promise. ~সন্তান *n* member of a respectable family; gentleman. ~সমাজ *n* polite/refined society; society of cultured/decent people. ~স্ত, ~স্থ *adj* (colloq) gentlemanlike; in the state of a gentleman; decent. ❑*n* prosperity; good fortune; good; politeness; civility. ~স্থতা *n*=~স্ত. ~স্ত/~স্থতা নেই be not proper; it is no good ....: এখানে থাকার আর ~স্থতা নেই.

ভদ্রা *n fem* (of ভদ্র) **1** gentlewoman; lady. **2** (astrol, astron) the second, the seventh and the twelfth day of a lunar fortnight (considered as inauspicious). ~ পড়া *vi* be hindered/ obstructed; have a setback/ hitch/ impediment. ~ভদ্র *n* good and bad/evil; respectable and disreputable. ~সন *n* **1** homestead. **2** throne. **3** palace. ভদ্রে (vocative of ~) my good lady; your ladyship.

ভদ্রোচিত *adj* gentlemanly; gentlemanlike; ladylike; courteous; suitable/right for a gentleman/gentlewoman; decent; respectable.

ভনভন *n* (onom) buzz; humming; drone . ~ করা, ভনভনানো *vi* buzz; drone; hum. ভনভনানি *n* buzz; drone; humming. ভনভনে *adj* buzzing; droning.

ভব *n* **1** worldly existence; world. **2** being; state of being; existence; life. **3** coming into existence; birth; production; origin. **4** God; deity. **5** Shiva. **6** welfare; prosperity; well-being. **7** obtaining; acquisition. **8** excellence. **9** becoming. ❑*adj* (used as a *suff*) produced; originating from. ~কারণ *n* the creator; God; the first cause. ~কারা *n* prison of worldly existence. ~কান্তার wilderness of worldly existence. ~ঘুরে *adj* roving/roaming about the world; vagrant; wandering; vagabond. ❑*n* vagabond; vagrant; wanderer; tramp. ~ঘুরেমি *n* vagabondage; vagabondism; vagrancy; wandering. ~জল *n* water (ocean) of worldly existence. ~তারণ *adj* delivering from worldly existence; giving salvation. ~তারিণী *fem.* ❑*n* goddess Durga. ~ত্রয় *n* world; earthly existence. ~নাশিনী *adj fem* destroying worldly existence; delivering from births. ~পার *n* deliverance from worldly existence. ~পারাবার *n* ocean of worldly existence. ~বন্ধন *n* bond/bondage of worldly existence. ~বারিনিধি=~পারাবার. ~ভয় *n* fears of worldly existence/re-birth. ~ভয়তারণ, ~ভয়বারণ *n, adj* (one) who delivers/protects from the evils of worldly existence. ~ভাব *n* love of worldly existence. ~ভার *n* burden of the world (as borne by God); burden of worldly existence. ~ভীরু *adj* afraid of worldly existence/ re-birth. ~ভূত *adj* being the origin/ source of all being. ~মোচন *n* releasing from worldly existence. ~রস *n* delight in worldly existence. ~লীলা *n* activities of one's mortal life. ~লীলা সাঙ্গ করা /হওয়া *vi* die; give up the ghost; breathe one's last; join one's ancestors. ~লোক, ~সংসার *nn* world; worldly existence. ~সন্ততি *n* uninterrupted series of births and transmigration's. ~সমুদ্র, ~সাগর, ~সিন্ধু *nn*=~পারাবার. ভবান্তর *n* another existence. ভবার্ণব *n*=~পারাবার. ভবের খেলা=~লীলা.

ভবতী *adj fem* respectable; venerable.

ভবদীয় *adj* your; yours.

ভবন *n* **1** place of abode; home; house; dwelling; residence; palace; building. **2** coming into existence; birth; production. **3** (used as a *suff*) act of being reduced to: ঘনী~, প্রস্তরী~. ~দ্বার *n* palace-gate. ~শিখী *n* domesticated peacock. ~স্বামী *n* lord of a house; paterfamilias. ~নীয় *adj* to be about to become/ be/ happen.

ভবভূতি *n* special powers of Shiva.

ভবাদৃশ *adj* (archaic) any one like your honour/ you. ভবাদৃশী *fem.*

ভবানী *n fem* Shiva's wife, goddess Durga.

ভবারাধ্য *adj* respected/ worshipped by the whole world. ❑*n* God.

ভবিতব্য *adj* inevitable; ineluctable. ❑*n* the inevitable; destiny. ~তা *n* inevitability; inevitable consequence; necessity ; fate; destiny.

ভবিতা *adj* becoming; being; what is ought to become/be ; future; imminent. ❑*n* future. ভবিত্রী *fem.*

ভবিষ্ণু *adj* **1** what is ought to become/ be; imminent; future. **2** faring well; thriving.

ভবিষ্য *adj* future; imminent; impending; coming. ❑*n* future. ~ তহবিল, ~-নিধি *nn* provident fund. ~ পুরাণ *n* one of the 18 Puranas. ~ সূচনা *n* presage.

ভবিষ্যৎ *adj* future; coming; later. ❑*n* **1** future; futurity; destiny. **2** consequence: এর ~ ভালো হবে না. **3** prospect; outlook: ~ খোয়ানো. **4** (gram) future tense. ~ কাল *n* **1**=~ (4). **2** future time. ভবিষ্যতে *adv* in future.

ভবিষ্যদ্দৃষ্টি *n* foresight; prevision; prescience; farsightedness. ভবিষ্যদ্দ্রষ্টা *n* seer; prophet; soothsayer; clairvoyant.

ভবিষ্যদ্বক্তা *n* prophet; soothsayer; clairvoyant; diviner.

ভবিষ্যদ্বাক্য, ভবিষ্যদ্বাণী *n* prophesy; prediction; prognostic; forecast. ভবিষ্যদ্বাণী করা *vt* prophesy; predict; forecast; foretell; presage; prognosticate. ভবিষ্যদ্বাদী *adj* predicting future events; prophesying.

ভবী *n fem* pertinacious person. ~ ভোলবার নয় A pertinacious person is not amenable to persuasion.

ভব্য *adj* **1** well-behaved; polite; courteous; mannerly; well-bred; so suave. **2** quiet; soft spoken; gentle; affable. **3** honest; righteous; pious. **4** auspicious; fortunate; benefactory. **5** civil; civilized; refined. **6** likely to be; future; about to be/become. ভব্যা *fem.* ~তা *n* **1** courtesy; politeness; (good) manners; gentleness; quietness; suavity; good budding; civility; refinement; urbanity; gentility; affability. **2** futurity. ~রূপ *n* good figure/ form.

ভভম, ভভম্ভম *n* (onom) boom; roll; thunder.

ভয় *n* fear; alarm; dread; apprehension; dismay; danger; peril; distress; fright; horror; terror; awe; panic; consternation; scare; diffidence. **~ করা** *vt* fear; be afraid; take fright/alarm; dread; be scared. **~ খাওয়া** *vi* be frightened alarmed/ scared; get a fright; flinch; cringe (at); show the white feather; cower; quail; be startled. **~ খাওয়ানো** *vt* frighten; scare; give a fright; dismay; shock; daunt; cow; overawe. **~খেকো** *adj* cowardly; chickenhearted; faint-hearted; nerveless; craven. **~ জন্মানো** *vi*=~ খাওয়ানো. **~ দেখানো** *vt* threaten; hold out threats; intimidate; browbeat; bully. **~ পাওয়া** =~ খাওয়া. **~ ভাঙা** *vi, vt* be free from fear; overcome fear; free from fear; dispel fear. **~ হওয়া** *vi* be stricken with fear; aprehend; be afraid of. **ভয়ে জড়সড় হওয়া** *vi* crouch (down) in fear; skulk; cringe (at); shrink back from fear; cower. **ভয়ে ভয়ে** *adv* timidly; fearfully; diffidently; timorously; warily; nervously. **~কর** *adj* causing fear; terrible; dangerous; fearful; awesome. **~কাতর, ~কাতুরে** *adjj* panicky; timid; fainthearted; nervous; sheepish; timorous; pusillanimous. **~ক্লিষ্ট** *adj* distressed with fear; frightened. **~চকিত** *adj* alarmed; aghast; terrified. **~ডর** *n* fear and anxiety. **~ডিণ্ডিম** *n* a drum used in battle. **~তরাসে** *adj*=~কাতর. **~তরাসী** *fem.* **~ত্রস্ত** *adj* trembling with fear; frightened. **~ত্রাতা** *n* saver from fear/danger. **~দ** *adj* inspiring fear; causing danger; frightening; fearful; dreadful; awesome; terrifying. **~দা** *fem.* **~নাশন** *adj* removing fear. **~নাশী** *adj*=~নাশন. **~নাশিনী** *fem.* **~নিমীলিতাক্ষ** *adj* having the eyes closed from fear. **~প্রতিকার** *n* removal of fear. **~প্রদ** =~দ. **~প্রদা** *fem.* **~প্রদর্শন** *n* act of threatening; intimidation; threats; menace. **~ প্রদর্শন করা** *vt* threaten; intimidate; bully; browbeat. **~প্রাপ্ত** *adj* frightened; scared. **~পূর্ণ** *adj* frightened; fearful; terrified; dismayed. **~বিধায়ী**=~কর. **~বিপ্লুত** *adj* fled/ fleeing through fear. **~বিহ্বল** *adj* disturbed/ agitated with fear; terror-stricken; pain-stricken; awe-stricken; unmanned; unstring; overawed. **~বিহ্বলতা** *n* terror; panic; horror; terrified state; state of alarm. **~ভ্রষ্ট**=~বিপ্লুত. **~ভীত** *adj* terrified; alarmed; horrified; petrified. **~শীল** *adj* of a timorous disposition; timid. **~শূন্য** *adj* fearless; dauntless; intrepid. **~শোকসমাবিষ্ট** *adj* filled with fear and sorrow. **~সন্ত্রস্ত** *adj* scared with fear. **~হারী** *adj* removing/ dispelling fear. **~হারিণী** *fem.* **~হীন**=~শূন্য. **~হেতু** *n* cause for fear; danger. **ভয়াক্রান্ত** *adj* overcome with fear. **ভয়াকুল, ভয়াতুর** *adjj* distressed with fear; afraid. **ভয়ান্বিত** *adj* filled with fear; alarmed. **ভয়ার্ত**=**ভয়াতুর**. **ভয়াভিভূত** *adj* overwhelmed with fear. **ভয়োপশম** *n* soothing/allaying of fear; encouragement. **ভয় নেই** don't fear; be not afraid. **ভয়ে পিঁপড়ার গর্তে লুকানো** (fig) cringe; cower; funk; loose one's nerve; chicken out. **ভয়ে ভক্তি** *n* respect out of fear.

ভয়ঙ্কর *adj* terrible; dreadful ; aweful; terrific; ghastly; fearful; horrible; horrendous; grisly; terrifying; awe-inspiring; shocking; frightful; eerie; monstrous; severe; formidable; fierce; tremendous. **ভয়ঙ্করী** *fem.*

ভয়ষা, ভয়সা=ভইষা

ভয়ানক *adj*=ভয়ঙ্কর. **~ রস** *n* (rhet) sentiment of terror. **~তা** *n* fearfulness; formidableness.

ভয়াপহ *adj* warding off fear/danger.

ভয়াবহ=ভয়ঙ্কর

ভয়াভয় *n* danger and security.

ভয়াল=ভয়ঙ্কর

ভয়ালু *adj* timid; afraid.

ভর *n* **1** weight; pressure; burden; load. **2** prop; support. **3** reliance; dependence: ভাগ্যের ওপর ~. **4** appearance; epiphany: তার উপর ঠাকুরের ~ হয়. **5** domination; influence; possession; control: ভূতের ~. **6** (phy) mass. **7** excess; abundance; large quantity; bulk; mass; intensity; overabundance: মানভরে, শ্রদ্ধাভরে. ❑*adj* **1** whole; entire: রাত~, ~ সংসার. **2** full; fully stuffed; brimful: ~পেট, bellyful. **3** advanced; mature: ~ সন্ধ্যা বেলা, ~ পোয়াতি. **4** measuring; amounting to: পোয়া~. **~ করা/দেওয়া** *vt* **1** place one's weight on; support one's self: লাঠিতে ~ করে দাঁড়ানো. **2** (of spirits, etc) possess; control; occupy: তার উপর জিন ~ করেছে. **~ হওয়া** *vi* be possessed. **ভরে** (used as a *suff* to form *advv*): আনন্দভরে, gladly, merrily; সাহসভরে, boldly. **~কেন্দ্র** *n* (geom) centroid. **~পুর** *adj* full to the brim; brimful; brimming over with; loaded; laden; packed; teeming ; replete; saturated; suffused; impregnated; imbued; charged. ❑*adv* to the full; to the utmost extent: ~পুর খাওয়া. **~বেগ** *n* (mech) momentum. **কৌণিক ~বেগ** *n* (mech) moment of momentum.

ভরণ *n* **1** filling; stuffing. **2** supporting; maintaining; nourishing. **3** salary; wages. **~পোষণ** *n* feeding, clothing and sheltering; maintenance; subsistence. **~পোষণ করা** *vt* provide with food, clothing and shelter; provide for; maintain; support. **~পোষণকারী** *n* provider; maintainer. **~পোষণোপায়** *n* means of subsistence/support; support; livelihood. **ভরণীয়, ~ণ্য** *adj* to be supported/ maintained/ borne. **ভরণী** *n* the second of the twenty-seven stars according to Hindu astronomy.

ভরত *n* skylark.

ভরতা=ভর্তা

ভরতি=ভর্তি

ভরদ্বাজ *n* skylark.

ভরন[১] *n* bronze.

ভরন,[২] **ভরনা** *n* **1** load; burden; charge. **2** support; prop. **~ দেওয়া**=ভর দেওয়া (⇒ ভর).

ভরন্ত *adj* full; replete; filled.

ভরপুর ⇒ ভর

ভরবেগ ⇒ভর

ভরভর *n* (onom) expressing thorough diffusion of perfume, etc. **ভরভরে** *adj* full to the brim; replete with.

ভরম[১] *n* (poet) dignity; self-respect; honour. **শরম ~** *n* modesty and self-respect.

ভরমে *adv* with deference; respectfully. **ভরমে ভরমে** *adv* before one loses one's honour; honourably.

ভরম[২] *n* **1** illusion; delusion; folly; distraction. **2** bewilderment; perplexity.

ভরসা *n* **1** reliance; trust; confidence; faith. **2** refuge; recourse; haven. **3** hope: আপনিই আমাদের একমাত্র ~. **4** courage; daring: ~ করে বলতে পারি, I dare say. **~ করা** *vi* rely/depend on; put one's confidence/ trust/ faith in; take refuge in; have recourse to. **~ ছাড়া** *vi* give up; lose at/ abandon hope; despair; loose heart. **~ থাকা** *vi* have (a) hope; have confidence/ trust/ faith in. **~ দেওয়া** encourage; hold out hope to; give encouragement; assure; promise support/help. **~ পাওয়া** *vi* be encouraged/ heartened/ reassured/ comforted/ buoyed up/ boosted/ emboldened. **~ যাওয়া** *n* lose hope.

ভরা[১] *vt, vi* **1** fill; stuff; pack in; cram; crowd. **2** insert; enclose: খামে চিঠি ~. **3** load; charge: জাহাজে মাল ~, বন্দুকে গুলি ~. **4** have the feeling of plenitude; be thoroughly pleased/satisfied: তার কথায় মন ভরে গেল. **5** be choked up (with); clog up: ময়লায় নর্দমাটা ভরে গেছে. **6** be filled congested/stuffed (with): সর্দিতে নাক ভরে গেছে. **7** teem (with); abound with: মাঠ লোকজনে ভরে গেল. 8 be replete with; be full to the brim: জোয়ারের জলে নদী ভরেছে. **9** supplement; add: এই টাকার সঙ্গে আরো কিছু টাকা ভরতে হবে. **10** be covered/smeared with: গায়ে ধুলা ~. **11** be diffused/ impregnated/ saturated/ imbued/ suffused with; diffuse; impregnate; permeate; imbue; saturate; suffuse: ফুলের গন্ধে বাতাস ভরে উঠেছে. **ভরে** (incomplete form used as a *prep* or *adj* over; covering; spreading over; to the full; to the point of satiety: কপোল ভরে শিশির ঝরে পড়ছে, পেট ভরে খাও. **ভরে আসা** *vi* **1** fill gradually; (begin to) fill out: তার গালদুটো ভরে আসছে. **2** swell with: অভিমানে তার বুক ভরে এলো. **3** be choked with: কান্নায় তার গলা ভরে এলো.

ভরা[২] *adj* **1** filled; stuffed; full; replete ; jammed; packed. crowded; crammed; congested; **2** loaded; charged. **3** brimful; brimming; (full to) overflowing; bursting; swollen: ~ নদী, ~ পেয়ালা. **4** teeming with; abounding in: মাছ~ পুকুর. **5** diffused/ suffused/ saturated/ impregnated /imbued with: জল~ চোখ, গন্ধে ~ হাওয়া, ভাবে ~ মন, brimful of ideas. **6** glutted; chock-ful (of), choked up; clogged up: ~ নর্দমা. **7** perfect; mature; prime: ~ যৌবন, the bloom/prime of youth. **8** advanced: ~ সাঁঝ. **9** deep; resonant; booming: ~ গলা. **~ জোয়ার** *n* flood-tide.

ভরা[৩] *n* **1** load; cargo; burden. **2** (fully) loaded boat/ vessel; barge. **~ই** *n* loading. **~ভুমি, ~বুড়ি** *n* sinking of a fully loaded vessel; shipwreck; wreck (also fig).

ভরাট *n* filling; earthwork in filling. ❑*adj* **1** thoroughly filled up. **2** deep; resonant; baritone; booming: ~ গলা. **~ হওয়া** *vi* **1** fill out: গাল ~ হওয়া. **2** fill up: পুকুর খাল ~ হওয়া. **ভরাটি** *n* flats; mud flats.

ভরানো *vt* cause to fill/ stuff/ pack/ load/ charge (⇒ ভরা); get filled/ stuffed/ packed/ charged.

ভরিত *adj* **1** filled; stuffed; loaded. **2** nourished; reared.

ভরিমা *n* **1** fullness; plenitude. **2** nourishing; rearing.

ভরি *n* unit of measure for precious metals equal to 180 grains.

ভর্জন *n* roasting ; frying. **ভর্জিত** *adj* roasted; fried.

ভর্তব্য *adj* to be supported/ maintained/ nourished.

ভর্তা[১] *n* **1** husband. **2** master; lord; chief. **3** maintainer; protector; preserver. **ভর্ত্রী** *fem* female supporter/nourisher; wife .

ভর্তা[২] *n* dish of boiled vegetables, fish, etc kneaded to a soft, moist mass and mixed with spices.

ভর্তি, ভরতি *n* admission; hire; employment; filling; stuffing replenishment. ❑*adj* **1** filled; stuffed; replete. **2** employed; hired; admitted into; enrolled: সেনাবাহিনীতে ~, স্কুলে ~, **~ করা** vt 1 fill; stuff replenish; load; pack. **2** employ; appoint: hire; admit; enroll.

ভর্তৃক *n* **1** husband. **2** lord; master; protector; nourisher; cherisher. **3** employer.

ভর্তৃদারক *n* king's son; crown prince. **ভর্তৃদারিকা** *fem* princess.

ভর্ৎসনা *n* **1** reproach; rebuke; censure; reprimand; scolding; chiding; reproof; tongue lashing; talking to; upbraiding. **2** invective; revilement; vituperation. **3** threat; menace. **~**

করা *vt* **1** reproach; rebuke; censure; reprimand; scold; upbraid; talk to. **2** revile; abuse; assail; lash out at; inveigh against. **3** threaten; menace. **ভর্ৎসক** *adj* one who rebukes/ reproaches/reviles/ threatens, etc. **ভর্ৎসনীয়** *adj* reprehensible; censurable; reproachable; blameworthy; condemnable; exceptionable. **ভর্ৎসিত** *adj* rebuked; reproached; reprimanded; scolded, etc. **ভর্ৎসিতা** *fem.*

ভল্ল *n* **1** bear. **2** kind of arrow/missile with a point of particular shape. **~ক** *n* bear. **~কী** *fem.*

ভল্লাত, ভল্লাতক, ভল্লিকা *nn* acajou; cashew-nut; marking-nut.

ভল্লুক, ভল্লূক *n* bear. **ভল্লুকা, ভল্লুকী** *fem.* **~জ্বর** *n* species of transitory fever.

ভস *n* (onom) expressing the noise of falling heap of sand or dust; sudden sinking of the foot into soft earth; splashing. **~ করে** *adv* at once; no sooner than...: চড়ার ওপর পা রাখতেই সেটা ~ করে নেমে গেল. **~ভস** *n* hiss; hissing (sound) ; fizz. **~ভসানো** *vi* hiss; fizz; sizzle. **~ভসানি** *n* hissing; sizzle; fizz. **~ভসে** *adj* hissing; fizzing; sizzling.

ভসম *n* (poet; archaic)=ভস্ম

ভস্কা, ভ্যাসকা *adj* **1** watery; insipid. **2** loose; flabby; boggy; slack.

ভস্ত্রা, ভস্ত্রকা, ভস্ত্রিকা *n* **1** bellows. **2** leathern bottle/vessel (used for carrying/ holding water).

ভস্ম *n* **1** ash; ashes; cinder; slag; clinker; calx. **2** cremated remains of a human body ashes. **~ করা** *vt* reduce/burn to ashes; calcine. **~চাপা** *adj* hidden/smouldering under ashes. **~সাৎ** *adj* reduced/ burnt to ashes; calcined. **~স্তূপ** *n* heap of ashes. **ভস্মাচ্ছন্ন, ভস্মাচ্ছাদিত** *adjj.* **1** covered/ smeared with ashes. **2** (fig) concealed; disguised. **ভস্মাধার** *n* ash-tray; win (as used for holding the ashes of a person whose body has been cremated); ash-bin; ash-can; ash-pan. **ভস্মাবশেষ** *n* remains of anythings burnt; remains of a cremated human body; ashes. **ভস্মাবৃত**=ভস্মাবছন্ন. **ভস্মিত** *adj* **1** burnt/ reduced to ashes. **2** (fig) ruined; destroyed. **ভস্মীকরণ** *n* reducing to ashes; (chem) calcination. **ভস্মীকৃত, ভস্মীভূত** *adj* = ভস্মিত. **ভস্মে ঘি ঢালা** (phrase) flog a dead horse.

ভা *n* **1** brightness; splendour; radiance; light. **2** ray.

ভাই *n* **1** brother. **2** cousin. **3** a near relative or an intimate friend. **4** (as a term of friendly address) gentleman; grandson/ grand-nephews. **~জ** *n fem* brother's wife; sister-in-law. **~ঝি, ~ঝী** *n fem* brother's daughter; niece. **~ঝি-জামাই** *n* niece's husband. **~দ্বিতীয়া** *n* a festival on the second day in the light half of the month of Kartik (on which sisters give entertainments to brothers and mark their foreheads with sandal-paste). **~পুত, ~পো** *nn* brother's son; nephew. **~পো-বৌ** *n fem* nephew's wife. **~ফোঁটা**=~ দ্বিতীয়া. **~বন্ধু, ~বেরাদর, ~ব্রাদার** *n pl* kinsman and relatives; one's own people. **~স্তা, ভাস্তা**=~পো. **~স্তি, ভাস্তি** = ~ঝি.

ভাইটামিন [E] *n* vitamin.

ভাইয়া *n* **1** (chiefly as a term of address)=ভাই. **2** an elder brother.

ভাউলিয়া, ভাউলে *n* small house-boat.

ভাও *n* **1** general condition/ tendency; trend. **2** price; rate. **3** determination; fixation.

ভাওয়া *vi* **1** (poet, archaic) shine; shine forth; appear; be splendid/ beautiful/ eminent/ bright/ luminous. **2** appear as; look like; pass for. **3** be; exist. **4** show; manifest; inhibit.

ভাং=ভঙ্গা

ভাংচি, ভাংচালি *nn* secret dissuasion; bad advice; (wrong) advice/ information given with the intention of discouraging one of the parties or causing rift between them; act of alienating sb secretly; breaking of friendship/ acquaintance/ old habit. **~ দেওয়া** *vt, vi* dissuade/ alienate/ discourage sb by giving him/her wrong advice/information; cause a rift; poison sb's mind against sb.

ভাংতি, ভাঙতি *n* small coins; change.

ভাঁওতা *n* bluff; deception; hoax; dodge; trick; gimmick; subterfuge; ruse. **~ দেওয়া** *vt* bluff; hoax; bilk; deceive; dodge; trick. **~বীজ** *n* bluffer; hoaxer; deceiver; dodger. **~বাজি** *n* bluffing; hoaxing; deception; dodging; trickery.

ভাঁওর *n* **1** trace; mark. **2** guess; seeing; noticing; recognition. **3** manner: কথার ~.

ভাঁওরানো *vt* **1** guess; notice; recognize; determine. **2** compare.

ভাঁজ *n* **1** (also geol) fold. **2** crease; plait; pleat. **3** wrinkle; contraction (of the forehead); furrow; crow's feet. **~ করা** *vt* fold; crease; plait; wrinkle; pucker (up); furrow. **~ হওয়া** *vi* fold; wrinkle; furrow. **~ন** *n* **1** practising vocal music. **2** folding.

ভাঁজা *vt* **1** practise vocal music; hum (a song, etc). **2** fold; crease. **3** exercise with: মুগুর ~. **4** brandish; wave. **5** shuffle (as playing cards). **6** scheme; exercise; hatch; cogitate: ফন্দি ~. **মুগুর ~** *vi* brandish/ exercise with. **সুর ~** *vi* practise vocal music; hum (a song, tune, etc.) **~ই-সেলাই** *n* (book-binding) folding and stitching.

ভাঁটা[১] *n* small wooden ball to play with.

ভাঁটা[২]**, ভাটা, ভাঁটি** *nn* **1** ebb; ebb-tide; low tide; ebbward direction of a stream; downstream direction; downward direction. **2** decline; ebb;

decrease. ~ দেওয়া *vi* row/sail with the ebb-tide. ~ পড়া/লাগা *vi* ebb; begin to ebb; be on the ebb; be at a low ebb; decline; be on the decline. সারাণি(ণী) ~ *n* end/cessation of the ebb-tide; slack water at ebb-tide.

ভাঁটাই=ভাঁটা[1]

ভাঁটি *n* **1** kiln (for buring bricks, etc). **2** oven ; furnace. **3** washerman's trough for boiling dirty clothes; vat; still. **4** distillery. **~খানা** *n* distillery; brewery; liquor-shop. **খোলা ~** *n* public house.

ভাঁড়[1] *n* court-jester; fool; clown; buffoon. **ভাঁড়ামি, ভাঁড়ামো** *n* jesting; buffoonery; drollery; clowning; tomfoolery; monkey tricks; horseplay. **ভাঁড়ামি/ ভাঁড়ামো করা** *vi* clown; play the fool; indulge in buffoonery/ horseplay.

ভাঁড়[2] *n* **1** earthen pot/ vessel. **2** case for containing barber's implements. **3** vessel for containing milk; pail.

ভাঁড়[3] *n* store; store-room; larder; pantry. **ভাঁড়ে মা ভবানী** completely exhausted store; utter indigence.

ভাঁড়াই=ভাঁড়ামি(⇒ ভাঁড়[1])

ভাঁড়ানো *vt* **1** deceive; bluff; bamboozle; beguile; hoodwink. **2** wheedle; cajole; fawn on. **3** impersonate; pass oneself off as; feign; pose aussume a false name/ identity: নাম/ পরিচয় ~.

ভাঁড়াভাঁড়ি *n* **1** deception bluffing; hanky-panky. **2** reciprocal swindling.

ভাঁড়ামি, ভাড়ামো, ভাড়াম⇒ ভাঁড়[1]

ভাঁড়ার *n* **1** store-house; store; store-room. **2** treasury; coffer; fund. **3** granary. **ভাঁড়ারি** *n* treasurer.

ভাঁতি *n* **1** splendour; light; lustre; radiance. **2** kind; sort.

ভাক্ত *adj* **1** of rice. **2** secondary; minor. **3** hypocritical; sanctimonious. **4** false. **5** of a devote; devotional.

ভাক *adj* (used as a *suff*) sharing: অংশ~.

ভাগ[1] *n* **1** division (also math). **2** apportionment; sharing out; partition. **3** part; piece; quarter; fraction; fragment. **4** share; portion; allotment. **5** a division of time: দিবা~, নিশা~. **6** region; part; side; spot; place: নিম্ন~. **7** fortune; lot; luck; fate. **8** inheritance. **9** (arith) numerator of fraction. **10** degree or 360th part of the circumference of a great circle. **~ করা** *vt* divide; distribute; allot; apportion; share out; partition. **~ দেওয়া** *vt* give a share/portion; allow to participate in: কাজের ~ দেওয়া. **~ পাওয়া** *vt* get a share/portion; be allowed to participate in. **~ নেওয়া** *vt* share; take a share; participate in. **~ ক্রিয়া** *n* (alg) dividend. **~চাষি** *n* share-cropper. **~ধেয়** *n* **1** share; portion. **2** revenue; share of a king; tax; impost. **3** lot; fortune; fate. ❑*adj* entitled to a share (as an his/ inheritor). **~ফল** *n* (arith) quotient. **~বাটোয়ারা** *n* apportioning; sharing. **~শেষ** *n* (arith) remainder. **~হর** *adj* taking a part; sharing. ❑ *n* co-heir. **~হার** *n* **1**(arith) (method of) division. **2** sharing; taking a share. **ভাগের মা গঙ্গা পায় না** (prov) what belongs to all belongs to none. **বাড়তি/বাড়ার ভাগ** in addition; moreover.

ভাগ[2] *n* (poet)=ভাগ্য

ভাগনা, ভাগনে *n* (coll)=ভাগিনেয়, **ভাগনি** *fem*=ভাগিনেয়ী

ভাগবত *n* **1** name of the most celebrated and popular of the 18 Puranas (especially dedicated to the glorification of Vishnu-Krishna). **2** follower /worshipper of Vishnu. **3** (derog) hypocrite; sanctimonious person. ❑*adj* **1** relating to/coming from Bhagabat. **2** divine; holy; sacred. **ভাগবতী** *adj fem* relating to devotion to God; devotional.

ভাগা[1] *vi* flee; run away; take to one's heels; escape; steal away; slip away; go off; make off.

ভাগা[2] *n* share; one of the equal parts of a thing; lot.

ভাগাড় *n* **1** ground for dumping dead cows. **ভাগাড়ে গরু পড়া** (fig) (people) scrambling for sth covetable as do vultures for a dead cow.

ভাগানো *vt* **1** put to flight; drive away; chase; rebuff; head off; send packing. **2** seduce; lore (away); entice; allure.

ভাগাভাগি *n* sharing out; apportionment/ partition among partners; allocation; distribution; deal; dispensation; division.

ভাগি *n* (poet; archaic)=ভাগ্য

ভাগিনা=ভাগিনেয়, **ভাগিনী** *fem*=ভাগিনেয়ী

ভাগিনী *fem* of ভাগী

ভাগিনেয় *n* (of a man) sister's son; (of a woman) son of one's husband's sister; nephew. **ভাগিনেয়ী** *fem* niece.

ভাগী[1] *adj* entitled to/ receiving/ possessing a share; partaking of; blessed with; concerned in; responsible for; participating in. ❑*n* partner; sharer; shareholder. **ভাগিনী** *fem*. **~দার** *n* **1**=~. **2** co-heir.

ভাগী[2] *adj* (poet) fortunate.

ভাগীরথী *n* the Ganges; one of the three main streams/ branches of it.

ভাগ্না, ভাগ্নে *n*(colloq)=ভাগিনেয়. **ভাগ্নি** *fem* = ভাগিনেয়ী. **~বউ, ~বৌ** *n fem* wife of a sister's son. **ভাগ্নিজামাই** *n* husband of a sister's daughter.

ভাগ্য *n* **1** fate; luck; chance; destiny; lot. **2** (good) fortune; happiness; welfare; good luck. **3** to be shared/divided; divisible. **~ক্রমে** *adv* in course of fortune; fortunately; luckily by chance. **~গণনা** *n* fortune telling; divination; soothsaying. **~গণনা করা** *vt* foretell; tell one's fortune; soothsay; divine. **~গণনাকারী** *n* fortuneteller; soothsayer; astrologer. **~গুণ** *n* good fortune. **~গুণে** *adv* **1** luckily; by a stroke of good luck/ fortune; by chance. **2** (iron) as luck would have it; because of one's ill-luck; unluckily. **~চক্র** *n* wheel of fortune; ever-changeful fortune. **~চক্রে** *adv* by a turn of fortune's wheel; in course of fortune. **~দেবতা** *n* god or goddess of fortune; destiny; (cf) the fates. **~দেবী** *fem.* **~দোষে** *adj* as ill luck would have it; unfortunately through bad luck. **~পরীক্ষা** *n* trial of luck. **~ পরীক্ষা করা** *vt* try one's luck. **~পুরুষ** *n* destiny ; the divine ordainer of fortune; providence. **~ফল** *n* fruits of one's acts in a former life; one's destiny; astrological reading of one's fortune. **~বক্তা** *n* good fortune; happiness; prosperity. **~বন্ত** *adj* fortunate; lucky; prosperous. **~বল** *n* strength of one's good fortune; fortune's favour. **~বান** =~বন্ত. **~বতী** *fem.* **~বিধাতা** =~পুরুষ. **~বিধাত্রী** *fem.* **~বিপর্যয়, ~বিপ্লব** *nn* reversal/ reverses of fortune; ill-luck; misfortune. **~বৈষম্য** *n* bad fortune; calamity. **~মন্ত** =~বন্ত. **~যোগ** *n* lucky/ fortunate juncture. **~রহিত** *adj* deserted by fortune; miserable. **~লিখন, ~লিপি** *n* one's foreordained fortune (believed by the Hindus to be written by Brahma on his forehead on the 6th day after birth); destiny. **~হীন** *adj* unfortunate; unlucky; luckless; ill-fated; ill-starred. **~হীনা** *fem.* ভাগ্যি *n* (colloq)=~. ❑*adv* luckily; it's fortunate that: ~ সে বাড়িতে ছিল. **ভাগ্যিস** *adv*=ভাগ্যি. **ভাগ্যের হাসিমুখ** *n* smiles of fortune. **ভাগ্যোদয়** *n* rise of fortune; dawning of one's good fortune; rising fortune.

ভাঙ, ভাঙ্গ=ভঙ্গা

ভাঙচি, ভাঙ্গচি *nn* ⇒ ভাংচি

ভাঙড়, ভাঙ্গড়, ভাঙ্গর *adj* addicted to bhang, drugs, etc. ❑*n* **1** bhang addict; addict. **2** Shiva. **~মতি** *adj* out of one's senses as a result of taking bhang.

ভাঙন[১]**, ভাঙ্গন** *n* **1** breaking; break; breach; act of breaking up. **2** erosion: নদীর কূলে ~. **3** rift; disunion; rent; crack; breach: সংসারে ~. **4** fissure; cleft: দেয়ালে ~. **5** deterioration; rift: বন্ধুত্বে ~. **6** disintegration; split: দলে ~. **7** beginning of downfall; decline; decay; breakdown; dissolution: রাজত্বের ~. **~ ধরা** *vi* begin to crumble/come off; disintegrate; erode; dwindle; fall to pieces; break up; crack; start cracking/ disintegrating; decline.

ভাঙন[২], ভাঙ্গন[২] *n* a species of flat fish.

ভাঙা, ভাঙ্গা *vt, vi* **1** break; be broken: গাছের ডাল ~. **3** crack; crumble; fall to pieces; come off; bring/pull down; demolish: দেয়াল ~. **4** fracture; be fractured: হাত/পা ~. **5** smash; dash: মাথা ~. **6** shatter; impair; ruin; deteriorate be shattered/ impaired/ ruined: স্বাস্থ্য ~. **7** erode; be eroded: নদীর পাড় ~. **8** give way. বাড়ির ভিত্তি ~/ভেঙে পড়া. **9** discontinue; break: অনশন ~. **10** break through; breach: শত্রুর ব্যূহ ~. **11** violate; infringe; transgress: আইন ~. **12** dissolve; bring/come to an end: সভা/বিবাহ ~. **13** sever; break off: সম্বন্ধ ~. **14** lose; shatter: আশা ~. **15** fall out (with sb); estrange; be estranged: বন্ধুত্ব ~. **16** disband; break up; disintegrate; be disintegrated: দল ~, সেনাদল ~. **17** disperse: দঙ্গল ~. **18** interrupt: ঘুম ~. **19** discourage; be discouraged/ dejected: মন ~. **20** bend; fold: কাগজটা ভাঙো. **21** obstruct ; impale: গতি ~. **22** become/ make hoarse; crack: গলা ~. **23** remove; dispel; be removed/ dispelled: ভয়/সন্দেহ ~. **24** grind; crash; pound; crunch: পাথর ~, গম ~, দাঁত দিয়ে কিছু ~. **25** open; unseal; unwrap; break open: প্যাকেট ~, দরজা ~. **26** debase; be debased; demean; degrade: কুল ~. **27** soothe; appease: মান ~. **28** sow dissension; alienate; break: ঘর ~. **29** disclose; divulge: কথাটা আমি নাই বা ভাঙলাম. **30** elaborate; give details; expand: ভেঙে বলা. **31** walk; cover; traverse; travel: পথ **~. 32** wade (through): জল/কাদা ~. ❑*adj* **1**=ভগ্ন (which ⇒). **2** breaking: হাড়~~ খাটুনি. **3** debased; weakened. **4** bad; ill: ~ কপাল. **5** broken; faulty: ~ ইংরেজি, ~ ছন্দ. **~ কপাল** *n* bad luck; ill fate. **~ কপাল জোড়া লাগা** (fig) to retrieve one's fortunes; prosper again after a setback. **~চুরা, ~চোরা** *adj* **1** broken; shattered; fragmented; crumbling; dilapidated. **2** uneven; jerky; rough: ~চোরা রাস্তা. **~নি** *n* **1**=ভাংচি. **2** small coins; change. ❑*adj fem* (also ~নী) given to intrigues; sowing dissension; prejudicing sb secretly against. **~নি দেওয়া** *vt*=ভাংচি দেওয়া. **ঘর ~নি** *n fem* woman sowing dissension among the members of a joint family. **~নে** *adj masc.*=~নী. **~নো** *vt* **1** cause to break/ grind/ split/ spoil. **2** change: টাকা ~নো. **3** cash: চেক ~নো. **~ভর্তি** *n* a whole number and its fraction. **~ভাঙা** *adj* **1** almost broken. **2** babbling; stuttering. **3** broken; imperfect: ~ ভাঙা হিন্দি. **~ভঙ্গি** *n* disruption; dissension; disintegration; prejudicing against; crumbling, dissuasion. **ভেঙে আসা** *vi* surge; rush at; scramble (for): চোখের নিমেষে জনতা ভেঙে আসে. **ভেঙে পড়া** *vi* **1**=ভেঙে আসা. **2** crumble; fall to pieces. **ভাঙে তো মচকায় না** (fig) would rather break than bend; be unyielding.

ভাঙ্গা *vi, vt, adj* (old lit)=ভাঙা

ভাঙ্গী *adj* addicted to bhang or hemp.

ভাজ=ভাইজ (⇒ ভাই)

ভাজক *n* (arith) divisior. ❑ *adj* dividing. **~ কলা** *n* (bot) meristem.

ভাজন *n* **1** division; dividing. **2** frying. **3** (used as a *suff*) object; receptacle: প্রণয়~, স্নেহ~. **4**

support; prop. **5** good/ worthy/ deserving person. **6** vessel; pot.

ভাজনা *adj* frying. **~খোলা** *n* fryer; frying; vessel; fry pan. **~খোলা থেকে আগুনে পড়া** out of the frying pan to the fire.

ভাজা *vt* fry; roast; scorch; parch. ❑*adj* fried; roasted; scorched; parched. ❑*n* a dish of anything fried. **~চাল** *n* fried rice. **~পোড়া** *adj* **1** burnt and fried. **2** fried rice, chick-pea, pea, potatoes, etc. **~ভাজা** *adj* **1** almost fried/roasted. **2** (fig) exasperated; extremely irritated; tormented; importuned; pestered; bothered; plagued; chafed: হাড় ~ভাজা. **~ভুজি** *n pl* fried dishes or snacks. **~ মাছটি উলটে খেতে জানে না** (fig) butter will/would not melt in sb's mouth.

ভাজি=ভাজা

ভাজিত *adj* **1** fried; roasted. **2** (arith) by (÷).

ভাজ্য *adj* **1** to be shared/distributed. **2** (arith) to be divided; divisible; dividable. ❑*n* (rith) dividend.

ভাট *n* **1** a particular mixed caste of hereditary panegyrics; professional singer of eulogies; bard. **2** wages; hire; rent; commission.

ভাটক *n* wages; rent; hire; charges; fare; freight; wages; fee.

ভাটকা *adj* stray; wandering; astray; strayed; lost. ❑*n* error; mistake; illusion; delusion. **ভুল~** *n* errors and omissions.

ভাটশালিক *n* the pied myna.

ভাটা, ভাঁটা *n* ebb; ebb-tide. **~ পড়া/লাগা** *vi* **1** ebb (away); begin to ebb; run down recede. **2** (fig) (begin to) decline; dwindle. **জোয়ার ~** *n* tides. **~নো** *vi* **1** ebb; be on the ebb. **2** (of strength fortune, etc.) decline; dwindle; be at a low ebb. **3** (of daytime) decline; become faint; wear on to/towards evening. **4** end; decay.

ভাটি[১]; ভাঁটি *n* **1**=ভাটা. **2** decline; end; even; eventide. **3** lower/low-lying region. **4** south. ❑*adj* mild; low; slight: ~ জ্বাল. **~ গাং** *n* a river on the ebb. **~ বেলা** *n* afternoon. **উজান ~** *n* **1** tides. **2** ups and downs; vicissitude. **3** acclivity and declivity; uneven land.

ভাটি[২] *n* **1** washerman's trough for boiling dirty clothes. **2** still (for making liquors); vat. **3** kiln: চুনের ~. **~খানা** *n* distillery; liquor-shop.

ভাটি[৩] *adj* southern; south. **~ বাংলা** *n* southern part of Bengladesh. **~য়াল** *adj* southern; belonging to the ebb tide; of/from the south: ~য়াল চাল, ~য়াল সুর.

ভাটিয়ারি *n* distiller; brewer. **~খানা** *n* **1** distillery. **2** liquor-shop; den of drunkards.

ভাটিয়ালি *n* a Bengali folk-musical mode: ~ গান.

ভাড়া *n* **1** hire; rent: গাড়ি~, বাড়ি~. **2** freight: রেল~. **3** wages: কুলি~. **4** capital; resource. ❑*adj* hired; rented; hackney. **~ করা** *vt* hire; rent; book **~ খাটা** *vi, vt* hire (out); let on hire; work for hire. **~ দেওয়া** *vt* **1** hire (out); let on hire let sth (to); put out on hire. **2** pay hire/ rent/charges/ freight/ wages/ fare. **~ নেওয়া** *vt*=~ করা. **~ পাওয়া** *vi* obtain the use or services of in return for fixed payment; be available on hire. **~টে** *adj* hired; rented; tenanted; hackney; mercenary. ❑*n* hireling; tenant of a hired/rented house; lessee. **~টে গাড়ি** *n* hackney-carriage; hackney-coach; cub.

ভাণা *vi* (old use, poet) say; tell.

ভাণ্ড *n* **1** vessel; pot; dish; receptacle; case; pitcher; jar; chest; box; vat; pail. **2** musical instrument. **3** capital (money); stock; treasure. **4** barber's razor-case. **5** body. **6** (chem) flask. **~পুট** *n* barber.

ভাণ্ডাগার *n* treasury; treasure.

ভাণ্ডানো *vt* (archaic) deceive; swindle; dodge, hoodwink.

ভাণ্ডার *n* **1** storehouse; store-room; store; depot; treasury; coffer. **2** granary; garner. **3** (arith) fund. **4** centre of a pond. **~করণিক** *n* store-clerk. **ভাণ্ডারে রাখা, ~জাত করা** *vt* store; garner. **~ পূর্ণ করা** *vt* fill one's coffer. **~সহায়ক** *n* depot assistant. **ভাণ্ডারা** *n* place or occasion for charitable distribution of rice/food. **ভাণ্ডারী** *n* **1** treasurer; store-keeper. **2** a particular Hindu family man.

ভাণ্ডিকা *n* (chem) cupel.

ভাণ্ডীর *n* **1** banian-tree. **2** a particular tree (also called ভাঁটগাছ).

ভাত[১] *n* **1** boiled rice. **2** putting rice into a child's mouth for the first time (one of Hindu sacraments). **~কাপড়** *n* food and clothing; maintenance. **~শালা** *n*=ভাণ্ডারা (⇒ ভাণ্ডার). **~ ছড়ালে কাকের অভাব হয় না** (prov) be liberal with your purse and they will liberal with support and flattery. **ভাতে~** *n* a dish of rice boiled with potatoes, lentil and other vegetables. **ভাতে মারা** *vt* deprive sb of his livelihood. **ভাতাসি** *n* aversion to rice due to over-eating.

ভাত[২] *adj* **1** shiny; appearing. **2** manifest; clearly revealed.

ভাতা *n* allowance; ration-money.

ভাতার *n* (sl) husband. **~খাকি, ~খাগি** *n fem* (term of abuse addressed to a married woman) widow; one who has devoured her husband. **~খোর** *n fem* (sl) a woman who has accepted the husbandship or someone other than her husband. **~পুত** *n* (sl) husband and son. **~পুতের মাথা খাওয়া** (term of abuse, curse) be bereaved of one's husband and son.

ভাতারি *adj fem* (term of abuse; vulg) accepting as husband: ভাই~, বাপ~.

ভাতি[1] *n* **1** splendour; brilliance; lustre; radiance. **2** manner; kind; type; bearing.
ভাতি[2] *adj* **1** rice-eating. **2** enslaved to another for one's food or maintenance: পর~.
ভাতিজা *n* brother's son; nephew. **ভাতিজি, ভাতিঝি** *n fem* brother's daughter; niece.
ভাতুড়ি *n* slough.
ভাতুড়ে *adj*=ভাতি[2] (2). ❑*n* wart; mole.
ভাতে *adj* boiled with rice. **আলু~** *n* potato boiled with rice.
ভাদর *n* (poet)=ভাদ্র, **ভাদুরে** *adj* of the month of Bhadra.
ভাদাল *n* **1** the creeper *gandha-bhadaliya*. **2** central part or marrow of the banana-tree; spathe of a plantain-tree before it shoots from the stem.
ভাদ্দর *n* (colloq)=ভাদ্র. **~বউ** =ভাদ্রবধূ. **ভাদ্দুরে** = ভাদুরে (⇒ ভাদর)
ভাদ্র, ভাদ্রপদ *n* the fifth month of the Bengali calendar (from the middle of August to the middle of September.
ভাদ্রবধূ *n fem* a younger brother's wife; sister-in-law.
ভান[1] *n* pretense; pretension; dissimulation; pretext; feigning; fakery; affectation.
ভান[2] *n* **1** splendour; glow; radiance; lustre. **2** knowledge; notion. **3** feeling. **4** beauty. **5** kind; sort.
ভাননে, ভানুনে *n* one who husks rice. **ভাননি, ভানুনি** *fem.*
ভানা *vt* **1** husk (rice). **2** grind; mill (wheat). **~কুটা** *n* husking and grinding. **~নো** *vt* cause to husk/grind/mill. **ধান~ কল** *n* husking machine; rice-mill.
ভানু *n* **1** the sun. **2** ray; beam. **3** Shiva. **4** king. **5** grace; beauty. **~কর** *n* ray of the sun. **~মতী** *adj fem* graceful; beautiful. ❑*n fem* daughter of the king of the Bhojas, celebrated for her knowledge of magic. **~মতীর খেলা/ খেল** *n* magic/ jugglery introduced by Bhanumati.
ভানুরী *n* one who husks rice.
ভান্তঃপ্রদেশ *n* (astron) interstellar space.
ভাপ *n* **1** steam; vapour. **2** heat; warmth. **3** fomentation. **~রা, ভাবরা** *n* steam; vapour. **ভাপ/ভাপরা দেওয়া** *vt* foment. **~সা** *adj* **1** sultry; muggy; stifling; frowzy. **2** musty; stuffy; fuggy; frowsty. **~সানি** *n* sultriness; mustiness. **~সানো** *vi* become sultry; swelter; give out a musty odour.
ভাপা *vi* steam; be slightly boiled. ❑*adj* cooked/ manufactured by the use of steam/vapour; steamed: ~ পিঠা. **~নো** *vt* steam; cook/boil by the use of steam. ❑*adj* = ভাপা *adj.*
ভাব *n* **1** any state of mind or body. **2** way of thinking or feeling. **3** sentiment. **4** emotion; passion: ভাবের উচ্ছ্বাস. **5** opinion. **6** native disposition; manner of being; temperament; character. **7** intention. **8** abstract idea; thought; imagination: ~জগৎ. **9** ecstasy; reverie: ভাবে বিভোর. **10** meditation; contemplation; cogitation: ~মগ্ন. **11** (phil) idea. **12** mood: ভাবান্তর **13** love; attachment; affection; friendship; amity: দুজনে গলায় গলায় ~. **14** peace: আড়ির পরে ~. **15** sense; inner significance; purport; meaning; implication; import: কবিতার ~. **16** acquaintance: তোমার সঙ্গে তো কতো লোকেরই ~. **17** form; shape: নব নব ~. **18** manner: mode; kind: এইভাবে, ওইভাবে. **19** conjecture; supposition. **20** seat of the feelings/ affections; heart; soul; mind. **21** that which is/exists; thing; substance; living creature. **22** becoming; being; existing; occurring; appearance. **23** turning/transition into. **24** state; condition; rank: স্থবির ~. **25** state of being anything: বাল~, the state of being a child, childhood: তনুতা~, state of thinness. **26** true condition/ state; truth; reality. **27** birth; origin. **28** manner of acting; conduct; behaviour. **29** (astron) state or condition of a planet. **30** an astrological house or lunar mansion. **31** (gram) mood. **32** wanton sport; dalliance. **~ করা** *vt* **1** be friends with ; make friends; make friends again; make friends with; make a friend of; make peace with; make acquaintance with; be on amicable terms with. **2** (old use) meditate; contemplate. **~ জাগা/লাগা** vi be under the spell of ecstasy; be affected with an idea/emotion. **~ রাখা** *vt* maintain friendly relations. **~ হওয়া** *vi* become friendly with; be acquainted with; be at peace with; become friendly; scrape an acquaintance with. **~গত** *adj* ideological; abstract; relating to inner significance/ underlying idea/content: নজরুলের ~গত বৈশিষ্ট্য. **~গতি, ~গতিক** *n* mood; attitude and bearing; outlook; inclination: তার ~গতিক ভালো নয়. **~গম্য** *adj* to be (or being) conceived by the mind. **~গম্ভীর** *adj* solemn; grave; full of weighty/ solemn ideas; serious; momentous; stately; ceremonial. **~গর্ভ** *adj* pregnant with ideas; impregnated with (deep) thoughts; profoundly thoughtful; having a deep meaning/significance; full of meanings. **~গ্রাহ্য** *adj* understanding the sense; appreciating the sentiment; capable of reading the inmost thoughts; appreciative; omniscient. **~গ্রাহ্য** *adj* to be conceived by the heart. **~ঘন** *adj* full of thoughts; compact: ~ঘন

ভাষা. ~চক্ষু *n* inner eye; thoughtful look; eyes of imagination ~চিত্র *n* inner thought/idea; conception (of a work of art). ~চৌর, ~চোর *nn* one who steals someone else's ideas. ~তন্ত্র *n* idealism. ~তান্ত্রিক *adj* idealistic. ~তান্ত্রিকতা *n* idealism. ~তরঙ্গ *n* emotional outburst; thought wave. ~তরল *adj* dilated/tremulous with emotion: ~তরল দৃষ্টি. ~ধারা *n* line of thinking; trend of thought. ~নিবিড় *adj*=~ঘন. ~পূর্ণ *adj*=~গর্ভ. ~প্রবণ *adj* sentimental; emotional; maudlin. ~প্রবণতা *n* sentimentalism; emotionalism; sentimentality. ~বাচক *adj* (gram) abstract. ~বাচ্য *n* neuter voice. ~বাদ *n* idealism. ~বাদী *n adj* idealist; idealistic. ~বিলাসী *adj* sentimental; idealistic; visionary. ~বিহ্বল *adj* overwhelmed with emotion; ecstatic; euphoric. ~বোধক, ~ব্যঞ্জক *adjj* signifying/ suggesting a thought or emotion. ~ব্যক্তি *n* expression of an emotion/a thought. ~ভক্তি *n* expression of reverence/respect. ~ভঙ্গি *n* = ~গতিক. ~ভরা *adj*=~গর্ভ. ~ভোলা *adj*=~বিহ্বল. ~ময় *adj*=~গর্ভ. ~মূর্তি *n* ideal/ imaginary shape or concept or form; image; inner form. ~রাখা *vt* maintain friendly relations. ~লহরী *n*=~তরঙ্গ. ~লেশহীন *adj* utterly blank; vacant; expressionless; impassive. ~শুদ্ধি *n* purity of mind/ thought. ~শূন্য *adj* void of affection/ attachment; expressionless. ~সঞ্চার *n* inception/ dawn/ genesis of an idea; transmission of an emotion /idea. ~সন্ধি *n* union/co-existence of two emotions. ~সমাহিত *adj* fixed/ collected in mind. ~সার *n* affection; love. ~হীন *adj* **1** meaningless. **2** blank; expressionless. ~সূচক *adj* = ~ব্যঞ্জক. ~স্থ *adj* being in love; enamoured; collected. ~স্থির *adj* fixed/rooted in the heart. ~স্নিগ্ধ *adj* heartily attached; affectionately disposed. ভাবের ঘরে চুরি (fig) tendency to keep up appearances and neglect the essentials.

ভাবক *adj* **1** thinking; imagining; fancying. **2** producing; creating. **3** promoting/ effecting one's welfare. ❑*n* **1** creator; producer. **2** sentiment; emotion; thought; meditation.

ভাবকানি, ভাবকি *n* **1** threat; scolding; reprimand. **2** grimaces.

ভাবড়া, ভাবরা, ভেবড়া, ভ্যাবড়া *adj* **1** scared; startled. **2** nonplussed; confused; dumbfounded. ~নো *vt* **1** score; startle; frighten. **2** nonplus; confuse; dumbfound.

ভাবন *n* **1** meditation; contemplation; thinking; cogitation; reflection; imagination; apprehension; conception; supposition. **2** consideration. **3** discussion; review. **4** (med) saturating any powder with fluid; infusion; steeping. **5** (Ayu) digestion. **6** ceremonial purification of a person; application of perfume etc; women's toilet. **7** dalliance; flirting. ভাবনীয় *adj* **1** conceivable; thinkable. **2** to be conceived/ imagined/ fancied/ supposed. **3** to be worried/ anxious about.

ভাবনা[১] *n* **1** thought; recollection; contemplation; meditation; imagination; fancy. **2** worry; anxiety. **3** idea; gist; substance.

ভাবনা[২] *n* **1**(med) repeated pulverization and purification/rectification of medicines etc; saturation. **2** (chem) infusion; maceration. ~ করা, ~য় পড়া *vi* worry; be worried.

ভাবনী, ভাবনি, ভাবুনী *nn fem* thoughtful woman; woman fond of/ attached to learning.

ভাবরা *n* ⇒ ভাপ

ভাবরানো, ভাবড়ানো *vi* be anxious/ worried/ confused/non- plussed.

ভাবা[১] *vi, vt* **1** think; cogitate. **2** meditate; contemplate; reflect. **3** recollect; remember: তুমি কি আমাকে একবারও ভাবো? **4** conceive; imagine. **5** consider; regard; judge; take (one) for: বন্ধু বলে ~. **6** intend; resolve: এখন কী ভেবে এসেছ? **7** contrive; devise: একটা কিছু উপায় ভাবো. **8** suppose; guess: তুমি কি ভাবছ সে আসবে? **9** worry (for): সামান্য কারণে এতো ভাবো কেন? ভেবেচিন্তে *adv* upon careful consideration; after serious thoughts; with sufficient reflection.

ভাবা[২] *vt* steam; freeze; congeal: ~ দই.

ভাবাচেকা=ভেবাচাকা(⇒ ভাবা)

ভাবাত্মক *adj*=ভাবগর্ভ(⇒ ভাব)

ভাবানুগ *adj* following the object; natural; simple.

ভাবানুষঙ্গ *n* association of ideas.

ভাবানো[১] *vt* cause to think; cause to worry; worry.

ভাবানো[২] *vt* **1** steam. **2** cause to thicken; curdle: দই ~.

ভাবান্তর *n* another state or condition; change of mental state/mood.

ভাবান্বিত *adj* thoughtful; worried; perturbed ; anxious.

ভাবাবিষ্ট *adj* lost or absorbed in thought/reverie/ ecstasy; overwhelmed with emotion.

ভাবাবেশ *n* absorption in thought/ reverie/ ecstasy; rapture; bliss; elation.

ভাবাভাস *n* **1** simulation of feeling/emotion. **2** faint hint of an emotion; paucity of emotion.

ভাবার্থ *n* **1** purport; gist; inner significance; substance. **2** intention; intent; spirit; purpose.

ভাবালু *adj* **1** thoughtful; compassionate; softhearted; commiserative. **2** sentimental. ~তা *n* sentimentalism; emotionalism.

ভাবি, ভাবী *n fem* brother's wife; sister-in-law. ~জান, ~জি *nn fem* (usually a form of address) respected sister-in-law.

ভাবিক *adj* **1** meaningful. **2** real; natural. **3** full of feeling/sentiment. **4** exciting. **5** future. **6** a figure of speech which consists in describing the part or future so vividly that it appears to be present.

ভাবিত *adj* **1** worried; anxious; troubled. **2** soaked in; obtained; got. **3** proved; established. **4** made to become; transformed into. **5** purified; cultivated. **6** (med) rectified: saturated; infused; macerated. **7** perfumed with; scented. **8** thought about; imagined; fancied; conceived; known; contemplated. **9** pervaded/ inspired by; occupied/ engrossed with; devoted to; intent upon.

ভাবিতাত্মা *adj* meditative; devout, holy ❑*n* saint; sage.

ভাবিনী *adj fem* worried; anxious. ❑*n fem* an attractive woman; an emotional or wanton woman.

ভাবী[1] *adj* about to be; future; imminent; predestined; inevitable; would be. বৈধ ~ **উত্তরাধিকারী** heir-apparent.

ভাবী[2] ⇒ভাবি

ভাবুক *adj* having a taste for the beautiful/ poetical; thoughtful; imaginative; intellectual; introspective; pensive, reflective. ❑*n* thoughtful/ reflective person; intellectual; philosopher. **~তা** *n* thoughtfulness; pensiveness; contemplativeness; imaginativeness. **~তাত্মক** *adj* impulsive: ~তাত্মক ভক্তি.

ভাবুনে *adj* **1** thoughtful; meditative; imaginative. **2** voluptuous; pleasure-seeking. **3** tongue-in-cheek; quippish; prankish: তোর মতো এমন ~ দেখিনি. **ভাবুনী** *fem.*

ভাবে (used as a suff) **1** (equivalent to Eng) -ly: সমান~; in ··· way: এই ~. **2** in the sense of: কথাটা কিভাবে বলল, বোঝা গেল না. **3** for ··· purpose: যে~ই এসে থাক. **4** in the guise of: এই ~ই যাও, তোমার পোশাকটা মন্দ কি?

ভাবোচ্ছ্বাস *n* outburst of emotion/ passion; surge of feeling; ecstasy; yearnings of the heart; impulses.

ভাবোদয় *n* rising of emotion/ passion; dawning of a thought/ an idea; inspiration.

ভাবোদ্দীপক *adj* thought -provoking; thought-inspiring; stimulating.

ভাবোদ্দীপন *n* awakening of an idea/a thought/an emotion.

ভাবোদ্রেক *n*=ভাবোদ্দীপন

ভাবোন্মত্ত *adj* beside oneself with an emotion/ idea/ a thought; worked up; keyed up; delirious; intoxicated with an idea/emotion; ecstatic.

ভাবোন্মাদ *adj* frenzied with emotion. ❑*n* frenzy; abandon; ecstasy; delirium; ebullience.

ভাবোন্মেষ *n*=ভাবোদয়

ভাব্য *adj* **1** about to be; what ought to be/become; inevitable. **2** conceivable; imaginable.

ভাম *n* **1** civet or zebet cat.

ভামা *n fem* angry/passionate woman; vixen.

ভামিনী *n* **1**=ভামা. **2** woman.

ভায় *vi* (poet) 3rd per **1** appear(s); seem(s). **2** shine(s); appear(s)/seem(s) pleasing/ likable.

ভায়রা, ভায়রা ভাই *nn* husband of one's wife's sister; brother-in-law.

ভায়া *n* brother; friend; comrade.

ভায়াদ *n* kinsmen.

ভার *n* **1** weight; load; gravity; heaviness. **2** pressure; burden: ঋণ~. **3** heavy work; toil; trouble; task imposed by someone; charge; trust: কাজের ~. **4** large quantity; collection; mass; heap; bulk: কেশ~. **5** responsibility; encumbrance: অফিসের ~. **6** excess. **7** bamboo pole borne on one's shoulders for carrying loads hanging from its either extremities; yoke; the quantity carried on such a yoke: এক ~ দই. **8** a weight put on a scale-pan to bring it into equipoise with the other scale-pan. **9** unit of weight=16000 tolas (তোলা). ❑*adj* **1** glum; gloomy; down in the dumps; heavy; heavy-laden; heavy-hearted; sad; distraught: মন ~. **2** difficult: hard: তাকে বোঝা ~. **3** unbearable; intolerable; miserable; burdensome: জীবন ~ হলো. **4** heavy; unbearable: কুসুমহার ~ হলো. **5** choked (with): গলা ~. **6** dreadfully still: পরিবেশ ~. **~ করা** *vi* become heavy-hearted/ gloomy; darken with sadness **~ ঘুচানো** *vi* free oneself from a burden/ responsibility; remove a load. **~ চাপানো/দেওয়া** *vt* burden; load; burden sb with; put a burden on; encumber; trouble; saddle; weigh down; overload; pressurize. **~বহন করা** *vi* carry burden/ load; shoulder a charge; bear the responsibility. **~ নেওয়া** *vt* carry burden/ weight/ goods; be loaded; take on or shoulder a responsibility/ charge/ burden/ task. **~কেন্দ্র** *n* (geom, mech) centre of gravity. **~ক্ষম** *adj* able to bear loads (as a ship). **~গ্রস্ত** *adj* burdened; encumbered; weighed down; saddled. **~গ্রাহী** *adj* bearing load. **~জীবী** *n* porter. **~বাহ, ~বাহক, ~বাহী** *nn* one who carries or shoulders a burden; porter; load bearer. ❑*adjj* carrying load/ weight/ burden. **~পড়া** *vi* be loaded; have a weight of responsibility **~ ফেলা** *vi* throw off a load/ weight. **~বাহন** *n* beast of burden; vehicle for loads; cart; wagon. **~বাহী ঘোড়া** *n* pack-horse; draught horse. **~বাহী পশু** *n* pack-animal; beast of burden; draught animal. **~মধ্য, ~মধ্যবিন্দু** *nn* centre of gravity. ~যষ্টি *n* pole/yoke for carrying loads. ~শঙ্কু *n* (mech) lever. ~সহ *adj* able to carry a great load; very strong/ powerful. ~সাম্য *n* balance of power; equilibrium. ~হীন *adj* **1** weightless; having no charge. **2** not loaded; light; not heavy; unburdened; feathery; buoyant.

ভারই=ভারুই

ভারত *n* **1** India; the republic of India; the Indian union. **2** descendant of Bharat (ভরত). **3** the Mahabharata. ~-গৌরব *adj* pride of India. ~ছাড়া *adj* **1** outside India. **2** not available in India. **3** outlandish ; exotic; queer; barbaric. **4** not mentioned in the Mahabharata. ~জাত *adj* produced in India. ~জুড়ে *adv* all over/ throughout India. ~জোড়া *adv, adj* all over India; all India. ~বর্ষ *n*=~ (1). ~বর্ষীয় *adj* of or dwelling in India; Indian. ~বাসী *adj* living in India; Indian. ❑*n* Indian. ~বাসিনী *fem.* ~ময় *adj* all over India. ~ মহাসাগর *n* the Indian Ocean. ~মাতা *n fem* India personified as the common mother of all Indians. ~রত্ন *n* jewel of India the title of highest honour conferred on eminent citizens by the President of India. ~রাষ্ট্র *n* the republic of India. ~ললনা *n fem* Indian woman. ~ সমুদ্র *n*=~ মহাসাগর. ~ সরকার *n* Indian Government; Government of India.

ভারতী *n* **1** speech; voice; word; eloquence; literary composition. **2** language. **3** message; narrative; news; report. **4** the goddess Saraswati. **5** one of the 10 orders of religious mendicants traced back to the pupils of Shamkaracharya (the members of which add the word Bharati to their names)

ভারতীয় *adj* Indian. ভারতীয়া *fem*. পশ্চিম ~ দ্বীপপুঞ্জ *n pl* the West Indies. পূর্ব-~ দ্বীপপুঞ্জ *n pl* the East Indies. ~করণ *n* Indianisation. ~তা *n* state of being Indian. ~তাপাদন *n*=~করণ.

ভারদ্বাজ *n* skylark. ❑*adj* coming from/relating to Bharadvaj.

ভারপ্রাপ্ত *adj* entrusted with charge/ responsibility of; in charge.

ভারভুর, ভারিভুরি *n* **1** ostentation; show; pretension; swank. **2** gravity; reserve; affected importance. **3** honour; prestige; dignity. **4** bossing; patronizing. **3** self-importance; self-assertion . ❑*adj* weighty; heavy.

ভারা *n* **1** scaffold. ~ বাঁধা *vt* build/ erect a scaffold. ~ভারা heaps/ plenty of.

ভারাক্রান্ত *adj* overloaded (as a ship); encumbered; afflicted (with); laden (with); weighted/burdened (with).

ভারার্পণ *n* **1** loading. **2** commitment of a charge; entrusting with a charge. **3** attaching of importance. ~ করা *vt* entrust sb with a charge; commit a charge.

ভারার্পিত *adj* entrusted with a charge.

ভারাবতরণ, ভারাবতারণ *n* taking down/removal of a load from.

ভারি *adv* great; very.

ভারিক *adj* heavy; swollen. ❑*n* porter; carrier.

ভারিক্কি, ভারিক্কে *adj* serious; grave; ponderous; imposing; serious-looking; solemn; having a condescending/patronizing air. ~ চাল ponderous movements; pompous/self important air; airs and graces. ভারিক্কী *fem.*

ভারিভুরি ⇒ ভারভুর

ভারী *adj* **1** heavy; heavily laden; weighty; hefty; ponderous. ~ শরীর. **2** difficult; hard; serious: ~ দায়িত্ব. **3** having an important/grave air; pompous: ~ চালচলন. **4** important; consequential; pretentious: ~ লোক. **5** gloomy: ~ আবহাওয়া/পরিবেশ. **6** afflicted; saddened; heavy; heavy-laden: ~ মন. **7** great; immense: ~ আনন্দ/দুঃখ. **8** full of/abounding in money: ~ পকেট. **9** (iron) nice; dear: ~ তো আমার বন্ধু ! **10** very; extremely; exceedingly: ~ ভালো ছেলে. **11** (iron) too much: আমাকে ~ সাহায্য করেছ. ❑*n* bearer; porter.

ভারুই *n* skylark; quail.

ভার্গী *n* kind of tree; *Clerodendrum siphonuntus*.

ভার্জিত *adj* roasted; fried.

ভার্যা *n fem* wife. ~ট *adj* living by the prostitution of a wife. ~পতি *n* man and wife.

ভাল[১] *n* **1** forehead, brow. **2** fate. **3** splendour, lustere.

ভালাই *n* good; welfare; benefit; weal.

ভালাবুরা=ভালোমন্দ (⇒ভালো)

ভালুক, ভালুক=ভল্লুক

ভালো, ভাল[২] *adj* **1** good; fair; excellent. **2** auspicious: ~ দিন. **3** healthy; whole; sound, in good health: শরীর ~ ? **4** harmless; safe. **5** honest; innocent: ~ মানুষ. **6** proficient; clever; efficient; able: বলতে-কইতে ~. **7** suitable: ~ ক্ষণ. **8** useful; helpful; serviceable: একজন ~ সহকারী, ~ ওষুধ. **9** genuine; authentic; bona fide; pure: ~ টাকা, ~ ঘি. **10** beneficial; wholesome: ~ উপদেশ/ পরামর্শ. **11** quiet; gentle. **12** great: ~ নামডাক. **13** many ; lot of; a great deal: আসরে ~ লোকসমাগম হয়েছিল; সে ~ খেতে পারে. **14** recovered from illness; cured: অসুখ ~ হওয়া. **15** rectified; redeemed corrected; reformed; reclaimed; improved: চরিত্র ~ করা. **16** official; true: তোমার ~ নাম কী? **17** flourishing: ~ ব্যবসা. **18** strong; authentic: ~ দলিল. **19** proper: এটা অনুরোধ করার ~ সময় নয়. **20** becoming; befitting: ~ পোশাক, ~ জবাব. **21** plentiful; sufficient: এবার ~ ফসল হয়েছে. ❑*adv* **1** well: ~ ভালো, এ-ও ~. **2** bravo: ~রে ~. **3** to/in a large number/ amount/ degree: ~ খাওয়া, আসরে লোকজন ~ আসা. ❑*n* **1** welfare; weal; prosperity: ~মন্দ. **2** (spelled ভাল) (archaic) beloved; husband. ❑*int* all right; well. ~ করা *vt* **1** do good; do one a good turn: পরের ~ করা.

2 do well: ওখানে না গিয়ে ~ করেছ. 3 cure; heal: রোগ ~ করা. 4 console; comfort; soothe ; solace: মন ~ করা. 5 improve; rectify; reform; reclaim: চরিত্র ~ করা. **~ করে** *adv* properly; clearly: ~ করে চলো; well; carefully; meticulously; minutely: কাজটা ~ করে করো; at ease: ~ করে বসো; soundly: ~ করে পেটাও. **~ খাওয়া** *vi* eat well; eat much; be accustomed to eat (and drink) choice things; be capable of eating much; eat good food. **~ চলা** (of vehicles, organizations, etc) run well/ smoothly/ properly; function; work/ function well/ smoothly; have sufficient means for subsistence/ other purposes. **~ চাওয়া** wish well. **~ থাকা** 1 be in good health. 2 be happy; have all that one could wish for; be comfortable. 3 live in prosperity; live like a lord; rolling in money: ঘুষের টাকায় সে বড়ো ~ আছে. 4 live honestly; live an honest life; behave (oneself): বড়ো সাহেবের বকুনি খেয়ে সে এখন ~ থাকবে; be quiet/gentle. 5 be in good condition: ওষুধ ছিটালে বইগুলি ~ থাকবে. **~ দেখানো** 1 look well. 2 look beautiful. 3 look healthy; seem to be in good health. 4 appear as becoming/befitting. 5 look honest. **~ বলা** *vt* 1 speak well. 2 speak well of; commend; approve. 3 laud; praise; acclaim; applaud. **~ মনে করা** *vt* think/ consider sth good/ proper/ right/ becoming. **~ মনে হওয়া** seem/ appear good/ proper/ right. **~ মানা** *vt* regard/ accept as good/ right. **~ লাগা** *vt* be to one's liking; appear good to sb; taste/sound/ seem good or well; like; relish; be fond of; enjoy; be attached to. **~ হওয়া** 1suit; fit ; be proper for: জামাটা তোমার ~ হয়েছে, কাজটা ~ হয়নি. 2 recover from illness; come round; be on one's legs; recuperate one's health; be cured: এই ওষুধটা খেলেই তুমি ~হয়ে যাবে. 3 prosper; thrive; be prosperous: তোমার ~ হোক. 4 improve; ameliorate: তার অবস্থা ~ হয়েছে. 5 be beneficial/ profitable; do good to: তার উপদেশে আমার ~ হয়েছে. 6 be corrected/ reformed/ reclaimed; be good: সে দিন দিন ~ হচ্ছে. 7 grow/ fall/ appear abundantly: গত বছর আম ~ হয়েছে, বৃষ্টি ~ হয়েছে. 8 assemble/come in large number: সভায় লোকসমাগম ~ হয়েছে. **~ হয়ে** *adv* 1 properly. 2 on recovery. 3 comfortably. **~ আপদ!** *int* dear me! what a pest! **~ কথা** *n* 1 good counsel ; profitable/good advice. 2 a good word. ❑*int* well. **~র মাথা খাওয়া** 1 (term of abuse) witness the death of one's most beloved one. 2 be ruined. **~মনে** *adv* well; properly; sincerely ; in good faith; open heartedly. **~মন্দ** *adj* 1good and bad; right and wrong. ❑*n* mishap; accident; death; calamity: তার যদি ~মন্দ কিছু ঘটে. 2 choice articles of food; delicacies. **~মানুষ** *n* 1 good man; good soul. 2 honest/ harmless man; guileless person. 3 harmless creature: গরুটি নিতান্ত ~মানুষ, ছেড়ে দিলেও পরের ক্ষতি করে না. 4 (derog) simpleton; addlehead; booby; dullard; blockhead. **~ মানুষ সাজা** pretend to be a good man/ innocent/ guileless. **~মানুষি** *n* 1 honest and blameless conduct; naiveté; simplicity; innocence. 2 (derog) pretence of honesty and innocence. **আর তোমার ~ হোক** (euphem) confound you! Devil take you! **~রে ~** *int* very well. **~য় ~য়** *adv* safely ; in safety; smoothly.

ভালোবাসা, ভালবাসা *n* love; liking; attachment; passion; affection; yearning; tender feelings; fancy; devotion; fondness; friendliness; reverence; amity. ❑*vt* love; like; be enamoured of; be in love with; lose one's heart to; care for; be taken with; have affection/ attachment/ fondness for; cherish; dote on.

ভাশুর *n* elder brother or cousin of one's husband; brother-in-law. **~ঝি** *n fem* daughter of such a brother-in-law. **~পো** *n* brother of such a brother-in-law. **~-ভাদ্রবৌ সম্পর্ক** (fig) from the rigid custom of Hindu women to keep themselves away from the sight of the elder brothers of their husbands.

ভাষ *n* 1 saying; statement; utterance; assertion; declaration; comment; speech. 2 commentary; annotation. **~ক** *n* speaker; talker. **ভাষিকা** *fem*.

ভাষণ *n* act of speaking; talking; speech; utterance; talk; lecture; statement. **~ দেওয়া** *vi* speak; deliver a speech/give a talk; lecture; give a lecture.

ভাষা[1] *n* 1 language; speech. 2 common or vernacular speech; dialect; any Indian Language other than Sanskrit. 3 expression. 4 statement; utterance; mode of speaking. **~চিত্রক** *n* play on words; conundrum. **~জ্ঞ** *adj* versed in languages. **~জ্ঞান** *n* language proficiency; command/ mastery of a language. **~তত্ত্ব** *n* philology; linguistics. **~তত্ত্বজ্ঞ, ~তত্ত্ববিৎ, ~তত্ত্ববিদ** *adjj* versed in philology/ linguistics. ❑*n* philologist; linguist. **~তাত্ত্বিক** *adj* philological; linguistic. ❑*n* philologist; linguist. **~তীত** *adj* beyond language/speech; ineffable; indescribable; inexpressible. **~ন্তর** *n* translation; rendering into another language. **~ন্তরিত** *adj* translated. **~ন্তরিত করা** *vt* render into another language; translate. **~বিজ্ঞান** *n* linguistics. **~বিজ্ঞানী** *n* linguist. **চলিত ~** *n* colloquial speech; one of the two modes of literary Bengali. **দেশী ~** *n* 1 native language. **মৃত ~** *n* dead language.

ভাষা[2] *vt, vi* (poet) 1express. 2 speak; sing; say; tell; announce; declare. 3 explain; comment.

ভাষাসম *n* bilingualism; a sentence so arranged that it may be either Sanskrit or Prakrit.

ভাষিত *adj* spoken; uttered; said. ❑*n* speech; language; talk.

ভাষী *adj* (often used as a *suff)* speaking; saying: বহু~, মন্দ~, ইংরেজি~.

ভাষ্য *n* **1** an explanatory work; commentary; exposition; explanation; annotation. **2** version: কর্তৃপক্ষের ~. ❑*adj* to be spoken/ said/ exposed/ expressed. **~কার** *n* writer of any commentary; commentator.

ভাস[১] **1**light; ray of light; lustre; brightness. **2** glory; splendour; majesty; beauty.

ভাস[২] *n* **1** cormorant. **2** vulture. **3** cock.

ভাসন্ত[১] *adj* splendid; beautiful.

ভাসন্ত[২] *adj* floating; drifting; afloat; adrift; buoyant.

ভাসমান[১] *adj*=ভাসন্ত[১]. **ভাসমানা***fem*

ভাসমান[২] *adj*=ভাসন্ত[২]. **ভাসমানা** *fem*

ভাসা *vi* **1** float; drift; swim; hover; be buoyant; be flooded/inundated/ submerged (with): মাঠ বন্যার পানিতে ভাসছে. **2** rise; occur to; strike/appear in: মনে ~. **3** (fig) be overflowing with. ❑*adj* floating; drifting; adrift. **~ ভাসা** *adj* **1** superficial; shallow; half-baked: ~ ভাসা জ্ঞান. **2** large; wide; fascinating and lovely: ~ ভাসা চোখ. **~ ভাসা জ্ঞান** *n* superficial knowledge.

ভাসাজাল *n* kind of large fishing net.

ভাসান *n* **1** floating. **2** immersion (as an image of a deity). **3** (also **~ গান**) kind of folk-song celebrating activities of some deities.

ভাসানো *vt* **1** float; waft; put a boat afloat/ adrift; launch a ship. **2** flood; inundate; overflow; bear down as the torrent does. **3** cause to rise/ appear/ strike. **4** immerse (as an image of a deity). **ভাসিয়ে নেওয়া** *vt* sweep (away).

ভাসী *adj* shining; brilliant.

ভাসুর=ভাশুর

ভাস্কর *n* **1** the sun. **2** sculptor. **3** fire.

ভাস্কর্য *n* sculpture.

ভাস্বতী *adj fem* shining; luminous; resplendent; bright; brilliant. **ভাস্বন** *mas.* **ভাস্বর** *n* shining; brilliant; resplendent; bright; incandescent. **~দীপ** *n* incandescent lamp.

ভাস্মন *adj* made/consisting of ashes; ashy.

ভি পি [E] *n* **1** V. P. (value payable). **2** Vice-President.

ভিক, ভিখ *n* (colloq)=ভিক্ষা

ভিকারি, ভিখারি=*n*= ভিক্ষুক. ❑*adj* ভিক্ষাজীবী (⇒ ভিক্ষা)

ভিক্ষা *n* **1** begging; asking; solicitation ; earnest request/ prayer; importuning. **2** any boon obtained by begging; alms; dole. **3** charitable/ gracious gift; service. **~ করা** *vt* **1** beg anything (esp alms). **2** live by begging. **3** wish for; desire; request/ pray earnestly; solicit; importune. **~ দেওয়া** *vt* give alms; dole (out); give/ grant (sth) charitably or condescendingly. **~চর** *adj, n* going about begging; mendicant. **~চর্যা** *n* living on alms; begging. **~জীবী** *adj* living by begging/on alms. ❑*n* mendicant. **~জীবিনী** *fem.* **~ন্ন** *n* food obtained as alms. **~পাত্র** *n* mendicant's bowl; alms-dish. **~প্রার্থী** *adj* begging alms. ❑*n* beggar. **~বৃত্তি**=~চর্যা. **~ভাণ্ড**=~পাত্র. **~র্থী** *n, adj* asking for alms; beggar; mendicant. **~র্থিনী** *fem.* **~লব্ধ** *adj* obtained by begging. **~শী** *adj* eating begged food. ❑*n* beggar. **~র চাল কাঁড়া আর আঁকাড়া** (fig) Beggars can't be choosers ; Don't look a gift horse in the mouth.

ভিক্ষু *n* **1** beggar; mendicant. **2** religious mendicant (esp a Brahmin in the fourth Asrama or period of his life when he subsists entirely on alms). **3** Buddhist mendicant/ monk. **4** disciple of Buddha. **~নী** *fem* Buddhist nun.

ভিক্ষুক *adj* begging; soliciting. ❑*n* beggar; mendicant; humble petitioner; a Brahmin of the middle order. **~ রমণী** *n fem* female mendicant; beggar-woman. **~ সম্প্রদায়** *n* beggardom. **ভিক্ষুকাশ্রম** *n* the fourth Asram or period of life of a Brahmin.

ভিখ *n* (colloq) alms. **~ মাগা**=ভিক্ষা করা. **গেঁয়ো যোগী ভিখ পায়না** (prov) A prophet is never honoured in his own country.

ভিখারি, ভিখারী, ভিখিরি (colloq) *n* = ভিক্ষুক. **ভিখারিনী** *fem.* **পথের ~** *n* **1** a street beggar. **2** (fig) pauper; utterly resourceless and indigent person.

ভিজন *n* getting wet in the rain.

ভিজা *vi* **1** get wet; be drenched (eg with rain); soak (in water); get soaked (through). **2** soften by being steeped in water or any other water. **3** soften emotionally; appease; indulge; pacify; please: মন ~. ❑*adj* **1** wet; drenched; dripping; soaked; saturated. **2** tearful; tear-stained, moist: ~ চোখ. **3** humid; damp; dewy; dank; misty; muggy; clammy: ~ হাত, ~ বাতাস. **~নো** *vt* make wet; soak; drench; douse; saturate; sodden; steep in water, etc; moisten; souse; damp; dampen. ❑*adj* soaked; drenched; moistened; saturated. **~ বিড়াল** *n* (fig) a wolf in ship's skin.

ভিজিট [E] *n* a physician's fee for a professional call or visit.

ভিজে (colloq) *adj* =ভিজা. **~ বেরাল**=ভিজা বিড়াল (⇒ বিড়াল)

ভিটকিলিমি *n* hypocrisy; imposture; deception; pranks.

ভিটা, ভিটি, ভিটে *n* **1** piece of ground on which a dwelling-house is built; foundation. **2** ancestral home. **~ছাড়া** *adj* ejected/ ousted from one's homestead or ancestral home; displaced from one's country. **~ছাড়া লোক** *n* displaced person. **~মাটি** =~. **~মাটি উচ্ছন্ন করা/চাটি করা** (fig) raze one's homestead to ground. **~য় ঘুঘু চরানো/সর্ষে বুনে দেওয়া** (fig) render a person homeless; ruin sb utterly; lay waste/ desolate sb's homestead.

ভিটামিন [E] *n* vitamin.

ভিটে ⇒ ভিটা

ভিড়, ভীড় *n* **1** crowd; throng; array; mob; mass; jam; swarm; host; multitude; the rabble. **2** assembly; assemblage; bevy; concourse; gathering ; galaxy: সুন্দরীদের ~. **3** rush; deluge: কাজের ~. **~ করা** *vi* crowd; throng; swarm; overcrowd; flock; huddle (together); mass; rush; teem. **~ ঠেলা** *vi* elbow/shoulder one's way through a crowd. **~ভাড়** *n* a large crowd.

ভিড়া *vi* **1** (of boats) come to the coast/bank ; draw up; come to lands; touch/get to (the bank, jetty, etc); touch at; cast anchor. **2** (of persons) associate with; join forces; team up; align; ally: দলে ~. **3** assemble; appear; gather: এ লোকটা আবার কোত্থেকে এসে ভিড়ল? **ভিড়ানো** *vt* **1** bring/ get to; bring to the coast/ bank ; moor; berth; anchor; dock; draw up. **2** cause to associate with; win over; coax sb (into).

ভিত *n* **1**foundation ; base; plinth. **2** wall; partition. **3** direction; side; point of the compass: চারি~. **4** place; spot. **5** shore; bank.

ভিতর *n* interior; inside; inner part; middle; interval; space of time. ❑*adj* inner; intimate; internal; inside inward. ❑*prep, adv* in; within; into; inside; in the midst of; amidst. **ভিতরের কথা/ খবর** *n* secret; inside story/ information. **ভিতরের ব্যাপার** *n* internal affair; secret. **~ দিক** *n* inside; inward direction/ portion. **~ বাড়ি** *n* female/inner apartments; gynaeceum. **~-বাহির** *n* the inside and the outside; ins and outs. **~-বাহির এক** *adj* sincere; candid ; frank; unpretended. **~বুদে** *adj* **1** uncommunicative; close-mouthed; tight-lipped; inarticulate; mousy. **2** dull; dull-witted; obtuse; dim-witted. **~-ভিতর, ভিতরে ভিতরে** *advv* at heart; inwardly; secretly; surreptitiously; underhandedly; under cover; covertly. **~ মহল**=~ বাড়ি. **ভিতরে** *prep, adv*=~.

ভিত্তি *n* **1**=ভিত (1,2). **2** cause; basis; ground. **3** fragment; portion; bit. **~প্রস্তর** *n* foundation-stone. **~ভূমি** *n* foundation; groundwork; basis; footing. **~মূল** *n* bottom of a foundation; base; plinth; bed rock; bed piece; substratum. **~স্থাপন করা** *v* lay the foundation of. **~শূন্য, ~হীন** *adjj* groundless; baseless; unfounded; flimsy; without foundation.

ভিদভিদে *adj* deceitful; tortuous.

ভিদা *n* splitting; bursting; destroying; destruction; cutting; boring; punching. ❑*vt*=ভেদা (⇒ ভেদ) **~নো**=ভেদানো (⇒ ভেদ).

ভিদ্য *adj* to be split/ burst open/ pierced/ split/ broken; capable of being pierced, split, etc. **~মান** *adj* piercing; splitting; cutting; breaking; bursting.

ভিন *adj* (colloq)=ভিন্ন. **~দেশ** *n* another country; foreign land. **~দেশী** *adj* foreign; exotic. ❑*n* foreigner; alien.

ভিন্দিপাল *n* short javelin/arrow thrown from the hand or shot through a tube.

ভিন্ন *adj* **1** other; different; separate; distinct; different from; other than. **2** split; torn; severed; broken; shattered; pierced; destroyed. **3** separated; isolated; segregated; estranged. **4** detached; disjoined; loosened; disunited; set at variance. **5** parted; partitioned; divided into parts. **6** opened; expanded; blown. **~ক্রম** *adj* out of order/ place; displaced. **~ জাতি** *n* different caste/ race. **~জাতীয়** *adj* of a different kind/sort; of a different nation/ caste/ tribe/ race. **~জাতীয়া** *fem.* **~তা, ~ত্ব** *nn* difference; otherness; state of being different from. **~ দেহ** *n* **1** another body. **2** wounded body. **~ ধাতু** *n* (fig) different stamp/ stuff. **~ ধাতুর লোক** man of a different stamp; man made of a different stuff. **~প্রকার** *adj* of a different kind/sort. **~ বর্ণ** *adj* of a different caste/tribe. **~ বর্ণ** *n* different colour. **~বাসী** *adj* (bot) dioecious. **~ বৃত্তি** *n* different occupation. **~ মত** *n* different opinion. **~মত** *adj* dissenting; disagreeing in opinion. **~ মতাবলম্বী** *adj* dissenting. ❑*n* dissenter. **~মতাবলম্বিনী** *fem.* **~ রুচি** *adj* having a different taste.

ভিন্নার্থ *n* different meaning. ❑*adj* having a different meaning; having different aims. **~ক** *adj* =~.

ভিমরাজ=ভৃঙ্গরাজ

ভিমরুল, ভীমরুল *n* hornet. **ভিমরুলের চাকে খোঁচা দেওয়া** stir up a hornet's nest; bring a hornet's nest about one's ears.

ভিয়ান, ভিয়েন (colloq) *n* making of sweetmeat; confection. **~ করা** *vt* make (sweetmeat). **~ ঘর** *n* a room for making sweetmeat; confectionery.

ভিয়োলা [E] *n* viola.

ভিরকুটি *n* **1**contraction of the brows; frown. **2** grimace. **3** audacity; impudence.

ভিরমি, ভির্মি *n* vertigo; dizziness; giddiness; fainting; swoon. **~ খাওয়া/লাগা** *vi* have vertigo; be dazed/stupefied; faint; swoon.

ভিল *n* a wild mountain race of India; member of that race.

ভিল্ল=ভিল. **ভিল্লী** *fem*

ভিষক *n* healer; physician. **~প্রিয়া** *n* the plant *Coccalus cordifolius.*

ভিসা [E] *n* visa.

ভিস্তি, ভিস্তী [P] *n* **1** leather-bag for carrying water; water-bag. **2** water-carrier. **~ওয়ালা**=~ (2).

ভীড় *n* ⇒ ভিড়

ভীত *adj* frightened; alarmed; terrified; afraid; anxious about. **ভীতা** *fem.* **~ করা** *vt* frighten; alarm; scare. **~চিত্ত** *adj* timid; faint-hearted; timorous; diffident; lily-livered; cowardly; unmanned.

ভীতি *n* fear; alarm; dread; fright; awe; horror; diffidence; timidity; dismay; consternation; misgiving; threat. **~কর, ~জনক, ~প্রদ** *adjj* causing/exciting fear; frightening; awe-inspiring; awful; fearful; alarming; dreadful; terrible; frightful; dreadful; terrifying. **~প্রদর্শক** *adj* threatening; menacing. **~প্রদর্শিকা** *fem.* **~প্রদর্শন করা** *vt* threaten; menace. **~বিহ্বল** *adj* terror-stricken; awe-stricken; intimidated; unmanned; overawed; horrorstricken; terrified ; aghast; petrified

ভীতু *adj* timid; cowardly; timorous; faint-hearted; chicken-hearted.

ভীম *adj* fearful; terrific; terrible; awful; formidable; tremendous. ❑*n* the second son of king Pandu. **ভীমা** *fem.* **~ একাদশী** *n* the eleventh day of the light half of the month of Magh. **~কর্মা** *adj* terrible in act; dreadful; very active. **~দর্শন** *adj* frightful in appearance. **~দ্বাদশী** *n* the twelfth day of the light half of the month of Magh. **~নাদ** *n* **1** a terrific sound. **2** lion. **~পরাক্রম** *adj* possessing formidable power/ prowess. **~পলশ্রী, ~পলাশী** *n* a particular Indian musical mode. **~বিক্রম** = ~পরাক্রম. **~বিক্রান্ত** *adj* terribly powerful/ courageous. **~বেগ** *n, adj* (of) fearful speed. **~মুখ** *adj* of fearful aspect/ appearance. **~সেন** *n* **1**= ~ (1). **2** a kind of camphor produced in Sumatra and Borneo.

ভীমরথী, ভীমরতি (colloq) *n* senility; dotage. **~গ্রস্ত** *adj* senile.

ভীমরুল ⇒ ভিমরুল

ভীমা ⇒ ভীম

ভীরু *adj* fearful; timid; cowardly; afraid of. **ভীরু** *fem.* **~ ব্যক্তি** *n* coward; poltroon; dastard; sneak; faint-heart. **~চিত্ত** *adj* faint hearted; timid; chicken-hearted. **~তা** *n* timidity; cowardice; fearfulness; dread of. **~প্রকৃতি, ~স্বভাব** *adjj* fearful/timid by nature; timorous.

ভীল=ভিল

ভীষণ *adj* terrifying; frightening; formidable; horrible; terrible; tremendous; severe; monstrous; hideous; grotesque; gruesome; outrageous; horrid; macabre. **~ আকার** *n* monstrous form. **~ আরাব** *n* terrific sound. **~তা, ~ত্ব** *n* terribleness; horribleness; monstrosity; awfulness; severity; tremendousness. **~দর্শন** *adj* terrific in appearance. **ভীষণাকার** *adj* monstrous in form; grotesque.

ভীষিত *adj* frightened; terrified.

ভীষ্ম *n* Name of a son of Shantanu and Ganga (in the Mahabharata). ❑*adj* terrible; dreadful. **ভীষ্মাষ্টমী** *n* the eighth day of the light half of the month of Magh. **ভীষ্মের প্রতিজ্ঞা** *n* an unalterable/resolute vow or pledge (like that of Bhishma); firm resolve.

ভুঁই *n* **1** the earth; soil ; ground. **2** territory; country; district. **3** place; site; situation. **4** agricultural land; field; land. **~চাঁপা** *n* kind of fragrant flower; *Kaemferia rotunda.* **~ফোড়, ~ফোঁড়** *adj* **1** upstart; mushroom. **2** baseless; imaginary; fanciful: ~ফোড় তত্ত্ব. ❑*n* upstart; parvenu; nouveau riche. **~মালী** *n* one of the Hindu sweeper community.

ভুঁইঞা, ভুঁইয়া, ভূঁইয়া *n* **1** landlord; landholder. **2** (hist) any one of the twelve feudal princes governing Bengal during the Mughal rule. **3** a particular family name.

ভুঁকা *vi* (archaic) pierce; prick. **~নো** *vt* push.

ভুঁড়া[১] *n* pea-pod.

ভুঁড়া[২] *n* **1** a bolster like container made of straw for preserving paddy. **2** the topmost part of a thatched roof.

ভুঁড়া[৩]**, ভুঁড়ো** *adj* powdered: ~ চুন.

ভুঁড়ি *n* **1** pot-belly; paunch; corporation. **2** (facet) belly. **3** pea. **~দার** *adj* pot-bellied. **~ হওয়া** *vi* grow pot-bellied.

ভুঁড়ে, ভুঁড়ো *adjj* pot-bellied; paunchy .

ভুঁদী *adj fem* of ভোঁদা

ভুঁদো=ভোঁদা

ভুক[১]**, ভুক-ভুক** *nn* (onom) suggesting a sound like that of liquid entering or passing out of a narrow-necked vessel.

ভুক[২]=ভুখ

ভুক[৩] *suff* eating; subsisting on: পিপীলিকা~.

ভুক্ত *adj* **1** eaten; enjoyed; made use of; possessed. **2** included/ incorporated/ comprised in: তালিকা~. **~পূর্ব** *adj* enjoyed before. **~ভোগ** *n* what has made use of/ used/ enjoyed/ suffered. **~ভোগী** *adj* having had similar suffering or experience in the past. ❑*n* sufferer. **~ভোজন** *n* rumination. **~শেষ, ভুক্তাবশিষ্ট, ভুক্তাবশেষ** *nn* ruminants of a meal; leavings.

ভুক্তন *n* **1** amends; rectification; correction; reparation. **2** entry. **3** enjoyment consumption.

ভুক্তি *n* **1** enjoyment; eating; consuming. **2** possession as one's own. **3** inclusion; incorporation; comprisal. **4** entry: অভিধানে/ খতিয়ানে ~. **5** a province under occupation; administrative division: তীর~.

ভুখ *n* **1** hunger. **2** thirst for worldly possessions. **~মিছিল, ভুখা-মিছিল** *nn* hunger-march. **ভুখা** *adj* hungry. **ভুখা ভগবান** *n* the hungry masses; the proletariat; the have-nots.

ভুগনি *n*=ভুগানি

ভুগা, ভোগা *vi, vt* suffer; experience; undergo; be rewarded/ requited for; sustain; suffer from; be afflicted/ harassed/ punished/ troubled with; pass through: কষ্টে ~, জ্বরে ~, তোমাকে আরো অনেক ভুগতে হবে. **~নো** *vt* cause to suffer/ undergo; give persistent/ constant trouble; afflict; trouble; harass; punish; torment; gall; chasten. **~নি** *n* suffering; affliction; trouble; torment; harassment.

ভুজ *n* **1** arm; hand. **2** side. **3** side of any geometrical figure; abscissa; arm: ত্রি~, চতুর্ভুজ. ❑*adj* having sides. **ভুজা** *fem:* দশ~. **~কোটর** *n* armpit. **~কোটি** *n* (germ) co-ordinates. **~পাশ, ~বন্ধন** *nn* snare/clasp of one's arms; embrace; hug; cuddle. **~পাশে /~বন্ধনে বাঁধা** *vt* clasp in one's arms; embrace; cuddle; hug. **~বল** *n* strength of one's arms; might; prowess. **~মধ্য** *n* breast. **~লতা** *n* a long slender arm. **~শিরঃ** *n* shoulder. **~স্তম্ভ** *n* paralysis of the arms. **অতি~** *n* (geom) hypotenuse. **চতুর্ভুজ** *n* (geom) quadrilateral. **ত্রি~** *n* (geom) triangle. **দশ~** *n* (geom) decagon. **পঞ্চ~** *n* (geom) pentagon. **বহু~** *n* (geom) polygon. **বিষম~** *n* (geom) scalene. **ষড়~** *n* (geom) hexagon. **সপ্ত~** *n* (geom) heptagon. **সম~** *n* (geom) equilateral. **সমদ্বি~** *n* (geom) isosceles.

ভুজং ভাজাং *n* false/flimsy arguments/ allurements/consolation: ~ দিয়ে টানা.

ভুজগ *n* **1** snake; serpent. **2** lecher; debauchee. **ভুজগী** *fem.* **ভুজগান্তক, ভুজগাশন** *nn* **1** serpent destroyer/serpent eater. **2** the Gadura. **3** peacock.

ভুজঙ্গ, ভুজঙ্গম *n* **1**=ভুজগ (1) . **2** tin; lead. **ভুজঙ্গিনী, ভুজঙ্গী , ভুজঙ্গমী** *fem* **1** female snake; serpent-maid. **2** malevolent/vicious woman. **~ভুক** *adj* serpent eating. ❑*n* **1** the Gadura. **2** peacock.

ভুজা *adj* fried: ভাজা~. **~ই** *n* frying.

ভুজাংশ *n* (astron) celestial longitude.

ভুজাগ্র, ভুজাদল *nn* hand.

ভুজান্তর *n* **1** other arm. **2** breast.

ভুজালি=ভোজালি

ভুঞা, ভুঁয়া, ভুইঞা=ভুঁইঞা

ভুঞ্জন *n* enjoyment ; eating; consumption.

ভুঞ্জা *vt, vi* (poet, archaic) **1** suffer; enjoy; experience. **2** eat; consume. **~নো** *vt* make/ cause sb to enjoy/ eat/ suffer.

ভুঞ্জিত *adj* eaten; enjoyed; suffered; undergone.

ভুটভাট, ভুটভুট, ভুটরভাটুর *nn* (onom) denoting sounds as gas moves through the bowels; rumbling in the bowels.

ভুট্টা *n* maze; mealie; (US) corn.

ভুড়ভুড় *n* (onom) suggesting sound of sth sinking slowly in muddy water; effervescence; bubble.

ভুড়ভুড়ি *n* effervescence; bubble; bubbling up; froth; foam. **~ ভাঙা** *vi* bubble; effervesce; ferment; bubble up; fizz; froth; foam.

ভুতড়ি, ভুতুড়ি *n*=ভুতি

ভুতি *n* inedible core and pulp of a jack-fruit.

ভুতুড়ে *adj* **1** relating to ghosts; done by ghosts; ghostly: ~ গল্প, ghost-story. **2** haunted: ~ বাড়ি. **3** ghostlike; spectral; spooky; wraithy; eerie; uncanny; weird: ~ পরিবেশ.

ভুনি, ভুনী *adj* fried. **~ খিচুড়ি** *n* a particular dish made cooked by frying rice and lentil in clarified butter.

ভুবঃ *n* (according to Hindu mythology) the second of the seven heavens; the eternal region; sky; firmament; atmosphere.

ভুবন *n* **1** world; earth; universe. **2** (myth) seven heavens and seven underworlds. **3** abode; residence. **4** a being; living creature; man; mankind. **~জয়ী** *adj* world conquering. **~ত্রয়** *n* the three worlds (heaven, earth and underworld). **~পাবন** *adj* world-purifying. **~পালক** *n* preserver of the worlds. **~বিখ্যাত** *adj* world-famous. **~বিজয়ী** *adj*=~জয়ী. **~বিজিত** *adj* known all over the world. **~ব্যাপী** *adj* worldwide; universal. **~ভুলানো** *adj* enchanting the whole world; holding the world under a spell. **~ময়** *adv* all over the world. **~মনোমোহিনী** *adj fem* captivating the minds of all people of the world. **~মোহন** *n* fascinating the whole world. **~মোহিনী** *fem.* **~হিত** *n* welfare of the world.

ভুবনেশ্বর *n* **1** lord of the world. **2** name of a sacred temple and city in India.

ভুবনেশ্বরী *n fem* **1** mistress of the world. **2** one of the ten manifestations of the goddess Durga.

ভুবর্লোক=ভুবঃ

ভুয়া, ভুয়ো *adj* unsubstantial; false; hollow; empty; unreal; flimsy; baseless; airy; illusory; vaporous.

ভুর *n* **1** illusion; delusion; error; misconception. **2** pretension; humbug. **~ ভাঙা** *vt* remove a wrong notion ; disillusion; open the eyes of; disabuse (of).

ভুরভুর *n* (onom) suggesting thorough diffusion with fragrance/ perfume; gratification arising from agreeable scent. ~ করা *vi* permeate (through). ❑*adj* charged/laden with; saturated with: গন্ধে ~. ভুরভুরে *adj* drunk; intoxicated; intoxicating.

ভুরা *n* kind of unrefined and coarse sugar. ❑*adj* powdery; free from moisture.

ভুরু *n* eyebrow.

ভুরো (colloq)=ভুরা

ভুল *n* **1** error; mistake; blunder; howler. **2** omission; oblivion; inadvertence; inattention; oversight; negligence. **3** delirium; wanderings: ~ বকা. ❑*adj* erroneous; mistaken; incorrect; wrong; inaccurate; improper; bad: ~ জবাব. ~ **করা** *vi* be in error; be mistaken; err; blunder; mistake/confess (one for the other); forget; be guilty of omission. ~ **বকা** *vi* become delirious; suffer from delirium; wander. ~ **ভাঙা** *vt,vi* **1** disillusion; open the eyes of; disabuse. **2** be disillusioned/ disabused; be freed from mistake/ error. ~ **হওয়া** *vi* be mistaken; fall into error; be wrong/incorrect. be inadvertent/ forgetful/ oblivious (of). ~**ক্রমে** *adv* by mistake. ~**চুক**, ~**ভাটকা**, ~**ভ্রান্তি** *nn* errors and omissions. **ঠিকে** ~ *n* **1** error in addition; error in fundamentals; silly mistake. **2** mistake in giving the full measure. ~ **করে** *adv*=~ক্রমে. ~**ন** *n* forgetfulness; forgetting. **ভুলের মাশুল দেওয়া** *vi* pay for one's mistake/ folly/ thoughtless act.

ভুলা, ভোলা *vi* , *vt* **1** forget; be forgetful; lose sight of; think no more of; fall/sink into oblivion; let bygones be bygones; efface from the memory; escape/slip one's memory. **2** omit. **3** mistake; err; blunder. **4** be indifferent/ callous to: আত্মসম্মান ~. **5** be enticed/ lured/ inveigled/ deceived/ tempted: প্রলোভনে ~. **6** be cajoled/ coaxed/ wheedled: মিষ্টিকথায় ~.**7** be charmed/ bewitched/ enchanted: চেহারা দেখে ~. **8** be consoled/ comforted/ soothed/ calmed: প্রবোধবাক্যে মন ভুলবে. **ভুলে যাওয়া** *vt* forget. **ভুলে-যাওয়া** *adj* forgotten; unremembered. **ভুলানো, ভোলানো** *vt* **1** cause to err/ mistake/ blunder; mislead; lead astray misguide; trip up. **2** cause to forget/omit. **3** entice; dupe; lure; inveigle; be guile; deceive; tempt; delude. **4** cajole; coax; wheedle. **5** charm; bewitch; enchant; put under a magic spell; enthrall. **6** console; comfort; soothe; calm. ❑*adj* **1** causing to err/mistake. **2** making forgetful. **3** enticing; alluring; tempting; beguiling; taking. **4** coaxing; seductive; bewitching; winning; charming; enchanting; fascinating. **5** consoling; comforting; soothing. ছেলে~ ছড়া *n* nursery rhyme.

ভুলানো, ভুলুনে *n* **1** one who charms/ bewitches/ tempts/cajoler/ wheedles/ entices/ lures. **2** deceiver; swindler; cheat. ❑*adj* enchanting; charming; insidious; fascinating; seducing; alluring; bewitching; captivating; enticing. **ভুলানি, ভুলানী, ভুলুনি, ভুলুনী** *fem.*

ভুলো *adj* **1** forgetful; oblivious; unmindful; absent-minded. **2** inexperienced; clumsy; inept. ❑*n* (term of endearment) Shiva.

ভুশ *n* (onom) suggesting **(a)** sound of dry; loose soil subsiding suddenly and easily; plank; **(b)** sound of springing up from under water, mire, etc; the sound made by a porpoise or other cetaceous animal when it rises out of water, also sound made by man/other animal which has dived on its coming to the surface. ~**ভুশ** *n* repeated of the above kind sound. ~**ভুশে** *adj* loose; floppy; *soundly;* friable.

ভুশণ্ডি, ভুশুণ্ডী, ভুশণ্ড, ভূষণ্ডী *nn* **1**(myth) an omniscient jackdaw/crow. **2** (usu facet) a very long lived person having wide experience.

ভুষা=ভুসা

ভুষি, ভুষী, ভুসি *n* husk; chaff; bran. ~ **মাল** *n* **1** refuse; waste matter; chaff; rubbish. **2** leguminous seeds like beans, peas, centils; pulse. ~**মালের খরিদদার** *n* **1** buyer/ customer of pulse. **2** (derog) contemptible customer. ~**মালের ব্যাপারী** *n* pulse merchant; pulse-dealer.

ভুষুড়ি *n*=ভুতি

ভুষুণ্ডি *adj* covered with: ধুলায় ~.

ভুষ্টিনাশ *n* annihilation; destruction; ruin.

ভুসা, ভুসো *n* **1** ashes of burnt rice, paper, etc. **2** soft. **3** lampblack (used as a collybrium and applied to eyelashes and eyelids). **4** ink. ❑*adj* sooty; ashen.

ভুসি ⇒ ভুষি

ভুসুণ্ডি, ভুসণ্ডী *n* kind of fire-arm.

ভূ *n* **1** the earth; world; universe; space. **2** underworld. **3** land; ground; soil; landed property: ~সম্পত্তি. **4** floor; pavement; piece of ground. **5** sacrificial fire. ~**কম্প**, ~**কম্পন** *nn* earthquake. ~**কম্পবিদ্যা** *n* seismography. ~**কম্পলিখ** *n* seismograph. ~**কর্ণ** *n* radius of the equator. ~**কেন্দ্রীয়** *adj* (astron) geocentric. ~**কেশ** *n* lichen; moss. ~**খণ্ড** *n* division/part of the earth; region; country. ~**গর্ভ** *n* bowels/ inside of the earth; subterranean region. ~**গর্ভস্থ**, ~**গর্ভস্থিত** *adjj* lying in the bowels of the earth; subterranean; underground. ~**গর্ভস্থ রেলপথ** *n* underground railway; tube-railway. ~**গহ্বর** *n* underground cavity/hole; cavern; underground chamber; subterranean. ~**গহ্বরবাসী** *adj* dwelling underground. ❑*n* dweller in an underground cell. ~**গোল**, ~**গোলবিদ্যা** *nn* geography. ~**গোলক** *n* (the terrestrial) globe. ~**চক্র** *n* equator; equinoctial line. ~**চর** *adj* going on/ inhabiting the earth:

living/moving on the earth; terrestrial. ~চাল, ~চালা, ~চালি *nn* earthquake. ~চিত্র *n* map. ~চিত্রাবলী *n* atlas. ~-চুম্বকত্ব *n* (phys) terrestrial magnetism. ~চ্ছায়া *n* 1 shadow of the earth; darkness. 2 eclipse. ~তত্ত্ব, ~তত্ত্ববিদ্যা *nn* geology. ~তত্ত্ববিদ, ~তাত্ত্বিক *nn* geologist. ~তত্ত্বীয় *adj* geological. ~তল *n* 1 surface of the earth; face/floor of the earth; ground. 2 the nether world. ~তলশয়ন *n* lying on the ground. ~তলশায়ী *adj* laid/lying upon the bare ground; fallen/prostrated on the ground; floored; knocked to ground. ~তলশায়িনী *fem.* ~তলস্থ, ~তলস্থিত *adjj* standing/being on the surface of the earth; terrestrial; earthly. ~তাত্ত্বিক *adj* geological. ~দান *n* gift of land. ~ত্বক *n* (geol) rust of the earth. ~দেব *n* divinity upon earth; Brahmin. ~ধন *n* "whose property is the earth"; king. ~ধর *n* 1 'earth-supporting' mountain. 2 serpent-demon Shaheshanaga. ~নিম্ন *n* the region underground. ❑ *adj* underground. ~নিম্ন তার *n* underground cable. ~পটল *n* (geog) crest of the earth. ~প *n* 'earth-protector'; king; prince. ~পতি *n* 'lord of the earth'; king; monarch; prince. ~পতিত *adj* fallen to the earth. ~পতিত হওয়া *vi* fall on/to the ground; prostrate oneself on the ground. ~পদ *n* tree. ~পরিধি *n* circumference of the earth. ~পর্যস্ত *adj* thrown on the ground. ~পাত *n* 1 following on the ground; falling down. 2 (geol) landslide; landslip. ~পতিত=~পর্যস্ত. ~পাতিত করা *vt* pull down/fell to the ground; knock to the ground; floor. ~পাল *n* 'earth-guardian'; king; prince. ~পুত্র *n* the planet Mars. ~পৃষ্ঠ *n* surface of the earth. ~পেন্দ্র *n* the greatest among kings. ~প্রদক্ষিণ *n* going around the earth; circumnavigation. ~প্রদক্ষিণ করা *vi* ambulate/ travel round the earth; rotate round the earth; circumnavigate. ~প্রকৃতি *n* (geog) configuration. ~বলয় *n* equator; circumference of the earth. ~বাসন *n* settlement. ~বিদ্যা *n* geology. ~বিদ্যাগত *adj* geological. ~বিদ্যাবিদ *n* geologist. ~বিষুব *n* equator. ~বিষুবরেখা *n* terrestrial equator. ~বৃত্ত *n* equatorial circle; equator. ~ভার *n* burden of the earth; burden of sins committed by mankind; burdensome charge of administering and protecting the earth. ~ভার হরণ করা *vt* redeem/ absolve the sins of mankind. ~ভারত *n* 1 India; all India. 2 earth; world. ~ভারতে *adv* any where. ~ভৃৎ *n* 'earth -supporter'; mountain; king; prince. ~মণ্ডল *n* terrestrial globe; orbis terrarium. ~রুহ *n* tree. ~লতা *n* earth worm. ~লুণ্ঠিত *adj* fallen/ prostrated on the ground; rolling/ wallowing on the ground. ~লুণ্ঠিতা *fem.* ~লুণ্ঠিত হওয়া *vi* roll/wallow on the ground; fall to the ground; prostrate oneself on the ground. ~লেপন *n* cow-dung; swabbing with a solution of cow-dung. ~লোক *n* terrestrial world; earth. ~শায়িত *adj* lying/ fallen on the earth. ~শয্যা *n* couch on the bare ground; base ground as one's bed. ~শায়িত *adj* laid/ knocked to the ground ; lying upon the bare ground; floored. ~শায়িতা *fem.* ~শায়ী *adj* lying on the bare ground. ~শায়িনী *fem.* ~সংস্কার *n* ground -preparation. ~সংস্থান *n* topography. ~সম্পত্তি *n* landed property; real estate. ~সুত *n* the planet mars. ~সুতা *n fem* Sita, wife of Rama. ~স্তর *n* (geol) stratum of the earth. ~স্পন্দ (geog) earth-tremor. ~স্বর্গ *n* heaven on earth ; earthly paradise. ~স্বামী *n* landlord; landholder. ~স্বামিনী *fem.*

ভূঃ *n* 1 world; earth. 2 land; ground. 3 (myth) the first of the seven regions.

ভুঁই *n*=ভুঁই. ~ আমলকি *n* the plant *Flacourita cataphracta*. ~ কদম্ব *n* a kind of *kadamba*. ~-কামড়ি *n* plant that creeps along the ground. ~-কুমড়া *n* liquorice. ~ছাতি *n* mushroom. ~জাম *n* a species of plant; *Premna herbacea*. ~পটোকা *n* fire-works.

ভুঁইয়া ⇒ ভুঁইঞা

ভূঁদি *n fem.* 1 fat; rotund; podgy; tubby. 2 pot-bellied. (⇒ ভোঁদা).

ভূগোল ⇒ ভূ

ভূঞা *n* 1 landlord; landowner. 2 feudal prince. ~ রাজা *n* feudal prince.

ভূত *n* 1 ghost of a deceased person; demon; bogy; bogey; goblin; spook; spectre; apparition. 2 spirit (good or evil). 3 one of the class of supernatural beings who attend on Shiva. 4 an element; one of the five elements: পঞ্চ~. 5 that which is/exists; any living being (divine, human, animal and even vegetable) 6 fact; matter of fact; reality. 7 the past: ~ভবিষ্যৎ. ❑*adj* 1 past; gone; become; been. 2 (used as *suff*) being; being like anything; consisting of; mixed/joined with; reduced to: অশ্মী~. 3 savage; wild; barbarian; uncivilized. ভূতা *n fem* . the fourteenth day of the dark-half of the month of Kartik. ~ ছাড়া *vi* be exorcised. ~ ছাড়ানো/ ঝাড়ানো/ তাড়ানো/ ভাগানো *vt* exorcise. ~ দেখা *vt* see an apparition; look as if one has seen a ghost; (fig) take fright. ~ নামানো *vt* 1 exorcise. 2 call up ghosts/ spirits in order to obtain messages from them (as by spiritualists). 3 raise the spirits. ভূতে ধরা/পাওয়া *vi* be possessed (by evil spirits). ভূতের ওঝা/রোজা *n* exorciser; ভূতের বাপের শ্রাদ্ধ *n* (fig) great and gross waste/extravagance; horrible mess; Pandemonium ; mob rule; chaos. ভূতের বেগার *n* profitless toil/venture; thankless job; wild-goose chase. ভূতের বোঝা *n* burden of the five elements/ existence. ভূতের ঝোঝা বয়ে মরা (fig) 1 shoulder a heavy responsibility in vain. 2 just exist; vegetate; live in vain. ঘাড়ে ~ চাপা

(fig) be possessed with an evil intention; be under an evil influence; be possessed; be obsessed. **সরিষার মধ্যে ~** a virus in the antidote. **ভূতের মুখে রাম নাম** (fig) saying or doing sth contrary to one's nature (esp evil nature); singing another tune. **~কাল** *n* past time; (gram) past/preterite tense. **~গণ** *n* **1** host of living beings. **2** multitude of spirits attending on Shiva. **~গত** *adj* **1** dissolved into the elements. **2** futile ; sterile; useless ; vain: ~গত পরিশ্রম. **~গ্রস্ত** *adj* **1** possessed by an evil spirit. **2** working/ moving mechanically as if possessed; dazed. **~গ্রস্তা** *fem.* **~গ্রাম** *n* multitude of spirits/ sinners. **~ঘ্ন** *adj* destroying spirits/ demons. **~চতুর্দশী** *n* the fourteenth day in the dark half of the month Kartik. **~তত্ত্ব** *n* **1** physics. **2** demonology. **~তত্ত্ববিদ** *n* proficient/ versed in demonology. **~ধাত্রী** *n fem* the earth. **~নাথ** *n* Shiva. **~নায়িকা** *n fem* 'leader of the Bhutas'; Durga. **~পক্ষ** *n* the dark lunar fortnight. **~পতি** *n* Shiva. **~পূর্ণিমা** *n* the day of full moon in the month Aswin (when the Bhutas are worshipped). **~পূর্ব** *adj* former; previous; ancient; erstwhile; late; prior; old. **~প্রেত** *n pl* (ghosts and) spirits collectively. **~বলি** *n* offering of food, etc to all created beings. **~বিজ্ঞান, ~বিদ্যা** *nn* knowledge of evil beings; demonology. **~ভবিষ্যৎ** *n pl* the past and the future. **~ভর্তা, ~ভৃৎ** *adjj* sustaining the elements/creatures. **~ময়** *adj* containing all beings; consisting of the five elements. **~যজ্ঞ**=~বলি. **~যোনি** *n* according to Hindu belief existence in the shape of ghosts after one's death. **~যোনি প্রাপ্ত হওয়া** *vi* become a ghost after one's death. **~শুদ্ধি** *n* **1** purification of the elemental/ mortal body. **2** knowledge; conscience. **~সংপ্লব** *n* flooding/ drowning of all creatures; universal deluge. **~সঞ্চার** *n* possession by evil spirits. **~সঞ্চার হওয়া** *vi* be possessed by evil spirits. **~সঞ্চারী** *n* forest conflagration. **ভূতাত্মা** *n* **1** elemental body; human body. **2** ghost; demon; spirit. **3** Brahma. **ভূতাবাস** *n* body (as the abode of elements). **ভূতাপেক্ষ** *adj* retrospective. **ভূতাবিষ্ট** *adj*=~গ্রস্ত. **ভূতাবেশ**=~সঞ্চার. **ভূতার্ত** *adj* tormented by demons. **ভূতার্থ** *adj* real; genuine; authentic.

ভূতল ⇒ ভূ

ভূতি *n* **1** eight divine powers of Shiva. **2** superhuman power (as attainable by the practice of austerity and magical rites.). **3** welfare personified. **4** ashes. **5** origin; birth. **6** prosperity; well-being; might; wealth; fortune. **7** ornament; decoration. **8** title of the Vaishyas. **~কর্ম** *n* any auspicious rite/ ceremony. **~কাম** *adj* desirous of wealth/ property.

ভূতিয়া *adj* of ghosts; ghostly.

ভূতুড়ে *n* **1** exorciser. **2** those who always live in the company of ghosts/ spirits.

ভূতোপহত=ভূতগ্রস্ত (⇒ ভূত)

ভূদেব, ভূধর, ভূপ, ভূপতি, ভূপতিত, ভূপদ, ভূপাতিত, ভূপাল ⇒ ভূ

ভূপালি, ভূপালী *n* an Indian musical mode.

ভূপেন্দ্র, ভূভার, ভূভারত, ভূভৃৎ ⇒ ভূ

ভূম *n* **1** province: বীর~, মান~. **2** land; ground. **3** field; plane: সম~,

ভূমণ্ডল ⇒ ভূ

ভূমধ্য *n* centre of the earth; bowels/ inside of the earth. **~সাগর** *n* the Mediterranean sea. **~সাগরীয়** *adj* Mediterranean.

ভূময় *adj* earthen; mud-built.

ভূমা *n* **1** the Supreme Being; the Omnipresent; God. **2** abundance; plenty; wealth; opulence; aggregate of all existing things; multitude; diversity. **3** sublimity. ❑*adj* most abundant/ opulent; plentiful. **~নন্দ** *n* most abundant delight; ecstasy; greatest/ sublime joy; joy in a sense of vastness.

ভূমি *n* **1** soil; ground; land; field; agricultural land. **2** earth; surface of the earth. **3** place; site; situation. **4** country; territory; district. **5** floor of a house; storey . **6** fit object/ person for; receptacle; subject; object: বিশ্বাস~. **7** (math) base of any geometrical figure. **8** part/ personification (played by an actor). **9** (yoga) step; stage; degree. **~কম্প** *n* earthquake. **~কুষ্মাণ্ড** *n* liquorice. **~খণ্ড** *n* region; country. **~গর্ভ** *n* bowels/ inside of the earth; subterranean region. **~গ্রহ** *n* land acquisition. **~চম্পক** *n*=ভুঁইচাঁপা. **~জ** *adj* produced from the earth; sprung from the ground; holding tenancy of land in piece of menial services. **~জ প্রজা** *n* villein. **~জম্বু** *n* species of plant; *Premna herbacea.* **~জীবী** *n* **1** farmer. **2** a Vaishya. **~তল** *n* surface of the earth; ground; floor. **~দান** *n* gift of land. **~নীচ** *n* (astron) pedigree. **~পতি, ~পাল** *nn* king. **~পৃষ্ঠ**=ভূপৃষ্ঠ (⇒ ভূ). **~বৃত্তি** *n* physiography. **~ভৃৎ**=ভূভৃৎ (⇒ ভূ) **~রাজস্ব** *n* land revenue. **~রুহ** *n* plant; tree. **~রেখা** *n* base-line. **~লুণ্ঠিত** =ভূলুণ্ঠিত (⇒ ভূ). **~লেখ্য** *n* land records. **~লেপন**=ভূলেপন (⇒ ভূ). **~শয্যা**=ভূশয্যা (⇒ ভূ). **~শায়িত**=ভূশায়িত (⇒ ভূ). **~শায়ী**=ভূশায়ী (⇒ ভূ). **~ষ্ঠ** *adj* **1** born. **2** standing/ remaining on the earth/ ground. **3** being/ lying in the earth; prostrated. **~ষ্ঠ হওয়া** *vi* **1** be born. **2** fall to the ground; prostrate oneself on the ground. **~সংস্কার** *n* land reform. **~সম্পত্তি** *n* =ভূসম্পত্তি (⇒ ভূ). **~সাৎ** *adj* fallen to the ground; razed to the ground. **~সাৎ করা** *vt* pull down to the ground; raze to the grounds; wipe out; lay waste; cavil; bulldoze; demolish; flatten. **~সুত** *n* the planet Mars

~স্খলন *n* landslip. ~স্থ, ~স্থিত *adj* lying/ standing/ situated on the ground.

ভূমিকা *n* **1** preface; introduction; preamble; prologue; introductory talk preceding a speech/ action. **2** an actor's part/ character. **3** role. **4** assumption of a dress/ disguise ; transfiguration. **5** earth; ground; soil. ~ গ্রহণ করা *vt* play/ take up a role; play the part of; act as.

ভূমিজ, ভূমিষ্ঠ ⇒ ভূমি

ভূমীন্দ্র *n* king; prince.

ভূম্যধিকারী *n* landlord; landholder.

ভূম্যুচ্চ *n* (astron) apogee.

ভূয়ঃ, ভূয় *adv* again and again; repeatedly; exceedingly; in a high degree. ❑*adj* more; abundant; repeated. ❑*n* abundance; excess.

ভূয়সী *adj fem* profuse; copious; repeated: ~ প্রশংসা. ভূয়ান *masc.*

ভূয়া=ভুয়া

ভূয়ান *adj*=ভূয়সী

ভূয়িষ্ঠ *adj* most abundant/ numerous/ great/ important; chief; principal. ~তা *n* abundance; plenty; multitude.

ভূয়োদর্শন, ভূয়োদর্শিতা *n* experience gathered through repeated direct perception; worldly wisdom; wide experience. ভূয়োদর্শনজনিত *adj* born of long and wide experience.

ভূয়োভূয় *adv*=ভূয়ঃ

ভূরি *adj* much; many; abundant; frequent; numerous; great; copious; profuse; excessive. ~ভোজন *n* **1** copious/ hearty meal; a surfeit (of). **2** feeding many people.

ভূর্জ *n* birch (tree). ~পত্র *n* **1** leaf made of birch bark for writing on. **2** birch-leaf.

ভূলোক *n* **1** the terrestrial world; earth. **2** country south of the equator.

ভূলুণ্ঠিত, ভূশয্যা ⇒ ভূ

ভূশণ্ডি, ভূশণ্ডী *n*=ভুশণ্ডি

ভূষণ *n* **1** decorating; adorning; ornament; decoration; embellishment. **2**(fig) glory; ornament: বিদ্বান দেশের ~. **3** (used as *suff)* having anything as ornament; adorned/ decorated with. ~ভূষণা *fem*: পুষ্প~. ~প্রিয় *adj* fondness of ornaments. ~প্রিয়তা *n* love of ornaments.

ভূষণীয় *adj* to be adorned/ decorated.

ভূষণ্ডী=ভুশণ্ডি

ভূষা *n* ornament; decoration.

ভূষিত *adj* adorned; decorated; embellished.

ভূষ্য=ভূষণীয়

ভূসম্পত্তি, ভূস্বর্গ, ভূস্বামী ⇒ ভূ

ভৃগু *n* **1** declivity ; slope; precipice; cliff; tableland; plateau. **2** name of one of the chief Brahminical families. **3** Shiva. **4** Parashuram, one of the three Ramas (son of jamadagni and sixth Avatara of Vishnu). ~পতি *n* 'chief of the Brahmans '; Parashuram. ~পাত *n* committing suicide by Precipitating one's self from a precipice. ~মান *adj* steep; sloping. ~রাম *n* parashuram. ~সুত *n* **1** the planet Venus. **2** Parashuram.

ভৃঙ্গ *n* **1** a species of large black bee; bumble bee. **2** a spicier of wasp. **3** fork-tailed shrike. **4** libertine. **5** a kind of tree. ~প্রিয়া *n* 'liked by bee's; the flowering creeper *Gaertnera racemosa*. ~রাজ *n* **1** 'bee-king'; bumble bee. **2** a large variety of the fork-tailed shrike; *Dissemerus paradises*. **3** the medicinal plant *Wedelia calendulacca*. **4** a famous Ayurvedic hair-tonic. ~রোল =ভিমরুল

ভৃঙ্গার *n* **1**a kind of pitcher or vase. **2** a vase used at the inauguration of a king. **3** cricket.

ভৃঙ্গারিকা *n* cricket.

ভৃঙ্গি, ভৃঙ্গী *n* one of Shiva's attendants.

ভৃত *adj* **1** borne; carried. **2** gained; acquired. **3** filled; full of. **4** hired; paid. **5** supported; maintained; nourished. **6** filled; full. ❑*n* hireling; hired servant/ labourer; mercenary. ~ক *adj* hired; receiving wages. ❑*n* **1** hire; wages. **2** hired labourer; servant; employee.

ভৃতি *n* **1** hire; wages; salary. **2** support; maintenance; nourishment. **3** bearing; carrying; bringing; fetching. **4** fullness; plenitude. **5** capital. ~জীবী, ~ভুক *adjj* enjoying/ receiving wages; wage-earning; salaried. ~ভুক সম্প্রদায় *n* salary-drawing class; salariat.

ভৃত্য *n* **1** servant; domestic servant; salaried employee. **2** dependent. **3** support; maintenance; wages. ❑*adj* to be nourished/ maintained. B□ujh *n fem.*

ভৃশ *adj* **1** abundant. **2** much; many; great. **3** frequent.

ভৃষ্ট *adj* fried; roasted. ভৃষ্টি *n* frying; roasting.

ভৃষ্টান্ন *n* fried rice.

ভেউ, ভেউভেউ *n* (onom) **1** bow-wow; bark; yap; yelp. **2** loud cry; whine. ~ করে কাঁদা *vi* cry one's heart/ eyes out; whine; cry bitterly.

ভেংচানি, ভেংচি *nn* grimace; mimicry; scowl. ভেংচি কাটা *vi*=ভেংচানো.

ভেংচানো *vi, vt* make/ pull a face/ faces (at sb); make grimaces; grimace; grin (at); scowl; mimic.

ভেঁপু *n* a kind of wind-instrument; flute; pipe; bugle; horn; hoot. ~ বাজানো *vi* blow the above instrument; pipe; flute; whistle; horn; hoot; trumpet; honk.

ভেক *n* frog. ভেকী *fem.* ~ভুক *n* snake.

ভেক[২]**, ভেখ** *n* **1** dress; garb. **2** disguise; guise. **3** garb of an ascetic, esp of a Vaishnava ascetic. **4** dissimulation; simulation; camouflage; sham; travesty; mask;

masquerade. ~ ধরা/ নেওয়া *vt* **1** take to asceticism, esp Vaishnava asceticism; put on the garb of a (Vaishnava) ascetic. **2** assume a disguise; sham; simulate; feign; affect; masquerade; pretend. ~**ধারী** *adj* **1** fake; sham; pseudo; mock; false; bogus; affected; hypocritical; pretending. **2** in the garb of a (Vaishnava) ascetic. ❑*n* sham; impostor; fake; hypocrite; poseur; humbug.

ভেকা, ভেকো, ভেক্কা *adj* **1** dumb founded; confused; bewildered; specified; confounded; flabbergasted; open-mouthed; thunderstruck. **2** foolish; silly; stupid; witless. **ভেকানো** *vi* be dumbfounded/ confounded etc. ~**চাকা**=~ (1).

ভেক ⇒ ভেক[2]

ভেঙচানো, ভেঙ্গচানো=ভেংচানো

ভেঙছি, ভেঙ্গচি= ভেংচানি

ভেঙানি, ভেঙ্গানি *n* grimace; mimicry.

ভেঙানো, ভেঙ্গানো *vi, vt* make faces; mimic.

ভেজা *vi, adj* =ভিজা. ~**নো** *vt, adj*=ভিজানো

ভেজানো *vt* **1** close (a door, window, etc) without bolting. **2** send. **3** set: আগুন ~. ❑*adj* closed (without bolting).

ভেজাল *n* **1** adulterant; contaminant; impurity. **2** trouble; tangle; hitch; snag; muddle pest. **2** trouble: কিছু করতে গেলেই প্রতিপদে ~. ❑*adj* adulterated; spurious; corrupt. ~ **দেওয়া/ মেশানো** *vt* adulterate; contaminate; corrupt; vitiate. ~ **বাধানো** *vt* cause/ create trouble; make a mess of; mess sth (up); get into a mess; get badly confused about sth; muddle(up); tie oneself in/up in/into knots. ~ **মেটানো** *vt* clear up the mess/ hitch ; clear up a difficulty; get rid of/ do away with a hitch.

ভেট *n* **1** a respectful present (made to a king); rich present; tribute; complimentary gift/ present (paid to a superior person) esp during an interview. **2** call; short visit. **3** meeting; union; interview. ~ **করা** *vi* call on; visit; meet.

ভেটকি *n* small freshwater fish that lives in rivers and ponds.

ভেটা *vi, vi* (poet) **1**= ভেট করা. **2** offer respectful presents; make sb a gift of sth.

ভেটেরা *n* inn-keeper; hotel-keeper; hotelier. ~**খানা** *n* **1** inn; tavern; caravan serai. **2** a place full of confused uproar; madhouse; babel.

ভেটেল *adj* (of boats) going with the ebb-tide; downstream.

ভেড়া[1] (colloq)=ভিড়া

ভেড়া[2] *n* **1** sheep; ram; lamb. **2** fool. **ভেড়ী, ভেড়ি** *fem* ewe. ~**র গোয়াল** *n* sheep-fold. ~**র গোয়ালে আগুন লেগেছে** (facet) A bad singer has started his musical baaing. ~**র ঠ্যাং** *n* sheep-shank. ~**র ডাক** *n* baa; bleat. ~**র পাল** *n* flock of sheep. ~**র মাংস** *n* sheep's flesh; mutton. ~**র লোম** *n* sheep's wool. ~ **চড়ানোর মাঠ** *n* sheeprun. ~**কান্ত** *n* **1** bell-wether. **2** tomfool; simpleton.

ভেড়ানো (colloq) = ভিড়ানো (⇒ ভিড়া)

ভেড়ি, বেড়ি *n* **1** embankment; dike. **2** embanked low land used as a fish-hatchery. ~ **বাঁধা** *vt* embank; dike. ~**ওয়ালা** *n* owner of an (embanked) fish-hatchery.

ভেড়ী, ভেড়ি *n fem* ewe.

ভেড়ুয়া, ভেড়ে, ভেড়ো *adj* **1** cowardly; gutless; craven. **2** sissified; hen-pecked. **3** foolish; asinine. ❑*n* **1** hen-pecked husband; sissy. **2** coward; craven. **3** fool; donkey . **4** pimp. **ভেড়ের ভেড়ে** *n* out-and-out coward.

ভেতো *adj* rice-eating; very fond of rice.

ভেদ *n* **1** breaking; splitting; cleaving; rending; tearing; piercing. **2** bursting asunder; opening; gaping; parting asunder. **3** basting forth/ out; expanding; blossoming; shooting out; sprouting. **4** separation; division; partition; part; portion. **5** disunion; schism; discussion; between; discord; disharmony; estrangement. **6** difference; disagreement; disunity; separation; antagonism; hostility. dissimilarity. **7** fissure; chasm; rupture; breach; hurt; injury. **8** distinction; difference; kind; sort; species; variety: রূপ~. **9** breaking open; disclosing; divulging; betrayal (of a secret); deciphering; expounding: রহস্য~, অর্থ~. **10** disturbance; interruption; violation; dissolution. **11** disuniting; winning over to one's side by sowing dissension. **12** change; alteration. **13** evacuation (of the bowels); diarrhoea. **14** penetration: ব্যূহ~. **15** secret. **16** (alg) variation; differentiation. **17** (biol) variety. **18** (phil) dualism; duality. ~ **করা** *vt* **1** break; split; cleave; pierce; rend. **2** differentiate. **3** discriminate. **4** divulge; decipher; penetrate; expose; expound. ~ **জন্মানো** *vi* sow dissension/ discord; estrange (from). ~**ক** *adj* **1** breaking into/ through; piercing. **2** making a difference. **3** distinguishing; defining. ❑*n* one who/ that which pierces/ cleaves/ pierce/ splits/ differentiates/ discriminates/ penetrates/ deciphers; determinative. ~**কর** *adj* breaking through/ down; souring dissension in/ among. ~**কারী** *adj* causing dissension/ discord/ disunion. ~ **জ্ঞান** *n* perception/ idea of a difference/ distinction; discrimination; partiality. ~**ন** *n* **1** the act of piercing/ cleaving/ breaking/ opening/ splitting/ separating; penetration. **2** bursting; parting asunder; breach; preacher. **3** disclosure; betrayal. ~**নীয়** *adj* **1** capable of being pierced/ split/ cleft/ penetrated; penetrable; vulnerable. **2** to be broken/ split/ cleft/ pierced/ divided. ~**নীতি** *n* policy of discrimination. ~**প্রত্যয়** *n* belief in dualism.

~বাদী one who maintains the duality of God and the universe. ~বমি *n* diarrhoea attended with vomiting; cholera. ভেদভেদা *vi* **1** split; cleave; break; cut/ rend asunder; pierce; penetrate; pass through. **2** open; expand. **3** disclose; betray. ~নো *vt* cause to split/ cleave/ penetrate. ভেদাভেদ *n* **1** disunion and union; dualism and non-dualism. **2** discriminatory treatment; discrimination.

ভেদিত *adj* broken; split; rent; cleft; pierced; penetrated.

ভেদী *adj* **1**=ভেদক (⇒ভেদ). **2** (used as a *suff*) rending; piercing: মর্ম~.

ভেদ্য *adj*=ভেদনীয়. ❑*n* excision.

ভেন্ডার [E] *n* vendor.

ভেপসা = ভাপসা (⇒ ভাপ)

ভেবরা, ভেবড়া *adjj* dumb-founded; stupefied; confounded. ~নো=ভাবরানো.

ভেবা, ভ্যাবা *adj* **1** confounded; nonplussed; dazed; bewildered; muddled. **2** utterly foolish; soft in the head; senseless; idiotic. ❑*n* dolt; blockhead; imbecile; half-wit; booby ; boob; ninny. ~ **গঙ্গারাম** *n* utter fool; tomfool; dunce. ~ **চাকা** *n* bewilderment; confusion; puzzlement; perplexity; stupefaction; shock; awe. ~**চাকা খাওয়া** *vi* be bewildered/ confounded/ puzzled/ perplexed/ awestruck/ stunned/ flabbergasted/ dumb founded/ stupefied/ struck dumb. ~**চাকা খাওয়ানো/ লাগানো** *vt* confound; bewilder; baffle; flabbergast; stupefy; nonplus. stun.

ভেরন গাছ *n* castor-oil plant; *Ricinus communis* or *Palma christi.*

ভেরি, ভেরী *n* kettle-drum.

ভেরুয়া=ভেড়ুয়া

ভেরে আসা *vi* be heavy: চোখ ঘুমে ভেরে আসে.

ভেরেণ্ডা *n*=ভেরনগাছ. ~ **ভাজা** (fig) idle; loaf; dawdle.

ভেল[1] *n* spurious; adulterated; counterfeit.

ভেল[2]=ভেলকি

ভেল[3] *vi past tense* (poet, archaic) became; happened.

ভেলকি, ভেলকিবাজি *n* **1** magic; conjuring tricks; prestidigitation; jugglery; conjuring; juggling; legerdemain; slight of hand; charm; spell; illusion; hocus-pocus. **2** deception. ~ **খাওয়ানো**=~ লাগানো. ~ **দেখানো** *vt* exhibit a magical show; perform magic; conjure; juggle. ~ **লাগা** *vi* be under a magic spell; be spellbound/ bewitched/ enchanted/ dazed. ~ **লাগানো** *vi* put under a magic spell; bewitch; cast a spell; enchant; beguile; daze; amaze; astound. ~**ওয়ালা** *n* magician; conjurer; juggler; prestidigitator; enchanter spellbinder.

ভেলকোনো **1**=ভেলকি দেখানো. **2** keep sb in the dark/ in ignorance (about sth) by trickery.

ভেলভেল=ফ্যালফ্যাল

ভেলসা *adj* soft; mild. ~ **তামাক** *n* mild tobacco.

ভেলা *n* raft; float. ~**য় সাগর পার হওয়া** (fig) accomplish an uphill task; do the impossible.

ভেল্কি = ভেলকি

ভেল্কোনো = ভেল্কোনো

ভেষজ *n* **1** drug; remedy; medicine; medicament. **2** medicine; medical science. ❑*adj* curing; healing; sanative: ~ গুণ. ~-**অধ্যাপক** *n* professor of medicine/ pharmacy. ~**করণ**, ~**কর্ম** *nn* preparation of drugs/ medicine; pharmacy. ~**তা** *n* healing power; curativeness. ~**বিজ্ঞান**, ~**বিদ্যা** *nn* pharmacy ; pharmacology. ~**লক্ষণ সংগ্রহ** *n* Materia Medica; pharmacopoeia. ~**শক্তি** drug potency. **ভেষজাঙ্গ** *n* anything taken with or after medicine. **ভেষজাগার, ভেষজালয়** *nn* druggist's/ apothecary's shop; pharmacy; dispensary. **ভেষজী** *n* pharmacist. **ভেষজ্য** *adj* curative; sanitary.

ভেস্ত [P] *n*=বেহেস্ত

ভেস্তা *adj* spoiled; foiled; upset; mixed. ~**নো** *vi* be spoiled/ foiled/ upset. **ভেস্তে যাওয়া** *vi* fail; founder; come to nothing/ naught; flunk.

ভৈক্ষ, ভৈক্ষ্য *n* anything obtained by begging; begged food; charity; alms. ~**চর্যা** *n* begging. ~**জীবী** *adj, n*=ভিক্ষুক.

ভৈরব *adj* frightful; terrible; horrible; formidably owe-inspiring. ❑*n* **1** a manifestation/ form of Shiva. **2** an Indian musical mode. **ভৈরবী** *fem* **1** a form of goddess Durga; one of the ten manifestations of Durga. **2** a female ascetic worshipping Shiva. **3** an Indian musical mode. **4** a turbulent woman; termagant; virago; fury. ~**চক্র** *n* Tantric drinking party.

ভৈল (poet. archaic)=ভেল

ভৈষজ, ভৈষজ্য *nn* **1** drug; medicine; remedy. **2** curativeness; healing efficacy. **3** administrating of drugs. ~ **উদ্যান** *n* garden of medicinal plants. ~ **বিদ্যা** *n* pharmacology.

ভৈষা=ভইষা (⇒ ভইষ)

ভো *int* o! ho! hullo.

ভোঁ[1] *n* (onom) **1** whistling; whizz; whizzing; whistle. **2** siren; whistle. **3** buzz (of bees, etc). ~ **দেওয়া** *vi* whistle. ~ **ভোঁ** *n* (onom) drone; continuous buzzing. ~ **ভোঁ করা** *vi* drone; buzz. **কান ~ ভোঁ করা** be filled with buzzing sound. **পকেট ~ ভোঁ করা** go clean/ stony/ flat broke; be penniless/ hard up/ skint; be (down) on one's uppers. **মাথা ~ ভোঁ করা** feel dizzy; (my) head is swimming. ~ **দৌড়** *n* hasty retreat/ flight; very swift/ quick run. ~ **দৌড় দেওয়া/ মারা** *vi* run at a break neck speed; run for life; cut and run; run for it.

ভোঁ[2]=ভোম

ভোঁতড়া, ভোঁদড়া *n* entrails.

ভোঁতা *adj* **1** blunt; edgeless: ~ ছুরি. **2** dull; heavy; ponderous: ~ বুদ্ধি. **3** discomfited; put out of countenance; abashed: ~ মুখ. **~ করা** *vt* blunt; dull; take away the edge of; put out of countenance; discomfit.

ভোঁদড় *n* civet-cat; otter.

ভোঁদা *adj* **1** fat corpulent; obese; blubbery; tubby; pudgy; rotund; stocky. **2** dull; dull-witted; feeble-witted; dumb. **ভুঁদি, ভুঁদী** *fem.*

ভোঁস-ভোঁস *n* **1** (onom) denoting noise of deep breathing (in sleep); wheeze. **2** snore.

ভোক *n* hunger. **~ছানি** *n* drowsiness/dizziness due to extreme hunger.

ভোক্তব্য *adj* **1** to be enjoyed/ eaten. **2** eatable; edible; enjoyable; sufferable.

ভোক্তা *adj* **1** eating; enjoying; experiencing; suffering; possessing. **2** one who enjoys/ eats; enjoyer; eater; sufferer; consumer. **ভোক্ত্রী** *fem.*

ভোগ *n* **1** feeling/ perception (of pleasure and pain); experiencing. **2** pleasure; delight. **3** enjoyment; enjoying. **4** eating; feeding on. **5** sexual enjoyment. **6** suffering; sustaining. **7** possession; wealth. **8** any object of enjoyment (as food, a festival, etc). **9** sensual pleasure. **10** food offering made to a deity. **11** affliction; trouble. **12** hire/ wages esp prostitution. **~ করা** *vt* **1** enjoy; use; eat and drink; enjoy meal; consume; make use of. **2** possess; take possession of. **3** enjoy carnally. **4** suffer; experience; sustain; undergo; be rewarded/ requited for. **~ দেওয়া** *vi* offer food offering; offer food and entertainment to a deity. **~গৃহ** *n* room for food-offering to a deity; women's apartments; harem. **~তৃষ্ণা** *n* desire of worldly enjoyments. **~দেহ** *n* 'the body of feeling'; the intermediate body which a dead person acquires after Shraddha (শ্রাদ্ধ) after cremation and with which, according to his works, he either enjoys happiness or suffers misery. **~বাসনা**=~তৃষা. **~বিলাস** *n* sensual/ worldly enjoyments; pleasures and luxury. **~বিলাসী** *adj* enjoying worldly pleasures and luxuries; voluptuous. ❑*n* voluptuary. **~বৃত্ত** *adj* passive. **~বৃত্তি** *n* passivity. **~ভূমি** *n* the place where people enjoy the reward of their works; heaven. **~রাগ**=~তৃষ্ণা. **~লালসা** *n* craving for sensual/ worldly pleasures. **~সাধন** *n* arduous endeavour to obtain pleasure; pleasure seeking. **~সুখ**=~বিলাস. **~স্থান** *n* **1** body. **2** women's apartments. **~স্পৃহা**=~তৃষ্ণা. **~স্বত্ব** *n* occupancy right.

ভোগবান *adj* devoted to enjoyments. **ভোগবতী** *fem.*

ভোগবতী *n* (myth) name of the Ganges as flowing in the nether world.

ভোগা[১] ⇒ ভুগা. **~নি**=ভুগানে (⇒ ভুগা). **~নো**=~নি (⇒ ভুগা)

ভোগা[২] *n* deception; cheating; swindling; hoaxing. **~ দেওয়া** *vt* deceive; cheat; swindle; hoax.

ভোগাকাঙ্ক্ষা *n*=ভোগতৃষ্ণা. **ভোগাকাঙ্ক্ষী** *adj* desirous of worldly enjoyment. **ভোগাকাঙ্ক্ষিণী** *fem.*

ভোগানে *adj* causing trouble/ suffering/ harassment; vexatious; toying; troublesome; verve-racking.

ভোগান্ত, ভোগান্তি *n* **1** end of enjoyment or suffering. **2** extreme suffering/ trouble; agony; extreme anguish; torment. **~ হওয়া** *vi* suffer/ be troubled greatly; be in anguish.

ভোগাবাস=ভোগগৃহ (⇒ ভোগ)

ভোগাভিলাষ=ভোগলালসা ⇒ ভোগ. **ভোগাভিলাষী** *adj* craving for sensual/ worldly pleasures; pleasure-seeking; voluptuous. **ভোগাভিলাষিণী** *fem.*

ভোগাভোগ *n* pleasure and its absence.

ভোগায়তন *n* **1** place of enjoyment. **2** the body.

ভোগার্হ *adj* fit for enjoyment; to be enjoyed/ possessed. **ভোগার্হা** *fem.*

ভোগাসক্ত *adj* attached to worldly/sensual pleasures; sybaritic *fem.* **ভোগাসক্তি** *n* attachment to worldly/ sensual pleasures; sybaritism.

ভোগী *adj* devoted to enjoyment; enjoying; eating. ❑*n* one who enjoys; sufferer; voluptuary; sybarite. **ভোগিনী** *fem.*

ভোগৈশ্বর্য *n* great fortune and happiness.

ভোগ্য *adj* **1** to be enjoyed/used; enjoyable. **2** to be suffered/endured. ❑*n* object of enjoyment; possession money. **ভোগ্যা** *fem adj*=~. ❑*n* prostitute. **~তা** *n* enjoyableness; usefulness.

ভোজ[১] *n* feast; banquet; meal; repast; dinner. **~ দেওয়া** *vt* give a feast to; feast; give a dinner; entertain at a dinner/feast. **নৈশ~, সান্ধ্য~** *nn* dinner; supper. **মধ্যাহ্ন ~** *n* lunch. **ভোজের পোশাক** *n* dinner-suit.

ভোজ[২] **1** the people of Yadu (যদু). **2** name of a king of the ancient Indian city of Dhara (ধারা), he was famous for his skill in magic. **3** magic; wizardry. **~পুর** *n* kingdom of Bhoj. **~পুরী** *n* native of Bhojpur. **~বাজি, ~বিদ্যা** *nn* magic; wizardry. **~বাজিকর** *n* magician; wizard; conjurer.

ভোজং, ভুজং *nn* bad advice ; evil counsel. **~ দেওয়া** *vt* win over by cajolery; coax into; persuade by flattery.

ভোজন *n* **1** eating; feeding. **2** feast. **3** food; meal. **~ করা** *vt* eat; take; dive; devour; feast. **~ করানো** *vt* feed; feast. **~ আগার, ভোজনাগার** *n* eating-house; dining-room/ hall; restaurant. **~ দক্ষিণা** *n* honorarium paid by a host to a Brahmin for the latter's condescending to eat the food offered by the former. **~পটু** *adj* capable of eating much; gluttonous; voracious. **~পাত্র** *n* dinner-plate. **~বিলাস** *n* indulgence in good eating; gourmandise. **~বিলাসী** *n* gourmand; gourmet. ❑*adj* fond of good eating; Epicurean. ভোজনার্থী *adj* desirous of food. ভোজনালয়, **~শালা**=ভোজনাগার. ভোজনাবশেষ=ভুক্তাবশেষ (⇒ভুক্ত).

ভোজবাজি ⇒ ভোজবাজি[2]

ভোজয়িতা *adj, n* feeding; one who feeds. ভোজয়িত্রী *fem.*

ভোজালি, ভোজালে *nn* a curved, short sword used by Gurkhas; Kukri.

ভোজী *adj* (used as a *suff*) eating; enjoying; feeding on: তৃণ~. ভোজিনী *fem.*

ভোজোৎসব *n* feast; banquet; dinner party.

ভোজ্য *adj* **1** to be eaten/ enjoyed. **2** eatable; edible. ❑*n* article of food; nourishment; store of provisions; dainty. **~দ্রব্য**, **~বস্তু** *nn* article of food.

ভোট[1] *n* Bhutan. ❑*adj* Bhutanese.

ভোট[2] [E]*n* vote; election; franchise; poll. **~ দেওয়া** *vt* cost/ record votes; vote; go to the polls. **~ নেওয়া** *vt* take votes; poll. **ভোটে দাঁড় করানো** *vt* nominate for election. **ভোটে দাঁড়ানো** *vi* stand for (parliament); face election; contest a seat (in parliament). **ভোটে দেওয়া** *vt* put to the vote. **~ গণনা** *n* counting of votes; poll. **~ গ্রহণ** *n* polling. **~গ্রহণ-নিযুক্তক** *n* polling agent. **~পত্রী** *n* ballot-paper. **~পেটী** *n* ballot-box. **~স্থান** *n* polling-booth; polling station. **ভোটার, ~দাতা** *nn* voter. **ভোটাধিকার** *n* suffrage. **ভোটাভুটি** *n* election; polling.

ভোম *adj* fuddled; besotted; stupefied: মদ টেনে/ নেশায় ~.

ভোমর[1] *n* drill; auger.

ভোমর[2], ভোমরা=ভ্রমর

ভোমা *adj* **1** foolish; witless; obtuse; bovine soft in the head. **2** bewildered; stupefied; dumbfounded; confounded. ❑*n* fool; tomfool.

ভোর *n* **1** morning; dawn; daybreak; sunrise. **2** end; close: এবার তোমার বাজি ~. **3** awakening; dawn ; dawning: নবযুগের ভোরে. ❑*adj* **1** lost; absorbed; rapt; engrossed: স্বপ্নে/ চিন্তায় ~. **2** fuddled; stupefied; besotted: নেশায় ~. **3** benumbed; numb; comatose; drowsy: প্রেমের আবেশে তনু ~. **~ করা** *vt* pass the night (without sleep); pass; spend: রাত ~ করা. **~ হওয়া** *vi* **1** dawn; begin to grow light. **2** come to a close/ an end; reach its close; end: দুখের রাত ~ হল. **3** be fuddled/ besotted/ stupefied; be benumbed; নেশায় ~ হওয়া. **~বেলা, ভোরের বেলা** *nn* time of daybreak. **ভোরে** *adv* at dawn; at the daybreak.

ভোরাই *n* morning hymn/ song; matin; matinal hymn. ❑*adj* morning; matinal.

ভোল *n* **1** disguise; guise; garb; (false) appearance; facade. **2** deception; deceit; trap; wile: দুষ্ট লোকের ~. **3** illusion; infatuation; fascination. **4** stupefaction; stupor; intoxication. **~ যাওয়া** *vi* be fascinated/ bewitched/ infatuated. **~ পাল্টানো/ ফেরানো** *vt* **1** change one's dress; improve one's appearance; appear a new guise. **2** (fig) improve one's social/ financial condition; advance socially.

ভোলা[1] ⇒ভুলা

ভোলা[2] *adj* **1** forgetful; oblivious; absent-minded; unmindful. **2** forgotten; lost; gone out of one's head. ❑*n* **1** utterly forgetful person. **2** Shiva.

ভোলানি, ভোলানী =ভুলানি, ভুলানী (⇒ ভুলানে)

ভোলানে=ভুলানে

ভোলানো=ভুলানো (⇒ ভুলা)

ভোল্টীয় *adj* (phys) voltaic.

ভৌগোলিক *adj* geographical. ❑*n* geographer.

ভৌত *adj* **1** elemental; material; physical; natural. **2** ghostly; eerie; ghostlike; spooky; haunted. ভৌতী *fem.* **~ধর্ম** physical property. **~বিজ্ঞান** *n* physical science.

ভৌতিক=ভৌত. **~ কাণ্ড** *n* ghostly affair; unintelligible affair. **~ গল্প** *n* ghost-story. **~ দেহ** *n* elemental/ material body. **~ নিয়ম** *n* law of nature; physical law. **~ পদার্থ** *n* material thing; matter. **~ বিদ্যা** *n* demonology. **~ ব্যাপার** *n* **1** physical phenomenon. **2** = **~কাণ্ড**.

ভৌতী ⇒ভৌতি

ভৌম *adj* **1** earthly; terrestrial; produced/ coming from the earth. **2** coming from the land (as revenue). ❑*n* **1** the planet Mars. **2** sky. ভৌমী *fem.* **~জল** *n* underground water. **~ দূরবীক্ষণ** *n* field glass. **~ পুষ্পদণ্ড** *n* (bot) scape. **~রত্ন** *n* coral.

ভৌমিক *n* **1** landlord; landowner; feudal prince. **2** a title. ❑*adj* earthly; related to the ground.

ভৌমী ⇒ ভৌম

ভ্যা, ভ্যা-ভ্যা *n* (onom) **1** baa; bleat. **2** loud weeping; howl; wail, ywol. **~ করা** *vi* baa; bleat.

ভ্যাংচানো=ভেংচানো

ভ্যাকসিন *n* [E] vaccine.

ভ্যাকা =ভেকা

ভ্যাজাল (colloq)=ভেজাল

ভ্যাদ *n* (onom) indicating a dull sound as of a blow on fall of sth soft; thud. **~ভ্যাদ করা** *vi* **1** give out a dull sound; fell soft/ spongy. **1** feel soft/ doughy/ spongy/ soggy/ boggy/ quaggy. **~ভ্যাদে** *adj* doughy; spongy; soggy; soft.

ভ্যাদান, ভ্যাদাল (also ~ **ব্যথা**) *n* afterpaint.

ভ্যানকা=ভেকা

ভ্যানভ্যান *n* (onom) buzz; drone. **~ করা** *vi* **1** buzz; drone. **2** complain continuously; drone; whine; talk sb's head off.

ভ্যাপসা=ভাপসা (⇒ ভাপ)
ভ্যাবড়া, ভ্যাবরা=ভেবরা
ভ্যাবা=ভেবা. ~**চ্যাকা**=ভেবাচাকা
ভ্যালসা=ভেলসা
ভ্যালা *adj* (iron) fine; nice; pretty: ~ ল্যাঠা তো. ❑*int* (iron) bravo! well done! ~রে মোর ভাই !
ভ্রংশ *n* **1** falling or slipping down/ off; fall; detachment. **2** decline; decay; downfall; ruin. **3** disappearance; cessation; loss: স্মৃতি~. **4** straying/ deviating from; deviation; abandonment. **5** deprivation of. **6** slip of tongue. **7** casting off: জাতি~. **8** (phys) displacement. ~**ন** *n* **1**= ~. **2** throwing down; causing to fall. ~**হার** *n* (phys) rate of displacement. **নীতি~** *n* demoralization; aberration; deviation from the rules; degeneration.
ভ্রংশিত *adj* **1** made to fall; thrown down. **2** deprived of. **3** detached; fallen. **4** cast off. **5** (phys) displaced.
ভ্রম *n* **1** error; mistake; blunder. **2** oblivion; omission; inadvertence; oversight. **3** illusion; (psych) hallucination. **4** whirl; whirlpool; whirlwind; eddy. **5** drill; auger; gimlet. ~ **করা** *vi* err; blunder; mistake; commit a mistake. ~ **হওয়া** *vi* be mistaken; overlook; be careless of. **ভ্রমে পড়া** *vi* be confused/ puzzled/ perplexed; be mistaken; fall into an error. ~ **নিরসন করা** *vt* remove a wrong notion; correct; set right; set straight; amend; rectify a mistake. ~**কৌতুক** *n* diversion through a series of errors. ~**ক্রমে** *adj* by mistake; inadvertently; in error. ~**জাল** *n* web of errors/ mistaken. ~**প্রবণ** *adj* fallible; erring. ~**প্রবণতা** *n* fallibility. ~**প্রমাদ** *n* errors and omissions. ~**বশত**=~ক্রমে. ~**সংশোধন** *n* rectification of errors. ~**সংশোধন করা** vt=~নিরসন করা. ~**সঙ্কুল** *adj* full of errors/ wrong notions; erroneous; mistaken.
ভ্রমণ *n* **1** travel; travelling; journey; wandering/ roaming about; peregrination; roving through; ambulation. **2** walk; walking: প্রাতঃ~ **3** revolution; rotation; turning round; whirl. ~ **করা** *vi* travel; journey; wander/ roam about; rove; itinerate; walk; rotate; revolve; move round; circulate. ~**কারী** *n* traveller; walker. ~**কারিণী** *fem.* ~**বৃত্তান্ত** *n* account of a journey; travels; travelogue. ~**শীল** *adj* travelling; itinerant; always on the move.
ভ্রমন্ত *adj* travelling.
ভ্রমমাণ *adj* travelling; migrant; itinerant; wandering; peripatetic; roving; revolving.
ভ্রমর *n* **1** a large dark bee; kind of bumble-bee; bee. **2** auger; gimlet. **3** gallant; libertine. **ভ্রমরী** *fem.* ~**কীট** *n* weevil. ~**কৃষ্ণ** *adj* as dark/ black as the bumble-bee. ~**গুঞ্জন,** ~**ঝঙ্কার** *n* buzzing/ humming of bumble-bees or bees.
ভ্রমরক *n* curl on the forehead.
ভ্রমা (poet) =ভ্রমণকরা
ভ্রমাত্মক *adj* erroneous; mistaken; illusive; illusory.
ভ্রমান্ধ *adj* blinded with errors/ illusions.
ভ্রমাসক্ত *adj* in error; mistaken.
ভ্রমি, ভ্রমী *n* whirlpool; eddy.
ভ্রষ্ট *adj* **1** dropped; fallen (down/ from/ off). **2** banished. **3** broken down; detached; decayed; ruined; disappeared; lost; gone. **4** strayed/ separated from; deviated; deprived of. **5** depraved; vicious. ❑*n* backslider; (fem) fallen/ unchaste woman. **ভ্রষ্টা** *fem.* ~**ক্রিয়** *adj* one who has omitted/ discontinued prescribed acts. ~**চরিত্র** *adj* characterless; depraved; degenerate; corrupt. ~**চরিত্রা** *fem* unchaste woman. ~**তা** *n* fallen/ detached/ decayed/ depraved state; depravity; deviation; aberration; corruption. ~**নিদ্র** *adj* deprived of sleep. ~**রাজ্য** *adj* fallen from/ deprived of a kingdom. ~**শ্রী** *adj* deprived of fortune. **ভ্রষ্টাচরণ** *n* wicked/ depraved/ evil practice; wrongdoing; corruption; vileness; ill conduct; misdeed; vicious activities. ~**চারী** *adj* given to wrongdoing; vicious; depraved; ill-conducted. **ভ্রষ্টাধিকার** *adj* fallen from office; dismissed.
ভ্রাজক *adj* causing to shine; making bright.
ভ্রাতা *n* brother (often used to designate a near relative/ intimate friend, esp as a term of friendly address); cousin.
ভ্রাতুষ্পুত্র *n* brother's son; nephew. **ভ্রাতুষ্পুত্রী** *n fem* brother's daughter; niece.
ভ্রাতুষ্পৌত্র *n* son of one's brother's son; grandson. **ভ্রাতুষ্পৌত্রী** *n fem* daughter of one's brother's son; granddaughter.
ভ্রাতৃ *n* (in compounds) = ভাই. ~**কন্যা**=ভ্রাতুষ্পুত্রী (⇒ভ্রাতুষ্পুত্র). ~**ঘাতক** *n* fratricide. ~**ঘাতী** *adj* fratricidal. ~**জ** =ভ্রাতুষ্পুত্রী. ~**জা**=ভ্রাতুষ্পুত্রী. ~**জায়া** *n fem* brother's wife; sister-in-law. ~**ত্ব** *n* fraternity; brotherhood. ~**দ্বিতীয়া** *n* festival on the second day in the lunar-half of the month of Kartik (on which sisters mark their brother's foreheads with sandalwood-paste and give them entertainments). ~**পুত্র**=ভ্রাতুষ্পুত্র. ~**পুত্রী** *n fem* ভ্রাতুষ্পুত্রী. ~**প্রেম** *n* fraternal/ brotherly love. ~**বৎ** *adv* like a brother. ~**বৎসল** *adj* affectionate towards one's brothers. ~**বৎসলা** *fem.* ~**বধ** *n* fratricide. ~**বধূ** =~জায়া. ~**ব্য** *n* cousin. ~**ভাব** *n* brotherly feeling; brotherliness. ~**শ্বশুর** *n* husband's eldest brother. ~**স্নেহ** *n* brotherly love. ~**হত্যা** *n* fratricide. ~**হন্তা** *n* fratricide.
ভ্রাত্রীয় *adj* brotherly; fraternal.
ভ্রান্ত *adj* **1** erroneous; mistaken; confused; illusive; illusory; wrong; false. **2** having a false notion; under an illusion; deluded.

ভ্রান্তি *n* **1** error; false notion/ impression; confusion; mistake; illusion. **2** (psych) delusion. **~কর, ~জনক** *adjj* causing error/ confusion; illusive; delusive; erroneous. **~জাল** *n* web of error. **~দর্শন** *n* erroneous perception. **~প্রদ**=~কর. **~বশত, ~বশে** *adv* by mistake; in error; inadvertently. **~বিনোদ** *n* diversion through a series of errors. **~মান্** *adj* mistaking anyone/ anything; erroneous; mistaken. **~মতী** *fem.* **~মান** *n* a particular figure of rhetoric (describing an error). **~মূলক** *adj* erroneous; mistaken; false; illusive. **~সঙ্কুল** *adj* full of errors; erroneous.

ভ্রামক *n* **1** magnet. **2** (phys) moment.

ভ্রামর *adj* relating/ belonging to a bee. ❑*n* kind of magnet or loadstone.

ভ্রাম্যমাণ *adj* **1** rotating; revolving. **2** travelling; itinerant: ~ বিক্রেতা. **3** mobile: ~ আদালত. **4** circulating: ~ পাঠাগার. **~ মূলধন** *n* capital floating.

ভ্রূ, ভ্রু *n* eyebrow; brow. **~কুঞ্চন, ~কুটি** *nn* contraction of the brows; frown. **~কুঞ্চন/~কুটি করা** *vi* knit the eyebrows; frown. **~কুটিকুটিল** *adj* contracted; frowning (as a face). **~ক্ষেপ** *n* glance; look; casting a glance; (fig) slightest heed. **~ক্ষেপ না করা** *vi* take no heed of; ignore completely; turn a deaf ear; disregard; turn a blind eye. **~ধনু** *n* bow of the eyebrows. **~বিভ্রম, ~বিলাস** *nn* playful movement of the eyebrows. **~ভঙ্গ, ~ভঙ্গি** *nn* =~কুটি; ~বিলাস. **~মণ্ডল** *n* arch of the eyebrow. **~মধ্য** *n* interval between the eyebrows. **~লতা** *n* 'brow-creeper'; an arched eyebrow. **~লেখা** *n* hachures. **~সঙ্কেত** *n* beckoning/ signal by moving the eyebrows.

ভ্রূণ *n* **1** embryo. **2** foetus; fetus. **~ঘ্ন** *adj, n* killer of an embryo; abortionist. **~জীব** *n* foetus. **~পত্র** *n* (bot) cotyledon. **এক~পত্রী** *n* monocotyledon. **দ্বি~পত্রী** *n* dicotyledon. **~বিদ্যা** *n* embryology. **~সম্বন্ধীয়** *adj* of/ relating to an embryo; embryonic; foetal; fetal. **~হত্যা, ~হনন** *nn* killing of an embryo. **~হত্যা করা** *vt* kill/ destroy an embryo; cause an unlawful abortion.

ম

ম *n* the twenty-fifth consonant of the Bengali alphabet. It is a voiced unspirated bilibial nasal consonant sound.

মই, মৈ *n* **1** ladder. **2** harrow. **~ দেওয়া** *vi* harrow a field. **গাছে তুলে দিয়ে ~ কেড়ে নেওয়া** (fig) let sb down after inciting him to sth; betray; leave in the lurch. **পাকা ধানে ~ দেওয়া** (fig) blast sb's hopes when they are about to be realized.

মউ, মৌ *n* honey. **~আলু** *n* sweet yam. **~চাক** *n* beehive; honeycomb. **~মাছি** *n* bee; honey-bee. **~মাছির চাক**=~চাক. **~মাছির রানী** *n fem* queen-bee. **~মাছি পালন** *n* apiculture; bee-keeping. **~লোভী** *adj* fond of honey.

মউজ, মওজ, মৌজ [A] *n* **1** wave; surge. **2** enjoyment; ecstasy. **~ করা** *vi* enjoy oneself. **মউজে/মৌজে আসা** *vi* be overjoyed. **মউজে/ মৌজে থাকা** *vi* be enjoying oneself; be in/go into ecstasy. **মউজি**=মগজি.

মউড় *n* tiara made of *sola* (sponge wood), worn by a Hindu bride.

মউত [A] *n* death.

মউতাত ⇒ মৌতাত

মউনি, মউনী *n* churn; churning-staff.

মউরলা *n* species of very small freshwater fish.

মউরি, মউরী=মৌরি

মউল=মৌল

মওকল, মোয়াক্কাল [A] *n* guardian; superintendent; trustee; delegate.

মওকা [A] *n* occasion; opportunity; contingency.

মওকুফ=মৌকুফ

মওজ=মউজ

মওজুদ=মজুত

মওড়া (colloq)=মহড়া

মওত=মউত

মওয়া *vi* churn; stir.

মওয়াজ্জমা=মোয়াজ্জমা

মওয়াজ্জল=মোয়াজ্জল

মওলবি, মওলবী=মৌলবি

মওলা, মাওলা, মৌলা [A] *nn* master; lord; Allah. **~না** *n* (lit our master); a title given to persons respected for their learning; a Muslim scholar possessing the highest degree from a theological school.

মওলুদ=মলুদ

মওসুম=মৌসুম

মকতব, মক্তব, মকতবখানা [A] *n* school; academy.

মকদুর [A] *n* power, means; resources; capacity; ability; possibility.

মকদ্দমা, মোকদ্দমা [A] *nn* **1** lawsuit; case; proceedings; litigation. **2** affair; subject; matter: একদিনের ~. **~ আনা** *vt* bring a lawsuit (against); bring to justice/treat; sue; proceed (against). **~ করা** *vi* bring/file a lawsuit; proceed (against); conduct a case; plead in a case; try/judge a case; enter into litigation; go to law. **~ তোলা** *vi* bring up a case for trial.

মকবরা, মকবেরা, মাকবেরা [E] *nn* tomb; mausoleum; sepulchre.

মকবুল [A] *adj* accepted; admitted; received; chosen.

মকমক *n* (onom) **1** suggesting suppressed anger. **2** croak of frogs. **3** growl. **রাগে ~ করা** *vi* fume; boil with rage; rage; seethe with anger. **মকমকা** *vi* **1** croak; growl; snarl. **মকমকি** *n* croak; growl; roar; scream; blare.

মকমল, মখমল [A] *n* velvet. **মখমলি পোকা** *n* the insect cochineal of various kinds.

মকর *n* **1** (myth) kind of sea-monster (sometimes confounded with the crocodile, shark, dolphin, etc; regarded as the emblem of Kamadeva). **2** emblem of Kamadeva (Hindu god of love). **3** (astrol) Capricorn. **4** an army of troops in the form of a Makara). **~কুণ্ডল** *n* earring shaped like a Makara. **~কেতন, ~কেতু** *nn* **1** 'having the Makara for an enblem' or 'having a fish on his banner'; Kamadeva, the god of love. **2** the sea. **~ক্রান্তি** *n* (astron) winter solstice. **~ক্রান্তিবৃত্ত** *n* (geog) tropic of Capricorn. **~ধ্বজ** *n* **1**=~কেতন. **2** (Ayu) a medicinal sublimate of sulphur, mercury and gold. **~ব্যূহ** *n* = ~ (4). **~মণ্ডল** *n* Tropic of Capricorn. **~রাশি** *n* (astrol) Capricorn. **~সংক্রান্তি** *n* (name of a festival marking) the transition of the sun from the Sagittarius to the Capricorn—in the month of Magh. **মকরাকর** *n* 'receptacle of Makaras', the sea. **মকরাক্ষ** *n* 'Makara-eyed'; name of a Rakshasa, a general of Ravana. **মকরাঙ্ক** **1** =~কেতু. **2** the sea. **মকরালয়** *n* ''abode of Makaras', the sea. **মকরাশ্ব** *n* having the Makara for a horse; Varuna (বরুণ). **মকরাস্য** *adj, n* Makar-faced.

মকরন্দ *n* honey; nectar.

মকররি=মুকররি (⇒ মুকরর)

মকরীয় *adj* of the Capricorn; of the Tropic of Capricorn. **~ শান্তবলয়** (geog) the calms of Capricorn.

মকরুহ [A] *adj* (according to Islamic law) detestable; abhorred; odious; detestable; unpleasant; disgusting

মকর্‌ররি [A] *adj* permanent; fixed; established; (of land) held on payment of fixed rent.

মকসদ *n* purpose, intention; object; aim; desire, wish; design.

মকসুদ *adj* intended; proposed. ❑*n* intent; object; aim; view; design.

মকাই, মক্কা *nn* Indian corn; maize.

মকান, মোকান [A] *n* house; dwelling; lodge; home; abode; place; habitation.

মকাম, মোকাম [A] *n* dwelling; station; place; abode; place of residence/encamping; site; situation; position; halt; occasion; opportunity; basis.

ম-কার *n* **1** ⇒ ম. **2** **~সাধন** *n* performance of the five essentials of the Tantric rituals (the words for which begin with letter ম, viz মদ্য, wine; মাংস, meat; মৎস্য, fish; মুদ্রা, coin; মৈথুন, sexual union).

মকুট=মুকুট

মকুফ, মকুফ, মকুব=মৌকুফ

মক্কর [A] *n* **1** design; sport; plot: আল্লাহর ~. **2** cunning; trick; cheating; deceit; fraud.

মক্কা[1] [A] *n* the city where the holy Kaaba is situated; Mecca; Makkah (⇒ কাবা).

মক্কা[2] ⇒ মকাই

মক্কি [A] *adj* Meccan.

মক্কেল [A] *n* client (of an advocate, attorney, etc). **~হীন** *adj* (of an advocate) briefless.

মক্তব ⇒ মকতব

মকশ, মকস [A] *n* exercise; practice; drawing the letters. **~ করা** *vt, vi* exercise; practise; imitate; copy.

মক্ষিকা, মক্ষী *n fem* fly; bee. **~মল** *n* wax. **~রানী** *n fem* queen-bee.

মখদম, মখদুম [A] *adj* served; honourable. ❑*n* teacher.

মখমল ⇒ মকমল

মখলুক [A] *n* creation; creature. **মখলুকাত** *n* things created; creatures.

মগ[1] [E] *n* mug.

মগ[2] *n* native of Myanmar/Burma or Arakan. **মগের মুল্লুক** *n* (fig) lawless country.

মগজ [P] *n* brain; brains; intelligence; intellect; head. **~ খালি করা** *vi* talk one's head off. **~ খেলানো** *vi* apply one's mind; beat/rack one's brain(s) (about sth); tax one's brain ; use one's brain(s).

মগজি [P] *n* edging; hem; hem-line; border. **~ সেলাই** *n* hemming-stitch.

মগডাল *n* topmost branch of a tree.

মগধ *n* the country of Magadha; South Bihar. **মগধি** *adj* relating to/coming from Magadha. ❑*n* a minister who sings the praises of a chief's ancestry.

মগন *adj* (poet, archaic)=মগ্ন

মগরব, মগরেব=মাগরিব

মগরা *adj* proud; haughty; insolent; obstinate; stubborn; cunning. **~মি** *n* haughtiness; insolence; obstinacy; stubbornness; cunning; artifice.

মগরুর [A] *adj* proud; arrogant; haughty.

মগরেব ⇒ মাগরিব

মগাই *adj* produced in Arakan/Burma; Arakanese; Burmese.

মগ্ন *adj* **1** plunged; sunk; immersed; drowned; submerged. **2** engrossed; lost; absorbed: চিন্তা~, ধ্যান~. **3** latent; dormant: ~চৈতন্য. **4** overwhelmed: শোক~. **~গিরি** *n* submarine mountain. **~চৈতন্য** *n* (psych) the subconscious. **~শৈল** *n* submarine rock.

মঘা *n* the tenth of the twenty-seven Nakshatras according to Hindu astronomy.

মঙ্গল *n* **1** welfare; good; benefaction; well-being; happiness; felicity; bliss. **2** anything auspicious or tending to a lucky issue (eg a good omen/ prayer/ benediction). **3** a good work. **4** Shiva. **5** the Mars. **6** Tuesday. **7** a kind of Bengali epic poem about popular deities. ❑*adj* auspicious; lucky. **~ করা** *vi* do good to. **~কর** *adj* auspicious; beneficent; propitious; doing good; beneficial; advantageous. **~কাব্য** *n*=~ (7). **~কামনা** *n* good wishes; good will. **~কাম, ~কামী** *adjj* well-wishing; wishing well to. **~কারী** *adj* causing welfare. ❑*n* one do who does good to others. **~কারিণী** *fem.* **~গীত** *n* solemn song. **~গ্রহ** *n* the Mars. **~ঘট** *n* a vessel full of water offered to the gods or placed in a house to win divine favour. **~চণ্ডী** *n fem* a manifestation of Durga. **~চ্ছায়** *n* the tree ficus infectoria. **~জনক**=~কর. **~তূর্য** *n* a musical instrument used at festivals. **~দায়ক** *adj* bestowing welfare; auspicious. **~দায়িনী** *fem.* **~দেবতা** *n* a tutelary deity. **~ধ্বনি** *n* an auspicious sound (eg marriage music). **~পাঠক** *n* a professional well-wisher or panegyrist. **~পাণি** *adj* having auspicious hands. **~প্রদ**=~দায়ক. **~বার** *n* Tuesday. **~ভেরী** *n* drum beaten on festive occasions. **~মন্দির** *n* auspicious house/temple. **~ময়** *adj* consisting of nothing but happiness; gracious; auspicious; benign; benignant. **~ময়ী** *fem.* **~সংবাদ, ~সমাচার** *nn* good news; news of well-being; (Christ) Gospel. **~সূচক** *adj* auguring good luck. **~সূত্র** *n* marriage thread. (tied round the wrists of the bride and the bridegroom). **~স্নান** *n* any solemn ablution. **মঙ্গলা** *n fem* **1** goddess Durga. **2** a devoted wife; a chaste woman. **মঙ্গলাকর** *n* mine of goodness. **মঙ্গলাকাঙ্ক্ষা**=~কামনা. **মঙ্গলাকাঙ্ক্ষী** = ~কামী. **মঙ্গলাকাঙ্ক্ষিণী** *fem.* **মঙ্গলাচরণ** *n* benediction; prayer for the success of anything; pronouncing a blessing. **মঙ্গলাচার** *n* repeating a prayer for success and observing other auspicious ceremonies. **মঙ্গলামঙ্গল** *n* good and evil; weal and woe. **মঙ্গলার্থ, মঙ্গলার্থে** *advv* for the sake of prosperity/happiness; for the good of. **মঙ্গলালয়** *adj, n* having an auspicious dwelling; temple.

মঙ্গলক *n* manganese.

মঙ্গলন *n*=মঙ্গলাচার (⇒ মঙ্গল)

মঙ্গলা *vi* (poet, archaic) observe auspicious ceremonies.

মঙ্গলেচ্ছা *n* benediction; felicitation.

মঙ্গলেচ্ছু *adj* wishing joy/prosperity.

মঙ্গলোৎসব *n* auspicious/solemn ceremony.

মঙ্গল্য *adj* **1** auspicious; lucky; conferring happiness. **2** beautiful; pleasant; agreeable. **3** pious; pure, holy. **মঙ্গল্যা** *n fem* Durga.

মঙ্গোল, মঙ্গোলীয় *n* Mongol. ❑*adj* Mongolian; Mongoloid; Mongol.

মচ *n* (onom) denoting sound of sudden breaking of bone, wood etc; crack; snap. **~মচ** *n* (onom) crunch; crackle; crackling; squeak (of shoes). **~মচানি** *n* crackling; squeak; cracking. **~মচানো** *vi* crack; cackle; squeak. **~মচে** *adj* **1** crisp; crunchy. **2** brittle; friable.

মচকা, মচকানি *nn* sprain; twist. **মচকানো** *vt, vt* sprain; twist; be sprained: হাত-পা মচকানো. **ভাঙে তো মচকায় না** ⇒ ভাঙা.

মচ্ছ, মচ্ছি *nn* fish.

মচ্ছব, মোচ্ছব=মহোৎসব

মচ্ছর *n* mosquito.

মছনদ=মসনদ

মছলত [A] *n* **1** counsel; advice; advisability: consultation. **2** cause; expediency; fitness.

মছলন্দ=মসলন্দ

মছলা, মসলা [A] *n* questions; problems; propositions; precepts of the Holy Prophet.

মছলি[1] *n* fish.

মছলি[2] *n* platform; shelf; scaffold.

মজকুর [A] *adj* mentioned; recorded; related; aforesaid. ❑*adj* statement; mention. **মজকুরি** *adj* process-serving.

মজদুর=মজুর. **মজদুরি**=মজুরি

মজন *n* **1** submersion; sinking; dip; plunge; submerging; submergence. **2** attachment; infatuation; crush.

মজনুন [A] *adj* possessed of an evil spirit; mad; insane; madly/desperately in love.

মজবুত [A] *adj* **1** strong; hard; stiff; solid; firm. **2** durable; fast; lasting. **3** fixed; immovable; permanent. **4** expert; efficient; adept; clever; adroit; skilful: আড্ডা দিতে ~, কাজকর্মে ~. **মজবুতি** *n* strength, firmness; solidity; durability.

মজযুব, মজুব [A] *adj* attracted; drawn; abstracted; absorbed/lost in (divine love); fanatic. ❑*n* one lost in divine love; a Godly person.

মজলিস, মজলিশ *n* **1** sitting; company; party; gathering. **2** meeting; congregation. **3** association; congregation; convention; society; club. **মজলিসি, মজলিশি** *adj* concerning a gathering/party; fit for a party;

capable of brightening up a party/gathering with pleasant/bearing: মজলিসি লোক/গল্প.

মজলুম [A] *adj* oppressed; wronged; injured; treated tyrannically. ❑*n* one who is treated wrongfully/ unjustly; the oppressed.

মজহব, মজহাব, মাজহাব [A] *n* religious school in Islam; creed; faith; doctrine; way of life. **মজহাবি** *adj* concerning religion; belong to a **~**.

মজা[১] [P] *n* **1** taste; flavour; deliciousness; delicacy; relish. **2** enjoyment; pleasure; comfort and luxury. **3** fun; sport; frolic; joke; banter; fun and games. **4** funny/ pleasant/ strange affair/ object/ incident. **5** (iron) affliction; distress; punishment; evil consequence. **~ উড়ানো** *vi* enjoy; revel; carouse. **~ করা** *vi* **1** amuse oneself; have fun; frolic; indulge in pleasures and frolics. **2** make fun of; poke fun at; pull sb's leg. **~ করে** *adv* **1** for/in fun; as a joke. **2** with relish; to one's heart's content. **~ চাখা/টের পাওয়া** *vi* feel/suffer the evil consequences; feel the pinch of; feel the weight/brunt of (an adventure, etc); get one's just deserts; take one's medicine. **~ চাখানো/টের পাওয়ানো** *vt* teach a good lesson; give one his deserts. **~ দেখা** *vi* take delight in sb's troubles; view sb's trouble with secret joy. **~ দেখানো**=~ চাখানো. **~ নেওয়া/ লোটা** *vi* enjoy; revel; have a gay, lively time; enjoy undue benefit from sth; wallow in sensual pleasures; be/live in clover; have the time of one's life; live it up. **~ পাওয়া** *vi* fall into the habit of; acquire a taste/longing for; come to relish. **~য় থাকা** *vi* amuse oneself; revel; enjoy oneself; have great fun; have a good time. **~ড়ে** *adj* full of fun; playful; amusing; frolicsome. **~র, ~দার** *adjj* **1** funny; amusing; interesting; droll; queer; surprising: মজার গল্প/কথা/লোক. **2** delicious; palatable; tasteful; savoury: ~দার খাবার.

মজা[২] *vi* **1** drown; be drowned: জলে ~. **2** go down; sink in/into sth: কাদায় ~. **3** silt up; be choked/clogged: পুকুর ~, নর্দমা ~. **4** sink in/into: পাপে ~, sink into vice. **5** be in deep water(s); run into trouble: এতোদিন ফাঁকে ফাঁকে বেড়িয়েছ, এবার মজেছ. **6** be fascinated/ charmed/ bewitched: রূপে ~. **7** fall/be in love: যে মজেছে সে বুঝেছে. **8** be head over heels in love; be infatuated with: কারো প্রেমে ~. **9** loose oneself in; be lost in; become engrossed in: বিষম মায়ায়/ঈশ্বরপ্রেমে ~. **10** be deceived/ tempted by; be deluded/ charmed with: ভবের মায়ায় ~, মিষ্টি কথায় ~. **11** ripen; mature: আচার ~. **12** be overripe; overripen: কলা ~. **13** ferment: তালের রস ~. **14** be utterly ruined/ kaput/ done for: ব্যবসায় মার খেয়ে সে মজল. ❑*adj* **1** overripe: ~ কলা. **2** silted up; derelict; clogged; choked up: ~ পুকুর, ~ নর্দমা. **~নো** *vt* **1** drown; submerge: বিধি বৃষ্টিতে দেশ ~ল. **2** bewitch; charm; entice; infatuate: রূপে মন ~নো. **3** while away; beguile (with): মিছা বেলা মজালাম. **4** bring disgrace/ shame on; tarnish; disgrace; dishonour; sully the good name of; bring into disrepute: কুল ~নো. **5** bring about sb's ruin/ undoing: এই লোকটাই আমাকে মজাবে. **6** silt up: পুকুর ~নো. **7** ferment: তালের রস ~নো. **8** ripen thoroughly; cause to mature thoroughly: আচার ~নো. **কুল ~নে** *adj, n* (one who brings) bringing disgrace on a family (by enticing a girl away from that family). **কুল ~নী** *fem* (one who brings) bringing disgrace on her family (be eloping). **দয়ে/দহে ~নো** *vt* **1** drown/throw into deep waters. **2** get sb into great trouble.

মজুদ, মজুত [A] *adj* **1** present; existent; ready at hand. **2** stored up; reserved; in reserve; hoarded; in store. **~ করা** *vi* store; hoard. **~ রাখা** *vt* keep ready at hand. **~ তহবিল** *n* reserve fund; reserve capital. **~দারি** *n* hoarder. **~দারি** *n* hoarding.

মজুমদার [P] *n* **1** (hist) revenue accountant of a district. **2** a family name.

মজুর, মজদুর [P] *n* labourer; workman; worker; porter. **~নী** *fem.* **~ গণ্ডগোল** *n* labour trouble. **~ সরদার** *n* foreman of a group of labourers; labour-leader.

মজুরা, মজুরি, মজুরী [P] *nn* **1** labour cost/ charges; wages (of a labourer); pay; hire. **2** labour; work. **মজুরি করা** *vi* work as a labourer.

মজ্জন *n* **1** sinking; diving; immersion; drowning; overwhelming; bathing. **2** marrow.

মজ্জমান *adj* sinking; drowning. **মজ্জমানা** *fem.*

মজ্জা *n* **1** marrow; bone-marrow. **2** (bot) pith. **3** (physiol) core. **4** (zoo) medulla. **~গত** *adj* pertaining to bone; deep-rooted; inveterate; bred-in-the bone; ingrained; deep-seated. **~গহ্বর** *n* (bot) pith cavity. **~রস** *n* semen.

মঞ্চ *n* **1** stage; platform; dais; rostrum. **2** raised seat; throne. **3** theatre; stage. **4** bedstead; couch. **5** pedestal; altar. **6** elevated platform/shed raised on bamboos in a field (where a watchman is stationed to protect the crop, cattle, birds, etc). **7** scaffold. **~ নির্দেশন, ~ নির্দেশনা** *nn* stage-direction. **~পীঠ** *n* seat on a platform. **~ভাষণ** *n* platform speech. **~মণ্ডপ** *n* a sort of temporary open shed; granary. **~ শিল্প** *n* stage-craft. **~শিল্পী** *n* stage-player; stage-decorator. **~সজ্জা** *n* stage-decoration. **~স্থ করা** *vt* produce/stage (a drama); enact. **মঞ্চমানায়ন** *n* production (of a drama). **মঞ্চমানারোহণ** *n* ascending a platform.

মঞ্চক=মঞ্চ

মঞ্ছনিকা *n* battering ram.

মঞ্চাল *n* realgar; red arsenic.

মঞ্জর *n* 1 cleansing by rubbing; brushing. 2 article for cleansing with.

মঞ্জরা *vi* (poet) blossom; sprout.

মঞ্জরি, মঞ্জরী *nn* 1 cluster of blossoms: পুষ্প~. 2 flower; bud. 3 shoot; sprout; sprig: আমের ~. 4 ear; spike: শস্য~, পুষ্প~. 5 foliage (as an ornament on buildings). **~জাল** *n* dense mass of buds/flowers. **~দণ্ড** *n* (bot) rachis; rhachis. **~পত্র** *n* (bot) bract.

মঞ্জরিত *adj* blossomed; budded; flowered; blown; in blossom; sprouted. **~ হওয়া** *vi* be in blossom; blossom; bud; flower; sprout.

মঞ্জা *n*=মঞ্জতৃণ

মঞ্জি, মঞ্জী *n* cluster of blossoms. **~ফলা** *n* banana.

মঞ্জিকা *n fem* harlot; courtesan.

মঞ্জিমা *n* beauty; elegance.

মঞ্জিল, মনজিল [A] *n* 1 a day's journey; stage. 2 hotel; serai. 3 dwelling house; lodging. 4 house; mansion. 5 storey (of a building). 6 destination; goal. 7 rank; dignity. 8 boundary. **মঞ্জিলে মাকসুদ** *n* destination; goal.

মঞ্জিষ্ঠা *n* the creeper Indian madder; *Rubia cordifolia.*

মঞ্জীর *n* anklet (with small jingling bells).

মঞ্জু *adj* beautiful; lovely; charming; pleasant; sweet; graceful; delicate. **~কেশী** *adj* having beautiful hair. **~কেশিনী** *fem.* **~গমন** *adj* going/walking gracefully. **~গমনা** *adj.* **~ঘোষ** *adj* uttering a sweet sound; sweet-sounding. ❑*n* 1 sweet sound. 2 one of the most celebrated Bodhisattvas among the northern Buddhists. 3 dove. **~ঘোষা** *adj fem.* **~নেত্র** *adj* fair-eyed. **~পাঠক** *adj* able to recite beautifully. ❑*n* parrot. **~ভাষী** *adj* sweetly speaking; honey-mouthed; fair-spoken. **~ভাষিণী** *fem.* **~স্বন**=~ঘোষ. **~হাসী** *adj* sweet-smiling. **~হাসিনী** *fem.*

মঞ্জুর [A] *adj* granted; approved of; admitted; accepted; sanctioned; permitted; chosen. **~ করা** *vt* grant; approve; admit; permit; accept; sanction; choose.

মঞ্জুরি, মঞ্জুরী [A] *n* sanction; approval; consent; permission; choice. ❑*adj* accepting; approving; sanctioning: ~ দস্তখত, **~ কমিশন** *n* grants commission.

মঞ্জুল *adj* beautiful; pleasing; lovely; charming. ❑*n* 1 bower; arbour. 2 a species of water-hen or gallinule. **~তা** *n* beauty; loveliness.

মঞ্জুশ্রী *n fem* 1 =মঞ্জুঘোষ (2) (⇒ মঞ্জু). 2 delicate/ charming grace/beauty; one possessing such grace/beauty.

মঞ্জুষা, মঞ্জূষা *nn* box; chest; case; basket; casket.

মট *n* (onom) suggesting a cracking or snapping sound; crack; snap. **~ করে** *adv* with a crack/snap. **~মট** *n* repeated cracks/ snaps. **~মট করে** *adv* freely; proudly; haughtily. **~মটে** *adj* very dry; arrogant.

মটকা[১] *n* 1 head; top. 2 topmost part of the surface of a thatched roof. **~ মারা** *vt* close up the opening at the centre of a thatched roof.

মটকা[২] *n* large earthen cask or barrel.

মটকা[৩] *n* a coarse variety of silk material.

মটকা[৪] *n* pose; posture; manner. **~ মারা** *vi* (fig) feign; pretend; pretend to be sleeping.

মটকানো *vt, vi* 1 twist/ wring/ break with a snap/ crack; snap; crack. 2 keep one's eyes half closed. **আঙ্গুল ~** *vi* snaps one's fingers. **ঘাড় ~** *vi* 1 wring (sb's) neck. 2 extort (from); squeeze sth out of sb. **আঙুল মটকে গালি দেওয়া** snap one's finger at sb (as an indication of one's intention to wring his neck) and curse him.

মটকি, মটকী *nn*=মটকা[২]

মটন [E] *n* mutton. **~চপ** *n* mutton-chop.

মটর[১] *n* pea. **~কলাই, ~কড়াই** *nn* pea. **~ডাল** husked pea-seeds used as food. **~দানা** *n* 1 grain/ seed of pea. 2 necklace/girdle comprising small pea-like balls. **~মালা** *n* necklace comprising small pea-like balls. **~শাক** *n* pea-plant eaten as a vegetable. **~শুটি** *n* pea-pod; green peas.

মটাৎ *n* (onom)=মট

মঠ[১] *n* 1 academy; college (esp for young Brahmins). 2 cloister; monastery; convent; abbey. 3 temple; shrine. **~ধারী, মঠাধিকারী, মঠাধ্যক্ষ** *nn* superintendent of a monastery; principal of a college, abbot, etc. **~ধারিণী, ~ধ্যক্ষা** *fem.*

মঠ[২] *n* sweetmeat made of flour mixed with cardamom, chilli powder, salt, camphor, etc and cooked in syrup.

মড়ক *n* pestilence causing great mortality; epidemic (of cattle, beasts, birds, etc); murrain. **~ লেগেছে** *vi* A pestilence has broken out; Death/ The epidemic is taking a heavy toll of lives. **~খোলা** *n* cremation ground.

মড়মড় *n* (onom) crash; crack. **~ করে ভেঙে পড়া** *vi* fall with a (great) crash; crash. **মড়মড়ে** *adj* rustling.

মড়া *n* dead body; corpse. **~খেকো, ~খেগো** *adj* scraggy; skinny; scrawny; starved: ~খেকো ঘোড়া. **~পোড়া**=মড়িপোড়া. **~র ওপর খাঁড়ার ঘা দেওয়া** *vi* (fig) strike a man when he is down; strike a dead horse; add insult to injury.

মড়িঘর *n* morgue.

মড়িপোড়া *adj* lending assistance in cremating dead bodies. ❑*n* such a Brahmin (considered as an outcast).

মড়ুঞ্চে *adj* whose offspring/new-born child dies.

মণি *n* **1** jewel; gem; precious stone; pearl; any ornament/ amulet. **2** (term of endearment) precious; treasure; darling: সোনা~, খুকু~. **3** peak point. ❑*adj* **1** best; greatest; glorious: রঘুকুল~. ~ক *n* mineral. ~কবিদ্যা *n* mineralogy. ~কঙ্কণ *n* bejewelled bracelet. ~কণ্ঠ *n* blue jay. ~কর্ণিকা *n* ear-ornament consisting of pearls/ jewels. ~কাচ *n* **1** crystal. **2** feathered part of an arrow. ~কাঞ্চন *n* gems and gold. ~কাঞ্চনযোগ *n* (fig) excellent combination/ union. ~কানন *n* wood/ grove containing jewels. ~কার *n* jeweller; lapidary. ~কুট্টিম *n* bejewelled house/ chamber. ~কুণ্ডল = ~কর্ণিকা. ~কুন্তলা *adj fem* having hair adorned with jewels. ~কূট *n* mountain containing jewels. ~কোঠা *n* room adorned with gems. ~খচিত *adj* studded/ adorned with gems. ~গ্রীব *adj* wearing a diamond necklace. ~দর্পণ *n* mirror adorned with/ consisting of jewels. ~দীপ *n* lamp adorned with jewels. ~দীপ্ত *adj* lit by precious stones. ~দ্বীপ *n* name of a mythical island in the ocean of nectar. ~পুর *n* name of a country. ~পুরী *adj* of/born in/produced in Manipur. ❑*n* native of Manipur. ~প্রভা *n* splendour of jewels. ~বন্ধ *n* wrist. ~বন্ধন *n* fastening of jewels. ~বীজ *n* pomegranate (tree). ~ভাণ্ডার *n* jewel-house. ~মণ্ডপ *n* crystal hall; hall on crystal pillars. ~মণ্ডিত *adj* set/studded with jewels or pearls. ~ময় *adj* full/formed/consisting of jewels; crystalline. ~মাণিক্য *n* gems and jewels; precious stones. ~মান *adj* adorned with jewels. ❑*adj* the sun. ~মালা *n* **1** string/necklace of jewels or pearls. **2** lustre; beauty. **3** kind of metre. ~মেখলা *adj* girdled with/surrounded by gems or jewels. ~যষ্টি *n* jewelled stick. ~রত্ন *n* precious stones. ~রাগ *n* colour of a jewel; vermillion; kind of ruby. ~সর, ~হার *nn*=~মালা. ~হারা ফণী *n* a snake which has lost the gems of its head; (fig) one who is inconsollably grief-stricken on account of losing his most precious treasure/beloved person.

মণিক *n* **1** gem; jewel; precious stone. **2** water-jar; pitcher.

মণিত *n* **1** sound of kissing; smack. **2** sound of pleasurable sensation made by women during sexual enjoyment.

মণিহারী=(old spelling of) মনিহারি

মণ্ড *n* **1** scum of boiled rice (or any grain). **2** gruel; starch; pulp; paste. **3** foam; froth. **4** pith; essence. **5** thick part of milk yoghurt; cream. **6** embolic myrobalan tree. **7** decoration; ornament. মণ্ডা *n fem* **1** sweet blob. **2** liquor.

মণ্ডক *n* sort of pastry of baked flour.

মণ্ডন *n* **1** adorning; decoration; embellishment; ornament. **2** toilet. **3** overlaying; inlaying; studding.

মণ্ডপ *n* **1** temple. **2** open hall/temporary shed (erected on festive occasions). **3** pavillion; tent. **4** arbour; bower. ❑*adj* drinking the scum of boiled rice or any other liquor. ~ প্রতিষ্ঠা *n* consecration of a temple.

মণ্ডরী *n* an insect of the family *Cystocirca gregaria* (= ঘুর ঘুরে).

মণ্ডল *n* **1** anything round. **2** disc (esp of the sun or moon). **3** circle; globe; orb. **4** ring; circumference; ball; wheel. **5** path/orbit of a heavenly body. **6** hallo (round the sun or moon). **7** ball for playing. **8** circular bandage (in surgery). **9** round mole/mark (caused by the finger-nail) on the body. **10** circular array of troops. **11** district; arrondissement; zone; region; village; locality; territory; province; country. **12** (also used as a *pl suff*)multitude; group; collection; congregation band; whole body; society; community; assemblage; company. **13** division/book of the Rigveda. **14** village headman; headman; leader; sheriff. **15** a ryot who collect revenues on behalf of the landlord. **16** (geom) zone. খণ্ড~ *n* sector/segment of a circle. ❑*adj* circular; round. ~নৃত্য *n* circular dance. ~পট্ট *n* (phys) zone plate. ~পরিদর্শক circle inspector. ~ভাগ *n* part of a circle. ~মধ্য *n* middle of a circle. আভা~ *n* (astron) corona. আলোক~ *n* photosphere. ইন্দু~ *n* disc of the moon. বর্ণ~ *n* Chromosphere. বায়ু~ *n* atmosphere. মণ্ডলাকার *adj* circular; spherical; round; globular. মণ্ডলাগ্র *adj* round-pointed. ❑*n* scimitar. মণ্ডলাধীশ *n* ruler of a country/province.

মণ্ডলক *n* **1** disc; circle; orb. **2** circular array of troops. **3** group; collection; heap; mass; troop; band; crowd. **4** cutaneous disease with spots. **5** mirror.

মণ্ডলিত, মণ্ডলায়িত *adjj* made round; circular.

মণ্ডলী *n* **1** (also used as a *pl suff*)=মণ্ডল (১১). **2** ring; circle. **3** snake. **4** the sun. ~করণ *n* rounding; gathering in a ball/circle; coil. ~কৃত *adj* curved; rounded; bent; made circular.

মণ্ডলেশ, মণ্ডলেশ্বর=মণ্ডলাধীশ (⇒ মণ্ডল)

মণ্ডা[১] *n* kind of sweetmeat; sweet blob.

মণ্ডা[২] *vt* (poet) decorate; adorn.

মণ্ডিত *adj* adorned; decorated; embellished. মণ্ডিতা *fem.* ~ করা *vt* adorn; decorate; embellish; overlay/stud (with).

মণ্ডূক *n* frog. **মণ্ডূকী** *fem.* **~গতি** *n* gait of a frog. **~পর্ণী** *n* the plant *Hydrocotyle asiatica*.

মণ্ডুর *n* rust of iron.

মণ্ডোদক *n* froth obtained from powdered rice; barm.

মৎ *pron* (archaic) my. **~কর্তৃক** by me. **~কৃত** *adj* done by me. **~পুত্র** *n* my son. **~প্রণীত** *adj* composed/written/compiled/done by me. **~পরায়ণ** *adj* selfish; egocentric.

মত *n* **1** opinion; view; remark. **2** consent; sanction; approval; approbation; commendation. **3** thought; idea; sentiment. **4** theory; doctrine; ism. **5** belief; faith; religion; creed; tenet. **6** prescription; rules; principles. **7** method; mode; means. **8** intention; design; purpose; wish. **~ করা** *vi* **1** agree (to); consent; acquiesce; assent; give one's consent; fall in with; accede (to). **2** intend. **~ করানো** *vt* persuade. **~ দেওয়া** *vi* **1**=~ করা (1). **2** give opinion; comment; opine. **3** advise. **4** approve. **~ নেওয়া** *vt* take/ seek/ obtain sb's opinion/ approval/ comment/ advice/ counsel. **~ পাওয়া** *vt* obtain sb's opinion/ approval. **~ বদলানো** *vt* change one's mind. **~ গ্রহণ** *n* poll. **~বাদ** *n* theory; doctrine; tenet; principle. **~বাদী** *adj n* adhering to/upholder of a particular theory/ doctrine/ tenet. **~বিরোধ, ~ভেদ** *nn* difference of opinion; disagreement; dissension. **মতাধিকার** *n* suffrage. **মতানৈক্য** =~বিরোধ. **মতান্তর** *n* another opinion/ creed/ sect; difference of opinion; a different/ contrary opinion/view/ doctrine/ theory. **মতান্তরে** *adv* in/according to another view/ theory. **মতাবলম্বন** *n* embracing a particular doctrine/ theory. **মতাবলম্বন করা** *vt* embrace/ uphold/ adhere to/profess/ accept a particular opinion/ view/ theory/ doctrine/ tenet/ creed/ religion. **মতাবলম্বী** *adj* holding the doctrine, view, etc of. ❑*n* adherent/ supporter/ upholder/ follower of a particular doctrine/ theory/ view/ opinion/ creed/ religion/ faith. **মতাবলম্বিনী** *fem.* **মতামত** *n* views for and against; opinion.

মতন, মতো *adj* **1** like; similar to; as: নদীর ~, আগের ~. **2** becoming; befitting; like: বীরের ~. **3** suiting; as desired; satisfying; after: মনের ~. **4** regarded/considered as; taken/ passing for; thought fit; approved: মনো~, পছন্দ~. ❑*prep* **1** for: আজকের ~, জন্মের ~, for good. **2** according to; in keeping with: কথা~. **করার/দেবার ~** to do/give.

মতলব [A] *n* **1** intention; motive; aim; purpose; object. **2** design; stratagem; plan; artifice; wile. **~ আঁটা** *vt* think out a plan; plan; scheme; hatch a plot; intrigue. **~ করা/ভাঁজা** *vt* design; contrive a plan/stratagem; design; scheme. **~ হাসিল করা** *vt* attain one's goal/object. **~বাজ** *adj* self-seeking; selfish; designing; scheming; artful; crafty; wily; perfidious; shady. ❑*n* self-seeker; plotter; schemer.

মতি[1] *n* **1** inclination; propensity; mentality. **2** intelligence; intellect. **3** memory. **4** heart: হৃষ্ট~. **5** desire; wish; design; intention: যদি তার ~ হয়. **6** devotion; attention: ধর্মে ~. **7** counsel; advice: কে দিয়েছে এ ~. **~ হওয়া** *vi* be inclined to; incline to; have a mind to. **~গতি** *n* 'mental course'; mode of thought; propensities; intentions and inclinations. **~চ্ছন্ন** *adj* **1** out of one's mind; not in one's right mind/ head. **2** evil-minded; waywarded; rakish; debauched; desolate; wayward. ❑*n* evil-mindedness; waywardness; folly; derangement; madness. **~চ্ছন্ন হওয়া** *vi* go astray; go off the rails; go mad; see things; rave; ramble. **~প্রকর্ষ** *n* superiority of mind; talent; cleverness. **~বিভ্রংস** *n* insanity; madness. **~বিভ্রম, ~ভ্রংশ, ~ভ্রম** *nn* **1** loss of memory. **2** loss of intellect/ judgement; confusion; error; misapprehension; lapse of judgement; aberration; delusion. **3** waywardness; delinquency; recalcitrance. **~ভ্রষ্ট, ~ভ্রান্ত** *adjj* **1** demented. **2** deranged; mad; crazy; unhinged; unbalanced; raving; barmy; loony; touched. **~ভ্রান্তি** *n*=~ভ্রম. **~মতো** *adv* according to one's inclination/ propensities. **~মত্তা** *n* intelligence; wisdom; sagacity; cleverness. **~মান** *adj* intelligent; wise; clever; discreet. **~মতী** *fem.* **~স্থিরতা, ~স্থৈর্য** *nn* firmness of resolve/mind; mental equipoise; sanity; level-headedness; sobriety; equilibrium; balance; composure. **~হীন** *adj* **1** deprived of sense; stupid. **2** lacking in devotion/ attention/ intention/ inclination. **~হীনতা** *n* **1** senselessness; stupidity; mindlessness; obtuseness; foolishness. **2** lack of devotion/ inclination, etc.

মতি[2]=মোতি. **~চুর, ~চূর**=মিহিদানা (⇒ মিহি)

মতিহারী **1** *n* name of a region in Bihar. **2** a variety of tobacco (grown in Matihari).

মতো (colloq) ⇒ মতি[1]

মৎকুণ *n* **1** bug. **2** beardless man. **3** elephant without tusks. **মৎকুণা** *fem.* pudendum of a young girl.

মৎত্রদ্দম [A] *n* translator; interpreter.

মৎফরেক্কা = মুতফরক্কা

মত্ত *n* **1** drunk; intoxicated; drunken; besotted. **2** excited (with joy); overjoyed; delighted. **3** excited by sexual passion/desire; in rut; ruttish (as an elephant). **4** furious; insane; mad; frenzied; maddened. **5** greatly proud of: ধন~. **6** absorbed/lost in: সঙ্গীতে ~. **7** addicted to; indulging in: ভোগবিলাসে ~. ❑*n* **1** cuckoo. **2** ruttish elephant. **3** buffalo. **4** madman. **মত্তা**

fem. ~গামিনী *n fem* woman with a rolling walk; bewitching/wanton woman. ~তা *n* **1** intoxication; sottishness. **2** great elation/joy; exhilaration; ebullience; ecstasy; song and dance; frenzy; delirium; flurry; thrill; fever pitch. **3** madness; derangement. **4** spasm; excitement furore; revelry; rage; feverish. enthusiasm. **5** addiction; absorbing preoccupation. **~দন্তী, ~বারণ, ~মাতঙ্গ, ~হস্তী** *nn* furious/ruttish elephant.

মৎলব=মতলব

মৎসর *n* **1** envy; jealousy; selfishness. **2** malice; spite; malevolence. **3** wrath; anger. **4** self-pity; self-deprecation. ❑*adj* **1** envious; jealous. **2** selfishness. **3** malicious; wicked; spiteful; malevolent; hostile. **4** greedy; base; mean. **মৎসরা** *fem.* **~ মানস** *adj* of envious disposition.

মৎস্য *n* **1** fish. **2** the first of the ten incarnation of Vishnu. **3** (astrol) Pisces. **মৎস্যা, মৎস্যী** *fem.* **~করন্তিকা** *n* fish-basket; any receptacle for fish. **~গন্ধা** *adj* having the smell of fish. ❑*n* Satyavati, mother of Vyasa. **~ঘণ্ট** *n* a highly seasoned dish of fish. **~জাত** *n* fishery product. **~জাল** *n* fishing-net. **~জীবী** *n* fisherman. **~ধানী** *n* fish-basket. **~ন্যায়** = মাৎস্যন্যায়. **~ পুরাণ** *n* name of one of the eighteen Puranas. **~বন্ধ** *n* fish-catcher; fisherman. **~বেধন, ~বেধনী** *nn* hook; angle. **~ব্যবসায়** *n* trade/profession of catching and selling fish. **~ব্যবসায়ী** *n* fisherman; fishmonger; fishdealer. **~রাজ** *n* fish-king; the best of fishes; *Cyprinus rohita.* **~সঙ্ঘ** *n* shoal of fish. **~ভোজী** *adj* fish-eating; feeding on fish. **মৎস্যাবতার**=~ (2). **মৎস্যাশী**=~ভোজী. **মৎস্যাসন** *n* a particular posture of yoga; fish-posture.

মৎস্যোদরী *n* 'sprung from a fish-belly'; Satyavati, mother of Vyasa.

মথ [E] *n* moth.

মথন *n* **1** stirring; churning; shaking; rubbing. **2** hurting; annoying; injury; destruction. **3** trampling; crushing. **4** (used as a *suff)* destroying: অসুর~. **~ করা** *vt* churn; stir; whirl round; shake; agitate; trouble; disturb; distress; destroy; trample; crush; rout.

মথনি *n* churning-rod.

মথা *vt* (archaic, poetic)=মথন করা (⇒ মথন)

মথিত *adj* churned; shaken; agitated; stirred; trampled; crushed; destroyed; routed. ❑*n* butter-milk churned without water. **~ করা** =মথন করা (⇒ মথন).

মথী *n* churning-stick.

মথুরা *n* an ancient city in India. **~ধাম** *n* city of Mathura.

মথ্যমান *adj* being churned/stirred up.

মদ *n* **1** any exhilarating/intoxicating drink; spirituous liquor; wine. **2** hilarity; rapture; excitement. **3** intoxication; inspiration. **4** insanity personified. **5** ardent passion for; sexual desire/ enjoyment; wantoness; lust; ruttishness; rut (esp of an elephant). **6** pride; arrogance; presumption; conceit of/about. **7** fluid/juice that exudes from the rutting elephants/stag's temples. **8** semen virile. **~ খাওয়া** *vi* drink wine; drink. **~ক** *n* an intoxicant consisting of opium, used for smoking. **~কর** *adj* intoxication. **~করী** *n* elephant in rut. **~কল** *adj* sounding/singing softly or indistinctly (as if intoxicated); drunk; intoxicated (with liquor/passion); ruttish; furious; mad. **~কলকোকিলকূজিত** *n* warbling of cuckoos during the breeding season. **~কলযুবতী** *n fem* young woman intoxicated with love. **~খোর** *adj* addicted to drinking. ❑*n* drunkard. **~গন্ধ, ~গন্ধা** *nn* intoxicating beverage. **~গর্ব** *n* insane vanity/ pride/ arrogance. **~গর্বিত, ~গর্বী** *adjj* intoxicated/mad with pride/vanity. **~গর্বিতা** *fem.* **~জ্বর** *n* fever of passion/pride. **~বারি** *n* temple-juice (of a ruttish elephant). **~বিক্ষিপ্ত** *adj* distracted by passion; ruttish; furious. **~বিহ্বল, ~বিহ্বলিত** *adjj* excited by passion; lustful; wanton. **~মত্ত** *adj* **1** wildly intoxicated; dead drunk. **2** drunk/ intoxicated/ mad with vanity/pride. **3** ruttish. **~মত্তা/ ~মত্ত হস্তী** *n* elephant in rut; furious elephant. **~মুকুলিত** *adj* half-closed with intoxication. **~মুকুলিতাক্ষী** *adj* with eyes half-closed with passion. **~মোহিত** *adj* stupefied by drunkenness. **~য়িতা** *adj fem* intoxicating. **~লেখা** *n* line formed by the rut-juice (on an elephant's temples). **~স্রাবী** *adj* emitting temple-juice (as a rutting elephant). **মদাকুল** *adj* agitated by passion/lust; furious with rut. **মদাঢ্য** *adj* rich in/filled with wine; intoxicated; drunk. **মদাতঙ্ক, মদাত্যয়** *n* disorder resulting from intoxication (as headache etc). **মদান্ধ** *adj* blind through drunkenness/ passion; infatuated; ruttish (as an elephant). **মদাবস্থা** *n* state of passion; ruttishness. **মদালস** *adj* lazy from drunkenness; indolent; languid; slothful. **মদালসা** *fem.* **মদালাপ** *n* sounds of love/joy; amorous conversation. **মদালাপী** *adj* uttering sounds of love/ joy. **মদালাপিনী** *fem.*

মদত, মদৎ, মদদ *n* help; aid; assistance; succour; reinforcement; cooperation. **~ করা/দেওয়া** *vt* help; assist; aid; cooperate with; reinforce. **~গার** *n* helper; ally; protector; assistant. **~গারি** *n*=~.

মদন *n* **1** Hindu god of love. **2** passion; love; sexual desire. **3** season of spring. **4** name of various plants. **5** bee; bumble bee. **6** act of intoxicating/exhilarating. ❑*adj* intoxicating. **মদনা** *fem* **1** any intoxicating drink; spirituous liquor. **2** musk. **3** lustful woman. **~কণ্টক** *n* erection of hair caused by a thrill of love. **~কলহ** *n* love-quarrel. **~ক্লিষ্ট** *adj* pained by love. **~ধর্ম** *n* coitus. **~পীড়া** *n* pain/ disquietude of love. **~পীড়িত** *adj* stricken with sexual desire/love; lovesick; lovelorn. **~পীড়িতা** *adj fem*. **~বশ** *adj* influenced by love; enamoured. **~বাণ** *n* shaft of Madana. **~মোহন** *n* 'infatuater of the god of love'; Sri Krishna. **~রিপু** *n* 'enemy of Kamadeva', Shiva. **~ললিত** amorously sporting/ dallying. **~লেখা** *n* love-letter. **~শর**=~বাণ. **মদনাতুর**=~পীড়িত. **মদনাবস্থা** *n* state of love. **মদনাশয়** *n* sexual desire.

মদনোৎসব *n* festival of Madana; vernal.

মদনোৎসুক *adj* pining/languid with love.

মদিনা **1** (lit) city. **2** city where the holy shrine of Prophet Muhammad (sm) is situated.

মদির *adj* intoxicating; exhilarating; delighting; lovely. ❑*n* wagtail (esp in the breading season). **~নয়ন** *adj* having intoxicating/ fascinating eyes; lovely-eyed. **~নয়না** *fem n* fascinating woman. **মদিরাক্ষ** = ~নয়ন. **মদিরাক্ষী** *fem*.

মদিরা *n* spirituous liquor; any inebriating drink; wine; nectar. **~গৃহ** *n* drinking-house; tavern. **~সব** *n* any intoxicating liquor.

মদিরেক্ষণা *adj*=মদিরনয়না (⇒ মদির)

মদিরোৎকট *adj* excited/intoxicated with spirituous liquor.

মদিরোন্মত্ত *adj* drunk with wine/spirituous liquor.

মদীয় *poss adj* (old use) my.

মদো, মোদো *adjj* pertaining to wine/spirituous liquor; alcoholic; spirituous; addicted to wine. ❑*n* drunkard.

মদোৎকট *adj* **1** excited by drink; intoxicated. **2** excited by passion; ruttish; furious. **3** arrogant. ❑*n* elephant in rut.

মদোদগ্র *adj* **1** much excited; furious. **2** arrogant; haughty.

মদোদ্ধত *adj* **1** intoxicated. **2** puffed up with pride; arrogant. **মদোদ্ধতা** *fem*.

মদোন্মত্ত *adj* intoxicated with passion or pride.

মদ্গুর=মাগুর

মদ্দ=মর্দ

মদ্দনা *n* (archaic) manliness; virility.

মদ্দা=মর্দা

মদ্দানি=মর্দানি

মদ্য *n* any intoxicating drink; vinous/spirituous liquor; wine. **~প, ~পায়ী** *adj* drinking/addicted to intoxicating liquor. ❑*nn* drunkard. **~পান** *n* drinking of intoxicating liquors. **~বিক্রেতা** *n* seller of intoxicating liquors; vintner; wine-merchant.

মদ্র *n* **1** an ancient country consisting of some districts of the modern Punjab. **2** joy; happiness.

মধু *n* **1** honey; nectar. **2** anything sweet (esp if liquid). **3** juice of the soma plant (সোম). **4** any sweet intoxicating drink; wine; spirituous liquor. **5** the month of Chaitra. **6** the season of spring. **7** name of an Asura. **8** liquorice. ❑*adj* sweet; delicious; pleasant; delightful; charming. **~ক** *n* **1** liquorice. **2** Asoka tree; *Jonesia asoka*. **3** Mahua tree; *Bassia latifolia*. **~কণ্ঠ** *adj* having a melodious/ mellifluous voice; soft-spoken; sweet-voiced. ❑*n* cuckoo. **~কর** *n* **1** bee. **2** lover; libertine. **3** the tree *Eclipta prostrata* (ভৃঙ্গরাজ). **~করী** *fem* female bee. **~করডম্বর** *n pl* swarm of bees. **~কোদক** *n* milk mixed with water. **~কোষ** *n* bee-hive; honeycomb. **~ক্রম** =~ কোষ. **~গন্ধ, ~গন্ধি, ~গন্ধিক** *adj* sweet-smelling. **~গ্রন্থি** *n* (bot) nectary. **~গ্রহ** *n* libation of honey. **~ঘোষ** *n* cuckoo. **~চক্র**=~কোষ. **~চন্দ্র, ~চন্দ্রমা, ~চন্দ্রিমা** *n* honeymoon. **~চ্ছন্দ** *n* name of the first of Vishvamitra's one hundred and one sons. **~জ** *adj* obtained from honey. ❑*n* earth; wax; sugar made from honey; sugar-candy. **~জাত** *adj* sprung/produced from honey. **~জালক**=~কোষ. **~জীব** *n* bee. **~জিহ্ব** *adj* honey-tongued; sweet-tongued; sweetly-speaking. **~তৃণ** *n* sugar-cane. **~ত্রয়** *n pl* the three sweet things (sugar, honey and clarified butter). **~ত্ব** *n* sweetness. **~দূত** *n* 'messenger of spring'; mango tree. **~দ্রুম**=**1** ~দূত. **2** Mahua tree. **~ধারা** *n* stream of honey. **~নাড়ি** *n* cell in a honeycomb. **~নিশি** *n* vernal/spring night; delightful night; wedding night. **~প** *adj* drinking sweetness; honey-drinking. ❑*n* large black bee. **~পর্ক** *n* mixture of honey; oblation of honey, curds and clarified butter. **~পর্কিক** *adj* presenting the offering of honey, etc. **~পর্ণী** *n* name of several plants (*Omelina arborea, Indigofera tinctoria, Cocculus cordifalus*, etc). **~পায়ী**=~প. **~পায়িনী** *fem*. **~পুরী** *n* city of Mathura. **~পুষ্প** *n* name of various plants *(Bassia latifolia, Acacia sirissa, Jonesia asoka, Minusopa elenga)*. **~পূর্ণ** *adj* full of honey; honeyed; very delicious; very sweet/charming. **~পেয়** *adj* sweet to drink. **~প্রমেহ** *n* diabetes. **~প্রাশন** *n* putting a little honey into the mouth of a new-born male child. **~প্রিয়** *adj* fond of honey/juice of flowers ❑*n* kind of plant (ভূমিজম্বু). **~বন** *n* **1** Indian cuckoo. **2** pleasure-garden. **~বর্ণ** *adj* honey-coloured; having an agreeable aspect. **~বল্লী** *n* liquorice; a kind of grape. **~বর্ষী** *adj* dropping/ raining sweetness; mellifluous. **~বহুলা** *n* the creeper *Gaertnera racemosa* (মাধবীলতা). **~বীজ** *n* pomegranate tree. **~ব্রত**=~কর. **~ভাষী** *adj* honey-tongued. ~ভুৎ=~কর. ~মক্ষিকা *n* bee. ~মতী *adj fem* **1** possessing/containing sweetness; sweet; pleasant; agreeable. **2** rich in honey; mixed in honey. ❑*n* **1** a particular step/ degree in yoga. **2** name of a river. **3** kind of metre. ~মান *adj masc.* ~মতীসিদ্ধি *n* attainment of a particular supernatural power. ~মত্ত *adj* drunk with wine/ honey; intoxicated/ excited by the spring. ~মদ *n* intoxication with wine. ~মদ্য *n* intoxicating drink made from honey or from the blossoms of *Bassia latifolia* (মহুয়া). ~ময় *adj* consisting of honey; sweet as honey; luscious. ~মাধবী *n* any spring flower abounding in honey; a particular species of flower; kind of intoxicating drink; wine. ~মাধবীক *n* any intoxicating drink. ~মালতী *n* kind of creeper. ~মাস *n* a spring month; month of Chaitra. ~মিশ্র *adj* mixed with honey/sweet milk. ~মূল *n* edible root of *Amorphophallus companulatus* (মৌ আলু). ~মেহ *n* diabetes mellitus. ~মেহী *adj* suffering from diabetes. ~যষ্টি, ~যষ্টিকা *nn* sugar-cane; liquorice. ~যামিনী=~নিশি. ~রস *n* juice of honey; sweetness; pleasingness; sugar-cane; wine palm (তাল); vine; bunch of grapes. ~রাতি=~নিশি. ~রিপু *n* enemy of Madhu; Sri Krishna. ~রিম *adj* sweet as honey; very sweet. ~রিমা *n* sweetness; suavity; charm. ~রুচি *adj* tasting sweet; honeyed. ~লিট, ~লেহ, ~লেহী *adj* licking honey. ❑*nn* bee. ~লুব্ধ, ~লোলুপ *adjj* longing after honey. ❑*nn* bee. ~শর্করা *n* honey and sugar. ~শাখ *n* *Bassia latifolia.* ~সখ *n* friend of spring; god of love. ~সর্পী *n* honey and clarified butter. ~সহায় *n* 'having spring for a companion; god of love. ~সূদন=~নিসূদন. ~স্রব *n* 'dropping sweetness'; name of several plants *(Bassia latifolia, Sanseviera roxburghiana,* etc); liquorice. ~স্বর=~কণ্ঠ.

মধুর *adj* **1** sweet; pleasant; delicious; amiable; charming; delightful. **2** sounding sweetly; uttering sweet cries; melodious; mellifluous; honeyed; sugary. ❑*n* **1** sweetness. **2** molasses. **3** poison. মধুরা *adj fem.* ~কণ্ঠ, ~কণ্ঠী *adjj* sweet-throated; singing sweetly. ~তা, ~ত্ব *n* sweetness; suavity; pleasantness; amiability; softness; charm. ~নিস্বন *adj* sweet-voiced. ~প্রকৃতি, ~স্বভাব *adjj* sweet-tempered. ~ভাষী *adj* speaking sweetly/kindly; soft-spoken. ~ভাষিণী *fem.* ~রাবী *adj* rumbling sweetly as a cloud. ~স্বন *adj* sweetly-sounding. ~স্বর *adj* sweet-voiced. মধুরাক্ষর *adj* speaking/sounding sweetly; melodious; mellow. মধুরাম্ল *adj* sweet and sour. মধুরালাপ *n* pleasant/ friendly conversation; amorous conversation; sweet/ melodious notes. ❑*adj* uttering sweet sounds.

মধুচ্ছিষ্ট *n* bees-wax.

মধূখ *n* bees-wax. ~ বতিকা *n* wax candle.

মধূৎসব *n* spring festival.

মধূদক *n* honey diluted with water; honey-water

মধূদ্যান *n* spring garden.

মধ্য *n* **1** middle. **2** waist; middle of the body. **3** middle finger. **4** (arith) mean. **5** (music) a particular measure. **6** midst; centre. **7** inside; interior. **8** middle of the sky. **9** space between. **10** midday. **11** meridian. **12** intermediate condition between. **13** belly; abdomen. **14** (music) mean-time. **15** cessation; pause; interval. ❑*adj* **1** middle; middlemost. **2** intermediate. **3** central. **4** standing between two. **5** impartial; neutral. **6** middle, ie being of a middle size/ kind/ quantity; middling; mediocre; medium; moderate: ~ বৃত্তি, middle course. **7** intervening; interim. **8** (with) mean. মধ্যা *fem.* উষ্ণতা *n* mean temperature. ~ক *n, adj* mean. ~কর্ণ *n* half diameter; radius. ~কাল *n* meantime. ~কালীন *adj* interim; ad interim. ~কোণ *n* (astron) mean anomaly. ~ক্ষামা, ~ক্ষীণা *fem* having a slender waist. ~গ *adj* going/being in the middle; of middling state. ❑*n* middleman. ~গা *fem.* ~গত *adj*=~গ. ~গগন *n* middle sky. ~গমন *n* (astron) culmination. ~গুণক *n* (math) modulus. ~চারী *adj* going in the midst/ among. ~চ্ছদা *n* (anat) diaphragm. ~জীবীয় *adj* (geol) Mesozoic. ~জ্যা *n* (astron) sign of the meridian. ~তঃ *adv* from/in the middle; centrally. ~তল *n* (astron) meridian plane. ~তা, ত্ব *nn* state of being in the middle; mediocrity. ~ত্বক *n* (bot) mesocarp. ~দন্ত *n* front tooth. ~দিন *n* midday. ~দেশ *n* **1** middle region/ space; central/ middle part of anything. **2** middle/ trunk of the body; waist; belly; abdomen. ~দেশীয় *adj* belonging to/living in the midland country; of midland origin. ~দেহ *n* middle/trunk of the body; belly. ~নগর *n* interior of a city. ~নতাংশ *n* (astron) meridian zenith distance. ~নিহিত *adj* placed in the middle; inserted; fixed into. ~নীচগমন *n* (astron) lower culmination. ~ন্দিন *n* midday; noon. ❑*adj*=মাধ্যন্দিন. ~পদলোপী (সমাস). *n* (gram) mode of forming compound words by deleting the word in the middle of other two. ~পন্থা *n* middle course; golden mean. ~পন্থী *adj.* ❑*adj* following the middle course; moderate. ❑*n* moderate. ~পর্দা, ~পরদা *n* middle lamella. ~পরিমাণ *n* middle measure/ magnitude. ~প্রবিষ্ট *adj* one who has stolen into another's confidence. ~বয়স, ~বয়সী, ~বয়স্ক *adjj* middle-aged. ~বয়সিনী, ~বয়স্কা *fem.* ~বর্তিতা *n* state of being in the middle/ inside; intermediary; mediation; intervention. ~বর্তী *adj* being in the middle/ between/

among; middle; central; intermediate; medial; intervening; mediate. ~বর্তিনী *fem.* ~বর্তী নিযুক্তক *n* handling agent. ~বর্তী হওয়া *vi* lie/go in the middle; mediate; intervene. ~বিত্ত *adj* middle-class. ~বিত্ত-মনোবৃত্তি *n* middle-class mentality; petty bourgeois mentality. ~বিত্ত শ্রেণী/ সম্প্রদায় *nn* middle class. ~বিধ *adj* mediocre; middling. ~বৃত্ত *n* **1** navel. **2** (astron) transit circle. ~ভাগ *n* middle part/ portion. ~ভাব *n* middle state/condition; mediocrity. ~মণি *n* **1** central/ principal gem of a necklace. **2** (fig) the most precious/ prominent person or thing; life and heart of the party etc; centre of attraction. ~মান *n* name of a musical measure. ~মিকা *n fem* young woman; maiden. ~যুগ *n* the Middle Ages. ~যুগীয় *adj* mediaeval. ~রাত্র, ~রাত্রি *n* midnight. ~রেখা *n* **1** middle line. **2** (astron) meridian. ~শরীর *n* (anat) trunk; torso. ~শায়ী *adj* lying within/in the middle. ~শিক্ষা *n* secondary education. ~শিক্ষা পরিষদ *n* Board of Secondary Education. ~শিরা *n* (bot) midrib. ~স্থ *adj* **1** being in the middle/ between/ among; standing between two persons/ parties; mediating; intermediate; intervening; medial; impartial; neutral. **2** of the interior/inside; inner; lying inside/in the interior/in the midst. ❑*n* **1** mediator; arbitrator; umpire; arbiter. **2** intermediary; middleman; go-between. **3** (math) meridian. মধ্যস্থা *fem.* ~ন্যায়পীঠ arbitral tribunal. ~স্থতা *n* **1** intermediate situation; being inside. **2** arbitration; mediation. **3** impartiality; indifference. ~স্থতা করা *vt* mediate; arbitrate. ~স্থল *n* middle place/region; middle; centre; middle of the body; waist; hip; inside; interior; midst. ~স্থান *n* middle space; air. ~স্থালি=স্থতা. ~স্থিত *adj* lying/ being in the middle/ among/ between/ inside; inside. মধ্যাঙ্গুলি *n* middle finger.

মধ্যখানে (used as a *case m*) **1** in the middle; in; within. **2** for nothing: ~ আমার টাকাগুলি গেল.

মধ্যন্দিন ⇒ মধ্য

মধ্যম *adj* **1** being/placed in the middle; middlemost; intermediate; medial; central. **2** of a middle kind/size/quality; middling; moderate. **3** middle-born; second. **4** standing between two persons/parties. ❑*n* **1** (music) the fourth note. **2** (music) the middlemost of the three scales. **3** the middle country. মধ্যমা *n fem* **1** waist; the middle: সুমধ্যমা. **2** womb. **3** a girl arrived at puberty. **4** middle finger. **5** (astron) mean. **6** (math) average. ~গ্রাম *n* (music) middle scale. ~জাত *adj* middle-born. ~পদ *n* middle term. ~পন্থা *n* middle course; moderateness; moderatism. ~পন্থী *adj* following the middle course; moderate. ~পাণ্ডব *n* middlemost of the five Pandavas; Arjuna. ~পুরুষ *n* (gram) second person. ~বয়স *n* middle age. ~বয়স্ক *adj* middle-aged. ~বয়স্কা *fem.* ~লোক *n* middle world; the earth. ~স্বর *n* (music) middle note. মধ্যাঙ্গুলি *n* middle finger.

মধ্যা *n fem* **1** middle finger. **2** young girl arrived at puberty. **3** middle term; mean of progression.

মধ্যাহ্ন *n* midday; noon. ~কাল *n* midday time; noon. ~কালীন *adj* of/at noon; midday; noonday; meridional. ~কালে at noon. ~ক্রিয়া *n* any one of the scriptural or other midday duties; midday meal; lunch. ~কৃত্য *n* midday duty/business/observance. ~তপন *n* midday sun. ~ভোজ, ~ভোজন *nn* midday meal; lunch; luncheon. ~ভোজন করা take one's midday meal; lunch. ~বেলা, ~সময় *n*=~কাল.

মধ্যে *prep* **1** in the middle; at the centre: মাঠের ঠিক ~. **2** in; within; into; inside: ঘরের ~. **3** between; in between; among: তিন ভাইয়ের ~ সে-ই বড়ো. **4** before; by: তিনি পাঁচটার ~ এসে পড়বেন. **5** within the (said) period; sometime back: ~ সে একবার এসেছিল. **6** at intervals. **7** as; as for: কাজের ~ তো এই? সে মানুষের ~ই নয়. **8** at heart: কার ~ কী আছে কে জানে? **9** more to sth/sb than meets the eye: এর ~ কথা আছে, পরে জানাব. ~ থেকে **1** from within; out of; from among: যতগুলি দরখাস্ত এসেছিল তার ~ থেকে. **2** for nothing: ~ থেকে তার ছাতাটা খোয়া গেল. ~ পড়া *vi* intervene: ~ পড়ে তিনি ঝগড়া মিটিয়ে দিলেন. ~ মধ্যে **1** from time to time; occasionally; once in a while; now and then: তিনি ~ মধ্যে আসেন. **2** at intervals; few and far between; sparsely: ~ মধ্যে গাছ লাগানো. **3** intermittently; every now and then: ~ মধ্যে সে জ্বরে ভোগে. ~ মধ্যেই often; off and on: ~ মধ্যেই সে রেগে ওঠে.

মধ্যোচ্চগমন *n* (astron) upper culmination.

মধ্যোন্নতি *n* (astron) meridian altitude.

মধ্বাসব *n* decoction of honey or of the *Bassia latifolia* (মহুয়া); sweet spirituous liquor.

মন[১] *n* **1** mind; heart. **2** intellect; intelligence; understanding; perception. **3** sense; conscience. **4** will. **5** spirit; spiritual principle. **6** thought. **7** imagination; invention. **8** excogitation; reflection. **9** opinion; consideration. **10** intention. **11** inclination; desire. **12** mood; mental state; temper; spirit. **13** affection; attachment; interest; feeling; attraction. **14** mentality. **15** memory. **16** attention. **17** earnestness; sincerity; devotion. **18** resolve; choice; decision. ~ আসন be inclined to; feel like: কাজে ~ আসা. ~ ওঠা (উঠা) be satisfied/pleased; achieve one's heart's desire; have all that one could wish for; be gratified: অল্পেতে তার ~ ওঠে না. ~ উঠে যাওয়া be fed up/disgusted with: তার উপর থেকে

আমার ~ উঠে গেছে. **~ কর-কর করা** be uneasy in one's mind; be troubled/agitated. **~ করা 1** resolve; make up one's mind; have a good mind to do sth; feel inclination for. **2** give one's mind to sth; direct one's attention to sth. **3** agree; condescend; consent: আপনি মনে করলে কাজটা হতে পারে. **~ কষা 1** take heart; nerve/ brace oneself; pluck up courage. **2** prove sb's thoughts; test sb's mind. **~ কাড়া** captivate the mind; win one's heart; bewitch; take/ catch the mind of; ravish. **~ কুড়ানো** compose one's mind; concentrate. **~ কেড়ে নেওয়া**=~ কাড়া. **~ কেমন করা** be uneasy in mind; be worried/ troubled/ agitated; be sick at heart. **~ খারাপ করা 1** feel sad/ distressed; become glum/ morose; grieve over sth; take sth to heart; cry one's heart out; pull a long face; despair; be upset. **2** make sad; upset; sadden; dampen. **~ খারাপ হওয়া** be out of humour; be unhappy; be out of sorts/ spirits; be in low/ poor spirits. **~ খোলা** open one's heart; unbosom oneself; speak one's mind; speak out/up; not to mince matters/mince one's words. **~ গড়া** be mentally prepared; brace oneself. **~ গলা** soften (with pity); relent; (heart) melt; take pity on. **~ গলানো** mollify; propitiate; appease; touch sb's feelings; melt sb's heart. **~ চলা** (of heart, thoughts) go; fly; be greatly attracted; feel the attraction of. **~ চাওয়া** be inclined to; have a mind to wish; will; desire. **~ চাঙা করা** cheer up; rejoice sb's heart; fortify; hearten; steel one's heart. **~ চুরি করা** steal sb's heart; bewitch; captivate; with the heart of. **~চোর, ~চোরা** *nn* captor of sb's heart; sweetheart. **~ ছড়ানো 1** give one's attention to too many things; let one's thoughts wander. **2** loose one's heart to many lovers; philander. **~ ছুটা (ছোটা)** lay for; feel a strong urge; have one's heart set on sth; set one's mind on sth (of mind/thoughts) wander. **~ ছোট করা** belittle; debase; demean; humiliate. **~ ছোট হওয়া 1** feel small; be mean; become niggardly/small-minded; be stricken with a sense of inferiority; feel inferior. **2** loose heart; be discouraged. **~ জানা** read sb's thoughts; know sb's mind. **~ জোগানো** humour; keep sb in good humour; pamper; flatter; curry favour with; fawn (on); comply with sb's orders/ desires; deny sb nothing; gratify sb's whims/ fancies; indulge. **~ জ্বলা** have heart-burning; smart with jealousy/ anger/ vexation; be consumed with envy/hatred/ greed; burn to avenge. **~ টলা 1** soften; yield; give in; relent; melt. **2** have a change of heart; waver; be of two minds; be in two minds; vacillate; hesitate; give way/ succumb to (temptation); be seduced; be swept of/ one's feet; be tempted; go off one's head: এমন রূপ দেখে মুনিরও ~ টলে. **~ টানা** attract; fascinate; incline; interest; appeal; stir sb's imagination. **~ টেকা** feel at ease/ comfortable; be in one's elements. **~ ঢালা** give one's mind to sth; give one's whole attention to sth; give all one's energy and attention to; apply one's mind to; be absorbed in. **~তরী** *n* the mind conceived of as a boat. **~ তিতো করা** vex; embitter; irritate; annoy; sour. **~ থাকা** have a liking for; care for; have interest in; feel love for; have the will; be attentive to. **~ থেকে 1** sincerely; from (the bottom of) one's heart; in all sincerity. **2** from memory; by/out of one's imagination. **~ দমা** be discouraged/ disheartened; lose heart; feel hopeless; have one's heart in one's boots. **~ দেওয়া 1** fall in love with; lose one's mind/one's energies (to sth/to doing sth); mind; direct the mind/ thoughts towards; think of: ~ দিয়ে কাজ করা. **3** be attentive to; pay attention/heed to: আমার কথায় ~ দাও. **~ ধসা**=~ দমা. **~ না মতি (ভ্রম)** (prov) The human mind is very unpredictable. **~ পড়া** take a fancy to; become fond of: ছেলেটিকে দেখে তার ~ পড়ে যায়. **~ পাওয়া 1** win sb's favour/love; win the heart of; ingratiate oneself with sb; curry favour with; please; satisfy: তার ~ পাওয়া সোজা নয়. **2** know sb's mind. **~ পোড়া** pine for; eat one's heart out; yearn for; waste away; be consumed. **~ ফেরা** be dissuaded/ disaffected/ put off/ disgusted. **~ ফেরানো** turn the mind from. **~ বসা 1** settle (down) to sth; take pleasure in; relish; take interest in: কাজে ~ বসা. **2** be to one's liking; be after one's heart. **~ বসানো** cause to settle (down) on; apply one's mind to; take sth up in earnest; concentrate (one's attention) on/upon. **~ বুঝা (বোঝা) 1** understand sb/sb's thoughts; read sb's thoughts; see through sb/sth. **2** realize; believe in; have faith: ~ বোঝ না তীর্থ করি. **~ বুঝানো** console; comfort; set one's mind at ease/rest; persuade. **~ ভরা** fill the mind/ heart; rejoice the heart; satisfy fully; gratify a person's hopes, desires, etc. **~ ভাঙা** be heart-broken/dejected/depressed; be in poor/low spirits. **~ ভাঙানো 1** break sb's heart; dishearten; discourage. **2** bias/ prejudice sb's mind against sb; poison a person's mind against sb; alienate; estrange; earwig. **~ ভার করা 1** be in bad humour; be sad/ depressed/ despondent/ glum/ gloomy/ down in the dumps; pull a long face; sulk; get sulky. **2** sadden; depress; dishearten; get sb down. **~ ভার হওয়া**=~ ভার করা (1). **~ভারী** *adj* gloomy; glum; sulky; cheerless; down in the mouth. **~ ভুলানো (ভোলানো) 1** charm/ captivate sb's mind; enchant; bewitch; fascinate; win sb's heart. **2** cajole; entice; wheedle into; soft-soap; falter. **~ভোলানো, ~ভুলানে** *adjj* **1** charming; fascinating. **2** flattering; honeyed; sugary; seductive; ingratiating. **~ভোলা** *adj* forgetful; oblivious; absent-minded; distracted; lost in thought; dreamy. **~ভ্রমরা** *n* (rhet) the mind conceived of as a bee. **~মরা** *adj* dejected; crestfallen; sulky; down-hearted; despondent; wretched; soul-sick; cast down; low. **~ মাতা** be thrilled/enchanted/ excited/ intoxicated/ drunk/ delirious oneself; bubble; bubble over. **~ মাতানো** *vi* enrapture; enchant; thrill; enthrall; delight; exhilarate; entrance; stimulate; animate; electrify; enthuse; intoxicate. **~মাতানো, ~মাতানে** *adjj* enchanting; thrilling; delightful; exhilarating; enthralling; stimulating; intoxicating. **~ মানা** be consoled/ consolable; agree/accept at heart. **~ যাওয়া** have a liking; like; take a fancy to: সে যাতে ~ যায় তাই করে, whatever takes/ attracts his/ her fancy. **~ রাখা**=~ জোগানো. **~ লাগা**=~ বসা. **~ লাগানো**=~ বসানো. **~ সরা** have a liking for; feel comfortable; at ease; be in one's elements; be willing to; feel like: ঘরে ~ সরে না. **~ হওয়া** be inclined to; be/feel disposed to; be willing/ ready. **~ হরা** win/ captivate the heart (of). **~ হাতড়ে দেখা** search one's heart/conscience. **~ হারানো** lose one's heart; be distracted; lose control of one's mind. **মনে আনা** remember; recall; bring/call sth to mind; think: অমন কথা মনেও আনবেন না. **মনে আসা/ওঠা** come suddenly into the mind; flash into/through one's mind; occur to/strike one; remember suddenly. **মনে করা 1** remember; recollect; recall; call/bring sth to mind; bring back to the mind; call up; recognize; look back upon. **2** think; consider; feel; count; regard; suppose. **3** have a mind/half a mind to do sth; resolve; decide. **মনে করে 1** without forgetting (do not forget to, etc) without fail: বইটা মনে করে এনো কিন্তু. **2** for what reason; with what purpose; why; what for: কী মনে করে এসেছো?. **মনে করানো** *vt* remind; jog sb's memory. **মনে জাগা**=মনে আসা. **মনে জানা** know/feel at heart; feel in one's bones; know in one's heart of hearts. **মনে ঠাঁই দেওয়া**=মনে স্থান দেওয়া. **মনে থাকা** remember; not forget; recall; be kept in mind. **মনে দানা কাটা** impress one's mind (indelibly); affect (the mind); fascinate; bring sth home to sb; touch; one's heart; stir. **মনে দাগ থাকা** have a (permanent) scar (of grief, etc) on the heart **মনে দাগ রাখা** leave a scar on the heart. **মনে দাগ লাগা** not to forget an insult, injury, etc. **মনে ধরা** be to one's liking; impress one's mind favourably; be after one's heart; like; have one's heart set on sth. **মনে নেওয়া 1** feel; consider. **2** like. **মনে পড়া 1**=মনে আসা. **2** ring a bell. **মনে পোষা/পুষে রাখা** keep/bear sth in mind; not to forget; nourish (feelings of hatred, etc). **মনে-প্রাণে** *adj* with all one's heart; in one's heart of hearts; from (the bottom of) one's heart. **মনে বিষ, মনের বিষ** *nn* malice; venom; spite; hatred; hate. **মনে বাজা** offend; shock; pain; be offended; take offence; take umbrage at sth; take amiss. **মনে বুঝা**=~ জানা. **মনে ভাবা** think; resolve. **মনে-মনে** *adv* in the thought; in thought/imagination. **মনে রাখা** remember; recall; not to forget; keep/bear in mind; retain in memory. **মনে লাগা 1**=মনে ধরা. **2**=মনে বাজা. **3** feel; suppose. **মনে স্থান দেওয়া 1** cherish; keep alive in one's heart; treasure (sth up in one's memory). **2** have/entertain the idea of sth; think of. **মনে হওয়া 1** think; suppose; feel; consider. **2** appear; seem: তাকে বয়সের তুলনায় বুড়ো মনে হয়. **3** occur; cross one's mind: কথাটা আমার মনে হলো. **মনের আগুন** mental anguish/ agony; heartache. **মনের কথা** one's secret thoughts, feelings and intentions; mind. **মনের কালি 1** vice; evil/ malicious thoughts. **2** ignorance. spiritual ignorance. **মনের গোল 1** doubt; suspicion; misgiving; distrust; mistrust; hesitation. **2** grudge; ill-will; discontent; malice; spite. **মনের জোর** (moral) courage; morale; firmness; nerve; guts; self-confidence; iron will; will power. **মনের ঝাল** grudge; revenge; resentment; ill-will; scorn; gall. **মনের ঝাল মেটানো** have/get one's revenge (on sb); satisfy a private spite. **মনের বিষ** malice; venom; spite; spitefulness; rancour. **মনের ব্যথা** mental pain; anguish. **মনের মতো/মতন** to one's liking; after one's own heart. **মনের ময়লা 1**=মনের কালি (1, 2). **2** mistrust; suspicion; misgiving. **মনের মানুষ** person after one's own heart; lover; favourite; sweetheart; idol. **মনের মিল** harmony; concord; understanding; adjustment; agreement. **মনের মিল হওয়া** be of one mind; be of the same mind; be in agreement; live in concord; get along (with sb); reach an understanding; see eye to eye; be on the same wavelength; be in harmony; live in perfect union. **মনের সাধ** heart's wish; mind's desire. **মনের সাধ মিটিয়ে** to one's heart content. **আপন মনে 1** by oneself; alone. 2 voluntarily; of one's own accord.

মন[২] **মণ** *n* a measure of unit (=40 seers which is about 82 lbs); maund. **~কষা** *n* system of calculating weight in terms of maunds, seer, etc. **~কে** *adv* for each maund; (in) every/each maund.

মনঃ (in compounds)=মন[১]. **~কল্পনা** *n* imagination; figment of imagination. **~কল্পিত** *adj* imagined; fancied; imaginary; fanciful; fictitious; fantastic. **~কষ্ট** *n* pain of mind; agony; anguish; heartache; torment; suffering;

distress; trouble; mortification. ~কষ্ট দেওয়া *vi* distress; torment; trouble; inflict pain/ suffering; hurt (in one's feelings); pain (sb's feelings); wound; mortify; grieve. ~কষ্ট পাওয়া *vi* be distressed/ tormented/ troubled/ pained/ hurt; suffer; be wounded/ mortified. ~ক্ষুণ্ন *adj* disappointed; saddened; displeased; disconsolate; offended; unhappy; disheartened; dejected; upset; cut up; mortified; grieved. ~ক্ষুণ্ন হওয়া *vi* be offended; take sth to heart; be disappointed/ displeased/ upset/ cut up/ hurt (in one's feelings); take sth amiss. ~পীড়া=~কষ্ট. ~পূর্ত *adj* to one's liking; after one's own heart; acceptable to; approved by; to one's satisfaction. ~প্রসাদ *n* serenity/ peace of mind. ~প্রাণ *n* all one's heart. ~প্রাণ দিয়ে চেষ্টা করা try heart and soul. ~প্রিয় *adj* dear to the heart. ~শক্তি *n* morale; resoluteness; strength of character. ~সমীক্ষক *n* psycho-analyst. ~সমীক্ষণ, ~সমীক্ষা *nn* psycho-analysis. ~সমীক্ষণ করা *vt* psycho-analyze. ~সমীক্ষামূলক *adj* psycho-analytic(al). ~সংযোগ *n* application of one's mind; concentration of mind. ~সংযোগ করা *vt* apply one's mind (closely) to; concentrate (on); direct one's thoughts to; be attentive to. ~সন্তাপ *n* mental anguish; grief. ~সমুন্নতি *n* high-mindedness. ~স্থ *n* abiding/dwelling in the heart; mental; determined; resolved; decided. ~স্থ করা *vt* resolve; decide; make up one's mind; intend; have a good mind to. ~স্থিরকরণ *n* act of strengthening/ confirming the mind. ~স্থৈর্য *n* firmness of mind.

মনকলা *n* 'imaginary banana'; imaginary banquet; wishful thinking; daydream; castles in the air.

মন-কষাকষি *n* strained relations; bad blood; mutual ill feelings; estrangement; bitterness; acrimony. ~ করা *vi* be at odds with sb; strain one's relations with; fall out (with sb).

মনকা-পাথর *n* agate.

মনকির-নকির [A] *n* names of two angels who according to Muslims, examine the souls of the departed in the grave.

মনক্কা, মনাক্কা *n* (A) species of raisin.

মন-খোলা *adj* open-hearted; frank; straight-forward; candid; above-board; free and frank.

মন-গড়া=মনঃকল্পিত (⇒ মনঃ)

মনছাল *n* red arsenic; realgar.

মনজিল ⇒ মঞ্জিল

মন-ঢালা *adj* hearty; generous; lavish; openhearted; whole-hearted.

মন-দেওয়া-নেওয়া *n* mutual love-making; courtship; love affair; romance. ~ করা be in love; court.

মনন *n* thinking; reflection; meditation; thought; intelligence; intellect; understanding. ~ করা *vi* think; reflect; meditate; conceive. ~শীল *adj* thoughtful; intellectual; reflective. মননীয় *adj* to be thought out; to be meditated on; conceivable; thinkable; understandable.

মনপবন *n* the mind conceived of as the wind; secret inclinations and intentions; wishes; longing. মনপবনের নাও *n* (in folk-tales) fairy-boat (which can be driven at any speed and in any direction as one wishes).

মন-প্রাণ=মনঃপ্রাণ (⇒ মনঃ)

মন-বাঞ্ছা=মনোবাঞ্ছা

মনমতো *adj* after one's own heart; to one's liking; desired; cherished.

মনমথ *n* (poet)=মন্মথ

মনমরা ⇒ মন

মনরক্ষা *n* compliance with one's orders/ desires; flattering; appeasement; indulging; fawning; ingratiation; cajolery; wheedling; pleasing. ~ করা=মন জোগানো (⇒ মন).

মনশ্চক্ষু *n* mind's eye; insight; imagination.

মনশ্চাঞ্চল্য *n* mental agitation/unrest; worry; anxiety; perturbation; concern.

মনসব [A] *n* dignity; office; post; station; magistracy. ~দার *n* (hist) **1** general serving the emperor in exchange of landed property. **2** officer/official of rank; functionary. **3** magistrate. ~দারি *n* rank or function of a mansabdar.

মনসা *n fem* **1** (myth) Hindu snake-goddess; protectress of men from the venom of snakes. **2** kind of cactus. ~মঙ্গল *n* kind of epic in honour of the goddess Manasa.

মনসিজ *n* 'heart-born'; love; god of love; Madana.

মনসুখ, মনসূখ [A] *adjj* cancelled; abolished; annulled; obliterated; erased; repealed; abrogated: আয়াতে ~.

মনসুন [A] *n* monsoon.

মনসুব, মনসুবা [A] *adj* related; allied; betrothed; surnamed; referred to; belonging to.

মনস্কাম, মনস্কামনা *nn* heart's wish; mind's desire.

মনস্তাপ *n* burning of the mind; mental pain; anguish; repentance; remorse.

মনস্তুষ্টি *n* **1** satisfaction of mind; heart's content; mental satisfaction; gratification; self-gratification; contentment; ease of mind. **2** mollification; adulation. ~কর *adj* satisfying; pleasing; gratifying; pleasurable.

মনস্থ=মনঃস্থ (⇒ মনঃ)

মনস্বী *adj* full of mind/sense; intelligent; clever; high-minded; magnanimous; wise; large; hearted; possessing mental calm/peace; endowed with great intellectual ability. মনস্বিনী

fem. মনস্বিতা *n* high-mindedness; magnanimity; great intellectual ability; intelligence; possession of mental calm/peace.

মনহুস [A] *adj* ill-omened; unlucky; unfortunate; abominable; dismal; bad.

মনাগুন=মনের আগুন (⇒ মন)

মনাছিব= মুনাসিব

মনান্তর *n* disagreement; dissension; strained relations; bitterness; bad blood; quarrel; difference of opinion; dispute; discord; conflict; controversy; rift; disharmony; squabble; wrangle.

মনাসিব=মুনাসিব

মনি-অর্ডার [E] *n* money-order. ~ **করা** *vt* send by money-order. ~ **করে/-যোগে** *adv* by money-order.

মনিব, মুনিব *n* **1** master; patron; employer. **2** landlord. **মনিবালী** *fem.* **মনিবানা,** ~**গিরি** *n* mastership; behaviour like a master; bossing.

মনিব্যাগ, মানিব্যাগ [E] *n* purse; wallet; money-bag.

মনিষ, মুনিষ *n* day-labourer; farmhand; farm-labourer; porter. ~**গিরি** *n* working as a farmhand/porter.

মনিষ্যি (dialect)=মনুষ

মনিহারি, মনিহারী *adj* dealing in stationery goods. ~**-দোকান** *n* stationery goods. ~**-দোকান** *n* stationery shop.

মনীষা *n* sharp intellect; intelligence; thought; wisdom; genius.

মনীষিত *adj* desired; wished.

মনীষিতা=মনীষ

মনীষী *adj* endowed with sharp intellect; intelligent; wise; thoughtful; sage. ❑ *n* man of intellect; learned/wise man; intellectual. **মনীষিণী** *fem.*

মনু *n* (myth) **1** any of the fourteen sons of Brahma. **2** Man par excellence/ representative man and father of the human race. **3** sacred text; incantation; spell. ~**সংহিতা** *n* collection of laws commonly known as 'the laws/ institutions of Manu'. ~**স্মৃতি** *n* Manu law-book.

মনুজ *n* Manu-born; man. ~**কুল** *n* human race. **মনুজা** *fem* woman. **মনুজেন্দ্র** *n* king; monarch.

মনুরা *n* (dialect) life.

মনুমেন্ট [E] *n* monument.

মনুষ্য *n* man; human being; mankind; humankind. ~**কৃত** *adj* man-made. ~**কণ্ঠ** *n* human voice. ~**খাদক** *adj* anthropophagous; man-eating. ❑*n* man-eating giant; ogre; cannibal. ~**খাদক ব্যাঘ্র** *n* man-eater. ~**গন্ধ** *n* human odour. ~**চরিত্র** *n* human character. ~**চিত্ত** *n* human heart. ~**জন্ম** *n* birth as a human creature; human life. ~**জাতি** *n* human race; mankind. ~**ত্ব** *n* humanity; state/ condition of man; manhood; humanness. ~**ত্বপূর্ণ** *adj* human; full of human qualities. ~**ত্ববর্জিত,** ~**ত্বহীন** *adj* devoid of humanity/ human quality; inhuman; brutal; inhumane. ~**দেহ** *n* human body. ~**ধর্ম** *n* law/ duty/ state/ character of man; humanity. ~**ধর্মা** *adj* having the nature/ character of man; human. ~**প্রকৃতি** *n* human nature. ~**বর্জিত** *adj* man-forsaken; uninhabited; desolate. ~**বসতি** *n* human habitation. ~**মূর্তি** *n* human figure/being/form; statue. ~**যজ্ঞ** *n* 'man-offering; act of devotion due to men; honouring of guests; hospitality. ~**রূপ** *n* human form. ~**লোক** *n* world of men. ~**সভা** *n* assembly/crowd/meeting-place of men. ~**সমাগম** *n* existence of men; gathering. ~**হীন** *adj* not inhabited by man; desolate. **মনুষ্যাবাস, মনুষ্যালয়** *nn* human habitation; human dwelling; house; human settlement; town; city; village.

মনুষ্যোচিত *adj* befitting/ becoming of man; humane.

মনো (in compounds)=মন[১]. ~**গত** *adj* existing/ passing/ concealed in the mind or heart; mental; inward. ~**গত ভাব** *n* **1** state of mind. **2** intention. ~**গতি** *n* 'heart's course; desire; wish. ~**গম্য** *adj* accessible to/conceivable by the mind. ~**গ্রাহী** *adj* captivating the mind; fascinating. ~**গ্রাহ্য** *n* to be grasped by the mind. ~**গ্লানি** *n* depression of mind. ~**জ** *adj* mind-born; born in/of the mind. ❑*n* god of love; love. ~**জগৎ** *n* realm/ sphere of the mind; realm of intellect/ imagination/ ideas/ thoughts/ fancy. ~**জ্ঞ** *adj* agreeable to the mind; pleasing; lovely; beautiful; charming. ~**দুঃখ** *n* heartache; mental affliction. ~**দুষ্ট** *adj* defiled with evil thoughts; depraved. ~**নয়ন** *n* choosing; choice; selection; nomination. ~**নয়ন করা** *vt* select; choose; nominate. ~**নিবেশ** *n* application of the mind; close attention. ~**নিবেশ করা** *vi* apply one's mind; pay close attention to; direct the mind/thoughts towards; apply/address oneself to; concentrate on. ~**নীত** *adj* chosen; selected; nominated; preferred; approved. ~**নীতা** *fem.* ~**নীত করা**=~নয়ন করা. ~**নীতক** *n* nominee. ~**নেত**=মনশ্চক্ষু. ~**বল্লভা** *n fem* beloved woman. ~**বাঞ্ছা,** ~**বাঞ্ছিত** *nn* heart's wish; mind's desire. ~**বাসনা**=~ বাঞ্ছা. ~**বিকার** *n* **1** aberration of the mind; mental perversion; neurosis; distraction. **2** (psych) emotion. **3** mental agitation. ~**বিচ্ছেদ**=মনান্তর. ~**বিজ্ঞান,**

~বিদ্যা *nn* psychology. ~বিদ্যাগত *adj* psychological. ~বিদ, ~বিজ্ঞানী *n n* psychologist. ~বিবাদ=মন-কষাকষি. ~বিরুদ্ধ *adj* 'opposed to thought'; incomprehensible. ~বৃত্তি *n* disposition/activity of the mind; mentality; attitude; volition; fancy. ~বেদনা, ~ ব্যথা *nn* mental pain; anguish. ~ব্যাধি *n* mental disease; psychosis; hypochondria. ~ব্যাধিগ্রস্ত *adj* mentally diseased; psychotic. ~ব্যাধির চিকিৎসক *n* psychiatrist. ~ব্যাধির চিকিৎসা *n* psychiatry. ~ভঙ্গ *n* **1** dejection; disappointment; despondency. **2** lethargy; languor; heart-sickness; discouragement. **3**=মনান্তর. ~ভব *n* 'mind-born'; god of love. ~ভাব *n* **1** mental state; attitude; predisposition. **2** intention; secret thoughts and feelings. ~ভার *n* burden of one's heart; heaviness of one's heart; grief; anger; distress. ~ভিনিবেশ *n* close application of mind. ~ভিপ্রায়. ~ভিরাম *adj* pleasing in mind; delightful. ~ভীষ্ট=~ভিপ্রায়. ~ভূ=~ভব=মনমত. ~মদ *n* arrogance; vanity; haughtiness. ~মধ্যে *adj* in one's heart; at heart; inwardly. ~ময় *adj* consisting of spirit/mind; spiritual; mental. ~ময় কোষ *n* (Hindu philosophy) the mental sheath (the second of the subtle sheaths in which the soul is encased). ~মালিন্য=মন-কষাকষি. ~মুগ্ধকর, ~মোহন *adjj* captivating/ fascinating the heart; charming; ravishing. ~মোহিনী *fem.* ~মৃগ *n* the heart conceived of as a deer. ~যায়ী *adj* going at will or wherever one likes. ~যোগ *n* attention; heed; application of the mind. ~যোগ দেওয়া *vi* pay attention to; apply one's mind/oneself; heed; take notice; mind; concentrate on; take cognizance of; mark. ~যোগহীন *adj* inattentive; careless; heedless. ~যোগিতা *adj* concentration; attentiveness; attention; application. ~যোগী *adj* attentive; intent; heedful; careful; mindful; awake to; wakeful; alive to. ~রঞ্জক *adj* pleasing to the mind; gratifying; delightful; lovely; diverting; heartening; charming; enchanting; flattering; adulatory. ~রঞ্জিকা *fem.* ~রঞ্জন *n* gratification of the heart; diversion; recreation; entertainment of the mind; adulation; pleasing. ❑*adj*=~রঞ্জক. ~রঞ্জিনী *fem.* ~রঞ্জন করা *vt* entertain the mind of; divert; please; amuse; delight; gratify; amuse; entertain; afford pleasure to. ~রথ *n* **1** the heart compared to a chariot. **2** heart's joy; wish; desire; fancy. ~রথগতি *adj* very fast; lightning-like; with lighting speed. ~রথ পূরণ, ~রথসিদ্ধি *nn* fulfillment of one's wish. ~রম *adj* gratifying the mind; attractive; pleasant; charming; beautiful. ~রমা *fem.* ~রাজ *n* affection; passion. ~রাজ্য *n* realm of mind/fancy. (⇒ ~জগৎ). ~লোভা *adj* alluring; charming; fascinating; enchanting. ~লৌল্য *n* whim; caprice; frisk of the mind; fantasy. ~হত *adj* disappointed. ~হর *adj* 'heart-stealing'; taking the fancy; fascinating; attractive; charming; beautiful. ~হরণ করা *vi* captivate the mind; fascinate; enchant. ~হরশাহী, ~হরসাহী *n* a style of kirtan (কীর্তন) songs. ~হরা *adj fem* of ~হর. ❑*n* **1** yellow jasmine. **2** a variety of sweetmeat. ~হতা=~হর. ~হারিত্ব *n* charm; loveliness; fascination. ~হারী=~হর. ~হারিণী *fem.*

-মন্ত *suff* =-বন্ত: শ্রী~, মূর্তি ~

মন্তব্য *n* comment; remark. ❑*adj* to be thought/considered. ~ করা *vt* comment; remark; make comments; pass a remark. ~পত্র *n* note-sheet. ~স্তম্ভ, মন্তব্যের ঘর *nn* (book-keeping) column of remarks.

মন্তর (colloq)=মন্ত্র. মন্তরে *adv* **1** by magic. **2** very quickly; in a trice; in an instant. মন্তরের চোটে=মন্ত্রবলে.

মন্তা *n* thinker; adviser; counsellor.

মন্তেক *n* [A] logic.

মন্ত্র *n* **1** sacred text/speech. **2** Vedic hymn/spiritual formula; portion of the Veda which contains the texts called Rik or Yaju or Sama. **3** sacred formula addressed to any individual deity. **4** mystical verse; magical formula; incantation; spell; charm. **5** consultation; conference; counsel; advice. **6** plan; design. **7** secret. **8** resolution; resolve; dicision. **9** principle; motto: জীবনের মূল~. ~ দেওয়া *vi* initiate sb into worship by teaching him the prescribed mystic and esoteric word(s) of prayer; counsel; give counsel; instigate. ~ নেওয়া *vi* be initiated into worship by learning from a *guru* the prescribed mystic and esoteric word(s) of prayer; be initiated into; take counsel. ~করণ *n* recital of a sacred text. ~কুশল *adj* experienced in counsel. ~কৃৎ *n* **1** composer of hymns. **2** counsellor; adviser. ~গুপ্তি *n* secret counsel; keeping a resolve/design/ plan secret. ~গুপ্তি-আইন *n* Official Secrets Act. ~গূঢ় *n* spy; secret agent. ~গৃহ *n* council chamber; cabinet. ~জল *n* water consecrated by charms/ sacred text. ~জিহ্ব *adj* having sacred text for tongues. ❑*n* fire. ~জ্ঞ *adj* knowing sacred text; experienced in counsel; knowing magical formula. ❑*n* learned Brahmin; priest; initiator; minister; secret agent. ~ণ, ~ণা *nn* consultation; deliberation; advising; counselling in private; counsel; advice; design; intrigue; instigation. ~ণা করা *vi* consult; deliberate; discuss; design; plan; intrigue; scheme. ~ণাগৃহ *n* council chamber; cabinet; private room/ house for consultation. ~ণাদাতা *n* adviser; counsellor; instigator.

~ণাদাত্রী *fem.* **~ণা-পরিষদ** *n* advisory council. **~ণাভবন**=~ণাগৃহ. **~ণালয়** *n* ministry. **~ণীয়** *adj* to be deliberated on. **~তন্ত্র** *n* spells and charms; incantations. **~দাতা** *n, adj* **1** spiritual guide/*guru* who initiates sb into worship by teaching him the prescribed mystic and esoteric formula/ words of prayer; spiritual teacher; **2** counsellor. **~দাত্রী** *fem.* **~দান করা**=~ দেওয়া. **~দর্শী** *adj* seeing/ knowing/ composing sacred text; skilled in counsel. **~স্রষ্টা** *n* seer/ composer of sacred text. **~পাঠ** *n* recitation of a sacred text. **~পূত** *adj* purified by sacred text; protected/ endured with protective power by means of incantation. **~প্রয়োগ** *n* magical means/ agency; employment of a sacred text/ spell. **~ফল** *n* fruit of counsel/ advice. **~বৎ** *adj* like magic. **~বল** *n* magical power; charm. **~বীজ** *n* seed (ie the first syllable) of a smell. **~বিদ**=~জ্ঞ. **~বিদ্যা** *n* science of mantras. **~ভবন**= ~গৃহ. **~ভেদ** *n* breach of counsel; betrayal of a design. **~মুগ্ধ** *adj* spell-bound. **~মুগ্ধা** *fem.* **~যোগ** *n* employment of a sacred text/ spell. **~শক্তি**=~বল. **~শিষ্য** *n* disciple of a guru; initiated disciple; initiate; ardent follower. **~শিষ্যা** *fem.* **~সাধন** *n* performance of an incantation in order to realize an end. **~সাধক** *n* performer of an incantation. **~সাধ্য** *adj* to be subdued/ effected by incantations/ spell; thoroughly versed in spells; succeeded in attaining one's goal by means of regular recitation of sacred text. **~সিদ্ধি** *n* attainment of one's goal/an end by regular recital of incantations; effect of a spell. **~সূত্র** *n* charm fastened on a string.

মন্ত্রি (in compounds)=মন্ত্রী. **~ত্ব** *n* office/ vocation of a minister or state; ministership; ministry. **~পরিষৎ/ পরিষদ** *n* cabinet; ministers (collectively). **~বর** *n* (term of courtesy) great minister; the hon'ble minister. **~মণ্ডলী, ~সভা**=~পরিষদ.

মন্ত্রিত *adj* **1** discussed; deliberated; determined; advised; counselled. **2** consecrated with sacred texts; enchanted; charmed.

মন্ত্রী *n* **1** minister; king's counsellor. **2** (in chess) queen. ❑*adj* counselling; advising. **মন্ত্রিণী** *fem.* **উপ~** *n* deputy minister. **প্রতি~** *n* minister of state. **প্রধান~** *n* prime minister. **মুখ্য~** *n* chief minister. **রাষ্ট্র~**=প্রতি~.

মন্থ *n* **1** churning; stirring round; shaking about; agitating. **2** churning-stick. **3** mixed beverage (usually parched barley meal stirred round in milk). **4** excretion of rheum. **5** a particular disease of the eye. **~গিরি** *n* the mountain Mandara (churning-mountain). **~জ** *n* butter. **~দণ্ড** *n* churning-stick. **~শৈল**=~দণ্ড. **~পাত্র, ~ভাণ্ড** *n* churning-vessel. **~রজ্জু** *n* churning string.

মন্থনী *n* churning-vessel (for yogurt or buttermilk).

মন্থর *adj* **1** slow; tardy; slack; leisurely; slow-footed; slow-moving; slow-paced; sluggish. **2** lazy; slothful; indolent. **3** bent; curved; crooked; hunchbacked. **4** bulky. **~ হওয়া** *vi* become slow; slow-moving. **~গামী** =~গতি. **~গামিনী** *fem.* **~ গতি** *n* slow motion.

মন্থরা *n fem* a hunchbacked female slave of Bharata's mother Kaikeyi.

মন্দ *adj* **1** slow; tardy; slow-moving; moving slowly/softly; loitering. **2** idle; lazy; sluggish in; apathetic; phlegmatic; indifferent to. **3** dull-witted; stupid; silly; foolish. **4** bad; wicked; mean; vile; evil: ~ লোক. **5** weak; slight; slack. **6** gentle: ~ হাওয়া. **7** dull; dim; faint: ~ আলো. **8** low: ~ স্বর. **9** feeble; weak: মন্দাগ্নি. **10** unhappy; miserable: ~ জীবন. **11** languid; ill; sick; indisposed; impaired: শরীরটা ~ যাচ্ছে. **12** unfavourable; adverse: ভাগ্য ~. **13** indigent; poor; impoverished: ~ অবস্থায় পড়া. **14** dull; meek: ~ধী. **15** dull; deteriorated; sluggish: ব্যবসা ~ যাচ্ছে. **16** harsh; rude; abrasive: ~ কথা/বাক্য. **17** scanty; poor; little small: ~ বেতনের চাকরি. **18** small in number/ quantity/ degree; negligible: বয়স তো নেহাত ~ হলো না. **19** drunken; addicted to intoxication. **20** ugly: ~ চেহারা. **21** cheap: দরে ~. **22** inferior: ~ জিনিস. ❑*n* **1** evil; harm; injury; bad: ~ হতে কতক্ষণ. **2** the planet Saturn. **~ করা** *vi* do harm to; cause injury to. **~ আচরণ** *n* misconduct; misdeed; misbehaviour. **~ কথা** *n* **1** abusive/filthy language; harsh/rude words. **2** reproach; rebuke; reprimand. **3** calumny; damaging/bad report. **~ কাজ** *n* misdeed; wicked; deed; disgraceful act; wrong. **~গ, ~গতি, ~গমন, ~গামী** *adjj* moving slowly; flowing slowly; slow-moving; slow. **~গামিনী** *fem.* **~ গতি** *n* slow motion. **~ চালচলন** *n* evil ways. **~তা, ~ত্ব** *nn* slowness; sluggishness; indolence; weakness; feebleness; littleness; insignificance; dullness; stupidity; badness; wickedness; vileness; unfavourableness; adverseness; illness; indisposition; inferiority ; ugliness; poverty; littleness. **~ধী** *adj* slow-witted. **~ন** *n* (mech) retardation. **~ নয় 1** not bad; moderate. **2** (iron) not a little; great deal: মজা ~ নয়. **~ ফল** *n* evil consequence; bad/unimportant results. **~ বল** *adj* having little strength; week. **~বায়ু** *n* breeze; zephyr. **~ বুদ্ধি** *n* **1** dull-witted; dull-headed; dullard. **2** wicked; vile; ill-natured; villainous; evil-minded. **~ বুদ্ধি** *n* **1** dullness; stupidity; obtuseness. **2** wickedness; evil thought. **~ভাগ, ~ভাগ্য** *adj* unfortunate; ill-fated;

unhappy; unlucky. ~ভাগা, ~ভাগ্যা, ~ভাগিনী *fem.* ~ ভাগ্য *n* bad luck; ill luck; misfortune. ~মতি=~বুদ্ধি. ~ মন্দ *adj* slow; gentle: ~ মন্দ সমীরণ. ❑*adv* slowly; gently. ~ সময় *n* bad/hard times. ~ সমীরণ=~ বায়ু. ~হাস, ~হাস্য *adjj* gently laughing; smiling. ~ হিল্লোল **1** *n* gentle stirring/quiver. **2** gentle waves; ripples. **মন্দাক্রান্তা** *n fem* name of a Sanskrit metre. ❑*adj* slowly advancing. **মন্দাগ্নি** *n* slowness of digestion; loss of appetite. ❑*adj* having weak digestion; dyspeptic. **মন্দানল**=~গ্নি. **মন্দানিল**=~বায়ু. **মন্দের ভালো** better than nothing; rather tolerable in the midst of a world of evils; the lesser of the two evils; passable; so-so.

মন্দা *adj* **1**=মন্দ. **2** (com) depressed; slumped: বাজার ~. **3** abated; lessened; slowed. ❑*n* **1** depression; slump. **2** abatement; reduction.

মন্দাকিনী *n fem* **1** (myth) the heavenly Ganges. **2** name of a Sanskrit metre.

মন্দাক্রান্তা ⇒ মন্দ

মন্দার *n* **1** the coral tree, *Erythrina indica* (also regarded as one of the five trees of paradise). **2** a white variety of calotropis. **3** kind of plant: ~পুষ্প. ~মালিকা *n* garland of *mandar* flowers.

মন্দি *n*=মন্দা

মন্দির *n* **1** temple; shrine; house of worship. **2** any waiting or abiding-place; habitation; dwelling; house; palace; abode: শয়ন~; ব্যাধি~. **3** town.

মন্দিরা *n* kind of small cup-shaped cymbals.

মন্দীভূত *adj* become slow/dull; lessened; diminished; abated; dimmed; (commerce) slumped. ~ করা *vi* slow down; lessen; be diminished; dim; abate; stump.

মন্দুরা *n* **1** stable for horses. **2** mattress; sleeping- mat.

মন্দোদরী *n fem* name of Ravana's favourite wife. ~মনোহর *n* Ravana.

মন্দোষ্ণ *adj* tepid; lukewarm. ~তা *n* gentle heat; warmth.

মন্দ্র *n* **1** low tone; low/base tone of the voice. **2** a kind of drum. ❑*adj* low; deep (of sound); hollow; rumbling; sounding/ speaking pleasantly. ~ ধ্বনি *n* rumbling sound; roaring.

মন্দ্রা *vi* (poet) roar.

মন্মথ *n* god of love; love. ~প্রিয়া *n fem* Kamadeva's wife Rati. ~শরাহত *adj* wounded with the shafts of love; love-sick. ~সখা *n* friend of Kamadeva/love; spring.

মন্বন্তর *n* **1** period/age of a Manu (মনু) (=4,320,000 human years). **2** great famine.

মফস্বল, মফঃস্বল *nn* [A] rural areas; countryside; subdivisions of a district; beyond head-quarters and interior of a district/sub-district.

মফিদ [A] *adj* profitable; useful; of use; beneficial; salutary; advantageous.

মফেল=মাহফিল

মবলগ [A] *n* **1** ready money; sum; quantity. **2** total. মবলগে *adv* in all; in total. ~বন্দি *n* total in words.

মম *poss adj* (poet) my.

ম-ম *adj* diffused/laden with (scent, etc). করা.

মমতা, মমত্ব *n* **1** affection; attachment; love; feeling of kinship. **2** interest. ~ করা *vt* love; be attached to; interest oneself in; consider as one's own. ~পূর্ণ, ~ময় *adjj* affectionate; loving; full of attachment. ~ময়ী *fem.* ~যুক্ত *adj* **1**=~পূর্ণ. **2** proud; arrogant. ~শূন্য, ~হীন *adjj* devoid of attachment/interest; indifferent; callous. ~শূন্যা, ~হীনা *fem.*

মমলেট [E] *n* omelet; omelette.

মমি [E] *n* dead-body preserved from decay (as in early Egypt); mummy.

ময় *suff* **1** full of; -ful; -ous; -some; -y: সৌন্দর্য~. **2** pervading; -wide: বিশ্ব~. **3** made of; consisting of; containing; abounding in: রত্ন~ মুকুট. **4** mixed with: বিষ~ ফল. -ময়ী *fem.*

ময়দা [P] *n* flour; meal; finest flour. ~কল *n* flour mill. ~ মাখা *vi* knead flour.

ময়দান [A] *n* plain; open field; area; battle field; ground; race course; parade ground.

ময়না[1] *n* myna; mynah.

ময়না[2] *n* kind of thorny plant; *Randia dumatorum.*

ময়না[3] **মায়না** [A] *n* inspection. ~ তদন্ত *n* post-mortem (examination); autopsy.

ময়মুরুব্বি [A] *n pl* guardians; patrons; protectors; elders.

ময়রা *n* confectioner. ~নি, ~নী *fem.* ~গিরি *n* profession of a confectioner. ~র দোকান *n* confectionery; sweetmeat shop.

ময়লা *n* **1** refuse; filth; soil; dust; dirt; garbage. **2** any bodily excretion/secretion; excrement; faeces; stool. **3** impurity (physical and moral): মনের ~. ❑*adj* **1** dirty; filthy; soiled. **2** (of complexion) not fair; dark. **3** not bright/clear; clouded; overcast: ~ আকাশ. **4** melancholy; gloomy: ~ মুখ. **5** crooked; impure: ~ মন. ~ করা *vt* soil; make dirty; dirty. ~টে *adj* slightly soiled; rather dark; darkish; rather gloomy. ~র গাড়ি *n* scavenger's cart/van/ train; night-soil cart. মনের ~ *n* impurity of the heart; crookedness.

ময়ান *n* mixing of ghee with dough. ~ দেওয়া *vi* knead with ghee.

ময়াল[1] *n* python.

ময়াল[2] [A] *n* kingdom; domain.

ময়ূখ *n* **1** ray of light; beam; lustre, brightness; flame. **2** beauty. ~মালা *n pl* rays. ~মালী *n* 'wreathed with rays'; the sun.

ময়ূর *n* peacock. ~ময়ূরী *fem* pea-hen. ~কণ্ঠী *n, adj* peacock-blue (sari or shawl). ~চূড়া, ~শিখা

nn **1** peacock's crest. **2** garden plant with red and yellow flowers; *Celosia cristata* (মোরগ ফুল). **~পঙ্খী** *n* boat shaped like a peacock. **~পুচ্ছ** *n* peacock's tail (feather). **~শাবক** *n* pea-chick.

মর *adj* mortal; perishable; transient. **~জগৎ** *n* world of death; (mortal) world. **~জীবন** *n* mortal life. **~মানব** *n* mortal (man). **~কুটে ~কট্টে** *adj* dying; withering. **মরামর** *n* mortals and immortals.

মরক=মড়ক

মরকত *n* emerald. **~কুঞ্জ** *n* emerald bower. **~বর্ণ** *n* emerald-green. **~মণি** *n* emerald gem. **~ময়** *adj* made of emerald.

মরক্কো *n* Morocco. ❑*adj, n* morocco (leather).

মরগেজ [E] *n* mortgage.

মরচে [P] *n* rust of iron. **~ ধরা/পড়া** *vi* rust.

মরজান [A] *n* coral; small pearl.

মরজি [A] *n* pleasure; wish; (sweet) will; desire; assent; consent; volition; choice. **~ হওয়া** *vi* like; please. **যদি তোমার ~ হয়** if you please; if you would. **যেমন তোমার ~** as you please. **~মাফিক** *adj, adv* according to the will/pleasure of; to the satisfaction of; satisfactorily; as and when one pleases.

মরণ *n* death; dying; passing away; decease; demise; cessation. ❑*int* (expression of shame or rebuke for) shame ! hell ! **~ আঘাত** *n* death-blow. **~ আর কি** It's death indeed ! for shame ! I would rather die ! what a nonsense! **~কামড়** desperate attempt. **~কাল** *n* time of death; last hour; dying moments. **~কালে হরিনাম** (fig) fruitless repentance for one's wickedness when one is dying; futile effort at the eleventh hour when almost all is lost. **~ছটফটানি** *n* death throes; death rattle. **~ডাক** *n* dying cry. **~ডাক ছাড়া/ ডাকা** (iron) be in one's death throes/ at one's last gasp. **~দশা** *n* time/ hour of death; last hour; last gasp; utter ruin. **~দশায় ধরা** be seized with a ruinous passion/folly. **~বাঁচন** *n* life and death. **~বাড় বাড়া** be excessively haughty/ vainglorious only to bring about one's fall. **~ভয়** *n* fear of death. **~ভীরু** *adj* afraid to die. **~শীল** *adj* liable to death; mortal. **~সঙ্কোচ** *n* rigor mortis. **~হীন** *adj* deathless; immortal. **মরণাত্মক** *adj* causing death. **মরণান্তক মরণান্তিক** *adjj* ending in death. **মরণাপন্ন; মরণাভিমুখ** *adj* dying; on the point of death; moribund. **মরণাপন্না, মরণাভিমুখী** *fem*. **মরণাশৌচ** *n* personal impurity caused by the death of a relative.

মরণীয় *adj* liable to die; doomed to death.

মরণোন্মুখ *adj* about to die; at death-door; dying; moribund.

মরত (poet)=মর্ত

মরতবা [A] *n* dignity; office; rank of honour; class; order; degree.

মরদ [A] *n* male; man; hero; fellow; husband; brave man; manly man. **~ আদমি** *n* gentleman; brave/ valiant man; tall strong man. **~কা বাত হাতি কা দাঁত** (prov) a gentleman's word is as good as ivory. **~বাচ্চা, মরদের বাচ্চা** *nn* son of a brave man; brave child. **~বাজ** *n, adj fem* lascivious (woman); lustful (woman); adulteress.

মরন্ত=মরণাপন্ন ⇒ মরণ

মরম *n* (poet) **1** heart. **2** any vital member/joint/ organ. **3** inmost feelings/ convictions: 'সই ~ কহিনু তোমারে'. **4** essence; gist. **5** intention; spirit import. **6** sympathy.

মরমর[1] *adj*=মরণাপন্ন ⇒ মরণ

মরমর[2] *n*=মর্মর

মরমিয়া, মরমী *adj* **1** mystic; mystical. **2** sympathetic friend; intimate; confidant.

মরশুম, মরসুম=মৌসুম

মরসিয়া, মর্সিয়া [A] *nn* **1** kind of elegiac song/poetry. **2** elegiac song sung in commemoration of the martyrdom of the Prophet's grandson Hazrat Imam Hossain.

মরহাবা, মারহাবা [A] *int* hail; welcome; bravo; God bless you !

মরহুম [A] *adj* dead; deceased; the late; one who has found mercy.

মরা *vi* **1** die; pass away; decease. **2** wither (away): গাছটা মরে গেছে. **3** evaporate: হাঁড়ির পানি মরে গেছে. **3** dry up: চোখের জল চোখেই মরে; পুকুর ~, কল্পনা মরে যাওয়া. **4** flow: কোথাকার জল কোথায় মরে. **5** suffer; be afflicted with; die ক্ষুধার জ্বালায় ~. **6** be extremely troubled/afflicted: ভেবে ~. **7** silt up: নদী ~. **8** be ruined/undone; come to naught: চাকরিটা গেলে নির্ঘাত মরবো. **9** decrease; dwindle; diminish; die down: তেজ ~. **10** be seized with; die: লজ্জায় ~. **11** be allayed; abate: ব্যথা ~. **12** be punished/severely dealt with; pay for: চালাকি করেছ কি মরেছ. **13** weaken; have one's appetite taken away; have poor appetite: পেট ~. **14** be spiritless; be crushed: দুঃখেকষ্টে মরে থাকা. **15** die away: আলো/বাতাস/শব্দ ~. ❑ *n* **1** death. **2**=মড়া usu. ❑*adj* **1** death.**2** dried up; silted: ~ নদী. **3** weak; spiritless; weakened: ~ মন. **4** faint; dim: ~ আলো. **5** parched; thirsty: ~ মাঠ. **6** withered: ~ গাছ. **7** skinny; flat: ~ পেট. **8** alloyed: ~ সোনা. **~ কটাল** *n* neap-tide. **~ কান্না** *n* wailing on account of bereavement; loud wailing; lamentation. **~ গাং/গাঙ** *nn* river at ebb-tide. **~ দেহ** *n* **1** dead body. **2** emaciated/lean/skinny body. **~পেট** anorexic. **~ পেট/নাড়া** *nn* stomach weakened on account of continuing under-feeding. **~ মরা** *adj* **1** moribund; spiritless; nearly dead. **2** shrivelled; emaciated; withered; shrunk. **~মাস** *n* dandruff; scurf. **~সোনা** *n* alloyed gold. **অনাহারে ~** *vi* die of hunger; starve (to death); famish. **জীয়ন্তে ~**

adj dead while alive. **মরমে ~** *vi* be extremely ashamed/mortified. **~র বাড়া গাল নেই 1** wishing sb's death is the ultimate curse. **2** extreme rebuke/curse. **~ মুখ দেখা** (form of swearing) you will see my/sb's dead face (unless you do sth). **মরতে মরতে বাঁচা** come back from the jaws of death. **মরে বাঁচা 1** to be relieved from suffering by death. **2** come back from the jaws of death. **মরে মরে** *adv* at the cost of one's health; with utmost strain and difficulty.

মরাই *n* large corn-bin made of bamboo, cane, etc; corn-loft; granary; magazine of corn.

মরাঠা *n* Maratha. ❑*adj* of Maharastra; Marathi.

মরাঠী *n* **1** native of Maharastra; Maratha. **2** Marathi (language). ❑*adj* of Maharastra; Marathi.

মরানো *vi* allow to evaporate=সবটা দুধই মরিয়ে ফেল্লে?

মরার=মরাই

মরাল *n* kind of duck or goose or flamingo; swan. **মরালী** *fem.* **~গামিনী** *adj fem* having the gait of a flamingo/ swan. ❑*n* a woman having such a gait. **~নিন্দিত** *adj* excelling even the swan (in beauty, etc). **~শাবক, ~শিশু** *nn* gosling; cygnet.

মরালী *n* row; line.

মরিচ *n* pepper; chilli; capsicum. **গোল~** *n* black pepper. **লঙ্কা~**; ⇒ লঙ্কা.

মরিচা=মরচে

মরি-মরি *int* (cry of profound admiration, wonderment, etc) aha; how excellent! superb!

মরিয়া *adj* desperate; death-defying; bold; devil-may-care. **~ লোক** *n* desperado.

মরীচি *n* ray of light; particle of light; shining mote/speck in the air. **~কা** *n* mirage; (fig) illusion. **~মালী** *adj* garlanded with rays; radiant. ❑*n* the sun.

মরু *nn* desert; wilderness; sandy waste. **~ঝঞ্ঝা, ~ঝটিকা, ~ঝড়** *nn* simoom; simoon. **~তরণী** *n* 'desert-boat'; camel. **~দ্বীপ** *n* oasis. **~পথ, ~পৃষ্ঠ, ~ভূ, ~ভূমি** *nn* =~. **~ময়** *adj* desert; full of deserts. **~যাত্রী** *n* desert-traveller. **~যাত্রীদল** *n* caravan. **~সাগর** *n* Dead-Sea. **~স্থল, ~স্থলী** *nn* desert spot; wilderness; desert.

মরুৎ, মরুত *n* **1** wind; air; breath; five winds of the body. **2** gods/deities in general. **~কর্ম, ~ক্রিয়া** *nn* breaking wind; flatulency. **~পথ** *n* path/region of the air.

মরুয়ত [A] *n* generosity; humanity; urbanity; affection; politeness; kindness; affability; benevolence: খাতির-~.

মরূদ্যান *n* oasis.

মর্কট *n* **1** monkey; ape. **2** spider. **3** (derog) man of stunted growth. **মর্কটী** *fem.* **~বাস** *n* cobweb.

মর্গ [E] *n* morgue.

মর্গেজ=মরগেজ. **~ দেওয়া** *vt* mortgage; hypothecate. **~গ্রাহী** *n* mortgagee. **~দাতা** *n* mortgager.

মর্চে=মরচে

মর্জি=মরজি

মর্টগেজ=মরগেজ

মর্তবা=মরতবা

মর্তবান [P] *n* jar for keeping preserves in; glazed earthen jar; vessel of the finest china/porcelain.

মর্তমান *n* a large variety of banana.

মর্তুকাম *adj* wishing to die.

মর্ত্য, মর্ত *n* **1** mortal; man. **2** world of mortals; earth. ❑*adj* mortal. **~তা** *n* mortality; human condition. **~ধর্ম** *n* laws/conditions of human life. **~ধাম, ~ভূমি ~লোক**=~ (2). **~বাসী** *n* inhabitant of the world; mortal; mankind. **~লীলা** *n* one's activities while living upon the earth.

মর্দ[1]=মর্দন

মর্দ[2] =মরদ

মর্দন *n* **1** trampling; thrashing; tormenting; paining; bruising. **2** pounding; crushing; grinding; kneading. **3** rubbing; fondling; massaging; massage. ❑*adj* (used as a *suff*) trampling; subduing; crushing: কালিয়~. **~ করা** *vt* trample; thrash; torment; pound; grind; crush; rub; fondle; massage; subdue.

মর্দমি=মর্দানি

মর্দল=মাদল

মর্দা=মরদ. **~না** *adj* manly; masculine; brave; male; relating to males. ❑*n* drawing room for men only.

মর্দানি [P] *n* (derog) manliness; masculinity; bravery; mannish behaviour. **~ করা** *vi* **1** make a show of one's manliness; display one's bravery. **2** (of women) behave in masculine/ mannish manner; romp.

মর্দানী, মদানি *n fem* masculine/mannish woman; hoyden; tomboy; amazon.

মর্দিত *adj* **1** trampled; thrashed; tormented; brushed. **2** pounded; crushed; ground; kneaded. **3** rubbed; fondled; massaged. **4** subdued. **~ করা**=মর্দন করা.

মর্দী *adj* crushing; pounding; grinding; destroying; subduing. **মর্দিনী** *fem.*

মর্ম *n* (⇒ মরম) **1** mortal spot; vulnerable point; any open/weak/sensitive/exposed part of the body. **2** inmost feelings/ convictions; heart. **3** joint of limbs; any joint/articulation. **4** core of anything; quick. **5** any vital member/ organ. **6** anything which requires to be kept concealed; secret. **7** secret quality; implication; hidden meaning; inner significance. **8** mystery. **9** essence; gist; substance. **10** underlying truth. **11** motive; intention. **~ জানা/বোঝা** *vt* know/bottom sb's heart; know sb's inner feelings/ convictions; know/ grasp the implication/ (inner) significance of; penetrate the secret/ mystery. **মর্মে আঘাত করা** *vt* wound sb's inmost feelings; cut/ touch sb to the quick; move sb deeply. **এই মর্মে** to this effect. **মর্মে মর্মে** with all one's heart; keenly; intensely; deeply. **~কথা** *n* **1** essence; gist; substance; implications. **2** innermost feelings/ convictions; yearning; longing; mystery. **~কাতরতা** *n* yearning; anguish; deep suffering. **~গ্রহ, ~গ্রহণ, ~ধারণ, মর্মাবধরণ** *n n* comprehension/ grasp of the significance/ essence/ implication. **~ অনুধাবন করা** *vt* grasp/ comprehend the significance/ implication/ essence/import. **~গ্রহণ/ ~ধারণ করা**=~ অনুধাবন করা. **~গ্রাহী** *adj* comprehending/ grasping us the significance/ implication; having a deep insight into; exceedingly acute/clever; sensitive; penetrating; discerning; perspicacious; compassionate; sympathetic. **~ঘাতী** *adj* cutting to the quick; causing intense suffering/ pain; heart-breaking; heart-rending. **~ঘাতিনী** *fem.* **~চ্ছিৎ**=~ঘাতী. **~জ্বালা** *n* hurt-burning; secret grudge/envy/agony/grief. **~জ্ঞ**=~গ্রাহী. **~জ্ঞান** *n* knowledge of a secret; grasp/ comprehension of the inner significance. **~দাহ**=~ জ্বালা. **~দাহী** *adj* wounding sb's feelings deeply; extremely agonizing; excessively poignant/ painful; cutting to the quick. **~ন্তুদ**= ~ঘাতী. **~পারগ** *adj* one who has penetrated into the interior of any matter; thoroughly conversant with. **~পীড়ক**=~দাহী. **~পীড়া** *n* pain in the innermost soul; mortification; heartache; mental anguish; heart-burning; envy. **~পীড়িত** *adj* sick at heart; grieved at heart; mortified. **~পীড়িতা** *fem.* **~বিদ, ~বিৎ**=~জ্ঞ. **~বিদারক, ~বিদারী** *adjj* heart-rending; heart-breaking. **~বিদ্ধ** *adj* piercing; poignant; cut to the quick. **~বেদনা, ~ব্যথা**=~পীড়া. **~বেদী**=~জ্ঞ. **~ভেদ** *n* piercing the heart; unraveling/ penetrating (a secret/mystery). **~ভেদ করা** *vt* **1** pierce the heart; rend the heart; drive into the heart. **2** fathom sb's heart; unravel/penetrate (a secret/mystery); comprehend the inner significance/ implications (of sth); decipher; make head or tail of. **~ভেদী** *adj* heart rending; pathetic; piercing. **~যন্ত্রণা**=~পীড়া. **~স্থল, ~স্থান** *nn* **1** vital part; vulnerable place/spot. **2** core of the heart; innermost recesses of the heart. **~স্পর্শী, ~স্পৃক** *adjj* touching (the vital); pathetic; moving; heart-breaking; stinging; piquant. **মর্মাঘাত** *n* death-blow; shock to one's heart/ feelings; deadly/ severe blow; very grievous hurt; home thrust. **মর্মান্তিক** *adj* heart-breaking; heart-rending; tragic; pathetic; piteous; very grievous/ fatal; cutting to the quick. **মর্মাবগত**=~জ্ঞ. **মর্মাবধারণ করা**=~গ্রহণ করা. **মর্মার্থ** *n* underlying significance; inner meaning/ significance; purport; essence; gist; substance; hidden meaning; sum and substance. **মর্মাহত** *adj* mortified; deeply grieved.

মর্মর[১] *n* marble. **~ পাথর, ~ পাষাণ, ~ প্রস্তর** *nn* marble stone.

মর্মর[২] *n* (onom) rustling (as leaves or garments); rustling sound; murmuring; murmur. **~ধ্বনি** =~. **~ করা** *vi* rustle; murmur.

মর্মরিত *adj* rustled. **~ হওয়া** *vi* rustle; be rustled; murmur.

মর্মিক=মর্মী

মর্মী *adj* versed in/acquainted/ familiar with anything (⇒ ~গ্রাহী). ❑*n* mystic.

মর্মোদ্‌ঘাটন, মর্মোদ্ধার, মর্মোদ্‌ভেদ *nn* exposition/ elicitation of the hidden meaning/underlying truth/ inner significance/ mystery. **~ করা** *vt* discover/ find the sense/ meaning of; elicit/ bring out/ penetrate the hidden meaning/ underlying truth/ inner significance/ mystery; reveal the secret of; puzzle out; make head or tail of.

মর্যাদা *n* **1** honour: dignity; prestige; respect. **2** cordial reception; preferential treatment: অতিথির ~. **3** decorum; grace; correctness: ~পূর্ণ আচরণ. **4** pride; distinction: ~বোধ. **5** rank; status: মন্ত্রীর ~. **6** good name; reputation: বংশের ~. **7** recognition; appreciation: প্রতিভার ~. **8** value; worth; importance: প্রতিশ্রুতির ~. **9** frontier; limit; bounds: আইনের ~. **~ দেওয়া** *vt* **1** honour; pay respect to ;respect. **2** receive/ treat cordially. **3** give the status of. **4** attach importance to; recognize the worth of; appreciate. **5** pay heed to; obey. **~ নষ্ট করা** *vt* dishonour; disgrace; defame; bring disgrace on; bring into disrepute; blemish; tarnish; taint; sully; bring shame upon. **~কর** *adj* respectable; honourable; creditable. **~পূর্ণ** *adj* dignified; graceful; decent; civil; decorous; seemly; well-bred. **~বান, ~শালী** = ~পূর্ণ. **~হানি** *n* dishonour; disgrace; defamation; indignity; blemish; disrepute; bad name; opprobrium; ignominy; slur; humiliation: **~হানি করা**=~ নষ্ট করা. **~হানিকর** *adj* damaging; dishonourable; shameful; ignominious; disgraceful; humiliating; defamatory; slighting; insulting.

মর্ষ, মর্ষণ *nn* **1** patience; endurance; enduring; forgiving; forbearance; tolerance; forgiveness. **2** destruction. **~কাম** *n* (psych) masochism. **~কামী** *n* masochist.

মর্ষিত *adj* borne; endured; forgiven. **~বান** *n* forgiving; enduring; patient; tolerant.

মর্সিয়া=মরসিয়া

মর্সুম *n* **1** =মৌসুম. **2** opportunity.

মল[1] 1 dust; filth; dirt; impurity (physical and moral). 2 any bodily excretion/ secretion; excreta; excrement; faeces; stool; dung. 3 stain; stigma; sin; vice. 4 gloom; melancholy. 5 rust; verdigris; dregs; dross; lees; scum. 6 evil thought; crookedness. **~গ** *n* washerman. **~ঘ্ন** *adj* removing dirty; cleansing. **~জ** *adj* arising from dirt/ filth. **~ত্যাগ** *n* defecation. **~ত্যাগ করা** *vi* 1 defecate; relieve/ ease oneself; evacuate (the bowels); pass stool; (children) soil; shit (sl). 2 (of inferior animals) excrete. **~ত্ব** *n* dirtiness; filthiness. **~দূষিত** *adj* soiled with dirt; filthy; fouled. **~দ্বার** *n* anus. **~দ্রাবী** *adj* dissolving impurity. **~নালী** *n* rectum. **~বাহী** *adj* carrying filth and soil; carrying stool/ excrement. **~ভাণ্ড** *n* large intestine; colon. **~ভুক** *adj* feeding on impurity. ❑*n* crow. **~ময়** *adj* full of dirt/filth; dirty; filthy. **~মূত্রপরিত্যাগ** *n* evacuation of faces and urine. **~যুক্ত** *adj* soiled; dirty. **~রোধ** *n* constipation of the bowels. **~শোধনাশয়, ~শোধনী** *nn* septic tank. **মলাকর্ষী** *n* sweeper; scavenger. **মলাশয়** *n* colon.

মল[2] *n* kind of bangle for the ankle; anklet.

মলন *n* 1 rubbing; smearing; anointing. 2 trampling; crushing; thrashing; threshing. 3 massaging; scrubbing.

মলম [A] *n* ointment; unguent; balm.

মলমল *n* variety of fine cotton fabric; muslin. **মলমলি** *adj* of muslin.

মলমাস *n* an intercalary mouth; (astrol) an inauspicious mouth for marriages, etc.

মলম্বা [A] *adv* plated; covered with gold/silver; bright; gilt; electroplating.

মলয় *n* 1 name of a mountain range on the west of Malabar; the western Ghats. 2 south wind; vernal breeze; wind (blowing) from Malaya). 3 Malabar. 4 a celestial grove (নন্দনকানন). ❑*adj* of the country Malabar. **~পবন, ~বায়ু, ~মাবুত, ~সমীর, ~সমীরণ,ময়লানিল** *nn*=~(2). **~জ** *adj* growing on the Malaya mountain. ❑sandal tree; sandal. **~জলীতল** *adj* cooled by the south wind. **ময়লাচল** *n* Malaya Mountain.

মলা[1]=ময়লা

মলা[2] *vt* 1 thresh: ধান ~. 2 pull; pinch; twist: কান ~. 3 trample; thrash. 4 rub; scrub; massage. **~ই** *n*=মলন. **~নো** *vt* cause to thresh/rub/ massage; get threshed/ pulled/ pinched/ rubbed/ scrubbed/ massaged.

মলাট *n* cover/ jacket of a book.

মলিদা [E] *n* 1 a fine woolen fabric/ cloth. 2 sweetmeat/ cakes made with wheat flour.

মলিন *adj* 1 dirty; filthy; impure; soiled; tarnished. 2 of a dark colour; dark; not fair: গায়ের রংটা একটু ~. 3 gloomy; sorrowful; sad; cheerless: ~ মুখ. 4 overcast; cloudy; clouded; gloomy: ~ আকাশ. 5 dim; faint: ~ আলো. 6 sinful; vicious; evil; impure: ~ মন. **~া** *fem.* **~তা, ~ত্ব** *nn* dirtiness; impurity; uncleanliness; gloom; blackness; wickedness; black mood; dimness; gloominess; sadness; darkness. **~প্রভ** *adj* whose light is obscured/clouded; dimmed. **~বদন, ~মুখ** *adjj* looking gloomy/ sad. **~বদনা, ~মুখী** *fem.*

মলিনিত *adj* dirtied; soiled; defiled; tainted; wicked; saddened.

মলিনিমা=মলিনতা (⇒মলিন)

মলিনীকৃত=মলিনিত

মলিম্লুচ *n* thief; robber.

মলুদ (শরীফ) [A] *n* celebration of the anniversary of the Holy Pophet's birth.

মল্ল *n* 1 wrestler; boxer; athlete; very strong man. 2 title of an ordinary soldier. ❑*adj* strong; robust. **~ক্রীড়া** *n* wrestling/boxing match; athletic sports; athletics. **~ক্রীড়া করা** *vi* wrestle; take part in athletics. **~ প্রতিযোগিতা** *n* wrestling contest; athletic tournament. **~নাগ** *n* name of Indra's elephant. **~বিদ্যা** *n* art of wrestling. **~বেশ** *n* wrestler's dress; (fig) fighting/ aggressive attitude. **~ভূ, ~ভূমি** *nn* 1 wrestling ground; arena. 2 battlefield. 3 district of Malbhum in west Bengal. **~যুদ্ধ** *n* wrestling/boxing match; pugilistic encounter. **~যুদ্ধ করা** *vi* wrestle. **~যোদ্ধা** *n* wrestler.

মল্লার *n* an Indian musical mode.

মল্লি, মল্লী *nn* a variety of jasmine; Arabian jasmine. **~কলি** *n* 1 bud of the Arabian jasmine. 2 Kind of earring.

মল্লিক [A] *n* title of the chief of a town or village; prince.

মল্লিকা *n* a variety of jasmine; *Jasminum Zambac*. **মল্লিকা , মল্লিকাখ্য** *nn* kind of goose.

মল্লী ⇒ মল্লি

মল্লু *n* bear.

মশ, মশমশ *nn* (onom) expressing the crumpling/ rustling sound occasioned by breaking dry leaves/ dry bread/ biscuit/ new shoes. **~মশ করা, ~মশানো** *vi, vt* rustle. **~মশনি** *n.* rustling.

মশক[1] *n* mosquito; gnat. **~দংশন** *n* mosquito-bite. **~সঙ্কুল** *adj* mosquito-infested; swarming with mosquitoes.

মশক[2] [P] *n* leather bag for carrying water; water bag.

মশকারা, মসকারা, মস্করা, মস্কারা *nn* [A] jest; joke; banter; fun; buffoonery; drollery; jesting; derision. **~ করা** *vi, vt* jest; joke; banter; poke fun (at); play the buffoon; make fun of; deride.

মশগুল [A] *adj* employed; occupied; busy; engaged; absorbed; engrossed; rapt; lost in.

মশলা, মসলা, মসল্লা *nn* 1 spices; seasoning; condiments. 2 ingredients: ঔষধের ~. 3 mortar.

4 materials: গল্পের ~. ~দার *adj* spicy; seasoned.

মশহুর [A] *adj* famous; celebrated; noted; well-known; illustrious.

মশা *n* mosquito. ডাঁশ ~ *n* gnat. ~ মারতে কামান দাগা/পাতা (fig) crush a butterfly on a wheel; *(cf)* storm in a teacup.

মশাই=মশায়

মশান *n* 1 elevated ground for burning dead bodies; crematorium. 2 official place for infliction of capital punishment.

মশায় *n* (colloq) (esp as a polite term of address) Sir; Mr: মুখুজ্যে~. ~-মশায় করা flatter; curry favour with; soft-soap.

মশারি, মশারী *nn* mosquito curtain/ net. ~ খাটানো *vi* rig up a mosquito curtain.

মশাল [A] *n* torch; flambeau; burner. ~চি, ~চী *nn* torch-bearer.

মশি, মশী *nn*=মসি

মশমশ ⇒ মশ

মসকারা ⇒ মশকারা

মসগুল=মশগুল

মসজিদ, মসজেদ [A] *n* mosque. জামে/ জুমা/ জুম্মা ~ *nn* congregational mosque.

মসনদ, মছনদ *n* throne. ~নশিন *adj* enthroned; sitting on the throne. ❑*n* reigning prince. মসনদী *adj* relating to the throne; royal; official.

মসনবি [A] *n* kind of metre/verse; poem written in this metre.

মসনে *n* (colloq)=মসীনা

মসমস=মশমশ

মসরুফ [A] *adj* engaged; busy; occupied; employed.

মসলত [A] *adj* advice; counsel; policy.

মসলন্দ [A] *n* 1 very finely-woven mat. 2 very fine rug.

মসলা ⇒ মশলা

মসলিন [A] *n* muslin.

মসায়েল *n pl*=মছলা

মসাহ্‌রা, মুসাহ্‌রা=মাসহারা

মসি, মসী *n* soot; lamp-black; ink. ~কূপী, ~ধান, ~ধানী, ~পাত্র, ~ভাণ্ড *nn* inkstand; inkpot. ~চিহ্নিত *adj* smeared/masked with ink ~কৃষ্ণ =~তুল্য.. ~জীবী *n* writer; scribe; clerk; journalist; (derog) pen-pusher. ~তুল্য, ~বৎ *adj* black as ink; inky; very black. ~নিন্দিত, ~লাঞ্ছিত *adjj* even blacker than ink/soot; very black; inky-black; jet-black; ebony-black; pitch-black. ~ময় *adj* 1 full of ink. 2 sooty; smudgy; inky; extremely dark.. ~ময়ী *fem.* ~লিপ্ত=~চিহ্নিত; very black/dark.

মসিনা, মসীনা *nn* linseed. ~ তৈল *n* linseed-oil.

মসিবত, মুসিবত [A] *n* misfortune; calamity; disaster; affliction; adversity; evil; ill; misery.

মসীল [A] *n* oppression; tyranny.

মসীহ [A] *n* Messiah; Christ.

মসুর, মসূর, মসুরি (colloq) *nn* a sort of lentil/pulse.

মসূরিকা, মসূরী *nn* smallpox.

মসৃণ *adj* 1 smooth; sleek; perfectly plain even; slippery. 2 soft tender: ~ আকাশ. 3 suave; mild; bland: ~ আলাপ-আলোচনা. 4 soothing: ~ রং. 5 easy; unobstructed; smooth; জীবনের পথ ~নয়. 6 (esp bot) glabrous. ~তা *nn* smoothness; sleekness; evenness; slipperiness; softness; tenderness; blandness; suavity.

মস্ক [A] *n* musk.

মস্কট *n* a variety of pomegranate.

মস্করা ⇒ মশকারা

মস্ত[1] *adj* 1 high; tall; lofty. 2 very large/big; huge; very broad/long; vast; enormous; gigantic; extensive: ~ বাড়ি/বাগান. 3 great; very distinguished/ influential/ powerful; very rich/opulent: ~ লোক. 4 big: ~ মামলা. 5 very serious: ~ সমস্যা. 6 elevated; noble: ~ আদর্শ. 7 very difficult: ~ দায়িত্ব. 8 very important: ~ প্রশ্ন. 9 of great value; precious: ~ কথা. 10 too much; excessive: ~ জ্বালা. 11 (iron) very little: কী ~ ত্যাগ ! ❑*adv* very; in high degree.

মস্ত[2] *n* head.

মস্ত[3] [P] *adj* drunk; intoxicated; drunk with the love of God.

মস্তক *n* 1 head; skull; cranium. 2 brain. 3 upper part of anything; top summit (esp of mountains or trees); tuft of leaves which grows at the top of various species of palm trees) crest. ~চ্যুত *adj* beheaded; decapitated; truncated. ~চ্যুতি, ~চ্ছেদ *nn* decapitation; beheading. ~চ্ছেদন করা *vt* behead; decapitate; truncate. ~বিশিষ্ট *adj* having a head; cephalous; headed. ~বিহীন, ~শূন্য, ~হীন *adjj* headless; truncated; acephalous. ~ ব্যবচ্ছেদ *n* cephalotomy. ~শূল *n* sharp/shooting pain in the head; headache. ~সংক্রান্ত *adj* cephalic. মস্তকাবরণ *n* covering for the head; headdress; cap; helmet; turban. মস্তকাভরণ *n* ornament for the head.

মস্তকোপরি *adj* on/over the head.

মস্তকোর্ধ্বে *adv* over the head; overhead.

মস্তাজির [A] *n* 1 tenant. 2 lessee.

মস্তান *n* 1 one drunk with the love of God. 2 rowdy; roughneck; hoodlum; hooligan; ruffian; মস্তানা 1 *adj* intoxicated; drunken. 2 arrogant; insolent. মস্তানী *fem.* মস্তানি, মস্তানী *nn* 1 drunkenness; intoxication. 2 hooliganism; ruffianism; rowdyism. 3 *fem* turbulent female of questionable moral; hellcat; rowdy whore.

মস্তাহাব, মোস্তাহাব [A] *adj* desirable; preferable.

মস্তিষ্ক *n* 1 brains; encephalon. 2 intellect; intelligence; brain. 3 memory. ~ খাটানো *vi* apply/tax one's brains. ~ আলোড়িত করা *vi* rack one's brains. ~ **বিকৃত করা** *vt* drive crazy; madden; puzzle. ~**প্রদাহ** *n* brain-fever; cephalitis; cerebritis. ~ **বিকৃতি** *n* insanity; mental disorder/derangement/ imbalance/ ailment; madness; folly; dementia. ~**বিজ্ঞান** *n* cerebrology. ~**বিজ্ঞানী** *n* cerebrologist. ~**যুক্ত** *adj* brainy; clever; brilliant. ~**শূন্য,** ~**হীন** *adj* brainless; stupid; dull-headed. **মস্তিস্কের কাজ** *n* function of brain; intellectual work; brainy job.

মস্তু *n* curd cream; whey.

মস্যাধার *n* ink-stand; ink-pot; ink-horn; ink-bottle.

মহকুমা *n* **1** formerly) subdivision of a district. **2** tribunal; court of justice. ~**-শাসক,** ~**-হাকিম** *n* subdivisional officer.

মহড়া [A] *n* **1** rehearsal; practice. **2** front; lead; position at front/in the front-line; forefront; fore; foreground. ~ **দেওয়া** *vt,* rehearse (parts in a play etc). ~ **নেওয়া/ ফেরানো/ রাখা/ রোখা** *vt* face; confront; face defiantly; bear the brunt (of); brave; breast; head up; spearhead; forge ahead.

মহৎ *adj* **1** great; noble; august; highminded: ~ ব্যক্তি , ~ উপন্যাস. **2** important; eminent; excellent; elevated; high. **3** large; big; vast; huge; ample; extensive. **4** numerous; considerable. **মহতী** *fem.* ~ **কুল** *n* distinguished/ noble family. ~ **সেবা** *n* service of the great; homage (rendered) to great men. ~ **স্থান** high place; lofty position.

মহতাব, মাহতাব *n* **1** moon. **2** moonlight. **3** a kind of fireworks.

মহতী *adj fem* ⇒ মহৎ

মহত্তম *adj superl* (of মহৎ) greatest; very great.

মহত্তর *adj comp* (of মহৎ) greater; very great; mighty; strong.

মহত্ত্ব *n* greatness; high rank/position; nobility; eminence; excellence; high-mindedness; generosity; abundance.

মহদ্‌ (in compounds)=মহৎ. ~**গুণ** *adj* possessing great virtues. ~**গৌরব** *n* great pride. ~**ভয়** *n* great danger; emergency. **মহদাশয়** *adj* high-minded; noble-natured; magnanimous; generous; great. **মহদাশা** *n* great expectation; high hope. **মহদাশয়া** *fem.* **মহাদাশ্রয়** *n* shelter/protection offered by the great.

মহনীয় *adj* to be honoured; praiseworthy; illustrious; glorious; honourable; adorable; venerable; noble; great. ~ **কীর্তি** *adj* of illustrious fame. ~ **মূর্তি** of a magnificent form/appearance.

মহন্ত, মোহান্ত *n* superior of a monastery/convent/ temple; abbot.

মহফিল, মহফেল=মাহফিল

মহব্বত [A] *n* love; friendship; affection.

মহম্মদ=মুহাম্মাদ. **মহম্মদীয়** *adj* Mohammedan.

মহরত, মহরৎ=মোহরৎ

মহরম, মহররম=মোহররম

মহরার=মুহরি[২]

মহর্লোক *n* (myth) the fourth of the seven worlds which rise one above the other.

মহর্ষি *n* great Rishi/ sage/ saint.

মহল [A] *n* **1** palace; palatial building; residence; house; mansion. **2** seraglio. **3** quarter; apartment; abode; place; station; location. **4** society: মহিলা~. **5** administrative division of an estate; taluk: খাস~. **6** *fem* wife; queen: মমতাজ~. ~**দার** *n* landlord. **মহলা** *adj* having a particular number of almost self-contained portions/ apartments: সাতমহলা ভবন.

মহলা [A] *n* rehearsal; practice; demonstration; test. ~ **দেওয়া** *vi* rehearse; practice; give a demonstration of; take a test.

মহলানাবিশ [P] *n* **1** head of a district. **2** a particular family name.

মহল্লক, মহল্লিক [A] *n* eunuch; attendant/ overseer of the women's apartments; chamberlain.

মহল্লা [A] *n* **1** quarter/part of a town; ward. **2** district. ~**দার** *n* headman of a district; resident of the same quarter.

মহা[১] *adj* (in compounds)=মহৎ (often translates the adjective 'general'). ~**অধিবক্তা** *n* advocate-general. ~**কচ্ছ** *n* sea. ~**কটিতটশ্রোণী** *adj fem* having large hips and buttocks. ~**কবি** *n* great/ classical/ epic poet. ~**কবি প্রয়োগ** *n* usage sanctioned by great poets. ~ **করণ** *n* secretariat of the government. ~**কর্ণ** *adj* having large ears. ~**কর্ষ,** ~**কর্ষণ** *nn* (phy) (force of) gravitation. ~**কর্ষাঙ্ক** *n* gravitation constant. ~**কর্ষীয়** *adj* gravitational. ~**কর্ষীয় একক** *n* gravitational unit. ~**কল্যাণক** *adj* very excellent. ~**কাব্য** *n* great/classical poem; epic (poem). ~**কাব্যিক,** ~**কাব্যীয়** *adj* epic; epical. ~**কায়** *adj* of great stature; large-bodied; bulky; huge; colossal; monstrous. ❑*n* elephant. ~**কার** *adj* great; extensive. ~**কারণ** *n* first cause. ~**কাল** *n* **1** form of Shiva in his character of destroyer (being then represented as black and of terrific aspect). **2** eternity; future. ~**কালী** *fem* a terribly destructive manifestation of goddess Durga. ~**কাশ** (astron) outer space; stellar sky; vast endless sky. ~**কাশচারণা** *n* space-travel. ~**কাশচারী** *n* astronaut; spaceman. ~**চারিণী** *fem.* ~**কাশযান** *n* spacecraft.. ~**কুল** *n* great/ noble family. ~**কুলীন** *adj* high-born; of noble/great family. ~**কুলীনতা** *n* noble birth. ~**কৃচ্ছ্র** *n* great penance. ~**কৃষ্ণ** *adj* very black. ~**খ্যাত** *adj* greatly renowned. ~**গমন** =~**প্রস্থান.** ~**গাণনিক** *n* accountant-general. ~**গুণ** *n* chief quality; cardinal virtue. ❑*adj* possessing great excellence; very meritorious; distinguished. ~**গুরু** *n* very venerable person (parents, religious initiator or husband). ~গ্রন্থ *n* great/sacred book. ~গ্রহ *n* name of Rahu (eclipse). ~গ্রীব *adj* long-necked. ❑*n* giraffe; camel. ~ঘোর *adj* very terrible/formidable. ❑*n* profound darkness. ~ঘোষ *adj* loud-sounding. ❑*n* loud sound. ~চক্র *n* great wheel; mystic circle/ assembly in the Shakta ceremonial. ~চণ্ড *adj, n* very passionate/ violent (man). ~চার্য *n* great teacher. ~চিকিৎসক *n* surgeon-general. ~চীন *n* great china. ~চ্ছায় *n* Indian fig tree. ~জই *adj* wearing a great braid/ coil of matted hair. ~জন *n* **1** great/ eminent/ illustrious/ virtuous man. **2** chief/head of a trade/ caste. **3** great merchant/ stockist/ wholesaler. **4** creditor; money-lender; usurer; capitalist. **5** any of the mediaeval poets who composed Kirtan songs about Radha and Krishna. ~জনী *n* usury; money-lending. ❑*adj* relating to usury/ money-lending; usurious. ~জনী করা *vi* practise usury; act as a money-lender. ~জনী-কারবার *n* money-lending business; banking; usury. ~জয় *n* great victory; triumph. ~জাগতিক *adj* cosmic. ~জাতি *n* great race/ nation; the plant *Gaertenera racemosa*. ~জ্ঞান *n* knowledge about reality; final knowledge; occult knowledge by dint of which a dead man can be brought back to life. ~জ্ঞানী *n* profoundly wise/learned; great sooth-sayer; possessing knowledge about ultimate reality. ~জ্যোতি *adj* having great splendour. ❑*n* Shiva. মহাঢ্য *adj* very rich/wealthy. ~তত্ত্ব *n* great principle. ~তপস্বী, ~তপা, ~তপাঃ *adjj* practising severe penance/ great religious austerities. ❑*n* great ascetic. ~তমঃ *n* gross (spiritual) darkness. ~তল *n* (myth) the sixth of the seven lower worlds/ regions under the earth inhabited by the Nagas, etc. ~তাপ *n* great heat. ~তিক্ত *adj* very bitter. ❑*n* the tree Nimb. ~তীক্ষ্ণ *adj* exceedingly sharp. ❑*n* marking-nut plant. ~তেজ *n* great heat/ spirit/vigour; a hero/ demigod. ~তেজ ~তেজস্বী, ~তেজা, ~তেজাঃ *adjj* highly spirited; vigorous; full of fire; fiery; of great splendour/ majesty. ~তেজস্বিনী *fem*. ~তৈল *n* human fat. ~ত্মা *adj* 'high-souled'; magnanimous; having a great/ noble nature; high-minded; noble; highly gifted; exceedingly wise; eminent; mighty; powerful; distinguished. ❑*n* the supreme spirit; great soul of the universe; the great principle ie intellect. ~ত্যাগ *n* great liberality/ generosity. ❑*adj* extremely liberal/ generous. ~ত্যাগী *adj*=~ত্যাগ. ~ত্রিশূল *n* great trident. ~দংষ্ট্র *adj* having great tasks/ fangs. ~দশা *n* influence of a predominant planet. ~দান *n* great gift. ~দেব *n* the great deity Shiva. ~দেবী *fem* **1** great goddess; Shiva's wife Parvati/ Durga. **2** chief wife of a king. ~দেশ continent. ~দেশীয় *adj* continental. ~দেশীয় দ্বীপ *n* (geog) continental island. ~দেহ *adj* having a great body. ~দ্ভুত *adj* very strange/ wonderful. ~দ্যুতি *adj* of great splendour; very bright/ glorious. ~দ্রাবক *adj* solution of sulphur; a kind of drug. ~দ্রুম *n* the tree *Figus religiosa* (অশ্বত্থ); great tree. ~দ্বন্দ্ব *n* great battle/ conflict. ~দ্বিজ=~ব্রাহ্মণ. ~দ্বীপ *n* great island. ~ধন *n* great wealth. ~ধনবান, ~ধনী *adj* very wealthy/rich. ~ধমনী *n* aorta. ~ধাতু *n* gold. ~ধিপাল *n* chancellor. ~ধ্যক্ষ *n* commissioner. ~নগর, ~নগরী *nn* great city; metropolis. ~নগরীয় *adj* metropolitan. ~নদ, ~নদী *nn* great river/stream. ~নন *adj* having a great mouth/face. ~নন্দ *n* **1** great bliss/delight. **2** great joy of deliverance from further transmigration; final emancipation. ❑*adj* highly delighted. ~নন্দা *fem* name of a river. ~নবমী *n* the ninth day in the lunar half of the month Ashwin. ~নাগরিক *n* mayor. ~নাটক *n* brilliant spectacle. ~নাদ *n* loud sound/cry; roaring; bellowing. ❑*adj* loud-sounding; roaring/bellowing loudly. ~নায়ক *n* great chief/leader. ~নাস *adj* having a great nose. ~নিদ্রা *n* great/eternal sleep; death. ~নিম *n* the tree *Melia bukajun*. (ঘোড়ানিম). ~নিরীক্ষক *n* Auditor-General. ~নির্বাণ *n* great Nirvana; total extinction of individual existence. ~নিশা *n* dead of night; midnight; dead hours of the night. ~নীলী *n* a blue variety of *Clitoria ternatea* (অপরাজিতা). ~নুভব, ~নুভাব *adj* high-minded; noble; generous; magnanimous; large-hearted. ~নুভবতা *n* high-mindedness; magnanimity; large-heartedness; generosity. ~নুরাগ *n* great love; excessive affection. ~ন্তক *n* death. ~পঙ্ক *n* great mire; cardinal sin. ~পথ *n* **1** high road; principal road. **2** death; passage into the next world. ~পদ্ম *n* **1** a particular high number. **2** one of the treasures of Kubera. **3** white lotus. ~পরাধ *n* great offence. ~পরিনির্বাণ *n* name of a Buddhist Sutra. ~পবিত্র *adj* greatly purifying. ~পাতক *n* great/deadly crime/sin. ~পাতকী *adj* guilty of one or more deadly sins. ~পাতকিনী *fem*. ~পাত্র *n* prime minister. ~পাপ *n* great crime. ~পাপিষ্ঠ, ~পাপী *nn* guilty of a great crime. ~পাপিষ্ঠা, ~পাপিনী *fem* ~পারিষদ *n* principal attendant. ~পীঠ *n* high seat. ~পুণ্য *adj* extremely favourable/ auspicious (as a day). ~পুরাণ *n* great Purana (eighteen Puranas composed by Vedavyasa). ~পুরুষ *n* **1** great/ eminent man. **2** great saint/ sage/ ascetic. **3** great soul; the supreme spirit. ~পূজা *n* solemn worship; great honour. ~পূত *adj* exceedingly pure. ~পৃথিবী *n* the great earth. ~পৌর্ণমাসী *n* a night in which Jupiter enters into conjunction with the full moon.

~প্রজাপতি *n* great lord of creatures; Vishnu. ~প্রতাপ *adj* very puissant. ~প্রতীহার *n* chief door-keeper. ~প্রপঞ্চ *n* great universe/visible world. ~প্রভ *adj* exceedingly brilliant/ splendid. ~প্রভাব *adj* exceedingly mighty/ powerful. ~প্রভু **1** great master; mighty lord; king; King. **2** very holy man/great saint. ~প্রয়াণ=~প্রস্থান. ~প্রলয় *n* **1** total annihilation of the universe at the end of a *kalpa*. **2** great conflict/ strife/ combat. ~প্রসাদ *n* great favour/ kindness; great present (of food, etc distributed among the persons present at the worship of an idol). ~প্রস্থান *n* setting out on the great journey; departing this life; dying. ~প্রস্থান করা *vi* set out on the great journey; depart from this life; die. ~প্রস্থানিক *n* relating to the great journey/dying. ~প্রাচীর *n* (anat) diaphragm. ~প্রাজ্ঞ *adj* very wise/ clever/ intelligent. ~প্রাণ *adj* **1** large-hearted; magnanimous. **2** (gram) aspirate. ~প্রাণা *fem.* ❑*n* (gram) an aspirate. ~প্রাণতা *n* **1** large-heartedness; magnanimity. **2** aspiration. ~প্রাণী *n* (colloq) life conceived as having an existence independent of the body; soul. ~প্রাব্রজ্যা *n* hard life of a wandering religious mendicant. ~ফল *n* great fruit/reward. ❑*adj* brining a rich reward. ~বংশ *n* great lineage/race. ~বক্ষাঃ *adj* broad-chested. ~বন *n* great forest. ~বল *adj* exceedingly strong; very powerful/mighty; very efficacious. ❑*n* **1** Buddha. **2** wind. **3** borax. ~বাক্য *n* great saying/maxim; saying of a great man. ~বারুণী *n* the festival on the thirteenth day of the moon's decrease in the month of Chaitra. ~বাহু *adj* long-armed; very strong; mighty. ❑*n* Sri Krishna. ~বিক্রম, ~বিক্রান্ত *nn* very valorous/ courageous. ~বিজ্ঞ *adj* very wise/ intelligent. ~বিদ্যা *n* class of personifications of the Shakti or female energy of Shiva; great/ exalted science; (facet) art of stealing. ~বিদ্যালয় *n* college. ~বিবর *n* (anat) foramen magnum. ~বিভ্রাট *n* great crisis/ confusion/ dilemma. ~বিষুব *n* vernal equinox. ~বিষুবরেখা *n* line of the vernal equinox. ~বিষুবসংক্রান্তি *n* transition of the sun in the Aries; day of this transition. ~বিহার *n* great Buddhist monastery. ~বীণা *n* a kind of lute. ~বীর *n* great hero. ~বীর্য *adj* very powerful/potent; of great strength/ energy. ~বেগ *adj* moving swiftly; flying swiftly; flowing rapidly; very fleet/ swift/ rapid. ~বৈদ্য *n* great/ chief physician; (iron) charlatan; quack. ~বৈর *n* great enemy. ~বোধি *n* great intelligence of a Buddha; highest/final knowledge. ~ব্যাধি *n* great/severe disease; black leprosy. ~ব্রাহ্মণ *n* great Brahmin; a priest who officiates at a *shraddha* or solemn ceremony in honour of deceased ancestor. ~ভয় *n* great danger/peril. ~ভাগ *adj* highly fortunate; very lucky; eminent in the highest degree; illustrious; noble-minded. ~ভাগ্য *n* great luck/happiness. ~ভাব *n* ecstatic state caused by profundity of love, devotion etc. ~ভিক্ষু *n* great monk; Gautama Buddha. ~ভুজ=~বাহু. ~ভূত *n* great element; gross element. ~ভৈরব *n* form of Shiva. ~মণ্ডল *n* great guild/ association/ concourse. ~মতি *adj* great; great-minded; having a great under-standing; clever. ~মদ *n* great pride/ intoxication; excessive/ violent rut. ~মনা, ~মনাঃ *adj* high-minded; magnanimous. ~মনস্বী=~মনা. ~মনস্বিনী *fem.* ~মন্ত্র *n* any very sacred/ efficacious text; great spell; very efficacious charm. ~মন্ত্রী *n* great/prime minister; chief counsellor. ~মহিম, ~মহিমান্বিত *adjj* truly great; majestic; possessing true greatness; most excellent/ glorious. ~মহিমান্বিতা *fem.* ~মহীরুহ *n* great/large tree. ~মহোপাধ্যায় *n* very great/ venerable teacher (title given to great Sanskrit scholars). ~মাংস *n* human flesh. ~মাত্য *n* prime minister. ~মাত্র *n* man of high rank; high official; prime minister; elephant-driver/- keeper. ~মানী *adj* **1** highly honourable/ venerable. **2** exceedingly proud. ~মানিনী *fem.* ~মান্য *adj* =~মানী (1); being in great honour with. ~মান্যা *fem.* ~মায়া *n* **1** illusion; divine power of illusion. **2** goddess Durga. **3** goddess Lakshmi. ~মায়াচ্ছন্ন *adj* overwhelmed with/enveloped in (divine) illusion; self-obliviously enmeshed in worldly affair. ~মার *n* great tumult/ hullabaloo. ~মারী *n* pestilence causing great mortality; ~মারী কাণ্ড *n* (facet) a great/ tumultuous affairs. ~মারীপীড়িত *adj* pestilence-stricken. ~মুনি *n* great sage/ ascetic. ~মূঢ় *adj* very foolish/ infatuated. ~মূর্খ *n* great fool. ~মূল্য *adj* very costly; precious. ~মেঘ *n* great/ dense cloud. ~মোহ *n* great confusion/ infatuation of mind. ~ম্ল *adj* very acid/ sour. ❑*n* fruit of the Indian tamarind. ~যশ, ~যশা *adjj* very renowned/ celebrated. ~যাত্রা=~প্রস্থান. ~যান *n* 'great vehicle' (name of the later system of Buddhist teaching said to have been first promulgated by Nagarjuna). ~যুদ্ধ *n* great war/ fight. ~যুগ *n* great yuga or yuga of the gods; great age. ~যোগী *n* great yogi; Shiva. ~যোদ্ধা *n* great warrior/soldier. ~রণ *n* great battle. ~রণ্য *n* great forest. ~রত্ন *n* precious jewel; most precious of all jewels. ~রথ, ~রথী *n* great charioteer. ~রব *adj* loud-sounding; uttering loud cries. ~রম্ভ *n* great enterprise/ undertaking. ~রহস্য *n* great secret/ mystery. ~রাজ *n* **1** great king; supreme sovereign; reigning prince; emperor. **2** (term of address for) a great ascetic/ bard/ Brahmin cook. ~রাজ্ঞী *fem* reigning queen; empress. ~রাজা *n* government title awarded to feudal princes, landlords, rich citizens etc. of India during the British rule; maharaja(h). ~রাজাধিরাজ *n* paramount sovereign; emperor; king of kings. ~রানা, ~রানা *nn* title of the rulers of Udaipur. ~রানী[1] *fem.* ~রানী[2] *n fem* empress; great queen; wife of a great king. ~রাত্র *n* time after midnight or near the close of night. ~রাত্রি *n* great night of the complete destruction of the world; time after midnight; solemn night. ~রাষ্ট্র *n* great kingdom/ country; land of Marathas in the west of India. ~রাষ্ট্রী *n* language of Maharastra; native of Maharastra; Marathi. ~রাষ্ট্রীয় *adj* of Maharastra. ~রুদ্র *n* an awe-inspiring form of Shiva. ~রূপ *adj* mighty in form. ~রোগ *n* severe illness; almost incurable disease; inveterate bad habit/ mannerism. ~রোগী *adj* suffering from a severe illness. ~রোগিনী *fem.* ~রোমা *adj* having large/ thick hair on the body; very hairy. ~রোষ *n* extreme anger. ~রৌদ্র *adj* very terrible. ~রৌরব *n* name of a hell. ~র্ঘ *adj* high-priced; very precious/ valuable/ costly expensive. ~র্ঘতা *n* costliness; preciousness; high value. ~র্ণব *n* mighty sea; ocean. মহার্থ *n* a great thing/ matter; weighty/ important meaning. ❑*adj* having great meaning; significant; important; weighty. ~লক্ষ্মী *n fem* great Lakshmi (Shakti of Narayana). ~লয়া *n fem* name of particular festival; day of the moon's change in the month of Bhadra and the last day of the Hindu lunar year. ~লিঙ্গ *n* 1 great Linga/ phallus. 2 Shiva. ~লোল *adj* excessively eager. ~শক্তি *n* 1 great strength/ prowess/ power. 2 name of Kartikeya and Durga. ❑*adj* very powerful/ mighty. ~শক্তিধর, ~শক্তিশালী *adj*=~শক্তি. ~শক্তিশালিনী. ~শঙ্খ *n* 1 great conch-shell. 2 (anat) temporal bone. 3 human bone. 4 frontal bone. ~শব্দ *n* great noise; loud sound/cry; tumult. ❑*adj* very noisy/loud. ~শয় *adj* having noble disposition; high-minded; magnanimous; noble; liberal. ❑*n* (term of courtesy affixed to the name of a gentleman) Mr: পাল ~শয়; (term of address) Sir. ~শয়া *fem* Mrs; Madam. ~শয়ন *n* great/ lofty bed/ couch. ~শয্যা *n* great/ lofty/ splendid couch. ~শল্ক *adj* large-scaled. ❑*n* kind of prawn/ sea crab. ~শস্ত্র *n* powerful weapon. ~শাখ *adj* having large branches. ~শান্তি *n* expiatory observance and recitation (for averting evil). ~শিরা *n* (anat) vena cava. ~শুক্তি *n* pearl muscle; mother of pearl. ~শুক্ল *adj* very white. ~শূদ্র *n* cowherd. ~শূন্য=~কাশ; great void. ~শূর *adj*=~শক্তি. ~শ্মশান *n* 1 great cemetery/ place for burning the dead. 2 city of Benaras. ~শ্রম *n* great hermitage. ~শ্রমণ *n* great religious mendicant; Gautama Buddha. ~শ্রী *n fem* name of Lakshmi. ~শ্বেত=~শুক্ল. ~শ্বেতা *n fem* name of Durga/ Saraswati. ~ ষষ্ঠ *n fem* a form of Durga. ~ষ্টমী *n* the great 8th; the eighth day in the light half of the month Ashwin; festival in honour of Durga. ~সঙ্কট *n* very troublesome/ intricate/ difficult problem or situation. ~সত্ত্ব *adj* having a great/ noble essence; noble; good; very powerful; mighty; steady; constant. ❑*n* great creature. ~সভা *n* great meeting/ association/ assembly; august gathering, (representative) legislative assembly; parliament; congress; large hall. ~সমষ্টি *n* grand total. ~সমারোহ *n* great pomp and grandeur. ~সমারোহে *adv* with much pomp and grandeur. ~সমুদ্র, ~সাগর *n* great sea; ocean. ~সাগরীয় *adj* oceanic. ~সাধক *n* great ascetic. ~সামন্ত *n* great vassal; war minister; commander-in-chief. ~সিংহ *n* great lion (*sharava*). ~সিন্ধু=~সমুদ্র. ~সিদ্ধি *n* great perfection; particular form of magical power. ~সুখ *n* great pleasure; copulation. ❑*n* Buddha. ~স্থবির *n* great elder; class of monks among Buddhists. ~স্রোত *n* alimentary canal. ~স্বন *n* loud sound; kind of drum. ❑*adj* loud-sounding.

মহা[2] *adj* (colloq) 1 terrible/ formidable: ~ আপদ. 2 great; excessive: ~ আনন্দ. 3 immense; large: ~ জঙ্গল.

মহান *adj masc* of মহৎ

মহানুপ্রাণতা=মহানুভবতা (⇒ মহা[1])

মহান্ত *n* 1=মহন্ত. 2 a devotee of Sri Krishna. 3 title of a head of a town/village.

মহাফেজ [A] *n* 1 guardian; keeper; guard; protector. 2 record keeper. ~খানা *n* record-room; archive. জাতীয় ~ *n* National Archive.

মহাভারত *n* 1 the Mahabharata, the great Indian epic. 2 great war of the Bharatas. 3 (fig) voluminous book, lengthy essay, etc. 4 great war: য়োরোপীয় ~. ~ অশুদ্ধ হওয়া (fig) occurrence of a serious fault/ lapse; be a disaster. ~ আরম্ভ করা (fig) begin an intolerably long harangue; begin interminable/ long-winded speech. মহাভারতীয় *adj* relating to/of the Mahabharata.

মহাল=মহল

মহি=মহী

মহিত *adj* honoured; celebrated; venerated.

মহিম[1] [A] *n* expedition; attack; battle.

মহিম[2] *adj* (in compounds)=মহিমা. ~ময় *adj* majestic; mighty; glorious; exalted. ~ময়ী *fem.*

মহিমা *n* 1 greatness; power; might; glory; exaltedness; majesty. 2 divine grace/ power. 3 magnitude. 4 influence: টাকার ~. 5 magical power of increasing one's size at will. ~কীর্তন *n* glorification; adulation; panegyric; eulogy. ~

কীর্তন করা *vi* sing the praises/ glory of; glorify; extol; exalt. মহিমান্বিত=মহিমময়. মহিমান্বিতা *fem*. ~ব্যঞ্জক *adj* expressive of grace/glory/majesty; glorious; gracious; majestic; magnificent. মহিমার্ণব *adj* as majestic/ glorious as the ocean; ocean of glory/ majesty/ grace.

মহিলা *n fem* lady; gentlewoman; woman. ~মজলিস, ~সঙ্ঘ *nn* woman's association/club. ~সমাজ *n* women's society; womenfolk.

মহিষ *n* **1** buffalo. **2** name of an Asura. ~ধ্বজ, ~বাহন *nn* Yama, the god of death. ~মর্দিনী *n fem* 'crusher of Mahisha; Durga. মহিষাসুর *n*=~(2).

মহিষা=ভইষা (⇒ ভইষ)

মহিষী *n fem* **1** female buffalo; buffalo-cow. **2** the first/consecrated wife of a king; any queen.

মহী *n* **1** earth. **2** ground; soil. ~ক্ষিৎ *n* King. ~জ *adj* earth-born; produced from the earth. ~তল *n* surface of the earth; soil; ground. ~ধর *n* mountain. ~ন, ~নাথ, ~ন্দ্র, ~প ~পতি, ~পাল *nn* king. ~রুহ *n* tree. ~লতা *n* earthworm.

মহীয়ান *adj* noble; very glorified; exalted; majestic. মহীয়সী *fem*.

মহুয়া *n* kind of flowering tree, its seeds or flowers (*Bassia latifolia*); mahua. ~র মউ/মধু *n* honey of mahua; butter obtained from mahua seeds.

মহুরী=মোহরার

মহুরী[1] *n* (archaic)=মৌরি

মহুরি[2] *n* flute.

মহেন্দ্র *n* **1** the great Indra, king of gods. **2** a mythological mountain range. মহেন্দ্রাণী *fem* Shaci, Indra's wife. ~কদলী *n* a species of banana. ~নগরী, ~পুরী *nn* city of Indra; Amaravati.

মহেশ, মহেশ্বর *nn* great lord/god; Shiva. মহেশানী, মহেশ্বরী *fem* goddess Durga. ~পুরী *n* Kailash, the city/abode of Shiva.

মহেষ্বাস *adj* having great skill in archery. ❑*n* great archer.

মহোৎসব *n* great festival; great rejoicing; grand gala; great communion of Vaishnavas singing kirtan songs and eating together.

মহোৎসাহ *n* great enthusiasm/energy/ zeal/ endeavour. ❑*adj* having great enthusiasm/ power/ energy/ zeal; very energetic/ enthusiastic. মহোৎসাহী *adj*=~. মহোৎসাহে *adj* with great enthusiasm/ zeal/ eagerness.

মহোদধি *n* great ocean.

মহোদয় *adj* **1** = মহানুভব. **2** highly prosperous/opulent; pre-eminent; highly fortunate; honourable; respected: মন্ত্রী~. ❑*n* (term of address) Sir. মহোদয়া *fem*.

মহোদর *n* large belly. ❑*adj* big-bellied. মহোদরী *fem*.

মহোদ্যম *n* great effort/ exertion. ❑*adj* very energetic/ diligent/ persevering; studiously occupied/ busily engaged in.

মহোদ্যোগ *n* great effort/ endeavour/ enterprise. ❑*adj* making great exertion; very laborious/ industrious.

মহোন্নত *adj* very high/ lofty; highly elevated/ exalted; greatly flouring/ prosperous. মহোন্নতি *n* great elevation; high rank/ position; great prosperity/ progress.

মহোপকার *n* great aid/ assistance/ benefit/ service; great good turn. ~ক, মহোপকারী *adjj* very beneficial/ serviceable/ benevolent; highly benign. ❑*n* great benefactor.

মহোরগ *n* great serpent; python.

মহৌষধ *n* very efficacious drug; sovereign remedy; panacea.

মহৌষধি, মহৌষধী *nn* **1** great/ very efficacious medicinal plant; any phosphorescent shrub/ creeper. **2** name of various medicinal plants.

মা[1] *n fem* **1** mother; mamma; mama; mum. **2** (of four-footed animals) dam. **3** goddess. **4** (term of address to) a young girl. ❑*int* expresses surprise; pain; ridicule; tiredness (also মা গো, ওমা). ~-ছা *n* mother and child. ~ঝি *n* mother and daughter. ~পো, ~বেটা *nn* mother and son. ~বাপ *n* **1** parents. **2** master, protector and guardian; only refuge. ~বাপগিরি *n* bossing; patronizing attitude. ~মরা *adj* motherless. ও ~ কী হবে? (exclamation) what will become of me? What is to be done now?

মা[2] *n* (music) the fourth note.

মাই *n* **1** (female) breast; teat; nipple. **2** milk from the breast. ~ খাওয়া *vt* suck one's mother's breast. ~ খাওয়ানো *vt* give (a child) the breast; suckle; nurse (one's baby) at the breast. ~ ছাড়া *vt* stop sucking (the breast). ~ ছাড়ানো *vt* wean (a baby). ~ ধরা *vt* begin to suck one's mother's breast. ~দিউনি *n fem* suckling nurse. ~দুধ *n* milk from the breast. ~ দেওয়া=~খাওয়ানো. ~পোষ *n* feeding-bottle. ~য়ের বোঁটা *n* nipple; teat.

মাইক, মাইক্রোফোন [E] *nn* mike; microphone.

মাইজ=মাজ[1]

মাইন [E] *n* mine (weapon).

মাইন(১) দার *n* (dial) salaried labourer/servant.

মাইনর, মাইনার *n* person not yet legally of age; minor. ❑*adj* (of schools) teaching from five to eight.

মাইনা=মাহিনা

মাইফেল *n* (colloq)=মাহফিল. মাইফেলি *adj* fond of parties; fun-loving; boisterous.

মাইয়া *n fem* (dial)=মেয়ে

মাইয়াত [A] *n* dead body.

মাইরি [E] *n fem* (in oaths) by Mary; believe me.

মাইল [E] *n* mile. **~পোস্ট** *n* [E] mile-post; milestone. **মাইলেজ, মাইলিজ** *nn* mileage.

মাউই, মাউই-মা *nn* mother-in-law or aunt-in-law of a brother/sister/cousin.

মাওলা, মাওলানা⇒মওলা

মাংনা=মাগনা (⇒ মাগন)

মাংস *n* flesh; meat. **~তুল্য** *adj* flesh-like. **~পেশি, ~পেশী** *nn* muscle. **~বিক্রেতা** *n* meat-seller; butcher. **~বৃদ্ধি** *n* increase/growth of flesh; accumulation of fat; adipose. **~ভোজী** *adj* flesh-eating; carnivorous; living on animal food. **~ভোজিনী** *fem.* **~ল** *adj* fleshy; plump; fat; adipose. **মাংসাদ, মাংসাশী** *adj* flesh-eating; carnivorous. **মাংসের দোকান** *n* meat shop; butcher's shop. **কুক্কুট~** *n* chicken; fowl. **গো~** *n* beef. **ছাগ~** *n* mutton. **পক্ষি~** *n* fowl; chicken. **বরাহ~** *n* pork. **বাছুরের ~** *n* veal. **মেষ ~** *n* mutton. **হরিণ~** *n* venison.

মাকড় *n* **1** spider; arachnid. **2** monkey; ape.

মাকড়শা *n* =মাকড় (1). **~র জাল** *n* spider's web; cobweb; gossamer.

মাকড়া *n* (colloq) **1** monkey; spider. **2** (derog) boy; fellow. **মাকড়ি** *fem.* ❑*adj* brick-red; pale red; mud-coloured: ~ রং.

মাকড়ি, মাকড়ী *nn* a variety of ear-ring.

মাকনা *n* young elephant with tusks. **~লা** *n* elephant of small stature and without tusks.

মাকাল *n* **1** a kind of creeper and its fruit which is eye-catching but contains offensive smelling inedible pulp. **2** (fig) (also **~ফল**) very handsome but worthless person.

মাকু *n* shuttle (of weavers).

মাকুন্দ *n, adj* adult male who has not grown his beard; beardless man.

মাক্ষিক *n* **1** honey. **2** pyrites. ❑*adj* relating to bees/ flies.

মাখন *n* butter. **~ তোলা** *vt* skim butter/milk. **~ দাগানো** *vt* clarify butter by boiling. **~ মাখানো** *vt* butter. **~তোলা দুধ** *n* skimmed milk; buttermilk. **~দাগানো ঘি** *n* clarified butter. **~বিক্রেতা** *n* butter-seller. **~বিক্রেতী** *fem* butter-wife; butter-woman. **~মাখানো** *adj* buttered; buttery.

মাখা *vt* **1** smear (with); spread; besmear with; cover/mark with; anoint; rub sth in: রুটিতে মাখন ~, তেল/ মলম ~, রং ~, কাদা ~. **2** dab; daub; coat (with): রং ~. **3** knead: ময়দা ~. **4** blend; mix with (spices, etc): মশলা দিয়ে তরকারি ~, দুধ দিয়ে ভাত ~. ❑*adj* smeared/ covered/ anointed/ mixed/ mingled/ tinged/ diffused/ impregnated with; kneaded; consecrated by: সুধা~. **~নো** *vt* cause to smear/ spread/ cover; get smeared/ covered with/ rubbed with/ kneaded. **~মাখি** *n* **1** thorough besmearing with: জলে-কাদায় ~মাখি. **2** mutual smearing; sprinkling (coloured water, etc) on each other: রং ~মাখি. **3** intimacy; close association; good terms; familiarity: বড়লোকের সঙ্গে ~মাখি. **~মাখি করা** *vi, vt* **1** associate (closely) with; hobnob with; frequent; consort with. **2** smear each other with; sprinkle on each other.

মাগ *n fem* (sl) wife.

মাগধ *adj* relating to/ born or produced/ customary among the Magadhas or the Magadha (মগধ) country. ❑*n* professional bard or panegyric of a king.

মাগধী *n* language of Magadha (one of the Prakit dialect). **অর্ধ~** *n* variety of the Magadhi dialect (being the language of the sacred literature of the Jains).

মাগন *n* begging; praying. **~কুড়ে** *n* beggar; mendicant. **মাগনা, মাংনা** *adj* obtained by begging; free (of cost); gratis; cost-free. ❑*adv* free of cost/ charge; free: মাগনা খাটা give free labour.

মাগফিরাত, মাগফেরাত [A] *nn* absolution; remission; pardon; forgiveness.

মাগরিব, মাগবের [A] *nn* sunset; evening; evening prayer.

মাগা, মাঙা, মাঙ্গা *vt* **1** beg; ask for; pray for; solicit. **2** admit; accept; accede; পরাজয় মেগে নেওয়া. **মেগে খাওয়া** *vi* live by begging.

মাগী *n fem* (sl) woman; prostitute. **~বাড়ি** *n* (sl) brothel. **~মিনসে** *n pl* man and woman; man and wife; couple.

মাগুর *n* variety of catfish.

মা-গোঁসাই *n fem* **1** wife of a religious preceptor; religious preceptress. **2** (facet) very harmless, innocent and ineffective person; ingenue.

মাগ্‌গি exorbitantly high in price; dear; sky-high; prohibitive; expensive; highpriced. **~গণ্ডা** *n* dearness and scarcity; sellers' market. **~গণ্ডার দিন/বাজার** *n* days of high price and scarcity. **~ভাতা** *n* dearness allowance.

মাঘ *n* the tenth month of the Bengali calendar (from the middle of January to the middle of February). **মাঘী** *adj* of the month of Magh. ❑*n* (also **মাঘী পূর্ণিমা**) day of full moon in the month of Magh. **এক মাঘে শীত যায় না** (prov) even if one opportunity to avenge oneself is missed, there will be plenty of others; *cf* there's as good fish in the sea as ever came out of it.

মাঙন=মাগন

মাঙনা=মাগনা (⇒ মাগন)

মাঙা=মাগা

মাঙ্গন[1]=মাগন

মাঙ্গন[2] *n* forced levy of money exacted from tenants by landlords (zamindars).

মাঙ্গলিক, মাঙ্গল্য *adj* conferring/ indicating happiness; auspicious; propitious. ❑*n* **1** any auspicious object/ ceremony. **2** welfare; propitiousness; weal; well-being. **3** good fortune.

মাঙ্গা[১]=মাগা
মাঙ্গা[২]=মাগ্‌গি
মাচা, মাচান *nn* **1** platform; dais; stage. **2** shelf. **3** scaffold. **4** shooting platform (usually up a tree). **5** raised seat. **6** bamboo-frame for carrying dead bodies to the crematorium.
মাছ *n* fish. **~ ধরা** *vt* catch fish; fish. **~ওয়ালা** *n* fishmonger. **~ওয়ালী** *fem* fish-woman. **~ধরা** *n* fishery. **~ধরা জাহাজ** *n* trawler. **~ধরা জাল** *n* fishing net. **~ধরা নৌকা** *n* fishing boat; trawler. **~ রাঙা, ~ রাঙ্গা** *nn* kingfisher. **নদীর ~** *n* river/fresh-water fish. **নোনা ~** *n* salted fish. **নোনা জলের ~** *n* salt-water fish. **পুকুরের ~** *n* fish reared in pond. **শুঁটকি ~** *n* dried fish. **সমুদ্রের ~** *n* marine fish. **মাছের কাঁটা** *n* fish-bone. **মাছের ঘেরি** *n* fishery. **মাছের চাষ** *n* pisciculture. **~ ঝুড়ি** *n* creel; fish-basket. **মাছের ডিম** *n* spawn; roe. **মাছের পুকুর** *n* fish-pond; hatchery. **মাছের বাজার** *n* fish-market. **মাছের ভেড়ি** *n* fishery-dam
মাছি *n* **1** fly. **2** foresight of a gun. **~টেপা** *adj* extremely stingy/miserly. **~মারা** *adj* (lit) fly-killing; (fig) blindly copying without exercising discretion; slavish: ~মারা কেরানি.
মাছুয়া *adj* (old use)=মেছো
মাজ[১] *n* (bot) pith within a stem; heart of a tree.
মাজ[২] *n* species of rush/sedge-like grass (*Saccharum sara/munja*) which is used for making rope.
মাজন *n* **1** wiping away; cleaning; rubbing; scouring; scrubbing; brushing; purifying; polishing. **2** cleansing substance; cleaner; tooth-powder/paste (also **দাঁতের ~**).
মাজহাব=মজহব
মাজা[১] *vt* wipe away; cleanse; purify; rub; scour; scrub; brush; polish. ❑*adj* cleansed; purified; rubbed; scoured; scrubbed; brushed; polished. মাজন *n* **~নো** *vt* cause to wipe away/ cleanse; get cleansed/ scoured/ scrubbed. **~ঘষা, ~ঘসা** *n* **1**=মাজন; washing. **2** meticulous cleansing and dressing; polish; refinement; care: চেহারার ~ঘষা. **3** training; cultivation; exercise; practice: কন্ঠের ~ঘষা. **4** finishing; finish; chiselling; meticulous correction/ revision; polish: elegance; improvement: লেখার/ ছবির ~ঘষা. **5** bargaining; haggling: অনেক ~ঘষার পর কেনা. ❑*adj* **1** polished; shiny; glossy; smooth. **2** polished; chiselled; trained; cultivated; refined; finished; sophisticated; urbane. **~ঘষা (করা)** *vt* **1** polish; gloss; finish; scour; scrape; scrub. **2** refine; polish; finish; smarten up; hone; round off; improve upon; chisel; cultivate; train; refine; better. **বাসন~ চাকর** *n* scullion. **বাসন~ ঝি** *n fem* scullery-maid.
মাজার [A] *n* shrine; tomb; grave; sepulchre.
মাজুন, মাজুম [A] *nn* an intoxicating drug prepared from the extract of hemp and sugar.
মাজুফল *n* gall-nut. **মাজুফলের রস** *n* gallic acid.
মাজুর [A] *adj* **1** dismissed. **2** helpless.
মাঝ *n* (colloq, dialect) **1** middle; centre. **2** inside; interior. **3** midst; company: বন্ধুদের মাঝে. **~খান**=~ (also ⇒ মধ্যস্থল). **~খানে**=মধ্যে. **~ থেকে**=মধ্যে থেকে; from the bottom of: অন্তরের ~ থেকে. **~দরিয়া** *n* mid-stream; mid-ocean; mid-sea. **মাঝামাঝি** *n* almost middle/ half. ❑*adj* almost middle/central; moderate; middling: মাঝামাঝি অবস্থা. ❑*adj* almost half-way; almost in/to the middle/centre; almost half. **মাঝার** *n* (poet, old use)=~. **মাঝারি** *adj* middling; moderate; of medium quality/ grade/ size.
মাঝি *n* **1** boatman; helmsman; steersman; boatswain. **2** (naut) midshipman. **3** (amongst Santal people) headman; man; Santal male; husband. **4** fisherman: **পদ্মা নদীর ~**. **~গিরি** *n* profession of a boatman/ helmsman. **~মাল্লা** *n* helmsman and his subordinate boatmen; crew. **~য়ান** *n* (amongst Santal people) wife of a headman; wife.
মাঝে=মধ্যে
মাঞ্জা *n* a glue mixed with powdered glass, etc for coating the string of a kite. **~ করা/ দেওয়া** *vt* coat a string with the above glue; sharpen.
মাঞ্জিষ্ঠ *adj* dyed with madder; red. ❑*n* red colour.
মাট *n* (in compounds) ground; earth. **~কলাই** *n* groundnut; monkey-nut. **~কোটা** *n* mud-built house consisting of two or more storeys.
মাটা=মেথি
মাটাপালাম *n* variety of coarse white fabric.
মাটাম *n* (try-) square. **~সই, ~সহি** *adjj* placed/set at right angle; perpendicular. **~ভাবে** *adv* straight; erect; uprightly; perpendicularly.
মাটি *n* **1** soil; dust; clay; mud. **2** ground. **3** floor; dirt. **4** foothold. **5** land; landed property. **6** earth; surface of the earth; world. **7** uselessness; futility; worthlessness. **~ করা** *vt* spoil; ruin; bungle; mar; make a mess/ hash of; mess up; fluff. **~ কাটা/কোপানো** *vi* dig; excavate; break up earth. **~ কামড়ে (পড়ে) থাকা** (fig) stick it out; persist doggedly; hang on; plod on. **~ খাওয়া** (fig) do sth deplorable/ regrettable/ disgraceful; do wrong. **~ খোঁড়া** *vi* dig. **~ তোলা** *vt* lift earth (from a hole, etc). **~ দেওয়া** *vt* bury; enter. **~ নেওয়া** *vi* fall to ground; eat dust. **~ ফেলা** *vt* **1** throw earth to fill up (a hole, etc). **2** start work at (a road, etc). **~ ভাপানো** *vi* (collog) idle; vegetate; loaf; laze (away). **~ মাখা** *vt* **1** knead clay. **2** besmear/smear with clay/ mud; soil. **~মাটি** *adj* clayey; muddy; musty. ❑*n* lassitude; sloth; languor. **~ মাড়ানো** *vi, vt* (colloq) visit; call; drop on. **~ লেপা** *vt* coat/plaster with mud or clay. **~ হওয়া** *vi* be spoiled/ ruined. **পায়ের তলার ~ সরে যাওয়া** (fig) lose one's foothold; be utterly helpless/ demoralized/enervated; be put out

of gear. ~ হয়ে যাওয়া *vi* hang one's head in/for shame. ~র খেলনা *n* earthen toy. ~র ঘর *n* mud-built house. ~র তেল *n* kerosene. ~র দর *n* nominal price; dirt cheap. ~র দরে কেনা buy sth dirt-cheap; buy sth for a (an old) song; have for the asking. ~র দরে বিকানো go for a song; go cheap. ~র দরে বিক্রি করা sell for a mere trifle. ~র দেয়াল *n* mud-built wall. ~র পুতুল *n* earthen doll. ~ বাড়ি=~র ঘর. ~র বাসন *n* earthenware; plate. ~র মানুষ *n* very gentle, forbearing and honest man; good soul; unassuming/self-effacing person. ~র মূর্তি *n* statue made of clay. ~র স্পর্শ পাওয়া fall to the ground. বিলাতি ~ *n* cement. বেলে ~ *n* sandy soil. শক্ত ~ *n* **1** hard soil. **2** (fig) tough/ stubborn/ intractable person. হাড় ~ করা *vi* die; eat dust.

মাটো *adj* **1** lazy; sluggish; slow; slack: ~ কাজ. **2** dark; lack-lustre; dull: ~ রং.. **3** uninteresting; dull: ~ খেলা.

মাঠ *n* **1** field; maidan. **2** (agricultural) land; field. **3** pasture; grazing ground. **4** playground; ground. **5** open space. ~গোঠ *n* fields and pastures. ~ঘাট *n* (lit) fields and landing-stages; (fig) every place. ~ ভাঙা traverse a field. মাঠে মারা যাওয়া *vi* (fig) be utterly lost; perish; leave no trace; be in vain; be an utter failure.

মাঠা[১] *n* **1** cream (of milk); butter. **2** buttermilk; whey. ~ তোলা *vt* skim the butter. ~তোলা দুধ *n* skimmed-mik.

মাঠা[২] *adj* **1** plain; blunt; dull: সাদা~. **2** muddy.

মাঠান[১] *n* arable land; plain.

মাঠান[২] *n fem* (used as term of address to a lady) venerable mother; madam.

মাড় *n* starch/scum of boiled rice or any grain. ~ গালা *vi* strain out starch (from boiled rice). ~ দেওয়া *vt* starch.

মাড়ওয়ারি, মাড়ওয়ারী=মাড়োয়ারি

মাড়ন *n* pounding; threshing; crushing.

মাড়া *vt* **1** pound: ঔষধ ~. **2** thresh: শস্য ~. **3** crush: আখ ~. ~ই *nn*=মাড়ন. ~নো *vt* tread, trample. ছায়া ~নো associate with; frequent; consort.

মাড়ি[১]=মাঢ়ী

মাড়ি[২] *n* concentrate of fruit-juice: কাঁঠালের ~.

মাড়ুয়া *n* (pejorative) **1**=মাড়োয়ারি. **2** a native of Western India; Hindustani.

মাড়োয়ারি *n* a native of Marwar/ Rajputana. ❑*adj* of/ relating to Marwar.

মাঢ়ি *n* **1** (bot) fibre/ germ of a leaf. **2** (anat) gum. ~র দাঁত *n* molar tooth.

মাণব *n* youth; lad; youngster. ~ক *n* **1** youth; lad; fellow. **2** (derog) littleman; manikin; dwarf.

মাণিক্য *n* ruby.

মাণ্ডলিক *adj* regional; provincial

মাত[১] *adj* charmed; enchanted; captivated; overwhelmed; swept off one's feet; intoxicated: গন্ধে/গানে/রূপে ~. ~ করা *vt* enchant; charm; intoxicate; overwhelm; replete; captivate. ~ হওয়া *vi* be charmed/intoxicated/ swept off one's feet.

মাত[২] [A] *n* (chess) checkmating; complete defeat of the opponent. ❑*adj* checkmated; completely defeated; routed. ~ করা *vt* checkmate; defeat thoroughly, rout; win ontright.

মাত[৩] *n* waste product; dross. ❑*adj* liquid: ~গুড়.

মাতওয়ারা=মাতোয়ারা

মাতঃ *n* (vocative) O mother.

মাতগুড় *n* drossy molasses; treacle.

মাতঙ্গ *n* elephant. মাতঙ্গি, মাতঙ্গিনী *fem.*

মাতন=মত্ততা (⇒ মত্ত)

মাতবর, মাতব্বর [A] *n* **1** chief; notable; headman; leader. **2** distinguished/influential man; somebody; man of position; bigwig. **3** busybody; swell-head; coxcomb; popinjay. ❑*adj* **1** leading; distinguished; influential; important; chief. **2** high-handed; conceited; domineering; self-important; presumptuous; consequential; pretentious. **3** trustworthy; reliable: ~ উকিল. **4** respectable.

মাতবরি, মাতব্বরি [A] *n* **1** leadership. **2** (derog) bossing; office of a headman/leader; posing as a distinguished/important/ influential man. **3** pompousness; self-importance; pomposity; airs; conceit; high-handedness; domineering/ master-ful/ overbearing manner. ~ করা *vi* domineer (over); be overbearing.

মাতম [A] *n* loud lamentation; wailing; mourning. মাতমি লেবাস *n* black clothes; mourning. মাতমি লেবাস পরা go into mourning.

মাতলামি, মাতলামো *nn* drunkenness; inebriation; revelry; carousal; racket; bacchanal; orgy.

মাতা[১] *n fem* mother; any woman fit to be regarded as one's mother or daughter: শ্বশ্রূ~, বধূ~. ~পিতা *n* mother and father; parents. ~পিতৃহীন *adj* parentless; orphan. ~পিতৃহীনা *fem.* ~মহ *n* maternal grandfather. ~মহী *fem* maternal grandmother.

মাতা[২] *vi* **1** be drunk/ intoxicated. **2** be excited/ overjoyed/ delighted/ frenzied/ mad/ maddened; become feverishly enthusiastic; run amuck; revel; run riot; bubble (over); be/go on the rampage; get excited; get on one's high horse; work oneself up into a frenzy; be crazy/ wild/ frenetic about. **3** be absorbed (in); enthuse over. **4** be in rut. **5** rise and swell by the action of fermentation;

ferment. **6** grow (too) luxuriantly; grow rank. **~নো** *vt* **1** intoxicate; inebriate. **2** stimulate; excite; enthuse; inflame; rouse; send sb mad; electrify; thrill. ❑*adj* intoxicating; maddening; exciting; soul-stirring sensational; stimulating; highly delightful. **~মাতি** *n* great excitement; frenzy; fever; fermentation; hysteria; furore; delirium; rampage; enthusiasm; fervour; craze; over enthusiasm. **~মাতি করা**=~. **~ল** *adj* drunk; besotted (by/with); intoxicated; inebriated; addicted to drinking; infatuated; beside oneself. ❑*n* drunkard; drunk; inebriate. **বদ্ধ ~ল** *adj* dead-drunk; blind-drunk. ❑*n* drunkard; heavy/ hard drinker.

মাতুয়া *n* dogmatism.

মাতুল *n* mother's brother/ cousin; maternal uncle. **মাতুলা, মাতুলানী, মাতুলী** *fem* wife of a maternal uncle. **~পুত্র** *n* son of a maternal uncle; cousin. **~পুত্রী** *n fem* daughter of a maternal uncle; cousin. **মাতুলালয়, মাতুলাশ্রম** *nn* home/ residence of a maternal uncle.

মাতৃ *n fem* (in compounds) mother. **~ক** *adj* coming from/ belonging to a mother; maternal; motherly; treated/ fostered as by one's mother; mothered: নদী ~ক দেশ. **~কল্প** *adj* deserving to be treated as one's mother; motherly; behaving as one's mothers. **~কা** *n fem* **1** mother. **2** maternal grandmother. **3** nurse. **4** sixteen divine mothers or personified energies of the principal Hindu deities. **5** any one of the alphabetical letters. **6** matron. **~কুল** *n* mother's line/ side. **~গণ** *n pl* (Hindu myth) eight divine female powers. **~গর্ভ** *n* mother's womb. **~গামী** *adj* one who has committed incest with his mother. **~গোত্র** *n* mother's family. **~ঘাতক, ~ঘাতী, ~ঘ্ন** *adjj* matricide. ❑*n* a matricide. **~তা** *n* state of a mother; motherhood. **~তুল্য(1)** = ~কল্প. **~দায়** *n* responsibility of performing the obsequies of one's deceased mother; mother's death. **~দায়গ্রস্ত** *adj* charged with onus of performing the obsequies of one's deceased mother. **~দুগ্ধ** *n* mother's milk. **~পক্ষ** *adj* belonging to mother's side/maternal line. **~পূজা** *n* act of adoring one's mother. **~বৎ**=~তুল্য. **~বৎ পরদারেষু** (phrase) one should look upon another's wife as one's mother. **~বধ** *n* matricide. **~বিয়োগ** *n* mother's death. **~ভক্ত** *adj* devoted/ deeply attached to one's mother. **~ভক্তি** *n* devotion/ deep attachment to one's mother. **~ভাষা** *n* mother-tongue. **~ভূমি** *n* motherland. **~রিষ্টি** *n* inauspicious conjunction of planets in one's horoscope foreboding danger to one's mother's life. **~শাসন** *n* matriarchy. **~শাসিত** *adj* matriarchal. **~শ্রাদ্ধ** *n* obsequies of one's deceased mother. **~সম, ~সমা**= ~তুল্য. **~সেবা** *n* services/ ministrations to one's mother. **~স্তন্য**= ~দুগ্ধ. **~স্তব, ~স্তোত্র** *nn* hymn of any of the divine mothers/ female deities; devotional hymn offered to one's mother. **~হত্যা** *n* matricide. **~হত্যাকারী, ~হন্তা** = ~ঘাতক. **~হত্যাকারিণী** *fem*. **~হীন** *adj* motherless. **~হীনা** *fem*.

মাতোয়ারা, মাতোয়ালা, মাতওয়ারা [A] *adjj* intoxicated; drunk; inebriated; beside oneself; rapt.

মাতোয়ালি=মুতওল্লী

মাত্তা [A] *n* gods; valuables; effects; chattels; furniture; merchandise: মাল ~.

মাত্র *n* measure; quantity; sum; size; duration. ❑*adj* **1** simple; mere: সে শিশু ~. **2** every; any: বাঙালি~ জানে. ❑*adv* **1** merely; only; simple: ~দুদিন. **2** just: এই~. ❑*prep* only for মুহূর্ত~. ❑*conj* as soon as: পত্র পাওয়া~ উত্তর দিয়ো.

মাত্রা *n* **1** measure (of any kind); quantity; size; duration; number; degree: জ্ঞানের ~. **2** limit: সবকিছুরই একটা ~ থাকা চাই. **3** unit of time; moment. **4** upper/ horizontal line of the Bengali or Nagari characters. **5** metrical unit; more; prosodical instant (ie the length of time required to pronounce a syllable). **6** musical unit of time. **7** right/ correct measure; order: ~জ্ঞান. **8** minute portion; particle; atom; trifle; dose: এক~ ঔষধ. **9** magnitude. **10** (math) dimension. **11** (phys) mass. **12** (mech) amplitude. **~ ছাড়ানো** *vi* go beyond the limit of (decency etc). **~গত** *adj* of/ relating to measure, dimension etc. **~ছন্দ** *n* metre measured by the number of prosodical instants. **~জ্ঞান** sense of proportion. **~তত্ত্ব** *n* (med) posology. **~তিরিক্ত, ~ধিক** *adjj* excessive; exorbitant; extravagant; too much; too many; overmuch; inordinate. **~বৃত্ত**= a Bengli poetical metre **~স্পর্শ** *n* material contact; concurrence of material elements. **~হীন** *adj* limitless; boundless; excessive.

মাত্রিক *n* materials; model; paragon. ❑*adj* **1** (used as a *suff*) containing a particular number of prosodical instant/ mora: দীর্ঘ~, ষন্মাত্রিক. **2** quantitative. **~ বিশ্লেষণ** *n* (chem) quantitative analysis. **মাত্রিকা** *n*=~.

মাৎস্য *adj* relating to/ coming from fish; fish-like; fishy. ❑*n*=মৎস্যপুরাণ (⇒ মৎস্য). **~ন্যায়** *n* the principle according to which larger fishes swallow up smaller ones; anarchy; free-for-all.

মাৎসর্য *n* envy; jealousy; spite.

মাথট *n* poll-tax; subscription; cess; capital levy.

মাথা *n* **1** head; skull. **2** top; crown; summit; peak; pinnacle; crest: গাছের/ পাহাড়ের ~. **3** tip: আঙ্গুলের ~. **4** end; extremity: কলমের ~. **5** prow (of a boat). **6** chief; head; headman; leading personality: গ্রামের ~.**7** bend; corner; end: রাস্তার

8 brain; intellect; talent; gift; good head: অঙ্ক ~ আছে. 9 hair: ~ ধোয়া. ❑*int* (expressing annoyance, anger, regret, failure, etc) (mere) nothing; pooh-pooh; damn; bosh. ~ **আঁচড়ানো** *vi* comb one's hair. ~ **উঁচু করা** *vt* 1 raise one's head; look up. 2 (fig) hold one's head; flourish; thrive; assert oneself; rise in revolt. ~ **উঁচু করে চলা** *vi* walk with head on high. ~ **উঁচু করে দাঁড়ানো** *vi* (fig) hold one's ground; not to give in to; hold one's head high. ~ **উড়ানো (ওড়ানো)** *vt* cut off/sever sb's head; behead; rip off sb's head; kill. ~ **কটকট করা** *vi* suffer from headache; have a bad headache. ~ **কাটা** *vt* disgrace; defame; put to shame. ~ **কাটা যাওয়া** *vi* be greatly ashamed; be put to shame; be shamefully disgraced; be exposed to disgrace. ~ **কাটা/কোটা/কুড়া/ কোড়া** *vt* 1 strike one's head (repeatedly) against the floor/ wall as a violent expression of grief. 2 implore (for); supplicate; beseech; adjure entreat (of). ~ **কেনা** *vi* have absolute power over; have under one's thumb. ~ **কোটাকুটি করা** *vi* 1 beg on one's knees. 2 grapple with. ~ **খাও** (in appeals, etc) (lit) you eat my head if you will/will not do this; (fig) for the love of me/God. ~ **খাওয়া** *vt* (fig) ruin; spoil; corrupt; lead astray; pervert; deprave. ~ **খাটানো** = ~ খেলানো. ~ **খারাপ করা** *vt* drive mad; madden; incense; unhinge; drive up the wall. ~ **খারাপ হওয়া** *vi* be/ become insane; go off mad; lose one's senses/mind; go out of one's mind. ~ **খেলা** *vi* have aptitude/ flair/ knack for: অঙ্কে/ দুষ্টামিতে ~ খেলা. ~ **খেলানো** *vi* give/ apply one's mind to; set one's wit to work; pore over; rack/ beat/ cudgel one's brain about. ~ **গরম করা** *vi* be angry; loose one's temper. ~ **গরম হওয়া** *vi* get angry/cross; have one's head turned; feel giddy; loose one's head. ~ **গুঁজে থাকা** *vi* have a poor shelter; take shelter somehow. ~ **গুঁড়া করা** *vi* break sb's head; brain. ~ **গুনতি** *n* counting of the number of people. ~ **গুণতি করা** *vi* count the heads/number of persons. ~ **গুলিয়ে দেওয়া** *vt* nonplus; bewilder; confound; daze. ~ **গুলিয়ে যাওয়া** *vi* be nonplussed/ dazed/ confounded; feel dizzy. ~ **ঘষা** *vi* rub the skull with soap, shampoo etc; shampoo. ~**ঘসা** *n* shampoo. ~ **ঘামানো**=~ খেলানো. ~ **ঘোরা** *vi* feel dizzy/giddy; have one's head turned. ~ **ঘোরানো** *vt* make one feel dizzy; daze; stagger; baffle; turn sb's head; (of sth) go to one's head. ~ **চাড়া দেওয়া** *vi* raise one's head; assert oneself; rise against; rebel; be come active; stir; be aroused: **প্রবৃত্তি** ~ চাড়া দেওয়া. ~ **চালা**=~ খেলানো; cogitate. ~ **চুলকানো** *vi* (fig) scratch one's head (as a sign of being perplexed). ~ **ঠাণ্ডা করা** *vi* (fig) calm oneself; calm down; come to one's senses; compose oneself; cool down/off. ~ **ঠাণ্ডা রাখা** *vi* keep one's head; keep cool; keep a cool head; be cool-headed; keep one's temper; master one's feelings. ~ **ঠিক করা** *vi* compose oneself. ~ **ঠেকানো** *vi* bow down before; make obeissance to. ~ **তুলে থাকা** *vi* hold one's head high. ~ **তুলে দাঁড়ানো** *vi* reveal itself; appear; crop up; become clearly visible. ~ **থাকা** *vi* have a good head for. ~ **দেওয়া** *vi* 1 sacrifice oneself; lay down one's life; pledge one's head. 2 pay attention to. ~ **ধরা** *vi* have a headache. ~ **নিচু করা** *vi* lower one's head in shame; be ashamed. ~ **নেওয়া** *vt* behead; put to the sword; take the life of. ~ **নোয়ানো** *vi* bow (down); yield (to); prostrate before; give in; give way; bend (to); hang one's head. ~ **পেতে নেওয়া** *vi* accept humbly; admit. ~ **ফাটা** *vi* have one's skull fractured. ~ **ফাটানো** *vi* break sb's head; strike one's head against. ~ **বাঁধা** *vi* dress hair; do up hair. ~ **বাঁধা দেওয়া/ বিকানো** *vi* enslave oneself to; sell one's soul (to); be head over heals in (debt, etc). ~ **ভাঙা**=~ ফাটানো. ~ **মাটি করা** *vi* waste/ abuse one's intelligence or intellect. ~ **রাখা** 1 save sb's life. 2 lie (down). ~ **হেঁট করা** *vi* 1 hang down one's head in shame; yield (to); bend (to); humiliate oneself. 2 bring disgrace on; bring shame on; disgrace: সে আমাদের সকলের ~ হেঁট করেছে. ~ **হেঁট করানো** *vi* humiliate; put to shame. ~ **হেঁট হওয়া** *vi* be disgraced; lose face; be humiliated; put to shame; be put out of countenance. ~**য় ওঠা** *vi* become audacious. ~**য় করা** *vi* 1 carry on one's head. 2 (fig) love/ respect/honour very highly. 3 (fig) make a great noise; create an uproar; raise the roof. 4 indulge too much; pamper. ~**য় কাপড় দেওয়া** *vi* veil one's head (with a portion of one's sari). ~**য় খেলা** *vi* pass through the head: কৌশল ~য় খেলা. ~**য় ঘোল ঢালা** *vi* disgrace; humiliate utterly; hold a person up to infamy; brand sb with infamy. ~**য় চড়া** *vi* 1= ~য় ওঠা. 2 (of liquor) go into one's head. 3 (path) go up in the brain: বায়ু ~য় চড়েছে. ~**য় ঢোকা** *vi* 1 be comprehensible/ intelligible to. 2 take sth into one's head: তার ~য় এই ধারণা ঢুকেছে যে. 3 be affected/ stricken with; be overcome by: ~য় ভয় ঢোকা. ~**য় ঢোকানো** *vi* 1 get sb to understand. 2 put sth into a person's head. ~**য় বুদ্ধি গজানো** *vi* begin to be intelligent; have a flash of wit; get intelligent. ~**য় রাখা** *vi* 1 treat with great respect/ cordiality/care; honour highly; think much of; look up to. 2 abide by/ observe with great care/ devotion. ~**য় মাথায়** *adj* 1 barely; just sufficient/ enough and no more. 2 end to end. ~**য় হাত দিয়ে পড়া** *vi* be unnerved; break down; be utterly dejected; drop with worries.

~য় হাত বুলানো *vi* **1** pass one's finger across one's/sb's forehead; caress. **2** cajole sb (into/out of doing sth); wheedle (into/ out of); coax (from/ into/out of). ~র উপর কেউ না থাকা have no guardian/ patron. ~র কাপড় টেনে দেওয়া=~য় কাপড় দেওয়া. ~র খুলি *n* skull; cranium. ~র ঘাম পায়ে ফেলা *vi* sweat and drudge. ~ ঘি *n* grey matter; brain. ~র ঝিকুর নড়া *vi* be tired of; go mad. ~র ঠাকুর *n, adj* very venerable/ dear (person); idol; apple of one's eye. ~র ঠিক না থাকা *vi* lose one's head; be out of one's mind/ not in one's right mind; take leave of one's senses. ~তালু *n* crown; top of the head. ~র দিব্য *n* adjuration; earnest/ solemn request. ~র রোগ *n* giddiness; vertigo. ~ওয়ালা *adj* brainy; brilliant; astute; acute. ~কামড়ানি *n* headache. ~খারাপ *adj* crazy; cranky; wild; mad; lunatic; deranged. ~খারাপ লোক *n* madman; crack-brain; crackpot. ~গরম *adj* hot-headed; short-tempered. ~ঘুরুনি, ~ঘোরা *nn* giddiness; vertigo. ~ধরা *n* headache. ~পাগলা=~খারাপ. ~পিছু, ~প্রতি *advv* per capita; per man; per head. ~ব্যথা *n* **1** headache. **2** concern; worry; responsibility. ~ভারী *n* heaviness in the head. ❑*adj* **1** thickheaded; dull; thickwitted. **2** top-heavy. ~মুণ্ড *n* head or tail. ~মুণ্ডু বুঝতে না পারা be unable to make head or tail of. ~ আর মুণ্ডু *int* ~মোটা *adj* thickheaded; dull; obtuse; block-headed ~ নেই তার ~ব্যথা make a fuss of sth; make much ado about nothing. কার ঘাড়ে দুটো ~ (as a challenge) Don't dare.... who has the audacity to.... ভালো ~ *n* sharp intelligence; good head. মোটা ~ dull wit/ head.

মাথাল[1] *adj* brainy; intelligent; brilliant.

মাথাল[2] *n* straw hat.

মাথি, মাথী *n* edible core of the head of certain palms.

মাথুর *adj* coming from/born in/belonging to Mathura (মথুরা). ❑*n* cycle of songs giving vent to the grief the people of Brindabana caused by Sri Krishna's departure to Mathura.

মাদক *adj* intoxicating; inebriant; addictive; stupefying: ~ দ্রব্য, drug. ❑*n* drug; intoxicant. ~ গ্রহণ/সেবন করা *vi* take drugs; drug oneself. ~তা *n* intoxicating property/ power; intoxication. ~বর্জন *n* abstention from drug-taking; prohibition. ~ বর্জন করা *vi* abstain from drug-taking. ~বিরোধী *adj* anti-drug. ~ সেবন *n* drug-addiction. ~সেবী *adj* addicted to drugs. ❑*n* drug-addict. মাদকাসক্ত = ~ সেবী. মাদকাসক্তি = ~ সেবন.

মাদল *n* kind of tom-tom or drum played by aborigines.

মাদানি *adj* relating to Medina; Medinite. ❑*n* **1** native of Medina. **2** one of Medinite origin.

মাদার *n* coral tree.

মাদি, মাদী [P] *adj* female; she: ~ হাতি. ❑*n* effeminate man.

মাদিয়ানা, মাদীয়ান [P] *n* mare. মাদিয়ানি *adj* effeminate.

মাদুর *n* mat.

মাদুলি, মাদুলী, মাদলি *nn* **1** amulet (usually shaped like a tom-tom). **2** kind of necklace made of gold.

মাদৃক, মাদৃশ *adv* (old use) like me; resembling me.

মাদ্রাজি, মাদ্রাজী *adj* of Madras. ❑*n* native of Madras.

মাদ্রাসা [A] *n* traditional Muslim religious school/ college; seminary.

মাধব *n* **1** Vishnu; Sri Krishna. **2** spring. **3** the month of Baishakh. ❑*adj* relating to honey; vernal. মাধবী *fem.* ~প্রিয়া *n* the goddess Lakshmi.

মাধবী, মাধবিকা *nn* **1** name of an evergreen creeper; *Gaertnera racemosa*, spring-creeper. **2** sacred basil. **3** kind of grass. **4** honey-sugar. ~কুঞ্জ *n* bower of spring-creeper. ~লতা=~.

মাধুকরী *n* **1** collecting alms after the manner of a bee (ie going from door to door). **2** alms obtained from five different places by the third class of mendicants. ~ বৃত্তি *n* begging from door to door like a bee.

মাধুরী *n* **1** sweetness; loveliness; deliciousness; pleasantness; amiableness; charm; exquisite charm; feeling of tender affection. **2** (rhet) grace of style. ~ময় *adj* full of sweetness, etc; lovely; graceful; tender; delicate.

মাধুর্য=মাধুরী. ~পূর্ণ=মাধুরীময় (⇒মাধুরী)

মাধ্যন্দিন *adj* of midday; meridianal. ~রেখা *n* (astron) the meridian.

মাধ্যম *adj* relating to the middle; middlemost. ❑*n* medium; vehicle: শিক্ষার ~.

মাধ্যমিক *adj* secondary; middling. ~ শিক্ষা *n* secondary education.

মাধ্যস্থ্য *n* intercession; mediation.

মাধ্যাকর্ষণ *n* (science) gravitation; gravity.

মাধ্যাহ্নিক *adj* belonging to/taking place at noon. ~ ক্রিয়া *n* midday rites.

মাধ্যিক *n* (bot) median.

মাধ্বী *n* **1** kind of intoxicating liquor (produced from honey. **2** fruit of the *Gaertnera racemosa* (মহুয়া). **3** grape.

মাধ্বীক *n* **1** kind of intoxicating liquor (produced from grapes). **2** honey. ~ ফল *n* of species of cocoa-nut. ~ মধুরা *n* species of date.

মান[1] *n* **1** measure; mearsuring; measurement; weighing. **2** unit of measure/ weight. **3** dimension; size; height; weight; length. **4** value; magnitude. **5** (alg) degree. **6** standard.

7 (music) rest; notation of time. ~ক্রম *n* precedence. ~চিত্র *n* map; chart. ~চিত্র-অভিক্ষেপ *n* (geog) stereographic projection. ~চিত্রকর, ~চিত্রকার *nn* cartographer. ~চিত্রবিদ্যা *n* cartography. ~চিত্রাঙ্কন *n* mapdrawing. ~চিত্রাবলী *n* maps; atlas. ~দণ্ড *n* measuring rod; measure; standard/ unit of measurement. ~বিন্দু *n* (phys) any of the fixed points (of a thermometer). ~মন্দির *n* observatory.

মান[2] *n* **1** honour; respect; consideration; regard. **2** fame. **3** dignity; pride. **4** vanity. ~ দেওয়া *vt* honour; treat with honour/ deference; respect. ~ রাখা *vt* respect; do honour to; heed; do the honours (to); save one's face. ~দ *adj* bestowing/conferring honour upon. মানদা *fem*. ~ন, ~না *nn* honouring; paying honour; showing respect; obeying; heeding; believing; observance; vowing; adoring; worshipping. ~নীয় *adj* to be honoured; deserving honour from; honourable; respectable; venerable. ~নীয়া *fem*. ~নীয়েষু (used as a polite form of addressing a letter) to an honourable person. ~নীয়াসু *fem*. ~পত্র *n* address (of honour). ~বর্জিত *adj* destitute of honour. ~মর্যাদা, ~সম্ভ্রম *nn* honour and dignity. ~মর্যাদা রক্ষা করা *vi* keep up/maintain one's dignity/ prestige. ~হানি *n* loss of honour; defamation libel. ~হানি করা *vt* defame; libel. ~হানিকর *adj* defamatory; libellous. ~হানির মকদ্দমা *n* defamation case; libel suit. ~হীন=~বর্জিত.

মান[3] *n* **1** wounded sense of honour; anger/ indignation excited by jealousy. **2** (esp in woman) caprice; sulking; huff caused by undesirable behaviour of a beloved person; tiff; pique. ~ করা *vi* sulk; huff; has tiff with; take a pique against sb. ~ ভাঙানো *vt* win over/ placate a beloved who is in a fit of pique/ huff. ~ ভরে *adv* in a fit of pique/ resentment. ~কলি *n* lover's quarrel; quarrel arising from jealousy. ~ভঙ্গ, ~ভঞ্জন *nn* allaying of one's/sb's huff; mollification of sb's resentment/ anger. ~ভঞ্জন-পালা *n* group of songs written about the mollification of Radha's sulking with Sri Krishna. ~ময়ী *adj fem* huffy; sulky; touchy.

মান[4], **মানকচু, মানকন্দ** *nn* varieties of arum.

মান[5] *suff* meaning; endowed with; possessing: বুদ্ধি~, কীর্তি~.

মানত, মানৎ [A] *nn* promise to offer a particular sacrifice to a deity on fulfillment of a prayer; vow. ~ করা *vi* vow; make a vow.

মানব *n* man; human being. ❑*adj* descended from/ belonging to man or Manu (the law-giver); human. মানবী *fem* womankind; woman; daughter of man. ~ক *n*=মানবক. ~চরিত্র *n* human nature/ character. ~ জাতি *n* human race; mankind; humankind. ~ জীবন *n* human life. ~তন্ত্র *n* humanism. ~তা, ~ত্ব *nn* humanity. ~ ধর্ম *n* religion of man; humanity. ~দ্বেষ *n* misanthropy. ~দ্বেষী *n* misanthrope. ~ প্রকৃতি *n* human nature. ~প্রেমিক *adj* humanist. ~লীলা *n* activities of a human being whilst existing upon the earth; existence as a human being. ~লীলা সংবরণ করা *vi* die; pass away; yield up the ghost; decease. ~ সমাজ *n* human society/ world; mankind. ~হীন *adj* having no human dweller; desolate; depopulated. ~ হৃদয় *n* human heart; human feelings; man's heart.

মানবিক *adj* human. ~ বিদ্যা *n* humanities.

মানবীয় *adj* human; humane.

মানবোচিত *adj* befitting a human being; humane; human.

মানস *n* **1** mind spirit; soul; mental powers. **2** feeling. **3** desire; intention; purpose. **4** name of a sacred lake and place of pilgrimage on mount Kailasa. **5** mental/ spiritual devotion. ❑*adj* belonging to the mind/ spirit; mental; spiritual; expressed in the mind; performed in thought (ie silent); tacit; conceived/ present in the mind; conceivable; imaginable. ~ করা *vi* desire; intend; purpose. ~ কন্যা *n fem* daughter born to one out of one's mind/fancy. ~জন্মা *n* mind-born; god of love. ~তা *n* mentality. ~ত্ব *n* state of spirit; spirituality; fulfilment of anything in mere thought. ~নয়ন, ~নেত্র *nn* mind's eye; inward eye; fancy; imagination. ~পট *n* canvas of the mind; imagination; fancy. ~পুত্র *n* son born to one out of one's mind/fancy; spiritual son. ~পুত্রী *fem* =~কন্যা. ~ প্রতিমা *n* image conceived in the mind; mental image. ~ বিজ্ঞান *n* mental science. ~ মন্দির *n* temple of one's mind. ~ রাজ্য realm of imagination/ fancy. ~লোচন =~নয়ন. ~সিদ্ধি *n* fulfilment of a desire/an intention; attainment of an end. মানসাঙ্ক *n* mathematical sum to be worked out mentally.

মানসিক *adj* mental; imaginary; fancied. ❑*n* sacrifice/offering promised to a deity on condition that one's prayer be granted. ~ করা *vi* promise a sacrifice/offering to a deity for the fulfilment of one's desire. ~ দেওয়া *vi* offer a promised sacrifice to a deity on fulfilment of a prayer.

মানসী *adj fem* conceived in the mind; fancied (⇒ মানস). ❑*n fem* woman/sweetheart of one's fancy.

মানা[1] *vt* **1** honour; respect; show respect to; revere: শিক্ষককে ~. **2** regard; consider; count: ভাগ্য বলে ~. **3** accept; be amenable to: প্রবোধ ~. **4** believe in: ঈশ্বর ~. **5** admit; acknowledge; own: দোষ ~, ঘাট ~. **6** obey; abide by; comply with: উপদেশ/নির্দেশ ~. **7** heed to: সে আমার কথা মানলো না. **8** acknowledge the authority of: উপরওয়ালাকে ~. **9** call on; cite: সাক্ষী ~. **10** observe: নিয়ম ~. **11** yield to: বাধা ~. **~নো** *vt* cause to honour/ respect/ acknowledge/ admit/ obey/ accept/ observe/ heed/ yield/ call on.

মানা[2] [A] *n* prohibition; forbidding; prevention; dissuasion. **~ করা** *vt* prohibit; forbid; prevent; dissuade; hinder.

মানান *n* becomingness; propriety; decorum; decorousness; beauty. ❑*adj* fitting; becoming; befitting; decorous; proper. **~সই** *adj*=~.

মানানো *vt* become; suit; befit; fit ; be suitable.

মানিক *n* ruby; jewel; precious object; (address of endearment) darling. ❑*adj* (chem) quantitative. **~জোড়** *n* **1** variety of egrets usually moving in pairs. **2** (often derog) pair of inseparable friends/ associates.

মানী *adj* **1** honoured; respected; honourable; respectable. **2** highly honoured/esteemed. **3** high-minded. **4** proud; haughty; vainglorious; touchy; particular about one's prestige/ dignity. **মানিনী** *fem* sulky; disdainful.

মানুষ *n* **1** man; human being; person. **2** human race. **3** grown-up person; adult. ❑*adj* belonging to mankind; human. **~ করা** *vt* rear; bring up; nurture; train sb to be a proper man. **~ হওয়া** *vi* be brought up; grow up; grow up into a proper man. **মানুষের মতো ~** proper man; great/ eminent person; ideal man; man of worth. **মানুষী** *n fem* woman; womankind. ❑*adj* human.

মানুষিক *adj* human.

মানুষ্য *n* human nature/condition; humanity; manhood.

মানে [A] *n* **1** meaning; intended sense; signification; import; sense; significance; implication. **2** motive; purpose; cause. **3** utility; use: তাকে বলার ~ কী? **~ করা** *vt* interpret; explain (the meaning of); elucidate; expound. **~ বোঝা** *vi* comprehend or understand the meaning/ motive/ intention/ import/ utility of. **~ বোঝানো** *vi* mean; signify; explain the meaning of; imply. **~ হওয়া** *vi* convey a meaning; serve a purpose; be of any use. **~ বই** *n* book of explanatory notes; key.

মানে-মানে *adv* whilst one's prestige/ dignity is still unimpaired.

মানোয়ার [E] *n* man-of-war. **মানোয়ারি** *adj* serving on board a man-of-war/ battleship; employed in the navy; naval.

মান্দার *n* (dial)=মন্দার

মান্দাস *n* raft; float.

মান্দ্য *n* **1** dearth; loss; decrease. **2** slowness; sloth; inertia; laziness; indolence. **3** weakness; dullness; feeble state (as of understanding/ digestion). **4** sickness; disease.

মান্ধাতা *n* name of a mythological king. **~র আমল** *n* time immemorial; time out of mind. **~র আমলের** antediluvian; dateless; antiquated; superannuated.

মান্য *adj* to be respected/ honoured; worthy of honour; respectable; venerable. ❑*n* **1** honour; respect; gift of honour; complimentary present; cordial reception: ~ দেওয়া. compliance; observance. **মান্যা** *adj fem.* **~ করা** *vt*=মানা[1]. **~গণ্য** *adj* respectable and important. **~ত্ব** *n* respectability; worthiness. **~বর** *adj* highly respectable/ honourable/ venerable. **~বরেষু** (used as a polite form of addressing a letter) to highly respectable person.

মাপ[1] *n* **1** measure; weight; dimension. **2** measuring; measurement. **3** pair of scales; balance. **~ নেওয়া** *vt* take measurements of; measure. **মাপে হওয়া** *vi* be of a particular measure/size; measure; fit in measurements. **~ক** *adj* serving as a measure of. ❑*n* weigher. **~কাটি, ~কাঠি** *nn* measuring-rod; measure; standard. **~জোক, ~জোখ** *nn* measurement(s); surveying. **~জোক করা** *vt* measure (minutely); survey. **~দড়ি** *n* measuring rope/tape. **~ন** *n* measuring; weighing; sounding; measurement. **~নদণ্ড** *n* measuring-rod. **~নযন্ত্র** *n* weighing-machine. **~নরজ্জু** *n* sounding-line; plumb-line. **~নী** *n* (geom) scale; ruler. **~সই, ~সহি** *adj, adv* conforming to particular measurements.

মাপ[2] [A] *n* pardon; excuse; exemption; immunity; absolution; remission. **~ করা** *vt* pardon; excuse; forgive; dispense with; exempt; remit (punishment); absolve.

মাপা *vt* **1** measure; weigh. **2** survey. **3** measure the length of; sound. **4** (fig) try to assess the importance/ weight of. ❑*adj* measured; weighed; surveyed; sounded; restrained; restricted; controlled: ~ কথা ~ খাওয়া. **~জোকা, ~জোখা** *adjj* measured; restricted; restrained; controlled; moderate. ❑*n* measuring; surveying. **~নো** *vt* cause to measure/survey/weigh/sound.

মাফ, মাফি=মাপ[2]

মাফলার [A] *n* muffler.

মাফিক [A] *adj* like; conformable; apt; analogous; concordant; conforming/according to. **~সই, ~সহি** *adj* **1** measured; made to measure; befitting. **2** according to; suitable; appropriate.

মাবুদ, মা'বূদ [A] *n* one of the appellations of Allah; (lit) one to be worshipped. ❑*adj* worshipped; adored.

মভৈঃ *int* be not afraid; don't fear. ❑*adj* expelling fear: ~ মন্ত্র.

মামড়ি *n* scab; slough. ❑*vi* scab; develop a scab.

মামদো (also ~ভূত) *n* (in fairy tales) ghost of a Muslim. **~বাজি** *n* bluster; bullying; rowdism.

মামলত [A] *n* **1** affair; business; transaction; negotiation; design; purpose: ~ হাসিল করা. **2** case/ suit in law. **3** substance; money.

মামলা [A] *n*=মামলত. **~ করা** bring/file a law-suit; proceed (against)/ enter into litigation. **~দার** *n* plaintiff. **~বাজ** *adj* litigious. **~বাজি** *n* litigiousness. **~মকদ্দমা** *n* litigation.

মামা[1] *n* brother/ cousin of one's mother; maternal uncle; uncle. **~ত, ~তো** *adjj* descended from one's maternal uncle; avuncular. **~ত ভাই/বোন** *n* cousin. **~বাড়ির আবদার,** unreasonable/capricious demand. **~শ্বশুর** *n* maternal uncle of one's husband or wife; uncle-in-law. **মায়ের কাছে ~বাড়ির গল্প করা** teach one's grandmother to suck eggs.

মামা[2] [A] *n fem* maid-servant; mother.

মামী *n fem* wife of a maternal uncle; aunt. **~শ্বাশুড়ি** *n fem* wife of a maternal uncle of one's husband or wife; aunt-in-law.

মামু *n (dial* or *facet)*=মামা[1]

মামুদা=মামদো

মামুর [A] *adj* **1** full; abundant; replete. **2** inhabited; populated; colonized; prosperous.

মামুলি, মামুলি [A] *adj* **1** customary; usual; conventional; traditional; traditionally/ conventionally fixed: ~ স্বত্ব easement. **2** common; ordinary; banal; hackneyed; trite; stock: ~ কথা. **3** paltry; negligible: ~ ব্যাপার/ খরচা. **4** current. **~ ধরন** *n* usual custom/ practice.

মায় *prep* [A] together with; with; inclusive of; along with; to.

মায়না=মাহিনা

মায়া *n* **1** illusion; unreality; material world; physical/ phenomenal nature; Maya. **2** hallucination; delusion; unreal/ illusory image; phantom; apparition. **3** deception; deceit; fraud; duplicity; trick. **4** witchcraft; magic. **5** disguise. **6** affection; attachment. **7** fascination; infatuation. **8** compassion. **~ করা** *vi* think/ treat with affection; be attached to; have/ take compassion on; be filled with compassion for; be reluctant to lose: চাকরির ~ করা. **~য় ভোলা** *vi* be duped by sorcery/illusion; be beguiled/ infatuated/ charmed. **~ উপবন** *n* enchanted garden. **~কর, ~কার** *nn* conjurer; juggler. **~কানন**=~ উপবন. **~কান্না** *n* affected sympathy/ sorrow; crocodile tears. **~গতি** *n* bond(s) of affection. **~ঘোর** *n* spell of illusion/ delusion/ infatuation/ enchantment. **~জাল** *n* network/ cobweb/ spell of illusion/ infatuation/ enchantment. **~জীবী** *n* conjurer; magician; juggler. **~ডোর** *n* bond of affection/ attachment. **~ত্মক** *adj* (essentially) illusory; delusive; disguised; illusive. **~দণ্ড** *n* magic wand. **~ধর, ~ধারী** *adjj* possessing illusion; skilled in magic; disguised; hypocritical. **~পাশ**=~জাল. **~বদ্ধ** *adj* strongly held under illusion; greatly attached/infatuated. **~বন্ধন** *n* bond of illusion/ affection/ attachment/ infatuation. **~কল** *n* power of illusion. **~বশ** *adj* fondly attached; under the spell of illusion/ infatuation; subject to attachment/ affection. **~বাদ** *n* the doctrine affirming the world to be illusion. **~বাদী** *adj* upholding the doctrine of Maya; illusionistic. ❑*n* illusionist. **~বিদ্যা** *n* magic; sorcery; jugglery. **~বী** *adj* **1** possessing illusion/ magical powers; employing deceit; deceiving/ deluding others. **2** illusory; creating illusions. **3** enchanting; infatuating: ~বী আলো. ❑*n* enchanter; conjurer; juggler; wizard; magician; sorcerer. **~বিনী** *fem* enchantress; witch; sorceress. **~মমতা** *n* love and attachment/ affection; affection and compassion. **~ময়** *adj* consisting of illusion; formed of/creating illusion; illusive; unreal; magical; deceptive; enchanting; infatuating; bewitching. **~ময়ী** *fem.* **~মুক্ত** freed from affection/ attachment; disenchanted; disillusioned. **~মৃগ** *n* illusory antelope; phantom deer. **~মোহ** *n*=~ঘোর. **~রজ্জু** =~ডোর. **~রাজ্য** *n* realm created by magic; realm of enchantment.

মায়াবসান *n* end/expulsion of ignorance.

মায়াবান *adj* **1** affectionate; loving; enchanting. **2** having magical powers; employing deceit; sly; cunning. **মায়াবতী** *fem.*

মায়িক *adj* illusory; creating illusion; practising deceit; deceiving others. ❑*n* conjurer; juggler.

মায়ী *adj* **1** artful; skilled in art/enchantment; cunning; deceptive; illusory. **2** subject to illusion. ❑*n* magician; conjurer; juggler.

মায়ূর *adj* belonging to/coming from a peacock; made of peacock's feathers.

মার[1] *n* **1** death; destruction: সত্যের ~ নেই. **2** killing; destroying; slaying. **3** pestilence. **4** beating; striking; flogging; thrashing. **5** loss: টাকা ~ যাওয়া. **~ খাওয়া** *vi* be beaten/ flogged. **~ দেওয়া** *vt* beat; flog; thrash. **~কাট** *n* fighting and bloodshed; tumult; tumultuous affray/ brawl; turbulence; uproar; frenzy; feverish haste and fuss. **~কুটে, ~কুটো** *adjj* given to beating at the slightest pretext; furious. **~খেকো** *adj* (one) who is often flogged; used to beating. **~ধর** *n* beating; thrashing; beating and arresting (as by the police). **~পিট** *n* riot; fray; affray; turbulence; mêlée; brawl; beating; flogging. **~মুখী, ~মুখো** *adj* about to strike/hurt;

violent; aggressive; belligerent; bellicose; pugnacious; threatening; menacing; jingoistic. ~মূর্তি *n* aggressive/ menacing/violent appearance. ❑*adj* about to hurt/strike; bellicose; violent; threatening.

মার[২] *n* **1** the Evil of temptation according to the Buddhists. **2** Hindu god of love; passion of love. **3** obstacle; hindrance.

মারওয়ারি *adj* of Marwar. ❑*n* native of Marwar; Marwari; language of Marwar.

মারক *n* any deadly disease; plague; pestilence. ❑*adj* destructive; pestilential.

মারকত *adj* belonging to an emerald; having any of the qualities/properties of emerald; coloured like an emerald.

মারণ *n* **1** killing; slaying; slaughter; death; destruction. **2** a magical ceremony having for its object the destruction of an enemy. **3** calcination. **4** beating. **মারণাস্ত্র** *n* weapon of destruction. **মারিত** *adj* killed; slain; destroyed.

মারপেঁচ, মারপ্যাঁচ *nn* **1** shrewd trick; stratagem. **2** shrewd/ tricky twist or turn; quibbling; sophistry; equivocation: কথার ~.

মারফত, মারফৎ [A] *prep* through by the hand of; by; per; through the medium of. **~দার** *n* one through whom sth is sent; agent.

মারবেল=মার্বেল

মারহাট্টা=মরাঠা

মারহাবা=মরহাবা

মারা *vt* **1** kill; slay. **2** strike (with); hit: বল ~, লাঠি ~. **3** beat; flog. **4** fire; shoot: গুলি ~. **5** drive in; pierce with; push into; implant: চাকু ~, পেরেক ~(rivet). **6** join; glue; attach; nail affix: তক্তা ~, টিকিট ~. **7** throw; explode: বোমা ~. **8** evaporate; condense; dehydrate; dry: জল ~, রস ~. **9** pick; rob; steal: পকেট ~. **10** earn; gain: দালালিতে সে অনেক টাকা মেরেছে। **11** sink; founder: তুফানে নৌকো ~ গেল. **12** bar; obstruct; block: পথ ~. **13** eliminate; eradicate; destroy; exterminate: বিষ ~. **14** cause to lose; degrade: জাত ~. **15** obtain by unfair means; misappropriate; defalcate: টাকা ~. **16** utter; fetch: হাঁক ~. **17** adopt (a certain posture): গুড়ি ~, ঘাপটি ~. **18** tuck: মালকোচা ~. **19** deal: ঘুসি ~, deal sb a blow. **20** afflict; distress: কথায় ~. **21** ruin: এবারের খরায় আমাকে মেরেছে. **22** sew up: তালি ~. **23** paste: লেবেল ~. **24** close up; fill up: ফাঁক ~. **25** win/earn (esp by a fluke): লটারি ~. **26** deprive of: অন্ন/রুজি ~. **27** eat; gobble. **28** give out; emit: জেল্লা ~. **29** blunt; dull: ধার ~. **30** hem: কোণ ~, মুড়ি ~. **31** adopt; have recourse to; exhibit: চাল ~. **32** apply; give: ঠেনা ~, ফুঁক ~, ঢু ~. **33** go beyond; cross. **34** peg, picket, stake: খুঁটা ~. **35** paint; apply: পোতিনা/ চিকা ~. **36** calcine: পারা/ লোহা ~. **37** cut; make: সিঁধ ~. **38** indulge in: গল্প ~. ❑*adj* attached; joined; inlaid with; overlaid/ encrusted with: মার্বেল-~. **~ধরা** *vt* beat; flog; castigate. **~ পড়া** *vi* be killed; be destroyed; be lost/ ruined. **~ যাওয়া** *vi* **1** die. **2** be lost: অনেকগুলি টাকা ~ গেল. **~মারি** *n* scuffle; affray; riot; brawl. **~মারি করা** *vi* scuffle; come to blows; skirmish; exchange blows; fight each other; brawl; fight it out; tussle.

মারাঠা=মরাঠা

মারাঠি=মরাঠী

মারাত্মক *adj* deadly; fatal; murderous; terrific; inconsolable: ~ শোক.

মারি, মারী *nn* epidemic disease; pestilence; plague. **~গুটিকা** *n* pustule/vesicle of smallpox. **~ভয়**=~.

মারীচ *n* name of a Raksha (রাক্ষস) or demon as mentioned in Indian mythologies or folk tradition.

মারুত *n* wind; air; god of wind; vital air; breath.

মারুতি *n* son of the wind-god; Hanuman.

মারেফাত, মারফত [A] *n* spiritual knowledge; realization; (suffism) union with God. **মারফতি** *adj* spiritual; mystic; secret; esoteric.

মারোয়াড়ি=মারওয়ারি

মার্কা [E] *n* mark; sign; brand. **~ দেওয়া** *vi* put a mark on; mark; brand. **~মারা** *adj* marked; branded; notorious.

মার্কিন [E] *adj* American; of the USA. ❑*n* **1** USA; America; American. **2** Kind of coarse white fabric.

মার্কেট [E] *n* market. **মার্কেটিং** *n* marketing.

মার্গ *n* **1** way; road; path; track; route; course. **2** anus; passage; channel. **3** seeking; search; hunting; tracing out. **4** way; manner; method; custom; means. **~সঙ্গীত** *n* classical music.

মার্গণ *n* **1** seeking; asking; desiring; requiring; investigating; investigation; research; inquiry. **2** begging; solicitation.

মার্গাখ্যায়ী *n* guide.

মার্গিক *n* traveller; wayfarer.

মার্গিত *adj* sought; searched (through); hunted after; pursued.

মার্গ্য *adj* to be sought/ searched for.

মার্চ [E] *n* **1** (the month of) March. **2** march.

মার্জক *n* cleaner. ❑*adj* cleaning.

মার্জন *n* **1** wiping away; cleaning; scouring; scrubbing; cleansing by rubbing/ brushing. **2** polishing; chiselling. **3** purifying; absolution. **4** sound of a drum. **মার্জনা** *n* **1**=~. **2** pardon; forgiving. **মার্জনা করা** *vt* **1** wipe away; clean; scour; scrub; cleanse by rubbing etc.; polish; chisel. **2** purify; absolve. **3** forgive; pardon; excuse. **মার্জনাহীন** *adj* unforgiving; relentless.

মার্জনী *n* broom; besom; brush; towel; napkin. **~য়** *adj* **1** to be cleansed/ rubbed/ scrubbed/ purified. **2** pardonable; excusable; forgivable.

মার্জার *n* **1** cat; tomcat. **2** polecat; civet cat. **মার্জারিকা, মার্জারী** *fem* she-cat.

মার্জিত *adj* **1** wiped; rubbed; swept; scrubbed; cleansed; purified. **2** polished; chiselled; refined; cultured; elegant; chaste: ~ রুচি, ~ ভাষা. **3** absolved; forgiven; chastened. **মার্জিতা** *fem*. ~ **করা**=মার্জনা করা (⇒ মার্জন)

মার্জিন [E] *n* margin.

মার্তণ্ড *n* the sun. ~**তাপ** *n* heat of the sun.

মার্তিক *adj* made of clay/loam; earthen.

মার্বল, মার্বেল *nn* marble.

মার্সিয়া=মরসিয়া

মাল[1] [A] *n* **1** riches; wealth; property; possession. **2** merchandise; goods; stock; wares; effects. **3** rent; revenue; land holding rented directly from the government. **4** thing. ~ **কাটা** *vi* (of goods) sell (well). ~**আমাওয়াত** *n* property left by a deceased person; unclaimed property. ~**কড়ি** *n* money; fund; wherewithal; means. ~**ক্রোক** *n* distraint. ~**ক্রোক করা** *vt* distrain. ~**ক্রোকি পরওয়ানা** *n* distraint warrant. ~**কোটা,** ~**খানা** *n* **1** treasury. **2** store-house; store-room; warehouse. ~ **খালাস করা** *vi* unload. ~**গাড়ি** goods-train; wagon; luggage-van. ~**গুজার** *n* tenant; subject; landholder; landlord; one who pays revenue. ~**গুজারদার** *n* tenant paying revenue directly to the landlord. ~**গুজারি** *n* land revenue; revenue assessment; rent paid in money; payment of rent and taxes. ~**গুদাম** *n* warehouse; store-house. ~**চালান** *n* delivery/shipment of goods. ~**জমি** *n* rented land; land holding rented directly from the government. ~**জামিন** *n* **1** security for property. **2** security in property. **3** surety. ~**জামিনি** *n* security for rent/debt. ~**জাহাজ** *n* cargo-boat; cargosteamer. ~ **তোলা** *vi* store goods. ~**দার** *adj* wealthy; rich; moneyed. ~**দারি** *n* wealthiness; wealth. ~**পত্র** *n pl* goods; luggage; goods and chattels; (personal) effects; merchandise. ~ **বোঝাই** *adj* loaded; (of ships) laden. ~ **বোঝাই করা** *vi* load; lade. ~**মশলা,** ~**মসলা** *n pl* ingredients; materials. ~**মাত্তা** *n pl* wealth; goods and effects; properties.

মাল[2] [A] *n* (sl) wine; liquor; booze. ~ **টানা** *vi* drink (alcoholic liquor); booze.

মাল[3] *n* **1** name of an Indian tribe; member of the tribe. **2** wrestler. **3** healer of poisonous snakebites (also ~বৈদ্য); snake-charmer. ~**কচ্ছ,** ~**কোঁচা** *nn* loin-cloth worn by tucking it tightly between one's legs like a suspender. ~**কোঁচা আঁটা/ দেওয়া/ মারা** *vi* tuck one's loin-cloth lightly between one's legs like a suspender. ~**ভূম** *n* land of the Mals; a district in West Bengal. ~**শাট,** ~**সাট** *n* **1**=~কচ্ছ. **2** bragging and vaunting (as by a fighter/ wrestler); slapping of one's arms etc as one gets ready to attach. ~**শাট মারা** *v* **1**=~কোঁচা মারা. **2** brag; vaunt; slap one's arms etc as one gets ready to attack.

মাল[4] *n* (poet, archaic)=মালা

মালক *n* coconut-shell.

মালকোশ,মালকৌশ, মালকোষ *n* name of an Indian raga (musical mode).

মালচক্রক *n* knee-pan.

মালঝাপ *n* name of a Bengali metre.

মালঞ্চ *n* flower-garden; arbour; bower.

মালতী *n* Kind of jasmin or its plant; *Jasminum grandiflorum*. ~**ফল** *n* nutmeg.

মালপুয়া, মালপোয়া *nn* a saucer-shaped sweetmeat made of flour/rice-powder-fried in ghee or oil and then dipped in sugar-juice.

মালপোকা *n* a kind of insect which eats into the top of a coconut-tree and lives there; *Astinae oryctes*.

মালব *n* name of an Indian musical mode.

মালবৈদ্য=মাল[3] (3)

মালভূম, মালভূমি *n* table land; plateau.

মালয় *n* **1** Malaya. **2** sandal-tree (also ~তরু).

মালসা *n* small earthen basin/bowl. **মালসি** *n* a smaller malsa.

মালসি *n* name of an Indian musical mode.

মালা[1] *n* **1** wreath; garland; crown. **2** necklace. **3** string of beads; rosary; chaplet. **4** row; series; line; regular succession. ~**কর,** ~**কার** *nn* garland-maker; gardener; florist. ~ **গাঁথা** *vi* form into a wreath; wreathe sth into; make (flowers etc) into a wreath. ~ **জপা** *vi* tell one's beads. ~**চন্দন** *n* garlands and sandal-paste (with which an adorable person is received). ~**চন্দন দেওয়া** *vi* receive with garlands and sandal-paste. ~**বদল** *n* exchange of garments/ necklaces (as done by Hindu brides and bridegrooms at a wedding); marriages; ~ **বদল করা** *vi* exchange garlands/ necklaces; marry.

মালা[2] *n* coconut-shell; coconut-shell cut into the shape of a tumbler.

মালাই[1] *n* film/ cream of milk. ~**বরফ** *n* ice-cream.

মালাই[2] *n* Malayan.

মালাইচাকি *n* knee-pan; knee-cap; patella.

মালাউন [A] *adj* cursed; excommunicated; driven out of society; accused. ❑*n* Satan.

মালাবার *n* Malabar. **মালাবারী** *adj* of Malabar. ❑*n* native of Malabar.

মালামাল *n pl* goods; luggage; personal effects.

মালিক [A] *n* **1** owner; proprietor; possessor. **2** Master; lord; King. **3** the Supreme Being; God. **4** husband. **5** occupier. **6** (commence) principal. ~**হীন** *adj* ownerless; derelict.

মালিকানা *n* **1** ownership; proprietorship; right to possession; title. **2** annual/ monthly allowance paid to the landlord; fee/rent to be paid to a proprietor; royalty; proprietary dues. ❑*adj* proprietary; relating to the title; like an owner. **মালিকানা রসুম** *n* proprietary dues. **মালিকানা স্বত্ব** *n* proprietary right.

মালিকা *n* **1** garland. **2** necklace.

মালিকি, মালিকী *n* **1**=মালিকানা (⇒ মালিক) absolute right.

মালিকুল মউত, মালেকুল মওত [A] *nn* angel of death.

মালিনী *n fem* of মালী.

মালিন্য=মলিনতা (⇒মলিন).

মালিশ, মালিস *nn* **1** massage; rubbing. **2** unguent; oil etc for rubbing/massage. **~ করা** *vt* rub; massage.

মালী *n* gardener; florist. ❑*adj* garlanded; encircled/surrounded by; crowned.

মালুম [A] *n* feeling; sensation; perception. ❑*adj* known; apparent; clear. **~ করা/পাওয়া** *vi, vt* know; apparent; clear. **~ করা/পাওয়া** *vi, vt* know; feel; perceive; sense. **~ হওয়া** *vi* seem; appear; become felt/known; be sensed/ perceived.

মালুমকাঠ *n* main mast (of a ship).

মালো *n* fisherman (by caste).

মালোপমা *n* (rhet) a particular figure of speech consisting of a string of comparisons.

মাল্য *n* **1** wreath; garland; chaplet. **2** crown. **3** flower. **~বান** *adj* wearing a garland; crowned with garland; garlanded. **~বতী** *fem*. **~দান** *n* garlanding.

মাল্লা [A] *n* sailor, seaman; boatman; oarsman.

মাশুক [A] *n* beloved; sweetheart.

মাশুল, মাসুল [A] *n* tariff; fee; tax; duty; fare; freight; charge; custom; excise; postage.

মাশুলচোর *n* notorious thief.

মাষ[1], মাষকলাই *nn* kind of pulse having seeds marked with black and grey spot.

মাষ[2], মাষক, মাষা *nn* particular weight of gold (= about of grains troy).

মাস *n* month. **মাসে, মাসে-মাসে** *adv* every month; monthly. **~কাবার** *n* close of a calendar month; (commerce) month-closing accounts. **~কাবারি** required at the close of a month; sufficient for a month; monthly. **~জাত** *n* one month old child. **~পয়লা, ~পহেলা** the first day of a month. **~বৃদ্ধি** *n* intercalary month. **~ভর** *adj* throughout the month. **~মাহিনা** monthly wages/salary. **মাসান্ত** *n* the last day of a month; month's end.

মাসতুত, মাসতুতো *adj* descended from a sister/cousin-sister of one's mother or mother-in-law; avuncular. **~ ভাই/বোন** *n* cousin.

মাসশাশুড়ি *n fem* sister/ cousin-sister of one's mother-in-law; aunt-in-law.

মাসশ্বশুর *n* husband of a মাসশাশুড়ি; uncle-in-law.

মাশহরা, মাসহারা [A] *n* monthly allowance/ stipend.

মাসাশ *n* (dial)=মাসশাশুড়ি

মাসি, মাসিমা, মাসিমাতা *n fem* sister/cousin-sister of one's mother; aunt.

মাসিক *adj* monthly. ❑*n* *1* monthly (journal). **2** menses; periods; monthlies. **~ পত্রিকা**=~ (1).

মাসুল ⇒ মাশুল

মাস্টার [E] *n* master. **মাস্টারি** *n* (act/ profession of) teaching.

মাহ [P] *n* month. **মাহে রমজান** *n* month of Ramadan.

মাহফিল [A] *n* party revelling in music and dance; meeting; musical soiree; assembly; congregation.

মাহতাব, মাহাতাব [P] *nn* the moon.

মাহাজনিক *adj* **1** fit for great persons/ merchants. **2** relating to a creditor; usurious. **3** commercial.

মাহাত্মিক *adj* belonging to an exalted person; glorious; majestic. **মাহাত্মিকী** *fem*.

মাহাত্ম্য *n* **1** magnanimity; light-mindedness; exalted state/ position; majesty; dignity; glory; excellence; nobility; greatness; sublimity. **2** peculiar efficacy/ virtue of any divinity/shrine etc; charm: অর্থের ~.

মাহাফা, মহাপ [A] *nn* small covered litter; palanquin.

মাহিনা, মাহিয়ানা [P] *nn* monthly wages/salary. **মাহিনার/মাইনের চাকর** (derog) paid servant.

মাহিষ *adj* belonging/ relating to a buffalo or buffalo-cow.

মাহিষ্য *adj*=মাহিষ. ❑*n* name of a Hindu caste.

মাহুত *n* keeper and driver of an elephant; mahout.

মাহেন্দ্র *adj* relating/belonging to great Indra. **~ক্ষণ** *n* (astrol) most auspicious conjunction of stars for commencing any work.

মিউ, মিউ *n* (onom) mew. **~মিউ করা** *vi* mew.

মিউজিয়ম [E] *n* museum.

মিউনিসিপ্যাল [E] *adj* municipal. **মিউনিসিপ্যালিটি** *n* municipality.

মি. [E] *n* Mr

মিচকে *adj* cunning; insidious; crafty; artful; foxy; sly; wily; slick; simulating.

মিছকিন [A] *adj* poor; miserable; wretched; indigent; needy; humble. ❑*n* poor people.

মিছরি, মিছরী [A] *nn* sugar-candy. **~র ছুরি** *n* (fig) sweet verbal stab; sugar-coated words. **~র পানা** *n* a cold-drink/ cordial made of sugar-candy.

মিছা, মিছে (colloq)=মিথ্যা. **~মিছি** *adv*=মিথ্যা

মিছিল [A] *n* **1** procession; cortege. **2** papers/ records of a lawsuit.

মিজরাব, মেজরাপ [A] *nn* kind of thimble used by instrumentalists; musical plectrum.

মিজান [A] *n* balance; pair of scales; measure. 2 total; addition; sum: ~ দেওয়া/ মেলানো.

মিঞা [P] *n* 1 master; lord; husband. 2 (also ~সাহেব) an appellation of courtesy affixed to the name of a man; Mr; Sir. ~-বিবি *n* husband and wife.

মিট *n* 1 settlement; compromise: reconciliation. 2 (accounts) balancing; paying off; compounding. ~ করা *vt* 1 settle; compromise; reconcile. 2 balance (an account); pay off (a bill) ; compound (a loss); make up. ~ হওয়া *vi* 1 be compromised/ reconciliated/settled. 2 be balanced/paid off/ made up/ compounded. ~মাট *n* reconciliation; compromise; settlement. ~মাট করা *vt* reconcile; compromise; settle/ patch up (a difference/ dispute etc). ~মাট হওয়া *vi* be reconciled/ compromised/ settled.

মিটমিট *n* (onom) blink; twinkle; wink; flicker; blinking; twinkling. ~ করা *n* blink; twinkle; wink; flicker. মিট্‌মিটে *adj* 1 blinking; hypocritical; sly. মিটমিটে শয়তান *n* a dissembling witch/ rogue; a wolf in a sheepskin. মিটমিটানি *n* ~. ~নো *vi*=~ করা.

মিটা *vi* 1 be accomplished/ finished/ done: কাজ/ দায়িত্ব ~. 2 be relieved/ removed: দুঃখ ~. 3 be satisfied/ fulfilled/ satiated/ slaked: সাধ ~. 4 be reconciled/ compromised/ settled/ patched up: বিবাদ ~. 5 (accounts) be balanced. 6 be compensated/ compounded: লোকসান ~. 7 be paid off/ settled. দাবি/ পাওনা ~. ~নো *vt* 1 accomplish; finish; complete; do. 2 relieve; remove: 3 satisfy; fulfil; satiate; slake. 4 reconcile; compromise; settle; patch up. 5 (accounts) balance. 6 compensate; compound. 7 pay off; settle.

মিটার[1] *n* meter: বৈদ্যুতিক ~.

মিটার[2] *n* metre (unit of measuring length).

মিটিং [E] *n* meeting.

মিটিমিটি *adv* (onom) blinkingly; flickering dimly: ~ তাকানো, ~ জ্বলা. ❑*adj* twinkling; blinking; winking; flickering (dimly). ~ করা *vi* twinkle; blink; wink; flicker (dimly).

মিটিরমিটির *n* (onom)=মিটমিট (extensive).

মিঠা *adj* 1 sweet; delicious; palatable. 2 melodious; mellifluous; suave; bland; pleasant; charming: ~ সুর / কথা. 3 capable of producing a sweet and soft effect: সেতারের ~ হাত. 4 fresh: ~ জল. ~ই *n* sweetmeat; candy. ~ইওয়ালা *n* confectioner; candyman. ~ইয়ের দোকান *n* sweetmeat-shop. ~কড়া *adj* 1 (of tobacco) mild; moderately strong; (of words) suave yet cutting to the quick. ~খিলি *n* betel-leaf rolled into a cone together with lime, betel-nut, sweetening, etc. ~জল, ~পানি *nn* freshwater.

মিডিয়ম [E] *n* medium.

মিড় *n* (music) slur.

মিত *adj* 1 measured; moderate; temperate; abstemious. 2 mild; scanty; frugal; little; limited by. ~বাক *adj* speaking measuredly or little; reticent; reserved; economical in speech; taciturn. ~ব্যয়, ~ব্যয়িতা *nn* frugality; thrift; economy. ~ব্যয়ী *adj* frugal; spending little; economical; thrifty. ~ভাষী=~বাক. ~ভাষিণী *fem*. ~ভাষিতা=~ব্যয়িতা. ~ভোজন *n* moderate food; scanty diet; temperance in food and drink; abstemiousness. moderate eating. ~ভোজী *adj* eating sparingly; moderate in diet; abstemious. ~হাসিনী *adj fem* smiling. মিতাক্ষর *adj* having measured syllables; metrical; short and comprehensive (in speech). মিতাচার *n* temperance; abstemiousness. মিতাচারী *adj* temperate; abstemious. মিতাচারিণী *fem*. ~চারিতা=মিতাচার. মিতার্থ *n* measured meaning. ❑*adj* of measured meaning; speaking with caution. মিতাশন, ~হার *nn*=~ভোজন. মিতাশি, মিতাহারী *adjj*=~ভোজী. মিতাশিতা=~ভোজন

মিতকনে *n* bridesmaid; best maid.

মিতবর *n* groomsman; best man.

মিতা *n* friend; pal; boon companion; crony; ally; associate; namesake. ~লি, ~লী *nn* friendship; companionship; fellowship.

মিতাক্ষরা *n* name of an ancient Hindu treatise on the law and rules of inheritance.

মিতি *n* 1 measure; measuring; weight; -metry: ত্রিকোণ~. 2 knowledge.

মিতিন *n fem* wife of a crony (মিতা); woman friend of a man.

মিতে (colloq)=মিতা

মিত্র *n* 1=মিতা. 2 the sun. মিত্রা *fem*=মিতিন. ~তা, ~ত্ব *nn*=মিতালি. ~ঘাতী, ~ঘ্ন *adjj* 'friend-killing'; treacherous. ~দ্রোহ, ~দ্রোহিতা *nn* injury/ betrayal of a friend; treachery to one's ally/ party. ~দ্রোহী *adj* seeking to injure a friend; hostile/ treacherous to one's friend. ❑*n* betrayer of a friend; false/ treacherous friend. ~দ্রোহিণী *fem*. ~দ্বেষী *adj* hating/ injuring a friend; treacherous friend. ~বৎসল *adj* affectionate towards friends; devoted to friends. ~ভাব *n* friendly disposition. ~ভেদ *n* separation of friends; breach of friendship. ~লাভ *n* acquisition of friends/ friendship.

মিত্রাক্ষর *n* rhymed verse.

মিথস্ক্রিয় *adj* interactive. মিথস্ক্রিয়া *n* interaction.

মিথুন *n* 1 pair (male and female); couple. 2 pairing; copulation. 3 (astrol) Gemini; the twins.

মিথোজীবিতা *n* (biol) symbiosis.

মিথোনির্দেশ *n* cross reference.

মিথ্যা *n* 1 lie; falsehood; falsity. ❑*adj* 1 wrong; incorrect; false; untrue: ~ কথা. 2 baseless fanciful; imaginary; got-up; unsubstantial: ~ অভিযোগ, ~ ভয়. **3** fruitless; vain; purposeless; useless; bootless; futile: ~ আলোচনা, ~ চেষ্টা. **4** affected; sham; feigned: ~ ব্যাধি. causeless; unprovoked: ~ ক্ষোভ. ❑*adv* for nothing; falsely; wrongly; incorrectly; improperly; in vain; deceitfully; untruly; only apparently; not in reality; fruitlessly; to no purpose. **~ কথা** *n* lie. **~কথা বলা** *vi* tell a lie. **~চরণ, ~চার** *nn* false/treacherous behaviour; hypocrisy; improper conduct; false play; dissimulation; treachery. **~চারী** *adj* acting falsely/ hypocritically; given to false play hypocritical; dissimulating. ❑*n* rogue; hypocrite. **~চারিণী** *fem.* **~চারিতা** *n*=~চরণ. **~ জ্ঞান, ~ ধারণা** *nn* false/ wrong conception/ notion/ idea/ impression; error; mistake. **~ দর্শন** *n* false appearance. **~ দৃষ্টি** *n* false doctrine; heresy; atheism. ❑*adj* having false notion; mistaken; erroneous. **~ নিরসন** *n* elimination of falsehood; denial by oath. **~পবাদ** *n* false accusation/blame; scandal; calumny. **~প্রিয়** *adj* addicted to lying; mythomaniac. **~বচন** *n* telling an untruth. **~বর্ণন** *n* false account; misrepresentation. **~বাক্য** *n* false statement; lie. **~ বাদ** *n* **1**=~বাক্য. **2** false blame/ accusation; calumny. **3** untruthfulness. **~বাদিতা** *n* untruthfulness. **~বাদী** *adj* lying; untruthful. ❑*n* liar. **~বাদিনী** *fem.* **~ভাষণ, ~ভাষিতা** *nn* lying; untruthfulness; false statement. **~ভাষী**=~বাদী. **~ভাষিণী** *fem.* **~মতি** *n* false opinion; error. **~মিথ্যা** *adv*=~. **~ সাক্ষী** *n* false/ tutored witness; perjury. **~ সাক্ষ্য** *n* false/ tutored witness; perjury. **~ সাক্ষ্য দেওয়া** *vi* give/ bear false witness; perjure. **~র জাহাজ/ ঝুড়ি/মরাই** *n* ship/ship-load/ basket of lies; given to telling lies unscrupulously; habitual liar. **~র তোড়/স্রোত** *n* spate of lies.

মিথ্যুক *adj* given to telling lies; untruthful. ❑*n* liar.

মিথ্যে (colloq)=মিথ্যা

মিনতি *n* humble prayer; earnest request; prayer; begging solicitation; entreaty; appeal earnest request. **~ করা** *vi* pray/ request humbly; beg; entreat; solicit; supplicate; implore; beseech; adjure; plead/ appeal for; pray. **~পূর্ণ** *adj* begging; supplicatory; imploring; appealing; entreating; imploring.

মিনসা, মিনসে *n* (sl) grown-up man; man; husband.

মিনা [P] *n* enamel; enamelling. **~ করা** *vt* enamel. **~করা** *adj* enamelled. **~কার** *n* enameller. **~কারি** *n* enamelling.

মিনার [A] *n* minaret; turret; tower; monument.

মিনি[১] *adj, pref* without; except; lacking in: ~ সুতোর মালা. **~মাগনা** *adj* cost-free.

মিনি[২] [E]=mini.

মিনিট [E] *n* sixtieth part of an hour/ degree; minute; moment. **মিনিটে মিনিটে** *adj* every minute/ moment; at short intervals.

মিনমিন *n* (onom) **1** faintness; indistinctness. **2** weakness; timidity. **3** mumble; mumbling. **4** nasal sound. **~ করা** *vi, vt* mumble; speak faintly/ hesitatingly/ timidly/ indistinctly. **মিনমিনে** *adj* mumbling; speaking faintly/ hesitatingly; faint-hearted; faint; weak.

মিয়া=মিঞা

মিয়ানো *vi* **1** lose crispness: খই/মুড়ি ~. **2** loose energy/vigour; dwindle; decline; wither; flag; slacken; become flaccid/limp. ❑*adj* no longer crisp; bereft of energy/vigour; limp; gutless; flaccid; spent.

মির, মীর [A] *nn* **1** commander; chieftain; grandee; nobleman. **2** a Muslim family name. **~দা**=মির্ধা. **~বহর** *n* admiral of the fleet. **~মুনশি** *n* chief clerk; head clerk; chief secretary. **~যা**=মির্জা.

মিরগেল=মৃগেল

মিরাস, মিরাশ [A] *n* patrimony; hereditary estate; bequest; ancestral property; legacy. **~-ইজারা** *n* lease/settlement of land to be enjoyed hereditarily. **মিরাসি, মিরাশি** *adjj* inherited; hereditary.

মিরাসি [A] *n* singer by hereditary profession.

মির্জা, মীর্জা [P] *nn* prince; Grande; son of a nobleman; a Muslim family name.

মির্জাই, মীর্জাই [P] *nn* kind of jacket with long, loose sleeves; quilted coat.

মির্ধা, মিরধা [P] *nn* headman of a village; messenger; a Muslim family name.

মিল[১] *n* **1** union; concord; combination; connection; intimacy harmony; agreement; unison: মনের ~, কথা ও কাজের ~, মতের ~, সুরের ~. **2** joining; fitting: তক্তা ~ খাওয়ানো. **3** similarity; likeness; resemblance: চেহারার ~. **4** balancing: হিসাবের ~. **5** rhyme: ছন্দের ~. **6** friendly terms; reconciliation; good terms: reconcilement: ওই পক্ষের ~. **~ করা** *vt* unite; combine; connect; add (up); harmonize; balance; reconcile; bring together; rhyme. **~ খাওয়া** *vi* unite/mix with; accord; be in harmony. **~ খাওয়ানো** *vt* join; unite; bring into harmony. **~ থাকা** *vi* be on good term with; be in agreement/ harmony. **~ দেওয়া** *vt* add; rhyme; find out a rhyme for. **~ রাখা** *vi* be intimate with; be on good terms with. **~ হওয়া** *vi* agree; be in harmony; be reconciled; be balanced; tally; be fitting; fit; rhyme. **~জুক, ~জুল** *nn* harmony; accord; association. **~মিলাও, ~মিশ** *nn* good/friendly terms; amicability. **~যুক্ত** *adj* rhyming.

মিল[২] [E] *n* mill; factory.

মিলন *n* **1** coming together; meeting; contact; union. **2** accord; unity; harmony alliance. **3**

reconciliation; reconcilement. **4** meeting/union of lovers; wedding; bridal. **~মন্দির** *n* assembly room/hall. **~সাধন** *n* act of uniting; union. **~স্থান** *n* meeting-place; tryst. **মিলনান্ত, মিলনান্তক** *adjj* ending happily/in union. **মিলনান্তক নাটক** *n* comedy.

মিলমিলা, মিলমিলে *nn* measles.

মিলাদ=মলুদ

মিলানো *vi* disappear; dissolves; melt away; vanish; bade: হাওয়ায় মিলিয়ে যাওয়া; সন্দেশ মুখে মিলিয়ে যায়.

মিলিত *adj* **1** united; combined; connected; mixed; furnished; joint. **2** assembled; gathered; met. **3** procured. **~ করা** *vt* unite; combine; mix; connect; join; mix; assemble; cause meet. **~ হওয়া** *vi* meet; assemble; gather. **~দল** *n* (bot) gamopetalous. **~বৃত্তি** *n* (bot) gamosepalous.

মিল্লত, মিল্লাত *nn* [A] **1** religion; faith. **2** nation.

মিশ[1] *n* mixing; blending; unision; mixtue; harmony; accord; agreement. **~ খাওয়া** *vi* be mixed/ blended; agree; harmonize; accord. **~ খাওয়ানো** *vt* mix; blend; harmonize; recognize; put in harmony with; adapt; accord; attune.

মিশ[2]=মিস

মিশন [E] *n* mission. **মিশনারি** *n, adj* missionary.

মিশমিশ=মিসমিস

মিশর=মিসর

মিশি=মিসি

মিশুক *adj* sociable; companionable.

মিশ্র *adj* **1** mixed; blended; combined; mingled. **2** manifold; diverse; various. ☐*n* **1** (arith) mixed (fraction). **2** (math) compound. (chem) mixture. **~ক** *n* **1** compounder; blender; mixer; adulterator. **2** ingredient of a compound. **~কবিদ্যা** *n* art of compounding medicines. **~জাতি** *adj* being of mixed birth/breed; one whose parents belong to different castes. **~ণ** *n* mixing; blending; compounding; mixture; addition; adulteration; amalgamation. **~ণবিধি** *n* process of mixing/ blending/ compounding. **~নীয়** *adj* to be mixed/ mingled; miscible. **~তা** *n* mixedness; mixture. **~ পদার্থ** *n* mixture; compound. **~ বর্ণ** *adj* being of a mixed colour. **~বাসী** *adj* (bot) polygamous. **~ সুর** *n* (music) mixed mode.

মিশ্রি=মিছরি

মিশ্রিত *adj* mixed; blended (with); compounded; adulterated; amalgamated. **~ করা** *vt* mix; blend; compound; adulterate; amalgamate.

মিষ্ট *adj* sweet; dainty; delicate; delicious; pleasing; pleasant. ☐*n* sweet meat; sweets. **~তা, ~ত্ব** *nn* sweetness; suavity; deliciousness. **~ভাষী** *adj* fair-speaking; soft-spoken; honey-tongued. **~ভাষিণী** *fem*. **~ভোজন** *n* eating of dainties. **~মুখ** *n* **1** a light repast of sweets: ~মুখ করা, take a light repast of sweets. **2** sweet/ pleasant speech: ~মুখে বলা, say sth gently/sweetly/pleasingly. **মিষ্টান্ন** *n* sweet meat; sweets; a sweet dish prepared by boiling rice in milk. **মিষ্টালাপী** *adj*=~ভাষী. ☐*n* pleasant talker/conversationalist.

মিস[1] *adj* inky; very dark; murky. **~কালো** *adj* jet-black; pitch-black; coal-black. **মিসমিসে** *adj* as black/dark as ink; inky.

মিস[2] [E] *n, fem* Miss.

মিসওয়াক [A] *n* softened stick used for cleaning teeth; tooth-brush.

মিসকাল [A] *n* a particular weight of gold.

মিসকিন=মিছকিন

মিসমার [A] *adj* demolished; raze; ruined. **~ করা** demolish; destroy; raze; ruin.

মিসর [A] *n* Egypt. **মিসরি, মিসরীয়** *adjj* Egyptian. ☐*nn* Egyptian.

মিসি *n* a dentifrice made of roasted tobacco, green vitriol, etc.

মিসিবাবা [E] *n* (used by domestic servants) missy.

মিসিল [A] *n* **1** file. **2** record.

মিস্টার [E] *n* Mister; Mr.

মিস্ত্রি, মিস্ত্রী *nn* (Pg) **1** mechanic; machine foreman; skilled/chief mechanic or artisan; artisan. **2** mason. **3** carpenter; joiner.

মিহনত [A] *n* labour; toil; industry; diligence, application; difficulty. **মিহনতি** *adj* toiling; laborious; industrious. ☐*n* labourer.

মিহরাব [A] *n* the principal place in the mosque, where the Imam prays; niche.

মিহি [P] *adj* **1** fine; fine-spun: ~ কাপড়. **2** soft; faint; effeminate: ~ গলা/সুর. **3** finely pulverized: ~ গুঁড়া. **4** delicate; subtle: ~ কাজ. **~দানা** *n* kind of sweetmeat consisting of very small globules.

মিহির *n* the sun.

মীড়=মিড়

মীন *n* **1** fish. **2** (astrol) the Pisces. **~কেতন, ~ধ্বজ** *nn* 'fish-bannered'; Hindu god of love. **~পেটি** *n* fishery. **~পোষ** *n* pisciculture. **~মীনাক্ষ** *adj* marked with a fish-eye. **মীনাক্ষী** *n fem* **1** name of a female deity worshipped in Deccan. **2** a daughter of Kubera.

মীমাংসক *adj* deciding; determining; decisive. ☐*n* **1** investigator; arbiter; arbitrator. **2** follower of the Mimangsa system of philosophy.

মীমাংসন *n* settlement; deciding; investigation. **মীমাংসনীয়, মীমাংসিতব্য** *adjj* to be settled/ examined/ investigated/ decided.

মীমাংসা *n* **1** solution (of a problem, etc). **2** settlement/arbitration (of a dispute); clearing up/settling (of complication, doubt, etc). **3** determination (of truths etc). **4** decision. **5**

compromise. **6** disposal (of an affair). **7** name of one of the three great divisions of orthodox Hindu philosophy (also ~-দর্শন). ~ **করা** *vt* solve; settle; decide; determine; arbitrate; dispose of; clear up; effect a compromise.

মীমাংসিত *adj* solved; settled; decided; determined; arbitrated; compromised.

মীলন *n* closing (said of eyes and flowers).

মীলিত *adj* closed; partly opened.

মুই *pron* (archaic, dial) I.

মুকদ্দমা=মকদ্দমা

মুকদ্দস [A] *adj* holy; consecrated; sanctified; hallowed.

মুকরর, মুকররর [A] *adjj* established; fixed; confirmed; determined; agreed upon; permanent. **মুকররি** *adj*=মকররি.

মুকানো (colloq)=মুখানো.

মুকাবিলা [A] *n* confrontation; encounter; comparison; collision; confronting; contest; meeting face to face; facing. ~ **করা** *vi* face; meet face to face; encounter; confront; settle/ decide after face to face discussion.

মুকুট *n* **1** crown; diadem; tiara. **2** (bot) corona. ~ **পরা** *vi* put on/wear a crown. ~ **পরানো** *vt* crown. ~**-পরা** *adj* crowned; wearing a diadem.

মুকুতা (poet) মুক্তা

মুকুতি (poet) = মুক্তি

মুকুন্দ *n* Vishnu (giver of liberation).

মুকুর *n* mirror; looking glass. ~**-দূরবীক্ষণ** *n* (phys) reflecting telescope.

মুকুল *n* bud. **মুকুলা** *vi* bud; blossom; flower; effloresce; be in bloom; (of flowers) bloom; blow. **মুকুলাবরণ** *n* (bot) bud-scale. **মুকুলিত** *adj* budded; full of blossoms; blooming; efflorescent. **মুকুলিতা** *fem.* **মুকুলোদগম** *n* budding.

মুক্ত *adj* **1** loosened; let loose; set free; relaxed; slackened; opened; open. **2** liberated; delivered; emancipated; freed from earthly bondage/ ties/ attachments: ~ পুরুষ. **3** released; freed: কারা~. **4** free; unobstructed; unhindered; unrestricted; left free: ~ পথ/গতি. **5** unbiased; unprejudiced; dispassionate; unaffected: ~ মন. **6** relieved of; rescued/ liberated from: ভয়~. **7** acquitted; discharged; freed: দায়~. **8** liberal; bountiful: ~হস্ত; cured of; recovered from: রোগ~. **9** unbolted; open: ~দ্বার. **10** sent forth; emitted; discharged; poured out; hurled; thrown: জ্যা~; হস্ত~. **11** shed (as tears). **12** extricated: বিপদ~. **13** untied; bare; unsheathed: ~কৃপাণ. **14** delivered from/ of: গর্ভ~. **15** removed; cleared: মকড়ি ~ হওয়া. ~ **করা** *vt* loose; let loose; loosen; free; set free; let go; slacken; release; liberate (from); deliver (from); spare; let live; allow to depart; dismiss; despatch; send forth; shed; emit; utter; discharge; throw; hurl; cast; shoot; untie; extricate; acquit; cure of; open; unbolt; unfasten; unsheathe; rescue; relieve (of); remove; clear; free from obstacles/ restrictions; exempt. ~**কচ্ছ** *adj* one who lets the hem of the loin-cloth hang down/ loose: (fig) hurrying excessively and ludicrously. ❑*n* a Buddhist. ~**কঞ্চুক** *adj* (of snake) that has cast its skin. ~**কণ্ঠ** *adj* loud. ~**কণ্ঠে** *adv* loudly; in a loud voice; speaking freely/ unhesitatingly; liberally; with all one's might. ~**কেশ** *adj* having the hair dishevelled/ hanging down. ~**কেশী** *adj*=~কেশ. ❑*n* goddess Kali. ~**চক্ষু** *adj* having the eyes opened. ~ **ছন্দ** *n* free verse. ~**তা**, ~**ত্ব** *nn* being liberated from existence; emancipation. ~**দ্বার** *n* open door. ~**নগরী** *n* undefended/ open/ liberated city. ~**পুরুষ** *n* liberated/ emancipated soul. ~**বন্দর** *n* free port. ~ **বাতাস** *n* open air. ~ **বুদ্ধি** *n* unfettered intellect/ mind. ❑*adj* having an unfettered mind. ~**বেণী** *adj* having the hair not tied up in a chignon; wearing one's hair in flowing plaits. ❑*n* **1** flowing plait of hair. **2** confluence of Tribeni at Allahabad. ~ **হস্ত** *adj* open-handed; liberal; generous; munificent. ~**হস্ততা** *n* open-handedness; liberality; generosity. ~**হস্তে** *adv* liberally; generously.

মুক্তা *n* pearl. ~**কলাপ** *n* ornament made of strings of pearl. ~**খচিত** *adj* studded/ set/ inlaid with pearls. ~**গার** *n* pearl-oyster. ~**গর্ভ** *adj* containing pearls; pearly. ~**ঝুরি**, ~**বর্ষী** *adj* sprinkling/ raining pearls. ❑*nn* a medicinal herb (acalypha indica). ~**তুল্য** *adj* pearl-like; pearly. ~**ফল** *n* pearl; camphor. ~**বলি**, ~**বলী** *nn* pearl necklace; string/ collection of pearls. ~**ময়** *adj* made/ consisting of pears. ~**মালা**, ~**লতা** *nn*=~বলি. ~**শুক্তি** *n* pearl-oyster. ~**সার** *n* pearl of the first water. ~**স্ফোট** *n* pearl-oyster. ~**হার** *n*=~বলি. ❑*adj* taking no food.

মুক্তি *n* **1** setting/ becoming free; release. **2** freedom. **3** liberation; deliverance from; final liberation/ emancipation; final beatitude. **4** throwing; casting; hurling; shooting; sending. **5** discharge. **6** acquittal. **7** recovery: রোগ~. **8** loosening; unbolting; opening. **9** end; termination: গ্রহণ ~. **10** delivery from/ of: গর্ভ~. **11** freedom from obstruction/restrictions. **12** rescue; relief: ভয়~. **13** unsheathing: কোষ~. **14** exemption. ~ **দেওয়া**=মুক্ত করা (⇒ মুক্ত). ~ **পাওয়া** *vi* attain salvation; gain freedom; be set free; be freed/ rescued/ released; be acquitted/ discharged; be extricated; be let loose/ loosened; recover; be cured; be emancipated/ liberated; become independent/ free; be freed from obstruction/ restrictions; be unbolted; be unsheathed; be delivered from/of. **~দ, ~দাতা** *n, adj* one who liberates/ frees/ acquits/ delivers/ releases/ extricated/ rescues/ lets loose/ relieves/ cures/ emancipates; one who gives salvation; liberator; rescuer; emancipator; deliverer; saviour. **~দা, ~দাত্রী** *fem.* **~দান, ~প্রদান** *nn* freeing; releasing; rescuing; setting free; deliverance; liberating; emancipating; relieving; act of giving salvation; extrication; acquittal; curing; discharging. **~দায়ক** *adj* liberating; emancipating; delivering; releasing etc. **~নামা, ~পত্র** *nn* deed of release; deed of reconveyance; passport. **~পদ** *n* place of deliverance. **~প্রার্থী** *adj* seeking liberation/ emancipation/ deliverance/ acquittal/ release etc. **~প্রার্থিনী** *fem.* **~ফৌজ** *n* army of liberation; the Salvation Army. **~মার্গ** *n* way of salvation/ liberation. **~লাভ** *n* attainment of salvation/ liberation/ freedom; release; acquittal; relief; rescue; deliverance; extrication; recovery. **~স্নান** *n* ceremonial bathing (esp in the Ganges) on termination of an eclipse.

মুখ *n* **1** face; visage; countenance; appearance. **2** mouth. **3** entrance; aperture; egress: গুহা~. **4** opening: ফোড়ার ~. **5** introduction; commencement; outset; beginning: উন্নতির ~. **6** end; extremity; head: রাস্তার ~. **7** tip; point: সুচের ~. **8** outlet: নালার ~. **9** outfall; embouchure; mouth: নদীর ~. **10** direction; quarter: ঘরের মুখে. **11** snout/ muzzle of an animal. **12** mouth/spout of a vessel. **13** fore part; front; van (of an army). **14.** upper part/top/head of anything. **15** eloquence; gift of the gab: মুখের ~. **16** impertinence; acrimonious speech; sharp caustic tongue: তোমার ভারি ~ হয়েছে দেখছি. **17** hope: অনেক বড়ো ~ করে এসেছিলাম. **18** honour; prestige: সে তো তোমার ~ রাখল না. **19** the chief/principal/ best. **20** nipple (of a breast). **21** source/ cause/ occasion of. **21** tongue; speech; language: দুর্মুখ. **~ আলগা করা** *vi* let loose one's tongue; speak out; open one's mouth. **~ উজ্জ্বল করা** *vi* bring glory/ credit to; do credit to. **~ করা** *vi* **1** flare up; fume. **2** snap at; scold (peevishly). **~ কুটকুট করা** *vi* **1** (of mouth) itch. **2** (fig) have an itch for speaking/ to speak. **~ কুটকুটানো** *vi* have an itch in the mouth. **~ খাওয়া** *vi* be rebuked/ scolded/ reprimanded. **~ খারাপ করা** *vi* utter abusive/ foul/ filthy words. **~ খিঁচানো** *vi* grimace; make grimaces; make faces (at); growl. **~ খোলা** *vi* open one's mouth; begin to speak. **~ গোঁজ গোঁজ করা, ~ গোঁজ করে থাকা** *vi* pull a long face; be down in the mouth. **~ চলা** *vi* be eating/ speaking/ scolding (continually). **~ চাওয়া** *vi* be dependent on sb; play second fiddle; lean on sb; wait for; be considerate about/ partial to sb. **~ চুন করা** *vi* turn pale (for fear, shame, etc); be shamefaced/ sheepish/ discomfited; loose face. **~ চুলকানো**=~ কুটকুট করা. **~ চেয়ে বসে থাকা**=~ চাওয়া. **~ চোকানো** *vi* (of mouth) water. **~ ছুটানো**=~ আলগা করা. **~ ছোট করা** *vi* discountenance; disgrace; discredit; put to shame; cut down to size. **~ ঝামটা দেওয়া** *vi* jaw at; remonstrate angrily; scold. **~ টিপে/ টিপেটিপে হাসা** *vi* smile in amusement; laugh up one's sleeve. **~ ঢাকা** *vi* cover one's face; veil oneself. **~ তাকানো**=~ চাওয়া. **~ তুলতে না পারা** *vi* be put out of countenance; be mortified/ abashed. **~ তুলে চাওয়া. ~ তোলা** *vi* **1** look up. **2** (fig) smile on: ভাগ্য মুখ তুলে চেয়েছে. **~ থাকা** *vi* have one's face saved; have appearances kept up. **~ থুবড়ে পড়া** **1** fall flat on one's face. **2** (fig) fall flat. **~ দেখা** *vi* (fig) see ceremonially the face of sb (esp of a bride) for the first time. **~ দেখানো** **1** show one's face; put in an appearance. **2** show ceremonially the face of a bride. **~ দেখাতে না পারা** *vi* be unable to show one's face; be put out of countenance. **~ নষ্ট করা** *vi* speak/ plead in vain. **~ নষ্ট হওয়া** *vi* have one's advice/ request turned down; meet with a rebuff. **~ নাড়া দেওয়া** *vi* jaw at; scold; rebuke; rail at; chide. **~ পোড়ানো** *vi* disgrace; scandalize. **~ ফসকানো** *vi* (of words, remarks, etc) slip off one's tongue. **~ ফেরানো** *vi* **1** turn away; look in another direction (in disgust, displeasure, etc). **2** become unfavourable/ hostile to. **~ ফোটা** *vi* begin to speak (esp for the first time); utter. **~ ফোলানো** *vi* pout one's lips; pull a long face. **~ বন্ধ করা** *vi* **1** hold one's tongue; shut one's month. **2** shut sb's month; silence; gag; muzzle; cut short. **~ বাঁকানো** *vi* turn one's nose up (in disgust, displeasure, etc); make a wry face. **~ বাড়া** *vi* become vocal; become too bold/ impertinent. **~ বাড়ানো** *vi* **1** look out of (the window, etc). **2** cause to be impudent/ cheeky. **~ বিগড়ানো** *vi* have a bad taste in the mouth; develop expensive tastes. **~ বোজা** *vi* shut one's mouth; keep one's mouth shut; keep mum. **~ ব্যাদান করা** *vi* gape; open one's mouth wide. **~ ভার করা**=~ গোঁজা করা. **~ ভেংচানো** *n* grimace; make faces. **~মারা** *vi* **1** close (a joint, etc). **2** take away sb's appetite by feeding him too much sweets. **3** put out of countenance; silence. **~ রক্ষা করা, ~ রাখা** *vi* save one's / sb's face; keep up appearances. **~ লাল করে দেওয়া** *vi* slap sb on the face. **~ লাল হওয়া** *vi* become red with anger/ embarrassment; flush up; go red; flush crimson; blush. **~ লুকানো** *vi* hide one's face. **~ শুকানো** *vi* look/ turn pale. **~ সামলানো** *vi* hold one's tongue; speak guardedly; keep one's mouth shut; save one's breath; keep one's counsel. **~ সিটকানো** *vi* turn one's nose up at; shrink from. ~ সেলাই করা *vi* keep mum. ~ সেলাই করে দেওয়া *vi* sew up/ seal sb's lips; silence. ~ হওয়া *vi* 1 (of boils, etc) open. 2 learn to take liberties in speech; become impudent; be unrestrained in speech; form a habit of scolding: এখন তার ভারি ~ হয়েছে. মুখে আগুন *n* wishing sb's death. মুখে আনা *vi* utter. মুখে আসা *vi* have (sth) on the tip of one's tongue. ~ মুখে করা *vi* put into one's mouth. ~ মুখে খই ফোটা *vi* be chattering excessively; talk nineteen to the dozen; be eloquent; have a ready tongue. মুখে জল আসা *vi* have one's mouth watering. মুখে জল দেওয়া *vi* 1 wash one's face. 2 give water to sb (after fasting or to quench his thirst). 3 put the water of the Ganges into the mouth of a dying person. মুখে দড় *adj* given to tall talks; all talk. মুখে দেওয়া *vi* 1 put into sb's mouth; feed. 2 eat. মুখে ফুলচন্দন পড়া (used as a good wish) have your tongue blessed for having made a favourable prophecy. মুখে ফেলা *vi* throw into one's mouth. মুখে-মুখে *adv* 1 by word of mouth; orally; viva voce. 2 extemporarily; impromptu; off-hand. 3 being talked about: তার কথা সবার মুখে-মুখে. 4 defiantly to one's face; in retort: মুখে-মুখে কথা বলা. 5 side by side: মুখে-মুখে জোড়া দেওয়া. ~ মুখে-মুখে চোপা করা *vi* retort defiantly. মুখে রোচা *vi* be agreeable to one's taste; relish; be to one's liking. মুখের উপর to sb's face; defiantly. মুখের কথা *n* oral promise; word of mouth; (fig) very easy job. মুখের কথা খসানো *vi* state what desired, etc; name. মুখের ছাঁদ *n* the cut of one's jib; type of face. মুখের তোড় *n* gift of the gab; eloquence; rhetoric; spate of words; fluency. মুখের ভয়ে for fear of scolding/sharp or caustic tongue. মুখের মতো *adj* fitting: মুখের মতো জবাব. মুখের মিষ্টি *n* sweet words. মুখের সামনে *adv* openly; to one's face. কোন মুখে has/have he/ I the face to. খোতা মুখ ভোঁতা করা put an end to one's tall talk; give a fitting reply; discomfit; humble sb's pride. খোতা মুখ ভোঁতা হওয়া be humiliated; get one's just deserts; eat humble pie. যত বড়ো ~ নয় তত বড়ো কথা be intolerably impertinent/ cheeky. ~আলগা *adj* having a loose tongue; unable to keep a secret. ~কমল *n* lotus-like face. ~কান্তি *n* beauty/grace face. ~ক্ষতি *n* sore in the mouth. ~গহ্বর *n* mouth. ~চন্দ্র *n* moon-like face. ~চন্দ্রিকা *n* ceremonial viewing of each other's face by a bride and a bridegroom at a wedding. ~চপল *adj* loquacious; garrulous. ~চাপল্য *n* loquacity. ~চাপা *adj* tongue-tied; uncommunicative; reticent. ~চুন *n* pale face (for fear/shame etc). ~চোরা *adj* shy; timid; bashful; tongue-tied. ~ছুট *adj*=~-আলগা. ~ছোপ *n* shyness; bashfulness. ~চ্ছটা, ~চ্ছবি *nn* glamour/beauty of a face; complexion. ~ঝামটা *n* jawing; abuse; scolding. ~ঢাকা *n* veiling. ~তাড়া, ~নাড়া *nn*=~ঝামটা. ~দেখানি *n* gift offered on seeing the face of a bride for the first time. ~ধোয়া *n* washing one's face. ~নিঃসৃত, ~নির্গত *adjj* issuing/emerging from sb's mouth/face. ~পঙ্কজ=~কমল. ~পট *n* veil. ~পত্র *n* 1 preface; preamble; introduction. 2 mouthpiece. ~পদ্ম=~কমল. ~পাত *n* 1 commencement; inception; inauguration. 2 opening/ top plait of a folded cloth. 3 front; outward show. ~পাত্র *n* spokesman; leader (of a delegation). ~ পোড়া *n* 1 (in abuses) disgraceful/ scandalous person; rascal; scoundrel. 2 (showing affection) mischievous person; imp. 3 kind of monkey (হনুমান). ~পুড়ি *fem.* ~প্রক্ষালন=~ধোয়া. ~ প্রসাদ *n* light of the countenance; graciousness of aspect. ~ প্রসাধন *n* decorating/ painting the face. ~ফাঁস=~-আলগা. ~ফোড় *adj* outspoken. ~বন্ধ *n* preface. ~বর্ণ *n* colour of the face. ~বাদ্য *n* musical instrument sounded with the mouth. ~বিবর *n* mouth. ~বৈরস্য *n* bad taste in the mouth. ~ব্যাদান *n* act of opening the mouth wide; gaping. ~ভঙ্গি *n* act of making wry faces. ~ভার *n* sulkiness; ill humour; glumness. ~ভেংচানি *n* glumness; distortion of the face. ~মণ্ডল *n* face. ~মধু *n* 1 honeyed words. 2 saliva; spittle. ~ মারুত *n* breath. ~মার্জনা *n* washing/ cleansing the mouth. ~মিষ্ট *adj* honey-mouth; sweet-lipped. ☐*n* sweet/suave language. ~রক্ষা *n* face-saving. ~রন্ধ্র *n* mouth of a flute. ~রাগ, ~রুচি *n* colour of the face. ~রেখা *n* feature; mien; air. ~রোচক *adj* tasty; palatable; savoury; appetizing. ~রোচক আলাপ/কথাবার্তা *n* small talk; gossip; tittle-tattle. ~রোচক কথা *n* pleasant/ flattering words. ~লাবণ্য *n*=beauty of countenance. ~শশী=~চন্দ্র. ~শুদ্ধি, ~শোধন *nn* cleansing/ purifying the mouth; deodorization of the mouth by chewing betel-leaves, etc. ~শোভা *n* brilliancy of the face. ~শোষ *n* dryness of the mouth. ~শ্রী= ~লাবণ্য. ~সর্বস্ব *adj* efficient in tall talk (but not in action). ~সর্বস্ব ব্যক্তি *n* mere talker; windbag. ~সাপট *n* tall talk; boasting. ~স্থান *n* headquarters. ~স্রাব *n* (flow of) saliva.

মুখজ *adj* produced from/in the mouth. ☐*n* Brahmin.

মুখটি[১] *n* cork; stopper; cap; lip.

মুখটি[২]=মুখোপাধ্যায়

মুখতসর=মোখতসর

মুখবাসন *n* mouth-perfuming.

মুখর *adj* 1 talkative; garrulous; loquacious; voluble. 2 acrimonious in speech; quarrelsome; sharptongued; shrewish; foul-mouthed; scurrilous; speaking harshly/

abusively. **3** noisy; tinkling (as an anklet etc); loud; clamorous. **4** sounding; resonant/ eloquent with; expressive of; reverberating; resounding. মুখরা *fem.* ☐*n* shrew; vixen; termagant. ~তা *n* talkativeness; garrulity; noisiness. মুখরিত *adj* resonant/ eloquent with; full of noise; resounding; reverberating. মুখরিতা *fem.*

মুখসাট *n* **1** jawing; abuse; scolding. **2** tall talk; bragging.

মুখস্থ *adj* **1** committed to memory; memorized; learnt by heart. **2** lying in/within the memory. ~ করা *vt* memorize; commit to memory; learn by heart. ~ বলা *vt* speak from memory; say by rote. ~ বিদ্যা *n* learning by rote; rote-learning; book-learning.

মুখস্থিত *adj*=মুখস্থ (2)

-মুখা=-মুখো

মুখাকৃতি *n* 'form of the countenance'; mien; look; facial features; face.

মুখাগ্নি *n* fire put into the mouth corpse at the time of lighting the funeral pile.

মুখাচ্ছাদন *n* cover/ veil for the face; face-cloth (of a corpse).

মুখানি *n* (poet)=মুখখানি

মুখানো *vi* be eager/ready; crane one's neck in eagerness/ expectation: ছেলেটা যাবার জন্যে মুখিয়ে আছে.

মুখাপেক্ষা *n* waiting for others' order/ word; dependence upon another. মুখাপেক্ষী *adj* dependent upon; hanging on; at the mercy of. মুখাপেক্ষিণী *fem.* মুখাপেক্ষী হওয়া *vi* depend upon; hang on; be at the mercy of মুখাপেক্ষী ব্যক্তি *n* dependent; hanger-on; satellite. মুখাপেক্ষিতা *n* dependence; act of hanging on.

মুখাবয়ব=মুখাকৃতি

মুখামুখি, মুখোমুখি *adj* face-to-face; head-on; frontal; facing one another; end on: ~ লড়াই. ☐*n* altercation; wrangle. ☐*adv* face to face (with); vis-a-vis; tête-à-tête; eyeball to eyeball.

মুখামৃত *n* **1** saliva. **2** moisture of the mouth (said in connection of kissing). **3** wise saying/ soothing words of a saint/ great man.

মুখি *n* sprout/ eye of an arum. ~কচু=~.

-মুখী *suft* having the face of; faced=পোড়া~, রাবণ~.

মুখুজ্জে=মুখোপাধ্যায়

-মুখো *suff* **1** having the face of; faced: কালা~, ঘোড়া~. **2** facing: দক্ষিণ~. **3** towards: ঘর ~.

মুখোপাধ্যায় *n* a family name of some Bengali Brahmins.

মুখোমুখি ⇒ মুখামুখি

মুখোশ, মুখোস *nn* **1** mask. **2** disguise; hypocrisy; dissimulation. ~ পরা *vi* wear a mask; masquerade; disguise oneself; dissimulate. ~ খোলা *vi* unmask; throw off one's mask. ~ পরানো *vi* mask; disguise.

মুখ্য *adj* first; principal; chief; eminent; major. ~ আধিকারিক *n* chief officer. ~ ও অবর কর্মী *n* officers and men. ~কর্ম *n* (gram) direct object. ~কুণ্ডলি *n* (phys) primary coil. ~ক্রিয়া *n* primary action; (gram) principal verb. ~ খরচ *n* prime cost. ~ত *adj* principally; chiefly; particularly. ~তা, ~ত্ব *nn* pre-eminence; superiority; highest rank/ position. ~ নিরীক্ষক *n* chief auditor. ~ নির্বাহক *n* chief executive. ~মন্ত্রী *n* chief minister. ~ মহাধ্যক্ষ *n* chief commissioner. মুখ্যাঙ্ক *n* (math) cardinal number. মুখ্যার্থ *n* primary meaning of a word.

মুগ *n* kind of pulse; *Phaseolus mungo.*

মুগা *n* **1** kind of silk worm; *Muga coccoon.* **2** kind of coarse silk spun by the above silk worms.

মুগুর *n* hammer; mallet; any hammer-like weapon/implement; club; cudgel; rammer.

মুগ্ধ *adj* **1** charmed; fascinated; enchanted; infatuated; bewitched; captivated; spellbound. **2** perplexed; bewildered. **3** foolish; ignorant; innocent; artless; inexperienced; simple; naive. **4** engrossed; absorbed; entranced: ধ্যান~. মুগ্ধা *fem.* ~ করা *vt* enchant; charm; fascinate; captivate; infatuate; bewitch. ~বোধ *n* 'instructing the ignorant'; name of a celebrated Sanskrit Grammar by Vopa-deva.

মুগ্ধা *n fem* young and beautiful female.

মুঘল=মোগল

মুচকানো *vt vi* sprain; cause to sprain; twist; be wricked; wrick. মুচকি/ মুচকে হাসা *vi* turn one's lips in a derisive/ suppressed smile; smile. মুচকি/মুচকে হাসি *n* smile.

মুচড়ানো *vt* twist; contort; wring; wrench; wriggle.

মুচমুচ, মুচমুচে (onom) denoting a softer sound than মচমচ and মুচমুচে respectively.

মুচলেকা [T] *n* bond; recognizance (of criminals); agreement; written obligation. ~ দেওয়া *vi* furnish a bond; enter into a recognizance.

মুচি[১]**, মুচী** *nn* worker in animal leather; shoe-maker; cobbler; tanner. মুচিনী *fem.*

মুচি[২] *n* **1** crucible. **2** tiny saucer-shaped earthen vessel (for making cakes etc). **3** green coconut within which there is no water and no kernel.

মুচকুন্দ *n* a variety of champak flowers; *Pterospermum suberifolium.*

মুচুটী *n* **1** closed hand; fist. **2** snapping the fingers. **3** pair of forceps.

মুচ্ছুদ্দি, মুচ্ছুদ্দী=মুৎসুদ্দী

মুছলমান=মুসলমান

মুছা *vt* wipe; mop; swab; rub out; obliterate; erase; efface; expunge. ~**নো** *vt* cause to wipe, etc.

মুজতাহিদ [A] *n* religious director; supervisor/ superintendent in religious matters; prelate. ☐*adj* striving; contending.

মুজদা [P] *n* good news; good tidings.

মুজরা, মুজরো [A] *n* **1** trial of professional singing and dancing. **2** allowance; premium. **3** deduction.

মুজা=মোজা

মুজাদ্দিদ [A] *n* revivalist; renewer; modernist; saint; reformer.

মুজাহিদ [A] *n* warrior in the defence of true faith; crusader.

মু'জিয়া=মোজেজা

মুঞ্জ *n* species of rush/sedge-like grass; *Saccharum sara/munja*.

মুঞ্জরণ *n* blossoming; sprouting.

মুঞ্জরা=মঞ্জরা

মুঞ্জরিত=মঞ্জরিত

মুঞ্জরী=মঞ্জরী

মুট=মুঠ

মুটে *n* porter. ~**মজুর** *n* labourers; (derog) menial/ low-grade worker.

মুঠ, মুঠা, মুঠি, মুঠো *n* **1** clenched hand; fist. **2** handful. **3** hilt; handle; haft. **4** firm hold; grif. ~**মুঠ, মুঠামুঠা, মুঠিমুঠি, মুঠোমুঠো** *n* handfuls of. **মুঠার মধ্যে** *adv* under one's control.

মুড়কি, মুড়কী *n* parched rice coated with boiled sugar, honey or molasses.

মুড়ন *n* shaving.

মুড়নি, মুড়ুনি *n* shaving the head (as a punishment).

মুড়মুড় *n* (onom) denoting a softer sound than মড় মড়.

মুড়া[1]**, মুড়ো** *n* **1** head of a fish or an animal. **2** stump (of a tree); pollard. **3** extremity; end: রাস্তার ~, কাজের ~. **4** tip; corner: কাপড়ের ~. **5** torn piece of cloth. ~**মুড়ি, মুড়োমুড়ি** *adv* from beginning to end; from top to bottom.

মুড়া[2] *adj* **1** shaven; bald; shorn: ~ মাথা. **2** worn-out; decayed: ~ ঝাঁটা/খেংড়া. **3** lopped; pollarded: ~ গাছ. **4** dehydrated: ~ মাখন. **5** unadorned; naked; graceless; bare: ~ দালান. **6** blunt: ~ কোদাল.

মুড়া[3] *vt* **1** cover; wrap; enclose: কাগজে ~. **2** wind round; ravel: আঙুলে সুতা ~. **3** fold: বিছানা ~. **4** double up: হাঁটু ~. **5** contort; twist; bend: শরীর ~. **6** adorn.

মুড়া[4] *vt* **1** shave: মাথা ~. **2** eat off the top (of); pollard; lop: গাছ ~.

মুড়ানো *vt* **1** shave; get shaved. **2** pollard; lop; cause to pollard/ lop. ☐*adj* **1** shaven. **2** pollarded; lopped.

মুড়ামুড়ি *n* **1** repeated twisting/ bending/ contortion. **2** (fig) haggling; bargaining.

মুড়ি[1] *n* cereal of rice parched on hot sand.

মুড়ি[2] *n* **1** severed head (of fish, goat, etc). **2** counterfoil: ~চেক, চেক~. ~**ঘণ্ট** *n* a highly seasoned dish prepared with the head of a fish, goat, etc.

মুড়ি[3]**, মুড়ো** *n* **1** covering; wrapping: চাদর ~. **2** folded edge/ hem of cloth, etc. ~ **দেওয়া** *vi* cover/ wrap oneself with: চাদর ~ দেওয়া; hem. ~-**সেলাই** *n* hem; hem-stitch. ~-**সেলাই করা/ দেওয়া** *vi* hem; hem-stitch.

মুড়ো (colloq) ⇒ মুড়া[1], মুড়ি[3]

মুণ্ড *n* (shaven) head. ~ **ঘুরে যাওয়া** have one's head turned; be confused/dazed perplexed/ bewildered: রূপ দেখে ~ ঘুরে যাওয়া. ~**চ্ছেদ,** ~**চ্ছেদন** *nn* beheading; decapitation. ~**চ্ছেদ/** ~**চ্ছেদন করা** *vi* behead; decapitate. ~**পাত করা** *vi* **1** behead. **2** (fig) ruin; shower abuse on. ~**মালা** *n* string of human heads. ~**মালী** *adj* wearing a string of human heads. ~**মালিনী** *fem.* ☐*n* goddess Kali. **মুণ্ডাকার** *adj* shaped like a head; (bot) capitate.

মুণ্ডক *n* **1** shaver; barber. **2** head.

মুণ্ডন *n* shaving the head; tonsure.

মুণ্ডা *adj* shaved; shorn; bald. ☐*n* name of a tribe; Munda.

মুণ্ডিত *adj* shaved; bald; shorn; lopped; cropped. ~ **করা** *vt* **1** shave; shear; crop; tonsure. **2** pollard; lop. ~ **কেশ,** ~ **মস্তক** *adjj* shaven-headed.

মুণ্ডী *n*=মুণ্ড. ☐*adj* headed.

মুণ্ডু ⇒ মুণ্ড

মুত *n* (vulg) urine; piss. **মুতা** *vi* urinate; pass urine. **মুতানো** *vt* cause to urinate; relieve.

মুতওয়ালি, মুতওল্লী [A] *nn* trustee; superintendent; treasurer (of a mosque).

মুতফরাক্কা [A] *adj* miscellaneous; dispersed; scattered. ☐*n* sundries.

মুতাবিক, মোতাবেক [A] *adv* in accordance to; according to; corresponding to; conforming to.

মুৎসুদ্দি, মুৎসুদ্দী [A] *n* clerk; accountant.

মুথা *n* kind of grass with bulbous roots; Cyperus rotundis.

মুদা *vt* close; shut: চক্ষু ~.

মুদাফত [A] *n* former owner (of land).

মুদামি [A] *adj* permanent. ~ **বন্দোবস্ত** *n* permanent settlement.

মুদারা *n* (music) middle octave.

মুদি *n* grocer. ~**নী** *fem.* ~**খানা,** ~**র দোকান** *nn* grocer's shop.

মুদিত *adj* **1** delighted; pleased. **2** closed; shut: ~ কলি. ~ **করা** *vt* close; shut.

মুদী ⇒ মুদি

মুদ্গ ⇒ মুগ

মুদ্গর ⇒ মুগুর

মুদ্দই [P] *n* **1** plaintiff. **2** adversary.

মুদ্দত, মুদ্দৎ [A] *nn* **1** time; interval of time; length of time; duration; long time. **2** term. **মুদ্দতি, মুদ্দতী** *adjj* continuing/ enforced for a fixed period; periodical. **মুদ্দতি হুণ্ডি** *n* bill payable after date.

মুদ্দালেহ [A] *n* defendant.

মুদ্দাফরাস ⇒ মুর্দা

মুদ্রক *n* printer.

মুদ্রণ *n* **1** printing; impression; stamping. **2** sealing up; closing. **~ করা** *vt* print; stamp; impress. **~ ও নিদর্শ বিভাগ** *n* Press and Forms Department. **~ নিবন্ধ** *n* press register. **~ নিবন্ধক** *n* press registrar. **~ব্যয়** *n* printing cost. **~শোধক** *n* press corrector; proof-reader. **~শোধন** *n* press correction; proof-reading.

মুদ্রলিখ *n* typewriter. **মুদ্রলেখক** *n* typist.

মুদ্রা *n* **1** money; coin; piece of money; wealth. **2** seal; stamp; signet; stamping; sealing; seal-ring; signet-ring. **3** impression; stamp; print; mark. **4** name of particular positions/ interwinings of the fingers (24 in number, commonly practised by Hindus in religious worship). **6** pose/ posture of dancing; gesture. **7** mannerism. ~দোষ. **~কর** *n* printer. **~কর প্রমাদ** *n* printing mistake. **~কার** *adj* nummular. **~ক্ষর** *n* typewriter. **~ক্ষরযন্ত্র** *n* typewriter. **~ক্ষরিক** *n* typist. **~ঙ্কন** *n* stamping; sealing; impression. **~ঙ্কিত** *adj* stamped; sealed; impressed; marked. **~ঙ্কিত করা** *vt* stamp; seal; impress; mark. **~তত্ত্ব, ~বিজ্ঞান** *nn* numismatics. **~দোষ** *n* mannerism. **~বিজ্ঞানী** *n* numismatist. **~মান** *n* money standard. **~মূল্য** *n* value of a coin/ currency. **~মূল্য হ্রাস** *n* depreciation/ devaluation of a currency. **~যন্ত্র** *n* printing machine. **~যন্ত্রালয়** *n* printing press. **~রক্ষক** *n* keeper of seals; treasurer. **~লিপি** *n* lithograph. **~শঙ্খ** *n* (chem) litharge. **~স্ফীতি** *n* inflation (of money). **কাগজি ~** *n* paper money. **নিদর্শন ~** *n* token coin.

মুদ্রিকা *n* **1** coin. **2** printed letter.

মুদ্রিত *adj* **1** stamped; impressed; sealed; printed; marked. **2** closed; shut. **~ করা** *vt* stamp; impress; seal; print; mark; close; shut. **~ক** *n* press; publication. **~ক-বিবাচন** *n* press censorship. **~নয়ন, ~নেত্র** *adjj* having the eyes closed. **~নয়নে, ~নেত্রে** *advv* with closed eyes.

মুনকির [A] *n* one who denies; atheist.

মুনফা ⇒ মুনাফা

মুনশি, মুন্সী [A] *n* **1** writer; scrivener; secretary; clerk; amanuensis; tutor; language teacher. **2** a title of respect. **~আনা, ~য়ানা** *n* **1** clerk-like. **2** skill in drafting/ composition; erudition; skill; virtuosity; calligraphy's penmanship. **~গিরি** *n* clerkship; teachership; secretaryship. **খাস~** *n* private secretary.

মুনসিফ, মুনসেফ [A] *n* judge; subordinate judge. **মুনসেফি** *n* **1** office of a munsiff. **2** relating to a munsiff. ~গিরি=মুনসেফি (1).

মুনাক্কা ⇒ মনক্কা

মুনাজাত, মোনাজাত [A] *n* prayer; supplication; hymns. **~ করা/ পড়া** *vi* sing hymns; implore Allah; supplicate.

মুনাফা [A] *n* profit; advantage; gains. **~ লোটা** *vi* profiteer. **~খোর, ~বাজ** *adj* given to profiteering; profiteer. **~খোরি, ~বাজি** *nn* profiteering.

মুনাফিক, মুনাফেক, মোনাফেক [A] *n* hypocrite; dissembler; enemy at heart; infidel. **মুনাফেকি** *n* hypocrisy; dissimulation affectation; pretence.

মুনাসিব [A] *adj* proper; suitable; fit; becoming; convenient; meet; expedient; pertinent; apposite; agreeable; to one's liking/ choice.

মুনি *n* sage (practising ascetical meditation); ascetic; hermit; seer; saint. **~র আশ্রম** *n* hermitage. **~বর** *n* the best of sages. **~বাক্য** *n* saying/ utterance of a sage. **~ব্রত** *n* observing a Muni's vows; keeping perpetual silence. **~স্থান** *n* abode of Munis/ ascetics. **নানা ~র নানা মত** many men many opinions; sages differ.

মুনিব ⇒ মনিব

মুনিয়া *n* a tiny Indian bird; amadavat.

মুনিষ ⇒ মনিষ

মুনীন্দ্র *n* great sage/ ascetic.

মুন্সিফ ⇒ মুনসিফ

মুন্সী ⇒ মুনশি

মুফঃস্বল ⇒ মফস্বল

মুফতি [A] *n* Muslim jurist/ law officer; expounder of Muslim law.

মুফুত, মুফৎ [P] *adj* gratis; free; acquired without cost/labour; given away without return/ benefit. ❑*adv* without payment; gratuitously; free of cost.

মুবারক [A] *adj* blessed; auspicious; sacred; august; holy; happy; fortunate. ❑*n* blessing; congratulation; felicitation. ❑*int* welcome; all hail ! **~বাদ** *n* congratulation; good wishes; wishing success. ❑*int* may it be fortunate ! hail !

মুমিন [A] *n* believer. ❑ *adj* faithful; believing.

মুমুক্ষা *n* desire of liberation from desire of final emancipation. **মুমুক্ষু** *adj* desirous of final emancipation; eager to be free from; striving after emancipation.

মুমূর্ষা *n* desire of death; impatience of life. **মুমূর্ষাবস্থায়** *adv* in a dying state; on the point of death.

মুমূর্ষু *adj* **1** about to die; dying; moribund. **2** wishing to die. **~ দশা** *n* dying state. **মুমূর্ষুক্তি** *n* dying declaration.

মুয়াজ্জল [A] *adj* hasty; expedient. **মহর ~** marriage portion payable at the time of marriage.

মুয়াজ্জিন [A] *n* one who calls Muslims to pray; muezzin.

মুরগা (dial) ⇒ মোরগ

মুরগি, মুরগী [P] *n fem* hen; (neutral) fowl; chicken. **মুরগির ছানা** *n* chick; chicken. **চীনা ~** *n* guineafowl.

মুরচা, মুরুচা [P] *n* line of entrenchment; fortification; battery.

মুরছা (poet) ⇒ মূর্ছা

মুরজ *n* kind of drum; tambourine.

মুরতি (poet) ⇒ মূর্তি

মুরদ [A] *n* **1** manhood; prowess. **2** ability; strength; power.

মুরব্বি, মুরুব্বি *n* **1** elders; superiors. **2** guardian; patron; protector; supporter; head; fosterer. **~গিরি, ~য়ানা** *n* patronization; bossing. **~গিরি/ ~য়ানা করা/ ফলানো** *vi* lord it over; assume officiously the post of a guardian/ leader; assume the condescending air of a patron. **~র জোরে** on carpet consideration.

মুরলি, মুরলী *n* flute; pipe.

মুরশিদ [A] *n* spiritual teacher; guide; monitor; head of a religious order; instructor. **মুরশিদি** *n* kind of spiritual song.

মুরাকেবা [A] *n* meditation; contemplation.

মুরারি *n* Sri Krishna, enemy of Mura (the demon).

মুরি *n* drain; gutter; sewer.

মুরিদ, মুরীদ [A] *n* disciple; follower; student. **~ করা** *vt* make a disciple; admit into a religious order. **মুরিদি, মুরিদী** *n* discipleship.

মুরুব্বি ⇒ মুরব্বি

মুরোত ⇒ মুরদ

মুর্গি ⇒ মুরগি

মুর্তজা [A] *adj* chosen; selected; agreeable; a title of Hazrat Ali (ra) the fourth caliph of Islam.

মুর্দা [P] *n* dead body; corpse. **~ফরাশ** *n* undertaker.

মুর্শিদ ⇒ মুরশিদ

মুলতবি, মুলতুবি [A] *adj* postponed; adjourned; delayed; pending; deferred; held in abeyance: ~ পাওনা, ~ আইন, ~ সভা. **~ করা/ রাখা** *vt* postpone; put off; adjourn; defer; hold in abeyance.

মুলতান[১] *n* name of an Indian musical mode.

মুলতান[২] *n* a city in the Punjab. **মুলতানি** *adj* of Multan.

মুলা, মুলো *n* radish.

মুলাকাত, মোলাকাত [A] *n* meeting; interview; visit; encounter. **~ করা** *vt* meet; pay a view; have an interview with.

মুলানো *vi* bargain; haggle.

মুলুক, মুল্লুক [A] *n* country; kingdom; region; territory; dominion; realm.

মুলো ⇒ মুলা

মুল্ক ⇒ মুলুক, **মুল্কি** *adj* national; political; indigenous. **মুল্কি কাগজ** *n* country/ indigenous paper.

মুশকিল, মুসকিল [A] *n* difficulty; hardship; complicacy; trouble; hitch; rub; fix. **~ বেঁধেছে** There is a difficulty/ complicacy/ trouble/ hitch/ fix. **~ আসান** *n* removal of difficulty/ trouble. **মুশকিলে পড়া** *vi* fall into difficulty; get into a trouble; be involved in an intricacy.

মুশতারি [A]*n* the planet Jupiter.

মুশল=মুষল

মুশায়েরা [A] *n* meeting of poets.

মুষড়ানো *vi* **1** be down-hearted/ dejected/ depressed/ discouraged. **2** wither. ❑*adj* down-hearted; dejected; depressed; discouraged.

মুষল *n* **1** pestle (esp of a husking-tree which is operated in the seesaw manner of a mortar). **2** mace; club; mallet. **~ধার, ~ধারা** *nn* torrential downpour. **~ধারায়/ ~ধারে বৃষ্টি পড়া** rain in torrents/ cats and dogs.

মুষা *n* crucible.

মুষ্ক *n* testicle; scrotum. **~গ্রন্থি** *n* testicles. **~চ্ছেদন করা** *vt* castrated. **ছিন্ন~** *adj* castrated.

মুষ্টামুষ্টি *n* fighting with fists; fisticuffs.

মুষ্টি *n* **1** clenched hand; fist. **2** handful: এক ~ চাল. **3** handle; hilt; haft. **4** firm hold; grip. **5** box; fisticuff; blow; buffet. **~গত** *adj* gripped; firmly held/ controlled. **~ঘাত** *n* blow with the fist. **~পাত** *n* pummelling; boxing; **~প্রহার** =~ঘাত. **~বদ্ধ** *adj* clenched; closed: ~বদ্ধ হাত, having a hand/ hands clenched/ closed. **~ভিক্ষা** *n* handful of rice/ other cereals given in charity; alms. **~মেয়** *adj* only a handful of; a little/ few. **~যুদ্ধ** *n* boxing; buffeting; pugilistic encounter. **~যুদ্ধ করা** *vt* engage in a boxing contest; practice boxing. **~যোগ** *n* empiric/ popular remedy. **~যোদ্ধা** *n* boxer; pugilist. **মুষ্ট্যাঘাত**=~ঘাত. **মুষ্ট্যাঘাত করা** *vt* box; buffet.

মুসব্বর [A] *n* aloe.

মুসম্মৎ, মোসাম্মৎ [A] *n fem* a title prefixed to the names of females; lady; Miss or Mrs. ❑*adj* named; called.

মুসলমান [P] *n* Muslim; follower of Islam. **~ধর্ম** *n* Islam. **মুসলমানি, মুসলমানী** *adj* Islamic; Muslim (attrib). ❑*n* **1** circumcision. **2** the Muslim faith. **3** *fem* muslim woman.

মুসলিম [A] *n* Muslim; one who professes Islam. ❑(attrib) Muslim: ~ সভ্যতা.

মুসা [A] *n* Moses.

মুসাফা [A] *n* shaking hands with.

মুসাফির, মুসাফের [A] *n* traveller; passenger; stranger; (colloq) beggar. **~খানা** *n* inn; sarai;

rest house. মুসাফিরি *n* travelling; moving from place to place.

মুসাবিদা, মুসাবেদা [A] *n* sketch; (first) draft; first copy. ~ **করা** *vt* draft.

মুসিবত ⇒ মসিবত

মুসুরি ⇒ মসুর

মুস্কিল ⇒ মুশকিল

মুহতাজ, মোহতাজ *adj* needy; poor; indigent.

মুহরি[1], **মুহুরি** *n* **1** end of a sleeve/ leg of a pair of trousers; border. **2** drain; gutter; sewer; gullet; aqueduct; conduit. **3** strainer covering the mouth of a drain, etc. **4** nut of a bolt.

মুহরি[2], **মুহুরি** [A]*n* clerk; scribe; writer; amanuensis. ~**গিরি** *n* clerkship.

মুহাজির, মুহাজের *n* emmigrant; refugee; evacuee. **মুহাজিরিন** *pl.*

মুহাদ্দিস [A] *n* one having the knowledge of tradition/ sayings of the Holy Prophet; narrator; believer in tradition.

মুহাম্মদ, মুহম্মদ, মোহাম্মদ *n* the Holy Prophet Muhammad (sm).

মুহুঃ *adj* again (and again); repeatedly; now and again.

মুহুরি, মুহুরী=মুহরি[1] ও মুহরি[2]

মুহুর্মুহু *adv. adj* again and again; time and again; at every moment; constantly; repeated; constant; incessant.

মুহূর্ত *n* moment; instant; any short space of time; a particular division of time (=48 minutes); point of time. ~**কাল** *n* a moment; a while. ~ **মধ্যে** in a moment/ an instant; presently; in a triee/ jiffy; in two licks. ~**মাত্র** *n* only a moment. ❑*adv* only for a monent/ while. **মুহূর্তেক** *adv* for a moment. **এই মুহূর্তে** *adv* at this moment; just now; at once; immediately.

মুহ্যমান, মোহ্যমান *adj* stupefied; benumbed; stunned; extremely afflicted; bewildered. **মুহ্যমানা** *fem.*

মূক *adj* dumb; speechless; mute; silent; dumbfounded. ~**তা** *n* dumbness; muteness. ~-**বধির** *adj* deaf and dumb. ~-**বধির ব্যক্তি** *n* deaf-mute.

মূঢ় *adj* **1** stupefied; bewildered; perplexed; confused; uncertain/ at a loss about. **2** stupid; foolish; dull; silly; simple; ignorant. **3** mentally obsessed; infatuated. **4** indolent. **5** gone astray/ astray. ~**তা** *n* **1** bewilderment; perflexity; confusion. **2** ignorance; folly; stupidity. **3** infatuation. ~**ধী,** ~**মতি** *adjj* 'silly-minded'; simple; foolish.

মূত্র *n* urine. ~**কুণ্ড** *n* urinal. ~**কৃচ্ছ্র** *n* painful micturition; strangury. ~**ত্যাগ করা** *vi* urinate; pass urine/ water; piss; make water. ~**দোষ** *n* urinary disease. ~**ধানী**=~কুণ্ড. ~**নালী** *n* urethra. ~**নালী-প্রদাহ** *n* urethritis. ~**নিঃসরণ** *n* discharge of urine; urination. ~**নিরোধ** *n* obstruction/ retention of urine. ~**পথ** *n* urinary passage; urethra. ~**পুট** *n* lower belly. ~**বর্ধক,** ~**ল** *adjj* diuretic. ~**বর্ধক ঔষধ** *n* diuretic. ~**যন্ত্র** *n* (biol) kidney. **মূত্রাধার, মূত্রাশয়** *nn* bladder. **মূত্রাধিকারোগ** *n* diabetes.

মূরছা ⇒ মুরছা

মূরতি (poet)=মূর্তি

মূর্খ *adj* **1** stupid; foolish; dull; silly. **2** illiterate; uneducated; ignorant; inexperienced. ❑*n* stupid person; fool; idiot; dunce; illiterate/ uneducated person; inexperienced person. ~**তা** *n* stupidity; foolishness; illiteracy; lack of education; ignorance; inexperience; dulness. ~ **তা প্রকাশ করা** betray one's stupidity/ ignorance. ~**তাসূচক** *adj* betraying/ indicative of stupidity/ gross ignorance. ~**পণ্ডিত** *n* learned fool.

মূর্ছন *n* **1** fainting; swooning; syncope. **2** calcimining quicksilver with sulpher. **3**=মূর্ছনা.

মূর্ছনা *n* (music) modulation; melody; regulated rise or fall of sounds through the scale.

মূর্ছা *n* fainting; swoon; stupor; syncope. ❑*vi* (poet)=~ যাওয়া. ~ **যাওয়া** *vi* faint; swoon; become senseless/ unconscious. ~**গত,** ~**প্রাপ্ত** *adjj* fainted; swooned; lying unconscious. ~**গত বাই** *n* hysteria. ~**তুর** *adj* faint; fainted. ~**পন্ন**=~গত. ~**প্রাপ্তি** *n* fainting; swooning. ~**বায়ু,** ~**রোগ** *nn* epilepsy; syncope. ~**বায়ুগ্রস্ত** *adj* epileptic; syncopic; syncoptic. ~**ভঙ্গ** *n* passing off of faintness; recovery of consciousness from a fainting fit.

মূর্ছিত *adj* **1** fainted; swooned; stupefied; insensible. **2** intensified; augmented; increased; pervaded: অধরে ~ হাসি. **মূর্ছিতা** *fem.* ~ **হওয়া** *vi* faint; swoon; be stupefied; become unconscious/corporeal.

মূর্ত *adj* **1** embodied; incarnate; formed; corporeal; substantial; material. **2** concrete. **3** (phys) real. **4** palpable; tangible; visible; manifest. ❑*n* (phy) real image. ~ **হওয়া** *vi* assume from; be embodied/ incarnate; become tangible/ manifest/ visible palpable.

মূর্তি *n* **1** any solid body or materials. **2** embodiment; manifestation; incarnation. **3** form; shape; figure; appearance; person. **4** idol; image; statue. ~**ধর, ধারী** *adjj* having a body; corporeal; incarnate. ~ **ধারণ,** ~ **পরিগ্রহ** *n* incarnation; embodiment. ~**ধারণ/** ~ **পরিগ্রহ করা** *vi* assume a material body/ form; incarnate; assume a particular appearance. ~**পূজক** *n* idolator (*fem* idolatress); image-worshipper. ~**পূজা** *n* adoration of images; idolatry. ~**প্রতিষ্ঠা** *n* setting up of idols. ~**মন্ত,** ~**মান** *adjj* incarnate; corporeal; embodied; personified; visible; manifest; downright; mischievous: ~মান বদমাশ. ~**মতী** *fem.*

মূর্ধন্য *adj* (gram) cerebral: ~ণ. ❑*n* (gram) cerebral sound/ letter; a cerebral.

মূর্ধা *n* head. **~ভিষিক্ত** *adj* having the head sprinkled; anointed; consecrated; universally acknowledged. ❑*n* consecrated king.

মূর্বা, মূর্বী *nn* kind of hemp from which bow-strings are made.

মূল[১] *n* **1** root; foot/ lower part/ bottom of anything: বৃক্ষ~. **2** bulb; bulbous plant. **3** basis; foundation. **4** cause; origin. **5** beginning; commencement. **6** original text: ~ থেকে অনুবাদ. **7** roots of various plants. **8** capital; principal: সুদেমূলে. **9** (math) root; factor of a quantity. **10** (phil) element. ❑*adj* **1** original; first; fundamental; basic. **2** principal; primary; chief; main; real. **3** capital; principal. **অবরোহ ~** *n* (bot) hanging root. **অস্থানিক ~** *n* (bot) adventitious root. **প্রধান/ মুখ্য ~** *n* (bot) tap root. **~ উপাদান** *n* essential element. **~একক** *n* fundamental unit. **~ক** *n* **1** radish. **2** (chem) radical. **~কণা** *n* molecule. **~কর্ম** *n* **1** original/ principal work. **2** employment of roots for magical purposes. **~কার** *n* author of an original work. **~কারণ** *n* first/ original/ primary cause; root-cause; real cause. **~কেন্দ্র** *n* **1** principal centre; headquarters. **2** (commerce) head office. **3** (geom) radical centre. **~গত** *adj* basic; fundamental; radical. **~ গায়েন** *n* leading singer of a chorus. **~ গ্রন্থ** *n* original text/ manuscript. **~চ্ছেদ, ~চ্ছেদন** *nn* cutting away the roots; cutting up by the roots. **~চ্ছেদ/ ~চ্ছেদন করা** *vi* cut away the roots; cut up by the roots. **~জ** *adj* growing from a root; radical; formed at the roots of trees. **~জ প্রেষ** *n* (bot) root-pressure. **~জীবী** *adj* (bot) root parasite. **~ত** *adv* on the root; from the beginning; originally; primarily; basically; fundamentally; **~তা, ~ত্ব** *nn* state of being a root/ foundation/ source. **~তত্ত্ব** *n* principle; basic/ fundamental truth; first principle. **~ত্র** *n* (bot) root-cap. **~দ** *n, adj* (alg) rational (quantity). **~দ্রব্য** *n* basic thing; capital; stock. **~ধন** *n* capital; principal investment. **~ ধর্ম** *n* fundamental properties. **~ নীতি** *n* fundamental policy; basic/ first; principle. **~পদার্থ** *n* (science) elements. **~ প্রকৃতি** *n* **1** original/ elemental nature. **2** (philo) original root/ germ out of which matter or all apparent forms are evolved; primary cause. **~ ফল** *n pl* roots and fruits. **~ ভিত্তি** *n* foundation; ground-work; bed-rock; primary basis. **~ভূত** = মূলীভূত. **~ মধ্যরেখা** *n* (astron) prime meridian. **~ মন্ত্র** *n* **1** primary/ principal/ fundamental text; spell. **2** guiding principle; motto; creed; firm; resolve. **~ রশ্মি** *n* (phys) direct ray. **~ রস** *n* (rhet) primary sentiment (⇒ রস). **~রোম** *n* (bot) root-hair. **~ শিকড়** *n* main root. **~ সূত্র** *n* fundamental rule/ principal. **~ স্রোত** *n* fountain-head of a river; principal current. **মূলে** *adv* at the root/ base; originally; basically; in the beginning. **মূলে ভুল করা** get hold of the wrong end of the stick.

মূল[২] *n* (poet)=মূল্য. **~ করা** *vi* bergain; fix the price.

মূল[৩] *n* name of the seventeenth (or nineteenth) lunar mansion. **~ ত্রিকোণ** *n* (astrol) the third astrological house.

মূলক *suff* rooted in; springing from; causing; exhibiting; having a tendency towards; quality of: বর্ণনা~, বিভ্রান্তি~.

মূলাকর্ষণ *n* pull by the root. **~ করা** *vi* pull by the root.

মূলাক্ষ *n* (geom) radical axis.

মূলাধার *n* name of a mystical circle situated above the generative organs; navel.

মূলিক *adj* **1** original; principal; primary; fundamental. **2** living on roots.

মূলী *adj* having a root. ❑*n* plant; tree.

মূলীভূত *adj* become a root; become a source/ origin; lying at the root; fundamental; basic.

মূলোচ্ছেদ, মূলোৎপাটন *nn* cutting/ digging up the roots; utter destruction; eradication; extirpation. **~ করা** *vi* destroy utterly; eradicate; uproot; root out; extirpate.

মূল্য *n* **1** price; cost; rate. **2** value; worth. **3** wages; salary; payment for services rendered; remuneration; hire-charge; here. **4** capital stock. **~ দেওয়া** *vi* give a price of; remunerate; value; esteem; appreciate/ recognize the value/ worth of. **~-অনুসার** *adj* ad valorem. **~জ্ঞাপক** *n* quotation (of prices). **~ নির্ধারণ, ~ নিরূপক** *adjj* appraising; evaluating. ❑*n* appraiser; evaluator. **~ নির্ধারণ/ ~ নিরূপণ করা** *vi* appraise; evaluate. **~পত্র** *n* (commerce) bill. **~বান** *adj* valuable; precious; costly. **~ বিবর্জিত** *adj* devoid of price; worthless. **~বৃদ্ধি** increase/ rise in price; appreciation. **~বেদন (-পত্র)** quotation of price/ charge. **~হীন** *adj* valueless; worthless; futile; useless. **~হ্রাস** *n* fall in value; depreciation. **মূল্যানুসার** *adj* ad valorem. **মূল্যানুসারে** *adv* according to value/ price; ad valorem. **মূল্যাবধারণ/ মূল্যায়ন করা** *vi* assess/ estimate the price/ value of; evaluate; appraise. **বর্তমান ~** present worth.

মূষ[১]**, মূষিক** *n* rat; mouse. **মূষা** *fem.*

মূষ[২] *n* crucible.

মৃগ *n* **1** deer; fawn; gazelle; antelope; stag; musk-deer. **2** forest animal; wild beast. **3** game of any kind. **মৃগী** *fem* doe. **কস্তুরী~** *n* musk-deer. **কৃষ্ণসার ~** *n* black antelope. **চিত্র~** *n* spotted deer. **শাখা~** *n* monkey. **~চর্ম, ~ছাল** *nn* deer-skin. **~তৃষা, ~তৃষ্ণা, ~তৃষ্ণিকা** *nn* mirage. **~নয়না, ~নেত্রা, ~লোচনা** *adjj fem* fawn-eyed. **~নাভি** *n* musk. **~পতি** *n* lion. **~পালক** *n* shepherd. **~মদ** *n* musk. **~য়া** *n* hunting; chase. **~য়া করা** *vi* hunt. **~য়া করতে যাওয়া** *vi* go for hunting. **~য়াকারী** *adj* hunter; huntsman. **~রাজ**

n lion. ~**শিরঃ** *n* name of the third (or fifth) Nakshatra containing three stars. ~**শিরা**, ~**শীর্ষ** *nn* the Nakshatra Mriga. ~**শিশু** *n* fawn. ~**শৃঙ্গ** *n* stag's horn. **মৃগাক্ষী**=~নয়না. **মৃগাঙ্ক** *n* 'deer-marked'; the moon. **মৃগাঙ্কমৌলি**, **মৃগাঙ্কশেখর** *nn* names of shiva. **মৃগাজিন** *n* deer-skin. **মৃগাজীব** *n* professional hunter.

মৃগী *n* epilepsy.

মৃগেন্দ্র *n* lion.

মৃগেল *n* species of large fresh-water fish; *Cyprinus mrigala.*

মৃণাল *n* **1** stalk of the lotus/ water-lily. **2** edible fibrous root of some kinds of lotus. ~**কোমল** *adj* delicate like a lotus-fibre. ~**নিন্দিত** *adj* excelling even a lotus-stalk in beauty/ delicateness. ~**বাহু**, ~**ভুজ** *fem* having arms as delicate as a lotus-stalk.

মৃণালিনী *n fem* lotus plant; group of lotuses.

মৃণালী *n* lotus.

মৃত *adj* **1** dead; deceased; defunct; departed. **2** lifeless; inanimate. **3** extinct: ~ আগ্নেয়গিরি. ~**ক** *n* **1** dead man; corpse. **2** impurity contracted through the death of a relation. ~**কল্প**, ~**প্রায়** *adjj* almost dead; apparently dead; well-nigh dead; dying; moribund. ~**গর্ভা** *adj fem* whose fetus dies. ~**জন** *n* dead man. ~**দার** *adj* one whose wife is dead. ~**দার ব্যক্তি** *n* widower. ~**দেহ** *n* dead body; corpse. ~**বৎসা** *adj fem* whose offspring/ new-born child dies. ~**সঞ্জীবনী** *adj* (capable of) reviving the dead. ❑*n* anything (esp a remedy) capable of reviving the dead. **মৃতাশৌচ**=~ক(2).

মৃৎ *n* (in composition) earth; clay; loam. ~**কর** *n* potter. ~**কাণ্ডজ** *n* (bot) radical leaf. ~**ক্ষয় রোধ** prevention of soil erosion. ~**পাত্র** *n* earthen pot/ vessel; earthenware. ~**পিণ্ড** *n* clod of earth; lump of clay. ~**শিল্প** *n* potter's art; pottery; clay-modelling. ~-**সংরক্ষণ** *n* soil conservation.

মৃত্তিকা *n* earth; clay; loam; mud; soil; ground; the earth; the world. **বাহিত** ~ *n* (geog) transported soil. ~**গঠিত** *adj*=মৃন্ময়. ~**গর্ভ** *n* bowels of the earth; underground place; underground. ~**চূর্ণ** *n* powdered earth; mould. ~**নির্মিত**=মৃন্ময়. ~**পাত্র**, ~**ভাণ্ড**=মৃৎপাত্র (⇒ মৃৎ). ~**ভোজন** *n* geophagy. ~**ভোজী** *adj* geophagus.

মৃত্যু *n* **1** death; demise; decease; loss of life. **2** Hindu god of death; Yama. ~**কবল** *n* jaws of death. ~ **কামনা** *n* desire of death; death-wish. ~ **কামনা করা** desire to die; desire sb's death. ~**কামী** *adj* desirous of dying; desirous of sb's death; wishing to die. ~**কাল** *n* hour/ time of death; dying moment. ~**কালীন** *adj* pertaining to the hour of death/ dying moments. ~**কালীন এজাহার** *n* dying statement/ declaration. ~**কালে হরিনাম** *n* death-bed repentance. ~গ্রাস=~কবল. ~**গ্রাসে পতিত হওয়া** *vi* fall into the jaws of death; die; be killed. ~**চিন্তা** *n* thoughts about death. ~**চিহ্ন** *n* sign of death/ being dead. ~**জিৎ** *n* conquerer of death. ~**ঞ্জয়** *adj* who has overcome death; deathless; immortal. ❑*n*. Shiva. ~**ঞ্জয়ী** *adj* overcoming death. ~**তুল্য** *adj* death-like; deadly. ~**দ** *adj* death-giving; fatal. ~**দণ্ড** *n* death-sentence; capital punishment. ~**দণ্ড দেওয়া** *vt* sentence to death; award capital punishment (to). ~**দণ্ডে দণ্ডিত হওয়া** be sentenced to death. ~**দূত** *n* messenger of death. ~**ভয়** *n* fear of death. ~**ভীত** *adj* afraid of death. ~**মুখ**=~কবল. ~ **যন্ত্রণা** *n* death-agony; throes of death. ~**যোগ** *n* probability of occurrence of death. ~**রাজ** *n* god of death. ~**লক্ষণ**=~চিহ্ন. ~**লোক** *n* world of death. ~**শয্যা** *n* death-bed. ~**হীন** *adj* deathless; immortal; everlasting. ~**হেতু** *n* cause of death.

মৃদঙ্গ *n* kind of drum resembling a tom-tom; tabor. **মৃদঙ্গী** *n* one who plays the ~.

মৃদু *adj* **1** soft; delicate; mild; tender; gentle; pliant; supple. **2** slight; moderate; light. **3** slow: ~ গতি. **4** weak; feeble; dim. **5** not loud; low. **6** meek; effeminate. **7** noiseless; stealthy: ~ পায়ে. **8** not sharp/ keen: ~ ধার. ~**কর্ম**, ~**ক্রিয়া** *nn* softening; mollifying. ~ **গতি** *n* gentle/ slow motion. ❑*adj* moving/ going softly/ slowly/ gently; having a soft/ gentle gait. ~ **গতিতে** *adv* with a gentle/ slow motion; moving gently/ slowly/ softly. ~**গমনা** *adj fem*=~গতি. ~**গামী** *adj*=~গতি. ~**গামিনী** *fem.* ~**গম্ভীর** *adj* low and deep; rumbling. ~**গুঞ্জিত** *adj* murmuring/ humming softly. ~-**চারুভাষী** *adj* emitting soft and sweet sounds. ~**জল** *n* soft water. ~**জিহ্ব** *adj* having a soft tongue. ~**তা**, ~**ত্ব** *nn* softness; gentleness; mildness; tenderness; weakness. ~**নাদ**, ~**নাদী** *adjj* low-sounding. ~**নাদিনী** *fem.* ~ **পবন**, ~ **বায়ু** *nn* gentle breeze. ~**পাণি** *adj* having delicate hand. ~**ভাষী** *adj* speaking sweetly. ~**ভাষিণী** *fem.* ~**মন্দ** *adj* **1** low and sweet: ~মন্দ ধ্বনি. **2** moving gently and pleasantly: ~মন্দ হাওয়া. **3** (iron) light but sharp: ~মন্দ আঘাত. ❑*adv* slowly; gently and pleasantly. ~**রোমশ** *adj* (bot) downy. ~**স্পর্শ** *n* gentle touch. ❑*adj* soft to the touch. ~**স্বভাব** *n* gentle nature. ❑*adj* of gentle nature. ~**স্বর** *n* low voice. ~**স্বরে** *adv* in a low voice; in a whisper. ~**হৃদয়** *adj* tender-hearted.

মৃদুল *adj* soft; mild; gentle; tender. **মৃদুলা** *fem.*

মৃদ্ভাণ্ড =মৃৎপাত্র (⇒ মৃৎ)

মৃন্ময় *adj* **1** made of earth/ clay; earthen; mud-built. **2** (geog) argillaceous. **মৃন্ময়ী** *fem.* ~ **তলানি** *n* (geog) terrigenous deposit. ~ **পাত্র**=মৃৎপাত্র (⇒ মৃৎ). ~**মূর্তি** *n* image made of clay; clay-model. ~ **শিল্প**=মৃৎশিল্প (⇒ মৃৎ).

মে [E] *n* (the month of) May. ~ **দিবস** *n* May Day.

মেউ, মেও=মিউ. ~ **ধরা** (fig) take risks; bell the cat; run the gauntlet; bear the brunt.

মেওয়া [P] *n* fruit. ~**ওয়ালা** *n* fruiterer; fruit-seller. ~**ওয়ালী** *fem* fruiteress.

মেকি, মেকী [A] counterfeit; spurious; false; faked; face (attrib); forged; artificial; dissimulating: ~লোক; fake: ~ কথা. ❑*n* fake.

মেখলা *n* (ornamental) girdle; belt; zone; band; fillet; sword-belt or guard.

মেখেজুখে *adv* mixing properly: ~ খাওয়া.

মেগাফোন [E] *n* megaphone.

মেঘ *n* **1** cloud. **2** mass; multitude. **3** name of an Indian musical mode. ~ **করা** *vi* cloud (over): আকাশে ~ করেছে, the sky clouded over. ~ **কাটা** *vi* (of cloud) clear away; pass away: ~ কেটেছে, The clouds have cleared away. ~ **জমা** *vi* cloud; (of sky) become clouded. ~ **হওয়া** *vi* cloud. **অলক-/ উর্ণা-/ কুণ্ডল-**~ cirrus. **অলকান্তর-**~ cirro-stratus. **আস্তর-**~ stratus. **কোদালে/ কুড়ুলে** ~ mackerel sky. **জলো-**~, **ঝড়ো/ ঝঞ্ঝা-**~ nimbus. **পুঞ্জ-**~ cumulus. **পুঞ্জালক-**~ cirro-cumulus. **ভাঙা**~ scattered clouds. **রাঙা/ সিঁদুরে** ~ crimson-coloured cloud (which presages a storm). **হাঁড়িয়া** ~ dark mass of cluds. **হিঙ্গুলে** ~=রাঙা ~. ~**কজ্জল** *adj* darkened by thick mass of clouds; gloomy; ovarcast. ~**খণ্ড** *n* cloudlet. ~**গম্ভীর** *adj* deep as (the rumbling) of a cloud. ~**গর্জন** *n* roar/ rumble of clouds; thundering; thunder. ~**জ**, ~**জাত** *adjj* born of clouds. ~**জাল** *n* thick clouds; mass of clouds. ~**জ্যোতি** *n* flash of light; lightening. ~**ডম্বর** *n* thunder; roar/ rumble of clouds; thunder-clap. ~**ডম্বর শাড়ি** *n* sari having the colour of a nimbus; dark blue sari. ~**তিমির** *n* darkness resulting from a clouded sky; cloudy/ rainy weather. ~**দীপ** *n* lightening. ~**দুন্দুভি** *n* rumbling/ clap of thunder. ~**দূত** *n* 'cloud-messenger'; title of a celebrated poem by Kalidasa. ~**নাদ** *n* roar/ rumble of clouds; thunder. ❑*adj* roaring/ rumbling like thunder. ~**নাদী** *adj* sounding like thunder. ~**নির্ঘোষ** *n* rumbling of clouds; thunder. ~**পঙ্‌ক্তি** *n* line/ succession of clouds. ~**পুষ্প** *n* 'cloud-blossom'; water. ~**বর্ণ** *adj* having the low of a cloud. ~**বর্ত্ম** *n* atmosphere. ~**বহ্নি** *n* lighting. ~**বাহন** *adj* having clouds for a vehicle. ❑*n* Indra. ~**বাহী** *adj* producing clouds. ❑*n* smoke. ~**বিতান** *n* 'cloud-canopy'; expanded mass of clouds. ~**বিস্ফূর্জিত** *n* rumbling of clouds; thundering. ~**মণ্ডল** *n* atmosphere. ~**মণ্ডিত** *adj* overcast with clouds; cloudy; cloud-capped. ~**মন্দ্র** rumbling of clouds. ~**মন্দ্রস্বর** *n* thunderous voice. ~**ময়** *adj* formed/ consisting of clouds; clouded; cloudy. ~**মল্লার** *n* name of a Raga (রাগ). ~**মার্গ** *n* atmosphere. ~**মালা** *n* mass/ succession of clouds. ~**মালী** *adj* 'cloud-wreathed'; cloud-capped. ~**মেদুর** *adj* (darkness) dense with clouds; rendered cool for being overcast with clouds. ~**যোনি** *n* smoke. ~**রব**=~**মন্দ্র**. ~**রাগ**=~(3). ~**রাজি**, ~**রেখা** *nn* line of clouds. ~**লা** *adj* overcast with clouds; cloudy. ~**শ্যাম** *adj* dark as a cloud. ~**সঙ্ঘাত** *n* assemblage/ multitude of clouds. ~**স্তনিত** *adj* thunderous. ❑*n* thunder. **মেঘাগম** *n* break/ advent of the monsoon; rainy season. **মেঘাচ্ছন্ন** *adj* overcast/ covered/ overspread with clouds. **মেঘাড়ম্বর** *n* thunder. **মেঘাত্যয়** *n* autumn. **মেঘাবৃত**=মেঘাচ্ছন্ন.

মেচক *n* light green.

মেচেতা, মেছতা, মেছেতা *n* freckles. ~**পড়া** *vi* be freckled.

মেছুনি, মেছোনি, মেছুনী *n fem* fish-woman; fisherman's wife.

মেছেতা ⇒ মেচেতা

মেছো *n* fisherman; fisher; fish-monger. ❑*adj* **1** fishy: ~ গন্ধ. **2** fish-eating; piscivorous: ~ কুমির. **3** relating to fish: ~ বাজার. ~ **ঘেরি** *n* fish-garth; fish-weir. ~**বাজার**, ~**হাটা** *nn* **1** fish-market. **2** (iron) noisy place.

মেজ[১] [P] *n* table; desk.

মেজ[২], **মেজো** *adj* **1** second-born: ~ ভাই. **2** second in order of age/ seniority: ~ সাহেব.

মেজবান [P] *n* host; entertainer. **মেজবানি** *n* hospitality.

মেজমেজ, ম্যাজম্যাজ *n* (onom) denoting; feeling of sickness/ lethargy/ indolence/ lassitude/ malaise/ indisposition. **গা** ~ **করা** *vi* not feel well; ache all over. **মেজমেজে, ম্যাজম্যাজে** *adjj* lethargic; indolent.

মেজর *n* (in army) Major.

মেজরাব ⇒ মিজরাব

মেজাজ [A] *n* **1** mood (of mind). **2** temperament; disposition; frame of mind; nature; constitution; humour. **3** fit of ill-humour; temper. ~ **করা** *vi* show temper; give oneself airs. ~ **খারাপ করা** *vi* **1** spoil one's temper; get on one's nerves. **2** get/ fly into a temper. be angry; get out of temper. ~ **খারাপ থাকা** *vi* be out of humour. ~ **খারাপ হওয়া** *vi* run out of temper; loose one's temper. ~ **ঠাণ্ডা রাখা** *vi* keep one's head cool. ~ **ঠাণ্ডা করা** *vi* cool down; humour. ~ **দেখানো**=~ করা. ~ **ভালো থাকা** *vi* be in good humour. ~ **ভালো হওয়া** *vi* recover one's good humour. **খারাপ** ~ ill humour. **খিটখিটে** ~ *n* short temper; peevish/ bilious temperament. **খোশ** ~ *vi* good humour; cheerful temperament. **চড়া** ~ *n* choleric/ haughty/ firy temperament; hot temper. **টেঁড়া** ~ *n* pigheadedness; peevishness; hot-headedness. **ঠাণ্ডা** ~ *n* cool head; composure; even-temperedness; cool-headedness. **নরম/ নেক** ~ *n* good nature, good humour; light-heartedness; geniality; affability; amiability. **বদ** ~=খিটখিটে ~. **ভালো** ~ *vi* good humour; high spirits. রুক্ষ ~=খিটখিটে মেজাজ. হাসি খুশি ~ *n* jolly/ jovial temperament; joviality. **মেজাজি, মেজাজী** *adjj* **1** having a particular/ typical temperament: বদ মেজাজি. **2** moody; haughty; touchy; changeable, vainglorious; choleric; edgy; short-tempered; hot-headed. **3** stylish: মেজাজি ব্যাপার.

মেজে, মেঝে *nn* floor.

মেট [E] *n* **1** (naut) mate. **2** gangsman; foreman of a group of labourers. **3** prisoner appointed task-master of fellow-prisoners.

মেটা=মিটা

মেটুলি, মেটে *nn* liver of a goat/ sheep/ cow taken as food.

মেটে *adj* **1** made of earth/ clay; earthen: ~ কলস. **2** mud-built: ~ ঘর. **3** plastered with clay/ terra-cotta: এক~. **4** mud-coloured; muddy: ~ রং. **5** earthy: ~ গন্ধ. ~ **সাপ** *n* a non-venomous mud-coloured snake. ~ **সিঁদুর** *n* miniam; read lead.

মেঠাই=মিঠাই

মেঠো *adj* **1** of field; passing through a field: ~ পথ. **2** befitting an open field; demagogic; rabble-rousing: ~ বক্তৃতা. **3** rustic; boorish; insolent; churlish: ~ আচরণ. ~ **পথ** *n* path through an open field made by frequent movement of people; track; pathway; footpath. ~ **বক্তৃতা** *n* harangue; demagogy; pep talk. ~ **সুর** *n* country/ pastoral/ rustic tune.

মেড়মেড় *n* dullness (of colour). **মেড়মেড়ে** *adj* dull; lacklustre; mat.

মেড়া *n* **1** ram. **2** fighting ram. **3** henpecked husband.

মেডাল, মেডেল [E] *n* medal.

মেডিকাল, মেডিকেল [E] *adj* medical.

মেড়ুয়া=মেড়ো

মেড়ো *n* (derog) native of Marwar; Marwari; up-countryman of India.

মেঢ্র *n* **1** ram. **2** penis. ~**চর্ম**, ~**ত্বক** *nn* fore-skin; prepuce.

মেথর [P] *n* scavenger; sweeper. **মেথরানী** *fem.* ~**গিরি** *n* sweeper's job/ profession.

মেথি[1] *n* pillar in the middle of the threshing-floor to which oxen are bound.

মেথি[2], **মেথিকা, মেথী** *nn* fenugreek plant or its seed.

মেথি[3], **মেথী** ⇒ মাথি

মেদ *n* fat; marrow. ~**জ** *adj* produced from fat. ☐*n* bone. ~**বৃদ্ধি** *n* growth of fat; obesity; corpulence.

মেদা, মেদা মারা *adj* lacking in vigour/ energy; spiritless; effeminate; gutless; spineless. ☐*n* milksop; sissy; ninny.

মেদিনী *n fem* earth, world; soil; ground.

মেদুর *adj* **1** gentle; unctuous: ~ পবন. **2** smooth; soft; bland. **3** think; dense; thick like/ with; full of: মেঘ~.

মেধ *n* animal sacrifice; offering; oblation; sacrifice.

মেধা *n* mental power/ vigour; intelligence; intellect; (good) memory. ~**বান**, ~**বী** *adjj* intelligent; gifted; endowed with a good memory. ~**বতী**, ~**বিনী** *fem.*

মেধ্য *adj* fit for a sacrifice/ oblation; free from blemish; sacrificial.

মেনি, মেনী *n fem* female cat; pussy(-cat). ☐*adj* female: ~ বিড়াল. ~**মুখো** *adj* shy; bashful; timid.

মেম [E] *n fem* European woman; madam. ~**সাহেব**, ~**সাব** *nn* European woman; mem-sahib; madam.

মেম্বর, মেম্বার [E] *n* member.

-**মেয়** *adj* measurable; countable; calculable; estimable; discernable; cognizable.

মেয়াদ ⇒ মিয়াদ

মেয়ে *n fem* **1** daughter. **2** little girl; girl. **3** woman. ☐*adj* female; she: ~ হাতি; effeminate. ~**ছেলে** *n* woman; womankind; womenfolk. ~**মর্দ**, ~**মদ্দ** (colloq) *nn pl* men and women; husband and wife. ~**মর্দানি** *n fem* manly woman; Amazon. ~**মানুষ**=~ছেলে. ~**মুখো** *n* (of men) effeminate; timid; sheepish; womanly; womanish. ~**লি**, ~**লী** *adj* of women; feminine; womanly; girly; womanish; effeminate. ~**র চূড়া** *n* jewel of woman. ~**লোক** *n* woman; (derog) female.

মেরজাই ⇒ মির্জাই

মেরাপ [A] *n* **1** temporary shed built of straw, bamboo-poles, etc. **2** covering.

মেরামত [A] *n* repair; mending; reparation; reconditioning. ~ **করা** *vt* repair; mend; get repaired; recondition. ~ **হওয়া** *vi* be repaired/ mended. **মেরামতি** *adj* needing repairs; of repairing/ mending; to be repaired: মেরামতি ~. ☐*n* **1** repair; repairs; repairing; mending. **2** cost/ charges of repairing/ mending.

মেরু *n* **1** either of the two ends of the axis of the earth; pole. **2** backbone; spine. **3** the central/ the most prominent bead in a rosary. **4** the most prominent finger-joint in particular positions of the fingers. ~**করণ** *n* polarization. ~-**চুম্বকমাত্র** *n* (ply) pole-strength. ~**জ্যোতি** *n* polar lights; aurora polaris. ~**দণ্ড** *n* vertebral/ spinal column; spine; backbone. ~**দণ্ডহীন** *adj* invertebrate; (both lit and fig) spineless. ~**দণ্ডহীন প্রাণিবর্গ** *n pl* the invertebrata. ~**দণ্ডী** *adj* vertebrate. ~**দণ্ডী প্রাণিবর্গ** *n pl* the vertebrata. ~**প্রদেশ** *n* polar region. ~**প্রভা**=~জ্যোতি. ~**রেখা** *n* earth's axis; polar point. **উপাক্ষ**-~**রেখা** *n* the earth's axis minor. **পরাক্ষ**-~**রেখা** *n* the earth's axis major. **কু**~ *n* South Pole; Antarctica. **সু**~ *n* North Pole.

মেল[1] [E]*n* (postal) mail. ~**ট্রেন** *n* mail-train.

মেল[২] *n* **1** assemblage; meeting; gathering. **2** union; junction; association. **3** heredity of a family considered for matrimonial purposes: ফুলিয়া ~. **4** intercourse; mating (esp of domestic animal). **5** eye-salve; antimony.

মেলক *n* one who unites.

মেলন ⇒ মিলন

মেলা[১] ⇒ মিলা. ~**নো**=মিলানো (⇒ মিলা)

মেলা[২] *vi* **1** open: চোখ ~. **2** spread: কাপড় ~. **3** present; expose: দৃষ্টির সামনে মেলে ধরা. ~**নো** *vt* cause to open/ spread/ expose.

মেলা[৩] **1** fair; exhibition: বৈশাখী ~. **2** crowd; assembly; assemblage; gathering; concourse: বহু মানুষের ~. **3** society; company; association: কবিদের ~. **4** a particularly high number. ❑*adj, adv* great (in number/ quantity/ expanse); vast; abundant; numerous; lot of; great deal of; very: ~ লোক, ~ ঝামেলা, ~ দূর.

মেলানি *n* **1** crowd; assemblage; gathering. **2** union; meeting. **3** society; association. **4** parting; farewell; farewell greeting. **5** parting gift; present; gift.

মেলামেশা *n* social intercourse/ communication; (intimate) association; friendly terms; familiarity. ~ **করা** *vi* associate with; communicate socially with; rub shoulders with; make friend with.

মেলেচ্ছ (colloq)=ম্লেচ্ছ

মেশা=মিশা. **মেশানো**⇒ মিশানো (⇒ মিশা)

মেশামেশি= মিশামিশি(⇒ মিশা)

মেশিন [E] *n* machine.

মেষ *n* **1** sheep. **2** ram. **3** (astrol) the Aries. **মেষী, মেষিকা** *fem* ewe. ~**চর্ম** *n* sheep-skin. ~**তুল্য,** ~**বৎ** *adjj* sheepish. ~**পাল** *n* **1** flock of sheep. **2** shepherd. ~**পালক** *n* shepherd. ~**মাংস** *n* mutton. ~**যূথ** *n* flock of sheep. ~**শাবক** *n* lamb.

মেস [E] *n* company of persons taking meals together; mess. ~**বাড়ি** *n* mess-building; mess.

মেসো *n* husband of one's mother's sister/ cousin-sister; uncle.

মেস্ক [A] *n* musk.

মেহ *n* urine.

মেহগনি [E] *n* mahogany.

মেহন *n* **1** penis. **2** urine. **3** act of passing urine. **4** copulation.

মেহনত, মেহন্নত [A] *nn*=মিহনত. ~ **করা** *vi* toil; labour; work/ endeavour laboriously; exert oneself; sweat; make heavy weather of; go to great trouble. **মেহনতানা** *n* wages of labour; labour charge.

মেহমান [P] *n* guest. ~**খানা** *n* guest-house; guest-chamber. ~**দার** *n* host; entertainer. ~**দারি** *n* hospitality. **মেহমানি** *n* hospitality; entertainment; banquet.

মেহেদি *n* henna.

মেহেরবান [P] *adj* kind; loving; affectionate; generous. **মেহেরবানি** *n* kindness; favour.

মেহরাব ⇒ মিহরাব

মৈ ⇒ মই

মৈত্র *adj* coming from/ given by/ belonging to a friend; friendly; amicable; benevolent; affectionate; kind. ❑*n* **1** alliance based on good-will; friendship. **2** association. **3** friend. **4** a title of Brahmins.

মৈত্রী *n* friendship; friendliness; benevolence; good will. ~**ভাব**=~.

মৈত্রেয় *adj*=মৈত্র. ❑*n* মৈত্র (4).

মৈত্র্য ⇒ মৈত্রী

মৈথিল *n* king of Mithila. ❑*adj* relating belonging to Mithila. ~ **ভাষা** *n* language of Mithila.

মৈথিলী *n fem* **1** language of Mithila. **2** Sita (daughter of Janak, King of Mithila), wife of Rama. **2** woman of Mithila.

মৈথুন *n* copulation; coitus; sexual intercourse; cohabitation.

মৈনাক *n* name of a mythological mountain.

মোকদ্দমা ⇒ মকদ্দমা

মোকরর ⇒ মুকরর. **মোকররি** ⇒ মুকররী

মোকান [A] *n* house; dwelling; residence; home; abode; lodging.

মোকাবা [A] *n* toilet-box.

মোকাবিলা, মোকাবেলা=মুকাবিলা

মোকাম [A] *n* **1** station; halt; place of encamping; site. **2** dwelling; residence; abode; mansion. **3** (commerce) place of origin; trading-station; trading-post. **4** dignity. ~ **করা** *vi* stay; halt; put up; stop; settle; dwell; abide.

মোকুব ⇒ মৌকুফ

মোক্তসর ⇒ মোখতসর

মোক্তার [A] *n* legally appointed representative; attorney; agent; mukhtar; assignee. ~**কার** attorneyship. ~**নামা** *n* power-of-attorney; written authority. **মোক্তারি** *n* mukhtarship; attorneyship. **মোক্তারি করা** *vi* practise as a mukhtar/ attorney. **আম**~ *n* general agent. **খাস** ~ *n* special agent.

মোক্ষ *n* **1** emancipation; liberation; release from worldly existence/ transmigration; final/ eternal emancipation. **2** final beatitude; salvation of the soul. **3** death. **4** liberation of an eclipsed/ occulted planet; end of an eclipse. ~**ণ** *n* **1** liberating; emancipating; releasing. **2** rescuing; setting at liberty. **3** loosing; untying. **4** shedding. **5** causing to flow. **6** acquittance of an obligation. **7** casting; shooting; hurling. **8** effusion; bleeding. ~**ণ করা** *vi* free/ deliver from; liberate/ emancipate (from transmigration); loosen; untie; undo; detach; shed; cause to flow; cast; shoot; hurt; bleed; let blood; release. ~**ণ-প্রভার** *n* redemption charges. ~ণীয় *adj* to be liberated/ emancipated/ rescued. ~দ *adj* liberating; emancipating; giving final beatitude/ salvation of the soul. ~দা *fem.* ~দাতা *adj*=~দ. ❑*n* redeemer of the soul; giver of eternal emancipation; liberator. ~দাত্রী *fem.* ~দায়ক =~দ. ~দায়িকা, ~দায়িনী *fem.* ~ধাম *n* abode of eternal bliss. ~পথ *n* way/ means of emancipation. ~প্রাপ্তি, ~লাভ, ~সাধন *n n* attainment of eternal bliss/ emancipation. ~লাভ করা *vi* attain eternal bliss/ salvation/ emancipation.

মোক্ষম [A] *adj* unfailing; strong; irrefutable; undeniable; fatal; terrible: ~ অস্ত্র/ যুক্তি/ ঔষধ.

মোক্ষিত *adj* liberated; set free; emancipated.

মোগল [P] *n* Moghal. ❑*adj* Moghal. মোগলানী *n fem.* মোগলাই *adj* of the Moghals.

মোচ, মোছ *n* **1** moustache; mustache. **2** tip; point; nib: কলমের ~. মোচে তা দেওয়া *vi* **1** twist moustache to make it curl. **2** (fig) challenge; vaunt; brag.

মোচক *adj* relieving; liberating; emancipating. ❑*n* one who relieves (pain, etc).

মোচড় *n* **1** twist; wring; contortion; wrench. **2** wriggle; constraint; pressure. **3** (mech) torsion. ~ দেওয়া *vt* **1** twist; wring; contort; wrench. **2** put (undue) pressure on; constrain. মোচড়ানো=মুচড়ানো. ~-মোচড়ি *n* **1** repeated twisting/ wringing/ contortion/ wrenching. **2** wriggling. **3** persisting solicitation; higgling; importunity. ~-মোচড়ি করা *vt* **1** twist; wring; wrench; contort. **2** wriggle. **3** solicit/ higgle persistently; importunate.

মোচন *n* **1** liberating; emancipating; liberation; release. **2** loosing; loosening; untying: বন্ধন~. **3** shedding: অশ্রু~, পত্র~. **4** discharge; shooting; darting: শর~. ❑dispelling; removing; alleviation: দুঃখ~. ~ করা *vt* release; loosen; untie; set free; shed; discharge; shoot; dispel; alleviate; remove; wipe (away).

মোচনীয় *adj* to be released/ loosened/ untied/ set free/ discharged/ dispelled/ alleviated/ removed/ wiped; removable; that can be effaced/ blotted.

মোচা *n* cone of the banana. মোচাকার *adj* conical. ~খোলা *n* skin of the cone of the banana. ~চিংড়ি *n* prawn.

মোচিত *adj* relieved;loosened; untied; set free; discharged; dispelled; alleviated; removed; wiped; shed.

মোচ্য ⇒ মোচনীয়

মোছা ⇒ মুছা. ~নো=মুছানো

মোজা [P]*n* stocking; sock. গরম ~ *n* woolen socks. ফুল-~ *n* socks that come up to the knee; stocking. হাত-~ *n* gloves. হাফ~ *n* socks.

মোজাইক [E] *n* mosaic.

মোজেজা, মাজেজা [A] *n* miracle.

মোট[1] *n* **1** load; burden; bundle; luggage; baggage. **2** bale. ~ঘাট *n* luggage; baggage ~ঘাটসমেত bag and baggage. ~বাহক *n* porter.

মোট[2] *n* total; aggregate; sum total. ❑*adj* total; aggregate. ~দেওয়া *vt* add up; total. মোটের উপর on the whole; on an average; generally.

মোট[3] *adj* true; essential. ~ কথা **1** the sum and substance; the long and the short of it. **2** as a matter of fact; in point of fact; in fact; in short: ~ কথা, তাকে বাদ দিয়ে কিছু হবার নয়.

মোটর [E] *n* motor; motor-car. ~-গাড়ি *n* motor-car. ~গাড়ি চালানো *vi* drive a motor-car. ~গাড়ির চালক, ~-চালক *nn* motor-driver; motorist. ~মিস্ত্রি *n* motor-mechanic. ভাড়াটে ~-গাড়ি *n* taxi; taxi-cab.

মোটা *adj* **1** fat; corpulent; stout; bulky; big; obese; heavy; fleshy; plump. **2** thick; coarse: ~ কাপড়/ চাল. **3** voluminous; thick; massive: ~ বই. **4** handsome; high: ~ বেতন. **5** grave; hoarse; husky: ~ গলা. **6** large: ~ আয়. **7** blunt; dull: ~মাথা/ বুদ্ধি. **8** plain; simple: ~ কথা. **9** gross; rough; ordinary: ~ দাগ, ~ কাজ. **10** vulgar: ~ রুচি. ~ ভাত-কাপড় *n* plain living. ~নো, ~ হওয়া *vi* grow fat; put on flesh/ weight; fatten (up). ~মুটি *adj* **1** rough: ~মুটি হিসাব/ ধারণা. **2** moderate; middling: ~মুটি অবস্থা. **3** cursory: ~মুটি পাঠ. ❑*adj* approximate; nearly; roughly; grossly; moderately; on the whole; cursorily: ~মুটি এক বছর. ~সোটা *adj* stout and strong; burly; plump.

মোটে *adv* **1** in total; altogther; in all. **2** only; at all; only now; just now: ~তো আমরা এলাম. ~ই *adv* at all: ~ই না, not at all.

মোড় *n* turn; bend; crossing. ~ নেওয়া *vi* turn; bend.

মোড়ক *n* packet; wrapping; wrapper; carton; paper cover.

মোড়ন *n* **1** wrapping; covering. **2** bending; twisting.

মোড়ল *n* **1** village headman. **2** (iron) leader; ring-leader. মোড়লি *n* **1** position and function of a headman. **2** (iron) over bearing/ masterful manner; unnecessary bossing; domineering attitude.

মোড়া[1] *vt* ⇒ মুড়া[3], মুড়া[4]

মোড়া[2] *n* wicker stool.

মোড়ানো ⇒ মুড়ানো

মোড়ামুড়ি ⇒ মোচড়ামুচড়ি (⇒ মোচড়)

মোণ্ডা ⇒ মণ্ডা[1]

মোতা ⇒ মুতা (⇒ মুত). ~নো=মুতানো (⇒ মুত)

মোতাওয়াল্লি=মুতওয়ালি

মোতাবেক =⇒ মুতাবিক

মোতায়েন [A] *adj* posted; stationed; appointed; fixed; assigned; deputed; posted on guards. ~ করা/ রাখা *vt* post; station; appoint; depute; post on guard; keep ready at hand.

মোতি *n* pearl.
মোতিচুর ⇒ মিহিদানা (⇒ মিছি)
মোতিয়া *n* kind of small sweet-scented flower like the jasmine.
মোত্তাকি, মুত্তাকি [A] *adj* abstemious; God-fearing; pious; sober; temperate.
মোদক *n* **1** small round sweet-meat; any sweet-meat. **2** (Ayu) kind of pill. ❑*adj* invigorating; exhilarating.
মোদন *n* gladdening; delighting; gratifying.
মোদিত *adj* **1** pleased; delighted. **2** perfumed; scented; filled with fragrance.
মোদের *pron* (poet)=আমাদের
মোদ্দা [A] *adj* true; essential; main; gross. ❑*conj* but; nevertheless; however; in short: যাই বলো, ~ সুযোগটা হাতছাড়া কোরো না. **~ কথা** in point of fact; the long and the short of it; the chief thing; after all.
মোনা *n* pestle of a foot-driven husking-tree.
মোনাজাত ⇒ মুনাজাত
মোনাফেক ⇒ মুনাফিক
মোনাসেব ⇒ মুনাসিব
মোবারক ⇒ মুবারক
মোম [P] *n* beewax; wax. **~ মাখানো** *vt* wax. **~জামা, ~ঢাল** *nn* wax-cloth. **~দান, ~বাতিদান** *nn* candlestick. **~বাতি** *n* wax candle. **~বাতিবিক্রেতা** *n* wax-candler. **মোমের কাগজ** *n* wax-paper. **মোমের পুতুল** *n* wax-doll.
মোমিন ⇒ মুমিন
মো-মো ⇒ ম-ম
মোয়া ⇒ মোদক (1). **ছেলের হাতের ~** (fig) sth very easily obtainable; trifle.
মোয়াজ্জিন ⇒ মুয়াজ্জিন
মোর *pron* (poet) ⇒ আমার
মোরগ [P] *n* cock; fowl; chicken. **মুরগি, মুরগী** *fem.* **মোরগের ঝুঁটি** *n* cock's-comb. **মোরগের ডাক** *n* cock-a-doodle; crow. **~ফুল** *n* canna.
মোরব্বা [A] *n* preserve; confection; jam; preserved fruit.
মোরা *pron* (poet) ⇒ আমরা
মোরাকাবা ⇒ মুরাকেবা
মোরে *pron* (poet) ⇒ আমাকে
মোর্শেদ ⇒ মুরশিদ
মোলাকাত ⇒ মুলাকাত
মোলায়েম [A] *adj* soft; tender; gentle; smooth; mild; suave: ~ কাপড়, ~ কথা.
মোলাহেজা [A] *n* looking into; inspection; contemplating; consideration; notice; regard; examination.
মোল্লা [A] *n* **1** a very learned man; doctor. **2** priest. **3** school master. **4** judge; jurist; mullah. **~গিরি** *n* profession/ office of a mullah. **~তন্ত্র** *n* government by/ dominated by mullahs. **~র দৌড় মসজিদ পর্যন্ত** (derog) A mullah's knowledge does not extend beyond the mosque; one's knowledge is limited by one's station of l...

মোষ ⇒ মহিষ
মোষড়ানো ⇒ মুষড়ানো
মোসলমান ⇒ মুসলমান
মোসলেম ⇒ মুসলিম
মোসাফের=মুসাফির
মোসাম্মৎ ⇒ মুসম্মৎ
মোসাহেব [A] *n* **1** (originally) companion. **2** flatterer; sycophant; hanger on; toady; fawner; adulator. **মোসাহেবি** *n* flattery; adulation; fawning; soft-soap; obsequiousness; blandishments. **মোসাহেবি করা** *vi* indulge in flattery; be servile; fawn; carry favour with; adulate; massage sb's ego; toady; flatter; pander to.
মোহ *n* **1** (phil) darkness/ delusion of mind (preventing the discernment of truth and leading to believe in the reality of worldly objects); ignorance. **2** loss of consciousness; bewilderment; perplexity; distraction; infatuation; delusion; error; folly. **3** fainting; stupefaction; swoon. **4** deep attachment; dotage. **~ নিরসন করা** *vi* dispel illusion/ darkness of mind/ folly/ delusion; disillusion; disenchant. **~ক, ~কর** *adjj* causing illusion/ ignorance/ folly; infatuating; bewildering; enchanting; fascinating; illusive; causing to faint. **~গ্রস্ত** *adj* **1** deluded; mentally obsessed; infatuated (by love). **2** stupefied; bewildered; bewitched; enchanted. **3** fascinated; fondly attached. **4** fainted; swooned. **~ঘোর** *n* spell/ darkness of illusion/ delusion/ ignorance/ infatuation/ mental obsession. **~ঘোরে** *adj* under the spell of illusion/ ignorance. **~জনক**=~ক. **~জাল** *n* snare/ mesh of (worldly) illusion. **~তিমির**=~ঘোর. **~নিদ্রা** *n* slumber/ stupor coused by illusion; thoughtless confidence. **~পাশ**=~জাল. **~বদ্ধ** *adj* caught in the snare of illusion/ infatuation/ ignorance. **~বন্ধ, ~বন্ধন** *nn* bondage of illusion/ ignorance/ worldly attachment/ infatuation. **~ভঙ্গ** *n* disillusionment; disenchantment; recovery from a fainting fit. **~মদ** *n* pride caused by illusion/ ignorance. **~মন্ত্র** *n* spell/ charm causing infatuation/ delusion. **~ময়** *adj* illusive; illusory; full of illusious; enchanting; bewitching. **~মুগ্ধ** *adj* deluded; enchanted; bewitched; infatuated; beguiled. **~মুদ্গর** *n* 'hammer of ignorance/ infatuation', title of a work of Shankaracharya intending to dispel illusion.
মোহড়া ⇒ মহড়া
মোহতাজ ⇒ মুহতাজ
মোহন *n* **1** charming; enchanting; tempting; temptation; infatuating; seduction; bewitching. **2** the being deluded/ infatuation; enchantment; delusion. **3** stupor. ❑*adj* infatuating; enchanting; captivating;

charming. মোহনা, মোহনী *fem.* ~চূড়া *n* enchanting top-knot/ crest. ~ভোগ *n* kind of sweetmeat. ~মালা *n* variety of gold necklace. ~-মূর্তি *n* fascinating figure.

মোহনা, মোহানা *nn* mouth (of a river); estuary; outlet.

মোহনিয়া *adj* (poet) ⇒ মোহন

মোহনীয় *adj* producing delusion; exquisite; enchanting.

মোহন্ত ⇒ মহন্ত

মোহম্মদ ⇒ মুহাম্মদ

মোহর [P] *n* **1** gold coin. **2** seal; stamp.

মোহরত [A] *n* **1** ceremonial beginning/ renewal: হিসাবের খাতা ~. **2** opening ceremony: নতুন ছবির ~. **3** practice; skill; experience.

মোহররম [A] *n* **1** the first month of the Hijra year. **2** the tenth of the month of Muharram, observed in memory of the martyrdom of Imam Hossain and his companions.

মোহরার ⇒ মুহরি[২]

মোহা *vi* (poet) ⇒ মোহিত করা (⇒ মোহিত)

মোহাজের ⇒ মুহাজির

মোহাদ্দেস ⇒ মুহাদ্দিস

মোহানা ⇒ মোহনা

মোহান্ত ⇒ মহন্ত

মোহান্ধকার ⇒ মোহঘোর (⇒ মোহ)

মোহাফেজ ⇒ মহাফেজ

মোহাম্মদী, মোহাম্মদীয় *n,adj* Mohammedan; Muslim.

মোহাররম ⇒ মোহররম

মোহিত *adj* infatuated; deluded; enraptured; enchanted; charmed; bewitched; fascinated. ~ করা *vt* infatuate; delenchant; charm; captivate; bewitch; fascinate; hypnotize. মোহিতা *fem.*

মোহিনী *adj fem*=মোহন. ❑*n fem* **1** fascinating/ enchanting woman; woman of bewitching beauty/ personal charm. **2** (myth) an exquisitely bewitching figure of a woman assumed by Narayana to deprive the Asuras of the nectar (অমৃত) churned out of the ocean. **3** (also ~বিদ্যা) hypnotism; witchcraft; sorcery; enchantment. **4** dancer. ~মায়া *n* enchanting illusion. ~শক্তি *n* charm; magic spell; hypnotic power; power of enchanting/ bewitching.

মোহ্যমান ⇒ মুহ্যমান

মৌ ⇒ মউ

মৌকুফ [A] *adj* abolished; remitted; exempted; condoned. ❑*n* remission; exemption; condonation. ~ করা *vt* abolish; remit; exempt; condone; leave off. মৌকুফি খাজনা *n* revenue/ rent held in abeyance.

মৌক্তিক *n* pearl.

মৌখিক *adj* **1** oral; verbal; viva voce. **2** phoney; sham: ~ ভালোবাসা. **3** windy; sham: ~ বড়াই. ~ উপাসনা *n* oral prayer. ~ চুক্তি *n* verbal agreement/ contract. ~ পরীক্ষা *n* viva voce (test/ examination); oral test/ examination. ~ বন্ধু *n* false friend. ~ ভক্তি *n* insincere devotion.

মৌচাক ⇒ মউ

মৌজ ⇒ মউজ

মৌজা [A] *n* village; place; district; group of villages regarded as an administrative unit (for land administration).

মৌজুদ ⇒ মজুদ

মৌটুসকি *n fem* honey-tongued woman.

মৌত ⇒ মউত

মৌতাত *n* **1** pleasant stupor caused by drinking/ drugging; intoxication; inebriation; tipsiness. **2** drinking wine/ taking drugs at routine hours. **3** craving for liquor/ drugs at routine hours as felt by drinkers/ drug-addicts. ~ করা/ চড়ানো *vi* drink alcohol/ take drugs at the fixed hour; booze. ~ ছুটে যাওয়া *vi* be roused from stupor. ~ ধরা *vi* get intoxicated. ~ লাগা *vi* begin to craving for liquor/ drugs. মৌতাতের সময় *n* fixed hour for taking drugs/ drinking alcohol.

মৌন *n* silence; taciturnity. ❑*adj* observing silence; silent; taciturn. ~ত্যাগ *n* breaking silence. ~ ত্যাগ করা *vi* break silence. ~ধারী *adj* observing silence. ~বৃত্তি *n* observing a vow of silence. ~ব্রত *n* vow of silence. ~ব্রতী =~ধারী. ~ ভঙ্গ =~ ত্যাগ. ~ভাব *n* silence; reticence. ~ভাব ধারণ করা *vi* keep silence. ~ মূর্তি *n* silent figure. ~ সম্মতি *n* tacit consent. ~স্বভাব *adj* taciturn; uncommunicative; reticent; non-vocal; reserved. মৌনাবলম্বন করা *vi* make a vow of silence; keep silent. মৌনাবলম্বী *adj*=~.

মৌনী *adj* **1** observing silence; silent; taciturn; reticent. **2** speechless: বিস্ময়ে ~. **3** mute: ~ প্রকৃতি.

মৌমাছি ⇒ মউমাছি (⇒ মউ)

মৌরলা ⇒ মউরলা

মৌরসি, মৌরুসী [A] *adj* hereditary; ancestral; patrimonial; ~ settled hereditarily: ~ পাট্টা. ~ স্বত্ব *n* hereditary right.

মৌরি *n* aniseed.

মৌরী *n* bow-string.

মৌর্য *n* name of a dynasty; Maurya dynasty.

মৌল[১] *adj* derived from roots; basic; radical; fundamental; elemental; primary. ❑*n* (science) element. ~ নীতি *n* basic/ fundamental principle/ policy. ~ পদার্থ *n* (science) element. ~ শিক্ষা *n* basic education.

মৌল[২] *n* **1** bud; blossom. **2**=মহুয়া

মৌলবি, মৌলভি [A] *nn* learned man; professor; Muslim doctor of law.

মৌলা ⇒ মওলা

মৌলানা ⇒ মওলানা (⇒ মওলা)

মৌলি, মৌলী *n* **1** diadem; crown; crest. **2** head; top. **3** top-knot; hair ornamented and braided round the head.

মৌলিক *adj* derived from a root; original; fundamental; basic; primary; radical; primitive; prime: ~ সংখ্যা. ~তা originality. ~পদার্থ *n* (science) element. ~ সংখ্যা *n* prime number.

মৌলী *adj* crowned; diademed.

মৌসুম [A] *n* **1** season; period. **2** the monsoon; the rains; rainy season. **মৌসুমি, মৌসুমী** *adj* seasonal; periodical. **মৌসুমি বায়ু** *n* the monsoon.

ম্যাও ⇒ মিউ. ~ **ধরা** ⇒ মেও ধরা (⇒ মেউ)

ম্যাগাজিন [E] *n* **1** magazine; periodical publication. **2** chamber for holding cartridges to be fed into the breech of rifle/ gun; magazine.

ম্যাচ[১] [E] *n* matcher; match-box.

ম্যাচ[২] [E] *n* contest; match.

ম্যাজম্যাজ ⇒ মেজমেজ

ম্যাজিক [E] *n* magic. ~-**লন্ঠন** *n* magic lantern.

ম্যাজিশিয়ান [E] *n* magician.

ম্যাজিস্ট্রেট [E] *n* Magistrate.

ম্যাজেন্টা [E] *n* magenta.

ম্যাটম্যাট, ম্যাড়ম্যাড় ⇒ মেড়মেড়

ম্যাদা ⇒ মেদা

ম্যানেজার [E] *n* manager (*fem* manageress). **ম্যানেজারি** *n* managership. **ম্যানেজারি করা** *n* act as a manager; manage.

ম্যান্ডারিন [E] *n* mandarin (chinese).

ম্যাপ [E] *n* map. ~ **দেখা** *vi* read a map. ~ **রচনা করা** draw a map.

ম্যালেরিয়া [E] *n* malaria. ~**ঘটিত** *adj* malarial. ~-**জ্বর** *n* malarial fever.

ম্রক্ষণ *n* **1** rubbing in; anointing. **2** ointment; oil.

ম্রিয়মাণ *adj* **1** dying; moribund. **2** distressed; dejected; glum; melancholy; sad; sorrowful; gloomy. **ম্রিয়মাণা** *fem*.

ম্লান *adj* **1** pale; haggard; faded. **2** withered; shrivelled; shrunk. **3** sad; cheerless; dejected; sorrowful; glum; melancholy. **4** weak; exhausted; languid; feeble; fatigued; wornout. **5** dim; darkened; gloomy; mat; lack-lusture; tarnished. **6** unhappy. ~**তা**, ~**ত্ব, ম্লানি, ম্লানিমা** *nn* withered/ faded condition; depression; dejectedness; languor; paleness; pallor; haggardness; sadness; melancholy; dimness; withering; fading; dullness; glumness; gloominess. ~**ছায়া** *n* shadow of gloom. ~ **দৃশ্য** *n* distressing sight. ~ **মুখ** *n* sad/ darkened countenance. ❑*adj* having a darkened countenance. ~**মুখে** *adj* with a sad/ gloomy face; dejectedly; glumly; cheerlessly. **ম্লানায়মান** *adj* getting pale/ dim/ dull/ dim/ haggard; withering; shrivelling; fading.

ম্লায়মান *adj* fading; darkening; languishing; withering; away.

ম্লিষ্ট *adj* **1** withered; faded; faint. **2** spoken indistinctly/ barbarously; indistinct.

ম্লেচ্ছ *n* **1** foreigner; non-Aryan; barbarian. **2** man of an outcast race; any person who does not speak Sanskrit and does not conform to usual Hindu Institution. **3** Greek settler of India. **4** wicked/ bad man; sinner. **5** (linguistics) barbarism; slang. ❑*adj* wicked; barbarous. ~**জাতি** *n* a man belonging to *mlecchas*; barbarian, savage; mountaineer. ~**তা** *n* condition of barbarians; barbarism. ~ **দেশ**, ~**মণ্ডল** *nn* foreign/ barbarous country. **ম্লেচ্ছাচার** *n* customs and practices of *mlecchas*; barbarous practice; non-Hindu customs and practices. **ম্লেচ্ছাচারী** *adj* adopting the customs and practices of *mlecchas*; practising non-Hindu/ evil customs; barbarous; barbaric.

ম্লেচ্ছিত *n* **1** foreign tongue. **2** (linguistics) barbarism.

য

য *n* the twenty-sixth consonant of the Bengali alphabet.

যই=জই

যক *n* (colloq) **1**=যক্ষ. **2** closely guarded riches of an extremely miserly person; mammon; miser's hoard: ~ রেখে যাওয়া. **3** extremely miserly person; scrooge; mammonist; curmudgeon. ~ **আগলানো** *n* hoard treasure; be stingy/ miserly. ~ **দেওয়া** *vt* **1** inter ceremonially a living child together with one's riches in the belief that the ghost of the child would guard the riches. **2** (facet) cheat sb of his money. **যকের ধন** *n* **1** riches guarded by a ghost. **2** miser's hoard.

যকাত=জাকাত

যকৃৎ *n* liver. ~ **কোষ** *n* hepatic cyst. ~ **প্রদাহ** *n* hepatitis.

যক্ষ *n* **1** name of a class of semi-divine beings (attendants of Kuvera). **2** ghost; spirit. **3** (iron) extremely miserly person; scrooge. **যক্ষী, যক্ষিণী** *fem*. ~**পুরী** *n* city of Kuvera (কুবের). ~**বিত্ত** *n* riches like those of Yaksha; riches that one guards but cannot make use of. ~**রাজ** *n* Kuvera, the king of Yakshas.

যক্ষনি, যক্ষুনি (colloq)=যখনই

যক্ষ্মা *n* pulmonary disease; consumption; tuberculosis. **রাজ**~ *n* phthisis.

যখন *conj* when; while; whilst; as; whereas; because; since. ~**ই, যখনি** *conj* whenever; as soon (as); no sooner (than): তুমি ~ই বলবে, আমি চলে আসব. ~**কার** *adj* of a particular/ specified time; the time of which: সে ~কার কথা বলছে

~কার যা তখনকার তা every work has its own time; everything must be done in its own proper time. **~-তখন** *adv* at all times; in (season) and out of season; (much too) frequently (and often vexatiously); whenever one likes; every now and then; at any hour or times: সে ~-তখন আসে. ❑*adj* **1** inopportune: ~-তখন আসা. **2** critical: রোগীর ~-তখন অবস্থা. **~ যেমন তখন তেমন** as the occasion/ situation demands.

যজন *n* **1** act of worshipping; worship. **2** act of sacrificing; sacrifice. **~-যাজন** *n* act of worshipping or sacrificing on behalf of one's ownself and on behalf of others; ministration.

যজমান *n* person paying the cost of a sacrifice; instituter of a sacrifice. **যজমানে** *adj* performing sacrifices on behalf of others: ~ বামুন.

যজুঃ, যজুর্বেদ *n* the Yajurveda ('the sacrificial Veda'). **যজুর্বেদ্য** *adj* familiar with the Yajurveda. **যজুর্বেদীয়** *adj* relating to the Yajurveda.

যজ্ঞ *n* **1** worship; devotion; prayer; act of devotion/worship. **2** sacrifice; oblation; offering; burnt offering. **3** (fig) great and pompous affair/ceremony. **~কর্ম** *n* sacrificial rite/ceremony. **~কুণ্ড** *n* a hole in the ground for receiving the sacrificial fire. **~কৃৎ** *adj* worshipping; performing a sacrifice. **~ডুমুর** *n* variety of figs; *Figus glomerata*. **~ধূম** *n* smoke of sacrificial fire. **~পশু** *n* sacrificial animal; victim. **~পাত্র** *n* sacrificial vessel. **~বেদি** *n* altar for sacrifice. **~ভূমি, ~শালা, ~স্থল, ~স্থান** *nn* place for sacrifice. **~সূত্র** *n* sacrificial thread/cord. **যজ্ঞাগ্নি, যজ্ঞানল** *nn* sacrificial fire. **যজ্ঞাঙ্গ** *n* part/means/instrument/requisite of sacrifice. **যজ্ঞান্ত** *n* end/conclusion of a sacrifice.

যজ্ঞীয় *adj* suitable/fit for sacrifice; sacrificial.

যজ্ঞেশ্বর *n* lord of sacrifice; Vishnu.

যজ্ঞোপবীত *n* investiture of youths of the three twice-born castes with the sacred thread; (in later times) the thread itself.

যৎ[১] (in composition) *pron*=যদ্. **~কালে** *conj* at the time when; when; whilst. **~কিঞ্চিৎ, ~সামান্য** *adj* (only) a little; very little; paltry; insignificant; meagre. **~পরোনাস্তি** *adj* extreme; utmost. ❑*adv* extremely; exceedingly.

যৎ[২] *n* name of an Indian musical measure.

যত[১], যতো *conj, adj, adv* **1** as many/much: ~ আসে ~ যায়. **2** all; whatever; whatsoever: ~ দলবল নিয়ে হাজির, সে-ই ~ নষ্টের মূল. **3** the more: ~ পায়, তত চায়. **4** as: ~ দিন যাচ্ছে, সে বুঝতে পারছে. **~ই** (emphatic of ~) however (much): ~ই চেষ্টা কর, however hard you try; ~ই সামান্য হোক, however little it may be. **~কাল** *adv, conj* as long (as); so long. **~কিছু** *adj, adv* whatever; whatsoever; every thing. **~ক্ষণ**=~কাল. **~ক্ষণ না** *prep, conj* till; until. **~খানি** *adj, adv* as far(as); as much/many (as); as long (as); so far (as): আমি ~খানি জানি. **~গুলি, ~গুলো** *adj, adv* as many (as); all the + *noun* + that ..: এখানে ~গুলি বই আছে. **~টা, ~টুকু**=~খানি. **~দিলো** *adj, adv* as long (as); so long; as many days (as); till: সে ~দিন না ফেরে. **~দূর** *adj, adv* as far (as). **~বার** *adj, adv* every time that; as many times (as); as often (as): আমি ~বার এখানে এসেছি. **~ নষ্টের গোড়া** the root of all evils/mischief. **~ বড়ো মুখ নয় তত বড় কথা** (fig) audacious utterance; have the effrontery to; get above oneself.

যত[২] *adj* restrained; controlled; held in; governed. **~চিত্ত** *adj* restrained in mind. **~ব্রত** *adj* observing vows; firm of purpose. **~যতাত্মা** *adj* self-restrained.

যতন *n* (poet)=যত্ন

যতি[১] *n* **1** (prosody) pause; caesura. **2** (gram) stop. **3** (music) pause. **~চিহ্ন** *n* punctuation-mark. **~পাত, ~ভঙ্গ** *nn* metrical fault/breach. **~ভ্রষ্ট** *adj* wanting the caesura.

যতি,[২] যতী *n* ascetic; devotee; hermit. **যতিনী** *fem.*

যতেক *adj, conj* (archaic, poet) as many/much; all: ~ বাসনা মোর.

যতেন্দ্রিয় *adj* having the organs of sense restrained; chaste; pure.

যত্ন *n* **1** effort; exertion; energy; zeal; trouble; pains; care; endeavour. **2** labour; laborious effort; toil; diligence. **~ করা/নেওয়া** *vi* **1** exert one's self; endeavour; take pains; make effort; perseve; attend to carefully; look after; mind; take care of. **2** labour; toil; strive to obtain; strive after; **~ত, ~পূর্বক** *adv* through/with effort; diligently; zealously; carefully; laboriously; with care. **~বান, ~শীল** *adjj* making effort; taking pains about; diligent; strenuous; careful; heedful; mindful; assiduous; attentive; zealous. **~বতী, ~শীলা** *fem*.

যত্র *adv, conj* where; wherein; wherever; whither; in/to whichever place; as much (as). **~তত্র** *adv* anywhere; here and there; everywhere; at random; anywhere and everywhere: ~তত্র ময়লা ফেলা. **~ আয় তত্র ব্যয়** spending as much as one earns.

যথা *adv, adj, conj* **1** in which manner/way; as; according as; like. **2** as for instance/ example; namely. **3** as it is/was. **4** that; so that; in order that. **5** as soon as. **6** because; since. **7** according to what is right/ proper; properly; correctly. **8** to the utmost degree/ amount/ number. **9** right; proper; fitting. **যথাংশ** *adv* according to shares/ portions; in due proportion; proportionately. ❑*n* quota. **~কথা** *n* true statement. **~কর্তব্য** *adj* proper to be done;

proper duty. ❑*adv* in accordance with one's duty; as one's duty warrants. **~কাম** *adj* conformable to desire. ❑*adv* acting according to desire/ wish; as one likes; at pleasure; conformably according to wish. **~কামী** *adj* self-willed; headstrong; obstinate. **~কাল** *n* proper time (for anything); suitable moment. **~কালে** *adv* in due time; at the right/ usual/ proper/ suitable time; in time; in due course; in good time. **~ক্রমে** *n* in due order. **~ক্রমে** *adv* in due/ regular order/ succession; successively; respectively. **~গত** *adv* **1** as (previously) gone. **2** as come; as one came. **~গুণ** *adv* according to qualities/endowments. **~জাত** *adj* just as born; stupid, foolish; barbarous; outcast. **~জ্ঞান** *adv* to the best of one's knowledge/judgement; according to (one's) knowledge. **~তথ** *adj, adv* conformable to truth/the exact state of the case; exact; accurate; precise; right; in conformity with truth/reality; precisely; exactly; fitly; duly. **~তথা**=যত্রতত্র (⇒ যত্র). **~দিষ্ট** *adj, adv* corresponding to what has been enjoined/directed; complying with/obedient to the order; according to a direction/instruction. **~দৃষ্ট** *adv* as seen/observed. **~নিয়ম, ~নিয়মে** *adv* in accordance with the rule/law/ formalities; duly; in due form. **~নুপূর্ব** *adv* according to a regular series; successively; respectively; conforming to the regular/due order/succession/sequence. **~ন্যায়** *adv* according to rule/justice; rightly; fitly. **~পূর্ব** *adv* as before/previously; in succession; one after another. **~পূর্ব তথা পর** no change in the condition/state; (iron) as bad as ever. **~বৎ** *adv* **1** duly; properly; rightly; suitably. **2** as before; without change. **~বিধি, ~বিহিত** *adj, adv* formal; formally; as is prescribed/due; in accordance with the rule/law/ formalities/ prescription. **~ভাগ** *n* prorate. **~ভিপ্রেত, ~ভিমত, ~ভিরুচি** *adv* as wished/intended/desired; according to one's desire/wish; as one pleases. **~মূল্য** *adj, adv* worth the price; according to price. **~যথ** *adj* precise; accurate; fit; exact. ❑*adv* **1** in a proper manner; as is fit/proper; suitably; rightly; fitly. **2** one after another; according to the due order/sequence/succession. **3** accurately; exactly; rightly; justly; precisely; correctly. **~যথভাবে** *adv*=~যথ. **~যোগ্য** *adj* proper; fit; as one deserves; suitable; fitting; just; becoming; consonant with propriety; as is fit. **~যোগ্যভাবে** *adv* in a befitting manner; properly; fitly; suitably. **~রণ্যং তথা গৃহম্** (fig) no change in the condition. **~রীতি** *adv* as usual; according to usage/custom/practice; duly. **~রুচি** *adj* according to liking/pleasure/ inclination/ taste. **~শক্তি** *adv* to the utmost of one's power; to the best of one's abilities; as much as one can. **~শাস্ত্র** *adv* according to precept/rule; according to the codes of law; conforming to scriptures. **~শ্রুত** *adv* as heard. **~সময়** *n* right/proper time. **~সময়ে** *adv* at the proper time. **~সম্ভব** *adv* as far/much/many as possible. **~সর্বস্ব** *n* whatever one possesses; one's entire possessions. **~সাধ্য**=~শক্তি. **~সাধ্য চেষ্টা করা** try one's best/utmost. **~স্থান** *n* right/proper place. **~স্থিত**=~বৎ.

যথায় *adv* where; wherein.

যথার্থ *adj* true; genuine; right; just; accurate; exact; correct; real; authentic: actual; proper. **~ত** *adv* truly; justly; accurately; exactly. **~তা** *n* truth; genuineness; correctness; exactness; authenticity; veracity; accuracy; exactitude.

যথেচ্ছ, যথেচ্ছা *advv* according to wish; at will/pleasure; as one pleases/wishes/ desires/ likes/chooses. **যথেচ্ছাচার** *n* willfulness; indiscipline; reckless conduct; recklessness. **যথেচ্ছাচারী** *adj* willful; reckless; wayward; self-willed; wild. **যথোচ্ছাচারিণী** *fem.*

যথেপ্সিত *adj* wished for. ❑*adv* according to wish/desire; as desired.

যথেষ্ট *adj* enough; sufficient; abundant; profuse. ❑ *adj* at pleasure; according to wish/inclination.

যথোক্ত *adv* as said/told previously.

যথোচিত, যথোপযুক্ত *adjj*=যথাযোগ্য (⇒ যথা). **~রূপে** =যথাযোগ্যভাবে

যথোপযোগী *adj*=যথাযোগ্য (⇒ যথা)

যদবধি *adv, conj* since which time; up to which time; till when; since when; from which time.

যদি *conj* if; in case that; provided that; when; since; lest: নেবে ~ এখনি নাও. **~ই** *adv, conj* even if; if perforce. **~ও, ~চ** *conj* though; although; even if/though. **~না** *conj* unless; if not. **~বা** *conj* if; even if; if perforce; or; if.

যদু *n* (myth) name of an ancient Indian hero. **~কুল** *n* family of Yadu/Yadavas. **যদুনাথ, ~পতি** *nn* chief/lord of the Yadavas/Yadus. **~বংশ** *n*=~কুল. **~মধু** *n* (derog) the man in the street, Tom, Dick and Harry; common man/run.

যদৃচ্ছ *adv*=যদৃচ্ছাক্রমে

যদৃচ্ছা *n* **1** self-will; spontaneity; free-will; one's pleasure. **2** accident; chance. **~ক্রমে** *adv* according to one's own desire/will; freely; spontaneously; voluntarily; at pleasure. **~প্রবৃত্ত** *adj* voluntary; spontaneous; free. **~লব্ধ** *adj* obtained by chance/accidentally/without effort/at will. **~লাভ** *n* obtaining what one desires.

যদ্দিন=যতদিন (⇒ যত)

যদ্ভবিষ্য *adj* who says 'what will be will be', fatalistic; resigned. ❑*n* unenterprising person.

who relies on fate and is heedless of the present; fatalist.

যদ্যপি=যদিও

যন্তর *n* (colloq)=যন্ত্র

যন্ত্র *n* **1** instrument; apparatus; machine; machinery; engine; mechanical contrivance; appliance; implement; device; tool. **2** organ: শ্বাস~. **3** surgical instrument. **4** musical instrument. **5** mystical diagram supposed to possess occult powers. **6** grindstone. **~কৌশল** *n* mechanical device; mechanism. **~কৌশলী** *n* mechanical engineer; technician; mechanic. **~গৃহ** *n* manufactory. **~চালক** *n* machineman; operator. **~চালনা** *n* operation of a machine. **~তন্ত্র** *n pl* tools and materials. **~নির্মাণ** *n* machine-making. **~নির্মাণকৌশল** *n* art of making machines/tools. **~নির্মাণবিদ্যা** *n* mechanical engineering. **~নির্মাতা** *n* tool-maker; machinist; mechanician. **~পাতি** *n* machinery; tools and implements. **~পেষণী** *n* grindstone. **~প্রকৌশল** *n* mechanical engineering. **~প্রকৌশলী** *n* mechanical engineer. **~বিজ্ঞান** *n* mechanics; mechanical engineering. **~বিজ্ঞানবিদ** *n* mechanic; mechanical engineer; machinist. **~বিদ, ~বিৎ** =~বিজ্ঞানবিদ. **~বিদ্যা**=~বিজ্ঞান. **~শালা** *n* machine-room; machine-shop; tool-house. **~শিল্প** *n* industry. **~শিল্পী** *n* **1** mechanic; mechanical engineer. **2** instrumentalist. **যন্ত্রের ন্যায়** like a machine/robot/an automaton. **অণুবীক্ষণ ~** *n* microscope. **দূরবীক্ষণ ~** *n* telescope. **বাষ্প~** *n* steam-engine. **মুদ্রা~** *n* printing machine. **শিল্প~** *n* tool. **সীবন~** *n* sewing-machine.

যন্ত্রক *n* **1** turn's wheel; lathe. **2** grindstone.

যন্ত্রণা *n* **1** pain; affliction; anguish; agony; suffering; torment; torture; pang. **2** trouble; pest. **~ দেওয়া** *vi* pain; torment; afflict; torture; hurt; cause pain; trouble; gale; anguish. **~ পাওয়া** *vi* be pained/anguished/afflicted; agonized; writhe; be in pain/anguish. **~কর, ~জনক, ~দায়ক** *adjj* painful; agonizing; hurtful; sore; troublesome; tormenting; anguishing; distressing; cruel; grievous. **~কাতর, ~ক্লিষ্ট** *adjj* in pain; suffering; tormented; tortured; agonized; anguished; distressed; afflicted. **~দাতা** *adj* tormenting; torturing. ☐*n* tormentor; torturer. **~দাত্রী** *fem.*

যন্ত্রিত *adj* **1** restrained; curbed. **2** fettered; bound; confined.

যন্ত্রী *n* **1** (music) instrumentalist. **2** machineman; operator; artisan. **3** director. **4** conspirator; plotter; machinator; wire-puller; intriguer.

যব *n* **1** barley; barley-corn. **2** (palmistry) figure/mark on the hand resembling a barley-corn. **3** a measure of length. **4** an unit of weight.

যবক্ষার *n* **1** carbonate of potash. **2** potassium nitrate. **~জান** *n* nitrogen.

যবদ্বীপ *n* Java. **~দ্বীপবাসী** *n, adj* Javanese. **~দ্বীপীয়** *adj* Javanese; Javan.

যবন *n* **1** Ionian Greek; Greek. **2** non-Hindu. **3** (taboo) Muslim. **যবনী** *fem.*

যবনানী *n pl* scripts of the (Ionian) Greek settlers of ancient India.

যবনিকা *n* **1** screen; curtain. **2** (theatre) drop-curtain. **3** যবনী (⇒ যবন). **~ উত্তোলন করা** *v* **1** draw the curtains; raise the drop-curtain. **2** reveal; disclose. **~পতন, ~পাত** *nn* drop of a curtain (between the acts/at the end of a play); (fig) termination/shelving (of an affair). **~পাত করা** *vi* (fig) draw a curtain over sth. **~র অন্তরালে** behind the scenes; in camera.

যবসুরা *n* malt liquor.

যবাগূ *n* boiled barley; gruel made of barley.

যবুথবু=জবুথবু

যবে *adv, conj* (old use) when.

যবোদর *n* a lineal measure (= $\frac{1}{8}$ inch).

যম[1] *n* **1** self-control; forbearance; restraint; any great moral rule or duty. **2** self-restraint (as the first of the eight means of attaining mental concentration).

যম[2] *n* **1** the Hindu god of death. **2** death. **3** the planet Saturn. **4** annihilator; killer; destroyer. **5** antidote: রোগের ~. **যমী** *fem* Yama's twin-sister. **যমে ধরা** *vi* be at death's door; be in the jaws of death; die; be seized with a ruinous passion. **যমের অরুচি** *n* an utterly repugnant person. **যমের দোসর** *n* a second Yama; a very fearful person. **যমের বাড়ি** *n*=যমের মুখ; to the jaws of death. **~কিঙ্কর** *n* Yama's servant/messenger. **~ঘর** *n*=যমালয়. **~জয়ী, ~জিৎ** *adj* who has conquered Yama; deathless; immortal. **~জাঙ্গাল** *n* the Milky Way. **~দণ্ড** *n* Yama's rod; (fig) death-like mortification. **~দূত** *n* **1** Yama's messenger/minister (employed to bring departed spirits to Yama's judgement-seat and thence to their final destination). **2** (fig) messenger carrying a bad news. **3** (fig) person of monstrous appearance. **~দ্বার** *n* Yama's south gate; gates of death/hell; death's door; death. **~দ্বারে যাওয়া** *vi* die; meet one's death; join one's ancestor. **~দ্বিতীয়া** *n* the second day in the light half of the month Kartik. **~পুকুর** *n* a vow observed by unmarried Hindu girls in the month of Kartik. **~পুরী** *n* city/abode of Yama. **~ভগিনী** *n* the river Yamuna. **~যন্ত্রণা, ~যাতনা** *nn* torment inflicted by Yama; death-agony; pangs of death; deathly/terrible affliction. **~রাজ** *n* king Yama, the lord of death.

যমক *n* 1 religious obligation/observance; restraint. 2 twin; twins. 3 (rhet) repetition in the same stanza of words or syllables similar in sound but different in meaning; paronomasia. 4 (bot) connate leaf. ❑*adj* twin; twin-born; doubled; twofold.
যমজ *adj* twin-born; twin. ❑*n* twins.
যমন *n* restraining; governing.
যমল *adj* twin; paired; doubled. ❑*n* singer in a duet. **~-গান** *n* duet (song).
যমানিকা, যমানী *nn* plant with acrid seeds used in medicine; *Ptychotis ajowan.*
যমালয় *n* city/abode of Yama. **যমালয়ে দেওয়া/ পাঠানো** *vi* 1 send to the jaws of death, give the death blow to; dispatch; bump off. 2 destroy/spoil utterly. **যমালয়ে যাওয়া** *vi* die; be killed; join one's ancestors; perish; give up the ghosts; be damned.
যমিত *adj* restrained; checked.
যমী *adj* self-controlled. ❑*n* one who restrains himself or subdues his senses.
যমুনা *n* the river Jamuna.
যযাতি *n* (myth) name of a celebrated monarch of the lunar race.
যশ *n* fame; renown; celebrity; good name; glory; (good) reputation; honour; credit. **~ গাওয়া** *vi* sing sb's praises; glorify; celebrate sb's fame; eulogize; acclaim; laud; extol; exalt. **~মান** *n* fame and honour. **~স্কর** *adj* conferring glory on; glorious for; bringing fame/renown. **~স্কাম** *adj* desirous of fame/glory; ambitious. **~স্কামনা** *n* desire of fame/renown. **~স্বী** *adj* illustrious; famous; celebrated. **~স্বিনী** *fem.*
যশঃ=যশ. **~কীর্তন** *n* spreading abroad/ proclaiming the glory (of sb). **~কীর্তন করা** = যশ গাওয়া. **~ক্ষয়** *n* loss of fame/reputation; disgrace; discredit. **~খ্যাপন** =~কীর্তন. **~পটহ** *n* drum; double drum. **~শেষ** *n* death. **~স্তম্ভ** *n* monument of fame/glory.
যশদ *n* zinc.
যশো *n* (in compound)=যশ. **~গান, ~গাথা** *n* song of praise; eulogy; panegyric. **~গান গাওয়া**=যশ গাওয়া (⇒ যশ). **~দ** *adj* conferring fame/renown. ❑*n* quicksilver. **~দা** *fem.* ❑*n* Sri Krishna's foster-mother. **~দাদুলাল, ~দানন্দন** *n* Sri Krishna (son of Yashoda). **~ধন** *n* fund/stock of fame. ❑*adj* one whose wealth is fame; renowned; famous. **~ভাগী** *adj* rich in glory; famous; renowned. **~ভাগ্য** *n* luck/destiny to earn fame. **~মণ্ডিত** *adj* crowned with fame. **~মতী**=~দা. **~মন্দির** *n* temple of fame. **~ময়** *adj* glorious; famous. **~ময়ী** *fem.* **~রশ্মি** *n* splendour of glory. **~রাশি** *n* heap/mess of glory; great fame; wide celebrity. **~রেখা** *n* (palmistry) line of fame. **~লিপ্সা** *n* greed for fame; thirst for glory. **~লিপ্সু** *adj* greedy for fame. **~লাভ করা** *vi* earn fame; attain glory. **~হর** *adj* depriving of reputation. **~হানি** = যশঃক্ষয় (⇒ যশঃ). **~হীন** *adj* shorn of glory.
যষ্টি *n* 1 any support; staff; stick; walking-stick, prop; wand; rod; mace; club; cudgel. 2 pole; pillar; perch. 3 stem; stalk; branch; twig. 4 anything thin or slender: অঙ্গ~, ভুজ~. 5 string; thread (esp of pearls). 6 crutch: খঞ্জের ~. 7 liquorice. **~গ্রহ** *adj* carrying a stick/staff. **~ প্রহার করা** *vt* cudgel; flagellate. **~মধু** *n* liquorice.
যষ্টিকা *n* 1 string of pearls. 2 staff; stick; club. 3 a particular pearl ornament/necklace. 4 liquorice.
যহুর [A] *n* manifestation; appearing.
যা[১] *n fem* wife of one's husband's brother; sister-in-law.
যা[২] *second pers imper* of যাওয়া (used as an exclamation) oh; dear me; nonsense; blast it! **ঐ যা, গেল যা** *int* (expressing mild regret/ disgust) oh dear!
যা[৩] *pron* (colloq) which; what; that; whichever; whatever: তুমি যা জানো, বলো. **যা-ই** *pron* whatever; whichever: সে যা-ই বলুক .... **যা কিছু** *pron* whatever; everything. **যাচ্ছে তাই** *adj, adv* whatever one pleases; utterly contemptible/ bad/ugly/ worthless: যাচ্ছেতাই লোক. **যা-তা** *n* nonsense: কী যা-তা বলছ ! ❑*adj* 1 worthless; contemptible; shoddy; trashy; deplorable; lousy: যা-তা খাবার/বই. 2 aweful; horrible; beastly, messy: যা-তা অবস্থা. 3 wayward; bizarre; strange; whimsical: যা-তা চিন্তা. **যা হবার** *adj* inevitable. **যা হোক** *adv* however; in any case.
যাই *conj, adv* since; because; just as; as soon as: ~ বললে তাই তো শুনলাম.
যাও *second pers imper* of যাওয়া (used to express protest/ disapprobation/ remonstrance/ derisive incredulity): stop it! **আরে ~, ~ যাও,** I want no more of your nonsense! dash it! what do I care ?
যাওন *n* going; departure; setting out; exit; parting; leaving.
যাওয়া *vi* 1 go; leave: আপনি কবে যাবেন ? 2 depart; leave: ট্রেন আজ যাবে না. 3 move: নতুন বাড়িতে কবে যাচ্ছেন ? 4 set out; start: আমরা এখনই যাচ্ছি. 5 elapse; pass: সময় যাচ্ছে. 6 proceed; advance: তুমি যাও, আমি পরে আসছি. 7 be terminated; end; come to an end: তাঁর চাকরিটা গেল. 8 die; pass away; be gone: বাবা তো গেলেন. 9 be lost; perish; be destroyed: জীবন/চোখের দৃষ্টি/ রাজ্য ~. 10 broach; attack: আলোচনা করতে গিয়ে বলেছিলাম. 11 suffice/be enough for: এ-চালে আর কতদিন যাবে ? 12 last: শার্টটা বেশি দিন যাবে না. 13 wear out; wear away: জুতোর তলাটা একেবারে গেছে. 14 be sold; sell: মালটা আজ কততে

যাচ্ছে? **15** be spent: শুধু শুধু অনেকগুলি টাকা গেল! **16** work; function; run: ঘড়িটা ঠিক যাচ্ছে না, শরীর ভালো যাচ্ছে না, I am not keeping well. **17** pass off: জ্বর ~. **18** be attracted: দৃষ্টি ~. **19** be inclined: মন ~. **20** (used after many verbs to complete or modify their meanings): বলে ~, পড়ে ~, করে ~, উঠে ~. ❑*n* =যাওন. **~-আসা** *n* coming and going; frequenting; visiting; intercourse; access. **যেতে বসা** *vi* be on the point of being ruined/lost/destroyed.

যাঁতা = জাঁতা

যাঁতি = জাঁতি

যাঁহা (also **~তক**) *adv, conj* where; as far as; as soon as; just as.

যাকাত [A] *n* charity; alms.

যাকে *pron* whom. **~তাকে** *n* **1** (to) a complete stranger; (to) a nobody: ~তাকে ধরে তো আর মেয়ে দেওয়া যায় না. **2** inept/ inexperienced person; novice; raw recruit; booby; greenhorn: ~তাকে দিয়ে কি কাজ হয়? **3** unworthy/ unfit person: ~তাকে ও-সকল কথা বলা ঠিক হয়নি.

যাগ=যজ্ঞ

যাচক *n* one who asks/prays (for); petitioner; beggar; mendicant. **যাচিকা** *fem.*

যাচন[১], যাচনা *n* begging; soliciting; asking (also in marriage); prayer; request; petition; entreaty for; solicitation of. **যাচনা করা** *vi* ask/beg (for); solicit; entreat; implore; pray for.

যাচন[২]=যাচাই. **~দার** *n* one who estimates the quality and value of a thing; appraiser; estimator.

যাচা[১] (⇒ যাচন[১])

যাচা[২] *vi* estimate/determine the quality, value etc. of sth; appraise; evaluate; compare; try (out); put to test; assay; verify. **~ই** *n* appraisal; valuation; estimation; comparison; test; trial; verification; testing; assay. **~ই করা** *v* = ~. **~নো** *vt* have/get sth appraised/ evaluated/ assayed etc.

যাচিত *adj* **1** asked; begged; solicited for; **2** entreated; importuned. **3** asked in message. **4** required; requisite; necessary. **~ক** *adj* borrowed. ❑*n* anything borrowed. **~ব্য** *adj* to be asked for.

যাচিতা *n* petitioner; suitor; wooer. **যাচিত্রী** *fem.*

যাচ্ছেতাই ⇒ যা[৩]

যাচ্ঞা = যাচন[১]

যাচ্য *adj* to be asked for. **~মান** *adj* being asked for.

যাজক *n* **1** priest; clergyman; cleric. **2** one who offers sacrifices/oblations; sacrificer. **~তন্ত্র** *n* hierocracy. **~তা, ~বৃত্তি** *nn* priesthood; clericity; vocation of a priest. **~ সম্প্রদায়** *n* priesthood; clerical order; the clergy.

যাজন *n* **1** act of conducting a religious service in the capacity of a priest. **2** sacrificing for others; act of performing a sacrifice. **~ বৃত্তি** *n* **1**=যাজক বৃত্তি (⇒ যাজক). **2** stipend/allowance given to a priest; benefice.

যাজনিক *adj* priestly; clerical; ecclesiastical. ❑*n* priest.

যাজি, যাজ্য *nn*=যাজক

যাজিকা *n fem* priestess; clergy woman.

যাজ্ঞসেনী *n fem* Draupadi, daughter of king Yajnasena (of the Mahabharata).

যাজ্ঞিক *n* **1** one versed in sacrificial ritual; priest. **2** sacrificer. ❑*adj* relating/ belonging to sacrifice; sacrificial.

যাঠা *n* cudgel; hammer; iron cudgel used as a weapon in war in ancient time.

যাতনা *n* acute pain; torture; torment; agony. **~কর, ~দায়ক** *adjj* painful; agonizing.

যাতব্য *adj* approachable; vulnerable; accessible; assailable.

যা-তা ⇒ যা[৩]

যাতায়াত *n* **1** coming and going; frequentation; access; visit. **2** movement; plying; run: ট্রেন-~, জাহাজ-~. **3** traffic: লোক-~. **~ করা** *vi, vt* come and go; frequent; move; run; ply. **~ খরচ** *n* travelling expenses/allowance. **যাতায়াতের পথ** *n* route; thoroughfare; itinerary; passage.

যাত্রা *n* **1** going; setting off; journey. **2** march; campaign; expedition: যুদ্ধ~. **3** voyage: সমুদ্র~. **4** movement. **5** flight: আকাশপথে ~. **6** leaving; departure: গাড়ির ~র সময়. **7** going on a pilgrimage. **8** festive train; procession: রথ~, দোল~. **9** feast; festival. **10** support of life; livelihood; maintenance: জীবন~. **11** intercourse: জগদ্~, worldly intercourse **12** way; means; expedient. **13** passing away time. **14** time; occasion: এ-~ তুমি বেঁচে গেলে. **15** sort of dramatic entertainment (popular in Bengal). **16** (christ) exodus. **~ করা** *vi, vt* **1** set out (on a journey); set out for; leave; move out; depart; strike camp; start/go on a journey. **2** (fig) begin; start: এখান থেকেই ~ করা যাক. **3** stage/act in an open-air drama (⇒ 15 above). **~ গাওয়া** *vi* sing/play in an open-air opera. **~ দেওয়া** *vi* arrange for staging an open-air drama; commission an open-air theatrical company . **~ওয়ালা** *n* performer in an open-air drama. **~গান** *n* **1** open-air opera/drama; open-air performance. **2** song contained in an open-air opera. **~দল** *n* open-air theatrical company. **~পুস্তক** *n* (Christ) Exodus. **~-ফল** *n* fruit of a pilgrimage/an expedition. **~বিরতি, ~ভঙ্গ** *nn* halt; stop. **~র অধিকারী** *n* proprietor (who is also the manager and director) of a theatrical company. **~র প্রাক্কালে** on the eve of departure **~র সঙ** *n* clown; buffoon; ridiculous actor.

যাত্রিক *adj* relating to journey/march. ❑*n* traveller, pilgrim; voyager.

যাত্রী *n* goer; traveller; passenger; voyager. ❑*adj* **1** moving; going; travelling. **2** carrying/transporting passengers: ~ নৌকা, passenger-boat.

যাত্রীবাহী *adj* carrying passengers. **~ জাহাজ** *n* passenger-ship.

যাথাতথ্য *n* correctness; authenticity; veracity; accuracy; reality.

যাথার্থ্য=যথার্থতা (⇒ যথার্থ)

যাদঃপতি *n* **1** ocean (lord of sea animals). **2** Varuna, the Hindu sea-god.

যাদব *adj* **1** relating to/descended from king Yadu. **2** descendant of king Yadu; Sri Krishna. **যাদবী** *fem* goddess Durga.

যাদু[১] *n* (term of endearment esp for children) darling; sweet; angel. **~ধন, ~মণি** *nn*=~.

যাদু[২]=জাদু

যাদৃক, যাদৃশ্, যাদৃশ *adjj, conjj* (archaic) as like; which like; like which; such; as. **যাদৃশী** *fem*. **যাদৃশী ভাবনা যস্য সিদ্ধির্ভবতি তাদৃশী** (Sanskrit phrase) as one contemplates, so one gains; like thought like success.

যাদৃচ্ছিক *adj* at will; at one's pleasure; spontaneous; voluntary: ~ মেলামেশা.

যান *n* **1** vehicle of any kind; carriage; waggon; vessel; ship; litter; palanquin. **2** path; course; way; route. **3** journey; travel; going; moving marching; riding. **4** (with Buddhists) vehicle/method of arriving at knowledge, means of release from repeated births. **~বাহ, ~বাহন** *n* transport; conveyance; vehicle. **~শালা** *n* coach house; garage.

যান্ত্রিক *adj* mechanical; versed in machines/mechanical engineering/machine operating. ❑*n* mechanic; machinist; machine-man; operator. **~তা** *n* mechanical behaviour; mechanization.

যাপক *adj, n* one who spends/passes (as time).

যাপন *n* passing; spending (as time); living: জীবন ~, বসন্ত ~. **~ করা** *vt* pass; spend; live; pass through.

যাপনীয় *adj* to be spent (as time)/passed/lived.

যাপা *vt*=যাপন করা

যাপিত *adj* spent (as time); passed; lived.

যাপ্য *adj* **1**=যাপনীয়. **2** incurable; chronic: ~ রোগ. **3** confidential; to be kept secret.

যাব[১]=জাব

যাব[২]=যাবক

যাবক *n* **1** lac/red dye prepared from the cochineal insect; lac-dye. **2** kind of paddy. **3** unripe barley. **~-রেখা** *n* line along the border of the foot of a woman drawn with lac-dye.

যাবচ্চন্দ্রদিবাকর *adv* as long as the sun and the moon will exist; for ever; eternally; perpetually.

যাবজ্জীবন *adj* during the whole of life; for life. ❑*adj* life-long; lasting for life. **~ কারাদণ্ড** *n* imprisonment for life; life-term; life sentence.

যাবৎ *conj* until; till; for; during: চার দিন ~ সে অসুস্থ. ❑*adv* as long (as); as far as; as much as: ~ দেহে প্রাণ আছে. ❑*adj* all; entire; whatever: গ্রামের ~ লোক.

যাবতীয় *adj* all; one and all; whatever: ~ বিষয়সম্পত্তি.

যাবন *adj* relating to the Yavanas (⇒ যবন); of Ionian Greeks; Greek; non-Hindu; (taboo) Muslim. ❑*n* olibanum.

যাবনিক *adj*=যাবন

যাম *n* the eighth part of the day (=three hours; period/watch of three hours). **~ঘোষ** *n* **1** jackal. **2** cock. **3** one who proclaim the watches. **~বতী** *n fem* night. **যামার্ধ** *n* half of a Yama.

যামল *n* pair.

যামি, যামী *n* **1** night. **2** woman of rank/respectability. **3** wife. **4** sister; female relation. **5** daughter.

যামিনী *n fem* night. **~নাথ** *n* 'beloved/husband of night' the moon. **~ভূষণ** *n* the moon. **~যোগে** *adv* by/at night.

যাম্য *adj* **1** relating/belonging to Yama (যম). **2** southern; southerly. **~বৃত্ত** *n* south pole. **যাম্যায়ন** *n* (astron) the sun's progress; south of the equator; winter solstice.

যাম্যোত্তর *n* (astron) meridian. **~গমন** *n* (astron) transit. **~বৃত্ত** *n* (astron) meridian line/circle.

যায় *n* **1** list; inventory; catalogue. **2** account; sake: কিসের যায়ে ছেড়ে দেব? **~ করা** *vi* make a list/an inventory.

যায়-যায় *adv, adj* on the point of going; on the point of dying/collapsing.

যাযাবর *adj* having no fixed/permanent abode; nomadic; vagrant; wandering; gypsy. ❑*n* **1** nomad. **2** vagrant mendicant; saint. **~ জাতি** *n* nomads; gypsies; wandering tribes. **~ পক্ষী** *n* migratory birds; birds of passage.

যার *pron* of what/which; of whom; whose. **~তার** of sb of no importance; of an ordinary person. **~পর নাই** *adj* extreme. ❑*adv* extremely.

যালিম=জালিম

যাহা *pron* (old style)=যা. **~তাহা**=যা-তা (⇒ যা)

যাহিল=জাহিল

যিগর=জিগর

যিজিয়া=জিজিয়া

যিনি *pron* (honorific) who.

যিয়াদা [A] *adj* more; additional; too much; excessive.

যিয়াফত [A] *n* feast; banquet; convivial entertainment.

যিয়ারত [A] *n* pilgrimage; visiting (a shrine).

যিশু, যীশু *nn* Jesus.

যুঁই *n* jasmine.

যুকতি, যুক্‌তি (archaic, poet)=যুক্তি

যুক্ত *adj* **1** joined; attached; enclosed. **2** fastened; harnessed; yoked. **3** united; federated; amalgamated. **4** furnished/ endowed/ filled/ supplied/ provided with; accompanied by; possessed of; invested with; possessing: বারান্দা~, শ্রী~. **5** absorbed in; attentive to: চিন্তা~. **6** come in contact with. **7** added to; increased by: লবণ~. **8** fitted; adapted: চাকা~. **9** connected with. **10** employed; engaged in; set to work; occupied with: কর্মে ~. **11** absorbed in deep meditation; concentrated; attentive: যোগ~. **12** (math) added: পাঁচ ~ সাত = বার. **13** compound: যুক্তাক্ষর. **14** conforming to: যুক্তি~. **15** (astron) being in conjunction with. **16** seized/ affected/ stricken with: অনুরাগ~, ক্রোধ~. **17** containing; having: ত্রুটি~, চর্বি~. ❑*n* (math) plus. **যুক্তা** *fem*. **~করা** *vt* join; attach; enclose; unite; fasten; furnish/supply/provide/fill with; invest with; add; fit; adapt; connect; engage. **~ হওয়া** *vi* join; be attached to/enclosed in. **~কর** *n* folded hands. ❑*adj* having one's hands folded. **~করে** *adv* with folded hands. **~দল** *adj* (bot) gamopetalous. **~ প্রচেষ্টা** *n* joint/united effort. **~প্রদেশ** *n* the United Provinces (in India). **~বৃতি** *adj* (bot) gamocepalous. **~বেণী** *n* **1** confluence of the Ganges, the Jamuna and the Saraswati near Allahabad. **2** plaited hair. **~রাজ্য** *n* the United Kingdom. **~রাষ্ট্র** *n* the United states (of America). **~রাষ্ট্রীয়** *adj* federal. **~রাষ্ট্রীয় বিচারালয়** *n* federal court . **~ শাসন** *n* joint government. **~ স্বাক্ষর** *n* joint signature. **যুক্তাক্ষর** *n* compound/conjunct letter.

যুক্তি *n* **1** reasoning; argument; logic; proof; judgement. **2** cause; reason; ground; motive. **3** induction; deduction from circumstances. **4** consultation; counsel; advice. **5** plan; scheme; strategy; contrivance; trick; cunning device. **6** joining; union; junction; connection; combination. **7** federation; amalgamation: unification. **~ আঁটা/করা** *vi* contrive; intrigue together; plan; scheme; consult; take counsel together. **~ দেওয়া** *vi* **1** argue; adduce reason; give reasons; make out a case for; show; prove one's point; demonstrate. **2** counsel; give counsel; advise. **~ দেখানো** =~ দেওয়া (1). **~ নেওয়া** *vi* hold/take counsel with sb; consult; confer with sb; take advice; take one's cue from; be advised by. **~দাতা** *n* counsellor; adviser; mentor; (derog) instigator. **~দাত্রী** *fem*. **~পূর্বক** *adv* with due deliberation; advisedly; purposely; calculatedly; thoughtfully; after due thought; after careful consideration; after conferring (with). **~ প্রদর্শন করা** =~ দেওয়া (1). **~বাদ** *n* rationalism. **~বাদী** *adj* rationalist; reasonable; sensible; rationalistic; amenable to reason. **~বাদী লোক** *n* rationalist; freethinker; reasonable person. **~বিদ্যা** *n* logic. **~বিরুদ্ধ** *adj* unreasonable; irrational. **~যুক্ত, ~সঙ্গত, ~সম্মত, ~সহ** *adjj* conforming to reason; based on argument; sensible; logical; reasonable; advisable. **~যুক্ততা** *n* reasonableness; advisability; suitability; propriety; fitness. **~শাস্ত্র** *n* logic. **~শূন্য, ~হীন** *adjj* unreasonable; irrational; groundless; causeless. **~সিদ্ধ** *adj* logical; reasonable; valid; sound.

যুক্ত্যাভাস *n*=rationalization.

যুগ *n* **1** pair; couple; brace. **2** yoke; team. **3** period of twelve years. **4** an age of the world; long mundane period of years (সত্য, ত্রেতা, দ্বাপর, কলি). **5** (astron) epoch. **6** era; age; great length of time: আর কতো ~ অপেক্ষা করবো? **7** times: যুগের হাওয়া. **8** generation: এ-যুগের ছেলেমেয়ে. **9** a measure of length (= 4 cubits). **~কীলক** *n* pin of a yoke. **~ক্ষয়** *n* end of an era/age; destruction of the world; universal dissolution causing the world to be created anew. **~ধর্ম** *n* spirit of the age/times; zeitgeist; trend/characteristics of the age/times. **~ধর্মপালন** *n* adoption of/following the trend of the age. **~ন্ধর** *n adj* holding/ bearing the yoke. ❑*n* **1** pole of a carriage; wood to which the yoke is fixed. **2** (fig) person who represents the spirit of an age. **~প্রবর্তক** *n* maker of an age/epoch. **~সন্ধি** *n* transition of an age. **~সন্ধিকাল** *n* transition period. **~সন্ধিকালীন** *adj* transitional. **যুগান্ত** *n* **1**=~ক্ষয়. **2** a radical revolution bringing in a new era. **যুগান্তকারী** *adj* epoch-making. **যুগান্তর** *n* another age/generation; new age; epoch-making revolution. **যুগাবতার** *n* divine incarnation of the age; greatest teacher/ preceptor of the age.

যুগপৎ *adj* simultaneous. ❑*adv* at the same time; simultaneously. **যুগপত্তা** *n* simultaneity.

যুগল *n* pair; couple; brace; team: নয়ন~, হংস~. **~তারা, ~তারকা** *nn* (astron) double star. **~বন্দি** *n* music played by two instrumentalists; duet. **~মূর্তি** *n* picture of Radha and Krishna united in love; picture of any divine couple.

যুগান = যোগান

যুগী *n* name of a Hindu caste.

যুগ্ম *n* **1** pair; couple; brace. **2** (astrol) sign of the zodiac Gemini. **3** double *sloka* (শ্লোক). ❑*adj* **1** joint. **2** (arith) even. **~তারা** *n* (astron) binary star. **~দর্পণ** *n* bi-mirror. **~সচিব** *n* joint secretary. **~সম্পাদক** *n* joint editor/ secretary.

যুগ্যি (dial)=যোগ্য

যুঝা *vi* fight; struggle; battle; give battle; be locked in a struggle; tussle; cross swords; contend/vie (with); scuffle. **~নো** *vt* cause to fight/struggle. **~যুঝি** *n* engagement; encounter; tussle; combat; duel; dispute; contention; fighting; strife.

যুটি *n* **1** pair; couple; brace. **2** *fem* one of a pair; partner. ☐*adj fem* of a particular age: সম~.

যুড়া *vt*=জুড়া

যুড়ি=জুড়ি

যুৎ=জুৎ

যুত *adj* attached; posed of; added; united/combined/joined/connected/ filled/ covered with; accompanied by: শ্রী~, গুণ~.

যুতা *n*=জুতি

যুতি[১] *n* addition; uniting; junction; union/ meeting with.

যুতি[২] *n* (astron) occultation. **~কাল** *n* syndic period.

যুদ্ধ *n* war; battle; struggle; fight; fighting; strife; conflict; encounter; combat; contest; tournament; warfare. **~ করা** *vt, vi* war; wage war; fight (with/for/against); battle; make war; take up arms; take the field; carry on war/hostilities; give battle; encounter; battle with; engage in battle; contend; contest; be locked in a struggle; cross swords; struggle; join battle; strive hard. **যুদ্ধে নামা** *vi* make war; go to war; declare/wage war; take up arms; join the war. **~-ঋণ** *n* war-loan. **~কারী** *adj* making war; fighting. ☐*n* fighter. **~কারিণী** *fem.* **~কাল** *n* time of war. **~কালীন** *adj* wartime. **~কুশল** *adj* skilled in warfare; military; martial; warlike. **~কৌশল** *n* military tactics; strategies; art of warfare. **~ক্ষেত্র** *n* battle-field. **~জয়** *n* victory (in war). **~জয়ী** *adj* victorious (in war/battle). **~জয়ী ব্যক্তি** *n* victor (in war); victorious person. **~জাহাজ** *n* warship; battleship; man-of-war. **~জিৎ** =~জয়ী. **~নাদ** *n* battle-cry. **যুদ্ধংদেহি** *adj* warlike; belligerent; warmongering; pugnacious. **যুদ্ধংদেহি ভাব** *n* bellicosity; belligerence; militancy; pugnacity; jingoism. **~নিপুণ** =~কুশল. **~নীতি** *n* rules and regulations of war; tactics of war; war policy; law of war. **~পটু** =~কুশল. **~পরাঙ্মুখ** *adv* averse from fighting. **~পোত**=~ জাহাজ. **~-প্রাঙ্গণ** *n* front. **~প্রিয়** *adj* bellicose; martial; war-like; soldierly. **~বন্দি** *n* prisoner of war. **~বাজ** *adj* warmongering. **~বাজ ব্যক্তি** *n* war-monger; militarist. **~-বিগ্রহ** *n* warfare; hostilities; bloodshed. **~বিদ্যা** *n* art of warfare; science of war; military art/science/tactics. **~বিধ্বস্ত** *adj* war-torn. **~বিভাগ** *n* War Department; war office; Defence Department. **~বিরতি** *n* cease-fire; cessation of war/hostilities; truce; armistice. **~বিশারদ** *adj* skilful in war. ☐*n* military expert. **~-বীর** *n* war-hero: valiant man; warrior. **~যাত্রা** *n* military expedition/campaign. **~রীতি** =~নীতি. **~শান্তি, ~শেষ** =cessation of war; armistice; truce. **~সচিব** *n* Defence Secretary/ Minister. **~সজ্জা** *n* battle-dress; military uniform/dress; armament; military equipment; preparation for war. **~সাধ** *n* desire to fight. **~সামগ্রী** *n* military equipment; implement of war. **~স্থল** *n* battle-ground. **যুদ্ধাজীব** *n* fighter; soldier; warrior. **যুদ্ধাবসান** =~শান্তি. **যুদ্ধার্থ** *adv* for war; to fight. **যুদ্ধার্থী** *adj* desirous of war; seeking war. **এলোমেলো ~** *n* skirmish. **হাতাহাতি ~** *n* battle-royal.

যুদ্ধোদ্যম *n* (vigorous and active) preparation for war; war effort.

যুদ্ধোদ্যোগ *n* beginning of hostilities; acts of war.

যুদ্ধোন্মত্ত *adj* fierce/frantic in battle; frenziedly fighting; aggressive; belligerent; warmongering.

যুদ্ধোন্মাদ *n* craze for war; war-neurosis; bellicosity.

যুদ্ধোন্মুখ *adj* on the war-path; bellicose.

যুদ্ধোপকরণ *n* arms and ammunition; war materials.

যুধিষ্ঠির *n* 'firm/steady in battle'; name of the eldest son of Pandu.

যুধ্যমান *adj* (engaged in) fighting; belligerent.

যুনানী=ইউনানী

যুব, যুব-জন *nn*=যুবক. **~জানি** *adj* having a young wife. **~রাজ** *n* crown prince; heir-apparent. **~রাজত্ব, ~রাজ্য** *nn* rank of an heir-apparent. **~রাজ্ঞী, ~রানী** *nn fem* wife/consort of a crown prince. **~সম্প্রদায়** *n* young people; youth (collectively). **~ সম্মেলন** *n* youth conference.

যুবক *adj* young; youthful; adult. ☐*n* young man; youth. **যুবতি, যুবতী** *fem n* young woman; girl.

যুবা = যুবক. **~কাল, ~বয়স** *n* youth; young age.

যুযুৎসা *n* desire for war/fighting; pugnacity; combativeness; bellicosity.

যুযুৎসু[১] *adj* wishing to fight; eager for battle; pugnacious. ☐*n* combatant.

যুযুৎসু[২]=জুজুৎসু

যুযুধান *adj* (engaged in) fighting. ☐*n* fighter; warrior.

যূথ *n* **1** herd; flock; troop; band; host; multitude; (great) number; flock; pack; flight; swarm. **2** group. **~চর, ~চারী** *adj* going about in troops; gregarious. **~নাথ, ~পতি, ~পাল** *nn* lord/leader of a herd/band/troop. **~বদ্ধ** *adj* grouped; herded. **~ভ্রষ্ট** *adj* fallen out/strayed from a herd. **যূথা** *fem.* **~ভ্রষ্ট পশু** *n* stray; straying.

যূথি, যূথিকা, যূথী *nn* kind of jasmine; *Jasminum auriculutum.*

যূপ, যূপকাষ্ঠ *nn* a smooth post/stake to which the sacrificial victim is fastened; sacrificial post/stake.

যুষ *n* soup; broth; pease-soup; decoction.

যে[1] *conj* that: সে বলল যে তুমি আসবে.

যে[2] *rel pron* **1** who; which; that: আমার ভাই, যে আমাকে প্রায়ই বলে ... যে একবার এখানে এসেছে .... **2** the *noun/pron* + that/who/which: যে-বাড়িটি তুমি কিনেছ ... যে-ছেলেটি গতকাল এসেছিল ... **যে-অবধি** *adv* since; ever: যে-অবধি সে এখানে এসেছে... **যে আজ্ঞা** as you please, sir; all right, sir; that's right, sir; I am at your command. **যে-কজন** all those; all the ... who... **যে-কটি** the few... that: যে-কটি ছেলে পরীক্ষা দিয়েছে. **যে-কথা সেই কাজ** true to one's word. **যে-কারণে** for which reason; the reason why; wherefore. **যে কালে** *conj* when; while; whilst. **যে-কেউ** *n, pron* anyone; anybody; whoever. **যে-কে-সেই** as before; (always) the same. **যে কোনো-কিছু** *n, pron* anything (whatever). **যে-কোনো জন, যে-কোনোটি** any one. **যে-কোনো স্থান** any place. **যে-কোনো স্থানে** *adv* anywhere; wherever: সে যে-কোনো স্থানে যাক... **যেটুকু** the little ... that. **যেদিন** the day (on which). **যে-পর্যন্ত** *conj* upto the time when; till; upto which; upto which time. **যে-পর্যন্ত না** until. **যেবা** *prop* whoever; whichever. **যে যে** *rel pron* all who; all which. **যে-সে** *pron* any man in the street; the common run of mankind; anybody; Tom, Dick and Harry; everybody: এমন কথা তো যে-সে বলতে পারে. ❑*adj* ordinary; common; vulgar; commonplace; humdrum: সে তো আর যে-সে লোক নয়.

যে[3] (particle added to certain sentences to give special stylistic effect). **1** (expresses the cause): তুমিও যে উঠলে, তবে আমি যাই. **2** (expresses doubt/uncertainty): কী যে হবে? **3** (expresses certainty and disappointment): সে যে আর এলো না. **4** (interrogation/enquiry): বইটা ফেরত দিলি না যে? **5** (amazement): এই যে! তুমি যে! **6** (remonstrance/ reproof): তুই যে বড়ো ওকে মারলি? তুমি যে আবার সেখানে গিয়েছিলে? **7** (disgust/ disappointment): আবার জ্বরটা উঠল যে. **8** (emphasis): খুশিতে বুক ভরে ওঠে যে. **9** (disagreement/ disapproval): কী যে বলো!

যেই *conj* the moment that ...; just as; as soon as: ~ তাকে কথাটা বললাম, ... ❑*pron* whoever: কথাটা ~ বলুক, ভালোই বলেছে.

যেখান *n* which/whichever place. **~কার** *adj* from which place; whence: ~কার মানুষ সেখানে. **যেখানে** *adv, conj* where; wherever. **যেখানে-সেখানে** *adv* here and there; everywhere; hither and thither; pell-mell; all over the shop.

যেতে বসা ⇒ যাওয়া

যেথা *adv* where. **~কার** =যেখানকার (⇒ যেখান). **~য়**=~. **~সেথা**=যেখানে-সেখানে (⇒ যেখান)

যেন *prep* **1** like: যাচ্ছে যেন হাতি. ❑*adv* as; as if; as though/it were: সে মুখ খুললো, যেন কিছু বলবে. ❑*conj* **1** that: সে যেন দীর্ঘজীবী হয়, May he live long; এ ব্যাপারে যেন কোনো ভুল-বোঝাবুঝি না থাকে, I wish there to be no misunderstanding on this matter. **2** so that: দেখো অযথা সময় নষ্ট কোরো না যেন. **3** accepting/supposing that; I admit; very well: তাই যেন হলো. **4** I cannot recall it; it escapes me for the moment: কী যেন নাম. **কী যেন তাকে বলো,** what d'you call him/her/it/them. **কী যেন তার নাম** what's his/her/its their name. **যেন-তেন** *adj* of any sort/kind; of a sort; of sorts; indifferent. **যেন-তেন প্রকারে(ন)** *adv* some-how; by some means or other; by fair means or foul; by hook or by crook; negligently; perfunctorily.

যেমতি, যেমত *adv, conj* as; as like; such as; like.

যেমন *adj, adv, conj* **1** as for instance/ example; namely; such as. **2** like: ~ বাবা তেমনি ছেলে, like father like son. **3** as; as soon as; just as; as much as; as like as: ~ বলা তেমনি কাজ, no sooner said than done. ❑*int* (expression of mild protest/ reproach/ surprise/ disagreement/ doubt) really: তুমিও ~! **~ই** *adj* whatever: ~ই হোক না কেন নিতেই হবে. ❑*adv* as soon as; in a trice: ~ই গেল অমনি এল. **~-তেমন** = যেন -তেন. **~-তেমন করে** = যেন -তেন প্রকারে. **~ কর্ম তেমন ফল** (prov) as you sow so you reap; sow the wind and reap the whirlwind. **~ দেবা তেমনি দেবী** like husband, like wife.

যেমনি=যেমনই (⇒ যেমন)

যেরূপ=যেমন

যেহেতু *conj* since; because; whereas; considering that.

যো[1]=জো

যো[2] *conj* as. **যো হুকুম** as you command; I am at your beck and call.

যোক্তব্য *adj* to be joined/ yoked/ united.

যোক্তা *adj* to one who joins/ yokes/ unites.

যোক্ত্র *n* **1** any instrument for tying/ fastening; rope; halter; thong. **2** (fig) provision; resource: চাকরির ~ নেই. **3** (fig) facility; convenience: কাজে ~ নেই.

যোখা = জোখা (⇒ জোখ)

যোগ *n* **1** union; junction; combination; contact with; mixing; mixture; blending. **2** connection; relation; association; contact. **3** cooperation; concert: এক যোগে. **4** abstract meditation and mental obstruction practised as a system (as taught by Patanjali and called the Yoga philosophy); yoga. **5** application/ concentration of the thoughts; abstract contemplation; meditation; self-concentration.

6 (math) addition; sum; total. 7 act of yoking/ attaching/ joining/ harnessing/ putting to (of horses). 8 fixing (as of an arrow on the bow-string). 9 putting on (of armour). 10 remedy; cure: হঠ~. 11 means; expedient; device; way; manner; method. 12 trick; stratagem; fraud; deceit. 13 employment; use; application; performance. 14 acquisition; gain; profit; wealth; property. 15 occasion; opportunity; chance: লাভের ~. 16 putting together; arrangement; disposition; regular succession. 17 fitting together; fitness; propriety; suitability. 18 medium; by: ডাকযোগে. 19 path; route; by: বিমানযোগে, নৌকাযোগে. 20 particular time; by: রাত্রিযোগে. 21 (astron) constellation; asterism. 22 (astrol) conjunction; lucky conjuncture; auspicious time; possibility of occurrence: বিষ্কুম্ভ ~, বিবাহের ~. 23 festival: একটা মস্ত ~ আছে. 24 union of the individual soul with the universal soul. 25 exertion; endeavour; zeal; diligence; industry; care; attention. 26 devotion; pious seeking after God. 27 (gram) connection of words together; syntactical dependence of a word; construction. 28 (linguistics) connection of a word with its root; original/ etymological meaning (as opposed to রূঢ়ি). 29 (math) plus sign. 30 undertaking; business; work. **~ করা** *vt, vi* unite; join; add; associate; mix; blend; practise yoga; apply; attach; fix; turn/ direct/ concentrate/ (the mind, thoughts etc); connect; bring together. **~ দেওয়া** *vt, vi* join; participate in; take up an employment; report as for duty; associate with; unite; add. **~ক্রিয়া** *n* (alg) components. **~ক্ষেম** *n* 1 attainment/ acquisition of unattained things and preservation of what is attained; security/ secure possession of what has been acquired; acquisition and preservation of property. 2 welfare; prosperity; substance; livelihood. 3 charge for securing property (from accidents); insurance. 4 property destined for pious uses and sacrifices. 5 indivisible inheritance. **~দান করা** *vi* join (math); report as for duty; take up an employment; associate with; participate in; side with; take part in. **~ধারী** *adj* absorbed in deep meditation. ❑*n* Shiva. **~নিদ্রা** *n* 1 state of half meditation; half sleep; yogic trance. 2 sleep of Vishnu at the end of a yoga; Vishnu's sleep personified as a goddess and said to be a form of Durga. **~নিষ্ঠ** *adj* devotedly meditative; absorbed in meditation. **~পট্ট** *n* cloth thrown over the back and knees of a devotee during meditation. **~পথ** *n* road leading to yoga. **~পদ** *n* state of self-concentration/ meditation. **~পীঠ** *n* particular posture during meditation. **~ফল** *n* result of addition; sum; (phys) summation. **~বল** *n* force of devotion; supernatural power. **~বাহী** *adj* 1 uniting; connecting. 2 acting as a medium; helping to maintain contact. 3 (chem) catalytic. ❑*n* medium. **~বাহ্য** *n* 1 quicksilver. 2 alkali. **~বিদ, ~বিৎ** *adj* conversant with the yoga; knowing the right means/ proper methods; follower of the yoga doctrines. **~ভঙ্গ, ~ভ্রংশ** *nn* interruption of (yogic) meditation; failing in yogic practice/ meditation. **~ভ্রষ্ট** *adj* interrupted/ foiled in yogic practice/ meditation; lured away/ fallen from spiritual heights attained by means of yoga. **~মায়া** *n fem* power of God in the creation of the world personified as a deity; name of Durga; magical power of abstract meditation. **~মার্গ** = ~পথ. *n* **~যুক্ত** *adj* immersed in deep meditation; absorbed in yoga. **~রূঢ়** *adj* (gram) having a special as well as an etymological and general meaning (said of certain words). **~শাস্ত্র** *n* any work on the yoga doctrine. **~সাজশ** *n* collusion; complicity; connivance; conspiracy. **~সাজশে** *adv* in collusion with; with the connivance of. **~সাধন** *n* unification; blending; mixture; joining; practice of yoga. **~সাধন করা** *vi* unite; mix; blend; join; combine; reconcile; incorporate; unify; couple; fuse. **~সাধনা** *n* practice of yoga. **~সার** *n* universal remedy. **~সিদ্ধ** *adj* perfected by means of yoga; successful in attaining spiritual perfection by means of yoga. **~সিদ্ধি** *n* attainment of spiritual perfection through yoga; obtaining the fruit of yogic practice. **~স্থ** *adj* absorbed in meditation.

যোগাকর্ষণ *adj* molecular attraction; cohesion.

যোগাচার *n* observance of the yoga.

যোগাড় *n* 1 preparation; arrangement; provision. 2 procurement; collection; obtaining; securing. **~ করা** *vi* procure; secure; get; obtain; array for; make preparation for; collect; manage; supply. **~ করে দেওয়া** *vi* procure for another; make available; find for; provide sth (for sb); provide sb with sth; furnish. **~যন্ত্র** *n* preparations; arrangements. **~ যন্ত্র করা** *vi* make arrangements/ preparations; arrange (for); manage; shift for oneself. **যোগাড়ে** *adj* 1 adept in procurement/ getting things done; adept/ employed in making preparations and arrangements. 2 full of resources; capable of shifting for oneself; cute; smart; dodgy; shifty. ❑*n* 1 resourceful person; shifty fellow; dodger. 2 assistant; hodman; hod-carrier.

যোগান *n* 1 supply; purveyance; stock; flow: কথার ~. 2 assistance; help: কাজে ~. **~দার** *n* 1 supplier; purveyor. **2** assistant; helper. **3** hod-carrier; hodman. ~ **দেওয়া** *vi* supply; purvey; procure. **যোগানো** *vi* **1** supply; purvey. **2** find; to be found: কথা যোগানো. **3** flatter; adulate; humour; puff: মন যোগানো. **যোগানের নিয়ম** *n* law of supply. **যোগাভ্যাস** *n* practice of yoga.

যোগাযোগ *n* **1** contact; touch; intercourse: তার সঙ্গে ~ রেখো, keep in touch with him. **2** relation; connection; association; communion: দুটি ঘটনার মধ্যে কোনো ~ নেই. **3** communication. **4** consistency: শুরু ও শেষের মধ্যে ~. **5** co-operation: দুজনের যোগাযোগে কার্যসম্পাদন. **6** conjuncture: শুভ ~. ~ **করা** *vi* contact; get into communication with. ~ **রক্ষা করা** *vi* maintain contact with; keep in touch with. ~ **স্থাপন করা** *vi* establish/ make contact with; get in contact with (sb); reach (sb) (by message/ telephone). ~ **ব্যবস্থা** *n* communication system. **গণ**~ *n* mass communication.

যোগারূঢ় ⇒ যোগ

যোগালে = যোগাড়ে (২)

যোগাসন *n* seat/ mode of sitting suited to profound meditation/ yoga; yoga posture.

যোগাসীন *adj* seated in yogic meditation. **যোগাসীনা** *fem*

যোগিনী *n fem* (of যোগী) **1** female demon or any being endowed with magical power. **2** fairy/ witch/ sorceress represented as sixty-four in number and as created by Durga and attendant on her or on Shiva. **3** female ascetic. **4** (with Buddhists) woman representing any goddess who is the object of adoration. **5** (astrol) a particular conjunction of stars.

যোগিবেশ, যোগীবেশ *n* conventional garb of a *yogi*/ an ascetic.

যোগিয়া *n* name of an Indian musical mode.

যোগী *n* **1** contemplative saint; ascetic; devotee. **2** follower of the yoga system; yogi. **3** name of a mixed caste. **4** selfless devotee (to any cause): কর্ম~. ~**ন্দ্র**, ~**শ**, ~**শ্বর** *nn* **1** master/ adept in the yoga. **2** Shiva. **3** Yajnavalkya. ~**ন্দ্র-বাসনা** *adj* coveted by *yogis*.

যোগে *prep* through; by means of; through the agency of; in cooperation with. ~**যাগে** *adv* **1** somehow; with great difficulty; the hard way. **2** by chance; through a favourable opportunity.

যোগ্য *adj* **1** fit/ qualified for; able/ equal to; capable (of); deserving; suitable; worthy: ~ লোক. **2** eligible; able; competent; efficient. **3** becoming; befitting: রাজার ~. **4** merited; deserved: ~ পুরস্কার/শাস্তি. **5** proper; right: ~ কাজ. **যোগ্যা** *fem*. ~**তা** *adj* qualification; ability; suitability; fitness; propriety; suitableness; eligibility; competence; capability; efficiency; worth; merit; aptness. ~**তানুসারে** *adv* according to/in order of merit. ~**তাপত্র** *n* certificate of merit/ competence.

যোজক *n* (geog) isthmus. ❑*adj* joining; linking; uniting; coupling. ~ **স্ক্রু** *n* binding screw.

যোজন *n* **1** joining; yoking; linking; mixing; blending; uniting. **2** use; application; arrangement; preparation. **3** mental concentration; directing the thoughts to. **4** employment: সৈন্য~. **5** investment: অর্থ~. **6** erecting; constructing; building; fixation; implantation; assembling: ধনুকে শর~. **7** junction; combination; union. **8** grammatical construction. **9** stage or yojan (ie distance traversed in one harnessing or without unyoking, sometimes regarded as 4/5 miles). ~ **করা**=যোগ করা (⇒ যোগ). ~**গন্ধা** *n* musk. ~**ভার** *n* (chem) combining weight. **যোজনা** =1 ~ (18). **2** plan; planning.

যোজনীয় *adj* to be joined/ combined/ united; to be set at work; to be used/ employed; to be connected with.

যোজয়িতব্য *adj* to be joined/ connected/ furnished with; to be made use of/ chosen/ selected.

যোজয়িতৃ *n* one who joins/ connects; setter (of precious stones).

যোজিত *adj* **1** joined; linked; mixed; blended; arranged; connected; put together; composed. **2** supplied/ furnished with. **3** used; employed; applied. **4** appointed to; charged with. **5** tied/ fastened to; put/ placed in; fixed; implanted. **6** invested.

যোজ্য=যোজনীয়

যোঝা (colloq)=যুঝা

যোট=জোট

যোটক *n* **1** combination; constellation; union. **2** combination for matrimonial purposes: রাজ~. **3** pair; one of a pair. ~ **মেলা** *vi* **1** be found agreeable for matrimonial purposes; combine well for matrimonial purpose; be supplied with a pair; be paired.

যোটা=জুটা. ~**নো**=জুটানো

যোড়=জোড়

যোড়া=জোড়া. ~**নো**=জোড়ানো

যোত=জোত

যোতা=জোতা

যোত্র *n* **1** the cord that fastens the yoke of a plough to the neck of an ox; fastening; tie; rope. **2** yoke. **3** resource; means; provision. **4** property. **5** assistance; help. **6** refuge; shelter. ~**সম্পন্ন** *adj* of means/ property; wealthy; well-to-do; well-off; affluent. ~**হীন** *adj* insolvent; impecunious; badly off.

যোদ্ধা *n* soldier; fighter; warrior; combatant.

যোদ্ধৃ *n*=যোদ্ধা. ~ **জাতি** *n* warlike/ martial race. ~**পতি** *n* general; commander. ~**পুরুষ** *n*=যোদ্ধা.

~বর্গ *n pl* warriors/ soldiers (collectively); fighting men; men at arms. ~বেশ *n* military dress; dress/ attire of a soldier; regimentals.

যোধ *n* **1**=যোদ্ধা. **2** war; battle; fighting. ~পতি *n* commander; general. ~সংরাব *n* mutual defiance of combatants; challenge.

যোধন *n* **1** war; battle; fighting. **2** battle-cry. **3** arms; military equipment's.

যোধী *adj* fighting; combating. ❑*n* combatant; warrior; conqueror.

যোনি, যোনী *nn* **1** female organ of generation; vulva; vagina. **2** place of birth; origin; source; spring; fountain. **3** birth; race; stock; caste; form of existence/ station fined by birth: দেব~, প্রেত~. **4** (archaic) animal.

যোয়ান১=যমানিকা

যোয়ান২=জোয়ান

যোয়াল=জোয়াল

যোশ [P] *n* excitement; heat: zeal; effervescence; enthusiasm; passion; emotion.

যোষিৎ *n* (young) woman; wife; girl; maiden. ~পুংস্ক *adj* (bot) gynandrous.

যোহর=জোহর

যোহরা = জোহরা

যো-হুকুম (phrase) as you command; at your command. যো-হুকুমের দল *n pl* flock of flatterers; obsequious followers.

যৌক্তিক *adj* **1** logical; reasonal. **2** suitable; fit; proper.

যৌগ *n* (chem) compound.

যৌগপদ্য *n* simultaneousness.

যৌগিক *adj* **1** compound; composite; complex; mixed. **2** (gram) having an etymological meaning. **3** (math) compound. **4** of yoga; yogic. ~ অনুবীক্ষণ *n* compound microscope. ~ অর্থ *n* (linguistics) derivative meaning. ~ কাচ *n* compound lens. ~ ক্রিয়া *n* **1** (gram) compound verb. **2** yogic performance. ~ পদার্থ *n* compound substance; compound. ~ বাক্য *n* compound sentence. ~ শব্দ *n* word having an etymological meaning; derivative. ~ সংখ্যা *n* mixed/ complex number.

যৌতুক *n* property given at marriage; dowry; marriage portion. ~ দেওয়া *n* bestow a dowry upon; dower; give a present. ~ প্রথা *n* dowry system. ~হীন *adj* portionless.

যৌথ *adj* joint; united; combined. ~ কারবার *n* joint stock business/ company. ~ চেষ্টা *n* united/ combined effort. ~ পরিবার *n* joint family. ~ স্বাক্ষর *n* joint signature.

যৌন *adj* **1** sexual; conjugal: ~ মিলন. **2** vaginal; biogenetic. **3** venereal: ~ রোগ. ~তা *n* sexuality.

যৌবন *n* youth; youthfulness; adolescence; puberty; manhood. ~কণ্টক *n* eruption/ pimples on the face. ~কাল *n* period of youth; grown-up stage. ~চাঞ্চল্য *n* restlessness of youth. ~জ্বালা (ardour of) youthful passions. ~দর্প *n* juvenile pride/indiscretion. ~দশা =~কাল. ~প্রাপ্ত *adj* arrived at manhood. ~প্রাপ্তা *fem* arrived at womanhood. ~বান *adj* young; youthful. ~বতী *fem.* ~ভার *n* 'burden of youth'; bloom of youth. ~মত্ত *adj* intoxicated with (the pride of) youth. ~মত্তা *fem.* ~লক্ষণ *n* sign of youth; grace; loveliness. ~শ্রী *n* beauty of youthfulness. ~সম্পন্ন *adj* full of youth; youthful. ~সম্পন্না *fem.* ~সহচর *n* friends/ companion of one's youth; confidant. ~সহচরী *fem.* ~সুখ *n* joys fo youth/ love. ~সুলভ *adj* usual for youth; youthful. ~স্থ *adj* being in the (bloom of) youth; arrived at puberty; marriageable. যৌবনারম্ভ *n* prime of youth; first bloom of youth; juvenility. যৌবনারূঢ় *adj* one who has arrived at adolescence/ puberty. যৌবনাবস্থা *n* state of youth; youthfulness; puberty.

যৌবনোদয় *n* appearance/ beginning of youth.

যৌবরাজিক *adj* relating/ belonging to an heir-apparent.

যৌবরাজ্য *n* rank/ office/ rights of a heir-apparent; right of succession to kingdom. ~ প্রদান করা, যৌবরাজ্যে অভিষিক্ত করা *vi* instal as a crown prince.

য়

য় *n* a letter of the Bengali alphabet. Originally it is the same letter as য. Its use in the initial position is limited to certain words of foreign origin and then it represents the sound of 'y'.

য়ুনানি, য়ুনানী=ইউনানি

য়োরোপ, য়ুরোপ=Europe. য়োরোপীয়, য়ুরোপীয় *nn, adjj* European.

র

র১ *n* the twenty-seventh consonant of the Bengali alphabet. ~ ফলা *n* the sign (্র) placed under a letter to form a conjunct letter. It is a voiced unaspirated alveolo trilled sound.

-র২ *suff* used to form possessive case: লাঠি~ বাড়ি, ঢাকা~ রাস্তা.

রই রই=রৈ রৈ

রইস [A] *n* chief; head; noble man; prince. ❑*adj* noble; leading; great; big: ~ লোক.

রওজা [A] *n* mausoleum; garden.

রওনা, রওয়ানা [P] *n* **1** going; departure; leaving; proceeding; setting out. **2** dispatch; sending. ~ **করা** *vt* dispatch; see off; send; send off. ~ **হওয়া** *vi* set out (on a journey); depart; leave.

রওয়া, রহা *vi* **1** remain; stay: কিছুই তো রইল না. **2** be: কোথায় রইল তার জারিজুরি? **3** stop: রও, আর এগিয়ো না. **4** wait: রও, আমি আসছি. **5** accompany: তুমি আমার সঙ্গে রইবে. **6** have: ঢাকায় তার দুটি বাড়ি রয়েছে. **7** pass time: সে কষ্টে রয়েছে. **8** be in: সে পালিয়ে রয়েছে, he is in hiding. **9** be at: মন তো ঘরে রয় না. **10** be in possession of: টাকা কি চিরদিন রয়? **11** exist: ঈশ্বর তো রয়েছেন. **12** last: এ রং কতদিন রইবে? **13** be saved/ preserved: দুর্ভিক্ষে প্রাণ রইল না.

রওয়াক=রোয়াক

রওশন [P] *adj* bright; lighted; illuminated; splendid; luminous; shining; conspicuous; manifest.

রওশনি, রওশনী [P] *n* light; splendour; brightness; illumination; eyesight.

রং১, রঙ১ *n* **1** colour; paint; dye; hue; pigment. **2** complexion. **3** (of playing cards) suit; one of a suit; trump; trump-suit. **4** exaggeration. ~ **ওঠা** *n* lose colour; fade; come out. ~ **করা** *vt* colour; dye; paint; apply colour to; put colour on. ~ **খেলা** *n* sport with colour; sprinkle red colour (at festive occasions). ~ **চড়ানো** *vi* put colour on; colour; exaggerate; embellish; embroider; dress up; play up. ~ **ফোটা** *vi* look bright; show off. ~ **বদলানো** *vi* change colour; change one's manner; be fickle ~ **হওয়া** *vi* take on colour; colour. ~**ওয়ালা** *n* dealer in paints. ~**চং**, ~**চঙ** *n* variegation in colouring; motley mixture of colours. ~**চঙে** *adj* motely; variegated; colourful; multicoloured; chequered; many-coloured; gaudy. ~**ঢং/ঢঙ** =রঙ্গচঙ্গ (⇒ রঙ্গ). ~**দার** *adj* coloured; showy; fine; painted. ~**বেরং** *adj* variegated in colours; diverse; motley; various; colourful. ~**মহল** *n* apartment for festive enjoyments; building dedicated to voluptuous enjoyments; sleeping apartment; drawing room; pleasure-house; theatre. ~**রেজ**=রংরেজ.

রং২, রঙ২=রঙ্গ১

রং৩=রঙ্গ২

রংরুট [E] *n* recruit.

রংরেজ [P] *n* dyer.

রক১ *n* (colloq)=রোয়াক. ~**বাজ** *adj* loafing; idle; gossipy.

রক২ [P] *n* roc (of fairy tales).

রকদস্তি [P] *n* schedule of boundaries.

রকবা [A] *n* area; survey. ~**বন্দি** *n* statement of area.

রকম [A] *n* **1** kind; sort; variety: পাঁচ ~ ফল. **2** manner; way; style; fashion; method: এ-~ করে হবে না. **3** figure; item; number: ~ওয়ারি. ❑*adv* about; nearly; approximately: দু আনা ~ অংশ. ~**ওয়ারি** *adv* item by item; in detail. ~**ফের** *n* type; category; variety; sort: ব্যবসার ~ফের. ~-**রকম** *adj* of various kinds; of various/ different sorts/ fashions/ kinds; various; varied: variegated; multifarious; manifold: ~-রকম খাবার. ~**সকম** *n* (derog) **1** ways; manner; movements; attitude; behaviour: তার ~সকম ভালো লাগছে না. **2** condition; symptoms: রোগীর ~সকম সুবিধের নয়. **রকমারি** =~-রকম. **কী** ~ how? **হরেক** ~ ⇒ হরেক.

রকার ⇒ র১

রকেট [E] *n* rocket.

রক্ত *n* **1** blood. **2** family. **3** red colour. ❑*adj* **1** red; crimson; reddened; blood-red. **2** coloured; dyed; painted. **3** (of eyes) blood-shot; reddened. **4** excited; affected with passion/ love; impassioned; charmed/ enamoured with; attached/ devoted to; fond of. ~ **গরম করা** *vt, vi* **1** make one's blood boil; incense; inflame; excite; arouse. **2** boil with rage; be/ become angry; fly into a rage; loose one's temper; fly off the handle. ~ **গরম থাকা** *vi* **1** retain blood-heat. **2** be still young/ full-blooded. ~ **গরম হওয়া** *vi* get excited; loose one's temper: তার ~ গরম হয়ে উঠেছে, His blood is up. ~ **চড়া** *vi* (of blood) rush to one's head. ~ **জমাট করা** *vi* curdle one's blood; make one's blood run cold; terrify; unnerve; (sl) put the wind up (sb). ~ **জমাট হওয়া** *vi* freeze; feel one's blood run cold/ one's knees knock/ one's hair stand on end. ~ **জল করা** *vi* (fig) work hard to the impairment of one's health; sweat blood; strain every nerve. ~ **ঝরা** *vi* **1** (of blood) flow. **2** (of people) bleed. ~ **ঠাণ্ডা হওয়া** =~ জমাট হওয়া: আমার ~ ঠাণ্ডা হয়ে গেল, My blood ran cold. ~ **দেওয়া** *vi* **1** donate blood. **2** give/ transfuse blood; give blood transfusion. **3** shed one's blood (e.g. for one's country). ~ **নেওয়া** *vi* **1** draw sb's blood (for blood test). **2** take revenge; spill blood. ~ **পড়া**=~ ঝরা. ~ **বন্ধ করা** *vi* stop bleeding. ~ **হওয়া** *vi* gain blood. ~-**অতিসার** *n* blood-dysentery; bloody flux. ~ **আঁখি** *n* blood-shot eyes; wrath; menace; angry look. ❑*adj* having blood-shot eyes; threatening; wrathful; blazing. ~**ক** *n* **1** blood. **2** red-coloured cloth. ~**কণিকা** *n* blood corpuscle. **লোহিত** ~**কণিকা** *n* red corpuscle. **শ্বেত** ~**কণিকা** *n* white corpuscle. ~**কণ্ঠ** *n* sweet-voiced. ~**কন্দল** *n* coral. ~**কমল** *n* red lotus. ~**করবী** *n* kind of flower and its plant; *Nerium odorum*. ~**কাঞ্চন** *n* kind of flower and its plant; *Baubinia variegata*. ~**কুমুদ** *n* red lotus. ~**ক্ষয়** *n* loss of blood; bloodshed. ~ **করা**

vi shed/ spill blood. **~ক্ষয়** *n* loss of blood. **~ক্ষয়ী** *adj* causing or involving loss of blood; sanguinary; bloody; destructive. **~ক্ষরণ** *n* blood-letting; bleeding. **~খদির** *n Acacia catechu*. **~গঙ্গা** *n* **1** river of blood; heavy bleeding. **2** blood-bath; great massacre. **~গরম** *adj* hot-headed; irascible; hot-blooded. **~চক্ষু** =~-আঁখি. **~চন্দন** *n* red sandal. **~চাপ** *n* blood-pressure. **~চিতা** *n* kind of plant and its red flowers; *Plumbago rosea*. **~চূর্ণ** *n* red powder; vermilion **~ চোষা** *vi* suck blood. **~চোয়া** *adj* blood-sucking. ❑*n* blood-sucker (animal and extortioner); vampire. **~চোষা বাদুড়** *n* vampire-bat. **~ ছুটা/ছোটা** *vi* (of blow) flow. **~জবা** *n* red china rose. **~জিহ্ব** *n* having a ruddy tongue; red-tongued. **~জ্বরা** *n* fever due to infusion of new blood. **~ জমাট করা** *adj* blood-curdling. **~ জল করা** *adj* hard-earned; earned by the sweat of one's brow. **~তঞ্চন** *n* clotting of blood. **~দর্শন** *n* blood-shed. **~ দর্শন করা** *n* shed sb's blood. **~দান** *n* donation of blood; blood-transfusion; shedding one's blood; blood-sacrifice. **~ দান করা** *vi* donate blood; transfuse blood; shed one's blood. (eg for one's country. **~দুষ্টি, ~দোষ, ~দূষণ** *nn* blood-poisoning; pyaemia; corrupting/ vitiating the blood. **~ধাতু** *n* red chalk; ruddle; red ochre. **~নদী** =~গঙ্গা. **~নয়ন** =~-আঁখি. **~নাসিক** *adj* bloody-nosed. ❑*n* owl. **~ নিশান** *n* red flag. **~নেত্র** =~-আঁখি. **~প** *adj* blood-drinking; blood-sucking. **~পত্রিকা** *n* red leave; *Boerhavia diffusa*. **~পদ্ম**=~কমল. **~পল্লব** *n Jonesia asoka*. **~পাত** *n* blood-shed; haemorrhage; bleeding. **~পাত করা** *vi* shed/ spill blood. **~পাত হওয়া** *vi* bleed. **~পাদ** *adj* red-footed. ❑*n* parrot. **~ পান করা** *vi* (also fig) suck/ drink sb's blood. **~পিণ্ড** *n* **1** lump of clotted/ congealed blood. **2** embryo. **~পিণ্ডালু** *n* species of red yam. **~পিত্ত** *n* a particular disturbance of the blood caused by bile; plethora; spontaneous haemorrhage from the mouth/ nose; haematemesis. **~পিপাসা** *n* blood-lust; blood thirstyness; thirst for blood. **~পিপাসু** *adj* blood-thirsty. **~পুষ্প** *n* red flower. ❑*adj* red-flowered; bearing red flowers. **~প্রদর** *n* flow of blood from the womb; bloody catamenia. **~প্রবাহ** *n* stream of blood. **~প্রেষ** *n* blood-pressure. **~ফল** *adj* the Indian fig-tree; banian. **~বৎ** *adj* blood-like; blood-red. **~বমন** *n* blood-vomiting; haematemesis. **~বমন করা** *n* vomit blood. **~বর্ণ** *n* red colour; colour of blood. ❑*adj* red-coloured; ruddy; blood-red; crimson. **~বসন** *n* red-coloured/ crimson-coloured cloth; red garments/ clothes; religious mendicant. ❑*adj* clad/ dressed in red; wearing red garments. **~বসনা** *fem*. **~বসনা নারী** woman in red/crimson. **~বহ** *adj* blood-carrying. **~বহা** *fem*. **~বহা নাড়ি** *n* vein; artery. **~বাস**=~বসন. **~বাহ** *n* blood-vessel. **~বাহী**=~বহ. **~বাহিনী** *fem*. **~বিকার** *n* alteration/ deterioration of blood. **~বিদ্রধি** *n* boil filled with blood. **~বিন্দু** *n* drop of blood. **~বীজ** *n* **1** (myth) name of a demon, each drop of whose blood, as soon as it fell to the ground, would instantly produce an identical demon. **2** pomegranate. **~বীজের ঝাড়** *n* **1** (derog) a large family which never becomes extinct or which cannot be exterminated. **2** bugs. **~বর্ধক, ~বর্ধন** *adj* blood-increasing. **~বৃদ্ধি** *n* increase of blood (in the body). **~বৃন্তা** *n*=শেফালি. **~বৃষ্টি** *n* flow/ dropping of blood. **~বেগনি, ~বেগুনি** *n, adj* violet; purple. **~ভাণ্ডার** *n* blood-bank. **~মস্তু** *n* serum. **~মত্ত** *adj* drunk/ satiated with blood; bloodthirsty. **~মাংস** *n* flesh and blood. **~মাংসের শরীর** *n* human body; flesh and blood. **~মাংসের সম্পর্ক** *n* blood-relation. **~মোক্ষক** *adj* blod-letting. **~মোক্ষণ** *n* blood-letting. **~মোক্ষণ করা** *n* draw blood from; bleed; let blood. **~রঞ্জিত** *adj* blood-stained; dyed in red. **~রস** *n* plasma. **~রাগ** *n* crimson glow/ colour. **~রাগমণি** *n* onyx. **~রেখা** *n* streak of blood; streak of crimson light/ colour. **~রেণু** *n* red powder; vermilion; bud of *Butea frondosa* (পলাশ). **~লোচন** *n* **1**=~-আঁখি. **2** pigeon. **~শূন্য** *adj* bloodless; anaemic; pale. **~শূন্যতা** *n* bloodlessness; anaemia; palour; paleness. **~শোধক** purifying blood. **~শোধন** *n* purification of blood. **~শোষক** *ajd*=~চোষা. **~ শোষণ করা** *n* suck blood. **~শোষা** *n* kind of lizard (popularly believed to suck blood from distance). **~শোষী** *adj*=~চোষা. **~শোষিণী** *adj*. **~সংবহন** *n* circulation of blood. **~সংবহনতন্ত্র** *n* circulatory system. **~সঞ্চয়** *n* congestion. **~সঞ্চার** *n* blood-transfusion. **~সঞ্চলন, ~সঞ্চালন** *nn*=~সংবহন. **~স্নান** *n* blod-bath; large-scale slaughter. **~স্থালি** *n* 'blood-receptacle'; any organ containing/ secreting blood; heart; blood vessel. **~স্রাব** *n* flow of blood; haemorrhage. **~স্রোত** *n* stream/ flow of blood. **~স্বল্পতা** *n* anaemia. **~হীন**=~শূন্য. **রক্তাংশুক** *n* red ray of light; red garment. **রক্তাক্ত** *adj* **1** sprinkled/ besmeared with blood. **2** blood-stained: রক্তাক্ত শার্ট. **3** bleeding: রক্তাক্ত মুখ. **4** bloody: রক্তাক্ত যুদ্ধ. **5** dyed/ painted in crimson; crimson: রক্তাক্ত আকাশ. **রক্তাক্ষ** *n* **1** blood-shot eyes; red eyes. **2** pigeon. **3** Indian crane. **4** buffalo. ❑*adj* red-eyed; having red blood-shot eyes; fearful; dreadful. **রক্তাঙ্গ** *adj* 'red-bodied'. ❑*n* **1** bug. **2** coral. **3** saffron. **রক্তাতিসার** =~-অতিসার. **রক্তাধর** *n* crimson lip. **রক্তাধার** *n* skin. **রক্তাধিক্য** *n* plethora. **রক্তাভ** *adj* having a crimson glow; reddish; ruddy; crimson; pink; ruby; flushed; reddened. **রক্তাভাব** *n* lack of enough blood; anaemia. **রক্তামাশয়** =~-অতিসার. **রক্তাম্বর**=

~বসন. রক্তাম্বু *n* serum. রক্তারক্তি *n* bloodshed; profuse bleeding; bloody scuffle. রক্তালু=~পিণ্ডালু. রক্তাশয় =~স্থালি. রক্তের অক্ষরে লেখা *adj* written in blood. ☐*v* shed one's own blood for. রক্তের দামে কেনা *adj* bought at the expense of blood/ life; blood-bought. ☐*v* buy at the expense of blood. রক্তের নেশা = ~পিপাসা. রক্তের সম্পর্ক/ সম্বন্ধ *n* blood-relationship.

রক্তি *n* **1** lovingness; pleasingness. **2** affection; attachment.

রক্তিম=রক্তাভ (⇒ রক্ত). রক্তিমা *n* redness; red/ crimson glow; flush; ruddiness.

রক্তোৎপল *n* red lotus.

রক্তোপল *n* red chalk; red ochre/ orpiment.

রক্ষ১ *adj* protecting; defending; guarding. **2** protection; safety; guarding.

রক্ষ২=রক্ষ

রক্ষঃ (in compounds) *n* (myth) evil being; demon; name of an anthropophagous race of India; Rakshasa. ~কুল *n* Rakshasa race. ~পুরী *n* Lanka, the city of Rakshasas. ~সভা *n* assemblage/ multitude of Rakshasas.

রক্ষক *adj* protecting; guarding; watching, defending. ☐*n* protector; guardian; keeper; watcher; guard; defender; guardsman; caretaker; maintainer; saviour; custodian; preserver.

রক্ষণ *n*=রক্ষা. ☐*adj* (used as a *pref*)=রক্ষক. ~শীল *adj* conservative. রক্ষণাবেক্ষণ *n* maintenance; care; custody; supervision; guarding; preservation. রক্ষণাবেক্ষণ করা *vi* maintain; look after; take care of; supervise; preserve; guard. রক্ষণাবেক্ষণাধীন *adj* in one's care/custody; under one's guardianship/ supervision/ tutelage.

রক্ষণীয় *adj* to be guarded/ preserved/ protected (from); to be taken care of/ maintained/ deposited; preservable; maintainable; capable of being protected/ taken care of.

রক্ষণোপায় *n* means of safety.

রক্ষা *n* **1** protection; guarding; defense; preservation; maintenance; care; security; upkeep. **2** rescue; escape; saving; safety; redemption; deliverance; relief; release; salvage: বিপদ থেকে ~. **3** observance; keeping; adherence; compliance; fulfillment; redemption; discharge: প্রতিশ্রুতি ~. ☐*v* (poet)=~ করা. ~ করা *vt* **1** protect; defend; take care of; look after; tend; guard; maintain; preserve; keep (up). **2** rescue; save; redeem; relieve; deliver; salvage. **3** observe; keep; fulfil; redeem; discharge; comply with; adhere to. **4** deposit; retain. ~ পাওয়া *vi* be saved/ relieved/ rescued etc; escape. ~ নেই no escape. ~কবচ, ~বন্ধ *nn* an amulet believed to have occult power to protect the wearer; safeguard. ~কর *adj* defensive. ~কর্তা =রক্ষক. ~কর্ত্রী *fem*. ~কালী *n* a manifestation of the goddess Kali. ~গৃহ *n* lying-in-chamber. ~ছিটকিনি *n* safety-catch. ~বর্ণ *n* (zoo) protective colouration. ~মন্ত্র *n* incantation chanted for protection against evil. ~র্থ *adv* for the sake of protection.

রক্ষি *n* (in compounds)=রক্ষী. ~গৃহ *n* guard-room. ~জন, ~বর্গ *nn pl* assemblage/ force of policemen; assemblage of guards/ sentinels. ~সৈন্য *n* guard; sentinel.

রক্ষিকা *n fem*=রাখি. ☐*adj fem* protecting.

রক্ষিণী *n fem* of রক্ষী

রক্ষিত *adj* **1** protected; saved; preserved. **2** guarded; maintained; rescued; taken care of; tended. **3** observed; redeemed; fulfilled. **4** deposited; retained. রক্ষিতা *fem*.

রক্ষিতব্য *adj* to be guarded/ protected/ taken care of/ kept (off).

রক্ষিতা[১] *n* protector; guard; watch; sentinel. ☐*adj* protecting; guarding; preserving. রক্ষিত্রী *fem*.

রক্ষিতা[২] *n fem* kept woman; mistress; concubine.

রক্ষী=রক্ষক

রক্ষো *n* (in compounds)=রক্ষঃ. ~ঘ্ন *adj* driving back/ destroying Rakshasa. ~জননী *n* producing Rakshasa; night. ~নাথ, ~রাজ *nn* lord of Rakshasa; Ravana.

রক্ষ্য=রক্ষণীয়

রগ [P] *n* **1** vein; artery. **2** temple. ~ টিপ টিপ করা *vi* have a morbid throbbing of temples. ~ঘেঁসে *adj* gracing the temple. ~-চটা *adj* short-tempered; irascible; bad-tempered; ill-tempered; testy; choleric; canton Kerous.

রগড়[১] *n* fun; joke; banter; jest; pleasantry; prank; drollery. ~ করা *vi* joke; crack/ make a joke; banter; jest; kid; pull one's leg; make fun (of); poke fun at; play pranks on (sb). ~ দেখা *vi* **1** see/ enjoy fun; have fun. **2** take delight in another's trouble/ misfortune.

রগড়[২] *n* rubbing; friction; abrasion; scratch; massage. রগড়ানো *vt* rub; grate; grind; massage; chafe; fret; curry (a horse, etc).

রগড়া-রগড়ি *n* **1** mutual/ repeated rubbing; polishing; chafing; abrasion; traction; scraping. **2** importunity; higgling; wrangling.

রগুড়ে *adj* jocular; droll; funny; prankish; quippish; comic; comical; waggish; amusing.

রগবত, রগবৎ [A] *n* inclination; affection; attraction.

রগরগ *n* brightness; loudness of colour; glare. ~ করা *vi* (of colour) be loud/ florid; dazzle; রগরগে *adj* (of colour) loud; bright; florid; lurid; gaudy.

রঘু *n* name of a mythological king and ancestor of Rama. **~কুল** *n* dynasty/ line of king Raghu. **~কুলতিলক** *n* 'ornament of the Raghu's daynasty'; Rama. **~কুলপতি, ~নাথ, ~পতি, ~বর, ~মণি** *nn* names of Rama. **~নন্দন** *n* son/ descendant of Raghu. **~বংশ**=~কুল.

রঙা *adj* (used as a *suff*) indicating possession of (certain number of) colour or colours: দো~, রক্ত~.

রঙানো *vt* dye; colour; paint.

রঙিন, রঙীন *adj* coloured; painted; dyed; variegated, gay; lively; ornate; flowery; ornamented; gaudy.

রঙিলা *adj* **1** gaudy; showy; gay; dappled; variegated; red; bright; fine. **2** addicted to pleasure; jovial; buxom.

রঙ্ক *adj* **1** niggardly; avaricious. **2** poor; miserable; hungry. **3** mean; base. **4** intoxicated with; wild; ecstatic; excited: রতি~.

রঙ্গ১ *n* **1** fun; joke; jest; banter; prank; drollery; pleasantry; frolic; entertaining show. **2** pleasure; joy; diversion; mirth; gaiety; delight; enjoyment: ভেসে যায় রঙ্গে. **3** caprice; trick: কত ~ জানো তুমি. **~ করা 1** joke; poke fun at; crack/ make a joke. banter; jest; kill; pull one's leg; stage a comic show; make a song (of). **2** enjoy oneself; lead a life of pleasure. **~ দেখা** *vi* see/ enjoy fun; have fun; take delight in another's trouble/ misfortune. **~ দেখানো** *vi* **1** give an entertaining show. **2** make one suffer/ pay for; pay one off; punish deservedly.

রঙ্গ২ *n* **1**=রং১ (1-3). **2** place for public entertainment or for dramatic exhibition; theatre; stage; arena; play-house. **3** field of battle. **4** tin. **5** variety enjoyment; dramatic performance. **6** athletic contest; tournament. **7** artistic/ affected pose or movement; affectation. **8** manner; fashion; mode; style. **9** battle; struggle; action. **~ক** *n* pigment; colouring matter; dye. **~রঙ্গে** = রংচঙে. **~চিত্র** *n* colour. **~জ** *n* vermilion. **~জীবক** *n* dyer; painter. **~চঙ্গ** *n* fun and frolic; wily/ artful gestures and postures; dalliance; buffoonery; flippancy. **~দার** *adj* funny; amusing; facetious; droll; showy. **~ন** *n* **1** painting. **2** name of a flower; Ixora coccinea. **~পূর্ব** *n* infra-red. **~প্রিয়** *adj* fun-loving; fond of making fun/ cracking jokes; jocular; jovial; funny. frolicsome. **~প্রিয়া** *fem*. **~প্রিয়তা** *n* love of fun/ merriment. **~ভঙ্গ** *n* antic(s). **~ভূমি** *n* place of acting; stage; theatre; arena; battlefield; wrestling-ground. **~মঞ্চ** *n* stage. **~মণ্ডপ** *n* theatre; play-house. **~মহল**=রংমহল (⇒ রং১). **~মাণিক্য** *n* ruby. **~রস** *n* fun and frolic; jocularity; badinage; wit and humour. **~রেজ**=রংরেজ. **~শালা** *n* theatre; play-house. **~সাজ** [P] *n* **1** dyer; colour-manufacturer. **2** painter. **~স্থল**=~ভূমি.

-রঙ্গ৩, রঙ্গা = রঙা. **জলরঙ্গ** (জলরঙা) *adj* water-coloured.

রঙ্গাজীব *n* **1** dyer. **2** painter. **3** actor; dancer; player. **4** colour-manufacturer.

রঙ্গানো=রঙানো

রঙ্গাবতার *n* actor; stage-player.

রঙ্গালয় *n* theatre.

রঙ্গিত *adj* **1** coloured. **2** embellished; handsome; pretty; ornate.

রঙ্গিন, রঙ্গিল=রঙিন

রঙ্গিনী *adj fem.* **1**=রঙ্গপ্রিয়া (⇒ রঙ্গ). **2** sportive; gay; frolicsome. **3** enamoured; passionate; impassioned. **4** coloured; painted. **5** taking frenzied delight in: রণ~.

রঙ্গিল *n* **1**=রঙ্গ. **2** colourfulness; beauty; loveliness.

রঙ্গিলা=রঙিলা

রঙ্গী 1=রঙ্গপ্রিয় (⇒ রঙ্গ). **2** enamoured.

রঙ্গীন=রঙিন

রঙ্গোত্তর (Phys) *adj* ultra-violet.

রচক=রচয়িতা

রচন *n* act of making/ forming/ arranging; preparing/ composing; building; composition; formation; creation.

রচনা *n* **1** arrangement; composition: কেশ ~. **2** disposition. **3** production; preparation; fabrication. **4** literary production; work; essay; composition. **5** arrangement of troops; array. **6** contrivance; invention. **7** building; construction: গৃহ ~. **8** management; accomplishment. **9** putting on; wearing (of garments). **10** stringing flowers/ garlands: মাল্য ~. **~ করা** *vt* arrange; compose; dispose; prepare; produce; fashion; form; make; construct; build; create; write. **~কৌশল** *n* method/ style of making/ composition. **~চৌর** *n* plagiarist. **~নৈপুণ্য** *n* skill in making/ building/ composition, style. **~পদ্ধতি, ~প্রণালী**=~কৌশল. **~শৈলী** *n* (esp literary) style. **কেশ ~***n* hair-do; hair-style. **কেশ ~ করা** *vi* do up/ dress one's hair.

রচনীয় *adj* to be composed/ arranged/ written/ disposed.

রচয়িতা *n* author; composer; writer; maker; builder; constructor; creator. **রচয়িত্রী** *fem*.

রচা vt=রচনা করা (⇒ রচনা). ❑*adj*=রচিত

রচিত *adj* composed; written; arranged; prepared; made; fashioned; built; constructed; produced; placed; inserted; inlaid on/in .

রজ, রজঃ *n* **1** dust. **2** pollen of flowers. **3** menstrual excretion. **4**=রজোগুণ. **রজঃকণা** *n* grain of dust.

রজক *n* washerman. **রজকী, রজকিনী** *fem* washer-woman.

রজত *n* silver. ❑*adj* silver-coloured; whitish; made of silver; silvery. **~কান্তি** *adj* silver-white. **~গিরি** *n* the mountain Kailasa. **~জয়ন্তী** *n* silver jubilee. **~দ্যুতি, ~ধবল, ~বর্ণ, ~শুভ্র** *adjj* silver-white; silver-coloured; silvery. **~প্রস্থ**=~গিরি. **~মুদ্রা** *n* silver coin. **~মূল্য** *n* price paid in silver coins. **রজতাঙ্গুরীয়** *n* silver-ring.

রজন *n* resin; rosin; gamboge.

রজনী, রজনি *n* night. **~কর, ~কান্ত, ~নাথ** *nn* the moon. **~গন্ধা** *n* tuberose. **~চর** *adj* wandering in the night. ❑*n* night-rover; thief; Rakshasa; nocturnal animal. **~জল** *n* night-dew; hoar-frost. **~মুখ** *n* evening. **~যোগে** *adv* by/at night.

রজস্বলা *n fem* in menses; menstruating; marriageable.

রজোগুণ *n* (phil) the second of the three *gunas* or qualities; it is sometimes identified with *tejas* (তেজস); it is said to predominate in air, and to be active, urgent and variable. **~জনিত** *adj* due/ produced by the quality of *rajas*. **~দর্শন** *n* (first) appearance of the menstrual excretion. **~বন্ধ** *n* menopause; suppression of menstruation. **~বল** *n* **1** darkness. **2** power of the quality of *rajas*.

রজ্জু *n* rope; cord; string; line; cable. **~পথ** *n* ropeway. **~বদ্ধ** *adj* fastened with a rope; tied with cords; bound with ropes; roped; corded; stringed. **~ভ্রম** *n* fallacy of mistaking (snakes etc) for a rope.

রঞ্জক১ *n* **1** dyer; colourist; painter. **2** dye; paint; colouring substance. **3** exciter of affection, etc; stimulus. ❑*adj* exciting passion/ love; pleasing; charming. **~ দ্রব্য, ~ পদার্থ** *nn* dye; paint; colouring substance; pigment.

রঞ্জক২ *n* gunpowder. **~ ঘর** *n* magazine of a gun; touch-hole.

রঞ্জন *n* **1** dyeing; colouring; painting; colouration. **2** pleasing; charming; rejoicing; delighting; conciliating; befriending. **3** lover. **4** red sandalwood. ❑*adj* charming; pleasing; entertaining; rejoicing; delighting; conciliating; delightful. **~ দ্রব্য** *n* any colouring substance. **~ প্রণালী** *n* process of dyeing/ colouring. **~ বিদ্যা** *n* art of dyeing/ colouring; art of pleasing.

রঞ্জন–রশ্মি *n* Röntgen rays; x-rays.

রঞ্জনী *adj fem*=রঞ্জন. ❑*n* **1** turmeric. **2** saffron. **3** red arsenic. **4** indigo plant.

রঞ্জনীয় *adj* to be dyed/ coloured/ painted; to be pleased/ rejoiced.

রঞ্জা *vt* (poet) dye; paint; colour.

রঞ্জিকা *n, adj fem* of রঞ্জক

রঞ্জিত *adj* **1** coloured; dyed; painted; tinted; illumined. **2** charmed; enchanted; entertained. **~ করা** *vt* colour; dye; paint; tint; illumine.

রঞ্জিনী=*adj fem*=রঞ্জনী

রটন, রটনা *n* **1** rumour. **2** circulation of a report/ rumour. **3** publicity; announcement; propagation; proclamation. **4** scandalous report; idle rumour; hearsay; canard; gossip. **~ করা** *vi* rumour; noise it abroad; announce; circulate; give publicity to; bruit it abroad.

রটা *vi* be in circulation; be bruited abroad/ about; be noised around; be gossiped; be made public; be rumoured. **রটানো**=রটনা করা (⇒ রটন). **যা রটে তার কিছু বটে** (fig) There is some truth in a rumour.

রটানি = রটন

রটানে *n* rumour-monger; tale-bearer; tale-teller; gossip.

রটিত *adj* rumoured; bruited (about); noised abroad/ around; gossiped; reported; made public; circulated. **~ হওয়া**=রটা.

রড [E]*n* rod (esp one of metal).

রড় *n* run to flee. **~ দেওয়া** *vi* be on the run; show a clean pair of heals; flee; bolt away.

রড়া *vi* (old use)=রড় দেওয়া (⇒ রড়). **~রড়ি** *n* running helter-skelter.

রণ *n* war; combat; fight; conflict; battle. **~ করা** *vt, vi* fight; combat; wage war; battle. **~ দেওয়া** *vi* give/ offer battle. **~কামী** *adj* desirous of war; wishing to fight; belligerent; militant. **~কুঠার** *n* battle-axe. **~কুশল** *adj* skilled in warfare; martial; warlike. **~কুশলা** *fem*. **~কৌশল** *n* art of warfare; military tactics/ skill. **~ক্ষেত্র** *n* battle-field. **~চণ্ডী** *n fem* goddess Chandi esp when engaged in fighting demons; violent bad tempered woman; termagant. **~চতুর** *adj* skilled in warfare. **~চাতুর্য** *n* military skill/ tactics; skill in warfare; military genius. **~জয়** *n* victory in battle. **~জয়ী, ~জিৎ** adjj victorious in war/ battle. **~ঢক্কা** *n* war-drum. **~তরঙ্গ** *n* tumult of war/ battle. **~তরি, ~তরী** *nn* warship; battleship. **~তূর্য** *n* war-drum. **~দক্ষ** =~কুশল. **~দক্ষতা** =~চাতুর্য. **~ধীর** *adj* steady in war ❑*n* great hero. **~নাদ** *n* war-cry. **~নিপুণ**=~চতুর. **~নিপুণা** *fem*. **~নৃত্য** *n* war-dance. **~নৈপুণ্য**=~চাতুর্য. **~পণ্ডিত** *adj* skilled in warfare; experienced in the art/ ways of war; skilful in war. **~পাণ্ডিত্য** *n* military expertise/ talent/ genius. **~পোত**=~তরী. **~প্রণালী** *n* method of warfare; strategy. **~প্রিয়** *adj* fond of war/ battle; warlike. **~বাদ্য** *n* military musical instrument; martial music; musical band. **~বেশ** *n* fighting attire; military uniform; belligerent approach/ attitude. **~ভঙ্গ** *n* retreat from the battle-field; decampment. **~ভঙ্গ দেওয়া** *vi* retreat/ flee from the battle-field; take flight; beat a (hasty) retreat; decamp. **~ভূমি** *n* battle-field; battle-ground. **~ ভেরি, ~ভেরী** *nn* battle-drum. **~মত্ত** *adj* fierce/ frantic in battle; frenziedly fighting. **~মুখ** *n* jaws of battle; van of battle/ an army; eager for battle; bellicose. **~মুখো** *adj* bellicose; eager for battle; warlike. **~মুখী** *fem*. **~যাত্রা** *n* military expedition/

campaign. ~রঙ্ক *adj* **1** tired of fighting; exhausted in combat. **2** eager for battle; longing for battle. ❑*n* elephant exhausted in battle. ~রঙ্গ *n* **1** fun/ delight of fighting. **2** battle-field. **3** craze for fighting; bellicosity. ❑*adj* fond of fighting. ~রঙ্গী *adj* fierce in battle. ~রঙ্গিণী *fem*. ~রসিক *adj* fond of fighting; desirous of fighting. ~লক্ষ্মী *n fem* fortune of war; goddess of battle. ~শয্যা *n* battle-field as one's death-bed. ~শিক্ষা *n* art/ science of war. ~শৃঙ্গ = ~ভেরি. ~সঙ্কুল *adj* in a state of war; engaged in war. ❑*n* confusion/ noise of battle; mixed/ tumultuous combat. ~সজ্জা, ~সাজ *nn* battle-dress; military uniform; armament; military equipment; warlike preparations; military accoutrements. ~স্তম্ভ *n* tower of victory. ~স্থল *n* battle-ground. ~হস্তী *n* war-elephant. ~হুঙ্কার *n* battle-cry; war-cry.

রণৎ *adj* sounding; ringing; rattling. ~কার *n* ringing/ rattling/ clanking sound.

রণন *n* (onom)=রণৎকার (⇒ রণ্য)

রণপা ⇒ রনপা

রণরণ *n* (onom) **1** twang; twanging; clatter; clangour; rattle. **2** humming; buzz (of mosquitoes). **3** mosquito; gnat. **4** regret for sth lost. **5** rattling of arms.

রণরণি *n* (onom) **1** rattle of arms. **2** tinkle of ornaments.

রণরণিকা *n* great anxiety/ longing.

রণাগ্র *n* front/ van of a battle.

রণাঙ্গন *n* battle-field; battle-arena.

রণাভিযান *n* military expedition/ campaign.

রণিত *adj* sounded; sounding; ringing; tinkled; tinkling. ❑*n* any ringing/ rattling sound; tinkle. ~ করা/ হওয়া *vi* sound; resound; ring; rattle; tinkle; twang.

রণোৎকট *adj* furious/ mad in battle.

রণোৎসাহ *n* eagerness for battle; prowess in battle.

রণোদ্যম *n* eagerness/ preparation for battle.

রণোন্মত্ত *adj* fighting furiously; mad in battle.

রণ্ড *n* man who dies without male issue. ❑*adj* **1** faithless. **2** widower. ~ক *n* barren tree.

রত *n adj* intent upon; engaged in; fond/ enamoured of; devoted/ attached/ disposed/ addicted to; employed/ absorbed in. ~কূজিত *n* lascivious murmur.

রতন *n* (poet)=রত্ন. ~চুড়, ~চুর *n* a particular ornament for the wrist, palms and fingers. ~মণি *n* greatest jewel. রতনে~ চেনে *(prov)* one can pick up one's like easily; birds of a feather flock together.

রতি[১] *n* **1** pleasure; enjoyment; attachment; delight (in); fondness (for). **2** (pleasure of) love; sexual passion/ union; amorous enjoyment. **3** sexual intercourse. **4** one of the two wives of the Hindu love-god Kama. ~কর্ম, ~ক্রিয়া *n* sexual intercourse; copulation. ~কান্ত *n* lover of Rati, Kamadeva. ~কুহর, ~গৃহ, ~মন্দির *nn* **1** pudenda. **2** pleasure-house. ~গুরু *n* **1** husband. **2** Kamadeva. ~পতি *n* Kamadeva. ~মদ *n* wine of sexual passion. ~রঙ্ক *adj* love-sick. ~শক্তি *n* virile power; manly power.

রতি[২] *n* **1** smallest measure of weight (= 1.875 grain). **2** (fig) very small/ tiny amount; wee; a wee bit; mite. এক~ a mite of a: এক~ মেয়ে.

রত্তি=রতি[২]

রত্ন *n* **1** jewel; gem; treasure; precious stones. **2** wealth; riches; goods; anything valuable or precious of its kind: পুত্র~, an excellent son. ~কুম্ভ *n* jar set with jewels. ~কূট *n* name of a mountain. ~কোষ *n* treasure of jewels. ~খচিত *adj* studded/ inlaid/set with gems. ~খনি *n* mine for precious stones. ~গর্ভ *adj* filled with precious stones; containing jewels; set with jewels. ❑*n* the sea. ~গর্ভা *adj fem* giving birth to excellent children. ❑*n* the earth. ~জীবী *n* jeweller; lapidary. ~দ্বীপ *n* coral island; treasure island. ~প্রভা *n* glitter/ splendour of jewels. ~প্রসূতী, ~প্রসবিণী, ~প্রসবিত্রী, ~প্রসূ *adjj fem* yielding gems; giving birth to excellent children. ~বণিক *n* jeweller; dealer in gems/ jewels. ~বতী *adj fem* abounding in/ decorated with precious stones/ pearls. ❑*n* the earth. ~বর *n* best of precious stones; gold. ~বর্ষুক *n* the mythical chariot Pushpak (supposed to rain/pour out jewels). ~বান *adj* abounding in/ decorated with precious stones/ gems. ~বৃক্ষ *n* coral. ~মণ্ডিত *adj* bedecked with jewels; bejewelled; studded/ inlaid with jewels. ~ময় *adj* made/ consisting of jewels; studded with precious stones. ~ময়ী *fem*. ~মালা *n* jewel necklace; pearl necklace. ~মালী *adj* adorned with a necklace of jewels. ~মুখ্য *n* chief of jewels; diamond. ~রাট =~মুখ্য. ~রাজি *n* string of pearls; jewels; gems. ~সিংহাসন *n* throne bedecked/ studded with jewels. রত্নাকর *n* jewel-mine; sea; ocean. রত্নাচল=~কূট, রত্নাবলি *nn* string of pearls; necklace of jewels; gems. রত্নাভরণ, রত্নালঙ্কার, রত্নালংকার *nn* jewel ornament; ornament of precious stones. রত্নালোক *n* lustre/ brilliance of a gem.

রথ *n* **1** chariot; car; two wheeled war-chariot. **2** any vehicle or equipage or carriage. **3** the chariot of Juggernaut. **4** festival of Juggernaut going in a chariot for a sea-bath. ~ টানা *vi* draw a chariot (esp the chariot of Juggernaut). ~ দেখা *vi* witness the festival of Juggernaut. ~কর, ~কার *n* chariot-maker; chariot-builder; wheelwright. ~গুপ্তি *n* fence of wood/ iron protecting a war-chariot from collision etc. ~ঘোষ *n* rattling/ rumbling of a chariot. ~চক্র *n* chariot-wheel. ~চর্যা *n* travelling/ going by carriage (frequently); chariot-course. ~চরণ, ~পাদ *nn* chariot-wheel. ~চালক *n* charioteer; coachman; carriage-driver. ~টানা *n* drawing a chariot. ~বাহক=~চালক. ~বেগ *n* speed of a chariot. ~যাত্রা *n* the festive procession of the car of Juggernaut. ~যুগ *n* chariot yoke. ~যুদ্ধ *n* fight on chariots. ~শালা *n* coach-house; carriage-shed. ~শ্রেণী *n* row of chariots. ~সারথি *n* charioteer. ~স্বামী *n* owner of a chariot/ carriage; charioteer. রথাঙ্গ *n* **1** any part of chariot. **2** chariot-wheel. **3** the bird ruddy goose. **4** discus. রথাঙ্গপাণি *n* 'having the discus in his hand'; Vishnu. রথারূঢ় *adj* mounted on a chariot. রথারূঢ়া *fem.* রথারোহণ *n* mounting/ ascending a chariot. রথারোহণ করা *vi* mount/ ascend a chariot. রথারোহী *adj* riding/ mounting a chariot/ vehicle. ❑*n* one who fights from a chariot; charioteer; rider/ passenger of any vehicle. রথারোহিণী *fem.* ~ দেখা ও কলা বেচা (fig) kill two birds with one stone. রথের মেলা *n* fair held on the occasion of the festival of Juggernaut.

রথিক, রথিন=রথী

রথী *n* carriage-driver; driver/ owner of a car/ chariot; charioteer; car-fighter; champion; hero; leader; lord. ~তম *n* chief of charioteers.

রথো *adj* **1** trashy: ~ মাল. **2** good-for-nothing; worthless: ~ লোক.

রথ্যা *n* **1** carriage-road; highway; street. **2** number of carriages/ chariots.

রদ[১] [A] *adj* nullified; abrogated; annulled; revoked; stayed; rejected; refuted; repealed. ❑*n* abrogation; nullification; revocation; stay. ~ করা *vt* nullify; abrogate; revoke; repeal; annul; stay; return; reject. ~-বদল *n* change; alteration; modification; additions and alterations; reshuffle: মন্ত্রীসভার ~-বদল. রদের হুকুম *n* stay order.

রদ[২] *n* tooth. রদন *n* **1**=~. **2** tooth-bite. রদনী *n* elephant.

রদি, রদ্দি [A] *adjj* trashy; rejected; worthless; waste; bad; shoddy; cheap; lousy; indifferent; good-for-nothing; shabby: ~ মাল ~ লোক.

রদ্দজওয়াব [P] *n* rejoinder.

রদ্দা [A] *n* stroke with the arm on the nape of another's neck. ~ দেওয়া/ মারা *vi* strike the nape of sb's neck with one's arm; seize sb by the neck and drive away.

রদ্দি ⇒ রদি

রনপা, রণপা *n* stilt.

রনরন=রণরণ

রন্ধন *n* cooking; cookery. ~ কার্য, ~ ক্রিয়া=~. ~ করা *vt* cook; dress (as food). ~কর্তা *n* cook. ~ গৃহ, ~শালা *nn* kitchen; cook-house. ~ পাত্র *n* cooking utensil. রন্ধনাগার, রন্ধনালয়=গৃহ

রন্ধনী *n*=রাঁধুনি

রন্ধিত *adj* cooked; dressed.

রন্ধ্র *n* **1** slit; split; hole; opening; aperture; chasm; fissure; cavity. **2** fault; defect; flaw; imperfection; weak part. **3** bore (of a gun). **4** name of the 8th astrological mansion. রন্ধ্রক *n* borer. ~-ক্যামেরা *n* pin-hole camera. ~গত *adj* entered into the hole/slit. ~গত শনি (astrol) location of the Saturn in the eighth zodiacal house of one's horoscope causing one's death; imminent death.

রপ্ত *n* [A] practice; familiarity; habitude. ❑*adj* accustomed; habituated; thoroughly learnt/ mastered; acclimatized. ~ করা *vt* master; learn thoroughly; be accustomed/ habituated to; get used to; be familiar with.

রপ্তানি, রপ্তানী [P] *n* export. ❑*adj* exported. ~ করা *vt* export. ~-বাণিজ্য *n* export-trade. ~শুল্ক *n* export duty.

রপ্তে রপ্তে *adv* gradually; by degrees; slowly.

র ফলা ⇒ র

রফা [A] *n* **1** settlement; compromise; compromise agreement; deciding. **2** finish; destruction. ~ করা *vi* settle; compromise; decide; come to terms with; set at rest; reach a settlement; make a compromise. ~দফা *n* deciding; settling. ❑*adj* settled. ~নামা *n* deed of compromise. দফা~ *n* destruction; discomfiture; wreck; ruin; rack and ruin; demolition; desolation. দফা-~ করা *vt* destroy; wreck; ruin; discomfit; demolish; smash; finish; knock out; undo; shatter.

রব[১] *n* **1** (of birds) song; singing. **2** hum; humming. **3** sound; clamour; noise; outcry; hue and cry. **4** rumour. **5** response. ~ উঠেছে A rumour is in the air; Rumour has it; There is a rumour that ... . ~ করা *vi* make a noise; sing; hum; cry; cry aloud; make a sound. ~রবা *n* hey day.

রব[২] [A] *n* lord; protector; God; preserver; master .

রবাব [A] *n* kind of violin.

রবার [E] *n* rubber.

রবাহূত *adj* come uninvited at a feast on hearing a report of it; unwelcome.

রবি[১] *n* the sun; sun-god. ~কর *n* sunbeam; sunray; sunshine; sunlight. ~করোজ্জ্বল *adj* brightened with sunrays; sunny; bright with sunlight. ~কান্ত *n* sun-stone. ~কিরণ *n* sunbeam. ~চক্র *n* particular astronomical diagram (the sun represented as a man carrying stars on the various parts of his body). রবিচ্ছবি *n* sun's radiance. রবিজ *n* 'sun-born'; the planet Saturn. ~নীচ *n* (astron) perihelion. ~বর্ষ *n* solar year. ~বার, ~বাসর *nn* sunday. ~মণ্ডল *n* orb of the sun. ~মার্গ *n* the ecliptic. ~রশ্মি =~কর.

রবি[২], রবী *n* [A] spring; spring harvest. ~খন্দ, ~শস্য *nn* spring harvest. ~উল আউয়াল *n* the fourth month of the Hizri year.

রভস *n* **1** passion; eager desire (for); great delight; upsurge of emotion. **2** haste; impetuosity; vehemence; hurry; zeal; speed. **3** (sexual) union; intercourse. **4** fun; pleasure; hilarity; joke; pleasantry.

রম[১] *adj* pleasing; delighting; dear; beloved. ❑*n* lover; husband; spouse.

রম[২] *n* [E] rum.

রমক *adj* toying amorously; dallying; sporting. ❑*n* lover; suitor.

রমজান *n* [A] ninth lunar month of the Hizri calendar; the month of fasting.

রমণ *n* **1** copulation; coitus; sexual union; dalliance; amorous sport. **2** sport; enjoyment; pleasure. **3** hinder parts; pudenda. **4** Kamadeva, the Hindu god of love. **5** lover; husband. **6** man. ~ করা *vi* have sexual intercourse with; copulate; dally amorously; indulge in sports/ enjoyment.

রমণী *n fem* woman; beautiful young woman; mistress; wife. ~কুল, ~জন *n* womenfolk; womankind. ~জনসুলভ *adj* womanly; woman-like; womanish. ~দুর্লভ *adj* beyond the reach of women. ~মোহন *adj* one who captures the fancy of women or casts a magic spell on them. ~মোহন পুরুষ *n* lady-killer. ~রত্ন *n* jewel of a woman. ~সুলভ = ~জনসুলভ.

রমণীয় *adj* pleasant; enjoyable; delightful; charming; agreeable; beautiful.

রমরমা *adj* prosperous; booming; thriving.

রমা[১] *vi* (poet)=রমণ করা

রমা[২] *n fem* **1** mistress; wife; beautiful young woman; sweetheart; lady-love. **2** name of Lakshmi, the goddess of wealth. **3** splendour; good luck; opulence; fortune; pomp. ~কান্ত, ~ধর, ~নাথ, ~পতি, ~প্রিয় *nn* lover/ husband of Rama; Vishnu.

রমিত *adj* **1** delighted; gladdened; rendered happy. **2** sported with. **3** sexually enjoyed; dallied. রমিতা *fem.*

রমেশ *n* lord of Rama; Vishnu.

রম্বস [E] *n* (geom) rhombus.

রম্ভা *n fem* **1** plantain; banana; banana-tree. **2** (myth) name of a celebrated Apsara. **3** name of the goddess Gauri (গৌরী). ~তৃতীয়া *n* name of the third day of the first half of the month of the Jaistha (so called because Hindu women on this day imitate Rambha, who bathed on the same day with particular ceremonies). **3** nothing; hoax; a mare's nest.

রম্ভোরু *n* woman having thighs (smooth and tapering) like (the stem of) a plantain tree. ❑*adj* full; round; lovely.

রম্য *adj* to be enjoyed; enjoyable; pleasant; delightful; beautiful. রম্যা *fem.* রম্যতা *n* pleasantness; loveliness; beauty. ~রচনা *n* belles-letters.

রম্যা *n fem* **1** night. **2** kind of lotus.

রয় *n* **1** quick motion; speed; swiftness. **2** current; stream of a river.

রয়না *n* kind of tree; *Amoora rohitaka.*

রয়ানি, রয়ানী *n* **1** a folk-song based on the mythological story of the goddess Manasa. **2** wailing; lamentation.

রয়িষ্ঠ *adj* fleetest; very vehement/ swift.

রয়ে বসে *adj* taking one's time (over); slowly; little by little; without hurry.

রয়ে রয়ে *adv* from time to time; every now and then; off and on; intermittently.

রলা *n* **1** slick. **2** cylindrical piece of tree-stump.

রশনা *n* **1** ornament worn as a girdle by a woman. **2**=রসনা. **3** robe; cord; strap.

রশা *n* thick rope/ cord. ~রশি *n* ropes and cords of various sizes; cordage.

রশি *n* **1** cord; rope; string. **2** gunter's chain/ scale. ~গির *n* chainman.

রশ্মি *n* **1** ray; beam. **2** rope; cord; strap; string. **3** rein; bridle. **4** eyelash. ~গুচ্ছ *n* bundle of rays. ~জাল *n* net/ garland of rays. ~পাত *n* shedding of rays; radiation. ~পুঞ্জ *n* heap/ mass of rays. ~মণ্ডল *n* circle/ garland of rays. ~ময় *adj* formed/ consisting of rays. ~মালী *adj* encircled/ garlanded with rays. নভো~,. মহাজাগতিক ~ *nn* cosmic rays.

রশ্মীয় *adj* radial. ~ কেন্দ্র *n* (phy) optical centre.

রস *n* **1** sap/ juice of plants; juice of fruit. **2** any liquid/ fluid; liquid solution: চিনির ~. **3** savour; flavour; taste: মধুর ~. **4** exudation: তালের ~. **5** best/ finest/ prime part of anything; essence; marrow: অন্ন~. **6** water; liquor; drink; syrup. **7** any mixture; elixir; draught; potion. **8** soup; broth. **9** constituent fluid/ essential juice of the body; serum; chyle: ~রক্তে পুষ্ট হয়ে .... **10** lymph; mucus; phlegm: দেহে রসাধিক্য. **11** semen virile; seminal fluid. **13** pus: ফোড়ার মুখ দিয়ে ~ পড়ছে. **14** water. **15** (rhet) taste/ character of a work; feeling/ sentiment prevailing in a work: শৃঙ্গার ~, অদ্ভুত ~. **16** serenity. **17** pleasure; delight; enjoyment. **18** love; affection; desire; strong attachment. **19** interest; sense of humour: এমন ~হীন লোক আর দেখিনি. **20** fun; jest; banter; wit and humour; hilarity. **21** charm; grace; beauty. **22** inner significance; purport: রসজ্ঞ ব্যক্তি. **23** arrogance; vanity; audacity; pride: তার ভারী ~ হয়েছে. **24** mercury; quicksilver (sometimes regarded as the quintessence of the human body). **25** myrrh. **26** any mineral or metallic salt. **27** metal/ mineral in a state of fusion. **28** monetary resources; money: ছেলেটি ভালো কিন্তু গোড়ায় ~ নেই. **29** poison. **30** disease. **31** quality. **32** wine. **33** (Vaishnava phil) disposition of the heart/ mind; religious sentiment (there are five *rasas* or *ratis* forming the five degrees of *bhakti* or devotion). **34** morbid exudation: ঘায়ের ~. **~ করা** *vi* **1** make fun of; jest; banter. **2** make a liquid solution of; extract/ obtain juice from. **~ জমা/ নামা** *n* become swollen (with dropsy etc): পায়ে ~ নেমেছে. **~ পাওয়া** *vi* find interest in; be amused/ enthused by sth. **~ ফুরানো** *vi* run out of funds. **~ হওয়া** *vi* **1** become juicy/ succulent. **2** (sl) became audacious/ arrogant/ vain. **~ করা** *n* a sweet and juicy drop of the kernel of coconut. **~কর্পূর** *n* perchloride of mercury; corrosive sublimate. **~কলা** *n* **1** singing/ sweet voice. **2** art of entertainment. **~কলি** *n* streak of mud (resembling a bud) painted on the bridge of the nose by Vaishnavas. **~কষ, ~কস** *n* **1** moisture. **2** sweetness and grace. **~কষহীন** *adj* dry and outspoken; dull; jejune; dreary; insipid; dismal. **~কাঙ্গালি** *adj* love-lorn; pining with love. **~কেশর**=~কর্পূর. **~ক্রিয়া** *n* application of fluid remedies/ fomentation's etc. **~গর্ভ** *adj* juicy; succulent; sappy; humorous; witty; flavoury; absorbing; spicy; delicious; savoury; delectable. ❑*n* **1** cinnabar. **2** collyrium made from the juice of Curium *xanthorrhiza*. **2** ointment made from the calx of brass. **~গোল্লা** *n* a sweet and juicy drop made of curd and flour. **~গ্রহ** *adj* apprehending flavours; having a taste for enjoyment. **~গ্রহণ** *n* appreciation. **~গ্রহণ করা** *vt* **1** taste; relish; enjoy. **2** (rhet) appreciate; be discerning; judge. **~গ্রাহী** *adj* capable of appreciation; appreciative; discerning; perceptive; sensitive. **~ঘন** *adj* **1** (rhet) zestful; very interesting; racy; absorbing. **2** full of juice; juicy. **রসজ** *n* **1** blood. **2** molasses. **রসজ্ঞ** *adj* appreciative; knowing tastes/ the taste of; familiar with. ❑*n* poet/ any writer who understands the rasas; connoisseur. রসা *fem*. **রসতা** *n* knowledge of flavours; experience; familiarity with; poetical skill/ taste; discrimination; judgement. **~জ্ঞান** *n* capability of appreciation; connoisseurship; good taste; sense of humour; flair. **রসজ্ঞ ব্যক্তি** *n* connoisseur; expert. **~ধাতু** *n* mercury. **~পূর্ণ**=~গর্ভ. **~বড়া** *n* sweet juicy drop made of pulped pigeon-pea. **~বড়ি** *n* (med) a pill containing mercury. **~বতী** *adj fem* **1**=~বন্ত. **2** graceful; lovely. **~বন্ত** *adj* **1** full of juice/ sap; juicy; succulent; moist. **2** charming; elegant; graceful; lovely. **3** possessing love and other rasas; impassioned; full of feeling; affected by emotions of love, jealousy, etc; witty; spirited. **~বাত** *n* rheumatic affection in the joints affected with swelling. **~বান**=~বন্ত. **~বেত্তা** = রসজ্ঞ. **~বোধ** =~জ্ঞান. **~ভঙ্গ** *n* interruption/ cessation of passion or sentiment; interruption of a spicy topic; artistic flaw; interruption of enjoyment (usually by coarseness). **~ভরা** =~গর্ভ. **~ময়** *adj* **1** formed of juice; liquid. **2** whose essence is taste; savoury. **3** delightful; charming; absorbing; full of wit and humour; full of flavour. **~মরা** *adj* dry; insipid; jejune. **~রঙ্গ** *n* fun; frolic; pleasantry; witticism. **~রচনা** *n* humours/ witty writing. **~রাজ** *n* **1** the most witty and humorous man. **2** Sri Krishna. **3** mercury. **4** antimony. **~শালা** *n* chemical laboratory/ workshop. **~শাস্ত্র** *n* **1** poetics; rhetoric. **2** alchemy. **~শোধন** *n* **1** purification of mercury. **2** borax. **~সিদ্ধ** *n* alchemist; chemist. **~সিন্দূর** *n* sulphide of mercury; sort of factitious cinnabar. **রসস্থ** *adj* stricken with excess of phlegm/ lymph/ mucus; succulent; juicy. **~স্ফীত** *adj* (bot) turgid. **~স্ফীতি** *n* (bot) turgidity; turgescence. **~স্রাব** *n* (bot) exudation. **~হীন** *adj* dry; uninteresting; sapless; dull; insipid.

রসদ [P] *n* **1** store of grain laid in for an army; provisions. **2** food. **3** rations. **4** supplies. **5** allowance of food. **6** (fig) means; monetary resources; expenses.

রসন *n* **1** tasting; taste, flavour; savour. **2** tongues as the organ of taste.

রসনা *n* tongue; palate. **রসনাগ্র** *n* tip of the tongue. **~মল** *n* impurity on the tongue. **~মূল** *n* root of the tongue.

রসনেন্দ্রিয় *n* organ of taste; tongue.

রসম, রসুম *n* [A] settled mode; established usage; precept. **~ ও রেওয়াজ** *n* custom and usage.

রসা[১] *n* **1** the earth. **2** tongue. **3** porcupine. **4** lower world; hell. **5** vine; grape. **~তল** *n*=~ (4). **রসাতলে দেওয়া** *vi* (fig) ruin/ destroy utterly. **রসাতলে যাওয়া** *vi* (fig) be ruined/ destroyed utterly.

রসা[২] *n* **1** meat-soup; gravy (of meat/ fish). **2** fruit-juice.

রসা[৩] *n* rope; cord; a 120 feet long rope. **~রসি** *n* cordage; ropes.

রসা[৪] *vi* **1** become juicy/ sappy. **2** ripen; mature; mellow. **3** become slightly rotten/ petrified. **4** soften; become moist; moisten: মাটি রসেছে. **5** be stricken with excess of phlegm/ lymph/ in the body; swell: চোখ-মুখ রসেছে. ❑*n* **1** *adj* juicy; succulent; mellow; ripe: ~ আম. **2** slightly rotten/ petrified/

decomposed; overripe: ~ মাছ. ~রসা *adj* moderately juicy.

রসাই=রসুই

রসাঞ্জন *n* 1 vitriol of copper or a sort of collyrium prepared from it with the addition of curcuma or from the calx of brass with amomum xanhorrhiza or from lead ore. 2 antimony; stibnite.

রসাতল ⇒ রসা[১]

রসাত্মক *adj* 1 having juice for its essence; characterized sapidity/ savour; sappy; juicy. 2 (rhet) tasteful; elegant; charming; beautiful; witty; humorous; flavoury. রসাত্মিকা *fem*.

রসাধিক্য *n* excess of juice/ flavour; morbid excess of phlegm/ lymph/ mucus in the body.

রসান *n* 1 act of steeping in juice. 2 wetting; moistening. 3 act of polishing gold, etc. 4 a polishing substance (containing alum, sulphur, nitre, etc). 5 a stone rubbing against which gold, etc are polished; polishing stone. 6 spicy/ piquant remark added to give flavour to speech; mockery; derision; cutting remark.

রসানি *n* 1 fluid; secretion; discharge; exudation. 2 broth; soup.

রসানো *vt* 1 make juicy; wet; moisten; melt. 2 (fig) soften; melt; affect; appeal to; move the feelings: মন ~. 3 make interesting by adding piquant/ spicy remarks. রসিয়ে *adv* with gusto/ zest; humorously.

রসাবেশ *n* affected state of the mind; ecstasy; bliss; beatitude.

রসাভাস *n* 1 (rhet) mere semblance/ false attribution/ improper manifestation of a sentiment. 2 (rhet) impropriety.

রসাম্ল *n* vinegar made from fruit; sour sauce; tamarind sauce.

রসায়ন *n* 1 chemistry. 2 a medicine supposed to prevent old age and prolong life; elixir; elixir vitae. 3 buttermilk. 4 poison. রসায়নজ্ঞ, রসায়নবিদ *adjj* versed in chemistry. ❑*n* chemist. ~বিদ্যা, ~শাস্ত্র *nn* chemistry. রসায়নাগার *n* chemical laboratory.

রসায়নী *adj* chemical; versed in chemistry. ❑*n* chemist; chemical scientist. ~বিদ্যা *n* science of chemistry.

রসা, রসালো *adj* 1 juicy; succulent; tasteful; delicious; palatable; sappy. 2 humorous; witty; spicy; piquant; racy: ~ আলাপ. 3 savoury; sweet; mellifluous; melodic; tuneful; sweet-sounding; harmonious: ~ গীত. ❑*n* 1 mango tree. 2 kind of grass.

রসালসা *n* (anat) artery.

রসালাপ *n* humorous/ witty/ amorous conversation; causerie; tête-à-tête; chitchat; pleasantries; badinage. ~ করা *vi* indulge/ be engaged in humorous/ witty/ amorous conversation; gossip; chat.

রসাস্বাদ, রসাস্বাদন=রসগ্রহণ (⇒ রস)

রসি=রশি

রসিক *adj* 1 having a discriminating taste; aesthetic; appreciative; having a sense of humour; sensitive; perceptive. 2. witty; humorous; jocose; amusing; facetious; ~ লোক. 3 versed in the art of love-making; lustful; gallant; sensual: ~ নাগর. ❑*n* 1 connoisseur; lover of art. 2 humourist; wit. রসিকা *fem*. রসিকতা *n* joke; jest; badinage; pleasantry; humorous/ amorous frolic; (sense of) humour; wit. ~ নাগর *n* gallant; ladies' man; philander.

রসিত *adj* 1 tasted. 2 having taste/ flavour/ sentiment, covered/ overlaid with gold; gilded; plated.

রসিদ, রসীদ [P] *n* receipt; acknowledgment. ~ কাটা *vi* write out a receipt.

রসিয়া *n, adj* (old use, poet)=রসিক

রসুই *n* cooking. ~ করা *vt* cook. ~ঘর, ~শালা *nn* kitchen.

রসুন[১] *n* garlic.

রসুন[২] *vi imper* please wait/ stop.

রসুম=রসম

রসুল *n* [A] messenger; prophet. রসুলুল্লাহ, রসুলে-খোদা *nn* messenger of God.

রসেন্দ্র *n* mercury.

রসোত্তম *n* 1 kind of lentil; *Phaseolus mungo*. 2 mercury.

রসোত্তীর্ণ *adj* (rhet) having the intended flavour effectively established; successful as a work of art. ~ হওয়া *vi* succeed as a work of art; come off.

রসোদ্‌গার *n* (Vaishnava lit) recollection of the bliss of union; longing for reunion.

রহমত, রহম [A] *nn* mercy; kindness; grace; pity; compassion. রহম করা *vi* take pity; feel pity for.

রহমান [A] *adj* most merciful; most forgiving. ❑*n* one of the appellations of Allah.

রহস্য *n* 1 secret; mystery; riddle. 2 secret doctrine; subtle/ recondite point; esoteric teaching. 3 jest; fun; pleasantry; joke. ~ করা *vi* 1 make fun; joke; jest; poke fun at; trifle; chaff; banter. 2 mystify; puzzle; be enigmatic. রহস্যচ্ছলে *adv* jokingly; in jest; jestingly; for/in fun. রহস্যজ্ঞ *adj* having a deep insight into; exceedingly astute/ clever; acquainted with the secret of. ~ভেদ *n* disclosure/ revelation/ exposure of a secret or mystery. ~ ভেদ করা *vi* disclose/ reveal/ divulge/ expose / solve/ unveil/ lay bare/ unmask/ bring to light a secret or mystery. ~ভেদী *adj* (capable of/ engaged in) unveiling/ discovering/ solving a secret or mystery. ~ময় *adj* mysterious; secret; hard to comprehend; enigmatic; mystic; esoteric; unfathomable. রহস্যাবৃত *adj* shrouded/ veiled in mystery; mysterious; secret; occult. **রহস্যালাপ** *n* **1** humorous/ witty/ amorous conversation. **2** confidential talk; tête-à-tête; secret conference. **রহস্যালাপ করা** *vi* **1** be engaged in humorous/ witty/ amorous conversation. **2** confer secretly; talk confidentially.

রহস্যোদ্‌ঘাটন, রহস্যোন্মোচন *n* ⇒ রহস্য

রহস্যোপন্যাস *n* detective novel.

রহিত *adj* **1** left; quilted; forsaken; deserted. **2** repealed; abolished; withdrawn; stayed; abrogated; held over; stopped; postponed; discontinued. **3** (used as a *suff*) destitute/ devoid/ deprived/ void of; separated/ free from: বিচারবুদ্ধি~. **4** wanting; absent. **~ করা** *vt* repeal; abolish; withdraw; abrogate; annul; revoke; stop; discontinue; postpone; stay; hold over.

রহিম, রহীম [A] *adj* (very) merciful.

রা[1] *n* **1** (colloq)=রব. **2** word; utterance. **~ করা/ কাড়া/ তোলা/ দেওয়া/ সরা** *vi* **1** make a/any sound by the mouth; utter a/any word; respond; answer. **2** protest; complain. **সাত চড়ে ~ না করা** not to utter a word/ complain/ remonstrate/ protest even when slapped/ hit repeatedly; be long-suffering; be forbearing.

রা[2] *suff* (used to form the *pl* of a *n* or *pron*): ছেলেরা, তোমরা.

রাই[1] *n* mustard. **~ সরিষা** *n*=~.

রাই[2] *n fem*=রাধিকা. **~কিশোরী** *n fem* young Radhika.

রাইফেল [E] *n* rifle.

রাইয়ত=রায়ত

রাও *n* =রায়

রাং, রাঙ, রাঙ্গ *nn* tin. **~ঝাল** *n* soldering with tin. **~ঝাল করা** *vt* solder with tin. **রাংতা** *n* tinfoil; tinsel. **~মিস্ত্রি** *n* tinker.

রাংচিতা *n* lead-wort.

রাঁড় *n fem* **1** widow. **2** prostitute; slut; concubine. **~-খোড়** *adj* lascivious; licentious; one who visits harlots. **~বাজ**=~খোড়. **~বাজি** *n* going after harlots; licentiousness. **~ রাখা** *vi* keep a prostitute. **রাঁড়ের বাড়ি** *n* brothel.

রাঁড়া *adj* barren. ❑*n* barren tree/ woman.

রাঁড়ি *n fem* (vulg) widow.

রাঁদা [P] *n* carpenter's plane.

রাঁধন *n* cooking.

রাঁধনি=রাঁধুনী

রাঁধা *vt* cook. ❑*adj* cooked. ❑*n* cooking. **~নো** *vt* get cooked. **~-বাড়া** *n* cooking and serving at table.

রাঁধুনি *adj* cooking. ❑*n* **1** cook. **2** kind of plant used in seasoning; *Carum roxburghianum*. **~ বামুন** *n* Brahmin cook.

রাকা *n* the full moon; day of full moon. **~শশী** *n* the full moon. **~পতি** *n* the moon.

রাকাত [A] *n* part of the prayer which includes standing, bending and two prostrations.

রাক্ষস *n* **1** [myth] a Rakshas/ demon in general; evil/ malignant demon. **2** member of an anthropophagous race; cannibal. **3** (facet) glutton. **4** (also ~বিবাহ) one of the eight forms of marriage; violent seizure/ rape of a girl after the defeat/ destruction of her relatives. ❑*adj* belonging to/ like a Rakshas; demonia; infested by demons. **রাক্ষসী** *fem*. **~ প্রকৃতি** *adj* ferocious/ fiendish/ malevolent by nature. **~ বিবাহ**=~ (4). **রাক্ষুসী বেলা** *n* the terminal one-eighth part of the daytime. **পেটে ~ সেঁদুনো** (fig) have a wolf in one's stomach; have a wolfish appetite. **রাক্ষুসে** *adj* **1**=~. **2** wolfish; ravenous: রাক্ষুসে ক্ষুধা. **3** monstrous; huge; gigantic: রাক্ষুসে মুলা.

রাক্ষসেন্দ্র *n* Rakshasa-king, Ravana.

রাক্ষসেশ্বর=রাক্ষসেন্দ্র

রাখন *n* **1** keeping. **2** depositing.

রাখনি, রাখনী *n* **1** keeping; maintaining **2** upkeep; maintenance. **3** wages of a shepherd.

রাখা *vt* **1** place; put; keep; lay: বইটা টেবিলে রাখো. **2** save; protect; preserve; help; shelter; guard: এবার তোমাকে কে রাখবে? **3** redeem; rescue; deliver: রাখে খোদা মারে কে? **4** keep intact; defend; maintain; keep up: সাহস ~, আত্মসম্মান ~. **5** wear; grow: দাড়ি/ টিকি ~. **6** keep alive; let live: এমন শত্রু ঘরে রাখতে নেই. **7** prevent; check; restrain: সে যেমন খেপেছে, তাকে রাখবে কে? **8** put into; deposit: ব্যাঙ্কে টাকা ~. **9** not let go; detain; keep back; prevent from leaving/ going forward: ওকে আর রেখো না. **10** give refuge/ asylum to: প্রাণসখা, রাখো পায়ে. **11** engage; employ: চাকর ~. **12** rear; tame; bring up: মুরগি/ কুকুর ~. **13** leave: ছাতাটা রেখে সে চলে গেল. **14** keep in store: ছেলেদের খাবার দাবার কিছু ~ উচিত. **15** keep for sale: আমাদের দোকানে ডিম রাখি না. **16** refrain from mentioning/ uttering; leave sb/ sth alone: আমার কথা রাখো, অন্য কথা বলো. **17** stop: নৌকা কোথায় রাখবে? **18** keep up; maintain: ঠাঁই ~. **19** heed; pay heed to; obey; comply with: অনুরোধ ~: আমার কথা রাখো. **20** fulfil; keep; observe: (নিজের) কথা/ প্রতিশ্রুতি ~. **21** have; nourish: আক্রোশ/ রাগ/ ভয়/ হিংসা ~. **22** save: দুর্দিনের জন্য কিছু টাকা রেখো. **23** pawn; receive as a pawn: ঘড়িটা রেখে যদি কিছু টাকা পাওয়া যায়. **24** give: নাম ~. **25** please; gratify; carry favour with: মন ~. **26** look after; tend; herd: রাখাল গরু রাখে. **27** leave behind; forget to bring/ take: বইটা বাড়িতে রেখে এসেছি. **28** maintain for one's enjoyment; keep: রক্ষিতা ~. **29** buy: ঝুড়িটা ফেরিওয়ালার কাছ থেকে রেখেছি. **30** set apart: অতিথির জন্য খাবার ~. **31** put by; set by; lay by/ aside: মেয়ের বিয়ের জন্য কিছু রাখছ তো? **32** take settlement; take on lease: জমি ~. **33** adopt: নিঃসন্তান লোকটি একটি ছেলে রেখেছে. **34**

cherish; keep up: মনে আশা রেখো. **35** park; pull on: গাড়ি কোথায় রাখব? **36** bear: কথাটা মনে রেখো. **আটকে ~** *vt* detain; keep back; prevent from leaving/ going forward. **কথা ~** *vi* **1** keep one's word/ promise. **2** comply with/ obey/ accede to one's request. **করে ~** *vt* get/ have sth done/ completed beforehand. **চোখ ~***v* keep an eye/ watch on. **জমিয়ে ~** *vt* lay by/ aside; pile up; accumulate; save up; store up; **ধরে ~** detain; hold back; shut up; collect: বৃষ্টির পানি ধরে ~. **নাম ~** *vi* **1** leave behind a lasting reputation; make/ win a name for oneself. **2** act upto the reputation of: বাপের নাম ~. **3** give a name to; name; christen; designate. **পা ~** *vi* set foot in; cross the threshold; enter; pop in. **পায়ে ~** *vt* treat/ favour/ shelter graciously; not to desert. **ফেলে ~** *vt* put off; abandon; leave; neglect. **বলে ~** *vi* tell before-hand; forewarn; warn. **ভাব ~** *vi* maintain friendly relations; be on good terms with **মন/ মনে ~** *vi* ⇒ মন. **মাথায় ~** *vi* ⇒ মাথা. **মান~**⇒ মান. **রেখে দেওয়া** *vi* **1** keep: টাকাটা তুমি রেখে দাও. **2** (as an expression of impatience, irritation, etc) stop talking about; not to give/ care a damn for: damn your ...: রেখে দাও তোমার গালভরা গল্প! **সাজিয়ে ~** *vi* keep/ arrange/ display/ put in order. **রেখে যাওয়া** *vt* leave behind.

রাখানো *vt* cause/ make sb to keep/lay.

রাখারাখি *n* **1** placing sth once here once there. **2** mutual protection. **3** secretiveness; hush-hush state.

রাখাল *n* cowherd; shepherd; herdsman. **~বালক** *n* cowboy. **~রাজ, ~ রাজা** *n* Sri Krishna. **রাখালি** *n* profession/ wages of a cowherd/ shepherd. ❑*adj* of cowherds/ shepherds; pastoral. **রাখালি গান** *n* pastoral (song); bucolic;

রাখি, রাখী *n* piece of thread which one ties round wrist of another in order to safeguard the latter from all evils. **~ পূর্ণিমা** *n* the full moon day of the month of Shravan. **~ বন্ধন** *n* act/ festival of tying a rakhi round the wrist of another.

রাগ[১] *n* **1** anger; huff; rage; fury; heat; wrath; passion; inflammation. **2** any feeling/ passion. **3** love/ affection/ sympathy (for); vehement desire (of); inclination, interest/ delight/ joy (in). **4** attachment to worldly pleasures/ enjoyments. **6** affection. **7** enmity; hostility. **8** indignation; sulking; wounded sense of honour; anger excited by jealousy. **~ করা** *vi* **1** be angry; rage; burst into anger; be in/ get into a huff; get/ grow angry; sulk; take offence/ umbrage/ exception/ amiss; pout; resent. **2** scold; reproach; admonish; reprimand. **~ দেখানো** *vi* show temper. **~ লাগা/ হওয়া** *vi* be angry/ offended: এতে ~ লাগে, It makes one angry/ makes one's blood boil. **~ত** *adj* angry; bitter; angered; fuming. **~তভাবে** *adv* angrily; in anger; with a show of rage. **~-দ্বেষ** *n* **1** malice; hatred. **2** love and hatred. **রাগা=~** করা. **রাগান্ধ** *adj* blind with passion/ desire/ rage: **রাগান্বিত** *adj* **1** angered; angry; furious; affected by passion/ desire. **~ পড়া** *vi* cool down; calm (down) **~রঙ্গ** *n* amorous play. **~ সামলানো** *vi* control one's temper.

রাগ[২] *n* **1** colour; hue; tint; dye; paint. **2** red hue/ colour/ tinge. **~চূর্ণ** *n* red powder. **~রক্ত** *n* crimson. **~রঞ্জিত** *adj* coloured. **~লেখা** *n* streak/ line of paint; stroke; mark of dye. **রাগারুণ** *adj* reddish; tawny.

রাগ[৩] *n* **1** particular musical mode/ order of sound/ formula. **2** note; harmony; melody. **~প্রধান** *adj* based on classical modes. **~মালা** *n* string/ series of musical modes.

রাগারাগি *n fem* scolding; wrangling; bitterness; bad blood.

রাগিণী *n fem* (secondary) musical mode.

রাগী *adj* **1** short-tempered; quick-tempered; choleric; irascible; testy; firy; hot-headed; edgy.

রাঘব *n* **1** descendant of Raghu; Ramchandra. **2** species of a very large fish. **~প্রিয়া, ~বাঞ্ছা** *nn fem* Sita, the wife of Rama. **~ বোয়াল** *n* **1**=~ (2). **2** (fig) man of high social standing who is a virulent extortioner of people; leading criminal (who generally manages to escapee punishment). **রাঘবানুজ** *n* Lakshmana, the younger brother of Rama. **রাঘবারি** *n* Ravana, the enemy of Rama.

রাঙ=রাং. **~চিতা** = রাংচিতা. **~ঝাল**=রাংঝাল. **রাঙতা** = রাংতা. **~মিস্ত্রি** = রাংমিস্ত্রি

রাঙন *n* a kind of flower; rangan.

রাঙা, রাঙ্গা *adj* **1** red; crimson; scarlet. **2** flushed; red: লজ্জায় ~. **3** (of elder brothers and sisters) occupying a particular (generally lower) position in the scale of seniority: ~ দাদা. **4** fair; fair-complexioned: ~বৌ. **~ আলু** *n* variety of sweet potato. **~নো** *vt* stain/ dye (red/ crimson/ scarlet); colour; brighten; cause to flush. **~ বাস** *n* cloth dyed in red ochre. **~ মুখ** *adj* red-faced. ❑*n* **1** face turned crimson with rage. **2** European. **~মুলা** *n* red reddish; (fig) handsome but worthless man.

রাঙি, রাঙ্গি, রাঙ্গী *n* a small sieve.

রাঙ্গ=রাং

রাঙ্গা ⇒ রাঙা

রাজ *n* **1** (in compounds only) king; sovereign; lord; chief. **2** (in compounds only) anything the best/ chief of the kind: ঋতু~, কবি~. **3** rule; government: ব্রিটিশ ~. ❑*adj* shining; radiant. **~-আজ্ঞা** *n* king's edict; royal decree. **~ঋষি** = রাজর্ষি. **রাজক** *adj* illuminating; irradiating; splendid. ❑*n* petty/ little king; petty prince; number of kings. **~কথা** *n* history of kings.

~কদম্ব *n* kind of Kadamba; *Nauclea cadamba*. ~কন্যা *n fem* king's daughter; princess. ~কবি *n* court-poet; poet-laureate. ~কর = রাজস্ব. ~কর্তৃ *n* king-maker; those who place the king on the throne. ~কর্ম *n* business/ duty of a king; king's service; state affairs; government service; public service. ~কর্মচারী *n* officer/ servant of the state; public servant; government officer. ~কার্য =~কর্ম. ~কীয় *adj* royal; regal; kingly; princely; magnificent. ~কুমার *n* king's son; prince. ~কুমারী *fem*=~কন্যা. ~কুল *n* **1** royal family; king's race; dynasty. **2** kings. ~কুলবধূ *n fem* woman of the royal family. ~কুলোদ্ভব *adj* born from a race of kings; royal descendant; princely-born. ~কোষ *n* (royal/ government) treasury. ~ক্ষমা *n* amnesty. ~গদি *n* royal seat; throne. ~গামী *adj* devolving/ escheating to the king (as property etc to which there are no heirs). রাজগি *n* kingship; kingdom. রাজগির *n* king's palace. ~গুরু *n* king's minister/ counsellor; spiritual guide of a king/ royal family. ~গুহ্য *n* king's mystery. ~গৃহ *n* king's house; palace. ~গ্রীব *n* species of small fish. ~ঘাতক *n* regicide. ~চক্রবর্তী *n* sovereign king; emperor; suzerain. ~চিহ্ন *n* insignia of royalty; organs of generation. ~ছত্র, ~চ্ছত্র *n* **1** umbrella which is officialy held over the head of a king. **2** insignia of royalty. **3** administration of a state/ kingdom. ~জম্বু *n* species of berry. ~জোটক *n* best astrological combination for matrimonial purposes. ~টিকা, ~টীকা *n* holy mark painted on the forehead of a king at coronation. রাজড়া *n* petty prince/ king; vassal. ~তক্ত, ~তখ্‌ত *n* throne. ~তনয় *n* king's son; prince. ~তনয়া *fem* princess. ~তন্ত্র *n* monarchy. ~তন্ত্রবাদী *n* royalist. ~তপস্বী=রাজর্ষি. ~তিলক =~টিকা. ~ত্ব *n* kingdom; state; domain; kingship; royalty; sovereignty; rule; government; reign; sway; predominate. ~ত্ব করা *vi, vi* reign; rule; govern; predominate; dominate; domineer. ~ত্বকাল *n* (period of) reign; rule; regime. ~দণ্ড *n* **1** king's sceptre/ authority. **2** punishment inflicted by a king/ law-court. ~দত্ত *adj* given/ conferred by a king/ government. ~দত্ত সম্মান *n* royal/ official/ government honour. ~দন্ত *n* principal/ front tooth. ~দম্পতি, ~দম্পতী *n* royal couple. ~দরবার *n* royal court; court of justice. ~দর্শন *n* royal audience; sight of a king. ~দার *n* king's wife; queen. ~দুলাল *n* prince. ~দুলালী *fem* princess. ~দুহিতা=~কন্যা. ~দূত *n* ambassador; royal envoy/ courier. ~দ্বার *n* king's gate; gate of a royal palace. ~দ্বারে *adv* before a king; in a royal court. ~দ্রোহ, ~দ্রোহিতা *n* high treason; sedition; rebellion; insurrection; insurgence. ~দ্রোহী *adj* seditious; insurgent; treasonous. ❑*n* rebel against the king/ established authority; traitor; insurgent; seditionist. ~দ্রোহিণী *fem*. ~ধর্ম *n* king's duty; rules/ laws relating to kings. ~ধানী metropolis; capital; king's residence. ~নন্দন =~তনয়. ~নন্দিনী *fem*=~কন্যা. ~নাবী *n* royal/ state navy. ~নামা *n* genealogical tree/ chronology/ chronicle of a royal line/ dynasty. ~নিয়ম *n* royal statute; law; politics. ~নীতি *n* politics; state-craft; royal conduct/ policy. ~নীতিক *adj* political. ❑*n* politician. ~নীতিজ্ঞ *adj* versed in politics/ statesmanship. ❑*n* politician; statesman. ~নৈতিক *adj*=~নীতিক. ~নীল *n* emerald. রাজন্য *n* (feudal) prince; man of the regal/ military tribe. রাজন্যক *n* a number/ assemblage of warriors. ~পট্ট *n* **1** royal crown. **2** throne. **3** royal charter. **4** kind of precious stone/ diamond of inferior quality. ~পত্নী *n fem* king's wife; royal consort; queen. ~পথ *n* king's highway; public road/ street/ thoroughfare; main road. ~পদ *n* office/ rank of a king; kingship; royalty. ~পরিচ্ছদ *n* royal robes/ attire/ dress. ~পাট *n* royal throne. ~পাত্র *n* **1** king's counsellor; minister. **2**=~পুরুষ. ~পুত *n* Rajput (inhabitant of Rajputana in India). ~পুতনী, ~পুতানী *fem*. ~পুত্র =~কুমার. ~পুত্রিকা, ~পুত্রী *fem*. ~পুর, ~পুরী *n* residence/ palace of a king; capital city of a king; (fig) magnificent palace/ city/ residence. ~পুরুষ *n* **1** royal servant/ minister; king's/ government officer. **2** police officer. **3** member of the royal household. ~প্রমুখ *n* a government title given to the leading feudal chief of India, vested with powers similar to that of a governor. ~প্রসাদ *n* royal favour; royal patent; any grant/ document granted by royal favour. ~প্রাসাদ *n* royal residence/ palace. ~বংশ *n* family of kings; dynasty. ~বংশী *n* (member of) a lowly Hindu caste. ~বংশীয় *adj* born of a royal family; of royal descent/ blood; dynastic. ~বংশীয় *fem* ~বন্দী *n* political prisoner. ~বর্ত্ম =~পথ. ~বাটি, ~বাটী, ~বাড়ি =~প্রাসাদ. ~বালা =~কন্যা. ~বিদ্রোহ =~দ্রোহ. ~বিদ্রোহী=~দ্রোহী. ~বিধি *n* royal state/ decree; law. ~বিপ্লব *n* political revolution. ~বৃত্ত *n* conduct/ occupation of a king. ~বৃত্তি *n* bounty. ~বেশ *n* royal garment. ~বৈদ্য *n* physician to a king/ queen; prince of physician. ~বৈর *n* sedition. ~ভক্ত *adj* devoted to one's sovereign/ state government; loyal. ~ভক্ত ব্যক্তি *n* loyalist. ~ভক্তি *n* loyalty (to one's sovereign). ~ভবন =~প্রাসাদ; government house. ~ভয় *n* fear of being punished by a king/ court of justice. ~ভাগ *n* landlord's share. ~ভাষা *n* king's language; state language. ~ভিষক =~বৈদ্য. ~ভৃত্য *n* king's servant; royal servant/ minister; government servant. ~ভোগ *n* king's meal; royal repast; a sweet and juicy drop made of curd. ~ভোগ্য *adj* fit to be eaten/ used/ enjoyed by a king. ~মজুর *n* mason's labourer; hodman; mason. ~মন্ত্রী *n* king's counsellor; royal minister; minister of state; cabinet member. ~মহল *n* king's palace; inner apartments of a palace. ~মহিষী *n fem* chief wife of a king; queen-consort. ~মাতা *n fem* king's mother; queen-mother. ~মান্য *n* present conventionally due from a tenant to landlord. ~মার্গ =~পথ. ~মিস্ত্রি, ~মিস্ত্রী *n* mason; architect. ~মুকুট *n* royal crown; diadem; kingship. ~মুদ্রা *n* royal signet/ seal. ~যক্ষ্মা *n* a kind of dangerous disease; tuberculosis; pulmonary consumption. ~যজ্ঞ *n* royal offering; king's sacrifice. ~যোগ *n* **1** particular stage in abstract meditation. **2** constellation under which princes are born; configuration of planets, etc at birth denoting a person destined for kingship. ~যোগ্য *adj* befitting a king; suitable for royalty; princely. ~যোটক *n* (astrol) the most auspicious constellation (as found in the horoscopes of the bride and the bridegroom); the most suitable union; the most advantageous concidence. ~যোষিৎ *n fem*=~দার. ~রক্ত *n* royal blood. ~রাজ *n* **1** king of kings; supreme sovereign; emperor. **2** name of Kubera (কুবের). **3** God. ~রাজড়া *n* princes and princelings/ princely persons; kings and princes; (derog) very wealthy/ influential/ affluent persons. ~রাজেশ্বর *n* king of kings; emperor. ~রাজেশ্বরী *fem* empress. ~রানী =~মহিষী. ~র্ষি *n* royal Rishi/ saint; saint of royal descent. ~লক্ষণ *n* royal token; sign of royalty; any mark on the body, etc indicating a future king. ~লক্ষ্মী *n fem* fortune/ prosperity of a king (personified as a goddess); royal sovereignty/ majesty. ~লিখা, ~লেখ, ~লেখ্য *nn* king's writing; royal letter/ edict. ~শক্তি *n* power of a king/ government; majesty/ influence of a king. ~শয়ন, ~শয্যা *n* king's couch; royal seat/ throne. ~শাসন *n* **1** king's rule; punishment inflicted by a king. **2** royal edict/ order. ~শেখর =~চক্রবর্তী. ~শ্রী =~লক্ষ্মী. ~সংস্করণ *n* deluxe edition (of a book). ~সদন =~প্রাসাদ. ~সন্নিধান *n* royal presence. ~সভা *n* royal court/ assembly; darbar. ~সম্পদ *n* royal/ princely treasures/ riches. ~সরকার *n* royal government/ court. ~সর্প *n* species of large serpent; ming-cobra. ~সাক্ষিক *adj* testified by the king (as a document). ~সাক্ষী *n* (law) approver. ~সাযুজ্য *n* close union with the king; sovereignty. ~সিংহাসন *n* throne; kingship. . ~সূয় *n* great sacrifice performed at the coronation of a king (by himself and his tributary princes). ~সেবা *n* royl service. ~সেবী *n* royal servant. ~স্ব *n* property of a king; tax/ rent/ revenue payable to a king/ the government; revenue. ~স্বঘটিত, ~স্ব-সংক্রান্ত *adjj* fiscal; financial. ~স্ব-পর্ষদ *n* board of revenue. ~স্ব-সচিব *n* finance secretary/ minister/ member. ~হংস *n* kind of goose/ swan; flamingo; gander. ~হংসী *fem* goose, swan. ~হত্যা *n* regicide. ~হন্তা *n* regicide. ~হন্ত্রী *fem*. ~হস্তী *n* royal elephant; excellent elephant. ~হাঁস=~হংস. ~হাসের বাচ্চা *n* gosling.

রাজ[২] *n* mason (⇒ ~মিস্ত্রি).

রাজ[৩] *n* state; government.

রাজন্ *n* (vocative) o king !

রাজস, রাজসিক *adjj* **1** belonging/ relating to the quality of rajas (⇒ রজোগুণ); endured with/ influenced by the quality of passion; passionate. **2** magnificent; majestic; princely.

রাজা *n* **1** king; monarch; prince; sovereign ruler. **2** government title of honour (in medieval and British India); Raja. **3** lord; man of magnificent and towering personality. **4** (chess) king. ~ করা *vt* make sb great/ very wealthy. ~-উজির *n pl* king and his minister; (fig) very wealthy and influential men; highups; the nobs. ~উজির মারা *n* tell cock-and-bull stories about one's capabilities and importance; talk big. রাজাজ্ঞা, ~দেশ = রাজ-আজ্ঞা (⇒ রাজ). রাজাধিকার *n* royal prerogative; monarch's territory. ~ধিরাজ *n* king of kings; paramount sovereign; suzerain. ~নুকম্পা, ~নুগ্রহ *nn* royal favour/ grace/ mercy; favour/ grace/ mercy shown by a government. ~নুগৃহীত *adj* favoured by the king. ~নুগৃহীতা *fem*. ~নুচর *n* monarch's servant/ follower/ attendant. ~নুমোদিত *adj* approved by the king. ~ন্তঃপুর *n* inner apartments of a monarch's residence. ~-প্রজা *n* king and his subjects. ~বলি, ~বলী *nn* genealogical tree of a dynasty. ~বাবু *n* His Majesty the king; princely gentleman. রাজাভরণ *n* king's ornament; regalia. ~রাজড়া = রাজরাজড়া (⇒ রাজ). ~র হাল *n* great opulence; princely luxury; milk and honey রাজার হালে থাকা *n* roll in wealth; live like a prince. ~ই *adj* fit for/ worthy of/ due to a king; royal; noble. ~সন *n* royal seat; throne.

রাজা[২] *vi* (poet) exist; be present; shine; be resplendent; glitter.

রাজি[১], রাজী *n* (used as a *suff*) line; row; streak; range.

রাজি[২] [A] *adj* willing; agreed; pleased; contented; satisfied. ~ করা(নো) *vt* make sb agree; persuade; win over; argue into; prevail on; enlist; cajole; coax. ~ হওয়া *vi* agree; assent; accede to; consent; acquiesce; be satisfied. ~নামা *n* deed of compromise/ consent; (law) joint petition of rival parties consenting to compromise. নিম~ *adj* half/ almost willing.

রাজিত *adj* illuminated; resplendent; brilliant; adorned; embellished.

রাজীব *n* (blue) lotus. **~লোচন** *adj* lotus-eyed; blue-eyed.

রাজেন্দ্র *n* lord of kings; supreme sovereign; emperor. **রাজেন্দ্রানী** *fem* empress.

রাজেশ্বর=রাজেন্দ্র

রাজোপজীবী=রাজানুজীবী (⇒ রাজ)

রাজোপাধি *n* title of king; little conferred by a king. **~ক** *adj* titled.

রাজ্ঞী *n fem* queen; wife of a king.

রাজ্য *n* **1** kingdom; realm; state; domain; territory. **2** reign; rule; kingship; sovereignty; royalty; empire. **3** (fig) large quantity/ expanse; immensity; infinity; world; universe: রাজ্যের তফাত, world of difference; রাজ্যের দুঃখ. **~ করা** *vi* reign; rule. **~খণ্ড** *n* portion of a kingdom/ country/ state; state; kingdom; country. **~ক্ষেত্র** *n* territory. **~চ্যুত** *n* fallen from sovereignty; dethroned; deposed. **~চ্যুত করা** *vt* dethrone; depose; drive out from one's kingdom. **~চ্যুতি** *n* dethronement; dispossession/ removal from one's kingdom. **~তন্ত্র** *n* science/ theory of government. **~ত্যাগ** *n* abandonment of rule/ government; abdication. **~ত্যাগ করা** *n* abandon one's rule; abdicate; give up the throne; leave one's country. **~পরিষদ** *n* council of states. **~পাল** *n* (in India) (title of the) governor of a state. **~পালন** *n* administration of a state/ kingdom. **~পালন করা** *vi* govern/ rule a state/ kingdom. **~ভার** *n* weight of (the duties) government; burden of governing a state. **~ভোগ** *n* possession of sovereignty. **~ভোগ করা** *vi* enjoy sovereignty. **~ভ্রংশ**=~চ্যুতি. **~ভ্রষ্ট**=~চ্যুত. **~রক্ষা** *n* protection/ defence of a kingdom. **~রক্ষা করা** *vi* defend/ protect a kingdom/ state. **~লক্ষ্মী** *n* good fortune of a kingdom. **~লাভ** *n* succession to the throne; obtainment of sovereignty. **~লাভ করা** *vi* obtain sovereignty; win a kingdom. **~লোভ** *n* desire for royalty; greed for the throne; greed for expansion of one's territory. **~লোভী** *adj* desirous of royalty; greedy of expanding one's territory. **~ শাসন** =~ পালন. **~শ্রী** =~লক্ষ্মী. **~ সরকার** *n* (in India) state government. **~সুখ** *n* pleasure of royalty; enjoyment of kingdom. **~সংস্থিতি, ~স্থিতি** *nn* government. **~হারা** =~চ্যুত. **রাজ্যাধিকার** *n* authority over a kingdom; right/ title to a sovereignty. **রাজ্যাধিকারী, রাজ্যাধিপতি** *nn* lord/ ruler of a kingdom. **রাজ্যাপহরণ** *n* taking away of a kingdom; usurpation. **রাজ্যাপহরণ করা** *vi* usurp a throne; capture/ acquire/ take possession of another's realm/ country by force. **রাজ্যাপহারক, রাজ্যাপহারী** *adj* one who usurps a throne; one who captures/ takes possession of another's kingdom/ country unlawfully. ❑*n* usurper. **রাজ্যাভিলাষ** *n* desire for a kingdom; ambition to rule; desire for expanding one's territory. **রাজ্যাভিলাষী** *adj* desirous of a kingdom; having ambition to rule; desirous of expanding one's territory. **রাজ্যাভিষিক্ত** *adj* inaugarated to a kingdom; crowned. **রাজ্যাভিষিক্ত করা** *vt* crown sb king; invest sb with kingdom; enthrone. **রাজ্যাভিষেক** *n* inauguration to a kingdom; coronation.

রাজ্যেশ্বর *n* king. **রাজ্যেশ্বরী** *fem* queen.

রাঢ় *n* ancient name of the part of Bengal lying on the western bank of the Ganges. **রাঢ়ী, রাঢ়ীয়** *adj* of Rada.

রাণা=রানা

রাণী=রানী

রাত *n* (colloq) night. **~ করা** *vi* be far on in the day; stay up late. **~ কাটানো** *vi* pass a night; stay overnight. **~ জাগা** *vi* stay up far into the night; keep late hours; stay/ sit up late. **~ জেগে কাজ করা** *vi* sit up and work late at night; burn the midnight oil. **~ হওয়া** *vi* get dark. **~কানা** *adj* night-blind; nyctalopic. **~চোরা** *adj* wandering by night. ❑*n* thief; nocturnal animals. **~দিন** *n* day and night. ❑*adv* night and day; ceaselessly. **~ভর, ~ভোর** *adv* all night long; nightlong; all night (long). **রাতারাতি** *adv* overnight; whilst there is still light; within a very short time: রাতারাতি ভোল পাল্টানো.

রাতা *adj* (archaic) red. ❑*n* (dial) cock.

রাতি, রাতিয়া *nn* (poet)=রাত

রাতুল *adj* red; blood-red; crimson.

-রাত্র *n* (in compounds)=রাত্রি: অহো~.

রাত্রি *n* night; nightfall; night-time; darkness; night-tide. **~ হয়েছে** It is night. **~কাল** *n* night-time. **~কালীন** *adj* nightly; nocturnal. **~কালে** *adv* at/by night. **~চর, ~ঞ্চর** *adjj* active at night; wandering by night; nocturnal: ~চর পাখি, night-bird. ❑*nn* thief; robber; demon; Rakshas; watchman. **~জল** *n* dew. **~জাগর** *adj* night-watching; keeping vigil; keeping awake by night. **~জাগরা** *fem*. **~জাগরণ** *n* night-watching; vigil; staying awake. **~ জাগরণ করা** *vi* keep vigil; stay awake; keep away by night. **~বাস** *n* **1** act of passing the night; night-rest; staying overnight. **2** night-dress; nightgown; nightie; nighty. **~বাস করা** *vi* stay over night. **~বেলা** *adv* at/by night. **~ভর, ~ভোর** =রাতভর (⇒ রাত). **~যোগে** =~বেলা. **~শেষ** *n* close/ end of the night; remainder/ last part of night.

রাত্র্যন্ধ *adj* night-blind; nyctalopic. ❑*n* night-blind; nyctalops. **~তা** *n* night-blindness; nyctalopia.

রাধা, রাধিকা *nn fem*. (myth) name of a celebrated cowherdess or gopi, beloved by Sri Krishna. **রাধাকান্ত** *n* lover of Radha; Sri Krishna. **রাধাচক্র** *n* discuss/ quoit of Sri,

Krishna. ~নাথ *n* lord of Radha; Krishna. **রাধাপদ্ম** *n* **1** white lotus. **2** sunflower. ~**বল্লভ**, ~**মাধব**, ~**রমণ** =রাধাকান্ত. ~**বল্লভী লুচি** *n* small saucer-shaped pancake made of kneaded flour stuffed with paste of pigeon-pea.

রাধে *n* (vocative)=রাধা. ~**কৃষ্ণ**, ~**মাধব** *nn* Radha and Krishna. ❑*int* expressing disgust, abhorrence, etc.

রান [P] *n* thigh; upper part of leg: মুরগির ~.

রানা[1] *n* **1** king. **2** title of the ruler of Udaypur.

রানা[2] *n* **1** balustrade/ raised terrace on either side of the flight of steps of a pond. **2** bench on either side of a flight of steps at the entrance of a house.

রানার [E] *n* (postal) runner.

রানী *n fem* queen.

রান্ধন *n* (archaic, dial)=রাঁধন. **রান্ধনী**=রাঁধুনি

রান্ধা *n, vt* (archaic, dial)=রাঁধা

রান্না *n* cooking. ~ **করা** *vt* cook. ~**ঘর** *n* kitchen. ~**বান্না**, ~**বাড়া** *nn* cooking and serving at table.

রাব[1] *n* treacle

রাব[2] *n* (poet)=রব[1]

রাবড়ি *nn* a sweetmeat prepared by condensing films of milk.

রাবণ *n* name of the ruler of Lanka, whose destruction by Rama forms the subject of Ramayana; Ravana. ~**চ্ছত্র** *n* medusa (fish). ~**পুরী** *n* abode of Ravana; Lanka. ~**মুখা**, ~**মুখো** *adj* fierce; ferocious; savage. **রাবণারি** *n* Ravan's enemy; Rama. **রাবণের চিতা/ চুলি** *nn* **1** quenchless fire. **2** ceaseless affliction; eternal torment.

রাবণি *n* son of Ravana; Meghnad.

রাবার = রবার

রাবিশ [E] *n* rubbish. ❑*adj* trashy. ❑*int* nonsense.

রাবী [A] *n* narrator; reciter: হাদিসের ~.

রাম *n* (myth) **1** seventh incarnation of Vishnu, son of Dasharatha, the hero of the Ramayana. **2** (derog) fellow: মস্ত~, হাঁদা~, কেবল~, বাঁটুল~. **3** so-and-so. **4** ordinary person (⇒ ~-শ্যাম). ~ **কহ/ বলো**, ~ *int* expressing/ disgust/ abhorrence, slight. ❑*adj* **1** pleasing; pleasant; charming; lovely; beautiful. **2** foremost; glaring specimen: মদ্দা~, বোকা~. **3** large; big: ~দা, ~ছাগল, ~ শিঙ্গা. **4** small: ~ বেগুন. ❑*adv* utterly; extremely: ~ কুঁড়ে. ~**কদলী** *n* species of large banana which becomes red when ripe. ~**কর্পূর** *n* species of fragrant grass. ~**কান্ত** *n* (facet) stick; rod. ~**কেলি**, ~**কেলী** *nn* an Indian musical mode. ~**খড়ি** *n* kind of red-tinged writing-chalk. ~**চন্দ্র**=~ (1). ~**ছাগল** *n* species of large goat. ~**দা** *n* kind of large chopper (used in beheading animals). ~**ধনু** *nn* rainbow. ~**ধূন** *n* song in glory of Rama. ~**নবমী** *n* the ninth day in the light half of the month of Chaitra (being the birthday of Rama). ~**পাখি** *n* (iron) cock; fowl. ~**বেগুন** *n* king of wild plant resembling egg-plant; *Colanum ferox*. ~**রাজত্ব**, ~**রাজ্য** *nn* **1** reign/ rule/ realm of Ram. **2** ideal realm/ rule; realm of absolute peace and prosperity; utopia. ~, ~-**রাম** *int* expressing: disgust/ regret/ surprise; my God ! ❑*n* salutation. ~**লীলা** *n* dramatic representation of the life and exploits of Rama. ~**শিঙ্গা**, ~**শিঙে** (colloq) *nn* funnel-shaped wind instrument/ mouthpiece made of a buffalo's horn. ~**শ্যাম** *n* Tom, Dick and Harry. ~ **না হতে রামায়ণ** (fig) doing things in the wrong order; taking the effect before the cause; putting the cart before the horse. **না ~ না গঙ্গা** (fig) neither this, nor that; irreverent. **সেই ~ও নেই, সেই অযোধ্যাও নেই** O the times ! O the manners !

রামা *n fem* (beautiful) woman; any young and charming woman; mistress; wife.

রামাইৎ *n* name of a Vaishnava sect.

রামায়ণ *n* Valmiki's celebrated epic. ~**কার** *n* author of the Ramayana.

রামায়েত = রামাইৎ

রামাশ্যামা = রামশ্যাম (⇒ রাম)

রায়[1] [A] *n* judgement; judicial pronouncement; verdict: ~ **দেওয়া** *vi* deliver/ pronounce a judgement.

রায়[2] *n* **1** a Hindu title. **2** chief; lord; king; prince. ❑*adj* large; big; long: ~বাঁশ. **রায়ী** *fem* princess; queen. ~**জাদা** *n* son of a Rai; prince. ~**বাঁশ** *n* long bamboo pole/ staff. ~**বেঁশে** *n* **1** foot soldier with a long bamboo staff. **2** kind of dance with staffs. ~**বাঘিনী** *n fem* **1** royal tiger. **2** extremely terrible woman; virago; termagant; hellcat. ~**বাহাদুর**, ~**সাহেব** *nn* official titles once conferred on important Hindu citizens. ~**রায়ান** *n* **1** (Hist) title of the finance minister in Muslim India. **2** chief of chiefs, a title conferred on very important Hindu citizens.

রায়ট [E] *n* riot

রায়ত, **রায়ৎ** [A] *nn* **1** tenants; peasants (of a landlord); tenant of a piece of agricultural land; ryot. **2** subjects. **3** cultivator. **রায়তি**, **রায়তী** *adj* relating to tenants/ ryots; settled permanently and hereditarily on a tenant/ ryot. ❑*n* **1** tenancy. **2** tenure. **3** holding of real estate.

রাশ[1] *n* **1** heap; mass; pile; group; multitude; number; quantity. **2** (astrol) birth-sign; sign of the zodiac; nature; temperament. ~**নাম** *n* name according to one's astrological birth-sign. ~**পাতলা** *adj* frivolous; flippant; light-headed. ~**ভারি**, ~**ভারী** *adjj* reserved in speech and manner; grave; grim; imposing; grand; solemn. ~**হালকা** =~পাতলা.

রাশ[2] *n* reins; bridle. ~ **আলগা করা** *vi* (lit and fig) give free rein/ the reins to sb/sth. ~ **ছাড়া** =~ আলগা করা: কল্পনার ~ ছাড়া, give the rein(s) to one's imagination. ~ টানা *vi* (lit and fig) draw rein; keep a tight rein on sb/sth.

রাশি =1 রাশ[১] (1, 2). 2 (math) number; term; quantity. 3 (alg) unknown quantity; element (of a determinant). ~ কৃত =রাশীকৃত. ~ চক্র *n* zodiacal circle; zodiac; horoscope. ~ নাম *n* name given to a child taken from the sign under which he is born. ~ভাগ *n* fraction. ~ভোগ (কাল) *n* passage of the sun or moon or any planet through the sign of a planet. ~মালা *n* (math) expression. ~রাশি heaps of.

রাশীকৃত *adj* made into a heap; heaped/ piled up; accumulated; amassed; collected.

রাষ্ট্র *n* 1 state; kingdom; realm; dominion; country. 2 wide publicity; propagation; proclamation. ❑*adj* widely circulated/ proclaimed; noised abroad. ~ করা *vt* circulate/noise aboard; proclaim widely; shout from the roof-tops; blaze aboard; trumpet (forth). ~জন nation. ~জনিক *adj* national. ~তাত্ত্বিক *adj* political. ~দূত *n* ambassador; envoy. ~নায়ক *n* statesman; ruler/ popular leader of a state. ~নিযুক্তক *n* chargé d' affaires. ~নিয়োগাধিকার *n* Public Service Commission. ~নীতি *n* politics. ~নৈতিক *adj* political. ~পতি *n* president of a state. ~পুঞ্জ *n* group/ union of nations; league of nations. ~বিপ্লব *n* political strife; (political) revolution. ~ ভাষা *n* state language. ~ মণ্ডল *n* commonwealth. ~সংসদ *n* state council; parliament. ~সঙ্ঘ, ~সংঘ *n* United Nations Organization. রাষ্ট্রাধীন *adj* territorial. রাষ্ট্রায়ত্ত *adj* nationalized. রাষ্ট্রায়ত্ত করা *vt* nationalize.

রাষ্ট্রিক *adj* pertaining to a state/ country; national; territorial; state.

রাষ্ট্রীয়=রাষ্ট্রিক. ~করণ *n* nationalization.

রাস[১] *n* 1 festival of dancing in honour of Sri Krishna and his dances with the Gopis (গোপী). 2 uproar; noise; din. ~ক্রীড়া, ~যাত্রা, ~লীলা *nn*=~ (1). ~পূর্ণিমা *n* full moon night of the month of Kartik. ~বিহারী *n* Sri Krishna. ~মঞ্চ, ~মণ্ডপ, ~মণ্ডল *n* platform on which the festival of ras is held.

রাস[২]=রাশ[২]

রাসকেল [E] *n* rascal.

রাসন *adj* gustatory.

রাসভ *n* ass; he-ass. রাসভী *fem* she-ass. ~নাদ *n* braying of an ass; hee-haw. ~নিন্দিত *adj* putting even the ass to shame; worse than the ass; creaky. ~নিন্দিতকণ্ঠ *n* voice the harshness of which would put even the ass to shame; creaky voice. ~বৎ *adj* asinine; ass-like.

রাসায়নিক *adj* of chemistry; chemical; versed in chemistry. ❑*n* one versed in chemistry; chemist; chemical. ~ আসক্তি *n* chemical affinity. ~ দ্রব্য *n* chemical. ~ পরীক্ষক *n* chemical examiner. ~ সম্মিলন *n* chemical combination.

রাস্তা [P] *n* 1 road; thoroughfare; way; street; path; lane. 2 manner. ~ দেখা *vi* 1 go one's way(s). 2 find a solution/ an answer. ~ দেখানো *vi* 1 show sb the door; dismiss. 2 show the way (to); guide. ~ ধরা *vi* follow (sb/ a road); set out. ~ খরচ *n* travelling expenses. ~ঘাট *n* roads and highways. ~ বন্ধ হওয়া *vi* (of roads, means of livelihood, etc) be blocked. ~র ধার *n* roadside; wayside. ~র লোক *n* 1 stranger: ~র লোককে একথা বলা যায় না. 2 casual acquaintance. সদর ~ *n* main road; open way. সরকারি ~ *n* public road; highway.

রাস্না *n* kind of orchid; *Vanda roxburghii*. ~গোত্রীয় *adj* orchidaceous; orchideous.

রাহ =রাহা

রাহমত=রহমত

রাহা [P] *n* road; way; passage; path. ~খরচ *n* travelling expenses. ~গির *n* traveller; wayfarer. ~গুজার *n* road; path; passage. ~জান *n* highwayman; robber. ~জানি *n* highway robbery. ~বর, রাহবর *n* guide; conductor. ~বরি, রাহবরি *nn* guidance; conducting.

রাহিত্য *n* absence; lack; want; annulment.

রাহী [P] *n* traveller; wayfarer.

রাহু *n* 1 (myth) name of a demon who is supposed to seize the sun and the moon and thus cause eclipse. 2 (astron) ascending node. 3 (fig) evil influence; (one who causes) ruin. ~র দশা *n* 1 (astrol) phase of the influence of the ascending node as indicated by one's horoscope. 2 (fig) period marked with calamity/ misery/ misfortune/ want etc. ~গ্রস্ত *adj* 1 (astron) eclipsed. 2 fallen under the influence of an evil person; obscured; fallen into obscurity. ~গ্রাস *n* 1 eclipse. 2 evil influence.

রি, রে *nn* (music) second note of the Indian gamut.

রিং [E] *n* ring; small hoop. ~ করা *vt* ring up.

রিকশ, রিকশা *nn* rickshaw. ~চালক *n* rickshaw-driver.

রিকাব = রেকাব

রিকাবি = রেকাবি

রিক্থ *n* property left at death; inheritance; wealth; possessions. ~গ্রহ *adj* receiving an inheritance; inheriting property. ❑*n* inheritor. ~ভাগী, ~হারী=~গ্রহ রিক্থী *adj* inheriting property. ❑*n* heir.

রিক্ত *n* 1 empty; void; emptied; hollow; hollowed; bare; bared. 2 vacant. 3 poor; destitute; indigent; penniless. 4 (in compounds) destitute/ devoid of; free from; without: মেঘ~. রিক্তা *fem*. ~ করা *vt* empty; leave sb destitute; rob; plunder. ~তা *n* emptiness; destitution; vacuity. ~তৌল *n* tare.

~পাণি, ~হস্ত *nn* empty hand. ❑*adjj* empty-handed; having nothing in the hand; bringing no present; broke; penniless; fundless.

রিক্তা *n fem* the 4th, 9th and 14th day of the lunar fortnight.

রিক্তি *n* vacancy.

রিক্রুট [E] *n* recruit. **রিক্রুটিং** *n, adj* recruiting.

রিঙ্খণ, রিঙ্গণ *nn* **1** sliding; crawling; slipping. **2** fall; disgrace; downfall.

রিঙ্গিত *adj* sliding; shed; slipped off. **রিঙ্গিতা** *fem.*

রিজক, রেজেক [A] *n* food; support; sustenance; subsistence; daily bread.

রিজার্ভেশন [E] *n* reservation.

রিটর্ন, রিটার্ন [E] *n, adj* return: ~ টিকেট.

রিঠা, রিঠে (colloq) *nn* **1** soapnut. **2** kind of small fish.

রিনঝিন, রিনিঝিনি, রিনিকিঝিনি, রিনিকিঝিনিকি *nn* (onom) jingling; jingle; tinkle (as of ornaments).

রিপিট [E] *n* rivet. ~ **করা** *vt* rivet.

রিপু[1] *n* **1** enemy; adversary; foe. **2** any one of the six inherent/ cardinal passions of man (viz sex-passion, anger, greed, infatuation, vanity and envy, collectively ষড়~. **3** (astrol) hostile planet. **~জয়, ~দমন** *nn* subjugation/ conquest of an enemy; subjugation/ subduing of one's inherent vices. ~ **দমন করা** *vi* subdue/ subjugate/ tame passions/ inherent vices. **~জয়ী** *adj* vanquishing/ destroying one's cardinal passions/ inherent vices/ foes. ❑*n* subduer of one's enemies, etc. **~পরতন্ত্র, ~পরবশ, ~বশ** *adj* ruled by/ giving oneself to one's passions/ inherent vices; vicious.

রিপু[2]=রিফু

রিপোর্ট [E] *n* report. ~ **করা** *vi* report (against). ~ **পেশ করা** *vi* submit a report. **রিপোর্টার** *n* reporter.

রিফাইনারি [E] *n* refinery.

রিফু [A] *n* darning; mending darn. ~ **করা** *vt* darn; mend. **~কর্ম** *n* darning. **~গর** *n* darner. **~গরি, ~গিরি** *n* darning.

রিবেট [E] *n* rebate.

রিভলবার, রিভলভার [E] *n* revolver.

রিম [E] *n* ream (of paper).

রিমঝিম, রিমিঝিমি *nn* (onom) patter (of rain).

রিযক = রিজক

রিয়াইত, রিয়াত = রেয়াত

রিয়া [A] *n* hypocrisy; affectation; pretense; outward/ affected/ simulated devoutness; sanctimony. **~কারি** *n* show of devoutness/ holiness.

রিরংসা *n* desire of pleasure/ sexual enjoyment; lasciviousness; lustfulness; lust. ~ **বৃত্তি** *n* sex instinct; lust; strong sexual desire.

রিরংসু *adj* wishing for sexual pleasure; wanton; lustful.

রিরি *n* (onom) expressing feeling of abhorrence, anger, etc. **(ঘৃণায়/ রাগে) গা ~ করা** get/ have the shivers; revolt against; sick at; turn one's stomach; shudder at; recoil at; get one's dander up; simmer with (rage, etc).

রিল [E] *n* reel.

রিলিফ [E] *n* relief.

রিশতা [P] *n* relationship; kinship; connection; affinity; alliance. **~দার** *n* relation; kinsman.

রিষ *n* envy; grudge; malice. **রিষারিষি** *n* mutual envy/ grudge/ malice; rivalry.

রিশালা=রিসালা

রিষ্ট, রিষ্টি *nn* injury; damage; failure; miscarriage; bad luck; misfortune; sin, woe; (astrol) evil planetary aspect/ influence.

রিষ্টওয়াচ [E] *n* wrist-watch.

রিসওয়াত, রিশওত [A] *n* bribe; illegal gratification.

রিসালা [A] *n* **1** troop of horses; cavalry; squadron. **2** treatise; tract. **~দার, রিসালদার** *n* officer of cavalry; commander of a squadron.

রিহার্সাল [E] *n* rehearsal (of a dramatic performance. etc). ~ **দেওয়া/ দেওয়ানো** *vt* rehearse.

রীত *n* (dail, poet)=রীতি

রীতি *n* **1** method; custom; usage; mode; practice; convention; way; manner. **2** rule. **3** nature; natural property; disposition; propensity. **4** general course (of events, etc); order. **5** style (of speaking/ writing); diction. **6** fashion; go; way: যুগের ~. **~ক্রমে** *adv* in keeping with the custom/ rule/ practice/ usage/ form; as usual; customarily; formally; in due form; conventionally. **~জ্ঞ** *adj* acquainted with established customs/ usage's. **~নীতি** *n pl* manners and customs. **~পদ্ধতি**=~নীতি. **~বিরুদ্ধ** *adj* **1** contrary to custom/ usage; contrary to one's nature/ habit; contrary to rule; irregular; contrary to a particular style/ manner/ fashion/ way; unconventional; **2** unidiomatic. **~মতো** *adv* **1** in keeping with custom/ usage/ practice/ rule/ form; customarily; formally; conventionally. **2** quite; completely; altogether; really; truly; thoroughly; soundly: ~মতো ভালো, ~মতো সুস্থ মানুষ. **~সম্মত, ~সিদ্ধ** *adj* **1** regular; according to rule; customary; fashionable; formal. **2** idiomatic.

রীম=রিম

রীল=রিল

-রু *suff* indicating likeness: ঘোড়া~, তুলা~.

রুই[1] *n* kind of very large fresh-water fish; *Cyprinus rohitaka.* **~কাতলা** *n* **1** rui and katla. **2** (lit and fig) big fish; big shot.

রুই[2] *n* white ant.
রুইতন [Du] *n* diamond (of playing cards).
রুকসত=রোখসত
রুকু [A] *n* bowing the head and the body in prayer.
রুক্ষ *adj* **1** rough; uneven; rugged: ~ পথ. **2** rude; unkind; harsh; cruel: ~ ব্যবহার/ ভাষা~. **3** hard; arid: ~ মাটি. **4** not greasy/ oily: ~ চামড়া. **5** unpleasant/ disagreeable/ not soft (to the sight, smell, etc). **6** angry; haughty: ~ দৃষ্টি. **~তা** *n* roughness; aridity; harshness; dryness; unkindness; acerbity; rudeness. **~ভাষী** *adj* speaking roughly; sharp-tongued; rough-spoken; foul-mouthed; rude. **~স্বভাব** *adj* haughty; arrogant; cross-grained; rude; uncivil; unrefined; ill-mannered.
রুখা[1] *vi* **1** get angry; flare up; burst into anger; snarl; gnarl; gnash. **2** be on the point of attacking; advance menacingly; shake the fist at; threaten. **3** stop: গাড়ি ~. **4** resist; intercept; prevent, interrupt; hinder; detain; check; oppose; obstruct; block; impede; restrain; oppose.
রুখা[2] *adj* **1** dry; rough; harsh; not oily; unbuttered; moistless; arid: ~ চুল/ মাথা. **2** plain; simple: ~ ভাত. **3** sapless; juiceless. **4** angry; rude; insolent; haughty; curt; blunt. **5** not provided with food; without board: ~ মাইনের চাকর.
রুখু, রুখো *adjj* (colloq)=রুখা[2]
রুগি, রুগী *adjj* (colloq)=রোগী
রুগ্‌ণ *adj* ill; diseased; unwell; sick; sickly; infirm; emaciated; debilitated; indisposed; ailing; in poor health; morbid; weak: ~ শরীর. রুগ্‌ণা *fem.* **~তা** *n* illness; sickness; ailment; disease; malady; morbidity.
রুচা *vi* be agreeable to one's taste/ liking; please; suit one's taste; have a taste for; be to one's liking.
রুচি *n* **1** taste; liking; relish; pleasure; appetite; zest; gusto; propensity; inclination: আহারে ~, শিল্পে ~. **2** good taste; choice: লোকটার ~ আছে. **3** desire; longing. **4** light; lusture; glow; splendour; colour; beauty; complexion: মুখ~, দন্ত~. **~কর** *adj* **1** appetizing; tasty; savoury; palatable; delectable; delicious. **2** in good taste; tasteful; graceful; refined, elegant; pleasant; attractive; decent. **~তা** *n* taking pleasure in; fondness/ taste for. **~বাগীশ** *adj* (usually derog) fastidious; overfastidious; finicky; fussy; puritanical; prudish; squeamish. **~বিরুদ্ধ** *adj* contrary to one's taste/ liking; in bad/ poor taste; in the worst of taste; tasteless; inelegant; indecent; indecorous; vulgar. **~ভেদ** *n* difference of taste. **~ভেদে** *adv* according to different tastes; according to difference in taste/ liking. **~র** *adj* **1** bright; brilliant; radiant; splendid. **2** beautiful; pleasant; charming. **3** sweet; dainty; nice. **রুচিরা** *fem.*
রুচিত *adj* **1** bright; brilliant; glittering. **2** pleasant; agreeable; sweet; delicate; dainty.
রুচিরা *n* name of a Sanskrit metre.
রুচ্য *adj* **1**=রুচিকর (⇒ রুচি). **2**=রুচিত
রুজ [E] *n* **1** rouge. **2** red oxide powder (used in polishing gold and silver).
রুজি [P] *n* daily sustenance; daily food/ allowance; livelihood; maintenance; wages; employment. **~-রোজগার** *n* earnings; income. **~-রোজগার করা** *vi* earn one's living/ one's livelihood/ one's daily bread; obtain an employment.
রুজু [A] *n* **1** return; bent; reference; appeal; inclination. **2** submission; filing; placing. ❑*adj* **1** submitted; preferred; filed; brought before a court. **2** faced; turned towards: মন ~ করা. **3** facing; straight. **~ করা** *vt* **1** submit; prefer; file; bring before a court: মামলা ~ করা. **2** turn; incline; dispose; concentrate: আল্লাহর প্রতি মন ~ করা. **~ দেওয়া** *vt* compare (accounts etc.) **~ হওয়া** *vi* submit oneself to; address oneself to. **~-রুজু** *adj* facing/ confronting each other.
রুটি, রুটী *n* bread; loaf; food; sustenance; livelihood. **~ গড়া** *vi* make bread (by kneading, rolling); make loaves; cook bread. **~ বেলা** *vi* roll bread into (into the shape of a saucer). **~ মারা** *vi* (fig) deprive sb of one's livelihood. **~ সেঁকা** *vi* bake bread. **~ওয়ালা** *n* baker. **~র কারখানা** *n* bakery. **~-রোজগার** *n* livelihood.
রুটিন [E] *n* routine. **~-বাঁধা** *adj* rigidly fixed; regular; routine; monotonous: ~-বাঁধা কাজ, routine duties: ~-বাঁধা জীবন.
রুণুঝুণু =রুনুঝুনু
রুদিত *adj* wept; lamented; weeping; crying; lamenting; wet with tears.
রুদ্ধ *adj* **1** shut; closed; covered; bolted: ~ দ্বার/গৃহ. **2** confined; incarcerated: কারা~. **3** obstructed; checked; blockaded: গতি ~, পথ ~. **4** suppressed: ~ ক্রন্দন. **5** suspended; choked: ~ নিঃশ্বাস/ স্পন্দন. **6** held back; withheld; kept back. **7** invested; besieged. **8** intercepted; arrested; prevented. **9** motionless; still: ~ বাতাস. **10** stagnant: ~ জল. **~ করা** *vt* close; bolt; shut; cover; incarcerate; lock up; confine in; obstruct; check; arrest; intercept; stop; restrain; prevent; keep back; withhold; blockade; besiege; invest; block up; conceal; veil; obscure; stop up; fill; suspend; suppress; choke. **~ কক্ষ** *n* closed room. **~ কক্ষে সভা/ আলোচনা** *n* meeting/ conference with/ behind closed door. **~কণ্ঠ** *adj* having one's voice choked. **~কণ্ঠে** *adv* with a choked

voice. ~গতি *adj* having one's motion arrested; obstructed; blockaded; stopped. ~তাপ *adj* (phys) adiabatic. ~দৃষ্টি *adj* having the sight impeded (by tears etc). ~দ্বার *adj* having the door(s) closed; close-door. ~দ্বার আলোচনা *n* secret session. ~প্রবাহ *adj* obstructed in (its) flow. ~মুখ *adj* having the mouth filled/ stuffed. ~শ্বাস *adj* breathless; panting; out of breath; gasping with bated breath. ~শ্বাসে *adv* breathlessly; with bated breath. pantingly; gasping for breath.

রুদ্র n **1** manifestation of Shiva as a destroyer. **2** (myth) a class of beings described as eleven in number. ❑*adj* terrible; dreadful; terrific; furious; howling; horrible; roaring. **রুদ্রাণী** *n fem* Rudra's wife, goddess Durga. ~জ *adj* produced from Rudra. ❑*n* quicksilver. ~ভাব *n* fierceness; terribleness; dreadfulness. ~মূর্তি *adj* having terrible/ terrific appearance; awful; awe-inspiring. **রুদ্রাক্ষ** *n* kind of berries (*Elaeocarpus ganitrus*) used as rosaries. **রুদ্রাক্ষমালা** *n* rosary composed of *rudrakshas*. **রুদ্রাক্রীড়** *n* 'Rudra's pleasure-ground'; cemetery/ burning-ground for corpses.

রুধা *vt*=রুদ্ধ করা (⇒ রুদ্ধ)

রুধির *n* **1** blood. **2** kind of precious stone. **3** the planet Mars. ❑*adj* red; blood-red; bloody. ~ পান/ শোষণ করা *vi* drink/ suck another's blood; (fig) extract money oppressively from; extort. ~ধারা *n* stream of blood. ~পাত *n* flow of blood. ~পায়ী *adj* blood-drinking; blood-sucking; extortionary. ~প্লাবিত *adj* swimming with/ soaked in blood. ~রঞ্জিত *adj* smeared/ covered with blood; bloody. ~স্নান *n* (lit and fig) blood-bath. ~স্রোত=~ধারা. **রুধিরাক্ত**=~রঞ্জিত. **রুধিরাখ্য** *n* carnelian (stone). **রুধিরাপ্লুত** *adj* drenched with blood; bloody.

রুনঝুন, রনুরনু, রুনুঝুনু, রুনুরুনু *nn* (onom) sweet jingling tinkling (as of the bells of a dancer's anklets).

রুপা *n* silver. ~র চাকতি *n* **1** (facet) silver coin. **2** (iron) bribe; money. ~লি *adjj* silver-coloured; silvery; silver-white; argentine.

রুপিয়া, রুপেয়া *n* rupee.

রুপো *n* (colloq)=রুপা. ~লি =রুপালি

রুবাই, রুবাঈ [A] *n* stanza of four lines; quatrain; a Persian verse-form. ~য়াত, ~য়াৎ *n pl* quatrains; Rubaiyyat.

রুম [E] *n* room.

রুমঝুম, রুমুঝুমু *nn* (onom) sweet jingle/ tinkle of anklets, musical instruments, etc.

রুমাল [P] *n* handkerchief; towel; napkin.

রুয়া[1] *vt* sow; plant. ❑*adj* sown; planted. ~নো *vt* get sown/ planted.

রুয়া[2] *n* large strip of bamboo used in thatching roofs.

রুঢ় *adj* **1** rough; harsh; rude haughty; insolent. **2** (gram) expressing a conventional meaning which is not directly connected with the etymology; used in conventional sense: ~ শব্দ. **3** (gram) conventional; traditional; popular: ~ অর্থ. **4** high; noble; great. **5** widely known; diffused; current; notorious; famous. **6** grown; developed; sprung up; produced. ~তা *n* roughness; rudeness; harshness; haughtiness; insolence. ~ পদার্থ *n* element. ~মূল *adj* firmly planted.

রুল[1] [E] *n* rule; ruling; law; precedent. ~ করা *vi* make a law. ~ জারি করা/ দেওয়া give/ issue a ruling; rule; give as a decision.

রুল[2] *n* **1** straight length of wood, plastic, metal, etc used in drawing straight lines; ruler. **2** baton; truncheon: পুলিশের রুলের গুঁতা. **3** (printed/ drown) straight line. ~ করা *vt* mark with straight lines; rules. ~ টানা *vi* make (a line/ lines) on paper (with a ruler); make parallel lines on (paper); rule.

রুলি *nn* thin bangle for the wrist.

রুলিং [E] *n* (law) ruling.

রুশনী=রওশনি

রুষা =রুষ্ট হওয়া

রুষিত, রুষ্ট *adj* offended; angered; irritated; furious; angry; enraged. **রুষিতা, রুষ্টা** *fem*. ~ করা *vt* offend; irritate; anger; enrage; incense; infuriate. ~ হওয়া *vi* be offended/ angry/ enraged; become angry/ furious; fume; burst into anger.

রুসুম **1**=রসম. **2** taxes; fees; duties; postage. **রুসুমাত** *n* traditional rites performed at a wedding.

রুহ [A] *n* spirit; soul; life; essence of anything; vital principal. **রুহানি** *adj* spiritual. **রুহানিয়াত** *n* spirituality.

রুহিতন = রুইতন

রূঢ়ি *n* **1** (gram) more amplified/ conventional/ popular meaning of words; employment of a word in such a meaning. **2** birth; production; rise; emergence; increase; development. **3** fame celebrity; notoriety. ~ শব্দ *n* word used in its conventional sense.

রূপ *n* **1** form; shape; figure. **2** any outward appearance/phenomenon/colour. **3** handsome form; loveliness; grace; beauty; splendour. **4** body; build. **5** nature; character; peculiarity; feature; mark; sign; symbol. **6** sort; type; kind: কি~. **7** colour; hue; complexion. **8** likeness; image; reflection. **9** (gram) any form of a noun/ verb (as inflected by declension or conjugation). **10** mode; manner, way: এ~, সে~. **11** (phil) concept; precept. ~ করা *vt* (gram) conjugate or decline. ~কথা *n* fairy tale; folk-tale; legend. ~কার *n* maker of images; moulder; sculptor; artist; dresser (esp of actors actresses). ~কৃৎ *adj* making forms/ figures. ~গুণ *n pl* beauty and merits. ~চাঁদ *n* (facet) silver coin; money; means. ~জ *adj* originating from/ caused by beauty; physical: ~জ মোহ. ~ত *adv* according to form. ~তত্ত্ব *n* 1 (linguistics) morphology. 2 aesthetics. ~তৃষ্ণা *n* thirst/ craving for beauty. ~দক্ষ *adj* 1 proficient in shaping/ moulding; creative; artistic. 2 adept in assuming disguises. 3 proficient in using make-up. ~দস্তা *n* pewter. ~ধর *adj* having the shape/ form of. ~ ধারণ করা *vi* assume the form/ shape of; disguise oneself as; assume the disguise of; appear as; play the role of (a dramatic character). ~ধারী *adj* 1 bearing a form; assuming a shape; disguised as; appearing as; impersonating. 2 embodied; corporeal. 3 endowed with beauty. ~ধারিণী *fem*. ~ পরিগ্রহ(ণ) করা *vi* take shape. ~বতী *adj fem* endowed with beauty; beautiful; lovely. ~বন্ত, ~বান *adjj* handsome; handsomely formed; beautiful. ~ভেদ *n* diversity/ variety of forms/ manifestations; variation. ~মাধুরী, ~মাধুর্য *nn* charm of beauty; good looks. ~মুগ্ধ, ~মোহিত *adjj* infatuated with; infatuated/ fascinated by beauty. ~মুগ্ধা, ~মোহিতা *fem*. ~মোহ *n* infatuation; fascination for beauty. ~যৌবন *n* youth and beauty. ~যৌবনসম্পন্ন *adj* full of youth and beauty; young and handsome. ~যৌবনসম্পন্না *fem*. ~রসগন্ধস্পর্শ *n* colour and taste and smell and palpability. ~রাশি *n* uncommon/ stunning/ great beauty; charmed. ~লাবণ্য *n* charm of personal beauty; gracefulness; glamour. ~শালী *adj* possessed of beauty; handsome; beautiful . ~শালিনী *fem*. ~সী *adj fem*=~বতী. রূপে *adv* in beauty/ form. ❑*suff* meaning; in the manner of the; as; -ly: বন্ধু~, দৃঢ়~. রূপে গুণে *adv* in beauty and talent. রূপের অপ্সরী/ ডালি/ তিলোত্তমা/ ধচুনি *nn* 1 woman of uncommon beauty; paragon of beauty; beauty queen. 2 (derog, iron) utterly ugly woman; repulsive/ hideous figure.

রূপক *n* (rhet) 1 figure of speech; metaphor; comparison; allegory. 2 a particular type of figure of speech. ❑*adj* having form; metaphorical; figurative. ~ বাক্য, ~ শব্দ *nn* figurative expression.

রূপা = রুপা

রূপাজীবা, রূপাজীবী *adjj fem* living by prostitution. ❑*nn* prostitute; harlot.

রূপান্তর *n* 1 different form/ shape/ nature. 2 change of form/ shape/ nature; transformation; metamorphosis. 3 translation. ~ করা/ ঘটানো *vt* 1 change the appearance, shape, quality or nature; transform; metamorphose. 2 translate.

রূপান্তরিত *adj* 1 changed into a different form/ shape; transformed. 2 (geol) metamorphic. ~ করা = রূপান্তর করা (⇒ রূপান্তর).

রূপায়ণ *n* 1 representation; shopping; forming. 2 depiction; narration. 3 embodiment. 4 dramatic impersonation. ~ করা *vt* depict; portray represent; play (the role of); impersonate; shape; give a shape/ form to; materialize.

রূপায়িত *adj* embodied; materialized; represented; shaped; narrated; depicted; portrayed; delineated; impersonated. ~ করা =রূপায়ণ করা. ~ হওয়া *vi* materialize; take a shape; be embodied/ represented/ depicted.

রূপালী=রুপালি

রূপি *n* rupee.

রূপিণী *adj fem* of রূপী

রূপিয়া *n* rupee.

রূপী[1] *adj* (used as a *suff*) having the form/ nature/ character of; characterized by; appearing as; disguised as: নর~, বহু~.

রূপী[2] *n* kind of ruddy-faced monkey.

রূপোপজীবিনী *n fem* prostitute.

রূপ্য *n* silver. রূপ্যাধ্যক্ষ *n* mint-master.

রূহ্ =রুহ

রে[1] = রেখা

রে[2] *int* 1 (vocative particle generally used contemptuously or to express disrespect, affection or threat) O, hey, ho. 2 expresses surprise, regret, pain, sorrow, etc: oh, ah.

রেউচিনি, রেউচিনী *nn* Indian rhubarb.

রেওয়া [P] *n* annual balance-sheet.

রেওয়াজ [A] *n* 1 usage; custom; fashion; currency; practice; prevalence; vogue. 2 practice of music. ~ করা *vi* practice (esp music). ~ থাকা *vi* be in vogue/ fashion; be current; be prevalent; be the practice of; be in practice. ~ হওয়া *vi* come into fashion/ vogue; become fashionable.

রেওয়ায়েৎ [A] *n* narration; tradition; legend.

রেঁদা, র‍্যাঁদা *nn* carpenter's plane.

রেক[1]=র‍্যাক

রেক[2] *n* wick container for measuring grain (about 1 kg).

রেক[3] *n* (colloq)=রেখা

রেকাত=রাকাত

রেকাব [A] *n* stirrup; train. ~দার *n* an attendant when riding; companion.

রেকাবি, রেকাবী [P] *n* (small) dish.

রেখ *n* (generally in compounds)=রেখা

রেখক *n* tracer.

রেখন *n* cross.

রেখা *n* 1 line; streak; scratch; stripe. 2 continuous line; row; range; furrow; series. 3 mark. 4 faint sign; thin like: গোঁফের ~. 5 (phys) rulings. ~ টানা *vi* draw a line. ~কার *adj* linear; striped. ~গণিত *n* geometry. ~ঙ্কন *n* drawing of lines; lineation. ~ঙ্কিত *adj* striped; furrowed; linear; lineated; striated. ~চিত্র *n* linedrawing; rough sketch. ~ন্যাস *n* outline; sketch. ~পাত

=~ স্কন. ~পাত করা *vi* draw a line; make an impression (as on one's mind); impress.

রেখিত *adj* crossed: ~ চেক

রেচক *adj* **1** purging; purgative; laxative; aperient. **2** (bot) excretory. ☐*n* **1** purgative; laxative; aperient. **2** (in yoga) breathing out; exhalation.

রেচন *n* **1** evacuation of bowels; purging; purgation; emptying. **2** (bot) excretion. **3** (in yoga) exhalation. ~ **করা/ করানো** *vt* evacuate bowels; purge. ~**তন্ত্র** *n* excretory system. ~**যন্ত্র** *n* excretory organ.

রেচিত *adj* emptied; purged; cleared; evacuated.

রেজগি, রেজকি [P] *n* small coins; change; silver bits.

রেজাই [A] *n* quilt; coverlet; kind of wrapper stuffed with carded cotton.

রেজাল্ট [E] *n* result.

রেজিস্টার[1] [E] *n* register.

রেজিস্ট্রার[2] [E] *n* registrar.

রেজিস্ট্রি, রেজিস্টারি *nn* registration; registry; register. ☐*adjj* registered. ~ **করা** *vt* register. ~-অফিস *n* registry (office). ~**কৃত** *adj* registered. ~**খাতা,** ~**বই** *nn* register.

রেজেক=রিজক

রেঞ্চ [E] *n* wrench.

রেট [E] *n* rate; price; speed.

রেডি [E] *adj* ready. ~ **করা/ করানো** *vt* make ready. ~ **হওয়া** *vi* get ready.

রেডিও, রেডিয়ো [E] *nn* radio. ~**গ্রাম** *n* radiogram.

রেডিয়াম [E] *n* radium.

রেডিয়েটার [E] *n* radiator.

রেড়ি *nn* castor-oil seed or plant. ~**র তেল** *n* castor-oil.

রেণু *n* **1** dust; grain/ atom of dust. **2** pollen of flowers; spore. **3** powder of anything. ~**সার** *n* camphor.

রেণুক, রেণুকা *nn Piper aurantiacum* (a fragrant medicinal fruit of bitter and pungent taste).

রেত[1] *n* stream of a river.

রেত[2] *n* (colloq) carpenter's file; rasp.

রেতঃ *n* semen; virile. ~**পাত** *n* emission/ ejaculation of semen.

রেতি, রেতী *nn*=রেত[2]

রেনেসাঁস [F] *n* renaissance.

রেপ [E] *n* rape.

রেফ *n* **1** (র্) this sign on Bengali letters to indicate a preceding 'r' sound. **2** upright antenna/ hair on heads of some creatures: দ্বি~.

রেফারি, রেফারী [E] *nn* referee.

রেবতী *n fem* the last of the twenty-seven Nakshatras according to Hindu astronomy.

রেবা *n* name of a river in south India (also called Narmada).

রেয়াজ=রেওয়াজ

রেয়াত, রেয়াৎ [A] *n* exemption; remission; concession; relaxation, indulgence; favour; show of respect; regard. ~ **করা** *vt* exempt; grant concession. relax; remit; (show) favour; respect.

রেয়াতি, রেয়াতী [A] *adjj* **1** concessional; remitted; relaxed. **2** favoured person.

রেয়ো *adj* arrived uninvited/ on hearing the report of a feast; uninvited. ~**ভাট** *n* beggar arrived uninvited on the report of a feast.

রে-রে-রে-রে *n* (onom) battle-cry of robbers.

রেল [E] *n* rail; railway train/ carriage; railway line; rail line. ~**ইঞ্জিন** *n* railway engine. ~**ওয়ে** *n* railway. ~**গাড়ি** *n* train. ~**চালক** *n* railway engine-driver. ~**পথ** *n* railroad; railway. ~**যোগে** *adv* by rail/ train. ~**লাইন** *n* rail line; railroad. ~**স্টেশন** *n* railway station.

রেলিং, রেলিঙ [E] *nn* railings.

রেশ *n* **1** lingering faint resonance of a sound/ note gradually dying out; faint echo: সঙ্গীতের ~. **2** faint feeling/ memory of sth; faint trace: মুখের ~. **3** faint sign: গোঁফের ~.

রেশম [P] *n* silk. ~ **কীট** *n* silk-worm. ~ **গুটি** *n* cocoon. ~ **বিজ্ঞান,** ~ **শিল্প** *nn* sericulture. রেশমি, রেশমী *adj* of silk; silk; silken.

রেশালা =রিসালা

রেষ *n* (colloq)=রিষ

রেস [E] *n* race; racing. ~ **দেওয়া** *vi* compete in speed; race. রেসের ঘোড়া *n* race-horse racer.

রেসালা=রিসালা

রেসুড়ে *n* racing man; race-goer; race-addict.

রেস্ত [Pg] *n* capital; funds; means; where withal; provision of money; sth left (of money); shift. ~-**শূন্য** *adj* having no capital; without provisions; out of funds; shiftless.

রেস্তোরাঁ [F] *n* restaurant.

রেহন, রেহান, রেহেন [A] *nn* mortgage; pawn; pledge. ~ **দেওয়া/ রাখা** *vt* mortgage; pawn. ~**দার** *n* mortgagee. ~**নামা** *n* deed of mortgage. ~**বন্ধ** *adj* mortgaged; pledged; in/ at pawn. রেহনাবন্ধ=~বন্ধ.

রেহাই [P] *n* exemption; escape; liberation; deliverance; relief; release; discharge. ~ **দেওয়া** *vt* exempt; acquit; release; discharge; relieve; set at liberty; set free. ~ **পাওয়া** *vi* be released/ discharged/ acquitted/ set free/ set at liberty; escape; be relieved; be exempted from.

রেহেল [A] *n* a stand for the Qoran; bookstand.

রৈ *n* sound; noise. রৈ রৈ *n* tumult; uproar; hullabaloo.

রৈখিক *adj* linear; lineal; lineate.

রোঁ, রোঁয়া *n* **1** (short) hair on the body of men and animals; down. **2** nap (of cloth, etc); short hairs/ fibres; bristles; wool. **3** soft feathers of a bird. রোঁয়া ওঠা *vi* (esp of dogs) suffer from mange. রোঁয়া-ওঠা *adj* mangy.

রোঁদ [E] *n* round; beat; prescribed circuit. রোঁদে বাহির হওয়া *vi* go on a round; patrol.

রোঁয়া ⇒ রোঁ

রোএর্দাদ = রোয়েদাদ

রোক[1] *n* (colloq)=রোখ

রোক[2] *n* cash; cash-purchase; ready money; cash and carry. ❑*adj* ready: ~ টাকা. ~ঋণ *n* cash credit. ~থোক *adj* in hard cash; cash down; in ready money. ~শোধ *n* cash-payment (of bills, etc). ~স্থিতি *n* cash-balance.

রোক[3] *n* **1** obstruction; barrier: obstacle; hindrance; impediment. **2** stopping; prevention; stop; interruption. **3** embargo.

রোক[4] [P] *n* (in chess) check.

রোক[5] [P] *n* **1** frontage; facade; facing. **2** vantage. রোকের *adj* advantageous: রোকের জমি/ জায়গা, advantageous site.

রোকড় *n* **1** cash-book; cash-account: রোকড়ে তোলা. **2** ready money; cash. **3** gold and silver ornaments; jewellery; stock. রোকড়ের কুটি/ কুঠি *n* banking house. রোকড়ের দোকান *n* banker's shop.

রোকসৎ=রোখসত

রোকা[1], **রোক্কা** [A] *nn* **1** hand-note; slip; note; chit; billet; short letter. **2** scrap of paper; piece. ~-হুণ্ডি *n* note of hand; bank-draft.

রোকা[2]=রোখা. ~ল=রোখাল

রোখ[1] *n* **1** stubborn resolve/ desire; aggressiveness; spiritedness; determination; stubbornness; fury; rage; turbulence; vehemence; ferocity; passion. **2** growth: গাছের ~. ~ চাপা *vi* filled with fury; be seized with a strong desire/ violent passion/ stubborn resolution. ~ দেখানো *vi* show/ exhibit spiritedness/ strong resolve (affected or impotent).

রোখ[2]=রোক[5]

রোখসত, রোখসৎ [A] *nn* **1** leave; permission. **2** dismissal; discharge. **3** compromise; settlement. **4** licence; indulgence; leave of absence. ❑*adj* dismissed; discharged: ~হওয়া. ~ চাওয়া *vi* ask leave; request for indulgence. ~ দেওয়া *vi* give leave; permit; dismiss; bid farewell; discharge. ~ হওয়া *vi* take leave; depart; be dismissed.

রোখা[1], **রোখাল** *adjj* stubborn; obstinate; headstrong; spirited; willful; self-willed; unruly.

রোখা[2]=রুখা[1]

রোগ *n* **1** disease; sickness; illness; infirmity ailment; morbidity; affliction; disorder; malady. **2** vice; incorrigible bad practice/ addiction: পরচর্চা তার প্রধান ~. ~ সারা *vi* **1** recover from a disease; be cured of a disease; come round; recuperate; get well. **2** be freed from a vice. ~ সারানো *vi* **1** cure (an illness); restore to health; make well. **2** break a habit; cure bad habit. ~ হওয়া *vi* be attacked with a disease; be/fall ill; be affected/ afflicted with; go down with; contract a disease. ~ক্লিষ্ট *adj* ill; attacked/ affected by a disease; afflicted. ~গ্রস্ত *adj* seized with any disease/ sickness; ailing; diseased; sick. ~ঘ্ন *adj* removing disease. ❑*n* medicine. ~চিকিৎসা *n* treatment of a disease. ~যোগ *n pl* ailments. ~জনক *adj* causing disease; unwholesome; (bot) pathogenic. ~জীবাণু *n* bacterium (*pl* bacteria), bacillus (*pl* bacilli); virus; germ. ~জীর্ণ *adj* worn-out/ run down by disease; wasted. ~দুর্বল *adj* weakened by disease; debilitated. ~নাশক, ~নাশন *adjj* destroying/ removing disease; curative; therapeutic. ~নিদান *n* cause of a disease. ~নিদানতত্ত্ব *n* pathology. ~নির্ণয় *n* diagnosis. ~ভয় *n* fear of disease. ~প্রতিষেধ *n* treatment; therapeutics; remedy; antidote. ~ভোগ *n* suffering from disease. ~মুক্ত *adj* freed/ cured/ recovered from disease; free from disease. ~মুক্ত করা =~ সারানো. ~মুক্ত হওয়া =~ সারা. ~মুক্তি *n* recovery (from a disease); restoration to health. ~যন্ত্রণা, ~যাতনা *nn* agonies of disease. ~লক্ষণ *n* sign/ symptom of a disease. ~শম, ~শান্তি *n n* alleviation/ cure of a disease; recovery from sickness. ~-শয্যা *n* sick-bed. ~শীর্ণ *adj* work out by disease. ~শোক *n pl* disease and bereavement. ~হ, ~হা, ~হর *adj* taking away disease; curative. রোগাক্রান্ত *adj* attacked/ afflicted by a disease; ill; diseased. রোগাতঙ্ক *n* pathophobia. রোগার্ত *adj* afflicted by disease/ ailment. রোগে ধরা/ পড়া *vi*=~ হওয়া.

রোগন [P] *n* oil; butter; grease; polish; sleekness.

রোগা *adj* **1**=রুগ্ন. **2** thin; lean; slight; delicate; feeble; weak; debilitated; skinny; emaciated. ~ হওয়া *vi* grow thin; become emaciated; waste away; be weakened; slim down; ~টে *adj* frail. ~পটকা *adj* lean and feeble; lanky.

রোগী *adj* sick; diseased; ailing; suffering from a disease. ❑*n* patient; sick man. রোগিণী *fem.*

রোগোপশম *n* alleviation/ cure of disease; abatement of a disease.

রোচক *adj* **1** giving an appetite; pleasing; agreeable; tasteful; palatable; delicious. **2** brightening; enlightening. ❑*n* **1** hunger; appetite. **2** stomachic; stimulant.

রোচনা *n* **1** a particular yellow pigment obtained from the bile of cows (also গো~). **2** hand some woman. **3** red lotus.

রোচা *vi* (colloq)=রুচা

রোচিষ্ণু *adj* **1** shining; bright; brilliant; splendid. **2** giving an appetite; tasteful. **3** elegant.

রোচ্য *adj* =রোচক

রোজ [P] *n* **1** day; date. **2** daily ways: দশ টাকা রোজে কাজ করে. **3** daily supply: রোজের দুধ. ❑*adv* daily; everyday: সে ~ আসে. **~ করা** *vi* arrange for the daily supply (of): দুধ ~ করা. **~করা, ~বাঁধা** *adjj* arranged for daily supply. **~কার** *adj* **1** of every day; daily: ~কার বাজার. **2**=~গার. **~কিয়ামত** *n* **1** the Last Day; day of judgement/ resurrection; doomsday. **2** scene of trouble/ distress; great calamity; confusion. **~গার** *n* earning; income; wages; employment. **~গার করা** *vi* earn; be employed. **~গারি, ~গারী, ~গেরে** *adjj* earning: ~গারি লোক. **~নামচা, ~নামা** *nn* diary; journal; daily account book. **~রোজ** *adv* every day; daily; always; day by day. **~হাসর** day of resurrection.

রোজা[১] [P] *n* fast; fasting; **~ করা/ রাখা** keep/ observe a fast. **~ খোলা** *vi* break a fast. **~ ভাঙা** *vi* break a fast before time; kill a fast. **~দার** *adj, n* fasting (person). **~দারি** *n* fasting.

রোজা[২]=ওঝা

রোজিনা [P] *n* daily wages/ allowance/ earnings; stipend.

রোটি = রুটি. **~কা** *n* slice of bread.

রোড [E] *n* road.

রোথো=রথো

রোদ, রোদ্দুর (colloq)*nn* =রৌদ্র

রোদন *n* crying; weeping; lamentation; wailing. **~ করা** *vi* cry; weep; lament; wail. **~শীল** *adj* crying; weeping; wailing; lamenting. **~শীলা** *fem.*

রোদসী *n fem* heaven and earth. ❑*adj fem*=রোদনশীলা (⇒ রোদন).

রোধ *n* **1** stopping; checking; obstructing; impeding; besieging; restraining; suppressing; preventing; blockading. **2** obstruction; hindrance; check; resistance; blockade. **3** dam; embankment. **4** shore; bank. **5** mountain slope; flank; side. **6** (phys) resistance. **~ করা** *vt* obstruct; check; arrest; stop; restrain; hinder; resist; prevent; keep back; avert; keep off; repel; shut; lock up; confine in. **~ক** *adj* stopping; holding back; restraining; obstructive; blocking; hindering; resistant. **~কুণ্ডলী** *n* (phys) resistance-coil. **~ থার্মোমিটার** *n* (phys) resistance thermometer. **~ন** *n*=~ (1,2). ❑*adj*=~ক. **রোধাঙ্ক** *n* (phys) specific resistance.

রোধা (colloq)*vt* =রুদ্ধ করা (⇒ রুদ্ধ)

রোধিত *adj* obstructed; hindered; blockaded; blocked; resisted; stopped.

রোধী *adj*=রোধক (⇒ রোধ). **রোধিনী** *fem*

রোধঃ *n* bank; embankment; dam; mound; wall; shore.

রোনাজারি *n* crying; lamentation; wailing.

রোপণ *n* **1** plantation; sowing. **2** putting; fixing; placing; setting: ধনুকে শর ~. **~ করা** *vt* **1** plant; sow. **2** place; fix; put; set. **~যন্ত্র** *n* sowing-machine.

রোপণীয় *adj* **1** to be planted/ sowed. **2** to be set (up)/ placed/ fixed/ put.

রোপা *vt* plant; sow. ❑*adj* transplanted: ~আমন.

রোপিত *adj* **1** planted; sown; sowed. **2** fixed; aimed (as an arrow).

রোবাইয়াত [A] *n*=রুবাইয়াৎ (⇒ রুবাই)

রোম[১] *n* hair (on the body of men and animals); (esp) short hair; bristles; wool; down; nap; feathers; fur. **~কূপ** *n* pore of the skin. **~গুচ্ছ** *n* tuft of hair; tail of the yak used as a chowrie (cf চামর). **~জ** *adj* produced from hair/ wool; woolen. **~রাজি** *n* streak/ row/ line of hair (esp on the abdomen of women just above the navel, said to denote puberty). **~বান** *adj* possessed of/ covered with hair. **~বিকার, ~বিক্রিয়া** *nn* bristling/ erection of the hair of the body. **~শ** *adj* hairy; woolly; shaggy; furry. **~হর্ষ** *n* bristling of the hair of the body; thrill (caused by joy, pain, cold, etc); horripilation; goose flesh. **~হর্ষণ** *n*=~হর্ষ. ❑*adj* thrilling; horrible. **~হর্ষ হওয়া** *vi* feel a thrill of joy/ horror; have the hair of the body erect.

রোম[২] [E] *n* Rome. **~ক, রোমান** *nn, adjj* Roman.

রোমন্থ, ~ন *nn* rumination. **~ করা** *vi* ruminate; chew the cud. **রোমন্থক** *n* ruminant.

রোমাঞ্চ=রোমহর্ষ (⇒ রোম[১]). **~কর** *adj* thrilling; hair-raising; exciting; sensational.

রোমাঞ্চিত *adj* thrilled; athrill; excited.

রোমান ⇒ রোম[২]

রোমান্টিক [E] *adj, n* romantic.

রোমান্স [E] *n* romance.

রোমীয় *adj* of Rome; Roman. **~ সম্প্রদায়** *n* Roman Church.

রোমোদ্গম, রোমোদ্ভেদ *nn* **1** growth/ sprouting of hair. **2**=রোমহর্ষ (⇒ রোম[১]).

রোয়া[১] *n* segment/ section of a fruit; replum.

রোয়া[২] *vt* (colloq)=রুয়া[১]. **~নো**=রুয়ানো

রোয়া[৩] *vi* cry; weep.

রোয়াক [A] *n* raised terrace in front part of a building.

রোয়েদাদ [P] *n* award (of a share). **সাম্প্রদায়িক ~** *n* communal award.

রোরুদ্যমান *adj* weeping violently/ intensely. রোরুদ্যমানা *fem.*

রোল[১] *n* **1** noise; cry; uproar; outcry; sound. **2** tinkling (of metallic ornaments).

রোল[২] [E] *n* roll (of names).

রোলার [E] *n* roller. **~ দেওয়া** *vt* beat/ flatter with a roller; roll; use a roller.

রোশন=রওশন. ~গির *n* lamp-lighter. ~চৌকি *n* orchestra of sanai (সানাই) and other instruments.

রোশনাই, রোশনি=রওশনি

রোষ *n* anger; wrath; rage; passion; fury. ~কষায়িত *adj* reddened with anger. ~কষায়িতলোচনে *adv* with eyes red with anger/ angry look; in anger; looking angrily. ~দগ্ধ *adj* burning with wrath. ~দাহ *n* wrath; fury. ~দীপ্ত, ~প্রদীপ্ত *adjj* inflamed with passion; livid/ burning with rage. ~পরুষ, ~রুক্ষ *adjj* rough/ harsh through wrath. ~শান্তি *n* appeasement of anger. রোষাকুলিত *adj* perplexed/ troubled by passion. রোষাগ্নি, রোষানল *nn* fire of anger/ rage/ passion; terrible anger/ fury. রোষান্বিত, রোষাবিষ্ট *nn* filled with anger/ wrath. রোষান্বিতা, রোষাবিষ্টা *fem.* রোষালাপ *n* exchange of angry words.

রোষা *vi* be angry/ furious; be offended/ irritated/ exasperated; flare up; fly into a rage.

রোষাল *adj* angry; wrathful; furious; passionate.

রোষিত *adj* angered; enraged; exasperated; irritated.

রোস, রোসো *vi, imper* wait.

রোসমৎ = রুসুমাৎ (⇒ রুসুম)

রোস্ট [E] *n* roast.

রোহ *n* **1** rising; mounting; sitting/ standing on; ascending; riding. **2** sprouting; germination. **3** shoot; sprout; bud; blossom. ~ণ=~ (1, 2).

রোহিণী *n fem* **1** (astron, astrol) name of the ninth Nakshatra or lunar asterism and of the lunar day belonging to it; it is personified as the daughter of Daksha and as the favourite wife of the Moon. **2** lightning. **3** young girl (aged between 2 years and 9 years 11 months and 21 days). **4** (red) cow. **5** (bot) climber. ❑*adj* **1** red. **2** climbing.

রোহিত *adj* red; reddish. রোহিতা *fem.* ❑*n* **1** kind of large fresh-water fish. **2** Indian redwood. **3** kind of deer. **4** blood. **5** saffron. রোহিতাশ্ব *n* **1** fire. **2** (myth) name of a son of king Harishchandra.

রোহী *adj* mounting; ascending; growing; climbing.

রৌক্ষ্য *n*=রুক্ষতা (⇒ রুক্ষ)

রৌদ্র *n* **1** heat; warmth; sunshine; the sun. **2** name of Yama, the Hindu god of death. **3** (rhet) sentiment of wrath/ fury. **4** wrath. **5** cold season of the year; winter. ❑*adj* **1** violent; impetuous; fierce; wild. **2** relating to/ belonging to/ coming from Rudra or the Rudras. ~ ওঠা *vi* (of the sun) rise: ~ উঠেছে, The sun is up. ~ পড়া *vi* (of the sun) go down; decline. ~ পোয়ানো/ পোহানো *vi* bask in the sun; take a sun-bath; sun oneself; sunbathe. ~ লাগানো *vt* put in/ expose (oneself, etc) to the rays of the sun; sun. রৌদ্রে দেওয়া *vt*=~ লাগানো; spread in the sun to dry. রৌদ্রে বসা *vi* sit in the sun. ~তা *n* wild/ savage state; dreadfulness. ~তাপ *n* heat from the sun. ~তাপদগ্ধ, ~দগ্ধ *adj* sunburnt; sun-burned; sun-drenched. ~দংষ্ট্রা *adj* having terrible tusks/ fangs. ~দর্শন *adj* fierce-looking; of dreadful appearance; terrific. ~পক্ব *adj* sun-baked; cooked by the sun. ~ময় *adj* sunny; bright with sunlight. ~রস *n* (rhet) sentiment of wrath/ fury. ~সেবন করা =~ পোয়ানো. ~স্নান *n* sunbath. ~স্নান করা *vi* sunbathe.

রৌদ্রোজ্জ্বল *adj* bright with/ shining in the sunlight; dazzling; sun-drenched; clear.

রৌপ্য *n* silver; argent. ~চক্র *n* **1** silver bracelet/ ring. **2** (fig) money. ~জয়ন্তী *n* silver jubilee. ~নির্মিত *adj* made of silver. ~ময় *adj* consisting/ made of silver; silvern; silvery. ~মুদ্রা *n* silver coin. ~মুদ্রাসমূহ *n pl* silvers. ~মূল্যে *adv* in exchange of silver(s)/ money. রৌপ্যালঙ্কার *n* silver ornament; (pl) silvers.

রৌরব **1** name of one of the Hindu hells. **2** terrible agony/ affliction; hell. ❑*adj* fearful.

রৌশন *adj, n*=রওশন; রওশনী

র‍্যাঁদা ⇒ রেঁদা

র‍্যাক [E] *n* rack (wooden/ metal framework).

র‍্যাপার [E] *n* wrapper.

ল

ল[1] *n* the twenty-eighth letter of the Bengali alphabet. It is a voiced unaspirated alveolar lateral sound. ~ফলা *n* ল placed under another consonant to form a conjunct letter.

ল[2] [E] *n* law; jurisprudence: 'ল' পড়া, 'ল'-এর ছাত্র.

লওয়া (lit colloq)*vt* (=নেওয়া) **1** take; take hold of: টাকাটা লও. **2** catch; seize; capture; gain possession of; snatch/ take away: ঘড়িটা চোর লইয়া গেল. **3** carry (with oneself); bear: কলঙ্ক লয়ে বেড়ানো. **4** follow: সদ্‌দৃষ্টান্ত/ সোজা পথ ~. **5** have recourse to; turn to: তোমাকে হারিয়ে আমি কী লয়ে থাকব? **6** take (with oneself); accompany (sb): সঙ্গে ~. **7** utter; pronounce; recite: আল্লাহর নাম ~. **8** buy: বাজার থেকে জিনিসপত্র ~. **9** collect: খাজনা ~. **10** take for cooking: আজ মাত্র পাঁচজনের চাল লইও. **11** borrow: মহাজনের কাছে টাকা ~. **12** obey; abide by; accept; take; listen to: আমার কথা লও, ও পথে যেয়ো না. **13** be to one's liking: ওটা আমার মনে লয় না. **14** get; have; eat or drink; allow oneself: ছুটি ~, পরামর্শ ~, পাতে দই ~, প্রশিক্ষণ ~.

ব্যবসায়ে শরিক ~, বাড়ি ~, কোথায় যাওয়ার জন্য টেক্সি ~ (= hire). **15** receive; accept; take: এই শার্টটার জন্য সে ২০০ টাকা লইয়াছে. **16** subscribe to; take: পত্রিকা ~. **17** need; require; take: সময় ~. **18** take (down): নোট ~. **19** find out; take; inquire: মাপ ~, সংবাদ ~. **20** treat/ regard in a specified way; take: সহজভাবে ~. **21** accept responsibility for; take: ক্লাস ~. **22** wear, assume: ভেক ~. **23** take to; adopt: সন্ন্যাস ~. **24** test: পড়া ~. **25** accept: নিয়ন্ত্রণ ~. **26** supervise: শ্রমিকদের কাজ ~. ~নো *vt* cause to take/ carry/ bear/ follow.

লওয়াজিম, লওয়াজিমা [A] *n pl* necessaries; requisites; essentials; ingredients; baggage.

লং *n* (dial) cloves.

লংকা=লঙ্কা

লংক্লথ [E] *n* long cloth.

লংগরখানা=লঙ্গরখানা

লক *n* glued silk-thread.

লকট [E] *n* loquat.

লকপক *n* (onom) expressing greed. **~ করা** *vi* crave; itch for; pine/ sigh for. **লকপকে** *adj* avid; greedy; covetous; lustful.

লকর [A] *n* title; sur-name; by-name.

লকবক = লগবগ

লকলক =*n* (onom) expressing **(a)** lolling out greedily; vibrating like a serpents' tongue: জিহ্বা ~ করা; **(b)** quiver; flashing; brandishing; dangling: তরবারি/আগুনের শিখা ~ করা. **লকলকানি** *n* lolling; quivering; flashing; flickering; dangling; quiver; brandishing. **লকলকে** *adj* lolling; quivering; flashing; flickering; dangling; springing.

লকা =লক্কা

লকাটে *adj* like a locket.

লকেট [E] *n* locket.

লক্কড় *n* wood; cudgel; log; club. **~ঝক্কর, ~ মার্কা** *adj* ramshackle: ~ঝক্কড় গাড়ি.

লক্কা [P] *n* **1** kind of beautiful fan-tailed pigeon. **2** (iron) fop; coxcomb; dandy; popinjay.

লক্ত *n* alluvial accretion.

লক্ষ[1] *n* **1** look; glance; looking. **2** aim. **3** mark; sign; target; object; goal. **~ করা** *vt* **1** mark; observe; notice; note; cast a look; glance. **2** aim at; direct towards; have in view; mean; intend. **~ রাখা** *vi* keep an eye on; keep watch; be on watch; be on the watch for.

লক্ষ[2] *n* one hundred thousand. ❑*adj* numerous; countless. **~পতি** *n* man with a hundred thousand Taka; millionaire; very wealthy man. **~লক্ষ** *adj* innumerable; countless. **লক্ষাধিক** *adj* more than a hundred thousand.

লক্ষক *adj* (rhet) indicating; hinting; expressing indirectly/ elliptically/ by metonymy.

লক্ষণ *n* **1** mark; sign; symbol; token; trait; characteristic. **2** attribute; quality. **3** lucky mark; favourable sign. **4** symptom/ indication of disease. **5** definition; accurate description **6** designation; appellation. **7** omen; presage prognostic. **~যুক্ত** *adj* possessing/ characterized by a sign/ mark/ symptom/ indication; having a characteristic; indicative of; presaging; marked by.

লক্ষণা *n* **1**(rhet) use of a word for another word with a cognate meaning; indirect/ figurative sense of a word; elliptical expression. **2** implication.

লক্ষণাক্রান্ত=লক্ষণযুক্ত (⇒ লক্ষণ)

লক্ষণাত্মক *adj* relating to signs/ marks; symptomatic; characteristic.

লক্ষণীয় *adj* remarkable; noticeable; noteworthy; perceptible; visible; prominent; to be observed/ remarked/ noted.

লক্ষিত *adj* **1** noticed; observed; remarked; marked; seen; perceived; beheld; espied. **2** aimed at. **3** felt; considered; regarded. **4** recognized. **5** (rhet) expressed figuratively/ elliptically; implied; signified; vaguely expressed/ indicated. **লক্ষিতার্থ** *n* figurative/ implied meaning.

লক্ষ্মণ *n* (myth) name of a younger brother and companion of Rama.

লক্ষ্মী *n fem* **1** Hindu goddess of fortune and beauty. **2** fortune; wealth; riches; prosperity. **3** beauty; grace; charm; loveliness. **4** splendour; lustre. **5** success; happiness. **6** (as term of endearment) dear one; darling: একটু চুপ করে বসো, ~টি. ❑*adj* well-behaved and good-natured; good: ~ ছেলে, ~মেয়ে. **~কান্ত** *n* beloved of Lakshmi; Narayana. **~ছাড়া** *adj* 'bereft of grace and fortune'; wretched; miserable; poor; uncouth; scoundrelly; wicked. ❑*n* scapegrace; rascal; scamp; scalawag; wretch; scoundrel; villain. **~ছাড়ী** *fem*. **~টি** =~(6). **~পেঁচা** *n* kind of owl said to be the vehicle of Lakshmi. **~মন্ত, ~বান** *adj* **1** possessed of fortune/ good luck; wealthy; prosperous; lucky; rich. **2** handsome; beautiful; graceful. **~বিলাস** *n* **1** kind of fine cloth. **2** a particular Ayurvedie hair oil. **~মণি, ~মণিটি** *nn* (term of endearment) dear; darling; treasure. **~শ্রী** *n* good fortune; prosperity; Lakshmi's favour; affluence; opulence; easy circumstances. **~সনাথ** *adj* endowed with beauty/ fortune. **~স্বরূপিণী** *adj fem* appearing as Lakshmi incarnate; endowed with all the qualities of Lakshmi. **~র বরপুত্র** *n* fortune's favourite. **~র বরযাত্রী** *n pl* (fig)fair weather friends. **~র ভাণ্ডার** *n* inexhaustible store.

লক্ষ্য *adj* to be marked/ observed/ remarked/ noticed/ perceived; observable; perceptible; intended; aimed at. ❑*n* aim; object; objective; purpose; end; intention; goal; targets. **~চ্যুত** -

adj missing the mark; failing to hit the target; stray; erratic; beside the mark; wide of the mark. ~চ্যুত হওয়া *vi* **1** miss the mark. **2** be/ fall wide of the mark. **3** go astray; deviate. ~ত *adj* apparently; openly. ~দর্শক *n* (phys) view-finder. ~বেধ, ~ভেদ *nn* hitting a mark/ bull's eye. ~বেধ/ ~ভেদ করা *vi* hit the mark. ~বেধী, ~ভেদী *adj* capable of hitting the mark; accurate; precise; unerring. ❑*n* marksman. ~ভ্রষ্ট= ~চ্যুত .~সিদ্ধি *n* attainment of an object. ~স্থল target; mark. ~হীন *adj* aimless.

লক্ষ্যীকৃত *adj* aimed at.

লখ, লখলাইন *nn* glued thread of silk.

লখা *vt* (poet, archaic)=লক্ষ করা (⇒ লক্ষ[১])

লগন *n* (poet)= লগ্ন .

লগবগ *n* (onom) expressing the movement of a long slender object; dangling; swinging; unsteadiness: ঢেঙ্গা লোকটা ~ করে চলে গেল. লগবগে *adj* dangling; swinging; leggy; lanky; unsteady; moving hither and thither.

লগা, লগি *n* **1** pole of bamboo, etc, esp one for propelling a boat; punt-pole. **2** crooked stick for pulling down fruit, etc. ~ ঠেলা *vi* punt.

লগিত *adj* =লগ্ন

লগুড় *n* heavy stick; staff; club; cudgel; mallet. লগুড়াঘাত করা *vt* strike/ beat with a cudgel or club; cudgel; club.

লগেজ=লাগেজ

লগ্ন *adj* **1** attached (to); adhered; adhering/ clinging to. **2** sticking/ remaining in. **3** fixed on. **4** clasping; touching. **5** intent on. **6** following closely. **7** meeting; intersecting; meeting: পরস্পর ~রেখা. লগ্না *fem.* ❑*n* **1** rising of the sun or of the planets. **2** the moment of the sun's entrance into a zodiacal sign. **3** auspicious moment/ time fixed upon as lucky for beginning to perform anything. **4** decisive moment/ time for action. **5** (astron) ascendant. **6** bard/ minstrel (who awakens the king in the morning). ~ হওয়া *vi* **1** attach/ stick/ cling/ adhere to; be attached to; meet; come in contact; cut; follow closely. **2** (of an auspicious moment) arrive. ~ কাল *n* auspicious time/ moment (pointed out by astrologers). ~ জ্যা *n* (geom) tangent. ~দিন, ~দিবস *nn* auspicious day. ~পত্র, ~পত্রিকা *nn* paper on which the auspicious moment for marriage, etc is written down. ~ভুজ *n* (astron) ascensional difference. ~ভ্রষ্ট *adj* failing to begin one's work at the auspicious a moment; who has missed the opportune moment. ~ মণ্ডল *n* the zodiac. ~ মুহূর্ত *n* auspicious moment for a marriage. ~ শুদ্ধি *n* auspiciousness of the signs, etc for the commencement of any contemplated work.

লগ্নক *n* surety; bail; bondsman.

লগ্নি *nn* investment of money (in business/ enterprise); lending money at interest; usury. ~ করা *vt* invest; lay out; lend at interest.

লঘিমা *n* **1** lightness; levity; absence of weight. **2** kind of supernatural faculty of assuming excessive lightness at will. **3** slight; disrespect .

লঘিষ্ঠ[১] *adj* most light/ quick; very light/ quick; lightest.

লঘিষ্ঠ[২] *adj* lowest; smallest; minimum; least. ~ উষ্ণতা *n* minimum temperature. ~ থার্মোমিটার *n* minimum thermometer. ~ সাধারণ গুণনীয়ক/ গুণিতক (abbr ল. সা. গু.) (arith)lowest/ least common multiple.

লঘীয়ান *adj* more/ very light or quick; less heavy; lighter; smaller; very small; lower.

লঘুলিপিক *n* stenographer.

লঘু *adj* **1** not heavy; light. **2** quick; swift; light; prompt; active: ~ পদে. **3** not difficult; light; easy; not heavy: ~ দায়িত্ব. **4** light in the stomach; easily digested/ digestible. **5** easy in mind; light hearted; frivolous; care-free. **6** short (in time). **7** small; minute; slight; insignificant; little. **8** (of persons) weak; feeble; mean; vile; contemptible; wretched; humble; low. **9** (of things) worthless; trivial; watery; liquid . **10** not serious; venial: ~ পাপ. **11** easily understood; easy; light: ~ পাঠ. **12** (prosody) light or short (as a vowel or syllable).**13** (gram) easily pronounced syllable. **14** soft; gentle (as sound).**15** minor. ~ অনুপাত *n* (arith) ratio of less inequality. ~করণ = লঘূকরণ. ~কায় *adj* light-bodied; slender; short (in stature); slightly built. ~ক্রিয়া *n* **1** small matter; trifle. **2** urination. ~ গতি *n* quick step; swiftness. ❑*adj* swift; having a swift step; nimble-footed. ~গামী *adj* moving with quiet gentle steps; moving nimbly; quick-moving; fleet-footed. ~গামিনী *fem.* ~গুণক *n* (math) reduction factor. ~ চতুষ্পদী *n* name of a metre. ~চিত্ত, ~চেতা *adj* light-minded; little minded; fickle; light-hearted; light-headed; frivolous; flippant. ~চিত্তা *fem.* ~জাতি *n* low caste; inferior race/ tribe. ~ জ্ঞান *n* contempt; slight; disregard. ~ জ্ঞান করা *vi* think lightly of; treat with contempt; look down upon; slight; disregard. ~তা, ~ত্ব *nn* **1** quickness; promptness; agility; dexterity. **2** lightness; ease; facility. **3** feeling of ease/ bodily freshness. **4** prosodial shortness. **5** smallness; littleness; meanness; insignificance. **6** light-mindedness; levity; thoughtlessness; wantonness; frivolity; flippancy. **7** want of rank/ dignity; humbleness; disregard; disrespect. ~ তাল *n* (music) kind of measure. ~ত্রিপদী *n* name of a metre. ~নির্মাণ *n* light works. ~ পঞ্চমূল *n* a particular compound of five different roots. ~পথ্য *n* light food/ diet. ~পাক *adj* easy of digestion; easily digested; light. ❑*n* gentle heat; slow fire. ~পাচ্য *adj* easily digestible. ~পাপ *n* venial sin; trivial offence. ~পায়ে *adj* light-footedly; nimbly; softly; with quiet, gentle steps . ~প্রকৃতি =~চিত্ত. ~প্রমাণ *adj* of little magnitude; short. ~ প্রযত্ন *adj* using little effort; indolent; impotent. ~বন্ধনী *n* sign of parenthesis; the first bracket. ~ বৃত্ত *n* small circle. ~বৃত্তি *adj* having a light nature; light in conduct/ behaviour; light-minded; ill-done; mismanaged. ❑*n* vile/ mean practice. ~ ভাব *n* light state; lightness; ease; facility. ~ভাবে *adv* lightly; light-heartedly; carelessly. ~ ভার *n* light burden. ❑*adj* not heavy; light. ~ভোজন *n* light repast; slight refreshment; light and easily digestible meal. ~ মস্তিষ্ক *n* cerebellum. ❑*adj* light-headed; dull-headed; frivolous. ~লঘু *adj* gentle; sweet; soft. ❑*adv* gently; sweetly; softly. ~স্ফীতি *n* nip tide. ~স্বর *n* (gram) short vowel. ~হস্ত *adj* light-handed; ready-handed; dexterous; nimble-fingered; dexterous in archery.

লঘূকরণ *n* **1** lightening; simplification. **2** commutation; attenuation. **3** (math) reduction. **4** (chem) dilution. লঘূকৃত *adj* lightened; simplified; commuted; attenuated; reduced; diluted.

লঙ্কা[১] *n* capsicum; chilli; long/ red pepper. ~বাটা *n* paste of chillies. ~মরিচ=~. ~র ঝাল *n* hotness/ hot taste of chillies.

লঙ্কা[২] *n* **1** Sri Lanka. **2** (myth) the city of Lanka (renowned as the capital of the great demon king Ravana). ~কাণ্ড *n* **1** canto of the Ramayana narrating the destruction of Lanka. **2** (fig) conflagration; tumultuous; affray; great upheaval; convulsion; turmoil; rummage. ~দহন, ~দাহন *nn* burning of Lanka by Hanumana. ~পতি, ~ধিপতি *nn* lord of Lanka; Ravana. ~পুরী *n* city of Lanka.

লঙ্কেশ, লঙ্কেশ্বর *n*=লঙ্কাপতি (⇒ লঙ্কা)

লঙ্গ[১] *n* (colloq) cloves.

লঙ্গ[২] [P] *adj* lame. ❑*n* lameness.

লঙ্গরখানা [P] *n* place where cooked food is distributed among the poor; gruel-kitchen.

লঙ্ঘন *n* **1** leaping; jumping; scaling over; leaping over; stepping across; crossing; traversing. **2** violation; transgression; infringement; dereliction; non-observance; non-compliance. **3** fasting. **4** passing. **5** insult; offence; injury; wrong. ~ করা *vt* **1** leap over; cross; traverse; step over; scale over. **2** overstep; transgress; violate; neglect; infringe; fail to perform; not to abide by/ comply with; disobey; disregard.

লঙ্ঘা *vt* (poet) = লঙ্ঘন করা. ~নো *vt* cause to leap over/ traverse/ violate.

লঙ্ঘিত *adj* **1** left over; crossed; scaled; passed over; traversed. **2** violated; overstepped; disregarded; transgressed; not complied with/ abided by/ observed; infringed.

লঙ্ঘনীয় *adj* **1** to be crossed/ left over/ passed over/ traversed. **2** to be violated/ transgressed/ disregarded.

লচপচ, লচলচ *nn* (onom) expressing the slow movement of a full-blown youthful woman. লচপচে, লচলচে *adj* sluggish; languid; indolent; leisurely.

লছমী, লছিমী *nn* (poet, archaic)=লক্ষ্মী

লজঞ্চুস, লজেঞ্চুস [E] *n* lozenge.

লজঝড় *adj* **1** indolent; lethargic; slothful. **2** worthless; good for nothing; trashy: ~লোক, ~মাল. **3** unmanageable: unwieldy; cumbersome: ~ বোঝা. **4** miserly: niggardly.

লজিক [E] *n* logic.

লজিজ [A] *adj* sweet; delicious; tasteful, savoury; nice; delightful; piquant.

লজ্জত [A] *n* taste; flavour; joy; pleasure; deliciousness; enjoyment.

লজ্জমান *adj* feeling abashed; bashful; timid.

লজ্জা *n* **1** shame; bashfulness; modesty; sense of delicacy; embarrassment. **2** hesitation; diffidence. **3** disgrace. ~ দেওয়া *vt* shame; put to shame; put out of countenance; discountenance; embarrass; confuse. ~ পাওয়া *vi* be ashamed; blush; feel shame; be abashed/ discountenanced; be embarrassed; feel timid; hesitate; feel diffident. ~বোধ করা *vi* feel shame; feel diffident; feel self-conscious; feel uncomfortable. ~কর, ~জনক *adj* causing shame; disgraceful; shameful. ~জনিত *adj* due to/ born of bashfulness/ modesty/ sense of delicacy. ~দৃষ্টি *n* bashful glance. ~নত, ~নম্র *adj* bending down with bashfulness; coy. ~ন্বিত *n* possessed of shame; modest; bashful. ~বনত *adj* bending down the face with shame/ bashfulness; stooping low with shame/ bashfulness/ modesty. ~বনত মুখে *adv* shame-facedly; bashfully; coyly. ~বহ *adj* causing shame; disgraceful. ~বান *adj* ashamed; bashful; embarrassed; perplexed. ~বতী *fem.* ~বতী লতা *n* the sensitive plant; *Mimosa pudica*. ~বিনম্রানন *adj* bending down the face with shame/ bashfulness. ~বোধ *n* (feeling of) shame; sense of disgrace; sentiment of shame/ modesty; modesty. ~বিহীন/ রহিত *adjj* void/ destitute of shame; shameless; immodest; impudent. ~শীল *adj* of modest disposition; bashful; humble; coy; shy. ~শীলা *fem.* ~শূন্য ~হীন=~বিহীন. ~শূন্যা, ~হীনা *fem.* ~শূন্যতা, ~হীনতা *nn* immodesty; shamelessness.

লজ্জালু *adj* shy; coy; bashful; timid. ❑*n* *Mimosa pudica*.. ~ **লতা** *n* *Mimosa pudica*.

লজ্জিত *adj* ashamed; abashed; embarrassed; put to shame; discountenanced.

লট, লট্ট *adjj* lewd.

লটক *n* **1** crook; scoundrel; knave. **2** frivoler; rattle-head.

লটকা *vt, vi* hang; dangle. ~**নো** *vt* **1** hang; hang up: ফাঁসিতে ~নো, দেয়ালে ছবি ~নো. **2** suspend; keep waiting; delay: কাজটা আর কতদিন লটকে রাখবে? **3** post: বিজ্ঞপ্তি/ পোস্টার ~নো.

লটকান *n* kind of fruit-tree.

লটখট, লটখটি *n* trouble; bottleneck; hitch; snag; complication. **লটখটে** *adj* vexatious; crafty; troublesome.

লটপট, লটাপট *nn* (onom) expressing **(a)** amorous movement; wallowing in sensual pleasure; **(b)** flapping loosely. ❑*adj* **1** flapping loosely; tumbling down. **2** lewd; lascivious; wanton; whorish. **লটপটে** *adj*=**লটপটানি** *n* **1** lewdness; lechery; love-making; promiscuity. **2** flapping; dangling; hanging. **লটপটানো** *vi* **1** flap; dangle; hang; swing; tumble down. **2** wallow (in sensual pleasures); have a good time; be intimate with.

লটবহর *n* accoutrements; luggage; outfit; baggage; impedimenta.

লটরচটর *n* pretended hurry; fuss.

লটরপটর=লটপট

লটা *n* **1** lock of hair. **2** kind of sour fruit; *Caesalpinia bonducella*. **3** kind of sparrow. **4** safflower. ❑*adj fem* lewd.

লটারি [E] *n* lottery.

লটুয়া *adj* lustful; lewd.

লড্ডু, লড্ডুক *nn* kind of sweetmeats rolled into balls.

লড় *n* (archaic) running; bolting; bold. ~ **দেওয়া** *vi* bolt (off); take to one's heels; jump (upon).

লড়ন[১] *n* (archaic)=নড়ন

লড়ন[২] *n* fight; fighting; combat.

লড়বড়ে *adj* (old use) নড়বড়ে

লড়া *vt,vi* fight; combat; struggle; whistle; encounter; wrangle; clash with: give battle; go to war; quarrel; vie with; contend. ~**ই** *n* battle; war; fight; quarrel; fighting; wrestling; contest; enmity; hostility; encounter; engagement; contention; vying. **লড়াই করা**=~. **লড়াইবাজ** *n* war monger. ~**কু** *adj* quarrelsome; contentious; pugnacious; militant. ~**নো** *vt* cause to fight/ contend; lead an army to the battle; play; set. ~**লড়ি** *n* **1** fighting; skirmish; scuffle; contention. **2** running helter-skelter.

লড়ি *nn* stick; staff.

লড়িয়ে, লড়ুয়ে *adjj* fighting; militant; military; bellicose; warlike. ❑*nn* fighter; combatant; militant. ~ **মনোবৃত্তি** *n* fighting spirit. ~ **মোরগ** *n* gamecock; fighting cock.

লণ্ডভণ্ড *adj* disarrayed; messed up; chaotic; at sixes and sevens; confounded; disrupted. ~ **করা** *vt* utterly disarray/ disrupt/ confound; upset; throw into disarray/ confusion.

লতা *n* **1** creeper. **2** any creeping/ winding plant or twining tendril. ~**কুঞ্জ**, ~**গৃহ**, ~**মণ্ডল** *nn* creeper-bower; arbour of creepers. ~**নে** *adj* creeping . ~**নো** *vi* (of a creeper) creep along/ up; stretch/ extend along/ up. ❑*adj* slender and graceful: ~নো বাহু. ~**পনস** *n* water-melon. ~**পাতা** *n* creepers and herbs. ~**পাশ** *n* snare/ festoon of creeper. ~**প্রতান** *n* tendril. ~**বিতান** *n* canopy made of creepers. ~**য়িত** *adj* grown along the ground/ on supports as a creeper; creeping along up; stretching/ extending along up. ~**বেষ্টন** *n* embrace. ~**বেষ্টিত** *adj* encircled by creepers.

লতিয়ে পড়া =নেতিয়ে পড়া (⇒ নেতানো). **লতিয়ে যাওয়া** *vi* **1** creep along/ over. **2** grow slender.

লতি *n* **1** lobe of the ear. **2** (bot) sucker: কচুর ~.

লতিকা *n* delicate/ slender creeper or small winding tendril (to which the graceful curve of a slim figure is compared).

লণ্ঠন [E] *n* lantern.

লন্ড্রি [E] *n* laundry.

লপচপানি *n* brag; tall talk; bombast.

লপটানো *vi* **1** entwine; cling to twine; be entangled/ involved (in). **2** wrap; fold (together): বিছানা লপটে রাখা, পাখির ডানা ~.

লপটালপটি *n* hugging; embracing; love-making.

লপরচপর *n* noise made while eating; crunching and lapping.

লপলপ *n* (onom) lapping (of the tongue); sound made in eating/ devouring liquid things.

লপেটা *n* kind of vamped slippers.

লপ্‌সি *n* **1** a gruel of rice, pulses, etc. **2** a drink made of milk or butter milk. **3** gruel of rice, vegetables, etc.

লপ্টানো =লপটানো. **লপ্টামি** *n* **1** hugging; clinging. **2** folding.

লপ্ত *adj* attached; joined; connected. ❑*n* stretch. **একলপ্তে** *adv* at a stretch; contiguously.

লফজ [A] *n* word; term; saying; language; speech; dialect; idiom.

ল ফলা ⇒ ল[১]

লব *n* (math) **1** numerator. **2** a minute division/ time. **3** particle; bit; little piece; fraction. ~**লেশ** *n* trace.

লবঙ্গ *n* clove tree; clove. ~**কলিকা** *n* clove. ~**লতা**, ~**লতিকা** *n* **1** a creeper bearing fragrant flowers; *Limonia scandens*. **2** kind of sweetmeat. **3** modest and charming female.

লবডঙ্কা *n* (hum) nothing; zero; mare's nest; cipher; nullity.

লবণ *n* salt; common salt. ❑*adj* saline; salty; salt; briny. ~**খনি** salt mine. ~**ছাড়া** *adj* salt free. ~**তা** *n* saltness; brinishness. ~**জল** *n* salt-water; saline water. ~**পোড়া** *adj* over-mixed with salt; over-salted. ~**সমুদ্র** *n* (myth) salt sea. **লবণাক্ত** *adj* smeared/ over spread with salt; salted; saline; saltish; containing too much salt. **লবণাত্মক** *adj* salty. **লবণাম্বু** *n* salt water. **লবণাম্বুধি, লবণাম্বুরাশি** *nn* sea; ocean. **লবণাম্ল** *n* (chem) muriatic acid; (raw) hydrochloric acid. **খনিজ** ~ *n* rock salt.

লবণচুষ =লজঞ্চুস

লবান=লোবান

লবেজান [P] *adj* (feeling like) dying; extremely distressed/ harassed; high-strung. ~ **করা** *vt* distress; torture; torment; leave half-dead.

লবেদা [P] *n* cloak; wrapper; outer garment; gown; water-proof cloak.

লবেদার *adj* foppish; elegant; fashionable.

লব্‌জ =লফজ

লব্জ =লফজ

লব্ধ *adj* 1 obtained; gained; received; attained; earned; acquired; caught; got at. 2 (mech)resultant. **লব্ধা** *fem.* ~**কাম** *adj* one who has gained his wishes; having one's desire fulfilled; gratified. ~**কীর্তি** *adj* one who has gained fame/ glorious; illustrious; famous. ~**গুণ** *n* (biol) acquired character. ~**প্রতিষ্ঠ** *adj* renowned. ~**প্রবেশ** *adj* one who has entered. ~**বর্ণ** *adj* 1 lettered; learned. 2 famous; renowned. ~**বিদ্যা** *adj* one who has acquired knowledge/ wisdom; learned; educated.

লব্ধি *n* 1 gain; profit. 2 obtaining; acquisition; gaining. 3 (mech) resultant. ~**নির্ণয়** *n* (mech) composition (of velocity).

লব্ধোদয় *adj* one who has received birth/ origin; one who has attained prosperity.

লভ্য *adj* 1 to be found/ met with/ obtained. 2 obtainable; acquirable; procurable; attainable; available; capable of being earned as profit; capable of being reached/ attained. 3 profit; gains. 4 interest.

লম্পট *adj* covetous; greedy; lustful; lascivious; licentious; libertine; debauched; lewd; profligate. ❑*n* libertine; lecher; dissolute person; debauchee.

লম্ফ *n* leap; spring, jump; hop; skip; bound. ~ **দেওয়া/মারা** *vi* leap; spring; jump; bound. ~**ঝম্প** *n* 1 repeated jumping/ leaping. 2 (fig) excessive haste/ fuss; bragging; bravado; vaunting. ~**ন** *n* jumping; leaping; springing. ~**দান,** ~**প্রদান** *nn*=~ন. **এক লম্ফে** at a leap. **লম্ফে লম্ফে** *adv* by leaps and bounds.

লম্ব *adj* 1 (geom) perpendicular; vertical; orthogonal. 2 hanging down; pendant; dangling; plumb; upright; straight. 3 (geog) orthographic(al). ❑*n* (geom) perpendicular. ~ **অভিক্ষেপ** *n* (geom) orthographic projection; orthography. 2 (geom) orthogonal projection. ~**কর্ণ** *adj* having pendulous ears; long eared. ❑*n* 1 ass. 2 rabbit. 3 goat. 4 elephant. ~**কায়** *adj* tall; lunky. ~**চ্ছেদ** (geom) normal section. ~**চুঞ্চু** *adj* long-beaked. ~**ন** *n* hanging down; causing to hang down. 2 (astron, phys) parallax. ~**ন-পদ্ধতি** *n* (phys) parallax method. ~ **বিন্দু** *n* (geom) orthocentre. ~**বৃত্ত** (astron) vertical circle. ~**মান** *adj* hanging; suspended; pendant; dependant. ~**সূত্র** *n* (mech) plumb-line.

লম্বরদার *n* leader of tenants entrusted with the charge of collecting revenue from other tenants.

লম্বা *adj* 1 long; tall; long-continued; lengthy. 2 incessant; continuous; uninterrupted: ~ ঘুম, ~ বৃষ্টি. 3 (fig) boastful; grandiloquent. ❑*n* vertical/ downward length. ~ **করা** *vt* 1 lengthen; extend. 2 lay prostrate on the ground by beating .~ **দেওয়া** *vi* decamp; take to one's heels; flee; run away; skip off; make off. ~ **হওয়া** *vi* lay oneself down; prostrate oneself; lie prostrate; stretch oneself out (on); lie on at full length. ~**ই** *n* length; measure of length. ~**ই-চওড়াই** *n* 1 (measure) of length and breadth. 2 boastful/ grandiloquent talk; bluster; bragging. **লম্বাংশ** *n* polar distance. ~ **কথা** *n* tall/ big/ boastful talk; vaunt; bluster. ~ **চাল** *n* extravagance; prodigality; excessive pomp (usually beyond one's means); swagger; swank. ~**টে** *adj* slightly tall; tallish; longish. ~**লম্বি** *adv* lengthwise; lengthways.

লম্বিকা *n* uvula; epiglottis.

লম্বিত *adj* hanging (down); pendant; suspended; flowing; dangling; glided down; clinging/ adhering to; supported/ nested on. ~ **বেণী** *n* long plait of hair; pigtail.

লম্বে *adv* (colloq) in length.

লম্বোদর *adj* having a large/ protuberant belly; pot-bellied; corpulent. ❑*n* Hindu god Ganesha .

লম্বৌষ্ঠ *adj* having a large/ prominent under-lip. ❑*n* camel.

লয় *n* 1 (music) time/ tempo (regarded as of three kinds). 2 dissolution; destruction; universal dissolution; extinction; annihilation. 3 death. 4 melting/ disappearance/ dissolution/ fusion in. ~ **করা** *vt* destroy; annihilate. ~ **দেওয়া** *vt* set/ maintain the tempo. ~ **হওয়া** *vi* melt; dissolve; liquefy; be dissolved/ destroyed/ annihilated/ absorbed. ~**কাল** *n* time of destruction/ dissolution. ~**ক্রিয়া** *n* 1 universal destruction/ annihilation. 2 (music) setting the tempo. ~**নৃত্য** *n* dance of destruction. ~মাফিক *adj* **1** at the right/ opportune time/ moment . **2** (music) in time. ~শুদ্ধ *adv* (music) performed in clear/ right time. ~হীন *adj* out of time.

লরি [E]*n* lorry.

ললজিহ্ব *adj* lolling the tongue; moving the tongue to and fro; fierce; savage; blood-thirsty.

ললন *n* **1** sporting; playing; dalliance; play. **2** amorous sport. **3** lolling/ moving (of the tongue).

ললনা *n fem* **1** (beautiful) woman. **2** woman. **3** tongue. ~প্রিয় *adj* **1** dear to women. **2** loving one's wife.

ললন্তিকা *n* long pendulous necklace.

ললাট *n* **1** forehead; brow; front. **2** destiny; fate; luck. ~ক *n* beautiful/ large brow. ~তট *n* slope/ surface of the forehead. ~দেশ *n* region of the forehead. ~পট্ট *n* flat surface of the forehead; large forehead. ~ভূষণ *n* ornament for the forehead; tiara; fillet. ~রেখা *n* line on the forehead supposed to indicate long life; wrinkled/ corrugated brow. ~লিখন, ~লিপি *nn* lines written on the forehead; destiny.

ললাটিকা *n* **1** ornament worm on the forehead. **2** coloured sectarial mark (of sandal-paste, clay, etc) on the forehead.

ললাম *n* = ললাটিকা. ❑*adj* beautiful; charming; eminent / best of its kind.

ললিত *adj* **1** charming; lovely; beautiful; pleasant. **2** gentle; soft. **3** artless; innocent. **4** desired; wished for. **5** quivering; tremulous. **6** playing; amorous; voluptuous; wanton. **7** (of speech) suave; bland. **ললিতা** *fem.* ❑*n* **1** languid gestures in a woman (expressive of amorous feelings). **2** dance of Indian dancing girls. **3** name of an Indian musical mode. **4** sport; dalliance; artlessness; grace; charm. ~কলা *n* fine arts; a fine art.

ললিতা *n fem* **1** goddess Durga. **2** name of a companion of Radha. **3** woman; wanton woman.

লশকর [P] *n* **1** army; encampment; camp; crowd. **2** naval soldier; sailor. **3** soldier.

লশন, লসুন *nn* (archaic) garlic.

লস *n* (phys) viscosity.

লসিকা *n* lymph. ~তন্তুবৃদ্ধি *n* lymphatic growth. ~নালী *n* lymph (atic) vessel. ~য়নী *adj* lymphatic.

লস্সি *n* milk-shake; a drink made of yoghurt.

লস্কর = লশকর

লহনা *n* dues; amount outstanding; dues other than rent.

লহমা [A] *n* minute; moment; twinkle of an eye; short while.

লহর *n* **1** (large) wave; billow; breaker surf. **2** row; coil.

লহরি, লহরী = লহর. ~লীলা *n* surfing.

লহা *vt* (old use) = লওয়া

লহু[1] *n* blood.

লহু[2] *adj* (old use) = লঘু

লা[1] *n* (dial) = lac.

লা[2] *int* (used to call attention or to express surprise, interrogation, contempt, etc by women amongst themselves) hey; ho ! hoy; there ! now: হাঁ লা; কেন লা.

লা[3] [A] *adj* (used as a *pref)* no; not; without; by no means; there is not; has the meaning of the English *prefs* un-, in-, ir-, im-: লা-ওয়ারিশ, লাচার, লা-শরিক.

লা[4] *n* (old use, dial) boat.

লাই[1] *n* (too much) indulgence; latitude; pampering. ~ দেওয়া *vt* indulge too much; pamper.

লাই[2] = parched rice.

লাই[3] = লেই

লাই[4] *n* intoxication; pleasant drowsiness. ঘুমের ~ *n* drowsiness.

লাইকেন [E] *n* (bot) lichen.

লাইট [E] *n* light.

লাইন = [E] **1** line: ~ টানা, রাজনীতির ~. **2** railway. **3** system: কাজের ~. **4** opportunity; outlet: অনেক চেষ্টা করেও সে কোনো ~ খুঁজে পেল না. **5** profession: এটা তার ~ নয়. ~ দেওয়া/ বাঁধা *vi* line up; stand in a queue; queue up. ~বাঁধা *adj* lined up; arrayed.

লাইনিং [E] *n* lining (as of a coat).

লাইফ [E] *n* life. ~ বেল্ট *n* life-belt. ~ বোট *n* life-boat. ~ সাইজ *n* life size.

লাইবেল [E] *n* libel.

লাইব্রেরি, লাইব্রেরী [E] *n* library.

লাইলাক [E] *n* lilac.

লাইলাতুল কদর [A] *n* night of power; the twenty seventh night of the month of Ramadan when the Qoran began to be revealed.

লাইসেন্স [E]*n* licence. ~বিহীন *adj* unlicenced.

লাউ *n* bottle-gourd. ~ডগা *n* **1** tender shoot of the bottle-gourd plant. **2** kind of very slender and venomous green snake. ~মাচা *n* scaffold/ trellis for supporting bottle-gourd plant. **লাউয়ের খোলা** *n* shell of bottle-gourd.

লাউঞ্জ [E] *n* lounge.

লাউডস্পিকার [E] *n* loudspeaker.

লাওয়ারিশ [A] *adj* leaving no heir; heirless.

লাকড়ি *n* wood; fuel wood.

লাক্ষণিক *adj* **1** expressing figuratively/ indirectly; figurative; metaphorical; secondary. **2** symptomatic. **3** versed in soothsaying; oracular. ~ অর্থ = লক্ষিতার্থ (⇒ লক্ষিত).

লাক্ষা *n* lac; shellac. ~ কীট *n* an insect producing lac. ~ রস *n* lac dye.

লাক্ষিক *adj* dyed with lac; lacquered.

লাখ = লক্ষ[২]. **~ কথার এক কথা** (fig) an utterance of incomparable/ immeasurable worth; an invaluable comment.

লাখরাজ, লাখেরাজ *adj n* rent-free (land). **~ জমি** *n* freehold. **~দার** *n,adj* holding of (holder of) rent-free land.

লাখো-লাখো *adj* many lakhs of; in lakhs; countless; innumerable; myriad; numberless.

লাগ *n* **1** touch; contact . **2** nearness; contiguity. **3** whereabouts. **4** reach. **~ পাওয়া** *vt* find; reach; track down; locate; meet. **লাগাসই** *adj* appropriate; fitting; suitable.

লাগন *n* **1** contact; union. **2** feeling of pain.

লাগা *vi, vt* **1** touch; come in contact with: গায়ে হাওয়া লাগা. **2** stick; be/ become joined/ fastened with; be attached/ affixed: খামে টিকেট ~, আটা ~. **3** smear; soil; cover: গায়ে কাদা/ ময়লা/ ধুলা ~. **4** suit; be appropriate/ suitable/ right/ fit; be proper for: কাপড় গায়ে ~, শব্দটি বাক্যের মধ্যে বেশ লেগে গেছে. **5** compete with; match; touch; bear/ stand comparison with: এই ছবির কাছে অন্য ছবি কোথায় লাগে? **6** need; stand in need of: আমার কিছুই লাগবে না. **7** join; take up (as duty); start (work); start in (on sth/ to do sth); set about sth: তাহলে এখনই কাজে ~ যাক. **8** be engaged in; be deeply absorbed in; devote oneself to; be engrossed in: এখন তিনি মকদ্দমাতেই লেগেছেন. **9** begin; start; commence: সে ভাবতে লেগেছে, রাত ৮টায় গ্রহণ লেগেছে. **10** win; make; secure: কাজটার জন্য সে অনেক চেষ্টা করেছে, কিন্তু লাগল না. **11** feel; be felt as; feel like; appear; seen: অদ্ভুত ~ appear/ sound strange: ক্ষুধা ~, গরম/শীত ~, মজা ~, taste delicious. **12** hurt; wound; feel pain; be felt as painful: আমার লাগছে, ফোঁড়াটায় লাগছে. **13** quarrel; dispute; pick a quarrel with: সে নিরীহ মানুষ, তার সঙ্গে ~ কেন. **14** pester; importune; tease; torment; plague; nag: ওর পেছনে লেগো না তো. **15** break out: যুদ্ধ/ বিবাদ ~. **16** clash; begin to quarrel; come to blows: দুই পক্ষে খুব লেগে গেল. **17** catch; break out: ঘরে আগুন ~. **18** be attracted/ interested; concentrate: কাজে মন ~. **19** stop at; come to anchor; bring (a boat) to anchor; touch at: ঘাটে নৌকা ~. **20** take/ strike root; become rooted: সেদিনের বৃষ্টিতে বেগুন চারাগুলি সব লেগেছে . **21** have effect; bear fruit: আমার কথা কোনো কাজেই লাগল না. **22** occur; take place: গ্রহণ লেগেছে. **23** be stuck; stick: জাহাজখানা চড়ায় লেগেছে, চাবিটি তালায় লেগে গেছে, গলায় কাঁটা লাগা, কাঁটায় লেগে জামা ছেঁড়া, tear one's dress on a thorn. **24** be pricked: গোলাপ তুলতে গিয়ে হাতে কাঁটা লেগেছে. **25** close; shut: দরজাটা লাগছে না. **26** gather: ভিড় লাগা. **27** take; require; need: সেখানে যেতে দুদিন লাগে. **28** cost, involve: বইগুলো কিনতে যা লাগে দেব, খরচ ~. **29** work; be effective: ওষুধটা লেগেছে. **30 come** true: তার ভবিষ্যদ্‌বাণী লেগেছে. **31** be held; take place: আগামী মাসে মেলা লাগবে. **32** pursue; hound; shadow; chase; follow: তার পেছনে পুলিশ লেগেছে. **33** pierce; hit: বুকে তীর/ গুলি লেগেছে. **34** strike; fall on: ঘুসি/ বেত ~. **35** be of use: এটা কী কাজে লাগবে. **36** fall under the evil influence of: শনি ~. **37** be close/ contiguous: দুটি বাড়ি গায়ে গায়ে ~. **38** be caught/ overtaken by (disease): সর্দি লাগা, catch cold. **39** be seized with: ভিরমি ~. **40** come off: ফাঁকা জায়গায় গান লাগে না. **লেগে থাকা** *vi* stick at/ to; pursue doggedly/ resolutely; continue at. **আগুন ~** *vi* **1** catch/ take fire; be on fire. **2** (fig) (of violence) flare up. **উঠে পড়ে ~** *vi* be up and doing; engage doggedly in; harass; hound. **এঁড়ে ~** *vi* suffer from rickets. **গলায় ঘা ~** *vi* have sth stuck on one's neck; choke over one's food. **গায়ে ~** *vi* **1** be hurt; take offence; take sth amiss. **2** be in contact with. **3** feel pain in the body; have aches and pain all over. **গায়ে মাংস ~** *vi* put on flesh. **ঘোর/ ঘুর ~** *vi* feel dizzy; be tipsy. **ঘুম ~** *vi* feel drowsy/ sleepy. **চমক ~** *vi* be amazed; marvel at. **(মুখে) চুনকালি ~** *vi* be disgraced; disgrace oneself; loose face; demean oneself; lose one's reputation. **চোখ ~** *vi* **1** (of eyes) be stuck with excretion. **2** be under the influence of an evil eye. **জোড়া ~** *vi* **1** stick (together); fit. **2** (of animals) mate; couple. **3** be healed: ভাঙা মন জোড়া লাগে না. **তাক ~** *vi* gape (at sb/ sth); be amazed; gasp with surprise; stare with astonishment; marvel. **কালে তালা ~***vi* be deafened. **দাঁতি ~** *vi* have the jaws tightly locked; have lock-jaw. **দাঁতে দাঁত ~** *vi* clench one's teeth with cold. **দিন ~** *vi* be at death's door. **নজর ~** *vi* **1** = চোখ ~ (2). **2** incur sb's hatred. **3** become an object of sb's envy/ greed. **পাক/ প্যাঁচ ~** *vi* strike/ come upon a snag. **পিছু/ পেছু ~** *vi* **1** find fault (with) continually; oppose. **2** harass; tease; torment. **3** hound; follow; shadow. **বিষয় ~** *vi* choke over one's food. **ভাব ~** *vi* be under the spell of an ecstasy; be lost in reverie. **ভেল্কি ~** *vi* **1** be bewildered/ bewitched/ dazed/ amazed; **2** be under a spell. **মনে ~***v* ⇒ মন.

লাগাও *adj* adjoining; contiguous; lying side by side.

লাগাড় *n* (also **নাগাড়,** which is more usual) continuity; stretch; uninterruptedness. ❑*adj* continuous; constant; incessant; uninterrupted. **এক লাগাড়ে** *adv* at a stretch; continuously; continually; uninterruptedly; incessantly; constantly.

লাগাতার *adj* continuous; incessant: uninterrupted: ~ হরতাল. ❑*adv* continually; uninterruptedly; incessantly.

লাগান *n* supply.

লাগানি-ভাঙানি *n* malicious and secret report against sb; backbiting.

লাগানো *vt* **1** affix; attach; stick; join: খামে টিকেট ~, বইয়ে মলাট ~. **2** cause to touch; bring into contact with: গায়ে গা ~. **3** expose (oneself) to: রোদ হিম ~. **4** apply; rub (on/ with): আঁঠা ~, ওষুধ/মলম ~.**5** strike with; use; inflict: বেত/ মার ~. **6** cause; instigate; excite. **7** fasten (with); shut; close; make fast; secure; fix: হুড়কা ~, দরজা ~. **8** apply (oneself/ one's mind to sth/ to doing sth): মনটাকে ভালো করে লাগাতে পারলে কোনো কাজই কঠিন নয়. **9** plant; sow: গাছ ~. **10** employ; engage; set (sb/ oneself) to doing sth; make use of: কাজে (লোক) ~. পড়ায় মন ~. **11** invest; lay out; lend at interest: ব্যবসায়ে/ সুদে টাকা ~.**12** apply/ coat with (paint, etc); cover with; smear sth on/ over/ with: রং ~. **কাদা ~** soil. **13** poison a person's mind against sb; report (against) maliciously and secretly; report sth in the way of scandal/ malice: লাগিয়ে লাগিয়ে তার কান ভারী করেছে. **14** complain: বাবা বুঝি লাগিয়েছেন ? **15** bring to; bring to anchor; cast anchor; stop: ঘাটে নৌকো ~, গাড়ি দ্বারে ~. **16** use appropriately; put: শব্দটা বাক্যের মধ্যে লাগাও দেখি কেমন লাগে. **17** impute to; smear; cast (a slur, etc): চরিত্রে কলঙ্ক /দাগ ~. **18** set: আগুন ~. **19** set: টেবিল ~. **20** take; spend: অনেক সময় ~. **21** cost: খরচ ~. **22** inspire; fill with; strike: ভয় ~. **23** make (giddy/ dizzy): ভিরমি ~. **আগুন ~** *vi* **1** set fire to .**2** sow dissension; excite quarrels. **উস্কি ~** *vt* instigate; incite; foment. **ঘুম ~** *vi* go to sleep. **(মুখে) চুনকালি ~** *vi* disgrace; expose to disgrace; sully sb's reputation; bring shame upon; put to shame; smear. **তাক ~** *vt* amaze; flabbergast; stagger; stun; astound. **তালা ~** *vt* lock; fit with a lock. **কানে তালা ~** *vi* deafen. **দম ~** *vi* **1** wind (as a watch). **2** have a long puff at (a pipe, etc). **নজর ~** *vt* **1** look covetously. **2** cast an evil eye. **3** make eyes at; look amorously at. **পাক/ প্যাট ~** *vt* **1** twist; spin. **2** complicate; throw obstacles in the way of. **ভেল্কি ~** *vi* dumfound; bamboozle; make fool of; bewitch.

লাগাম [P] *n* bridle; rein. **~ কামড়ানো** *vi* champ the bit. **~ টানা** *vt* **1** rein in (a horse); draw; rein. **2** keep a light rein on sb/ sth; restrain; curb; bridle; check; control. **~ ধরা** *vi* hold/ take the reins. **~পরানো** *vi* **1** bridle. **2** (fig) bridle; rein. **~ ছাড়া** *adj* (lit and fig) unbridled.

লাগায়েৎ, লাগায়েত [A] *prep* = নাগাদ

লাগাল = নাগাল

লাগালাগি *n* backbiting; accusations; insinuation. **~ করা** *vi* backbite; sow dissension; report slanderously.

লাগি *prep* (old use, dial poet) for; for the sake of; on account of.

লাগুন [E] *n* lagoon.

লাগেজ [E] *n* luggage.

লাগোয়া = লাগাও

লাঘব *n* **1** decrease; reduction; diminution. **2** lightness; levity; ease; relief. **3** skill; alacrity; dexterity: হস্ত-~. **4** derogation of dignity; sleight; disrespect. **5** lack of weight/ consequence. **6** swiftness; rapidity; speed. **~ করা** *vt* **1** decrease; reduce; diminish; lower; deflate; minimize; lessen; lighten; reduce the weight of. **2** relieve . **3** humiliate; belittle; denigrate. **~ হওয়া** *vi* decrease; lessen; diminish; decline; drop; fall; dwindle.

লাঙট, লাঙ্গট = লেঙট

লাঙল, লাঙ্গল *nn* plough. **~ চষা/ টানা /দেওয়া** *vt* plough. **~ টানা** *adj* drawing a plough. **~দণ্ড** *n* pole/ beam/ shaft of a plough. **~ রেখা** *n* furrow. **লাঙলের ফাল** *n* ploughshare.

লাঙ্গুল *n* tail (of beasts). **~হীন** *adj* tailless.

লাচাড়ী *n* name of a Bengali metre suitable for dancing; song composed in this metre.

লাচার [P] *adj* helpless; resourceless; poor; compelled; pressed.

লাচি, লাছি *nn* bunch; tuft: এক ~ পাট.

লাজ[1] *n* (clolloq) = লজ্জা. **লাজের মাথা খেয়ে** *adv* shamelessly.

লাজ[2] *n* fried/ parched grain (esp rice grain). **~ পেয়া** *n* water with parched grain; rice gruel. **~ মণ্ড** *n* scum of parched grain.

লা-জওয়াব, লাজবাব [A] *adjj* rendered speechless; silenced; confuted; disconcerted; having no reply to give. **~ করা** *vt* render speechless; silence; confound.

লাজুক *adj* shy; bashful; timid; coy; modest; diffident.

লাঞ্ছন *n* **1** mark; sign; token. **2** mark of ignominy; stain; spot. **3** name; appellation. **4** flag; banner. ❑*adj* (in compounds) marked/ characterized by; furnished/ provided with.

লাঞ্ছনা *n* reproach; rebuke; reprimand; disgrace; harassment; insult; indignity; ignominy. **~ করা** *vt* reproach; rebuke; reprimand; admonish; disgrace; insult; subject to indignities; persecute; harass.

লাঞ্ছিত *adj* **1** marked; decorated; characterized by; endowed/ furnished with; bearing a particular emblem/ sign. **2** reproached; rebuked; reprimanded; disgraced; harassed; insulted; persecuted. **3** stained; tarnished; spotted; soiled. **লাঞ্ছিতা** *fem.*

লাট[1] [E] *n* **1** governor; governor-general (also বড়ো ~); military governor জঙ্গি ~: **2** lord. **~ করা** *vt* promote to a very high rank. **ছোট ~** *n* provincial governor; lieutenant governor. **~ বেলাট** *n pl* (iron) lords and nobles; bigwigs.

লাট[2] [E] **1***n* parcel of an estate. **2** parcel of land (esp agricultural) marked out for administrative purpose. **3** set of things offered together for sale; lot . **4** rent payable on a specific day. ~**বন্দি** *adj* (of land) marked out for auction (to realize arrears of rent); divided in lots. ~**বন্দি করা** (also ~ করা) divide into lots; mark out for auction.

লাট[৩] *adj* **1** (of clothes) having the crease spoiled; crumpled; ruffled; shabby; rumpled. **2** prostrate on the ground. ❑*n* worn-out clothes. ~করা *vt* crumple; ruffle; rumple. ~ **খাওয়া** *vi* **1**(of measles, etc) sink. **2** (of kites) behave awkwardly and refuse to keep flying; spin. **মেরে ~ করা** *vt* knock sb senseless/ reeling to the ground; knock down. ~ **ভাঙা** *adj* =~.

লাট[৪] *n* pillar; steeple: অশোক ~. জয়ৎ ~ *n* victory column.

লাটাই *n* reel; bobbin; spool.

লাটিম, লাটু, লাট্টু *n* top. ~ **ঘোরানো** *vt* spin a top.

লাঠানো *vt* beat with a stick/ rod chasten; birch; thrash; batter; cudgel.

লাঠালাঠি *n* **1** fighting with staffs/ sticks. **2** serious quarrel. ~ **করা** *vi* fight one another with staffs/ sticks; come to blows.

লাঠি *n* stick; staff. ~ **খেলা** *v* fight with sticks as a sport; practise fighting with sticks. ~**পেটা করা** *vt* hit with a stick; birch; thrash; trounce. ~ **বাজি করা** *vi* fight with sticks; lead a violent life. ~ **মারা** = ~পেটা করা. ~**ঠেঙ্গা**, ~**সোটা** *nn pl* sticks of different sizes. **লাঠিয়াল** *n* (skilled) fighter with sticks; ruffian; gangster; hoodlum. **লাঠিয়ালি** *n* skill in the profession of fighting with sticks.

লাড্ডু = লড্ডু

লাড়ু = লড্ডু. ~ **পাকানো** *vi* **1** roll sweetmeat. **2** (fig) complicate; bungle; make a mess of. ~ **গোপাল** **1** figure of Sri Krishna as a child in a creeping state and carrying a sweetmeat in one of his hands. **2** (hist) particular posture for physical punishment.

লাথ = *n* (dial) = লাথি

লাথি *n* kick; leg. ~ **ওঁচানো** *vt* aim a kick. ~ **খাওয়া** *vi* be kicked; receive a kick. ~ **দেওয়া/মারা** *vt* kick; give sb a kick. ~ **লাগা** *vi* be touched by sb's foot. ~**খেকো** *adj* one who is always killed for his misdeeds; vile; abject; base; ignoble.

লাদ[১] = নাদ

লাদ[২] = নাদা

লাদা *vt* load. ~**ই** *n* load; burden: cargo.

লাদি = নাদি

লাদাবি [A] *adj* unclaimed.

লানত [A] *n* curse; imprecation; abuse; execration. ~ **করা/ দেওয়া** *vi* curse; imprecate.

লান্সনায়েক *n* (in the Army) brevet naik (⇒ নায়েক).

লাপাত্তা *adj* traceless; vanished.

লাফ = লম্ফ. ~ **ঝাঁপ** = লম্ফঝম্ফ. **লাফানি** *n* leaping; jumping; skipping; frisking; fretting; hopping; bounding; bounce. ~**নে** *adj* frisking; jumping; hopping; fretful. **লাফানো** *vi* leap; jump; skip. hop; bounce; fret; bound. **লাফানি** *n* jumping; frisking; flouncing; fuss. **লাফালাফি করা** *vi* frisk gambol; flounce; caper; cut caper(s); be impatient; fret; fuss. **লাফালাফি -ঝাঁপাঝাঁপি** *n* frolic.

লাব, লাবক *nn* a variety of perdix (*Perdix chinesis*).

লাবড়া *n* dish of mixed vegetables.

লাবণ *adj* of salt; saline; salt; salted.

লাবণি, লাবণী *n* (poet) = লাবণ্য

লাবণিক *adj* = লাবণ. ❑*n* salt-seller.

লাবণ্য *n* **1** beauty; loveliness; grace; charm . **2** saltness; taste/ property of salt. ~**বর্জিত** *adj* graceless; ugly; plain. ~**ময়** *adj* having a charming/ graceful figure; graceful; lovely. ~**ময়ী** *fem.* ~**শ্রী** *n* great beauty. **লাবণ্যার্জিত** *adj* obtained through beauty. ❑*n* gift presented to a bride at her marriage by her father-in-law and mother-in-law.

লাবণ্যোজ্জ্বল *adj* resplendent in beauty.

লাভ *n* **1** obtaining; getting; attaining; attainment; acquisition. **2** gain; profit; benefit; advantage; earning. **3** income; interest; utility. ~ **করা** *vt* **1** obtain; gain; attain; secure; receive; take; find; have; reap; benefit; gain possession of. **2** make a profit; benefit. **3** earn. ~ **হওয়া** *vi* **1** come/ turn out as a profit/ income. **2** be of use/ utility/ interest: এতে আমার লাভ কী? ~**কর**, ~**জনক** *adjj* profitable; fruitful; gainful; lucrative. ~**বান** *adj* one who has gain/ advantage/ profit/ benefit ~ **বান হওয়া** *vi* profit; benefit from/ by; get benefit; be the beneficiary; gain from. ~**ক্ষতি**, ~ **লোকসান**, **লাভালাভ** *nn* profit and loss; gain and detriment. **লাভাংশ** *n* dividend. **লাভে** *adv* at profit. **লাভে মূলে** *adv* including principal and profit/ interest.

লাভা [E] *n* lava.

লামা *n* (Tibetan) lama.

লাম্পট্য *n* lewdness; dissoluteness; lasciviousness; debauchery; profligacy; licentiousness; wantonness.

লায়েক [A] *adj* **1** worthy; deserving; proper; suitable. **2** able; capable; qualified; competent. **3** grown-up; of full age. **4** (derog) grown-up enough to be a libertine. ~**জমি** *n* cultivable land.

লার্ভা [E] *n* larva.

লাল[১] *adj* **1** red; reddened. **2** flushed. **3** red hot; enraged; angry. ❑*n* red; redness; flush. ~**চে** *adj* reddish. ~ **জমি** *vi* very fertile land. ~ **রতন**, ~ **রত্ন** *nn* ruby. ~ **করা** *vt* redden; dye/ paint red. ~ **বাতি জ্বালা** *vi* go into liquidation;

become bankrupt; collapse; crash. ~ হওয়া *vi* **1** redden; flush; become red. **2** be very angry; fly into a passion. **3** be ripe.

লাল[২] *n* **1** infant boy; darling; dear. **2** son. ❑*adj* beloved. ~**মোহন** *n* kind of sweetmeat made of curd.

লাল[৩] *n* saliva; slaver; spit; slobber; spittle. ~ **কাটা/ঝরা** *vi* **1** (of a baby) slobber. **2** slaver; salivate. ~ **গড়ানো / পড়া** *vi* salivate in sleep. ~ **ফেলা** *vi* spit.

লালচ *n* greed; covetousness; avarice; temptation. ~ **দেওয়া** *vt* tempt; allure; entice. **লালচি, লালচে** *adj* greedy; covetous.

লালন *n* **1** act of bringing up carefully; breeding; upbringing; rearing; nurture. **2** fond; cherishing: আশা-~. ~**পালন** *n* careful upbringing. ~ **করা** *vt* **1** bring up; breed; foster; nurture; nurse; rear/tend carefully. **2** cherish fondly; nurture. ~-**পালন করা** *vt* nourish and bring up; rear.

লালস *adj* eagerly longing for; ardently desirous of; greedy; covetous; lustful; delighting/absorbed in. ❑*n*=লালসা.

লালসা *n* longing; ardent desire; fond attachment/ devotion to; greed; covetousness; avidity; lust; eagerness.

লালসানি *n* slaver; discharge.

লালসীক *adj* slobbery; slippery.

লালা[১] *n*=লাল[৩]. ~**ক্লিন্ন** *adj* wet with saliva. ~**গ্রন্থি** *n* salivary gland. **লালায়িত** *adj* hankering after; craving/ yearning for; covetous; coveting . **লালায়িত হওয়া** *vi* hanker after; crave for; yearn for; after; covet; set one's heart upon. ~**স্রাব** *n* flow of saliva; salivation.

লালা[২] *n* (title or polite form used in addressing certain non Bengali gentlemen) Master; grandee; Sir; Mr.

লালাটিক *adj* relating to fate/ destiny or the forehead. ❑*n* ornament worn on the forehead; tiara.

লালি *n* redness; blush; reddening flush; crimson.

লালিকা *n* **1** jesting/ evasive reply. **2** equivoque. **3** parody.

লালিত *adj* **1** carefully brought up/ tended/ reared; nurtured. **2** fondly cherished. ~**পালিত** *adj* nourished and brought up.

লালিত্য *n* **1** grace; beauty; charm. **2** sweetness; suavity.

লালিম *adj* **1** flushed; crimson; ruby; rosy; flush. **2** red; reddish; ruddy. **লালিমা** *n* **1** glow; bloom; blush; flush. **2** redness; ruddiness; high colour; red tint.

লালী *n* ⇒ লালি. ❑*adj*=লালিম

লাশ, লাস [P] *n* human carcass; dead body; corpse.

লা-শরিক [A] *adj* having no partner.

লাস[১] ⇒ লাশ

লাস[২]=লাস্য

লাস[৩] [E] *n* last (for making shoes on).

লাস্য *n* **1** dancing (as practised by woman); dance. **2** amorous gestures. ~**ময়ী** *adj fem* (given to)dancing; glamorous; seductive.

লিক[১]**, লিখ** *n* traces of carriage wheels (left on roads). ~ **ধরা** *vt* follow the track/ beaten path.

লিক[২] *n* (colloq)=লিকি

লিকলিক *n* (onom) expressing great thinness/ slenderness. ~ **করা** *vi* flash. **লিকলিকে** *adj* thin; slender; willowy; gangling; wiry.

লিকার [E] *n* liquor.

লিকি *n* nit; egg of louse; young louse.

লিক্ষা=লিখি

লিখন *n* **1** writing; composing. **2** drawing; tracing. **3** piece of writing; letter; note; chit; script; manuscript. ~**পঠন** *n* reading and writing. ~**প্রণালী,** ~**ভঙ্গি** *nn* style/ mode of writing or composing.

লিখা, লেখা *vi, vt* **1** write; compose; copy; write to. **2** draw; trace; describe; sketch. **3** delineate; paint; engrave; inscribe. **4** mark; scratch. ~**জোখা** *n* accounts; score; reckoning. **লিখানো** *vt* cause to write/ compose/ draw; get sth written/composed; teach one how to write. ~**পড়া** *n* **1** reading and writing; studies; education. **2** agreement in black and white. **3** legally registered agreement . ~**পড়া করা** *vi* **1** read and write; study; receive education. **2** enter into/ draw up a written agreement. **3** execute a legally registered agreement. ~**লিখি** *n* writing; exchange of letters; correspondence. ~**লিখি করা** *vi* write to one another; exchange letters; make repeated representation in writing; be in correspondence with. **লিখে ওঠা** *vt* finish writing. **লিখে দেওয়া** *vi* **1** write for sb. **2** execute a deed of gift. **লিখে রাখা** *vt* note; put down in writing; jot down; write down; record. **এক কলম লিখে দেওয়া** *vi* put it down in writing (as a guarantee for authenticity).

লিখিত *adj* **1** written; composed; copied. **2** drawn; described. **3** inscribed; engraved; delineated. **4** foreordained; ordained. ~ **জবানবন্দি** *vi* written deposition.

লিখিতব্য *adj* to be written; worth writing about.

লিখিয়ে *adj* skilful in writing/ describing/ delineating. ❑*n* writer; author; composer.

লিঙ্গ *n* **1** mark; sign; token; badge; emblem. **2** (gram) gender. **3** sign of sex; penis; organ of generation; phallus; esp that of Shiva worshipped in the form of a stone. ~**দেহ,** ~**শরীর** *nn* subtle body. ~**পূজা** *n* phallic worship; phallicism; phallism. ~**বৃত্তি** *adj* making a livelihood by false appearance/ assumed outward marks. ❑*n* religious hypocrite. ~মূর্তি *n* phallic emblem. লিঙ্গায়েত *n* community worshipping the phallus of Shiva.

লিঙ্গী *adj* having a mark/ sign; wearing a distinguishing mark. ❑*n* hypocrite.

লিচু *n* lychee; litchi.

লিটার [E] *n* litre.

লিডার [E] *n* leader.

লিথো, লিথোগ্রাফি [E] *n* lithography.

লিপন = লেপন

লিপস্টিক [E] *n* lipstick.

লিপা = লেপা. ~পোঁছা *vt* clean and wash; polish.

লিপি *n* **1** writing: ললাট~. **2** script; alphabet. **3** letter; note; epistle; missive. **4** painting; drawing. ~কর *n* writer; scribe; penman; copyist; amanuensis; composer of letters. **~কর প্রমাদ** *n* slip of the pen; error committed by a copyist. **~কলা, ~কৌশল** *n* **1** penmanship; art/ style of writing. **2** calligraphy. **লিপিকা** *n* (short) letter; chit; note. **~কার** =কর. **~চাতুর্য** =~কলা. **~বদ্ধ, ~ভুক্ত** *adj* recorded; entered. **~বদ্ধ/ ~ভুক্ত করা** *vt* record; place on record; write/ include in a letter/ book etc; note. **~বিদ্যা** *n* **1** art of letter-writing. **2** calligraphy. **3** penmanship.

লিপ্ত *adj* **1** smeared/ anointed/ daubed with; soiled with. **2** involved/ implicated in; engaged/ employed in. **3** sticking/ adhering to. **4** joined; connected. **5** (zoo) webbed. **~পদ, ~পাদ** *adj* webfooted. **~হস্ত** *adj* having the hands smeared/ stained.

লিপ্যন্তর *n* transliteration. **~ করা** *vt* transliterate.

লিপ্সা *n* desire to gain; wish to acquire/ obtain; longing/ yearning for; avidity; covetousness. **~ করা** *vi* long/ yearn for; desire; covet.

লিপ্সু *adj* wishing to gain/obtain; desirous of; longing for; avid; covetous.

লিভার[1] [E] *n* liver. **লিভারের দোষ** *n* liver complaint/ trouble.

লিভার[2] [E] *n* lever.

লিমনেড, লেমনেড [E] *n* lemonade.

লিরিক [E] *n* lyric.

লিলানো = লিলানো

লিল্লা, লিল্লাহ [A] *adv* for God's sake; in the name of God.

লিসপিস *n* (onom) itch; itching: **হাত ~ করা** *vi* have an itch for; itch for.

লিস্ট, লিস্টি (colloq) [E] *nn* list; roll; inventory. **~ করা** *vi* make a list of. **~ভুক্ত** *adj* listed; enlisted.

লীগ [E] *n* league.

লীঢ় *adj* licked; tasted; devoured.

লীন *adj* **1** dissolved/ absorbed in; merged in; disappeared; vanished. **2** clung/pressed closely together; attached/devoted to. **3** lying/ resting on. **4** (phys) latent. **লীনা** *fem.* **~তাপ** *n* (phys) latent heat.

লীয়মান *adj* vanishing; disappearing; melting; fading; dissolving; evanescing.

লীলা *n* **1** play; sports; diversion; pastime; amusement. **2** mere sport/ play; child's play; ease/ facility in doing anything. **3** amorous play/ gestures. **4** mere appearance; semblance; pretense; disguise; sham. **5** grace; beauty; charm; elegance; loveliness. **~কমল** *n* a woman's toy-lotus. **~কলহ** *n* lover's quarrel; sham-fight; quarrel/ dispute in play. **~কানন** *n* pleasure garden. **~কুঞ্জ** *n* pleasure grove. **~ক্ষেত্র** pleasure ground; field of activities. **~খেলা** *n* (mere) sport; amusement; diversion. **~খেলা সাঙ্গ করা/ হওয়া** *vi* **1** die; breathe one's last; pass away; give up the ghost; depart this life. **2** (iron) give up one's (criminal) activities and surrender. **~গতি** *n* elegant bearing. **~গৃহ, ~গেহ** *nn* pleasure house; place of amusement/ sport. **~চঞ্চল** *adj* playful; frolicsome; rompy. **~তনু** *n* formed/ assumed for mere sport/ pleasure. **~পদ্ম**=~কমল. **~বতী** *adj fem* possessed of grace/ beauty, graceful; charming; playful; coquettish; lively. ❑*n* beautiful and charming woman. **~ভূমি** =ক্ষেত্র. **~ময়** *adj* playful; sportive; blissful; joyful; gleeful. ❑*n* the playful one (said of God). **~ময়ী** =~বতী. **~য়িত** *adj* having assumed a beautiful pose/ posture; graceful; elegant; shapely; dallying. **~শেষ, ~সংবরণ, ~সাঙ্গ** *nn* end of one's life; death. **~স্থল, ~স্থলী, ~ স্থান**=~ ক্ষেত্র.

লীলোদ্যান *n* pleasure-garden of gods.

লু *n* very hot wind; simoom.

লুই *n* kind of very soft woolen wrapper.

লুকাচুপি, লুকোচুপি *nn* hiding; concealment. **~ করা** *vi* conceal; hide; cover up; hush up; keep back/ secret.

লুকাচুরি, লুকোচুরি *n* (lit and fig) hide-and-seek. **~ খেলা** *vi* play at hide-and-seek; dodge.

লুকানি= লুকাচুরি

লুকানো *vt, vi* **1** hide; go in hiding; keep out of side; remain invisible; hole up. **2** hide; conceal; cover (up) veil; curtain; mask; enshroud; camouflage; wrap. ❑*adj* hidden; concealed.

লুক্কায়িত *adj* gone into hiding; concealed; hidden; disappeared; screened; unrevealed. **~ হওয়া** *vi* go into hiding; hide; disappear; keep out of sight.

লুঙ্গি *n* a kind of loin-cloth.

লুচি *n* kind of soft, thin, fine saucer-shaped bread fried in ghee.

লুচ্চা *adj* lewd; wicked; mean; low; corrupt; debauched; profligate; lecherous; lascivious. ❑*n* rake; profligate; libertine; lecher; debauchee; wicked man. **লুচ্চামি** *n* lewdness; profligacy; lasciviousness; rascality; knavery; lechery; depravity; debauchery.

লুঞ্চিত *adj* **1** plucked; pulled. **2** uprooted; eliminated.

লুট, লুঠ *nn* **1** plunder; loot; rapine; robbery; reckless misappropriation; ravage; pillage. **2** booty; prize; spoils; swag (vulg). **3** scattering sth before a crowd to be picked up: হরির~. **~ করা** *vt* **1** plunder; loot; rob; ruin; take by storm; misappropriate recklessly; spoil. **2** enjoy greatly: মজা ~ করা. **3** captivate; enthral: হৃদয় ~করা. **লুটের মাল** *n* booty; plunder; prize; gain. **~তরাজ, ~পাট** *nn* plundering; pillage; sack; plundering and looting; havoc; devastation; ravage. **~তরাজ/ ~পাট করা** *vi* plunder; pillage; sack; ravage.

লুটা, লোটা *vt, vi* **1** =**লুট করা** (⇒ লুট). **2** roll; toss about; sprawl; wallow; tumble; go down reeling; welter; hang down loosely; flow: মাটিতে ~, চুল পিঠে লুটোচ্ছে. **লুটানো** *vi, vt* **1** cause to plunder/ rob. **2**=~ (2). **3** cause to roll; let flow; loosen. **~পুটি** *n* rolling (up on the ground); wallowing; weltering; tumble and toss; sprawling. **~পুটি খাওয়া** *vi* roll; toss about; wallow.

লুটেরা *adj* one who robs/ plunders; plundering rapacious. ❑*n* robber; plunderer.

লুটেল *n*=লুটেরা

লুটোপুটি *n*([colloq) =লুটাপুটি (⇒ লুটা)

লুঠ ⇒ লুট

লুঠিত =লুণ্ঠিত

লুড়া *n* faggot; fagot (⇒ নুড়া).

লুড়ি (dial) *n* =নুড়ি

লুন (dial) *n* =নুন

লুণ্ঠক *adj* robbing; plundering; pillaging. ❑*n* robber; plunderer; pillager; thief.

লুণ্ঠন *n* **1** plunder; robbing; robbery; pillaging; sacking; loot; ransacking . **2** derivation (of pleasure) in a great measure: আনন্দ ~. **~ করা**=লুট করা (⇒ লুট).

লুণ্ঠিত *adj* **1** plundered; pillaged; sacked; ransacked; stolen; robbed; looted; ravaged. **2** rolling (on the ground); flowing; sprawling; wallowing; lying prostrate. **লুণ্ঠিতা** *fem*.

লুপ্ত *adj* **1** hidden; invisible; concealed. **2** no longer existing; extinct; defunct; obsolete; missing; gone out of currency/ practice; abolished: ~ প্রজাতি, ~ আইন. **3** covered/ wrapped. **4** disappeared; suppressed; annihilated; lost; destroyed. **5** (gram) dropped; elided. **6** [bot] abortive. **~ করা** *vt* hide; conceal; cause to disappear; abolish; suppress; annihilate; destroy; elide; efface. **~ হওয়া** *vi* become hidden/ concealed/ invisible; become extinct/ obsolete; go out of currency/ practice; be covered/ wrapped; disappear; be destroyed/ annihilated. **~প্রায়** *adj* almost hidden/ invisible/ covered/ extinct/ obsolete/ defunct/ destroyed/ abortive; obsolescent. **~বুদ্ধি** *adj* utterly perplexed; confounded; flabbergasted. **~রত্ন** *n* hidden treasure. **লুপ্তাঙ্গ** *n* (bot) abortive organ.

লুপ্তি *n* **1** hiding; concealment; invisibility. **2** extinction; obsoleteness; abolition; obsolescence; annihilation; destructiveness. nonexistence; demise; disappearance; suppression.

লুপ্তোদ্ধার *n* recovery/ reclamation of a thing lost/ destroyed/ ruined; discovery of a hidden/ secret thing.

লুপ্তোপমা *n* (rhet) kind of simile wanting/ omitting the particle of comparison.

লুফা *vt* **1** catch sth before it touches the ground; catch/ get/ hold of; take a catch. **2** (fig) receive/ accept eagerly: বইটি ক্রেতারা লুফে নিয়েছে. **লুফানো** *vt* cause to catch/ take a catch. **~লুফি** *n* throwing and catching (of a ball and other things) **~লুফি করা** *vi* **1** throw sth to each other and catch it. **2** scramble for.

লুব্ধ *adj* **1** greedy; covetous; avaricious; desirous of; longing for; avid. **2** tempted; allured; enticed. **লুব্ধা** *fem* ❑*n* **1** lustful man; libertine. **2** hunter. **3** sirus; dogstar. **~ করা** *vt* tempt; allure; entice. **~ক** =~. **~ দৃষ্টি, ~ নয়ন** *nn* covetous/ greedy eyes. ❑*adj* looking greedily. **~প্রকৃতি, ~মতি** *adj* of a greedy nature; covetous. **লুব্ধাশয়** =~ প্রকৃতি.

লুলা[১] *n* **1** paw. **2** (derog) hand. ❑*adj* having no hands; crippled.

লুলা[২] *vt, vi* (poet) move to and fro; roll about; stir.

লুলিত *adj* **1** moved/ tossed about; agitated; swinging to and fro; dangling; fluttering; heaving; waving; tremulous. **2** disarranged; dishevelled.

লূ =লু

লূতা *n* spider; arachnid . **~জাল, ~তন্তু** *nn* cobweb; spider's web. **~তন্তুবৎ** *adj* gossamer; as light as gossamer flimsy.

লেই *n* paste; glue.

লেওড়া *n* (vulg) penis.

লেং, লেঙ, *n* (sl) leg; shank. **~ বাড়ানো** *vi* step forward. **~ মারা** *vt* trip (up); [fig] betray suddenly; play a trick on.

লেংচা[১] *n* a kind of sweetmeat made of curd.

লেংচা[২] *adj* lame; limping. ~নি *n* limping. ~নো *vt* limp.

ল্যাংটা, লেঙটা *n* 1 naked; nude. 2 bare; destitute.

লেংটি =লেঙ্গটি

লেংড়া[১] *n* an excellent variety of mango.

লেংড়া[২]=লেংচা[২]. ~নো = লেংচানো

লেক =lake.

লেকচার *n* lecture; (iron) harangue. লেকচার দেওয়া *vi* lecture; harangue. ~শোনা *vi* attend a lecture. লেকচারার lecturer.

লেখ *n* 1 writing; piece of writing. 2 letter; epistle. 3 calculation; reckoning . 4 line. 5 (arith) graph. ❑*adj* (to be) written.

লেখক *n* 1 writer; scribe; author. 2 copyist. 3 painter. লেখিকা *fem* authoress. ~স্বত্ব *n* copyright.

লেখকানু *n* 1 insignificant writer; scribbler. 2 copyist; scribe; pen-pusher.

লেখন = লিখন

লেখনিক *n* 1=লেখক. 2 one who makes a deputy sign a document (from inability to sign).

লেখনী *n* 1pen/ pencil. 2 painter's brush. 3 anything to write with. ~ চালনা করা *vi* write (esp books). ~প্রসূত *adj* coming out of/ produced by pen.

লেখনীয় *adj* to be written/ painted/ drawn/ transcribed.

লেখা *vi*=লিখা . ❑*adj* written. ❑*n* 1 writing; piece of writing; article: essay: আপনার ~টা আমি পড়েছি. 2 handwriting. 3 letter. 4 scratch; stroke; streak; line; stripe; furrow: চন্দ্র~, বিদ্যুল্লেখা. 5 delineation; painting; drawing. 6 number; account; reckoning; count. ~জোকা =লিখাজোকা. লেখানো =লিখানো. ~পড়া= লিখাপড়া. ~লেখি=লিখালেখি.

লেখিকা = ⇒ লেখক

লেখিত *adj* 1= লিখিত. 2 caused to be written.

লেখ্য *adj* 1= লেখনীয়. 2 used in writing only; written: ~ ভাষা. ❑*n* 1 writing; letter; epistle; script; manuscript. 2 any written document; deed; record. 3 inscription. 4 drawing; painting; copying; picture. 5 signature. ~কৃত *adj* done in writing; signed; executed. ~ক্রিয়া *n* scarification. ~দায়ক *n* record-supplier. ~নিবন্ধক *n* registrar of assurances. ~পত্র *n* deed; document; letter. ~ প্রাপক *n* record finder. ~ প্রামাণিক *n* notary pubic. ~রক্ষক record-keeper. লেখ্যস্থান *n* office. লেখ্যাগার *n* record room.

লেখ্যোপকরণ *n* writing material (eg ink, pen, paper, etc).

লেঙ ⇒ লেং

লেঙট ⇒লেঙ্গট

লেঙটা ⇒ লেংটা

লেঙুড় ⇒ লেঙ্গুড়

লেঙুড়া ⇒ লেংড়া

লেঙ্গ = লেং

লেঙ্গচা = লেংচা

লেঙ্গচানো = লেংচানো

লেঙ্গট *n* a tiny loincloth worn by wrestlers and some ascetics in the fashion of a suspensor.

লেঙ্গটি *n* a tiny piece of cloth covering the private parts.

লেঙ্গড়া = লেংড়া

লেঙ্গি = লেং

লেঙ্গুড় *n* tail.

লেচি *nn* lump of dough (to be rolled and then fried of baked).

লেজ *n* 1 tail. 2 (fig) hind part of anything; rear; rump: দলের ~. জাহাজের/নৌকার ~ *n* stern. ~ গুটানো *vi* 1 (fig) be defeated; knuckle under; take it lying down; eat humble pie. 2 turn tail; run away with tail between the legs. ~ ধরে চলা *vi* follow servility; tag along/after/behind. ~ মাড়ানো *vi* twist sb's tail, (fig) annoy; treat on the toes of; get on the nerves of. ~ মোটা হওয়া *vi* be puffed up/ over bearing; give oneself airs; get too big for one's boots. ~ খেলা *vi* do sth cunningly. লেজে খেলানো *vt* harass sb by giving false hope/ keeping in suspense; hold out/ after a carrot to sb. ~কাটা শিয়াল *n* (iron) disgraced person who advises others to follow his ways. লেজে গোবরে *adj* panic-stricken; unnerved; petrified; getting/having the wind up. ~ঝোলা *adj* long-tailed. ~সাট *n* flap of a bird's or animal's tail.

লেজা[১] (colloq) *n* 1 tail of a fish. 2 hind part of anything . ~মুড়া, ~মুড়ো *n* the whole thing; alpha and omega. ~মুড়া বাদ দিয়ে *adj* 1 omitting the unnecessary details. 2 leaving the beginning and the end.

লেজা[২] [E]*n* spear; lance; javelin; pick.

লেজার [E] *n* ledger.

লেজুড় (colloq) *n* 1 tail; rear; rump. 2 what is attached/ affixed to the rear end; tail-piece. 3 (iron) degrees; titles. ~ বৃত্তি *n* servile/slavish following; toeing the line; sycophancy; subservience.

লেট [E] *n* delay. ❑*adj* late. ~ করা *vi* be late.

লেটা = লেঠা

লেটার-বক্স [E] *n* letter-box.

লেঠা *n* 1 trouble; difficulty; fix; crisis; snag. 2 an species of small soft fish.

লেঠেল *n* (colloq) = লাঠিয়াল ⇒ লাঠি

লেড [E] *n* (in printing) (plate of) lead.

লেডি[১] [E] *n fem* lady.

লেন্ডি[২], লেন্ডী *n* paria dog.

লেডি কেনি *n* kind of sweetmeat made by frying curd (named after Lady canning).

লেডী = লেডি

লেড়কা (dial) *n* boy; child; youngster; babe; son.

লেন্ডিপেন্ডি *n* (colloq) small children; kiddies.

লেডি, লেন্ডি *nn* piece of string for spinning a top.

লেদা *n* cow-dung. ~**ড়ু**, ~**ড়ে** *n* lazy; slothful; indolent.

লেদাপোকা *n* cutworm.

লেন [E] *n* lane.

লেনদেন, লেনাদেনা *nn* act of giving and taking; transaction; exchange; dealing; bargain.

লেন্স [E] *n* lens.

লেপ[1] *n* **1** coating; smearing; daubing; anointing; plastering. **2** anything smeared on; layer/coating of paint, etc; ointment; plaster; wash. **লেপা** *vt* smear/besmear/coat wash/ with; anoint with; taint; stain; plaster. ❑*adj* coated; smeared; besmeared; anointed; washed with (med). **লেপানো** *vt* cause to be coated/ plastered/smeared/anointed.

লেপ[2] [P] *n* quilt stuffed with cotton; coverlet. **লেপের ওয়াড়** *n* quilt case.

লেপক *n* one who smears/applies coating or wash; plasterer.

লেপটানো *vt*, *vi* **1** cling/adhere to; stick: জামাটা গায়ে লেপ্টে আছে. **2** smudge. **3** make smudges on. **4** be smeared with. **5** intertwine; fold; wrap. ❑*adj* tight; close-fitting; sticking; sticky/ smudged .

লেপন *n* **1** smearing; coating; anointing; plastering; spreading on. **2** ointment; plaster; coat of paint, etc. ~ **করা** *vt*=লেপা (⇒লেপ [1]).

লেফট-রাইট [E] *n* left-right.

লেফটেনেন্ট, লেপ্টেনেন্ট [E]*n* lieutenant.

লেফাফা [A] *n* envelope; cover; enclosure; wrapper. ~**দুরস্ত**, ~**দোরস্ত** *adj* outwardly/formally meticulous; suave; glib; slick.

লেবরেটরি [E] *n* laboratory.

লেবাস [A] *n* apparel; clothes; dress; attire; costume; guise.

লেবু [A] *n* lemon; lime.

লেবেল [E] *n* label. ~ **আঁটা/মারা/লাগানো** *vt* label. ~**-আঁটা** *adj* labelled.

লেভার [E] *n* lever.

লেভি [E] *n* levy.

লেমনেড = লিমনেড

লেলা *adj* fool; dunce; simpleto; booby; wilting. ~**ক্ষেপা**, ~**খেপা**, ~**খ্যাপা** *adj* **1** crackbrained, touched (in the head); crackpot; unhinged. **2** tomfool; blockhead.

লেলানো *vt* let (a dog, etc) loose (on sb/sth); incite to attack; instigate.

লেলিহ, লেলিহান *adj* **1** frequently; licking/ darting out the tongue. **2** blazing; flashing; fiery: ~ শিখা.

লেশ *n* small part/portion; particle; atom/little bit/slight trace of; shadow of. ~**মাত্র** *adj* (used chiefly in the negative) even the faintest trace/shadow of; even an iota/bit of.

লেস [E] *n* lace. ~ **পরানো/বসানো** *vt* trim/ decorate with a lace: lace; enlace.

লেহ্ =লেহন. ~**নীয়** *adj* to be licked; lickable; to be lapped/licked up/eaten by licking.

লেহন *n* licking; tasting/lapping with the tongue. ~ **করা** *vt* lick; lap; lick at; taste; sip; take any food by licking/lapping. ~**কারী** *adj* licking/ lapping. ❑*n* licker.

লেহাজ [A] *n* **1** respect; regard; honour; deference. **2** courtesy; good manners; modesty; shame.

লেহী *adj* = লেহনকারী. ❑*n* licker.

লেহ্য *adj* = লেহনীয়. ❑*n* sipped food.

লৈখিক *adj* **1** relating to/used in writing; written (not oral). **2** (alg) graphical. **3** literary.

লৈঙ্গ, লৈঙ্গিক *adj* **1** relating to penis or gender. **2** sexual.

লো = লা[2]

লোক *n* **1** wide space or world; the universe; any division of the universe; sphere; region; tract: ত্রি~. **2** the earth; world of human beings. **3** inhabitants of the world; mankind; folk; people; public; men. **4** person; human being. **5** company; community. **6** ordinary life; worldly affairs. **7** common practice/usage. **8** servant; porter: সঙ্গে ~ আছে ? না থাকে একজন ডাকো. **9** caste: তারা কী লোক ? ~ **হাসানো** *vi* be the object of public ridicule; make oneself a laughing-stock; make oneself the butt of the (town, etc). **লোকে বলে** they/people say; it is said. ~**কথা**, ~**কাহিনী** *nn* popular tale/legend; folktale; folklore. ~**কান্ত** *adj* liked by every one; pleasing to all; popular. ~**গণক** *n* census enumerator. ~**গণনা** *n* census. ~**গতি** *n* way of the world; actions of men. ~**গাথা** *n* verse/song handed down orally; ballad. ~**গুরু** *n* teacher of the world; instructor of the people. ~**চক্ষু** *n* eyes of men; eye of the world; the sun. ~**চক্ষুতে** *adj* in the eyes of the people/public. ~**চক্ষুর আগোচরে** *adv* underhand; underhandedly; under cover. ~**চক্ষুর সমক্ষে** *adv* publicly; openly. ~**চর** *adj* wondering through the worlds. ~**চরিত্র** *n* way/proceedings of the world; human character. ~**জ** *adj* of the community. ~**জন** *n* people (at large); one's followers/ associates/ supporters; suite; train of followers; retinue. ~**জিৎ** *adj* winning conquering the world/any region; winning/ heaven. ❑*n* conqueror of the world; name of Buddha. ~**জ্ঞ** *adj* knowing the world; understanding men. ~**জ্ঞতা** *adj* knowledge of mankind/the world. ~**ত**, ~**তঃ** *adv* by men; from people; in the eyes/ opinion or from the viewpoint of the public; as usual/customary in the world. **~ধর্মত** *adv* in the eyes/opinion of people and religion; from the point of view of religion as popularly understood. **~তন্ত্র** *n* system/course of the world. **~তন্ত্রবাদ** *n* democracy. **~ত্রয়** *n pl* the three worlds (heaven, earth and atmosphere/lower regions). **~দেখানো** *adj* falsely demonstrative: false; makebelieve; phoney; feigned; simulated; sham; for effect; ostentatious; superficial; hollow. **~ধর্ম** *n* worldly matter/condition. **~নায়ক** *n* leader of men. **~নিন্দা** *n* public scandal/ censure; infamy; reproach/ censure of the world; public shame; obloquy. **~নিন্দিত** *adj* generally censured; infamous. **~নীতি** = লোকাচার. **~পরম্পরা** *n* succession of generations; transition from generation to generation of people/from man to man; tradition. **~পরম্পরাগত** *adj* transmitted/handed down from generation to generation of people; traditional. **~পাবক** *n* redeemer/purifier of the world. **~পাল** *n* guardian of the world; king; (myth) any one of the eight presiding deities of the eight corners of the universe. **~পালক** *adj* protecting the world. ❑*n* king; sovereign. **~পালন করা** *vi* look after the welfare of the people/subjects; rule; administer. **~পিতামহ** *n* great forefather of mankind; (according to Hindu notion) Brahma. **~পূজিত** *adj* honoured by the world; universally revered. **~প্রবাদ** *n* popular talk; common saying; commonly used expression; hearsay; rumour. **~প্রশাসন** *n* public administration. **~প্রসিদ্ধ** *adj* celebrated in the world; universally known. **~প্রসিদ্ধ** *n* universal establishment/ reception (of a custom, etc); general prevalence; universal fame. **~প্রিয়** *adj* popular. **~প্রিয়তা** *n* popularity. **~বন্ধু** *n* friend of all; philanthropist. **~বল** *n* strength of one's supporters/ followers; one's men/supporters collectively; manpower. **~বহির্ভূত** *adj* lying outside the human society; not to be found amongst men; unusual; rare; uncommon. **~বচন, ~বাদ** *n* public rumour; people's talk; talk of the world. **~বার্তা** *n* world's news; popular report/rumour. **~বাহিত** *adj* drawn/ pulled by men. **~বাহ্য** *adj* **1** excluded from the world/society; excommunicated. **2** singular; eccentric. **3** to be pulled/ drawn by men. **~বিদ্বিষ্ট** *adj* hated by the people. **~বিরাগ** *n* aversion/ displeasure of the people. **~বিশ্রুত** *adj* universally celebrated; famous. **~বিশ্রুতি** *n* worldwide fame; notoriety. **~ব্যবহার** = লোকাচার. **~মত** *n* public opinion. **~বৃত্তান্ত** *n* events/ occurrences of the world; course/proceedings of the world. **~ব্রত** *n* general practice; general mode of life. **~ব্যবহার** = লোকাচার. **~মত** *n* public opinion. **~মাতা** *n fem* mother of the world; goddess Lakshmi. **~যশ** =~বিশ্রুতি. **~যাত্রা** *n* business and traffic of men; worldly affairs; conduct of men. ordinary actions; worldly existence; career in life; support of life. **~রক্ষা** *n* protection of the people . **~রঞ্জক** *adj* popular. **~রঞ্জন** *n* pleasing the world; satisfying men; gaining public confidence; public entertainment. **~লজ্জা** *n* fear of public disgrace. **~লশকর, ~লস্কর** *n* retinue; following; attendants. **~লীলা** *n* worldly activities. **~লৌকিকতা** *n* social formalities/ amenities. **~শিক্ষক** = ~গুরু. **~শিক্ষা** *n* mass education; public instruction. **~শ্রুতি** *n* **1** = বিশ্রুতি. **2** popular report. **~সংখ্যা** *n* population. **~সঙ্গীত** *n* folk-song. **~সভা** *n* house of the people. **~সমাকীর্ণ** *adj* crowded; teeming with people; thickly populated. **~সমাগম** *n* gathering/collection of people; assemblage. **~সমাজ** *n* human society; public; community. **~সাধারণ** *n* (general) public; common man. ❑*adj* common (as a topic). **~সাহিত্য** *n* folk literature. **~সিদ্ধ** *adj* world established; current among the people; usual; common; universally admitted; generally received. **~সীমান্তবর্তী** *adj* passing beyond ordinary limits; extraordinary; supernatural. **~সেবক** *n* social welfare worker. **~সেবা** *n* social (welfare) service. **~স্থিতি** *n* **1** duration/ existence of the world. **2** human society/habitation. **3** universal law; generally established rule. **~হিত** *n* public welfare/good. **~হিতকর** *adj* beneficial to the world/mankind/public; promoting the well-being of the people. **~হিতকর কার্য** *n* public welfare service/work. **~হিতব্রত** *n* philanthropy; devotion to the service of mankind. ❑*adj* (also **~হিতব্রতী**) dedicated to public service; devoted to public welfare work; benevolent; philanthropic. **~হিতৈষণা** *n* benevolence; altruism; philanthropy. **~হিতৈষী** *adj* benevolent; altruistic; philanthropic. **~ হিতৈষিণী** *fem.* **লোকাকীর্ণ** =~সমাকীর্ণ. **লোকাচার** *n* usage/ practice of the world; general/ popular custom; common/ popular/ practice. **লোকাচার-বিরুদ্ধ** *adj* contrary to popular practice; opposed to prevalent custom/ usage. **লোকাতিগ/ লোকাতিশয়** =~সীমান্তবর্তী. **লোকাতীত** *adj* extraordinary; uncommon; extramundane; supernatural; superhuman; miraculous. **লোকানুরাগ** *n* love of mankind; universal love/benevolence. **লোকান্তর** *n* another/the next world; future life; the hereafter; death. **লোকান্তরগত, লোকান্তরগামী** *adjj* dead; deceased. **লোকান্তরগতা, লোকান্তরগামিনী** *fem.* **লোকান্তরগতি, লোকান্তরগমন** *nn* going to the other world; eternal journey; death. **লোকান্তরপ্রাপ্ত, লোকান্তরিত** = লোকান্তরগত. **লোকান্তরপ্রাপ্তা, লোকান্তরিতা** *fem.* **লোকান্তরিত**

হওয়া *vi* die; pass away. লোকান্তরপ্রাপ্তি = লোকান্তরগতি. লোকাপবাদ = লোকনিন্দা. লোকাভাব *n* want of men/workers; thin population. লোকাভিলষিত *adj* universally; coveted; generally liked. লোকায়ত *adj* materialistic; atheistic; secular. ❑*n* materialist; system of atheistic philosophy (taught by Charvaka); materialism. লোকায়ত রাষ্ট্র *n* secular state. লোকায়তিক *adj* materialistic. ❑*n* materialist; atheist. লোকারণ্য *n* vast crowd of people; great concourse of people. (লোকে) লোকারণ্য হওয়া *vi* teem with a vast multitude of people; be crowded/ packed/ swarming with. লোকালয় *n* human habitation/ settlement; colony; town; village; human society. লোকালয়ে মুখ দেখানো *vi* have the face to move in society; show one's face to the public. লোকালোক *n* **1** the world and the non-world. **2** (myth) a belt/circle of mountains surrounding the outermost of the seven seas and dividing the visible world from the region of darkness. **3** horizon.

লোকন *n* act of seeing/looking/viewing.

লোকমা [A] *n* morsel; mouthful; bit.

লোকসান *n* loss; damage; harm; detriment. ~ করা *vi* cause/suffer a loss; damage; harm; ~ দেওয়া *vt* suffer/incur a loss; lose.

লোকাল বোর্ড [E] *n* local board.

লোকিত *adj* seen; be beheld; viewed.

লোকেশ *n* **1** lord of the world; Brahma. **2** king.

লোকোত্তর *adj* unusual; uncommon; extraordinary; phenomenal; exceptional; outstanding; prodigious.

লোকোপকার *n* good of the people; public benefit/advantage.

লোচন *n* **1** eye. **2** seeing; looking; viewing. **3** illuminating; commentary. ~ গোচর *n* range/horizon of the eye. ❑*adj* being within the range of the eye; visible. ~পথ *n*=~গোচর. ~প্রান্ত *n* corner of an eye. ~রঞ্জন *n* pleasing to the eye; lovely. ~লোভন *adj* eye catching; attractive; extremely beautiful. ~লোচনানন্দ *n* delight of the eye; cynosure.

লোচ্চা = লুচ্চা

লোটন[1] *n* **1** ground tumbler (pigeon). **2** hair worn in a loosely hanging bun. ❑*adj* (of hair in a bun) loosely hanging.

লোটন[2] **1** লুণ্ঠন. **2** rolling; wallowing; sprawling.

লোটা[1] *vt, vi*=লুটা. ~নো = লুটানো

লোটা[2] *n* small pot for holding water.

লোড়া=নোড়া

লোণা=লোনা

লোদা *n* boggy land. ❑*adj* soft; infirm; soggy; quaggy. ~ চর *n* infirm soil.

লোধ, লোধ্র *n* a kind of tree; symplocos racemosa. ~রেণু *n* a cosmetic powder prepared from the bark of the above tree.

লোনা *adj* salty; saltish; saline; salted: ~ মাছ. ❑*n* damaging coating on walls, etc caused by moisture/ damp; excess of salinity in soil/ water/ air. ~ ধরা *vi* be affected with a damaging coating caused by damp; (of boat) be damaged by salinity.

লোপ *n* **1** destruction; abolition; annihilation; suppression. **2** extinction. **3** disappearance; absence. **4** concealment. **5** (gram) dropping; elision. ~ করা *vt* destroy; annihilate; abolish; cause to disappear; suppress; waste; lay waste. **2** conceal; hide. **3** elide. ~ পাওয়া/হওয়া *vi* be destroyed/ suppressed/ abolished; become extinct/ obsolete; disappear; vanish; be concealed/ hidden; be elided. ~প্রাপ্ত=লুপ্ত.

লোপাট *n* utter destruction; annihilation; plunder; sacking; pillage; depredation; ravage; abduction; secret removal. ~ করা *vt* destroy utterly; annihilate; plunder; sack; pillage; depredate; hide/ conceal thoroughly; carry off; cart off; remove; stealthily; make away with.

লোফা = লুফা. ~লুফি = লুফালুফি

লোবান *n* kind of incense; frankincense; benzoin; olibanum. ~দানি *n* censer; receptacle for incense.

লোভ *n* **1** greed; avidity; eager desire for; Longing after; covetousness; cupidity; avarice lucre. **2** allurement; enticement; temptation . ~ করা *vi* be greedy of; covet; desire greatly/ eagerly; long for; have a strong desire/ inclination for; hanker after/ for; lust for/after; thirst for worldly possessions. ~ জন্মানো *vi* **1** be tempted; feel greedy; overcome by greed. **2** make sb greedy; tempt; allure. ~ দেখানো *vt* tempt; allure; entice. ~ সংবরণ করা *v* check/ control one's greed; resist temptation. ~জনক =~নীয়. ~ন *n* allurement; enticement; temptation. ❑*adj* alluring; enticing; attracting; tempting; attractive; fascinating. ~নীয় *adj* covetable; alluring; seducing; seductive; attractive; charming; lucrative: ~নীয় চাকরি. ~মোহিত *adj* beguiled by covetousness/ avarice. ~শূন্য *adj* free from avarice/ greed. লোভা *adj*=~ন. লোভাকৃষ্ট *adj* attracted by greediness/ covetousness. লোভাতুর, লোভার্ত , লোভান্বিত *adj* stricken with extreme greed; avaricious; greedy; possessed of covetousness. লোভে *adv* from greediness/ desire. লোভে পড়া *vi* fall into a temptation; become greedy of; fall a prey to greediness. লোভে পাপ পাপে মৃত্যু (prov) temptation leads to sin and sin to death; avarice leads to vice and vice to death.

লোভিত *adj* allured; enticed; seduced.

লোভী *adj* covetous; avaricious; desirous of; eager after; greedy; longing for; avid; easily tempted/ allured; greedy of worldly possessions.

লোভ্য *adj* to be desired/ longed for; desirable; covetable; alluring; seductive.

লোম =রোম (⇒ all the compounds at that entry).

লোমনাশক *adj n* depilatory.

লোম-ফোঁড়া *n* boil in a hair follicle.

লোমহর্ষক *adj* causing the hair to bristle; exciting a thrill of joy/ terror; thrilling; hair-raising; terrifying; horrifying; horrendous; bloodcurdling.

লোয়াজিমা = লওয়াজিমা

লোর *n* (poet) tears.

লোল *n* **1** moving hither and thither; agitated; unsteady; restless. **2** shaking; rolling; tossing; dangling; swinging. **3** desirous; lustful; greedy; eagerly; longing for/desirous of. **4** changeable; transient; inconstant; fickle. **5** loose; hanging; flabby; baggy; flaccid. **~কুন্তল** *adj* having dangling/ pendant earrings. **~চর্ম** *adj* shrivelled; wizened. **~চক্ষু** *adj* having a rolling eye; looking wantonly upon. **~জিহ্বা** *adj* having a rolling/ restless tongue; insatiable; greedy; fluttering; blazing: ~জিহ্বা অগ্নি. **~তা, ~ত্ব** *nn* movableness; restlessness; fickleness; wantonness; cupidity; eager desire. **~নেত্র, ~নয়ন, ~লোচন** *adj* having rolling eyes. **~লোল** *adj* being in constant motion; ever restless. **লোলাঙ্গী** *adj fem* past one's prime; having a flaccid body. **লোলাপাঙ্গ** *adj* having tremulous/ quivering outer corners (said of eyes).

লোলক *adj* pendant; swinging. ❑*n* a jewel for the nose.

লোলা *n* **1** tongue. **2** greediness.

লোলানো *vt* move to and fro; all about; shake; swing.

লোলিত, লোলায়মান *adj* moving; shaken; agitated; tremulous; rolling; having.

লোলুপ *adj* very desirous/ covetous/ eager; ardently longing for; greedy; avid. **~তা** *n* eager desire/ longing for; cupidity; greediness; lust; avidity.

লোষ্ট,লোষ্ট্র *nn* **1** lump of earth/ clay; clod. **2** (fig) trifle. **~বৎ** *adj, adv* like a clod; as valueless as a clod.

লোহ[১] *n* **1** iron. **2** any metal. **3** weapon. **~কান্ত** *n* magnetic iron.

লোহ[২] *n* (archaic) tears.

লোহা *n* iron. **~চুর** *n* iron filings; iron dust/ rust; pulverized iron. **~র কারখানা** *n* iron foundry; smithy. **~র** *n* blacksmith. **~র জিনিস** *n* hardware. **~ লক্কড়** *n* iron, timber and similar materials. **আকরিক ~** *n* iron-ore. **কড়া** *n* steel. **কান্ত ~** *n* magnetic iron. **ঢালাই ~** *n* cast iron. **নরম ~** *n* soft iron; pig-iron. **পেটা/মুগুা ~** *nn* wrought iron.

লোহিত *n* **1** red; redness. **2** blood. ❑*adj* red; reddish; red coloured. **~ক** *n* ruby. **~ চন্দন** *n* saffron. **~লোচন, লোহিতাক্ষ** *adj* red-eyed; having eyes reddned with anger/ passion. **রক্তকণিকা** *n* red blood corpuscle. **~ সাগর** *n* the Red sea. **লোহিতাঙ্গ** *adj* red-limbed. ❑*n* red limb; the planet Mars. **লোহিতানন** *n* red face. ❑*adj* red-faced. **লোহিতায়ন** *n* copper.

লোহু, লৌ *nn* blood.

লৌকতা *n* (colloq) =লৌকিকতা

লৌকিক *adj* **1** worldly; terrestrial; mundane; temporal; not sacred; earthy. **2** belonging to/ occurring in ordinary life; common; usual; customary; general. **3** formal. **লৌকিকতা** *n* **1** worldliness; general prevalence; usual custom. **2** formality; civilities; politeness courtesy. **3** formal gift given to sb, esp on a ceremonial occasion. **4** mundane affairs. **লৌকিকতা (রক্ষা) করা** *vi* comply with necessary formalities whilst dealing with sb; mind one's manners.

লৌল্য *n* **1** restlessness; unsteadiness; fickleness; inconsistency. **2** lustfulness; eagerness; greediness; passion; ardent longing.

লৌহ *n* **1** iron; steel. **~ কণ্টক** *n* anchor. **2** metal. **~কার** *n* blacksmith. **~কিট্ট** *n* rust. **~ঘটিত** *adj* ferrous; chalybeate. **~চূর্ণ** =লোহাচূর. **~নির্মিত** *adj* made of iron/ steel. **~বর্ত্ম** *n* railway. **~ভাণ্ড** *n* iron vessel; metal mortar. **~ময়** made of iron/ steel. **~মল** *n* rust. **~শৃঙ্খল** *n* iron-chains; fetters.

লৌহিত্য *n* redness; red colour.

ল্যাং=লেং

ল্যাংচা = লেংচা[১],লেংচা[২]. **~নো** = লেংড়ানো

ল্যাংবোট [E] *n* **1** longboat. **2** slow-moving cargoboat. **3** (iron) constant companion/ follower; drag; encumbrance.

ল্যাজ =লেজ

ল্যাজা =লেজা[১], লেজা[২]

ল্যাঠা = লেঠা

ল্যান্ডস্কেপ [E] *n* landscape.

ল্যাবড়া *adj* garrulous; talkative.

ল্যাভেন্ডার [E] *n* lavender.

ল্যাম্প [E] *n* lamp.

ল্যারিংক্স [E] *n* larynx. **ল্যারিঙ্কাইটিস** *n* laryngitis.

ল্যালা = লেলা

ব

ব (অন্তঃস্থ)

ব *n* the twenty-ninth consonant of the Bengali alphabet. It has lost its original sound *(va)* and become completely assimilated with ব (*ba*). ~ **ফলা** *n* ব placed under or by the side of another consonant to form conjunct letter.

শ

শ[1] *n* the thirtieth consonant of the Bengali alphabet. It is a voiceless, unaspirated post dental fricative sibilant or spirant sound.
শ[2] *n* (colloq) =শত
শওকত [A] *n* dignity; magnificence; grandeur; pomp; power; might.
শওয়াল [A] *n* the tenth month of the Hijri year.
শওহর [P] *n* husband.
শংকর=শঙ্কর
শংসন *n* **1** praise; compliment; eulogy. **2** benediction. **3** recitation; reciting. **4** report; announcement; communication.
শংসা =শংসন. ~ **পত্র**, ~ **লেখ** *nn* testimonial; certificate; citation.
শংসিত *adj* **1** praised; celebrated. **2** said; told. **3** wished; desired.
শংস্য *adj* **1** to be praised; praiseworthy. **2** to be recited.
শক *n* **1** name of a white-skinned race/ tribe; the scythian race; a scythian. **2** an era introduced by king Shaka in 78 AD; any era. **শকাব্দ** *n* =~ (2). **শকারি** *n* enemy subduer of the shakas; Vikramaditya, an ancient Indian king.
শকট *n* vehicle; cart; waggon; car; carriage. ~ **চালক** *n* carter; driver; coachman; carman. **গো-** ~ *n* bullock cart. **বাষ্পীয়** ~ *n* railway train.
শকটিকা *n* small cart; child's cart; toy-cart.
শকতি *n* (poet)=শক্তি
শকরকন্দ [P] *n* sweet potato.
শকল *n* **1** chip; fragment; splint; log; piece; bit. **2** scales of fish. **3** bark; (bot) bast. ~ **তন্তু** *n* bast fibre.
শকলী *n* fish.
শকাব্দ=শক
শকার =শ. ~ **বকার** *n* filthy words beginning with শ and ব; filthy/ vile/ language; invective. ~**বকার করা** *vt* revile; abuse; abusing; inveigh against; vituperate.
শকারি=শক
শকুন *n* **1** vulture. **2** bird. **3** bird of good or bad omen. ~**জ্ঞ** *adj* knowing omens. ~ **জ্ঞান**, ~ **তত্ত্ব** *nn* knowledge of birds/ omen; augury.
শকুনি *n* **1** (large) bird. **2** vulture. **3** brother of queen Gandhari (in the Mahabharata). **4** (fig) a relative who, by giving evil counsel, leads a family to ruin.
শকুন্ত *n* **1** bird. **2** vulture. **3** blue jay. ~**লা** *n fem* (myth) name of a daughter of the Apsara Menaka by Viswamitra.
শকুল, সকুল *nn* kind of fresh-water fish.
শক্ত *adj* **1** hard; strong; stiff: ~ লাঠি. **2** obdurate; stubborn; obstinate; tough: সে বড়ো ~ লোক. **3** severe; rigorous; strict; rigid: ~ নিয়ম. **4** niggardly; stingy: খরচের বেলায় ~. **5** difficult; baffling: ~ শব্দ. **6** harsh; unkind; cruel: ~ কথা/ বাক্য. **7** tricky; puzzling; complex; intricate; impenetrable; unfathomable: ~ সমস্যা/ প্রশ্ন, অতি অচিন্তনীয়কে ধারণা করা বড়োই ~. **8** delicate; uphill; arduous; formidable: ~ দায়িত্ব. **9** incurable; serious; stubborn; sharp; severe; sore; excruciating: ~ অসুখ, ~ ব্যথা. **10** cruel; heartless; relentless; harsh; meriless: তার ওপর এতো ~ হয়ো না. **11** durable; tight: ~ বাঁধন. **12** firm; steady: ~ পায়ে হাঁটো. **13** able; capable; competent .**14** fit for work; skilled; adept; efficient; skilful: তার বিষয়সম্পত্তি এবার ~ হাতে পড়েছে. **15** hard to deceive/ win over; clever: ~ ব্যবসায়ী. **16** powerful; mighty; strong. **17** diligent; tough; hard-working. ~**খানি** *n* (fig) very hard taskmaster; very stubborn/ obstinate man. ~ **পাল্লায় পড়া** *vi* be up against more than one's match. **শক্তের ভক্ত নরমের যম** (fig) sb who flatters a strong opponent but tyrannizes over the weak.
শক্তি *n* **1** power; strength; might; force. **2** ability; capability. **3** energy. **4** effort. **5** faculty. **6** skill; capacity for; power over. **7** effectiveness/ efficacy (of a remedy); potency (as of homeopathic medicines). **8** regal power; powerful state. **9** personal pre-eminence. **10** power/ signification of a word. **11** energy/ active power of a deity personified as his wife and worshipped by the Shakta sect of Hindus under various names. **12** the goddess Durga. **13** the goddess Lakshmi. **14** creative power/ imagination (of a poet). ~**কর** *adj* giving strength; invigorating; tonic; stimulating. ~**ক্ষয়** *adj* loss of strength / power/ energy; loss of men (of an army). ~**ধর** *adj* powerful; strong; mighty. ❑*n* name of Kartikeya, the commander-in-chief of the heavenly forces. ~**পূজা** *n* Shakti-worship. ~ **প্রয়োগ করা** *vi* apply force. ~ **বর্গ** *n pl* states influential in international affairs/ taking part in a war; powers. ~**বিহীন** *adj* powerless; weak; impotent. ~**বিহীনা** *fem*. ~ **মত্তা** *n* strength; powerfulness; forcefulness; possession of full vigour; efficacy. ~**ময়**, ~**মান** *adj* powerful; strong; vigorous; forceful; mighty; able. ~**ময়ী**, ~**মতী** *fem*. ~**শালিতা** =মত্তা. ~**শালী** =~ময়. ~**শালিনী** *fem*. ~ **শেল** *n* (myth) name of a deadly missile. ~**সঞ্চয়** *n* accumulation of strength/ power; increase in strength; preservation of

energy. ~ সঞ্চয় করা *vi* gain strength. ~ সঞ্চয় করা *vt* strengthen; invigorate; brace up; energize; reinforce; infuse strength in. ~সম্পন্ন =~ময়. ~সম্পন্না *fem*. ~সামর্থ্য *n* power and capabilities; abilities. ~সাম্য *n* balance of power. ~হীন =বিহীন. ~হীনতা *n* powerlessness; weakness; impotence ~র নিত্যতা *n* (phys) conservation of energy. অব্যক্ত ~ *n* potential energy. গতি~ *n* kinetic energy.

শক্তু *n* coarsely ground meal; grit; grouts (esp of barley-meal).

শক্য *adj* capable of being (done); possible; able; practicable; feasible. ~তা *adj* possibility; practicability; feasibility; capability; capacity.

শক্র *n* Indra, the king of gods. শক্রাণী *fem* Indra's wife.

শখ [A] *n* **1** desire; longing; interest; fondness. **2** hobby; fancy; liking: টিকেট জমানোর ~. **3** amusement; pleasure; one's own accord/ choice: শখের চাকরি. ~ করা *vi* desire; choose/ invite/ undertake voluntarily; do sth for pleasure/ amusemant; fancy; have a fancy for.

শঙ্কনীয় *adj* to be feared/ suspected/ distrusted.

শঙ্কর *adj* causing prosperity; auspicious; beneficent. ☐*n* **1** Shiva. **2** species of large sea-fish. শঙ্করী *fem* goddess Durga.

শঙ্কা *n* **1** fear; apprehension; alarm; terror; dread; care. **2** distrust; suspicion; misgiving. ~ করা *vi* fear; apprehend; be anxious/ apprehensive; dread; suspect; distrust; be afraid of; be in doubt /uncertain about. ~কুল *adj* bewildered by fear/ doubt; perturbed; greatly frightened; full of misgiving. ~কুলা *fem*. ~ন্বিত *adj* apprehensive; filled with fear; afraid. শঙ্কান্বিতা *adj*. ~ময় *adj* full of doubt/ uncertainty; fearful; afraid. ~ময়ী *fem*. ~শীল *adj* of hesitating/ diffident disposition. ~শূন্য *adj* free from apprehension/ doubt/ misgiving; fearless. ~সূচক *adj* fearful; dreadful; fearsome. ~স্পৃষ্ট *adj* touched with fear; seized with alarm. ~হর, ~হরণ *adj* expelling fear/ misgiving. ~হরা *fem*. ~হীন = শূন্য. ~হীনা *fem*.

শঙ্কিত *adj* **1** alarmed; apprehensive; suspicious; distrustful; afraid of; anxious about; frightened; fearful; timorous; perturbed. **2** feared; apprehended. **3** doubted; doubtful.

শঙ্কু[1]=শঙ্কিত

শঙ্কু[2] *n* **1** peg; nail; wedge; spike. **2** stake; pillar; post. **3** hand of a clock. **4** forceps. **5** arrow; spear; dart. **6** pin/ gnomon of a dial. **7** probe. **8** prod. **9** skewer. **10** (geom) cone. **11** fibre/ vein of a leaf. **12** measure of twelve fingers. **13** measuring rod. ~কর্ণ *n* an ass (having pointed ears). ~চ্ছেদ *n* (goem) conic section. ~দোলক *n* (mech) conical pendulum. ~পট্ট *n* seen-dial.

শঙ্খ *n* **1** shell; conch-shell. **2** conch-bangle. **3** temple (of the face). **4** a particular high number (said to = a hundred billion). ~ক *n* **1** conch-shell. **2** temporal bone; forehead. **3** disease of the head. ~কার *n* **1** worker in shells; shell-cutter. **2** a particular Hindu caste. ~চক্রগদাপদ্মধারী *adj n* Vishnu (having a conch, a discus, a mace and a lotus). ~চিল, ~চিল্ল *nn* species of white breasted kite; falco cheela. ~চূড়া *n* king-cobra. ~চূর্ণ *n* shell- power. ~ চূর্ণী *n fem* evil spirit of woman who has died when her husband was still alive; female ghoul. ~দ্রাবক *n* (chem) aqua regia. ~ধ্বনি, ~নাদ *nn* sound of a conch/ horn. ~ধ্বনি/ ~নাদ করা *vi* blow a conch-shell. ~নখ *n* kind of nail. ~বণিক *n* dealer and worker in articles of conch-shells. ~বলয় *n* shell-bracelet. ~বিষ *n* white arsenic; ratsbane. ~মালা *n* **1** shell-necklace. **2** garland of bones. ~মুখ *n* alligator. ~শুভ্র *adj* shell-white.

শঙ্খিনী *n fem* **1**=শঙ্খচূর্ণী (⇒ শঙ্খ). **2** one of the four sexual classes into which women are divided. **3** mother of pearl.

শঙ্খী *n* **1** Vishnu (possessing a conch). **2** worker in shells. **3** the ocean. ☐*adj* possessing a conch; bearing shells.

শচি, শচী *n fem* **1** name of the wife of Indra. **2** name of the mother of Chaitanya (চৈতন্য).

শজনে *n* (colloq) =শাজিনা

শজারু *n* procupine.

শজিনা *n* horse-raddish. ~খাড়া *n* the edible stem of this plant.

শটকা *n* **1** long flexible tube of a hookah. **2** hookah; hubble-bubble. **3** slip of bamboo used in catching certain species of fish.

শটকানো = সটকানো

শটকে *n* (colloq)=শতকিয়া (⇒ শত)

শটল *n* putrefaction; rotting/ decomposition.

শটি *nn* the plant *Curcuma zedoaria;* zedoary. ~ফুড *n* a barley-like powder produced from zedoary.

শটিত *adj* putrefied; rotten; decomposed.

শঠ *adj* false; deceitful; fraudulent; wicked; malignant. ☐*n* cheat; rogue; false husband/ lover. ~তা, ~তাচরণ *nn* roguery; depravity; deceit; swindling; wickedness; wicked/ roguish conduct; knavery; false play; sharp practice; crookedness; slyness; chicanery. ~তা করা *vt* , *vi* deceive; play false; swindle; chicane.

শণ *n* a kind of hemp/ flax. ~ তন্তু *n* thread/ string made of the fibre of hemp. ~পাট *n* san hemp. শণে তৈরি *adj* hempen; flaxen. শণের নুড়ি *n* sheaf of fibres of flax; (fig) grey hair.

শত *n* ,*adj* hundred. ❑*adj* many; innumerable. ~**ক** *n* **1** hundred. **2** aggregate of one hundred similar things: গীতি ~. **3** century; amount of a hundred. ❑*adj* consisting of a hundred; comprising/ amounting to a hundred. ~**করা** *adj*, *adv* percent. ~**করা হার/ হিসাব** *n* percentage. ~**কিয়া** *n* table of numbers upto one hundred. ~**কোটি** *n* , *adj* **1** thousand million; billion. **2** countless; innumerable. ~**খণ্ড** *n* hundred pieces. ❑*adj* broken into/ reduced to/ torn to (hundred) pieces; tattered; ~**খণ্ড করা** *vt* break into a hundred pieces. ~**গুণ** *n* hundred times. ❑*adj* hundred-fold; hundred times; hundred times of. ❑*adv* to / by hundred times; many/ countless times; in/ to a great degree/ extent; far. ~**গুণে** *adv*=~গুণ. ~**গুণিত** *adj* increased a hundred fold; hundred times longer. ~**গ্রন্থি** *adv* patched at hundred places; tattered. ❑*n* *durva* grass. ~**ঘ্নী** *n* (myth) a particular deadly missile. ~**চেষ্টা** *n* utmost effort. ~**চ্ছিদ্র**, ~**চ্ছিন্ন** *adjj* having a hundred holes/ openings; torn at hundred places; tattered. ~**জীবী** *adj* living a hundred years. ~**তম** *adj* /hundredth. ~**তমী** *fem*. ~**দল** *n* lotus-flower. ~**দ্রু** *n* the river sutlej. ~**ধা** *adj* in/ to a hundred divisions; in a hundred ways; a hundred-fold; into a hundred parts/ pieces. ~**ধার** *adj* / having a hundred streams/edges/ points; hundred-edged. ❑*n* thunderbolt. ~**ধারে** *adv* in hundred/ innumerable streams. ~**পদী** *n* **1** centipede. **2** scorpion. **3** earwig. ~**পুষ্প** *adj* having a hundred flowers; many-flowered. ~**বর্ষ** *n* hundred years. ~**বার্ষিক** *adj* centennial. ~**বার্ষিক উৎসব** *n* centenary. ~**ভিষা** *n* name of a constellation. ~**মারী** *n* **1** a man who has killed a hundred. **2** (iron) a bad physician who has killed a hundred patients; charlatan; quack. ~**মুখ** *n* a hundred mouths/ openings. ❑*adj* **1** having a hundred apertures/ outlets; proceeding/ in hundred ways; having a hundred ways/ issues. **2** (fig) voluble; glib; garrulous. ~**মুখী** *n* besom. ~**মুখে** *adv* volubly; glibly; highly: ~মুখে প্রশংসা করা. ~**মূলী** *n* species of asparagus. ~**রূপা** *adj* having a hundred/ many forms or shapes. ❑*n fem* name of the daughter and wife of Brahma. ~**শ**, ~**শঃ** *adj* by/ in hundreds; a hundred times; hundred times over; over and over again. ~**সহস্র** *n*, *adj* hundred thousand. ❑*adj* many; innumerable; countless. **শতাংশ** *n* a hundredth part; one hundred parts; one percent. ~**শতাব্দ**, **শতাব্দী** *nn* hundred years; century. **শতায়ু**, **শতায়ুঃ**=~জীবী. **শতায়ু ব্যক্তি** *n* centenarian. **প্রতি ~** *adj* percent.

শতরঞ্চ শতরঞ্চ [A] *nn* chess.

শতরঞ্জি, **শতরঞ্চি** [A] *nn* kind of checkered carpet.

শতেক *adj* one hundred; nearly/ approximately a hundred; many hundred; many; innumerable; hundreds of. ~**খাকি**, ~**খাগি** *nn fem* (vulg) (in swearing) cursed women who has seen the death of a hundred near ones. ~**খোয়ারি** *n fem* (vulg) (in swearing) cursed woman who will have to suffer many misfortunes.

শত্তুর *n* (colloq)=শত্রু

শত্রু *n* enemy; foe; adversary; opponent; rival. ~**ঘ্ন** *adj* destroying enemies. ❑*n* name of the youngest brother of Rama. ~**জন** *n* enemy. ~**জয়** *n* conquering an enemy. ~**জয়ী**, ~**ঞ্জয়ী**, ~**জিৎ** *adjj* victorious over enemies. ~**তা**, ~**ত্ব** *nn* enemity; hostility; antagonism; animosity. ~**তাচরণ** *n* hostile conduct; hostility; disaffection. ~**তাচরণ করা** *vi* be hostile to; bear malice. ~**দমন** *n* subduing enemies. ~**নাশ** *n* destruction of enemies. ~**পক্ষ** *n* side/ part of an enemy; adversary; enemy party; opponent. ~**মর্দন** *n* crushing/ destroying enemies. ~**মিত্রভেদ** *n* discrimination between one's enemies and friends. ~**সঙ্কুল** *adj* full of enemies. ~**র মুখে ছাই** (fig) woe unto my enemies.

শনশন *n* (onom) expressing the sound of wind or sth rushing through the air; whiz; scream; whistle.

শনাক্ত, **সনাক্ত** [P] *n* recognition; identification. ~ **করা** *vt* recognize; identify.

শনি *n* **1** planet Saturn or its regent (fabled as the offspring of the sun). **2** Saturday. **3** enemy. ~**বার** *n* Saturday. ~ **ধরা/ লাগা** *vi* (astrol) be under the influence of Saturn; fall on evil days. ~**র দশা** *n* (astrol) influence of Saturn; (fig) state of utter distress/ruin. ~**র দৃষ্টি** *n* **1**(astrol) aspect of Saturn. **2** (fig) evil eye; state of utter distress/ ruin evil days.

শনৈঃশনৈঃ *adv* gradually; quietly; gently; slowly; by and by; little by little.

শনৈশ্চর *n* the planet Saturn or its regent.

শপ [A] *n* **1** kind of large mat. **2** line; rank; row.

শপতি *n* (poet)=শপথ

শপথ *n* **1** oath; vow; promise. **2** swearing; curse. ~ **করা** *vi* take an oath; swear; vow; promise; swear an oath. ~ **করানো** *vt* cause to take an oath; swear; administer the oath to sb ~ **করে/ পূর্বক** *adv* on/ under oath; with oaths; on one's oath. ~**পূর্বক ত্যাগ করা** *vt* give up/ renounce on oath; abjure. ~**করণ** *n* swearing; taking an oath. ~**পত্র** *n* written testimony on oath; affidavit. ~**প্রমাণক** *n* commissioner of affidavits.

শপাৎ *n* (onom) expressing a hissing/ brushing sound (as of a whip); swish; whang. ~ **করে** *adv* with a whang .

শপাশপ *n* (onom) 1 repeated swishing sound; whang. 2 sound of gulping liquid food. □*adv* 1 repeated with a whang. 2 quickly and greedily.
শপ্ত *adj* cursed.
শফ *n* hoof.
শফরী=সফরী
শব, শবদেহ 1 *nn* dead body; corpse; 2 water. **~দহন, ~ দাহ, ~দাহন** *nn* cremation (of a corpse). **~ দাহ করা** *vi* burn a dead body; cremate. **~দাহক** *n* one who cremates; cremator. **~দাহন চুল্লি** *n* cremator; incinerator. **~দাহ স্থান** *n* elevated place for burning dead bodies; crematorium. **~ পরীক্ষা** *n* post-mortem; autopsy. **~ পরীক্ষা করা** *vi* make a post-mortem of; autopsy. **~ ব্যবচ্ছেদ** *n* dissection of a dead body. **~ ব্যবচ্ছেদ করা** *vi* dissect a dead body. **~যাত্রা** *n* funeral procession. **~যান** *n* bier. **~রূপা** *adj* corpselike. **~ সৎকার** *n* obsequies; funeral rites; cremation; burial. **~ সৎকার করা** *vi* perform the obsequies of; cremate; bury. **~ সমাধি** *n* burial. **~সাধন**(1) *n* magical ceremony/ rite performed with a corpse. 2 (fig) dreadful endeavour to achieve sth. **শবাকার** *n* 1 *adj* corpselike; looking like a corpse. **শবাগার** *n* morgue. **শবাগ্নি** *n* funeral fire. **শবাচ্ছাদন (বস্ত্র)** *n* shroud: winding-sheet. **শবাধার** *n* coffin. **শবানুগমন করা** *vi* follow a corpse to the funeral place. **শবানুগামী, শবানুযাত্রী** *nn* one who follows a corpse to the funeral place; mourner. **শবাসনা** *adj fem* mounted on a corpse. □*n* goddess Kali.
শবনম, শবনাম [P] *n* 1 dew. 2 kind of fine linen.
শবর *n* wild hunting tribe of India; member of this tribe; hunted. **শবরী** *fem*.
শবল *adj* variegated; brindled; dappled; spotted.
শবলা, শবলী *fem*. □*n* spotted cow; cow of plenty. **শম্বলিত** *adj*=~.
শবে কদর [P] *n*=লাইলাতুল কদর
শবে বরাত [P] *n* the fifteenth night of Shaban (the eighth month of the Hijri year), which is celebrated by Muslims as the night of fate.
শব্দ *n* 1 sound; noise; voice; tone. 2 cry; call: পাখির ~ . 3 word. 4 speech; language. **~ করা** *vi* utter a sound; raise the voice; cry aloud; call; make a noise. **~কর, ~কারী** *adj* making a sound/noise; sounding; sonorous; crying; calling. **~কোষ** *n* dictionary; lexicon. **~গত** *adj* being/ residing in a word (as a poetical meaning). **~গুণ** *n* quality of sound; excellence of the sound/ form (of a poem). **~গ্রহ** *n* receiver of sound; ear. **~ চাতুর্য** *n* skill in words; cleverness of diction; eloquence. **~চিত্র** *n* sound picture; imagery. **~চোর** *n* plagiarist. **~তত্ত্ব** *n* philology; phonetics; morphology **~ তরঙ্গ** *n* sound-wave. **~ তাত্ত্বিক** *adj* philological; morphological. □*n* philologist; phonetician. **~প্রকরণ** *n* orthography. **~বহ** *adj* conveying sounds/ sound-wave. □*n* air. **~ বিদ্যা** *n* grammar; philology. **~ বিন্যাস** *n* arrangement of words; syntax. **~বিভূতি** *n* stock of words; diction; copiousness/ richness of vocabulary. **~বিরোধ** *n* contradiction. in words; seeming contradiction. **~বৃত্তি** *n* function of word. **~বেদী** *adj* hitting an unseen (but heard) object. **~বেধ্য** *adj* to be shot at without being seen. **~বোধ** *n* knowledge derived from verbal testimony. **~ব্রহ্ম** *n* 'word-Brahma'; the Veda considered as a revealed sound/ word and identified. with the Supreme Being (cf Logos). **~ভেদী** =বেধী. **~ময়** *adj* full of sound; noisy; wordy. **~যোনি** *n* 1 origin/ source of a word. 2 (gram) root. **রূপ** *n* nature/ quality of a sound; grammatical form of a word. **~ শক্তি** *n* force/ signification of a word; power of words; different imports of a word. **~শাস্ত্র** *n* grammar; philology. **~শূন্য** *adj* soundless; noiseless; speechless; silent. **~সমুদ্র, ~সাগর** *nn* sea/ treasure of words. **~সৌকর্য** *n* facility of expression. **~সৌষ্ঠব** *n* elegance of words; graceful style. **শব্দাড়ম্বর** *n* high-sounding words; verbosity; bombast **শব্দাতীত** *adj* beyond the reach of sound (applied to the Supreme). **শব্দাবিধান** *n* sound-receptacle; ear. **শব্দানুকরণ, শব্দানুকৃতি** *nn* imitation of sounds; onomatopoeia. **শব্দানুরূপ** *n* conformity to/ imitation of sound. **শব্দানুশাসন** *n* grammar. **শব্দাম্বুধি** =~সমুদ্র. **শব্দায়মান** *adj* in the state of making sounds; sounding; resounding. **শব্দার্থ** *n* sound and sense; nature/ meaning of sounds; meaning of a word; word-meaning. **শব্দালঙ্কার** *n* embellishment of the sound (of a sentence by rhyme, alliteration, etc); figure of speech depending for its pleasingness on sound/ words. **শব্দাবলী** *n* collection of paradigms of declension. **টু~** *n* faintest sound. **ভীম ~** *n* loud sound.
শব্দিত *adj* sounded; cried; uttered; called; named; resounded; filled with sound.
শম¹ *n* 1 good. 2 happiness.
শম² *n* 1 tranquility; calm; peace; rest; equanimity; quietism. 2 absence of passion; abstraction from eternal objects through intense meditation; conquest of desire. 3 cessation; desistance; mitigation; alleviation; pacification; alloyment; extinction. 4 alleviation/ cure of a disease; convalescence. 5 final happiness; emancipation from all the illusions of existence. **~ক** *adj* pacifying; mitigating. □*n* pacifier peace-maker. **~তা** =~.
শমন¹ [E] *n* summons.
শমন² *n* 1 calming; tranquillizing; soothing; allaying; extinguishing; appeasing;

pacification. **2** peace of mind; tranquillity; calm. **3** malediction. **4** reviling. **5** (the god of) death; Yama. **6** killing; slaying; immolation. **শমনী** *fem* night. ~**দ্বার** *n* death's door; death. ~**ভান**, ~**সদন** *nn* abode of death; death's door. ~**সদনে গমন করা** *vi* die; give up the ghost; join one's ancestors. ~**সদনে প্রেরণ করা** *vt* kill; strike dead; dispatch; smite

শমনীয় *adj* to be tranquillized; consolable; soothing.

শময়িতা *n* **1** alleviator; tranquillizer. **2** killer; destroyed. **শময়িত্রী** *fem.*

শমশের [P] *n* sword.

শমস্‌-উল-উলামা, শামসুল উলামা *nn* the sun of the learned (a little conferred on very learned people).

শমিত *adj* **1** appeased; allayed. **2** relieved; cured. **3** relaxed; intermitted. **4** repressed; restrained. **5** callused; quelled.

শমী[১] *adj* tranquil; pacific; incapable of any emotion; calm; restrained; one who has subdued/ mastered passions; continent. **শমিনী** *fem.*

শমী[২] *n* kind of tree; prosopis spicigera. ~**গর্ভ** *n* fire. ~ **ধান্য** *n* sami grain; any pulse/ grain growing in pods.

শম্পা *n* lightning.

শম্বর *n* **1** kind of deer. **2** name of demon. **3** kind of fish. ~**সূদন** *n* destroyer of Shambara; god of love. **শম্বারি** *n* enemy of Shambara; god of love.

শম্বু, শম্বূ *n* bivalve shell.

শম্বুক, শম্বূক *n* **1** =শম্বু. **2** snail. **3** shell; conch. ~**গতি** *n* snail-like pace/ movement; snail's pace; procrastination; slowness; sluggishness. ❑*adj* sluggish; slow; snail-paced. ~**গতিতে** *adv* at a snail's pace.

শম্ভূ *n* Shiva.

শয়খ=শেখ

শয়তান [A] *n* **1** Satan; the Devil; rogue; devil; mischief-maker; fiend; villain; rascal. **2** (as a term of endearment) mischievous fellow; imp. **শয়তানি** *n* **1** wickedness; devil's tricks; mischief; malice; devilry. **2** (in endearment) mischieviousness. ❑*adj* devilish; diabolical; wicked; evil; satanic; miscivious. **শয়তানি করা** *vi* play the devil with; do evil; be up to some devilry. **শয়তানি** *n fem* wicked/ fiendish woman.

শয়ন *n* **1** lying down; rest; repose; resting. **2** sleeping; sleep. **3** bed; couch; sleeping-place. **4** sexual intercourse; copulation; cohabitation. ~ **করা** *vi* lie (down); recline; repose; rest; go to sleep; lie down to sleep; fall sleep; sleep together; go to bed/ sleep with; sleep with. ~**কক্ষ**, ~**কুটির**, ~**গৃহ** *nn* bed-room; bed-chamber. ~**কাল** *n* bed-time. ~**মন্দির** =~কক্ষ. ~**রচনা** *n* preparation of a bed/ couch. **শয়নাকাঙ্ক্ষা** *n* desire to sleep; sleepiness. **শয়নাগার**=~কক্ষ.

শয়নীয় *adj* to be slept/ laid on; fit/ suitable for sleep or rest. ❑*n* bed; couch.

শয়ান *adj* lying down/ at length; resting; sleeping; prostrate; asleep. **শয়ানা** *fem.* ~ **রেখা** *n* (bot) horizontal live.

শয়ালু *adj* sleeping; inclined to sleep; sluggish; slothful. ❑*n* **1** dog. **2** jackal. **3** boa.

শয়িত *adj* reposed; lying; sleeping; asleep. ~**বান**=~. **শয়িতবর্তী** *fem.*

শয্যা *n* **1** bed; bedding; couch; cot; sofa. **2** lying; reposing; sleeping. **3** resting place. ~ **করা** *vi* make the beds. ~ **নেওয়া** *vi* take to one's bed; become bedridden. ~ **পাতা** *vi* make a bed. ~**কণ্টক**, ~ **কণ্টকী** *nn* an illness in which one fell, as if one's bed is a bed of thorns. ~**কাল** *n* sleeping-time. ~**গত** *adj* gone to bed; lying on a couch; bedridden; confined to bed. ~**গতা** *fem.* ~**গৃহ** *n* bed-chamber. **শয্যাচ্ছাদন** *n* bed covering; counterpane; sheet; bedspread; bedsheet. ~**তল** *n* bed; couch. ~**পার্শ্ব**, ~**প্রান্ত** *nn* end of a bed; bedside. ~ **রচনা** *n* preparation of a bed. ~ **রচনা করা** *vi* make a bed. ~**শায়ী** =~গত. ~**শায়িনী** *fem* . ~**সঙ্গী**, ~**সহচর** *nn* bed-fellow; husband; paramour. ~**সঙ্গিনী**, ~**সহচরী** *fem* wife; concubine. ~**স্তরণ** =~চ্ছাদন.

শর[১] *n* **1** arrow; shaft; dart. **2** sort of reed/ grass; *Saccharum sura* (used for arrows). ~**ক্ষেপ** range of an arrow-shot. ~**ক্ষেপ(ণ)** / ~ **নিক্ষেপ করা** *vi* shoot an arrow. ~**জ**. ~**জন্মা** *n* ' born in a clump of reed; Kartikeya. ~**জাল** *n* dense mass/ multitude of arrows. ~**ধি** *n* quiver. ~**বন** *n* thicked/ clump of reeds. ~**বর্ষণ** *n* shower of arrows. ~**বর্ষণ করা** *vi* shower arrows. **শরবিদ্ধ** *adj* hit pierced with arrows. ~**বৃষ্টি** =~বর্ষণ. **শরব্য** *n* butt/ mark for arrows; target. ~**মল্ল** *n* archer. **শয্যা** *n* couch formed of arrows (esp for a dead/ wounded warrior); (fig) battle-field. ~**সন্ধান** *n* taking aim with an arrow. ~**সন্ধান করা** *vi* take aim with an arrow; shoot an arrow. **শরাঘাত** *n* arrow-shot; wound caused by an arrow. **শরাঘাত করা** *vi* strike/ wound with an arrow. **শরাভ্যাস** *n* practice with bow and arrow; practice of archery. **শরারোপণ** *n* planting an arrow on a bow. **শরাশ্রয়** *n* quiver. **শরাসন** *n* bow. **শরাহত** *adj* wounded by an arrow.

শর[২]=সর

শরচ্চন্দ্র *n* the autumnal moon.

শরণ *n* **1** shelter; place of shelter/ refuge / rest; hut; house; abode; resort; retreat. asylum; home; habitation. **2** refuge; recourse; protection. **3** protector. ~ **নেওয়া** *vi* take shelter; come/ go for shelter; go to sb for protection; seek refuge with; have recourse to.

শরণাগত, শরণাপন্ন *adj* come for protection/ shelter. ❑*nn* one who comes for refuge/ protection; refuge; fugitive. **শরণাগতা, শরণাপন্না** *fem.* **শরণার্থী** *adj* seeking refuge/ protection. ❑*n* refugee.

শরণ্য *adj* **1** affording shelter; yielding help/ protection. **2** needing shelter/ protection; seeking refuge with. ❑*n* one/ what affords protection/ defence; refuge. **শরণ্যা** *fem* the goddess Durga. **শরণ্যতা** *n* (condition of) affording protection.

শরৎ (কাল) *n* autumn; time/ season of autumn. **~কালীন** *adj* autumnal. **~চন্দ্র** =শরচ্চন্দ্র.

শরদ [P] *n* kind of stringed musical instrument.

শরদিন্দু *n* autumnal moon. **~নিভ** *adj* like the autumnal moon. **~নিভানন** *adj* having a face resembling the autumnal moon. **~নিভাননা** *fem.* **~বিনিন্দিত** *adj* more beautiful than the autumnal moon.

শরবত, শরবৎ [A] *n* beverage; cold drink; sherbet.

শরবতী *n* variety of lemon.

শরভ *n* **1** kind of deer. **2** a fabulous animal said to be stronger than a lion. **3** young elephant. **4** locust. **5** grasshopper. **6** camel.

শরম [P]*n* shame; modesty; bashfulness; coyness. **~ করা/লাগা** *vi* feel shame; be ashamed/ abashed; feel ashamed; blush; be bashful. **শরমার্ত** *adj* perplexed with shame; abashed; flushed with shame; bashful.

শরমিন্দা [P] *adj* ashamed; blushing; bashful; modest.

শরা[1] *n* shallow earthen plate/ lid; earthen ware vessel; flat cover; platter.

শরা[2] [A] *n* law; laws of equity; the divine code of life; dogma. **~শরিয়ত** *n* Islamic law/ code of life; revealed law; laws and statutes; justice.

শরাকত, শিরকত, শুরাকাত [A] *nn* partnership; society; company.

শরাফত, শরাফৎ [A] *n* nobility; civility; good manners; politeness.

শরাব [A] *n* wine; spirit; spirituous liquor. **~খানা** *n* tavern; distillery; public house. **~খোর** *n* drunkard; alcoholic; tippler. **~খোরি** *n* drunkenness; imbibing; alcoholism; drinking wine/ alcohol.

শরাবন তহুরা [A] *n* pure drink; divine wine.

শরাবি, শরাবী [A] *adj* intoxicated. ❑*n* drunkard.

শরিক [A] *n* partner; associate; participant.; accomplice; ally. ❑*adj* joint; united. **~ হওয়া** *vi* be a partner; partake; join; participate. **শরিকান** [A] *n pl* partners. **শরিকানা** *n* share (of a joint-owner or partner); part; joint-ownership; partnership.

শরিকি, শরিকানি [A] *adj* jointly owned.

শরিফ, শরীফ [A] *adj* noble; eminent; honourable; highborn; gentle; holy; sacred; aristocratic. ❑*n* chief of tribe/ caste; aristocrat.

শরিয়ত, শরীয়ত [A] *nn* revealed law; law statute; ordinance; justice; equity.

শরিয়তি [A] *adj* legal; conform to revealed law; law abiding; dogmatic.

শরীর *n* body; bodily frame; physique; one's own person; any solid body. **~গত** *adj* bodily; physical; lying within the body; of the body. **~গ্রন্থি** *n* bone-joint. **~গ্রহণ** *n* assumption of a bodily form. **~জ** *adj* produced from/ belonging to/ performed with the body; bodily; physical. ❑*n* **1** offspring; son. **2** sickness. **3** lust; god of love. **~জা** *fem.* **~ত্যাগ** *n* abandonment of the body; renunciation of life. **~ ধারণ করা** *vi* assume a bodily form/ shape; take one's birth in the world. **~পতন, ~পাত** *nn* collapse of the body; impairment/ loss of health; death. **~পাত করা** *vi* impair one's health; sacrifice one's life; die. **~বদ্ধ** *adj* endowed/ invested with a body. **~ভাক্** *adj* embodied being. **~রক্ষক, ~রক্ষী** *nn* body-guard. **~সংস্কার** *n* purification of the body; decoration/ adorning of the person. **~স্থ** *adj* existing in the body; bodily; physical; lying within the body.

শরীরী *adj* having a body; embodied; corporeal; living. **শরীরিণী** *fem.*

শর্কর *n* pebble; small stone.

শর্করা *n* **1** sugar; ground/ candied sugar. **2** gavel; grit; pebble; shingle; gravelly mould / soil. **3** potsherd. **4** gravel (as a disease); calculus; concretion . **~বৎ, ~বান,** *adj* sugary; gravelly; granular; gritty. **~মিশ্রিত** *adj* sugared.

শর্করিক, শর্করিল *adj* sugary; sugared; gritty; gravelly; stony; impregnated with gritty/ gravelly particles.

শর্কী [A] *adj* eastern; oriental.

শর্ত [A] *n* condition; stipulation; term; provision; agreement; wager; bet. **~ করা** *vi* make an agreement/ stipulation; stipulate; lay a wager; bet. **~সাপেক্ষ** *adj* conditional. **~সাপেক্ষ** *adv* conditionally. **~হীন** *adj* unconditional; unqualified. **শর্তাধীনে** *adj* conditional. **এই শর্তে** on this condition. **বিনা শর্তে** unconditionally; without condition.

শর্তা *n* nut- cracker.

শর্ব *n* Shiva. **শর্বাণী** *fem* Durga.

শর্বরী *n* **1** night. **2** woman.

শর্ম *n* **1** bliss; joy; delight; comfort; happiness. **2** good; welfare.

শর্মণ *n* common surnane of Brahmins.

শর্মা *n* **1**=শর্মন. **2** (in vaunts, etc) I; I the speaker myself.

শর্ষে *n* (colloq) mustard seed.

শলভ *n* grasshopper; locust.

শলা[1] *n* long pin/ stick of metal or wood. **2** pike; arrow; shaft. **3** (med) probe. **4** skewer.

শলা[2] [A] *n* **1** counsel; advice. **2** concord; peace. **~পরামর্শ** *n* (mutual) consultation; counsel. **~পরামর্শ করা** *vi* consult; take advice; hold/ take with sb; take counsel together. **~পরামর্শ দেওয়া** *vt* advice; counsel.

শলাকা *n* **1** any small stake/ stick; rod; twig. **2** rib (of an umbrella). **3** bar (of a cage/ window). **4** pencil; brush. **5** piece of bamboo. **6** chip; splinter; splint. **7** match; thin piece of wood. **8** peg; pin; arrowhead; needle. **9** (med) probe. **10** quill of a procupine.

শলি[1] **শলী** *nn* a dry measure of corn.

শলি[2] =শলাকা

শলিতা=সলিতা

শল্ক *n* **1** fish-scale. **2** bark (of a tree). **3** chip; shaving; portion. **শল্কল**=~.

শল্য *n* **1** stake; stick; rod; peg; pin . **2** arrow; arrow-head. **3** thorn. **4** (med) probe; anything tormenting/ causing pain. **5** bone. **6** fence; boundary. **7** porcupine. **8** (bot) spine. **~ক** *n* **1** porcupine. **2** the thorny shrub *Vauguieria spenosa*. **~কণ্ঠ** *n* porcupine. **~কর্তা, ~চিকিৎসক** *nn* surgeon. **~চিকিৎসা** *n* surgery; surgical treatment/ operation. **~তন্ত্র** = surgery. **~বিদ** *n* surgeon. **~বিদ্যা** *n* surgery.

শল্যোদ্ধার *n* extraction of arrows and thorns.

শল্ল, শল্লক *nn* **1** scale. **2** bark (of a tree). **3** frog. **~কী** *n* **1** porcupine. **2** kind of tree; *Boswellia thurifera*.

শশ, শশক *nn* **1** hare; rabbit. **2** markings on the moon. **3** man of mild character easily led (one of the four classes into which men are divided by erotic writers). **4** lodhra tree; *Symplocos racemosa*. **5** gun-myrrh. **~ধর** *n* **1** the moon. **2** camphor. **~বিষাণ, ~শৃঙ্গ** *nn* (lit) hare's horn; impossibility; absurdity; mare's nest. **~ব্যস্ত** *adj* frantically hurrying; frightened; alarmed; panicky. ❑*adv* hurrying; frantically. **~লাঞ্ছন** *n* the moon.

শশম = সসম

শশাঙ্ক =*n* hare-marked; the moon. **~রেখা, ~লেখা** *nn* lunar crescent; digit of the moon.

শশি *n* (in compounds)=শশী. **~কর** *n* moon beam; moon-light; moonshine. **~কলা** *n* (digit of) the moon. **~কাণ্ড** *n* **1** moon-stone. **2** white lotus-flower opening at night. **~প্রভু** *adj* shining like the moon; radiant as the moon. ❑*n* pearl. **2** white esculent water-lily. **~প্রভা** *n* moon -light; the moon. lusture. **~বদনা** *adj fem* moon-faced. **~ভাষণ** *n* 'moon-decorated'; Shiva. **~মুখ** *adj* moon-faced. **~রেখা** *n* digit of the moon. **~শেখর** *n* 'having the moon as diadem'; Shiva.

শশী *n* the moon.

শষ্কুলী *n* a large round cake (composed of ground rice, sugar and sesame).

শষ্প, শস্প *nn* (young/ sprouting) grass. **~শয্যা** *n* bed of grass. **~শ্যাম** *adj* grown green with tender grass. **শষ্পাবৃত** *adj* covered with young grass.

শসন *n* slaughtering; killing.

শসা *n* cucumber.

শস্ত্র *n* **1** weapon (which is to be wielded by the hand and not thrown). **2** sword; an instrument for cutting/ wounding; knife; dagger. **3** instrument; tool. **4** iron; steel. **5** surgical instrument. **~ক** *n* **1** iron. **2** knife. **~কর্ম** *n* surgical operation. **~কার, ~কারক** *nn* armourer. **~চিকিৎসক** *n* surgeon. **~চিকিৎসা** *n* surgery. **~জীবী** *adj* living by arms. ❑ *n* professional soldier. **~ত্যাগ** *n* abandoning/ throwing away a weapon. **~ধর, ~ধারী, ~পাণি** *adj* bearing arms/ weapons; armed. ❑*n* soldier. **~ধরা, ~ধারিণী** *fem*. **~বিদ্যা** *n* military science; science of archery. **~বিহীন** *adj* unarmed. **~ভৃৎ** =~ধর. **শস্ত্রাগার** *n* armoury; arsenal. **শস্ত্রাজীব** =জীবী.

শস্ত্রী *adj* having weapons; bearing arms; armed with a sword. ❑*n* knife; small weapon.

শস্প ⇒ শষ্প

শস্য *n* **1** corn; grain; cereal. **2** crop(of corn); harvest. **3** kernel (of fruits). **4** (bot) albumen (also সস্য) **~ক্ষেত্র** *n* corn-field. **~চ্ছেদক** *n* reaper; harvester. **~চ্ছেদন করা** *vt* reap. **~চ্ছেদন যন্ত্র** *n* reaping-machine; reaper. **~পূর্ণ** *adj* full of/ grown with corn. **~পেষণ করা** *vi* grind corn; husk. **~পেষণ-যন্ত্র** *n* corn-mill; husking-machine. **~প্রদ** *adj* yielding corn; fertile. **~ভোজী** *adj* feeding on corn; graminivorous (of pests) destroying corn by eating it up. **~মঞ্জরী** *n* ear of corn; corn-stalk. **~খালী** *adj* 'corn-wreathed'; abounding in corn/ crops. **~ল** *adj* abounding in crops; (of fruits) full of kernel; pulpy; (bot) albuminous. **~সালী** = পূর্ণ. **~শালিণী** *fem*. **~শূক** *n* awn of grain. **~শ্যামল** *adj* green with abundant corn. **~শ্যামলা** *fem*. **~ সংগ্রহ করা** *vt* harvest; procure corn/ cereals. **~ সংগ্রহের কাল** *n* harvest-time; harvest. **~সংস্থান** *n* storing/ storage of corn. **শস্যাগার** *n* granary; grange. **শস্যাধার** *n* corn-bin.

শহদ [A] *n* honey; nectar.

শহর [P] *n* town; city. **~ কোতোয়াল** *n* chief of city police. **~তলি, ~তলী** *nn* outskirts of a town/ city; suburb; environs. **~স্থ** *adj* of/ living in a town/ city; urban.

শহরৎ=শোহরৎ

শহাদত=শাহাদাত

শহিদ, শহীদ [A] *n* martyr. **~ হওয়া** *vi* be martyred; attain martyrdom; die a martyr. **~ত্ব** *n* martyrdom. **শহীদান** *n pl* martyrs.

শহিদি, শহীদি *adj* of martyrs: ~ দর্জা/ মৃত্যু.

শহুরে *adj* living in a town/ city; urban; urbane; (derog) townish; townly; (attrib) city; town. ❑*n* (derog) townee. ~ **জীবন** *n* urban life; town-fife. ~ **হাওয়া** *n* (usually derog) influence of a town/ city. ~**পনা** *n* (derog) affected urbanity; townish airs and graces.

শা *n* (colloq)=শাহ. ~ **খরচে** *adj* prodigal; extravagant; lavish; wasteful. ~**জিরা** *n* long black cumin. ~**নজর** *n* solemn rite of the bride and the bridegroom looking at each other at a Muslim wedding.

শাঁ *n* (onom) **1** expressing noise of rushing water or a flying arrow; hissing; swish; whizz.

শাঁই শাঁই *n* (onom) **1** expressing noise of violent wind or flying arrow; whizz. **2** wheeze.

শাঁক, শাঁখ *nn* conch; conch-shell; shell. ~ **বাজানো** *vi* blow a conch(-shell). ~ **আলু** *n* white esculent fruit shaped almost like a conch-shell. ~**চুন্নি**, ~**চূর্ণী** =শঙ্খচূর্ণ (⇒শঙ্খ). **শাঁখে ফুঁ পাড়া**=~ বাজানো. **শাখের করাত** *n* **1** a saw ford cutting conch-shells. **2** (fig) sth which cuts both ways; dilemma.

শাঁকালু, শাঁখালু =শাঁখ-আলু (⇒শাঁক)

শাঁখা *n* conch-bracelet. **শাঁখারি** *n* **1** dealer/ worker in articles of conch-shells. **2** (member of a) Hindu caste dealing and working in articles of conch-shells. **শাঁখারিণী** *fem.*

শাঁখিনী *n fem* **1**=শঙ্খিনী

শাঁট, শাঁটন *nn* husking: ঢেঁকির ~.

শাঁটা *vt* husk.

শাঁড়া=ষাঁড়া

শাঁপি=শামি

শাঁ শাঁ *n* (onom) expressing noise of violent wind or quick movement.

শাঁস *n* **1** kernel; pulp. **2** pith; core; marrow. **3** (fig) solid worth; grey matter: তার মগজে ~ আছে. **4** wealth; riches; means; substance. **শাঁসালো** *adj* **1** abounding in kernel; pulpy; pithy. **2** full of solid worth; brainy; substantial; wealthy.

শাক *n* potherb; vegetable; greens; vegetable food. ~**পাতা** *n* greens; vegetables. ~**ভাত** *n* dish of only rice and greens; (fig) very/ poor/ simple food; poor meal. ~**সবজি** *n* green vegetables; potherb. ~**সবজির ক্ষেত** *n* kitchen garden. ~ **শাকান্ন** =~ ভাত . **শাকাশী** *adj* herbivorous. **শাকাহারী** *n* vegetarian. ~ **দিয়ে মাছ ঢাকা** (fig) a futile attempt at concealing a serious offence. **বোঝার ওপর শাকের আঁটি** (fig) the last straw.

শাকট *adj* relating/ belonging to a cart; going in a cart; drawing a cart.

শাকর [P] *n* sugar.

শাকরেদ=শাগরেদ. **শাকরেদি** =সাগরেদি.

শাকাটিক *adj*=শাকট. ❑*n* Carter.

শাকুনিক *adj* relating to birds/ omens ominous. ❑*n* **1** bird-catcher; fowler. **2** augur.

শাকুল *adj* **1** derived from/ relation to birds/ omens. **2** having the nature of a bird. **3** ominous; portentous. ❑*n* **1** bird-catcher. **2** augury; omen. ~**বিদ** *n* augur. ~**বিদ্যা** *n* augury.

শাক্ত *adj* relating to power/ energy; relating to the Shakti or divine energy under its female personification. ❑*n* worshipper of Shakti (often identified with Durga).

শাক্য *n* name of a tribe of landowners and Kshatriyas in Kapilavastu. ~**মুনি**, ~**সিংহ** *nn* Gautama Buddha.

শাখা *n* **1** (lit and fig) branch. **2** bough; ramus. **3** limb of the body; arm or leg. **4** wing of a building. **5** division; subdivision; section; part. **6** branch/ school of the Veda. **7** offshoot. ~**কলম** *n* (bot) cutting. **শাখাগ্র** *n* **1** top of a branch. **2** finger. **শাখাচ্যুত** *adj* fallen/ detached from a branch. ~**নগর** *n* suburb. ~**নদী** *n* branch; tributary. **শাখান্তরাল** *n* position screened off by the branches of a tree. ~**প্রশাখা** *n pl* branches and twigs off a tree; off shoots; ramifications. ~**বিন্যাস** *n* (bot) branching; ramification. ~**বিলীন** *adj* settled/ sitting on branches. ~**মৃগ** *n* monkey. ~**সীন** *adj* sitting on branches. ~**স্থ** *adj* standing/ bein on branches.

শাখী *adj* having branches; branched. ❑*n* tree.

শাগরেদ [P]*n* disciple; pupil; apprentice; scholar; follower; trainee; attendant.

সাগরেদি *n* discipleship; pupillage; apprenticeship; sycophancy. ~ **করা** *vi* act as a disciple/ pupil; become a follower/ disciple of; dance attendance on; toad to(sb).

শাঙন *n* (poet)=শ্রাবণ

শাঙ্কর *adj* relating/ belonging to Shiva; relating to/ derived from Shankaracharya.

শাঙ্খ *adj* relating to/ made of conch or any shell.

শাজাদা=শাহজাদা

শাট *n* man's loin-cloth; strip of cloth; dhoti.

শাটার [E] *n* shutter.

শাটিন [E] *n* satin.

শাটী *n* sari.

শাঠ্য *n* deceit; guile; roguery; dishonesty; wickedness.

শাড়ি. শাড়ী *n* sari.

শাণিত *adj* **1** sharpened on a grindstone; whetted; sharp. **2** (fig) stimulated; sharp; poignant; cutting (to the quick); acute: ~ বুদ্ধি, ~ ক্ষুধা, ~ বাক্য.

শাত *adj* **1**=শাণিত. **2** feeble; slender; thin; emaciated. **3** lovely; glamorous; splendid. ~**ন** *n* **1** causing to fall/ decay; felling; hearing; cutting. **2** polishing; planing. **3** destroying; ruining. ~**ন করা** *vt* cut off; clip; polish; plane; trim.

শাদা=সাদা

শাদি, শাদী [P] *n* marriage; wedding. ~ **করা** *vt* marry; wedused. ~**য়ানা** *n* festivities; festive music at marriage or other joyous occasions; rejoicings. ❑*adj* relating to marriage/ rejoicings.

শাদ্বল *n* place abounding in young grass; grassy spot. ❑*adj* grassy; verdant; green.

শান[1] *n* **1** whetstone; grindstone; touchstone. **2** sharpness. খর~. **3** saw. ~ **দেওয়া** *vt* **1** whet; sharpen. **2** stimulate; made poignant. ~**ওয়ালা** *n* whetter; sharpener. ~**পাথর**=~.

শান[2] [A] *n* paved/ cemented floor. ~ **বাঁধানো** *vt* pave.

শান[3] [A] *n* **1** condition; state; circumstance. **2** dignity; quality; nature; disposition. **3** importance; pomp; lusture; eminence; glory; grandeur. ~**দার** *adj* splendid; grand; pompous; stately. ~**শওকত** *n* splendour; pomp and show; glory. **শানে নজুল/ নযুল** *n* circumstances of revelation (of Qoranic verses).

শান[4] *n* =মশাল

শানক, শানকি [A]*nn* earthen plate.

শানা[1] *n* armour.

শানা[2] [A] *n* **1** comb-like part of the loom. **2** comb.

শানা[3], **শানানো** *vi* be satisfied/ gratified: অতো অল্পে কি তার ~য়?

শানাই= সানাই

শানানো[1]=শান দেওয়া (⇒ শান)

শানানো[2] ⇒ শানা[3]

শান্ত *adj* **1** peaceful; pacified; serene; appeased; tranquil; quietened; self-composed; poised; impassive; calm; calmed. **2** free from passions; undisturbed. **3** gentle; mild; friendly; kind. **4** composed; gratified; satisfied. **5** abated; subsided; ceased; stopped; extinguished; averted. **6** soft; pliant. **7** rendered ineffective; innocuous; harmless. **8** come to an end; gone to rest; deceased; died; dead; departed. **9** purified; cleansed. **10** allayed. ~ **করা** *vt* quieten; calm; pacify; appease; satisfy; gratify; soothe; allay; alleviate; assuage; propitiate; put at rest; ease; console; solace; comfort; placate. ~**চিত্ত**, ~**চেত্তা** *adjj* tranquil minded; composed in mind; calm. ~**জ্বর** *adj* one whose fever/ grief is alleviated. ~ **তা** *n* quietness; calmness; freedom from passion. ~**তোয়** *adj* having calm/ still waters; gently flowing. ~**দান্ত** *adj* mild and moderate. ~**প্রকৃতি** *adj* gentle-natured; mild-natured; having a calm disposition; serene; even-tempered. ~ **বলয়** *n* (geog) a region/ belt of calms. ~ **ভাব** *n* **1** mental calm/ tranquillity; impassivity; serenity;; self-composure; poise; phlegm. **2** lull; calm. ~**মনা:** *adj* composed in mind. ~ **মূর্তি** *n* tranquil appearance; calm. ❑*adj* having a tranquil appearance; tranquil; calm. ~ **রস** *n* (rhet) sentiment of quietism/ tranquility. ~ **রূপ** =~ মূর্তি. ~**শিষ্ট** *adj* gentle and polite. ~ **স্বভাব** =~ প্রকৃতি.

শান্তি *n* **1** peace; tranquility; calm; quiet; peace/ calmness of mind; quietude. **2** absence of passion. **3** averting of pair. **4** alleviation (of evil/ pain); removal: আপৎ ~. **5** abatement; cessation. **6** pause; breach; interruption. **7** any expiatory/ propitiatory rite for averting evil/ calamity. **8** satisfaction; gratification: ক্ষুধা ~. **9** peace; welfare; prosperity; weal; good fortune; each; comfort; happiness; bliss. **10** rest. **11** death; destruction. **12** appeasement; pacification. ~**কর** *adj* causing peace/ prosperity; soothing; restful. ~**করণ** *n* averting of an evil. ~**কর্ম** *n* any action for averting evil. ~**জনক** =~কর. ~**জল** *n* propitiatory water. ~**নিকেতন** *n* abode of peace. ~**পুরী** *adj* produced at Shantipur in west Bengal; current/ used in Shantipur; born/ living at Shantipur. ❑*n* a very fine handloom fabric produced at Shantipur. ~**পুরে** *adj* (colloq) =~পুরী. ~**পূর্ণ** *adj* peaceful; peaceable; restful; quiet; tranquil; calm. ~**প্রিয়** *adj* peace-loving. ~**বিধায়ক** *adj* peace-making; pacifying. ❑*n* peace-maker. ~**ভঙ্গ** *n* breach of the peace. ~ **ভঙ্গ করা** *vi* disturb the peace of; create disturbances; disturb. ~**ভঙ্গকারী** *adj* disturbing (the peace); creating disturbance; disturbing. ❑*n* trouble-maker; peace-breaker. ~**ময়** =~পূর্ণ, ~**ময়ী** *fem.* ~**রক্ষক** *n* peace-officer; policeman; defender of the peace. ~**রক্ষা** *n* peace-keeping. ~ **রক্ষা করা** *vi* maintain peace. ~ **স্থাপন করা** *vi* make peace (with); bring about peace (with); restore friendly relations; pacify. ~**স্বস্ত্যয়ন** *n* propitiatory ablation. ~**হীন** *adj* agitated; disturbed; unquiet; restless.

শাপ *n* **1** curse; malediction; imprecation. **2** oath; ban; interdiction. ~ **দেওয়া** *vt* curse; pronounce/ utter a curse on sb; imprecate; damn; swear at. ~**গ্রস্ত** *adj* seized by/ suffering from/ lying under a curse; cursed; accursed. ~ **প্রদান** *n* utterance of a curse. ~ **বিমোচন** *n* deliverance from a curse. ~ **বিমোচন করা** *vi* free/ deliver/release from a curse. ~**ভ্রষ্ট** *adj* fallen/ expelled (from heaven) by a curse. ~**ভ্রষ্টা** *fem.* ~**মুক্ত** *adj* freed from a curse. ~**মুক্তি**, ~**মোচন**=~ বিমোচন. ~**শাপান্ত** *n* vehement and repeated cursing. **শাপা** *vt*=~ দেওয়া. **শাপান্ত** *n* **1** end of a curse or of the period of its effect. **2** spell of vehement cursing.

শাপলা *n* variety of water-lily.

শাপিত *adj* cursed.

শাপী = শাপগ্রস্ত (⇒ শাপ)

শাফা [A] *n* cure; healing; recovery.

শাফায়ত, শাফায়ৎ [A] *n* intercession; recommendation.
শাব = শাবক
শাবক *n* young of any animal; child.
শাবর *adj* relating to the shabaras (শবর).
শাবল *n* crowbar.
শাবাজ *n* royal falcon.
শাবান [A] *n* the eighth month of the Hijri year.
শাবাশ [P] *int* bravo; excellent; well done.
শাব্দ *adj* **1** expressed in words; oral; verbal; based on sounds; nominal. **2** relating to sound; acoustic. **3** sonorous.
শাব্দিক *adj* **1** relating to sounds/ words; verbal; sonorous. **2** prolix; verbose. ❑*n* one conversant with words; grammarian; lexicographer; philologist. **~তা** *n* verbosity; prolixity.
শাম[1] [P] *n* evening.
শাম[2] [A] *n* Syria.
শামপান = সাম্পান
শামলা[1] *adj* (of complexion/ skin) not fair; black; dark.
শামলা[2] [P] *n* **1** a narrow kind of shawl for tying round the head/ waist. **2** end of a turban. **3** kind of turban.
শামা[1] [A] *n* lamp; candle. **~দান** *n* candle-stick; candle-holder. **~পোকা** *n* small, greenish insects which are attracted by light.
শামা[2], **শামি** *n* iron ferrule/ covering (of a stic, etc).
শামি-কাবাব *n* kind of kabab, made of flat rounded cakes of mince-meat.
শামিক্স *n* slaughter-house.
শামিয়ানা [P] *nn* canopy; awning; pavilion.
শামিল [A] *adj* **1** included; annexed; connected: গ্রামটি পূর্বে এই জেলার ~ ছিল. ২ equivalent/ similar to; almost the same as; tantamount to: রাজদ্রোহের ~. **3** blended with; mingled.
শামী[1] = শামি (⇒ শামা[2])
শামী[2] *adj* Syrian.
শামুক *n* snail; shell; conch. **~খোলা, ~ভাঙ্গা** *nn* large species of bird. **~চুন** *n* shell-lime. **শামুকের খোলা** *n* snail-shell; conch-shell.
শায়ক *n* arrow; shaft; dart.
শায়িত *adj* **1** knocked down; felled; struck down. **2** laid down. **শায়িতা** *fem.*
শায়ী *adj* **1** lying down; reclining; resting; abiding. **2** fallen: সমর ~. **শায়িনী** *fem.*
শায়েস্তা [P] *adj* **1** subdued; chastened; broken; tamed; punished; rectified; corrected. **2** gentle; docile; polite; well-boed. **3** proper; suitable; worthy; honourable. **~ করা** *vt* **1** punish; chasten; subdue; tame; break; master; correct; rectify. **2** teach.
শারঙ্গ, শারঙ্গী *nn* a stringed musical instrument akin to the violin.
শারদ, শারদীয় *adjj* produced/ growing in autumn; autumnal. **শারদী, শারদীয়া** *fem.*
শারদা *n fem* **1** goddess Durga. **2** goddess Saraswati. **3** kind of vina or lute.
শারাব=শরাব
শারি[1], **শারিকা** *nn fem* kind of bird; myn (h); *shalik*=(শালিক).
শারি[2] *n* chessman; piece at chess; kind of die/ small cube used in games with dice.
শারীর *adj* bodily; corporeal; physical; anatomical; physiological. **~তত্ত্ব, ~বিধান, ~বৃত্ত, ~বৃত্তি** *nn* physiology. **~সংস্থান, ~স্থান** *nn* anatomy.
শারীরিক *adj* relating to the body; bodily; corporeal; contained in the body; material; physical.
শার্কর *adj* **1** made of sugar; sugary. **2** gravelly; stony.
শার্ঙ্গ *adj* made of horny; horny; corneous. ❑*n* bow (esp that of Vishnu). **~ধর, ~পাণি, শার্ঙ্গী** *nn* one armed with a bow; Vishnu.
শার্ট [E] *n* shirt. **ফুল ~** *n* shirt with long sleeves. **হাওয়াই ~** *n* Hawaii shirt; bush-shirt. **হাফ ~** *n* shirt with half sleeves.
শার্দূল *n* **1** panther; leopard; tiger. **2** (as a *suff*) best; excellent; preeminent. **শার্দূলী** *fem.* **~বিক্রীড়িত** *n* name of a Sanskrit metre. **~ললিত** *n* name of Sanskrit metre.
শার্শি, শার্সি = শাশি
শাল[1] *n* shawl.
শাল[2] *n* **1** sal tree; *Vatica robusta*; its valuable timber. **2** large pike for impalement of criminals: শালে চড়ানো. **3** name of large fish. **4** heart-rending affliction/ grief; agony. **5** deafening. **6** enclosure; fence; court. **7** rampart; wall. **8** workshop: কামার~. **~কোঁড়া** *n* young sal tree. **~নির্যাস** *n* resinous exudation of the sal tree. **~প্রাংশু** *adj* as high as a sal tree. **শালে দেওয়া/ চড়ানো** *vt* impale.
শালগম [P] *n* turnip.
শালগ্রাম, শালগ্রাম শিলা *nn* a sacred stone worshipped by the Vaishnavas and supposed to be pervaded by the presence of Vishnu (it is a black stone and chiefly found near village shalgram situated on the river Gandaki).
শালতি *n* dugout made of the trunk of a sal tree; canoe.
শালা[1] *n* **1** brother/ cousin brother of one's wife; brother-in-law. **2** (vulg) fellow; guy. **3** (used as a term of abuse) dirty fellow. **~জ, ~বউ** *nn fem* wife of a brother-in-law; sister-in-law.
শালা[2] *n* (used as a *suff*) house; mansion; building; hall; large room; appartment; shed; workshop; stable; establishment; store; repertory: অতিথি~, পান্থ~, পাঠ~, রন্ধন ~ গো~. কর্ম~.

শালি *n* a variety of autumnal paddy/ rice. ~ **জমি** *n* paddy field. ~ **ধান,** ~ **ধান্য** *nn* autumnal paddy.

শালিক *n* kind of small yellow-breasted singing bird (⇒ শারি[১]).

শালিকা *n* house; repository.

শালী[১] *n fem* **1** sister/ cousion sister of one's wife; sister-in-law. **2** (vulg) woman; slut; hussy.

-শালী[২] *adj* possessing; abounding in; full of; possessed of; amply provided/ furnished with; conversant with; distinguished for: ধন~, বল~, সৌভাগ্য~. ~**শালিনী** *fem.*

শালীন *adj* **1** bashful; modest; shy. **2** decorous; decent; polite; courteous. ~**তা** *n* **1** bashfulness; modesty; shyness. **2** decency; decorum; politeness; courteous. ~**তাবর্জিত** *adj* devoid of modesty; immodest; indecent; indecorous; impolite.

শালু *n* kind of red-coloured cotton fabric.

শালুক, শালূক *nn* **1** lotus; water-lily. **2** esculent root of different kinds of lotus.

শাল্মলি, শাল্মলী, শাল্মল *nn* **1** seemul or silk-cotton tree; *Bombax heptaphyllum.* **2** name of a mythological island.

শাশবিবি *n fem* mother-in-law.

শাশি [E] *nn* sash; window-pane.

শাশুড়ি *n fem* mother-in-law; aunt-in-law.

শাশ্বত, শাশ্বতিক *adjj* eternal; constant; perpetual; everlasting; immortal. **শাশ্বতী** *fem.*

শাসক *n* ruler; governor; chastiser; subduer; teacher; instructor; repressor; administer; controller. ~**বর্গ** *n* governing body. ~**মণ্ডলী** *n* governing body; administrative body; administration; government. ~ **সম্প্রদায়** *n* ruling class.

শাসন *n* **1** rule (over); government; dominion; administration; reign; management. **2** subjugation; subdual. **3** punishing; punishment; chastisement; correction. **4** order; enactment; command; edict; decree. **5** control; repression: ইন্দ্রিয়~. **6** jurisdiction. **7** instruction; teaching. ~ **করা** *vt* **1** govern; rule; dominate; administer; reign subdue. **2** chastise; punish; inflict punishment; correct; censure; chasten; discipline. **3** control; repress; restrain. **4** command; bid; order; direct; enjoin; decree. ~**কর্তা** *n* ⇒ শাসক. ~**কর্ত্রী** *fem.* ~**কৃত্যক** *n* administrative service. ~**তন্ত্র** *n* constitution (of a state); form of government. ~**তান্ত্রিক** *adj* relating to the form of government; constitutional; administrative. ~**পত্র** *n* edict; decree. ~**প্রণালী** *n* system of government. ~**যন্ত্র** *n* government machinery. ~**হর,** ~**হারক,** ~**হারী** *nn* messenger; envoy. **শাসনাধীন** *adj* governed (by); under jurisdiction (of); under rule (of); politically dependent (on); under domination (of). **শাসনে আনা** *vt* subdue; subjugate; bring under control; subject.

শাসনীয় *adj* to be chastised/ corrected; deserving punishment; punishable; to be controlled/ governed; governable; controllable.

শাসা *vt*=শাসন করা (⇒ শাসন). ~**নি** *n* threat; threatening; menace; growl; fulmination.

শাসানো *vi* threaten; menace; fulminate; scowl; utter threats; gnarl; snarl.

শাসি=শাশি

শাসিকা *n fem* (of শাসক)

শাসিত *adj* governed; ruled; subdued; administered; controlled; repressed; disciplined; punished; chastised; chastened; restrained; directed; instructed. **শাসিতা** *fem.*

শাসিতা *n* punisher; chastiser; ruler; governer; commander; teacher; instructor. **শাসিত্রী** *fem.*

শাস্তর *n* (colloq)=শাস্ত্র

শাস্তা *n* **1** শাসিতা. **1** Gautama Buddha.

শাস্তি *n* punishment; correction; sentence; severe affliction; ordeal. ~ **দেওয়া** *vt* punish; sentence; afflict. ~ **নেওয়া** *vi* accept punishment; kiss the rud. ~ **পাওয়া** *vi* be punished/ sentenced/ chastised/ chastened/ penalized/ castigated; get/meet with one's deserts. ~**বিধান** *n* infliction of punishment/ penalty; punishment; penalization; imposition of punishment. ~**বিধান করা** *vi* inflict/impose punishment; sentence; condemn. ~**ব্যবস্থা** *n* punitive measures; provision for punishment; penalty. ~**মূলক** *adj* punitive; penal; corrective; disciplinary.

শাস্ত্র *n* **1** order; command; precept; rule. **2** (esp Hindu) scripture. **3** teaching; instruction; direction; advice. **4** any instrument of teaching; manual/ compendium/ treatise of rules; book; religious/scientific treatise; sacred book/ composition of divine authority. ~**কার,** ~**কৃৎ** *n* author of a *shastra/* scripture/ treatise. ~**চর্চা** *n* study of scriptures. ~ **চর্চা করা** *vi* study scriptures. ~**জ্ঞ,** ~**জ্ঞানী** *adj* acquainted with/ versed in scriptures; learned. ❑*n* specialist. ~**জ্ঞান** *n* knowledge of the scriptures. ~ **তত্ত্ব** *n* truth (taught) in the scriptures. ~**তত্ত্ব** *adj* knowing thoroughly a scripture; understanding the truth of a scripture. ~**তঃ** *adv* according to the scriptures/ prescribed rules. ~**দর্শী** =~জ্ঞ. ~**নিন্দা** *n* reviling/ denying/ denunciation of the authority of the scriptures. ~**নিষিদ্ধ** *adj* forbidden by scriptures; unscriptural. ~**পারদর্শী,** ~**প্রবীণ** *adj* thoroughly versed in the scriptures. ~**প্রসঙ্গ** *n* subject of the scriptures. ~**বচন** *n* gospel truth; scriptural teaching. ~**বর্জিত** *adj* free from all rule/ law. ~**বহির্ভূত** *n* not contained in the scriptures; unscriptural. ~**বিদ,**

~বিৎ *adj*=~জ্ঞ. ~বিধান *n* precept of the scriptures. ~বিধানোক্ত *adj* prescribed by sacred precept. ~বিধি *n* holy rite; scriptural prescription/ injunction; sacred ritual. ~বিপ্রতিষিদ্ধ *adj* forbidden by/contrary to the scripture. ~বিপ্রতিষেধ *n* opposition to the scriptures; any act contrary to sacred precept. ~বিমুখ *adj* disinclined to learning; averse from study. ~বিরুদ্ধ *adj* opposed/ contrary to the scriptures; unscriptural. ~বিরোধ *n* opposition to sacred precept; incompatibility of different works. ~বিহিত *adj* 1 enjoined/ prescribed by the scriptures. 2 conform to the scriptures. ~বুদ্ধি *n* learning (derived) from the scriptures. ~ব্যাখ্যা *n* exposition/ explanation of the scriptures. ~ব্যুৎপত্তি *n* perfect conversancy/ knowledge of the scriptures. ~মতি *adj* learned in the scriptures; having a well-informed mind. ~মর্ম *n* secret/ purport of the scriptures. ~সঙ্গত, ~সম্মত *adjj*=~বিহিত. ~সিদ্ধ *adj* established by the scriptures; lawful. শাস্ত্রাচরণ *n* observance of sacred precepts; study of the scriptures. শাস্ত্রাতিক্রম *n* transgressing the scriptures; violation of sacred precepts. শাস্ত্রানুমত, শাস্ত্রানুমোদিত *adjj*=~বিহিত. শাস্ত্রানুযায়ী *adj* conform to the scriptures; scriptural. ❑*adv* in accordance with conformity to the scriptures or sacred precepts. শাস্ত্রানুশীলন =~চর্চা. শাস্ত্রানুষ্ঠান *n* observance of the scriptures. শাস্ত্রানুসার *n* conformity to the scriptures. শাস্ত্রানুসারে *adv*=শাস্ত্রানুযায়ী. শাস্ত্রাভিজ্ঞ *adj* versed in the scriptures. শাস্ত্রার্থ *n* object/ purport of a book; precept of the scriptures; significance/ meaning of the scriptures. শাস্ত্রালাপ *n* discussion about scriptural questions. শাস্ত্রালাপ করা *vi* discuss/ talk about the scriptures; discuss any technical subject. শাস্ত্রালোচনা *n* discussion about/ study of the scriptures. শাস্ত্রালোচনা করা *vi* discuss/ study the scriptures; discuss any technical subject.

শাস্ত্রী *adj* versed in the scriptures; learned ❑*n* teacher of sacred books/ science; learned man; a title given to man versed in the scriptures.

শাস্ত্রীয় *adj* taught in/ agreeable to/ belonging to the scriptures; conformable to sacred precepts; legal. ~ বচন *n* scriptural saying; sacred precept; gospel truth.

শাস্ত্রোক্ত *adj* declared/ enjoined by the scriptures; sanctioned by/ mentioned in the scriptures.

শাস্য=শাসনীয়

শাহ [P] *n* king; prince; monarch; king at chess; a title assumed by Muslim holy men. ~জাদা *n* prince. ~জাদি *n fem* princess. ~নজর = শানজর (⇒ শা). ~রগ *n* jugular vein. শাহানশাহ *n* king of kings; emperor.

শাহাদাত [A] *n* evidence; witness; testimony. 2 martyrdom. ~ অঙ্গুলি *n* forefinger.

শাহানা[1] *n* name of an Indian musical mode.

শাহানা[2] [P] *adj* royal; princely; regal. ❑*n* wedding dress.

শাহি [P] *adj* royal; kingly; imperial; regal. ~ তক্ত/তখ্ত *nn* royal seat; throne.

শাহিদ [A] *n* witness.

শাহিন [P] *n* royal white falcon.

শিউলি[1] *n* (colloq)=শেফালি

শিউলি[2] *n* a man whose profession it is to incise the head of the date-palm to obtain its juice.

শিওর *n* (colloq)=শিয়র

শিওরানো *vi* (colloq)=শিহরানো

শিং *n* horn. ~ দেখানো/ নাড়া/ বাঁকানো *vi* 1 aim one's horns threateningly. 2 (fig) become audaciously aggressive; intimidate; look threatening; shake the fist at; look daggers. ~ ভেঙে বাছুরের দলে ভেড়া throw off all self-esteem to associate with youngsters.

শিংশপা= শিশু[2]

শিক [P] *n* skewer; spit; any long and thin piece of metal; window-bar. ~কাবাব *n* shish kebab.

শিকড় *n* (bot) root. ~ গাড়া *vi* (lit, fig) take/ strike root; (fig) become established; be firmly established.

শিকড়ে *adj* having roots.

শিকদার [P] *n* 1 (hist) soldier using a long musket. 2 (hist) magistrate; justice of the peace. 3 (hist) an administrative title. 4 a particular family name.

শিকনি *n* mucus of the nose. ~ ঝাড়া *vi* blow one's nose. ~ ঝরা/পড়া *vi* (of the nose) run: তার ~ পড়ছে, His nose runs.

শিকম [P] *n* belly; measurement round the belly; girth.

শিকরা, শিকরে [A] *nn* kind of falcon.

শিকল, শিকলি (colloq) *nn* chain; fetters; shackles. ~ আঁটা/ পরানো, শিকলে বাঁধা *vt* chain; enchain; fasten with chain(s); fetter; put in chains/ fetters.

শিকলের আংটা/ কড়া *n* link.

শিকস্তি[1] [P] *n* running hand; kind of writing in Persian or Urdu.

শিকস্তি[2] [P] *adj* broken. ~ জমি *n* land devoured by a river, etc.

শিকা *n* reticulate bag made of strings/ wires roept hanging form the wall or the ceiling. শিকে ছেঁড়া *vi* (fig) gain by a stroke of luck; win by a fluke; fall to one's lot. শিকেয় ওঠা *vi* (fig) be shelved/ pigeonholed. শিকেয় তোলা *vi* (fig) shelve; pigeonhole; table.

শিকায়ত, শিকায়েত [A] *n* 1 complaint; lamentation; illness. 2 accusation.

শিকার *n* [P] **1** hunting; chase. **2** prey; game. **3** victim: ষড়যন্ত্রের ~. **4** plunder; booty. ~ **করা** *vi vt* hunt; prey upon; ensnare; catch; go out hunting. ~ **হওয়া** *vi* be hunted; become a victim of; fall a prey to. **শিকারে যাওয়া** *vi* go out hunting.

শিকারি, শিকারী *adj* (relating to) hunting. ☐*n* hunter; huntsman; fowler. ~ **কুকুর/ কুত্তা** *n* hunting dog; hound. ~ **পশু/ পাখি** *n* beast/ bird of prey. **পক্ষি** ~ *n* fowler.

শিকি=সিকি

শিকথ=সিকথ

শিক্য=শিকা

শিক্ষক *n* teacher; tutor; trainer; professor; preceptor; instructor. **শিক্ষিকা** *fem.* ~**তা** *n* teaching; tuition; instruction; pedagogy; tutorship. ~**তা করা** *vi* teach; work/ act as a teacher. ~**সমিতি** *n* teachers' association/ council.

শিক্ষণ *n* **1** act of learning; study; acquiring knowledge. **2** teaching; instruction (in); training. ~**কৃত্যক** *n* education service. ~**তত্ত্ব** *n* educational theory. ~**শিক্ষা** *n* teachers' training.

শিক্ষণীয় *adj* to be taught; to be learnt; instructive; edifying.

শিক্ষয়িতা *n* teacher; instructor. **শিক্ষায়িত্রী** *fem.*

শিক্ষা *n* **1** learning; study; knowledge; art; skill; education. **2** teaching; instruction. **3** lesson; precept; moral. **4** chastisement; punishment. **5** practice. **6** breeding. **7** the science which teaches proper articulation and pronunciation of Vedic texts. ~ **করা** *vt* learn; study; acquire knowledge; practise. ~ **দেওয়া** *vt* **1** teach; impart knowledge; instruct; educate; give lessons in; train; coach; school. **2** (iron) punish/ reprove severely; teach sb a lesson; take sb to task. ~ **নেওয়া** *vi* take lessons (from). ~ **পাওয়া** *vi* **1** receive education/ instruction/ training; learn; take courses; acquire knowledge/ learning. **2** (iron) receive reproof/ punishment; be taught a lesson. ~**অধিকর্তা** *n* Director of Public Instruction. ~**গুরু** *n* teacher; initiator; religious preceptor; mentor. ~ **গ্রহণ করা** *vi* receive education/ instruction/ training; take lessons from. ~**দাতা** =~গুরু. ~**দাত্রী** *fem.* ~ **দান করা** =~ দেওয়া. ~**দীক্ষা** *n* education and culture; breeding; schooling; grounding; learning. ~**ধিকার** *n* Education Directorate. ~**ধীন** *adj* studying under; being taught by; receiving education; under training; apprenticed. ~**নবিস** *n* apprentice; probationer; novice; learner; beginner. ~**নবিসি** *n* apprenticeship; probation; novitiate. ~**নবিসি করা** *vi* serve one's apprenticeship; be apprenticed to; be on probation; study under. ~**নীতি** *n* education policy. ~**নৈপুণ্য** *n* aptitude for learning; teaching ability. ~ **পরিষদ** *n* education board. ~**পীঠ** *n* seat of learning. ~**প্রণালী** *n* system/ method of teaching/ training/ education; pedagogy. ~**প্রদ** *adj* instructive; educative: illuminating; enlightening; edifying; didactic. ~**প্রাপ্ত** *adj* educated; trained; literate; cultivated. ~**বিভাগ** *n* Education Department. ~**বিস্তার** *n* spread of education. ~ **বিস্তার করা** *vi* spread/ propagate education; disseminate knowledge. ~ **মন্ত্রণালয়** *n* Ministry of Education. ~**র্থী** *adj* desirous of learning; seeking knowledge/ education/ instruction/ training. ☐*n* student; trainee; learner; scholar; pupil; freshman; apprentice; novice. ~**লাভ** *n* acquisition of knowledge; learning. ~ **লাভ করা** =~ পাওয়া. ~ **সংস্কার** *n* educational reforms. ~ **সচিব** *n* education secretary. ~ **সভা,** ~ **সমিতি** *nn* council of education. ~ **সম্বন্ধীয়** *adj* educational. **উচ্চ** ~ *n* higher education. **উচ্চ মাধ্যমিক** ~ higher secondary education. **কলেজি** ~ *n* college education. **কারিগরি** ~ *n* technical training. **প্রাথমিক** ~ *n* primary education. **লোক**~ *n* public instruction. **স্ত্রী**~ *n* female education.

শিক্ষিকা *n fem* ⇒শিক্ষক

শিক্ষিত *adj* educated; cultured; instructed; taught; trained; practised; skilled; schooled; literate. **শিক্ষিতা** *fem.* ~ **সমাজ,** ~ **সম্প্রদায়** *nn* educated class; intelligentsia.

শিখ *n* Sikh.

শিখণ্ড, শিখণ্ডক, শিখণ্ডিক *nn* **1** peacock's tail. **2** crest; plume; tuft. **3** tuft/ lock of hair left on the crown or sides of the head at tonsure. **4** peacock.

শিখণ্ডী *adj* wearing a tuft/ lock of hair; tufted; crested. ☐*n* **1** peacock. **2** peacock's tail. **3** cock. **4** arrow. **5** Vishnu. **6** son of Drupada (in the Mahabharata). **7** (fig) one from behind whose cover some misdeed is done. **শিখণ্ডিনী** *n fem* pea-hen.

শিখন= শিক্ষণ

শিখর *n* **1** peak point. **2** top/ summit (of a tree). **3** edge/ point of a sword. **4** pinnacle; turret; end; spire; apex; vertex; crest. **5** a ruby-like gem. **6** bud of the Arabian jasmine. **শিখরা** *fem.* ~**দশনা** *adj fem* having teeth resembling the buds of the Arabian jasmine. ~**বাসিনী** *adj fem* dwelling in a peak (of the Himalayas). ☐*n* goddess Durga.

শিখরী *adj* pointed; peaked; crested; tufted. ☐*n* **1** (peaked) mountain. **2** hill-post; stronghold. **3** tree. **4** (mech) pyramid. **শিখরিণী** *fem* **1** excellent/ eminent woman. **2** dish of curds and sugar with spices. **3** Arabian jasmine. **4** the plant *Jasminum sambac.*

শিখা[১] *n* **1** top; sharp end; point; spike; peak; summit; pinnacle; projection; end. **2** (pointed) flame; beam; ray of light. **3** tuft/ lock of hair on the crown of the head; crest; top-knot; plume. **4** branch which takes root. **5** point/ tip of the foot. **~ধর, ~ধারক, ~ধারী** *adj* having a sharp end/ point; having a topknot. ☐*n* peacock. **~বান** *adj* flaming; burning. **জারক ~** *n* oxidizing flame. **বিজারক ~** *n* reducing flames.

শিখা² *vt* learn; study; practise; undergo training. ☐*adj* that which has been learnt/ studied/ practised; mastered; acquired. **~নো** *vt* teach; educate; groom; instruct; train; tutor; coach. ☐*adj* that which has been taught; tutored; trained; schooled; advised; instructed. **~নো সাক্ষী** *n* tutored/ primed witness.

শিখি *n, adj* (in compounds)=শিখী. **~কণ্ঠ, ~গ্রীব** *nn* blue vitriol. **~ধবজ** *adj* fire-marked. ☐*n* **1** smoke. **2** Kartikeya. **~পুচ্ছ** *n* peacock's tail. **~বাহন** *n* Kartikeya.

শিখিনী *n fem* (of শিখী) pea-hen.

শিখী *adj* having a tuft/ lock of hair on the top of the head. ☐*n* **1** peacock. **2** fire. **3** cock. **4** mountain. **5** tree.

শিগগির (colloq)=শীঘ্র

শিঙ, শিঙ্গ=শিং. **শিঙাল, শিঙেল** *adjj* horned. **শিঙানো** *vi* **1** grow horns. **2** gore.

শিঙা, শিঙ্গা *n* horn; bugle; trumpet. **~ ফোঁকা** *vi* (sl) die; kick the bucket.

শিঙাড়া, শিঙ্গাড়া *nn* **1** kind of stuffed snack shaped like a water nut. **2** water nut.

শিঙি, শিঙ্গি *nn* species of fresh-water fish (kind of sheat-fish); *Saccobranches fossils.*

শিঙ্গেল *adj* horned.

শিঙ্ঘান *n* mucus of the nose.

শিঞ্জিল, শিঞ্জিতে¹ *n* tickling; sounding; tinkling of metallic ornament.

শিঞ্জিতে² *adj* tinkled; tinkling; jingling; rattling; sounding; sounded; resounded (with).

শিঞ্জিনী *n* **1** anklet. **2** bow-string. **3** tinkling rings worn round the toes/ feet. **4** (math) sine.

শিটা, শিটে (colloq) *nn* dregs; dross; sediment.

শিটি=সিটি

শিঠা=শিটা

শিত *adj* **1** sharpened; sharp; pointed; whetted. **2** slender; slim; thin.

শিতান=শিথান

শিতি *adj* **1** white. **2** black; dark-blue. **~কণ্ঠ** *adj* dark-necked; white necked. ☐*n* **1** Shiva. **2** peacock. **3** gallinule.

শিথলানো *vt* loosen; slacken; slip-(off).

শিথান *n* **1** place/ position at the head of a person lying. **2** pillow (for the head).

শিথিল *adj* **1** loose; flabby; baggy; flaccid: ~ অঙ্গ/ চর্ম. **2** weak; feeble; worn-out; languid; tired: ~ দেহ. **3** dishevelled; unfastened; untied: ~ কেশপাশ. **4** lose; not strict: ~শাসন. **5** slow; tardy; slowed down; relaxed; slackened; leisurely: ~ গতি. **6** slovenly; blowzy; careless; neglectful; poky; slipshod; dowdy: ~ বেশবাস. **~তা** *n* looseness; slackness; laxity; slowness; laziness; relaxation; inertia; carelessness; slovenliness; neglectfulness. **~ প্রযত্ন** *adj* careless; negligent; perfunctory unmindful of; lacking in carefulness/ earnestness in one's work; casual.

শিন্নি *n* (colloq)=শিরনি

শিব *n* **1** Shiva, the third god of the Hindu Triad. **2** good; weal; welfare. **3** happiness. **4** liberation; final emancipation. **5** sacred writings. ☐*adj* good; auspicious; propitious; gracious; favourable; benign; kind; benevolent; friendly. **~কর, ~ঙ্কর** *adj* causing happiness/ prosperity; auspicious; propitious. **~ কীর্তন** *n* act of praising/ celebrating Shiva. **~ চতুর্দশী** *n* the fourteenth day of the dark half of the month of Magh (kept as a festival in honour of Shiva). **~ জ্ঞান** *n* knowledge of what is fortunate/ auspicious moment. **~ত্ব** *n* **1** nature of Shiva; state/ condition (of a person absorbed in) Shiva. **2** immortality. **~ত্ব প্রাপ্তি** *n* death. **~নেত্র** *n* upturned eyes of Shiva; eyes become upturned on the eve one's death. ☐*adj* having upturned eyes (on the eve one's death). **~পুরী** *n* the city of Benaras. **~ পূজা** *n* worship/ adoration of Shiva. **~বাহন** *n* bull. **~রাত্রি** *n* night of. ~ চতুর্দশী (a popular Hindu fast and festival in honour of Shiva). **~রাত্রির সলতে** *n (fig)* the only son; the sole surviving descendant. **~লিঙ্গ** *n* Shiva's genital organ or Shiva worshipper in the form of a phallus. **~লোক** *n* Shiva's heaven (on Kailas). **সাযুজ্য**=~ত্ব. **শিবালয়** *n* temple of Shiva. ~ গড়তে বাঁদর গড়া (fig) do evil in one's attempt to do sth good.

শিবা *n* **1** goddess Durga. **2** jackal; vixen.

শিবানী *n fem* wife of Shiva (=Durga).

শিবি *n* **1** beast of prey. **2** birch tree.

শিবিকা *n* palanquin; litter; palkee; sedan; sedan-chair. **~রোহী** *adj* going in a palanquin/sedan. **~রোহিণী** *fem.*

শিবির *n* **1** entrenchment for the protection of an army; camp; encampment. **2** royal camp/residence. tent in a royal camp; any tent. **~ সন্নিবেশ** *n* encampment **~ স্থাপন করা** *n* pitch a tent/ tents; encamp.

শিবেতর *adj* malignant; inauspicious.

শিম *n* legume; bean; kidney bean.

শিমুল *n* silk-cotton tree. **~ তুলা** *n* silk-cotton; kapok; cotton wool. **~ ফুল** *n* (fig) very handsome but worthless person.

শিম্ব, শিম্বা, শিম্বি, শিম্বিকা, শিম্বী *nn* **1**=শিম. **2** pod.

শিয়র *n* **1** place/ position at the head of a person lying. **2** (fig) imminence: শিয়রে শমন

শিয়া [A] *n* a follower of Hazrat Ali; Shiah. ~ মজহাব *n* Shiah sect.
শিয়াকুল *n* kind of wild thorny plant; *Zigypas aenoplia*.
শিয়ান, শিয়ানা = সেয়ানা
শিয়াল *n* jackal; fox. শিয়ালী *fem*. ~ কাঁটা, শিয়াকাঁটা *n* a wild thorny plant; *Argemone mexicana*. ~ ফাঁকি *n* hoodwinking. শিয়ালের যুক্তি *n* mischievous counsel/ plan. সব শিয়ালের এক রা (fig) people of the same sort will raise the same cry.
শির[1] *n* 1 head. 2 cranium. 3 upper end/ highest part of anything; top; peak; summit; pinnacle; acme. 4 forepart/ van (of an army). 5 chief; foremost; first. ~জ *n* hair of the head. ~দাঁড়া *n* backbone; spinal column. ~শ্ছেদ(ন) *n* cutting off the head; decapitation; beheading ~শ্ছেদ(ন) করা *n* cut off the head; decapitate behead. ~স্ক, ~স্ত্র, ~ স্ত্রাণ *nn* cap; helmet; turban; head-dress; hat. শিরে সংক্রান্তি *n* (fig) imminent danger.
শির[2] *n*=শিরা
শিরঃ=শির[1]. ~কপালী *n* religious mendicant who carries about a human skull. ~কম্প(ন) *n* act of shaking the head; nod; vertigo; dizziness. ~কোণ *n* vertical angle. ~পীড়া *n* headache. ~শূল *n* violent headache.
শিরক=শেরেক
শিরনাম, শিরোনাম [P] *n* title; address; superscription; heading; caption.
শিরনি, শিরনী [P] *n* sweetmeat; sweet dish prepared by boiling rice in milk with sugar etc.
শিরপা [P]*n* 1 turban of honour awarded by a prince, etc. 2 reward; prize.
শিরপেচ [P]*n* 1 bejewelled/ embroidered turban. 2 ornament worn in the turban.
শিরশির *n* (onom) expressing: a tingling/ thrilling/ uncanny sensation; tingle; thrill; tickling; quiver. ~ করা *vi* tickle; tingle; quiver.
শিরশ্ছেদ, শিরস্ক, শিরস্ত্র, শিরস্ত্রাণ ⇒ শির[1]
শিরা[1] *n* 1 vein; artery; tendon; nerve; any tubular vessel of the body. 2 (bot) costa. ~জাল *n* network of vessels/ veins. ~বিন্যাস *n* venation. ~ল *adj* 1 having numerous/ large veins; veined; venose. 2 (bot) costate. ❑*n* name of particular fruit (*Averrhoa carambola*).
শিরা[2] [P]*n* syrup.
শিরাজ [A] *n* lamp; candle. শিরাজাম মুনিরা *n* brilliant lamp (a title of the prophet Muhammed).
শিরাজি, শিরাজী [P] *adj* relating to/ produced in Shiraj (in Iran). ❑*n* wine (produced in Shiraj).
শিরানা *n*=শিখান
শিরালি *n* horn-blowing religious mendicant.
শিরিন [P] *adj* sweet; pleasant; gentle.
শিরিশ, শিরিস [P] *nn* glue. ~ কাগজ *n* sand paper; glass paper.
শিরীষ *n* rain-tree; *Acacia sirissa*.
শিরো *n* (in compounds)=শির[1]. ~গৃহ *n* top-room; room on the top of a house. ~দেশ *n* (region of the) head; crown; top. ~ধার্য *n* to be borne on the head; to be greatly honoured; to be obeyed/ complied with; to be accepted with humility/ reverence. ~ধার্য করা *vt* bear on one's head; obey/ accept with humility/ reverence or submissively. ~ধি *n* neck. ~বিরেচন *n* snuff; errhines. ~বেষ্ট(ন) *n* turban. ~ভূষণ *n* 1 head ornament. 2 (fig) object of glory/ reverence; a reverend/ excellent person. ~মণি *n* 1 jewel worn on the head. 2 title of honour conferred on Sanskrit scholars. 3 the chief (of); reverend person. ~মালী *adj* garlanded with skulls. ❑*n* Shiva. ~রত্ন= ~মণি. ~রুহ *n* hair of the head. ~স্থি *n* skull.
শিরোনাম, শিরোনামা =শিরনাম
শিরোপা=শিরপা
শির্নি=শিরনি
শিল *n* 1 stone slab/ flat mortar for grindings pieces; flat stone for sharpening tools. 2 hail; hailstone. 3 gleaning; gathering stalks/ ears of corn. ~ পড়া *vi* hail.
শিলওয়ার = সালওয়ার
শিলা *n* 1 stone; rock; crag. 2 hailstone; hail. 3 lower mill-stone. 4 lower timber of a door. 5 top of the pillar supporting a house. 6 red arsenic. ~কুট্টক *n* stone-cutter's chisel/ hatchet. ~খণ্ড *n* stone; pebble. ~গৃহ *n* grotto. ~জতু *n* bitumen; asphalt; benzoin. ~তল *n* surface of a rock; floor paved with stone. ~ত্মজ *n* iron. ~ধাতু *n* chalk; yellow ochre; red chalk. ~পট্ট *n* stone slab (for sitting or grinding. ~পুত্র *n* grindstone. ~ফলক =~পট্ট. ~বর্ষণ, ~বৃষ্টি *nn* hail; hailstorm; shower of stones. ~বর্ষী *adj* raining stones. ~ময় *adj* made of stone; stony; rocky. ~মূর্তি *n* stone statue. ~রস *n* benzoin; incense. ~লিপি *n* stone inscription.
শিলীন্ধ্র *n* 1 plantain tree. 2 mushroom. 3 flower of the plantain tree.
শিলীন্ধ্রী *n* 1 kind of bird. 2 earth. 3 kind of jasmine.
শিলীপদ=শ্লীপদ
শিলীভূত *adj* fossilized; turned to stone; petrified.
শিলীমুখ *n* 1 arrow. 2 bee.
শিল্প *n* 1 art; fine art; artistry. 2 work of art. 3 craft; handicraft. 4 industry. 5 arts and crafts. ~-অধিকর্তা *n* Director of Industries. ~কর্ম *n* work of art; artistry; handicraft. ~কলা *n* fine arts. ~কলাবিদ *adj* versed in fine arts. ~কার *n* artist; artisan; handicraft man; mechanic; painter. ~কুশল *adj* skilled in handicraft/ artistic work;

artistic. ~কুশলা *fem.* ~কুশলতা, ~কৌশল *nn* artistic skill; artistry; technical skill; method/technique of a work of art. ~গৃহ *n* workshop; workroom; manufactory; atelier; studio. ~জাত *adj* industrial; manufactured. ~জীবী *adj* living by art, etc. ❑*n* artisan; craftsman; mechanic; artist. ~জীবিনী *fem.* ~প্রদর্শনী *n* art/ industrial exhibition. ~বিদ্যা *n* industrial/ technical art; science of arts/ mechanics; craft; handicraft; fine art. ~বিদ্যালয় *n* industrial/ technical school; art school; school of fine arts. ~বিধি *n* rule of art; industrial act. ~ মন্ত্রণালয় *n* ministry of industry. ~যন্ত্র *n* machine. ~যান্ত্রিক *n* industrial engineer. ~যোজন *n* industrialization. ~যোজিত *adj* industrialized. ~রসায়নী *n* industrial chemist. ~শালা *n* 1=~গৃহ. 2 museum of arts and crafts. ~শাস্ত্র =~বিদ্যা. শিল্পায়ন *n* industrialization. শিল্পায়িত *adj* industrialized. শিল্পালয় *n* art institute. বাস্তু ~, স্থাপত্য ~ *nn* architecture. শ্রম~ *n* industry. সুকুমার/ সূক্ষ্ম ~ *n* fine art.

শিল্পিক *adj* artistic. ❑*n*=শিল্পকার (⇒ শিল্প)

শিল্পী *n*=শিল্পকার (⇒ শিল্প). ~য় *adj* industrial.

শিল্পোন্নত *adj* industrialized.

শিল্পোন্নতি *n* industrial development.

শিশ, শিস *n* (onom) whistle; hum; chirp. ~ দেওয়া *vi* whistle; hum, chirp. ~ধ্বনি *n* (ling) sibilant.

শিশমহল [P] *n* glass house; house adorned with glass; apartment fitted with mirrors.

শিশা [P] *nn* 1 glass. 2 mirror; looking glass. 3 bottle. 4 glass pane.

শিশি *n* [P] small bottle; phial made of glass.

শিশির *n* 1 dew; hoarfrost. 2 cool/ dewy season; winter. ~কণা *n* dew drop. ~কাল *n* cool season. ~ধৌত, ~সিক্ত *adjj* washed/ wet with dew; dewy. ~পাত *n* dewfall. ~বিন্দু *n* dew drop. ~স্নাত *adj* bathed in dew; dewy; wet with dew. শিশিরাঙ্ক *n* (phys) dew point.

শিশু[1] *n* child; infant; young of any animal; boy under eight years of age; lad under sixteen. ❑*adj* young; infantile. ক *n* 1 child; young. 2 porpoise; *Dolphinus gangeticus*. ~ কন্যা *n fem* infant daughter. ~কাল *n* (time of) infancy; childhood. ~ক্রন্দন *n* weeping/crying of a child/ infant. ~ক্রীড়া *n* child's play. ~তা, ~ত্ব *nn* childhood; infancy; childishness. ~পাঠ *n* juvenile reader. ~পাঠ্য *adj* intended/ fit for juvenile readers; juvenile. ~পাল 1 *n* name of the king of Cedis inhabiting a country in central India. ~পালক *n* protector of children. ~পুত্র *n* infant son. ~প্রকৃতি, ~স্বভাব *nn* childlike nature; simplicity. ❑*adj* childlike; simple as a child. ~ভাব *n* state of childhood; infancy. ~মার *n* 1 Gangetic porpoise/ dolphin. 2 (astron) Ursa Minor. ~ শশী *n* crescent. ~শিক্ষা *n* child/ juvenile education. ~সন্তান *n* infant child. ~ সাহিত্য *n* children's/ juvenile literature. ~ সাহিত্যিক *n* author of juvenile literature. ~সুলভ *adj* childlike; simple; innocent; natural for a child. ~ হত্যা *n* infanticide. ~হত্যাকারী *n* infanticide. ~ হৃদয় *adj* childlike; innocent; naive; ingenuous.

শিশু[2] *n* the tree *Dalbergia sissoo*.

শিশ্ন[3] *n* male genital organ; penis. শিশ্নোদরপরায়ণ *adj* addicted to lust and gluttony.

শিষ *n* 1 ear of corn; stalk; stem; flower-spike. 2 flame. 3 head; skull.

শিষ্ট *adj* 1 well-behaved; well-bred mannerly; gentle; polite; courteous; good natured; civil; disciplined. 2 educated; cultured; learned. 3 elegant; chaste. 4 righteous; left; remaining; residual. শিষ্টা *fem.* ~তা *n* 1 politeness; civility; gentleness; courtesy; courteousness; decorum; (good) manners. 2 refinement; culture; learning; elegance. 3 righteousness. ~ পর্বত *n* (geog) relict mountain. ~ প্রয়োগ *n* practice of the learned; idiomatic usage. ~ বায়ু *n* residual air. ~ ব্যবহার = শিষ্টাচার. ~ সম্ভাষণ *n* polite/ courteous address/ greeting. ~ সাহিত্য *n* polite literature. শিষ্টাচার, শিষ্টাচরণ *nn* 1 good manners; proper behaviour; courtesy; polite behaviour; etiquette; civility. 2 practice/ conduct of the learned or virtuous. 3 formality. শিষ্টাচারবিরুদ্ধ *adj* opposed/ contrary to good manners; opposed to the practice of the virtuous; unmannerly; impolite discourteous; unrefined; ill-behaved. শিষ্টাচারবিরুদ্ধতা *n* discourtesy; discourteousness; bad/ poor manners; incivility. শিষ্টাচারসম্মত *adj* courteous; mannerly; urbane, civilized; well-mannered; gracious. শিষ্টাচারী *adj* observant of the rules of etiquette; well-behaved; courteous; civil; amiable; gentlemanly; civilized.

শিষ্টি *n* command; order; direction; correction.

শিষ্য *n* disciple; pupil; scholar; (devoted) follower. শিষ্যা *fem.* ~তা, ~ত্ব *nn* discipleship; pupilage.

শিস ⇒ শিশ

শিস্তি [P] *n* thimble.

শিহরন *n* thrill; shudder; shiver; excitement; titillation; horripilation.

শিহরা, শিহরানো *vi* (feel a) thrill; shudder; shiver; be excited; feel thrills.

শিহরিত *adj* thrilled; cited; shivering; shuddering; titillated; trembling; quivering.

শীকর *n* fine/ drizzling rain; drizzle; spray; mist. ~কণা *n* drop of rain/ water. ~বর্ষী *adj* raining in fine drops; drizzling.

শীগগির (colloq)=শীঘ্র

শীঘ্র *adj* quick; swift; rapid; speedy; prompt. ❑*adv* quickly swiftly; rapidly; promptly; speedily. ~কারী *adj* acting/ operating speedily; prompt (in action). ~গতি, ~গামী *adj* going/ moving/ running quickly; nimble-footed; fast; swift; fast-moving. ~চেতন *adj* having quick intellect; very sagacious. ~তা *n* swiftness; speed; rapidity; promptness. ~বুদ্ধি *adj* quick-witted. ~বেধী *adj* shooting quickly. ❑*n* good archer. শীঘ্রায়মান=~গতি.

শীত *n* **1** cold season; winter. **2** cold; coldness; chill; cold weather; chilliness. ❑*adj* cold; cool; chilly; frigid; apathetic. ~ করা/ ধরা/লাগা *vi* feel cold; shiver with cold. ~ কাটানো *vi* winter. ~ কেটেছে winter is at end; be relieved of the sensation of cold. ~ পড়েছে winter has set in; it is cold (today). ~ক *n* refrigerator. ~কর *adj* causing coolness. ❑*n* the moon. ~কাঁটা *n* goose-flesh caused by (sudden) sensation of cold. ~কাতর, ~কাতুরে *adj* over-sensitive to cold. ~কাতরতা *n* over-sensitiveness to cold. ~কাল *n* cold season; winter (season); cold weather. ~কালীন *adj* belonging to/ produced in the cold season; winter; wintry. ~কিরণ *n* the moon. ~ন *n* refrigeration. ~পিত্ত *n* nettle rash. ~প্রধান দেশ *n* cold country. ~বস্ত্র *n* warm clothes; winter garment; woolen clothes. ~ভীরু *adj* afraid of cold. ~ময়ূখ, ~রশ্মি *nn* the moon. শীতাংশু *n* 'cold-rayed' the moon. শীতাকুল *adj* benumbed with cold; frozen. শীতাগম *n* advent of cold/ winter. শীতাতপ *n* cold and heat; winter and summer. শীতাতপনিয়ন্ত্রণ *n* air-conditioning. শীতাতপনিয়ন্ত্রিত *adj* air-conditioned. শীতাতপসহিষ্ণু *adj* resistant to cold and heat. শীতাদ্রি *n* snowy mountains; the Himalayas. শীতাধিক্য *n* excess of cold. শীতার্ত *adj* suffering from/ stricken with cold; shivering with cold. শীতার্দ্র *adj* cold and humid. শীতালু=শীতার্ত. শীতে কাঁপা *vi* shiver with cold.

শীতল[১] *adj* **1** cold; cool; cooling; chilly; frosty; shivering. **2** soothing; free from passion: ~ কথা. **3** soothed; warmed up: প্রাণ ~. ~ করা *vt* cool; make cold; assuage; soothe. ~তা, ~ত্ব *nn* coldness; cool; insensitivity; apathy; indifference. ~ পাটি *n* kind of mat very cool and soothing to lie on. ~স্তম্ভ *n* hibernation. ~স্পর্শ *adj* cool to the touch. ❑*n* (fig) soothing touch.

শীতল[২] *n* a Hindu religious rite observed in the evening: ~ দেওয়া.

শীতলা *n fem* **1** small-pox. **2** the goddess inflicting small-pox.

শীতলীকরণ *n* cooling; making cool.

শীতলীভবন *n* cooling; getting cool.

শীতুড়ি *n* winter clothes.

শীতোষ্ণ *adj* cold and hot; tepid. ~ বলয় *n* (geog) temperate zone.

শীত্যভাব *n* cold state; becoming cool; coldness.

শীৎকার, শীৎকৃতি *nn* a sound made by drawing in the breath (to express any sudden thrill of pleasure or pain and especially pleasurable sensations during sexual enjoyment).

শীধু *n* **1** spirituous liquor distilled from molasses; rum (or any similar spirit). **2** (fig) nectar. ~গন্ধ *n adj* (having the) smell of rum/ spirituous liquor. ~প, ~ পায়ী *adjj* drinking spirits. ❑*nn* drunkard. ~পান *n* drinking of spirits.

শীর্ণ *adj* **1** lean; emaciated; thin; slender. **2** withered; faded; shrivelled; shrunk. শীর্ণা *fem.* ~ কায় *adj* lean-bodied; scraggy; emaciated; leggy; lanky; slight. ~তা, ত্ব *nn* thinness; leanness; emaciation.

শীর্ষ *n* **1** head; skull. **2** tip; top; apex; summit; pinnacle. **3** fore-part; front. **4** (math) vertex. **5** the highest/ first/ most distinguished place. ~ক *adj* having a particular title; styled; entitled; headed. ~ কোণ *n* (geom) vertical angle. ~ বেচ্ছদ(ন) *n* decapitation. ~স্থ *adj* being/ situated on the head/ top. ~স্থান *n*=~. ~স্থান অধিকার করা *vi, vt* stand first; top the list. ~স্থানীয় *adj* highest; foremost; topmost; first; chief; most distinguished; top-ranking. ~স্থানীয় ব্যক্তিরা *n pl* top people.

শীল[১] *n* **1** nature; disposition; character; tendency; natural disposition. **2** habit; custom; usage; natural or acquired way of living/ acting; practice; conduct; behabiour. **3** good disposition/ character; moral conduct; piety; integrity; virtue; morality. **4** a particular Hindu family name. ❑*adj* (used as a *sufi*) habituated/ accustomed/ disposed/ addicted to; practising; natured: গুণ~, পুণ্য~, দান~. শীলা *fem.* ~তা *n* disposition; inclination; customary practice; morality; virtuousness. ~ধর্ম *n* morality. ~ পত্র *n* character certificate. ~ পরিচয় *n* character-roll. ~বাণ্ *adj* possessed of a good disposition/ character; well-conducted; moral. ~বতী *adj.* ~ব্রত *adj* possessed of virtue/ good conduct. ❑*n* (Buddhist) ceremonial practices.

শীল[২] [E] *n* (zool) seal.

শীলন *n* repeated practice; constant study.

শীলিত *adj* practised; exercised; refined.

শীশা ⇒ শিশা. ~গর *n* glass maker. ~গরি *n* glass making.

শীষ= শিষ

শু [E] *n* shoe.

শুকা *vi, vt* smell. ❑*adj* smelled. ~নো *vt* cause to smell.

শুঁটকা, শুটকো (colloq) *adj* dry; dried; shrivelled; thin; lean; withered.

শুঁটকি, শুঁটকী *adjj* **1** dried: ~ মাছ **2** emaciated and shrivelled. ❑*n* dried fish.

শুঁটি *nn* pod; legume.

শুঁঠ *n* dried ginger.

শুঁড় *n* **1** proboscis. **2** trunk (of the elephant, boar, etc). **3** shout (of the tortoise). **4** antenna/ feeler (of an insect). **5** (facet) mouth including the neck (of human beings). **~ বাড়ানো** *n* stretch out ones proboscis/ trunk/ snout/ antenna; crane one's neck.

শুঁড়ি১ *adj* very narrow: ~ পথ

শুঁড়ি২ *nn* distiller and vendor of spirituous liquors (considered as a mixed caste); wine-seller; taverner. **~খানা, ~র দোকান** *nn* tavern; liquor-shop; wine-shop; public house. **~র সাক্ষী মাতাল** one offender bears out another.

শুঁয়া, শুঁয়ো (colloq) *n* **1** own. **2** antenna; feeler. **~ পোকা** *n* caterpillar; chrysalis.

শুক *n* **1** parrot. **2** name of a son of Vyasa. **~নাস** *adj* having a nose like a parrot's beak.

শুকতারা *n* the planet Venus.

শুকনা, শুকনো (colloq) *adj*=শুষ্ক. **~ কথায় চিঁড়ে ভেজে না** (fig) mere words cannot accomplish a thing; mere words cannot butter bread. **~ বরফ** *n* dry ice.

শুকর=শোকর

শুকা (colloq)=শুখা

শুকানো *vi,vt* **1** dry (up) (out): খালবিল শুকিয়ে গেছে, চুল/ কাপড় ~. **2** emaciate; be emaciated: রোগে ~. **3** wither; be withered: ফুল ~. **4** heal; be healed: ঘা ~.

শুক্কুর *n* (colloq)=শুক্র

শুক্ত *n* sour liquor or gruel.

শুক্তা, শুক্তো *nn* dish of bitter vegetables; bitter curry.

শুক্তি, শুক্তিকা *n* **1** oyster; pearl-oyster; oyster; oyster shell. **2** conch-shell. **3** portion of a skull. **~জ, ~বীজ** *nn* pearl.

শুক্র *n* **1** the planet Venus or its regent. **2** semen; virile; seed of animals; sperm. **3** name of the preceptors of the Daityas. **~কর** *adj* producing semen. **~ জ, ~ভূ** *adjj* produced from (one's own) semen. ❑*n* one's own son. **~তারল্য** *n* spermatorrhoea; involuntary seminal discharge. **~বার, ~বাসর** *n* Friday. **শুক্রাচার্য** *n* sage Shukra=~ (3). **শুক্রাণু** *n* spermatozoid. **শুক্রাশয়** *n* testes.

শুক্ল *adj* **1** white; whitish. **2** pure; spotless; clean; unsullied. **3** grey; hoary. **4** light; clear; fair. ❑*n* **1** white (the colour). **2** bright half of a lunar month. **3** butter. **শুক্লা** *fem* the goddess Saraswati. **~কর্মা** *adj* pure in action/ conduct. **~ কেশ** *adj* white -haired. **~তা, ~ত্ব** *nn* whiteness. **শুক্লাতিথি** *n* any day of the ~ পক্ষ. **~ পক্ষ** *n* the fortnight during which the moon is increasingly visible till it attains fullness. **~ পক্ষীয়** *adj* relating to the light half of the month. **~ মণ্ডল** *n* white circle/ globe; region of cornea. **শুক্লাম্বর** *n, adj* (having a) white garment; clad in white. **শুক্লাম্বরা** *fem.*

শুক্লিমা *n* whiteness; white colour.

শুখতা, শুখতি *nn* weight lost in dryness.

শুখা *adj* **1** dry; sapless. **2** rude; harsh; rough: ~ কথা. **3** exclusive of bed and board: ~ মাইনের কাজ. ❑*n* **1** drought: হাজা~. **2** rickets. **3** tobacco mixed lime used as quid; roasted tobacco used in bidis (বিড়ি).

শুঙ্খ, শুঙ্খা *nn* =শুঁয়া

শুচি *adj* **1** pure; clean; clear. **2** holy; immaculate; unsullied; undefiled; innocent; honest; virtuous. **3** white; brilliantly white. **4** bight; gleaming; radiant. ❑*n* **1** fire. **2** the sun. **3** purity; virtue; purification; honesty. **~তা, ত্ব** *nn* purity; clearness; uprightness; honesty; virtue; cleanliness; sanctity; holiness; immaculateness; whiteness. **~দ্রুম** *n* holy tree; sacred fig-tree. **~বাই, ~বায়ু** *nn* hysterical mania for cleanliness and sanctity. **~বায়ুগ্রস্ত** *adj* suffering from a hysterical mania for cleanliness. **~ব্রত** *adj* virtuous in conduct; (of gods) whose observances are pure/ holy. **~শুভ্র** *adj* bright with sanctity/ virtuousness. **~স্মিত** *adj* smiling brightly; having a pure smile; accompanied by a bright/ pure smile. **~স্মিতা** *fem.*

শুজনি, শুজনী *nn* diapered bedcover.

শুণ্ঠি, শুণ্ঠী *nn* dried ginger.

শুণ্ড=শুঁড়. **~ধর** *n* elephant.

শুণ্ডিকা *n* uvula; epiglottis.

শুণ্ডী *n* **1** distiller; seller of spirituous liquors. **2** elephant.

শুদ্ধ *adj* **1** faultless; free from error; flawless; immaculate; correct; blameless; accurate; right; exact; according to rule. **2** pure; true; clean; purified; holy; sanctified; rectified; consecrated; sacred. **3** genuine; simple; mere; only; unmodified. **4** complete; entire: দেশ~ লোক. **5** unqualified; unmitigated. **6** veritable; unequalled. **7** bright; white. clear. ❑*adv* only; merely. **~ শুদ্ধা** *fem.* **~ করা** *vt* purify; clean; correct; amend; rectify; sanctify; consecrate; cleanse; clear; remove impurity or anything noxious. **~চিত্ত** *adj* pure-minded; pure at heart; pure-hearted; virtuous/ chaste in mind. **~চিত্ততা** *n* pure-mindedness; purity of mind. **~ চৈতন্য** *n* pure intelligence. **~তা** *n* purity; correctness; faultlessness; flawlessness; chastity; genuineness; holiness; sacredness. **~ধী, ~বুদ্ধি** *adjj*= ~চিত্ত. **~ বর্ণালি** *n* (phys) pure spectrum. **~ ভাব** *n* purity of mind. **~মতি**=~চিত্ত. **~বেশ** *adj* dressed in clean garments. ~লেখ *n* fair copy. ~ সংখ্যা *n* abstract number. ~সত্ত্ব *adj* having a pure character; innocent; guileless; pure-souled. **শুদ্ধাচার** *adj* practising virtue/ cleanliness; pure in practices and observances; virtuous; righteous. ☐*n* practice of virtue; virtuousness; cleanliness; rectitude; correct/ faultless conduct. **শুদ্ধাচারিতা** *n*=শুদ্ধাচার. **শুদ্ধাচারী** *adj*=শুদ্ধাচার. **শুদ্ধাচারিণী** *fem.* **শুদ্ধাত্মা** *adj* pure-minded. **শুদ্ধানন্দ** *n* pure joy. **শুদ্ধান্ত** *n* private/ women's apartments; harem. **শুদ্ধান্তবাসিনী** *n fem* keeping constantly to the women's apartments/ harem. **শুদ্ধাভা** *n* pure light. **শুদ্ধাশুদ্ধ** *n pl* right and wrong; sacred and profane; correct and incorrect; pure and impure.

শুদ্ধি *n* **1** cleansing; purification; rectification; purgation. **2** purity; correctness; correction; making true; amendment; accuracy; genuineness; truth. **3** clearness; certainty. **4** holiness; freedom from defilement; sanctification; innocence. **5** purificatory rite. ~কর *adj* causing purity; purifying; correcting. ~তি *n* list of errors; errata; corrigenda.

শুধরানো *vi, vt* rectify; correct; mend one's ways; remedy; set right/ straight; be rectified/ corrected/ set right/ mended.

শুধা[১] *adj* (dial)=শুধু

শুধা[২] *vt* pay back; repay; settle; discharge.

শুধা[৩], **শুধানো** *vi, vt* ask; inquire.

শুধু *adj* **1** only; mere: ~ কথা. **2** empty; bare; plain: ~ হাতে, ~ চোখে. ☐*adv* only; merely; just; simply; continuously: সারাদিন ধরে ~ বৃষ্টি হচ্ছে, সে ~ চোখ তুলে তাকাল. ~ **শুধু** *adv* **1** for nothing: এখানে ~ শুধু আসা. **2** in vain: তুমি ~ শুধু খেটে মরছ.

শুনা, শোনা *vt* **1** hear; listen to; give ear; lend an ear; hearken; **2** heed; pay heed to; comply with; obey: ছেলেটা কথা শোনে না. ☐*adj* heard; learnt indirectly by hearing from others; listened to; hears about/ of; orally transmitted/ communicated. ~ **কথা** *n* hearsay; rumour; report. **শুনানো** *vt* **1** make one hear; tell; inform. **2** cause to obey/ comply with/ heed. **কথা ~নো** *vi* **1** make sb obey. **2** give sb a piece of one's mind; revile; rebuke; censure; criticize; take to task; chide; scold; tongue-lash; lecture. **গল্প ~নো** *vi* tell sb a story. **গান ~নো** *n* sing sb a song; sing before sb. **শুনিয়ে (শুনিয়ে) বলা** *vi* speak in sb's hearing. **শুনানি** *n* (law) hearing. **শুনানির দিন/ তারিখ** *n* day/ date of hearing. **মামলার শুনানি হবে** The case will come up for hearing. **শুনিবা মাত্র** *adv* directly upon hearing.

শুভ *adj* **1** auspicious; favorable; fortunate; prosperous. **2** good; suitable; fit; useful; suitable; beneficial; benefactory. **3** splendid; bright; beautiful; handsome. ☐*n* **1** good; good fortune; auspiciousness; happiness; bliss; prosperity; welfare. **2** benefit; service; good/ virtuous action. **3** beauty; charm. **শুভা** *fem.* ~**কর** *adj* causing welfare; auspicious; fortunate; beneficial; benefactory. ~**কর্ম, ~কার্য** *nn* good/ virtuous act; auspicious action/ work; solemn/ religious rite/ ceremony/ function. ~ **কামনা** *n* well-wishing; good wishes. ~**ক্ষণ** *n* auspicious/ lucky moment. ~**গ্রহ** *n* auspicious/ favourable planet; lucky star. ~**ঙ্কর**=~কর. ~**ঙ্করা** *fem.* ~**ঙ্করী** *n fem* **1** name of Parvati. **2** system of arithmetical calculation introduced by Shuvankar. ~**ঙ্করীর ফাঁকি** *n* jugglery with figures. ~**দ, ~দায়ক** =~কর. ~**দা** *fem.* ~**দিন** *n* auspicious/ luck day ~**দৃষ্টি** *n* **1** favourable/ kind/ auspicious look. **2** solemn rite of the bride and bridegroom looking at each other at a Hindu wedding. ~**প্রদ** =~কর. ~**ফল** *n* happy/ auspicious result or outcome; good/ happy consequence. ~ **মুহূর্ত** =~ক্ষণ. ~ **লক্ষণ** *n* auspicious sign/ mark/ omen. ~**লগ্ন** =~ক্ষণ. ~ **সংবাদ** *n* good news. ~**সূচক** *adj* auspicious; propitious. ~**সূচন(া)** *n* auspiciousness; auspicious beginning; good start. **শুভাকাঙ্ক্ষা** *n*=~ কামনা. **শুভাকাঙ্ক্ষী** *adj* well-wishing. ☐*n* well-wisher. **শুভাকাঙ্ক্ষিণী** *fem.* **শুভাগমন** *n* kind/ welcome visit; auspicious coming. **শুভাদৃষ্ট** *n* good luck/ fortune. **শুভাদৃষ্টবশত** *adv* fortunately; luckily. **শুভানুধ্যায়ী** =শুভাকাঙ্ক্ষী. **শুভানুধ্যায়িনী** *fem.* **শুভানুষ্ঠান** *n* auspicious/ solemn ceremony or function. **শুভান্বিত** *adj* endowed with prosperity/ good fortune; happy; prosperous. **শুভার্থী** *adj* **1** desirous of prosperity/ welfare. **2**=শুভাকাঙ্ক্ষী. **শুভার্থিনী** *fem.* **শুভাশীর্বাদ, শুভাশিস** *nn* good wishes; benediction; blessing; congratulation. **শুভাশুভ** *n* weal and woe; good and evil. ☐*adj* pleasant and unpleasant; agreeable and disagreeable; prosperous and unfortunate; good and evil.

শুভেক্ষণ *adj* having auspicious/ fair eyes. **শুভেক্ষণা** *fem.*

শুভেতর *adj* other than auspicious; unlucky; unfortunate; evil; bad.

শুভ্র *adj* **1** white; hoary; grey; white-coloured. **2** clear; spotless; immaculate. **3** radiant; shining; splendid; beautiful. **4** pure; chaste; unblemished; virtuous: ~ চরিত্র/ মন. ☐*n* **1** whiteness. **2** tale. **3** sandal. **শুভ্রা** *fem.* ~**কান্তি** *n* spotless/ radiant beauty. ☐*adj* fair-complexioned. ~**কায়** *adj* fair-skinned; white. ~**কেশ** *n* grey/silvery hair. ☐*adj* hoary; grey-haired; grizzled. ~**মৌলি** *adj* white-crested. **শুভ্রাংশু** *n* white ray. ☐*n* the moon.

শুমার [P] *n* counting; enumeration; calculation; estimate. **আদমশুমারি** *n* census.

শুয়া[১] *n* parrot.

শুয়া[২], শুয়ো=শুঁয়াপোকা (⇒ শুঁয়া)

শুয়া[৩] *vi* **1** lie down; go to bed; recline; rest; repose; sleep. **শুয়ে পড়া** *vi* lie down; go to bed. **2** prostrate; succumb. **~নো** *vt* **1** lay down; put; settle; set. **2** force to lie prostate; knock down to the ground. **শুয়ার, শুয়োর** (colloq)=শূকর. **শুয়ারের খোঁয়াড়** *n* pigsty; piggery. **শুয়ারের গোঁ** *n* pigheadedness. **শুয়ারের পাল** *n* flock of swine.

শুরু [A] *n* beginning; start; commencement; inception. **~ করা/** *vt* begin; start; commence; institute; take the lead; inaugurate. **~ হওয়া** *vi* begin; start; commence. **~ থেকে শেষ** from beginning to end.

শুরুয়া [P] *n* broth; soup.

শুলফা, সুলফো (colloq) *nn* sowa (*Anethum sowa*).

শুলুক [A] *n* way; mode; manner; usage; treatment; clue. **~ সন্ধান** *n* technique; method; secrets; ins and outs. **~ সন্ধান করা** *vi* search for a clue/ weak point; make a secret search for sth.

শুল্ক *n* **1** tax; duty on import/ export; customs; toll; tariff duty. **2** marriage-portion; nuptial gift; dowry. **~শালা, শুল্কালয়** *n* customs house; toll-house. **শুল্কাধীন** *adj* bonded. **শুল্কাধীন পণ্যাগার** *n* bonded warehouse.

শুশনি *n* cress.

শুশুক *n*=শিশুক (২) (⇒ শিশু)

শুশ্রূষা *n* nursing (of the sick); attendance (upon); service. **~ করা** *vt* nurse. **~কারী** *adj* nursing; attending. ❑*n* male nurse. **~কারিণী** *fem* nurse; (nursing) sister. **~ প্রণালী** *n* nursing.

শুষা = শোষণ করা (⇒ শোষণ)

শুষির = সুষির

শুষ্ক *adj* **1** dry; dried: ~ গোময়/বস্ত্র. **2** arid; parched: ~ মা, ~ ওষ্ঠ. **3** dried up: ~ জলাশয়. **4** withered sear; sere: ~ পুষ্প. **5** emaciated; shrunk; shrivelled; pale: ~ মুখ, ~ ত্বক. **6** sapless; pithless: ~ কাষ্ঠ. **7** useless; fruitless; dull; Vain; groundless; unprofitable; pointless; empty; vapoury: ~ বাক্য, ~ তর্ক. **8** harsh: ~ কণ্ঠ. **9** merely formal: ~ভদ্রতা. **~কণ্ঠ** *adj* having a parched throat. **~তা** *n* dryness: aridity. **~দেহ** *adj* having an emaciated body; wasted. **~ পরীক্ষা** *n* (chem) dry test.

শূক *n* **1** awn of grain. **2** bristle; spicule; spike; bristle/ sharp hair of insects. **3** larva. **~কীট** *n* caterpillar; chrysalis. **~ঘ্ন** *adj* larvicide. **~ধান্য** *n* any awned/ bearded grain. **~পদ** *n* (zoo) chaetopod. **~শিম্বী** *n* cowhedge plant.

শূকর *n* hog; boar; swine; pig. **শূকরী** *fem* swine. **~ছানা ~শাবক** *nn* young pig; porket. **~পালক** *n* swineherd; pig-driver. **শূকরের মাংস** *n* pork. **বন্য~** *n* wild boar.

শূদ্র *n* fourth or lowest of the four Hindu castes; Shudras; Shudra. **শূদ্রা** *fem* female Shudra. **শূদ্রাণী** *fem* female Shudra; wife of a Shudra. **শূদ্রী** *fem* wife of a Shudra.

শূন *adj* (archaic, poet)=শূন্য

শূন্য *n* **1** (math) zero; cipher; nothing; naught. **2** space; heaven; atmosphere. **3** void; vacuum empty/ lonely/ deserted place; desert. **4** vacuity; nonentity; absolute non-existence (esp with Buddhists). ❑*adj* **1** empty; void. **2** hollow; barren; desolate; deserted. **3** vacant (as a look or state); absent; absent-minded; having no certain object/ aim; distracted. **4** possessing nothing; empty; wholly destitute. **5** wholly alone/ solitary; having no friends/ companions. **6** (used as a *suff*) void of; free from; destitute of; wanting; lacking; -less; -un. **7** non-existent; absent; missing. **8** indifferent; insensible. **শূন্যা** *fem*. **~কুম্ভ** *n* **1** empty pitcher. **2** (derog) man of no worth/ substance; man of straw. **~ক্রান্তি-রেখা** *n* (astron) actinic line. **~গর্ভ** *adj* empty; hollow; vain; unsubstantial; insincere: ~গর্ভ কথা. **~চিত্ত** *adj* vacant-minded; absent-minded; thinking of nothing. **~তা** *n* emptiness; loneliness; desolateness; vacancy (of gaze); distraction; absence/ want (of); nothingness; non-existence; non-reality; illusory nature; indifference. **~ দৃষ্টি** *n* vacant/ blank look. **~ পথ** *n* sky; air; aerial route. **~ পানে** *adv* towards the sky. **~বাদ** *n* (Buddhist) doctrine of the non-existence (of any spirit either Supreme or human); nihilism. **~বাদী** *adj* Buddhistic; Buddhist; atheistical; nihilistic. ❑*n* affirmer of a void (ie, of the non-existence of any Spirit, divine or human); Buddhist; atheist; nihilist. **~ভাগী** *n* noncontributory partner. **~ ভাব** *n* state of being empty; emptiness. **~ মন** =~ চিত্ত.. **~মনে** *adv* in a vacant mood. **~মার্গ** =~পথ. **~ যাত্রা** *n* flight. **~স্থান** *n* empty/ vacant place or space; gap; blank. **~হস্ত** *adj* empty-handed; broke; financially hard-up; not carrying any weapon. **~ হস্তে** *adj* empty-handedly; without (having any money; without carrying any weapon. **~হৃদয়**=~চিত্ত.

শূন্যীকরণ *n* making empty; laying waste; evacuation.

শূন্যীকৃত *adj* emptied; laid waste; turned into a desert; evacuated.

শূপকার *n* cook.

শূয়ার *n* =শূকর

শূর *adj* strong; powerful; valiant; brave; heroic. ❑*n* strong/ mighty/ valiant man; warrior; champion; hero. **~তা, ~ত্ব** *nn* heroism; bravery; valour. **~ম্মন্য** *n* bully.

শূরোচিত *adj* befitting a hero; heroic; gallant.

শূর্প *n* winnowing basket/ fan; kind of wicker receptacle which, when shaken about, serves as a fan for winnowing corn. **~কর্ণ** *adj* having ears like winnowing fans. ❑*n* **1** elephant. **2** Ganesha. **~নখা** *adj* having fingernails like winnowing fans. ❑*n* name of the sister of Ravana.

শূর্পী *n* small winnowing fan.

শূল *n* **1** sharp iron pin/ stake; spike; spit (on which meat is roasted). **2** pointed dart; lance; pike; spear; trident of Shiva. **3** stake for impaling criminals. **4** sharp/ acute pain (esp that of colic or gout); inflammation. **5** flag; banner. **6** death. **শূলে চড়ানো/ দেওয়া** *vt* impale (as a criminal). **~ঘ্ন** *adj* removing sharp pain/ colic; anodyne. **~ধর, ~ধারী** *adjj* bearing a spear (applied to Rudra-Shiva). **~নাশক, ~নাশন** *adjj* removing pain in the stomach. **~পক্ব** *adj* skewered/ spitted and roasted. **~পাণি** *adj* holding a spear/ trident in one's hand. ❑*n* Shiva. **~বিদ্ধ** *adj* pierced with a spear/ trident; skewered; spitted. **~বেদনা, ~ব্যথা** *n* sharp pain; colic pain. **~হস্ত**=~পাণি. **শূলাকৃতি** *adj* like a pike trident/ spear. **শূলাগ্র** *n* point of a pike/ stake/ trident; pike head. **~নি** *n* pain; ache; inflammation; itching. **~নো** *vi* become painful; ache; inflame; have an itching (for).

শূলী=শূলপাণি (⇒ শূল). **শূলিনী** *adj fem*

শূল্য *adj* roasted on a spit. ❑*n* roasted meat.

শৃগাল=শিয়াল. **শৃগালিকা, শৃগালী** *fem*. **~কণ্টক**=শিয়াল-কাঁটা. **~কোলি** *n* sort of jujube; Zizyphus oenoplia.

শৃঙ্খল *n* **1** chain; fetters; irons. **2** system; rule; order; arrangement. **3** discipline. restrain. **~নিয়ম** *n* (math) chain-rule. **শৃঙ্খলা** *n* **1** discipline. **2** method; system. **3** arrangement; orderliness; disposition. **4** due order/ succession; sequence. **5** concatenation. **শৃঙ্খলাবদ্ধ** *adj* **1** disciplined; orderly; systematic; methodical. **2** chained; fettered. **শৃঙ্খলাহীন** *adj* disorderly; undisciplined; confused; unsystematic; haphazard; chaotic; unmethodical; disorganized; muddled.

শৃঙ্খলিত *adj* chained; fettered; bound; confined.

শৃঙ্গ *n* **1** horn; antler. **2** top/ summit (of a mountain); peak; crag. **3** summit of a building; pinnacle; turret. **4** any peak; projection; lofty object; elevation; point; end; extremity. **5** cusp/ horn of the moon. **6** highest point; acme; height/ perfection of anything. **7** syringe; water-engine. **~ধর** *n* mountain. **~ধ্বনি** *n* sound of a (musical) horn. **ক্ষুদ্র ~** *n* cornicle. **শৃঙ্গাকার** *adj* horn-shaped; corniform.

শৃঙ্গার *n* **1** (rhet) erotic sentiment (one of the nine Rasas). **2** love; sexual passion/ desire/ enjoyment. **3** dress suitable for amorous purposes; elegant dress; fine garments; finery. **4** fragrant powder for the dress or person.

শৃঙ্গী[১] *adj* **1** horned; erected; peaked. **2** tusked; having a sting. **শৃঙ্গিনী** *fem* cow.

শৃঙ্গী[২] *n* **1** species of fish (⇒ শিঙি). **2** mountain. **3** horned beast.

শেওড়া *n* name of a small, crooked, ugly tree; *Trophis aspera*.

শেওলা=শৈবাল

শেঁকো *n* white arsenic.

শেখ [A] *n* **1** Sheik(h). **2** venerable old man. **3** a particular Muslim family name.

শেখর *n* **1** crown; diadem; crest. **2** chaplet/ wreath of flowers worn on the top of the head. **3** peak; summit. **4** (fig) the highest part/ chief/ head/ best/ most beautiful of: কবি~.

শেখা *vt* (colloq)=শিখা[২]. **~নো**=শিখানো

শেজ[১] *n* bed.

শেজ[২] *n* lamp within a chimney; lantern.

শেঠ *n* **1** merchant (prince); banker; eminent man; president/ foreman of guild. **2** a particular family name.

শেফালি, শেফালী, শেফালিকা *nn* a white fragrant autumnal flower and its tree *Vitex negundo*.

শেমিজ [E] *n* chemise.

শেয়াকুল=শিয়াকুল

শেয়ান(া)=সেয়ান(া)

শেয়ার [E] *n* share.

শেয়াল=শিয়াল

শের [E] *n* tiger; lion; brave man. **~নর** *n* brave man. **~বাবর** *n* lion.

শেরওয়ানি *n* kind of long coat worn by men.

শেরি [E] *n* sherry.

শেরিফ [E] *n* sheriff.

শেরেক [A] *n* infidelity; polytheism; paganism; belief in the plurality of God.

শেরেকি [A] *n* association of partners to God; polytheism.

শেরে-খোদা [P] *n* lion/tiger of God.

শেল[১] *n* sharp-pointed mythical missile (⇒ শল্য). **বুকে ~সম বাজা** cut sb to the heart/ quick.

শেল[২] [E] *n* shell (to be fired from a gun).

শেষ *n* **1** end; issue; conclusion; finish; close; termination; completion. **2** residue; leavings; surplus; balance; the rest; remainder. **3** death; destruction; ruin. **4** solution; settlement: সমস্যার ~. **5** rear; backside; back-end; last/ lowest position or place; rearmost/ backmost place or position: সবার শেষে. **6** name of a mythological thousand-headed serpent regarded by Hindus as an emblem of eternity. ❑*adj* last; remaining (out of/ from); left (from); concluding; final; ultimate; lowest; rearmost. **~ করা** *vt* **1** end; put an end to; conclude; bring to an end; finish; wind up; make an end of;

complete; terminate. **2** destroy; ruin; kill; do sb in (sl). ~ **হওয়া** *vi* **1** end; come to an end; conclude; be concluded/ finished; close; run out; cease; stop; lapse; expire. **2** be ruined/ killed/ destroyed. ~ **অবস্থা,** ~**দশা** *nn* last/ final stage; fag end; point of death; dying stage. ~**কালে** *adv* at last; in the end. ~**চুম্বকত্ব** *n* (phys) residual magnetism. ~**ত**=~কালে. ~**নাগ**=~(6). ~**পাদ** *n* last quarter. ~**বয়ঃ** *adj* old. ~**বয়সী** *fem.* ~ **বিচার** *n* the Last Judgement. ~ **বিচারক** *n* Final Judge. ~**বিচারের দিন** *n* the Day of Judgement; Judgement Day; the Last Judgement; Doomsday. ~**ভাগ** *n* rest/ remaining/ last part; remaining portion. ~ **মুহূর্ত** *n* last moment; eleventh hour. ~ **রক্ষা** *n* taking care that an undertaking is brought to a conclusion; that which saves the situation at the last moment. ~ **রক্ষা করা** *vi* save the situation. ~ **রাত্রি** *n* last watch of the night; small hours. **শেষাবস্থা**=~ অবস্থা. **শেষাশেষি** *adv* at the last moment; at last; at long last; at the eleventh hour; ultimately; finally; in the end. **শেষে** *adj* in the end; in conclusion; at last; towards the close; last; ultimately; finally.

শেষোক্ত *adj* last-named; last-mentioned; mentioned last of all.

শেহালা=শৈবাল

শৈক্ষ *n* apprentice.

শৈত্য *n* coldness; frigidity; cold; chilliness; chill.

শৈথিল্য *n* looseness; laxity; flaccidity; slackness; relaxation; weakness; negligence; inattention; dilatoriness; remission; decrease; diminution; slowness; tardiness; dishevelled/ blowzy state.

শৈব *adj* relating/ belonging/ sacred to the god Shiva; worshipping/ following Shiva; coming/ derived from Shiva. ❑*n* worshipper/ follower of Shiva.

শৈবলিত *adj* covered with moss (⇒ শৈবাল).

শৈবলিনী *n* river.

শৈবাল *n* kind of duck-weed or green moss-like plant growing in pools; lichen; alga (*pl* algae).

শৈবালিত=শৈবলিত

শৈল *n* **1** mountain; hill. **2** rock; stone; crag. ❑*adj* made of stone; stony; rocky; stone-like. ~**কন্যা** *n* daughter of the mountain; Parvati. ~**জ** *adj* 'mountain-born'; made of stone; born of/ grown on a mountain/ hill; mountainous; hilly. ~**জা** *fem.* **শৈলা** *n fem* goddess Durga. ~-**তত্ত্ব** *n* petrology; petrography. ~**তনয়া**=~কন্যা. ~**ময়** *adj* hilly; mountainous. ~**শিরা** *n* ridge. ~**সুতা** *n*=~জা. **শৈলাগ্র** *n* mountain top. **শৈলান্তরীপ** *n* promontory.

শৈলী *n* **1** style. **2** habit; custom; manner of acting/ living; practice; usage.

শৈলেন্দ্র *n* chief/ lord of mountains; the Himalayas.

শৈলেয় *adj* rocky; stony; mountain-like; hard; produced in mountains/ rocks. ❑*n* bitumen; benzoin; storax. **শৈলেয়ী** *n fem* Parvati.

শৈলোৎক্ষেপ-বৃষ্টি *n* (geog) relief-rain.

শৈল্য *adj* rocky; stony; hard.

শৈশব *n* childhood; infancy; babyhood; pupilage; period under age (ie under sixteen); babyhood; childhood days. ~ **কাল**=~. ~**কালীন** *adj* of infancy/ childhood days. ~ **কালোচিত** *adj* proper for infancy/ childhood; babyish; childish; child-like. ~**লীলা** *n* childhood activities. ~**সঙ্গী** *n* companion/ friend of one's childhood. ~ **স্মৃতি** *n* memories/ reminiscence(s) of one's childhood. **শৈশবাবধি** *adj* from childhood. **শৈশবাবস্থা**=~.

শোঁ, শোঁ-শোঁ *nn* (onom) whiz; swish; scream (of wind); whirr.

শোঁকা *vt* (colloq)=শুঁকা. ~**নো**=শুঁকানো

শোক *n* **1** mourning; lamentation; grieving. **2** sorrow; affliction; anguish; pain; trouble. ~ **করা** *vt, vi* mourn; grieve (for/ over); lament. ~**গাথা,** ~**গীতি** *nn* dirge; elegy. ~**গ্রস্ত** *adj* bereaved; grief-stricken; grieved; mourning. ~**চিহ্ন** *n* sign/ token of mourning. ~**জনক** *adj* causing sorrow; lamentable; woeful; distressing; sad; distressful; sorry. ~**জর্জরিত,** ~**জীর্ণ** *adjj* afflicted with sorrow; downcast with grief; grief-laden. ~**তাপ** *n* physical and mental agony; misery; desolation. ~**তপ্ত** *adj* consumed by sorrow/grief. ~**নাশ** *n* removal of grief. ~**পরায়ণ** *adj* wholly given up to sorrow. ~**পরিপ্লুত** *adj* overwhelmed with sorrow. ~**প্রবাহ** *n* flow/ upsurge/ outburst. intensity of grief. ~**বিকল** *adj* overwhelmed with grief/ sorrow. ~**বিনাশন** *adj* removing/ destroying sorrow. ~**বিবর্ধন** *adj* increasing grief. ~**বিহ্বল**=~বিকল. ~**ব্যঞ্জক** *adj* indicating grief/ mourning; mournful; doleful; lugubrious. ~**ভার** *n* weight/ burden of sorrow. ~**ময়** *adj* consisting/ full of sorrow. ~**মূর্ছিত** *adj* stupefied/ stunned by grief. ~**সঙ্গীত** *n* elegy; dirge. ~**সন্তপ্ত** *adj* bereaved; consumed by grief. ~**সভা** *n* condolence meeting. ~**সাগর** *n* sea of sorrow; ocean of trouble. ~**সূচক**=~ব্যঞ্জক. **শোকাকুল** *adj* overwhelmed/ filled/ overcome with grief. **শোকাগ্নি** *n* fire of sorrow; violent grief; burning fire of grief. **শোকাচ্ছন্ন**=শোকাকুল. **শোকাতুর** *adj* afflicted with grief. **শোকানল** =~শোকাগ্নি. **শোকাপনোদন** *n* removal of grief. **শোকাবহ** ~জনক. **শোকাবিষ্ট**=~শোকাকুল. **শোকাবেগ** =~প্রবাহ. **শোকাবেশ** *n* fit/ paroxysm of sorrow. **শোকাভিভূত** *adj* afflicted/ overwhelmed with grief **শোকার্ত**=~ শোকাতুর. **শোকার্তি** *n* visitation/ affliction by sorrow.

শোকোচ্ছ্বাস *n* outburst of grief.

শোকোদ্দীপ্ত *adj* agitated/ excited by sorrow/ grief.

শোকর [A] *n* thanks; gratitude; gratefulness. ~ করা *vt, vi* thank; return thanks; be grateful. ~গুজার *adj* thankful; grateful. ~গুজারি *n* thanksgiving; thankfulness; gratitude.

শোকরানা [A] *n* (acknowledgment of) gratitude; thanksgiving.

শোচন, শোচনা *nn* mourning; grieving; lamentation; regret; repentance. ~ করা *vi, vt* grieve (for/ over); mourn; lament; regret; repent.

শোচনীয় *adj* lamentable; deplorable; pitiable; sad; regrettable; sorry; mournful; woeful; miserable; grievous. ~তা *n* deplorableness; grievousness; wretchedness;

শোচ্য *adj* to be lamented; deplorable; miserable.

শোণক, শোনাক *nn* kind of shrub and its fruit; *Bignonia indica*.

শোণিত *n* 1 blood. 2 saffron. ❑*adj* red. ~কণা, ~কণিকা *nn* (anat) blood-corpuscle; small drop of blood. ~ ধারা *n* flow/ stream of blood. ~পাত *n* bloodshed; haemorrhage. ~পায়ী *adj* blood-sucking. ~পায়ী প্রাণী *n* blood-sucker. ~পিত্ত *n* haemorrhage. ~পিপাসা *n* blood-thirstiness; blood-lust. ~পিপাসু *adj* blood-thirsty. ~প্রবাহ=~ধারা. ~বর্ষী *adj* flowing with blood. ~মোক্ষণ *n* blood-letting. ~রঞ্জিত *adj* blood-stained; smeared with blood; bloody. ~শিরা *n* vein; artery; blood-vessel. ~শোধক *adj* blood-purifying. ~শোধন *n* purification of blood. ~শোষণ *n* sucking of blood; (fig) extortion. ~স্নাত *adj* bathed in blood. ~স্নান *n* blood-bath. ~স্রাব *n* haemorrhage. শোণিতাক্ত, শোণিতাদিগ্ধ=~রঞ্জিত.

শোণিকা *n* redness; crimson; red glow/ tinge; flush.

শোথ *n* swelling; dropsy; morbid intumescence. ~ নামা *vi* have (dropsical) swelling.

শোধ *n* 1 payment; repayment; acquittance; clearing off (dues). 2 retaliation; revenge; vengeance. ~ করা *vt* pay; repay; settle. ~ তোলা *vi* take revenge (upon); avenge; have one's revenge (on). retaliate; square accounts with sb; take vengeance on. ~ দেওয়া *vt* 1 pay back; repay; pay requite sth/sb (with sth); make requital. 2=~ তোলা. ~ নেওয়া=~ তোলা. ~ যাওয়া *vi* be paid/ repaid. ~বোধ *n* 1 settling/ balancing of accounts; settlement. 2 having one's revenge on sb; squaring up with sb; measure for measure; tit for tat; requital. ~বোধ হওয়া *vi* be quit. শোধ্য *adj* 1 payable; repayable; due. 2 to be cleansed/ purified/ refined/ corrected. জন্মের ~ *adj* for ever/ good.

শোধক *adj* purificatory; purifying; sanctifying; corrective; cleansing; refining; rectifying; reformative; repaying. ❑*n* 1 purifier. 2 (arith) subtrahend.

শোধন *n* 1 cleaning; purifying; cleansing; refining; purification; rectification; correction; sifting. 2 amendment; revision; reformation; reclamation. 3 payment; repayment; acquittance. ~ করা *vt* 1 purify; rectify; clean; cleanse; refine. 2 amend; correct; reform; revise.

শোধনী *adj* fem=শোধক. ❑*n* broom; brush.

শোধনীয় *adj* 1 to be cleansed/ purified/ rectified/ refined/ corrected/ amended. 2 capable of being cleansed/ purified/ rectified. 3 to be paid/ repaid/ discharged; payable; repayable; due.

শোধরানো (colloq)=শুধরানো

শোধা=শোধ করা (⇒ শোধ)

শোধাক্ষম *adj* insolvent. ~তা *n* insolvency. ~-নিবন্ধক *n* registrar of Insolvency.

শোধিত *adj* 1 purified; cleansed; rectified; refined. 2 corrected; amended; revised; reclaimed; reformed. 3 paid; repaid; settled; discharged.

শোধ্য ⇒ শোধ

শোনা (colloq)=শুনা. ~নো=শুনানো

শোফ *n* inflammatory/ morbid swelling.

শোফার [F] *n* chauffeur.

শোভন *adj* 1 beautiful; lovely; brilliant; splendid; correct; right; decorous; decent; becoming. 3 graceful; excellent; elegant. শোভনা *fem*.

শোভনীয় *adj* beautiful; splendid.

শোভমান *adj* looking beautiful/ decorous; existing/ being present beautifully. শোভমানা *fem*. ~ হওয়া *vi* shine; be resplendent (with).

শোভা *n* splendour; brilliance; lustre; beauty; grace; loveliness; embellishment; glamour; beautiful show. ~ করা *vt* adorn; beautify; embellish; grace. ~ পাওয়া *vi, vt* 1 look beautiful/ decorous; shine; be resplendent. 2 behave; become: এমন কথা তোমার মুখে ~ পায় না. ~ হওয়া *vi* look beautiful/ decorous; be adorned/ graced; have a beautiful show. ~কর *adj* beautifying; embellishing; adorning; decorative; giving glamour/ grace to. ~ময় *adj* full of lustre/ beauty; beautiful; graceful; glamorous. ~যাত্রা *n* procession. ~যাত্রা করে যাওয়া *vi* go in a procession. ~যাত্রা বের করা *vi* take out a procession. ~যাত্রী *n* processionist. ~শূন্য, ~হীন *adj* having no beauty; unsightly; plain; unseemly; unaesthetic.

শোভাঞ্জন *n* horse-radish.

শোভিত *adj* splendid; beautiful; embellished/ adorned by; decked (in); decorated; graced.

শোভী *adj* 1 beautifying; adorning; embellishing; adding grace to. 2 brilliant;

beautiful; splendid; resplendent with. শোভিনী *fem*.

শোয়া (colloq)=শুয়া. **~নো**=শুয়ানো. **~বসা** *n* **1** (lit) lying and sitting. **2** (fig) deportment; bearing. **3** association; social intercourse. **~বসা করা** *vi* live with another as neighbours/ in the same society; frequent; associate with; hobnob (together/ with sb).

শোর [P] *n* noise; outcry; tumult; uproar. **~ তোলা** *vi* raise an uproar; make a noise; hoot; kick up a row; clamour (for). **~গোল** *n* hue and cry; clamour; disturbance; tumult; uproarious noise; agitation.

শোরা [P] *n* nitre; salt-petre. **~ঘটিত** *adj* nitric.

শোল *n* species of large tubular fish (= শকুল).

শোলা *n* sponge wood.

শোষ *n* **1** dryness; desiccation; drying up. **2** (med) pulmonary consumption. **3** (med) sinus. **4** thirst. ❑*adj* dried up within: ~ আঁখ. **~-কাগজ** *n* blotting-paper.

শোষক *adj* **1** absorbing; absorbent; drying up; sucking up. **2** exploiting; extorting. ❑*n* **1** absorbent; absorber. **2** exploiter; extortioner; sponger.

শোষণ *n* **1** absorption; drying up; drying; parching; suction; desiccation; withering. **2** exploitation; extortion. **~ করা** *vt* **1** absorb; suck in; dry up; desiccate; parch; wither. **2** exploit; extort.

শোষা=শোষণ করা

শোষানি *n* difficulty in breathing.

শোষিত *adj* **1** absorbed; dried/ sucked up; desiccated; emptied; exhausted; drained. **2** exploited; subjected to extortion.

শোহরত [A] *n* **1** announcement; proclamation; publishing; report; advertising. **2** fame; renown; reputation. ঢোল~ *n* proclamation by beat of drums.

শোহিনী *n* name of an Indian musical mode.

শৌক্তিকেয়, শৌক্তেয় *adjj* relating to a pearl; pearly. ❑*n* pearl.

শৌক্ল্য *n* whiteness; white.

শৌখিন, শৌখীন [A] *adjj* **1** given to luxury/ niceties; luxurious; voluptuous; having refined/ delicate taste; pleasure-seeking: ~ লোক. **2** (pleasing to/ gratifying) fancy; fine; dainty; delicate: ~ জিনিস, fancy goods. **~তা** *n* luxury; luxuriousness; pleasure seeking; inclination to niceties; possession of refined/ delicate taste; daintiness.

শৌচ *n* **1** cleanness; purity; cleanliness. **2** purification (esp from defilement caused by the death of a relation). **3** self-purification. **4** cleansing/ washing of one's posteriors after evacuation of bowels. **~ করা** *vi* **1** cleanse/ purify one's body and mind. **2** cleanse after evacuation of bowels. **~কর্ম, ~ক্রিয়া** *nn*=~.

শৌণ্ড *adj* **1** addicted to drinking; drunk; intoxicated; drunken; inebriate. **2** being the pride of; celebrated: দান~.

শৌণ্ডিক=শুঁড়ি. **শৌণ্ডিকালয়** *n* liquor-shop; tavern; public house.

শৌণ্ডী=শুঁড়ি

শৌভিক *n* magician; juggler.

শৌর্য *n* heroism; valour; prowess; might. **~বীর্য** *n* strength and courage; gallantry; guts; exploits; mettle; intrepidity. **~শালী** *adj* courageous; valiant; heroic; valorous; intrepid; gallant. **~শালিনী** *fem*.

শৌল্ক, শৌল্কিক *adjj* relating to tolls/ taxes/ customs; levied (as tax). ❑*nn* customs-house officer; superintendent of customs/ tolls; toll collector.

শ্মশান *n* **1** elevated place for burning dead bodies; crematorium; burning-ground; cemetery/ burial place for the bones of cremated corpses. **2** (fig) desolate/ cheerless place, house, etc. **~কালী** *n* a form of Durga (as the presiding deity of crematoria). **~চারী** *adj* roaming/ dwelling in or frequenting burning-grounds. **~চারিণী** *fem*. **~পুরী, ~ভূমি**=~. **~বন্ধু** *n* one who accompanies and carries a dead body to the burning ground. **~বাসী** *adj* dwelling in burning-grounds. **~বাসিনী** *fem*. **~বৈরাগ্য** *n* momentary abandonment of worldly desires at the sight of a burning-ground. **~সাধন** *n* magical rites performed in a burning-ground to obtain control over evil spirits. **শ্মশানালয়** *n* place for burning the dead; burning-ground. **শ্মশানালয়বাসী** *adj* inhabiting burning-grounds. ❑*n* spectre; ghost. **শ্মশানে পরিণত করা** turn into/ reduce to a desolate desert; devastate; lay waste; ravage.

শ্মশ্রু *n* beard; hairs of the beard. **~ধারী** *adj* wearing a beard. **~মণ্ডিত, ~ল, ~শোভিত** *adjj* covered with beard; bearded. **~শূন্য, ~হীন** *adjj* beardless.

শ্যাম *adj* **1** black; dark-coloured; dark blue/ brown/ grey/ green; verdant; sable; cloud-cloured. **2** having a swarthy/ dark complexion (considered as a mark of beauty. ❑*n* **1** Sri Krishna. **2** black; blue; green. **3** Indian cuckoo. **শ্যামা** *fem*. **~কান্তি** *n, adj* (having a) sweet swarthy/ dark complexion or colour; dark-coloured; luscious green; verdant. **~বর্ণ** *n* **1** dark blue/ bottle-green colour; green/ dark colour; sweet swarthy complexion. ❑*adj* dark-coloured; having a dark sweet complexion. **~ল** *adj* dark-coloured; green; cloud-coloured; swarthy. **~লা, ~লী** *fem*. **~লা বসুন্ধরা** *n fem* the (mother) earth green with crops and vegetation. **~লতা** *n* **1** darkness; blackness; dark colour; verdancy; green (colour); verdure; greenness. **2** dark complexion. **~সুন্দর** *adj* dark and beautiful. ❑*n* Sri Krishna. **শ্যামাঙ্গ** *adj* black-bodied; having a dark complexion; dark-complexioned. **শ্যামাঙ্গী, শ্যামাঙ্গিনী** *fem.* **~ রাখি না কুল রাখি** have to choose between one's lover and infamy on the one hand and one's husband and good name of one's family on the other; (fig) be between the horns of a dilemma.

শ্যামক, শ্যামাক *nn* kind of cultivated millet; pancium.

শ্যামলিত *adj* darkened; obscured; become green; frumentaceum.

শ্যামলিমা=শ্যামলতা (⇒ শ্যাম)

শ্যামলী *n fem* dark-coloured cow.

শ্যামা *n fem* **1** uncommonly beautiful woman having a dazzlingly bright creamy complexion; slender woman; belle; beauty. **2** dark-complexioned woman; brunette. **3** goddess Kali (a form of Durga). **4** Indian cuckoo. **5** river Jamuna. **6** name of various plants. **~ পোকা** *n* green-coloured winged insect found in late autumn. **~ লতা** *n* the plant *Ichonocarpus frutescena*.

শ্যামায়মান *adj* darkening; getting dark; getting/ becoming green.

শ্যাম্পেন [F] *n* champagne.

শ্যালক=শালা[১]

শ্যালাজ=~শালাজ (⇒ শালা)

শ্যালিকা, শ্যালী=শালী[১]. শ্যালীপতি=ভায়রা

শ্যেন *n* hank; falcon; eagle; any bird of prey. শ্যেনী *fem.* **~চক্ষু, ~চক্ষুঃ, ~দৃষ্টি** *adjj* hawk-eyed; falcon-eyed; eagle-eyed. **~দৃষ্টিতে লক্ষ করা** *vt* watch like a law.

শ্রথন=শ্রন্থন

শ্রদ্দধান *adj* having faith; trustful; believing; respectful; reverent.

শ্রদ্ধা *n* **1** respect; reverence; honour; admiration; loyalty; esteem. **2** trust; faith; confidence; trustfulness: তার সামর্থ্যের প্রতি আমার ~ আছে. **3** desire; wish; inclination: খেতে ~. **4** devotion: ধর্মে ~. **~ করা** *vt* revere; esteem; love and respect; admire; have confidence/ faith in; trust; honour; to look upon. **~ন্বিত, ~বান, ~যুক্ত, ~লু, ~শীল** *adjj* respectful; regardful; deferential; having faith/ confidence in; faithful; believing. **~ভাজন, ~স্পদ** *adjj* respectable; respected; august; reverend; esteemed; venerated; honourable; revered. ❑*n* object of reverence; reverend person. **~স্পদা** *fem.* **~ভাজনেষু, ~স্পদেষু** (form of address in letters) respected sir.

শ্রদ্ধেয় *adj* honourable; respectable; venerable; reverend; trustworthy; credible. **শ্রদ্ধেয়া** *fem.* **~তা** *n* respectability; trustworthiness; credibility.

শ্রবণ *n* **1** hearing; that which is heard; audition; listening (to). **2** ear. **~ করা** *vt* hear; listen/ attend to; give ear to; be attentive; learn/ hear anything about. **~গোচর** *n* range of hearing. ❑*adj* being within hearing. **~ পথ** *n* ear-passage; ear; hearing. **~ বহির্ভূত** *adj* incapable of being heard; inaudible. **~বিবর** *n* auditory passage; ear. **~মধুর, ~মনোহর** *adjj* sweet to hear. **~মূল** *n* root of the ear. **~যোগ্য** *adj* worth hearing/ listening to; audible. **~সুখকর** *adj* pleasant to the ear. **শ্রবণাতিক্রান্ত, শ্রবণাতীত**= ~বহির্ভূত.

শ্রবণীয় *adj* to be heard; worth hearing; audible.

শ্রবণেন্দ্রিয় *n* organ/ sense of hearing; ear.

শ্রব্য *adj*= শ্রবণীয়. **~কাব্য** *n* poem intended to be heard, ie excluding drama. **~তা** *n* audibility.

শ্রম *n* **1** labour; toil; exertion; effort. **2** hard work; diligence; assiduity; industry; application; pains; trouble. **3** fatigue; weariness; exhaustion. **4** rigour: স~ কারাদণ্ড. **~ করা** *vi* labour; toil; make effort; exert one's self; do hard work; apply oneself diligently/ assiduously; do physical/ manual labour; strive; work hard; strenuous; toilsome; fatiguing. **~কর** *adj* causing fatigue/ trouble; painstaking; **~কাতর** *adj* reluctant to toil; lazy; sluggard. **~ক্লান্ত** *adj* exhausted with fatigue. **~খিন্ন** *adj* depressed by fatigue. **~জ** *n* produced by toil/ industry; industrial. **~জ দ্রব্য** *n* industrial product. **~জনক**=~কর. **~জল** *n* sweat; perspiration. **~জীবী** *adj* earning one's livelihood by manual labour; working-class. ❑*n* labourer; workman; industrial worker. **~জীবীসঙ্ঘ** *n* trade union. **~জীবী সমাজ** *n* working class. **~নাশ** *n* removal of fatigue. **~নাশক** *adj* dispelling fatigue. **~বণ্টন, ~বিভাগ** *nn* division of labour. **~বিমুখ**=~কাতর. **~ মন্ত্রণালয়** *n* Ministry of labour. **~ মহাধ্যক্ষ** *n* Labour Commissioner. **~লব্ধ** *adj* obtained/ earned by toil/ industry. **~লভ্য** *adj* obtainable by effort/ endeavour/ application. **~শিল্প** *n* industry. **~শীল, ~সহিষ্ণু** *adj* laborious; diligent; industrious; assiduous; painstaking; hard-working. **~শীলতা, ~সহিষ্ণুতা** *nn* industry; endeavours; diligence; assiduity. **~সাধ্য** *adj* to be accomplished by exertion; laborious; toilsome; strenuous. **~সিদ্ধ** *adj* accomplished by exertion/ labour; laboured. **~স্বীকার করা** *vi* take trouble/ pains. **~ হরণ**=~নাশ. **শ্রমাপনয়ন, শ্রমাপনোদন** *nn* dispelling fatigue. (**শ্রমাপনয়ন/ শ্রমাপনোদন করা** *vi* allay/ remove fatigue; refresh; freshen up. **অনুৎপাদক ~** *n* unproductive labour. **উৎপাদক ~** *n* productive labour.

শ্রমণ *n* Buddhist monk/ mendicant; ascetic.

শ্রমিক *n*=শ্রমজীবী (⇒ শ্রম). **~ আন্দোলন** *n* labour movement. **~ গোলযোগ** *n* labour unrest/

trouble. ~ **দল** *n* gang of labourers; (pol) Labour Party. ~ **সঙ্ঘ** *n* trade union.

শ্রমী *adj*=শ্রমশীল (⇒ শ্রম)

শ্রমোপজীবী *adj*=শ্রমজীবী (⇒ শ্রম) **শ্রমোপজীবিনী** *fem.*

শ্রাদ্ধ *n* **1** Hindu ceremony in honour and for the benefit of dead relatives; *sraddha*, obsequies; gifts/ offerings at a *sraddha*. **2** (iron) extravagant use/ spending; waste; squandering: টাকার ~. **3** (iron) vituperation. **4** (iron) undesirable affair. **5** (fig) utter ruin; exacerbation; cruel persecution. ~ **করা** *vi, vt* **1** perform the *sraddha* rites/ ceremonies. **2** (iron) squander; use/ spend extravagantly; fritter (away); dissipate; waste: টাকার ~ করা, play ducks and drakes with one's money. **3** revile; vituperate; inveigh against; swear like a trooper. **4** ruin utterly; wreck. ~ **খাওয়া** *vi* partake of the feast given on the occasion of a *sraddha* ceremony. ~ **গড়াবে** (sl) the undesirable affair will go a long way; the affair will be attended with (unpleasant) consequences. ~**কর্ম**, ~**কার্য**, ~**ক্রিয়া** *nn* *sraddha* rite; obsequies. ~**দেব** *n* any god presiding over *sraddha* rites; Yama. ~**শান্তি** *n* *sraddha* and similar rites so that the manes may enjoy blessed peace. **ভূতের বাপের** ~ (fig) utter confusion; mess; jumble; madhouse; bedlam.

শ্রাদ্ধিক *adj* relating to a *sraddha*. ❑*n* **1** recipient of *sraddha* oblations. **2** present given at a *sraddha*.

শ্রাদ্ধীয় *adj*=শ্রাদ্ধিক

শ্রান্ত *adj* tired; fatigued; exhausted; wearied. ~ **করা** *vt* tire; fatigue; exhaust; (make) weary. ~**কায়** *adj* having a tired/ exhausted body. ~**ক্লান্ত** *adj* wearied and exhausted; extremely tired/ exhausted. ~**গতি** *n* languid movement. ❑*adj* languid; slow-moving. ~**দেহ**=~কায়. ~**শয়ান** *adj* lying down wearied. ~**হৃদয়** *adj* wearied/ distressed in mind.

শ্রান্তি *n* fatigue; tiredness; weariness; exhaustion. ~**কর**, ~**জনক** *adj* fatiguing; tiring; wearisome; laborious; exhausting. ~**হর** *adj* removing/ allaying exhaustion/ fatigue/ weariness; refreshing. ~**হীন** *adj* untiring; tireless; indefatigable.

শ্রাবণ[১] *n* the fourth month of the Bengali calendar. ~-**ধারা** *n* incessant rain/ downpour of the month of *Shravan*. **ধারা**-~*n* *Shravan*, the month of incessant rain/ downpour.

শ্রাবণ[২] *adj* auditory; relating to/ perceived by the ear.

শ্রাবণী *n* day of full-moon in the month of *Shravan*.

শ্রাবিত *adj* caused to be heard; communicated; proclaimed, announced.

শ্রাব্য=শ্রবণীয়

শ্রী *n* **1** light; lustre; radiance; splendour; glory; beauty; grace; loveliness. **2** prosperity; welfare; good fortune; success; auspiciousness; wealth; treasure; riches. **3** high rank; power; might; majesty; royal dignity. **4** appearance; manner; style; attitude: কথার ~. **5** an appellation prefixed before the names of eminent persons or to that of a sacred thing or place: ~মধুসূদন, ~ক্ষেত্র. **6** name of an Indian musical mode. **7** name of Lakshmi (as goddess of prosperity and beauty and wife of Vishnu. **8** name of Saraswati (goddess of learning). **9** fame; renown. **10** intellect. ~**কণ্ঠ** *n* name of Shiva. ~**করকমল** *n* lotus-like auspicious hand. ~**করকমলেষু** (form of addressing a person respectfully, in a letter) to your/ his lotus-like auspicious hands. ~**কান্ত** *n* ''beloved by Shri'; Vishnu. ~**ক্ষেত্র** *n* Puri in Orissa. ~**খণ্ড** *n* sandal-tree; sandal. ~**ঘর** *n* (iron) prison; gaol; jail; cooler. ~**ঘরবাস** *n* imprisonment; confinement; captivity; incarceration. ~**চরণ** *n* auspicious foot. ~**চরণেষু** (form of addressing a venerable person, in a letter) to your/ his auspicious feet. ~**চরণকমল** *n* lotus-like auspicious foot. ~**চরণকমলেষু**=~চরণেষু. ~**পঞ্চমী** *n* the fifth day of the bright fortnight of the month of Magh (a festival in honour of Saraswati). ~**পতি** *n* name of Vishnu. ~**পথ** *n* royal road; highway. ~**পদ**, ~**পদপঙ্কজ**, ~**পদপল্লব**, ~**পাদ**, ~**পাদপদ্ম** *nn*=~চরণ. ~**ফল** *n* wood-apple (tree). ~**বৎস** *n* **1** name of Vishnu. **2** a mark/ curl of hair on the breast of Vishnu. ~**বৎসলাঞ্ছন** *n* Vishnu. ~**বৃদ্ধি** *n* prosperity; increase in wealth; advancement; growth; progress. ~**বৃদ্ধি লাভ করা** *vi* prosper; thrive; flourish; improve. ~**বৃদ্ধি সাধন করা** *vt* improve; cause to prosper/ thrive; promote prosperity/ wealth; advance; enrich; better, ameliorate. ~**ভ্রষ্ট** *adj* fallen from/ bereft of prosperity; in decline; impoverished; deprived of beauty/ grace/ glamour; decayed. ~**ভ্রষ্টা** *fem.* ~**মৎ** *adj* **1** beautiful; charming; lovely; pleasant; splendid; glorious. **2** possessed of fortune; fortunate; auspicious; wealthy; prosperous; eminent; illustrious; venerable (prefixed like Sri before the names of eminent persons and celebrated works). ~**মতী** *fem.* **1** an appellation prefixed before the names of Hindu women. **2** name of Radha (as a noun). ~**মন্ত**=~মৎ. ~**মান** *adj* (often prefixed before the name of a junior person)=~মৎ. ~**মুখ** *n* **1** beautiful/ auspicious face. **2** the word শ্রী written on the back of letter. ~**মূর্তি** *n* image or personification of Vishnu; image of Lakshmi;

any idol. ~যুক্ত, ~যুত, ~ল *adjj* happy; fortunate; famous; illustrious; wealthy (prefixed as an honorific title to the names of men). ~যুক্তা *fem.* ~রাগ=~ (6). ~শূন্য, ~হীন *adjj* deprived of beauty/ grace; ugly; wretched; miserable; ill-looking.

শ্রুত *adj* **1** heard; listen to; heard about/ of; transmitted orally. **2** known; famous; celebrated. ~কীর্তি *adj* one whose fame is heard about; famous. ~ধর, ~লিখন, ~লিপি, ~লেখক=শ্রুতিধর, শ্রুতিলিখন, শ্রুতিলিপি, শ্রুতিলেখক respectively (⇒ শ্রুতি).

শ্রুতি *n* **1** hearing; listening; audition. **2** organ/ power of hearing; ear. **3** that which is heard/ perceived by the ear; sound; noise. **4** rumour; report; hearsay; news; intelligence. **5** sacred knowledge; legend; the Veda. **6** (music) a particular division of the octave; quarter tone/ interval (twenty two of these are enumerated). ~কটু, ~কঠোর *adjj* harsh to the ear; unmelodious; grating; jarring; cacophonic. ~গম্য, ~গোচর *adjj* perceptible by the ear; audible. ~ধর *adj* retaining what has been heard; having a good memory. ❑*n* such a person. ~পথ *n* range of hearing; ear; earshot. ~মধুর *adj* pleasant to the ear; melodious. ~মূল *n* root of the ear. ~লিখন *n* (act of writing to) dictation; shorthand writing; stenography. ~লিপি *n* script written to dictation/ by shorthand. ~লেখক *n* writer taking dictation; shorthand writer; stenographer. ~সুখকর *adj* pleasant to hear/ the ear. ~স্মৃতি *n* the Veda and human tradition or law. ~হারী *adj* captivating the ear.

শ্রূয়মাণ *adj* being heard.

শ্রেঢ়ী *n* **1** (math) progression. **2** (math) series. ~ব্যবহার *n* rules of progression. ধারাবাহিক ~, বিপরীত ~ *nn* harmonic progression. ~গুণ ~ *n* geometrical progression. সমান্তর ~ *n* arithmetical progression.

শ্রেণী, শ্রেণি (in compounds) *n* **1** line; row; range; series; succession. **2** (alg) series. **3** troop; flock; multitude; number; swarm. **4** company (of artisans following the same business); community. **5** class: সামাজিক ~. **6** class (of school, college, etc); form. **7** division. **8** (phys) grade. ~করণ *n* classification; grading. ~কৃত *adj* classified; graded; made into a row; forming rows/ lines. ~ফল *n* (alg) sum of series. ~বদ্ধ, ~বিন্যস্ত *adjj* arranged in a line/ row; alined; aligned; arrayed; (bot) classified. ~বন্ধ, ~বিন্যাস *nn* formation of a row/ line; classification. ~বন্ধ পদ্ধতি, ~বন্ধ প্রণালী *nn* system of alignment/ arrayment/ classification. ~বন্ধসূত্র *n* principles of classification. ~বিভাগ *n* classification; division into classes/ communities/ castes/ groups. ~ভুক্ত *adj* included into a particular line/ class/ group.

শ্রেয় *adj* **1** better (than); more splendid/ beautiful; more excellent / distinguished; superior; preferable. **2** most excellent; best. **3** propitious; well disposed to; auspicious; fortunate; conducive to welfare/ prosperity; beneficial; proper. ❑*n* **1** the better state; the better fortune/ condition. **2** good; benefit; welfare; bliss; fortune; happiness. **3** bliss of final emancipation; felicity; beatitude. **4** virtue; religion. ~স্কর *adj* making better/ superior; causing/ securing fortune; conducive to happiness; salutary; wholesome; beneficial. ~স্করী *fem.* ~স্কাম *adj* desirous of welfare/ prosperity.

শ্রেয়ঃ=শ্রেয়. ~কল্প *adj* almost the best.

শ্রেয়ান *adj* better; superior; beneficial; good; excellent; more beneficial. শ্রেয়সী *fem.*

শ্রেয়ো=শ্রেয় (in compounds). ~জনক=শ্রেয়স্কর. ~র্থী *adj* desirous of good/ felicity/ bliss; ambitious. ~লাভ *n* attainment of good/ virtue/ bliss/ felicity.

শ্রেষ্ঠ *adj* **1** most excellent; best; first; chief. **2** best of/ among/ in respect of. **3** most splendid/ beautiful; most beautiful of/ among. **3** greatest; superior; better. শ্রেষ্ঠা *fem.* ~তম *adj* the very best; the most excellent. ~তর *adj* more excellent; better than. ~তা, ~ত্ব *n* superiority; eminence; excellence; pre-eminence.

শ্রেষ্ঠী=শেঠ

শ্রোণি *n* hip and loins; buttocks; posteriors. ~চক্র *n* pelvis. ~তট *n* slope of the hips. ~দেশ *n* region of the hips. ~ফলক *n* hip and loins. ~বিম্ব *n* round hips; waist-band. ~সূত্র *n* string worn round the loins.

শ্রোতব্য *adj* to be heard/ listened to; worth hearing; audible.

শ্রোতা *n* hearer; listener. শ্রোত্রী *fem.*

শ্রোতৃবর্গ, শ্রোতৃমণ্ডলী *n pl* audience.

শ্রোত্র *n* **1** ear. **2** the Veda.

শ্রোত্রিয় *adj* versed in the Veda/ conversant with sacred knowledge. ❑*n* **1** Brahmin versed in the Veda/ conversant with sacred knowledge; theologian; divine. **2** (one of) a class of Brahmins who are not *kulins* (কুলীন).

শ্রৌত *adj* **1** relating to hearing/ the ear; audible; auditory. **2** relating to the sacred tradition; prescribed by/ founded on/ conformable to the Veda. ❑*n* three sacred fires collectively.

শ্লক্ষ্ণ *adj* **1** slippery; smooth. **2** polished; fine; refined; bland; tender. ~তা *n* smoothness.

শ্লথ=শিথিল. ~গতি *adj* slow-moving; sluggish; leisurely. ~ন *n* relaxation. ~বন্ধন *adj* loose;

loosened. ~বৃন্ত *adj* having a loose stalk; falling. ~সন্ধি *adj* having weak joints.

শ্লাঘনীয় *adj* praiseworthy; laudable; commendable. ~তা *n* praiseworthiness.

শ্লাঘা *n* **1** pride; vaunt; boasting. **2** praise; commendation. আত্ম~ *n* self-praise; boasting; exaltation.

শ্লিপ [E] *n* slip.

শ্লিষ্ট *adj* **1** embraced; clasped; entwined. **2** clinging/ adhering to; adhering closely; fitting tight; joined together; united; connected; attached. **3** (rhet) connected so as to be susceptible of a double interpretation; equivocal. ~ প্রয়োগ *n* equivocation. ~রূপক *n* (rhet) ambiguity as a metaphor.

শ্লীপদ *n* swelled leg; elephantiasis.

শ্লীল *adj* decent; polite; courteous; modest; decorous. ~তা *n* decency; politeness; courtesy; modesty; decorum. ~তাহানি *n* violation of modesty; outraging modesty (of a woman); rape; sexual assault.

শ্লেট=স্লেট

শ্লেষ *n* **1** connection; junction; (sexual) union. **2** (rhet) double meaning; equivoque; ambiguity; paranomasia; pun; hidden meaning. **3** irony; insinuation; ridicule; sarcasm; mockery. **4** adhering/ clinging to; embracing; embrace. ~ করা *vi* insinuate (against); direct an ironical/ sarcastic remark (at/ against); ridicule; deride.

শ্লেষোক্তি *n* expression having a double meaning; sarcasm; insinuation; ironical/ insinuating remark.

শ্লেষ্মা *n* mucus; phlegm; rheum; phlegmatic humour; catarrh. বুকে ~ জমা have congestion in one's chest. ~ ঝরা *vi* have one's nose running. ~ঘটিত *adj*=শ্লৈষ্মিক. ~ ধাতু *n* phlegmatic humour.

শ্লৈষ্মিক *adj* mucous; phlegmatic; catarrhal; rheumatic. ~ ঝিল্লি *n* mucous membrane.

শ্লোক *n* **1** poem; stanza; couplet; distich. **2** proverb; maxim. **3** fame; renown; glory; praise; hymn of praise: পুণ্য~. শ্লোকাত্মক *adjj* versified.

শ্ব *n* dog. ~দন্ত *n* canine tooth. ~বৃত্তি *n* **1** dog-like behaviour; servility; servitude; mean/ clinging/ obsequious/ flattery; toadyism. **2** gaining a livelihood by manual labour; servitude.

শ্বশুর *n* father-in-law; uncle-in-low. শাশুড়ি *fem.* ~ঘর *n* a woman's father-in-law's or husband's house. ~ঘর করা *vi* (of a woman) lead a married life (in one's father-in-law's/ husband's house). ~বাড়ি, শ্বশুরালয় *nn* a man's father-in-law's house. ~ মন্দির *n* (facet)=~বাড়ি.

শ্বশ্রূ (মাতা) *n fem* mother-in-law; aunt-in-law.

শ্বসন *n* **1** breathing; respiration; hissing; panting; breath. **2** air wind. ~তন্ত্র *n* respiratory system. কৃত্রিম ~ *n* artificial respiration.

শ্বসমান *adj* breathing (heard); respiring; panting.

শ্বসিত *adj* breathed; sighed; possessed of breath/ life.

শ্বা *n* dog. ~দন্ত *n* canine tooth.

শ্বান *n* dog. ❑*adj* canine.

শ্বাপদ *n* beast of prey; wild beast. ❑*adj* relating/ belonging to a wild best. ~সঙ্কুল, ~সমাকীর্ণ *adjj* frequented/ infested by wild beasts.

শ্বাস *n* **1** breath; respiration; breathing; aspiration. **2** affection of the breath; hard breathing; asthma; asthmatic spasm. **3** (last) gasp. ~ ওঠা *vi* be at one's last gasp; be attacked with a spell of asthma spasms. ~ ছাড়া *n* breathe out; exhale; respire; sigh; heave a sigh. ~ নেওয়া *vi* breathe in; draw breath; inhale. ~কষ্ট *n* breathing trouble; dyspnœa; difficulty of breathing; hard breathing of a dying person. ~কাশ *n* 'breath-cough'; asthma. ~কার্য, ~ক্রিয়া *nn* breathing; respiration. ~কেন্দ্র *n* respiratory centre. ~গ্রহণ *n* inhalation. ~ গ্রহণ করা=~ নেওয়া. ~ত্যাগ *n* exhalation. ~ ত্যাগ করা=~ ছাড়া. ~ধারণ *n* suppression/ suspension of breath. ~নালী *n* windpipe; trachea. ~পথ *n* respiratory passage. ~ প্রশ্বাস *n* respiration; breathing. ~যন্ত্র *n* respiratory organ. ~রোগ *n* any disease characterized by breathing trouble; pulmonary disease. ~রুদ্ধ *adj* suffocated; choked. ~রুদ্ধকর *adj* suffocating; choking. ~রোধ *n* obstruction of the breath; oppression of the chest; suffocation; choking; bated breath. ~রোধ করা *vt* suffocate; choke; make breathless; smother: stifle; asphyxiate. ~রোধ হওয়া *vi* be suffocated/ choked/ asphyxiated; choke; become breathless. ~রোধক=~রুদ্ধকর. শ্বাসারি *n* (Ayu) a plant used as a cure for breathing trouble; *Costus speciosus*.

শ্বেত *n* white (colour). ❑*n* white; bright; dressed in white; (of hair) grey. শ্বেতা *fem.* ~কায় *adj* white-bodied; white-complexioned. ~কুষ্ঠ *n* white leprosy; leucoderma. ~কেশ *n* white hair. ~চর্ম *n* white skin. ❑*adj* white-skinned. ~দ্বীপ *n* **1** name of a mythological abode of the blessed. **2** (facet) British Isles. ~পাথর, ~প্রস্তর *nn* marble. ~প্রদর *n* leucorrhoea. ~ রক্তকণিকা *n* white corpuscle. ~মণ্ডল *n* sclerotic coat. ~শুভ্র *adj* very white; snow-white. ~সর্ষপ *n* white mustard. ~সার *n* starch. ~হস্তী *n* (lit fig) white elephant. শ্বেতাভ *adj* whitish; having a white glow/ tinge. শ্বেতাম্বর *n* white garment. ❑*adj* clad in white.

শ্বেতি, শ্বেতী *nn* white leprosy; leucoderma.

ষ

ষ *n* the thirty-first consonant of the Bengali alphabet. It is an unvoiced unaspirated post-dental fricative sound; allophone of শ.

ষট্ *n, adj* (in compounds) six. **~ক** *n* sextet(te); hexad. **~কর্ণ** *n* six ears. ❑*adj* six-eared; heard by six ears (said of secret counsel which has been unfortunately heard by a third person). **~কর্ম** *n* the six duties of Brahmins (study, teaching the Veda, offering sacrifices, conducting them for others, giving and accepting gifts). **~কোণ** *n, adj* six-angled (figure); hexagon (al). **~চক্র** *n* the six mystical circles of the body. **~চত্বারিংশ** *n, adj* forty-six(th). **~চত্বারিংশৎ** *n, adj* forty-six. **~চত্বারিংশত্তম** *adj* forty-sixth. **~চত্বারিংশত্তমী** *fem.* **~চরণ** *adj* six-footed. ❑*n* **1** louse. **2** bee. **~ত্রিংশ** *n, adj* thirty-six(th). **~ত্রিংশৎ** *n, adj* thirty-six. **~ত্রিংশত্তম** *adj* thirty-sixth. **~ত্রিংশত্তমী** *fem.* **~পঞ্চাশ** *n, adj* fifty-six(th). **~পঞ্চাশৎ** *n, adj* fifty-six. **~পঞ্চাশত্তম** *adj* fifty-sixth. **~পঞ্চাশত্তমী** *fem.* **~পদ** *adj* six-footed; hexapod. ❑*n* bee. **~পদী** *fem.* **~ষষ্ট** *adj* sixty-sixth. **~ষষ্টি** *n, adj* sixty-six. **~ষষ্টিতম** *adj* sixty-sixth. **~ষষ্টিতমী** *fem.* **~সপ্ততি** *n, adj* seventy-six. **~সপ্তমিতম** *adj* seventy-sixth.

ষড়্ *n, adj* (in compounds) six. **~ঋতু** *n* the six seasons. **~গুণ** *adj* six times; sixfold. **~জ** *n* name of the first of the seven primary notes of music. **~দর্শন** *n* the six systems of Hindu philosophy. **~ধা** *adj* six-edged; of six kinds/ manners; six times. ❑*adv* in six kinds/ manners; six times. **~বর্গ**=~রিপু. **~বিংশ** *adj* twenty-sixth. **~বিংশতি** *n, adj* twenty-six. **~বিংশতিতম** *adj* twenty-sixth. **~বিংশতিতমী** *fem.* **~বিধ** *adj* of six sorts; sixfold. **~ভুজ** *adj* six-armed; six-sided; hexagonal. ❑*n* hexagon. **~যন্ত্র** *n* conspiracy; intrigue; secret plot. **~যন্ত্র করা** *vi* conspire; hatch a conspiracy; plot; intrigue. **~যন্ত্রকারী** *adj* conspiring; intriguing. ❑*n* conspirator; plotter; intriguer. **~রস** *n* six flavours/ tastes. **~রিপু** *n* the six inner foes/ faults of men.

ষড়ঙ্গ *n* the six principal parts of the body (ie two arms, two legs, head and waist); six limbs/ branches; the six limbs or works auxiliary to the Veda.

ষড়শীতি *n, adj* eighty-six. **~তম** *adj* eighty-sixth. **~তমী** *fem.*

ষড়ানন *n* six mouths/ faces; Kartikeya, the commander of the heavenly forces. ❑*adj* six-mouthed; sixfaced.

ষণ্ড *n* **1** bull; ox. **2** eunuch; hermaphrodite. **ষণ্ডা** *adj* as obstinate and hefty as a bull; robust; hefty; bull-headed. ❑*n* ruffian; hoodlum; brute.
ষণ্ডামর্ক, ষণ্ডামার্ক *n* **1** (myth) Shanda and Amarka, two roughish and godless teachers. **2** rowdy; brute; ruffian; hoodlum. ❑*adj* savage; savage-looking; brutish; ferocious. **ষণ্ডামি** *n* hooliganism; rowdyism; savagery ruffianism; thuggery.

ষণ্ণবতি *n, adj* ninety-six. **~তম** *adj* ninety-sixth. **~তমী** *fem.*

ষণ্মাস *n* period of six months; half a year. **ষণ্মাস্য** *adj* six months old; capable of being done in six months.

ষত্ব *n* state of the letter or sound sha (ষ); substitution of ষ for স. **~বিধান, ~বিধি** *nn* (gram) rules governing the substitution of ষ for স. **~ণত্ব** *n* substitution of ষ for স and ণ. for ন **~ণত্বজ্ঞান** *n* (lit) knowledge of the right use of the letters ষ and ণ; (fig) common sense; judgement.

ষষ্টি *n, adj* sixty. **~তম** *adj* sixtieth. **~সহস্র** *n, adj* sixty thousand.

ষষ্ঠ *adj* sixth. **ষষ্ঠাংশ** *n* one sixth; sixth part.

ষষ্ঠী *n fem* **1** name of a Hindu goddess supposed to protect children. **2** the sixth day of the bright fortnight. **3** (gram) the sixth or genitive case. **~ তৎপুরুষ** *n* (gram) kind of compound of which the first member would (if uncompounded) be in the genitive case. **~তলা** *n* place for the worship of goddess Shashthi. **~বাটা** *n* Hindu ceremonial gift sent to a son-in-law on the eve of জামাই~ (⇒জামাই). **~বুড়ি** *n fem* goddess Shashthi. **~র কৃপা** *n* obtaining a child through the grace of goddess Shashthi; being blessed with many children.

ষাঁড় *n* ox; bull. **ষাঁড়াষাঁড়ি** *n* **1** fight between two bulls. **2** (also ষাঁড়াষাঁড়ির বান) floods/ tidal wave roaring like two bellowing bulls engaged in fighting each other; surging flood-water/ waves. **ষাঁড়ের গোবর/ নাদ** *nn* good-for-nothing; scamp; scallywag; nev'r-do-well; worthless fellow. **ষাঁড়ের গোঁ** *n* bull-like obstinacy; bull-headedness. **গোকুলের ~** *n* wilful/ wayward man; self willed person; gadabout. **ধর্মের ~** *n* wildly wayward man allowed to move scot-free.

ষাট[১] *n, adj* sixty.

ষাট[২] *int* May goddess Shashti (ষষ্ঠী) be with you for your safety; God forbid!

ষাণ্মাসিক *adj* six-monthly; half-yearly.

ষেট, ষেটে *nn*(colloq)=ষষ্ঠী. **ষেটের (কোলের) বাছা** (used by way of blessing) favoured child of

Shashthi. **ষেটেরা** *n* Hindu ceremony performed on the sixth day of a child's birth.

ষোড়শ *n* **1** sixteen. **2** aggregate of sixteen kinds of gifts given at a *shraddha* (শ্রাদ্ধ). ❑*adj* sixteen; sixteenth. **~উপচার**=ষোড়শোপচার. **~কলা** *n* sixteen digits of the moon. **~দান** *n*=~(2). **~ মাতৃকা** *n* sixteen divine mothers. **ষোড়শাংশ** *n* sixteenth part; one-sixteenth. **ষোড়শাঙ্গ** *adj* having sixteen parts/ ingredients.

ষোড়শী *adj fem* (of ষোড়শী) sixteen years old. ❑*n* **1** sixteen years old girl. **2** name of the one of the ten Mahavidya (মহাবিদ্যা).

ষোড়শোপচার *n* sixteen different articles necessary for a perfect worship; sixteen acts of homage. **ষোড়শোপচারে** *adv* **1** with all the necessary sixteen articles. **2** (fig) lavishly; thoroughly.

ষোল *n, adj* sixteen. **~ আনা** *n* sixteen *annas* (আনা); one Taka/ Rupee. ❑*adj* total; whole; complete. ❑*adv* totally; wholly; completely; thoroughly. **~ই** *n, adj* sixteenth (of a month). **~ কড়াই কানা** *adj* totally useless/ defective/ false. **~কলা** *n* the sixteen digits of the moon. **~কলায়** *adv* thoroughly; completely; in every respect: বাপের স্বভাব একেবারে ~কলায় পেয়েছে. **~কলায় পূর্ণ হওয়া 1** be in full bloom. **2** (iron) be thoroughly fulfilled.

ষ্টক, ষ্টকিং, ষ্টীম, ষ্টীমার, ষ্টীল, ষ্টেট, ষ্টেশন, ষ্টোভ, ষ্ট্যান্ডার্ড, ষ্ট্যাম্প, ষ্ট্রীট=স্টক, স্টকিং, স্টিম, স্টিমার, স্টিল, স্টেট, স্টেশন, স্টোভ, স্ট্যান্ডার্ড, স্ট্যাম্প, স্ট্রিট

স

স[১] *n* the thirty-second consonant of the Bengali alphabet. It is an unvoiced unaspirated pre-alveolar sound; allophone of শ.

স[২] *pref* (expressing junction, conjunction, possession, similarity, equality) with; together/ along with; accompanied by; added to; having; possessing; containing; having the same: সসম্মান, সশিষ্য, সজাতীয়, সতীর্থ.

সই[১] *n fem* (colloq)=সখী

সই[২] [A] *n* signature; impression/ mark given as a substitute for signature: টিপ~. **~ করা/ দেওয়া** *vi* sign; put one's signature; put an impression/ mark as a substitute for signature. **তাই ~** let it be.

সই[৩] *adj* capable of hitting the mark; possessing marksmanship.

সই[৪] *adj* just (enough); right. **~-সই** *adj, adv* not more not less; just enough.

সই[৫] [A] *suff* indicating **(a)** able to; -able; -ible: টেক~, জুত~; **(b)** up to: মাথা~, বুক~; **(c)** conforming to: মাপ~, পছন্দ~.

সই[৬] *suff* laid: মাটি~, জল~.

সইস *n* =সহিস

সওগাত, সওগাৎ [P] *n* (rich) present; gift.

সওদা [P] *n* trade; traffic; purchase; marketing; bargaining; goods; wares; merchandise. **~ করা** *vi* buy; purchase; strike a bargain. **~গর** *n* trader; merchant (prince). **~গরি, ~গরী** *n* profession of a merchant; commerce; trade. ❑*adj* mercantile; commercial. **~গরি করা** *vi* work as a merchant; follow the occupation of a trader; trade. **~গরি অফিস** *n* merchant office; mercantile firm. **~গরি মাল** *n* merchandise. **~পত্র, ~পাট, ~সুলুপ** *nn* traffic; barter; goods; wares; purchases.

সওয়া[১] *vt* **1** bear; suffer; endure; sustain. **2** tolerate; stand: অন্যায় ~. **3** be inured (to): গা~. **4** brook: অপমান ~. **5** get acclimatized to: আবহাওয়া ~. **~নো** *vt* cause to bear/ suffer/ endure/ sustain; inure; acclimatize.

সওয়া[২], **সোয়া** *n, adj* one and one-fourth; one and a quarter. **~ ঘণ্টা** *n* an hour and a quarter. **~ দুই** *n* two and a quarter. **~ দুটো বাজে** It is a quarter past two.

সওয়াব=সোয়াব

সওয়ার [P] *n* rider; passenger; traveller on horse back; horseman; cavalry-man; trooper. ❑*adj* mounted; riding. **~ হওয়া** *vi* ride; mount. **ঘোড়~** *n* rider; horseman.

সওয়ারি [P] *n* **1** conveyance; vehicle; carriage; mount. **2** rider; passenger. **3** riding; cavalcade. **4** bridge (of string instruments). ❑*adj* mounted; riding. **~ হওয়া** *vi* mount; board a vehicle; ride.

সওয়াল [A] *n* **1** question; inquiry; query. **2** petition; application. **3** request; demand; proposition. **4** problem. **5** cross examination. **~ করা** *vt* question; inquire; plead/ argue (on behalf of a plaintiff); cross-examine; ask; beg. **~ জবাব** *n* question and answer; argument and counter-argument. **~ জবাব করা** *n* argue; plead; discuss.

সং[১] *n*=সঙ

সং[২] *pref*=সম

সংকট, সংকটোত্তীর্ণ, সংকর, সংকরীকরণ, সংকর্ষণ, সংকলক, সংকলন, সংকলিত, সংকল্প, সংকল্পিত, সংকীর্ণ, সংকীর্তন, সংকীর্তিত, সংকুচিত, সংকুল, সংকুলান, সংকেত, সংকোচ, সংগীত, সংগুপ্ত, সংগূঢ়, ⇒ সঙ্কট, সঙ্কটোত্তীর্ণ, সঙ্কর, সঙ্করীকরণ, সঙ্কর্ষণ, সঙ্কলক, সঙ্কলন, সঙ্কলিত, সঙ্কল্প, সঙ্কল্পিত, সঙ্কীর্ণ, সঙ্কীর্তন, সঙ্কীর্তিত, সঙ্কুচিত, সঙ্কুল, সঙ্কুলান, সঙ্কেত, সঙ্কোচ, সঙ্গীত, সঙ্গুপ্ত, সঙ্গূঢ়

সংক্রম *n* 1 going/ entering together. 2 course; progress. 3 transition; passage/ transference to; transit. 4 passage of the sun/ a planet through the zodiacal sign. 5 bridge.

সংক্রমণ *n* 1 going/ meeting together; union with; entrance into. 2 transference to; transferring. 3 entrance; appearance; commencement. 4 (med) infection; contagion. 5 transmission (of a practice/ virtue/ vice). 6 the sun's passage from one sign of the zodiac to another. ~ **করা** *vi* 1 come together; meet; encounter. 2 come near; approach; appear. 3 enter (a constellation). 4 go/ pass over or through; transit. 5 (med) infect. 6 be transmitted (into). ~ **কাল** *n* (astron) time of transmit. ~ **যন্ত্র** *n* transit instrument.

সংক্রমণিকা *n* gallery.

সংক্রমিত *adj* 1 conducted; led to. 2 transferred; changed. 3 infected; transmitted; communicated. 4 transited (from one zodiacal sign to another). ~ **হওয়া** *vi* 1 enter. 2 (of diseases) infect; be transmitted. 3 (of patients) be infected. 4 be influenced by; acquire (as a practice). 5 (astron) pass/ make a transit from one zodiacal sign to another.

সংক্রান্ত *adj* 1 (used as a *suff)* of; relating/ pertaining to; regarding; as regards; concerning. 2 gone/ come together; passed/ transferred from.

সংক্রান্তি *n* 1 (astron) passage of the sun/ a planet from one sign/ position in the heavens to another. 2 last day of a Bengali month: চৈত্র~.

সংক্রাম=সংক্রম. ~**ক** *adj* 1 infections; contagious. 2 wide; broad; extensive. ~**ক বিষ** *n* virus. ~**রোগ** *n* infectious disease.

সংক্রামণ=সংক্রমণ (⇒ সংক্রম)

সংক্রামিত=সংক্রমিত

সংক্ষিপ্ত *adj* abbreviated; condensed; summarized; abridged; shortened; reduced; curtailed; short; brief; concise. ~ **করা**=সংক্ষেপ করা. ~**তা** *n* conciseness; shortness; brevity; concision. ~-**নির্ধার** *n* summary assessment. ~-**বিচার** *n* summary trial. ~**সার** *n* summary; abstract; précis; synopsis.

সংক্ষুব্ধ *adj* violently agitated/ shaken/ disturbed; extremely aggrieved/ troubled/ concerned/ perturbed/ mortified.

সংক্ষেপ *n* 1 summarization; condensation; abridgement; compression; shortening; abbreviation; reduction; curtailment. 2 summary; précis; synopsis; abstract; compendium; epitome; brief exposition; essence; quintessence. 3 conciseness. ~ **করা** *vt* summarize; compress; condense; abridge; shorten; curtail; abbreviate; reduce. **সংক্ষেপণ** *n*=~ (1). ~**ত**, ~**তঃ**, **সংক্ষেপে** *adv* in short/brief; briefly; in few words; in fine; in substance; in a word.

সংক্ষেপিত=সংক্ষিপ্ত

সংক্ষোভ *n* violent shock/ jolt; agitation; commotion; disturbance; great perturbation/ concern/ aggrievement.

সংখ্যক *adj* numbering; amounting to; numbered: ৫ ~ ধারা.

সংখ্যা *n* 1 number; sum; total; numeral; (math) figure. 2 reckoning; calculation; enumeration. 3 term. ~ **করা** *vt* enumerate; count; estimate; calculate; sum up; reckon. ~ **হওয়া** *vi* be capable of being enumerated/ counted/ numbered; be countable. ~ **গণনা** *n* enumeration; counting. ~**গরিষ্ঠ** *adj* larger in number; (being in the/ a) majority. ~**গরিষ্ঠতা** *n* majority. ~**গুরু** *adj* large/ larger in number; enjoying a majority. ~**গুরু (~গরিষ্ঠ) সম্প্রদায়** *n* majority community. ~**জ্যোতিষ** *n* numerology. ~**ত** *adj* counted; enumerated; numbered; calculated; reckoned. **সংখ্যাতীত** *adj* innumerable; countless; numberless. **সংখ্যান** *n* enumeration; calculation; counting; numbering. ~**নুপাতে** *adv* in proportion to number. ~**পন** *n* estimation; enumeration; calculation. ~**পাত** *n* writing down a number. ~**বাচক** *adj* expressive of/ denoting number; numeral. ~**মাত্র** *n* mere enumeration. ~**মান** *n* measure. ~**মাপন** *n* measurement. **সংখ্যায়ক** *n* enumerator; calculator. ~**লঘিষ্ঠ** *adj* smallest in number. ~**লঘু**, ~**ল্প** *adj* small in number; minority; smaller in number. **সংখ্যাল্প প্রতিবেদন** *n* minority report. ~**লঘু/ ~লঘিষ্ঠ সম্প্রদায়** *n* minority community. ~**শব্দ** *n* numeral. ~**সূচক**=~বাচক.

সংখ্যেয় *adj* countable; to be numbered/ enumerated/ calculated; calculable.

সংগ [P] *n* stone. ~**তরাশ** *n* stone-cutter; sculptor. ~**দিল** *adj* hard-hearted; merciless. ~**সার, সংগেসার** *adj* stoned (to death). **সংগে মর্মর** *n* marble.

সংগঠক *n* organizer.

সংগঠন *n* organization; organized body. ~ **করা** *vt* organize.

সংগঠিত *adj* organized. ~ **করা** *vt* organize.

সংগর *n* parole.

সংগমন *n* concurrence.

সংগামী *adj* concurrent.

সংগীত=সঙ্গীত

সংগৃহীত *adj* 1 collected; gathered; raised: ~ অর্থ/ তহবিল. 2 compiled: ~ শব্দাবলী. 3 picked; culled: ~ ফুল.

সংগোপন, সংগোপিত=সঙ্গোপন, সঙ্গোপিত respectively.

সংগ্রহ, সংগ্রহণ *nn* 1 collecting; collecting; gathering; raising: চাঁদা ~, গল্প ~. 2 anthology; compilation: শব্দ~. 3 collected: রচনা~ 4

accumulation; conglomeration; agglomeration. **5** culling; picking: পুষ্প~; taking; obtaining; acquisition. **~ করা** *vt* collect; gather; raise; compile; accumulate; obtain; acquire; assemble; cull; pick. **~কার, ~কারী** *adj* collecting; gathering; compiling; accumulating; culling. ❑*nn*=সংগ্রাহক.

সংগ্রহীতা=সংগ্রাহক. **সংগ্রহীত্রী** *fem.*

সংগ্রাম *n* **1** struggle: জীবন~. **2** war; battle; hostile encounter; fight; combat; conflict. **~ করা** *vi, vt* struggle; fight; make war; combat; engage in a war/ battle; encounter. **~শীল** *adj* engaged in war; struggling; combative; militant; never shy of fighting/ struggling.

সংগ্রামী=সংগ্রামশীল (⇒ সংগ্রাম). **~ মনোবৃত্তি** *n* fighting spirit; will to struggle.

সংগ্রাহ *n* grasping; forcible seizure; fist; clenching the fist. **~ক** *n* gatherer; compiler; collector; raiser; culler. **সংগ্রাহিকা** *fem.*

সংঘটন, সঙ্ঘটন *nn* **1** occurrence; happening; incident. **2** act of causing. **3** union/ junction with; assemblage.

সংঘটিত *adj* **1** brought about; come about. **2** assembled/ brought together. **~ হওয়া** *vi* happen; come about; be brought about; occur; take place; supervene.

সংঘট্ট *n* **1** rubbing/ clashing together; friction; collision. **2** conflict; rivalry. **3** junction/ union with. **~ণ** *n* encountering; close contact/ union. **2**=~.

সংঘট্টিত *adj* **1** rubbed/ struck together/ against; kneaded. **2** collected; assembled.

সংঘর্ষ *n* **1** rubbing together; friction; collision. **2** mutual attrition; rivalry; conflict; clash; strife. **~ন**=~. **~ জনিত** *adj* caused by collision/ friction.

সংঘাত *n* **1** striking/ dashing together; crushing. **2** clash; collision; conflict; strife; combat; war. **3** (mech) impact. **~-বল** *n* (mech) resultant force. **~-রেখা** *n* (mech) line of impact. **সরল সমক্ষ ~** *n* (mech) direct impact.

সংঘুষিত, সঙ্ঘুষ্ট *adjj* sounded; proclaimed; resonant.

সংঘৃষ্ট *adj* rubbed with/ together; collided.

সংচারাজ্ঞা *n* transit visa.

সংচিতি *n* reserve.

সংচূর্ণন *n* grinding to powder; trituration; comminution.

সংচূর্ণিত *adj* completely pulverized/ comminuted; cut/ broken to pieces; triturated. **~ করা** *vt* grind to powder; comminute; pulverize; triturate.

সংচেতনা *n* synaesthesia.

সংজ্ঞা *n* **1** name; appellation; title; technical term; designation. **2** consciousness. **3** clear knowledge/ conception/ motion/ understanding. **4** (loose) definition. **~ দেওয়া** *vt* name; designate; give name/ appellation. **~ পাওয়া** *vi* recover consciousness. **~ হারানো** *vi* lose consciousness; fall senseless; faint; swoon. **~কেন্দ্র** *n* sensory centre. **~তন্ত্র** *n* sensory system. **~ত** *adj* understood; well-known; conscious. **~ন** *n* consciousness; perception. **~নাশ** *n* loss of consciousness; fainting. **~নাশক** *adj* rendering unconscious/ senseless. **~বাচক** *adj* **1** (gram) proper. **2** appellative. **~বাচক বিশেষ্য** *n* proper noun. **সংজ্ঞার্থ** *n* definition; technical meaning. **~লাভ** *n* recovering/ regaining consciousness. **~লোপ**=~নাশ. **~হারা, ~হীন** *adjj* senseless; unconscious.

সংজ্ঞাপন *n* apprising; informing; announcement; advertisement.

সংজ্ঞিত *adj* made known; communicated; name; termed; defined.

সংজ্বর *n* great heat/ fever.

সংদিল=সংগদিল (⇒সংগ)

সংনমন *n* compression.

সংনমিত *adj* compressed.

সংনম্য *adj* compressible.

সংনির্ণয় *n* judgement.

সংনির্ণীত *adj* adjudged.

সংপরিবর্তন *n* modification.

সংপাতবিন্দু *n* (geom) point of concurrency.

সংপুট, সংপূরক, সংপৃক্ত, সংপৃক্তি, সংপৃষ্ট, সংপ্রশ্ন, সংপ্লব = সম্পুট, সম্পূরক, সম্পৃক্ত, সম্পৃক্তি, সম্পৃষ্ট, সম্প্রশ্ন, সম্প্লব

সংবৎ *n* **1** year. **2** year introduced by Vikramaditya (in 58 BC) or Shalibahana (in 56 BC). **~সর** *n* a whole/ full year; year.

সংবদন *n* conversation; communication; discourse.

সংবরণ *n* **1** keeping back; checking; containing; restraint; prevention. **2** concealment; covering; closing; concealing; closing. **~ করা** *vt* **1** keep back; check; restrain; stop; contain; prevent: লোভ ~ করা. **2** cover; conceal; dress/ tie properly; put on/ wear properly.

সংবরা *vt* (poet)=সংবরণ করা

সংবর্ত *n* **1** rolling up; destruction; periodical destruction/ dissolution of the world; cataclysm. **2** rain-cloud; the cloud that appears to destroy the world. **সংবর্তক** *n* **1** submarine fire. **2** world-destroying clouds.

সংবর্তি, সংবর্তিকা *nn* wick.

সংবর্ধক *adj* **1** augmenting; increasing; promoting. **2** receiving respectfully.

সংবর্ধন, সংবর্ধনা *nn* **1** (respectful) reception; hearty/ warm reception; greeting; welcome. **2** prospering; thriving; complete growth; growing up. **3** furthering; promoting; fostering; rearing up. **4** augmenting; increasing. **সংবর্ধনা করা/ দেওয়া** *vt* receive warmly; accord a respectful/—

hearty reception; welcome warmly; do the honours.

সংবর্ধিত *adj* 1 brought to complete growth; brought up; reared; raised; cherished; completely grown/ developed. 2 warmly received/ greeted; felicitated; one to whom a warm reception has been accorded. সংবর্ধিতা *fem.*

সংবলিত *adj* joined/ mixed with; containing; bearing; possessed of; attended by.

সংবহ *n* guiding; conducting. ~ন *n* circulation: রক্ত~.

সংবাদ *n* 1 information; news; report; message. 2 conversation; colloquy with: সখী~. 3 narrative; story. ~দাতা *n* press reporter; newspaper correspondent. ~পত্র *n* newspaper. ~পত্র বিক্রেতা *n* news-agent. ~পত্রসেবী *n* journalist. ~-প্রতিষ্ঠান, ~ সরবরাহ প্রতিষ্ঠান *nn* news agency. ~বহ, ~বাহক, ~বাহী *n* messenger; courier. ~বাহক পায়রা *n* carrier-pigeon.

সংবাদিকা *n* miscellaneous news.

সংবাদী *adj* 1 conversing; talking. 2 (music) of a harmonizing with the principal one. 3 (pol) responsivist. ❑*n* interlocutor.

সংবার *n* obstacle; impediment; closure. ~ণ *n* warding off; keeping back.

সংবাস *n* (common) dwelling; house; cohabitation.

সংবাহ *n* 1 carrying/bearing along (loads). 2 guiding; conducting; circulation: রক্ত~. 3 rubbing the body; massage; carrying (as of a horse); shampooing. ~ক *adj* 1 load-carrying. 2 circulating. 3 massaging. ❑*n* 1 porter; conveyer; transporter. 2 masseur. 3 that which circulates. সংবাহিকা *fem.* ~ন=~. ~ন করা *vt* 1 carry (loads); convey; bear. 2 carry/ move/ rub along the body. 3 massage; curry; shampoo. সংবাহাগার *n* massage clinic/ parlour.

সংবাহিত *adj* 1 carried. 2 circulated; conducted; guided. 3 massaged; carried; shampooed.

সংবিগ্ন *adj* worried; agitated; concerned; disturbed; flurried; terrified.

সংবিৎ, সংবিদ *n* 1 consciousness. 2 intellect; understanding. 3 stipulation; agreement. 4 name; appellation. ~ পাওয়া *vi* regain/ recover consciousness. ~ হারানো *vi* lose consciousness; faint; fall senseless. ~পত্র *n* deed of agreement. ~ লঙ্ঘন *n* breach of agreement.

সংবিত্তি *n* 1 perception; feeling; sense; consciousness. 2 understanding; intellect.

সংবিদা *n* contract; deed of agreement.

সংবিদিত *adj* 1 known; recognized; understood. 2 informed.

সংবিধা, সংবিধান *n* 1 arrangement; disposition; management; prescription. 2 constitution of a state. 3 (biol) adaptation. সংবিধান-সভা *n* constituent assembly.

সংবিধি *n* statute. ~বদ্ধ *adj* statutory.

সংবিভক্ত *adj* divided; distributed; separated.

সংবিভাগ *n* 1 sharing with others; partition; distribution; bestowing. 2 rationing; rations. ~-নিয়ামক *n* controller of rationing. ~-পত্র *n* ration card.

সংবিষ্ট *adj* 1 seated. 2 asleep; sleeping. 3 absorbed; hypnotized.

সংবীক্ষণ *n* perceiving; search; inquiry; observation.

সংবীত *adj* 1 covered over; clothed; mailed; armoured. 2 covered/ surrounded/ furnished with. 3 concealed/ obscured by; hidden; invisible; wrapped round; unseen.

সংবৃত *adj* 1 covered; shut up; enclosed/ enveloped in; surrounded/ accompanied/ protected by. 2 concealed; laid aside; kept secured. 3 restrained; suppressed; retired; withdrawn: ~ আত্মা. 4 contracted; compressed; closed: ~ স্বর. ~ চুল্লি *n* muffled furnace.

সংবৃতি *n* 1 covering; concealing; keeping secret. 2 closure. 3 dissimulation; hypocrisy.

সংবৃত্ত *adj* 1 become; grown. 2 happened; occurred; passed. 3 concealed. সংবৃত্তা *fem.*

সংবৃত্তি *n* 1 fulfilment. 2 being; becoming; happening; existence.

সংবেগ *n* 1 violent agitation; excitement; flurry. 2 vehemence; intensity.

সংবেদ *n* sensation; perception; consciousness. ~ন=~. ~নশীল *n* sensitive; susceptible; sensory; sensorial. ~নশীলতা *n* sensitiveness; sensitivity. ~নীয় *adj* to be perceived/ felt. সংবেদ্য *adj* to be known/ understood/ learnt/ felt; intelligible; perceptible by senses; sensible. সংবেদ্যতা *n* intelligibility; perceptibility.

সংবেশ *n* 1 lying down; sleeping. 2 sitting. ~ক *n* hypnotist; mesmerist. ~ন *n*. 1 hypnosis; hypnotism; mesmerism. 2 lying down; sleeping. 3 sexual union; coition.

সংবেশিত *adj* hypnotized. ~ করা *vt* hypnotize.

সংব্যবহার *n* transaction.

সংভরণ *n* supplies; rationing. ~পত্র *n* ration card.

সংভার, সম্ভৃত *n* stock (of goods). ~-গণন *n* stock-taking. ~-বহি *n* stock-book; ledger.

সংভৃত, সম্ভৃতি *adj* stored; requisitioned; indented. ~-আধিকারিক *n* indenting officer. ~ক *n* indent.

সংভৃতি *n* storing; storage; requisitioning; indenting; indenture. ~পত্র *n* indent.

সংযত *adj* 1 self-controlled; self-possessed; self-contained; restrained; disciplined; self-restrained; continent. 2 moderate; temperate; sparing. 3 checked; controlled; repulsed;

curbed; subdued; prevented; suppressed. **4** modest; gentle; demure. ~ **করা** *vt* **1** restrain; control; govern; discipline; regulate. **2** restrict; temper; moderate. **3** suppress; prevent; check; repulse ; subdue; curb. ~**চিত্ত** *adj* controlled in mind; one whose mind is tranquil/ collected; temperate; self-restrained; abstemious. ~**বাক** *adj* restrained in speech; taciturn; reticent; sparing/ reserve in speech. **সংযতাহার** *adj* temperate in eating; sparing in food and drink.

সংযতেন্দ্রিয় *adj* having the senses/ passions controlled; continent.

সংযম *n* **1** restraint; continence; control (of the senses); self-control; discipline; temperance; self-restraint. **2** check; curb; restraint: বেগ~. **3** moderation; sparingness: বাক~. **4** subdual; control: ইন্দ্রিয়~. **5** modesty; demureness; gentleness: আচরণে ~. **6** concentration of mind. **7** fasting and other rites observed on the eve of a holy occasion. ~-**করা**=সংযত করা (⇒ সংযত). ~**ন** *n* curbing; checking; restraining; self-control; subduing; regularization; disciplining; tempering; moderation; controlling.

সংযমিত *adj* restrained; controlled; checked; subdued; disciplined; regulated; prevented; repulsed; curbed; tempered.

সংযমী *adj* one who subdues his passions; who/ what restrains/ curbs/ subdues; practising self-control/ discipline; self-restrained; moderate; temperate; abstemious; reserved; sparing; modest; demure.

সংযাত, সংজাত *adj* gone together; proceeded together.

সংযাত্রা *n* procession; travelling together.

সংযাত্রিক *n* processionist. ~ **দল** *n* procession.

সংযাত্রী *adj* going in a procession; travelling together. ❑*n* processionist; traveller.

সংযুত *adj* **1** composite. **2**=সংযুক্ত.

সংযুক্ত *adj* **1** joined/ bound together; tied; fettered; conjoined; linked; attached. **2** united; combined; connected; related. **3** admixed; amalgamated. **4** federated; federal. **5** placed/ put/ fixed in. **6** accompanied/ attended by. **সংযুক্তা** *fem.* ~ **করা** *vt* join/ bind together; tie; connect; unite; combine; place/ put/ fix in; link; conjoin; federate.

সংযুক্তি=সংযোজন

সংযুতি *n* composition.

সংযোগ *n* **1** connection; conjunction; combination; addition; relation; attachment; association. **2** union; absorption. **3** contact. **4** joining; linking. **5** admixture. **6** intercourse; communication; liaison. **7** close application: মনঃ~. ~ **সাধন করা** *vi* join; together; unite; link; couple; connect; bring together; fix on; piece/ attach together; connect; combine. ~ **স্থাপন করা** *vi* establish contact; get into touch. ~**ধর্মী** *adj* synthetic. ~**নিয়ম** *n* (with) associative law. ~**বিয়োগ** *n* addition and subtraction. ~**সাধক** *adj* joining; uniting; connecting. **সংযোগাধিকারিক** *n* liaison officer.

সংযোগী *adj* **1** being in contact/ connection; closely connected with; united. **2** joining; connecting; uniting.

সংযোজক *adj* **1** joining together; bringing together/ about; connecting; uniting; what/ that which joins/ attaches/ admixes/ unites/ amalgamates/ adds. **2** (gram). copulative. ~ **অব্যয়** *n* copulative conjunction.

সংযোজন *n* joining/ uniting with; linking; attachment; amalgamation; addition; admixture; unification. ~ **করা** *vt* join; link; attach; admix; add; amalgamate; assemble; connect. **সংযোজনা** *n* **1**=~. **2** arrangement.

সংযোজিত *adj* joined; conjoined; attached; linked; united; connected; assembled; mixed; amalgamated; admixed. ~**ব্য** *adj* to be joined/ united/ attached.

সংরক্ষক *n* guardian; keeper; protector; conserver; preserver; conservator; guard; custodian; defender; curator; one who arranges for reservation.

সংরক্ষণ *n* **1** guarding; watching; custody. **2** preservation; protection; safe-keeping; conservation; defence; safe-guard. **3** reservation. ~ **করা** *vt* guard; watch over; preserve; conserve; protect; defend; save from; keep; secure; reserve. ~ **নীতি** *n* protectionism. ~**শীল** *adj* conservative; protectionist. **সংরক্ষণাগার** *n* conservatory; preservatory; depository. **ধর্ম**~ *n* defence of faith. **বাণিজ্য**~ *n* protectionism. **শক্তি**~ *n* conservation of energy. **সতীত্ব** ~ *n* preservation of chastity.

সংরক্ষণীয় *adj* to be protected/ guarded; conservable; preservable; defendable; defensible.

সংরক্ষা=সংরক্ষণ

সংরক্ষিত *adj* protected; preserved; taken care of; conserved; guarded; defended; safeguarded; reserved.

সংরক্ষী *adj* one who guards. ❑*n* guardian; keeper.

সংরব্ধ *adj* **1** agitated; excited; enraged; furious; exasperated. **2** encouraged. **3** fast; swift.

সংরম্ভ *n* **1** vehemence; impetuosity; intensity; agitation; flurry. **2** excitement; zeal; enthusiasm; eagerness; ardent desire. **3** anger; fury; wrath (against).

সংরম্ভী *adj* angry; furious; inflamed; irritable; wrathful. **সংরম্ভিনী** *fem.*

সংরাধন *n* act of conciliating/pleasing by worship; perfect concentration of mind; meditation.

সংরাব *n* clamour; uproar; tumult.

সংরুদ্ধ *adj* stopped completely; obstructed hindered; confined; besieged; held; closed; sealed; detained; surrounded by.

সংরূঢ় *adj* grown; sprung up; sprouted.

সংরোধ *n* complete obstruction/opposition; hindrance; stop; restraint; prevention; restriction; confinement.

সংলগ্ন *adj* **1** closely attached; being in contact with; adhering; sticking to/in; adjoining; clinging to. **2** (math) adjacent. ~ **হওয়া** *vi* cling to; attach to; adhere to; be adjacent/ fixed to; adjoin.

সংলাপ *n* dialogue; conversation; friendly discussion.

সংলিপ্ত=সংলগ্ন

সংশপ্তক *n* an army which is determined to fight to the last.

সংশয় *n* doubt; uncertainty; hesitation; irresolution; suspicion; apprehension; scepticism; fear; concern. **~কর, ~জনক** *adj* causing doubt/risk; dubious. **~স্থ** *adj* being uncertainty; doubtful. **সংশয়াকুল** *adj* greatly troubled by doubt/ suspicion/ hesitation; greatly afraid of/ concerned about/ apprehensive of; beset with doubt. **সংশয়াত্মক** *adj* dubious; doubtful; uncertain. **সংশয়াত্মা** *adj* having a doubtful mind; sceptic; apprehensive. **~ন** *adj*=সংশয়ী. **সংশয়ান্বিত, সংশয়াপন্ন, সংশয়াবিষ্ট** *adjj* beset with doubt; doubtful about; suspicious; apprehensive; afraid; hesitating; uncertain; sceptical. **সংশয়পনোদন** *n* removal of doubt/ suspicion. **সংশয়ালু** *adj* disposed to doubt; doubtful/ sceptical about.

সংশয়িত *adj* irresolute; doubtful about. **সংশয়িতা** *fem.* **~ব্য** *adj* to be called in doubt; dubious; problematical.

সংশয়ী *adj* given to doubt/ suspicion; doubtful; dubious; fearful; apprehensive; sceptical by nature.

সংশিত *adj* **1** ready; prepared for/ resolved upon. **2** made ready; well-prepared; all right; accomplished; completed. **3** decided; firmly adhered to; rigid (as a vow). **~ব্রত** *adj* firmly adhering to a vow; faithful to an obligation; honest; virtuous.

সংশুদ্ধ *adj* completely purified/ cleansed; pure; clean.

সংশুদ্ধি *n* perfect purification/ purity; cleaning (the body); acquittal; acquittance; correction; rectification.

সংশোধক *adj* purifying; cleaning; rectifying; correcting; revising. ❑*n* purifier; cleaner; reformer; rectifier; corrector; reclaimer from evil ways.

সংশোধন *n* (thorough) purification/ rectification/ correction/ reformation/ revision/ amendment. ~ **করা** *vt* purify; rectify; correct; reform; revise; amend; cleanse thoroughly. ~ **অধিকারী** *n* revising authority. **~বাদ** *n* (pol) revisionism. **~বাদী** *n* revisionist. **সংশোধনাগার** *n* reformatory; house of correction.

সংশোধনীয় *adj* to be purified/ purged/ cleansed/ corrected/ revised/ amended/ reformed; reformable; amendable; corrigible; rectifiable; revisable.

সংশোধিত *adj* completely cleaned and purified; amended; reformed; corrected; rectified; revised; modified.

সংশোধ্য=সংশোধনীয়

সংশ্রয় *n* **1** conjunction; combination; connection; association. **2** refuge; shelter; asylum. **3** reference/ relationship to. **4** system.

সংশ্রয়ী *adj* having recourse to; seeking protection.

সংশ্রিত *adj* joined/ united with; leaning against; clinging to; resorted to; sought for refuge/ protection; clung to; embraced.

সংশ্রুত *adj* well heard; learnt.

সংশ্লিষ্ট *adj* **1** clasped/ pressed together; contiguous; coherent; closely connected with; attached; related with; associated/ associating with. **2** concerned; involved/ included in: ~ ব্যক্তি. **3** synthetic. **4** affiliated. ~ **করা** *vt* associate; include; affiliate; involve; attach; connect. ~ **আধিকারিক** *n* attached officer.

সংশ্লেষ *n* **1** junction; union; connection; close contact with; adhesion; attachment; association; relation; involvement. **2** synthesis. **3** (bot) conjugation. **~ণ** *n* **1** synthesis. **2** joining ; connecting; bond; cement. **~ণী** *adj* synthetic.

সংসক্ত *adj* **1** adhered/ stuck together; sticking fast; closely connected; united; coherent; cohering; adhering; closely connected; related. **2** (phys) tenacious. ~ **হওয়া** *vi* adhere/ stick together; stick fast; cohere.

সংসক্তি *n* **1** cohesion. **2** adherence; attachment; connection; relation; contact; intimacy; intercourse. **3** addiction/ devotion to. **4** chemical affinity.

সংসদ, সংসৎ *n* **1** assembly; parliament. **2** association; council; meeting; congress; session. **~সচিব** *n* parliamentary secretary. **~-সদস্য** *n* member of the parliament.

সংসরণ *n* **1** going about; walking/ wandering through; passing through. **2** highway; principal road.

সংসর্গ *n* **1** association; contact; connection; intercourse. **2** sexual union/ intercourse; cohabitation. **3** commingling; commixture; conjunction. **4** society; company; fellowship. ~ **করা** *vi* associate/ mix with; mingle with; cohabit; have sexual intercourse with; be intimate with; fraternize with. ~ **ছাড়া** *vi* give up company; dissociate oneself from. **সংসর্গজ** *adj* produced by union/ contact. ~ **দোষ** *n* fault/ evil consequence of association (with bad people). ~ **লিপ্সা** *n* longing for sb's company; sexual desire. **সংসর্গাভাব** *n* (logic) universal negation.

সংসর্প, সংসর্পণ *nn* **1** creeping; gliding; sneaking. **2** equable/ gentle motion. **3** expansive.

সংসর্পী *adj* creeping; moving gently along; floating/ swimming about; extending.

সংসার *n* **1** the world; secular life; worldly life; mundane existence. **2** domestic life; family. **3** earthly attachment and interests. **4** marriage. **5** housekeeping; household; married couple. ~ **করা** *vi* **1** lead domestic life; manage domestic affairs. **2** (of men) marry; take a wife; get married. **3** (of women) act as one's housewife; live with. ~ **চালানো**=~ করা (১). ~ **ত্যাগ করা** *vi* renounce the world. ~ **পাতা** *vi* set up a household (esp by marrying). ~**-অরণ্য, ~-কানন** *nn* world/ domestic life compared to a forest. ~ **কামনা** *n* desire for the joys of the world/ earthly enjoyments/ conjugal life; desire to lead domestic life; desire to set up a household. ~ **কারা(গার)** *n* world/ married life as a prison. ~ **গুরু** *n* world's guru; god of love. ~ **চক্র** *n* world compared to a wheel. ~ **জ্ঞান** *n* worldly wisdom; practical knowledge. ~ **ত্যাগ** *n* renunciation of the world. ~ **ত্যাগী** *adj* one who has renounced the world. ~ **ধর্ম** *n* domestic life/ duties; family life. ~ **পথ** *n* road of the world. ~ **পার** *n* next world. ~ **বন্ধন** *n* bonds/ fetters of the world. ~ **বাসনা**=~ কামনা. ~ **মরু** *n* world as a desert. ~ **যাত্রা** *n* earthly/ daily life; domestic life; livelihood. ~ **লীলা** *n* mortal/ worldly/ human life. ~ **সমুদ্র** *n* ocean-like world. ~ **সুখ** *n* joys of the world; happiness of domestic life. **সংসারারণ্য**=~ অরণ্য. **সংসারার্ণব**=~ সমুদ্র. **সংসারাশ্রম** *n* order/ state of a householder. **সংসারাশ্রমে প্রবেশ করা** *vi* settle down to married life; marry and settle down; start to live the life of a householder; enter the world. **সংসারাসক্ত** *adj* engrossed in earthly pleasures and interests. **সংসারাসক্তি** *n* attachment to worldly pleasures and interests.

সংসারী *adj* leading a family life; worldly; attached to mundane existence; mundane. ~ **লোক** *n* family man. **ঘোর** ~ *adj* **1**=সংসারাসক্ত (⇒সংসার). **2** deeply concerned with family and worldly interests.

সংসিক্ত *adj* well sprinkled / moistened.

সংসিদ্ধ *adj* **1** fully / thoroughly performed/ accomplished. **2** dressed; prepared. **3** attained; won. **4** innate, instinctive; natural. **4** one who has attained beatitude.

সংসিদ্ধি *n* **1** complete accomplishment/ fulfilment; perfection; success. **2** perfect state; beatitude; final emancipation. **3** healing; cure; recovery. **4** natural state/ quality; nature.

সংসূচিত *adj* indicated; shown; displayed.

সংসৃতি *n* course; revolution; passage (through).

সংসৃষ্ট *adj* **1** related; associated/ connected with; involved in; belonging to; affiliated (with). **2** mixed of various kinds.

সংসৃষ্টি *n* **1** union; combination; association; intercourse. **2** (rhet) association of two distinct metaphors in close proximity in one sentence.

সংস্করণ *n* **1** edition. **2** (rare) correction; revision.

সংস্কর্তা *n* **1** one who prepares/ dresses/ cooks. **2** purifier; reformer.

সংস্কার *n* **1** purification; cleansing; embellishment; adornment. **2** making ready; preparation; dressing (of food). **3** refining (of metals). **4** polishing (of gems). **5** cleansing the body; toilet; attire. **6** any purificatory ceremony; sacrament; ceremony performed on a dead body; sacred/ sanctifying ceremony (one which purifies from the taint of sin contracted in the womb). **7** making sacred; hallowing; consecration. **8** correction; amendment: ভ্রম~. **9** revision: গ্রন্থ~. **10** reformation; reforms. **11** repair; mending. **12** faculty of memory; mental impression/ recollection. **13** impression on the mind of acts done in a former state of existence. **14** mental conformation/ creation of the mind; irrational belief/ notion; prejudice; superstition; stock knowledge. **15** innate knowledge/ feeling; instinct; intuition. ~ **করা** *vt* **1** purify; cleanse; embellish; adorn; press; dress; refine; polish. **2** reform. **3** correct; revise; elaborate; amend. **4** repair; mend. **5** form/ arrange according to sacred precepts; hallow; consecrate; purify/ reclaim sacramentally. ~**ক** *adj* purifying; consecrating; making ready. ❑*n* **1** reformer. **2** purifier; cleaner; sacramental; purifier/ reclaimer. **3** mender; repairer; repairman. **4** cleaner; dresser. **5** corrector; reformer. **সংস্কারক** *adj* produced by purificatory rites; superstitions. ~ **বদ্ধ** *adj* bound by superstitions/ prejudices/ instincts/ stock notions. ~বর্জিত, ~হীন *adjj* **1** free from superstition/ prejudice/ stock notions. **2** without purificatory rites; a man of one of the three Hindu classes who has not been a recipient of initiation with the sacred thread or of the other purificatory ceremonies (and hence becomes an outcaste). ~বাদ *n* the doctrine that the world may be made better by human effort; maliorism. ~ সাধন করা *vi*=~ করা. সংস্কারাচ্ছন্ন *adj* blinded by superstitions/ prejudices/ stock notions. অন্ধ~ *n* blind/ irrational notion; prejudice. গৃহ~ *n* house-repair; (daily) cleansing of a house. বেশ~ *n* tidying up of one's dress; dressing.

সংস্কৃত *adj* **1** purified; consecrated; sanctified; hallowed; initiated. **2** cleansed; dressed. **3** reformed; polished; embellished; adorned; elegant; highly decorated. **4** mended; repaired. ❑*n* Sanskrit. ~জ্ঞ *adj* versed in Sanskrit.

সংস্কৃতি *n* **1** culture. **2** purification; reformation; perfection; hallowing; consecration. ~বান *adj* cultured.

সংস্ক্রিয়া *n* any purificatory rite or consecration.

সংস্থা *n* **1** establishment; association; guild; society; authority; club. **2** established order; position; location; situation.

সংস্থান *n* **1** constitution: অঙ্গ~. **3** provision: অর্থের ~. **3** being; existence. life. **4** shape; structure; build; form; appearance; construction; formation. **5** orderly placing arrangement. **6** (biol) distribution.

সংস্থাপক *adj* fixing firmly; establishing. ❑*n* founder; architect. সংস্থাপিকা *fem.*

সংস্থাপন *n* establishment; foundation; setting up. ~ করা *vt* establish; found; set up. ~ মন্ত্রণালয় *n* ministry of establishment.

সংস্থাপয়িতা *n*=সংস্থাপক. সংস্থাপয়িত্রী *fem.*

সংস্থিত *adj* **1** placed; laid; rested; lying; sitting; being in/ on. **2** abiding; remaining; standing; left standing. **3** arranged; stationed. **4** shaped; formed.

সংস্থিতি *n* **1** living in/ with/ near; standing/ sitting on. **2** established order. **3** nature; quality; condition; property. **4** duration; continuance in the same state/ condition; constancy. **5** form; shape; existence.

সংস্পর্শ *n* close/ mutual contact; touch; connection; association; concern; conjunction. সংস্পর্শে আসা *vi* come in/ into contact with; come into close relation with; get in touch with; come upon. সংস্পর্শে থাকা *vi* have connection with; associate with; keep in touch with; keep company with; consort with.

সংস্পৃষ্ট *adj* touched; brought into contact; closely united with; touching; contacted; contiguous; affected/ afflicted by; visited; defiled by.

সংস্ফুট *adj* bursting open; blossomed; blown.

সংস্মৃত *adj* remembered; collected; called to the mind.

সংস্মৃতি *n* remembering; remembrance; recollection.

সংস্রব *n* connection; relation; association; company; concern; contact; touch; influence. ~ এড়ানো *vi* shun/avoid the company of; keep away from. ~ থাকা *vi* have. connection with; be involved in. ~ রাখা *vi* associate with; keep in touch with; keep connection with; have relation with. ~হীন *adj* having no connection/ concern with; out of touch; unrelated; irrelevant. সংস্রবে আসা come into close relation with; come in/ into contact with. সংস্রবে থাকা have connection with; associate with; keep in touch with; consort with.

সংহত *adj* **1** struck together; closely joined/ mixed with; contiguous; coherent; combined; compacted. **2** solid; firm; compact; condensed; integrated; united; composite. **3** crystallized. ~ করা *vt* strike together; make solid; unite solidity; crystallize; consolidate; intensify; harden; buttress. ~ বর্তনী *n* closed circuit.

সংহতি *n* **1** compactness; solidity; crystallization; firmness. **2** integration; solidarity; complete union; firm/ alliance. **3** (phys) molecular attraction. **4** (phys) agglomeration. ~ নষ্ট করা *vi* cause to disintegrate; undermine the solidarity (of). ~বাদ *n* collectivism.

সংহনন *n* **1** killing; destroying; destruction. **2** compactness; glaciation.

সংহরণ *n* **1** destroying; destruction; killing. **2** withdrawal; revocation. **3** contraction. ~ করা *vi* **1** destroy; kill. **2** fetch back; withdraw; revoke; retract. **3** contract.

সংহর্তা *n* one who destroys/ withdraws/ revokes. ❑*adj* destroyed; killed. সংহর্ত্রী *fem.*

সংহর্ষ *n* bristling/ erection of the hair of the body; thrill of delight; joy; pleasure; sexual excitement.

সংহার *n* destruction; killing; slaughter. **2** universal destruction. **3** end; conclusion; termination; close; finish. **4** withdrawal; revocation; retraction. **5** contraction; abridgement. **6** dressing up. ~ করা=সংহরণ করা. সংহারক *adj* destroying; destructive; slaying; ruinous. ❑*n* destroying. ~ কাল *n* time of the destruction of the world. ~ মূর্তি *n* image/ embodiment of destruction/ annihilation; terrifying appearance.

সংহারা *vt* (poet)=সংহরণ করা

সংহারী *adj*=সংহারক (⇒ সংহার). সংহারিণী *fem.*

সংহিত *adj* joined; put together; endowed with; combined.

সংহিতা *n* **1** collection; any methodically arranged collection of texts/ verses. **2** the real continuous text of the Vedas as formed out of the *padas* of separate words by proper phonetic changes (according to various schools); various Hindu law-books; Samhita. **3** code. **~কার** *n* compiler/ author of a Samhita or law-book; lawgiver. **~বদ্ধ** *adj* codified.

সংহূতি *n* shouting/ calling out together; clamour.

সংহৃত *adj* **1** collected; accumulated; drawn/ brought together. **2** destroyed; killed. **3** withdrawn; revoked. **4** contracted; shrunk. **5** abridged.

সংহৃতি *n* **1** collection; accumulation. **2** destruction (of the universe); conclusion; end. **3** contraction; abridgement.

সংহৃষ্ট *adj* bristling; shuddering; thrilled; glad; delighted.

সঁপা *vt* (colloq)=সমর্পণ করা

সক *n* (archaic)=শখ

সকড়ি *n* scraps/ leavings of a meal. **2** rice. **3** things which have come in contact with rice/ cooked food.

সকণ্টক *adj* **1** having thorns; thorny; prickly. **2** troublesome; perilous.

সকরকন্দ [P] *n* sweet potato.

সকরুণ *adj* **1** compassionate; tender. **2** lamentable; pitiable; piteous; full of pity; pathetic; woeful.

সকর্ণ *adj* having ears.

সকর্দম *adj* muddy; soiled.

সকর্মক *adj* (gram) transitive. **~ ক্রিয়া** *n* transitive verb.

সকল *adj* all; entire; whole. ❑*pron* all; everybody; everything. ❑*suff* denoting; plurality: লোক~. **~ দিক দিয়ে** in all respects; all things considered, taking all possibilities into account. **সকলেই** *pron* one and all; everybody. **সকলের প্রিয়** loved by all; favourite with everyone.

সকাণ্ড *adj* (bot) having a stem; caulescent.

সকাতর *adj* afflicted; distressed; sorrowful; intent; aggrieved; stricken with grief; extremely solicitous; pitiful. **সকাতরে** *adv* distressfully; plaintively; sorrowfully; very solicitously / intently.

সকাম *adj* **1** acting or purpose; purposeful. **2** lustful. **~ ধর্ম** *n* religion practised with an end in view/ from interested motives.

সকারী *adj* active.

সকাল *n* **1** morning; dawn; daybreak. **2** haste hurry. **~ হওয়া** *vi* dawn: ~ হচ্ছে, Day is beginning to break/ dawning. **~ বেলা** *adv*=সকালে. **~ সকাল** *adj* betimes; soon; quickly; early. **সকালে** *adv* (early) in the morning; at dawn/ daybreak; early.

সকাশ *n* presence; vicinity; nearness; propinquity. **সকাশে** *adv* in the presence of; before; near.

সকুটম্ব *adj* together with one's friends and relations.

সকুণ্ডল *adj* decorated with/ wearing ear-rings.

সকোপ *adj* full of anger; enraged; displeased. **সকোপে** *adv* angrily.

সকৌতুক *adj* **1** full of fun/ amusement; funny; droll; amusing; playful mischievous : ~ হাস্য. **2** amused : ~ দৃষ্টি. **সকৌতুকে** *adj* playfully; mischievously; amusedly.

সক্তু *n* flour of fried barley or gram.

সক্রিয় *adj* active; practical : ~ অংশগ্রহণ. **~তা** *n* activeness; initiative.

সক্রোধ=সকোপ

সক্ষম *adj* able; capable; competent; able-bodied; active; energetic. **~ তা** *n* ability; capability; competence; activeness; vigour; vitality.

সক্ষোভ *adj* offended; grieved ; agitated; distressed.

সখ=শখ

সখা *n* (boon) companion; assistant; confidant; (bosom/ intimate) friend; chum. **সখী** *fem* female friend/ companion; woman's confidante; mistress. **~জন** *n* female friend(s). **~ভাব** *n* **1** behaviour like a confidante. **2** system of Vaishnava worship in which the devotee regards himself as a confidante of Sri Krishna.

সখিতা, সখিত্ব, সখ্য *nn* friendship; companionship; intimacy (with); fellowship; alliance. **সখ্যস্থাপন করা** *vi* make friends with; enter into alliance with.

সখেদ *adj* having grief. **সখেদে** *adj* sadly; woefully.

সখ্য ⇒ সখিতা

সগর্ব *adj* proud; arrogant; exalted; elated; haughty; boastful. **সগর্বে** *adj* proudly; haughtily; arrogantly.

সগর্ভ *adj* **1** pregnant; impregnated by; big with child. **2** (of a brother) of same blood (ie) by the same mother and father. **সগর্ভা** *n fem.*

সগুণ *adj* **1** having qualities/ attributes/ properties; having good qualities/ virtues; virtuous. **2** possessing three primary qualities (ie সত্ত্ব, রজঃ and তম); worldly. **3** furnished with a string/ cord.

সগোত্র *adj* being of the same family/ clan; kindred; agnate; homogeneous; related to. ❑*n* kinsman of the same family; distant kinsman; agnate. **সগোত্রা** *fem* kinswoman. **~ বিবাহ** *n* endogamous marriage.

সগৌরবে *adj* proudly; gloriously; with dignity; honourably.

সঘন *adj* **1** thick; dense; solid. **2** clouded; cloudy. সঘনে *adv* ceaselessly; incessantly; repeatedly.

সঘর *n* family of equal social standing for matrimonial purpose.

সঙ, সং *n* **1** clown; joker; buffoon; bumpkin. **2** mask; farce grotesque spectacle/ procession; buffoonery. ~ করা *vi* play the fool/ buffoon; behave/ act like a clown. ~ সাজা *vi* dress up as a clown.

সঙিন, সঙীন=সঙ্গিন

সঙ্কট, সংকট *n* **1** dangerous/ critical situation; crisis; strait; great difficulty; critical condition; knotty problem; tight corner; crux. **2** narrow path/ passage; gorge; strait; defile; pass. **3** crowd. ☐*adj* crowded together; impassable; narrow; dense; impervious. ~কাল *n* critical time; crisis; hard times. ~সঙ্কুল *adj* dangerous; perilous; critical. সঙ্কটস্থ *adj* being in difficulties. ~স্থল *n* (geog) isthmus. সঙ্কটাপন্ন *adj* beset with difficulties; greatly endangered; imperilled. সঙ্কটাবস্থা *n* critical situation; tight corner. উভয় ~ *n* dilemma.

সঙ্কটোত্তীর্ণ, সংকটোত্তীর্ণ *adj* released from difficulties.

সঙ্কর, সংকর *n* **1** mixing together; commingling; intermixture; confusion (esp of castes/ races); offspring of a mixed marriage; half-breed; half-caste; mongrel. **2** hybrid. ☐*adj* half-bud; hybrid; cross-bred. সঙ্করজ, ~জাত *adjj* born from a mixed caste. ~ ধাতু *n* alloy; base metal.

সঙ্করীকরণ, সংকরীকরণ *n* mixing together; confusing; hybridization.

সঙ্কর্ষণ, সংকর্ষণ *n* **1** drawing near; attraction; pull. **2** drawing out extraction. **3** ploughing; cultivation.

সঙ্কলক, সংকলক *n* compiler; collector; accumulator.

সঙ্কলন, সংকলন *n* collection; compilation; addition; heaping together. ~ করা *vt* collect; compile; add; accumulate; heap together. ~গ্রন্থ *n* compilation.

সঙ্কলয়িতা=সঙ্কলক. সঙ্কলয়িত্রী *fem.*

সঙ্কলিত, সংকলিত *adj* collected; compiled; accumulated; added.

সঙ্কল্প, সংকল্প *n* **1** will; volition; desire; purpose; definite intention/ decision/ wish (for); determination; resolve. **2** solemn vow to do sth (taken esp on the eve of a religious worship); resolution. **3** conception/ idea/ notion formed in the mind/ heart. ~ করা *vi* wish; long for; be desirous of; will; purpose; resolve; intend; aim at; strive after; be determined; make up one's mind; vow; take a solemn vow to do sth (esp on the eve of a religious worship). ~বদ্ধ *adj* determined; resolved; decided; resolute; bent (upon). ~-বিকল্প *n* desire and doubt; hesitation; misgiving; qualm. ~সাধন, ~সিদ্ধি *n n* accomplishment of an object; attainment of one's desire. ~সাধন/ ~সিদ্ধ করা *vi* accomplish an object; attain one's goal/ desire/ object.

সঙ্কল্পিত, সংকল্পিত *adj* desired; wished for; intended; purposed; determined; resolved on; passed/ adopted as a resolution.

সঙ্কাশ *n, adj* (used as a *suff)* having the appearance of; (looking) like: তুষার~.

সঙ্কীর্ণ, সংকীর্ণ *adj* **1** narrow; ungenerous; meager. **2** mixed; commingled; confused; crowded with. **3** polluted; adulterated; born of a mixed marriage. **4** sprinkled; scattered; strewn; spread; diffused. ~চিত্ত, ~চেতা(ঃ), ~মনা(ঃ) *adj* narrow-minded; small-minded; mean; petty. ~চিত্ততা *n* narrow-mindedness; meanness; pettiness. ~জাতি *adj* of mixed birth/ caste; impure through illegal intermarriage. ~তা **1** narrowness; smallness. **2** meanness; pettiness. ~হৃদয়, সঙ্কীর্ণাত্মা *adjj*=~চিত্ত. সঙ্কীর্ণাবস্থা *n* straitened reduced circumstances; impecuniousness; indigence.

সঙ্কীর্তন, সংকীর্তন *n* **1** praise; celebration; glorification; singing in praise (of God/ any deity). **2** song in praise of God/ any deity; hymn. **3** description. ~ করা *vi, vt* **1** praise; celebrate; glorify; sing the praise (of); sing in praise of God/ any deities; hymn. **2** mention/ relate fully; announced; proclaimed.

সঙ্কীর্তিত, সংকীর্তিত *adj* **1** praised; celebrated; glorified. **2** mentioned fully; narrated.

সঙ্কুচিত, সংকুচিত *adj* **1** contracted; shrunk; crinkled; shrivelled: ~ভ্রূ/ চর্ম. **2** narrowed : ~ পথ. **3** closed; shut : ~ পক্ষ. **4** curtailed; reduced : ~ব্যয়. **5** miserly; niggardly : ~ হস্ত. **6** drawn back; diffident; hesitating : ~ কণ্ঠে. **7** cowering; cowered : ভয়ে ~. **8** (phys) compressed. ~ করা *vt* **1** contract. **2** curtail; reduce. **3** close; shut. **4** curtail; reduce; cut down; narrow. **5** cause to shrink/ hesitate/ cower. **6** (phys) compress. ~ হওয়া *vi* **1** contract; shrink; close; shrivell. **2** be curtailed/ reduced. **3** be niggardly/ miserly. **4** draw back; shrink; become diffident; cower; hesitate. **5** (phys) be compressed.

সঙ্কুল, সংকুল *adj* (used as a *suff*) crowded together; filled/ thronged/ mingled/ affected with; abounding in; possessed of; infested with.

সঙ্কুলান, সংকুলান *n* sufficiency; adequacy. ~ হওয়া *vt* suffice / be sufficient (for); be adequate.

সঙ্কেত, সংকেত *n* **1** intimation; hint; allusion; preconcerted sign/ signal/ gesture; presage; beckoning; beck; token. **2** secret tryst for lovers. **3** (phys) formula. **4** rule. **5** clue. **6** code. ~ **করা** *vi* beckon; signal; gesture. ~**দেওয়া** *vi* (give a) hint; hint (at); presage; make a signal. **সঙ্কেতক** *n* (ling) signifier. **সঙ্কেতন** *n* (ling) signification. ~**স্থান** *n* place appointed for meeting; rendezvous. **সঙ্কেতে** *adv* by a sign/ hints/ allusions.

সঙ্কোচ, সংকোচ *n* **1** contraction. **2** curtailment : ব্যয়~. **3** shrinking. **4** shyness; timidity; cowering; diffidence; hesitation. (phys) compression. **6** closing; shutting up. ~ **করা** *vt* , *vi* **1** curtail; cut down; reduce. **2** hesitate; be shy (of); be diffident; feel hesitation. ~ **বোধ করা** *vi*=~ করা (২). ~**ক** *adj* contracting; curtailing; causing to shrink/ shrivel up; astringent. ~**ন** *n* **1** contraction. **2** curtailment. **3** shrinking. **4** shutting; closing. 5 (phys) compression. **6** abridgement. ~**নশীল** *adj* contractile. ~**নীয়** *adj* to be limited/ restricted; contractible. ~**শূন্য**, ~**হীন** *adjj* ; **1** unhesitating; candid; free; straightforward; ingenuous. **2** unabashed; unscrupulous shameless.

সঙ্ক্রম, সঙ্ক্রমণ, সঙ্ক্রমিত, সঙ্ক্রান্ত, সঙ্ক্রান্তি, সঙ্ক্রাম, সঙ্ক্রামিত, সঙ্ক্ষিপ্ত, সঙ্ক্ষুব্ধ, সঙ্ক্ষেপ, সঙ্ক্ষেপিত, সঙ্খ্যক, সঙ্খ্যা, সঙ্খেয় = সংক্রম, সংক্রমণ, সংক্রমিত, সংক্রান্ত, সংক্রান্তি, সংক্রাম, সংক্রামিত, সংক্ষিপ্ত, সংক্ষুব্ধ, সংক্ষেপ, সংক্ষেপিত, সংখ্যক, সংখ্যা, সংখেয়

সঙ্গ[1] *n* **1** association; intercourse; company. **2** contact; touch. ~ **করা** *vi* associate with; mix (with); keep company with. ~ **দেওয়া** *vi* keep sb company. ~ **পাওয়া** *vi* enjoy the company of; come into contact with. ~ **গুণ** *n* (influence of) good company/ association. **2** (iron) vices of evil company. ~ **ত্যাগ** *n* abandonment of association/ attachment. ~ **ত্যাগ করা** *vi* part company (with sb); end a relationship. ~**দোষ** *n* vices of evil company; influence of bad company. ~ **রোধ** *n* quarantine.

সঙ্গ[2]=সংগ

সঙ্গত *adj* **1** come together; met; encountered; joined; united. **2** fitted together; allied with; friendly to; proper; suitable; apposite; just; according with; fit for; reasonable; conforming to; consistent with; compatible. ❑*n* **1** (music) accompaniment; agreement; harmony; tuning up. **2** frequent meeting; intercourse; alliance; association. ~ **করা** *vt* **1** accompany; play an accompaniment to. **2** tune up.

সঙ্গতি *n* **1** coming together; meeting with; association; intercourse; society; alliance; company. **2** congruity; appropriateness; fitness; applicability; propriety; consistency; reasonableness; justness; coherence. **3** provision; wealth; fund; riches; means: অর্থের ~. **4** sexual union. ~ **করা** *vi* make provision for; fit out/ up; provide sb with sth; provide sth (for sb). ~ **থাকা** *vi* **1** has coherence/ consistency; be consistent (with) agree. **2** have means. ~ **বজায় রাখা** *vi* **1** maintain coherence/ consistency. **2** maintain unity/ harmony. ~**পন্ন**, ~**শালী**, ~**সম্পন্ন** *adjj* having means; well-to-do; moneyed; wealthy. ~ **প্রবণতা** *n* adaptability. ~**হীন** *adj* **1** poor; hard up; resourceless. **2** inconsistent; incoherent; incongruous.

সঙ্গম *vi* **1** coming together; meeting; union; intercourse; association. **2** sexual intercourse. **3** confluence (of rivers). **4** concourse : জন~.

সঙ্গিন [P] *adj* **1** hard; difficult; heavy. **2** serious; critical. **3** weighty; severe; strong. ❑*n* bayonet

সঙ্গিনী *n fem* (of সঙ্গী)

সঙ্গী *n* companion; associate; accomplice; comrade; mate. **সঙ্গিনী** *fem.*

সঙ্গীত, সংগীত *n* music; song; concert; chorus. ~**চর্চা** *n* practice/ cultivation of music. ~**জ্ঞ** *adj* versed/ skilled in music. ❑*n* musician. ~**প্রিয়** *adj* fond of music. ~**প্রিয় ব্যক্তি** *n* lover of music. ~**বিদ্যা**, ~**শাস্ত্র** (science of) music. ~ **বিদ্যালয়** *n* music school. ~ বিশারদ=~জ্ঞ. ~**মুখর** *adj* resounding with music. ~ **মুগ্ধ** *adj* enchanted by music. ~ **লহরি** *n* wave of music. ~**শালা** *n* music-hall. ~ **শিক্ষক** *n* music teacher. ~ **শিক্ষয়িত্রী**, ~ **শিক্ষিকা** *fem.* **সঙ্গীতানুরাগ** *n* love for music. **সঙ্গীতানুরাগী** *adj* fond of music. **সঙ্গীতানুরাগিণী** *fem.* **সঙ্গীতানুশীলন, সঙ্গীতাভ্যাস**=~চর্চা. **সঙ্গীতানুশীলন/ সঙ্গীতাভ্যাস করা** *vi* practice music. **সঙ্গীতালোচনা** *n* study/ cultivation of music; discussion about music. **জাতীয়** ~ *n* national anthem/ song. **প্রভাত** ~ *n* morning song; matin. **যন্ত্র**~ *n* instrumental music. **শেষ**~ *n* last/ dying song; swan song.

সঙ্গীন=সঙ্গিন

সঙ্গুপ্ত, সংগুপ্ত *adj* well hidden; concealed; kept secret.

সঙ্গূঢ়, সংগূঢ় *adj* completely concealed/ hidden from view.

সঙ্গে *prep* **1** with; in the company of; along with; together with. **2** in possession of. **3** in comparison with. ~ **সঙ্গে** *adj* **1** (always) in the company of; close; nearby: ~ সঙ্গে থাকা. **2** (always) in one's possession : ~ সঙ্গে রাখা. **3** as soon as; no sooner than; at once; টাকাটা সে ~ সঙ্গে দিয়ে দিল.

সঙ্গোপন, সংগোপন *n* perfect secrecy; complete hiding/ concealment. **সঙ্গোপনে, সংগোপনে** *adv* secretly; furtively; covertly; surreptitiously; underhand; under cover; in strict privacy; in/ with great secrecy.

সঙ্গোপিত, সংগোপিত *adj* (perfectly) hidden/ concealed.

সঙ্ঘ *n* **1** association; society; community; company; guild; club. **2** any collection/ assembly; heap; multitude; quantity; crow; host; number. **3** clerical community; congregation; church. **4** (Buddhist) the whole community/ collective body/ brotherhood of works. ~**ক্রিয়াবাদ** *n* collectivism. ~**চারী** *adj* going in flocks/ shoals; gregarious. ~**জীবী** *adj* living in company; belonging to a vagrant band. ❑*n* hired labourer; porter. ~**বদ্ধ** *adj* united; incorporated concerted; combined.

সঙ্ঘটন, সঙ্ঘটিত, সঙ্ঘট্ট, সঙ্ঘর্ষ, সঙ্ঘাত, সঙ্ঘুষিত, সঙ্ঘৃষ্ট = সংঘটন, সংঘটিত, সংঘট্ট, সংঘর্ষ, সংঘাত, সংঘুষিত, সংঘৃষ্ট

সঙ্ঘারাম *n* Buddist convent/ monastery (⇒ সঙ্ঘ).

সচকিত *adj* startled; alarmed; timid; on the alert; alerted.

সচঞ্চল *adj* agitated; restless; excited.

সচন্দন *adj* together with sandal wood paste.

সচরাচর *adj* usually; generally; commonly; customarily; often.

সচল *adj* moving; mobile; active; current; effective; locomotive. ~ **করা** *vt* put/ set in motion; activate.

সচিত্র *adj* garnished/ together with pictures; illustrated; painted; variegated.

সচিব *n* secretary; counsellor; companion.

সচেতক *n* (pol) whip. **মুখ্য** ~ *n* chief whip.

সচেতন *adj* **1** sentient animate; rational; sensible. **2** conscious; living; aware; alive; **3** vigilant; alert. ~**তা** *n* consciousness; awareness sensibility. ~ **দৃষ্টি** *adj* vigilant; alert. ~ **থাকা** *vi* be on the alert/ look-out; exercise vigilance; be aware/ vigilant/ alive.

সচেষ্ট *adj* making effort/ exertion; active.

সচ্চরিত্র *adj* having a good character; virtuous; chaste; morally excellent. ❑*n* good conduct. **সচ্চরিত্রা** *adj fem.* ~**তা** *n* good conduct; virtuousness; moral excellence; chastity.

সচ্চিদানন্দ *n* existence and thought and joy; name of the one self-existent Spirit. ❑*adj* eternal, omniscient and blissful.

সচ্চিন্তা *n* good thought.

সচ্ছল *adj* well-to-do; well-off;solvent. ~**তা** *n* well-to-do/ well-offstate; comfort; ease.

সচ্ছিদ্র, সছিদ্র *adj* **1** having hole(s); porous; perforated. **2** having defects; faulty.

সজদা=সেজদা

সজন *adj* together with men/ people; frequented/ inhabited by men. ❑*n* man of the same family; kinsman.

সজনী *n fem* confidante; sweet-heart; lady-love.

সজল *adj* possessing/ containing water; watery; wet; humid; tearful. ~ **নয়নে** *adv* with tears in one's eyes. ~ **মেঘ** *n* rain-closed; nimbus.

সজাগ *adj* wakeful; awake; vigilant; aware; conscious; on the alert; alive.

সজাতি *adj* belonging to the same tribe/ caste/ class/ kind; similar. ❑*n* son of a man and woman of the same caste.

সজাতীয় *adj* of the same caste/ kind/ species; homogeneous, like; similar; kindred; resembling. **সজাতীয়া** *fem.* ~**তা** *n* homogeneity; similarity.

সজারু=শজারু

সজিনা=শজিনা

সজীব *adj* **1** having life; alive; living; animate. **2** vivacious; lively; fresh; invigorated. ~ **করা** *vt* animate; vivify; rejuvenate; invigorate; activate.

সজোরে *adj* forcefully; forcibly; violently; by violence.

সজ্জন[১] *n* good/ virtuous/ wise/ honest man. ❑*adj* well-born; respectable; virtuous; amiable.

সজ্জন[২] *n* equipment; preparation; caparisoning an elephant.

সজ্জা *n* **1** dress; decoration. **2** equipment; armour; mail. **3** preparation. **4** furnishings; fittings and furniture; outfit; accoutrements. **5** arraying. ~**কক্ষ**, ~**গৃহ** *nn* dressing-room; green-room.

সজ্জিত *adj* **1** dressed; decorated; ornamented; adorned **2** equipped; prepared; (made) ready for/ to. armed. **3** furnished. **4** arrayed. **সজ্জিতা** *fem.* ~ **করা** *vt* **1** dress; decorate; adorn. **2** equip; prepare; fit out; arm; made ready for. **3** furnish. **4** array.

সজ্জীকরণ *n* **1** dressing; decoration; adorning; adornment. **2** equipping; arming; accoutrement; preparation. **3** furnishing. **4** arraying.

সজ্জাকৃত, সজ্জীভূত *adj* =সজ্জিত

সজ্ঞান *adj* conscious; aware; in one's senses.

সজ্ঞানে *adv* consciously; knowingly.

সঞ্চকী *n* **1** moulder.

সঞ্চয় *n* **1** collection; gathering; accumulation. **2** heap; hoard; storage; store; stock. **3** saving; savings. ~ **করা** *vt* gather together; accumulate; collect; acquire; pile/ heap up; amass; save; store; stock. ~ **কোষ** *n* secondary/ storage cell. ~**ন** *n* **1**=~. **2** compilation. **3** selected works; anthology: প্রবন্ধ ~ন. ~**নী** *n* magazine. ~**শীল** *adj* in the habit of saving; provident; thrifty; frugal; sparing. ~**শীলতা** *n* habit of saving; frugality; thrift; providence; sparingness; parsimony.

সঞ্চয়িতা *n* collection/ selection (of poems).

সঞ্চয়ী *adj* (given to) saving; thrifty; frugal; sparing; accumulating. **~ হিসাব** *n* savings account.

সঞ্চরণ *n* going together/ through; passing over from; passage; motion; movement; roaming; circulation. **~ করা** *vi* go/ wander about; roam; walk about; drive/ ride in/ on; go in/ through; enter; traverse; pervade; pass over to; pass from one to another; move; circulate. **~শীল** *adj* disposed to move/ ramble about; (engaged in) moving / circulating/ roaming; mobile; ambulatory.

সঞ্চরমান *adj* on the move; in the state of moving/ roaming; roving; rambling; passing; wandering.

সঞ্চরা *vi* (poet)=সঞ্চরণ করা

সঞ্চরিত *adj* moved; circulated; passed; set in motion; handed round. **~ হওয়া**=সঞ্চরণ করা.

সঞ্চরিষ্ণু *adj* disposed to move / ramble about.

সঞ্চালন *n* moving about; movement; circulation; trembling; fluttering; shaking; agitation.

সঞ্চলিত *adj* moved; circulated; shaken; agitated; quivering; trembling; fluttering. **~ হওয়া** *vi* move about/ to and fro; oscillate; quiver; travel; flutter; circulate.

সঞ্চায়ক *adj* accumulating. ❑*n* accumulator. **~ ব্যাটারি** *n* secondary/ storage battery.

সঞ্চার *n* **1** walking about; wandering; roaming; driving; riding; any motion; movement; gait. **2** transit; passage. **3** passing over; transition; transference. **4** (astrol) passage / entrance of the sun into a new sign. **5** transmission (of disease); contagion. **6** infusion: প্রাণ~. **7** arousing; excitation; incitation; inciting; impelling: ভয়~. **8** pervasion; diffusion: আলোক~. **9** accumulation; collection: মেঘ~. **10** transfusion: রক্ত~. **11** advent; beginning; appearance; onset; oncoming: যৌবন~. **~ করা** *vt* convey; transmit; transfer; communicate; infuse; transfuse; inspires incite; arouse. **~ক** *adj* transferring; communicating; inspiring; arousing; inciting; awakening. ❑*n* leader; guide. **~ণ** *n* =~.

সঞ্চারিত *adj* **1** caused to go; moved; set in motion. **2** impelled; driven; guided. **3** transmitted; communicated. **4** inspired; excited; incited; roused. **5** infused. **6** transfused. **7** transited (to another zodiac sign). **8** accumulated; collected. **9** begun; set in. **~ করা** *vt* **1** transmit; transfuse; communicate; rouse; incite; infuse. **2** cause; set in; bring; set in motion; cause to pass through/ go; lead. **~ হওয়া** *vi* **1** wander/ walk about; move; roam; go in/ through; enter. **2** traverse; pervade. **3** issue from; ensue. **4** be transmitted/ communicated. **5** be roused/ incited/ infused with. **6** be transfused. **7** make a transit. **8** (astron, astrol) make a transit to another zodiacal sign.

সঞ্চারী *adj* **1** going together / about; going hither and thither; roaming; wandering; moving in; in motion; passing. **2** going/ passing from one to another. **3** transmitted; infectious; contagious; hereditary. **4** penetrating into. **5** passing away; transitory; adventitious; unsteady; inconstant; temporary; evanescent. **6** influencing; impelling; inciting; rousing; setting in motion. **7** infusing; transfusing. **8** (music) ascending and descending. ❑*n* **1** (music) the third line/ step of an Indian musical mode (রাগ). **2** (rhet) passing sentiment which accompanies the principal sentiment in a piece of poetical composition; transitory sentiment. **সঞ্চারিণী** *adj, fem.*

সঞ্চালক *adj* one who moves/ guides/ controls/ initiated. ❑*n* guide; initiator; mover. **সঞ্চালিকা** *fem* .

সঞ্চালন *n* moving; agitating; shaking; waving; inducing; excitation; arousal. **~ করা** *vt* move; agitate; set in motion; circulate; wave; shake.

সঞ্চলিত *adj* moved; agitated; set in motion; waved; induced; excited; aroused. **সঞ্চলিতা** *fem.*

সঞ্চিত *adj* piled together; gathered; collected; accumulated; heaped up; amassed; hoarded; saved; stored. **সঞ্চিতা** *n* selected works; anthology.

সঞ্চীয়মান *adj* being gathered/ collected/ accumulated/ saved/ stored.

সঞ্চেয় *adj* to be gathered/ collected/ accumulated/ saved.

সঞ্জনন *n* production; creation; generation; growth; development; effecting. **সঞ্জননা**=~.

সঞ্জাত *adj* born; produced; grown; arisen; become; sprung; evolved; appeared.

সঞ্জাব [P] *n* living; fringe.

সঞ্জীবন *adj* making alive; animating; bringing to life; infusing/ restoring life; rejuvenating; life-giving; refreshing. ❑*n* infusion/ restoration of life; animation; reanimation; rejuvenation. **সঞ্জীবনী** *adj fem.* ❑*n* kind of elixir.

সঞ্জীবিত *adj* vivified; enlivened; animated; rejuvenated.

সট *n* (onom) expressing; speed and suddenly. **~ করে** *adv* in trice; in a flash.

সটকা *n* **1** (long slender pipe or tube of a) hookah. **2** fishing-rod.

সটকান *n* decampment; slip; getaway; escape. **~ দেওয়া** *vi* decamp; escape; slip; flee; break out (of); give the slip to sb.

সটকানো *vi* =সটকান দেওয়া

সটাং, সটান *adj* **1** (lying) straight (ahead); horizontal: ~ রাস্তা. **2** lying at length: ~ হওয়া.

3 perfectly erect; tight; taut: ~ চামড়া. ❑*adj* 1 straight ahead; straightway; forthwith; in a straight manner: ~ পাড়ি দেওয়া. 2 erectly; uprightly: ~ দাঁড়ানো, stand erect/ upright/ length wise; flat: ~ শুয়ে পড়া, ~ পড়ে যাওয়া, fall full length.

সটীক *adj* accompanied / explained by a commentary; annotated.

সঠিক *adj* perfectly right / genuine; correct/ accurate; exact: ~ খবর. ❑*adj* quite correctly / exactly / accurately: ~ বলো দেখি কী হয়েছিল. ~ভাবে *adj* =~.

সডাক *adj* inclusive of postage.

সড় [A] *n* 1 (derog) secret consultation. 2 (derog) secret entente/ understanding/ agreement. 3 intrigue; scheme; plot; conspiracy. ~ করা *vi* 1 have secret consultation/ conference; confer secretly. 2 enter into a secret entente/ understanding/ agreement; arrange secretly (with). 3 hatch a plot; intrigue/ conspire (with).

সড়ক *n* highway; road; avenue; street.

সড়কি *n* lance; spear; javelin. ~ওয়ালা *n* spearman.

সড়গড় *adj* thoroughly learnt/ mastered/ accustomed/ habituated; committed to memory; memorized; learnt by rote. ❑*n* practice; committing sth to memory; ability to read; recite fluently. ~ করা *vt* learn/ master thoroughly; get thoroughly accustomed (to)/ habituated (with); memorize; learn by heart; learn by rote; commit to memory; keep at one's fingertips; read / recite fluently.

সড়সড় *n* (onom) expressing (a) quick gliding movement of reptiles, etc; (b) slipperiness; (c) itching sensation. ~ করা *vi* 1 (of reptiles, etc) glide past. 2 itch. 3 be titillated / tickled. সড়সড়ানি *n* 1 gliding movement. 2 itching; tickling; titillation. ~ করে *adv* slippingly; suddenly.

সড়াক, সড়াৎ *nn* (anom) expressing: sudden quick movement.

সৎ[1] *adj* 1 honest; virtuous; good; excellent. 2 having existence. 3 real; actual; true; right. 4 lasting; enduring. 5 solemn; charitable. ❑*n* God. ~ কথা *n* good conversation. ~ কবি *n* good / true poet. ~কর্ম, ~কার্য, ~ক্রিয়া *nn* good work; virtuous act; virtue. ~কার *n* 1 kind treatment; honour; favour. reverence; hospitality. 2 obsequies; cremation: শব ~কার. ~ করা *vt* 1 receive and treat cordially/ respectfully; entertain generously. 2 perform obsequies; cremate. ~কৃত *adj* honoured; treated with respect/ hospitality; entertained; worshipped; adored. ~কৃতি *n* 1 doing good; virtue; morality. 2 kind treatment; hospitality; hospitable reception. ~পথ, ~মার্গ *nn* good/ right way; correct/ virtuous conduct; orthodox doctrine. ~পথাবলম্বী, ~পথাশ্রয়ী *adj* taken/ following the virtuous course; virtuous; righteous. ~ পরামর্শ *n* good counsel/ advice. ~পাত্র *n* 1 worthy bridegroom. 2 worthy person; righteous/ just person. ~পুত্র *n* good/ virtuous son. ~ প্রতিগ্রহ *n* acceptance of gifts from virtuous men. ~প্রসঙ্গ *n* religious topic. ~সংসর্গ ~সঙ্গ *nn* intercourse/ association with the good; good company. ~সঙ্গ করা, ~সঙ্গে থাকা *vi* associate with the good; keep good company. ~সঙ্গে কাশী বাস, অসৎসঙ্গে সর্বনাশ (prov) good company brings one heavenly bliss whilst evil company brings ruin. ~সাহস *vi* moral courage. ~স্বভাব *vi* good nature. ❑*adj* good-natured; virtuous; of amiable disposition.

সৎ[2] *adj* (used as a *pref)* 1 related through another wife of one's husband or through another husband of one's wife; step: ~ ছেলে. 2 having one parent in common; half: ~ বোন. 3 related by another marriage; step. ~ ছেলে, ~ বেটা *n* step-son. ~ বাপ *n* step-father. ~ বোন *n* half-sister; step-sister. ~ ভাই *n* half-brother; step-brother. ~ মা *n* step-mother. ~ মেয়ে *n* step-daughter. ~ শাশুড়ি *n* step-mother-in-law.

সতত *adv* always; even; constantly; perpetually; continually; at all hours; ceaselessly; incessantly.

সততা *n* honesty; integrity; goodness; uprightness; probity; rectitude; candour.

সতর=সতের

সতরঞ্চ, সতরঞ্জ=শতরঞ্জ

সতরঞ্চি, সতরঞ্জি=শতরঞ্জি

সতর্ক *adj* cautious; careful; watchful; alert. ~ করা *vt* caution; warn. ~ থাকা *vi* be careful/ cautious; be on the alert / one's guard. ~তা *n* carefulness; cautiousness; watchfulness; vigilance; alertness. ~ দৃষ্টি রাখা *vi* keep a careful watch on; watch (over) sth.

সতর্কীকরণ *n* cautioning; warning.

সতর্কীকৃত *adj* cautioned; warned.

সতা=সতিন, ~ই *n fem* step-mother. ~তো =সৎ[2].

সতিন, সতিনী (archaic) *nn fem* women who has the same husband with another woman or whose husband has other wives; fellow-wife; female rival. ~কাঁটা *n* son/ daughter of one's fellow-wife, who is regarded as one's thorn in the flesh. ~ঝি *n fem* step-daughter. ~পো *n* step-son.

সতী *n fem* 1 good and virtuous/ faithful wife; chaste / devoted wife. 2 faithful wife who burns herself with her husband's corpse. 3 (myth) Sati, the Daughter of Daksha and wife of Shiva. ❑*adj fem* (of a wife) intently devoted to one's husband; chaste. ~গিরি *n* (iron) show / affectation of chastity demonstrated by a wife; (false) pride of chastity / honesty. ~ত্ব *n* wifely fidelity; chastity of a wife. ~ত্বনাশ *n* violation of chastity; rape. ~ নাশ করা *vt* rape; violate. ~ত্ব রক্ষা করা *vi* preserve one's chastity. ~দাহ *n* Hindu practice of widows burning themselves with their husband's corpses; suttee; sati. ~ধর্ম=~ত্ব. ~পনা= গিরি. ~লক্ষ্মী *n fem* a very chaste and pleasing wife who brings fortune to her husband; virtuous wife. ~সাধ্বী *n fem* perfectly chaste / faithful wife. ~সাবিত্রী *n fem* a wife as chaste and faithful as Sabitri.

সতীন=সতিন

সতীর্থ *adj* having read in the same class; fellow-student; class-fellow

সতৃণ *adj* grown with grass; grassy.

সতৃষ্ণ *adj* **1** having thirst; thirsty. **2** desirous; yearning; eager; wistful; longing: ~ দৃষ্টি.

সতেজ *adj* **1** vigorous; energetic; animated; spirited; reinvigorated; resusciated; blooming; bouncing. **2** (of trees, etc) luxuriant. **3** emphatic; forceful. সতেজে *adv* vigorously; energetically. animatedly; spiritedly; luxuriantly; emphatically; forcefully.

সতের *n* , *adv* seventeen. ~ই *n, adj* (the) seventeenth (day of a month).

সত্তম *adj* very good/ right; most virtuous; the best / first / chief of: কবি~.

সত্তর *n, adj* seventy.

সত্তা *n* **1** existence; being. **2** eternal existence; reality. **3** excellence. **4** honesty; goodness; integrity; goodness. **5** origin; birth.

সত্ত্ব *n* **1** being; existence. **2** entity. **3** reality. **4** true essence; nature; disposition of mind; character. **5** spiritual essence; spirit; mind. **6** vital breath; life; consciousness; strength (of character); firmness; energy; resolution; courage; self-command; good sense; magnanimity. **7** quality of purity/ goodness; (regarded as the highest of the three *gunas*). **8** material/ elementary substance; matter; thing. **9** living/ sentient being; creature; animal. **10** juice; extract; marrow; preparation made of juice/ essence: আম~. ~গুণ *n* the quality of purity/ goodness (⇒ 7 above). ~বান *adj* **1** endowed with/ possessed of the true essence. **2** endowed with life; living; existent. **3** energetic; courageous; resolute. ~স্বামিত্ব *n* ownership; proprietary right.

সত্ত্বেও *prep* in spite of; despite; notwithstanding.

সত্য *adj* **1** true; real; actual; genuine; right; correct. **2** sincere; honest; truthful; faithful; virtuous; good. **3** successful; effectual; valid. ❑*n* **1** truth; reality; genuineness. **2** solemn assertion; vow; oath; promise. **3** quality of goodness/ purity/ knowledge. **4** (myth) the first of the four *yugas* or ages. ~ করা *vi* take a solemn vow; take an oath; promise. ~ বলা *vi* speak/ tell the truth; speak the right thing. ~ই *adv* truly; indeed; verily; certainly. ~ কথন *n* speaking the/ of truth; truthfulness. ~ কথা *n* truth. ~ কথা বলা *vi* speak the truth. ~কাম *adj* truth-loving. ❑*n* lover of truth. ~ঙ্কার *n* **1** promise. **2** making true/ good; ratification of a contract/ bargain. **3** earnest money. ~ত *adv* in truth; truly; really; in truth. ~তা *n* truth; veracity; genuineness; authenticity; reality. ~নারায়ণ *n* name of particular divinity (called Satyapir in Bengal). ~নিষ্ঠ *adj* given up to truth; thoroughly honest; true to one's word/ vow. ~নিষ্ঠা *n* truthfulness; devotion to truth; integrity. ~পথ *n* path of virtue; right path. ~পরায়ণ=~নিষ্ঠ. ~পরায়ণতা=~নিষ্ঠা. ~ পালন করা *vi* keep/ fulfil one's promise/ vow. ~পীর=~নারায়ণ. ~প্রতিজ্ঞ *adj* true/ faithful to a promise. ~প্রিয় *adj* devoted to truth; truth-loving. ~ বাক্য *n* true speech; veracity; truth. ❑ *adj* true in speech. ~বাদিতা *n* truthfulness. ~বাদী *adj* speaking the truth; truthful. ~বাদিনী *fem* ~বান *adj* truthful; veracious. ~ব্রত *n* vow of truthfulness. ❑*adj* devoted to a vow of truth; strictly truthful. ~ ভঙ্গ *n* breach of vow/ promise/ trust. ~ ভঙ্গকারী *adj* treacherous; unfaithful. ❑*n* traitor. ~মূলক *adj* based on truth; true. ~যুগ *n* =~(4). ~ রক্ষা *n* keeping a promise/ one's word. ~লোক *n* (myth) the highest of the seven worlds. ~ সত্য *adv* really; indeed; verily; in truth. ~সন্ধ *adj* true to engagements; keeping one's agreement/ promise; faithful; truthfulness. সত্যাকৃতি *n* conclusion/ ratification of an agreement/ bargain. সত্যাখ্যাত *adj* verified. সত্যাখ্যান *n* verification. সত্যাখ্যান করা *vt* verify. সত্যাগ্রহ *n* **1** earnest endeavour for the establishment of the reign of truth. **2** (pol) passive resistance; Satyagraha. সত্যাগ্রহ করা *vi* offer passive resistance. সত্যাগ্রহী *n* determined champion of truth/ the reign of truth; one offering passive resistant. সত্যাচরণ *n* guileless conduct. সত্যানুরাগ *n* devotion to/ love for truth. সত্যানুরাগী *adj* devoted to truth; truth-loving. সত্যানুরাগিণী *fem*. সত্যানুসন্ধান *n* search for truth. সত্যানুসন্ধায়ী *adj* searching for truth. সত্যানৃত *n* **1** truth and falsehood. **2** commerce; trade. সত্যাপন *n* verification; ratification; speaking/ observing the truth. সত্যাপন করা *vt* verify; affirm; take an oath. সত্য বলতে কি to speak the truth. সত্যাসত্য *n* =সত্যানৃত. আপাত~ *adj* true on the surface; plausible. ❑*n* verisimilitude; plausibility. তিন ~ *n* an oath/ promise thrice uttered to make it inviolable.

সত্যি *n, adj* (colloq)=সত্য. ~কার, ~কারের *adj* true; real; genuine. ~কারভাবে *adj* truly; really.

সত্র *n* 1 great soma sacrifice. 2 alms house; asylum; hospital. 3 session (of legislative assembly, higher court, etc). 4 wood; forest. ~কালে *adv* in sessions. ~স্থ *adj* in session. দণ্ড~ *n* sessions.

সত্রাস *adj* terrified; terror-stricken. সত্রাসে *adv* with terror or fear; in a fright.

সত্বর *adj* quickly; swiftly; hurriedly; speedily; expeditiously; promptly; fast. সত্বরে=~.

সদ্ *adj* (in compounds)=সৎ[১]

সদ *adj* (in compounds)=সৎ[১]. ~নুষ্ঠান *vi* 1 performance of a solemn rite. 2 good/ charitable deed/ work. ~ন্তঃকরণ *n* good/ honest heart; good purpose. ~ন্তঃকরণে *adv* with a good heart/ purpose. ~ভিপ্রায় *n* good/ noble purpose/ intention; honest intention. ~র্থ *n* positive sense; true/ correct meaning. ~র্থক *adj* positive; having a good significance. ~সৎ *adj* good and bad; having the nature both of entity and non-entity. ~সৎজ্ঞান *n* conscience. ~সৎভাব *n* reality and unreality; truth and falsehood. ~সদ্বিবেচনা *n* discrimination between true and false or between good and bad. সদাচার *n* practice of good men; virtuous conduct; good manners; approved usage. সদাচারনিষ্ঠ, সদাচারপরায়ণ, সদাচারী *adjj* virtuous (in practice); practising whatever is enjoined by scriptures; good-mannered; upright. সদাত্ম *adj* possession a good nature; good; virtuous. সদালাপ *n* conversation on a good/ pious/ spiritual topics; amiable/ good conversation. সদালাপী *adj* given to conversation on good/ pious/ spiritual topic; good conversationalist. সদাশয় *adj* of a good/ noble mind; noble-hearted; kind-hearted; magnanimous. সদাশয়তা *n* kind-heartedness; noble-mindedness; magnanimity; amiability.

সদকা [A] *n* alms; sacrifice; gifts to the poor; propitiatory offerings.

সদন *n* 1 dwelling; residence; house; home; seat. 2 presence; nearness: রাজ~.

সদমা [A] *n* shock; blow; injury.

সদম্ভ *adj* arrogant; haughty; boastful; proud. সদম্ভে *adv* arrogantly; haughtily; boastfully; proudly.

সদয় *adj* kind; merciful; compassionate; gentle; gracious; charitable; benignant. ~চিত্ত *adj* kind-hearted. ~ভাবে *adv* kindly; mercifully; gently.

সদর [A] *n* 1 headquarters. 2 principal city of a district. 3 first place/ seat; seat of government. 4 outer portion/ apartment of a residential building. ❑*adj* 1 principal; chief. 2 outer. 3 of/ situated in the headquarters of a district . 4 open: ~ জায়গা. ~-অন্দর *n* inner and outer apartment. ~-অন্দর নেই (fig) there is no privacy in anything here. ~আলা *n* subordinate judge. ~ কাছারি *n* headquarters; head office. ~ জমা *n* revenue to be paid to the government. ~ দরজা *n* main gate (of a building). ~ দেওয়ানি আদালত *n* chief civil court. ~ ফর্দ *n* front page/ leaf. ~ রাস্তা *n* main road/ street. ~ মোকাম *n* headquarters.

সদরি [P] *n* waistcoat; jacket.

সদর্প=সদম্ভ

সদলবলে *adv* attended by one's friends and followers/ one's retinue; in force; mustering strong.

সদস্য *n* member. সদস্যা *fem.* ~তা, ~পদ *nn* membership. ~প্রধান *n* leader of a legislative assembly; leader of the house.

সদা *adv* always; ever; every time; continually; perpetually. ~কাল *adv* =~. ~গতি *adj* always in motion. ❑*n* wind. ~নন্দ *adj* feeling/ giving perpetual bliss. ever cheerful. ❑*n* perpetual bliss. ~নন্দময় *adj* =~নন্দ. ~ব্রত *n* place/ institution for charitable distribution of food etc.; alms-house. ~শিব *adj* always kind; always happy/ prosperous. ❑*n* Shiva. ~সর্বদা *adv* always; ever.

সদাই, সদায়=সওদা

সদাগর=সওদাগর

সদিচ্ছা *n* good/ noble intention or will. ~প্রণোদিত *adj* actuated by a good/ noble intention or will; well-intentioned.

সদিয়াল [P] *n* commander of one hundred soldiers.

সদুক্তি *n* good word.

সদুত্তর *n* good/ honest reply; satisfactory/ proper/ correct/ right answer.

সদুদ্দেশ্য *n* good/ noble purpose or intention. ~পূর্ণ *adj* well-meaning; well-meant; well-intentioned. সদুদ্দেশ্যে *adv* with a good/noble purpose or intention; with good intentions.

সদুপদেশ *n* good/ wise advice or counsel; moral advice.

সদুপদেষ্টা *n* good/ wise adviser or consellor; moral instructor.

সদুপায় *n* honest/ good/ fair/ virtuous/ fair means; suitable/ appropriate means.

সদৃশ *adj* 1 (also used as a *pref)* similar (to); like; resembling. 2 identical; equal. ~ কোণ *adj* (geom) equiangular. ~ ত্রিভুজ *n* similar triangle. ~ বিধান *n* homeopathy.

সদ্গতি *n* good/ happy state or fortune; final beatitude; spiritual salvation. 2 obsequies; cremation. 3 way of good men. 4 (hum) proper disposal. ~ করা *vt* 1 perform obsequies; create. 2 (hum) dispose of. ~ লাভ করা *vi* 1 enjoy happy state after death; attain final beatitude; be properly cremated. **2** (hum) be disposed of.

সদ্‌গুণ *n* good/ noble quality; virtue.

সদ্‌গুরু *n* good (religious) teacher/ instructor.

সদ্‌গোপ *n* name of a Hindu caste (milkman class); member of this caste.

সদ্ধর্ম *n* **1** true religion; good law; true justice. **2** Buddhist doctrines.

সদ্‌বংশ *n* good/ noble family or race. **~জাত** *adj* born in/ descended from/ sprung from a good or noble family or race; well-born; of noble birth; nobly born.

সদ্‌বক্তা *n* eloquent speaker; good orator.

সদ্‌বিচার *n* just/ wise decision; equity; (true) justice.

সদ্‌বিচারক *n* good/ wise/ equitable judge.

সদ্‌বিবেচক *adj* gifted with judgement and penetration; judicious; sagacious; sane; discreet; prudent.

সদ্‌বিবেচনা *n* judgement and penetration; sagacity; discernment; judiciousness; discretion; discreteness; discrimination; acumen. **~ করা** *vt* think/ decide/ judge sagaciously or discreetly; discriminate; show discrimination.

সদ্‌বিম্ব *n* (phys) true image.

সদ্‌বুদ্ধি *n* **1** good sense; good nature; goodness. **2** good/virtuous design. **3** good advice/ counsel. **4** right sort of intelligence. ❑*adj* wise; sensible; judicious.

সদ্‌বৃত্ত *adj* honest; possessing good habits; right-minded; upright; having a good character; high-minded; conscientious. ❑*n* good conduct; behaviour of good men.

সদ্‌বৃত্তি *n* **1** good conduct/ disposition. **2** honest occupation.

সদ্‌ব্যবহার *n* **1** good behaviour/ treatment; conscientious treatment. **2** proper/ good use. **~ করা** *vi* **1** behave well/ oneself; treat sb well/ courteously. **2** make good use of; turn sth to good account; use well/ in the best way.

সদ্‌ব্যয় *n* **1** proper use: সময়ের ~. **2** proper/ useful spending: টাকার ~. **~ করা** *vt* **1** use properly. **2** spend properly/ usefully.

সদ্‌ভাব *n* **1** friendship; amity; friendly relations; affection to. **2** goodness; kindness.

সদ্ম *n* abode; dwelling; house; place.

সদ্য, সদ্য *adv* in the very moment; at once; immediately; on the same day; recently; just; forthwith; without delay. **~পক্ব** *adj* **1** freshly cooked. **2** newly gathered; fresh; early: **~পক্ব ফল**, early fruit. **~পর্যুসিত** *adj* one day old. **~পাতী** *adj* quickly falling/ dropping; liable to fall as soon as rising; (fig) very transitory/ sort-lived. **~প্রসূত** *adj* newborn; very recently born; just born. **~প্রসূতা** *fem*. **~বিগত** *adj* recently past. **~প্রাণহর, ~প্রাণহারী** *adj* quickly destroying vigour. **~হরা, ~হারিণী** *fem*. **~সদ্য** *adv* immediately; at once; just; very recently; then and there. **~স্নাত** *adj* one who has taken his/ her bath just now; newly bathed. **~স্নাতা** *fem*.

সদ্যস্ক, সদ্যস্তন *adj* today's; of that day; new; recent. ❑*n* calf.

সদ্‌যুক্তি *n* good reasoning; good advice/ counsel.

সদ্যো *adv* (in compounds)=সদ্য

সদ্যোজাগ্রৎ *adj* just awakened.

সদ্যোজাত *adj* newly born; newborn.

সদ্যোমাংস *n* fresh flesh.

সদ্যোমৃত *adv* just/ recently dead.

সধন *adj* **1** wealthy; possessing riches; opulent. **2** together with riches.

সধবা *n* wife whose husband is alive. ❑*adj* having one's husband alive.

সধর্ম *n* same nature/ qualities. ❑ *adj* having the same nature/ qualities; equal; like; subject to the same law. **~চারিণী** *n fem* legal/ virtuous wife. **~ত্ব** *n* the having a similar nature; homogeneousness.

সধর্মা, সধর্মী *adj* **1** having the same duties/ nature; having similar properties; resembling; like; equal to. **2** following the same trade/ religion. **সধর্মিণী** *n fem* legal/ virtuous wife.

সন [A] *n* (calendar) year; era. **~সন** *adv* annually. **~হাল** *n* current year.

সনদ, সনন্দ [A] *n* certificate; testimonial; diploma; credential; proof; warrant; charter; document; (deed of) grant.

সনসন=শনশন

সনাক্ত ⇒ শনাক্ত

সনাতন *adj* **1** eternal; perpetual; permanent; everlasting. **2** primeval; ancient; very old. ❑*n* **1** Vishnu. **2** Brahma. **3** Shiva. **~ ধর্ম** *n* **1** eternal religion/ form of religion. **2** Hindu religion and tradition; the very ancient form of Hinduism. **সনাতনী** *adj* following the eternal religion/ ancient form of Hinduism; orthodox. ❑ *n* name of Durga.

সনাথ *adj* having a master/ protector; protected by; having a lord/ husband; occupied by; possessed of; furnished/ endowed with; accompanied by: শশি~ যামিনী.

সনাম *adj* having the same name as.

সনির্বন্ধ *adj* pertinaciously solicitous; insistent; importunate; eager. **~ অনুরোধ** *n* earnest request; entreaty.

সনীড় *adj* **1** having the same nest; closely related/ united; kindred with nest.

সনে *prep* (poet, archaic)=সঙ্গে

সনেট [E] *n* sonnet.

সন্ত *n* saint; ascetic.

সন্তত *adj* 1 stretched/ extended along; spread over. 2 continuous. 3 uninterrupted; lasting; eternal.

সন্ততি *n* 1 uninterrupted succession; lineage; race; progeny; offspring; descendant. 2 expanse; continuity; uninterruptedness; continuum. 3 continuous line/ series/ flow; heap; mass; multitude. 4 density; intensity.

সন্তপ্ত *adj* 1 greatly heated/ inflamed; burnt up; red-hot; molten; melted. 2 oppressed; pained; tormented; distressed. wearied; fatigued; aggrieved; afflict. 3 running a temperature. ~ করা *vt* 1 oppress; distress; torment; afflict; grieve. 2 inflame; burn; scorch; make very hot; cause to be heated. ~ হৃদয়ে *adv* with an afflicted/ distressed/ aggrieved heart.

সন্তরণ *n* swimming; notation. ~ করা *vi* swim. ~কারী *n* swimmer. ~কারিণী *fem.* ~দক্ষ, ~পটু *adjj* skilled in swimming.

সন্তর্পণ *n* act of satiating/ refreshing; refreshment.

সন্তর্পণে *adv* very cautiously/ carefully; with circumspection.

সন্তলন=সন্তোলন

সন্তান *n* offspring; son or daughter; progeny; lineage; descendant. ~ ধারণ *n* pregnancy; childbearing. ~ ধারণ করা *vi* be pregnant; conceive; be big with child. ~ পালন *n* up bring; breeding; rearing. ~ পালন করা *vi* bring up/ nurse a child. ~ প্রসব *n* childbirth; childbearing; delivery; labour. ~ প্রসব করা *vi* give birth to a child; deliver/ bear a child; bring forth a child. ~বতী *n fem* one who has borne a child. ~বান *n masc* one to whom child is born. ~বাৎসল্য *n* affection/ love for children. ~সন্ততি *n* children; descendants; offspring. ~সম্ভবা *adj fem* pregnant; expecting; big with child; expectant. ~সম্ভাবনা *n* pregnancy. ~হীন *adj* childless. ~হীনা *adj.* কন্যা~ *n fem* daughter. পুত্র~ *n* son.

সন্তানোচিত *adj* becoming a son or daughter; filial.

সন্তানোৎপাদন *n* reproduction; procreation. ~ করা *n* beget a child; procreate; generate offspring.

সন্তাপ *n* 1 becoming very hot; great/ burning heat; glow; fire. 2 affliction; pain; sorrow; anguish; distress; grief; mortification; bereavement. 3 regret; repentance. ~ক্লিষ্ট=সন্তপ্ত. ~ণ *n* burning; paining; afflicting.

সন্তাপিত=সন্তপ্ত

সন্তুষ্ট *adj* satisfied; contented; well pleased; delighted with; gratified; propitiated. সন্তুষ্টা *fem.* ~ করা *vt* satisfy; please; propitiate; gratify; make contented; rejoice. ~ চিত্তে *adv* with a contented heart; contentedly; happily.

সন্তুষ্টি=সন্তোষ

সন্তোলন *n* act of singeing lightly in oil or butter.

সন্তোষ *n* satisfaction; contentedness; contentment; gratification; propitiation. ~ উৎপাদন/ প্রদান/ সাধন করা=সন্তুষ্ট করা. ~জনক, ~দায়ক, ~দায়ী, ~প্রদ *adjj* satisfactory. ~পূর্বক *adv* with satisfaction/ pleasure.

সন্ত্রস্ত *adj* frightened; alarmed; trembling with fear; panic-stricken; awed; afraid of; terrified; greatly perturbed.

সন্ত্রাস *n* terror; great fear/alarm; terrorism. ~ক *adj* terrorizing. ❑*n* terrorist. ~বাদ *n* terrorism. ~বাদী *adj n* terrorist. সন্ত্রাসের রাজত্ব *n* reign of terror.

সন্ত্রাসিত *adj* frightened; alarmed; terrorized; terrified; panic-stricken.

সন্ত্রাসী *adj.n* terrorist.

সন্দংশ, সন্দংশিকা, সন্দংশী *nn* pair of tongs/ pincers/ nippers; forceps; pliers; small shears.

সন্দর্ভ *n* dissertation; treatise; essay; musical/ literary composition; book; collection.

সন্দর্শন *n* 1 act of looking steadfastly; gazing; viewing; seeing; beholding. 3 inspection; surveying; careful/minute observation; consideration. ~ করা *vt* behold; view; consider; supervise; inspect; observe (minutely/ carefully).

সন্দষ্ট *adj* bitten; pressed closely together; pinched; ripped.

সন্দিগ্ধ *adj* full of suspicion/ doubt; inclined to suspect; suspicious; dubious; doubtful; suspected; uncertain. ~চিত্ত, ~চেতা ~মনা *adj* having a suspicious/ doubtful mind; suspicious; sceptical distrustful. ~তা *n* dubiousness; distrust; dubiety; unbelievingness; suspicion; uncertainty.

সন্দিষ্ট *adj* pointed out; assigned; stipulated; promised.

সন্দিহান *adj* =সন্দিগ্ধ

সন্দীপক *adj* inflaming; exciting; kindling; arousing.

সন্দীপন *n* kindling; exciting; inspiring; excitation; inflaming; arousing; arousal; incitation. ❑*adj* =সন্দীপক

সন্দীপনী *adj fem* =সন্দীপক

সন্দীপিত, সন্দীপ্ত *adjj* lighted up; kindled; inflamed; excited; flaming; burning; enkindled; incited; roused.

সন্দেশ *n* 1 communication of intelligence; message; information; errand; news; tidings; report. 2 order; command; direction. 3 present; gift. 4 kind of dry sweets made of posset, ~ওয়ালা *n* manufacturer/ seller of the aforesaid sweetmeat. ~বহ, ~হর *n n* messenger; envoy.

সন্দেহ *n* **1** doubt; suspicion; uncertainty. **2** (rhet) a figure of speech expressing doubt. ~ করা *vt* doubt; suspect. ~জনক *adj* causing doubt/ suspicion; suspicious; doubtful; dubious; suspect. ~জনকভাবে *adv* suspiciously. ~দোলা *n* vacillation; wavering; hesitation. ~দোলায় দোলা *vi* vacillate; waver; float in sea of doubt; have misgivings. ~ নেই there is no doubt; without doubt; no doubt; doubtlessly. ~ বাই *n* suspicious nature; propensity to suspect foul play, conspiracy, etc. ~বাদ *n* scepticism. ~বাদী *n* sceptic. ~ভঞ্জন *n* removal of doubt/ misgivings/ suspicion; resolution of doubt. ~ ভঞ্জন/নিরসন করা *vi* remove resolve a doubt/ misgiving. ~স্থলে *adv* in case of doubt/ uncertainty. সন্দেহাকুল *adj* perturbed by doubt. সন্দেহের অতীত beyond doubt; above suspicion. সন্দেহের পাত্র suspect. সন্দেহের বিষয় matter of doubt. সন্দেহের লেশ *n* shadow of of doubt; faint trace of doubt.

সন্ধান *n* **1** search; quest; pursuit; discovery; research. **2** trace: তার কোনো ~ পাওয়া গেল? **3** mystery. **4** secret entrance. **5** planning; fixing on: শর ~. **6** joint; point of contact; joining; uniting. **7** (chem) fermentation; manufacture of fermented liquors. ~ করা *vt* **1** search (for); look for; (try to) trace; research; hunt (for); seek; go in quest for; chase after; pursue. **2** fix on; plant; place; join. **3** discover. **4** ferment. ~ নেওয়া *vi* inquire about/ concerning. ~ পাওয়া *vi* find/ get a trace (of); find out; locate; trace; detect. ~ হওয়া *vi* be searched/ traced; be found out/ detected/ located/ spotted/ discovered. ~পুস্তক *n* book of reference. ~সুলুক *n* **1** information; trace; news. **2** inquiry; exploration; investigation. **3** secrets; contrivance. ~সূত্র *n* clue.

সন্ধানিত *adj* **1** searched; looked for; pursued. **2** bound together; joined; fixed; placed; planted.

সন্ধানী, সন্ধায়ী *adj* engaged in searching; searching; investigative; sharp; piercing; penetrating; keen; inquisitive; curious. সন্ধানী আলো *n* search-light. সন্ধানী দুরবিন *n* collimating telescope.

সন্ধি *n* **1** junction; connection; combination; union (with); unification. **2** association; intercourse (with). **3** agreement; compact; alliance; league; reconciliation; compromise; peace between/ with; making a treaty of peace; negotiating alliance. **4** (gram) euphonic junction of final and initial letters; *sandhi*. **5** (anat) joint; articulation. **6** contrivance; management. **7** place/ point of connection or contact; juncture; hinge; boundary; boundary line. **8** critical juncture; crisis; opportune moment. **9** interstice; crevice; interval. **10** interval between day and night; twilight. **11** wall; cavity/ hole/ breach in wall made by a housebreaker. **12** seam; fold. **13** period at the expiration of each Yuga or age. **14** space between heaven and earth; horizon. **15** juncture/ division of a drama. **16** secret; mystery: যে জানে স্বপ্নের ~. **17** reasoning; argument. ~ করা **1** conclude a treaty; make a compact; sign (a) peace; enter into an alliance; heal the breach; compromise. ~কাষ্ঠ *n* wood below the top of a gable. ~ক্ষণ *n* juncture of two ages/ moments/ periods. ~চৌর *n* burglar. ~ত *adj* **1** joined/ fastened together; put to/on; fixed; united with. **2** allied; covenanted; concluded (as an alliance). **3** prepared; mixed together; fermented. ~ত পদ *adj* (zoo) jointed leg. ~পদ *adj* (zoo) arthropod. ~পত্র *n* written covenant; written agreement of peace. ~পূজা *n* worship of Durga in autumn at the juncture of the eighth and the ninth lunar day. ~প্রদাহ *n* arthritis. ~বদ্ধ *adj* united; joined; bound by a treaty/an agreement; covenanted. ~বন্ধ *n* ligaments/sinews of the joints. ~বন্ধন *n* ligament; tendon. ~বন্ধনী *n* ligament. ~বাত *n* gout; rheumatism. ~বিগ্রহ *n* peace and war. ~বিচ্ছেদ *n* (gram) disjoining of *sandhi*. ~বেলা *n* twilight; evening. ~ভঙ্গ *n* **1** joint-fracture; dislocation of a joint. **2** violation of a treaty/covenant; disruption of alliance. ~মুক্ত *adj* dislocated. ~ যুক্ত *adj* articulated. ~স্থল *n* juncture. ~হারক=~চৌর. কপাট-~ *n* hinge-joint. বিসর্গ~ *n* (gram) euphonic junction of a বিসর্গ with a vowel or consonantal sound, or of a consonantal sound with a vowel sound. স্বর-~ *n* (gram) euphonic junction of two vowel sounds.

সন্ধিৎসা *n* **1** desire to know/inquire; inquisitiveness; curiosity. **2** wish to make peace/form an alliance with.

সন্ধিৎসু *adj* **1** inquisitive; curious. **2** wishing to make peace/form an alliance with.

সন্ধুক্ষিত *adj* kindled; inflamed.

সন্ধেয় *adj* to be joined/united/connected with; to be reconciled/made peace or alliance with.

সন্ধ্যা *n* **1** juncture of day and night; twilight; evening; dusk; nightfall. **2** religious acts performed at the three divisions of the day; evening prayer. **3** period which proceeds a Yuga or age of the world; transition period. **4** time (of performance): দু~ খাওয়া. **5** beginning: কলির ~. **6** close; closing period: জীবন~. ~ করা *vi* **1** be late in the evening; be overtaken by evening: ~ করে বাড়ি ফিরো না. **2** perform evening rites; say one's prayer (at the three divisions of the day). ~-আহ্নিক *n* rites performed in the evening and during the day.

~-উপাসনা *n* worship performed in the evening/at the three divisions of the day. ~ংশ *n* period at the end of each Yuga. ~কাল *n* evening-time; twilight-time. ~কালিক, ~কালীন *adjj* belonging to evening-time/twilight-time; vesper-time; evening. ~কালে *adv* in the evening. ~কৃত্য *n* evening rites. ~-গোধূলি *n* evening twilight; dusk. ~তারা *n* evening star; Vesper. ~ত্রয়=তিন সন্ধ্যা. ~দীপ *n* evening lamp. ~বন্দনা *n* morning and evening hymns and acts of worship. ~ ভাষা *n* esoteric/hermetic language. ~রাগ, ~লোক *nn* red glow of twilight; twilight-ray. ~শঙ্খ *n* evening conch-shell. ~ সময়=~কাল. তিন ~, ত্রি~ *nn* three divisions/periods of the day (morning, noon and evening).

সন্নত *adj* curved; inclined; stooping/bowing to; bent; bowed before; revered; deepened; sunk in; depressed; bent down through sorrow; dispirited.

সন্নাত *n* bending down; stooping; lowness; depression; inclination; leaning towards; submission; humility toward.

সন্নদ্ধ *adj* **1** bound/fastened/tied together; bound; girt. **2** armed; mailed; armoured; equipped; accoutred. **3** harnessed. **4** prepared; ready. **5** arrayed; aligned; lined-up. **6** ready to discharge water (said of a cloud). **7** wearing amulets; provided with charms. **8** sticking/clinging/adhering to; adjoining; bordering; near.

সন্না=সন্দেশ

সন্নাহ *n* armours; mail; equipment; coat of mail; accoutrements; harness. **সন্নাহ্য** *adj* armed; armoured; ready for battle.

সন্নিকট *adj* **1** very proximate/near. **2** imminent; approaching: ~ মৃত্যু. ❑*adv, prep* **1** very near; close to/by: নগর-~. **2** before; in the presence of: রাজ-~. **সন্নিকটে** *adj*=~.

সন্নিকর্ষ *n* nearness; proximity; close contact; nieghbourhood; approximation; vicinity; connection to; relation with. ~ণ *n* **1**=~. **2** (math) approximation.

সন্নিকৃষ্ট *adj* drawn together/near; contiguous; proximate; near; imminent.

সন্নিধান *n* **1** juxtaposition. **2** nearness; vicinity; proximity; contiguity. **3** presence. **4** placing down; depositing. **5** place of deposit; receptacle; gathering-place; custody. **সন্নিধানে** *adj* near; in the presence of; in possession/custody of; in (close) proximity/vicinity to.

সন্নিধি=সন্নিধান

সন্নিপতিত *adj* **1** flown/fallen down; descended. **2** met together; assembled. **3** appeared; arrived.

সন্নিপাত *n* **1** falling in/down together; collapse; utter ruin/fall/destruction. **2** meeting; encounter; contact/collision with. **3** conjunction; aggregation; combination; mixture. **4** (Ayu) a complicated derangement of the three humours; typhoid. ~ন *n* causing to fall together; combination; conjunction.

সন্নিবদ্ধ *adj* firmly bound together/on; closely connected with/attached to; planted/covered with; firmly tied/shut/set.

সন্নিবন্ধ(ন) *n* binding firmly together/on; tying together; binding fast.

সন্নিবিষ্ট *adj* **1** seated down together; assembled. **2** fixed in/on; set in order; arrayed; arranged; inserted; entered into. **3** sticking/resting/contained in. **4** entered deeply into; absorbed/engrossed in; occupied with. **3** contiguous; neighbouring.

সন্নিবৃত্ত *adj* turned/come back; returned; withdrawn desisted; stopped; ceased.

সন্নিবৃত্তি *n* returning; coming back; desisting from; forbearance; avoiding.

সন্নিবেশ *n* **1** putting down together; insertion; inclusion. **2** setting; orderly placing; stationing; arreyment; arrangement; encampment; setting up; pitching. **3** assembling together; assembly; assemblage; construction; composition; fabrication. **4** seat; position; place; situation. ~-দোষ *n* (astron) error of judgement.

সন্নিবেশিত=সন্নিবিষ্ট

সন্নিভ *adj* (used as a *pref)* like; similar to; resembling; equivalent to.

সন্নিযুক্ত *adj* confirmed (in a post); attached; appointed; employed. ~ শল্যচিকিৎসক *n* house surgeon.

সন্নিযোগ *n* confirmation (in a post); attachment; appointment; employment.

সন্নিহিত *adj* **1** deposited; fixed; laid up; placed. **2** near; close; proximate; contiguous; present; at hand; approaching. **3** (geom) adjacent. ~মান *n* (geom) close approximation.

সন্যস্ত *adj* **1** deposited; consigned; intrusted. **2** thrown-down; laid aside. **3** given up; relinquished; abandoned; deserted.

সন্ন্যাস *n* **1** renunciation of the world; (profession of) asceticism; ascetic mendicancy. **2** laying aside; resignation; abandonment. **3** apoplexy. **4** deposit; trust. ~ গ্রহণ করা *vi* take to asceticism; become an ascetic; renounce the world.

সন্ন্যাসী *n* ascetic; devotee; religious mendicant. **সন্ন্যাসিনী** *fem.* অনেক ~তে গাজন নষ্ট (prov) Too many cooks spoil the broth.

সন্মার্গ *n* right path/way

সপ [A] *n* kind of large mat.

সপক্ষ *adj* **1** siding with; taking the same side; supporting; favourable. **2** feathered (as an arrow). ❑*n* partisan; friend; supporter;

adherent. ~তা *n* supporting; favouring. ~তা করা *vt* support; back. সপক্ষে *adv* in support of; in favour of.

সপত্ন *n* rival; adversary; enemy. ~তা *n* rivalry; enmity.

সপত্নী[১] *n fem* another wife of one's husband; fellow-wife or mistress; female rival. ~কন্যা *n fem* step-daughter. ~পুত্র *n* step-son.

সপত্নী[২] *adj, adv* with wife/wives; accompanied by/attended with wife or wives.

সপরিকর *adj* attended by a retinue.

সপরিজন *adj* accompanied by/attended with one's family. ❑*adv* with one's family.

সপরিবার, সপরিবারে *advv*=সপরিজন

সপর্দ=সোপর্দ

সপসপ *n* (onom) expressing **(a)** sound of gulping liquid food; **(b)** thoroughly wet: ভিজে ~, dripping wet; wet to the skin; **(c)** repeated swishing sound: ~ করে চাবুক কষা.

সপসপে *adj* dripping/thoroughly wet; wet to the skin; moist; damp.

সপাং, সপাৎ=সপাৎ

সপাদ *adj* **1** having feet; footed; legged. **2** with a quarter; increased by one-fourth.

সপাসপ=শপাশপ

সপিণ্ড *n* kinsman connected by the offering to the *pinda* (ball of rice, flour, etc offered to the deceased ancestors); near kinsman.

সপিণ্ডকরণ *n* **1** obsequial rites to be performed at the end of the first year of death. **2** (hum) utter destruction/undoing.

সপিনা [E] *n* subpoena. ~ জারি করা/ধরানো/পাঠানো *vt* (summon with a) subpoena. ~ পাওয়া *vi* be subpoenaed.

সপুত্র *adj* having/accompanied by a son or children. ❑*adv* with one's son. ~ক *adv* together with one's son.

সপুষ্পক-উদ্ভিদ *n* phanerogam.

সপেটা [E] *n* fruit of the sapota.

সপ্ত *n, adj* seven. ~ক *n* **1** collection/aggregate of seven; heptad. **2** the seven notes collectively of an octave. ~চত্বারিংশ *n, adj* forty-seven; forty-seventh. ~চত্তারিংশৎ *n* forty-seven. ~চত্তারিশত্তম *adj* forty-seventh. ~চত্তরিংশত্তমী *fem.* ~চ্ছদ *n* kind of tree; *Astonia scholaris.* ~তল *adj* seven-storied. ~তি *n, adj* seventy. ~তিতম *adj* seventieth. ~তিতমী *fem.* ~ত্রিংশ *n, adj* thirty-seven; thirty-seventh. ~ত্রিংশৎ *n* thirty-seven. ~ত্রিংশত্তম *adj* thirty-seventh. ~ত্রিংশত্তমী *fem.* ~দশ *adj* seventeen(th). ~দশী *fem n, adj* seventeen years old (girl). ~দ্বীপ *n* (myth) the seven divisions of the earth. ~দ্বীপা *adj fem* consisting of the seven divisions of the earth. ❑*n* earth. ~ধা *adj* in seven parts/ways; by seven times. ~ধাতু *n* seven constituent elements of the body. ~নবতি *n, adj* ninety-seven. ~নবতিতম *adj* ninety-seventh. ~নবতিতমী *fem.* ~পঞ্চাশ *adj* fifty-seventh. ~পঞ্চাশৎ *n* fifty-seven. ~পঞ্চাশত্তম *adj* fifty-seventh. ~পঞ্চাশত্তমী *fem.* ~পত্র, ~পর্ণ *nn*=~চ্ছদ. ~পদী *adj* consisting of seven feet, parts, etc; seven-footed; heptapodic; heptametrical. ❑*n* the seven steps round the sacred fire at the Hindu marriage ceremony. ~পাতাল *n* (myth) seven regions under the earth/underworlds. ~বিংশৎ *n* twenty-seven. ~বিংশতি *n, adj* twenty-seven. ~বিংশতিতম *adj* twenty-seventh. ~বিংশতিতমী *fem.* ~ম *adj* seventh. ~মী *adj fem.* ❑*n* **1** seventh lunar day of the fortnight. **2** the seventh case, ie the locative or its terminations. ~মী-তৎপুরুষ *n tatpurusha* compound of which the first member is supposed to be in a locative case. ~যোজী *adj* (chem) heptavalent. ~রথী *n* the seven great charioteers of the Mahabharata. ~রথীবেষ্টিত *adj* surrounded by the seven great charioteers (of the Mahabharata); (fig) surrounded by innumerable enemies/opponents. ~র্ষি *n* **1** seven ancient great sages of India. **2** seven stars of the constellation Ursa Major. ~মণ্ডল *n* Ursa Major. ~লোক, ~স্বর্গ *nn* (myth) the seven worlds. ~শত *n, adj* seven hundred. ~শলাক, শলাকা *n* kind of astrological diagram used for indicating auspicious days for marriages. ~ষষ্টি *n, adj* sixty-seven. ~ষষ্টিতম *adj* sixty-seventh. ~ষষ্টিতমী *fem.* ~সপ্ততি *n, adj* seventy-seven. ~সপ্ততিতম *adj* seventy-seventh. ~সপ্ততিতমী *fem.* ~সমুদ্র, ~সাগর, ~সিন্ধু *nn* (myth) the seven seas. ~সুর, ~স্বর *nn* seven notes of an octave. সপ্তা *n* (colloq)=সপ্তাহ. সপ্তাশীতি *n, adj* eighty-seven. ~শিতিতমী *fem.* সপ্তাস্র *adj* heptagonal; septangular. ❑*n* heptagon. সপ্তাহ *n* seven days; week. সপ্তাহকাল *n* period of seven days; week. সপ্তাহকালমধ্যে *adv* within seven days; in a week's time.

সপ্রতিবন্ধ *adj* conditional.

সপ্রতিভ *adj* possessed of quick discernment/presence of mind; smart; bright; clever; intelligent; resourceful; cute; quick-witted; alert; having one's wits about one; unembarrassed; 'not to be embarrassed'.

সপ্রমাণ *adj* having proof/evidence; authentic; proved; vindicated. ~ করা *vt* prove; justify; vindicate; demonstrate.

সফর[১] [A] *n* travel; journey; voyage; tour. ~ করা *vi* travel; go on a journey; journey; tour; visit. ~সূচি *n* tour programme. সফরে বের হওয়া *vi* go on a tour/journey.

সফর[২] [A] *n* the second month of the Hijri year.

সফরি [P] *adj* concerning a journey; travelling. ❑*n* provisions for a journey; traveller.

সফরী *n* kind of tiny fish.
সফল *adj* having good results; fruitful; successful; productive; profitable. ~ **করা** *vt* make fruitful/successful; make good; carry through; accomplish; make effective. ~ **হওয়া** *vi* succeed; triumph; be successful; become fruitful; accomplish; prosper; be successful in; score a success; make it; bear fruit. ~**কাম**, ~ **মনোরথ** *adjj* successful in attaining/ realizing one's desire or end. ~**তা** *n* success; successfulness; profitableness; effectiveness; achievement; fruitfulness.
সফিনা=সপিনা
সফেদ *adj* [P] white. **সফেদা** *n* **1** chalk. **2** flour. **3** white lead; ceruse. **4** kind of fruit.
সফেদি *n* [P] **1** whiteness. **2** whitewash. **3** white of an egg. ~ **করা/ধরানো/লাগানো** *vi* whitewash.
সফেন *adj* foamy; frothy.
সব[১] *adj* all; whole; entire; every. ❑*pron.* all; everything; everybody; whatever one possessed. ❑*pref* meaning plurality /multitude. ভাই~. ~**চিন** *adj* (iron) familiar with everything/everybody; all-knowing. ~**চিন ব্যক্তি** *n* know-all. ~**জান**, ~**জান্তা** *adjj* professing to have knowledge of everything; all-knowing. ❑*n* know-all ~**শুদ্ধ**, ~**সুদ্ধ** *adv* including everything/all; in total; all told; with everything; en bloc: all told. **সবাই** *pron* all; every one; one and all. **সব্যাকার**, **সবার** *adj* of every body/all; owned/shared by all; common; public; universal.
সব[২]=সাব
সবংশে *adv* with the entire family.
সবক [A] *n* lesson; lecture. ~ **দেওয়া** *vi* instruct; teach a lesson.
সবজজ ⇒ সাব
সবজা [P] *n* greenness; verdure; green; herbage
সবজি, **সবজী** *nn* potherb; green-stuffs; vegetables. ~**ওয়ালা** *n* green-grocer; vegetable vender. ~-**বাগ**, ~**বাগান** *n* vegetable garden; kitchen garden.
সবনম=শবনম
সবর=সবুর
সবরি আম *n* guava.
সবরি কলা *n* a superior quality of banana.
সবর্ণ *adj* **1** of the same caste/ class/ tribe. **2** having the same colour/appearance; similar; like; equal to. **3** (gram) belonging to the same class of sounds; homogeneous to. **4** endogamous. **সবর্ণা** *fem.* ❑*n* **1** one of the same caste/class/tribe. **2** (gram) letter/sound from the same phonetical group. ~ **বিবাহ** *n* marriage of the people of the same castes; endogamy.
সবল *adj* powerful; strong; forceful; able; fit (for work); invigorated: রোগের পরে ~ হওয়া; rally from an illness; rally one's strength: recovered. **সবলা** *fem.* ~**তা** *n* strength; power; vigour; fitness; force. **সবলে** *adv* forcefully; forcibly.
সবলুট, **সবলোট** *adj* dissolute; rakish; debauched; profligate; self-indulgent; pleasure-seeking. ❑*n* **1** rake; profligate; debauchee. **2** know-all.
সবস্ত্র *adj* together with wearing clothes.
সবাক *adj* talking. ~**চিত্র** *n* talking-picture; talkie; talking film.
সবাত-শ্বসন *n* (bot) aerobic respiration.
সবাধ *adj* harassed; annoyed; strained; afflicted. ~ **গতি** *n* (mech) constrained motion.
সবান্ধব *adj* accompanied by one's friends and relatives. ❑*adj* (together) with one's friends and relatives. **সবান্ধবে** *adv*=~.
সবাস *adj* **1** clothed; dressed. **2** scented; perfumed. **3** having a dwelling.
সবিকল্প *adj* having/admitting of an alternative or option or doubt; optional; doubtful. ~ **জ্ঞান** *n* **1** (phil) duality; awareness of distinction between the knower and the knowable. **2** (logic) awareness of distinction between adjective and substantive.
সবিকাশ *adj* **1** shining; radiant. **2** developed; elaborated.
সবিগ্রহ *adj* having body/form; embodied.
সবিতা *n* **1** sun; sun-deity. **2** God. **3** stimulator; vivifier; rouser. **সবিত্রী** *fem* mother; female producer.
সবিতৃমণ্ডল *n* orb of the sun.
সবিদ্য *adj* learned. **সবিদ্যা** *fem.*
সবিনয় *adj* modest; humble; polite. ~ **নিবেদন** *n* humble submission. ~ **প্রার্থনা** *n* humble petition/request/prayer. ~**নিবেদনমিদং** (old use) It is humbly submitted that.... **সবিনয়ে** *adv* humbly; politely; modestly.
সবিভ্রম *adj* employing amorous/coquettish glances; coquettish; wanton.
সবিরাম *adj* intermittent. ~ **জ্বর** *n* intermittent fever.
সবিলাস *adj* acting coquettishly; wanton; amorous.
সবিশেষ *adj* **1** detailed; elaborate: ~ বর্ণনা. **2** particular; uncommon; unusual; extraordinary. **3** earnest; special: ~ অনুরোধ. ❑*adj* in detail; elaborately; at length; particularly; exceptionally; exceedingly.
সবিষাদ *adj* having despondency; despairing; dismayed.
সবিস্তর *adj* diffuse; complete; abundant.
সবিস্তার *adj* **1** detailed; elaborate. **2** fully extended: ~ প্রসারণ. ❑*adv* to the full extent; in detail; at length; elaborately **সবিস্তারে** *adv*=~.
সবিষ *adj* poisonous.

সবিস্ময় *adj* surprised; perplexed; amazed; astonished; wondering. **সবিস্ময়ে** *adv* in surprise; amazedly; wonderingly.

সবীজ *adj* containing seed or germ; seeded. ~ **উদ্ভিদ** *n* spermaphyta.

সবুজ [P] *adj* **1** green. **2** unripe. **3** fresh. **4** young; tender-aged. ❑*n* **1** green; verdure. **2** young person; youngman; young people. ~ **কণিকা** *n* (bot) chlorophyll corpuscle.

সবুর [A] *n* patience; endurance; self-restraint; resignation; submission. ~ **করা** *vi* have/keep patience; wait; endure; exercise self-restraint. **সবুরে মেওয়া ফলে** (prov) patience has its reward; patience pays/succeeds.

সবে[1]=সবাই (⇒ সব)

সবে[2] *adv* **1** merely; only. **2** just now/then: ~ সন্ধ্যা হলো **3** in all; all told: ~ধন.

সবেবরাত=শবেবরাত

সব্জি=সবজি

সব্বাই *pron* (colloq)=সবাই (⇒ সব)

সব্য *adj* **1** right. **2** left. **3** southern. ~**সাচী** *adj* one who can draw a bow with both hands; ambidextrous. ❑*n* ambidexterer; Arjuna of Mahabharata. ~**সাচিতা** *n* ambidexterity.

সব্যাজ *adj* artful; fraudulent; false; deceitful.

সব্রীড় *adj* bashful; modest.

সভক্তি *adj* devoted; respectful; dedicated.

সভঙ্গ *adj* (bot) crenate.

সভয় *adj* fearful; apprehensive; afraid; timid. **সভয়ে** *adv* with fear; fearfully; anxiously; timidly.

সভর্তৃকা=সধবা

সভা *n* **1** meeting; assembly; gathering; congregation; reunion; conference; council; convention; get-together. **2** social party; committee; society; good society; club; union; association. **3** place for public meetings; large assembly-room/hall; palace; court of a king/ justice; council-chamber. **4** assemblage. গুণাবদমাসের ~. ~ **আহ্বান করা** *vi*=~ ডাকা. ~ **করা** *vi* **1** hold a meeting; assemble; meet. **2** hold court; sit in court. ~ **চলছে** The meeting is in progress/under way. ~ **ডাকা** *vi* convene/call a meeting. ~ **বসেছে** The meeting has commenced. **2** The court has sat. ~ **ভাঙলো** **1** The meeting is over/ended/done with. **2** The court has risen. ~**কক্ষ** *n* assembly-hall; council-room; committee-room; meeting room. ~**কবি** *n* court-poet. ~**গৃহ**=~কক্ষ. ~**জন** *n* **1** member of an audience; people present at a meeting; assembly; gathering. **2** member of an assembly/court/council/association; courtier. ~**তল** *n* venue/place of a meeting; floor of an assembly house/hall. ~**ধিবেশন** *n* meeting; session; sitting. ~**নায়ক** *n* president of an assembly; chairman; chairman of a legislative council. ~**নেত্রী** *n fem* chairperson/ president of a meeting, association, assembly, etc. ~**পণ্ডিত** *n* Brahmin scholar retained in court; court-pundit. ~**পতি**=~নায়ক. ~**পতিত্ব** *n* presidentship; chairmanship; presidency. ~**পতিত্ব করা** *vt* preside (over); chair. ~**ভঙ্গ** *n* break-up/dissolution of a meeting; rising of a court. ~**ভবন** *n* assembly/council/ society/court house; association hall; auditorium. ~**মঞ্চ** *n* podium; rostrum. ~**রম্ভ** *n* commencement of a meeting; beginning of a session. ~**সদ**, ~**সৎ** *nn* **1** member of a council/ committee/ conference/ an assembly. **2** courtier. **3** (law) assessor. ~**সমিতি** *n* meetings and associations. ~**সীন** *adj* sitting in/presiding at a council or court of justice; sitting at a meeting. ~**স্থ** *adj* being at an assembly/a court. ~**স্থল**=~তল.

সভার তৌল *n* laden weight.

সভ্য *adj* suitable to good society; courteous; polite; refined; civilized; not vulgar; decorous; mannerly; elegant. ❑*n* member (of a club/parliament/an association/an assembly). **সভ্যা** *fem.* ~ **করা** *vt* **1** enroll as a member. **2** civilize. ~ **হওয়া** *vi* **1** become/be enrolled as a member. **2** be civilized; become courteous/ polite. ~ **জগৎ** *n* **1** civilized society/world. **2** refined/cultured society. ~**তা** *n* **1** politeness. refinement; good manners/breeding; courtesy; civility. **2** civilization; culture. ~**তাভিমানী** *adj* proud (often arrogantly) of one's culture/ civilization/refinement. ~**তাভিমানিনী** *fem.* ~**পদ** *n* membership. ~**পদ ত্যাগ করা** *vi* resign membership. ~**ভব্য** *n* **1** courteous and gentle; well-mannered; affable; civil: ~ভব্য ছেলে. **2** fit for civilized society; decent: ~ভব্য পোশাক. ~**সমাজ**=~জগৎ

সম[1] *pref* denoting; with, together with, along with, together, altogether. It expresses union, conjunction, thoroughness, intensity, completeness, etc.

সম[2] *adj* **1** even; smooth; flat; plain; level; parallel; uniform. **2** same; equal; similar; like; equivalent; like to; identical/homogenous with. **3** always the same; constant; unchanged; fair; impartial **4** having the right measure; regular; right; normal; straight. **5** equable; neutral; impartial; indifferent. **6** equally distant from extremes; ordinary; common; middling. **7** just; upright; good; straight; honest. **8** complete; whole entire. ❑*n* **1** (music) term point of a measure. **সমা** *fem.* ~**ক** *n* (arith) mean. ~**কক্ষ** *adj* equal; having equal weight/strength; equipotential; evenly balanced; match: সে তোমার ~কক্ষ নয়. ~**কক্ষা** *fem.* ~**কক্ষ লোক** *n* compeer. ~**কক্ষতা** *n* equality; parity. ~কন্যা *n fem* suitable maiden; girl fit to be married. ~কাম *n* homosexuality. ~কামিনী *n* a homosexual woman. ❑*adj* lesbian. ~কামী *n* homosexnal person. ❑*adj* homosexual. ~কারী *adj* counter-availing. ~কাল *n* the same time/age/moment. ~কালবর্তী *adj* contemporary. ~কালিক, ~কালীন *adj* **1** contemporary. **2** simultaneous. ~কালিক-সমীকরণ *n* simultaneous equation. ~কালে *adv* at the same time; in the same age; simultaneously. ~কেন্দ্রিক *adj* concentric. ~কোণ *n* (geom) right-angle. ~কোণী, ~কৌণিক *adj* right-angled. ~কোণীয় *adj* (geog) orthogonal. ~ক্ষেত্র-অভিক্ষেপ *n* equal area projection. ~গুণ, ~গুণবিশিষ্ট *adjj* of like virtues/ quality/ character. ~গুণশ্রেঢ়ী *n* (math) geometrical progression. ~ঘন *adj* homogeneous. ❑*n* (geom) regular solid. ~চতুরস্র, ~চতুর্ভুজ *adj* square. ❑*nn* equilateral tetragon. ~চিত্ত *adj* evenminded; possessing equanimity; equable. ~চ্ছেদ *adj* having an equal denominator; having equal divisions. ❑*n* (phys) plane section. ~জাতি, ~জাতিক, ~জাতীয় *adjj* equal in kind; homogeneous. ~জাতিত্ব, ~জাতিকতা, ~জাতীয়তা *n n* homogeneity. ~তল *adj* plain; level; flat; smooth. ❑*n* **1** plain. **2** (geom) plain surface/figure; plane. ~তলভূমি *n* plain; even/level ground. ~তা *n* **1** equality; sameness; equivalence; similarity; identity with. **2** fairness; impartiality towards. **3** uniformity; straightness. **4** liveliness; flatness. **5** equanimity. **6** equableness; normal condition. ~তীত *adj* quite past/gone by. ~তুল, ~তুল্য *adjj* comparable; equal; equivalent; of equal value; equipotential; parallel. ~তুল্যা *fem.* ~ত্বরণ *n* (mech) uniform acceleration. ~ত্রিভুজ *n* (geom) equilateral triangle. ~দর্শন *adj* **1** of similar appearance. **2**=~দর্শী. ❑*n* impartiality; equity; fair-mindedness; equanimity. ~দর্শিতা *n*=~দর্শন. ~দর্শী *adj* **1** looking impartially on; regarding all things impartially. **2** impartial in consideration/ treatment; fair-minded; equitable; equitable in dispensation of justice; impartial. ~দুঃখ, ~দুঃখী *adjj* feeling pain in common with another; compassionate; sympathizing; sympathetic. ~দুঃখিনী *fem.* ~দুঃখসুখ *adj* sharing grief and joy with another; indifferent to pain and pleasure; justice; impartial. ~দর্শিনী *fem.* ~দূরবর্তিতা *n* equal distance; equidistance. ~দূরবর্তী *adj* equidistant. ~দূরবর্তিনী *fem.* ~দৃষ্টি *n* act of looking on all equally/impartially; impartiality; impartial view. ❑*adj* even-eyed; impartial. ~দ্বিবাহু, ~দ্বিভুজ *nn* isosceles. ~দ্বিবাহু ত্রিভুজ *n* isosceles triangle. ~ধর্ম *adj* of equal nature/character; resembling. ~পদ *n* equal rank. ~পদস্থ *adj* equal in rank/ office/ status/dignity/authority ~পরিণত *adj* (biol) homogenous. ~পদস্থা *fem.* ~পাঠী *n* classmate; class-fellow; fellow-student. ~পাঠিনী *fem.* ~পার্শ্বীয় *adj* (bot) collateral. ~পৃষ্ঠ *adj*=~তল. ~প্রবাহ *n* (phys) direct current. ~প্রভ *adj* having equal splendour. ~প্রাণ *adj* inseparably united (in feeling, thought, etc); intimate: ~প্রাণ বন্ধু, bosom friend. ~প্রাণা *fem.* ~প্রাণতা *n* intimacy; communion; affinity. ~প্রেষ *n* (phys) uniform pressure. ~প্রেষরেখা *n* (geog) isobar. ~বয়সী, ~বয়স্ক *adjj* of equal age; of the same age; contemporaneous; coeval. ~বয়স্কা *fem.* ~বর্ণ *adj* of the same colour; being of the same/equal caste. ~বর্ত-কোণ *n* (phys) angle of polarization. ~বর্তন *n* (phys) polarization. ~বর্তাক্ষ *n* (phys) axis of polarization. ~বর্তিত *adj* polarized. ~বর্তিত করা *vt* polarize. ~বর্তিতা *adj* equidistance; equality. ~বর্তী *adj* acting uniformly; being equal/equidistant. ~বর্তিনী *fem.* ~বর্তুল *n* (geom) cylinder. ~বর্ষণ *n* raining equally. ~বর্ষণরেখা (geog) isohyet. ~বাহু *adj* equilateral. ~বিন্দু *n* (geom) concurrent. ~বুদ্ধি *adj* esteeming all things alike; indifferent; fair-minded; impartial. ❑*adj* fair-mindedness. ~বৃত্ত *adj* uniformly round. ~বৃত্তি *adj* **1** (bot) homogeneous. **2** of an equal/even temper; equable; fair; moderate. ❑*n* equanimity; even temper. ~বেগ *n* uniform velocity. ~বেদনা, ~ব্যথা *nn* sympathy; fellow-feeling; compassion; commiseration. ~বেদী, ~ব্যথী *adjj* suffering equal pain; sympathetic; compassionate; commiserative. ~বেদী কম্পন *n* sympathetic vibration. ~ভাগ *n* equal share. ~ভাগী *adj* sharing equally. ❑*n* equal partner. ~ভাব *n* equability; homogeneousness; similarity; sameness; same/similar state of mind; same or similar state/condition/manner. ❑*adj*=~ভাবাপন্ন. ~ভাবাপন্ন *adj* of like nature/ property; of the same or similar state/ condition/manner; having the same/ similar state of mind; similar; same; equable. ~ভাবাপন্ন জলবায়ু *n* equable climate. ~ভাবে *adv* equally; in the same/similar manner or way; uniformly; unchangingly. ~ভূমি *n* even ground; plain. ❑*adj* level; flat; plain; razed to the ground. ~ভূমি করা *vt* level; raze to the ground. ~ভোগবাদ *n* communism. ~মণ্ডল *n* temperate zone. ~মাত্র *adj* (alg) homogeneous. ~মাত্রিক *adj* **1** of the same size/measure. **2** of the same prosodical measure. ~মালভূমি *n* (geog) tableland; plateau. ~মুখ *adj* (mech, of forces) like. ~মূল *adj* (arith) equivalent. ~মূল্য *adj* of the same/equal price or value or rate; equivalent. ~মূল্যে *adv* at par; at the same of equal price/rate. ~রাশি *n* (arith) even number. ~রূপ *adj* of the same form; alike in form/manner; uniform; homomorphic; homomorphous. ~রূপতা *n* uniformity. ~রেখা *adj* forming an even line; straight. ~রৈখিক *adj* collinear. ~লয় *n* synchronism. ❑*adj* synchronous. ~শোধন *n* (math) equation. ~শ্রেণী *n* same class/ race/ family/rank. ~শ্রেণীভুক্ত *adj* belonging to the same class/ race/ family/ rank. ~ষড়্ফলক *n* (geom) cube. ~সংযোগ *n* (bot) cohesion. ~সংস্থ *adj* homologous. ~সংস্থান *adj* (biol) homogeneous. ❑*n* (phys) equilibrium. ~সত্ত্ব *adj* consubstantial; (bot) homogeneous. ~-সম *adj* equal. ❑*adj* end to end. ~সাময়িক *adj* contemporary; contemporaneous. ~সুখদুঃখ= ~দুঃখসুখ. ~সূত্র *n* **1** prime & vertical circle. **2** one and the same straight line: ~সূত্রে অবস্থান. **3** one and the same bond/string: ~ সূত্রে গ্রথিত. **4** one and the source/means: ~সূত্রে জানা. ~সূত্রস্থ *adj* situated on the same diameter; living at the antipodes. ~স্থল *n* even/level ground. ~স্বর *adj* having the same tone/accent. ❑*n* same voice. ~স্বরে *adv* in unison; with one voice. ~স্বামিত্ব *n* equal authority/ownership. ~হার=~মূল্য. **সমাংশ** *n* equal share. **সমাশংক** *adj* (chem) isomerous. **সমাংশিক** *adj* consisting of equal parts. **সমাংশে** *adv* in equal parts/ shares/portions. **সমাকার, সমাকৃতি** *adjj* of similar shape and form; similar; like; isomorphous. **সমাক্ষ** *adj* coaxial. **সমাক্ষরেখা** *n* parallel of latitude. **সমাক্ষর** *adj* having the same number of syllables. **সমাঙ্গ** *adj* regular. **সমানুপাত** *n* (math) equal ratio; proportion. **সমানুপাতিক** *adj* relating to proportion; proportionate. **সমানুপাতিকপ্রতিনিধিত্ব** *n* proportional representation. **সমানুরূপ** *adj* (geom) directly similar. **সমান্তর** *n* **1** equal distance. ❑*adj* (arith & alg) equidistant. **2** (geom) parallel. **সমান্তরতা** *n* equidistance; parallelism. **সমান্তররেখা** *n* parallel line. **সমান্তরশ্রেঢ়ী** *n* arithmetical progression. **সমান্তরশ্রেণী** *n* arithmetic series. **সমান্তরাল** *adj* parallel. **সমান্তরাল ক্ষেত্র** *n* parallelogram. **সমান্তরালতা** *n* parallel; parallelism. **সমান্তরাল রেখা** *n* parallel line. **সমান্তরাল সরল রেখা** *n* parallel straight line. **সমার্থক** *adjj* having the same meaning; synonymous. **সমার্থক শব্দ** *n* synonyms.

সমক্ষ *adj* lying before; present; visible; direct. ~তা *n* visibility. ~ দর্শন *n* act of seeing with the eyes; ocular evidence. ~ দৃষ্টি *n* direct vision. ~ বর্ণালীবীক্ষণ *n* direct vision spectroscope. **সমক্ষে** *adv* before one's eyes; in the sight/presence of; manifestly; visibly.

সমগ্র *adj* all; entire; whole; complete; total; exhaustive; overall; each; every. ~তা *n* totality; whole; entirely; wholeness; total; sum. ~ বিস্তার *n* overall width. ~ সূচি *n* exhaustive list. ~ভাবে *adv* on the whole; fully: entirely; thoroughly.

সমঙ্গ *n* (zoo) imago.

সমজ=সমঝ

সমঝ *n* understanding; comprehension; knowledge; discernment; conception. ~দার *adj* intelligent; prudent; wise; capable of appreciating; understanding; sympathetic; considerate ❑*n* connoidiscernment; perspicaciousness;sseur. ~দারি *n* understanding; connoisseurship; sympathy; considerateness. **সমঝানো, সমঝা** *vt* **1** make clear; explain; account for; make sb understand/ feel/ appreciate; convince; instruct; advise. **2** warn; correct; remonstrate with; scold; take to task; chastise.

সমঞ্জস *adj* **1** proper; fit; right; appropriate; just; correct. **2** sound; good; excellent. **3** consistent; well-balanced; fitting. **4** (geom) harmonic.

সমত্ত=সোমত্ত

সমধিক *adj* excessive; superabundant; superfluous; exceeding; exceedingly great; overmuch; considerable; many. ❑*adv* excessively; exceedingly; overmuch.

সমন [E] *n* summons. ~ জারি করা/দেওয়া/পাঠানো *vi* serve/issue a summons. ~ ধরানো *vi* serve summons.

সমনস্ক *adj* endowed with understanding.

সমন্ত্রক *adj* accompanied with sacred verses; charmed.

সমন্বয় *n* **1** adjustment; agreement; harmony. **2** co-ordination. **3** combination; synthesis. **4** connected sequence/consequence. ~ করা *vt* **1** adjust; bring into agreement; reconcile; bring, about harmony/ agreement; harmonize. **2** co-ordinate. **3** make a synthesis of; synthesize; synthesize. ~ন, ~বিধান, ~সাধন *nn* adjusting; adjustment; co-ordinating; co-ordination; harmonization; act of bringing into agreement.

সমন্বয়িত *adj* adjusted; well-balanced; reconciled; co-ordinated; concerted; balanced; regulated; made consistent; unified; brought into agreement; synthesized; synthetised.

সমন্বিত *adj* **1**=সমন্বয়িত. **2** possessing; attended with; endowed with; full of; mixed with: নানা গুণ~.

সমবধান *n* great attention.

সমবস্থ *adj* **1** in/of the same/similar condition; in the same position/state as before. **2** standing/remaining firm; steady. **সমবস্থা, সমবস্থান** *n* same/similar condition/state; unchanged position/state; status quo; resting; abiding in.

সমবায় *n* **1** coming/meeting together; contact; concourse; congress; assemblage; collection; crowd; aggregate. **2** co-operation. **3** (mech) combination. **4** conjunction (of heavenly bodies). **5** (phil) perpetual; co-inherence; inner/intimate relation; constant/intimate union; inseparable concomitance. **6** collision. ☐*adj* united; assembled: ~ হওয়া. **~-সমিতি** *n* co-operative society.

সমবায়ী *adj* **1** co-operative. **2** closely connected/united; concomitant; inhercut in. **3** aggregated; combined; capable of combining; component; constituent. **~ কারণ** *n* inseparable/ inherent connection; material/ substantial cause.

সমবেত *adj* come together; met; assembled; united; combined; collected; all. **~ করা** *vt* bring together; assemble; combine; unite. **~ হওয়া** *vi* come/meet/mix/assemble together; be united (in); gather. **~ভাবে** *adv* unitedly; in a body.

সমভিব্যাহার *n* (old use) association; company. **সমভিব্যাহারে** *adj* in the company of; accompanied by.

সমভিব্যাহারী *adj* (old use) accompanying. **সমভিব্যাহারিণী** *fem.*

সময় *n* **1** time. **2** time of the clock: তিনটার ~, at three o'clock. **3** particular time; part of day; time (of): সন্ধ্যার ~, in the evening. **4** point/ period of time: সেই সময়, at that time. **5** appointed/ proper time; right moment for doing anything: এটা কি রাগের ~? **6** opportunity; suitable/opportune time; occasion; time; season: ~ বুঝে চেষ্টা করা, এটা খেলার ~. **7** (working) hours; time: অফিসের সময়, বিপদের ~, hour of danger. **8** times: সুসময়, good days, good hour. **9** period; time; age; reign; regime: সাহজাহানের ~. **10** leisure; time: আমার এতটুকু ~ নেই. **11** juncture; circumstance; case; condition; state: এই সময়ে. **12** days of life; longevity; time: তার ~ ফুরিয়েছে, his time is up; his (last) hour has come/struck. **13** last hour; dying day: তার ~ হয়েছে— চলে গেছে. **14** established custom; usage; convention; conventional rule/usage; practice; observance. **15** sign; hint; indication. **~ করা** *vi* make/find time (for); fix time (for); find leisure (for). **~ বুঝে চলা** *vi* **1** keep up with the times. **2** see how the wind blows; play safe; lock before one leaps; watch one's step. **3** swim with the tide; jump on the bandwagon; follow the line. **~ দেওয়া** *vi* give/allow sb time. **~ দেখা** *vi* read the clock/time. **~ নষ্ট করা** *vi* **1** waste/kill time; while away the time. **2** let go/loose an opportunity. **~ পাওয়া** *vi* get/find time/leisure; be given/allowed time. **~ বলা** *vi* tell the time (of clock). **~ হয়েছে** It is time; One's days are numbered. **~-অসময়** *n* proper and improper time. **~-অসময় নেই** in season and out of season; at all hours. **~ক্রমে** *adv* in course of time. **~জ্ঞান** *n* sense of time; punctuality. **~ থাকতে** while there is time. **~ নিরূপণ করা** ascertain the time of; fix the time for. **~নিরূপণ-তালিকা** *n* time-table. **~নিষ্ঠ** *adj* punctual. **~নিষ্ঠা** *n* punctuality. **~মতো** *adv* at the right time; in time. **~রক্ষক** *adj* keeping time. ☐*n* time-keeper. **~-রেখা** *n* date-line. **~ সময়** *adv*=সময়ে সময়ে. **~সেবক, ~সেবী** *adjj* time-serving. ☐*nn* time-server. **সময়ানুসারে** *adv* **1** according to a fixed/particular time; in time. **2** according to the age/time; according to the demand of the passing state/condition; keeping up with the time; following the trend of the age. **সময়ান্তর** *n* another/some other time. **সময়ান্তরে** *adj* at another/some other time. **সময়ে সময়ে** *adv* at times; from time to time; occasionally; now and then. **সময়ে ও অসময়ে** *adj* in season and out of season; at all times; in joy and sorrow. **অত্যল্প সময়ে** *adv* in no time. **কাজের ~** *n* time for work; working hours. **একটার ~** (at) one o'clock. **বর্তমান ~** *n* present times. **বসন্তের ~** (in) spring; springtime; spring season. **ভালো ~** *n* good times; opportune moment. **সন্ধ্যার ~** (in) the evening; evening time. **স্থানীয় ~** *n* local time. **মরবার ~ না থাকা** be pressed for time.

সময়োচিত, সময়োপযোগী *adjj* timely; opportune; well-timed.

সমর *n* war; battle; hostile encounter; conflict; struggle; fight. **~কৌশল** *n* strategy; tactics; soldiership. **~ক্ষেত্র, ~ভূমি** *nn* battle-field; battle-ground; arena. **~শায়ী** *adj* killed in a battle/action; fallen in fight. **~শায়িনী** *fem.* **~সজ্জা, ~সাজ** *nn* battle-dress; military accouterment; war equipment; preparation for war; military preparedness. **~স্থল, সমরাঙ্গন** = ~ক্ষেত্র. **সমরানল** *n* war regarded as fire; flames of war; conflagration of war. **সমরাস্ত্র** *n* war-weapon.

সমর্থ *adj* **1** able; capable; competent; suitable/fit (for); able-bodied; match (for). **2** of full age and able to earn: ~ ছেলে. **3** of full age and fit for marriage: ~ মেয়ে. **সমর্থা** *fem.*

সমর্থক *adj* supporting; seconding; corroborating. ☐*n* supporter; seconder; upholder; defender; backer; ally; champion.

সমর্থন *n* **1** supporting; support; seconding; upholding; backing; countenancing; endorsement; championship. **2** confirmation. **3** corroboration; vindication; justification. **সমর্থনা**=~. **~ করা** *vt* support; second; uphold; champion; bolster up; back; shore up;

countenance; endorse; defend; confirm; corroborate.

সমর্থনীয় *adj* to be supported/ seconded/ upheld/ backed/ countenanced/ endorsed; supportable; defensible; tenable; justifiable.

সমর্থিত *adj* supported; seconded; upheld; backed; bolstered up; endorsed; confimred; corroborated; countenanced. **সমর্থিতা** *fem.*

সমর্পণ *n* act of placing/throwing upon; delivering/ handing completely over; rendering; consigning; presenting; bestowing; dedication; act of committing to the charge/custody of; surrender; making over; bestowal; presentation. **~ করা** *vt* deliver over; consign; impart; give (away); bestow; hand (over); make over; commit (to the custody of); surrender; pass (over); render relinquish (sth/to sb); yield up. **~কারী** *adj* yielding; surrendering; bestowing; relinquishing. ❑*n* giver; one who makes over/ render/imparts/commits to the custody of or charge of; surrenderer; on who yields up/hands over. **~কারিণী** *fem.*

সমর্পা *vt* (poet)=সমর্পণ করা

সমর্পিত *adj* made over; consigned to; placed/fixed in or on; given; committed to the charge/custody of; yielded up; rendered; imparted.

সমল *adj* dirty; foul; impure; filthy; sinful. ❑*n* excrement.

সমষ্টি *n* totality; aggregate; sum; total; sum total; collectiveness. **~করণ** *n* totaling; totalization; addition; (phys) aggregation. **~গত** *adj* collective. **~গতভাবে** *adv* collectively.

সমষ্টীভূত *adj* totalled; aggregated; collective.

সমস্ত *adj* combined; compounded; compound; united; whole; all; entire; collected. ❑*n* whole; aggregate of all the parts. **~পদ** *n* (gram) compound word.

সমস্যমান *adj* (gram) under the process of being compounded; to be compounded.

সমস্যা *n* problem; (difficult) question; puzzle; riddle; intricate situation; point at issue; fix. **~পূরণ/~ সমাধান করা** *vi* solve a problem; settle an issue; puzzle out. **~পূর্ণ, ~মূলক, ~সঙ্কুল** *adjj* problematic; puzzling; intricate; vexatious; tangled; complicated; enigmatic.

সমা *adj fem* of সম

সমাকলন *n* integral calculus.

সমাকর্ষ(ণ) *n* drawing near; attraction.

সমাকর্ষী *adj* drawing together; attracting.

সমাকীর্ণ *adj* strewn over; bestowed; overspread; completely covered (with); pervaded/infested with; full of.

সমাকুল *adj* **1** crowded together; crowded/filled with; replete with; full of; abounding in. **2** greatly agitated/confounded; troubled; confused; flurried; bewildered; perturbed. **3** full of misgivings. **~তা** *n* great agitation/ confusion/ bewilderment/ trouble of mind; perturbation.

সমাকৃত *adj* brought/collected together.

সমাক্রান্ত *adj* trod/stepped upon; pressed/ borne sown; overrun; attacked; assailed; seized upon.

সমাখ্যা(ন) *n* **1** name; appellation. **2** explanation; interpretation. **3** fame; celebrity.

সমাখ্যাত *adj* **1** proclaimed; declared. **2** acknowledged as; called; named; famed; celebrated; notorious; renowned.

সমাগত *adj* come together; met; encountered; assembled; gathered; arrived. **সমাগতা** *fem.* **~ হওয়া** *vi* come together; meet; be united with; assemble; gather; come to/near; arrive at; approach.

সমাগতি=সমাগম

সমাগম *n* coming (together); encounter/ meeting (with); approach; arrival; assemblage; assembly (of); gathering. **জন~** *n* gathering; concourse of people. **অবৈধ জন~** *n* unlawful assembly.

সমাঘ্রাত *adj* well smelled.

সমাচার *n* news; information; message; report; tradition.

সমাচ্ছন্ন *adj* **1** completely covered with; thoroughly enveloped/ overcast. **2** thoroughly overwhelmed/ besotted: চিন্তা~. **সমাচ্ছন্না** *fem.* **~তা** *n* state of being completely covered/ overcast; state of confusion; confusedness; bewilderment; sottishness; inebriation.

সমাজ *n* **1** (human) society. **2** community; class; nation; race. **3** meeting; assembly; association; congregating; congress; gathering; conclave; company; collection. **4** any one of the divisions of biological history; species; kingdom: পক্ষি~. **~কর্ম** *n* social work. **~কল্যাণ** *n* social welfare. **~চ্যুত** *adj* ostracized; outcaste; socially boycotted. **~চ্যুত করা** *vt* ostracize; cast sb out of society; boycott socially. **~চ্যুত ব্যক্তি** *n* outcaste. **~চ্যুতি** *n* expulsion/ exclusion from society; social ostracism; excommunication; social boycott. **~জ্ঞতা** *n* knowledge of the society. **~তত্ত্ব** *n* sociology. **~তন্ত্র** *n* socialism. **~তন্ত্রী** *adj* socialist; socialistic. ❑*n* socialist. **~তাত্ত্বিক** *adj* sociological. ❑*n* sociologist. **~তান্ত্রিক**=~ তন্ত্রী. **~নীতি** *n* social laws/ principles; sociology. **~পতি** *n* headman/ leader of a society; social leader. **~পতিত**=~চ্যুত. **~পাঠ** *n* social studies. **~বদ্ধ** *adj* **1** (of people) social; living in societies. **2** (of animals) gregarious. **~বন্ধন** *n* social ties; bonds of society; social constraints; social obligations. **~বহির্ভূত** *adj* outside the society;

extra-social; unsocial. **~বহিস্কৃত**=~চ্যুত. **~বিজ্ঞান, ~বিদ্যা** *nn* sociology. **~বিজ্ঞানী** *n* social scientist; sociologist. **~বিধি** *n* social rule/ law. **~বিরুদ্ধ, ~বিরোধী** *adjj* antisocial. **~ব্যাধি** *n* social malady. **~রহিত**=~চ্যুত. **~শক্তি** *n* power of the society. **~শাসন** *n* rule/ authority of the society; social laws/ rules; administration of the society. **~শিক্ষা** *n* social studies . **~শৃঙ্খল** *n* bonds of society. **~শৃঙ্খলা** *n* social discipline. **~সংস্কার** *n* social reform. **~সংস্কার করা** *vi* reform a society. **~সংস্কারক** *n* social reformer. **~সেবক** *n* social worker. **~সেবা** *n* social work/ service. **~হিত** *n* welfare of the society. **~হিতকর, ~হিতকারী** *adjj* beneficial for the society. **~হিতৈষণা** *n* act of doing good of the society; philanthropy. **~হিতৈষী** *adj* philanthropic; humanitarian. ❑*n* philanthropist. **~হিতৈষিণী** *fem.*

সমাদর *n* **1** great respect; veneration. **2** great/ deep appreciation. **3** very hearty/ warm/ cordial/ respectful reception: অতিথির ~. **3** warm felicitation/ greetings. **4** zealous/ enthusiastic reception or welcome: বইয়ের ~. **5** passionate love/ fondness for; enthusiasm for: ফুটবলের ~. **~ করা** *vt* receive very heartily/ warmly/ cordially/ respectfully/ enthusiastically/ zealously; entertain cordially/ generously; love passionately; be enthusiastic about; felicitate; appreciate deeply; think highly of. **~নীয়** *adj* admirable; venerable; estimable; to be appreciated.

সমাদৃত *adj* very heartily/ warmly/ cordially/ respectfully/ enthusiastically/ zealously received; deeply appreciated; respected; venerated; highly esteemed/ valued; thought of highly; in high esteem; highly popular. **সমাদৃতা** *fem.*

সমাধা *n* completion; accomplishment; termination; settlement; end. **~ করা** *vt* complete; accomplish; settle; conclude; end.

সমাধান *n* **1** solution; unravelling; resolution. **2**=সমাধা. **~ করা** *vt* solve; resolve; unravel; settle; puzzle out; riddle.

সমাধি *n* **1** tomb; grave; vault. **2** mausoleum; sepulchral monument; sanctuary/ tomb of a saint. **3** burial; internment. **4** intense absorption; trance. **5** intense application; intentness; concentration of the thoughts; profound/ abstract meditation; intense contemplation. **6** self-absorbed spiritual meditation during which the meditator loses his/ her identity and becomes one with the Supreme Being; religious vow of intense devotion or self-imposed abstraction. **7** (fig) end. **~ক্ষেত্র** *n* burial-ground; cemetery; grave. **~প্রস্তর** *n* tombstone.**~ফলক** *n* epitaph. **~বল** *n* force of meditation. **~ভঙ্গ** *n* interruption/ disturbing of meditation. **~ভঙ্গ করা** disturb/ interrupt meditation; give up meditation. **~মগ্ন** *adj* absorbed in meditation. **~মন্দির** *n* tomb; mausoleum; sepulchral monument. **~স্তম্ভ** *n* tombstone; monument. **~স্থ** *adj* absorbed in meditation; buried. **~স্থ করা** *vt* bury; lay in the grave; inter. **~স্থল, ~স্থান**=~ক্ষেত্র.

সমাধ্যায়ী *adj* reading the same subject/ in the same class. ❑*n* fellow-student; class-mate.

সমান *adj* **1** equal; same; identical; one:=তারা দুজনেই ~. **2** alike; similar; uniform; like to: তার ~ কেউ নেই. **3** level; flat: ~ রাস্তা. **4** unchanging; unchanged. **5** moderate; middling. **6** (sl) thoroughly chastised: মার খেয়ে ~. ❑*n* one of the five vital airs of the body. **~ করা** *vt* **1** make similar/ equal/ alike/ identical; equalize; even (up). **2** level; flatten; smooth; plane; make uniform; straighten; dress: জমি/কাপড় ~ করা. **3** adjust; correct: ঘড়ি ~ করা. **4** chastize thoroughly: মেরে ~ করা. **~কারক** *adj* making all things equal/ the same; levelling. **~কালীন** *adj* simultaneous; contemporaneous. **~ত্ব** *n* equality (with). **~ধর্মী** *adj* having the same qualities; similar to. **~বল** *adj* of equal strength. **~সমান** *adj* **1** equal; equivalent; equal in strength; equalized; alike; equally balanced. **2** even; evenly contested; drawn: খেলা ~-সমান. **3** neither more nor less; half-and-half: ~-সমান ভাগ. **4** (gambling) quits. **~-সমান দ্বন্দ্ব** *n* even match; neck and neck struggle.

সমানাধিকরণ *n* **1** same predicament/ category; common substratum. **2** grammatical agreement in case; same case-relation. ❑*adj* **1** being in the same category/ predicament. **2** being in the same case-relation (with). **3** co-existent. **সমানাধিকার** *n* equal rights and privileges for all. **সমানাধিকারতন্ত্রতা, সমানাধিকারবাদ** *nn* communism. **সমানাধিকারী** *adj* enjoying equal rights and privileges.

সমানে[1] *adv* with honour/ dignity; honourably.

সমানে[2] *adv* ceaselessly; non-stop; at a stretch; incessantly. **~-সমানে** *adj* evenly contested. **~-সমানে লড়াই** *n* even match.

সমাপক *adj* finishing; completing; fulfilling.

সমাপতন *n* coincidence.

সমাপন *n* completion; completing; conclusion; end; ending; close; finishing; finish; fulfilment. **~ করা** *vt* end; bring to an end; complete; conclude; finish; put an end to; close; terminate; fulfil. **~ হওয়া** *vi* end; close; be finished/ concluded/ completed; come to an end; be fulfilled. **~ সঙ্গীত** closing/ concluding song.

সমাপনী *adj* closing; concluding. **~য়** *adj* to be finished/ concluded/ completed.

সমাপিকা *adj fem* **1**=সমাপক. **2** (gram) finite. **~ ক্রিয়া** *n* finite verb.

সমাপিত, সমাপ্ত *adjj* completed; finished; ended; concluded; closed; accomplished; fulfilled. **~ করা**=সমাপন করা. **~ হওয়া**=সমাপন হওয়া.

সমাপ্তি=সমাপন

সমাবতল *n* (phys) plano-concave.

সমাবরণ *n* occultation.

সমাবর্তন *n* **1** convocation (of a university/ institution). **2** (hist) return home of a (Brahmin) student after completing his studies in the house of a preceptor. **3** returning.

সমাবিষ্ট *adj* **1** occupied; possessed by; filled with. **2** engrossed; absorbed; possessed. **3** assembled; collected.

সমাবৃত *adj* covered all over; concealed; enveloped; wrapt in; surrounded/ beset with; protected/ guarded by; encircled by.

সমাবৃত্ত *adj* returned.

সমাবেশ *n* **1** assemblage; gathering; meeting. **2** absorption; engrossment. **3** co-existence; simultaneous occurrence: নানা গুণের ~.

সমাবেশিত *adj* **1** brought together; placed; fixed; inserted. **2** absorbed; engrossed.

সমামেল *n* confederation.

সমায়াত *adj* come; arrived.

সমাযোগ *n* union; conjunction; connection; contact with.

সমারব্ধ *adj* undertaken; taken in hand; begun.

সমারম্ভ *n* **1** beginning; commencement. **2** enterprise.

সমারূঢ় *adj* **1** mounted/ ridden by; one who has mounted/ ascended. **2** ceremoniously/ solemnly installed (upon): সিংহাসনে ~. **সমারূঢ়া** *fem*.

সমারোহ *n* **1** pomp; grandeur; splendour; magnificence; fanfare; éclat; pageant; pageantry; parade. **2** crowd; grand assemblage: মেঘের ~. **3** ascending; mounting; riding upon. **~ করা** *vi* give a display of pomp/ grandeur; make a splendid arrangement; put on a show; make a splash. **~পূর্ণ** *adj* pompous; grandiose; ostentatious; spectacular; ambitious. **~পূর্বক, সমারোহে** *advv* pompously; ostentatiously; with great éclat; in grand style; in a grandiose manner.

সমালোচক *n* critic; reviewer. **সমালোচিকা** *fem*.

সমালোচন, সমালোচনা *n* **1** criticism; review. **2** censure; animadversion. **সমালোচনা করা** *vt* **1** criticize; review; write a review; pass judgement on; comment on. **2** find fault with; censure; animadvert (on).

সমালোচিত *adj* criticized; reviewed; censured; animadverted.

সমালোচ্য *adj* to be reviewed/ criticized; under review; open to criticism; censurable.

সমাশ্রয় *adj* support; shelter; place of refuge; asylum; dependence on.

সমাশ্রিত *adj* taking refuge with; leaning on; resting/ dependent on; leaned on; resorted to.

সমাস *n* **1** (gram) composition of words; compound word. **2** combination; condensation. **~ করা** *vi* form a compound. **~ ভাঙা** *vi* resolve a compound into its components. **~বদ্ধ** *adj* compound. **~বহুল** *adj* abounding in compounds. **সমাসার্থ** *n* sense of a compound.

সমাসক্ত *adj* attached (to); addicted (to); intent upon; devoted to; occupied with.

সমাসক্তি *n* sticking/ adhering closely to; attachment; devotion.

সমাসঙ্গ *n* **1**=সমাসক্তি. **2** joining; union; connection.

সমাসন্ন *adj* **1** near; proximate; close to. **2** reached; attained; approached.

সমাসীন *adj* seated/ installed; sitting.

সমাসোক্তি *n* (rhet) concise speech (a figure of speech by which the proceedings of any object spoken of are indicated by describing the similar action or attributes of another object).

সমাহত *adj* struck down; wounded; killed.

সমাহরণ *n* **1** collection; combination; accumulation; combination; gathering. **2** concentration. **~ করা** *vt* bring together; collect; assemble; combine; gather.

সমাহর্তা *n* collector. **সমাহর্ত্রী** *fem*.

সমাহার *n* **1** collection; assemblage; aggregation; combination; summing up; sum; totality; multitude. **2** abbreviation. **3** (gram) compounding of words; compound. **~ করা**=সমাহরণ করা.

সমাহিত *adj* **1** buried; interred. **2** put/ placed in or upon; fixed; placed; deposited. **3** composed; collected; concentrated (as the thoughts upon); one who has collected his thoughts or is fixed in abstract meditation; lost in meditation; quite devoted to; intent upon. **4** steadfast; firm; devout. **~ করা** *vi* bury; inter; lay in the grave. **~চিত্ত** *adj* having the mind absorbed in sth; collected; composed.

সমাহৃত *adj* brought together; collected; fetched; gathered; assembled; concentrated.

সমাহৃতি *n* collecting; assembling.

সমাহ্বয় *n* **1** challenge; conflict. **2** setting animals to fight for sport; betting.

সমিতি *n* association; society; council; club; committee. **বণিক-~** *n* chamber of commerce.

সমিদ্ধ *adj* set alight/ on fire; lighted; kindled; ignited; inflamed; excited.

সমিধ *n* firewood, fuel, log of wood, faggot, grass, etc, used as fuel; oblation to fuel; firewood for kindling a sacrificial fire.

সমিন্ধন *n* **1** igniting; kindling. **2** fuel; firewood.

সমীকরণ *n* **1** act of making even; levelling; putting on a level with; equalization; equalizing. **2** (alg) equation. **3** (arith) reduction of fractions to a common denominator. **4** assimilation. ~ **করা** *vt* make even; level; put on a level with; equalize; (alg) equate; (arith) reduce (fractions) to a common denominator. **সমকালীন/যুগপৎ** ~ *n* simultaneous equation. **সমীকরণের মান** *n* (alg) root.

সমীকৃত *adj* **1** made even; levelled; put on a level with. **2** (alg) equated. ~ **কাল** *n* (arith) equated time.

সমীক্ষ, সমীক্ষ্য *n* complete investigation. ~**ণ** *n* looking at/ about thoroughly; search; close investigation; scrutiny; research; deliberation. ~**ণ করা** *vt* investigate; look at/ inspect thoroughly; examine; inquire into; consider well; scrutinize. **সমীক্ষা** *n* **1** thorough/ close inspection; deep insight; understanding; intellect; investigation; search; inquiry. **2** essential nature/ truth/ principle. **সমীক্ষ্যকারিতা** prudence; circumspection; discretion; caution; foreside. **সমীক্ষ্যকারী** *adj* prudent; judicious; discreet; cautious; circumspect. **সমীক্ষ্যকারিণী** *fem.*

সমীক্ষিত *adj* considered; investigated; thoroughly viewed/ observed; searched; scrutinized; researched; scanned; deliberated.

সমীচীন *adj* proper; correct; appropriate; just; right; reasonable; prudent; wise.

সমীপ *adj* proximate; close by; at hand; contiguous; adjacent; approaching; imminent. ❑*n* nearness; proximity; vicinity; presence; imminence. ~**বর্তী**, ~**স্থ** *adj* near; close by; approaching. **সমীপে** *adj* near; close to; before; in the presence of; to; towards.

সমীভবন *n* equation; equalization. **সমীভূত** *adj* equalized.

সমীর, ~**ণ** *nn* wind; air; breeze.

সমীরিত *adj* **1** stirred; tossed; moved; thrown. **2** sent forth; uttered.

সমীহ *n* show of respect; deference; regard; hesitation caused by awe. ~ **করা** *vt* treat with deference; look up to; defer to. ~ **না করা** not to pay respect to; ignore; disregard; disdain; scorn. **সমীহা** *n* wish; desire.

সমুখ *n*, *adj* (colloq)=সম্মুখ

সমুচয়=সমুচ্চয়

সমুচিত *adj* well suited; fit; right; proper; adequate; condign: ~ শাস্তি.

সমুচ্চ *adj* **1** lofty; high. **2** elevated; exalted: ~ মর্যাদা. **3** very loud; vociferous: ~ শব্দ.

সমুচ্চয় *n* **1** aggregation; accumulation; collection; assemblage; multitude; aggregate; totality. **2** (gram) conjunction of words/ sentences; conjunctive sense. **3** (rhet) a figure of speech (the joining together of two or more independent things associated in idea with some common action).

সমুচ্চার(ণ) *n* utterance; pronunciation.

সমুচ্ছল, সমুচ্ছলিত *adjj* jerked up; waved (above); overflowing; brimful; brimming; rippling.

সমুচ্ছিন্ন *adj* torn up; uprooted; eradicated; utterly destroyed.

সমুচ্ছেদ(ন) *n* utter destruction; extermination; annihilation; complete eradication/ extirpation; ejection.

সমুচ্ছায় *n* rising; increase; growth; height; high degree; elevation; erection.

সমুচ্ছ্রিত *adj* well raised; elevated; surging; high; exalted; powerful.

সমুচ্ছ্রিতি *n* augmentation; increase; growth.

সমুচ্ছ্বসিত *adj* breathed/ sighed deeply; breathing deeply; swollen; welled up; overflowed; impassioned; swelled.

সমুচ্ছ্বাস *n* heavy expiration; sighing; emotional/ passionate outburst; strong emotion/ passion; bursting forth; great delight.

সমুজ্জ্বল *adj* shining; radiant; splendid; brilliant.

সমুৎকর্ণ *adj* eager to hear; all ears.

সমুৎকীর্ণ *adj* **1** completely perforated/ pierced. **2** deeply engraved/ inlaid.

সমুৎক্রম *n* going upwards; rise; ascent.

সমুৎক্রোশ *n* crying out loud; clamour.

সমুত্থ *adj* risen; rising up; appearing; sprung/ produced/ derived from. **সমুত্থান** *n* **1** rising; getting up; swelling; augmentation; increase; flourishing. **2** origin. **3** (Christ) resurrection.

সমুত্থিত *adj* risen; raised (as dust); towering above (as a peak); surging (as waves); gathered (as clouds); sprung from; (Christ) risen from the dead. **সমুত্থিতা** *fem.* ~ **হওয়া** *vi* rise/ get up; tower up; gather (as clouds); come forth; spring from; appear; become visible; rise from the dead.

সমুৎপত্তি *n* origin; birth; rise.

সমুৎপন্ন *adj* arisen; produced; begotten (by); occurred; happened; taking place; sprung up.

সমুৎপাটন *n* tearing out/ away; severing; detaching; uprooting; pulling up; eradication.

সমুৎপাটিত *adj* uprooted; eradicated; torn out/ away; utterly destroyed; extirpated; ejected.

সমুৎফুল্ল *adj* **1** highly delighted; exultant; elated; ecstatic; overjoyed. **2** blooming; fully developed.

সমুৎসাদন=সমুৎপাটন

সমুৎসাদিত=সমুৎপাটিত

সমুৎসুক *adj* very eager/ curious; anxious; anxiously desirous; longing for.

সমুৎসৃষ্ট *adj* altogether shed forth; given away; wholly given up/ abandoned.

সমুদয় *n* **1** collection; combination; assemblage; multitude; aggregate; aggregation; totality; whole. **2** success; prosperity; rising. **3** group. ❑*adj* whole; all; entire; total.

সমুদায় *n*=সমুদয় (1). ❑*adj*=সমুদয়.

সমুদিত *adj* gone up; risen; elevated.

সমুদীরণ *n* uttering; pronouncing; reciting.

সমুদীরিত *adj* uttered; pronounced; recited.

সমুদ্গত *adj* risen up; come forth; appeared; sprouted.

সমুদ্গম *n* going up; rising; ascending; sprouting.

সমুদ্গীত *adj* sung out loud; chanted loudly.

সমুদ্গীর্ণ=সমুদীরিত

সমুদ্দিষ্ট *adj* designated as; named; called; referred to.

সমুদ্দুর *n* (colloq)=সমুদ্র

সমুদ্দেশ *n* complete description; reference. **সমুদ্দেশে** *adv* to; towards; with regard to.

সমুদ্ধত *adj* **1** uplifted; elevated; towering; heaving; violent; swelling. **2** arrogant; puffed up with pride; impudent.

সমুদ্ধরণ *n* **1** extricating; uprooting; lifting; eradication; extirpation; delivery; rescue. removal. **2** quotation.

সমুদ্ধর্তা *adj* one who lift up/ raises/ extricated from; extirpator; deliverer; rescuer.

সমুদ্ধার *n* **1** extraction from; extrication from any danger; rescue; delivery; removal. **2** quotation.

সমুদ্ধৃত *adj* drawn up; lifted; taken from; quoted.

সমুদ্ধৃতি=সমুদ্ধরণ

সমুদ্ভব *n* production; origin; birth.

সমুদ্ভাবনা *n* invention; creation; coinage.

সমুদ্ভাবিত *adj* invented; created; coined.

সমুদ্ভাসন *n* lighting up; illuminating; brightening.

সমুদ্ভাসিত *adj* lighted up; brightened; illuminated; flooded with light.

সমুদ্ভূত *adj* sprung up; born; originated; risen; produced; derived/ evolved from.

সমুদ্যত *adj* **1** lifted up; raised. **2** ready/ eager for action; prepared to; about to; on the point of.

সমুদ্যম *n* great effort/ exertion; setting about; readiness to/ for.

সমুদ্যমী *adj* exerting one's self; strenuous; zealous; eager.

সমুদ্যোগ *n* thorough preparation; setting about.

সমুদ্র[১] *n* sea; ocean. ❑*adj* marine. **~-উদ্ভিদ** *n* sea-weed. **~কফ**=~ফেন. **~কল্লোল** *n* ocean wave. **~কান্তা** *n* river. **~গ** *n* ocean-going; sea-going; seafaring; flowing towards the sea. ❑*n* **1** seafarer; seaman. **2** river. **~গমন** *n* going/ voyaging by sea; sea-roving. **~গর্ভ** *n* sea-bottom; womb of the sea. **~গামী**=~গ. **~চর** *adj* (boil) pelagic. **~চোর**, **~চৌর** *nn* pirate. **~চৌর্য** *n* piracy. **~জাত** *adj* sea-born. **~তট** *n* sea-coast. **~তীর** *n* sea-shore. **~তীরবর্তী** *adj* coastal. **~নেমি** *adj* surrounded by the ocean (as the earth). **~পথ** *n* sea-route; sea-way. **~পথে** *adv* by sea. **~পৃষ্ঠ** *n* sea-level; surface of the sea. **~ফেন** *n* sea-foam; bone of the cuttle fish. **~বলয়া**, **~বলয়াঙ্কিতা**, **~মেখলা** *adjj* sea-girdled; sea-girt. **~বসনা** *adj* sea-clothed; sea-girt. **~বহ্নি** *n* submarine fire. **~বায়ু** *n* sea-breeze; sea-air; sea-wind. **~বাহিত** *adj* sea-borne. **~বেলা** *n* sea-beach; flood-tide. **~মন্থন** *n* (myth) churning of the ocean by gods and demons. **~যাত্রা** *n* sea-voyage. **~যাত্রা করা** *vi* make/ go on a sea-voyage. **~যান** *n* sea-going vessel; ship. **~যুদ্ধ** *n* naval battle. **~সঙ্গম** *n* confluence of a river with the ocean. **~সৈকত** *n* sea-beach. **~স্নান** *n* sea-bathing; ablution in the sea. **~স্রোত** *n* ocean-current. **সমুদ্রাম্বরা**= ~বসনা. **সমুদ্রে ঝাঁপ দেওয়া** (fig) brave/ face a great danger. **সমুদ্রে পাদ্য অর্ঘ্য**, **সমুদ্রে বিন্দুপাত** (fig) a drop in the ocean. **সমুদ্রের ঢেউ** *n* ocean-waves; billow. **অকূল সমুদ্রে পড়া** (fig) **1** be all/ completely at sea; be at a loss. **2** be in great danger. **সফেন ~** *n* foamy sea.

সমুদ্র[২] *adj* stamped; sealed; marked; printed.

সমুন্নত *adj* **1** high; lofty; elevated. **2** noble; sublime; proud; exalted; dignified.

সমুন্নতি *n* **1** rising; elevation; increase; growth; swelling; prosperity. **2** eminence; high position; exaltation.

সমুন্নয়(ন) *n* raising; elevating; developing; lifting.

সমুপগম *n* going near; approach.

সমুপচিত *adj* collected; heaped; accumulated; abundant.

সমুপস্থিত *adj* appeared; arrived; come close to; approaching; imminent.

সমুপেত *adj* come; arrived.

সমুল্লাসিত *adj* gleaming; brilliant; shining; delighted.

সমুল্লেখ(ন) *n* writing down; mention.

সমূল *adj* having roots; together with the root; entire. **~ক** *adj* having a cause; having a foundation/ basis; genuine: ~ক আশঙ্কা. **সমূলে** *adv* root and branch; entirely; thoroughly; completely: সমূলে নির্মূল করা.

সমূহ *n* (also used as a *pl suff*) collection; assemblage; multitude; aggregate; heap; number; totality; sum: বৃক্ষ~. ❑*adj* **1** many; much; numerous; great: ~ ক্ষতি. **2** tremendous; terrible: ~ বিপদ.

সমৃদ্ধ *adj* very successful/ prosperous/ flourishing; affluent; wealthy; enriched; rich; full-grown; abundant; plenteous. **সমৃদ্ধা** *fem.* **~ করা** *vt* enrich.

সমৃদ্ধি *n* great prosperity/ success; growth; increase; thriving; fortune; perfection; excellence; plenty; abundant. **~শালী, ~সম্পন্ন**=সমৃদ্ধ. ~**শালিনী, ~সম্পন্না** *fem.*
সমেত *adj* together with; with; possessed of; including; inclusive of.
সমোচ্ছ্বাস-রেখা *n* co-tidal lines.
সমোত্তল *adj* (phys) plano-convex.
সমোন্নতি-রেখা *n* contour (line).
সমোষ্ণ-রেখা *n* (geog) isotherm.
সম্পতিত *adj* fallen; flown/ rushed/ run together.
সম্পত্তি *n* property; assets; possessions; real estate. **~শালী**=সম্পৎশালী. **চলিত ~** *n* liquid assets.
সম্পদ, সম্পৎ *n* **1** good fortune; riches; wealth; prosperity; possessions; treasure; property; belongings; real estate. **2** blessing; glory; pride: তিনি আমাদের দেশের ~. **3** proud/ glorious acquisition; benefit; attainment; advantage: সাহস তার বড়ো ~. **4** excellence; riches: ভাব~. **~শালী** *adj* wealthy; affluent; rich; substantial; prosperous; moneyed; well-to-do. **~শালিনী** *fem.*
সম্পন্ন *adj* **1**=সম্পদশালী. **2** accomplished; completed; effected; performed. **3** excellent; perfect. **4** (used as a *suff*) endowed/ furnished with; possessed of; become; turned into: রূপগুণ~. **সম্পন্না** *fem.*
সম্পর্ক *n* relation; association; contact; touch; connection; union; intercourse; concern; company; kinship. **~ রাখা** *vi* maintain relation; have relations with; keep connection; associate with; keep company with; observe the formalities of kinship. **~ না রাখা** break of relations; have no dealings. **~ স্থাপন করা** *vi* get in contact (with); make contact (with); contact; enter into an alliance. **~শূন্য, ~হীন** *adjj* unrelated; irrelevant; unconnected; having no concern (with); having no kinship with.
সম্পর্কিত, সম্পর্কীয় *adjj* related; connected/ concerned with; having kinship (with); relating to; having affinity (with). **সম্পর্কিতা, সম্পর্কীয়া** *fem.*
সম্পাত *n* **1** fall; drop; swift descent: অশনি~. **2** taking place; happening; occurrence; appearance: বিপদ-~. **3** falling upon; incidence: আলোক~. **4** collision; concussion. **5** curse; malediction. **6** (astron) procession of the equinox. **~বিন্দু** *n* point of incidence.
সম্পাদক *adj* effecting; performing; accomplishing; executive. ❑*n* **1** performer. **2** editor (of a newspaper). **3** secretary (of an association). **4** executive. **সম্পাদিকা** *fem.* **~তা** *n* editorship.
সম্পাদকীয় *adj* editorial. **~ স্তম্ভ** *n* editorial column.
সম্পাদন *n* performance; accomplishment; execution; carrying out; effecting; making. **~ করা** *vt* perform; accomplish; carry out; effect; execute. **সম্পাদনা** *n* editing. **সম্পাদনা করা** *vt* edit.
সম্পাদনীয় *adj*=সম্পাদ্য
সম্পাদিত *adj* **1** performed; carried out; executed; accomplished; fulfilled. **2** edited.
সম্পাদ্য *adj* to be performed/ carried out/ executed/ accomplished. ❑*n* (geom) problem.
সম্পীড়ন *n* **1** compression; pressing; squeezing. **2** oppression.
সম্পুট(ক) *n* **1** hemispherical bowl. **2** round covered case/ box/ casket (for jewellery). **3** screwed receptacle made of paper or tree-leaves; cornet.
সম্পূরক *n* completing; filling; supplementing; supplementary. **~ কোণ** *n* (geom) supplementary angle; supplement.
সম্পূরণ *n* completion; fulfilment; supplementation. **~ করা** *vt* complement; supplement; fulfil; complete.
সম্পূরণীয় *adj* to be filled/ supplemented/ complemented/ fulfilled.
সম্পূরিত *adj* filled; quite full; filled with; supplemented.
সম্পূর্ণ *adj* **1** completed; accomplished; fulfilled; finished; completely filled/ full; full of; completely endowed/ furnished with. **2** complete; whole; entire; thorough; total. **3** (derog) downright: ~ বদমাইশি. ❑*adv* completely; wholly; entirely; thoroughly; fully; totally; quite. **~ করা** *vt* complete; finish; accomplish; fulfil; fill completely; round off. **~তর** *adj* more filled; very full; fuller. **~তা** *n* completion; completeness; fullness; complete fullness; thoroughness; perfection; wholeness; entirety; totality; plenitude. **~ভাবে, ~রূপে** *advv*=~.
সম্পূর্তি *n* completion; fulfilment.
সম্পৃক্ত *adj* **1** related/ connected with; joined/ united with; having concern with; concerned with. **2** mixed together; combined; blended; inlaid; interspersed. **3** saturated. **~তা** *n* relation; connection; concern; union; joining; saturated; inlaying.
সম্পৃক্তি=সম্পৃক্ততা. **অতি~** *n* over-saturation.
সম্পোষ্য *adj* to be well-nourished/ supported.
সম্প্রচার *n* wide circulation; broadcast; broadcasting. **~ কেন্দ্র** *n* broadcasting station.
সম্প্রচারিত *adj* broadcast; widely circulated.
সম্প্রতি *adv* now; now-a-days; recently; at this moment; at present; in these days; in present times; of late; just.
সম্প্রতিপত্তি *n* **1** correct conception; right understanding. **2** agreement; admission;

assent; concurrence; acknowledgement; affirmation.

সম্প্রতিপন্ন *adj* recognized; acknowledged; agreed upon; assented to.

সম্প্রতীতি *n* 1 certain knowledge. 2 renown; fame.

সম্প্রদত্ত *adj* 1 given over; transmitted; handed down; bestowed; conferred. 2 given in marriage. **সম্প্রদত্তা** *fem.*

সম্প্রদাতা *adj, n* 1 one who gives/ delivers over/ bestows/ confers; bestower; presenter. 2 one who gives away the bride ceremonially to the charge of the bridegroom.

সম্প্রদান *n* 1 act of giving/ handing over; presenting; bestowing (also in marriage; granting; allowing; bestowal. 2 gift; present; donation. 3 (gram) case (also ~কারক). ~ **করা** *vt* give/ hand over; present; bestow; grant; allow; deliver wholly over; give completely up; impart; give in marriage.

সম্প্রদায় *n* 1 (religious) sect; community. 2 society; brotherhood; school: লেখক ~. 3 race: মনুষ্য ~. 4 band; company; group: গুণ্ডা ~. ~**ভুক্ত** *adj* belonging to a particular sect/ community/ society/ brotherhood/ race/ band.

সম্প্রদায়ী *adj* communalist.

সম্প্রদেয় *adj* to be given/ bestowed/ handed over. ~ **পত্র** *n* negotiable instrument.

সম্প্রধারণ *n* determination; deliberation; deciding on the propriety or impropriety of anything.

সম্প্রয়োগ *n* 1 application; employment. 2 investment.

সম্প্রসারণ *n* expansion; extension; development.

সম্প্রসারিত *adj* expanded; extended; developed. ~ **করা** *vt* expand; extend; develop.

সম্প্রাপ্ত *adj* well reached/ attained; obtained; gained.

সম্প্রাপ্তি *n* attainment; acquisition; gain.

সম্প্রীত *adj* completely satisfied/ pleased; delighted.

সম্প্রীতি *n* 1 complete satisfaction; joy; delight (in); pleasure. 2 good will; friendship with; friendly terms; amity; love; attachment; affection.

সম্বৎ, সম্বৎসর=সংবৎ, সংবৎসর respectively.

সম্বদ্ধ *adj* 1 bound/ tied together; joined; connected; related; united; affiliated; amalgamated; having kinship with. 2 shut; closed. 3 coherent.

সম্বদ্ধীকরণ *n* affiliation; amalgamation.

সম্বন্ধ *n* 1 binding/ joining together; close connection/ union/ association; conjunce; inherence; concern; connection with; relation to; affinity. 2 personal connection (by marriage); kinship; fellowship; relationship; intercourse; association; friendship; intimacy (with). 3 marriage proposal/ negotiation. ~ **করা** *vt* negotiate a marriage; make negotiations for a marriage. ~ **থাকা** *vi* have connection/ relation/ concern/ relationship/ kinship/ intercourse (with); belong to; be connected with/ related to. ~ **রাখা** *vi* 1 maintain relations with; stay in contact with; keep up with. 2 observe formalities of kinship/ relationship. ~**পদ** *n* (gram) a word in the possessive case; genitive. ~**সূচক** *adj* expressing relation; relational; related. **সম্বন্ধে** *adj* (used as a *prep*) concerning; about; regarding; in relations to; as for.

সম্বন্ধী *adj* related to; connected with; relating/ belonging to; concerning. ❑*n* wife's (elder) brother/ cousin-brother; brother-in-law. ~**করণ** *n* affiliation. ~**য়** *adj*=~.

সম্বর *n* kind of deer; chamois.

সম্বরণ=সংবরণ

সম্বরা[1]=সংবরা

সম্বরা[2] *n* spices singed in oil or butter and mixed with any cooked dish by re-boiling. ~ **দেওয়া** *vt* re-boil (a cooked dish) by mixing with spices singed in oil or butter.

সম্বর্ধনা=সংবর্ধনা

সম্বর্ধিত=সংবর্ধিত

সম্বল *n* 1 provender/ provisions for a journey; stock for travelling; viaticum. 2 resources; provision; fund; capital (money); (total) savings. 3 support; prop; (last) resort. ~ **করা** *vi* resort to; have recourse to; depend/ bank on. ~**শূন্য**, ~**হীন** *adjj* resourceless; destitute; beggared; indigent; penniless; insolvent.

সম্বলিত=সংবলিত

সম্বাদী=সংবাদী

সম্বাধ *n* 1 hindrance; impediment. 2 pressure; affliction; distress; annoy. 3 crowd; throng.

সম্বিত, সম্বিৎ=সংবিৎ

সম্বুদ্ধ *adj* wide awake; wise; prudent; clever; perfectly enlightened. ❑*n* name of a Buddha; deified sage.

সম্বুদ্ধি *n* 1 perfect knowledge/ perception. 2 calling out to (a person in the distance); making one's call heard.

সম্বোধ *n* perfect knowledge/ understanding; perception. ~**ন** *n* 1 calling to; address; form of address. 2 awaking; arousing. 3 (gram) vocative case or its termination. ~**ন করা** *vt* call to; address; accost. ~**পদ** *n* (gram)=~ (3). **সম্বোধা** *vt* (poet)=~ন করা.

সম্বোধি *n* perfect knowledge/ enlightenment. ~**ত** *adj* 1 fully warned; duly apprised. 2 called; addressed.

সম্ভব *adj* 1 possible; probable; likely. 2 arisen/ produced/ originated from; born of; made of;

grown in: অগ্নি~. ❑*n* **1** birth; production; origin; source; being produced from. **2** cause; reason; occasion. **সম্ভবা** *adj fem.* **~ত** *adv* probably; possibly; likely; perhaps; may be. **~পর** *adj*=~. **সম্ভবাতীত** *adj* beyond all possibilities; improbable; unlikely. **সম্ভাব্য** *adj* probable. **সম্ভাব্যতা** *n* possibility; feasibility.

সম্ভাবন *n* **1** worship; honour; respect; esteem; regard. **2** imagination; supposition; assumption. **সম্ভাবনা** *n* **1** probability; likelihood. **2** (rhet) a figure of speech.

সম্ভাবনীয় *adj* to be assumed/ supposed; possible; probable; potential. **~তা** *n* possibility; probability; potentiality.

সম্ভাবিত *adj* **1** possible; probable; likely; fit for; suited; adequate. **2** thought highly of; esteemed; honoured; respected.

সম্ভাব্য[১]=সম্ভব্য (⇒ সম্ভব). **2** contingent. **~ অনুদান** *n* contingency grant. **~ আদেয়ক/ মূল্যপত্র** *n* contingent bill. **~তা** *n* possibility; probability; likelihood; contingency. **~ প্রভার/ব্যয়** *n* contingency charges.

সম্ভার *n* **1** thing; article; load of things. **2** provision; necessaries; materials; requisite; collection of things required for any purpose; heap. **3** preparation. **4** fullness; completeness.

সম্ভাষ=সম্ভাষণ. **সম্ভাষা** *vi, vt*=সম্ভাষণ করা

সম্ভাষণ *n* discourse; talk; conversation with; greeting; addressing; hail. **~ করা** *vt, vi* converse with; greet; address; hail; accost; speak to; salute. **~নিপুণ** *adj* skilled in conversation.

সম্ভাষিত *adj* spoken/ conversed with; greeted; addressed; accosted; hailed; saluted. ❑*n* talk; conversation.

সম্ভাষী *adj* talking; conversing; addressing.

সম্ভূত *adj* **1** born/ produced/ arisen/ proceeding from; made/ composed of; sprung/ evolved from; originated. **2** caused (by): অবিবেচনা~. **সম্ভূতা** *fem.*

সম্ভূতি *n* **1** origin; production; birth. **2** great/ super-human power; manifestation of might.

সম্ভৃত *adj* **1** stored; stocked; laden; filled; collected; accumulated; assembled; concentrated. **2** provided; supported; well maintained; nourished. **3** carried; borne (in the womb).

সম্ভৃতি *n* **1** prevision; preparation. **2** complete maintenance; support; nourishment. **3** fullness; plenitude.

সম্ভেদ *n* **1** breaking; piercing; cleavage; disjunction; separation; division.

সম্ভোগ *n* **1** complete enjoyment; pleasure; delight (in). **2** carnal/ sensual enjoyment; sexual union with. **~ করা** *vt* enjoy; (esp carnally); have sexual intercourse with.

সম্ভ্রম *n* **1** awe; deference; respect. **2** honour; dignity; nobility; modesty; prestige. **~ উদ্রেক করা** *vi* inspire respect/ awe. **~ করা** *vt* treat with deference; defer to; respect; revere. **~শালী** *adj* honourable; respectable; noble; dignified; venerable; decent; august. **~শালিনী** *fem* **~হানি করা** *vi* dishonour; outrage modesty of.

সম্ভ্রান্ত *adj* respectable; honoured; noble; of noble birth; aristocratic; high-born. **~ ব্যক্তি** *n* respectable/ high-born/ honoured person; aristocrat. **~তন্ত্র** *n* government by aristocrats; aristocracy. **~ বংশীয়** *adj* born in a noble family; of a noble/ aristocratic family; high-born. **~বংশীয়া** *fem.* **~ সমাজ, ~ সম্প্রদায়** *nn* aristocracy; nobility.

সম্মত *adj* **1** consenting; willing; ready; acquiescent. **2** agreed/ consented/ assented to; approved/ sanctioned/ permitted by; conforming to: বিধি~. **3** accepted; admitted: সর্ববাদি~. **~ হওয়া** *vi* agree; assent to; approve; give consent; acquiesce; accept. **সম্মতা** *fem.*

সম্মতি *n* consent; assent; acquiescence; approval; concurrence; willingness; approbation; permission; sanction. **~ দেওয়া** *vi* consent; assent; give consent; permit; approve; concur. **~ পাওয়া** *vi* obtain/ get consent/ permission (of); get approved. **~ দান, ~ প্রদান** *nn* consent; assent; approval.

সম্মদ *n* exhilaration; happiness; delight.

সম্মর্দ *n* **1** pressure; friction. **2** meeting; encounter; battle; war. **~ন** *n* rubbing; friction.

সমন্দি = সম্বন্ধী

সম্মাদ *n* great exhilaration; intoxication; frenzy.

সম্মান *n* **1** honour; respect; homage; reverence; deference; deferential treatment; respectful and cordial reception. **2** prestige; dignity; credit. **~ করা/দেওয়া/দেখানো** *vt,vi* respect; show respect; pay respects; honour; revere; look up to; defer to; pay homage to; receive cordially and with respect; reverence; show deference to; treat with deference. **~ নষ্ট করা** *vi* dishonour; disgrace; discredit; bring disgrace upon; take away one's good name. **~ পাওয়া** *vi* be honoured. **~ হারানো** *vt* lose honour/ prestige/ credit; be disgraced; fall into disrepute; disgrace oneself; demean oneself; get a bad name; lose one's reputation; degrade oneself. **~জনক** *n* honourable; creditable. **~ন(1)** *n* act of honouring; homage; worshipping; respectful felicitation. **~পূর্বক, ~পুরঃসর** *adv* respectfully. **~ভাজন** *adj* honourable; respectable; respected. **~রক্ষা** *n* preservation of honour. **~লাঘব** *n* dishonour; indignity; humiliation; disrepute. **~ লাঘব করা** *vi* dishonour; show disrespect; disparage; belittle; deprecate; defame; malign. **~লাভ** *n* winning honour/ credit; gaining reputation/ respectability. ~হানি *n* loss of honour/ prestige/ credit; dishonour; indignity; defamation; disrepute; discredit. **সম্মানার্হ, সম্মানাস্পদ**=~ভাজন.

সম্মানিত *adj* honoured; treated with reverence/ respect; honourable; venerable; respected; respectable.

সম্মানী *adj* having a sense of honour; respectable. ❑*n* honorarium. ~য় *adj* to be honoured/ respected; honoured; respected.

সম্মার্জক *adj* sweeping; cleansing; purifying. ❑*n* sweeper.

সম্মার্জন *n* act of sweeping/ cleansing thoroughly; cleansing; scouring; purifying; brushing; scrubbing.

সম্মার্জনী *n* broom; besom; scouring-brush; scrubbing-brush; mop; swab.

সম্মার্জিত *adj* well cleansed/ swept; scoured; brushed.

সম্মিত *adj* **1** measured (out); meted. **2** measuring so much; just so much. **3** of the same measure/ extent; equal; like; same.

সম্মিলন *n* **1** mingling/ meeting together; mixture; union; amalgamation; assemblage; junction. **2** gathering; conference; meeting; rally.

সম্মিলনী *n* association; club; society.

সম্মিলিত *adj* assembled; collected; united; joined; amalgamated; rallied. ~ভাবে *adv* unitedly; in a body.

সম্মিশ্র *adj* commingled; mixed together; joined; connected. ~ণ *n* commingling; mixing together; mixture.

সম্মিশ্রিত *adj* mixed together; mingled; intermixed (with).

সম্মুখ *adj* facing; fronting; confronting; being face to face/ in front of/ opposite to; present; before the eyes; lying in the front; frontal; anterior; facing one another; opposite. ❑*n* front; forepart. ~ কোণ *n* (geom) subtended angle. ~বর্তী *adj* lying in front; facing; confronting; opposite; anterior; approaching. ~বর্তিনী *fem*. ~ যুদ্ধ, ~ সংগ্রাম, ~ সমর *nn* face-to-face fight; frontal attack; open fight. ~স্থ=~বর্তী. **সম্মুখে** *adv* before; in front of; in presence of; opposite to; face to face.

সম্মুখীন *adj*=সম্মুখবর্তী (⇒ সম্মুখ). ~ হওয়া *vt* face; confront; encounter; come face to face with; approach.

সম্মূঢ় *adj* completely stupefied; astounded; perplexed; bewildered; unconscious; senseless.

সম্মূর্ছন *n* **1** stupefaction; insensibility; fainting away. **2** increase; expansion; spreading.

সম্মূর্ছিত *adj* stupefied; senseless; unconscious.

সম্মৃষ্ট=সম্মার্জিত

সম্মেলক *adj* one who gathers/ collects/ organizes; organizing.

সম্মেলক=সম্মিলন

সম্মোহ *n* stupefaction; bewilderment; confusion; insensibility; unconsciousness; ignorance; folly; illusion of mind. ~ক *adj* stupefying; infatuating; bewitching; fascinating; hypnotizing. ~ন *n* fascination; illusion; deluding; infatuation; leading astray; hypnosis; hypnotism. ❑*adj* deluding; infatuating; hypnotizing; hypnotic; leading astray. **সম্মোহিনী** *adj fem.*

সম্মোহিত *adj* stupefied; bewildered; infatuated; fascinated; enraptured; charmed; hypnotized; enchanted. **সম্মোহিতা** *fem.* ~ করা *vt* stupefy; bewilder; infatuate; fascinate; enrapture; charm; hypnotize; enchant.

সম্যক *adj* **1** entire; whole; thorough; complete; all. **2** correct; accurate; proper; true; right. **3** uniform; same; identical. **4** pleasant; agreeable. **5** in one line; straight. ❑*adv* completely; wholly; thoroughly; by all means; correctly; truly; properly; fully; in the right way/ manner; well; duly. ~তা, ~ত্ব *nn* completeness; perfection; rightness; perfect manner. ~পাঠ *n* right pronunciation; correct reading. ~ পালন *n* right/ due protection or maintenance. ~ প্রণিধান *n* true/ profound meditation or attention. ~ প্রয়োগ *n* right use/ employment; due practice. ~ প্রবৃত্তি *n* right action/ function (of the senses). ~ সঙ্কল্প *n* right resolve. ~ সম্বুদ্ধি, ~ সম্বোধ *nn* complete enlightenment. ~ স্মৃতি *n* right recollection.

সম্যগ *adj* (in compounds)=সম্যক. ~-আজীব *n* right living. ~-উক্ত *adj* properly/ accurately said. ~ জ্ঞান *n* right/ complete/ full knowledge. ~ দর্শন *n* right perception/ insight. ~দর্শী *adj* possessed of true insight. ~ দৃষ্টি *n*=~ দর্শন. ❑*adj*=~দর্শী. ~ বাক *n* right speech. ~ বোধ *n* right understanding. ~ বৃত্তি *n* right discharge of duties.

সম্রাজ্ঞী *n fem* empress; queen.

সম্রাট *n* emperor; paramount ruler/ sovereign.

সযত্ন *adj* careful; meticulous; making efforts; painstaking; diligent; endeavouring to; cordial. **সযত্নে** *adv* carefully; meticulously; with care; diligently; painstakingly; cordially.

সয়তান=শয়তান

সয়লাব [P]*n* flood; deluge; inundation; torrent.

সয়া[১] [E]*n* soy; soya. ~বিন=soy(a) bean.

সয়া[২] *n* husband of a lady friend/ confidant.

সর *n* thin layer on milk or any other similar substance; film. ~পুরিয়া *n* kind of sweetmeat made of fried and stuffed milk-film. ~ভাজা *n* sweetmeat made of fried milk-film.

সরকার *n* **1** lord; master. **2** owner. **3** king's court; government; ruler; regime. **4** estate; property. **5** superintendent; purchasing/ collecting clerk. **6** team leader of folk song *kabi*.

সরকারি, সরকারী *adj* belonging to the state/ government; governmental; public. ~ **অভিশংসক** *n* public prosecutor. ~ **আদেশ** *n* government order. ~ **উকিল** *n* government pleader. ~ **চাকরি** *n* government service. ~ **নিয়ন্ত্রণাধীন** *adj* government controlled; under government control. ~ **প্রতিবেদক** *n* public reporter. ~ **প্রতিবেদন** *n* government report. ~**বিদ্যালয়** *n* government school. ~ **কৌসুলি** *n* government counsel. ~ **রাস্তা** *n* public road; highway. ~ **সাহায্য** *n* subsidy; grants in aid. ~ **সুযোগসুবিধা** *n* government facilities.

সরগম *n* gamut; descending scale.

সরগরম *adj* **1** zealous; ardent; full of high spirits/ enthusiasm and excitement; active. **2** in a bustle; lively; feverish; packed and noisy; uproarious; excite. ~ **করা** *vt* excite; inflame; stir; work up; animate; enthuse; thrill; electrify; galvanize.

সরজমিন, সরেজমিন [P] *n* scene of occurrence; venue of an affair; confines.

সরঞ্জাম [P] *n* **1** equipment; implements; provisions, furnishings; fittings; outfit; accoutrements; appurtenances; accessories; paraphernalia. **2** preparation; arrangement.

সরট *n* lizard; chameleon.

সরণ *n* **1** going; moving; running. **2** iron rust. ~**শীল** *adj* moving; gliding; sliding.

সরণি, সরণী *n* road; path; way; avenue.

সরতা *n* (dial) kind of scissors for cutting betel-nuts.

সরদল, সরদাল [P]*n* lintel.

সরদার [P] *n* chief; commander; leader; headman; chieftain; village magistrate. ~**নি,** ~**নী** *fem.* ~ **দফতরি** *n* binding foreman. ~-**পড়ুয়া** *n* a senior pupil assisting in school discipline and teaching; monitor.

সরদারি [P] *n* headship; leadership; chieftaincy; bossing; sway. ~ **করা** *vi* **1** act as a headman/ chieftain. **2** behave in masterful/ overbearing manner; boss; domineer; lord it over; browbeat; be overbearing.

সরদি, সর্দি [P] *n* cold; catarrh: সরদি ঝরছে/পড়ছে, The nose runs. ~ **ঝাড়া** *vi* blow one's nose. ~ **লাগা/ হওয়া** *vi* catch (a) cold; have a cold. ~**গরমি** *n* sunstroke; heatstroke.

সরদেওয়াল, সরদেয়াল *n* wall behind a house.

সরন্ধ্রতা *n* porosity.

সরপুঁটি *n* kind of fresh-water fish.

সরপুরিয়া ⇒ সর

সরপেচ [P] *n* an ornament worn in the turban.

সরপোশ, সরপোষ [P] *n* cover; lid.

সরফরাজ [P] *adj* **1** exalted; august. **2** delighted. ❑*n* (iron) great/ an important man; self-important person; saucy fellow; busybody; meddler; Nosey Parker.

সরফরাজি *n* overbearing manner; officiousness; sauciness; bossing; meddling.

সরবৎ=শরবত

সরবন্দ [P] *n* turban.

সরবরাহ [P] *n* supply; amount supplied; purveying. ~ **করা** *vt* supply; purvey. ~**কার,** ~**কারী** *n* supplier; purveyor.

সরভাজা ⇒ সর

সরম=শরম

সরল *adj* **1** straight. **2** outstretched. **3** simple; easy. **4** right; correct. **5** upright; sincere; honest; candid; artless; guileless; naive. **6** plain; inornate. **7** free from intricacies. ❑*n* **1** a species of pine tree; deodar. **2** (math) simplification. **সরলা** *adj fem.* ~ **করা** *vt* simplify. ~ **অণুবীক্ষণ** *n* simple microscope. ~ **আচরণ** *n* plain dealing. ~ **কোণ** *n* straight angle. ~ **গতি** *n* direct motion. ~**চিত্ত** *adj* simple-hearted; simple-minded. ~**তা** *adj* simplicity; uprightness; honesty; straightness; plainness; inornateness; candour; naiveté; easiness; naturalness; innocence; ease. ~**তাপূর্ণ** *adj* simple; candid; artless; plain; naive; honest; straightforward; natural; unaffected; innocent; ingenuous. ~ **দোলক** *n* simple pendulum. ~ **দোলন** *n* (phy) simple harmonic motion. ~ **প্রকৃতি** *adj* simple-natured; candid; ingenious; unpretentious; sincere; credulous; unsophisticated; innocent; simple-hearted. ~**বর্গীয়** *adj* (bot) coniferous. ~**বুদ্ধি,** ~**মতি,** ~**মনা** *adj* simple-hearted; sincere; ingenuous; straightforward. ~ **রেখা** *n* straight line. ~**রেখাক্রমে** *adv* in a straight line. ~**রৈখিক** *adj* formed of straight lines; rectilinear; rectilineal. ~**রৈখিক ক্ষেত্র** *n* (geom) rectilineal figure. ~**স্বভাব** =~প্রকৃতি. ~**হৃদয়, সরলান্তকরণ** *adjj* =~বুদ্ধি. **সরলাক্ষ** *n* (zoo) simple eye. **সরলান্ত্র** *n* large intestine; rectum.

সরলিত *adj* straightened; straight.

সরলীকরণ *n* simplification; making straight.

সরলীকৃত *adj* simplified.

সরলোন্নত *adj* upright; steep; vertical; perpendicular.

সরষে *n* (colloq)=সরিষা

সরস *adj* **1** juicy; containing sap; pithy. **2** moist; wet. **3** fresh; new. **4** elegant; beautiful; charming; beautiful; gracious. **5** tasty; succulent; savoury. **6** expressive of poetical sentiment; witty; humorous; funny. **7** passionate; impassioned; enamoured. **সরসা** *fem.* ~**তা** *n* freshness; succulence; wit; humour; novelty; juiciness.

সরসর *n* (onom) rustle; rustling.
সরসিজ *n* lotus.
সরসী *n* pool; pond; lake.
সরস্বতী *n* **1** Hindu goddess of eloquence and learning. **2** a title of proficiency in literature. **সরস্বতীর বরপুত্র** favoured son of goddess Saraswati; (fig) man of great learning.
সরহদ্দ [P] *n* boundary; border; frontier; confines; perimeter. **~বন্দী** *n* determination of boundary.
সরহস্য *adj* possessing anything secret/ mystical; mysterious.
সরা[১]=শরা[১]. **ধরাকে ~ জ্ঞান করা** get above oneself; get too big for one's boots.
সরা[২]=শরা[২]
সরা[৩] *vi* **1** move; move away/ aside; stir; withdraw: সে এখান থেকে কিছুতেই সরবে না. **2** issue forth; come out; flow out: মুখে কথা সরে না. **3** come in and go out; flow; pass: জানলা খুলে দাও, বাতাস সরবে. **4** slip away; decamp: সুযোগ পেয়ে চোর সরে পড়েছে. **5** be willing to work: কাজে হাত সরে না. **6** be willing/ inclined: মন ~. **7** move facilely: কলম কিছুতেই সরছে না. **8** use. **~নো** *vt* **1** take aside; remove; withdraw; transfer; recall; dismiss: চাকরি থেকে ~. **2** dislodge; take away/ off. **3** steal; defalcate.
সরাই [P] *n* inn; caravanserai; temporary lodging for travellers. **~খানা**=~.
সরাগ *adj* having colour; reddened; enamoured; impassioned; passionate; flushed with passion.
সরাপ=শরাব
সরাল *n* a species of wild duck.
সরাসর, সরাসরি [P] *adv* **1** wholly; entirely; from beginning to end; from one end to the other. **2** directly; straightway; straight ahead. **3** outright; summarily; in a cursory manner: প্রস্তাবটা তিনি সরাসরি নাকচ করে দিলেন. ❑*adj* direct; straight; outright; summary. **~ নির্ধার** *n* summary assessment. **~ বিচার** *n* summary justice/ trial.
সরিক=শরিক
সরিকানা=শরিকানা
সরিকানি=শরিকানি
সরিৎ *n* river; stream.
সরিয়ত=শরিয়ত
সরিষা *n* mustard; mustard-seed. **~ ক্ষেত** *n* field of mustard. **~ গাছ** *n* mustard. **~-তৈল** *n* mustard-oil. **ভিটায় ~ বোনা** (fig) ruin sb utterly by destroying his homestead.
সরীসৃপ *n* any creeping animal; reptile.
সরু *adj* **1** slender; thin; dainty; delicate; threadlike; wispy; slim; willowy; wiry; withy. **2** not coarse; fine; fine-spun: ~ চাল/ কাপড়. **3** narrow: ~ রাস্তা. **4** pointed: ~ ডগা. **5** subtle; delicate; fine: ~ কাজ. **6** fine; sharp; shrill; sweet; soft: ~ গলা. **7** keen; sharp; acute; fine; hairsplitting: ~ বুদ্ধি. **~ গলা** *n* **1** thin/ longish neck. **2** fine/ sweet/ soft voice.
সরূপ *adj* having the same shape/ form; like; similar; resembling. **সরূপতা** *n* likeness; similarity.
সরেজমিন ⇒ সরজমিন. **সরেজমিনে** *adv* right on the spot. **সরেজমিনে তদন্ত/তহকিফ** *n* investigation on the spot; local investigation.
সরেস *adj* fine; excellent; best; prime.
সরোকার [P] *n* concern; relation; right.
সরোজ *n* lotus.
সরোজিনী *n* a pond abounding in lotus; multitude of lotus.
সরোদ [P] *n* name of a stringed musical instrument; lyre. **সরোদী** *n* lyre-player.
সরোবর *n* lake; large pond.
সরোরুহ *n* lotus.
সরোরোধ *n* bank of a lake.
সরোষ *adj* angry; enraged. **সরোষে** *adv* angrily; wrathfully.
সর্গ *n* **1** primary creation; creation of matter/ the world. **2** begetting; procreation. **3** nature; natural property; disposition; tendency. **4** chapter; book; section; canto. **5** division of physical history; kingdom. **~বন্ধ** *n* poem/ composition divided into sections/ cantos; epic. **উদ্ভিদ~** *n* vegetable/ plant kingdom. **প্রাণি~** *n* animal kingdom. **মণিক~** *n* mineral kingdom.
সর্জ *n* *sal* tree; *Vatica robusta*, resin of *sal* tree. **~রস** *n* incense; resin.
সর্জন *n* **1** creation; creating. **2** abandoning; ceding; giving up. **সর্জনা** *n* originality; creativity.
সর্জি, সর্জিকা, সর্জী *nn* fuller's earth. **~কা ক্ষার** *n* carbonate of soda.
সর্ত=শর্ত
সর্দল=সরদল
সর্দার=সরদার
সর্দি=সরদি
সর্প *n* snake; serpent; serpent-demon. **সর্পী,** সর্পিণী *fem.* **~গতি** *n* (wrestling) a snake's tortuous movement. **~গন্ধা** *n* ichneumon plant. **~দংশন** *n* snakebite. **~দংষ্ট্রিকা, ~দন্ত** *nn* fang of a snake. **~দষ্ট** *adj* bitten by snake. **~ফণা** *n* snake's hood. **~ভুক** *n* snake-eater; peacock. **সর্পাঘাত** *n* snakebite. **সর্পাশন**=~ভুক.
সর্পণ *n* act of creeping/ gliding; stealing away; moving softly; going tortuously; movement; motion.
সর্পি, সর্পিঃ *nn* clarified butter; sacrificial ghee.
সর্পিল *adj* **1** serpentine; winding; zigzag; meandering; tortuous. **2** spiral.
সর্পী *adj* creeping; gliding; moving slowly; crawling; reptile. সর্পিণী *fem.*
সর্ব *adj* all; whole; entire; every; complete; thorough; universal; total; of all sorts;

manifold. ❑*n* **1** name of Shiva. **2** express. **~ংসহ** *adj* all-bearing; all-enduring; bearing everything patiently. **~ংসহা** *fem.* **~ংহর** *adj* carrying/ taking away everything. **~কর্তা** *n* maker/ creator of all; God. **~কর্ম** *n* all kinds of works/ rites/ occupations. **~কর্মী** *adj* doing every work; practising/ understanding every occupation. **~কাম** *n* all kinds of desires. ❑*adj* wishing everything; fulfilling all wishes; possessing everything wished for . **~কামী** *adj*=~কাম. **~কাম্য** *adj* loved/ desired by all. **~কাল** *n* all times. **~কালীন** *adj* belonging to all times/ seasons; perpetual; all-time; of all time; working/ covering whole-time; whole-time. **~কালে** *adv* at all times; always; ever. **~ক্ষণ** *n* all time; all the time; the whole time. ❑*adv* every moment; always; ceaselessly; for ever. **সর্বগ, ~গত, ~গামী** *adjj* all-pervading; omnipresent. ❑*n* spirit; soul. **সর্বগা, ~গত, ~গামিনী** *fem.* **~গতি** *n* refuge of all. **~গন্ধ** *n* all kinds of perfumes. ❑*adj* containing all odours. **~গুণ** *n* every good quality; every excellence; all qualities. **~গুণবিধি, ~গুণাকর, ~গুণাধার** *nn* repository of all virtues/ good qualities. ❑*adjj*=~গুণসম্পন্ন. **~গুণসম্পন্ন, ~গুণান্বিত, ~গুণী, ~গুণোপেত** *adjj* endowed with every excellence; gifted with every good quality; possessing all excellence/ virtues. **~গ্রাস** *n* act of devouring/ grabbing everything; total eclipse. **~গ্রাসী** *adj* swallowing all; all-devouring; all-grabbing; voracious; rapacious. **~গ্রাসিনী** *fem.* **~গ্রাহী** *adj* all embracing; universal. **~জগৎ** *n* the whole world; universe. **~জন** *n* every person. **~জনকল্যাণ**=~জনহিত. **~জনপ্রিয়** *adj* dear to everyone; beloved of all; universally popular. **~জনমনোহর** *adj* pleasing to everyone. **~জনস্বীকৃত** *adj* universally/ unanimously admitted/ accepted. **~জনহিত** *n* universal good/ welfare; public good/ welfare. **~জনহিতকর** *adj* beneficial to/ good for all; universally good. **~জনীন** *adj* salutary to every one; relating/ belonging to everyone; universal; public; common. **~জনীনতা** *n* universality. **~জিৎ** *adj* all-conquering; all-surpassing; excellent. **সর্বজ্ঞ** *adj* all-knowing; omniscient. **~জ্ঞতা, ~জ্ঞত্ব** *nn* omniscience. **~ত, ~তঃ** *adv* from all sides; in every direction; everywhere; entirely; wholly; thoroughly; completely; in everything; by all means; in all ways. **~তন্ত্র** *adj* universally acknowledged; admitted by all schools. **সর্বতোভাবে** *adv* in every way/ respect/ manner; by all means; in all respects. **সর্বতোমুখ** *adj* facing in all directions; turned everywhere. **~ত্যাগ** *n* complete renunciation. **~ত্যাগী** *adj* all-renouncing; all-sacrificing. **~ত্যাগিনী** *fem.* **সর্বত্র** *adv* everywhere; always; in every case; at all times; ever; in all directions. **~ত্রগ, ~গামী** *adjj* all-pervading; omnipresent; capable of reaching/ going everywhere. **~ত্ব** *n* wholeness; totality; completeness. **~থা**=~তোভাবে. **~দমন** *adj* all-subduing; all-timing. **~দর্শন** *adj* all-viewing **~দর্শী** *adj* all-seeing. **~দর্শিনী** *fem.* **~দা** always; at all times; ever. **~দুঃখক্ষয়** *n* destruction of all pain; final emancipation from all existence. **~দুঃখহর** *adj* removing all pain/ afflictions. **~দেশীয়** *adj* coming from/ existing in/ found in every country; international; universal; country-wide. **~দ্রব্য** *n* all things. **~দ্রষ্টা** *adj* all-seeing. **~ধন** *n* all one's property. **~ধর্মসমন্বয়** *n* synthesis/ harmonization of all religions. **সর্বধা** *adj* all-containing. **~নাম** *n* pronoun. **~নাশ** *n* complete loss/ ruin; destruction of everything; great danger/ calamity; utter ruin/ destruction; great harm. **~নাশ করা** *vt* ruin utterly; undo (sb); destroy completely/ totally; cause a great harm/ calamity/ danger. **~নাশ হওয়া** *vi* lose everything; be undone; be ruined/ destroyed utterly; be harmed greatly; be placed in a great danger/ calamity. **~নাশা, ~নেশে** *adj* (colloq)=~নাশী. ❑*n* one who ruins a person by exposing him to shame; blither; shameless person. **~নাশী** *adj* all-destroying; causing complete/ total destruction; ruinous; disastrous; destructive; fatal; catastrophic. ❑*n fem*=~নাশা. **~নাশিনী** *adj fem.* **~নিয়ন্তা** *n* all-subduer; one who controls everything; all in all; the Supreme Ruler; God. **~নিয়ন্ত্রী** *fem.* **~পথীন** *adj* going in every direction. **~প্রকার** *adj* of all kinds/ sorts/ varieties; all-round. **~প্রকারে** *adv* in every manner/ respect/ way. **~প্রথম** *adj* first; foremost. **~প্রধান** *adj* most important/ distinguished; foremost; chief of all; pre-eminent; supreme; chief; principal. **~প্রযত্ন** *n* all efforts. **~প্রযত্নে** *adv* with all one's might; to the best of one's ability. **~প্রাণ দিয়ে** *adv* with all one's soul. **~প্রাপ্তি** *n* attainment of all things. **~প্রিয়** *adj* dear to/ beloved of all; popular with all; universally popular. **~বাদিসম্মত** *adj* approved by all disputants; universally admitted; unanimously agreed/ accepted; unanimous. **~বিখ্যাত** *adj* celebrated by all. **~বিদ** *adj* all-knowing; omniscient. ❑*n* the Supreme Being. **~বিদ্য** *adj* possessing all science; omniscient. **~বিদ্যা** *n* all science/ knowledge. **~বিধ**=~প্রকার. **~বিনাশ** *n* entire destruction; complete ruin. **~বিষয়ে** *adj* in all matters/ subjects/ respects; in everything. **~বিষহর** *adj* counteracting all poisons. **~বিষহর ঔষধ** *n* antidote for all poisons. **~বেদী** *adj* omniscient. **~ব্যাপক** *adj* general. **~ব্যাপিকা** *fem.* **~ব্যাপিতা, ~ব্যাপিত্ব** *nn* universality; omnipresence; ubiquitousness. **~ব্যাপী** *adj* all-pervading; embracing all particulars; omnipresent; ubiquitous. ~ব্যাপিনী *fem.* ~ভক্ষ *adj* eating/ devouring everything; omnivorous. ❑*n* fire. ~ভুক *adj* all-devouring; omnivorous. ~ভূত *n* all created beings. ~ভূতাত্মা *n* soul of all beings. ~ভোগ্য *adj* to be enjoyed by all. ~মঙ্গল *adj* universally auspicious. ❑*n* all that in auspicious. ~মঙ্গলময় *adj* source of all good. ~মঙ্গলময়ী *fem* . ~মঙ্গলা *n fem* source of all good; name of goddess Durga. ~ময় *adj* **1** comprehending all; all-containing. **2** all-pervading; ubiquitous; universal; omnipresent. **3** all in all; all-powerful; omnipotent; supreme: ~ময় কর্তা. ~ময়ী *fem.* ~যত্ন *n* every effort. ~যত্নে *adj* making every possible effort. ~রস *n* every taste/ flavour; saline flavour. ~রূপ *adj* of all kinds. ~রোগ *n* all kinds of diseases. ~রোগহর *adj* counteracting/ curing all diseases. ~রোগহর ঔষধ *n* cure-all; panacea. ~লক্ষণ *n* all auspicious marks. ~লোক *n* the whole world/ universe/ people; every one; all beings; all and sundry; everybody. ~শক্তি *n* entire strength. ~শক্তি দিয়ে *adv* with all one's might. ~শক্তি প্রয়োগ করা *vi* exert one's utmost; apply total/ utmost strength/ power; do everything in one's power. ~শক্তিমান *adj* All-powerful; Almighty; Omnipotent; Allah. ~শরীর *n* the whole body. ~শান্তি *n* universal tranquillity/ calm. ~শাস্ত্রজ্ঞ *adj* versed in all branches of learning/ all sciences/ all scriptures. ~শুভঙ্কর *adj* auspicious to all. ~শূন্য *adj* completely empty. ~শূন্যতা *n* complete void. ~শেষ *adj* last of all; ultimate; final. ~শেষে *adv* last of all; at last. ~শোকবিনাশী *adj* removing all sorrows/ grieves. ~শ্রেষ্ঠ *adj* best of all; highest; supreme. ~সংহার *adj* all destroying. ❑*n* universal destruction. ~সংহারী *adj*=~সংহার. ~সঙ্গত *adj* suited to/ for all. ~সমক্ষে *adv* before everybody; in presence of all; publicly; in public; openly . ~সম *adj* equal in all respects; congruent. ~সমতা *n* sameness/ identity with all things/ in every respect; complete identity/ equality; impartiality/ equality towards everything. ~সময়, ~সময়ে *adv* at all times; all the time; always; every time; ever. ~সমর্থিত=~সম্মত. ~সম্পন্ন *adj* provided with everything. ~সম্ভব *n* source of everything. ~সম্মত *adj* unanimous. ~সম্মতি *n* approval/ agreement/ consent of all; common consent. ~সম্মতিক্রমে *adv* unanimously; with unanimous approval/ support. ~সহ=~ংসহ. ~-সাকল্যে *adv* in all; in total; in the aggregate; as a whole; collectively. ~সাক্ষী *n* witness of everything. ~সাধন *n* accomplishing everything. ~সাধারণ *adj* common to all. ❑*n* public; people. ~সামান্য *adj* common to all. ~সাম্য *n* equality in all respects. ~সার *n* essence/ cream of the whole. ~সিদ্ধ *adj* accomplished in every respect. ~সিদ্ধি *n* accomplishment of every object; attainment/ realization of all desires/ ends; complete success. ~সুলভ *adj* easy to be obtained by everyone. ~স্রষ্টা *n* the creator of all. ~স্ব *n* the whole of a person's property/ possessions; one's all; entire property. ~স্বহরণ *n* seizure/ confiscation of all one's property; robbing one of all one's belongings. ~স্বান্ত *adj* robbed of one's all belongings; utterly ruined. ~স্বামী *n* owner/ master of all. ~হর *adj* appropriating everything; all-destroying. ~হরণ=~স্বহরণ. ~হারী *adj* all-seizing. ~হিত *adj* useful/ beneficial to all. সর্বাংশ *n* all parts. সর্বাংশে *adv* in every part; in all respects; thoroughly; perfectly; completely. সর্বাগ্র *adj* first; foremost; lying in the forefront. সর্বাগ্রে *adj* first of all; in the forefront; in the foremost part. সর্বাঙ্গ *n* the whole body; all the limbs. ~সুন্দর *adj* beautiful in every member/ limb; perfectly/ completely beautiful; beautiful in all respects/ every part. সর্বাঙ্গসুন্দরী *fem.* সর্বাঙ্গীণ, সর্বাঙ্গীন *adjj* covering/ pervading/ thrilling the whole body; considering all aspects/ every limb; thorough; total; complete; comprehensive. সর্বাঙ্গে *adv* all over the body; all over; in all parts/ respects; in every part; thoroughly; totally; completely. সর্বাণী *n* name of goddess Durga. সর্বাতিশায়ী *adj* surpassing everything. সর্বাত্মক *adj* all out; with all one's soul; complete; total all-pervading; comprehensive; supreme; sovereign. সর্বাত্মা *n* the universal soul; the whole being/ nature. সর্বাদি *n* beginning/ first of all things. সর্বাদৃত *adj* well-received by all; dear to all; universally popular. সর্বাদ্য *adj* first of all; having existed the first. সর্বাধিক *adj* most of all; most; greatest; utmost; largest; highest. সর্বাধিকারী *adj* all-powerful; all in all. সর্বাধিক্য *n* superiority to all/ everything. সর্বাধিনায়ক *n* commander-in-chief. সর্বাধিপত্য *n* universal sovereignty. সর্বাধ্যক্ষ *n* general superintendent; director general. সর্বানুকারী *adj* all-imitating. সর্বানুভূত *adj* all-perceiving. সর্বানুভূতি *n* universal experience. ❑*adj* all-perceiving. সর্বানুমতি *n* consent of all. সর্বান্ত *n* end of everything. সর্বান্তঃকরণে *adv* wholeheartedly; with all one's heart; heart and soul; willingly and completely. সর্বান্তর্যামী *adj* one who knows every heart. ❑*n* universal soul. সর্বাপেক্ষা *adv* of all; beyond all; above all. সর্বাবয়ব=সর্বাঙ্গ. সর্বাভরণভূষিত *adj* adorned with all ornaments. সর্বাভিসন্ধী *n* cynic; calumniator. সর্বার্থ *n* all things/ objects; all manner of things; all matters; all senses. সর্বার্থকুশল *adj* skilful in all matters. **সর্বচিন্তক** *adj* thinking about everything. **সর্বার্থসাধক** *adj* effecting/ fit for everything; realizing everything; supplying all needs; fulfilling all desires. **সর্বার্থসাধিকা** *fem*. **সর্বার্থসাধন** *adj*=সর্বার্থসাধক. ❑*n* means of accomplishing everything. **সর্বার্থসিদ্ধি** *n* accomplishment of all aims. **সর্বাশী** *adj* omnivorous. **সর্বাহ্ণ** *n* the whole day. **সর্বাহ্ণিক** *adj* daily.

সর্বেশ্বর *n* lord of all; universal monarch; Supreme Lord; God; Shiva. ❑*adj* supreme; sovereign; having sovereign authority over everything. **~বাদ** *n* pantheism. **~বাদী** *adj* pantheistic. ❑*n* pantheist.

সর্বেসর্বা *adj* all in all; predominant; invested with absolute authority.

সর্বোৎকর্ষ *n* pre-eminence over all.

সর্বোচ্চ *adj* highest (of all); most high.

সর্বোত্তম, সর্বোত্তর *adjj* best of all; choicest; most excellent.

সর্বোপরি *adv* above all; on the topmost place; uppermost.

সর্বোষধি *n* all (kinds of) medicinal herbs.

সর্ষপ=সরিষা

সলওয়া [A] *n* quail.

সলজ্জ *adj* feeling shame/ modestly; bashful; embarrassed; abashed; modest; coy; ashamed.

সলজ্জিত *adj* ashamed; abashed.

সলতে=সলতা

সলমা [A] *n* band of embroidery. **~চুমকি** *n* spangled embroidery.

সলা=শলা[২]

সলাজ=সলজ্জ

সলাম, সলামত=সালাম, সালামত

সলি=শলি[১]

সলিকা [A] *n* **1** good disposition; good taste; careful observation of rules of etiquette. **2** dexterity; address; skill.

সলিতা [A] *n* slender wick.

সলিয়ে-বলিয়ে *adj* by persuasion.

সলিল *n* water. **~সমাধি** *n* watery grave; drowning; (fig) utter/ irrevocable loss.

সলিলী *adj* of water; watery.

সলীল *adj* playing; sporting (not in earnest); playful; mocking; sneering; coquettish; sportive.

সলুক [A] *n* intercourse; association; familiarity. ⇒ **শলুক**.

সলোভ *adj* greedy; avaricious.

সল্মা=সলমা

সল্লকী *n* porcupine; hedgehog.

সল্লা=শলা[২]

সশঙ্ক *adj* fearful; doubtful; timid; shy; suspicious. **~চিত্ত** *adj* fearful at heart. **সশঙ্কে** *adv* fearfully; timidly; timorously; diffidently.

সশঙ্কিত *adj* (incorrect)=সশঙ্ক

সশব্দ *adj* having sound/ noise; full of cries; sounding; loud; noisy; clamorous. **সশব্দে** *adv* with noise; noisily; loudly; clamorously.

সশরীর *adj* with the body; embodied. **সশরীরে** *adv* **1** in the mortal body; alive: সশরীরে স্বর্গগমন. **2** in person; bodily: সশরীরে আগমন.

সশস্ত্র *adj* having arms; armed; in arms.

সশিষ্য *adj* attended by pupils/ disciples.

সশ্রদ্ধ *adj* respectful; deferential; trustful.

সশ্রম *adj* wearied; rigorous: ~ কারাদণ্ড.

সশ্রীক *adj* lovely; beautiful; splendid.

সশ্লেষ *adj* ambiguous; having a double meaning; sarcastic; ironical.

সসংকোচ *adj* diffident; timorous; hesitating; shy. **সসংকোচে** *adv* diffidently; timorously; hesitatingly.

সসংজ্ঞ *adj* conscious; having sense; sensible.

সসংশয় *adj* doubting; doubtful; uncertain; dubious.

সসজ্জ *adj* adorned; dressed up. **সসজ্জা** *fem*.

সসত্ত্ব *adj* possessing energy/ vigour; containing living creatures/ animals. **সসত্ত্বা** *fem* containing an embryo; pregnant. **সসত্ত্বাবস্থা** *n* pregnancy.

সসন্তান *adj* together with children/ offspring.

সসপেন্ড [E] *adj* suspended.

সসম [P] *adj* sixth.

সসম্ভ্রম *adj* deferential; respectful; regardful. **সসম্ভ্রমে** *adv* with deference; respectfully.

সসম্মান *adj* respectful; honourable; reverential. **সসম্মানে** *adv* with respect/ honour; respectfully; honourably; (academic) with honours.

সসাক্ষিক *adj* (happening) before witnesses.

সসাগর *adj* together with/ inclusive of the oceans. **সসাগরা** *fem*. **সসাগরা ধরণী** *n* the earth inclusive of the oceans; the whole earth.

সসাজ=সসজ্জ

সসার [E] *n* saucer; an UFO.

সসীম *adj* **1** finite; having a limit. **2** terminating.

সসেমিরা *adj* bewildered; stupefied; dazed: ~ হয়ে থাকা.

সসৈন্য *adj* with/ commanding an army; with guards, armies and equipages. **সসৈন্যে** *adv*=~.

সসৌষ্ঠব *adj* lovely; gracious; shapely.

সস্তা *adj* cheap. **~দরে, ~য়** *advv* cheap; on the cheap. **~য় কেনা/বেচা** *vi* buy/ get/ sell sth on the cheap/ cheaply. **~য় বিক্রি হওয়া** *vi* go cheap. **~য় কিস্তিমাত করা** *vt* obtain sth without efforts; win cheap applause; win a cheap victory. **~র তিন অবস্থা** (fig) cheap and nasty/ shoddy.

সস্ত্রীক *adj, adv* with wife; attended/ accompanied by one's wife.

সস্নেহ *adj* **1** affectionate; loving. **2** oily; greasy. **সস্নেহে** *adv* affectionately; lovingly; with affection; tenderly.

সস্পৃহ *adj* filled with desire/ longing; longing (for); desirous (of); expressing a desire.

সস্মিত *adj* smiling; laughing. **~ বদন** *n* smiling face. ❑*adj* having a smiling face. **~বদনা** *fem*. **~ বদনে** *adv* with a smiling face.

সস্য *n* (bot) endosperm.

সস্বেদ *adj* moist with sweat; perspiring; exuding.

-সহ[১] *adj* (used as a *suff)* expressing (capable of) bearing, enduring, overcoming: যুক্তি~, ভার~.

-সহ[২] *prep* (used as a *suff)* with; together with; along with; in the company of; including: পুত্রকন্যা~, ভাড়া~.

সহ[৩] *pref* expressing with, along/ together with, in company, in common, jointly, in concert, at the same time/ simultaneous with. **~অধিকর্তা** *n* assistant director. **~কর্মী** *n* colleague; co-worker; associate. **~কার** *n* **1** assistance; co-operation. **2** (kind of fragrant) mango tree; mango blossom. **~কারিতা** *n* assistance; co-operation. **~কারী** *adj* assisting; assistant; co-operating; concurrent; sub-. ❑*n* assistant; co-worker; concurrent agent. **~কারিণী** *fem*. **~কারী সচিব** *n* assistant secretary. **~কারী প্রধান শিক্ষক** *n* assistant headmaster. **~কারী সম্পাদক** *n* sub-editor; assistant secretary. **~কৃৎ** *adj* assisting; co-operating. ❑*n* assistant. **~গ** *n* (alg) co-efficient. **~গমন** *n* going with; accompanying; a widow's going with her deceased husband, ie burning herself with his dead body. **~গমন করা** *vi* go with/ together; accompany; burn oneself with one's own husband's funeral pyre. **~গামী** *adj* **1** going together/ with; accompanying; concurrent. **2** burning oneself with one's deceased husband. **~গামিনী** *fem*. **~গামী হওয়া**=~গমন করা. **~ঘটন** *n* concurrence. **~ঘটমান** *adj* concurrent. **~চর, ~চারী** *adjj* going with/ together accompanying; associating with; belonging together; (gram) correlative. ❑*n* companion; follower; friend; associate; confidant; attendant. **~চরী, ~চারিণী** *fem* confidante; mistress; female companion/ friend. **~চার (বাদ)** *n* (phil) parallelism. **~জাত** *adj* born together/ at the same time; born from the same mother; twin-born; equal in age; innate; inborn; natural; congenital; inherent. **~জাত অধিকার** *n* birthright. **~জাত প্রবৃত্তি/বৃদ্ধি/সংস্কার** *n* instinct. **~দূত** *n* attaché. **~ধর্ম** *n* community of law/ duty; common usage/ characteristic. **~ধর্মচারিণী, ~ধর্মিণী** *nn fem* a wife who shares duties; lawful/ legitimate wife. **~ধর্মী** *adj* following the same faith/ religion/ customs; having common properties/ virtues/ propensities/ functions. ❑*n* co-religionist. **~ধূরী** *n* colleague. **~নর্তন, ~নৃত্য** *nn* act of dancing together. **~পথিক, ~পথী** *adj* going by the same road. ❑*n* companion on a journey; fellow-traveller. **~পাঠী** *n* fellow-student; class-mate; class-fellow. **~পাঠিনী** *fem*. **~প্রধান** *n* deputy chief. **~প্রধান শিক্ষক** *n* assistant headmaster. **~প্রধান শিক্ষিকা** *fem* assistant headmistress. **~বাস** *n* dwelling together; common abode; cohabitation; living as husband and wife. **~বাস করা** *vt* live/ dwell together; cohabit; live as man and wife. **~বাসী** *adj* (bot) monoecious. **~ব্যাপ্ত** *adj* co-extensive. **~ব্যাপ্তি** *n* co-extension. **~ভাব** *n* **1** being together; companionship; community. **2** inseparability; concomitance. **3** co-existence. **~ভাবী** *adj* **1** connected together; coherent. **2** concomitant. **3** helping; assisting. ❑*n* friend; partisan; adherent. **~ভেদ** *n* (alg) joint variation. **~মরণ** *n* dying together; burning with the corpse of husband; concremation; suttee. **~মরণে যাওয়া** *vi* die together; burn oneself with the corpse of one's husband. **~মৃতা** *adj fem* woman who has burnt herself with her dead husband. **~যাত্রা** *n* travelling together. **~যাত্রী, ~যায়ী** *adjj* accompanying; going/ travelling together. ❑*n* companion; fellow-traveller. **~যাত্রিণী** *fem*. **~যাত্রী হওয়া** *vi* go/ journey/ travel together; accompany. **~যোগ, ~যোগিতা** *nn* co-operation. **~যোগিতা করা** *vi* co-operate (with); associate (with). **~যোগী** *adj* co-operating; associating; associate: ~যোগী অধ্যাপক. ❑*n* associate; co-worker; colleague; co-operator; comrade. **~যোগিনী** *fem*. **~যোগী প্রধান শিক্ষক** *n* joint headmaster. **~যোগী সম্পাদক** *n* associate editor. **~যোগে** *adv* (together) with; mixed with; in co-operation with. **~যোজন** *n* co-ordination. **~যোজিত** *adj* co-ordinated. **~যোদ্ধা** *n* fellow-soldier; brother-in-arms. **~-শিক্ষক** *n* assistant master/ teacher. **~-শিক্ষিকা** *fem* assistant mistress. **~সমীকরণ** *n* (alg) simultaneous equation. **সহাধিকার ক্ষেত্র** *n* concurrent jurisdiction. **সহাধীক্ষক, সহাধ্যক্ষ** *n* assistant superintendent; vice-principal. **সহাধ্যয়ন** *n* studying together; companionship in study. **সহাধ্যায়ী** =~পাঠী. **সহানুগমন** =~মরণ. **সহানুভূতি** *n* sympathy; fellow-feeling; compassion. **সহানুভূতিশীল** *adj* sympathetic/ compassionate (by nature). **সহানুভূতিসম্পন্ন** *adj* sympathetic; compassionate. **সহাবস্থান** *n* co-existence. **সহার্থ** *n* accompanying/ accessory matter or meaning. **সহার্থক** *adj* having the same object/ meaning; synonymous.

সহজ *adj* **1** simple; easy; natural; effortless; smooth; plain; easily understood; not difficult; handy; elementary. **2** born/ produced together or at the same time; congenital; innate; hereditary; original; natural; inborn; instinctive; inherent. ❑*n* natural state/ disposition. ~ উপায় *n* simple/ easy means. ~ কথা *n* plain language; straight answer; simple matter. ~ কর্ম/কাজ *n* easy task. ~গম্য *adj* easily accessible; easy to understand. ~ জ্ঞান *n* instinct. ~তর *adj* easier. ~ ধার্মিক *adj* innately religious. ~ পথ *n* straight way. ~প্রবণ *adj* **1** easily done; simple; easy. **2** pliable, pliant; ductile; flexible; submissive; plastic. ~প্রবণতা *n* **1** easiness; facility. **2** pliability; flexibility; pliancy; malleability. ~ বিশ্বাস *n* credulity; innate conviction. ~ বিশ্বাসী *adj* credulous; naive; gullible. ~বোধ্য *adj* easily understood/ intelligible/ comprehensible. ~মিত্র *n* natural friend/ ally. ~ যান, ~ ধর্ম *nn* form of worship practised by a Vaishnava or Buddhist community. ~লভ্য *adj* easily obtainable/ available. ~লব্ধ *adj* easily obtained; within reach; accessible. ~ লোক *n* **1** simple man. **2** simpleton; gullible person. ~ শত্রু *n* natural enemy. ~ সাধন =~ যান. সহজে *adv* **1** easily; at ease; effortlessly; without effort; with ease; swimmingly; handily; conveniently. **2** usually; generally; ordinarily: এমনটি সহজে দেখা যায় না.

সহজিয়া *adj* natural; innate. ❑*n* (also ~ ধর্ম)=সহজযান (⇒ সহজ).

সহজেতর *adj* other than natural; not innate/ inherent/ congenital; unnatural; accidental.

সহন *n* enduring; suffering; toleration; patience; forbearance; patient endurance. ~শীল *adj* of a patient disposition; tolerant; patient; enduring; forbearing. ~শীলা *fem*. ~শীলতা *n* patience; forbearance; tolerance; patient endurance.

সহনীয় *adj* bearable; tolerable; sufferable; endurable; pardonable.

সহবত, সহবৎ [A] *n* **1** companionship; society; company; association; intercourse; carnal intercourse; cohabitation. **2** good manners (learnt in society); courtesy. ~ করা *vi* keep company with; cohabit; copulate. ~দুরস্ত *adj* fit for good company; decent.

সহবর্তি *adj* attending; accompanying. ❑*n* companion; attendant.

সহর=শহর

সহরৎ=শোহরৎ

সহর্ষ *adj* joyful; glad. সহর্ষে *adv* joyfully; gladly.

সহর্ষিত=সহর্ষ

সহল [A] *adj* easy; simple; not difficult. সহলে *adv* gently.

সহসা *adv* suddenly; all on a sudden; precipitately; quickly; immediately; at once; unexpectedly; in a flash.

সহস্র *n, adj* thousand. ❑*adj* countless; innumerable; many and diverse. ~ক *adj* thousand headed. ❑*n* millennium. ~কর, ~কিরণ *adj* thousand-rayed. ❑*n* the sun. ~তম *adj* thousandth. ~তমী *fem*. ~দ্রংষ্ট্র *adj* thousand-toothed. ❑*n* sort of sheat-fish. ~দল *adj* having a thousand petals; thousand-petalled. ~দৃক *adj* thousand-eyed ❑*n* Indra. ~ধা *adv* in a thousand ways/ parts; in countless/ manifold ways; thousand fold. ~ধার *adj* having a thousand edges. ~ধারা *n* cascade falling in innumerable streams; river flowing in a great many streams. ~ধারে *adj* in a thousand streams. ~নয়ন *adj* thousand-eyed. ❑*n* Indra. ~পতি *n* chief of a thousand (villages). ~পত্র *adj* thousand-petalled. ~পদ *adj* thousand-footed; having a thousand columns. ❑*n* millipede; Vishnu; the sun. ~প্রকার *adj* innumerable kinds of; manifold; many and diverse. ~ প্রকারে *adv* in a thousand/ countless ways or manners. ~বার *adv* thousand times; countless/ many times. ~বৃত্ত *n* (geom) auxiliary circle. ~লোচন =~নয়ন. ~শ *adv* by thousands. ~শীর্ষ *adj* thousand-headed; hydra-headed. ❑*n* Narayana. সহস্রাংশু =~কর. সহস্রাক্ষ =~নয়ন. সহস্রাধিক *adj* more than a thousand. সহস্রার *adj* thousand-spoked. ❑*n* kind of cavity said to be found in the top of the head and to resemble a lotus reversed (fabled as the seat of the soul).

সহস্রী *n*=সহস্রপতি (⇒ সহস্র)

সহা = সওয়া. ~নো = সওয়ানো

সহায় *n* **1** companion; follower; adherent; ally; assistant; helper; supporter; patron. **2** help; aid; assistance; support; patronization; prop; recourse; resource. ~ক *adj* helpful; helping; assisting; supporting; accessory; patronizing; subsidiary; auxiliary; useful; beneficial; abetting; (gram) auxiliary. ~ক ক্রিয়া *n* auxiliary verb. ~তা *n* = ~(1). ~তা করা *vt* aid; help; assist; succour; lend a hand; benefit; promote; further; subserve; support; sustain; prop; bolster up; patronize; abet; stand by; side with; render assistance ~তাকারী *adj*=~ক. ❑*n* helper; assistant; helping hand; abettor; accomplice. ~তাকারিণী *fem*. ~সম্পত্তি *n* resources; wherewithal; means. ~সম্বল *n* friends to turn to and resources to fall back on.

সহাস্য *adj* laughing; smiling. ~ বদনে, ~ মুখে *advv* with a smiling face; laughingly.

সহি [A] *n* **1** = সই[২]. **2** endorsement. ~দাতা *n* endorsers; signatory.

সহিংস *adj* violent.

সহিত *prep* with; along/ together with. ❑*adj* joined; conjoined; united; accompanied/ attended by; containing.

সহিলি, সহেলি *nn* woman's female companion; handmaid; damsel; female friend; confidante.

সহিষ্ণু *adj* patient; enduring; having fortitude; stoical; tolerant. **~তা** *n* patience; fortitude; toleration; tolerance; endurance.

সহিস [A] *n* groom; horse-keeper.

সহিসালামত [A] *adj* safe and sound.

সহুরে = শহুরে

সহৃদয় *adj* **1** kind; kind-hearted; good-hearted; full of feeling; sensible; large-hearted: ~ ব্যক্তি. **2** hearty; cordial; sincere: ~ অভ্যর্থনা. **3** sympathetic; appreciative; compassionate; considerate: ~ বিবেচনা/ বিচার. ❑*n* learned man. **সহৃদয়া** *fem.* **~তা** *n* kindness; kind-heartedness; good-heartedness; sympathy; compassion; amiability.

সহেলি ⇒ সহিলি

সহোদর *adj* **1** co-uterine; born of the same womb/ mother. **2** closely resembling; similar. ❑*n* uterine brother. **সহোদরা** *fem* uterine sister.

সহ্য *adj* **1** endurable; tolerable; bearable; sufferable. **2** endured; tolerated; borne; suffered. ❑*n* tolerance; endurance; fortitude; patience. **~ করা** = সওয়া. **~গুণ** *n* quality of bearing patiently; forbearance. **সহ্যাতীত** *adj* unbearable; intolerable; insupportable; insufferable; unendurable. **সহ্যের সীমা** the limit of one's patience; a limit to one's patience.

সা *n* (music) first and eighth of the notes in the musical octave.

সাইকেল [E] *n* bicycle.

সাইক্লোন [E] *n* cyclone.

সাইজ [E] *n* size.

সাইত, সাইদ [A] *nn* **1** first cash sale of the day; auspicious beginning. **2** prosperity; felicity.

সাইন[1] (trig) [E] *n* sine.

সাইন[2] [E] *n* sign. **~বোর্ড** *n* signboard.

সাইম [E] (bot)*n* cyme.

সাইমুম [A] *n* a hot pestilential wind.

সাইরেন [E] *n* siren.

সাউ *n* merchant (by caste/ profession); money-lender. **~কারি** *n* **1** pretence of honesty/ innocence. **2** money-lending; trading.

সাং abbr. of সাকিন

সাংকেতিক= সাঙ্কেতিক

সাংক্রামিক *adj* contagious; communicable; infectious.

সাংখ্য *adj* numeral; relating to number. ❑*n* name of one of the three great divisions of Hindu philosophy (ascribed to the sage Kapila); Sankhya system of philosophy.

সাংখ্যিক = সংখ্যা

সাংগ্রামিক *adj* relating to war; warlike; martial.

সাংঘাতিক = সাঙ্ঘাতিক

সাংদৃষ্টিক *adj* visible/ perceptible at the same time; synoptic; evident; undeniable.

সাংবৎসর, সাংবৎসরিক *adjj* yearly; annual; perennial; occurring every year; continuing for a year; lasting/ occupying a year.

সাংবাদিক *adj* pertaining to news; journalistic. ❑*n* journalist. **~তা** *n* journalism. **~তা করা** *vi* work as a journalist; be engaged in journalism.

সাংযাত্রিক *n* voyaging merchant; one who trades by sea.

সাংশয়িক *adj* dubious; doubtful; hazardous.

সাংসর্গিক *adj* produced by/ resulting from contact/ intercourse; contagious.

সাংসারিক *adj* **1** connected with/ dependent on mundane existence; worldly; earthly. **2** domestic; familial. **~ জ্ঞান** *n* worldly wisdom.

সাংসিদ্ধিক *adj* effected naturally; natural; innate; native; self-existent; absolute.

সাংস্থানিক *adj* belonging/ relating to a common place of abode. ❑*n* fellow-countryman (or countrywoman).

সাঁ, সাঁই[1]=শাঁ

সাঁই[2] *n* religious preceptor/ associate/ teacher; God. ⇒ স্বামী.

সাঁইত্রিশ *n, adj* thirty-seven.

সাঁইসাঁই=শাইশাই

সাঁওতাল *n* name of an aboriginal tribe of Bangladesh and India.

সাঁকো *n* a mate-shift narrow pathway over a canal made of bamboo or wood often hazardous.

সাঁচা, সাঁচি, সাঁচ্চা=সাচ্চা

সাঁজ **1** (colloq) *n*= সন্ধ্যা. **2** evening lamp: ~ দেওয়া.

সাঁজা *n* fermenting agent used in making curd/ yoghurt; rennet.

সাঁজাল *n* fumigation by burning cowdung, hay, etc to expel mosquitoes.

সাঁজোয়া, সাজোয়া *n* armour; coat of mail. **~ গাড়ি** *n* armoured car.

সাঁঝ (colloq) *n*=সন্ধ্যা

সাঁঝাল = সাঁজাল

সাঁট *n* **1** hint; sign; gesture: ~ বোঝা. **2** brevity; concision; terseness; conciseness. **~লিপি** *n* shorthand. **সাঁটে** *adv* succinctly; concisely; in short/ brief; briefly.

সাঁটা *vt, vi* **1** fix or attach firmly/ tightly. **2** seize/ hold firmly. **3** grip. **4** constrict: বুকপিঠ সেঁটে ধরেছে. **5** husk. **6** cut; clip; (facet) gorge oneself with; gormandize. ❑*adj* fixed/ attached firmly or tightly; held/ seized/ gripped firmly.

সাঁড়াশি, সাঁড়াশী *n* pincers; forceps; tongs. **পাক-~** *n* vice. **~-অভিযান** *n* pincer-movement.

সাঁতরানো *vi* swim.

সাঁতলানো *vt* singe lightly in oil or butter. ❑*adj* lightly singed in oil or butter.

সাঁতার *n* swimming; natation. ~ **কাটা/দেওয়া** *n* swim. ~ **কাটার পুকুর** *n* swimming pool. ~**-জল,** ~**-পানি** *nn* mass of water so deep that one has to swim to cross it; deep water.

সাঁতারু *n* (expert) swimmer.

সাঁধানো *vt* enter; penetrate.

সাঁপি *n* roundish part at the front of a sacrificial post into which the neck of a beast is put.

সাকরেদ, সাগরেদ=শাগরেদ

সাকল্য, সাকুল্য *n* totality; completeness; entireness; whole; total amount/ number. **সাকল্যে, সাকুল্যে** *adv* in toto; in all.

সাকাঙ্ক্ষ *adj* having a wish/ desire; wishing; desirous; longing.

সাকার *adj* having form; having any shape/ definite figure, corporeal; bodied. **সাকারা** *fem.* ~**-উপাসনা** *n* form of worship in which deities are conceived as having forms; idolatry. ~**বাদ** *n* doctrine upholding the worship of God in visible forms.

সাকারোপাসক *n* idolator. ❑*adj* idolatrous.

সাকারোপাসনা = সাকার-উপাসনা(⇒ সাকার)

সাকিন [A] *n* place of one's residence; address.

সাকী [A] *n* **1** cup-bearer; page-boy.

সাক্ষর *adj* **1** literate. **2** containing syllables/ letters. ~**তা** *n* literacy.

সাক্ষাৎ *adj* **1** visible; manifest. **2** in bodily form; incarnate; appearing in person: ~ যম. **3** equal to; resembling: ~ দেবতা. **4** immediate; direct. ❑*n* **1** interview; call; meeting; audience: রাজ~. **2** (visible) presence: ঈশ্বরের ~. ~ **করা** *vi* visit; call on; pay a visit to; interview; meet; pay a call on. ~ **পাওয়া** *vi* be able to meet (with); have a meeting with; happen to meet (with); be in communion (with); be able to commune (with). ~**কর্তা,** ~**কারী** *adj* one who sees everything. ❑*n* **1** visitor; interviewer. **2** eye-witness. ~**কারিণী** ~**কার** *n* **1** interview; meeting. **3** realization; evident/ intuitive perception. ~**প্রার্থী** *adj, n* one who asks for/ seeks an interview with; visitor. ~**প্রার্থিনী** *fem.* ~**ভেদ** *n* (arith) direct variation. ~ **সম্বন্ধ** *n* direct relation; outward/ formal relation. ~ **সম্বন্ধে** *adv* directly. **সাক্ষাতে** *adv* face to face; in one's presence.

সাক্ষি= সাক্ষী

সাক্ষিগোপাল *n* (fig) helpless witness; puppet.

সাক্ষী *n* witness; eye-witness. ~ **পড়ানো** *vi* prime/ tutor a witness. ~ **মানা** *vi* cite sb as a witness; call upon sb as a witness. ~**র কাঠগড়া** *n* witness-box; witness-stand. ~**র জবানবন্দি** *n* deposition/ examination of a witness. ~**র জেরা** *n* cross-examination of a witness. ~**সাবুদ** *n* witness and evidence.

সাক্ষ্য *n* witness; evidence; testimony; attestation; deposition. ~ **দেওয়া** *vi* bear witness; give witness (on behalf of); depose; testify; give evidence.

সাগর *n* sea; ocean. ~**গর্ভ** *n* sea-bed. ~**গামী** *adj* ocean-going. ~**গামিনী** *fem.* ~**ছেঁচা মানিক** (fig)*n* precious jewel. ~**পার** *n* seashore; other shore/ side of a sea. ~**পারে** *adj* on the seashore; beyond seas; abroad; across the sea; overseas. ~**বক্ষ** *n* sea-level. ~**মেখলা** *adj* sea-girt. ❑*n* earth. ~**শাখা** *n* arm of the sea. ~**সঙ্গম** *n* place where a river (esp the Ganges) falls into a sea; estuary. **সাগরাঙ্ক** *n* sea-level. **সাগরাম্বরা** *adj fem* sea-clad. **সাগরালয়** *adj* living in the ocean. ❑*n* name of Varuna.

সাগু *n* sago. ~**দানা** *n* grain of sago; sago.

সাগ্নিক *adj* possessing/ maintaining a sacred fire; associated with witnessed by Agni. ❑*n* Brahmin who maintains perpetual sacred fire.

সাগ্রহ *adj* eager; persistent; earnest; pertinacious; intent; wistful. **সাগ্রহে** *adv* eagerly; persistently; earnestly; intently; with pertinacity.

সাঙ্কর্য *n* mixing/ blending together confusedly; confusion; mixture.

সাঙ্কেতিক *adj* consisting of signs; symbolic (al); emblematical. ❑*n* (arith) practice.

সাঙ্ক্রামিক=সাংক্রামিক

সাঙ্ক্ষেপিক *adj* abridged; concise; short; contracted.

সাঙ্খ্য=সাংখ্য

সাঙ্গ *adj* **1** having limbs/ a body; together with the limbs. **2** complete; entire. **3** concluded; finished; completed; ended. ~ **করা** *vt* conclude; finish; complete; end. ~ **হওয়া** *vi* end; come to an end; conclude. ~**রূপক** *n* (rhet) kind of metaphor.

সাঙ্গা, সাঙা *nn* re-marriage.

সাঙ্গাত, সাঙাত *nn* (sl) **1** bosom friend; intimate companion; pal. **2** accomplice. **সাঙ্গাতি, সাঙাতি** *fem.*

সাঙ্গীকরণ *n* assimilation.

সাঙ্গোপাঙ্গ *n pl* friends and followers/ associates; cronies; rabble.

সাঙ্ঘাতিক *adj* serious; fatal; mortal; terrible; tremendous. ❑*adv* very; extremely.

সাচি *adv* crookedly; awry; obliquely; askance; sideways. ~**বর্তন** (phys) *n* diffraction.

সাচিবিক *adj* secretarial.

সাচীকৃত *adj* made crooked; bent sideways; distorted; averted.

সাচ্চা *adj* true; genuine; real; pure; upright; righteous: ~ লোক.

সাজ *n*=সজ্জা. ~**গোজ** *n* (meticulous) dressing. ~**ঘর** *n* green room. ~**ন** *n* dressing; decoration; embellishment. ~**ন্ত** *adj* fitting; beautifying; decorative; proper. ~**সজ্জা** *adj* **1** dressing; trappings; finery; full dress; make-up. **2** equipment; equipage; outfit; accoutrements. **3**

fittings and furniture; furnishings. **~সরঞ্জাম** *n* equipment; outfit; equipage; furnishings.

সাজশ [P] *n* conspiracy; intrigue; confederacy; collusion: যোগ~.

সাজা[1] [P] *n* punishment; penalty; chastisement; correction; requital; retribution. **~ দেওয়া** *vt* punish; chastise; award punishment. **~ নেওয়া** *vi* receive/ accept punishment; kiss the rod. **~ পাওয়া** *vi* be punished.

সাজা[2] *vi* **1** dress (oneself); embellish oneself. **2** dress up (as); disguise oneself: সে দস্যু সেজেছে. **3** make up; take up the role of: সে হ্যামলেট সেজেছে. **4** pretend to be; assume a false dress/ appearance; pass oneself off as; pose as: সাধু ~. **5** equip oneself; get ready; be prepared: যুদ্ধের জন্যে ~. **6** prepare; process; get ready: পান/তামাক ~. **7** become; behave; befit: এমন কথা তাকে সাজে না. ❑*adj* **1** disguised/ appearing as; pretending. **2** prepared; processed. **~নো** *vt* **1** dress; embellish; decorate; adorn; beautify: বিয়ের কনে ~নো. **2** lay out; arrange artistically: বাগান ~নো. **3** disguise; dress up. **4** cast (for the part of): নাটকে রাজা ~নো. **5** fit out; rig (with): জাহাজ ~নো. **6** equip; arm: সেনাদল ~নো. **7** arrange; place in order; array; dispose: বইগুলি সাজাও. **8** fabricate; concoct; cook up: মামলা ~নো. **1** prepare; process; get prepared: কল্কে ~নো. ❑*adj* **1** dressed; embellished; decorated; adorned. **2** artistically laid out. **3** disguised. **4** placed in order; arranged; arrayed. **5** fabricated; cooked-up; concocted.

সাজাত্য *n* community of race with; equality of kind; homogeneity; kindredness.

সাজি[1] *n* kind of high-rimmed, usually round wicker-tray or wicker-basket.

সাজি[2], **সাজি মাটি** *nn* fuller's earth.

সাজো *adj* today's; fresh; recent: ~ দই/কাপড়. ❑*adv* recently; afresh: ~ ভানা. ❑*n*=~বাসী. **~বাসী** *n* **1** system of washing clothes, etc with fuller's earth within a few hours. **2** washerman who washes clothes in the aforesaid manner.

সাট[1]=সাঁট

সাট[2] *n* (sl) collusion; conspiracy; mutual understanding.

সাটিন [E] *n* satin.

সাটী=শাটী

সাড় *n* sensitivity; sensibility; sensation; feeling; consciousness.

সাড়ম্বর *adj* pompous; grandiose; high-falutin; showy; ostentatious. **সাড়ম্বরে** *adv* pompously; ostentatiously.

সাড়া *n* **1** response; answer; reaction: তার কোনো ~ নেই. **2** sound; noise. **3** excitement; hubbub; great animation; flurry; flushed: সারা বাড়িতে ~ পড়ে গেছে. **4** sign of existence; throbbing: প্রাণের ~. **5** word; speech; voice: তার মুখে ~ নেই. **~শব্দ** *n*=~.

সাড়ি, সাড়ী=শাড়ি

সাড়ে *adj* joined with a half; plus/ increased by one half: ~ তিন, three and half; বেলা ~ তিনটা, half past three; ~ তিন টাকা, three and a half Takas; ~ তিন মাইল, three and a half miles, three miles and a half.

সাত *n, adj* seven. **~ই** *adj* (of the days of a month) seventh. ❑*n* the seventh day of a month; the seventh. **~ কথার এক কথা** (fig) a weighty remark. **~ কথা শোনানো** (fig) lecture sb for; scold; lash out; rebuke. **~কাণ্ড** *adj* consisting of/ divided into seven cantos; lengthy. ❑*n* grandiose affair. ❑*adv* at great length; in detail. **~কাণ্ড রামায়ণ** *n* (fig) lengthy/ detailed account or narrative. **~ খুন মাপ** (fig) (said of a favourite person) act of keeping one's eyes closed to all offences/ failings. **~ঘাটের জল খাওয়ানো** put to great trouble; harass. **~ চড়ে রা না করা** (fig) be long-suffering/ extremely meek; take every insult/ oppression lying down. **~চল্লিশ** *n, adj* forty-seven. **~জন্মে** *adv* (ever) ever in the long past/ future. **~তবক** *adj* seven-storied. **~তাড়াতাড়ি** *adv* with an excessive haste; post haste; at the double. **~ নকলে আসল খাস্তা** (fig) repeated imitations makes the origin lose its identity. **~নরী** *adj* having seven tiers/ strings: ~নরী হার. **~নলা** *adj* seven-barrelled. **~পাঁচ** *adj* various; many and diverse; multifarious. ❑*adv* about this and that: ~পাঁচ ভাবা. **~পুরুষ** *n* seven generations; the long past and future. **~ষট্টি** *n, adj* sixty-seven. **~সতের** *adj* various; diverse. **~সমুদ্র তের নদীর পার** (fig) (in folktales) a place where a human being can hardly go; a place beyond the (corners of the) world. **সাতে নেই, পাঁচেও নেই** (fig) perfectly disinterested/ aloof; having no concern with.

সাতত্য *n* continuity; constancy; uninterruptedness.

সাতা *n* the seven of playing-cards.

সাতাত্তর *n, adj* seventy-seven.

সাতানব্বই, সাতানব্বুই (colloq) *n, adj* ninety-seven.

সাতান্ন *n, adj* fifty-seven.

সাতাশ *n, adj* twenty-seven.

সাতাশি, সাতাশী *n, adj* eighty-seven.

সাতাশে *n* twenty-seventh day of a month; the twenty-seventh. ❑*adj* (of the days of a month) twenty seventh.

সাতিশয় *adj* excessive; overmuch; extreme; exceeding. ❑*adv* excessively; extremely; exceedingly; overmuch.

সাতই *n, adj* (colloq)=সাতই (⇒ সাত)

সাত্তা *n* (colloq)=সাতা

সাত্ত্বিক *adj* **1** related to/ endowed with the quality of Sattva (সত্ত্বগুণ), ie 'purity' or 'goodness'. **2** pure; true; genuine; honest; good; virtuous. **3** dispassionate; disinterested; unconcerned about the consequence; unaffected: ~ পূজা. **~ ভাব** *n* **1** quality of Sattva; disinterestedness; purity; goodness. **2** state of body caused by some natural emotion (constituting a class of 8 *Bhavas* holding middle place between *Shayi* and *Vyabhichari-bhavas).*

সাথ *prep* (dial)=সাথে. ❑*n* company: সাথের মানুষ.

সাথী *n* companion; associate: সঙ্গী~.

সাথে *prep* with; in company of.

সাদর *adj* cordial; respectful; attentive/ devoted to. **সাদরে** *adv* cordially; respectfully; attentively.

সাদা [P] *adj* **1** white. **2** simple; plain; sincere; artless; guileless; candid: ~ মন. **3** white; white-skinned: ~ আদমি. **4** unadorned; frank; categorical; unequivocal; plain; straightforward: ~ কথা. **5** blank; unwritten: ~ কাগজ. **6** unblurred; clear; naked: ~ চোখ. ❑*n* white colour; white-skinned people; white race. **~ কথা** *n* plain words. **~ কাগজ** *n* white/ blank paper. **~টে** *adj* whitish. **~ দিল** *adj* artless; simple. **~মাটা, ~মাঠা, ~সিধা, ~সিধে** (colloq) *adj* **1** candid; plain; straightforward; simple; simple-hearted; unassuming; straight. **2** categorical; unequivocal; downright. **3** ordinary; bald; unadorned; unornamented. **4** dull; drab; uninteresting. **~কে কালো এবং কালোকে ~ করা** (fig) lie shamelessly; lie in one's teeth/ throat. **সই করা ~ কাগজ** (fig) carte blanche.

সাদি[1], **সাদী**[1] *n*=শাদি

সাদি[2], **সাদী**[2] *n* horseman; charioteer; elephant-rider.

সাদিক [A] *adj* true; sincere; faithful; veracious; just; (a man) of his word.

সাদিয়ানা=শাদিয়ানা (⇒ শাদি)

সাদৃশ্য *n* likeness; similarity; resemblance; analogy; affinity; image; portrait.

সাধ *n* **1** desire; longing; wish; craving; passion; ambition; aspiration; solicitation. **2** volition; will; free will; (one's own) accord: ~ করে বিপদ ডাকা. **3** fancy; choice: সাধের জিনিস. **5** name of a ceremony for giving desired articles of food to a pregnant woman: ~ খাওয়া. **6** option. **~ করা** *vt* desire; long (for); set one's heart upon; covet; lust for/ after; crave; hanker for/ after; hunger for/ after; pine for; itch for/ after; yearn for. **2** choose; volunteer (for); opt (for). **~ করে** *adj* voluntarily; of one's own accord; willingly; freely; wilfully. **~ মেটা** *vt* **1** be satiated. **2** (iron) be fed up/ sick of. **~-আহ্লাদ** *n* tender longing; yearning; desire or enjoyment.

সাধক *adj* **1** efficient; effective; productive of; accomplishing; adapted to any purpose. **2** austerely endeavouring to achieve an end; engaged in austere worship of God; practising ascetic austerities. ❑*n* worshipper (of God); votary; devotee; one who practises ascetic austerities. **সাধিকা** *fem*. **~তা** *n* efficacy.

সাধন *n* **1** accomplishment; performance; attainment; fulfilment; realization; completion; perfection. **2** worship; adoration; austere ascetic practice. **3** austere endeavour. **4** means; instrument; tool; agent; implement; apparatus; expedient. **~ করা** *vt* accomplish; attain; perform; complete; realize by dint of austere/ arduous endeavour. **~ ক্রিয়া** *n* act of performance. **~ নিষ্ঠা** *n* devotion to austere ascetic practice. **~পত্র** *n* instrument. **~-ভজন** *n* religious prayer and meditation/ worship religious practice.

সাধনা *n* **1** worship; adoration; austere ascetic practice. **2** austere/ arduous endeavour or practice: সাহিত্য ~. **3** austerities. **4** austere vow/ difficult goal: এ বড়ো কঠিন ~. **~ করা** *vi* **1** worship God; be engaged in austere ascetic practices. **2** endeavour austerely/ arduously; strive; struggle; exert one's powers; strain.

সাধনী *n* means; expedient.

সাধনীয় *adj* **1** to be performed/ accomplished/ attained. **2** to be formed (as words). **3** to be acquired (as knowledge).

সাধর্ম্য *n* similarity; likeness; resemblance; similitude; affinity; community.

সাধা *vt* **1** bring about; accomplish (a desired thing); effect; fulfil; complete; execute. **2** form (as words). **3** practise: গলা ~. **4** attain/ effect an object; be successful; succeed; prosper; realize; attain one's object; obtain one's wishes. **5** gain; obtain; acquire; procure. **6** endeavour/ practise austerely or arduously: মন্ত্র ~. **7** offer: ঘুষ ~. **8** invite; ask for: সেধে বিপদে পড়া. **9** put forward; offer; create: বাদ ~. **10** volunteer; come forward; do sth with a good grace; make the first advances: সেধে কথা বলা. **11** entreat; implore; request earnestly; implore; prevail upon sb: তাকে কতো সাধলাম, সে কিছুতেই রাজি হলো না. **12** try to appease/ pacify: পায়ে ধরে সাধা. ❑*adj* **1** practised; seasoned: ~ গলা. **2** offered lovingly; heed out for acceptance: ~ ভাত. **~নো** *vt* **1** cause to endeavour/ practise arduously or austerely. **2** make sb to practise. **3** cause to implore/ request earnestly. **~সাধি** *n* entreaty; plea; earnest request; importunity. **~সাধি করা** *vt* entreat; implore; make repeated requests.

সাধারণ *adj* **1** general; common; belonging/ applicable to all or many; common to all: ~ সভা. **2** ordinary; usual; trite; banal: ~ কথা. **3** public: ~ গ্রন্থাগার. **4** universal: ~ মত. **5** trifling; venial: ~ অপরাধ. **6** generic: ~ নাম. ❑*n* public; people; commonalty. **সাধারণী** *fem*. **~ কৃত্যক** *n* general service. **~ত, ~তঃ** *adv* generally; usually; commonly; ordinarily. **~তা, ~ত্ব** *n* commonness; ordinariness; banality; universality. **~তন্ত্র** *n* republic. **~তন্ত্রবাদী, ~তন্ত্রী** *nn, adjj* republican. **~ ধর্ম** *n* common quality; general property/ characteristic. **~ভাবে** *adv* generally; usually; in general terms; ordinarily; commonly. **~ শিক্ষা** *n* general education. **সাধারণ্য** *n* **1** commonness; universality. **2** general properties/ characteristics. **3** public; people; commonalty.

সাধিকা *adj, n fem* ⇒ সাধক

সাধিত *adj* **1** brought about; accomplished; performed; attained; completed. **2** (gram) derived; formed: ~ শব্দ. **3** practised/ endeavoured austerely or arduously. **4** proved. **~ ধাতু** *n* derivative verb. **~ শব্দ** *n* derivative.

সাধিত্র *n* means; tool; instrument; apparatus; appliance.

সাধিষ্ঠ *adj* most proper/ right; most honest.

সাধু *adj* **1** good; excellent; virtuous; honest; pious; righteous; honourable; saintly. **2** well-born; noble; of honourable/ respectable descent. **3** correct; pure; refined; classical: ~ ভাষা. **4** proper; appropriate; idiomatic; elegant; chaste; polite: ~ প্রয়োগ. ❑*n* **1** saint; holy man; ascetic. **2** trader; usurer; money-lender. ❑*int* excellent ! bravo! **~গিরি** *n* show of righteousness; simulation of piety/ goodness/ honesty; sanctimoniousness. **~তা** *n* **1** honesty; uprightness; goodness; righteousness; saintliness; piety; virtuousness; integrity; piousness. **2** correctness; excellence. **3** nobility. **~তাচরণ** *n* good conduct; honest/ virtuous/ upright/ good behaviour; practice of piety/ virtue. **~বাদ** *n* applause; accolade; praise; approbation; approval; thanksgiving. **~বাদ দেওয়া** *vt* applaud; praise; acclaim; thank. **~বৃত্ত** *adj* having good manners; virtuous; honest. **~ ভাষা** *n* classical language; elegant/ polished/ chaste language (one of the two styles of Bengali prose (cf চলিত ভাষা). **~শীল** *adj* righteous; virtuously inclined; virtuous. **~সঙ্গ, ~সংসর্গ** *nn* association with the good/ saints and ascetics; company of saints and ascetics; good company. **~সম্মত** *adj* approved by the good; honest; virtuous. **~সাবধান** (lit) O merchant, beware of the thief/ swindler; (fig) beware of the danger.

সাধে *adv* of one's own accord; willingly; for nothing: ~ কি আর বলি ...?

সাধ্য *adj* **1** within one's power; within the range of one's capability. **2** capable of being done/ accomplished/ attained; practicable; feasible; attainable. **3** to be accomplished/ brought about/ fulfilled/ effected/ attained. **4** to be proved/ demonstrated. **5** curable. ❑*n* **1** capability; feasibility; attainability; range of one's capability: সাধ্যের বাইরে, beyond one's power. **2** (logic) major term. **~তা** *n* practicableness; feasibility; curableness; attainability. **~পক্ষে** *adv* to the best of one's ability; as much as one can do. **~পাল** *n* bailiff. **~বহির্ভূত** *adj* beyond the range of one's capability; beyond one's power. **~মতো, ~মতে, সাধ্যানুরূপ, সাধ্যানুযায়ী** *adv*=~পক্ষে. ❑*adj* within one's power; within the range of one's capability. **~সাধনা** *n* earnest plea/ entreaty; repeated importunities/ solicitations. **সাধ্যাতিরিক্ত, সাধ্যাতীত** *adj*=~বহির্ভূত. **সাধ্যানুসারে** *adv*=~পক্ষে. **সাধ্যাবয়ব** *n* (logic) major term. **সাধ্যাসাধ্য** *adj* practicable and unpracticable.

সাধ্বী *adj fem* of সাধু. ❑*n* chaste/ virtuous woman; faithful wife.

সান=শান

সানক, সানকি [A] *nn* earthenware plate/ dish.

সানন্দ *adj* joyful; glad; happy; pleased. **সানন্দে** *adv* joyfully; gladly; with delight/ pleasure; readily; cheerfully; happily.

সানপেটা *adj* paved; concrete.

সানা[1]=শানা[1]

সানা[2] *vt* knead.

সানাই [P] *n* kind of wooden flute.

সানানো *vt* cover; suffice: এতো অল্পে সানায় না.

সানি [A] *adj* second. ❑*n* match; equal; the second. **~ বিচার** *n* retrial.

সানু *n* table-land; mountain-ridge; plateau; foot of a hill.

সানুকম্প *adj* full of pity; compassionate; tender; kind.

সানুকূল *adj* agreeable; favourable.

সানুচর *adj* having attendants; with followers.

সানুজ *adj* accompanied by/ along with a younger brother.

সানুদেশ=সানু

সানুনয় *adj* entreating; imploring; full of entreaty/ supplication; begging; beseeching; supplicatory. **~ প্রার্থনা** *n* humble prayer; supplication. **সানুনয়ে** *adv* imploringly; entreatingly.

সানুনাসিক *adj* nasal; nasalized; singing through the nose.

সানুভব *adj* subjective.

সানুমান *n* mountain.

সানুরাগ *adj* full of love; feeling/ betraying passion; affectionate; loving; enamoured.

সান্টিং [E] *n* shunting.

সান্ত *adj* 1 finite; limited. 2 ending in 'স'.

সান্তর *adj* having space/ an interval/ interstices.

সান্তরাল *adj* having an interval.

সান্তারা [Pg] *n* an orange-like fruit.

সান্ত্রী [E] *n* sentry; armed guard/ watchman; soldier on guard.

সান্ত্বন *n* consolation; soothing with kind words; act of appeasing; solace.

সান্ত্বনা *n*=সান্ত্বন. ~ দেওয়া *vt* console; comfort; solace; soothe; address kindly/ gently. ~কারী, ~দাতা *nn* one who consoles/ comforts; comforter. ~কারিণী, ~দাত্রী *fem*. ~দান=সান্ত্বন. ~দায়ক, ~প্রদ *adj* consoling; comforting; soothing; consolatory; solaceful. ~বাক্য *n* comforting/ consolatory speech or words.

সান্ত্বনিত *adj* comforted; consoled; soothed.

সান্ত্বনীয় *adj* to be comforted/ consoled/ soothed.

সান্দ্র *adj* 1 thick; solid; compact; dense; intense. 2 unctuous; viscid; oily; viscous. 3 smooth; soft; tender; bland. ~তা *n* thickness; denseness; density; intensity; viscosity. ~তাঙ্ক *n* coefficient of viscosity. ~তামাপক *n* viscometer.

সান্ধা(নো) *vt* (old use) enter; penetrate.

সান্ধ্য *adj* of evening; relating to the evening twilight; vespertine. ~-তারকা, ~ তারা *n* evening star; vesper. ~ দীপ *n* evening-lamp. ~ পরিচ্ছদ *n* evening dress. ~ বায়ু, ~ সমীরণ *nn* evening breeze. ~ ভোজন *n* evening meal; dinner. ~ ভ্রমণ *n* evening walk. ~ সঙ্গীত *n* evening song. ~ সম্মিলনী, ~ সম্মেলন *nn* evening party. সান্ধ্যাকাশ *n* evening sky.

সান্নিধ্য *n* nearness; vicinity; presence; proximity; closeness; company: বন্ধুর ~. ~ এড়ানো *vi* give a wide berth to.

সান্নিপাতিক *adj* 1 complicated (esp applied to a dangerous illness produced by a combined derangement of the three humours). 2 coming into close contact/ conjunction; coalescing. ~ জ্বর *n* typhoid; enteric fever.

সান্ন্যাসিক *n* religious mendicant.

সান্বয় *adj* 1 related to; closely connected with. 2 with grammatical connections made explicit: ~ টীকা.

সাপ *n* snake; serpent. সাপিনী *fem*. ~খোপ, ~টাপ *nn* snakes and similar animals. ~ও মরে, লাঠিও না ভাঙে accomplish a difficult job without sustaining any loss or damage. ~ হয়ে কাটা আর ওঝা হয়ে ঝাড়া (fig) to hunt with the hound and run with the hare. সাপে নেউলে (সম্পর্ক) (fig) perpetual enmity as that existing between the snake and the mongoose; eternal enmity. সাপের ছুঁচো গেলা (fig) involvement in a nasty affair which cannot now be shaken off; a bitter pill to swallow. সাপের পাঁচ পা দেখা (fig) get extremely audacious as if one has come into possession of some rare power; get above oneself. সাপের লেজে পা দেওয়া (fig) to antagonize a powerful man; provoke a deadly enemy. সাপের হাই/হাঁচি বেদেয় চেনে (fig) A jeweller knows the shine of a gem. সাপের হাঁড়ি (fig) virago; hellcat; termagant; fury.

সাপট *n* (omon) 1 violent stroke (as with a tail); flam. 2 loud bragging; bullying; vaunt. 3 violence; fury; rage: বাতাসের ~.

সাপটা *adj* 1 ordinary; drab; flat: ~ জলপান. 2 in lump; gross: ~ দর. ❑*adv* in lump and without discrimination: ~ কেনা.

সাপটানো *vt* hug; clasp; embrace; cradle in one's arms; cuddle.

সাপটাসাপটি *n* mutual hugging/ clasping. ❑*adj* locked in an embrace.

সাপত্ন, সাপত্ন্য *n* 1 half-brother; rival; enmity. 2 enmity/ rivalry among the wives of the same husband. 3 relationship of children born from different wives of the same husband. ❑*adj* born from a rival or fellow-wife.

সাপরাধ *adj* having faults; criminal; guilty.

সাপুড়ে *n* snake-charmer.

সাপেক্ষ *adj* 1 relative. 2 depending/ dependent on; subject to; governed by a particular stipulation; presupposing/ requiring anything. ~তা, সাপেক্ষ্য *nn* relativity. সাপেক্ষানুমান *n* (logic) mediate interference.

সাপোট=সাপট

সাপ্টা=সাপটা

সাপ্তপদীন *n* friendship; intimacy.

সাপ্তাহিক *adj* weekly. ❑*n* weekly magazine.

সাফ [A] *adj* 1 clean; cleansed; pure; clear. 2 clear-cut; frank; unequivocal; precise: ~ কথা. 3 innocent. 4 apparent; obvious. 5 thorough; obvious: ~ মিথ্যা. 6 empty; emptied; cleaned out: পকেট ~. 7 plain; simple. 8 feed of obstruction; cleared: পালাবার পথ ~. 9 decimated; completely destroyed; annihilated: বংশ ~. 10 unconditional. ❑*adv* clearly; cleanly; entirely; completely; thoroughly. ~ করা *vt* 1 clean; cleanse; purify; wash. 2 make clear. 3 eliminate; annihilate; destroy utterly. 4 clean out; empty. পকেট ~ করা pick sb's pocket. ~ কথা *n* clear-cut words; final words. ~ কবালা *n* deed of conveyance/ outright sale. ~ জবাব *n* straight answer; sharp retort; complete denial. ~ সাফ *adv* plainly; openly; flatly.

সাফল্য *n* success; fruitfulness; result; profitableness. ~মণ্ডিত *adj* crowned with success; successful.

সাফা [A] *adj* pure; clean; clear; brilliant; polished. ❑*n* name of a hill near Mecca. **~ই** *n* **1** purity; cleanliness; clearness. **2** cleansing. **3** exculpation; vindication of innocence; exonerative explanation. **সাফাই গাওয়া** *vt* plead innocence; plead not guilty. **সাফাই দেওয়া** *vt* advance arguments to vindicate innocence. **সাফাই সাক্ষী** *n* witness vindicating the innocence of the accused.

সাফায়াত=শাফায়াত

সাব- [E] *pref* sub-. **~ইনস্পেক্টর** *n* sub-inspector. **~এডিটর** *n* sub-editor. **~কমিটি** *n* sub-committee. **~জজ** *n* sub-judge. **~রেজিস্ট্রার** *n* sub-registrar.

সাবকাশ *adj* having leisure/ an opportunity. ❑*n* leisure; good opportunity.

সাবড়ানো=সাবাড় করা

সাবধান *adj* attentive; careful; heedful; cautious; on the alert; on one's guard. ❑*n int* be careful; take care; be on guard. **~ করা** *vt* caution; warn. **~তা** *n* carefulness; cautiousness; alertness; heedfulness; attention. **সাবধানের মার নেই** (prov) safe bind safe find. **সাবধানে** *adv* carefully; cautiously; attentively.

সাবধানী *adj*=সাবধান

সাবন *n* **1** solar day. **2** solar month. ❑*adj* solar: ~ মাস.

সাবমেরিন [E] *n* submarine.

সাবয়ব *adj* having a body/ parts; corporeal. **~ত্ব** *n* the being composed of parts; corporeality.

সাবলীল *adj* effortless; easy; facile; smooth; artistic; playful. **~তা** *n* effortlessness; facility; playfulness; case.

সাবশেষ *adj* having a remainder; incomplete.

সাবহিত *adj* giving attention: attentive; cautious.

সাবাড় *adj* **1** finished. **2** thoroughly consumed/ spent: eaten up. **3** killed; murdered; done in; utterly ruined/ destroyed. **~ করা** *vt* **1** finish. **2** spend/ consume thoroughly. **3** kill; slay; murder; do in; ruin/ destroy utterly.

সাবান [A] *n* soap. **~ মাখা/মাখানো** *vt* soap. **একখণ্ড গোটা ~** *n* cake of soap. **এক চাকা গোটা ~** *n* soap-ball. **এক টুকরো ~** *n* piece of soap. **~ কৌটা** *n* soap-case; soap-dish. **~তুল্য** *adj* saponaceous; soap. **~ভবন** *n* (chem) saponification. **সাবানের ফেনা** *n* soap-suds; lather.

সাবালক *adj* of age. **সাবালিকা** *fem*. **~ হওয়া** *vi* come of age; reach majority; attain adulthood. **~ত্ব** *n* full age; adulthood; majority. **সাবালকী** =~ত্ব.

সাবাস = শাবাশ

সাবিত্রী *n fem* name of a verse/ prayer addressed to Savitri (সাবিতৃ) or the Sun.

সাবু *n* (dial)=সাগু

সাবুদ, সাবুৎ [A] *n* firmness; constancy; proof; evidence; testimony; demonstration. ❑*adj* firm; constant; confirmed: ঈমান ~. **~ করা** *vt* prove; demonstrate; vindicate; correct; confirm.

সাবেঈন [A] *n* Sabian.

সাবেক [A] *adj* former; prior; preceding; foregoing; old; ancient; past; original; first. **~কেলে** *adj* old-fashioned; out-moded; out-dated. **সাবেকি, সাবেকী** *adj* of old; old-fashioned; dated; of old school; obsolete; moth-eaten.

সাবেত, সাবিত [A] *adj* firm; steady; immovable; resolute. constant. **~ করা** *vt* prove; verify; confirm; establish.

সাব্যস্ত *adj* **1** adjudged; adjudicated; ascertained. **2** decided; fixed; resolved. **~ করা** *vt* **1** adjudge; adjudicate; ascertain. **2** decide; fix; resolve; settle.

সাম *n* **1** (also ~বেদ) one of the three principal Vedas; 'Veda of chants'. **2** hymn/ psalm of the Samveda. **3** conciliation; negotiation.

সামগ্রিক *adj* general; total.

সামগ্রী *n* complete collection/ assemblage of implements or materials; thing; article; apparatus; baggage; goods and chattels; effects; things.

সামগ্র্য *n* totality; entirety; completeness.

সামঞ্জস্য *n* **1** fitness; propriety. **2** congruity. **3** harmony; agreement; symmetry; adjustment; mutual understanding. **~ বিধান করা** *vt* harmonize; adjust: bring into agreement.

সামনা *n* front; face; forepart; surface usually presented. **~সামনি** *adj, adv* face-to-face with; facing each other; in presence of.

সামনে *prep* in front of; before; in the face of; facing; opposite to; on the face/ surface of.

সামন্ত *n* **1** vassal; feudatory prince; chief of a district. **2** minister. **3** leader; general; captain; champion; commander, chieftain. **~চক্র, ~তন্ত্র** *nn* feudal system; feudalism. **~ নৃপতি** *n* feudal prince. **~ রাজ্য** *n* feudal state; dependency.

সামন্তরিক = সামান্তরিক

সামবায়িক *adj* co-operative; belonging to/ frequenting an assembly. ❑*n* **1** minister; counsellor; member of an assembly. **2** co-operator; member of a co-operative society.

সাময়িক *adj* **1** temporary; provisional; periodic; periodical. **2** seasonable; timely: ~ ব্যবস্থা. **3** current: ~ খবর; published periodically: ~ পত্র. **~ উত্তেজনা** *n* momentary excitement/ impulse; heat/ spur of the moment. **~ উত্তেজনাবশে** on the spur/ in the heat of the moment. **~ পত্রিকা** *n* periodical. **সাময়িকী** *n* **1** current event/ topic. **2** periodical.

সামরিক *adj* relating to war; military; martial; war-like. ~ **আইন** *n* martial law. ~ **আদালত** *n* martial law court. ~ **জাতি** *n* martial race. ~ **দণ্ডবিধি** *n* martial law. ~ **পোত** *n* warship. ~ **বিচারালয়** *n* court-martial. ~ **শক্তি** military power/ strength. ~ **শিক্ষা** *n* military training.

সামর্থ্য *n* **1** ability; capacity; capability; efficiency. **2** fitness. **3** strength; power. ~ **বাধ** *n* efficiency bar.

সামলা=শামলা

সামলানো *vt* **1** save; protect; keep safe; guard. **2** check; restrain: লোভ ~. **3** manage; manage to keep in the proper place: কাপড় ~. **4** tide over; surmount: রোগ/বিপদ সামলে ওঠা. **5** wield: তরবারি ~.

সামাই[1] *n* patience.

সামাই[2] *n* **1** holding capacity. **2** room; space.

সামাজিক *adj* **1** social. **2** pertaining to social formalities: ceremonious; formal. **3** sociable; companionable: ~ লোক. ~**তা** *n* formalities; sociableness; formal gift. ~**তা করা** *vi* do/ perform social duties; observe formalities; meet social obligations; bestow a gift on a ceremonial occasion. ~ **প্রথা** *n* social customs. ~ **মৃত্যু** *n* civil death.

সামান [P] *n* necessaries; furniture; apparatus; tools; instruments.

সামান্তরিক *n* parallelogram. ~-**সূত্র, বল**-~ *nn* (mech) parallelogram of forces.

সামান্য *adj* **1** universal; general; generic. **2** shared by others; joint; common (to). **3** common; common-place; vulgar; ordinary; insignificant; banal; trite; low: ~ লোক. **4** very small in number/ amount/ degree; paltry. **5** (math) vulgar. ❑*n* **1** (logic) genus. **2** common/ generic property. **সামান্যা** *fem.* ~**ত** *adj* generally; in general. ~**তা**, ~**ত্ব** *nn* state of generality; ordinariness; commonness. ~ **ধর্ম** *n* common/ general/ general property or characteristic. ~ **ভগ্নাঙ্ক**, ~ **ভগ্নাংশ** *n* vulgar fraction. ~ **মিশ্র** *n* (chem) mechanical mixture. ~ **লক্ষণ** *n* general definition; common/ general/ generic character or sign. ~-**লক্ষণা** *n* intuition. ~ **সমীকরণ** *n* (alg) single equation. **সামান্যাভিধান** *n* connotation.

সামান্যা *n fem* common female; prostitute.

সামান্যীকরণ *n* generalization.

সামাল *n* **1** protection. **2** check. **3** patience. ❑*int* beware; take care; be on guard. ~ **করা/দেওয়া** *vt* check; manage; manage to keep in position/ safe/ steady.

সামিয়ানা=শামিয়ানা

সামিল=শামিল

সামীপ্য *n* nearness; proximity; contiguity; presence; company; neighbourhood.

সামুদয়িক *adj* collective; entire; total; general; comprehensive.

সামুদ্র *adj* relating to the sea; oceanic; marine; maritime. ❑*n* **1** impression/ mark on the body. **2** mariner; voyager; sailor. ~ **জলবায়ু** *n* maritime/ oceanic climate.

সামুদ্রক *adj* **1**=সামুদ্র. **2** relating to marks on the body; relating to good or bad fortune. ❑*n* art of interpreting marks on the body; palmistry. ~ **বিদ্যা** *n* palmistry.

সামুদ্রিক *adj*=সামুদ্র. ~ **উদ্ভিদ** *n* seaweed; sea-plant. ~ **জাতি** *n* maritime race. ~ **জীব** *n* pelagic deposit. ~ **দস্যু** *n* pirate. ~ **বাণিজ্য** *n* maritime trade; sea trade. ~**যাত্রা** *n* voyage.

সামূহিক *adj* collective.

সাম্পান *n* sampan.

সাম্প্রতিক *adj* recent; current; contemporary; present.

সাম্প্রদায়িক *adj* communal; sectarian. ~**তা** *n* communalism; sectarianism. ~ **দাঙ্গা** *n* communal riot. ~ **বাটোয়ারা** *n* communal award.

সাম্য *n* **1** equality; evenness; equilibrium; equipoise; equal/ normal state. **2** similarity; similitude. **3** balance; mental equilibrium. **4** communism. ~**কেন্দ্র** *n* centre of equilibrium. ~**বাদ** *n* communism. ~**বাদী** *n, adj* communist; communistic. ~ **বিন্দু** *n* (geom) similitude. ~ **রক্ষা** *n* maintenance of balance/ equilibrium.

সাম্রাজ্য *n* empire. ~**বাদ** *n* imperialism. ~**বাদী** *n, adj* imperialist; imperialistic.

সাম্রাজ্যিকতা *n* imperialism.

সাযুজ্য *n* **1** intimate union; communion with. **2** identification; absorption; unification; oneness. **3** one of the four grades of salvation; absorption into the divine essence.

সায়[1] *n* consent; assent: ~ দেওয়া.

সায়[2] *n* termination. ❑*adj* ended. ~ **করা** *vt* end; finish: গান যখন ~ করা হলো.

সায়ংকাল *n* evening; even-tide. **সায়ংকালীন** *adj* of the evening; evening; vespertine. **সায়ংকালীন প্রার্থনা** *n* evening prayer.

সায়ংকৃত্য *n* prayer and other things to be done in the evening; evening service.

সায়ংসন্ধ্যা *n* **1** evening prayer. **2** evening twilight.

সায়ক=শায়ক

সায়ন *n* (astron) declination; equinox.

সায়ন্তন=সায়ংকালীন (⇒ সায়ংকাল)

সায়মাশ *n* evening meal; supper.

সায়র *n* (poet) sea; large pond.

সায়া [P] *n* petticoat.

সায়াহ্ন *n* eventide; evenfall; evening. ~**কাল**=সায়ংকাল. ~**কৃত্য**=সায়ংকৃত্য.

সায়ুধ *adj* furnished with arms; armed.

সায়েব *n* (colloq)=সাহেব

সায়ের [A] *n* walk; excursion; taking the air; perambulation; strolling.

সায়েল, সায়িল *n* [A] petitioner; applicant; beggar; mendicant.

সায়েলি *n* begging; mendicancy.
সায়েস্তা=শায়েস্তা
সার[১] *n* **1** core/ pith/ solid interior of anything; sap. **2** substance/ essence/ marrow/ cream/ essential part of anything; quintessence; extract; best part. **3** firmness; power; vigour; energy; spirit. **4** real meaning; main point: ~ কথা. **5** compendium; summary; epitome; gist; substance. **6** dung; manure; fertilizer. **7** worth; value; wealth; property; riches; goods. ☐*adj* precious; valuable; good; sound; best; excellent; essential; true; real; inner. **~ করা** *vt* regard sth as the best/ sole object; choose as the sole object of pursuit; go all out for; set one's heart on. **~ বোঝা** *vt* regard sth as the best/ sole object of pursuit. **~ দেওয়া** *vt* manure; use manure/ fertilizer. **~ কথা** *n* gist; sum and substance; essence; burden. **~বুড়, ~গাদা, ~ডোবা** *n* dung-hill; manure-pit. **~গর্ভ** *adj* substantial; rich in content. **~গুণ** *n* chief/ principal virtue. **~গ্রন্থ** *n* compendium; manual; vademecum. **~গ্রাহী** *adj* capable of extracting/ apprehending the essence/ best part of sth. **~জ** *n* (fresh) butter. **~ত** *adj* essentially. **~তা, ~ত্ব** *nn* firmness; solidity; worth; values. **~বত্তা** *n* substantiality; real worth; merit; inner substance; hardness. **~বর্জিত** *adj* devoid of substance; sapless; pithless. **~বস্তু** *n* essence; inner substance; quintessence; core; gist. **~বান** *adj* substantial; nourishing; hard; solid; firm; strong; valuable; precious; sappy; pithy; full of substance; fertile; essential. **~ভূত** *adj* being the chief thing; best; most excellent; substantial. **~মর্ম** *n* précis; gist; essence. **~মাটি** *n* marl; manure. **~লোহ** *n* steel. **~শূন্য, ~হীন** *adj* devoid of value; worthless; sapless; pithless. **~সংগ্রহ, ~সঙ্কলন** *nn* collection/ compilation of the substantial/ best specimens; compendium. **উদ্ভিজ্জ ~** *n* vegetable manure. **খনিজ ~** *n* mineral fertilizer. **প্রাণিজ/প্রাণী-~** *n* animal fertilizer. **মিশ্র ~** *n* compost.
সার[২] *n* row; line. **~ দেওয়া** *vi* arrange in a row; array; line (up). **~বন্দি**=সারিবন্দি.
সার[৩] *n* (rhet) climax.
সারং *n* name of a stringed instrument.
সারগম=সার্গম
সারঙ *n* name of a musical mode.
সারঙ্গ *n* **1**=সারঙ. **2** name of a stringed instrument. **3** a variety of spotted deer. ☐*adj* of variegated colour; dappled. **সারঙ্গা, সারঙ্গী** *fem.*
সারঙ্গী *n* **1**=সারঙ্গ (2). **2** a sarangi-player.
সারণি, সারণী *n* **1** stream; channel; water-pipe. **2** table. **সারণিত** *adj* tabled. **সারণিকরণ, সারণীকরণ** *n* tabling. **সারণিবদ্ধ, সারণীবদ্ধ** *adj* tabular. **সারণিভুক্ত, সারণীভুক্ত** *adj* tabled.
সারণিক *n* traveller.
সারথি *n* charioteer; driver of a car; coachman.
সারথ্য *n* office of a charioteer/ coachman charioteering.
সারদা=শারদা
সারবন্দি=সারিবন্দি
সারমেয় *n* dog. **সারমেয়ী** *fem* bitch.
সারল্য *n* simplicity; straightness; rectitude; sincerity; honesty (⇒ সরলতা).
সারস *n* a kind of bird with a long neck and beak; kingstork.
সারসী *n* **1** Indian/ Siberian crane; stork. **2** swan. **সারসী** *fem.*
সারসন *n* **1** belt; girdle. **2** woman zone/ girdle (said to be formed of 25 strings).
সারস্বত *adj* **1** relating/ belonging to Saraswati (the goddess or the river). **2** learned; eloquent. **~ সমাজ** *n* learned people/ society.
সারস্বতোৎসব *n* festival in honour of Saraswati.
সারা[১] *vt* **1** hide; conceal; keep in a safe place: গয়নাগুলি সে সেরে রেখেছে. **2** finish; accomplish; conclude: কাজ ~. **3** give; apply; utter: হাঁক ~. **4** kill; finish off; destroy: ডাকাতরা তাকে সেরে ফেলেছে. **5** mend; repair: ঘড়ি ~. **6** cure; heal; be cured; restored/ improved; restore; improve; recover; come round: রোগ ~, স্বাস্থ্য ~, রোগী সেরে উঠেছে. **7** ruin; undo: অনিয়মই তাকে সেরেছে. **8** correct; rectify: ভুল ~, স্বভাব ~. ☐*adj* **1** finished; tired; weary; harassed; exhausted; ready to drop; fatigued; dead-tired: খুঁজে খুঁজে ~. **2** repaired; mended. **3** corrected. **~নো** *vt* **1** mend; repair. **2** rectify; correct. **3** cure; heal; restore; improve.
সারা[২] *adj* whole; entire; all. **~ক্ষণ** all the time. **~ জীবন** all life; throughout the whole of one's life. **~ দিন** all day; all day long; the whole day. **~ বৎসর** all (the) year round; at all times of the year; the whole year. **~ বেলা** throughout the whole of the forenoon/ afternoon; throughout the whole of the period/ time. **~ মাস** throughout the whole of the month. **~ রাত** all night (long); the whole night; throughout the whole night. **~ সকাল** the whole morning. **~ সন্ধ্যা** the whole evening.
সারাংশ *n* substance; summary; essence; gist; abstract; précis; pith.
সারাৎসার *n* essence; quintessence; the best (of).
সারানি, সারাণি *n* end. **~ ভাঁটা** *n* end/ cessation of ebb tide; slack water at ebb tide.
সারালো=সারাবান (⇒ সার)
সারি[১] *n* row; line; column; range; string; series. **~বন্দি** *adj* arranged in a row/ line; alined; aligned; arrayed. **~ সারি** *adv* in rows/ lines; serially; rows of.
সারি[২] *n* kind of folk-song in Bangladesh sung esp by boatmen.

সারি[৩], **সারিকা, সারিগামা, সারিন্দা**=শারি[১], শারিকা, সারেগামা, সারঙ্গ (2) respectively.
সারী=শারী
সারূপ্য *n* **1** sameness/ similarity of form; identity of appearance; resemblance; likeness; conformity with. **2** assimilation to/ conformity with the deity (one of the grades of beatitude).
সারেং[১], **সারেঙ**[১]=সারং
সারেং[২], **সারেঙ**[২] [P] *n* boatswain; serang.
সারেগামা *n* (music) **1** the first four notes in the musical octave. **2** musical notation. **3** elementary lessons in music; (fig) elementary knowledge.
সারেঙ ⇒ সারেং
সারেঙ্গ=সারেং
সারেঙ্গী=সারঙ্গী
সারেজাহান [P] *n* the whole world.
সারেসার *adv*=সারি সারি (⇒ সারি[১])
সারোদ্ধার *n* extraction of the true significance; essence; essential point; core. **সারোদ্ধারে** *adv* in brief; in short; in a nutshell.
সার্কাস [E] *n* circus. ~ **দেখানো** *vi* hold/ give a circus-show. ~-**খেলোয়াড়** *n* showman of a circus. **সার্কাসি** *adj* of circus.
সার্কুলার [E] *n* circular.
সারগম *n* (music) octave, gamut.
সার্চ [E] *n* search. ~**লাইট** *n* searchlight.
সার্জন [E] *n* surgeon
সার্জেন, সার্জেন্ট [E] *n* sergeant; police-sergeant.
সার্ট [E] *n* shirt.
সার্টিফিকেট [E] *n* certificate. ~ **দেওয়া** *vt* give (one) a certificate; certify.
সার্থ *adj* **1** having meaning/ purport; significant; meaningful; important. **2** having property; wealthy; opulent. **3** successful. **4** useful. ❑*n* **1** travelling company of traders/ pilgrims; caravan. **2** companion. **3** troop; collection of men. **4** multitude of similar animals; herd; flock. **5** member of any company. **6** firm. ~**নিবন্ধক** *n* registrar of firms. ~**বাহ** *n* **1** leader/ conductor of a company; merchant; trader. **2** company of/ caravan of traders/ merchants. **3** guide.
সার্থক *adj* having meaning; significant; meaningful; successful; useful; effective; realized; gratified. ~**জন্মা** *n* successful in life. ~**তা**, ~**ত্ব** *nn* significance; success; use; utility; efficacy; effectiveness; realization; gratification. ~**নামা** *adj* one who has fully justified his name; renowned; famous.
সার্ধ *adj* one and half; plus one half.
সার্ব *adj* relating to all; fit/ good for all; universal; general. ~**কালিক** *adj* of/ belonging to all times; suited to all seasons; everlasting; eternal; perpetual. ~**জাতিক** *adj* relating/ belonging to all nations; international; universal. ~**জাতিকতা** *n* **1** universal/ international brotherhood. **2** universality; internationalism. ~**জাতিক ভ্রাতৃত্ব**=~জাতিকতা (1). ~**ত্রিক** *adj* of all places; all-pervading; omnipresent. ~**দেশিক**, ~**দেশীয়** *adjj*=সর্বদেশীয় (⇒ সর্ব). ~**ধাতুক** *adj* applicable to the whole of a radical term or to the complete form of the verbal base. ~**নামিক** *n* relating to a pronoun/ pronominal. ~**ভৌম** *adj* relating to/ consisting of/ ruling over the whole earth; known throughout the world; comprising the whole world; supreme; sovereign; world-wide; having world-wide fame. ❑*n* emperor; universal monarch; sovereign (ruler). ~**ভৌমত্ব** *n* sovereignty. ~**রাষ্ট্রিক** *adj* pertaining to all states; international; universal. ~**লৌকিক** *adj* prevailing throughout/ common to the whole world; known by/ permitted by every one; common; universal.
সার্বিক *adj* **1** general; overall; universal. **2** whole; total.
সার্ভে [E] *n* survey. ~**য়ার** *n* surveyor.
সার্ষপ *adj* made of/ derived from mustard.
সার্সি, সার্শী=শার্শি
সাল[১]=শাল
সাল[২] [P] *n* **1** year; era. ~**তামামি** *n* **1** year-closing. **2** annual report/ review. **3** annual accounts/ balance-sheet.
সালওয়ার *n* trousers; breeches; pantaloon.
সালগম *n* turnip.
সালঙ্কার, সালংকার *adj* **1** having ornaments/ decorations; decorated; adorned; embellished with ornaments; ornamented; rich in ornament. **2** (of language) ornate; full of flowery language. **সালঙ্কারা** *fem*.
সালতি=শালতি
সালন, সালুন *nn* curry.
সালমমিছরি *n* salep.
সালসা [Pg] *n* Ayurvedic tonic; elixir.
সালাত [A] *n* prayer; supplication; benediction.
সালাদ [E] *n* salad.
সালাম [A] *n* **1** peace. **2** salutation. **3** good-bye. ~ **আলাইকুম** peace be with you. ~ **করা** *vt* salute. ~ **দেওয়া** salute; send one's compliments; express the desire to call on a person. ~ **নেওয়া** accept and return salutation (of). ~ **ফিরানো** finish the prayer.
সালামত [A] *adj* safe; well; sound. ❑*n* safety; peace; security; well-being; health.
সালামতি *n*=সালামত
সালামি, সালামী [A] *n* **1** salutation; reception; welcome. **2** present; gift.
সালার [P] *n* commander; chief; leader; general; captain.
সালিক[১]=শালিক
সালিক[২] [A] *n* traveller; devotee.

সালিয়ানা [P] *n* annual grant/ stipend/ fee/ rent. ❑*adj* annual; yearly. ❑*adj* annually.

সালিশ, সালিস [A] *n* third person; arbitrator; mediator; arbiter; judge. **~নামা** *n* deed of award; award by arbitration. **সালিশের রায়** *n* arbitrament; arbitrement.

সালিশি, সালিসি *n* arbitration; mediation. ❑*adj* arbitral; under arbitration. **~ করা** *vt* arbitrate; mediate.

সালু=শালু

সালুক=শালুক

সালিক=সালিক[২]

সালোকসংশ্লেষ *n* photosynthesis.

সালোক্য *n* form of salvation which enables one to live with God in the same heaven.

সালোয়ার=সালওয়ার

সার্শি, সার্শি *nn*=শার্শি

সাশ্রয় *n* cut in expenditure; saving; economy.

সাশ্রু *adj* tearful; shedding tears; full of tears; with tears. **~নয়ন, ~লোচন** *adjj* having tearful eyes. **~নয়নে, ~লোচনে** *advv* with tearful eyes.

সাষ্টাঙ্গ *adj* performed with eight limbs/ members (as a reverential prostration of the body so as to touch the ground with the hands, breast, forehead, knees and feet). **সাষ্টাঙ্গে** *adv* touching the ground with one's eight limbs; lying at full length with one's face to the ground.

সাহঙ্কার, সাহংকার *adj* proud; arrogant; conceited; full of pride/ vanity. **সাহঙ্কারে, সাহংকারে** *advv* proudly; conceitedly; haughtily.

সাহচর্য *n* companionship; fellowship; society; association; company; cooperation; help.

সাহজিক *adj* innate; natural; instinctive.

সাহস *n* boldness; daring; temerity; courage; bravery; intrepidity; audacity. **~ করা** *vi* dare; brave; venture; make bold; hazard; down the gauntlet.

সাহসিক *adj* bold; daring; impetuous; brave; courageous; audacious; intrepid; rash. **~তা** *n*=সাহস.

সাহসী=সাহসিক. **~ হওয়া** *vi* be brave/ courageous/ audacious; dare; venture. **সাহসিনী** *fem*.

সাহানা=শাহানা[১]

সাহাবি, সাহাবী [A] *n* one of the companions of the Holy Prophet.

সাহায়ক *adj* subsidiary.

সাহায্য *n* **1** help; assistance; aid; support; succour; backing; patronization; lift. **2** gratuitous gift; donation. **3** (derog) abatement; collaboration. **~ করা** *n* help; assist; give assistance; aid; support; back; lend a hand; give help; succour; patronize; donate; abet; collaborate. **~কারক, ~কারী** *adjj* helping; assisting; aiding; supporting; helpful; patronizing, conducive; abetting; collaborating ancillary. ❑*n* helper; assistant; help; helping hand; partner; supporter; patron; collaborator abettor. **~কারিণী** *fem*. **~কৃত** *adj* helped; aided; assisted; supported. **~ দান** *n* give of help assistance. **~ দান করা**=~ করা. **~ দেওয়া**=~ করা. **~ পাওয়া/লাভ করা** *vt* get help/ assistance be helped/ aided/ succoured. **~প্রাপ্ত** *ad* aided; in receipt of help/ assistance aid. **~প্রাপ্ত স্কুল** *n* aided school; school in receipt of grant-in-aid. **~প্রার্থী, ~-ভিখারি** *nn* one who seeks help. **~প্রার্থিনী** *fem* **সাহায্যার্থ, সাহায্যার্থে** *adv* in aid of; for help.

সাহারা [A] *n* **1** desert. **2** the Sahara.

সাহিত্য *n* **1** literature; polite literature; belles-lettres. **2** composition; writing. **3** association; connection; combination; society. **~কলা** *n* art of literary composition. **~ক্ষেত্র** *n* field/domain of literature. **~ চর্চা** *n* literary pursuit/ discussion. **~ চর্চা করা** *vt* cultivate/ study literature; engage oneself in literary pursuits. **~জগৎ** *n* world of letters; literary world. **~জীবী** *n* literary man; man of letters; litterateur. **~বীর, ~রথী** *nn* eminent great man of letters. **~বৃত্তি, ~ব্যবসায়** *nn* literary profession. **~ব্যবসায়ী**=~জীবী. **~-ভাণ্ডার** *n* storehouse/ repertory of literature. **~শাস্ত্র** *n* literature; literary art; study of literature. **~ শিল্প**=~কলা. **~সভা** *n* literary society/ gathering/ world. **~ সমাজ** *n* literary world. **~ সমালোচক** *n* critic (of literature); literary critic. **~ সমালোচনা** *n* literary criticism. **~সেবক** *n*=~সেবী. **~ সেবা** *n* pursuit/cultivation of literature; devotion to literature. **~ সেবা করা** *vt* pursue/cultivate literature; devote oneself to literature. **~সেবী** *adj* devoted to literature; devotedly pursuing/ cultivating/studying/ composing literature. ❑*n* devotee/servant of literature; writer; author; literary man. **সাহিত্যাকাশ** *n* firmament of literature. **সাহিত্যাচার্য** *n* doctor of literature; great teacher of literature; great literary scholar; great author. **সাহিত্যাধ্যাপক** *n* professor of literature. **সাহিত্যানন্দ** *n* pleasures of literature. **সাহিত্যানুরাগ** *n* love of literature. **সাহিত্যানুরাগী** *adj* devoted to literature. ❑*n* lover of literature. **সাহিত্যানুরাগিণী** *fem*. **সাহিত্যানুশীলন**=সাহিত্যচর্চা. **সাহিত্যামোদ**=সাহিত্যানন্দ. **সাহিত্যামোদী**=সাহিত্যানুরাগী. **সাহিত্যালোচনা** *n* literary discussion; study of literature. **সাহিত্যালোচনা করা** *vt* discuss literature

সাহিত্যিক *adj* literary. ❑*n* man of letters; literary man; author; writer; litterateur.

সাহু, সাহুকারি=সাউ, সাউকারি respectively.

সাহেব *n* **1** gentleman. **2** master; lord; ruler **3** (used as) a title of courtesy; Mr; Sir: মৌলবি জনসন ~. **4** proprietor; boss; chief: অপিসের বড়

~. **5** Englishman; European. সাহেবা *fem* lady; woman of rank. ~ সাজা *vi* adopt/assume the English/European dress and style of living. ~-পাড়া *n* English/European quarter (in a town or village). ~-মেম *n* an Englishman and an Englishwoman; a European and a European woman; English/European couple. সাহেবান *n pl* gentlemen; masters. কালা ~ *n* (derog) dark-complexioned man adopting/assuming the dress and the style of an Englishman/ a European; sham Englishman; Anglo-Indian.

সাহেবি *adj* like the English/ Europeans; English; European. ❑*n* English/ European dress or style of living as adopted by foreigners; Englishness; Europeanism; English/ European life-style. ~য়ানা *n*=~.

সাহেবী=সাহেবি

সিংদরজা=সিংহদরজা (⇒ সিংহ)

সিংহ *n* **1** lion. **2** (astrol) Leo. **3** hero; eminent person. **4** (in compounds) chief/lord of (to express excellence of any kind: পুরুষ~. সিংহী, সিংহিনী *fem* lioness. ~কেশর *n* lion's mane. ~গ্রীব *adj* lion-necked. ~তুল্য *n* lion-like; leonine. ~দরজা, ~দ্বার *nn* principal/chief gate; any gate/entrance; palace-gate. ~ধ্বনি, ~নাদ *n* roar of a lion; lion's roar; war-cry. ~নাদ করা *vi* roar like a lion; yell out a war-cry. ~পুরুষ *n* lion of a man; lion-hearted man; exceptionally powerful and valiant man. ~বাহিনী *adj fem* riding on a lion (said of Durga). ~-বিক্রম *n* prowess like that of lion; great prowess. ~বিক্রান্ত *adj* valiant as a lion. ~বিবর *n* lion's den. ~ভাগ *n* lion's share. ~রাশি *n* (astrol) Leo. ~শাবক, ~শিশু *nn* lion's cub.

সিংহল *n* island of Ceylon (Sri Lanka).

সিংহলী *adj* Ceylonese. ❑*n* Ceylonese; Ceylonese language.

সিংহাসন *n* throne. ~চ্যুত, ~ভ্রষ্ট *adj* fallen from the throne; dethroned. ~চ্যুত করা *vt* dethrone; depose. ~চ্যুতি *n* dethronement; deposition. ~ত্যাগ *n* abdication. ~ ত্যাগ করা *vt* abdicate the (throne) সিংহাসনারূঢ় *adj* seated on a throne; enthroned; reigning. সিংহাসনে আরোহণ করা/বসা *vt* ascend the throne. সিংহাসনে বসানো *vt* enthrone.

সিঁচা, সেঁচা=সেচা

সিঁড়ি, সিঁড়ী *n* stairs; flight of steps; staircase; ladder. ~ বাওয়া/ভাঙা *vi* run up/down the stairs.

সিঁথা, সিঁথি *n* parting (of hair on one's head). ~ কাটা *vt* part one's hair.

সিঁদ=সিঁধ

সিঁদুর *n* vermilion; red lead; mercuric sulphide. চীনা ~ *n* vermilion. মেটে ~ *n* red lead.

সিঁদুরে *adj* bright scarlet; vermilion. ~ মেঘ দেখে ঘর পোড়া গরু ভয় পায় (prov) Once bitten twice shy.

সিঁধ *n* hole/breach/cavity in a wall made by a housebreaker. ~ কাটা/দেওয়া *vi* break into a house. ~ দিয়ে চুরি করা *vi* burgle; commit burglary (by making holes/breaches in the wall). ~কাটি, ~কাঠি *n* burglar's tool/rod used in making holes/breeches in the wall. ~চুরি *n* housebreaking; burglary.

সিঁধেল (চোর) *n* a thief who enters a house by a hole made in the wall.

সিক=শিক. ~কাবাব=শিককাবাব.

সিকতা *n* sand; gravel; sandy soil. ~ময় *adj* sandy; full of sand; gravelly.

সিকনি=শিকনি

সিকলি=শিকল

শিকা[1]=শিকা

সিকা[2] *n*=সিকি

সিকি, সিকে[1] (colloq) *n* coin valuing a quarter of a taka or rupee; one-fourth part. ❑*adj* onefourth of; a quarter of; quarter-. সিকি অংশ/ভাগ *n* one-fourth part; quarter.

সিকে[2] =শিকা

সিক্কা [A] *n* name of an obsolete rupee-coin of the Indian sub-continent. বিরাশি ~র ওজন *n* **1** a seer (0.933 kg) of 82 *sikkas* (0.957 kg). **2** unusually heavy.

সিক্ত *adj* **1** wet; wetted; moist; moistened. **2** (fig) tearful. সিক্তা *fem*. ~ করা *vt* wet; moisten. ~তা *n* moistness; vapour; mist; humidity; wet.

সিকথ *n* wax. ~ করগুক *n* pomade.

সিক্‌নি=শিকনি

সিগন্যাল [E]*n* signal.

সিগারেট [E] *n* cigarette. ~ খাওয়া *vt* smoke a cigarette.

সিঙাড়া, সিঙ্গাড়া=শিঙাড়া

সিজ *n* a kind of spurge (*Euphorbia nerrifolia*).

সিজদা=সেজদা

সিজা, সিঝা *vi* be boiled in water. ~নো *vt* boil in water. ❑*adj* boiled in water. ~পোড়া *adj* boiled and burnt.

সিজিল [A] *n* arrangement, orderliness; order; method.

সিঞা *vt* sew (up). ~নো *adj* sewed.

সিঞ্চন *n* sprinkling; watering; spraying. ~ করা *vt* sprinkle; water; spray; scatter in small drops; besprinkle/moisten with.

সিঞ্চা *vt* (poet)=সিঞ্চন করা (⇒ সিঞ্চন)

সিঞ্চিত *adj* sprinkled; sprayed; watered; soaked by sprinkling (spraying). সিঞ্চিতা *fem*.

সিট [E] *n* seat.

সিটকানো *vt* turn up/contract in contempt, disgust, abhorrence, etc: নাক ~.

সিটা=শিটা

সিটি[1] *n* whistle; steam-whistle. ~ দেওয়া *vi* whistle.

সিটি[2] [E] *n* city.

সিটে=শিটে ⇒ শিটা

সিন্ডিকেট [E] *n* syndicate.

সিত *adj* 1 white. 2 pale; bright; light. সিতা *fem.* ~কণ্ঠ *adj* white-necked. ❑*n* gallinule. ~কর *adj* white-rayed. ❑*n* 1 moon. 2 camphor. ~পক্ষ *n* 1 light half of a month. 2 goose. সিতাংশু *n* moon; camphor.

সিতা *n* sugar. ~খণ্ড *n* sugar in lumps; lump-sugar; sugar candy. ~ভোগ *n* kind of sweetmeat made of sugar, flour, milk curds, etc.

সিতান=শিথান

সিতার [P] *n* =সেতার

সিতারা [P] *n* star.

সিতি *n* 1 white. 2 blue; black. ~কণ্ঠ *adj* having a white throat; dark-necked. ❑*n* 1 Shiva. 2 peacock. 3 gallinule. ~মা *n* 1 whiteness. 2 blackness.

সিতোপল *n* white stone; chalk ;crystal.

সিথান=শিথান

সিদরাতুল মুনতাহা [A] *n* a stop in the seventh heaven; tree of knowledge in Paradise.

সিদ্দিক [A] *n* friend. সিদ্দিকিন *n pl* friends. ~ করা *vt* chastise; discipline; chasten; give sb a good thrashing.

সিদ্ধ *adj* 1 boiled; cooked by boiling; parboiled; boiled for sterilization/cleaning. 2 profusely sweating and utterly fatigued; broiling; broiled: গরমে ~ হওয়া. 3 accomplished; effected; fulfilled; gained; realized; performed; obtained; acquired: উদ্দেশ্য ~ হওয়া. 4 one who has attained the highest object; having attained divine grace through austere religious practice; beatified; perfected; become perfect. 5 endowed with supernatural faculties. 6 illustrious; sacred; holy; divine. 7 thoroughly skilled/versed in; proficient; expert. 8 proved; substantiated; amenable to. 9 valid. 10 prepared, cooked; dressed. 11 admitted to be true/right; established; settled. 12 resulting from: যুক্তি~. ❑*n* 1 (myth) one of a class of demi-gods. 2 holy personage or great saint (esp one who has attained one of the states of beatitude). 3 great adept in magic; one who has acquired supernatural powers. 4 boiled eatables. সিদ্ধা *fem.* ~ করা *vt* 1 boil; cook by boiling; parboil; boil for sterilization/ cleaning. 2 cause to sweat profusely. 3 attain; accomplish; fulfil; perform; gratify. 4 make sb expert/ proficient in. ~ হওয়া *vi* 1 be boiled/ cooked. 2 be fulfilled/ gratified/ effected/ accomplished/ successful; have success; hit a mark. 3 attain one's aim/object. 4 attain the highest object; become perfect; attain beatitude. 5 be valid/admissible; hold good; be proved/ demonstrated/ established/ demonstrated. ~ চাল *n* parboiled rice. ~কাম *adj* having the wishes fulfilled; successful. ~তা, ~ত্ব *nn* 1 perfection; perfect state. 2 condition of a Siddha. 3 establishment/ validity of a rule/doctrine. ~পীঠ *n* holy place where at least one million immolations, ten million burnt-offerings and innumerable religious services have taken place. ~পুরুষ *n* 1 holy personage/saint who has attained perfection. 2 master (in any field). ~মনস্কাম, ~মনোরম=~কাম. ~হস্ত *adj* adept; thoroughly skilled/expert/proficient. সিদ্ধান্ন *n* parboiled/ cooked rice.

সিদ্ধাই *n* divine grace/supernatural power obtained through austere religious practice; beatitude.

সিদ্ধান্ত *n* 1 decision; conclusion; resolution. 2 demonstrated conclusion of an argument. 3 settled opinion/doctrine; dogma; axiom; received/admitted truth. 4 theory. 5 (math) deduction. 6 fired/established/canonical text-book or received scientific treatise on any subject. 7 judgement. ~ করা *vi* decide; conclude; resolve; deduce; draw a conclusion (from). সিদ্ধান্তে উপনীত হওয়া/পৌঁছা *vi* come to a / reach the conclusion.

সিদ্ধার্থ *adj* one who has accomplished an aim/object; successful. ❑*n* name of the great Buddha.

সিদ্ধি *n* 1 supreme felicity; bliss; beatitude; complete sanctification (by penance, etc); final emancipation; perfection. 2 accomplishment; fulfilment; complete attainment (of an object); performance; success; hitting of a mark. 3 prosperity; personal success; fortune. 4 attainment of proficiency/skill/knowledge. 5 leaves and shoots of hemp; bhang. ~ খাওয়া *vt* chew and swallow bhang; drink a beverage of pulped bhang. ~ ঘোঁটা *vt* stir pulped bhang in milk, coconut-milk, etc in order to make a beverage. ~দ *adj* conferring beatitude/felicity. ~দাতা *adj*=~দ. ❑*n* name of Ganesha. ~দাত্রী *fem* a form of Durga. ~লাভ *n* acquirement of success/ perfection. ~ লাভ করা=সিদ্ধ হওয়া (⇒ সিদ্ধ).

সিদ্ধেশ্বরী *n fem* name of a Hindu goddess.

সিধা, সিধে *adj* 1 straight; direct; lying continually onward; not curved; circuitous; shortest: ~ রাস্তা. 2 easy; simple; straightforward: ~ কথা. 3 chastened; disciplined; corrected; chastised. ❑*adv* 1 straight: ~ চলা. 2 straightway; at once; directly: শোনামাত্র ~ দৌড়ানো. ❑*n* gift of uncooked eatables arranged on a tray. ~ করা

vt chastise; discipline; chasten; give sb a good thrashing.

সিধানো *vt* enter; penetrate.

সিন=সীন

সিনা [P] *n* breast; bosom; chest.

সিনান *n* (poet)=স্নান

সিনেট [E] *n* senate.

সিনেমা [E] *n* cinema; motion picture; film; cinema house. ~ **দেখা** *vt* see a film; go to the pictures. ~**ভক্ত** *n* film-fan. ~**শিল্পী** *n* film-artist. ~**স্টার** *n* film-star.

সিন্দুক [A] *n* chest; safe.

সিন্দুর=সিঁদুর

সিন্ধি, সিন্ধী *adj* of Sindh; inhabiting Sind. ❑*n* native of Sind; language of Sind; Sindi.

সিন্ধু *n* **1** ocean; sea. **2** river; stream. **3** the Indus. **4** province of Sind. **5** name of an Indian musical mode. ~**কর্দম** *n* ooze. ~**ঘোটক** *n* walrus.

সিন্নি *n* (colloq)=শিরনি

সিপ=ছিপ

সিপাই *n* (colloq)=সিপাহি

সিপারা [P] *n* one of the 30 chapters of the Qoran.

সিপাহসালার *n* general; commander; commander-in chief.

সিপাহি, সিপাহী [P] *n* soldier; messenger of a court; sepoy; constable. ~**বিদ্রোহ** *n* sepoy-mutiny.

সিফত, সিফাৎ [A] *n* quality; attribute.

সিভিল [E] *adj* civil. ~ **কোর্ট** *n* civil court. ~ **সার্জন** *n* civil surgeon. ~ **সার্ভিস** *n* civil service.

সিম=শিম

সিমুম=সাইমুম

সিমেন্ট [E] *n* cement.

সিম্ফনি [E] *n* symphony.

সি-মোরগ [P] *n* name of a fabulous bird (of the size of thirty birds); griffin; eagle.

সিয়ন *n* sewing; stitch.

সিয় [P] *adj* black; dark; sombre.

সিয়ান *adj*=সেয়ান

সিয়ানো *vt* sew; stitch.

সিয়াম [A] *n* fast; fasting.

সিরকা=সির্কা

সিরসির=শিরশির

সিরা [P] *n* syrup.

সিরাজ [A] *n* lamp; candle. **সিরাজাম মুনিরা** *n* brilliant lamp.

সিরাতুল মুস্তাকিম [A]*n* direct road; right way.

সিরিঞ্জ [E]*n* syringe.

সিরিশ [P]*n* glue. ~ **কাগজ** *n* sand-paper; glass-paper.

সিরিস্তা=সেরেস্তা

সির্কা *n* [P] vinegar.

সির্নি=শিরনি

সিল[১] *n* (zool) seal.

সিল[২], **সীল** *n* seal. ~ **করা** *vt* seal; set a seal on. ~**-করা** *adj* sealed. ~**মোহর** *n* seal containing a name or any other sign.

সিলাই=সেলাই

সিলিং [E]*n* ceiling.

সিল্ক [E]*n* silk.

সিসৃক্ষা *n* wish/purpose to create.

সিসৃক্ষু *adj* wishing/purposing to create.

সীতা *n fem* **1** furrow; track/line of a plough-share. **2** Sita, the heroine of the Ramayana. ~ **পতি** *n* Rama, the husband of Sita. ~**ভোগ**=সিতাভোগ(⇒ সিতা).

সীৎকার=শীৎকার

সীধু=শীধু

সীন [E]*n* scene (of a drama); scenery.

সীবন *n* sewing; stitching; embroidery. ~ **করা** *vt* sew; stitch. ~**-শিল্প** *n* embroidery; art of sewing.

সীবনী *n* needle; awl.

সীমন্ত *n* **1** parting (of hair). ~**ক** *n* red lead; vermilion.

সীমন্তিনী *n fem* **1** a woman of whose husband is alive. **2** woman; wife. ~**শাসন** *n* (facet) petticoat government; gynocracy.

সীমন্তোন্নয়ন *n* a Hindu custom observed by women in the fourth or sixth month of pregnancy.

সীমা *n* **1** boundary; landmark; border; frontier. **2** limit; bounds: আনন্দের ~ নেই. **3** end; termination: দুঃখের ~ নেই. ~ **অতিক্রম করা** *vi* go beyond the limit (of); go too far; transgress. ~ **কর** *n* terminal tax/cess. ~**না** *n* **1** border; boundary; bounds; boundary-line; periphery. **2** end; termination; extremity. ~ **নির্ণয় করা** *vt* mark off/determine bounds (of); demarcate; delimit; mark/fix the limits of. ~ **নির্দেশ করা** *vi*=~ নির্ণয় করা. **সীমান্ত** *n* border; boundary; frontier; bounding-line; bounds. **সীমান্ত-প্রদেশ** *n* frontier province; frontiers. **সীমান্ত বাণিজ্য** *n* frontier trade. **সীমান্তরক্ষী** *n* frontier guard. **সীমান্তরক্ষী বাহিনী** *n* border security force. ~**ন্তর** *n* other frontier/boundary. ~**-পরিসীমা** *n* limit; end: ~ পরিসীমা নেই, there are no bounds; know(s) no bounds; ... no end of; ... without end. ~**বদ্ধ** *adj* confined within/restricted to limits; limited; restricted. ~**বন্ধন** *n* limitation. ~**বিবাদ** *n* litigation about boundary. ~**লঙ্ঘন**=সীমোল্লঙ্ঘন. ~**শূন্য,** ~**হীন** *adjj* limitless; unlimited; boundless; endless; infinite. ~**সন্ধি** *n* meeting point of two boundaries. ~**-স্তম্ভ** *n* boundary-post; boundary-pillar. ~**স্থ** *adj* limiting.

সীমার [A] *n* **1** person who did the cruel act of slaying Iman Hussain at the battle of Karbala. **2** (fig) a very cruel person.

সীমিত *adj* limited; bounded. ~ **সঙ্ঘ** *n* limited company.

সীমিকা *n* semicolon.
সীমোল্লঙ্ঘন *n* transgressing of a boundary; passing a frontier; trespass. ~ **করা** *vi* transgress a boundary; go beyond (a limit/boundary); pass a frontier; trespass.
সীরা *n* plough.
সীস *n* lead; stick of blacklead within a pencil. ~**ক**=~. ~**শ্বেত** *n* white lead. ~**সিন্দূর** *n* minium.
সীসা, সীসে (colloq) *n* lead. **সীসাঞ্জন** *n* galena.
সু- *pref* denoting good, excellent, right, auspicious, virtuous, beautiful, easy, well, sweet, very, much, rightly, greatly, easily, etc: সুজন, সুখবর.
সুই, সুঁই *n* needle; awl.
সুইচ [E]*n* switch.
সুইপার [E]*n* sweeper.
সুটি=শুটি
সুড়ি=শুঁড়ি
সুদরি *adj* (colloq)=সুন্দরী
সুঁদি *n* water-lily; lotus.
সুকঠিন *adj* very difficult/tough/hard/stiff.
সুকণ্ঠ *adj* sweet-voiced; having a melodious voice. **সুকণ্ঠী** *fem.*
সুকতলা=সুখতলা
সুকন্দক *n* onion.
সুকন্যা *n fem* beautiful/virtuous girl; good daughter.
সুকর *adj* easy to be done; easy for. ~**তা** *n* easiness; feasibleness.
সুকানি, সুকানী [A]*n* steerman/quartermaster of a steamer.
সুকর্ম *n* good work. **সুকর্মা** *adj* performing good works; virtuous. ❑*n* good/expert artificer/ artist/ architect.
সুকল্পিত *adj* well-planned; well-thought out.
সুকান্ত *adj* very handsome.
সুকান্তি *n* handsome appearance.
সুকীর্তি *n* good praise; wide fame/renown.
সুকুমার *adj* **1** very tender/delicate/ soft/young: ~মতি বালক. **2** very beautiful/graceful; fine. ❑*n* delicate youth. **সুকুমারী** *fem.* ~**কলা,** ~**বিদ্যা,** ~**শিল্প** *nn* fine arts. ~**ত্ব** *n* delicacy; tenderness; fineness. ~**বৃত্তি** *n* tender/fine sensibility; artistic bent of mind. ~**মতি** *adj* tender-hearted; innocent as a child; pure in heart; of tender age. ~**শিল্পী** *n* artist; artiste.
সুকৃৎ *adj* doing good; benevolent; virtuous; pious.
সুকৃত *n* **1** good/righteous deed; meritorious act; virtue; moral merit. **2** benefit, bounty; friendly aid; favour. **3** fortune; auspiciousness; reward; recompense. ❑*adj* well done/ made/ formed/ executed; well arranged; adorned; made good; well-conducted; virtuous; fortunate. ~ **কর্ম** *n* good/ meritorious act. ❑*adj* doing good deeds; virtuous.
সুকৃতি *n* good/correct conduct; kindness; virtue; practice of religious austerities; good luck; piety; welfare; weal.
সুকৃতী *adj* **1** doing good actions; virtuous; generous. **2** prosperous; fortunate.
সুকৃত্য *n* good/clever/righteous act; right/ virtuous action.
সুকেশ *adj* having beautiful hair. **সুকেশা, সুকেশী, সুকেশিনী** *fem.*
সুকোমল *adj* very soft/tender.
সুকৌশল *n* good contrivance/ device/ artifice/ stratagem; cleverness; ingenuity; cunning; trickery; skilfulness. **সুকৌশলে** *adv* cleverly; artfully; skilfully; cunningly; adroitly.
সুকৌশলী *adj* clever; artful; skilful; deft; ingenious; cute; crafty; cunning; shrewd.
সুক্ত *n* (colloq)=সুক্তা
সুক্তা, সুক্তানি, সুক্তো *nn* dish of bitter vegetables.
সুখ *n* **1** ease; easiness; comfort; prosperity. **2** pleasure; joy; bliss; happiness; delight; contentment. ~**কর,** ~**জনক,** ~**দ,** ~**দায়ক,** ~**প্রদ** *adj* causing or giving pleasure/ happiness/ delight; comfortable; happy; pleasant; delightful; easeful; blissful; pleasurable; joyful. ~**দা,** ~**দায়িকা,** ~**দাত্রী** *fem.* ~**চর** *adj* going/ moving easily. ~**জ,** ~**জাত** *adj* born/produced easily; pleasure-born. ~**দুঃখ** *n* pleasure and pain; joy and sorrow; weal and woe. ~**দুঃখময়** *adj* consisting of pleasure and pain. ~**দৃশ্য** *adj* pleasant to see; beautiful to look at. ~**ধাম** *n* abode of joy; heaven. ~**পর** *adj* fond of ease/ comfort; intent on enjoyment. ~**পাঠ্য** *adj* readable at ease. ~**প্রশ্ন** *n* inquiry as to welfare. ~**বাদ** *n* Epicureanism. ~**বাদী** *adj,n* Epicurean ~**বাস,** ~**বাসর** *nn* pleasant/ comfortable abode. ~**বিধান করা** *vi* provide for ease and comfort/ happiness. ~**বেদন** *n* consciousness of pleasure. ~**বুভুক্ষু** *n* pleasure-hungry; pleasure-seeking. ~**বোধ** *n* feeling of comfort/ happiness. ~**বোধ করা** *vt* feel comfortable/ happy. ~**ভাক,** ~**ভাগী** *adjj* possessing/ sharing happiness; happy; fortunate. ~**ভাগিনী** *fem.* ~**ভোগ** *n* enjoyment of pleasure. ~ **ভোগ করা** *vt* enjoy happiness/ joy/bliss; enjoy ease and comfort. ~**ভোগী** *adj* enjoying pleasure/ joy/ happiness/ bliss; enjoying ease and comfort; blissful; happy. ~**ভোগ্য** *adj* easy to be enjoyed/ disposed. ~**ময়** *adj* full of joy and pleasure; delightful; full of ease. ~**রবি** *n* sun of joy/happiness. ~**রাত্রি** *n* **1** quiet, comfortable night. **2** night of new moon (when there is a festival in honour of Lakshmi). ~**লেশ** *n* little pleasure; trace/ bit/ jot of ease/ comfort/ happiness. ~**শয়ন,** ~**শয্যা** *nn*

placid rest/ sleep; comfortable bed/ couch; bed of pleasure; bed of roses. ~শায়িত *adj* sleeping/ lying comfortably (on). ~শায়ী *adj* sleeping/ resting pleasantly. ~শান্তি *n* happiness and peace. ~শ্রাব্য, ~শ্রুতি *adj* agreeable/ pleasing to the ear; pleasant to hear; melodious/sweet to the ear. ~সংবাদ *n* 'a piece of happy news'. ~সমুদ্র, ~সাগর, ~সিন্ধু *nn* ocean of pleasure; endless happiness/ bliss. ~সমৃদ্ধি *n* happiness and prosperity. ~সম্পদ, ~সম্পৎ *n* happiness and riches; milk and honey. ~সাধ্য *adj* easy to be accomplished/ attained. ~সুপ্ত *adj* comfortably asleep; resting well; sweetly sleeping. ~সুপ্তি *n* placid/quiet sleep. ~সূর্য=~রবি. ~সেবা *n* pleasure seeking; hedonism; dissipation. ~সেবী *adj* pleasure-seeking; hedonism; dissipated; sensuous. ❑*n* pleasure seeker; hedonist; sensualist. ~সেব্য *adj* easy of access. ~সৌভাগ্য *n* happiness and riches. ~স্পর্শ *adj* agreeable to the touch; pleasant to the feelings. ~স্বপ্ন *n* happy/pleasant dream; dream of happiness. ~স্মৃতি *n* happy memory/ recollection. ❑*adj* full of happy memories. ~স্বচ্ছন্দতা, ~স্বাচ্ছন্দ্য *nn* happiness and ease; milk and honey; easy circumstances. ~স্বাচ্ছন্দ্যে*adv* in comfort and happiness; in easy/flourishing circumstances. সুখানুভব, সুখানুভূতি=সুখবোধ. সুখান্ত *n* end of happiness. ❑*adj* ending in happiness. সুখান্বেষণ *n* search/ quest for pleasure/ comfort/ happiness. সুখান্বেষী *adj* searching for/ seeking pleasure/ comfort/ happiness; pleasure-seeking. সুখাপন্ন *adj* one who has attained/ gained happiness; happy; delighted. সুখাবহ *adj* bringing/ conferring pleasure; delightful; pleasurable. ~ভিলাষ *n* desire of pleasure. ~রোহণ *adj* easy to be ascended. সুখার্ত *adj* affected by joy. সুখার্থ *adj* for the sake of ease/pleasure. সুখার্থী *adj* seeking/ wishing for pleasure/ happiness. সুখাশা *n* hope of pleasure/ enjoyment. সুখাসন *n* comfortable seat. সুখাসীন *adj* comfortably seated. সুখে *adv* with/at ease; comfortably; happily; gladly; contentedly; blissfully; in bliss. সুখে থাকতে ভূতে কিলায় (fig) act of inviting unnecessary troubles. সুখের কাঁটা *n* (fig) obstacle to happiness. সুখের পায়রা *n* (fig) fairweather friend; person of happy-go-lucky temperament.

সুখী *adj* happy; glad; delighted; comfortable; content; satisfied; blessed; given to luxury. সুখিনী *fem.*

সুখেচ্ছা *n* hope/desire of happiness.

সুখেচ্ছু *adj* desirous of happiness.

সুখৈশ্বর্য *n* happiness and riches; prosperity.

সুখোৎপত্তি *n* realization/occurrence of pleasure.

সুখোৎপাদন *n* production of happiness.

সুখোৎসব *n* festival of pleasure; festive occasion; gala.

সুখোদয় *n* dawn/dawning of happiness/ affluence.

সুখোষ্ণ *adj* pleasantly warm; tepid.

সুখ্যাত *adj* very renowned; famous; well-known.

সুখ্যাতি *n* good report; celebrity; fame; praise; good reputation. ~ করা *vt* praise; acclaim; laud.

সুগঠন *n* good/fine shape. ❑*adj* well-shaped; fine-built; strong-built.

সুগঠিত *adj* **1**=সুগঠন. **2** well-formed; well-constructed; well-organized.

সুগত *adj* going well; one who has fared well. ❑*n* Buddha.

সুগতি *n* **1** good/happy condition; welfare; happiness; bliss. **2** secure refuge.

সুগন্ধ *n* fragrant smell; fragrance; sweet smell/aroma; perfume. ❑*adj* fragrant; sweet-smelling; aromatic. ~পূর্ণ, ~ময় *adj* fragrant; aromatic; perfumed. ~বহ *n* wind; breeze.

সুগন্ধি *adj* sweet-smelling; fragrant. ❑*n* perfume; fragrance.

সুগভীর *adj* very deep; profound; fathomless.

সুগম *adj* **1** easy to be traversed; easy of access; easily accessible. **2** easy to be ascertained/ understood; easy to understand/ learn. **3** easy; practicable. সুগমন, সুগম্য *adjj* easily traversed/ passed; easy of access.

সুগম্ভীর *adj* very grave/serious; very deep.

সুগহন *adj* very thick/ close/ impervious/ deep.

সুগীত *n* good song. ❑beautifully rendered; well-sung.

সুগুণ *n* good quality.

সুগুপ্ত *adj* well guarded; well hidden/concealed; kept very secret.

সুগুপ্তি *n* good protection; great secrecy.

সুগূঢ় *adj* well guarded/concealed; very secret.

সুগৃহীত *adj* held firmly; seized; grasped; clung/adhered to . ~নামা *adj* one whose name is invoked auspiciously.

সুগ্রহ *adj* easy to be obtained.

সুগ্রাহী *adj* sensitive (as of a photo-cell).

সুগোল *adj* well rounded; rotund.

সুঘট *adj* easy contrived/accomplished.

সুঘটন *n* good arrangement/joining.

সুঘটিত *adj* well joined/ united/ contrived/ arranged.

সুঘোষ *adj* making a loud noise; very noisy.

সুচ *n* needle; awl.

সুচক্র *adj* having beautiful wheels.

সুচতুর *adj* very clever/skilful/sly/cunning. সচতুরা *fem.*

সুচরিত *n* good character/conduct/behaviour; virtuous actions. ❑*adj* virtuous; moral; good charactered. সুচরিতা *fem.* সুচরিতেষু to you/him of good character (form of polite address in a letter); my dear. সুচরিতাসু *fem.*

সুচরিত্র=সুচরিত. সুচরিত্রা *fem*

সুচর্মা *adj* having beautiful skin/bark.

সুচারু *adj* very lovely/beautiful; pleasing; delightful; very neat. ~তা *n* loveliness; great beauty. ~রূপে *adv* beautifully; perfectly; nicely.

সুচিক্কণ *adj* **1** very smooth. **2** beautiful; lovely; fine; bright; glossy.

সুচিত্রিত *adj* **1** well-painted; well-decorated. **2** nicely delineated; well-described.

সুচিন্তা *n* good/pious/deep/high thought; due consideration/reflection; pious/high thinking.

সুচিন্তিত *adj* well thought about; well weighed/ considered; carefully/judiciously considered; well-thought; well-thought-out; well-planned; well-devised. ~ পরিকল্পনা *n* well-thought-out plan.

সুচির *adj* very/too long; lasting for a long time: ~ রাত্রি. ~ কালে *adv* in a very long time. সুচিরে *adv* after a very long time.

সুচিরায়ু *n* god; divinity.

সুচিরেপ্সিত *adj* ever-desired; long-desired. সুচিরেপ্সিতা *fem.*

সুচিত *adj* distinctly marked.

সুচেতা *adj* **1** merry; of cheerful temperament; happy; contented. **2** having great intelligence; sapient. **3** well-minded; benevolent. **4** careful; cautious.

সুছন্দ, সুছাদ *adjj* well-shaped; artistically shaped; having an artistic style.

সুজন *adj* good/ virtuous/ pious/ benevolent/ kind/honest person; good soul. ~তা *n* goodness; kindness; benevolence.

সুজনি=শুজনি

সুজন্ম *n* noble/auspicious birth. সুজন্মা *adj* of noble/auspicious birth.

সুজলা *adj fem* having good/sweet water; well-watered; watered by numerous rivers.

সুজাত *adj* **1** nobly born; noble; well-born; well grown. **2** of an excellent kind/nature; fine; beautiful. সুজাতা *fem.*

সুজি *n* flour in fine granules; coarsely ground flour; semolina; semola.

সুজিৎ *adj* easily overcoming.

সুজিত *n* easy conquest.

সুজেয় *adj* easily conquerable.

সুঝ *n* foresight; vision; perception; understanding: বুঝ~. সুঝা *vt* understand; perceive.

সুট [E]*n* suit: ~কোট. ~ পরা *vi* put on suit/ European dress. ~কেস *n* suitcase. ~-পরা *adj* wearing a suit.

সুট করা [E]*v* suit: জামাটা গায়ে ~ করেছে.

সুটকি=শুঁটকি

সুঠাম *adj* well-built; shapely; well-shaped; having a well-built body; robust; vigorous; brawny; husky; beautiful.

সুড়ং, সুড়ঙ্গ=সুরঙ্গ

সুড়সুড় *n* (onom) denoting tickling/ titillating sensation. ~ করা *vi* tickle. সুড়সুড়ানি, সুড়সুড়ি *n* tickle; titillation. সুড়সুড়ি দেওয়া *vt* tickle; titillate. ~ করে *adv* stealthily; surreptitiously; silently: ~ করে পলায়ন.

সুড়ুৎ *n* (onom) denoting **(a)** sound of gulping liquid; **(b)** sound of fleeing suddenly. ~ করে *adv* **1** at one gulp. **2** pronto; in a flash.

সুডৌল, সুঢপ *adjj* **1** shapely; well-shaped. **2** symmetrical.

সুত *n* son; child; offspring. সুতা *fem* daughter.

সুতনু *adj* very thin/slender; having a beautiful body; graceful; handsome; shapely. ☐*n* beautiful/well-shaped body.

সুতরী *n fem* woman possessing a beautifully slim body; belle; beauty.

সুতপা, সুতপাঃ *adjj* practising severe austerity. ☐*n* **1** ascetic; hermit. **2** sun.

সুতপ্ত *adj* very hot; much heated; very severe.

সুতরাং *conj, adv* so; therefore; hence; consequently.

সুতলি *n* very thin thread/string; fibre of yarn.

সুতহিবুক *n* junction of the fourth and fifth astrological houses (said to be suitable for marriages).

সুতা[1] *n fem* ⇒ সুত

সুতা[2] *n* **1** thread; yarn; cotton thread. **2** a measure of length (= ·25 inch). ~কৃমি=সূত্রকৃমি.

সুতার[1] *adj* (having a) delicious (taste); tasty. ☐*n* delicious taste.

সুতার[2]=সূত্রধর

সুতি, সুতী *adjj* made of cotton thread/yarn.

সুতিক্ত *adj* very bitter.

সুতীক্ষ্ণ *adj* **1** very sharp/pungent. **2** acutely painful; severe; cutting. **3** very keen. **4** harsh; strident; shrill.

সুতীব্র *adj* piercing; very sharp; deafening; biting; very keen.

সুতুঙ্গ *adj* very lofty/tall.

সুতুলি=সুতলি

সুতো *n* (colloq)=সুতা[2]

সুদ [A]*n* interest (on loan); usury. ~ কষা *vi* calculate/find out interest. ~ হওয়া *vi* accrue interest. ~খোর *adj* living on usury; usurious. ☐*n* usurer. ~সমেত *adv* with interest. সুদে খাটানো *vt* lay out/invest on interest. সুদে ধার দেওয়া *vt* lend on interest. সুদের ~, চক্রবৃদ্ধি ~ *nn* compound interest.

সুদক্ষ *adj* very skilful/capable/clever/ strong/ deft/proficient. সুদক্ষা *fem.*

সুদক্ষিণ *adj* very courteous/polite/generous/ liberal. **সুদক্ষিণা** *fem.*
সুদন্ত *adj* having good/ handsome teeth. ❑*n* good tooth. **সুদন্তী** *adj fem.*
সুদর্শন *adj* good-looking; beautiful; handsome; lovely; pleasing to the eye. ❑*n* (also ~ **চক্র**) circular weapon of Vishnu-Krishna. **সুদর্শনা** *fem.*
সুদায় *n* endowment; good/auspicious gift.
সুদারুণ *adj* very cruel/terrible/dreadful.
সুদিঠি=সুদৃষ্টি
সুদিন *n* clear/fine/auspicious day; happy day; happiness; good times.
সুদী, সুদি *adjj* relating to usury; usurious. ~ **কারবার** *n* usury.
সুদীপ্ত *adj* shining bright.
সুদীর্ঘ *adj* very long; very lengthy.
সুদুর্লভ *adj* very difficult to be attained; very rare/ scarce.
সুদুশ্চর *adj* very difficult of access; inaccessible.
সুদুষ্কর *adj* very difficult to be done; most arduous.
সুদুস্তর *adj* very difficult to be crossed/passed.
সুদূর *adj* very remote/distant; far-off. ~ **ব্যবধান** *n* very great distance; far cry. ~**পরাহত** *adj* foredoomed to failure; very unlikely; likely once in a blue moon; hardly possible.
সুদৃঢ় *adj* very firm/hard/steady; strong; very tenacious; absolutely unwavering.
সুদৃশ্য *adj* clearly visible; looking beautiful; handsome; lovely; pleasing to the eye.
সুদ্ধ *adv* **1** including; together with: পৃথিবী~ লোক. **2** even: তার বউ~ তার নিন্দা করে.
সুধন্বা *adj* having an excellent bow; proficient in archery. ❑*n* great archer. **সুধন্বী** *fem.*
সুধর্ম *n* good law; justice; duty.
সুধা *n* **1** good drink; beverage of the gods; nectar. **2** nectar/honey of flowers. **3** milk; moonlight. **4** lime; white-wash. ~ **ঢালা** *vi* **1** pour nectar. **2** (fig) sweeten; flatter; please; console; comfort. **সুধাংশু**, ~**কর** *nn* moon. ~**ধবল**, ~**ধবলিত** *adjj* white as plaster; white washed; plastered; stuccoed. ~**নিধি** *n* moon. ~**পাত্র** *n* container/receptacle of nectar. ~**বর্ষণ**, ~**বৃষ্টি** shower of nectar. ~**বর্ষণ/~-বৃষ্টি করা** *vi* **1** shower/rain/sprinkle nectar. **2** (of the moon) scatter moonlight. **3** flatter; please; comfort; console. ~**বর্ষী** *adj* **1** raining/showering nectar. **2** (fig) comforting; consoling; pleasing; flattering. ~**ময়** *adj* **1** consisting of nectar. **2** (fig) very sweet/pleasing/flattering/ comforting; mellifluous; sweet-flowing. **3** (of a person) well-behaved; charming. ~**ময়ী** *adj.* ~**মাখা** *adj* filled with/soaked in nectar; nectarine; delicious; lovely; mellifluous; very sweet: ~মাখা কণ্ঠ/বচন. ~**মুখ** *n* lovely face. ❑*adj* lovely-faced; sweet; honeyed. ~**মুখী** *fem.* ~**সমুদ্র**, ~**সিন্ধু** *nn* sea/ocean of nectar. ~**সিক্ত** *adj* soaked with nectar; (fig) very sweet/ pleasant; honeyed. ~**স্বর** *adj* having a sweet voice; honey-tongued.
সুধা=শুধা^{৩}. ~**নো**=শুধানো(⇒ শুধা^{৩})
সুধার *adj* well pointed; cutting; very sharp.
সুধারা *n* good disposition/ system; improvement. ❑*adj* streaming beautifully.
সুধী *adj* wise; having a good understanding; learned; sensible; clever; judicious; erudite; religious; pious. ❑*n* wise/ learned/ erudite man.
সুধীর *adj* very considerate/ wise; unperturbed; calm and collected/ composed; firm; resolute. ~**তা** *n* calmness; tranquility; firmness; steadiness.
সুধ=শুধ
সুনজর *n* favour; blessing; consideration; favourable view. **সুনজরে দেখা** *vi* look favourably on. **সুনজরে পড়া** *vi* find favour with sb; take/ catch the fancy of.
সুনন্দ *adj* pleasing well; delighting; delightful. **সুনন্দা** *adj.*
সুনয়ন *adj* having beautiful eyes; fair-eyed. **সুনয়না** *fem.*
সুনসান *adj* desolate; deserted; quiet; still; hushed.
সুনাম *n* good reputation/ name; fame; renown; good will.
সুনিদ্রা *n* good/ sound/ peaceful sleep.
সুনিপুণ *adj* very skilled/ adroit; highly efficient/ competent.
সুনিভৃত *adj* very secret/ private.
সুনিয়ত *adj* well-governed; well-disciplined; very regular.
সুনিয়ন্ত্রণ *n* good control/ discipline/ regulation.
সুনিয়ন্ত্রিত *adj* well-disciplined; well-governed; well-controlled; well-managed; well-restrained; well-regulated.
সুনিয়ম *n* good law/ rule/ principle; good management.
সুনিরূপিত, সুনির্ণীত, সুনির্দিষ্ট, সুনির্ধারিত *adjj* clearly/ firmly/ nicely/ categorically defined or fined or demarcated; well-defined; definite; clear-cut; specific; distinct.
সুনির্মল *adj* perfectly pure/ clear; perfectly fresh; immaculate; pellucid.
সুনিশ্চয় *n* firm resolve. ❑*adj*=সুনিশ্চিত.
সুনিশ্চিত *adj* perfectly sure/ certain; well-ascertained/ fired/ determined/ settled; thoroughly positive/ assured/ convinced. ❑*adv* surely; certainly; assuredly; positively.
সুনীতি *n* good conduct/ behaviour; good policy; wisdom; discretion; good morals; excellent principle.

সুনীল *adj* very blue/ black; dark; dark blue.

সুন্দর *adj* beautiful; handsome; lovely; charming; agreeable; pleasing; pleasant; good-looking; fine; nice; pretty; graceful; sweet; elegant. **সুন্দরী** *fem.* **~ করা** *vt* beautiful; embellish; improve.

সুন্দরী *adj* ⇒ সুন্দর. ❑*n* **1** beautiful woman/ girl; beauty; belle. **3** kind of timber-tree or its timber grown in Sundarbans; sundri.

সুন্নত, সুন্নৎ [A] *n* **1** tradition of the Holy Prophet. **2** ordinance of the religion; religious ceremony. **3** circumcision. **~ করা** *vi, vt* circumcise; be circumcised.

সুন্নি [A] orthodox Muslim; follower of the sunnat-ul-jama'at sect; sunni: sunnite.

সুপ [E] *n* soup.

সুপক্ক *adj* **1** well-cooked; thoroughly boiled. **2** thoroughly ripe; matured. **3** well-experienced.

সুপণ্ডিত *adj* profoundly learned/ erudite; well-versed.

সুপথ, সুপন্থা *n* **1** good road. **2** virtuous course; good conduct; honest path/ way/ means.

সুপথ্য *n* good/ wholesome/ hygienic food or diet.

সুপর্যাপ্ত *adj* very plentiful; very spacious.

সুপাচ্য *adj* easily digestible.

সুপাত্র *n* **1** good/ worthy/ fit/ deserving person or bridegroom or match. **2** beautiful cup/ receptacle. **সুপাত্রী** *fem* good/ worthy/ fit/ deserving/ desirable female or bride, excellent bride.

সুপারি *n* betel-nut; areca-nut.

সুপারিন্টেন্ডেন্ট [E] *n* superintendent.

সুপারিশ [P] *n* recommendation. **~ করা** *vt* recommend. **~-পত্র** *n* letter of recommendation. **সুপারিশি** *adj* recommending; recommendatory.

সুপুত্র *n* good/ worthy/ excellent son. **সুপুত্রী** *fem* good/ excellent/ worthy daughter.

সুপুরি *n* (colloq)=সুপারি

সুপুরুষ *n* handsome/ well-built man. ❑*adj* handsome; well-built.

সুপ্ত *adj* **1** fallen asleep; sleeping; slept; asleep. **2** dormant: ~ আগ্নেয়গিরি. **3** latent: ~ প্রবৃত্তি.

সুপ্তি *n* **1** sleep; deep sleep. **2** dormancy. **3** latency. **4** sleepiness; drowsiness.

সুপ্তোত্থিত *adj* arisen from sleep.

সুপ্রকাশ *adj* very/ distinctly visible; manifest.

সুপ্রচ্ছন্ন *adj* well-concealed.

সুপ্রজনবিদ্যা *n* eugenics.

সুপ্রণালী *n* good method/ rule/ custom.

সুপ্রতিপন্ন *adj* well-established.

সুপ্রতিভা *n* fine intelligence/ intellect.

সুপ্রতিষ্ঠ, সুপ্রতিষ্ঠিত *adj* **1** well-established; standing firm; well-founded; firmly settled down. **2** famous; very celebrated; well-reputed. **3** (mech) stable. **সুপ্রতিষ্ঠিতা** *fem.*

সুপ্রতিষ্ঠা *n* **1** firm position. **2** good reputation; fame. **3** installation; establishment; consecration.

সুপ্রতীত *adj* well-known.

সুপ্রতুল *adj* abundant; plentiful.

সুপ্রভ *adj* very bright/ splendid; glorious; beautiful.

সুপ্রভাত *n* **1** beautiful dawn/ daybreak; earliest dawn; fine/ auspicious morning. **2** (fig) dawn/ dawning of fortune. **3** (as a greeting) good morning.

সুপ্রযুক্ত *adj* well-applied; very appropriately used.

সুপ্রয়োগ *n* good/ proper application; appropriate use; good/ profitable utilization.

সুপ্রশস্ত, সুপ্রসারিত *adjj* **1** very spacious/ commodious; widely extended; **2** free from obstacles; unbound; open: চলার পথ ~.

সুপ্রসন্ন *adj* very bright/ serene (as the face or mind); very gracious/ favourable/ kind; highly pleased/ satisfied; very propitious. **~ হওয়া** *vi* favour; smile on/ upon: ভাগ্য ~ হওয়া.

সুপ্রসব *n* easy/ smooth parturition/ delivery.

সুপ্রসাদ *n* extreme graciousness/ propitiousness.

সুপ্রসিদ্ধ *adj* well-known; renowned; celebrated; very famous. **সুপ্রসিদ্ধা** *fem.*

সুপ্রাতঃ *n* fine morning.

সুপ্রাপ্য *adj* easily obtainable/ available.

সুপ্রিয় *adj* dear; beloved; very pleasant.

সুপ্রীত *adj* very delighted; well-pleased with.

সুফল *n* good effect/ result/ fruit. ❑*adj* yielding much/ good fruit; fruitful. **সুফলা** *fem.* **~দায়ক, ~প্রসূ** *adj* yielding good result; producing good effect; fruitful.

সুফলা *adj fem* yielding much/ abundant fruits; abundantly/ richly fructiferous; highly fertile/ productive.

সুফী [A] *n* a sect of Muslim devotees; Muslim mystics; abstemious person; Sufi. ❑*adj* belonging/ relating to the Sufi sect; mystic. **~বাদ** *n* Sufism.

সুবচন *n* good speech; eloquence; good/ wise saying; epigram; maxim; adage; sweet words; salutary wards/ counsel; sweet words.

সুবদন *adj* having a handsome/ beautiful/ pretty face; fair-faced. **সুবদনা, সুবদনী** *fem.*

সুবদ্ধ *adj* bound fast; firmly closed; clenched.

সুবন্দোবস্ত, সুবন্দেজ *nn* good management/ arrangement.

সুবর্ণ *n* **1** gold; gold coin. **2** money; wealth; property. **3** a particular weight of gold. **4** good caste. ❑*adj* **1** of a beautiful/ good colour; brilliant in hue; bright; golden; yellow. **2** made of gold. **3** of a good tribe/ caste. **সুবর্ণা** *adj.*

~খচিত, ~গঠিত, ~নির্মিত *adj* studded/ inlaid/ set with gold. ~ গৈরিক *n* red ochre. ~জয়ন্তী *n* golden jubilee. ~চম্পক *n* yellow-flowering *champak*. ~পদক *n* gold-medal. ~পদকপ্রাপ্ত ব্যক্তি *n* gold-medallist. ~প্রতিমা *n* gold/ golden image; (fig) very beautiful (female) figure/ person. ~বণিক *n* Hindu community originally trading in gold and carrying on banking business; member of this community. ~বর্ণ *adj* golden-coloured. ~ বর্ণা *fem.* ~ময় *adj* made/ consisting of gold. ~ময়ী *fem.* ~রেখা, ~লেখা *nn* streak of gold. ~ সুযোগ *n* golden opportunity.

সুবলিত *adj* well-built; very powerful/ strong.

সুবহ, সুলেহ *adj* easy to be drawn/ carried; portable. ~তা *n* portability.

সুবহ্ *n* [A] morning; dawn; day-break. সুবহে/ সুবে উম্মিদ *n* dawn of hope. সুবহে/ সুবে কাযিব *n* the time just before day-break; light before day-break. সুবহে/ সুবহে সাদেক *n* dawn of day.

সুবহান আল্লাহ [A] *int* God be praised; Good God !

সুবা, সুবে [A]*n* province. ~দার *n* governor of a province; military commissioned officer. ~দারি *n* governorship of a province.

সুবাতাস *n* favourable wind.

সুবাদ *n* relation; connection. এই সুবাদে in this connection; thus related/ connected; thanks to.

সুবাস *n* sweet smell/ odour; fragrance; aroma; perfume.

সুবাসিত *adj* well-scented/ perfumed. ~ করা *vi* perfume; scent. ~ তেল *n* perfumed/ scented oil.

সুবিচার *n* justice; equity; good/ impartial/ wise/ correct judgement. ~ করা *vi* do justice; judge rightly/ impartially/ wisely; meet out justice. ~ক *n* good/ wise/ impartial judge.

সুবিজ্ঞাত *n* well-known.

সুবিদিত *adj* well-known; well understood.

সুবিধা *n* **1** advantage; opportunity; convenience; facility; excellent/ advantageous/ favourable means or circumstance. ~ নেওয়া *vi* take advantage of; avail oneself of an opportunity/ advantage. ~জনক *adj* advantageous; convenient; opportune. ~প্রাপ্ত *adj* placed in an advantageous position; put to an advantage; privileged. ~বাদ *n* opportunism. ~বাদী *adj, n* opportunist. ~মতো *adv* conveniently; at one's convenience. ~-সুযোগ *n* opportunities; facilities.

সুবিধান *n* good order/ arrangement/ regulation/ rule.

সুবিধি *n* good rule/ ordinance/ law.

সুবিনয়, সুবিনীত *adjj* well-educated; well-bred; very modest/ polite; well-behaved.

সুবিন্দু *n* zenith.

সুবিন্যস্ত *adj* well-arranged; well-arrayed; well spread out; orderly; nicely laid out/ displayed.

সুবিপুল *adj* very large/ giant/ numerous/ spacious; huge; immense. সুবিপুলা *fem.*

সুবিমল *adj* perfectly clear/ pure; immaculate.

সুবিশাল=সুবিপুল

সুবিস্তর *adj* very extensive/ large; very great/ intense; abundant.

সুবিস্তীর্ণ, সুবিস্তৃত *adjj* well spread/ laid out; very extensive/ large/ broad; far-flung; vast.

সুবিহিত *adj* well done/ performed/ carried out/ arranged; richly provided with; well supplied.

সুবুদ্ধি *n* good sense/ understanding/ inclination; prudence; discretion; conscientiousness. ❑*adj* good and wise; clever; prudent; conscientious; intelligent; sensible.

সুবৃত্ত *adj* **1** well rounded; beautifully globular/ round. **2** virtuous; good; well-conducted.

সুবৃষ্টি *n* good rain.

সুবৃহৎ *adj* very big/ large; huge; immense; gigantic.

সুবে *n* ⇒ সুবা

সুবেদী *adj* sensitive; perceptive; ~ সমালোচনা.

সুবেশ *n* fine dress/ garment. ❑*adj* well-dressed; well-clad; wearing fine clothes; beautifully dressed.

সুবেশী *adj*=সুবেশ

সুবোধ *n* right intelligence; good understanding/ sense. ❑*adj* easy to be understood; easily taught; easy; well-behaved; docile; sensible. সুবোধ্য *adj* easily understood/ intelligible; lucid; clear.

সুবোশাম *adv* morning and evening (⇒ সুবহ্).

সুব্যক্ত *adj* very clear/ bright; very plain/ distinct/ manifest; clearly expressed; perfectly manifest.

সুব্যবস্থা *n* good arrangement/ management; good provision; good settlement.

সুব্যবস্থিত *adj* well-arranged; well-managed; steady; standing firm.

সুব্রত *adj* strict in observing religious vows; very religious/ virtuous. সুব্রতা *fem* virtuous wife.

সুভক্ষ্য *adj* good to eat; pleasing to the palate; tasteful. ❑*n* excellent food.

সুভব্য *adj* very polite/ courteous/ good-mannered.

সুভাষিত *adj* spoken well/ eloquently. ❑*n* good/ eloquent speech; witty saying.

সুভাষী *adj* speaking friendly words; eloquent; silver-tongued; soft-spoken. সুভাষিণী *fem.*

সুভাস *adj* shining beautifully; brilliant.

সুভিক্ষ *n* abundant supply of provisions; plenty. ❑*adj* having good food/ abundant supply of provisions.

সুভূষণ *adj* well adorned/ decorated. **সুভূষণা** *fem.*

সুমঙ্গল *n* good fortune; great blessing/ benefit. ❑*adj* bringing good fortune; very auspicious.

সুমত *n* good advice/ counsel; good intention.

সুমতি *n* good mind/ disposition; benevolence; good sense: তার ~ হয়েছে, He came back to his senses. Good sense dawned on him.

সুমধুর *adj* very sweet/ tender/ gentle; very delicious; very pleasant; very melodious.

সুমধ্যম *adj* slender-waisted. **সুমধ্যমা** *n fem* graceful woman.

সুমন *n* flower.

সুমনা *adj* good-minded; well-disposed; benevolent; gracious; favourable; wise; large-hearted; learned.

সুমন্ত্রণা *n* good advice/ counsel.

সুমন্ত্রিত *adj* well-advised; wisely planned.

সুমন্দ *adj* very slow/ dull; gentle.

সুমহৎ, সুমহান *adjj* very great; noble; magnificent; magnanimous; high-minded. **সুমহতী** *fem.*

সুমার=শুমার. **~নবিশ** *n* accountant.

সুমিত *adj* well fixed; moderate; restrained; well measured out.

সুমিতি *n* moderation; moderateness; restraint.

সুমিষ্ট=সুমধুর

সুমীমাংসা *n* good/ right/ wise decision or settlement.

সুমীমাংসিত *adj* wisely/ correctly/ nicely/ happily decided or settled.

সুমুখ[1] *n* (colloq)=সম্মুখ

সুমুখ[2] *n* good/ beautiful face or mouth. ❑*adj* fair-faced; handsome.

সুমেধা *adj* having a good understanding; sensible; intelligent.

সুমেরু *n* 1 name of a mythological mountain. 2 North Pole. **~প্রভা** *n* Aurora Borealis. **~বৃত্ত** *n* Arctic circle. **~-মহাসাগর** *n* Arctic ocean.

সুযুক্তি *n* 1 good reasoning/ argument. 2 good advice/ counsel.

সুযোগ *n* favourable juncture; good opportunity; opportune moment; chance; favourable/ convenient time. **~-সুবিধা** *n* facilities. **~-সন্ধানী** *adj* seeking an opportunity; opportunist. ❑*n* opportunist. **সুযোগের প্রতীক্ষা করা** bide one's opportunity/ time.

সুযোগ্য *adj* very competent/ capable/ worthy/ deserving. **~সুযোগ্যা** *fem.*

সুযোজনা *n* good arrangement/ disposition.

সুয়া *a fem* (colloq) favourite; dearly loved by one's husband: ~ রানী.

সুয়ো *adj* (colloq)=সুয়া

সুর[1] *n* 1 (musical) note; tone; sound; melody; key time. 2 voice: মিহি সুরে কথা বলা. 3 accent. **~ করা** *vi* 1 set to music: গানে ~ করা. 2 tune (as a musical instrument). 3 read/ recite in singsong voice/ manner: ~ করে পড়া. **~ বদলানো** 1 change the tune of (a musical instrument). 2 (fig) sing another tune; change one's tune; sing small. 3 pass to another tune/ pitch in singing. **~ বাঁধা** *vi* tune up; adjust the strings etc. (of a musical instrument) to the right pitch. **~ ভাঁজা** *vi* hum a note/ strain/ tune. **~ মিলানো** *vi* bring into harmony/ agreement with, attune to. **~ কম্প** *n* trembling of tone. **~কার** *n* one who sets/ puts sth to music; composer of music. **~জ্ঞান, ~বোধ** *nn* sense of music. **~বোধহীন** *adj* tonedeaf. **~বাহার** *n* a stringed musical instrument. **~শিল্পী** *n* musician; artistic; singer (songstress). **~স্রষ্টা** *n* composer. **এক সুরে বাঁধা** *adj* in unison/ in tune/ concord.

সুর[2] *n* 1 god; divinity; deity. 2 the sun. 3 sage; learned man. **সুরী** *fem.* **~কন্যা** *n fem* daughter of a god; celestial female. **~গুরু** *n* preceptor of the gods, Brihaspati. **~ধুনী, ~নদী** *nn* the Ganges, river of the gods. **~পতি** *n* Indra, the lord of the gods. **~পুর, ~পুরী, ~লোক** *nn* city of the gods; heaven. **~বালা**=~কন্যা. **~বৈরী, ~রিপু** *nn* enemy of the gods; an Asura; demon. **~সুন্দরী ~সুরাঙ্গনা** *n fem* lovely celestial female; Apsara. **সুরারি**=~বৈরী. **সুরালয়**=~পুর. **সুরাসুর** *n* gods and Asuras.

সুরকি, সুরখি [P]*nn* brick-dust.

সুরক্ত *adj* 1 deeply dyed; deep red; crimson. 2 strongly affected/ impassioned; deeply attached.

সুরক্ষা *n* careful protection.

সুরক্ষিত *adj* well-protected; carefully guarded; well-defended; fortified; well-preserved. **সুরক্ষিতা** *adj fem.*

সুরঙ্গ[1] *n* tunnel; hole.

সুরঙ্গ[2] *adj* bright-coloured; vermilion; cinnabar. ❑*n* 1 good colour/ dye. 2 orange tree. **সুরঙ্গা** *n* crystal.

সুরঞ্জিত *adj* deeply coloured/ dyed.

সুরৎ [A] *n* 1 form; figure; shape; face; countenance; aspect; appearance. 2 manner; condition; plight; circumstance. **~ পাল্টানো/ বদলানো** *vt, vi* 1 change; transform; metamorphose; change figure. 2 disguise; personate; feign. **~ বিগড়ানো** *vt* disfigure; deform. **~ওয়ালী** *adj fem* pretty; possessing beauty. **~হাল** *n* 1 statement of facts/ circumstances of a case; written declaration; deposition; on-the-spot investigation. 2 present condition; state of affair.

সুরত[1] *n* amorous/ sexual pleasure or intercourse; coition. ❑*adj* very attached/ enamoured. **সুরতা** *fem.*

সুরত[১]=সুরৎ
সুরতি[১] *n* great enjoyment/ delight; embrace.
সুরতি[২]=সুর্তি
সুরব *n* **1** sweet/ melodious voice/ note. **2** good name/ reputation; renown.
সুরবল্লী *n* an astringent herb; oldenlandia umbellata.
সুরবাহার *n* ⇒ সুর[১]
সুরভি *n* **1** sweet smell; fragrance; perfume; any sweet-smelling substance. **2** name of a fabulous cow. ❑*adj* sweet-smelling; fragrant; perfumed; aromatic. সুরভিত *adj* filled with sweet scents; perfumed. সুরভিতা *fem.*
সুরভী=সুরভি[২]
সুরমা=সুর্মা
সুরমা *adj fem* **1** very beautiful/ graceful/ lovely/ charming. **2** a river in Bangladesh.
সুরম্য *adj* very pleasant/ beautiful; stately; magnificent: ~ অট্টালিকা.
সুরস *adj* **1** rich in water; juicy; well-flavoured; sapid; savoury. **2** sweet; lovely; charming. ❑*n* suit juice. সুরসাল *adj* sweet/ succulent.
সুরসিক *adj* having a very discriminating/ discerning/ fine taste; very witty/ humorous. সুরসিকা *fem.* ~ ব্যক্তি *n* man full of taste/ feeling; man of excellent taste/ wit; humourist.
সুরা *n* spirituous liquor; wine; alcohol. ~পাত্র *n* wine-glass; wine cup; decanter. ~পান *n* drinking. ~ পান করা *vi* drink (wine/ liquor/ alcohol); tipple; booze. ~পানাভ্যাস *n* habit of drinking. ~পানমত্ত, ~পানোদ্দীপ্ত, ~পানোন্মত্ত *adj* drunk; drunken; tipsy; besotted; dead-drunk; sottish. ~পানোন্মাদ *n* drunkenness; intoxication; sottishness; inebriation; tipsiness. ~পায়ী *adj* addicted to drinking; alcoholic; tipsy. ❑*n* drunkard; drunk; bloat; tippler. ~রঞ্জিত *adj* (of eyes) reddened on account of drinking; flushed with drinking. ~সব *n* beer/ spirituous liquor produced by the fermentation of unripe corn. ~সার *n* alcohol; rectified spirit of wine. খাঁটি/ নির্জল ~সার *n* absolute/ pure alcohol. বিশুদ্ধ/ শোধিত ~সার *n* rectified spirit.
সুরাইয়া [A] *n* the pleiades.
সুরাখ [P] *n* hole; orifice. ❑*adj* perforated; having holes.
সুরাঙ্গনা *n* ⇒ সুর[২]
সুরাসুর *n* ⇒ সুর[২]
সুরাহা *n* **1** right path; proper way. **2** good/ adequate remedy; way out; escape: বিপদের ~. **3** solution; issue; answer: সমস্যার ~. **4** opportunity. **5** good arrangement/ provision: টাকার ~. ~ করা *vi* **1** find an adequate remedy. **2** solve; resolve. **3** manage; make good arrangement/ provision for. **4** find a way out. **5** devise a good expedient/ means.
সুরাই, সুরাহি [A] *nn* goblet; long-necked flask.
সুরী *n fem* ⇒ সুর[২]
সুরু=শুরু
সুরুক=শুলুক
সুরুচি *n* good/ refined/ fine taste. ~বান, ~সম্পন্ন *adjj* of refined/ fine taste; of refined culture; cultured; tasteful.
সুরুচির *adj* shining brightly; radiant; brilliant; splendid; beautiful.
সুরুয়া=শুরুয়া
সুরূপ *adj* well-formed; handsome; beautiful; good-looking. সুরূপা *fem.*
সুরেখা *n* auspicious mark/ sign.
সুরেণু *n* mote.
সুরেন্দ্র *n* Indra, king of the gods.
সুরেলা *adj* melodious; musical; dulcet.
সুরেশ্বর *n* lord of the gods; Brahma, Shiva; Indra. সুরেশ্বরী *fem* goddess Durga.
সুর্কি, সুর্কী=সুরকি
সুর্খ [P] *adj* red.
সুর্তি[১] [P] *n* lottery; raffle. ~ খেলা *vi* play at lottery; have a game of lottery; cast lots.
সুর্তি[২] *n* a preparation of powdered tobacco taken with betel leaves.
সুর্মা [P] *n* collyrium; antimony reduced to fine powder for applying to the eyes. ~দানি *n* small box for holding collyrium.
সুলক্ষণ *n* good/ auspicious mark or sign. ❑*adj* bearing good/ auspicious marks on one's person; auspicious. সুলক্ষণা *adj fem.* সুলক্ষণাক্রান্ত *adj*=~.
সুলক্ষিত *adj* well examined/ observed; carefully observed.
সুলতান [A] *n* king; sovereign; emperor; sultan. সুলতানা *fem* queen; empress; sultana. সুলতানাত, সালতানাত *n* empire; kingdom; realm; dominion; sultanate.
সুলতানি, সুলতানী [A] *adj* regal; royal; princely; relating to the sultans. ❑*n*=সুলতানাত.
সুলভ, সুলভ্য *adj* easily accessible/ obtainable/ available; feasible; easy; common; trivial; cheap. সুলভতা *n* state of being easily available/ obtainable; triviality; cheapness. সুলভে *adv* cheaply.
সুললিত *adj* very playful/ wanton/ charming; very sweet/ lovely/ melodious/ pleasant/ musical; delicately soft/ flexible.
সুলিখিত *adj* well-written; perspicuous; pleasant to read.
সুলুক=শুলুক
সুলুপ [E] *n* sloop; light boat; sloop-of-war.
সুলেখ *adj* having/ forming clear lines; clearly written.
সুলেখক *n* good writer/ author. সুলেখিকা *fem.*
সুলোচন *adj* having beautiful/ fine eyes; fine eyed. সুলোচনা *fem.*
সুলোহিত *adj* very red. ❑*n* beautiful red colour.
সুশান্ত *adj* very calm/ placid.
সুশাসক *n* good/ wise ruler.

সুশাসন *n* good/ wise rule or government.

সুশাসিত *adj* well governed/ regulated; wisely governed/ ruled; well-disciplined; kept under good discipline; well-controlled; well-restrained. **সুশাসিতা** *fem.*

সুশিক্ষা *n* good education/ training/ advice.

সুশিক্ষিত *adj* well-educated; well-trained; well taught/ disciplined; well-instructed. **সুশিক্ষিতা** *fem.*

সুশীত, সুশীতল *adjj* very cold/ cooling; freezing; frigid.

সুশীল *adj* good-tempered; having an amiable disposition; good-natured; gentle; having a good character; virtuous. **সুশীলা** *fem.* **~তা** *n* good morals; natural amiability; gentleness.

সুশৃঙ্খল *adj* orderly; regular; systematic; methodical. **~ভাবে** *adv* in an orderly manner; in good order; systematically; methodically; regularly. **সুশৃঙ্খলা** *n* orderliness; good discipline; regularity; order; orderly arrangement.

সুশৃঙ্খলিত *adj*=সুশৃঙ্খল

সুশোভন *adj* very handsome/ beautiful/ decorous; splendid; excellent. **সুশোভনা** *adj.*

সুশোভমান *adj* shining beautifully; handsome; splendid.

সুশোভিত *adj* very beautifully decorated/ adorned/ bedecked; beautified. **সুশোভিতা** *fem.*

সুশ্রাব্য *adj* pleasing to the ear; melodious; sweet.

সুশ্রী, সুশ্রীক *adjj* handsome; beautiful; lovely; comely; pretty.

সুশ্লিষ্ট *adj* closely adhering; close; tight; well joined.

সুষনি *n* an edible aquatic herb.

সুষম *adj* **1** balanced; well-balanced; well-proportioned; regular; even; beautiful; splendid. **~ খাদ্য** *n* balanced diet. **সুষমা** *n* exquisite beauty; splendour; sweet grace. **সুষমাময়** *adj* very beautiful/ graceful. **সুষমাময়ী** *fem.*

সুষির *adj* perforated; pierced; hollow. ❑*n* **1** hollow; hole; cavity. **2** (also **~ যন্ত্র**) wind instrument. **~তা** *n* hollowness.

সুষুপ্ত *adj* fast asleep; sleeping soundly.

সুষুপ্তি *n* deep/ sound sleep.

সুষুম্না (Ayu) *n* a particular artery or vein of the body (lying between those called *ida* and *pingala* and supposed to be one of the passages for the breath or spirit. **~কাণ্ড** *n* spinal chord. **~শীর্ষক** *n* medula oblongata.

সুষ্ঠু *adj* good; apt; fit; proper; excellent; nice; immaculate; smooth. **~ভাবে** *adv* well; fitly; duly; aptly; excellently; nicely; smoothly.

সুসংবাদ *n* good news/ tidings.

সুসংবৃত *adj* well covered/ veiled/ dressed; wrapped up/ concealed in.

সুসংবৃদ্ধ *adj* well thriven; very prosperous.

সুসংযত *adj* well restrained/ controlled; well composed; well governed/ disciplined.

সুসংযুত, সুসংযুক্ত *adjj* closely joined/ united; well composed/ knit together.

সুসংস্কৃত *adj* well-refined; beautifully adorned/ decorated; well cooked/ prepared; well-arranged; very refined/ polite/ civil/ polished.

সুসংস্থিত *adj* well situated; standing firmly; well brought together; well-arranged.

সুসংহত *adj* firmly joined/ combined; closely united; pressed against each other; thoroughly consolidated; well compacted; well knit together.

সুসংহতি *n* great compactness/ consolidation.

সুসঙ্গত *adj* very harmonious/ apt/ proper/ pertinent/ apposite/ appropriate.

সুসঙ্গতি *n* good harmony/ concord; great pertinence/ appositeness.

সুসজ্জ, সুসজ্জিত *adj* well-dressed; well-equipped; well-decorated; well-furnished. **সুসজ্জিতা** *fem.*

সুসজ্জীকৃত, সসজ্জীভূত=সুসজ্জ. **সুসজ্জীকৃতা** *fem.*

সুসন্তান *n* good/ worthy child.

সুসভ্য *adj* highly civilized/ refined.

সুসম *adj* perfectly level/ smooth.

সুসমঞ্জস *adj* perfectly harmonious/ coherent/ congruous.

সুসময় *n* favourable/ prosperous times; good days; opportune/ suitable/ favourable moment.

সুসমাচার *n* **1** good news/ tidings. **2** (Christ) Gospel.

সুসমাপ্ত *adj* well finished/ done.

সুসমাহিত *adj* very intent/ attentive; having the mind intently fixed/ absorbed on an object or a subject; fallen into a trance.

সুসমৃদ্ধ *adj* very wealthy/ prosperous; very abundant.

সুসম্পন্ন *adj* well finished/ supplied; well-executed; well-performed; completed; carried out. **~ করা** *vt* perform/ execute thoroughly or nicely; complete; do thoroughly; carry through.

সুসম্বদ্ধ *adj* coherent; consistent.

সুসহ *adj* easy to be borne/ suffered; fairly tolerable.

সুসাধিত=সুসম্পন্ন

সুসাধ্য *adj* easy to do/ accomplish/ execute performed.

সুসার *n* **1** good essence/ sap/ substance; (financial) ease; plenty; abundance. **2** good arrangement; solution; settlement: কাজের ~ করা.

সুসিক্ত *adj* thoroughly wet/ drenched; soaked; very moist; sodden; dripping.

সুসিদ্ধ *adj* 1 well cooked; thoroughly boiled. 2 thoroughly accomplished/ fulfilled. 3 valid; thoroughly demonstrated/ proved.

সুস্থ *adj* 1 healthy; faring well; sound; fit; well; hearty; blooming. 2 sane; rational; mentally sound: ~ চিন্তা, ~ মন. 3 calm; untroubled; in normal state; unperturbed; peaceful: ~ জীবন. ~ করা *vt* cure; heal; remedy; bring round. ~ হওয়া *vi* 1 get well; yet better; recover; recuperate. 2 come round: মেজাজ ~ হওয়া. ~কায়, ~দেহ, ~দেহী *adjj* healthy; sound of body; robust; able-bodied; fit. ~-চিত্ত *adj* sane; mentally sound; of sound mind; sound of/ in mind; in possession of one's faculties; enjoying mental peace. ~তা *n* health; healthiness; soundness of body or mind; welfare.

সুস্থিত *adj* 1 well established. 2 unshaken (as a heart). 3 being in good condition; well off; easy; comfortable; healthy; prosperous; wealthy; well-established; well-placed (in life). 4 stable; enjoying mental equilibrium.

সুস্থিতি *n* 1 good condition; excellent position; well-being; welfare. 2 stability; equilibrium.

সুস্থির *adj* 1 very firm/ steady; stable; resolute; cool; perfectly calm/ composed. 2 firmly settled/ ascertained/ fixed. ~তা *n* steadiness; coolness; calmness; firmness; stability; calm; tranquility.

সুস্নাত *adj* well purified by bathing; one who has duly performed his ablutions. সুস্নাতা *fem.*

সুস্নিগ্ধ *adj* 1 very smooth/ soft/ gentle. 2 very loving/ tender. সুস্নিগ্ধা *fem.*

সুস্পর্শ *adj* very pleasant to the touch; very soft/ tender.

সুস্পষ্ট *adj* very clear/ distinct/ manifest; evident; thoroughly revealed/ exposed; explicit; categorical. ~রূপে *adv* very clearly; categorically; explicitly; distinctly; in unmistakable terms.

সুস্মিত *adj* smiling sweetly. সুস্মিতা *fem.*

সুস্বন *adj* very loud. ❑*n* loud noise; sweet sound/ note/ melody.

সুস্বপ্ন *n* good/ lucky/ pleasant/ happy dream.

সুস্বর *adj* sweet-voiced; harmonious; melodious. ❑*n* right note/ accent; sweet vice.

সুস্বাদ *adj* having a good taste; well-flavoured; sweet; delicious; tasty. ❑*n* good/ pleasant/ delicious taste.

সুস্বাদু *adj*=সুস্বাদ

সুহাস *adj* having a pleasant smile; pleasantly/ charmingly smiling. সুহাসিনী *fem.*

সুহিত *adj* very fit/ suitable; very salutary/ beneficial. সুহিতা *fem.*

সুহৃদ *n* friend; ally; well-wisher. ❑*adj* kind-hearted. ~বর *n* excellent friend/ ally/ well-wisher. ~সম্মত *adj* friendly.

সুহৃদয় *adj* good-hearted; friendly.

সূক্ত *n* 1 Vedic hymn. 2 wise saying.

সূক্তি *n* good/ friendly speech; wise saying; beautiful verse/ stanza.

সূক্ষ্ম *adj* 1 minute; small; short; narrow; thin. 2 fine; delicate. 3 acute; hair-splitting; subtle; keen: ~ বুদ্ধি. 4 nice; exact; precise: ~ বিচার. 5 subtle; atomic; intangible; astral: ~ শরীর. 6 (mech.) sensitive (of balance). 7 low; low-pitched. 8 very sly; sharp. ~ কীট *n* (zoo) animalcule. ~ কোণ *n* (geom) acute angle. ~কোণী *adj* acute-angled. ~গ্রাহী *adj* delicate; sensitive; susceptible. ~তা *n* minuteness; fineness; delicateness; subtlety; narrowness; sharpness; keenness; sensitiveness; pointedness; great slyness; imperceptibility (by the senses). ~দর্শিতা, ~দর্শিত্ব *nn* quick-sightedness; acuteness; wisdom; keen-sightedness; sagacity; minute and equitable justice; keen discernment; insight; scrutiny. ~দর্শী *adj* quick-sighted; keen-sighted; sharp-sighted; of acute discernment; quick; intelligent; scrutinizing; sagacious; judging minutely and with perfect equity. ~দর্শিনী *fem* ~ দেহ *n* (philo) subtle/ body; astral body. 2 (biol) infusorial. ~দেহী জীবাণু *n* (biol) infusoria. ~ধার *adj* 1 very cutting/ sharp; sharp-edged; incisive; trenchant. 2 flowing/ falling in a very fine stream. ~বস্ত্র *n* fine cloth. ~বিচার *n* minute and equitable judgement; fine discernment; hair-splitting scrutiny. ~বুদ্ধি *n* keen/ fine intelligence; intellectual acumen. ❑*adj* keenly intelligent; sharp witted; discerning; keen-minded; penetrating. ~ভূত *n* subtle element. ~মান *n* (geom) close approximation. ~ শরীর=~ দেহ. সূক্ষ্মাগ্র *adj* pointed; sharp-pointed. সূক্ষ্মাতিসূক্ষ্ম, সূক্ষ্মানুসূক্ষ্ম *adj* extremely fine/ acute/ keen/ thin/ pointed/ delicate/ subtle; hair-splitting; impalpable; fine-drawn; ethereal; very penetrating/ discerning; infinitesimal; microscopic; minuscule.

সূচ *n*=সুচ

সূচক *adj* (also used as a *suff*) indicating; pointing to/ out; showing; designating; expressing; commencing; foreboding; presaging. ❑*n* 1 (alg) index. 2 indicator. 3 manager/ chief actor of a company. ~ শ্রেণী *n* (alg) exponential series. ~ সংখ্যা *n* index number. ~ সূত্র *n* (alg) exponential theorem.

সূচন *n* 1 indication; communication; expression; pointing out. 2 signalling; hinting.

সূচনা *n* 1 beginning; commencement; start; inception. 2 introduction; preface; preamble. 3 presage; foreboding. 4=সূচন. ~ করা *vt* 1 begin; start; commence. 2 introduce; preface; make an introduction. 3 indicate; hit signal;

communicate; show; reveal; betray; point out. 4 forbode; presage.

সূচনীয় *adj* to be pointed out/ indicated.

সূচি *n* 1 needle; any sharp-pointed instrument; awl. 2 indicator (as of a measuring instrument). 3 table of contents; index; list; inventory; catalogue. **~কর্ম, ~শিল্প** *n n* needlework; embroidery. **~খণ্ড** *n* frustum. **~খাত** *vi* pyramid; cone. **~জীবী** *n* tailor. **~নিবদ্ধ** *n* index register. **~পত্র** *n* table of contents; index. **~ভেদ্য** *adj* 1 capable of being pierced with a needle. 2 very dense/ compact; palpable (as darkness): ~ভেদ্য অন্ধকার, pitchblack/ murky/ inky darkness. **~মুখ** *adj* as pointed as a needle; having a pointed end; pin-pointed; very sharp. ❑*n* point of a needle.

সূচিকা=সূচি. **~ভরণ** (Ayu) *n* a drug containing a minute quantity of snake-poison.

সূচিত *adj* 1 pointed out; indicated; hinted; communicated; shown; betrayed; made known by. 2 begun; started; commenced; initiated.

সূচী=সূচি

সূচ্য=সূচনীয়

সূচ্যগ্র *n* point of a needle; as much land as is pierced by the point of a needle; very little; iota; inch. ❑*adj* very little. **~পরিমাণ, ~পরিমিত** *adjj*=~.

সূত *adj* born; engendered; one that has brought forth (young). সূতা *fem.* ❑*n* 1 royal herald/ bard. 2 carpenter.

সূতা=সুতা

সূতি *n* birth; production; parturition; delivery. সূতিকা *n fem* 1 woman who has recently brought forth a child; lying-in woman; a cow that has recently calved. 2 puerperal sickness/ diarrhoea. সূতিকাগার, **~গৃহ** *nn* lying-in chamber. **~জ্বর** *n* puerperal fever.

সূতি, সূতী=সুতি

সূত্র *n* 1 fibre; thread; yarn; cord; string; wire. 2 line; stroke. 3 sacred thread/ cord (worn by the first three classes of Hindus). 4 rule; direction; law. 5 short sentence; aphoristic rule; aphorism: বেদান্ত~, পাণিনির ~. 6 rubric; summary introduction of a subject-matter; argument: আলোচনার ~. 7 (alg) formula. 8 principle: মূল ~. 9 (of dramas) prologue; introduction; commencement; beginning. 10 link; connection: কর্ম~. 11 clue; trail: রহস্যের ~. 12 tie; bond: পরিণয়~. 13 brief hint/ point: তার কথার ~ ধরে … . 14 chain; series: চিন্তা~. **~কার** *n* author of a sutra; manual; aphorizer; aphorist. **~কৃমি** *n* thread-worm; *(pl)* oxyurides. **~ধর** *n* carpenter; joiner. **~ধার** *n* 1=~ধর. 2 stage-manager; principal actor (who superintends the whole performance. **~পাত** *n* commencement; start; beginning; inception. **~পাত করা** *vt* commence; begin; start; initiate. **~পাত হওয়া** *vi* begin; commence; start. সূত্রাকার *adj* filiform.

সূদন *n* killing; destroying; slaying; destruction. ❑*adj* killing; destroying.

সূপ *n* sauce; broth; soup. **~কার** *n* cook.

সূর *n* 1 the sun. 2 wise/ learned man.

সূরী *n* learned man; sage; scholar. ❑*adj* learned; astute; wise; clever.

সূর্প=শূর্প

সূর্য *n* the sun; sun-god. **~কমল** *n* sunflower; heliotrope. **~কর, ~কিরণ** *nn* sunbeam; (ray of) sunshine; sunlight. **~করোজ্জ্বল** *adj* sunlit; bright with sunlight; sunny; sunshiny. **~কান্ত** *n* sun-stone; sun-crystal; burning-glass; flint-glass. **~কেন্দ্রীয়** *adj* heliocentric. **~গ্রহণ** *n* solar eclipse. **~ঘড়ি** *n* sundial. **~তেজ** *n* heat of the sun. **~দেব** *n* sun-god. **~পক্ব** *adj* sunburnt; sunbaked; cooked by the heat of the sun. **~পূজা** *n* sun-worship; heliolatry. **~বংশ** *n* (myth) solar race of Kings. **~প্রভ** *adj* bright as the sun. **~প্রভা**=~কর. **~বংশধর** *n* descendant of the solar race. **~বংশীয়** *adj* belonging to the solar race. **~বিম্ব** *n* disc of the sun. **~ভক্ত** *n* sun-worshipper. **~মণি**=~কান্ত. **~মণ্ডল** *n* orb/ disc of the sun. **~মুখী** *n* sunflower. **~রশ্মি**=~কর. **~লোক** *n* solar system/ region. **~সারথি** *n* Sun's charioteer. **~স্নান** *n* sunbath. সূর্যাবর্তী *adj* heliotropic. সূর্যাবৃত্তি *n* heliotropism. সূর্যালোক *n* sunlight; sunshine. সূর্যাস্ত *n* sunset; sundown. সূর্যাস্তকালে *adv* at sunset/ sundown.

সূর্যোদয় *n* sunrise. **~কালে** *adv* at sunrise.

সূর্যোপাসক *n* sun-worshipper.

সূর্যোপাসনা *n* sun-worship.

সৃক্বণী *n* corner of the lips.

সৃজন *n* creation; production; making; designing; institution; formation. **~ করা** *vt* create; produce; bring into existence; make; form; institute; design. **~কর্তা** *n* creator; maker; God; producer; designer. **~কর্ত্রী** *fem.* **~শক্তি** *n* creativity; creative power. **~শীল** *adj* creative.

সৃজনী *adj* creative. **~শক্তি**=সৃজনশক্তি (⇒ সৃজন).

সৃজা *vt* (poet)=সৃজন করা

সৃজিত=সৃষ্ট

সৃজ্যমান *adj* being created; nascent.

সৃতি *n* wandering; transmigration. **~বিদ্যা** *n* kinematics.

সৃপ্ত *adj* slipped (out of); crept.

সৃষ্ট *adj* created; brought forth; produced; made; formed; designed; instituted. **~জীব** *n* created being.

সৃষ্টি *n* 1=সৃজন. 2 sth created/ made/ instituted. 3 universe. **~ করা**=সৃজন করা. **~কর্তা**=সৃজনকর্তা. **~কর্ম, ~কার্য, ~ক্রিয়া** *nn* creation of the world; work of creation; creative work. **~কৌশল, ~চাতুর্য** *n* (wonderful) art of creation; manner/

method of creation. ~ক্ষমতা *n* creative power/ faculty. ~ছাড়া *adj* not to be found anywhere in God's creation; bizarre; odd; outlandish; eccentric; strange. ~তত্ত্ব *n* cosmology; cosmogony. ~নাশ *n* destruction of the universe. ~নাশ করা *vi* destroy/ dissolve the universe; undo everything. ~নাশা, ~নাশী *adjj* undoing everything; nihilistic; vandalistic; ruinous; destructive. ~নাশিনী *fem.* ~নৈপুণ্য *n* creative ability; skill in creation. ~বাদ *n* doctrine of creation; cosmogony. ~বৈচিত্র্য *n* (wonderful) diversity of the creation. ~রক্ষা *n* preservation of the creation. ~রক্ষা করা *vi* preserve and maintain the creation ~লোপ=~নাশ. ~স্থিতি-প্রলয় *n* creation, preservation and dissolution (of the universe).

সে *pron* 1 he. 2 she. 3 it. ❑*adj* that: সে ব্যক্তি, সে শহর.

সেই *adj* that; that very: ~ রাত. ❑*pron* that person/ thing; that; that time. ❑*adv* 1 after all: ~ তো এলে, তবে দেরি করলে কেন? 2 long ago: ~ যে গেল, ফেরার নামটি নেই. ❑*con* as; so; no sooner than: যেই এল, ~ চলে গেল. ~খান=সেখান. ~জন = সেজন. ~ থেকে *adv* from that time; thenceforth; from that (thing).

সেঁউতি[1], **সেঁউতী** *n* bailing vessel/ bucket.

সেঁউতি[2], **সেঁওতি** *n* kind of indigenous white rose.

সেঁকো, সেঁকো বিষ *nn* arsenic.

সেঁজুতি *n* evening-lamp.

সেঁতসেঁতে *n* (onom) expressing dampness/ wetness/ humidity. ~ করা *vi* be damp/ dank. স্যাঁতসেঁতে *adj* damp; dank; moist.

সেঁধানো *vt, vi* 1 drive into. 2 enter; penetrate; get into.

সেক *n* fomentation. ~ দেওয়া *vt* foment.

সেকরা [P] *n* goldsmith; silversmith. সেকরানী *fem.*

সেকা *vt* 1 warm slowly in heat. 2 toast; bake: রুটি ~. ❑*adj* toasted; baked.

সেকাই *n* (trig) secant.

সেকাল *n* past; past/ bygone days; ancient times; days of yore. ~ ও একাল *n* past and present. সেকালে *adv* at that time; then; in those days.

সেকেন্ড *n, adj* second. ~ হওয়া *vi* stand second. এক সেকেন্ডে in a second/ trice. ~হ্যান্ড *adj* second hand.

সেকেন্দর, সেকান্দর [P] *n* Alexander the great.

সেকেন্দরি, সেকেন্দারী *adj* of king Sekandar Shah. ~ গজ *n* lineal measure in which 1 yard is equal to 3 inches.

সেকেলে *adj* 1 of ancient times; ancient; old; of the past. 2 out-of-date; old-fashioned; outmoded; antiquated; archaic; back-dated; dated. ~ লোক/ বস্তু *nn* back number; anachronism.

সেক্রেটারি [E] *n* secretary.

সেখ=শেখ

সেখান *n* that place. ~কার *adj* of that place. ~ থেকে *adv* from there/ that place. সেখানে *adv* there; at/ in/ to that place.

সেগুন *n* teak; teak-wood.

সেঙাৎ, সেঙ্গাত *nn*=সাঙ্গাত

সেচ *n* 1 sprinkling; watering; spraying; bailing. 2 irrigation. ~কর *n* irrigation tax/ cess. ~ন *n*=~. ~ন করা=সেচা. ~কৃত্যক *n* irrigation service. সেচনযন্ত্র *n* spray. ~নী *n* spray; sprinkling apparatus; watering-can; bail; bale; bailing bucket/ vessel. সেচা *vt* 1 spray; sprinkle. 2 water. 3 bail/ bale out. 4 bail water (out). 5 lift a small quantity from the bottom; fish up/ out. 6 dredge.

সেজ[1] *n* bed.

সেজ[2], **সেজো** *adj* 1 third in order of birth; third-born: ~ছেলে. 2 third in order of seniority: ~ সাহেব.

সেজন *n* 1 that person. 2 the Supreme Being; God.

সেজদা [A] *n* prostration; bowing in prayer so as to touch the ground with the forehead. ~ করা/ দেওয়া *vi* prostrate; adore.

সেজা, সেজানো, সেঝা, সেঝানো=সিজা, সিজানো, সিঝা, সিঝানো respectively.

সেট [E] *n* set: গয়নার ~. ❑*adj* fixed in position; set. ~ করা *vt* put; fix; set.

সেটকানো=সিটকানো

সেটেলমেন্ট [E] *n* settlement.

সেতার [P] *n (n)* a stringed musical instrument; sitar. ~বাদক, সেতারী *nn* one who plays the aforesaid instrument; setarist.

সেতু *n* bridge; causeway; dam; dike; culvert. ~ বাঁধা *vi* build a bridge (over); join by means of bridge; bridge; span. ~বন্ধ *n* 1 forming of a causeway/ bridge; dam; bridge. 2 the ridge of rocks extending from Ramesvar on the South-Eastern coast of India to Sri Lanka. ~বন্ধন *n* construction of a bridge/ dam; bridge: dam.

সেথা, সেথায়=সেখানে

সেথো *n* companion; traveller's professional companion and guide. ~গিরি *n* act/ profession of accompanying/ guiding a traveller.

সেন *n* 1 commander; hero: ভীম~. 2 a Hindu family name.

সেনসর [E] *n* censor.

সেনসাস [E] *n* census.

সেনা *n* 1 soldier. army; serviceman; armed forces; troop/ band/ body of men; troop of soldiers. ~গ্র, ~গ্রভাগ *nn* front/ van of an army. ~গ্রগামী *adj* going at the front of an army. ❑*adj* general. ~ঙ্গ *n* component part of an army. ~চর *n* soldier; warrior. ~জীব, ~জীবী=~চর. ~ধিকারিক *n* army/ military officer. ~ধিপ, ~ধ্যক্ষ, ~নায়ক *nn* commander of an army; general

~নিবাস *n* army quarters; cantonment; barracks; garrison. ~নিবেশ করা *vi* array/ station soldiers. ~নী, ~পতি=~ধিপ. প্রধান ~পতি *n* commander-in-chief. ~পতিত্ব, ~পত্য *nn* commandership; generalship; command. ~পতিত্বে *adj* under sb's command. ~বাস *n* camp; cantonment. ~ব্যূহ *n* battle-array. ~ভঙ্গ *n* breaking of an army; rout; disorderly fight; debacle. ~মুখ=~গ্র. ~শিবির *n* army encampment; cantonment. পশ্চাদ্বর্তী ~ *n* rear party of an army. পুরোবর্তী ~ *n* vanguard; advance party of an army.

সেন্ট [E] *n* scent.

সেন্সর = সেনসর

সেন্সাস = সেনসাস

সেপাই=সিপাহী

সেপায়া [P]*n* tripod.

সেপ্‌টেম্বর, সেপ্টেম্বর [E] *n* September.

সেবক[1] *adj* **1** revering; worshipping; following. **2** serving; waiting upon; nursing. ❑*n* **1** worshipper; votary; follower. **2** servant; attendant; nurse; sick-nurse; waiter. সেবিকা *fem.* ~সমিতি *n* organization of social works. সেবকাধম *n* the humblest of servants; obsequious servant.

সেবক[2] *n* sewer.

সেবন[1] *n* **1** indulgence in; practice/ employment of; devotion/ addiction to; fondness for: গঞ্জিকা ~. **2** act of taking/ eating/ drinking/ smoking: ঔষধ ~. **3** waiting upon; attendance; serving; service. **4** worship; reverence; adoration; revering. ~ করা *vt* take; eat; drink; smoke; enjoy; use; employ; have.

সেবন[2] *n* sewing; darning; stitching.

সেবনীয় *adj* **1** to be taken/ eaten/ drunk/ smoked/ enjoyed/ used/ employed/ had/ made use of. **2** to be honoured/ revered/ worshipped; honourable; worthy of being worshipped. **3** to be served/ waited upon/ obeyed; worthy of being served/ nursed.

সেবমান *adj* **1** honouring; worshipping; revering. **2** serving; attending upon. **3** nursing.

সেবা **1** service; serving. **2** nursing; waiting upon. **3** worship; homage; reverence; devotion to. **4** addiction to; indulgence in; practice/ employment/ frequent enjoyment of. **5** taking; eating; drinking; smoking. ❑*vi* =~ করা. ~ করা *vi* **1** serve. **2** wait upon; nurse. **3** worship; honour; obey. **4**=সেবন করা. ~ইত *n* votary; worshipper; priest and beneficiary of a temple or religious institution. ~কর্ম, ~কার্য *n* service; domestic service; attendance; nursing. ~দাস *n* **1** servant. **2** (derog) lackey; stooge. ~দাসী *fem.* **1** maidservant. **2** maiden dedicated to the service of a temple/ religious institution. **3** woman who serves an ascetic or a Vaishnava devotee or the head of a religious institution. **4** (iron) concubine. ~ধর্ম *n* sacred task of serving others; social service looked upon as a religion. ~য়ত, ~য়েত=~ইত. ~বৃত্তি *n* livelihood gained by service. ~ব্রত *n* social service as a religion. ❑*adj* devoted to humanitarian service.

সেবিত *adj* **1** enjoyed; taken; eaten; drunk; smoked. **2** served; waited upon. **3** nursed. **4** worshipped.

সেবিতব্য=সেবনীয়

সেবী *adj* (used as a *suff)* **1** one who serves/ waits on; serving; waiting on. **2** enjoying; practising; employing; addicted to; fond of. **3** one who nurses; nursing. **4** worshipping.

সেব্য=সেবনীয়

সেমই=সেমতি

সেমতি *adv* (archaic) like that; as.

সেমাই *n* kind of vermicelli which is cooked with milk and sugar.

সেমিকোলন [E] *n* semicolon.

সেমিজ=শেমিজ

সেমিটিক [E] *n* Semitic.

সেমিনার [E] *n* seminar.

সেয়ান, সেয়ানা *adjj* **1** shrewd; sly; clever; conscious. **2** feigning. **3** of age; adult: ~ মেয়ে. ~ পাগল *n* one feigning madness; feigning madman; one who has a method in one's madman. সেয়ানে সেয়ানে কোলাকুলি (fig) find/ meet one's match; diamond cuts diamond.

সের *n* a Bengali measure of weight (=o. 933 kg); seer. ~কিয়া *n* table of counting by seers. ~কে *adv* in/ for each seer. সেরা, সেরী *adjj* weighing so many pounds: দশ~.

সরকশ [P] *n* refractory; rebellious; obstinate.

সেরা[1] *adj* best; excellent; choicest.

সেরা[2], **সেরী** *adjj* ⇒ সের

সেরূপ *adj* of that form/ kind. ❑*adv* **1** so; as much. **2**=সেরূপে. সেরূপে *adv* in that manner/ way.

সেরেফ *adj, adv* (A) only; alone; mere; merely; sheer; purely; excessively; unmixed.

সেরেস্তা, সেরেশতা [P] *n* **1** office. **2** department. ~দার *n* office superintendent; headclerk; record-keeper; chief clerk. ~দারি *n* office/ post of a headclerk/ office superintendent.

সেলাই *n* sewing; stitching; stitch; seaming; darning; seam. ~ করা *vt* sew; stitch; darn; seam. ~ খোলা *vt, vi* unsew; unstitch; get unsewn. সেলাইয়ের ফোঁড় *n* stich. চণ্ডীপাঠ থেকে জুতা ~ পর্যন্ত all kinds of job.

সেলাখানা [P]*n* aruroury; arsenal.

সেলাম *n* সালাম

সেলামি=সালামি

সেলুন [E] *n* saloon; barber's shop.

সেলুলয়েড [E] *n* celluloid.

সেলেখানা=সেলাখানা

সেলেট [E] *n* slate.

সেস [E] *n* cess; tax; local rate.

সেসন, সেশন [E] *n* session; (law) sessions. ~ জজ *n* sessions-judge. সেসনে পাঠানো *vt* commit to/ send up to the sessions. **2** academic session.

সেহা [P] *n* account book; entry showing payment of rent. ~ করা *vt* enter/record rent-receipt. ~নবিশ, ~নবিস *n* accountant; book-keeper. ~বহি *n* account book.

সেহাই [P] *n* ink. ~ কলম *n* ink and pen; writing.

সেহেতু *conj* for that reason; because of that; that is why.

সেহেরা *n* a garland worn on the forehead by the bride and the bridegroom at the marriage ceremony.

সেহেরি [A] *n* food taken by Muslims a little before dawn during the fasting month of Ramadan.

সেহেলি=সহিলি

সৈ=সই

সৈকত *n* sea-beach; sand-bank; sandy shore/ soil; bank; shore. ❑*adj* sandy; gravelly.

সৈনাপত্য *n* command of an army; generalship; commandership.

সৈনিক *n* **1** soldier; army-man; fighter. **2** guard; sentinel. ❑*adj* belonging/ relating to an army; military; martial. ~ জীবন *n* profession/life of/as a soldier; army/military life. ~ পুরুষ *n* soldier; fighting man; fighter. ~ বৃত্তি *n* profession of a soldier; military profession. ~বৃত্তি অবলম্বন করা *vi* become a soldier.

সৈনিকোচিত *adj* soldier-like; soldierly; befitting a soldier.

সৈন্ধব *adj* **1** relating to the sea; oceanic; marine; aquatic. **2** belonging to/produced in/coming from the Indus or Sind. ❑*n* rock-salt; salt. ~ লবণ *n*=~.

সৈন্য *n* **1** soldier; serviceman; army; armed forces. **2** sentinel; guard. ❑*adj* belonging to/proceeding from an army. ~দল *n* army; regiment; troops. ~নিবাস *n* barracks. ~ পরিচালন, ~ সঞ্চালন *nn* manoeuvre; command of an army. ~ পরিচালনা করা *vt* command/ manoeuvre/ lead an army. ~বাস *n* camp of an army. ~ যোজন *n* mobilization (of an army). ~ সমাবেশ *n* concentration/array of troops. ~ সমাবেশ করা *vt* concentrate/ array/ station/ mobilize troops. ~সামন্ত *n* armed forces and vassals; army; soldiers; troops; armed forces.

সৈন্যাধ্যক্ষ *n* commander of an army; general; commander-in-chief. প্রধান সৈন্যাধ্যক্ষ *n* commander-in-chief. স্থায়ী ~ *n* standing army.

সৈমন্তিক *n* red-lead.

সৈয়দ [A] *n* **1** descendant of the holy Prophet. **2** lord; master; prince; chief.

সোঁওয়াব=সোয়াব

সোঁ=শোঁ

সোঁটা *n* thick stick/staff; cudgel.

সোঁত[1] *n* (dial)=স্রোত. সোঁতা *n* very thin stream.

সোঁত[2] *adj* entire; whole.

সোঁদা *adj* **1** smelling like dry earth wetted with rain-water. **2** sweet.

সোঁদাল *n* kind of plant with yellowing flowers; *Cursia fistula.*

সোচ্চার *adj* loud; clamorous; strident; vociferous. ~ হওয়া *vi* be loud; raise one's voice.

সোচ্ছ্বাস *adj* **1** enthusiastic. **2** breathing hard; panting.

সোজা *adj* **1** straight; not curved: ~ লাঠি. **2** simple; simple-hearted; honest; upright; virtuous: ~ মানুষ. **3** chastened; chastised; disciplined; coerced: মার খেয়ে ~ হওয়া. **4** easy: কাজটা ~ নয়. **5** easy to understand; plain: কথাটার মানে খুব ~. **6** lying straight in front of: নাক-~. **7** lying continually onward: রাস্তাটা ~ চলে গেছে. **8** shortest; not circuitous; direct: ~ পথ. **9** straightforward; unequivocal; plain: ~ কথা. ❑*adv* straight ahead; continuously onward. ~ করা *vt* chasten; chastise; coerce; correct; teach a lesson to; rectify. ~ হওয়া *vi* be chastened/corrected/chastised. ~সুজি *adv* **1** plainly; categorically; straight; outspokenly; straightforwardly; unequivocally. **2** by the straight/shortest route; straightway; straightly; directly; in a direct course.

সোটা=সোঁটা

সোডা [E] *n* soda; sodium carbonate; sodium bicarbonate; washing soda. ~ ওয়াটার *n* soda water.

সোত=সোঁত

সোৎকণ্ঠ *adj* having an ardent desire; ardently longing for; eager; anxious.

সোৎপ্রাস *adj* derisive; ironical; scornful.

সোৎসব *adj* festive; with festivity; ceremonial.

সোৎসাহ *adj* ardent; zealous; enthusiastic; energetic. সোৎসাহে *adv* enthusiastically; ardently; zealously; with enthusiasm; energetically.

সোৎসুক *adj* yearning/longing for; anxious about.

সোদর *n* (colloq) সহোদর

সোদ্বেগ *adj* agitated; disturbed; anxious; fearful.

সোদ্যম *adj* energetic; enterprising.

সোদ্যোগ *adj* energetic; zealous.

সোনা *n* **1** gold; gold-ornament. **2** (as a term of endearment) precious; treasure. ❑*adj* **1** golden; yellow; gold-coloured. **2** sweet; precious; gentle-natured: ~ মেয়ে. ~ কষা *vi* test gold by streak. ~চাঁপা *n* = সুবর্ণচম্পক (⇒ সুবর্ণ). ~দানা *n* gold ornament; riches. ~ব্যাঙ *n* a species of yellow frog; golden frog. ~মুখ *n* sweet face; fair and bright face; happy face. ❑*adj* having a sweet/bright/fair face; fair-faced. ~মুখী *fem* of ~মুখ. ☐*n* senna. ~মুখ করে *adv* with an expression of happiness/ delight; delightedly. ~য় সোহাগা (fig) 1 a happy match; perfect/most desirable union. 2 (iron) alliance of two vile persons. ~র অঙ্গ *n* golden body; excellent form. ~র কাঠি, রূপার কাঠি (folk-tales) wands of gold and silver; means of keeping alive or killing. ~র খনি *n* goldmine. ~র গহনা *n* gold ornaments. ~র জল ⇒ gold ink; gold paint. ~র পাত *n* gold-leaf. ~র পাথর বাটি (fig) an absurdity; a mare's nest. ~র বাট *n* gold bar. ~র বেনে=সুবর্ণবণিক. ~র সংসার *n* a happy and prosperous family. ~রু *n* goldsmith. ~লি, ~লী *adj* golden; gold-coloured; gilded. ~লি আঁশ *n* golden fibre; jute. ~লি কালি *n* gold ink. ~লি চুল *n* golden hair. ~লি চুলওয়ালা *adj* golden-haired. ~লি জরি *n* gold-thread. ~লি মাছ *n* goldfish. কাঁচা/পাকা সোনা *n* pure/unalloyed gold. কেলে ~ *n* (term of endearment) a dark-complexioned son; Sri Krishna. মেকি ~ *n* counterfeit gold.

সোপকরণ *adj* together with the implements; properly equipped.

সোপচার *adj* with all articles of food and clothing required to be offered in religious worship.

সোপর্দ, সোপরদ্দ [P] *n* charge; care; keeping; giving over; trust; commitment; delivery; submission; resignation. ~ করা *vt* 1 give in charge; consign; entrust. 2 send up/commit for trial.

সোপাধিক *adj* 1 having some peculiar attribute/distinguishing title. 2 restricted by some condition/limitation/stipulation.

সোপান *n* stairs; step; staircase; ladder; escalator. ~পঙ্‌ক্তি, ~শ্রেণী, সোপানাবলি *nn* line/flight of stairs; staircase.

সোফা [E] *n* sofa.

সোবহানাল্লাহ=সুবহান আল্লাহ

সোবে [A] *n* doubt.

সোম *n* 1 the moon. 2 Monday. 3 name of a plant (said to be the climbing plant *Sacrostema viminalis* or *Asclepias acida*). 4 juice of the Soma plant. ~বার *n* Monday. ~রস *n* juice of the Soma plant. ~রাজ *n* name of a plant. ~লতা *n* the Soma plant.

সোমত্ত *adj fem* (colloq) of age; grown-up; marriageable; of marriageable age.

সোয়াদ *n* (dial)=স্বাদ

সোয়ামি *n* (dial)=স্বামী

সোয়ার=সওয়ার

সোয়ারি=সওয়ারি

সোয়াল=সওয়াল

সোয়াস্তি *n* (dial, colloq)=স্বস্তি

সোর=শোর. ~-শরাবত, ~-সরাবত *n* noise; tumult; disturbance. ~গোল, ~সার *n* hue and cry; clamour; hullabaloo; uproar.

সোরপোষ [P] *n* cover; lid.

সোরা=শোরা

সোরাই, সোরাহি=সুরাই

সোলা, শোলা *n* sponge-wood. ~র টুপি *n* sola hat.

সোলে [A] *n* compromise. ~ করা *vi* compromise. ~নামা *n* deed of compromise.

সোসর *adj* 1 (archaic) equal; like; equal in power/ strength. 2 collaborator.

সোসাইটি [E] *n* society.

সোহবত [A] *n* 1 companionship; society; company; association. 2 conversation. 3 intercourse; carnal intercourse; cohabitation. ~ করা *vi* 1 keep company with. 2 cohabit; copulate.

সোহম, সোহং (phrase) I am He. সোহংবাদ *n* the philosophical doctrine that identifies God with individual soul.

সোহরৎ=শোহরত

সোহাগ *n* 1 love; affection; tender feelings; 2 caress; amorous caress; fondling; petting. ~ করা *vt* 1 treat with affection. 2 caress; caress amorously; fondle; pet.

সোহাগা *n* borax.

সোহাগী, সোহাগিনী *adjj* enjoying love of; beloved. ☐*n* woman loved much by her husband.

সোহিনী=শোহিনী

সৌকর্য *n* easiness of performance; facility of doing.

সৌকুমার্য *n* tenderness; delicacy; great beauty/ grace; great softness; attractive youth/ youthfulness.

সৌক্ষ্ম্য *n* minuteness; fineness; subtlety.

সৌখিন, সৌখীন=শৌখিন

সৌগন্ধ, সৌগন্ধ্য *nn* fragrance; sweet smell; perfume; aroma.

সৌগন্ধিক *n* dealer in perfumes. ☐*adj* sweet-scented; fragrant.

সৌজন্য *n* 1 goodness; kindness; friendliness; courtesy; good manners; civility. 2 compliments : ~ সংখ্যা/ কপি, complimentary copy.

সৌজাত্য *n* good birth. ~বিদ্যা *n* eugenics.

সৌদামিনী *n* lightning; electricity.

সৌধ *n* palace; fine house; stuccoed mansion; edifice. ~কিরীটিনী *adj fem* adorned with numerous palaces. ~চূড়া, ~মৌলী, ~শিখর *nn* top/turret of a palace.

সৌন্দর্য *n* beauty; loveliness; gracefulness; elegance; grace. ~গর্ব, ~গরিমা *nn* pride of beauty. ~গর্বিত *adj* proud of beauty. ~গর্বিতা *fem.* ~জনিত *adj* caused by beauty. ~বর্ধক *adj* enhancing/augmenting beauty; embellishing; adding to grace/ charm. ~পূর্ণ, ~মণ্ডিত *adj* highly beautiful; graceful; beauteous; exquisite; gorgeous; ravishing. ~ভার, ~সম্ভার

nn great beauty. ~মত্ত *adj*=~গর্বিত. ~ময়=~পূর্ণ. ~ময়ী *fem*. ~শালী, ~সম্পন্ন=~পূর্ণ. ~শালিনী, ~সম্পন্না *fem*. ~হীন *adj* devoid of beauty; ugly; graceless; ungainly; hideous. ~হীনা *fem*.

সৌপ্তিক *adj* connected with/relating to sleep; nocturnal. ❑*n* attack on sleeping men; nocturnal combat.

সৌবর্ণ *adj* golden.

সৌভাগ্য *n* good luck; good fortune; success; prosperity; happiness. ~ক্রমে *adv* by good luck; luckily; fortunately. ~বলে, ~বশত, ~বশে= ~ক্রমে. ~বান *adj* lucky; fortunate; prosperous. ~বতী *fem*. ~মদ *n* intoxication (produced) by happiness/prosperity. ~রবি, ~সূর্য *nn* great fortune/prosperity; lucky star. ~লক্ষ্মী *n fem* (myth) goddess of fortune; good fortune personified. ~শালী=~বান. ~শালিনী *fem*.

সৌভিক *n* juggler; conjurer; wizard; magician.

সৌভ্রাত্র *n* good brotherhood; fraternity.

সৌমনস্য *n* satisfaction of mind; gladness; cheerfulness.

সৌমিত্র, সৌমিত্রি *n* son of Sumitra.

সৌম্য *adj* **1** placid; gentle; mild; mentally balanced. **2** cool and moist. **3** dignified; unruffled. **4** beautiful; majestic. ❑*n* (vocative) good/excellent sir. ~তা *n* gentleness; placidity; mildness; beauty; graciousness. ~দর্শন *adj* pleasant to look at; good-looking; handsome; majestic; dignified; unruffled; having a calm/placid appearance. ~ভাব *n* mental calm/equilibrium; placidity. ~মূর্তি *adj* = ~দর্শন. ❑*n* calm/ placid/ unruffled appearance; handsome figure. সৌম্যাকৃতি *n* = ~ মূর্তি.

সৌর *adj* relating to/belonging to/coming from the sun; solar; haliolatrous. ❑*n* worshipper of the sun. ~কর, ~কিরণ *n* sunbeam; sunlight; sunshine. ~কলঙ্ক *n* sun-spot. ~কাল *n* solar time. ~চিকিৎসা *n* sun-bath. ~জগৎ *n* solar region/sphere/system. ~দিন, ~দিবস *n* solar day. ~বৎসর, ~বর্ষ *nn* solar year; astronomical/ equinoctial/ natural year. ~বর্ণালী *n* solar spectrum. ~মণ্ডল=~জগৎ. ~মাস *n* solar month.

সৌরভ *n* fragrance; perfume; aroma. সৌরভান্বিত *adj* fragrant; perfumed; sweet-scented.

সৌরাজ্য *n* good sovereignty; good government.

সৌষ্ঠব *n* **1** beauty; grace; decorum; excellence. **2** beautiful symmetry; shapliness: অঙ্গ~. **3** smoothness; extreme skilfulness; cleverness: কাজের ~. সৌষ্ঠবান্বিত *adj* graceful; beautiful; decorous; shapely; handsome.

সৌসাদৃশ্য *n* close/nice similarity or resemblance.

সৌহার্দ, সৌহার্দ্য, সৌহৃদ্য *nn* good-heartedness; affection; friendship for/with; fellow-feeling; cordiality. ~পাশ, ~বন্ধন *nn* bond/tie of friendship.

স্কন্দ *n* (myth) Kartikeya, the god of war.

স্কন্ধ *n* **1** shoulder; upper part of the back or region from the neck to the shoulder-joint (of man and animal). **2** stem/trunk of a tree. **3** chapter; section (of a book); canto. **4** part; division (of an army). স্কন্ধে করা/ নেওয়া/ বহন করা *vt* shoulder; take up/carry upon one's shoulders. ~দেশ *n* region of the shoulder; shoulders.

স্কন্ধী *adj* having a big stem. ❑*n* tree.

স্কলারশিপ [E] *n* scholarship.

স্কুল [E] *n* school. ~ পালানো *vi* play truant. স্কুলে যাওয়া *vi* (in case of a student) go to school; (in case of others) go to the school. স্কুলের ছুটি *n* school holiday. স্কুলের শিক্ষা *n* school education. স্কুলের সময় *n* school hours.

স্ক্রু, স্ক্রুপ [E] *nn* screw. ~ আঁটা *vt* screw (up); fasten/tighten with a screw(s). ~ খোলা *vt* unscrew; come unscrewed; open/ loose/ detach by screwing. মাথার ~ ঢিলা থাকা have a screw loose.

স্খলন *n* **1** falling; fall; falling into. **2** stumbling; tottering; tripping; unsteady gait; slipping; act of slipping off. **3** mistake; blundering; lapse; error; aberration; act of going astray. **4** mumbling; faltering; stammering; slip of the tongue; stuttering; unguarded utterance of undesirable things. **5** displacement (of argument). **6** discharge; emission (of semen). **7** shedding; act of coming off/getting detached; loosening; detachment.

স্খলিত *adj* **1** fallen. **2** stumbling; stumbled; tripping; unsteady. **3** dropping; falling; dripping; trickling down. **4** stammering; faltering (speech); stuttering; mumbling. **5** erring; failing; blundering; aberrant; gone astray. **6** intoxicated; drunk; shed; detached; loosened; slipped (off); slipping; come off. ~ হওয়া *vi* **1** fall; be shed; come off; get detached/loose; loosen; slip off. **2** stumble; trip; totter; loose one's foot; waver; fluctuate. **3** drop/slip (down); trickle down. **4** stammer; falter (as speech); make mistakes; blunder; err; fail; go astray; aberrant. স্খলিতা *fem*. ~কণ্ঠ *adj* mumbling; stuttering; stammering; faltering. ~গতি *adj* having an unsteady gait; tottering; staggering. ~চরণ, ~পদ *adjj* stumbling; having unsteady steps; stumbled. ~ চরণে, ~ পদে *adv* with unsteady steps; faltering by. ~বচন, ~বাক্য *adjj* making mistakes in speaking; stammering; faltering; blundering. ~মতি *adj* erring in judgement; weak-minded.

স্খালন *n* **1** felling; shedding; detaching; loosening. **2** extenuation. **3** removal; absolution. **4** washing: পদ~. ~ **করা** *vt* **1** fell; shed; detach; loosen. **2** extenuate; remove; absolve . **3** wash.

স্খালিত *adj* **1** felled; shed; detached; loosened. **2** extenuated; removed; absolved. **3** washed. **স্খালিতা** *fem.*

স্টার্চ [E] *n* starch.

স্টার্লিং [E] *n* sterling. ~**-স্থিতি** *n* sterling balance.

স্টিম [E] *n* steam. **অতিতাপিত** ~ *n* superheated steam. **স্টিমার** *n* steamer. **স্টিমার ঘাট** *n* steamer-station; pier; wharf.

স্টুয়ার্ড [E] *n* steward.

স্টেথিসকোপ [E] *n* stethoscope.

স্টেশন [E] *n* station.

স্টোভ [E] *n* stove.

স্টোর [E] *n* store.

স্ট্যাম্প [E] *n* stamp. ~**-পরিদর্শক** *n* stamp reporter. ~**বিক্রেতা** *n* stamp vendor.

স্তন *n* **1** female breast. **2** teat; dug; udder. **3** nipple. ~**ত্যাগ** *n* weaning. ~**দুগ্ধ** *n* breast-milk. ~**ন্ধয়**=~প. ~**ন্ধয়ী** *fem.* ~**প**, ~**পায়ী** *adjj* sucking the breast. ❑*nn* suckling; breast-fed infant. ~**পা**, ~**পায়িকা** *fem.* ~**বৃন্ত** *n* nipple. ~**ভার** *n* swelling bosom. ~**মণ্ডল** *n* orb/projection of the female breast. ~**মুখ**, **স্তনাগ্র** *nn* nipple. **স্তনাংশুক** *n* cloth covering the breasts. **স্তনান্তর** *n* **1** the space between the breasts; centre of the chest. **2** a mark on the breast (superstitously supposed to be indicating future widowhood). **3** another breast.

স্তনন *n* **1** sounding; sound; noise. **2** rumbling of clouds. **3** groaning; breathing hard.

স্তনিত *adj* sounding; thundering; reverberating; resounding. ❑*n* **1** thunder; rumbling of clouds. **2** loud groaning.

স্তন্য *n* milk; breast-milk. ❑*adj* contained in the female breast. ~**জীবী**=~**পায়ী**. ~**ত্যাগ** *n* ceasing to drink a mother's milk; being weaned. ~ **ত্যাগ করা** *vi* cease to suck mother's breast/ give suck to baby; be weaned. ~ **ত্যাগ করানো** *vt* wean. ~**দাত্রী** *adj fem* suckling. ❑*n* mother; wet-nurse. ~**দান** *n* the giving of milk from the breast. ~ **দান করা** *vt* suckle. ~**পান** *n* sucking of milk from the breast. ~ **পান করা** *vi* (of a baby) suck its mother's breast: ~**পায়ী** *adj* sucking milk from the breast; unweaned; mammalian. ~**পায়ী প্রাণী** *n* mammal. ~**পায়ী প্রাণিবর্গ** *n* Mammalia. ~**পায়ী শিশু** *n* suckling.

স্তব *n* praise; eulogy; song of praise; hymn; panegyric; glorification; adulation. ~ **করা** *vt.vi* praise; sing in praise of; glorify; eulogize; celebrate; adulate. ~**গান**, ~**ন** *nn* praising; songs of praise; adulation. ~**পাঠ** *n* recital of a song of praise/a hymn. ~**স্তুতি** *n* praise and solicitation; adoration; adulation.

স্তবক *n* **1** cluster (of blossoms); bunch (of flowers); bouquet; nosegay. **2** tuft. **3** stanza; chapter/section (of a book). **4** collection; multitude; quantity. **5** tassel. **6** cyme.

স্তবকিত *adj* clustered; bunched together/up; full of blossoms.

স্তব্ধ, **স্তব্ধীভূত** *adjj* **1** immovable; paralysed; (rendered) motionless; stunned; stupefied; senseless; fallen/lying in a stupor; dazed. **2** stiff; rigid; stiffened. **স্তব্ধতা** *n* motionlessness; stiffness; stupefaction; immovability; torpor; immobility; quietude.

স্তম্ব *n* **1** clump/tuft of grass; clump; bunch; cluster. **2** the post to which an elephant is tied.

স্তম্ভ *n* **1** post; pillar; column. **2** stem (as of a tree). **3** fixedness; stiffness; rigidity; torpor; paralysis; stupefaction; motionlessness. **4** stagnation; stagnancy. **5** becoming hard/ solid; stoppage; obstruction; suppression; magical arresting of any feeling/force (as of hunger, thirst or of the forces of fire, water, etc). **6** support; propping; strengthening. ~**ক** *adj* stopping; arresting. ❑*n* (geom) cylinder. ~**কর** *adj* **1** causing obstruction; hindering; impeding. **2** causing stiffness; paralysing; stupefying. ~**ন** *n* **1** stiffening; making rigid/ immovable; stopping; arresting; checking; restraining; stupefaction; becoming stiff/rigid. **2** stopping/arresting (by magical means). **3** astringent; styptic. ~**লিপি** *n* epitaph. **স্তম্ভাকার** *adj* shaped like a pillar; cylindrical; columnal.

স্তম্ভিত *adj* **1** stiffened; paralyzed; benumbed; stupefied; astounded; stunned; rendered motionless. **2** stopped; brought to a standstill; suppressed; restrained; made stagnant. **স্তম্ভিতা** *fem.* ~ **করা** *vt* **1** stupefy; benumb; paralyze; stiffen; stun; astound; render motionless. **2** stop; bring to a stand-still; suppress; restrain. ~ **হওয়া** *vi* be dumbfounded; be struck dumb with amazement.

স্তর *n* **1** layer. **2** stratum. **3** bed. **4** tier. **5** lamina. ~**নতি** *n* dip of a strata. ~**বিন্যাস** *n* stratification. ~**মেঘ** *n* stratus. **স্তরায়ন** *n* stratification. **স্তরে স্তরে** *adv* in layers; in tiers; layer by layer. **স্তরে স্তরে স্থাপিত** stratified; tiered.

স্তরিত *adj* stratified; laminate(d). ~ **বস্তু** *n* laminated core. **স্তরণ** *n* lamination.

স্তরীভূত *adj* stratified. ~ **শিলা** *n* (geog) stratified rock.

স্তবক *n* **1**stanza. **2** a bunch (of flower). **3** hymn.

স্তাবক *adj* praising; extolling; flattering. ❑*n* panegyrist; praiser; eulogizer; adulator; flatterer. ~**তা** *n* flattery; adulation; servility; blandishment.

স্তাম্ভিক *adj* (minerl) columnar.

স্তিমিত *adj* **1** still; calm; tranquil; motionless; immobile; unmoving; fixed. **2** wet; moist; damp. **3** dim; faint: ~ প্রদীপ. ~ **নয়ন,** ~ **নেত্র** *adjj* having the eyes intently fixed. ~ **নয়নে,** ~ **নেত্রে** *advv* looking fixedly; gazingly.

স্তুত *adj* praised; eulogized; hymned; glorified; celebrated; recited with praise (as a hymn); flattered; propitiated; adulated.

স্তুতি *n* praise; eulogy; hymn; panegyric; commendation; adulation; glorification; propitiation; propitiatory speech. ~ **করা** *vi* praise; laud; glorify; eulogize; extol; celebrate in song/hymns; sing in praise of; flatter; propitiate. ~**পাঠক** *n* panegyrist; bard; herald. ~**প্রিয়** *adj* fond of praise/flattery/adulation. ~**বাণী,** ~**বাদ** *nn* laudatory speech; eulogy; encomium.

স্তূপ *n* **1** heap; pile. **2** mound; low hill. **3** Buddhist monument; tope. ~/**স্তূপাকার করা** *vt* heap; pile up. ~ **পর্বত** *n* block mountain. ~**মেঘ** *n* cumulus. **স্তূপাকার, স্তূপাকৃতি** *adj* collected in a heap; piled up.

স্তূপীকৃত *adj*=স্তূপাকার (⇒ স্তূপ)

স্তোক[1] *n* **1** praise. **2** temptation; enticement. **3** consolation; false hope/assurance/promise: ~ দিয়ে রাখা. ~**বাক্য** *n* false/insincere assurance; blandishments; cajolery; blarney.

স্তোক[2] *adj* little; slight. ~**নম্র** *adj* little bent down; slightly depressed.

স্তোতা *adj* praising; worshipping. ❑*n* **1** panegyric . **2** captive. **3** worshipper.

স্তোত্র *n* eulogy; praise; hymn of praise; encomium. ~ **পাঠ করা** *vt* recite a hymn of praise. ~ **গাথা** *n* hymn/song of praise; hymn.

স্তোভ *n* **1** torpor; paralysis; stupefaction. **2** blarney.

স্ত্রী *n fem* **1** wife. **2** married woman. **3** woman; female. ~**-আচার** *n* traditional rites performed at a wedding by women whose husbands are alive. ~**গমন** *n* going to women; sexual intercourse with one's wife. ~**ঘাতক,** ~**ঘাতী** *adjj* murderer of a woman/wife. ~**চরিত্র** *n* doings of woman; woman's character. ~**চিত্তহারী** *adj* captivating the heart of woman. ~**চিহ্ন** *n* female organ. ~**চৌর** *n* libertine. ~**জন** *n* womankind. ~**জননী** *adj* bringing forth (only) daughters. ~**জন্ম** *n* birth as a woman. ~**জাতি** *n* female sex; fair sex; womankind. ~**জাতীয়** *adj* feminine; female. ~**জিত** *adj* ruled by a woman/wife; henpecked. ~**জীবী** *adj* one who lives by (prostitution of) his wife or other women. ~**ত্ব** *n* womanhood; wifehood; femininity; womanly function and duties. ~ **ত্যাগ করা** *vt* desert/divorce a wife. ~**দ্বেষ** *n* misogyny. ~**দ্বেষী** *adj* misogynous. ❑*n* misogynist; woman-hater. ~**ধন** *n* wife's personal property; dowry; dot; portion. ~**ধর্ম** *n* **1** duty of a woman. **2** menstruation; menses. ~**নির্জিত**=~জিত. ~**পণ্যোপজীবী** *adj* one who lives by keeping prostitutes. ~ **পরিগ্রহ করা** *vt* take a wife; marry. ~**-পুং ধর্ম** *n* duties of husband and wife. ~**পুরুষ** *n* man and wife; male and female; husband and wife. ~**প্রত্যয়** *n* feminine suffix. ~**প্রধান** *adj* dominated by women. ~**-প্রস**=~জননী. ~**প্রিয়** *adj* dear to woman. ~**বশ,** ~**বশ্য** *adjj* subject to woman; ruled by a woman; henpecked; uxorious. ~**বুদ্ধি** *n* (usually derog) female understanding. ~**ভাব** *n* effeminacy. ~**ময়** *adj* effeminate. ~**মায়া** *n* woman's craft. ~**মূর্তি** *n* female figure. ~**রত্ন** *n* jewel of woman/wife; excellent woman/wife. ~**রোগ** *n* female disease. ~**লিঙ্গ** *n* **1** feminine gender. **2** female organ. ~**লোক** *n* woman. ~**শিক্ষা** *n* female education. ~**সংসর্গ,** ~**সঙ্গ,** ~ **সঙ্গম,** ~ **সম্ভোগ,** ~ **সহবাস,** ~ **সেবা** *n n* intercourse with wife/ woman; sexual connection/ intercourse. ~**সভা** *n* assembly of women. ~**সুলভ** *adj* womanly; womanish; feminine; effeminate. ~**স্বভাব** *n* nature of woman; effeminacy. ❑*adj* effeminate. ~**স্বাধীনতা** *n* female liberty; freedom of women; female emancipation. ~**হত্যা** *n* murder of a wife/woman. ~**হরণ** *n* forceful abduction of a woman. ~**হারী** *n* forceful abductor of a woman.

স্ত্রৈণ *adj* **1** female; feminine; relating to/ belonging to women; subject to/ ruled by women. **2** uxorious; henpecked. ❑*n* henpecked husband.

–**স্থ** *adj* (used as a *suff*) **1** standing; abiding; deposited/ contained in; being located/ situated in; arrived at; come of; staying. **2** existing or being in/or/among; occupied with; engaged in; devoted to.

স্থগন *n* **1** act of covering/ hiding; concealment. **2** adjournment; postponement; suspension. **3** stopping; cessation; standing still.

স্থগিত *adj* **1** stopped; interrupted; brought to a standstill; ceased. **2** adjourned; postponed; put off; suspended; discontinued; **3** covered; concealed; hidden.

স্থপতি *n* architect; master builder; mason. ~ **কর্ম** *n* masonry. ~ **বিজ্ঞান,** ~ **বিদ্যা** *nn* architecture.

স্থবির *adj* **1** old; ancient; venerable. **2** infirm; decrepit; powerful; firm; solid; thick. ❑*n* **1** old man. **2** (with Buddhists) Elder. **স্থবিরা** *n fem* old woman. ~**তা,** ~**ত্ব** *nn* decrepitude; infirmity; stagnation; inertia; lethargy; doldrums; sloth; inaction.

স্থল *n* **1** place; spot; site; location; locality; scene; venue. **2** (dry) land; ground; shore; firth earth. **3** condition; circumstance; situation; case: এমন স্থলে আপনি কী করতেন. **4** place; stead; position: তার স্থলে তুমিই যাও. **5** matter;

subject; point; object; point: বিবাদ~. ~কমল *n* flower of *Hibiscus mutabilis*. ~কমলিনী *n fem Hibiscus mutabilis*. ~কুমুদ *n Nerium odorum*. ~গত *adj* gone/left on dry land. ~চর, ~চারী *adjj* living/moving on (dry) land; land (attrib). ~জ *adjj* growing/living on (dry) land. ~পথ *n* road by land; land-route. ~পথে *adj* by land; over land. ~পদ্ম=~কমল. ~বাণিজ্য *n* land-trade. ~বায়ু *n* land-breeze. ~বিহঙ্গ *n* land bird. ~বিশেষে *adv* as the case may be; in some cases/places; wherever opposite/ appropriate. ~ভূমি *n* land. ~ভাগ *n* solid part of the earth's surface; land. ~যুদ্ধ *n* land-fight. ~সঙ্কট *n* isthmus. ~স্থ *adj* **1** standing on dry ground. **2**=স্থলাভিষিক্ত. **স্থলাভিষিক্ত** *adj* placed in other's position/post; substitute; deputizing. **স্থলাভিষিক্ত হওয়া** *vi* succeed; replace; supplant; take the place of; step into the shoes of. **স্থলে** *adv* in the place of.

স্থলী *n* **1** place; site; location. **2** (dry) land; ground; shore. **3** (anat) bladder. (bot) sac. ~য় *adj* **1** relating/belonging to dry land; terrestrial. **2** belonging to a place; local. **3** belonging to a situation/case.

স্থাণু *n* **1** stump; stem; trunk; stake post; pile; pillar; peg. **2** nest of white ants. **3** Shiva. ❑*adj* standing firmly; stationary; firm; motionless; fixed; immovable. ~বৎ *adj* like a pillar.

স্থান *n* **1** place; spot; location; scene; venue. **2** dwelling; abode; house. **3** region; domain; locality; province; sphere; country; station; rank; office; position; dignity; degree: তাঁর ~ অতি উচ্চে. **4** state; condition; situation; circumstances; case. **5** place; room; stead. **6** place for; proper/right place; scope. **7** receptacle of; repository; shelter; container. **8** (phil, geom) space. **9** holy place. ~চ্যুত *adj* fallen/ removed from a place or office; displaced; dislocated; removed; dislodged. ~চ্যুতি *n* displacement; removal; dislocation; dislodgment. ~ ত্যাগ করা *vi* quit/leave a place; remove; go away; depart; withdraw; slip away. ~প্রাপ্তি *n* obtainment of a place/ situation. ~বহুল *adj* spacious; roomy; commodious. ~বিচরণ *n* topography. ~ভ্রষ্ট = ~চ্যুত. ~মাহাত্ম্য *n* greatness/glory of a place; influence of a place; divine virtue (supposed to be) inherent in a sacred spot. ~সঙ্কুলান *n* accommodation; provision of space. ~ সঙ্কুলান হওয়া *vi* be accommodated. **স্থানাঙ্ক** *n* (math) co-ordinate. **স্থানাঙ্ক-পরিবর্তন** *n* transformation of co-ordinates. **স্থানান্তর** *n* another place. **স্থানান্তরে যাওয়া** *vi* go to another place; remove; shift. **স্থানান্তরণ** *n* transfer. **স্থানান্তরিত** *adj* transferred; shifted; removed to another place. **স্থানাপন্ন** *adj* officiating. **স্থানাভাব** *n* want of space/ room/ accommodation. **স্থানে** *adv* in place of; instead of; in lieu of. **স্থানে স্থানে** *adv* at places; here and there; sporadically. **পিতৃস্থানে** acting as a father.

স্থানিক *adj* belonging to a place/site; local; regional.

স্থানীয় *adj* having its place in; being in; local; occupying the place of; representing: পিতৃ~. ~কাল *n* local time.

স্থাপক *adj*=স্থাপয়িতা. **স্থাপকা** *fem*.

স্থাপত্য *n* architecture; building; erecting; masonry. ~ কলা, ~ শিল্প *nn* art of architecture. ~ বিজ্ঞান, ~ বিদ্যা *nn* science of architecture. ~ শিল্পী *n* architect; mason.

স্থাপত্যিক *adj* architectural.

স্থাপন *n* **1** establishing; establishment; founding; foundation; raising; instituting; institution; placing; putting; depositing; installation. **2** fixing; application: দৃষ্টি~. **3** setting (up). **4** maintaining; preserving; storing; keeping. ~ করা *vt* **1** establish; found; raise; institute; place; put; set (up); deposit; install. **2** fix; apply; maintain; preserve; store; keep. **স্থাপনা** *n*=~.

স্থাপনীয় *adj* to be fixed/ established/ erected/ set up/ founded/ raised/installed/ deposited.

স্থাপয়িতব্য *adj*=স্থাপনীয়

স্থাপয়িতা *n* one who places/puts/installs; founder; establisher; institutor. **স্থাপয়িত্রী** *fem*.

স্থাপিত *adj* established; founded; raised; instituted; put; placed; installed; deposited; fixed; stored; set up; instituted; lodged; settled.

স্থাপ্য *adj*=স্থাপনীয়

স্থাবর *adj* standing still; not moving; fixed; stationary; immovable; stable; immobile. ~-জঙ্গম *n* everything stationary and movable or inanimate and animate. ~ ও অস্থাবর *adj* movable and immovable. ❑*n* movables and immovables. ~তা *n* fixedness; immobility. ~ সম্পত্তি *n* immovable property; movables; real estate.

স্থায়িতা, স্থায়িত্ব *nn* constancy; durability; stability; permanency; durableness; steadiness; fixity; invariableness; unchangeability; immobility.

স্থায়িভাব *n* **1**=স্থায়িতা. **2** (rhet) lasting or durable state of mind or feeling. **স্থায়িভাবে** *adv* abidingly; permanently; stably; lastingly.

স্থায়ী *adj* **1** lasting; permanent; constant; enduring; abiding; being in a particular place; resident; firm; unalterable; everlasting; perpetual; stable; immobile. **2** standing: ~ কমিটি. **3** fixed: ~ আমানত.

স্থাল, স্থালী *nn* vessel; receptacle; plate; cup; bowl; dish; caldron; pot; culinary utensil.

স্থিত *adj* standing; situated; located; resting/abiding/remaining in; staying; fixed; present; firm; unwavering; static. ~তা, ~ত্ব *nn* being in a place. ~ধী *adj* steady-minded; firm; unmoved; calm. ~প্রজ্ঞ *adj* firm in judgement and wisdom; calm; contented. স্থিতাবস্থা *n* status quo; standstill. স্থিতাবস্থা-চুক্তি *n* standstill agreement.

স্থিতি *n* 1 standing upright/ firmly; staying; location; remaining; stay; abiding; residence; sojourn in/at. 2 continuance in being; maintenance of life; continued existence. 3 permanence; duration. 4 stability; fixity. 5 maintenance; sustenance. 6 (mech) equilibrium. 7 (book-keeping) balance. ~কাল *n* duration. ~পত্র *n* balance-sheet. ~বিদ্যা, ~বিজ্ঞান *nn* statics. ~শীল *adj* stable; durable; firm; static; permanent; durable; lasting; abiding; fixed. ~শীলতা *n* stability; permanence; durableness. ~স্থাপক *adj* elastic. ~স্থাপকতা *n* elasticity.

স্থিতীয় *adj* static.

স্থিত্যধিকার *n* locus standi; recognized position.

স্থির *adj* 1 firm; hard; solid; compact; strong. 2 fixed; immovable; motionless; still; calm; unperturbed; tranquil. 3 unflactuating; durable; permanent; lasting; changeless; perpetual. 4 resolute; unwavering; steady; stationary. constant; steadfast. 5 fixed; settled; ascertained. 6 ❑*adv* surely; for certain; fixedly. ~ করা *vt* 1 make steady. 2 fix; settle; determine; ascertain. ~চিত্ত, ~চেতা *adj* firm-minded; single-minded; steady; resolute; unwavering; firm. ~তা *n* 1 stability; steadfastness; permanence; moral firmness; constancy; tranquility. 2 motionlessness; stationariness. 3 certainty; fixity. ~ তারা *n* (astron) fixed star. ~ দৃষ্টি *n* fixed/ steadfast look; gaze. ~নিশ্চয় *adj* convinced; firmly resolved; definite; confident. ~প্রতিজ্ঞ *adj* resolute; firmly resolved; firm; determined. ~বুদ্ধি *adj* steady-minded; resolute; steadfast; even-minded; staid. ~ মতি *n* firm mind; steadfastness. ❑*adj*=~ বুদ্ধি. ~ যৌবন *n* perpetual youth. ❑*adj* possessing perpetual youth; ever youthful; unaging. ~যৌবনা *adj fem*. ~ সিদ্ধান্ত *n* firm resolve/decision; conclusive finding/ascertainment. স্থিরাঙ্ক *n* (mech) co-efficient of elasticity. স্থিরায়ু *adj* long-lived.

স্থিরীকরণ *n* fixation; determination; ascertainment; settlement; decision; settling.

স্থিরীকৃত *adj* fixed; determined; ascertained; settled; decided; resolved.

স্থূণা *n* post; pillar; beam; column; stake.

স্থূল *adj* 1 fat; corpulent; bulky. 2 large; thick; stout; massive; big; huge. 3 coarse; gross; rough; approximate; not detailed/precisely defined; clumsy. 4 dense; dull; stolid; stupid; doltish; naïves; ignorant. 5 flat; broad; snub. 6 ordinary; banal; vulgar. 7 tangible; material; gross. ~ কথা *n* substance; the long and the short (of it); broad meaning. ~কায় *adj* large-bodied; corpulent; hefty; bulky; fat; obese. ~ কোণ *n* (geom) obtuse angle. ~কোণী *adj* obtuse-angled. ~গ্রীব *adj* thick-necked. ~চর্ম *adj* thick-skinned; insensitive; unfeeling. ~চর্মী *n*=~চর্ম. ❑*adj* pachyderm. ~ চাপ *n* bow-like instrument used for cleaning cotton. ~তা, ~ত্ব *nn* 1 largeness; bigness; bulkiness; corpulence; obesity; fatness. 2 flatness; thickness; broadness; coarseness; naïveté; grossness; vulgarity; dullness; plainness. ~ দৃষ্টি *n* superficial observation; plain eyes; plain/superficial looks. ❑*adj*=~দর্শী. ~দর্শী *adj* thick-witted; dim-witted; dull; dull-witted; obtuse; imperceptive. ~দেহ *adj*=~কায়. ~ধী *adj* dull-witted; stupid. ~নাস, ~নাসিক *adjj* thick-nosed; snub-nosed. ❑*nn* boar. ~নাস ব্যক্তি *n* snub-nose. ~বস্ত্র *n* coarse clothes. ~ বিষয় *n* gross/material object. ~বুদ্ধি *adj* dull-witted; dull-headed; thick-headed. ~বুদ্ধি ব্যক্তি *n* dullard. ~ মান *n* (geom) rough approximation. ~ রূপ *n* gross material form/frame. ~ শরীর *n* gross/material and perishable body. ~ হস্ত *n* large and coarse hand. স্থূলাঙ্গ=~কায়. স্থূলান্ত্র *n* large intestine.

স্থূলোদর *adj* pot-bellied; abdominous.

স্থৈতিক *adj* potential. ~ শক্তি *n* potential energy.

স্থৈর্য *n* 1 calmness; tranquillity; patience; sangfroid. 2 perseverance; steadfastness; constancy. 3 firmness; solidity; fixedness; stability; immobility; steadiness.

স্থৌল্য=স্থূলতা (⇒ স্থূল)

স্নাত *adj* bathed; washed; cleansed; immersed. ~ক *n* Brahmin youth who has returned home after completing his studies under a religious teacher; graduate. ~কোত্তর *adj* postgraduate.

স্নান *n* bathing; washing; ablutions; bath; religious or ceremonial lustration. ~ করা *vi* bathe; take a bath. ~ করানো *vt* bathe; wash. ~কক্ষ, ~গৃহ, ~ঘর, ~শালা *nn* bathroom. ~বস্ত্র *n* bath-dress; wet cloth. স্নানাগার *n* bathroom. স্নানাহার *n* bathing and eating. স্নানাহ্নিক *n* bathing and prescribed daily prayer. আতপ~ *n* sunbath. ঘর্ম~ *n* drenching with perspiration. প্রাতঃ~ *n* a bath early in the morning. বাষ্প~ *n* vapour bath. রৌদ্র~, সূর্য~=আতপ~.

স্নানীয় *adj* fit/suitable for bathing; used in ablution. ❑*n* anything used in bathing.

স্নানোদক *n* bath-water.

স্নানোপকরণ *n* accessory of a bath; any utensil used in bathing.

স্নায়বিক *adj* nerval; nervous. ~ **দৌর্বল্য** *n* nervous debility.

স্নায়বীয় *adj* nervous.

স্নায়ু *n* **1** nerve. **2** ligament; sinew; tendon. ~**দৌর্বল্য** *n* nervous debility. ~**প্রদাহ** *n* neuritis. ~**মণ্ডল,** ~**মণ্ডলী** *nn* nervous system. ~**ময়** *adj* sinewy. ~**যুদ্ধ** *n* war of nerves. ~**শূল** *n* neuralgia. ~**স্পন্দ** *n* beat of the nerves; pulse.

স্নিগ্ধ *adj* **1** soft; mild; bland; gentle; agreeable; sweet; lovely; charming . **2** pleasant; cooling; cool; cooled; refreshing. **3** oily; greasy; fat. **4** sticky; viscous; viscid; unctuous; slippery; smooth. **5** loving; tender; affectionate; friendly: ~ কণ্ঠ. স্নিগ্ধা *fem.* ~**কর** *adj* cooling; smoothing; repressing. ~**কান্তি** *adj* having a soft/agreeable complexion; having a glossy/bright colour. ~**জ্যোতি** *adj* having a tender lustre. ~**তা** *n* **1** softness; gentleness; mildness; blandness; sweetness. **2** smoothness; coolness; cool. **3** unctuousness; oiliness; greasiness. ~**দৃষ্টি** *n* pleasant/gentle look. ❑*adj* looking lovingly/ tenderly. ~**বর্ণ**=~কান্তি. ~**শ্যামল** *adj* verdant; pleasantly green.

স্নিগ্ধোজ্জ্বল *adj* glowing softly; sweet and lustrous.

স্নিগ্ধোষ্ণ *adj* oily and warm.

স্নেহ *n* **1** oil; grease; fat; fatty substance. **2** fattiness; oiliness; unctuousness; greasiness; lubricity; viscidity. **3** affection; love; tenderness; attachment (to); fondness (for). ~ **করা** *vt* love; be attached to/fond of; has affection for; feel affection towards. ~**গর্ভ** *adj* affectionate; tender; loving. ~**দ্রব্য,** ~**পদার্থ** *nn* fatty/oily/greasy substance. ~**পাত্র** *n* (worthy) object of love/affection; beloved person. ❑*adj* worthy of/deserving affection/ love. ~**পাত্রী** *fem.* ~**পালিত** *adj* brought up with affection/tenderness. ~**পুত্তলি** *n* object of love/affection; idol. ~**পরায়ণ,** ~**পূর্ণ,** ~**প্রবণ** *adjj* full of affection; affectionate; tender; loving. ~**পূর্ব** *adj* affectionately; tenderly; fondly. ~**প্রবণতা** *n* affection; tenderness. ~**প্রীতি** *n* love and affection. ~**বন্ধন** *n* bonds of love/affection. ~**বদ্ধ** *adj* bound by love/affection. ~**বান,** ~**ময়,** ~**শালী,** ~**শীল** *adjj*=~পরায়ণ. ~**বতী,** ~**ময়ী,** ~**শালিনী,** ~**শীলা** *fem.* ~**ভাজন**=~পাত্র. ~**বচন** *n* words of love/affection. ~**মমতা** *n* love and affection; deep attachment. ~**মাখা** *adj* affectionate; loving. ~**সঞ্চার** *n* upsurge/ infusion of love or affection. ~**সম্ভাষ** *n* kind conversation. ~**সার** *n* marrow. ~**সিক্ত** *adj* affectionate; loving. ~**সুধা** *n* nectar of love/ affection. ~**শূন্য,** ~**হীন** devoid of love/affection; unloving; unkind. ~**স্পর্শ** *n* loving/ affectionate love; touch of love/ affection. **স্নেহার্দ্র** *adj* softened with love/affection. **স্নেহালিঙ্গন** *n* loving/affectionate embrace. **স্নেহাশীর্বাদ** *n* affectionate blessing. **স্নেহাস্পদ**=~পাত্র.

স্নৈগ্ধ্য *n*=স্নিগ্ধতা (⇒ স্নিগ্ধ)

স্নো [E] *n* snow.

স্পঞ্জ [E] *n* sponge.

স্পন্দ *n*=স্পন্দন

স্পন্দন *n* throbbing; throb; quiver; pulse; tremor; motion; activity; pulsation; palpitation; quivering; twitching; trembling; agitation; beat. **2** (mech) vibration. ~**ময়** *adj* throbbing; quivering; pulsating; tremulous. ~**ময়ী** *fem.* ~**রহিত,** ~**শূন্য,** ~**হীন** *adjj* motionless; still; immobilized; torpid; spellbound. **নাড়ির** ~ *n* pulse-beat. **নেত্র**~ *n* quivering of eyelids.

স্পন্দিত *adj* **1** quivering; trembling; pulsating; shaking; beating; throbbing; vibrating; palpitating. **2** pulsated; shaken; throbbed; quivered; vibrated. **স্পন্দিতা** *fem.* ~ **হওয়া** *n* quiver; throb; twitch; tremble; vibrate; quake; palpitate; throb with life; pulsate; beat; shake.

স্পর্ধা *n* **1** daring; audacity; defiance; vaunting arrogance; insolence. **2** courage; emulation; rivalry. **3** envy. ~ **করা** *n* **1** vaunt; rant and bluster; give oneself airs; swagger; boast; pheme oneself. **2** defy; emulate; dare; challenge; venture; flout; hurl defiance at.

স্পর্ধিত, স্পর্ধী *adjj* **1** defiant; audacious; daring; plucky; spirited; bold; intrepid. **2** arrogant; vaunting; bragging; boasting. **3** emulating.

স্পর্শ *n* touch; sense of touch; contact. ~ **করা** *vt* touch; feel with the hand; lay the hand on; stroke; come into contact. ~**ক** *adj* touching; feeling. ❑*n* (geom) tangent. ~**কাতর** *adj* sensitive; touchy. ~**কাতরতা** *n* sensitivity. ~**কোণ** *n* angle of contact. ~**ক্রামক,** ~**ক্রামী** *adjj* contagious. ~**ক্ষম** *adj* capable of touch; tangible. ~**জ্যা** *n* (geom) tangent. ~**তন্মাত্র** *n* subtle element of tangibility (or of air). ~**ন** *n* touching; handling; contact. ~**নীয়** *adj* to be touched/felt/perceived. ~**নেন্দ্রিয়** *n*=স্পর্শেন্দ্রিয়. ~**বর্ণ** *n* any one of the twenty five consonants from ক্ to ম্; stop. ~**বিন্দু** *n* point of contact. ~**মণি** *n* touchstone; kind of philosopher's stone (supposed to turn everything it touches to gold). ~**রেখা** *n* tangent; touch-line. ~**লজ্জা** *n* the sensitive plant, *Mimosa pudica*. ~**সুখ** *n* pleasure of touch. ❑*adj* pleasant to the touch. **স্পর্শানুভূতি** *n* sense of touch; tactual perception. **স্পর্শাসহ, স্পর্শাসহিষ্ণু** *adjj* sensitive to/intolerant of touch. **স্পর্শাসহত্ব** *n* sensitivity to touch.

স্পর্শিনী *adj fem* ⇒ স্পর্শী. ❑*n* (geom) tangent. ~-**বল** *n* tangent force. ~**বেগ** *n* tangential velocity.

স্পর্শী *adj* 1 touching; reaching/ penetrating to: মর্ম~. 2 tangential; contagious. **স্পর্শিনী** *fem.* ~য়=স্পর্শনীয় (⇒ স্পর্শ). ~য়া *fem.*

স্পর্শেন্দ্রিয় *n* organ/sense of touch; skin.

স্পষ্ট *adj* clear; clearly perceived/discerned; distinctly visible; distinct; evident; plain; intelligible; manifest; express categorical; obvious; explicit; outspoken; positive. ❑*adv* dearly; distinctly; evidently; expressly; categorically; obviously; explicitly; positively; outspokenly; plainly. ~ করা *vt* make clear/evident; clarify; elucidate; explain. ~ কথা *n* plain speech; straight-forward; language. ~ত, ~তঃ *advv*=~. ~তা *n* clearness; distinctness; evidence; obviousness; transparency; clarity; lucidity; intelligibility; perspicuity. ~ দিবালোকে *adv* in broad daylight. ~বক্তা, ~বাদী, ~ভাষী *adjj* plain-spoken; outspoken; frank in speech; straightforward. ~বক্তী, ~বাদিনী, ~ভাষিণী *fem.* ~বাদিতা, ~ভাষিতা *n* outspokenness; frankness; in speech; straight-forwardness; plain speaking. **স্পষ্টাক্ষরে** *adv* in distinctly legible letters; in clear terms; in plain words; categorically; expressly; explicitly. **স্পষ্টার্থ** *adj* clear in meaning; distinct. **স্পষ্টাস্পষ্টি** *adj* very clear; outspoken; express; categorical. ❑*adv* very clearly; quite plainly; outspokenly; in clear terms; unequivocally; categorically; expressly.

স্পষ্টীকরণ *n* making clear; elucidation; clarification.

স্পষ্টীকৃত *adj* made clear; elucidated; clarified; exposed.

স্পার্শন *adj* tactile.

স্পিরিট [E] *n* spirit.

স্পৃশ্য *adj* to be touched/felt; tangible; sensible; tactile.

স্পৃষ্ট *adj* 1 touched; felt with the hand; handled. 2 affected/afflicted/possessed by. 3 defiled. 4 (gram) formed by complete contact of the organs of utterence: ~ ধ্বনি. বিদ্যুৎ ~ *adj* shocked by electricity.

স্পৃহণীয় *adj* desirable; attractive; covetable; lik(e)able.

স্পৃহা *n* (eager) desire; covetousness; envy; longing for; pleasure/ delight in; liking; inclination. ~হীন *adj* free from all desires/ longings; averse; uninclined; loath; reluctant.

স্পেকুলেশন [E] *n* speculation.

স্প্রিং [E] *n* spring. ~তুলা *n* spring-balance.

স্ফটিক *n* crystal; quartz. ~তুল্য *adj* crystal-like; crystalline. ~নির্মিত, ~ময় *adjj* consisting/ made of crystal; crystalline. ~পাত্র *n* crystal vessel. ~প্রভ *adj* glittering like crystal; crystalline; transparent. ~ স্তম্ভ *n* crystal pillar. ~ হর্ম্য *n* crystal palace. **স্ফটিকালোক** *n* quartz lamp.

স্ফটিকারি *n* alum.

স্ফাটিক=স্ফটিকনির্মিত (⇒ স্ফটিক)

স্ফার *n* shock; slap; bang; opening; widening; expanse; width. ~ণ *n* 1 trembling; quivering; throbbing; vibration. 2 expansion; opening; widening; manifestation. 3 bragging; boasting; swagger.

স্ফারিত *adj* 1 opened wide; widened; expanded; widely diffused. 2 throbbing; vibrating.

স্ফিংস [E] *n* Sphinx.

স্ফীত *adj* 1 swollen; enlarged; inflated; bloated; puffed up; expanded: ~ বক্ষ. 2 thriving; flourishing; prosperous; rich; well off; abounding in; full of. 3 dense; heavy. 4 much; abundant; numerous. ~ করা *vt* fatten; swell; strengthen; increase; augment; expand. ~ হওয়া *vi* 1 swell; grow fat; increase; become bulky; expand; bloat; be inflated. 2 thrive; prosper; flourish; be puffed up. ~কায় *adj* corpulent; swelled up; inflated; bulky; fat-bodied. ~তা *n*=স্ফীতি.

স্ফীতি *n* 1 bulkiness; enlargement; swelling; expansion; inflation. 2 prosperity; flourishing condition.

স্ফুট *adj* 1 open; opened. 2 burst open; expanded; blossomed; blown; blooming: ~ কুসুম. 3 plain; distinct; evident; manifest; express explicit; apparent. 4 pierced; bored: দন্ত~. ~ কোণ *n* (astron) true anomaly. ~তা *n* manifestness; openness; distinctness. ~ন *n* 1 bursting; opening; expanding; blooming; blossoming. 2 cracking (of the joints, etc). 3 boiling; effervescence. 4 manifestation; expression. 5 piercing; boring. ~নাঙ্ক *n* boiling-point. ~নোন্মুখ *adj* on the point of bursting open/blooming/boiling. ~বাক *adj* speaking distinctly/frankly.

স্ফুটিত *adj* 1 burst; budded; blown; bloomed; blooming. 2 unfolded; manifested. 3 pierced; bored. 4 boiled.

স্ফুরণ *n* 1 trembling; throbbing; vibration; pulsation; quivering. 2 springing; breaking forth; starting into view; expansion. 3 manifestation; unfolding; expression; awakening. 4 flashing; twinkling; glittering; coruscation; glow; shine; glitter.

স্ফুরা *vi* (poet)=স্ফুরিত হওয়া

স্ফুরিত *adj* 1 quivering; throbbing; trembling; palpitating; quivered; trembled. 2 flashing; glowing; glittering; shining; glittered; flashed. 3 broken forth; burst into view; suddenly arisen/appeared. 4 manifested; expressed; plainly displayed/exhibited. 5 swollen; swelled. 6 awakened; excited. ~ হওয়া *vt* 1 tremble; throb; quiver; twitch; palpitate. **2** flash; glitter; gleam; glisten; twinkle; glow; shine; be brilliant/distinguished. **4** dart; bound; rebound; spring. **5** break forth; burst out plainly/visibly; start into view; be evident/manifest. **6** be awakened/incited. **স্ফুরিতাধর** *n* trembling/quivering lips. ❑*adj* having trembling/ quivering lips.

স্ফুলিঙ্গ *n* spark; fire-brand. **~ ছড়ানো** *vi* emit sparks; spark. **~-মোক্ষণ** *n* spark-discharge. **স্ফুলিঙ্গান্তর** *n* spark-gap.

স্ফূর্ত *adj* bloomed; unfolded; manifested; expressed; revealed; uttered; revealed.

স্ফূর্তি *n* **1** merriment; fun; amusement; joviality; hilarity; sprightliness; cheerful enthusiasm/ energy. **2** breaking forth visibly; sudden appearance/ display; manifestation; revelation; looming; unfolding; expression; utterance. **3** quivering; throb; throbbing; palpitation; tremor; vibration. **~ করা** *vi* rejoice; jubilate; revel; frolic; engage in merriment. **~ পাওয়া** *n* **1** have fun; amuse oneself; have one's fling. **2** feel invigorated/energized. **3** break forth; be evident/manifest. **~জনক** *adj* cheering; exhilarating; thrilling; winsome; cheery. **~ব্যঞ্জক, ~সূচক** *adjj* cheerful; blithe; blitheful; sprightly; lively; jovial; hilarious; vivacious; merry; beaming; good-humoured. **~মান** *adj* thrilling (with joy/excitement); tremulous; agitated. **~লাভ** *n* blossoming; opening; bloom. **~ সহকারে** *adv* cheerfully; vivaciously; merrily.

স্ফোট, স্ফোটক *n* swelling; boil; tumour; abscess; furuncle; pustule; pimple.

স্ফোটন *n* **1** breaking/splitting asunder; crushing; destroying. **2** piercing; boring; rending; cleaving. **3** revealing; unfolding; expressing. **4** (chem) ebullition.

স্ফোটনী *n* instrument for splitting or cleaving; auger; gimlet; awl.

স্ফোটনোন্মুখ *adj* about to bloom.

স্মর *n* **1** Kam-deva, the Hindu god of love. **2** memory; remembrance. ❑*adj* remembering; recollecting: জাতি~. **~দশা** *n* state of the body produced by love. **~বীজ** *n* **1** a fabulous fish (regarded as Kama's emblem). **2** male organ. **~হর** *n* 'destroyer of love'; Shiva. **স্মরাতুর** *adj* love-sick.

স্মরণ *n* **1** remembering; recollection; remembrance; reminiscence; calling to mind; memory. **2** mental recitation (of the name of a deity); calling upon the name of a god. **3** reflection; meditation. **4** request/summons to come: আপনি আমাকে ~ করেছেন? **5** (rhet) rhetorical recollection. **~ করা** *vt* **1** remember; recollect; call sth to mind; bear in mind; bring sth to mind; recall sth to the memory; think of; be mindful of. **2** reflect; meditate. **3** recite. **4** request/summon to come. **~ করানো** *vt* remind; call to remembrance; suggest; put sb in mind of sth. **~ হওয়া** *vt* occur to the mind; rise in one's memory; be recollected/remembered; come to remember. **~/স্মরণে থাকা** *vi* be borne in mind; be remembered. **~/স্মরণে রাখা** *vt* keep/bear in mind; remember; retain in memory; recall. **~কাল** *n* period to which memory may extend; living memory. **~চিহ্ন** *n* keepsake; memento; memorial. **~পট** *n* canvas of memory. **~পটে/ ~ পথে উদিত হওয়া** *vi* flash into/through one's mind; occur to; come into (sb's mind) **~পথ** *n* road of memory. **~লিপি** *n* reminder; memorandum. **~শক্তি** *n* memory; retentive capacity of mind. **~শক্তিহীন** *adj* lacking in memory; having poor memory. **স্মরণাতীত** *adj* immemorial; forgotten; beyond the reach of memory. **স্মরণাতীত কাল** *n* time immemorial. **স্মরণার্থ** *adv* for reminding/ remembering. **স্মরণার্হ** *adj* memorable.

স্মরণিক *adj* memorial. ❑*n* remembrance; souvenir. **স্মরণিকা** *n fem* souvenir; relic; memorabilia.

স্মরণীয় *adj* to be remembered; memorable. **~ বিষয়সমূহ** *n* memorable things/events; memorabilia.

স্মরা *vt* (poet)=স্মরণ করা (⇒ স্মরণ)

স্মরোদ্দীপক *adj* erotic; arousing sexual desire; aphrodisiac.

স্মরোদ্দীপন *n* sexual desire/excitement.

স্মরোন্মাদ *n* amorous intoxication/folly.

স্মর্তব্য *adj* to be remembered; memorable.

স্মার *n* memo.

স্মারক *adj* recalling; reminding. *nn* **~নিধি** *n* memorial fund. **~পত্র, ~লিপি** *nn* memorandum; reminder; memento. **~স্তম্ভ** *n* memorial column; monument.

স্মারণ *n* reminding; calling to mind; causing to remember.

স্মারিত *adj* reminded; called to mind; recalled to recollection.

স্মার্ত *adj* **1** relating to memory; memorial. **2** recorded in/based on the *Smriti* (⇒ স্মৃতি); based on tradition; prescribed/sanctioned by traditional land or usage; legal. **3** versed in tradition. ❑*n* **1** orthodox Brahmin versed in/guided by traditional law and usage. **2** law-giver.

স্মিত *n* smile; gentle laugh. ❑*adj* **1** smiled; smiling. **2** blossomed; blown; blooming. **~বদন, ~মুখ** *nn* smiling face. ❑*adj* having a smiling face. **~মুখে** *adv* with a smiling face. **স্মিতানন**=~বদন. **স্মিতাননা** *adj fem.*

স্মৃত *adj* remembered; recollected; called to mind.

স্মৃতি *n* **1** remembrance; reminiscence; memory; calling to mind. **2** thinking; meditation. **3** souvenir; memento. **4** the whole body of Hindu sacred tradition. **5** the whole body of Hindu codes of law. **~কথা** *n* memoirs; reminiscences. **~কর্তা, ~কার, ~কারক** *adj* law-giving. ❑*n* law-giver. **~চারণ** *n* reminiscence. **~চিহ্ন, ~নিদর্শন** *nn* memento; memorial; souvenir. **~পট**=স্মরণপট. **~পথ**=স্মরণপথ. **~ফলক**=স্মরণপট. **~বার্ষিকী** *n* anniversary. **~বিভ্রম** *n* confusion/ loss of memory. **~ভাণ্ডার** *n* memorial fund. **~ভ্রংশ** *n* loss of memory; dementia; oblivion; loss of consciousness/ discretion. **~ভ্রষ্ট** *adj* one whose memory has been lost; suffering from dementia. **~মন্দির** *n* tomb; mausoleum. **~মান** *adj* having a good memory; bright; intelligent. **~মতী** *fem.* **~রক্ষা** *n* commemoration. **~ রক্ষা করা** *vi* commemorate. **~ রক্ষার্থ** *adv* in commemoration of; keep/honour the memory of. **~লোপ** *n* temporary obstruction/failure of memory; forgetfulness. **~শক্তি** *n* retentive faculty. **~শাস্ত্র** *n* law-book; code. **~সঙ্গত, ~সম্মত** *adjj* confirming to/approved by law. **~স্তম্ভ** *n* tombstone; monumental column/pillar. **~হর** *adj* causing loss of memory. **~হীন** *adj* destitute of memory; oblivious; forgetful. **~হেতু** *n* cause of recollection; impression on the mind; association of ideas.

স্যন্দ *n* **1** going; flowing; running; streaming. **2** trickling; oozing; fluxion; exudation. **3** speed; rapid motion; velocity. **~ন** *n* **1** filtration. **2** exudation. **3** trickling perspiration. **4** chariot. **5** going; velocity.

স্যন্দিত *adj* filtered; exuded; flowing; running; streaming.

স্যন্দী *adj* **1** flowing; running. **2** oozing; trickling; dropping/ emitting liquid.

স্যমীক *n* **1** ant-hill. **2** cloud. **3** kind of tree.

স্যাঁতসেঁত=সেঁতসেঁত

স্যাঙাৎ, স্যাঙ্গৎ, স্যাঙ্গত, স্যাঙ্খাত=সাঙ্গাত

স্যাতলা=শেওলা

স্যাণ্ডেল [E] *n* sandal.

স্যার [E] *n* sir.

স্যূত *adj* sewn; woven; stitched; joined; fabricated; sewn/woven together.

স্যূতি *n* **1** sewing; stitching; weaving. **2** bay/sac.

স্রংসন *n* **1** falling; loosening; causing to fall. **2** (geog) fault. **~ উপত্যকা** *n* rift valley. **~ন**=~(1).

স্রংসিত *adj* caused to fall/slip down; loosened.

স্রংসী *adj* becoming loose; falling down; slipping off.

স্রক, স্রজ *n* wreath of flowers; garland. **স্রকচন্দন** *n* wreath of flowers and sandal-paste.

স্রগ্ধর *adj* wearing a garland. **স্রগ্ধরা** *fem.* **স্রগ্ধরা** *n* kind of Sanskrit metre.

স্রব, স্রবণ *nn* **1** streaming; flowing (off); oozing; exudation. **2** fountain; spring.

স্রষ্টা *n* creator; God; maker; author.

স্রষ্টৃত্ব *n* creatorship.

স্রস্ত *adj* fallen (from); dropped; slipped; loosened; relaxed; hanging down. **~তা** *n* laxity; flaccidity. **~দেহ** *adj* having relaxed/ languid limbs.

স্রাব *n* **1** discharge. **2** oozing; exudation; flow. **3** miscarriage. **~ক** *adj* exuding; shedding; causing to flow.

স্রাবী *adj* streaming; flowing; dripping.

স্রুত *adj* flowed out; having flowed from; flowing; streaming; distilled; exuded; oozed.

স্রুতি *n* stream; flow; effusion; fall; course; outflow; distillation; exudation.

স্রেফ=সেরেফ

স্রোত *n* current/bed of a river; stream; torrent; watercourse. **~জল** *n* flowing water; river. **~স্বতী, ~স্বিনী** *nn fem* river. **স্রোতে ভেসে যাওয়া** drift down a stream; drift away. **স্রোতে গা ভাসিয়ে দেওয়া** go with the stream.

স্রোতঃ = স্রোত. **~পথ** *n* drain.

স্রোতো *n* (in compounds)=স্রোত. **~জল**=স্রোতজল (⇒ স্রোত). **~ঞ্জন** *n* antimony. **~বহ, ~বহা** *nn* river. **~বাহিত** *adj* carried by the current. **~বেগ** *n* rush of current. **~হীন** *n* currentless; stagnant; still.

স্লাইস [E] *n* slice.

স্লিপ [E] *n* slip.

স্লিপার [E] *n* slipper.

স্লেট [E] *n* slate (for writing on). **~পাথর** *n* slate.

স্লো [E] *adj* slow.

স্ব *adj* own; one's own (applicable to all the three persons according to context). ❑*pron* oneself. ❑*n* **1** one's self; self; ego; human soul. **2** man of one's own people/tribe; relative; kinsman. **3** one's own goods; wealth; property; riches. **স্ব স্ব** *adj* relating to each distributively; respective: **স্ব স্ব কর্তব্য. স্ব স্ব প্রধান** each independent and self-sufficient; each considering himself/ herself most important.

স্বঃ *n* heaven.

স্বকপোলকল্পনা *n* figments of imagination.

স্বকপোলকল্পিত *adj* invented by one's fancy; fictitious; imaginary; fanciful.

স্বকর্ম *n* one's own work/ deed/ duty/ business/ occupation; function. **~কৃৎ** *adj* doing one's work, etc.

স্বকাম *n* narcissism. ❑*adj* selfish.

স্বকামী *adj* following one's own wish; self-pleasing; self-loving; selfish.

স্বকার্য=স্বকর্ম

স্বকাল *n* one's own time; proper time.

স্বকীয় *adj* **1** own; one's own; belonging to one's self/family/people; personal; original. **2** (math) intrinsic. ~তা *n* originality. ~ সহায়ক *n* personal assistant.

স্বকুল *n* one's own family/race/kin.

স্বকৃত *adj* done/ performed/ built/ composed/ created by oneself. ~ভঙ্গ *adj* one who has lowered one's family by entering into a prohibitive matrimonial alliance.

স্বখাত *adj* dug by oneself. ~সলিল *n* (fig) consequences of one's own action/deed.

স্বগত *adj* 1 belonging to one's self; passing in one's own mind; subjective. 2 (spoken) to oneself; apart. 3 (drama) aside. ~ভেদ *n* (biol) differentiation.

স্বগতোক্তি *n* soliloquy.

স্বগৃহ *n* one's own house/ residence.

স্বগ্রাম *n* one's own/native village. ~বাসী *n* co-villager.

স্বঘর *n* 1=স্বগৃহ. 2 one's own family.

স্বচক্ষে *adv* with one's own eyes.

স্বচ্ছ *adj* transparent; very clear; pellucid; crystal clear; crystalline; lucid. ~ কাগজ *n* tracing paper. ~তা *n* perfect clearness; transparency; purity; lucidity; perspicuity. ~দৃষ্টি *n* clear sight/vision. ❑*adj* clear-sighted. ~পত্র *n* talc. ~মণি *n* crystal. ~ সলিল *adj* containing clear/ transparent water. ~ সলিলা *fem.*

স্বচ্ছন্দ *n* one's own/ free will; one's choice/ fancy. ❑*adj* ease; at ease; frees; independent; uncontrolled; spontaneous; enjoying freedom of will/ liberty of choice; comfortable; facile; acting at pleasure. ~ বোধ করা *vi* feel comfortable/at ease. ~গতি *n* easy/ natural/ free/ unrestrained movement. ❑*adj* moving at ease/freely. ~চর, ~চারী *adjj* moving about at will; independent. ~চিত্ত *adj* at ease; nonchalant; carefree. ~চিত্তে *adv* with an easy heart; without demur; readily; willingly; gladly. ~তা=স্বাচ্ছন্দ্য. ~বিহার *n* ramble; promenade; wandering. স্বচ্ছন্দানুবর্তিতা *n* individuality; liberty. স্বচ্ছন্দানুবর্তী *adj* independent; free; at ease. স্বচ্ছন্দে *adv* at ease; at one's own will/pleasure; freely; at pleasure; easily; spontaneously; as one pleases; at pleasure.

স্বজন *n* one's own people; own kindred; one's own man; kinsman or kinswoman; relative; relation; kith and kin; friend; member of one's own family. স্বজনী *fem.* ~তা *n* relationship to/with. ~ত্যাগ *n* disownment/desertion of one's own people. ~ত্যাগী *n*, *adj* one who has disowned/deserted his own people. ~প্রিয় *adj* attached to one's own people. ~প্রিয়তা, ~প্রীতি *nn* love or attachment to one's own people; nepotism. ~দ্বেষ, ~বিচ্ছেদ, ~বিবাদ, ~বিরোধ *nn* discord/strife/conflict with one's own people; rift between relations/friends.

স্বজাত *adj* self-begotten.

স্বজাতি *n* one's own kind/ family/ caste/ community/ race/nation. ~দ্রোহ, ~বিরোধ *nn* hostility to/revolt against one's own people /community/ nation/ race/ caste. ~দ্রোহী *adj* hostile to/rebellious against one's own people/ race/ community/ caste/nation. ~দ্রোহিণী *fem.* ~প্রীতি, ~প্রেম *nn* love of one's own people/ nation/ community. ~প্রেমিক *adj* attached to one's own people/ nation/ community. ~সুলভ *adj* natural to one's nation/ caste/ community/ kind.

স্বজাতীয়, স্বজাত্য *adj* relating/ belonging to one's own kind/ class/ race/ nation/ community. স্বজাতীয়া *fem.*

স্বজ্ঞা *n* intuition.

স্বত=স্বতঃ

স্বতঃ *adj* of one's own self; of one's own accord; by/in/of oneself or itself; spontaneously. ~ক্রিয় *adj* automatic. ~প্রবৃত্ত *adj* self-acting; voluntary; actuated/acting by oneself. ~প্রমাণ *adj* self-evident; axiomatic. ~সিদ্ধ *adj*=~প্রমাণ. ❑*n* axiom. ~স্ফূর্ত *adj* spontaneous. ~ স্ফূর্ততা, ~ স্ফূর্তি *nn* spontaneity; spontaneousness.

স্বতন্ত্র *adj* 1 independent; free; self-dependent. 2 separate; secluded; aloof. 3 different; another: ~ বিষয়. 4 (anat) sympathetic. স্বতন্ত্রা *fem.* ~তা *n*=স্বাতন্ত্র্য. ~ স্নায়ুতন্ত্র *n* sympathetic nerve system. ~ভাবে *adv* separately; independently.

স্বতন্ত্রিক *adj*=স্বতন্ত্র

স্বতো *adv* (in compounds)=স্বতঃ. ~চ্ছ্বাস*n* self-expression; sprightliness; liveliness; gaiety; alacrity. ~জ্জ্বল, ~দীপ্ত *adjj* naturally bright/brilliant; self-luminous; luminescent. ~দহন *n* spontaneous combustion. ~বৃত্তি *n* spontaneity.

স্বত্ব *n* (proprietary) right; ownership; right to possession; claim; lawful claim; title. ~ত্যাগ relinquishment of right. ~ত্যাগপত্র *n* relinquishment of right. ~নিয়োগ *n* assignment. ~নিয়োগী *n* assignee. ~নিয়োজক *n* assignor. ~নিরসন *n* expropriation. ~পত্র *n* title-deed; title. ~বান *adj* having proprietary right; having a right/claim to; entitled. ~ভোগী *n*, *adj* beneficiary. ~লোপ *n* abolition of right. ~লোপনীতি *n* (Indian hist) Doctrine of Lapse. ~শূন্য *adj* having no right/claim. ~সাব্যস্ত *n* establishment/determination of title/right. ~সাব্যস্তের মামলা *n* title-suit. ~স্বামিত্ব *n* proprietary right; right and ownership. ~হানি *n* loss of proprietary right. ~হেতু *n* ground/cause of proprietary right. স্বত্বাধিকার *n* proprietary right; ownership and possession. স্বত্বাধিকারী *adj* rightfully owning/possessing. ❑*n* proprietor; owner. স্বত্বাধিকারিণী *fem.* স্বত্বাভাব *n* non-existence of proprietary right. স্বত্বার্থন *n* claim; act of laying claim to. স্বত্বার্থী *n* claimant. স্বত্বের দলিল=~পত্র. স্বত্বের মামলা *n* title-suit.

স্বদল *n* =স্বপক্ষ

স্বদেশ *n* one's own country/ home; homeland; nativeland; mother country; fatherland. ~ত্যাগ *n* leaving one's native country; migration; emigration. ~ত্যাগী *adj* one who has left one's native land; emigrating; migrating. ❑*n* emigrant; émigré; migrator. ~ত্যাগিনী *fem.* ~দ্রোহ, ~দ্রোহিতা *nn* hostility to/revolt against one's native land; treason. ~দ্রোহী *n* hostile to/ rebellious against one's native land. ~দ্রোহিণী *fem.* ~প্রিয় *adj* attached/devoted to one's native land. ~প্রীতি, ~প্রেম, ~ভক্তি *n n* patriotism; love of one's native land. ~প্রেমিক, ~প্রেমী, ~ভক্ত *adj* attached to one's native land; patriotic. ❑*n* patriot. ~বৎসল *adj*=~প্রেমিক. ~বৎসলতা, ~বাৎসল্য *nn*=~প্রীতি. ~লক্ষ্মী *n* mother country. ~সেবক *n* servant/devotee of one's native land. ~সেবা *n* service of/devotion to one's native land. ~সেবী *adj* serving one's native country. ~হিতৈষণা *n* desire of doing good to one's native land. ~হিতৈষী *adj* desirous of doing good to one's native land; public-spirited. ❑*n* patriot; public-spirited citizen. ~হিতৈষিণী *fem.* স্বদেশানুরক্ত, স্বদেশানুরাগী *adjj*=~প্রেমিক. স্বদেশানুরক্তা, স্বদেশানুরাগিণী *fem.* স্বদেশানুরক্তি, স্বদেশানুরাগ *n*=~প্রীতি.

স্বদেশী *adj* of/made in one's native land; home-made; indigenous; native; home-grown. ❑*n* (hist) Indian national movement favouring home industries and boycott of foreign goods; *swadeshi*. স্বদেশিনী *fem.* ~ করা *vi* participate in *swadeshi*. ~য় *adj* of/born in/made in one's native land. স্বদেশিনা *fem.* ~শিল্প *n* home-industry.

স্বধর্ম *n* **1** one's own religion. **2** the religion or the rights and duties of one's own forefathers/ race/ class/ caste. **3** characteristics/ function of one's race/ caste/ class. **4** one's own duty. **5** one's natural calling/ trade. **6** peculiar property; peculiarity. ~চ্যুত *adj* **1** apostate. **2** fallen from/ neglecting one's own duty. ~চ্যুত ব্যক্তি *n* apostate. ~চ্যুতি, ~ত্যাগ *nn* **1** apostasy; abandoning one's own religion. **2** dereliction/neglect of one's own duty. ~ত্যাগ করা *vi* **1** abandon one's own religion; apostatize. **2** neglect one's own duty/natural calling. ~ত্যাগী *adj* apostate; negligent of one's own duty. ~ত্যাগিনী *fem.* ~নিরত, ~নিষ্ঠ, ~পরায়ণ *adjj* devoted to/abiding in/practising one's own religion or duty. ~নিরতা, ~নিষ্ঠা, ~পরায়ণা *fem.* ~নিষ্ঠা, ~পরায়ণতা *nn* devotion to one's own religion/duty. ~পালক *adj* =~নিরত. ~পালিকা *fem.* ~পালন *n* observation of one's own religion. ~ পালন করা *vi* abide in/observe/defend one's own religion or duty. ~পালনরত, ~রত *adjj* engaged in observance/ defence of one's religion; abiding in one's own religion/duty; practising one's own natural calling/ function. ~ভ্রষ্ট *adj*=~চ্যুত. ~স্খলন *n*=~চ্যুতি.

স্বন *n* sound; noise. ~ন *n* sounding; ringing; reverberation. ~বিদ্যা *n* acoustics. ~মাপক sonometer.

স্বনাম *n* one's own name. ~খ্যাত, ~ধন্য, ~প্রসিদ্ধ *adjj* celebrated/known by one's own name; renowned; famous. স্বনামে বেনামে using one's own name and under names of others; under one's real name and pseudonyms.

স্বনিত *adj* sounded; sounding; rung; rattling; rambling.

স্বনির্ভর *adj* self-reliant. ~তা *n* self-reliance.

স্বনিষ্ঠ *adj* true to oneself.

স্বন্বয় *n* co-ordination.

স্বপক্ষ *n* one's own party/team; man of one's party; friend.

স্বপক্ষীয় *adj* of/belonging to one's own party or team. স্বপক্ষীয়া *fem.*

স্বপন *n* (poet)=স্বপ্ন

স্বপ্ন *n* **1** dream; dreaming. **2** (fig) fancy; reverie; vision; musing; dreaminess. ~ দেখা *vi* dream (a dream); have a dream; fancy; vision. ~ ভাঙা *vi* awake from a dream; have one's fancy/fanciful hope fritter away; have one's dream/vision shattered. ~কল্প *adj* dream-like. ~ঘোর *n* dreaminess; trance; obsession caused by a dream/vision. ~চারিতা *n* somnambulism; dream-walking. ~চারী *adj* somnambulant. ❑*n* somnambulist. ~চারিণী *fem.* ~জগৎ *n* dreamworld; dreamland; world of dream. ~জাল *n* web of dreams; continuous reverie. ~তত্ত্ব *n* science/theory of dream; interpretation of dreams; oneirology. ~দর্শন *n* dreaming; vision in a dream. ~দর্শী, ~দ্রষ্টা *adjj* dreaming; visionary. ❑*nn* dreamer; visionary. ~দর্শিনী *fem.* ~দৃষ্ট *adj* seen in a dream. ~দোষ *n* nocturnal pollution. ~প্রয়াণ *n* setting out in a dream; dream-journey. ~বৎ *adj* dream-like; dreamy; visionary; moony. ~বিচার *n* interpretation of dreams. ~বৃত্তান্ত *n* narration of dreams. ~ভাষিত *adj* said in a dream. ~ময়, স্বপ্নীল (poet) *adj* full of dreams; dreamy; visionary; consisting of dreams. ~ময়ী *fem.* ~রহস্য *n* secret of dreams. ~লোক=~জগৎ. ~লব্ধ *adj* obtained/appeared in a dream. স্বপ্নাতীত *adj* undreamt of; beyond one's dream; quite unexpected. স্বপ্নাদিষ্ট *adj* divinely commanded/inspired in a dream. স্বপ্নাদেশ *n* divine command/inspiration received in a dream. স্বপ্নাদ্য *adj* **1**=~লব্ধ. **2** dream-like.

dreamy. স্বপ্নাবস্থা *n* state of dreaming; trance; reverie. স্বপ্নাবিষ্ট *adj* under the spell of a dream; into a trance; dreamy; deeply dreaming. স্বপ্নাবেশ *n* spell of a dream; dreaminess. স্বপ্নাবির্ভাব *n* appearance in a dream. স্বপ্নেও না দেখা/ ভাবা (fig) not even to dream of. জাগ্রৎ ~, দিবা~ *nn* day-dreaming; reverie.

স্বপ্নোত্থিত *adj* awakened from a dream.

স্বপ্নোদিত *adj* appeared in a dream.

স্বপ্রকাশ *adj* clear/evident by itself; self-luminous; self-revealed; self-manifested.

স্বপ্রচার *n* propaganda; self-propaganda; self-advertisement ; self-aggrandizement.

স্বপ্রণীত *adj* composed/ compiled/ written by oneself; self-composed.

স্বপ্রধান *adj* self-dependent; independent.

স্ববশ *adj* self-controlled; independent; free;

স্ববিবেক *n* discretion.

স্বভাব *n* **1** nature; innate/ inherent disposition; own condition/ state of being. **2** natural quality; property; character. **3** instinct. impulse. **4** conduct; behaviour; habit; practice. **5** original/ normal/natural state or condition. ~কবি *n* poet by nature; born poet; poet of nature. ~কৃপণ *adj* miserly/niggardly by nature; naturally mean. ~কৃপণতা, ~কার্পণ্য *nn* innate miserliness/stinginess. ~গত *adj* natural; normal; innate. ~গুণ *n* natural quality/ property/ function; innate/ characteristic/ normal quality. ~গুণে *adv* by nature. ~চরিত্র *n* character and conduct/ practice; innate and acquired nature. ~জ, ~জনিত, ~জাত *adjj* produced by natural disposition; innate; natural; instinctive. ~ত, ~তঃ *advv* naturally; by nature. ~দুর্বৃত্ত *adj* habitual offender; born criminal. ~প্রকৃতি *n* character and conduct; temperament; disposition. ~বর্ণনা *n* description of nature/phenomenal world. ~বাদ *n* naturalism. ~বাদী *n, adj* naturalist. ~বিরুদ্ধ *adj* unnatural; abnormal; contrary/opposed to (one's) nature. ~-শোভা *n* natural beauty; scenic splendour. ~সঙ্গত, ~সম্মত *adjj* natural; inherent; innate; native; inbred; inborn; instinctive; habitual. ~সিদ্ধ *adj* **1**=~সঙ্গত. **2** obvious; self-evident. **3** self-made. ~সুন্দর *adj* beautiful by nature. ~সৌন্দর্য *n*=~শোভা. ~সুলভ=~সঙ্গত. ~স্বাধীন *adj* independent by nature.

স্বভাবী *adj* normal.

স্বভাবোক্তি *n* **1** (rhet) detailed poetical description of an object of nature. **2** statement of the exact nature (of anything); accurate description of the properties (of things).

স্বমত *n* one's own/free opinion.

স্বয়ং *pron* **1** oneself (myself, yourself, himself, etc). **2** (in compounds) self. ❑*adv* by own self; personally; voluntarily. ~কৃত *adj* made/ performed/ effected/ committed/ composed by one's self; natural; spontaneous. ~ক্রিয় *adj* automatic. ~চল *adj* automobile. ~চল যান *n* automobile. ~দত্ত *adj* self-given. ~প্রকাশ *adj* self-manifesting. ~প্রজ্জ্বলিত *adj* self-kindled. ~প্রভ *adj* self-shining. ~প্রভা *fem.* ~বর *n* self-choice; election of a husband by a bridegroom at a public assembly of suitors. ❑*adj* self-choosing. ~বরা *n fem* **1** a girl who chooses her husband by herself. **2**=~বর. ~বরণ *n* free choice of a husband. ~লিখ *adj* self-registering; self-recording. ~শ্রেষ্ঠ *adj* self-important. ~সম্পূর্ণ *adj* **1** self-sufficient: খাদ্যে ~সম্পূর্ণ. **2** self-contained: ~সম্পূর্ণ বাসগৃহ. ~সিদ্ধ *adj* perfect in itself; having realized one's end by one's own effort. ~সিদ্ধা *fem.*

স্বয়মধিগত *adj* self-acquired.

স্বয়মর্জিত *adj* acquired/ gained by oneself.

স্বয়ম্বর *n, adj*=স্বয়ংবর (⇒ স্বয়ং)

স্বয়ম্ভর *adj* self-supporting; self-sustaining.

স্বয়ম্ভু, স্বয়ম্ভূ *adjj* self-existent; self-born. ❑*n* Brahma.

স্বর *n* **1** sound; noise. **2** voice; tone of voice. **3** tone of the musical scale; accent; pitch. **4** vowel. ~কম্প *n* (music) beat; trembling of tone. ~কম্পন *n* tremor/ modulation of voice. ~কক্ষ *n* voice box. ~গ্রাম *n* musical scale; gamut. ~গ্রাম সাধা *vi* practise scales. ~তন্ত্রী *n* vocal chords. ~ধরযন্ত্র *n* gramophone; phonograph. ~নিবেশ *n* (music) temperament; tuning. ~পরিবর্ত change/modulation of the voice. ~বর্ণ *n* vowel. ~বিকার *n* hoarseness; huskiness. ~বিজ্ঞান *n* phonology. ~বিবর্ত= ~বিকার. ~বৃত্ত *n* system of versification measured by the number of syllables in each foot (each open and closed syllable being of equal value). ~ভক্তি *n* (gram) vowel insertion. ~ভঙ্গ *n* morbid hoarseness of voice. ~ভঙ্গি *n* modulation of voice; intonation. ~ভেদ *n* indistinctness of utterance; hoarseness. ~মাধুর্য *n* sweetness of voice. ~মাপক *n* sonometer. ~যন্ত্র *n* larynx. ~লহরী *n* waves/ ripples of musical notes. ~লিপি *n* musical notation. ~লোপ *n* aphasia. ~সঙ্গতি *n* **1** (gram) vowel harmony. **2** (music) chord. ~সন্ধি *n* (gram) junction/coalition of vowels.

স্বরচিত *adj* composed/written/contrived/ made by oneself; self-composed.

স্বরাজ self-government; Home Rule; autonomy; independence; swaraj.

স্বরাজ্য *n* **1** own dominion/kingdom/state. **2** independent dominion; sovereignty.

স্বরাট *n* God.

স্বরানুকরণ *n* mimicking one's voice.

স্বরাষ্ট্র *n* own kingdom/state. ~ মন্ত্রণালয় *n* Ministry of Home Affairs. ~ মন্ত্রী *n* Home Minister. ~ সচিব *n* Home Secretary.

স্বরিত *adj* **1** caused to sound; sounded; voiced; uttered. **2** having an accent; accentuated. ❑*n* kind of mixed tone produced by a combination of high and low tone.

স্বরুচি *n* one's own will/ pleasure.

স্বরূপ *n* one's own form/ shape; own condition; nature; peculiarity; characteristic; real/ true nature or condition; natural/ normal state or condition. ❑*adj* similar; like; true; real. **~ চিন্তা** *n* meditation about oneself; introspection; self-contemplation; self-reflection. **~ত, ~তঃ** *adv* **1** in one's own form; according to one's own form. **2** by itself; in reality; by nature; truly; really. **~তা, ~ত্ব** ~ *nn* state of one's own form/ nature; identity of form/ nature. **~নির্ণয়** *n* determination of real character/ nature; ascertainment of true form/ nature. **~লক্ষণ** *n* characteristic. **~সম্বন্ধ** *n* identical relation. **স্বরূপে** *adv*.

স্বর্গ *n* heaven; (according to Hindu scripture) heavenly bliss; paradise. **~কাম, ~কামী** *adjj* desirous of heaven. **~গঙ্গা, ~ঙ্গ** *n* Milky way; Galaxy; the celestial Ganges. **~গত** *adj* gone to heaven; dead. **~গতি, ~গমন** *nn* going to heaven; death. **~গামী** *adj* going to heaven. **~গামিনী** *fem*. **~চ্যুত** *adj* fallen/ descended from heaven. **~জিৎ** *adj* winning heaven. **~তরু** *n* tree of heaven. **~দ্বার** *n* heaven's gate. **~ধাম** *n* heaven. **~নরক** *n* heavens and hells. **~পতি** *n* lord of heaven; Indra. **~পুরী** *n* heaven. **~প্রদ** *adj* procuring paradise. **~প্রাপ্তি** *n* attainment of heaven. **~বধূ** *n fem* celestial nymph; *apsara*. **~বাস** *n* residence in heaven. **~বাসী** *adj* residing in heaven; departed; late. **~ভোগ** *n* enjoyment of heaven/ beatitude. **~মন্দাকিনী**= ~গঙ্গা. **~মার্গ** *n* road to heaven. **~রাজ্য** *n* kingdom of heaven. **~লাভ**=~প্রাপ্তি. **~ লাভ করা** *vi* attain heaven; go to the happy hunting grounds. **~লোক** *n* celestial world; heaven. **~শ্রী** *n* glory of heaven. **~সাধন** *n* means of attaining heaven. **~সুখ** *n* heavenly bliss; bliss of heaven; beatitude. **~স্থ, ~স্থিত** *adjj* dwelling in heaven; dead. **স্বর্গাধিপতি** *n* lord of heaven. **স্বর্গারূঢ়** *adj* ascended to heaven. **স্বর্গারোহণ** *n* ascension to heaven. **স্বর্গার্থ** *adv* for the sake of heaven. **স্বর্গবাস** *n* abode in heaven. **~ হাতে পাওয়া** (fig) attain happiness and riches of all description; attain supreme joy/ happiness. **স্বর্গে তোলা** (fig) praise/ extol to the skies. **স্বর্গে বাতি দেওয়া** *vi* **1** continue one's line of descent by procreation. **2** light a lamp/ torch in honour of one's deceased forefathers and elevate it on a pole in the air. **স্বর্গে যাওয়া** *vi* go/ ascend to heaven; die.

স্বর্গীয় *adj* relating/ belonging to heaven; leading to heaven; heavenly; celestial; divine; dead. **স্বর্গীয়া** *fem*. **~ পিতা** *n* one's late father; heavenly father.

স্বর্ণ *n* gold; aurum. **~ উপকূল** *n* gold-coast. **~কণা, ~কণিকা** *nn* particle/ grain of gold. **~কমল** *n* red lotus. **~কার** *n* gold-worker; goldsmith. **~খচিত** *adj* studded/ inlaid/ set with gold. **~খনি** *n* goldmine. **~গর্ভা** *adj fem* **1** very fertile. **2** (said of a mother) giving birth to brilliant sons and daughters. **~ছাতার** *n* Indian goldfinch. **~চূড়** *adj* gold-crested. ❑*n* blue joy. **~জ** *n* the metal tin. **~পদ্ম** *n* red lotus. **~পত্র** *n* gold-leaf; gold-foil. **~পত্র-তড়িদ্‌বীক্ষণ** *n* gold-leaf electroscope. **~পিঞ্জর** *n* gold/ golden cage. **~পুষ্প** *n* the plant and flower *champaka*. **~প্রতিমা** *n* gold/ golden image (fig) very beautiful female; figure/ person. **~প্রসূ** *adj* exceptionally fertile; auriferous. **~বণিক** *n* gold merchant; money changer. **~বর্ণ** *adj* gold-coloured; golden. **~ভূমি** *n* auriferous land (fig) richly fertile land/ soil. **~ভূষণ** *n* gold ornaments. **~মণ্ডিত** *adj* gilded; gilt; covered with gold-leaf. **~ময়** *adj* consisting/ made of gold; golden. **~ময়ী** *fem*. **~মাক্ষিক** *n* golden pyrites. **~মান** *n* gold standard. **~মৃগ** *n* **1** golden deer; phantom deer; illusory antelope. **2** illusion; mirage. **~রেখা** *n* gold streak (on a touchstone). **~রেণু** *n* gold-dust. **~লতা** *n* gold creeper; *Cardiospermum halicacabum*. **~সিন্দুর** *n* (Ayu) a particular medicinal preparation containing mercury. **~সুযোগ** *n* golden opportunity. **~সূত্র** *n* gold-thread; gold-wire. **স্বর্ণাক্ষর** *n* letter of gold. **স্বর্ণাক্ষরে লেখা** *adj* written in letters of gold. **স্বর্ণাঙ্গুরি, স্বর্ণাঙ্গুরী, স্বর্ণাঙ্গুরায়, স্বর্ণাঙ্গরীয়ক** *n* gold ring. **স্বর্ণাভ** *adj* golden. **স্বর্ণাভরণ, স্বর্ণালঙ্কার** *n* gold ornament.

স্বর্বধূ *n fem* celestial woman; *apsara*.

স্বর্বেশ্যা *n fem* courtesan of heaven; *apsara*.

স্বর্লোক *n* (world of) heaven.

স্বলেখন *n* autograph.

স্বল্প *adj* very little/ few; minute; only a little/ few; short; bit. **~তা** *n* fewness; smallness; scarcity; scantiness; paucity. **~দৃষ্টি** *adj* very shortsighted. **~বল** *adj* extremely weak/ feeble. **~ব্যয়** *n* very little expenditure. **~ব্যয়ে** *adv* at a low/ small cost or expense; cheaply; at little cost. **~ভাষী** *adj* speaking very little; reticent; reserved; tight-lipped; laconic; non-vocal. **~ভাষিণী** *fem*. **~শরীর** *adj* having a very diminutive body; small in stature. **~স্মৃতি** *adj* having a short memory. **স্বল্পায়ু** *adj* short-lived. **স্বল্পাহারী** *adj* subsisting on meagre/ scanty meal; abstemious.

স্বশাসন *n* autonomy; self-government; self-control.

স্বশাসিত *adj* autonomous; self-governing; self-governed; self-controlled.

স্বসংবিদ *n* knowledge of one's own/ true essence. ❑*adj* knowing one's self.

স্বসংবৃত *adj* self-guarded.

স্বসংবেদন *n* knowledge of oneself; self-knowledge.

স্বসা *n* sister.

স্বস্তি *n* 1 well-being; good; weal; fortune; luck; success. 2 ease; relief: ~র নিঃশ্বাস. 3 benedictory incantation. 4 contentment; peace; freedom from anxiety. ~ক *n* 1 any lucky auspicious object. 2 kind of mystical cross/ mark made on persons or things to denote good luck; *swastika*. 3 particular mode of sitting practised by *yogis*. 4 kind of cake. ~কর, ~দায়ক *adjj* relieving; comfortable; careful; palliative. ~ পরিষদ *n* security council. ~বচন *n* benedictory words; incantation; benediction. ~বাচন *n* recital/ utterance of the benedictory incantation. ~মুখ *adj* wishing joy/ happiness. ❑*n* bard; Brahmin. ~হীন *adj* restless; peaceless; without respite; having no respite; unrelieved; uneasy; restive; fitful. ~কাসন *n*=~ (3). ~র নিঃশ্বাস ফেলা heave a sigh of relief. সুখের চেয়ে ~ ভালো (prov) Peaceful poverty is better than worried affluence.

স্বস্ত্যয়ন *n* 1 religious service performed for fighting out evils, remission of sins, recovery from evils, etc. 2 blessing; benediction.

স্বস্থ *adj* self-abiding; sound; well; contented; healthy (in body and mind); composed; self-sufficient; confident. ~চিত্ত *adj* sound in mind. ~তা *n* well-being; health; ease.

স্বস্থান *n* one's own place; own home.

স্বস্রীয় *n* sister's son; nephew. **স্বস্রীয়া** *fem* sister's daughter; niece. ❑*adj* of a sister.

স্বহস্ত *n* one's own hand. ~গত *adj* fallen into/ being in one's own hand. **স্বহস্তাক্ষর** *n* one's hand-writing. **স্বহস্তে** *adv* by one's own hand.

স্বাক্ষর *n* one's own hand-writing; signature; autograph. ~ করা *vt* sign.

স্বাক্ষরিত *adj* signed.

স্বাগত *n, adj* welcome. ~ জানানো *vt* welcome. ~ ভাষণ *n* welcome address. ~ সম্ভাষণ *n* warm greetings.

স্বাগতিক *adj* 1 inquiring. 2 host: ~ দেশ

স্বাচ্ছন্দ্য *n* 1 freedom of the will; liberty of choice; freeness. 2 ease; comfort; facility.

স্বাজাতিক *adj* relating to one's countrymen/ caste/ community/ race/ nation; nationalistic; communal. ~তা *n* nationalism.

স্বাজাত্য *n*=স্বাজাতিকতা

স্বাতন্ত্র্য *n* freedom of the will; independence; separateness; distinction; freedom; aloofness; seclusion; originality; difference.

স্বাতি, স্বাতী *n* 1 name of the star Arcturus (as forming the fifteenth lunar asterism). 2 (myth) one of the wives of the Sun.

স্বাদ *n* 1 taste; flavour; savour; relish. 2 gustation; tasting. 3 beauty/ charm (of a poem). ~ গ্রহণ, ~ন *nn* tasting; licking; enjoying; gustation. ~ গ্রহণ করা *vt* taste; relish; enjoy. ~গ্রাহী *adj* tasting. ~হীন *adj* tasteless; insipid; flat; unsavoury; flavourless.

স্বাদিত *adj* tasted; relished.

স্বাদু *adj* tasty; pleasant to the taste; sweet; savoury; palatable; dainty; delicious; agreeable; charming. ~তা *n* sweetness; savouriness.

স্বাদেশিক *adj* 1 of one's mother country; national; patriotic nationalistic. 2 indigenous; native; home. ~তা *n* patriotism; nationalism.

স্বাধিকার *n* one's own right/ office/ jurisdiction/ territory/ privilege; autonomy.

স্বাধিষ্ঠান *n* one's own place; one of the six mystical circles of the body.

স্বাধীন *adj* free; independent; unrestricted; unrestrained. ~ করা *vt* free; liberate; set free. ~ হওয়া *vi* be free/ independent; win freedom. ~তা *n* freedom; independence. **স্বাধীনতা দিবস** *n* Independence Day. ~ভাবে *adv* freely; independently.

স্বাধ্যায় *n* recitation/ repetition/ study of the Veda.

স্বাধ্যায়ী *adj* reciting/ repeating the Veda. ❑*n* repeater/ student of the Veda.

স্বানুবন্ধ *adj* (geom) self-conjugate.

স্বানুভব *n* one's own personal experience/ observation.

স্বানুরূপ *adj* resembling one's self; suited to one's character.

স্বাপ্নিক *adj* of dream; visionary; dreamy. ❑*n* dreamer; visionary.

স্বাবমাননা *n* self-contempt.

স্বাবলম্ব, স্বাবলম্বন *n* self-help; self-reliance; self-support.

স্বাবলম্বিতা=স্বাবলম্ব

স্বাবলম্বী *adj* self-reliant; self-supporting; having recourse to self-help. **স্বাবলম্বিনী** *fem.*

স্বাভাবিক *adj* natural; normal; usual; native; innate; spontaneous; original; peculiar; inherent; instinctive; characteristic. ~তা *n* naturalness; usualness; spontaneity.

স্বাভাষিকতা *n* love of/ attachment to one's own language.

স্বাভিলষিত, স্বাভীষ্ট *adj* coveted/ desired by one's self.

স্বামি *n* (in compounds)=স্বামী. ~জী *n* title of saints/ great ascetics; spiritual preceptor. ~তা, ~ত্ব *n* ownership; mastership; lordship; proprietorship; rule; authority. ~নী *n fem* mistress; proprietress; lady. ~সেবা *n* service of a master; respect/ reverence for a master or husband. ~হীন *adj* ownerless; masterless. ~হীনা *adj fem* (of a woman) who has lost her husband; widowed.

স্বামী *n* **1** husband. **2** lord; owner; proprietor; master; employer. **3** chief; commander. **4** king; prince. **5** spiritual preceptor; learned Brahmin.

স্বায়ত্ত *adj* dependent on oneself; being under one's control; self-controlled; self-possessed; self-governing. ~শাসন=স্বশাসন. ~শাসিত= স্বশাসিত.

স্বায়ত্তীকরণ *n* subjection to oneself.

স্বায়ম্ভুব *adj* relating to/ derived from the self-existent.

স্বারাজ্য *n* independent rule; uncontrolled dominion; sovereignty; state of self-effulgence.

স্বার্জিত *adj* self-acquired.

স্বার্থ *n* **1** self-interest; one's own affair/ cause; personal matter/ advantage; one's own aim/ object. **2** one's own property/ substance. ❑*adj* meaningful; significant: বাক্যের ~ একক. ~চিন্তক *adj* selfish; self-interested; egocentric; self-seeking. ~চিন্তা *n* selfish thoughts; self-seeking; self-concern; selfishness; egoistic; egotistic. ~ত্যাগ *n* self-sacrifice; self-denial; self-abnegation. ~ তাগ করা *vi* sacrifice one's own interests. ~ত্যাগী *adj* self-sacrificing; self-denying; unselfish; selfless. ~পর, ~ পরায়ণ *adjj*=~ চিন্তক. ~পরতা, ~ পরায়ণতা *n* selfishness; egotism; egoism. ~বুদ্ধি *n* selfish motive/ thought. ~বুদ্ধিপ্রণোদিত *adj* actuated/ prompted by a selfish motive/ thought. ~ময় *adj* **1** full of selfishness. **2** absorbed in one's own interests/ affairs. ~লিপ্সু *adj* wishing to gain one's own object; self-seeking. ~শূন্য *adj* selfless; unselfless; disinterested. ~সাধন, ~সিদ্ধি *n* accomplishment of one's own object/ desire; realization of one's own interests. ~সাধনতৎপর *adj* intent on/upon accomplishing one's own object/ desire. ~ সিদ্ধ হওয়া *vi* have one's object/ desire accomplished. ~হীন=~ শূন্য. স্বার্থান্ধ *adj* blinded with selfishness/ self-interest; blindly/ unscrupulously self-seeking. স্বার্থান্বেষণ *adj* self-seeking. স্বার্থান্বেষী *adj* self-seeking; self-intent; egoistic. স্বার্থান্বেষী ব্যক্তি *n* self-seeker; egoist. স্বার্থান্বেষিণী *fem.* স্বার্থে *adv* in the interest of; for the sake of.

স্বার্থিক *adj*=স্বার্থচিন্তক (⇒ স্বার্থ)

স্বার্থোদ্ধত *adj* shamelessly/ arrogantly/ blatantly self-seeking.

স্বার্থোন্মত্ত *adj* madly self-seeking.

স্বাস্থ্য *n* health; hygiene; ease; comfort; peace; sound state (of body/ soul). ~-অধিকর্তা *n* Director of Public Health. ~কর *adj* healthy; salubrious; salutary; health-giving; hygienic; wholesome; conducive to health; health-promoting. ~করী *fem.* ~কর স্থান *n* health-resort; health station. ~কৃত্যক *n* health services. ~দায়ক, ~দায়ী=~কর. ~দায়িকা, ~দায়িনী *fem*. ~নিবাস *n* sanatorium. ~নাশ *n* impairment of health; ill health. ~ পরিদর্শক *n* sanitary inspector. ~বান *adj* healthy; sound; hale; well; hearty; blooming. ~বিদ্যা *n* hygiene. ~বিধান *n* sanitation; hygiene; measures for recovery/ improvement of health. ~বিধান করা *vi* measures for recovery/ improvement of health. ~বিধি *n* science of/ rules for healthy living; hygiene. ~ব্যবস্থা *n* sanitation. ~ভঙ্গ *n* ruin/ wreck of health; poor/ ill health. ~ভঙ্গ হওয়া *vi* be in poor health. ~ভূমি=~কর স্থান. ~ মন্ত্রণালয় *n* Ministry of Health. ~ মন্ত্রী *n* Minister of Health. ~রক্ষা *n* preservation of health. ~লাভ *n* recovery (of health); recuperation; rally. ~-সম্পদ *n* health considered as wealth. ~সম্পন্ন=~বান. ~হানি=~নাশ. ~হীন *adj* in ill/ poor health; sickly; wan. ~হীনা *fem.* স্বাস্থ্যাধিকারিক *n* health officer. স্বাস্থ্যান্বেষণ *n* search for health; attempt to recuperate one's health. স্বাস্থ্যান্বেষী *adj* anxious to recuperate/ concerned about one's health; valetudinarian.

স্বাস্থ্যোদ্ধার *n* restoration to health; recovery; recuperation; rally. ~ করা *vi* get well; rally; recuperate (one's health); recover.

স্বাহা *n* **1** exclamation used in making oblations to the gods (hail ! hail to). **2** (myth) oblation (personified). **3** wife of *Agni* (অগ্নি).

স্বীকরণ *n* **1** making one's own; appropriating; accepting. **2**=স্বীকার.

স্বীকর্তব্য *adj* **1** to be accepted. **2** to be agreed/ assented to.

স্বীকার *n* **1** acceptance: নিমন্ত্রণ ~. **2** assent; agreement; promise; consent; acquiescence: সাহায্য করতে ~. **3** owning; recognition: বন্ধুত্ব ~. **4** confession: দোষ~. **5** courting; accepting; inviting upon oneself: দুঃখ~. **6** acknowledgement; admission; admittance: কৃতজ্ঞতা ~. **7** sustaining: ক্ষতি~. ~ করা *vt* **1** accept. **2** assent; agree to; consent; promise; acquiesce. **3** own; recognize. **4** confess. **5** court; invite upon oneself. **6** admit; acknowledge. **7** sustain. ~ হওয়া *vi* agree; accept; consent.

স্বীকারী *n* acceptor.

স্বীকারোক্তি *n* confession.

স্বীকার্য *adj* to be agreed/ assented to; to be accepted; acceptable; admissible; to be owned/ confessed; to be recognized/ acknowledged; acknowledgeable. ❑*n* (geom) postulate. ~রূপে *adv* admittedly.

স্বীকৃত *adj* accepted; admitted; assented to; promised; consented; agreed; acknowledged; recognized; owned; confessed; acquiesced. **~ বিষয়** *n* **1** admitted fact. **2** (geom) postulate.

স্বীকৃতি *n* **1** recognition; acknowledgement. **2** admission; admittance; acceptance. **3** agreement; consent; acquiescence. **4** confession; owning.

স্বীয় *adj* relating/ belonging to one's self; own; proper; peculiar.

স্বেচ্ছা *n* one's own wish/ will; free will; self-will; volition. **~কৃত** *adj* voluntarily/ wilfully done; voluntary; wilful; intentional; deliberate; intended. **~ক্রমে** *adv* of one's own accord; voluntarily; deliberately; wilfully; intentionally; freely; purposely; by choice of one's free will; at pleasure; according to one's own will. **~চার** *n* wilfulness; wantonness; self-will; aberration; capriciousness; waywardness; caprice; whim; whimsy. ❑*adj* acting as one likes; wilful; wanton; self-willed; wayward; whimsical; capricious. **~চারিতা** *n*=~চার. **~চারী** *adj*=চার. **~চারিণী** *fem.* **স্বেচ্ছাধীন, স্বেচ্ছানুবর্তী** *adjj* subject to one's free will; self-willed; wilful; opinionated; headstrong; wayward; froward. **স্বেচ্ছাধীনা, স্বেচ্ছানুবর্তিনী** *fem.* **স্বেচ্ছানুবর্তিতা** *n*=~চার. **~পূর্বক** *adv*=~ক্রমে. **~প্রণোদিত, ~প্রবৃত্ত, ~রত** *adjj* actuated/ prompted by one's own will; voluntary; spontaneous; deliberate. **~প্রদত্ত** *adj* voluntarily given. **~মতো** *adj* according to one's own will/ wish; at pleasure. **~য়** *adv*=~ক্রমে. **~মৃত্যু** *n* voluntary/ deliberate courting of death. ❑*adj* having death in one's own power; dying at one's own will: **~সেবক** *n* volunteer. **~সেবিকা** *fem.*

স্বেদ *n* **1** sweat; sweating; perspiration. **2** warm vapour; steam. **3** warmth; heat fomentation. **~গ্রন্থি** *n* sweat-gland. **~জ** *adj* generated by perspiration; perspiratory. **~জনক** *adj* causing/ inducing sweat; perspiratory. **~জল, ~বারি** *n* sweat; perspiration. **~বিন্দু** *n* drop of sweat; bead of perspiration. **~সিক্ত** *adj*=স্বেদাক্ত. **~স্নান** *n* vapour-bath. **~স্রাব, ~স্রুতি** *nn* profuse sweating/ perspiration. **স্বেদাক্ত, স্বেদাপ্লুত, স্বেদার্দ্র** *adjj* drenched/ damp with sweat; sweaty; in a sweat.

স্বেদন *n* **1** sweating; perspiring. **2** softening; fomenting.

স্বেদোদগম *n* breaking out of perspiration.

স্বৈর *n* wilfulness; arbitrariness; despotism; act of doing as one pleases; dissoluteness; waywardness; unrestrained exercise of one's will. ❑*adj* acting at will; self-willed; acting as one likes; wilful; independent; unrestrained; arbitrary; unrestricted; despotic; autocratic; dissolute; wayward; capricious. **~চার** *n* **1**=~. **2** autocracy. **~চারী** *adj*=~. **~চারিণী** *fem.* **~তন্ত্র** *n* autocracy; despotism. **~তা** *n*=~. **~বর্তী, ~বৃত্ত** *adjj*=~. **~বৃত্তি** *n*=~. **স্বৈরা, স্বৈরাচার** *n, adj*=~. **স্বৈরাচারী** *adj*=~. **স্বৈরিতা** *n*=~. **স্বৈরী** *adj*=~. **স্বৈরিণী** *fem* unrestrained/ wayward (esp said of unchaste women). ❑*n* wayward/ profligate woman; prostitute; whore.

স্বোদর *n* one's own belly. **~পূরক** *adj* filling only one's belly; thinking only of eating; selfish. **~পূরণ** *n* filling of one's own belly; eating one's fill.

স্বোপার্জিত *adj* self-acquired; earned/ acquired by oneself; deliberately invited upon oneself.

হ

হ *n* the thirty-third and last consonant of the Bengali alphabet. It is a voiced aspirated glottal fricative sound (or voiced glottal aspirated sound without stop).

হইচই *n* (onom) very loud uproar; hullabaloo; clamour; fuss; ado; commotion; fracas; rumpus. **~ করা** *vi* raise a very loud uproar; make noise; be noisy; fuss noisily. **~ করে বেড়ানো** *vi* gad about; gallivant about/ off.

হইতে *prep* (old style)=হতে

হইয়া *prep* (old style)=হইয়া

হই হই *n* (onom) hullabaloo; bedlam; hue and cry; noisiness; clamorousness; hubbub; hurly-burly; tumult. **~ করা** *vi* clamour; raise the roof; vociferate; raise a hue and cry.

হওন *n* **1** being; happening; occurrence. **2** birth. **3** becoming. **4** sufficing.

হওয়া *vi* **1** be; become: মন্ত্রী ~. **2** arise; come into existence; be created; exist. **3** happen; occur: কী হবে কে জানে. **4** take place: সভা ~. **5** come; arrive: যখন সময় হবে. **6** be accumulated; come into; be earned/ gained: তার টাকা হয়েছে, He has made money. **7** increase; augment; grow; add to: এখন বয়স হয়েছে,. **8** advance: বেলা হলো. **9** set in: সন্ধ্যা ~, রাত হয়েছে, It is night; It is getting dark. **10** suffice; be sufficient/ adequate for: এতো অল্প টাকায় কী হবে? **11** be fine/ suitable; do: সে সময়মতো এলে হয়. **12** turn into: রক্ত জল ~. **13** be finished/ completed; accomplished/ performed: এ কাজটা কয় ঘণ্টায় হলো? **14** fall: এক পশলা বৃষ্টি হয়ে গেল, বৃষ্টি ~, rain. **15** cover; extend over: জ্বর কতদিন হলো? How long is he/ she running a temperature; তিন ঘণ্টা হলো আমি এসেছি, It is three hours since I came. **16** elapse: এক মাস হলো তার দেখা নেই. **17** become one's own/ one's property: পর কি কখনো আপন হয়? **18** be born: তার একটি ছেলে

হয়েছে. **19** grow: এবার খুব ধান হয়েছে; be seized/ attacked with: আমার খুব ভয় হয়, I am afraid ....; তার জ্বর হয়েছে, He has a fever. **20** bear a particular relation to: সে আমার আত্মীয় হয়, He is my relation. **21** fit: শার্টটা ঠিক হয়েছে? **22** be likely (to happen): তা হবে. **23** be spoiled: তবেই হয়েছে. **24** be obtained/ procured: তার একটা চাকরি হয়েছে, He has got a job. **25** be done: এমন জায়গায় এমন কথা বলতে হয় না. **হয় আর কি, হয় হয়** on the point of being done; about to happen. **হয়কে নয় করা** deny what is obvious. **হয়ে আসা 1** come near the close; be about to end/ terminate. **2** be dying; be in the last gasp; be at the point of death: ওর হয়ে এসেছে, আর বেশি দেরি নেই. **হলো বলে** be about to be completed/ accomplished; be almost ready.

হংস *n* **1** goose; gander; swan; flamingo; drake. **2** a poetical/ mythical bird. **3** kind of ascetic. **4** one of the vital airs. **5** soul; spirit. **হংসী** *fem* female goose; duck. **~গদ্গদা** *adj fem* prattling like a swan. ❑*n* sweetly speaking woman. **~গমন** *n* gait of a swan/ goose. **~গমনা, ~গামিনী** *adjj fem* walking like a swan. ❑*n* graceful woman. **~ডিম্ব** *n* duck's egg. **~ধ্বনি** *n* **1** cackling/ cry of a goose or swan. **2** an Indian musical mode. **~নাদ** *n*=~ধ্বনি(1). **~নাদী** *adj* making a noise like a goose/ swan; cackling. **~নাদিনী** *adj fem*=~নাদী. ❑*n* graceful woman. **~পাঁতি** *n* line/ flight of goose or swan; flock of wild geese, etc. **~বলাকা** *n* kind of crane. **~বাহন** *adj* riding on a swan/ geese. ❑*n* Brahma. **~বাহিনী** *n fem* goddess Saraswati. **~মালা**=~পাঁতি. **~মিথুন** *n* couple of geese/ swans. **~রথ** *n adj*=~বাহন. **~রাজ** *n* **1** large gander. **2** maiden-hair fern. **~রুত** *n*=~ধ্বনি. ❑*adj*=~নাদী. **~শাবক** *n* duckling. **হংসাণ্ড** *n*=~ডিম্ব. **হংসাবলী** *n*=~পাঁতি. **হংসারূঢ়** mounted on a swan. ❑*n* Brahma. **হংসারূঢ়া** *fem*.

হংসোদক *n* clear water; kind of cordial liquor.

হক [A] *n* **1** truth. **2** justice; equity; right; rectitude. **3** just claim; lot; portion; duty. **4** the deity; God. ❑*adj* just; right; true. ❑*adv* rightful. **~ আদায় করা** *vt* perform one's duty; render one his due. **~কথা** *n* just/ right words. **~দাবি** *n* rightful claim. **~দার** *adj* rightful; having right/ claim (to). **~ নাহক** rightly or wrongly. **~পরস্ত** *n* worshipper of God; pious man. **~ মারা** *n* usurp a right; deprive sb of his right. **~ সাচেত করা** *vi* prove one's claim. **~সফা** *n* right of preemption.

হকচকানো *vi* be nonplussed; not knowing which way to turn; be flabbergasted; wobble; fatter; flounder; be taken aback.

হকার [E] *n* hawker; pedlar; huckster. **খবরের কাগজের ~** *n* newsboy.

হকারি *n* hucksterу; pedlary.

হকি [E] *n* hockey.

হকিকত [A] *n* **1** truth; fact; reality. **2** state; condition. **~নামা** *n* account; narration.

হকিয়ত [A] *n* proprietary right; ownership right.

হকুক [A] *n* rights; dues; privileges.

হক্কানি [A] *adj* true; just; genuine.

হজ, হজ্ব [A] *n* pilgrimage to Mecca. **~ করা** *vi* go on a pilgrimage to Mecca. **~যাত্রী** *n* pilgrim (to Mecca).

হজম [A] *n* **1** digestion. **2** (iron) misappropriation; embezzlement. **3** (fig) act of accepting meekly/ swallowing: অপমান ~. **~ করা** *vt* **1** digest. **2** (iron) misappropriate; embezzle. **3** (fig) put up with; stomach; swallow: গালি ~ করা.

হজমি, হজমী [A] *adj* digestive. **~ গুলি** *n* digestive pill.

হজরত, হযরত [A] *n* **1** dignity. **2** a title applied to a great man; lord; master.

হজ্জাম *n* [A] **1** barber; shaver; hair dresser. **2** phlebotomist; circumciser.

হট *n* (onom) indicating; suddenness/ quickness/ rashness. **~ করে** *adv* hastily; abruptly; impetuously; suddenly.

হটর-হটর *n* (onom) indicating difficult/ heavy movement. **~ করে চলা** *vi* trudge; stagger along; stumble along/ about; plod on.

হট হট *n* (onom) expressing the idea of gadding about. **~ করে বেড়ানো** *vi* gad about; go roaming.

হটা *vi* **1** move backwards/ aside; retreat; fall back; retire; recede. **2** be driven back/ repulsed/ defeated. **3** back out; shrink from. **~নো** *vt* drive backward; repel; push back; foil; put off/ back; remove.

হটকা *adj* lanky: ঢেঙা ~.

হট্ট *n* market; fair. **~গোল** *n* confused uproar; din; babel; bedlam; hullabaloo. **~বিলাসিনী** *n fem* wanton woman; prostitute. **~মন্দির** *n* (facet) market place; thatched stall/ booth.

হঠ *n* **1** violence; force. **2** obstinacy; pertinacity; imprudence; rashness. **3** retreat; withdrawal. **4** defeat: ~ না মানা. **~কারিতা** *n* **1** imprudence; rashness; insolence; impetuosity; foolhardiness; indiscretion. **2** violence; force. **3** immodesty; incivility; discourtesy; disrespect. **~কারী** *adj* **1** imprudent; rash; impetuous; foolhardy; indiscreet; hasty; thoughtless; ill-advised; injudicious. **2** insolent; impudent. 3 violent; headstrong; unruly; wild. **~কারিণী** *fem*. **~যোগ** *n* kind of forced or abstract meditation (forcing the mind to withdraw from external objects); performed with great self-torture. **~যোগী** *n* adherent of the Hatha-yoga.

হঠা=হটা

হঠানো=হটানো

হঠাৎ *adv* suddenly; all of a sudden; abruptly. **~কার** *n*=হঠকারিতা (⇒ হঠ). **~নবাব** *n* upstart; parvenu; nouveau riche.

হড়কা *adj* slippery. ❑*n* sudden hard pull; tug. **~নি** *n* slipping; sliding; gliding. **~নো** *vi* slip; slide; slither.

হড়গড়ানে, হড়গড়ে *adjj* slipping; sloping; sough; uneven; up and down.

হড়গড়ানো *vi* slip; roll down; stumble.

হড়বড় *n* volubility; logorrhea; prolixity; gibberish; gobbledygook; verbiage; jabber; jabbering. **হড়বড়ানি** *n*=~. **হড়বড়ানো** *vt* gibber; gabble; jabber; speak in a hurried and inarticulate manner.

হড়বড়ে *adj* **1** voluble; jabbering; gabby; effusive; torrential. **2** over-hasty.

হড়মড়ে *adj* rustling; breaking short; brittle.

হড়হড় *n* (onom) **1** slipperiness. **2** rattling. **3** rambling: **~ করা** *vi* be slippery/ slithery; slip. **হড়হড়ানো** *vi, vt* **1**=~ করা. **2** drag forcefully. **~ করে** *adv* slippingly; suddenly.

হড়হড়ে *adj* slippery.

হজ্জিক *n* sweeper. **হজ্জিকা** *fem.*

হণ্ডা, হণ্ডিকা, হণ্ডী *nn* urn; (cooking) pot.

হত *adj* **1** smitten; killed; slain. **2** destroyed; ruined; undone; ended; gone. **3** lost. **4** struck; beaten. **5** injured; marred; hurt; wounded; hit by. **6** visited/ afflicted/ tormented by; suffering from; struggling with. **7** destitute/ bereft of; less. **8** frustrated; foiled; baffled. **9** struck off (as a head.) **10** whirled up; raised (as dust). **11** miserable; wretched; hopeless. **~গৌরব** *adj* deprived/ bereft/ shorn of glory; past all glory. **~চিত্ত, ~চেতন, ~চৈতন্য** *adj* bereft of sense; mad; dispirited; unconscious; stupefied; perplexed; confounded; flabbergasted. **হতচ্ছাড়া** *adj* wretched; miserable; graceless; reckless and dissipated. **হতচ্ছাড়া লোক** *n* wretch; rascal; scapegrace; rogue. **~জীবন** *n* blighted/ wrecked life. ❑*adj*=~জীবিত. **~জীবিত** *adj* deprived of life/ hope; overcome with despair. **~জ্ঞান** *adj*=~চিত্ত. ❑*n* contempt; scorn; slight; disdain; disregard. **~জ্ঞান করা** *vt* contemn; despise; look down upon; sneer at; think nothing of; make light of. **~ত্রপা** *adj fem* devoid of shame; shameless. **~পুত্র** *adj* one whose son(s) have been killed. **~প্রভ** *adj* dimmed in lusture; bereft of beauty; lack-lustre; dull. **~প্রায়** *adj* almost/ nearly killed. **~বল, ~বীর্য** *adjj* one who has lost his virility/ vigour; rendered vigourless/ powerless; impotent; weakened; enervated. **~বুদ্ধি, ~ভম্ব** *adjj* confounded; dumbfounded; stunned; taken aback; agape; flabbergasted; stupefied; dazed; thunderstruck. **~বুদ্ধিকর** *adj* amazing; bewildering; perplexing; stunning; staggering; disconcerting; confounding. **~ভাগা, ~ভাগ্য** *adjj* ill-starred; ill-fated; luckless; unfortunate; wretched; miserable. ❑*n* wretch; poor fellow. **~ভাগিনী, ~ভাগী** *fem.* **~মান** *adj* humbled; disgraced; slighted; dishonoured; humiliated; shamefaced. **~মূর্খ** *n* excessive fool; blockhead; tomfool; dunce; imbecile. **~-শ্রদ্ধ** *adj* having lost one's faith in/ reverence for; disgusted; displeased; disenchanted; fed up. **~শ্রদ্ধা** *n* irreverence; disrespect; disesteem; disregard; apathy; loath; slight; despise; disdain; neglect. **~শ্রী** *adj* whose prosperity is blighted; reduced to penury; deprived/ shorn of one's grace/ beauty/ glory; fallen on evil days. **~হৃদয়** *n* cursed/ broken heart. ❑*adj* broken-hearted. **হতাদর** *n* neglect; slight; disregard; apathy; insult; disrespect; lack of cordial/ warm reception. ❑*adj* neglected; slighted; insulted; not received with cordialility/ warmth. **হতাশ্বাস** *adj* hopeless; in despair; disheartened; despondent; discouraged; dismayed; crestfallen. **হতাহত** *adj, n* dead and wounded.

হতাশ *adj* disappointed; cast down; low; crestfallen; down in the mouth; disenchanted; disillusioned; frustrated; let down; disgruntled; despondent; dejected. **~ করা** *vt* disappoint; let down; disenchant; frustrate; dishearten; discourage; cast down. **~ হওয়া** *vt* be disappointed/ disenchanted/ dejected/ hopeless; despair; yield to despair; lose/ give up/ abandon all hope. **হতাশা** *n* disappointment; frustration; disenchantment; disillusionment; dejection; despondency; low spirits; dismay; hopelessness; despair; dashed hopes.

হতে *prep* from; since; of.

হতোদ্যম *adj* one whose efforts are crushed; broken in purpose; dispirited; dejected; dismayed; low-spirited; cast down; despondent.

হতোস্মি *int* I am undone.

হতুকি *n* (dial)=হরীতকী

হত্তেল *n* (dial)=হরিতাল

হত্যা *n* **1** killing; slaying; slaughter; murder; massacre. **2** persistent squatting at the temple of a deity for obtaining divine favour. **~ করা** *vt* kill; slay; smite; hit; murder; put to death; massacre. **~ দেওয়া** *vi* **1** squat at the temple of a deity for obtaining divine favour. **2** (fig) solicit doggedly; supplicate; beseech; implore; entreat. **~কাণ্ড** *n* murder; massacre; carnage; instance of homicide. **হত্যাকারী** *n* killer; slayer; homicide; murderer. **~কারিণী** *fem* murderess. **হত্যাপরাধ** *n* offence of homicide/ murder; culpable homicide amounting to murder. **হত্যাপরাধী** *adj* guilty of murder/ homicide. ❑*n* homicide; murderer. **হত্যাপরাধিনী** *fem.*

হদ [A] *n* limit; boundary; extent; bar.

হদিস, হদিশ [A] *n* **1** whereabouts: তার কোনো ~ পেলে? **2** clue; trace; information: চুরির ~. **3** means; way: মুক্তির ~. **4** first taste/ glimpse: সুখের ~.

হদ্দ [A] *n*=হদ. ❑*adj* extreme: ~মজা. ❑*adv* at most; in all; not exceeding: ~ দশ বিঘা. **~ করা** *vi* do one's best/ utmost; leave no stone unturned. **~ জবাব** *n* rejoinder. **~ তলব** *n* total demand. **~মুদ্দ** *adj* at best; at the most. **~মুদ্দ হয়ে** *adv* headlong; precipitately; like wildfire.

হনন *n*=হত্যা. **হননীয়** *adj* to be struck/ beaten/ killed; worthy of death.

হনহন *n* (onom) expressing; walking/ moving at a great speed. **~ করে, হনহনিয়ে** *adv* at full speed; the double; apace; posthaste; (in) double-quick (time).

হনু, হনূ *nn* **1** jaw; jawbone, mandible. **2**=~মান. **~মান** *n* **1** entellus. **2** (myth) name of a celebrated monkey-chief who was an ally of Ramchandra; *Hanumana.*

হন্তদন্ত *adj* flurried; nervous; flustered; fussed-up; high-strung. **~ হয়ে** *adv* in a flurry of alarm/ excitement; pantingly; excitedly; all in a fluster.

হন্তব্য *adj* to be slain/ killed; to be punished with death; fit to be killed/ slain.

হন্তা *n* killer; slayer; murderer; robber; assassin; disturber; obstacle; destroyer. ❑*adj* killing; slaying; murdering. **হন্ত্রী, ~রক** *n, adj*= ~.

হন্দর [E] *n* hundredweight.

হন্য *adj*=হন্তব্য. **~মান** *adj* being killed/ slain/ destroyed.

হন্যা, হন্যে (colloq) *adj* **1** murderous; madly ousting to kill/ slay/ murder/ bite/ beat/ attack. **2** frenzied; frantic; frenetic; berserk. **3** rabid: ~ কুকুর. **~ হয়ে** *adv* frenziedly; hysterically; like mad.

হপ্তা [P] *n* week; seven days. **~ হপ্তা** *adv* every/ each week.

হবন *n*=হোম

হবনী *n* sacrificial ladle; hole made in the ground for the sacrificial fire. **~য়** *adj* to be offered with fire; sacrificial. ❑*n* oblation; clarified butter.

হবা *n fem*=হাওয়া

হবি *n*=হবিঃ. **~স্য, ~ষ্যি** (colloq) *nn* sunned rice boiled in clarified butter for oblation. **~ষ্য/ ~ষ্যি করা** *vi* eat (nothing but) boiled sunned rice and clarified butter. **~ষ্যান্ন**=~ষ্য. **~ষ্যালী** *adj* eating sacrificial food/ rice boiled in clarified butter.

হবিঃ *n* oblation; burnt offering; anything offered as an oblation with fire.

হবু *adj* would-be; to-be; future.

হবুচন্দ্র *n* name of an utterly stupid king of folk tales. **~ রাজার গবুচন্দ্র মন্ত্রী 1** a king and his minister, both utterly stupid. **2** (fig) a stupid person and his equally stupid companion.

হব্য *n*=হবিঃ. ❑*adj* to be offered as an oblation; sacrificial; fit to be offered as an oblation.

হম্বা *n*=হাম্বা

হম্মাম *n*=হামমাম

হ-য-ব-র-ল *n* disorder; confusion; mess; topsy-turvydom; muddle. ❑*adj* **1** topsy-turvy; mess; in a state of disorder; messed up: ~ হয়ে থাকা. **2** dumbfounded; flabbergasted; confounded: তার কথা শুনে আমি তো ~.

হযরত=হজরত

হয়[1] *n* horse; stallion.

হয়[2] *vi* third person present and indicative of হওয়া. **~কে নয় করা** (fig) deny what is evident; undo/ unsettle a settled fact. **~-হয়** *adj* imminent; impending; forthcoming.

হয়[3] *con* either: ~ আমি নয় তুমি. **~ নয়** *con* either ... or.

হয়তো, হয়ত *adv* perhaps; possibly; probably; perchance; may be.

হয়রান [A] *adj* **1** fatigued; tired; weary; exhausted. **2** harassed; disturbed; worried; exasperated; badgered. **~ করা** *vt* **1** tire; weary; fatigue; exhaust; enervate. **2** harass; disturb; badger; exasperate; torment; bedevil.

হয়রানি [A] *n* **1** fatigue; tiredness; weariness; exhaustion; lassitude. **2** harassment; exasperation; annoyance; pestering; vexation; exacerbation.

হর[1] *n* **1** (myth) Shiva, the destroyer. **2** (arith) denominator; divisor. ❑*adj* taking away; carrying (off); removing; destroying; ravishing; captivating; allaying; killing; robbing: দুঃখ~. **হরা** *adj fem.* **~গৌরী** *n* form of Shiva and Parvati conjoined. **~চূড়ামণি** *n* Shiva's crest-gem; moon. **হরণ** *n* **1** robbing; plunder; pilferage; stealing. **2** abduction; taking away; carrying off. **3** removing; allaying; removal; elimination; destruction. **4** (arith) division. **হরণ করা** *vt* **1** rob; plunder; pilfer; lift; steal. **2** take away; carry off; abduct; seize; deprive of. **3** remove; allay; destroy; dispel; frustrate; annihilate. **4** conquer; win(over). **5** outdo; eclipse; surpass. **6** enrapture; charm; fascinate: মন ~ করা. **7** protract; delay: কাল ~ করা, gain time. **8** (arith) divide. **হরণ-পূরণ** *n* division and multiplication. **~-হর বমবম** *int* (myth) a sound uttered in honour of Shiva.

হর[2] [P] *adj* every; each; any; all. **~ওকত** *adv* =হরবকৎ. **~করা** *n* running footman; messenger; courier; emissary; peon; runner; postal messenger; postman. **~বিসম** *n* all/ various kinds. **~ঘড়ি** *adv* every hour; always; every now and then; often. ~তরফ *n* all/ various directions. ~দম *adv* every moment; always; non-stop; often; incessantly; continuously; every now and then. ~বোলা *n* one who mimicks or is capable of mimicking every voice/ sound/ note; mimic.

হরকত, হরকৎ [A] *nn* **1** hindrance; interruption; obstacle; impediment; obstruction. **2** fault; misdemeanour. **3** motion; gesture; action. ~করা *vi* act unproperly; do an improper thing.

হরগিজ, হরগেজ [P] *adv* ever; on any account.

হরণ ⇒ হর[১]

হরতন [Du] *n* hearts (of playing-cards).

হরতাল *n* stoppage of all works in protest throughout wide area; hartal; general strike.

হরদম ⇒ হর[২]

হরপ, হরফ [A] *nn* **1** a letter of the alphabet. **2** speech; talk. **3** character; type. ~-ঢালাই *n* type-casting. ~-ঢালাইয়ের কারখানা *n* type-foundry.

হরবকৎ, হরবখত [A] *advv* every time; always.

হরবোলা ⇒ হর[২]

হররা *n* noisy outburst; gales; roars; screams; shrieks: হাসির ~.

হরষ *n* (poet)=হর্ষ

হরষিত *adj* (poet)=হর্ষিত

হরা[১] *adj fem*=হর[১]

হরা[২] *vt*=হরণ করা ⇒ হর[১]

হরি *n* **1** (myth) name of Sri Krishna/ Narayana/ Vishnu/ Shiva. **2** sun. **3** moon. ❑*adj* fawn-coloured; yellow; reddish brown; tawny; pale yellow; fallow; bay (applied to horses). ~গুণ *n*=~নাম. ~গুণগান *n* act of singing the glory of Hari. ~ ঘোষের গোয়াল *n* **1** cowhouse of Hari Ghosh (ie the guest-house of a famous wealthy man of Calcutta–which used to be always packed with idlers who were fed by him out of charity). **2** (fig) topsy-turvydom; Pandemonium; shambles. ~চন্দন *n* yellow sandal. ~জন *n* **1** (lit) Hari's people/ flock; Hindu untouchable; Hariyan. ~দাস *n* slave/ worshipper of Hari. ~ধ্বনি *n* loud shouting of the name of Hari. ~নাম *n* name of Hari. ~নাম করা *vi* utter/sing the name of Hari. ~নামের ঝুলি/ ঝোলা *n* bag to hold the rosary used in keeping count of singing the name of Hari. ~ নামের মালা *n* rosary for keeping count of singing the name of Hari. ~প্রিয় *adj* liked/ loved by Hari. ~প্রিয়া *fem*. ❑*n* Lakshmi. ~প্রেম *n* devotion to/ love of Hari. ~বর্ষ *n* (myth) one of the 9 divisions of the Jambu-dvip (জম্বুদ্বীপ). ~বাসর *n* **1** any eleventh lunar day, which is a day of fast. **2** (facet) fasting. ~বাসর করা *vi* (facet) go without food; fast. ~বোল *n, int* loud shouting of the name of Hari; shout the name of Hari. ~ভক্ত *adj* devoted to/ worshipping Hari. ❑*n* devotee/ worshipper of Hari. ~ভক্তি *n* devotion to/ worship of Vishnu. ~ভক্তি উবে যাওয়া *vi* (facet) have one's high esteem/ confidence lost. ~র লুট, ~লুট *nn* scattering of *batasha* (বাতাসা) in honour of Hari for the congregation of devotees to pick up. ~সঙ্কীর্তন, ~সংকীর্তন *n* act of pronouncing/ repeating the name of Hari; singing in chorus in praise of Hari. ~সভা *n* assembly to sing the glory of Hari. ~হর *n* **1** Hari and Shiva conjoined. **2** form of deity consisting of Vishnu and Shiva. ~হর মূর্তি=~হর (2). ~হরাত্মা *adj* (of two friends, etc) inseparably united; intimate; bosom. হরি ~ *int* O Hari ! O Hari ! (uttered to express disgust, amagement, etc).

হরিণ *n* deer; antelope; fawn; stag; buck; gazelle. হরিণী *fem*. female deer; doe. ~ছানা, ~শাবক, ~শিশু *nn* fawn.. ~নয়না, ~লোচনা, হরিণাক্ষী *adjj* gazelle-eyed; deer-marked. ❑*n* moon. ~মাংস *n* venison. ~শৃঙ্গ *n* stag's horn; antler.

হরিণ-বাড়ি *n* **1** presidency gaol of Calcutta. **2** house of correction; gaol; jail.

হরিৎ *n* green (colour); verdure. ❑*adj* green; greenish; verdant. ~কপিশ *adj* yellowish-brown.

হরিত *n, adj*=হরিৎ. ~ক *adj* greenish. হরিতাশ্ম *n* **1** emerald; turquoise. **2** sulphate of copper; blue vitriol.

হরিতাল *n* **1** yellow orpiment; sulphuret of arsenic. **2**=হরিয়াল. ~ভস্ম *n* calyx of yellow orpiment.

হরিতালিকা, হরিতালী *nn* Milky-Way.

হরিদ্রা *n* turmeric. ~বর্ণ *n, adj* yellow. ~ভ *adj* yellowish.

হরিন্মণি *n* emerald.

হরিয়াল *n* kind of pigeon of yellowish green colour; *Columba hurriyala*.

হরিদ্বর্ণ *adj,n* green; green-coloured; of a yellowish golden colour.

হরিষ *n* (poet)=হর্ষ. হরিষে-বিষাদ sudden onset of sorrow/ calamity in midst of joy or merry-making; joy turned into sorrow.

হরীতকী *n* yellow myrobalan tree and its fruit.

হরেক [P] *adj* many and diverse; different; assorted. ~ রকম *adj* of various kinds; assorted.

হরেদরে *adv* on an average; on the whole.

হর্তা *adj* one who carries off/ robs/ abducts/ steals/ destroys/ kills/ removes/ allays. ❑*n* robber; thief; destroyer; dispeller; remover. হর্ত্রী *fem*. ~কর্তা *n* **1** destroyer and creator. **2** (fig) absolute ruler; dictator; supreme authority; all in all. ~কর্তাবিধাতা *n* **1** creator, preserver and destroyer. **2** (fig)=~কর্তা.

হর্ম্য *n* palace; large house; mansion; edifice; large and beautiful building. ~চূড়া, ~শিখর,

~শেখর *nn* spire. ~তল *n* flat roof/ upper room of a palace/ mansion.

হর্যক্ষ *n* lion.

হর্ষ *n* **1** joy; pleasure; happiness; delight; mirth. **2** erection; bristling: রোম~. **হর্ষক** *adj* thrilling; delighting; gladdening. ~কর *adj* causing joy/ happiness. **হর্ষণ** *n*= ~. ❑*adj* causing the hair of the body to stand erect; thrilling with joy/ pleasure; gladdening; pleasant; delightful. ~ধ্বনি, ~নাদ, ~রব *nn* shout/ cry of joy; hurrah. ~প্রকটন, ~প্রকাশ *nn* expression of joy/ delight. ~বর্ধক *adj* delighting; delightful; thrilling; delightsome. ~বিকশিত *adj* blooming/ beaming with joy/ delight. ~বিহ্বল *adj* agitated with joy; overjoyed; beside oneself with joy.

হর্ষিত *adj* **1** gladdened; delighted; charmed; pleased; happy. **2** made to stand erect; bristling.

হর্ষোচ্ছ্বাস *n* ecstasy; rapture; elation.

হর্ষোদয় *n* rise of joy; occurrence of pleasure.

হল[১] *n* **1** (gram) a technical expression for all the consonants or any consonant. **হলন্ত** *adj* ending in a consonant; consonantal; ending with a ~ (্). ~ মিল *n* (prosody) masculine rhyme. ~বর্ণ *nn* consonant. ~শব্দ *n* closed syllable.

হল[২] *n* plough. ~কর্ষক *adj* guiding/ driving a plough. ❑*n* tiller (of law); ploughman; farmer. ~কর্ষণ *n* ploughing; tillage. ~কর্ষণ করা *vi* plough; till (land); cultivate. ~চালক=~কর্ষক. ~চালনা=~কর্ষণ. ~দণ্ড *n* shaft/ pole of a plough. ~ধর, ~ভৃৎ *nn* **1** ploughman; cultivator. **2** (myth) Balarama, the elder brother of Sri Krishna (carrying a peculiar weapon shaped like a plough-share). ~ভৃতি *n* ploughing; agriculture. **হলায়ুধ** *n* 'plough-weaponed; Balarama.

হল[৩] [E] *n* hall.

হল[৪] [A] *n* gilding; solving; solution. ~ করা *vt* gild; solve; dilute. ~-করা *adj* gilt; gilded.

হলকা [A] *n* **1** ring; circle; loop. **2** assembly; fraternity: হলকায়ে জিকর. **3** circuit of a village; ward. **4** flock; troop: হাতির ~. **5** sudden hot wave: আগুনের ~.

হলকুম [A] *n* wind-pipe; throat.

হলদি, হলদী *n, adj* (colloq)=হলুদ

হলদে *n, adj* (colloq) yellow. ~টে *adj* yellowish.

হলন্ত ⇒ হল[১]

হলফ, হলপ [A] *nn* oath; solemn swearing. ~ করা *vi* take an oath. ঈশ্বরের নামে ~ করা swear by God. ~ করানো/ দেওয়া *vi* administer an oath. ~ করে বলা *vi* swear to. ~নামা *n* declaration on oath; affidavit. **হলফান** *adv* on oath.

হলহল *n* (onom) indicating excessive looseness/ slackness. **হলহলে** *adj* very loose/ slack; baggy.

হলাহল *n* (myth) kind of deadly poison.

হলী=হলধর (⇒ হল২)

হলুদ *n* **1** turmeric. **2** yellow. ❑*adj* yellow.

হল্য *adj* cultivable; arable. **হল্যা** *fem*. ❑*n* cultivated land.

হল্লা *n* **1** uproar; tumult; hullabaloo. **2** assault; attack. ~ করা *vi* make a noise/ riotous uproar/ hullabaloo; be noisy; pick up a row.

হসন *n* laughing; smiling; laughter; laugh; smile.

হসন্ত[১] *n* the sign (্) indicating the consonantal ending of a letter. ❑*adj*=হলন্ত (⇒ হল্ (1).

হসন্ত[২] *adj* **1** laughing; smiling. **2** blooming.

হসন্তিকা *n* portable fire-vessel; small fire-place.

হসিত *adj* **1** laughing; smiling. **2** blooming.

হস্ত *n* **1** hand. **2** forearm. **3** elephant's trunk. **4** measure of length from the elbow to the tip of the middle finger (= 18 inches); cubit. **5** position of the hand. ~কণ্ডূতি, ~কণ্ডূয়ন *nn* **1** (lit) itching of the hand. **2** (fig) strong desire to do sth by the hand, esp to beat or write. ~কমল *n* lotus carried in the hand; lotus-like hand. ~কুশল *adj* dexterous; skilful hand. ~কৃত *adj* made with the hand. ~কৌশল *adj* **1** skill of hand; manual dexterity. **2** sleight of hand. **3** palming. ~ক্ষেপ(ণ) *n* interference; intervention; intrusion; meddling. ~ক্ষেপ(ণ) করা *vi* set one's hand to; interfere (with); meddle; intervene. ~গত *adj* come hand; fallen into one's possession; procured; obtained; secured. ~গত করা *vt* secure possession of; procure; obtain; get hold of; seize; appropriate; get in/on hand. ~গির=~কুশল. ~গ্রাহ্য *adj* to be taken by hand. ~চালনা *n* movement of hand. ~চালনা করা *vi* **1** move one's hand. **2** (iron) beat; flog. ~চ্যুত *adj* fallen from one's hand; slipped from/ out of one's hand; passed out of one's possession/ control/ hand; escaped. ~চ্যুত হওয়া *vi* fall from one's hand; slip out of one's hand; pass out of one's hand/ possession/ control; escape. ~চ্যুতি *n* slipping out of one's hand. ~চ্ছেদন *n* amputation of a hand. ~তল *n* (palm of the) hand. ~তাল *n* clapping the hands together. ~দ্বয় *n* the two hands; both hands. ~ধারণ *n* holding by the hand; supporting; helping. ~ ধারণ করা *vi* hold by the hand; hold sb's hand. ~পদ, ~পাদ *nn* hands and feet. ~ প্রসারণ করা *n* stretch out/ extend one's hand. ~বর্তী *adj* being/ remaining in the hand; seized; held; caught hold of. ~বিন্যাস *n* position of the hands. ~ভ্রষ্ট=~চ্যুত. ~মৈথুন *n* masturbation. ~যুগল *n* the two hands. ~রেখা *n* line on the hand/ palm. ~রেখা

পাঠ করা *vi* tell (sb's) fortune from the lines on the palm; read sb's hand/ palm. **~রেখাবিদ** *n* palmist; ch(e)irologist. **~লাঘব** *n* lightness; manual readiness; cleverness; sleight of hand. **~লাঘব করা** *n* palm. **~লিখিত** *adj* written by hand; hand-written. **~লিখিত পুঁথি** *n* manuscript. **~লিপি, ~লেখ** *nn* **1** handwriting. **2** manuscript. **~লিপি-বিশেষজ্ঞ** *n* expert in handwriting; ch(e)irographer. **~শিল্প** *n* handicraft; hand-work; handiwork. **~শিল্পশিক্ষক** *n* instructor in manual work; manual instructor. **~শিল্পী** *n* handicraftsman; artisan. **~সূত্র** *n* bangle/ ornament/ piece of thread put on the wrist of a girl before her wedding. **~স্থ, ~স্থিত** *adjj* being in/ held with the hand; held. **হস্তাক্ষর** *n* handwriting. **হস্তাক্ষর-বিশেষজ্ঞ**=~লিপি-বিশেষজ্ঞ. **হস্তাঙ্গুলি** *n* finger. **হস্তাঞ্জলি** *n* hands joined together and hollowed. **হস্তান্তর** *n* **1** transfer to another's hand/ possession/ control; handing over. **2** (law) convergence. **3** another hand. **4** transfer to another hand. **হস্তান্তর করা** *vt* transfer to another's hand/ control/ possession; hand sth over (to). **হস্তান্তরিত** *adj* **1** transferred to another's hand/ possession/ control; handed over. **2** transferred to another hand. **হস্তান্তরের দলিল** *n* deed of conveyance. **হস্তাবর্তন** *n* passing one's hand lightly (and caressingly). **হস্তাবলেপ** *n* swearing by hand. **হস্তামলক** *n* fruit/ seed of the myrobalan in the hand. **হস্তামলকবৎ** *adj, adv* (fig) already in one's grasp; very palpable; clear; clearly; palpably. **হস্তার্পণ** *n* **1** laying hands on; setting one's hand to. **2**=~ক্ষেপ. **হস্তার্পণ করা** *vi* **2** lay hands on; **2**=~ক্ষেপ করা.

হস্তবুদ [P] *n* **1** accounts of past and present. **2** descriptive rent-roll (of an estate). **3** total annual income of an estate.

হস্তি *n* (in compounds)=হস্তী. **~দন্ত** *n* tusk of an elephant; ivory. **~দন্তখচিত** *adj* inlaid with ivory. **~মদ** *n* exudation from an elephant's temples. **~মূর্খ** *n* blockhead; tomfool. **~যূথ** *n* herd of elephants. **~শালা** *n* elephant-stable. **~শুন্ড** *n* elephant's trunk.

হস্তিনী *n fem* **1** female elephant. **2** a woman of a particular class (one of the four classes into which women are divided, described as having thick lips, thick hips, thick fingers, large breasts, dark complexion, and strong sexual passion).

হস্তিপ *n* elephant-keeper; elephant-driver.

হস্তী *n* elephant.

হস্তোদক *n* water held in the hand.

হা *int* expressing grief, suffering pain, anger, astonishment, satisfaction, disapproval, etc; ah ! alas ! oh ! ha ! well !

হাই *n* **1** yawn. **2** (dial) demand: তার বড়ো ~. **~তোলা** *vi* yawn.

হাইকোর্ট [E] *n* High Court.

হাইড্রোজেন [E] *n* hydrogen.

হাইদর=হায়দার

হাইফেন [E] *n* hyphen. **~ দেওয়া** *vi* hyphen; hyphenate.

হাইল [A] *n*=আল

হাইস্কুল [E] *n* high school.

হাউই [P] *n* sky-rocket. **~ বাজি** *n* rocket for fireworks display.

হাউজ [A] *n* basin of a fountain; reservoir; cistern.

হাউমাউ *n* **1** loud cry; wail; loud complaint. **2** hue and cry. **~ করা** *vi* **1** make a loud/ uproarious complaint; wail; bawl; yowl. **2** raise a hue and cry. **~খাঁউ** fy to fi fum.

হাউনি=হাবেলি

হাউস[1] [P] *n* desire; lust; inordinate desire. **~ করা** *vi* desire eagerly.

হাউস[2] [E] *n* house. **~-সার্জন** *n* house surgeon.

হাওজ=হাউজ

হাওদা [A] *n* litter (used on an elephant or camel, in which the ladies travel); open seat on an elephant.

হাওয=হাউজ

হাওয়া[1] [A] *n* Eve.

হাওয়া[2] *n* **1** air; wind; breeze; weather; climate . **2** (fig) contact; influence: বদলোকের ~. **3** (fig) atmosphere; trend; general tendency: পাশ্চাত্য শিক্ষার গুণে এখানকার ~ বদল হয়ে গেছে. **4** evil spirit: বাচ্চার গায়ে ~ লেগেছে. **5** rumour. **~-অফিস** *n* meteorological office. **~ই** *adj* aerial; airy; pneumatic. **~ই খবর** *n* rumour; gossip. **~ই জাহাজ** *n* aeroplane; airplane. **~ই মিঠাই** *n* candy-floss. **~ করা** *vt* fan. **~ খাওয়া** *vi* **1** take an airing; walk about idly; enjoy fanning; air oneself. **2** go without food; fast; eat Barmecide's feast. **3** loaf; idle (away/ about); dawdle (away). **~ গাড়ি** *n* motor-car; car. **~ চলা** *vi* (of wind) blow; be airy/ breezy. **~ দেওয়া** *vi* **1** fan; blow the cool. **2** aerate. **3** (fig) excite/ foment (a quarrel); fan. **4** (facet) decamp. **~ পাওয়া** *vi* **1** get air. **2** (fig) sense; get: বিপদের ~ পাওয়া. **3** (fig) come in contact (of); be influenced (by). **4** get stimulus. **~ ফেরা** *vi* (of conditions) change. **~-বদল** *n* change of air/ climate. **~ বদল করা** *vi* change climate; undergo a change of condition. **~-বন্দুক** *n* air-gun. **~ ভরা** *vi* pump up; inflate. **~য় উড়ে যাওয়া** *vi* be very lean/ thin; be so light as to be blown away by the wind. **~র বেগে যাওয়া** *vi* run/ ride/ drive. like the wind. **~র সঙ্গে লড়াই করা** *vi* quarrel with the wind; be ready to quarrel; seek occasion for a quarrel. **~ লাগা** *vi* **1** get air; be airy. **2** (fig) get stimulus. **3** (fig) come in contact (of); be influenced (by). **4** swell out: পালে হাওয়া লেগেছে, The sails swelled out. **~ লাগতে না দেওয়া** *vt* keep closed; keep off. ~

হওয়া *vi* scamper off; disappear; run away as fast as the wind; evaporate; vanish (into the air); decamp .

হাওয়াল=হাওলা

হাওর *n* extensive marsh/ fen.

হাওলা [A] *n* **1** custody; charge; care; possession. **2** (also ~ জমি) piece of land held under fixed terms and conditions. ~ **করা** *vt* commit to the charge/ charge of; consign; make over. ~**দার** *n* one who holds a piece of land under fixed terms and conditions.

হাওলাত, হাওলাৎ [A] *nn* **1** borrowing; loan; debt. **2** custody; things given in charge. ~ **করা** *vi* borrow. ~ **দেওয়া** *vt* lend. ~**বরাত** *n* borrowing and fining a future point of time for payment.

হাওলাতি, হাওলাতী *adj* borrowed; taken on loan.

হাঁ[1] *particle, int* yes.

হাঁ[2] *n* **1** (expanse of) open mouth; yawn; gape; open-mouthed stare. **2** opening; mouth; aperture; orifice; chasm: গুহার ~. ~ **করা** *vi* **1** open one's mouth. **2** stare with open mouth; gape. **3** be wide open; yawn; gape: গর্তের মুখ ~ করে আছে. ~ **হওয়া** *vi* become wide open; gape. ~-**হওয়া** *adj* gaping.

হাঁ[3], **হাঁগা, হাঁগো** *int* used in addressing a person familiarly; my dear.

হাঁইফাঁই=হাঁসফাঁস

হাঁউমাউ=হাউমাউ

হাঁক *n* loud call/ shout/ cry; yell. ~ **দেওয়া/ পাড়া** *vi* call/ shout loudly; yell; roar; bawl; bellow; utter a loud cry; hoop. ~**ডাক** *n* **1** repeated loud calls/ shouts; **2** wide reputation of being wealthy and powerful; prestige; dominance; reputation as a powerful man. ~**ডাক পাড়া** *vi* raise a hue and cry; vociferate. ~ **পাড়াপাড়ি** *n* repeated shouting; outcry; yelling.

হাঁকড়ানো *vt* **1** drive very proudly/ speedily: গাড়ি ~. **2** brandish/ move with éclat; beat severely with: চাবুক ~. **3** build (ostentatiously) for oneself: তেতলা বাড়ি ~.

হাঁকন *n* shouting; yelling.

হাঁকপাক *n* fidgets; nervousness; uneasiness. ~ **করা** *vi* fidget; be nervous/ uneasy.

হাঁকা *vi, vt* shout; call/ announce/ declare loudly; yell. ~**হাঁকি** *n* repeated loud calling/ shouting; yelling; vociferation. ~**হাঁকি করা** *vi* call/ shout loudly and repeatedly; yell; vociferate; cry repeatedly.

হাঁকানো[1]=হাঁকড়ানো

হাঁকানো[2] *vt* drive out; oust; turn out; chase away; send away; throw out.

হাঁকার=হাঁক

হাঁকুপাকু=হাঁকপাক

হাঁচন *n* sneezing.

হাঁচা *vi* sneeze. ~**নো** *vt* cause to sneeze.

হাঁচি *n* sneeze.

হাঁটকানো *vt* **1** rummage (in/ through/ among). বইয়ের আলমারি ~. **2** make a mess of in course of rummaging.

হাঁটন *n* walking.

হাঁটা *vi* walk; stroll; go for a walk. ❑*n* walk; walking. ~**নো** *vt* (cause to) walk; teach (esp a baby) how to walk. ~**পথ** *n* **1** way to be covered by walking. **2** path/ route for walking. ~**পথে** *adj* on foot. **হাঁটাহাঁটি** *n* repeated walking/ visits on foot; constant walking; travelling to and fro. **হাঁটাহাঁটি করা** *vi* go (to)/ visit repeatedly on foot; walk to and fro; shuttle.

হাঁটু *n* knee. ~ **গাড়া/ পাড়া/ পাতা** *vi* be on one's knee; kneel down; bend the knee; genuflect. ~ **জল** *n* knee-deep water.

হাঁটুনি *n* walk; walking.

হাঁড়ল *n* large hole.

হাঁড়া *n* large cooking pot.

হাঁড়ি *n* (earthen) pot/ boiler; cooking pot. ~**কুড়ি** *n* kitchen utensils; pots and pitchers. ~ **খাওয়া** *vi* steal food from a cooking pot. ~**খেকো** *adj* one who steals food from a cooking pot. ~**খাকি** *fem.* ~ **ঠেলা** *vi* stave away in the kitchen. ~**পানা** *adj* **1** pot-like; chubby. **2** glum; sullen. ~**মুখ** *n* **1** large round face. **2** sullen looks. ~**র খবর** *n* internal information; ins and outs. **কেলে** ~ *n* cooking pot turned black on account of being used in cooking for a long time.

হাঁড়িচাচা *n* Indian tree-pie.

হাঁড়িয়া *n* an inferior liquor obtained from fermented rice.

হাঁড়ী=হাঁড়ি

হাঁদা *adj* **1** fat; potbellied; corpulent; broad in the beam. **2** dull-witted; stupid; idiotic; imbecile; obtuse; half-witted; blockheaded. ~-**পেটা** *adj* pot-bellied. ~**রাম** *n* dunce; prince of idiots; blockhead; dullard; dunderhead.

হাঁপ *n* (onom) **1** sigh. **2** laboured breathing; gasp; panting; asthmatic spasm; whoop. ~ **ওঠা** *vi* be out of breath; breathe hard; pant; gasp for breath; be seized with an asthmatic spasm. ~ **ছাড়া** *vi* utter/ heave a sigh (of relief); breathe freely; sigh. ~ **ছাড়ার অবকাশ** *n* breathing-time; breathing-space; respite; reprieve; breathing spell. ~ **ছেড়ে বাঁচা** *vi* (fig) breathe again; heave a sigh of relief; be relieved. ~**টান** *n* whoop; asthmatic spasm; gasping. ~ **ধরা**=~ ওঠা. ~ **ফেলা**, ~ **ছাড়া, হাঁপানো** *vi.* **1** pant; gasp for breath. **2** (fig) fidget.

হাঁপানি *n* **1** panting. **2** asthma. ~ **ওঠা**=হাঁপ ওঠা (⇒ হাঁপ). ~-**কাস**, ~-**কাসি** *n* asthma. ~**রোগী** *n* asthmatic patient.

হাঁস *n* duck; drake; gander; goose; swan. ~**কল** *n* hasp; hatch.

হাঁসফাঁস *n* **1** laboured breathing. **2** fidget. **~ করা** *vi* **1** gasp for breath; breathe with difficulty. **2** fidget; be nervous.

হাঁসিয়া[1] *n* **1** a curved large knife fixed at right angle in a piece of wood on which one sets while cutting fish, vegetables, etc. **2** sickle.

হাঁসিয়া *n*=হাশিয়া

হাঁসী *n fem* duck; goose.

হাঁসুলি *n* crescent-shaped ornament worn round the neck.

হাঁ-হাঁ *int* used to prevent/ interrupt suddenly; oh no ! ❑*particle* yes, yes; of course.

হ্যাঁ *particle* (colloq) yes; yea; yeah.

হাকিক *n* carnelian.

হাকিম[1] *n*=হকিম

হাকিম[2] *n* **1** judge; magistrate; deputy magistrate. **2** ruler; master.

হাকিমি *n* magistracy. ❑*adj* magisterial.

হাগন *n* (sl) defecation.

হাগা *vi* (sl) defecate; shit; evacuate the bowels; relieve oneself. ❑*n* **1** defecation; shit; excrement; stool. **2** bowel movement. **~নো** *vt* evacuate another's bowels; purge. **~ পাওয়া** *vi* have a bowel movement. **~মোতা** *n* defecation and urination; call of nature. ❑*vi* defecate and urinate; relieve oneself.

হাঘর *n* **1** low family. **2** destitute; homeless person.

হাঘরে *adj* **1** born of a low/ indigent family. **2** homeless; destitute; indigent; vagabond.

হাঙর, হাঙ্গর *n* shark.

হাঙ্গামা, হাঙ্গাম [P] *n* **1** riot; disturbance; disorder; tumult; uproar; affray. **2** assault; raid; inroad. **3** difficulty; hitch; trouble. **~ করা/ বাঁধানো** *vi* riot; create a difficulty/ disturbance; brew trouble/ mischief.

হাজত[1], **হাজৎ** *nn* (police) custody; guardroom for under-trial prisoners; (police) lock-up. **হাজতে দেওয়া/ রাখা** *vt* give sb into custody; send to police custody. **~ হওয়া** *vi* be in custody. **~খানা** *n*=~.

হাজত[2] *n* revenue held in abeyance.

হাজরা [P] *n* **1** commander of a thousand. **2** headman of a village. **3** a particular family name.

হাজরি [A] *n* **1** presence; attendance; appearance; audience. **2** breakfast; dinner. **~ খাওয়া** *vi* have breakfast. **ছোট ~** *n* breakfast. **বড় ~** *n* dinner.

হাজা *vi* **1** rot/ be spoilt; be/ being drenched in water for a long time; putrefy/ decay in water: ধান ~. **2** be affected with chilblains: হাত-পা ~. ❑*n* **1** decay/ decomposition/ putrefaction due to long submersion in water. **2** excessive rainfall or flood. **3** sore caused by excessive use of water; chilblain. **4** retting; rating; rotting. **~নো** *vt* **1** soak; soften/ spoil/ rot by soaking or exposure to moisture; ret; rate; rot: পাট ~নো. **2** flood; inundate: দেশ ~নো. ❑*adj* **1** retted; rated; ratted: ~নো পাট. **2** flooded; inundated. **~নো মজানো** *vt* rot by soaking; submerge and spoil. **~মজা** *adj* (of a pond) dried up and slimy; derelict; rain/ flood and draught.

হাজাম *n* **1**=হজ্জাম. **2** professional circumciser. **~ত, ~ৎ** *nn* **1** shaving; hair dressing. **2** circumcision.

হাজ্জাম *n*=হাজাম

হাজার [P] *n, adj* thousand. ❑*adv* however much; as much as. **~ বললেও** even if repeated a thousand times/ times without number; however much one repeats. **~ হাজার, হাজারে হাজারে** thousands of; innumerable; countless. **হাজারে একটা** one in a thousand.

হাজারি, হাজারী *nn*=হাজরা

হাজি [A] *n* person who has performed pilgrimage to Mecca; Haji.

হাজির [A] *adj* present; ready at hand; appeared; in attendance. **~ করা(নো)** *vt* present; produce; lay before; make ready; summon. **~ থাকা** *vi* be present; wait on; be in attendance. **~ হওয়া** *vi* be present; be at hand; attend; be at the service of; be ready. **~জবাব** *adj* ready with an answer; ready-witted; pert. **~জবাবি** *n* readiness in replying; repartee. **~জামিন** *n* offering bail/ security for the appearance of another in court; bondsman. **~জামিনি** *n* security for personal appearance; giving bail for another. **গর~** *adj* absent; not present.

হাজিরা [A] *n* presence; attendance; appearance; audience; muster-roll; roll-call. **~ নেওয়া** *vi* mark attendance; call the roll; call out the names (of). **~-খাতা, ~-বই** *nn* attendance register.

হাজিরি=হাজিরা

হাজী=হাজি

হাজ্জাম=হাজাম

হাট *n* **1** market; market-place. **2** fair. **3** disturbingly noisy place; madhouse. **4** abundance; plenty; galaxy: রূপের ~. **5** assemblage; concourse: বোকার ~. **~ করা** *vi* **1** go to (the) market for buying and selling; do one's marketing; provide oneself with necessaries. **2** open fully/ wide; open to public view; lay bare: দরজা/ হৃদয় ~ করা. **3** make a mess of: টেবিলটা যা ~ করে রেখেছ. **~ বসা** *vi* (of a market) be held; be. **~ বসানো/ মেলানো** *vi* **1** establish/ set up a market. **2** (fig) (cause to) assemble; make a loud disturbing noise; kick up/ make a din/ racket. **~বার** *n* market-day. **ভাঙা ~** *n* **1** market/ fair on the point of closing; deserted market. **2** (fig) fag end; close; last stage. **হাটে হাঁড়ি ভাঙা** *vi* (fig) disclose/ reveal sb's guilt/ wrong-doing in public; expose/ unmask sb; make public sb's wrong-doing; noise sth abroad. কেঁদে ~ করা *vi* cry uproariously; scream and wail.

হাটুরে *n* market-man; market-woman; market. ❑*adj* **1** going to market for buying/ selling: ~ লোক. **2** carrying goods (and people) to the market: ~ নৌকা.

হাডুডু, হাডু-ডুডু *nn* a Bengali outdoor game; *kabadi.*

হাড্ডি *n* (colloq) bone. **~সার** *adj* skinny; skin and bone; reduced to a skeleton.

হাড় *n* **1** bone. **2** (fig) most sensitive part; marrow: ~ জ্বলে যাওয়া. **3** (fig) core; heart: হাড়ে হাড়ে টের পাওয়া. **4** (fig) secret; details: ~হদ্দ. **5** (fig) ability; capability: ও কাজ তার হাড়ে হবে না. **~ এক ঠাঁই মাস এক ঠাঁই করা** give a thorough beating; thrash soundly; thrash the life out of sb. **~ কাটে ত মাস কাটে না** (said of a blunt knife) It cuts bone by its heaviness, but does not cut flesh. **~ কালি করা** (fig) **1** exhaust/ exasperate utterly (with affliction/ toil); wear sb out; lacerate; torment; sweat. **~ কালি হওয়া** *vi* (fig) be utterly exhausted/ exasperated (with affliction/ toil); sweat blood. **~ গুড়া করা** (fig) beat soundly; give sb a good hiding/ smashing; blow; thrash the living daylights out of. **~ জুড়ানো** (fig) **1** relieve; give/ bring relief to. **2** be/ feel relieved. **~ জ্বালানো** (fig) trouble in the extreme; torment; exacerbate; pester. **~ ভাঙ্গা** *vi* beat severely/ black and blue. **~ ভাজা ভাজা হওয়া** (fig) be tired of; be worn out (by sth); be weary (of). **~ মাটি করা** *vi* (fig) die; give up the ghost. **~মাস আলাদা করা**= ~ এক ঠাঁই মাস এক ঠাঁই করা. **হাড়ে দূর্বা গজানো** (fig) be extremely lazy. **হাড়ে বাতাস লাগা** (fig) feel relieved. **হাড়ে-মাসে জড়ানো** (fig) be inseparably connected. **~কাট** *n*=হাড়িকাঠ. **~কৃপণ, ~কিপ্টে** *nn* extremely miserly/ niggardly, close-fisted; extremely stingy. **~কৃপণ লোক** *n* penny pincher; skinflint. **~গোড়** *n* bones (collectively). **~জিরজিরে** *adj* skeletal; worn to a shadow; scrawny; skinny; scraggy. **~জ্বালানে** *adj* (fig) pestilential; pestilent; extremely annoying; nerve-racking; importunate. **~পাকা, ~পেকে** *adj* **1** hardened; weather-beaten; seasoned; veteran. **2** skinny; wasted; wiry. **3** extremely precocious; inveterate. ❑*n* veteran; old-timer. **~পাজি, ~-বজ্জাত, ~-বদমাস** *adjj* wicked to the bones; out-and-out wicked. ❑*nn* out-and-out rogue/ rascal/ crook. **~-ভাঙা** *adj* extremely toilsome; back-breaking. **~হদ্দ** *n* all particulars/ information. **হাড়ে হাড়ে** *adv* to the bone; to one's cost. **হাড়ে হাড়ে টের পাওয়া** (fig) feel the pinch of.

হাড়গিলা, হাড়গিলে (colloq) *n* **1** adjutant (bird). **2** (fig) long-necked; long-legged thin person; scrag.

হাড়ি *n*=হাড়ী

হাড়ি কাঠ, হাড়িকাঠ *n* wooden frame-work to which the neck of a sacrificial animal is fixed at the time of immolation. **হাড়ি কাঠে গলা দেওয়া** (fig) brave/ face certain death.

হাড়ী *n* a scheduled cast amongst Hindus; member of this caste. **হাড়িনী** *fem.*

হাত *n* **1** hand. **2** fore-arm. **3** cubit; half a yard. **4** (fig) control; authority; power; influence; possession. **5** (fig) manipulation; hand: এতে তার কোনো ~ ছিল না. **5** reach; clutched. **~ আসা** (fig) develop the habit of; become expert. **~ ওঠানো** *vi* **1** (fig) give up; refrain from; forgo; desist; relinquish; keep the hands off; stop. **2** pray. **3** salute. **4** slap; beat. **~ কচলানো** *vi* wring one's hands (in regret or to curry favour). **~ করা** *vt* (fig) with sb over; gain the favour of; persuade sb by argument; bring into one's possession/ under one's control. **~ কামড়ানো** *vi* bite one's hand in disappointment/ frustration; squirm; repent; regret; wriggle (from discomfort, shame or embarrassment). **~ খালি করা** *vi* be empty-handed/ hard up/ broke; empty the hands of money. **~ খালি হওয়া** *vi* be hard up/ penniless. **~ গোনা** *vi* read sb's hand/ palm. **~ গোটানো** *vi* (fig) take off one's hand; cease participating in a work; keep from doing sth; let things take their course; stand aloof; do nothing; let pass; relax one's efforts; sit idle. **~ চলা** *vi* **1** raise one's hand to strike; beat; slap. **2** work quickly with one's hands; be dexterous/ dextrous. **~-চালানো** *vi* beat/ belabour with one's hands; cuff; slap. **2** hurry the work; speed up; quicken the pace of work. **~ চুলকানো** *vi* (fig) itch for; long for. **~জোড় করা** *vi* **1** join the hands. **2** beg with folded hands; entreat earnestly; apologize/ solicit/ salute with folded hands; supplicate; implore; beseech; reverence. **~ জোড়া থাকা** *vi* (fig) be fully occupied; have one's hands full. **~ ঝটকানো** *vi* twitch; give a jerk to the hand. **~ ঝোলানো** *vi* **1** lay hands on; lift/ raise a hand/ one's hand against sb; beat with hand; deal/ strike a blow (to sb) with one's hand; assault; raise one's hand (to vote for or against or to express one's assent to); rise one's hand to support a person/ proposal. **~ থাকা** *vi* **1** have a hand (in sth). **2** be skilful in using one's hands; have a light hand. **~ দিয়ে** *adv* **1** with hand; by the hands. **2** by hand; through: কারো ~ দিয়ে পাঠানো. **~ দিয়ে হাতি ঠেলা** (fig) accomplish a stupendous task by humble means. **~ দেওয়া** *vi* **1** touch with one's hand; lay hand on. **2** meddle; interfere with; encroach upon. **3** undertake; take up; take in hand; let one's hand to. **4** lend a hand;

support; assist; help. কপালে ~ দেওয়া (fig) become utterly dejected and stupefied at one's ill-luck; despair; be hopeless; be confounded. গালে হাত দেওয়া (fig) be dejected or amazed. ~ দেখা *vi* 1 read sb's hand/ pulse; tell the fortune of. 2 feel the pulse. ~ দেখানো *vi* 1 show the hand to a fortune-teller. 2 let the physician feel the pulse. ~ দোলানো=~ ঝোলানো. ~ ধরা *vi* grasp sb's hand; take by the hand; protect; aid; shake hands with sb. ~ ধরাধরি করে চলা *vi* walk hand in hand. ~ ধুয়ে বসা *vi* 1 be hopeless; despair. 2 keep the hands off; relinquish; leave off; dissociate oneself. ~ ধোয়া *vi* wash one's hands off. ~ নাড়া *vi* move hand; move one's hand (at sb). ~ নিশপিশ করা *vi* itch for. ~ পড়া *vi* be touched/ handled. 2 be taken in hand; be undertaken. 3 be interfered with. ~ পাকানো *vi* get one's hands used to sth by practice; become skilled/ seasoned by practice; get one's hand in; get used to; be trained. ~-পা চালানো *vi* set oneself to work; labour hard. ~-পা ঠাণ্ডা হয়ে যাওয়া *vi* swoon; faint; be cast down/ utterly dejected; be dying. ~-পা চলা *vi* have the ability to work; be strong enough to work. ~-পা না আসা/ওঠা *vi* be afraid; be diffident; take fright; loose courage; be paralysed. ~-পা ছেড়ে দেওয়া *vi* give up; resign oneself; loose heart; relax one's efforts. ~-পা পেটের মধ্যে ঢোকা/ সেঁধনো *vi* be terrified/ terribly shaken/ horrified/ terror-stricken. ~-পা বাঁধা *vi* bind sb hand and foot. ~-পা বাঁধা থাকা *vi* be helpless/ powerless. ~-পা বেঁধে জলে ফেলে দেওয়া *vi* consign to utter misery; throw/ fling to the jaws of death; ruin sb's life knowingly. ~-পা বের করা *vi* exaggerate; make a mountain out of a molehill; fabricate. ~ পাতা *vi* extend the hand; stretch out one's hand; beg; pray; earnestly request/ ask for help or monetary assistance; beseech; appeal for; solicit; importune. ~ পৌঁছানো *vi* have access; reach. ~ ফসকানো *vi* slip through one's fingers; miss the mark. ~ ফেরানো, ~বদল করা/ হওয়া *vv* change hands. ~ বাঁধা *vi* 1 tie sb's hands; render sb unable to do a thing. 2 have no leisure; be much engaged in business; have one's hands full. ~ বাড়ানো *vi* 1 stretch out the hand; endevour to get sth; gain possession of. 2 extend a helping hand; help; land a hand. ~ বোলানো *vi* pass one's hand lightly (and caressingly over sth)); caress; coak; feel. গায়ে ~ বোলানো *vi* 1 caress; give a affectionate/ loving touch; stroke; pet; comfort. 2 pacify; propitiate; console with adulatory words and caressing; win over; cajole. মাথায় ~ বোলানো *vi* 1 stroke sb's head. 2 woo; make oneself pleasant to sb; wheedle (into/ out of); cheat by cajolery; inveigle sb into (doing sth). ~ মুঠা করা *vi* clench the fist. ~ মেলানো *vi* 1 shake hands with; close a bargain. 2 join hands with. ~-লাগা *vi* be touched; be felt. ~ লাগানো *vi* 1 handle; touch; lay hands on. 2 lend a hand. 3 slap. ~ সড়সড় করা *vi* itch (for). ~কড়া, ~কড়ি *nn* handcuff. ~কড়ি দেওয়া/ পরানো *vt* handcuff. ~করাত *n* handsaw. ~কষা *adj* stingy; niggardly; close-fisted. ~কাটা *adj* 1 having one's arm(s) amputed; armless. 2 (of shirts, etc) sleeveless. ~খরচ *n* pocket money. ~খালি *adj* 1 empty-handed; broke. 2 wearing no ornaments in one's hands. 3 having no work on one's hand; unoccupied. ~খোলা *n* lavish; bountiful; free-handed; prodigal; unsparing; extravagant. ~ঘড়ি *n* watch. ~চিঠা *n* hand-note; short letter/ note; receipt; chit. ~চুলকানি *n* itching of the hand. ~ছাড়া *adj* out of hand; out of possession/ control; lost. ~ছাড়া হওয়া *vi* go out of hand. ~ছানি *n* beckoning with the hand. ~ছানি দেওয়া *vt* beckon (with the hand). ~টান *n* 1 stinginess; frugality. 2 pilfering habit; kleptomania. ~ঠার=~ছানি. ~তালি *n* (hand-) clapping; applause. ~তালি দেওয়া *vi* clap one's hands; applaud. ~তোলা *n* a thing obtained out of sb's favour; charitable gift. ~ধরা *adj* very obedient to; servile; subservient; obsequious. ~পা বাঁধা *adj* utterly helpless; inescapably bound to. ~-ফেরতা *adv* through various/ several hands. ~বদল *n* change of hands. ~ বদলাবদলি *n* mutual exchange. ~বাক্স *n* cash-box; hand-box. ~-বাড়ানি *n* han(d)sel. ~বাড়ি, ~লণ্ঠন *nn* portable lamp. ~ভারী *adj* stingy; close-fisted. ~ মাথায় রাখা *n* (fig) swear by the head of. ~ মেলানো *n* 1 shake hands with. 2 close a bargain; give one's hand on a bargain. 3 join hands. ~মোজা *n* gloves. ~যশ *n* reputation for efficiency (of physicians, lawyers, artisans, etc). ~সই *n* (good) marksmanship. ~সাফাই *n* 1 sleight of hand; expertness; skill; skilfulness. 2 thievishness; deftness in pilfering with the hand. হাতে *adv* 1 at sb's hand; out of one's hand: কারো হাতে খাওয়া. 2 by hand; through: চিঠি তার হাতে পাঠিয়ো. 3 on hand; at hand; ready to hand. হাতে করা=হাতে নেওয়া. হাতে-কলমে *vi* practically; by direct practice and training. হাতে-কলমে করা *vi* have practical experience. ~-খড়ি *n* 1 sacrament of initiation into one's studies; first lesson in writing to a child. 2 (fig) initiation into a work; introduction (to); commencement of apprenticeship; initial stage of learning (a trade, etc.). হাতে-গড়া *adj* 1 hand-made. 2 (fig) brought up/ built (up) by oneself. হাতে চাঁদ দেওয়া *vi* (fig) fulfil sb's wildest wish/ desire; pamper to. হাতে চাঁদ পাওয়া *vi* (fig) obtain sth beyond one's wildest dream. **হাতে জল না গলা** *vi* (fig) be extremely close-fisted. ~ **থাকা** *vi* **1** be in one's possession/ under one's control; possess; hold in reserve; have in hand; remain (in hand). **3** be at hand. **4** be friendly to; be well-disposed to. **হাতে ধরা** *vi* (fig) importunate/ solicit very ardently; supplicate; implore. **হাতে নয় ভাতে মারা** (fig) subdue/ weaken not by beating but by starving. **হাতে-নাতে** *adv* in the very act of doing; red-handed. **হাতে নেওয়া** *vi* **1** take/ hold in one's hand. **হাতে পড়া** *vi* come to hand. **2** undertake; take up. **হাতে পাওয়া** *vi* (fig) get under one's control; wind sb round one's (little) finger. **হাতে পাঁজি মঙ্গলবার** (fig) ready proof. **হাতে বেড়ি পড়া** *vi* **1** to be hand-cuffed. **2** to be arrested by police on a criminal charge. ~ **মাথা কাটা** *vi* (fig) become very haughty; be intoxicated with one's power/ authority; become tyrannical. **হাতের ঢিল ছুড়ে দিলে আর ফেরে না** (prov) A shot in the locker once thrown will not come back. **হাতের পাঁচ** *n* last resort. **হাতের পুতুল** *n* puppet; cat's paw; pawn. **হাতের লক্ষ্মী পায়ে ঠেলা** (fig) throw away one's fortune. **হাতে স্বর্গ পাওয়া** (fig) be blessed with an unexpected stroke of luck. **হাতে হাত মিলানো** *vi* shake hands. **হাতে হাত রাখা** *vi* put one's hand into that of another; promise. **হাতে-হাতে** *adv* **1** (from) hand to hand; by hand; with hand; by; by the hands. **2** quickly; readily; directly; in no time: হাতে-হাতে ফল পাওয়া. **3** promptly. **4** red-handed: হাতে-হাতে ধরা. **কাঁচা হাত** *n* inexperienced/ unskilled worker; raw/ poor hand. **খালি হাত** *n* empty hand; unornamented hand; bare hand. **খালি হাতে** *adv* empty-handed; with bare hands. **ছোট হাতের অক্ষর** *n* small letter (of the Roman alphabet). **পাকা হাত** *n* experienced/ skilled worker; old hand. **বড়ো হাতের অক্ষর** *n* capital letter (of the Roman alphabet).

হাতড়ানো *n* **1** grope; feel. **2** appropriate to oneself; misappropriate.

হাতল *n* handle.

হাতা[1] *n* **1** ladle. **2** sleeve (of a coat, shirt, etc). ~ **করে তোলা** *vt* ladle out. ~ **গুটানো** *vi* roll up one's sleeves. **ফুল-হাতা** *adj* having sleeves up to wrists. **হাফ-হাতা** *adj* having sleeves up to elbow only; short-sleeved.

হাতা[2] [A] *n* **1** limits; boundary; confines; precincts: বাড়ির ~. **2** (fig) control.

হাতানো *vt* **1** appropriate to oneself; misappropriate; defalcate. **2** rummage through. **3** seize; take possession of; swindle; make free with; clean sb out; walk off with; pinch.

হাতাহাতি *n* scuffle (with hands); hand-to-hand fight; fisticuffs; exchange of blows. ❑*adj* hand-to-hand. ~ **লড়াই** *n* hand-to-hand fight.

-হাতি[1] *adj* (used as a *suff)* **1** measuring as many cubits (half a yard): বারো~ শাড়ি. **2** directed towards the right or the left hand: ডান~ রাস্তা.

হাতি[2] *n* **1** elephant. **2** (fig) a very bulky/ corpulent/ gigantic/ hefty person. ~ **পোষা** *vi* **1** keep an elephant. **2** (fig) keep a white elephant. ~**র খোরাক** *n* **1** elephant's feed. **2** (fig) very expensive upkeep/ maintenance. **3** Gargantuan meal. ~**র দাঁত** *n* tusk; ivory. ~**র শুঁড়** *n* trunk.

হাতিচোক *n* artichoke.

হাতিনা *n* (dial) verandah.

হাতিয়ার *n* **1** tool; hand-tool. **2** weapon; arms. ~**বন্দ** *adj* carrying arms on one's person; armed.

হাতিশাল *n* elephant-stable.

হাতী=**হাতি**[2]

হাতুড়ি, হাতুড়ী *n* hammer.

হাতুড়ে *adj* quack; charlatanic; shoddy. ❑*n* quack; charlatan; quacksalver; mountebank. ~**গিরি,** ~ **চিকিৎসা** *n* quackery; charlatanism; quack remedies. ~ **চিকিৎসক** *n* quack (physician); charlatan.

হাদিস, হাদীস [A] *n* Hadith; sayings, doings and precepts of Prophet Muhammad(sm); Prophetic tradition in Islam.

হাধিক *int* fie ! shame ! out upon ! what a pity !

হানা *vt* **1** drive (a weapon, etc); throw; cast; hurl; heave; fling; lob; launch; bandy: বাক্যবাণ ~. **2** shoot: তীর ~. **3** dart: দৃষ্টি ~. **4** flash: বিজলি ~. ❑*n* **1** attack; invasion; assault: শত্রুর ~. **2** raid: পুলিশের ~. ❑*adj* haunted: ~বাড়ি. ~ **দেওয়া** *vi* **1** raid; invasion. **1** haunt. ~**দার** *adj* invading; occupying. ❑*n* invader; raider. ~**দার বাহিনী** *n* invading army. ~**বাড়ি** *n* haunted house. ~**হানি** *n* mutual fighting; in fighting; dash; scramble; clash.

হানাফি *n* follower of Imam Abu Hanifa.

হানি *n* **1** loss; damage; impairment; injury; decrease; harm; diminution; failure. **2** deficit; insufficiency; shortcoming. ~ **করা** *vi* damage;' destroy; injure; impair. ~ **নাই** (there is) no harm. ~**কর** *adj* detrimental; injurious; harmful; destructive.

হানিমুন [A] *n* honeymoon.

হাপর *n* **1** furnace (esp of a smith); forge. **2** seedbed. **3** kind of basket for keeping fish alive in water.

হাপিত্যেশ *n* **1** yearning; hankering; longing; craving; pining. **2** regret; repentance. ~ **করা** *vi* **1** hanker for/ after; yearn for/ after; crave; pine for; starve for; languish for; long for. **2** regret; repent.

হাপুস *n* (onom) indicating: the sound of eating noisily. ~**হুপুস করে** *adv* (of eating) greedily; noisily. ~ **নয়ন** *n* tearful eyes. ~ **নয়নে** *adv* streaming with tears. ~ নয়নে কাঁদা *vi* cry one's eyes out; weep copiously; dissolve in tears.

হাফ [E] *adj* half. ~আখড়াই *n* kind of Bengali song-tournament. ~গেরস্ত *n* demirep. ~টাইম *n* half time. ~টিকিট *n* concessional ticket (for children). ~টোন *n* half-tone. ~ডে, ~রোজ *n* half-holiday; half-time.

হাফিজ, হাফেজ *n* **1** guardian; protector. **2** one who knows the whole Qoran by heart.

হাব *n* coquettish gestures of women. ~ভাব *n* **1** coquettish gestures; coquettishness; dalliance. **2** demeanour; attitude: তার ~ভাব ভালো নয়.

হাবজা *n* trash; refuse; rubbish. ❑*adj* trashy; worthless. ~গোবজা *n* hodge-podge.

হাবড় হাটি *n* **1** mud; sludge; slush; slime. **2** trash.

হাবড়া *adj* garrulous; talkative.

হাবলা *adj* dull-witted; stupid; idiotic.

হাবশি, হাবসি *n* Abyssinian; Negro.

হাবা *adj* **1** dumb. **2** stupid; dull; doltish; dull-witted; idiotic; silly. ❑*n* (also ~ লোক) fool; idiot; booby; jackass; rattle-head; simpleton. ~ গঙ্গারাম *n* boob; addle-head; half-wit; dunce; dullard; dunderhead. ~গবা *adj* simple-minded, simple-headed; addlepated; feeble-minded.

হাবাত[1]=হাভাত

হাবাত[2] *n* loss; ruin. মূলে ~ *n* loss/ ruin at the very outset; total loss/ ruin.

হাবাল *n*=হাওলা

হাবিজাবি *n* **1** rubbish; riff-raff; scum; rubble; trash. **2** nonsense; stuff and nonsense; abracadabra; balderdash.

হাবিব [A] *n* friend; beloved; sweetheart; comrade.

হাবিয়া [A] *n* the lowest region of hell.

হাবিলদার [P] *n* a petty military officer.

হাবুজখানা [P] *n* prison.

হাবুডুবু *n* **1** frantic effort of a drowning person to keep above water. **2** (fig) struggle to escape sth. **3** (fig) deep absorption/ involvement. ~ খাওয়া *vi* **1** struggle frantically to keep afloat. **2** (fig) be over head and ears; be deeply engrossed/ involved; be up to the/ one's ears; in (work, etc).

হাবেলি, হাবেলী [A] *n* **1** dwelling; house; large and spacious building; residential house. **2** row of residential houses; lines.

হাভাত *n* **1** one without means of procuring one's daily food; utterly indigent/ wretched person; starveling; beggar. **2** indigence; abject property. ❑*adj*=হাভাতে. **হাভাতে** *adj* having no means to procure one's daily food; utterly indigent/ wretched; beggarly.

হাম[1] [A]*n* measles. ~ লাট খেয়েছে measles have receded.

হাম[2] [P]*adj* similar; mutual. ~ছায়া *n* neighbour. ~দম *n* friend. ~দর্দ *n* sympathizer; fellow sufferer; partner in adversity; condoler. ❑*adj* sympathetic. ~দর্দি *n* sympathy; condolence. ~দিল *n* friend; crony. ~রাহ *n* companion; fellow traveller/ passenger. ~রাহি *n* **1**=~রাহ **2** companionship; company; society in travelling.

হামড়ি=হুমড়ি

হামবড়, হামবড়া *n* self-important; self-conceited; egotistic(al); bumptious; pretentious; pompous. **হামবড়াই** *n* self-importance; pompousness; conceit;

হামবাগ [E] *n* dishonest/ deceitful person; humbug.

হামলাহ [A] *n* attack; onset; assault; storm; charge; invasion; raid; riot. ~ করা *vt* attack; assault; storm; invade; assail; launch an attack; kick up a row.

হামলানো *vi* (of a cow) low loudly for the calf.

হামা, হামাগুড়ি *n* movement on all fours; crawl; crawling. ~ টানা, ~গুড়ি দেওয়া *vi* move on all fours; crawl.

হামান [P] *n* mortar. ~দিস্তা *n* mortar and pestle.

হামাম=হাম্মাম

হামাল [A]*n* burden; load; pregnancy; fruit of the womb; foetus.

হামিলা, হামেলা *adj fem* [A] pregnant.

হামেশা [P]*adv* always; ever; continually; perpetually; incessantly.

হামেহাল [P]*adv* in and out of season; at all times; ever; always.

হাম্বা *n* (onom) low. ~রব করা *vi* low.

হাম্বির, হাম্বীর *n* name of an Indian musical mode.

হাম্মাম [A] *n* hot bath; Turkish bath; bagnio; hammam.

হায় *int* ah ! alas ! oh ! fie ! shame! ~ হায় করা *vi* groan; moan; be afflicted. ~রে কপাল alack; alack-a-day.

হায়ওয়ান [A] *n* animal; beast; brute; stupid fellow; blockhead.

হায়ওয়ানিয়াত [A]*n* beastliness; brutality; animal nature.

হায়ন *n* (calendar) year; era.

হায়া [A] *n* modesty; shame; shyness; bashfulness.

হায়াত [A] *n* life; existence.

হার[1] *n* necklace; garland; wreath; string. ~ গড়া *vt* make a necklace. ~ গাঁথা *vt* weave a garland; weave flowers into a wreath.

হার[2] *n* defeat. ~ মানা/ স্বীকার করা *vi* acknowledge defeat. ~ হওয়া *vi* be defeated/ beaten. ~জিৎ *n* victory and defeat; success and failure.

হার[3] *n* **1** division. **2** rate; proportion. পরিবর্ত~~ *n* rate of exchange. শতকরা ~ *n* rate per hundred; percentage. **হারাহারি** *adj* proportionate; average; pro rata.

হারক *adj* taking; seizing; removing; ravishing; robbing; stealing; captivating. ❑*n* **1** divisor. **2** thief; robber.

হারকাত *n* defeated team (in a game).

হারমদ, হারমাদ=হর্মাদ

হারমোনিয়াম, হার্মোনিয়ম [E] *n* harmonium.

হারা *vi* **1** be defeated/ beaten. **2** lose (a game, etc). ❑*adj* (used as a *suff*) having lost; deprived/ bereft/ bereaved of; -less: গৃহ~; মাতৃ~. **~নো** *vt* **1** lose; miss: টাকা ~নো, সুযোগ ~নো. **2** defeat; beat; vanquish; triumph over. ❑*adj* lost; missing. **~নো-প্রাপ্তি** *n* what has been lost and what has been found; lost and found. **~নো সূত্র** *n* missing link/ clue.

হারাবলী *n* string of pearls.

হারাম [A] *adj* **1** unlawful; forbidden; prohibited; wrong. **2** sacred: ~ শরিফ, sacred precincts. **~ খাওয়া** *vi* receive the wages of iniquity; get money by unlawful means; take bribe. **~খোর** *n* one who lives on the wages of iniquity/ unlawful gains; corrupt person; usurer. **~জাদা** *n* **1** illegitimate; bastard. **2** rogue; scoundrel; swine. **~জাদি** *fem.*

হারামি, হারামী [A] *n, adj* illegitimate; bastard; wicked; villain.

হারি *n* defeat; vanquishment; setback.

হারিকেন [E] *n* hurricane (lantern).

হারিত *adj* **1** robbed; carried off. **2** lost; relinquished; made away with.

-হারী *adj* (used as a *suff*) **1** robbing; stealing; carrying away. **2** ravishing; captivating; exceeding; surpassing; attracting; charming; fascinating. **-হারিণী** *fem.*

হারেম [A] *n* women's apartment; harem.

হার্টফেল [E] *n* heart-failure.

হার্দ, হার্দ্য *n* love; kindness; affection. ❑*adj* relating to/ being in the heart.

হার্দিক *adj* relating to/ being in the heart; cordial; cardiac; tender; affection.

হার্মোনিয়ম⇒ হারমোনিয়াম

হার্য *adj* to be taken away/ carried off/ robbed/ appropriated/ taken/ borne.

হাল[1] *n* plough; metal hoop; tire. **~ চালানো/ দেওয়া/ বাওয়া** *vt* plough; till. **~ পরানো** *vt* tire.

হাল[2] [A] *n* **1** state; condition; circumstance; situation. **2** present time. **3** case. **4** spiritual ecstasy. **5** statement; narrative. ❑*adj* modern; current; present. **~খাতা** *n* (festival on the occasion of ceremonial opening of a) fresh account-book/ ledger (opened usually on the New Year's Day) for coming year. **~চাল** *n* **1** circumstances; state. **2** trend; tendency. **3** attitude; bearing; posture. **~ নিকাশ** *n* accounts of current income and expenditure; current balance-sheet. **~বকেয়া** *n* current arrears; arrears of the current year. **~ফিল** *adv* at present; recently; of late. **~হকিকত** *n* state of affairs; real state/ condition. **রাজার ~** *n* regal splendour; life of a king; milk and honey. **রাজার হালে থাকা** live like a lord; never have had it so good; be rolling in money. **হাড়ির হাল** *n* wretched/ squalid condition.

হাল[3] *n* helm; rudder. **~ ধরা** *vi* steer.

হালকা *adj* **1** not heavy; light; of short weight: ~ শরীর, ~ ধাতু. **2** easily digested; light: ~ খাবার, light meal/ repast. **3** negligible; trifling; frivolous; paltry; petty; worthless; unimportant: ~ বিষয়/ ব্যাপার. **4** mild; gently blowing; gentle: ~ হাওয়া. **5** care-free; cheerful; light: ~ মন. **6** airy; light: ~ কথা. **7** gentle; delicate; light: ~ ছোঁয়া/ স্পর্শ. **8** nimble; nimble-handed; nimble-footed; agile; lively; lithe: ~ পদক্ষেপ. **9** not deep; easily disturbed: ~ ঘুম. **10** wanton; light; frivolous: ~ মেয়েমানুষ, ~ স্বভাব. **11** dizzy; delirious; light: মাথা ~ বোধ হওয়া. **12** not serious; easily done; not difficult to bear; light: ~ বই/ গান, ~ কাজ, ~ শাস্তি. **~ করা** *vt* **1** lighten; disburden; relieve; ease; disencumber: মন ~ করা. **2** reduce the amount of; lighten; ease (of). facilitate: কাজ ~ করা. **~ভাবে গ্রহণ করা** *vi* take/ treat lightly; take it/ things easy.

হালাক [A] **1** *adj* ruined; destroyed. **2** slayed; killed. **3** harassed; exhausted; nagged. **~ করা** *vt* **1** ruin; destroy; slay; kill; harass; fatigue; exhaust; nag (at).

হালাল [A]*adj* legal; lawful; right; admissible; legitimate; showing religious sanction; killed as prescribed by Islamic law. **~ করা** *vt* make lawful; slaughter according to the Muslim way.

হালি *n* (group of) four.

হালিক *adj* of relating to a plough. ❑*n*=হালী[1] and হালী[2].

হালিয়া=হেলে

হালী[1] *n* ploughman.

হালী[2] *n* helmsman; steerman.

হালুইকর *n* confectioner; sweetmeat-seller.

হালুম *n* (onom) (facet) roar of a tiger; growl.

হালুয়া [A] *n* kind of sweet-meat made of flour, ghee and sugar, etc.

হাল্কা=হালকা

হাল্লাক=হালাক

হাশর, হাসর [A] *n* resurrection; doomsday; meeting; gathering; congregation. **রোজ ~** *n* day of resurrection.

হাশিয়া [A] *n* **1** hem; border. **2** margin (of a book); marginal note.

হাশিশ, হাশীশ [A] *n* hashish; cannabis; bhang.

হাস *n* laugh; smile.

হাসনাহেনা, হাসনুহানা *n* kind of very sweet-scented white flower that blooms in the evening.

হাসপাতাল [E] *n* hospital.

হাসা *vi* **1** laugh; smile. **2** taunt; deride; ridicule; laugh down. **3** (fig) be illuminated; shine; scintillate; glitter; glow. **~নো** *vt* **1** make sb laugh/ smile. **2** cause to deride/ ridicule; be an object of ridicule/ derision; be the butt of. **~হাসি** *n* **1** laughter; screams/ shrieks of laughter; guffaw. **2** derision; ridicule; mockery; raillery; taunt; jeer. **~হাসি করা** *vi* **1** laugh together derisively. **2** laugh at; deride; laugh down; ridicule; laugh in/ up one's sleeve; snigger (at/ over). **হেসে ওড়ানো** *vt* laugh away; laugh to scorn. **হেসে কুটিকুটি হওয়া** *vi* giggle; laugh one's head off; convulse with laughter. **হেসেখেলে** *adv* **1** in a happy-go-lucky manner; playfully; like a dream; cheerily; merrily; in fun and games. **2** easily; swimmingly; with ease; smoothly. **হেসেহেসে** *adv* smilingly.

হাসি *n* **1** laugh; laughter; smile. **2** scorn; ridicule; mockery; derision: ~র পাত্র. **3** (fig) brightness; splendour: চাঁদের ~. **~ পাওয়া** *vi* feel inclined to smile (a derisive smile); feel inclined to laugh in one's sleeves; be amused; be titillated. **~কান্না** *n* smiles and tears; joys and sorrows; alternate joy and sorrow. **~খুশি** *adj* cheerful; gay; jolly; vivacious; lively; cheery; sunny; merry. ❑*n* jollity; gaiety; cheerfulness; liveliness; vivacity; good nature; good humour. **~ঠাট্টা, ~তামাশা, ~মস্করা** *n* banter; joke; fun; badinage; pleasantry; joking; jest. **~ঠাট্টা/ ~তামাশা করা** *vi* banter, badinage; poke fun at; make fun of; jest; pull sb's leg. **~মুখ** *n* smiling face. **~মুখে** *adv* with a smiling face; readily; gladly; with a good grace; willingly; ungrudgingly; freely; graciously. **~র কথা** *n* amusing/ ludicrous/ ridiculous/ funny affair, proposal, thing, etc. **~র গররা** *n* roars/ gales/ screams/ shrieks of laughter. **~র ঘটা/ ছটা** *n* glow/ glitter of a smile; mirth; screams of laughter. **~র পাত্র** *n* object of ridicule/ derision; butt of. **~র বস্তু** *n* laughing stock. **মুখে~ ফোটা** *vi* **1** smile; beam with satisfaction; grin (with delight); be all smiles; smile broadly. **2** (of a face) be wreathed in smiles. **অট্ট~** *n* laud laughter; horse-laugh. **কাষ্ঠ~, দেঁতো ~** *nn* forced smile. **দেখন ~** *n* ready smile. **বিদ্রূপের হাসি** *n* derisive laughter. **মধুর/ মিষ্টি ~** *n* sweet smile. **মুচকি ~** *n* smile; suppressed laugh. **ম্লান ~** *n* sad smile; bitter smile.

হাসিন [A] *adj* beautiful; handsome; elegant; comely; charming. **হাসিনা** *fem*.

হাসিনী *adj fem* (used as a *suff*) smiling/ laughing (in the manner indicated): মৃদুমন্দ~.

হাসিল [A] *n* acquisition; accomplishment; result; gain. ❑*adj* accomplished; performed; realized; fulfilled. **~ করা** *vt* accomplish; perform; realize; get; acquire; obtain; gain; produce.

হাস্য *n* laugh; laughter; smile. **~ করা** *vi* laugh; smile; laugh/ smile derisively. **~কর, ~জনক** *adjj* provoking laughter; causing to laugh; ridiculous; laughable; ludicrous; funny; comical; farcical. **~কৌতুক, ~পরিহাস** *nn* pleasantry; badinage; banter; jest; humour; buffoonery; drollery. **~চ্ছটা** *n* gales of laughter; mirth. **~দীপ্ত, ~প্রদীপ্ত** = হাস্যোজ্জ্বল. **~ধ্বনি, ~রব** *n* shrieks/ screams of laughter. **~পরিহাস**= ~কৌতুক. **~বিচ্ছুরিত** *adj* lit up with a smile. **~ময়** *adj* smiling; beaming; happy; pleasant; cheerful; prepossessing. **~ময়ী** *fem*. **হাস্যমুখ** = হাসিমুখ (⇒ হাসি). **~রঞ্জিত** *adj* brightened with smile; beaming. **~রস** *n* (rhet) sense of humour; sentiment of mirth; comic. **~রসাত্মক** *adj* comical; humorous; funny. **~রসাত্মিকা** *fem*. **~রসাত্মক নাটক** *n* farce; comedy. **~রসাভিনেতা** *n* comic actor; comedian. **~রসিক** *n* wit; humorist; witty/ jocose person; comic actor/ singer; comedian; jester; buffoon; comic artist. ❑*adj* humorous; witty; funny; jocose; droll; comic; jocular. **~রসিকা** *fem*. **~লহরী** *n* gales of laughter. **~সংবরণ করা** *vi* suppress/ check laughter. **হাস্যালাপ** *n* pleasantry; badinage; chit-chat. **হাস্যাস্পদ** = হাসির পাত্র (⇒ হাসি).

হাস্যোজ্জ্বল *adj* brightened/ lit up with smile; smiling; beaming.

হাস্যোদ্দীপক, হাস্যোদ্রেককর *adjj*=হাস্যকর (⇒ হাস্য)

হা-হতোস্মি *int* alas, I am undone/ lost !

হা হা[1] *int* repeated *ha* (⇒ হা); lamentation; wailing. **~ করা** *vi* **1** lament/ grieve/ wail loudly. **2** be desolate/ empty: ঘরটা ~ করছে. **~ করে ওঠা** *vi* **1** burst into loud lamentation/ wailing. **2** be filled with grief; feel great distress; bleed for. **~কার** *n* general/ great/ loud lamentation; wailing; consternation; desolation; grieving. **~কার করা** *vi* lament/ bewail loudly; beat one's breast; cry one's heart out; bleed (for).

হাহা[2] *n* (onom) loud laughter; Ha ! Hah ! howl of derision; roars of laughter; guffaw. **~ করা** *vi* laugh loudly; roar with laughter; guffaw; give a coarse/ boisterous laughter. **~ করে ওঠা** *vi* burst into a guffaw/ noisy laughter.

হা-হুতাশ *n* profound regret/ repentance; compunction; remorse; contrition. **~ করা** *vi* repent/ regret deeply; mourn; lament; bewail; rue; deplore.

হিং, হিঙ *n* asafœtida.
হিং টিং ছট *n* (facet) meaningless words resembling Sanskrit words in sound; gibberish; abracadabra; mumbo jumbo; balderdash.
হিংসক *adj* given to killing/ harming others; noxious; malevolent; envious; spiteful; malicious; jealous. ❑*n* **1** noxious animal; beast of prey. **2** enemy. **3** killer.
হিংসন=হিংসা
হিংসা *n* **1** malice; spite; envy; jealousy; malevolence. **2** injury; harm; mischief; wrong; violence. **3** killing; slaughter. ~ **করা** *vt* **1** envy; be jealous of; bear sb malice; bear malice towards; have a spite against. **2** kill; slay; injure; harm; destroy; wish to injure. **~ত্মক** *adj* malicious; spiteful; violent; malevolent; envious. **~দ্বেষ** *n* ill will; malice; envy and hatred; spite; spitefulness; rancour. **~পরায়ণ, ~লু** *adjj*=হিংসক.
হিংসিত *adj* **1** hurt; injured; killed; destroyed; slain. **2** envied; begrudged.
হিংসুক, হিংসুটে *adj* envious; jealous; spiteful. ❑*n* envious/ spiteful person.
হিংস্র *adj* fierce; cruel; ferocious; brutal; savage; hurtful; injurious; mischievous; murderous; destructive; felt. **~ক** =~. **~তা** *n* ferocity; cruelty; fierceness; savagery; mischieviousness; brutality. ~ **পক্ষী** *n* bird of prey. ~ **পশু** *n* beast of prey.
হিঁচড়ানো *vi, vt* **1** drag forcefully; trail; pull along; **2** trail along; graze along/ against.
হিঁদু *n* (colloq) Hindu.
হিঁয়ালি *n*=হেঁয়ালি
হিকমত, হিকমৎ *n* **1** wisdom; knowledge; skill; cleverness. **2** device. **3** power; strength; might; ability; efficiency.
হিকমতি, হিকমতী [A] *adj* clever; resourceful; shrewd; skilful; ingenious; efficient.
হিক্কা *n* hiccup; hiccough. ~ **ওঠা** *vt* have the hiccups. ~ **তোলা** *vt* hiccup.
হিঙুল, হিঙ্গুল *n* cinnabar.
হিঙ্গ, হিঙ্গু *n* asafetida.
হিচকা=হিক্কা
হিজড়া, হিজড়ে (colloq) *n* hermaphrodite; eunuch. **হিজড়ানি, হিজড়ি** *fem.*
হিজরত [A] *n* **1** migration; flight. **2** flight of the Holy Prophet from Mecca to Medina in 622 A.D.
হিজরা, হিজরি, হিজরী [A] *n* Muslim era counted from 622 AD; hegira; hejira.
হিজল *n* kind of tree; *Barringtonia acutungula.*
হিজলি বাদাম *n* cashew-nut.
হিজিবিজি *adj* illegible; scrawly; scribbly. ❑*n* scribble; scrawl; scrabble. ~ **আঁকা/ লেখা** *vi* scrawl; scrabble; scribble.
হিঞ্চা, হিঞ্চে=হেলেঞ্চা
হিটলারি *adj* of/ like Hitler; violent; rabid; fiery; insane; lunatic; mad; frenetic: ~ কাণ্ডকারখানা/ মেজাজ.
হিড়হিড় *n* (onom) indicating: rapid and violent dragging along/ falling down; noise of such dragging/ falling. ~ **করে** *adv* violently; by storm; headlong.
হিড়িক *n* **1** passing popular excitement; craze; rage; the latest thing; passing fad; fashion: পাড়ায় পাড়ায় রবীন্দ্রজয়ন্তীর ~. **2** mad rush: বিদেশ যাওয়ার ~. **3** great pressure: কাজের ~. **4** noisy, disorderly crowd; commotion; hurly-burly; rush: ঈদের ~.
হিত *n* anything useful/ suitable/ salutary/ proper; good; benefit; advantage; service; welfare; well-being; weal. ❑*adj* **1** beneficial; advantageous; salutary; wholesome; suitable; agreeable for/ to. **2** put; placed; laid (upon); set (up); established. ~ **করা** *vi* do good to; benefit; help; be of value/ help; avail; profit. **~কথা** *n* friendly advice; salutary instruction; good/ salutary/ beneficial advice or teaching. **~কর** *adj*=~. **~করী** *fem.* **~কাম, ~কামী** *adj* wishing well to; desirous of benefiting. **~কামনা** *n* desire for another's welfare; well-wishing. **~কামনা করা** *v* wish sb good. **~কারী** *adj*=~. **~কারিণী** *fem.* **~বচন, ~বাক্য** *nn* friendly advice; good counsel. **~বাদী** *adj* speaking good counsel/ friendly advice; telling beneficial/ salutary words. ❑*n* friendly counsellor/ adviser. **~বাদিনী** *fem.* **~সাধন করা**=~ করা. **হিতাকাঙ্ক্ষা**=~কামনা. **হিতাকাঙ্ক্ষী,** *adjj*=~কাম. ❑*n* well-wisher. **হিতাকাঙ্ক্ষিণী** *fem.* **হিতার্থী** *adj* desiring/ seeking one's (own) welfare or advantage. ❑*n* well-wishes. **হিতার্থিনী** *fem.* **হিতার্থে** *adj* for sake of another's welfare. **হিতাহিত** *n* good and evil; right and wrong. ❑*adj* advantageous and disadvantageous. **হিতাহিতজ্ঞান** *n* knowledge of what is good (right) and what is evil (wrong); power of distinguishing right and wrong; moral sense. **হিতাহিতজ্ঞানশূন্য** *adj* frenzied; insane; frenetic; berserk. **হিতাহিতজ্ঞানশূন্য হয়ে** *adv* frenziedly; in a frenzy (of); hysterically. **হিতাহিত বিবেচনা করা** *vi* discriminate between good and evil/ right and wrong; distinguish good and evil.
হিতেচ্ছা, হিতৈষণা *nn* wishing well; good-will; good-wishes; desire/ disposition to do good to; benevolence;
হিতৈষী *adj* well-wishing; desiring another's welfare; benevolent. ❑*n* well-wisher. **হিতৈষিণী** *fem.*
হিতোক্তি *n* good advice.
হিতোপদেশ=হিতকথা (⇒ হিত). **~ক** *adj* giving good/ salutary/ beneficial advice. ❑*n* good adviser/ preceptor/ counsellor.

হিতোপদেষ্টা=হিতোপদেশক (⇒ above)

হিদায়ত, হিদায়েত, হেদায়েত *n* [A] instruction; guidance; righteousness. ~ করা *vt* **1** instruct; guide. **2** discipline; guide towards the right path. ~ পাওয়া *vi* be guided; accept instruction.

হিন্তাল *n* marshy date tree; *Phoenix/ Elate paludosa.*

হিন্দি *n* Hindi (language).

হিন্দু [P] *n* Hindu; Hindoo. ❑*adj* of Hindu/ Hinduism. ~ত্ব *n* quality/ state of being Hindu; Hinduism. ~ধর্ম *n* Hindu religion. ~ধর্মাবলম্বী *n* Hindu. ~ধর্মাবলম্বিনী *fem*. ~য়ানি *n* (iron) practices, rites and sacraments of Hinduism. ~সমাজ *n* Hindu society/ community; Hindus (collectively). ~স্তান, ~স্থান *n* Hindustan; India. ~স্তানি, ~স্থানী *adj* Indian; inhabiting upper/ central India; Hindustani. ❑*n* Hindustani (language).

হিন্দোল *n* **1** swing; swinging cradle/ hammock. **2** ornamental swing/ litter in which figures of Sri Krishna are carried during the Swing-festival (ঝুলন) in the bright half of the month of Sravan (শ্রাবণ); Swing-festival. **3** name of an Indian musical mode.

হিপ হিপ হুররে [E] *int* Hip, hip, hurrah.

হিফাজত=হেফাজত

হিবা [A] *n* gift; bequest; grant; present. ~ করা *vt* bequeath; execute a deed of gift; make a gift. ~নামা *n* deed of gift.

হিবুক *n* fourth astrological house.

হিব্রু [E] *n* Hebrew.

হিম *n* **1** cold; frost; dew; coldness; hoar-frost; snow; chill. **2** cold season; winter. **3** sandal tree. ~ পড়ছে *vi* Dew is collecting. ~ঋতু *n* winter season. ~কর *adj* causing/ producing cold; cold. ❑*n* moon. ~ক্ষয়িত *adj* glaciated. ~গর্ভ *adj* laden with snow. ~গিরি *n* the Himalayan mountain. ~গৃহ, ~ঘর *n* cold store/ storage; room furnished with cooling appliances. ~ঘ্ন *adj* keeping off snow. ~জ *adj* produced in the Himalayan mountain. ~জ্যোতিঃ *adj* cold-rayed (as the moon). ~ঝঞ্ঝা *n* hailstorm; blizzard. ~দ্যুতি=~জ্যোতি. ~ধ্বস্ত *adj* withered by cold; frostbitten; frost-nipped. ~ নিবারণ করা *vi* keep/ ward off or prevent cold. ~-বিমুক্ত *adj* freed from cold. ~পাত *n* fall of snow. ~বর্ষী *adj* snowy; frosty; freezing. ~বৎ, ~বান *adjj* having frost/ snow; frosty; snowy; icy; snow-clad. ❑*nn* the Himalayas. ~বারি *n* cold water. ~বাহ *n* glacier. ~মণ্ডল *n* Arctic/freezing zone. ~মিশ্র *n* freezing mixture. ~মুকুট *n* ice-cap. ~রেখা *n* snowline. ~শয়ন *n* (zoo) hibernation. ~শিলা *n* hailstone; iceberg. ~শীতল *adj* very cold/ frosty; freezing. ~শৈল *n* **1** iceberg. **2** the Himalayas. ~সংহতি *n* mass of ice/ snow; deep snow. ~সংহনন *n* glaciation. ~সাগর *n* sea of snow. হিমাংশু *adj* cool-rayed. ❑*n* moon. হিমাগম *n* approach a cold; beginning of winter; advent of the cold season/winter. হিমাগার *n* cold storage. হিমাঙ্ক *n* freezing point. হিমাঙ্গ *n* body bereft of blood-heat; frozen/ lifeless body. ❑*adj* having a frozen/ lifeless body. হিমাচল *n* the Himalayas. হিমাচ্ছন্ন *adj* snow-covered; snow-clad. হিমাদ্রি *n* the Himalayas mountain. হিমানী *n* mass/ collection of snow; ice; snow. হিমানী-সম্প্রপাত *n* avalanche. হিমানিল *n* cold/ frosty wind. হিমান্ত *n* end of the cold season. হিমাম্বু *n* cold water. হিমায়ক *n* refrigerator. হিমায়ন *n* refrigeration. হিমায়িত *adj* refrigerated; frozen. হিমায়িত করা *vt* refrigerate; deep-freeze. হিমার্ত *adj* pinched/ afflicted/ stricken with cold; frozen; suffering from cold. হিমালয় *n* abode of cold; the Himalayas range of mountains. হিমালয়নন্দিনী *n fem* goddess Durga.

হিমশিম, হিমসিম *n* extreme exhaustion/ fatigue; bewilderment; trouble. ~ খাওয়া *vi* **1** be in deep waters/ great difficulties; be in a predicament; be up to the/ one's ears in work, etc; get out of one's depth. **2** be almost fainting with exhaustion/ fatigue/ harassment; be bewildered; have a hard/ thin time (of it). **3** cower in fear.

হিমিকা *n* hoar-frost.

হিম্মত, হিম্মৎ [A] *n* spirit; mind; resolution; bravery; courage; power; magnanimity. ~জিগর *n* lion-hearted man; daredevil.

হিয়া *n* (poet)=হৃদয়

হিরণ *n* gold.

হিরণ্ময় *adj* golden; gold-coloured. হিরণ্ময়ী *fem*.

হিরণ্য *n* gold. ~কণ্ঠ *adj* gold-necked; golden-voiced. ~গর্ভ *n* **1** golden fetus. **2** Brahma. ❑*adj* full of gold; auriferous. ~দ *adj* yielding gold. হিরণ্যা *n fem* earth. ~বর্ণ *adj* gold-coloured. ~ময় *adj* made of gold. ~মালী *adj* having a golden garland.

হিরাকস [P] *n* green vitriol; sulphate of iron.

হিল [E] *n* heel.

হিলমিল *n* (onom) expressing zigzag movement of water. ~ করা *vi* stream/ flow in a zigzag; meander.

হিলা *vi* (old style) lean; droop.

হিলিমিলি *adj* zigzag; stripy; striped; variegated; checkered.

হিল্লা, হিল্লে [A] (colloq) *n* **1** stratagem; artifice; device. **2** means; way out; ways and means; expedient: সমস্যার ~. **3** disposal; arrangement: কাজের ~, মেয়ের বিয়ের ~. **4** remedy: রোগের ~. **5**

provision: ভবিষ্যতের ~. 6 provide with an employment: ছেলেটার একটা ~ হলেই বাঁচি. 7 clue; trace: চুরির ~. settlement: 8 বিবাদের ~. ~ **করা** *vt* **1** find a solution/ a way out; solve; resolve; **2** dispose of; arrange for. **3** find a remedy/ cure; redress. **4** provide for; provide with an employment. **5** find a clue; trace; unravel; disentangle. **6** settle.

হিল্লোল *n* **1** swing. **2** wave; surge; wavy/ surging motion.

হিষ্টিরিয়া=হিস্টিরিয়া

হিস *n* (onom) hiss; fizz. **~হিস** *n* hissing; fizzing. **~হিস করা** *vi* hiss; fizz.

হিসসা, হিস্যা, হিস্‌সে (colloq), **হিস্যে** (colloq) [A] *nn* **1** share; part; lot; portion. **2** co-sharer; co-owner; partner: বড়ো ~. **~ করা** *vt* share; distribute; divide; apportion. **~দার** *n* sharer; share holder; partner. **~দারি** *n* partnership; sharing.

হিসহিস⇒হিস

হিসাব [A] *n* **1** counting; reckoning. **2** calculation; computation. **3** account(s). **4** accounting. **5** estimate. **6** rate. **7** (fig) explanation. **8** (fig) consideration; deliberation; sense: এই হিসাবে. **~ করা** *vt* **1** calculate; compute; estimate. **2** (fig) consider; deliberate. **3** (fig) take into account. **4** make up an account. **~ চাওয়া** *vi* **1** ask for accounts/ an estimate (of). **2** (fig) demand an explanation; call/ bring to account. **~ চুকানো** *vi* **1** settle up accounts; clear accounts; quit scores; be quits; cry quits; close an account with. **2** (fig) settle one's account (with); balance/ square accounts (with sb); pay/ settle/ wipe off old scores. **~ দেওয়া** *vi* **1** submit/ tender accounts/ an estimate. **2** give/ render an account. **~ নেওয়া** *vi* take an account from. **~ মিটানো**=~ চুকানো. **~ মেলা** *vi* (of accounts) tally with; correspond; agree. **~ মেলানো** *vt* compare accounts; balance accounts. **~ রাখা** *vt* keep accounts; register in account books. **হিসাবে ধরা/ নেওয়া** *vi* **1** include in calculation/ accounts/ counting/ reckoning/ an estimate. **2** take into account; consider. **~কিতাব** *n* (detailed) accounts/ calculation. **~নবিশ** *n* accountant; ledger-writer. **~নিকাশ** *n* **1** accounting; accounts; detailed reckoning. **2** (fig) explanation. **~ পরীক্ষক** *n* auditor. **~ পরীক্ষা** *n* audit. **~ পরীক্ষা করা** *vi* audit. **~রক্ষক** *n* account keeper; accountant. **এই হিসাবে** on this account; in this sense. **কোন হিসাবে ?** **1** on which account? **2** at what rate? **3** on what ground; by what logic? **কোনো হিসাবেই না** on no account; not on any account; in no case.

হিসাবি, হিসাবী *adjj* **1** of/ relating to accounts; accountable. **2** calculating; cautious; circumspect. frugal; economical; thrifty.

হিস্টিরিয়া [E] *n* hysteria. **~গ্রস্ত** *adj* hysteric; hysterical.

হি হি *n* (onom) expressing (a) violent shivering in cold; (c) giggling noise; cackle. **~ করা** *vi* **1** shiver violently. **2** giggle; cackle.

হীন *adj* **1** bereft/ deprived of; devoid/ divested/ destitute of; lacking; free from; less. **2** poor; little; low; vile; bad; base; lowly; mean. **3** inferior to; weaker than, brought low; lower; broken down in circumstances; degraded; humiliated; lowered; humble; poor; indigent; undignified; indigent: ~ অবস্থা. **4** miserable; decreased; diminished; dim; dull. **হীনা** *fem.* **~ করা** *vt* debase; humiliate; degrade; lower; make poor/ indigent. **~কর্ম** *n* low practices; vile deeds/ practice. **~কর্মা** *adj* **1** engaged in low practices; doing vile/ hateful deed; employed in a lowly/ base work. **2** neglecting/ omitting customary rites/ religious acts. **~কুল** *n* low family. ❑*adj* of a low family; base-born; plebeian. **~ গুণ** *adj* of inferior virtue/ merit. **~চরিত, ~চরিত্র** *nn* base/ mean conduct. ❑*adjj* depraved; mean-natured; vile. **~চেতা** *adj* mean-minded. **~জ, ~জন্মা** *adjj* low-born. **~জাতি** *adj* of low caste; outcaste; degraded; vile. **~তা, ~ত্ব** *nn* **1** defectiveness; deprivation; destitution; privation; poverty; misery. **2** lack; shortage; want/ absence of: চরিত্র~তা. **3** meanness; vileness; low state; hatefulness; humility; humiliation; indignity. **~তাব্যঞ্জক** *adj* indicating meanness; ignoble; disgraceful; undignified; lowly. **~প্রকৃতি** *adj* mean-natured; vile; ignoble; small-minded; sordid. **~প্রভ** *adj* dim; lustreless; lack-lustre; bleary. **~প্রাণ** *adj* **1** mean-minded. **2** dying; sluggish; torpid. **~প্রাণা** *fem.* **~বর্ণ** *adj* of low caste; outcaste. **~বল** *adj* deficient in strength; weak; feeble; weakened; enfeebled. **~বীর্য** *adj*=~বল. **~বাদী** *adj* **1** contradicting. **2** speechless; dumb. **~বুদ্ধি** *adj* **1** of weak understanding; dull-witted. **2** having evil/ vile thoughts; wicked; vicious. **~বৃত্তি** *adj* of base conduct; employed in a vile/ lowly occupation. ❑*n* vile/ lowly occupation. **~ বেশ** *n* shabby dress. ❑*adj* shabbily dressed. **~ভাব** *n* indigence; misery; penury; lowliness. **~মতি, ~মনা** *adjj* mean-minded; suffering from inferiority complex. **~মন্যতা, ~মানস** *nn* inferiority complex. **~যান** *n* 'simpler/ lesser vehicle'; name of the earliest system of Buddhist doctrine. **~রূপ** *adj* deficient in form/ beauty. **~শক্তি**=~বল. **হীনাঙ্গ** *adj* defective in limb; crippled; mutilated; lame. **হীনাবস্থ** *adj* poor; indigent; in a miserable state; in reduced/ straitened circumstances. **হীনাবস্থা** *n* poverty; indigence; reduced/ straitened circumstances; evil days; miserable/ wretched state; low life.

হীরক *n* diamond. **~খচিত** *adj* with a diamond in it; set with diamonds. **~ চূর্ণ** *n* diamond-dust; diamond-powder. **~ জয়ন্তী** *n* diamond-jubilee; diamond anniversary (of a marriage)/ wedding.

হীরা, হীরে (colloq) *n* diamond. **~মণি** *n* diamond as a precious stone. **~র খনি** *n* diamond ore; diamond mine. **~র টুকরা** *n* **1** piece of diamond. **2** (fig) very bright person; jewel. ❑*adj* very intelligent and promising; very bright; jewel of a: ~র টুকরা ছেলে. **~র ধার** *n* (fig) great sharpness/ acuteness/ keenness of mind, intelligence etc. **কাচ-কাটা ~** *n* glass-cutter.

হীরাকস=হিরাকস

হীরামন *n* (in folk-tales) name of a talking parakeet.

হীল [E] *n* heel.

হুইপ [E] *n* whip (also) of a political party.

হুইল [E] *n* wheel.

হুইসল, হুইসেল [E] *n* whistle.

হুইস্কি [E] *n* whisky.

হুংকার=হুঙ্কার

হুঁ *n* (onom) expressing: assent, acknowledgement, willingness, doubt, acceptance, consent, doubt etc; yes; aye; hmm.

হুঁকা, হুঁকো [A] *n* hookah; hubble-bubble. **~নলিচা শুদ্ধ** lock, stock and barrel; root and branch. **~ পানি বন্ধ করা** *vi* boycott sb; excommunicate. **~বরদার** *n* servant who prepares the hookah; hookah-bearer. **হুঁকারি** *n* hookah-smoker; hookah-addict.

হুঁশ *n* [P] **1** sense; consciousness; judgement; understanding; discretion; good sense; sensation. **2** caution; cautiousness. **~ আসা** *vi* regain consciousness; come to oneself. **~ হওয়া** *vi* **1** regain consciousness. **2** come to one's senses; recover one's senses; come to one's self. **3** become cautious/ prudent.

হুঁশিয়ার *adj* **1** cautious; alert; watchful; careful; discreet; prudent. **2** intelligent; attentive; clever. **~ করা** *vt* warn; give notice; caution. **~ হওয়া** *iv* be alert; be on the guard; be careful/ cautious/ prudent.

হুঁশিয়ারি *n* caution; cautiousness; cautioning; watchfulness; alertness; discretion; prudence. **~ সঙ্কেত** *n* cautionary signal.

হুক [E] *n* hook.

হুকমত, হুকমৎ=হুকুমত

হুকুম [A] *n* **1** order; command. **2** decree; rule; statute; law; ordinance; sanction; decision. **3** article (of faith); precept. **4** authority; jurisdiction. **5** permission. **~ করা** *vi* order; command; decree; award; sentence; enjoin. **~ চালানো** *vi* exercise authority; rule; govern. **~ জারি করা** *vi* issue an order/ injunction. **হুকুম তামিল/ পালন করা** *vi* execute/ carry out an order; comply with an order. **~ দেওয়া** *vi* give/ pass an order; order; command; give permission; permit; issue an injunction. **~ অমান্য/ খেলাপ করা** *vi* infringe/ violate an order; disobey. **~দার** *int* (in the army & police) a call of challenge by the sentry; who comes there. **~নামা** *n* written orders/ decree; warrant; permit; writ of command. **~বরদার** *n* person who carries out order. ❑*adj* obedient. **~বরদারি** *n* carrying out orders; obedience to orders. **~ রদ করা** *vi* cancel/ revoke/ repeal/ withdraw an order/ permission/ decree/ consent etc. **যো ~** as you command (indicating cringing audience).

হুকুমত, হুকুমৎ [A] *n* government; sovereignty; dominion; jurisdiction; sway; authority; power; rule.

হুক্কাহুয়া *n* (onom) bark of foxes.

হুঙ্কার *n* (onom) roar; roaring; bellowing; menacing cry; growl. **~ ছাড়া/ দেওয়া** *vi* roar; growl; yell; thunder against/ out. **হুঙ্কারা** *vi* (poet)=~ ছাড়া.

হুঙ্কারিত, হুঙ্কৃত *adj* roared; yelled; growled; roaring.

হুজরা [A] *n* **1** small room; cell; closet; private room. **2** a private room for prayer or meditation.

হুজুক, হুজুগ *nn* **1** passing popular trend; craze. **2** rumour. **3** fashion. **~ ছড়ানো** *vi* spread a rumour; gossip. **~ তোলা** *vi* raise a rumour; noise it about/ abroad/ around; rumour. **হুজুগে** *adj* **1** given to participating madly in a passing popular trend/ excitement; hysterical; easily excitable; given to accepting madly a passing fashion. **2** given to indulging in rumours. **হুজুগে মাতা** *vi* participate/ involve oneself in a passing popular trend/ excitement; follow the crowd; swim with the tide.

হুজুর *n* **1** presence; presence of a superior authority. **2** master; honoured person. ❑*int* Your Majesty; Your Highness; Sir; Your Lordship; Your Excellence; Your Honour.

হুজ্জত, হুজ্জৎ [A] *n* **1** altercation; disputation; argument; dispute. **2** hubbub; row; quarrel; trouble. **~ বাঁধানো** *vi* create a row/ trouble; pick a quarrel.

হুজ্জতি, হুজ্জতী *adj* quarrelsome; contentious; troublesome; rowdy; factious.

হুট *n* (onom) expressing: suddenness, rashness, quickness, contempt, etc. **~ করে**

adv hastily; abruptly; impetuously; rashly; all on a sudden.

হুটপাট, হুটোপাটি *n* noisy play; frisking; gambol; romping; play of romps; wild/ merry prank; prancing. ~ **করা** *vi* frisk; gambol; romp; cavort; play noisily.

হুড় *n* noisy crowd; confused crowd of people; disorderly crowd; stampede. ~ **করা** *vi* crowd and shove each other in a disorderly manner; crowd together; stampede; run amuck; dust up; struggle confusedly; go/ be on the rampage. ~**দঙ্গল** *n* melee; confused struggle; rampage; stampede.

হুড়কা[১], হুড়কো[১] (colloq) *n* latch; bolt. ~ **আটা/ দেওয়া** *vt* latch; bolt.

হুড়কা[২], হুড়কো[২] (colloq) *adj fem* afraid of cohabiting with one's husband; shunning one's husband's company.

হুড়মুড় *n* (onom) sound indicating: movement of a surging crowd; headlong fall; sudden crumbling of a large and heavy object. ~ **করে** *adv* with crash; suddenly. ~ **করে (ভেঙে) পড়া** *vi* **1** crash; fall with a crash; crumble down noisily. **2** fall headlong. **3** scramble (for).

হুড়হুড় *n* (onom) rumbling (of clouds or of the bowels). **হুড়হুড়ে (গুড়গুড়ে)** *adj* rumbling.

হুড়া, হুড়ো (colloq) *n* **1** push; vigorous push; shove. **2** cudgel. ~ **লাগানো** *vt* **1** shove. **2** cudgel. ~**তাড়া** *n* **1** goad; urging; prod; spur; drive. **2** haste; hurry. ~**তাড়া করা** *vi* **1** goad; prod; urge; spur; drive. **2** hasten; hurry. ~**হুড়ি** *n* **1** mutual shoving (in a crowd); tumult; melee; jostling. **2** noisy gambolling/ playing. ~**হুড়ি করা** *n vi* **1** shove one another noisily; scramble (for); run amuck; rush violently; jostle each other. **2** gambol/ play noisily.

হুড়ুক *n* (onom) **1** speed; rush. **2** sudden tug/ pull.

হুড়ুদ্দম *n* (onom) violent movement; romping; commotion; turbulence; rumpus; welter; stir.

হুড়ুম[১] *n* **1** (colloq) kind of fried rice.

হুড়ুম[২] *n* (onom) noisy/ disorderly movement. ~ **করে** *adv* abruptly; impulsively; precipitately; (at) full tilt. ~**দুড়ুম** *n* tumult; unruliness; turbulence; rumpus.

হুণ্ডি *n* bill of exchange; cheque; bank-draft; note of hand. ~ **কাটা/ দেওয়া** *vi* issue a bill of exchange. ~ **ভাঙানো** *vi* cash a bill of exchange. ~**গ্রাহক** *n* drawer. ~**প্রেরক** *n* drawee. **উপযোজক** ~ *n* accomodation bill. **খাড়া/ দর্শনী** ~ *n* bill on demand. **মেয়াদি/ মুদ্দতি** ~ *n* bill payable after date.

হুতাশ[১] *n* oblation-fire; fire.

হুতাশ[২] *n* despair; dismay; fear; dejection; worry. **হুতাশে** *adv* in despair/ dismay; desperately; fretfully; in anguish.

হুতাশন=হুতাশ[১]

হুতুম, হুতোম *n* the largest and ugliest species of owl.

হুদ্দা, হুদ্দো [A] (colloq) *n* jurisdiction; limit; precincts (of a building).

হুদ্ হুদ [A] *n* hoopoe; a crested bird.

হুনর [P] *n* excellence in any art; skill; art; accomplishment; cleverness; knowledge; attainment; virtue.

হুনরি, হুনরী *adj* skilful; clever; excellent; relating to handicrafts. ❑*n* **1** skilfulness. **2** one skilled in handicrafts; artisan. ~ **কাজ,** ~ **কর্ম** *nn* crafts; handicrafts.

হুপ *n* (onom) whoop. ~ **করে** *adv* suddenly; all on a sudden; abruptly; rashly.

হুপিংকাশি [E] *n* whooping-cough.

হুপো *n* (onom) hoopoe.

হুবহু [P] *adj* identical; exactly similar. ❑*adv* exactly.

হুম *n* (onom) sound expressing consent, prohibition, hesitation, etc.

হুমকি *n* threat; intimidation; menace; thunder. ~ **দেওয়া** *vi* threaten; give/ utter a threatening; menace; intimidate.

হুমড়ি *n* headlong fall; tumble; falling prone; stumbling. ~ **খাওয়া** *vi* fall headlong/ prone; tumble; stumble. ~ **খেয়ে পড়া** *vt* (fig) scramble (for); scrimmage; be mad about.

হুর, হুরি [A] *n fem* black-eyed nymph; virgin of paradise.

হুরমত [A] *n* dignity; honour; respect; reputation.

হুল *n* sting; antenna. ~ **ফোটানো/ বেঁধানো** *vt* sting.

হুলস্থুল *n* tumultuous confusion; hullabaloo; uproar; tumult; turbulence. ~ **কাণ্ড/ ব্যাপার** *n* tumultuous affair.

হুলা ⇒ হুলো

হুলাহুলি *n* (onom) **1**=উলু (ধ্বনি). **2** uproar; tumult; commotion.

হুলিয়া [A] *n* **1** police circular containing the description of personal features of an accused who is absconding. **2** appearance; features; distinctive marks; identity.

হুলু(ই) (also ~ধ্বনি, ~রব)=উলু

হুলুস্থুল=হুলস্থুল

হুলো, হুলোবিড়াল *nn* tomcat. **হুলী** *fem.*

হুল্লোড় *n* **1** revelry; carnival; merryment; festivity; frolic. **2** crowd. **3** hurly-burly; uproar; hullabaloo; tumult.

হুশ[১]=হুঁশ. হুশিয়ার=হুঁশিয়ার

হুশ[২]=হুস[২]

হুস, হুসহুস *nn* (onom) hissing sound; hiss; fizz. ~**হুস করা** *vi* hiss; fizz. ~**হুস করে** *adv* with a hissing sound.

হুহু *n* (onom) sound expressing (a) noise made by a strong wind; howl; whistle; (b) feeling of emptiness/ dejection: আমার মন ~ করছে, There is an aching void in my heart.

হুঙ্কার, হূঙ্কার *n* (onom) roar; thunder.

হুন, হূণ *n* Hun.

হৃৎ *n* (in compounds) heart. **~কন্দর** *n* inmost part of the heart; bottom of one's heart. **~কমল** *n* the heart compared to a lotus. **~কম্প(ন)** heart-throb; palpitation. **~পঙ্কজ, ~পদ্ম**=~কমল. **~পিণ্ড** *n* heart. **~পীড়া** *n* oppression of the heart; heart disease. **~প্রিয়** *adj* dear to the heart. **~শূল** *n* angina pectoris; heartache. **~স্পন্দন** *n* heartbeat.

হৃত *adj* **1** taken (away); stolen; looted; robbed; seized; plundered. **2** fascinated; charmed; ravished. deprived/ bereft of; having lost; -less. **~ধন** *adj* spoiled of wealth. **~বাস** *adj* deprived of clothes. **~বিত্ত** *adj* stripped of everything; deprived of one's property. **~রাজ্য** *adj* stripped of a kingdom. **~সর্বস্ব** *adj* robbed/ stripped of all personal property; entirely ruined. **হৃতাধিকার** *adj* deprived of an office/ right; turned out; dispossessed; ousted; deprived of one's privilege/ possessions; cashiered.

হৃদ্ *n* heart. **~গত** *adj* gone to/ being in the heart; lying in the innermost recesses of one's heart; cherished; dear; pleasant; coming to mind; conceived. **~ঘাত** *n* heartbeat. **~ধরা কলা** *n* (anat) pericardium. **~দেশ** *n* region of the heart. **~বিলাসী, ~বিহারী** *adj* wandering in the heart; injoying the inner beauty; inward-looking. **~বোধ** *n* feeling; insight; sympathetic understanding; gut reaction; sensitivity. **~যন্ত্র**=হৃৎপিণ্ড. **~রোগ** *n* heart disease; cardiac complaint.

হৃদয় *n* **1** heart; mind; soul. **2** heart/ centre/ core/ essence or best/ dearest/ most/ secret part of sth. **~-আকাশ, ~-গগন** *nn* heart compared to the sky; expanse of the heart; generous heart. **~কন্দর** *n*=হৃৎকন্দর (⇒ হৃৎ). **~গত** *adj*=হৃদ্গত (⇒ হৃদ্). **~গ্রাহী** *adj* captivating the heart; fascinating; very pleasant/ charming. **~গ্রাহিণী** *fem*. **~ঙ্গম** *adj* touching the heart. **~ঙ্গম করা** *vt* realize; perceive; appreciate; be aware of; feel deeply; grasp; understand. **~জ** *adj* born of/ originating in the heart; belonging to the heart. **~ত** *adj*=হৃদ্গত (⇒ হৃদ্). **~তন্ত্রী** *n* heartstring. **~তোষিণী** *adj fem* pleasing to the heart. **~দর্পণ** *n* mirror of one's heart. **~দাহী** *adj* heart-burning. **~দেশ** *n* region of the heart. **~দৌর্বল্য** *n* weakness of heart; faintheartedness. **~দ্রবকর** *adj* melting the heart; pathetic; touching. **~নাথ** *n* lord of one's heart; beloved. **~নিধি** *n* treasure of one's heart; dearest object. **~পট** *n* heart conceived as a piece of canvas. **~পদ্ম**=হৃৎকমল (⇒ হৃৎ). **~পারাবার** *n* heart compared to the ocean. **~পিঞ্জর** *n* heart conceived as a cage; the inmost recesses of the heart. **~পীড়া** *n* heartache. **~প্রিয়** *adj* dear to the heart; beloved. **~বল** *n* moral courage; resoluteness; moral fibre; will power; iron will; mental vigour; character. **~বল্লভ** *adj* beloved of the heart; husband; lover; sweetheart. **~বল্লভা** *fem* wife; mistress of the heart. **~বান** *adj* generous; tender-hearted; large-hearted; kind; magnanimous; bighearted; warm-hearted. **~বিদারক, ~বিদারী, ~বেধী, ~ভেদী** *adjj* heart rending; pathetic; heart-piercing; heart-breaking; cutting to the quick. **~বীণা** *n* heart conceived as a lyre. **~বৃত্তি** *n* disposition/ inclination of heart; sensibility; feeling. **~বেদনা, ~ব্যথা** *nn* heart-pang; heart-ache; mental anguish; grief; affliction; secret grudging; heart burning; pining for love. **~ভাবক** *adj* **1** emotional; passionate; ardent. **2** moving; stirring; affecting; emotive. **~ভূষণ** *n* ornament of heart; very dear. **~মণি** *n*=~নিধি. **~মন্দির** *n* heart conceived as a shrine; sacred and secret abode of the heart. **~রত্ন**=~নিধি. **~রাজ্য** *n* kingdom of heart; inner world; world of ideas. **~লক্ষ্মী** *n fem* mistress; beloved; sweetheart; wife. **~শূন্য** *adj* heartless; unfeeling; merciless; cruel. **~শূল, ~শেল** *nn* **1** heartache; heartbreak; grief. **2** angina pectoris. **~সমুদ্র, ~সাগর, ~সিন্ধু** *nn*=~পারাবার. **~সর্বস্ব** *n* sole lord of one's heart; darling; husband; presiding deity. ☐*adj* very sentimental; wearing one's heart on/ upon one's sleeve. **~স্থ** *adj* being in the heart. **~স্থল, ~স্থলী, ~স্থান** *nn* breast; region (of the heart). **~স্পর্শী** *adj* touching/ moving/ moving the heart; very pathetic/ appealing. **~হারী** *adj* revishing/ fascinating the heart; captivating. **~হারিণী** *fem*. **~হীন**=~ শূন্য. **~হীনতা** *n* heartlessness. **হৃদয়াকাশ** *n*=~-আকাশ. **হৃদয়ানন্দ** *n* heart's joy. **হৃদয়ানুগ** *adj* gratifying the heart. **হৃদয়ালু**=~বান. **হৃদয়াসন** *n* heart conceived as a seat; altar of one's heart. **হৃদয়িক, হৃদয়ী** = হৃদয়বান. **হৃদয়েশ, হৃদয়েশ্বর** *nn* lord/ master of one's heart; lover; husband. **হৃদয়েশা, হৃদয়েশ্বরী** *fem* mistress/ lady of one's heart; wife. **হৃদয়োচ্ছ্বাস** *n* great outburst of emotion; outpourings of the heart; strong emotion. **হৃদয়োন্মাদকর** *adj* bewitching hearts; sout-stirring; intoxicating.

হৃদাকাশ *n*=হৃদয়-আকাশ (⇒ হৃদয়)

হৃদি *n* (in compounds and poet) heart. **~পদ্মাসন** *n* heart conceived as a lotus to sit upon; lotus-seat of the heart. **~শয়** *adj* lying/ remaining in the heart.

হৃদ্য *adj* **1** being in the heart; internal; inward; inmost; innermost. **2** pleasing/ dear to the heart; beloved; cherished; pleasant; charming; lovely. **3** pleasant to the stomach; dainty; savoury. **4** hearty; cordial; loving; sincere; amicable. **~তা** *n* heartiness; cordiality; agreeableness; delightfulness; pleasantness; amicability; sincerity.

হৃষিত *adj*=হৃষ্ট

হৃষীকেশ *n* Vishnu; Sri Krishna.

হৃষ্ট *adj* thrilled with rapture; rejoiced; glad; pleased; cheerful; merry; delighted; happy; gladdened. **~চিত্ত, ~চেতন** *adj* rejoiced in heart. **~চিত্তে** *adv* gladly; joyfully; cheerfully; with a happy mind; happily. **~তুষ্ট** *adj* pleased and satisfied. **~পুষ্ট** *adj* happy and well-fed; happy and fat; buxom; plump. **~রোমা** *adj* having the hair of the body bristling/ thrilling. **হৃষ্টান্তঃকরণ** = ~চিত্ত.

হে (*vocative particle*) oh ! ho ! ❑*int* used to express contempt, disapprobation, ill-will or envy.

হেই, হেঁই *int* (sl) indicating: earnest appeal/ solicitation: ~বুড়ো তোর পায়ে পড়ি.

হেঁইয়ো *int* a call to exertion as in heaving.

হেঁকোচ=হ্যাকোচ

হেঁচকা *n* sudden pull/tugs; yank. ❑*adj* sudden and forceful: ~ টান. **~ টান মারা** *vt* give a jerk; pull suddenly; yank. **~নি** *n* sudden pull; yank; jerk.

হেঁচকি[১] *n*=হেঁচকানি (⇒ হেঁচকা)

হেঁচকি[২] *n*=হিক্কা

হেঁচড়ানি *n* dragging.

হেঁচড়ানো *vt*=হিচড়ানো

হেঁজিপেঁজি *adj* most ordinary; nondescript; of no importance; commonplace; run-of-the-mill; vulgar; inconsequential; measly; obscure. **~ লোক** *n* man in the street; nobody; riffraff; scum; dregs of society.

হেঁট *adj* **1** bent down; bowing down: ~মুণ্ড, bowing/ bending down the head. **2** stooping: ~ হয়ে প্রণাম করা. ❑*n* bottom; underneath: হেঁটে কাটা. **~ করা** *vt* **1** bend; bow: মাথা ~ করা, bow to, submit one's self, incline the head. **2** bring down; topple; overturn; turn upside down. **3** disgrace; bring disgrace on; shame; bring shame on sb. **লজ্জায় মাথা ~ করা/ হওয়া** hang one's head (in/ for shame).

হেঁড়ে, হেঁড়েল *adjj* **1** large and round like a cooking pot; bloated; rotund: ~ মুখ. **2** deep and harsh; croaky; raucous, raspy: ~ গলা.

হেঁতাল *n*=হিন্তাল. **হেঁতালের বাড়ি** *n* stick made of the timber of this tree.

হেঁয়ালি *n* puzzle; riddle; enigma; mystification: ~ রাখো.

হেঁশেল, হেঁসেল *n* kitchen.

হেঁসো=হাসিয়া

হেকমত=হিকমত

হেকারত [A] *n* contempt; disdain; scorns. **~ করা** *vt* despise; hate. **হেকারতের দৃষ্টিতে দেখা** look down upon; hate.

হেকিম, হকীম [A] *n* **1** physician; doctor. **2** sage; philosopher. **হকিমানা** *adj* physician-like; sage-like. ❑*n* practice of medicine.

হেকিমি, হকীমী [A] *adj* relating to the Muslim system of medicine. ❑*n* practice of the Muslim system of medicine.

হেঙ্গাম=হাঙ্গাম

হেট *int* (onom) gee, gee-up; go on; go faster.

হেড [E] *n* head; intelligence. ❑*adj* (in compounds) head; chief. **~ক্লার্ক, ~বাবু** *nn* headclerk. **~মাস্টার** *n* headmaster.

হেডিং [E] *n* heading.

হেতাল বেদনা, হেতাল ব্যথা *nn* after pains.

হেতু *n* **1** cause; reason. **2** logical reason/ deduction/ argument; reason for an inference; logic. **3** motif; purpose; object: আপনার এখানে আসার ~? **4** origin; prime cause. **5** second member of the five-member Indian syllogism. ❑*adv* by reason of; on account of; because of; caused/ effected/ actuated/ impelled/ attracted by: লোভ~. **~তা, ~ত্ব** *n* state of being a cause; causation; existence of cause/ motif; causativeness. **~দুষ্ট** *adj* inconceivable by reasons; unreasonable. **~বাদ** *n* statement of reasons/ argument; assigning a cause; argument; reasoning; preamble of a law; disputation. **~বিদ্যা** *n* logic; dialectics; teleology. **~মান** *adj* having a reason/ cause; provided with reasons/ proofs; well-founded; proceeding from a cause; accompanied with arguments. **~যুক্ত** *adj* provided with reasons; well-founded. **~রূপক** *n* (rhet) metaphor accompanied with reasons. **~শূন্য** *adj* devoid of reason; unfounded. **এই ~** because of this; for this reason/ purpose; on account of this; by virtue of this.

হেতুক *adj* **1** causing; effecting. **2** caused/ effected/ conditioned by. **3** destined for. ❑*n* cause; instrument; agent.

হেতের *n*=হাতিয়ার. **হাতে-হেতেরে** *adv* practically.

হেত্বাভাস *n* (logic) mere appearance of a reason; fallacious semblance of an argument; fallacious widdle term; fallacy.

হেথা, হেথায় *adv* (poet) here.

হেদাতি, হেদায়তি *adjj* guided (to the right path).

হেদানো *vi* (sl) become extremely distressed for being separated from one's lover/ an object; very much long for; pine for; waste away.

হেদায়েত=হিদায়ত

হেদে *int* (archaic) (used in addressing) O.

হেন *adj* such; like; such like. **~তেন** *adj* worthless; contemptible.

হেনস্তা, হেনস্থা *nn* slight; harassment; neglect; persecution; distress. **~ করা** *vt* persecute; harass; slight; distress; torment; gall; worry.

হেনা [A] *n* henna.

হেপা *n* **1** pressure; duress: ~য় পড়ে কাজ করা. **2** trouble; toublesome burden/ charge; stress; strain; brunt: কারবারের ~. **3** opportunity: সেও এই ~য় আখের গুছিয়ে নিল. **~ পোয়ানো/ সামলানো** *vi* bear a troublesome burden; execute a troublesome charge; face the music; bear the brunt of.

হেপাজত=হেফাজত

হেফজ [A] *n* learning by memory; memory. **~ করা** *vt* commit to memory; learn by heart.

হেফাজত [A] *n* guarding; preserving; custody; security; safety; care; charge. **~ করা** *vt* preserve; guard; defend. **হেফাজতে দেওয়া** *vt* commit to the charge/ custody/ care of.

হেবা=হিবা

হেম *n* gold. **~কান্তি** *adj* having a golden lusture/ complexion. **~কার** *n* goldsmith. **~কুম্ভ, ~ঝারি** *nn* gold jar. **~পুষ্প** *n* *champaka* flower. **~প্রতিমা** *n* golden statue/ image. **~প্রভ**=~কান্তি. **~লতা** = স্বর্ণলতা. **হেমাঙ্গ** *adj* having golden limbs/ parts; golden. **হেমাঙ্গিনী, হেমাঙ্গী** *fem.* **হেমাদ্রি** *n* = সুমেরু. **হেমাভ** *adj* having golden glow; looking like gold.

হেমন্ত *n* the season comprising the two months of Kartik and Agrahayan of Bengali year; autumn; the cold season.

হেমায়েল শরিফ [A] *n* small Qoran suspended to the neck as an amulet.

হেয় *adj* **1** fit to cast off; comptemtible; despicable. **2** base; vile; abject; hateful. **3** slighted. **~ করা** *vt* belittle; decry; discredit; revile; denigrate. **~জ্ঞান** *n* contempt; slight; scorn; disdain; neglect. **~ জ্ঞান করা** *vt* scorn; pooh-pooh; sneer at; look down upon; regard as contemptible; despise; make light of.

হেরফের *n* **1** alteration/ modification (to a slight degree); change; difference. **2** manipulation (as in a balance-sheet). **3** inconsistency: কাজে ও কথায় ~. **~ করা** *vt* alter slightly; modify; differentiate; manipulate; work a change; vary.

হেরা *vt* (poet) see; behold.

হেরেম [A] *n* women's apartment.

হেলন^1 *n* act of slighting; disregard; contempt.

হেলন^2 *n* leaning; slanting; inclination; slant; tilt.

হেলা^1 *n* **1** disrespect; contempt; slight; disdain. **2** neglect; negligence. **3** ease. **~ করা** *vt* **1** disrespect; treat with contempt; slight; despise; scorn; ignore; disdain. **2** neglect; be negligent; default: কাজে ~ করা. **~ফেলা** *n* utter neglect/ negligence/ disrespect; dilly-dallying; dawdling. **~ফেলা করা** *vt* **1** slight; scorn; disrespect; neglect. **2** dilly-dallying; dawdle (away). **~ফেলা করে** *adv* without any effort; negligently; dilly-dallying; dawdling. **~য়** *adv* with ease; without effort; easily; effortlessly; standing on one's head. **3** through negligence/ carelessness: ~য় হারানো.

হেলা^2 *vi* lean; slant; incline; tilt; tip. ❑*adj* leaning/ slanting/ inclining to; sloping. **~নো** *vt* cause to lean/ slant/ incline; bend; tilt; tip. **হেলে-দুলে** *adv* swinging sideways; in a waddling fashion. **হেলে-দুলে চলা** *vi* waddle. **~হেলি** *n* leaning against each other.

হেলে^1 *adv*=হেলায় (⇒ হেলা^1)

হেলে^2 *n* ploughman; peasant; rustic. ❑*adj* one who guides a plough; used in ploughing. **~চাষা** *n* peasantry.

হেলে^3 *n* a non-venomous snake.

হেলেঞ্চা *n* kind of herb.

হেলেম [A] *n* clemency; gentleness; toleration; mildness; gentleness.

হেষা, হেষনি *nn*=হ্রেষা

হেস্তনেস্ত [P] *n* finalization; final settlement; finish. **~ করা** *vt* put an end to; make an end of; resolve; finalize; see through; settle finally.

হৈ *int* ho.

হৈ চৈ=হই চই

হৈম^1 *adj* consisting/ made of gold; golden. **~কিরণ, ~দ্যুতি** *nn* golden lustre.

হৈম^2 *adj* wintry; caused/ produced by snow or ice.

হৈমন্ত *adj* wintry; relating to/ suitable to/ growing in winter/ autumn; autumn(al). ❑*n* winter. **হৈমন্তী** *adj fem.*

হৈমন্তিক *adj*=হৈমন্ত. ❑*n* **1** autumn paddy. **~ চন্দ্র** *n* harvest moon.

হৈমবত *adj* Himalayan. **হৈমবতী** *n fem* goddess Durga; Parvati.

হৈয়ঙ্গবীন *n* clarified butter prepared from yesterday's milking; fresh butter.

হৈরিক *n* adamant. ❑*adj* adamantine.

হো *int* ho; O; oh ! ah !

হোঁচট *n* stumble. **~ খাওয়া** *vi* stumble. **হোঁতকা, হোঁৎকা** *adj* (derog) **1** corpulent; fat and ugly; bloated; bloated with overeating. **2** dull-witted; obstinate; thick-headed. **~ পেটুক** *n* bloated glutton.

হোঁদড় *n* hyena.

হোঁদল *adj* pot-bellied; corpulent; paunchy; podgy. **~কুতকুত, ~কুৎকুৎ** *n* corpulent and dark-complexioned person/ beast.

হোগল, হোগলা *nn* **1** species of aquatic grass used in building the walls of huts and in making mats. **2** mat made of the above plant.

~কুঁড়ি, ~গুঁড়ি *nn* pollen of the flowers of the above plant.

হোটেল [E] *n* hotel; inn; eating-house; restaurant. ~**ওয়ালা** *n* hotel-keeper; hotelier; inn-keeper; manager/ owner of an eating-house/ restaurant. ~**ওয়ালী** *fem.*

হোড়[1] *n* **1** kind of boat. **2** stolen goods. **3** a Hindu family name.

হোড়[2] *n* **1** mud; slime. **2** inundation; flooding.

হোড়া *n* thief.

হোতা *n* **1** sacrificer; priest (who at a sacrifice invokes the gods or recites the Rigveda. **2** instigator: দুষ্কর্মের ~.

হোত্র *n* sacrificing; burnt-offering; oblation with fire.

হোত্রী *n*=হোতা. ~**য়** *adj* relating/ belonging to a sacrificing priest (হোতা).

হোথা, হোথায় *adv* (poet) there.

হোম *n* act of making an oblation to the gods by casting clarified butter into the fire; oblation (with fire); burnt-offering; sacrifice. ~**কুণ্ড** *n* hole in the ground for the sacred fire for oblation. ~**ধান্য** *n* sesamum. ~**ধূম** *n* smoke of a burnt-offering. ~**ধেনু** *n* cow yielding milk for an oblation. ~**ভস্ম** *n* ashes of a burnt-offering. **হোমাগ্নি, হোমানল** *nn* sacrificial fire.

হোমরাচোমরা *adj* (iron) prominent and important and well-to-do; august; eminent. ❑*n* (also ~ ব্যক্তি) bigwig; somebody; high-up; notability; mogul; big gun; VIP; big noise.

হোমিওপ্যাথ [E] *n* homoeopath.

হোমিওপ্যাথি [E] *n* homoeopathy. ~**ক** *adj* homoeopathic.

হোমী *adj* offering; presenting an oblation.

হোয়াক *n* (onom) involuntary sound made whilst vomiting.

হোরা *n* (astrol) hour. ~**কোণ** *n* hour angle. ~**চক্র**, ~**বলয়** *n* hour circle. ~**বিজ্ঞান** *n* astrology.

হোরি, হোলি, হোলী *nn* Hindu spring festival at the approach of the vernal equinox.

হোল্ডল [E] *n* hold-all; a traveller's bag in which he holds his beds and other things.

হোশ=হুঁশ

হো হো *n* (onom) noise of a very loud laughter; ha ! ha! ~ **করে ওঠা/ হাসা** *vi* burst into a very loud laughter; guffaw. ~ **করে বেড়ানো** *vi* sow one's wild oats.

হৌজ=হাউজ

হৌস [E] *n* mercantile firm; (commercial) house; trading establishment.

হ্যাংলা *adj* **1** repulsively/ shamelessly greedy. **2** lewd. **3** lanky; leggy. ~**পনা**, ~**মি** *nn* shameless greed; repulsive greediness.

হ্যাঁ=হাঁ

হ্যাঁকোচ *n* (onom) rattling sound of a vehicle; rattle. ~ **ক্যাকোচ করা** *vi* rattle along.

হ্যাঁচকা=হেঁচকা

হ্যাজাক *n* kind of gas-lamp.

হ্যাট [E] *n* hat. ~**ধারী** *adj* wearing a hat; hatted.

হ্যাদানো=হেদানো

হ্যাদে=হেদে

হ্যাপা=হেপা

হ্যান্ডনোট [E] *n* note of hand; hand-note; promissory note; IOU. ~ **কাটা** *vt* write out/ issue an IOU/ hand-note.

হ্যান্ডবিল [E] *n* handbill.

হ্যাভারসাক *n* [E] haversack; a soldier's bag for carrying provisions.

হ্রদ *n* lake; lagoon; large pond; pool.

হ্রসিমা *n* shortness; smallness.

হ্রস্ব *adj* short; small; dwarfish; little; low; low-pitched; abbreviated; shortened; reduced; small in amount. ~**জ্যোতি** *adj* dim. ~**তা**, ~**ত্ব** *n* shortness; smallness. ~**তেজা** *adj* weak; enfeebled. ~**দীর্ঘজ্ঞান** *n* (fig) common sense; horse sense; gumption. ~**স্বর** *n* (phonetics) short vowel.

হ্রস্বীকরণ *n* shortening; abbreviation; reduction.

হ্রাদ *n* sound; noise.

হ্রাস *n* diminution; shortening; decrease; reduction; deterioration; curtailment; waning; detriment. ~ **করা** *vt* reduce; decrease; diminish; shorten; curtail. ~ **পাওয়া/হওয়া** *vi* decrease; be diminished/ reduced/ curtailed/ lessened; diminish; become short/ small; wane. ~**প্রাপ্ত** *adj* reduced; diminished; decreased; waned; abated; diminutive. ~**প্রাপ্ত হওয়া** *vi*=~ পাওয়া. ~**বৃদ্ধি** *n* **1** rise and fall: মূল্যের ~বৃদ্ধি. **2** waning and waxing: চন্দ্রকলার ~বৃদ্ধি. **3** appreciation and depreciation. **4** aggravation and diminution: রোগের ~বৃদ্ধি.

হ্রী *n* modesty; shyness; bashfulness; shame; timidity. ~**মান** *adj* bashful; modest; ashamed; shy; timid; embarrassed. ~**মতী** *fem.*

হ্রেষা, হ্রেষাধ্বনি *nn* (onom) neighing (of a horse); whinnying. ~**ধ্বনি করা** *vi* neigh.

হ্লাদ, হ্লাদন *nn* gladness; delight; pleasure; joy.

হ্লাদিত *adj* gladdened; delighted; joyful; refreshed.

হ্লাদিনী *adj fem* **1** refreshing; gladdening; exhilarating; comforting. **2** treated with/ brought up with excessive indulgence; doted on; pet; beloved. ❑*n* (Vaishnava phil) a particular *shakti* (শক্তি); Radha.

হ্লাদী *adj*=হ্লাদিনী

memoranda

memoranda